Nancy. Phillips
46 Craibe Road.
Kingussie
Inverness-shire
PH21. 1PB

CHAMBERS

LARGE PRINT DICTIONARY

CHAMBERS

LARGE PRINT DICTIONARY

CHAMBERS

CHAMBERS
An imprint of Chambers Harrap Publishers Ltd
7 Hopetoun Crescent, Edinburgh EH7 4AY

Reprinted 1999

This dictionary is based on *Chambers Paperback Dictionary*, 1998

We have made every effort to mark as such all words which we believe to be trademarks. We should also like to make it clear that the presence of a word in the dictionary, whether marked or unmarked, in no way affects its legal status as a trademark.

ISBN 0-550-10007-5

The editorial contributions to this dictionary of George Davidson, Anne Seaton and Catherine Schwarz are acknowledged with thanks.

Typeset by Chambers Harrap Publishers Ltd, Edinburgh
Printed and bound in Great Britain by
Caledonian International Book Manufacturing Ltd, Glasgow

Contents

Preface

Chambers Large Print Dictionary is based on the text of *Chambers Paperback Dictionary* published in 1998. Up to date and easy to use, this dictionary provides a wide selection of the words most likely to be met with in everyday life. Definitions are clear and succinct, and many examples are included which show the words in use in phrases and sentences.

Help has been given with the spelling of parts of verbs, plurals of nouns, and comparatives and superlatives of adjectives:

(a) where a letter is doubled (as in *tan*, *tanning*, *tanned*: *big*, *bigger*, *biggest*) or where doubt about doubled letters could arise (as in *benefit*, *benefiting*, *benefited*);

(b) where a final *-y* or *-o* might cause difficulty (as *fairy*, *fairies*; *silly*, *sillier*, *silliest*; *tomato*, *tomatoes*);

(c) with all present participles of verbs ending in *-e*, most of which simply drop the *-e* before *-ing* (as in *mine*, *mining*; but *die*, *dying*, and *singe*, *singeing*).

Where the past tense of an irregular verb is different from the past participle, both forms are of course given in the dictionary. Where only the past participle is given, the past tense is to be understood as being the same as the past participle.

In this dictionary, words such as *realise* and *realisation* are spelled *-ise* and *-isation*, but it is equally correct to spell them *-ize* and *-ization*.

Contributors

Publishing Manager
Elaine Higgleton

Editorial Team
Sandra Anderson, Penny Hands,
Megan Thomson

Pre-press Department
Siri Hansen, Louise McGinnity

Abbreviations used in the Dictionary

abbrev.	abbreviation
adj(s).	adjective(s)
adv(s).	adverb(s)
and/or	'and' or 'or' — both or either
cap.	capital
cent.	century
coll.	colloquial(ly)
comp.	comparative
conj.	conjunction
conn.	connected (with), connection
contr.	contracted
dial.	dialect
Dict.	dictionary
dim.	diminutive
E.	East
e.g.	(L. *exempli gratia*) for example
esp.	especially
fem.	feminine
fol.	following
i.e.	(L. *id est*) that is
imit.	imitative
imper.	imperative
incl.	including
infin.	infinitive
infl.	influenced
interj.	interjection
masc.	masculine
mod.	modern
N.	North
n(s).	noun(s)
neut.	neuter
n.pl.	noun plural
opp.	opposed, opposite
orig.	origin, original(ly)
p.	penny, pence
pa.p.	past participle
pass.	passive
pa.t.	past tense
perh.	perhaps
pfx.	prefix
pl.	plural
pr.p.	present participle
pr.t.	present tense
prep.	preposition
prob.	probably
pron.	pronounced
pron(s).	pronoun(s)
®	registered trademark
R.C.	Roman Catholic
S.	South
sfx.	suffix
sing.	singular
sq.	square
superl.	superlative
usu.	usual(ly)
v(s), vb(s).	verb(s)
v(s).i.	verb(s) intransitive
v(s).t.	verb(s) transitive
vulg.	vulgar(ly)
W.	West

Abbreviations of names of languages or regions

Afr.	African
Amer.	American
Austr.	Australian
Celt.	Celtic
Dan.	Danish
Du.	Dutch
Engl.	English
Fr.	French
Gael.	Gaelic
Ger.	German
Gk.	Greek
Heb.	Hebrew
Ir.	Irish
It.	Italian
Jap.	Japanese
L.	Latin
M.	Middle
M.E.	Middle English
Norw.	Norwegian
N.Z.	New Zealand
O.	Old
O.E.	Old English
Pers.	Persian
Port.	Portuguese
Russ.	Russian
S. Afr.	South African
Scand.	Scandinavian
Scot.	Scottish
Sp.	Spanish
Swed.	Swedish
Turk.	Turkish
U.S.(A.)	United States
W.	Welsh

Pronunciation Guide

Accented syllables are shown by putting a stress mark after the accented syllable, thus: *ban'dit*, *dis-pel'*, *dis-gust'ing*.

Vowels and diphthongs in accented syllables

Sound			Examples	Pronunciation
ā	as in	fate, bare	name, hair	*nām*, *hār*
ä	as in	father, far	grass, harm	*gräs*, *härm*
a	as in	sat	bad, have	*bad*, *hav*
ē	as in	me, fear	lean, here	*lēn*, *hēr*
e	as in	pet	red, said	*red*, *sed*
ī	as in	mine, sire	side, hire	*sīd*, *hīr*
i	as in	bid	pin, busy	*pin*, *biz'i*
ō	as in	mote, more	bone, floor	*bōn*, *flōr*
o	as in	got	shot, shone	*shot*, *shon*
ö	as in	all, for, more	lawn, horn, floor	*lön*, *hörn*, *flör*
o͞o	as in	moon, poor	fool, tour	*fo͞ol*, *to͞or*
oo	as in	foot	full, would	*fool*, *wood*
ū	as in	mute, pure	tune, endure	*tūn*, *in-dūr'*
u	as in	bud	run, love	*run*, *luv*
û	as in	her	heard, bird, world, absurd	*hûrd*,*bûrd*,*wûrld*,*ȧb-sûrd'*
ow	as in	house, hour	mount, sour	*mownt*, *sowr*
oi	as in	boy	buoy, soil	*boi*, *soil*

Vowels of unaccented syllables

These are marked with a dot to show that they are not pronounced as distinctly as in accented syllables: *in'fȧnt*, *sī'lėnt*, *bish'ȯp*, *om'ni-bu̇s*.

Consonants

b, *d*, *f*, *h*, *j*, *k*, *l*, *m*, *n*, *p*, *r*, *s*, *t*, *v*, *w* and *z* are pronounced as in standard English.

The following other symbols are used:

Sound			Examples	Pronunciation
ch	as in	cheap	church	*chûrch*
g	as in	good	game	*gām*
H	as in	loch	pibroch	*pē'bro*H
hw	as in	where	what	*hwot*
ng	as in	sing	rang, longer	*rang*, *long'gėr*
sh	as in	shine	shape, sugar	*shāp*, *shoog'ȧr*
th	as in	thin	theme, health	*thēm*, *helth*
TH	as in	then	though, bathe	TH*ō*, *bā*TH
y	as in	yet	young, feature	*yung*, *fē'tyu̇r* (or *fē'chu̇r*)
zh	as in	azure	measure, vision	*mezh'u̇r*, *vizh'(ȯ)n*

Additional sounds in foreign words

an^g and *on^g* are French nasal vowels, as in *vin blanc*. ' is used where a pronunciation with *ė* is possible, but not obligatory, in French, as **timbre** *tan^{g}br'*.

A

a, an *ȧ*, *ȧn*, or emphatic *ā*, *an*, *adjs.* the indefinite article (**a** is used before words starting with the sound of a consonant, e.g. *a dog, a year, a ewe*; **an** is used before words beginning with the sound of a vowel, e.g. *an ear, an honour*) **1** one. **2** any. **3** each, every.

A1 *ā'wun'*, *adj.* **1** classed as A1 in Lloyd's Register of ships. **2** (*coll.*) very good.

aback *ȧ-bak'*, *adv.* (of sails) pressed backward against the mast by the wind.
taken aback taken by surprise and rather upset.

abacus *ab'ȧ-kus*, *n.* a counting-frame.

abaft *ȧ-bäft'*, *adv.* **1** on the stern part of a ship. **2** behind.—*prep.* behind.

abandon *ȧ-ban'dȯn*, *v.t.* **1** to give up. **2** to desert. **3** to yield (oneself) without restraint (to): *to abandon oneself to despair.*—*n.* careless freedom of action.
aban'doned *adj.* **1** completely deserted. **2** very wicked.
aban'donment *n.* the act of abandoning.

abase *ȧ-bās'*, *v.t.* to humble:—*pr.p.* **abas'ing**. **abasement** *n.*

abash *ȧ-bash'*, *v.t.* to make ashamed or confused; to disconcert.

abate *ȧ-bāt'*, *v.t.* **1** to make less. **2** to deduct.—*v.i.* to grow less:—*pr.p.* **abat'ing**.
abate'ment *n.* **1** the act of abating. **2** the sum or quantity abated.

abattoir *a'bȧt-wä*, *-bät'-*, *-wä'*, *n.* a public slaughterhouse.

abbacy *ab'ȧ-si*, *n.* **1** the office of an abbot. **2** an abbey:—*pl.* **abb'acies**.
abbé *ab'ā*, *n.* **1** orig. the French name for an abbot. **2** a priest or clergyman.
abbess *ab'es*. See **abbot**.
abbey *ab'i*, *n.* **1** a convent under an abbot or abbess. **2** the church now or formerly attached to it:—*pl.* **abb'eys**.
abbot *ab'ȯt*, *n.* the male head of an abbey:—*fem.* **abb'ess**.

abbreviate *ȧ-brē'vi-āt*, *v.t.* **1** to shorten. **2** to abridge:—*pr.p.* **abbrē'viating**.
abbreviā'tion *n.* **1** the act of shortening. **2** a part of a word used for the whole.

ABC *ā-bē-sē'*, *n.* **1** the alphabet. **2** a table of information alphabetically arranged, e.g. a railway timetable. **3** a course of basic instruction: *the ABC of bicycle maintenance.*

abdicate *ab'di-kāt*, *v.t.* and *v.i.* formally to give up (office or dignity):—*pr.p.* **ab'dicating**.
abdicā'tion *n.*

abdomen *ab-dō'mėn*, or *ab'*, *n.* **1** the belly. **2** the part of the body below the chest.
abdom'inal *(-dom'-) adj.*

abduct *ab-dukt'*, *v.t.* **1** to take away by fraud or violence. **2** to kidnap.
abduc'tion *n.*

abeam *ȧ-bēm'*, *adv.* on the beam, or in a line at right angles to a vessel's length.

aberration *ab-ėr-ā'sh(ȯ)n*, *n.* **1** act of wandering from the right path or from the normal way of behaving. **2** a mental lapse.

abet *ȧ-bet'*, *v.t.* to give encouragement or aid to (used chiefly in a bad sense):—*pr.p.* **abett'ing**; *pa.p.* **abett'ed**.
abett'or, abett'er *ns.*

abeyance *ȧ-bā'ȧns*: **in abeyance** **1** undecided for the present: *The matter was left in abeyance.* **2** left unfilled for the time being: *The office of president was in abeyance.*

abhor *ȧb-hör'*, *v.t.* **1** to detest, loathe. **2** to shun, reject utterly:—*pr.p.* **abhorr'ing**; *pa.p.* **abhorred'**.
abhorr'ence *n.*
abhorr'ent *adj.* hateful: *Deceit was abhorrent to him.*

abide *ȧ-bīd'*, *v.t.* to endure, tolerate: *I cannot abide an unpunctual person.*—*v.i.* (*old-fashioned*) to dwell; to stay:—*pr.p.* **abid'ing**; *pa.t.* **abode'** or **abid'ed**.
abide by to adhere to, act according to: *to abide by one's promise*; to abide by the terms of the treaty.

ability. See **able**.

abject *ab'jekt*, *adj.* cowering, miserable.
ab'jectly *adv.* **ab'jectness** *n.*

abjure *ȧb-jōōr'*, *v.t.* to swear to give up or to leave for ever:—*pr.p.* **abjur'ing**.

ablaze *ȧ-blāz'*, *adv.*, *adj.* (not used before a noun) **1** burning strongly. **2** very bright.

able *ā'bl*, *adj.* **1** having enough strength, power, or means (to do a thing). **2** skilful, talented, clever.
ability *ȧ-bil'i-ti*, *n.* **1** the quality of being able. **2** power (physical or mental). **3** sufficient strength, skill, etc. (to do something):—*pl.* **abil'ities**; *opp.* **inabil'ity**.
a'bly *adv.*
a'ble-bod'ied *adj.* having a strong body.
able seaman, able-bodied seaman

(*abbrev*. **A.B.**) one able to perform all the duties of seamanship and having a higher rating than the ordinary sailor.
See also **disable**.

ablution *ȧ-blōō'sh(ȯ)n*, *n*. (often in *pl*., usu. *humorous*) act of washing, esp. the body.

abnormal *ab-nör'mȧl*, *adj*. **1** not normal. **2** very unusual.
abnormal'ity *n*. (*pl*.-**ies**).
abnor'mally *adv*.

aboard *ȧ-bōrd'*, *bōrd'*, *adv*. or *prep*. **1** on board. **2** in, or into (a ship, a train, etc.).

abode[1] *ȧ-bōd'*, *n*. a dwelling-place, house.
of no fixed abode without a permanent address.

abode[2]. See **abide**.

abolish *ȧ-bol'ish*, *v.t.* **1** to put an end to, to do away with. **2** to annul.
aboli'tion *n*.
aboli'tionist *n*. one who seeks to abolish anything, e.g. capital punishment or (*history*) slavery.

A-bomb *ā'bom*, *n*. an atomic bomb.

abominate *ȧ-bom'in-āt*, *v.t.* to loathe, detest extremely:—*pr.p*. **abom'inating**.
abom'inable *adj*. hateful, detestable.
abom'inably *adv*.
abominā'tion *n*. **1** loathing. **2** anything disgusting or detestable.
abominable snowman a large ape-like creature supposed to inhabit the snows of Tibet (also **yeti**).

aborigines *ab-ȯ-rij'in-ēz*, *n.pl*. the original or native inhabitants of a country:—*sing*. **aborig'ine** *(-rij'i-nē)*, *slang abbrev*. **ab'ō**:—*pl*. **ab'ōs**.
aborig'inal *adj*. earliest, primitive.—*n*. one of the aborigines.

abort *ȧ-bort'*, *v.i.* **1** to miscarry in birth. **2** to cease to develop before development is complete. **3** to come to nothing.—*v.t.* **1** to terminate the development of (a foetus), or a pregnancy in (a female). **2** to put a stop to, abandon (a project, etc.).
abor'tion *n*.
abor'tive *adj*. unsuccessful: *an abortive attempt*.

abound *ȧ-bownd'*, *v.i.* **1** to be in plentiful supply. **2** to be rich (in), well supplied (with).
See also **abundance**.

about *ȧ-bowt'*, *prep*. **1** round on the outside of. **2** all round. **3** here and there in. **4** on (one's person). **5** belonging to, as a quality. **6** near (place, time, size, etc.). **7** concerning.—*adv*. **1** around. **2** near. **3** nearly. **4** here and there. **5** on the opposite tack. **6** in the opposite direction: *to face about*.
be about to to be on the point of.
time, turn, about alternately, in turn.
week, day, etc. **about** every alternate week, day, etc.

above *ȧ-buv'*, *prep*. **1** on or to the upper side of. **2** higher than. **3** more than. **4** too proud or too good to descend to.—*adv*. **1** overhead. **2** in a higher position, order, or power. **3** at an earlier point in a writing.
above'-board *adj*. open, honourable.

abrade *ȧ-brād'*, *v.t.* **1** to rub off (skin, etc.). **2** to wear down by friction:—*pr.p*. **abrad'ing**.
abrasion *ȧ-brāzh'(ȯ)n*, *n*. **1** the act of rubbing off. **2** an injury caused by scraping or rubbing.
abrā'sive *(-ziv, -siv) adj*. **1** scraping. **2** of speech, behaviour, etc., tending to hurt other people's feelings.—*n*. something that abrades (as emery).

abreast *ȧ-brest'*, *adv*. **1** with fronts in a line. **2** side by side. **3** up with: *abreast of the times*.

abridge *ȧ-brij'*, *v.t.* to shorten:—*pr.p*. **abridg'ing**.
abridg'ment (sometimes **abridge'ment**) *n*.

abroad *ȧ-bröd'*, *adv*. **1** over a wide area. **2** out of doors; at large. **3** in, or to, another country or other countries.—*n*. another country or other countries: *letters from abroad*.

abrogate *ab'rȯ-gāt*, *v.t.* to set aside, to do away with (e.g. a law):—*pr.p*. **ab'rogating**.
abrogā'tion *n*.

abrupt *ȧ-brupt'*, *adj*. **1** the opposite of gradual. **2** steep. **3** sudden, hasty. **4** (of style) passing suddenly from one thought to another. **5** (of manners) ungracious, rude.
abrupt'ly *adv*. **abrupt'ness** *n*.

abscess *ab'ses*, *n*. an inflamed area or swelling, containing pus, formed within a tissue of the body.

abscond *ȧb-skond'*, *v.i.* to run away secretly, esp. in order to escape the law.

absent *ab'sėnt*, *adj*. **1** away, not present. **2** not existing. **3** inattentive.—*v.t.* *(ȧb-sent')* to keep (oneself) away (from e.g. a meeting).
ab'sence *n*. **1** the state of being away. **2** want (of). **3** inattention.
absentee' *(-tē') n*. **1** one who is absent. **2** one who makes a habit of being away from his estate, office or employment.—Also *adj*. (used only before a noun).
absentee'ism *n*. the practice of being absent from duty.
ab'sently *adv*.

ab'sent-mind'ed *adj.* inattentive to what is happening round one.

absence of mind forgetfulness, inattention.

absinth(e) *ab'sinth, n.* **1** wormwood. **2** a liqueur containing (orig. at least) extract of wormwood.

absolute *ab'sȯl-ūt,* or *-o͞ot, adj.* **1** free from limits or restrictions. **2** not limited by rules or laws: *an absolute monarch.* **3** complete, certain: *absolute proof.*

ab'solutely *adv.* **1** without restriction. **2** completely.—*interj.* *(-ūt'-, -o͞ot'-)* certainly, I agree.

absolute alcohol water-free alcohol.

absolute zero the lowest possible temperature, approximately -273°C.

absolution. See **absolve**.

absolve *ȧb-zolv',* or *-solv', v.t.* **1** to set free, release (from a promise or duty, or from blame). **2** to pardon. **3** to acquit:—*pr.p.* **absol'ving.**

absolution *ab-sȯl-ū'sh(ȯ)n,* or *-o͞o'-, n.* **1** setting free from punishment. **2** forgiveness, esp. forgiveness of sins formally declared by a priest.

absorb *ȧb-sörb',* or *-zörb', v.t.* **1** to suck in, soak up (liquids, etc.). **2** to take in (information, etc.). **3** to take up the whole attention of. **4** to use fully (a person's energies, etc.). **5** to take over (other businesses, etc.).

absor'bent *adj.* and *n.* (something) able to absorb (*def. 1*).

absorb'ency *n.*

absorp'tion *n.* **1** the act of absorbing. **2** entire occupation of mind.

abstain *ȧb-stān', v.i.* to keep oneself away (from), refrain (from).

abstain'er *n.* one who abstains, esp. from drinking alcohol.

absten'tion *n.* the act of refraining (from).

abstinent *ab'stin-ėnt, adj.* keeping oneself from indulgence (e.g. in alcohol).

ab'stinence *n.*

abstemious *ȧb-stēm'i-ůs, adj.* taking little food or drink, indulging in few pleasures.

abstem'iously *adv.*

abstem'iousness *n.*

abstention, abstinence, etc. See **abstain**.

abstract *ȧb-strakt', v.t.* **1** to draw away or out. **2** to remove quietly. **3** to summarise.—*adj. (ab'strakt)* **1** (of a noun) denoting a quality or condition: *Redness, courage, justice, poverty, are abstract nouns.* **2** (of art) concerned more with design, colour, shape, etc., than with faithful representation.—*n.* a summary.

abstract'ed *adj.* absent-minded.

abstract'edly *adv.*

abstrac'tion *n.* **1** the act of abstracting. **2** absence of mind.

in the abstract in theory.

abstruse *ȧb-stro͞os', adj.* difficult to understand, obscure: *abstruse reasoning.*

abstruse'ness *n.*

absurd *ȧb-sûrd', adj.* **1** unreasonable. **2** ridiculous.

absurd'ness, absurd'ity (*pl.* **-ies**) *ns.*

absurd'ly *adv.*

abundance *ȧ-bun'dȧns, n.* plentiful supply.

abund'ant *adj.* **1** plentiful. **2** rich (in).

abund'antly *adv.* more than sufficiently: *abundantly obvious.*

abuse *ȧ-būz', v.t.* **1** to use wrongly. **2** to betray (e.g. a confidence). **3** to injure. **4** to reproach, scold violently:—*pr.p.* **abus'ing.**—*n.* *(ȧb-ūs')* **1** ill or wrong use. **2** unjust use. **3** harsh, offensive language. **4** an evil practice or custom.

abus'ive *(-ūs'-) adj.* rudely scolding or reproachful.

abus'ively *adv.* **abus'iveness** *n.*

See also **misuse**.

abut *ȧ-but', v.i.* **1** to be joined at end or side (with *on (to), upon, against*). **2** to border (on):—*pr.p.* **abutt'ing**; *pa.p.* **abutt'ed.**

abysmal *ȧ-biz'mȧl, adj.* **1** very deep or great: *abysmal ignorance.* **2** (*coll.*) very bad: *abysmal behaviour.*

abyss *ȧ-bis', n.* a bottomless depth, chasm.

acacia *ȧ-kā'sh(y)ȧ, n.* a thorny plant, a wattle.

academic, etc. See **academy**.

academy *ȧ-kad'ėm-i, n.* **1** a college giving special training: *a military, naval academy.* **2** a society for the encouragement of science or art. **3** esp. in Scotland, a (usu. secondary) school:—*pl.* **acad'emies.**

academ'ic *adj.* **1** of a college or university. **2** scholarly. **3** theoretical as opposed to practical.—*n.* one pursuing a scholarly career, e.g. as a university teacher.

academ'ical *adj.* academic.—*n.* (in *pl.*) university cap and gown.

academ'ically *adv.*

academician *ȧ-kad-ė-mish'ȧn, n.* (esp. with *cap.*) a member of an academy (*def.* 2), e.g. an artist elected to the Royal Academy in London.

acanthus *ȧ-kan'thůs, n.* **1** a prickly-leaved plant. **2** an ornament resembling its leaves, used in architecture.

accede *ak-sēd', v.i.* **1** to come into office. **2** to give consent: *I cannot accede to your*

request:—*pr.p.* **acced'ing**.
See also **accession**.

accelerate *ak-sel'ėr-āt*, *v.t.* **1** to increase the speed of. **2** to cause to happen sooner.—*v.i.* to move faster:—*pr.p.* **accel'erating**.
accelerā'tion *n.* **1** increase of speed. **2** the rate of change of velocity.
accel'erator *n.* **1** something that accelerates, e.g. a lever, pedal, etc. for regulating the speed of a machine. **2** an apparatus for giving high energy to atomic particles.

accent *ak'sėnt*, *n.* **1** (usu. in *pl.*) tone of the voice. **2** a stress on a syllable or word. **3** a mark (') to show this stress. **4** in certain languages, any of several marks placed over letters to indicate quality of sound. **5** the kind of pronunciation typical of a particular region, class, etc. **6** emphasis.—*v.t.* *(ȧk-sent')* **1** to stress. **2** to mark with an accent (*defs. 3, 4*).
accent'uate *v.t.* **1** to emphasise. **2** to make more obvious:—*pr.p.* **accent'uating**.
accentuā'tion *n.*

accept *ȧk-sept'*, *v.t.* **1** to take (something offered). **2** to take upon oneself (e.g. responsibility). **3** to acknowledge as true: *I accept your story of what happened.* **4** to agree to. **5** to undertake to pay: *to accept a bill of exchange*.
accept'able *adj.* **1** satisfactory (to someone). **2** pleasing.
accept'ably *adv.*
accept'ance *n.* **1** act of accepting. **2** approval.
acceptā'tion *n.* a meaning, esp. the generally understood meaning of a word, etc.
accept'ed *adj.* generally approved of or believed in.

access *ak'ses*, *n.* **1** a means or right of approach, contact, or use. **2** entrance. **3** an increase. **4** an attack or fit: *an access of rage*.
access'ible *adj.* **1** able to be reached. **2** open or available (to):—*opp.* **inaccessible**.
accessibil'ity *n.*
accession *ȧk-sesh'(ȯ)n*, *n.* **1** a coming into esp. high office, e.g. the position of king or queen: *Charles II's accession to the throne*. **2** an addition: *accessions to the library*.

accessory *ȧk-ses'ȯr-i*, *adj.* **1** additional. **2** (*law*; also **access'ary**) taking part as a helper in a crime.—*n.* **1** anything additional (*esp.* in *pl.*): *her handbag, scarf and other accessories*; *The car was fitted with useful accessories*. **2** (*law*; also **access'ary** *pl.* **-ies**) one who aids a crime:—*pl.* **access'ories**.

accident *ak'si-dėnt*, *n.* **1** an unexpected event. **2** chance. **3** a mishap or disaster.
accident'al *adj.* happening by chance.—*n.* (*music*) a sharp, flat, or natural not in the key signature.
accident'ally *adv.*
chapter of accidents a series of unfortunate happenings.

acclaim *ȧ-klām'*, *v.t.* **1** to applaud. **2** to hail: *He was acclaimed as the finest sprinter of his generation.*—*n.* enthusiastic approval.
acclamā'tion *n.* (a shout of) applause, enthusiastic agreement or approval.

acclimatise *ȧ-klī'mȧ-tīz*, *v.t.* to accustom to a new climate or new surroundings:—*pr.p.* **acclim'atising**.
acclimatisā'tion *n.*

acclivity *ȧ-kliv'i-ti*, *n.* an upward slope:—*pl.* **accliv'ities**.

accolade *ak'ȯ-lād*, *n.* **1** orig. an embrace, now a light touch on each shoulder with the flat of a sword performed in making a man a knight. **2** any recognition of merit.

accommodate *ȧ-kom'ȯd-āt*, *v.t.* **1** to make suitable. **2** to adjust. **3** to supply (with). **4** to oblige. **5** to provide with a place to stay. **6** to find, or be, a place for (something):—*pr.p.* **accomm'odating**.
accomm'odating *adj.* obliging.
accommodā'tion *n.* **1** lodging. **2** room, space (for).

accompany *ȧ-kum'pȧn-i*, *v.t.* **1** to go with. **2** to escort. **3** to exist or occur along with. **4** to perform a musical accompaniment to or for:—*pr.p.* **accom'panying**; *pa.p.* **accom'panied**.
accom'paniment *n.* **1** something that accompanies. **2** music played to support a soloist, etc.
accom'panist *n.* one who plays music for a soloist.

accomplice *ȧ-kum'plis*, or *-kom'-*, *n.* a helper, esp. in crime.

accomplish *ȧ-kum'plish*, or *kom'-*, *v.t.* **1** to finish. **2** to fulfil; to achieve.
accom'plished *adj.* highly skilled.
accom'plishment *n.* **1** finishing, completion. **2** achievement. **3** a special skill.

accord *ȧ-körd'*, *v.i.* to agree (with), be in keeping (with).—*v.t.* to grant, give to (a person).—*n.* agreement.
accord'ance *n.* agreement.
accord'ingly *adv.* therefore.
according to **1** in agreement with: *He acted according to his promise*. **2** as said or told by: *according to the witness*.
of one's own accord without being

prompted to do it by someone else.
with one accord with spontaneous unanimity.

accordion *ȧ-kör'di-ȯn*, *n.* a musical instrument with bellows, keyboard, and metal reeds.
accord'ion-pleat'ing *n.* pleating with very narrow folds.

accost *ȧ-kost'*, *v.t.* to go up to and speak to, esp. in an unfriendly, or a sexually suggestive, way.

account *ȧ-kownt'*, *v.i.* **1** to give a reason (for). **2** to be a reason (for). **3** to deal with, get rid of (with *for*).—*n.* **1** a counting. **2** a statement of money due. **3** (usu. in *pl.*) a record of money received and spent. **4** a person's money, deposited in a bank or post-office, that he can add to or withdraw. **5** an arrangement with a shop, etc., by which one pays a bill e.g. monthly, rather than at the time of purchase. **6** story; report. **7** sake: *on my account* (for my sake, because of me).
account'able *adj.* **1** able to be explained. **2** responsible (*for* something, *to* someone).
account'ant *n.* one who is trained to keep accounts.
account'ancy *n.* the work of an accountant.
bring, call, to account to demand an explanation from.
by all accounts in everyone's opinion.
on account of because of.
on no account not for any reason.
take into account to consider as part of the problem: *I'll take his illness into account when marking his test.*
take (no) account of (not) to take into consideration.
turn to (good) account to turn to one's advantage.

accoutrements *ȧ-ko͞o'tėr-mėnts*, *n.pl.* **1** dress. **2** military equipment.

accredit *ȧ-kred'it*, *v.t.* to give authority to.
accred'ited *adj.* having power to act on behalf of some person or group of persons.

accrue *ȧ-kro͞o'*, *v.i.* **1** to come as a natural result (from). **2** to fall naturally (to a person) as a right:—*pr.p.* **accru'ing**; *pa.p.* **accrued'**.

accumulate *ȧ-kūm'ūl-āt*, *v.t.* to pile up, to amass.—*v.i.* to increase or pile up greatly through time:—*pr.p.* **accum'ulating**.
accumulā'tion *n.* **1** the act of piling up. **2** a mass or pile.
accum'ulative *adj.* heaping up.
accum'ulātor *n.* **1** a thing or person that accumulates. **2** an electric battery that can be recharged by sending a reverse current through it. **3** the part of a computer, etc. that stores numbers.

accurate *ak'ūr-it*, *adj.* **1** exactly right. **2** exact:—*opp.* **inaccurate**.
acc'uracy *n.* **acc'urately** *adv.*

accursed *ȧ-kûrs'id*, *adj.* **1** lying under a curse. **2** doomed. **3** extremely wicked.

accuse *ȧ-kūz'*, *v.t.* to make, or bring, a charge against: *They accused him of stealing*:—*pr.p.* **accus'ing**.
accusā'tion *n.* the charge brought against anyone.
accused *ȧ-kūzd'*, *n.* or *n.pl.* the person(s) accused in a court of law.

accustom *ȧ-kus'tȯm*, *v.t.* to make (someone, oneself) used (to): *I've had to accustom myself to getting up early*.
accus'tomed *adj.* **1** usual. **2** used (to).

ace *ās*, *n.* **1** the one in dice, cards, dominoes, etc. **2** an outstanding expert: *He's an ace with a rifle*; *a flying ace*. **3** in tennis, a serve that cannot be returned.—*adj.* (used only before a noun) expert: *an ace snooker-player*.
within an ace of barely avoiding.

acerbity *ȧ-sûr'bi-ti*, *n.* **1** bitterness, sourness. **2** harshness.

acetic acid *ȧ-sē'tik* (or *-set'-*) *as'id*, vinegar.

acetylene *ȧ-set'i-lēn*, *n.* a gas used for welding, etc., made from water and calcium carbide.

ache *āk*, *n.* a continued pain.—*v.i.* **1** to be in continued pain or continuously painful. **2** to long, pine (for, to do):—*pr.p.* **ach'ing.**
ach'ing *n.* and *adj.*

achieve *ȧ-chēv'*, *v.t.* **1** to carry out, perform. **2** to gain, win:—*pr.p.* **achiev'ing.**
achieve'ment *n.* **1** performance. **2** gaining. **3** a deed to be admired.

acid *as'id*, *adj.* **1** sharp; sour. **2** sarcastic.—*n.* **1** a sour substance. **2** (*chemistry*) a substance that turns blue litmus red, combines with a base to form a salt, etc.
acid'ify *v.t.* and *v.i.* to (cause to) become acid (*def. 1*):—*pr.p.* **acid'ifying**; *pa.p.* **acid'ified.**
acid'ity, ac'idness *ns.*
acid'ulate *v.t.* to make slightly acid:—*pr.p.* **acid'ulating.**
acid rain rain containing sulphur and nitrogen compounds and other pollutants.
acid test **1** a test for gold by acid. **2** a searching test.

acknowledge *ȧk-nol'ij*, *v.t.* **1** to own as true. **2** to confess. **3** to announce receipt of: *to acknowledge a letter*:—*pr.p.* **acknowl'edging.**
acknowl'edg(e)ment *n.* **1** admission.

2 confession. **3** (a sign of) recognition. **4** (an expression of) thanks.

acme *ak'mē, -mi, n.* the top or highest point: *the acme of perfection.*

acne *ak'nē, -ni, n.* a common skin disease with pimples.

acolyte *ak'ȯ-līt, n.* **1** a minor church officer. **2** an attendant; a follower.

acorn *ā'körn, n.* the fruit of the oak.

acoustic *ȧ-kōōs'tik, adj.* (usu. used before a noun) **1** having to do with hearing, or with sound. **2** used in hearing. **3** worked, set off, by sound: *an acoustic mine.* **4** (of musical instruments) not electric: *an acoustic guitar.*

acous'tics *n. pl.* properties (e.g. of a room or hall) which make hearing in it good or bad.—*n.sing.* the science of sound.

acquaint *ȧ-kwānt', v.t.* (with *with*) **1** to make (oneself) familiar with: *New members should acquaint themselves with the club rules.* **2** to inform (a person) about: *Acquaint her with your plans as soon as you can.*

acquaint'ance *n.* **1** (slight) personal knowledge of, familiarity with, someone or something. **2** a person, or the persons, known (slightly) to one.

acquaint'anceship *n.* acquaintance (*def. 1*).

be acquainted 1 to know one another (slightly). **2** (with *with*) to have some personal knowledge of.

acquiesce *ak-wi-es', v.i.* **1** to agree. **2** (with *in*) to accept: *to acquiesce in this plan:*—*pr.p.* **acquiesc'ing.**

acquies'cence *n.* **acquies'cent** *adj.*

acquire *ȧ-kwīr', v.t.* to gain; to get.

acquire'ment *n.* something learned or got by effort.

acquisition *a-kwi-zi'sh(ȯ)n, n.* **1** the act of acquiring. **2** something acquired. **3** a useful gain.

acquis'itive *adj.* eager to get possessions.

acquis'itiveness *n.*

acquit *ȧ-kwit', v.t.* to declare innocent:—*pr.p.* **acquitt'ing**; *pa.p.* **acquitt'ed.**

acquitt'al *n.* a freeing from an accusation.

acquit oneself to conduct oneself, do one's part: *He acquitted himself well in the debate.*

acre *ā'kėr, n.* **1** a measure of land, 4840 sq. yards (0.405 hectare). **2** (in *pl.*) lands, estates.

acreage *ā'kėr-ij, n.* the number of acres in a piece of land.

acrid *ak'rid, adj.* **1** unpleasantly bitter in taste or smell. **2** angry, bitter.

acrid'ity, ac'ridness *ns.*

acrimony *ak'ri-mon-i, n.* bitterness of feeling or speech.

acrimōn'ious *adj.*

acrobat *ak'rō-bat,* or *-rō-, n.* one who performs gymnastic feats.

acrobat'ic *adj.*

acrobat'ics *n.pl.* acrobatic feats.

acronym *ak'rō-nim, n.* a word made from the first letters or syllables of other words e.g. *NATO* is an acronym of *N*orth *A*tlantic *T*reaty *O*rganisation.

across *ȧ-kros', prep.* **1** from side to side of. **2** on, or to, the other side of.—Also *adv.*

acrostic *ȧ-kros'tik, n.* a poem or puzzle in which the first or last letters of each line, taken in order, spell a word or a sentence.

acrylic *ȧ-kril'ik, adj.* (of a material) synthetically produced from **acrylic acid.**—Also *n.*

act *akt, v.i.* **1** to do something. **2** to produce an effect (on). **3** to behave: *If this happened, how would you act?* **4** to perform (e.g. on the stage). **5** to pretend. **6** to serve (as). **7** (with *for*; law, etc.) to represent.—*v.t.* **1** to perform. **2** to imitate or play the part of.—*n.* **1** a deed. **2** the very process (of doing something). **3** a law. **4** a section of a play.

act'ing *n.* **1** action. **2** performing.—*adj.* carrying out the duties of, esp. for a time: *the acting president.*

action *ak'sh(ȯ)n, n.* **1** a deed. **2** operation: *The machine is not in action.* **3** a battle. **4** a gesture. **5** a lawsuit. **6** the events (of a play, etc.). **7** the mechanism (e.g. of a watch).

ac'tionable *adj.* liable to be the subject of a lawsuit.

act'ivate *v.t.* **1** to make active. **2** to make radioactive:—*pr.p.* **act'ivating.**

active *ak'tiv, adj.* **1** energetic; nimble. **2** busy. **3** causing action. **4** in force:—*opp.* **inactive.**

act'ively *adv.* **act'iveness** *n.*

act'ivist *n.* one who believes in strong political action.

activ'ity *n.* **1** activeness. **2** action, motion. **3** occupation:—*pl.* **activ'ities**; *opp.* **inactivity.**

act'or *n.* one who performs in plays, etc.:—*fem.* **act'ress.**

action replay the repeating, often in slow motion, of a piece of television film.

action station a post to be manned

during, or in readiness for, battle or other operation.

actual *ak'tū-ȧl, adj.* **1** real; existing in fact. **2** present, current.
actual'ity *n.* **1** reality. **2** (in *pl.*) present conditions or facts:—*pl.* **actual'ities**.
act'ually *adv.* really; in fact.

actuary *ak'tū-ȧr-i, n.* one who makes the calculations in an insurance office:—*pl.* **act'uaries**.
actuarial *ak-tū-ā'ri-ȧl, adj.*

actuate *ak'tū-āt, v.t.* **1** to put in motion. **2** to move (a person) to a particular action:—*pr.p.* **act'uating**.

acumen *ak'ū-mėn,* or *ȧ-kū', n.* sharpness, quickness of understanding.

acupuncture *ak'ū-punk-chůr, n.* a method of relieving pain, etc. by sticking pins into the patient's skin at various points.

acute *ȧ-kūt', adj.* **1** sharp-pointed. **2** keen: *acute hearing.* **3** shrewd. **4** very great, severe: *acute disappointment.* **5** (of a disease) coming to a crisis rather than lasting.
acute'ly *adv.* **acute'ness** *n.*
acute accent a mark (´) over a vowel.
acute angle an angle less than a right angle.

ad *ad, n.* Short for **advertisement**.

adage *ad'ij, n.* an old saying, proverb.

adamant *ad'ȧ-mȧnt, n.* orig. diamond or other very hard material.—*adj.* refusing to yield.

Adam's apple *ad'ȧmz ap'l, n.* the hard projection in front of the throat.

adapt *ȧ-dapt', v.t.* **1** to make suitable (*for*, e.g. a purpose; *to*, e.g. circumstances). **2** to alter so as to fit new circumstances, environment, etc.—Also *v.i.*
adapt'able *adj.* **1** that may be adapted. **2** (of a person) able and willing to fit in with different circumstances.
adaptabil'ity *n.*
adaptā'tion *n.* **1** the act of adapting. **2** something adapted.
adapt'er, adapt'or *n.* an attachment enabling a piece of apparatus to be put to a new use, or to be fitted to something else when it is not otherwise the right size or shape.

add *ad, v.t.* **1** to put (one thing) to (another). **2** to find the sum of (also *v.i.*). **3** to say further: *He apologised, adding that it would not happen again.*
addi'tion *n.* **1** the act of adding. **2** the thing added.
addi'tional *adj.* **1** that is added. **2** extra.
add'itive *n.* a substance added to food, etc.
adden'dum *n.* something added to e.g. a statement, book:—*pl.* **adden'da**.
add to to increase.
add up 1 to calculate the sum of. **2** to come (to) in total. **3** to make sense.

adder *ad'ėr, n.* a small poisonous snake found wild in Britain, a viper.

addict *ad'ikt, n.* one who is dependent on, finds it impossible to give up, a habit, vice, etc., e.g. drug-taking.
addict'ed *adj.* enslaved to, dependent on (with *to*).
addic'tion *n.*
addict'ive *adj.* inclined to cause dependence.

addition, additive, etc. See **add**.

addle *ad'l, v.t.* **1** to make rotten. **2** to confuse:—*pr.p.* **add'ling**.
add'led *adj.* **1** rotten. **2** confused.

address *ȧ-dres', v.t.* **1** to speak or write to: *Address him by his first name, as George, as 'Doctor'; Address your remarks to the chairman.* **2** to put a name and address on (an envelope, etc.).—*n.* **1** a speech. **2** (*old-fashioned*) manner, bearing. **3** (in *pl.*) (*old-fashioned*) courtship. **4** the number (or name) of the house, the name of the street, town, etc. where one lives, and to which mail is directed.
addressee' *(-ē') n.* the person to whom a letter is addressed.
address oneself to 1 to turn one's energies to. **2** to address (a person).

adduce *ȧ-dūs', v.t.* to quote as proof, evidence or example:—*pr.p.* **adduc'ing**.

adenoids *ad'ėn-oidz, n.pl.* swollen tissue at the back of the nose.

adept *ad'ept, ȧ-dept', adj.* completely skilled.—*n.* an expert.

adequate *ad'i-kwit, adj.* **1** sufficient (for). **2** equal (to a task, etc.). **3** satisfactory:—*opp.* **inadequate**.
ad'equacy *n.*
ad'equately *adv.* **ad'equateness** *n.*

adhere *ȧd-hēr', v.i.* **1** to stick (to). **2** to remain loyal (to):—*pr.p.* **adher'ing**.
adher'ence *n.* steady loyalty.
adher'ent *n.* a follower, supporter.
adhesion *ȧd-hē'zh(ȯ)n, n.* the process or state of sticking.
adhes'ive (*-hēs'-* or *-hēz'-*) *adj.* sticky. —*n.* a substance (e.g. gum, glue) used to make substances stick to each other.

ad hoc *ad hok, adj.* (of a committee or other body) set up for this very purpose.

adieu *ȧ-dū', interj.* farewell.—*n.* a farewell:—*pl.* **adieus** or **adieux** *(ȧ-dūz')*.

ad infinitum *ad in'fin-ī'tům,* for ever.

adipose *ad'i-pōs, adj.* fatty.

adjacent *ȧ-jā'sėnt, adj.* lying next (to).
adjac'ency *n.*

adjective *aj'ik-tiv*, *n*. a word that describes a noun (e.g. a *red* flower; an *upper* room; The air is *cool*).
adjectīv'al *adj*.

adjoin *ȧ-join'*, *v.t.* to lie next to.—*v.i.* to lie side by side, in contact.

adjourn *ȧ-jûrn'*, *v.t.* to discontinue (a meeting) in order to continue it at another time or place.—Also *v.i.*
adjourn'ment *n*.

adjudge *ȧ-juj'*, (esp. *law*) *v.t.* **1** to pronounce; to decide. **2** to award, assign (costs, etc.)

adjudicate *ȧ-jōō'di-kāt*, *v.t.* to give judgment on.—*v.i.* **1** to pronounce judgment. **2** to act as judge in a competition:—*pr.p.* **adju'dicating**.
adjudicā'tion *n*. **adju'dicātor** *n*.

adjunct *a'jungkt*, *n*. a thing joined or added.

adjure *ȧ-jōōr'*, *v.t.* to command solemnly, request earnestly:—*pr.p.* **adjur'ing**.

adjust *ȧ-just'*, *v.t.* **1** to rearrange or alter to suit new circumstances. **2** to regulate (a machine, etc.).—*v.i.* to alter one's behaviour, adapt (to a new environment, etc.).
adjust'able *adj*. **adjust'ment** *n*.

adjutant *a'joo-tȧnt*, *n*. an officer who assists a commanding officer.
adjutancy *a'joo-tȧn-si*, *n*. rank of an adjutant.

ad-lib *ad-lib'*, *v.i.* to say something in a speech, play, etc. without preparation, esp. to fill up time.—Also *v.t.*:—*pr.p.* **ad-libb'ing**; *pa.p.* **ad-libbed'**.—*adv*. (**ad lib**) without limit; freely.—*adj*. and *adv*. (done) without preparation.

administer *ȧd-min'is-tėr*, *v.t.* **1** to govern. **2** to manage. **3** to carry out (the law, justice, etc.). **4** to give (e.g. medicine, a rebuke).
admin'istrate *v.t.* to govern, manage:—*pr.p.* **admin'istrating**.
administrā'tion *n*. **1** the process of administering. **2** (the people responsible for) management or government.
admin'istrative *(-trȧ-) adj*.
admin'istrātor *n*.

admirable, etc. See **admire**.

admiral *ad'mir-ȧl*, *n*. (an officer of) the highest naval rank.
Ad'miralty *n*. the government office that manages the navy and its business.

admire *ȧd-mīr'*, *v.t.* **1** to have a high opinion of. **2** to look at with approval:—*pr.p.* **admir'ing**.
ad'mirable *(-mir-) adj*. **1** worthy of approval. **2** extremely good.
ad'mirably *adv*. extremely well.
admirā'tion *(-mir-) n*.
admir'er *n*. **1** one who admires someone or something. **2** a lover or suitor.
admir'ing *adj*. **admir'ingly** *adv*.

admission. See **admit**.

admit *ȧd-mit'*, *v.t.* **1** to allow to enter. **2** to have room for. **3** to acknowledge, confess.—*v.i.* to allow (with *of*): *This admits of no other explanation*:—*pr.p.* **admitt'ing**; *pa.p.* **admitt'ed**.
admiss'ible (esp. *law*) *adj*. allowable:—*opp*. **inadmissible**.
admiss'ion *n*. **1** the act of admitting. **2** admittance. **3** something confessed or acknowledged.
admitt'ance *n*. the right to enter.
admitt'edly *adv*. unquestionably.

admixture *ȧd-miks'chůr*, *n*. (the act of mixing in) an additional ingredient.

admonish *ȧd-mon'ish*, *v.t.* **1** to reprove. **2** to warn.
admoni'tion *n*. **1** reproof. **2** warning.
admon'itory *adj*.

ad nauseam *ad nö'si-ȧm, adv* excessively.

ado *ȧ-dōō'*, *n*. trouble, fuss:—*pl*. **ados'**.

adobe *ȧ-dō'bi*, *n*. **1** a sun-dried brick. **2** a house made of such bricks.

adolescent *ad-ȯ-les'ėnt*, *adj*. growing out of childhood, becoming adult.—*n*. a person at this stage of life.
adoles'cence *n*. the period between childhood and maturity.

adopt *ȧ-dopt'*, *v.t.* **1** to take (a child of other parents) as one's own. **2** to take up (e.g. an opinion, a habit). **3** to choose. **4** to approve.
adop'tion *n*.
adop'tive *adj*. by adoption: *his adoptive father.*

adore *ȧ-dōr'*, *-dör'*, *v.t.* **1** to love intensely. **2** to worship:—*pr.p.* **ador'ing**.
ador'able *adj*. worthy of being adored.
adorā'tion *n*. **1** great love. **2** worship.
ador'er *n*.
ador'ing *adj*. **ador'ingly** *adv*.

adorn *ȧ-dörn'*, *v.t.* to deck, make beautiful.
adorn'ment *n*. decoration; ornament.

adrenaline *ȧ-dren'ȧ-lin*, *n*. a hormone produced in response to fear, anger, etc., preparing the body for quick action.

adrift *a-drift'*, *adj*. (not used before a noun) and *adv*. drifting, floating.

adroit *ȧ-droit'*, *adj*. skilful.
adroit'ly *adv*. **adroit'ness** *n*.

adulation *ad-ū-lā'sh(ȯ)n*, *n*. excessive praise.
ad'ulātory *adj*.

adult *ad'ult*, *ȧ-dult'*, *adj*. **1** fully grown. **2** mature.—*n*. a grown-up person.

adulterate *ȧ-dul'tėr-āt*, *v.t.* to make impure by mixing in something else:—*pr.p.* **adult'erating**.
adulterā'tion *n.*

adultery *ȧ-dul'tėr-i*, *n.* sexual intercourse between a husband and a woman who is not his wife, or between a wife and a man who is not her husband.
adul'terer *n.*:—*fem.* **adul'teress**.
adul'terous *adj.*

advance *ȧd-väns'*, *v.t.* **1** to propose, suggest, put forward. **2** to promote. **3** to encourage the progress of. **4** to supply or pay beforehand. **5** to make earlier (the time of an appointment, etc.).—*v.i.* **1** to go forward. **2** to make progress:—*pr.p.* **advanc'ing.**—*n.* **1** progress. **2** improvement. **3** a loan. **4** (often in *pl.*) an approach towards friendship, etc.—*adj.* (used only before a noun) **1** made or given before due. **2** (of e.g. military force) sent forward in front of main force.
advanced' *adj.* far on in development or progress.
advance'ment *n.* **1** progress. **2** promotion.
in advance 1 beforehand. **2** before due.
in advance of 1 before. **2** farther forward than.

advantage *ȧd-vän'tij*, *n.* **1** superiority over another. **2** gain, benefit. **3** (*lawn tennis*) the first point gained after deuce.—*v.t.* to benefit, profit:—*pr.p.* **advan'taging**.
advanta'geous *(-tā'jŭs) adj.*
advantā'geously *adv.*
take advantage of 1 to use the opportunity given by (a happening or condition). **2** to use (e.g. a person) unfairly for one's own ends.
to advantage 1 in a way that shows the good qualities clearly. **2** in a way that brings profit.
See also **disadvantage**.

advent *ad'vent*, *n.* **1** coming, or arrival. **2** (*cap.*) a period of preparation for the nativity of Christ, including four Sundays before Christmas.
adventi'tious *adj.* accidental.

adventure *ȧd-ven'chŭr*, *n.* **1** a strange or exciting experience. **2** excitement, risk.
adven'turer *n.* **1** one who seeks adventure. **2** one who seeks his fortune by discreditable means:—*fem.* **adven'turess**.
adven'turous *adj.*
adven'turously *adv.*

adverb *ad'vûrb*, *n.* a word added to a verb, adjective, or other adverb to show time, manner, place, degree, etc. (e.g. *Yesterday* he looked *more carefully* in the drawer, and *there* he found the *very* small key).
adver'bial *adj.* **adver'bially** *adv.*

adversary *ad'vėr-sȧr-i*, *n.* **1** an opponent. **2** an enemy:—*pl.* **ad'versaries**.

ad'verse *ad'vûrs*, *adj.* **1** acting against one: *adverse winds, circumstances.* **2** expressing disapproval: *adverse criticism.*
ad'versely (or *vûrs'*) *adv.*
adver'sity *n.* misfortune (*pl.* **-ies**).

advert[1] *ȧd-vûrt'*, *v.i.* to refer (to).

advert[2] *ad'vûrt*, *n.* short for **advertisement**.

advertise *ad'vėr-tīz*, or *-tīz'*, *v.t.* **1** to make known publicly. **2** to draw attention to the merits of.—*v.i.* to issue a public notice, esp. a request (for):—*pr.p.* **ad'vertising**.
advert'isement *(-ûr'tiz-,-ûr'tis-) n.*
advertis'er *(-tīz'-) n.*

advice *ȧd-vīs'*, *n.* **1** recommendation to a person about what he should do. **2** a formal notice.
advis'able *(-vīz'-) adj.* (of action) wise:—*opp.* **inadvisable**.
advisabil'ity *n.*
advise *ȧd-vīz'*, *v.t.* **1** to give advice to. **2** to recommend: *I advised her to buy it; Do you advise buying now?* **3** to inform (usu. with *of*):—*pr.p.* **advis'ing**.
advis'edly *(-id-li) adv.* after careful consideration.
advis'er *n.* one who advises.
advis'ory *adj.*

advocate *ad'vȯ-kit*, *-kāt*, *n.* **1** one who pleads the cause of another, esp. in a court of law in Scotland. **2** a supporter: *an advocate of reform.* **3** (*cap.*) the Holy Spirit.—*v.t.* *(-kāt)* to plead in favour of, recommend:—*pr.p.* **ad'vocating**.
advocacy *ad'vȯ-kȧ-si*, *n.* **1** the work or part of an advocate. **2** pleading for something; recommendation.

adze *adz*, *n.* a carpenter's tool with a thin arched blade with its edge at right angles to the handle.

aegis *ē'jis*, *n.* **1** protection. **2** patronage.

aeon, eon *ē'ȯn*, *n.* **1** an age. **2** a very long time.

aerate *ā'ėr-āt*, *ār'-*, *v.t.* to put air, or a gas, into:—*pr.p* **aer'ating**.

aerial *ā'ėr-i-ȧl*, *ār'-*, *adj.* of, in, or from, the air.—*n.* a wire or rod (or set of these) able to send or receive radio waves, etc.

aerie *ā'ėr-i*, *ār'-*, *ī'ri*, *n.* the nest of any bird of prey, esp. of an eagle.—Also **aery**, **eyrie, eyry**.

aero- *ā-ėr-ō*, *ār-*, (as part of a word) air.
aerobatics *ā-ėr-ō-bat'iks*, *ār-*, *n.sing.* the art of performing stunts in an aircraft.—*n.pl.* such stunts.
aerobic *ā-ėr-ō'bik*, *ār-*, *adj.* (of an or-

ganism) requiring oxygen from the air for life.

aerō'bics (also **Aerobics®**) *n.sing.* a system of rhythmic exercise aimed at increasing the body's oxygen consumption.

aerodrome *ā'ėr-ō-drōm*, *ār'-*, *n.* a landing and maintenance station for aircraft.

aerodynamics *ā-ėr-ō-dī-nam'iks*, *ār-*, *n.sing.* the study of forces acting on bodies in motion in air.

aerodynam'ic *adj.*

aerofoil *ā'ėr-ō-foil*, *ār'-*, *n.* an air-resisting surface—wing, plane, aileron, etc.

aerogramme, **aerogram** *ā'ėrō-gram*, *ns.* an airmail letter, designed to be folded, sealed and sent without an envelope.

aeronaut'ics *n.sing.* the science or art of navigation in the air.

aeroplane *ā'ėr-ō-plān*, *ār'-*, *n.* a flying machine, heavier than air, with planes or wings.

aerosol *ā'ėr-ō-sol*, *ār'-*, *n.* **1** a liquid, e.g. an insecticide, in a container under pressure. **2** the container.

aerospace *ā'ėr-ō-spās*, *ār'*, *n.* (the science of flight through) the earth's atmosphere and the space beyond.

aery. See **aerie**.

aesthete *ēs'thēt*, or *es'-*, *n.* one who has a great love of beauty and the arts.

aesthet'ic *(-thet') adj.* **1** of beauty or good taste. **2** beautiful, tasteful.

aesthet'ically *adv.*

aesthetics *es-thet'iks*, or *ēs-*, *n.sing.* the study or principles of the fine arts.

afar *ȧ-fä'*, *adv.* from, at, or to, a distance—usu. **from afar**, **afar off**.

affable *af'ȧ-bl*, *adj.* **1** easy to talk to. **2** cheerful and pleasant.

affabil'ity *n.* **aff'ably** *adv.*

affair *ȧ-fār'*, *n.* **1** business, concern: *What she does is her own affair.* **2** (in *pl.*) business dealings. **3** a love affair. **4** a thing; an occurrence.

affect¹ *ȧ-fekt'*, *v.t.* **1** to act upon. **2** to change. **3** to move the feelings of: *He was deeply affected by the story.*

affect'ing *adj.* having power to move the feelings: *an affecting performance.*

affect² *ȧ-fekt'*, *v.t.* **1** to make a pretence of: *He affected grief.* **2** to adopt deliberately: *She affects a flamboyant style of dress.*

affectā'tion *n.* insincere or unnatural behaviour; pretence.

affect'ed *adj.* **1** inclined to behave unnaturally so as to impress. **2** sham.

affection *ȧ-fek'sh(ȯ)n*, *n.* **1** love, friendship. **2** (*old-fashioned*) a disease.

affec'tionate *adj.* loving.

affec'tionately *adv.*

affiance *ȧ-fī'ȧns*, *v.t.* to betroth:—*pr.* p. **affī'ancing**.

affidavit *af-i-dā'vit*, *n.* a written declaration on oath.

affiliate *ȧ-fil'i-āt*, *v.t.* to attach (to), connect (with), as a minor college to a university:—*pr.* p. **affil'iating**.

affiliā'tion *n.*

affinity *ȧ-fin'i-ti*, *n.* **1** relationship by marriage. **2** close relationship. **3** similarity, likeness. **4** attraction, liking:—*pl.* **affin'ities**.

affirm *ȧ-fûrm'*, *v.t.* to state positively.

affirmā'tion *n.*

affirm'ative *adj.* **1** affirming. **2** saying yes. **3** not negative.—Also *n.*

affirm'atively *adv.*

affix *ȧ-fiks'*, *v.t.* to attach (with *to, on, upon*).—*n. (af'iks)* a prefix or suffix.

afflict *ȧ-flikt'*, *v.t.* to give continued pain or distress to.

afflic'tion *n.* **1** (a cause of) distress. **2** an ailment.

affluent *af'lōō-ėnt*, *adj.* wealthy.—*n.* a stream flowing into a river or lake.

aff'luence *n.* wealth.

afford *ȧ-fōrd*, *-förd'*, *v.t.* **1** to yield, produce. **2** (with *can*) to bear the expense or risk of: *Can we afford a new car?*; *We cannot afford to miss this chance.*

afforest *a-for'ist*, *v.t.* to turn into forest by planting young trees.

afforestā'tion *n.*

affray *ȧ-frā'*, *n.* a fight; a brawl.

affright *ȧ-frīt'*, *v.t.* to frighten.

affront *ȧ-frunt'*, *v.t.* to insult openly.—*n.* an insult.

afield *ȧ-fēld'*, *adv.* out, abroad.

far afield a long way from home.

aflame *ȧ-flām'*, *adv.*, *adj.* (not used before noun) **1** flaming. **2** glowing.

afloat *ȧ-flōt'*, *adv.*, *adj.* (not used before a noun) **1** floating. **2** at sea. **3** free from debt: *A loan would keep the company afloat.*

afoot *ȧ-foot'*, *adv.*, *adj.* (not used before a noun) **1** astir. **2** in progress.

aforesaid *ȧ-fōr'sed*, or *-för'*, **aforementioned** *-men'sh(ȯ)nd*, *adjs.* said or named before.

afraid *ȧ-frād'*, *adj.* (not used before a noun) **1** struck with fear. **2** frightened (of). **3** unwillingly inclined to think (that).

afresh *ȧ-fresh'*, *adv.* anew, again.

Afrikaner *af-ri-kän'ėr*, earlier **Afrikan'der** *ns.* one born in South Africa of white parents (esp. of Dutch descent).

Afrikaans *af-ri-käns'*, *n.* one of the two

official languages of S. Africa, developed from 17th cent. Dutch.

Afro-Asian *af'rō-ā'zhyȧn, -sh(i-)ȧn, -shyȧn, adj.* **1** of, consisting of, Africans and Asians. **2** of Asian origin but African citizenship. **3** of mixed Asian and African blood.

aft *äft, adj.* and *adv.* **1** behind. **2** near or towards the stern of a vessel.

after *äf'tėr, prep.* and *adv.* **1** behind in place. **2** later (than).—*prep.* **1** following, in search of. **2** in imitation of. **3** according to.—*adj.* (used only before a noun) **1** behind in place. **2** later in time. **3** more toward the stern of a vessel.

af'tercare *n.* care given to someone after a period of treatment.

af'ter-effect *n.* an effect that comes after an interval or when the first effect has passed.

af'ter-life *n.* a life after death.

af'termath *n.* later consequences (esp. if bad).

afternoon' *n.* the time between noon and evening (*adj.*, *äf'*).

af'tershave *n.* a lotion used on the face after shaving.

af'terthought *n.* a later thought, or the action resulting from it.

af'terwards *adv.* later.

after all **1** in spite of everything: *after all, she's still young*. **2** everything considered.

again *ȧ-gen', ȧ-gān', adv.* **1** once more. **2** in addition. **3** moreover. **4** (*old*) back, in return.

against *ȧ-genst', ȧ-gānst', prep.* **1** in the opposite direction to. **2** in opposition to. **3** in contact or in collision with.

agate *ag'ėt, n.* precious stone formed of layers of quartz of various tints.

agave *ȧ-gā'vi, n.* an American aloe-like plant, a source of sisal.

age *āj, n.* **1** the time during which a person or thing has lived or existed. **2** later years of life. **3** a period in the development of the earth or man: *another ice age; the Bronze Age*. **4** (*coll.*) a long time (often in *pl.*).—*v.i.* to grow old.—*v.t.* to make old:—*pr.p.* **ag'ing** or **age'ing**; *pa.p.* **aged** *(ājd)*.

aged *ā'jid, adj.* **1** advanced in age. **2** *(ājd)* of the age of.—*n.pl.* *(ā'jid)* old people.

age'less *adj.* never growing old.

of age aged 18 or over.

agency. See **agent**.

agenda *ȧ-jen'dȧ, n.* (a list of) things to be discussed, etc., at a meeting, etc.

agent *ā'jėnt, n.* **1** one authorised to transact business for another. **2** the person or thing that is active in producing a result: *Petroleum can be used as a cleaning agent*.

a'gency *n.* the office or business of an agent:—*pl.* **a'gencies**.

by, through, the agency of by the action of.

agglomeration *ȧ-glom-ėr-ā'sh(ȯ)n, n.* a heap, mass.

aggrandise *ȧ-gran'dīz,* or *ag'-, v.t.* to make greater in power, rank, etc:—*pr.p.* **aggrand'ising**.

aggrandisement *ȧ-gran'diz-mėnt, n.*

aggravate *ag'rȧ-vāt, v.t.* **1** to make worse. **2** to provoke, irritate:—*pr.p.* **agg'ravating**.

agg'ravāting *adj.* **aggravā'tion** *n.*

aggregate *ag'ri-gāt, v.t.* and *v.i.* to collect into a mass; to accumulate.—*v.t.* (*coll.*) to amount to:—*pr.p.* **agg'regating**.—*adj.* *(-it, -āt)* formed of parts collected in a mass.—*n.* **1** the sum total. **2** a mass consisting of rock fragments. **3** any material added to cement to make concrete.

aggregā'tion *n.*

in the aggregate considered as a whole.

aggression *ȧ-gresh'(ȯ)n, n.* **1** first act of hostility. **2** hostile behaviour.

aggress'ive *adj.* inclined to attack first, quarrelsome.

aggress'ively *adv.* **aggress'iveness** *n.*

aggress'or *n.*

aggrieved *ȧ-grēvd', adj.* (unhappy because) unjustly treated.

aggro *ag'rō,* (*slang*) *n.* hostility, violence, between groups, gangs, etc.

aghast *ȧ-gäst', adj.* stunned with horror.

agile *aj'īl,* (*U.S.*) *aj'il, adj.* active, nimble.

agility *ȧ-jil'i-ti, n.* nimbleness.

aging. See **age**.

agitate *aj'i-tāt, v.t.* **1** to shake; to stir violently. **2** to disturb, excite.—*v.i.* to stir up public feeling (for): *to agitate for reform of the law*:—*pr.p.* **ag'itating**.

ag'itated *adj.* anxious, excited.

agitā'tion *n.* **1** disturbance. **2** excitement. **3** stirring up of public feeling.

ag'itator *n.*

aglow *ȧ-glō', adv., adj.* (not used before a noun) bright, glowing, with colour or warmth.

agnostic *ag-nos'tik, ȧg-, n.* one who holds that we know (and can know) nothing of God, or of anything beyond the material world.

agnosticism *ag-nos'ti-sizm, ȧg-, n.*

ago *ȧ-gō', adv.* (a certain length of time) into the past.

agog *ȧ-gog'*, *adv.*, *adj.* (not used before a noun) eager; excited.

agony *ag'ȯ-ni*, *n.* extreme suffering:—*pl.* **ag'onies**.

ag'onise *v.i.* to struggle mentally, worry unduly: *to agonise over a problem*:—*pr.p.* **ag'onising**.

ag'onised *adj.* registering extreme pain: *an agonised cry*.

ag'onising (or *-īz'-*) *adj.* extremely painful.

agrarian *ȧ-grā'ri-ȧn*, *adj.* relating to land, or its management.

agree *ȧ-grē'*, *v.i.* **1** to get on with one another. **2** to come to a decision that both or all accept. **3** to think the same as (with *with*). **4** to consent (to). **5** to suit (with *with*): *Heat does not agree with him*:—*pr.p.* **agree'ing**; *pa.p* **agreed'**.

agree'able *adj.* **1** pleasant. **2** pleasing (to). **3** in favour of (with *to*). **4** willing.

agree'ableness *n.* **agree'ably** *adv.*

agreed' *adj.* agreed upon: *an agreed syllabus*.

agree'ment *n.* **1** state of agreeing. **2** a bargain or contract.

agriculture *ag'ri-kul-chu̇r*, *n.* the cultivation of land.

agricul'tural *adj.*

agricul'turalist *n.* one who is an expert in agriculture.

aground *ȧ-grownd'*, *adv.*, *adj.* (not used before a noun) (of ships) (stuck) on the sea-bed, etc., in shallow water.

ague *ā'gū*, *n.* **1** a fever coming in fits. **2** a fit of shivering.

ahead *ȧ-hed'*, *adv.* **1** farther on. **2** in advance (of). **3** on, onward.

ahoy *ȧ-hoi'*, *interj.* a call used in hailing at sea.

aid *ād*, *v.t.* to help, assist.—*n.* **1** help. **2** anything that helps. **3** a helper.

aid and abet (*law*) to assist and encourage (an illegal act).

aide *ād*, *n.* a confidential assistant to a person of senior rank.

aide-de-camp *ād'dė-kon^g*, *n.* an officer attending a general, king, governor, etc.:—*pl.* **aides'-de-camp** *(ād')*.

AIDS *ādz*, *n.* acquired immune deficiency syndrome.

ail *āl*, *v.i.* to be ill.

ail'ment *n.* an illness, discomfort.

What ails you? What is the matter?

aileron *ā'lėr-on*, *el'ėr-on^g*, *n.* a flap at the rear of aeroplane wings.

aim *ām*, *v.i.* **1** to try to hit (with *at*). **2** to try to (with *at*): *to aim at increasing output*. —*v.t.* **1** to point, throw, etc. (at). **2** to purpose, try (to do).—*n.* **1** act of, or skill in, aiming. **2** a purpose, object, intention.

aim'less *adj.* without purpose.

aim'lessly *adv.* **aim'lessness** *n.*

take aim to direct a gun or missile at an object.

ain't *ānt*, (*coll.*) contracted form of *are not, am not* or *is not*; also *has not, have not*.

air *ār*, *n.* **1** the mixture of gases we breathe, the atmosphere. **2** the space overhead. **3** an appearance, look: *The house had an air of neglect*. **4** a melody. **5** (in *pl.*) affectation.—*v.t.* **1** to expose to the air so as to freshen or dry. **2** to express, esp. insistently: *to air one's opinions*.

air'y *adj.* **1** well supplied with fresh air. **2** light, or otherwise like air. **3** light-hearted, flippant. **4** fanciful:—*comp.* **air'-ier**; *superl.* **air'iest**.

air'ily *adv.* **air'iness** *n.*

air'ing *n.* **1** exposure to air or heat. **2** a short walk, etc., in the open air.

air'less *adj.* **1** still, windless. **2** stuffy.

air arm the branch of the fighting services that uses aircraft.

air bag a bag that inflates automatically in a collision to protect the occupants of a car.

air'-bed *n.* an inflatable mattress.

air'borne *adj.* **1** transported by air. **2** in the air, off the ground.

air'-condi'tioning *n.* (apparatus for) cleaning, and controlling the temperature of, the air in a building, etc.

air corridor the route through the air to which a pilot must confine himself.

air'craft *n.* any machine for flying in the air:—*pl.* **air'craft**.

aircraft carrier a ship from which aircraft can take off and on which they may alight.

air'-cushion *n.* an inflatable cushion.

air'field *n.* an area, usu. with hangars, etc., where (esp. military) aircraft can land and take off.

air force a force organised for war in the air.

air'gun *n.* a gun that discharges missiles by means of compressed air.

air hostess a stewardess who looks after aircraft passengers.

air lift a transport operation carried out by air.

air line (a company that owns) a regular air transport service.

air'liner *n.* a large passenger-aircraft.

air'-lock *n.* **1** a small chamber in which pressure of air can be raised or lowered. **2** a bubble in a pipe interfering with flow of liquid.

air mail **1** the system of carrying mail by air. **2** mail carried by air.

air'man *n.* an aviator, flyer.
air'plane *n.* (*U.S.*) an aeroplane.
air pocket a region of thinner air, in which aircraft drop.
air'port *n.* an aerodrome where commercial aircraft arrive and depart.
air raid a raid by enemy aircraft.
air'-screw *n.* the propeller of an aircraft.
air'-sea rescue the combined use of aircraft and high-speed launches in sea rescue.
air'ship *n.* a lighter-than-air craft.
air'strip *n.* a strip of ground used as a (temporary) runway.
air'tight *adj.* so tight as not to admit air.
air'way *n.* **1** a passage for air, e.g. into the lungs. **2** a regular route for air travel.
air'worthy *adj.* in a condition for safe flying:—*comp.* **air'worthier**; *superl.* **air'worthiest.**
in the air **1** vague: *Our plans are still in the air.* **2** being generally considered, talked about as possible: *Prison reform is in the air.*
off, on, the air (not) being broadcast by radio.

aisle *īl, n.* **1** a passage between rows of seats in a cinema, church, etc. **2** in a church, a part divided off, usu. by pillars, from the nave, choir or transept.

aitchbone *āch'bōn, n.* **1** the bone of the rump. **2** the cut of beef over this bone.

ajar *ȧ-jä', adv.* partly open.

akimbo *ȧ-kim'bō, adv.* or *adj.* (not used before a noun) with hand on hip and elbow bent outward.

akin *ȧ-kin', adj.* **1** related by blood. **2** similar in nature.

alabaster *al'ȧ-bäs-tėr,* or *-bäs'-, n.* a whitish, translucent material easily carved, used for ornamental objects.

à la carte *ä lä kät',* according to the bill of fare—each dish chosen and priced separately.

alacrity *ȧ-lak'ri-ti, n.* briskness, cheerful readiness.

à la mode *ä lä mōd',* according to the fashion.

alarm *ȧ-läm', n.* **1** warning of danger: *to sound, raise, the alarm.* **2** sudden fear. **3** a contrivance to rouse from sleep or to attract attention: *alarm-clock, fire-alarm.*—*v.t.* to fill with fear.
alarm'ing *adj.* **alarm'ingly** *adv.*
alarm'ist *n.* one who is too much inclined to expect trouble.

alas *ȧ-las', interj.* exclamation of grief.

alb *alb, n.* in R.C. churches, a white linen vestment reaching to the feet.

albatross *al'bȧ-tros, n.* a large, web-footed sea bird of the Southern Ocean.

albino *al-bē'nō, n.* a person or animal whose skin and hair are white, because of a lack of colouring pigment:—*pl.* **albi'nos.**

album *al'bum, n.* **1** a blank book for photographs, autographs, etc. **2** a long-playing record or a set of these.

albumen *al-bū'min,* or *al'-, n.* white of egg.
albū'minous *adj.*

alchemy *al'ki-mi, n.* (*history*) the early stage of chemistry, its chief aims being to change other metals into gold, and to discover the elixir (see this word) of life.
al'chemist *n.* one who studies alchemy.

alcohol *al'kȯ-hol, n.* an intoxicating liquid made by the fermentation of sugar, etc.
alcohol'ic *adj.* of, like, containing, caused by, alcohol.—*n.* a person who has a craving for alcohol and drinks too much.
al'coholism *n.* **1** the condition of an alcoholic. **2** alcoholic poisoning.

alcove *al'kōv, n.* a recess.

alder *öl'dėr, n.* a tree related to the birch, usu. growing in moist ground.

alderman *öl'dėr-mȧn, n.* in English boroughs, an official next in rank to the mayor.

ale *āl, n.* **1** another name for beer. **2** the name given to beer produced by a particular fermentation process.
ale'house *n.* a place where ale is sold.

alert *ȧ-lûrt', adj.* **1** watchful. **2** brisk.—*n.* a warning of danger.—*v.t.* to warn to be ready.
alert'ly *adv.* **alert'ness** *n.*
on the alert on the watch (for).

alfalfa *al-fal'fȧ, n.* lucerne.

alfresco *al-fres'kō, adv.* and *adj.*, in the fresh or cool air.

alga *al'gȧ, n.* a seaweed or related plant:—*pl.* **algae** (*al'jē* or *-gē*).

algebra *al'ji-brȧ, n.* a method of calculation using letters to represent numbers.
algebrā'ic, -al *adjs.*

algorithm *al'gȯ-ri*TH*m, n.* (*computers*) a set of procedures for making a calculation.

alias *ā'li-ȧs, n.* an assumed name:—*pl.* **a'liases.**—*adv.* also known as.

alibi *al'i-bī, n.* **1** a plea that a person charged with a crime was elsewhere when it was committed. **2** (*coll.*) an excuse.

alien *āl'yėn,* or *ā'li-ėn, adj.* **1** foreign. **2** contrary (to): *Unkindness was alien to his gentle nature.*—*n.* **1** a foreigner. **2** one of foreign birth who has not been naturalised.

alienate *āl'yėn-āt*, *ā'li-ėn-āt*, *v.t.* **1** to make (a person) feel unfriendly to one. **2** to turn (a person's affections) away from another person, etc.:—*pr.p.* **ā'lienating**.

alienā'tion *n.*

alight[1] *ȧ-līt'*, *v.i.* **1** to come down from a horse, out of a vehicle, etc. **2** to land, settle (on, upon):—*pa.p.* **alight'ed**.

alight[2] *ȧ-līt'*, *adv.*, *adj.* (not used before a noun) on fire.

align *ȧ-līn'*, *v.t.* **1** to bring into line. **2** (with *oneself*) to take a side in an agreement, politics, etc.: *to align oneself with the rebels*.

align'ment *n.*

alike *ȧ-līk'*, *adj.* (not used before a noun) like, having resemblance.—*adv.* in the same manner: *He treated all his children alike*.

aliment *al'i-mėnt*, *n.* food.

alimen'tary *adj.*

alimentary canal the passage for food in animals, including the gullet, stomach, intestines, etc.

alimony *al'i-mȯ-ni*, *n.* an allowance paid by a husband to his wife, or by a wife to her husband, to provide support, when they are legally separated.

alive *ȧ-līv'*, *adj.* **1** (not used before a noun) living, not dead: *Victoria was still alive in 1900*. **2** brisk. **3** alert. **4** busy, crowded (with).

alive to conscious of: *He was alive to the dangers of the situation*.

alkali *al'kȧ-lī*, *n.* a soluble salt with basic (see **base**[1]) qualities:—*pl.* **al'kali(e)s**.

alkaline *al'kȧ-līn*, or *-lin*, *adj.*

all *öl*, *adj.* **1** the whole of. **2** every one of.—*adv.* **1** wholly. **2** completely: *all-powerful*. **3** entirely.—*pron.* **1** the whole. **2** everything.

all'-clear' *n.* a signal that danger is over.

All-Hall'ow(s) *(-hal'o(z))* *n.*(*sing.*) All Saints' Day.

all'-round' *adj.* (good) in all aspects: *an all-round sportsman*.

all at once suddenly.

all but very nearly.

All Fools' Day April 1.

all in **1** everything included (*adj.* **all'-in'**). **2** (*coll.*) exhausted.

all in all considering everything.

all right **1** yes, agreed. **2** safe and sound. **3** good enough.

All Saints' Day November 1.

All Souls' Day November 2.

all there mentally sound or alert.

all up at an end, with no further hope.

at all in the least degree.

for good and all finally.

in all in total.

allay *ȧ-lā*, *v.t.* to make less, relieve: *to allay someone's fears*:—*pa.p.* **allayed'**.

allege *ȧ-lej'*, *v.t.* to assert without proof:—*pr.p.* **alleg'ing**.

allegation *a-lė-gā'sh(ȯ)n*, *n.*

allegiance *ȧ-lē'jȧns*, *n.* **1** the duty of a subject to his sovereign. **2** loyalty.

allegory *al'ė-gor-i*, *n.* a story with a second or hidden meaning:—*pl.* **all'egȯries**.

allegor'ical *adj.* **allegor'ically** *adv.*

allegro *a-lā'grō*, or *-leg'-*, *adv.*, *adj.* (*music*) brisk(ly), rapid(ly).—Also *n.* (pl. **-os**).

alleluia(h) *al-i-lōō'yä*, *interj.* and *n.* same as **halleluiah**.

allergy *al'ėr-ji*, *n.* **1** abnormal sensitiveness of the body to substances usu. harmless. **2** (*coll.*) dislike:—*pl.* **all'ergies**.

aller'gic *adj.* (with *to*) **1** affected in a bad way by (certain substances). **2** (*coll.*) feeling dislike towards.

alleviate *ȧ-lē'vi-āt*, *v.t.* to make lighter, lessen (e.g. pain):—*pr.p.* **allē'viating**.

alleviā'tion *n.*

alley *al'i*, *n.* **1** a walk in a garden between hedges. **2** a narrow passage in a city. **3** an enclosure for skittles, etc.:—*pl.* **all'eys**.

alliance, **allied**, **allies**. See **ally**.

alligator *al'i-gā'tȯr*, *n.* a reptile of the crocodile group found mainly in America.

alliteration *ȧ-lit-ėr-ā'sh(ȯ)n*, *n.* the repeating of the same *sound* (not necessarily the same *letter*) at the beginning of two or more words in close succession, as '*s*even *g*rave and *s*tately *c*edars'.

allit'erāte *v.i.*:—*pr.p.* **allit'erating**.

allit'erative *adj.*

allocate *al'ȯ-kāt*, *v.t.* **1** to give as a share (to). **2** to set apart (for a purpose):—*pr.p.* **all'ocating.**

allocā'tion *n.*

allot *ȧ-lot'*, *v.t.* **1** to distribute in portions. **2** to give to (someone) as his share:—*pr.p.* **allott'ing**; *pa.p.* **allott'ed**.

allot'ment *n.* **1** the act of allotting. **2** a share. **3** a piece of ground let out for spare-time cultivation.

allow *ȧ-low'*, *v.t.* **1** to permit: *Smoking is not allowed*; *I allowed him to go*. **2** to admit: *We must allow that he was under stress*. **3** to give (a person a sum of money) esp. at regular intervals. **4** to add or deduct in estimating.—*v.i.* **1** to permit, admit (of): *His silence allows of only one explanation*. **2** to take into consideration when planning, judging, etc. (with *for*): *to allow for emer-*

gencies, for someone's youth.

allow'able *adj.*

allow'ance *n.* a fixed sum given or quantity allowed.

make allowance for to allow for.

make allowances for to be lenient towards, judge kindly.

See also **disallow**.

alloy *à-loi'*, *v.t.* **1** to mix (one metal) with another. **2** to make less perfect: *There is always something to alloy one's pleasure*: —*pa.p.* **alloyed** *(à-loid').*—*n.* *(al'oi)* **1** a mixture of two or more metals. **2** anything that makes quality poorer.

allspice *öl'spīs*, *n.* the (powdered) berries of a West Indian species of myrtle, used as a spice.

allude *à-lūd'*, or *-lo͞od'*, *v.i.* to refer (to) indirectly or in passing: *He alluded to my previous statements*; *That remark of his alludes to my previous statement*:—*pr.p.* **allud'ing**.

allu'sion *n.* (an) indirect reference.

allu'sive *(-siv) adj.* **1** containing an allusion. **2** full of allusions.

allure *à-lūr'*, or *-lo͞or'*, *v.t.* to draw on by, or as if by, a lure (see this word):—*pr.p.* **allur'ing**.—*n.* ability to charm.

allure'ment *n.* **1** fascination, charm. **2** the act of alluring. **3** something serving to tempt or encourage.

allur'ing *adj.* **allur'ingly** *adv.*

allusion, allusive. See **allude**.

alluvium *à-lū'vi-ùm*, or *-lo͞o'-*, *n.* earth, sand, gravel, etc., carried along by rivers and deposited on lower lands:—*pl.* **allu'via**.

allu'vial *adj.*

ally *à-lī'*, *v.t.* to join by marriage, friendship treaty, etc:—*pr.p.* **ally'ing**; *pa.p.* **allied'**. —*n.* *(al'ī)* **1** a state, etc., united by treaty. **2** a helper or loyal friend:—*pl.* **all'ies** *(-īz)*.

allī'ance *n.* union by treaty, etc.

allied *al'īd* or *à-līd'*, *adj.* **1** joined by treaty. **2** related.

Alma Mater *al'mà mā'tėr*, *n.* one's university or school.

almanac *öl'mà-nak*, *n.* a calendar with information about various events.

almighty *öl-mī'ti*, *adj.* having all might or power.

the Almighty God.

almond *äl'mond*, *n.* the fruit, (esp. its kernel) of the almond tree, related to the peach but with a dry husk instead of flesh.

almoner, almonry. See **alms**.

almost *öl'mōst*, *adv.* nearly.

alms *ämz*, *n.pl.* money, etc., given to the poor.

almoner *al'mòn-ėr*, or *ä'mòn-*, *n.* **1** one who distributes alms. **2** a social worker attached to a hospital to help and advise patients.

al'monry *(al'* or *ä')* *n.* a place where alms are distributed:—*pl.* **al'monries**.

aloe *al'ō*, *n.* a plant of the lily family used in medicine:—*pl.* **al'oes** (as *n.sing.* the name of a drug obtained from aloe leaves).

aloft *à-loft'*, *adv.* **1** overhead. **2** at or to a (great) height. **3** above the deck, or at the masthead.

alone *à-lōn'*, *adj.* (not used before a noun) by oneself, solitary.—*adv.* **1** by oneself. **2** only.

along *à-long'*, *adv.* **1** in the direction of the length of something. **2** onward. **3** in the company (of) (with *with*).—*prep.* **1** in the direction of the length of. **2** at a point in the extent of.

alongside' *prep.* to or at the side of; beside.—*adv.* **1** to or at the side of something or someone. **2** close to a ship's side.

all along all the time.

aloof *à-lo͞of'*, *adv.* at a distance.—*adj.* showing aloofness.

aloof'ness *n.* unwillingness to associate freely with others.

aloud *à-lowd'*, *adv.* **1** loudly. **2** not in a whisper or merely in one's mind.

alp *alp*, *n.* a high mountain.

al'pine *adj.* of the high mountains: *alpine flowers*.

al'penstock *n.* a long spiked stick used by climbers.

alpaca *al-pak'à*, *n.* **1** a kind of llama, with long silky wool. **2** cloth made of its wool.

alpenstock. See **alp**.

alpha *al'fà*, *n.* **1** the first letter of the Greek alphabet. **2** the chief star of a constellation. **3** a mark given for excellent work.

alpha and omega the beginning and the end.

alphabet *al'fà-bet*, *n.* the letters of a language arranged in order.

alphabet'ical *adj.* **alphabet'ically** *adv.*

al'phabetise *v.t.* to put in alphabetical order:—*pr.p.* **al'phabetising**.

alpine. See **alp**.

already *öl-red'i*, *adv.* previously, or before the time being spoken of.

Alsatian *al-sā'sh(y)àn*, *n.* a large wolf-like dog.

also *öl'sō*, *adv.* in addition, besides.

al'so-ran *n.* **1** a racehorse which has not been placed in the first three. **2** an unsuccessful or unimportant person.

altar *öl'tȧr, n.* **1** a high place or structure on which sacrifices were once offered. **2** in Christian churches, the table on which the Eucharist is consecrated.
al'tarpiece *n.* a work of art placed above and behind the altar.

alter *öl'tėr, v.t.* to make different; to change.—*v.i.* to become different.
al'terable *adj.* **alterā'tion** *n.*

altercation *öl-tėr-kā'sh(ȯ)n, n.* a noisy dispute, a quarrel.

alter ego *al'tėr eg'ō,* or *ē'gō,* **1** a second self. **2** a bosom friend.

alternate *öl'tėr-nāt, v.t.* to use, do, etc. by turns.—*v.i.* to happen, act, etc. by turns:—*pr.p.* **al'ternating.**—*adj. (öl-tûr'nit)* coming, or following, by turns.
alter'nately *adv.* **alternā'tion** *n.*
alter'native *adj.* (usu. used before a noun) **1** offering a choice of a second possibility. **2** offering a different system from the accepted or conventional one: *alternative society, technology.*— *n.* **1** a second possibility. **2** one of two (or sometimes more) possibilities.
alter'natively *adv.*
al'ternātor *n.* a generator supplying alternating current.
alternating current an electric current that at intervals reverses its direction.

although *öl-*TH*ō', conj.* **1** admitting that. **2** in spite of the fact that.

altimeter *al-tim'ė-tėr, n.* an instrument for measuring height above sea-level, etc.
altitude *al'ti-tūd, n.* height, esp. above sea-level.

alto *al'tō, n.* **1** the highest male voice (counter-tenor). **2** the lowest female voice (contralto) or boy's voice. **3** a singer having such a voice:—*pl.* **al'tos.**—Also *adj.*

altogether *öl-tȯ-ge*TH*'ėr, adv.* completely.

altruism *al'trōō-izm, n.* living or acting for the good of others.
al'truist *n.*
altruis'tic *adj.* **altruis'tically** *adv.*

alum *al'ȧm, n.* a mineral salt containing aluminium, used in dyeing.
alumina *ȧ-lū'min-ȧ,* or *-lōō', n.* the oxide of aluminium.
aluminium *a-lū-min'i-ȧm,* or *-lōō-, n.* a light metal resembling silver.—Also **alu'minum** (*U.S.*).

alumnus *ȧ-lum'nȧs, n.* a pupil, student, of a school or university:—*pl.* **alum'nī.**

always *öl'wāz, adv.* **1** at all times. **2** continually. **3** in any case.

am. See **be.**

amalgam *ȧ-mal'gȧm, n.* a mixture, esp. of mercury with other metals.
amal'gamate *v.t.* to unite (e.g. business firms).—*v.i.* **1** to unite (with). **2** to blend:—*pr.p.* **amal'gamating.**
amalgamā'tion *n.*

amass *ȧ-mas', v.t.* and *v.i.* to gather in a large quantity, accumulate.

amateur *am'ȧ-tėr, -tyȧr, n.* one who practises an art, takes part in a sport, etc. for the love of it, not for professional gain.—*adj.* **1** not professional. **2** amateurish.
amateur'ish *adj.* not very skilful.

amatory *am'ȧ-tȯr-i, adj.* of love.

amaze *ȧ-māz', v.t.* to astonish greatly:—*pr.p.* **amaz'ing.**
amaze'ment *n.* great astonishment.
amaz'ing *adj.* **amaz'ingly** *adv.*

Amazon *am'ȧ-zȯn, n.* **1** one of a nation of female warriors in Greek legend. **2** a masculine or large, strong woman.

ambassador *am-bas'ȧ-dȯr, n.* **1** a minister of the highest rank representing a state in another country. **2** a representative, messenger:—*fem.* **ambass'adress.**
ambassado'rial *adj.*

amber *am'bėr, n.* **1** a fossil resin, used for ornaments, etc. **2** its yellowish colour.

ambidextrous *am-bi-deks'trȧs, adj.* able to use both hands equally well.

ambience *am'bi-ėns, n.* environment, atmosphere.
am'bient *adj.* surrounding.

ambiguous *am-big'ū-ȧs, adj.* having more than one possible meaning.
ambigū'ity *n.* **1** uncertainty of meaning. **2** an ambiguous word or statement:—*pl.* **ambigū'ities.**
ambig'uously *adv.* **ambig'uousness** *n.*

ambition *am-bish'(ȯ)n, n.* desire for power, honour, fame, excellence.
ambi'tious *adj.* **ambi'tiously** *adv.*
ambi'tiousness *n.*

ambivalence *am-biv'ȧ-lėns, n.* the co-existence (e.g. in one person) of contradictory feelings towards something.
ambiv'alent *adj.*

amble *am'bl, v.i.* **1** to walk, move, at an easy pace. **2** (of a horse, etc.) to move lifting two feet on one side together:—*pr.p.* **am'bling.**—*n.* an easy pace.

ambrosia *am-brō'z(h)i-ȧ, n.* in Greek mythology, the food of the gods.
ambro'sial *adj.*

ambulance *am'būl-ȧns, n.* **1** a vehicle for the sick and injured. **2** a mobile army hospital.

ambuscade *am'bȧs-kād, n.* ambush.
am'bush *am'boosh, n.* **1** concealment in order to make a surprise attack. **2** a group

of people so hidden. **3** the attack so made.—*v.t.* to attack from an ambush.

ameliorate *ȧ-mēl'yȯr-āt*, *v.t.* and *v.i.* to make, or to become, better:—*pr.p.* **amel'iorating**.
ameliorā'tion *n.*

amen *ä-men'*, *ā-*, *interj.* so be it (said at the end of a prayer).

amenable *ȧ-mēn'ȧ-bl*, *adj.* easy to lead or persuade.
amenabil'ity, **amen'ableness** *ns.*

amend *ȧ-mend'*, *v.t.* to correct, improve.
amend'ment *n.* **1** correction. **2** improvement. **3** an alteration proposed on a bill, motion, etc.
make amends to make good a loss, to make up (for).

amenity *ȧ-mēn'i-ti*, or *-men'*, *n.* **1** pleasantness of situation, etc. **2** (in *pl.*) attractive features of locality (e.g. parks):—*pl.* **amen'ities**.

American *ȧ-mer'i-kȧn*, *adj.* of *America*, esp. of the United States.—*n.* a native of America.

amethyst *am'i-thist*, *n.* a violet quartz.

amiable *ām'yė-bl*, or *-i-ȧ-bl*, *adj.* **1** good-natured; friendly. **2** likable.
amiabil'ity, **am'iableness** *ns.*
am'iably *adv.*
amicable *am'i-kȧ-bl*, *adj.* (e.g. of an agreement between parties) friendly.
am'icableness, **amicabil'ity** *ns.*
am'icably *adv.*
amity *am'i-ti*, *n.* **1** friendship. **2** goodwill.

amice *am'is*, *n.* a strip of fine linen worn by R.C. priests at mass.

amid *ȧ-mid'*, **amidst** *ȧ-midst'*, *preps.* **1** in the middle of. **2** among.
amid'ships *adv.* halfway between the stem and the stern of a ship.

amiss *ȧ-mis'*, *adj.* (not used before a noun) **1** wrong. **2** out of order.—*adv.* badly.
take amiss to resent.

amity. See **amiable**.

ammeter *am'i-tėr*, *n.* an instrument for measuring an electric current.

ammo *am'ō*, (*coll.*) *n.* short for **ammunition**.

ammonia *ȧ-mō'ni-ȧ*, *n.* **1** a sharp-smelling gas, very soluble in water. **2** a solution of ammonia gas in water.
ammo'niac, **ammonī'acal** *adjs.*
ammo'niated *adj.* containing ammonia.

ammonite *am'ȯ-nīt*, *n.* a fossil shell shaped like a tightly-coiled ram's horn.

ammunition *am-ū-nish'(ȯ)n*, *n.* **1** powder, shot, shells, bombs, etc. **2** material used against opponents in an argument.

amnesia *am-nē'zh(y)ȧ*, or *-zi-ȧ*, *n.* loss of memory.

amnesty *am'nis-ti*, *n.* a general pardon, esp. for hostile acts against the government:—*pl.* **am'nesties**.

amoeba *ȧ-mē'bȧ*, *n.* a tiny creature composed of one cell only, variable in shape:—*pl.* **amoe'bae** *(-bē)*.

amok *ȧ-mok'*, **amuck** *ȧ-muk'*: **run amok**, **amuck** to rush about frenziedly, murdering and destroying.

among *ȧ-mung'*, **amongst** *ȧ-mungst'*, *preps.* **1** amidst. **2** in the group of. **3** to each of.

amoral *a-mor'ȧl*, or *ā-*, *adj.* incapable of distinguishing between right and wrong.

amorous *am'ȯr-ůs*, *adj.* **1** inclined to love. **2** showing love.
am'orously *adv.* **am'orousness** *n.*

amorphous *ȧ-mör'fůs*, *adj.* shapeless.

amount *ȧ-mownt'*, *v.i.* **1** to come in total (to). **2** to be equal in effect (to): *This action amounts to rebellion.*—*n.* **1** a sum. **2** a quantity.

ampere *am'per*, short form **amp** *amp*, *ns.* the unit by which an electric current is measured.

ampersand *am'pėr-sand*, *n.* a name for the character &, 'and'.

amphetamine *am-fet'ȧ-mēn*, *n.* a type of drug used as a stimulant.

amphibian *am-fib'i-ȧn*, *n.* **1** an animal that spends part of its life in water, part on land (e.g. a frog). **2** an aircraft able to take off from, or alight on, land or water. **3** a vehicle for use on land or water.—Also *adj.*
amphib'ious *adj.* adapted to life, or to use, on land and on or in water.

amphitheatre *am'-fi-thē-ȧ-tėr*, *n.* **1** an oval or circular building with rows of seats rising from an open space (the arena). **2** anything like an amphitheatre in form.

ample *am'pl*, *adj.* **1** large. **2** enough. **3** in generous quantity.
am'pleness *n.*
am'plifier *(-fī-ėr)* *n.* **1** something that enlarges. **2** a device for increasing the power of electric currents, as in a radio, for increasing sound.
am'plify *v.t.* **1** to make larger. **2** to add details to: *He amplified his previous statement*:—*pr.p.* **am'plifying**; *pa.p.* **am'plified**.
amplificā'tion *n.*
amplitude *am'pli-tūd*, *n.* **1** largeness, ampleness. **2** the maximum variation from its central position of a vibration, oscillation, sound wave, etc.
am'ply *adv.*

ampoule *am'pōōl*, *n.* a small usu. glass container of medicine for injection.

amputate *am'pū-tāt*, *v.t.* to cut off (e.g. a limb):—*pr.p.* **am'putating**.
amputā'tion *n.*

amuck. See **amok**.

amulet *am'ū-lit*, *n.* an object worn as a charm against evil.

amuse *ȧ-mūz'*, *v.t.* **1** to entertain pleasantly. **2** to arouse mirth in:—*pr.p.* **amus'ing**.
amuse'ment *n.* **1** something that entertains. **2** enjoyment. **3** mirth.
amus'ing *adj.* **amus'ingly** *adv.*

an. See **a**.

anachronism *ȧn-ak'rȯn-izm*, *n.* **1** in writing, etc., the error of placing something in a time earlier or later than the period to which it belongs, e.g. mentioning a clock striking in a story of ancient Rome. **2** something that seems out of date in the modern world.
anachronist'ic *adj.*

anaconda *an-ȧ-kon'dȧ*, *n.* a large South American water-snake.

anaemia *ȧ-nē'mi-ȧ*, *n.* bloodlessness.
anae'mic *adj.* **1** suffering from anaemia. **2** feeble, without brightness or spirit.

anaesthesia. See **anaesthetic**.

anaesthetic *an-is-thet'ik*, *-ēs-thet'ik*, *adj.* producing loss of consciousness or loss of feeling.—*n.* a substance that does this.
anaesthesia *(-thēz'yȧ)* *n.* loss of consciousness or of sensation, esp. artificially induced.
anaesthet'ics *n.sing.* the branch of medicine dealing with anaesthesia.
anaes'thetise *(-ēs')* *v.t.* to give an anaesthetic to:—*pr.p.* **anaes'thetising**.
anaes'thetist *(-ēs')* *n.* a doctor who gives the anaesthetic to a patient before a surgical operation, etc.

anagram *an'ȧ-gram*, *n.* a word or sentence formed from the letters of another, e.g. 'live' for 'evil' or 'Flit on, cheering angel' for 'Florence Nightingale'.

analgesia *an-ȧl-jē'zi-ȧ*, *n.* painlessness.
analge'sic *(-sik)* *n.* a remedy that lessens pain.—Also *adj.*

analogous, analogue. See **analogy**.

analogy *ȧn-al'ȯ-ji*, *n.* **1** resemblance in certain respects: *the analogy between the gills of a fish and the lungs of an animal.* **2** reasoning from similar cases:—*pl.* **anal'ogies**.
anal'ogous *adj.* similar.
analogue *an'ȧ-log*, *n.* something analogous.

analyse *an'ȧ-līz*, *v.t.* **1** to break up (a whole) into its parts, as, e.g., a sentence into clauses or a chemical compound into its elements. **2** to examine the nature of: *to analyse a problem.* **3** (esp. *U.S.*) to psychoanalyse (see **psyche**):—*pr.p.* **an'alysing**.
analysis *ȧ-nal'i-sis*, *n.* **1** act of analysing. **2** (esp. *U.S.*) psychoanalysis:—*pl.* **anal'yses** *(-sēz)*.
an'alyst *(-list)* *n.* **1** one who analyses, e.g. chemicals. **2** (esp. *U.S.*) a psychoanalyst.
analyt'ical *(-lit'-)* *adj.* analysing.

anarchy *an'ȧr-ki*, *n.* **1** absence or failure of government. **2** confusion.
anar'chical *(-ki-kȧl)* *adj.*
an'archist *n.* **1** one whose ideal society has no form of government. **2** one who tries to overturn government by violence.

anathema *ȧ-nath'ė-mȧ*, *n.* **1** a solemn curse. **2** a hated person or thing.

anatomy *ȧ-nat'ȯ-mi*, *n.* (the science of) the structure of the body and its parts.
anatom'ical *adj.* **anatom'ically** *adv.*
anat'omist *n.*

ancestor *an'ses-tȯr*, or *an'sis-*, *n.* one from whom a person is descended, a forefather:—*fem.* **an'cestress**.
ances'tral *(-ses')* *adj.*
an'cestry *n.* (one's line of descent from) one's ancestors:—*pl.* **an'cestries**.

anchor *ang'kȯr*, *n.* **1** something thrown overboard to hold a ship, etc. in position, esp. a device with barbs that stick into the bed of the sea, etc. **2** anything that gives steadiness.—*v.t.* to fix by an anchor.—Also *v.i.*
anch'orage *n.* a place for anchoring.
anch'orman **1** someone relied on in any enterprise. **2** one who steers a television discussion, etc.
at anchor anchored.
cast anchor to let down the anchor.
weigh anchor to take up the anchor; to sail away.

anchorite *ang'kōr-īt*, *n.* a hermit:—*fem.* **anch'oress**.

anchovy *an'chȯ-vi*, *n.* a small Mediterranean fish of the herring family:—*pl.* **an'chovies**.

ancient *ān'shėnt*, *adj.* **1** very old. **2** belonging to times long past, esp. before the fall of the Roman Empire.—*n.* **1** an aged man. **2** one who lived in ancient times.

ancillary *an-sil'ȧr-i*, *adj.* helping or related, but less important.—Also *n.* (*pl.* **-ies**).

and *and*, *conj.* showing addition, repetition, or result—used to connect words, phrases, clauses, or sentences.

andante *an-dan'tā*, *adv*. and *adj*. (*music*) moderately slow(ly), and even(ly).

android *and'roid*, *n*. in science fiction, a robot in human form.

anecdote *an'ik-dōt*, *n*. a brief account of an interesting incident.

anemometer *an-i-mom'it-ėr*, *n*. an instrument for measuring wind velocity.

anemone *ȧ-nem'ȯ-ni*, *n*. a flower related to the buttercup, windflower.
See also **sea anemone**.

aneroid *an'ė-roid*, *adj*. (of a barometer) in which pressure of air is measured without use of mercury or other fluid.

anew *ȧ-nū*, *adv*. afresh; again.

angel *ān'jėl*, *n*. **1** a divine messenger. **2** a guardian spirit.
angel'ic *(an-) adj*. **angel'ically** *adv*.
angel'ica *n*. an aromatic plant whose candied stalk is used to decorate cakes, etc.

angelus *an'ji-lus*, *n*. **1** a short act of worship repeated at morning, noon, and night. **2** a bell rung to announce the time of it.

anger *ang'gėr*, *n*. great displeasure; wrath. —*v.t.* to make angry.
ang'ry *adj*. **1** excited with anger. **2** inflamed. **3** threatening (e.g. of the sky):—*comp*. **ang'rier**; *superl*. **ang'riest**.
ang'rily *adv*. **ang'riness** *n*.

angina (pectoris) *an-jī'nȧ (pek'tȯr-is)*, a heart disease with attacks of intense pain.

angle[1] *ang'gl*, *n*. **1** a corner. **2** a space between two straight lines, or three surfaces, meeting in a point, or between two surfaces meeting in a line. **3** a point of view.—*v.t.* to give (an account, e.g. of news) in such a way as to suit a particular point of view:—*pr.p*. **ang'ling**.
ang'ular *adj*. **1** having an angle or angles. **2** thin, bony.
angular'ity *n*.

angle[2] *ang'gl*, *v.i*. **1** to fish with rod and line. **2** to scheme (for).
ang'ler *n*. **ang'ling** *n*.

Angles *ang'glz*, *n. pl*. a north German tribe who founded settlements in Britain and from whom England took its name.
Ang'lican *(-kȧn) adj*. of the Church of England.
ang'licise *(-sīz) v.t*. to make English or more like English: *to anglicise the pronunciation of a French word*:—*pr.p*. **ang'licising**.
Anglo-, anglo- *ang'glō-*, *-glȯ-*, (as part of a word) English.
ang'lophile *(-fīl) n*. one who admires the English.—Also *adj*.
anglophil'ia *(-fil'-) n*. such admiration.
ang'lophobe *(-fōb) n*. one who dislikes the English.—Also *adj*.
anglophō'bia *n*. such dislike.
Ang'lo-Sax'on *n*. **1** Old English, the earliest form of the English Language. **2** a Germanic settler in England or southern Scotland.—Also *adj*. (applied also to English-speaking people generally).

angora *ang-gō'rȧ*, *-gö'-*, *n*. a goat, cat, or rabbit, with long silky hair.

angostura *ang'gȯs-tūr'ȧ*, *n*. the aromatic bark of a S. American tree, orig. used medicinally.

angry. See **anger**.

angstrom *ang'strȯm*, *n*. a unit of measurement for wavelengths.

anguish *ang'gwish*, *n*. very great pain of body or mind, agony.
ang'uished *adj*.

angular, **angularity**. See **angle**[1].

aniline *an'i-lēn*, *-lin*, *-līn*, *n*. oily liquid from coal tar, used in dyeing, etc.—Also *adj*.

animadvert *an-i-mad-vûrt'*, *v.i*. (with *on*) to express criticism of.
animadver'sion *(-vûr'sh(ȯ)n) n*.

animal *an'i-mȧl*, *n*. **1** a being having life, sensation, and motion at will, distinguished from a plant, which has life, but apparently not sensation or voluntary motion. **2** one of the lower animals as opp. to man.—Also *adj*.
an'imate *v.t*. **1** to give life to. **2** to make lively. **3** to inspire, motivate. **4** to cause (a cartoon figure, etc.) to move:—*pr.p*. **an'imating**.—*adj*. *(-it)* living:—*opp*. **inanimate**.
an'imated *adj*. **1** (depicting figures) moving as if alive: *an animated doll, cartoon*. **2** lively: *an animated discussion*.
animā'tion *n*.

animosity *an-i-mos'i-ti*, *n*. **1** strong dislike. **2** hostility.

aniseed *an'i-sēd*, *n*. the seed of anise, a plant of Mediterranean regions.

ankle *angk'l*, *n*. the joint connecting the foot and leg.
ank'let *n*. an ornament or covering for the ankle.

annals *an'ȧlz*, *n. pl*. historical records.

anneal *ȧ-nēl'*, *v.t*. to bring (glass or metals) to a proper condition by means of strong heat and gradual cooling.

annex *ȧ-neks'*, *v.t*. **1** to add; to attach. **2** to take possession of (e.g. another's territory).—*n*. *(an'eks)* an additional building (also spelt **annexe**).
annexā'tion *n*.

annihilate *ȧ-nī'hil-āt*, *v.t.* **1** to destroy utterly. **2** to crush by look or word.
annihilā'tion *n.*

anniversary *an-i-vûr'sȧr-i*, *n.* the day of the year on which an event (e.g. a birthday or wedding) occurred or is commemorated:—*pl.* **anniver'saries**.—Also *adj.*

annotate *an'ȯ-tāt*, *v.t.* to make notes on:—*pr.p.* **ann'otating**.
annotā'tion *n.*

announce *ȧ-nowns'*, *v.t.* **1** to make known publicly. **2** to be evidence of: *A familiar smell announced the goat's return*:—*pr.p.* **announc'ing**.
announce'ment *n.*
announc'er *n.* one who announces, esp. who introduces items of a radio or television programme.

annoy *ȧ-noi'*, *v.t.* **1** to anger slightly. **2** to tease:—*pr.p.* **annoy'ing**; *pa.p.* **annoyed'**.
annoy'ance *n.* **annoy'ingly** *adv.*

annual *an'ū-ȧl*, *adj.* yearly.—*n.* **1** a plant that lives only one year. **2** a book that is one of a series published yearly.
ann'ually *adv.*
annuity *ȧ-nū'i-ti*, *n.* a payment made each year during a given period (usu. the receiver's life):—*pl.* **annū'ities**.
annū'itant *n.* one who receives an annuity.

annul *ȧ-nul'*, *v.t.* **1** to cancel, abolish. **2** to declare not valid (see this word):—*pr.p.* **annull'ing**; *pa.p.* **annulled'**.
annul'ment *n.*

annular *an'ū-lȧr*, *adj.* ring-shaped.

Annunciation *ȧ-nun-si-ā'sh(ȯ)n*, *n.* the Angel's salutation to the Virgin Mary (Luke i. 28), March 25 (Lady Day) in the Christian Calendar.

anode *an'ōd*, *n.* the conductor through which an electric current enters a battery, etc.

anodyne *an'ȯ-dīn*, *n.* **1** a medicine that relieves pain. **2** something that calms or soothes.

anoint *ȧ-noint'*, *v.t.* **1** to smear with ointment or oil. **2** to consecrate with oil.

anomaly *ȧ-nom'ȧ-li*, *n.* something that is unusual, irregular, not normal:—*pl.* **anom'alies**.
anom'alous *adj.* irregular, not normal.

anon[1] *ȧ-non'*, *adv.* **1** immediately. **2** soon.

anon[2] *ȧ-non'*, short for **anonymous**.

anonymous *ȧ-non'i-mu̇s*, *adj.* without the name of the author, contributor, etc.
anon'ymousness, **anonym'ity** *ns.*
anon'ymously *adv.*

anorak *an'ȯ-rak*, *n.* a waterproof jacket, usu. warm and hooded.

anorexia nervosa *an-ȯr-eks'i-ȧ nėr-vō'-zȧ*, an emotional illness causing the sufferer to refuse food and become sometimes dangerously thin.

another *ȧn-u*TH*'ėr*, *adj.* **1** a different (thing or person). **2** one more of the same kind.—Also *pron.*
one another each other.

answer *än'sėr*, *n.* **1** a reply. **2** a reply in the form of an action: *His answer to this was to draw his sword*. **3** the solution of a problem.—*v.t.* **1** to reply or respond to. **2** to say in response. **3** to act in response to: *to answer the bell*. **4** to satisfy (e.g. someone's requirements).—*v.i.* **1** to reply. **2** to be responsible (for). **3** to suffer (for e.g. a fault). **4** to correspond (to e.g. a description).
an'swerable *adj.* **1** able to be answered. **2** responsible: *I will be answerable to you for his good behaviour*. **3** deserving the blame (for).

ant *ant*, *n.* a small insect, related to bees, wasps, etc., commonly thought of as very industrious.
ant'eater *n.* any of several long-snouted, sticky-tongued ant-eating animals.
ant(s')'-eggs *n.pl.* pupae, not eggs, of ants.
ant'-hill *n.* a hillock built as nest by ants.

antagonist *an-tag'ȯn-ist*, *n.* one who strives against another, an opponent.
antagonist'ic *adj.* **1** unfriendly, hostile. **2** opposed (to).
antagonist'ically *adv.*
antag'onise *(-īz)* *v.t.* to arouse opposition or hostile feelings in:—*pr.p.* **antag'onising**.
antagonisā'tion *n.*
antag'onism *n.* hostility; opposition.

Antarctic *ant-äk'tik*, *adj.* of south pole or south polar regions.
Antarctic Circle an imaginary circle round the south pole at a distance of about 23 degrees.

ante- *an-ti-*, *pfx.* before (place or time).
antechamber *an'ti-chām'bėr*, **an'te-room** *-ro͞om*, *ns.* a room leading into a larger one.
an'tedate *v.t.* **1** to date before the true time. **2** to be of an earlier date than (something else):—*pr.p.* **an'tedating**.

antecedent *an-ti-sēd'ėnt*, *adj.* previous, prior (to).—*n.* **1** a noun, clause, etc., to which a following pronoun refers. **2** (in *pl.*) the previous history of a person or thing.

antechamber. See **ante-**.

antedate. See **ante-**.

antediluvian *an-ti-di-lōō'vi-ȧn*, or *-lū'*, *adj.* **1** existing or happening before Noah's Flood. **2** (*humorous*) aged.

antelope *an'ti-lōp*, *n.* swift, graceful animal related to the goat:—*pl.* **an'telope(s)**.

antenatal *an-ti-nā'tl*, *adj.* before birth.

antenna *an-ten'ȧ*, *n.* **1** a feeler or horn in insects, etc. **2** a system of conductors used for sending out or receiving electromagnetic waves. **3** an aerial:—*pl.* **antenn'ae** *(-ē)*, (*radio,* etc.) **antenn'as**.

anterior *an-tē'ri-ȯr*, *adj.* more to the front.

anteroom. See **ante-**.

anthem *an'thėm*, *n.* **1** a piece of music for a church choir, usu. set to words from Scripture. **2** any song of praise or gladness.

anther *an'thėr*, *n.* the part of the stamen in a flower that contains the pollen.

anthology *an-thol'ȯ-ji*, *n.* a chosen collection of pieces of poetry or prose:—*pl.* **anthol'ogies**.

anthol'ogist *n.* one who makes an anthology.

anthracite *an'thrȧ-sīt*, *n.* a kind of coal that burns nearly without flame.

anthrax *an'thraks*, *n.* a deadly disease of sheep and cattle that may be given to man.

anthrop(o)- (as part of a word) man.

anthropoid *an'thrȯ-poid*, or *-thrō'*, *adj.* man-like (applied esp. to the highest apes).—Also *n.*

anthropology *an-thrȯ-pol'ȯ-ji*, *n.* the study of mankind.

anthropol'ogist *n.*

anti- *an-ti*, *pfx.* **1** against. **2** the opposite of.

anti-air'craft *adj.* used to fight against enemy aircraft.

anticlī'max *n.* the opp. of a climax, a dull or disappointing ending after mounting excitement or interest.

an'ticlock'wise *adj., adv.* in the opposite direction to that in which clock hands move.

anticy'clone *n.* the opp. of a cyclone, a spiral flow of air out from an area of high atmospheric pressure.

an'tifreeze *n.* a chemical with a low freezing point, added to the water in a car's radiator to stop it freezing.

antihistamine *(-his'tȧ-min), n.* a drug used to treat allergies.

antimacassar *(-mȧ-kas'ȧr) n.* a covering to protect chair backs, etc. (orig. to protect from *Macassar* hair oil).

an'ti-personnel' *adj.* intended to destroy military personnel (see this word) or other people.

antipers'pirant *n.* a substance that helps to prevent perspiration.—Also *adj.*

anti-semit'ic *adj.* hating or opposing Semites (Jews).

anti-sem'itism *n.*

antisō'cial *adj.* **1** against the welfare of the community, etc.: *Vandalism is antisocial.* **2** not showing fondness for the company of others.

antitox'in *n.* a substance formed in the body that fights against poisons due to bacteria.

an'ti-trade' *n.* a wind that blows in the opposite direction to the trade wind.

antibiotic *an-ti-bī-ot'ik*, *adj.* and *n.* (a chemical compound, e.g. penicillin) used to stop the growth of bacteria that cause disease.

antibody *an'ti-bod-i*, *n.* a substance produced in (e.g.) the human body to fight bacteria, etc.:—*pl.* **an'tibodies**.

antic *an'tik*, *n.* (usu. in *pl.*) a caper, an odd or unexpected action.

anticipate *an-tis'i-pāt*, *v.t.* **1** to act before, forestall (another person or thing). **2** to foresee. **3** to expect.—*v.i.* to speak, act, before the appropriate time:—*pr.p.* **antic'ipating**.

anticipā'tion *n.* **anti'cipātory** *adj.*

anticlimax, **anticlockwise**, **anticyclone**. See **anti-**.

antidote *an'ti-dōt*, *n.* **1** something given to act against poison. **2** anything that prevents evil (with *against, for, to*).

antifreeze, **antihistamine**, **antimacassar**. See **anti-**.

antimony *an'ti-mȯn-i*, *n.* an element, a brittle, bluish-white metal.

antipathy *an-tip'ȧth-i*, *n.* strong dislike (*to, against, between*):—*pl.* **antip'athies**.

antipathet'ic *adj.*

anti-personnel, **antiperspirant**. See **anti-**.

antipodes *an-tip'ȯ-dēz*, *n.pl.* or *n.sing.* an opposite point on the globe, esp. (with *cap.*) Australia and New Zealand, being opposite Europe.

antipodē'an *adj.*

antiquary *an'ti-kwȧr-i*, *n.* one who studies relics of the past:—*pl.* **an'tiquaries**.

antiquar'ian *(-kwār') adj.* connected with the study of antiquities.—*n.* an antiquary.

an'tiquated *adj.* grown old or out of fashion.

antique *an-tēk'*, *adj.* **1** old. **2** old-fashioned.—*n.* **1** anything very old. **2** a piece of old furniture, etc., sought by collectors.

antiquity *an-tik'wi-ti*, *n.* **1** ancient times, esp. those of the ancient Greeks and Romans. **2** great age. **3** something remaining from ancient times:—*pl.* **antiqu'ities**.

antirrhinum *an-ti-rī'nu̇m*, *n.* snapdragon.

anti-semitic. See **anti-**.

antiseptic *an-ti-sep'tik*, *n.* a substance that destroys bacteria (e.g. in a wound) or prevents their growth.—Also *adj.*

antisocial. See **anti-**.

antithesis *an-tith'i-sis*, *n.* **1** the direct opposite (of). **2** sharp contrast:—*pl.* **antith'eses** *(-sēz)*.

antitoxin, **anti-trade**. See **anti-**.

antler *ant'lėr*, *n.* a deer's horn or a branch of it.

antonym *an'tȯ-nim*, *n.* a word opposite in meaning to another:—*opp.* **synonym**.

anus *ā̄n'u̇s*, *n.* the lower opening of the alimentary canal or digestive system.

anvil *an'vil*, *n.* an iron block on which metals are hammered into shape.

anxious *angk'shu̇s*, *adj.* **1** agitated by hope and fear. **2** causing fear and uneasiness. **3** eager: *anxious to please, anxious for a change.*

anx'iously *adv.* **anx'iousness** *n.*

anxiety *ang-zī'i-ti*, *n.* **1** anxiousness. **2** eagerness, concern. **3** cause of worry: —*pl.* **anxi'eties**.

any *en'i*, *adj.* and *pron.* one, no matter which.—*adv.* at all.

an'ybody *pron.* any person.

an'yhow *adv.* **1** in any way. **2** in any case. **3** in a careless way. **4** in an untidy state.

an'yone *pron.* any person.

an'ything *pron.* a thing of any kind.

an'yway *adv.* nevertheless; in spite of that.

an'ywhere *adv.* in any place at all.

Anzac *an'zak*, *n.* a soldier from Australia or New Zealand (orig. First World War).

aorta *ā-ör'tȧ*, *n.* the great artery that carries blood from the heart to different parts of the body.

apace *ȧ-pās'*, *adv.* swiftly.

apart *ȧ-pät'*, *adv.* **1** aside. **2** in, into pieces.

apart from except for.

apartheid *ȧ-pät'(h)īd*, *n.* keeping people of different races apart by making them live in different areas, etc.

apartment *ȧ-pät'mėnt*, *n.* **1** a room in a house. **2** (usu. in *pl.*) a set of rooms.

apathy *ap'ȧ-thi*, *n.* want of feeling or interest.

apathet'ic *adj.* **apathet'ically** *adv.*

ape *āp*, *n.* **1** a monkey, esp. a large one with little or no tail. **2** one who copies another person.—*v.t.* to imitate:—*pr.p.* **ap'ing**.

aperient *ȧ-pē'ri-ėnt*, *n.* a laxative medicine.

aperitif *ȧ-per'i-tēf*, *n.* an alcoholic drink taken as an appetiser.

aperture *ap'ėr-tyu̇r*, *-chu̇r*, *n.* an opening.

apex *ā'peks*, *n.* the summit, top, tip:—*pl.* **āpexes, apices** *(ā'pi-sēz)*.

ā'pical *(-pi-kl) adj.*

aphid *a'fid*, *ā'fid*, **aphis** *af'is*, *ā'fis*, *ns.* a greenfly, etc:—*pl.* **aphides** *(af'i-dēz, ā'fi-dēz)*.

aphorism *af'ȯr-izm*, *n.* a short, well-expressed saying.

aphrodisiac *af-rō-diz'i-ak*, *rȯ-*, *n.* a drug, etc. that increases sexual desire.—Also *adj.*

apiary *āp'i-ȧr-i*, *n.* a place where bees are kept:—*pl.* **ap'iaries**.

ap'iarist *n.* one who keeps bees.

ap'iculture *(-cul-chu̇r) n.* bee-keeping.

apical, **apices**. See **apex**.

apiece *ȧ-pēs'*, *adv.* to or from each one.

aplomb *ȧ-plom'*, *n.* self-possession, coolness.

apocalypse *ȧ-pok'ȧ-lips, n.* **1** a revelation, esp. of divine mysteries, as that (with *cap.*) granted to St. John. **2** (with *cap.*) the last book of the New Testament, dealing with this. **3** an event of great violence and grandeur.

apocalyp'tic *adj.*

Apocrypha *ȧ-pok'rif-ȧ*, *n.* fourteen books left out of the Protestant Old Testament.

apoc'ryphal *adj.* **1** unlikely to be true. **2** (with *cap.*) of the Apocrypha.

apogee *ap'ȯ-jē*, *n.* **1** the point at which a planet, moon, etc. is furthest from the body round which it revolves. **2** a highest point, culmination.

apologetic. See **apology**.

apology *ȧ-pol'ȯ-ji*, *n.* **1** an expression of penitence. **2** an argument in defence of a belief, etc.:—*pl.* **apol'ogies**.

apologetic *ȧ-pol-ȯ-jet'ik*, *adj.* penitently acknowledging one's fault.

apologet'ically *adv.*

apol'ogise *v.i.* to express regret for a fault:—*pr.p.* **apol'ogising**.

apoplexy *ap'ȯ-pleks-i*, *n.* loss of sensation and power of motion due to bursting or stoppage of a blood-vessel.

apoplec'tic *adj.*

apostasy, **apostacy** *ȧ-pos'tȧ-si*, *n.* abandonment of one's religion, principles, or party.

apos'tate *n.* one guilty of apostasy.

apostle *ȧ-pos'l*, *n.* **1** one sent to preach the gospel, esp. one of the twelve disciples of Christ. **2** the principal champion of a new

cause.
apostolic *a-pos-tol'ik*, *adj.*

apostrophe *à-pos'trò-fi*, *n.* a mark (') showing the omission of a letter or letters in a word (e.g. *can't* for *cannot*) or indicating the possessive case (as in *the boy's coat*).

apothecary *à-poth'ik-àr-i*, *n.* one who dispenses drugs and medicines:—*pl.* **apoth'ecaries.**

appal *à-pöl'*, *v.t.* to terrify, dismay:—*pr.p.* **appall'ing**; *pa.p.* **appalled'**.
appall'ing *adj.* **appall'ingly** *adv.*

apparatus *ap-àr-ā'tùs*, *n.* **1** set of tools or instruments. **2** equipment.

apparel *à-par'ėl*, *n.* clothing.—*v.t.* to dress:—*pr.p.* **appar'elling**; *pa.p.* **appar'elled.**

apparent *à-par'ėnt*, *adj.* **1** easy to see, evident: *It is apparent from your performance that you are out of practice.* **2** seeming, but not real: *This photograph gives you an apparent squint.*
appar'ently *adv.* as it seems.

apparition *ap-àr-ish'(ò)n*, *n.* **1** an appearance, esp. of a supernatural being. **2** a ghost.

appeal *à-pēl'*, *v.i.* **1** to call upon for help, sympathy, etc. (with *to*): *G. appealed to K. for support.* **2** to object to an official decision made concerning oneself, esp. to take a case one has lost to a higher court. **3** to be pleasing (to): *The idea appeals to me.*—Also *n.*
appeal'ing *adj.* **1** imploring. **2** arousing sympathy or liking.
appeal'ingly *adv.*
appell'ant *n.* one who appeals to a higher court.

appear *à-pēr'*, *v.i.* **1** to become visible. **2** to come into view. **3** to arrive. **4** to present oneself. **5** to be published. **6** to seem (to be).
appear'ance *n.* **1** the act of appearing. **2** form, aspect, outward look. **3** outward show: *an appearance of truth.*
See also **apparition, apparent.**

appease *à-pēz'*, *v.t.* **1** to pacify, esp. by granting demands. **2** to satisfy (e.g. hunger, curiosity):—*pr.p.* **appeas'ing.**
appease'ment *n.*

appellant. See **appeal.**

appellation *ap-il-ā'sh(ò)n*, *n.* a name or title.

append *à-pend'*, *v.t.* to add, attach.
append'age *n.* something appended.
appendicī'tis *n.* inflammation of the appendix in the body.
append'ix *n.* **1** something added, as information at the end of a book or document. **2** a narrow tube leading from the large intestine.—*pl.* **append'ixes, append'ices** *(-i-sēz)*.

appertain *ap-ėr-tān'*, *v.t.* to belong (to). See also **appurtenance.**

appetite *ap'it-īt*, *n.* **1** natural desire. **2** desire for food. **3** hunger (with *for*).
app'etiser *(-īz-ėr) n.* something to whet the appetite.
app'etising *adj.*

applaud *à-plöd'*, *v.t.* **1** to praise by clapping the hands. **2** to praise loudly.—Also *v.i.*
applause' *(-plöz') n.* praise loudly expressed, esp. by clapping.

apple *ap'l*, *n.* the fruit of the **apple tree**, a tree related to the rose.
apple of the eye **1** the pupil of the eye. **2** something especially dear.
apple-pie order perfect order.

appliance, applicant, etc. See **apply.**

appliqué *ap-le'ka*, *n.* a type of ornamental needlework, with small pieces of fabric sewn on to a larger surface.

apply *à-plī'*, *v.t.* **1** to put close (to). **2** to use in dealing with: *to apply force to the jammed door.*—*v.i.* **1** to make a formal request (to someone for something, e.g. a job). **2** to have a bearing, come into use: *The rule does not apply in this case.* **3** to have reference to, affect: *The order does not apply to me*:—*pr.p.* **apply'ing**; *pa.p.* **applied'** *(-plīd)*.
applī'ance *n.* **1** a utensil, device, machine, etc. **2** a fire engine.
app'licable (or *-plik'-*) *adj.* able to be applied, relevant (to): *The law is applicable to all drivers*:—*opp.* **inapplicable.**
applicabili'ity, applicableness *ns.*
app'licant *n.* one who applies.
applicā'tion *n.* **1** act of applying. **2** a remedy (e.g. an ointment) applied to the body. **3** diligent effort or attentive study. **4** a request (for employment, etc.).
applied science science put to use, generally industrial.
apply oneself to give one's full attention and energy (to a task, to doing something).

appoint *à-point'*, *v.t.* **1** to fix: *to appoint a day for the meeting.* **2** to choose (a person) for an office or employment.
appoint'ed *adj.* **1** fixed. **2** furnished: *a luxuriously appointed flat.*
appoint'ment *n.* **1** the act of appointing. **2** an engagement. **3** a position, job. **4** (in *pl.*) equipment, furnishing.

apportion *à-pōr'sh(ò)n*, or *-pör'-*, *v.t.* to divide in shares.

apposite *ap'òz-it*, *adj.* suitable, appropriate: *an apposite remark*:—*opp.*

inapp'osite.
app'ositely *adv*. **app'ositeness** *n*.

appraise *à-prāz'*, *v.t.* **1** to set a price on. **2** to judge, estimate, the quality of:—*pr.p.* **apprais'ing**.
apprais'al *n*.

appreciate *à-prē'shi-āt*, *v.t.* **1** to know the value of. **2** to understand. **3** to value highly.—*v.i.* to rise in value:—*pr.p.* **ap-prē'ciating**.
apprē'ciable *adj*. capable of being perceived or noticed:—*opp*. **inapprē'ciable**.
apprē'ciably *adv*. to an extent that can be noticed.
appreciā'tion *n*. **1** estimating the value (of something). **2** understanding (of). **3** realisation of the good qualities (of). **4** a talk or article describing these. **5** an increase in value.
apprē'ciative *adj*. showing appreciation (of).
See also **depreciate**.

apprehend *ap-ri-hend'*, *v.t.* **1** to arrest. **2** to understand. **3** to fear.
apprehen'sion *ap-ri-hen'sh(ȯ)n*, *n*.
apprehen'sive *adj*. anxious, timid.

apprentice *à-pren'tis*, *n*. one bound to another to learn a trade or art.—*v.t.* to bind as an apprentice:—*pr.p.* **appren'ticing**.
appren'ticeship *n*. **1** the state of an apprentice. **2** the term for which he is bound.

apprise *à-prīz'*, *v.t.* to inform:—*pr.p.* **ap-pris'ing**.

approach *à-prōch'*, *v.t.* **1** to draw near to. **2** to be nearly equal to. **3** to speak to (a person) for the purpose of getting him to do something.—*v.i.* to come near.—*n.* **1** a coming near. **2** a way leading (to). **3** advance, overture (often in *pl.*).
approach'able *adj*. **1** that can be approached. **2** ready to listen and be friendly.

approbation *ap-rȯ-bā'sh(ȯ)n*, *n*. approval.

appropriate *à-prō'pri-āt*, *v.t.* **1** to take as one's own, take possession of. **2** to set apart for a purpose:—*pr.p.* **appro'priat-ing**.—*adj.* *(-pri-it)* **1** suitable. **2** proper: *Make your complaint to the appropriate authority*:—*opp*. **inappropriate**.
appro'priately *adv*. suitably.
appro'priateness *n*.
appropriā'tion *n*. **1** the act of appropriating. **2** assignment (of money) to a purpose.

approve *à-prōōv'*, *v.t.* **1** to speak or think well of. **2** to give permission for, sanction.—*v.i.* (with *of*) to be pleased or satisfied with, think well of:—*pr.p.* **ap-prov'ing**.
approv'al *n*.
approv'ing *adj*. **approv'ingly** *adv*.
approved school (till 1969) a state school for young people who had broken the law.
on approval (of goods, etc.) taken for trying out, without obligation to buy.
See also **approbation**, **disapprove**.

approximate *à-proks'im-it*, *adj*. nearly (esp. not intended to be completely) correct or accurate.—*v.i.* *(-im-āt)* to come very near, in quantity, quality, etc. (to):—*pr.p* **approx'imating**.
approx'imately *adv*.
approximā'tion *n*. **1** the fact of approximating (to). **2** a figure, estimate, etc., that is not exact but near enough for the purpose.

appurtenance *à-pûr'tėn-àns*, *n*. **1** something which belongs, as a part, or as a right or privilege. **2** (in *pl.*) equipment.

après-ski *ap'rā-skē'*, *n*. (the evening period of, or clothes suitable for) amusements after skiing.—Also *adj*.

apricot *ā'pri-kot*, *ap'-*, *n*. an orange-coloured fruit of the plum kind.

April *ā'pril*, *n*. fourth month of the year.
April fool the victim of a hoax on the 1st of April, All Fools' Day.

apron *ā'prȯn*, *n*. **1** a garment made of cloth, leather, etc. worn to protect the front of one's clothing. **2** a short cassock worn by a bishop, etc. **3** the hard surface on which planes stand, at an airport. **4** a part of a stage that projects into the auditorium.

apropos *a-prȯ-pō'*, *adv.*, *adj*. appropriate(ly): *His entrance came, was, apropos.*—*prep*. (also **apropos of**) in reference to: *Apropos (of) your holiday, what are your travel arrangements?*

apse *aps*, *n*. a semicircular recess, esp. at the east end of the choir of a church.

apt *apt*, *adj*. **1** liable (to). **2** suitable, appropriate: *an apt quotation*. **3** clever (at):—*opp*. **inapt**.
ap'titude *n*. **1** fitness. **2** talent (for).
apt'ly *adv*. **apt'ness** *n*.

aqua vitae *a'kwà vē'tī*, *-vī'tē*, *n*. **1** an old name for alcohol. **2** brandy, whisky, etc.

aqu(a)- *a-kw(a)-*, (as part of a word) water.
aqualung *a'kwà-lung*, *n*. a light-weight diving apparatus, with compressed-air supply carried on the back.
aquamarine *ak-wà-mà-rēn'*, *n*. a bluish-green precious stone, or its colour.
a'quaplane *n*. a board on which one stands and is towed behind a motor boat.—*v.i.* **1** to ride on an aquaplane. **2** (of a vehicle) to move, skid, on a film of water:—*pr.p.* **a'quaplaning**.

aquarium *ȧ-kwā'ri-ŭm*, *n.* a tank or tanks for keeping water animals.
aquatic *ȧ-kwat'ik*, *adj.* living, growing or taking place (e.g. sports), in water.
aquatint *ak'wȧ-tint*, *n.* a method of etching on copper, using *aqua fortis*, nitric acid.
aqueduct *ak'wi-dukt*, *n.* a bridge carrying water, e.g. taking a canal across a valley.
aqueous *ā'kwi-ŭs*, *adj.* watery.

aquiline *ak'wil-īn*, or *-in*, *adj.* curved like an eagle's beak.

Arab *ar'ȧb*, *n.* **1** one of the inhabitants of Arabia, etc. **2** an Arabian horse.—Also *adj.*
Arabian *ȧ-rā'bi-ȧn*, *n.*, *adj.* (a native) of Arabia.
Arabic *ar'ȧ-bik*, *n.* the language of Arabia.
Arabic numerals 1, 2, 3, etc.

arabesque *ar'ȧ-besk*, *n.* **1** a standing position in ballet with one leg extended behind. **2** a curly, intertwined type of decoration.

arable *ar'ȧ-bl*, *adj.* fit for growing crops:—*opp.* **inar'able**.

arbiter *ä'bit-ėr*, *n.* **1** a judge, arbitrator. **2** a person having control over (with *of*): *Who are the arbiters of women's fashions?*
ar'bitrate *v.i.* to act as arbitrator:—*pr.p.* **ar'bitrating**.
arbitrā'tion *n.*
ar'bitrator *n.* one who decides between parties in a dispute.

arbitrary *ä'bi-trȧr-i*, *adj.* **1** (of a decision, etc.) made at random, based on a whim rather than on rational argument. **2** wilful, capricious.
ar'bitrarily *adv.* **ar'bitrariness** *n.*

arbitrate *etc.* See **arbiter**.

arboreal *ä-bōr'i-ȧl*, *-bör'-*, *adj.* **1** living in trees. **2** adapted for this.
arboriculture *ä'bȯ-ri-kul-chŭr*, *n.* forestry, growing of trees.

arbour *ä'bȯr*, *n.* a seat in a garden shaded by branches of trees, etc.

arc *äk*, *n.* **1** a part of the circumference of a circle or other curve. **2** a luminous discharge of electricity across a gap.
arc'-lamp, **arc'-light** *ns.* a lamp in which the source of light is an electric arc.

arcade *ä-kād'*, *n.* a covered, arched walk, esp. one with shops on both sides.

arcane *ä-kān'*, *adj.* hidden, mysterious.

arch[1] *äch*, *n.* **1** a curved structure of stone or other material, able to bear a load. **2** a monument in the form of an arch. **3** anything like an arch in shape. **4** the raised part of the sole of the foot.—*v.t.* to curve, raise in an arch.—Also *v.i.*
arch'way *n.* an arched passage.

arch[2] *äch*, *adj.* mischievous, playful, esp. in an affected way.
arch'ly *adv.* **arch'ness** *n.*

arch- *äch-* (*äk-* in some words taken straight from Greek), *pfx.* chief, often in a bad sense: *arch-enemy*.

archaeology *ä-ki-ol'ȯ-ji*, *n.* the study of people of earlier times, esp. before written history, from the remains of their buildings, weapons, etc.
archaeolog'ical *adj.* **archaeol'ogist** *n.*

archaic *ä-kā'ik*, *adj.* (esp. of language) no longer in common use.

archangel *äk-ān'jėl*, *n.* a chief angel.

archbishop *äch-bish'ȯp*, *n.* a chief bishop.
archbish'opric *n.* the see, or office, of an archbishop.

archdeacon *äch-dē'kȯn*, *n.* the chief deacon, the ecclesiastic next under the bishop.

archduke *äch'dūk'*, *n.* the title of the former ruling princes of Austria:—*fem.* **archduch'ess** *(-duch')*.
archduch'y (*pl.* **-ies**), **archduke'dom** *ns.*

archer *ä'chėr*, *n.* one who shoots with a bow and arrows.
ar'chery *n.* shooting with the bow.

archetype *ä'ki-tīp*, *n.* **1** a prototype (see this word). **2** an absolutely typical example.
archetyp'al *adj.*

archipelago *ä-ki-pel'ȧ-gō*, *n.* a group of islands:—*pl.* **archipel'ago(e)s**.

architect *ä'ki-tekt*, *n.* one who plans and designs buildings.
architecture *ä'ki-tek-chŭr*, *n.* **1** the art of building. **2** a style of building: *modern architecture*.
architec'tural *adj.*

archives *ä'kīvz*, *n.pl.* **1** a place in which government, or other, records, esp. documents, are kept. **2** public records.
arch'ivist *(-iv-)* *n.* a keeper of archives.

Arctic *äk'tik*, *adj.*, *n.* (of) the north pole or north polar regions.—*adj.* (without *cap.*) very cold.
Arctic Circle an imaginary circle round north pole at a distance of about 23 degrees.

ardent *ä'dėnt*, *adj.* fiery, passionate.
ar'dently *adv.*
ar'dour *n.* **1** warmth of passion or feeling. **2** eagerness.

arduous *ä'dū-ŭs*, *adj.* requiring much hard work, laborious.
ar'duously *adv.* **ar'duousness** *n.*

are[1] *ä*, *n.* a unit of measurement, 100 sq. metres.

are[2]. See **be**.

area *ā'ri-ȧ*, *n.* **1** a surface or an enclosed space. **2** sunken space round the basement of a building. **3** extent, range.

arena *ȧ-rē'nȧ*, *n.* **1** a sanded space in an ancient amphitheatre where gladiators, etc., fought. **2** a space, surrounded by seats, for contests, displays, etc. **3** a place of action or conflict.

arête *a-ret'*, *n.* a sharp ridge on a mountain.

argon *ä'gon*, *n.* an element, a colourless, odourless, inert gas.

argosy *ä'gȯ-si*, *n.* a large merchant vessel richly laden:—*pl.* **ar'gosies**.

argot *ä'gō*, *n.* slang, originally that of thieves and vagabonds.

argue *ä-gū*, *v.i.*, *v.t.* to debate dispute.—*v.t.* **1** to prove, or try to prove, by reasoning (that). **2** to be evidence of, imply. **3** to persuade (*into, out of*): *Try to argue him out of his decision to go*:—*pr.p.* **ar'guing**; *pa.p.* **argued** *(ä'gūd)*.

ar'guable *adj.* **1** capable of being proved by argument: *It is arguable that he was not to blame*. **2** doubtful, debatable: *Whether he was to blame is arguable*.

ar'gument *n.* **1** a discussion, dispute. **2** a reason, or reasoning, supporting (or against) an opinion, etc.: *an argument for, in favour of, communism*. **3** an outline of the subject (of e.g. a book).

argumen'tative *adj.* fond of arguing.

aria *ä'ri-ȧ*, *n.* a song, air, in a cantata, oratorio, or opera, for one voice.

arid *ar'id*, *adj.* **1** dry, parched. **2** (of e.g. a discussion) fruitless, without result.

arid'ity, ar'idness *ns.*

aright *ȧ-rīt*, *adv.* in a right way.

arise *ȧ-rīz'*, *v.i.* **1** to rise up. **2** to come into being, occur: *if the need, question, etc., arises*. **3** to spring (from):—*pr.p.* **aris'-ing**; *pa.t.* **arose'**; *pa.p.* **arisen** (*ȧ-riz'n*).

aristocracy *ar-is-tok'rȧs-i*, *n.* **1** government by the nobility. **2** the upper classes generally. **3** persons of great distinction within a particular profession, etc:—*pl.* **aristoc'racies**.

aristocrat *ar'is-tȯ-krat*, or *ȧr-is'-*, *n.* a member of the aristocracy.

aristocrat'ic *adj.* **aristocrat'ically** *adv.*

arithmetic *ȧ-rith'mėt-ik*, *n.* the art of counting and reckoning by figures.

arithmet'ical *adj.*

arithmet'ically *adv.*

arithmetician *(-mė-tish'ȧn)* *n.* one skilled in arithmetic.

ark *äk*, (*Bible*) (often with *cap.*) *n.* **1** the sacred chest in which the Tables of the Law were kept (Exodus xxv. 10–16). **2** the vessel in which Noah escaped the Flood (Genesis vi.–viii.).

arm[1] *äm*, *n.* **1** the part of the body between the shoulder and the hand. **2** the sleeve of a garment. **3** a projecting support at the side of a chair. **4** anything similar to an arm in shape or function. **5** a branch, e.g. of a military service. **6** power: *the arm of the law*.

arm'chair *n.* a chair with arms at each side.—*adj.* with no practical experience: *an armchair critic of football*.

arm'ful *n.* as much as the arms can hold.

arm'let *n.* a band round the arm.

arm'pit *n.* the hollow under the arm at the shoulder.

with open arms with a hearty welcome.

arm[2] *äm*, *v.t.* to supply with arms.—*v.i.* to take arms, make ready for war.

armament *ä'mȧ-mėnt*, *n.* **1** (often in *pl.*) equipment for war, e.g. the guns, etc., of a ship, aeroplane or tank. **2** the act of arming.

armed *ämd*, *adj.* **1** carrying a gun. **2** supplied with weapons.

armour *ä'mȯr*, *n.* **1** (*history*) protective clothing of metal. **2** defensive steel- or iron-plating. **3** vehicles, esp. tanks, with armour and guns, and the forces that fight in them.

ar'moured *adj.* **1** protected by armour. **2** supplied with armoured vehicles.

ar'mourer *n.* a maker or repairer of, or one who has charge of, armour.

ar'moury *n.* the place in which arms are made or kept:—*pl.* **arm'ouries**.

arms *ämz*, *n. pl.* **1** weapons. **2** a coat of arms (see this).

army *ä'mi*, *n.* **1** a large body of people armed for war. **2** a body of people banded together in a special cause: *the Salvation Army*. **3** a great number:—*pl.* **ar'mies**.

ar'mour-plat'ed *adj.* strengthened with plates of specially hardened steel.

lay down arms to surrender.

up in arms **1** armed for battle. **2** ready for hot argument, defiant.

armada *ä-mä'dȧ*, *n.* a fleet of armed ships.

armadillo *ä-mȧ-dil'ō*, *n.* a small American animal with an armour of bony plates:—*pl.* **armadill'os**.

armament. See **arm**[2].

armistice *ä'mis-tis*, *n.* a ceasing of hostilities, a truce.

armorial *ä-mōr'i-ȧl*, *-mör'-*, *adj.* relating to heraldry.

armorial bearings the design in a coat of arms.

armour, **armourer**, **arms**, **army**, etc. See **arm²**.

aroma *ȧ-rō'mȧ*, *n.* a sweet smell.
aromat'ic *adj.* **1** fragrant. **2** spicy.
aromather'apy the treatment of ailments using oils from plants and flowers.
aromather'apist *n.*

arose. See **arise**.

around *ȧ-rownd'*, *prep.* **1** on all sides of. **2** here and there in. **3** (esp. *U.S.*) near to (a time, place, etc.).—*adv.* **1** on every side. **2** in a circle. **3** somewhere near. **4** here and there. **5** in existence.

arouse *ȧ-rowz'*, *v.t.* **1** to awaken. **2** to give rise to: *to arouse suspicion*:—*pr.p.* **arous'ing**.

arpeggio *ä-pej'i-ō*, *n.* a chord of which the notes are given, not together, but in rapid succession:—*pl.* **arpegg'ios**.

arraign *ȧ-rān*, *v.t.* **1** to put (a prisoner) on trial. **2** to accuse or complain of publicly.
arraign'ment *n.*

arrange *ȧ-rānj'*, *v.t.* **1** to put in order. **2** to settle. **3** (*music*) to adapt (a composition) for performance by instruments or voices different from those for which it was orig. written.—*v.i.* to come to an agreement (with a person):—*pr.p.* **arrang'ing**.
arrange'ment *n.* **1** setting in order. **2** an agreement, a settlement. **3** a plan. **4** a piece of music arranged as described above.

arrant *ar'ȧnt*, *adj.* (used only before a noun) downright, thoroughgoing: *arrant nonsense*; *an arrant thief*.

arras *ar'ȧs*, *n.* a tapestry hung round the walls of rooms.

array *ȧ-rā'*, *n.* **1** an impressive or orderly collection, arrangement or display. **2** (esp. fine) clothing.—*v.t.* to dress, adorn, or equip.

arrear *ȧ-rēr'*, *n.* (usu. in *pl.*) something that remains unpaid or undone.
in arrears not up to date (e.g. in payments).

arrest *ȧ-rest'*, *v.t.* **1** to stop, hinder (progress, etc.). **2** to seize by legal authority. **3** to catch the attention of.—*n.* **1** stoppage. **2** seizure by warrant.

arrive *ȧ-rīv'*, *v.i.* **1** to reach a destination. **2** to come to (a solution, decision, etc.; with *at*). **3** (*coll.*) to obtain success:—*pr.p.* **arriv'ing**.
arriv'al *n.* **1** the act of arriving. **2** a person or thing that arrives.

arrogance *ar'ȯ-gȧns*, *n.* a great show of superiority or importance.
arr'ogant *adj.* **1** overbearing. **2** haughty.
arr'ogāte *v.t.* to assign, esp. without justification (something to oneself or someone else):—*pr.p.* **arr'ogating**.

arrow *ar'ō*, *n.* **1** a straight, pointed weapon shot from a bow. **2** any arrowshaped object, esp. a sign indicating direction.

arrowroot *ar'ō-rōōt*, *n.* a starchy food obtained from roots of certain tropical plants.

arse *äs*, (*slang*) *n.* the buttocks.

arsenal *ä'si-nȧl*, *n.* a government-owned place where weapons and ammunition are stored or manufactured.

arsenic *ä's(ė)nik*, *n.* **1** an element metallic grey in colour. **2** a highly poisonous compound of this element and oxygen.

arson *ä'sȯn*, *n.* the crime of wilfully setting on fire (e.g. a house).

art¹. See **be**.

art² *ät*, *n.* **1** human skill: *produced by art and not by nature*. **2** knack: *the art of making a little go a long way*. **3** taste and skill: *the art of the painter in creating this effect*. **4** painting, sculpture, etc. **5** rules, methods: *the art of war*. **6** (in *pl.*) the non-scientific university subjects. **7** craft, cunning.
art'ful *adj.* **1** cunning. **2** skilful.
art'fully *adv.* **art'fulness** *n.*
artist *ä'tist*, *n.* one who practises an art, esp. painting, sculpture, etc.
artis'tic *adj.* **1** (of a person) having the gifts of an artist. **2** showing good taste:—*opp.* **inartistic**.
artis'tically *adv.*
ar'tistry *n.* artistic skill.
art'less *adj.* **1** simple. **2** without cunning.
art'lessly *adv.* **art'lessness** *n.*
See also **artefact**, **artifice**, **artisan**.

artefact, **artifact** *ä'ti-fakt*, *n.* (*archaeology*) an object made by human workmanship.

artery *ä'tėr-i*, *n.* **1** a tube or vessel that carries blood away from the heart. **2** any main route of communication (e.g. a road):—*pl.* **ar'teries**.
arterial *ä-tēr'i-ȧl*, *adj.* of, or like, an artery.

artesian *ä-tē'zhȧn*, *-zi-ȧn*, *adj.* indicating a type of well in which water rises in a borehole by internal pressure.

arthritis *ä-thrī'tis*, *n.* inflammation of a joint.
arthritic *(-thrit'ik) adj.*

artichoke *ä'ti-chōk*, *n.* either of two plants, one thistle-like with large scaly heads, parts of which can be eaten, the other of the sunflower family (**Jerusalem artichoke**, the name having developed from

It. *girasole,* sunflower) with potato-like tubers.

article *ä'ti-kl, n.* **1** a separate object. **2** (in *pl.*) an agreement made up of clauses: *articles of apprenticeship.* **3** a section of a document. **4** a literary composition in a newspaper, etc., dealing with a particular subject. **5** the name given in grammar to *the* (**definite article**) and *a* or *an* (**indefinite article**).—*v.t.* to bind (an apprentice, etc.) by articles:—*pr.p.* **ar'ticling**.

articulate *ä-tik'ū-lāt, v.t.* to pronounce in distinct syllables.—*v.i.* to speak distinctly:—*pr.p.* **artic'ulating**.—*adj.* *(-it)* able to express one's thoughts clearly:—*opp.* **inarticulate**.

artic'ulated *adj.* **1** having parts connected by joints. **2** in connected sections, as **articulated truck**, etc., a vehicle with detachable cab which, when attached, can move at an angle to the rest.

artic'ulately *adv.* **artic'ulateness** *n.*

articulā'tion *n.* **1** a joining of bones. **2** (distinct) utterance.

artifact. See **artefact**.

artifice *ä'ti-fis, n.* **1** a device; a trick. **2** skill; trickery.

artificer *ä-tif'is-ėr, n.* a craftsman.

artificial *ä-ti-fish'ȧl, adj.* **1** made by art, not natural. **2** not real. **3** (of a person) not natural in manner.

artificial'ity *n.* **artific'ially** *adv.*

artillery *ä-til'ėr-i, n.* **1** big guns. **2** the soldiers who manage them.

artisan *ä-ti-zan',* or *ä'-, n.* a skilled workman.

artist, **artistic**, etc. See **art**[2]

artiste *ä-tēst', n.* a public performer.

arum lily *ā'rŭm lil'i,* a tall, white decorative house plant.

Aryan *ā'ri-ȧn, adj.* **1** of a large group of peoples of Europe and Asia whose languages can be shown to have developed from one ancient parent language. **2** (as used in Hitler's Germany) non-Jewish. —Also *n.*

as *az, ȧz, conj.* **1** while, when. **2** because. **3** in the same way that. **4** though: *Young as I am, I understand.* **5** in the position or character of: *He excels both as a teacher and as a scholar.*—*adv.* **1** used in comparisons, e.g. the first *as* in *as soon as I can.* **2** for instance.—*pron.* who, which, that.

as for, as to concerning.

as if, as though as it would be if.

asbestos *az-bes'tos, n.* a mineral that will not burn, fibrous and capable of being woven.

ascend *ȧ-send', v.i.* **1** to climb up. **2** to rise.—*v.t.* **1** to go up. **2** to mount.

ascend'ancy, ency *n.* control (over).

ascend'ant, -ent *adj.* rising.

ascension *ȧ-sen'sh(ȯ)n, n.* a rising up.

ascent' *n.* **1** an act, or way, of ascending. **2** an act of rising, a rise. **3** a slope, gradient.

Ascension day the festival held on the Thursday ten days before Whitsunday, commemorating Christ's ascent to heaven.

in the ascendant supreme, in a controlling position.

ascertain *as-ėr-tān', v.t.* **1** to find out. **2** to make certain.

ascertain'able *adj.* **ascertain'ment** *n.*

ascetic *ȧ-set'ik, n.* one who endures severe bodily hardships, or denies himself much, esp. as a religious discipline.—Also *adj.*

ascet'ically *adv.* **ascet'icism** *n.*

ascribe *ȧ-skrīb', v.i.* to attribute, consider as belonging (to): *The play was wrongly ascribed to Shakespeare*:—*pr.p.* **ascrib'ing**.

ascrib'able *(-skrīb'-) adj.*

ascrip'tion *(-skrip'-) n.* act of ascribing.

Asdic *az'dik, n.* an apparatus for locating submarines, etc., by means of ultrasonic waves echoed back from them.

asepsis *ā-sep'sis, n.* the absence, or elimination (e.g. by sterilisation of dressings, etc.) of the bacteria that cause sepsis.

asep'tic *adj.* **asep'tically** *adv.*

asexual *ā-seks'ū-ȧl, adj.* **1** without sex. **2** not depending on sex.

ash[1] *ash, n.* **1** a timber tree with silvery bark. **2** its hard white wood.

ash[2] *ash, n.* **1** (often in *pl.*) the dust of anything burnt. **2** (in *pl.*) the remains of the human body, esp. when burnt. **3** (often in *pl.*) a sign of repentance or sorrow.

ash'en *adj.* **1** grey like ash. **2** very pale.

ash'y *adj.*

Ash Wednesday the first day of Lent.

the Ashes symbolically, the ashes of English cricket carried home by the victorious Australians in 1882, and contended for at each test-match series.

ashamed *ȧ-shāmd', adj.* (rarely used before a noun) feeling shame.

ashlar *ash'lä, n.* (stonework built of) square-cut stones.

ashore *ȧ-shōr', -shör', adv.* on shore.

Asian *ā'sh(i-)ȧn, ā'shyȧn, -zh-, adj.* belonging to Asia.—*n.* a native of Asia.—Also **Asiatic** *(ā-shi-at'ik, -zhi-)*.

aside *ȧ-sīd', adv.* **1** on or to one side. **2** apart.—*n.* words spoken by an actor which the other persons on the stage are supposed not to hear.

asinine *as'in-īn*, *adj*. stupid.
asininity *as-in-in'i-ti*, *n*.

ask *äsk*, *v.t.* **1** to request, beg. **2** to put a question to. **3** to inquire what is: *to ask the time, the way*. **4** to invite.—*v.i.* to make request or inquiry (for, about).
ask after to ask about the progress or welfare of.

askance *ȧ-skans'*, *adv*. sideways.
eye, **look at**, **or view**, **askance** to look at with suspicion.

askew *ȧ-skū'*, *adv*. and *adj*. (not used before a noun) to one side.

aslant *ȧ-slänt'*, *adv*. and *adj*. (not used before a noun) slanting(ly).

asleep *ȧ-slēp'*, *adv*. and *adj*. (not used before a noun) **1** sleeping. **2** dead. **3** (of limbs) numbed.

asp *asp*, *n*. a small poisonous snake.

asparagus *ȧs-par'ȧ-gus*, *n*. a plant of which the young shoots are a table delicacy.

aspect *as'pekt*, *n*. **1** the way something appears, either to one's eye or one's mind. **2** view, point of view. **3** direction of facing.

aspen *as'pėn*, *n*. the trembling poplar.

asperity *as-per'i-ti*, *n*. **1** harshness, sharpness (e.g. of manner). **2** bitter coldness (of weather).

aspersion *ȧs-pûr'sh(ȯ)n*, *n*. slander, damaging criticism: *to cast aspersions on someone*.

asphalt *as'fölt, -falt*, *n*. a dark, hard substance, used for paving, road-making, roofing, etc.

asphodel *as'fō-del*, *n*. **1** a plant of the lily family. **2** in Greek legend, a plant associated with the dead.

asphyxia *as-fiks'i-ȧ*, *n*. suffocation; cessation of life due to lack of oxygen in the blood.
asphyx'iate *v.t.* to suffocate:—*pr.p.* **asphyx'iating**.
asphyxiā'tion *n*.

aspic *as'pik*, *n*. a savoury meat jelly containing fish, game, etc.

aspidistra *as-pi-dis'trȧ*, *n*. a plant with large thick leaves, often grown in a pot.

aspirant. See **aspire**.

aspirate *as'pir-it*, *n*. the sound of the letter *h*.—*v.t.* *(-āt)* to pronounce with an *h*, as in *house*:—*pr.p.* **as'pirating**.

aspire *ȧs-pīr'*, *v.i.* **1** (with *to* or *after*) to desire eagerly. **2** to have high aims:—*pr.p.* **aspir'ing**.
aspirant *as-pīr'ȧnt*, *as'pir-ȧnt*, *n*. one who aspires, a candidate.
aspirā'tion *n*. **1** ambition. **2** eager desire.

aspirin *as'pir-in*, *n*. a type of drug that lessens pain.

ass *as*, *n*. **1** a small horse-like animal, a donkey. **2** a stupid person.

assagai. Same as **assegai**.

assail *ȧ-sāl'*, *v.t.* to attack suddenly, or again and again, with force, energy, arguments, etc.
assail'ant *n*. one who attacks.

assassin *ȧs-as'in*, *n*. **1** (*history*) one of a military and religious order who carried out secret murders. **2** one who assassinates.
assass'inate *v.t.* to murder (esp. a politically important person) by violence:—*pr.p.* **assass'inating**.
assassinā'tion *n*.

assault *ȧ-sölt'*, *n*. an attack, esp. a sudden one.—*v.t.* to make an assault on.

assay *ȧ-sā'*, *v.t.* to find the proportion of a metal in (an ore or alloy).—Also *n*.

assegai *as'ė-gī*, *n*. spear used by tribes of southern Africa.

assemble *ȧ-sem'bl*, *v.t.* **1** to call together. **2** to collect. **3** to put together the parts of (a machine).—*v.i.* to meet together:—*pr.p.* **assem'bling**.
assem'blage *n*. a collection of persons or things.
assem'bly *n*. **1** the act of assembling. **2** a gathering of persons for a particular purpose:—*pl.* **assem'blies**.
assembly line the machines and workers necessary for the manufacture of an article, arranged in such a way that each article can follow the one before through all the necessary processes without a break.

assent *ȧ-sent'*, *v.i.* to agree (to).—*n*. saying 'yes', agreement.

assert *ȧ-sûrt'*, *v.t.* **1** to declare strongly. **2** to defend (e.g. one's right): *He managed to assert his right to be present at the discussion*.
assertion *ȧ-sûr'sh(ȯ)n*, *n*. **1** the act of asserting. **2** a firm statement.
asser'tive *adj* inclined to make assertions, or to assert oneself.
assert oneself to refuse to have oneself or one's opinions ignored.

assess *ȧ-ses'*, *v.t.* **1** to value for taxation. **2** to estimate the value, power, etc, of: *to assess one's chances, one's opponent*.
assess'ment *n*.
assess'or *n*. **1** an assistant or adviser to a judge or magistrate. **2** one who assesses taxes.

assets *as'ets*, *n.pl.* (orig. *sing.*) the property of a deceased person, or a debtor, or a merchant, etc.

asset (*false sing.*) **1** an item of property. **2** something advantageous: *His charming voice is an asset.*

asseverate *ȧ-sev'ėr-āt*, *v.t.* to declare solemnly:—*pr.p.* **assev'erating**.
asseverā'tion *n.*

assiduity *as-i-dū'i-ti*, *n.* constant attention and effort.
assid'uous *adj.* diligent, persevering.
assid'uously *adv.* **assid'uousness** *n.*

assign *ȧ-sīn'*, *v.t.* to allot, give: *They assigned the task to us*; *Committee-members were assigned seats on the platform.* **2** to fix, appoint (a place or time). **3** to ascribe.
assignation *a-sig-nā'sh(ȯ)n*, *n.* an appointment to meet, esp. a lover.
assignee *as-in-ē'*, or *-sīn-*, *n.* one to whom a right or property is assigned.
assignment *(-sīn'-)* *n.* **1** the act of assigning. **2** (orig. *U.S.*) a task allotted.

assimilate *ȧ-sim'il-āt*, *v.t.* **1** to make similar (to). **2** (of plants and animals) to digest (food). **3** to take in (knowledge):—*pr.p.* **assim'ilating**.
assimilā'tion *n.*

assist *ȧ-sist'*, *v.t.* to help.—*v.i.* to be present (at a ceremony).
assis'tance *n.*
assis'tant *adj.* helping.—*n.* **1** a helper, esp. one appointed to help. **2** one who sells goods and helps customers in a shop.

assize *ȧ-sīz'*, *n.* **1** (*Scot.*) a jury. **2** (in *pl.*) till 1971, sittings of a court in English counties at which cases were tried by judges on circuit (i.e. travelling around) and a jury.

associate *ȧ-sō'shi-āt*, *v.t.* **1** to join in friendship or partnership. **2** to connect in thought.—*v.i.* **1** to keep company (with). **2** to unite:—*pr.p.* **asso'ciating**.—*adj.* *(-āt, -ȧt)* allied or connected.—*n.* *(-āt, -ȧt)* a companion, friend, partner, or ally.
associā'tion *(-si-* or *-shi-)* *n.* **1** a society. **2** union or combination.
Association football the game played by the rules of the Football Association, shortened to **soccer** *(sok'ėr)*.

assonance *as'ȯn-ȧns*, *n.* similarity of (usu. vowel-) sound between words, etc. as with *mate* and *shape*.

assort'ed *ȧ-sört'id*, *adj.* mixed in kind, miscellaneous (**ill-**, **well-assorted** going badly, well, together).
assort'ment *n.* a variety, mixture.

assuage *ȧ-swāj'*, *v.t.* **1** to soothe, ease (e.g. pain). **2** to satisfy (e.g. hunger):—*pr.p.* **assuag'ing**.

assume *ȧ-sūm'*, *-sōōm'*, *v.t.* **1** to put on (e.g. a disguise). **2** to take upon oneself (e.g. responsibility). **3** to take for granted, suppose to be a fact:—*pr.p.* **assum'ing**.
assum'ed *adj.* **1** pretended. **2** taken for granted.
assumption *ȧ-sum(p)'sh(ȯ)n*, *n.* **1** the act of assuming. **2** something taken for granted.
assuming that if one can take it as true that.
Assumption of the Virgin in the R.C. church, a festival (August 15) commemorating the taking up of the Virgin Mary, body and soul, into heaven.

assure *ȧ-shōōr'*, *v.t.* **1** to tell (someone) positively (that). **2** to make (someone) sure (of). **3** to ensure. **4** to insure (someone's life):—*pr.p.* **assur'ing**.
assur'ance *n.* **1** a feeling of certainty. **2** confidence. **3** a solemn declaration or promise. **4** insurance (in the case of *life assurance* only).
assured' *adj.* **1** certain. **2** confident.
assur'edly *(-id-li)* *adv.* certainly.

aster *as'tėr*, *n.* **1** a perennial plant with flowers like stars, the Michaelmas daisy. **2** also (*China aster*) a related summer annual.
as'teroid *n.* one of a large number of small planets, most of which move in orbits between Mars and Jupiter.
as'terisk *n.* a star-shaped mark, used in printing, etc., to point out a note, show the omission of words, etc., thus *.
See also **astro-**.

astern *ȧ-stûrn'*, *adv.* towards the stern or hinder part of a ship.

asteroid. See **aster**.

asthma *as(th)'mȧ*, *n.* a disorder of the organs of breathing, with painful gasping, coughing, etc.
asthmat'ic *adj.* **asthmat'ically** *adv.*

astigmatism *ȧ-stig'mȧ-tizm*, *n.* a sight defect in which the eye fails to bring rays of light from one source to a common focus.

astir *ȧ-stûr'*, *adv.*, *adj.* (not used before a noun) **1** on the move, stirring. **2** out of bed.

astonish *ȧ-ston'ish*, *v.t.* to strike with surprise or wonder, to amaze.
aston'ishing *adj.* **aston'ishment** *n.*

astound *ȧ-stownd'*, *v.t.* to amaze, astonish, utterly.

astrakhan *as-trȧ-kan'*, *n.* **1** lambskin with curled wool. **2** a fabric in imitation of it.

astray *ȧ-strā'*, *adv.* or *adj.* (not used before a noun) out of the right way, straying.

astride *ȧ-strīd'*, *prep.* with legs on each side of.—*adv.* **1** with legs on each side. **2** with legs apart.

as'tringent *ȧ-strin'jėnt*, *adj.* **1** drawing together body tissues. **2** (of manner, etc.) stern, severe.
astrin'gency *n.* **astrin'gently** *adv.*

astro- *as-tro-*, (as part of a word) star.
astrology *ȧs-trol'ȯ-ji*, *n.* the study of the stars and their supposed influence on the lives of human beings.
astrol'oger *n.* **astrolog'ical** *adj.*
astronomy *ȧs-tron'ȯ-mi*, *n.* a study of the stars and heavenly bodies (a later and more scientific study than astrology).
astron'omer *n.*
astronom'ical *adj.* **1** of, concerned with, astronomy. **2** (of numbers) very large.
astronom'ically *adv.*
astronaut *as'trō-nöt*, *n.* one who travels in space.
astronaut'ics *n.sing.* the science of travel in space.
astrophys'ics *n.sing.* the physical and chemical analysis of the stars.
astrophys'ical *adj.* **astrophys'icist** *n.*

astute *ȧs-tūt'*, *adj.* shrewd; cunning.
astute'ly *adv.* **astute'ness** *n.*

asunder *ȧ-sun'dėr*, *adv.* into parts.

asylum *ȧ-sīl'ŭm*, *n.* **1** (a place of) refuge, esp. for fugitives. **2** (*old*) an institution for the care of the unfortunate, esp. the insane.

asymmetry *ā-sim'ė-tri*, *n.* lack of symmetry.
asymmet'rical *adj.*

at *at*, *prep.* expressing exact position in space, time, etc.

ate. See **eat**.

atheism *ā'thi-izm*, *n.* disbelief in the existence of God.
a'theist *n.* one who disbelieves in God.
atheist'ic(al) *adjs.* **atheist'ically** *adv.*

athlete *ath'lēt*, *n.* one who is good at sports that need speed, strength and agility.
athlet'ic *(-let'-)* *adj.* **1** of athletics. **2** strong, vigorous.
athlet'ics *(-let'-)* *n. pl.* sports such as running, jumping, or others that show physical strength and skill.—*n.* sing. the practice of these.
athlete's foot a contagious disease of the foot caused by a fungus.

athwart *ȧ-thwört'*, *prep.* across.

Atlantic *ȧt-lan'tik*, *adj.* of the Atlantic Ocean.—*n.* the ocean between Europe, Africa, and America.

atlas *at'lȧs*, *n.* a book of maps.

atmosphere *at'mȯs-fēr*, *n.* **1** the gases that surround the earth or any of the heavenly bodies. **2** any surrounding feeling or influence.
atmospher'ic *(-fer'-)* *adj.*
atmospher'ics *n.pl.* in radio reception, disturbing signals caused by atmospheric conditions.

atoll *at'ol*, *ȧ-tol'*, *n.* an island formed of a belt of coral enclosing a lagoon.

atom *at'ȯm*, *n.* **1** the smallest part of an element that can take part in a chemical change, once thought to be indivisible, but now known to be composed of still smaller particles (electrons, etc.). **2** anything very small: *There is not an atom of truth in that story.*—Also *adj.*
atom'ic *adj.* **1** of an atom. **2** driven by atomic power: *atomic submarine*.
at'omise *v.t.* to reduce to fine particles or atoms:—*pr.p.* **at'omising**.
at'omiser *n.* an instrument for reducing liquids to a fine spray.
atom(ic) bomb a bomb in which the explosion is caused by the splitting of nuclei of atoms of certain elements, e.g. uranium.
atomic energy nuclear energy (see **nucleus**).
atomic pile. See **pile**.
atomic power power for making electricity, etc., obtained by splitting atomic nuclei.

atonal *ā-tōn'ȧl*, *a-*, *adj.* not in any key.
atonal'ity *(-tȯn-al')* *n.*

atone *ȧ-tōn'*, *v.i.* to make amends (for); to make up (for):—*pr.p.* **aton'ing**.
atone'ment *n.* amends; reparation.

atrocious *ȧ-trō'shus*, *adj.* extremely cruel or wicked.
atro'ciously *adv.* **atro'ciousness** *n.*
atroc'ity *n.* **1** an atrocious act. **2** atrociousness:—*pl.* **atroc'ities**.

atrophy *at'rȯf-i*, *n.* wasting away of an organ of the body.—Also *v.t.* and *v.i.*:—*pr.p.* **at'rophying**; *pa.p.* **at'rophied**.

atropine *at'rȯ-pin*, *n.* the poison present in belladonna (see this).

attach *ȧ-tach'*, *v.t.* **1** to fasten (to something). **2** to join (oneself to): *He attached himself to our party*. **3** to add: *to attach a condition to a promise*. **4** to attribute (importance, significance, etc.) to: *I attach no importance to his opinion*.
attached' *adj.* **1** fastened, joined, added (to). **2** fond of (with *to*).
attach'ment *n.* **1** something attached, e.g. an extra part to enable a machine to do special work. **2** a feeling or tie of affection. **3** legal seizure (of goods).

attaché *ȧ-tash'ā*, *n.* a junior member of an ambassador's suite.

attach'é-case *n.* a rectangular hand case, e.g. for documents.

attack *ȧ-tak'*, *v.t.* **1** to fall upon, intending to injure or overcome. **2** to speak or write against.—*n.* **1** an act of attacking physically or verbally. **2** a confident firmness in performing (music, etc.). **3** a fit (of illness).

attain *ȧ-tān'*, *v.t.* **1** to reach or gain by effort. **2** to arrive at.—*v.i.* (with *to*) to come to or arrive at (aim, possession, state).
attain'able *adj.*
attain'ment *n.* **1** act of attaining. **2** the thing attained. **3** an accomplishment in learning: *a man of great attainments.*

attainder *ȧ-tān'der*, *n.* loss of civil rights because of treason.

attar *at'ȧr*, *n.* a fragrant oil got esp. from roses.

attempt *ȧ-tem(p)t'*, *v.t.* to try.—*n.* **1** an endeavour, effort. **2** an attack: *an attempt on someone's life.*

attend *ȧ-tend'*, *v.t.* **1** to wait on or accompany (an important person). **2** to be present at. **3** to wait for.—*v.i.* to give heed, listen.
atten'dance *n.* **1** the act of attending. **2** presence. **3** the number of persons attending.
atten'dant *adj.* accompanying: *attendant circumstances* (circumstances at the time of an action, event).—*n.* one who attends, a servant.
attention *ȧ-ten'sh(ȯ)n*, *n.* **1** notice, heed: *to attract, call, pay, give, attention.* **2** steady application of the mind. **3** care. **4** erect position with hands by the sides and heels together.
atten'tive *adj.* **1** listening or observing. **2** courteous:—*opp.* **inattentive**.
atten'tively *adv.* **atten'tiveness** *n.*

attenuate *ȧ-ten'ū-āt*, *v.t.* and *v.i.* **1** to (cause to) become thinner or weaker. **2** to reduce in force or value:—*pr.p.* **atten'-uating**.

attest *ȧ-test'*, *v.t.* to testify or bear witness to, e.g. by signature.
attestā'tion *n.*

attic *at'ik*, *n.* a room in the roof of a house.

attire *ȧ-tīr'*, *v.t.* to dress:—*pr.p* **attir'ing.**—*n.* clothing.

attitude *at'i-tūd*, *n.* **1** posture; position. **2** state of thought or feeling: *What is your attitude to corporal punishment?*
strike an attitude to assume a pose, esp. an affected one.

attorney *ȧ-tûr'ni*, *n.* one who has legal power to act for another:—*pl.* **attor'neys**.
Attorney General the chief law officer of the state in England.
district attorney (*U.S.*) a public prosecutor for a district.

attract *ȧ-trakt'*, *v.t.* **1** to draw (to): *What attracts you to medicine as a career?* **2** to allure. **3** to draw forth, obtain: *I could not attract her attention.*
attrac'tion *n.*
attrac'tive *adj.* pleasing, alluring.
attrac'tively *adv.* **attrac'tiveness** *n.*

attribute *ȧ-trib'ūt*, *v.t.* **1** to consider as belonging (to): *This poem is attributed to Shelley.* **2** to consider to be caused by: *I attribute his failure to lack of effort:*—*pr.p.* **attrib'uting.**—*n.* *(at'ri-būt)* a quality, esp. one always thought of as belonging to a person or thing.
attrib'utable *adj.*
attribū'tion *n.* the act of attributing.

attrition *ȧ-tri'sh(ȯ)n*, *n.* wearing down by, or as if by, friction.

attune *ȧ-tūn'*, *v.t.* to accustom (to):—*pr.p.* **attun'ing**.

atypical *ā-tip'i-kl*, *adj.* not typical.

aubergine *ō'bėr-zhēn*, *n.* a plant with an oval purple fruit, eaten as a vegetable.

auburn *ö'bu̇rn*, *adj.* reddish brown.

auction *ök'sh(ȯ)n*, *n.* a public sale in which articles are sold to the person who 'bids' or offers the highest price.—*v.t.* to sell thus.
auctioneer' *n.* one who is licensed to sell by auction.

audacious *ö-dā'shu̇s*, *adj.* **1** daring, bold. **2** impudent.
audā'ciously *adv.*
audā'ciousness, audac'ity *(-das'-)* *ns.*

audible *öd'i-bl*, *adj.* able to be heard:—*opp.* **inaudible**.
aud'ibleness, audibil'ity *ns.*
aud'ibly *adv.*
aud'ience *n.* **1** a ceremonial interview. **2** an assembly of people who listen or watch.
aud'it *n.* an examination of accounts by authorised person(s).—Also *v.t.*
audi'tion *n.* a hearing to test a performer.
aud'itor *n.* **1** a hearer. **2** one who audits accounts.
auditor'ium *n.* the space allotted to the audience in a public building.
aud'itory *adj.* connected with hearing.
aud'iō-engineer' *n.* one concerned with broadcasting sound.
aud'iō-ty'pist *n.* one who types from a recording.
audiō-vis'ual *(-viz'-)* **aids** films, recordings, etc. used in teaching.

au fait *ō fā'*, familiar (with a subject).

auger *ö'gėr*, *n.* a carpenter's tool for boring holes.

aught *öt*, *n.* a whit, anything.

augment *ög-ment'* *v.t.*, *v.i.* to increase.
augmentā'tion *n.*

augur *ö'gür*, *v.t.* to foretell.—*v.i.* (of things) to promise (well, ill).
augury *ö'gur-i*, *n.* (*pl.* **-ies**).

august *ö-gust'*, *adj.* **1** inspiring reverence. **2** dignified. **3** majestic.

auk *ök*, *n.* a sea bird with short wings found in northern seas.

auld lang syne *öld lang sīn*, (*Scot.*) 'old long since', the dear distant past.

aunt *änt*, *n.* **1** a father's or a mother's sister. **2** an uncle's wife.

au pair *ō pār'*, a young person from abroad, usually a woman, who does light housework in return for pocket money and lodgings.

aura *ör'ȧ*, *n.* a particular feeling, air or atmosphere.

aural *ör'ȧl*, *adj.* of the ear.
aur'ally *adv.*

au revoir *ō rė-vwä'* (goodbye) till we meet again.

auricle *ör'i-kl*, *n.* either of the two upper cavities (hollow divisions) of the heart.

aurora *ö-rō'rȧ*, *-rö-'*, *n.* **1** (usu. *cap*) dawn. **2** a display of coloured bands of light, caused by high-speed particles thrown out from the sun.
aurora borealis *(bō-ri-āl'is*, or *bö-)* the northern aurora, or 'northern lights'.
aurora australis *(ös-trā'lis)* the 'southern lights', seen near the south pole.

auscultation *ös-kul-tā'sh(ȯ)n*, *n.* listening to the lungs and heart with a stethoscope.

auspices *ös'pis-is*, *n.pl.*: **under the auspices of** under the patronage, with the official encouragement, of.
auspicious *ös-pi'shus*, *adj.* **1** having good omens of success. **2** favourable, fortunate:—*opp.* **inauspicious**.
auspi'ciously *adv.* **auspi'ciousness** *n.*

austere *ös-tēr'*, *adj.* **1** stern. **2** strictly upright. **3** simple in a bare, severe way.
austere'ness, auster'ity *(-ter'-)* *ns.*
austere'ly *adv.*

Australasian *ös-trȧ-lā'sh(i-)ȧn*, *-shyȧn*, *-zh-*, *adj.* of Australia, New Zealand and the nearby S. Pacific Islands.— *n.* a native of these parts.

Australian *ös-trā'li-ȧn*, *adj.* of Australia.—*n.* a native of Australia.

Austrian *ös'tri-an*, *adj.* of Austria.—*n.* **1** a native of Austria. **2** the type of German spoken there.

authentic *ö-then'tik*, *adj.* **1** genuine. **2** unquestionably true.
authen'tically *adv.*
authen'ticate *v.t.* **1** to prove genuine. **2** to make valid or legal:—*pr.p.* **authen'ticating**.
authenticity *(-tis'-)* *n.* genuineness.

author *ö'thȯr*, *n.* (*masc.* or *fem.*) **1** the writer of a book, article, etc. **2** the creator or beginner (of anything):—*fem.* **auth'oress**.
auth'orship *n.*

authorise *ö'thȯr-īz*, *v.t.* **1** to give permission for: *to authorise a holiday*. **2** to give power, right to: *They authorised her to buy balls for the club*:—*pr.p.* **au'thorising**.
authorisā'tion *n.*
Authorised Version the 1611 translation of the Bible.

authority *ö-thor'i-ti*, *n.* **1** legal power or right. **2** personal power due to one's office or to one's character. **3** a book or person quoted because regarded as very reliable or important. **4** permission. **5** a body or board in control. **6** (in *pl.*) persons in power:—*pl.* **author'ities**.
authoritā'rian *adj.* insisting on obedience to authority.
author'itative *adj.* coming from one who has authority or power, or who has knowledge.
author'itatively *adv.*

aut(o)- (as part of a word) **1** for oneself. **2** by oneself. **3** (**auto-**) same as **auto**.
autism *ö'tizm*, *n.* an abnormality in mental development that affects the sufferer's ability to relate to other people.
autis'tic *adj.* of, suffering from this.
aut'o short for **automatic** and **automobile**.
autobiography *ö-tȯ-bī-og'rȧf-i*, *n.* the life of a person written by himself or herself:—*pl.* **autobiog'raphies**.
autobiog'rapher *n.*
autobiograph'ic(al) *adjs.*
autocrat *öt'ȯ-krat*, *n.* a ruler or other person whose word is law.
autocrat'ic *adj.* **1** of, suited to, an autocrat: *an autocratic manner*. **2** expecting to be obeyed.
autocrat'ically *adv.*
aut'ocross *n.* a motor race over fields and rough tracks.
Autocue® *ö'tȯ-kū*, *n.* a device showing a television speaker the text of what he or she is to say.
autograph *ö'tȯ-gräf*, *n.* **1** one's own handwriting. **2** a signature.—*v.t.* to write one's signature in or on.
automatic *ö-tȯ-mat'ik*, *adj.* **1** self-acting, working of itself. **2** of a firearm, loading itself from an attached magazine and/or able to continue firing as long as

there is pressure on the trigger (also *n.*). **3** not conscious, done without thinking: *His action was automatic, for his thoughts were on something else.*

automat'ically *adv.*

automatic teller machine an electronic panel set into the exterior wall of a bank, etc. from which one can obtain cash or information about one's bank account.

automation *ö-tȯ-mā'sh(ȯ)n, n.* extensive use of machines, esp. of electronic devices for controlling other machines.

autom'aton *(-ȧ-tȯn) n.* **1** a robot or other self-operating machine. **2** a human being who acts like a machine and without intelligence:—*pls.* **autom'atons, -ata.**

automobile *ö'tȯ-mō-bēl,* or *-bēl', n.* a motor car.

autonomy *ö-ton'ȯ-mi, n.* self-government.

auton'omous *adj.* having self-government.

autopsy *ö'top-si,* or *-top'-, n.* examination of a body after death:—*pl.* **aut'opsies.**

autumn *ö'tum, n.* the third season of the year, in northern regions from August or September to October or November.

autum'nal *adj.*

auxiliary *ög-zil'yȧr-i, adj.* helping, additional: *auxiliary forces.*—*n.* **1** a helper. **2** (*grammar*; also **auxiliary verb**) a verb that forms tenses of other verbs (e.g. He *is* going; she *has* gone; I *shall* go). **3** (esp. in *pl.*) a soldier serving with another nation:—*pl.* **auxil'iaries.**

avail *ȧ-vāl', v.t.* to help, benefit, in achieving a purpose, etc.—Also *v.i.*—*n.* use, benefit.

avail'able *adj.* **1** that can be used or obtained. **2** within reach, accessible.

avail'ableness, availabil'ity *ns.*

avail oneself of to take advantage of, use.

of little, no, avail of little, no, use in achieving what one wants.

avalanche *av'ȧl-änsh, n.* a mass of snow and ice sliding down from a mountain.

avant-garde *a-vän^g-gäd', n.* those who take a leading part in a new movement.—Also *adj.*

avarice *av'ȧr-is, n.* eager desire for wealth.

avaricious *av-ȧ-ri'shus, adj.* extremely greedy.

avari'ciously *adv.* **avari'ciousness** *n.*

avast *ȧ-väst', interj.* (*at sea*) stop!

avenge *ȧ-venj', -venzh', v.t.* **1** to take revenge for (an injury): *He avenged his brother's death.* **2** to take revenge on behalf of (a person): *We shall avenge the murdered king:*—*pr.p.* **aveng'ing.**

aveng'er *n.*

avenue *av'in-ū, n.* **1** a tree-bordered approach to a house in its grounds. **2** a street or road. **3** a means, way of reaching: *an avenue of escape*; *avenues to success.*

aver *ȧ-vûr', v.t.* to declare, assert:—*pr.p.* **averr'ing**; *pa.p.* **averred'.**

average *av'ėr-ij, n.* the result obtained by dividing a sum of quantities by their number: *The average of the four numbers 1, 5, 8, and 10 is 2446.*—*adj.* **1** midway between extremes. **2** ordinary.—*v.t.* to fix, reach, an average of.—*v.i.* to form an average:—*pr.p.* **av'eraging.**

averse *ȧ-vûrs', adj.* (not used before a noun) disinclined or opposed (with *to* or *from*).

averse'ness *n.*

aver'sion *n.* **1** dislike. **2** the object of dislike.

avert' *v.t.* **1** to turn (e.g. eyes, thoughts) away from something or aside. **2** to prevent, ward off.

aviary *ā'vi-ȧr-i, n.* a place for keeping birds:—*pl.* **a'viaries.**

aviation *a-vi-ā'sh(ȯ)n, n.* the science of flying in aircraft.

a'viātor *n.*

avid *av'id, adj.* greedy, eager.

avid'ity *n.* **av'idly** *adv.*

avocado *av-ȯ-kä'dō, n.* a pear-shaped green tropical fruit (also **avocado pear**):—*pl.* **avoca'dos.**

avocation *av-ȯ-kā'sh(ȯ)n, n.* **1** a distraction or hobby. **2** (*wrongly*) a vocation.

avoid *ȧ-void', v.t.* **1** to escape, keep clear of. **2** to shun.

avoid'able *adj.* **avoid'ance** *n.*

avoirdupois *av-ėr-dė-poiz',* or *av'-, adj.* or *n.* (according to) the system of weights in which the lb. equals 16 oz.

avow *ȧ-vow', v.t.* **1** to declare openly. **2** to confess.

avowed' *adj.* acknowledged, declared.

avow'al *n.* **1** a declaration. **2** a frank admission.

avuncular *ȧ-vung'kūl-ȧr, adj.* of, like, an uncle.

await *ȧ-wāt', v.t.* **1** to wait or look for. **2** to be in store for.

awake *ȧ-wāk', v.t.* to rouse from sleep, or from inaction.—*v.i.* to cease sleeping:—*pr.p.* **awak'ing**; *pa.t.* **awoke', awaked'**; *pa.p.* **awok'en, awaked'.**—*adj.* (not used before a noun) **1** not asleep. **2** watchful, vigilant.

awak'en *v.t.* and *v.i.* **1** to awake. **2** to

rouse into interest or attention.
awak'ening *n.*
awake to fully aware of.

award *ȧ-wörd'*, *v.t.* **1** to grant, bestow. **2** to give, assign, legally.—*n.* **1** judgment. **2** portion, payment, prize assigned.

aware *ȧ-wār'*, *adj.* (rarely used before a noun) **1** informed. **2** conscious (of).
aware'ness *n.*

awash *ȧ-wosh'*, *adj.* (not used before a noun) **1** (of e.g. a deck) with waves washing over. **2** covered with water. **3** tossed by the waves.

away *ȧ-wā'*, *adv.* **1** from a place, or from the person speaking. **2** absent. **3** continuously: *They worked away till dark.* **4** at once, without waiting: *Fire away with your questions*!; *straight away.* **5** into nothing: *The money dwindled away.*
away with (him, etc.)**!** take (him, etc.) away!
do away with 1 to make an end of. **2** to abolish.
make away with 1 to steal and escape with. **2** to destroy.

awe *ö*, *n.* **1** reverence and wonder. **2** fear.—*v.t.* to strike with fear or wonder:—*pr.p.* **aw'ing.**
awe'some *adj.* causing awe.
awe'struck *adj.* struck with awe.
aw'ful *adj.* **1** terrible. **2** inspiring respect. **3** (*slang*) very great.
aw'fully (*coll.*) *adv.* very, greatly.
aw'fulness *n.*

awhile *ȧ-hwīl'*, *-wīl*, *adv.* for a short time.

awkward *ök'wȧrd*, *adj.* **1** clumsy; not graceful. **2** embarrassing. **3** difficult to deal with.
awk'wardly *adv.* **awk'wardness** *n.*

awl *öl*, *n.* a pointed instrument for boring small holes, esp. in leather.

awning *ön'ing*, *n.* a canvas covering, e.g. in front of a shop, to give shelter from sun or rain.

awoke, awoken. See **awake**.

awry *ȧ-rī'*, *adj.* (not used before a noun) crooked.—*adv.* **1** crookedly. **2** not the way desired, wrong: *The whole scheme went awry.*

axe, (*U.S.*) **ax** *aks*, *n.* a tool for hewing or chopping:—*pl.* **ax'es**.—*v.t.* **1** to cut down, reduce. **2** to dismiss as not required:—*pr.p.* **ax'ing.**
an axe to grind a purpose of one's own to serve.

axial. See **axis**.

axiom *aks'i-ȯm*, *aks'yȯm*, *n.* **1** a truth or statement that needs no proof. **2** an accepted principle or rule.
axiomat'ic *adj.*

axis *aks'is*, *n.* **1** the line, real or imaginary, about which a body rotates, or about which the parts of a figure, etc. are arranged. **2** a fixed line adopted for reference. **3** an alliance:—*pl.* **axes** *(aks'ēz).*
ax'ial *adj.* of, relating to, an axis.

axle *aks'l*, *n.* the pin or rod on which a wheel turns.

ay, aye *ī*, *adv.* yes; indeed.—*n.* **aye** *(ī)* a vote, or one who votes, in favour:—*pl.* **ayes.**

aye, ay *ā*, *adv.* **1** ever. **2** always.

azalea *ȧ-zāl'yȧ*, *-i-ȧ*, *n.* a shrubby plant like a rhododendron.

azure *a'zhu̇r*, *ā'-*, *-zūr*, *adj.* **1** sky-coloured. **2** clear, cloudless.

ayatollah *ī-ȧ-to'lȧ*, *n.* a religious leader in Iran.

B

babble *bab'l*, *v.i.* **1** to talk indistinctly or continually. **2** (of water) to make a murmuring sound. **3** to tell a secret or secrets (to):—*pr.p.* **babb'ling**.

babe. See **baby**.

babel *bāb'ėl*, *n.* **1** (see *Genesis xi*) a confused mixture (of sounds). **2** a scene of noise and confusion.

baboon *bȧ-bōōn'*, *n.* a large monkey with long face, large canine teeth, short tail.

baby *bā'bi*, **babe** *bāb*, *ns.* **1** an infant. **2** (*slang*) a girl:—*pls.* **ba'bies, babes**.
bā'byhood *n.* the time of being a baby.
bā'byish *adj.*
bā'by-sitter *n.* one who remains in the house with a child while its mother or usual guardian goes out.

Bacchus *bak'us*, *n.* the Roman god of wine.

bachelor *bach'ė-lȯr*, *n.* an unmarried man.
Bachelor of Science, etc. a person who has taken a university degree in science, etc.

bacillus *bȧ-sil'us*, *n.* a rod-shaped or (*loosely*) other bacterium causing disease:—*pl.* **bacill'i** *(-ī)*.

back *bak*, *n.* **1** the hind part of the body in man, and the upper part in animals. **2** the part in the rear. **3** the curved part of the outside of a book. **4** (*football*, etc.) one of the players behind the forwards. **5** a covering, etc. put on the back of something.—*adj.* **1** lying at the back. **2** due some time ago: *back pay*. **3** out of date: *a back number of a magazine.*—*adv.* **1** to the place from which the person or thing came. **2** to a former time or condition. **3** in return: *He gave back blow for blow.*—*v.t.* **1** to move back. **2** to give a back to. **3** to help, support (a person, etc.) (often **back up**). **4** to bet on.—*v.i.* **1** to move back. **2** (of wind) to change in the direction opposite to that of the movement of the hands of a clock.
back'er *n.* one who supports another in an undertaking, e.g. with money.
back'bench'er *n.* a member of parliament who does not hold any important office.
back'biting *n.* speaking evil of (a person) behind his back.
back'blocks (*Austr.*) *n.pl.* thinly settled country, esp. far from seacoast or river.
back'bone *n.* **1** the spine. **2** chief support. **3** firmness.
back'date' *v.t.* **1** to put an earlier date on (a cheque, etc.). **2** to make payable from a date in the past:—*pr.p.* **back'dat'ing**.
back'-fire *n.* the ignition of gas in an internal-combustion engine's cylinder at the wrong time, or *within* a gas-burner instead of at an outlet.—Also *v.i.* (**back-fire'**):—*pr.p.* **back-fir'ing**.
back'ground *n.* **1** the space behind the principal figures of a picture. **2** previous happenings that explain an event. **3** someone's origin, education, etc.
back'hand *n.* **1** a stroke made, shot played, with the hand turned backwards. **2** writing with the letters sloping backwards.
back'hand(ed) *adjs.* and *advs.*
back'hand'er (*coll.*) *n.* a bribe.
back number an out of date copy or issue, or person, or thing.
back'pay *n.* pay that is overdue.
back-ped'al *v.i.* to reverse one's opinion, course of action, etc.:—*pr.p.* **back-ped'alling**; *pa.p.* **back-ped'alled**.
back-seat driver a person with no responsibility who gives much advice.
back'side' *n.* the rump, bottom.
backslide' *v.i.* to fall back into sin or error:—*pr.p.* **backslid'ing**.
back'space *v.i.* to move a typewriter carriage or computer cursor backwards:—*pr.p.* **back'spacing**.—*n.* the key used for backspacing.
backstage' *adv.* behind a theatre stage.—Also *adj.*
back'stairs *adj.* secret or underhand.
back'street *n.* a street away from the main street.—*adj.* illegal or secret: *a backstreet abortion.*
back'stroke *n.* **1** a backhand stroke. **2** (*swimming*) a stroke made when on the back.
back'track *v.i.* **1** to return the way one came. **2** to reverse one's previous opinion.
back'wash *n.* **1** a backward current, e.g. that of a receding wave. **2** a reaction or (often unintentional) repercussion.
back'water *n.* **1** a river pool not in the main stream. **2** a place not affected by what is happening in the world outside.
back'woods *n.pl.* forest or uncultivated country.
back down to give up one's opinion, claim, etc.
back out **1** to move out backwards. **2** to withdraw from a promise, etc.
back up see **back** *v.t.* (*def. 3*) (*n.* **back'-up**).

back water to keep a boat steady or make it move backwards by reversing the action of the oars.

break the back of 1 to burden too heavily. **2** to complete the heaviest part of (a task).

put one's back into to do with all one's strength.

put someone's back up to anger someone.

take a back seat to take an unimportant position.

backward *bak'wȧrd*, *adv.* and *adj.* **1** towards the back. **2** on the back. **3** towards the past. **4** from a better to a worse state.—*adj.* **1** late in developing or in becoming civilised. **2** dull, stupid. **3** shy, bashful.

back'wardness *n.* **back'wards** *adv.*

bacon *bā'kȯn*, *n.* the back and sides of pig salted, dried, etc.

save (some)one's bacon (to enable someone) to come off unharmed, though with difficulty.

bacteria *bak-tē'ri-ȧ*, *n.pl.* organisms visible only under a microscope found in countless numbers in decomposing matter, in air, soil and its products, and in living bodies. Their activities are essential to plant and animal life, but some are the germs of disease:—*sing.* **bactē'rium.**

bacteriol'ogy *n.* the study of bacteria.

bacteriol'ogist *n.*

bad *bad*, *adj.* **1** not good. **2** wicked. **3** hurtful. **4** rotten: *a bad egg*. **5** faulty: *a bad guess*. **6** worthless: *bad money*. **7** painful. **8** unwell. **9** severe, serious:—*comp.* **worse** *(wûrs)*; *superl.* **worst** *(wûrst)*.

bad'ly *adv.*:—*comp.* **worse**; *superl.* **worst.**

bad'ness *n.*

bad blood ill-feeling.

bad debt a debt that will never be paid.

go to the bad to go to moral ruin.

bade. See **bid.**

badge *baj*, *n.* a mark, emblem, or ornament giving some information about the wearer.

badger *baj'ėr*, *n.* a burrowing animal of the weasel family.—*v.t.* to pursue as dogs hunt the badger, to pester or worry.

badinage *bad-in-äzh*, *bad'in-ij*, *n.* light playful talk, banter.

badminton *bad'min-tȯn*, *n.* a game played with shuttlecocks.

baffle *baf'l*, *v.t.* **1** to check, hinder or make useless: *to baffle an attempt*. **2** to bewilder, be too difficult for (a person):—*pr.p.* **baff'ling.**

baff'ling *adj.*

bag *bag*, *n.* **1** a sack, pouch. **2** a measure of quantity. **3** the quantity of fish, game, etc., secured by a sportsman.—*v.t.* **1** to put into a bag. **2** to kill (game). **3** to seize, secure, or steal.—*v.i.* to hang like an empty bag:—*pr.p.* **bagg'ing**; *pa.p.* **bagged.**

bagg'y *adj.* loose like an empty bag: *baggy trousers*:—*comp.* **bagg'ier**; *superl.* **bagg'iest.**

bag and baggage with all one's belongings, equipment.

let the cat out of the bag to let out the secret.

bagatelle *bag-ȧ-tel'*, *n.* **1** a trifle, something of little importance. **2** a game played on a board with balls and a cue or some similar device for propelling the balls.

baggage *bag'ij*, *n.* **1** the tents, provisions, etc., of an army. **2** a traveller's luggage.

bagpipe *bag'pīp*, *n.* (often in *pl.*) a wind instrument, a bag fitted with pipes.

bail[1] *bāl*, *v.t.* to set (a person) free by giving security for his appearance in court when required (with *out*).—*n.* **1** money given as security for this. **2** the person who gives it.

go bail to act as bail (for a person).

bail[2] *bāl*, *n.* one of the cross pieces laid on the top of the wicket in cricket.

bail[3] *bāl*, *v.t.* **1** to clear (a boat) of water with shallow buckets, etc. **2** to scoop (water) (out) from a boat.—Also **bale** (*pr.p.* **bal'ing**).

bail (more usu. **bale**) **out** to escape from an aeroplane by parachute.—See also **bail**[1] *v.t.*

Bailey bridge *bā'li brij*, a prefabricated bridge quickly put up.

bailie *bāl'i*, *n.* in Scotland, the title of a magistrate presiding, esp. formerly, in a burgh court.

bailiff *bāl'if*, *n.* **1** a sheriff's officer. **2** a person who manages an estate, or a farm, etc., for its owner.

bairn *bārn*, (*Scot.* and *dial.*) *n.* a child.

bait *bāt*, *n.* **1** food put on a hook to make fish bite. **2** anything intended to attract or allure.—*v.t.* **1** to put food as a lure on (hook), in (trap). **2** to set dogs on (a bear, badger, etc.). **3** to tease unkindly, annoy.

baize *bāz*, *n.* a coarse woollen cloth, often green.

bake *bāk*, *v.t.* **1** to dry, harden, or cook by the heat of the sun or of fire. **2** to cook in an oven.—*v.i.* to be or become very hot; to become baked:—*pr.p.* **bāk'ing.**

bak'er *n.* one who bakes bread, etc.

bak'ery *n.* a place where baking is done, or where bread, cakes, etc. are sold:—*pl.* **bak'eries.**

bak'ing *n.* things baked.

a baker's dozen thirteen.

baking powder a powder containing a carbonate (such as *baking soda*) and an acid substance (such as *cream of tartar*) used to make cakes, etc. rise.

baking soda a white powder, sodium bicarbonate.

baksheesh *bak'shēsh*, *n*. a present of money.

balalaika *bä-lȧ-lī'kȧ*, *n*. a musical instrument with a triangular body and a guitar neck.

balance *bal'ȧns*, *n*. **1** a weighing instrument with two dishes or scales hanging from a beam supported in the middle. **2** steadiness. **3** steadiness, calmness, of mind. **4** the sum required to make the two sides of an account equal. **5** the sum due on an account.—*v.t.* **1** to make, or keep, steady. **2** to weigh in one's mind (against something else). **3** to make the debtor and creditor sides of (an account) agree.—*v.i.* **1** to have equal weight or power, etc. **2** to hesitate or waver (between):—*pr.p.* **bal'ancing.**

balance sheet a paper showing a summary and balance of accounts.

balance wheel a wheel in a watch regulating the beat.

in the balance undecided, uncertain.

on balance having taken everything into consideration.

balcony *bal'kȯn-i*, *n*. **1** a platform projecting from the wall of a building. **2** in theatres, etc., an upper floor or gallery:—*pl.* **bal'conies.**

bald *böld*, *adj.* **1** without hair (or feathers, etc.) on the head (or top). **2** bare, plain: *a bald statement*.

bald'ing *adj.* going bald.

bald'ly *adv.* in a bare or plain way.

bald'ness *n.*

balderdash *böl'dėr-dash*, *n*. nonsense.

bale[1] *bāl*, *n*. a, usu. large, tight bundle of goods or material.—*v.t.* to make into bales:—*pr.p.* **bal'ing.**

bale[2]. Same as **ball[3]**.

baleful *bāl'f(oo)l*, *adj.* **1** having evil results: *a baleful influence*. **2** full of hate: *a baleful expression*.

balk, **baulk** *bö(l)k*, *n*. an unploughed ridge.—*v.t.* **1** to check, hinder. **2** to baffle.—*v.i.* **1** to pull up, stop (at an obstacle). **2** to refuse to act in a particular way: *He agreed to the plan, but balked at telling such an unkind lie*.

ball[1] *böl*, *n*. **1** anything roughly the shape of a sphere. **2** a round or roundish object used in games. **3** a bullet. **4** a rounded part of the body: *the ball of the thumb*.

ball'-bearing *n.* **1** (in *pl.*) in machinery, a device for lessening friction by making a revolving part turn on loose steel balls. **2** one of the balls.

ball'cock *n.* a valve in a cistern, shut or opened by the rise or fall of a floating ball.

ball'-point *n.* and *adj.* (a pen) having a tiny ball as the writing point.

have the ball at one's feet to have success within reach.

no ball (*cricket*) a ball bowled in a way judged to be contrary to rule.

on the ball **1** quick, alert. **2** up-to-date with a situation.

ball[2] *böl*, *n*. a formal gathering for dancing.

ball'room *n.*

have a ball (*coll.*) to have a good time.

ballad *bal'ȧd*, *n*. **1** a simple poem in stanzas of two or four lines telling a story. **2** a simple, often sentimental, song.

ball'admonger *(-mung-gėr)* *n.* a dealer in, or composer of, ballads.

ballast *bal'ȧst*, *n*. **1** heavy matter placed in a ship to keep it steady when it has no cargo. **2** anything that gives steadiness.—*v.t.* to make or keep steady.

in ballast without cargo.

ballerina *bal-ė-rē'nȧ*, *n*. a female ballet-dancer:—*pl.* **ballerin'as.**

ballet *bal'ā*, *n*. **1** a theatrical performance of dancing with intricate steps and mime, often telling a story. **2** the art of dancing in this way. **3** the troupe that performs such dancing.

balletomane *bȧ-let'ō-mān*, *n*. a ballet enthusiast.

ball'et-dancer *n.*

ballistics *bȧ-lis'tiks*, *n.sing.* the science of objects (e.g. bullets, rockets) fired through the air.

ballis'tic *adj.*

ballistic missile a missile guided for part of its course but falling as an ordinary projectile.

balloon *bȧ-lo͞on'*, *n*. **1** a large bag, made of light material and filled with a gas lighter than air—often with car (*def. 3*) attached. **2** a toy of similar form, made of thin rubber and filled with air.—*v.i.* **1** to travel by balloon. **2** to puff out like a balloon.

ballot *bal'ȯt*, *n*. **1** a piece of paper, ball, etc. put into a box for secret voting. **2** this method of voting.—*v.i.* **1** to vote by ballot. **2** to draw lots (for):—*pr.p.* **ball'oting;** *pa.p.* **ball'oted.**

ballyhoo *bal-i-ho͞o'* (or *bal'-*), (*coll.*) *n.* **1** noisy or sensational advertising. **2** outcry.

balm *bäm*, *n*. **1** an oily, fragrant substance. **2** ointment. **3** anything that heals or soothes pain.

balm'y *adj.* **1** fragrant. **2** soothing:—*comp.* **balm'ier**; *superl.* **balm'iest**.

balm'iness *n.*

balmoral *bal-mor'ȧl*, *n.* a flat Scottish bonnet.

balmy. See **balm**.

balsa *bal'sȧ, böl'sȧ*, *n.* a tropical American tree with very light wood.

balsam *böl'sȧm*, *n.* **1** a fragrant liquid resin or resin-like substance obtained from certain trees. **2** a flowering garden annual.

baluster *bal'ŭs-tėr*, *n.* a small pillar supporting a stair rail, etc.

bal'ustrade *n.* a row of balusters joined by a rail.

bamboo *bam-bōō'*, *n.* a gigantic grass with hollow, jointed, woody stems.

bamboozle *bam-bōō'zl*, *v.t.* **1** to deceive. **2** to confuse completely, mystify:—*pr.p.* **bambooz'ling.**

ban *ban*, *n.* a prohibiting, forbidding.—*v.t.* **1** to forbid. **2** to disapprove of strongly:—*pr.p.* **bann'ing**; *pa.p.* **banned.**

banal *bȧ-näl'*, *bā'nȧl*, *adj.* commonplace, trivial: *The speaker made a few banal remarks and sat down.*

banal'ity *n.* (*pl.* **-ies**).

banana *bȧ-nä'nȧ*, *n.* **1** a gigantic tropical tree. **2** its yellow fruit.

be, go bananas (*slang*) to be, go crazy.

band[1] *band*, *n.* (usu. in *pl.*) anything that binds or fetters—now usu. **bond(s)**.

band[2] *band*, *n.* **1** a strip of cloth, etc. to put round anything. **2** a stripe of different colour or material crossing a surface. **3** (in *pl.*) two linen strips hanging in front from the collar of a clergyman or barrister. **4** (*radio*, etc.) a group of frequencies or wavelengths. **5** a separately recorded section of a record.

bandage *ban'dij*, *n.* **1** a strip for winding round an injury. **2** an adhesive plaster for dressing and protecting a wound.—Also *v.t.*:—*pr.p.* **band'aging**.

band'box *n.* a box for millinery, etc.

band[3] *band*, *n.* **1** a number of persons united for a purpose. **2** a body of musicians (esp. wind, percussion).—*v.t.* and *v.i.* to associate, unite: *They banded themselves together to oppose him.*

band'master *n.* the conductor of a band of musicians.

bands'man *n.* a musician in a band.

band'stand *n.* a platform for out-of-door musicians.

jump, leap on the bandwagon to join in any popular and successful movement in the hope of benefiting from it.

bandage. See **band**[2].

bandana, bandanna *ban-dan'ȧ*, *n.* a silk or cotton coloured handkerchief.

bandbox. See **band**[2].

bandicoot *ban'di-ko͞ot*, *n.* **1** a very large rat of India, etc. **2** a small pouched, insecteating animal of Australia, etc.

bandied. See **bandy**[1].

bandit *ban'dit*, *n.* **1** an outlaw. **2** a robber. **3** a gangster:—*pl.* **ban'dits**, **banditti** *(-dit'ē)*.

bandoleer, **bandolier** *ban-dȯ-lēr'*, *n.* a shoulder belt, esp. for holding cartridges.

bandy[1] *ban'di*, *v.t.* **1** to strike, throw, to and fro. **2** to give and take (e.g. blows, words, reproaches):—*pr.p.* **ban'dying**; *pa.p.* **ban'died**.

bandy[2] *ban'di*, *adj.* (of legs) bent outward at the knee:—*comp.* **ban'dier**; *superl.* **ban'diest**.

bandy-legg'ed *adj.*

bane *bān*, *n.* **1** ruin, woe. **2** the source or cause of evil.

bane'ful *adj.* hurtful, destructive.

bane'fully *adv.* **bane'fulness** *n.*

bang *bang*, *n.* **1** a heavy blow. **2** a sudden loud noise.—*v.t.* **1** to beat. **2** to slam.—*v.i.* **1** to make a loud noise. **2** to slam.—*adv.* (*coll.*) **1** exactly: *bang on two o'clock.* **2** absolutely: *bang up-to-date*.

bang'er *n.* **1** (*coll.*) a decrepit old car. **2** (*slang*) a sausage.

bang goes (*coll.*) that's the end of.

go with a bang to go well, be a success.

bangle *bang'gl*, *n.* a ring worn on arm or leg.

banian. See **banyan**.

banish *ban'ish*, *v.t.* **1** to exile. **2** to drive away: *banish fears*.

ban'ishment *n.*

banister *ban'is-tėr*, *n.* Same as **baluster**.

banjo *ban'jō*, or *-jō'*, *n.* a musical instrument of the guitar kind:—*pl.* **ban'jo(e)s**, **-jo(e)s'**.

bank[1] *bangk*, *n.* **1** a mound, ridge. **2** the margin of a river, lake, etc. **3** rising ground in the sea.—*v.t.* (often with *up*) **1** to enclose, strengthen, with a bank. **2** to cover (a fire) so as to make it burn more slowly.—*v.t.* and *v.i.* (of aircraft) to tilt in turning.

bank[2] *bangk*, *n.* **1** a place where money is deposited, lent, exchanged. **2** a place for storing other valuable material (e.g. **blood bank**, where blood plasma is kept).—*v.t.* to put into a bank.—*v.i.* to have a bank account.

bank'er *n.* **1** one employed in banking. **2** the stake-holder in certain gambling

games.
bank'ing *n.* and *adj.*
bank book a book recording money deposited in, or withdrawn from, a bank.
banker's card a cheque card.
bank holiday a day (often also a public holiday) on which banks are closed.
bank note a note issued by a bank, which passes as money.
bank rate formerly, the rate at which the Bank of England was prepared to discount (see this word) bills of exchange.
bank on to rely, reckon, on.
break the bank to win from the casino management the sum fixed as the limit it is willing to lose on one day.

bank[3] *bangk*, *n.* a row or collection of rows (e.g. of oars, instruments, keys on a typewriter).

bankrupt *bangk'rupt*, *n.* one who fails in business.—*adj.* **1** insolvent. **2** having none left (with *of*, *in*).—*v.t.* to make bankrupt.
bank'ruptcy *n.* (*pl.* **-ies**).

banner *ban'ėr*, *n.* **1** a military flag. **2** a large strip of cloth bearing a slogan, etc.
banner headline one right across a newspaper.

banning, **banned**. See **ban**.

bannock *ban'ȯk*, *n.* a flat cake, esp. a plain one.

banns *banz*, *n. pl.* a proclamation of intention to marry.
forbid the banns to object formally to a proposed marriage.

banquet *bang'kwit*, *n.* **1** a feast. **2** a ceremonial dinner, with speeches.—*v.t.* and *v.i.* to give, or to share in, a feast:—*pr.p.* **ban'queting**; *pa.p.* **ban'queted**.

banshee *ban'shē*, *n.* a fairy who wails before a death in the family to which she is attached.

bantam *ban'tȧm*, *n.* a small variety of domestic fowl, notable for courage.
ban'tamweight *n.* a boxer not heavier than 8 st. 6 lb. (about 53.5kg.) (amateur 8 st. 7 lb. (about 54kg.)) or less than 8 st. (about 51kg.)

banter *ban'tėr*, *v.t.* to tease good-humouredly.—*n.* **1** humorous ridicule. **2** jesting.

banyan, **banian** *ban'yȧn*, *n.* an Indian fig tree with rooting branches.

baptise *bap-tīz'*, *v.t.* **1** to dip in, or sprinkle with, water as a religious ceremony. **2** to give a name to, christen:—*pr.p.* **baptis'ing**.
bap'tism *(-tizm)* *n.* **baptis'mal** *adj.*
Bap'tist *n.* one of a religious sect that approves of adult baptism only.
baptism of fire an ordeal, such as a soldier's first experience of battle.

bar *bär*, *n.* **1** a rod of solid substance. **2** a bolt. **3** a hindrance. **4** a bank of sand, gravel, at the mouth of a river, etc. **5** a counter across which drinks are served. **6** a counter at which articles of one kind are sold. **7** a public house. **8** the rail dividing off the judge's seat at which prisoners stand to be charged or sentenced. **9** the lawyers who plead in court. **10** a division in music.—*v.t.* **1** to fasten with a bar. **2** to shut out. **3** to hinder (from):—*pr.p.* **barr'ing**; *pa.p.* **barred**.—*prep.* barring.
barr'ing *prep.* except for, excepting.
bar code an arrangement of thick and thin lines on the wrapping of products in shops, containing information which can be read by a computer.
bar'maid, **-man**, **-person**, **-tender** *ns.* attendants who serve at the bar of a public house or hotel.
called to the bar admitted as barrister or advocate.

barb *bärb*, *n.* **1** the beard-like jag near the point of an arrow, fish-hook, etc. **2** a pointed or hurtful remark.—*v.t.* to arm with barbs.
barbed *adj.* having or containing a barb or barbs: *a barbed arrow*; *barbed comments*.
barbed wire wire with sharp points at intervals, used for fencing, etc.

barbarous *bär'bȧr-ůs*, *adj.* **1** uncivilised. **2** brutal.
barbār'ian *n.* **1** an uncivilised person. **2** a cruel, brutal person.—Also *adj.*
barbar'ic *(-bar')* *adj.* **1** uncivilised. **2** (of e.g. ornaments) primitive but rich and splendid.
bar'barism *n.* state of being uncivilised.
barbar'ity *n.* **1** barbarousness. **2** a barbarous act:—*pl.* **barbar'ities**.
bar'barousness *n.*

Barbary ape *bär'bȧr-i āp*, a small tailless ape found in Africa and Gibraltar.

barbecue *bär'be-kū*, *n.* **1** a framework for grilling meat, etc. over a charcoal fire. **2** a social entertainment in the open air, at which food is barbecued.—*v.t.* to cook on a barbecue:—*pr.p.* **bar'becuing**; *pa.p.* **bar'becued**.

barber *bär'bėr*, *n.* a person who shaves faces and cuts hair.

barberry *bär'bėr-i*, *n.* a thorny shrub with yellow flowers and usu. red berries:—*pl.* **bar'berries**.

barbiturate *bärb-it'ūr-it*, *n.* a sedative or soporific drug.

barcarol(l)e *bär'kȧ-rōl*, *n.* a gondolier's boating song.

bard *bärd*, *n.* **1** a poet and singer among the Celts. **2** a poet.
bard'ic *adj.*

bare *bār*, *adj.* **1** uncovered, naked. **2** empty. **3** (used only before a noun) mere, only, without anything in addition: *his bare needs.*—*v.t.* to strip, uncover:—*pr.p.* **bar'ing**.
bare'ly *adv.* **1** scantily, with little. **2** scarcely, only just: *barely enough food.*
bare'ness *n.*
bare'back *adj.* (also **bare'backed**) and *adv.* without saddle.
bare'faced *adj.* **1** without beard, etc. **2** undisguised, impudent: *a barefaced lie.*
bare'foot(ed) *adjs.* and *advs.*
bare'head'ed *adj.* and *adv.*

bargain *bär'gin*, *n.* **1** an agreement. **2** something bought cheaply.—*v.i.* to haggle about price, about the terms of an agreement, etc.—*v.t.* to make it a condition of an agreement (that something should be done).
bargain for to expect, be prepared for.
bargain on to depend on.
into the bargain in addition, besides.

barge *bärj*, *n.* a flat-bottomed boat, used on rivers and canals.—*v.i.* **1** to move clumsily (about). **2** to bump (into). **3** to push one's way (into) rudely:—*pr.p.* **barg'ing**.
bargee' *(-ē')* *n.* a bargeman.

baritone *bar'i-tōn*, *n.* (a singer with) a deep-toned male voice between bass and tenor.—Also *adj.*

barium *bā'ri-um*, *n.* an element, a whitish metal.
barium meal a mixture of barium sulphate administered in order to make the alimentary canal visible in X-ray pictures.

bark[1] *bärk*, *n.* **1** the short, explosive sound made by a dog, wolf, etc. **2** a similar sound. **3** (*coll.*) a harsh cough.—*v.i.* **1** to yelp like a dog. **2** to speak sharply or abruptly.
bark'er *n.* a person who stands advertising wares, a show, etc., in a loud voice to passers-by.
bark up the wrong tree to be on the wrong scent, to have, and act on, the wrong idea.

bark[2], **barque** *bärk*, (*poetry*) *n.* a boat.

bark[3] *bärk*, *n.* the corky and other material than can be peeled from a woody stem, such as a branch, tree trunk.—*v.t.* to strip bark or skin from: *He barked his shin.*

barley *bär'li*, *n.* a grain used for food and for making malt liquors and spirits.
barley sugar sugar candied by melting and cooling to make a sweetmeat.
barley water a drink for invalids, made from pearl barley.

barm *bärm*, *n.* the froth of beer or other fermenting liquor.
barm'y *adj.* **1** frothy. **2** (*slang*) crazy:—*comp.* **barm'ier**; *superl.* **barm'iest**.

barmaid, etc. See **bar**.

bar mitzvah *bär mits'vȧ*, **1** a Jewish boy who has reached the age (13) of religious responsibility. **2** the festivities celebrating this event.

barn *bärn*, *n.* a building in which grain, hay, etc. are stored.
barn dance **1** a dance held in a barn. **2** a lively country dance in polka rhythm.
barn owl an owl, buff-coloured above, white below.
barn'stormer *n.* **1** a touring actor, esp. one who rants. **2** a travelling speaker.

barnacle *bär'nȧ-kl*, *n.* a shellfish that sticks to rocks and ship bottoms.

barograph *bar'ō-gräf*, *n.* a barometer that makes a record of changes in the pressure of the atmosphere.

barometer *bȧ-rom'i-tėr*, *n.* an instrument by which the weight or pressure of the atmosphere is measured and changes of weather are indicated.
baromet'ric *adj.*

baron *bar'on*, *n.* **1** a title of rank, lowest in the House of Lords. **2** a foreign noble of similar grade. **3** (in *pl.*) under the feudal system, the chief holders of land from the Crown, later the great lords generally. **4** a powerful person: *a newspaper baron.*
bar'oness *n.* a baron's wife, or a lady holding a baronial title in her own right.
bar'onet *n.* the lowest British title that can be passed on to an heir (see **sir**).
bar'onetcy *n.* the rank of a baronet:—*pl.* **bar'onetcies**.
barōn'ial *adj.* **1** of a baron. **2** (*architecture*) of a style imitating that of old castles.
bar'ony *n.* the rank or land of a baron:—*pl.* **bar'onies**.

barperson. See **bar**.

barque. Same as **bark**[2].

barrack[1] *bar'ȧk*, *n.* (usu. in *pl.*) a building for housing soldiers.

barrack[2] *bar'ȧk*, *v.i.* to shout in an unfriendly way, cheer mockingly.—Also *v.t.*
barr'acking *n.* and *adj.*

barrage *bar'äzh*, *-azh'*, *n.* **1** an artificial bar across a river. **2** a barrier formed by artillery fire, or by captive (see this word) balloons. **3** an overwhelming number or amount at one time: *a barrage of questions.*

barrel *bar'ėl, n.* **1** a wooden container made of curved staves bound with hoops. **2** a metal container of similar shape. **3** the quantity held by such containers. **4** anything long and hollow (e.g. the tube of a gun).

barr'elled *adj.*

barrel organ an instrument for playing tunes by means of a revolving cylinder set with pins which operate keys and thus admit air to a set of pipes.

barren *bar'ėn, adj.* **1** incapable of bearing offspring. **2** unfruitful. **3** (of land) bare, desolate. **4** unprofitable: *a barren discussion.*

barr'enly *adv.* **barr'enness** *n.*

barricade *bar'i-kād, n.* a barrier quickly put up to block e.g. a street.—*v.t.* **1** to block (e.g. a street) thus. **2** to shut (e.g. oneself) away behind a barrier:—*pr.p.* **barr'icading.**

barrier *bar'i-ėr, n.* **1** a defence against attack. **2** any obstacle that keeps things, etc. apart.

barrier cream a skin cream that prevents dirt, *etc.* from entering the pores.

barring, barred. See **bar.**

barrister *bar'is-tėr, n.* one qualified to plead at the bar in English or in Irish law courts.

barrow[1] *bar'ō, n.* a small wheeled vehicle used to carry a load.

barrow boy a fruit seller with a barrow.

barrow[2] *bar'ō, n.* a mound raised over a grave in former times, a tumulus.

bartender. See **bar.**

barter *bär'tėr, v.t.* **1** to give (one thing) in exchange (for another). **2** to give away for unworthy gain.—Also *v.i.* and *n.*

basal. See **base**[1].

basalt *bas'ölt, bas-ölt', n.* the name for certain dark-coloured rocks thrown up as lava from volcanoes.

basalt'ic *adj.*

base[1] *bās, n.* **1** a foundation, support. **2** the lowest part. **3** the chief ingredient or substance in a mixture. **4** a substance added for a purpose that is not the main purpose of the mixture (e.g. to give it bulk). **5** a place from which a military or other action is carried on, headquarters. **6** the line (or surface) on which a plane (or solid) figure is regarded as standing. **7** (*chemistry*) a substance that turns red litmus blue, reacts with an acid to form a salt, etc. **8** the number on which a system of numbers (e.g. of logarithms) is founded.—*v.t.* to found (on):—*pr.p.* **bas'ing;** *pa.p.* **based** *(bāst).*

bās'al *adj.* of, or situated at, the base, esp. of the skull.

base'less *adj.* **1** without a base. **2** groundless, without reason: *a baseless fear, claim.*

base'ment *n.* the lowest storey of a building, below street level.

bas'ic *adj.* **1** of, forming, like, a base. **2** fundamental, essential: *a basic principle.*—*n.* (in *pl.*) fundamental principles.

base rate the rate, determined by a bank, on which it bases its lending rates of interest.

Basic English an English vocabulary of a very few of the most useful words.

basic slag a by-product in the manufacture of steel, used as manure.

base[2] *bās, adj.* **1** low. **2** mean, vile, worthless. **3** (of money) counterfeit, imitation.

base'ly *adv.* **base'ness** *n.*

baseball *bās'böl, n.* a game played with bat and ball, the American national game since 1865.

baseless, basement. See **base**[1].

basely, baseness. See **base**[2].

bash *bash, v.t.* **1** to beat or smash in. **2** to attack maliciously.—*n.* **1** a heavy blow. **2** a dint.

have a bash (*coll.*) to make an attempt (at).

bashful *bash'f(oo)l, adj.* shy, lacking confidence.

bash'fulness *n.* **bash'fully** *adv.*

basic. See **base**[1].

Basic *bās'ik, n.* a computer language using simple English and algebra (also **BASIC**).

basil *baz'il, n.* an aromatic herb.

basin *bās'n, n.* **1** a wide, open dish. **2** a bowl in a toilet, etc.: *a washhand basin.* **3** any hollow place containing water, as a dock. **4** the area drained by a river and its tributaries.

basis *bās'is, n.* same as **base**[1] esp. in the sense of a foundation for something not material: *Their friendship rested on the basis of trust:*—*pl.* **bas'es** *(-ēz).*

bask *bäsk, v.i.* **1** to lie (in warmth or sunshine). **2** to enjoy: *He basked in the approval of his friends.*

basket *bäs'kit, n.* a container of plaited or interwoven twigs, rushes, etc.

bas'ketful *n.*

bas'ketball *n.* a game in which goals are scored by throwing a ball into a raised net (orig. a basket).

bas'ketwork *n.* any material made of interlaced twigs, etc.

Basque *bäsk, n.* one of a people inhabiting the western Pyrenees in Spain and France, or their language.—Also *adj.*

bas-relief *bas'-ri-lēf, bä'*, *n.* sculpture in which the figures do not stand out far from the background.

bass[1] *bās*, *n.* (*music*) **1** the lowest part sung or played. **2** a bass singer. **3** a bass instrument, esp. (*coll.*) a double bass.—Also *adj*.

bass[2], basse *bas*, *n.* a fish related to the perch:—*pl.* **bass, basse, bass'es**.

basset *bas'it*, *n.* a hound like a dachshund, but bigger and with very long ears.

bassinet(te) *bas'i-net*, *n.* **1** a hooded basket used as a cradle. **2** a form of pram.

bassoon *bȧ-sōōn', -zōōn'*, *n.* a woodwind instrument which gives a very low sound.
bassoon'ist *n.*

bast *bäst*, *n.* **1** the inner bark, esp. of the lime tree. **2** fibre. **3** matting.

bastard *bäs'tȧrd*, *n.* **1** a child born of parents not married to each other. **2** (*vulg.*; showing anger, dislike, sympathy, etc.) a person: *a cruel bastard*; *an unlucky bastard.*—Also *adj*.

baste[1] *bāst*, *v.t.* to beat with a stick:—*pr.p.* **bast'ing**.
bast'ing *n.*

baste[2] *bāst*, *v.t.* to drop fat or butter over (roasting meat, etc.):—*pr.p.* **bast'ing**.

baste[3] *bāst*, *v.t.* to sew slightly or with long stitches, to tack:—*pr.p.* **bast'ing**.

bastinado *bas-ti-nā'dō*, *v.t.* to beat esp. on the soles of the feet (an Eastern punishment):—*pa.p.* **bastinā'doed**.

bastion *bas'ti-ȯn, bas'tyȯn*, *n.* **1** a part sticking out at the angle of a fortification. **2** a defence, stronghold.

bat[1] *bat*, *n.* **1** a shaped piece of wood, etc. for striking the ball in cricket, baseball, table-tennis, etc. **2** a batsman.—*v.i.* to use a bat.—Also *v.t.*:—*pr.p.* **batt'ing**; *pa.p.* **batt'ed**.
batt'er, bats'man *ns.*
batt'ing *n.* **1** the use of a bat. **2** cotton, etc., fibre prepared in sheets.
off one's own bat on one's own initiative.

bat[2] *bat*, *n.* a mouse-like flying animal with very long arm and hand bones, the finger bones supporting its 'wings' as the ribs do an umbrella.
batt'y (*coll.*) *adj.* crazy:—*comp.* **batt'ier**; *superl.* **batt'iest**.

bat[3] *bat*, *v.t.* to flutter, wink (an eyelid, eye):—*pr.p.* **batt'ing**; *pa.p.* **batt'ed**.

batch *bach*, *n.* the quantity of bread baked, or of anything made or got ready, at one time.

bated breath. See **breath**.

bath *bäth, bath*, *n.* **1** water into which to dip the body. **2** a large container, usu. fitted with taps and a waste pipe, for bathing in. **3** (also **bath'tub**) a smaller container for water, esp. without taps, etc., for bathing in. **4** (often in *pl.*) an artificial pool, house, or building in which one may bath or bathe. **5** the exposing of the body to sunlight, mud, etc. **6** liquid, sand, etc., into which something is put for heating, washing, etc.:—*pl.* **baths** *(bäTHz, baths).*—*v.t.* and *v.i.* to wash in a bath.
bath'house *n.* **bath'room** *n.*
Order of the Bath an order of knighthood.
See also **Bath, bathe**.

Bath *bäth*, *n.* a city in Avon, S.W. England, with Roman *baths*.
Bath bun a rich sweet bun.
Bath chair (also without *cap.*) an invalid's wheeled chair.

bathe *bāTH*, *v.t.* **1** to wash gently. **2** to moisten (with, in).—*v.i.* to take a bath or bathe:—*pr.p.* **bath'ing**.—*n.* a swim or dip.
bath'er *n.* **bath'ing** *n.*

bathyscaphe *bath'i-skāf*, **bathyscope** *-skōp*, **bathysphere** *-sfēr*, *ns.* types of observation chamber for natural history work under water.

batik *bat'ik*, *n.* a method of dyeing patterns on cloth by waxing certain areas so that they remain uncoloured.

batman *bat'mȧn*, *n.* an officer's servant.

baton *bat'ȯn*, *n.* **1** a staff or truncheon, esp. of a policeman. **2** (*music*) a conductor's stick.

batsman. See **bat[1]**.

battalion *bȧ-tal'yȯn*, *n.* a large body of soldiers.

batten[1] *bat'n*, *v.i.* **1** (often with *on*) to feed gluttonously. **2** (with *on*) to live well at the expense of: *He battened on his generous aunt*.

batten[2] *bat'n*, *n.* **1** sawn timber used for flooring. **2** in ships, a strip of wood used to fasten down the hatches.—*v.t.* to fasten with battens (often with *down*).

batter[1]. See **bat[1]**.

batter[2] *bat'ėr*, *v.t.* **1** to beat with blow after blow. **2** to wear, spoil, with beating or by use.—*n.* (*cooking*) eggs, milk, flour, etc. beaten together into a paste.
battered *adj.* **1** often violently assaulted: *a battered wife.* **2** (*cooking*) covered with batter.
batt'ery *n.* **1** a number of pieces of artillery. **2** a unit group of artillery and the people manning it. **3** a series of two or more electric cells arranged, or a single cell constructed, to produce, or store,

a current. **4** a similar arrangement of other apparatus. **5** an arrangement of cages in which laying hens are kept. **6** a similar arrangement of compartments for rearing pigs, cattle, etc. **7** (*law*) assault by blow or touch:—*pl.* **batt'eries**.

batt'ering-ram *n.* a large beam with a metal head, formerly used in war for battering down walls.

batting. See **bat**[1,3].

battle *bat'l, n.* **1** a contest between opposing armies. **2** a fight between persons or animals.—*v.i.* **1** to fight. **2** to struggle (with *with, against,* or *for*):—*pr.p.* **battl'ing**.

batt'leaxe *n.* **1** an axe once used in battle. **2** (*coll.*) an unpleasant domineering woman.

batt'le-cry *n.* **1** a shout in battle. **2** a slogan.

batt'lefield *n.* the place where a battle is or has been fought.

battle royal a fight or argument of great fierceness, or one in which many take part.

batt'le-scarred *adj.* bearing marks of damage in battle.

batt'leship *n.* a heavily armed and armoured warship.

half the battle anything that brings one well on the way to success.

join, do, battle to fight.

battledore *bat'l-dōr, -dör, n.* a light bat for striking a shuttlecock.

battlement *bat'l-mėnt, n.* (often in *pl.*) a wall or parapet with openings for firing from.

batty. See **bat**[2].

bauble *bö'bl, n.* **1** a trifling trinket. **2** a toy. **3** a court jester's stick.

baulk. See **balk**.

bauxite *bök'sīt, -zīt, n.* an aluminium ore, found at *Les Baux* (near Arles), etc.

bawdy *bö'di, adj.* vulgar, coarse: *bawdy songs*:—*comp.* **baw'dier**; *superl.* **baw'diest**.

bawl *böl, v.i.* and *v.t.* to shout or cry out loudly.—*n.* a loud cry or shout.

bay[1] *bā, adj.* reddish brown.—*n.* a bay horse.

bay[2] *bā, n.* a wide inlet of the sea, etc.

bay[3] *bā, n.* **1** the space between two columns, partitions, etc. **2** a recess. **3** a compartment in an aircraft.

bay window a window forming a recess.

sick bay a ship's, etc., hospital.

bay[4] *bā, n.* **1** a laurel tree. **2** (in *pl.*) a garland or crown of victory, orig. of laurel.

bay leaf a type of laurel leaf, dried and used as a seasoning in cooking.

bay[5] *bā, n.* the deep cry of hounds when hunting.—*v.i.* (esp. of large dogs) to bark:—*pa.p.* **bayed**.

hold, keep, at bay to fight off, keep from overwhelming one.

stand, be, at bay to be in a position of having to turn and face an enemy, a difficulty, etc.

bayonet *bā'ȯn-it, n.* a stabbing instrument of steel fixed to the muzzle of a rifle.—*v.t.* to stab with a bayonet:—*pr.p.* **bay'oneting**; *pa.p.* **bay'oneted**.

bayonet fitting one for a light bulb, etc., in which prongs are fitted into slots and twisted to secure the bulb.

bay window. See **bay**[3].

bazaar *bȧ-zär', n.* **1** an Eastern marketplace. **2** a shop, etc., where miscellaneous goods are sold. **3** a sale of work.

bazooka *bȧ-zōō'kȧ, n.* a weapon consisting of a long tube that launches a projectile with an explosive head.

be *bē, v.i.* **1** to live. **2** to exist. **3** to occur.—*v.* used to form tenses of other verbs, as in *I am going, they were walking*:—*pr.p.* **bē'ing**; *pa.p.* **been** *(bin)*; *pr.t.* (*sing.*) **am, art, is,** (*pl.*) **are**; *pa.t.* (*sing.*) **was, wert, was,** (*pl.*) **were** *(wėr).*

being *bē'ing, n.* **1** existence. **2** any person or thing existing.

be- *pfx.* **1** around, on all sides, thoroughly, etc., as in *besmear*, to smear over. **2** used to form words from *adjs.*, as in *befoul*, to make foul. **3** to call or treat as (something), as in **befriend**—see this word.

beach *bēch, n.* the shore of a sea or lake, esp. when sandy or pebbly.—*v.t.* to drive or haul (a boat) up on the beach.

beach'comber *(-kōm-ėr) n.* **1** a long rolling wave. **2** a drunken loafer in Pacific seaports. **3** a settler on a Pacific island who lives by pearl-fishing and gathering jetsam. **4** a person who gathers jetsam.

beach'head *n.* an area on a seashore in enemy territory seized by an advance force and held to cover the main landing.

beacon *bē'kȯn, n.* **1** a fire on a high place used as a signal, esp. formerly of danger. **2** anything that warns of danger, e.g. a sign or light marking rocks, shoals, etc. **3** a sign marking a street crossing. **4** a radio transmitter that sends out signals to guide shipping or aircraft.

bead *bēd, n.* **1** a little ball of glass, etc., strung with others in a rosary or a necklace. **2** a drop of liquid. **3** a bubble. **4** the foresight of a gun.

bead'y *adj.* (of eyes) small and bright:—*comp.* **bead'ier**; *superl.* **bead'iest**.

tell, count, one's beads to say one's prayers.

beadle *bēd'l*, *n.* **1** a mace-bearer. **2** an officer with minor duties of a church, college, etc.

beady. See **bead**.

beagle *bē'gl*, *n.* a small dog, often used in hunting hares (**bea'gling**).

beak *bēk*, *n.* **1** the bill of a bird. **2** anything pointed or projecting. **3** the nose.

beaker *bēk'ėr*, *n.* **1** (*old*) a large drinking-bowl or cup. **2** a straight-sided mug without a handle. **3** a deep glass vessel used in chemistry.

beam *bēm*, *n.* **1** a long straight piece of timber, etc. for building, etc. **2** one of the pieces of timber or metal placed from side to side in forming a ship's frame. **3** the greatest width of a ship or boat. **4** the part of a balance from which the scales hang. **5** a shaft or ray (of light, etc.). **6** a radio signal sent out along a narrow course to guide aircraft.—*v.i.* to smile broadly.—*v.t.* and *v.i.* to transmit (radio signals).

off the beam 1 off the course indicated by a radio beam. **2** (*coll.*) inaccurate.

on her beam ends (of a ship) so much inclined to one side that the beams become nearly upright.

on one's beam ends at the end of one's resources in money, etc.

on the beam 1 in the direction of a ship's beams, at right angles to her course. **2** on the course indicated by a radio beam.

bean *bēn*, *n.* **1** the name of several pod-bearing plants and their seeds. **2** a seed of such plants, used as food. **3** the bean-like seeds of other plants, e.g. coffee.

bean sprouts the young shoots of certain kinds of bean, used as a vegetable, esp. in Chinese cookery.

full of beans in high spirits.

not have a bean (*coll.*) to have no money.

spill the beans. See **spill**.

bear[1] *bār*, *v.t.* **1** to carry. **2** to support. **3** to heave, thrust (back). **4** to endure. **5** to behave or conduct (oneself). **6** to bring forth or produce (offspring, an idea, etc.) (*pa.p.* **born** *(börn)* in passive uses, as in *He was born in America*):—*pr.p.* **bear'ing**; *pa.t.* **bore** *(bōr, bör)*; *pa.p.* **borne** *(bōrn, börn)*.

bear'able *adj.* that can be endured.

bear'er *n.* **1** one who, or something that, bears. **2** one who helps to carry a body to the grave. **3** a carrier, messenger, or (in India) personal attendant.

bear'ing *n.* **1** manner, posture, etc. **2** direction, situation, position (of one object with regard to another). **3** connection with: *This has no bearing on the question.* **4** (usu. in *pl.*) a part of a machine that bears friction, because another part turns or moves in it.

bear down 1 to swoop (on). **2** to press down (on) or downward.

bear fruit 1 to produce fruit. **2** to have the desired result.

bear hard, heavily, on someone to be difficult for someone to endure.

bear in mind. See **mind**.

bear out to support, confirm: *This bears out what you said.*

bear up to keep up one's courage.

bear with to be patient with.

be borne in upon someone to be impressed on someone's mind.

bring to bear to bring into use or operation (with *on, upon, against*): *They brought pressure to bear on him to leave the country.*

find, get, one's bearings 1 to find one's position with reference to e.g. a known landmark. **2** to come to understand a new situation.

lose one's bearings to become uncertain of one's position.

bear[2] *bār*, *n.* **1** a heavy animal with shaggy hair and hooked claws. **2** (with *cap.*) the name of two northern groups of stars, the Great and the Little Bear.

bear'-bait'ing *n.* the former sport of setting dogs to attack a tethered bear.

bear garden 1 an enclosure where bears are kept. **2** a rough, noisy place or scene.

bear'skin *n.* **1** the skin of a bear. **2** a high fur cap worn by the Guards in England.

bearable. See **bear**[1].

beard *bērd*, *n.* **1** the hair that grows on the chin and cheeks. **2** something that suggests this. **3** a tuft of prickles on ears of corn.—*v.t.* **1** to take by the beard. **2** to face deliberately, oppose boldly.

beard'ed *adj.* **beard'less** *adj.*

bearer, bearing. See **bear**[1].

beast *bēst*, *n.* **1** an animal, as opposed to man. **2** a (esp. large) four-footed animal. **3** a brutal person.

beast'ly *adj.* **1** like a beast in actions or behaviour. **2** coarse. **3** (*coll.*) disagreeable:—*comp.* **beast'lier**; *superl.* **beast'liest**.

beast'liness *n.*

See also **bestial**.

beat *bēt*, *v.t.* **1** to strike repeatedly. **2** to strike (e.g. bushes) to rouse game. **3** to overcome. **4** to be too difficult for. **5** to mark (time) with a baton, etc. **6** to mix (eggs, etc.) thoroughly with a whisk, etc.—*v.i.* **1** to move with regular strokes. **2** to throb. **3** (of waves) to dash (on, against):—*pr.p.* **beat'ing**; *pa.t.* **beat**; *pa.p.* **beat'en.**—*n.* **1** a stroke, or its sound, as of a clock, a metronome, a piece of music or the pulse. **2** a round or course: *a policeman's beat.*

beat'en *adj.* **1** made smooth or hard by treading: *a beaten path.* **2** shaped by hammering. **3** overcome, defeated. **4** mixed with a whisk, etc.

beat'er *n.*

beat'ing *n.* **1** a thrashing. **2** a throbbing. **3** the rousing of game.

beat music popular music with a very pronounced rhythm.

beat about the bush. See **bush**.

beat a retreat to withdraw in a hurry.

beat down 1 to reduce (the price) by haggling. **2** to force (a person) to take a lower price.

beat one's brains to make a great effort to think of, or to remember, something.

beat the clock to do or finish something within the time allowed.

beat up 1 to collect (e.g. recruits, helpers). **2** to injure by repeated punching, kicking, etc.

dead beat completely exhausted.

beatify *bē-at'i-fī*, *v.t.* to make, or declare to be, blessed or happy:—*pr.p.* **beat'tifying**; *pa.p.* **beat'ified.**

beatif'ic, *al adjs.* **1** making very happy. **2** expressing happiness: *a beatific smile.*

beatif'ically *adv.*

beatificā'tion (*R.C.* Church) *n.* declaration by the Pope that a person is blessed in heaven, the first step to canonisation.

beating. See **beat**.

beatitude *bē-at'i-tūd*, *n.* **1** heavenly happiness. **2** (in *pl.*) the sayings of Christ in *Matthew v.,* declaring certain classes of persons to be blessed.

beatnik *bēt'nik*, *n.* a person (*orig.* one of a group of U.S. poets or writers) who dresses and behaves in a deliberately unconventional way.

beau *bō*, *n.* **1** a boyfriend or lover. **2** a dandy:—*pl.* **beaux** *(bōz)*; *fem.* **belle** (see this word).

beau ideal *bō ī-dē'ȧl*, a person one considers of the highest excellence.

beauteous, beautiful, etc. See **beauty**.

beauty *bū'ti*, *n.* **1** a quality very pleasing to eye, or ear, etc. **2** a woman or girl having such a quality. **3** an object, etc., attractive-looking or very good (sometimes *ironic*: *The black eye he got was a beauty*):—*pl.* **beau'ties**.

beauteous *bū'tyu̇s*, *-ti-u̇s* (chiefly in poetry) *adj.*

beautician *bū-tish'(ȧ)n*, *n.* a person whose business it is to make people more beautiful, e.g. by manicuring, face-massaging, etc.

beautiful *adj.* **beau'tifully** *adv.*

beau'tify *(-fī)* *v.t.* **1** to make beautiful. **2** to adorn:—*pr.p.* **beau'tifying**; *pa.p.* **beau'tified.**

beauty queen a girl or woman who is voted the most attractive in a competition (**beauty contest**).

beaver *bēv'ėr*, *n.* **1** a gnawing animal noted for its skill in damming streams. **2** its fur. **3** a hat made of its fur.

beav'erboard (® with *cap.* in U.S.) *n.* a building board of wood fibre.

beaver away (*coll.*) to keep busily working (at).

becalm *bi-käm'*, *v.t.* **1** to calm. **2** to make motionless (esp. a ship).

becalmed' *adj.*

became. See **become**.

because *bi-koz'*, *bi-kȯz'*, *conj.* for the reason that.

because of on account of.

beck *bek*, *n.* **1** a sign with the finger. **2** a nod.

at someone's beck and call always ready to serve and obey someone.

beckon *bek'ȯn*, *v.t.* and *v.i.* to summon by making a sign or nodding (to).

become *bi-kum'*, *v.i.* **1** to come to be. **2** to be the fate (of): *What has become of it?*; *What is to become of me?*—*v.t.* to suit or befit:—*pr.p.* **becom'ing**; *pa.t.* **becāme'**; *pa.p.* **become'**.

becom'ing *adj.* **1** suitable (to). **2** suiting attractively: *a becoming hat.*

becom'ingly *adv.*

bed *bed*, *n.* **1** a piece of furniture, or a place, to sleep on. **2** the channel of a river. **3** a plot in a garden. **4** a place in which anything rests, a foundation. **5** a layer.—*v.t.* **1** to put to bed. **2** to plant in a bed:—*pr.p.* **bedding;** *pa.p.* **bedd'ed.**

bedd'ing *n.* **1** mattress, bedclothes, etc. **2** litter for cattle.

bed'clothes *n.pl.* sheets, blankets, etc.

bed'cover *n.* an upper cover for a bed.

bed'fellow *n.* **1** a sharer of the same bed. **2** a person or thing associated with another.

bed'pan *n.* a wide, shallow bowl into which an ill person may urinate, etc. without getting out of bed.

bed'ridden *adj.* permanently in bed because of age or sickness.

bed'rock *n.* **1** the solid rock underneath soil or rock fragments. **2** the lowest layer. **3** the foundation, basis. **4** hard essential facts.
bed'room *n.* a room for sleeping in.
bed'side *n.* the place or position next to a bed.—Also *adj.*: *a bedside table*.
bed'sit, bedsitt'er *ns.* a single room (*usu.* rented) for eating and sleeping (and often cooking) in.
bed'spread *n.* a cover put over a bed during the day.
bed'stead *n.* a frame for supporting a bed.
bed and board food and lodging.
a bed of roses any easy or comfortable place.
lie in the bed one has made to take the consequences of one's own acts.

bedaub *bi-döb'*, *v.t.* to smear.—*pa.p.* **bedaubed'**.

bedevil *bi-dev'l*, *v.t.* **1** to torment. **2** to bewitch. **3** to muddle, spoil:—*pr.p.* **bedev'illing**; *pa.p.* **bedev'illed**.

bedlam *bed'lăm*, *n.* (a place of) uproar.

bedouin *bed'ōō-in*, *n.* a tent-dwelling Arab.

bedraggled *bi-drag'ld*, *adj.* soiled as by dragging in the wet or dirt.

bee *bē*, *n.* **1** a four-winged insect, related to wasps and ants, esp. (**honey-bee**) the insect that makes honey. **2** (esp. *U.S.*) a social gathering for work or entertainment: *a sewing bee*.
bee'hive *n.* a box in which bees are kept, of straw-work, wood, etc.—*adj.* like a dome-shaped beehive.
bees'wax *n.* the yellowish, solid substance produced by bees, and used by them in making their cells.
bee in one's bonnet an idea that has become fixed in one's mind.
make a bee-line for to take the most direct road to.

Beeb *bēb*, *n.*, *coll.* for **BBC** (British Broadcasting Corporation).

beech *bēch*, *n.* a forest tree with smooth silvery bark and small nuts.
beech mast the nuts of the beech tree, which yield a valuable oil.
copper beech a variety of beech with purplish-brown leaves.

beef *bēf*, *n.* **1** (the flesh of) a bull, cow, etc. **2** muscle as opp. to brain.
beef'y *adj.* **1** like beef. **2** fleshy, heavy:—*comp.* **beef'ier**; *superl.* **beef'iest**.
beef'iness *n.*
beef'burger *n.* a fried or grilled round flat cake of finely chopped meat.
beefeater *bēf'ēt-ėr*, *n.* **1** a yeoman of the sovereign's guard. **2** a warder of the Tower of London.
beef tea the juice of chopped beef, taken by invalids.

beehive See **bee**.

been. See **be**.

beer *bēr*, *n.* an alcoholic drink made by fermentation from malted barley, flavoured with hops.
beer'y *adj.*:—*comp.* **beer'ier**; *superl.* **beer'iest**.
beer'iness *n.*
beer and skittles idle enjoyment.
small beer 1 weak beer. **2** trivial affairs. **3** an unimportant person.

beeswax. See **bee**.

beet *bēt*, *n.* a plant with a round or carrot-shaped root, one variety (**red beet**) used as food, another (**sugar beet**) as a source of sugar.
beet'root *n.* the root of the (usu. red) beet.

beetle[1] *bē'tl*, *n.* an insect with four wings, the front pair hard and horny and forming a cover for the hind pair.
beetle off (*coll.*) to scurry away.

beetle[2] *bē'tl*, *n.* a heavy wooden mallet used for driving wedges, etc.

beetle[3] *bē'tl*, *v.i.* (of e.g. a cliff) to jut, stick out, hang over:—*pr.p.* **beet'ling**.

beetle-browed *bē'tl-browd*, *adj.* **1** with projecting, heavy eyebrows. **2** scowling, sullen.

befall *bi-fōl'*, *v.t.* to happen to (a person or thing).—*v.i.* to happen:—*pr.p.* **befall'ing**; *pa.t.* **befell'**; *pa.p.* **befall'en**.

befit *bi-fit'*, *v.t.* to be suitable to, fitting, right for:—*pr.p.* **befitt'ing**; *pa.p.* **befitt'ed**.
befitt'ing *adj.* **befitt'ingly** *adv.*

befogged *bi-fogd'*, *adj.* (of a person) confused.

before *bi-fōr'*, *prep.* **1** in front of. **2** earlier than. **3** in preference to. **4** better than.—*adv.* **1** in front. **2** earlier.—*conj.* earlier than the time when.
before'hand *adv.* before the time, esp. as preparation.

befoul. See **be-**.

befriend *bi-frend'*, *v.t.* **1** to act as a friend to. **2** to help.

beg *beg*, *v.i.* to ask alms or charity.—*v.t.* to ask earnestly (for):—*pr.p.* **begg'ing**; *pa.p.* **begged**.
beggar *beg'ăr*, *n.* **1** one who lives by begging. **2** a mean fellow. **3** (*playfully*) a rogue, rascal.—*v.t.* to make very poor:—*pr.p.* **begg'aring**; *pa.p.* **begg'ared**.
begg'arly *adj.* **1** poor. **2** mean.

begg'arliness *n*.
beggar description to be greater than the speaker can find words to describe.
beg off to be or cause to be excused from a punishment, a duty, etc.
beg the question to take for granted the very point that is required to be proved.
beg to differ to disagree.
go a-begging to find no claimant or purchaser.

began. See **begin**.

beget *bi-get'*, *v.t.* **1** (of a male parent) to procreate. **2** to cause: *to beget ill-feeling*:—*pr.p.* **begett'ing**; *pa.t.* **begot'**; *pa.p.* **begott'en**.

beggar, beggarly, etc. See **beg**.

begin *bi-gin'*, *v.i.* **1** to arise (from). **2** to be the first to do something. **3** to open, start, commence.—Also *v.t.*:—*pr.p.* **beginn'ing**; *pa.t.* **began'**; *pa.p.* **begun'**.
beginn'er *n*. **beginn'ing** *n*.
to begin with 1 at first. **2** firstly.

begonia *bi-gōn'yȧ, -i-ȧ*, *n*. a greenhouse plant usually with pink flowers and often with coloured leaves.

begot, begotten. See **beget**.

begrudge *bi-gruj'*, *v.t.* to grudge, envy: *She begrudged him his success*:—*pr.p.* **begrudg'ing**.

beguile *bi-gīl'*, *v.t.* **1** to cheat (of, out of, something). **2** to lead by deception (into), to deceive: *He was beguiled into buying the faked antique*. **3** to charm, amuse:—*pr.p.* **beguil'ing**.

begum *bē'gum, bā'*, *n*. a Muslim princess or lady of rank.

begun. See **begin**.

behalf *bi-häf'*, *n*. sake, account, part: *acting in, on, my behalf*; *on behalf of the members of the club*.

behave *bi-hāv'*, *v.t.* to conduct (oneself) well: *If you come, you must behave yourself.*—*v.i.* **1** to conduct oneself well. **2** to conduct oneself (well, badly, etc.). **3** (of persons, things) to act in response to something done or happening: *How did he behave when told the news?*:—*pr.p.* **behav'ing**.
behaved' *pa.p.* used in phrases **well (ill, badly) behaved**, showing, esp. as a habit, good (bad) manners or conduct.
behaviour *bi-hāv'yȯr*, *n*. **1** conduct, manners. **2** response to what is done or happens.
be (up)on one's best behaviour to be trying to conduct oneself well.
See also **misbehave**.

behead *bi-hed'*, *v.t.* to cut off the head of.
behead'ing *n*.

beheld. See **behold**.

behest *bi-hest'*, *n*. **1** a command. **2** bidding.

behind *bi-hīnd'*, *prep*. **1** at the back of. **2** at the far side of. **3** in support of, encouraging. **4** in a direction backward from. **5** later than. **6** less good than.—*adv*. **1** at the back, in the rear. **2** backward. **3** past.
behind'(hand) *adv*. or *adj*. late, in arrears (with e.g. work, payments).

behold *bi-hōld'*, *v.t.* **1** to see, observe. **2** to look at.—*v.i.* to look:—*pa.t.* and *pa.p.* **beheld'**.
behold'en *adj*. obliged, indebted, grateful (to).
behold'er *n*.

beholden. See **behold**.

beho(o)ve *bi-hōv', -hōōv'*, *v.t.* now only in the phrase **it beho(o)ves,** it is right or necessary for: *It behoves you to show gratitude*.

beige *bāzh*, *n*. **1** a fabric made of undyed wool. **2** the colour of this. **3** now, a pinkish buff colour.

being. See **be**.

belabour *bi-lā'bȯr*, *v.t.* to beat soundly.

belated *bi-lāt'id*, *adj*. happening late or too late.

belay *bi-lā'*, *v.t.* to fasten (a rope) by coiling it round a **belay'ing-pin** or short rod:—*pr.p.* **belay'ing**; *pa.p.* **belayed'**.

belch *belch*, **belsh**, *v.t.* and *v.i.* **1** to give out wind by the mouth. **2** (of a gun, volcano, etc.) to throw out violently.

beleaguer *bi-lēg'ėr*, *v.t.* to lay siege to.

belfry *bel'fri*, *n*. the part of a steeple or tower in which bells are hung:—*pl*. **bel'fries**.

Belgian *bel'jȧn*, *n*. and *adj*. (a native) of *Belgium*.

belie *bi-lī*, *v.t.* **1** to prove false. **2** to fail to act up to (e.g. a promise). **3** to give a false picture of:—*pr.p.* **bely'ing**; *pa.p.* **belied'**.

belief. See **believe**.

believe *bi-lēv'*, *v.t.* **1** to regard (something) as true. **2** to trust (a person), accepting what he says as true. **3** to think, suppose.—*v.i.* to have faith (in):—*pr.p.* **believ'ing**.
belief' *n*. **1** faith. **2** trust.
believ'able *adj*. **believ'er** *n*.
See also **disbelieve**.

belittle *bi-lit'l*, *v.t.* **1** to make to seem small. **2** to speak slightingly of:—*pr.p.* **belitt'ling**.

bell[1] *bel*, *n*. **1** a hollow vessel of metal struck by a tongue or clapper. **2** other device for giving a ringing sound. **3** anything bell-shaped, as the bell of a harebell, etc. **4** the sound of a bell.—*v.t.* to provide with a bell.

bell'-tent *n.* a bell-shaped tent.

bell'-tower *n.* a tower built to contain bells.

sound as a bell in perfect condition.

bell^2 *bel, v.i.* (esp. of stag) to bellow, roar.

belladonna *bel-ȧ-don'ȧ, n.* **1** deadly night-shade, a plant, all parts of which are poisonous. **2** the drug prepared from it.

belle *bel, n.* **1** a beautiful girl. **2** the most beautiful lady at a dance, etc.
See also **beau.**

bellicose *bel'i-kōs, ạdj.* warlike, quarrelsome.

belligerent *bi-lij'ėr-ėnt, adj.* **1** carrying on war. **2** warlike: *a belligerent attitude.—n.* a nation or person waging war.

bellig'erence *n.* **bellig'erently** *adv.*

bellow *bel'ō, v.i.* **1** to roar like a bull. **2** to make a loud outcry.—Also *v.t.—n.* **1** the roar of a bull. **2** any deep sound or cry.

bellows *bel'ōz, n.pl.* or *n.sing.* an instrument for making a current of air to be directed on to e.g. a fire.

belly *bel'i, n.* **1** the part of the body between the breast and the thighs. **2** the interior of anything. **3** the bulging part of anything:—*pl.* **bell'ies.**—*v.t.* and *v.i.* to swell out:—*pr.p.* **bell'ying**; *pa.p.* **bell'ied.**

bell'yfull *n.* a quantity sufficient or more than sufficient.

belong *bi-long', v.i.* **1** to go along (with). **2** to be the property of (with *to*). **3** to be a native, member, etc., of (with *to*).

belong'ings *n.pl.* possessions.

beloved *bi-luvd', adj.* much loved (by, of).—*adj.* and *n.* *(bi-luv'id)* very dear (person).

below *bi-lō', prep.* **1** beneath. **2** underneath. **3** not worthy of.—*adv.* **1** in a lower place. **2** on earth.

belt *belt, n.* **1** a girdle, strip, or band of leather, cloth, etc. **2** a zone, a region. **3** a seat-belt.—*v.t.* **1** to surround with a belt. **2** to thrash with a belt.—*v.i.* (*coll.*) to go quickly.

belt'ed *adj.* **1** (of a knight, earl) wearing a ceremonial belt. **2** having a belt. **3** (of an animal) marked with a band of different colour.

belt'ing *n.* a thrashing.

belt out (*coll.*) to sing, etc. vigorously or enthusiastically.

belt up (*slang*) to be quiet.

under one's belt firmly secured or in one's possession.

bemoan *bi-mōn', v.t.* to lament.

bemused *bi-mūzd', adj.* **1** dazed. **2** absorbed.

bench *bench, -sh, n.* **1** a long seat, form. **2** a mechanic's work-table. **3** a judge's seat.

bench'mark *n.* anything used as a standard or point of reference.

bend *bend, v.t.* **1** to curve (e.g. a bow). **2** to make crooked. **3** to force to submit: *to bend a person to one's will.* **4** to apply closely: *to bend one's energies to the job.* **5** to turn, direct (e.g. steps, eyes).—*v.i.* **1** to be crooked or curved. **2** to stoop. **3** to lean. **4** to submit (with *to, before, towards*):—*pa.t.* and *pa.p.* usu. **bent** (but *on one's* **bend'ed** *knees*).—*n.* a curve.

bent *adj.* **1** (*coll.*) dishonest, immoral. **2** (*slang*) homosexual.

bent'wood *n.* wood artificially curved for chair-making, etc.

be bent on to be determined on: *bent on going*; *bent on reform.*

the bends caisson disease (see this).
See also **bent**^{2}.

bene- *ben-i-*, (as part of word) well.

beneath *bi-nēth', prep.* under, below.—Also *adv.*

beneath contempt not even worth despising.

beneath one unworthy of one, not in keeping with one's dignity.

benediction *ben-i-dik'sh(ȯ)n, n.* **1** a prayer asking for the divine blessing. **2** blessedness.

benefaction *ben-i-fak'sh(ȯ)n, n.* **1** a good deed. **2** a grant or gift.

ben'efactor (or *-fak'*) *n.* **1** one who gives friendly help. **2** one who makes a gift to a charity:—*fem.* **ben'efactress** (or *-fak'*). See also **beneficence**, etc.

benefice *ben'i-fis, n.* a church office to which property or revenue is attached, as that of a rector or vicar.

beneficence *bi-nef'i-sėns, n.* active kindness, charity.

benef'icent *adj.*

beneficial *ben-i-fish'ȧl, adj.* useful, advantageous, having good results.

benefic'ially *adv.*

benefic'iary *n.* one who receives a gift, legacy, advantage, etc.:—*pl.* **benefic'iaries.**
See also **benefaction**, etc.

benefit *ben'i-fit, n.* **1** something good to receive or have done to one. **2** an advantage. **3** a performance at a theatre, game, etc. at which proceeds go to one player. **4** a right under an insurance scheme: *unemployment benefit.—v.t.* to do good to.—*v.i.* to gain advantage (from, by):—

pr.p. **ben'efiting**; *pa.p.* **ben'efited**.

benevolence *ben-ev'ol-ens, n.* **1** the will to do good. **2** kindness. **3** generosity.

benev'olent *adj.* **1** charitable, generous. **2** feeling kindly, wishing well.

benev'olently *adv.*

Bengali *ben-gö'lē, n.* and *adj.* (a native) of Bengal.

benign *bi-nīn', adj.* **1** favourable (*opp.* **malign.**) **2** (*medical*) not malignant. **3** gracious. **4** kindly.

benignant *bi-nig'nant, adj.* kind; gracious.

benig'nity *n.* **1** goodness of disposition. **2** kindness and graciousness.

benign'ly *bi-nīn'li, adj.*

bent[1]. See **bend**.

bent[2] *bent, n.* a leaning, tendency, inclination of the mind.

to the top of one's bent as much as one likes.

bent[3] *bent, n.* any stiff or wiry grass.

bentwood. See **bend**.

benumbed *bi-numd', adj.* (esp. of feelings) deadened, numb.

benzene *ben'zēn, n.* a liquid hydrocarbon obtained from coal tar.

benzine *(-zēn) n.* a mixture of hydrocarbons got from petroleum, used as solvent of grease, etc., and for motor fuel.

ben'zol(e) *n.* crude benzene, used as a motor spirit.

bequeath *bi-kwēth', v.t.* **1** to leave (personal estate) by will. **2** to hand down.

bequest *bi-kwest', n.* **1** an act of bequeathing. **2** a legacy.

bereave *bi-rēv', v.t.* to deprive (of), esp. by death:—*pr.p.* **bereav'ing**; *pa.p.* **bereaved'** or **bereft'**.

bereaved' *adj.* deprived by death of a relative, etc.

bereave'ment *n.*

bereft. See **bereave**.

beret *ber'ā, n.* a round, flat, soft cap.

berg *bûrg, n.* **1** a hill, mountain. **2** an iceberg.

beriberi *ber'i-ber'i, n.* an Eastern disease, due to lack of vitamin B.

berry *ber'i, n.* **1** a small juicy fruit. **2** a coffee bean:—*pl.* **berr'ies**.

berserk *ber-sûrk', -zûrk', adj.* (not usu. used before a noun) violently angry, mad.—Also *adv.*

berth *bûrth, n.* **1** a ship's station in port. **2** a sleeping-place in a ship, etc. **3** a job, place of employment.—*v.t.* to moor a ship.

give a wide berth to to keep well away from.

beryl *ber'il, n.* a precious stone of which emerald and aquamarine are varieties.

beryll'ium *n.* a light steely element.

beseech *bi-sēch', v.t.* **1** to beg, entreat. **2** to beg for:—*pa.t.* and *pa.p.* **beseeched'** or **besought'**.

beset *bi-set', v.t.* **1** to attack on all sides. **2** to surround: *beset with troubles*:—*pr.p.* **besett'ing**; *pa.t.* and *pa.p.* **beset'**.

besetting sin the sin that most often tempts and gets the better of one.

beside *bi-sīd', prep.* **1** by the side of, near. **2** over and above, in addition to.—Also *adv.*

besides *bi-sīdz', prep.* over and above, in addition to.—Also *adv.*

be beside oneself to be frantic with anxiety, fear, or anger.

beside the point irrelevant.

besiege *bis-ēj', v.t.* **1** to set armed forces round (e.g. a town) in order to force it to surrender. **2** to throng round. **3** to assail (with requests, questions):—*pr.p.* **besieg'ing**.

besieg'er *n.*

besmear. See **be- (1)**.

besmirch *bi-smûrch', v.t.* to soil, dirty.

besom *bē'zom, biz'om, n.* a bunch of twigs for sweeping, a broom.

besotted *bi-sot'id, adj.* foolishly infatuated (with).

besought. See **beseech**.

bespatter *bi-spat'er, v.t.* to sprinkle with dirt or anything moist.

bespeak *bi-spēk', v.t.* to show: *His action bespeaks great courage*:—*pa.t.* **bespōke'**; *pa.p.* **bespoke'** and **bespōk'en**.

bespoke *bi-spōk', adj.* **1** (also **bespok'en**) ordered (as boots, clothes, etc.). **2** (of a tailor, etc.) making clothes, etc., to order.

best *best, adj.* (used as *superl.* of **good**) good in the highest degree.—*n.* **1** one's utmost effort. **2** the highest perfection. **3** the best part.—*adv.* (*superl.* of **well**) **1** in the highest degree. **2** in the best manner.—*v.t.* to get the better of.

best-before date a date on the packaging of a product, indicating when it should be used by.

best man the bridegroom's attendant at a wedding.

bestsell'er *n.* **1** (a book) which sells in large numbers. **2** the author of a bestselling book.

bestsell'ing *adj.*

for the best 1 with the best intentions. **2** with the best results all things considered.

had best would be best to.

put one's best foot foremost to make one's best effort.

bestial *best'yȧl, -i-ȧl, adj.* **1** brutal. **2** depraved.

bestial'ity *n.* **best'ially** *adv.*

bestir *bi-stûr'*, *v.t.* to rouse to action (esp. oneself):—*pr.p.* **bestirr'ing**; *pa.p.* **bestirred'**.

bestow *bi-stō'*, *v.t.* **1** to place, or store, put away. **2** to give (with *on*).

bestow'al *n.*

bestrew *bi-stro͞o'*, *v.t.* to scatter (with):—*pa.t.* **bestrewed'**; *pa.p.* **bestrewed'**, **bestrown'**, **bestrewn'**.

bestride *bi-strīd'*, *v.t.* **1** to stride over. **2** to sit or stand across:—*pr.p.* **bestrīd'ing**; *pa.t.* **bestrid'**, **bestrode'**; *pa.p.* **bestrid'**, **bestridd'en**.

bet *bet*, *n.* a wager, money staked to be lost or won.—*v.t.* and *v.i.* to lay or stake, as a bet:—*pr.p.* **bett'ing**; *pa.t.* and *pa.p.* **bet** or **bett'ed**.

bett'er *n.* **bett'ing** *n.*

beta *bē'tȧ, n.* **1** the second letter of the Greek alphabet. **2** a mark given for work which is less good than that marked alpha.

be'ta-block'er *n.* a drug that reducs heart-rate.

betake *bi-tāk'*, *v.t.* to take (oneself), to go: *He betook himself to church*:—*pa.t.* **betook'**; *pa.p.* **betak'en**.

betel *bē'tl, n.* the leaf of the betel-pepper, which is chewed in the East along with certain nut-like seeds and lime.

bête noire *bet nwär* a person or thing that one particularly dislikes.

bethink *bi-thingk'*, *v.* (with *oneself*) to call to mind:—*pa.t.* and *pa.p.* **bethought** *(bi-thöt')*.

betide *bi-tīd'*, (*old*) *v.t.* to happen to: *Woe betide him.*—*v.i.* to happen, come to pass:—*pr.p.* **betid'ing**.

betimes *bi-tīmz'*, *adv.* in good time.

betoken *bi-tō'kn*, *v.t.* to be evidence of, show.

betook. See **betake**.

betray *bi-trā'*, *v.t.* **1** to give up treacherously (e.g. friends, secrets). **2** to deceive. **3** to show signs of: *to betray anxiety*.

betray'al *n.* **betray'er** *n.*

betroth *bi-trō*TH'(or *-trōth'*), *v.t.* to promise in marriage.

betrōth'al *n.* **betrōthed'** *n.* and *adj.*

better[1], etc. See **bet**.

better[2] *bet'ėr, adj.* **1** (used as *comp.* of **good**) good in a greater degree. **2** preferable. **3** improved. **4** stronger in health.—*adv.* (as *comp.* of **well**) well in a greater degree.—*n.* (esp. in *pl.*) a superior—*v.t.* **1** to improve. **2** to surpass.

bett'erment *n.* improvement.

be better than one's word to do more than one had promised.

better half (*playfully*) a spouse.

better off 1 richer. **2** happier.

get the better of 1 to outwit. **2** to overcome.

had better would be wiser to.

the better part of most of.

think better of (it) to change one's mind about (it).

between *bi-twēn'*, *prep.* and *adv.* **1** in, to, through, or across an interval of space, time, etc. **2** to and from. **3** connecting. **4** by combined action of. **5** part to (one), part to (the other).

between'-times, **-whiles** *advs.* at intervals.

between you and me, between ourselves in confidence.

betwixt *bi-twikst'*, *prep.* and *adv.* between.

betwixt and between neither the one nor the other.

bevel *bev'l, n.* **1** a slant on an edge or surface. **2** an instrument for measuring angles.—*v.t.* to form with a bevel or slant:—*pr.p.* **bev'elling**; *pa.p.* **bev'elled**.

beverage *bev'ėr-ij, n.* a drink.

bevy *bev'i, n.* **1** a flock of birds, esp. of quails. **2** a company, esp. of ladies:—*pl.* **bev'ies**.

bewail *bi-wāl'*, *v.t.* to wail, lament.

beware *bi-wār'*, *v.i.* to be on one's guard (with *of, lest*, etc.): *Beware of the dog.*—Also *v.t.*: *Beware the hidden danger*. Used only in *imper.* and in *to beware, shall, should, must*, etc., *beware*.

bewilder *bi-wil'dėr, v.t.* to perplex, puzzle.

bewil'derment *n.* perplexity.

bewitch *bi-wich'*, *v.t.* **1** to cast a spell on. **2** to fascinate, charm.

bewitch'ing *adj.* **bewitch'ingly** *adv.*

bey *bā, n.* a governor or ruler:—*pl.* **beys**.

beyond *bi-yond'*, *prep.* **1** on the farther side of. **2** farther on than. **3** later than. **4** other than. **5** out of the reach, range, power, etc. of: *beyond help, understanding, one's strength, one's means.*—*adv.* farther away.

be beyond caring, etc., to be too tired, esp. emotionally, to care, etc.

be beyond one to be too much for one to do, to understand, etc.

the back of beyond a very remote place.

the (Great) Beyond the hereafter.

bi- *bī-*, *pfx.* **1** two. **2** twice. **3** in two parts.

biannual *bī-an'ū-ȧl, adj.* half-yearly.

bias *bī'ȧs, n.* **1** a greater weight on one

side. **2** a leaning to one side. **3** prejudice. **4** the line or direction diagonally across the grain or warp of a fabric: *silk cut on the bias.*—*v.t.* **1** to give a bias to. **2** to prejudice:—*pr.p.* **bī'as(s)ing**; *pa.p.* **bī'as(s)ed.**

bias binding (*needlework*) a narrow strip of fabric cut on the bias.

bib *bib*, *n.* **1** a cloth, etc. put under a child's chin. **2** the top part of an apron, etc.

bibb'er *n.* one who drinks much (as in *wine-bibber*).

Bible *bī'bl*, *n.* **1** the sacred writings of the Christian Church, consisting of the Old and New Testaments. **2** (also without *cap.*) a book containing these. **3** (without *cap.*) an authoritative book.

biblical *bib'li-kl*, *adj.*

bibliography *bib-li-og'răf-i*, *n.* a descriptive list of books of one author, or on one subject, etc.

bibliog'rapher *n.*

bibliograph'ic(al) *adjs.*

bibliomania *bib-li-ō-mā'ni-ȧ*, *n.* a mania for collecting rare books.

bibulous *bib'ū-lus*, *adj.* too fond of alcoholic drink.

bicameral *bī-kam'ėr-ȧl*, *adj.* (of a parliament) consisting of two houses.

bicarbonate *bī-kär'bȯn-it*, *n.* **1** a substance containing hydrogen, oxygen, carbon and a metal. **2** sodium bicarbonate.

bicentenary *bī-sen-tēn'ȧr-i*, or *-ten'*, *n.* a two hundredth anniversary:—*pl.* **bicenten'aries.**—Also *adj.*

biceps *bī'seps*, *n.* the muscle in front of the upper arm, starting at two different points in the shoulder.

bicker *bik'ėr*, *v.i.* **1** to keep on quarrelling about small things. **2** to quiver, as a flame. **3** to gurgle, as running water.

bicuspid *bī-kus'pid*, *n.* a premolar tooth.

bicycle *bī'si-kl*, *n.* a vehicle, driven by pedals or a motor, with two wheels and a seat.—*v.i.* to ride a bicycle:—*pr.p.* **bi'cycling.**—Also **bike** (*coll.*):—*pr.p.* **bik'ing.**

bid *bid*, *v.t.* **1** to tell to (do something). **2** (*old*) to invite: *to bid someone to a feast.* **3** to wish: *to bid someone good morning.* **4** to offer to pay at an auction. **5** to call in a card game: in senses **1**, **2**, **3** *pr.p.* **bidd'ing**; *pa.t.* **bade** (*bad, bād*); *pa.p.* **bidd'en**; in senses **4**, **5** *pr.p.* **bidd'ing**; *pa.t.* and *pa.p.* **bid.**—*v.i.* to state a price (*for* a contract).—*n.* **1** an offer of a price. **2** a call at cards. **3** an attempt to obtain: *He made a bid for power.*

bidd'able *adj.* obedient, docile.

bidd'er *n.*

bidd'ing *n.* **1** the making of bids. **2** command: *at my bidding.*

bid fair to seem likely (to).

bide *bīd*, *v.t.* to wait for; chiefly in **bide one's time**, to wait for a good opportunity.

bidet *bē'dā*, *n.* a basin on a low pedestal for washing the genital area, etc.

biennial *bī-en'i-ȧl*, *-yȧl*, *adj.* **1** lasting two years. **2** happening once in two years.—*n.* a plant that flowers only in its second year, then dies.

bienn'ially *adv.*

bier *bēr*, *n.* a carriage or frame of wood for carrying the dead to the grave.

bifocal *bī-fō'kȧl*, *adj.* (of spectacles for near and distant vision) having two focuses.—*n.* (in *pl.*) bifocal spectacles.

big *big*, *adj.* **1** large, great. **2** important. **3** pompous:—*comp.* **bigg'er**; *superl.* **bigg'est.**

bigg'ish *adj.* rather big.

big game large animals that are hunted.

big name a celebrity.

big shot a bigwig.

big'wig *n.* a person of importance.

talk big to talk as if one were important.

bigamy *big'ȧm-i*, *n.* the crime of having two wives or two husbands at once.

big'amist *n.* **big'amous** *adj.*

bight *bīt*, *n.* **1** a wide bay. **2** a coil of rope.

bigot *big'ȯt*, *n.* one who blindly and obstinately supports a cause, party, etc.

big'oted *adj.*

big'otry *n.* bigoted attitude or conduct.

bijou *bē'zhōō*, *adj.* small and neat.

bike. See **bicycle**.

bikini *bi-kē'ni*, *n.* a woman's scanty two-piece swimming-costume.

bilateral *bī-lat'ėr-ȧl*, *adj.* **1** having two sides. **2** affecting two sides, countries, etc.: *a bilateral agreement.*

bilberry *bil'bėr-i*, *n.* a shrub with a dark blue berry:—*pl.* **bil'berries.**

bile *bīl*, *n.* **1** a yellowish-green thick bitter fluid in the liver. **2** bad temper.

bilious *bil'yus*, *adj.* **1** of, due to, or affected by, too much bile. **2** (esp. of colours) unpleasant, often resembling bile.

bil'iousness *n.*

bilge *bilj*, *n.* **1** the bulging part of a cask. **2** the broadest part of a ship's bottom. **3** filth such as collects there. **4** (*coll.*) nonsense.

bilingual *bī-ling'gwȧl*, *adj.* **1** written in two languages. **2** speaking two languages (e.g. English and Welsh) equally well.

bilious, etc. See **bile.**

bilk *bilk, v.t.* **1** to avoid paying (debt, creditor). **2** to avoid, slip away from.

bill[1] *bil, n.* **1** a kind of battleaxe. **2** a tool with a long blade, used in cutting hedges.
bill'hook *n.* a bill having a hooked point.

bill[2] *bil, n.* **1** a bird's beak. **2** a sharp promontory.—*v.i.* to join bills as doves do.
bill and coo to caress fondly.

bill[3] *bil, n.* **1** a draft of a proposed law. **2** an account of money owed for goods, etc. **3** a bill of exchange (see below). **4** (*U.S.*) a banknote. **5** a placard or advertisement.—*v.t.* **1** to send an account to. **2** to announce by bill.
bill'sticker, bill'poster *ns.* one who sticks up bills or placards.
bill of exchange a written order from one person (the *drawer*) to another (the *drawee*) desiring the latter to pay to a named person a sum of money on a certain future date.
bill of fare a menu.
bill of lading a paper signed by the master of a ship which makes him responsible for the safe delivery of the goods listed in it.

billabong *bil'ȧ-bong, n.* (*Austr.*) **1** a branch of a river flowing out of the main stream. **2** a waterhole, pond.

billet *bil'it, n.* **1** a note. **2** a lodging, esp. for a soldier. **3** (*coll.*) a post, job.—*v.t.* to lodge (e.g. soldiers):—*pr.p.* **bill'eting**; *pa.p.* **bill'eted**.

billet-doux *bil'i-do͞o', n.* a love-letter:—*pl.* **billets-doux** *(bil'i-do͞oz')*.

billiards *bil'yȧrdz, n.* sing. a game played with a cue and balls on a table with pockets at the sides and corners.
bill'iard *adj.*

billie. See **billy**.

billion *bil'yȯn, n.* in Britain, France, etc., a million millions (1 000 000 000 000 or 10^{12}): in U.S., now often in Britain, a thousand millions (1 000 000 000 or 10^9).

billow *bil'ō, n.* a great wave of the sea swelled by wind.—*v.i.* to roll as in waves.
bill'owy *adj.*

billy, billie *bil'i, n.* an Australian bushman's can for cooking or making tea (also **bill'ycan**):—*pl.* **bill'ies**.
bill'y-goat *n.* a male goat.

biltong *bil'tong, n.* (*S. Afr.*) sun-dried meat in tongue-shaped strips.

bimetallic *bī-mi-tal'ik adj.* formed of two metals.

bimonthly *bī-munth'li, adj.* and *adv.* **1** once in two months. **2** twice a month.

bin *bin, n.* a receptacle for corn, bottled wine, dust, etc.

binary *bī'nȧr-i, adj.* **1** consisting of two. **2** of or relating to the binary system.
binary system a system of numbers based on two digits, 0 and 1.

bīnd *bīnd, v.t.* **1** to tie with a band, bandage, or bond. **2** to make fast (to). **3** to sew a border on. **3** to fasten together and put a cover on (a book). **4** to make (a person) swear or promise (to do something). **5** to oblige (a person to do something):—*pa.t.* and *pa.p.* **bound** *(bownd)*.
bind'er *n.* **1** one who binds books. **2** a reaping-machine, or the part of one, that binds grain into sheaves as it cuts it.
bind'ing *adj.* **1** restraining. **2** compelling; obligatory.—*n.* **1** the act of binding. **2** anything that binds. **3** the covering in which the leaves of a book are fixed.
-bound as part of a word, restricted to or by, as *housebound, fogbound*.
bind over to subject to legal obligation (e.g. to appear in court, to behave well).
bound to 1 obliged to. **2** sure to.
bound up in giving all one's interest and affection to.

bingo *bing'gō, n.* a game of chance using numbers.

binoculars *bin-ok'ūl-ȧrz,* or *bīn-, n.pl.* field-glasses (see **field**).

bi(o)- *bī(-ō)-* (as part of a word) **1** life. **2** living thing(s).

biochemistry *bī-ō-kem'is-tri, n.* the chemistry of living substances.
biochem'ical *adj.* **biochem'ist** *n.*

biodegradable *bī-ō-di-grād'ȧ-bl, adj.* (of substances) able to be broken down into parts by bacteria.

biography *bī-og'rȧf-i, n.* a written account of a person's life:—*pl.* **biog'raphies**.
biog'rapher *n.* **biograph'ic, -al** *adjs.*

biology *bī-ol'ȯ-ji, n.* the science of living things (animals and plants).
biolog'ical *adj.* **biolog'ically** *adv.*
biol'ogist *n.*
biological clock the innate mechanism which regulates the physiological rhythms of an organism.
biological warfare methods of fighting involving the use of disease bacteria.

bionics *bī-on'iks, n.* sing. **1** the use of biological principles in the design of computers, etc. **2** the replacement of parts of the body with electronic or mechanical devices.
bion'ic *adj.* of or using bionics.

biopsy *bī'op-si, n.* the removal and examination of tissue, etc. from a living body for diagnostic purposes:—*pl.* **bi'opsies**.

bipartite *bī-pärt'īt, adj.* affecting two parties (as a treaty or agreement).

biped *bī'ped*, *n*. animal with two feet.

biplane *bī'plān*, *n*. an aeroplane with two sets of wings, one above the other.

birch *bûrch*, *n*. **1** a valuable timber tree with smooth white bark. **2** a rod for punishment, made of birch twigs.—*v.t.* to flog.

bird *bûrd*, *n*. a general name for feathered animals.

bird's-eye view 1 a general view from above. **2** a summary (of a subject).

Biro® *bī'rō*, *n*. a type of ball-point pen:—*pl*. **Bi'ros**.

birth *bûrth*, *n*. **1** coming into the world. **2** lineage: *of noble birth*. **3** beginning.

birth control the control of reproduction by contraceptives.

birth'day *n*. (the anniversary of) the day on which one is born.

birth rate the ratio of births to population.

birth'right *n*. the right one may claim by birth.

give birth (to) to produce, bear (young).

biscuit *bis'kit*, *n*. **1** a crisp piece of dough baked in small flat cakes. **2** (*U.S.*) a soft round cake. **3** pottery after first baking but not yet glazed.—*adj*. pale brown.

bisect *bī-sekt'*, *v.t.* to cut into two equal parts.

bisexual *bī-seks'ū-ȧl*, *adj*. **1** sexually attracted to both males and females. **2** having both male and female sexual organs.—*n*. a bisexual person.

bisexual'ity *n*.

bishop *bish'ȯp*, *n*. **1** a Christian clergyman in spiritual charge of a group of churches or diocese. **2** one of the pieces in chess.

bish'opric *n*. **1** the office of a bishop. **2** a diocese.

bismuth *biz'mu̇th*, or *bis'-*, *n*. a brittle reddish-white element.

bison *bī'sȯn*, *n*. a large wild ox; there are two species, the European, almost extinct, and the American, commonly called buffalo.

bit¹ *bit*, *n*. **1** a small piece. **2** a coin, esp. small. **3** a short time. **4** a small tool for boring. **5** the part of the bridle that a horse holds in its mouth.

bit by bit gradually.

do one's bit to take one's share in a task.

take the bit in one's teeth to tackle a problem determinedly, throwing off control.

bit². See **bite**.

bit³ *bit*, *n*. (*computers*) the smallest unit of information.

bitch *bich*, *n*. **1** the female of the dog, wolf, and fox. **2** (*abusively*) a woman.—*v.i.* to make unpleasant comments.

bitch'y *adj*. spiteful, unpleasant:—*comp*. **bitch'ier**; *superl*. **bitch'iest**.

bite *bīt*, *v.t.* and *v.i.* **1** to seize or tear with the teeth. **2** to pierce with the mouth parts, as an insect. **3** to eat into with a chemical. **4** (of an implement) to grip:—*pr.p.* **bit'ing**; *pa.t.* **bit**; *pa.p.* **bitt'en**.—*n*. **1** a grasp by the teeth. **2** a puncture by an insect. **3** a mouthful. **4** a small meal.

bit'er *n*.

bit'ing *adj*. causing pain: *a biting wind*; *a biting remark*.

bitter *bit'ėr*, *adj*. **1** biting or acid to the taste. **2** painful. **3** harsh.

bitt'erly *adv*. **bitt'erness** *n*.

bitt'ers *n.pl*. a liquid prepared from bitter herbs or roots.

bitt'ersweet *n*. a nightshade.—*adj*. unpleasant and pleasant at the same time.

the bitter end the very end, however painful.

bittern *bit'ėrn*, *n*. a bird like the heron.

bitumen *bĭt'ū-min*, or *bi-tū'*, *n*. an inflammable substance consisting mainly of hydrocarbons, such as certain kinds of naphtha, petroleum, asphalt.

bivalve *bī'valv*, *n*. and *adj*. (an animal) having a shell in two valves or parts, as an oyster has.

bivouac *biv'oo-ak*, *n*. resting at night in the open air (esp. by soldiers).—Also *v.i.*:—*pr.p.* **biv'ouacking**; *pa.p.* **biv'ouacked**.

bi-weekly *bī-wēk'li*, *adj*. occurring once in two weeks or twice a week.—*n*. a bi-weekly publication:—*pl*. **bi-week'lies**.

bizarre *bi-zär'*, *adj*. odd, fantastic.

blab *blab*, *v.i.* **1** to talk much. **2** to tell tales.—*v.t.* to let out (a secret):—*pr.p.* **blabb'ing**; *pa.p.* **blabbed**.

black *blak*, *adj*. **1** of the darkest colour. **2** without colour. **3** dismal. **4** sullen. **5** horrible. **6** foul. **7** under trade union ban. **8** (usu. **Black**) dark-skinned, esp. of African, W. Indian or Australian Aboriginal origin.—*n*. **1** black colour. **2** absence of colour. **3** (usu. **Black**) a dark-skinned person, esp. one of African, W. Indian or Australian Aboriginal origin.—*v.t.* **1** to make black. **2** to put under trade union ban.

black'en *v.t.*, *v.i.* to make, become, black.

black'ing *n*. a substance used for blacking leather, etc.

black'ly *adv*. **black'ness** *n*.

black'-and-white' *adj*. **1** partly black and partly white. **2** not in colour (*TV*). **3** consisting of, or considering only, extremes.

black art black magic (see **magic**).

black'ball *v.t.* to reject (someone) in voting (by putting a black ball into a ballot box, or otherwise).

black'-beet'le *n.* a cockroach (not a true beetle).

black'berry *n.* a very dark-coloured fruit on a trailing prickly stem, usu. growing wild:—*pl.* **black'berries.**—*v.i.* to gather blackberries:—*pr.p.* **black'berrying;** *pa.p.* **black'berried.**

black'bird *n.* a dark-coloured bird of the thrush family.

black'board *n.* a dark-coloured board for writing on in chalk.

black box 1 an instrument for detecting earthquakes or underground explosions. **2** an electronic unit which records all the flight details in an aircraft.

black bread rye bread.

black'cock *n.* the male of the **black grouse,** a grouse of N. England and Scotland.

black'curr'ant *n.* a shrub related to the gooseberry, with small black fruit.

black eye an eye with discoloration round it due to a blow, etc.

black flag a pirate's flag.

blackguard *blag'ärd, n.* a scoundrel, a low, evil person.—*v.t.* to abuse, revile.

black'guardly *adj.*

black ice a thin, transparent layer of ice on a road.

black'lead *n.* graphite.

black'leg *n.* a person willing to work during a strike.

black list a list of people suspected, not approved of, etc. (*v.t.* **black'-list**).

black'mail *v.t.* **1** to extort money by threatening to reveal something the victim wants to keep secret. **2** to force (into doing something) by threats.—Also *n.*

black'mailer *n.*

black Maria a prison van.

black market illegal buying and selling at high prices of goods that are scarce, rationed, etc.

black'out *n.* **1** darkness produced by putting out all lights. **2** a period of unconsciousness or loss of memory. **3** a complete stoppage of communications, etc.

black pudding a sausage of suet, blood, etc.

black sheep a disreputable member of a family or group.

black'smith *n.* a smith working in iron.

black'thorn *n.* a dark-coloured thorny shrub bearing sloes.

black and blue badly bruised.

be black in the face to have the face purple through anger, effort, etc.

in black and white 1 in writing or print. **2** in no colours but black and white.

in someone's black books. See **book.**

in the black solvent, not in debt.

bladder *blad'ėr, n.* **1** a thin bag stretched by filling with liquid or air. **2** the receptacle for the urine in the body.

blade *blād, n.* **1** the flat part of a leaf or petal, esp. a leaf of grass or corn. **2** the cutting part of a knife, sword, etc. **3** the flat part of an oar, propeller, fan, etc. **4** a dashing fellow.

blaeberry *blā'bėr-i, n.* a bilberry:—*pl.* **blae'berries.**

blame *blām, v.t.* **1** to criticise, express disapproval of. **2** to consider the responsibility as belonging to: *I blame the wet road for the skid.*—*n.* **1** finding of fault. **2** responsibility for something bad.

blame'less *adj.* innocent.

blame'lessly *adv.* **blame'lessness** *n.*

blame'worthy *adj.* worthy of blame.

blame'worthiness *n.*

be to blame (for) to be responsible (for an unfortunate happening).

blanch *blänch* or *-sh, v.t., v.i.* to make, or grow, white.—*v.t.* (*cookery*) to immerse (vegetables, etc.) briefly in boiling water.

blancmange *blä-monzh', n.* a jelly-like pudding prepared with milk.

bland *bland, adj.* **1** soothing. **2** mild. **3** polite.

bland'ly *adv.* **bland'ness** *n.*

blandish *bland'ish, v.t.* to flatter, coax.

bland'ishment *n.* **1** (usu. in *pl.*). flattering or coaxing action or speech. **2** (in *pl.*) soft, agreeable words or caresses.

blank *blangk, adj.* **1** (of paper) without writing or marks. **2** (of a tape, etc.) not recorded on. **3** empty. **4** expressionless.—Also *n.*

blank'ly *adv.* **blank'ness** *n.*

blank cartridge one without a bullet.

blank cheque one on which the sum to be paid has not been entered.

blank verse unrhymed verse.

draw a blank. See **draw.**

blanket *blang'kit, n.* **1** a warm, usu. woollen, covering for a bed, or one used as a garment by American Indians, etc. **2** a covering generally.—*adj.* covering a group of things: *a blanket agreement.*—*v.t.* to cover with, or as with, a blanket:—*pr.p.* **blank'eting;** *pa.p.* **blank'eted.**

blare *blār, v.i.* (of e.g. a trumpet) to sound loudly:—*pr.p.* **blar'ing.**—Also *n.*

blarney *blär'ni, n.* pleasant talk or flattery.

blasé *blä'zā, adj.* bored with pleasures through having had too many.

blaspheme *blas-fēm'*, *v.i.* **1** to speak irreverently (of God, etc.). **2** to swear:—*pr.p.* **blasphem'ing.**
blasphem'er *n.*
blasphemous *blas'fėm-ŭs*, *adj.*
blas'phemy *(-fėm-i) n.*

blast *bläst*, *n.* **1** a gust of wind. **2** a forcible stream of air. **3** the sound of a wind instrument. **4** an explosion, or the strong wave of air spreading out from it.—*v.t.* **1** to blight, wither. **2** to ruin, destroy. **3** to tear apart by an explosion.
blast'ed *adj.* **1** blighted, withered. **2** cursed, damned.
blast'ing *n.*
blast furnace a smelting furnace into which hot air is blown.
blast'-off *n.* the (moment of) launching of a rocket-propelled missile or space capsule.

blatant *blāt'ȧnt*, *adj.* **1** glaring, obvious: *a blatant lie.* **2** vulgarly showy.

blather. Same as **blether**.

blaze[1] *blāz*, *n.* **1** a rush of light or flame. **2** an outburst (e.g. of anger). **3** a bright display.—*v.i.* to burn, shine brightly:—*pr.p.* **blaz'ing.**
blaz'er *n.* a light sports jacket, usu. bright or distinctive in colour.
blaze away to go on without pause firing gun(s), speaking angrily, etc.

blaze[2] *blāz*, *n.* **1** a white mark on an animal's face. **2** a guiding mark made on a tree.
blaze a trail **1** to show a forest track by marking trees. **2** to lead the way in any change or development.

blaze[3] *blāz*, *v.t.* to proclaim, spread abroad:—*pr.p.* **blaz'ing.**

blazer. See **blaze**[1].

blazon *blā'zn*, *v.t.* **1** to make public, to publish. **2** to display very obviously:—*pr.p.* **bla'zoning**; *pa.p.* **bla'zoned.**

bleach *blēch*, *v.t.* and *v.i.* to whiten, to take out, or lose, colour.—*n.* a substance that bleaches.
bleaching powder powder for bleaching, esp. chloride of lime.

bleak *blēk*, *adj.* **1** dull and cheerless. **2** cold, unsheltered.
bleak'ly *adv.* **bleak'ness** *n.*

bleary *blēr'i*, *adj.* (of eyes) sore and red:—*comp.* **blear'ier**; *superl.* **blear'iest.**—Also **blear.**
bleary-eyed' *adj.*

bleat *blēt*, *v.i.* to cry as a sheep.—Also *n.*

bled. See **bleed**.

bleed *blēd*, *v.i.* **1** to lose blood. **2** to die in battle. **3** to lose sap:—*v.t.* **1** to draw blood or sap from. **2** to extort money from:—*pa.t.* and *pa.p.* **bled.**
bleed'ing *n.* and *adj.*

bleep *blēp*, *v.i.* to make a high-pitched sound.—Also *n.*
bleep'er *n.* a device, e.g. a pager, which bleeps.

blemish *blem'ish*, *n.* a stain or defect.—*v.t.* to spoil.

blench *blench* or *-sh*, *v.i.* to shrink, flinch.

blend *blend*, *v.t.* to mix together, esp. with good result.—*v.i.* to go well together (as colours).—*n.* a mixture.
blend'er *n.* (*cookery*) an electric machine for mixing ingredients.
blend'ing *n.* and *adj.*

bless *bles*, *v.t.* **1** to pronounce holy. **2** to ask God to show favour to. **3** to make happy:—*pa.p.* and *adj.* **blessed** (*blest*; *adj.* usu. *bles'id*) or **blest.**
bless'edly *adv.* **bless'edness** *n.*
bless'ing *n.* **1** a wish or prayer for happiness or success. **2** any cause of happiness. **3** approval.

blest. See **bless**.

blether *bleTH'ėr*, *v.i.* to chatter foolishly.
bleth'erskate, (*U.S.*) **blath'erskite** *ns.* a talkative fool.

blew. See **blow**.

blight *blīt*, *n.* **1** a disease in plants that withers them. **2** anything that spoils.—*v.t.* **1** to cause to wither. **2** to bring to nothing: *His letter blighted our hopes.*
blight'er *n.* a scamp, wretch.
planning blight a fall in value, and hence neglect, of property in an area due to uncertainty about the official plans for the area's future.

blighty *blī'ti*, (*military slang*) *n.* home, the home country.

blind *blīnd*, *adj.* **1** without sight. **2** not noticing. **3** unable to understand or to foresee. **4** concealed. **5** without an opening: *blind wall.* **6** (of flying, landing, etc.) solely by means of instruments.—*n.* **1** something to mislead. **2** a window screen.—Also *v.t.*
blind'ed *adj.* made blind.
blind'ing *adj.* tending to make blind.
blind'ly *adv.* **blind'ness** *n.*
blind'fold *adj.* with the eyes bandaged so as not to see.—Also *v.t.*
blind alley **1** a passage without an exit. **2** a job with no prospects.
blind'man's-buff' *n.* a game in which one person is blindfolded and tries to catch the others.
blind spot **1** the point on the retina of the eye on which no images are formed. **2** an area which cannot easily be seen (e.g. by a car driver) because of an obstruction (e.g. the car window frame).

3 any matter about which one always shows lack of understanding.
blind to unable to see or appreciate.
bake blind to bake (a pastry case) without its filling.

blink *blingk*, *v.i.* **1** (of a light) to twinkle or wink rapidly. **2** (of eyelids) to move rapidly up and down.—*v.t.* to move (the eyelids) rapidly up and down.—*n.* **1** a glimpse. **2** a gleam.
blink'ers *n.pl.* leather flaps on a bridle preventing a horse from seeing sideways.
on the blink (of something electrical, mechanical, etc.) (going) out of order.

bliss *blis*, *n.* the highest happiness.
bliss'ful *adj.* **bliss'fully** *adv.*
bliss'fulness *n.*

blister *blis'tėr*, *n.* **1** a thin bubble on the skin, containing watery matter. **2** a similar spot on any surface.—*v.t.* to raise a blister or blisters on.—Also *v.i.*:—*pr.p.* **blis'tering**; *pa.p.* **blis'tered.**

blithe *blī*TH, *adj.* gay, light-hearted.
blithe'ly *adv.* **blithe'ness** *n.*

blitz *blits*, *n.* (from Ger. *Blitzkrieg*, lightning war) any sudden, vigorous attack.—*v.t.* to make such an attack (on.)

blizzard *bliz'ȧrd*, *n.* a blinding storm of wind and snow.

bloated *blōt'id*, *adj.* swollen or puffed out, esp. after eating too much.
bloat'er *n.* a herring partly dried in smoke.

blob *blob*, *n.* **1** a drop of liquid. **2** a small, shapeless mass.

bloc *blok*, *n.* a group, combination, of nations, or of parties, etc., who have an interest or purpose in common.

block *blok*, *n.* **1** a mass of wood or stone, etc., usu. flat-sided. **2** a piece of wood on which a person is beheaded. **3** a piece of wood used for chopping on, for printing (illustrations) or as a toy (for building). **4** (*machinery*) a pulley with its framework, or the framework alone. **5** a connected group of houses. **6** a compact group or set (e.g. of shares, seats). **7** an obstruction or barrier.—*v.t.* **1** to obstruct: *She blocked his path.* **2** to hinder. **3** to stop (a ball) with a bat resting upright on the ground.
block'age *n.* an obstruction.
block capital, letter a capital letter written in imitation of printing type (e.g. those in NAME).
block'head *n.* a stupid fellow.
block'house *n.* a small temporary fort.
block system a system of signalling by which no train can enter a section of the railway till the previous train has left it.

blockade *blȯ-kād'*, *n.* blocking every approach to a place by land or sea.—Also *v.t.*:—*pr.p.* **blockad'ing**; *pa.p.* **blockad'ed.**
blockade'-runn'er *n.* a person or ship that passes through a blockading force.

blockage. See **block.**

bloke *blōk*, *n.* (*coll.*) a man.

blond *blond*, *adj.* **1** light-coloured. **2** fair-haired.—Also **blonde.**
blonde *blond*, *n.* and *adj.* (of) a woman with fair complexion and light-coloured hair.

blood *blud*, *n.* **1** the red fluid in the arteries and veins. **2** shedding of blood. **3** royal or aristocratic descent. **4** descent. **5** relationship. **6** a dandy. **7** temper: *His blood was up.*
blood'ed *adj.* **1** having been in battle. **2** initiated.
blood'less *adj.* **1** anaemic. **2** without spirit or emotion. **3** without the shedding of blood.
blood'y *adj.* **1** stained with blood. **2** murderous, cruel. **3** (*bad language*) annoying (sometimes used without meaning):—*comp.* **blood'ier**; *superl.* **blood'iest.**
blood'ily *adv.* **blood'iness** *n.*
blood bath a massacre.
blood'curdling *adj.* **1** terrifying. **2** horrible.
blood donor a person who gives blood for use in transfusion.
blood group any one of the kinds into which human blood is classified.
blood heat the normal temperature of human blood (about 37° Centigrade, 98° Fahrenheit).
blood'hound *n.* a large, keen-scented hound, used for tracking.
blood-'poisoning *n.* any one of several diseases caused by bacteria, etc. in the blood.
blood pressure the pressure of the blood on the walls of the blood-vessels.
blood'shed *n.* the shedding of blood, slaughter.
blood'shot *adj.* (of eyes) red, inflamed with blood.
blood sports those in which animals are killed.
blood'stained *adj.* stained with blood.
blood'stream *n.* the blood flowing through the body.
blood'thirsty *adj.* **1** eager to kill, cruel. **2** (of a film, etc.) showing bloodshed or violence.
blood'thirstiness *n.*
blood'-vessel *n.* any of the tubes in the body through which the blood flows.

bloody Mary a cocktail of vodka and tomato juice.

blood'y-mind'ed *adj.* (*coll.*) deliberately uncooperative or awkward.

in hot (or **cold**) **blood** while under (or free from) excitement or passion.

bloom *blōōm*, *n.* **1** a blossom, flower. **2** the state of flowering. **3** freshness, perfection. **4** rosy colour. **5** the powder on the rind of fresh fruits.—*v.i.* to flower.

bloom'ing *adj.* flourishing.

blossom *blos'ŏm*, *n.* **1** a flower, esp. of a fruit tree. **2** such flowers collectively: *the apple blossom.*—*v.i.* **1** to put forth flowers. **2** to flourish, prosper.

blot *blot*, *n.* **1** a spot or stain. **2** something which spoils something else: *a blot on the landscape.*—*v.t.* **1** to spot or stain. **2** to dry with blotting-paper:—*pr.p.* **blott'ing**; *pa.p.* **blott'ed**.

blott'er *n.* a pad or book of blotting-paper.

blott'ing-paper *n.* soft, unglazed paper used for sucking up ink.

blot out 1 to hide from sight, or conceal from memory. **2** to destroy completely.

blotch *bloch*, *n.* a discoloration on skin.—Also *v.t.*

blotched, **blotch'y** (*comp.* **-ier**; *superl.* **-iest**), *adjs.*

blouse *blowz*, *n.* a woman's usu. loose outer garment for the upper part of the body.

blow[1] *blō*, *n.* **1** a stroke or knock. **2** a sudden misfortune.

blow[2] *blō*, *v.i.* **1** (of a current of air) to be in motion. **2** to drive air (upon or into). **3** to breathe hard. **4** to spout, as a whale.—*v.t.* **1** to drive by a current of air. **2** to sound (a wind instrument). **3** to drive air into. **4** (of insects) to lay eggs on.—*pa.t.* **blew** (*blōō*); *pa.p.* **blown** (*blōn*).

blown *adj.* out of breath.

blow'y *adj.* windy:—*comp.* **blow'ier**; *superl.* **blow'iest**.

blow'-dry' *v.t.* to dry (hair) with a hand-held hair-drier, simultaneously arranging it by brushing:—*pr.p.* **blow'-dry'ing**; *pa.p.* **blow'-dried'**.

blow'fly *n.* a fly that lays eggs on meat, etc., esp. the bluebottle.

blow'hole *n.* **1** a breathing hole in ice for whales, etc. **2** a whale's nostril. **3** a vent for the escape of gas.

blow'lamp *n.* a portable lamp for aiming a very hot flame at a particular spot.

blow'out *n.* **1** the bursting of a car tyre. **2** a violent escape of gas, etc.

blow'pipe *n.* **1** a pipe through which air or gas is blown on a flame to increase its heat. **2** a tube from which an arrow is blown.

blow'torch *n.* a blowlamp.

blow over to pass over or away.

blow up 1 to shatter, or be shattered, by explosion. **2** to lose one's temper. **3** to fill with air or a gas. **4** to scold. **5** to enlarge (e.g. a photograph) (*n.* **blow'-up**).

blowzy *blowz'i*, *adj.* **1** fat and red. **2** dishevelled:—*comp.* **blowz'ier**; *superl.* **blowz'iest**.—Also **blows'y**.

blubber *blub'ėr*, *n.* the fat of whales and other sea animals.—*v.i.* to weep noisily.

bludgeon *bluj'ŏn*, *n.* a short stick with a heavy end for striking.—Also *v.t.*

blue *blōō*, *adj.* **1** of the colour of the sky or the deep sea. **2** dismal. **3** depressed. **4** indecent. **5** pornographic: *a blue film.*—*n.* **1** the sky. **2** the sea. **3** a blue colour or paint. **4** a blue powder or liquid used in washing clothes. **5** (a distinction given to) one who has represented his university in athletics, etc.

blu'ish *adj.* slightly blue.

bluey *blōō'i*, *n.* an Australian bushman's bundle.

blue'bell *n.* **1** the wood hyacinth. **2** (often *blōō'bel'*) in Scotland and N. England the harebell.

blue'-book *n.* a parliamentary report (from its blue paper wrapper).

blue'bottle *n.* **1** a large fly with blue abdomen. **2** the blue cornflower.

blue'-coll'ar *adj.* relating to manual work or workers.

blue pencil a pencil for correcting or censoring.—*v.t.* (**blue'-pen'cil**) to mark out with blue pencil:—*pr.p.* **blue'-pen'cilling**; *pa.p.* **blue'-pen'cilled**.

Blue Peter a blue flag with a white square in the centre hoisted as a sign that a ship is about to sail.

blue'print *n.* a detailed plan of work to be carried out.

blue ribbon 1 the ribbon of Knights of the Garter. **2** any great prize.

blue stocking a highly educated woman.

from (or **out of**) **the blue** without warning.

once in a blue moon very seldom.

(the) blues 1 low spirits. **2** a very slow dismal song, of Black American origin.

bluff[1] *bluf*, *adj.* rough, hearty, frank in manner.—*n.* a steep cliff, esp. along sea-shore or river.

bluff'ness *n.*

bluff[2] *bluf*, *v.t.* and *v.i.* to deceive, or try to deceive, by pretending to have something (e.g. good cards) that one does not have.—Also *n.*

blunder *blun'dėr*, *v.t.* **1** to make a bad

mistake. **2** to stumble about.—Also *n.*

blunderbuss *blun'dėr-bus, n.* **1** a short handgun with a wide bore. **2** a stupid person.

blunt *blunt, adj.* **1** having a dull edge or point, not sharp. **2** rough, outspoken.—*v.t.* to make less sharp or painful.

blunt'ly *adv.* **blunt'ness** *n.*

blur *blûr, n.* **1** a smudge, smear. **2** a dimness.—*v.t.* **1** to blot. **2** to dim.—*v.i.* to become unclear, smudged.—*pr.p.* **blurr'ing**; *pa.p.* **blurred**.

blurb *blûrb, n.* a publisher's description of a book, usu. printed on the jacket.

blurt *blûrt, v.t.* (with *out*) to say suddenly or without thinking of the effect or result.

blush *blush, n.* a red glow on the skin caused by shame, etc.—*v.i.* to show shame, joy, etc., by growing red in the face.

blush'er *n.* a cosmetic for adding pink colour to the cheeks.

bluster *blus'tėr, v.i.* **1** to make a noise like a blast of wind. **2** to bully, swagger.—Also *n.*

blus'terer *n.* **blus'tering** *adj.* and *n.*

blus'teringly *adv.*

blus'tery *adj.* noisily windy.

boa *bō'ȧ, n.* **1** a kind of large snake (especially the **boa-constric'tor**) that kills by winding itself round its prey. **2** a long wrap of fur or feathers for the neck.

boar *bōr, bör, n.* a male (esp. wild) pig.

board *bōrd, börd, n.* **1** a broad and thin strip of timber. **2** a table for food. **3** meals: *bed and board.* **4** an official group of persons: *a board of directors.* **5** (in *pl.*) the stage. **6** a sheet of stiff material, e.g. for binding books.—*v.t.* **1** cover with boards. **2** to supply with meals (and lodging) at a fixed price. **3** to enter (a ship, etc.), esp. by force.—*v.i.* to lodge and take meals.

board'er *n.* **board'ing** *n.* and *adj.*

board'ing-house *n.* a house where boarders live.

board'ing-school *n.* a school in which board and lodging as well as instruction are given.

above board open(ly) (see also **aboveboard** at **above**).

across the board applying in all cases.

on board on, or in, a ship, plane, etc.

go by the board to be discarded, lost.

sweep the board to win every point in a game or contest.

boast *bōst, v.i.* to talk with too much pride (of, about).—*v.t.* to have, possess proudly: *The house boasts a fine view.*—*n.* **1** an expression of pride. **2** a subject of pride.

boast'ful *adj.* **boast'fully** *adv.*

boast'fulness *n.* **boast'ing** *n.*

boat *bōt, n.* **1** a small open craft usu. moved by oars. **2** a ship. **3** a dish shaped like a boat: *a gravy-boat.*—*v.i.* to sail about in a boat.

boat'ing *n.* and *adj.*

boat'-hook *n.* a metal hook fixed to a pole, for pulling or pushing a boat.

boat'man *n.* a man in charge of a boat:—*pl.* **boat'men.**

boat train a train taking passengers to or from a ship in dock.

in the same boat in the same difficult situation.

boatswain *bō'sn, n,* an officer who looks after a ship's boats, rigging, etc.—Also **bo'sun, bosun** *bo'sn.*

bob[1] *bob, v.i.* **1** to move up and down. **2** to curtsy.—*v.t.* to cut (hair) so that it does not fall beyond the neck:—*pr.p.* **bobb'ing**; *pa.p.* **bobbed.**—*n.* **1** a short jerky movement. **2** the weight on a pendulum, plumb line, etc. **3** a bobbed hair-style.

bob'sled, bob'sleigh *(-slā) ns.* **1** a short sledge. **2** a sleigh made up of two of these, usu. with one common seat. **3** a racing sledge for two or more, with steering mechanism and brakes.

bob'tail *n.* a short or cut tail.

bob[2] *bob, (coll.) n.* a shilling (5 pence):—*pl.* **bob.**

bobbin *bob'in, n.* a reel or spool for winding thread, wire, etc.

bobby *bob'i, n. (coll.)* a policeman:—*pl.* **bobb'ies.**

bobsled, bobtail, etc. See **bob**[1].

bode *bōd*: **bode ill, well** to be an omen of or foretell bad, good fortune.

bodice *bod'is, n.* a close-fitting part of a woman's dress covering the trunk.

bodily. See **body**.

bodkin *bod'kin, n.* **1** a small dagger. **2** a large blunt needle.

body *bod'i, n.* **1** the whole frame of a man or animal. **2** a corpse. **3** the main part of anything. **4** a mass. **5** (*coll.*) a person. **6** a group of persons considered as acting as one:—*pl.* **bod'ies.**

bod'ied *adj.* having a body of a certain kind: *strong-bodied.*

bod'ily *adj.* of the body.—*adv.* as one whole and completely: *to remove bodily.*

body blow a serious setback.

bod'yguard *n.* a guard to protect (esp. an important person).

body language communication by means of attitudes, facial expressions, gestures, etc.

body stocking a one-piece skin-tight undergarment for women.

bod'ywork *n.* the outer frame of a motor vehicle.

Boer *bōōr*, *n.* a South African of Dutch descent.—Also *adj.*

boffin *bof'in*, *n.* (*coll.*) a scientist.

bog *bog*, *n.* spongy ground, a marsh.—*v.i.* (often **bog down**) to sink, or be hindered in movement or progress, in, or as if in, a bog:—*pr.p.* **bogg'ing**; *pa.p.* **bogged.**—Also *v.t.*

bogg'y *adj*:—*comp.* **bogg'ier**; *superl.* **bogg'iest.**

bogg'iness *n.*

bogey[1] *bō'gi*, (*golf*) *n.* the score, for a hole or for the full round, of an imaginary good player, Colonel *Bogey*:—*pl.* **bo'geys.**

bogey[2]. See **bogie.**

bogey[3]. See **bogy.**

boggle *bog'l*, *v.i.* **1** to be amazed. **2** to make difficulties (about) (or with *at*):—*pr.p.* **bogg'ling.**

bogie, bogey *bō'gi*, *n.* **1** a low truck. **2** a four- or six-wheel truck supporting part of a long vehicle, e.g. a locomotive body, and making it able to run on a curved track:—*pl.* **bo'gies, bo'geys.**

bogus *bō'gus*, *adj.* sham, not genuine.

bogy, bogey *bōgi*, *n.* **1** a goblin. **2** something specially dreaded. **3** the devil:—*pl.* **bo'gies, bo'geys.**

Bohemian *bō-hē'mi-ȧn*, *n.* **1** a Czech. **2** (usu. without *cap.*) one who lives in a free and easy way, taking no notice of conventional rules of behaviour.—Also *adj.*

boil[1] *boil*, *v.i.* and *v.t.* to turn rapidly from liquid to vapour.—*v.i.* **1** to bubble up. **2** to be hot. **3** to be angry.—*v.t.* to cook by boiling.

boil'er *n.* a vessel in which water is heated or steam is produced.

boil'ing-point *n.* the temperature at which a liquid turns to vapour.

boil[2] *boil*, *n.* an inflamed swelling.

boisterous *bois'tėr-us*, *adj.* wild, noisy, exuberant, stormy.

bois'terously *adv.* **bois'terousness** *n.*

bolas *bō'lȧs*, *n. sing.* or *pl.* a thong, weighted with balls, thrown so as to curl round an animal's legs and hobble it.

bold *bōld*, *adj.* **1** daring. **2** impudent. **3** spirited. **4** striking, well-marked.

bold'ly *adv.* **bold'ness** *n.*

make so bold (as to) to venture (to), take the liberty (of).

bole *bōl*, *n.* the round stem of a tree.

bolero *bȯ-lā'rō*, *n.* **1** a Spanish dance. **2** the music for it. **3** (usu. *bol'ė-rō*) a short jacket-like bodice:—*pl.* **boleros.**

boll *bol*, *n.* a round seed-vessel as in cotton, flax, poppy, etc.

bollard *bol'ȧrd*, *n.* a short post on a wharf or ship round which ropes are fastened.

bolster *bōl'stėr*, *n.* **1** a long round pillow. **2** a pad, prop.—*v.t.* **1** to prop up. **2** to aid:—*pr.p.* **bol'stering.**—Also **bolster up.**

bolt[1] *bōlt*, *n.* **1** a bar to fasten a door, etc. **2** an arrow. **3** a thunderbolt. **4** a stout pin. **5** a roll of cloth.—*v.t.* **1** to fasten with a bolt. **2** to swallow hastily.—*v.i.* to go away fast (like an arrow from a bow).

a bolt from the blue an unexpected happening.

bolt upright upright, and straight as an arrow.

bolt[2] *bōlt*, *v.t.* to sift (flour).—Also **boult.**

bomb *bom*, *n.* **1** a hollow case containing explosive or other harmful material, thrown or dropped. **2** (*coll.*) a great deal of money.—*v.t.* to drop or throw bombs on.—*v.i.* (*slang*) of a play, etc., to fail badly, to be a flop.

bomber *bom'ėr*, *n.* **1** an aeroplane built for bombing. **2** a person who drops or throws bombs.

bomb'proof *adj.* strong enough to resist bombs.

bomb'shell *n.* **1** formerly, a bomb. **2** startling, often bad, news.

bombard *bom-bärd'*, *v.t.* **1** to attack with artillery. **2** to batter or pelt (with).

bombardier *(-bȧr-dēr')* *n.* **1** the person in a bombing aeroplane who aims the bombs. **2** a corporal in the artillery.

bombard'ment *n.*

bombast *bom'bast*, *n.* pompous language.

bombas'tic *adj.* **bombas'tically** *adv.*

Bombay duck *bom'bā duk*, a small Indian fish, dried and eaten with curries.

bona fide *bō'na fīd'ā*, genuine(ly).

bona fides genuineness.

bonanza *bȯn-an'zȧ*, *n.* (a source or period of) prosperity.

bonbon *bon'bon*, *bon^g'bon^g*, *n.* a sweetmeat.

bond *bond*, *n.* **1** something that binds. **2** something that unites people. **3** a written promise to pay a sum of money, usu. by a certain date. **4** (in *pl.*) captivity.—*v.t.* to bind, connect, or cause to stick together.

bond'ing *n.* the forming of an attachment between a mother and her newborn child.

bonded store or **warehouse** a warehouse where goods are kept until customs or other duty on them is paid.

bondage *bon'dij*, *n.* **1** slavery. **2** the state of being completely under the control of another person.

bone *bōn*, *n.* **1** a hard substance forming the skeleton of higher animals. **2** (in *pl.*) the skeleton. **3** (in *pl.*) any framework.—*v.t.* to take the bones out of (e.g. meat):—*pr.p.* **bon'ing**; *pa.p.* **boned**.

boned *adj.* **1** with bones removed: *boned fish*. **2** (often as part of a word) having bones: *a small-boned girl*.

bony *bō'ni*, *adj.* **1** full of, or like, bones. **2** having large bones or little flesh:—*comp.* **bo'nier**; *superl.* **bo'niest**.

bon'iness *n.*

bone china china in making which ashes of burnt bones are used.

bone dry absolutely dry.

bone idle extremely lazy.

bone meal ground bones.

bone'-sett'er *n.* one who, without the normal surgeon's training, treats broken or displaced bones.

bare bones the basic facts.

bone of contention a cause of argument or quarrelling.

bone to pick with a grievance against (a person).

make no bones about to have no hesitation, scruple, about.

bonfire *bon'fīr*, *n.* a fire in the open air.

bonnet *bon'it*, *n.* **1** a headdress fastened by strings. **2** (*Scot.*) a cap. **3** the cover of a motor-car engine, etc.

bonny, **bonnie** *bon'i*, *adj.* **1** pretty. **2** healthy-looking. **3** fine:—*comp.* **bonn'ier**; *superl.* **bonn'iest**.

bonsai *bon'sī*, *n.* **1** the art of growing specially-cultivated dwarf trees in a shallow pot. **2** such a tree so grown.

bonus *bō'nus*, *n.* **1** an addition to the sum due as interest, dividend, or wages. **2** something extra:—*pl.* **bo'nuses**.

bony. See **bone**.

boob[1] *bo͞ob, (coll.) v.i.* to make a mistake.—Also *n.*

boob[2] *bo͞ob*, (*coll.) n.* (usu. in *pl.*) a woman's breast.

booby *bo͞o'bi*, *n.* **1** a stupid person. **2** a kind of gannet:—*pl.* **boo'bies**.

booby prize a prize for the lowest score, etc.

boo'by-trap *n.* **1** a trap for the unwary, such as something put above a door so as to fall on the person who opens the door. **2** a bomb or mine made to look like something harmless.

book *book*, *n.* **1** a number of sheets of paper (esp. printed) bound together. **2** a literary composition, bound and covered. **3** the words of a musical drama. **4** a record of bets. **5** (in *pl.*) records, e.g. of a business.—*v.t.* **1** to note in a book. **2** of police, a football referee, to enter (the name of an (alleged) offender) in a book. **3** to engage in advance.—*v.i.* to buy a ticket (for).

book'ie (*coll.*) *n.* a bookmaker.

book'ing *n.* a reservation.

book'ish *adj.* fond of reading.

booklet *n.* a small (paper-covered) book.

book'binding *n.* putting the covers on books.

book'binder *n.*

booking office an office where tickets are sold.

book'keeping *n.* keeping accounts.

book'keeper *n.*

book'maker *n.* a professional betting man who takes bets and pays winnings.

book'mark *n.* something put in a book to mark a page.

book plate a label pasted inside the cover of a book, with owner's name, etc.

book'stall *n.* a stand where books, etc. are sold.

book token a card that can be exchanged for books of the value shown on it.

book'worm *n.* **1** a grub that eats holes in books. **2** a person who reads continually.

be in someone's good (or **bad** or **black**) **books** to be in (or out of) favour with someone.

bring to book to make (a person) explain, or suffer for, his conduct.

get one's books to be dismissed.

take a leaf out of another's book to follow someone else's example.

boom[1] *bo͞om*, *n.* **1** a pole by which a sail is stretched, a microphone is held, etc. **2** a chain or bar stretched across a harbour. **3** an inflatable barrier used to control (e.g. oil) pollution at sea.

boom[2] *bo͞om*, *v.i.* to make a hollow sound, as of the sea.—Also *n.*

boom[3] *bo͞om*, *v.i.* to become suddenly prosperous.—*n.* a sudden increase in business, etc.

boom town a suddenly prosperous town.

boomerang *bo͞om'ė-rang*, *n.* **1** a curved wooden missile used by natives of Australia, so balanced that, when thrown to a distance, it returns to the thrower. **2** an act or action that recoils on the doer.—Also *v.i.*

boon[1] *bo͞on*, *n.* a blessing, thing to be thankful for.

boon[2] *bo͞on*: **boon companion** a close friend, whose company one enjoys.

boor *bo͞or*, *n.* a coarse, ill-mannered person.

boor'ish *adj.*

boost *bo͞ost*, *v.t.* **1** to push up. **2** to increase, improve.—*n.* **1** a push up. **2** something that encourages or helps. **3** an increase.

boost'er *n.* **1** a person or thing that boosts. **2** a device for increasing or renewing power, force, etc. **3** part of a system producing movement at high speed, e.g. first stage of a rocket that works by several stages.

boot[1] *bo͞ot*, *n.* **1** a covering for the foot and lower part of the leg, usu. of leather. **2** a place for luggage in a motor car.—*v.t.* **1** to put boots on. **2** to kick.

bootee *bo͞ot-ē'*, *n.* **1** a woollen boot for a baby. **2** a lady's short boot.

boots *n. sing.* a hotel servant who may clean boots.

boot'legger *n.* **1** one who smuggles alcoholic liquor (orig. in leg of long boot). **2** an illegal dealer.

boot'leg *v.t.*, and *v.i.* (*pr.p.* **boot'legging**; *pa.p.* **boot'legged**), and *adj.*

have one's heart in one's boots to be in terror.

boot[2] *boot*, (*old word*) *n.* advantage.

boot'less *adj.* (of an action) useless.

to boot in addition.

bootee. See **boot**[1].

booth *bo͞o*TH, or *-th*, *n.* **1** a tent at a fair. **2** a covered stall. **3** an enclosed, or partly-enclosed, compartment for voting in, for a public telephone, etc.

bootleg, bootlegger. See **boot**[1].

bootless. See **boot**[2].

booty *bo͞ot'i*, *n.* spoil, plunder.

booze *bo͞oz*, *v.i.* to drink deeply:—*pr.p.* **booz'ing**.—*n.* **1** alcoholic drink. **2** a drinking bout.

booz'y *adj.*:—*comp.* **booz'ier**; *superl.* **booz'iest**.

borax *bō'raks*, *bö'*, *n.* a mineral compound, found as a salty crust on shores of certain lakes, used as cleansing agent, etc.

bo'ric, boracic *(bȯ-ras'ik) adjs.*

border *bör'dėr*, *n.* **1** the edge of anything. **2** the boundary of a country, esp. (with *cap.*, also in *pl.*) that between England and Scotland. **3** flower bed in a garden.—*v.i.* to come near, to lie on the border of (with *on, upon*).

bor'derer *n.* one who lives on the border of a country.

bor'derland *n.*

bore[1] *bōr*, *bor*, *v.t.* **1** to pierce by a rotating tool so as to form a round hole. **2** to make (a hole) thus. **3** to thrust against (as one racehorse against another):—*pr.p.* **bor'ing**.—*n.* **1** a hole made by boring. **2** the hollow tube of a gun. **3** the diameter of the tube.

bore'hole *n.* a hole bored in the earth's crust for obtaining water, oil, samples, etc.

bore[2] *bōr*, *bor*, *v.t.* to weary, seem dull to:—*pr.p.* **bor'ing**.—*n.* a tiresome person or thing.

bore'dom *n.* the state of being bored.

bor'ing *adj.* uninteresting, dull.

bore[3]. See **bear**[1].

bore[4] *bōr*, *bor*, *n.* a tidal flood which rushes up the estuaries of certain rivers.

boric. See **borax**.

born, borne. See **bear**[1].

boron *bō'ron*, *bö'-*, *n.* an element found in borax, etc.

borough *bur'ȯ*, *n.* **1** a town with a corporation and special privileges granted by royal charter. **2** a town that sends representatives to parliament.

county borough a borough of 100000 inhabitants or more.

See also **burgh**.

borrow *bor'ō*, *v.t.* **1** to take on loan. **2** to adopt (words) from another language.

borr'ower *n.* **borr'owing** *n.*

borsch(t) *börsh(t)*, *ns.* a Russian soup with beetroot, etc.

borstal *bör'stȧl*, *adj.* applied to a system of training delinquents while they are in custody.—Also *n.*

borzoi *bōr'zoi*, *n.* a Russian hound bred orig. for hunting wolves.

bosh *bosh*, *n.* nonsense.—Also *interj.*

bosom *booz'-*, *bo͞oz'ȯm*, *n.* the breast.—*adj.* intimate: *bosom friend.*

boss[1] *bos*, *n.* a knob or stud.

boss[2] *bos*, *n.* the master, manager.—*v.t.* **1** to manage. **2** to order about.

boss'y *adj.* inclined to order others about:—*comp.* **boss'ier**; *superl.* **boss'iest**.

boss'iness *n.*

bo'sun, bosun. See **boatswain**.

botany *bot'ȧn-i*, *n.* the science of plants.

botan'ic, -ical *adjs.*

bot'anist *n.* one skilled in botany.

botanic garden(s) a public park stocked with native and foreign plants.

botch *boch* *n.* **1** a clumsy patch. **2** ill-finished work.—*v.t.* **1** to mend clumsily. **2** to do badly.

both *bōth*, *adj.* and *pron.* **1** the two. **2** the one and the other.—*conj.* (or *adv.*) as well, equally.

bother *bo*TH*'ėr*, *v.t.* **1** to annoy. **2** to worry.—Also *n.* and *interj.*

botherā'tion *n.* and *interj.* (*coll.*)

both'ersome *adj.*

bothy, bothie *both'i*, *n.* a hut, esp. one

shared by farm servants:—*pl.* **both'ies**.

bottle *bot'l*, *n.* **1** a hollow narrow-necked vessel for holding liquids. **2** its contents. **3** (*slang*) courage.—*v.t.* to put into bottles:—*pr.p.* **bott'ling**.
bottle bank a skip for glass refuse only.
bott'le-green *adj.* dark green.
bott'leneck *n.* **1** a narrow part of a road apt to become very crowded with traffic. **2** any stage of a process where progress is obstructed.
bottle up to keep in, repress (e.g. one's feelings).

bottom *bot'ȯm*, *n.* **1** the lowest part of anything. **2** the part of the body on which one sits. **3** the seat of a chair. **4** the hull of a ship, hence the ship itself. **5** the bed of the sea, etc.
bott'omless *adj.* very deep.
at bottom in reality.
be at the bottom of to be the real cause of.
bottom out of prices, etc., to reach and settle at the lowest level.
get to the bottom of to discover the explanation of, or real facts of.

botulism *bot'ū-lism*, *n.* a type of foodpoisoning, caused by bacteria in infected sausages, tinned food, etc.

boudoir *bōōd'wär*, *n.* a lady's private sittingroom.

bough *bow*, *n.* a branch of a tree.

bought. See **buy**.

boulder *bōl'dėr*, *n.* a large stone, often one rounded by the action of water.

boulevard *bōōl'ė-vär(d)*, *n.* a broad road lined with trees.

boult. See **bolt²**.

bounce *bowns*, *v.i.* **1** to spring suddenly. **2** to rebound like a ball. **3** (*coll.*) of a cheque, to be returned unpaid from a bank because of lack of money in the account.—*v.t.* to make (e.g. a ball) rebound:—*pr.p.* **bounc'ing**.—Also *n.* **bounc'ing** *adj.* big, strong, and lively.
bounc'y *adj.*:—*comp.* **bounc'ier**; *superl.* **bounc'iest**.

-bound. See **bind** and **bound⁴**.

bound¹. See **bind**.

bound² *bownd*, *v.t.* to limit, restrain, or surround.—Also *n.* (usu. in *pl.*).
boun'dary *n.* the line by which an area is marked off:—*pl.* **boun'daries**.
bound'less *adj.* having no limit, vast.
out of bounds outside the permitted area.

bound³ *bownd*, *v.i.* to spring or leap.—*n.* a spring or leap.

bound⁴ *bownd*, *adj.* ready to go to, on the way to (usu. with *for*): *bound for the North.*
-bound as part of a word, on the way to, as *northbound.*

bounty *bown'ti*, *n.* **1** generosity in giving. **2** something generously given. **3** a sum given to encourage e.g. the production of a commodity:—*pl.* **boun'ties**.
boun'teous (*-ti-ůs*, or *-tyůs*), **boun'tiful** *adjs.* **1** generous. **2** plentiful.

bouquet *bōōk'ā*, or *-ā'*, *n.* **1** a bunch of flowers. **2** the perfume of wine.

bourgeois *bōōr'zhwä*, *n.* one of the **bourgeoisie** (*bōōr'zhwä-zē* or *-zē'*), the middle class of citizens.—Also *adj.*

bout *bowt*, *n.* **1** a period, spell, fit (of). **2** a contest.

boutique *bōō-tēk'*, *n.* a small fashionable, esp. clothes, shop, or a similar department in a shop.

bovine *bō'vīn*, *adj.* **1** of cattle, **2** dull.

bow¹ *bow*, *v.i.* **1** to bend: *to bow before the storm.* **2** to submit: *He bowed to his fate.* **3** to bend the head or the body in greeting a person, etc.—*v.t.* **1** to bend. **2** to weigh down, crush.—Also *n.*

bow² *bō*, *n.* **1** anything in the shape of an arch, as the rainbow. **2** a springy curved rod bent by a string, by which arrows are shot. **3** a rod with horsehair by which the strings of a violin, etc. are sounded. **4** a looped knot of ribbon, etc.
bow'-legged' *adj.* having bandy legs.
bow'man *n.* an archer.
bow window a curved window.
have two strings to one's bow to have more than one choice, plan, etc.

bow³ *bow*, *n.* the fore part of a ship—often used in *pl.*

bowdlerise *bowd'lėr-īz*, *v.t.* to expurgate (a book, etc.):—*pr.p.* **bowd'lerising**.

bowel *bow'ėl*, *n.* **1** (usu. in *pl.*) the entrails, intestines. **2** (in *pl.*) the inside of anything.

bower *bow'ėr*, *n.* **1** an arbour. **2** a boudoir.
bower'-bird *n.* an Australian bird that makes a bower ornamented with feathers, shells, etc.

bowie-knife *bō'i-nīf*, *n.* a long heavy sheathed knife, designed by Colonel *Bowie* (d. 1836):—*pl.* **bow'ie-knives**.

bowl¹ *bōl*, *n.* **1** a wooden ball used for rolling along the ground. **2** (in *pl.*) a game played on a green with bowls having a bias.—*v.i.* **1** to play at bowls. **2** to speed smoothly (along). **3** to deliver ball(s), in cricket.—*v.t.* **1** to deliver (a ball) in cricket. **2** to put (a batsman) out thus.
bowl'er *n.* **bowl'ing** *n.*
bowl'ing-alley *n.* a long narrow covered rink for skittles:—*pl.* **bowl'ing-alleys**.

bowl'ing-green *n.* a smooth green for bowls.
bowl over 1 to knock down. **2** to overcome with emotion.
bowl[2] *bōl*, *n.* **1** a basin for holding liquids. **2** a round hollow part (e.g. of a tobacco pipe).
bowler[1]. See **bowl**[1].
bowler[2] *bōl'ėr*, *n.* a hard, felt hat.
bowline *bō'līn*, *n.* **1** a rope to keep a sail close to the wind. **2** (also **bowline knot**) a knot used to tie a bowline so that it will not slip or jam, and also used in rock-climbing, etc.
bowsprit *bō'sprit*, *n.* a strong spar projecting over the bows of a ship.
box[1] *boks*, *n.* **1** an evergreen shrub. **2** a small tree with hard wood. **3** a case for holding something. **4** a (Christmas) present. **5** in a theatre, a group of enclosed seats.—*v.t.* **1** to put into boxes. **2** (usu. with *up*) to enclose, shut in uncomfortably.
Boxing day the first weekday after Christmas day.
box junction an area at a road junction, criss-crossed with yellow lines, which a vehicle may not enter unless its exit is clear.
box office 1 a theatre booking office. **2** receipts from a play, etc. **3** an attraction as judged by the money taken.
box pleat a kind of double pleat.
box the compass to name the 32 points in order and backwards.
the box (*coll.*) (the) television.
box[2] *boks*, *n.* a blow on the ear with the hand.—*v.t.* to strike with the hand.—*v.i.* to fight with the fists.
box'er *n.* **box'ing** *n.*
box'ing-glove *n.* a boxer's padded glove.
boxer[1]. See **box**[2].
boxer[2] *boks'ėr*, *n.* a medium-sized dog with smooth brown hair, orig. a German police dog.
boy *boi*, *n.* **1** a male child. **2** a servant.
boy'hood *n.* time of being a boy.
boy'ish *adj.*
Boys' Brigade an organisation of boys to promote reverence, discipline, etc.
Boy Scout. See **Scout**.
boycott *boi'kot*, *v.t.* **1** to shut out from all social or business dealings. **2** to refuse to take part in, deal with, etc.—Also *n.*
brace *brās*, *n.* **1** anything that draws together and holds tightly. **2** a pair, couple. **3** a piece of wire fitted over the teeth to straighten them. **4** (in *pl.*) straps for supporting the trousers. **5** a rope for turning a yard (see this word) of a ship.—*v.t.* **1** to tighten. **2** to strengthen: *He braced himself for the struggle*:—*pr.p.* **brac'ing**.
brac'ing *adj.* **1** strengthening. **2** filling with energy: *bracing sea air*.
bracelet *brās'lit*, *n.* **1** an ornament worn round the wrist. **2** (*coll.*) a handcuff.
bracken *brak'ėn*, *n.* a fern, esp. the commonest British fern.
bracket *brak'it*, *n.* **1** a support for a shelf, etc. **2** a small shelf. **3** a number of people grouped according to income. **4** (in *pl.*) in writing or printing, the marks, such as () or [], used to enclose one or more words.—*v.t.* **1** to enclose by brackets. **2** to group together (similar or equal things):—*pr.p.* **brack'eting**; *pa.p.* **brack'eted**.
brackish *brak'ish*, *adj.* (of water) saltish.
bract *brakt*, *n.* a leaf-like part at the base of a flower.
brad *brad*, *n.* a small nail.
brad'awl *n.* an awl to pierce holes.
brae *brā*, (*Scot.*) *n.* a hill slope.
brag *brag*, *v.i.* to boast:—*pr.p.* **bragg'ing**; *pa.p.* **bragged**.— *n.* a boastful statement.
braggart *brag'ȧrt*, *n.* a boaster.
Brahman, -min *brä'man, -min*, *ns.* a Hindu of the highest or priestly caste.
Brah'manism or **-min-** *ns.* the worship of the god **Brah'ma**.
braid *brād*, *v.t.* to plait or entwine.—*n.* a narrow band (of hair, threads, etc.) made by plaiting or entwining.
braille *brāl*, *n.* a system of printing for the blind, using raised dots.
brain *brān*, *n.* **1** a greyish substance, the part of the nervous system within the skull. **2** (often in *pl.*) cleverness, intelligence, the mind.—*v.t.* to dash out the brains of.
brain'y *adj.* clever:—*comp.* **brain'ier**; *superl.* **brain'iest**.
brain'iness *n.*
brain child a person's favourite theory, invention, etc.
brain death the cessation of function of the brain, considered by some an indication of death.
brain storm 1 a sudden mental disturbance. **2** a brain wave.
brain'-teaser *n.* a difficult puzzle or problem.
brain'wash *v.t.* to force a person to conform, confess, etc., by subjecting him to indoctrination or mental pressure.
brain'washing *n.*
brain wave a sudden bright idea.
brains trust a group of experts, esp. one answering questions in public.
braise *brāz*, *v.t.* to stew in a closed dish:—*pr.p.* **brais'ing**.

brake[1] *brāk*, *n.* a thicket.

brake[2] *brāk*, *n.* a device to slow down the motion of a wheel or vehicle.—Also *v.i.* and *v.t.*:—*pr.p.* **brak'ing.**

bramble *bram'bl*, *n.* **1** the blackberry bush. **2** (*Scot.*) a blackberry.

bran *bran*, *n.* the inner husks of grain sifted from the flour.

branch *bränch*, or *-sh*, *n.* **1** a limb of a tree. **2** any offshoot from a parent stem (e.g. of road, railway, family). **3** a department of a business, etc.—*v.i.* to spread out as a branch or branches (with *out, off, from*).

brand *brand*, *n.* **1** a piece of wood burning or partly burned. **2** a mark stamped with a hot iron. **3** a make, quality (of goods). **4** a sword.—*v.t.* **1** to mark with a hot iron. **2** to fix a mark of disgrace upon.

brand'-new *adj.* very new.

brandish *brand'ish*, *v.t.* to wave (e.g. a weapon).

brandy *bran'di*, *n.* a strong spirit distilled from wine:—*pl.* **bran'dies.**

bran'dy-snap *n.* a thin, crisp biscuit, flavoured with ginger and orig. brandy.

brass *bräs*, *n.* **1** an alloy of copper and zinc. **2** (*slang*) money. **3** (usu. in *pl.*) memorial tablets of brass. **4** boldness, impudence. **5** the brass instruments in an orchestra. **6** the players of these.

brass'y *adj.* **1** like brass. **2** impudent. **3** harsh in tone:—*comp.* **brass'ier;** *superl.* **brass'iest.**

brass'ily *adv.* **brass'iness** *n.*

brass band a band of players of (mainly) brass wind instruments.

brass hat (*slang*) a high-ranking officer.

brass neck (*coll.*) cheek, effrontery.

brass plate a nameplate on a door.

brass'-rubbing *n.* **1** copying the design on a brass plate by covering it with paper and rubbing it with wax, chalk, etc. **2** the copy so made.

See also **brazen.**

brassiere *bras'i-ėr*, *n.* a woman's undergarment supporting the breasts.

brat *brat*, *n.* a scornful name for a child.

bravado *bräv-ä'dō*, *n.* **1** a show of bravery. **2** bold pretence.

brave *brāv*, *adj.* **1** courageous. **2** noble. **3** finely dressed.—*v.t.* **1** to meet boldly. **2** to face (it out):—*pr.p.* **brav'ing.**—*n.* a Red Indian warrior.

brave'ly *adv.* **brav'ery** *n.*

bravo *brä'vō'*, *interj.* well done!

brawl *bröl*, *n.* a noisy quarrel.—Also *v.i.*

brawn *brön*, *n.* **1** muscle, esp. of the arm or leg. **2** strength. **3** potted meat from pig's flesh.

brawn'y *adj.*:—*comp.* **brawn'ier;** *superl.* **brawn'iest.**

brawn'iness *n.*

bray *brā*, *n.* the cry of the ass.—Also *v.i.*

brazen *brā'zn*, *adj.* **1** of brass. **2** impudent.—*v.t.* to face (a situation) with impudent boldness: *to brazen it out.*

brazier *brāz'yėr*, *brāzh'(y)ėr*, *n.* a worker in brass.

brazier[1]. See **brazen.**

brazier[2] *brāz'yėr*, *brāzh'(y)ėr*, *n.* a pan for hot coals.

Brazilian *brȧ-zil'yėn*, *adj.* of Brazil, in South America.—*n.* a native of Brazil.

breach *brēch*, *n.* **1** a break or gap. **2** a breaking (of law, promise, etc.). **3** a quarrel.—*v.t.* to make an opening in.

breach of the peace a riot, disturbance.

bread *bred*, *n.* **1** food made of flour or meal baked. **2** food. **3** (also **bread and butter**) livelihood.

bread'winner *n.* one who earns a living for a family.

bread'fruit tree a tree of the South Sea Islands, whose starchy fruit is eaten baked or roasted.

on the breadline with barely enough to live on.

breadth. See **broad.**

break *brāk*, *v.t.* **1** to divide into parts by force. **2** to shatter. **3** (also **break in**) to tame, train (e.g. a horse). **4** to check (e.g. a fall). **5** to interrupt (e.g. silence). **6** to cure (someone of a habit). **7** to tell (news).—*v.i.* **1** to fall in pieces. **2** to dawn. **3** of a voice, to change (usu. fall) in pitch. **4** to change direction (as a cricket-ball):—*pa.t.* **brōke;** *pa.p.* **brōk'en** (see this word).—*n.* **1** an opening. **2** a pause. **3** (*billiards*) a series of successful strokes. **4** (*cricket*) change of direction of a ball. **5** (*coll.*) a stroke of luck (good or ill); a chance or opportunity.

break'able *adj.*—Also *n.* (in *pl.*).

break'age *n.* the act of breaking, or its results.

break'er *n.* **1** a person or thing that breaks. **2** a wave broken on rocks or beach.

break'down *n.* **1** collapse. **2** an accidental stoppage. **3** (also **nervous breakdown**) a period of depression, great anxiety, etc. **4** an analysis.

breakdown gang, vehicle a squad of men, a vehicle, to remove wreckage.

break'neck *adj.* reckless.

break'-out *n.* See **break out.**

breakfast *brek'fȧst*, *n.* the first meal of the day.—*v.i.* to take this.

breast *brest*, *n.* **1** the front of the human or animal body between the neck and belly. **2** either of the two milk-producing glands on this part of a woman's body. **3** the affections.—*v.t.* **1** to oppose. **2** to go up: *to breast a hill.* **3** in running, to touch (the finishing tape) with the breast.

breast'feed *v.t.* and *v.i.* to feed (a baby) with milk from the breast:—*pa.p.* **breast'fed.**

breast'plate *n.* armour for the breast.

make a clean breast to confess fully.

breath *breth*, *n.* **1** the air drawn into and then sent out from the lungs. **2** life. **3** an act of breathing. **4** a faint breeze.

breathalyser *breth'ȧl-īz-ėr*, *n.* a device which indicates the amount of alcohol in a person's breath.

breath'less *adj.* **1** out of breath. **2** having difficulty in breathing. **3** very eager or excited.

breath'lessly *adv.* **breath'lessness** *n.*

with bated breath with breathing checked by awe, anxiety, or excitement (*bate v.t.* same as *abate*).

breathe *brēTH*, *v.i.* **1** to draw in and let out from the lungs breath or air. **2** to rest or pause. **3** to live.—*v.t.* **1** to draw in (e.g. air) or send out from the lungs. **2** to whisper. **3** to let (a horse) recover breath:—*pr.p.* **breath'ing.**

breath'er *(-ēTH') n.* **1** a spell of exercise. **2** a rest to recover breath.

breath'ing *n.* and *adj.*

bred. See **breed.**

breech *brēch*, *n.* the back part, esp. of a gun.

breeches *brich'iz*, *n.pl.* trousers, esp. ones coming just below the knee.

breech birth a birth in which the buttocks of the baby come first.

breech'es-buoy *n.* a life-saving apparatus in part like a pair of breeches.

breed *brēd*, *v.t.* **1** to produce (offspring). **2** to train or bring up. **3** to raise: *He breeds horses.* **4** to cause: *Idleness breeds discontent.*—*v.i.* **1** to produce offspring. **2** to be produced:—*pa.t.* and *pa.p.* **bred.**—*n.* **1** offspring. **2** kind, race, or species: *a rare breed of dog.*

breed'ing *n.* **1** act of producing. **2** education and training. **3** good manners.

breeze *brēz*, *n.* **1** a gentle wind. **2** a quarrel.

breez'y *adj.* **1** windy. **2** bright, lively:—*comp.* **breez'ier**; *superl.* **breez'iest.**

breez'ily *adv.* **breez'iness** *n.*

brethren. See **brother.**

Breton *bret'ȯn*, *n.* a native of Brittany (*Bretagne*), France.—*adj.* of Brittany.

breviary *brēv'i-ȧr-i*, *brēv'yȧr-*, *n.* a book containing the daily service of the R.C. Church:—*pl.* **brev'iaries.**

brevity. See **brief.**

brew *bro͞o*, *v.t.* **1** to make (beer, ale). **2** to make (tea). **3** to plot.—*v.i.* **1** to brew beer, etc. **2** to be in preparation: *Mischief was brewing.*—*n.* **1** something brewed. **2** an amount, quality, or variety of something brewed.

brew'er *n.*

brew'ery *n.* place for brewing:—*pl.* **brew'eries.**

briar[1], **brier** *brī'ėr*, *n.* **1** a prickly shrub. **2** a wild rose bush.

briar[2], **brier** *brī'ėr*, *n.* **1** the white heath, from whose root tobacco pipes are made. **2** a pipe of this wood.

bribe *brīb*, *n.* a gift offered to persuade a person to do something, usu. dishonest.—Also *v.t.*:—*pr.p.* **brib'ing.**

brib'ery *n.* giving or taking bribes.

bric-à-brac *brik'ȧ-brak*, *n.* interesting, often treasured, odds and ends.

brick *brik*, *n.* **1** (a block of) baked or 'burned' clay for building. **2** (*slang*) one who is cheerful and helpful in troubles.

brick'bat *n.* **1** a piece of brick, esp. as a missile. **2** an insult.

brick'layer *n.* one who builds with bricks.

drop a brick to make a tactless blunder.

bride *brīd*, *n.* a woman about to be married, or newly married.

bridal *brīd'ȧl*, *adj.* of a bride or wedding.

bride'groom *n.* a man about to be married, or newly married.

brides'maid *(brīdz') n.* an unmarried woman attending the bride at a wedding.

bridge[1] *brij*, *n.* **1** a structure to carry traffic over a river, etc. **2** the narrow raised platform for the captain of a ship. **3** the bony part of the nose. **4** the support of the strings of a violin.—*v.t.* to be, or to build, a bridge over:—*pr.p.* **bridg'ing.**

bridge'head *n.* **1** a fortification on the enemy side of a river. **2** any advanced position seized in enemy territory.

bridging loan a short-term loan, usu. for a large sum and at a high rate of interest, provided esp. for house purchase.

bridge[2] *brij*, *n.* a card game, played by two against two, the hand of the declarer's partner always being exposed.

bridle *brī'dl*, *n.* **1** the harness about the head of a horse to which the reins are attached. **2** any restraint.—*v.t.* to restrain.—*v.i.* to toss the head proudly like

a restive horse (often with *up* and *at*): *She bridled (up) at this remark*:—*pr.p.* **brid'-ling**.
bridle path, road a path for riders and horses.

brief *brēf*, *adj*. short.—*n*. **1** a short statement (esp. in a lawsuit, of a client's case). **2** (in *pl.*) close-fitting pants or underpants.—*v.t.* to give detailed instructions to.
brief'ly *adv*. **brief'ness, brev'ity** *ns*.
hold a brief for to speak in favour of.
in brief in few words.

brier. See **briar**[1,2].

brigade *bri-gād'*, *n*. **1** a body of troops consisting of two or more regiments, or battalions, etc. **2** a uniformed band organised for a purpose.
brigadier' *(-dēr')* *n*. a rank in the army, or a person of this rank.

brigand *brig'ȧnd*, *n*. a robber, esp. one of a band in unsettled or remote country.

bright *brīt*, *adj*. **1** shining. **2** clear. **3** cheerful. **4** clever.
bright'en *v.t.* and *v.i.* to make, or become, bright or brighter.
bright'ly *adv*. **bright'ness** *n*.

brilliant *bril'yȧnt*, *adj*. **1** sparkling. **2** splendid. **3** talented.—*n*. a fine diamond.
brill'iantly *adv*.
brill'iance, brill'iancy *ns*.
brilliantine *bril'yȧn-tēn*, *n*. a dressing to make the hair glossy.

brim *brim*, *n*. **1** the edge of a river, lake, cup, etc. **2** the rim of a hat.—*v.i.* to be full to the brim:—*pr.p.* **brimm'ing**; *pa.p.* **brimmed**.
brim'ful *adj*. full to the brim.
brim over to overflow.

brimstone *brim'stōn*, *n*. sulphur.

brindle(d) *brin'dl(d)*, *adjs*. brownish or grey, marked with streaks.

brine *brīn*, *n*. very salt water.
brin'y *adj*. very salt:—*comp*. **brin'ier**; *superl*. **brin'iest**.
brin'iness *n*.
the briny the sea.

bring *bring*, *v.t.* **1** to fetch, to lead or carry (to a place). **2** to cause to come (e.g. rain, relief), to result in. **3** to put before a court of law, etc.: *to bring an action against someone*:—*pa.t.* and *pa.p.* **brought** *(brö̇t)*.
bring about to cause.
bring forth to give birth to, produce.
bring home to to prove to, to show clearly to.
bring in 1 to introduce. **2** to produce as profit. **3** to pronounce (a verdict).
bring off to achieve (something attempted).
bring oneself to persuade oneself (to).
bring out 1 to make clear, reveal. **2** to publish.
bring round 1 to restore from unconsciousness. **2** to win over.
bring to to restore to consciousness.
bring up 1 to rear or educate. **2** to introduce to notice: *Bring up the matter at the meeting*. **3** to vomit.
bring up the rear to come last.

brink *bringk*, *n*. the edge or border of a steep place or of a river.
on the brink of on the point of, very near.

briny. See **brine**.

briquette *bri-ket'*, *n*. a brick-shaped block of fuel made of coal dust.

brisk *brisk*, *adj*. **1** lively. **2** active.
brisk'ly *adv*. **brisk'ness** *n*.

brisket *brisk'it*, *n*. the part of the breast of an animal next to the ribs, when considered as food.

bristle *bris'l*, *n*. a short, stiff hair.—*v.i.* **1** to stand erect or stiffly as bristles do. **2** to show anger:—*pr.p.* **brist'ling**; *pa.p.* **brist'led** *(bris'ld)*.
brist'ly *adj*.:—*comp*. **brist'lier**; *superl*. **brist'liest**.
brist'liness *n*.
bristle with to be full of.

Britannia *bri-tan'yȧ*, *n*. **1** Britain. **2** a female figure personifying it.

British *brit'ish*, *adj*. of Britain or the Commonwealth.

Briton *brit'ȯn*, *n*. **1** one of the early inhabitants of Britain. **2** a native of Great Britain.

brittle *brit'l*, *adj*. **1** easily broken. **2** frail.
britt'leness *n*.

broach *brōch*, *n*. a boring tool.—*v.t.* **1** to pierce (a cask). **2** to open up (a subject).

broad *brö̇d*, *adj*. **1** wide. **2** large, spacious. **3** coarse: *a broad story*. **4** of, in, a strong dialect: *a broad accent*. **5** full: *broad daylight*. **6** clear: *a broad hint*. **7** general, without going into detail: *a broad outline*.—*n*. (in Norfolk) a lake-like expansion of a river.
broad'en *v.t.* and *v.i.* to make, or become, broad or broader.
broad'ly *adv*.
broad'ness, breadth *(bredth)* *ns*.
broad arrow a mark (⬆) stamped on British government property, including clothing worn by convicts.
broad'cast *v.t.* **1** to scatter (seed) by hand. **2** to make widely known. **3** to send out by radio, television (entertainment programmes, news, messages, etc.) (also *v.i.*):—*pa.t.* and *pa.p.* **broad'cast**.—Also *n*. and *adj*.

broad'caster *n.* **broad'casting** *n.*
broad'cloth *n.* a fine woollen cloth.
broad jump (*U.S.*) long jump.
broad'loom *n.* carpet woven on a wide loom.—Also *adj.*
broad'-mind'ed *adj.* **1** ready to allow others to think or act as they choose without criticising them. **2** tolerant, not prejudiced.
broad'sheet *n.* a newspaper printed on large sheets of paper.
broad'side *n.* **1** the side of a ship. **2** firing of all the guns on one side of a ship of war. **3** a strongly critical attack.
broad'sword *n.* a cutting sword with a broad blade.

brocade *brȯ-kad'*, *n.* a silk material having a design on it that appears raised.

broccoli *brok'ȯ-li*, *n.* (also **sprouting broccoli**) a hardy variety of cauliflower with green or purple florets.

brochure *brō'shoor, brȯ-shōōr'*, *n.* a pamphlet.

brock *brok*, *n.* a badger.

brogue *brōg*, *n.* **1** a stout shoe. **2** a characteristic, esp. Irish, accent.

broil[1] *broil*, *n.* a noisy quarrel.

broil[2] *broil*, *v.t.* to grill.—*v.i.* to be very hot.
broil'er *n.* a quickly-reared young chicken sold ready for broiling.

broke[1] *brōk*, (*coll.*) *adj.* having no money, penniless.

broke[2]. See **break**.

broken *brō'kn*, *pa.p.* of **break**.—*adj.* **1** incomplete. **2** interrupted. **3** irregular. **4** imperfect: *He speaks broken English.* **5** ruined.
brok'enly *adv.* with voice unsteady.
brok'en-down' *adj.* not in working order, or good condition, or health.
brok'en-heart'ed *adj.* overcome by grief.
broken home the home of children whose parents are divorced or have separated.
brok'en-wind'ed *adj.* (of a horse) having difficulty in breathing.

broker *brō'kėr*, *n.* one employed to buy and sell for others.
brok'erage *n.* **1** the business of a broker. **2** commission charged by a broker.

bromide *brō'mīd*, *n.* **1** a compound of bromine, esp. one used as a sedative. **2** a trite, commonplace remark.
bromine *brō'mēn, -min*, *n.* a liquid giving off strong fumes.

broncho, bronco *brong'kō*, (*U.S.*) *n.* a half-tamed horse:—*pl.* **bron'chos, bron'cos.**

bronchus *brongk'us*, *n.* either of the main forks of the windpipe:—*pl.* **bronch'i** *(brongk'ī)*.
bronch'ial *adj.*
bronchitis *brong-kī'tis*, *n.* inflammation of the lining of bronchial tubes.

brontosaurus *bron-tȯ-sö'rus*, *n.* a four-footed dinosaur, found fossil in U.S.A.

bronze *bronz*, *n.* **1** an alloy of copper and tin. **2** its colour. **3** a bronze medal.—Also *adj.*
bronzed *adj.* **1** coated with bronze. **2** sunburned.
Bronze Age the period between the Stone and Iron Ages, in which tools and weapons were made from bronze.
bronze medal in athletics competitions, etc., the medal awarded as third prize.

brooch *brōch*, *n.* an ornamental clasp with an attached pin fitting into a hook.

brood *brōōd*, *v.i.* **1** to sit as a hen on eggs. **2** to hang or hover (over). **3** to think anxiously for some time.—*n.* **1** offspring. **2** the number hatched at once.—*adj.* for breeding, as in *brood* mare, etc.
brood'y *adj.* **1** (of hen bird) ready to brood. **2** deep in anxious thought:—*comp.* **brood'ier**; *superl.* **brood'iest**.

brook[1] *brook*, *n.* a small stream.

brook[2] *brook*, *v.t.* to bear, endure.

broom *brōōm*, *n.* **1** a shrub of the pea family with yellow flowers. **2** a long-handled sweeping-brush.
broom'stick *n.* the handle of a broom.

broth *broth*, *n.* a soup, esp. one containing vegetables and barley or rice.

brothel *broth'ėl*, *n.* a house where people pay for sex.

brother *bru*TH*'ėr*, *n.* **1** the name given to a male child by the other children of his parents. **2** a close friend. **3** a fellow member of any group:—*pl.* **broth'ers, breth'ren** (the latter esp. used of fellow members of religious bodies, etc.).
broth'erhood *n.* **1** the state of being a brother. **2** an association of men for any purpose.
broth'erly *adj.* like a brother, kind.
broth'erliness *n.*
broth'er-in-law *n.* **1** the brother of a husband or wife. **2** a sister's husband. **3** a husband's or wife's sister's husband:—*pl.* **broth'ers-in-law**.

brought. See **bring**.

brow *brow*, *n.* **1** the eyebrow. **2** the forehead. **3** the edge (of a hill).
brow'beat *v.t.* to bully:—*pa.t.* **brow'beat**; *pa.p.* **brow'beaten**.

brown *brown*, *adj.* **1** of dark colour, between red and yellow. **2** sunburnt.—Also *n.*—*v.t.* **1** to roast brown. **2** to make brown.—*v.i.* to become brown.

brownie *brown'i*, *n.* **1** a friendly goblin. **2** (with *cap.*; in full **Brownie Guide**) a junior Girl Guide. **3** a kind of rich, chewy chocolate cake.

brown bread bread made of unsifted wheat flour, or of other darkish material.

brown coal lignite.

a brown study deep thought.

browse *browz*, *v.i.* **1** to feed (on shoots or leaves of plants). **2** to read here and there.—*v.t.* to feed on:—*pr.p.* **brows'ing**.

brucellosis *brōō-sėl-ō'sis*, *n.* a disease of animals, esp. cattle, that can be transmitted to man through infected milk.

bruise *brōōz*, *v.t.* to inflict a bruise on by striking.—*v.i.* to become bruised:—*pr.p.* **bruis'ing**.—*n.* an injury with discoloration of the skin made by anything heavy and blunt.

bruis'er *n.* **1** a boxer. **2** a tough, a bully.

brunette *brōō-net'*, *n.* a woman with brown or dark hair.

brunt *brunt*, *n.* **1** the shock or force of a blow. **2** the chief strain: *to bear the brunt of.*

brush *brush*, *n.* **1** an instrument with bristles, wire, hair, for cleaning, scrubbing, painting. **2** a bushy tail. **3** a light passing touch. **4** a skirmish. **5** a thicket. **6** (*Austr.*) forest and undergrowth. **7** backwoods.—*v.t.* **1** to pass a brush over. **2** to remove by sweeping.—*v.i.* to pass with light contact.

brushed *adj.* of cloth, with the surface roughened: *brushed denim.*

brush'wood *n.* **1** loppings and broken branches. **2** a thicket.

brush up **1** to freshen one's appearance. **2** to refresh one's knowledge of.—*n.* **brush'-up**.

brusque *broosk, brusk, adj.* blunt and abrupt in manner.

brusque'ly *adv.* **brusque'ness** *n.*

Brussels sprouts *brus'lz sprowts*, a variety of cabbage with sprouts on the stem like tiny cabbages.

brute *brōōt*, *adj.* **1** of the lower animals. **2** without fine feeling. **3** stupid. **4** cruel. —*n.* **1** one of the lower animals. **2** (*sometimes playfully*) a cruel person.

brut'al *adj.* **1** like a brute. **2** very cruel.

brut'alise *v.t.* to make brutal:—*pr.p.* **brut'alising**.

brutal'ity (*pl.* **-ies**) *n.* **brut'ally** *adv.*

brut'ish *adj.* **1** brutal. **2** stupid.

brut'ishly *adv.* **brut'ishness** *n.*

bubble *bub'l*, *n.* **1** a thin-walled floating ball in air or liquids, or in solids a cavity, filled with air or gas. **2** something empty or insubstantial.—*v.i.* **1** to rise in bubbles. **2** to form bubbles:—*pr.p.* **bubb'ling**; *pa.p.* **bubb'led**.

bubb'ly *adj.*:—*comp.* **bubb'lier**; *superl.* **bubb'liest**.—*n.* (*coll.*) champagne.

bubb'liness *n.*

bubonic plague *bū-bon'ik plāg* a form of plague characterised by swellings in the groin or armpit.

buccaneer *buk-ȧ-nēr'*, *n.* **1** a 17th-century pirate in the West Indies. **2** an adventurer.

buck *buk*, *n.* **1** the male of deer, goat, hare, rabbit. **2** a dashing fellow. **3** a counter in poker. **4** (*U.S.*) a dollar.—*v.i.* **1** (of a horse) to attempt to throw the rider by rapid jumps into the air. **2** (*coll.*) to resist.

bucked *adj.* (*coll.*) cheered.

buck'skin *n.* a soft leather made of deerskin or sheepskin.

buck tooth a projecting tooth.

buck up (*slang*) **1** to hurry. **2** to cheer up.

pass the buck to shift the responsibility to someone else.

bucket *buk'it*, *n.* a vessel for holding water.—*v.i.* (*coll.*) (of rain) to pour heavily:—*pr.p.* **buck'eting**; *pa.p.* **buck'eted**.

buckle *buk'l*, *n.* **1** a fastening for a strap or band, consisting of a rim and, usu., a movable tongue. **2** a curled or warped state.—*v.t.* **1** to fasten with a buckle. **2** to prepare (oneself) for action.—*v.t.* and *v.i.* **1** to warp. **2** to bend or crumple (of a metal object—e.g. a wheel, a girder):—*pr.p.* **buck'ling**.

buck'ler *n.* a small shield.

buckle to, down to apply oneself.

buckram *buk'rȧm*, *n.* coarse linen, cotton, etc., stiffened with size (see **size**[2]).

bucolic *bū-kol'ik*, *adj.* having to do with country life.

bud *bud*, *n.* a shoot of a tree or plant, containing undeveloped leaves, or flower(s), or both.—*v.i.* **1** to put forth buds. **2** to begin to grow:—*pr.p.* **budd'ing**; *pa.p.* **budd'ed**.

budd'ing *adj.* beginning to develop: *a budding poet.*

nip in the bud to destroy at its very beginning.

Buddha *bood'ȧ*, *n.* the Enlightened, a title applied to the founder of the Buddhist religion or **Buddh'ism**.

Buddh'ist *n.* a believer in Buddhism.

budge *buj*, *v.i.* and *v.t.* to move or stir:—*pr.p.* **budg'ing**; *pa.p.* **budged**.

budgerigar *buj'ėr-i-gär*, *n.* a small parrot or lovebird (orig. Australian), often kept as a pet.—Also (*coll.*) **budg'ie**.

budget *buj'it, n.* any plan showing how money is to be spent, esp. a statement and programme put before parliament by the Chancellor of the Exchequer.—*v.i.* **1** to prepare a plan of expenditure. **2** to allow (for) in a budget.—Also *v.t.*:—*pr.p.* **budg'eting**; *pa.p.* **budg'eted**.
budg'etary *adj.*

buff *buf, n.* **1** white leather from which the grain surface has been removed. **2** a light yellow (also *adj.*). **3** (*coll.*) bare skin. **4** an enthusiast.

buffalo *buf'à-lō, n.* **1** a large kind of ox, esp. one used in Asia to draw loads, etc. **2** a fierce African ox. **3** (*U.S.*) the American bison:—*pl.* **buff'aloes**.

buffer *buf'ėr, n.* a device for deadening the force with which a moving body strikes something.
buffer state a neutral state lying between two rival states.

buffet[1] *buf'it, n.* a blow with the hand or fist, a slap.—*v.t.* **1** to strike with the fist. **2** to battle against. **3** to knock about: *buffeted by the waves, by fate*:—*pr.p.* **buff'eting**; *pa.p.* **buff'eted**.

buffet[2] *büf'ā, n.* **1** a refreshment bar. **2** a self-service meal, usu. cold, set out on tables.

buffoon *bù-fōōn', n.* a clown; a fool.
buffoon'ery *n.*

bug *bug, n.* **1** an insect, esp. one that infests houses and beds. **2** a disease germ. **3** a, usu. mechanical, defect. **4** a craze, enthusiasm. **5** a concealed listening device.—*v.t.* **1** (*coll.*) to irritate. **2** to place a concealed listening device in:—*pr.p.* **bugg'ing**; *pa.p.* **bugged**.

bugbear *bug'bār, n.* something one fears or hates.

bugger *bug'ėr,* (*vulg.*) *n.* a term of abuse, sometimes kindly, often nearly meaningless.—*interj.* (*vulg.*) expressing annoyance.

buggy *bug'i, n.* **1** a light one-horse vehicle. **2** (*coll.*) a motor vehicle. **3** a child's push-chair:—*pl.* **bugg'ies**.

bugle *bū'gl, n.* **1** a hunting-horn, orig. a buffalo horn. **2** a wind instrument, used chiefly for military signals.
bu'gler *n.*

build *bild, v.t.* to form or construct.—*v.i.* to rely (on, upon):—*pa.p.* **built**.—*n.* form, make: *a man of heavy build*.
build'er *n.*
build'ing *n.* **1** the art or business of erecting houses, etc. **2** anything built.
building society a society that advances money for houses.
built'-in' *adj.* forming a permanent part of a building, etc.: *built-in cupboards*.
built'-up *adj.* covered with houses, etc.: *a built-up area*.
build up to form, strengthen, gradually (as a business, reputation).

bulb *bulb, n.* **1** an underground bud, with roots on the under side, as in onions, narcissi, etc. **2** an electric light globe.
bul'bous *adj.* **1** having, growing from, a bulb. **2** like a bulb, e.g. in shape; swollen.

bulge *bulj, n.* a swelling.—*v.i.* to swell out:—*pr.p.* **bulg'ing**; *pa.p.* **bulged**.

bulk *bulk, n.* **1** size. **2** great size. **3** large quantity. **4** the greater part.—*v.i.* **1** to be in bulk. **2** to be of importance.
bulk'y *adj.*:—*comp.* **bulk'ier**; *superl.* **bulk'iest**.
bulk'iness *n.*
in bulk 1 (of cargo) loose in the hold, not packaged. **2** in large quantities.

bulkhead *bulk'hed, n.* a partition between one part of a ship's interior and another.

bull[1] *bool, n.* **1** the male of the ox family and of whale, walrus, elephant, moose. **2** (*slang*) nonsense, rubbish.—*adj.* male.
bull'ock *n.* a young bull, or a male animal reared solely to produce beef.
bull'dog *n.* a dog of great courage, formerly used to bait bulls.
bull'fight *n.* in Spain, etc., a spectacle in which a bull is goaded to fury by mounted men with lances, and finally killed by a swordsman on foot.
bull'finch *n.* a red-breasted finch.
bull'frog *n.* a large N. American frog.
bull ring the enclosure in which a bullfight takes place.
bull's-eye *n.* **1** the centre of a target. **2** the shot that hits it. **3** a hard, striped, peppermint sweet. **4** a small circular opening or window.
bull terrier a breed of dog with a smooth coat, orig. a cross between bulldog and terrier.
take the bull by the horns to tackle a difficulty.

bull[2] *bool, n.* a former letter, with seal attached, from the Pope.

bulldog. See **bull**[1].

bulldoze *bool'dōz, v.t.* **1** to force by threats, etc. (into doing something). **2** to force (one's way). **3** to use a bulldozer on:—*pr.p.* **bull'dozing**.
bull'dozer *n.* a tractor for clearing obstacles and levelling ground.

bullet *bool'it, n.* a metal ball fired from a small firearm (rifle, pistol, etc.).
bull'et-proof *adj.* through which a bullet cannot force its way.

bulletin *bool'i-tin, n.* an official report of news, or of a patient's progress.

bullfight, etc. See **bull**[1].

bullion *bool'yȯn, n.* gold and silver in the mass not made into coins.

bullock. See **bull**[1].

bully[1] *bool'i, n.* a cruel and boastful tormentor of the weak.:—*pl.* **bull'ies**.—*adj.* (*coll.*) excellent.—*v.t.* **1** to torment, domineer over. **2** to force (into doing something):—*pr.p.* **bull'ying**; *pa.p.* **bull'ied**.

bully[2] *bool'i,* **bully-beef** *bool'i-bēf, ns.* canned or pickled beef.

bulrush *bool'rush, n.* a tall strong rush.

bulwark *bool'wȧrk, n.* **1** a rampart. **2** the side of a ship above the deck. **3** any means of defence.

bum (slightly *vulg.*) *n.* the buttocks.

bumblebee *bum'bl-bē, n.* a large, loud-humming wild bee, a humble bee.

bump *bump, v.i.* **1** to knock. **2** to jolt.—*v.t.* to strike against or on.—*n.* **1** a dull, heavy blow. **2** a lump or swelling.

bump'er *n.* **1** a bar on a motor car to lessen the shock of collision. **2** a glass filled to the brim. **3** anything very large (also *adj.*).

bump'y *adj.*:—*comp.* **bump'ier**; *superl.* **bump'iest**.

bumpkin *bump'kin, n.* an awkward, clumsy rustic.

bumptious *bump'shus, adj.* full of one's own importance.

bump'tiously *adv.* **bump'tiousness** *n.*

bun *bun, n.* **1** a kind of sweet cake. **2** a rounded mass of hair.

bunch *bunch* or *-sh, n.* **1** a number of things fastened or growing together. **2** a cluster. **3** a group.—*v.i.* to cluster.—*v.t.* to make a bunch of.

bundle *bun'dl, n.* a number of things bound together.—*v.t.* to make into bundles.—*v.t.* and *v.i.* to (cause to) go hurriedly or in confusion (away, off, out):—*pr.p.* **bun'dling**.

bung *bung, n.* the stopper of the hole in a barrel.

bungalow *bung'gȧ-lō, n.* **1** a lightly-built house of one storey in India. **2** a house of one storey.

bungle *bung'gl, n.* **1** anything clumsily done. **2** a task or job badly carried out.—Also *v.t.* and *v.i.*:—*pr.p.* **bung'ling**.

bung'ler *n.*

bunion *bun'yȯn, n.* a swelling on the first joint of the great toe.

bunk[1] *bungk, n.* **1** a sleeping-berth in a ship's cabin. **2** a narrow bed, esp. one of a pair fixed one above the other (also **bunk bed**).

bunk'er *n.* **1** a large box esp. for stowing coals. **2** a hollow containing sand on a golf course.—*v.t.* to put fuel into.—*v.i.* to take in fuel.

bunk'ered *adj.* **1** in a bunker. **2** in difficulties.

bunk[2]. See **bunkum**.

bunkum *bung'kum, n.* nonsense—also **bunk**.

bunny *bun'i,* (*coll.*) *n.* a rabbit:—*pl.* **bunn'ies**.

bunsen burner *boon'sėn, bun'sėn bûrn'ėr,* a gas burner in which air mingles with the gas and produces a smokeless flame of great heating power.

bunting *bunt'ing, n.* **1** a thin cloth for flags. **2** flags, esp. a ship's.

buoy *boi, n.* a floating anchored mark, acting as a guide, as a warning, or as a mooring point for boats.—*v.t.* (usu. with *up*) to keep afloat, or to raise the spirits of.

buoy'ancy *n.* **1** ability to float lightly on water or in the air. **2** cheerfulness, ability to recover good spirits quickly.

buoy'ant *adj.* **1** tending to float or rise. **2** cheerful.

bur[1], **burr** *bûr, n.* the prickly case round the seed(s) of certain plants, sticking readily to things it touches.

bur[2], **burr** *bûr, n.* the rough sound of *r* pronounced in the throat, as it is in Northumberland.

burble *bûr'bl, v.i.* to talk much, saying little, esp. from excitement:—*pr.p.* **bur'bling**.

burden[1] *bûr'dn, n.* **1** a load. **2** cargo. **3** something difficult to bear. **4** a responsibility.—*v.t.* **1** to load. **2** to oppress.

bur'densome *adj.* **1** heavy. **2** causing weariness or discomfort.

burden[2] *bûr'dn, n.* **1** a refrain of a song. **2** the chief idea expressed in a statement, etc.: *The burden of his complaint was that he was underpaid.*

bureau *bū'rō, bū-rō', n.* **1** a combined writing table and chest of drawers. **2** an office for collecting and supplying information:—*pl.* **bureaux**, **-reaus** *(-rōz)*.

bureaucracy *bū-rok'rȧ-si, n.* government by officials, responsible only to their chiefs:—*pl.* **bureauc'racies**.

bur'eaucrat *n.* one who practises or favours bureaucracy.

bureaucrat'ic *adj.*

burgess *bûr'jis, n.* a citizen, esp. a freeman, of a borough.

burgh *bur'ȯ, n.* a spelling of **borough** (in Scotland).

burgher *bûr'gėr, n.* an inhabitant of a

borough or burgh.

burglar *bûrg'lȧr*, *n*. one who breaks into a house, etc. (until 1969, by night) to steal.
burg'lary *n.*:—*pl.* **burg'laries**.
bur'gle *v.t.*:—*pr.p.* **burg'ling**.

burial. See **bury**.

burlesque *bûr-lesk'*, *n.* a comic and exaggerated imitation in writing or acting.—Also *v.t.*:—*pr.p.* **burlesqu'ing**.

burly *bûr'li*, *adj.* big and sturdy:—*comp.* **bur'lier**; *superl.* **bur'liest**.

Burmese *bûr-mēz'*, *adj.* of *Burma* or its language.—*n*. a native, or the language, of Burma.

burn[1] *bûrn*, *n*. a small stream.

burn[2] *bûrn*, *v.t.* **1** to destroy or injure by fire. **2** to expose to great heat.—*v.i.* **1** to be on fire. **2** to feel great heat or passion:—*pa.t.* and *pa.p.* **burned**, **burnt**.—*n.* a hurt or mark caused by fire.
burn'er *n.* the part of a lamp or gas jet from which the flame arises, or the whole fixture.
burn'ing *n.* and *adj.*
burnt offering something burned on an altar as a sacrifice.
burn one's boats to destroy one's means of retreat, stake everything on success.

burnish *bûr'nish*, *v.t.* to make bright by rubbing.

burnt. See **burn**[2].

burr. Same as **bur**[1,2].

burrow *bur'ō*, *n.* a hole dug by certain animals for shelter.—*v.i.* to make, live in, holes underground.

bursar *bûr'sȧr*, *n.* **1** one who keeps the purse, a treasurer (esp. of a college). **2** in Scotland, a student helped by the funds of an endowment.

burst *bûrst*, *v.t.* to break open or in pieces suddenly.—*v.i.* **1** to fly open or break in pieces. **2** to come, go, suddenly or violently (into, out of). **3** to break (into): *to burst into tears, song,* etc.:—*pa.t.* and *pa.p.* **burst**.—*n.* **1** a sudden outbreak. **2** a spurt.

bury *ber'i*, *v.t.* **1** to hide in the ground. **2** to place (e.g. a dead body) in a grave, the sea, etc. **3** to cover, hide. **4** to put (something) out of one's mind:—*pr.p.* **bur'ying**; *pa.p.* **bur'ied**.
bur'ial *n.*
bury the hatchet to stop quarrelling.

bus *bus*, *n.* a large public road vehicle for many passengers:—*pl.* **bus'es**.

bush *boosh*, *n.* **1** a shrub thick with branches. **2** wild uncultivated country.
bush'y *adj.* thick and spreading:—*comp.* **bush'ier**; *superl.* **bush'iest**.
bush'iness *n.*
bush'man *n.* **1** a settler in uncleared land. **2** one of an aboriginal race in S. Africa:—*pl.* **bush'men**.
bush'ranger *(-rānj-) n.* in Australia, one who leads a lawless life in the bush.
beat about the bush to approach a subject in an indirect way.

bushel *boosh'l*, *n.* a dry measure of 8 gallons.
hide one's light under a bushel to conceal one's talents or abilities.

busier, **busiest**, **busily**. See **busy**.

business *biz'nis*, *n.* **1** trade, profession, or work. **2** one's concern or affair. **3** one's duty. **4** a matter or affair.
bus'inesslike *adj.* practical, methodical, alert and prompt.
bus'inessman *n.* a person who works in commerce:—*fem.* **bus'inesswoman**.

busk *busk*, *v.i.* to entertain (as a musician, an actor) in the street.
busk'er *n.*

bust *bust*, *n.* **1** a sculpture of the head and breast of a person. **2** (the measurement round) a woman's chest.

bustle[1] *bus'l*, *v.i.* to busy oneself noisily or fussily:—*pr.p.* **bust'ling**.—Also *n.*

bustle[2] *bus'l*, *n.* a frame or pad making a skirt hang back from the hips.

busy *biz'i*, *adj.* **1** fully employed. **2** active. **3** diligent:—*comp.* **bus'ier**; *superl.* **bus'iest**.—*v.t.* to occupy (oneself):—*pr.p.* **bus'ying**; *pa.p.* **busied** *(biz'id).*
bus'ily *adv.*
bus'yness *n.* state of being busy.—See also **business**.
bus'ybody *n.* a meddling person:—*pl.* **bus'ybodies**.

but *but, prep.* **1** only. **2** except.—*conj.* **1** on the other hand. **2** nevertheless. **3** except that.—*adv.* only: *There is but one objection.*

butcher *booch'ėr*, *n.* one whose business is to kill cattle, etc., for food, or who deals in their flesh.—*v.t.* **1** to kill for food. **2** to kill cruelly.
butch'ery *n.* great slaughter.

butler *but'lėr*, *n.* **1** a servant who has charge of the liquors, plate, etc. **2** the principal male servant of a household.

butt[1] *but*, *v.i.* and *v.t.* to push or strike with the head, as a goat does.—Also *n.*
butt in to interrupt, interfere.

butt[2] *but*, *n.* a large cask.

butt[3] *but*, *n.* **1** a mark for archery practice. **2** a victim of ridicule, target for the wit of others. **3** (in *pl.*) a shooting range.

butt[4] *but*, *n.* **1** the thick and heavy end. **2** the stump.

butter *but'ėr*, *n.* an oily substance made from cream by churning.—*v.t.* to put butter on.

butt'ery *adj.* **butt'eriness** *n.*

butt'ercup *n.* a cup-like golden yellow flower.

butt'er-fing'ers *n.* a person who tends not to catch e.g. a ball, or to drop things.

butt'erfly *n.* **1** an insect with large beautiful wings. **2** a cheerful, flighty person:—*pl.* **butt'erflies**.

butt'ermilk *n.* the milk left after the butter has been separated from the cream by churning.

butter up to flatter.

buttery[1]. See **butter**.

buttery[2] *but'ėr-i*, *n.* a storeroom for provisions, esp. liquors:—*pl.* **butt'eries**.

buttock *but'ȯk*, *n.* either half of the rump of the body behind.

button *but'n*, *n.* **1** a knob or disc of metal, bone, etc., used as a fastening, ornament, or badge. **2** a small knob pressed to operate something.—*v.t.* **1** to fasten by means of buttons. **2** to close (up) tightly:—*pr.p.* **butt'oning**; *pa.p.* **butt'oned**.

butt'onhole *n.* **1** the hole or slit into which a button is passed. **2** a flower or flowers worn in it.—*v.t.* to detain in talk (orig. *buttonhold*):—*pr.p.* **butt'onholing**.

butt'ons *n. sing.* a page in a hotel, etc.

buttress *but'rės*, *n.* **1** a support built on to the outside of a wall. **2** any prop.—*v.t.* to prop or support.

buxom *buk'sȯm*, *adj.* plump and attractive.

buy *bī*, *v.t.* **1** to purchase for money. **2** to bribe. **3** to get in exchange for something:—*pr.p.* **buy'ing**; *pa.p.* **bought** *(böt)*.

buy'er *n.*

buzz *buz*, *v.i.* **1** to make a noise like that of insects' wings. **2** to hover (about).—*v.t.* to fly very low over or very close to.—Also *n.*

buzz'er *n.* an electrical or other apparatus producing a buzzing sound.

buzz word a word well-established in a particular jargon, its use implying specialised knowledge.

buzzard *buz'ȧrd*, *n.* a large bird of prey.

by *bī*, *prep.* **1** at the side of. **2** via. **3** denoting the agent, means, etc.: *done by me.* **4** measured in terms of: *by the yard.* **5** (of time) at or before. **6** during: *by day.*—*adv.* **1** near. **2** past. **3** in reserve.—Also *adj.* and *pfx.*

by'-election *n.* an election during the sitting of parliament to fill one seat.

by'gone *adj.* past.—*n.* (in *pl.*) **1** past causes of ill-will. **2** household articles of the past.

by'pass *n.* a side track to avoid an obstruction or a busy area.—*v.t.* to avoid by taking such a route.

by'path *n.* a secluded or indirect path.

by'-pro'duct *n.* a product formed during the making of something.

C

cab *kab*, *n.* **1** a carriage for hire, horse-drawn or **(taxi-cab)** motor-driven. **2** a driver's shelter on a vehicle.
cabby, **cabbie** *kab'i*, *n.* the driver of a cab (*def. 1*):—*pl.* **cabb'ies**.

cabal *kȧ-bal'*, *n.* **1** a group plotting secretly together. **2** the plot itself.

cabaret *kab'ȧ-rā*, *n.* **1** a restaurant with variety turns. **2** an entertainment given in such a restaurant.

cabbage *kab'ij*, *n.* **1** a vegetable with leaves forming a head. **2** a dull, inactive person.

cabbie, cabby. See **cab**.

caber *kāb'ėr*, *n.* a long, heavy pole tossed by Highland athletes.

cabin *kab'in*, *n.* **1** a hut or cottage. **2** a small room, esp. in a ship. **3** the part of an aircraft in which the passengers travel.
cab'in-boy (*hist.*) *n.* a boy who waits on the occupants of a ship's cabin.
cabin crew the members of an aircraft's crew who look after the passengers.
cabin cruiser a motor-boat with one or more cabins.

cabinet *kab'in-it*, *n.* **1** a case, or piece of furniture, for holding articles of value. **2** (often *cap.*) a selected number of the chief ministers who govern a country.
cab'inetmaker *n.* one who makes fine wooden furniture.

cable *kā'bl*, *n.* **1** a strong rope or chain for hauling or tying anything, esp. a ship's anchor. **2** a wire for carrying electric current. **3** a cablegram.—*v.t.* and *v.i.* to send or telegraph by cable:—*pr.p.* **ca'bling**.
ca'ble-car *n.* a carriage, either hanging from a moving cable (in a **ca'bleway**) or running on rails and pulled by a moving cable (in a **ca'ble-rail'way**), used as a means of transport up hills, etc.
ca'blegram *n.* a telegram sent by cable.
cable television the transmission of television programmes to people's houses by cable.

caboodle *kȧ-bōō'dl*, (*coll.*) *n.* lot, crowd, collection: *the whole caboodle*.

caboose *kȧ-bōōs'*, (*U.S.*) *n.* the van on a freight train for the train crew.

cacao *kȧ-kä'ō*, or *kȧ-kā'ō*, *n.* **1** the tropical tree from whose seeds cocoa and chocolate are made. **2** the seeds themselves.

cache *kash*, *n.* **1** a hiding-place for treasure, stores, etc. **2** treasure, stores, hidden.

cachou *kash'ōō*, *n.* a sweet used to perfume the breath.

cackle *kak'l*, *n.* the sound made by a hen or goose: talk or laughter like this.—Also *v.i.*:—*pr.p.* **cack'ling**.

cacophony *kȧ-kof'ȯ-ni*, *n.* an unpleasant combination of sounds:—*pl.* **cacoph'onies**.
cacoph'onous *adj.*

cactus *kak'tus*, *n.* a prickly plant whose stem stores water and does the work of leaves:—*pl.* **cac'ti** *(-tī)*, **cac'tuses**.

cad *kad*, *n.* a mean, low fellow.
cadd'ish *adj.*

cadaver *kȧ-dav'ėr*, *n.* a human corpse.
cadav'erous *kȧ-dav'ėr-us*, *adj*, thin, haggard.

caddice. See **caddis**.

caddie, caddy *kad'i*, *n.* one who carries clubs for a golfer:—*pl.* **cadd'ies**.—*v.i.* to act as a caddie:—*pr.p.* **cadd'ying**; *pa.p.* **cadd'ied**.
caddie car, cart, a little two-wheeled cart for carrying golf clubs upright.

caddis, caddice *kad'is*, *n.* the larva of the **caddis-fly**, which lives in water in a **cadd'is-case**, a silken sheath covered with bits of wood, stone, etc.

caddy[1] *kad'i*, *n.* a small box for tea:—*pl.* **cadd'ies**.

caddy[2]. See **caddie**.

cadence *kā'dėns*, *n.* rise and fall of sound: rhythm.

cadet *kȧ-det'*, *n.* **1** a younger son. **2** a student in a military or naval school.

cadge *kaj*, *v.t.* and *v.i.* to beg, sponge:—*pr.p.* **cadg'ing**.
cadg'er *n.* **1** a hawker. **2** a sponger.

cadmium *kad'mi-um*, *n.* an element, a white metal resembling tin.

Caesarian *siz-ār'i-ȧn*, *n.* (also without *cap.*) a Caesarian operation.
Caesarian operation, section the delivery of a baby by cutting through the walls of the abdomen.

caesium *sēz'i-um*, *n.* an element, a soft metal used in electron tubes, etc.

café *caf'ā*, *n.* a restaurant.
café au lait *(ō lā)* white coffee.
café noir *(nwär)* black coffee.

cafeteria *ka-fi-tēr'i-ȧ*, *n.* a self-service restaurant with a counter.

caffeine *kaf'ēn*, *n.* a stimulating substance present in coffee and tea.

caftan, **kaftan** *kaf'tan*, *n.* a type of long, flowing dress or robe, often brightly-coloured.

cage *kāj*, *n.* **1** a box of wire and wood, etc. for holding birds or animals. **2** a lift in a mine, etc.—*v.t.* to put or imprison in a cage:—*pr.p.* **cag'ing**.
cage'bird *n.* a bird suitable for keeping in a cage.

cagey, **cagy** *kā'ji*, (*coll.*) *adj.* **1** secretive. **2** wary, cautious:—*comp.* **cag'ier**; *superl.* **cag'iest**.
cag'ily *adv.* **cag'iness** *n.*

cagoul(e) *kȧ-gōōl'*, *n.* a lightweight waterproof anorak.

cagy. See **cagey**.

cahoots *kȧ-hōōts'*: **in cahoots** working together for a bad or dishonest purpose.

cairn *kārn*, *n.* **1** a heap of stones. **2** a small Scottish terrier.
cairn'gorm' *n.* brown or yellow quartz found in the Cairngorm Mountains.

caisson *kās'ȯn*, *kȧ-sōōn'*, *n.* **1** an ammunition chest or wagon. **2** a structure for keeping out the water while the foundations of a bridge are being built.
caisson disease a disease (also known as **the bends**) caused by a sudden change from higher air pressure to lower, as in coming up out of a caisson (*def.* 2).

cajole *kȧ-jōl'*, *v.t.* **1** to coax. **2** to cheat by flattery:—*pr.p.* **cajol'ing**.
cajol'ery *n.*

cake *kāk*, *n.* **1** a baked piece of usu. sweetened or flavoured dough. **2** a flattened hard mass: *a cake of soap*.—*v.t.* and *v.i.* to form into a cake:—*pr.p.* **cak'ing**.

calabash *kal'ȧ-bash*, *n.* **1** the dried shell of the melon-like fruit of a tree of tropical America, used for holding liquids. **2** a gourd.

calamine *kal'ȧ-mīn*, *-min*, *n.* **1** zinc carbonate. **2** a pink powder containing zinc carbonate or zinc oxide, used in soothing lotions.

calamity *kȧl-am'i-ti*, *n.* a great misfortune:—*pl.* **calam'ities**.
calam'itous *adj.*

calcium *kal'si-ùm*, *n.* an element, a metal of which one compound (*calcium carbonate*) forms marble, limestone, chalk, and coral.
calcif'erous (*-sif'*) *adj.* containing lime.
cal'cify *v.t.* and *v.i.* to make or become limy:—*pr.p.* **cal'cifying**; *pa.p.* **cal'cified**.

calculate *kal'kū-lāt*, *v.t.* **1** to count or reckon. **2** to think out. **3** (*U.S.*) to plan. **4** (*U.S.*) to think, suppose:—*pr.p.* **cal'culating**.
cal'culated *adj.* deliberate.
cal'culating *adj.* selfishly scheming.
calculā'tion *n.*
cal'culātor *n.* **1** a machine which makes mathematical calculations. **2** a table or book of tables.
calculated to 1 likely to. **2** intended to.
calculate on to base one's plans or forecasts on.
See also **incalculable**.

calculus *kal'kū-lùs*, *n.* **1** a stone-like mass which may form in certain parts of the body (*pl.* **cal'culī**). **2** a mathematical system of calculation, as one that studies the changes in a constantly varying quantity (*pl.* **cal'culuses**).

Caledonian *kal-i-dō'ni-ȧn*, *adj.* of the Highlands, or of Scotland.—Also *n.*

calendar *kal'in-dȧr*, *n.* **1** a table showing the months, weeks, and days. **2** a list or record of events in chronological order.

calender *kal'in-dėr*, *n.* a press with rollers for finishing the surface of cloth, paper, etc.—Also *v.t.*

calf[1] *käf*, *n.* **1** the young of the cow, elephant, whale, etc. **2** calfskin leather:—*pl.* **calves** *(kävz)*.
calve *käv*, *v.t.* and *v.i.* to bring forth (a calf):—*pr.p.* **calv'ing**.
calf'skin *n.* a hide or leather of a calf.

calf[2] *käf*, *n.* the thick fleshy part at the back of the leg below the knee:—*pl.* **calves** *(kävz)*.

calibre, **caliber** *kal'i-bėr*, *n.* **1** the size of the bore of a tube or gun. **2** (of a person) degree of excellence or importance.
cal'ibrāte *v.t.* **1** to mark the scale on (a measuring instrument). **2** to check or adjust the scale of (a measuring instrument):—*pr.p.* **cal'ibrating**.
calibrā'tion *n.*

calico *kal'i-kō*, *n.* a cotton cloth first brought from *Calicut* in India:—*pl.* **cal'icos**, **-oes**.—Also *adj.*

calif. Same as **caliph**.

calipers. See **callipers**.

caliph *kal'if*, or *kā'lif*, *n.* the name taken by successors of Mohammed.
cal'iphate *n.* the office, rank, or government of a caliph.

calk. See **caulk**.

call *köl*, *v.i.* **1** to shout loudly. **2** to make a short visit. **3** to telephone.—*v.t.* **1** to name. **2** to summon. **3** to describe as: *to call someone an ass*. **4** to telephone.—*n.* **1** a summons or invitation. **2** a demand. **3** a short visit. **4** a telephone connection or conversation, or a request for one. **5** a cry, esp. of a bird. **6** need, reason: *You*

have no call to be offended by this.
call'er *n.*
call'ing *n* **1** crying. **2** naming. **3** summoning. **4** trade, profession.
call'-box *n.* a small compartment or construction containing a telephone for public use.
call'-boy *n.* a boy who calls the actors when they are wanted on the stage.
call'-girl *n.* a prostitute.
call in question to challenge, dispute.
call off 1 to cancel. **2** to order to stop attacking: *call your dog off, call off the attack.*
call on 1 to visit. **2** (also **call upon**) to request, urge.
call out to instruct (workers) to come on strike.
call someone to account to demand an explanation from someone.
call up 1 to summon, esp. to the armed forces (*n.* **call'-up**). **2** to bring into memory.

calligraphy *kȧl-ig'rȧ-fi, n.* (beautiful) handwriting.

callipers, calipers *kal'i-pėrz, n. pl.* compasses suitable for measuring the inside or outside diameter of objects.
cal(l)iper (splint) *n.* a support for a leg, consisting of two metal rods.

callous *kal'ụs, adj.* **1** hardened. **2** unfeeling, cruel, hard-hearted.—*n.* a callosity.
call'ously *adv.* **call'ousness** *n.*
callos'ity *n.* a hard thickening of the skin:—*pl.* **callos'ities**.

callow *kal'ō, adj.* not mature, inexperienced.

callus *kal'ụs, n.* a callosity.

calm *käm, adj.* **1** still or quiet. **2** not anxious or flustered.—*n.* **1** absence of wind. **2** tranquillity.—*v.t.* **1** to make calm. **2** to quiet.
calm'ly, *adj.* **calm'ness** *n.*

calomel *kal'ō-mel, n.* the popular name of a chloride of mercury, used in medicine.

calorie *kal'ȯr-i, n.* **1** a measure of heat. **2** a great calorie.
great, large, calorie a unit used in measuring the heat- or energy-producing value of food.

calumny *kal'ụm-ni, n.* **1** false accusation. **2** slander:—*pl.* **cal'umnies**.
calum'niāte *v.t.*:—*pr.p.* **calum'niating**.

Calvary *kal'vȧ-ri, n.* **1** the name of the place where Christ was crucified. **2** a representation of Christ's crucifixion:—*pl.* **Cal'varies**.

calve, calves. See **calf**[1,2].

Calvinism *kal'vin-izm, n.* the teaching of the religious reformer, John *Calvin.*
Cal'vinist *n.* **Calvinist'ic** *adj.*

calyces. See **calyx**.

calypso *kȧ-lip'sō, n.* a West Indian folk song, telling of current events and made up as the singer goes along:—*pl.* **calyp'sos**.

calyx *kal'iks,* or *kā'liks, n.* the outer covering or cup of a flower:—*pl.* **calyxes** or **calyces** *(-sēz).*

camaraderie *kam-ȧ-räd'ėr-ē, n.* the spirit of comradeship, friendliness.

camber *kam'bėr, n.* a slight curve on an upper surface (e.g. of a deck, bridge, aeroplane wing, road).

camcorder *kam'körd-ėr, n.* a video camera and video recorder combined in one handheld unit.

came. See **come**.

camel *kam'ėl, n.* an animal with one, or two, humps on its back, used as a beast of burden and for riding.
camel('s) hair **1** the hair of the camel. **2** the hair of a squirrel's tail, used for paint brushes.

camellia *kȧ-mēl'yȧ,* or *-mel',* or *-i-ȧ, n.* an evergreen shrub, native of eastern Asia, grown for its beautiful waxy flowers.

cameo *kam'i-ō, n.* an engraved gem in which the design is in relief:—*pl.* **cam'eos**.

camera *kam'ėr-ȧ, n.* **1** the apparatus in which a photographer exposes a sensitive plate or film. **2** (*television*) the apparatus that receives the picture and turns it into electrical impulses for sending out.
cam'eraman *n.*
in camera (of a law case) tried in secret.

camisole *kam'i-sōl, n.* a woman's underbodice with narrow shoulder straps.

camomile *kam'ō-mīl, n.* a type of plant, or its dried flowers, used in medicine.

camouflage *ka'moo-fläzh, n.* something, e.g. a special colouring or covering, which makes a person, animal, building, etc. difficult to see against its background.—*v.t.* to disguise with camouflage:—*pr.p.* **cam'ouflaging**.

camp[1] *kamp, n.* **1** the ground on which tents are pitched. **2** military quarters, barracks. **3** a group of huts, etc. in which people stay for a time for some purpose: *a holiday camp.* **4** a party or side.—*v.i.* to settle or stay in tents.
camp'er *n.* **1** one who goes camping. **2** a motor vehicle built or converted for living in.

camp bed, **camp chair**, **camp stool** a bed, chair, stool, that can be folded up when not in use.
camp follower one not a soldier who follows in the rear of an army.

camp[2] *kamp*, *(slang) adj.* **1** (deliberately) effeminate. **2** absurdly old-fashioned, exaggerated, etc. **3** homosexual.—*n.* camp behaviour, etc.

campaign *kam'-pān'*, *n.* **1** the operations of an army while in the field in one area or for one purpose: *the Burma campaign in the Second World War.* **2** organised action in support of a cause.—*v.i.* to serve or work in a campaign.
campaign'er *n.*

campanile *kam-pȧn-ē'lā*, *n.* a bell-tower, esp. one apart from the church:—*pl.* **campaniles** *(-ē'lāz)* or sometimes It. **campanili** *(-ē'lē).*

campanula *kam-pan'ū-lȧ*, *n.* a plant with bell-shaped flowers.

camphor *kam'fȯr*, *n.* a strongly scented solid oil, obtainable from the camphor laurel of India, China, and Japan, or manufactured.
cam'phorāted *adj.* treated, saturated, with camphor.

campus *kam'pu̇s*, *n.* college or university grounds.

can[1] *kan*, *kȧn*, *v.* **1** be able to, know how to: *I can swim.* **2** be allowed to: *You can go if you like*:—*pa.t.* **could** *(kood).*

can[2] *kan*, *n.* **1** a vessel for holding liquids. **2** a closed container of tin-plate in which food is preserved.—*v.t.* to preserve in cans:—*pr.p.* **cann'ing**; *pa.p.* **canned**.
cann'ery *n.* a factory where goods are canned:—*pl.* **cann'eries**.

Canadian *kȧ-nā'di-ȧn*, *adj.* of *Canada*.—*n.* a native of Canada.

canal *kȧn-al'*, *n.* **1** an artificial watercourse, esp. for ships. **2** a passage in the body carrying fluids, etc.: *the alimentary canal.*
can'alise *v.t.* to direct into a channel, or towards an end, or to give an outlet to: *to canalise one's energies into working for disarmament*:—*pr.p.* **can'alising**.

canard *ka-när(d)'*, *n.* a false rumour.

canary *kȧ-nā'ri*, *n.* a yellow domesticated variety of a kind of singing finch found in the *Canary* Islands:—*pl.* **canar'ies**.

cancan *kan'kan*, *n.* a wild, high-kicking dance of French origin.

cancel *kan'sėl*, *v.t.* **1** to strike out by crossing with lines. **2** to mark with a postmark. **3** to withdraw (e.g. an order, a subscription). **4** to put off (something planned):—*pr.p.* **can'celling**; *pa.p.* **can'celled**.
cancellā'tion *n.*
cancel out to make ineffective by having an exactly opposite effect: *The benefits and drawbacks of the scheme cancel each other out.*

cancer *kan'sėr*, *n.* **1** a malignant growth. **2** any evil that gradually destroys.
can'cerous *adj.*
See also **carcinogenic**.

candelabrum *kan-di-lä'bru̇m*, *n.* a branched and ornamented candlestick:—*pl.* **candela'bra**—also used as *sing.* with *pl.* **candela'bras**.

candid *kan'did*, *adj.* frank, open, sincere.
can'didly *adv.*
can'didness, **can'dour** *(kan'dȯr)*, *ns.*

candidate *kan'di-dit*, *-dāt*, *n.* one who offers himself for an office or honour.
candidature *kan'di-di-chu̇r*, **candidacy** *kan'di-dȧ-si* *(pl.* **-ies**), *ns.*

candied. See **candy**.

candle *kan'dl*, *n.* a cylinder of wax, tallow, etc., surrounding a wick.
can'dlestick *n.* a holder for a candle.
can'dlewick *n.* a tufted cotton material, used for bedspreads, etc.
burn the candle at both ends to exhaust one's strength (e.g. by working early and late).
not fit to hold a candle to very much less good, etc., than.

Candlemas *kan'dl-mȧs*, *n.* **1** the R.C. festival of the purification of the Virgin Mary, on 2nd February, when candles are blessed. **2** a quarter day in Scotland.

candour. See **candid**.

candy *kan'di*, *n.* **1** (also **sugar-candy** *shoog'ȧr-kan'di*) a sweatmeat made of sugar. **2** (*U.S.*) any sweet:—*pl.* **can'dies.**—*v.t.* and *v.i.* to preserve in, or coat with, sugar:—*pr.p.* **can'dying**; *pa.p.* **can'died**.

candytuft *kan'di-tuft*, *n.* a plant with flowers growing in tufts.

cane *kān*, *n.* **1** the stem of a small palm, large grass, etc. **2** a rod. **3** a walking-stick.—*v.t.* to beat with a cane:—*pr.p.* **can'ing**.
cane'-su'gar *n.* sugar obtained from the sugar cane.

canine *kān'īn*, *kan'*, *adj.* like or of a dog.
canine teeth in man, four sharp-pointed teeth between the incisors and premolars.

canister *kan'is-tėr*, *n.* a box or case, usu. of metal, for holding tea, shot, etc.

canker *kang'kėr*, *n.* **1** a sore in which pus forms. **2** a fungus disease in trees. **3** inflammation in horses' feet. **4** eczema of dogs' ears. **5** anything that corrupts or destroys.—Also *v.t.* and *v.i.*

cannabis *kan'ȧ-bis, n.* a narcotic drug got from the hemp plant.

cannibal *kan'i-bȧl, n.* **1** a person who eats human flesh. **2** an animal which eats members of its own species.
cann'ibalism *n.* **cannibalist'ic** *adj.*

cannon *kan'ȯn, n.* **1** any type of old firearm discharged from a carriage or mount (modern firearms of this type are called *guns*). **2** a large, rapid-firing gun fitted to an aircraft, etc. **3** a stroke in billiards—an oblique hit from one ball to another:—*pl.* of firearm in certain cases **cann'on.**—*v.i.* to hit and rebound as a ball in a cannon at billards:—*pr.p.* **cann'oning**; *pa.p.* **cann'-oned**.
cann'onball *n.* a ball, usu. iron, formerly shot from a cannon.
cannon fodder people regarded merely as material to be used in war.

cannot *kan'ot, v.* **1** am, is, or are, unable to. **2** am, is, or are, not allowed to.

canny *kan'i,* (*Scot.*) *adj.* **1** shrewd. **2** cautious, careful. **3** gentle:—*comp.* **cann'ier**; *superl.* **cann'iest**.
cann'ily *adv.* **cann'iness** *n.*

canoe *kȧ-nōō', n.* a light narrow boat driven by means of a paddle.—*v.i.* to go in a canoe:—*pr.p.* **canoe'ing**; *pa.p.* **canoed'**.
canoe'ist *n.*

canon *kan'ȯn, n.* **1** a law or rule of the church. **2** the books of the Bible accepted by the Christian Church. **3** a cleric belonging to a cathedral. **4** a list of saints. **5** a musical composition in which one part follows another in imitation. **6** a rule, standard.
canon'ical *adj.*
canon'icals *n.pl.* official dress of the clergy.
can'onise *v.t.* to place in the canon or list of saints:—*pr.p.* **can'onising**.
canonisā'tion *n.*

canon. See **canyon**.

canopy *kan'ȯ-pi, n.* a covering hung over a throne, bed, etc.:—*pl.* **can'opies.**—*v.t.* to cover with a canopy:—*pr.p.* **can'opying**; *pa.p.* **can'opied**.

cant[1] *kant, n.* **1** hypocritical, insincere speech. **2** the special language of a class or group: *thieves' cant.*—Also *v.i.*

cant[2] *kant, n.* **1** an inclination, slope. **2** a toss or jerk.—*v.t.* and *v.i.* **1** to toss suddenly. **2** to tilt.

can't *känt*, abbrev. of **cannot**.

cantaloup(e) *kan'tȧ-lōōp, n.* a small, ribbed variety of musk melon.

cantankerous *kȧn-tang'kėr-ůs, adj.* **1** quarrelsome. **2** cross and unreasonable.
cantan'kerously *adv.*
cantan'kerousness *n.*

cantata *kan-tä'tȧ, n.* a musical dramatic work sung by a chorus as a concert performance.

canteen *kan-tēn', n.* **1** a small container used by soldiers for holding water, etc. **2** a refreshment room in barracks, factory, etc. **3** a case for cutlery.

canter *kan'tėr, n.* an easy gallop.—Also *v.t., v.i.*

Canterbury bell *kan'tėr-bėr-i bel,* a variety of campanula.

canticle *kan'ti-kl, n.* **1** a song. **2** a hymn.

cantilever *kan'ti-lēv-ėr, n.* a large bracket for supporting balconies, stairs, etc.
cantilever bridge one composed of projecting arms built out from the piers and meeting in the middle of the span.

canto *kan'tō, n.* a division of a long poem:—*pl.* **can'tos**.

canton *kan'tȯn, kan-ton', n.* **1** a district. **2** one of the Swiss federal states.
canton'ment *n.* (pron. *kȧn-tōōn'mėnt* in army). **1** the temporary quarters of troops. **2** formerly in India, a permanent military town.

canvas *kan'vȧs, n.* **1** a coarse cloth made of hemp or flax, etc., used for sails, tents, etc., and for painting on. **2** the sails of a ship.
under canvas 1 with sails spread. **2** in tents.

canvass *kan'vȧs, v.t.* and *v.i.* to go round asking for (support, votes, custom, etc.).
can'vasser *n.*

canyon *kan'yȯn, n.* a deep gorge or ravine between high steep banks, worn by rivers.—Also **can'on**.

caoutchouc *kow'chook, n.* raw rubber, the latex or juice of rubber trees.

cap *kap, n.* **1** a soft hat, with or without a peak. **2** a cover or top, e.g. of a pen. **3** a person capped for a team. **4** a contraceptive device. **5** a small paper disc enclosing an explosive substance.—*v.t.* **1** to cover with a cap. **2** to confer a degree on. **3** (*sport*) to admit to a team. **4** to outdo: *K. capped R.'s performance with a better one*:—*pr.p.* **capp'ing**; *pa.p.* **capped**.
cap in hand 1 humbly. **2** begging humbly.
to cap it all as the last and worst of a series of bad things.

capable *kāp'ȧ-bl, adj.* **1** able, clever in practical ways. **2** clever, etc. enough to: *He is capable of doing better than he does.* **3** bad enough to: *He is capable of letting someone else take the blame.* **4** made so as to be able to: *a car capable of doing 90*

miles an hour:—*opp.* **incap'able**.
cap'ableness, **capabil'ity** (*pl.* **ies**), *ns.*

capacious *kȧ-pā'shus, adj.* roomy, wide.

capacitor *kȧ-pas'i-tȯr, n.* an apparatus for collecting and storing electricity.

capacity *kȧ-pas'i-ti, n.* **1** power of holding, containing. **2** volume. **3** mental ability. **4** position: *in his capacity as a leader.* **5** greatest possible extent: *filled to capacity*; *working to capacity*:—*pl.* **capac'-ities**.
See also **incapacitate**, **incapacity**.

cape[1] *kāp, n.* a long, loose, sleeveless outer garment, or a somewhat shorter one attached to a coat or cloak.

cape[2] *kāp, n.* a head or point of land running into the sea.

caper[1] *kā'pėr, n.* the pickled flower-bud of the caper shrub, used in sauces.

caper[2] *kā'pėr, v.i.* **1** to leap or skip. **2** to frolic.—*n.* **1** a leap. **2** a prank. **3** (*coll.*) any activity, esp. if bad or dishonest.

capercailzie *ka-pėr-kāl'(y)i, n.* a large kind of grouse.

capillary *kȧ-pil'ȧr-i, kap'il-ȧr-i, adj.* (of a tube) having a very small bore.—*n.* **1** a tube with a fine bore. **2** (in *pl.*) the tiny vessels that join veins to arteries:—*pl.* **capillaries**.

capital[1] *kap'it-ȧl, adj.* **1** of the head. **2** involving the loss of the head or of life: *capital punishment.* **3** chief, principal. **4** (*old-fashioned*) excellent.—*n.* **1** the chief town or seat of government. **2** a capital letter. **3** the money for carrying on a business. **4** possessions bringing in income.
cap'italise *v.t.* to write in capital letters.—*v.i.* (with *on*) to make capital out of:—*pr.p.* **cap'italising**.
cap'italism *n.* control of money and business by capitalists.
cap'italist *n.* one who has much money in business concerns.—Also *adj.*
capital expenditure spending on buildings, machines, etc.
capital gains profits from the sale of assets.
capital goods producer goods.
capital letter a letter of the type used at the beginning of sentences, etc.
capital levy a tax on capital.
capital ship a warship of the largest and strongest class.
make capital out of to turn to one's advantage.

capital[2] *kap'it-ȧl, n.* the top part of a column, etc.

capitulate *kap-it'ūl-āt, v.i.* to yield, surrender:—*pr.p.* **capit'ulating**.
capitulā'tion *n.*

capon *kā'pȯn, n.* a castrated cock bred for use as food.

caprice *kȧ-prēs', n.* **1** an unreasonable change of mind or mood. **2** a whim. **3** a fanciful and sprightly work in music, etc.
capri'cious *(-ri'shus) adj.* **1** full of caprice. **2** changeable.
capri'ciously *adv.* **capri'ciousness** *n.*

capsicum *kap'si-kum, n.* **1** the fruit of a tropical shrub, also called **red** or **green pepper**. **2** the dried fruit of related shrubs, which yield paprika and cayenne pepper.

capsize *kap-sīz', v.t.* to upset, overturn (a boat).—Also *v.i.*:—*pr.p.* **capsiz'ing**.
capsīz'al *n.*

capstan *kap'stȧn, n.* a machine turned by bars used for winding e.g. a ship's cable.

capsule *kap'sūl, n.* **1** the dry seedbox of a plant. **2** a covering, or container, of an organ within the body. **3** a small gelatine case for a dose of medicine, etc. **4** a closed metal container. **5** a space capsule (see this under **space**.)

captain *kap'tin, n.* **1** the commander of a ship or aircraft. **2** a rank in the army and navy, or a person of this rank. **3** the leader of a team or club.—*v.t.* to be captain of (a team, etc.).
cap'taincy *n.* the rank or role of captain.

caption *kap'sh(ȯ)n, n.* a newspaper heading, or a note accompanying an illustration, cinematograph picture, etc.

captious *cap'shus, adj.* ready to find fault.
cap'tiously *adv.* **cap'tiousness** *n.*

captivate *kap'tiv-āt, v.t.* to charm:—*pr.p.* **cap'tivating**.
cap'tivating *adj.* charming.

captive *kap'tiv, n.* a prisoner.—*adj.* **1** kept a prisoner. **2** unable to refuse what is offered: *a captive audience.* **3** held by a rope (as a balloon).
captiv'ity *n.* the state of being a prisoner, caged, etc.
cap'tor *n.* one who captures.
cap'ture *v.t.* **1** to take by force, skill, etc., to seize. **2** to take possession of (e.g. attention, imagination):—*pr.p.* **cap'-turing**.—Also *n.*

car *kär, n.* **1** a vehicle on wheels, esp. an automobile. **2** (as part of a word) a railway carriage: *a dining-car.* **3** the part of a balloon that carries passengers.

carafe *kȧ-räf', n.* a glass bottle for water or wine.

caramel *kar'ȧ-mėl, n.* **1** sugar melted and browned, used for colouring or flavouring. **2** a sweet made with sugar, butter, etc.

carat *kar'ȧt, n.* **1** a measure of weight for gems. **2** a unit in stating the fineness of gold: *18-carat gold means an alloy in which 18 out of 24 parts are pure gold.*

caravan *kar'ȧ-van, -van', n.* **1** a company travelling together for safety, esp. across a desert. **2** a house on wheels.
caravanserai *kar-ȧ-van'sėr-ī, n.* an inn or enclosed court where desert caravans stop.—Also **caravan'sarai, -sary.**

caraway *kar'ȧ-wā, n.* a plant with spicy-tasting seeds.

carbide. See **carbon**.

carbine *kär'bīn, n.* a short light musket.

carbon *kär'bȯn, n.* an element, of which pure charcoal is an example, occurring also as diamond and graphite.
carbide *kär'bīd, n.* a compound of carbon with another element, esp. calcium carbide.
carbohydrate *kär-bō-hī'drāt, n.* a compound of carbon, hydrogen, and oxygen, e.g. sugars, starches.
carbolic acid *kär-bol'ik as'id*, an acid from coal tar, used as a disinfectant.
car'bonate *n.* a salt containing carbon, oxygen, and a metal.
carbonif'erous *adj.* producing coal.
carbon copy 1 a duplicate of writing or typescript made by means of **carbon paper**, a paper coated with lamp black, etc. **2** an exact copy or imitation.
carbon dating a method of determining the age of e.g. wood, by measuring the amount of one type of carbon it contains.
carbon dioxide a gas present in the air, and breathed out by animals and absorbed by plants.
carbon monoxide a colourless, odourless, very poisonous gas.

Carborundum® *kär-bȯr-un'dum, n.* a compound of silicon and carbon used as an abrasive.

carboy *kär'boi, n.* large bottle with a frame of basketwork.

carbuncle *kär'bung-kl, n.* **1** a red precious stone (a garnet). **2** an inflamed ulcer.

carburettor *kär'bū-ret-ȯr* (or *-ret'-*), **carburetter** *n.* a part of an internal-combustion engine in which air is mixed with fuel in vapour form.

carcass, carcase *kär'kȧs, n.* **1** the dead body of an animal. **2** (*disrespectfully*) a live human body. **3** the framework of anything.

carcinoma *kä-si-nōm'ȧ, n.* a cancer.
carcin'ogen *(-sin'ŏj-ėn) n.* a substance capable of causing cancer.
carcinogen'ic *adj.*

card[1] *kärd, n.* **1** a small piece of pasteboard with figures for playing a game, or with greeting, invitation, etc. **2** (in *pl.*) game(s) played with cards.—*v.t.* to write (information) on a card.
card'board *n.* a stiff, finely finished pasteboard.—Also *adj.*
card'-sharp'er *n.* one who makes a business of cheating at cards played for money.
on the cards not improbable.

card[2] *kärd, n.* an instrument for combing wool, etc.—*v.t.* to comb (wool, etc.).

cardamom, cardamum *käd'ȧ-mum, ns.* the dried aromatic seeds of the cardamom plant, used as a spice.

cardiac *kär'di-ak, adj.* of the heart.

cardigan *kär'di-gȧn, n.* a knitted woollen jacket.

cardinal *kär'din-ȧl, adj.* **1** principal. **2** of chief importance.—*n.* one of the dignitaries next in rank to the Pope in the R.C. Church.
cardinal numbers numbers expressing how many (1, 2, 3, etc.).
cardinal points the four chief points of the compass—north, east, south, west.
cardinal virtues justice, prudence, temperance, fortitude.

cardio- *kär'di-ō-*, (as part of a word) heart.
car'diograph *(-gräf) n.* an instrument for recording movements of the heart.
cardiology *(-o'lȯ-ji) n.* the science that deals with the structure, functions, and diseases of the heart.

care *kār, n.* **1** worry. **2** cause of worry. **3** keeping: *in my care.* **4** attention and pains: *Do it with care.*—*v.i.* **1** to be anxious (for, about). **2** to be willing (to). **3** to have a fondness (for). **4** to look after, provide (for):—*pr.p.* **car'ing.**
care'ful *adj.* **1** taking care or pains. **2** full of anxiety.
care'fully *adv.* **care'fulness** *n.*
care'less *adj.* **care'lessness** *n.*
car'er *n.* one who is responsible for looking after an ill, disabled or otherwise dependent person.
care'free *adj.* having no worries.
care label a label on a garment giving instructions on washing, etc.
care'taker *n.* one put in charge of anything, esp. a building.—*adj.* put in charge until a replacement is found: *a caretaker government.*
care'worn *adj.* worn out by anxiety.

take care to be cautious, watchful, painstaking, etc.
take care of to look after.

career *kȧ-rēr*, *n.* **1** a rush. **2** progress through life, esp. advancement in business or profession.—*v.i.* to move rapidly and wildly.

caress *kȧ-res'*, *v.t.* to touch gently, to fondle.—Also. *n.*

caret *kar'ėt*, *n.* a mark, ^, to show where to insert something omitted.

cargo *kär'gō*, *n.* a ship's or aeroplane's load:—*pl.* **car'goes**.

caribou *kar-i-bōō'*, *kar'*, *n.* the American reindeer.

caricature *kar'i-kȧ-tyůr*, *-chůr*, *n.* a likeness so exaggerated as to appear ridiculous.—Also *v.t.*:—*pr.p.* **car'icaturing**.
caricatur'ist *n.*

caries *kā'ri-ēz*, *n.* decay, esp. of teeth.

carillon *ka'ril-yȯn*, or *-ril'*, *n.* **1** a set of bells for playing tunes. **2** a melody played on them.

carmine *kär'mīn*, *-min*, *n.* purplish red.—Also *adj.*

carnage *kär'nij*, *n.* slaughter.

carnal *kär'nȧl*, *adj.* **1** of physical, esp. sexual, desires and pleasure. **2** not spiritual.

carnation *kär-nā'sh(ȯ)n*, *n.* a garden flower, a variety of pink.

carnelian. Same as **cornelian**.

carnival *kär'ni-vȧl*, *n.* **1** merrymaking before Lent in R.C. countries. **2** a fairlike entertainment.

Carnivora *kär-niv'ȯ-rȧ*, *n. pl.* flesh-eating animals.
car'nivore *(-vōr, -vör)* *n.* a carnivorous animal.
carniv'orous *adj.* flesh-eating.

carob *kar'ȯb*, *n.* **1** a pod-bearing Mediterranean tree. **2** a chocolate substitute made from its fruit.

carol *kar'ȯl*, *n.* a song of joy or praise, esp. at Christmas.—*v.i.* to sing:—*pr.p.* **car'olling**; *pa.p.* **car'olled**.

carotid *kȧ-rot'id*, *adj.* of the two great arteries of the neck.

carouse *kȧr-owz'*, *n.* **1** a drinking-bout. **2** a noisy revel.—Also *v.i.*:—*pr.p.* **carous'ing**.
carous'al *n.* **1** a carouse. **2** a feast.

carp[1] *kärp*, *v.i.* (with *at*) to find fault with small errors or misdeeds.

carp[2] *kärp*, *n.* a type of freshwater fish.

carpal *kär'pȧl*, *adj.* and *n.* (a bone) of the wrist.

carpenter *kär'pin-tėr*, *n.* a worker in wood, esp. as used in building houses.—Also *v.i.*
car'pentry *n.* the work of a carpenter.

carpet *kär'pit*, *n.* **1** the woven covering of floors, stairs, etc. **2** an expanse (e.g. of growing flowers).—*v.t.* **1** to cover with or as with, a carpet. **2** to put on the carpet (*def. 2*):—*pr.p.* **car'peting**; *pa.p.* **car'peted**.
car'peting *n.* carpet material.
on the carpet **1** under discussion. **2** up before someone in authority for reprimand.

carriage *kar'ij*, *n.* **1** the act, or cost, of carrying. **2** a vehicle for carrying, esp. horse-drawn or on a railway. **3** behaviour, bearing.
carr'iageway *n.* (part of) a road used by vehicles.
carriage forward with the cost of conveying not prepaid.
carriage free free of charge for transport.
carriage paid with the cost of conveying prepaid.

carrier. See **carry**.

carrion *kar'i-ȯn*, *n.* **1** dead animal flesh. **2** anything vile.

carrot *kar'ȯt*, *n.* **1** a vegetable with a sweet reddish or yellowish tapering root. **2** an incentive, enticement.
carr'oty *adj.* (of hair) carrot-coloured.

carry *kar'i*, *v.t.* **1** to convey or transport. **2** to bear. **3** to support. **4** to hold (oneself, one's head, etc.): *Carry yourself less stiffly.* **5** to take by force. **6** to approve by a majority: *The motion was carried.*—*v.i.* (of a gun shot, sound, etc.) to travel (a certain distance):—*pr.p.* **carr'ying**; *pa.p.* **carr'ied**.
carr'ier *n.* **1** one who carries, esp. for payment. **2** a container for carrying. **3** one who passes on an infectious disease without himself having any symptoms.
carrier bag a plastic, etc. bag for carrying shopping, etc.
carrier pigeon a pigeon that carries messages, trained to return home.
carr'ycot *n.* a small portable cot.
carried away unable to control oneself because of excitement, etc.
carry all before one to overcome all resistance.
carry on **1** to manage (e.g. a business). **2** (*coll.*) to behave badly or foolishly (*n.* **carr'y-on'**). **3** to continue (with).
carry one's point to get one's plan or view accepted.
carry out, through to accomplish.
carry the day to gain the victory.

cart *kärt*, *n.* a two-wheeled vehicle for carrying loads.—*v.t.* to convey in a cart.

cart'age *n.* the act, or cost, of carting.
car'ter *n.* one who drives a cart.
cart'wheel *n.* **1** the wheel of a cart. **2** a sideways somersault.
put the cart before the horse to reverse the natural or sensible order.

carte *kärt*: **à la carte** (of a meal) chosen dish by dish.

carte-blanche *kärt'-blon^g^sh'*, *n.* freedom to act as one thinks best.

cartel *kär-tel'*, *n.* a combination of business firms.

cartilage *kär'ti-lij*, *n.* **1** in man and animals, a firm elastic substance, gristle. **2** a piece of this.

cartography *kär-tog'rȧ-fi*, *n.* map-making.
cartog'rapher *n.*

carton *kär'tȯn*, *n.* a box of thin pasteboard.

cartoon *kär-to͞on'*, *n.* **1** a preparatory drawing on strong paper to be transferred to a fresco, tapestry, etc. **2** any large drawing. **3** a drawing satirising, making fun of, someone or something. **4** a cinematograph film made by photographing a succession of drawings.
cartoon'ist *n.*

cartridge *kär'trij*, *n.* **1** a case containing the charge for a gun. **2** a small container which can be easily put into a machine, holding e.g. film, ink, or tape.

carve *kärv*, *v.t.* **1** to cut into designs, shapes, or pieces. **2** to cut up (meat):—*pr.p.* **car'ving.**
car'ver *n.* **1** one who carves. **2** a carving-knife.
car'ving *n.*
carve out 1 to hew out. **2** to gain by one's exertions: *He carved out a career for himself.*

cascade *kas-kād'*, *n.* **1** a waterfall. **2** an arrangement of pieces of apparatus in which each feeds into the next.—*v.i.* to fall in cascades:—*pr.p.* **cascad'ing.**

cascara *kas-kä'rȧ*, *n.* a Californian bark used as a laxative.

case¹ *kās*, *n.* **1** state or condition. **2** an instance, example: *two cases of mumps in the town.* **3** a person under medical treatment. **4** a legal trial. **5** a statement of facts or arguments. **6** (*grammar*) a form of a noun, pronoun, or adjective expressing its relation to other words in the sentence (in Old English, Latin, Russian, etc., different cases have different endings; compare *who*, *whom*, *whose*).
in any case 1 under any circumstances. **2** whatever the other facts or circumstances.
in case lest, for fear.
make out a case to argue convincingly.

case² *kās*, *n.* **1** a covering, box, or sheath. **2** a cabinet for displaying things in. **3** a suitcase. **4** the boards and back of a book.—Also *v.t.*:—*pr.p.* **cas'ing.**
case'-hard'ened *adj.* unfeeling, callous.
case'-knife *n.* a knife kept in a sheath.
case'ment *n.* **1** a window frame. **2** a window that opens on hinges.

cash *kash*, *n.* **1** coin or money. **2** ready money.—*v.t.* to turn into or exchange for money.
cashier *kash-ēr'*, *n.* one who has charge of the receiving and paying of money.
cash'-and-carr'y *n.* a store (often wholesale) where goods are sold cheaply for cash and taken away by the buyer.
cash dispenser an automatic teller machine.
cash'phone *n.* a coin-operated payphone.
cash'-reg'ister *n.* a till recording the amount put in.
hard cash, spot cash ready money.

cashew *kȧ'sho͞o*, *kȧ-sho͞o'*, *n.* **1** a tropical American tree. **2** its nut.

cashier¹ *kash-ēr'*, *v.t.* to dismiss from a post in disgrace.

cashier². See **cash**.

cashmere *kash'mēr*, *n.* (a shawl, fabric, made from) fine *Kashmir* goats' hair.—Also *adj.*

casino *kȧ-sē'nō*, *n.* a building with public dance halls, gaming tables, etc.:—*pl.* **casi'nos.**

cask *käsk*, *n.* a hollow round vessel for holding liquor, made of staves bound with hoops.

casket *käs'kit*, *n.* **1** a small case for holding jewels, etc. **2** (*U.S.*) a coffin.

cassava *kȧ-sä'vȧ*, *n.* the West Indian name of the plant from which tapioca is obtained.

casserole *kas'ė-rōl*, *n.* a vessel in which food is both cooked and served.—Also *v.t.*:—*pr.p.* **cass'eroling.**

cassette *kȧ-set'*, *n.* a container for film or magnetic tape.

cassock *kas'ȯk*, *n.* **1** a long robe worn by clergy and choristers. **2** a shorter garment, worn under the pulpit gown by Scottish clergymen.

cast *käst*, *v.t.* **1** to throw. **2** to shed, drop. **3** to mould or shape (esp. metal). **4** to give (an actor) a rôle in a play (as):— *pa.p.* **cast.**—*n.* **1** a throw. **2** the distance thrown. **3** a squint of the eye. **4** matter ejected by an earthworm, or by a hawk, etc. **5** the company of actors taking the parts in a play. **6** a rigid casing, e.g. of plaster of Paris and gauze, for holding a broken bone

in place while it sets.
cast'ing *n.* **1** the act of casting or moulding. **2** something that is cast.
cast'away *n.* a shipwrecked person.
casting vote the deciding vote of the chairman of a meeting when the other votes are equally divided.
cast'-i'ron *n.* an iron-carbon alloy with impurities.—*adj.* **1** of cast-iron. **2** rigid, unyielding. **3** very strong.
cast'-off *adj.* laid aside or rejected.—Also *n.*
cast down discouraged, depressed.
cast in the teeth of to fling as a reproach against.
cast lots to draw lots.
cast off **1** to throw off, to set aside as useless. **2** to untie (the mooring lines of a boat). **3** to finish (knitting) with an edge that will not run. **4** to disown.
cast on to make stitches.
cast up **1** to add up. **2** to bring up as a reproach.

castanets *kas'tȧ-nets*, *n. pl.* two hollow shells of ivory or hard wood struck together as accompaniment to dances and guitars.

caste *käst*, *n.* a social class, esp. in India.

castellan, castellated. See **castle**.

caster. Same as **castor**.

castigate *kas'tig-āt*, *v.t.* **1** to punish. **2** to criticise severely:—*pr.p.* **cas'tigating**.
castigā'tion *n.*

castle *käs'l*, *n.* **1** a fortified house or fortress. **2** the residence of a prince or nobleman. **3** a mansion. **4** a piece in chess.
castellan *kas'tel-ȧn*, *n.* the governor of a castle.
cas'tellāted *adj.* having turrets and battlements like a castle.
castles in the air, or **in Spain**, day-dreams, schemes that cannot be carried out.

castor *käs'tȯr*, *n.* **1** a small wheel on legs of furniture. **2** a vessel with perforated top for pepper, sugar, etc.—Also **cas'ter**.

castor-oil *käs'tȯr-oil'*, *n.* an oil from a tropical plant, used as medicine and for other purposes.

castrate *kȧ-strāt*, *v.t.* to remove the sexual organs of:—*pr.p.* **castrat'ing**.
castrā'tion *n.*

casual *kaz(h)'ū-ȧl*, *adj.* **1** chance. **2** offhand. **3** careless. **4** informal. **5** employed occasionally, not regularly (also *n.*): *casual labour.* **6** occasional: *casual work*.
cas'ually *adv.* **cas'ualness** *n.*
cas'ualty *n.* **1** a person (or thing) lost by wounds, death, desertion (or breakage), etc. **2** the casualty department of a hospital:—*pl.* **cas'ualties**.

casuistry *kaz'ū-is-tri*, *kazh'*, *n.* **1** quibbling. **2** reasoning (e.g. about one's duty) esp. if not straightforward or completely honest.
cas'uist *n.* **casuist'ic(al)** *adjs.*

cat *kat*, *n.* **1** a small wild or pet animal. **2** any large wild animal (as a tiger, lion) related to it. **3** a spiteful woman. **4** short for **cat-o'-nine'-tails**.
catt'y *adj.* spiteful, nasty:—*comp.* **catt'ier**; *superl.* **catt'iest**.
cat-and-dog *adj.* quarrelsome.
cat'call *n.* a shrill whistle or loud cry expressing disapproval.—Also *v.i.*
cat'gut *n.* a kind of cord made from the intestines of sheep and other animals, used for violin strings, surgical ligatures, etc.
cat'kin *n.* a spike or tuft of small flowers, as in the willow, hazel, etc.
cat-o'-nine'-tails *n.* a whip with nine knotted cords or lashes.
cat's'-paw *n.* **1** a light breeze. **2** a dupe or tool (from the fable of the monkey who used the paws of a cat to draw chestnuts out of the fire.)
cat'suit *n.* a woman's close-fitting one-piece trouser suit.
cat'walk *n.* a narrow walk, often high off the ground, e.g. on a bridge.

cata- *kat-ȧ-*, *pfx.* down.

cataclysm *kat'ȧ-klizm*, *n.* **1** a flood of water. **2** a violent upheaval.

catacomb *kat'ȧ-kōm*, *-ko͞om*, *n.* an underground burial-place.

catafalque *kat'ȧ-falk*, *n.* the structure on which a coffin rests during the lying-in-state.

catalogue *kat'ȧ-log*, *n.* a list of names, books, etc.—*v.t.* to put in a catalogue:—*pr.p.* **cat'aloguing**.

catalysis *kȧ-tal'i-sis*, *n.* the hastening, or slowing down, of a chemical change by a substance which itself undergoes no permanent chemical change.
cat'alyst (or **catalytic agent**) *n.*
catalyt'ic *adj.*

catamaran *kat-ȧ-mȧ-ran'*, *n.* **1** a raft of logs lashed together. **2** a swift sailing-boat with two hulls side by side.

catapult *kat'ȧ-pult*, *n.* **1** an old war machine for throwing stones, etc. **2** a forked stick with an elastic string fixed to the prongs for throwing small missiles.

cataract *kat'ȧ-rakt*, *n.* **1** a waterfall. **2** cloudiness of the lens of the eye causing blindness.

catarrh *kȧt-är'*, *n.* a discharge of fluid caused by inflammation of a mucous membrane.

catastrophe *kȧt-as'trȯ-fi*, *n.* **1** a sudden disaster. **2** a great misfortune.
catastroph'ic *adj.* **catastroph'ically** *adv.*

catcall. See **cat**.

catch *kach*, *v.t.* **1** to take hold of (a thing in motion). **2** to trap. **3** to entangle. **4** to attract (a person's attention). **5** to hit: *The ball caught him on the ear.* **6** to succeed in hearing. **7** to be in time for. **8** to surprise, detect: *I caught him stealing.* **9** to take (a disease) by infection:—*pa.p.* **caught** (*köt*).—*n.* **1** anything that seizes or holds. **2** a snare. **3** a haul of fish. **4** anything worth catching. **5** a song in which the parts are caught up by different voices in turn.
catch'er *n.*
catch'ing *adj.* **1** infectious. **2** attractive.
catch'y *adj.* attractive and readily remembered, as a tune, etc.:—*comp.* **catch'ier**; *superl.* **catch'iest**.
catchment area, **basin** the area from which a river or a reservoir draws its water supply.
catch'penny *n.* a worthless thing, intended merely to gain money.—Also *adj.*
catch'word *n.* **1** among actors, the cue. **2** the first word of a page given at the bottom of the page before. **3** any word or phrase taken up and repeated.
catch fire to ignite, to begin to burn.
catch it to get a scolding.
catch on **1** to understand. **2** to become popular.
catch out **1** to put out at cricket by catching the ball. **2** to catch, detect, in error, or doing something (esp. bad).
catch sight of to get a glimpse of.
catch the eye to attract attention.
Catch 22 denoting a situation in which one can never win or in which all possible actions have undesirable consequences.
catch up **1** to come level (with), overtake. **2** to get up-to-date. **3** to snatch up hastily.

catechise *kat'i-kīz*, *v.t.* **1** to teach by question and answer. **2** to question searchingly:—*pr.p.* **cat'echising**.
cat'echism *n.* **1** a book (esp. religious) of instruction by means of question and answer. **2** a series of probing questions on any subject.
cat'echist, **cat'echīser** *ns.*

category *kat'ė-gȯr-i*, *n.* a class or division consisting of things (or people) of the same kind:—*pl.* **cat'egories**.
categor'ical *adj.* absolute, definite, explicit: *a categorical refusal to help*.
categor'ically *adv.*
cat'egorise *v.t.* to put into a category or categories, to classify:—*pr.p.* **cat'egorising**.

cater *kā'tėr*, *v.i.* to provide food, entertainment, facilities, etc. (for).
cat'erer *n.* **cat'ering** *n.*

caterpillar *kat'ėr-pil-ȧr*, *n.* the grub of a butterfly or moth.—*adj.* moving on endless belts: *a caterpillar tractor*.

caterwaul *kat'ėr-wöl*, *n.* **1** the shriek or cry of the cat. **2** any similar noise.—Also *v.i.*
cat'erwauling *n.*

catgut. See **cat**.

cathedral *kȧth-ēd'rȧl*, *n.* the principal church of a diocese, with the bishop's throne.

Catherine-wheel *kath'ė-rin-hwēl*, *n.* **1** an ornamented circular window. **2** a firework which rotates in burning.

cathode *kath'ōd*, *n.* the conductor through which an electric current leaves a battery, etc.
cathode rays streams of electrons.
cathode ray tube a device in which a narrow beam of electrons strikes against a screen, as in a television set.

catholic *kath'ȯl-ik*, *adj.* **1** universal. **2** of the R.C. Church. **3** including all or much: *catholic tastes*:—*n.* (*cap.*) an adherent of the R.C. Church.
cathol'icism *n.* the tenets of the R.C. Church.
catholic'ity (*-is'-*) *n.* **1** the quality of affecting, or including, all or much. **2** breadth of view.

catkin, **catsuit**. See **cat**.

cattle *kat'l*, *n.pl.* grass-eating animals, esp. oxen, bulls, and cows.
cattle cake concentrated feed in block shape for cattle.

catty, **catwalk**. See **cat**.

Caucasian *kö-kā'z(h)i-ȧn*, *n.* and *adj.* (a person) of the white race of man.

caught. See **catch**.

cauldron *köl'drȯn*, *n.* a large pot.

cauliflower *kol'i-flow(-ė)r*, *n.* a variety of cabbage whose white flower head is eaten.

caulk, **calk** *kök*, *v.t.* to make (e.g. a ship) watertight by pressing oakum, etc. into the seams.

cause *köz*, *n.* **1** the action, happening, etc., that produces an effect. **2** motive. **3** reason. **4** a legal action. **5** an aim for which an individual or party works.—*v.t.* **1** to produce. **2** to bring about. **3** to lead (a person to do something):—*pr.p.* **caus'ing**.

causeway *köz'wā*, **causey** *köz'i*, *ns.* a raised pathway.

caustic *kös'*, *kos'tik*, *adj.* **1** burning. **2** bitter, severe, cutting: *caustic comments.*—*n.* a substance that burns or wastes away the skin and flesh.
caus'tically *adv.* **caus'ticness** *n.*
caustic soda. See **soda**.

cauterise *kö'tėr-īz*, *v.t.* to burn with a caustic or a hot iron:—*pr.p.* **caut'erising**.
cauterisā'tion *n.*

caution *kö'sh(ȯ)n*, *n.* **1** care, heedfulness. **2** a warning.—*v.t.* to warn.
cau'tionary *adj.* containing warning.
cau'tious *adj.* **1** careful. **2** watchful. **3** prudent:—*opp.* **incautious**.
cau'tiously *adv.* **cau'tiousness** *n.*

cavalcade *kav-ȧl-kād'*, *kav'*, *n.* a procession of persons, esp. on horseback.

cave *kāv*, *n.* a hollow place in a rock.
cave'man *n.* **1** one, esp. of the Stone Age, who lives in a cave. **2** one who behaves violently, esp. towards women:—*pl.* **cave'men**.
cave in to give way, collapse (*n.* **cave'-in**):—*pr.p.* **cav'ing in**.

cavern *kav'ėrn*, *n.* a deep hollow place in rocks.
cav'ernous *adj.* **1** hollow. **2** full of caverns.

caviar(e) *kav-i-är'*, *kav'i-är*, *n.* **1** salted roe of sturgeon, etc. **2** something too fine for the vulgar taste.

cavil *kav'il*, *v.i.* to make trifling objections:—*pr.p.* **cav'illing**; *pa.p.* **cav'illed**.— Also *n.*

cavity *kav'it-i*, *n.* **1** a hollow place, a hole. **2** a decayed hollow in a tooth:—*pl.* **cav'ities**.

cavort *kȧv-ört'*, *v.i.* to prance, bound.

cayenne *kā-en'*, *n.* a type of red pepper.

cayman *kā'mȧn*, *n.* an alligator, esp. of South American kind:—*pl.* **cay'mans**.

cease *sēs*, *v.t.* and *v.i.* to stop:—*pr.p.* **ceas'ing**.—Also *n.*
cease'less *adj.* never ceasing.
ceas'ing, **cessā'tion** *(ses-)*, *ns.*
cease'-fire' *n.* **1** an end to hostilities. **2** an order for, or time of, this.
See also **incessant**.

cedar *sē'dȧr*, *n.* a cone-bearing evergreen with hard, sweet-scented wood.

cede *sēd*, *v.t.* to yield or give up to another:—*pr.p.* **ced'ing**.
ce'ding, **cession** *se'sh(ȯ)n*, *ns.*

cedilla *sė-dil'ȧ*, *n.* a mark put under the letter *c* (ç) to show that it is to have the sound of *s*.

Ceefax® *sē'faks*, *n.* the teletext service of the British Broadcasting Corporation.

ceiling *sēl'ing*, *n.* **1** the inner roof of a room. **2** the upper limit. **2** the limiting height for a particular aircraft.

celandine *sel'ȧn-dīn*, *n.* **1** (*greater celandine*) a plant of the poppy family. **2** (*lesser celandine*) a kind of buttercup.

celebrate *sel'i-brāt*, *v.t.* **1** to perform (a rite, e.g. mass). **2** to hold festivities in honour of (a happy or important event):—*pr.p.* **cel'ebrating**.—Also *v.i.*
cel'ebrated *adj.* famous.
celebrā'tion *n.* an act of celebrating.
celeb'rity *n.* **1** fame. **2** a well-known person:—*pl.* **celeb'rities**.

celery *sel'ėr-i*, *n.* a vegetable with long juicy stalks.
celer'iac *n.* a variety of celery with a swollen root, eaten as a vegetable.

celestial *sėl-est'yȧl*, *adj.* heavenly.

celibacy *sel'i-bȧs-i*, *n.* an unmarried state.
cel'ibate *(-bȧt)* *adj.* **1** living single. **2** bound by vow not to marry.—Also *n.*

cell *sel*, *n.* **1** a small room, e.g. in a prison or monastery. **2** a unit of living matter. **3** the unit of an electrical battery in which chemical action takes place. **4** a small group in a larger organisation, esp of political activists.
cell'ular *adj.* consisting of, or containing, cells, or tiny hollow spaces.
cell'ulose *(-ōs)* *n.* the chief substance in the cell walls of plants.
cell phone a pocket telephone for use in a cellular radio system based on a network of transmitters.

cellar *sel'ȧr*, *n.* **1** an underground room, esp. one for stores, e.g. for wine. **2** a stock of wines.
cell'arage *n.* **1** cellars. **2** charge for storing in cellars.

cello, **'cello** *chel'ō*, *n.* for **violoncello**:—*pl.* **cell'os**, **'cell'os**.
cell'ist, **'cell'ist** *n.* for **violoncellist**.

cellophane *sel'ō-fān*, *n.* a transparent wrapping material.

cellular. See **cell**.

cell'ulite *n.* body fat which makes the skin look dimpled.

celluloid *sel'ū-loid*, *n.* a hard elastic substance made from gun-cotton and camphor, etc.

cellulose. See **cell**.

Celt *kelt*, *selt*, *n.* one of the group of peoples who speak, or once spoke, Celtic.
Cel'tic *adj.* of the Celts.—*n.* a group of related languages incl. Welsh, Irish, Gaelic.

cement *si-ment'*, *n.* **1** anything that makes two bodies stick together. **2** mortar.—*v.t.* to join firmly.

cemetery *sem'i-tri*, *n.* ground set apart for burial of the dead:—*pl.* **cem'eteries**.

cenotaph *sen'ō-täf*, *n.* a monument to one who is buried elsewhere.

censor *sen'sȯr*, *n.* **1** an official who examines written and printed matter with power to delete any of the contents. **2** a stern critic.—Also *v.t.*

censō'rious *adj.* fault-finding.

censo'riously *adv.* **censo'riousness** *n.*

cen'sorship *n.* the office or action of a censor.

censure *sen'shůr*, *v.t.* **1** to blame. **2** to condemn as wrong:—*pr.p.* **cen'suring**.—Also *n.*

census *sen'sůs*, *n.* an official counting of a country's inhabitants.

cent *sent*, *n.* a coin worth the hundredth part of a dollar, rand, etc.

per cent see **per**.

cent(i)- *sent-(i)*, (as part of a word) **1** a hundred. **2** a hundredth part.

centaur *sen'tör*, *n.* a creature in Greek story, half man, half horse.

centenary *sen-tēn'ȧr-i*, or *-ten'-*, or *sen'-tin-*, *n.* a hundredth anniversary:—*pl.* **centenaries**.—Also *adj.*

centenā'rian *n.* one who is a hundred years old.

centigrade *sen'ti-grād*, *adj.* divided into a hundred degrees, as the *centigrade*, or *Celsius* (from name of Swed. astronomer) *thermometer*, in which freezing point of water is zero and boiling point of water is 100.

centigram(me) *sen'ti-gram*; **centilitre** *sen'ti-lē-tėr*; **centimetre** *sen'ti-mē-tėr*, *ns.*

centipede *sen'ti-pēd*, *n.* a small crawling creature with many joints, most of the joints bearing one pair of legs.

central, **centralise**, etc. See **centre**.

centre *sen'tėr*, *n.* the middle point, or middle, of anything.—*v.t.* and *v.i.* to place, or to be, in the centre:—*pr.p.* **cen'tring** *(-tėr-)*.

cen'tral *adj.* **1** belonging to, or close to, the centre. **2** principal.

cen'tralise *v.t.* **1** to bring to, collect at, one place, esp. at the middle, or the most important, point. **2** to bring under one control: *to centralise the government*:—*pr.p* **cen'tralising**.

centralisā'tion *n.*

central heating heating of a building by water, steam, or air, from one source.

central locking in a vehicle, the automatic locking of all the doors by the locking of the driver's door.

central processor the part of a computer which performs the calculations, etc.

centre in, **round**, etc., to be collected, concentrated in, round, etc.

centri- *sen-tri-*, (as part of a word) centre.

centrif'ugal (also *-fūg'*) *adj.* **1** tending away from a centre. **2** using or produced by **centrifugal force** (by which objects revolving round a centre tend to move outwards, away from the centre).

centrip'etal *adj.* tending towards a centre.

century *sen'tū-ri*, *n.* **1** a period of a hundred years. **2** a hundred runs in cricket:—*pl.* **cen'turies**.

ceramic *sėr-am'ik*, *adj.* of ceramics or a ceramic.—*n.* **1** potter's clay or a modern substitute. **2** (in *pl.*) the articles made by a potter.

ceram'ics *n.sing.* the art of pottery.

cereal *sē'ri-ȧl*, *n.* **1** (usu. in *pl.*) grain used as food, as wheat, barley. **2** a food prepared from such grain.

cerebellum. See **cerebrum**.

cerebrum *ser'i-brům*, *n.* the front and larger part of the brain.

cerebell'um *n.* the hinder and lower part of the brain.

cer'ebro-spin'al *adj.* of the brain and spinal cord.

ceremony *ser'i-mȯ-ni*, *n.* **1** a sacred rite. **2** a formal act. **3** pomp or formality:—*pl.* **cer'emonies**.

ceremō'nial *adj.* relating to ceremony.—*n.* a system of ceremonies.

ceremō'nially *adv.*

ceremō'nious *adj.* carefully formal or polite.

certain *sûr'tin*, *-tn*, *adj.* **1** sure, without doubt. **2** never failing in action or result. **3** some, or one, not definitely named, or not known to the listener(s): *certain MPs*; *a certain Mrs. Smith*.

cer'tainly *adv.*—*interj.* yes, of course.

cer'tainty *n.* **1** something which cannot be doubted. **2** something which is sure to happen. **3** freedom from doubt:—*pl.* **cer'tainties**.

certificate *sėr-tif'i-kit*, *n.* **1** a written declaration of some fact. **2** a testimonial of character.—*v.t.* *(-kāt)* to give a certificate to:—*pr.p.* **certif'icating**.

cer'tifiable *adj.* that, who, can be certified (esp. as insane).

certificā'tion *n.*

cer'tify *v.t.* **1** to declare formally. **2** to guarantee:—*pr.p.* **cer'tifying**; *pa.p.* **cer'tified**.

cervix *sûr'viks*, *n.* the neck of the womb.
cervical *(sėr-vī'kl)* **smear** the collection of a sample of cells from the cervix, and the examination of these cells under a microscope as a test for early cancer.

cessation. See **cease**.

cession. See **cede**.

cesspool *ses'pōōl*, **cesspit** *ses'pit*, *ns.* a pool or pit for collecting filthy water.

chafe *chāf*, *v.t.* **1** to make hot by rubbing. **2** to fret or wear by rubbing.—*v.i.* to fret or rage:—*pr.p.* **chaf'ing**.

chaff *chäf*, *chaf*, *n.* **1** the husks of corn as threshed or winnowed. **2** good-humoured teasing.—*v.t.* to tease good-naturedly.

chaffinch *chaf'inch*, *-sh*, *n.* a songbird of the finch family.

chagrin *sha'grin*, *n.* vexation, annoyance.—*v.t.* to vex, annoy:—*pr.p.* **chag'rining**.

chain *chān*, *n.* **1** a series of links or rings passing through one another. **2** a series. **3** anything that binds. **4** a measure 66 feet (20.1 metres) long. **5** (in *pl.*) fetters.—*v.t.* **1** to fasten. **2** to fetter.
chain gang a gang of convicts chained together.
chain mail armour made of iron links.
chain reaction a process whose product starts off other similar processes.
chain store one of a number of shops linked under the same ownership.

chair *chār*, *n.* **1** a movable seat for one, with a back to it. **2** the seat or office of a person in authority, e.g. one who conducts a meeting. **3** the position of a professor.—*v.t.* **1** to carry in in triumph. **2** to preside at (a meeting).
chair'lift *n.* a series of seats hanging from a moving cable, for carrying skiers etc. up a mountain.
chair'man, **-woman**, **-person** *ns.* one who presides at a meeting.

chalet *shal'ā*, *n.* **1** a summer hut in mountains for herdsmen, etc. **2** a wooden house. **3** a small, usu. wooden, house for holiday-makers.

chalice *chal'is*, *n.* **1** a cup or bowl. **2** a communion cup.

chalk *chök*, *n.* **1** white rock, a soft limestone. **2** a chalk-like substance used for writing.
chalk'y *adj.* **chalk'iness** *n.*

challenge *chal'inj*, *v.t.* **1** to summon to a contest. **2** to express objection to (a juryman or jury, a decision, etc). **3** to claim or arouse (e.g. attention):—*pr.p.* **chall'enging**.—*n.* **1** a summons to a contest. **2** an objection. **3** a task which tests one's powers.
chall'enger *n.* **chall'enging** *adj.*

chamber *chām'bėr*, *n.* **1** a room. **2** the place where an assembly meets. **3** a law-making body. **4** the back end of the bore of a gun.
cham'bermaid *n.* a female servant in charge of bedrooms.
chamber music **1** music suitable for a room as opp. to a large hall. **2** music for strings, with or without piano or wind.
chamber of commerce an association in a town or district to watch over business interests.

chamberlain *chām'bėr-lin*, *n.* **1** an officer managing the household of a king or nobleman. **2** the treasurer of a corporation.

chameleon *kȧ-mēl'yȯn*, or *-i-ȯn*, *n.* a small lizard able to change colour.

chamfer *cham'fėr*, *n.* a bevelled edge or corner.—Also *v.t.*

chamois *sham'wä*, *n.* **1** an Alpine antelope. **2** (*pron. sham'i*) a soft leather orig. made from its skin (also **shamm'y**):—*pl.* **cham'ois.**

champ *champ*, *v.i.* to make a snapping noise with the jaws in chewing.—*v.t.* to chew.
champing at the bit impatient to act.

champagne *sham-pān'*, *n.* **1** a white sparkling wine from *Champagne* in France, or elsewhere. **2** any other wine from Champagne.

champion *cham'pi-ȯn*, *n.* **1** one who fights for himself or for another. **2** one who defends a cause. **3** in games, a competitor who has defeated all others.—*adj.* first-class.—*v.t.* to defend, to support.
cham'pionship *n.*

chance *chäns*, *n.* **1** something that happens for no known reason. **2** something thought of as causing unplanned events: *Chance brought them to the spot at the same moment.* **3** risk. **4** opportunity. **5** possibility.—*v.t.* to risk.—*v.i.* to happen:—*pr.p.* **chanc'ing.**—*adj.* (used only before a noun) happening accidentally.
chanc'y *adj.* (*coll.*) risky, uncertain:—*comp.* **chanc'ier**; *superl.* **chanc'iest**.
an even chance equal probability for and against.
chance on, **upon** to happen to find or meet.
the chances are the probability is.

chancel *chän'sl*, *n.* the (traditionally eastern) part of a church containing altar, sanctuary and choir, orig. separated from the nave by a screen of lattice-work.

chancellor *chän'sėl-ȯr*, *n.* **1** a chief minister. **2** the head of a university.
chancellery *chän'sė-lė-ri*, or *-slė*, *n.* **1** the department of a chancellor. **2** the office attached to an embassy, etc.

Chancellor of the Exchequer the chief minister of finance in the British government.

Lord (**High**) **Chancellor** the speaker of the House of Lords and head of the judiciary.

chancery *chăn'sėr-i*, *n.* a division of the High Court of Justices.

chandelier *shan-dė-lēr'*, *n.* a frame with branches for holding lights.

chandler *chand'lėr*, *n.* **1** a candle maker. **2** a dealer in candles. **3** a dealer generally.

change *chānj*, *v.t.* **1** to exchange (for). **2** to put, take, another in place of. **3** to give or get smaller coin for.—*v.t.* and *v.i.* **1** to make, or to become, different. **2** to alter (with *from*, *to*, *into*). **3** to put different clothes on (someone), or put on different clothes. **4** to go from one train, etc., to another: *I have to change trains*; *I change at Crewe*:—*pr.p.* **chang'ing**.—*n.* **1** alteration. **2** something different. **3** small coins. **4** money given back when too much is handed over as payment. **5** variation (see **ring²**).

change'able *adj.* **1** changing often. **2** fickle.

change'ableness, **changeabil'ity** *ns.*

change'ling *n.* a child taken or left in place of another, esp. by fairies.

change hands to pass into different ownership.

channel *chan'l*, *n.* **1** the bed of a stream. **2** a passage of deeper water through which ships can sail. **3** a strait or narrow sea: *the English Channel.* **4** a groove, furrow, etc. **5** a means of sending information, etc. **6** (*radio, etc.*) a path for signals in one direction.—*v.t.* **1** to furrow, groove. **2** to direct (e.g. one's energies) into a particular activity, etc.:—*pr.p.* **chann'elling**; *pa.p.* **chann'elled**.

chant *chänt*, *v.t.* to recite in a singing manner.—*n.* **1** a kind of sacred music in which a number of syllables are recited to one tone. **2** anything chanted.

chanty. Same as **shanty²**.

chaos *kā'os*, *n.* complete disorder or confusion.

chaot'ic *adj.* **chaot'ically** *adv.*

chap¹ *chap*, *v.i.* (of skin) to crack in cold weather:—*pr.p.* **chapp'ing**; *pa.p.* **chapped**.

chapped *adj.*

chap² *chap*, *n.* a fellow.

chap³, **chapfallen**. See **chop²**.

chapel *chap'ėl*, *n.* **1** a place of Christian worship not belonging to the established church of the country. **2** one attached to a house or institution. **3** a part of a church with its own altar.

chaperon(e) *shap'ė-rōn*, *n.* a lady under whose care a girl appears in society.—Also *v.t.*:—*pr.p.* **chap'eroning**.

chaplain *chap'lin*, *n.* a clergyman attached to a ship, regiment, institution, or family.

chap'laincy *n.* the office of chaplain.

chapter *chap'tėr*, *n.* **1** a main division of a book. **2** the canons of a cathedral. **3** an organised branch of a society (e.g. of freemasons).

chapter house a building or room where a chapter meets.

char¹ *chär*, *v.t.* and *v.i.* to scorch:—*pr.p.* **charr'ing**; *pa.p.* **charred**.

char² *chär*, *v.i.* to do house cleaning:—*pr.p.* **charr'ing**; *pa.p.* **charred**.

char'woman *n.* a woman employed for this purpose.

character *kar'ăk-tėr*, *n.* **1** a letter or mark. **2** nature, qualities. **3** strength of mind and purpose: *a man of character.* **4** an odd, eccentric person. **5** a person in a play or novel.

char'acterise *v.t.* **1** to be characteristic of, to distinguish, mark: *Good taste characterises her*. **2** to describe (as):—*pr.p.* **char'acterising**.

characterīsā'tion *n.* **1** creation of character(s) in a play or novel. **2** description.

characteris'tic *adj.* typical (of a person, etc.): *He showed characteristic unwillingness to say what he thought.*—*n.* a typical quality.

characteris'tically *adv.*

character actor an actor who often plays the part of an eccentric or unusual person.

charade *shȧ-räd'*, *n.* a game in which the syllables of a word, and then the whole word, are acted.

charcoal *chär'kōl*, *n.* the black part of partly burned wood, etc.

charge *chärj*, *v.t.* **1** to load. **2** to fill (with). **3** to fill with electricity. **4** to command. **5** to accuse. **6** to ask as the price. **7** to record as debt in, against: *Charge it to my account, to me.* **8** to attack at a rush.—*v.i.* **1** to ask payment (for). **2** to attack at a rush:—*pr.p.* **charg'ing**.—*n.* **1** load. **2** cost. **3** the powder, or powder and shot, for e.g. a gun. **4** a quantity of electricity. **5** care. **6** something looked after (e.g. a child). **7** control. **8** command. **9** an accusation. **10** an attack at a rush.

charge'able *adj.* **1** (making one) liable to be charged: *If he does that, he is chargeable with fraud*; *a chargeable offence.* **2** that should, or may, be charged:

This expense is chargeable to the firm's account.

charg'er *n.* **1** a large flat dish. **2** a horse ridden in battle.

charge card a card which entitles one to make purchases on credit in a particular shop.

be in charge of to control and be responsible for.

give (someone) in charge to hand (a person) over to the police.

chargé-d'affaires *shär-zhā-dä-fer', n.* an ambassador's deputy:—*pl.* **chargés-d'affaires.**

charily, chariness. See **chary**.

chariot *char'i-ot, n.* a vehicle used in ancient warfare or racing.

charioteer' *n.* a chariot driver.

charisma *kȧ-riz'mȧ, n.* **1** spiritual power given by God. **2** a gift or personal quality which makes one able to impress others.

charity *char'i-ti, n.* **1** love. **2** kindly feeling. **3** the giving of money, etc. to the poor. **4** a fund or institution whose purpose is to give such help:—*pl.* **char'ities.**

char'itable *adj.* **char'itably** *adv.*

charlatan *shär'lȧ-tȧn, n.* a quack.

charlotte *shär'lot, n.* a kind of fruit tart.

charm *chärm, n.* **1** a spell. **2** something thought to have magical power. **3** attractiveness.—*v.t.* **1** to influence by a charm. **2** to delight.

charmed *adj.* **1** protected, as by a spell. **2** delighted.

charm'er *n.*

charm'ing *adj.* very attractive.

charm'ingly *adv.*

chart *chärt, n.* **1** a map of part of the sea, with its coasts, shoals, depth, etc. **2** a table giving information—*v.t.* **1** to make a chart of. **2** to plan out on or with a chart.

charter *chärt'ėr, n.* a formal writing giving titles, rights, or privileges, esp. one granted by the sovereign or government.—*v.t.* to let or hire, as a ship or aircraft, on contract.

chartered accountant one qualified under the regulations of the Institute of Accountants.

charter flight a flight made in an aeroplane hired by a particular group of people.

charwoman. See **char²**.

chary *chār'i, adj.* unwilling to risk (with *of*): *Be chary of lending money to him.* **2** cautious:—*comp.* **char'ier**; *superl.* **char'iest.**

char'ily *adv.* **chari'ness** *n.*

chase *chās, v.t.* **1** to pursue. **2** to hunt. **3** to drive (away):—*pr.p.* **chas'ing.**—*n.* **1** pursuit. **2** hunting.

give chase to run after someone.

chasm *kazm, n.* a deep opening, gulf.

chassis *shas'ē, n.* **1** the frame, wheels, machinery (but not body) of a motor car, etc. **2** an aeroplane's landing-carriage:—*pl.* **chassis** *(shas'iz).*

chaste *chāst, adj.* **1** virtuous sexually. **2** pure in taste and style.

chaste'ly *adv.*

chaste'ness, chas'tity *(chas') ns.*

chasten *chās'n, v.t.* **1** to make better by punishment, suffering, etc. **2** to keep from being too great: *This failure chastened his pride.*

chastise *chas-tīz', v.t.* **1** to punish. **2** to beat:—*pr.p.* **chastis'ing.**

chas'tisement (*-tiz-*, or *-tīz'-*) *n.*

chastity. See **chaste**.

chasuble *chaz'-* or *chas'ū-bl, n.* a sleeveless vestment worn by the priest when celebrating mass.

chat¹ *chat, v.i.* to talk in an easy, friendly way:—*pr.p.* **chatt'ing**; *pa.p.* **chatt'ed.**—Also *n.*

chatt'y *adj.*:—*comp.* **chatt'ier**; *superl.* **chatt'iest.**

chatt'ily *adv.* **chatt'iness** *n.*

chat'-show *n.* a programme on which invited personalities talk informally with the host.

chat² *chat, n.* a small bird of the thrush family.

château *shä'tō, n.* a (French) castle:—*pl.* **châ'teaux** *(-tōz).*

chatelaine *shat'ė-lān, n.* the mistress of a castle or house.

chattel *chat'ėl, n.* an item of property, usu. in *pl.* as in **goods and chattels**, all movable property.

chatter *chat'ėr, v.i.* **1** to talk idly or quickly. **2** (of birds) to utter rapid short notes. **3** (of teeth) to knock together.—*n.* idle talk.

chatt'erbox *n.* a talkative person.

chatty. See **chat¹**.

chauffeur *shō'fėr, n.* one employed to drive a private motor car.

chauvinism *shō'vin-izm, n.* an unreasonable belief in the superiority of one's own nation, sex, etc.

chauv'inist *n.* **chauvinis'tic** *adj.*

cheap *chēp, adj.* **1** low in price. **2** of small value. **3** vulgar.

cheap'en *v.t.* **1** to lower the price of. **2** to make vulgar, worthy of contempt, etc.

cheap'ly *adv.* **cheap'ness** *n.*

cheat *chēt, v.t.* **1** to deceive. **2** to swindle.—Also *v.i.* and *n.*

check[1] *chek*, *v.t.* **1** to stop. **2** to hinder. **3** to find fault with (a person). **4** to look at or test (a calculation, apparatus, etc.) to see that it is correct, accurate, working properly, etc.—*n.* **1** a sudden stop. **2** something that hinders progress. **3** (*chess*) a position in which the king is open to attack. **4** a test of correctness, accuracy, etc. **5** (a fabric with) a pattern of squares.
checked *adj*.
check'list *n.* a list of things to be checked or done.
check'mate *n.* (*chess*) a position from which the king cannot escape.—*v.t.* **1** to put (one's opponent's king) in this position. **2** to put a final stop to:—*pr.p.* **check'mating**.
check'-out *n.* the desk where one pays for goods bought in a supermarket, etc.
check in, **out** to record one's arrival at, or departure from, work, a hotel, etc.
check up (*n.* **check'-up**) **1** to investigate. **2** to examine.

check[2], **checkered**, **checkers**. See **cheque**.

cheek *chēk*, *n.* **1** the side of the face below the eye. **2** impudence.
cheek'y *adj.*:—*comp.* **cheek'ier**; *superl.* **cheek'iest**.
cheek'ily *adv.* **cheek'iness** *n.*
cheek'bone *n.* the bone ridge below the eye.

cheep *chēp*, *v.i.* to chirp, as a young bird.—Also *n.*

cheer *chēr*, *n.* **1** a shout of approval or welcome. **2** (*old*) state of mind: *Be of good cheer.*—*v.t.* **1** to encourage (with *on*). **2** to applaud.
cheer'ful *adj.* **1** in good spirits, happy. **2** lively. **3** ungrudging.
cheer'fully *adv.* **cheer'fulness** *n.*
cheer'less *adj.* **1** gloomy. **2** without comfort.
cheer'y *adj.* lively, merry:—*comp.* **cheer'ier**; *superl.* **cheer'iest**.
cheer'ily *adv.* **cheer'iness** *n.*

cheese *chēz*, *n.* the curd of milk pressed into a hard mass.
cheese'-par'ing *n.* stinginess.—Also *adj.*

cheetah *chē'tȧ*, *n.* an African and Indian animal like the leopard, used in hunting.

chef *shef*, *n.* a cook, esp. a head cook.
chef d'œuvre *(shā dûvr')* *n.* a masterpiece:—*pl.* **chefs** *(shā)* **d'œuvre**.

chemical, **chemist**, etc. See **chemistry**.

chemistry *kem'is-tri*, *n.* the science that deals with the properties of substances and the ways in which they act on, or combine with, each other.
chem'ical *adj.* of chemistry or chemical(s).—*n.* a substance used in a chemical process, either in research or in industry.
chem'ist *n.* **1** a scientist who studies chemistry. **2** a pharmacist.
chem'ō- (or *kē'*-) (as part of a word) chemical.

chenille *shė-nēl'*, *n.* a soft, velvety fabric.

cheque (*U.S.* **check**) *chek*, *n.* a written order on a printed form telling a bank to pay money to a person named.
chequ'ered, **check'ered** *adj.* **1** marked with squares. **2** partly good, partly bad; with ups and downs: *a chequered career*.
chequ'ers, (more often) **check'ers** *n.sing.* the game of draughts.
cheque book a book of cheque forms.
cheque card a card issued by a bank guaranteeing that the holder's cheques (up to a certain limit) will be honoured.

cherish *cher'ish*, *v.t.* **1** to protect and love. **2** to have in the mind or heart: *to cherish a hope, an idea, a feeling*.

cheroot *shė-rōōt'*, *n.* a cigar not pointed at either end.

cherry *cher'i*, *n.* a tree, or its small, usu. red, fruit:—*pl.* **cherr'ies**.

cherub *cher'ŭb*, *n.* **1** a winged creature with human face. **2** a beautiful child:—*pl.* **cher'ubs**, **cher'ubim** *(-oo-)*.
cheru'bic *(-ōō'bik) adj*.

chervil *chûr'vil*, *n.* a plant with aromatic leaves used as a herb.

chess *ches*, *n.* a game for two played with pieces (**chess'men**) on a chequered board (**chess'board**).

chest *chest*, *n.* **1** a large strong box. **2** the part of the body between the neck and the abdomen.
chest of drawers a set of drawers fitted in a single piece of furniture.

chesterfield *chest'ėr-fēld*, *n.* **1** a long overcoat. **2** a heavily padded sofa.

chestnut *ches'nut*, *n.* **1** an edible nut in a prickly husk (the *Spanish* or *sweet chestnut*). **2** the tree that bears it. **3** a stale joke.—*adj.* reddish-brown.
See also **horse chestnut**.

chevron *shev'rȯn*, *n.* the V-shaped band on the sleeve of a non-commissioned officer's coat.

chew *chōō*, *v.t.* to break (food) up with the teeth.—Also *n.*
chew'y *adj.*:—*comp.* **chew'ier**; *superl.* **chew'iest**.
chew'ing-gum *n.* a preparation made from sweetened and flavoured gum.
chew the cud 1 to chew a second time food already swallowed (as a cow does). **2** to think deeply.

chic *shēk, adj.* stylish.—Also *n.*
chicanery *shi-kā'nė-ri, n.* dishonest cleverness in argument.
chick *chik, n.* a baby bird.
chick'en *n.* **1** a young hen, etc. **2** the flesh of a fowl. **3** a chicken-hearted person (also *adj.*)
chick'en-heart'ed *adj.* cowardly.
chick'enpox *n.* a contagious disease with fever and blister-like spots.
chick'weed *n.* a garden weed liked by fowls and cage birds.
chicory *chik'ȯ-ri, n.* **1** a plant with blue flowers. **2** its carrot-like root (ground to mix with coffee).
chide *chīd, v.t.* to scold, rebuke:—*pr.p.* **chid'ing**; *pa.t.* **chīd'ed, chid**; *pa.p.* **chīd'ed, chidd'en, chid**.
chīd'ing *n.* and *adj.*
chief *chēf, adj.* **1** head. **2** most important.—*n.* **1** the head of a clan or tribe. **2** the head of a department or business.
chief'ly *adv.* mainly.
chief'tain *(-tin) n.* the head of a clan.
chiffon *shif'on, shē-fon^g, n.* a thin gauzy material.
chilblain *chil'blān, n.* a red swelling, esp. on hands and feet, in cold weather.
child *chīld, n.* **1** a very young person. **2** a son or daughter:—*pl.* **chil'dren** *(chil').*
child'hood *n.* the state or time of being a child.
child'ish *adj.* **1** like the ways or interests of a child. **2** silly.
child'ishly *adv.* **child'ishness** *n.*
child'like *adj.* like a child, innocent.
child'birth *n.* the process of a mother giving birth to a child.
child's play an easy task.
chili. Same as **chilli**.
chill *chil, n.* **1** coldness. **2** a cold that causes shivering.—Also *adj.*—*v.t.* and *v.i.* to make, or to grow, cold.—*v.t.* to discourage: *to chill someone's enthusiasm.*
chill'y *adj.* cold:—*comp.* **chill'ier**; *superl.* **chill'iest**.
chill'ness, chill'iness *ns.*
chilli *chil'i, n.* the pod of a capsicum, used in sauces, etc., or, dried and ground, as cayenne pepper:—*pl.* **chill'i(e)s**.
chime *chīm, n.* **1** a set of bells tuned in a scale. **2** the ringing of bells in succession. **3** the bell(s) in a clock with which it strikes the hour.—Also *v.t.* and *v.i.*:—*pr.p.* **chim'-ing**.
chimney *chim'ni, n.* a passage for the escape of smoke, etc., from a fireplace or furnace.
chim'ney-pot *n.* a pipe at the top of a chimney to increase draught.
chim'ney-piece *n.* a shelf over the fireplace.
chim'ney-stack *n.* **1** a group of chimneys carried up together. **2** a very tall chimney.
chim'ney-stalk *n.* a chimney-stack (*def.* 2).
chim'ney-sweep *n.* one who cleans chimneys.
chimpanzee *chim-pan-zē', also chim', n.* an African ape, the most man-like of the apes.
chin *chin, n.* the jutting part of the face below the mouth.
china *chīn'ȧ, n.* fine kind of earthenware orig. made in *China*, porcelain.
china clay a fine white clay used in making porcelain, kaolin.
chinchilla *chin-chil'ȧ, n.* **1** a small rodent of South America. **2** its soft grey fur.
chine *chīn, n.* a piece of the backbone (esp. of a pig) with adjoining flesh for cooking.
Chinese *chīn-ēz', n.* **1** a native of *China* (*pl.* **Chinese**'). **2** the language of China.—Also *adj.*
Chinese lantern a paper lantern.
chink[1] *chingk, n.* a narrow opening.
chink[2] *chingk, n.* clink, as of coins.—Also *v.i., v.t.*
chintz *chints, n.* cotton printed in several colours.
chip *chip, v.t.* to strike small pieces off.—Also *v.i.*:—*pr.p.* **chipp'ing**; *pa.p.* **chipped**.—*n.* **1** a small piece chipped off, or (in e.g. china) place damaged in this way. **2** a small piece of potato fried. **3** a counter used in games. **4** a minute piece of silicon or other material on which one or more microcircuits can be printed (also **mi'crochip**).
chip in to interrupt, interpose.
chipmunk *chip'mungk, n.*' a small striped North Amer. squirrel.
chiropodist *ki-rop'ȯ-dist* (also *shi-, chi-*) *n.* one who treats corns, bunions, etc.
chirop'ody *n.* the treatment of corns, etc.
chiropractor *kī-rō-prak'tȯr, n.* one who heals certain disorders of the body by adjusting the position of the bones of the spine, etc.
chirp *chûrp, n.* the sharp, thin sound of certain birds and insects.—Also *v.i.*
chirp'y *adj.* **1** lively. **2** merry:—*comp.* **chirp'ier**; *superl.* **chirp'iest**.
chirp'ily *adv.* **chirp'iness** *n.*
chisel *chiz'ėl, n.* a tool with a cutting edge at the end.—*v.t.* to cut, carve, etc. with a chisel:—*pr.p.* **chis'elling**; *pa.p.* **chis'-elled**.

chit[1] *chit, n.* **1** a brief note. **2** an order or pass.—Also **chitt'y** (*pl.* **chitt'ies**).

chit[2] *chit, n.* (*slightingly*) a girl.

chivalry *shiv'ȧl-ri, n.* **1** the customs of feudal knights. **2** bravery and courtesy.
chiv'alrous *adj.* showing the qualities of an ideal knight, generous, courteous, etc.
chiv'alrously *adv.*

chive *chīv, n.* a herb like the leek and onion, used as flavouring.

chivy, **chivvy** *chiv'i, v.t.* **1** to chase. **2** to keep urging on, harass, annoy:—*pr.p.* **chiv(v)'ying**; *pa.p.* **chiv(v)'ied**.

chlorine *klö', klō'rēn, n.* an element, a yellowish-green gas with a suffocating smell—used in bleaching, disinfecting, etc.
chlo'ride *n.* any of certain compounds of chlorine (e.g. common salt, *sodium chloride*, which consists of chlorine and sodium).
chlo'rinate *v.t.* to treat with chlorine or a compound of chlorine (as in purifying water):—*pr.p.* **chlor'inating**.
chlorinā'tion *n.*
chloroform *klor'ȯ-förm, n.* a colourless liquid used as an anaesthetic.
chlor'ophyll *(-ȯ-fil) n.* the colouring matter of the green parts of plants.

chock *chok, v.t.* to fix with a wedge.—*n.* a wedge to keep e.g. a cask from rolling.
chock'-a-block', **chock'-full'** *adjs.* quite full.

chocolate *chok'ȯ-lit, n.* **1** a paste made from pounded seeds of the cacao tree. **2** a beverage or sweet made from this.—Also *adj.*

choice *chois, n.* **1** the act or power of choosing. **2** the thing chosen. **3** alternative.—*adj.* worthy of being chosen.

choir *kwīr, n.* **1** a chorus or band of singers. **2** the part of a church where the singers stand.
See also **choral** under **chorus**.

choke *chōk, v.t.* **1** to throttle. **2** to interfere with the breathing of. **3** to block.—*v.i.* to have the breathing checked by something in the throat:—*pr.p.* **chok'ing.**—*n.* **1** the action or sound of choking. **2** a device which controls the flow of air, etc.
chok'er *n.* a close-fitting necklace.

cholera *kol'ėr-ȧ, n.* a highly infectious deadly disease with bilious vomiting, etc.

cholesterol *kȯ-les'tėr-ol, n.* a fatty alcohol found in body tissues and fluids.

chomp *chomp, v.t.* and *v.i.* to munch noisily.

choose *chōōz, v.t.* **1** to take (one thing) rather than another. **2** to select (also *v.i.*). **3** to want, prefer, decide: *If he chooses to resign, let him*:—*pr.p.* **choos'ing**; *pa.t.* **chose** *(chōz)*; *pa.p.* **chos'en**.

choos'y, **choos'ey** *adj.* difficult to please, choosing with (too) great care:—*comp.* **choos'ier**; *superl.* **choos'iest**.
See also **choice**.

chop[1] *chop, v.t.* **1** to cut with a sudden blow. **2** to cut into small pieces:—*pr.p.* **chopp'ing.**—*n.* a slice of mutton or pork containing a rib.
chopp'er *n.* **1** one who, or somethat that, chops. **2** (*coll.*) a helicopter.
chopp'y *adj.* (of sea) running in irregular waves:—*comp.* **chopp'ier**; *superl.* **chopp'iest**.
chopp'iness *n.*

chop[2] *chop, n.* used in *pl.* **chops**, the jaws, mouth of an animal.—Also **chap(s)**.
chop'fallen (or more usu. **chap'-**) *adj.* dejected.

chop[3] *chop, v.i.* to shift, change direction.
chop and change to keep changing.

chopper, **choppy**. See **chop**[1].

chopsticks *chop'stiks, n.pl.* two small sticks of wood, ivory, etc., used by Chinese instead of a fork.

choral, **chorale**. See **chorus**.

chord[1] *körd, n.* (*music*) a number of notes sung or played together.

chord[2] *körd, n.* **1** an old alternative spelling of cord (*spinal, vocal, chord*). **2** (*geometry*) a straight line joining any two points on a curve.

chore *chōr, chör, n.* a piece of housework, or other hard or dull job.

choreography *kor-i-og'rȧ-fi, n.* **1** the art of arranging dances. **2** the arrangement of a ballet, etc.
choreog'rapher *n.*

chorister. See **chorus**.

chortle *chört'l, v.i.* to give a low deep laugh:—*pr.p.* **chort'ling.**—Also *n.*

chorus *kōr'ủs, kör', n.* **1** a group of singers. **2** the singers and dancers in a show. **3** the refrain of a song.—*v.t.* to sing or say together.
chor'al *adj.* to be sung by a choir.
chorale *(-äl') n.* a simple, slow tune for a psalm or hymn.
chor'ister *(kor') n.* a member of a choir.

chose, **chosen**. See **choose**.

chough *chuf, n.* the red-legged crow.

chow *chow, n.* a dog of a prob. Chinese breed.

Christ *krīst, n.* Jesus of Nazareth.
christen *(kris'n) v.t.* **1** to baptise in the name of Christ. **2** to give a name to.
Christendom *(kris'n-) n.* the part of the world in which Christianity is the recognised religion.
Christian *kris'chȧn, n.* a follower of

Christ.—Also *adj.*
Christian'ity *n.* **1** the religion of the followers of Christ. **2** the spirit of this religion.
Christian name a personal name given (as at christening), in addition to the surname; a forename.
Christian Science a religion which includes belief in healing by faith without medicine.

Christmas *kris'mȧs, n.* an annual festival in memory of the birth of Christ, held on December 25.
Christmas box (*old*) a box with a Christmas gift.
Christmas Eve (the evening of) December 24.
Christmas tree a fir, pine or artificial tree decorated at Christmas.

chromatic *krō-mat'ik, adj.* **1** of colours. **2** (*music*) proceeding by semitones: *chromatic scale*.
chrome *n.* **1** chromium, or a chromium compound. **2** something plated with chromium.
chrō'mium *n.* an element, a non-rusting metal whose compounds have beautiful colours.
chrō'mosome *n.* one of the rod-shaped bodies into which a cell nucleus divides, and in which the genes are located.

chron(o)- *kron(-ō)-*, (as part of a word) time.
chron'ic *adj.* **1** (esp. of a disease) lasting a long time. **2** constant, continual.
chron'ically *adv.*
chronicle *kron'i-kl, n.* a record of events in order of their happening.
chron'icler *n.* a writer of a chronicle.
chronograph *kron'ȯ-gräf, n.* an instrument for taking exact measurements of time (e.g. a stop watch).
chronological order the order in which events happened or will happen.
chronology *krȯn-ol'ȯ-ji, n.* order in time.
chronometer *krȯn-om'ė-tėr, n.* a very accurate form of timepiece.

chrysalis *kris'ȧ-lis, n.* **1** the pupa stage in the life-history of butterflies and moths which do not form cocoons. **2** the hard, often golden-coloured, skin covering the pupa.

chrysanthemum *kris-an'thė-mum, n.* an autumn garden flower related to the daisy, corn marigold, etc.

chub *chub, n.* a small fat river fish.
chubb'y *adj.* short and thick, plump.
chubb'iness *n.*

chuck[1] *chuk, n.* **1** the call of a hen. **2** a word of endearment.

chuck[2] *chuk, v.t.* **1** to pat gently (under the chin). **2** to throw.
chuck'er-out *n.* one who puts out undesirable people.

chuckle *chuk'l, n.* a quiet laugh.—Also *v.i.*:—*pr.p.* **chuck'ling**.

chum *chum, n.* a close companion.
chumm'y *adj.* (*coll.*) friendly:—*comp.* **chumm'ier**; *superl.* **chumm'iest**.
chumm'ily *adv.* **chumm'iness** *n.*

chunk *chungk, n.* a thick piece of anything, as wood, bread, etc.

church *chûrch, n.* **1** a building for public worship. **2** (*cap.*) the whole body of Christians.
churchwar'den *n.* **1** a layman who looks after the interests of a parish or church. **2** a long clay pipe.
church'yard *n.* the burial ground round a church.

churl *chûrl, n.* an ill-bred, surly person.
churl'ish *adj.*
churl'ishly *adv.* **churl'ishness** *n.*

churn *chûrn, n.* **1** a machine for making butter. **2** a large milk can.—*v.t.* **1** to make (butter). **2** to shake violently.—Also *v.i.*

chute *shōōt, n.* a sloping channel for sending down water, rubbish, etc.

chutney *chut'ni, n.* an East Indian sauce of mangoes, chillies, etc.

cicatrix *sik'ȧ-triks, n.* a scar over a wound that is healed:—*pl.* **cic'atrixes, cicatrī'cēs**.

cider *sī'dėr, n.* an alcoholic drink made from apples.

cigar *si-gär', n.* a roll of tobacco leaves for smoking.
cigarette' *n.* finely cut tobacco rolled in thin paper.

cinch *sinch, n.* **1** a horse's belly-band or girth. **2** (*coll.*) something done with ease. **3** (*coll.*) a certainty.

cinder *sin'dėr, n.* **1** partly burned coal. **2** (in *pl.*) ashes. **3** anything charred by fire.

cine- *sin'i-*, (as part of a word) moving picture.
cin'e-cam'era *n.* a camera for taking moving pictures.

cinematograph *sin-i-mat'ō-gräf, n.* an apparatus for projecting moving pictures.
cin'ema *n.* **1** a building in which motion pictures are shown. **2** (with *the*) the art, or business, of making motion pictures.

Cingalese. See **Sinhalese**.

cinnamon *sin'ȧ-mȯn, n.* the spicy bark of a tree of the laurel family in Ceylon.

cipher *sī'fėr, n.* **1** (*arithmetic*) the character 0. **2** a nonentity. **3** a monogram. **4** a secret way of writing or code.

circle *sûr'kl, n.* **1** a figure bounded by one line every point of which is equally distant from the centre. **2** a ring. **3** a company or group (of people).—*v.t.* to move round.—*v.i.* to move in circles:—*pr.p.* **cir'cling**.
cir'clet *n.* a little circle, esp. as ornamental headband.
See also **circular, circulate, encircle**.

circuit *sûr'kit, n.* **1** a journey or course round. **2** a journey or tour made regularly by judges, preachers, salesmen, etc. **3** the places on such a journey or tour. **4** the path of an electric current.
circū'itous *adj.* roundabout, not direct.
cir'cuitry *n.* the plan of, or components of, an electrical circuit.

circular *sûr'kū-lȧr, adj.* **1** round. **2** (of reasoning) leading back to where it started.—*n.* a notice, etc. sent to a number of persons.
cir'cularise *v.t.* to send circular(s) to:—*pr.p.* **cir'cularising**.
circular'ity *n.*
circular saw a steel disc with teeth for sawing wood, metal, etc., usu. power-driven.

circulate *sûr'kū-lāt, v.t.* and *v.i.* **1** (to cause) to go round in a fixed path. **2** (to cause) to go about generally; to spread:—*pr.p.* **cir'culating**.
circulā'tion *n.* **1** the act of moving in a closed path (as the blood in the veins). **2** the sale of a book or periodical.
cir'culatory *adj.*

circum- *sėr-kum'-, sûr'kum-,* (as part of a word) about, round.

circumcise *sûr'kum-sīz, v.t.* **1** to remove the foreskin of (a male). **2** to perform a similar operation on (a female):—*pr.p.* **cir'cumcising**.
circumcis'ion *n.*

circumference *sėr-kum'fėr-ėns, n.* the boundary line, esp. of a circle.

circumflex *sûr'kum-fleks, n.* an accent (ˆ), orig. showing rising and falling of the voice, on a vowel or syllable.—Also *adj.*

circumlocution *sûr-kum-lō-kū'sh(ȯ)n, n.* a roundabout phrase or way of speaking.

circumnavigate *sûr-kum-nav'i-gāt, v.t.* to sail round (esp. the world):—*pr.p.* **circumnav'igating**.
circumnavigā'tion *n.*
circumnav'igator *n.*

circumscribe *sûr-kum-skrīb', sûr', v.t.* **1** to draw a line round. **2** to draw (one figure) so as to enclose another, the outer touching the inner at as many points as possible. **3** to confine, restrict:—*pr.p.* **circumscribing**.

circumspect *sûr'kum-spekt, adj.* looking round on all sides, cautious, prudent.
cir'cumspectly *adv.*
circumspec'tion, cir'cumspectness *ns.*

circumstance *sûr'kum-stans, n.* **1** a fact or event. **2** (in *pl.*) the time, place, etc. of an act or event. **3** the state of one's affairs: *in bad circumstances* (poor). **4** ceremony: *pomp and circumstance.*
circumstantial *(-stan'shȧl) adj.* giving details that make the story look like the truth.
circumstantial evidence evidence that makes a conclusion seem likely though it does not give direct proof.

circumvent *sûr-kum-vent', v.t.* **1** to prevent (a person) from carrying out a plan. **2** to outwit (a person).

circus *sûr'kus, n.* **1** a travelling show with performances by horsemen, acrobats, animals, etc. **2** (esp. in street names) a group of houses in a circle.

cistern *sis'tėrn, n.* a tank, etc., for storing water or other liquid.

citadel *sit'ȧ-dėl, n.* a fortress in or near a city.

cite *sīt, v.t.* **1** to summon, esp. to appear in court. **2** to quote as an example or as proof.—*pr.p.* **cit'ing**.
citā'tion (*sī-,* or *si-*) *n.* **1** something quoted. **2** a summons to appear in court. **3** official recognition of an achievement, brave act, etc.

citizen *sit'i-zėn, n.* **1** an inhabitant of a city or town. **2** a member of a state.
cit'izenship *n.* the status, and the rights and or duties, of a citizen.
See also **civic, civil, city**.

citron *sit'rȯn, n.* the fruit of the citron tree, resembling a lemon.
citric acid the acid to which lemons and certain other fruits owe their sourness.
citrus fruit a citron, lemon, orange, lime, etc.

city *sit'i, n.* **1** a large town. **2** a town with a corporation or cathedral. **3** the business centre or orig. area of large town:—*pl.* **cit'ies**.
the City that part of London regarded as the centre of business.

civet *siv'it, n.* a perfume obtained from the **civet(-cat)**, a small flesh-eating animal of Africa, India, etc.

civic *siv'ik, adj.* of a city or citizen.
civ'ics *n.sing.* the study of one's duties as a citizen.

civil *siv'il, adj.* **1** of the state or community: *civil affairs.* **2** of ordinary citizens, ordin-

ary, as opposed to military or ecclesiastical: *in civil life.* **3** (of law cases) concerned with rights and the remedy of injuries other than criminal. **4** polite (*opp.* **unciv'il**).
civ'illy *adv.*
civil'ity *n.* politeness:—*opp.* **incivility**.
civil'ian *n.* one engaged in civil as distinguished from military pursuits.
civilise *siv'il-īz, v.t.* **1** to change the ways of (a primitive people) to those found in a more advanced type of society. **2** to make more refined and polite:—*pr.p.* **civ'ilising**.
civilisā'tion *n.* **1** the state of being civilised. **2** civilised peoples.
civil defence protection of the civilian population against the effects of enemy attack in wartime.
civil engineer. See **engineer**.
civil liberties the rights of a citizen according to the law of the country.
civil list the expenses of the sovereign's household.
civil servant a member of the **civil service**, the paid service of the state, not including navy, army, and air force.
civil war a war between citizens of the same state.

clad *klad, adj.* **1** clothed. **2** covered: *an ivy-clad wall*; *an armour-clad warship.*—*v.t.* to cover, face (one material) with another:—*pr.p.* **cladd'ing**; *pa.p.* **clad**.
cladd'ing *n.*
See **clothe**.

claim *klām, v.t.* **1** to demand as a right. **2** to assert (often with *that*).—*n.* **1** a demand for something supposed due. **2** a demand for payment of compensation, etc. **3** an assertion (that something is a fact). **4** a piece of land allotted e.g. to a miner.
claim'ant *n.* one who makes a claim.
lay claim to make a claim (to).
See also **disclaim**.

clairvoyance *klār-voi'ȧns, n.* the power of seeing things not present to the ordinary senses.
clairvoy'ant *n.* and *adj.*

clam *klam, n.* **1** a shellfish with two shells hinged together. **2** a silent or secretive person.

clamber *klam'bėr, v.i.* to climb by grasping with hands and feet.—Also *n.*

clammy *klam'i, adj.* moist and sticky (and usu. cold):—*comp.* **clamm'ier**; *superl.* **clamm'iest**.
clamm'iness *n.*

clamour *klam'ȯr, n.* **1** a loud demand. **2** uproar.—Also *v.i.*
clam'orous *adj.* **1** noisy. **2** making loud demands.
clam'orously *adv.*

clamp *klamp, n.* a piece of timber, iron etc. used to fasten things together or to strengthen a framework.—*v.t.* to fasten with a clamp.
clamp down on to stop the activity of, suppress.

clan *klan, n.* a tribe or group of families under a single chieftain, commonly having the same surname.
clann'ish *adj.* closely united and showing little interest in people not of the clan or group.
clans'man *n.* a member of a clan.

clandestine *klan-des'tin, -tīn, klan', adj.* secret, hidden.

clang *klang, v.i.* to produce a loud, deep, ringing sound.—Also *v.t.* and *n.*
clangour *klang'gȯr, n.* a loud, ringing noise.

clank *klangk, n.* a sound such as is made by a heavy chain.—Also *v.i.* and *v.t.*

clannish, etc. See **clan**.

clap *klap, n.* **1** a sudden blow. **2** the noise made by two things striking together. **3** a burst of sound, e.g. thunder.—*v.t.* **1** to strike, thrust, together. **2** (*Scot.*) to pat with the hand. **3** to applaud with the hands. **4** to put suddenly: *to clap a person in prison.*—Also *v.i.*:—*pr.p.* **clapp'ing**; *pa.p.* **clapped**.
clapp'er *n.* the tongue of a bell.
clap'trap *n.* **1** insincere, empty words. **2** nonsense.
clap eyes on to catch sight of.

claret *klar'it, n.* a red wine of Bordeaux.

clarify *klar'i-fī, v.t.* and *v.i.* to make, or become, clear:—*pr.p.* **clar'ifying**; *pa.p.* **clar'ified**.
clarificā'tion *n.*

clarinet *klar-in-et'*, or *klar', n.* a wind instrument, usu. of wood.
clarinett'ist *n.*

clarion *klar'i-ȯn, n.* a clear, rousing note.
clarion call a clear, loud call to action.

clarity. See **clear**.

clash *klash, n.* **1** a loud noise as of weapons striking together: **2** a fight or disagreement.—*v.i.* **1** to dash noisily (against, into). **2** to disagree. **3** to take place at the same time. **4** not to look well together, with.—*v.t.* to strike noisily together.

clasp *kläsp, n.* **1** a fastening made of linking parts. **2** a bar on a medal ribbon. **3** an embrace. **4** a grasp, handshake.—*v.t.* **1** to fasten with a clasp. **2** to grasp. **3** to embrace.

clasp'-knife, *n.* a knife whose blade folds into the handle.

class *kläs, n.* **1** a group of persons or things alike in some way. **2** a division according to quality, etc. (e.g. *first class*). **3** the system of dividing people into social classes, as upper, middle, lower. **4** a number of students or scholars taught together.—*v.t.* to place in a class.

classify *klas'i-fī, v.t.* **1** to arrange in classes. **2** to put into a class or category (see also **classified** *adj.*):—*pr.p.* **class'-ifying**; *pa.p.* **class'ified**.

classificā'tion *n.*

class'ified *adj.* **1** (of information) on the secret list. **2** (of a road) entitled to receive a government grant.

class'-con'scious *adj.* very much aware of belonging to a certain class in society.

class legislation laws favouring one section of the community.

class'mate *n.* a pupil in the same class.

class war a struggle between different classes in the community.

classical *klas'i-kl, adj.* **1** (of literature) considered to be of the highest class. **2** of ancient Greece or Rome, or both.

class'ic *adj.* standard, stock: *the classic example* (the example usu. given).

the classics classical literature, esp. that of Greece and Rome.

classify, etc. See **class**.

clatter *klat'ėr, n.* **1** a rattling noise: *the clatter of pots and pans.* **2** noisy talk.—Also *v.i.* and *v.t.*

clause *klöz, n.* **1** part of a sentence with subject and predicate. **2** a section of a contract, will, or act.

claustrophobia *klös-trō-fō'bi-ȧ, n.* dread of narrow or closed places.

claustropho'bic *adj.*

clavicle *klav'i-kl, n.* the collar-bone.

claw *klö, n.* **1** the hooked nail of an animal or bird. **2** the leg of a crab, insect, etc., or its pointed end or pincer.—*v.t.* to scratch or tear with the claw(s).

clay *klā, n.* **1** a soft, sticky, earthy material. **2** earth in general. **3** the human body.

clay'ey *adj.*:—*comp.* **clay'ier**; *superl.* **clay'iest**.

claymore *klā'mōr, -mör, n.* a large sword formerly used by Scottish Highlanders.

clean *klēn, adj.* **1** free from dirt. **2** pure. **3** guiltless. **4** neat. **5** complete (e.g. *a clean sweep*). **6** (of a driving licence) without endorsements for motoring offences.—*adv.* **1** quite. **2** entirely.—*v.t.* and *v.i.* to make, or to become, clean.

clean'er *n.*

cleanly[1] *klēn'li, adv.* **clean'ness** *n.*

cleanly[2] *klen'li, adj.* clean, esp. as a habit:—*comp.* **clean'lier**; *superl.* **clean'-liest**.

clean'liness *(klen') n.*

cleanse *klenz, v.t.* to make clean or pure:—*pr.p.* **cleans'ing**.

cleans'er *n.* that which cleanses, e.g. a liquid which removes make-up.

clean'-cut' *adj.* **1** neat. **2** neat and respectable in appearance.

clean'-limbed' *adj.* well-proportioned, handsome.

clean'-sha'ven *adj.* without beard or moustache.

a clean slate **1** a fresh start. **2** a record without a stain on it.

a clean sweep. See **sweep**.

have clean hands to be free from guilt.

make a clean breast of to own up to (something).

clear *klēr, adj.* **1** bright, undimmed: *a clear light.* **2** free from obstruction or difficulty. **3** plain, distinct: *clear writing.* **4** easily understood. **5** obvious: *It is clear that he will not help us.*—*adv.* **1** plainly. **2** wholly. **3** away from: *Stand clear of the gates!*—*v.t.* **1** to make clear. **2** to empty. **3** to free from suspicion, acquit. **4** to leap, or pass, by or over. **5** to make a profit of: *He cleared £50 on the deal.* **6** to set (a ship) free for sailing.—*v.i.* to become clear.

clear'ly *adv.*

clear'ness, **clarity** *(klar'i-ti) ns.*

clear'ance *n.* **1** the act of clearing. **2** a certificate that a ship has satisfied all demands of the custom house and has permission to sail. **3** the distance between two objects, or between a moving and a stationary part of a machine.

clear'ing *n.* **1** the act of making clear. **2** land cleared of wood, etc., for cultivation.

clear'-cut *adj.* **1** with clear outline. **2** plain and definite.

clear'way *n.* a stretch of road on which motorists are forbidden to stop.

clear out **1** to get rid of. **2** to empty. **3** to go away (also **clear off**).

clear up to make, or become, clear.

See also **clarify**.

cleat *klēt, n.* **1** a wedge. **2** a piece of wood nailed across something to keep it firm. **3** a projecting piece of wood or metal with two arms to which ropes are made fast.

cleave[1] *klēv, v.t.* **1** to split. **2** to make (a way through):—*pr.p.* **cleav'ing**; *pa.t.* **cleft**, **clōve**; *pa.p.* **cleft**, **clō'ven**.

cleav'age *n.* **1** the act of splitting. **2** the way in which two things are split or divided. **3** the hollow between the breasts.

cleav'er *n.* a butcher's chopper.
cleft *n.* **1** an opening made by splitting. **2** a crack, chink.
cloven hoof **1** a hoof, like those of cows, sheep, etc., which is divided, not solid. **2** a sign of the devil or of an evil nature.

cleave[2] *klēv*, *v.i.* **1** to stick. **2** to remain faithful (to):—*pr.p.* **cleav'ing**; *pa.p.* and *pa.t.* **cleaved.**

clef *klef*, *n.* (*music*) a sign on the stave fixing the pitch of the notes.

cleft. See **cleave**[1].

clematis *klem'ȧ-tis*, *n.* a creeping plant.

clement *klem'ėnt*, *adj.* **1** merciful. **2** (of weather) mild (*opp.* **inclement**).
clem'ency *n.*

clementine *kle'mėn-tēn*, *-tīn*, *n.* a type of small orange.

clench *klench*, or *-sh*, *v.t.* **1** to close tightly (e.g. fist, teeth). **2** to grasp.

clergy *klûr'ji*, *n.* the ministers of the Christian, or sometimes another, religion.
cler'gyman *n.* one of the Christian clergy, a regularly ordained minister.
cler'ic *n.* a clergyman.
clerical *kler'ik-ȧl*, *adj.* of the clergy.

clerical[1]. See **clergy**.

clerical[2]. See **clerk**.

clerk *klärk (U.S. klûrk)*, *n.* **1** one who leads the responses in the English Church service. **2** an official in charge of correspondence, records, transactions of a court or corporation. **3** one who deals with letters, accounts, etc. in an office.
cler'ical *(kler')* *adj.* of a clerk or of one who copies: *a clerical error*.
clerk'ess *n.* a female clerk.
clerk of works one who superintends the erection of a building, etc.

clever *klev'ėr*, *adj.* **1** able. **2** skilful.
clev'erly *adv.* **clev'erness** *n.*

cliché *klē'shā*, *n.* a phrase too often used.

click *klik*, *n.* a short, sharp sound like a tick.—Also *v.i.*

client *klī'ėnt*, *n.* **1** one who employs or consults a lawyer, broker, etc. **2** a customer.
clientele, **clientele** *klē-ong-tel*, *klī-ėn-tel'*, *n.* a group of clients.

cliff *klif*, *n.* **1** a high steep rock. **2** the steep side of a mountain.
cliff'-hanger *n.* **1** a very exciting adventure or contest. **2** an ending (of an episode) that leaves one in suspense.

climate *klī'mit*, *n.* **1** the weather conditions of a region (temperature, moisture, etc.). **2** the (e.g. economic) conditions in a country, etc.
climat'ic *adj.* **climat'ically** *adv.*

climax *klī'maks*, *n.* **1** the highest point. **2** the most dramatic moment.

climb *klīm*, *v.i.* or *v.t.* **1** to go up, rise, ascend, esp. with difficulty. **2** (of plants) to ascend by clinging to (an object).—*v.i.* to slope upward.—*n.* **1** ascent. **2** a place to be climbed.
climb'er *n.* **climb'ing** *n.* and *adj.*
climb down **1** to come down, esp. using hands and feet. **2** to become more humble, take back what one has said (*n.* **climb'-down**)

clime *klīm*, (*rather poetical*: often in *pl.*) *n.* **1** region. **2** climate.

clinch *klinch*, or *-sh*, *v.t.* **1** to fasten (a nail) by bending down the point. **2** to settle or confirm (an argument, a bargain).—*v.i.* to grapple (with).—*n.* **1** the act of clinching. **2** in boxing, a position in which the boxers hold each other with their arms. **3** a passionate embrace.

cling *kling*, *v.i.* **1** to stick close. **2** to be fond of and too dependent on a person (with *to*). **3** to refuse to give up: *to cling to a belief*.—*pa.t.* and *pa.p.* **clung.**
cling'film *n.* thin transparent plastic material used to wrap food.

clinic *klin'ik*, *n.* **1** a private hospital. **2** a place where out-patients are treated or advised.
clin'ical *adj.* **1** of or involving patients. **2** having to do with observing in a cool, unemotional way.

clink[1] *klingk*, *n.* a ringing sound made by striking metal, etc.—Also *v.i.* and *v.t.*
clink'er *n.* hard cinder formed in furnaces.

clink[2] *klingk*, *n.* (*coll.*) prison.

clip[1] *klip*, *v.t.* **1** to cut with shears. **2** to trim. **3** to shorten (words) in speaking indistinctly:—*pr.p.* **clipp'ing**; *pa.p.* **clipped.** —*n.* a smart blow.
clipp'er *n.* **1** a type of fast sailing-ship. **2** (in *pl.*) a tool for clipping.
clip someone's wings to take away from (a person) power to reach his ambition.

clip[2] *klip*, *v.t.* to fasten with a clip:—*pr.p.* **clipp'ing**; *pa.p.* **clipped.**—*n.* a fastener for holding (e.g. papers) together.

clique *klēk*, *n.* a group of people who are friendly with each other but exclude others.
cliqu'ish, **cliquey**, **cliquy** *adjs.*

cloak *klōk*, *n.* **1** a loose outer garment. **2** something which hides one's activities, intentions, etc.—*v.t.* **1** to put a cloak on. **2** to cover. **3** to hide.

cloak'room *n.* **1** a room for coats, hats, etc. **2** a lavatory.

clock *klok*, *n.* an instrument for measuring time.

clock'wise *adv.* in the direction of the movement of the hands of a clock:—*opp.* **anticlockwise**.

clock'work *n.* **1** the machinery of a clock. **2** machinery as steady and regular as that of a clock.

clock in, **on**, **out**, **off** to register the time of arrival at, or of leaving, work.

clock up (*coll.*) to reach (a certain speed, score, etc.).

like clockwork very steadily, without faults or hitches.

round the clock for all of a twenty-four hour day.

clod *klod*, *n.* **1** a thick lump, esp. of earth. **2** a stupid fellow.

clod'hopper *n.* **1** a rustic. **2** a lout.

clog *klog*, *n.* **1** a block of wood that hinders movement. **2** anything that hinders. **3** a shoe with a wooden sole. **4** a wooden shoe. —*v.t.* to choke and stop:—*pr.p.* **clogg'ing**; *pa.p.* **clogged**.

cloister *klois'tėr*, *n.* **1** a covered arcade forming part of a monastery or college. **2** a monastery or nunnery.

clois'tered *adj.* living away from the busy world.

clone *klōn*, *n.* a group of identical organisms reproduced from a single parent cell. —*v.t.* to produce a clone:—*pr.p.* **clon'ing.**

close[1] *klōs*, *adj.* **1** to shut up. **2** with no opening. **3** hot and airless. **4** stingy (also **close'-fist'ed**). **5** near, in time or place. **6** intimate: *a close friend*. **7** unwilling to tell much, secretive. **8** (of argument, examination, etc.) careful, with no weak spots.—*n.* **1** a narrow entry off a street. **2** the enclosed place round a cathedral.

close('ly) *advs.* **close'ness** *n.*

close call, **shave** a narrow escape.

close harmony harmony in which the notes of the chords are close together.

close'-knit' *adj.* (of a community, etc.) closely united in friendship, etc.

close season the time of the year when it is illegal to kill certain game or fish.

close'-up *n.* a photograph or film taken near at hand and thus big in scale.

See also **close**[2].

close[2] *klōz*, *v.t.* **1** to shut. **2** to end. **3** to conclude (e.g. a bargain).—*v.i.* **1** to come together. **2** to grapple (with). **3** to agree (with). **4** to come to an end:—*pr.p.* **clos'-ing.**—*n.* a pause or stop.

closure *klōzh'ür*, *n.* **1** the end, closing (of something). **2** the stopping of a parliamentary debate by vote of the House.

closed circuit an electrical circuit in which there is a complete path, with no break, for the current to flow along.—*adj.* (with *hyphen*; of television) transmitted and reproduced for a special audience, not sent out to the general public.

closed shop a factory, etc. in which only members of a trade union, or a particular trade union, will be employed.

close down **1** to shut up. **2** to bring, or come, to an end (*n.* **close'-down**).

closet *kloz'it*, *n.* **1** a recess off a room. **2** a small private room.—*v.t.* to shut up in, or take into, a room for a conference:—*pr.p.* **clos'eting**; *pa.p.* **clos'eted**.

clot *klot*, *n.* **1** a mass stuck together of soft or fluid matter, as blood. **2** a fool.—*v.t.* and *v.i.* to form into clots:—*pr.p.* **clott'ing**; *pa.p.* **clott'ed**.

cloth *kloth*, *n.* **1** woven material from which garments, coverings, etc., are made. **2** a piece of this. **3** a tablecloth.

clothe *klō*TH, *v.t.* **1** to cover with garments. **2** to provide with clothes:—*pr.p.* **cloth'ing** (-TH-); *pa.t.*, *pa.p.* **clōthed** (-TH-), **clad**.

clothes *klō*TH*z*, *n.pl.* garments.

clothier *klō*TH*'i-ėr*, *n.* one who makes or sells clothes.

clothing *klō*TH*'ing*, *n.* clothes.

cloud *clowd*, *n.* **1** a mass consisting of tiny particles of water, often in a frozen state, floating in the atmosphere. **2** a great number. **3** a great volume (of dust or smoke). **4** something causing gloom.—*v.t.* **1** to overspread with clouds. **2** to darken. **3** to stain.—*v.i.* to become clouded or darkened.

cloud'y *adj.* **1** darkened with clouds. **2** gloomy. **3** not clear or transparent:—*comp.* **cloud'ier**; *superl.* **cloud'iest**.

cloud'ily *adv.* **cloud'iness** *n.*

cloud'burst *n.* a sudden heavy shower of rain over a small area.

under a cloud in trouble or disgrace.

clout *klowt*, *n.* **1** a piece of cloth. **2** a blow. **3** (*coll.*) influence, power.

clove[1] *klōv*, *n.* the flower bud of the **clove tree**, dried as a spice.

clove[2] *klōv*, *n.* a segment of a bulb, as garlic.

clove[3], **cloven**. See **cleave**[1].

clover *klōv'ėr*, *n.* a plant with leaves in three parts, used for fodder.

clov'erleaf *n.* a traffic arrangement in which one road passes above another and the roads connecting the two are in the pattern of a four-leaved clover.

live in clover to live luxuriously.

clown *klown*, *n.* **1** a buffoon, jester, in a circus, etc. **2** one who behaves ridiculously

and without dignity, a fool.
clown'ish *adj.*

cloy *kloi*, *v.t.* to weary with too much (esp. of sweetness):—*pr.p.* **cloy'ing**; *pa.p.* **cloyed**.

club *klub*, *n.* **1** a heavy stick. **2** a bat or stick used in certain games (e.g. golf, hockey). **3** a number of persons meeting for study, games, etc. **4** the place where these people meet. **5** (in *pl.*) one of the four card suits (marks on Spanish cards are club-shaped).—*v.t.* to beat with a club.—*v.i.* to join (together), put money into a joint fund, for some purpose:—*pr.p.* **clubb'ing**; *pa.p.* **clubbed**.

cluck *kluk*, *n.* **1** the call of a hen to her chickens. **2** any sound like it.—Also *v.i.*

clue *klōō*, *n.* anything that helps to lead to the solution of a mystery, puzzle, etc.

clump *klump*, *n.* a cluster (e.g. of trees or shrubs).—*v.i.* to walk heavily.

clumsy *klum'zi*, *adj.* **1** awkward in shape or movement. **2** tactless, not skilfully made or carried out: *a clumsy apology*:—*comp.* **clum'sier**; *superl.* **clum'siest**.
clum'sily *adv.* **clum'siness** *n.*

clung. See **cling**.

cluster *klus'tėr*, *n.* **1** a bunch. **2** a group.—Also *v.i.* and *v.t.*

clutch[1] *kluch*, *v.t.* **1** to grasp. **2** to hold tightly.—*n.* **1** control (usu. in *pl.*): *to fall into his clutches.* **2** a device by which two moving parts of a machine may be connected or disconnected.

clutch[2] *kluch*, *n.* **1** a brood of chickens. **2** a number of eggs on which a bird sits at one time.

clutter *klut'ėr*, *n.* **1** confusion, untidiness. **2** a collection of objects in a crowded or muddled state.—*v.t.* **1** to put in a crowded, muddled way. **2** (also **clutter up**) to cover or fill in an untidy or crowded way.

co- *kō-*, *pfx.* meaning working, living, etc. together.

coach *kōch*, *n.* **1** a large, four-wheeled carriage. **2** a railway carriage. **3** a bus for tourists, etc. **4** a private tutor. **5** a trainer in athletics.—*v.t.* to prepare (a person) for examination, contest, etc.
coach'man *n.* the driver of an old horse-drawn carriage.

coagulate *kō-ag'ū-lāt*, *v.t.* and *v.i.* (to cause) to become a thickened mass:—*pr.p.* **coag'ulating**.
coagulā'tion *n.*

coal *kōl*, *n.* a black mineral (formed long ago from wood) that will burn.—*v.t.* and *v.i.* to supply with, or take in, coal.
coal'-bunk'er *n.* a box for holding coal.
coal'-face *n.* the exposed surface of coal in a mine.
coal'field *n.* a district where there is coal to be mined.
coal'-gas *n.* the mixture of gases obtained from coal, used for lighting and heating.
coal'-mine, -pit *n.* a mine or pit from which coal is dug.
coal'-tar *n.* a thick, black liquid formed e.g. when gas is made from coal.
haul over the coals to scold, reprimand.
See also **collier**.

coalesce *kō-ȧl-es'*, *v.i.* to grow together, unite:—*pr.p.* **coalesc'ing**.
coalesc'ence *n.*
coalition *kō-ȧl-ish'(ȯ)n*, *n.* an alliance, esp. of states or of political parties.

coarse *kōrs*, *körs*, *adj.* **1** common. **2** rough. **3** rude.
coarse'ly *adv.* **coarse'ness** *n.*
coars'en *v.t.* and *v.i.* to make, or become, coarse.
coarse'-grained' *adj.* **1** large in grain, as wood. **2** lacking in fine feelings.

coast *kōst*, *n.* the border of land next to the sea.—*v.i.* **1** to sail along or near a coast. **2** to travel downhill in a vehicle without using an engine.
coast'al *adj.* of the coast.
coast'er *n.* **1** a vessel that sails along the coast. **2** a mat for a glass, mug, or the like.
coast'guard *n.* **1** a man, or (now also) woman, employed to watch the coast for smugglers, ships in distress, etc. **2** coastguards as a body.
the coast is clear there is no obstacle or danger in the way.

coat *kōt*, *n.* **1** an outer garment with sleeves. **2** the hair or wool of an animal. **3** any covering (e.g. one of paint).—*v.t.* to cover with a coat or layer.
coat'ing *n.* a covering.
coat of arms a family badge or crest.
coat of mail a piece of armour for the upper part of the body made of metal plates or of linked metal rings.

coax *kōks*, *v.t.* to persuade by flattery, patient and gentle treatment, etc.

cob *kob*, *n.* **1** a short-legged strong horse. **2** a male swan. **3** (also **cob'nut**) a large hazelnut. **4** a corncob.

cobalt *kō'bölt*, *n.* an element, a silver-white metal, with compounds that give a blue colouring matter.

cobble[1], **cobblestone** *kob'l(stōn)* *ns.* a rounded stone used in paving.

cobble[2] *kob'l, v.t.* **1** to mend (shoes, etc.). **2** to patch or mend. esp. badly:—*pr.p.* **cobb'ling.**
cobb'ler *n.* one who mends shoes.

coble, cobble[3] *kōb'l, kob'l, ns.* a small flat-bottomed fishing-boat.

cobra *kō'brȧ, kob'rȧ, n.* a poisonous snake which swells out its neck so that it resembles a hood.

cobweb *kob'web, n.* **1** the spider's web. **2** anything flimsy.

coca *kō'kȧ, n.* a shrub whose leaves yield **cocaine** *(kō-kān')*, a drug sometimes used as a local anaesthetic and also taken by drug-addicts.

cochineal *koch'i-nēl, n.* a scarlet dye, from dried bodies of an insect found on a cactus in Mexico, etc.

cock *kok, n.* **1** the male of birds, esp. of the domestic fowl. **2** a weathercock. **3** a tap for liquor. **4** the hammer in the lock of a gun.—*v.t.* **1** to set upright. **2** to draw back the cock of (a gun). **3** to tilt up (e.g. the brim of a hat).
cock'er (spaniel) *n.* a small kind of spaniel.
cock'erel *n.* a young cock.
cock'y *adj.* conceited, cocksure, too confident:—*comp.* **cock'ier**; *superl.* **cock'iest**.
cock'iness *n.*
cock-and-bull story an absurd, unbelievable one.
cock'chafer *(-chā-fėr) n.* a large greyish-brown beetle.
cock'crow, -ing *n.* early morning.
cock'fight *n.* a fight between gamecocks.
cock'fighting *n.*
cock'pit *n.* **1** a pit or enclosed space where gamecocks fought. **2** a place where many battles have been fought. **3** a compartment in an aircraft for the pilot, etc., in a small ship for the steersman, in a racing car for the driver(s).
cock'sure *adj.* **1** very sure. **2** too confident.
cock'tail *n.* a mixture of drinks, used as an appetiser.

cockade *kok-ād', n.* a rosette worn on the hat as a badge.

cockatoo *kok-ȧ-to͞o', n.* a parrot with a large crest.

cockchafer, cocker, cockerel, cockfight, etc. See **cock**.

cockle *kok'l, n.* a shellfish with a hinged, heart-shaped shell.
cock'leshell *n.* **1** the shell of a cockle. **2** a frail boat.

cockney *kok'ni,* (also *cap.*) *n.* a native of the City of London:—*pl.* **cock'neys.**

cockpit. See **cock**.

cockroach *kok'rōch, n.* a household pest, a beetle-like insect.

cocksure, cocktail, cocky. See **cock**.

coco *kō'kō, n.* a palm tree (*pl.* **cō'cōs**) producing the **co'conut**, a large nut containing a white solid lining and a clear liquid.
coconut matting matting made from the husk of the coconut.

cocoa *kō'kō, n.* **1** the seed of the cacao tree. **2** a powder and drink made from the seeds.

cocoon *kȯ-ko͞on', n.* the silk sheath spun by many insect larvae, e.g. silkworms, and by spiders for their eggs.

cod *kod,* **codfish** *kod'fish, ns.* a food fish of northern seas.
cod'ling *n.* a small cod.
cod'-liver oil an oil obtained from cod's liver.

coddle *kod'l, v.t.* to pamper, over-protect, treat as an invalid:—*pr.p.* **codd'ling.**

code *kōd, n.* **1** a collection of laws or of rules: *the Highway Code.* **2** a standard of behaviour: *code of conduct.* **3** a secret system of words, letters, or symbols.
cōd'ify *v.t.* to classify, arrange in an orderly way:—*pr.p.* **cod'ifying;** *pr.p.* **cod'ified.**
code'-name, -number *ns.* a name, number, used for convenience, secrecy, etc. instead of a person's real name.

codicil *kod'i-sil, n.* a short addition to a will or treaty.

codify. See **code**.

co-education *kō-ed-ū-kā'sh(ȯ)n, n.* education of pupils or students of both sexes in the same school or college.
co-educā'tional *adj.*

coerce *kō-ûrs', v.t.* to compel (a person, an action): *I coerced him into going*; *to coerce obedience:*—*pr.p.* **coer'cing.**
coer'cion *kō-ûr'sh(ȯ)n, n.*

co-exist *kō-egz-ist', -igz-, v.i.* to exist at the same time.
co-exist'ence *n.*
peaceful co-existence living peacefully beside people who hold different views from oneself.

coffee *kof'i, n.* a drink made from the ground beans of the **coffee tree**.
coff'ee-bar, -house, -room, -shop, -stall *ns.* a place where coffee, etc. is served.
coff'ee-table *n.* a small, low table.

coffer *kof'ėr, n.* a chest for holding money or treasure.
coff'er-dam *n.* a watertight structure

used for building the foundations of bridges, etc., under water.

coffin *kof'in, n.* a box for a dead body.

cog *kog, n.* **1** a tooth on a wheel. **2** a person or thing having a necessary but subordinate part in an organisation, etc.
cogged *adj.*
cog'wheel *n.* a toothed wheel.

cogent *cō'jėnt, adj.* convincing, to the point: *a cogent argument, reason.*

cogitate *koj'i-tāt, v.i.* to turn a thing over in one's mind, ponder.—Also *v.t.*:—*pr.p.* **cog'itating.**
cogitā'tion *n.*

cognac *kon'yak, n.* a French brandy.

cognisance *kog'niz-ėns,* or *kon'-*: **take cognisance of** to notice, take into consideration.

cogwheel. See **cog.**

cohabit *kō-hab'it, v.i.* to dwell together as, or as if, husband and wife.

cohere *kō-hēr', v.i.* to stick together:—*pr.p.* **coher'ing.**
cohēr'ent *adj.* clear and logical: *He was able to give a coherent account of what had happened:—opp.* **incoherent.**
coher'ency, coher'ence *ns.*
cohē'sion *n.* the act or state of sticking together.

coiffeur *kwäf-ûr', n.* a hairdresser.
coiffure *kwäf-ür', n.* a style of hairdressing.

coil *koil, v.t.* and *v.i.* to wind in rings.—*n.* **1** a length (e.g. of rope) wound in rings. **2** one of these rings, or anything similar. **3** a type of contraceptive device.

coin *koin, n.* a piece of stamped metal used as money.—*v.t.* **1** to make metal into (money). **2** to gain (money) quickly in great quantity. **3** to invent (a word, phrase).
coin'age *n.* **1** the act of making (money, a new word, etc.). **2** the money used in a country. **3** a newly-coined word or phrase.

coincide *kō-in-sīd', v.i.* **1** to occur at the same time. **2** to be identical. **3** to agree: *This coincides with what he told us:*—*pr.p.* **coincid'ing.**
coin'cidence *(-sid-) n.* the accidental, but striking, happening of one event at the same time as, or following, another.
coincident'al *adj.* **coincident'ally** *adv.*

coir *koir, n.* the strong fibre of the coconut.

coke *kōk, n.* a fuel obtained by driving off gases from coal.

colander, cullender *kul'ėnd-ėr,* or *kol', n.* a strainer for draining off liquids, a bowl or the like with holes in the bottom.

cold *kōld, adj.* **1** the opposite of hot. **2** chilly. **3** unfriendly.—*n.* **1** lack of heat; chilliness. **2** cold weather. **3** an illness with catarrh, sneezing, etc.
cold'ly *adv.* **cold'ness** *n.*
cold'-blood'ed *adj.* **1** having blood (like that of a fish) which takes the same temperature as the surroundings of the body. **2** cruel, unfeeling.
cold cream a cream-like ointment used to cool, etc., the skin.
cold feet lack of courage.
cold front the surface of an advancing mass of cold air where it meets a mass of warmer air.
cold'-shoul'der *v.t.* to give the cold shoulder to.
cold sore a blister or group of blisters on or near the mouth, caused by a virus.
cold war. See **war.**
give someone the cold shoulder to show that one is unwilling to be friendly with (a person).
in cold blood deliberately.
leave one cold to fail to impress.
pour, throw cold water on to discourage.

coleslaw *kōl'slö, n.* a salad made from raw cabbage.

colic *kol'ik, n.* severe pain in the abdomen caused e.g. by flatulence.

coliseum. Same as **colosseum.**

collaborate *kol-ab'ȯr-āt, v.i.* **1** to work together on the same piece of work. **2** to work along (with) treacherously:—*pr.p.* **collab'orating.**
collaborā'tion *n.* **collab'orator** *n.*

collage *kol-äzh', n.* (the art of making) a picture consisting of miscellaneous pieces of material pasted on to a background.

collapse *kȯl-aps', v.i.* **1** to fall down. **2** to break down. **3** to become unable to continue:—*pr.p.* **collaps'ing.**—Also *n.*
collaps'ible, -able *adj.* (of e.g. boat, chair) able to be folded up.

collar *kol'ȧr, n.* **1** a band or chain worn round the neck: *a dog's collar.* **2** the part of a garment at the neck.—*v.t.* (*coll.*) to seize.
coll'ar-bone *n.* either of two bones joining the breast bone and shoulder-blade.

collate *kȯ-lāt', v.t.* **1** to examine and compare (things which are similar, e.g. reports, evidence). **2** to gather together, arrange in order, and check for completeness, correctness of order, etc.: *Photocopy and collate this report:*—*pr.p.* **collat'ing.**

colleague *kol'ēg, n.* a person with whom one is associated in a profession or occupation.

collect *kol-ekt', v.t.* **1** to bring together. **2** to gather (payments or contributions). **3** to put (one's thoughts) in order. **4** to go for and remove.—*v.i.* **1** to gather together. **2** to grow in quantity: *Water collects in the rain-barrel.—n. (kol'ekt)* a short prayer of one sentence.

collec'ted *adj.* **1** composed, cool. **2** (of a writer's works) gathered together in one book or set of books.

collect'edness *n.*

collec'tion *n.* **1** the act of collecting. **2** the gathering of contributions. **3** the money collected. **4** a set of objects, etc., collected. **5** a range of new fashion clothes shown by a clothes-designer.

collec'tive *adj.* of a number of people, or states, etc., taken together as one group; combined.

collect'or *n.* one who collects, e.g. tickets, money, specimens.

collective bargaining negotiation on pay, conditions, etc. by a body of workers and an employer.

collective security a policy according to which the security of each is guaranteed by all.

colleen *kol'ēn, kȯ-lēn', n.* a girl.

college *kol'ij, n.* **1** a learned society: *the college of surgeons.* **2** a society or building that is part of a university. **3** a place where certain subjects may be studied: *agricultural college.*

collegiate *kȯ-lē'ji-it, adj.*

college of education a college where teachers are trained.

collide *kol-īd', v.i.* **1** to dash together. **2** to clash:—*pr.p.* **collid'ing.**

colli'sion *(-i') n.* **1** a crash, violent meeting (of e.g. two vehicles). **2** a clash, conflict (between e.g. views, purposes, persons).

collie *kol'i, n.* a breed of sheepdog originating in Scotland.

collier *kol'yėr, n.* **1** one who works in a coal-mine. **2** a ship that carries coal.

coll'iery *n.* a coal-mine:—*pl.* **coll'ieries.**

collop *kol'ȯp, n.* a slice of meat.

colloquy *kol'ȯ-kwi, n.* a conversation:—*pl.* **coll'oquies.**

collō'quial *adj.* of, used in, common informal conversation.

collo'quially *adv.*

collō'quialism *n.* an expression used in ordinary, informal talk.

collusion *kȯ-lōō'zh(ȯ)n,* or *-lū', n.* a secret agreement to deceive.

colon[1] *kō'lon, n.* a punctuation mark (:).

colon[2] *kō'lon, n.* the greater portion of the large intestine.

colonel *kûr'nėl, n.* a rank in the army, or an officer of this rank.

colonnade *kol-ȯn-ād', n.* a row of columns, or of trees, placed at regular intervals.

colony *kol'ȯn-i, n.* **1** a group of people who settle together in another country. **2** the settlement so formed. **3** a collection of animals, birds, living together:—*pl.* **col'onies.**

colon'ial *(-ōn') adj.*

col'onise *v.t.* to establish a colony in (a place):—*pr.p.* **col'onising.**

colonisā'tion *n.* **col'onist** *n.*

colossus *kȯl-os'ůs, n.* **1** a gigantic statue. **2** anything gigantic.

coloss'al *adj.*

colossē'um *n.* a large place of entertainment, esp. a large open-air theatre (now in ruins) in Rome.

colour *kul'ȯr, n.* **1** a quality which an object has only when light falls on it (e.g. redness, blueness, etc.). **2** paint. **3** race or race-mixture other than Caucasian. **4** an appearance of truth: *to give colour to a statement.* **5** vividness. **6** (in *pl.*) a flag (*sing.*, see **troop**).—*v.t.* **1** to put colour on, stain, paint. **2** to exaggerate. **3** to affect: *Fear of loss coloured his attitude to the problem.—v.i.* to blush.

col'ouring *n.* **colo(u)rā'tion** *n.*

col'oured *adj.* **1** having colour. **2** belonging to a dark-complexioned race.

col'ourful *adj.* **1** full of colour. **2** vivid.

col'ourless *adj.* **1** without colour. **2** not vivid, lively, or interesting.

colour bar refusal to treat coloured people in the same way as white.

col'our-blind *adj.* unable to distinguish certain colours.

local colour. See **local.**

off colour **1** faded. **2** not at one's best, ill.

come off with flying colours to win triumphantly.

come out in one's true colours to show one's real character.

colt *kōlt, n.* a young horse.

colt'ish *adj.* **1** like a colt. **2** frisky.

colts'foot *n.* a yellow-flowered plant of early spring.

columbine *kol'ům-bīn, n.* a plant of the buttercup family with flowers like a group of pigeons.

column *kol'ům, n.* **1** a stone or wooden pillar used to support or adorn a building. **2** a long, narrow body of troops. **3** an upright row of figures. **4** a vertical section of a page of print.

col'umnist *(-nist) n.* a person who writes regular articles for a newspaper.

coma *kō'mȧ, n.* a long-continuing unconscious state.

com'atose *(-tōs) adj.* **1** drowsy. **2** in a coma.

comb *kōm, n.* **1** a toothed instrument for separating and cleaning hair, wool, flax, etc. **2** the crest of some birds. **3** cells for honey.—*v.t.* **1** to arrange, or clean, with a comb. **2** to search (a place) thoroughly (for something).

comb'er *n.* a long foaming wave.

combat *kom'bat,* or *kum', v.t.* to fight or struggle against, oppose:—*pr.p.* **com'-bating**; *pr.p.* **com'bated**.—*n.* a struggle.

com'batant *adj.* and *n.* (one who is) fighting.

com'bative *adj.* quarrelsome.

combe. Same as **coomb**.

combine *kȯm-bīn', v.t.* **1** to join together in one whole. **2** to unite. **3** to possess together: *He combines stupidity with cunning.*—*v.i.* **1** to come into close union. **2** (*chemistry*) to unite and form a compound:—*pr.p.* **combin'ing**.—*n.* *(kom'-bīn)* **1** an association of trading companies. **2** a combine harvester.

combinā'tion *n.* **1** union. **2** a motor bicycle with sidecar. **3** the series of letters or numbers that must be set in order on the dials of a **combination lock**, e.g. on a safe, to open it.

combinā'tions *n. pl.* an undergarment combining vest and drawers.

combine harvester a machine that both harvests and threshes.

combustible *kȯm-bust'i-bl, adj.* **1** liable to take fire and burn. **2** excitable:—*opp.* **incombustible**.—*n.* anything that will take fire.

combustion *kȯm-bus'ch(ȯ)n, n.* burning.

spontaneous combustion burning caused by heat produced in the substance itself.

come *kum, v.i.* **1** to move towards this place (opp. of *go*). **2** to draw near. **3** to reach, stretch (to). **4** to arrive. **5** to amount (to). **6** to become: *to come loose*:—*pr.p.* **com'-ing**; *pa.t.* **came**; *pa.p.* **come**.

com'er *n.* one who comes (usu. with *adj.*; e.g. *newcomer, late-comer, all comers*).

come'-back *n.* **1** a return to popularity, etc. **2** cause or chance to complain.

come'-down *n.* **1** loss of rank. **2** a disappointment.

comeup(p)'ance (*coll.*) *n.* deserved punishment.

come about to happen.

come across **1** to meet. **2** to find by chance.

come back to return to popularity, office, etc.

come by to obtain.

come down **1** to descend. **2** to be reduced. **3** to lose money and position: *to come down in the world*.

come home to one to touch (one's interests, feelings) closely.

come in for to receive (e.g. abuse).

come into to fall heir to.

come of to be the result of.

come of age to reach the age at which one is considered to be an adult.

come out **1** to become known. **2** to be published. **3** to make a first appearance in fashionable society. **4** to go on strike.

come round to recover from a faint, ill-humour, etc.

come to **1** to recover consciousness or sanity. **2** to amount to.

come to pass (*old*) to happen.

to come future (e.g. *in days to come*).

comedy *kom'i-di, n.* a play of a pleasant or amusing kind:—*pl.* **com'edies**.

comē'dian *n.* **1** an actor of comic parts. **2** an entertainer who tells jokes, etc.:—*fem.* **comedienne** *(kom-ē-dē-en')*.

comely *kum'li, adj.* pleasing, good-looking:—*comp.* **come'lier**; *superl.* **come'-liest**.

come'liness *n.*

comet *kom'it, n.* a heavenly body usu. with a shining tail.

comfit *kum'fit, n.* a sweetmeat.

comfort *kum'fȯrt, v.t.* **1** to help (someone in pain or distress). **2** to cheer.—*n.* **1** encouragement. **2** quiet enjoyment. **3** anything that makes one feel more at ease, or happier, or better able to bear misfortune. **4** the state of feeling comfortable:—*opp.* **discomfort**.

com'fortable *adj.* **1** in comfort, at ease. **2** giving comfort.

com'forter *n.* **1** one who comforts. **2** (*cap.*) the Holy Spirit. **3** a woollen scarf. **4** a dummy teat for a baby to suck.

comic *kom'ik, adj.* **1** of comedy. **2** causing mirth.—*n.* **1** (*coll.*) an amusing person. **2** a paper containing stories told mainly in pictures.

com'ical *adj.* funny.

comic paper a comic (*def. 2*).

comic strip a strip of small pictures showing stages in a story.

comma *kom'ȧ, n.* in punctuation, the mark (,).

inverted commas marks of quotation ("—", '—').

command *kȯm-ȧnd', v.t.* **1** to order. **2** to have authority over. **3** to have within sight: *The house commands a fine view over the bay.*—*n.* **1** an order. **2** control. **3** the thing commanded, over which one has command. **4** ability or understanding.

commandant' *n.* an officer who has the command of a place or of a body of troops.
commandeer' (orig. *Afrikaans*) *v.t.* **1** to seize for military use. **2** to seize for any purpose.
command'er *n.* **1** one who commands. **2** (the rank of) any of several officers in the armed forces.
command'er-in-chief' *n.* the officer in supreme command of an army, or of the entire forces of the state.
command'ing *adj.* **1** impressive: *He has a commanding appearance.* **2** with a wide view: *a commanding position on the hill.*
command'ment *n.* a command, esp. of God.
command'o *n.* **1** a unit of specially trained troops for tasks requiring special courage, skill, and initiative. **2** one serving in such a unit:—*pl.* **comman'dos.**

commemorate *kȯ-mem'ȯ-rāt,* *v.t.* **1** to honour the memory of by a solemn celebration. **2** to serve as a memorial of:—*pr.p.* **commem'orating.**
commemorā'tion *n.*
commem'orative *adj.*

commence *kȯm-ens', v.i., v.t.* to begin:—*pr.p.* **commenc'ing.**
commence'ment *n.*

commend *kom-end', v.t.* **1** to entrust: *I commend him to your care.* **2** to praise.
commend'able *adj.* praiseworthy.
commendā'tion *n.* praise.

commensurate *kȯ-men'sho͞o-rȧt,* *adj.* equal in size, importance, etc.; in proportion (to something else).

comment *kom'ent, n.* a remark, observation, criticism.—Also *v.i.*
comm'entary *n.* **1** a series of comments. **2** a description of a ceremony, etc. by one who is watching it (also **running commentary**):—*pl.* **comm'entaries.**
comm'entate *v.i.* to give a commentary:—*pr.p.* **comm'entating.**
comm'entātor *n.*

commerce *kom'ûrs, n.* **1** interchange of goods between nations or people, trade on a large scale. **2** dealings.
commer'cial *adj.* **1** of commerce. **2** (of radio, TV, etc.) paid for by advertisements.—*n.* a radio or television advertisement.
commercial traveller the travelling representative of a business firm.

commingle *kȯ-ming'gl, v.t.* and *v.i.* **1** to mingle. **2** to mix (with):—*pr.p.* **comming'ling.**

commiserate *kȯ-miz'ėr-āt, v.t.* and *v.i.* to feel or express sympathy (with):—*pr.p.* **commis'erating.**
commiserā'tion *n.*

commissar *kom-i-sär', n.* **1** in the former U.S.S.R., the head of a government department. **2** in the former U.S.S.R., a **political commissar,** a person in charge of political education esp. in the armed forces.
commissariat *(-sā'ri-ȧt) n.* the department in charge of provisions, e.g. for an army.

commission *kȯ-mish'(ȯ)n, n.* **1** the act of committing. **2** a document conferring authority. **3** something to be done by one person on behalf of another. **4** an order esp. for a work of art. **5** the fee paid to an agent for transacting business. **6** a body of persons appointed to investigate something.—*v.t.* **1** to give a commission to or for. **2** to empower.
commissionaire' *n.* a doorkeeper in uniform.
commiss'ioner *n.* **1** a representative of the government in a district or department. **2** a member of a commission.
commission agent a bookmaker.
commissioned officer an officer in the army, navy, or air force, respectively of or above the rank of second lieutenant, sub-lieutenant, pilot officer.
in, out of, commission 1 in, or not in active use. **2** ready, or not ready, for action.
commit *kȯ-mit', v.t.* **1** to give as a trust, entrust. **2** (with *to*) to put in (e.g. the grave, the flames). **3** to send (to prison). **4** to become guilty of (a crime, etc.). **5** to bind, pledge (oneself): *to commit oneself to help, to the cause of peace:*—*pr.p.* **committ'ing;** *pa.p.* **committ'ed.**
commit'ment *n.* **1** the act of committing. **2** an obligation, promise.
committ'al *n.* the act of committing.
committ'ed *adj.* pledged to do, or to support, something.
committ'ee *n.* a number of persons, selected from a larger body, to see to some special business.
commit to memory to learn by heart.
commit to writing to set down in writing.

commodious *kȯ-mō'di-ůs, adj.* spacious.

commodity *kȯ-mod'i-ti, n.* an article or product used in trade:—*pl.* **commod'ities.**

commonwealth *kom'ȯn-welth,* *n.* **1** the whole body of the people. **2** a form of government in which the power rests with the people. **3** an association of states, as the Commonwealth of Australia or the (British) Commonwealth of Nations.

commotion *kȯ-mō'sh(ȯ)n, n.* **1** confused and noisy action. **2** a disturbance.

communal. See **commune¹**.

commune¹ *kom'ūn, n.* **1** in France, etc., a small division of the country. **2** a group of people living together, sharing work, etc.
commū'nal (or *kom'-*) *adj.* **1** of a community. **2** shared.

commune² *kȯ-mūn', v.i.* to talk together:—*pr.p.* **commū'ning**.

communicate *kȯ-mū'ni-kāt, v.t.* **1** to give, pass on (a disease, emotion, etc.). **2** to make known, tell.—*v.i.* **1** to get in touch, talk (with). **2** to have a connecting door. **3** to partake of Holy Communion:—*pr.p.* **commū'nicating**.
commū'nicable *adj.* (esp. of a disease) able to be passed on.
commū'nicant *n.* one who partakes of Holy Communion.
communicā'tion *n.* **1** an act, or means, of conveying information. **2** a piece of information. **3** a letter, message, etc. **4** (in *pl.*) the means of sending messages or of transporting e.g. troops and supplies.
commū'nicative *adj.* inclined to give information, not reserved.
communion *kȯ-mūn'yȯn, n.* **1** fellowship, esp. religious. **2** (*cap.*; also **Holy Communion**) the celebration of the Lord's Supper.

communiqué *kom-ū'ni-kā, n.* an official announcement.

communism *kom'ū-nizm, n.* **1** a social system under which there is no private property, everything being held in common by the community. **2** (also *cap.*) the system under which the state owns all the means of production.
comm'unist *n.* (also *cap.*) one who believes in communism.—Also *adj.*

community *kȯ-mūn'i-ti, n.* **1** a group of people living in one place. **2** the public in general:—*pl.* **commun'ities**.
community charge a tax related to property, charged according to the number of residents, to pay for local public services.

commute *kȯ-mūt', v.t.* **1** to cxchange (a punishment) for one less severe. **2** to exchange or substitute (one thing for, into, another).—*v.i.* (orig. *U.S.*) to travel regularly between home in the suburbs and work in the city:—*pr.p.* **commut'ing**.
commut'er *n.*

compact¹ *kȯm-pakt', adj.* **1** closely placed or fitted together. **2** with much in a small space. **3** firm. **4** brief.—*v.t.* to press closely together.
compact disc a small audio disc on which digitally recorded sound is registered as a series of pits that are readable by a laser beam.

compact² *kom'pakt, n.* **1** a bargain or agreement. **2** a treaty.

companion¹ *kȯm-pan'yȯn, n.* **1** a friend or associate. **2** one paid to accompany or live with and help another.—*adj.* **1** accompanying. **2** matching.
compan'ionable *adj.* pleasant to have as a companion.
compan'ionship *n.* **1** the state of being companions, or of having companion(s). **2** friendly feeling.
See also **company**.

companion² *kȯm-pan'yȯn, n.* (on a ship) a window frame through which light passes to a lower deck or cabin.
compan'ion-ladder, -way *ns.* the ladder or stair from an upper to a lower deck or to a cabin.

companionable, -ship. See **companion¹**.

company *kum'pȧ-ni, n.* **1** a group of people, e.g. of guests. **2** persons united for trade, etc., a business firm. **3** part of a regiment. **4** the crew of a ship. **5** companionship:—*pl.* **com'panies**.
keep someone company to accompany, stay with, a person for companionship or to prevent loneliness.
part company to go separate ways.

comparable, -ative. See **compare**.

compare *kȯm-pār', v.t.* **1** to set (things) together to see how far they agree or disagree, are similar or dissimilar, etc. **2** to set (one thing) beside another for this purpose: *Compare my drawing with yours.* **3** to represent as similar to: *She compared him to a bull in a china shop.*—Also *v.i.*:—*pr.p.* **compar'ing**.
comparable *kom'pȧr-ȧ-bl, adj.* **1** of the same kind or on the same scale (with *with*). **2** worthy to be compared (to):—*opp.* **incomparable**.
compar'ative *adj.* **1** judged by comparing with something else: *When the children tired of playing express trains, we had comparative quiet.* **2** (*grammar*) denoting the degree of adjective or adverb between positive and superlative (e.g. *blacker, taller, farther, better, more courageous, more carefully*) (also *n.*).
compar'atively *adv.*
compar'ison *n.* the act of comparing.
beyond compare much better than any other.
compare notes to discuss and compare views, impressions, etc.
there is no comparison between A

and B A is not good (etc.) enough to be compared with B.

comparison. See **compare**.

compartment *kȯm-pärt'mėnt*, *n.* a separate part or division, e.g. of a railway carriage.

compass *kum'pȧs*, *n.* **1** limits. **2** the range of pitch possible to a voice or instrument. **3** an instrument consisting of a magnetised needle, used to find directions. **4** (in *pl.*) an instrument with two movable legs, for drawing circles, etc.—*v.t.* **1** to pass or go round. **2** to achieve, bring about: *to compass his downfall*.

compassion *kȯm-pash'(ȯ)n*, *n.* sorrow for the sufferings of another.
compassionate *kȯm-pash'(ȯ)n-it*, *adj.*
compass'ionately *adv.*

compatible *kȯm-pat'ibl*, *adj.* **1** able to live or associate happily together. **2** not contradictory: *The two statements are compatible.* **3** in keeping or agreement (with):—*opp.* **incompatible.**
compatibil'ity *n.* **compat'ibly** *adv.*

compatriot *kȯm-pā'tri-ȯt*, or *pat'*, *n.* a fellow-countryman.

compeer *kȯm-pēr'*, *kom'*, *n.* **1** one who is equal e.g. in age, rank. **2** a companion.

compel *kȯm-pel'*, *v.t.* to force: *to compel someone to go*:—*pr.p.* **compell'ing**; *pa.p.* **compelled'**.
compell'ing *adj.* forcing action, consideration, attention, belief, etc.
See also **compulsion.**

compendium *kȯm-pen'di-ŭm*, *n.* **1** a summary, abstract. **2** a collection of games in one box:—*pl.* **compen'diums, -dia.**

compensate *kom'pėn-sāt*, *v.t.* to make up to (someone) for loss or wrong.—*v.i.* to make up (for):—*pr.p.* **com'pensating.**
compensā'tion *n.* **1** payment, etc., to make up for loss or injury. **2** (*U.S.*) reward for service.

compère *kom'per*, *n.* one who introduces items of an entertainment.—Also *v.t.*:—*pr.p.* **com'pèring.**

compete *kȯm-pēt'*, *v.i.* to strive for e.g. a prize, to try to beat others:—*pr.p.* **compet'ing.**
competi'tion *(-pėt-i')* *n.* **1** an act of competing. **2** a contest for a prize. **3** rivalry.
compet'itive *adj.* **1** (of an examination, sports, etc.) in which a reward goes to the one, or ones, who does, or do best. **2** fond of competing, eager to win. **3** (of prices) as low as, or lower than, those of one's competitors.
compet'itor *n.* **1** one who competes. **2** a rival.

competent *kom'pi-tėnt*, *adj.* **1** capable. **2** legally qualified:—*opp.* **incompetent.**
com'petence, **com'petency** *ns.* **1** capability. **2** qualification as required by law. **3** sufficiency (e.g. of money to live on).
com'petently *adv.*

competition, etc. See **compete.**

compile *kȯm-pīl'*, *v.t.* to make (a book, etc.) by collecting materials from other books, reports, etc.:—*pr.p.* **compil'ing.**
compilā'tion *n.* **compil'er** *n.*

complacent *kȯm-plā'sėnt*, *adj.* **1** showing satisfaction. **2** showing too much satisfaction with oneself, etc. and unawareness of dangers, etc.
complā'cence, complā'cency *ns.*
complā'cently *adv.*

complain *kȯm-plān'*, *v.i.* **1** to express pain, sense of injury (*of* or *about*). **2** to state a grievance.
complain'ant *n.* one who complains.
complaint' *n.* **1** a statement of one's sorrow or dissatisfaction. **2** an ailment.

complaisant *kȯm-plā'zȧnt*, *adj.* ready to give in to others.
complai'sance *n.*

complement *kom'pli-mėnt*, *n.* **1** that which completes or fills up. **2** the full number or quantity (e.g. *a ship's complement*, the full number of officers and crew). **3** the angle that must be added to a given angle to make up a right angle.
complement'ary *adj.* together making up a whole, or a right angle.

complete *kȯm-plēt'*, *adj.* **1** whole. **2** perfect, absolute: *a complete idiot.* **3** thorough: *a complete overhaul.* **4** finished:—*opp.* **incomplete.**—*v.t.* **1** to finish. **2** to make perfect:—*pr.p.* **complet'ing.**
complete'ness *n.* the state of being whole, perfect, thorough.
comple'tion *n.* **1** the act of finishing. **2** the state of being finished.

complex *kom'pleks*, *adj.* **1** composed of many parts. **2** complicated, difficult.—*n.* **1** a set of repressed emotions and ideas which affect a person's behaviour. **2** (*loosely*) an uncontrollable, irrational reaction to, or feeling (about). **3** a group of buildings, etc. forming a unit: *a shopping, sports, complex*.
complex'ity *n.* **com'plexly** *adv.*

complexion *kȯm-plek'sh(ȯ)n*, *n.* **1** colour or look of the skin, esp. of the face. **2** general appearance or character.

compliance, **compliant**. See **comply.**

complicate *kom'pli-kāt*, *v.t.* to make (more) complex or difficult:—*pr.p.* **com'plicating.**
complicā'tion *n.* **1** an additional circum-

stance making a situation more difficult. **2** an additional disease making recovery from a first disease more difficult.

complicity *kom-plis'i-ti*, *n.* the state of being an accomplice: *He denied complicity in his brother's crime.*

See also **complex**.

compliment *kom'pli-mėnt*, *n.* **1** an expression of praise or flattery. **2** (in *pl.*) greetings.—*v.t.* **1** to pay a compliment to. **2** to congratulate (on).

compliment'ary *adj.* **1** flattering, praising. **2** given free: *a complimentary ticket*.

comply *kom-plī'*, *v.i.* to act in the way that someone else has commanded or wished:—*pr.p.* **comply'ing**; *pa.p.* **complied'**.

complī'ance *n.*

compli'ant *adj.* **1** yielding. **2** obliging.

component *kȯm-pō'nėnt*, *adj.* forming one of the parts of a whole.—Also *n.*

comport *kȯm-pōrt'*, *-pört'*, *v.t.* to bear, behave (oneself).

compose *kȯm-pōz'*, *v.t.* **1** to form by putting parts together. **2** to make up, be the parts of. **3** to set in order or at rest (e.g. one's thoughts, face). **4** to settle (e.g. a dispute). **5** to create (esp. in literature or music).—Also *v.i.*:—*pr.p.* **compos'ing**.

composed' *adj.* quiet, calm.

compos'er *n.* a writer, esp. of a piece of music.

com'posite *adj.* made up of two or more distinct parts.—*n.* (also **composite flower**) a flower, such as that of the daisy, which is made up of a central head of tiny flowers, or 'tube florets', surrounded by a ring of tiny white or coloured flowers, or 'ray florets'.

composi'tion *(kom-)* *n.* **1** the act of composing. **2** material, ingredients. **3** a mixture, compound. **4** a work in literature, music, or painting. **5** the manner in which parts of such a work are combined.

compos'itor *n.* one who puts together type for printing.

com'post *n.* a mixture of rotting vegetation for manure.

compō'sure *(-zhėr)* *n.* calmness, self-possession.

See also **component**.

compos mentis *kom'pos ment'is* of sound mind.

compost. See **compose**.

compound[1] *kȯm-pownd'*, *v.t.* **1** to mix or combine. **2** to make worse.—*adj.* *(kom'pownd)* **1** composed of a number of parts. **2** not simple.—*n.* **1** a mass made up of a number of parts. **2** (*chemistry*) a substance formed from two or more elements.

compound interest. See **interest**.

compound[2] *kom'pownd*, *n.* an enclosure round a house or factory (in India, etc.), or for labourers (S. Africa).

comprehend *kom-prė-hend'*, *v.t.* **1** to understand. **2** to include.

comprehen'sible *adj.* capable of being understood:—*opp.* **incomprehensible**.

comprehen'sion *n.* the act or power of understanding:—*opp.* **incomprehension**.

comprehen'sive *adj.* taking in, including, much.

comprehen'sively *adv*.

comprehen'siveness *n.*

comprehensive school a secondary school, serving a particular area, that provides education for all levels and types of pupil.

compress *kȯm-pres'*, *v.t.* **1** to press together. **2** to force into a narrower space.—*n.* *(kom'pres)* **1** a pad used in surgery to apply pressure to any part. **2** a folded cloth applied to the skin.

compress'ible *adj.* that may be compressed.

compress'ion *kom-presh'(ȯ)n*, *n.* **1** the act of compressing. **2** the state of being compressed. **3** the stroke that compresses the gases in an internal-combustion engine.

comprise *kom-prīz'*, *v.t.* **1** to contain, include. **2** to consist of:—*pr.p.* **compris'ing**.

compromise *kom'prȯ-mīz*, *n.* a settlement of differences in which both sides yield something.—*v.t.* to involve in scandal, suspicion, etc.—*v.i.* to make a compromise:—*pr.p.* **com'promising**.

com'promised *adj.* brought under suspicion.

com'promising *adj*.

comptroller *kȯn-trōl'ėr*, *n.* older form of **controller**.

compulsion *kȯm-pul'sh(ȯ)n*, *n.* **1** the act of compelling. **2** coercion. **3** an impulse (to do something unreasonable or not sensible).

compul'sive *adj.* of, arising from, an irrational impulse.

compul'sory *adj.* that must be done or carried out.—*n.* a compulsory exercise in e.g. an ice-skating competition:—*pl.* **compul'sories**.

compunction *kȯm-pungk'sh(ȯ)n*, *n.* **1** uneasiness of conscience, scruple: *He had no compunction about keeping the money.* **2** remorse.

compute *kȯm-pūt'*, *v.t.* **1** to calculate. **2** to estimate:—*pr.p.* **comput'ing**.

computā'tion *n.*
comput'er *n.* an electronic machine which can perform calculations, handle and store information, and control equipment.
comput'erise *v.t.* to cause to be handled or controlled by a computer:—*pr.p.* **comput'erising**.

comrade *kom'rid, kum'rid, n.* **1** a close companion. **2** a fellow communist or socialist.
com'radeship *n.*

con[1] *kon, v.t.* to study carefully:—*pr.p.* **conn'ing**; *pa.p.* **conned**.

con[2], **conn** *kon, v.t.* to direct the steering of (a ship):—*pr.p.* **conn'ing**; *pa.p.* **conned**.
conn'ing-tow'er *n.* the place on a warship or submarine from which orders for steering, etc. are given.

con[3] *kon, v.t.* to trick, play a *con*fidence trick on:—*pr.p.* **conn'ing**; *pa.p.* **conned**.
con'-man *n.* one who plays **con'-tricks** on people.

con[4]. See **contra**.

concave *kon-kāv', kon', adj.* curved inwards (opposed to *convex*).—Also *n.*
concave'ness, concav'ity *(-kav'), ns.*

conceal *kȯn-sēl', v.t.* **1** to hide. **2** to keep secret.
conceal'ment *n.*

concede *kȯn-sēd', v.t.* **1** to admit (e.g. a point in an argument). **2** to grant (e.g. a right).—*v.i.* to admit (that):—*pr.p.* **conced'ing**.
See also **concession**.

conceit *kȯn-sēt', n.* **1** too high an opinion of oneself. **2** a fancy.
conceit'ed *adj.* having a high opinion of oneself.

conceive *kȯn-sēv', v.t.* **1** to become pregnant with. **2** to form in the mind. **3** to imagine.—Also *v.i.*:—*pr.p.* **conceiv'ing**.
conceiv'able *adj.*:—*opp.* **inconceiv'able**.
conceiv'ably *adv.*
See also **conception**.

concentrate *kon'sėn-trāt, v.t.* **1** to bring to one place: *He concentrated his forces at the point where he hoped to break through.* **2** to give (all one's energies, etc.) to one purpose (with *on*). **3** to make stronger (e.g. a liquid by removing some of the water).—*v.i.* to give all one's attention to one thing:—*pr.p.* **con'centrating**.—*n.* concentrated animal feed.
concentrā'tion *n.*
concentration camp a place where political prisoners, etc. are imprisoned.

concentric *kȯn-sent'rik, adj.* having a common centre.

conception *kȯn-sep'sh(ȯ)n, n.* **1** the act of conceiving. **2** the formation in the mind (of an idea). **3** an idea (also **con'cept**).
concep'tualise *v.t.* to form a concept of:—*pr.p.* **concep'tualising**.

concern *kȯn-sûrn', v.t.* **1** to have to do with. **2** to make uneasy or worried. **3** to interest, trouble (oneself): *Do not concern yourself about his future.*—*n.* **1** something that concerns or belongs to one. **2** anxiety. **3** a business.
concerned' *adj.* anxious.
concern'ing *prep.* about.

concert *kon'sėrt, n.* a musical entertainment.—*v.t. (kȯn-sûrt')* to arrange, plan.
concert'ed *adj.* **1** arranged beforehand. **2** carried out by people acting together: *a concerted attack*.
concertina *kon-sėr-tē'nȧ, n.* a musical wind instrument with bellows and keys.
concerto *kȯn-chûr'tō, n.* a long piece of music for solo instrument with orchestral accompaniment:—*pl.* **concer'tos**.
in concert together.

concession *kȯn-sesh'(ȯ)n, n.* **1** the act of conceding or granting. **2** a grant, esp. of land. **3** something yielded or allowed.

conch *kongk, konch, n.* a kind of sea-shell.

conciliate *kȯn-sil'i-āt, v.t.* to win over (someone previously unfriendly or angry):—*pr.p.* **concil'iating**.
conciliā'tion *n.*
concil'iatory *adj.* intended, showing a desire, to conciliate: *a conciliatory manner*.

concise *kȯn-sīs', adj.* **1** brief. **2** in few words.
concise'ly *adv.* **concise'ness** *n.*

conclave *kon'klāv, n.* **1** an assembly of cardinals. **2** any private or secret assembly.

conclude *kȯn-klōōd', v.t.* **1** to end. **2** to decide. **3** to arrange (a treaty).—*v.i.* **1** to end. **2** to form a final judgment:—*pr.p.* **conclud'ing**.
conclud'ing *adj.* final.
conclusion *kȯn-klōō'zh(ȯ)n, n.* **1** the end. **2** judgment.
conclusive *(-klōō'siv) adj.* **1** final. **2** convincing (*opp.* **inconclusive**).
conclus'ively *adv.* **conclus'iveness** *n.*
in conclusion finally.

concoct *kȯn-kokt', v.t.* to make up (as a dish in cookery, or an untrue story).
concoc'tion *n.* **1** a mixture (esp. a dish of food). **2** a made-up story.

concomitant *kȯn-kom-i-tȧnt, adj.* accompanying, occurring together with.

concord *kon'körd, or kong', n.* **1** agreement. **2** a combination of pleasant sounds.
concord'ance *n.* an index or dictionary

of the words or passages of a book or author.

concourse *kon', kong'kōrs, -kȯrs, n.* **1** a crowd. **2** the act of crowding together. **3** a large open space in a building, etc.

concrete *kon'krēt,* or *-krēt', adj.* **1** (the opposite of *abstract*) denoting a thing, not a quality or state. **2** made of (building) concrete.—*n.* a mixture of limc, sand, pebbles, etc., used in building.
concreteness *n.*
concre'tion *n.* a solid mass formed from a collection of material.

concur *kȯn-kûr', v.i.* to agree: *I cannot concur with you in this opinion*:—*pr.p.* **concurr'ing**; *pa.p.* **concurred'**.
concurr'ent *adj.* **1** agreeing. **2** meeting in the same point. **3** coming or existing together.
concurr'ence *n.*
concurr'ently *adv.* at the same time: *three sentences of six months, to run concurrently*.

concussion *kȯn-kush'ȯn, n.* **1** violent shaking. **2** temporary injury to the brain caused by a heavy blow on the head.

condemn *kȯn-dem', v.t.* **1** to blame. **2** to sentence to punishment. **3** to declare to be unfit to use.
condemnā'tion *n.*
condemned cell a cell for a prisoner under sentence of death.

condense *kȯn-dens', v.t.* to make smaller in volume, size.—*v.i.* **1** to be reduced to smaller size, etc. **2** (of vapour) to turn to liquid:—*pr.p.* **condens'ing**.
condensā'tion *n.* **1** the act of condensing. **2** liquid formed from vapour.
condens'er *n.* a capacitor (see this).
condensed milk milk made thicker, and smaller in quantity, by evaporation, and sugared.

condescend *kon-di-send', v.i.* **1** to act patronisingly, treat a person as if one is better than he is. **2** to make oneself humble, forget one's dignity.
condescend'ing *adj.* patronising.
condescen'sion *n.*

condiment *kon'di-mėnt, n.* a seasoning used at table to give flavour to food.

condition *kȯn-dish'(ȯ)n, n.* **1** (in *sing.* or *pl.*) the state in which a person or thing is: *in a liquid condition*; *good housing conditions.* **2** something that must exist or happen or be done before something else can or will. **3** a term in an agreement.—*v.t.* **1** to affect or control. **2** to put, cause to be, in a good condition: *to condition one's hair*.
condi'tional *adj.* depending on certain conditions (e.g. *a conditional sale* of a house is one that will be completed only if certain things happen or are done).
condi'tionally *adv.*
condi'tioner *n.* a substance or apparatus that brings e.g. hair, the air, into a good or desired condition.
in, out of, condition in good, bad, condition.
on condition that if, and only if, (something is done).

condom *kon'dom, n.* a contraceptive rubber sheath worn by a man.

condole *kȯn-dōl', v.i.* to express sympathy (with someone):—*pr.p.* **condol'ing**.
condol'ence (or *kon'*) *n.*

condone *kȯn-dōn', v.t.* to excuse, forgive (an offence, wrong):—*pr.p.* **condon'ing**.

condor *kon'dȯr, n.* a large vulture found among the Andes of S. America.

conducive *kȯn-dūs'iv, adj.* tending, helping, towards: *Late nights are not conducive to good health*.

conduct *kȯn-dukt', v.t.* **1** to lead. **2** to convey (water, etc.) **3** to direct (e.g. an orchestra). **4** to manage (e.g. a business). **5** to behave (oneself). **6** to transmit (heat, electricity).—*n.* *(kon'dukt)* **1** management. **2** behaviour.
conduct'or *n.* **1** the person or thing that conducts. **2** a director of orchestra or choir. **3** one in charge of, and who collects fares on, a bus, etc. (*fem.* **conduct'ress**). **4** a substance that transmits electricity, heat, etc.

conduit *kon'dit, n.* a channel or pipe to convey water or (also *kon'dū-it*) covering electrical wiring.

cone *kōn, n.* **1** a solid figure with a vertex, and a base that is a circle or an ellipse. **2** the fruit of the pine, fir, etc. **3** anything cone-shaped.
con'ical *(kon') adj.* cone-shaped.

coney. Same as **cony**.

confection *kȯn-fek'sh(ȯ)n, n.* **1** a sweet. **2** a fancy article of women's clothing, esp. a hat.
confec'tioner *n.* one who makes or sells sweets or cakes.
confec'tionery *n.* **1** the shop or business of a confectioner. **2** sweets:—*pl.* **confec'tioneries**.

confederacy. See **confederate**.

confederate *kȯn-fed'ėr-it, n.* **1** an ally. **2** an accomplice.—Also *adj.*
confed'eracy *n.* **1** a league, alliance. **2** a conspiracy:—*pl.* **confed'eracies**.
confederā'tion *n.* **1** a league, esp. of princes, states, etc. **2** an association.

confer *kȯn-fûr'*, *v.t.* to give, esp. formally (e.g. an honour).—*v.i.* **1** to consult each other. **2** to carry on a discussion:—*pr.p.* **conferr'ing**; *pa.p.* **conferred'**.
con'ference *n.* a meeting for discussion.

confess *kȯn-fes'*, *v.t.* **1** to acknowledge, admit. **2** to make known (sins to a priest).—*v.i.* to make a confession.
confessed' *adj.* admitted.
confess'ion *n.* acknowledgment of a crime or fault.
confess'ional *n.* **1** the seat or recess where a priest hears confessions. **2** the institution of hearing confessions.
confess'or *n.* a priest who hears confessions and grants absolution.
confession of faith the creed of a church or sect.

confetti *kȯn-fet'ē*, *n. pl.* bits of coloured paper thrown e.g. at weddings.

confidant(e). See **confide**.

confide *kȯn-fīd'*, *v.i.* to tell secrets or private thoughts: *He confided in his brother*.—*v.t.* **1** to tell (secrets, plans, thoughts, etc. to someone). **2** to entrust (something, to someone's care):—*pr.p.* **confid'ing**.
confidant' *(-fid-)* *n.* one to whom secrets are told:—*fem.* **confidante'** *(-ant')*.
con'fidence *n.* **1** trust or belief. **2** a piece of information given in the belief that it will not be passed on. **3** self-reliance. **4** boldness.
con'fident *adj.* **1** trusting firmly. **2** bold.
confiden'tial *adj.* **1** secret, not to be told to others. **2** entrusted with secrets: *confidential secretary*.
confiden'tially *adv.*
confid'ing *(-fīd'-)* *adj.* trustful, unsuspicious.
confidence trick (*U.S.* **game**) the trick of a swindler who first gains a person's trust and then persuades him to hand over money.
in confidence as a secret, confidentially.
in someone's confidence told someone's secrets

confine *kon-fīn'*, *v.t.* **1** to limit, keep within limits: *They succeeded in confining the fire to a small area.* **2** to shut up, imprison:—*pr.p.* **confin'ing.**—*n.pl.* *(kon'fīnz)* limits, boundaries.
confine'ment *n.* **1** the state of being shut up or imprisoned. **2** being in bed at the birth of a child.

confirm *kȯn-fûrm'*, *v.t.* **1** to strengthen: *This confirmed his resolve.* **2** to make (a person) more firm (e.g. in a belief.) **3** to show (a statement) to be true. **4** to admit to full communion (in a Christian church).
confirma'tion *n.*
confirmed' *adj.* **1** settled in a habit or way of life: *A confirmed drunkard, bachelor.* **2** shown to be true.

confiscate *kon'fis-kāt*, *v.i.* to seize (having authority to do so), esp. as a penalty.—*pr.p.* **con'fiscating**.
confiscā'tion *n.*

conflagration *kon-flȧ-grāsh'(ō)n*, *n.* a great fire.

conflict *kon'flikt*, *n.* a struggle, contest.—*v.i.* *(kȯn-flikt')* to contradict each other: *The two accounts of what had happened conflicted.*
conflict'ing *adj.* **1** clashing. **2** contradictory.

confluence *kon'floo-ėns*, *n.* a flowing together, or the place of meeting, of rivers.

conform *kȯn-fȯrm'*, *v.i.* **1** to behave, dress, worship, etc. in the way that most other people do. **2** to be similar (to), have the same shape as: *to conform to a pattern*.
conformā'tion *n.* form, shape, or structure.
conform'er, **conform'ist** *ns.* one who conforms, esp. with the worship of the established church.—See also **nonconformist**.
conform'ity *n.* **1** likeness. **2** agreement (to, with). **3** obedience, compliance: *in conformity with her wishes*.

confound *kȯn-fownd'*, *v.t.* **1** to mix completely, confuse. **2** to throw into disorder. **3** to puzzle and surprise greatly.
confound'ed *adj.* (*coll.*) horrible, very annoying.
See also **confuse**.

confront *kȯn-frunt'*, *v.t.* **1** to face in a hostile manner: *Enemies, difficulties, etc. confront me.* **2** to bring (a person) face to face (with e.g. accusers, evidence, anything unpleasant to him).
confrontā'tion *n.*

confuse *kȯn-fūz'*, *v.t.* **1** to throw into disorder. **2** to perplex, bewilder. **3** to embarrass. **4** to fail to realise the difference between, mix up:—*pr.p.* **confus'ing**.
confused' *adj.* **confus'ing** *adj.*
confū'sion *n.* **1** disorder. **2** mixing up. **3** bewilderment. **4** embarrassment.

confute *kȯn-fūt'*, *v.t.* to prove to be false or wrong:—*pr.p.* **confut'ing**.

congeal *kȯn-jēl'*, *v.t.* and *v.i.* **1** to freeze. **2** to solidify, as by cold.

congenial *kȯn-jēn'i-ȧl*, *adj.* **1** (of people) having the same tastes and interests, in sympathy. **2** pleasant, suited to one: *a congenial task*.

congenital *kȯn-jen'i-tȧl, adj.* (of diseases or deformities) born with a person.
congen'itally *adv.*

conger *kong'gėr, n.* a large sea eel.

congested *kȯn-jest'id, adj.* **1** (of a part of the body) having too much blood. **2** overcrowded.
congestion *kȯn-jest'sh(ȯ)n, n.* **1** an accumulation of blood in part of the body, or of traffic in one place. **2** overcrowding.

conglomeration *kon-glom-ėr-ā'sh(ȯ)n, n.* a collection (of things of mixed kind).

congratulate *kȯn-grat'ū-lāt, -grach', v.t.* **1** to express one's joy to (a person) because of a success he has had. **2** to think (oneself) lucky: *He congratulated himself on his escape*:—*pr.p.* **congrat'ulating.**
congratulā'tion *n.* **congrat'ulatory** *adj.*

congregate *kong'grė-gāt, v.t.* and *v.i.* to gather together:—*pr.p.* **con'gregating.**
congregā'tion *n.* **1** a gathering. **2** a body of people in a church for a service, or belonging to a church.
Congregā'tionalism *n.* a form of church government in which each congregation manages all its own affairs.

congress *kong'gres, n.* **1** an assembly of diplomats or delegates. **2** (*cap.*) the legislature or parliament of the United States, etc.
congressional *kon-gresh'on-al, adj.*
con'gressman, -woman *ns.* a member of Congress, esp. of the House of Representatives.

congruent *kong'groo-ėnt, adj.* of two geometrical figures, coinciding at all points when one is fitted on top of the other.
con'gruous *adj.* suitable, appropriate.—See also **incongruous.**
congru'ity *(-grōō') n.*

conical. See **cone.**

conifer *kon'i-fėr, n.* a cone-bearing tree, as the fir, etc.
conif'erous *adj.* cone-bearing.

conjecture *kȯn-jek'chůr, n.* an opinion formed on slight evidence; a guess:—*v.t.* to infer on slight evidence; to guess:—*pr.p.* **conjec'turing.**
conjec'tural *adj.*

conjugal *kon'joo-gȧl, adj.* of marriage.

conjugate *kon'joo-gāt, v.t.* to give the different parts of (a verb):—*pr.p.* **con'jugating.**
conjugātion *n.* **1** the act of conjugating. **2** the different parts of a verb.

conjunction *kȯn-jungk'sh(ȯ)n, n.* **1** union, combination. **2** a word that connects sentences, clauses, or words (e.g. *and, but*).

conjuncture *kȯn-jungk'chůr, n.* **1** combination of circumstances. **2** a crisis.
in conjunction with (acting) together with.

conjunctivitis *con-jungk-tiv-ī'tis, n.* inflammation of the inside of the eyelid and surface of the eye.

conjure *kun'jėr, v.i.* by swiftness of hand, etc., to perform tricks that seem magical.—*v.t.* **1** to command (a devil or spirit). **2** to produce as if by magic. **3** *(kȯn-jōōr')* to tell solemnly, implore: *She conjured him not to say anything*:—*pr.p.* **conjuring.**
con'juror, con'jurer *n.*
a name to conjure with the name of an important, very influential, person.
conjure up to bring up in the mind (a picture, etc.).

conn. See **con²**.

connect *kȯn-ekt', v.t.* **1** to tie or fasten together, join, link. **2** to establish a communication link between (e.g. on the telephone): *I am trying to connect you.* **3** to associate in the mind, think of together.—Also *v.i.*
connect'ed *adj.* **1** joined. **2** (of statement) logically arranged, easy to follow:—*opp.* **disconnected.**
connec'tion, connex'ion *n.* **1** something that connects. **2** the state of being connected. **3** (also in *pl.*) a circle of people associated with one, esp. in business. **4** opportunity to change trains, buses, etc. on a journey without much delay. **5** a relative.
connec'tive *adj.* joining.
in this connection when we are considering this.

conning-tower. See **con²**.

connive *kȯn-īv', v.i.* to wink (at a crime, etc.), make no attempt to hinder it:—*pr.p.* **conniv'ing.**
conniv'ance *n.*

connoisseur *kon-ės-ûr',* or *-is-ūr', n.* **1** an expert critic of art, music, etc. **2** one who knows all about something: *a connoisseur of wine.*

connotation *kon-ȯt-ā'sh(ȯ)n, n.* what is suggested by a word in addition to its simple meaning.

connubial *kȯ-nū'bi-ȧl, adj.* of marriage.

conquer *kong'kėr, v.t.* **1** to gain by force. **2** to overcome.—Also *v.i.*
con'queror *n.*
con'quest *kong'kwest, n.* **1** the act of conquering. **2** something won by force or effort.

consanguinity *kon-sang-gwin'it-i, n.* relationship by blood.
consanguin'eous *adj.*

conscience *kon'shėns, n.* **1** the knowledge or sense of right and wrong. **2** conscientiousness. **3** scruple: *He had no conscience about dismissing the men.*
conscientious *kon-shi-en'shůs, adj.* **1** guided by conscience. **2** careful and earnest.
conscien'tiously *adv.*
conscien'tiousness *n.*
conscientious objector one who objects on grounds of conscience, esp. to military service.
in all conscience fairly and reasonably.
prisoner of conscience one imprisoned for his religious, political, etc. beliefs.

conscious *kon'shůs, adj.* aware of oneself and one's surroundings: *The patient was conscious.* **2** aware or having knowledge (of); aware (that): *He was conscious of their disapproval, conscious that they disapproved.* **3** deliberate, intentional: *He made a conscious effort to please.*
con'sciously *adv.*
con'sciousness *n.* **1** feelings, thoughts, mind in its widest sense. **2** awareness. **3** the waking state of the mind.

conscript *kon'skript, n.* one enrolled by the state to serve in the armed forces, etc.—*v.t.* *(kȯn-skript')* to compel to enlist.
conscrip'tion *n.*

consecrate *kon'si-krāt, v.t.* **1** to set apart for a holy use. **2** to make (e.g. a custom) be regarded as sacred. **3** to devote: *He consecrated himself to the cause of peace*:—*pr.p.* **con'secrating.**
consecrā'tion *n.*

consecutive *kȯn-sek'ū-tiv, adj.* following one after the other in regular order: *on two consecutive days.*
consec'utively *adv.*

consensus *kȯn-sen'sůs, n.* **1** general trend: *The consensus of opinion is that we should do this.* **2** agreement.

consent *kȯn-sent', v.i.* to agree (to).—*n.* **1** agreement. **2** permission.

consequence *kon'si-kwėns, n.* **1** a result. **2** importance: *The small error is of no consequence.* **3** social standing.
con'sequent *adj.* following, esp. as a natural result.
con'sequently *adv.*
consequential *kon-si-kwen'sh(ȧ)l, adj.* **1** following as a result. **2** self-important.
See also **inconsequent, inconsequential.**

conserve *kȯn-sûrv', v.t.* to keep from damage, decay, or loss:—*pr.p.* **conser'ving.**—*n.* something preserved, as fruits in sugar.
conserv'ancy *n.* a board with authority to control a port, river, or to protect trees, wildlife, etc.:—*pl.* **conserv'ancies.**
conservā'tion *n.* the act of conserving old buildings, the countryside, wild animals, etc.
conservā'tionist *n.* one who encourages or practises conservation.
conser'vatism *n.* **1** (*cap.*) the opinions and principles of a Conservative. **2** dislike of change, esp. sudden or extreme change.
conser'vative *adj.* **1** (*loosely*) moderate, understated: *a conservative estimate.*—*n.* **1** (*politics; cap.*) a member or supporter of the Conservative Party. **2** one who dislikes change.
Conservative Party 1 a political party advocating support of established customs and institutions, opposition to socialism, and favouring free enterprise. **2** its representatives in parliament.
conservatory *n.* **1** a greenhouse. **2** a similar room, attached to a house and used as a lounge:—*pl.* **conser'vatories.**

consider *kȯn-sid'ėr, v.t.* **1** to think. **2** to think about carefully. **3** to take into account. **4** to regard as: *I consider you very foolish.* **5** to pay attention to the comfort, wishes, etc. of (someone).—Also *v.i.*
consid'erable *adj.* fairly large, great, or important:—*opp.* **inconsiderable.**
consid'erably *adv.*
consid'erate *adj.* thoughtful about others:—*opp.* **inconsiderate.**
considerātion *n.* **1** the act of thinking about something. **2** a fact to be taken into account in making a decision, etc.: *The size of the train fare is a consideration.* **3** compensation or reward. **4** thoughtfulness for others.
consid'ering *prep.* taking into account: *Considering his deafness, he manages to understand very well.*
in consideration of in return for.
take into consideration to make allowance for in considering a situation or problem.

consign *kȯn-sīn', v.t.* **1** to entrust (to e.g. a person's care). **2** to put in, commit (to e.g. the grave, the flames). **3** to send by rail, etc.
consignee' *n.* one to whom anything is consigned or sent by a **consign'or.**
consign'ment *n.* **1** the act of consigning. **2** a load (of goods).

consist *kȯn-sist', v.i.* to be composed (of).
consist'ency (*pl.* **-ies**), less commonly **consist'ence,** *ns.* **1** the degree of thickness: *the consistency of treacle.* **2** the state of being consistent. **3** agreement, harmony.

consist'ent *adj.* **1** not contradictory: *The two statements are consistent*; *The second statement is consistent with the first.* **2** always (acting, thinking) according to the same principles: *He was consistent in his opposition to war*:—*opp.* **inconsistent**.

consis'tently *adv.* **1** always in the same way. **2** invariably.

console[1] *kȯn-sōl'*, *v.t.* **1** to give comfort to. **2** to lessen the grief or disappointment of:—*pr.p.* **consol'ing**.

consolā'tion *n.*

consolation match, **prize**, **race**, etc. a match, prize, race, etc., for those who have been unsuccessful.

See also **inconsolable**.

consort *kon'sört*, *n.* **1** a wife or husband. **2** an accompanying ship.—*v.i. (kȯn-sört')* to keep company (with).

consortium *kȯn-sört'yum*, *-i-um*, *n.* an association, union, etc. (for a special purpose) of international bankers or businessmen:—*pl.* **consort'ia**, **-iums**.

conspicuous *kȯn-spik'ū-ůs*, *adj.* catching the eye, very noticeable:—*opp.* **inconspicuous**.

conspic'uously *adv.*

conspire *kȯn-spīr'*, *v.t.* **1** to plot or scheme together. **2** (of e.g. events) to work together (to bring about a result):—*pr.p.* **conspir'ing**.

conspiracy *kȯn-spir'ȧ-si*, *n.*:—*pl.* **conspir'acies**.

conspir'ator *n.* **conspiratōr'ial** *adj.*

constable *kun'stā-bl*, or *kon'*, *n.* a police officer.

constab'ulary *n.* a police force:—*pl.* **constab'ularies**.

Chief Constable an officer commanding the police force in an administrative area.

constant *kon'stȧnt*, *adj.* **1** unchanging. **2** never stopping. **3** faithful (*opp.* **inconstant**).

con'stancy *n.*

con'stantly *adv.* **1** very often. **2** always.

constellation *kon-stėl-ā'sh(ȯ)n*, *n.* a group of stars.

consternation *kon-stėr-nā'sh(ȯ)n*, *n.* astonishment, dismay.

constipate *kon'stip-āt*, *v.t.* to stop up (esp. the bowels):—*pr.p.* **con'stipating**.

constipated *adj.* **constipā'tion** *n.*

constitute *kon'stit-ūt*, *v.t.* **1** to appoint. **2** to form, make up:—*pr.p.* **con'stituting**.

constit'uency *n.* the voters, or area, represented by a member of parliament:—*pl.* **constit'uencies**.

constit'uent *adj.* **1** helping to form. **2** able to make laws: *a constituent assembly.*—*n.* **1** a necessary part. **2** one of those who elect a representative to parliament.

constitū'tion *n.* **1** the natural condition of body or mind: *He had a strong constitution and survived a lot of hardship.* **2** a set of rules governing a society. **3** the principles and laws according to which a country is governed.

constitū'tional *adj.* **1** born in one: *a constitutional weakness.* **2** legal. **3** reigning, but controlled by law of the land: *a constitutional monarch*:—*n.* a walk for the sake of one's health.

constrain *kȯn-strān'*, *v.t.* to force (a person to do something).

constrained' *adj.* forced, embarrassed: *a constrained smile*.

constraint' *n.* **1** compulsion. **2** loss of freedom of action. **3** a reserved or embarrassed manner.

constrict *kȯn-strikt'*, *v.t.* **1** to press together tightly, squeeze: *His collar constricted his neck.* **2** to restrict.

constrict'or *n.*

construct *kȯn-strukt'*, *v.t.* **1** to build, make. **2** to draw: *to construct a triangle*.

construc'tion *n.* **construc'tional** *adj.*

construc'tive *adj.* **1** having to do with making, not with destroying (opp. of *destructive).* **2** pointing out something that should be done: *a constructive suggestion*.

construc'tor *n.*

put a (wrong) construction on to take a (wrong) meaning out of.

construe *kȯn-strōō'*, *v.t.* **1** to translate. **2** to interpret, explain: *Do not construe my silence as meaning approval*:—*pr.p.* **constru'ing**.

consul *kon'sůl*, *n.* **1** one of two chief magistrates in ancient Rome. **2** an agent who looks after his country's affairs in a foreign country.

con'sūlar *adj.*

con'sūlate *n.* the office or residence of a consul.

consult *kȯn-sult'*, *v.t.* to ask advice or information from.—*v.i.* (of a doctor or lawyer) to give professional advice.

consult'ant *n.* one who gives professional advice.—Also *adj.*

consultā'tion *n.*

consul'tative *adj.* for consultation or discussion only.

consult'ing *adj.* (of a doctor or lawyer) who gives advice.

consume *kȯn-sūm'*, *v.t.* **1** to destroy, e.g. by fire. **2** to eat. **3** to waste or spend.—*v.i.* to waste away:—*pr.p.* **consum'ing**.

consum'er *n.*

consumption *kȯn-sum(p)'sh(ȯ)n*, *n.*

1 the act of consuming. **2** the amount consumed. **3** (*old*) tuberculosis of the lungs.
consumer(s') goods goods to be used, without further manufacturing process, to satisfy human needs.

consummate *kon'sum-āt*, *v.t.* to complete: —*pr.p.* **con'summating**.—*adj.* (*kon-sum'it*) complete, perfect: *He was a consummate actor*.

consumption, See **consume**.

contact *kon'takt*, *n.* **1** touch. **2** meeting. **3** nearness, allowing passage of electric current or passing on of disease. **4** a place where electric current may be allowed to pass. **5** a person who has been in the company of someone with an infectious disease. **6** a go-between.—*v.t.* and *v.i.* to bring, come, into touch, connection, with.
contact lens a, usu. plastic, lens worn in contact with the eyeball instead of spectacles.

contagious *kon-tā'jus*, *adj.* spreading from one person to another: *a contagious disease*; *Excitement is contagious*.
contā'gion *n.*

contain *kon-tān'* *v.t.* **1** to enclose. **2** to include. **3** to keep (an enemy force) from moving. **4** to restrain: *He could not contain his anger*.
contain'er *n.* **1** a receptacle. **2** that in which goods are enclosed for transport.
contain'erise *v.t.* to put (freight) into large standard sealed containers:—*pr.p.* **contain'erising**.
container port, terminal a place where containers are loaded into specially-designed **container ships**.
See also **contents**.

contaminate *kon-tam'i-nāt*, *v.t.* to make impure by touching or mixing (with something):—*pr.p.* **contam'inating**.
contaminā'tion *n.*

contemplate *kon'tem-plāt*, *v.t.* **1** to look at attentively. **2** to intend: *I contemplate going to France*.—*v.i.* to think seriously, meditate:—*pr.p.* **con'templating**.
contemplā'tion *n.*
con'templātive *adj.* (or *-tem'plà-*).

contemporary *kon-tem'po-rar-i*, *adj.* **1** living, happening at, belonging to, the same period. **2** of the same age. **3** (*loosely*) of the present day.—Also *n.* (*pl.* **-ies**).

contempt *kon-tempt'*, *n.* (with *for*) scorn, very low opinion.
contempt'ible *adj.* **1** despicable, deserving scorn. **2** mean.
contempt'uous *adj.* haughty, scornful.
contempt'uously *adv.*
contempt of court disobedience or lack of respect shown to or in a law court.

contend *kon-tend'*, *v.i.* to struggle (against).—*v.t.* to say, maintain (that).
contention *kon-ten'sh(o)n*, *n.* **1** strife. **2** a quarrel. **3** debate. **4** an opinion strongly supported in debate.
conten'tious (*-shus*) *adj.* quarrelsome.

content¹ *kon-tent'*, *adj.* (not used before a noun) **1** satisfied. **2** quietly happy.—*n.* satisfaction—often 'heart's content':—*opp.* **discontent**.—*v.t.* to satisfy, please.
content'ed *adj.* content.
content'edly *adv.* **content'ment** *n.*

content² *kon'tent*, *n.* **1** the information, etc. conveyed in a speech, etc. **2** the amount of something contained in something else. **3** (in *pl.*) things contained. **4** the list of subjects treated in a book.

contention, -ious. See **contend**.

contest *kon-test'*, *v.t.* **1** to argue against. **2** to fight for.—*n.* (*kon'*) **1** a struggle for superiority or victory. **2** strife. **3** debate.
contest'ant *n.* one who contests.

context *kon'tekst*, *n.* the parts of something written or spoken that go before and follow a passage under consideration and may fix its meaning: *This statement, taken out of its context, gives a wrong impression of the speaker's opinions*.
in this context in this particular connection.

contiguous *kon-tig'ū-us*, *adj.* touching, very near.
contigū'ity *n.*

continent¹ *kon'ti-nent*, *n.* **1** one of the great divisions of the land surface of the globe. **2** (**the Continent**) the mainland of Europe.
continent'al *adj.* **1** characteristic of the continent of Europe, European. **2** characteristic of a great land area: *a continental climate*.
continental breakfast a light breakfast of coffee and rolls.
continental quilt a type of quilt used instead of blankets.

continent² *kon'ti-nent*, *adj.* **1** not indulging desire or passion. **2** able to control the excretion of urine, etc.:—*opp.* **incontinent**.
con'tinence *n.*

contingent *kon-tin'jent*, *adj.* (of a happening) dependent (on some other happening or circumstance).—*n.* a quota or group, esp. of soldiers.
contin'gency *n.* a chance happening:—*pl.* **contin'gencies**.
contingency plan a plan made in case a particular situation should arise.

continue *kȯn-tin'ū*, *v.t.* **1** to go on with (*opp.* **discontinue**). **2** to resume, begin again.—*v.i.* **1** to last or endure. **2** to go on, esp. after a break:—*pr.p.* **contin'uing.**
contin'ual *adj.* **1** unceasing. **2** frequent.
contin'ually *adv.*
contin'uance *n.* going on without interruption: *The continuance of the drought may cause a water shortage.*
continuā'tion *n.* **1** going on. **2** beginning again. **3** something that increases or carries on. **4** a further instalment of a story, etc.
contin'ued *adj.* **1** uninterrupted. **2** unceasing. **3** in instalments.
continū'ity *n.* **1** the state of being continuous. **2** a complete scenario of a motion picture. **3** the correct or consistent ordering of scenes in a film, etc.
contin'uous *adj.* joined together, or going on, without interruption.
contin'uum *(-ū-ŭm)* *n.* something which is continuous, without ends or parts.

contort *kȯn-tört'*, *v.t.* to twist or turn violently.
contor'tion *n.* a violent twisting.
contor'tionist *n.* one who practises contorted positions as entertainment.

contour *kon'tōōr*, *n.* outline.
contour line a line drawn on a map through all points at the same height above sea level.
contour map a map in which the shape of land is shown by contour lines.

contra *kon'trȧ*, *prep.* against.—*n.* an argument against (usu. **con**).

contraband *kon'trȧ-band*, *adj.* excluded by law, prohibited.—*n.* smuggled or prohibited goods.

contraceptive *kon-trȧ-sep'tiv*, *n.* and *adj.* (a drug, device) which prevents the conceiving of children.
contracep'tion *n.*

contract *kȯn-trakt'*, *v.t.* **1** to draw together, make smaller. **2** to promise in writing (to do something). **3** to become liable to pay (a debt). **4** to take (a disease). **5** to form (a habit).—*v.i.* **1** to shrink, become less. **2** to bargain (for).—*n.* *(kon'trakt)* an agreement in writing, a bond.
contrac'tion *n.* **1** the act of contracting. **2** a word shortened in speech or spelling.
contract'or *n.* one who promises to do work or furnish supplies at a fixed rate.
contrac'tual *adj.*

contradict *kon-trȧ-dikt'*, *v.t.* **1** to deny, declare to be untrue. **2** to accuse (a person) of a misstatement. **3** to be contrary to: *His second statement contradicts his first.*
contradic'tion *n.* **1** a denial. **2** a statement contradicting, not in keeping with, another.
contradict'ory *adj.* **contradict'oriness** *n.*

contralto *kȯn-tral'tō*, *n.* (a person with) the lowest musical voice in women:—*pl.* **contral'tos.**—Also *adj.*

contraption *kȯn-trap'sh(ȯ)n*, *n.* a contrivance, makeshift machine.

contrary *kon'trȧ-ri*, *adj.* **1** opposite. **2** unfavourable: *contrary winds.* **3** contradictory. **4** *(kon-trā'ri)* perverse, self-willed (*comp.* **contra'rier**; *superl.* **contra'riest**). —*n.* an opposite:—*pl.* **con'traries.**
contrariness *n.*
on the contrary no, the very opposite is true.
to the contrary supporting an opposite statement, view, or contradictory fact, etc.: *It may be true; there is no evidence to the contrary.*

contrast *kȯn-träst'*, *v.i.* to show marked difference from: *His words contrast with his deeds.*—*v.t.* to compare so as to show differences.—*n.* *(kon'träst)* **1** unlikeness in things compared. **2** a thing showing a marked unlikeness (to another).

contravene *kon-trȧ-vēn'*, *v.t.* to disregard, break (a law):—*pr.p.* **contraven'ing.**
contraven'tion *n.*

contretemps *kon^g'trė-ton^g*, *n.* **1** something that happens at an awkward moment. **2** a hitch.

contribute *kȯn-trib'ūt*, *v.t.* **1** to give along with others. **2** to write (an article published in a magazine, etc.).—*v.i.* **1** to give something. **2** to help to bring about: *His gaiety contributed to his popularity*:—*pr.p.* **contrib'uting.**
contribū'tion *n.* something contributed.
contrib'utor *n.*
contrib'utory *adj.* contributing: *a contributory cause; a cause contributory to his downfall.*

contrite *kon'trīt*, *adj.* penitent, deeply sorry for something one has done.
con'triteness, contri'tion *(-tri')* *ns.*

contrive *kȯn-trīv'*, *v.t.* **1** to plan. **2** to invent. **3** to manage (to do something):—*pr.p.* **contriv'ing.**
contriv'ance *n.* **1** an act of contriving. **2** the thing contrived (esp. something mechanical). **3** a plan or scheme.

control *kȯn-trōl'*, *n.* **1** restraint, check: *Please keep the dog under control.* **2** authority, command. **3** a lever or wheel for controlling movements. **4** an experiment done for use as, or anything else which will provide, a standard of comparison for other experiments.—*v.t.* **1** to keep

in check, restrain. **2** to govern:—*pr.p.* **controll'ing**; *pa.p.* **controlled'**.
controll'er *n.* **1** one who, or something that, controls. **2** one who checks the accounts of others.
control panel a panel with switches, gauges, and dials, for operating and checking the functioning of a machine, etc.
control tower a building at an aerodrome from which take-off and landing instructions are given.

controversy *kon'trȯ-vėr-si, kȯn-trov'*, *n.* **1** a discussion of opposing views. **2** strife in words:—*pl.* **controversies**.
controver'sial *(-shȧl) adj.* **1** of controversy. **2** not unquestionably true, open to dispute (e.g. a statement).
controvert'ible *adj.* able to be denied or disproved:—*opp.* **incontrovertible**.

conundrum *kȯn-un'drụm*, *n.* **1** a riddle. **2** a puzzling question.

conurbation *kon-ûr-bā'sh(ȯ)n*, *n.* a group of towns forming a single built-up area.

convalesce *kon-vȧl-es'*, *v.i.* to regain strength after illness:—*pr.p.* **convales'-cing**.
convales'cent *adj.* and *n.*
convales'cence *n.*

convection *kȯn-vek'sh(ȯ)n*, *n.* conveyance of heat through liquids and gases by means of currents due to the movement of the heated parts.
convector (heater) *n.* a heater which works by convection.

convene *kȯn-vēn'*, *v.i.* and *v.t.* to come, or call, together:—*pr.p.* **conven'ing**.
convēn'er *n.* one who convenes a meeting.
See also **convent, convention**.

convenient *kȯn-vēn'yėnt*, *adj.* **1** suitable. **2** handy. **3** easy to use or to reach:—*opp.* **inconvenient**.
conven'ience *n.* **1** suitableness, handiness. **2** any means of giving ease or comfort.
conven'iently *adv.*
convenience food food prepared before sale so as to require little or no preparation before eating.
at your convenience when it suits you, gives you little trouble.
marriage of convenience a marriage made for the sake of practical advantages, usu. money.
public convenience a public toilet.

convent *kon'vėnt*, *n.* a house for nuns (or monks), a nunnery (or monastery).

conventicle *kon-vent'i-kl*, *n.* an illegal gathering, esp. religious, esp. in the 17th century.

convention *kȯn-ven'sh(ȯ)n*, *n.* **1** an assembly, esp. of representatives for some common purpose. **2** a temporary treaty. **3** an agreement. **4** established usage.
conven'tional *adj.* **1** customary. **2** bound by the accepted standards of conduct, manners, or taste. **3** formal. **4** not natural, impulsive, or original.

converge *kȯn-vûrj'*, *v.i.* to move towards, or meet in, one point or value:—*pr.p.* **conver'ging**.
conver'gence *n.* **conver'gent** *adj.*

converse[1]. See **convert**.

converse[2] *kȯn-vûrs'*, *v.i.* to talk easily, not formally:—*pr.p.* **convers'ing**.
conversā'tion *n.* talk.
conversā'tional *adj.*
conversa'tionalist *n.* one who excels in conversation.

convert *kȯn-vûrt'*, *v.t.* **1** to change from one thing into another. **2** to change from one religion to another, or from a sinful to a holy life. **3** to alter (into). **4** to turn (to another purpose): *to convert to one's own use*.—*n. (kon'vėrt)* a converted person.
con'verse *adj.* opposite.—Also *n.*
convert'er *n.* **1** one who converts. **2** an apparatus for making a change in an electric current (also **convertor**).
convert'ible *adj.* **1** that may be converted. **2** exchangeable at a fixed price for gold or other currency.—*n.* a car with a folding top.
convertibil'ity *n.*

convex *kon-veks', kon'*, *adj.* curved on the outside, the reverse of *concave*.
convex'ity *n.*

convey *kȯn-vā'*, *v.t.* **1** to carry. **2** to transmit. **3** to communicate. **4** to make over (property) legally.
convey'er, -or *n.* (also *adj.*).
convey'ance *n.* **1** the act of conveying. **2** a vehicle of any kind. **3** (*law*) the act of transferring property. **4** the writing which transfers it.
convey'ancer *n.* a lawyer who carries out transference of property.
convey'ancing *n.* the branch of the law dealing with the transfer of property.
conveyor belt an endless, moving belt of rubber, metal, etc., carrying articles, e.g. from one part of a building to another.

convict *kȯn-vikt'*, *v.t.* to prove, pronounce, guilty.—*n. (kon'vikt)* one found guilty of crime, esp. one condemned to penal servi-

tude.
convic'tion *n.* **1** the act of convicting. **2** strong belief.

convince *kȯn-vins'*, *v.t.* to persuade (a person) that something is true:—*pr.p.* **convin'cing.**
See also **conviction.**

convivial *kȯn-viv'i-ȧl*, *adj.* social, jovial.
convivial'ity *n.* **conviv'ially** *adv.*

convoke *kȯn-vōk'*, *v.t.* to call together:—*pr.p.* **convok'ing.**
convocā'tion *n.* **1** the act of convoking. **2** an ecclesiastical or university assembly.

convolvulus *kȯn-vol'vū-lu̇s*, *n.* a twining or trailing plant with trumpet-shaped flowers.

convoy *kon'voi*, *v.t.* to accompany for protection.—*n.* **1** a fleet of merchantmen escorted by ships of war. **2** a column of military supplies, or other vehicles, etc.

convulse *kȯn-vuls'*, *v.t.* **1** to shake violently: *to convulse with laughter, pain.* **2** to cause violent laughter in: *The thought convulsed him.*
convul'sion *n.* **1** any involuntary contraction of the muscles causing violent spasms. **2** any violent disturbance. **3** (in *pl.*) fits of laughter.
convuls'ive *adj.* **convuls'ively** *adv.*

cony (*pl.* **-ies**), **coney** (*pl.* **-eys**) *kō'ni*, *kun'i*, *n.* a rabbit.

coo *ko͞o*, *v.i.* **1** to make a sound as a dove. **2** to talk caressingly:—*pr.p.* **coo'ing**; *pa.p.* **cooed** *(ko͞od)*.—Also *n.*

cooee *ko͞o'ē*, **cooey** *ko͞o'i*, *n.* a call to attract attention, orig. the signal-call of Australian aborigines in the bush.

cook *kook*, *v.t.* **1** to prepare (food) by heating. **2** to alter, make false (accounts, etc.).—*n.* one who cooks.
cook'er *n.* a stove for cooking.
cook'ery *n.* the art or practice of cooking.

cookie *kook'i*, *n.* **1** a kind of bun. **2** (*U.S.*) a biscuit.

cool *ko͞ol*, *adj.* **1** slightly cold. **2** calm. **3** indifferent. **4** impudent.—*v.t.* and *v.i.* to make, or grow, cool or cooler.
cool'er *n.* **1** anything that cools. **2** a vessel for cooling.
cool'ly *adv.* **cool'ness** *n.*
cool'-head'ed *adj.* not easily excited, able to act calmly.

coolie, cooly *ko͞ol'i*, *n.* an Indian or Chinese hired labourer:—*pl.* **cool'ies.**

coomb, combe *ko͞om*, *n.* **1** a deep little wooded valley. **2** a hollow in a hillside.

coon *ko͞on*, *n.* **1** a raccoon. **2** a sly fellow. **3** (*derogatory*) a Negro.

coop *ko͞op*, *n.* **1** a wicker basket. **2** a box for fowls or small animals.—*v.t.* to shut up in a coop or elsewhere.—Also **coop up.**

cooper *ko͞op'ėr*, *n.* one who makes tubs, casks, etc.
coop'erage *n.* **1** the work or workshop of a cooper. **2** the sum paid for a cooper's work.

co-operate *kō-op'ėr-āt*, *v.i.* to work together for a purpose:—*pr.p.* **co-op'erating.**
co-operā'tion *n.*
co-op'erative *adj.* willing to co-operate, helpful.—*n.* an enterprise owned by the workers in it.
co-operative society a profit-sharing association of consumers for the cheaper purchase of goods or for other trading purposes.

co-opt *kō-opt'*, *v.t.* to elect into a body by the votes of its members.

co-ordinate *kō-ör'di-nāt*, *v.t.* **1** to adjust (a movement, an action) so that it works in smoothly (with other movements or actions). **2** to make (e.g. movements, efforts) work smoothly together:—*pr.p.* **co-or'dinating.**
co-ordinā'tion *n.*

coot *ko͞ot*, *n.* a waterfowl with a white spot on the forehead.

cop *kop*, (*slang*) *v.t.* to catch:—*pr.p.* **copp'ing**; *pa.p.* **copped.**
cop, copp'er (*slang*) *ns.* a policeman.

copal *kō'pal*, *n.* a hard resin got from many tropical trees.

cope[1] *kōp*, *v.i.* to struggle (with) successfully, manage:—*pr.p.* **cop'ing.**

cope[2] *kōp*, *n.* a long cloak, orig. with a hood, worn by clergy.
cope'-, cop'ing-stone *ns.* **1** the stone that tops a wall. **2** the finishing touch.
cop'ing *n.* the topmost course (see this word) of masonry of a wall.

copious *kō'pi-u̇s*, *adj.* plentiful, overflowing.
cō'piously *adv.* **cō'piousness** *n.*

copper[1] *kop'ėr*, *n.* **1** an element, a metal of a red colour. **2** (usu. in *pl.*) a coin made of copper or a substitute. **3** a vessel made of copper, as a clothes-boiler.
copp'erplate *n.* **1** a plate of polished copper on which something has been engraved. **2** faultless handwriting.

copper[2]. See **cop.**

coppice *kop'is*, **copse** *kops*, *ns.* a wood of low trees for cutting from time to time.

copra *kop'rȧ*, *n.* the dried kernel of the coconut, yielding coconut oil.

copse. See **coppice.**

copulate *kop'ū-lāt, v.i.* to have sexual intercourse (with):—*pr.p.* **cop'ulating**.
copulā'tion *n.*

copy *kop'i, n.* **1** an imitation. **2** a reproduction. **3** an individual specimen of a book. **4** a model for imitation. **5** matter for printing. **6** material for a newspaper writer: *This is good copy*:—*pl.* **cop'ies.**—*v.t.* **1** to make a copy of. **2** to imitate.—*v.i.* to crib work of e.g. a schoolfellow:—*pr.p.* **cop'ying**; *pa.p.* **cop'ied**.
cop'ybook *n.* a writing or drawing book with models for imitation.
cop'yright *n.* the sole right to reproduce a literary, dramatic, musical, or artistic work—also to perform, translate, film, or record such a work.—*adj.* protected by copyright.
cop'ywriter *n.* a writer of copy (esp. advertisements) for the press.
blot one's copybook to make a bad mistake in behaviour, etc.

coquet, **coquette** *ko-ket', v.i.* to flirt:—*pr.p.* **coquett'ing**; *pa.p.* **coquett'ed.**—*n.* (**coquette**) a woman who likes to flirt.
coquett'ish *adj.*

coracle *kor'ȧ-kl, n.* an old kind of rowing-boat made from skins stretched over basketwork.

coral *kor'ȧl, n.* a hard substance of various colours, made up of skeletons of a kind of tiny animal, gradually built up from the bottom of the sea to form a **coral reef** or **island**.

cor anglais *kor on^g'glā*, a type of oboe.

cord *körd, n.* **1** thin rope or thick string. **2** something resembling this. **3** anything that binds.
cord'age *n.* a quantity of ropes.
cord'ite *n.* a smokeless explosive, so called from its cord-like appearance.

cordial *kör'di-ȧl, adj.* **1** hearty, sincere. **2** warm, affectionate.—*n.* **1** anything which revives or comforts. **2** an invigorating or sweetened drink.
cordial'ity *n.* warmth of feeling or the expression of it.
cord'ially *adv.*

cordite. See **cord**.

cordon *kör'don, -dȯn, n.* **1** a cord or ribbon given as a badge of honour. **2** a line of sentries or policemen to prevent access to an area.—*v.t.* (or **cordon off**) to enclose with a cordon.
cordon bleu *kor-don^g blû, adj,* (of a cook or cookery) of a very high standard.

corduroy *kör-dù-roi', n.* **1** a thick ribbed cotton fabric. **2** (in *pl.*) trousers of this.

core *kōr, kör, n.* **1** the inner part of anything, esp. fruit. **2** the part of a nuclear reactor containing the fissile material.—*v.t.* to take out the core of:—*pr.p.* **coring**.

co-respondent *kō-rė-spond'ėnt, n.* (*law*) a person charged with adultery, along with the petitioner's wife or husband, who is the *respondent*.

corgi *kör'gi, n.* a Welsh breed of dog with fox-like head and short legs:—*pl.* **cor'gis**.

cork *körk, n.* **1** the outer bark of the cork tree (an oak of S. Europe, N. Africa, etc.). **2** a stopper, esp. of cork.—*adj.* made of cork.—*v.t.* to stop with a cork, to plug.
corked *adj.* (of wine) spoiled by a faulty cork.
cork'screw *n.* a screw for drawing corks from bottles.—*adj.* like a corkscrew in shape.

corm *körm, n.* the short, bulb-like underground stem of the crocus, etc.

cormorant *kör'mȯ-rȧnt, n.* a web-footed sea bird, known for its large appetite.

corn[1] *körn, n.* **1** a grain, hard particle. **2** seeds of cereal plants or the plants themselves; (in England) wheat, (in Scotland, Ireland) oats, (in North America) maize. **3** anything banal or trite.—*v.t.* to sprinkle with grains of salt, preserve with salt.
corned *adj.* salted—e.g. **corned beef** (now also cooked and canned).
corn'y *adj.* of or like corn, esp. *def. 3*:—*comp.* **corn'ier**; *superl.* **corn'iest**.
corn'cob *n.* (the long woody centre of) the ear of maize.
corn'crake *n.* a bird with a harsh croaking cry, living in cornfields.
corn exchange a market where grain is sold.
corn'flour *n.* finely ground flour esp. of maize.
corn'flower *n.* a blue-flowered plant of cornfields.

corn[2] *körn, n.* a small hard growth chiefly on the foot.
tread on someone's corns to hurt someone's feelings.

cornea *kör'ni-ȧ, n.* the transparent horny membrane that forms the front covering of the eye.
cor'neal *adj.*

cornelian *kör-nēl'yȧn, n.* a red stone used in jewellery.

corner *kör'nėr, n.* **1** the point where two lines or surfaces meet. **2** a secret place. **3** an awkward position, difficulty. **4** in association football, a free kick from the corner flag. **5** a business operation by which a few gain control of the whole available supply of something.—*v.t.* **1** to put in a corner. **2** to put in an embarrassing

position from which escape is difficult. **3** to gain control of the supplies of (something)—*v.i.* to turn a corner.
cor'nerstone *n.* **1** a stone that joins the two walls of a building at a corner, esp. one built into the corner of the foundation. **2** something of the greatest importance.
turn the corner to get past a difficulty or danger.

cornet[1] *kör'nit, n.* **1** an instrument of brass, with three valves, more tapering than the trumpet. **2** any cone- or funnel-shaped object.

cornet[2] *kör'nit, n.* till 1871, a cavalry officer who carried the colours.

cornice *kör'nis, n.* plaster moulding round a ceiling.

Cornish *kör'nish, adj.* of *Cornwall.—n.* the people or former language of Cornwall.

corny. See **corn**[1].

corolla *kȯr-ol'ȧ, n.* the inner covering of a flower, composed of petals.

corollary *kȯr-ol'ȧr-i, n.* a consequence, something that follows from something else:—*pl.* **coroll'aries**.

coronary *kor'ȯ-nȧ-ri, n.* a **coronary thrombosis**, a heart disease caused by the blockage of one of the **coronary arteries** which supply blood to the wall of the heart:—*pl.* **cor'onaries**.

coronation *kor-ȯn-ā'sh(ȯ)n, n.* the act of crowning a sovereign.

coroner *kor'ȯ-nėr, n.* an officer of the Crown who enquires into the causes of accidental or suspicious deaths.

coronet *kor'o-net, n.* **1** a small crown. **2** an ornamental headdress.

corporal[1] *kör'pȯ-rȧl, n.* a non-commissioned officer below a sergeant, or his rank.

corporal[2] *kör'pȯ-rȧl, adj.* **1** of, relating to, the body. **2** not spiritual.
corporal punishment beating, etc.

corporate *kör'pȯ-rit, adj.* **1** legally joined to form a body or corporation. **2** united: *The success was due not to one man but to corporate effort.*
corporā'tion *n.* **1** a body, such as a business company with power given to it by law to act as one individual. **2** a town council. **3** (*coll.*) a large paunch.
corporate spirit willingness to work with others for the good of all.

corps *kōr, kör, n.* **1** a division of an army. **2** an organised group:—*pl.* **corps** *(kōrz, körz).*

corpse *körps, n.* a dead body, esp. of a human being.
corpulence *kör'pū-lėns,* **corpulency** *-lėn-si, ns.* fleshiness, fatness.
cor'pulent *adj.*
corpuscle *kör'pus-l,* or *-pus'l, n.* a cell lying in a fluid such as the blood plasma.

corral *kȯr-al', n.* **1** an enclosure for cattle, etc. **2** in an encampment, an enclosure made by placing wagons in a circle.—*v.t.* **1** to form (wagons) into a corral. **2** to put in a corral:—*pr.p.* **corrall'ing**; *pa.p.* **corralled'**.

correct *kȯr-ekt', v.t.* **1** to remove faults from. **2** to mark errors in. **3** to set (a person) right. **4** to punish.—*adj.* **1** free from faults. **2** true:—*opp.* **incorrect**.
correc'tion *n.* **correct'ly** *adv.*
correct'ive *adj.* intended to, having the power to, set right.—Also *n.*
See also **incorrigible**.

correlate *kor'i-lāt, v.i.* (of facts, etc.) to be related to one another.—*v.t.* to show a relationship between (facts, etc.):—*pr.p.* **corr'elating**.
correlā'tion *n.*

correspond *kor-is-pond', v.i.* **1** to be in agreement (with): *His promises do not correspond with his actions.* **2** to be similar in some way: *The American Congress corresponds to the British Parliament.* **3** to communicate by letter (with).
correspond'ence *n.* **1** agreement. **2** similarity, likeness. **3** communication by letters. **4** letters, etc.
correspond'ent *n.* **1** one with whom another exchanges letters. **2** one who contributes letters or news to a newspaper, etc.

corridor *kor'i-dȯr, n.* **1** a passageway, esp. one off which rooms open. **2** a narrow strip of land serving as a passageway.
corridor carriage, train a carriage, train, with a corridor from end to end.

corrie *kor'i, n.* a rounded hollow in a mountain.

corrigendum *kor-i-jen'dum, n.* a mistake requiring correction:—*pl.* **corrigen'da**.

corroborate *kȯ-rob'o-rāt, v.t.* to support, confirm: *She corroborated her sister's story*; *The witness's statement was corroborated by other evidence*:—*pr.p.* **corrob'orating**.
corroborā'tion *n.*
corrob'orative *adj.* tending to confirm or support: *corroborative evidence*.

corroboree *kȯ-rob'ȯ-rē, n.* **1** a dance of Australian aborigines. **2** a song for this. **3** a festive gathering.

corrode *kȯ-rōd', v.t.* to eat away (as rust, chemicals, etc. do).—*v.i.* to be eaten away:—*pr.p.* **corrod'ing**.
corrosion *kȯ-rō'zh(ȯ)n, n.*

corro'sive *(-siv, -ziv) adj.* eating away as an acid does.—Also *n.*

corrugate *kor'oo-gāt, v.t.* to wrinkle or draw into folds:—*pr.p.* **corr'ugating**.

corrugā'tion *n.*

corrugated iron sheet iron rolled into a wavy shape for the sake of strength.

corrupt *kȯr-upt', v.t.* **1** to cause (fruit, flesh, etc.) to go bad. **2** to make morally rotten. **3** to bribe.—*v.i.* to rot.—*adj.* **1** putrid, bad. **2** wicked. **3** dishonest.

corrupt'ible *adj.* **1** that may be corrupted. **2** capable of being bribed:—*opp.* **incorruptible**.

corrup'tion *n.* **1** rottenness. **2** evilness. **3** bribery. **4** an altered form of a word: *Caterpillar is probably a corruption of Old French chatepelose, a 'hairy cat'.*

corsage *kör-säzh', kör', n.* **1** the bodice or waist of a woman's dress. **2** a small bouquet for pinning on to a dress.

corsair *kör'sār n.* a pirate, or pirate ship.

corselet. Same as **corslet**.

corset *kör'sit, n.* a close-fitting stiff inner bodice.

corslet, **corselet** *körs'lit, n.* **1** armour for the body. **2** a form of corset.

cortege *kör-tezh', n.* a procession, esp. a funeral procession.

corundum *kȯ-run'dum, n.* a very hard mineral, forms of which include sapphire, ruby, emery.

coruscate *kor'ŭs-kāt, v.i.* to sparkle:—*pr.p.* **cor'uscating**.

coruscā'tion *n.*

corvette *kör-vet', n.* an escort vessel, specially designed for protecting convoys against submarine attack.

cos *kos, n.* a long-leafed type of lettuce.

cosh *kosh, n.* a small club.—*v.t.* to hit with a cosh.

cosmetic *koz-met'ik, adj.* **1** designed to increase the beauty of the face, etc. **2** intended to hide defects, improve superficially.—*n.* a preparation for increasing beauty.

cosmos *koz'mos, n.* the universe.

cos'mic *adj.*

cos'monaut *n.* an astronaut, esp. Russian.

cosmopolitan *koz-mȯ-pol'i-tȧn, n.* **1** a citizen of the world. **2** a person who is free from national prejudices.—*adj.* **1** at home in all places. **2** belonging to all parts of the world. **3** containing people from all parts of the world: *New York is a cosmopolitan city.*

cosmic rays streams of very fast moving particles (*def. 2*) coming from outer space.

cossack *kos'ak, n.* one of a people in south-eastern Russia, famous as horsemen.

cosset *kos'it, v.t.* to pamper:—*pr.p.* **coss'eting**; *pa.p.* **coss'eted**.

cost *kost, v.t.* **1** to bring (a certain price). **2** to be valued at (a certain price). **3** to take, require, as if in payment: *The victory cost many lives.* **4** to estimate the cost of producing (something):—*pa.t.* and *pa.p.* **cost** (*defs. 1-3*), **cost'ed** (*def. 4*):—*n.* **1** what is paid or suffered to obtain anything. **2** (in *pl.*) expenses of a lawsuit.

cost'ly *adj.* **1** expensive, of great cost. **2** valuable:—*comp.* **cost'lier**; *superl.* **cost'liest**.

cost'liness *n.*

costermonger *kos'tėr-mung-gėr*, **coster** *ns.* a seller of apples and other fruit, etc., from a barrow.

costliness, **costly**. See **cost**.

costive *kos'tiv, adj.* constipated.

costume *kos'tūm, n.* **1** dress. **2** a woman's outer dress.

costum'er, **costum'ier** *ns.* one who makes or deals in costumes.

costume jewellery jewellery made of inexpensive materials, not real gems.

costume play, etc., one in which actors wear dress of an earlier period.

cosy *kō'zi, adj.* **1** snug. **2** comfortable:—*comp.* **cos'ier**; *superl.* **cos'iest**.—*n.* a covering for a teapot:—*pl.* **cos'ies**.

co'sily *adv.* **cos'iness** *n.*

cot[1] *kot, n.* a small dwelling, a cottage.

cot[2] *kot, n.* a small bed or crib.

cot death the sudden, unexplained death in sleep of an apparently healthy baby.

coterie *kō'tė-ri, n.* a number of people interested in the same things who tend to exclude other people.

cottage *kot'ij, n.* **1** a small house. **2** a country residence.

cott'ager *n.* one who lives in a cottage, esp. a labourer.

cottage cheese a soft, white, loose cheese made from skim milk.

cotton *kot'n, n.* **1** a soft substance like fine wool, the hairs covering the seeds of cotton plants. **2** yarn or cloth made of cotton.—Also *adj.*

cotton gin a machine for separating the seeds from the fibre of cotton.

cotton grass a sedge with long, silky hairs.

cott'ontail *n.* the ordinary American rabbit.

cotton wool **1** cotton in its raw or woolly stage. **2** loose cotton pressed in a sheet used to absorb fluid or to protect an injury. **3** too great protection from the discomforts of life.

cotton on (to) (*coll.*) to understand.

couch[1] *kowch*, *v.t.* **1** to lay down on a bed. **2** to express (in words.) —*n.* **1** a bed. **2** a padded piece of furniture for resting on.

couch[2] **(-grass)** *kowch, kōōch, (-gräs)*, *n.* a grass related to wheat, a troublesome weed.

cougar *kōō'gȧr*, (esp. *U.S.*) *n.* a puma.

cough *kof*, *v.i.* to expel air with a harsh sound.—Also *n.*

could. See **can**[1].

council *kown'sil*, *n.* a body of people meeting to talk over questions and to make decisions or laws.

coun'cillor *n.* a member of a council.

council house a house primarily for renting built by a local authority, e.g. a county council.

council tax a tax based on property value.

counsel *kown'sil*, *n.* **1** advice. **2** a barrister or advocate.—*v.t.* to advise, recommend:—*pr.p.* **coun'selling**; *pa.p.* **coun'selled.**

coun'sellor *n.* one who counsels.

keep one's own counsel to keep one's intentions secret.

take counsel with to discuss problem(s) with.

count[1] *kownt*, *n.* a foreign noble equal in rank to an English earl:—*fem.* **count'ess** a lady of the rank of, or the wife of, a count or earl.

coun'ty *n.* a division of a country, state, etc.:—*pl.* **coun'ties.**

county borough. See **borough**.

county council a council for managing the affairs of a county.

county town the town in which the public business of a county is done.

count[2] *kownt*, *v.t.* **1** to name the numbers up to: *to count twenty.* **2** to find the total number of. **3** to consider: *I count you as one of my friends.*—*v.i.* **1** to name the numbers (to). **2** to be considered. **3** to be important: *Every effort will count.*—*n.* **1** the act of numbering. **2** the number counted. **3** a particular charge brought against a prisoner, etc.

count'er *n.* **1** one who, or something that, counts. **2** a token used in reckoning. **3** a table on which money is counted or goods laid.

count'less *adj.* very many.

count'down *n.* a counting backwards to check progress towards the beginning of an event, regarded as zero.

count'ing-house *n.* a room where accounts are kept.

count for much, little, etc. **1** to be important, unimportant, etc. **2** to have much, little, etc., effect on the result.

count on 1 to rely on (a person). **2** to expect, depend on (a happening).

count out 1 not to include. **2** to say that (a boxer) is the loser because he cannot get up within a count of ten seconds.

out for the count unconscious, exhausted.

countenance *kown'tin-ȧns*, *n.* **1** the face. **2** good will, support.—*v.t.* to favour, encourage:—*pr.p.* **coun'tenancing.**

out of countenance embarrassed, abashed.

counter[1]. See **count**[2].

counter[2] *kown'tėr*, *adv.* in the opposite direction.—*adj.* contrary, opposite.—*v.t.* to meet or answer (a stroke or move) by another.

counteract' *v.t.* to act against, hinder, undo the effect of.

counterac'tion *n.*

coun'ter-attack *n.* an attack in reply to an attack.—Also *v.i.* and *v.t.*

coun'ter-attrac'tion *n.* a rival attraction.

counterbal'ance *v.t.* to balance by weight on the opposite side.—Also *n.* *(kown')*.

coun'tercharge *n.* an accusation made in opposition to another.

coun'ter-claim *n.* a claim made in opposition to another.

coun'ter-clock'wise *adv.* anticlockwise.

coun'ter-esp'ionage *n.* activities directed against the enemy's spy system.

coun'terfoil *n.* a coupon detached from a bank cheque, etc., and kept by the giver.

coun'ter-intell'igence *n.* (an organisation carrying out) measures aimed at preventing an enemy from obtaining information.

coun'termarch *v.i.* to march back or in an opposite direction.—Also *n.*

coun'ter-measure *n.* an action taken to prevent, or to try to undo the effect of, another action.

coun'ter-mō'tion *n.* a proposal in opposition to a motion already made.

coun'ter-offen'sive *n.* a counter-attack.

coun'terpart *n.* **1** a duplicate of a legal document. **2** a person or thing very like another.

coun'terplot *n.* a plot intended to frustrate another plot.

coun'terpoise *v.t.* **1** to weigh against. **2** to act in opposition to with equal effect:—*pr.p.* **coun'terpoising.**—*n.* an equally heavy weight in the other scale.

coun'ter-proposal *n.* one which proposes an alternative to a proposal already made.

coun'ter-revolū'tion *n.* a revolution undoing a previous revolution.

countersign' *v.t.* **1** to sign on the opposite side. **2** to sign in addition to another, so as to certify that a document is genuine.

coun'tersign *n.* a military password.

counterfeit *kown'tėr-fit, -fēt, v.t.* **1** to imitate. **2** to copy unlawfully (e.g. money). **3** to forge.—Also *n.* and *adj.*

counterfoil. See **counter**[2].

countermand *kown-tėr-mänd', v.t.* **1** to recall or to stop (e.g. an order for goods) by a command contradicting one already given. **2** to cancel (a command).

counter-march, etc. See **counter**[2].

counterpane *kown'tėr-pān, n.* a cover for a bed.

counterpart, etc. See **counter**[2].

counter-tenor *kown'tėr-ten'ȯr, n.* a male voice higher than a tenor, or a person with such a voice.—Also *adj.*

countess. See **count**[1].

country *kun'tri, n.* **1** districts where there are fields, moors, etc., as opposed to towns and built-up areas. **2** the land in which one was born or in which one lives. **3** a nation:—*pl.* **coun'tries**.

coun'trified, coun'tryfied *adj.* looking, sounding, acting, like (that of) someone who lives in the country.

coun'try-and-west'ern *n.* a popularised form of music derived from the rural folk-music of the United States.—Also *adj.*

country cousin a relative or person from the country, unaccustomed to the town or its ways.

country dance a dance in which partners are arranged in opposite lines or a circle of couples.

coun'try-folk *n.pl.* the people who live in the country.

coun'try-house, -seat *ns.* a landowner's large house in the country.

coun'tryman *n.* **1** one who lives in the country. **2** one born in the same country as another:—*fem.* **coun'trywoman**.

coun'tryside *n.* the parts of the country other than the towns and cities.

go to the country to hold a general election.

county. See **count**[1].

coup *kōō, n.* **1** a sudden successful stroke, trick, or move. **2** a coup d'état.

coup d'état *(dā-tä')* a sudden and violent change in government.

coupé *kōō-pā', n.* a covered two-door motor-car.

couple *kup'l, n.* **1** something that joins two things together. **2** two of a kind together. **3** a pair. **4** a few.—*v.t.* **1** to join. **2** to associate in thought:—*pr.p.* **coup'ling**.

coup'let *n.* two lines of verse, one following the other, that rhyme with each other.

coup'ling *n.* **1** a link for joining together, e.g. railway carriages. **2** an appliance for transmitting motion in machinery.

coupon *kōō'pon, n.* **1** a part of a ticket, etc. that can be torn off. **2** a piece cut from an advertisement, etc., entitling one to something, e.g. a gift. **3** a betting form, such as a **football coupon**, in which one enters one's forecast of the results of matches.

courage *kur'ij, n.* the quality that makes people able to meet dangers without giving way to fear, bravery.

courā'geous *(-jus) adj.* brave, fearless.

courā'geously *adv.* **courā'geousness** *n.*

courgette *koor-zhet', n.* a small marrow.

courier *kōō'ri-ėr, n.* **1** a messenger. **2** a state messenger. **3** a travelling attendant, e.g. of people on a tour.

course *kōrs, körs, n.* **1** the path in which anything moves. **2** a channel for water. **3** the direction to be followed: *to fly on course*. **4** the ground over which a race is run, golf is played, etc. **5** usual progress or development: *The disease has followed its normal course.* **6** line of action: *Your best course would be to go to the police.* **7** a series, as of lectures, etc. **8** a division of a meal. **9** a row of bricks or stones in a wall.—*v.t.* **1** to run through or over. **2** to hunt (game) with greyhounds.—*v.i.* to move with speed:—*pr.p.* **cours'ing**.

cours'ing *n.*

a matter of course something that will, would, naturally, certainly, happen.

in due course when the natural time for it comes.

in the course of during.

of course naturally, needless to say.

court *kōrt, kört, n.* **1** a space enclosed in some way. **2** one surrounded by house(s). **3** persons who form a sovereign's suite or council. **4** attentions with the aim of winning favour, affection, etc: *to pay court to someone.* **5** (*law*) the place where legal cases are heard. **6** the judges and officials who preside there.—*v.t.* **1** to pay attentions to. **2** to woo. **3** to try to gain (e.g. attention, applause).

court'ier *n.* **1** a member of a sovereign's court. **2** a flatterer.

court'ly *adj.* having fine manners:—*comp.* **court'lier**; *superl.* **court'liest**.

court'ship *n.* wooing.

court'house *n.* a building where the law

courts are held.

court'-mar'tial *(-shȧl) n.* a court held by officers of the armed forces to try offences against service discipline:—*pl.* **courts'mar'tial**, *(coll.)* **court'=mar'tials.**—Also *v.t.*:—*pr.p.* **court'=mar'tialling**; *pa.p.* **court'-mar'tialled.**

court'yard *n.* a court or enclosed ground beside or within a house.

courteous *kûrt'yùs, adj.* polite, considerate and respectful.

court'eously *adv.* **court'eousness** *n.*

courtesy *kûrt'i-si, n.* **1** courteous behaviour. **2** a courteous act:—*pl.* **court'-esies.**

courtier, **courtly**, etc. See **court**.

cousin *kuz'n, n.* **1** the son or daughter of one's uncle or aunt (**full cousin**, **first cousin**), or any descendant of either. **2** also any of various other relations not in the same direct line as oneself.

cove *kōv, n.* **1** a small inlet of the sea, a bay. **2** a cavern or rocky recess.

coven *kuv'ėn, n.* a gathering of witches.

covenant *kuv'ė-nȧnt, n.* an agreement between two people or two parties to do, or to refrain from doing, something.—*v.t.* to agree by covenant (to do something).

Covenant'er (*Scot.*) *n.* one who signed or was loyal to an agreement for the defence of Presbyterianism.

Coventry *kov', kuv'ėnt-ri*: **send to Coventry** to shut out from one's company, refuse to speak to, etc.

cover *kuv'ėr, v.t.* **1** to put or spread something on, over, or about. **2** to clothe. **3** to hide. **4** to protect e.g. by insurance. **5** to include. **6** to be sufficient for. **7** to travel over: *to cover 40 miles in a day.* **8** to point a gun, etc. directly at. **9** to investigate, report on.—*n.* **1** something that covers, hides, protects. **2** undergrowth, thicket concealing game, etc.

cov'erage *n.* **1** the area covered. **2** the items included by an insurance policy, news reporting, etc.

cov'ering *n.* something which covers.

cov'ert *adj.* secret, concealed.—*n.* **1** a place that gives concealment. **2** a thicket.

cov'ertly *adv.* secretly.

covering letter a letter to explain documents enclosed with it.

cover point (*cricket*) the player who supports point and stands to his right.

cover up **1** to cover completely. **2** to conceal (something wrong or dishonest) (*n.* **cov'er-up**).

coverlet *kuv'ėr-lit, n.* a bedcover.

covert. See **cover**.

covet *kuv'it, v.t.* to desire or wish for eagerly (esp. something belonging to someone else):—*pr.p.* **cov'eting**; *pa.p.* **cov'eted.**

cov'etous *adj.* **1** very desirous. **2** greedy, grasping.

cov'etousness *n.*

covey *kuv'i, n.* **1** a brood or hatch (of partridges). **2** a small flock of game birds.

cow[1] *kow, n.* the female of bovine and certain other animals, as the elk, elephant, whale, etc.

cow'boy *n.* **1** (*U.S.*) a man who has charge of cattle on a ranch. **2** (*coll.*) a slighting term for an often inadequately qualified person providing inferior services.

cow'catch'er (*U.S.*) *n.* an apparatus on the front of railway engines to throw off obstacles.

cow'herd *n.* one who herds cows.

cow'hide *n.* **1** the hide of a cow made into leather. **2** a whip made of cowhide.

cow'pox *n.* a disease which appears in pimples on the teats of the cow, the matter from the pimples being used for vaccination against smallpox.

cow[2] *kow, v.t.* to subdue, frighten with threats.

coward *kow'ȧrd, n.* **1** one who turns tail, one without courage. **2** often applied to one who brutally takes advantage of the weak.

cow'ard, **cow'ardly** *adjs.*

cow'ardice, **cow'ardliness** *ns.*

cowboy, **cowcatcher**. See **cow**[1].

cower *kow'ėr, v.i.* **1** to crouch down or shrink back through fear, etc. **2** to crouch timidly.

cowherd, **cowhide**. See **cow**[1].

cowl *kowl, n.* **1** a cap or hood. **2**. a monk's hood. **3** a cover for a chimney, etc. **4** an engine bonnet. **5** a cowling.

cowl'ing *n.* the casing of an aeroplane engine.

cowpox. See **cow**[1].

cowrie, **cowry** *kow'ri, n.* a seashell used among primitive peoples as money and as a magical object:—*pl.* **cow'ries**.

cowslip *kow'slip, n.* a kind of primrose, common in pastures.

cox *koks, n.* a coxswain, esp. of a racing-boat.—Also *v.t.*

coxcomb *koks'kōm, n.* **1** a strip of red cloth notched like a cock's comb, which jesters used to wear. **2** a fop, conceited dandy.

coxswain *kok'sn*, or *kok'swān, n.* **1** one who steers a boat. **2** a petty officer in charge of a boat and crew.

coy *koy, adj.* coquettishly bashful.
coy'ly *adv.* **coy'ness** *n.*

coyote *ko-yō'ti, (U.S.) kī-ōt'i, kī'ōt, n.* a small wolf (*prairie wolf*) of N. America.

coypu *koi'pōō, n.* a large S. American beaver-like water animal which has established itself in East Anglia.

cozy. *U.S.* form of **cosy**.

crab[1] *krab, n.* a sea animal with shell and five pairs of legs, the first pair bearing claws.
catch a crab in rowing, to fail to dip the oar correctly and thus lose balance.

crab[2] *krab, n.* **1** a wild bitter apple (also **crab apple**). **2** a sour-tempered person.

crabbed *krab'id, adj.* **1** ill-natured (also **crabb'y**:—*comp.* **crabb'ier**; *superl.* **crabb'iest**). **2** (of handwriting) badly-formed, cramped.

crack *krak, v.i.* and *v.t.* **1** to make, or cause to make, a sudden sharp sound. **2** to break open (e.g. a nut). **3** to break partly, but not into pieces.—*v.t.* **1** to break a compound (e.g. petroleum) into simpler compounds. **2** to make (a joke).—*n.* **1** a sudden sharp splitting sound. **2** a chink. **3** a flaw. **4** a blow. **5** a biting, witty comment. **5** an expert.—*adj.* (*coll.*) very good: *a crack shot*.
cracked *adj.* **1** damaged. **2** crazy.
crack'er *n.* **1** a thin crisp biscuit. **2** a small tube of paper, usu. containing a gift, paper hat, etc., which comes apart with a bang when the ends are pulled.
crack down (on) to take firm action (against something) (*n.* **crack'down**).
crack up **1** to praise: *It's not all it's cracked up to be.* **2** to fail suddenly, to go to pieces.

crackle *krak'l, v.i.* to give out slight but frequent cracks:—*pr.p.* **crack'ling**.—Also *n.*
crack'ling *n.* the rind of roast pork.
crack'ly *adj.* brittle:—*comp.* **crack'lier**; *superl.* **crack'liest**.

cradle *krā'dl, n.* **1** a bed in which a child is rocked. **2** infancy. **3** a frame of various kinds, e.g. one under a ship that is being built or repaired.—*v.t.* to lay or hold as if in a cradle:—*pr.p* **crad'ling**.

craft *kräft, n.* **1** cunning. **2** skill. **3** an art, skilled trade. **4** (as *pl.*) boats, ships. **5** a (small) ship.
craft'y *adj.* cunning:—*comp.* **craft'ier**; *superl.* **craft'iest**.
craft'ily *adv.* cunningly, secretly.
craft'iness *n.*
crafts'man *n.* one skilled at making something.
crafts'manship *n.* skill in making.

crag *krag, n.* a rough steep rock.
cragg'ed, **cragg'y** (*comp.* **cragg'ier**; *superl.* **cragg'iest**) *adjs.*

cram *kram, v.t.* **1** to stuff, fill very full (with). **2** to stuff (into). **3** to stuff the memory with.—*v.i.* **1** to eat greedily. **2** to stuff the memory with facts for an examination:—*pr.p.* **cramm'ing**; *pa.p.* **crammed**.

cramp *kramp, n.* **1** a painful contraction of the muscles. **2** a tool with a movable part which can be screwed tight so as to press things together. **3** a cramp-iron.—*v.t.* **1** to put where there is not enough space. **2** to restrict, hamper: *Lack of money cramped our efforts.* **3** to fasten with a cramp-iron.
cramped *adj.* **1** without enough room. **2** (of handwriting) small and closely-written.
cramp'-īron *n.* a piece of metal bent at both ends for binding things together.
cramp'on *n.* **1** a grappling-iron. **2** an iron plate with spikes, for the foot, for hill-climbing, pole-climbing, etc.

cran *kran, n.* a measure of quantity of herrings just landed, containing about 1000 on an average.

cranberry *kran'bėr-i, n.* **1** the red acid berry of a small evergreen shrub. **2** the shrub:—*pl.* **cran'berries**.

crane *krān, n.* **1** a large wading bird, with long legs, neck, and bill. **2** a machine for raising heavy weights.—*v.t.* or *v.i.* to stretch out (the neck):—*pr.p.* **cran'ing**.
crane'-fly *n.* a fly with very long legs, the daddy-longlegs:—*pl.* **crane'-flies**.
cranes'bill, **crane's'bill** *n.* a wild geranium.

cranium *krā'ni-ŭm, n.* **1** the skull. **2** the bones enclosing the brain:—*pl.* **cra'nia**, **-iums**.
crā'nial *adj.* of the cranium.

crank *krangk, n.* **1** a device for passing on motion, esp. for changing motion to and fro into motion round and round. **2** an odd notion. **3** a person with odd notions. **4** an ill-tempered person.—*v.t.* to set going by turning a crank.
crank'y *adj.* **1** shaky. **2** full of odd notions. **3** cross:—*comp.* **crank'ier**; *superl.* **crank'iest**.
crank'iness *n.*

cranny *kran'i, n.* **1** a chink, small narrow opening (e.g. in a wall). **2** a hole:—*pl.* **crann'ies**.

crap *krap, (vulg.) n.* **1** faeces. **2** nonsense, rubbish.

crape *krāp, n.* a thin silk fabric with wrinkled surface, usu. dyed black.

crash *krash, n.* **1** a noise as of things breaking or falling on something hard. **2** a collision. **3** a serious business or other failure.—*v.i.* **1** to fall to pieces with a loud noise. **2** to be violently driven (against, into). **3** to land in such a way as to be damaged or destroyed. **4** to gatecrash.—Also *v.t.*
crash'dive' *v.i.* of a submarine, to dive very fast.—Also *v.t.*:—*pr.p.* **crash'div'ing.**
crash helmet a cushioned safety head-dress worn by racing-motorists, motor-cyclists, and airmen.
crash'-land' *v.i.* of an aircraft, to make a landing with the undercarriage up.—Also *v.t.*

crass *kras, adj.* **1** thick. **2** coarse. **3** stupid.

crate *krāt, n.* an openwork container, now usu. made of wooden slats, for packing crockery, carrying fruit, etc.—Also *v.t.*:—*pr.p.* **crat'ing.**

crater *krā'tėr, n.* **1** the bowl-shaped mouth of a volcano. **2** a hole made in the ground by the explosion of a shell, bomb, etc.

cravat *krȧ-vat', n.* a kind of scarf or necktie worn by men.

crave *krāv, v.t.* **1** to beg earnestly for. **2** to long for. **3** to require:—*pr.p.* **crav'ing.**
crav'ing *n.* desire, longing.

craven *krāv'n, n.* a coward.—*adj.* cowardly, spiritless.

craw *krö, n.* the crop or first stomach of fowls.

crawfish. See **crayfish**.

crawl *kröl, v.i.* **1** to move as a snake does. **2** to move on hands and knees. **3** to behave in a much too humble manner. **4** to move very slowly. **5** to be covered with crawling things.—*n.* **1** a slow pace. **2** an alternate overhand swimming stroke.

crayfish *krā'fish*, **crawfish** *krö'fish, n.* **1** a freshwater shellfish. **2** the small spiny lobster.

crayon *krā'ȯn, n.* **1** a coloured pencil of chalk, wax or pipeclay, for drawing. **2** a drawing in crayons.

craze *krāz, v.t.* to make (a person) mad:—*pr.p* **craz'ing.**—*n.* a foolish enthusiasm, fashion, hobby.
craz'y *adj.* **1** frail. **2** mad. **3** made of irregular pieces (as a quilt or pavement). **4** (*coll.*) very enthusiastic (about):—*comp.* **craz'ier**; *superl.* **craz'iest.**
craz'ily *adv.* **craz'iness** *n.*

creak *krēk, v.i.* to make a sharp, grating sound, as of a hinge.—Also *n.*
creak'y *adj.* (*comp.* **-ier**; *superl.* **-iest**).
creak'iness *n.*

cream *krēm, n.* **1** the fatty substance that forms on milk. **2** the best part of anything. **3** any cream-like preparation or refreshment (e.g. *cold cream, ice cream*).—*v.t.* **1** to take the cream (off). **2** to make cream-like.—*v.i.* to form cream, become cream-like.
cream'ery *n.* a place where butter and cheese are made:—*pl.* **cream'eries.**
cream'y *adj.* full of or like cream:—*comp.* **cream'ier**; *superl.* **cream'iest.**
cream'iness *n.*
cream of tartar purified tartar from wines, an ingredient in baking powders.

crease *krēs, n.* **1** a mark made by folding or doubling anything. **2** (*cricket*) a line showing the position of batsman or bowler. —*v.t.* to make creases in.—*v.i.* to become creased:—*pr.p.* **creas'ing.**

creasote. See **creosote**.

create *krē-āt', v.t.* **1** to bring into being. **2** to give rise to. **3** to give a rank, etc. to: *to create a man a peer*:—*pr.p.* **creat'ing.**
creā'tion *n.* **1** the act of creating. **2** something created. **3** the universe.
creā'tive *adj.* able to create, imaginative.
creativ'ity *n.* **creā'tor** *n.*
creature *krē'chůr, n.* **1** something that has been created, esp. an animal. **2** a human being. **3** a person ruled by the will of another.
the Creator God.

crèche *kresh, n.* a public nursery for children.

credence *krē'dėns, n.* belief.
credentials *krė-den'shlz, n. pl.* evidence, esp. written evidence, of trustworthiness or authority.
credible *(kred'-) adj.* that may be believed:—*opp.* **incredible.**
credibil'ity, cred'ibleness *ns.*
cred'ibly *adv.*
cred'it *n.* **1** belief. **2** good reputation. **3** sale on trust. **4** time allowed for payment. **5** the side of an account on which payments received are entered. **6** (in *pl.*) (the list of) the names of people who have helped make a film, etc.—*v.t.* **1** to believe. **2** to enter on the credit side of an account. **3** to think (a person) has: *I do not credit him with much sense*:—*pr.p.* **cred'iting;** *pa.p.* **cred'ited.**
cred'itable *adj.* bringing honour.
cred'itor *n.* one to whom money is owed.
cred'ulous *adj.* believing too easily:—*opp.* **incredulous.**
cred'ulousness, credu'lity *ns.*
credit card a card allowing one to pay for purchased articles at a later date.
be a credit to to bring honour to.

give credit to 1 to believe (a story). **2** to admit that (a person) has earned praise (for some action).

creed *krēd*, *n.* a summary of one's religious, or other, beliefs.

creek *krēk*, *n.* **1** a small inlet or bay, or the tidal estuary of a river. **2** in America and Australia, a small river.

creel *krēl*, *n.* a basket, esp. for fish.

creep *krēp*, *v.i.* **1** to move on or near the ground. **2** to move slowly or stealthily. **3** to grow along the ground or on supports, as a vine. **4** to fawn or cringe. **5** to shudder:—*pa.t.* and *pa.p.* **crept**.—*n.* **1** a crawl. **2** (in *pl.*) horrible shrinking.

creep'er *n.* a creeping plant.

creep'y *adj.* causing creeps, weird:—*comp.* **creep'ier**; *superl.* **creep'iest**.

creep'ily *adv.* **creep'iness** *n.*

cremation *krem-ā'sh(ȯ)n*, *n.* the act of burning, esp. of the dead.

cremate' *v.t.*:—*pr.p.* **cremat'ing**.

crematōr'ium *n.* a place where cremation is done.

creosote *krē'ȯ-sōt*, **creasote** *krē'ȧ-sōt*, *n.* an oily liquid obtained from wood tar.—*v.t.* to treat (e.g. wood) with creosote as a preservative:—*pr.p.* **cre'osoting**.

crêpe *krāp*, *n.* **1** a crape-like fabric. **2** rubber rolled in thin crinkly sheets. **3** a pancake.

crêpe'-de-chine' *(-dė-shēn')* *n.* a crape-like fabric, originally of silk.

crêpe paper a type of thin crinkled paper.

crepitation *krep-i-tā'sh(ȯ)n*, *n.* a sound that can be heard in the lungs in certain diseases.

crept. See **creep**.

crescendo *kresh-en'dō*, *adv.* gradually increasing in force or loudness.—Also *n.* (*pl.* **-dos**).

crescent *kres'ėnt*, *adj.* shaped like the new or old moon.—*n.* something of this shape, e.g. a curved row of houses.

cress *kres*, *n.* a plant with sharp-tasting leaves used in salads.

crest *krest*, *n.* **1** the comb or tuft on the head of a cock or other bird. **2** the summit, highest part (e.g. of a hill, a wave). **3** a plume of feathers on top of a helmet. **4** a badge or emblem.

crest'fallen *adj.* dejected, very much disappointed.

cretin *kre'tin*, or *krē'*, *n.* a person suffering from cretinism.

cre'tinism *n.* a disease caused by the fact that the thyroid gland does not work properly, one symptom (if the disease is not treated) being mental deficiency.

cretonne *kret-on'*, or *kret'*, *n.* a strong printed cotton fabric used for curtains or for covering furniture.

crevasse *krė-vas'*, *n.* a crack or split, esp. a cleft in a glacier.

crevice *krev'is*, *n.* **1** a crack. **2** a narrow opening.

crew[1] *kroo͞*, *n.* **1** a company, gang, mob. **2** those who man a ship. **3** the group of people in charge of an aeroplane in flight or a travelling bus, train, etc.

crew[2]. See **crow**.

crib *krib*, *n.* **1** a manger. **2** a stall for oxen. **3** a child's bed. **4** (*coll.*) a key or literal translation used by school pupils.—*v.t.* to steal or copy (another's work):—*pr.p.* **cribb'ing**; *pa.p.* **cribbed**.

crick *krik*, *n.* a cramp of the muscles, esp. of the neck.

cricket[1] *krik'it*, *n.* an insect related to the grasshopper, the male of which makes a chirping noise with his wing-covers.

cricket[2] *krik'it*, *n.* **1** an outdoor game played with bats, a ball, and wickets, between two sides of eleven each. **2** (*coll.*) fair play.

crick'eter *n.*

cried, **crier**. See **cry**.

crime *krīm*, *n.* **1** act(s) punishable by law. **2** an offence, sin.

criminal *(krim'-)* *adj.* **1** concerned with crime: *criminal law*; *a criminal lawyer.* **2** guilty of crime. **3** of the nature of crime.—*n.* one guilty of crime.

criminal'ity *n.* **crim'inally** *adv.*

criminol'ogy *n.* the study of crime and criminals.

criminol'ogist *n.*

crimp *krimp*, *v.t.* **1** to press into folds or pleats. **2** to give a corrugated appearance to. **3** to make crisp.

crimson *krim'zn*, *n.* a deep purplish red colour.—Also *adj.*

cringe *krinj*, *v.i.* **1** to crouch with fear. **2** to behave too humbly:—*pr.p.* **cringing**.

crinkle *kring'kl*, *v.t.* to wrinkle, crimp.—*v.i.* to wrinkle up:—*pr.p* **crink'ling**.—*n.* a wrinkle.

crink'ly *adj.* wrinkly:—*comp.* **crink'lier**; *superl.* **crink'liest**.

crinoline *krin'o-lin*, *n.* **1** a stiff fabric of horsehair and flax, used to make skirts stick out. **2** a petticoat or skirt on hoops of steel wire.

cripple *krip'l*, *n.* a lame or disabled person.—Also *adj.*—*v.t.* **1** to lame. **2** to deprive of power or strength:—*pr.p.* **cripp'ling**.

crisis *krī'sis, n.* **1** the time of greatest importance or danger. **2** the decisive moment. **3** a time of great difficulty or distress. **4** the turning-point (of a disease):—*pl.* **crises** *(krī'sēz)*, or (*coll.*) **cri'sises**. See also **critical**.

crisp *krisp, adj.* **1** (of hair) curling. **2** having a wavy surface. **3** dry and brittle. **4** (of air) bracing. **5** (of e.g. style) firm, decided.—*v.t.* to make crisp.
crisp'ly *adv.* **crisp'ness** *n.*
crisp'y *adj.*:—*comp.* **crisp'ier**; *superl.* **crisp'iest**.
crisp'iness *n.*

criss-cross *kris'kros, n.* **1** a mark formed by two lines in the form of a cross. **2** a network of crossing lines.—Also *adj., adv., v.t.* and *v.i.*

criterion *krī-tē'ri-on, n.* a standard used, referred to, in judging:—*pl.* **critē'ria**.

critic *krit'ik, n.* **1** one who judges literary or artistic work. **2** one who finds faults.
crit'ical *adj.* **1** of criticism. **2** judging good and bad points. **3** fault-finding. **4** of a crisis. **5** of great(est) importance: *Help arrived at the critical moment.* **6** dangerous: *a critical shortage of food.*
crit'ically *adv.*
crit'icise *v.t.* **1** to give an opinion of, or judgment on (something). **2** to find fault with:—*pr.p.* **crit'icising**.
crit'icism *n.*

croak *krōk, v.i.* **1** to utter a low hoarse sound, as a frog or raven. **2** to grumble. **3** (*slang*) to die.—Also *n.*
croaky *adj.*:—*comp.* **croak'ier**; *superl.* **croak'iest**.

crochet *krō'shā, n.* a handcraft like knitting, done with a small hook.—Also *v.i.* and *v.t.*:—*pr.p.* **cro'cheting** *(krō'shā-ing)*; *pa.p.* **cro'cheted** *(krō'shād)*.

crock[1] *krok, n.* a pot or jar.
crock'ery *n.* earthenware and china vessels.

crock[2] *krok, n.* **1** an old horse. **2** a broken-down or useless person, car, etc.
crock up (*coll.*) to break down in health.

crocodile *krok'ȯ-dīl, n.* **1** a large reptile found in the rivers of Asia, Africa, South America, and northern Australia. **2** a double file of schoolchildren.
crocodile tears sham tears, hypocritical grief.

crocus *krō'kus, n.* a plant with brilliant yellow, purple, or white flowers, growing from a corm.

croft *kroft, n.* **1** a small piece of enclosed land esp. for growing crops. **2** a small farm.
croft'er *n.*

croissant *krwä'sonᵍ, n.* a crescent-shaped roll.

cromlech *krom'lek, n.* a circle of upright stones.

crone *krōn, n.* a withered old woman.

crony *krōn'i, n.* a close companion:—*pl.* **crōn'ies**.

crook *krook, n.* **1** a bend. **2** a staff bent at the end, as a shepherd's or bishop's. **3** a swindler.—*v.t.* and *v.i.* to bend into a hook.
crook'ed *(-id) adj.* **1** not straight. **2** dishonest. **3** *(krookt)* bent like a crook.
crook'edly *adv.* **crook'edness** *n.*

croon *krōōn, v.t.* and *v.i.* **1** to sing or hum in an undertone. **2** to sing quietly in a very sentimental manner.—Also *n.*
croon'er *n.*

crop *krop, n.* **1** a hunting-whip with a loop instead of a lash. **2** a mode of cutting the hair short. **3** the total growth or quantity harvested. **4** the craw of a bird.—*v.t.* **1** to cut off the top or ends of. **2** to cut short. **3** to raise crops on:—*pr.p.* **cropp'ing**; *pa.p.* **cropped**.
crop up to come up (in conversation), happen, unexpectedly.

cropper *krop'ėr, n.* **1** a fall. **2** a failure.
come a cropper to have a fall.

croquet *krō'kā, n.* a game in which wooden balls are driven by mallets through series of arches set in the ground.

croquette *kroket', n.* a fried ball or cake of minced meat or fish.

crosier, crozier *krō'zhyer, n.* the staff of a bishop or abbot.

cross *kros, n.* **1** a gibbet, consisting of two beams, one placed across the other. **2** (the symbol of) the Christian religion. **3** the sufferings of Christ. **4** any lasting cause of suffering or unhappiness. **5** a hybrid: *a cross between a bulldog and a terrier.* **6** a monument in a street, often a cross, where proclamations are made, etc.—*v.t.* **1** to make the sign of the cross over. **2** (to cause) to pass from one side to the other of. **3** to thwart, oppose the wishes of (a person). **4** to breed from (two different species of an animal or plant). **5** to draw two lines across (a cheque) to show that it may be paid only to a bank account.—*v.i.* **1** to lie or pass across. **2** to meet and pass.—*adj.* **1** lying across. **2** ill-tempered. **3** hybrid.
cross'ing *n.* **1** the act of going across, or of opposing the wishes of another, etc. **2** the place where a roadway, etc., may be crossed.
cross'ly *adv.* in an ill-tempered way.
cross'wise *adv.* across, transversely.
cross'bar *n.* a horizontal bar, usu.

between upright supports.

cross'-benches *n.pl.* seats in Parliament for members (**cross'-benchers**) who do not wish to vote either on the Government side or on the Opposition.

cross'bones *n.pl.* two thigh bones laid across each other—forming, with the skull, an emblem of death or piracy.

cross'bow *n.* a bow placed crosswise on a *stock* or wooden bar, with devices for pulling back the string and shooting the arrow.

cross'breed *n.* a breed produced by the crossing of different breeds.

cross'bred *adj.*

cross'-coun'try *adj.* **1** across a country. **2** across fields, etc., not on roads.

cross'-exam'ine *v.t.* **1** to test the evidence of (a witness on the other side) by questioning him. **2** to question searchingly: *—pr.p.* **cross'-exam'ining.**

cross'-examinā'tion *n.*

cross'-eyed *adj.* having a squint.

cross'fire *n.* lines of gunfire from two, or more, points crossing each other.

cross'-grained' *adj.* **1** (of wood) with irregular grain. **2** ill-natured and unwilling to do what other people want.

cross'patch *n.* an ill-natured person.

cross'piece *n.* a piece lying across something else.

cross'-ply (tyre) *n.* a tyre in which the layers of fabric in the body of the tyre are wrapped so as to cross each other diagonally.

cross'-pur'pose *n.* an opposing purpose or plan (**be at cross-purposes** to misunderstand each other, to be unconsciously talking of different things, working on different plans, etc.)

cross'-question *v.t.* to cross-examine.

cross'-ref'erence *n.* a reference from one part of a book to another (e.g. *crawfish.* See *crayfish*).

cross'road *n.* **1** a road crossing the principal road. **2** (in *pl.*) the place of crossing of two roads. **3** a point where an important choice of action has to be made.

cross'-sec'tion *n.* **1** a section made by cutting across (e.g. across a pipe at right angles to the length). **2** a sample showing all the important parts: *A cross-section of British opinion on a subject would show what people of different social classes, doing different kinds of work, thought about it.*

crossword (puzzle) *n.* a word-puzzle in which a square is to be filled with words reading across and down found from clues.

cross out to draw a line through.

on the cross diagonally.

crosse. See **lacrosse.**

crotchet *kroch'it, n.* **1** a note in music, equal to half a minim (♩). **2** a queer notion or opinion, an odd habit.

crotch'ety *adj.* **1** having crotchets, cranky. **2** ill-tempered.

crouch *krowch, v.i.* **1** to bend down or lie close to the ground. **2** to cringe.

croup[1] *kro͞op, n.* the rump of a horse.

croup[2] *kro͞op, n.* a children's disease causing breathing difficulties and a harsh cough.

croupier *kro͞o'pi-ėr,* or *-pi-ā, n.* one who collects the money at the gaming-table.

crow *krō, n.* **1** the name given to a number of large birds, generally black, including raven, rook, hooded crow, and carrion crow. **2** the carrion crow in particular. **3** the cry of a cock. **4** an infant's cry of joy.—*v.i.* **1** to croak. **2** to cry as a cock or happy baby. **3** to boast:—*pa.t.* **crew** *(kro͞o)* or **crowed**; *pa.p.* **crowed.**

crow'bar *n.* a large iron lever bent at the end like the beak of a crow.

crow's'-foot *n.* a wrinkle at the outer corner of the eye:—*pl.* **crow's'-feet.**

crow's'-nest *n.* **1** a shelter at the masthead of a ship for a lookout man. **2** any high lookout point.

as the crow flies in a straight line.

crowd *krowd, n.* **1** a number of persons or things closely pressed together, without order. **2** people in general. **3** (*coll.*) a set of people, friends.—*v.t.* **1** to fill by pressing together. **2** to fill too full. **3** to give too little space.—*v.i.* **1** to press on. **2** to swarm, throng.

crowd'ed *adj.*

crown *krown, n.* **1** a circular head-ornament, esp. as a mark of royalty or honour. **2** the sovereign. **3** governing power in a monarchy. **4** the top, e.g. of head, hat, hill. **5** a gold, etc. cap fitted over a broken or bad tooth. **6** (*old*) a coin worth 25p.—*v.t.* **1** to set a crown on. **2** to reward, finish happily: *Success crowned her efforts.*

crown colony a colony without representative government, governed directly by the home government.

crown land land belonging to the sovereign.

crown prince in some countries, the heir to the throne:—*fem.* **crown princess.**

crozier. Same as **crosier.**

crucial *kro͞o'shal, adj.* **1** testing. **2** of the greatest importance, decisive: *This was the crucial test; He came at the crucial moment.*

See also **crux.**

crucible *kroo͞'si-bl, n.* a pot for melting metals, etc.

cruciform *kroo͞'si-förm, adj.* cross-shaped.

crucify *kroo͞'si-fī, v.t.* **1** to put to death on a cross. **2** to torture. **3** to treat harshly, hold up to scorn:—*pr.p.* **cru'cifying**; *pa.p.* **cru'cified**.
cru'cifix *n.* a figure or picture of Christ on the cross.
crucifix'ion *n.* death on the cross, esp. (usu. *cap.*) that of Christ.

crude *kroo͞d, adj.* **1** not prepared, unrefined: *crude oil*. **2** blunt, tactless: *a crude statement*; *crude behaviour*.
crude'ness, **crud'ity** (*pl.* **-ies**) *ns.*

cruel *kroo͞'ėl, adj.* **1** pleased at causing pain. **2** merciless. **3** very painful: *cruel sufferings*.
cru'elly *adj.* **cru'elty** (*pl.* **-ies**) *n.*

cruet *kroo͞'it, n.* a small jar or bottle for sauces, salt, pepper, etc.
cru'et(-stand) *n.* a frame for holding cruets.

cruise *kroo͞z, v.i.* **1** to sail, fly, or wander to and fro. **2** to go at cruising speed:—*pr.p.* **cruis'ing**.—*n.* a voyage from place to place for pleasure or in search of enemy ships, etc.
cruis'er *n.* a fast medium-sized warship.—See also **cabin cruiser** at **cabin**.
cruising speed **1** (*aircraft*) the speed at which the engine works most efficiently and economically. **2** (*motor car*) the best speed for a long drive.

crumb *krum, n.* a fragment or morsel, esp. of bread.
crumb'y, **crumm'y** *adj.* **1** in, or covered with, crumbs. **2** (*coll.*) not good, inferior, unpleasant, etc.:—*comp.* **-ier**; *superl.* **-iest**.

crumble *krum'bl, v.t.* to break into crumbs.—*v.i.* **1** to fall into small pieces. **2** to decay:—*pr.p.* **crum'bling**.
crum'bly *adj.* apt to crumble, brittle:—*comp.* **crum'blier**; *superl.* **crum'bliest**.

crummy. See **crumb**.

crumpet *krump'it, n.* a flat soft cake.

crumple *krump'l, v.t.* **1** to crush into folds or wrinkles. **2** to crease.—*v.i.* **1** to become wrinkled. **2** (usu. **crumple up**) to collapse:—*pr.p.* **crum'pling**.

crunch *krunch*, or *-sh, v.t.* **1** to crush with the teeth or underfoot. **2** to chew (anything hard) and so make a noise.—*n.* **1** a noise of crunching. **2** (*coll.*) the testing moment, real trial of strength

crupper *krup'ėr, n.* **1** a strap of leather fastened to the saddle and passing under the horse's tail to keep the saddle in its place. **2** the hind part of a horse.

crusade *kroo͞-sād', n.* **1** (*history*) a military expedition of Christians to win back the Holy Land from the Muslims. **2** a continued vigorous effort to help forward a (good) cause.—*v.i.* to take part in a crusade:—*pr.p.* **crusad'ing**.
crusad'er *n.*

crush *krush, v.t.* **1** to break, or crumple. **2** to squeeze together. **3** to overwhelm, subdue: *to crush one's enemies*.—*v.i.* to push one's way (past, etc.).—*n.* **1** a tightly packed crowd. **2** a drink made of the juice of crushed fruit.
crush'-barrier *n.* a barrier put up to keep back a crowd.

crust *krust, n.* **1** the hard rind or outside coating e.g. of bread, pie. **2** the outer part of the earth.—*v.t.* to form a crust on.—*v.i.* to form a crust.
crust'y *adj.* **1** having a crust. **2** surly, irritable:—*comp.* **crust'ier**; *superl.* **crust'iest**.
crust'ily *adv.* **crust'iness** *n.*

crustacean *krus-tā'shȧn, n.* any animal of the class including crabs, lobsters, barnacles, etc.

crutch *kruch, n.* **1** a staff with a crosspiece at the head to support a lame person. **2** any support or prop.

crux *kruks, n.* **1** a difficult point. **2** the essential point: *That is the crux of the matter, of the problem*.

cry *krī, v.i.* **1** to utter a shrill loud sound. **2** to shed tears.—*v.t.* **1** to utter loudly. **2** to announce in public. **3** (*old*) to offer for sale by crying:—*pr.p.* **cry'ing**; *pa.p.* **cried**.—Also *n.*:—*pl.* **cries**.
cri'er *n.*
cry'ing *adj.* **1** that cries. **2** demanding to be put right: *a crying evil*.
a far cry a great distance.
cry down to speak slightingly of.
cry off to cancel an engagement or agreement.
cry up to praise.
in full cry in full pursuit, used of dogs in a hunt.

cryo- *krī'ō-* (as part of a word) of very low temperatures.

crypt *kript, n.* an underground cell or chapel.
cryp'tic *adj.* **1** secret. **2** very difficult to understand: *a cryptic saying*.
cryp'to- (as part of a word) hidden.
cryp'to *n.* a secret member of a party:—*pl.* **cryp'tos**.

crystal *kris'tl, n.* **1** a clear quartz. **2** (a piece of) a solid material (e.g. salt or ice) whose atoms are arranged in a regular pattern. **3** anything bright or clear. **4** cut glass. **5** a

vessel of cut glass. **6** glassware.
crys'tal, **crys'talline** *adjs.* consisting of crystal, or like crystal in clearness.
crys'tallise *v.t.* and *v.i.* **1** to form into crystals. **2** to make or become definite or clear: *His thoughts about the matter had not had time to crystallise.*—*v.t.* to cover with a coating of sugar crystals:—*pr.p.* **crys'tallising**.
crystallisā'tion *n.*

cub *kub*, *n.* **1** the young of certain animals, as foxes, etc. **2** (*often slightingly*) a young boy or girl. **3** (*cap.*) a **Cub Scout**, a boy belonging to the junior section of the Scout Association.—*v.i.* to bring forth young:—*pr.p.* **cubbing**; *pa.p.* **cubbed**.

cube *kūb*, *n.* **1** a solid body having six equal square faces. **2** the third power of a quantity (e.g. 8 = 2 × 2 × 2 = the cube of 2).—*v.t.* to raise to the third power:—*pr.p.* **cub'ing**.
cū'bic *adj.* **1** of a cube (also **cū'bical**). **2** of the third power or degree. **3** equal in volume to a cube whose edge is the stated length: *a cubic centimetre*.
cub'ism *n.* an attempt in painting to express the artist's emotions by putting different views of an object into the same picture and using geometrical shapes.
cube root the number of which a given number is the cube (e.g. 2 is the cube root of 8).

cubicle *kū'bi-kl*, *n.* a small place partitioned off from a larger room.

cubism. See **cube**.

cubit *kū'bit*, *n.* a measure used long ago, equal to the length of the arm from the elbow to the tip of the middle finger (18 to 22 inches, 46 to 56cm).

cuckoo *kook'ōō*, *n.* a bird that cries 'cuckoo', and that puts its eggs in the nests of other birds.

cucumber *kū'kum-bėr*, *n.* a creeping plant, with long fruit used as a salad and pickle.

cud *kud*, *n.* food brought from the first stomach of a ruminating animal (e.g. a cow) back into the mouth and chewed again.

cuddle *kud'l*, *v.t.* to hug, to fondle:—*pr.p.* **cudd'ling**.—Also *v.i.* and *n.*
cudd'ly *adj.*:—*comp.* **cudd'lier**; *superl.* **cudd'liest**.

cudgel *kuj'l*, *n.* a heavy staff, a club.—*v.t.* to beat with a cudgel:—*pr.p.* **cudg'elling**; *pa.p.* **cudg'elled**.
take up the cudgels for (someone) to defend (a person) vigorously.

cue[1] *kū*, *n.* **1** the last words of another actor's speech, or a noise or movement, etc., serving as a sign to an actor to speak, etc. **2** a hint about how to act or behave: *In condemning the action the Press took their cue from the Government spokesman.*

cue[2] *kū*, *n.* **1** a pigtail. **2** a tapering rod used in playing billiards, snooker, etc.

cuff[1] *kuf*, *n.* a blow with the open hand.—Also *v.t.*

cuff[2] *kuf*, *n.* **1** the end of the sleeve near the wrist. **2** a covering for the wrist.
cuff'-link *n.* one of a pair of ornamental fasteners for shirt cuffs.
off the cuff without planning or rehearsal.

cuirass *kwi-ras'*, or *kū-*, *n.* a covering, orig. of leather, to defend breast and back.

cuisine *kwi-zēn'*, *n.* (the art of, or a style of) cookery.

cul-de-sac *kul'-dė-sak*, *n.* a street closed at one end.

culinary *ku'lin-ȧr-i*, *kū'*, *adj.* of, used in, the kitchen or in cookery.

cull *kul*, *v.t.* **1** to select. **2** to pick, gather. **3** to pick out and destroy as superfluous, etc. (as seals, deer) (also *n.*).

cullender. Same as **colander**.

culminate *kul'mi-nāt*, *v.i.* **1** to reach the highest point. **2** to reach the greatest development: *The disturbances culminated in a battle with knives*:—*pr.p.* **cul'minating**.
culminā'tion *n.*

culottes *koo-lots'*, *n.pl.* loose-fitting, usu. knee-length, shorts, looking like a skirt.

culpable *kul'pȧ-bl*, *adj.* deserving blame.
culpabil'ity, **cul'pableness** *ns.*
cul'pably *adv.*

culprit *kul'prit*, *n.* **1** one who is at fault. **2** a criminal. **3** (*Eng. law*) a prisoner accused but not yet tried.

cult *kult*, *n.* **1** a system of religious belief. **2** a sect. **3** great devotion to: *the cult of physical fitness*.

cultivate *kul'ti-vāt*, *v.t.* **1** to till or prepare (ground) for crops. **2** to grow (a crop). **3** to develop, or improve, by care or study: *to cultivate good manners.* **4** to encourage (e.g. science, friendship). **5** to seek the company of (a person).
cultivā'tion *n.* **1** the art or practice of cultivating. **2** a refined, cultivated state.
cul'tivator *n.* an implement for breaking up ground, esp. among crops.
culture *kul'chur*, *n.* **1** cultivation. **2** educated refinement. **3** a type of civilisation: *Bronze Age culture*.
cul'tural *adj.* **cul'turally** *adv.*
cul'tured *adj.* **1** cultivated. **2** well educated, refined.

culvert *kul'vert, n.* an arched watercourse under a road, etc.

cumber *kum'bėr, v.t.* **1** to get in the way of. **2** to burden uselessly.
cum'bersome, **cum'brous** *adjs.* **1** heavy, unwieldy. **2** burdensome.

cummerbund *kum'ėr-bund, n.* a sash worn around the waist.

cumulative *kūm'ū-lāt-iv, adj.* becoming greater by additions: *Frequent small doses have a cumulative effect*; *cumulative evidence*.

cunning *kun'ing, adj.* **1** skilful, clever: *a cunning device for opening the high window.* **2** crafty, sly.—*n.* **1** skill. **2** craftiness, slyness.

cup *kup, n.* **1** a drinking-vessel. **2** the amount contained in a cup. **3** anything cup-shaped. **4** an ornamental vessel used as a prize.—*v.t.* **1** to form into the shape of a cup. **2** to hold in something cup-shaped:—*pr.p.* **cupp'ing**; *pa.p.* **cupped**.
cup'ful *n.* as much as fills a cup:—*pl.* **cup'fuls**.
cupboard *kub'ȯrd, n.* a place for keeping food, dishes, etc.
cup'-tie *n.* one of a series of games in a competition in which the prize is a cup.

Cupid *kū'pid, n.* the Roman god of love.
cupid'ity *n.* desire for wealth, greed.

cupola *kū'pȯ-lȧ, n.* **1** a rounded vault on the top of a building. **2** a dome, esp. a small one.

cupri- *kūp'ri-*, **cup'ro-** *-rō-* (as part of a word) of or containing copper.
cup'rō-nick'el *n.* an alloy of copper and nickel.—Also *adj.*

cur *kûr, n.* **1** a mongrel dog. **2** a surly, rude, or cowardly person.

curate *kūr'it, n.* a Church of England cleric assisting a rector or vicar.

curative. See **cure**.

curator *kū-rā'tȯr, n.* one in charge of something, e.g. of a place where things are shown, such as a museum.

curb *kûrb, n.* **1** a chain or strap attached to the bit for holding back a horse. **2** a check or restraint: *to put a curb on his wild enthusiasm.* **3** another spelling (esp. *U.S.*) of **kerb**.—*v.t.* to restrain or check.

curd *kûrd, n.* **1** milk thickened by acid. **2** (often in *pl.*) the solid part of milk, as distinguished from the whey.
curd'le *v.t.* and *v.i.* to turn into curd:—*pr.p.* **curd'ling**.
curdle someone's blood to horrify someone.

cure *kūr, n.* **1** the action of healing. **2** something that heals or makes well.—*v.t.* **1** to heal. **2** to rid (someone of e.g. a bad habit). **3** to preserve, as by drying, salting etc.:—*pr.p.* **cur'ing**.
cur'able *adj.*:—*opp.* **incurable**.
cur'ative *adj.* intended to, likely to, cure.—*n.* a remedy.

curfew *kûr'fū, n.* **1**. (*history*) the ringing of a bell as a signal to put out fires and lights. **2** an order forbidding people to be in the streets after a certain hour.

curio *kū'ri-ō, n.* a rare and curious article:—*pl.* **cū'rios**.

curious *kū'ri-ůs, adj.* **1** anxious (to find out). **2** inquisitive. **3** strange, odd.
curios'ity *n.* **1** inquisitiveness. **2** eagerness to find out. **3** something strange and rare: —*pl.* **curios'ities**.

curl *kûrl, v.t.* to twist into ringlets, to coil.—*v.i.* **1** to form curls, curves, or spirals. **2** to play at the game of curling.—*n.* **1** a ringlet of hair, etc. **2** a wave, bend, or twist.
curl'iness *n.*
curl'ing *n.* a game played on ice.
curl'y *adj.*:—*comp.* **curl'ier**; *superl.* **curl'iest**.

curlew *kûr'lū*, or *-lōō, n.* a moorland bird with long curved bill, long legs, and a plaintive cry.

curling, etc. See **curl**.

currant *kur'ȧnt, n.* **1** a small black raisin or dried seedless grape. **2** the fruit of any of several shrubs.

currency. See **current**.

current *kur'ėnt, adj.* **1** passing from person to person: *This story is current.* **2** present: *the current month.*—*n.* **1** a stream of water or air. **2** a flow of electricity. **3** course: *the current of events*.
curr'ently *adv.*
curr'ency *n.* **1** the fact, time, of being current. **2** money of a country (*pl.* **-ies**).
current account a bank account from which money may be withdrawn by cheque.

curriculum *kůr-ik'ū-lům, n.* a course, esp. of study at school or university:—*pl.* **curric'ulums**, or **-la**.
curriculum vitae *(vē'tī)* a brief account of a person's life, education, experience, interests, etc.

curry[1] *kur'i, n.* **1** a seasoning of turmeric and mixed spices. **2** a stew flavoured with it:—*pl.* **curr'ies**.—*v.t.* to cook with curry:—*pr.p.* **curr'ying**; *pa.p.* **curr'ied**.

curry[2] *kur'i, v.t.* **1** to dress (leather). **2** to rub down and dress (a horse):—*pr.p.* **curr'ying**; *pa.p.* **curr'ied**.
curr'ier *n.*
curry favour to seek favour by flattery.

curse *kûrs*, *v.t.* **1** to wish that evil may fall upon (someone). **2** to vex or torment.—*v.i.* to swear:—*pr.p.* **curs'ing.**—Also *n.*
cursed *kûrst*, *adj.* **1** under a curse. **2** *(kûr'sid)* hateful.

cursive *kûr'siv*, *adj.* (of handwriting) flowing, with letters joined.

cursor *kûr'sėr*, *n.* a flashing device that appears on a VDU screen to show position e.g. of the end of the last entry.
cursory *kûr'sȯr-i*, *adj.* running quickly over, hasty: *He gave it a cursory glance.*
cur'sorily *adv.*

curt *kûrt*, *adj.* rudely brief: *a curt refusal.*
curt'ly *adv.* **curt'ness** *n.*

curtail *kûr-tāl'*, *v.t.* **1** to cut short. **2** to make less (e.g. powers, privileges):—*pr.p.* **curtail'ing**; *pa.p.* **curtailed'**.
curtail'ment *n.*

curtain *kûr't(i)n*, *n.* the hanging drapery at a window, around a bed, etc.—*v.t.* to enclose, or furnish, with curtains.

curtsy, **curtsey** *kûrt'si*, *n.* a bow made by women by bending the knees:—*pl.* **curt'sies, -seys.**—*v.i.* to make a curtsy:—*pr.p.* **curt'sying, -seying**; *pa.p.* **curt'sied, -seyed.**

curve *kûrv*, *n.* **1** a bend. **2** a line that is not straight yet includes no angles, like part of the edge of a circle.—*v.t.* to bend into a curve.—*v.i.* to bend or move in a curve:—*pr.p.* **cur'ving.**
cur'vature *(-vȧ-chůr) n.* curving: *curvature of the spine.*
cur'vy *adj.*:—*comp.* **cur'vier**; *superl.* **cur'viest.**

cushion *koosh'ȯn*, *n.* **1** a case filled with soft stuff, for resting on. **2** anything that softens a blow.—*v.t.* to act as a cushion for, against.

cushy *koosh'i*, *adj.* easy and comfortable: *a cushy job*:—*comp.* **cush'ier**; *superl.* **cush'iest.**

cuss *kus*, (*slang*) *n.* **1** a curse. **2** a fellow.
cuss'ed *adj.* **1** cursed. **2** obstinate.
cuss'edness *n.* determination not to do what someone wants to be done.

custard *kus'tȧrd*, *n.* **1** milk, eggs, etc. sweetened and baked together. **2** a cooked mixture of milk and **custard powder**, a preparation containing sugar, cornflour, flavouring, etc.

custody *kus'tȯ-di*, *n.* **1** care, keeping: *in the custody of her mother.* **2** imprisonment: *The accused is in custody.*
custō'dian *n.* one who keeps, guards, takes care of, something.

custom *kus'tȯm*, *n.* **1** what one is in the habit of doing. **2** common usage. **3** regular trade or business. **4** (in *pl.*) duties on imports and exports. **5** (in *pl.*) the government department that collects these duties. **6** (in *pl.*) a custom house.
cus'tomary *adj.* usual, habitual.
cus'tomarily *adv.*
cus'tomer *n.* **1** a person who buys from one. **2** (*slang*) a person.
cus'tom-built', -made' *adjs.* made to order.
custom house the place where duties on exports and imports are collected.
customs union states united as a single area for purposes of customs duties.
go through (the) customs to have one's luggage (checked and) passed by the customs authorities.

cut *kut*, *v.t.* **1** to make a slit in. **2** to cleave or pass through. **3** to fell, hew, mow, trim. **4** to make by cutting. **5** to wound or hurt. **6** to shorten (e.g. a writing). **7** to divide (a pack of cards), or to draw (a card) from the pack. **8** to refuse to recognise (an acquaintance). **9** to reduce (e.g. a price). **10** to intersect (a line). **11** to stay away from: *to cut a class.* **12** to strike (a ball) obliquely to the off side by a sharp movement. **13** to make (a ball) spin.—*v.i.* **1** to make a cut. **2** to intersect. **3** to move quickly (through). **4** (*slang*) to run away. **5** (in motion pictures) to cease photographing:—*pr.p.* **cutt'ing**; *pa.p.* **cut.**—*n.* **1** a slit or opening made by cutting. **2** a wound made with something sharp. **3** a stroke or blow. **4** a thrust with a sword. **5** the way a thing is cut. **6** the shape and style (of clothes). **7** a piece (of meat). **8** any other act of cutting.
cutt'er *n.* **1** the person or thing that cuts. **2** a small swift vessel.
cutt'ing *n.* **1** a piece cut off a plant for planting to grow a new plant. **2** a passage cut from a newspaper. **3** a passage cut (e.g. through rock, for a road or railway).—*adj.* (of a remark) cruel, hurtful.
cut'-and-dried' *adj.* **1** (e.g. of opinions) ready-made. **2** arranged very exactly beforehand: *His plans were cut-and-dried.*
cut glass. See **glass.**
cut'-throat *n.* an assassin.
a cut above rather better than.
be cut out, up. See **cut out, up.**
cut back 1 to return in the course of a play, film, etc. to something that happened earlier (*n.* **cut'back**). **2** to reduce or decrease (*n.* **cut'back**). **3** to prune (e.g. roses).
cut both ways to have or result in both advantages and disadvantages.
cut corners 1 to round corners in the quickest (but dangerous) way. **2** to do a

job in the quickest way.

cut dead to ignore the presence of (someone).

cut down 1 to take down by cutting. **2** to reduce: *to cut down expenses.*

cut in 1 to say, interrupting a speaker. **2** to intrude. **3** having left a line of traffic, to break into it again farther forward.

cut off 1 to destroy. **2** to get between (a person, etc.) and a point he wishes to reach. **3** to stop: *to cut off supplies.*

cut off with a shilling to disinherit.

cut one's teeth (of a baby) to have the teeth grow through the gums.

cut out 1 to shape by cutting (*n.* **cut'-out**). **2** to get rid of: *to cut out waste.* **3** to take the place of, supplant (a rival). **4** to disconnect from the source of power. **5** (of e.g. an engine) to fail, stop (*n.* **cut'-out**). **6** (**be cut out**) to be suited to be (with *for, to be*): *He was not cut out for a parson.*

cut up 1 to carve. **2** to criticise severely. **3** (**be cut up**) to be distressed.

cut up rough to make a fuss, show annoyance.

short cut a shorter, quicker way.

cute *kūt, adj.* **1** knowing, shrewd, cunning. **2** (*U.S.*) quaintly pleasing.

cuticle *kū'ti-kl, n.* **1** the outermost or thin skin. **2** the skin at the inner edge of a finger- or toenail.

cutlass *kut'lȧs, n.* a short, broad sword, with one cutting edge.

cutler *kut'lėr, n.* one who makes or sells knives.

cut'lery *n.* knives, forks, spoons.

cutlet *kut'lit, n.* **1** a small slice of meat (mutton, veal, pork) with rib or other bone attached, fried or broiled. **2** other food made up in similar shape.

cutter, etc. See **cut**.

cuttlefish *kut'l-fish, n.* a ten-armed sea creature able to give out a black, inky liquid when attacked.

cyanogen *sī-an'ō-jėn, n.* a poisonous gas, a compound of carbon and nitrogen.

cy'anide *n.* a compound of cyanogen with a metal or metals (the cyanides are poisonous).

cybernetics *sī-bėr-net'iks, n.sing.* the study of communication and control in living bodies, computers, etc.

cybernet'ic *adj.*

cyclamate *sīk'la-māt, sik', n.* a very sweet substance formerly used as a sweetening agent.

cyclamen *sik'lȧ-mėn, n.* a plant of the primrose family, with nodding flowers and petals bent back.

cycle *sī'kl, n.* **1** a period of time in which events happen in a certain order, and which constantly repeats itself: *the cycle of the seasons.* **2** any series of events that repeats itself constantly. **3** a series of poems, songs, etc. centring round a person or event. **4** a bicycle.—*v.i.* to ride a bicycle:—*pr.p.* **cy'cling**.

cy'clic *adj.* **1** contained in a circle: *a cyclic quadrilateral.* **2** (also **cy'clical**) of, in, cycles.

cy'clist *n.* a person who rides a bicycle.

cycles per second. See **hertz**.

cyclone *sī'klōn, n.* **1** a system of winds blowing round a centre of low pressure. **2** (*loosely*) a wind storm.

cyclop(a)edia. Same as **encyclopaedia**.

cyclostyle *sī'klō-stīl, n.* an apparatus for making copies of a writing.—Also *v.t.*:—*pr.p.* **cy'clostyling**.

cygnet *sig'nit, n.* a young swan.

cylinder *sil'in-dėr, n.* **1** a roller-shaped object. **2** applied to many parts of machinery of this shape, solid or hollow.

cylin'drical *adj.* cylinder-shaped.

cylinder head the closed end of the cylinder of an internal-combustion engine.

cymbal *sim'bȧl, n.* a hollow brass, plate-like, musical instrument, beaten with a stick or together with another.

cynical *sin'ik-ȧl, adj.* unwilling to recognise goodness.

cyn'ically *adv.*

cyn'ic *n.* one who takes a low view of human nature.

cynicism *sin'i-sizm, n.* **1** a cynical attitude. **2** a cynical remark.

cypress *sī'prės, n.* an evergreen tree whose branches used to be carried at funerals.

cyst *sist, n.* a bladder or bag-like or small blister-like structure formed in the body.

cystī'tis *n.* inflammation of the bladder.

czar, czarina. Same as **tsar, tsarina**.

Czech *chek, n.* **1** a native or citizen of the *Czech Republic.* **2** (*formerly*) a native or citizen of *Czechoslovakia.* **3** the language of the *Czech Republic.*—Also *adj.*

D

dab[1] *dab*, *v.t.* **1** to strike gently with something soft or moist. **2** to peck:—*pr.p.* **dabb'ing**; *pa.p.* **dabbed**.—*n.* **1** a gentle blow. **2** a small lump of anything soft or moist. **3** a small flounder (fish).

dab[2] *dab*, *n.* an expert person.—Also **dab hand**.

dabble *dab'l*, *v.i.* **1** to move a hand, foot, beak, etc. in water. **2** to do anything in a trifling way:—*pr.p.* **dabb'ling**.
dabb'ler *n.*

dachshund *daks'hoond*, *däks'hoont*, *n.* a type of small long-bodied dog with very short legs.

dacoit, **dakoit** *dȧ-koit'*, *n.* in India and Burma, one of a band of robbers.

dad *dad*, **daddy** *dad'i*, *ns.* affectionate names for father:—*pls.* **dads**, **dadd'ies**.
daddy-long'legs *n.* the crane-fly.

dado *dā'dō*, *n.* the lower part of a room wall when decorated in a different way from the rest:—*pl.* **da'do(e)s**.

daffodil *daf'ȯ-dil*, *n.* a yellow-flowered spring plant that grows from a bulb.

daft *däft*, *adj.* **1** silly. **2** reckless.

dagger *dag'ēr*, *n.* **1** a short sword for stabbing. **2** a mark of reference (†).
at daggers drawn ready to fly at each other and fight.

dago *dā'gō*, *n.* (*not polite*) a man of Spanish, Portuguese, or Italian origin:—*pl.* **dā'goes**.

daguerreotype *dȧ-ger'ō-tīp*, *n.* an early photograph taken on a silver, or silvered copper, plate.

dahlia *dāl'yȧ*, (*U.S.*) *däl'yȧ*, *n.* a garden plant with large brightly-coloured flowers.

Dáil *doil*, *n.* the lower house of the legislature of the Republic of Ireland.

dailies, **daily**. See **day**.

dainty *dān'ti*, *adj.* **1** pleasant to the taste. **2** small or fragile and pretty or charming:—*comp.* **dain'tier**; *superl.* **dain'tiest**. —*n.* something choice to eat:—*pl.* **dain'ties**.
dain'tily *adv.* **dain'tiness** *n.*

dairy *dā'ri*, *n.* **1** the place where milk is kept, and butter and cheese are made. **2** a shop supplying milk:—*pl.* **dai'ries**.
dai'ry-farm *n.*
dai'rymaid *n.* **dai'ryman** *n.*

dais *dā'is*, *dās*, *n.* a raised floor at the end of a hall.

daisy *dā'zi*, *n.* a composite plant having heads with white or pink rays and a yellow disc:—*pl.* **dai'sies**.

dakoit. See **dacoit**.

dale *dāl*, *n.* low ground between hills.
dales'man *n.* a man of the dales of northern England, esp. Yorkshire.

dally *dal'i*, *v.i.* **1** to idle. **2** to play (with):—*pr.p.* **dall'ying**; *pa.p.* **dall'ied** *(dal'id)*.
dall'iance *n.*

Dalmatian *dal-mā'sh(ȧ)n*, *n.* a dark-spotted white dog.

dam[1] *dam*, *n.* **1** an embankment to hold backwater. **2** the body of water thus held in check.—*v.t.* **1** to hold back by means of a dam. **2** (with *up* or *back*) to control (emotion, tears):—*pr.p.* **damm'ing**; *pr.p.* **dammed**.

dam[2] *dam*, *n.* a mother, usu. of animals.

damage *dam'ij*, *n.* **1** injury. **2** loss. **3** the value of what is lost. **4** (*coll.*) cost. **5** (in *pl.*) payment due to one person for loss or injury suffered through fault of another.—*v.t.* to harm.—*v.i.* to suffer injury:—*pr.p.* **dam'aging**.

damask *dam'ȧsk*, *n.* a material, now usu. of linen, with a woven design.
damask rose a pink rose from which a fragrant substance for perfumery is got.

dame *dām*, *n.* **1** the title of a lady of the same rank as a knight. **2** (*slang*) a woman. **3** the comic, vulgar old woman of pantomime (played by a man).

damn *dam*, *v.t.* **1** to condemn. **2** to sentence to eternal punishment.—*n.* an oath, a curse.
dam'nable *adj.* **1** hateful. **2** (*coll.*) annoying.
damnā'tion *n.* eternal punishment.
damned *damd*, *adj.* **1** sentenced to everlasting punishment. **2** hateful.
damning *dam'ing*, *adj.* leading to conviction or to ruin: *damning evidence.*

damp *damp*, *n.* **1** moist air. **2** in mines, any gas other than air (e.g. **fire-damp**—see this word).—*v.t.* **1** to wet slightly. **2** to discourage.—*adj.* moist, moderately wet.
damp'en *v.t.* and *v.i.* to make or become damp.
damp'er *n.* **1** a movable plate for controlling the draught, e.g. in a stove. **2** a depressing person, thing, or happening. **3** bread in a flat cake, esp. when baked over a camp fire.
damp'ness *n.*

damsel *dam'zėl*, *n.* a young woman.

damson *dam'z(ȯ)n*, *-sȯn*, *n.* a small dark-coloured plum.

dan *dan*, *n.* **1** in judo, etc., a level of proficiency (usu. 1st rising to 10th). **2** a person who has gained such a level.

dance *däns*, *v.i.* **1** to move in time, usu. to music. **2** to move lightly and gaily. **3** (of eyes) to sparkle.—Also *v.t.*:—*pr.p.* **dan'cing**.—*n.* **1** a series of steps in time to music. **2** a social gathering at which people dance. **3** a tune to accompany dancing.

dan'cer *n.* **dan'cing** *n.* and *adj.*

dance attendance on (someone) to hang about (someone) ready to carry out his wishes.

lead someone a dance to cause someone needless trouble and difficulty.

dandelion *dan'di-lī-ȯn*, *n.* a common plant with leaves with jagged tooth-like edges, and yellow flower.

dander *dan'dėr*, *n.* anger (in the phrase **get someone's dander up**).

dandle *dan'dl*, *v.t.* to bounce (a small child) on one's knee:—*pr.p.* **dan'dling**.

dandruff *dand'ruf*, *n.* a scaly scurf on the skin under the hair.

dandy *dan'di*, *n.* a person who pays (too) much attention to dress:—*pl.* **dan'dies**.

Dane *dān*, *n.* a native of Denmark.

Danish *dān'ish*, *adj.* belonging to Denmark.—*n.* the language of the Danes.

danger *dān'jėr*, *n.* **1** circumstance(s) that may result in harm or injury. **2** peril. **3** risk.

dan'gerous *adj.* **1** very unsafe. **2** (of a person) not to be trusted.

dangle *dang'gl*, *v.i.* **1** to hang loosely. **2** to follow (after someone), to hang (about, around someone).—*v.t.* **1** to hold swaying loosely. **2** to keep before a person's mind (a hope, prize, temptation, etc.):—*pr.p.* **dang'ling**.

Danish. See **Dane**.

dank *dangk*, *adj.* moist, wet.

danseuse *dong-sûz'*, *n.* a female dancer, esp. a ballet dancer.

dapper *dap'ėr*, *adj.* **1** neat, smart. **2** little and active.

dapple *dap'l*, *adj.* marked with spots (also **dapp'led**).

dapp'le-grey, *adj.* (of a horse) of grey colour with darker spots.—Also *n.*

dare *dār*, *v.t.* to be bold enough to: *I dare not go*:—*3rd pers. sing.* **dare(s)**; *pr.p.* **dar'ing**; *pa.t.* **durst, dared**; *pa.p.* **dared**. —*v.t.* **1** to be bold enough (to): *I dare to contradict.* **2** to take the risk of boldly: *I dare the steep ascent.* **3** to challenge: *I dare you to do it*:—*3rd pers. sing.* **dares**; *pr.p.* **dar'ing**; *pa.t.* and *pa.p.* **dared**.—*n.* a challenge.

dar'ing *adj.* **1** bold. **2** courageous.—*n.* boldness.

dare'-devil *n.* a rash, venturesome fellow.—*adj.* reckless.

I dare say I suppose.

dark *därk*, *adj.* **1** without light. **2** gloomy. **3** blackish. **4** difficult to understand. **5** secret: *to keep something dark.* **6** evil: *dark deeds.*—Also *n.*

dark'en *v.t.* and *v.i.* to make, or become dark or darker.

dark horse a person about whom little is known.

be in the dark about to know nothing about.

the Dark Ages the period in Europe between the late 5th century and the 10th, or later.

darling *där'ling*, *n.* **1** one dearly loved. **2** a favourite.—Also *adj.*

darn *därn*, *v.t.* to mend (clothes, etc.) with crossing rows of stitches.—*n.* the place so mended.

dart *därt*, *n.* **1** a pointed weapon or toy for throwing with the hand. **2** anything that pierces.—*v.t.* and *v.i.* to send, or to move, with speed.

darts *n.sing.* a game in which darts are thrown at a board (**dart'board**).

dash *dash*, *v.t.* **1** to throw, thrust, violently, esp. so as to break. **2** to ruin: *This dashed his hopes.* **3** to depress: *Nothing could dash his spirits.*—*v.i.* to rush.—*n.* **1** a rush. **2** a short race. **3** a small quantity: *whisky and a dash of soda.* **4** a mark (—) at a break in a sentence. **5** liveliness, spirit.

dash'ing *adj.* **1** spirited. **2** showy.

dash'board *n.* **1** a board in the front part of a vehicle to keep off splashes of mud, etc. **2** a board with dials in front of the driver's seat in a car, etc.

dastard *das'tȧrd*, *n.* a mean coward.—Also *adj.*

das'tardly *adj.* (of conduct, a person) cowardly and treacherous.

data *dā'tȧ*, *n.pl.* (often treated as *n.sing.*) facts given:—*sing.* **dā'tum**.

databank *n.* (*computers*) a library of files, possibly including databases.

database *n.* (*computers*) a collection of systematically stored files that are often connected with each other.

data processing the handling of information by computers.

data protection safeguards to protect the privacy and security of data.

date[1] *dāt*, *n.* **1** a statement of time (or time and place) of writing, sending, etc., noted

on a letter, book, document. **2** the time of an event. **3** (*coll.*) an appointment or engagement. **4** (*coll.*) the person with whom one has the appointment.—*v.t.* to give a date to.—*v.i.* **1** to have a beginning: *This practice dates from the first century A.D.* **2** to become old-fashioned-looking:—*pr.p.* **dāt'ing.**
dāt'ed *adj.* old-fashioned.
date line the line east and west of which the date differs by one day—the 180th meridian.
out of date, out'-of-date' **1** old-fashioned. **2** (of a ticket, etc.) no longer valid.
up to date, up'-to-date' **1** to the present time. **2** in touch with the latest ideas or practices.

date[2] *dāt*, *n.* the fruit of the **date palm**, a talltree with leaves at the top, growing in the tropics.

datum. See **data.**

daub *döb*, *v.t.* **1** to smear. **2** to paint without skill.—Also *n.*

daughter *dö'tėr*, *n.* a female child.
daugh'ter-in-law *n.* a son's wife:—*pl.* **daugh'ters-in-law.**

daunt *dönt*, *v.t.* **1** to frighten. **2** to discourage.
daunt'less *adj.* not to be daunted.
daunt'lessly *adv.* **daunt'lessness** *n.*

dauphin *dö'fin*, *n.* formerly, the eldest son of the King of France.

davit *dav'it*, *n.* one of a pair of pieces of timber or iron to raise a boat over a ship's side or stern.

Davy-lamp *dā'vi-lamp*, *n.* the safety-lamp for miners invented by Sir Humphry *Davy* (1778–1829).

Davy Jones's locker *dā'vi jōn'ziz lok'ėr*, the sea, as the grave of drowned men.

dawdle *dö'dl*, *v.i.* **1** to waste time. **2** to move slowly:—*pr.p.* **dawd'ling.**
dawd'ler *n.* **dawd'ling** *n.* and *adj.*

dawn *dön*, *v.i.* **1** to become day. **2** to begin to appear.—*n.* **1** daybreak. **2** a beginning. —Also **dawn'ing.**
dawn (up)on one to become suddenly clear to one.

day *dā*, *n.* **1** the period from sunrise to sunset. **2** the period from midnight to midnight. **3** the hours spent at work (*working day*). **4** lifetime: *in my great-grandfather's day.* **5** time of influence, activity, etc.
daily *dā'li*, *adj.*, *adv.* (of) every day.—*n.* **1** a paper published every day. **2** a servant who does not sleep in the house:—*pl.* **dai'lies.**
day'-book *n.* a book in which money transactions are entered at once.
day'break *n.* dawn, the first appearance of light.
day'-dream *n.* a fanciful plan, or imaginary pleasant event(s).—*v.i.* to make the former, or to experience the latter, in one's mind.
day'light *n.* light of day.—Also *adj.*
day'-release' *n.* time off from work for education.—Also *adj.*
day school a school held during the weekday, as opposed to a night school, a boarding school, or a Sunday school.
day'time *n.* the hours between sunrise and sunset.
day by day over a succession of days.
day in, day out every day for an indefinite time.
lose, or **win, the day** to lose, or win, the fight.
the other day not long ago.

daze *dāz*, *v.t.* to stun, stupefy:—*pr.p.* **daz'ing.**—*n.* a bewildered state.
dazed *dāzd*, *adj.*

dazzle *daz'l*, *v.t.* **1** to daze or overpower with a strong light. **2** to amaze by beauty or cleverness:—*pr.p.* **dazz'ling.**

de- *dē-*, *di-*, *pfx.* **1** down, as in **depose.** **2** away from, as in **derail.** **3** completely, as in **denude.** **4** used to form words undoing an action, as in **decentralise, decompress.**

deacon *dē'kȯn*, *n.* **1** in episcopal churches, a member of the clergy under priests. **2** a church officer. **3** in Scotland, the master of an incorporated company.
dea'coness *n.* a woman who helps the clergy in social work.

deactivate *dē-akt'i-vāt*, *v.t.* to make (a bomb etc.) inoperative:—*pr.p.* **deact'ivating.**

dead *ded*, *adj.* **1** without life. **2** without the appearance of feeling of life. **3** (of a ball) out of play. **4** complete: *a dead loss.* **5** exact: *dead centre.* **6** completely accurate. **7** not working.—*adv.* completely.
dead'en *v.t.* to lessen, weaken (e.g. pain).
dead'ly *adj.* **1** causing death. **2** very great: *deadly earnestness:*—*comp.* **dead'lier;** *superl.* **dead'liest.**—*adv.* extremely.
dead'liness *n.*
dead'(-and)-alive' *adj.* dull, not active.
dead'-beat' *adj.* completely exhausted.
dead'-end' *n.* a pipe, road, etc., closed at one end.
dead heat a race in which two or more competitors are equal.
dead language one no longer spoken by ordinary people.
dead letter **1** one undelivered and un-

claimed at the post office. **2** a law which has been made but is not enforced.

dead'line *n.* the very latest time for finishing something.

dead'lock *n.* a standstill resulting from a failure to agree.

dead'pan *adj.* **1** showing no emotion. **2** in mock seriousness.

dead'-weight' *n.* a cumbersome weight.

be dead set against to be utterly opposed to.

the dead dead person(s).

See also **death, die**[1].

deaf *def, adj.* **1** unable to hear. **2** refusing to listen: *deaf to his plea for mercy*.

deaf'en *v.t.* **1** to make deaf. **2** to daze with noise. **3** to make (e.g. walls) soundproof.

deaf'ness *n.*

deaf'-mute' *n.* one who is deaf and dumb.

deal[1] *dēl, n.* **1** a portion, amount: *a great, good, deal.* **2** the act of dividing cards. **3** a bargain, arrangement.—*v.t.* **1** to divide, to distribute. **2** to deliver (e.g. a blow).—*v.i.* **1** to do business (with). **2** to trade (in). **3** (with *with*) to act towards: *You have dealt unfairly with me.* **4** to distribute cards:—*pa.p.* **dealt** *(delt).*

deal'er *n.*

deal'ings *n.pl.* transactions, often business: *I have no dealings with him.*

deal with to tackle and settle (e.g. a task, a problem, or the person causing it).

deal[2] *dēl, n.* **1** a fir or pine board of a standardsize. **2** softwood.—*adj.* of deal.

dean *dēn, n.* **1** a cathedral clergyman who presides over the canons. **2** also the title of people holding other important offices in the church, universities, colleges, etc.

dear *dēr, adj.* **1** high in price. **2** beloved.—*n.* one who is beloved.—*adv.* at a high price.

dear'ly *adv.* **dear'ness** *n.*

dearth *dûrth, n.* scarcity.

death *deth, n.* dying, end of life.

death'ly *adj.* like death:—*comp.* **death'lier**; *superl.* **death'liest**.

death'less *adj.* living for ever.

death'bed *adj.* last minute: *a deathbed repentance*.

death'-blow *n.* a blow that causes death or the end.

death duties part of the value of the possessions left by a dead person paid to the government.

death penalty punishment of a crime by death.

death rate the proportion of deaths to the population.

death roll, toll a list of the dead, or the number of dead (e.g. in an accident).

death's-door *n.* the point of death.

death's-head *n.* the skull of a human skeleton.

death'-trap *n.* an unsafe structure or a dangerous place.

death warrant 1 an order for the execution of a criminal. **2** something that causes an end to e.g. a plan, hope.

death'watch *n.* **1** a watch by a dying person. **2** (also **death-watch beetle**) an insect that makes a ticking noise.

be in at the death 1 in hunting, to be up on the animal before the dogs have killed it. **2** to be present at the finish or climax of anything.

See also **dead, die**[1].

deb. Short for **débutante**.

débâcle, debacle *dā-bäk'l', di-bak'l, n.* a complete break-up, collapse, or failure.

debar *di-bär', v.t.* to shut out, prevent (from): *People under 18 are debarred from voting*:—*pr.p.* **debarr'ing**; *pa.p.* **debarred'**.

debase *di-bās', v.t.* **1** to make of less value, or less high quality. **2** to make (oneself) less highly thought of by others:—*pr.p.* **debas'ing**.

debased' *adj.* **1** lowered in quality. **2** degraded, wicked.

debate *di-bāt', n.* **1** a discussion, esp. a formal one before an audience. **2** an argument.—Also *v.t.* and *v.i.*:—*pr.p.* **debat'ing**.

debat'able *adj.* requiring discussion because perhaps not correct: *a debatable point*; *debatable statements*.

debauch *di-böch', v.t.* to make morally bad.—*n.* a fit of drunkenness or debauchery.

debauched' *adj.*

debauch'ery *n.* great indulgence in sensual pleasures.

debenture *di-ben'chur, n.* a written acknowledgment of a debt, issued by a company.

debilitate *di-bil'i-tāt, v.t.* to make weak:—*pr.p.* **debil'itating**.

debil'ity *n.* bodily weakness:—*pl.* **debil'ities**.

debit *deb'it, n.* an entry on the debtor side of an account.—*v.t.* to enter on the debtor side of an account:—*pr.p.* **deb'iting**; *pa.p.* **deb'ited**.

debit card a card which can be used to transfer money directly from a customer's bank account to the retailer's.

debonair *deb-ö-nār', adj.* cheerful and with pleasant manners.

debouch *di-bowch'*, *v.i.* to come out from a narrow pass or confined place.

debrief *dē-brēf'*, *v.t.* to gather information from (a spy, an astronaut, etc.) after a mission.

débris *dāb'rē*, **debris** *deb-rē'* (or *deb'*-), *ns.* **1** ruins, rubbish. **2** rocky fragments.

debt *det*, *n.* **1** what one owes to another. **2** the state of owing or being under an obligation: *He is in debt*; *I am in your debt for this help*.

debt'or *n.* one who owes a debt.

debt of honour a gambling debt or other debt which one ought to pay although not legally required to do so.

debug *dē-bug'*, *v.t.* **1** to remove concealed listening devices from. **2** to put right faults in (a mechanism, esp. in an aeroplane or a computer):—*pr.p.* **debugg'ing**; *pa.p.* **debugged'**.

debunk *dē-bungk'*, (*slang*) *v.t.* to take away an undeserved good reputation from (a person or thing).

début, debut *dā'bū*, or *-bū'*, *n.* a first public appearance on the stage, in society, etc.

débutante, debutante *deb'ū-tȧnt*, *n.* a girl making her first appearance at the fashionable parties, etc. of high society.

deca- *dek'ȧ-*, *pfx.* ten, ten times, as e.g. in the following:

decade *dek'ād*, *n.* a series of ten years.

decagram *n.* 10 grams.

decalogue *dek'ȧ-log*, *n.* the Ten Commandments.

decametre *n.* 10 metres.

decadence *dek'ȧ-dens*, *n.* falling away from high standards in morals or in the arts.

dec'adent *adj.*

decaffeinate *dē-kaf'in-āt*, *v.t.* to remove caffeine from (coffee etc.):—*pr.p.* **decaff'einating**.

decagram, decalogue, etc. See **deca-**.

decamp *di-kamp'*, *v.t.* to make off, esp. secretly.

decant *di-kant'*, *v.t.* **1** to pour off, leaving sediment. **2** to pour from one vessel to another.

decant'er *n.* an ornamental bottle for holding decanted liquor.

decapitate *di-kap'i-tāt*, *v.t.* to behead:—*pr.p.* **decap'itating**.

decapitā'tion *n.*

decarbonise *dē-kär'bon-īz*, *v.t.* to remove carbon or carbon dioxide from:—*pr.p.* **decar'bonising**.

decathlon *dek-ath'lȯn*, *n.* a two-day contest of ten events held at the modern Olympic Games since 1912.

decay *di-kā'*, *v.i.* **1** to fall in ruins. **2** to rot. **3** to fall into a worse state.—Also *n.*

decayed' *adj.* **1** rotted. **2** having lost position, power or money.

decease *di-sēs'*, *n.* death.

deceased' *adj.* dead.—*n.* the dead person referred to.

deceit *di-sēt'*, *n.* **1** the act of deceiving. **2** fraud.

deceit'ful *adj.* **1** deceiving. **2** insincere.

deceit'fully *adv.* **deceit'fulness** *n.*

deceive *di-sēv'*, *v.t.* **1** to mislead. **2** to cheat:—*pr.p.* **deceiving**.

deceiv'er *n.*

See also **deception.**

decelerate *dē-sel'ėr-āt*, *v.t.* and *v.i.* to slow down:—*pr.p.* **decel'erating**.

December *di-sem'bėr*, *n.* the twelfth (Roman tenth) month.

decent *dē'sėnt*, *adj.* **1** proper (*opp.* **indecent**). **2** fairly good. **3** (*coll.*) kindly, not severe.

dē'cency *(-sėn-si) n.* **dē'cently** *adv.*

decentralise *dē-sen'trȧl-īz*, *v.t.* to transfer from a central body (e.g. the central government) or position, to local centres:—*pr.p.* **decen'tralising**.

decentralisā'tion *n.*

deception *di-sep'sh(ȯ)n*, *n.* **1** the act of deceiving. **2** something that deceives.

decep'tive *adj.* misleading: *Appearances may be deceptive*.

decep'tively *adv.* **decep'tiveness** *n.*

deci- *des'i-*, *pfx.* one-tenth, as in the following:

decimate *des'i-māt*, *v.t.* (of disease or slaughter) to reduce greatly in number (in Roman times, to slay every tenth man):—*pr.p.* **dec'imating**.

dec'ibel *n.* a unit of loudness of sound.

decigram *n.* $\frac{1}{10}$ gram.

decimetre *n.* $\frac{1}{10}$ metre.

decide *di-sīd'*, *v.t.* to end, to settle.—*v.t.*, *v.i.* to (cause one to) make up one's mind:—*pr.p.* **decid'ing**.

decid'ed *adj.* **1** settled. **2** clear, definite: *a decided advantage.* **3** resolute.

decid'edly *adv.* definitely, very much.

deciduous *di-sid'ū-ůs*, *adj.* shedding leaves, or antlers, etc.

decigram, etc. See **deci-**.

decimal *des'i-m(ȧ)l*, *adj.* **1** numbered by tens. **2** in which each unit is a tenth of, or ten times, the value of some other unit.—*n.* a decimal fraction.

dec'imalise *v.t.*, *v.i.* to change from a non-decimal to a decimal system of measurement:—*pr.p.* **dec'imalising**.

decimal fraction a fraction expressed as so many tenths, hundredths, thousandths,

etc., and written as shown:— 0.1 = $\frac{1}{10}$, 2.33 = $2\frac{33}{100}$, etc.
decimal place the position of a digit to the right of a decimal point.
decimal point the point (.) that follows the whole units from a decimal fraction.

decimate, decimetre, etc. See **deci-**.

decipher *di-sī'fėr*, *v.t.* to read (secret writing), or make out (something that is not clear).
deciph'erable *adj.*:—*opp.* **indeciph'-erable**.

decision *di-sizh'(ȯ)n*, *n.* **1** the act of deciding. **2** a judgment. **3** firmness (*opp.* **indeci'sion**): *to act with decision.*
decī'sive *adj.* **1** deciding, putting an end to a contest, dispute, etc.: *a decisive battle*; *a decisive fact.* **2** showing decision and firmness: *a decisive manner*:—*opp.* **indecī'sive**.
decī'sively *adv.* **decī'siveness** *n.*

deck *dek*, *v.t.* to adorn.—*n.* **1** a platform extending from one side of a vessel to the other. **2** a floor in a bus, etc. **3** (*U.S.*) a pack of cards. **4** the turntable of a record-player. **5** the part of a tape-recorder or computer on or in which the tapes are placed to be played.
deck'-chair *n.* a light collapsible chair of spars and canvas.

declaim *di-klām'*, *v.i.* **1** to make a speech in a very formal, or in a passionate, manner. **2** to speak violently (against someone).—Also *v.t.*
declamation *dek-lȧ-mā'sh(ȯ)n*, *n.*
declamatory *di-klam'ȧ-tȯr-i*, *adj.*

declare *di-klār'*, *v.t.* **1** to announce formally: *to declare war.* **2** to say firmly, assert. **3** to name (goods in one's possession) at a custom house. **4** (*bridge*) to name (trump suit) or call (no trump).—*v.i.* (*cricket*) to end an innings before ten wickets have fallen:—*pr.p.* **declar'ing**.
declaration *dek-lȧ-rā'sh(ȯ)n*, *n.* **1** a firm statement. **2** a formal announcement.
declared *di-klārd'*, *adj.* clearly and firmly stated: *his declared intention.*
declare oneself to say which side one is on, or what one is going to do.
declare for (or **against**) to say that one supports (or opposes).

declassify *dē'klas'i-fī*, *v.t.* to take off the secret list:—*pr.p.* **declass'ifying**; *pa.p.* **declass'ified**.

declension. See **decline**.

decline *di-klīn'*, *v.i.* **1** to bend, or slope, down. **2** to become less strong, or good, etc. **3** to refuse.—*v.t.* **1** to refuse. **2** to give the various cases of (a noun or adjective) (*n.* in this sense **declen'sion**):—*pr.p.* **declin'ing**.—*n.* **1** a down slope. **2** a gradual loss of strength, etc.

declivity *di-kliv'i-ti*, *n.* a down slope:—*pl.* **decliv'ities**.

decode *dē-kōd'*, *v.t.* to turn (a coded message) into ordinary language:—*pr.p.* **decod'ing**.

decommission *dē-cȯm-ish'(ȯ)n*, *v.t.* to take (a warship etc.) out of operation:—*pr.p.* **decommiss'ioning**.

decompose *dē-kȯm-pōz'*, *v.t.* to separate into parts or elements.—*v.i.* to decay, rot:—*pr.p.* **decomposing**.
decomposition *n.*

decompress *dē-kȯm-pres'*, *v.t.* to decrease the pressure on, esp. gradually.
decompression *(-presh'(ȯ)n) n.*

decontaminate *dē-kȯn-tam'in-āt*, *v.t.* to free (a place, clothing, a person) from poisonous chemicals, dangerous radiation, etc.:—*pr.p.* **decontam'inating**.
decontaminā'tion *n.*

decontrol *dē-kȯn-trōl'*, *v.t.* to remove (esp. official) control from:—*pr.p.* **decontroll'-ing**; *pa.p.* **decontrolled**.—Also *n.*

décor *dā'kör*, *n.* the decoration and arrangement of a stage or room.

decorate *dek'ȯ-rāt*, *v.t.* **1** to make look beautiful or striking by adorning. **2** to put paint, wallpaper, etc. on the walls, etc. of (a room, etc.). **3** to give a medal or badge to, as a mark of honour:—*pr.p.* **dec'orating**.
decorā'tion *n.*
dec'orative *adj.* ornamental, beautiful.
dec'orator *n.* one who decorates houses, etc.

decorous *dek'ȯ-rus*, *adj.* **1** behaving in a proper way. **2** quiet and dignified:—*opp.* **indec'orous**.
decorum *di-kōr'um, -kör'*, *n.* **1** polite and dignified behaviour. **2** good taste.

decoy *di-koi'*, *v.t.* to lure into a trap.—*n.* *(dē'koi)* anything intended to lead into a snare.

decrease *di-krēs'*, *v.i.* to become less.—*v.t.* to make less:—*pr.p.* **decreas'ing**.—Also *n. (dē'krēs)*.

decree *di-krē'*, *n.* **1** an order, edict or law. **2** a judgment, decision.—*v.t.* **1** to order, command (something). **2** to give a decision or order (that).—Also *v.i.*:—*pr.p.* **decree'ing**; *pa.p.* **decreed'**.
decree nisi a divorce decree that becomes absolute unless cause is shown that it should not.

decrepit *di-krep'it*, *adj.* **1** infirm through old age. **2** broken-down, or almost in ruins.
decrep'itness, decrep'itude *ns.*

decry *di-crī*, *v.t.* **1** to belittle. **2** to express disapproval of:—*pr.p.* **decry'ing**; *pa.p.* **decried'**.

dedicate *ded'i-kāt*, *v.t.* **1** to consecrate (to some sacred purpose). **2** to devote wholly or chiefly: *He dedicated his life to this good work.* **3** to inscribe (esp. a book, to someone):—*pr.p.* **ded'icating**.
dedicā'tion *n.*

deduce *di-dūs'*, *v.t.* to conclude from facts one knows or assumes: *From the height of the sun I deduced that it was about ten o'clock*:—*pr.p.* **deduc'ing**.
deduc'tion *n.*

deduct *di-dukt'*, *v.t.* to subtract (from).
deduc'tion *n.* the amount subtracted.

deduction. See **deduce**, **deduct**.

deed *dēd*, *n.* **1** an act. **2** an exploit. **3** a legal document.
See also **do**[1].

dee-jay, **deejay** *dē'jā*, *-jā'*, *n.* a disc-jockey.

deem *dēm*, *v.t.* to judge, think.

deep *dēp*, *adj.* **1** going, or placed, far down or far in. **2** plunged (in, e.g. difficulties). **3** engrossed (in, e.g. study). **4** intense, strong (e.g. learning, sleep, grief, colour). **5** low in pitch. **6** secretive, cunning.—*adv.* far in, into: *deep in the forest.*—*n.* (with *the*) the sea.
deep'en *v.t.* **1** to make deeper. **2** to increase.—*v.i.* to become deeper.
deep'ly *adv.*
deep'ness, **depth** (see this word) *ns.*
deep'-dyed *adj.* very great—in a bad sense.
deep'-freeze' *n.* a type of low-temperature refrigerator which freezes food quickly and can preserve it for a long time.—Also *v.t.*
deep'-laid' *adj.* (of e.g. a plan) carefully made.
deep'-seat'ed *adj.* firmly rooted: *a deep-seated prejudice.*
in deep water in difficulties.

deer *dēr*, *n.* a cud-chewing animal with antlers (usu. in the male only):—*pl.* **deer**.
deer forest a wild tract (not necessarily woodland) reserved for deer.

deface *di-fās'*, *v.t.* to disfigure, spoil the appearance of:—*pr.p.* **defac'ing**.
deface'ment *n.*

defame *di-fām'*, *v.t.* to speak evil of:—*pr.p.* **defam'ing**.
defamation *def-ȧ-mā'sh(ȯ)n*, *n.*
defam'atory *adj.* slanderous.

default *di-fölt'*, *v.i.* to fail to do something one ought to do, as, e.g. to appear in court, to pay money.—Also *n.*
default'er *n.*

defeat *di-fēt'*, *v.t.* to win a victory over.—*n.* **1** overthrow in battle. **2** loss of a game, race, etc.
defeat'ism *n.* a frame of mind in which one expects and accepts defeat.
defeat'ist *adj.* and *n.*

defecate *dē'fi-kāt*, *v.i.* to empty the bowels:—*pr.p.* **de'fecating**.
defecā'tion *n.*

defect *dē'fekt*, *n.* a fault, flaw.—*v.i.* *(di-fekt')* to desert a country, political party, etc. to go to or join another.
defec'tion *n.* **1** desertion. **2** failure in duty.
defec'tive *adj.* **1** faulty. **2** incomplete.—*n.* a person not having normal mental or physical powers.
defec'tor *n.*
See also **deficient**, **deficiency**.

defence. See **defend**.

defend *di-fend'*, *v.t.* **1** to guard, protect, against attack. **2** to argue in favour of.
defend'ant (*law*) *n.* a person accused or sued.
defend'er *n.*
defence (*U.S.* **defense**) *di-fens'*, *n.* **1** a defending. **2** a means of protection. **3** an accused person's plea, or (*law*) his party. **4** those defending the goal in football, etc.
defence'less *adj.*
defens'ible *adj.* possible to defend: *a defensible position*; *a course of action that is defensible*:—*opp.* **indefens'ible**.
defens'ive *adj.* **1** protective. **2** resisting attack.
on the defensive in a defensive position or state.

defer[1] *di-fûr'*, *v.t.* to put off to another time:—*pr.p.* **deferr'ing**; *pa.p.* **deferred'**.
defer'ment *n.*

defer[2] *di-fûr'*, *v.i.* to yield (to the wishes or opinions of another, or to authority):—*pr.p.* **deferr'ing**; *pa.p.* **deferred'**.
deference *def'ėr-ėns*, *n.* **1** yielding to the judgment or opinion of another. **2** courteous willingness to do this.
deferen'tial *(-en'shȧl)* *adj.* showing deference or respect.
deferen'tially *adv.*

defiance, **defiant**. See **defy**.

deficient *di-fish'ėnt*, *adj.* wanting, lacking.
defic'iency *n.* **1** a lack. **2** the amount lacking:—*pl.* **defic'iencies**.
def'icit (or *-fis'*) *n.* the amount by which a sum of money etc. is less than the sum required.
deficiency disease one due to lack of an essential (as a vitamin) in diet—e.g. rickets, scurvy.

defile[1] *di-fīl'*, *v.i.* to march off in file:—*pr.p.* **defil'ing.**—*n.* *(dē'fīl, di-fīl')* a narrow pass, in which troops can march only in file.

defile[2] *di-fīl'*, *v.t.* **1** to make unclean. **2** to corrupt:—*pr.p.* **defil'ing.**
defile'ment *n.*

define *di-fīn'*, *v.t.* **1** to fix the bounds or limits of. **2** to outline clearly. **3** to fix, or to state, the meaning of:—*pr.p.* **defin'ing.**
defin'able *(-fīn') adj.*:—*opp.* **indefin'able.**
def'inite *(-in-it) adj.* **1** fixed, certain. **2** exact. **3** clear:—*opp.* **indef'inite.**
def'initely *adv.* **def'initeness** *n.*
defini'tion *n.* **1** an explanation of the exact meaning of a word or phrase. **2** sharpness of outline.
defin'itive *adj.* **1** decisive, settling once for all. **2** final.
definite article. See **article.**

deflate *dē-flāt'*, *v.t.* **1** to let gas out of (e.g. a tyre). **2** to reduce in importance, self-confidence, etc.:—*pr.p.* **deflat'ing.**
deflā'tion *n.* **1** the act of deflating. **2** a decrease in the amount of money available within an economy, and a consequent drop in trade, etc.

deflect *di-flekt'*, *v.t.* to turn aside (from).
deflec'tion, deflex'ion *n.*

deforest *dēfor'ist*, *v.t.* to make bare of forests or trees.
deforestā'tion *n.*

deform *di-förm'*, *v.t.* **1** to spoil the shape of. **2** to make ugly.
deformā'tion *(dē-) n.* change of shape.
deformed' *adj.* misshapen, abnormally formed.
deform'ity *n.* **1** a part abnormal in shape. **2** the state of being badly shaped:—*pl.* **deform'ities.**

defraud *di-fröd'*, *v.t.* **1** to cheat. **2** to deprive (of) by dishonest means.

defray *di-frā'*, *v.t.* to pay the expenses of.

defrost *dē'frost'*, *v.t.* **1** to remove frost or ice from. **2** to thaw.

deft *deft*, *adj.* skilful, quick and neat.
deft'ly *adv.* **deft'ness** *n.*

defunct *di-fungkt'*, *adj.* dead.—*n.* a dead person.

defuse *dē-fūz'*, *v.t.* **1** to remove the fuse from. **2** to make harmless:—*pr.p.* **defus'ing.**

defy *di-fī'*, *v.t.* **1** to challenge. **2** to resist boldly:—*pr.p* **defy'ing;** *pa.p.* **defied'.**
defy'ing, defi'ance *(-fī') ns.*
defi'ant *adj.* **defi'antly** *adv.*
defi'er *n.*

degenerate *di-jen'ėr-it*, *adj.* having lost high moral and/or physical qualities.—*n.* a person, plant, etc. that is degenerate.—*v.t.* *(-āt)* to become much less good or admirable:—*pr.p.* **degen'erating.**
degen'eracy *(-ȧs-i)*, **degenerā'tion** *ns.*

degrade *di-grād'*, *v.t.* **1** to lower in rank. **2** to punish by depriving of office. **3** to make low, contemptible:—*pr.p.* **degrad'ing.**
degradation *deg-rȧ-dā'sh(ȯ)n*, *n.*

degree *di-grē*, *n.* **1** rank. **2** a title given by a university (gained by examination or as an honour). **3** a unit of temperature. **4** one 360th part of a complete revolution: *There are 90 degrees in a right angle.* **5** amount: *with some degree of certainty.*
by degrees gradually.
in a high degree (small degree) to a great (small) extent.
third degree an American police method of extorting a confession by bullying, etc.
to a degree to a great extent.

dehydrate *dē-hī'drāt, dē'hī-drāt*, *v.t.* **1** to dry (foodstuffs). **2** to deprive of fluid:—*pr.p.* **dehydrating.**
dehydrā'tion *n.*

de-ice *dē-īs'*, *v.t.* to prevent formation of, or to remove, ice:—*pr.p.* **de-ic'ing.**
de-ic'er *n.*

deify *dē'i-fī*, *v.t.* to treat, or worship, as a god:—*pr.p.* **dē'ifying;** *pa.p.* **dē'ified.**
deificā'tion *n.*
dē'ity *n.* **1** a god or goddess. **2** (*cap.*; with *the)* God:—*pl.* **dē'ities.**

deign *dān*, *v.i.* to condescend (to), do, as a favour: *to deign to reply.*—*v.t.* to give as a favour: *to deign a reply.*

deities, deity. See **deify.**

déjà vu *dā'zhä vü'*, the feeling of having experienced before something that is in fact being experienced for the first time.

deject *di-jekt'*, *v.t.* to cast down in spirits, make gloomy.
dejec'ted *adj.* **dejec'tedly** *adv.*
dejec'tedness, dejec'tion *ns.*

delay *di-lā'*, *v.t.* **1** to put off to another time. **2** to hinder.—*v.i.* to put off time:—*pr.p.* **delay'ing;** *pa.p.* **delayed'.**—Also *n.*

delectable *di-lekt'ȧ-bl*, *adj.* delightful, pleasing.
delect'ableness *n.* **delect'ably** *adv.*
delectā'tion *n.* delight.

delegate *del'i-gāt*, *v.t.* **1** to send as a representative. **2** to entrust: *to delegate power to a person or assembly:*—*pr.p.* **del'egating.**—*n.* *(-git, -gāt)* an elected representative.
delegā'tion *n.* **1** a body of delegates. **2** the act of delegating.

delete *di-lēt'*, *v.t.* to blot out, erase:—*pr.p.* **delet'ing.**
delē'tion *n.*

deleterious *del-i-tē'ri-ůs*, *adj.* hurtful or destructive.

delf, delft *delf(t)*, **Delft'ware** *ns.* a kind of earthenware orig. made at *Delft*, Holland.

deliberate *di-lib'ėr-āt*, *v.t.* to weigh well in one's mind.—*v.i.* **1** to consider the reasons for and against. **2** to reflect:—*pr.p.* **delib'erating.**— *adj.* *(-it)* **1** intentional. **2** cautious, unflurried: *his deliberate way of working.*
delib'erately *adv.* **delib'erateness** *n.*
deliberā'tion *n.* **1** careful thought. **2** calmness, coolness: *moving with deliberation.* **3** (in *pl.*) formal discussions.

delicate *del'i-kit*, *adj.* **1** pleasing to the senses, esp. the taste. **2** dainty. **3** of very fine texture. **4** frail. **5** requiring careful handling (e.g. a problem). **6** deft. **7** very finely made for very careful work: *a delicate instrument*:— *opp.* **indel'icate.**
del'icately *adv.* **del'icateness** *n.*
del'icacy *n.* **1** fineness. **2** sensitiveness. **3** great tactfulness. **4** great skill. **5** the quality of requiring great care. **6** frailness. **7** something delightful to eat (*pl.* **del'icacies**).

delicatessen *del-i-kȧ-tes'n*, *n.* **1** cooked meats, pâtés, unusual foods, etc. **2** a shop selling these.

delicious *di-lish'ůs*, *adj.* **1** highly pleasing to the taste. **2** giving exquisite pleasure.
deli'ciously *adv.* **deli'ciousness** *n.*

delight *di-līt'*, *v.t.* to please highly.—*v.i.* to have or take great pleasure (in).—*n.* great pleasure.
delight'ful *adj.* **delight'fully** *adv.*

delimit *dē-lim'it*, or *di-*, *v.t.* to fix the limits of:—*pr.p.* **delim'iting**; *pa.p.* **delim'ited.**

delineate *di-lin'i-āt*, *v.t.* **1** to sketch, show by drawing. **2** to describe:—*pr.p.* **delin'eating.**
delineā'tion *n.*

delinquent *di-ling'kwėnt*, *adj.* **1** not carrying out one's obligations. **2** guilty of misdeeds.—Also *n.*
delin'quency *n.* **1** failure in duty. **2** minor law-breaking. **3** misdeed (*pl.* **delin'quencies**).

delirious *di-lir'i-ůs*, *adj.* **1** wandering in mind, light-headed. **2** wild with excitement.
delir'iousness, delir'ium *ns.* **1** the state of being delirious. **2** wild excitement.

deliver *di-liv'ėr*, *v.t.* **1** to set free (from). **2** to rescue. **3** to bring and hand to another: *to deliver parcels.* **4** to deal (a blow), send (e.g. a ball). **5** to pronounce, speak (a judgment, a sermon). **6** to help (a woman) in giving birth to a child. **7** to assist at the birth of (a child).
deliv'erance *n.* rescue, freeing.
deliv'ery *n.* the act or manner of delivering:—*pl.* **deliv'eries.**

dell *del*, *n.* a hollow, usu. with trees.

delphinium *del-fin'i-ům*, *n.* any of various kinds of branching plants with irregular, usu. blue, flowers.

delta *del'tȧ*, *n.* **1** the fourth letter of the Greek alphabet. **2** a tract of land formed at the mouth of a river, in shape like the Greek capital delta, .

delude *di-lo͞od'*, *-lūd'*, *v.t.* to deceive:—*pr.p.* **delud'ing.**
delusion *di-lo͞o'zh(o̊)n*, or *-lū'*, *n.* a false belief, esp. as a symptom of mental illness.

deluge *del'ūj*, *n.* **1** flood. **2** a great quantity.—*v.t.* to fill, overwhelm, with a great quantity:—*pr.p.* **del'uging.**

delusion. See **delude.**

de luxe *di looks'*, very luxurious or elegant.

delve *delv*, *v.t.*, *v.i.* to dig.—*v.i.* to seek patiently and carefully (for e.g. information):—*pr.p.* **delv'ing.**

demagogue *dem'ȧ-gog*, *n.* a political orator who appeals to the passions and prejudices of the people.

demand *di-mänd'*, *v.t.* **1** to ask, or ask for, firmly or sharply. **2** require: *This problem demands careful thought.*—*n.* **1** an urgent request. **2** a question. **3** an urgent claim: *demands on one's time.* **4** desire shown by consumers (for goods).
demand'ing *adj.* requiring much effort, ability, attention, etc.
on demand when asked for.

demarcation *dē-märk-ā'sh(o̊)n*, *n.* **1** the marking or describing of boundaries or limits. **2** the strict marking off of work to be done by one kind of craftsmen from that to be done by craftsmen of other trades.

demean *di-mēn'*, *v.t.* to lower in dignity (usu. *demean oneself*).

demeanour *di-mēn'ėr*, *n.* manner, bearing.

demented *di-ment'id*, *adj.* out of one's mind.
dementia *di-men'shȧ*, *n.* a loss of normal mental ability and functioning.

demerit *dē-mer'it*, *n.* a fault, shortcoming.

demesne *di-mān'*, or *-mēn'*, *n.* land which is one's property and in one's own use.

demi- *dem'i*, *pfx.* half, as in:
demigod *dem'i-god*, *n.* **1** one whose nature is partly divine. **2** a man regarded with worshipful admiration.

demilitarised zone *dēmil'it-ȧr-īzd zōn*, an area between opposing forces from which all troops have been removed.

demise *di-mīz'*, *n.* death.

demob *dē-mob'*, (*coll.*) *v.t.* short for **demobilise**:—*pr.p.* **demobb'ing**; *pa.p.* **demobbed'**.—*n.* (*coll.*) short for **demobilisation**.

demobilise *dē-* or *di-mōb'il-īz*, or *-mob'*, *v.t.* **1** to disband (e.g. an army). **2** (*coll.*) to discharge (a person) from an armed service:—*pr.p.* **demob'ilising**.
demobilisā'tion *n.*

demo *de'mō*, (*coll.*) *n.* a demonstration (*def. 4*):—*pl.* **de'mos**.

democracy *di-mok'rȧ-si*, *n.* (a country having) a form of government in which the people have power freely to elect representatives to carry on the government:—*pl.* **democ'racies**.
dem'ocrat *(dem')* *n.* **1** one who believes in democracy as a principle. **2** (*cap.*) a member or supporter of the **Democratic party** (one of the two great political parties in United States).
democrat'ic *adj.* **1** of democracy. **2** believing in equal rights and privileges for all.
democrat'ically *adv.*

demolish *di-mol'ish*, *v.t.* **1** to lay in ruins. **2** to destroy, put an end to.
demoli'tion *(dem-)* *n.*

demon *dē'mȯn*, *n.* an evil spirit, a devil.
demoniac *di-mō'ni-ak*, *adj.* **1** possessed by an evil spirit. **2** frantic.—Also *n.*
demoniacal *dē-mȯ-nī'ȧ-kl*, *adj.*

demonstrate *dem'ȯn-strāt*, *v.t.* **1** to show or point out clearly. **2** to prove.—*v.i.* to make a public expression of opinion: *A crowd collected to demonstrate against the new taxes*:—*pr.p.* **dem'onstrating**.
demonstrā'tion *n.* **1** proof beyond doubt. **2** a practical display or exhibition. **3** a display of emotion. **4** a public expression of opinion, as by a mass-meeting, a procession, etc.
demon'strative *adj.* **1** pointing out. **2** proving with certainty. **3** in the habit of showing one's feelings.
dem'onstrator *n.* **1** a teacher or assistant who helps students with practical work. **2** a person who takes part in a public demonstration.

demoralise *di-mor'ȧl-īz*, *v.t.* to take away confidence and courage, to throw into confusion:—*pr.p.* **demor'alising**.
demoralisā'tion *n.*

demote *dē-mōt'*, *v.t.* to reduce in rank:—*pr.p.* **demoting**.
demo'tion *n.*

demur *di-mûr'*, *v.i.* to object (with *at*):—*pr.p.* **demurring**; *pa.p.* **demurred'**.

demure *di-mūr'*, *adj.* quiet, modest, shy (sometimes affectedly so).

demurred, demurring. See **demur**.

den *den*, *n.* **1** the lair of a wild beast. **2** a haunt (of vice or of great poverty). **3** a private room or retreat.

denationalise *dē-nash'(ȯ)n-ȧl-īz*, *v.t.* to return from state to private ownership:—*pr.p.* **denat'ionalising**.

denial. See **deny**.

denier *den'i-ėr*, *n.* a unit of silk, rayon, and nylon yarn weight.

denigrate *den'i-grāt*, *v.t.* to attack the good reputation of, defame:—*pr.p.* **den'igrating**.

denim *den'im*, *n.* **1** a cotton fabric. **2** (in *pl.*) a denim garment, esp. jeans.

denizen *den'i-zn*, *n.* an inhabitant (human or animal).

denominate *di-nom'in-āt*, *v.t.* **1** to give a name to. **2** to call, name:—*pr.p.* **denom'inating**.
denominā'tion *n.* **1** a name or title. **2** a class of units in money, weights, measures: *First reduce 7 tons and 5 cwt. to the same denomination.* **3** a religious body.
denominā'tional *adj.* of denominations (*def. 3*).
denom'inator *n.* in a vulgar fraction, the number below the line.

denote *di-nōt'*, *v.t.* **1** to be the sign of. **2** to mean:—*pr.p.* **denot'ing**.

dénouement, denouement *dā-nōō'-mon^g*, *n.* **1** the unravelling of a plot or story. **2** the outcome.

denounce *di-nowns'*, *v.t.* **1** to inform against or accuse publicly. **2** to notify formally termination of (a treaty, etc.):—*pr.p.* **denounc'ing**.
See also **denunciation**.

dense *dens*, *adj.* **1** thick, close, compact. **2** very stupid.
dense'ly *adv.* **dense'ness** *n.*
dens'ity *n.* **1** the quality of being dense. **2** the mass of unit volume of a substance:—*pl.* **dens'ities**.

dent *dent*, *n.* a small hollow made by pressure or a blow.—Also *v.t.*

dental *den'tȧl*, *adj.* **1** of, or for, the teeth. **2** (of a sound) produced with the aid of the teeth.
dentate *den'tāt*, *adj.* **1** toothed. **2** notched.
dentifrice *den'ti-fris*, *n.* a substance for cleaning the teeth.
dentine *den'tēn*, *n.* the substance of

which teeth are mainly composed.
dentist *den'tist*, *n.* one who takes out, etc., or cares for, teeth.
den'tistry *n.* a dentist's work.
denture *den'chůr*, *n.* a set of teeth, esp. artificial.

denude *di-nūd'*, *v.t.* **1** to make bare. **2** to strip (of): *land denuded of vegetation:*—*pr.p.* **denud'ing.**
denudā'tion *n.* the wearing away of rocks by water, etc.

denunciation *di-nun's(h)i-ā'sh(ȯ)n*, *n.* the act of denouncing or accusing.
denun'ciātor *n.* one who denounces.

deny *di-nī'*, *v.t.* **1** to declare not to be true. **2** to reject. **3** to refuse: *He denied me food:*—*pr.p.* **deny'ing**; *pa.p.* **denied'**.
denī'al *n.*
deny oneself to do without (things that one desires or needs).

deodorise *dē-ō'dȯ-rīz*, *v.t.* to take the smell from:—*pr.p.* **deō'dorising.**
deō'dorant, deō'doriser *ns.* a substance that destroys or conceals smells.

depart *di-pärt'*, *v.i.* **1** to go away. **2** to die. **3** (with *from*) to cease to follow: *to depart from one's original plan.*
depart'ed *n.* and *adj.* (one who is) dead.
depar'ture *(-chůr) n.*
a new departure (the beginning of) a new course of action.

department *di-pärt'mėnt*, *n.* **1** a part. **2** a section of an administration (e.g. *the Department of Justice*), university, office, shop.
department'al *adj.*

depend *di-pend'*, *v.i.* **1** (*old*) to hang down (from). **2** to rely (on). **3** to receive necessary support from (with *on*). **4** (of a future happening, etc.) to be decided by: *Its success depends on your efforts.*
depend'able *adj.* trustworthy.
depend'ent *adj.*:—*opp.* **independ'ent.**
depend'ant *n.* one who is kept, supported, by another.
depend'ence *n.* **1** the state of being dependent. **2** reliance, trust.
depend'ency *n.* a colony without self-government:—*pl.* **depend'encies.**

depict *di-pikt'*, *v.t.* **1** to paint. **2** to describe.

depilatory *di-pil'ȧ-tȯr-i*, *adj.* taking hair off.—Also *n.* (*pl.* **-ies**).

deplete *di-plēt'*, *v.t.* **1** to empty (of). **2** to reduce in number or amount:—*pr.p.* **deplet'ing.**
deplē'tion *n.*

deplore *di-plōr'*, *-plör'*, *v.t.* to express disapproval and regret about (something):—*pr.p.* **deplor'ing.**
deplor'able *adj.* **1** sad. **2** very bad.
deplor'ableness *n.* **deplor'ably** *adv.*

deploy *di-ploi'*, *v.t.* to spread out (troops) so as to form a longer front.—Also *v.i.*
deploy'ment *n.*

depopulate *di-pop'ū-lāt* (or *dē-*), *v.t.* to reduce greatly the population of (a region):—*pr.p.* **depop'ulating.**
depopulā'tion *n.*

deport[1] *di-*, *dē-pōrt'*, *-pört'*, *v.t.* to send (an alien, criminal) out of the country.
deportā'tion *n.*

deport[2] *di-pōrt'*, *-pört'*, *v.t.* to behave (oneself).
deport'ment *n.* bearing, behaviour.

depose *di-pōz'*, *v.t.* **1** to remove from a high position (e.g. from that of king). **2** to testify on oath:—*pr.p.* **depos'ing.** See also **deposition.**

deposit *di-poz'it*, *v.t.* **1** to put or set down. **2** to entrust for safe keeping: *to deposit money in a bank.*—*n.* **1** solid matter that has settled down in a liquid. **2** money put in a bank. **3** money given as a guarantee or as the first part of a payment.
depos'itory *n.* a place where anything is deposited:—*pl.* **depos'itories.**

deposit account a bank account in which money deposited gains interest but from which transfers of money cannot be made by cheque.

deposition *dēp-ȯ-zish'(ȯ)n*, *n.* **1** a written testimony used as evidence in court. **2** removal (from office). **3** the act of depositing.

depot *dep'ō*, *dē'pō*, *n.* **1** a storehouse. **2** a military station or headquarters. **3** (*U.S.*) a railway station.

deprave *di-prāv'*, *v.t.* to make bad or worse, to corrupt:—*pr.p.* **deprav'ing.**
depraved' *adj.* evil, corrupt.
depraved'ness, deprav'ity *(-prav')*, *ns.* great wickedness.

deprecate *dep'ri-kāt*, *v.t.* to express disapproval of (an action or a condition or state):—*pr.p.* **dep'recating.**

depreciate *di-prē'shi-āt*, *v.t.* **1** to lower the value of. **2** to speak slightingly of.—*v.i.* to fall in value:—*pr.p.* **depre'ciating.**
depreciā'tion *n.* **depre'ciatory** *adj.*

depredation *dep-rė-dā'sh(ȯ)n*, *n.* **1** the act of robbing, robbery. **2** destructive action suggesting robbery: *the sea's depredations on the land.*

depress *di-pres'*, *v.t.* **1** to press down. **2** to lower. **3** to lessen the activity of (e.g. trade). **4** to cast a gloom over, make unhappy.
depressed' *adj.* **depress'ing** *adj.*

depression *di-presh'(ȯ)n, n.* **1** a lowering. **2** a hollow. **3** low spirits. **4** lack of activity in trade. **5** a region of low pressure: *a depression over the Atlantic.*
depress'ive *n.* one who suffers from periods of depression.—Also *adj.*

deprive *di-prīv', v.t.* (with *of*) to take something away from: *This move deprived the fugitive of his means of escape.*
depriv'al *n.*
deprivation *dep-riv-ā'sh(ȯ)n, n.* **1** depriving. **2** loss. **3** hardship.
deprived' *(-prīvd) adj.* underprivileged.

depth *depth, n.* **1** deepness. **2** a deep place. **3** intensity, strength: *the depth of her feelings.*
depth'-charge *n.* a bomb that explodes under water.
in depth thoroughly, in detail.
out of one's depth **1** in water where one cannot touch the bottom. **2** in a situation with which one cannot deal.
See also **deep, deepness.**

depute *di-pūt', v.t.* **1** to appoint (a person) as one's substitute. **2** to make over (one's authority to a person as deputy):—*pr.p.* **deput'ing.**
deputā'tion *n.* persons appointed to represent and speak on behalf of others.
dep'utise *v.i.* to act as deputy.—*v.t.* to make a deputy:—*pr.p.* **dep'utising.**
dep'uty *n.* **1** one appointed to act for another. **2** a delegate:—*pl.* **dep'uties.**

derail *dē-rāl', v.t.* to cause to leave the rails.

derange *di-rānj', v.t.* **1** to put out of place, or out of working order. **2** to make insane:—*pr.p.* **derang'ing.**
deranged' *adj.* **derange'ment** *n.*

derate *dē-rāt', v.t.* to relieve, wholly or partly, from payment of local rates:—*pr.p.* **derat'ing.**
derāt'ing *n.* and *adj.*

Derby *där'bi, n.* **1** an annual horse race held on Epsom Downs. **2** (without *cap.*) a race or contest attracting much local interest (*pl.* **derb'ies**).

deregulate *dē-reg'ū'-āt, v.t.* to remove controls from (a business etc.):—*pr.p.* **dereg'ulating.**
deregula'tion *n.*

derelict *der'ė-likt, adj.* abandoned, left to decay.—Also *n.*
derelic'tion *n.* **1** abandoning. **2** neglect (of duty).

deride *di-rīd', v.t.* to laugh at, mock:—*pr.p.* **derid'ing.**
derision *di-rizh'(ȯ)n, n.* **1** mockery. **2** a laughing-stock.
derī'sive *(-siv) adj.* mocking.
derī'sory *adj.* **1** derisive. **2** ridiculous.

derive *di-rīv', v.t.* **1** to draw, take (from a source or origin). **2** to trace (a word) to its root.—*v.i.* to come, arise (from):—*pr.p.* **deriv'ing.**

derivation *der-i-vā'sh(ȯ)n, n.* **1** the tracing of a word to its root. **2** source. **3** descent.
deriv'ative *adj.* derived from something else, not original.—*n.* a word, substance, formed from another word, substance.

dermatitis *dûr-mȧ-tī'tis, n.* inflammation of the skin.

dermatol'ogy *n.* the science that is concerned with the skin and its diseases.
dermatol'ogist *n.*

derogate *der'ȯ-gāt, v.i.* to take away (from authority, dignity, merit, etc.).
derog'atory *adj.* **1** lowering to one's dignity, etc. **2** scornful, disparaging.
derog'atorily *adv.* **derog'atoriness** *n.*

derrick *der'ik, n.* **1** an apparatus like a crane for lifting weights. **2** a framework over an oil well that holds the drilling machinery.

dervish *dûr'vish, n.* a member of any of various Muslim religious orders, usu. vowed to poverty, some practising howling, others violent dancing.

desalinate *dē-sal'in-āt, v.t.* to take salt out of (esp. sea water):—*pr.p.* **desal'inating.**
desalinā'tion *n.*

descant *des'kant, n.* in music, an accompaniment above the tune.—*adj.* denoting a musical instrument of a higher pitch than most others of the same family.—*v.i. (diskant')* to talk at length about (with *on*).

descend *di-send', v.i.* **1** to climb down. **2** to pass to a lower place or condition. **3** (with *on, upon*) to invade. **4** to be derived.—*v.t.* to go down.
descend'ant *n.* an offspring, near or distant.
descent' *n.* **1** the act of descending. **2** a slope. **3** an attack. **4** lineage.

describe *di-skrīb', v.t.* to trace out, draw: *to describe a circle.* **2** to give an account of:—*pr.p.* **describing.**
description *di-skrip'sh(ō)n, n.* **1** the act of describing. **2** an account of anything in words. **3** a sort or kind.
descrip'tive *adj.*
See also **indescribable.**

descry *di-skrī', v.t.* to espy, notice, see:—*pr.p.* **descry'ing**; *pa.p.* **descried'.**

desecrate *des'i-krāt, v.t.* **1** to treat without reverence. **2** to profane:—*pr.p.* **des'ecrating.**
desecrā'tion *n.*

desert[1] *di-zûrt', n.* something (usu. bad) that is deserved—often in *pl.*

desert[2] *di-zûrt'*, *v.t.* to leave, forsake.—*v.i.* to run away, esp. from the army.
desert'er *n.* **deser'tion** *n.*

desert[3] *dez'ėrt*, *n.* **1** a place where there is too little water, and little or no plant life. **2** a desolate place.—Also *adj.*

deserve *di-zûrv'*, *v.t.* to earn by one's actions, to merit:—*pr.p.* **deserv'ing.**
deserv'ing *adj.* worthy.
deserv'edly *(-id-li) adv.* justly.
See also **desert**[1].

déshabillé. Same as **dishabille.**

desiccate *des'i-kāt*, *v.t.* **1** to dry up. **2** to preserve by drying:—*pr.p.* **des'iccat'ing.**
desiccā'tion *n.*

design *di-zīn'*, *v.t.* **1** to prepare a plan of. **2** to intend.—*n.* **1** a preliminary sketch, plan in outline. **2** a plan formed in the mind. **3** intention. **4** arrangement of forms and colours.
des'ignate *(-ig-nāt) v.t.* **1** to point out. **2** to name. **3** to be a name for. **4** to appoint:—*pr.p.* **des'ignating.**—*adj. (-nit, -nāt)* appointed to office but not yet installed (placed after noun, e.g. *ambassador designate*).
designā'tion *n.* **1** a pointing out. **2** a name. **3** a title.
design'edly *(-id-li) adv.* intentionally.
design'er *n.* **1** one who makes designs or patterns. **2** a plotter.
design'ing *adj.* artful, scheming.—*n.* the art of making designs or patterns.
have designs on to be trying or planning to get (something) for oneself.

desire *di-zīr'*, *v.t.* **1** to long for. **2** to ask:—*pr.p.* **desir'ing.**—*n.* **1** an earnest longing or wish. **2** a request.
desir'able *adj.* **1** worthy of desire. **2** pleasing.
desir'ableness, desirabil'ity *ns.*
desir'ous *adj.* wishful.

desist *di-zist'*, *sist'*, *v.i.* to stop (often with *from*): *Make him desist from trying to open it.*

desk *desk*, *n.* **1** a piece of furniture for use when writing or reading. **2** a public information, etc., counter. **3** a department in a newspaper office: *the sports desk.*

desolate *des'ȯ-lāt*, *v.t.* **1** to lay waste, empty of people, make ruinous. **2** to make wretched:—*pr.p.* **des'olating.**—*adj. (des'-ȯ-lit)* **1** very lonely or barren. **2** joyless.
desolā'tion *n.*

despair *di-spār'*, *v.i.* to lose hope (of).—*n.* **1** hopelessness. **2** something that causes one to despair.
despair'ing *adj.* **despair'ingly** *adv.*
See also **desperate.**

despatch. Same as **dispatch.**

desperado *des-pėr-ä'dō*, *-ā'dō*, *n.* **1** a reckless fellow. **2** a ruffian:—*pl.* **desper-a'do(e)s.**

desperate *des'pėr-it*, *adj.* **1** despairingly reckless. **2** hopeless. **3** (*coll.*) extremely bad.
des'perately *adv.* **des'perateness** *n.*
desperā'tion *n.* **1** a state of despair. **2** recklessness.

despicable *des'pik-ȧ-bl*, or *-pik'*, *adj.* contemptible, worthless.
despicably *adv.* **despicableness** *n.*
despise *di-spīz'*, *v.t.* **1** to look upon with contempt. **2** to scorn:—*pr.p.* **despis'ing.**

despite *di-spīt'*, *prep.* in spite of.

despoil *di-spoil'*, *v.t.* **1** to strip completely (of possessions). **2** to rob.

despond *di-spond'*, *v.i.* to be without hope, dejected.
despond'ence, despond'ency *ns.*
despond'ent *adj.*
despond'ently, despond'ingly *advs.*

despot *des'pot*, *n.* **1** a ruler with absolute power. **2** a tyrant.
despot'ic, -al *adjs.* **despot'ically** *adv.*
des'potism *n.* **1** absolute power. **2** tyranny.

dessert *di-zûrt'*, *n.* fruits, sweets, etc., served at the end of a meal.
dessert'spoon *n.* a spoon between a tablespoon and a teaspoon in size.

destine *des'tin*, *v.t.* to set apart for a certain use, state, etc.: *He destined this money to pay for a library*; *a son who was destined for the Church*:—*pr.p.* **des'tining.**
destinā'tion *n.* the place to which one, anything, is going.
des'tined *adj.* **1** bound (for a place). **2** intended. **3** having as one's fate: *destined to succeed*; *destined to be hanged.*
des'tiny *n.* unavoidable fate:—*pl.* **des'-tinies.**

destitute *des'ti-tūt*, *adj.* **1** in utter want. **2** (with *of*) entirely lacking in: *destitute of common sense.*
des'tituteness, destitū'tion *ns.*

destroy *di-stroi'*, *v.i.* to ruin, to do away with, to kill:—*pr.p.* **destroy'ing**; *pa.p.* **destroyed'.**
destroy'er *n.* **1** a person or thing that destroys. **2** a small fast warship armed with torpedoes, etc.
destruc'tible *adj.* able to be destroyed:—*opp.* **indestructible.**
destructibil'ity *n.*
destruction *di-struk'sh(ȯ)n*, *n.* **1** act of destroying. **2** ruin.
destruc'tive *adj.* **1** causing destruction. **2** ruinous, deadly: *destructive to animals*; *destructive of happiness.* **3** merely

negative: *destructive criticism.*
destruc'tively *adv.* **destruc'tiveness** *n.*
destruc'tor *n.* a furnace for burning up refuse.

desultory *des'ul-tȯr-i, adj.* **1** jumping from one thing to another: *desultory reading.* **2** rambling: *desultory remarks.*
des'ultorily *adv.* **des'ultoriness** *n.*

detach *di-tach', v.t.* **1** to unfasten. **2** to separate (from). **3** to send off (e.g. troops) on special service.—Also *v.i.*
detach'able *adj.*
detached' *adj.* **1** unconnected. **2** free from emotion, unprejudiced: *a detached attitude to the problem.*
detach'ment *n.* **1** the act of detaching. **2** the state of not being influenced by emotion or prejudice. **3** a body (e.g. of troops).

detail *dē'tāl, di-tāl', v.t.* **1** to tell fully, give all the facts of. **2** to choose, set (a person, to do a particular job).—*n.* **1** a small part. **2** an item.
detailed *adj.* giving many details.
in detail point by point, item by item.

detain *di-tān', v.t.* **1** to delay, stop. **2** to keep in custody.
detainee' *(-ē') n.* one held in custody.
detention *di-ten'sh(ȯ)n, n.* **1** act of detaining. **2** being detained. **3** imprisonment. **4** keeping in school as punishment.

detect *di-tekt', v.t.* **1** to find (someone in the act of). **2** to discover the presence or fact of: *to detect a smell of gas.*
detec'table, -ible *adj.* **detec'tion** *n.*
detec'tive *n.* a person who tracks criminals or watches suspected persons.—Also *adj.*
detec'tor *n.* an apparatus that detects (e.g. electric waves, metal).

détente *dā-tong̃t', n.* a lessening of hostility between nations.

detention. See **detain**.

deter *di-tûr', v.t.* to frighten or prevent (from doing something):—*pr.p.* **deterr'ing**; *pa.p.* **deterred'**.
deterrent *di-ter'ėnt, adj.* having the effect of deterring.—Also *n.* (now esp. applied to a nuclear weapon).

detergent *di-tûr'jėnt, n.* a material that cleanses (usu. not including soap).—*adj.* cleansing.

deteriorate *di-tē'ri-ȯ-rāt, v.t.* to make worse.—*v.i.* to grow worse:—*pr.p.* **dete'riorating.**
deteriorā'tion *n.*

determine *di-tûr'min, v.t.* **1** to fix or settle: *The committee were to determine the course to be taken.* **2** to cause (a person) to decide (to). **3** to find out exactly: *He tried to determine what had gone wrong:*—*pr.p.* **deter'mining**.
determinā'tion *n.* **1** the act of determining. **2** fixed purpose. **3** firmness of character.
deter'mined *adj.* **1** fixed or settled. **2** firm in purpose.
See also **indeterminate.**

deterrent, etc. See **deter**.

detest *di-test', v.t.* to hate intensely.
detestā'tion *(dē-) n.*
detest'able *(di-) adj.* extremely hateful.
detest'ableness *n.* **detest'ably** *adv.*

dethrone *di-thrōn', v.t.* **1** to remove from a throne. **2** to depose:—*pr.p.* **dethron'ing.**
dethrone'ment *n.*

detonate *det'ȯ-nāt, dē'tȯ-nāt, v.i., v.t.* to explode, cause to explode, violently:—*pr.p.* **det'onating.**
detonā'tion *n.*
det'onator *(-ā-tȯr) n.* a substance or device that sets off an explosion.

detour *dā'tōōr, dē', di-tōōr', n.* **1** a winding (e.g. of a river). **2** a roundabout way.
make a detour to go by a roundabout way.

detract *di-trakt', v.i.* to take away (from), lessen, esp. reputation or worth.
detract'or *n.* **detrac'tion** *n.*

detriment *det'ri-mėnt, n.* harm, damage, disadvantage (in phrases, *without detriment to, to the detriment of*).
detrimen'tal *adj.* and *n.* (something) disadvantageous or damaging.

de trop *di trō', (of a person) in the way, unwelcome.

deuce[1] *dūs, n.* **1** a card of die with two spots. **2** (*lawn tennis*) a situation in which one side must gain *two* successive points to win the game, or two successive games to win the set—i.e. at three points each ('forty all'), at four, etc., points each, or at an equal number of games each.

deuce[2] *dūs, n.* the devil.

Deutschmark *doich'märk,* **Deutsche Mark** *doich'ė märk, ns.* the unit of German currency.

devalue *dē-val'ū, v.t.* to reduce the value of:—*pr.p.* **deval'uing.**
devaluā'tion *n.*

devastate *dev'ȧs-tāt, v.t.* **1** to lay waste. **2** to overwhelm (a person) with grief:—*pr.p.* **dev'astating.**
dev'astating *adj.* overwhelming.
devastā'tion *n.*

develop *di-vel'ȯp, v.t.* **1** to bring to a more advanced state. **2** to show gradually (e.g. a disease, a habit). **3** to open (an attack). **4** to make (a photograph) visible by treating the film or plate with chemicals or electrically.—*v.i.* **1** to grow to a more advanced state. **2** to come gradually into being:—*pr.p.* **devel'oping**.

devel'oper *n.* **devel'opment** *n.*

developing country now the more usu. term for an underdeveloped country.

deviate *dē'vi-āt*, *v.i.* to turn aside (from a norm):—*pr.p.* **de'viating**.

dē'viant *n.* and *adj.* **deviā'tion** *n.*

devious *dē'vi-us*, *adj.* **1** roundabout: *devious paths.* **2** rather dishonest: *by devious methods.*

de'viously *adv.* **de'viousness** *n.*

device. See **devise**.

devil *dev'l*, *n.* **1** (*cap.*) the spirit of evil, Satan. **2** any evil spirit. **3** a wicked person. **4** a drudge.—*v.t.* to season highly and broil.—*v.i.* to drudge for another, esp. a lawyer or author:—*pr.p.* **dev'illing**; *pa.p.* **dev'illed**.

dev'ilish *adj.* **1** very wicked. **2** (*coll.*) very great (also *adv.*).

dev'ilment *n.* mischief.

dev'ilry *n.* conduct, or an action, worthy of a devil:—*pl.* **dev'ilries**.

dev'il-may-care *adj.* reckless.

devious. See **deviate**.

devise *di-vīz'*, *v.t.* **1** to invent, contrive. **2** to plan, scheme:—*pr.p.* **devis'ing**.

devi'ser *n.*

device *di-vīs'*, *n.* **1** a contrivance, invention. **2** a plan. **3** an emblem. **4** a motto. **5** (in *pl.*) inclinations: *Leave him to his own devices.*

devoid *di-void'*, *adj.* (with *of*) free from, completely without: *devoid of fear, of meaning.*

devolve *di-volv'*, *v.i.* **1** to fall as a duty: *This task will devolve upon you.* **2** to be passed over or down.—*v.t.* **1** to give as a duty. **2** to pass over or down:—*pr.p.* **devolv'ing**.

dēvolū'tion (or *dev-*, or *-lōō'*) *n.* the act of devolving, esp. the delegation of certain powers to regional governments by a central government.

devote *di-vōt'*, *v.t.* to give up wholly: *to devote one's life, one's energies, to the cause of peace*:—*pr.p.* **devot'ing**.

devot'ed *adj.* warmly loyal: *a devoted friend.*

devotee' *(-tē')* *n.* an enthusiast for, supporter (of): *a devotee of racing.*

devō'tion *n.* **1** strong loyalty or affection. **2** (in *pl.*) prayers.

devour *di-vowr'*, *v.t.* **1** to eat up greedily. **2** to take in eagerly by eye and mind.

devout *di-vowt'*, *adj.* **1** pious. **2** earnest.

devout'ly *adv.* **dēvout'ness** *n.*

dew *dū*, *n.* tiny drops of moisture deposited from the air on cooling, esp. at night.

dew'y *adj.*:—comp. **dew'ier**; *superl.* **dew'iest**.

dew'iness *n.*

dexterity *deks-ter'i-ti*, *n.* **1** skill, esp. with the hands. **2** mental skill.

dex'terous, **dex'trous** *adj.* skilful.

dhow *dow*, *n.* an Arab sailing ship.

diabetes *dī-ȧ-bē'tēz, -tiz*, *n.* any of several diseases, characterised e.g. by intense thirst, or by too much sugar in the urine and blood.

diabetic *(-bet'ik, -bē'tik)* *adj.* of diabetes.—*n.* a sufferer from diabetes.

diabolic(al) *dī-ȧ-bol'ik(-ȧl)*, *adjs.* **1** devilish. **2** very bad.

diacritic *dī-ȧ-crit'ik*, *n.* a mark added to a letter to show its exact sound or value (e.g. the dot of *ȧ*).

diadem *dī'ȧ-dem*, *n.* a band worn round the head as a badge of royalty.

diaeresis, **dieresis** *dī-ēr'i-sis, -er'*, *n.* a mark (¨) placed over the second of two vowels to show that each is to be pronounced separately, as *naïve*:—*pl.* **di(a)er'esēs**.

diagnosis *dī-ȧg-nō'sis*, *n.* a conclusion as to what is wrong reached by examining a patient, a situation, etc.:—*pl.* **diagnō'sēs**.

di'agnose *(-nōz)* *v.t.* to recognise (a disease, etc.) from symptoms:—*pr.p.* **di'agnosing**.

diagnos'tic *(-nos')* *adj.*

diagonal *dī-ag'ȯ-nȧl*, *adj.* stretching from one corner to an opposite corner.—*n.* a straight line so drawn.

diag'onally *adv.*

diagram *dī'ȧ-gram*, *n.* a figure or plan showing briefly the facts of a statement that is difficult to follow or remember.

diagrammat'ic *adj.*

dial *dī'ȧl*, *n.* **1** the face of a watch or clock. **2** a plate with a movable index used for various purposes (e.g. on a gas, electric, meter). **3** the numbers and moving disc on a telephone.—*v.t.* to turn a telephone dial in such a way as to connect with (a number).—Also *v.i.*:—*pr.p.* **dī'alling**; *pa.p.* **dī'alled**.

dialling code a group of numbers dialled in order to direct a call to a particular telephone exchange.

dialect *dī'ȧ-lekt*, *n.* a form of a language used by a particular district or class.

dialogue *dī'ȧ-log*, *n.* a conversation, esp. in a play or novel.

dialysis *dī-al'i-sis*, *n.* the removal of impurities from the blood by means of a machine (**kidney machine**).

diameter *dī-am'ė-tėr*, *n.* a straight line drawn from side to side of, and passing through the centre of, a circle.
diamet'ric, **-al** *adjs.* (as if at opposite ends) of a diameter: *The two are diametrical* (*i.e. complete*) *opposites*.
diamet'rically *adv.*

diamond *dī'ȧ-mȯnd*, *n.* **1** a crystal form of pure carbon, extremely hard. **2** a four-sided figure with all sides equal but angles not right angles. **3** a playing card with red mark(s) of this shape. **4** a diamond-shaped area.—Also *adj.*
diamond wedding, **jubilee** the sixtieth anniversary of a wedding or other important event.
rough diamond **1** an uncut diamond. **2** a worthy but unpolished person.

diaper *dī'ȧ-pėr*, (esp. *U.S.*) *n.* a baby's nappy.

diaphanous *dī-af'ȧ-nus*, *adj.* transparent—now usu. because fine, delicate.

diaphragm *dī'ȧ-fram*, *n.* **1** a thin dividing membrane. **2** the midriff, the part separating chest from abdomen. **3** a contraceptive device a woman fits over her cervix.

diarist. See **diary**.

diarrhoea, (*U.S.*) **diarrhea** *dī-ȧ-rē'ȧ*, *n.* too frequent emptying of the bowels with too much liquid in the faeces.
diarrh(o)ē'ic *adj.*

diary *dī'ȧ-ri*, *n.* a daily record of events:—*pl.* **di'aries**.
dī'arist *n.* one who keeps a diary.

diatribe *dī'ȧ-trīb*, *n.* an angry harangue (against someone or something).

dibble *dib'l*, *n.* a pointed tool used for making holes to put seed or plants in.—Also **dibb'er**.

dice *dīs*, *n.* a small cube with numbered faces used in games and gambling:—*pl.* **dice**.—*v.i.* to play with dice.—*v.t.* **1** to mark with squares. **2** to cut into small cubes:—*pr.p.* **dic'ing**.

dichotomy *dī-kot'ȯ-mi*, *n.* a sharp division into two opposed groups, classes, etc.:—*pl.* **dichot'omies**.

dickey[1], **dicky**[1] *dik'i*, *n.* **1** a seat at the back of carriage, motor car. **2** a false shirt-front:—*pl.* **dick'eys**, **dick'ies**.

dicky[2], **dickey**[2] *dik'i*, (*coll.*) *adj.* shaky:—*comp.* **dick'ier**; *superl.* **dick'iest**.

dicky-bird *dik'i-bûrd*, *n.* a child's word for a (small) bird.

Dictaphone® *dik'tȧ-fōn*, *n.* a machine for recording, and later dictating, letters, etc.

dictate *dik-tāt'*, *v.t.* **1** to say or read for another to write. **2** to lay down with authority: *to dictate terms to a defeated enemy*. **3** to make necessary: *Circumstances dictated this course of action.*—*v.i.* to give orders (to):—*pr.p.* **dictat'ing**.—*n.* *(dik'-tāt)* an order.
dictā'tion *n.* **1** the act of dictating. **2** something read for another to write down.
dictā'tor *n.* an all-powerful ruler.
dictā'torship *n.*
dictatō'rial *(-tȧ-)* *adj.* **1** like a dictator. **2** overbearing: *his dictatorial manner*.
dictatō'rially *adv.*

diction *dik'sh(ȯ)n*, *n.* **1** one's manner of speaking. **2** choice of words.

dictionary *dik'sh(ȯ)n-ȧ-ri*, *n.* **1** a book containing the words of a language alphabetically arranged, with their meanings, etc. **2** a work containing other information alphabetically arranged:—*pl.* **dic'tionaries**.

dictum *dik'tum*, *n.* a saying, esp. a considered opinion:—*pl.* **dic'ta**.

did. See **do**[1].

didactic, **-al** *di-dak'tik*, *-ȧl*, or *dī-*, *adjs.* **1** intended to teach. **2** pompous. **3** moralising.

diddle *did'l*, *v.t.* to swindle:—*pr.p.* **didd'ling**.

die[1] *dī*, *v.i.* **1** to stop living. **2** to wither:—*pr.p.* **dy'ing**; *pa.p.* **died** *(dīd)*.
die'hard *n.* **1** one who keeps up a vain resistance. **2** an extreme conservative.
be dying for (*coll.*) to want very much.
be dying to (*coll.*) to be very keen to.
die away to fade from sight or hearing.
die out to become extinct.

die[2] *dī*, *n.* **1** a dice. **2** a device for stamping coin, etc., or for cutting metal:—*pl.* (gaming) **dice** *(dīs)*; (stamping) **dies** *(dīz)*.
the die is cast an irrevocable step has been taken.

dieresis. See **diaeresis**.

diesel (engine) *dēz'l (en'jin)*, an internal-combustion engine in which heavy oil (**diesel oil**) is ignited by heat produced by compression.
dies'el-elec'tric *adj.* using power obtained from a diesel-operated electric generator.
dies'el-hydraul'ic *adj.* using power transmitted by means of one or more mechanisms filled with oil.

diet[1] *dī'ėt*, *n.* **1** food. **2** food planned or prescribed, esp. as a means of losing weight.—*v.i.* to take food according to rule because of illness, in order to slim, etc.—*v.t.* to put on a diet:—*pr.p.* **di'eting**; *pa.p.* **di'eted**.
dī'etary, **dietet'ic** *adjs.* of a diet or diets.

dietet'ics *n. sing.* the science of regulating diet.
dieti'cian *n.* an expert on diet.

diet² *dī'ėt*, *n.* an assembly, council, or parliament.

differ *dif'ėr*, *v.i.* **1** (with *from*) to be unlike. **2** (often with *with*, *from*) to disagree (with):—*pr.p.* **diff'ering**; *pa.p.* **diff'ered**.
diff'erence *n.* **1** what makes one thing unlike another. **2** a quarrel. **3** the amount by which one quantity or number is greater than another.
diff'erent *adj.* not the same (with *from*).
differential *dif-ėr-en'shl*, *n.* a price or wage difference.
differentiate *dif-ėr-en'shi-āt*, *v.t.* **1** to mark, be, a difference: *This slight difference in colour differentiates A from B; This differentiates A and B.* **2** to see, describe, the difference: *Look at the specimens and try to differentiate A and B.*—*v.i.* **1** to see, describe the difference (between): *Try to differentiate between A and B.* **2** to make a difference (between two people, etc.), e.g. to treat one with more generosity than the other:—*pr.p.* **differen'tiating**.
differentiā'tion *n.*

difficult *dif'i-kůlt*, *adj.* **1** not easy. **2** requiring hard work. **3** hard to please, or to persuade: *She is a difficult person.*
diff'iculty *n.* **1** hardness, laboriousness. **2** an obstacle, objection: *He is suitable otherwise but his age is a difficulty.* **3** something that cannot be easily understood. **4** (in *pl.*) troubles, esp. money troubles:—*pl.* **diff'iculties**.

diffident *dif'i-dėnt*, *adj.* lacking self-confidence, shy.
diff'idence *n.* **diff'idently** *adv.*

diffraction *di-frak'sh(ȯ)n*, *n.* the spreading of light and other rays passing through a narrow opening, or by the edge of an object.

diffuse *di-fūz'*, *v.t.* and *v.i.* to spread in all directions:—*pr.p.* **diffus'ing**.—*adj.* *(di-fūs')* **1** widely spread, **2** using many words.
diffused' *(-fūzd') adj.*
diffu'sion *(-fū'zh(ȯ)n) n.*

dig *dig*, *v.t.* **1** to turn up (e.g. earth) with a spade, etc. **2** to make (a hole) thus. **3** to poke or thrust:—*pr.p.* **digg'ing**; *pa.p.* **dug**.—Also *v.i.*—*n.* **1** a thrust, a poke, a jibe. **2** an archaeological excavation. **3** (in *pl.*; *coll.*) lodgings.
digg'er *n.*
digg'ings *n.pl.* a place where digging or mining is carried on.
dug'out *n.* **1** a boat made by hollowing out the trunk of a tree. **2** a rough dwelling or shelter, *dug out* of a slope or bank or in a trench.

digest *di-* or *dī-jest'*, *v.t.* **1** (of an animal or plant body) to break down food in the mouth, stomach, etc. **2** to endure patiently (e.g. an insult). **3** to think over (e.g. unpleasant news).—*v.i.* to undergo digestion.—*n.* *(dī'jest)* **1** an orderly summary of any written matter. **2** a magazine consisting of extracts from other sources.
digest'ible *adj.* that may be digested:—*opp.* **indigest'ible**.
digestion *di-jes'ch(ȯ)n*, or *dī-*, *n.* **1** the act of digesting. **2** the ability to digest.—See also **indigestion**.
digest'ive *adj.*—*n.* (also **digestive biscuit**) a type of sweet wholemeal biscuit.

digger, digging(s). See **dig**.

digit *dij'it*, *n.* **1** a finger or toe. **2** any of the figures 0 to 9.
dig'ital *adj.*
digital clock, watch one without the normal face, time being indicated directly by numbers.
digital computer an electronic calculating machine using arithmetical digits.

digitalis *dij-i-tā'lis*, *n.* a powerful heart stimulant obtained from dried leaves of the common foxglove.

dignify *dig'ni-fī*, *v.t.* to confer honour on—sometimes undeserved honour: *a cottage dignified by the name of 'Four Winds House'*:—*pr.p.* **dig'nifying**; *pa.p.* **dig'nified**.
dig'nified *adj.* showing dignity.
dig'nitary *n.* a person holding high office, esp. in the church:—*pl.* **dig'nitaries**.
dig'nity *n.* **1** stateliness of manner; manner showing a sense of one's own worth or of the solemnity of the occasion (*opp.* **indig'nity**). **2** high rank:—*pl.* **dig'nities**.
beneath one's dignity degrading, in one's own estimation at least.
be on one's dignity to be ready to take offence at any slight.

digress *di-* or *dī-gres'*, *v.i.* to wander from the point, or from the main subject.
digression *(-gresh'ȯn) n.*

dike, dyke *dīk*, *n.* **1** a trench, or the earth dug out and thrown up. **2** a ditch. **3** a mound raised to prevent flooding. **4** (*Scot.*) a wall.

dilapidated *di-lap'i-dāt-id*, *adj.* in a state of disrepair, neglected, very shabby.
dilapidā'tion *n.*

dilate *di-*, or *dī-lāt'*, *v.i.* **1** to become larger, to swell out. **2** (with *on, upon*) to comment at length upon.—*v.t.* to cause to dilate:—

pr.p. **dilat'ing.**
dilā'tion, dilatā'tion *ns.* enlargement.

dilatory *dil'ȧ-tȯr-i, adj.* **1** inclined to delay. **2** delaying, putting off.
dil'atoriness *n.*

dilemma *di-*, or *dī-lem'ȧ, n.* a position in which each of two (or more) courses is equally undesirable.

dilettante *dil-ē-tan'ti, n.* **1** one who dabbles in an art or science. **2** a lover of the arts, connoisseur.

diligent *dil'i-jėnt, adj.* earnestly working hard, industrious.
dil'igence *n.* **dil'igently** *adv.*

dilly-dally *dil'i-dal'i, v.i.* to loiter, trifle:—*pr.p.* **dilly-dall'ying**; *pa.p.* **dilly-dall'ied.**

dilute *di-*, or *dī-lūt'*, or *-lo͞ot', v.t.* **1** to lessen the strength, etc., of, by mixing, esp. with water. **2** to increase the proportion of unskilled to skilled among (workers in an industry):—*pr.p.* **dilut'ing.**—*adj.* reduced in strength, weak.
dilu'tion *n.*

dim *dim, adj.* **1** not bright or distinct. **2** not seeing, or understanding, etc., clearly: —*comp.* **dimm'er**; *superl.* **dimm'est.**— *v.t.* and *v.i.* to make, or become, dark:—*pr.p.* **dimm'ing**; *pa.p.* **dimmed.**
dim'ly *adv.* **dimness** *n.*
dim'wit (*coll.*) *n.* a stupid person.
take a dim view to disapprove (of).

dime *dīm, n.* a Canadian and U.S. coin worth 10 cents.

dimension *di-*, *dī-men'sh(ȯ)n, n.* measure in length, breadth, or thickness.
-dimen'sional (as part of a word) having a stated number of dimensions: *a three-dimensional model.*

diminish *di-min'ish, v.t.* and *v.i.* to make, or become, less.
See also **diminution.**

diminuendo *di-min-ū-en'dō, adj.* and *adv.* (*music*) gradually letting the sound die away.—Also *n.* (*pl.* **-os**, **-oes.**)

diminution *dim-in-ū'sh(ȯ)n, n.* lessening.
dimin'utive *adj.* very small.—*n.* a word formed from another to express a little one of the kind (e.g. *codling* from *cod*).
See also **diminish.**

dimmer, etc. See **dim.**

dimple *dim'pl, n.* a small hollow, esp. on the surface of the body.—*v.i.* to form dimples.—*v.t.* to mark with dimples:—*pr.p.* **dimp'ling.**

dimwit. See **dim.**

din *din, n.* a loud continued noise.—*v.t.* to repeat loudly and persistently in order to teach:—*pr.p.* **dinn'ing**; *pa.p.* **dinned.**

dine *dīn, v.i.* to take dinner.—*v.t.* to give dinner to:—*pr.p.* **din'ing.**
din'er *n.* **1** one who dines. **2** a restaurant car on a train (also **din'ing-car**).
din'ing-room *n.* a room used for meals.
See also **dinner.**

ding-dong *ding'-dong, n.* the sound of bells.—*adj.* (e.g. of an argument, fight, etc.) stubbornly contested with alternate success and failure.

dinghy *ding'gi, n.* a small rowing-boat or ship's tender:—*pl.* **din'ghies.**

dingo *ding'gō, n.* the native dog of Australia:—*pl.* **din'goes.**

dingy *din'ji, adj.* **1** shabby, dirty-looking. **2** not bright:—*comp.* **din'gier**; *superl.* **din'giest.**
din'gily *adv.* **din'giness** *n.*

dinner *din'ėr, n.* **1** the main meal of the day. **2** a formal gathering to eat dinner, often with speeches.
dinn'er-jacket *n.* a man's usu. black jacket for formal occasions.

dinosaur *dī'nȯ-sör, n.* a usu. large extinct reptile.

dint *dint, n.* **1** the mark of a blow. **2** force: *He managed to do it by dint of perseverance.*—*v.t.* to make a dint in.

diocese *dī'ȯ-sēs, -sis, n.* a bishop's district.
diocesan *dī-os'is-n, -iz-n, adj.* of a diocese.

dip *dip, v.t.* **1** to plunge for a moment. **2** lower and raise again (as a flag).—*v.i.* **1** (with *into*) to take a casual glance at, or brief interest in. **2** to slope downwards:—*pr.p.* **dipp'ing**; *pa.p.* **dipped.**—*n.* **1** a down slope, a hollow. **2** a bath(e). **3** a candle made by dipping a wick in tallow. **4** a liquid in which something is dipped.
dipp'er *n.* **1** a ladle. **2** a bird that dives for food. **3** (*cap.*) the Plough.

diphtheria *dif-thē'ri-ȧ, n.* an infectious throat disease in which the air passages become covered with a leathery membrane.

diphthong *dif'thong, n.* **1** two vowel sounds (represented by one letter or by two) pronounced as one syllable, as in *boy* (=*bo-i*), *now* (=*na-oo*), *my* (=*ma-i*). **2** (*loosely*) two letters expressing one sound, as *ph* in *photograph*, *ea* in *dead*, *eo* in *people.* **3** either of the symbols æ, œ.

diploma *di-plō'mȧ, n.* a document conferring an honour or a privilege.
diplomacy *di-plō'mȧ-si, n.* **1** the art of negotiating with foreign countries or looking after one's country's affairs in a foreign country. **2** skill and tact in carrying out any negotiations or in hand-

ling people.
dip'lomat *n.* **1** one involved in diplomacy (*def. 1*). **2** (also **diplō'matist**) one showing skill and tact in handling people.
diplomat'ic *adj.* **diplomat'ically** *adv.*

dipper, dipping. See **dip**.

dipsomania *dip-sō-mā'ni-ȧ, n.* an irresistible craving for strong drink.
dipsomā'niac *n.*

dire *dīr, adj.* dreadful.

direct *di-rekt', dī'rekt, adj.* **1** straight, not roundabout. **2** (of manner) straightforward, frank. **3** in an unbroken line of descent:—*opp.* **indirect**.—*v.t.* **1** to turn in a particular direction: *to direct one's steps towards, one's attention towards, one's remarks to a person.* **2** to show (a person) the way (to). **3** to mark (an envelope, etc.) with a name and address. **4** to instruct, order. **5** to control, regulate: *to direct operations.*
direc'tion *n.* **1** the act of aiming, or turning, towards something. **2** the region in which something lies. **3** the line or course in which anything moves. **4** guidance. **5** command. **6** (in *pl.*) instructions: *directions for use.*
direc'tive *n.* a general instruction as to procedure issued by a higher authority.
direct'ly *adv.* **1** in a direct manner. **2** almost at once.
direct'ness *n.*
direct'or *n.* **1** a person or thing that directs. **2** one of a group of persons who manage the affairs of a business.
direct'ory *n.* a book giving names and addresses, and sometimes telephone numbers:—*pl.* **direct'ories**.
direct current an electric current flowing in one direction only.
direct speech speech reported in the exact words of the speaker as opp. to indirect speech (see this).
direct tax income tax (also property tax, if any) as opp. to indirect tax (see this).

dirge *dûrj, n.* a funeral song or hymn.

dirigible *dir'i-ji-bl, -ij', n.* a balloon or airship that can be steered.

dirk *dûrk, n.* a Highland dagger.

dirt *dûrt, n.* mud, dust, dung, etc.
dirt'y *adj.* **1** not clean. **2** soiled. **3** unclean morally. **4** stormy: *dirty weather*:—*comp.* **dirt'ier**; *superl.* **dirt'iest**.—*v.t., v.i.* to soil, become soiled, with dirt:—*pr.p.* **dirt'ying**; *pa.p.* **dirt'ied**.
dirt'ily *adv.* **dirt'iness** *n.*
dirt track **1** a motor-cycle racing track with earthy or cindery surface. **2** any poorly constructed road or track with an earthy or stony surface.

dis- *dis-, pfx.* usu. reversing the meaning of the rest of the word (e.g. **disbelieve, discontent**).

disable *dis-ā'bl, v.t.* **1** to take away the ability or strength of. **2** to cripple:—*pr.p.* **disa'bling**.
disabil'ity *n.* **1** the thing that prevents one from doing something, esp. a physical handicap. **2** lack of power, esp. legal, to act:—*pl.* **disabil'ities**.
dis'abled *adj.* having a disability, esp. a physical handicap.
disa'blement *n.* the act of disabling or state of being disabled.

disabuse *dis-ȧ-būz', v.t.* to undeceive or set right: *Disabuse him of this idea.*:—*pr.p.* **disabus'ing**.

disaccord *dis-ȧ-körd', n.* lack of accord, disagreement.

disadvantage *dis-ȧd-vän'tij, n.* a drawback, unfavourable circumstance.
disadvan'taged *adj.* not having what the majority of people around one have, e.g. homeless, in poverty, etc.
disadvantā'geous *(-jus) adj.*
at a disadvantage in an unfavourable position.

disaffect *dis-ȧ-fekt', v.t.* to make discontented or unfriendly.
disaffect'ed *pa.p., adj.* discontented, disloyal.
disaffect'edness, disaffec'tion *ns.*

disagree *dis-ȧ-grē', v.i.* **1** to differ. **2** to quarrel. **3** (of food) to cause indigestion: *Onions disagree with me.*
disagree'able *adj.* unpleasant.
disagree'ably *adv.* **disagree'ment** *n.*

disallow *dis-ȧ-low', v.t.* to refuse to allow or admit (e.g. a claim).

disappear *dis-ȧ-pēr', v.i.* **1** to vanish from sight. **2** to fade out of existence.
disappear'ance *n.*

disappoint *dis-ȧ-point', v.t.* **1** to fall short of the hopes of: *This disappointed Mary.* **2** to fail to fulfil: *This disappointed her hopes.*
disappoint'ment *n.*

disapprobation. See **disapprove**.

disapprove *dis-ȧ-prōōv', v.i.* to have an unfavourable opinion (of).—Also *v.t.*:—*pr.p.* **disapprov'ing**.
disapprov'al, disapprobā'tion *ns.*
disapprov'ing *adj.* **disapprov'ingly** *adv.*

disarm *dis-ärm', v.t.* **1** to take away weapons from. **2** to make (an unfriendly person) feel friendly.—*v.i.* to get rid of or reduce national armaments.
disarm'ament *n.* reduction of, or doing away with, fighting forces or equipment.
disarm'ing *adj.* gaining goodwill or

friendliness: *a disarming smile.*
disarm'ingly *adv.*

disarrange *dis-ȧ-rānj'*, *v.t.* to disturb the arrangement of, put in order:—*pr.p.* **disarrang'ing.**

disarray *dis-ȧ-rā'*, *n.* **1** disorder. **2** state of being incompletely dressed.

disassociate *dis-ȧ-sō'shi-āt*, *v.t.* to dissociate:—*pr.p.* **disasso'ciating.**

disaster *diz-äs'tėr*, *n.* **1** an unfortunate event. **2** great misfortune.
disas'trous *adj.* very unfortunate, ruinous.
disas'trously *adv.* **disas'trousness** *n.*

disavow *dis-ȧ-vow'*, *v.t.* **1** to deny that one has: *He disavowed knowledge of the affair.* **2** to refuse to admit responsibility for.

disband *dis-band'*, *v.t.* to disperse, break up (esp. an army).—Also *v.i.*
disband'ment *n.*

disbelieve *dis-bi-lēv'*, *v.t.* not to believe.—Also *v.i.* (with *in*):—*pr.p.* **disbeliev'ing.**
disbelief' *n.*

disburse *dis-bûrs'*, *v.t.* to pay out:—*pr.p.* **disburs'ing.**
disburs'al, disburse'ment *ns.*

disc, disk *disk*, *n.* **1** a flat, thin, circular body. **2** a gramophone record. **3** (**disk**) (*computers*) a device for storing information, consisting of a disk or disks. **4** a pad of cartilage between vertebrae.
disk drive (*computers*) part of a computer system that records data onto and retrieves data from disks.
disc'-jockey *n.* a person who introduces and plays records (esp. of popular music) on radio, television, etc.

discard *dis-kärd'*, *v.t.* and *v.i.* **1** to throw away (a card) as useless. **2** to get rid of.

discern *di-sûrn'*, *di-zûrn'*, *v.t.* to distinguish clearly by the eye or understanding.
discern'ible *adj.* **discern'ibly** *adv.*
discern'ing *adj.* having insight and understanding.
discern'ment *n.*

discharge *dis-chärj'*, *v.t.* **1** to unload (cargo). **2** to set free. **3** to acquit. **4** to dismiss. **5** to fire (a gun). **6** to let out (e.g. smoke). **7** to perform (duties). **8** to pay (a debt):—*pr.p.* **discharg'ing.**—*n.* (also *dis'-*) **1** unloading. **2** acquittal. **3** dismissal. **4** firing. **5** giving out. **6** performance. **7** payment.

disciple *dis-ī'pl*, *n.* one who believes in the teaching of another.

discipline *dis'i-plin*, *n.* **1** training in an orderly mode of life. **2** order kept by means of control (*opp.* **indis'cipline**). **3** penance. **4** a branch of learning, sport, etc.—*v.t.* **1** to bring under control. **2** to punish, chastise:—*pr.p.* **dis'ciplining.**
disciplinā'rian *n.* one who enforces strict discipline.
dis'ciplinary (or *-plin'-*) *adj.* **1** of discipline. **2** punishing, intended to enforce control: *take disciplinary action.*

disclaim *dis-klām'*, *v.t.* to deny, refuse to acknowledge.
disclaim'er *n.* a denial.

disclose *dis-klōz'*, *v.t.* to lay open, reveal:—*pr.p.* **disclos'ing.**
disclō'sure *n.* **1** the act of disclosing. **2** something that is disclosed.

disco *dis'kō*, *n.* a discothèque:—*pl.* **dis'cos.**

discolour *dis-kul'ȯr*, *v.t.* **1** to spoil the colour of. **2** to stain.—Also *v.i.*
discolo(u)rā'tion *n.*

discomfit *dis-kum'fit*, *v.t.* **1** to abash, embarrass. **2** to defeat:—*pr.p.* **discom'fiting**; *pa.p.* **discom'fited.**
discom'fiture *n.*

discomfort *dis-kum'fȯrt*, *n.* lack of comfort, uneasiness.

discommode *dis-kȯ-mōd'*, *v.t.* to inconvenience:—*pr.p.* **discommod'ing.**

discompose *dis-kȯm-pōz'*, *v.t.* to agitate, fluster:—*pr.p.* **discompos'ing.**
discompo'sure *n.*

disconcert *dis-kȯn-sûrt'*, *v.t.* to embarrass, take aback.

disconnect *dis-kȯ-nekt'*, *v.t.* **1** to separate. **2** to detach, disjoin.
disconnect'ed *adj.* **1** separated. **2** (of speech, writing) rambling.
disconnec'tion *n.*

disconsolate *dis-kon'sȯ-lit*, *adj.* forlorn, dejected.
discon'solately *adv.* **discon'solateness** *n.*

discontent *dis-kȯn-tent'*, *n.* **1** dissatisfaction. **2** ill-humour.
discontent'ed *adj.* **1** dissatisfied. **2** fretful.
discontent'edly *adv.*
discontent'edness, discontent'ment *ns.*

discontinue *dis-kȯn-tin'ū*, *v.t.* **1** to leave off, stop. **2** to put an end to.—Also *v.i.*:—*pr.p.* **discontin'uing.**
discontin'uance, discontinuā'tion *ns.*
discontinu'ity *n.* lack of continuity.
discontin'uous *adj.* not continuous, interrupted.

discord *dis'körd*, *n.* **1** disagreement, quarrelling. **2** a loud and/or inharmonious sound.
discord'ant *adj.* **1** disagreeing. **2** harsh.
discord'ance, discord'ancy (*pl.* **-cies**), *ns.*

discothèque, **-theque** *dis'kō-tek*, *n.* **1** a club for dancing to music from gramophone records. **2** the equipment and records used to provide such music.

discount *dis'kownt*, *n.* a sum taken off a price or account, benefiting the payer.—*v.t.* *(dis-kownt')* **1** to leave out of consideration. **2** to allow for exaggeration in (e.g. a story). **3** to buy or sell (e.g. a bill of exchange not yet due) deducting from the price the value of interest for the time it has still to run.

at a discount **1** below par. **2** not in demand.

discountenance *dis-kown'tėn-ȧns*, *v.t.* to show disapproval of:—*pr.p.* **discoun'tenancing**.

discourage *dis-kur'ij*, *v.t.* **1** to dishearten. **2** to persuade against (with *from*): *The rain discouraged him from going camping.* **3** to hinder. **4** to oppose:—*pr.p.* **discour'aging**.

discour'agement *n.* **discour'aging** *adj.*

discourse *dis-kōrs'*, *-körs'*, *dis'*, *n.* a speech, a sermon.—*v.i.* *(dis'-kōrs'*, *-körs')* **1** to talk. **2** to hold forth (upon):—*pr.p.* **discours'ing**.

discourteous *dis-kûr'tyůs*, *adj.* not polite, rude.

discour'teousness, **discour'tesy** (*pl.* **-sies**), *ns.*

discover *dis-kuv'ėr*, *v.t.* **1** to find by chance. **2** to find out.

discov'erer *n.*

discov'ery *n.* **1** a finding out. **2** (*old*) exploration. **3** a thing discovered:—*pl.* **discov'eries**.

discredit *dis-kred'it*, *n.* **1** loss of good reputation: *I know something to his discredit.* **2** doubt. **3** disbelief.—*v.t.* **1** to disbelieve. **2** to make unbelievable. **3** to disgrace:—*pr.p.* **discred'iting**; *pa.p.* **discred'ited**.

discred'itable *adj.* disgraceful.

discred'itably *adv.*

discreet *dis-krēt'*, *adj.* **1** prudent, wise. **2** not saying anything to cause trouble:—*opp.* **indiscreet**.

discreet'ness *n.*

discretion *dis-kresh'(ȯ)n*, *n.* **1** discreetness. **2** liberty to act as one thinks fit.

at the discretion of left to the judgment or will of (someone).

discrepancy *dis-krep'ȧn-si*, *n.* disagreement, inconsistency: *I noticed some discrepancy between, a number of discrepancies in, the two accounts of what happened:*—*pl.* **discrep'ancies**.

discrep'ant *adj.*

discrete *dis-krēt'*, *adj.* separate.

discretion. See **discreet**.

discriminate *dis-krim'i-nāt*, *v.t.* to be the difference between (often with *from*): *These markings discriminate the one bird from the other.*—*v.i.* **1** to observe a difference (between). **2** (with *in favour of*, *against*) to treat favourably or unfavourably:—*pr.p.* **discrim'inating**.

discrim'inating *adj.* **1** making distinctions. **2** showing good judgment.

discriminā'tion *n.* **1** the act of discriminating. **2** the ability to recognise small differences. **3** good judgment.

discrim'inatory *adj.* not treating all people alike.

discursive *dis-kûr'siv*, *adj.* wandering from the point.

discus *dis'kůs*, *n.* a heavy disc thrown in athletic competitions.

discuss *dis-kus'*, *v.t.* to talk about.

discussion *dis-kush'(ȯ)n*, *n.*

disdain *dis-dān'*, *v.t.* **1** to think it unworthy of oneself: *I disdain to take the money.* **2** to scorn, reject.—*n.* **1** scorn. **2** haughtiness.

disdain'ful *adj.* **disdain'fully** *adv.*

disease *diz-ēz'*, *n.* (an) illness of mind or body.

diseased' *adj.*

disembark *dis-im-bärk'*, *v.t.* to set ashore.—*v.i.* to land.

disembarkā'tion *(-em-)* *n.*

disembody *dis-im-bod'i*, *v.t.* to separate (e.g. the spirit) from the body:—*pr.p.* **disembod'ying**; *pa.p.* **disembod'ied**.

disembowel *dis-im-bow'ėl*, *v.t.* to take the inside out of:—*pr.p.* **disembow'elling**; *pa.p.* **disembow'elled**.

disenchant *dis-in-chänt'*, *v.t.* to free from enchantment or from a pleasant false belief.

disenchant'ment *n.*

disencumber *dis-in-kum'bėr*, *v.t.* to free from something that hampers or burdens.

disengage *dis-in-gāj'*, *v.t.* **1** to separate, disjoin. **2** to free.—*v.i.* (of opponents) to withdraw from hostile positions:—*pr.p.* **disengag'ing**.

disengaged' *adj.* **1** separated. **2** freed. **3** not occupied or engaged. **4** not in a job.

disengage'ment *n.*

disentangle *dis-in-tang'gl*, *v.t.* **1** to free from entanglement. **2** to unravel:—*pr.p.* **disentang'ling**.

disentang'lement *n.*

disestablish *dis-is-tab'lish*, *v.t.* to deprive (a church) of state support.

disestab'lishment *n.*

disfavour *dis-fāv'ȯr, n.* **1** displeasure, disapproval. **2** the state of being out of favour: *He was in disfavour because he had stayed out late.*

disfigure *dis-fig'ůr, v.t.* to spoil the beaty of, to deface:—*pr.p.* **disfigur'ing.**
disfig'urement, disfigūrā'tion *ns.*

disfranchise *dis-fran'chīz, v.t.* to take the right to vote away from:—*pr.p.* **disfran'-chising.**

disgorge *dis-görj', v.t.* **1** to vomit. **2** to throw out with violence. **3** to give up (what one has wrongfully seized):—*pr.p.* **disgorg'ing.**

disgrace *dis-grās', n.* **1** the state of being out of favour. **2** a cause of shame. **3** dishonour.—*v.t.* **1** to dismiss from favour or office. **2** to bring shame upon:—*pr.p.* **disgrac'ing.**
disgrace'ful *adj.* very bad, shameful.
disgrace'fully *adv.* **disgrace'fulness** *n.*

disgruntled *dis-grun'tld, adj.* dissatisfied and sulky.

disguise *dis-gīz', v.t.* **1** to conceal by a change of dress, etc. **2** to hide (e.g. one's intentions):—*pr.p.* **disguis'ing.**—*n.* dress and/or make-up intended to conceal who the wearer is.

disgust *dis-gust', n.* **1** loathing. **2** indignation. **3** feeling of sickness.—*v.t.* to arouse these feelings in (someone).
disgust'ing *adj.* **disgust'ingly** *adv.*

dish *dish, n.* **1** a vessel in which food is served. **2** the food in a dish.—*v.t.* **1** to put in a dish, for table. **2** (*coll.*) to defeat or ruin.
dish aerial a large aerial, shaped like a dish, used e.g. in satellite television.
dish up 1 to serve. **2** to present (something presented before): *to dish up old arguments.*

dishabille *dis-a-bēl', n.* **1** carelessness of dress. **2** undress.—Also **déshabillé'** *(dā-zä-bēyā).*

dishearten *dis-här'tn, v.t.* to take courage or hope away from, depress.

dishevel *di-shev'el, v.t.* to disorder, make untidy, as hair:—*pr.p.* **dishev'elling;** *pa.p.* **dishev'elled.**

dishonest *dis-on'ist, adj.* **1** not honest. **2** cheating. **3** insincere.
dishon'estly *adv.* **dishon'esty** *n.*

dishonour *dis-on'ȯr, n.* disgrace, shame.—*v.t.* **1** to deprive of honour. **2** to disgrace. **3** to refuse payment of (e.g. a cheque).
dishon'ourable *adj.* **dishon'ourably** *adj.*

disillusion *dis-i-lōō'zh(ȯ)n,* or *-lū', n.* setting free from false pleasant belief or view.— *v.t.* to do this, to undeceive.
disillu'sioned *adj.* free from illusions, esp. taking a cynical view of life.
disillu'sionment *n.*

disincentive *dis-in-sen'tiv, n.* something that discourages one from trying, or that stands in the way of progress.

disinclination *dis-in-kli-nā'sh(ȯ)n, n.* unwillingness.
disincline' *v.t.* to make unwilling (to do, for):—*pr.p.* **disinclin'ing.**
disinclined' *adj.* unwilling (to do, for).

disinfect *dis-in-fekt', v.t.* to destroy disease germs in.
disinfect'ant *n.* anything that destroys the causes of infection.
disinfec'tion *n.*

disingenuous *dis-in-jen'ū-ůs, adj.* not frank or open, crafty.
disingen'uousness *n.*

disinherit *dis-in-her'it, v.t.* to take away from (a person) the right to inherit: —*pr.p.* **disinher'iting;** *pa.p.* **disinher'-ited.**

disintegrate *dis-in'ti-grāt, v.i.* **1** to come to pieces. **2** to crumble.—Also *v.t.*:—*pr.p.* **disin'tegrating.**
disintegrā'tion *n.*

disinter *dis-in-tûr', v.t.* **1** to take out of a grave. **2** to bring (e.g. something hidden, forgotten) to view:—*pr.p.* **disinterr'ing;** *pa.p.* **disinterred'.**
disinter'ment *n.*

disinterested *dis-in'tris-tid, adj.* not influenced by private feelings or selfish motives.
See also **uninterested.**

disjoin *dis-join', v.t.* to separate what has been joined.
disjoint' *v.t.* **1** to put out of joint. **2** to separate united parts.
disjoint'ed *adj.* not properly connected: *some disjointed remarks.*
disjoint'edly *adv.* **disjoint'edness** *n.*

disk. See **disc.**

dislike *dis-līk', v.t.* to be displeased with, to disapprove of:—*pr.p.* **dislik'ing.**—Also *n.*

dislocate *dis'lȯ-kāt, v.t.* **1** to put out of joint. **2** to throw out of order (e.g. traffic, plans):—*pr.p.* **dis'locatlng.**
dislocā'tion *n.*

dislodge *dis-loj', v.t.* **1** to drive from a place of rest, hiding, or defence. **2** to knock accidentally out of place:—*pr.p.* **dislodg'ing.**

disloyal *dis-loi'ȧl, adj.* false, faithless.
disloy'ally *adv.* **disloy'alty** *n.*

dismal *diz'mȧl, adj.* gloomy, cheerless.
dis'mally *adv.* **dis'malness** *n.*

dismantle *dis-man'tl, v.t.* **1** to strip of furniture, fittings, etc. **2** to pull down, or take to pieces:—*pr.p.* **dismant'ling**.

dismay *dis-mā', v.t.* to daunt, discourage or upset (a person).—Also *n.*

dismember *dis-mem'bėr, v.t.* **1** to tear limb from limb. **2** to tear to pieces.
dismem'berment *n.*

dismiss *dis-mis', v.t.* **1** to send away. **2** to put away (from one's thoughts). **3** to remove from office or employment. **4** (*law*) to put out of court, to discharge.
dismiss'al *n.*
dismiss'ive *adj.* showing a lack of interest.

dismount *dis-mownt', v.i.* to come off a horse, etc.—*v.t.* **1** to remove from a support, etc. **2** to unhorse.

disobedient. See **disobey**.

disobey *dis-ȯ-bā', v.t.* to neglect, or refuse, to do what is commanded.
disobedient *dis-ȯ-bēd'yėnt, adj.* neglecting, or refusing, to obey.
disobē'dience *n.* **disobē'diently** *adv.*

disoblige *dis-ȯ-blīj', v.t.* to show disregard for the claims or wishes of (a person):—*pr.p.* **disoblig'ing**.
disoblig'ing *adj.* unwilling to consider or to act according to the wishes of others.
disoblig'ingly *adv.*

disorder *dis-ör'dėr, n.* **1** lack of order, confusion. **2** a disturbance, breach of the peace. **3** a disease.—*v.t.* **1** to disarrange. **2** to upset health (physical or mental) of.
disor'dered *adj.*: *a disordered mind.*
disor'derly *adj.* **1** out of order, in confusion. **2** irregular, lawless.
disor'derliness *n.*

disorganise *dis-ör'gȧn-īz, v.t.* **1** to destroy the arrangement of. **2** to throw into disorder:—*pr.p.* **disor'ganising**.
disorganisā'tion *n.*

disorientate *dis-ō'ri-ėn-tāt, -ör', v.t.* to make uncertain as to whereabouts and direction:—*pr.p.* **disor'ientating**.

disown *dis-ōn', v.t.* to refuse to acknowledge as belonging to oneself.

disparage *dis-par'ij, v.t.* to talk slightingly of:—*pr.p.* **dispar'aging**.
dispar'agement *n.* **dispar'agingly** *adv.*

disparate *dis'pȧr-it, adj.* very different.

disparity *dis-par'i-ti, n.* inequality, difference (in age, amount, etc.):—*pl.* **dispar'ities**.

dispassionate *dis-pash'(ȯ)n-it, adj.* free from passion, cool, unbiassed: *a dispassionate observer; a dispassionate statement of the difficulties.*
dispass'ionately *adv.*

dispatch, **despatch** *dis-pach', v.t.* **1** to send (e.g. a messenger). **2** to put to death. **3** to deal with (e.g. business) quickly.—*n.* **1** a sending away (e.g. of mail). **2** haste. **3** a message. **4** (in *pl.*) state papers (military, diplomatic, etc.)
dispatch box a box for holding dispatches or valuable papers.
dispatch rider a carrier of dispatches on motor-cycle, etc.

dispel *dis-pel', v.t.* to drive away, make disappear (e.g. fears, darkness):—*pr.p.* **dispell'ing**; *pa.p.* **dispelled'**.

dispensable, etc. See **dispense**.

dispense *dis-pens', v.t.* **1** to give out, distribute, in portions (e.g. alms, favours). **2** to deal out, administer: *He sat under a palm tree dispensing justice to the tribe.* **3** (also *v.i.*) to make up (prescriptions):—*pr.p.* **dispens'ing**.
dispens'er *n.*
dispens'able *adj.* that may be done without:—*opp.* **indispensable**.
dispensary *dis-pens'ȧr-i, n.* a place where medicines are given out:—*pl.* **dispens'aries**.
dispensation *dis-pen-sā'sh(ȯ)n, n.* **1** the act of dealing out. **2** an act of divine Providence. **3** permission to neglect a rule.
dispense with to get rid of, or do without: *to economise by dispensing with two assistants.*

disperse *dis-pûrs', v.t.* **1** to scatter in all directions. **2** to spread (e.g. news). **3** to cause to vanish.—*v.i.* **1** to separate. **2** to spread. **3** to vanish:—*pr.p.* **dispers'ing**.
dispers'al, disper'sion *ns.*

dispirit *dis-pir'it, v.t.* to discourage.
dispir'ited *adj.* dejected.

displace *dis-plās', v.t.* **1** to disarrange, shift. **2** to remove from office. **3** to take the place of:—*pr.p.* **displac'ing**.
displace'ment *n.* **1** a putting or being out of place. **2** the quantity of water displaced by a floating body.
displaced person 1 one taken from his country as slave labour. **2** a refugee.

display *dis-plā', v.t.* to show.—*n.* **1** exhibition. **2** a show intended to attract notice.

displease *dis-plēz', v.t.* **1** to anger slightly. **2** to be disagreeable, e.g. artistically, to:—*pr.p.* **displeas'ing**.
displeased' *adj.*
displeasure *dis-plezh'ūr, n.* **1** anger. **2** disapproval.

disport *dis-pōrt', -pört', v.t.* to amuse (oneself).—*v.i.* to frolic.

dispose *dis-pōz', v.t.* **1** to arrange. **2** to make inclined: *This disposed him to make*

light of what had happened:—*pr.p.* **dispos'ing**.
dispos'able *adj.* able to disposed of.
dispos'al *n.* **1** arrangement. **2** getting rid (of). **3** right of using, etc.: *I put a car at his disposal*.
disposed' *adj.* **1** inclined (*opp.* **indisposed'**). **2** having a certain feeling (towards): *well-, ill-disposed towards his neighbours*.
dispose of **1** to arrange what is to be done about. **2** to get rid of.
See also **disposition** (from a different root).

disposition *dis-pȯ-zish'(ȯ)n*, *n.* **1** arrangement. **2** bestowal by will (of one's property etc.). **3** natural tendency, temper: *The child has a placid disposition*.

dispossess *dis-pȯz-es'*, *v.t.* to put out of possession (of), deprive (of).

disproof *dis-prōōf'*, *n.* **1** the act of disproving. **2** proof that something is not true.

disproportion *dis-prȯ-pōr'sh(ȯ)n*, *-pör'*, *n.* lack of proportion (in size, importance, etc.).
dispropor'tionate *adj.* too large or too small in relation to something else.
dispropor'tionately *adv.*

disprove *dis-prōōv'*, *v.t.* to prove to be not true, false, wrong:—*pr.p.* **disprov'ing**.
See also **disproof**.

dispute *dis-pūt'*, *v.t.* **1** to argue about. **2** to argue against. **3** to resist, contest.—Also *v.i.*:—*pr.p.* **disput'ing**.—*n.* **1** a contest in words. **2** a quarrel.
disput'able (also *dis'*) *adj.* **1** that may be disputed. **2** not certain:—*opp.* **indisputable**.
disput'ant (or *dis'*), **disput'er** *ns.*
disputā'tion *n.* an argument.
disputa'tious *(-ā'shus) adj.* inclined to argue.

disqualify *dis-kwol'i-fī*, *v.t.* **1** to take away a qualification or right from. **2** to make unfit for some purpose:—*pr.p.* **disqual'ifying**; *pa.p.* **disqual'ified**.
disqualificā'tion *n.*

disquiet *dis-kwī'it*, *n.* **1** unrest. **2** uneasiness. **3** anxiety.—*v.t.* to make uneasy, worry:—*pr.p.* **disquī'eting**; *pa.p.* **disquī'eted**.
disquī'eting *adj.* **disquī'etude** *n.*

disquisition *dis-kwi-zish'(ȯ)n*, *n.* a long discourse.

disregard *dis-ri-gärd'*, *v.t.* to pay no attention to.—*n.* **1** lack of attention. **2** neglect (of—also with *for*).

disrepair *dis-ri-pār'*, *n.* the state of being out of repair.

disrepute *dis-ri-pūt'*, *n.* bad repute.
disrep'utable *adj.* **1** disgraceful. **2** of low character. **3** not respectable.
disrep'utably *adv.*

disrespect *dis-ri-spekt'*, *n.* **1** lack of respect. **2** discourtesy. **3** rudeness.
disrespect'ful *adj.* **disrespect'fully** *adv.*

disrobe *dis-rōb'*, *v.t.* to undress:—*pr.p.* **disrob'ing**.

disrupt *dis-rupt'*, *v.t.* and *v.i.* to break up, throw into disorder (e.g. a meeting, traffic, friendly relations).
disrup'tion *n.*
disrup'tive *adj.* causing a break-up, separation, disorder.

dissatisfy *dis-sat'is-fī*, *v.t.* **1** to fail to satisfy. **2** to make discontented:—*pr.p.* **dissat'isfying**; *pa.p.* **dissat'isfied**.
dissatisfac'tion *n.*

dissect *di-sekt'*, *v.t.* **1** to cut into parts for examination. **2** to study and criticise (e.g. a man's character or motives).
dissec'tion *n.* the act or the art of cutting in pieces for careful study.

dissemble *di-sem'bl*, *v.t.* to disguise, mask: *He dissembled his true motives*.—Also *v.i.*:—*pr.p.* **dissem'bling**.
dissem'bler *n.*

disseminate *di-sem'in-āt*, *v.t.* to spread abroad (e.g. news, information):—*pr.p.* **dissem'inating**.
disseminā'tion *n.*

dissent *di-sent'*, *v.i.* **1** to refuse to agree. **2** to hold opinions different (from e.g. those of the church established by law).— Also *n.*
dissen'sion *n.* **1** disagreement. **2** strife.
dissent'er *n.* a member of a sect which has broken away from an established church.
dissen'tient *(-sh'ėnt) n.* one who disagrees.—Also *adj.*

dissertation *dis-ėr-tā'sh(ȯ)n*, *n.* a long formal piece of writing or talk.

disservice *dis-sûr'vis*, *n.* injury, an ill turn.

dissever *di(s)-sev'ėr*, *v.t.* **1** to sever. **2** to separate.

dissident *dis'i-dėnt*, *n.* one who disagrees, esp. with a government.—Also *adj.*

dissimilar *di(s)-sim'i-lȧr*, *adj.* unlike.
dissimilar'ity *n.* (*pl.* **-ties**.).

dissimulate *di-sim'ū-lāt*, *v.t.* to conceal or disguise (e.g. one's feelings).—Also *v.i.*:—*pr.p.* **dissim'ulating**.
dissimulā'tion *n.*

dissipate *dis'i-pāt*, *v.t.* **1** to dispel, make disappear (e.g. fog, fears). **2** to squander, waste.—Also *v.i.*:—*pr.p.* **diss'ipating**.

diss'ipated *adj.* indulging too much in drinking and other pleasures.
dissipā'tion *n.* **1** scattering. **2** wasteful spending (e.g. of money, energy). **3** intemperance. **4** frivolous amusement.

dissociate *di-sō'shi-āt, v.t.* **1** to separate. **2** to separate in thought (from). **3** (with *oneself from*) to refuse to give one's support to.—Also *v.i.*:—*pr.p.* **dissō'ciating.**

dissolute *dis'ol-ōōt, -ūt, adj.* loose in morals.
diss'olutely *adv.* **diss'oluteness** *n.*

dissolution. See **dissolve**.

dissolve *di-zolv', v.t.* **1** to melt. **2** to break up. **3** to put an end to (e.g. a parliament, a marriage).—Also *v.i.*:—*pr.p.* **dissolv'ing.**
dissolution *dis-ol-ōō'sh(o)n, -ū', n.*

dissonance *dis'o-nans, n.* **1** a discord, esp. one deliberately used in music. **2** disagreement.
diss'onant *adj.*

dissuade *di-swād', v.t.* to prevent (from) by advice or persuasion:—*pr.p.* **dissuad'ing.**
dissuā'sion *n.*

distaff *dis'täf, n.* the stick that holds the bunch of flax or wool in spinning.
distaff side the female part of a family.

distance *dis'tans, n.* **1** the space (between). **2** a far-off place or point: *in the distance.* **3** the scheduled duration of a boxing match, etc. **4** reserve of manner.
dis'tant *adj.* **1** far off, or far apart, in place or time. **2** not close: *a distant relation.* **3** reserved, not friendly: *Her manner was distant.*

distaste *dis-tāst', n.* dislike.
distaste'ful *adj.* disagreeable.
distaste'fully *adv.* **distaste'fulness** *n.*

distemper[1] *dis-tem'pėr, n.* **1** a method of painting using e.g. size instead of oil. **2** paint of this kind.—*v.t.* to paint in distemper.

distemper[2] *dis-tem'pėr, n.* **1** a disordered state of body or mind. **2** a disease, esp. of young dogs.

distend *dis-tend', v.t.* to stretch outwards.—*v.i.* to swell.
disten'sion *n.*

distil *dis-til', v.i.* to fall in drops.—*v.t.* **1** to let, or cause to, fall in drops. **2** to turn a liquid into vapour by heat, and then the vapour back to liquid again, as a means of purifying, etc. **3** to extract the spirit from anything by this method.—*pr.p.* **distill'ing**; *pa.p.* **distilled'.**
distillā'tion *n.* **distill'er** *n.*
distill'ery *n.* a place where distilling, esp. of whisky, is carried on:—*pl.* **distill'eries.**

distinct *dis-tingt', adj.* **1** separate. **2** different. **3** clear. **4** easily seen, heard, etc.:—*opp.* **indistinct'.**
distinc'tive, *adj.* **1** marking difference. **2** characteristic: *I recognised her from the back; she has a distinctive walk.*
distinction *dis-tingk'sh(o)n, n.* **1** difference. **2** outstanding merit. **3** a mark of honour.
distinct'ly *adv.* **distinct'ness** *n.*

distinguish *dis-ting'gwish, v.t.* **1** to mark off as different (often with *from*). **2** to make out, recognise. **3** to give distinction to.—*v.i.* to recognise a difference (between).
disting'uishable *adj.*:—*opp.* **indisting'uishable.**
disting'uished *adj.* **1** marked out (by). **2** eminent, famous.

distort *dis-tört', v.t.* **1** to twist out of shape. **2** to misrepresent: *to distort the truth.* **3** to make (sound) indistinct and harsh.
distor'tion *n.*

distract *dis-trakt', v.t.* **1** to draw away, esp. the mind or attention. **2** to trouble, perplex. **3** to make crazy.
distract'ed *adj.*
distrac'tion *n.* **1** perplexity. **2** agitation. **3** madness. **4** something that takes the mind off other, esp. more serious, affairs.
See also **distraught.**

distrait *dis-trā', adj.* absent-minded, inattentive because worried.

distraught *dis-tröt', adj.* **1** deeply agitated or worried. **2** crazy.

distress *dis-tres', n.* **1** extreme pain. **2** a cause of suffering. **3** misfortune or difficulty.—*v.t.* to cause pain or suffering to.
distress'ing *adj.* **distress'ingly** *adv.*

distribute *dis-trib'ūt, v.t.* **1** to divide among several, hand out. **2** to scatter (about a space):—*pr.p.* **distrib'uting.**
distribu'tion *n.* **distrib'utive** *adj.*
distrib'utor, -er *n.*

district *dis'trikt, n.* **1** territory marked off for administrative or other purpose. **2** a region.
district attorney. See **attorney.**
district nurse a nurse who attends to patients in their own homes.

distrust *dis-trust', n.* lack of trust or faith, suspicion.—*v.t.* to have no trust in.
distrust'ful *adj.* **distrust'fully** *adv.*
distrust'fulness *n.*

disturb *dis-tûrb', v.t.* **1** to throw into confusion. **2** to agitate, disquiet. **3** to interrupt.
disturb'ance *n.* **1** tumult, disorder. **2** interruption. **3** confusion (of arrangement, etc.). **4** the act of disturbing.
disturb'er *n.*

disunite *dis-ū-nīt'*, *v.t.* to separate, esp. in opinions or aims.—Also *v.i.*:—*pr.p.* **dis-unit'ing.**
disu'nity *(-ū'ni-) n.*

disuse *dis-ūs'*, or *dis'ūs*, *n.* the state of not being used.—*v.t.* *(dis-ūz')* to cease to use:—*pr.p.* **disus'ing.**

ditch *dich*, *n.* a trench dug in the ground, esp. for water.—*v.i.* **1** to dig ditches. **2** to crash-land in the sea.—*v.t.* **1** to drain by ditches. **2** to drive, throw, into a ditch. **3** to crash-land (plane) in the sea. **4** (*coll.*) to get rid of.
ditch'er *n.* a man or machine that makes, cleans, or repairs ditches.

dither *di*TH*'ėr*, *v.i.* to hesitate, be uncertain, act in a nervous hesitating way.—Also *n.*

ditto *dit'ō*, sometimes written **do.**, *n.* the same thing.—*adv.* in the same manner.

ditty *dit'i*, *n.* a little poem to be sung:—*pl.* **ditt'ies.**

ditty-bag *dit'i-bag*, *n.* a sailor's bag for needles, thread, etc.—Also **ditt'y-box.**

diurnal *dī-ûr'nȧl*, *adj.* of, performed in, or lasting, a day.

divan *di-van'*, *or dī'*, *n.* **1** a couch without back or sides. **2** a divan-bed.
divan'-bed' *n.* a type of bed without a fixed board at the head or foot, sometimes usable as a couch.

dive *dīv*, *v.i.* **1** to plunge into water or down through the air. **2** to go deeply (into):—*pr.p.* **div'ing.**—*n.* **1** a plunge. **2** a swoop.
div'er *n.* **1** one who dives. **2** one who works under water using special breathing equipment. **3** a duck-like diving bird.

diverge *dī-* or *di-vûrj'*, *v.i.* **1** to separate and go in different directions. **2** to differ (from a standard):—*pr.p.* **diverg'ing.**
diverg'ence *n.* **diverg'ent** *adj.*

divers *dīv'ėrz*, *adj.* several.

diverse *dī-vûrs'*, or *dī'*, *adj.* **1** different, unlike. **2** of various kinds.
diverse'ly *adv.* **diverse'ness** *n.*
diver'sity *n.* **1** diverseness. **2** point of difference:—*pl.* **diver'sities.**
diversify *dī-vûr'si-fī*, *v.t.* **1** to give variety to. **2** to begin to produce a variety of (goods, etc.).—Also *v.i.*:—*pr.p.* **diver'-sifying**; *pr.p.* **diver'sified.**

diversion. See **divert.**

divert *dī-*, *di-vûrt'*, *v.t.* **1** to change the direction, or route, of. **2** to turn (to another purpose). **3** to distract (the attention). **4** to amuse.
divert'ing *adj.* amusing.
diversion *di-vûr'sh(ȯ)n*, *n.* **1** a place where, or the route along which, traffic is diverted. **2** turning aside. **3** amusement, recreation. **4** a movement to mislead an opponent.

divest *dī-* or *di-vest'*, *v.t.* to strip or deprive (of anything).

divide *di-vīd'*, *v.t.* **1** to break up, or mark off, into parts. **2** to share (among). **3** to keep apart. **4** to cause (an assembly) to vote on a motion. **5** to find out how many times one number contains another.—Also *v.i.*:—*pr.p.* **divid'ing.**—*n.* a watershed.
div'idend *(-i-dend) n.* **1** the number that is to be divided. **2** interest on shares, etc.
divid'er *n.* **1** a person or thing that divides. **2** (in *pl.*) a two-pointed measuring instrument, similar to compasses.
divid'ing *adj.*, *n.*
division *di-vizh'(ȯ)n*, *n.* **1** the act of dividing. **2** a partition, barrier. **3** a section. **4** a part of a larger body, e.g. a constituency, an army unit. **5** separation. **6** difference in opinion, etc. **7** the finding how many times one number is contained in another.
divis'ible *adj.* able to be divided:—*opp.* **indivis'ible.**
divisional *di-vizh'ȯn-ȧl*, *adj.* of, or marking, a division.
divis'or *(-vīz') n.* the number that divides the dividend.

divine *di-vīn'*, *adj.* **1** of, belonging to, a god. **2** holy. **3** excellent.—*n.* a clergyman.—*v.t.* to perceive through keenness of understanding or insight:—*pr.p.* **divining.**
divinā'tion *(di-vi-) n.* **1** foretelling the future. **2** insight, intuition.
divi'ner *(-vī') n.* one who has, or claims, skill in finding hidden water or metals.
divin'ity *(di-vin'-) n.* **1** the nature of God. **2** a god or goddess (*pl.* **divin'ities**).
divi'ning-rod *n.* a rod, often of hazel, used by a diviner.

divisible, division, etc. See **divide.**

divorce *di-vōrs'*, *-vörs'*, *n.* **1** the legal ending of a marriage. **2** a complete separation.—*v.t.* **1** to dissolve the marriage of, or one's marriage with. **2** to separate:—*pr.p.* **divor'cing.**
divor'cee *(-sē) n.* a divorced person.

divulge *dī-vulj'*, or *di-*, *v.t.* **1** to let out (a secret). **2** to reveal (that):—*pr.p.* **divulg'-ing.**

dizzy *diz'i*, *adj.* **1** giddy. **2** confused. **3** causing giddiness:—*comp.* **dizz'ier**; *superl.* **dizz'iest.**
dizz'ily *adv.* **dizz'iness** *n.*

do[1] *dōō*, *v.t.* **1** to carry out, perform (e.g. one's duty, a piece of work, justice). **2** to perform some action on, as to clean (a room), cook (a steak), arrange (hair). **3** (*slang*) to swindle. **4** to make the round of: *to do all the picture galleries.*—*v.i.* **1** to act, behave: *Do as I do.* **2** to get along, fare: *He is doing well.* **3** to be sufficient: *Sixpence will do*:—*2nd sing.* (thou) **dost** *(dust)*, *3rd* (he, etc.) **does** *(duz)*, (formerly) **doth** *(duth)*; *pa.t.* **did**; *pr.p.* **do'ing** *(dōō')*; *pa.p.* **done** *(dun).*—**Do** is often used in place of other verbs, esp. to avoid repeating them (e.g. *I may not manage to go, but if I do, I hope to see John*); it is also used along with a more important verb (1) in questions (e.g. *Do you know where he is?*), (2) to give emphasis (e.g. *I do hope we win*), and (3) in sentences with 'not' (e.g. *I did not go*).—*n.* **1** a swindle. **2** a festivity:—*pl.* **do's** or **dos**.

doer *dōō'ėr, n.*

do'ing *n.* **1** (*coll.*) a scolding, a beating. **2** (in *pl.*) actions, behaviour. **3** (in *pl.*; *slang*) things necessary.

done *adj.* **1** finished. **2** exhausted.

do'-or-die' *adj.* desperate, regardless of cost or consequences.

do away with **1** to abolish. **2** (also **do for, in**) to kill, murder.

do proud to make (someone) feel flattered, to treat lavishly.

See also **deed**.

do², **doh** *dō, n.* (*music*) the first tone or keynote of the scale.

do³. See **ditto**.

docile *dō'sīl, adj.* (of a person, animal) easy to manage.

do'cilely *adv.* **docil'ity** *n.*

dock¹ *dok, n.* a weed with large leaves and a long root.

dock² *dok, v.t.* **1** to cut short. **2** to take something off (e.g. wages).—*n.* the part of a tail left after clipping.

dock³ *dok, n.* **1** the part of a harbour, etc. where ships load, unload, are repaired, etc. **2** (in *pl.*) the area surrounding this. **3** the box etc., in court where the accused is placed.—*v.t., v.i.* to put in, or enter, a dock.

dock'er *n.* one who works at the docks.

dock'yard *n.* an enclosure, esp. naval, with docks, slipways, stores, etc.

dry dock a dock that can be emptied of water so as to lay bare the hull of a ship for cleaning and repairs.

floating dock a floating form of dry dock.

docket *dok'it, n.* **1** a note on a document naming its contents. **2** a label. **3** a list of cases in court. **4** a permit or certificate.—*v.t.* to make a summary of, or a note of (contents):—*pr.p.* **dock'eting**; *pa.p.* **dock'eted**.

doctor *dok'tȯr, n.* **1** a man or woman trained to treat the sick. **2** one who has received from a university the highest degree in arts, science, etc.—*v.t.* **1** to treat as a doctor does. **2** to patch up. **3** to tamper with: *The drink was doctored*—i.e. something had been put into it.

doc'torate *n.* the degree of doctor.

doctrinaire *dok-tri-nār', adj.* **1** stubbornly and dogmatically following a theory, regardless of circumstances or consequences. **2** stubbornly dogmatic.

doctrine *dok'trin, n.* **1** a belief or teaching. **2** a set of beliefs on one subject.

doc'trinal (or *-trī'nȧl*) *adj.*

document *dok'ū-mėnt, n.* a paper containing information or proof or evidence.—*v.t.* (*dok'ū-mėnt*, or *-ment'*) **1** to supply with documents. **2** to prove by documents.

document'ary *adj.* of, or found in, documents.—*n.* a motion picture showing the facts of a particular human activity: *a documentary about pottery-making*:—*pl.* **document'aries**.

dodder *dod'ėr, v.i.* to shake, to totter, esp. because of old age.

dodge *doj, v.t.* **1** to avoid by a sudden movement: *She dodged the snowball.* **2** to avoid having to carry out (a duty), or to answer (a question), etc.—Also *v.i.*:—*pr.p.* **dodg'ing**.—*n.* **1** an act of dodging. **2** a trick.

dodg'er *n.*

dodg'y (*coll.*) *adj.* **1** tricky. **2** risky:—*comp.* **dodg'ier**; *superl.* **dodg'iest**.

Dodgem(s)® *doj'ėm(z), n.* (*pl.*) (also without *cap.*) an amusement in which drivers of small electric cars try to bump others without being bumped.

dodo *dō'dō, n.* a large extinct bird:—*pl.* **do'do(e)s**.

doe *dō, n.* the female of the fallow deer, antelope, rabbit, and hare.

doe'skin *n.* **1** the skin of a doe (deer). **2** a smooth, close-woven, woollen cloth.

doer, does. See **do¹**.

doff *dof, v.t.* to take off (e.g. a hat).

dog *dog, n.* **1** a domesticated, or wild, flesh-eating animal, esp. the male. **2** a mean scoundrel. **3** a gripping, or holding, device.—*adj.* **1** male: a *dog fox.* **2** bad, pretended: *dog French.*—*v.t.* to follow closely as a dog does:—*pr.p.* **dogg'ing**; *pa.p.* **dogged**.

dogg'ed *(-id) adj.* keeping on at what one is doing, determined, persistent.

dogg'edly *adv.* **dogg'edness** *n.*

dog'-collar *n.* **1** a collar for a dog. **2** a close-fitting collar worn by a clergyman.

dog days a supposedly hot part of July

and August, the period when the Dogstar rises with the sun.

dog'-eared *adj.* **1** (of the pages of a book) with a corner turned down like a dog's ear. **2** (of a book, etc.) with corners so bent. **3** scruffy, untidy.

dog'fight *n.* **1** a fight between dogs. **2** a single combat (esp. of aeroplanes).

dog'fish *n.* a small shark.

dog'rose *n.* a wild rose.

dogs'body *n.* a drudge:—*pl.* **dogs'-bodies.**

Dog'star *n.* Sirius, the brightest star in the heavens.

dog'-tired' *adj.* utterly exhausted.

dog violet the common scentless wild violet.

dog'-watches *n.pl.* on a ship, the watch 4–6 p.m. or 6–8 p.m., consisting of two hours only instead of four.

dog in the manger one who will not let others enjoy what he himself cannot use.

go to the dogs to go to ruin.

in the doghouse in disgrace.

the dogs greyhound racing.

doge *dōj*, or *dō'jā*, (*history*) *n.* the chief magistrate in Venice and Genoa.

dogged, doggedly. See **dog.**

doggerel *dog'ėr-ėl*, *n.* worthless verses, sometimes in irregular rhythm.

dogma *dog'mȧ*, *n.* **1** a doctrine laid down with authority, e.g. by the Church. **2** a settled opinion.

dogmat'ic, -al *adjs.* asserting positively in an overbearing manner.

dogmat'ically *adv.*

dog'matise *v.i.* to state one's opinion dogmatically or arrogantly:—*pr.p.* **dog'-matising.**

dog'matism *n.* dogmatic manner, attitude.

doh. See **do**^{2}.

doily *doi'li*, *n.* a small lace or lacy paper mat laid on or under dishes:—*pl.* **doi'lies.**—Also **doy'ley** (*pl.* **doy'leys**).

doings. See **do**^{1}.

dolce vita, la *dol'chā vē'tä, lä* the sweet life, a life of luxury.

doldrums *dol'drumz*, *n.pl.* **1** parts of the ocean about the equator where calms are frequent. **2** low spirits.

dole *dōl*, *n.* **1** a share. **2** state payment to an unemployed person.—*v.t.* to deal (out) in small amounts:—*pr.p.* **dol'ing.**

doleful *dōl'f(oo)l*, *adj.* sorrowful, gloomy.

dole'fully *adv.* **dole'fulness** *n.*

doll *dol*, *n.* a toy in human form.

doll'y *n.* **1** a little doll. **2** an instrument for turning or pounding, used in washing clothes, mining, etc.:—*pl.* **doll'ies.**

dollar *dol'ȧr*, *n.* a silver coin (=100 cents) of U.S.A., Canada, etc.

dollop *dol'ȯp*, *n.* a lump, shapeless mass.

dolly. See **doll.**

dolmen *dol'mėn*, *n.* a prehistoric table-like stone structure.

dolphin *dol'fin*, *n.* **1** a porpoise-like animal about 8 or 10 feet long. **2** a fish about 5 feet in length, noted for the brilliance of its colours when dying.

dolt *dōlt*, *n.* a dull or stupid fellow.

dolt'ish *adj.* dull, stupid.

Dom *dom*, *n.* a title given to certain Roman Catholic dignitaries, and to certain monks.

domain *dȯ-mān'*, *n.* **1** lands. **2** one's sphere of influence or of knowledge.

dome *dōm*, *n.* **1** a structure like a half sphere forming the roof of a building. **2** anything so shaped.

domed *adj.*

domestic *dȯ-mes'tik*, *adj.* **1** belonging to the house. **2** private. **3** (of animals) tame, sharing man's life. **4** not foreign: *the Government's domestic policies.*—*n.* a servant in the house.

domes'ticate *v.t.* **1** to make domestic. **2** to tame:—*pr.p.* **domes'ticating.**

domestic'ity *(-tis'-)* *n.* home life.

domestic science the household arts (such as catering, cookery, laundry-work) studied scientifically—now usu. known as **home economics.**

domicile *dom'i-sil, -sīl*, *n.* a person's legal place of residence.—*v.t.* to establish in a fixed residence:—*pr.p.* **dom'iciling.**

domicil'iary *(-sil'i-ȧr-i)* *adj.*

dominant *dom'in-ȧnt*, *adj.* **1** ruling, most important, most influential. **2** (of genes) very likely to be passed on to a child.

dom'inate *v.t.* **1** to be lord over, have a very strong influence over: *The stronger man dominates the weaker.* **2** to tower above: *The castle dominates the landscape.*—Also *v.i.* (sometimes *dominate over*):—*pr.p.* **dom'inating.**

dominā'tion *n.*

domineer' *v.i.* to be tyrannical, overbearing.

domineer'ing *adj.*

dominion *dȯ-min'yȯn*, *n.* **1** sovereignty. **2** rule. **3** a self-governing country of the British Commonwealth (with *cap.* as part of the official title of certain countries).

domino *dom'in-ō*, *n.* **1** a hooded cape. **2** an oblong piece of wood or plastic divided by a line into two parts, each part blank or marked with from one to six spots:—*pl.* **dom'inoes.**

dom'inoes *n.sing.* the game played with dominoes.

don[1] *don, n.* **1** a Spanish title, corresponding to English Sir, Mr. **2** a fellow of a college.

donn'ish *adj.* like a university don.

don[2] *don, v.t.* to put on (e.g. a coat):—*pr.p.* **donn'ing**; *pa.p.* **donned**.

donation *dō-nā'sh(ȯ)n, n.* a gift of money or goods to a fund or collection.

donāte' *v.t.* to give to a fund, etc.:—*pr.p.* **donat'ing**.

dō'nor *n.* a giver.

done. See **do**[1].

donkey *dong'ki, n.* an ass:—*pl.* **don'keys**.

don'key-en'gine *n.* a small auxiliary engine.

donkey jacket an outdoor jacket of thick hard-wearing material.

don'key-work *n.* drudgery.

donor. See **donation**.

don't *dōnt*, abbrev. of **do not**.

doodle *dōōd'l, v.i.* to make meaningless drawings or scribbles e.g. while thinking: —*pr.p.* **dood'ling**.—Also *n.*

doom *dōōm, n.* **1** judgment. **2** destiny. **3** ruin.—*v.t.* to condemn, destine (often in *pass.*, e.g. *The attempt was doomed to failure*).

dooms'day *n.* judgment day.

door *dōr, dör, n.* **1** the entrance into a building or room. **2** a hinged, usu. wooden, barrier which closes the entrance. **3** a means of approach: *the door to success*.

door'keeper *n.* one in charge of a door.

door'post *n.* the jamb or side piece of a door.

door'step *n.* a raised step leading to a door.

door'way *n.* an opening where there is or might be a door.

dope *dōp, n.* **1** a drug. **2** anything that dulls the mind or senses. **3** (*slang*) information.—Also *v.t.*:—*pr.p.* **dop'ing**.

do'pey, do'py *adj.* stupid, not able to think clearly:—*comp.* **do'pier**; *superl.* **do'piest**.

Doric *dor'ik, adj.* of a style of Greek architecture.—*n.* a broad dialect, esp. broad Scots.

dormant *dör'mȧnt, adj.* **1** sleeping. **2** not active: *a dormant volcano*.

dormer (window) *dör'mėr (win'dō)*, a small window jutting out from a sloping roof.

dormitory *dör'mi-tȯr-i, n.* a large sleeping-room with many beds:—*pl.* **dor'mitories**.

dormie. See **dormy**.

dormouse *dör'mows, n.* a squirrel-like gnawing animal related to mice:—*pl.* **dor'mice**.

dormy, dormie *dör'mi, (golf) adj.* said of a player when he is leading by as many holes as there are holes still to play.

dorsal *dör'sȧl, adj.* of the back.

dose *dōs, n.* **1** the quantity of medicine, etc., to be taken at one time. **2** anything disagreeable forced on one.—*v.t.* to give medicine in doses to:—*pr.p.* **dos'ing**.

dōs'age *n.* a method or rate of dosing.

doss *dos, (slang) n.* a bed.—*v.i.* **1** to lie (down) to sleep. **2** to sleep.

doss'-house *n.* a cheap lodging-house.

dossier *dos'i-ā, n.* a bundle of documents relating to one person or subject.

dost. See **do**[1].

dot[1] *dot, n.* **1** a small round spot. **2** the shorter of the two signal elements in Morse.—*v.t.* **1** to mark with dots. **2** to set (objects) here and there:—*pr.p.* **dott'ing**; *pa.p.* **dott'ed**.

dott'y *adj.* feeble, crazy:—*comp.* **dott'ier**; *superl.* **dott'iest**.

dot[2] *dot, n.* a dowry.

dotage, dotard. See **dote**.

dote *dōt, v.i.* **1** to show weak, or too great, affection for (with *on*). **2** to be weak-minded from old age:—*pr.p.* **dot'ing**.

dot'age *n.* the childishness of old age.

dot'ard *n.* one who is in his dotage.

doth. See **do**[1].

dotty. See **dot**[1].

double *dub'l, adj.* **1** twice as much: *double pay*. **2** consisting of two. **3** having two similar parts. **4** folded over. **5** deceitful, insincere.—*n.* **1** a person (or thing) so like another as to be mistaken for him (or it). **2** twice the amount, score, etc. **3** (in *pl.*) in tennis, etc, a game with two players on each side.—*v.t.* **1** to multiply by two. **2** to fold in two. **3** to pass, esp. to sail, round:—*pr.p.* **doub'ling**.

double agent a spy working for two opposing powers at the same time, but loyal only to one, or perhaps neither.

doub'le-barr'elled *adj.* **1** (of a gun) having two barrels. **2** with two possible meanings. **3** (of a surname) made up of two names.

double bass a stringed instrument, largest and deepest of the violin kind.

double bed one large enough for two people.

doub'le-breast'ed *adj.* (of a jacket or coat) having one half of the front overlapping the other.

double cream cream with more fat in it than single cream.

doub'le-cross, **doub'lecross** *v.t.* to swindle, deceive or betray (one for or with whom one was supposed to be swindling, etc. someone else).—Also *n.*
doub'le-deal'er *n.* a deceitful person.
doub'le-deal'ing *n.* deceit.
doub'le-deck'er *n.* a ship, vehicle, with two decks.
doub'le-dyed *adj.* deeply stained (with guilt).
doub'le-edged *adj.* with two cutting edges.
doub'le-faced *adj.* two-faced, insincere.
double glazing a double layer of glass in a window with an air-space between to keep heat in and noise out.
doub'le-quick *adj.* and *adv.* very quick(ly).
double standard the allowing of different standards of behaviour to different (groups of) people, esp. oneself as opposed to others.
double take an initial reaction to something, followed by a second reaction showing more surprise, etc.
doub'le-talk *n.* talk that sounds to the purpose but really tells nothing.
at the double running.
double back to turn sharply and go back in the direction one has just come from, usu. not by the same path.

doublet *dub'lit*, *n.* a close-fitting jacket formerly worn by men.

doubloon *dub-lōōn'*, *n.* an old Spanish gold coin.

doubt *dowt*, *v.i.* to be undecided in opinion.—*v.t.* **1** to distrust, suspect. **2** to be uncertain about: *I doubt the wisdom of your plan.*—*n.* **1** uncertainty. **2** suspicion.
doubt'er *n.*
doubt'ful *adj.* **1** feeling doubt, uncertain what to think, expect, etc. **2** able to be doubted, not clear: *The meaning is doubtful.* **3** questionable: *The wisdom of this action is doubtful.* **4** suspicious: *a doubtful character loitering outside.* **5** (of the future, a result, etc.) uncertain, but probably not good.
doubt'fully *adv.* **doubt'fulness** *n.*
doubt'less *adv.* **1** certainly. **2** probably.
no doubt certainly.

douche *dōōsh*, *n.* a jet of water directed on the body (inside or outside) from a pipe.

dough *dō*, *n.* a mass of flour or meal moistened and kneaded, but not baked.
dough'nut *n.* **1** a ring-shaped cake fried in fat. **2** a device of this shape.

doughty *dow'ti*, *adj.* **1** strong. **2** brave:—*comp.* **dough'tier**; *superl.* **dough'tiest**.
dough'tily *adv.* **dough'tiness** *n.*

dour *dōōr*, (chiefly *Scot.*) *adj.* **1** sullen. **2** harsh, grim. **3** obstinate.

douse, **dowse** *dows*, *v.t.* **1** to plunge into water. **2** to lower (a sail). **3** to put out:—*pr.p.* **dous'ing**, **dows'ing**.

dove *duv*, *n.* **1** a (esp. small type of) pigeon often used as an emblem of innocence, or gentleness. **2** one who seeks peace and conciliation rather than war or confrontation.
dove'cot *(-kot)*, **dove'cote** *(-kot, -kōt)*, *ns.* a building in which pigeons breed.
dove'tail *n.* a mode of joining by fitting wedge-shaped pieces (*tenons*) into like cavities (*mortises*).—*v.t.* to fit (one thing exactly into another).

dowager *dow'ȧ-jėr*, *n.* esp. in the ranks of the nobility, a title given to a widow to distinguish her from the wife of her husband's heir: *the dowager duchess*.

dowdy *dow'di*, *adj.* **1** not smart. **2** badly dressed:—*comp.* **dow'dier**; *superl.* **dow'diest**.

dower *dow'ėr*, *n.* **1** the part of a husband's property that goes to his widow. **2** a dowry. **3** natural gift(s).
dow'ered *adj.*
dowry *dow'ri*, *n.* the property a woman brings to her husband at marriage:—*pl.* **dow'ries**.

down[1] *down*, *n.* **1** soft feathers. **2** a soft covering of fluffy hairs.
Down'ie® *n.* a continental quilt.
down'y *adj.*:—*comp.* **down'ier**; *superl.* **down'iest**.

down[2] *down*, *adv.* **1** to, or in, a lower position or state. **2** to a smaller size, etc. **3** from an earlier to a later date. **4** away from a centre (capital, university, etc.). **5** in writing, type, etc.: *Put down what I dictate.* **6** on the spot, in cash: *£1 down and £3 later.*—*adj.* **1** moving in the direction indicated by *adv.* **down**: *the down train.* **2** descending: *on the down grade.* **3** depressed.—*prep.* **1** in a descent along, through, or by. **2** to or in a lower position on.—*v.t.* to knock or lay down.—*n.* (in phrase **ups and downs**) see **up**.
down'ward(s) *adv.* **1** from higher to lower. **2** from source to outlet.
down'ward *adj.*
down'-and-out' *adj.* and *n.* (a person) at the end of his resources, without money or hope.
down'-at-heel' *adj.* **1** having the back of the shoe trodden down. **2** shabby.
down'cast *adj.* **1** (of eyes) looking downwards. **2** depressed, dejected.
down'fall *n.* **1** fall, failure, ruin. **2** a fall of rain, snow, etc.
down'-heart'ed *adj.* discouraged.

down'hill' *adv., adj.* down the hill.
down-mar'ket *adj.* cheap or of poor quality.
down'pour *n.* a heavy fall of rain, etc.
down'right *adv.* **1** in plain terms. **2** thoroughly.—*adj.* **1** plain-spoken. **2** absolute: *a downright nuisance*.
down'stage' *adv.* towards the footlights.
down'stairs *adv.* in, or to, a lower storey.—Also *adj.*
down'-to-earth' *adj.* **1** sensible. **2** practical. **3** realistic.
down'trodden *adj.* trampled on, oppressed.
down in the mouth depressed, sad.
go down with to catch (a disease).

Downie®. See **down**[1].

downs *downz, n.pl.* an upland tract of pasture land.

Down's syndrome *downz' sin'drōm, n.* a medical condition, caused by a genetic abnormality, whose symptoms include mental retardation and flattened facial features.

downy. See **down**[1].

dowry. See **dower**.

dowse[1]. See **douse**.

dowse[2] *dowz, v.i.* to use a divining-rod:—*pr.p.* **dows'ing**.

doyley. See **doily**.

doze *dōz, v.i.* to sleep lightly or for short spells:—*pr.p.* **doz'ing**.—Also *n.*

dozen *duz'n, n.* a set of twelve.

drab *drab, n.* **1** thick grey cloth. **2** a grey or dull-brown colour.—*adj.* dull, uninteresting.
drab'ly *adv.* **drab'ness** *n.*

draft *dräft, n.* **1** a smaller body (of men, animals, things) selected from a larger. **2** (esp. *U.S.*) conscription. **3** an order for the payment of money. **4** a preliminary sketch.—*v.t.* **1** to draw an outline of. **2** to draw up in preliminary form. **3** to draw off (for a special purpose). **4** (*U.S.*) to conscript (soldiers).
drafts'man *n.* one who draws up documents, or (usu. **draughts'man**) plans, designs, etc.

drag *drag, v.t.* **1** to draw or pull by force or roughly. **2** to pull slowly. **3** to search (a river bed, etc.) with a drag-net or hook.—*v.i.* to move slowly and heavily:—*pr.p.* **dragg'ing**; *pa.p.* **dragged**.—*n.* **1** a net (**drag'-net**) or hook for dragging along to catch things under water. **2** anything that slows down, or interferes with progress. **3** the force on an aeroplane, etc., that tends to reduce forward motion. **4** (*coll.*) a very boring person or thing.

dragon *drag'ȯn, n.* **1** a winged reptile in old stories. **2** a fierce person. **3** a lizard of the E. Indies.
drag'onfly *n.* an insect with a long body and brilliant colours:—*pl.* **drag'onflies**.

dragoon *drȧ-gōōn', n.* a horse-soldier.—*v.t.* to force by bullying.

drain *drān, v.t.* **1** to draw (off, away, e.g. water). **2** to make dry. **3** to exhaust.—*v.i.* to flow off, or become dry, gradually.—*n.* **1** a watercourse. **2** a ditch. **3** a sewer. **4** something that causes a heavy outflow (e.g. of money): *This project is a major drain on our resources*.
drain'er *n.* a utensil on which articles are placed to drain.
drain'age *n.* the process, method, or system of draining.
drainage basin the area of land which drains into one river.

drake *drāk, n.* the male of the duck.

dram *dram, n.* **1** $\frac{1}{16}$ of an ounce. **2** a small drink, esp. of whisky.

drama *dräm'ȧ, n.* **1** a story or play for acting on the stage. **2** dramatic literature. **3** a series of deeply interesting events.
dramatic *drȧ-mat'ik, adj.* **1** of, or in the form of, a drama. **2** vivid, striking.
dramat'ically *adv.*
dramat'ics *n.pl.* **1** (also *n.sing.*) the production of plays. **2** exaggeratedly emotional behaviour.
dram'atise *v.t.* **1** to turn into the form of a play. **2** to make vivid and striking:—*pr.p.* **dram'atising**.
dramatisā'tion *n.*
dram'atist *n.* a writer of plays.
dram'atis perso'nae *(-sō'nē, -nī)* the characters of a play or dramatic event.

drank. See **drink**.

drape *drāp, v.t.* **1** to hang cloth in folds about. **2** to place (oneself) gracefully (over or around):—*pr.p.* **drap'ing**.—*n.* (in *pl.*; *U.S.* or *theatre*) curtains.
drāp'er *n.* a dealer in cloth, clothing, etc.
drāp'ery *n.* **1** cloth goods. **2** hangings. **3** a draper's business:—*pl.* **drap'eries**.

drastic *dräs'tik, adj.* **1** powerful in action (e.g. of a purgative). **2** violent, severe (e.g. of measures).
dras'tically *adv.*

draught *dräft, n.* **1** the act of drawing or pulling. **2** a deep drink. **3** a quantity (of fish) taken in a net. **4** a current of air. **5** the depth of water a ship requires to float freely. **6** a thick disc used in the game of draughts.—Also a spelling for **draft**.
draughts *n.sing.* a game played with draughts on a chequered board.
draugh'ty *adj.* full of currents of air:—

comp. **draugh'tier**; *superl.* **draugh'tiest**.

draugh'tily *adv.* **draugh'tiness** *n.*

draught animal one used for pulling heavy loads.

draught beer beer sold from the cask, not bottled.

draughts'man *n.* one who draws plans, designs, etc. or (usu. **drafts'man**) draws up documents.

draw *drö, v.t.* **1** to pull. **2** to bring or take out. **3** to deduce, form: *to draw conclusions.* **4** to make a picture of. **5** to describe. **6** to require (a depth of water) for floating. **7** (*sport*) to play (a game) in which neither person, side, wins. **8** to attract (a crowd). **9** (*history*) to disembowel (a criminal).—*v.i.* **1** to move (towards, or away from): *to draw near, back.* **2** to play a drawn game. **3** to practise sketching. **4** to draw lots: *Draw for partners:—pa.t.* **drew** *(dro͞o)*; *pa.p.* **drawn**.—*n.* **1** the act of drawing. **2** an attraction. **3** a drawn game. **4** the selection of winning tickets in a lottery.

draw'er *n.* **1** one who draws. **2** a sliding box in a chest of drawers or other piece of furniture. **3** (in *pl.*) an undergarment for the lower part of the body and legs.

draw'ing *n.* **1** representing objects by lines, shading, etc. **2** a picture so made.

draw'back *n.* a disadvantage.

draw'bridge *n.* a bridge that can be drawn up and let down.

draw'ing-pin *n.* a pin with a large flat head, for fastening paper on a board.

draw a blank **1** to get a lottery ticket that wins no prize. **2** to obtain no result.

draw, cast lots to decide on someone or something by drawing names out of e.g. a box.

draw on **1** to pull on (e.g. gloves). **2** to make a demand upon (e.g. one's money resources, one's imagination, a person—for something).

draw out **1** to prolong. **2** to make (someone) speak freely.

draw the line (at something) to refuse to do it, approve of it, etc.

draw up **1** to draft a (document). **2** to stop (as in driving a car). **3** to move closer.

drawing-room *drö'ing-room, -ro͞om, n.* (orig. *withdrawing-room*) **1** a room to which to withdraw after dinner. **2** a room for entertaining guests formally.

drawl *dröl, v.t.* and *v.i.* to speak, or utter, in a slow, lengthened tone.—Also *n.*

drawn. See **draw**.

dray *drā, n.* a low strong cart.

dread *dred, n.* great fear.—*v.t.* to fear greatly.

dread'ful *adj.* **1** producing great fear. **2** very bad, annoying.

dread'fully *adv.* **dread'fulness** *n.*

dreadnought *dred'nöt, n.* a type of battleship with heavy guns.

dream *drēm, n.* **1** thoughts, fancies, or a vision during sleep. **2** a daydream. **3** something very beautiful. **4** an unrealised ambition.—*v.i.* **1** to fancy events during sleep. **2** to think idly.—Also *v.t.:—pa.t.* and *pa.p.* **dreamed** or **dreamt** *(dremt)*.

dream'er *n.*

dream'y *adj.* **1** full of dreams. **2** fond of dreaming. **3** vague, dim, idle:—*comp.* **dream'ier**; *superl.* **dream'iest**.

dream'ily *adv.* **dream'iness** *n.*

dreary *drēr'i, adj.* **1** gloomy. **2** very dull:—*comp.* **drear'ier**; *superl.* **drear'iest**.

drear'ily *adv.* **drear'iness** *n.*

dredge[1] *drej, n.* an apparatus for bringing up material from the bottom of a river or sea.—*v.t.* to deepen (e.g. a river) by bringing up mud:—*pr.p.* **dredg'ing**.

dredg'er *n.* a vessel fitted with dredging apparatus.

dredge[2] *drej, v.t.* to sprinkle:—*pr.p.* **dredg'ing**.

dregs *dregz, n.pl.* **1** the grounds (of liquor). **2** anything worthless.

drench *drench* or *-sh, v.t.* **1** to give medicine to (an animal) by force. **2** to soak.—*n.* a dose of medicine forced down the throat.

drench'ing *n.* a soaking.

dress *dres, v.t.* **1** to straighten (e.g. a line of soldiers). **2** to prepare (food). **3** to treat, bandage (wound). **4** to clothe.—*v.i.* **1** to come into line. **2** to put on clothes.—*n.* **1** covering for the body. **2** a gown.

dress'er *n.* **1** one who dresses. **2** a kitchen sideboard.

dress'ing *n.* **1** anything applied (as manure to land, sauce or stuffing to food). **2** the bandage, etc. applied to a wound.

dress'y *adj.* **1** showy. **2** fond of stylish clothes:—*comp.* **dress'ier**; *superl.* **dress'iest**.

dress'ily *adv.* **dress'iness** *n.*

dress circle orig. the first gallery in a theatre, intended for people in evening dress.

dress'ing-gown *n.* a loose garment worn when one is not fully dressed.

dress'ing-table *n.* a table with a mirror and usu. drawers, usu. in a bedroom.

dress rehearsal the final rehearsal of a play, etc., for which the performers wear their costumes.

fancy dress clothes of another country, historical period, etc., worn e.g. at a **fancy dress ball**.

morning dress, **evening dress**, **full dress** dress for formal occasions.

dressage *dres'äzh*, *n.* the training of a horse in deportment and response to controls.

drew. See **draw**.

dribble *drib'l*, *v.i.* **1** to fall in small drops. **2** to allow saliva to trickle from the mouth. **3** (*football*, etc.) to move the ball along little by little.—*v.t.* **1** let fall in small drops. **2** to give out in small amounts. **3** (*football*, etc) to move (the ball) along little by little:—*pr.p.* **dribb'ling**.—Also *n.*

drib'let, **dribb'let** *n.* a drop, trickle, small quantity.

dried, **drier**. See **dry**.

drift *drift*, *n.* **1** a heap of matter driven together, as snow. **2** the direction in which a thing is driven. **3** the state of drifting. **4** the general meaning (of what is said).—*v.t.* to carry by drift.—*v.i.* **1** to be floated or blown along. **2** to be driven into heaps. **3** to wander or live without any definite aim.

drift'er *n.* **1** a fisherman or a fishing-boat that uses a drift-net. **2** one who drifts.

drift'-net *n.* a net which is allowed to drift with the tide.

drift'wood *n.* wood drifted ashore by the sea.

drill[1] *dril*, *v.t.* **1** to bore, pierce. **2** to train or teach (soldiers, pupils, etc.) by repeated practice. **3** to sow in rows.—*n.* **1** an instrument that bores. **2** exercise, esp. of soldiers. **3** an exercise that teaches by repetition. **4** practice. **5** a furrow with seeds or growing plants.

drill[2] *dril*, *n.* a stout twilled linen or cotton cloth.

drily. See **dry**.

drink *dringk*, *v.t.* **1** to swallow (a liquid). **2** to take (in) through the senses.—*v.i.* **1** to swallow a liquid. **2** to make a habit of taking too much intoxicating liquor:—*pa.t.* **drank**; *pa.p.* **drunk**.—*n.* **1** something to be drunk. **2** intoxicating liquor.

drink'er *n.*

drunk *adj.* showing the effects of having drunk too much alcoholic drink.—*n.* a drunk person.

drunk'ard *n.* one who drinks too much alcoholic liquor.

drunk'en, *adj.* **1** drunk. **2** in the habit of drinking too much alcohol. **3** caused by intoxication: *a drunken brawl.*

drunk'enly *adv.* **drunk'enness** *n.*

drink to to wish (someone or something) well while drinking something, esp. alcoholic.

drip *drip*, *v.i.* **1** fall in drops. **2** to let fall drops.—*v.t.* to let fall in drops:—*pr.p.* **dripp'ing**; *pa.p.* **dripped**.—*n.* **1** a drop. **2** a falling in drops. **3** apparatus for passing a liquid slowly and steadily into a vein.

dripp'ing *n.* something that falls in drops, as fat from meat in roasting.

drip'-dry' *adj.* (of a material or garment) which requires little or no ironing when allowed to dry hanging up.—*v.t.* and *v.i.* to dry in this way without moisture being squeezed out:—*pr.p.* **drip'-dry'ing**; *pa.p.* **drip'-dried'**.

drip'stone *n.* a moulding over doorways, etc. throwing off rain.

drive *drīv*, *v.t.* **1** to urge, hurry along. **2** to control or guide (e.g. a car). **3** to hit with force (e.g. a golf ball from a tee, a nail into wood, etc.). **4** to impel (a person to): *Despair may drive a man to drink.* **5** to carry on (a brisk trade). **6** to conclude, get agreement to (a bargain): *to drive a hard* (i.e. exacting) *bargain.*—*v.i.* **1** to press (forward). **2** to go in a vehicle. **3** to control the vehicle one is in. **4** to work hard (at):—*pr.p.* **driv'ing**; *pa.t.* **drove**; *pa.p.* **driv'en** *(driv').*—*n.* **1** an excursion in a vehicle. **2** a private road to a house. **3** a road with houses. **4** energy, push. **5** a campaign for some purpose. **6** a driving shot. **7** a driving mechanism.

driv'er *n.*

drive'-in *n.* a store, cinema, etc., where people are catered for while remaining in their motor cars.—Also *adj.*

drove *drōv*, *n.* **1** a number of cattle, or other animals, driven. **2** a large crowd (of people).

drov'er *n.* one whose job is to drive cattle.

be driving at to be trying to say or suggest.

drivel *driv'l*, *v.i.* to speak like an idiot:—*pr.p.* **driv'elling**; *pa.p.* **driv'elled**.—*n.* nonsense.

driv'eller *n.*

drizzle *driz'l*, *v.i.* to rain in small drops:—*pr.p.* **drizz'ling**.—*n.* a small, light rain.

drizz'ly *adj.*:—*comp.* **drizz'lier**; *superl.* **drizz'liest**.

droll *drōl*, *adj.* **1** odd. **2** amusing.

droll'ness, **droll'ery** (*pl.* **-eries**), *ns.*

dromedary *drom'i-dàr-i*, or *drum'*, *n.* a one-humped Arabian camel:—*pl.* **drom'-edaries**.

drone *drōn*, *n.* **1** the male of the honey bee. **2** one who lives on the labour of others, as the drone bee does. **3** a deep humming sound. **4** a bass pipe of a bagpipe. **5** a dull boring voice. **6** a monotonous tiresome speaker.—*v.i.* **1** to make a low humming sound. **2** to speak in a dull boring voice.—Also *v.t.*:—*pr.p.* **dron'ing.**

drool *drōōl*, *v.i.* **1** to slaver. **2** to drivel. **3** to show foolishly excessive fondness, pleasure or desire (with *over*).

droop *drōōp*, *v.i.* **1** to sink or hang down. **2** to grow weak or faint.

drop *drop*, *n.* **1** a small blob of liquid. **2** a small quantity. **3** a small round sweet. **4** a fall. **5** a steep descent. **6** a disappointment.—*v.i.* **1** to fall in drops. **2** to fall suddenly, or steeply—*v.t.* **1** to let fall. **2** to give up (e.g. a friend, a habit). **3** to utter or write in a casual manner: *to drop a remark, a note*:—*pr.p.* **dropp'ing**; *pa.p.* **dropped**.

drop'let *n.* a tiny drop.

dropp'er *n.* a device for giving liquid in drops.

dropp'ings *n.pl.* dung, excreta, of animals or birds.

drop kick (*Rugby*) a kick made as the ball, dropped from the hand, rebounds from the ground.

drop'-scene, **drop'-curtain** *ns.* a painted curtain lowered to hide all or part of the stage.

drop off to fall asleep.

drop out **1** to withdraw e.g. from a contest. **2** (*coll.*) to withdraw from one's academic course, the conventional way of life, etc. (*n.* **drop'-out**).

dropsy *drop'si*, *n.* an unnatural collection of water in any part of the body.

drop'sical *adj.*

dross *dros*, *n.* **1** small or waste coal. **2** refuse.

drought *drowt*, *n.* lack of rain or of water.

drove, **drover**. See **drive**.

drown *drown*, *v.i.* to die of suffocation in liquid.—*v.t.* **1** to kill thus. **2** to flood. **3** to overwhelm.

drowse *drowz*, *v.i.* **1** to be heavy with sleep. **2** to sleep lightly:—*pr.p.* **drows'ing**.

drow'sy, *drow'zi*, *adj.* sleepy:—*comp.* **drow'sier**; *superl.* **drow'siest**.

drow'sily *adv.* **drow'siness** *n.*

drub *drub*, *v.t.* to beat or thrash:—*pr.p.* **drubb'ing**; *pa.p.* **drubbed**.

drubb'ing *n.* a thrashing.

drudge *druj*, *v.i.* to do dull, very hard, or mean work:—*pr.p.* **drudg'ing.**—*n.* one who does such work.

drudg'ery *n.* hard or humble work.

drug *drug*, *n.* **1** any substance used in medicine. **2** a substance used to dull pain or give pleasant sensations.—*v.t.* and *v.i.* to dose with a drug or drugs:—*pr.p.* **drugg'ing**; *pa.p.* **drugged**.

drugg'ist (esp. *U.S.*) *n.* one who sells medicines, a pharmacist.

drug'-add'ict, *n.* one who has formed the habit of taking drugs.

drug'-store (*U.S.*) *n.* a shop which sells cosmetics, newspapers, soft drinks, etc. as well as medicines.

druid *drōō'id*, *n.* a priest among the ancient Celts of Britain and Gaul.

drum *drum*, *n.* **1** a percussion instrument, a membrane stretched on a round frame (cylinder or half sphere). **2** anything shaped like a drum, as a container for liquids. **3** (**ear'drum**) the membrane in the middle of the ear.—*v.i.* to beat or tap in rhythm.—*v.t.* to force (an idea, a lesson, into someone) by much repetition: —*pr.p.* **drumm'ing**; *pa.p.* **drummed**.

drumm'er *n.* **drumm'ing** *n., adj.*

drum'-ma'jor *n.* the marching leader of a military band.

drum'stick *n.* **1** the stick with which a drum is beaten. **2** the lower joint of the leg of a cooked fowl.

drunk, etc. See **drink**.

dry *drī*, *adj.* **1** without, or with too little, moisture, sap, rain, etc. **2** thirsty. **3** uninteresting. **4** (of humour, manner) unemotional, cold. **5** (of wine) not sweet:—*comp.* **drī'er**; *superl.* **drī'est.**—*v.t.* to free from water or moisture.—*v.i.* to become dry (also **dry up**):—*pr.p.* **dry'ing**; *pa.p.* **dried**.

drier, **dryer** *drī'ėr*, *n.* an apparatus, or substance, that dries or hastens drying.

dri'ly, **dry'ly** *adv.* **dry'ness** *n.*

dry battery, **dry-cell** (*electricity*) *ns.* a battery, cell, containing paste, not liquid.

dry'-clean *v.t.* to clean with chemicals, without water.

dry dock. See **dock**.

dry goods drapery, etc. as opp. to hardware or groceries.

dry ice solid carbon dioxide.

dry rot decay of timber caused by fungi which make it dry and brittle.

dry'salter *n.* a dealer in gums, dyes, tinned goods, etc.

dry'saltery *n.* (*pl.* **-ies**).

dryad *drī'ad, ad*, *n.* a wood nymph.

dual *dū'ȧl*, *adj.* **1** consisting of two separate parts: *dual carriageway*. **2** in the hands of two: *dual ownership*; *dual controls*.

du'al-pur'pose, *adj.* serving two purposes.

dual personality a condition in which an individual shows at different times two very different characters.

dub[1] *dub*, *v.t.* **1** to give a knighthood to, by touching each shoulder with a sword. **2** to nickname:—*pr.p.* **dubb'ing**; *pr.p.*

dubbed.
dubb'ing *n.* (or **dubb'in**) a grease for softening leather.

dub[2] *dub, v.t.* **1** to give (a film) a new sound-track (e.g. in a different language). **2** to add sound effects or music to (a film, etc.):—*pr.p.* **dubb'ing**; *pa.p.* **dubbed**.
dubb'ing *n.*

dubiety. See **dubious**.

dubious *dū'bi-ůs, adj.* **1** doubtful: *I am dubious about the wisdom of this action.* **2** probably not honest: *dubious dealings.*
dū'biousness, dūbī'ety *ns.*

ducal. See **duke**.

ducat *duk'ȧt, n.* an old gold coin.

duchess *duch'es, n.* **1** the wife or widow of a duke. **2** a woman of the same rank as a duke in her own right.
duch'y *n.* the territory of a duke:—*pl.* **duch'ies**.

duck[1] *duk, n.* **1** coarse cloth for small sails, sacking, etc. **2** (in *pl.*) trousers, etc., of this.

duck[2] *duk, v.t.* to dip for a moment in water.—*v.i.* **1** to dip or dive. **2** to lower the head suddenly.—Also *n.*

duck[3] *duk, n.* **1** a water bird, wild or domesticated, with short legs and broad flat bill. **2** a female duck (the male being a **drake**). **3** (*cricket*; orig. *duck's egg*) a score by a batsman of no runs.
duck'bill *n.* a platypus.
duck'ling *n.* a young duck.

duck[4] *duk, n.* a transport vehicle for land and water.

duct *dukt, n.* a tube or pipe for fluids, electric cable, etc.

ductile *duk'tīl, -til, adj.* capable of being drawn out into wire or threads.

dud *dud, adj.* and *n.* (a thing) that is useless, not working, etc.

dudgeon *duj'ȯn n.* resentment, anger.

due *dū, adj.* **1** owed. **2** expected according to timetable, promise, etc.: *The bus is due in three minutes.* **3** proper: *Take due care.*—*adv.* directly: *sailing due east.*—*n.* **1** what is owed. **2** what one has a right to. **3** (in *pl.*) charge, fee, toll.
dū'ly *adv.* **1** properly. **2** at the proper time.
due to 1 brought about by: *His success was due to hard work.* **2** because of, owing to: *The game was postponed due to frost.* (This use of *due to* is common but still felt by some people to be wrong, *because of* or *owing to* being preferred.)
See also **duty**.

duel *dū'ėl, n.* **1** a combat, under fixed conditions, between two people over a matter of honour, etc. **2** any contest (a physical struggle or a battle of wits) between two people or two sides.—Also *v.i.*:—*pr.p.* **dū'elling**; *pa.p.* **dū'elled**.
dū'ellist *n.*

duet *dū-et', n.* a musical composition for two performers.
duett'ist *n.*

duffel *duf'l, n.* a thick, coarse woollen cloth, with a thick nap.—Also **duff'le**.
duff'le-coat, duff'el-coat *n.* a usu. hooded jacket or coat made of duffel, usu. with toggles rather than buttons.

duffer *duf'ėr, n.* a stupid person.

duffle. See **duffel**.

dug[1] *dug, n.* a nipple or udder of a cow, etc.

dug[2], **dugout**. See **dig**.

duke *dūk, n.* a nobleman of the highest rank.
ducal *dū'kȧl, adj.* of a duke.
duke'dom *n.* the title, rank, or territories of a duke.
See also **duchess, duchy**.

dulcet *dul'sit, adj.* sweet.

dull *dul, adj.* **1** slow of hearing, of learning, or of understanding. **2** not bright or clear. **3** blunt. **4** not exciting or interesting.—*v.t.* or *v.i.* to make or to become dull.
dully *dul'li, adv.* **dull'ness** *n.*

duly. See **due**.

dumb[1] *dum, (orig. U.S.) adj.* very stupid.

dumb[2] *dum, adj.* **1** without the power of speech. **2** silent.
dumb'ly *adv.* **dumb'ness** *n.*
dumm'y *n.* **1** one who is dumb. **2** a sham article, e.g. in a shop. **3** a model of a human used for displaying clothes, etc. **4** an artificial teat for a baby to suck. **5** an exposed hand of cards, or the imaginary player of them. **6** (*football*, etc) a feint of passing or playing the ball:—*pl.* **dumm'ies**.—Also *adj.*
dumb'bell *n.* a double-headed weight swung in the hands to develop the muscles.
dumb show gesture without words.
dumb'-wait'er *n.* a movable table for food, dishes, etc. at meals.
dum(b)found' *v.t.*, **dum(b)found'er** *v.t.* to make speechless with amazement.

dummy. See **dumb**.

dump *dump, v.t.* **1** to set (down) heavily. **2** to discard, as on a rubbish heap. **3** to put quantities of (goods) at a low price on the market, esp. of another country.—*n.* **1** a thud or dull blow. **2** a place for rubbish.

dumpling *dump'ling, n.* a thick pudding or mass of soft paste.

dumps *dumps*, *n.pl.* (usu. with *the*) gloom, depression.

dumpy *dump'i*, *adj.* short and thick:—*comp.* **dump'ier**; *superl.* **dump'iest**.
dump'ily *adv.* **dump'iness** *n.*

dun[1] *dun*, *adj.* of a dark, brownish colour.—*n.* a dun horse.

dun[2] *dun*, *v.t.* to demand payment from:—*pr.p.* **dunn'ing**; *pa.p.* **dunned**.

dunce *duns*, *n.* a person slow at learning.

dunderhead *dun'dėr-hed*, *n.* a stupid person.

dune *dūn*, *n.* a low hill of sand.

dung *dung*, *n.* animal faeces, esp. when used as manure.
dung'hill *n.* a heap of dung.

dungaree *dung-gȧ-rē'*, or *dung'*, *n.* **1** a coarse cotton cloth. **2** (in *pl.*) trousers, with a bib, made of this cloth.

dungeon *dun'jȯn*, *n.* **1** (*orig.*) the principal tower of a castle. **2** a dark prison, esp. a cell under ground.

dunk *dungk*, *v.t.* to dip (a biscuit, etc.) in coffee, etc. when eating it.

duo *dū'ō*, *n.* a duet:—*pl.* **dū'os**.

duodecimal *dū-ō-des'i-ml*, *adj.* counting by twelves.

duodenum *dū-ō-dē'nům*, *n.* the first part of the small intestine, so called because about twelve finger-breadths long.
duodē'nal *adj.*

duologue *dū'ȯ-log*, *n.* a conversation between two.

dupe *dūp*, *n.* one who is cheated.—*v.t.* **1** to deceive. **2** to trick:—*pr.p.* **dup'ing**.

duple *dū'pl*, *adj.* **1** double. **2** having two beats to the bar.
duplex *dū'pleks*, *adj.* twofold, double.
duplicate *dū'pli-kit*, *adj.* exactly like.—*n.* **1** another thing of the same kind. **2** a copy.—*v.t.* *(dū'pli-kāt)* **1** to double. **2** to make an exact copy or copies of:—*pr.p.* **du'plicating**.
duplicā'tion *n.*
dū'plicātor *n.* a copying machine.
duplicity *dū-plis'i-ti*, *n.* deceit, double-dealing.
in duplicate in two copies.

durable *dūr'ȧ-bl*, *adj.* **1** able to last. **2** resisting wear.
dur'ableness, **durabil'ity** *ns.*
durā'tion *n.* the length of time anything continues.

durbar *dûr'bär*, *(India)* *n.* **1** an official reception. **2** a court.

duress *dū-res'*, or *dū'*, *n.* illegal force used to make a person do something.

during *dū'ring*, *prep.* **1** throughout the time of. **2** in the course of.

durra *doo'rȧ*, *n.* Indian millet.

durst. See **dare**.

dusk *dusk*, *n.* twilight, partial darkness.
dusk'y *adj.* **1** dark-coloured. **2** gloomy:—*comp.* **dusk'ier**; *superl.* **dusk'iest**.
dusk'ily *adv.* **dusk'iness** *n.*

dust *dust*, *n.* **1** fine particles of solid matter. **2** powdery matter carried in the air.—*v.t.* **1** to free from dust. **2** to sprinkle with a powdery substance.
dust'er *n.* a cloth for removing dust.
dust'y *adj.* covered with, containing, or like, dust:—*comp.* **dust'ier**; *superl.* **dust'iest**.
dust'ily *adv.* **dust'iness** *n.*
dust'bin *n.* a bin for household rubbish.
dust'-cover *n.* a loose paper book jacket.
dust'man *n.* one who clears away household refuse.
Red Duster *n.* the Red Ensign (see **Ensign**).
raise a dust to cause a commotion by complaining.
throw dust in the eyes of to deceive.

Dutch *duch*, *adj.* of the Netherlands, its people, or language.—Also *n.*
Dutch courage courage induced by alcoholic drink.
double Dutch any language unknown or not understood.
go Dutch (*coll.*) to pay each for himself.

duty *dū'ti*, *n.* **1** what one ought, morally or legally, to do. **2** action(s) required: *The duties of this post are few.* **3** a tax on goods:—*pl.* **du'ties**.
du'tiable *adj.* liable to be taxed.
du'tiful *adj.* attentive to duty.
du'tifully *adv.*
du'ty-free *adj.* free from tax.
on, off, duty actually at, not at, work.

duvet *dōō'vā*, *n.* a continental quilt.

dux *duks*, (*Scot.*) *n.* the top academic prize-winner in school or class:—*pl.* **dux'es**.

dwarf *dwörf*, *n.* an animal, plant, or person much below the ordinary height.—*v.t.* **1** to hinder from growing. **2** to cause to appear small.

dwell *dwel*, *v.i.* **1** to live (in a place). **2** (with *on*) to fix the attention on, to talk at length about:—*pr.p.* **dwell'ing**; *pa.p.* **dwelt** (or **dwelled**).
dwell'er *n.*
dwell'ing *n.* the house, hut, etc. where one lives.

dwindle *dwin'dl*, *v.i.* to grow less in size, waste away: *His fortune, his hopes, dwindled*:—*pr.p.* **dwind'ling**.

dye *dī*, *v.t.* **1** to stain. **2** to give a new colour to:—*pr.p.* **dye'ing**; *pa.p.* **dyed**.—*n.* **1** a colour. **2** a powder or liquid for col-

ouring garments, etc.
dy'er *n.* one who dyes cloth, etc.
dyed'-in-the-wool' *adj.* of firmly fixed opinions.
dye'(-)stuff *n.* material used in dyeing.
dye'-work(s) *n.*, *n.sing.* a factory where things are dyed.

dying. See **die**[1].

dyke. Same as **dike**.

dynamic(al) *dī-nam'ik(àl)*, *adjs.* **1** concerned with force. **2** (**dynamic**) of a person, forceful, very energetic.
dynam'ically *adv*.
dynam'ics *n.sing.* the science that deals with forces acting on bodies to produce or alter motion.
dy'namite *n.* a powerful explosive.
dy'namo *n.* (short for **dynamo-electric machine**) a machine which generates electric currents by means of the relative movement of conductors and magnets: —*pl.* **dy'namos**.

dynasty *din'às-ti*, or *dīn'*, *n.* a succession of rulers of the same family:—*pl.* **dyn'-asties**.
dynas'tic *adj*.

dysentery *dis'èn-tri*, *n.* an infectious disease with severe diarrhoea.

dyslexia *dis-leks'i-à*, *n.* great difficulty in learning to read or spell, not caused by lack of intelligence.
dyslex'ic *n.* and *adj*.

dyspepsia *dis-pep'si-à*, *n.* indigestion.
dyspep'tic *n.* and *adj*.

dystrophy *dis'trò-fi*, *n.* defective nutrition, and consequent deterioration, of bodily tissue, as in *muscular dystrophy* (see this under **muscle**).

E

each *ēch*, *adj.*, *pron.* every one of two or more.—*adv.* to or for each one; apiece.
each other used as the object when the action, etc., is between two or more people: *My brother(s) and I don't see each other very often.*

eager *ē'gėr*, *adj.* **1** anxious (to do, for). **2** keen.
ea'gerly *adv.* **ea'gerness** *n.*

eagle *ē'gl*, *n.* a large bird of prey noted for its keen sight.
ea'glet *n.* a young eagle.

ear[1] *ēr*, *n.* **1** the part of the head by means of which we hear. **2** the sense of hearing. **3** favourable attention: *She has the headmaster's ear*.
ear'ache *n.* a pain in the ear.
ear'drum. See **drum**.
ear'mark *n.* **1** an owner's mark on the ears of sheep, etc. **2** a distinctive mark.—*v.t.* **1** to put an earmark on. **2** to set aside (for a particular purpose).
ear'phone *n.* a device held in or over the ear for listening to the radio or telephone.
ear'-piercing, **ear'-splitting** *adjs.* very loud.
ear'ring *n.* an ornament attached to the lobe of the ear.
ear'shot *n.*: **within**, **out of**, **earshot** within, beyond, the distance at which a sound can be heard.
ear'wig *n.* an insect once supposed to creep into the ear.
set (people) by the ears to make (people) quarrel.

ear[2] *ēr*, *n.* a spike, e.g. of corn.

earl *ûrl*, *n.* a British nobleman ranking between a marquis and a viscount:—*fem.* **count'ess** (see **count**[1]).
earl'dom *n.* the title, rank, or territories of an earl.

early *ûr'li*, *adv.* **1** in the first part of a period of time, course, series: *early in his life*. **2** before the usual, expected, or agreed time.—*adj.* belonging to, happening, near the beginning (of the day, etc.), or in the distant past, or in the near future:—*comp.* **ear'lier**; *superl.* **ear'liest**.
ear'liness *n.*
early bird **1** an early riser. **2** one who gains by acting more promptly than his rivals.

earmark. See **ear**[1].

earn *ûrn*, *v.t.* **1** to gain by work. **2** to deserve.
earn'ings *n.pl.* wages.

earnest[1] *ûr'nist*, *adj.* serious.
ear'nestly *adv.* **ear'nestness** *n.*
in earnest **1** serious, not jesting: *I am in earnest when I say this.* **2** seriously, with energy, determination: *He set to work in earnest*.

earnest[2] *ûr'nist*, *n.* **1** money given in token of a bargain made. **2** a pledge.

ear-piercing, **earphone**, **earring**, **earshot**, **ear-splitting**. See **ear**[1].

earth *ûrth*, *n.* **1** (often *cap.*) the third planet in order from the sun. **2** the world. **3** soil. **4** dry land. **5** a burrow. **6** an electrical connection with the earth.—*v.t.* to connect to earth electrically.
earth'en *adj.* made of earth, or of baked clay.
ear'thy *adj.* **1** of, like, earth. **2** coarse:—*comp.* **ear'thier**; *superl.* **ear'thiest**.
earth'iness *n.*
earth'ly *adj.* **1** passed, happening, etc. on earth. **2** worldly. **3** possible on earth: *no earthly chance, use;* (used like a *pron.*; *coll.*) *I haven't an earthly* (chance, idea):—*comp.* **earth'lier**; *superl.* **earth'liest**.
earth'liness *n.*
earth'enware *n.* pottery coarser than china.
earth'quake *n.* a shaking of the earth's crust.
earth'work *n.* a fortification of earth.
earth'worm *n.* an animal with a ringed body and no backbone, living in damp earth.
go, run, to earth. See under **ground**.
on earth used for emphasis: *What on earth are you doing?*

earwig. See **ear**[1].

ease *ēz*, *n.* **1** freedom from pain, or from worry. **2** rest from work. **3** freedom from difficulty: *to do it with ease.* **4** naturalness: *ease of manner.*—*v.t.* **1** to free from pain, trouble or anxiety. **2** to lessen (e.g. pressure). **3** to manoeuvre very gradually (into, out of, a position).—*v.i.* to become less (also **ease off**):—*pr.p.* **eas'ing**.
eas'y *adj.* **1** free from pain, trouble, anxiety, difficulty. **2** (of manner) not stiff. **3** comfortable. **4** not strict. **5** (not used before a noun; *coll.*) having no strong preference:—*comp.* **eas'ier**; *superl.* **eas'iest**.—*interj.* be careful!

eas'ily *adv.* **eas'iness** *n.*
easy chair a soft, comfortable chair, usu. an armchair.
eas'y-go'ing *adj.* not inclined to worry.
at ease 1 without anxiety or embarrassment. **2** (*army*) (standing) with legs apart and hands clasped behind the back.
ill at ease, **ill-at-ease'** uncomfortable, embarrassed.

easel *ēz'l*, *n.* the frame on which painters support their pictures while painting.

easier, **easily**, etc. See **ease**.

east *ēst*, *n.* **1** the part of the heavens where the sun rises. **2** a region, etc. in this direction.—Also *adj.* and *adv.*
east'erly *adj.* **1** coming from the east. **2** looking towards the east.—Also *adv.*
east'ern *adj.* of, or towards, the east.
east'erner *n.* one who belongs to the east.
east'ernmost *adj.* farthest east.
east'ward *adv.* towards the east.
east wind a wind from the east.
the East the countries east of Europe.

Easter *ēst'ėr*, *n.* a Christian festival commemorating the resurrection of Christ.
Eas'tertide *n.* the time of Easter.

easy. See **ease**.

eat *ēt*, *v.t.* and *v.i.* to (chew and) swallow:—*pr.p.* **eat'ing**; *pa.t.* **ate** (*et* or *āt*); *pa.p.* **eaten** *(ēt'n)*.
eat'able *adj.* fit to be eaten.—*n.* (in *pl.*) food.
eats (*coll.*) *n.pl.* food.
eat into to waste away, corrode: *Acids eat into metal*.
See also **edible**, **inedible**.

eau-de-cologne *ō-dė-kō-lōn'*, *n.* a perfumed spirit first made in Cologne.

eaves *ēvz*, *n.pl.* the edge of a roof projecting beyond the wall.
eaves'drop *v.i.* to listen in order to overhear private conversation (with *on*):—*pr.p.* **eaves'dropping**; *pa.p.* **eaves'-dropped**.
eaves'dropper *n.*

ebb *eb*, *n.* **1** the going back of the tide. **2** a decline.—Also *v.i.*
ebb'-tide *n.* the ebbing tide.
at a low ebb in a poor or depressed state.
on the ebb ebbing or declining.

ebony *eb'ȯn-i*, *n.* a black wood almost as heavy and hard as stone.—*adj.* made of, black as, ebony.

ebullient *i-bul'yėnt*, *adj.* high-spirited, very enthusiastic.
ebull'iently *adv.* **ebull'ience** *n.*

eccentric *ek-sen'trik*, *adj.* **1** with axis or support not in the centre. **2** not concentric. **3** odd, not normal: *His behaviour is eccentric; an eccentric old man.*—*n.* an eccentric person.
eccen'trically *adv.*
eccentric'ity *(-tris'-)* *n.* **1** the state of being eccentric. **2** oddness of behaviour:—*pl.* **eccentric'ities**.

ecclesiastic *i-klē-zi-as'tik*, *n.* a priest, clergyman.
ecclesias'tic(al) *adjs.* of the church or clergy.

echelon *esh'ė-lon*, *n.* **1** a stepwise arrangement of troops, ships, etc. in parallel lines, each line being a little to the right or left of that in front of it. **2** a group of people at a particular level in an organisation, etc.

echo *ek'ō*, *n.* **1** a repetition of sound caused by the throwing back of sound waves from a surface which they strike. **2** an imitator:—*pl.* **echoes** *(ek'ōz)*.—*v.i.* to sound loudly with an echo.—*v.t.* **1** to repeat (sound, a statement). **2** to imitate:—*pr.p.* **ech'oing**; *pa.p.* **ech'oed** *(-ōd)*.

éclair *ā-klār'*, *n.* a long, light, cream-filled cake with usu. chocolate icing.

éclat *ā-klä'*, *n.* brilliance, dazzling effect.

eclectic *i-klek'tik*, *adj.* choosing the best ideas, etc. from a variety of sources.

eclipse *i-klips'*, *n.* **1** the disappearance of the whole or part of a heavenly body, e.g. of the sun when the moon comes between it and the earth. **2** loss of brilliancy, decline, downfall.—*v.t.* **1** to hide. **2** to darken. **3** to surpass: *His successes eclipsed those of his brother*:—*pr.p.* **eclip'sing**.
eclip'tic *n.* the apparent path of the sun among the fixed stars.

ecology *i-kol'ȯ-ji*, *n.* (the study of) the relationship between living things and their surroundings.
ecolog'ical *adj.*—**ecolog'ically** *adv.*
ec'o-friendly *adj.* not harmful to the environment.
ecol'ogist *n.* one who studies ecology.
e'cosystem *n.* a community of living things and their relationship to their surroundings.

economy *i-kon'ȯ-mi*, or *ē-*, *n.* **1** the thrifty management of money, etc. **2** organisation of money and resources: *the country's economy.* **3** a saving:—*pl.* **econ'omies**.
econom'ic (*ē-*, or *e-*) *adj.* **1** of, concerned with, economics. **2** profitable.
econom'ical *adj.* thrifty, not extravagant.
econom'ically *adv.*
econom'ics *n.sing.* the study of production and distribution of money and goods.
econ'omise (*i-*, or *ē-*) *v.i.* (with *on*) **1** to use money, supplies, etc. carefully. **2** to save:—*pr.p.* **econ'omising**.

econ'omist *n.* one who studies economics.

ecru *ek'rōō,* or *ā'-*, *n.* an off-white or fawn colour.—Also *adj.*

ecstasy *ek'stȧ-si, n.* **1** very great joy. **2** overpowering emotion or feeling. **3** (in *pl.*) expressions of joy:—*pl.* **ec'stasies**.
ecstat'ic *adj.* rapturous.
ecstat'ically *adv.* **ecstat'icness** *n.*

ecumenical *ēk-* or *ek-ū-men'ik-ȧl, adj.* of, or concerned with the unity of, the whole Christian church.

eczema *ek'si-mȧ, n.* a skin disease with an itchy rash, often caused by irritants.

eddy *ed'i, n.* a current of water or air running back against the main stream:—*pl.* **edd'ies.**—*v.i.* to move round and round:—*pr.p.* **edd'ying**; *pa.p.* **edd'ied**.

edelweiss *ā'dėl-vīs, n.* an alpine plant with woolly leaves and heads.

edge *ej, n.* **1** the border of anything. **2** the brink. **3** the cutting side of an instrument. **4** sharpness (e.g. of mind, appetite).—*v.t.* **1** to border. **2** to move little by little.—*v.i.* to move sideways:—*pr.p.* **edg'ing**.
edg'ing *n.* a border or fringe round a garment, etc.
edg'y *adj.* irritable:—*comp.* **edg'ier**; *superl.* **edg'iest**.
edg'ily *adv.* **edg'iness** *n.*
edge'ways, edge'wise *advs.* sideways.
have the edge on to have the advantage over.
on edge uneasy, nervous, irritable.

edible *ed'i-bl, adj.* **1** suitable as food. **2** fit to eat:—*opp.* **inedible**.
ed'ibleness, edibil'ity *ns.*

edict *ē'dikt, n.* a decree, order, command, of someone in authority.

edification. See **edify**.

edifice *ed'i-fis, n.* a large building.

edify *ed'i-fī, v.t.* to improve the mind or morals of:—*pr.p.* **ed'ifying**; *pa.p.* **ed'ified**.
edificā'tion *n.* **1** instruction. **2** progress in knowledge or in goodness.
ed'ifying *adj.* instructive, improving.

edit *ed'it, v.t.* to prepare for publication, or for broadcasting or telecasting.
edi'tion *n.* **1** number of copies of a book, etc., printed at a time. **2** the form in which they are published.
ed'itor *n.* **1** one who edits books, etc. **2** one who conducts a newspaper, periodical, etc.:—*fem.* (*rare*) **ed'itress**.
editō'rial *adj.* of or belonging to an editor.—*n.* an article in a newspaper written by an editor or leader writer.

educate *ed'ū-kāt, v.t.* to train and teach:—*pr.p.* **ed'ucating**.
educā'tion *n.*
educā'tional *adj.* **1** of education. **2** increasing knowledge and wisdom.
educā'tion(al)ist *ns.* a person who studies methods of educating.
ed'ucātive *adj.* tending to educate.
ed'ucātor *n.*

eel *ēl, n.* a fish with long smooth cylinder-shaped or ribbon-shaped body.

eerie *ē'ri, adj.* weird, causing fear:—*comp.* **ee'rier**; *superl.* **ee'riest**.
ee'rily *adv.* **ee'riness** *n.*

efface *i-fās', v.t.* **1** to rub out. **2** to remove, obliterate (from the memory, etc.). **3** (with *oneself*) to shun notice:—*pr.p.* **effac'ing**.

effect *i-fekt', n.* **1** result, consequence: *the unwelcome effects of overeating.* **2** impression produced: *His words had no effect on her; The combination of colours gave a pleasing effect; He doesn't really think that—he only said it for effect.* **3** (in *pl.*) goods, property: *his personal effects.* **4** (in *pl.*; *theatre*) sound and lighting devices.—*v.t.* to bring about: *to effect a reconciliation.*
effec'tive *adj.* **1** having power to produce, or producing, a desired result: *The new teaching methods have not proved effective; It will take a really effective speaker to persuade them.* **2** striking, pleasing: *The varied flowers made an effective display.*
effec'tively *adv.* **1** in an effective way: *He speaks effectively.* **2** really, practically: *The worst part of this job is effectively over.*
effec'tual *(-tū-ȧl) adj.* successful in producing the desired result: *Effectual measures were taken against drug-smuggling.*
in effect 1 (of a rule, etc.) in operation: *That law is no longer in effect.* **2** in reality: *In effect, our opinions differed very little.*
put into effect, give effect to to act in accordance with (a decision), put into operation (a law).
take effect to come into force: *This regulation does not take effect until June 9.*
to this, that effect with this, that meaning.
to the effect that meaning that.
See also **ineffective, ineffectual**.

effeminate *i-fem'in-it, adj.* **1** (of a man) behaving, etc. like a woman. **2** unmanly.
effem'inateness, effem'inacy *ns.*

effervesce *ef-ėr-ves', v.i.* **1** to froth up, give off bubbles of gas. **2** to be excited or very lively:—*pr.p.* **efferves'cing**.
efferves'cence *n.* **efferves'cent** *adj.*

effete *i-fēt', adj.* exhausted, worn out.

efficacious *ef-i-kā'shus, adj.* (esp. of a medicine, remedy) producing the result intended:—*opp.* **inefficacious**.
effica'ciousness, eff'icacy *(-kȧ-si), ns.*

efficient *i-fish'ėnt, adj.* **1** (of a person) capable, skilful. **2** satisfactory in use: *A knife does not make an efficient corkscrew.* **3** very practical: *an efficient method*:—*opp.* **inefficient**.
efficiency *i-fish'ėn-si, n.*
efficiently *i-fish'ėnt-li, adv.*

effigy *ef'i-ji, n.* **1** a likeness of a person (esp. sculptured). **2** the head on a coin:—*pl.* **eff'igies**.

effluent *ef'loo-ėnt, n.* **1** a stream that flows out of another stream or of a lake. **2** liquid industrial waste. **3** sewage.

effluvium *i-flōō'vi-ům, n.* disagreeable vapours, e.g. from decaying matter:—*pl.* **efflu'via**.

effort *ef'ȯrt, n.* **1** the expending of strength or energy; hard work. **2** an attempt. **3** a struggle.
eff'ortless *adj.* done, etc. apparently without effort.

effrontery *e-frunt'ėr-i, n.* impudence.

egg[1] *eg, n.* **1** a rounded body laid by a bird, etc. from which a young one is hatched. **2** such a body laid by a hen, used as food. **3** an ovum. **4** something resembling an egg.
egg'cup *n.* a small container for holding a boiled egg at table.
egg'-plant *n.* an aubergine.
egg'-timer *n.* a device like an hour-glass for timing the boiling of an egg.

egg[2] *eg, v.t.* (followed by **on**) to urge, encourage (a person to do something).

ego *e'gō, ē'gō, n.* the 'I,' or self—the part of a person that is conscious and thinks.
egocen'tric *adj.* self-centred.
e'goism *(-gō-izm) n.* **1** self-interest. **2** selfishness.
e'goist *n.* one who thinks and speaks too much about himself.
egoist'ic, -al *adjs.*
e'gotism *n.* a frequent use of the pronoun I, speaking much of oneself.
e'gotist *n.* an egoist, a boastful person.
egotist'ic, -al *adjs.*

egregious *i-grē'jyůs, adj.* outrageous, shocking: *an egregious lie*.

egress *ē'gres, n.* **1** the act of going out. **2** the way out.

Egyptian *i-jip'sh(ȧ)n, adj.* belonging to Egypt.—*n.* a native of Egypt.
Egyptol'ogy *n.* the science of Egyptian antiquities.

eider (duck) *ī'dėr (duk), n.* a northern sea duck with fine down on its breast.
ei'derdown *n.* **1** the down or soft feathers of the eider duck. **2** a quilt filled with this or other material.

eight *āt, n.* **1** the number next above seven (8 or VIII). **2** a set of eight things or persons, as the crew of an eight-oared racing boat. **3** the eighth hour after midday or midnight. **4** the age of eight years. **5** anything (e.g. a shoe, a playing-card) denoted by eight.—*adj.* **1** 8 in number. **2** eight years old.
eighth *ātth, adj.* **1** next after the seventh. **2** equal to one of eight equal parts.—Also *n.*
eighteen, *ā'tēn, ā-tēn', n.* and *adj.* eight and ten (18 or XVIII).
eighteenth *adj.* **1** next after the seventeenth. **2** equal to one of eighteen equal parts.—Also *n.*
eighty *ā'ti, n.* and *adj.* eight times ten (80 or LXXX).
eigh'ties *n.pl.* the numbers eighty to eighty-nine.
eigh'tieth *adj.* **1** next after the seventy-ninth. **2** equal to eighty equal parts.—Also *n.*

eisteddfod *ī-ste*TH'*vod, n.* **1** a congress of Welsh bards. **2** a meeting, in Wales, for competitions in music, poetry, drama, etc.

either *ī*'TH*ėr*, or *ē*'TH*ėr, adj.* (used only before a noun) **1** the one or the other. **2** the one and the other: *There are trees on either side of the road.*—*pron.* the one or the other.— *adv.* (in negative expressions) also: *He doesn't ski and he doesn't skate either*.
either ... or *conjs.* introducing alternatives: *You must either go to see him or send an excuse*; *Either Jim or Joe will go*.

ejaculate *i-jak'ū-lāt, v.t.* to utter, exclaim, suddenly.—*v.i.* to discharge semen:—*pr.p* **ejac'ulating**.
ejaculā'tion *n.* **ejac'ulatory** *adj.*

eject *i-jekt', v.t.* **1** to throw out. **2** to expel, dismiss.
ejec'tion *n.* the act of ejecting.
eject'or-seat *n.* an aeroplane seat that can be shot clear with its occupant in an emergency.

eke *ēk*: **eke out** **1** to make (something) seem sufficient by adding something else: *You could eke out the meat with plenty of potatoes.* **2** to manage to make (a scanty living):—*pr.p.* **ek'ing out**.

elaborate *i-lab'ȯr-āt, v.t.* to work out or describe in detail: *He elaborated his theory.*—*v.i.* to make detailed observations (on or upon):—*pr.p.* **elab'orating**.—*adj.* *(-it)* **1** very detailed or complicated. **2** (of style of dress, etc.) very formal or fashionable.

elab'orately *adv.* **elaborā'tion** *n.*

elapse *i-laps'*, *v.i.* (of time) to pass:—*pr.p.* **elap'sing**.

elastic *i-las'tik*, *adj.* **1** (of material) able to resume its original shape after being pulled or pressed out of shape. **2** springy:—*opp.* **inelas'tic**.—*n.* a fabric, esp. in ribbon form, made elastic by the weaving in of rubber strands.

elasticity *i-las-tis'i-ti*, or *ē-*, *n.*

elastic band a rubber band (see **rubber**).

elate *i-lāt'*, *v.t.* to make glad or proud:—*pr.p* **elat'ing**.

elat'ed *adj.* **elat'edly** *adv.*

elā'tion *n.* high spirits caused by success.

elbow *el'bō*, *n.* **1** the joint where the arm bends. **2** the part of a sleeve covering this. **3** any sharp bend.—*v.t.* **1** to push with the elbow. **2** to jostle.

el'bow-grease (*humorous*) *n.* hard work, esp. cleaning and polishing.

el'bow-room *n.* space enough for moving or acting.

elder[1] *el'dėr*, *n.* **1** a shrub or tree with purple-black fruit from which is made **elderberry wine**, etc. **2** a related shrub with red berries.

elder[2] *el'dėr*, *adj.* (usu. used before a noun and esp. of members of a family) older; senior: *my three elder sisters*; *the elder Pitt*; *Pliny the elder*.—*n.* **1** a person who is older: *the elder of the two sons*; *He's my elder by two years*; *Be polite to your elders*. **2** an older, more experienced member of a tribe, etc. **3** an office-bearer in presbyterian churches.

el'derly *adj.* getting old.

el'dest *adj.*, *n.* (one, usu. in a family, who is) oldest.

elder statesman an important senior member of a group.

elect *i-lekt'*, *v.t.* **1** to choose by vote. **2** to choose (to do something).—*adj.* (placed after a noun) chosen for office but not yet in it: *president elect*.—*n.pl.* (*old*, esp. *theology*) chosen people.

elec'tion *n.* the public choosing, or choice, of person(s) for office.

electioneer' *v.t.* to work to bring about the election of a candidate.

elec'tive *adj.* (of a post) filled by election.

elec'tor *n.* a person who has a vote at an election.

electoral *adj.* of elections or electors.

elec'torate *n.* all the electors taken together.

electric *i-lek'trik*, *adj.* **1** of, produced by, or worked by, electricity. **2** (of atmosphere) full of excitement.

elec'trical *adj.* (usu. used before a noun) relating to electricity.

elec'trically *adv.*

electrician *i-lek-trish'(å)n*, *e-*, *n.* an engineer specialising in electrical appliances and installations.

electricity *i-lek-tris'i-ti*, *e-*, *n.* the form of energy associated with the attraction and repulsion that takes place between particles, producing heat, light, power to drive machines, etc.

elec'trify *v.t.* **1** to pass electricity through. **2** to adapt for operation by electricity: *to electrify railways*. **3** to excite suddenly; to astonish:—*pr.p.* **elec'trifying**; *pa.p.* **elec'trified**.

electrificā'tion *n.*

electric blanket one containing electric wires, for heating a bed.

electric chair a chair used in electrocuting condemned criminals.

electric shock. See **shock**.

See also **electro**.

electro- *i-lek-trō-*, *-o-*, or *-ȯ-*, (as part of a word) of, caused by, electricity.

electrocar'diogram *n.* a trace made of the electrical changes in the heart as it beats.

electro-convulsive therapy a treatment for mental illness using the convulsive effect of electric shocks.

elec'trocute *(-kūt)* *v.t.* to put to death, or to kill accidentally, by electricity:—*pr.p.* **elec'trocuting**.

electrocū'tion *n.*

elec'trode *n.* a conductor through which a current of electricity enters or leaves a battery, an arc lamp, etc.

electroenceph'alogram *(-en-sef'å-lō-gram)* *n.* a trace made of the electrical impulses produced by the brain.

electrol'ysis *(-is-is)* *n.* the breaking-up of a chemical compound by electricity.

elec'tro(-)mag'net *n.* a piece of soft iron made magnetic by a current of electricity passing through a coil of wire wound round it.

electromagnetic waves a travelling disturbance in space, of which light waves and the waves used in radio are examples.

elec'tron *n.* a very light particle within the atom having the smallest possible charge of electricity.

electron'ic *adj.* of electrons or electronics.

electron'ics *n.sing.* a branch of physics dealing with electrons and their use in machines, etc.

electron microscope one that uses electrons to increase magnification.

elec'troplate *v.t.* to cover with silver or

other metal by means of electrolysis:—*pr.p.* **elec'troplating**.
elec'troplating *n.*
elec'trotype *n.* a printing plate made by coating a mould with copper by means of electrolysis.

elegant *el'i-gȧnt, adj.* **1** (e.g. of clothes) usu. expensive and in good taste. **2** dressed in such clothes. **3** graceful. **4** refined:—*opp.* **inelegant**.
el'egance, el'egancy (*pl.* **-cies**), *ns.*

elegy *el'i-ji, n.* song of mourning:—*pl.* **el'egies**.

element *el'i-mėnt, n.* **1** an essential or component part of anything. **2** a substance that cannot be split by chemical means into simpler substances: *Hydrogen, chlorine, iron, and uranium are elements.* **3** (in *pl.*) the first things to be learned in any subject. **4** (in *pl.*; *hist.*) the four substances earth, air, fire and water, of which the Earth, etc. was formerly thought to be composed. **5** (in *pl.*) the forces of nature, as wind and rain. **6** (*radio*) an electrode. **7** a resistance wire in an electric heater, etc.
elemen'tal *adj.* of, like, the forces of nature.
elemen'tary *adj.* **1** very simple. **2** concerned with early stages, basic.

elephant *el'i-fȧnt, n.* an animal with very thick skin, a trunk, and two ivory tusks.
elephan'tine *(-tīn) adj.* **1** very large. **2** clumsy.
white elephant a useless possession, esp. one costly or troublesome to maintain.

elevate *el'i-vāt, v.t.* **1** to raise to a higher position. **2** to raise in mind or morals. **3** to make more cheerful:—*pr.p.* **el'evating**.
elevā'tion *n.* **1** raising or being raised. **2** rising ground. **3** an angle measuring height. **4** height. **5** an architect's drawing of a side of a building. **6** nobility, dignity. **7** a dancer's ability to remain in the air.
el'evātor *n.* **1** (*U.S.*) a lift. **2** a hoist for goods. **3** a high storehouse for grain.

eleven *i-lev'n, n.* the number next above ten (11 or XI). **2** a set of eleven things or persons, as a football, hockey, or cricket team. **3** the eleventh hour after midday or midnight. **4** the age of eleven years. **5** any thing (e.g. a shoe) denoted by eleven.—*adj.* **1** eleven in number. **2** eleven years old.
elev'enth *adj.* **1** next after the tenth. **2** equal to one of eleven equal parts.—Also *n.*
at the eleventh hour at the last moment, in the nick of time.

elf *elf, n.* a tiny, mischievous fairy:—*pl.* **el'ves**.
elf'in, elf'ish *adjs.*

elicit *i-lis'it, e-, v.t.* to draw out from a person (information, an admission).

eligible *el'i-ji-bl, adj.* **1** qualified, esp. legally, to be chosen. **2** worthy to be chosen:—*opp.* **ineligible**.—Also *n.*
el'igibleness, eligibil'ity *ns.*

eliminate *i-lim'i-nāt, e-, v.t.* **1** to get rid of. **2** to omit, ignore:—*pr.p.* **elim'inating**.
eliminā'tion *n.*

élite *ā-lēt', n.*, sometimes *n.pl.*, the best or most important (of a class of people).
éli'tism *n.* (the belief in) the development of, or domination by, an élite.
éli'tist *n.*

elixir *i-lik'sėr, n.* a supposed liquid that would make people able to go on living for ever, or a substance that would turn base metals into gold.

Elizabethan *i-liz-ȧ-bē'thȧn, adj.* of Queen Elizabeth I (reigned 1558–1603) or her time.—*n.* a person of this period.

elk *elk, n.* the largest of all deer, found in the north of Europe and Asia.

ell *el, n.* an old measure of length, orig. taken from the arm.

ellipse *i-lips', n.* a regular oval (i.e. one which can be divided in two ways into two parts of the same size and shape).
ellip'tical *adj.*

elm *elm, n.* a tall tree with tough wood and corrugated bark.

elocution *el-ȯ-kū'sh(ȯ)n, n.* the art of speaking clearly and effectively.

elongate *ē'long-gāt, v.t.* to make longer:—*pr.p.* **e'longating**.
e'longāted *adj.* long and (usu.) narrow.
elongā'tion *n.*

elope *i-lōp', v.i.* to run away secretly, esp. with a lover:—*pr.p.* **elop'ing**.
elope'ment *n.*

eloquence *el'ȯ-kwens, n.* **1** the power of expressing emotion or thought in words that impress or move other people. **2** moving words.
el'oquent *adj.* (*opp.* **inel'oquent**).
el'oquently *adv.*

else *els, adv.* **1** otherwise. **2** except the person or thing mentioned.
elsewhere' *adv.* in, or to, another place.
or else or if not, or otherwise.

elucidate *i-lōōs'i-dāt, lūs', v.t.* to make clear, explain (e.g. something difficult or mysterious):—*pr.p.* **elu'cidating**.
elucidā'tion *n.*

elude *i-lōōd'*, *-lūd'*, *v.t.* **1** to escape or avoid by trick or nimbleness. **2** to escape the memory of (a person), to understand:—*pr.p.* **elud'ing.**
elu'sive *(-siv) adj.* **1** escaping often or cleverly. **2** hard to grasp or to express.

elver *el'vėr*, *n.* a young eel.

elves. See **elf**.

em-. See **en**.

emaciate *i-mā'shi-āt*, *v.t.* and *v.i.* to make, or become, very thin by loss of flesh:—*pr.p.* **emā'ciating.**
emā'ciated *adj.* **emaciā'tion** *n.*

emanate *em'ȧ-nāt*, *v.i.* to flow, come, out (from some source): *This information emanates from his family*:—*pr.p.* **em'anating.**
emanā'tion *n.* something given out by a substance, e.g. scent, rays.

emancipate *i-man'si-pāt*, *v.t.* to set free from slavery or other restraint or control:—*pr.p.* **eman'cipating.**
emancipā'tion *n.* **eman'cipator** *n.*

emasculate *i-mas'kū-lāt*, *v.t.* **1** to castrate. **2** to weaken, deprive of force:—*pr.p.* **emas'culating.** **emasculā'tion** *n.*

embalm *im-bäm'*, *v.t.* to preserve (a dead body) from decay by treatment with spices or drugs.

embankment *im-bangk'mėnt*, *n.* a bank or ridge made e.g. to keep back water or to carry a railway.

embargo *im-bär'gō*, *n.* **1** stoppage by authority of movement of ships in and out of a port, or of certain trade. **2** a ban (on something):—*pl.* **embar'goes.**—Also *v.t.*:—*pr.p.* **embar'going**; *pa.p.* **embar'goed.**

embark *im-bärk'*, *v.t.* to put on board ship.—*v.i.* **1** to go on board ship. **2** to start (on, upon any action): *to embark on a war.*
embarkā'tion *(em-) n.*

embarrass *im-bar'ȧs*, *v.t.* **1** to hinder, hamper. **2** to involve in (esp. financial) difficulty. **3** to confuse, make self-conscious.
embarr'assment *n.*

embassy *em'bȧs-i*, *n.* **1** an ambassador and his staff. **2** an ambassador's official residence. **3** a deputation:—*pl.* **em'bassies.**

embattle *im-bat'l*, *v.t.* to arrange in order for, or prepare for, battle:—*pr.p.* **embatt'ling.**
embatt'led *adj.*

embed *im-bed'*, *v.t.* to fix deeply (in something):—*pr.p.* **embedd'ing**; *pa.p.* **embedd'ed.**

embellish *im-bel'ish*, *v.t.* **1** to make beautiful with ornaments. **2** to increase the interest of (a story) by adding fictitious details.
embell'ishment *n.*

ember *em'bėr*, *n.* **1** a piece of live coal or wood. **2** (in *pl.*) smouldering remains of a fire.

embezzle *im-bez'l*, *v.t.* to take fraudulently (money that has been entrusted to one):—*pr.p.* **embezz'ling.**
embezz'lement *n.* **embezz'ler** *n.*

embitter *im-bit'ėr*, *v.t.* to make bitter or resentful.
embitt'ered *adj.* soured.

emblazon *im-blā'zȯn*, *v.t.* **1** to adorn (with heraldic devices, etc.). **2** to display, set out (a heraldic or other device) prominently.

emblem *em'blėm*, *n.* an object chosen to represent a quality, state, etc.: *The dove is the emblem of peace.*
emblemat'ic *adj.*: *The dove is emblematic of peace.*

embody *im-bod'i*, *v.t.* **1** to express, give form to: *The poet's feeling for beauty is embodied in this poem.* **2** to include. **3** to represent in living form: *Parker embodied my idea of fearless honesty*:—*pr.p.* **embod'ying**; *pa.p.* **embod'ied.**
embod'iment *n.*

embolden *im-bōld'n*, *v.t.* **1** to make bold. **2** to give (someone) courage (to do something).

embolism *em'bȯ-lizm*, *n.* the blockage of an artery by a blood-clot, etc.

emboss *im-bos'*, *v.t.* to ornament with raised design.
embossed' *adj.*

embrace *im-brās'*, *v.t.* **1** to take into one's arms with affection, to hug. **2** to take eagerly (e.g. an opportunity). **3** to adopt (a religion, cause, etc.). **4** to include: *The term 'man' often embraces men, women, and children.*—*v.i.* (of two people) to hug one another:—*pr.p.* **embracing.**—*n.* a hug.

embrasure *im-brā'zhůr*, *n.* an opening in a wall (e.g. for cannon), widening from within.

embrocation *em-brō-kā'sh(ȯ)n*, *n.* a lotion for rubbing on the body to ease muscular pain.

embroider *im-broid'ėr*, *v.t.* **1** to ornament with designs in needlework. **2** to add fictitious detail to (a story).—Also *v.i.*
embroid'ery *n.*:—*pl.* **embroid'eries.**

embroil *im-broil'*, *v.t.* **1** to involve (a person) in a quarrel (with another or others). **2** to throw into confusion.
embroil'ment *n.*

embryo *em'bri-ō, n.* **1** a young animal or plant in its earliest stages in seed, protective tissue, egg, or womb. **2** the beginning stage of anything:—*pl.* **em'bryos**.—Also *adj.*
embryol'ogy *n.* the science of the formation and development of the embryo.
embryol'ogist *n.*
embryon'ic *adj.* in an early stage of development.

emend *i-mend', v.t.* to correct errors in (esp. a book).
emendā'tion *n.*

emerald *em'ėr-ȧld, n.* **1** a green gemstone. **2** its colour.—Also *adj.*

emerge *i-mûrj', v.i.* **1** to rise out (from water, etc.). **2** to come out. **3** to become known:—*pr.p.* **emer'ging**.
emer'gence *n.* act of coming out.
emer'gency *n.* an unexpected happening or situation requiring immediate action:—*pl.* **emer'gencies**.
emer'gent *adj.* **1** coming out. **2** (of a nation) just independent.

emeritus *i-mer'i-tu̇s, adj.* (esp. of a professor; usu. placed after a noun) retired.

emery *em'ėr-i, n.* a very hard mineral used in powdered form for polishing.

emetic *i-met'ik, adj.* causing vomiting.—*n.* a medicine that causes vomiting.

emigrate *em'i-grāt, v.i.* to leave one's country and settle in another:—*pr.p.* **em'igrating**.
em'igrant *adj.* emigrating or having emigrated.—Also *n.*
emigrā'tion *n.*
émigré *em'i-grā, n.* one who leaves his country esp. for political reasons.

eminent *em'i-nėnt, adj.* **1** rising above others. **2** distinguished.
em'inence *n.* **1** a rising ground, hill. **2** distinction. **3** (*cap.*) a title of honour for a cardinal.
em'inently *adv.* very, obviously: *eminently suitable.*

emir *e-mēr', n.* a chieftain in Arabia or north Africa.
emir'ate (or *em'*) *n.* the office or lands of an emir.

emissary, emission. See **emit**.

emit *i-mit', v.t.* to give out (e.g. light, heat):—*pr.p.* **emitt'ing**; *pa.p.* **emitt'ed**.
emission *i-mish'(ȯ)n, n.*
em'issary *(em') n.* one sent on a mission (often secret or underhand):—*pl.* **em'issaries**.

emollient *i-mol'yėnt, adj.* softening.—*n.* a substance that softens or soothes.

emolument *i-mol'ū-mėnt, n.* (often in *pl.*) profit from employment, salary, fees.

emotion *i-mō'sh(ȯ)n, n.* **1** a (strong) feeling such as joy, love, fear, anger, jealousy. **2** agitation of mind or feelings.
emo'tional *adj.* **1** of the emotions. **2** easily affected by joy, love, fear, etc.
emo'tionally *adv.*
emo'tive *adj.* arousing emotion.

empathy *em'pȧ-thi, n.* the experiencing of another's feelings, etc. by exercise of one's own imagination.

emperor *em'pėr-ȯr, n.* the royal title of a head of an empire:—*fem.* **em'press**.
empire *em'pīr, n.* a widespread group of states, etc., under the same ruling power, not always an emperor.

emphasis *em'fȧ-sis, n.* **1** stress put on words. **2** importance given to something: *The emphasis of the talk was on the need to work hard:*—*pl.* **em'phases** *(-sēz).*
em'phasise *(-sīz) v.t.* to lay stress on:—*pr.p.* **em'phasising**.
emphat'ic *adj.* **1** expressed with emphasis. **2** firm and definite.
emphat'ically *adv.* **emphat'icness** *n.*

empire. See **emperor**.

empiric, empirical *em-pir'ik, -ȧl, adjs.* depending on, known by, experiment or experience.

emplacement *im-plās'mėnt, n.* a gun platform.

emplane *im-plān' v.i., v.t.* to go, put on board an aircraft:—*pr.p.* **emplan'ing**.

employ *im-ploi', v.t.* **1** to occupy the time or attention of. **2** to use. **3** to give work to.—*n.* employment, service: *He was in the employ of a foreign government.*
employed' *adj.* **1** having a job. **2** working.
employ'ee (or *-ē'*) *n.* one who works for an **employ'er**.
employ'ment *n.* **1** the act of employing. **2** the state of being employed. **3** an occupation, esp. regular trade, etc.

emporium *em-pō'ri-um, -pö', n.* **1** a central place to which goods are brought for sale. **2** a large shop.

empower *im-pow'ėr, v.t.* **1** to authorise: *I empowered him to draw the necessary money.* **2** to enable.

empress. See **emperor**.

empty *emp'ti, adj.* **1** having nothing inside. **2** unoccupied. **3** without, devoid (of): *empty of meaning.* **4** (of dreams, threats, etc.) having no practical result.—*v.t.* and *v.i.* to make, or become, empty:—*pr.p.* **emp'tying**; *pa.p.* **emp'tied**.—*n.* an empty bottle, etc.:—*pl.* **emp'ties**.
emp'tiness *n.*

emu *ē'mū*, *n.* an Australian running bird, related to the ostrich.

emulate *em'ū-lāt*, *v.t.* **1** to strive to equal or be better than. **2** to imitate:—*pr.p.* **em'ulating**.
emulā'tion *n.*

emulsion *i-mul'sh(ȯ)n*, *n.* a milky liquid prepared by mixing e.g. oil and water.
emul'sify *v.t.* to make an emulsion of:—*pr.p.* **emul'sifying**; *pa.p.* **emul'sified**.

en- *en-*, *pfx.* used to form verbs from nouns and adjectives, meaning (1) to put into, e.g. **encase**; (2) to bring into the condition of, e.g. **enslave**; (3) to make, e.g. **endear**. Before *b*, *p*, and sometimes *m*, *en-* becomes *em-*, e.g. **embed**, **empower**.

enable *in-ā'bl*, *v.t.* to make able:—*pr.p.* **enab'ling**.

enact *in-akt'*, *v.t.* **1** to act (a role, scene, etc.). **2** to decree by law (that). **3** to pass (a law).
enact'ment *n.* **1** the passing of a bill into law. **2** a law.

enamel *i-nam'ėl*, *n.* **1** a type of glass applied as coating to a metal or other surface and fired. **2** the natural coating of the teeth. **3** a glossy paint. **4** a glossy coating for the fingernails.—Also *v.t.*:—*pr.p.* **enam'elling**; *pa.p.* **enam'elled**.

enamour *in-am'ȯr*, *v.t.* used in the phrase **enamoured of, with**, in love with, or delighted with.

encamp *in-kamp'*, *v.i.* to settle in a camp.—Also *v.t.*
encamp'ment *n.* a place where troops, etc., are encamped.

encapsulate *en-kap'sū-lāt*, *v.t.* to express briefly but sufficiently:—*pr.p.* **encap'sulating**.

encase *in-kās'*, *v.t.* **1** to enclose in a case. **2** to surround, cover (with *in*):—*pr.p.* **encas'ing**.

enchain *in-chān'*, *v.t.* to put in chains.

enchant *in-chänt'*, *v.t.* **1** to put a spell or charm on. **2** to delight.
enchant'ed *adj.*
enchant'er *n.*:—*fem.* **enchant'ress**.
enchant'ment *n.*

encircle *in-sûrk'l*, *v.t.* **1** to surround (with). **2** to go or pass round:—*pr.p.* **encirc'ling**.

enclave *en'klāv*, *n.* a piece of territory entirely enclosed within foreign territory.

enclose *in-klōz'*, *v.t.* **1** to shut in. **2** to surround. **3** to put inside a letter or its envelope:—*pr.p.* **enclos'ing**.
enclosure *en-klō'zhůr*, *n.* **1** enclosing. **2** land surrounded by fence or wall. **3** something put in along with a letter.

encode *en-kōd'*, *v.t.* to put (a message, etc.) into code:—*pr.p.* **encod'ing**.

encomium *in-kō'mi-ům*, *n.* an expression of very high praise.

encompass *in-kum'pås*, *v.t.* **1** to surround. **2** to include. **3** to bring about.

encore *ong-kōr'*, *-kör'*, or *ong'*, *n.* a call for repetition of a performance, or for a further performance.—Also *v.t.* (*pr.p.* **encoring**) and *interj.*

encounter *in-kown'tėr*, *v.t.* **1** to meet. esp. unexpectedly. **2** to meet (difficulties, an enemy).—*n.* **1** a meeting. **2** a fight.

encourage *in-kur'ij*, *v.t.* **1** to give courage or hope to (someone). **2** to urge (a person to do something):—*pr.p.* **encour'aging**.
encour'agement *n.* **encour'aging** *adj.*
encour'agingly *adv.*

encroach *in-krōch'*: **encroach (up)on** **1** to intrude, esp. little by little, on (someone's land, rights, etc.). **2** to make a gradual advance into.
encroach'ment *n.*

encrust *in-krust'*, *v.t.* to cover with a crust or hard coating e.g. of precious materials.
encrustā'tion *n.*

encumber *in-kum'bėr*, *v.t.* **1** to hamper the movement of, to burden. **2** to load (e.g. an estate) with debt.
encum'brance *n.* something that burdens.

encyclical *in-sik'li-kål*, *n.* a letter from the Pope, circulated to all his bishops.—Also *adj.*

encyclopaedia *in-sī-klō-pē'di-å*, *n.* a reference work containing information on every branch of knowledge, or on one particular branch: *an encyclopaedia of jazz.*
encyclopae'dic *adj.* having a large amount of information on a great variety of subjects.

end *end*, *n.* **1** the last point or part. **2** the finish. **3** death. **4** result. **5** aim, purpose. **6** a fragment, an odd piece.—*v.t.* **1** to bring to an end. **2** to destroy.—*v.i.* **1** to come to an end. **2** to result (in). **3** (with *up*) to arrive, come, become, eventually.
end'ing *n.*
end'less *adj.* **1** continuous, because having the two ends joined: *an endless chain.* **2** going on for ever or for a very long time.
end'ways, **end'wise** *advs.* with the end forward.
at a loose end with nothing to do.
make (both) ends meet to live within one's income, not overspend.

no end (of) (*coll.*) very much (of).
on end 1 erect. **2** continuously.

endanger *in-dān'jėr*, *v.t.* to put in danger.
endangered species a species of animal threatened with extinction.

endear *in-dēr'*, *v.t.* to make dear or more dear.
endear'ing *adj.* arousing feelings of affection.
endear'ment *n.* **1** act of endearing. **2** a caress or word of love.

endeavour *in-dev'ȯr*, *v.i.* **1** to strive (to). **2** to attempt (to).—*n.* a strenuous attempt.

endemic *en-dem'ik*, *adj.* (e.g. of a disease) regularly found in a people or a district owing to local conditions.

endive *en'div*, *n.* a salad plant related to chicory.

endocrine *en'dȯ-krīn*, *adj.* (of a gland) making hormones and releasing them into the bloodstream.

endorse *in-dörs'*, *v.t.* **1** to write, esp. one's signature, on the back of (a cheque, etc.). **2** to note an offence on (a driving licence). **3** to give one's approval to, support (a statement, decision, etc.):—*pr.p.* **endor'sing.**
endorse'ment 1 the act of endorsing. **2** a note of an offence on a driving licence.

endow *in-dow'*, *v.t.* **1** to give a permanent income to (usu. an institution or part of one). **2** to give a talent, quality, etc. to: *Nature had endowed him with practical ability.*
endow'ment *n.*

endue *in-dū'*, *v.t.* (usu. in *pass.*) to endow, provide (with a quality):—*pr.p.* **endu'ing**; *pa.p.* **endued'**.

endure *in-dūr'*, *v.t.* **1** to bear with patience. **2** to undergo. **3** to tolerate.—*v.i.* **1** to remain firm. **2** to last:—*pr.p.* **endur'ing.**
endur'able *adj.* able to be borne.
endur'ance *n.* **1** the power of bearing, or of lasting. **2** the time through which something lasts.

endways, endwise. See **end.**

enema *en'ė-mȧ*, *n.* **1** a liquid medicine injected into the rectum. **2** an instrument for doing this.

enemy *en'i-mi*, *n.* **1** a person who hates or wishes to injure one. **2** an opponent (of): *an enemy of change*:—*pl.* **en'emies.**—*n.sing.* or *n.pl.* one's opponents in a war.—Also *adj.*
See also **enmity.**

energy *en'ėr-ji*, *n.* **1** the power (of electricity, etc.) to do work. **2** (often in *pl.*) a person's capacity for work, etc. **3** ability to act, or habit of acting, vigorously:—*pl.* **en'ergies.**
energet'ic *adj.* very active, vigorous.
energet'ically *adv.*
en'ergise *v.t.* to rouse to activity:—*pr.p.* **en'ergising.**

enervate *en'ėr-vāt*, *v.t.* to take strength or vigour from:—*pr.p.* **en'ervating.**

enfeeble *in-fē'bl*, *v.t.* to weaken:—*pr.p.* **enfee'bling.**
enfee'blement *n.*

enfold *in-fōld'*, *v.t.* **1** to wrap up (in, with, something). **2** to embrace.

enforce *in-fōrs'*, *-förs'*, *v.t.* **1** to compel obedience to: *to enforce a law, a command.* **2** to force (an action or way of acting): *He will now try to enforce payment of the money*:—*pr.p.* **enforc'ing.**
enforce'able *adj.* **enforce'ment** *n.*

enfranchise *in-fran'chīz*, *-shīz*, *v.t.* **1** to set free. **2** to give voting rights to:—*pr.p.* **enfran'chising.**
enfran'chisement (*-chiz-*, *-shiz-*) *n.*

engage *in-gāj'*, *v.t.* **1** to bind by a promise. **2** to hire: *to engage a workman.* **3** to reserve: *to engage a table for four.* **4** to take hold of, hold fast (e.g. attention, sympathy). **5** to join battle with. **6** (of part of a machine) to interlock with (another part). **7** to cause to interlock.—*v.i.* **1** to promise (to). **2** to take part (in): *to engage in smuggling.* **3** to join battle. **4** to interlock:—*pr.p.* **engag'ing.**
engaged' *adj.* **1** bound by promise (esp. to marry). **2** employed (in). **3** busy. **4** hired. **5** reserved. **6** occupied. **7** in battle (with). **8** interlocked.
engage'ment *n.*
engag'ing (*-gāj'*) *adj.* attractive.

engender *in-jen'dėr*, *v.t.* to cause (e.g. hatred, strife).

engine *en'jin*, *n.* **1** a machine in which heat or other energy is used to produce motion. **2** a locomotive.
engineer' *n.* **1** a person who designs or makes machinery. **2** one who designs, constructs, or manages, public works such as roads, railways, bridges, sewers, etc. (**civil engineer**) or who does similar work in the army. **3** an officer who manages a ship's engines. **4** (*U.S.*) an engine driver.—*v.t.* to arrange, bring about, by skill or cunning.
engineer'ing *n.* the art or profession of an engineer.
engine driver one who drives a locomotive.

English *ing'glish*, *adj.* belonging to England or its inhabitants or language.—*n.* the language of Britain, a great part of the British Commonwealth, and the U.S.A.

(**Old English**, the English language as spoken up till about A.D. 1100; **Middle English,** from then till about 1500; **Modern English,** from about 1500 onwards).

engraft *in-grăft'*, *v.t.* to graft, insert, introduce (into).

engrained. Same as **ingrained**.

engrave *in-grāv'*, *v.t.* **1** to cut (letters, etc.) on stone, wood, or metal, or to etch (them) with acid. **2** to ornament (a hard surface) thus. **3** to impress deeply (e.g. on the mind):—*pr.p.* **engrav'ing**.
engrav'er *n.* one who engraves.
engrav'ing *n.* **1** the art or act of an engraver. **2** a picture taken from an engraved plate, a print.

engross *in-grōs'*, *v.t.* **1** to take up the interest or attention of wholly. **2** to write in legal form.
engross'ing *adj.* very interesting.
engross'ment *n.*

engulf *in-gulf'*, *v.t.* to swallow up wholly.

enhance *in-häns'*, *v.t.* **1** to heighten, increase: *The fine clothes enhanced her beauty*:—*pr.p.* **enhan'cing**.

enigma *i-nig'mȧ*, *n.* a puzzling statement, person, or thing.
enigmat'ic *(en-ig-) adj.* puzzling.
enigmat'ically *adv.*

enjoin *in-join'*, *v.t.* to order (a person to do something).
See also **injunction**.

enjoy *in-joi'*, *v.t.* **1** to find pleasure in: *I enjoy skating.* **2** (with *oneself*) to experience pleasure: *to enjoy oneself.* **3** to experience (esp. a benefit—e.g. a long life, good health, a steady income).
enjoy'able *adj.* **enjoy'ment** *n.*

enlarge *in-lärj'*, *v.t.* **1** to make larger. **2** to reproduce on a larger scale (e.g. a photograph).—*v.i.* **1** to grow larger. **2** to say, write, more (with *(up)on*): *He enlarged upon his holiday plans*:—*pr.p.* **enlarg'ing**.
enlarge'ment *n.*

enlighten *in-līt'n*, *v.t.* to give information to (a person).
enlight'ened *adj.* wise through knowledge, free from prejudice.
enlight'enment *n.*

enlist *in-list'*, *v.t.* **1** to engage as a soldier, etc. **2** to obtain, make use of in a cause: *May I enlist your help in this effort to raise money?*—*v.i.* **1** to register for service, esp. as a soldier. **2** to enter heartily (in a cause, service).
enlist'ment *n.*

enliven *in-līv'n*, *v.t.* **1** to make active. **2** to make sprightly or cheerful.

en masse *on^g mas*, *adv.* all together in a body.

enmesh *in-mesh'*, *v.t.* to entangle (as if) in a net or mesh.

enmity *en'mi-ti*, *n.* unfriendliness, ill-will.

ennoble *i-nō'bl*, *v.t.* **1** to make noble in character. **2** to raise to the nobility:—*pr.p.* **enno'bling**.
enno'blement *(-nō'bėl-) n.*

ennui *on'wē*, *n.* boredom.

enormous *i-nör'mus*, *adj.* very large.
enor'mity *n.* **1** (an act of) great wickedness. **2** outrageousness: *the enormity of this remark.* **3** (*loosely*) enormousness:—*pl.* **enor'mities**.
enor'mously *adv.*
enor'mousness *n.* hugeness.

enough *i-nuf'*, *adj.* and *n.* (in the) quantity, number, degree, required.—Also *adv.*
well (good) enough quite well (good).

enquire. See **inquire**.

enrage *in-rāj'*, *v.t.* to make angry:—*pr.p.* **enrag'ing**.

enrapture *in-rap'chur*, *v.t.* to give great pleasure or delight to:—*pr.p.* **enrap'turing**.

enrich *in-rich'*, *v.t.* **1** to make rich. **2** to improve the quality of by adding something.

enrol(l) *en-rōl'*, *in-*, *v.t.* to enter in a roll, list, register, e.g. as pupil, member.—*v.i.* to register:—*pr.p.* **enrōll'ing**; *pa.p.* **enrōlled**.
enrōl'ment *n.*

en route *on^g rōōt*, on the way (for, to).

ensconce *in-skons'*, *v.t.* to settle (oneself, etc.) comfortably (in):—*pr.p.* **enscon'cing**.

ensemble *on^g-son^g'bl'*, *n.* **1** all the parts of a thing taken together. **2** a complete costume, outfit. **3** in opera, etc. a passage performed by all the singers who are on stage. **4** a group of musicians who perform together.

enshrine *in-shrīn'*, *v.t.* **1** to enclose in, or as if in, a shrine. **2** to cherish (e.g. in the memory):—*pr.p.* **enshrin'ing**.

enshroud *in-shrowd'*, *v.t.* to cover completely.

ensign *en'sīn*, *en'sin*, *n.* **1** the flag of a nation, regiment, etc. **2** (*hist.*) the lowest commissioned officer in the army or (*U.S.*) navy.

enslave *in-slāv'*, *v.t.* to make (a person) a slave, or to obtain great power over (him):—*pr.p.* **enslav'ing**.
enslave'ment *n.*

ensnare *in-snār'*, *v.t.* to catch in a snare:—*pr.p.* **ensnar'ing**.

ensue *in-sū'*, *v.i.* **1** to come after. **2** to result (from):—*pr.p.* **ensū'ing**; *pa.p.* **ensūed'**.

ensure *in-shōōr'*, *v.t.* to make sure, certain: —*pr.p.* **ensur'ing**.

entail *in-tāl'*, *v.t.* to bring as a result, require: *These alterations will entail great expense*.

entangle *in-tang'gl*, *v.t.* **1** to make tangled. **2** to involve (in difficulties). **3** to ensnare:—*pr.p.* **entang'ling**.
entang'lement *n.* **1** a tangled obstacle. **2** a difficult position.

entente *on^g-ton^gt*, *n.* an agreement between states.

enter *en'tėr*, *v.i.* **1** to go or come in. **2** to put down one's name (for a competition, etc.).—*v.t.* **1** to come or go into (a place). **2** to join or take part in. **3** to begin. **4** to enrol or record in a book. **5** (with *for*) to put (a person, animal, etc.) into (a competition, etc.).
enter into 1 to become a party to: *to enter into an agreement with someone*. **2** to take part heartily in. **3** to sympathise with (another's feelings). **4** to begin to discuss (a question). **5** to be a part, or an ingredient, of.
enter (up)on to begin.
See also **entry**, **entrance[1]**.

enteric *en-ter'ik*, *n.* typhoid fever.
enterī'tis *n.* inflammation of the intestines.

enterprise *en'tėr-prīz*, *n.* **1** something that is attempted (esp. if it requires boldness). **2** willingness to try new lines of action.
enterpris'ing *adj.* showing enterprise, adventurous.

entertain *en-tėr-tān'*, *v.t.* **1** to receive as a guest. **2** to amuse. **3** to hold in the mind or feelings: *to entertain a belief*; *to entertain a great dislike*.
entertain'er *n.* one who gives amusing performances professionally.
entertain'ing *adj.* and *n.*
entertain'ment *n.* **1** the act of entertaining. **2** something that entertains, as a party, a theatrical show. **3** amusement.

enthral(l) *in-thröl'*, *v.t.* **1** to hold as by a spell. **2** to delight:—*pr.p.* **enthrall'ing**; *pa.p.* **enthralled'**.
enthral'ment *n.*

enthrone *in-thrōn'*, *v.t.* to place on a throne, as king or bishop:—*pr.p.* **enthron'ing**.
enthrone'ment *n.*

enthusiasm *in-thū'zi-azm*, *n.* **1** intense interest in something. **2** a desire to help something forward: *enthusiasm for the cause of peace*.
enthuse' *v.t.* and *v.i.* (*coll.*) to make, be, become, enthusiastic:—*pr.p.* **enthus'ing**.
enthu'siast *n.* a person filled with enthusiasm.
enthusias'tic *adj.* **enthusias'tically** *adv.*

entice *in-tīs'*, *v.t.* **1** to tempt (into doing something) by arousing hope or desire. **2** to lead astray:—*pr.p.* **entic'ing**.
entice'ment *n.* **entic'ing** *adj.*

entire *in-tīr'*, *adj.* **1** whole. **2** complete.
entire'ly *adv.* **entire'ness** *n.*
entire'ty (or *-tīr'ė-ti*) *n.* **1** completeness. **2** the whole.

entitle *in-tī'tl*, *v.t.* **1** to give as a name to (e.g. a book). **2** to give (a person) a right (to something, or to do something):—*pr.p.* **entit'ling**.
entit'lement *n.*

entity *en'ti-ti*, *n.* **1** existence. **2** a thing that exists:—*pl.* **en'tities**.

entomb *in-tōōm'*, *v.t.* to bury.

entomology *en-tȯ-mol'ȯ-ji*, *n.* the science of insects.
entomolog'ical (*-loj'*) *adj.*
entomol'ogist *n.*

entourage *on^g'too-räzh*, *n.* followers.

entr'acte *on^g'trakt*, *n.* **1** the interval between acts in a play. **2** a piece of music etc. played then.

entrails *en'trālz*, *n.pl.* the internal parts of an animal's body, the bowels.

entrain *in-trān'*, *v.t.* and *v.i.* to put, or go, into a railway train (esp. of troops).

entrance[1] *en'trȧns*, *n.* **1** act of entering. **2** the right to enter. **3** a place of entering. **4** a door. **5** a beginning.
en'trant *n.* one who enters (esp. a competition, a profession, etc.).
See also **enter**, **entry**.

entrance[2] *in-träns'*, *v.t.* to fill with rapturous delight:—*pr.p.* **entran'cing**.

entrap *in-trap'*, *v.t.* to catch as in a trap:—*pr.p.* **entrapp'ing**.

entreat *in-trēt'*, *v.t.* to ask earnestly.
entreat'y *n.* (*pl.* **-ies**).

entrée *on^g'trā*, *n.* **1** the right of admission. **2** a dish served at dinner between main courses or as a main course.

entrench *in-trench'*, *-sh'*, *v.t.* **1** to dig trenches round (a place) for defence. **2** to establish (e.g. oneself) in a strong position.
entrench'ment *n.*

entrust *in-trust'*, *v.t.* **1** to give into the care of another: *I entrusted my jewellery, this secret, to her*. **2** to trust (with): *I entrusted her with the duty of locking up*.

entry *en'tri*, *n.* **1** act of going or coming in. **2** the right to enter. **3** a place of entering. **4** something written in a list, reference book, etc. **5** a person or thing, or (*n.pl.*) the total number of these, entered for a

contest, etc.
See also **enter**, **entrance**[1].

entwine *in-twīn'*, *v.t.* to twine (with, about, round):—*pr.p.* **entwin'ing**.

E-number *ē'num-bėr*, *n.* any identification code for food additives approved by the European Union.

enumerate *i-nū'mėr-āt*, *v.t.* **1** to count the number of. **2** to name one by one: *He enumerated my faults—laziness, vanity, etc.*:—*pr.p.* **enu'merating**.
enumerā'tion *n.*

enunciate *i-nun's(h)i-āt*, *v.t.* **1** to state formally. **2** to pronounce distinctly:—*pr.p.* **enun'ciating**.
enunciā'tion *n.*

envelop *in-vel'ȯp*, *v.t.* **1** to cover by wrapping. **2** to surround entirely:—*pr.p.* **envel'oping**; *pa.p.* **envel'oped**.
envelope *en'vėl-ōp*, *on'*, *n.* a wrapper or cover, esp. for a letter.
envel'opment *n.* act of enveloping.

enviable, **envious**. See **envy**.

environ *in-vī'rȯn*, *v.t.* to surround.
envi'ronment *n.* **1** surroundings. **2** surrounding conditions, esp. as influencing a person's development or growth. **3** the natural conditions in which we live.
environment'alism *n.* the movement to preserve the natural environment from pollution.
environmen'talist *n.*
envi'rons *n.pl.* outskirts (of a place).

envisage *in-viz'ij*, *v.t.* to picture to oneself; to contemplate or consider: *What alterations had you envisaged?*:—*pr.p.* **envis'aging**.

envoy *en'voi*, *n.* a messenger, esp. one sent to deal with a foreign government:—*pl.* **envoys**.

envy *en'vi*, *n.* **1** a feeling of discontent at another's well-being or success. **2** the object of such a feeling: *Her mink coat was the envy of her friends.*—*v.t.* **1** to feel envy towards. **2** to grudge:—*pr.p.* **en'vying**; *pa.p.* **en'vied**.
en'viable *adj.* that is to be envied.
en'vious *adj.* feeling, or showing, envy.

enzyme *en'zīm*, *n.* a substance produced by living cells that acts as a catalyst (see this word) in certain chemical changes.

eon. See **aeon**.

epaulet(te) *ep'ȯ-let*, *n.* a shoulder ornament on a uniform.

épée *ep'ā*, *n.* a sword with a sharp point and narrow blade, triangular in cross-section, used in fencing.

ephemeral *i-fem'ėr-ȧl*, *adj.* **1** lasting only for a day. **2** short-lived.

epic *ep'ik*, *n.* **1** a long poem telling a story of great deeds. **2** any story of great deeds.—*adj.* great, heroic.

epicentre *ep'i-sen-tėr*, *n.* the point on the earth's surface directly above the origin of an earthquake.

epicure *ep'i-kyūr*, *n.* a person of refined taste, esp. in food and drink.
epicure'an *(-rē')* *adj.*

epidemic *ep-i-dem'ik*, *n.* an outbreak of a disease that attacks large numbers at one time.—Also *adj.*

epidermis *ep-i-dûr'mis*, *n.* top skin, cuticle, covering the true skin.

epigram *ep'i-gram*, *n.* a short, neat saying in prose or verse.
epigrammat'ic *adj.*

epilepsy *ep'i-lep-si*, *n.* a disease of the nervous system with attacks of unconscienceness with or without convulsions.
epilep'tic *adj.* and *n.*

epilogue *ep'i-log*, *n.* **1** a speech at the end of a play. **2** the concluding section of a book, programme, etc.

epiphany *i-pif'ȧn-i*, *n.* a church festival (January 6) commemorating the showing of Christ to the Wise Men.

episcopacy *i-pis'kȯ-pȧs-i*, *n.* the government of the church by bishops.
epis'copal *adj.* **1** governed by bishops. **2** belonging to bishops.
episcopā'lian *adj.* of (government by) bishops.—*n.* a member of an episcopal church.

episode *ep'i-sōd*, *n.* an incident, or series of events, occurring in a longer story.

epistle *i-pis'l*, *n.* **1** (esp. *humorous*) a letter. **2** (*cap.*) in the Bible, a letter from an apostle.
epistolary *i-pis'tȯ-lȧr-i*, *adj.* of, or in a letter: *His epistolary style was dull.*

epitaph *ep'i-täf*, *n.* a tombstone inscription.

epithet *ep'i-thet*, *n.* **1** an adjective describing a familiar or important quality of its noun (e.g. the *blue* sky; Richard *Lionheart*). **2** a descriptive term, sometimes insulting.

epitome *e-pit'ȯ-mi*, *n.* **1** a short summary. **2** something that represents another on a small scale.
epit'omise *v.t.* **1** to condense. **2** to represent on a small scale:—*pr.p.* **epit'omising**.

epoch *ēp'ok*, (*U.S.*) *ep'*, *n.* an age in history.
ep'och-ma'king *adj.* great enough to affect the course of history and begin a new epoch.

equable *ek'wȧ-bl, adj.* **1** not extreme: *In an equable climate the temperature does not vary widely.* **2** not easily annoyed or agitated:—*opp.* **ineq'uable**.

equal *ē'kwȧl, adj.* the same in size, quantity, value, ability, etc.—*n.* one of the same age, rank, etc.—*v.t.* to be, or to achieve something, equal to:—*pr.p.* **ē'qualling**; *pa.p.* **ē'qualled**.
e'qualise *v.t.* and *v.i.* to make, or become, equal:—*pr.p.* **e'qualising**.
equality *ē-kwol'i-ti, n.* (*opp.* **inequality**).
e'qually *adv.*
equal to fit or able for: *Is he equal to this heavy task?*; *I do not feel equal to telling him the truth.*
equate *i-quāt'*, or *ē-*, *v.t.* **1** to state as equal (to). **2** to regard as in some way the same:—*pr.p.* **equat'ing**.
equā'tion *n.* **1** the act of equating. **2** in mathematics, etc., a statement that two things are equal or the same. **3** a formula expressing a chemical reaction.

equanimity *ē-kwȧ-nim'i-ti, ek-, n.* evenness of temper, calmness.

equate, **equation**. See **equal**.

equator *i-kwā'tȯr, n.* an imaginary circle passing round the globe, at an equal distance from N. and S. poles.
equatō'rial (or *-tö'-*) *adj.*
equatorial regions the hot parts of the earth near the equator.

equerry *ek'wė-ri, i-kwer'i, n.* **1** (*history*) an officer in charge of horses. **2** a male official attending a member of a royal family:—*pl.* **equerries**.

equestrian *i-kwes'tri-ȧn, adj.* **1** of horsemanship. **2** done, performed, etc. on horseback.—*n.* one who rides on horseback.

equi- *ē-kwi-, pfx.* equal.
equian'gular *adj.* having equal angles.
equidis'tant *adj.* equally distant (from).
equilat'eral *adj.* having all sides equal.

equilibrium *ē-kwi-lib'ri-ȯm, n.* a state of equal balance between weights or forces, or between opposing powers or influences, etc.

equine *ē'kwīn*, or *ek', adj.* of, of the nature of, a horse.

equinox *ē'kwi-noks*, or *ek', n.* the time when the sun crosses the equator, making night and day equal in length, about March 21 and September 23.
equinoc'tial *(-shȧl) adj.* of the equinoxes, or the time of these.
equinoctial gales high gales popularly supposed to be common about the times of the equinoxes.

equip *i-kwip', v.t.* to fit out with everything needed:—*pr.p.* **equipp'ing**; *pa.p.* **equipped'**.
equipage *ek'wi-pij, n.* carriage and attendants.
equip'ment *n.* **1** the act of equipping. **2** the clothes, apparatus, tools, machines, etc. necessary for a job, expedition, etc.

equitation *ek'wi-tā'sh(ȯ)n, n.* horse-riding.

equity *ek'wi-ti, n.* **1** fairness; the spirit of justice that helps in interpreting the law (*opp.* **inequity**). **2** (in *pl.*) ordinary shares:—*pl.* **eq'uities**.
eq'uitable *adj.* fair:—*opp.* **inequitable**.

equivalent *i-kwiv'ȧ-lėnt, adj.* equal in value, power, meaning, etc.—Also *n.*

equivocal *i-kwiv'ȯ-kȧl, adj.* **1** capable of meaning two or more things. **2** of uncertain nature.
equiv'ocate *v.i.* to use words of uncertain meaning esp. in order to mislead:—*pr.p.* **equiv'ocating**.
equivocā'tion *n.*

era *ē'rȧ, n.* an age, period, of a particular character, or dating from a particular event, etc.: *an era of reform*; *the Christian era.*

eradicate *i-rad'i-kāt, n.* to root out, get rid of completely:—*pr.p.* **erad'icating**.
erad'icable *adj.*:—*opp.* **inerad'icable**.
eradicā'tion *n.*

erase *i-rāz', v.t.* to rub out:—*pr.p.* **eras'ing**.
eraser *i-rā'zėr, n.*
erasure *i-rā'zhȯr, n.* rubbing out.

ere *ār*, (*old*) *prep., conj.*, before.

erect *i-rekt', adj.* **1** upright. **2** (of the penis) enlarged and hard.—*v.t.* **1** to set upright. **2** to build; to construct.
erec'tile *(-tīl) adj.* (of bodily tissue) able to become erect.
erec'tion *n.* **1** the act of erecting. **2** a building or structure. **3** a hardening and enlarging of the penis.
erect'ly *adv.* **erect'ness** *n.*

ergonomics *ûr-gȯ-nom'iks, n.sing.* the study of the conditions, efficiency, etc. of people at work.

ermine *ûr'min, n.* **1** the stoat. **2** its white winter fur, used with the black tail-tip attached for robes of judges, etc.

erode *i-rōd', v.t.* **1** (of acids, etc.) to eat away. **2** (of water, ice, wind, etc.) to wear away:—*pr.p.* **erod'ing**.
ero'sion *i-rō'zh(ȯ)n, n.*
ero'sive *(-siv) adj.*

erotic *i-rot'ik, adj.* of love or sexual desire.
erogenous *i-roj'i-nȯs*, **erotog'enous** *(er-ȯ-toj') adjs.* producing sexual excitement.

err *ûr, v.i.* **1** to go astray. **2** to make a mistake, be wrong. **3** to sin.
errat'ic *adj.* **1** wandering. **2** not dependable in conduct, etc.

erra'tum *(-rä')* *n.* an error in writing or printing:—*pl.* **erra'ta**.
erro'neous *(-rō')* *adj.* **1** wrong. **2** mistaken.
erro'neously *adv.* **erro'neousness** *n.*
err'or *n.* **1** a blunder, mistake. **2** wrongdoing.

errand *er'ȧnd, n.* **1** a short journey to fetch something, deliver a message, etc., esp. for someone else. **2** the object of a journey.

errant *er'ȧnt, adj.* (used only before a noun) **1** wrong, mistaken. **2** straying.
See also **knight-errant**.

erratic, erratum, etc. See **err**.

ersatz *ėr-zäts', ûr', adj.* substitute: *ersatz coffee.*

eruct *i-rukt'*, **eructate** *-āt, v.t.* to belch out.—Also *v.i.*:—*pr.ps.* **eruct'ing, eruct'ating**.
eructā'tion *n.*

erudite *er'ōō-dīt*, or *er'ū-*, *adj.* having learned much from books.
erudition *(-di')* *n.*

erupt *i-rupt', v.i.* **1** (of a volcano) to throw out lava, etc. **2** to break out, esp. violently.
erup'tion *n.* a bursting forth (e.g. of lava, of feeling, of spots on the skin).
erup'tive *adj.*

escalate *es'kȧ-lāt, v.i.* to increase rapidly in scale or intensity:—*pr.p.* **es'calating**.
es'calātor *n.* a moving staircase.

escalope *es'kȧ-lop, n.* a thin, boneless slice of meat, esp. veal.

escape *is-kāp', v.t.* **1** to get clear away from (e.g. custody). **2** to manage to avoid (e.g. punishment). **3** to slip from (the memory): *His name escapes my memory*, or *escapes me*:—*v.i.* **1** to gain freedom; to flee. **2** (of e.g. gas) to leak:—*pr.p.* **escap'ing**.—*n.* **1** an act of escaping. **2** a leakage.
es'capade *(-kȧ-)* *n.* a mischievous adventure.
escap'ism *(-kāp')* *n.* the tendency to escape from reality into daydreams, etc.
escap'ist *(-kāp')* *n.*
escape'ment *n.* a device controlling movement, e.g. in a watch.

escarpment *is-kärp'mėnt, n.* the steep side of a hill or rock.

escheat *is-chēt', n.* property that falls to the state for want of an heir.—Also *v.i.*

eschew *is-chōō', v.t.* to shun, avoid, abstain from (e.g. evil, violence).

escort *es'kört, n.* person(s), ship(s), etc., accompanying for protection, guidance, custody, or courtesy.—*v.t.* *(is-kört')* to attend as escort.

escutcheon *is-kuch'ȯn, n.* a shield on which a coat of arms is shown.

Eskimo *es'ki-mō, n.* (*now often offensive*) one of a people inhabiting the far north:—*pl.* **Es'kimo(s)**.—Also *adj.*

esoteric *es-ō-ter'ik, adj.* obscure, mysterious; known only to a few.

espalier *is-pal'yėr, n.* **1** a lattice on which to train fruit trees. **2** a fruit tree trained on stakes or lattice.

esparto *es-pär'tō, n.* a strong grass grown in Spain, N. Africa, etc., and used for making paper, etc.

especial *is-pesh'(ȧ)l, adj.* (used only before a noun) **1** beyond the ordinary: *with especial care.* **2** particular: *his especial merit.*
espec'ially *adv.* particularly, notably.
especially as for the important reason that.

Esperanto *es-pėr-an'tō, n.* a planned international language introduced in 1887.

espionage *es-pyȯn-äzh'*, or *es'*, *n.* **1** spying. **2** use of spies.

esplanade *es-plȧ-nād', n.* a level space for walking or driving, esp. at the seaside.

espouse *is-powz', v.t.* **1** (*old*) to give or take in marriage. **2** to support (a cause):—*pr.p.* **espous'ing**.
espous'al *n.* support (of a cause).

espresso *es-pres'ō, n.* (coffee made in) a machine in which pressure of steam is used to get maximum flavour from the coffee beans:—*pl.* **espress'os.**

esprit de corps *es-prē dė kör* **1** loyalty to the society to which one belongs. **2** public spirit.

espy *is-pī', v.t.* to catch sight of:—*pr.p.* **espy'ing**; *pa.p.* **espied'**.

esquire *es-kwīr'*, also *es'*, *n.* **1** (*orig.*) a squire, an attendant on a knight. **2** (*cap.*) a title of respect in addressing letters.—*abbrev.* **Esq**.

essay *es'ā, n.* **1** an attempt. **2** a written composition.—*v.t.* *(e-sā')* **1** to test (e.g. one's powers). **2** to attempt:—*pr.p.* **essay'ing**; *pa.p.* **essayed'**.
ess'ayist *n.* a writer of essays.

essence *es'ėns, n.* **1** the inner nature of anything, its most important quality. **2** a substance obtained from a plant, drug, etc. in concentrated form: *essence of peppermint.*
essential *i-sen'sh(ȧ)l, adj.* **1** absolutely necessary (*opp.* **inessential**). **2** (usu. used before a noun) basic, inner: *her essential good humour.* **3** (usu. used before a noun) of, being, or containing, an essence: *The leaves are crushed so as to extract their essential oil.*—*n.* something

indispensable.
essen'tially *adv.* basically, in inner nature: *She is an essentially selfish person.*
in essence basically, fundamentally.

establish *is-tab'lish, v.t.* **1** to settle firmly in a position. **2** to settle in business. **3** to found (e.g. a university, a business). **4** to cause people to adopt: *to establish a custom.* **5** to get people to accept as true, just, etc.: *to establish a fact, a claim.* **6** to make (a church) the recognised state church.
estab'lishment *n.* **1** the act of establishing. **2** a permanent civil or military force or commercial staff. **3** one's residence, household, and style of living. **4** the church established by law.
the Establishment the people holding important positions in a community.

estate *is-tāt', n.* **1** condition or rank. **2** total possessions. **3** property in land. **4** a piece of land developed for building. **5** (*old*) a political division of society.
estate agent one whose job is to sell houses and land.
estate'-car *n.* one with generous luggage-space and a rear door.

esteem *is-tēm', v.t.* **1** to value. **2** to regard with respect. **3** to consider to be.—*n.* (favourable) opinion; respect.
estimable *es'tim-ȧ-bl, adj.* worthy of respect.
es'timāte *v.t.* **1** to judge the worth of. **2** to calculate:—*pr.p.* **es'timating**.—*n.* *(-mit)* **1** an approximate calculation. **2** a statement of the probable cost of proposed work.
estimā'tion *n.* **1** a reckoning. **2** judgment, opinion.
See also **inestimable**.

estrange *is-trānj', v.t.* to make unfriendly: *The former friends were estranged by these events:*—*pr.p.* **estran'ging**.
estrange'ment *n.*

estuary *es'tū-ȧr-i, n.* the wide mouth of a river up which the tide flows:—*pl.* **es'tuaries**.

et cetera *et set'(ė-)rȧ*, usu. written **etc.** or **&c.**, Latin phrase meaning 'and the rest', 'and so on'.
etcet'eras *n.pl.* additional items.

etch *ech, v.t.* or *v.i.* **1** to make (designs) on metal, glass, etc., by using acid to eat out the lines. **2** to treat (metal, etc.) thus.
etch'ing *n.* the picture from an etched plate.

eternal *i-tûr'nȧl, adj.* **1** without beginning or end. **2** unchanging. **3** (*coll.*) never ceasing: *your eternal chattering.*
eter'nally *adv.*
eter'nity *n.* **1** an endless, or seemingly endless, time. **2** the state or time after death:—*pl.* **eter'nities**.

ether *ē'thėr, n.* **1** the clear, upper air. **2** the non-material medium formerly supposed to fill all space. **3** a colourless liquid used as a solvent of fats, etc., and as an anaesthetic.
ethe'real, ethe'rial *(i-thē') adj.* supernaturally delicate or fairy-like.

ethical *eth'ik-ȧl, adj.* **1** of morals. **2** morally right, or in keeping with high standards.
eth'ically *adv.* **eth'icalness** *n.*
eth'ics *n.sing.* the science of morals.—*n.pl.* moral principles.

ethnic *eth'nik, adj.* having, or relating to, a common race or cultural tradition.
eth'nically *adv.*
ethnic'ity *n.* racial status or distinctiveness.

ethnology *eth-nol'ȯ-ji, n.* the science that studies the varieties of the human race.
ethnolog'ical *adj.*

ethos *ē'thos, n.* the spirit or general attitude of a community, etc.

etiquette *et'i-ket*, or *-ket', n.* **1** forms of ceremony in society or at court. **2** the unwritten laws observed by members of a profession: *medical, legal, etiquette.*

etymology *et-i-mol'ȯj-i, n.* **1** the study of the derivation and original meaning of words. **2** the history of a particular word:—*pl.* **etymol'ogies**.
etymolog'ical *(-loj'-) adj.*

eu- *ū-, pfx.* well.

eucalyptus *ū-kȧ-lip'tus, n.* a large Australian evergreen tree, yielding timber, oils, gum.

Eucharist *ū'kȧ-rist, n.* (the bread and wine administered at) the sacrament of the Lord's Supper.

eugenic *ū-jen'ik, adj.* of, or bringing about, race improvement.
eugen'ics *n.sing.* the science of this.

eulogy *ū'lȯ-ji, n.* high praise, written or spoken:—*pl.* **eu'logies**.
eu'logise *v.t.* to praise:—*pr.p.* **eu'logising**.
eulogis'tic *adj.* full of praise.

eunuch *ū'nuk, n.* a castrated man.

euphemism *ū'fim-izm, n.* a mild expression for something that is disagreeable (e.g. *to fall asleep* for 'to die').
euphemis'tic *adj.*

euphony *ū'fȯ-ni, n.* pleasing sound.
euphō'nious *adj.*

euphoria *ū-fō'ri-ȧ, fö', n.* feeling (often irrational) of extreme cheerfulness.
euphor'ic *(-for') adj.*

Eurasian *ū-rā'zh(y)ȧn, -shȧn, adj.* **1** of mixed European and Asiatic descent. **2** of Europe and Asia.—Also *n.*

eureka *ū-rē'kȧ, interj.* I've found it.

European *ū-rȯ-pē'ȧn, adj.* belonging to Europe.—*n.* a native of Europe.

euthanasia *ū-thȧ-nāz'yȧ, n.* putting to death painlessly, esp. to end suffering.

evacuate *i-vak'ū-āt, v.t.* **1** to empty out the contents of. **2** to withdraw from (a fortified place, etc.). **3** to clear out (troops, inhabitants, etc.) from a town, etc.:—*pr.p.* **evac'uating**.
evacuā'tion *n.*
evacuee' *n.* a person removed in an evacuation.

evade *i-, ē-vād', v.t.* **1** to escape or avoid by trickery or skill. **2** to avoid answering (a question):—*pr.p.* **evad'ing**.
evasion *i-vā'zh(ȯ)n, n.* **1** the act of evading. **2** a trick or excuse used to evade.
evasive *i-vā'siv, adj.* **1** having the purpose of evading: *to take evasive action.* **2** not frank and direct: *evasive answers.*
eva'sively *adv.* **eva'siveness** *n.*

evaluate *i-,* or *ē-val'ū-āt, v.t.* to find the value of:—*pr.p.* **eval'uating**.
evaluā'tion *n.*

evanescent *ev-ȧn-es'ėnt, ē-vȧn-, adj.* **1** vanishing. **2** passing quickly away.
evanes'cence *(-es'ėns) n.*

evangelical *ē-van-jel'ik-ȧl, adj.* **1** of, in keeping with, the teachings of the gospel. **2** seeking the conversion of sinners.
evan'gelist *n.* **1** one who preaches the gospel. **2** a writer of a gospel (Matthew, Mark, Luke, or John).
evangelis'tic *adj.*

evaporate *i-vap'ȯr-āt, v.i.* **1** to pass off in vapour. **2** to vanish.—*v.t.* to turn into, drive off as, vapour:—*pr.p.* **evap'orating**.
evaporā'tion *n.*

evasion, evasive. See **evade**.

eve *ēv, n.* **1** the day (night) before a festival: *Christmas Eve.* **2** the time just before an event: *the eve of the battle.*

even[1] *ē'vn, adj.* **1** level. **2** smooth. **3** regular. **4** divisible by 2 without a remainder. **5** equal (in quantity, etc.). **6** (of temper) not easily ruffled, calm.—*v.t., v.i.* to make, or become, even or smooth (often with *out*).—*adv.* **1** still, yet: *even better.* **2** used also to emphasise something unexpected about an action, etc.: *He swam daily in winter, and even enjoyed it; Even Mary would not be so silly; He suspects even his friends.*
e'venly *adv.* **e'venness** *n.*
be even with to be revenged on.
even if whether or not.
even so nevertheless.
even though in spite of the fact that.

even[2] *ē'vn, n.* evening.
evening *ēv'ning, n.* **1** the close of the day. **2** the end of life.
evening dress clothes worn for formal occasions in the evening.
evening star a planet, esp. Venus, seen in the west after sunset.
e'vensong *n.* prayer said or sung at evening.
e'ventide *n.* **1** evening. **2** old age.

event *i-vent', n.* **1** something that happens, an incident or occurrence. **2** an item in a programme of sports.
event'ful *adj.* **1** full of events. **2** exciting.
eventual *(-ū-al) adj.* (used only before a noun) happening as an outcome; final.
eventual'ity *n.* a possible happening:—*pl.* **eventual'ities**.
event'ually *adv.* finally, at length.
at all events or **at, in, any event** in any case.
in the event of if (something) occurs.

ever *ev'ėr, adv.* **1** at all times: *happily ever after; growing ever weaker; ever since childhood; ever willing to help.* **2** at any time: *hardly ever; if ever I go; better than ever.* **3** (esp. *coll.*) used to give emphasis: *as politely as ever I can; ever so quietly; what ever did she say?*
ev'ergreen *adj.* always green.—*n.* a plant that remains green all the year.
everlast'ing *adj.* **1** endless. **2** eternal.—*n.* **1** eternity. **2** a flower that when dried may be kept for years unchanged.
everlast'ingly *adv.* **everlast'ingness** *n.*
evermore' *adv.* for ever.
for ever, forever 1 always, continually. **2** for all time.

every *ev'ri, adj.* **1** each of a number without exception. **2** all possible: *We made every effort.*
ev'erybody, ev'eryone *(ev'ri-) prons.* every person.
ev'eryday *adj.* **1** daily. **2** common, usual, ordinary.
ev'erything *pron.* **1** all things. **2** all.
ev'erywhere *ev'ri-hwār, adv.* in every place.
every other every second, each alternate: *every other day.*

evict *i-, ē-vikt', v.t.* to turn out, expel (esp. by legal process, from house or land).
evic'tion *n.*

evident *ev'i-dėnt, adj.* **1** clearly to be seen. **2** clear to the mind; obvious.
ev'idence *n.* **1** indication, a sign. **2** proof. **3** information in a law case.—*v.t.* to indicate, show, prove:—*pr.p.* **ev'idencing**.
ev'idently *adv.* obviously; apparently.

turn King's (Queen's) evidence (of an accomplice in a crime) to give evidence against his partner(s).

evil *ē'vl*, *ē'vil*, *adj.* **1** bad. **2** wicked.—*n.* **1** harm. **2** wickedness. **3** sin.—used to form *adjs.*, as **e'vil-mind'ed**, **e'vil-smell'ing**.
e'villy *adv.* **e'vilness** *n.*
e'vil-do'er *n.* one who does evil.
e'vil-eye' *n.* a supposed power to cause harm by a look.

evince *i-vins'*, *v.t.* to show (a quality, etc. that one has): *The child evinced remarkable powers of reasoning*:—*pr.p.* **evin'cing**.

eviscerate *i-vis'ėr-āt*, *v.t.* to tear out the bowels of:—*pr.p.* **evis'cerating**.

evocation, **evocative**. See **evoke**.

evoke *i-vōk'*, *v.t.* **1** to draw forth: *to evoke a reply, a storm of abuse.* **2** to call up in the mind (e.g. a memory, a picture):—*pr.p.* **evok'ing**.
evocā'tion *n.* **evoc'ative** *(-vok') adj.*

evolution, **evolutionary**. See **evolve**.

evolve *i-volv'*, *v.t.* **1** to develop, show, work out, gradually. **2** to give off (heat, etc.).—*v.i.* to develop gradually:—*pr.p.* **evolv'ing**.
evolution *ē-vȯl-ū'sh(ȯ)n*, or *-ōō'*, *U.S.* *ev'*, *n.* **1** gradual working out or development. **2** the teaching that higher forms of life have gradually arisen out of lower. **3** the giving off (e.g. of gas, heat). **4** (usu. in *pl.*) orderly movements of a body of troops, flock of birds, etc.
evolu'tionary *adj.*

ewe *ū*, *n.* a female sheep.

ewer *ū'ėr*, *n.* a large water jug with a wide spout.

ex- *eks-*, *pfx.* **1** former or late: *ex-president*; *his ex-wife.* **2** outside: *an ex-directory telephone number* (one not in the directory).

exacerbate *iks-as'ėr-bāt*, *v.t.* to make (e.g. a disease, pain, anger) worse:—*pr.p.* **exac'erbating**.
exacerbā'tion *n.*

exact *ig-zakt'*, *v.t.* **1** to compel payment of: *to exact a fine from the culprit.* **2** to insist upon having: *to exact obedience.*—*adj.* completely accurate; correct; precise:—*opp.* **inexact'**.
exact'ing *adj.* severe, demanding much from a person: *His boss is very exacting*; *exacting work*.
exac'tion *n.* **1** the act of exacting. **2** an unreasonable amount of work, money, etc. forced from someone.
exac'titude *(-ti-tūd) n.* correctness.
exact'ly *adv.* in an exact manner.—*interj.* I completely agree!
exact'ness *n.*

exaggerate *ig-'zaj'ėr-āt*, *v.t.* to cause (something) to appear, or to describe it as, greater, etc. than it is.—*v.i.* to go beyond the truth in describing something:—*pr.p.* **exagg'erating**.
exaggerā'tion *n.*

exalt *ig-zölt'*, *v.t.* **1** to elevate in rank, etc. **2** to praise, glorify.
exaltā'tion *n.* **1** elevation. **2** glorification. **3** rapture.
exal'ted *adj.* of high rank; noble.

exam. See **examine**.

examine *ig-zam'in*, *v.t.* **1** to test. **2** to question. **3** to look closely into:—*pr.p.* **exam'ining**.
examinā'tion *n.* **1** close inspection. **2** a test of knowledge (also **exam'**). **3** formal questioning.
examinee' *(-ē') n.* one who is examined.
exam'iner *n.*

example *ig-zäm'pl*, *n.* **1** a specimen. **2** something that serves to illustrate a fact, etc. **3** a person or thing that is either a pattern or a warning.
exem'plar *n.* a model; an example.
exemplary *ig-zem'plȧr-i*, *adj.* **1** worthy of imitation: *exemplary behaviour.* **2** serving as a warning: *exemplary punishment.*
exem'plify *v.t.* to be an example of:—*pr.p.* **exem'plifying**; *pa.p.* **exem'plified** *(-fīd)*.
exemplificā'tion *(-fi-kā') n.*
make an example of to punish as a warning to others.

exasperate *ig-zäs'pėr-āt*, *v.t.* to irritate very much indeed:—*pr.p.* **exas'perating**.
exasperā'tion *n.*

excavate *eks'kȧ-vāt*, *v.t.* **1** to scoop out (a hole). **2** to dig out (soil). **3** to lay bare (buried ruins, etc.) by digging:—*pr.p.* **ex'cavating**.
excavā'tion *n.*
ex'cavātor *n.* **1** one who excavates. **2** a machine used for excavating.

exceed *ik-sēd'*, *v.t.* **1** to go beyond: *to exceed the speed limit.* **2** to be greater than. **3** to be too great for. **4** to be better than.
exceed'ingly *adv.* very.
See also **excess**.

excel *ik-sel'*, *v.t.* to be better than.—*v.i.* to be very good (at, in):—*pr.p.* **excell'ing**; *pa.p.* **excelled'**.
excellence *ek'sė-lėns*, *n.* unusual goodness or worth.
Excellency *(ek'-) n.* a title of honour, esp. for ambassadors and governors.
excellent *(ek'-) adj.* **1** unusually good. **2** of great virtue, worth, etc.
excellently *(ek'-) adv.*

except *ik-sept'*, *v.t.* to leave out.—*prep.* leaving out: *Everyone cheered except me*; *The story is correct*, *except that it was John*, *not Jim*, *who fell in*.
excep'ting *prep.* except.
excep'tion *n.* **1** the act of excepting. **2** something not included. **3** something not according to the rule.
excep'tional *adj.* unusual, remarkable.
excep'tionally *adv.*
except for apart from.
take exception to, at 1 to object to. **2** to take offence at.

excerpt *ek'sėrpt*, *n.* a passage taken from a book, etc., an extract.

excess *ik-ses'*, *n.* **1** a going beyond what is usual, or what is proper. **2** an extreme amount: *an excess of generosity.* **3** the amount by which one thing is greater than another.—*adj.* additional to what is normal or allowable.
excess'ive *adj.* beyond what is usual, right or proper, immoderate.
excess'ively *adv.* **excess'iveness** *n.*
in excess of more than.

exchange *iks-chānj'*, *v.t.* **1** to give or give up in return for something else. **2** to give and receive: *to exchange blows*, *news*:—*pr.p.* **exchang'ing.**—*n.* **1** the giving and taking of one thing for another. **2** a conversation or dispute. **3** the building where merchants, etc., meet for business. **4** the changing of the currency of one country for that of another. **5** a central office where telephone lines are connected.
exchange'able *adj.*

exchequer *iks-chek'ėr*, *n.* **1** a national treasury. **2** (*cap.*) the government department in charge of the nation's finances. **3** one's funds, finances.

excise[1] *ek-sīz'*, *ek'*, *n.* **1** a tax on certain goods produced within the country, and on licences. **2** the department concerned with such taxes.
excis'able *(-sīz') adj.* on which excise duty has to be paid.
excise'man *n.* an officer collecting excise.

excise[2] *ik-sīz'*, *v.t.* to cut out or off:—*pr.p.* **excis'ing.**
excision *ik-sizh'(ȯ)n*, *n.*

excite *ik-sīt'*, *v.t.* **1** to rouse (e.g. feelings). **2** to rouse strong feelings, esp. of pleasurable anticipation, in (someone). **3** to stir up (e.g. rebellion). **4** to produce electric or magnetic activity in:—*pr.p.* **excit'ing.**
excit'able *(-sīt') adj.* easily excited.
excitabil'ity *(-sīt-) n.* **excit'ed** *adj.*
excite'ment *n.* excited state, or something that causes it.
excit'ing *adj.*

exclaim *iks-klām'*, *v.i.* to say suddenly and loudly.—Also *v.t.*
exclamā'tion *(eks-klȧm-) n.* an uttered expression of surprise, strong protest, etc.
exclam'atory *(-klam') adj.*
exclama'tion-mark *n.* the mark following and showing an exclamation (!).

exclude *iks-klōōd'*, *v.t.* **1** to shut out. **2** to thrust out. **3** to except:—*pr.p.* **exclud'ing.**
exclud'ing *prep.* not including.
exclu'sion *n.*
exclusive *iks-klōō'siv*, *adj.* **1** shutting or leaving out. **2** limited to one individual or group: *an exclusive right.* **3** limited to a high social group: *an exclusive club.* **4** fashionable and expensive. **5** single, sole: *Fishing was his exclusive interest*.
exclusive of not including, not taking into account.

excommunicate *eks-kom-ū'ni-kāt*, *v.t.* to expel from the communion of the church:—*pr.p.* **excommu'nicating.**
excommunicā'tion *n.*

excrement. See **excrete.**

excrescence *iks-kres'ėns*, *n.* an abnormal outgrowth, e.g. a wart.
excres'cent *adj.* growing out.

excrete *iks-krēt'*, *v.t.* to separate and discharge (waste matter):—*pr.p.* **excret'ing.**
excrement *eks'krė-mėnt*, *n.* useless matter, esp. solid, discharged from the body, dung.
excrēt'a *n.pl.* poisonous or waste substances expelled from a cell, a tissue, or an animal body.
excrē'tion *n.*
excrēt'ory *adj.*

excruciating *iks-krōō'shi-ā-ting*, *adj.* extremely painful.
excru'ciātingly *adv.*

exculpate *eks'kul-pāt*, *v.t.* to clear from the charge of a fault or crime:—*pr.p.* **ex'culpating.**
exculpā'tion *n.*

excursion *iks-kûr'sh(ȯ)n*, *n.* a trip, esp. for a number of people, for pleasure or other purpose.

excuse *iks-kūz'*, *v.t.* **1** to free (a person) from blame or guilt. **2** to overlook (a fault). **3** to free from a duty or obligation: *I excused him from coming to the meeting.* **4** to ask permission to absent (oneself):—*pr.p.* **excus'ing.**—*n.* *(iks-kūs')* a reason for excusing, esp. one given by the offender.
excus'able *(-kūz') adj.* (*opp.* **inexcusable**).

execrate *eks'i-krāt*, *v.t.* **1** to curse. **2** to detest:—*pr.p.* **ex'ecrating.**
ex'ecrable *adj.* abominable, very bad.

ex'ecrably *adv.*
execrā'tion *n.* a cursing.

execute *eks'i-kūt, v.t.* **1** to perform, carry out: *to execute a command; She executed a pirouette.* **2** to put to death by law:—*pr.p.* **ex'ecuting.**
exec'utant *(-ek'ū-) n.* one who performs, esp. as a musician.
execu'tion *(-kū') n.* **execu'tioner** *n.*
exec'utive *adj.* concerned with management, or with putting laws or regulations into effect.—*n.* **1** the branch of the government that puts the laws into effect. **2** a person, or body of persons, that directs and manages.
exec'utor *n.* the person appointed to see a will carried into effect:—*fem.* **exec'utrix.**
exec'utory *adj.*

exemplar, exemplary, exemplify. See **example.**

exempt *ig-zem(p)t', v.t.* to free from a duty which other people have to carry out (e.g. military service, payment of taxes).—*adj.* freed, excused (from).
exemp'tion *n.*

exercise *eks'ėr-sīz, n.* **1** training by exertion or use of the body or mind. **2** a written school task. **3** (esp. in *pl.*) a movement designed to train the body. **4** an act of worship.—*v.t.* **1** to train by use; to give exercise to. **2** to use: *to exercise care, common sense; to exercise one's right to vote.* **3** to worry: *He was exercised about the loss of time.*—*v.i.* to train, exercise the body:—*pr.p.* **ex'ercising.**

exert *ig-zûrt', v.t.* to bring into action (e.g. strength, influence).
exer'tion *n.* **1** the act of bringing into active use. **2** an effort.

ex gratia *eks grā'shi-ȧ,* as a favour, not out of obligation.

exhale *eks-hāl', eg-zāl', v.t.* and *v.i.* **1** to breathe out. **2** to give off, or to rise as, vapour, smell, etc.:—*pr.p.* **exhal'ing.**
exhalation *eks-(h)ȧ-lā'sh(ȯ)n, egz-ȧ-, n.*

exhaust *ig-zöst', v.t.* **1** to empty (a vessel, e.g. a cask). **2** to use up completely (e.g. air, one's supplies, one's strength). **3** to tire out. **4** to say all that can be said about (a subject of discussion).—*n.* **1** the part of an engine through which waste from the working fluid escapes. **2** the waste so escaping.
exhaus'ted *adj.* **1** used up. **2** empty. **3** extremely tired.
exhaus'tion *n.*
exhaus'tive *adj.* very thorough.

exhibit *ig-zib'it, v.t.* **1** to show. **2** to show to the public.—*n.* **1** (*law*) a document or an article produced in court to be used as evidence. **2** an article at an exhibition.
exhibi'tion *(eks-i-) n.* **1** a showing, display. **2** a public show, esp. of works of art, manufactures, etc. **3** an allowance towards support given to a student (usu. competed for).
exhibi'tionism *n.* purposely behaving in such a way as to attract attention to oneself.
exhibi'tionist *n.*
exhib'itor *n.* one who provides an exhibit for a display, etc.

exhilarate *ig-zil'ȧ-rāt, v.t.* to make merry or very lively:—*pr.p.* **exhil'arating.**
exhilarā'tion *n.*

exhort *ig-zört', v.t.* to urge strongly and earnestly.
exhortā'tion *(eg-zör-) n.*

exhume *ig-zūm, v.t.* to dig out (esp. a body from a grave):—*pr.p.* **exhum'ing.**
exhumā'tion *n.*

exigency *ig-zij'en-si, n.* (often in *pl.*) urgent need: *He was forced by the exigencies of the situation to sell his house:*—*pl.* **exig'encies.**

exiguous *ig-zig'ū-ůs, adj.* scanty, mean.

exile *eks'īl,* or *egz'īl, n.* **1** (one who experiences) long absence from country or home. **2** banishment.—*v.t.* to expel, send (someone) away, from his country:—*pr.p.* **ex'iling.**

exist *ig-zist', v.i.* **1** to be. **2** to live. **3** to continue to live.
exist'ence *n.*
exist'ent *adj.* existing, esp. now.
existen'tialism *n.* a philosophy emphasising freedom of choice and personal responsibility for one's own future and moral development.
existen'tialist *adj.* and *n.*

exit *eks'it, egz', n.* **1** a departure, esp. of a player from the stage. **2** death. **3** a way out.—*v.i.* to go out (the Latin word *exit* is used as a stage direction usu. *exit so-and-so,* so-and-so goes off).

exodus *eks'ȯ-důs, n.* a going out, esp. (*cap.*) that of the Israelites from Egypt.

ex officio *eks ȯ-fish'i-ō,* because, as a result, of one's office or position.

exonerate *ig-zon'ėr-āt, v.t.* to free from blame, acquit:—*pr.p.* **exon'erating.**
exonerā'tion *n.*

exorbitant *ig-zör'bi-tȧnt, adj.* (of prices or demands) very high or unreasonable.
exor'bitance, exor'bitancy *ns.*

exorcise *eks'ȯr-sīz, v.t.* to drive away (an evil spirit):—*pr.p.* **ex'orcising.**
ex'orcist *(-sist) n.*

exotic *ig-zot'ik*, *adj.* **1** introduced from a foreign country: *an exotic plant.* **2** (*coll.*) very unusual, colourful.—Also *n.*

expand *iks-pand'*, *v.t.* and *v.i.* **1** to spread out. **2** to make, or grow, larger. **3** to tell, or speak, in greater detail.
expanse' *n.* a wide area or extent: *He saw only an expanse of ocean.*
expan'sion *n.* expanding; increase in size or bulk.
expan'sive *adj.* **1** able to expand. **2** wide. **3** (of a person) expressing feelings freely, telling much.

expatiate *iks-pā'shi-āt*, *v.i.* to talk, write, at length (on a subject):—*pr.p.* **expa'tiating.**

expatriate *eks-pā'tri-āt*, *v.t.* to send (someone) out of his country; to exile (oneself):—*pr.p.* **expa'triating.**—*adj.* and *n.* *(-tri-it)* expatriated (person).
expatriā'tion *n.*

expect *iks-pekt'*, *v.t.* **1** to look forward to as likely to happen. **2** to look for as one's due: *I expect gratitude for my help.* **3** (*coll.*) to suppose.
expec'tant *adj.* looking or waiting for something to happen.
expec'tancy *n.* **1** the state of expecting. **2** hopefulness.
expectā'tion *(eks-)* *n.* **1** the state of expecting. **2** something expected. **3** (in *pl.*) the prospect of good fortune, esp. through a will.

expectorate *iks-pek'tȯ-rāt*, *v.t.* and *v.i.* **1** to expel (phlegm) by coughing, etc. **2** (*coll.*) to spit:—*pr.p.* **expec'torating.**
expectorā'tion *n.*

expedient *iks-pē'di-ėnt*, *adj.* suitable, advisable, advantageous (sometimes used of actions that are not very just or upright):—*opp.* **inexpedient.**—*n.* a contrivance, emergency measure.
expē'dience, expē'diency *ns.* **1** advisability. **2** a regard for what is advantageous to oneself.

expedite *eks'pi-dīt*, *v.t.* to hasten, speed up:—*pr.p.* **ex'pediting.**
expedi'tion *(-di')* *n.* **1** speed, promptness. **2** an organised journey with a purpose. **3** those making such a journey.
expedi'tionary *adj.* of an expedition.
expedi'tious *(-di')* *adj.* speedy.

expel *iks-pel'*, *v.i.* **1** to drive out. **2** to banish:—*pr.p.* **expell'ing**; *pa.p.* **expelled'.**
expulsion *iks-pul'sh(ȯ)n*, *n.*

expend *iks-pend'*, *v.t.* to spend (e.g. money, time, energy, on something).
expend'able *adj.* that may be sacrificed, esp. in war to gain e.g. time.
expen'diture *(-chůr)* *n.* **1** the act of expending. **2** money spent.
expense' *n.* **1** cost. **2** a cause of spending: *A house is a continual expense.* **3** (in *pl.*) sums spent in the execution of a commission, duty, etc.
expen'sive *adj.* costly, dear.

experience *iks-pē'ri-ėns*, *n.* **1** practical knowledge gained by trial or observation (*opp.* **inexperience**). **2** an event by which one is affected, from which one learns.—*v.t.* **1** to meet with, undergo. **2** to feel:—*pr.p.* **expe'riencing.**
expe'rienced *(-pē'-)* *adj.* taught by experience—skilful, wise.

experiment *iks-per'i-mėnt*, *n.* something done in the hope of making a discovery, or as a test.—*v.i.* **1** to search for knowledge by trial. **2** to do experiments (on, with).
experiment'al *adj.* **1** relating to, used for, based on, experiment. **2** done as an experiment: *an experimental flight.*
experiment'ally *adv.*

expert *eks'pûrt*, *adj.* skilled through training or practice: *She's expert at map-reading*; *an expert car-designer*; *expert advice*:—*opp.* **inexpert.**—*n.* one who is expert.
expertise *eks-pėr-tēz'*, *n.* expertness.
ex'pertly *adv.* **ex'pertness** *n.*

expiate *eks'pi-āt*, *v.t.* to pay the penalty of; to make up for (wrong one has done):—*pr.p* **ex'piating.**
expiā'tion *n.*

expire *iks-pīr'*, *v.i.* **1** to die. **2** to end: *My leave expires tomorrow.* **3** (of a ticket, licence, etc.) to become out of date:—*pr.p.* **expi'ring.**
expirā'tion *(eks-)* *n.* the act of expiring.
expi'ry *(-pī')* *n.* the end (of a period of time, or of an agreement—e.g. a truce—with a time limit).

explain *iks-plān'*, *v.t.* **1** to make clear, easy to understand. **2** to be, give, a reason for: *That explains his silence.*
explanation *eks-plȧ-nā'sh(ȯ)n*, *n.* **1** the act of explaining. **2** a statement, fact, etc., that explains.
explan'atory *(-plan')* *adj.* giving an explanation.
See also **explicable.**

expletive *eks-plē'tiv*, *n.* a meaningless oath or exclamation.

explicable *eks'plik-ȧ-bl*, or *iks-plik'*, *adj.* capable of being explained:—*opp.* **inexplicable.**

explicit *iks-plis'it*, *adj.* **1** distinctly stated: *explicit instructions.* **2** outspoken, leaving nothing to the imagination:—*opp.* **inexplicit.**
explic'itly *adv.* **explic'itness** *n.*

explode *iks-plōd'*, *v.t.* **1** to cause to blow up. **2** to show to be wrong, and reject (e.g. a theory).—*v.i.* **1** to burst with a loud report. **2** to burst out (e.g. into laughter). **3** (of a population, etc.) to increase with startling rapidity:—*pr.p.* **explod'ing**.
explosion *iks-plō'zh(ȯ)n*, *n.* **1** the act of exploding. **2** a sudden burst with a loud noise. **3** an outburst of feelings, etc. **4** a sudden startling increase.
explo'sive *(-plō'siv, ziv) adj.* **1** liable to explode. **2** bursting out with violence and noise. **3** (of a situation, etc.) fraught with danger.—*n.* something that will explode.
high explosive a material with very violent explosive effect.

exploit *eks'ploit*, *n.* a (daring) deed or action.—*v.t.* *(iks-ploit')* **1** to work, use (e.g. natural resources). **2** to make selfish gain out of (e.g. a person).
exploitā'tion *(eks-) n.* the act of exploiting.

explore *iks-plōr'*, *-plör'*, *v.t.* **1** to travel or search through for the purpose of discovery. **2** to examine thoroughly.—Also *v.i.*: —*pr.p.* **explor'ing**.
explorā'tion *(-plor-ā') n.*
explor'atory *(-plor'ȧ-) adj.* exploring, esp. investigating.
explor'er *n.*

explosion, explosive. See **explode**.

exponent *iks-pōn'ėnt*, *n.* **1** one who explains, is supporter of (a theory, belief). **2** one who shows the meaning and value of works of others (e.g. who interprets music by playing it). **3** (*mathematics*) a symbol showing the power to which a quantity is to be taken.
exponen'tial *adj.* (*mathematics*, etc.) involving an exponent, i.e. (of an increase, etc.) ever more rapid.
See also **exposition.**

export *iks-pōrt'*, *-pört'*, *v.t.* to carry or send (goods) out of a country.—*n.* *(eks'pōrt, -pört)* **1** the act of exporting. **2** something that is exported.
exportā'tion *n.* **export'er** *n.*

expose *iks-pōz'*, *v.t.* **1** to leave unprotected, lay open (to e.g. attack, the weather, observation). **2** to make publicly known (crime, folly, an imposter, etc.). **3** to exhibit to public view. **4** to subject (film, etc.) to the action of light:—*pr.p.* **expos'ing**.
exposé *iks-pō'zā*, *n.* a usu. outspoken account.
exposure *iks-pō'zhu̇r*, *n.* **1** exposing or being exposed. **2** lack of protection from harsh weather conditions. **3** the act of exposing photographic film or plate to light, or the length of time this is done.

exposition *eks-pȯ-zish(ȯ)n*, *n.* **1** a public exhibition. **2** a detailed explanation or account (of a subject).

expostulate *iks-post'ū-lāt*, *v.i.* **1** to protest, object. **2** to argue, remonstrate (with):—*pr.p.* **expos'tulating**.
expostulā'tion *n.*

expound *iks-pownd'*, *v.t.* **1** to present in detail (e.g. a theory). **2** to explain fully.

express *iks-pres'*, *v.t.* **1** to press or force out. **2** to put into words: *Try to express the idea more simply.* **3** (**express oneself**) to put one's thought, feeling, into words. **4** (of e.g. a look) to show (e.g. an emotion).—*adj.* (used only before a noun) clearly stated: *my express wish.* **2** sole, particular: *my express purpose in telephoning.* **3** delivered by special messenger. **4** travelling, operating at high speed.—*adv.* **1** with haste. **2** by express train or special messenger.—*n.* **1** a very fast train, etc. **2** a fast delivery service.
express'ion *(-presh'(ȯ)n) n.* **1** forcing out by pressure. **2** showing meaning, feeling, by means of language, art, one's face, etc. **3** the look on one's face. **4** show of feeling in the performance of music. **5** a word, phrase: *You use too many slang expressions.* **6** (*mathematics*) a group of symbols together indicating a quantity.
express'ive *adj.* **1** expressing, being evidence (of): *a look expressive of annoyance.* **2** expressing meaning or feeling clearly: *an expressive voice.*
express'ively *adv.* **express'iveness** *n.*
express'ly *adv.* **1** in clear words, definitely: *I told you expressly to put it away.* **2** purposely, solely: *I went expressly to tell her this.*
See also **inexpressible**.

expropriate *eks-prō'pri-āt*, *v.t.* to take (property) from its owner:—*pr.p.* **expro'-priating**.
expropriā'tion *n.*

expulsion. See **expel**.

expunge *iks-punj'*, *v.t.* to erase, take out (e.g. from a list):—*pr.p.* **expun'ging**.

expurgate *eks'pu̇r-gāt*, *v.t.* to remove anything supposedly harmful or offensive from (a book, etc.):—*pr.p.* **ex'purgating**.
expurgā'tion *n.*

exquisite *eks'kwi-zit*, or *iks-kwiz'*, *adj.* **1** (of e.g. workmanship) of great excellence. **2** very beautiful. **3** (of pain or pleasure) extreme.
ex'quisitely (or *-kwiz'*) *adv*.

ex-serviceman, -woman *eks-sûr'vis-mȧn, -woom-ȧn, ns.* one formerly in one of the fighting services.

extant *iks-stant'*, *adj.* still existing.

extempore *iks-tem'pȯ-ri*, *adv.* on the spur of the moment, without preparation.—*adj.* composed and delivered or performed in this way.
extemporā'neous, **extem'porary** *adjs.*
extem'porise *v.i.* to speak, or compose and play, extempore:—*pr.p.* **extem'-porising.**
extemporisā'tion *n.*

extend *iks-tend'*, *v.t.* **1** to stretch out. **2** to make longer: *to extend the time.* **3** to make cover a larger area or greater number of things: *to extend one's power, the meaning of a term.* **4** to hold out (e.g. the hand). **5** to offer (e.g. sympathy).—*v.i.* to stretch, reach.
exten'sion *n.* **1** the act of extending. **2** a part added, e.g. to a building. **3** a supplementary telephone line. **4** instruction provided by a university for students not actually attending it.
exten'sive *adj.* **1** wide: *an extensive area, search.* **2** large in amount: *extensive purchases, knowledge.*
extent' *n.* **1** length, area, or volume. **2** scope, range: *to the full extent of his power.*
extended play (of a gramophone record) usu. 7 in. (18cm.) in diameter, with several tracks.
to a certain, some, extent within certain limits: *This is to some extent true.*

extenuate *iks-ten'ū-āt*, *v.t.* to make (a crime, etc.) seem less serious by showing that there was some excuse for it:—*pr.p.* **exten'uating.**
extenuā'tion *n.*

exterior *iks-tē'ri-ȯr*, *adj.* **1** outer. **2** outside.—*n.* the outside (of something).

exterminate *iks-tûr'mi-nāt*, *v.t.* to destroy utterly (e.g. vermin in a building, etc.):—*pr.p.* **exter'minating.**
exterminā'tion *n.* **exter'minātor** *n.*

external *iks-tûr'nȧl*, *adj.* **1** outside; on the outside: *a lotion for external application.* **2** outside oneself: *the external world.* **3** (of trade) foreign.—*n.* (in *pl.*) the outward parts, circumstances, etc.

extinct *iks-tingkt'*, *adj.* **1** (of fire, life) out, gone, dead. **2** (of a volcano) no longer erupting. **3** (of a kind of animal, etc.) no longer existing.
extinc'tion *n.*

extinguish *iks-ting'gwish*, *v.t.* **1** to put out (a fire, a light). **2** to destroy (e.g. hope).
extin'guisher *n.* a spraying device for putting out fire.
See also **extinct.**

extirpate *eks'tûr-pāt*, *v.t.* to destroy totally, root out, exterminate:—*pr.p.* **ex'tirpating.**
extirpā'tion *n.*

extol *iks-tōl'*, *v.t.* to praise highly:—*pr.p.* **extoll'ing**; *pa.p.* **extolled'.**

extort *iks-tört'*, *v.t.* to obtain (from a person) by threats or violence: *to extort a promise, a confession, money.*
extor'tion *n.* **1** the crime or practice of extorting. **2** a much too great charge.
extor'tionate *adj.* (of a price) much too high.
extor'tioner *n.*

extra *eks'trȧ*, *adj.* **1** more than the usual or the necessary. **2** additional.—*adv.* unusually.—*n.* **1** what is extra. **2** something charged additionally. **3** a special edition of newspaper, etc. **4** a film actor temporarily engaged to be one of a crowd.

extra- *pfx.* outside; beyond.

extract *iks-trakt'*, *v.t.* **1** to draw out, esp. by force (e.g. a tooth, money, a confession). **2** to select (passages from a book, etc.). **3** to take out (a substance forming part of a mixture or compound) by chemical or physical means.—*n.* *(eks'trakt)* **1** anything drawn from a substance by heat, distillation, etc., as an essence. **2** a passage taken from a book, etc.
extrac'tion *n.* **1** the act of extracting. **2** descent: *He is of Greek extraction.*
extrac'tor *n.* **1** one who, or that which, extracts. **2** a fan or other device for removing stale air, etc. from a room, etc.

extracurric'ular *eks'trȧ-kur-ik'ū-lȧr*, *adj.* additional to the school or university curriculum.

extradition *eks-trȧ-dish'(ȯ)n*, *n.* delivering up by one government to another of fugitives from justice.
ex'tradite *(-trȧ-dīt)* *v.t.*:—*pr.p.* **ex'tra-diting.**

extramural *eks-trȧ-mūr'ȧl*, *adj.* (of teachers, teaching) connected with a university but not under its direct control.

extraneous *iks-trān'yus*, *adj.* coming from outside and not belonging: *extraneous matter in the soup.*

extraordinary *iks-trörd'nȧr-i*, or *-di-nȧr-*, *adj.* **1** not usual or regular. **2** wonderful, surprising. **3** (used after a noun) additional: *envoy extraordinary.*
extraor'dinarily *adv.*
extraor'dinariness *n.*

extra-sensory *eks-trȧ-sen'sȯ-ri*, *adj.* (of perceptive ability, etc.) beyond the scope of the normal senses.

extra-terrestrial *eks-trȧ-tėr-est'ri-ȧl*, *n.*, *adj.* (a being) coming from outside the planet Earth.

extravagant *iks-trav'à-gànt, adj.* **1** spending too freely. **2** wasteful. **3** (of e.g. grief, praise) too great.
extrav'agance *n.*
extravaganza *iks-trav-à-gan'zȧ, n.* a drama, display, outfit, etc. that is highly colourful and fanciful.

extravert. See **extrovert**.

extreme *iks-trēm', adj.* **1** (used only before a noun) far from the centre. **2** far from the ordinary or normal. **3** very great: *extreme pain.—n.* **1** the farthest point. **2** the highest degree: *foolish in the extreme.*
extreme'ly *adv.* **extreme'ness** *n.*
extrē'mism *n.* the views of an extremist.
extrē'mist *n.* a person who holds extreme views or is ready to use extreme measures.
extremity *(-trem'i-ti) n.* **1** the utmost limit; the highest degree. **2** great need or distress. **3** (in *pl.*) hands or feet:—*pl.* **extrem'ities**.
the extreme penalty death, execution.
extreme unction. See **unction**.

extricate *eks'tri-kāt, v.t.* **1** to free (from difficulties). **2** to disentangle:—*pr.p.* **ex'tricating**.
extricā'tion *n.*
See also **inextricable**.

extrovert *eks'trō-vûrt,* **extravert** *-trà-, n.* one whose interests are in matters outside himself, who communicates easily with others—opp. to *introvert.*—Also *adj.*

extrude *iks-trōōd', v.t.* to force or thrust out:—*pr.p.* **extrud'ing**.
extrusion *eks-trōō'zh(ȯ)n, n.*

exuberant *igz-ū'bėr-ànt,* or *-ōō', adj.* **1** luxuriant; overflowing. **2** showing, or in, high spirits.
exu'berance, exu'berancy *ns.*

exude *igz-ūd', v.t.* to give off by, or as if by, sweating:—*pr.p.* **exud'ing**.

exult *igz-ult', v.i.* **1** to rejoice greatly (at a happening). **2** to triumph (over e.g. a defeated rival).
exul'tant *adj.* **exultā'tion** *n.*

eye *ī, n.* **1** the bodily organ by which we see. **2** anything like an eye, as the hole of a needle, loop or ring for a hook, etc. **3** a bud on a potato tuber. **4** the calm centre of a cyclone:—*pl.* **eyes** *(īz).—v.t.* **1** to look at. **2** to observe closely:—*pr.p.* **eye'ing** or **ey'ing**; *pa.p.* **eyed** *(īd).*
eye'ball *n.* the globe of the eye.
eye'brow *n.* a hairy arch above the eye.
eye'lash *n.* one of the hairs that edge the eyelid.
eyelet. See below.
eye'lid *n.* the cover of the eye.
eye'liner *n.* a cosmetic for outlining the eye.
eye'-o'pener *n.* something astonishing.
eye'piece *n.* the lens or lenses of a telescope, etc. to which the eye is applied.
eye'shadow *n.* a coloured cosmetic for the eyelid.
eye'sight *n.* the power of seeing.
eye'sore *n.* something unpleasant to look at.
eye'tooth *n.* an upper canine tooth.
eye'wash *n.* **1** a lotion for the eye. **2** nonsense.
eye'witness *n.* one who sees a thing happen.
make eyes at to ogle.
see eye to eye with (someone) to agree with (someone).
with an eye to (something) with (something) in view.

eyelet *ī'lit, n.* a small hole for a lace or cord in a garment, sail, etc.

eyrie, eyry. Same as **aerie**.

F

fable *fā'bl, n.* **1** a short story, often with animal characters, intended to teach a moral lesson. **2** an untrue story.
fā'bled *(-bld) adj.* **1** mentioned in fable. **2** fictitious, imaginary.
fabulous *fab'ū-lus, adj.* **1** told of in fable. **2** imaginary. **3** very large, amazing. **4** (*coll.*) excellent.

fabric *fab'rik, n.* **1** cloth. **2** framework, structure (of a building, etc.).
fab'ricate *v.t.* to manufacture, make. **2** to make up (a false story, lie):—*pr.p.* **fab'-ricating.**
fabricā'tion *n.* **fab'ricator** *n.*

fabulous. See **fable**.

façade *fā-säd', n.* **1** the front of a building. **2** a deceptive appearance shown to the world: *He trembled behind a brave façade.*—Also **facade**.

face *fās, n.* **1** the front part of the head from forehead to chin. **2** any surface: *the rock face; the face of the earth.* **3** appearance. **4** impudence. **5** a grimace: *He made a face at me*:—*v.t.* **1** to be opposite to. **2** to turn towards. **3** to stand up to, resist. **4** to be forced to tackle (a difficulty). **5** to put a surface on.—*v.i.* **1** to turn the face. **2** to take, have, a direction: *to face east.* **3** to stand (up to):—*pr.p.* **fac'ing.**
face'less *adj.* **1** with concealed identity. **2** (*slightingly*) acting in a robot-like impersonal way.
facial *fā'shȧl, adj.* of the face.
fac'ing *n.* a coating or decoration of different material.
face'-lift *n.* **1** an operation aimed at smoothing and firming the face. **2** the improvement of the outside of a building.
face value **1** the value as stated on the face of a coin, etc. **2** apparent value (of e.g. a promise, a result).
in (the) face of **1** in spite of. **2** when forced to meet, deal with (e.g. opposition).
lose face to suffer loss of dignity.
on the face of it as it appears at first glance (often deceptively).
save one's face to avoid openly appearing foolish or wrong (*n.* and *adj.* **face'-saving**).
set one's face against to oppose strongly.

facet *fas'it, n.* **1** a side of a many-sided object, as a crystal. **2** an aspect of a subject.
fac'eted *adj.*

facetious *fȧ-sē'shus, adj.* funny, joking.

facial. See **face**.

facile *fas'īl, il, adj.* **1** easy: *a facile victory.* **2** usu. too easy, not deep, thorough, or well thought out: *facile emotions, conclusions.* **3** fluent: *a facile tongue.*
facil'itate *v.t.* to make easier:—*pr.p.* **facil'itating.**
facility *fȧs-il'i-ti, n.* **1** ease and quickness. **2** something that makes an action possible or easier (usu. in *pl.*, **facil'ities**; e.g. *facilities for cooking*; *transport facilities*).

facing. See **face**.

facsimile *fak-sim'i-li, n.* an exact copy.

fact *fakt, n.* **1** anything known to have happened or to be true. **2** (*loosely*) anything supposed to be true and used in argument. **3** reality.
fac'tual *adj.* of, or containing, facts.
as a matter of fact, in fact in reality.
the fact of the matter the plain truth.

faction *fak'sh(ȯ)n, n.* **1** a group of people (part of a larger group) acting together (mostly used in a bad sense). **2** strife between parties, e.g. in the state.
fac'tious *fak'shus, adj.* disloyal, rebellious.

factor *fak'tȯr, n.* **1** one who does business for another. **2** one of two or more quantities, which, when multiplied together, produce a given quantity: *2, 3, and 5 are factors of 30.* **3** any circumstance that influences the course of events.
fac'tory *n.* a building where goods are manufactured:—*pl.* **fac'tories.**

factotum *fak-tō'tum, n.* a person employed to do all kinds of work.

factual. See **fact**.

faculty *fak'ul-ti, n.* **1** a power of the mind (e.g. reason). **2** a natural power of the body (e.g. hearing). **3** ability, knack. **4** a group of related departments of study in a university: *the faculty of medicine.* **5** the members of a profession:—*pl.* **fac'ulties.**

fad *fad, n.* a whim, craze.
fadd'ish, fadd'y (*comp.* **-ier**; *superl.* **-iest**) *adjs.*
fadd'iness *n.*

fade *fād, v.i.* **1** to lose freshness, colour, or strength of body. **2** to die away.—*v.t.* to cause (an image or a sound) to become gradually less distinct or loud (also **fade out**) or more distinct or loud (also **fade in**):—*pr.p.* **fad'ing.**

faeces *fē'sēz, n.pl.* solid excrement.
faecal *fē'kȧl, adj.*

fag *fag, v.i.* **1** to become weary. **2** to work hard. **3** to be a schoolboy fag.—*v.t.* to weary:—*pr.p.* **fagg'ing**; *pa.p.* **fagged**.—*n.* **1** a schoolboy forced by tradition to do jobs for an older boy. **2** hard work unwillingly done. **3** (*slang*) a cigarette.
fag'-end *n.* **1** the butt of a cigarette. **2** *(-end')* the last, least good part.

fag(g)ot *fag'ȯt, n.* a bundle of sticks.

Fahrenheit *far'ėn-hīt, fär', adj.* (of a temperature scale or thermometer) having the freezing point of water marked at 32° and the boiling point at 212°.

fail *fāl, v.i.* **1** to become less strong. **2** (of heart) to stop (see **heart**). **3** to become less, or too little, in quantity: *The stream failed.* **4** to be unsuccessful: *The attack failed*; *He failed in his test.* **5** to neglect (to do something). **6** to become bankrupt.—*v.t.* **1** to be lacking to: *Words fail me.* **2** to disappoint or desert (a person). **3** to reject (an examination candidate) as not good enough. **4** to be rejected as not good enough in (an examination) (also *n.*).
fail'ing *n.* a fault, weakness.—*prep.* if the thing mentioned is lacking: *Failing help from outside, the fort must surrender.*—*adj.* that fails.
fail'ure *n.* **1** lack of success. **2** an unsuccessful person. **3** stoppage: *heart failure.* **4** neglect to carry out an action: *failure to reply.* **5** bankruptcy.
fail'-safe *adj.* incorporated, or with something incorporated, to prevent an accident in the case of a breakdown.
without fail definitely, certainly.

fain *fān,* (*old*) *adv.* gladly (only in *would fain do*, etc.)

faint *fānt, adj.* **1** lacking in strength. **2** dim. **3** lacking courage: *a faint heart.* **4** about to faint.—*v.i.* **1** to lose courage. **2** to swoon, become unconscious (also *n.*).
faint'ly *adv.* **faint'ness** *n.*
faint'-heart'ed *adj.* lacking in spirit, cowardly.

fair[1] *fār, adj.* **1** bright. **2** clear. **3** beautiful. **4** of a light hue. **5** free from clouds and rain. **6** (of promises, etc.) seeming good, but not sincere. **7** just: *a fair division of work.* **8** pretty good.—*v.i.* (of weather) to become clear.—Also *adv.*: *fair and square.*
fair'ly *adv.* **1** in a fair way. **2** completely, fully. **3** to some extent.
fair'ness *n.*
fair copy a corrected version free from errors.
fair'-spok'en *adj.* **1** pleasant, courteous. **2** pleasant, but insincere or deceitful.
fair'way *n.* **1** the channel by which vessels enter or leave a harbour. **2** any clear course. **3** the smooth turf of a golf-course between tee and green.
fair and square **1** honestly. **2** straight: *He hit him fair and square.*
play fair. See **play**.
the fair sex the female sex.

fair[2] *fār, n.* **1** a market of importance held at fixed times. **2** an exhibition of goods from different firms, countries, etc. **3** a bazaar for charity, etc., often with amusements.

fairy *fār'i, n.* an imaginary small being in human form:—*pl.* **fair'ies**.—*adj.* like a fairy, fanciful, delicate.
fair'yland *n.* the country of fairies.
fairy lights tiny coloured lights used as decorations.
fairy ring, circle a circle in a pasture due to fungi.
fairy story, tale **1** a story about fairies. **2** an untrue, unbelievable tale.

faith *fāth, n.* **1** trust, confidence. **2** trust in God. **3** a belief in religion. **4** a religion. **5** loyalty to one's promise: *to keep, break, faith with someone.*
faith'ful *adj.* **1** believing. **2** keeping one's promises. **3** loyal. **4** true, accurate.
faith'fully *adv.* **faith'fulness** *n.*
faith'less *adj.* **1** not believing, esp. in God. **2** false. **3** disloyal.
faith'-healing or **-cure** *n.* belief in, or a system or instance of, curing sickness through prayer and faith alone, without medicine, etc.
bad faith treachery.
in good faith with sincerity, not intending to deceive.
the faithful believers.
See also **fidelity**.

fake *fāk, v.t.* **1** to make (something that pretends to be more valuable than it is): *to fake a picture, a piece of old jewellery.* **2** to produce a false appearance of: *to fake a burglary*:—*pr.p.* **fak'ing**.—*n.* **1** something faked. **2** a person who fakes. **3** an impostor.—Also *adj.*

fakir *fa-kēr', fā'kir, n.* a (esp. Muslim) religious beggar in India, etc.

falcon *föl'kȯn, fö'kn, n.* a long-winged hawk that usu. strikes its prey from above, esp. one trained to hunt game.
fal'coner *n.* one who hunts with falcons.
fal'conry *n.* hunting with falcons.

fall *föl, v.i.* **1** to drop from a height. **2** to collapse. **3** to die in battle. **4** to be overthrown. **5** (of a beseiged place) to be captured. **6** (of wind, water) to go down, sink. **7** to become less high: *Prices fell.* **8** (of the face) to show disappointment. **9** (of the eyes) to be lowered. **10** (of an eye, glance) to come by chance (on). **11** to flow, or slope, downwards. **12** to hang down. **13** to yield to temptation. **14** to pass into any state, to become: *to fall asleep*; *to fall in love*; *to fall due.* **15** to occur. **16** to come (to one) as one's share, duty, etc. **17** to begin energetically: *to fall to work*, *to complaining* (see also **fall to** below):—*pr.p.* **fall'ing**; *pa.t.* **fell**; *pa.p.* **fall'en**.—*n.* **1** the act of falling. **2** overthrow. **3** a drop from a higher to a lower, or a better to a worse, position or state. **4** something that falls: *a fall of snow.* **5** (usu. in *pl.*) water descending. **6** (esp. *U.S.*) autumn.

fall'-out *n.* radioactive dust from a nuclear explosion or an atomic power plant.

fall back to retreat.

fall back (up)on 1 to retreat to. **2** to use, etc. (something) for want of something better.

fall behind 1 to make too little progress. **2** to get in arrears (with e.g. payments).

fall flat to fail completely, have no effect.

fall for 1 to fall in love. **2** to be fooled by (a trick).

fall foul of. See **foul**.

fall in to take places in ranks.

fall in with 1 to meet by chance. **2** to act in agreement with: *to fall in with his wishes.*

fall off 1 to become less good. **2** to die away. **3** to desert (from e.g. an allegiance).

fall on 1 to begin eagerly. **2** to begin to eat. **3** to attack.

fall on one's feet to be lucky.

fall out 1 to quarrel. **2** to happen. **3** to leave ranks.

fall over oneself to be in great haste or eagerness (to do something).

fall through to come to nothing.

fall to 1 to begin e.g. a task hastily and eagerly. **2** to begin to eat: *Bring in breakfast and fall to.*

fallacy *fal'ȧ-si*, *n.* **1** an unsound argument. **2** a false idea or belief:—*pl.* **fall'acies**.

fallacious *fȧ-lā'shus*, *adj.* **1** misleading, false. **2** not showing sound reasoning.

fallen. See **fall**.

fallible *fal'i-bl*, *adj.* liable to make mistakes, or to be mistaken:—*opp.* **infallible**.

fallibil'ity *n.*

fallow[1] *fal'ō*, *adj.* left uncultivated or unsowed for a time.—*n.* land left thus for a year or more.—*v.t.* to plough (land) without seeding it.

fallow[2] *fal'ō*, *adj.* yellowish-brown.

fallow deer a yellowish-brown deer smaller than the red deer.

false *föls*, *fols*, *adj.* **1** wrong. **2** purposely untrue: *to bear false witness.* **3** deceiving. **4** untruthful. **5** unfaithful. **6** not genuine or real. **7** (of teeth, etc.) artificial.

false'ly *adv.*

false'hood *n.* **1** lying, deceitfulness. **2** a lie.

false'ness, **fal'sity** *ns.*

falsify *föls'i-fī*, *fols'*, *v.t.* **1** to alter (a document) so as to deceive. **2** to represent incorrectly or falsely. **3** to disappoint (one's hopes):—*pr.p.* **fal'sifying**; *pa.p.* **fal'sified**.

fal'sifiable *adj.* **falsificā'tion** *n.*

play false. See **play**.

falsetto *föl-set'ō*, *fol-*, *n.* a forced voice of a range or register above the natural, esp. in a man:—*pl.* **falsett'os**.—Also *adj.*

falsifiable, **falsification**, **falsify**, **falsity**. See **false**.

falter *föl'tėr*, or *fol'*, *v.i.* **1** to stumble. **2** to speak with hesitation (also *v.t.*). **3** to waver.

fal'tering *adj.* **fal'teringly** *adv.*

fame *fām*, *n.* **1** reputation, esp. if good. **2** renown.

famed, **fām'ous** *adjs.* well-known, renowned.

fam'ously (*coll.*) *adv.* very well.

familiar *fȧ-mil'yȧr*, *adj.* **1** well-known: *a familiar sight.* **2** well-acquainted: *He was familiar with their customs.* **3** close, intimate: *a familiar friend.* **4** informal. **5** too free or intimate.—*n.* **1** a close friend. **2** an attendant spirit: *a witch's familiar*.

famil'iarly *adv.* **familiar'ity** *n.*

famil'iarise *v.t.* to make (a person) well-acquainted (with something):—*pr.p.* **famil'iarising**.

family *fam'i-li*, *n.* **1** parents and their children. **2** the children alone. **3** the descendants of one common ancestor. **4** a group of animals, plants, languages, etc. having a common origin:—*pl.* **fam'ilies**.

family planning birth control.

family tree a genealogical tree (see this).

famine *fam'in*, *n.* **1** extreme scarcity esp. of food. **2** hunger.

fam'ished *adj.* very hungry.

famous, famously. See **fame**.

fan[1] *fan*, *n.* **1** a moving device for causing a current of air. **2** a small hand device, usu. shaped like part of a circle, for cooling the face.—*v.t.* **1** to cool with a fan. **2** to increase the strength of: *This remark fanned the flames of his anger.* **3** to clean (grain) with a fan:—*pr.p.* **fann'ing**; *pa.p.* **fanned**.

fan'light *n.* a window above a door, esp. one shaped like a half circle.

fan'tail *n.* a pigeon with tail feathers spread out like a fan.
fan out to spread out in the shape of a fan.

fan[2] *fan, n.* (short for **fanatic**) an enthusiastic follower of some sport, or hobby, or public favourite.
fanatic *fȧ-nat'ik, n.* a person filled with unreasonably great enthusiasm for something.
fanat'ic(al) *adjs.* **fanat'ically** *adv.*
fanat'icism *(-is-izm) n.* excessive enthusiasm.

fancy *fan'si, n.* **1** power of the mind to imagine things, esp. things unlike reality. **2** an image in the mind. **3** an idea with little reality behind it. **4** a liking, inclination (for):—*pl.* **fan'cies**.—*adj.* ornamental, not plain:—*comp.* **fan'cier**; *superl.* **fan'ciest**.—*v.t.* **1** to picture, imagine. **2** to think without being sure. **3** to take or have a liking or inclination for. **4** to breed (animals, e.g. bird, or plants) so as to develop certain qualities:—*pr.p.* **fan'cying**: *pa.p.* **fan'cied**.
fan'cier *n.*
fan'ciful *adj.* **1** inclined to have fancies. **2** created by fancy.
fan'cifully *adv.*
fancy dress dress chosen according to fancy, e.g. to represent a character in history or fiction.

fanfare *fan'fār, n.* a flourish or call on trumpets or bugles.

fang *fang, n.* **1** a long pointed tooth. **2** a poison-bearing tooth of a snake. **3** the root of a tooth.
fanged *adj.* having fangs.

fanlight, fantail. See **fan**[1].

fantasia *fan-tā'zi-ȧ, fan-tȧ-zē'ȧ, n.* a musical composition in irregular form.

fantasy *fan'tȧ-zi, -si, n.* **1** fancy. **2** the forming of mental pictures, esp. when unreal. **3** an idea not based on reality:—*pl.* **fan'tasies**.
fan'tasise *v.i.* to have a fantasy or fantasies (about):—*pr.p.* **fan'tasising**.
fantas'tic *adj.* **1** unreal. **2** odd, unnatural. **3** unbelievable. **4** (*coll.*) great, excellent.—Also (*defs. 1,2*) **fantas'tical**.
fantas'tically *adv.*

far *fär, adj.* **1** distant. **2** more distant of two.—*adj.* **1** to, at, over, a great distance. **2** to, at, an advanced stage. **3** very much: *a far harder task*:—*comp.* **far'ther** (also, with additional meaning, **fur'ther**—see this word); *superls.* **far'thest** (also **fur'thest**), **far'thermost** (also **fur'thermost**).
far'away *adj.* **1** distant. **2** absent-minded, dreamy: *a faraway expression*.
Far East China, Japan, and other countries of E. and S.E. Asia.
far'-east'ern *adj.*
far'-fetched' *(-fecht') adj.* (of an argument, comparison, etc.) not natural, reasonable, or obvious.
far'-flung' *adj.* extending over a great distance.
far'-reach'ing *adj.* affecting a great number of things, affecting (things) to a great extent, etc.
far'-sight'ed *adj.* foreseeing what is likely to happen and preparing for it.
a far cry a long distance.
far and away, **by far** by a great deal.

farce *färs, n.* **1** a (style of) comedy depending on ridiculous situations. **2** something absurd. **3** a silly sham.
far'cical *(-si-kȧl) adj.* absurd.

fare *fār, v.i.* **1** (*old*) to travel. **2** to get on (well, ill). **3** (*old*) to be fed:—*pr.p.* **far'ing**.—*n.* **1** the price paid for travelling in a vehicle, ship, etc. **2** a passenger in a public conveyance. **3** food.
farewell' *interj.* goodbye.—*n.* **1** a well-wishing at parting. **2** departure.—*adj.* *(fār'wel')* **1** parting. **2** final.
fare with to turn out for: *I wonder how it fares with the travellers*.

farinaceous *far-i-nā'shu̇s, adj.* containing flour, meal, or starch.

farm *färm, n.* **1** a tract of land used for cultivation or pasturage. **2** land or water used for breeding animals (as *fox farm, oyster farm*).—*v.t.* **1** to cultivate (land). **2** to give, or to receive, a fixed payment in return for the right to collect (taxes). **3** to let or lease.—*v.i.* to run a farm.
farm'er *n.* **farm'ing** *n.* and *adj.*
farm'stead *n.* a farm with buildings belonging to it.
farm'yard *n.* the yard surrounded by farm buildings.
farm out to give work for which one is responsible to others to do.

farrago *fȧ-rä'gō,* or *-rā', n.* a confused mixture: *a farrago of lies*:—*pl.* **farra'goes**.

farrier *far'i-ėr, n.* **1** one who shoes horses. **2** one who treats horses' diseases.
farr'iery *n.* the farrier's art.

farrow *far'ō, n.* a litter of pigs.—*v.i.* or *v.t.* to bring forth (pigs).

farther, etc. See **far** and **further**.

farthing *fär'THing, n.* an old coin, the fourth of an old penny.

fascia *fā'shyȧ, n.* a dashboard (*def. 2*).

fascinate *fas'in-āt, v.t.* **1** to control by the eye as a snake does. **2** to charm, attract

irresistibly:—*pr.p.* **fas'cinating.**
fas'cinating *adj.* **fascinā'tion** *n.*

Fascism *fash'izm, n.* a system of right-wing, nationalistic government similar to that in Italy from 1922–1944, controlling everything and suppressing all criticism or opposition.
Fasc'ist *n.* and *adj.*

fashion *fash'(ȯ)n, n.* **1** the make or cut of a thing. **2** the exact shape in dress that is in favour at the time (also *adj.*) **3** the custom of the time. **4** manner: *He replied in an irritable fashion.—v.t.* **1** to make. **2** to shape, form (into, to).
fash'ionable *adj.* **1** following fashion or in use at the time. **2** following fashion in dress or living. **3** moving in high society.
after, in, a fashion **1** in a way. **2** to a certain extent.
in, out of, fashion fashionable, not fashionable.

fast[1] *fäst, adj.* **1** firm. **2** fixed. **3** steadfast: *a fast friend.* **4** (of a colour) unfading.—*adv.* **1** firmly. **2** sound: *fast asleep.*
fasten *fäs'n, v.t.* **1** to make fast. **2** to fix securely. **3** to attach.—Also *v.i.*
fastener *fäsn'ėr, n.* a clip, catch, or other means of fastening.
fas'tening *n.*
fast'ness *n.* **1** fixedness. **2** a stronghold, castle.
fasten (up)on **1** to direct (e.g. one's eyes) on. **2** to seize on (e.g. a fact, a statement). **3** to fix (something disagreeable—e.g. blame) on (someone).
make fast **1** to lock, bar. **2** to fasten up.
play fast and loose to act unscrupulously (from the name of a cheating game).

fast[2] *fäst, adj.* **1** quick, rapid. **2** (of a clock, etc.) showing a time in advance of the correct time. **3** dissipated.—Also *adv.*
fast food(s) types of food, such as chips, hamburgers, which can be prepared and served quickly.

fast[3] *fäst, v.i.* **1** to go hungry. **2** to eat no food, esp. as a religious duty.—Also *n.*
fast'ing *n.* and *adj.*

fasten, etc. See **fast**[1].

fastidious *fas-tid'i-ůs, adj.* **1** very critical, difficult to please (in e.g. one's taste in books, art, music). **2** very careful because easily disgusted: *fastidious about cleanliness.*
fastid'iously *adv.* **fastid'iousness** *n.*

fat *fat, adj.* **1** plump. **2** too plump. **3** fruitful, profitable:—*comp.* **fatt'er** *superl.* **fatt'est.**—*n.* **1** an oily substance under the skin. **2** solid animal oil. **3** the richest part of anything.
fatt'ed *adj.* made fat.
fat'ness *n.*
fatt'en *v.t., v.i.*, to make, or grow, fat.
fatt'y *adj.* containing, or like, fat:—*comp.* **fatt'ier**; *superl.* **fatt'iest**.
fatt'iness *n.*
fat-free' *adj.* (of food) having virtually all the fat removed.
fat'-head *n.* a stupid person.

fatal, etc. See **fate**.

fate *fāt, n.* **1** what is bound to happen, destiny, fortune. **2** ruin, death. **3** (*cap.*) any of the three goddesses controlling the birth, life, and death of man.
fat'al *(fāt') adj.* **1** causing death. **2** disastrous: *a fatal mistake.* **3** fateful.
fat'alism *n.* the belief that everything that is to happen has been prearranged, and that there is no good trying to influence events.
fat'alist *n.* **fatalist'ic** *adj.*
fatality *fȧ-tal'i-ti, n.* **1** the state of being unavoidable. **2** a death caused by accident:—*pl.* **fatal'ities**.
fated *fāt'id, adj.* **1** doomed. **2** destined (to): *He seemed fated to miss chances.*
fate'ful *adj.* important because deciding something: *The fateful day arrived.*

father *fä'THėr, n.* **1** a male parent. **2** an ancestor or forefather. **3** a protector. **4** a monk, priest, religious teacher. **5** the oldest member of any company. **6** one of the leading men in a city, etc. **7** the person who begins, founds, or first makes something: *J. L. Baird was the father of television.—v.t.* **1** to be the father of. **2** to be considered as the author or originator of.
fath'erhood *n.* the state of being a father.
fath'erly *adj.* of, like, or suitable in, a father.
fath'erliness *n.*
fath'er-in-law *n.* the father of one's husband or wife.
fath'erland *n.* one's native country.

fathom *faTH'ȯm, n.* a unit used in measuring depth = 6 feet, 1.83 m.—*v.t.* **1** to measure the depth of. **2** to understand, get to the bottom of.

fatigue *fȧ-tēg', n.* **1** weariness caused by hard work. **2** a soldier's task (not military) given to him as a punishment. **3** weakness (esp. of metals) caused by use.—*v.t.* and *v.i.* **1** to exhaust or become exhausted. **2** to weaken:—*pr.p.* **fatigu'ing**; *pa.p.* **fatigued'**.

fatuous *fat'ū-ůs, adj.* silly, idiotic.
fat'uousness, fatu'ity *ns.*

faucet *fö'sit, (U.S.) n.* a tap.

fault *fölt, folt, n.* **1** an error. **2** a blemish. **3** a slight offence. **4** (*geol.*) a fracture in the earth's crust.
fault'less *adj.* without fault, perfect.
fault'y *adj.* (*comp.* **-ier**; *superl.* **-iest**).
fault'iness *n.*
fault'-finder *n.* **fault'-finding** *n.* and *adj.*
at fault to blame, guilty.
find fault with to criticise, complain of (for *ns.* and *adj.*, see above).

faun *fön, n.* a Roman country god with a goat's legs and/or horns and a tail.
faun'a *n.* the animals (collectively) of a region or a period.

faux pas *fō pä,* a blunder, esp. something said that is indiscreet.

favour *fā'vȯr, n.* **1** goodwill. **2** approval. **3** a kind of deed. **4** the state of being approved: *in favour, out of favour.* **5** a knot of ribbons on a cake or worn at a wedding or an election:—*opp.* **disfavour** (*defs. 1,2, 4*).—*v.t.* **1** to regard with goodwill. **2** to be on the side of. **3** to prefer. **4** to be an advantage to, help towards: *The dark night favoured his escape.* **5** to oblige (with). **6** (*coll.*) to resemble.
fā'vourable *adj.* **1** showing goodwill or approval. **2** helpful, advantageous (to). **3** promising.
fā'vourably *adj.*
fā'voured *adj.* **1** preferred. **2** enjoying special advantages. **3** having a certain appearance (as in *ill-, well-, favoured*).
fā'vourite *n.* **1** a well, or best, liked person, thing, etc. **2** a person treated with too much friendliness. **3** one (esp. a horse) expected to win.
fā'vouritism *n.* unfair generosity to one rather than to another.
in favour of 1 in support of. **2** for the benefit of. **3** for the account of: *He drew a cheque in favour of John Smith.*

fawn¹ *fön, n.* **1** a young deer in its baby coat. **2** light yellowish-brown.—Also *adj.*

fawn² *fön, v.i.* **1** to show affection as a dog does. **2** to flatter in a too humble way (with *upon*).

fay¹ *fā, n.* a fairy.

fay². See **fey**.

fealty *fē'àl-ti, n.* loyalty of a vassal to his lord.

fear *fēr, n.* a painful emotion roused by danger or thought of danger.—*v.t.* **1** to expect with alarm. **2** to be regretfully inclined to think: *I fear you will not find him at home.*—*v.i.* to be afraid.
fear'ful *adj.* **1** full of fears, timid. **2** afraid (of something happening). **3** terrible. **4** (*coll.*) very bad.
fear'fully *adv.* **fear'fulness** *n.*
fear'less *adj.* daring, brave.
fear'some *adj.* causing fear, frightful.
for fear of in order not to: *for fear of losing it.*

feasible *fēz'i-bl, adj.* practicable, possible.
feas'ibleness, feasibil'ity, *ns.*

feast *fēst, n.* **1** an anniversary, esp. of a religious event, celebrated with solemnity or joy. **2** a large and rich meal. **3** rich enjoyment: *The scene was a feast for the eyes.*—Also *v.t.* and *v.i.*
festal *fes'tàl, adj.* **1** of, for, a feast. **2** gay.
See also **festival, festive,** etc.

feat *fēt, n.* a deed of great strength, skill, or courage.

feather *feTH'ėr, n.* **1** one of the growths that form the covering of a bird. **2** anything like a feather in appearance.—*v.t.* **1** to furnish or adorn with feathers. **2** to turn (an oar, etc.) edgewise to lessen air resistance. **3** to rotate (aircraft propeller blades, etc.) so as to reduce drag.
feath'ery *adj.* like feathers.
feath'eriness *n.*
feath'er-bed' *n.* a mattress filled with feathers.
feath'er-brain *n.* a frivolous person.
feath'erweight *n.* a boxer of not more than 9st (57.153kg).
a feather in one's cap an honour, cause for pride and pleasure.
feather one's nest to pile up wealth while holding a position of trust.
show the white feather to show cowardice.

feature *fē'chùr, n.* **1** a characteristic, quality. **2** a part of the face. **3** (in *pl.*) the face. **4** the main picture in a programme. **5** a special newspaper article.—*v.t.* and *v.i.* to give, or to have, an important part:—*pr.p.* **feat'uring.**
fea'tureless *adj.* with no points of interest.

February *feb'roo-àr-i, n.* the second month of the year.

feces (esp. *U.S.*). Same as **faeces**.

feckless *fek'lis, adj.* incompetent, inefficient.

fecund *fē'kùnd, adj.* fertile, fruitful.
fecund'ity *n.*

fed. See **feed¹**.

federal *fed'ėr-àl,* (of a union or government) in which several states, while independent in home affairs, combine for national or general purposes.
fed'eralist *n.* a supporter of a federal constitution or union.
fed'erate *v.t.* and *v.i.* to join in a league or federation:—*pr.p.* **fed'erating.**

fed'erated *adj.*
federā'tion *n.* a federal union, or the act of uniting in one.

fee *fē*, *n.* **1** the price paid for professional services. **2** a sum paid for a privilege: *entrance fee.*—*v.t.* to hire:—*pr.p.* **fee'ing**; *pa.p.* **feed**.

feeble *fē'bl*, *adj.* very weak.
fee'bleness *n.* **fee'bly** *adv.*
fee'ble-mind'ed *adj.* weak-minded.

feed[1] *fēd*, *v.t.* **1** to give food to. **2** to supply necessary material to: *to feed a fire.* **3** to satisfy or encourage: *to feed his vanity.* **4** to give cues to (a comedian). **5** to put (material) little by little (into e.g. a computer):—*pa.p.* **fed**.—Also *v.i.*—*n.* **1** food, esp. for cattle. **2** one who, something that, feeds or supplies. **3** a meal, esp. for a baby.
feed'er *n.* and *adj.*
feed'-back *n.* **1** a response providing useful information or guidelines for further development. **2** the returning of some of the sound from a loud-speaker to a microphone connected to it, causing a loud noise.
fed up (*coll.*) tired and disgusted.

feed[2], **feeing**. See **fee**.

feel *fēl*, *v.t.* **1** to become aware of by touch. **2** to examine by touch. **3** to grope (one's way). **4** to be conscious of. **5** to experience (e.g. an emotion):—*pr.p.* **feel'ing**; *pa.p.* **felt**.—Also *v.i.* and *n.*
feel'er *n.* **1** in animals, an organ with which to feel. **2** a remark or action to find out the opinions of others.
feel'ing *n.* **1** the sense of touch. **2** a sensation. **3** an impression. **4** consciousness of pleasure or pain. **5** emotion. **6** affection.—*adj.* experiencing, or showing, emotion.

feet. See **foot**.

feign *fān*, *v.t.* **1** to pretend to feel (e.g. sickness, grief). **2** to sham.
feigned *adj.*
feint *fānt*, *n.* **1** a pretence. **2** a movement intended to deceive.

felicity *fē-lis'i-ti*, *n.* **1** happiness. **2** skill or appropriateness (of phrase, expression).
felic'itate *v.t.* to congratulate:—*pr.p.* **felic'itating**.
felic'itous *adj.* **1** happy. **2** appropriate.

feline *fē'līn*, *adj.* of, like, a cat.

fell[1]. See **fall**.

fell[2] *fel*, *v.t.* **1** to strike to the ground. **2** to cut down.

fell[3] *fel*, *n.* **1** a hill. **2** moorland.

fell[4] *fel*, *n.* a skin.

fell[5] *fel*, *adj.* cruel, fierce, deadly.

fellow *fel'ō*, *n.* **1** a man. **2** a worthless person. **3** a companion and equal. **4** one of a pair. **5** one who holds a fellowship. **6** one who belongs to a (usu. learned) society.—*adj.* belonging to the same group or class: *fellow citizen, fellow-countryman.*
fell'owship *n.* **1** friendliness. **2** an association. **3** money left to a college for the support of graduates called fellows. **4** the position of fellow.
fell'ow-feel'ing *n.* sympathy.
fellow traveller **1** one who travels in the same vehicle. **2** a communist sympathiser.

felon *fel'on*, *n.* one guilty of a serious crime.
felo'nious (*-lō'-*) *adj.* **1** criminal. **2** wicked.
fel'ony *n.* a crime punishable by penal servitude or death:—*pl.* **fel'onies**.

felt[1]. See **feel**.

felt[2] *felt*, *n.* a woollen fabric made by pressure, not weaving.—*v.i.* to become like felt.—*v.t.* to make into, or make like, felt.

female *fē'māl*, *adj.* and *n.* **1** (one) of the sex that produces young. **2** (one) of the kind of flower that has a pistil and thus bears seeds. **3** (a plant) with such flowers only.

feminine *fem'i-nin*, *adj.* **1** of women. **2** like a woman. **3** (*grammar*) of the gender to which words denoting females belong.
fem'inism *n.* support of women's rights.
fem'inist *n.*

femur *fē'mur*, *n.* the thigh bone.
fem'oral (*fem'-*) *adj.* of the thigh.

fen *fen*, *n.* low marshy land often covered with water.
fenn'y *adj.* **fen'land** *n.*

fence *fens*, *n.* **1** a barrier for enclosing land. **2** a receiver of stolen goods.—*v.t.* to enclose with a fence.—*v.i.* **1** to practise fencing with sword or foil. **2** to give answers that tell nothing or promise nothing:—*pr.p.* **fenc'ing**.
fenc'er *n.* **1** a maker of fences. **2** one who practises fencing with sword or foil.
fenc'ing *n.* **1** the act of, or material for, putting up a fence. **2** the art of attack and defence with a sword, etc., practised with blunted weapons and protective clothing. **3** turning aside questions or arguments.

fend *fend*, *v.t.* to ward (off), turn aside: *to fend off a blow.*—*v.i.* to look after (with *for*): *to fend for oneself.*
fend'er *n.* **1** anything used as a guard against touching or collision. **2** a low metal guard round a hearth. **3** a mudguard. **4** (*U.S.*) a bumper (*def. 1*).

fennel *fen'el*, *n.* a plant with yellow flowers in parasol-shaped clusters, whose seeds and leaves are used as seasoning.

fenny. See **fen**.

feral *fē'răl,fer'ăl,adj.* wild, esp. if formerly domesticated.

ferment *fûr'mėnt, n.* **1** a substance that causes fermentation. **2** internal motion among the parts of a fluid. **3** agitation, tumult.—*v.t. (fėr-ment')* **1** to excite fermentation in. **2** to stir up.—*v.i.* **1** to undergo fermentation. **2** to seethe with excitement.
fermentā'tion *n.* **1** a slow change in an organic substance, usu. giving off heat and gas, e.g. the change of grape sugar to alcohol. **2** excitement.

fern *fûrn, n.* a plant with no flowers and beautiful feather-like leaves.

ferocious *fė-rō'shus, adj.* savage, fierce.
fero'ciously *adv.*
fero'ciousness, **feroc'ity** *(-ros'), ns.*

ferret *fer'it, n.* a half-tamed variety of polecat used to hunt out rabbits and rats.—*v.t.* to search (out) cunningly:—*pr.p.* **ferr'eting**; *pa.p.* **ferr'eted**.

ferri-, ferro- *pfxs.* of, containing, iron.
ferr'o-con'crete *n.* reinforced concrete.

ferrule *fer'ūl,-ōōl,-ul,n.* a metal ring or cap to strengthen the tip of a stick, umbrella.

ferry *fer'i, v.t.* to carry over water (or land) esp. along a regular route, by boat, ship, or aircraft:—*pr.p.* **ferr'ying**; *pa.p.* **ferr'ied**.—*n.* **1** a place of carriage across water. **2** a ferry boat:—*pl.* **ferr'ies**.

fertile *fûr'tīl, -til, adj.* **1** able to produce in great quantity. **2** inventive: *a fertile imagination*:—*opp.* **infer'tile**.
fer'tileness, **fertil'ity** *(-til'), ns.*
fer'tilise *(-til-īz) v.t.* **1** to make fertile. **2** to make capable of development:—*pr.p.* **fer'tilising**.
fertilisā'tion *n.* the act of fertilising.
fer'tiliser *(-īz-ėr) n.* a material used to make the soil more fertile.

ferule *fer'ōōl, -ūl, n.* a rod for punishment.

fervent *fûr'vėnt, adj.* **1** warm in feeling. **2** enthusiastic.
fer'vency *n.* **1** eagerness. **2** emotional warmth.
fer'vid *adj.* **1** very hot. **2** having burning desire or enthusiasm.
fer'vour *n.* warmth and earnestness.

festal. See **feast**.

fester *fes'tėr, v.i.* **1** to suppurate. **2** to rot. **3** to rankle: *The injustice festered in his mind.*

festival *fes'ti-văl, n.* **1** a joyful celebration. **2** a season of performances of music, etc.
fes'tive *adj.* **1** of a feast. **2** gay, merry.
festiv'ity *n.* **1** merrymaking, celebration. **2** gaiety:—*pl.* **festiv'ities**.

festoon *fes-tōōn', n.* a garland hung between two points.—*v.t.* to adorn, hang (with festoons, etc.)

fetal. See **foetus**.

fetch *fech, v.t.* **1** to go and get. **2** to bring. **3** to be sold for (a stated price). **4** to heave (a sigh). **5** to draw (a breath). **6** to deal (a blow).
fetch'ing *adj.* charming.

fête *fāt, fet, n.* a festive entertainment, esp. out of doors, usu. held to raise money.—*v.t.* to entertain lavishly, make much of (a person):—*pr.p.* **fêt'ing**; *pa.p.* **fêt'ed**.

fetid *fē'tid*, or *fet', adj.* stinking.

fetish *fet'ish, n.* **1** an object worshipped because a spirit is supposed to lodge in it, or for other reason. **2** something regarded with undue reverence.

fetlock *fet'lok, n.* **1** a tuft of hair that grows above a horse's hoof. **2** the part where this hair grows.

fetter *fet'ėr, n.* **1** a chain for the feet—used chiefly in *pl.* **2** anything that restrains.—*v.t.* **1** to put fetters on. **2** to restrain.

fettle *fet'l, n.*: **in fine/good fettle** in good condition or spirits.

fetus. See **foetus**.

feud *fūd, n.* **1** a deadly quarrel between families or clans. **2** a lasting quarrel.

feudal *fū'dăl, adj.* of or connected with the **feudal system**, the system in the Middle Ages by which vassals held lands from more important lords, being bound in return to fight for these lords in war.

fever *fē'vėr, n.* **1** (a disease, esp. infectious, marked by) great bodily heat and quickening of pulse. **2** extreme excitement, agitation, anxiety.
fe'vered *adj.*
fe'verish *adj.* **1** having a slight fever. **2** restlessly excited. **3** too eager.
fe'verishly *adv.* **fe'verishness** *n.*
fever pitch a state of great excitement or agitation.

few *fū, adj.* a small number of, not many.
a few a small number (of).

fey, fay *fā, adj.* **1** fated soon to die—a state said to be marked by high spirits. **2** supernatural.

fez *fez, n.* a, usu. red, brimless cap with black tassel:—*pl.* **fezz'es**.

fiancé (*fem.* **fiancée**) *fē-on^g'sā, n.* a person engaged to be married (with *my, your, his, her*).

fiasco *fi-as'kō, n.* a failure, orig. in a musical performance:—*pl.* **fias'cos, -coes**.

fiat *fī'at, n.* **1** a formal command. **2** a decree.

fib *fib*, *n.* a trivial lie.—Also *v.i.*:—*pr.p.* **fibb'ing**; *pa.p.* **fibbed**.

fibre *fī'bėr*, *n.* **1** a fine thread, or thread-like substance. **2** a material composed of fibres. **3** texture. **4** character: *moral fibre*.
fi'brous *adj*.
fi'breglass *n.* (a material made of) fine fibres of glass, used as insulation, etc.

fibula *fib'ū-lȧ*, *n.* the outer of the two bones from the knee to the ankle.

fickle *fik'l*, *adj.* **1** inconstant. **2** changeable.
fick'leness *n.*

fiction *fik'sh(ȯ)n*, *n.* **1** a made-up story. **2** a falsehood. **3** novels and stories in prose.
fic'tional *adj.* of fiction, not fact.
fictitious *fik-tish'ůs*, *adj.* imaginary.

fiddle *fid'l*, *n.* **1** a stringed instrument, esp. a violin. **2** a swindle, act of cheating.—*v.i.* **1** to play on a fiddle. **2** to make aimless movements (with). **3** to tinker (with). **4** to tamper (with). **5** to cheat (also *v.t.*):—*pr.p.* **fidd'ling**.
fidd'ler *n.*
fidd'ly *adj.* requiring much dexterity, awkward:—*comp.* **fidd'lier**; *superl.* **fidd'liest**.
play second fiddle to take a less important part than someone else.

fidelity *fi-del'i-ti*, or *fī-*, *n.* **1** loyalty. **2** faithfulness. **3** exactness in reproducing: *fidelity to the text, to the score*:—*opp.* **infidel'ity**.

fidget *fij'it*, *v.i.* to move uneasily, be restless:—*pr.p.* **fidg'eting**; *pa.p.* **fidg'eted**.—*n.* **1** one who fidgets. **2** (in *pl.*) nervous restlessness.

field *fēld*, *n.* **1** a piece of ground enclosed for tillage, pasture, or sport. **2** the scene (of a battle). **3** an expanse (e.g. *icefield*). **4** land yielding a natural product (e.g. gold, coal). **5** an area enclosed or marked off in some way. **6** a sphere of interest, knowledge, etc. **7** those taking part in a hunt or a horse race. **8** players or competitors.—*v.t.* **1** to catch or stop (a ball) and throw it to the appropriate place. **2** to put (a team) into the field to play.—*v.i.* to stand ready to stop the ball in cricket, baseball, etc.
field'er, **fields'man** *ns.*
field day **1** a day when troops are given exercises in the field. **2** any day of unusual bustle or importance.
field event an athletic event other than a race.
field'fare *n.* a type of thrush.
field'-glasses *n.pl.* a small double telescope.
field'-gun *n.* a light mobile cannon.
field hospital a temporary hospital near the scene of a battle.
field marshal the highest rank in the British army, or a person of this rank.
field-mouse. See **mouse**.
field work work done out of doors, e.g. surveying, or collecting facts or information.

fiend *fēnd*, *n.* **1** (*cap.*) Satan. **2** a devil. **3** a cruel person. **4** (*coll.*) an enthusiast.
fiend'ish *adj.* **fiend'ishness** *n.*

fierce *fērs*, *adj.* **1** angry, savage. **2** violent. **3** intense, eager: *fierce rivalry*.
fierce'ly *adv.* **fierce'ness** *n.*

fiery *fīr'i*, *adj.* **1** like, or of, fire. **2** blazing. **3** very red. **4** full of passion. **5** irritable:—*comp.* **fier'ier**; *superl.* **fier'iest**.
fier'ily *adv.* **fier'iness** *n.*
fiery cross a cross of two sticks, charred and dipped in blood, sent round to summon clansmen to arms.

fiesta *fē-es'tȧ*, *n.* **1** a saint's day. **2** a holiday. **3** festivity.

fife *fīf*, *n.* a small flute.

fifteen *fif'tēn*, *fif-tēn'*, *n.* and *adj.* five and ten (15 or XV).
fifteenth *adj.* **1** next after the fourteenth. **2** equal to one of fifteen equal parts.—Also *n.*
fifth *adj.* **1** next after the fourth. **2** equal to one of five equal parts.—Also *n.*
fifty *fif'ti*, *adj.* and *n.* five times ten (50 or L).
fif'ties *n.pl.* the numbers fifty to fifty-nine.
fif'tieth *adj.* **1** next after the forty-ninth. **2** equal to one of fifty equal parts.—Also *n.*
fif'ty-fif'ty **1** half-and-half. **2** (of chances) equal.
fif'ty-pence' (piece) a coin worth fifty pence.

fig *fig*, *n.* **1** a small tree bearing a pear-shaped fruit. **2** the fruit. **3** the smallest bit.

fight *fīt*, *v.i.* **1** to strive (for). **2** to contend in war or single combat.—*v.t.* **1** to engage in conflict with. **2** to win (one's way) by a struggle:—*pr.p.* **fight'ing**; *pa.p.* **fought** *(föt)*.—*n.* **1** a struggle. **2** a battle. **3** the will or strength to fight: *There was no fight left in him*.
fight'er *n.* **fight'ing** *adj.* and *n.*
fighting chance a chance of success given great effort.
fight shy of to avoid.

figment *fig'mėnt*, *n.* an invention (of the imagination).

figurative. See **figure**.

figure *fig'ůr*, *n.* **1** the form in outline. **2** a geometrical form. **3** a representation in drawing, etc., a diagram. **4** appearance. **5** a person noticed by the public: *a polit-*

ical figure. **6** a number, or the mark representing it. **7** price: *a high figure.* **8** a set of steps in a dance, or of movements in skating.—*v.t.* **1** to mark with a design. **2** to imagine. **3** (*coll.*) to conclude, assume.—*v.i.* to play a part (in):—*pr.p.* **fig'uring;** *pa.p.* **fig'ured.**

fig'urative *(fig'yůr-) adj.* of, or using, figures of speech.

fig'uratively *adv.*

fig'ured *adj.* marked with a design: *figured silk.*

fig'urehead *(fig'ůr-) n.* **1** a figure under a ship's bowsprit. **2** a leader who does not have the real power.

fig'urine *fig'yůr-ēn, n.* a small statuette.

figure skating ice-skating in prescribed patterns.

cut a figure to make an impressive appearance.

figure of speech an expression in which words are used in an unusual way for the purpose of making a striking effect (see **metaphor**).

figure out to come to understand by thought or study.

filament *fil'ȧ-mėnt, n.* a thread-like object, e.g. the conductor in an electric light bulb (made to glow by the passage of current).

filch *filch, v.t.* to steal (something small).

file¹ *fīl, n.* **1** a wire, etc., on which papers are strung. **2** a folder, cabinet, etc., in which papers are kept. **3** a list. **4** a line of soldiers ranged one behind one another.—*v.t.* **1** to put on, or in, a file. **2** to bring (a suit) before a law court.—*v.i.* to march, walk, in a file:—*pr.p.* **fil'ing.**

(in) single file, Indian file singly, one behind another.

file² *fīl, n.* a steel instrument with a rough surface for smoothing or rasping metals, etc.—*v.t.* to cut or smooth with a file:—*pr.p.* **fil'ing.**

fil'ing *n.* a particle rubbed off with a file.

filial *fil'yȧl, -i-ȧl, adj.* of, suitable to, a son or daughter.

fil'ially *adv.*

filibuster *fil'i-bus-tėr, n.* **1** a pirate, or one who makes war without authorisation. **2** (one who makes) a very long speech intended to hinder the passage of a law in a parliament, etc.—Also *v.i.*

filigree *fil'i-grē, n.* **1** ornamental work in which threads of precious metal are interlaced. **2** anything delicate.

Filipino *fil-i-pē'nō, n.* a native of the *Philippine Islands:*—*pl.* **Filipi'nos:**—*fem.* **Filipi'na.**

fill *fil, v.t.* **1** to make full. **2** to put (something) by degrees (into a container). **3** to put a filling in a cavity in (a tooth). **4** to satisfy (a requirement). **5** to occupy, or appoint a person to (a vacant post). **6** to occupy (time).—*v.i.* to become full.—*n.* as much as fills or satisfies.

fill'er *n.*

fill'ing *n.* anything used to fill up a hole, cavity, etc.

fill in **1** to occupy (time). **2** to complete (e.g. a form).

fillet *fil'it, n.* **1** a band worn round the head. **2** a thin narrow strip. **3** a boneless slice of fish or meat.—*v.t.* to bone:—*pr.p.* **fill'eting;** *pa.p.* **fill'eted.**

fillip *fil'ip, n.* encouragement, a stimulus.

filly *fil'i, n.* a young mare:—*pl.* **fill'ies.**

film *film, n.* **1** a thin skin or membrane. **2** the sensitive coating of a photographic plate. **3** a ribbon of celluloid with such a coating for ordinary photographs or for photographs for projecting by cinematograph. **4** a motion picture. **5** a slight haziness.—*v.t.* **1** to cover with a film. **2** to make a motion picture of.

fil'my *adj.* **1** very light and thin. **2** misty:—*comp.* **fil'mier;** *superl.* **fil'miest.**

Filofax® *fīlō-faks, n.* a personal organiser.

filter *fil'tėr, n.* **1** a device or apparatus for freeing a liquid from solid matter. **2** in photography, a device used to change the tone of certain colours. **3** a green arrow on a traffic light which allows one lane of traffic to move while the main stream is held up.—*v.t.* to purify by means of a filter.—*v.i.* **1** to pass through a filter, etc. **2** (of cars, etc.) to join a stream of traffic gradually. **3** (of a lane of traffic) to move in the direction shown by the filter. **4** (of news) to leak out.

fil'ter-bed *n.* a bed of sand, gravel, etc. used for filtering water or sewage.

See also **filtrate.**

filth *filth, n.* anything very dirty.

fil'thy *adj.:*—*comp.* **fil'thier;** *superl.* **fil'thiest.**

fil'thiness *n.*

filtrate *fil'trāt, v.t.* to filter:—*pr.p.* **fil'trating.**—*n.* a liquid that has been filtered.

fin *fin, n.* **1** an organ by which fish, etc. balance and swim. **2** a part of a mechanism like a fish's fin in shape or purpose.

finned, finn'y (*comp.* **-ier**; *superl.* **-iest**), *adjs.*

final *fī'nȧl, adj.* **1** very last, with no repetition to follow. **2** (of e.g. a decision) not to be questioned or altered.—*n.* **1** the last contest in a knock-out competition. **2** (in *pl.*) the last examination for a university degree, etc.

fin'ally *adv.*
fin'alise *v.t.* to put the finishing touches to:—*pr.p.* **fin'alising.**
final'ity *n.* the quality of being final and decisive.

finale *fi-nä'li, n.* **1** the end. **2** the last movement in a musical composition. **3** the last item in a concert.

finalise, finality. See **final.**

finance *fi-nans', fī-, n.* **1** money affairs, esp. of a state or public body. **2** (in *pl.*) money resources.—*v.t.* to provide money for:—*pr.p.* **financ'ing.**
finan'cial *(-shȧl) adj.* **finan'cially** *adv.*
finan'cier *(-si-) n.* one skilled in finance.
financial year any period of twelve months at the end of which accounts are balanced, esp. that ending on April 5.

finch *finch, -sh, n.* any of a number of sparrow-like birds.

find *fīnd, v.t.* **1** to come upon or meet with. **2** to discover. **3** to succeed in obtaining (e.g. time, courage, to do something, or money for something). **4** to declare after trial: *to find the prisoner guilty.*—*pr.p.* **find'ing;** *pa.p.* **found.**—*n.* something found, esp. of value or interest.
find'er *n.* **find'ing** *n.*
find oneself 1 to come to full mastery of one's natural powers. **2** to be in, arrive at.
find one's feet to become able to cope readily with new conditions.
find out 1 to discover by investigation or calculation. **2** to detect (a person) in crime or fault, or to discover his true character.

fine[1] *fīn, adj.* **1** excellent. **2** not coarse. **3** thin. **4** delicate. **5** slight, subtle: *a fine distinction* (a difference not easily seen or understood). **6** (*ironically*) of high quality, very great: *A fine mess you have made!* **7** containing a high proportion of precious metal: *fine gold.* **8** sharp, keen.—*v.t.* to make fine:—*pr.p.* **fin'ing.**—*adv.* **1** finely (usu. *coll.*). **2** with little time, space, to spare.
fine'ly *adv.* **fine'ness** *n.*
fin'ery *n.* fine or showy things.
fine arts painting, sculpture, etc.

fine[2] *fīn, n.* money to be paid as a punishment.—*v.t.* to impose a fine on:—*pr.p.* **fin'ing.**
in fine in conclusion, in short.

finesse *fi-nes', n.* **1** subtlety. **2** cunning strategy.—Also *v.i.*:—*pr.p.* **finess'ing.**

finger *fing'gėr, n.* **1** one of the five end parts of the hand. **2** anything finger-shaped. **3** a fingerbreadth. **4** any of the divisions of a glove covering the fingers.—*v.t.* **1** to toy or meddle with. **2** (*music*) to mark choice of fingers in playing.
fing'ering *n.* **1** touching. **2** the positioning of the fingers in playing music.
fing'er-board *n.* the part of a musical instrument on which the fingers are placed.
fin'gerbreadth *n.* a distance, height, measured by the breadth of a finger.
fin'germark *n.* a mark left on a surface by a finger.
fin'gernail *n.* the nail on a finger.
fing'erpost *n.* a signpost.
fing'erprint *n.* an impression of the ridges of the finger tip, which can be used as a means of identification.
fing'erstall *n.* a sheath for a finger.
a finger in the pie a share in something being done.
have (a subject) at one's fingertips to be perfect master of it.
put one's finger on to point out exactly: *to put one's finger on the cause of the trouble.*

finical *fin'i-kȧl, adj.* **1** fussy, too particular about small details. **2** (of things) with too much small detail.
fin'icking, fin'icky *adjs.* finical.

finish *fin'ish, v.t.* **1** to end. **2** to complete the making of. **3** to make perfect. **4** to use up, etc., whole, or remainder, of. **5** (*coll.*) to overcome or destroy. **6** to complete the education of (a girl) before introduction to society.—*v.i.* **1** to leave off. **2** to end (in, by).—*n.* **1** the end. **2** the last touch. **3** polish.
fin'ished *adj.* **1** not able for further effort, or capable of achieving further success. **2** (of e.g. a performance, performer) polished, excellent.

finite *fī'nīt, adj.* **1** having an end or limit (*opp.* **in'finite**). **2** applied to a part of a verb that has a subject (e.g. *He speaks*, but not *to speak*, or *speaking*).

Finn *fin, n.* a native of Finland.
Finn'ish *adj.*

finny. See **fin.**

fiord, fjord *fyörd, n.* a long, narrow, rock-bound inlet.

fir *fûr, n.* a cone-bearing tree valuable for its timber.
fir'-cone *n.*

fire *fīr, n.* **1** heat and light caused by burning. **2** burning fuel in a grate, etc. **3** destructive burning (e.g. of a house, forest). **4** brightness of a gem. **5** enthusiasm. **6** discharge of firearms.—*v.t.* **1** to set on fire. **2** to bake, dry, etc., by heat. **3** to fill with enthusiasm or inspiration: *The story fired his imagination.* **4** to shoot with (a gun, etc.) or shoot (a bullet, arrow, etc.). **5** to dismiss from a post.—*v.i.* to shoot with firearms:—*pr.p.* **fir'ing**.

fir'ing *n.* and *adj.*

fire'-alarm *n.* an apparatus for giving an alarm when fire breaks out.

fire'arm *n.* (usu. in *pl.*) a weapon discharged by an explosion.

fire'brand *n.* **1** a piece of wood on fire. **2** one who stirs up strife.

fire'-break *n.* a strip of land kept clear to stop the spread of a fire, e.g. in a forest.

fire'brick *n.* a brick made to resist high temperatures.

fire brigade a team of people employed to put out fires.

fire'-bucket *n.* a bucket containing sand or water for putting out fires.

fire'clay *n.* a clay used in making fire-bricks.

fire'-damp *n.* a gas that may catch fire in coal-mines.

fire engine a motor vehicle with equipment for fire fighting.

fire'-escape' *n.* an iron stairway or other special means of exit from a building for use in case of fire.

fire extinguisher an apparatus for putting out fires (containing water or chemicals) that can be carried by one person.

fire'fighter *n.* a member of a fire brigade.

fire'fly *n.* a beetle that gives off light by night.

fire'-ī'ron *(-ėrn)* *n.* a fireside implement—e.g. a poker—not necessarily made of iron.

fire'man *n.* **1** a man whose business it is to help in putting out fires. **2** a man who tends the fires, e.g. of a steam engine.

fire'place *n.* the place in a room where a fire is burned.

fire'-plug *n.* a hydrant for use in case of fire.

fire'proof *adj.* **1** that will not burn easily. **2** not easily cracked by strong heat.—*v.t.* to make fireproof.

fire'-rais'ing *n.* the crime of arson.

fire'wood *n.* wood for fuel.

fire'works *n.pl.* **1** a display of lights produced by exploding devices, usu. as entertainment. **2** the materials for this (*sing.* used for one article). **3** a display of temper, wit, etc.

firing line the area or troops within range of the enemy.

firing party, **squad** a detachment with the job of firing over the grave of someone buried with military honours, or of shooting someone sentenced to death.

catch fire to begin to burn.

hold one's fire to stop shooting.

under fire being fired at e.g. by enemy soldiers.

See also **fiery**.

firm[1] *fûrm, adj.* **1** fixed. **2** strong and steady. **3** resolute.

firm'ly *adv.* **firm'ness** *n.*

firm[2] *fûrm, n.* a business partnership or association.

firmament *fûr'mȧ-mėnt, n.* the sky.

first *fûrst, adj.* **1** before all others in place, time, or degree. **2** most eminent. **3** chief.—*adv.* before anything else, in time, space, rank, etc.

first'ly *adv.* in the first place, as the first point: *I can give three reasons for not going:—firstly, it is cold; secondly, it is wet; thirdly, I don't want to.*

first aid treatment of a wounded or sick person before the doctor's arrival.

first'-born *n.* the eldest child.—Also *adj.*

first'-class' *adj.* of the best quality.

first fruits **1** the fruits first gathered in a season. **2** the first profits or effects of anything.

first'-hand' *adj.* obtained directly: *a first-hand account of the event* (an account from someone who was present).

first lady the wife of the U.S. president.

first'-rate *adj.* of the highest excellence.

first water the first or highest quality—used esp. of diamonds and pearls.

firth *fûrth, n.* an arm of the sea, esp. a river mouth.

fiscal *fis'kȧl, adj.* **1** of, concerning, the public revenue. **2** of financial matters.—*n.* in Scotland, an officer who prosecutes in criminal cases in local and inferior courts—in full, *procurator-fiscal*.

fish *fish, n.* **1** an animal with a backbone that lives in water, and breathes through gills. **2** its flesh. **3** (*coll.*) a person: *He's a queer fish*:—*pl.* **fish**, or **fish'es**.—*v.i.* **1** to catch, or try to catch, fish. **2** to search (for) under water, etc. **3** to try artfully to obtain: *to fish for information, for an invitation.*—*v.t.* **1** to draw (out, up). **2** to fish in (a stream).

fish'ing *n.* and *adj.*

fish'er, **fish'erman** *ns.*

fish'ery *n.* **1** the business of catching fish. **2** a place for catching fish. **3** the legal right to take fish:—*pl.* **fish'eries**.

fish'y *adj.* **1** of fish. **2** like a fish. **3** (*coll.*) suspicious, or improbable:—*comp.* **fish'ier**; *superl.* **fish'iest**.

fish'iness *n.*

fish finger a small oblong cake of fish coated in batter or bread-crumbs.

fish'-hook *n.* a hook for catching fish.

fish'ing-line *n.* a cord used, with hook(s), etc., for catching fish.
fish'ing-rod *n.* a long, tapering, easily bent, rod, usu. in sections, used along with a fishing-line, etc.
fish'monger *n.* one who sells fish.
fish'-slice *n.* a broad-bladed implement for turning, or serving, fish.
have other fish to fry to have more important matters to attend to.

fishplate *fish'plāt, n.* an iron plate, one of a pair used to join railway rails.

fishy. See **fish**.

fissile *fis'īl, adj.* **1** that may be split. **2** capable of nuclear fission.
fission *fish'ȯn, n.* **1** splitting. **2** the splitting of the nucleus of an atom with great release of energy.
fiss'ionable *adj.* **1** (of nuclei) fissile. **2** (of material) having such nuclei.
fissure *fish'ür, n.* a narrow opening or split.
fission bomb the atomic bomb, whose energy comes from the splitting of nuclei of atoms.

fist *fist, n.* the closed or clenched hand.
fist'icuffs *n.* **1** boxing. **2** blows.

fit[1] *fit, adj.* **1** able (for). **2** suitable (for). **3** suitable or proper: *That is not a fit way to behave.* **4** in good health:—*comp.* **fitt'er**; *superl.* **fitt'est.**—*v.t.* **1** to be the right size or shape for (someone or something). **2** to be suitable for (e.g. an occasion). **3** to make (something) suitable.—Also *v.i.*:—*pr.p.* **fitt'ing**; *pa.p.* **fitt'ed.**—*n.* **1** a thing that fits: *Your jacket is a good fit.* **2** the way in which a thing fits: *The fit of it is good.*
fit'ly *adv.* suitably.
fit'ness *n.*
fitt'ed *adj.* **1** cut, sewn, etc. to fit exactly. **2** (of a cupboard, etc.) built to fit a particular space and attached to or built into the wall of a room.
fitt'er *n.* **1** one who fits clothes. **2** one who puts parts of machinery together.
fitt'ing *adj.* **1** that fits. **2** suitable.—*n.* **1** (usu. in *pl.*) a furnishing, fixture. **2** the trying on of an article of clothing so that it can be adjusted to fit the wearer.
fitt'ingly *adv.* suitably.
fit'ment *n.* a furnishing, esp. if built-in.
be fit to to be in a state to: *to be fit to scream with rage.*
fit out to provide with all necessary clothes, equipment, etc.

fit[2] *fit, n.* **1** an attack of illness, esp. epilepsy. **2** an attack (of laughter, etc.). **3** a passing mood: *a fit of gloom.*
fit'ful *adj.* coming in short spells.
fit'fully *adv.* **fit'fulness** *n.*
by fits and starts in bursts with intervals between.

five *fīv, n.* **1** the number next above four (5 or V). **2** a set of five things or persons. **3** the fifth hour after midday or midnight. **4** the age of five years. **5** any thing (e.g. a shoe, a playing-card) denoted by five.—*adj.* **1** 5 in number. **2** five years old.
fiv'er (*coll.*) *n.* a five-pound note.
five'-pence' (piece) a coin worth five pence.
See also **fifteen, fifth**, etc.

fives *fīvz, n. sing.* any of several games played in a walled court with a ball struck by the hand in a padded glove.

fix *fiks, v.t.* **1** to place firmly, attach firmly. **2** to direct steadily: *He fixed his eyes on the door.* **3** to settle definitely: *to fix the price.* **4** to make (a photograph) permanent by means of chemicals. **5** to put right, repair. **6** (*coll.*) to arrange (a matter) dishonestly, or to bribe or silence (a person or persons).—*n.* **1** (*coll.*) a difficulty. **2** (*slang*) a shot of heroin or other drug.
fixā'tion *n.* **1** the act of fixing. **2** emotional development that stops too early in life. **3** an obsession.
fix'ative *n.* something that sets colours.
fixed *adj.*
fix'edly *(-id-li) adv.* steadily, intently.
fixture *(-chür) n.* **1** a furnishing or article of furniture that is fixed in position. **2** an event arranged for a fixed time.
fixed stars stars which appear always to occupy the same position in the sky—opp. to *planets.*

fizz *fiz, v.i.* to make a hissing sound.—*n.* any frothy drink.
fizz'y *adj.*:—*comp.* **fizz'ier**; *superl.* **fizz'iest.**
fizz'iness *n.*
fizz'le *v.i.* to hiss or splutter:—*pr.p.* **fizz'ling.**
fizzle out 1 to splutter and go out. **2** to come to nothing.

fjord. See **fiord**.

flabbergast *flab'ėr-gäst,* (*coll.*) *v.t.* to stun with surprise.

flabby *flab'i, adj.* **1** soft, yielding. **2** hanging loose:—*comp.* **flabb'ier**; *superl.* **flabb'iest.**
flabb'ily *adv.* **flabb'iness** *n.*

flaccid *flak'sid, flas'id, adj.* hanging in loose folds, not firm, limp.

flag[1] *flag, v.i.* to grow tired or spiritless:—*pr.p.* **flagg'ing**; *pa.p.* **flagged.**

flag[2] *flag, n.* a plant with sword-shaped leaves—an iris, or a reed.

flag[3] *flag, n.* a piece of bunting, usu. with a design, used to show nationality, party, etc., to mark a position, or to send information.—*v.t.* to signal, or signal to, by flag or hand:—*pr.p.* **flagg'ing**; *pa.p.* **flagged**.

flag'ship *n.* the ship in which an admiral sails, and which carries the flag.

flag'staff, **flag'pole** *ns.* a pole on which a flag is hung.

flag down to signal (e.g. a car) to stop.

flag[4] *flag*, *n.* a flat paving-stone.

flagellation *flaj-ėl-ā'sh(ȯ)n*, *n.* whipping or scourging.

flagon *flag'ȯn*, *n.* a vessel with a narrow neck, handle, and lid, for liquids.

flagrant *flā'grȧnt*, *adj.* glaring, scandalous: *a flagrant error, fault, crime*.

fla'grancy *n.* **fla'grantly** *adv.*

flail *flāl*, *n.* an implement for threshing corn.—Also *v.t.*

flair *flār*, *n.* a talent, aptitude.

flak *flak*, *n.* **1** anti-aircraft fire. **2** strong criticism.

flake *flāk*, *n.* **1** a small layer or film. **2** a very small loose piece (e.g. of snow).—*v.t.* to form into flakes.—*v.i.* to come (off) in flakes:—*pr.p.* **flak'ing**.

flak'y *adj.*:—*comp.* **flak'ier**; *superl.* **flak'iest**.

flak'iness *n.*

flake out to collapse, faint, from weariness or illness.

flamboyant *flam-boi'ȧnt*, *adj.* **1** gorgeously coloured. **2** too showy. **3** intended to attract notice.

flame *flām*, *n.* **1** the gleam or blaze of fire. **2** heat of rage, etc. **3** love.—*v.i.* to break out in flame:—*pr.p.* **flam'ing**.

flam'ing *adj.* **1** brilliant. **2** violent.

flamm'able *adj.* inflammable, easily set on fire:—*opp.* **non-inflamm'able**.

flamingo *flȧ-ming'gō*, *n.* a water bird, pink or bright red, with long legs and neck:—*pl.* **flaming'o(e)s**.

flammable. See **flame**.

flan *flan*, *n.* an open tart with custard, fruit, or other filling.

flange *flanj*, *n.* an edge or rim, raised or sticking out.

flank *flangk*, *n.* **1** the side of an animal from ribs to thigh. **2** the side or wing of an army, fleet, etc.—*v.t.* **1** to pass round the side of. **2** to be situated at the side of.

flannel *flan'(ė)l*, *n.* **1** a warm soft cloth of wool or wool and other material. **2** (in *pl.*) a garment, esp. trousers, of this. **3** flattering or evasive words.

flannelette' *n.* a cotton imitation of flannel.

flap *flap*, *n.* **1** the blow, or the movement, of a broad loose object. **2** anything broad and hanging loose. **3** a movable part of an aircraft's wing that helps it e.g. to rise on take-off. **4** (*coll.*) a panic, fluster.—*v.t.* and *v.i.* **1** to move with a flap. **2** to beat (wings):—*pr.p.* **flapp'ing**; *pa.p.* **flapped**.

flare *flār*, *v.i.* **1** to burn with a glaring, unsteady light. **2** to widen out in a bell shape:—*pr.p.* **flar'ing**.—*n.* **1** an unsteady glare. **2** a flash. **3** a sudden bright light used as a signal, etc. **4** a gradual widening, esp. of skirt.

flare up **1** to blaze suddenly. **2** suddenly to show anger (*n.* **flare'-up**).

flash *flash*, *n.* **1** a very brief gleam of light. **2** a sudden short burst (e.g. of merriment). **3** an instant of time. **4** a distinctive mark on a uniform. **5** a brief news dispatch by telegraph. **6** in a film, a scene shown briefly as explanation or comment, esp. (**flash'-back**) a scene of the past.—*v.i.* **1** to shine out suddenly. **2** to burst out into violence.—*v.t.* to cause to flash.

flash'y *adj.* showy, trying to be smart:—*comp.* **flash'ier**; *superl.* **flash'iest**.

flash'ily *adv.* **flash'iness** *n.*

flash'-back. See **flash** (*def.* 6).

flash'-bulb *n.* a bulb producing flashlight for photography.

flash'light *n.* **1** a sudden, brief, very bright light used to take photographs. **2** an electric torch.

flask *fläsk*, *n.* a narrow-necked vessel for liquid or powder, of metal, glass, etc.

flat *flat*, *adj.* **1** smooth. **2** level. **3** stretched out. **4** (of e.g. lemonade) no longer sparkling. **5** tasteless. **6** no longer blown up: *a flat tyre*. **7** uninteresting, dull. **8** (*music*) lower than the pitch intended or mentioned. **9** downright: *a flat lie*. **10** (of shoes) not having a raised heel. **11** (of a battery) with little or no power in it:—*comp.* **flatt'er**; *superl.* **flatt'est**.—*n.* **1** a level part. **2** a plain. **3** land covered by shallow water. **4** a storey or floor of a house, esp. one, or part of one, as a separate residence. **5** (*music*) a character (♭) which lowers a note a semitone. **6** a flat tyre.

flat'ly *adv.* **flat'ness** *n.*

flatt'en *v.t.* and *v.i.* to make, or become, flat.

flat'fish *n.* a fish (e.g. a sole) with a flat body.

flat'-iron (*old*) *n.* an iron for smoothing cloth.

flat race a race over level ground.

flat rate a rate the same in all cases.

flat spin (*coll.*) a panic, flap.

flat out **1** at full speed. **2** using every effort.

flatten out **1** to make or become flat or

level. **2** to bring an aeroplane into a horizontal course after a climb or dive.

flatter[1], **flattest**. See **flat**.

flatter[2] *flat'ėr*, *v.t.* **1** to praise insincerely. **2** to represent (a person, thing, etc.) as better, etc., than he, it, etc., really is: *The photograph flatters him.* **3** to please (with false hopes).
flatt'erer *n.* **flatt'ering** *adj.*
flatt'ery *n.* false praise.

flatulence *flat'ū-lėns*, *n.* gas in the intestines.

flaunt *flönt*, *v.t.* and *v.i.* to show off.

flautist *flöt'ist*, *n.* a flute-player.

flavour *flā'vȯr*, *n.* **1** taste. **2** interest. **3** special quality.—*v.t.* to give flavour to.
flā'vouring *n.* any substance used to give a flavour.

flaw *flö*, *n.* **1** a break, crack. **2** a defect.
flaw'less *adj.* perfect.

flax *flaks*, *n.* **1** the fibres of a plant which are woven into linen cloth. **2** this plant.
flax'en *adj.* **1** of, like, flax. **2** light yellow: *flaxen hair*.

flay *flā*, *v.t.* to strip the skin off:—*pr.p.* **flay'ing**; *pa.p.* **flayed**.

fleet[1] *flēt*, *n.* **1** a number of ships, or aircraft, or motor cars, etc., in company. **2** a division of the navy, commanded by an admiral. **3** the navy.

fleet[2] *flēt*, *adj.* swift, nimble.
fleet'ly *adv.* **fleet'ness** *n.*

fleeting *flēt'ing*, *adj.* passing swiftly.

Fleet Street *flēt strēt*, the press (from the London street of that name which has many newspaper offices.)

Flemish *flem'ish*, *adj.* of Flanders (west Belgium and part of France), its people, or its language.—Also *n.*

flesh *flesh*, *n.* **1** the soft substance (muscle, etc.) that covers the bones of animals. **2** animal food. **3** the body. **4** the soft substance of fruit.
flesh'ly *adj.* of the body, not spiritual.
flesh'y *adj.* fat:—*comp.* **flesh'ier**; *superl.* **flesh'iest**.
flesh'iness *n.*
flesh and blood **1** human nature. **2** kindred, relations.
in the flesh **1** alive. **2** in person.

fleur-de lis *flûr'-dė-lē'*, or *-lēs'*, *n.* a flower-like ornament and heraldic device of the kings of France.

flew. See **fly**.

flex *fleks*, *v.t.* and *v.i.* to bend.—*n.* **1** a bending. **2** a cord, esp. of insulated wire.
flexible *fleks'i-bl*, *adj.* **1** easily bent. **2** easy to adapt. **3** willing to change one's mind:—*opp.* **inflex'ible**.
flex'ibleness, **flexibil'ity** *ns.*
flex'itime *n.* a system whereby a worker does an agreed number of hours' work at times partly of his own choosing.

flick *flik*, *v.t.* to strike lightly.—*v.i.* to look (through) a book, etc. casually or quickly.—*n.* a flip.

flicker *flik'ėr*, *v.i.* **1** to flutter. **2** to burn unsteadily.

flier. See **fly**.

flight[1] *flīt*, *n.* **1** the act of passing, flying, through the air. **2** the distance travelled thus. **3** a series (of steps). **4** a flock (of birds) flying together. **5** a volley (e.g. of arrows). **6** the passage (of time). **7** the soaring (of fancy). **8** a unit in the Air Force, equivalent of a platoon in the army.
flight'less *adj.* unable to fly.
flight'y *adj.* changeable, acting according to the whim of the moment:—*comp.* **flight'ier**; *superl.* **flight'iest**.
flight'iness *n.*
flight attendant a member of the cabin crew on a passenger aircraft.
flight'-lieuten'ant *n.* a rank in the Air Force, or a person of this rank.
flight'-recorder *n.* a device which records information about the working of an aircraft during flight.
in the first flight in the highest class.
See also **fly**.

flight[2] *flīt*, *n.* the act of fleeing.

flimsy *flim'zi*, *adj.* **1** thin. **2** easily torn. **3** weak: *a flimsy excuse*:—*comp.* **flim'sier**; *superl.* **flim'siest**.—*n.* (a copy on) thin paper.
flim'sily *adv.* **flim'siness** *n.*

flinch *flinch*, *-sh*, *v.i.* **1** to shrink back (from). **2** to wince.

fling *fling*, *v.t.* **1** to cast, toss, throw. **2** to put suddenly.—*v.i.* to rush, dash:—*pa.p.* **flung**.—*n.* **1** a throw. **2** a rather careless attempt. **3** a spell of dissipation or pleasure. **4** a lively dance.

flint *flint*, *n.* **1** a hard mineral from which sparks are easily struck with steel. **2** anything very hard or difficult to make an impression on

flip *flip*, *v.t.* and *v.i.* **1** to flick. **2** to flap:—*pr.p.* **flipp'ing**; *pa.p.* **flipped**.—*n.* **1** a flick. **2** a short flight.
flipp'er *n.* a limb for swimming, as in seals, etc.

flippant *flip'ȧnt*, *adj.* **1** quick and pert in speech. **2** frivolous.
flipp'ancy, **flipp'antness** *ns.*
flipp'antly *adv.*

flirt *flûrt*, *v.t.* to move (a light article) jerkily.—*v.i.* **1** to play at courtship. **2** to trifle (with).—*n.* a man, or esp. woman,

who is in the habit of flirting.
flirtā'tion *n.* **flirtā'tious** *(-shus) adj.*

flit *flit, v.i.* **1** to flutter on the wing. **2** to fly silently or quickly. **3** to depart. **4** (*Scot.*) to change one's house.—Also *v.t.*:—*pr.p.* **flitt'ing**; *pa.p.* **flitt'ed**.
flitt'ing *n.*

flitch *flich, n.* the side of a hog salted and cured.

flitter *flit'ėr, v.i.* to flutter.
flitt'ermouse *n.* a bat:—*pl.* **-mice**.

float *flōt, v.i.* **1** to be supported in or on a liquid. **2** to drift.—*v.t.* **1** to cause to float. **2** to launch (e.g. a scheme).—*n.* **1** a raft. **2** the cork on a fishing-line. **3** a low cart. **4** a type of small open-sided van used esp. for milk delivery. **5** a platform on wheels. **6** money provided esp. for giving change.
flo(a)tā'tion *n.* **float'ing** *adj.* and *n.*
floating dock. See **dock**.
floating voter a voter not attached permanently to any one party.

flock[1] *flok, n.* **1** a company, esp. of animals. **2** a Christian congregation.—*v.i.* to come in crowds.

flock[2] *flok, n.* **1** a lock of wool. **2** woollen or cotton refuse. **3** fine particles of wool, etc. applied to something to give a raised velvety surface.

floe *flō, n.* a field of floating ice.

flog *flog, v.t.* to beat, strike, lash:—*pr.p.* **flogg'ing**; *pa.p.* **flogged**.

flood *flud, n.* **1** a great flow of water. **2** a deluge. **3** the rise of the tide. **4** any great quantity.—*v.t.* **1** to overflow. **2** to cover, or fill, as if with a flood.—Also *v.i.*
flood'gate *n.* a sluice.
flood'lighting *n.* strong lighting from many points (*v.t.* **flood'light**:—*pa.p.* **flood'lit**).
flood'-tide *n.* the rising tide.

floor *flōr, flör, n.* **1** the part of a room on which one stands. **2** a platform. **3** a storey. **4** any levelled area.—*v.t.* **1** to make a floor in. **2** to throw on the floor. **3** (*coll.*) to defeat. **4** to stump: *This question floored him.*
floor'ing *n.* material for floors.

flop *flop, v.i.* to fall down suddenly:—*pr.p.* **flopp'ing**; *pa.p.* **flopped**.—*n.* **1** a fall. **2** a collapse. **3** (*coll.*) a failure.
flopp'y *adj.*:—*comp.* **flopp'ier**; *superl.* **flopp'iest**.
floppy disk (*computers*) a thin flexible disk used to store information.

flora *flō'rȧ, flö'rȧ, n.* **1** the plants of a region or of a period. **2** a list of these.
flo'ral *adj.* of flowers.
floret *flo'rit, n.* one of the closely packed small flowers that make up the head of certain plants such as daisies, broccoli, etc.
flo'rid *(flo') adj.* **1** flowery. **2** too bright in colour. **3** too richly ornamental.
flo'rist *(flo') n.* a cultivator or seller of flowers.

florin *flo'rin, n.* formerly, a cupro-nickel coin (orig. silver) worth 2 shillings (10 new pence).

florist. See **flora**.

floss *flos, n.* a loose downy or silky substance from a plant, or from the outer part of a silkworm cocoon. **2** fine embroidery silk.

flotation. See **float**.

flotilla *flo-til'ȧ, n.* a fleet of small ships.

flotsam *flot'sȧm, n.* goods lost by shipwreck and found floating on the sea, as opp. to *jetsam*.

flounce[1] *flowns, v.i.* to move suddenly or impatiently:—*pr.p.* **flounc'ing**.—Also *n.*

flounce[2] *flowns, n.* a hanging strip gathered and sewed to the skirt of a dress.

flounder[1] *flown'dėr, v.i.* **1** to struggle awkwardly. **2** to stumble helplessly in thinking or speaking.

flounder[2] *flown'dėr, n.* a small flat fish.

flour *flowr, n.* **1** finely ground meal of wheat or other grain. **2** any fine soft powder.—*v.t.* to sprinkle with flour.
flour'y *adj*:—*comp.* **flour'ier**; *superl.* **flour'iest**.
flour'iness *n.*

flourish *flur'ish, v.i.* **1** to grow luxuriantly. **2** to prosper. **3** to make ornamental strokes with the pen. **4** to show off.—*v.t.* to brandish in show or triumph.—*n.* **1** showy splendour. **2** a mark made by a bold stroke of the pen. **3** the waving of a weapon, etc. **4** a showy passage of music.
flour'ishing *adj.* thriving, prospering.

flout *flowt, v.t.* to jeer at, treat with contempt.

flow *flō, v.i.* **1** to run, as water. **2** to circulate, as blood. **3** to move smoothly. **4** to rise, as the tide. **5** to be in great quantity. **6** (of hair) to hang loose and waving.—Also *n.*
flow chart a chart showing the sequence of operations to be carried out in some process or activity.

flower *flow'ėr, flowr, n.* **1** the blossom of a plant, the part in which seed is formed. **2** the best of anything. **3** the prime of life.—*v.i.* **1** to blossom. **2** to flourish.
flow'ery *adj.* **1** full of, or adorned with, flowers. **2** using, or containing, many fine-sounding words, figures of speech, etc.:—*comp.* **flow'erier**; *superl.* **flow'er-**

iest.
flow'eriness *n*.

flown. See **fly**.

flu *flōō*, (*coll.*) *n*. abbrev. of **influenza**.

fluctuate *fluk'tū-āt*, *v.i.* **1** to move up and down or to and fro. **2** to vary:—*pr.p.* **fluc'tuating**.
fluctuā'tion *n*.

flue *flōō*, *n*. **1** a pipe for hot air, smoke, etc. **2** a small chimney.

fluent *flōō'ėnt*, *adj.* **1** able to express oneself quickly and easily: *He is a fluent speaker.* **2** coming quickly and easily: *He spoke to her in fluent French.*
flu'ency *n*. **flu'ently** *adv*.

fluff *fluf*, *n*. any soft, downy stuff.
fluff'y *adj.*:—*comp.* **fluff'ier**; *superl.* **fluff'iest**.

fluid *flōō'id*, *adj.* **1** flowing. **2** not solid, rigid or stable. **3** shifting. **4** changing.—*n*. a substance whose particles can move about with freedom—a liquid or gas.
flu'idness, fluid'ity *ns*.
fluid ounce one-twentieth of a pint.

fluke[1] *flōōk*, *n*. **1** a flounder. **2** a worm causing a liver disease, esp. in sheep.

fluke[2] *flōōk*, *n*. the part of an anchor that fastens in the ground.

fluke[3] *flōōk*, *n*. an accidental success.

flummox *flum'ȯks*, *v.t.* to perplex.

flung. See **fling**.

flunkey *flung'ki*, *n*. **1** a footman. **2** a cringing fellow:—*pl.* **flun'keys**.

fluor *flōō'ȯr*, *n*. a mineral containing fluorine—also **flu'orspar**.
fluores'cence *n*. the quality possessed by some varieties of fluor, etc., of giving out light under certain conditions.
fluores'cent *adj*.
flu'oridate, flu'oridise *vs.t.* to treat (drinking water) with a fluoride:—*pr.ps.* **flu'oridating, flu'oridising**.
fluoridā'tion *n*.
flu'oride *(-īd) n*. a compound of fluorine and another element.
flu'orine *n*. an element, a pale greenish-yellow gas.
fluorspar. See **fluor**.
fluorescent lighting brighter lighting obtained, for the same amount of electricity used as with ordinary lighting, by having fluorescent material in the lamp.

flurry *flur'i*, *n*. **1** a blast or gust. **2** agitation, bustle.—*pl.* **flurr'ies**.—*v.t.* to agitate, confuse:—*pr.p.* **flurr'ying**; *pa.p.* **flurr'ied**.

flush[1] *flush*, *n*. **1** a flow of blood to the face. **2** freshness, vigour: *in the first flush of youth*.—*v.i.* **1** to become red in the face. **2** to flow swiftly.—*v.t.* **1** to make red in the face. **2** to excite with joy: *flushed with victory*. **3** to cleanse by a rush of water.—*adj.* well supplied with money.

flush[2] *flush*, *adj.* having the surface level (with another surface).

flush[3] *flush*, *v.i.* (of birds) to start up and fly away.—*v.t.* **1** to rouse (game birds). **2** to force (out) from concealment.—*n*. a number of birds roused at one time.

flush[4] *flush*, *n*. a run of cards all of the same suit.

fluster *flus'tėr*, *n*. flurry, agitation.—*v.t.* to make hot and confused.

flute *flōōt*, *n*. **1** a musical wind instrument, a pipe with finger-holes and keys, blown through a hole in the side. **2** any of the curved vertical furrows (called **flut'ing**), e.g. on a pillar.—*v.i.* to play the flute.—*v.t.* to form grooves in:—*pr.p.* **flut'ing**.
flut'ist *n*.—See also **flautist**.

flutter *flut'ėr*, *v.i.* **1** to flap the wings. **2** to move in a quick irregular way. **3** to be in agitation or in uncertainty.—Also *v.t.*—*n*. **1** a quick irregular motion. **2** agitation. **3** a gamble.

flux *fluks*, *n*. **1** the act of flowing. **2** the act or state of changing. **3** a flow of matter. **4** a substance added to another to make it melt more readily.

fly *flī*, *v.i.* **1** to move through the air, esp. on wings or in an aircraft. **2** to move swiftly. **3** to pass away. **4** to flee. **5** to burst: *The glass flew into pieces.*—*v.t.* **1** to avoid, flee from. **2** to cause to fly. **3** to cross by flying. **4** to take by air:—*pr.p.* **fly'ing**; *pa.t.* **flew** *(flōō)*; *pa.p.* **flown** *(flōn)*.—*n*. **1** an insect with two transparent wings, esp. the common housefly. **2** a fish-hook dressed to suggest a fly. **3** a flap of material with buttonholes or a zip, e.g. on trousers. **4** a flap at the entrance to a tent. **5** a light double-seated carriage. **6** a fly-wheel. **7** (in *pl.*) in a theatre, the part above the stage from which the scenery etc. is controlled:—*pl.* **flies**.—*adj.* (*slang*) **1** smart, knowing. **2** cunning, sly.
fly'er, flī'er *n*.
fly'blown *adj.* **1** tainted with flies' eggs or maggots. **2** tainted.
flying boat a type of seaplane.
flying doctor a doctor, esp. orig. in remote parts of Australia, who can be called by radio and who flies to visit patients.
fly'ing-fish *n*. a fish that can leap from water and stay in the air for a short time.
fly'ing-fox *n*. a large bat.
flying officer a rank in the Air Force, or a person of this rank.
flying saucer a circular unidentified fly-

ing object, supposedly from outer space.
flying squad a body of police organised for fast action or movement or available for duty where needed.
flying start **1** in a race, a start in which the signal is given after the competitors are in motion. **2** a favourable beginning leading to an advantage over others or to rapid progress.
flying visit a very brief visit.
fly'leaf *n.* a blank leaf at the beginning or end of a book.
fly'over *n.* **1** a road or railway crossing above another. **2** a fly-past.
fly'paper *n.* a sticky or poisonous paper for destroying flies.
fly'-past *n.* a ceremonial flight of aircraft.
fly'weight *n.* a boxer not heavier than 8 st. (50.8 kg.).
fly'wheel a large heavy wheel applied to machinery to keep the speed even.
fly in the face of to defy, treat with contempt (person, custom, etc.)
fly in the ointment a minor bad thing that spoils something otherwise good.
fly out to break out in a rage.
let fly **1** to hurl, shoot. **2** (with *at*) to attack with missiles or words.
See also **flight**[1].

foal *fōl*, *n.* the young of the horse, ass, etc.—*v.i.*, *v.t.* to give birth to (a foal).

foam *fōm*, *n.* **1** froth. **2** bubbles on the surface of liquor. **3** (in poetry) the sea.—*v.i.* **1** to gather foam. **2** to run foaming (over, etc.). **3** to be in a rage.—*adj.* (used only before a noun; of a material) with many bubbles in it, sponge-like: *foam rubber*.

fob[1] *fob*, *v.t.* **1** to foist (off on). **2** to give (someone) something less good than he wanted: *I was fobbed off with excuses and promises*.

fob[2] *fob* *n.* **1** a small pocket for a watch. **2** a chain hanging from it.

focal. See **focus**.

fo'c'sle. Contr. form of **forecastle**.

focus *fōkŭs*, *n.* **1** a point in which rays of light, etc., come together (e.g. light rays after passing through a lens). **2** any central point:—*pl.* **fō'cuses**, **foci** *(fō'sī)*.—*v.t.* **1** to adjust (e.g. field-glasses) so as to get a clear picture. **2** to bring (a picture) up clearly e.g. by adjusting a projector. **3** to direct to one point or subject: *The accident focused public attention on the necessity for a new road*:—*pr.p.* **fō'cus(s)ing**; *pa.p.* **fō'cus(s)ed**.
fō'cal *adj.* having to do with a focus.
in (out of) focus placed so as to give (or not to give) a clear picture.

fodder *fod'ėr*, *n.* food for cattle.

foe *fō*, *n.* an enemy.
foe'man *n.* an enemy in war:—*pl.* **foe'-men**.

foetid *fē'tid*, *adj.* Same as **fetid**.

foetus, fetus *fē'tŭs*, *n.* the young animal in the egg or in the womb.
foe'tal, **fē'tal** *adjs.*

fog *fog*, *n.* **1** a thick mist. **2** confusion or bewilderment.—*v.t.* **1** to shroud in fog. **2** to make indistinct, or difficult to understand:—*pr.p.* **fogg'ing**; *pa.p.* **fogged**.
fogg'y *adj.*:—*comp.* **fogg'ier**; *superl.* **fogg'iest**.
fogg'iness *n.*
fog'-bank *n.* a dense mass of fog.
fog'horn *n.* **1** a horn sounded as a warning signal in foggy weather. **2** a deep, loud voice.

fogy, fogey *fō'gi*, *n.* someone with old-fashioned views:—*pl.* **fo'gies**, **fo'geys**.

foible *foi'bl*, *n.* a failing, weakness.

foil[1] *foil*, *v.t.* to defeat, baffle (a person, an attempt):—*pr.p.* **foil'ing**; *pa.p.* **foiled**.—*n.* a light, blunt-edged sword with a button at the point, used in fencing.

foil[2] *foil*, *n.* **1** a leaf or thin plate of metal. **2** a thin leaf of metal put under a precious stone to show it to advantage. **3** any thing or person that serves as contrast for something or someone else.

foist *foist*, *v.t.* to palm off (something undesirable on someone).

fold[1] *fōld*, *n.* **1** a doubling of anything upon itself. **2** a layer. **3** a crease.—*v.t.* **1** to lay in folds. **2** to bring (wings) close to the body, (arms) together and close to the body. **3** to clasp (one's hands). **4** to wrap up. **5** to embrace. **6** (*cookery*) to mix (in, together) lightly. **7** (of a business, etc.) to cease to operate (also with *up*).
fold'er *n.* a folding case for loose papers.
fold'ing *adj.* that can be folded.

fold[2] *fōld*, *n.* **1** an enclosure esp. for sheep. **2** a flock of sheep in a fold. **3** the Church, or a particular church.—*v.t.* to put into a fold.

foliage *fō'li-ij*, *n.* leaves.
folio *fō'li-ō*, *n.* **1** a leaf (two pages) of a book. **2** a page number. **3** a sheet of paper folded once. **4** a book having pages of the largest size. **5** a page in an account book, or two opposite pages numbered as one:—*pl.* **fō'lios**.

folk *fōk*, *n.* **1** people. **2** one's own family:—*pl.* **folk**, **folks**.
folk'lore *n.* the ancient beliefs, customs and traditions of the people.
folk'song, -tale *ns.* a song or story origi-

nating among the people and handed down by them.

follow *fol'ō, v.t.* **1** to go or come behind. **2** to pursue. **3** to come after. **4** to result from. **5** to go along (a road). **6** to practise (a profession). **7** to imitate. **8** to obey (the rules). **9** to act on (advice). **10** to keep the eye or mind fixed on. **11** to grasp or understand: *I do not follow your argument.*

foll'ower *n.*

foll'owing *n.* supporters.—*adj.* **1** coming after or behind. **2** about to be mentioned: *Pack the following articles:—3 cups, a spoon, sugar… .*—*prep.* after, as a result of.

follow up to follow (an action) with others intended to increase e.g. an advantage.

folly *fol'i, n.* **1** silliness or weakness of mind. **2** a foolish action or thing:—*pl.* **foll'ies**.

foment *fō-ment', v.t.* **1** to apply a (usu.) warm liquid or damp cloth to. **2** to stir up (e.g. strife).

fomentā'tion *n.* the act of fomenting, or the material used.

fond *fond, adj.* **1** foolish; *fond hopes.* **2** foolishly tender and loving. **3** very affectionate. **4** (with *of*) liking: *fond of animals, of sport, of boasting.*

fon'dle *v.t.* to caress:—*pr.p.* **fond'ling**.

fond'ly *adv.* **fond'ness** *n.*

fondant *fon'dånt, n.* a soft sweet that melts in the mouth.

fondle. See **fond**.

font *font, n.* the, usu. stone, receptacle for holding baptismal water.

food *fōōd, n.* **1** what one feeds on. **2** nourishment. **3** material for mental or spiritual activity: *That gave him food for thought.*

food poisoning illness caused by eating food made toxic by bacteria, etc.

food processor an electrical appliance for chopping, blending, etc. food.

food'stuff *n.* a material used as food.

fool[1] *fōōl, n.* **1** a person showing lack of ordinary sense. **2** a person of weak mind. **3** a jester.—*v.t.* to deceive.—*v.i.* **1** (also with *about, around*) to play the fool. **2** to trifle.

fool'ery *n.* foolish behaviour.

fool'hardy *adj.* foolishly bold, rash.

fool'hardily *adv.* **fool'hardiness** *n.*

fool'ish *adj.* **1** lacking common sense. **2** weak in intellect. **3** ridiculous.

fool'ishly *adv.* **fool'ishness** *n.*

fool'proof *adj.* **1** that even a fool could understand. **2** not likely to go wrong even if clumsily handled.

foolscap *fōōl'skap, fōōlz'kap, n.* writing or printing paper, $17 \times 13\frac{1}{2}$ in. (43×34 cm.), orig. bearing the watermark of a fool's cap and bells.

a fool's errand a silly errand or one without result.

a fool's paradise a state of happiness based on false beliefs or hopes.

play the fool to act deliberately in a foolish way.

fool[2] *fōōl, n.* crushed fruit stewed, mixed with cream and sugar.

foolhardy, foolscap, etc. See **fool**[1].

foot *foot, n.* **1** the part of the body on which an animal stands or walks. **2** the part of a garment covering the foot. **3** the lower part. **4** a measure, 12 inches (30.5 cm.) (orig. the length of a man's foot). **5** a division of a line of poetry:—*pl.* **feet** (**foot** in phrases such as *a ten-foot wall*).—*v.i.* (with *it*) to dance, to walk.—*v.t.* to pay (a bill):—*pr.p.* **foot'ing**; *pa.p.* **foot'ed**.

foot'ing *n.* **1** a foothold. **2** foundation. **3** position, conditions: *to be on a friendly footing with one's neighbours.*

foot'ball *n.* (a game with) a large ball for kicking.

foot'board *n.* a board for getting in and out of a vehicle, or one for a driver's feet.

foot'fall *n.* (the sound of) a footstep.

foot'hills *n.pl.* lesser heights below high mountains.

foot'hold *n.* **1** a place on which to stand. **2** a position from which to advance.

foot'light *n.* one of a row of lights in front of and on a level with the stage in a theatre, etc.

foot'loose *adj.* free to do as one pleases.

foot'man *n.* a servant in livery:—*pl.* **foot'men**.

foot'mark, foot'print *ns.* the mark of a foot.

foot'note *n.* a note at the foot of a page referring to something in the text above.

foot'pad *n.* a highwayman on foot.

foot'path *n.* a path or way for pedestrians only.

foot'plate *n.* the platform on which the driver of a locomotive engine stands.

footprint. See **footmark**.

foot'race *n.* a race on foot.

foot'rule *n.* a rule or measure marked in feet and inches.

foot'-soldier *n.* one who marches and fights on foot.

foot'sore *adj.* having painful feet because of much walking.

foot'step *n.* the mark, or sound, of a foot.

foot'wear *n.* boots and shoes.

foot-and-mouth disease a very serious, rapidly spreading, disease of cloven-footed animals (e.g. cows).

on foot 1 walking or running. 2 afoot, in progress, happening.

put one's foot down to take a firm stand, to oppose or support something strongly.

put one's foot in it to blunder.

set on foot to set in motion (e.g. a plan).

footling *fo͞ot'ling, adj.* silly, trivial.

foo yung. See **fu yung**.

fop *fop, n.* an affected dandy.

fopp'ish *adj.* **fopp'ishness** *n.*

for *fö̆r, fȯr, prep.* **1** because of (e.g. *He wept for shame).* **2** in payment of, or return for: *£2.50 for a book*; *a reward for his services.* **3** on behalf of: *Please do it for me.* **4** with a purpose as indicated: *He went for the milk*; *a case for holding books.* **5** through the space or time of: *For seven miles he met no one*; *he walked for two hours.—conj.* because.

for all that in spite of that.

forage *for'ij, n.* **1** food for horses and cattle. **2** provisions.—*v.i.* **1** to carry off fodder forcibly. **2** to rummage about (for what one wants):—*pr.p.* **for'aging**.

foray *for'ā, n.* a raid.

forbade. See **forbid**.

forbear[1] *fö̆r-bār', v.i.* **1** to be patient. **2** to refrain (from): *We must forbear from making any comment* (also with infinitive; e.g. *He forbore to comment*):—*pa.t.* **forbore'**; *pa.p.* **forborne'**.

forbear'ance *n.* patience, control of temper, long-suffering.

forbear'ing *adj.*

forbear[2]. Same as **forebear**.

forbid *fö̆r-bid', v.t.* **1** to command not (to do). **2** to prevent, make impossible:—*pa.t.* **forbade'** *(-bad')*; *pa.p.* **forbidd'en**.

forbidd'en *adj.* **1** prohibited. **2** unlawful.

forbidd'ing *adj.* causing dislike, unpleasant, rather frightening: *a forbidding appearance.*

forbore, **forborne**. See **forbear**.

force[1] *fōrs, fȯrs, n.* **1** strength, power, energy. **2** violence. **3** power (of an argument) to convince. **4** purpose, value. **5** operation: *The rule has never been put into force.* **6** a body of men and women prepared for action: *the police force.—v.t.* **1** to push, draw, thrust, etc. by force. **2** to gain by force: *to force an entry.* **3** to compel (a person, an action): *They forced him to go, forced a confession from him.* **4** to cause (a plant) to grow or ripen rapidly:—*pr.p.* **forc'ing**.

forced *adj.* **1** accomplished by great effort: *a forced march.* **2** unnatural: *His cheerfulness was rather forced.*

force'ful *adj.* powerful, vigorous.

force'fully *adv.* **force'fulness** *n.*

forc'ible *adj.* **1** having force. **2** done, carried out, by force.

forc'ibly *adv.* **forc'ibleness** *n.*

in force **1** in large numbers. **2** applying, having effect e.g. as part of the law.

force[2] *fōrs, fȯrs, v.t.* to stuff (e.g. a fowl):—*pr.p.* **forc'ing**.

force'meat *n.* meat chopped fine and highly seasoned, esp. for stuffing.

forceps *fȯr'seps, n.* a pincer-like instrument for holding or lifting.

ford *fōrd, fȯrd, n.* a place where water may be crossed on foot, on horseback, etc., or in a vehicle.—Also *v.t.*

fore *fōr, fȯr, adj.* front (as in *fore wing*, or *forewing*, etc.).—*n.* the front (in the phrase **to the fore**, in the front or an obvious place, prominent).—*adv.* at or towards the front of a ship.—*interj.* (*golf*) a warning cry to anybody in the way of the ball.

fore and aft lengthwise of a ship.

fore- *fōr-, fȯr-, pfx.* before.

forearm[1] *fōr'ärm, fȯr', n.* the part of the arm between elbow and wrist.

forearm[2] *fōr-ärm', fȯr-, v.t.* to arm or prepare beforehand.

forebear *fōr'bār, fȯr',* (orig. *Scot.*) *n.* ancestor.

forebode *fōr-bōd', fȯr-, v.t.* to be an omen of: *These early mishaps seemed to forebode a disastrous end to the expedition*:—*pr.p.* **forebod'ing**.

forebod'ing *n.* a feeling that something bad will happen.

forecast *fōr'käst, fȯr',* also *-käst', v.t.* and *v.i.* to tell beforehand, predict: *He forecast good weather for the next three days*:—*pa.t.* and *pa.p.* **forecast(ed)**.—Also *n.*

forecastle, fo'c'sle *fōk'sl, n.* the forepart of a ship under the maindeck, the quarters of the crew.

foreclose *fōr-klōz', fȯr-, v.t.* to take away from a person who has mortgaged property the right to redeem (the mortgage) and get his property back:—*pr.p.* **foreclos'ing**.

foreclos'ure *(-klōzh'ür) n.*

foredeck *fōr'dek, fȯr' n.* the forepart of a deck or ship.

foredoom *fōr-do͞om', fȯr-, v.t.* to doom beforehand.

forefather *fōr'fä-THėr', fȯr', n.* an ancestor.

forefinger *fōr'fing-gėr, fȯr', n.* the finger next to the thumb.

forefoot *fōr'foot, fȯr', n.* one of the front feet of a four-footed animal.

forefront *fōr'frunt, för'*, *n.* the very front.

forego[1] *fōr-gō', för-*, *v.t.* to go before—chiefly used in its *pr.p.* **forego'ing** and *pa.p.* **foregone'**.

foregone conclusion 1 a conclusion come to before study of the evidence. 2 an inevitable result.

forego[2] better **forgo** (see this word).

foreground *fōr'grownd, för'*, *n.* the part of a picture or view nearest the observer's eye.

forehand *fōr'hand, för'*, *adj.* made with the palm of the hand in front.—Also *n.*

forehead *for'id, -ed*, or *fōr'hed, för'*, *n.* the part of the head above the eyes, the brow.

foreign *for'in*, *adj.* **1** belonging to another country. **2** concerned with dealings with countries other than one's own: *the Foreign Office, foreign exchange, foreign correspondent.* **3** coming from an outside source: *a speck of dust or other foreign body in his eye.* **4** not in keeping with (with *to*): *Deceit was foreign to her nature.*

for'eigner *n.* a native of another country.

Foreign Office the government department dealing with foreign affairs.

forejudge *fōr-juj', för-*, *v.t.* to judge before hearing the facts and proof:—*pr.p.* **forejudg'ing**.

foreknowledge *fōr-nol'ij, för-*, *n.* knowledge of a thing before it happens.

foreland *fōr'lȧnd, för'*, *n.* a headland.

foreleg *fōr'leg, för'*, *n.* a front leg.

forelock *fōr'lok, för'*, *n.* the lock of hair on the forehead.

foreman *fōr'mȧn, för'*, *n.* an overseer:—*pl.* **fore'men**:—*fem.* **fore'woman** (*pl.* **fore'-women** *-wim-in*).

foremast *fōr'mäst, -mȧst, för'*, *n.* the mast that is next to a ship's bow.

foremost *fōr'mōst, för'*, *adj.* first in place, rank, or dignity.—Also *adv.*

forename *fōr'nām, för'*, *n.* a person's first name or Christian name.

forenoon *fōr'nōōn, fōr-nōōn', för-*, *n.* the part of the day before midday.

forensic *fö-ren'sik*, *adj.* belonging to courts of law or the investigation of crime.

forepart *fōr'pärt, för'*, *n.* the front, or the early, part.

forerunner *fōr'run-ėr, för'*, *n.* a person or thing that goes, or happens, before.

foresaid *fōr'sed, för'*, *adj.* already mentioned.

foresee *fōr-sē', för-*, *v.t.* or *v.i.* to see or know beforehand:—*pa.t.* **foresaw'**; *pa.p.* **foreseen'**.

foreshadow *fōr-shad'ō, för-*, *v.t.* to indicate (a coming event), as a shadow in front shows an approaching object.

foreshore *fōr'shōr, för'*, *n.* the space between the high and low water marks.

foreshorten *fōr-shört'n, för-*, *v.t.* **1** to cause (an object that sticks out towards the spectator) to appear as if shortened in the direction towards the spectator. **2** to draw, etc. (an object) so as to show this apparent shortening.

foresight *fōr'sīt, för'*, *n.* **1** the act of foreseeing. **2** the ability to see what is likely to happen. **3** prudence, care for the future. **4** a sight on the muzzle of a gun.

foreskin *fōr'skin, för'*, *n.* the loose skin round the penis.

forest *for'ist*, *n.* **1** a large tract of land covered with trees. **2** a preserve for large game: *a deer forest*.

for'ester *n.* one who has the charge of, or works in, a forest.

for'estry *n.* the art of cultivating forests.

forestall *fōr-stöl', för-*, *v.t.* **1** to act before (someone), and so hinder his plans. **2** to act before (something that is going to happen).

foretaste *fōr'tāst, för'*, *n.* a slight experience beforehand (of something pleasant or unpleasant).

foretell *fōr-tel', för-*, *v.t.* to tell before, to predict:—*pa.p.* **foretold'**.

forethought *fōr'thöt, för'*, *n.* prudent thought or care for the future.

foretold. See **foretell**.

forever. See **ever**.

forewarn *fōr-wörn', för-*, *v.t.* to warn beforehand.

forewing. See **fore**.

forewoman. See **foreman**.

foreword *fōr'wûrd, för'*, *n.* a preface.

forfeit *för'fit*, *v.t.* **1** to lose the right to by some fault or crime. **2** (*loosely*) to give up voluntarily (a right).—*n.* **1** a penalty for a fault. **2** a fine.

for'feiture *n.* **1** the act of forfeiting. **2** the thing forfeited.

forgave. See **forgive**.

forge[1] *förj, fōrj*, *n.* **1** a furnacc, csp. one in which iron is heated. **2** a smithy. **3** a place where anything is shaped or made.—*v.t.* **1** to form by heating and hammering. **2** to form. **3** to counterfeit (e.g. a signature).—*v.i.* to commit forgery:—*pr.p.* **forg'ing**.

forg'er *n.*

forg'ery *n.* **1** the making or altering of writing, or a picture, etc. with the intention of deceiving. **2** the writing, picture, etc. so produced:—*pl.* **forg'eries**.

forge[2] *fŏrj, fōrj, v.t.* to move steadily on: *to forge ahead*:—*pr.p.* **forg'ing**.

forget *fŏr-get', v.t.* **1** to put away from the memory. **2** to fail to remember, to neglect, omit:—*pr.p.* **forgett'ing**; *pa.t.* **forgot'**; *pa.p.* **forgott'en**.
forget'ful *adj.* **1** apt to forget. **2** not thinking (of e.g. duty, other people).
forget'fully *adv.* **forget'fulness** *n.*
forget'-me-not *n.* a small plant with blue flowers, regarded as the emblem of remembrance.
forget oneself to lose one's self-control or dignity.

forgive *fŏr-giv', v.t.* **1** to pardon, or cease to feel resentment against (a person). **2** to pardon, overlook (a fault).—Also *v.i.*:—*pr.p.* **forgiv'ing**; *pa.t.* **forgave'**; *pa.p.* **forgiv'en**.
forgive'ness *n.* pardon.
forgiv'ing *adj.* ready to pardon, merciful.

forgo *fŏr-gō'*, less correctly **forego**, *fōr-gō', fŏr-, v.t.* to give up, do without:—*pa.t.* **for(e)went'**; *pa.p.* **for(e)gone'**.

forgot, forgotten. See **forget**.

fork *fŏrk, n.* **1** a pronged instrument. **2** anything that divides into prongs or branches. **3** one of the branches into which a road or river divides, also the point of separation.—*v.i.* to divide into two branches.
forked, fork'y *adjs.* shaped like a fork.
fork-lift truck a power-driven truck with an arrangement of steel prongs which can lift and carry heavy packages and stack them where required.

forlorn *fŏr-lŏrn', adj.* **1** forsaken. **2** pitiful, wretched.
forlorn'ly *adv.* **forlorn'ness** *n.*

form *fŏrm, n.* **1** shape. **2** mode of arrangement. **3** condition, state: *water in the form of ice.* **4** a system (e.g. of government). **5** fixed procedure: *forms and ceremonies.* **6** a mere formality. **7** a partly blank statement to be filled with details. **8** a mould. **9** a bench. **10** a class in school. **11** the bed of a hare.—*v.t.* **1** to give shape to. **2** to make. **3** to conceive (an idea, opinion) in the mind. **4** to develop (a habit).—*v.i.* **1** to develop. **2** to take (up) position in (a particular arrangement.)
for'mal *adj.* **1** according to the fixed procedure. **2** marked by ceremony. **3** stiff, coldly correct:—*opp.* **infor'mal**.
for'mally *adv.*
for'malise *v.t.* **1** to make formal. **2** to make precise:—*pr.p.* **for'malising**.
formal'ity *n.* **1** formal quality. **2** a formal act:—*pl.* **formal'ities**.
formā'tion *n.* **1** the act of making. **2** something that is formed. **3** structure. **4** prearranged order: *to fly in formation.*
form'ative *adj.* giving form or shape: *the formative years of one's life*.
See also **formula, formulate**.

format *fŏr'mat, n.* **1** of books, etc., the size, shape, in which they are issued. **2** the style, arrangement and contents of a programme. **3** (*computers*) the description of the way data is, or is to be, arranged on a disk, etc. *v.t.* **1** to arrange a book, etc. into a specific format. **2** (*computers*) to arrange data for use on a disc, etc. **3** (*computers*) to prepare a disc, etc. for use by dividing it into sectors:—*pr.p.* **form'atting**; *pa.p.* **form'atted**.

formation, formative. See **form**.

former *fŏr'mėr, adj.* **1** before in time. **2** past. **3** first mentioned (of two).
form'erly in former, past, times.

formidable *fŏr'mi-dȧ-bl, mid', adj.* difficult to deal with.
formidableness *n.* **formidably** *adv.*

formula *fŏrm'ū-lȧ, n.* **1** a set form of words. **2** a rule expressed in algebraic symbols. **3** the composition of a substance expressed in chemical symbols:—*pl.* **form'ulas, form'ulae** *(-ē)*.
form'ulate *v.t.* **1** to express in definite form. **2** to make (a plan) in detail:—*pr.p.* **for'mulating**.

forsake *fŏr-sāk', v.t.* **1** to desert. **2** to give up:—*pr.p.* **forsāk'ing**; *pa.t.* **forsook'**; *pa.p.* **forsāk'en**.

forswear *fŏr-swār', v.t.* to renounce, esp. upon oath.—*v.i.* (also, as *v.t.*, **forswear oneself**) to swear falsely:—*pa.t.* **forswore'**; *pa.p.* **forsworn'** *(-ō-, -ö-)*.

fort *fōrt, fŏrt, n.* **1** a small fortress. **2** (in N. America) an outlying trading-station.
fortificā'tion *n.* **1** the art of strengthening a military position against attack. **2** (usu. in *pl.*) walls, etc. built to strengthen a position.
fortify *fŏr'ti-fī, v.t.* to strengthen, esp. against attack or in readiness for an effort or ordeal:—*pr.p.* **for'tifying**; *pa.p.* **for'tified**.
fortitude *fŏr'ti-tūd, n.* courage in enduring misfortune, pain, etc.
fortress *fŏr'tris, n.* a fortified place.
hold the fort to take charge temporarily.

forte[1] *fŏr'tā, n.* something in which one excels.

forte[2] *fŏr'ti, adj., adv.* (*music*) loud:—*superl.* **fortis'simo** very loud.

forth *fōrth, fŏrth, adv.* **1** forward. **2** onward. **3** out. **4** into the open.
forth'com'ing *adj.* **1** approaching in time. **2** ready when required. **3** (of a person) frank and sociable.

forth'right *adj.* **1** honest. **2** downright.
forthwith' *adv.* immediately.

fortieth. See **forty**.

fortification, **fortified**, **fortify**. See **fort**.

fortissimo. See **forte**[2].

fortitude. See **fort**.

fortnight *fört'nīt*, *n.* two weeks.

fortress. See **fort**.

fortuitous *för-tū'i-tùs*, *adj.* happening by chance.

fortune *för'chùn*, *n.* **1** whatever comes by chance, luck. **2** prosperity, success. **3** a large sum of money.
for'tunate *(-it) adj.* lucky.
for'tune-tell'er *n.* one who **tells fortunes**, i.e. foretells, or pretends to foretell, what will happen to people in the future.
for'tune-tell'ing *n.*

forty *för'ti*, *n.* and *adj.* four times ten (40 or XL).
for'ties *n.pl.* the numbers forty to forty-nine.
for'tieth *(-ti-ėth) adj.* **1** next after the thirty-ninth. **2** equal to one of forty equal parts.—Also *n.*
forty winks a short nap.
See also **four**.

forum *fōr'ùm*, *för'*, *n.* **1** a market place, esp. that in ancient Rome where business was done and law cases were settled. **2** a place, or opportunity, for discussion.

forward *för'wàrd*, *adv.* **1** near, or to, the front (also **forwards**). **2** ahead. **3** into view. **4** into consideration: *to bring forward a suggestion.*—*adj.* **1** near, or at, the front. **2** in an onward direction: *a forward movement.* **3** pert, bold.—*n.* a player in a forward position.—*v.t.* **1** to send on (e.g. a letter). **2** to help on (e.g. a plan).

forwent. See **forgo**.

fossil *fos'il*, *n.* **1** the remains of an animal or vegetable turned to stony substance (also *adj.*; used only before a noun). **2** an old-fashioned person or thing.
foss'ilise *v.t.* and *v.i.* to change into a fossil:—*pr.p.* **foss'ilising**.
fossil fuel any fuel such as coal, petroleum and natural gas, derived from fossilised matter.

foster *fos'tėr*, *v.t.* **1** to bring up. **2** to help to grow or develop, encourage.
fos'ter-broth'er, **-child**, **-daugh'ter** etc., *ns.* a child brought up with a family of different parentage.
fos'ter-fa'ther, **-moth'er**, **-pa'rent** *ns.* one who brings up a child in place of its father, mother.

fought. See **fight**.

foul *fowl*, *adj.* **1** filthy. **2** impure. **3** obscene. **4** stormy: *foul weather.* **5** against the rules: *a foul stroke.*—*v.t.* **1** to make foul. **2** to collide with. **3** to become entangled with.—*n.* a breach of the rules in a game.
foully *fowl'li*, *adv.* **foul'ness** *n.*
foul play **1** unfair action in a game. **2** dishonesty. **3** murder.
fall foul of **1** to come against. **2** to quarrel with. **3** to assault.
foul up **1** to (cause to) become blocked or entangled. **2** (*coll.*) to cause to fail or break down; to bungle (*n.* **foul'-up**).
See also **filth**.

found[1]. See **find**.

found[2] *fownd*, *v.t.* **1** to build or base: *a house founded on a rock*; *a story founded on fact.* **2** to start, establish, set up: *He left money to found a college.*
foundā'tion *n.* **1** the act of founding. **2** (often in *pl.)* the base of a building. **3** the basis: *The foundation of this rumour was a remark someone had misunderstood.* **4** a permanent fund for some special object.
found'er *n.*
foundation stone one of the stones forming the foundation of a building.
well founded **1** reasonable. **2** based on fact.

found[3] *fownd*, *v.t.* to form by melting and pouring into a mould, to cast.
found'er *n.*
found'ry *n.* the place where founding is carried on:—*pl.* **found'ries**.

founder[1] *fownd'ėr*, *v.i.* **1** to collapse. **2** to fill with water and sink.

founder[2,3]. See **found**[2,3].

foundling *fownd'ling*, *n.* a small child found deserted.

foundry. See **found**[3].

fount *fownt*, *n.* **1** a spring of water. **2** a source.
fount'ain *(-in) n.* **1** a structure for producing a jet or jets of water. **2** water spouting e.g. from this. **3** a spring or source.
fount'ain-head *n.* the source, the beginning.
fountain pen a pen having a reservoir for holding ink.

four *fōr*, *för*, *n.* **1** the number next above three (4 or IV). **2** a set of four things or persons. **3** the fourth hour after midday or midnight. **4** the age of four years. **5** any thing (e.g. a shoe, a playing-card) denoted by four.—*adj.* **1** 4 in number. **2** four years old.
fourth *adj.* **1** next after the third. **2** equal to one of four equal parts.—Also *n.*
four'teen (also *-tēn'*) *adj.* and *n.* four

and ten (14 or XIV).
four'teenth (also *-tēnth'*) *adj.* **1** next after the thirteenth. **2** equal to one of fourteen equal parts.—Also *n.*
four'-foot'ed *adj.* having four feet.
four'-hand'ed *adj.* of a game, played by four people.
four'-post'er *n.* a large bed with four posts on which to hang curtains.
four'score *adj.* four times a score—80.
four'some *adj.* in which four act together (also *n.*).
four'square' *adj.* **1** square. **2** presenting a firm, bold front to all.
on all fours **1** on hands and knees. **2** exactly like, strictly able to be compared (with).
See also **forty**.

fowl *fowl*, *n.* **1** a bird. **2** a bird of the poultry kind, a cock or hen. **3** the flesh of a fowl:—*pl.* **fowls**, **fowl**.
fowl'er *n.* one who shoots or snares wild-fowl.

fox *foks*, *n.* **1** an animal akin to the dog (*fem.* **vix'en**). **2** a cunning person.
fox'y *adj.*:—*comp.* **fox'ier**; *superl.* **fox'iest**.
fox'iness *n.*
fox'glove *n.* a plant (*Digitalis*) with flowers like glove fingers.
fox'hole *n.* a small hole in which one, or two, people can hide.
fox'hound *n.* a hound for hunting foxes.
fox terrier a terrier sometimes trained to unearth foxes.
fox'trot *n.* a dance to syncopated music.

foyer *fwä'yā*, *n.* (in theatres) a lobby, an anteroom for waiting, etc.

fracas *frak'ä*, *n.* **1** uproar. **2** a noisy quarrel:—*pl.* **frac'as** *(-äz)*.

fraction *frak'sh(ȯ)n*, *n.* **1** a fragment, a small part. **2** (the symbol for) any part of a unit, e.g. $\frac{2}{3}$, $\frac{5}{8}$.
frac'tional *adj.*

fractious *frak'shus*, *adj.* **1** ready to quarrel, cross, peevish. **2** difficult to manage.
frac'tiously *adv.* **frac'tiousness** *n.*

fracture *frak'chur*, *v.t.* to break or crack:—*pr.p.* **frac'turing**.—*n.* **1** the breaking of any hard body, esp. a bone. **2** the part broken.

fragile *fraj'īl*, *adj.* **1** easily broken. **2** frail. **3** delicate.
fragil'ity *n.*
See also **frail**.

fragment *frag'ment*, *n.* **1** a piece broken off. **2** a very small part.—*v.t.* and *v.i.* *(frag-ment')* to break into fragments.
frag'mentary (or *-men'*) adj. consisting of fragments.
fragmentā'tion *n.*

fragrant *frā'grant*, *adj.* sweet-scented.
frā'grance, **frā'grancy** *ns.*

frail *frāl*, *adj.* **1** very easily shattered. **2** weak in health. **3** morally weak.
frail'ness, **frail'ty** (*pl.* **frail'ties**), *ns.*

frame *frām*, *v.t.* **1** to form. **2** to put together. **3** to plan. **4** to articulate: *He could scarcely frame the words.* **5** to enclose in a frame. **6** to serve as a frame for. **7** to make (someone) the victim of a frame-up:—*pr.p.* **fram'ing**.—*n.* **1** a structure made to enclose or support anything. **2** the skeleton. **3** state (of mind).
fram'ing *n.*
frame'-up *n.* a false criminal charge with the production of false evidence.
frame'work *n.* the skeleton or outline of anything.

franc *frangk*, *n.* the standard unit of money in France, Belgium and Switzerland.

franchise *fran'chīz*, *-shīz*, *n.* a right granted, esp. that of voting for a member of Parliament or of selling a company's goods in a given area.

Franco- *frang'kō-*, (as part of a word) French.

frank *frangk*, *adj.* open, candid, outspoken.—*v.t.* to mark by means of a **franking-machine** to show that postage has been paid.
frank'ly *adv.* **frank'ness** *n.*

frankfurter *frangk'fûr-tėr*, *n.* a type of smoked sausage.

frankincense *frangk'in-sens*, *n.* a sweet-smelling resin from Arabia.

frantic *fran'tik*, *adj.* **1** mad. **2** furious. **3** desperate.
fran'tically *adv.* **fran'ticness** *n.*
See also **frenzy**.

fraternal *fra-tûr'nål*, *adj.* brotherly.
frat'ernise *v.i.* to associate as brothers or friends:—*pr.p.* **frat'ernising**.
frater'nity *n.* a society of people having common interests:—*pl.* **frater'nities**.
fratricide *frat'ri-sīd*, *n.* **1** one who kills his brother. **2** the murder of a brother.

fraud *fröd*, *n.* **1** deceit. **2** imposture. **3** dishonesty. **4** (*coll.*) a cheat, impostor. **5** something that is not what it pretends to be.
fraud'ulent *(-ū-lėnt) adj.*
fraud'ulently *adv.*
fraud'ulence, **fraud'ulency** *ns.*

fraught *fröt*, *adj.* **1** laden, filled (with). **2** anxious, distressed.

fray[1] *frā*, *n.* **1** a conflict. **2** a brawl.

fray[2] *frā*, *v.t.* **1** to ravel out the edge of. **2** to cause loose ends in by rubbing.—Also *v.i.* and *n.*
frayed *adj.* (of tempers) strained.

freak *frēk*, *n.* **1** a sudden caprice or fancy. **2** a prank. **3** an abnormal natural object or occurrence. **4** one who is wildly enthusiastic about something: *a film-freak.*—*adj.* (used only before a noun) abnormal: *a freak storm, result.*
freak'ish *adj.* **1** apt to change the mind suddenly. **2** very odd, like a freak.

freckle *frek'l*, *v.t.* to spot, colour with spots:—*pr.p.* **freck'ling.**—*n.* **1** a brownish-yellow spot on the skin. **2** any small spot.
freck'ly (*comp.* **-ier**; *superl.* **-iest**), **freck'led** *adjs.*

free *frē*, *adj.* **1** not bound. **2** at liberty. **3** not under a tyrannical government. **4** unrestrained. **5** frank. **6** ready: *free to confess.* **7** lavish. **8** not attached. **9** not having (esp. something bad) (also as part of a word): *free from pain*; *The roads were free of traffic*; *trouble-free.* **10** exempt (from). **11** without payment. **12** (of e.g. a translation) not word for word:—*comp.* **frē'er**; *superl.* **frē'est.**—*v.t.* **1** to set at liberty. **2** to release from anything that restrains. **3** to rid (with *from*, *of*):—*pr.p.* **free'ing**; *pa.p.* **freed**.
free'dom *n.* **1** liberty. **2** absence of control or interference by other person or persons. **3** absence of restraint on one's movements. **4** exemption from: *freedom from taxation.* **5** privileges connected with a city. **6** frankness, outspokenness.
free'ly *adv.* **free'ness** *n.*
freebooter. See separate entry.
free enterprise the carrying-on of business without interference from the government.
free fight a mixed-up fight in which a number of people take part.
free'-for-all' *n.* a race or contest open to anyone, or a free fight.
free'-hand *adj.* (of a drawing) done by hand alone, without the help of instruments.
free'-hand'ed *adj.* open-handed, liberal.
free'-heart'ed *adj.* **1** open-hearted. **2** generous.
free'hold *adj.* (of an estate) belonging to the holder or his heirs for all time, not just for a given number of years.
free'-lance' *adj.* working when and for whom one pleases, not for any one employer.—Also *n.*, *adv.* and *v.i.* (*pr.p.* **free'-lanc'ing**).
free'man *n.* **1** one who is free, not a slave. **2** one who has received the freedom of a city, etc.:—*pl.* **free'men.**
free'mason *n.* (also *cap.*) a member of a secret order whose aims are to encourage friendly feeling and mutual help.
free'masonry *n.* **1** (also *cap.*) the system and practices of the freemasons. **2** the sense of fellowship between or among people having the same interests.
free'-range' *adj.* **1** (of poultry) allowed to move about freely. **2** (of eggs) laid by such poultry.
free speech the right to express opinions of any kind.
free'-style *adj.* (of a competition, etc.) in which any style of action may be used.
free'thinker *n.* a person who wants to form his own opinions, esp. in matters of religion.
free trade foreign trade without customs duties or other restrictions.
free verse verse in lines of irregular length.
free'-wheel' *n.* the mechanism of a bicycle by which the back wheel can be disconnected and set free from the driving gear.—*v.i.* to use this mechanism, to coast.
free'-will' *n.* **1** liberty of choice. **2** power of acting freely.
a free hand liberty to choose for oneself, or to act as one thinks best.
free and easy informal.
free on board (F.O.B.) delivered to the vessel or other conveyance without charge.
make free with to take liberties with (a person, possessions of another).

freebooter *frē'bōōt-ėr*, *n.* a pirate.

freesia *frē'zi-ȧ*, *n.* a sweet-scented flower growing from a corm.

freeze *frēz*, *v.i.* **1** to become ice. **2** to become solid from cold. **3** to be very cold. **4** to become motionless, stiff: *to freeze with terror.* **5** to become fixed (to) by cold.—Also *v.t.*:—*pr.p.* **freez'ing**; *pa.t.* **froze**; *pa.p.* **frōz'en**.
freez'er *n.* a cabinet for keeping food at, or bringing it down to, a temperature below freezing-point.
freez'ing-point *n.* the temperature at which a liquid becomes solid—that of water being 0° centigrade (Celsius).

freight *frāt*, *n.* **1** the load, cargo, of a ship, etc. **2** the charge for transporting goods by water, land, or air.—*v.t.* to load.
freight'er *n.* a ship or aircraft used to carry freight.
freight'liner *n.* a train with specially designed containers and rolling-stock, used for the rapid transport of goods.

French (in names of things sometimes spelt **french**) *french*, *-sh*, *adj.* of France or its people.—*n.* the people or language of France.

French'man *n.* a native of France:—*fem.* **French'woman**.

French chalk a soft mineral (soapstone) used in dry-cleaning, etc.

French polish a varnish for furniture.

French window a long window opening like a door.

take French leave to depart secretly without warning.

frenetic *fri-net'ik*, *adj.* frantic, frenzied.

frenzy *fren'zi*, *n.* **1** a violent excitement. **2** a fit of madness:—*pl.* **fren'zies**.

fren'zied *adj.* **fren'ziedly** *adv.*

frequent *frē'kwėnt*, *adj.* coming or occurring often:—*opp.* **infre'quent**.—*v.i.* *(fri-kwent')* to visit often.

fre'quency *n.* **1** repeated occurrence. **2** commonness of occurrence. **3** the number per second of vibrations, waves, etc.:—*pl.* **fre'quencies**.

fre'quently *adv.* **frequent'er** *n.*

fresco *fres'kō*, *n.* a painting done on walls covered with damp plaster:—*pl.* **fres'co(e)s**.

fresh *fresh*, *adj.* **1** untired. **2** blooming, healthy. **3** new, newly-made, etc. **4** another: *a fresh chapter.* **5** (of wind) strong. **6** (of weather) cool, invigorating. **7** (*slang*) making unwanted advances. **8** cheeky. **9** (of butter) without salt. **10** (of food) not preserved.

fresh'en *v.t.* and *v.i.* to make, or become, fresh (often with *up*).

fresher. See **freshman**.

fresh'ly *adv.* **fresh'ness** *n.*

fresh'man *n.* a university student in his or her first year (also **fresh'er**):—*pl.* **-men**.

fresh'water *adj.* living in water that is not salt.

fret[1] *fret*, *v.t.* **1** to eat into. **2** to rub or chafe. **3** to wear away by rubbing. **4** to ripple (water). **5** to vex.—*v.i.* **1** to wear, fray. **2** to be discontented or unhappy. **3** to worry:—*pr.p.* **frett'ing**; *pa.p.* **frett'ed**.

fret'ful *adj.* peevish.

fret'fully *adv.* **fret'fulness** *n.*

fret[2] *fret*, *v.t.* to carve or make a network of straight lines on:—*pr.p.* **frett'ing**; *pa.p.* **frett'ed**.

fret'saw *n.* a saw with narrow blade and fine teeth, used for fretwork, etc.

fret'work *n.* **1** ornamental carved work. **2** perforated woodwork.

fret[3] *fret*, *n.* a short ridge on the finger-board of a guitar or other instrument.

friable *frī'ȧ-bl*, *adj.* apt to crumble, easily reduced to powder.

frī'ableness, **friabil'ity** *ns.*

friar *frī'ȧr*, *n.* a member or a mendicant (see this word) monastic order.

fri'ary *n* a convent of friars:—*pl.* **fri'aries**.

fricassee *frik-a-sē'*, *frik'*, *n.* a dish of fowl, rabbit, etc., cut up and served in sauce.—Also *v.t.*:—*pr.p.* **fricasseeing**; *pa.p.* **fricasseed**.

friction *frik'sh(ȯ)n*, *n.* **1** rubbing. **2** the resistance of a moving body to sliding, rolling, etc. caused by its surface and the surface of the body along which it moves. **3** disagreement, strife.

Friday *frī'di*, *n.* the sixth day of the week.

fridge *frij*, *n.* a refrigerator.

fried. See **fry**[1].

friend *frend*, *n.* **1** an intimate acquaintance, a well-wisher, helper, supporter. **2** (*cap.*) a Quaker.

friend'less *adj.* without friends.

friend'ly *adj.* **1** like a friend. **2** kind, showing friendship. **3** favourable:—*comp.* **friend'lier**; *superl.* **friend'liest**.

friend'liness *n.*

friend'ship *n.* **1** attachment from mutual liking. **2** friendly assistance.

friendly society an association for insurance against sickness, old age, etc.

frieze[1] *frēz*, *n.* a heavy woollen cloth.

frieze[2] *frēz*, *n.* a decorative band along the top of the wall of a room.

frigate *frig'it*, *n.* **1** orig. a light vessel driven by oars or sails. **2** at different periods, the name applied to different types of warship.

fright *frīt*, *n.* **1** sudden fear. **2** terror. **3** (*coll.*) a person of ridiculous appearance.

fright'en *v.t.* **1** to make afraid, alarm. **2** to scare (away, off).

fright'ful *adj.* **1** terrible, shocking. **2** (*coll.*) very great.

fright'fully *adv.* **fright'fulness** *n.*

take fright to become afraid.

frigid *frij'id*, *adj.* **1** frozen. **2** cold.

frigid'ity, **frig'idness** *ns.*

frigid zones the parts of the earth's surface within the Arctic and Antarctic circles.

frill *fril*, *n.* **1** a trimming made from a strip of cloth gathered along one side. **2** (in *pl.*) unnecessary adornment, or affectation.

frill'y *adj.*:—*comp.* **frill'ier**; *superl.* **frill'iest**.

fringe *frinj*, *n.* **1** a border of loose threads. **2** hair cut falling over the brow. **3** the border or outer edge of an area or group.—*v.t.* to border:—*pr.p.* **fring'ing**.—*adj.* (used only before a noun) **1** not quite part of a normal or orthodox form, group, etc.: *fringe medicine.* **2** in addition to e.g. one's salary: *fringe benefits.* **3** less common or popular: *fringe sports.*

Frisbee® *friz'bi, n.* a plastic saucer-shaped object made to skim through the air as a game.

frisk *frisk, v.i.* to gambol, leap playfully.—*v.t.* (*slang*) to search the pockets, etc., of (a person).
frisk'y *adj.* lively, frolicsome:—*comp.* **frisk'ier**; *superl.* **frisk'iest**.
frisk'ily *adv.* **frisk'iness** *n.*

fritter[1] *frit'ėr, n.* a piece of fruit, etc. fried in batter.

fritter[2] *frit'ėr, v.t.* (often **fritter away**) to squander, waste little by little.

frivolous *friv'ȯ-lus, adj.* **1** trifling, silly, not serious. **2** fond of gaiety.
friv'olously *adv.* **friv'olousness** *n.*
frivol'ity *n.* **1** silly, trifling nature: *the frivolity of this objection.* **2** something that is frivolous or gay:—*pl.* **frivol'ities**.

frizz, friz *friz, v.t.* and *v.i.* to form into, or become, small short crisp curls:—*pr.p.* **frizz'ing**; *pa.p.* **frizzed**.—*n.* **1** a curl. **2** a mass of curls.
frizzle *friz'l, v.t., v.i.,* to curl:—*pr.p.* **frizz'ling**.—Also *n.*
frizz'y *adj.* with many small curls:—*comp.* **frizz'ier**; *superl.* **frizz'iest**.

frizzle[1]. See **frizz**.

frizzle[2] *friz'l, v.t.* **1** to fry. **2** to scorch:—*pr.p.* **frizz'ling**.

fro *frō, adv.:* **to and fro 1** to a place and back again. **2** first in one direction, then in the other.

frock *frok, n.* **1** a monk's wide-sleeved garment. **2** a woman's or child's dress.
frock coat a double-breasted knee-length coat for men.

frog *frog, n.* a tail-less web-footed animal living part of its life in water, part on land.
frog'man *n.* a diver with devices like a frog's webbed feet attached to his own feet to help him in swimming under water.

frolic *frol'ik, n.* **1** a prank. **2** a merrymaking.—*v.i.* **1** to play pranks. **2** to be merry, have fun:—*pr.p.* **frol'icking**; *pa.p.* **frol'icked**.
frol'icsome *adj.* merry, playful.

from *from, prep.* **1** out of. **2** springing out of. **3** beginning at. **4** in or to a state of separation. **5** by reason of.

frond *frond, n.* a leaf, esp. of a palm or fern.

front *frunt, n.* **1** the face, or forepart, of anything. **2** the foremost line or position. **3** the scene of actual fighting. **4** the forces struggling for a political or other object, esp. if comprising a number of groups joining together for this purpose: *popular front.* **5** something worn on the chest. **6** demeanour, bearing: *to present a bold front to the enemy.* **7** land along the edge of sea, river, etc. **8** the bounding surface between two masses of air of different temperature, etc. **9** something used to conceal a dishonest or disreputable activity.—Also *adj.*—*v.t.* **1** to stand in front of or opposite. **2** to oppose face to face. **3** to add a front to.—*v.i.* to face.
front'age *n.* **1** the front part of a building, or the length of this. **2** the ground in front.
front'al *adj.* of, belonging to, or in, the front: *to make a frontal attack.*
front'-bench' *adj.* pertaining to the senior members of the Government or the opposition in Parliament.

frontier *frun'tēr, -tēr', n.* **1** the boundary of a country. **2** (chiefly *U.S.*) the border of settled country.—Also *adj.*
frontiers'man *n.* a dweller on a frontier.

frontispiece *frun'tis-pēs, n.* a picture in the front of a book before the text.

frost *frost, n.* **1** temperature at or below freezing point of water. **2** minute particles of ice on a surface.—*v.t.* to cover with frost or something that looks like frost.
fros'ted *adj.* frostlike in appearance (as glass that has been roughened).
fros'ty *adj.*:—*comp.* **fros'tier**; *superl.* **fros'tiest**.
frost'bite *n.* injury to part of the body by severe cold.
frost'bitten *adj.*

froth *froth, n.* foam.—*v.t.* to cause froth on.—*v.i.* to throw up froth.
froth'y *adj.* **1** full of froth. **2** like froth. **3** (of e.g. talk) empty, meaning little:—*comp.* **froth'ier**; *superl.* **froth'iest**.

frown *frown, v.i.* to wrinkle the brow in anger, disapproval, or deep thought.—Also *n.*
frown'ing *adj.* **1** disapproving. **2** gloomy.
frown (up)on to disapprove of.

frowsty *frow'sti, adj.* fusty:—*comp.* **frow'stier**; *superl.* **frow'stiest**.
frowzy, frowsy *frow'zi, adj.* **1** fusty. **2** dingy. **3** untidy, neglected:—*comp.* **frow'zier, -sier**; *superl.* **frow'ziest, -siest**.

froze, frozen. See **freeze**.

frugal *frōō'gȧl, adj.* **1** economical, thrifty. **2** costing little, scanty: *They lived on frugal fare.*
frugal'ity, fru'galness *ns.*
fru'gally *adv.*

fruit *frōōt*, *n.* **1** the product of the earth that is suitable for food. **2** the part of a plant that contains the seed(s). **3** product, result: *the fruit of his hard work.*—*v.i.* to produce fruit.

fruit'erer *n.* one who sells fruit.

fruit'ful *adj.* **1** producing much fruit. **2** producing good results.

fruit'less *adj.* useless, without result.

fruit'fully *adv.* **fruit'lessly** *adv*.

fruit'y *adj.* like fruit, esp. in taste:—*comp.* **fruit'ier**; *superl.* **fruit'iest**.

fruit cocktail a fruit salad of diced fruit.

fruit machine a gambling machine on which certain combinations of pictures of fruit, etc. must be got for a win.

fruit salad a mixture of pieces of fruit.

fruition *frōō-ish'(ȯ)n*, *n.* **1** (*orig.*) pleasurable use or possession. **2** realisation, attainment: *the fruition of our hopes*.

frump *frump*, *n.* a plain, dowdy woman.

frustrate *frus-trāt'*, or *frus'*, *v.t.* to thwart, to defeat, bring to nothing: *to frustrate one's efforts*:—*pr.p.* **frustrating**.

frustrat'ed (or *frus'*) *adj.* **1** thwarted. **2** filled with a sense of disappointment and discouragement, or dissatisfaction.

frustrā'tion *n.*

fry[1] *frī*, *v.t.* and *v.i.* **1** to cook in oil or fat. **2** to burn, scorch:—*pr.p.* **fry'ing**; *pa.p.* **fried**.—*n.* a dish of something fried:—*pl.* **fries**.

fry[2] *frī*, *n.* **1** a swarm of fishes just spawned. **2** young salmon in their second year.

small fry persons or things of little importance.

fuchsia *fū'shi-ȧ*, *n.* a shrub with long usu. red and purple, hanging flowers, native to South America.

fuck *fuk*, (*bad language*) *v.t.* and *v.i.* to have sexual intercourse (with).—Also *n.* and *interj*.

fuddle *fud'l*, *v.t.* **1** to stupefy with drink. **2** to confuse.—*v.i.* to drink far too much:—*pr.p.* **fudd'ling**.—Also *n.*

fuddy-duddy *fud'i-dud'i*, *n.* a fogy:—*pl.* **fudd'y-dudd'ies**.—Also *adj.*

fudge *fuj*, *n.* **1** nonsense. **2** a soft sweetmeat.—*v.t.* **1** to patch up. **2** to fake. **3** to render obscure:—*pr.p.* **fudg'ing**.

fuel *fū'ėl*, *n.* anything that feeds a fire, supplies energy, etc.—*v.t.* **1** to incite, stimulate.—*v.i.* to take in fuel:—*pr.p.* **fu'elling**; *pa.p.* **fu'elled**.

fugitive *fūj'i-tiv*, *adj.* **1** running away. **2** passing swiftly.—*n.* one who is running away: *a fugitive from justice*.

fugue *fūg*, *n.* a musical composition in which a theme or melody is taken up by a number of different parts or voices in turn.

fulcrum *ful'krum*, *fool'*, *n.* the prop or fixed point on which a lever moves:—*pl.* **ful'crums, ful'cra.**

fulfil *fool-fil'*, *v.t.* **1** to carry out (e.g. a command, a promise). **2** to satisfy (e.g. a requirement). **3** to realise completely: *This fulfilled his hopes*:—*pr.p.* **fulfill'ing**; *pa.p.* **fulfilled'**.

fulfil'ment *n.*

full[1] *fool*, *adj.* **1** holding as much as can be contained. **2** with plenty (of): *a purse full of money.* **3** complete: *a full year.* **4** swelling. **5** plump. **6** (of clothes) with ample material. **7** (with *of*) eager to talk (about something).—*adv.* **1** fully. **2** exactly, directly: *It hit him full in the face*.

full'y *adv.* completely.

full'ness *n.*

full'-blood'ed *adj.* **1** vigorous, hearty. **2** of unmixed blood.

full'-blown' *adj.* **1** (of a flower) fully opened out. **2** fully developed.

full dress the dress worn on occasions of ceremony.

full'-dress' *adj.* **1** important, formal. **2** with attention to every detail: *a full-dress investigation*.

full'-face' *adj.* showing the front of the face completely.—Also *adv.* and *n.*

full'(y)-fash'ioned (*-ȯnd*) *adj.* (of knitted garments) made so as to fit the curves of the body exactly.

full'-length' *adj.* **1** of the usual length. **2** (of e.g. a portrait) showing the whole length.

full moon (the time when) the whole moon (is) lit up.

full'-scale' *adj.* **1** carried out with all forces, equipment, etc. **2** covering everything.

full stop a point marking the end of a sentence.

full time the end of a football, etc. match.

full'-time' *adj.* for the whole of the working day, week, etc.

in full **1** without reduction: *paid in full.* **2** without abbreviation.

in the fullness of time at the proper or destined time.

to the full completely.

full[2] *fool*, *v.t.* to scour and thicken (cloth).

full'er *n.*

fulminate *ful'min-āt*, *v.i.* to speak violently (against): *He fulminated against these laws*:—*pr.p.* **ful'minating**.

fulsome *fool'sum*, *adj.* **1** overdone: *fulsome praise.* **2** disgusting.

fumble *fum'bl*, *v.i.* **1** to grope about awkwardly. **2** to use the hands awkwardly.—

v.t. **1** to handle awkwardly. **2** (*games*) to drop, fail to catch (the ball):—*pr.p.* **fum'bling.**
fum'bler *n.* **fum'bling** *n.* and *adj.*

fume *fūm, n.* smoke or vapour (often in *pl.*), esp. if strong smelling.—*v.i.* **1** to give off fumes. **2** to be in a rage:—*pr.p.* **fum'ing.**
fum'igate *v.t.* to expose to fumes, esp. in order to disinfect:—*pr.p.* **fum'igating.**
fumigā'tion *n.* **fum'igator** *n.*

fun *fun, n.* merriment, joking.
funny *fun'i, adj.* **1** full of fun, laughable. **2** perplexing, odd:—*comp.* **funn'ier**; *superl.* **funn'iest.**
funn'ily *adv.* **funn'iness** *n.*
funny bone a nerve in the elbow (because of the tingling sensation produced by a blow on it).
for fun, in fun as a joke.
make fun of to laugh at, ridicule.

function *fungk'sh(o̊)n, n.* **1** a formal social gathering (e.g. a public dinner). **2** the proper or expected activity or duty: *The function of the heart is to keep the blood circulating; One function of the Speaker of the House of Commons is to see that rules are observed.*—*v.i.* **1** to perform a function. **2** to operate.
func'tional *adj.* **1** of, or concerned with, a function: *A functional disease is one that affects the activity of an organ of the body.* **2** capable of acting. **3** (of e.g. a building) designed with a view to practical usefulness rather than attractive appearance.
func'tionary *n.* an official:—*pl.* **func'tionaries.**

fund *fund, n.* **1** a sum of money for a special purpose. **2** a store laid up: *a fund of stories, of common sense.* **3** (in *pl.*) money available for spending.

fundamental *fun-då-ment'ål, adj.* **1** underlying, essential: *fundamental principles.* **2** complete, affecting everything: *a fundamental change in his views.*—*n.* something that serves as a groundwork, an essential part.
fundament'ally *adv.* at bottom, essentially: *The men were fundamentally different: one fundamentally honest, the other thinking first of what would be most profitable.*

funeral *fū'nėr-ål, n.* (the ceremony of) burial or cremation.
funereal *fū-nē'ri-ål, adj.* **1** of, or suiting, a funeral. **2** dismal, mournful.

fungus *fung'gůs, n.* a plant that has no green colouring matter and has to live on dead or dying plants or animals—e.g. mushrooms, moulds:—*pl.* **fungi** *(fun'jī, -gī)*, **fun'guses.**
fungicide *fun'ji-sīd, n.* a substance that kills fungi.
fungicid'al *adj.*
fun'goid *adj.* fungus-like.

funicular (**railway**) *fū-nik'ū-lår (rāl'wā), n.* a cable-railway esp. one going up a hill.

funk *fungk, (coll.) n.* **1** a state of terror. **2** a coward.—*v.t.* and *v.i.* to shirk through fear.

funnel *fun'l, n.* **1** a passage for escape of smoke, etc. **2** a vessel, usu. a cone ending in a tube, for pouring fluids into bottles, etc.
funn'elled *adj.* having funnel(s).

funnily, funny, etc. See **fun.**

fur *fûr, n.* **1** the thick, soft, fine hair of certain animals. **2** their skins with the hair attached. **3** a garment, esp. a shoulder wrap, of fur. **4** a fur-like coating.
furred *adj.* having fur, or a fur-like coating.
furr'y *adj.* **1** covered with fur. **2** like fur:—*comp.* **furr'ier**; *superl.* **furr'iest.**
furr'iness *n.*
furr'ier *n.* a dealer in furs.

furbelow *fûr'bė-lō, n.* **1** a plaited border or flounce. **2** a showy ornament.

furbish *fûr'bish, v.t.* to rub until bright.
furbish up to restore, renovate (something old).

furious, -ly, -ness. See **fury.**

furl *fûrl, v.t.* to roll up.

furlong *fûr'long, n.* one-eighth of a mile (220 yds, 201.17m).

furlough *fûr'lō, n.* leave of absence.

furnace *fûr'nis, n.* an enclosed structure in which great heat is produced.

furnish *fûr'nish, v.t.* **1** to fit up (e.g. a room). **2** to supply (a person with something). **3** to provide (e.g. food, reasons, an excuse).
fur'nishings *n.pl.* fittings, esp. furniture.
furniture *fûr'ni-chůr, n.* movable objects, in e.g. a house, such as chairs, tables.

furore *fū-rōr'ā, -rör', fū'rōr, -rör, n.* **1** a craze. **2** wild general excitement, enthusiasm, or anger.

furrow *fur'ō, n.* **1** the trench made by a plough. **2** a groove. **3** a wrinkle.—*v.t.* **1** to form furrows in. **2** to wrinkle.—Also *v.i.*

further *fûr'*THė*r, adv.* **1** (*comp.* of **far**—see this word) at or to a greater distance or degree. **2** in addition.—*adj.* **1** more distant. **2** additional.—*v.t.* to help on (e.g. a plan).
fur'therance *n.* a helping forward.
fur'thermore *adv.* moreover, besides.
fur'thest, fur'thermost. See **far.**

furtive *fûr'tiv, adj.* **1** stealthy. **2** secret.
fur'tively *adv.* **fur'tiveness** *n.*

fury *fū'ri, n.* **1** rage. **2** violent passion. **3** madness. **4** a fierce, violent woman:—*pl.* **furies**.
fu'rious *adj.* **1** very angry. **2** violent.
fu'riously *adv.* **fu'riousness** *n.*

furze *fûrz, n.* gorse, whin.

fuse¹ *fūz, v.t.* **1** to join by melting together. **2** to unite into a whole. **3** to cause (something electrical) not to work because a fuse has melted.—*v.i.* **1** to be reduced to a liquid. **2** to blend. **3** (of something electrical) to stop working because of the melting of a fuse:—*pr.p.* **fus'ing**.—*n.* a bit of fusible metal inserted as a safeguard in an electric circuit.
fus'ible *adj.* that can be fused or melted.
fusion *fū'zh(ò)n, n.* **1** the act of melting. **2** a close union of things, as if melted together.
fusion bomb the hydrogen bomb, whose energy comes from the fusion of hydrogen nuclei to become helium nuclei.

fuse² *fūz, n.* any device for causing an explosion to take place at a certain time chosen, beforehand, esp. explosive material enclosed in a waterproof cord.—Also, esp. *U.S.*, **fuze**.

fuselage *fūz'ėl-äzh, n.* the body of an aeroplane.

fusilier, **fusileer** *fū-zi-lēr', n.* an old word for a type of musketeer, still used in the names of certain regiments.

fusillade *(-lād') n.* **1** a discharge of numbers of firearms together or continuously. **2** a volley (of missiles). **3** an outburst (e.g. of questions).

fusion. See **fuse¹**.

fuss *fus, n.* **1** unnecessary bustle or agitation. **2** complaints or protests.—*v.i.* to be agitated about unimportant things.—*v.t.* to agitate (a person).
fuss'y *adj.* **1** making a fuss. **2** in the habit of doing so. **3** too particular. **4** (of clothes, etc.) with too much trimming, etc.:—*comp.* **fuss'ier**; *superl.* **fuss'iest**.
fuss'ily *adv.* **fuss'iness** *n.*

fusty *fus'ti, adj.* having a mouldy, musty smell;—*comp.* **fus'tier**; *superl.* **fus'tiest**.
fus'tily *adv.* **fus'tiness** *n.*

futile *fū'tīl, -til, adj.* useless, producing no result.
fu'tilely *adv.*
fu'tileness, **futil'ity** *(-til'), ns.*

future *fū'chur, adj.* **1** about to be. **2** that is to come.—*n.* time to come.
futurity *fū-tū'ri-ti, n.* **1** time to come. **2** event(s) yet to come:—*pl.* **futur'ities**.

fuze. See **fuse²**.

fuzz *fuz, n.* **1** fine light particles, as dust. **2** fluff.—*v.t., v.i.* to cover, or become covered, with fine particles.
fuzz'y *adj.* **1** fluffy. **2** blurred:—*comp.* **fuzz'ier**; *superl.* **fuzz'iest**.
fuzz'ily *adv.* **fuzz'iness** *n.*

G

gab *gab*, (*coll.*) n. idle chatter.
gift of the gab a talent for talking.

gabardine. See **gaberdine**.

gabble *gab'l, v.i.* to talk very quickly:—*pr.p.* **gabb'ling**.—Also *n.*
gabb'ler *n.* **gabb'ling** *n.*

gaberdine *gab'ėr-dēn, n.* **1** (*history*) a loose cloak. **2** a twill fabric, esp. of cotton and wool. **3** a coat of this.—Also **gab'ardine**.

gable *gā'bl, n.* the triangular part of an outside wall of a building between the top of the side wall and the slopes on the roof.

gad *gad, v.i.* to rove restlessly or idly (often with *about*):—*pr.p.* **gadd'ing**; *pa.p.* **gadd'ed**.
gad'about *n.* a person who gads.

gadfly *gad'flī, n.* a blood-sucking fly that distresses cattle:—*pl.* **gad'flies**.

gadget *gaj'it, n.* a small (usu. clever) device or object.

Gael *gāl, n.* a Celt of the Scottish Highlands, Ireland or the Isle of Man.
Gaelic *gā'lik, adj.* of the Gaels.—*n.* a Celtic language, that of the Scottish Highlands *(gal'ik)* and Ireland *(gā'lik)*.

gaff[1] *gaf, n.* **1** a hook for landing large fish. **2** (*naut.*) a spar supporting fore-and-aft sail.

gaff[2] *gaf, n.*: **blow the gaff** to give away a secret.

gaffe *gaf, n.* a blunder, indiscretion.

gaffer *gaf'ėr, n.* **1** (*coll.*) an old man, orig. a respectful term. **2** the foreman of a squad of workmen.

gag *gag, v.t.* **1** to stop the mouth of (a person) forcibly. **2** to compel to keep silence.—*v.i.* **1** to joke. **2** to retch:—*pr.p.* **gagg'ing**; *pa.p.* **gagged**.—*n.* **1** something thrust into a person's mouth to force him to be silent. **2** a joke, hoax.

gage[1] *gāj, n.* **1** something thrown down as a challenge to fight. **2** a pledge.

gage[2]. See **gauge**.

gaggle *gag'l, n.* **1** a flock of geese. **2** a little group of people.

gaiety, gaily. See **gay**.

gain *gān, v.t.* **1** to earn. **2** to win. **3** to obtain. **4** to reach: *He managed at length to gain the shore.* **5** to have an increase of (e.g. weight, speed).—*v.i.* **1** to profit. **2** to improve, or appear better. **3** (of a clock, etc.) to go too fast.—*n.* **1** something gained. **2** profit. **3** an increase.
gain'er *n.*
gain'ful *adj.* profitable. **gain'fully** *adv.*
gain (up)on to overtake by degrees.

gainsay *gān-sā', gān'sā, v.t.* to contradict; to deny:—*pa.t.* and *pa.p.* **gainsaid** (*-sād', -sed'*, or *gān'*).

gait *gāt, n.* a person's way of walking.

gaiter *gā'tėr, n.* a covering for the lower leg, fitting over the shoe.

gala *gä'lȧ, n.* a festivity, fête.

galactic. See **galaxy**.

galantine *gal'ȧn-tēn, tin, n.* poultry, veal, etc., served cold in jelly.

galaxy *gal'ȧk-si, n.* **1** an independent group of stars. **2** a splendid gathering of people:—*pl.* **gal'axies**.
galac'tic *adj.*

gale *gāl, n.* a very strong wind.

gall[1] *göl, n.* **1** bile. **2** bitterness of feeling. **3** impudence.
gall bladder a bodily organ attached to the liver, that stores bile.
gall'stone *n.* a hard body formed in the gall bladder or bile ducts.

gall[2] *göl, n.* a growth produced by an insect, esp. on oaks.

gall[3] *göl, n.* a sore due to rubbing.—*v.t.* **1** to roughen, chafe, hurt by rubbing. **2** to irritate.
gall'ing *adj.* very annoying.

gallant *gal'ȧnt, adj.* **1** brave. **2** noble; splendid: *a gallant ship.* **3** attentive to ladies (also *gȧ-lant'*).—*n.* (*old*) **1** a man of fashion. **2** a suitor.
gall'antly *adv.* **gall'antness** *n.*
gall'antry *n.* **1** bravery. **2** attention, or a compliment, paid to a lady:—*pl.* **gall'antries**.

galleon *gal'i-ȯn, gal'yȯn,* (*history*) *n.* a large Spanish sailing ship.

gallery *gal'ėr-i, n.* **1** a long passage, or long narrow room. **2** an upper floor of seats, esp. (in a theatre) the highest. **3** the occupants of the gallery. **4** any body of spectators (e.g. at a golf match). **5** a room or building for exhibition of works of art. **6** a horizontal underground passage:—*pl.* **gall'eries**.
play to the gallery to play for the applause of the least cultured.

galley *gal'i, n.* **1** a long, low ship with one deck, moved by oars (and often sails). **2** a ship's kitchen. **3** (*printing*) an oblong tray holding type that has been arranged for printing. **4** (also **gall'ey-proof**) a sheet printed from a galley (or otherwise) for correction before the text is divided into pages:—*pl.* **gall'eys**.

galley slave 1 (*history*) a person forced to row in a galley. **2** an overworked person.

galling. See **gall**[3].

gallivant *gal'i-vant*, *v.i.* to gad about.

gallon *gal'ȯn*, *n.* a measure of quantity of liquid.

gallop *gal'ȯp*, *n.* a horse's swiftest pace.—*v.i.* and *v.t.* to go, or cause to go, at a gallop:—*pr.p.* **gall'oping**; *pa.p.* **gall'oped**.

gallows *gal'ōz*, *n.sing.* a wooden frame on which criminals are hanged:—*pl.* **gall'ows**.

gall'ows-bird *n.* a person who deserves hanging.

gallstone. See **gall**[1].

Gallup poll *gal'ŭp pōl* a method of testing public feeling or opinion by questioning a selection of the population.

galore *gȧ-lōr'*, *-lör'*, *adv.* in abundance.

galosh *gȧ-losh'*, **golosh** *n.* an overshoe, now usu. of rubber.

galumph *gȧl-umf'*, *v.i.* **1** to stride triumphantly. **2** to move clumsily.

galvanise *gal'vȧn-īz*, *v.t.* **1** to stimulate by an electric current. **2** to rouse suddenly to action. **3** to coat (e.g. iron) with zinc:—*pr.p.* **gal'vanising**.

galvanom'eter *n.* an instrument for measuring electric currents.

gambit *gam'bit*, *n.* **1** a chess opening in which a player sacrifices a pawn or piece in order to gain an advantage. **2** a move, esp. of this type, in conversation, in a transaction, etc.

gamble *gam'bl*, *v.i.* **1** to play cards, etc. for money. **2** to risk money, etc. on a result that depends on chance (with *on*). **3** to take chances (with).—*v.t.* to risk (money, etc.) on a venture:—*pr.p.* **gam'bling**.—*n.* (something that involves) a risk.

gambol *gam'bȯl*, *v.i.* to leap, skip:—*pr.p.* **gam'bolling**; *pa.p.* **gam'bolled**.

game[1] *gām*, *n.* **1** an amusement or sport. **2** (in *pl.*) athletic sports. **3** a contest in sport, or a division of it, or the number of points required for a win. **4** a scheme or plan. **5** animals, etc. hunted for sport. **6** the flesh of some of these.—*adj.* **1** of game animals. **2** plucky. **3** ready, willing (for).

game'ly *adv.* pluckily.

game'ster *n.* a gambler.

gam'ing *n.* gambling.

game'cock *n.* cock trained to fight.

game'keeper *n.* one who has care of game.

game preserve, **reserve**. See **preserve**, **reserve**.

game show a television quiz or game with prizes for winning contestants.

games'manship *n.* the art of beating one's opponent by attacking his morale.

game warden one who looks after game in a reserve, etc.

the game is up the scheme has failed.

game[2] *gām*, *adj.* lame.

gamete *gam'ēt*, *n.* either of the two cells, male or female, that unite in sexual reproduction.

gamin *gam'an*[g], *n.* **1** a street urchin. **2** a small roguish boy:—*fem.* **gamine** *(gȧm-ēn', gam').*—Also *adjs.* (the *fem. adj.* usu. means 'small, pert, with elfish charm').

gamma *gam'ȧ*, *n.* the third letter of the Greek alphabet.

gamma rays powerful radiation given off by radium and other radioactive substances.

gammon *gam'ȯn*, *n.* (meat from) the lower end of a smoked or cured leg of bacon.

gammy *gam'i*, (*coll.*) *adj.* (of a leg) lame:—*comp.* **gamm'ier**; *superl.* **gamm'iest**.

gamut *gam'ŭt*, *n.* **1** the whole range of a voice or instrument. **2** the full range of anything (e.g. of emotions).

gander *gan'dėr*, *n.* the male goose.

gang *gang*, *n.* **1** a number of labourers, etc. working together. **2** a band of criminals, or of roughs. **3** (*coll.*) a group of friends.

gang'ster *n.* a member of a gang of criminals or roughs.

gangling *gang'gling*, *adj.* lanky.

ganglion *gang'gli-ȯn*, *n.* **1** a small lump on the sheath of a tendon, esp. on wrist or ankle. **2** a nerve-centre.

gangplank *gang'plangk*, *n.* a wooden board for providing access to and from a ship.

gangrene *gang'grēn*, *n.* death of a part of the body.

gan'grenous *gang'grin-ŭs, adj.*

gangster. See **gang**.

gangway *gang'wā*, *n.* **1** a passage into, out of, or through, a place. **2** a movable bridge from ship to shore.

gannet *gan'it*, *n.* a large web-footed bird of northern seas, a solan goose.

gantry *gan'tri*, *n.* **1** orig. a stand for barrels. **2** a set of racks for bottles. **3** a platform for a travelling crane, etc. **4** a structure supporting railway signals:—*pl.* **gan'tries**.

gaol, **gaoler**. Spellings of **jail**, **jailer**.

gap *gap*, *n.* **1** a break, opening, vacant space. **2** a lack. **3** a difference, divergence.

gape *gāp*, *v.i.* **1** to open the mouth wide. **2** to stare, esp. with open mouth. **3** to be wide open:—*pr.p.* **gap'ing**.—Also *n.*

garage *gar'äzh, gar'ij, gȧ-räzh'*, *n.* **1** a small building in which to keep a car. **2** a building where motor vehicles are repaired, and petrol, oil, etc. is sold.—*v.t.* to keep (a car) in a garage:—*pr.p.* **garaging**.

garb *gärb*, *n.* dress, costume, esp. with regard to its style.—*v.t.* to clothe.

garbage *gär'bij*, *n.* refuse, rubbish.

garble *gär'bl*, *v.t.* to distort or muddle (facts, etc.):—*pr.p.* **garb'ling**.

garden *gär'dn*, *n.* **1** a piece of ground on which flowers, etc., are grown. **2** a fertile region. **3** (in *pl.*, sometimes *n.sing.*) a park.—*v.i.* to work in a garden.
 gardener *gärd'nėr*, *n.* **gard'ening** *n.*, *adj.*

gardenia *gär-dē'ni-ȧ*, *n.* a tropical shrub, with fragrant, usu. white, flowers.

gargantuan *gär-gan'tū-ȧn*, *adj.* huge.

gargle *gär'gl*, *v.t.*, *v.i.* to wash (the throat), preventing the liquid from going down by forcing out air against it:—*pr.p.* **garg'-ling**.—Also *n.*

gargoyle *gär'goil*, *n.* a spout, ending in a grotesque head, jutting out from a roof gutter.

garish *gār'ish*, *adj.* showy, gaudy.
 gar'ishly *adv.* **gar'ishness** *n.*

garland *gär'lȧnd*, *n.* a wreath of flowers or leaves.

garlic *gär'lik*, *n.* a plant with a bulb having a strong taste and smell.

garment *gär'mėnt*, *n.* any article of clothing.

garner *gär'nėr*, *n.* a granary, store.—*v.t.* to gather in; to collect.

garnet *gär'nit*, *n.* a precious stone, usu. red, resembling the seeds of the pomegranate.

garnish *gär'nish*, *v.t.* to adorn, decorate (a dish of food).—Also *n.*
 gar'nishing, **gar'nishment** *ns.*

garotte. See **garrotte**.

garret *gar'it*, *n.* a room just under the roof of a house.

garrison *gar'i-s(ȯ)n*, *n.* **1** a body of soldiers guarding a fortress. **2** the building housing them. **3** such a fortress, or fortified place.—*v.t.* to supply (town, etc.) with troops.

garrotte, **garotte** *gȧ-rot'*, *n.* a mode of putting criminals to death—orig. a string round the throat tightened by twisting a stick, later a brass collar tightened by a screw.—*v.t.* **1** to execute in this way. **2** to half strangle, in order to rob:—*pr.p.* **gar(r)ott'ing**; *pa.p.* **gar(r)ott'ed**.

garrulous *gar'ū-lus, -ū-*, *adj.* talkative.
 garru'lity *(-ōō', -ū')*, **garr'ulousness** *ns.*
 garr'ulously *adv.*

garter *gär'tėr*, *n.* **1** a band to support a stocking. **2** (*cap.*) (the badge of) the highest order of knighthood in Britain.

gas *gas*, *n.* **1** a substance in a condition in which it has no definite boundaries but will fill any space. **2** natural or coal gas, or other gas for lighting and heating. **3** (*U.S.*) gasolene (i.e. petrol). **4** (*coll.*) empty talk:—*pl.* **gas'es**.—*v.t.* to treat, poison, etc. with gas.—*v.i.* to talk gas, to chat:—*pr.p.* **gass'ing**; *pa.p.* **gassed**.
 gaseous *gā'shus, -si-us, gas'i-us*, *adj.* of, like, gas.
 gas'ify *v.t.* and *v.i.* to turn into gas:—*pr.p.* **gas'ifying**; *pa.p.* **gas'ified**.
 gasificā'tion *n.*
 gas'olene, **gas'oline** *(-ȯ-lēn)* (*U.S.*) *n.* petrol for vehicles, etc.
 gasom'eter *n.* a gas-holder.
 gass'y *adj.* containing gas:—*comp.* **gass'ier**; *superl.* **gass'iest**.
 gass'iness *n.*
 gas'-bag (*coll.*) *n.* a talkative person.
 gas chamber a room that can be filled with gas for killing people or animals.
 gas'-fitter *n.* one who fits buildings with apparatus for using gas.
 gas'-holder *n.* a storage tank for gas.
 gas'-mask *n.* a device covering nose, mouth, and eyes as a protection against poisonous gases.
 gas'-meter *n.* an instrument for measuring amount of gas used.
 gas'works *n.sing.* a place where gas is made.

gash *gash*, *v.t.* to cut deeply into.—*n.* a deep, open cut.

gasify, **gasolene**, etc. See **gas**.

gasp *gäsp*, *v.i.* **1** to struggle for breath. **2** to catch the breath. **3** (with *for*) to desire eagerly.—*v.t.* (also **gasp out**) to utter with gasps.—Also *n.*
 at the last gasp at the point of death or of giving up.

gassy, **gasworks**. See **gas**.

gastric *gas'trik*, *adj.* of the stomach.
 gas'tro-enterī'tis *n.* inflammation of the mucous membrane of the stomach and the intestines.
 gastronomy *gas-tron'ȯ-mi*, *n.* the art or science of good eating.
 gas'tronome *n.* one who studies gastronomy.

gate *gāt*, *n.* **1** a passage into a city, enclosure, large building. **2** a metal, wooden, etc. frame for closing an entrance. **3** at an airport, any of the numbered exits from which to board an aircraft. **4** the number of people who pay to get in to a football match, etc.; the total money paid for entrance.

gate'crasher *n.* a person who comes uninvited (e.g. to a party).

gate'crash *v.t.* and *v.i.*

gate'-house *n.* a house over, or near, the entrance to a city, college, etc.

gate'-keeper *n.* one in charge of a gate.

gate'-post *n.* a post supporting a gate.

gate'way *n.* **1** the opening or structure for containing a gate. **2** an entrance.

gâteau, **gateau** *gat'ō*, *n.* a rich cake, esp. with cream:—*pl.* **gât'eaux**, **gat'eaus** *(-ōz)*.

gather *gaTH'ėr*, *v.t.* **1** to collect, bring together. **2** to draw together. **3** to pick (e.g. flowers). **4** to pick up, accumulate. **5** in sewing, to draw up in puckers. **6** to learn, conclude: *I gather from that remark that you have been to Italy.*—*v.i.* **1** to come together. **2** to increase. **3** to suppurate.—*n.* a fold in cloth.

gath'ering *n.* **1** a meeting. **2** a crowd.

gather oneself together to collect all one's strength as if about to leap.

gauche *gōsh*, *adj.* **1** clumsy. **2** tactless.

gaucherie *gōsh'ė-rē*, *-rē'*, *n.* **1** clumsiness. **2** (a piece of) tactlessness:—*pl.* **gaucheries.**

gaucho *gow'chō*, *n.* a cowboy of the pampas of South America:—*pl.* **gau'chos.**

gaudy *göd'i*, *adj.* showy; vulgarly bright:—*comp.* **gaud'ier**; *superl.* **gaud'iest**.

gaud'ily *adv.* **gaud'iness** *n.*

gauge, *U.S.* **gage**, *gāj*, *n.* **1** a measuring device. **2** a standard of measure. **3** an instrument recording rainfall, or force of wind. **4** the distance between the rails of a railway line.—*v.t.* **1** to measure. **2** to estimate, judge:—*pr.p.* **gaug'ing, gag'ing**.

gaunt *gönt*, *adj.* **1** thin; haggard. **2** grim, desolate looking.

gauntlet[1] *gönt'lit*, *n.* **1** the iron glove of armour, formerly thrown down in challenge. **2** a long glove covering the wrist, or the part of it that does this.

throw down the gauntlet to give a challenge, be aggressive.

gauntlet[2] *gönt'lit*, *n.* **run the gauntlet** **1** to undergo the old punishment of having to run through a lane of e.g. soldiers who strike one as one passes. **2** to expose oneself to harsh treatment.

gauze *göz*, *n.* a thin transparent fabric.

gauz'y *adj.*:—*comp.* **gauz'ier**; *superl.* **gauz'iest**.

gear *gēr*, *n.* **1** equipment; tools. **2** harness. **3** tackle. **4** clothes. **5** (*dial.*) possessions. **6** any moving part or system of parts for transmitting (passing on) motion.—*v.t.* to adapt or fit (to a particular need, etc.).

gear'ing *n.* means of transmission of motion, esp. a group of toothed wheels.

gear'-lever a device for selecting, engaging, and disengaging gears.

gear'-wheel *n.* a wheel with teeth that transmit motion by acting on those of a similar wheel or on a chain.

high gear, **low gear** a gear which gives a high, or a low, number of revolutions of the driven part relatively to the driving part.

in, out of, gear connected, or not connected, with the motor.

geese. See **goose**.

geezer *gē'zėr*, (*slang*) *n.* a (esp. elderly) man, or person generally.

Geiger counter *gī'gėr kown'tėr*, an instrument used to detect the presence of radioactive substances.

geisha *gā'shȧ*, *n.* a Japanese girl trained to entertain by her conversation, playing, dancing, etc.

gel *jel*, *n.* a semi-solid, jelly-like substance.—*v.i.* **1** to form a gel. **2** (*coll.*) to take shape (also **jell**):—*pr.p.* **gell'ing**; *pa.p.* **gelled**.

gelatine *jel'ȧ-tin*, *n.* a colourless, odourless, and tasteless substance, prepared from bones, hides, etc.

gelatinous *jil-at'in-ůs*, *adj.*

gelding *gel'ding*, *n.* a castrated horse.

gelignite *jel'ig-nīt*, *n.* an explosive.

gem *jem*, *n.* **1** a precious stone, esp. when cut. **2** anything admirable, or flawless.

gemmol'ogy *n.* the study or science of gems.

gemmol'ogist *n.*

gem'stone *n.* a precious, or semi-precious, stone, esp. when uncut.

gendarme *zhon^g'därm*, *n.* in France, a military policeman:—*pl.* **gendarmes** (pron. as *sing.*).

gender *jen'dėr*, *n.* in grammar, any of (usu.) three classes (masculine, feminine, or neuter) into which nouns and pronouns are divided (e.g. the noun *drake* is masculine; the noun *vixen* is feminine; the pronoun *it* is neuter).

See also **common**.

gene *jēn*, *n.* any of the material units passed on from parent to offspring that decide the characteristics of the offspring.

genealogy *jēn-i-al'ȯ-ji*, or *jen-*, *n.* **1** the history of relationship and descent of families. **2** the pedigree of a person or

family:—*pl.* **geneal'ogies**.
genealog'ical *adj.*
genealogical tree a table in the form of a tree with branches showing several generations of a family.

genera. See **genus**.

general *jen'ėr-ȧl, adj.* **1** including, or affecting, every, or nearly every, person, thing, class or place, etc.: *A general election is one affecting every constituency.* **2** expressing a fact true of a number of examples: *He made the general statement that cuckoos leave their eggs in other birds' nests.* **3** including, or dealing with, a number of different things: *a general cargo*; *general knowledge*; *general science.* **4** common, widespread: *It is the general opinion that this move was a mistake.* **5** not going into detail: *Give me a general idea of your plans.* **6** (as part of an official title, often placed after a noun) chief: *a governor-general.—n.* **1** an army officer of high rank. **2** (esp. *R.C. Church*) the head of a religious order.
gen'eralise *v.i.* **1** to make a general statement: *Do not generalise from one example.* **2** to form an idea supposed to cover all cases:—*pr.p.* **gen'eralising**.
generalisā'tion *n.*
general'ity *n.* **1** the quality of being general. **2** a general statement. **3** the majority of people:—*pl.* **general'ities**.
gen'erally *adv.* **1** usually; on the whole: *a generally good report.* **2** in general: *disliked by people generally*.
general post office the head post office of a town or district.
general practice the work of a **general practitioner**, a doctor who deals with all types of cases.
in general considering most cases though not necessarily all.

generate *jen'ėr-āt, v.t.* to produce, bring into being (e.g. heat, electricity, hatred, ideas):—*pr.p.* **gen'erating**.
generā'tion *n.* **1** production or formation. **2** a single stage in natural descent. **3** the people of the same age or period.
gen'erative *adj.* (having the power) of generating or producing.
gen'erātor *n.* **1** a person or thing that generates. **2** a machine for producing gas, or (dynamo) one for making electricity.
generating station a building where electricity is made on a large scale.

generic. See **genus**.

generous *jen'ėr-ůs, adj.* **1** free in giving. **2** very ready to admit the worth of others. **3** large, not small or mean: *a generous gift*.
generos'ity *n.* (*pl.* **-ies**).
gen'erously *adv.* **gen'erousness** *n.*

genesis *jen'ės-is, n.* **1** origin. **2** (*cap.*) the first book of the Bible.
genet'ic *adj.* of, concerned with, origin or heredity.
genet'ics *n.sing.* the science of heredity.

genial *jē'ni-ȧl, adj.* **1** cheering. **2** kindly.
genial'ity, ge'nialness *ns.*
ge'nially *adv.*

genie *jē'ni, n.* in Arabian stories, a magical slave:—*pl.* **ge'nies** or **ge'nii** *(-ni-ī)*.

genital *jen'i-tȧl, adj.* **1** of the genitals. **2** of sexual reproduction.
gen'itals *n.pl.* the organs of sexual reproduction (also **genitā'lia**).

genius *jē'ni-ůs, n.* **1** outstanding powers of mind. **2** a person having such powers. **3** a natural ability: *a genius for saying the right thing.* **4** a (good or evil) spirit, supposed to preside over each person, place, and thing:—*pl.* **ge'niuses**, or (esp. *def. 4*) **ge'nii** *(-ni-ī)*.

genocide *jen'ō-sīd, n.* deliberate extermination of a race or people.

genre *zhon^g-r', n.* a kind, esp. of art or literature.

gent *jent, n.* a slang abbrev. of **gentleman**.

genteel *jen-tēl', adj.* **1** (orig.) well-bred. **2** too refined in manners.
genteelly *jen-tēl'li, adv.*

gentian *jen'shȧn, n.* an alpine plant, usu. blue-flowered.

gentile *jen'tīl, n.* anyone not a Jew.

gentle *jen'tl, adj.* **1** well-born. **2** mild in manners, disposition, or action. **3** soft. **4** quiet, low. **5** gradual: *a gentle slope*.
gent'leness *n.* **gent'ly** *adv.*
gentil'ity *n.* **1** good birth. **2** refinement, real or affected.
gent'leman *n.* **1** a man of good birth. **2** a man of good feeling and instincts, courteous and honourable. **3** (*politely*) a man:—*pl.* **gent'lemen**; *fem.* **gent'lewoman** (*pl.* **women**).
gent'lemanly *adj.* **gent'lemanliness** *n.*
gent'leman-at-arms *n.* a member of the royal bodyguard.
gentleman's (-men's) agreement one resting on honour, not on law.
gents *n.* a men's public toilet.

gentry *jen'tri, n.pl.* **1** the class of people next below the rank of nobility. **2** (*coll.*) people, esp. of a particular type: *the bookmaking gentry*.

genuflect *jen'ū-flekt, v.i.* to bend the knee in worship or respect.
genūflex'ion (also **genūflec'tion**) *n.*

genuine *jen'ū-in, adj.* **1** real, not artificial or fake: *genuine leather.* **2** sincere, honest: *a genuine desire to help*.
gen'uinely *adv.* **gen'uineness** *n.*

genus *jē'nu̇s, n.* a group of related animals or plants:—*pl.* **genera** *(jen').*
gener'ic *(jen-) adj.* **1** of, relating to, a genus. **2** (of name, term) applying to a group or class. **3** general.

geo- *jē-ō-, ji-o-* (as part of word) the earth.
geocen'tric *(-sen'trik) adj.* **1** having the earth as centre. **2** reckoned from the centre of the earth.
geography *ji-og'rȧ-fi, n.* the science that describes the surface of the earth and its inhabitants.
geog'rapher *n.*
geograph'ic(al) *(-raf') adjs.*
geograph'ically *adv.*
geographical mile. See **mile**.
geology *ji-ol'ȯ-ji, n.* the science of the history and development of the earth's crust.
geol'ogist *n.* **geolog'ic(al)** *adjs.*
geolog'ically *adv.*
geometry *ji-om'ė-tri, n.* a branch of mathematics dealing with lines, angles, figures.
geomet'ric(al) *adjs.* **geomet'rically** *adv.*
geometric(al) progression a series of numbers such that each is multiplied by a fixed number to supply the next, e.g. 1, 2, 4, 8, 16, 32, etc.

georgette *jör-jet', n.* a thin silk stuff.

geranium *jė-rā'ni-u̇m, n.* plant with seed-vessels like a crane's bill in shape, esp. with red flowers.

gerbil *jûr'bil, n.* a small, rat-like desert animal that can be kept as a pet.

geriatrics *jer-i-at'riks, n.sing.* the branch of medicine concerned with the diseases of old age.
geriat'ric *adj.*
geriatri'cian *n.* a specialist in geriatrics.

germ *jûrm, n.* **1** a very tiny form of animal or plant life that causes disease. **2** the tiny beginning of anything: *the germ of an idea.*
germ'icide *n.* a substance that destroys disease germs.
germ'ināte *v.i.* to begin to grow (esp. of a seed).—*v.t.* to cause to sprout:—*pr.p.* **germ'ināting.**
germinā'tion *n.*

german *jûr'mȧn, adj.* (following the noun) full: *cousin german.*
germane *jûr-mān', adj.* closely related; relevant: *That fact is not germane to the present argument.*

German *jûr'mȧn, adj.* of Germany or its people.—*n.* a native or inhabitant, or the language, of Germany:—*pl.* **Ger'mans.**
German'ic *adj.* **1** of Germany, the Germans, or the German language. **2** also of the language group called Germanic.—*n.* a group of related languages that includes English, German, Dutch, the Scandinavian languages, Gothic, etc.

gerrymander *jer-i-man'dėr, v.t.* to rearrange (voting districts) in favour of a particular party.

Gestapo *gė-stä'pō, n.* the secret police in Germany under the Nazis.

gestation *jes-tā'sh(ȯ)n, n.* (the time, from conception to birth, of) the carrying of young in the womb.

gesticulate *jes-tik'ū-lāt, v.i.* to make vigorous gestures, esp. when speaking:—*pr.p* **gestic'ulating.**
gesticulā'tion *n.*
gesture *jes'chu̇r, n.* **1** a movement of the head, hand, etc., to express an idea, feeling, etc. **2** an act done to express one's attitude or intentions: *a gesture of friendship, appreciation.*—Also *v.i:*—*pr.p.* **ges'turing.**

get *get, v.t.* **1** to obtain, gain, capture. **2** to fetch. **3** to receive. **4** to catch (a disease). **5** to cause to be in any condition or position: *to get the fire lit*; *to get oneself untidy*; *to get the nails out of the box.* **6** to persuade (a person to do something). **7** to make ready (e.g. dinner). **8** (*coll.*) to understand: *I don't get the joke.* **9** (*coll.*) to catch, attack, harm: *A bullet got him in the chest.* **10** (*coll.*) to irritate: *His laziness really gets me.*—*v.i.* **1** to (manage to) go, pass, reach, arrive, etc.: *When does the train get to London?*; *I got home late*; *He got in through the window.* **2** to become: *to get old, thirsty.* **3** (*coll. Scot.*) to manage, or to be allowed: *Did he get to go?*:—*pr.p.* **gett'ing**; *pa.t.* **got**; *pa.p.* **got**, (*U.S.*) **gott'en.**
get-at'-able *adj.* easy, possible, to reach.
get'away *n.* an escape.—Also *adj.*
get'-together *n.* a gathering, reunion.
get at 1 to reach. **2** to find out. **3** to hint at. **4** to bribe.
get away with 1 to escape with. **2** to do (something) without being reproved or punished.
get by 1 to manage, cope. **2** to be accepted as satisfactory.
get it across, over, through, to (someone) to make (someone) understand.
get off to be let off punishment.
get on with 1 to agree, be friendly, with. **2** to make progress with.
get over to recover from.
get round 1 to avoid (a difficulty). **2** to persuade, coax (a person).
get there to succeed.
get up 1 to rise. **2** to ascend. **3** to prepare. **4** to learn up. **5** to dress.

get up to to apply oneself to (esp. something mischievous).

gewgaw *gū'gö*, *n.* something showy and without value.

geyser *gē'zėr*, *n.* **1** a spring that shoots out hot water and steam. **2** a heater for bath water, etc.

ghastly *gäst'li*, *adj.* **1** death-like. **2** terrible. **3** (*coll.*) very bad:—*comp.* **ghast'lier**; *superl.* **ghast'liest**.
ghast'liness *n.*

ghee *gē*, *n.* an Indian clarified butter.

gherkin *gûr'kin*, *n.* a small cucumber.

ghetto *get'ō*, *n.* **1** the Jews' quarter in some cities. **2** a (usu. poor) area inhabited by any racial group:—*pl.* **ghett'os**.

ghost *gōst*, *n.* **1** a spirit, esp. of a dead person. **2** a faint suggestion: *a ghost of an idea, of a chance.* **3** one who writes another's books, speeches, etc. for him (also **ghost'-writer**).—*v.t.* and *v.i.* to write (another's books, etc.) for him.
ghost'ly *adj.*:—*comp.* **ghost'lier**; *superl.* **ghost'liest**.
ghost'liness *n.*
give up the ghost to die.

ghoul *gōōl*, *n.* **1** an Eastern demon said to prey on the dead. **2** a person excessively interested in gruesome things.
ghoul'ish *adj.*

giant *jī'ȧnt*, *n.* **1** a huge person in fairy stories. **2** an unusually big person or thing. **3** a person of great ability:—*fem.* **gi'antess**.
giga- *gī'gȧ-* (as part of a word) a thousand million times the unit named.
gigantic *jī-gan'tik*, *adj.* huge.
gigan'tically *adv.*

gibber *jib'ėr*, *v.i.* to utter senseless sounds.
gibberish *jib'ėr-ish*, *n.* **1** rapid, gabbling talk. **2** nonsense.

gibbet *jib'it*, *n.* a gallows with projecting arm from which to dangle corpses.

gibbon *gib'ȯn*, *n.* an ape with very long arms.

gibe. See **jibe**.

giblets *jib'lits*, *n. pl.* the internal eatable parts of a fowl, etc.

giddy *gid'i*, *adj.* **1** unsteady, light-headed, dizzy. **2** that causes giddiness: *a giddy height.* **3** flighty, impulsive:—*comp.* **gidd'ier**; *superl.* **gidd'iest**.
gidd'ily *adv.* **gidd'iness** *n.*

gift *gift*, *n.* **1** a thing given. **2** a bribe. **3** a good quality or ability given by nature.—*v.t.* **1** to present, give. **2** to endow (a person, with a talent).
gift'ed *adj.* very talented.
look a gift horse in the mouth to criticise a gift.

gig[1] *gig*, *n.* **1** a light, two-wheeled carriage. **2** a long, light boat.

gig[2] *gig*, (*coll.*) *n.* an engagement, of a band, etc. usu. for one performance only.

giga. See **giant**.

gigantic(ally). See **giant**.

giggle *gig'l*, *v.i.* to laugh in a nervous or silly manner:—*pr.p.* **gigg'ling**.—Also *n.*
gigg'ler *n.* **gigg'ling** *n.*, *adj.*
gigg'ly *adj.*:—*comp.* **gigg'lier**; *superl.* **gigg'liest**.
gigg'liness *n.*

gigolo *jig'ȯ-lō*, *n.* **1** a professional male dancing partner. **2** a young man living at the expense of an older woman, in return for his attentions:—*pl.* **gig'olos**.

gild *gild*, *v.t.* **1** to cover with gold or a gold-like substance. **2** to give a false appearance to:—*pa.p.* **gild'ed**, **gilt**.
gild'er *n.* **gild'ing** *n.*
gild the lily to adorn something that is already perfect.
See also **gilt**.

gill[1] *gil*, *n.* **1** in fish, an organ for breathing. **2** (in *pl.*; usu. *humorous*) the flesh around the jaw.

gill[2] *jil*, *n.* a measure, pint (0.14 litre).

gillie *gil'i*, *n.* esp. in Scotland, an attendant on a sportsman on a shooting or fishing trip:—*pl.* **gill'ies**.

gillyflower *jil'i-flow(-ė)r*, *n.* a name for various flowers that smell like cloves.

gilt *gilt*, *n.* a gold or gold-like substance used for gilding ornaments, etc.—Also *adj.*
gilt'-edged *adj.* **1** having gilded edges. **2** (of shares, etc.) safe to invest in, not risky.

gimbals *jim'bȧlz*, *n.pl.* a two-ring contrivance for supporting an object, such as a ship's compass, so that it remains horizontal.

gimcrack *jim'krak*, *adj.* shoddy, ill-made, frail.

gimlet *gim'lit*, *n.* a tool for boring holes, with screw point and crosspiece handle.
gim'let-eyed *adj.* very sharp-sighted and observant.

gimmick *gim'ik*, *n.* **1** an addition intended to make an article for sale seem more attractive. **2** a clever mechanical device. **3** a device or trick adopted to attract notice.

gin[1] *jin*, *n.* a shortened form of *geneva*, a spirit distilled from grain and flavoured with juniper berries, etc.

gin[2] *jin, n.* **1** a trap or snare. **2** a machine for separating cotton from its seeds.
gin trap a powerful, toothed trap.

ginger *jin'jėr, n.* **1** the underground stem of a plant in the E. and W. Indies, with a hot taste. **2** liveliness, stimulation.—*adj.* sandy, reddish.—*v.t.* to enliven (with *up*).
gin'gery *adj.*
ginger ale, **ginger beer** non-alcoholic effervescent drinks flavoured with ginger.
gin'gerbread *n.* a cake flavoured with treacle and usu. ginger.
gin'gersnap *n.* a ginger-flavoured biscuit (also **ginger nut**).

gingerly *jin'jėr-li, adv.* with extreme caution; very gently.—Also *adj.*
gin'gerliness *n.*

gingham *ging'ȧm, n.* checked or striped cotton cloth.

gipsy, **gypsy** *jip'si, n.* a member of a wandering people of Indian origin, a Romany:—*pl.* **-ies**.

giraffe *ji-räf', n.* an African animal with very long neck and forelegs.

gird[1] *gûrd, v.t.* **1** to encircle with, or as if with, a belt. **2** to fasten (on a sword) with a belt. **3** to prepare (oneself) for action: —*pa.t.* and *pa.p.* **gird'ed** or **girt**.
gird'er *n.* a great beam of wood, iron, steel, e.g. to support a floor, wall, roadway of a bridge.
girdle *gûrd'l, n.* **1** a waist belt or cord. **2** anything that encloses like a belt.

gird[2] *gûrd, v.i.* to gibe, jeer (at).

girdle[1]. See **gird**[1].

girdle[2]. Same as **griddle**.

girl *gûrl, n.* **1** a female child. **2** a young woman.
girl'friend *n.* **1** a female sexual or romantic partner. **2** a female friend, esp. of a woman.
girl'hood *n.* the state or time of being a girl.
girl'ish *adj.* of, like, a girl.
Girl Guide (now usu. **Guide**) a member of an organisation for girls, like the Scouts.

giro *jī'rō*, (also with *cap.*) *n.* **1** a system by which payment may be made through banks, post offices, etc. **2** (also **gi'ro-cheque**) a form like a cheque by which such payment is made. **3** (*coll.*) a system of social security payment (by giro-cheque).

girt. See **gird**[1].

girth *gûrth, n.* **1** a band fitted round a horse's belly, holding the saddle in position. **2** the measurement round something, as a tree, waist, etc.

gist *jist, n.* the main point or points: *Give me the gist of his argument*.

give *giv, v.t.* **1** to hand out or over. **2** to pay. **3** to yield as product or result. **4** to do; to do (something) to: *He gave a cry*; *I gave him a push*. **5** to provide: *to give help*; *to give a party*. **6** to render (e.g. thanks). **7** to pronounce (e.g. a decision). **8** to apply (oneself to something).—*v.i.* **1** to yield to pressure, etc. **2** to open, or lead, into (with *upon*, *on*, *into*):—*pr.p.* **giv'ing**; *pa.t.* **gave**; *pa.p.* **given** *(giv'n)*.
giv'en *adj.* stated: *under the given conditions*.
give'away *n.* something that accidentally betrays.
give away **1** to hand out as a present. **2** to give (the bride) to the bridegroom at a wedding ceremony. **3** to allow (something) to become known.
give in to yield.
given (that) considering (that).
given to in the habit of: *He's given to overeating*.
give oneself away to betray one's secret unawares.
give off to emit (a smell, etc.).
give out **1** to send out (e.g. a flash, a smell). **2** to announce. **3** to run short, be used up. **4** (of e.g. engine) to fail.
give over to cease.
give place to **1** to make room for. **2** to be succeeded by.
give the game, **show**, **away** to allow a secret, etc. to become known.
give up **1** to abandon. **2** to stop trying.
give way **1** to yield. **2** to collapse under strain.
See also **gift**.

gizzard *giz'ȧrd, n.* a stomach, esp. the second stomach of a bird.

glacé *gla'sā, adj.* **1** iced. **2** glossy.

glacial *glā'shȧl, -si-ȧl, adj.* **1** of, produced by, ice or glacier. **2** of an ice age. **3** (*coll.*) icy, very cold.
glaciā'tion *n.* **1** freezing. **2** formation of glaciers, or a time of this.
glacier *glas'i-ėr*, also *glās', n.* a mass of ice, fed by snow on a mountain, slowly creeping downhill.

glad *glad, adj.* **1** pleased. **2** giving pleasure:—*comp.* **gladd'er**; *superl.* **gladd'est**.
gladd'en *v.t.* to make glad, cheer.
glad'ly *adv.* **glad'ness** *n.*
glad'some (*poetic*) *adj.* joyful.
glad rags (*coll.*) one's best clothes.

glade *glād, n.* open space in a wood.

gladiator *glad'i-ā-tȯr, n.* in ancient Rome, a man who was trained to fight with other men or with animals for the amusement of spectators.

gladiolus *glad-i-ō'lŭs, n.* a plant with sword-shaped leaves and spikes of flowers, of different colours:—*pl.* **gladiō'luses, gladiō'lī.**

gladsome. See **glad.**

glamour *glam'ŏr, n.* fascination or charm, esp. with little reality behind it.

glam'orise *v.t.* to represent (something) as more attractive, romantic, etc. than it really is:—*pr.p.* **glam'orising.**

glam'orous *adj.* **glam'orously** *adv.*

glance *gläns, v.i.* **1** to fly obliquely (off): *The ball glanced off the edge of his bat.* **2** to give a very brief look (at). **3** to gleam, flash:—*pr.p.* **glan'cing.**—Also *n.*

gland *gland, n.* a cell or group of cells that takes substances from the blood and stores them for use, or in order that the body may get rid of them: *sweat glands.*

glandular *glan'dū-lăr, adj.*

glandular fever a feverish illness characterised by swollen glands and an increase in the blood's white corpuscles.

glare *glār, v.i.* **1** to give a dazzling light. **2** to stare fiercely:—*pr.p.* **glar'ing.**—Also *n.*

glar'ing *adj.* **1** fiercely bright. **2** very obvious: *a glaring error.*

glar'ingly *adv.*

glasnost *gläs'nost, n.* in Russia, the policy of openness and forthrightness.

glass *gläs, n.* **1** a hard, usu. breakable, material through which light can pass, made by fusing sand or similar substance with soda and lime or other chemicals. **2** an article made of glass, esp. a drinking vessel or a mirror. **3** (in *pl.*) spectacles.

glass'y *adj.* **1** of or like glass; smooth and shiny. **2** (of the eyes) cold, expressionless:—*comp.* **glass'ier;** *superl.* **glass'iest.**

glass'ily *adv.* **glass'iness** *n.*

glass'ful *n.* as much as fills a drinking glass:—*pl.* **glassfuls.**

glaze *glāz, v.t.* **1** to fit (e.g. a frame) with glass; to put windows in (a building). **2** to cover (pottery, food, etc.) with glaze. **3** to add a shiny surface to.—*v.i.* (e.g. of the eyes) to become glassy:—*pr.p.* **glaz'ing.**—*n.* **1** a glassy coating put on pottery. **2** a transparent coating of jelly or syrup for food. **3** any added shiny surface.

glaz'er *n.* a workman who glazes pottery, paper, etc.

glaz'ier *n.* one who sets glass in window frames, etc.

glaz'ing *n.* **1** the (fitting of) glass in windows. **2** glaze (see this).

glass fibre fibreglass (see **fibre**).

glass'house *n.* a greenhouse.

glass paper paper coated with powdered glass, for smoothing.

glass'ware *n.* household vessels made of glass.

cut glass fine glass shaped or ornamented by cutting or grinding.

plate glass glass in thick plates made by casting, rolling, grinding, and polishing.

glaze, glazier, etc. See **glass.**

gleam *glēm, v.i.* to shine faintly or very briefly.—Also *n.*

glean *glēn, v.t.* **1** to gather (grain) after the reapers. **2** to collect (what is thinly scattered, e.g. news, facts).—Also *v.i.*

glee *glē, n.* **1** gaiety; delight. **2** (*music*) a song in parts.

glee'ful *adj.* **1** merry. **2** triumphant.

glee'fully *adv.* **glee'fulness** *n.*

glen *glen, n.* **1** a narrow valley with a stream. **2** a depression among hills.

glib *glib, adj.* ready, fluent, and insincere: *a glib tongue:*—*comp.* **glibb'er;** *superl.* **glibb'est.**

glib'ly *adv.* **glib'ness** *n.*

glide *glīd, v.i.* **1** to move smoothly and easily. **2** to flow gently. **3** to fly a glider:—*pr.p.* **glid'ing.**—*n.* act of gliding.

glīd'er *n.* an aircraft without engine.

glimmer *glim'ėr, v.i.* to burn or shine, faintly.—*n.* a faint ray (of e.g. light, hope, understanding).

glimm'ering *n.* glimmer.

glimpse *glimps, n.* a very brief view.—*v.t.* to get a brief view of:—*pr.p.* **glimp'sing.**

glint *glint, v.i.* to gleam, sparkle.—Also *n.*

glissade *glēs-äd', glis-äd', v.i.* to slide, glide down:—*pr.p.* **glissad'ing.**—*n.* **1** act of sliding down a slope. **2** a gliding movement in ballet.

glisten *glis'n, v.i.* **1** to shine faintly. **2** to sparkle.

glitter *glit'ėr, v.i.* **1** to sparkle. **2** to be splendid or showy.—Also *n.*

glitt'ering, glitt'ery *adjs.*

glitz *glits, (coll.) n.* extravagant showiness.

glitz'y *adj.*

gloaming *glōm'ing, n.* twilight.

gloat *glōt, v.i.* to gaze, or think, with wicked or malicious joy: *He gloated over John's defeat.*

globe *glōb, n.* **1** a ball. **2** a sphere. **3** the earth. **4** a sphere representing the earth. **5** a spherical glass cover for a lamp.

glōb'al *adj.* **1** spherical. **2** affecting the whole world.

globular *glob'ū-lăr, adj.* globe-shaped.

globule *glob'ūl, n.* a drop.

globe'-trott'er *n.* one who goes sightseeing about the world.

glockenspiel *glok'ėn-s(h)pēl, n.* a musical instrument having a set of bells or bars played by hammers.

gloom *gloo͞m, n.* **1** partial darkness, dimness. **2** dismalness. **3** lowness of spirits.
gloom'y *adj.*:—*comp.* **gloom'ier**; *superl.* **gloom'iest**.
gloom'ily *adv.* **gloom'iness** *n.*

glorify *glō'ri-fī, glö', v.t.* **1** to make glorious. **2** to praise highly or too highly:—*pr.p.* **glo'rifying**; *pa.p.* **glo'rified**.
glorificā'tion *n.*
glo'ry *n.* **1** honour. **2** an object of great pride. **3** splendour. **4** a halo. **5** the bliss of heaven:—*pl.* **glo'ries**.—*v.i.* to boast about (with *in*):—*pr.p.* **glo'rying**; *pa.p.* **glo'ried**.
glo'rious *adj.* **1** noble; splendid. **2** (*coll.*) delightful.
glo'riously *adv.*
glory hole a cupboard, etc. containing an untidy collection of miscellaneous objects.

gloss[1] *glos, n.* an explanation of a hard word, etc.—*v.t.* to make remarks in explanation of (something).
gloss'ary *n.* a list of words with their meanings:—*pl.* **gloss'aries**.

gloss[2] *glos, n.* brightness as of a polished surface.—*v.t.* to give a gloss to.
gloss'y *adj.* smooth and shining:—*comp.* **gloss'ier**; *superl.* **gloss'iest**.—*n.* (*coll.*) a fashion magazine, etc. with glossy paper:—*pl.* **gloss'ies**.
gloss'ily *adv.* **gloss'iness** *n.*
gloss paint paint containing varnish, giving a hard, shiny finish.
gloss over to make light of, explain away (e.g. a mistake).

glossary. See **gloss[1]**.

glottis *glot'is, n.* the opening between the vocal cords.
glott'al *adj.*
glottal stop a speech sound made by closing the glottis (e.g. the sound made by some speakers instead of *t* in a word such as *water*).

glove *gluv, n.* **1** a covering for the hand, esp. with a sheath for each finger. **2** a boxing-glove.
glove compartment a shallow shelf at the front of a car, for holding gloves, etc.

glow *glō, v.i.* **1** to burn without flame. **2** to give out a steady light. **3** to tingle, or flush, with warmth or emotion.—Also *n.*
glow'ing *adj.* **1** that glows. **2** bright, vivid. **3** very enthusiastic.
glow'worm *n.* a beetle whose larvae and wingless females give out light.

glower *glow'ėr, v.i.* to stare angrily, scowl.

glowing, glowworm. See **glow**.

glucose *gloo͞'kōs, -kōz, n.* a kind of sugar obtained from fruit juices, etc., and present in the blood.

glue *gloo͞, n.* **1** an impure gelatine got by boiling animal refuse, used as an adhesive. **2** any of several synthetic substances used as adhesives.—*v.t.* to join with, or as if with, glue:—*pr.p.* **glu'ing**; *pa.p.* **glued**.
glu'ey *adj.*:—*comp.* **glu'ier**; *superl.* **glu'iest**.
glue'-sniffing *n.* the practice, dangerous and sometimes fatal, of inhaling the fumes of certain types of glue for their pleasurable effect.

glum *glum, adj.* **1** sullen. **2** gloomy.

glut *glut, v.t.* **1** to overfeed, cram. **2** to overstock (the market):—*pr.p.* **glutt'ing**; *pa.p.* **glutt'ed**.—*n.* a too great supply.
glutton *glut'(ȯ)n, n.* **1** one who eats too much. **2** (*coll.*) one who is eager (for something). **3** an animal related to the weasel.
glutt'onous *adj.* very greedy.
glutt'onously *adv.*
glutt'onousness, glutt'ony *ns.*

gluten *gloo͞'tėn, n.* a protein present in wheat flour.
glutinous *gloo͞'tin-u̇s, adj.* gluey, sticky.

glutton, etc. See **glut**.

glycerin(e) *glis'ėr-ēn, -in,* or *-ēn', n.* a sweet, sticky, colourless liquid got from fat.

gnarled *närld, adj.* knotty, twisted.

gnash *nash, v.t.* to grind (the teeth) in rage, etc.—*v.i.* (of teeth) to strike together.

gnat *nat, n.* any of various small (biting) flies.

gnaw *nö, v.t.* **1** to bite with a scraping or mumbling movement, or in agony or rage. **2** to wear (away). **3** to torment: *gnawed by a sense of guilt*.—Also *v.i.* (with *at*).

gnome *nōm, n.* **1** a dwarf, goblin. **2** an obscure manipulator of international finance, etc.

gnu *noo͞, nū, n.* a large antelope in S. and E. Africa.

go *gō, v.i.* **1** to move, pass. **2** to leave, depart. **3** (of mechanism) to act, work. **4** to turn out, happen, proceed. **5** to be spent, lost, etc.: *That's how the money goes.* **6** to give way, break. **7** to be in a stated condition: *to go barefoot, hungry.* **8** to attend regularly (with *to*): *Where does he go to school?* **9** to become: *to go mad.* **10** to be guided (by). **11** to stretch, extend, lead. **12** to be given, sold (to someone). **13** (*coll.*) to be a success. **14** to proceed with some activity: *I'll go for a walk*; *I'm going swimming*:—*pr.p.* **go'ing**; *pa.t.* **went** (orig. *pa.t.* of **wend**); *pa.p.* **gone** *(gon)*; *pr.t. 3rd sing.* **goes** *(gōz)*.—*n.* (all meanings *coll.*) **1** an attempt, turn (at). **2** a success. **3** energy:—*pl.* **goes**.

-go'er (as part of a word) a regular attender: *a theatre-goer*.

go'ing *n.* **1** the act of moving. **2** departure. **3** conditions of travel or action: *It was heavy going*.—*adj.* **1** in (successful) operation. **2** current.

gon'er *(gon'ėr)* (*slang*) *n.* a person or thing doomed, dead, broken, etc.

go'-ahead *adj.* energetic, enterprising.

go'-between *n.* one who carries messages between, or helps to make arrangements affecting, two people or parties.

go-gett'er *n.* an energetic person who gets what he seeks.

goings-on' *n.pl.* behaviour (esp. bad).

be going to to be about (to), to intend (to).

go back on to fail to act up to (a promise).

go down to be received (well, badly).

go down with to catch (a disease).

go for 1 to attack. **2** to be attracted by.

go in for (**something**) to make (something) one's study or occupation.

go off 1 to leave. **2** to become less good. **3** to explode.

go on 1 to continue. **2** to make a fuss. **3** to base one's opinion, etc. on.

go over 1 to look at, examine. **2** to list, discuss, perform, etc. in order.

go round 1 to be enough for everyone. **2** to circulate.

go through 1 to search, or to examine in order. **2** to experience (e.g. troubles). **3** to spend or use up (e.g. a fortune). **4** to rehearse, or to act or carry out, from beginning to end.

go through with to carry on with and finish.

go under to fail, be ruined.

go with 1 to be often in the company of. **2** to be a usual accompaniment of. **3** to be suitable, pleasing, with: *Do the red gloves go with your red hat?*

on the go busy, active.

goad *gōd*, *n.* **1** a sharp-pointed stick for driving cattle. **2** something that drives a person to action.—*v.t.* **1** to drive with a goad. **2** to urge on to action. **3** to torment, annoy.

goal *gōl*, *n.* **1** the winning-post. **2** the two upright posts between which the ball is sent in some games. **3** such a shot, or the point it gains. **4** an end, aim: *the goal of his ambition*.

goal'keeper (*coll.* **goal'ie**) *n.* the player who tries to prevent the ball from entering the goal.

goat *gōt*, *n.* a very agile, hairy, animal related to sheep.

goatee' *n.* a beard on thc chin only.

goat'-herd *n.* one who looks after goats.

get someone's goat to irritate someone.

gob *gob*, *n.* **1** (*slang*) the mouth. **2** a lump, clot, mass.

gobble *gob'l*, *v.t.* to swallow quickly.—*v.i.* to make a noise in the throat, as a turkey does:—*pr.p.* **gobb'ling**.

gobbledygook, **gobbledegook** *gob'l-di-gook*, *n.* pompous, or meaningless, talk.

goblet *gob'lit*, *n.* a large drinking-cup without a handle.

goblin *gob'lin*, *n.* a mischievous sprite.

go-cart. See **go-kart**.

god *god*, *n.* **1** a superhuman being with power over the lives of men. **2** (*cap.*) in religions such as the Jewish faith and Christianity, the creator and ruler of the world. **3** a person or thing considered of very great importance: *Money was his god*. **4** (in *pl.*) (the occupants of) the gallery of a theatre:—*fem.* **godd'ess**.

god'less *adj.* **1** not acknowledging God. **2** wicked.

god'ly *adj.* keeping God's laws, pious:—*comp.* **god'lier**; *superl.* **god'liest**.

god'liness *n.*

god'father, **god'mother** *ns.* one who, at a child's baptism, guarantees that the child will receive religious education.

god'child, **god'daughter**, **god'son** *ns.*

god'fearing *adj.* pious, religious.

god'forsaken *adj.* wretched; neglected.

god'send *n.* a very welcome piece of good fortune.

god'speed' (also with *cap*) *interj.*, *n.* a wish for good fortune, a speedy journey, etc., expressed at parting.

-goer, **goes**. See **go**.

goffer *gof'ėr*, *v.t.* to pleat or crimp.

goggle *gog'l*, *v.i.* **1** to stare, roll the eyes. **2** (of eyes) to bulge:—*pr.p.* **gogg'ling**.—*adj.* rolling; staring with surprise.—*n.* **1** a goggling look. **2** (in *pl.*) spectacles worn to protect the eyes.

go-go dancer *gō'gō däns'ėr* a female dancer who performs in night clubs and discothèques.

going. See **go**.

goitre *goi'tėr*, *n.* enlargement of the thyroid gland in the throat.

go-kart, **go-cart** *gō'kärt*, *n.* a low racing-vehicle made up of a frame, with wheels, engine and steering gear.—Also **kart**.

gold *gōld*, *n.* **1** a precious yellow metal, an element. **2** coins made of this. **3** anything precious. **4** the colour of gold. **5** a gold medal.—*adj.* **1** of gold. **2** of the colour of gold.

gold'en *adj.* **1** of gold. **2** of the colour of gold. **3** happy: *golden hours.* **4** very favourable: *a golden opportunity*.

gold'-digg'er *n.* **1** one who mines gold. **2** (*slang*) a woman who attaches herself to a man for the sake of the presents he gives her.

gold dust gold in fine particles.

golden eagle the common eagle, which has a slight golden gleam about its head and neck.

golden handshake a large sum given to an employee or member forced to leave a firm, etc.

golden mean a wise and moderate, not extreme, course of action.

golden syrup. See **syrup**.

golden wedding, **jubilee** the fiftieth anniversary of a wedding or other important event.

gold'-field *n.* a region where gold is found.

gold'finch *n.* a finch which has black, red, yellow, and white plumage.

gold'fish *n.* a Chinese and Japanese freshwater fish, golden-yellow in its domesticated state, brownish when wild.

gold leaf gold beaten very thin.

gold medal in athletics competitions, etc., the medal awarded as first prize.

gold mine **1** a mine from which gold is dug. **2** a source of great profit.

gold plate vessels and utensils of gold.

gold rush a rush to a new gold-field.

gold'smith *n.* a worker in gold and silver.

gold standard a standard consisting of gold (or of a weight in gold) in relation to which money values are reckoned.

as good as gold perfectly behaved.

golf *golf*, (*rarely*) *gof*, *n.* a game with a ball and a set of clubs, in which the ball is played along a course and into a series of small holes set in the ground at intervals.—Also *v.i.*

golf'er *n.* **golf'ing** *n.* and *adj.*

golf club **1** a club formed of people whose purpose is to play golf. **2** its premises. **3** (also **golf'-club**) the implement with which the golf ball is struck.

golf course, **golf links** the ground on which golf is played.

gollywog, **golliwog** *gol'i-wog*, *n.* (*old*) a doll with black face and bristling hair.

golosh. Same as **galosh**.

gondola *gon'dȯ-lȧ*, *n.* a long, narrow boat used on the canals of Venice.

gondolier (*-lēr'*) *n.* one who propels a gondola.

gone, **goner**. See **go**.

gong *gong*, *n.* a metal disc, usu. rimmed, that sounds when struck or rubbed with a drumstick.

good *good*, *adj.* **1** virtuous: *a good man.* **2** well-behaved. **3** kind, generous: *She was good to me.* **4** of high or satisfactory quality, ability, etc.: *good food*; *a good reason*; *a good doctor.* **5** pleasant: *a good time.* **6** beneficial: *Fruit is good for you*; *This ointment is good for warts.* **7** ample, sufficient; large in amount: *a good supply*; *a good deal of nonsense*; *a good number of mistakes.* **8** thorough: *a good cry*; *a good sleep.*:—*comp.* **bett'er**; *superl.* **best**.—*n.* **1** (opp. to **evil**) righteousness; virtuous actions. **2** something that increases happiness or success; welfare, benefit: *for your good.* **3** (in *pl.*) movable possessions. **4** (in *pl.*) merchandise. **5** (in *pl.*) freight as opposed to passengers: *a goods train*.

good'ness *n.*

good'ly *adj.* (used only before a noun; *old*) **1** fine. **2** ample.

good'y *n.* (usu. in *pl.*) a sweet, cake or other delicacy:—*pl.* **good'ies**.

good-bye', **goodbye'** *interj.* or *n.* contr. of 'God be with you', farewell:—*pl.* **goodbyes'**, **goodbyes'**.

good-day', **good day**, **good evening**, **good morning**, **goodnight'**, **good night** *interjs.* or *ns.* contr. from 'I wish you a good day', etc.

good'-for-noth'ing *adj.* worthless.—*n.* an idle, worthless person.

Good Friday the Friday of Passion Week.

good humour cheerfulness; an amiable mood.

good'-hu'moured *adj.* being in, or showing, good humour.

good'-look'ing *adj.* handsome, beautiful.

good nature kindness and readiness to be pleased.

good'-na'tured *adj.* showing good nature.

good Samaritan a person who helps one in time of trouble (St. Luke's gospel, X, 30–37).

good'y-good'y *n.*, *adj.* (a person who is) well-behaved from weakness rather than genuine virtue:—*pl.* **good'y-good'ies**.

goodwill', **good will** **1** a friendly attitude. **2** readiness, cheerful consent. **3** the good reputation that a business has built up.

as good as practically, all but: *He as good as told me to leave*.

be as good as one's word to fulfil one's promise.

for good (and all) permanently, for always.

give as good as one gets to do as much harm to one's opponent as he does to oneself.

good for you (him, etc.)**!** an expression of approval.

in good time early, with time to spare.

make good 1 to carry out (a promise, a boast). **2** to make up for (a loss). **3** to prove (an accusation). **4** to get on in the world. **5** to do well after a bad start.

no good useless; worthless.

gooey *gōō'i*, (*coll.*) adj. sticky, slimy:—*comp.* **goo'ier**; *superl.* **goo'iest**.

goofy *gōō'fi*, (*coll.*) *adj.* foolish:—*comp.* **goof'ier**; *superl.* **goof'iest**.

googly *gōōg'li*, (*cricket*) *n.* a ball that breaks in a different way from the way suggested by the bowler's action:—*pl.* **goog'lies**.

goose *gōōs*, *n.* **1** a web-footed animal like a duck, but larger. **2** a silly person:—*pl.* **geese** (*gēs*).

goose'-flesh *n.*, **goose'-pimples** *n.pl.* a puckering of the skin through cold, horror, etc.

goose'(-)step *n.* a method of marching with knees stiff and sole brought flat on the ground.—*v.i.* **goose'-step**:—*pr.p.* **goose'-stepping**; *pa.p.* **goose'-stepped**.

See also **gander, gosling**.

gooseberry *gōōz'bėr-i*, or *gōōs'*, *n.* **1** a prickly shrub with globe-shaped fruit. **2** the fruit itself. **3** an unwanted third person:—*pl.* **goose'berries**.

gopher *gō'fėr*, *n.* a name in America applied to various burrowing animals.

gore[1] *gōr*, *gör*, *n.* blood, esp. when clotted.

gor'y *adj.*:—*comp.* **gor'ier**; *superl.* **gor'iest**.

gor'ily *adv.* **gor'iness** *n.*

gore[2] *gōr*, *gör*, *v.t.* to pierce with horns, tusks, spear, etc.:—*pr.p.* **gor'ing**.

gore[3] *gōr*, *gör*, *n.* a triangular piece let into a garment to widen it.

gorge *görj*, *n.* **1** the throat. **2** a ravine.—*v.t.* and *v.i.* to swallow, or feed, greedily: —*pr.p.* **gor'ging**.

gorgeous *gör'jus*, *adj.* showy, splendid.

gor'geously *adv.* **gor'geousness** *n.*

gorgon *gör'gon*, *n.* **1** (*cap.*) any of three monsters in Greek legend whose look turned people to stone. **2** an ugly or terrifying woman.

gorilla *gor-il'a*, *n.* the largest of the apes.

gormandise *gör'man-dīz*, *v.i.* to eat too quickly and too much:—*pr.p.* **gor'mandising**.

gormless *görm'lės*, (*coll.*) *adj.* stupid.

gorse *görs*, *n.* furze or whin, a prickly shrub with yellow flowers.

gory. See **gore**[1].

gosling *goz'ling*, *n.* a young goose.

gospel *gos'pėl*, *n.* **1** the teaching of Christ. **2** a narrative of the life of Christ, esp. one of those in the New Testament. **3** (*coll.*) absolute truth.

gossamer *gos'a-mėr*, *n.* **1** fine threads made by a spider which float in the air or lie on bushes. **2** any very thin material.

gossip *gos'ip*, *n.* **1** one who goes about telling and hearing news or idle scandal. **2** idle talk about others.—*v.i.* to listen to and repeat such talk.

goss'iping *n.* and *adj.* **goss'ipy** *adj.*

got. See **get**.

Goth *goth*, *n.* one of a Germanic nation who invaded the Roman Empire.

Goth'ic *adj.* **1** of the Goths or their language. **2** of a style of architecture with pointed arches. **3** (of tales) gloomy, sinister.—*n.* the Gothic language or architecture.

gotten. See **get**.

gouge *gowj*, also *gōōj*, *n.* a chisel with hollow blade, for cutting grooves or holes.—*v.t.* **1** to scoop out, as with a gouge. **2** to force out, as the eye with the thumb:—*pr.p.* **gou'ging**.

goulash *gōō'lash*, *n.* a seasoned stew of meat and vegetables, etc.

gourd *gōōrd*, *n.* **1** a large fleshy fruit. **2** its rind used as a bottle, cup, etc.

gourmand *gōōr'mand*, *-mon^g*, *n.* a glutton. See also **gormandise**.

gourmet *gōōr'mā*, *n.* a person with a delicate taste in food, orig. in wines.

gout *gowt*, *n.* acute inflammation of smaller joints, esp. of the big toe.

gout'y *adj.*:—*comp.* **gout'ier**; *superl.* **gout'iest**.

gout'iness *n.*

govern *guv'ėrn*, *v.t.* **1** to rule (also *v.i.*). **2** to control (e.g. one's temper). **3** to guide, direct (e.g. a decision, a choice).

gov'erness *n.* a woman in charge of teaching children in their home.

government *guv'ėr(n)-mėnt*, *n.* **1** ruling or managing; control. **2** system of governing. **3** (often *cap.*) the persons appointed to rule a state, etc.: *steps taken by the* *government then in power.*—*adj.* of the government (*def. 3*): government bonds, stores, responsibility.

government'al *adj.*

gov'ernor *n.* **1** a ruler. **2** one who rules a colony, province, etc., or, in the U.S., a state. **3** the head of an institution, e.g. a prison. **4** a member of a committee governing a school, etc. **5** (*machinery*) a regulator, a contrivance for keeping speed constant.

gov'ernorship *n.*

Gov'ernor-Gen'eral *n.* the King's, Queen's, representative in a British dominion:—*pl.* **Gov'ernors-Gen'eral.**

gown *gown, n.* **1** a woman's dress. **2** an academic, a clergyman's, or an official, robe.

grab *grab, v.t.* **1** to seize or grasp suddenly. **2** to take possession of illegally:—*pr.p* **grabb'ing;** *pa.p.* **grabbed.**—*n.* **1** a sudden grasp or clutch. **2** a device for gripping an object, or material, in order to lift or haul it.

grace *grās, n.* **1** ease, elegance or refinement in shape, movement, manner or behaviour. **2** a pleasing quality. **3** mercy. **4** time in hand, or a delay granted, before a deadline, etc. **5** a short prayer before or after a meal. **6** a title used in addressing or speaking of a duke, a duchess, or an archbishop: *Your, His, Grace.* **7** (usu. *cap.*) in Greek legend, any of three beautiful sister goddesses.—*v.t.* **1** to adorn. **2** to honour (an occasion) by being present:—*pr.p.* **grac'ing.**

grace'ful *adj.* **grace'fully** *adv.*

grace'fulness *n.*

grace'less *adj.* **1** without grace. **2** having no sense of decency or of what is right.

gracious *grā'shůs, adj.* **1** courteous. **2** kind. **3** merciful.—*interj.* expressing surprise (also **good gracious, gracious me**).

gra'ciously *adv.* **gra'ciousness** *n.*

grace note a note not required for melody or harmony, added for effect.

be in someone's good (bad) graces to be in (not in) favour with someone.

with (a) good (bad) grace in an amiable (or an ungracious) way.

year of grace year of Christian era, A.D.

gradation. See **grade**.

grade *grād, n.* **1** step or degree in a scale e.g. of quality or of rank. **2** (esp. *U.S.*) a mark denoting quality, e.g. on a student's work. **3** (*U.S.*) a class in a school. **4** a slope. **5** a hundredth part of a right angle.—*v.t.* to arrange according to grade, e.g. according to size or quality.—*v.i.* to press or change from one thing to another through a series of intermediate stages; to merge:—*pr.p.* **grad'ing.**

gradation *grȧ-dā'sh(ȯ)n, n.* **1** a scale or series of steps. **2** arrangement according to grade. **3** passing from one colour, etc., to another by degrees.

gradient *grā'di-ėnt, n.* **1** the degree of slope (e.g. of a railway). **2** a slope.

gradual *grad'ū-ȧl, adj.* advancing or happening gently and slowly.

grad'ually *adv.*

grad'uate *v.t.* **1** to arrange in grades. **2** to mark (e.g. a thermometer scale) with divisions.—*v.i.* **1** to change gradually. **2** to receive a university degree, etc.:—*pr.p.* **grad'uating.**—*n.* *(grad'ū-it)* a person who has a university degree, etc.

graduā'tion *n.*

grade crossing (*U.S.*) a level crossing.

make the grade to do as well as necessary.

on the down, or **up, grade** falling or rising; failing or improving.

graffiti *grȧ-fē'ti, n.pl.* drawings, words, scribbled, painted, etc. on a wall.

graft[1] *grăft, v.t.* **1** to transfer (a shoot or part of one plant) to another so that it unites with it and grows. **2** to put (skin) from one part of the body on another part.—Also *n.*

graft[2] *grăft,* (*slang*) *n.* **1** profit by dishonest means, esp. in public life. **2** hard work.—Also *v.i.*

grail *grāl, n.* the platter used by Christ at the Last Supper.

grain *grān, n.* **1** a single small hard seed. **2** corn in general. **3** a hard particle. **4** a very small quantity. **5** the smallest British, etc., weight (equal to 1/7000 of a pound, or 0.0648 gram). **6** the arrangement and size of the fibres in wood, etc. or the pattern produced by them. **7** the direction of the threads in a fabric. **8** the side of leather from which the hair has been removed. **9** the particles in a photographic emulsion which go to compose the photograph.—*v.t.* to paint (wood) in imitation of natural grain.

grain'ing *n.*

against the grain **1** against the fibre of the wood. **2** against one's natural inclination.

See also **granary.**

gram. See **gram(me).**

grammar *gram'ȧr, n.* **1** (the study of) the rules for forming words and for combining words to form sentences. **2** a book that teaches this.

grammat'ical *adj.* **1** according to the rules of grammar. **2** of, relating to, grammar.

grammat'ically *adv.*
grammar school **1** (*orig.*) a school in which Latin grammar was taught. **2** a school giving an education specially suitable for pupils who go afterwards to a university.

gram(me) *gram, n.* a thousandth part of a kilogram(me).

gramophone *gram'ō-fōn, n.* an instrument for reproducing sounds by means of a needle on a revolving grooved disc.
gramophone record such a disc.

grampus *gram'pus, n.* any of various types of whale or dolphin, esp. the killer whale, known for spouting and puffing.

granary *gran'ȧr-i, n.* a storehouse for grain or threshed corn.

grand *grand, adj.* **1** of highest rank or importance. **2** noble, dignified. **3** magnificent, splendid; imposing. **4** (*coll.*) very good, very fine. **5** (as part of a word) of the second degree of parentage or descent, as **grand'father**, a father's or mother's father, **grand'child**, a son's or daughter's child; so **grand'mother**, **grand'son**, **grand'daughter**, etc.—*n.* **1** (*U.S. slang*) 1000 dollars. **2** a grand piano.
grand'ly *adv.* **grand'ness** *n.*
grandeur *grand'yur, n.* **1** splendour of appearance. **2** (of an idea, or of expression in words) loftiness.
grandil'oquent *adj.* **1** speaking grandly. **2** pompous.
grandil'oquence *n.* **grandil'oquently** *adv.*
gran'diose (*-ōs*, or *ōz*) *adj.* **1** grand or imposing. **2** pompous.
grandfather clock a clock with a long case standing on the ground (**grandmother clock** a smaller, similar clock).
grand'-mas'ter *n.* **1** an international chess champion or very skilled player. **2** (usu. **Grand Master**) the head of a religious order of knighthood or of the Freemasons, etc.
grand opera opera without spoken dialogue.
grand piano a large harp-shaped piano, with horizontal strings.
grand'sire (*old*) *n.* **1** a grandfather. **2** any ancestor.
grand slam the winning of all the tricks at bridge, etc.
grand'stand *n.* an erection with raised rows of seats giving a good view (e.g. of a racecourse).
grand total the complete total.

grange *grānj, n.* a country house with farm buildings attached.

granite *gran'it, n.* a hard rock composed of quartz and other minerals.

granny *gran'i, (coll.) n.* grandmother:—*pl.* **grann'ies**.

grant *gränt, v.t.* **1** to give (something applied or asked for): *to grant a right.* **2** to agree to (e.g. a request). **3** to admit as true: *I grant that I was stupid.*—*n.* **1** a giving or bestowing. **2** an allowance.
granted, granting (that) (even) if one can accept as true (that).
take for granted to assume, esp. without realising one is doing so.

granule *gran'ūl, n.* a little grain.
gran'ūlar *adj.*
gran'ūlāte *v.t.* **1** to break into small grains. **2** to make rough on the surface:—*pr.p.* **gran'ulating.**
granulā'tion *n.* **1** forming into grains. **2** tissue formed in a wound in early stage of healing.

grape *grāp, n.* a small smooth-skinned green or purple fruit from which wine is made.
grape'fruit *n.* a large yellow-skinned fruit related to the orange and lemon:—*pl.* **grape'fruit** or **grape'fruits.**
grape'shot *n.* shot that scatters on being fired.
grape'vine *n.* **1** the vine on which grapes grow. **2** an informal news network; rumour.
sour grapes something that one pretends is not worth having because one cannot obtain it.

graph *gräf, n.* diagram in which a line shows the changes in a variable quantity (e.g. rising and falling temperature).
graph'ic *adj.* **1** of writing or drawing. **2** of describing or picturing. **3** vivid: *a graphic account of an accident.* **4** (also **graph'ical**) of graphs.
graph'ically *adv.*
graph'ite *n.* a mineral, a form of carbon, known as 'blacklead', used in pencils.
graphol'ogy *n.* the study of handwriting.
graphol'ogist *n.*
graphic arts drawing, painting, engraving, etc.

grapnel *grap'nėl, n.* **1** a small anchor with several claws. **2** a grappling-iron.
grapp'le *n.* a grappling-iron.—*v.t.* to seize, hold, with a grapple.—*v.i.* **1** to struggle (with). **2** to try to deal (with, e.g. a problem):—*pr.p.* **grapp'ling.**
grapp'ling-i'ron *n.* an instrument for seizing and holding, esp. an enemy's ship.

grasp *gräsp, v.t.* **1** to seize and hold. **2** to understand.—*v.i.* **1** (with *at*) to try to seize. **2** (with *at*) to accept eagerly.—*n.* **1** grip. **2** power of seizing: *success was within his*

grasp. **3** power of understanding.
grasp'ing *adj.* avaricious; greedy.

grass *gräs*, *n.* **1** plants with long, narrow leaves and tubular stem, including wheat and other cereals, and the plants (hay when dried) on which cattle, sheep, etc. graze. **2** (*slang*) marijuana.—*v.i.* (*slang*) to inform against (with *on*).
grass'y *adj.* covered with grass:—*comp.* **grass'ier**; *superl.* **grass'iest**.
grass'iness *n.*
grass'hopper *n.* a hopping insect that feeds on plants, chirping by rubbing its wings.
grass'land *n.* land on which the chief natural vegetation is grass not trees.
grass roots **1** basic or fundamental matter. **2** the ordinary people, the voters.
grass snake a harmless ringed snake.
grass widow(er) a person temporarily separated from husband or wife.
let the grass grow under one's feet to loiter, delay.

grate[1] *grāt*, *n.* a framework of iron bars for holding a fire.
grat'ing *n.* a frame crossed by bars, used for covering or separating.

grate[2] *grāt*, *v.t.* **1** to rub (cheese, vegetables, etc.) into shreds with a grater. **2** to rub, grind.—*v.i.* **1** to make a harsh sound. **2** to irritate, annoy, jar (on):—*pr.p.* **grat'ing**.
grat'er *n.* an instrument with a rough surface for grating vegetables, etc.
grat'ing *adj.* jarring on the feelings, harsh, irritating.

grateful *grāt'fool*, *-fl*, *adj.* **1** thankful, appreciative of kindness. **2** (*old*) agreeable, pleasing.
grate'fully *adv.* **grate'fulness** *n.*
gratitude *grat'i-tūd*, *n.* thankfulness:—*opp.* **ingratitude**.
gratify *grat'i-fī*, *v.t.* **1** to please. **2** to satisfy:—*pr.p.* **grat'ifying**; *pa.p.* **grat'ified**.
grat'ifying *adj.* **gratificā'tion** *n.*

grating. See **grate**[1,2].

gratis *grā'tis*, *grat'is*, *adv.* for nothing, without payment.

gratitude. See **grateful**.

gratuity *grȧ-tū'i-ti*, *n.* **1** a money gift in return for service, a tip. **2** a lump sum given, esp. to a soldier, when discharged, etc.:—*pl.* **gratu'ities**.
gratū'itous *adj.* **1** done or given for nothing. **2** uncalled-for, without excuse: *a gratuitous insult*.
gratū'itously *adv.* **gratū'itousness** *n.*

grave[1] *grāv*, (*old*) *v.t.* and *v.i.* to engrave; to carve:—*pr.p.* **grav'ing**; *pa.p.* **graved** (or **grāv'en**).—*n.* a pit dug out, esp. one in which to bury the dead.
grave'digger *n.* one whose job is digging graves.
grave'stone *n.* a stone placed as a memorial at a grave.
grave'yard *n.* a place for graves.

grave[2] *grāv*, *adj.* **1** important, serious: *a grave responsibility*. **2** threatening, critical. **3** not cheerful; solemn.
grave'ly *adv.* **grave'ness** *n.*
grav'itate *v.i.* to be strongly attracted, hence to move (towards):—*pr.p.* **grav'itating**.
gravitā'tion *n.* **1** the act of gravitating. **2** the tendency of matter to attract and be attracted.
gravity *grav'i-ti*, *n.* **1** graveness—importance, seriousness, or solemnity. **2** gravitation, esp. the force by which bodies are attracted towards the earth.

grave accent *gräv ak'sėnt*, a mark (`) over a vowel.

gravel *grav'l*, *n.* small stones.—*v.t.* **1** to cover with gravel. **2** to puzzle completely:—*pr.p.* **grav'elling**; *pa.p.* **grav'elled**.
grav'elly *adj.*

gravity, gravitate. See **grave**[2].

gravy *grāv'i*, *n.* (a sauce made from) the juices from meat that is cooking.

gray. Same as **grey**.

graze[1] *grāz*, *v.t.* **1** to feed on (growing grass). **2** to put to feed. **3** (of land) to supply food for (animals).—*v.i.* to eat grass:—*pr.p.* **graz'ing**.
grazier *grā'zyėr*, *n.* one who grazes cattle for the market.
graz'ing *n.* **1** the act of feeding on grass. **2** pasture.

graze[2] *grāz*, *v.t.* **1** to pass lightly along the surface of. **2** to scrape skin from:—*pr.p.* **graz'ing**.—Also *n.*

grease *grēs*, *n.* **1** soft thick animal fat. **2** oily matter of any kind.—*v.t.* (*grēz*, *grēs*) to smear with grease, lubricate:—*pr.p.* **greas'ing**.
greas'y *grēz'i*, *grēs'i*, *adj.*:—*comp.* **greas'ier**; *superl.* **greas'iest**.
greas'ily *adv.* **greas'iness** *n.*
grease paint actors' make-up, composed of paint and e.g. tallow.

grebe *grēb*, *n.* a short-winged almost tailless freshwater diving bird.

Grecian. See **Greek**.

greed *grēd*, *n.* a too great appetite or desire, esp. for food or money.
greed'y *adj.*:—*comp.* **greed'ier**; *superl.* **greed'iest**.
greed'ily *adv.* **greed'iness** *n.*

Greek *grēk*, *adj.* of Greece, its people, or its language.—*n.* a native, inhabitant, or the language, of Greece.

Grecian *grē'sh(ȧ)n*, *adj.* Greek, esp. in style, design, shape, etc.

green *grēn*, *adj.* **1** of the colour of growing plants. **2** covered with grass, etc. **3** unripe. **4** young; inexperienced; easy to deceive. **5** pale, sick-looking, as with nausea or, conventionally, extreme envy. **6** concerned with the care of the environment.—*n.* **1** the colour of growing plants. **2** a small grassy patch of ground. **3** a member of the Green Party, an environmentalist. **4** on a golf-course, the prepared ground round the hole. **5** (in *pl.*) green vegetables.

green'ery *n.* **1** green plants. **2** foliage.

green'ness *n.*

green belt a strip of open land surrounding a town.

green'fly *n.* an aphis, plant louse:—*pl.* (*usu.*) **green'fly**.

green'grocer *n.* a dealer in vegetables.

green'horn *n.* an inexperienced youth, easily cheated (prob. orig. an ox with young horns).

green'house *n.* a building, usu. of glass, for plants.

greenhouse effect the warming-up of the earth's surface due to too much carbon dioxide in the atmosphere.

Green Party a political party concerned with conserving natural resources and decentralising political and economic power.

green'room *n.* a room in a theatre for actors when off stage, which orig. had walls coloured green.

have green fingers to be a skilful gardener.

the green-eyed monster jealousy.

the green light permission to go ahead.

greengage *grēn'gāj*, *n.* a greenish-yellow variety of plum.

greengrocer, **greenhorn**, etc. See **green**.

Greenwich (mean) time *grin'ij (mēn) tīm*, *gren'*, *-ich*, a reckoning of time in which the sun's crossing of the meridian 0° is taken as 12 noon. (0° passes through the former observatory at Greenwich.)

greet *grēt*, *v.t.* **1** to salute with good wishes. **2** to welcome. **3** to meet (eye, ear, etc.).

greet'ing *n.* **1** act or words on meeting. **2** (in *pl.*) a friendly message.

gregarious *gri-gā'ri-ŭs*, *adj.* **1** living in flocks. **2** fond of company.

gregā'riously *adv.* **gregā'riousness** *n.*

grenade *gri-nād'*, *n.* **1** a small bomb thrown by hand or shot from a rifle. **2** a glass projectile containing chemicals for putting out fires, etc.

grenadier *gren-ȧ-dēr'*, *n.* **1** (*orig.*) a soldier who threw grenades. **2** (in *pl.*, *cap.*) now title of first regiment of Foot Guards.

grew. See **grow**.

grey, **gray** *grā*, *adj.* **1** of a mixture of black and white; ash-coloured as hair that is losing its original colour. **2** having grey hair. **3** dull, dismal.—*n.* **1** a grey colour. **2** a grey horse.—*v.i.* to become grey (-haired).

grey'ly *adv.* **grey'ness** *n.*

grey'lag *n.* the common wild goose.

grey matter **1** the ashen-grey part of brain and spinal cord. **2** (*coll.*) brains.

greyhound *grā'hownd*, *n.* a tall, slender dog, with great speed and keen sight.

grid *grid*, *n.* **1** a grating. **2** a gridiron. **3** a network, e.g. of power-transmission lines.

griddle *grid'l*, *n.* a flat iron plate for baking or frying.—Also (*Scot.*, etc.) **girdle** *(gûrd'l)*.

gridiron *grid'ī-ėrn*, *n.* a frame of iron bars for cooking over a fire.

gridlock *grid'lok*, *n.* a situation where no progress is possible.

grid'locked *adj.*

grief. See **grieve**.

grieve *grēv*, *v.t.* to cause sorrow to.—*v.i.* **1** to feel sorrow. **2** to mourn:—*pr.p.* **griev'ing**.

grief *n.* deep sorrow, regret.

grief'-stricken *adj.* overwhelmed with grief.

griev'ance *n.* a real or fancied ground for complaint.

griev'ous *adj.* **1** painful. **2** causing sorrow.

griev'ously *adv.* **griev'ousness** *n.*

come to grief to meet disaster, fail.

griffin *grif'in*, **griffon**, **gryphon** *-ȯn*, *ns.* an imaginary animal, with lion's body and eagle's beak and wings.

grill *gril*, *v.t.* **1** to cook under or over direct heat. **2** to cross-examine severely.—*n.* **1** a grating. **2** a gridiron. **3** the part of a cooker in which food is grilled.

grille *gril*, *n.* **1** a lattice. **2** a grating in a convent or jail door.

grilse *grils*, *n.* a young salmon on its first return from salt water.

grim *grim*, *adj.* **1** cruel, unrelenting: *a grim master*; *grim necessity.* **2** terrible, horrible: *grim sights in the disaster area*; *a grim task.* **3** (*coll.*) very unpleasant. **4** resolute, unyielding: *grim determination.* **5** (of joke, smile) causing, expressing, horror not amusement:—*comp.* **grimm'er**; *superl.* **grimm'est**.

grim'ly *adv.* **grim'ness** *n.*

grimace *gri-mās'*, *n.* a twisting of the face, in jest, etc.—Also *v.i.*:—*pr.p.* **grimā'cing**.

grime *grīm*, *n.* sooty, greasy or ingrained dirt.
grim'y *adj*:—*comp.* **grim'ier**; *superl.* **grim'iest**.
grim'iness *n.*

grin *grin*, *v.i.* **1** to smile broadly, showing the teeth. **2** (*old*) to show the teeth in a snarl:—*pr.p.* **grinn'ing**; *pa.p.* **grinned**.—*n.* a broad smile.

grind *grīnd*, *v.t.* **1** to crush to powder. **2** to wear down, sharpen, etc. by rubbing. **3** to grate together, grit (the teeth). **4** to rub or crush with a twisting action. **5** to oppress (often **grind down**).—*v.i.* **1** to be rubbed together. **2** to jar or grate. **3** to work, drudge or study hard.—*pr.p.* **grind'ing**; *pa.t.* and *pa.p.* **ground** *(grownd)*.—*n.* **1** (*coll.*) hard, dull work or effort. **2** the action, sound, etc. of grinding.
grind'er *n.* **1** a person or machine that grinds. **2** a tooth that grinds food.
grind'stone *n.* a circular revolving stone for sharpening tools.
keep one's (or **someone's**) **nose to the grindstone** to toil, or force someone to toil, without ceasing.

grip *grip*, *n.* **1** firm hold with hand or mind. **2** power control: *in the grip of circumstances.* **3** the handle or part by which anything is grasped. **4** way of grasping. **5** a travelling bag or small case.—*v.t.* **1** to take fast hold of. **2** to hold the attention or interest of:—*pr.p.* **gripp'ing**; *pa.p.* **gripped**.
come to grips 1 to get into a close struggle (with). **2** (with *with*) to tackle (a problem).

gripe *grīp*, (*coll.*) *v.i.* to fret, complain:—*pr.p.* **grip'ing**.—*n.* (*coll.*) a complaint. **2** (in *pl.*) severe pain in the intestines.

grisly *griz'li*, *adj.* **1** frightful. **2** hideous:—*comp.* **gris'lier**; *superl.* **gris'liest**.
gris'liness *n.*

grist *grist*, *n.* corn for grinding.
bring grist to the mill to be a source of profit

gristle *gris'l*, *n.* a soft elastic substance in animal bodies, cartilage.
grist'ly *adj.*:—*comp.* **grist'lier**; *superl.* **grist'liest**.
grist'liness *n.*

grit *grit*, *n.* **1** hard particles e.g. of sand, stone, etc. **2** a coarse sandstone. **3** courage, spirit.—*v.t.* to sprinkle (icy roads) with grit to prevent skids:—*pr.p.* **gritt'ing**; *pa.p.* **gritt'ed**.
gritt'y *adj.*:—*comp.* **gritt'ier**; *superl.* **gritt'iest**.
gritt'ily *adv.* **gritt'iness** *n.*
grit one's teeth to close the teeth tightly, esp. in bracing oneself for something unpleasant.

grizzle *griz'l*, *v.i.* to grumble, fret:—*pr.p.* **grizz'ling**.

grizzled *griz'ld*, *adj.* grey, or mixed with grey.
grizz'ly *adj.* of a grey colour:—*comp.* **grizz'lier**; *superl.* **grizz'liest**.—*n.* the grizzly bear.
grizzly bear a large, fierce bear of N. America.

groan *grōn*, *v.i.* **1** to utter a deep sound of distress or disapproval. **2** to creak loudly. **3** to be afflicted by (with *under*). **4** (of a table) to be loaded with food.—*n.* a deep moan.

groat *grōt*, *n.* an old English silver coin.

grocer *grōs'ėr*, *n.* a dealer in tea, suger, and other household commodities.
groc'ery *n.* **1** shop, or business, of a grocer. **2** (in *pl.*) goods sold by grocers:—*pl.* **groc'eries**.

grog *grog*, *n.* a mixture of spirits and cold water, without sugar.
grogg'y *adj.* **1** slightly drunk. **2** weak from blows or illness:—*comp.* **grogg'ier**; *superl.* **grogg'iest**.

groin *groin*, *n.* **1** the place where the inner sides of the thighs meet the body. **2** the angular curve formed by the crossing of two arches.

groom *grōōm*, *n.* **1** one who has charge of horses. **2** an officer of the royal household. **3** a bridegroom.—*v.t.* **1** to clean, etc. (a horse's coat). **2** to make smart and neat: *a well-groomed appearance.* **3** to prepare (for political office, or stardom).
grooms'man *n.* the attendant on a bridegroom at his marriage.

groove *grōōv*, *n.* **1** a furrow, or long hollow, such as is cut with a tool or made spirally in a gramophone record to take the needle. **2** a fixed routine, rut.—*v.t.* to cut a groove in:—*pr.p.* **groov'ing**.
groo'vy (*slang*) *adj.* very good:—*comp.* **groo'vier**; *superl.* **groo'viest**.

grope *grōp*, *v.i.* to search (for something) as if blind or in the dark.—*v.t.* to search for by feeling: *to grope one's way*:—*pr.p.* **grop'ing**.

gross *grōs*, *adj.* **1** coarse. **2** very fat. **3** glaring: *a gross error.* **4** total, including everything.—*n.* **1** the whole taken together. **2** twelve dozen:—*pl.* **gross**.—*v.t.* to make a total profit of.
gross'ly *adv.* **1** coarsely. **2** very much: *grossly exaggerated.*

gross'ness *n.*
in gross in bulk, wholesale.

grotesque *grō-tesk'*, *adj.* fantastic, very odd and ugly.—Also *n.*
grotesque'ly *adv.* **grotesque'ness** *n.*

grotto *grot'ō*, *n.* **1** a cave. **2** an imitation cave:—*pl.* **grott'o(e)s**.

grouch. See **grouse²**.

ground¹. See **grind**.

ground² *grownd*, *n.* **1** the solid surface of the earth. **2** land. **3** a piece of land for special use: *a football ground.* **4** (in *pl.*) land attached to a house. **5** soil. **6** (in *pl.*) dregs, sediment. **7** foundation, basis. **8** (often in *pl.*) sufficient reason, justification: *What are the grounds for this accusation?* **9** the area forming the background of a picture, etc.—*v.t.* **1** to cause (a boat) to run aground. **2** to bring to the ground. **3** to debar (a pilot, or aircraft) from flying. **4** to fix, base. **5** to teach (someone) the first, most important, parts of a subject: *I tried to ground him in Latin.*—*v.i.* to reach or strike the ground.
ground'ed *adj.* prevented from flying.
ground'ing *n.* basic instruction.
ground'less *adj.* without foundation or reason.
ground floor the floor on (or nearly on) a level with the ground.
groundhog. See **marmot**.
ground'nut *n.* the peanut, a plant with pods that push down into the earth and ripen there.
ground plan **1** a plan of the lowest storey of a building. **2** a first or outline plan.
ground rent a rent paid to a landlord for the use of the ground.
ground'sheet *n.* a waterproof sheet spread on the ground by campers, etc.
grounds'man *n.* a man who takes care of a sports field, etc.
ground staff aircraft mechanics, etc., whose work is on the ground.
ground swell a broad, deep rolling of the ocean due to past storm, etc.
ground'work *n.* the foundation, first stages of, first work on, anything.
gain ground **1** to advance. **2** to make progress. **3** to become more widely held: *The idea that rebellion was necessary was now gaining ground.*
get off the ground to make a successful start.
give ground to fall back, retreat.
go to ground, **earth** to go into hiding.
lose ground to fall back, decline.
run to ground, **earth** to search out, find.
stand, **hold**, **one's ground** to stand firm.

groundsel *grown(d)'sėl*, *n.* a common yellow-flowered weed of waste ground.

groundsheet, **groundsman**, **groundwork**. See **ground**.

group *grōōp*, *n.* **1** a number of persons or things together. **2** a party or association. **3** a band of musicians, singers, etc. who perform (esp. popular) music together.—*v.t.* and *v.i.* to form into a group or groups.
group captain an air force officer.

grouse¹ *grows*, *n.* any of a number of moorland game birds, esp. the **red grouse**, a plump bird with a short curved bill, short legs, and feathered feet:—*pl.* **grouse**.

grouse² *grows*, *v.i.* to grumble:—*pr.p.* **grous'ing**.—Also **grouch**.—*n.* a grumble.

grove *grōv*, *n.* a small wood.

grovel *grov'l* or *gruv'l*, *v.i.* **1** to crawl on the earth. **2** to make oneself too humble. **3** to cower:—*pr.p.* **grov'elling**; *pa.p.* **grov'elled**.

grow *grō*, *v.i.* **1** to have life. **2** to develop. **3** to become larger, etc. **4** to become; to come gradually: *He grew angry*; *I grew to like him.*—*v.t.* to cause (e.g. plants) or allow (e.g. hair) to grow:—*pa.t.* **grew** *(grōō)*; *pa.p.* **grown** *(grōn)*.
grow'er *n.*
grown *adj.* **1** developed. **2** adult: *a grown man.*
grown'-up *adj.* grown, adult.—Also *n.*
growth *n.* **1** growing; the amount grown. **2** development. **3** a mass of tissue that grows in the body where it ought not to.
grow (up)on **1** (of a habit, etc.) to gain a greater hold on (a person). **2** to begin to seem attractive to (a person).
grow up **1** to become adult. **2** (of e.g. a custom) to become common.

growl *growl*, *v.i.* **1** to utter a deep, rough sound as a dog does. **2** to grumble in a surly way.—Also *n.*

growth. See **grow**.

groyne *groin*, *n.* a breakwater to check drifting of sand, etc.

grub *grub*, *v.i.* to dig in the dirt.—*v.t.* **1** (with *up* or *out*) to dig out of the ground. **2** to clear (ground) of roots, etc.:—*pr.p.* **grubb'ing**; *pa.p.* **grubbed**.—*n.* **1** the larva of a beetle, moth, etc. **2** (*slang*) food.
grubb'y *adj.* dirty:—*comp.* **grubb'ier**; *superl.* **grubb'iest**.
grubb'ily *adv.* **grubb'iness** *n.*

grudge *gruj*, *v.t.* to give, allow, suffer, etc. unwillingly: *I grudge the money*; *I grudge him his success*; *I don't grudge spending* *money in a good cause:—pr.p.* **grudg'-ing.**—*n.* a feeling of resentment (against someone) for a particular reason.

grudg'ing *adj.* unwilling: *a grudging admission; grudging admiration.*

grudg'ingly *adv.*

gruel *grōō'ėl, n.* a thin food made by boiling oatmeal in water or milk.

gru'elling *adj.* exhausting.

gruesome *grōō'sủm, adj.* horrible.

gruff *gruf, adj.* rough or abrupt in manner or sound.

gruff'ly *adv.* **gruff'ness** *n.*

grumble *grum'bl, v.i.* **1** to complain peevishly. **2** to murmur, growl, rumble:—*pr.p.* **grumb'ling,**—*n.* **1** the act or sound of grumbling. **2** a complaint.

grum'bly *adj:—comp.* **grum'blier**; *superl.* **grum'bliest**.

grum'bliness *n.*

grumpy *grum'pi, adj.* surly, cross:—*comp.* **grum'pier**; *superl.* **grum'piest**.

grum'pily *adv.* **grum'piness** *n.*

grunt *grunt, v.i.* to make a sound like a pig.—Also *n.*

gryphon. See **griffin**.

g-suit *jē'sūt, -sōōt, n.* a close-fitting suit with cells that can be inflated to prevent flow of blood away from the head, worn by airmen against black-out during high acceleration.

guanaco *gwä-nä'kō, n.* a S. American wild animal related to the llama:—*pl.* **guena'-co, guena'cos.**

guano *gwä'nō, n.* the dung of sea birds, used for manure.

guarantee *gar-ản-tē', n.* **1** a (esp. written) statement by a maker (of a car, watch, etc.) that he will replace his product or repair it free of charge if it becomes faulty within a certain period. **2** something that ensures that something else will follow: *Ability is no guarantee of success.* **3** something valuable handed over for keeping till a promise is fulfilled; a pledge. **4** an undertaking to be responsible for another person's fulfilling a promise.—*v.t.* **1** to give a guarantee in respect of. **2** to secure (against). **3** to promise. **4** to be responsible for (the truth of a statement, etc.):—*pr.p.* **guarantee'-ing**; *pa.p.* **guaranteed'**.

guarantor' (or *gar'*-) *n.* one who gives a guarantee.

guaranty *gar'ản-ti,* (*law*) *n.* guarantee:—*pl.* **guar'anties.**

guard *gärd, v.t.* **1** to protect from danger or attack. **2** to prevent from escaping. **3** to keep under restraint: *to guard one's tongue.—v.i.* to take precautions (against).—*n.* **1** a man or men stationed to watch and prevent from escaping, etc., or to protect. **2** one who has charge of a railway train. **3** state of watching: *on guard.* **4** posture of defence. **5** something that protects against injury, etc. **6** (in *pl.*; *cap.*; **Foot, Horse, Life Guards**) household troops (see **house**).

guard'ed *adj.* cautious: *guarded replies to searching questions.*

guard'ian *n.* **1** one who guards or takes care. **2** (*law*) one who has the care of the person, property, and rights of another.—*adj.* protecting.

guard'ianship *n.* protection, care.

guard'house, -room *ns.* a house or room for accommodation of guards.

guards'man *n.* a soldier of the Guards.

on (or **off**) **one's guard** on (or not on) the watch, prepared (or unprepared).

mount guard to go on guard duty.

guava *gwä'vả, n.* a tropical American tree with yellow, pear-shaped fruit.

gudgeon[1] *guj'ỏn, n.* **1** a pivot. **2** an iron pin. **3** a socket for a rudder.

gudgeon[2] *guj'ỏn, n.* **1** a small freshwater fish. **2** a person easily cheated.

guerrilla *gė-ril'ả, n.* a member of a small band acting independently and harassing an enemy army by raids, etc.—*adj.* of this kind of soldier or method of fighting.

guess *ges, v.t.* **1** to judge, form an opinion, when one has little or no evidence. **2** to hit on the correct answer, etc., in this way. **3** (esp. *U.S.*) to think, suppose.—Also *n.*

guess'timate *(-tim-it)* (orig. *humorous*) *n.* an *estimate* based on *guess*work rather than careful calculation.

guess'work *n.* process or result of guessing.

guest *gest, n.* a visitor received and entertained.

guest'house *n.* a small hotel.

guffaw *gu-fö', v.i.* to laugh loudly.—*n.* a loud laugh.

guide *gīd, v.t.* **1** to lead or direct. **2** to influence: *This guided me in my choice:—pr.p.* **guid'ing.**—*n.* **1** one who conducts travellers, tourists, etc. **2** someone or something that leads or directs one in any way. **3** a device to keep something moving along a particular line. **4** a guidebook. **5** (*cap.*) a Girl Guide (see **girl**).

guid'ance *n.* direction; leadership.

guide'-book a book of information for tourists.

guide dog a dog trained to lead blind people.

guide'line *n.* **1** a drawn line, or a rope, acting as a guide. **2** (esp. in *pl.*) an indication of present or future course.

guild *gild*, *n.* **1** in the Middle Ages, an association or union of merchants or of craftsmen of a particular trade. **2** an association for mutual aid.
guild'hall *n.* **1** the hall of a guild. **2** a town hall.

guilder *gil'dėr*, *n.* the standard coin of the Netherlands.

guile *gīl*, *n.* cunning, deceit.
guile'ful *adj.* crafty, deceitful.
guile'fully *adv.* **guile'fulness** *n.*
guile'less *adj.* artless, frank.
guile'lessly *adv.* **guile'lessness** *n.*

guillemot *gil'i-mot*, *n.* a diving bird with pointed bill and short tail.

guillotine *gil'ȯ-tēn*, *n.* **1** an instrument for beheading, recommended for use in the French Revolution by J.I. *Guillotin*, a doctor. **2** a machine for cutting paper, etc. **3** (in parliament) the practice of prearranging times for voting in order to limit discussion.—Also *v.t.*:—*pr.p.* **guill'otining**.

guilt *gilt*, *n.* **1** the state of having done wrong or of having broken a law. **2** a feeling that one has done wrong or is to blame.
guilt'less *adj.* innocent.
guilt'y *adj.* **1** having done a wrong thing: *guilty of murder.* **2** involving, or conscious of, wrongdoing: *a guilty act*; *a guilty conscience*:—*comp.* **guilt'ier**; *superl.* **guilt'iest**.
guilt'ily *adv.* **guilt'iness** *n.*

guinea *gin'i*, *n.* **1** an old English gold coin, first made of gold brought from *Guinea,* in Africa. **2** its value, finally 21s (£1.05).
guin'ea-fowl *n.* an African bird of the pheasant family, grey with white spots.
guin'ea-pig *n.* **1** a small South American rabbit-like animal sometimes used in laboratory research. **2** a human being used as subject of experiment.

guise *gīz*, *n.* appearance, esp. an assumed or false appearance: *The fox in the story came in the guise of a priest.*

guitar *gi-tär'*, *n.* a musical instrument with usu. six strings, plucked or twanged.
guitar'ist *n.*

gulch *gulch*, *gulsh*, (*U.S.*) *n.* a narrow rocky valley, gully.

gulf *gulf*, *n.* **1** a large inlet of the sea. **2** a very deep place. **3** a deep, usu. impassable, division (between e.g. persons).

gull¹ *gul*, *n.* a web-footed sea bird with long wings.

gull² *gul*, *v.t.* to deceive, dupe.
gullible *gul'i-bl*, *adj.* easily deceived.
gullibil'ity, **gull'ibleness** *ns.*

gullet *gul'it*, *n.* the tube by which food passes to the stomach.

gullible, etc. See **gull.**

gully *gul'i*, *n.* **1** a channel worn by running water, e.g. on a mountain side. **2** (*cricket*) the position between slips and point:—*pl.* **gull'ies**.

gulp *gulp*, *v.t.* and *v.i.* **1** to swallow eagerly, or with difficulty. **2** to gasp, choke, as if swallowing in this way.—Also *n.*

gum¹ *gum*, *n.* the firm fleshy tissue that surrounds the bases of the teeth.
gum'boil *n.* an abscess on the gum.

gum² *gum*, *n.* **1** a substance that is given out from certain plants, and hardens on the surface. **2** a plant gum or similar substance used as an adhesive, etc. **3** a transparent type of sweet. **4** chewing-gum.—*v.t.* to coat, or to join, with gum:—*pr.p.* **gumm'ing**; *pa.p.* **gummed.**
gumm'y *adj*:—*comp.* **gumm'ier**; *superl.* **gumm'iest**.
gumm'iness *n.*
gum'boot *n.* a rubber boot.
gum'-tree *n.* a tree yielding gum, etc., e.g. a eucalyptus tree.

gumption *gum(p)'sh(ȯ)n*, *n.* **1** shrewdness. **2** common sense.

gun *gun*, *n.* a tube-shaped weapon from which projectiles are discharged, usu. by explosion, e.g. a cannon, rifle, pistol, revolver, etc.
gunn'er *n.* **1** one who works a gun. **2** a private in the artillery. **3** an officer in charge of naval guns, etc.
gunn'ery *n.* the art of using guns, or the science of artillery.
gun'boat *n.* a small vessel fitted to carry one or more guns.
gun'-carriage *n.* the support on which an artillery weapon is mounted.
gun'-cotton *n.* an explosive, cotton soaked with acids.
gun dog a dog trained to help sportsmen shooting game.
gun'fire *n.* firing of gun(s).
gun'man *n.* an armed criminal.
gun'-metal *n.* **1** an alloy of copper and tin. **2** the dark grey colour of this alloy.
gun'powder *n.* an explosive mixture of saltpetre, sulphur, and charcoal.
gun'room *n.* an officers' mess in a warship.
gun'-running *n.* smuggling guns into a country.
gun'shot *n.* **1** the range of a gun. **2** a shot from a gun.
gun'smith *n.* one who makes or repairs guns.
gun down to shoot or kill with a gun, esp. ruthlessly:—*pr.p.* **gunn'ing down**; *pa.p.* **gunned down.**

stick to one's guns to hold to one's position in argument, etc.

gunwale *gun'l*, *n.* the upper edge of the hull of a small boat.

guppy *gup'i*, *n.* a small, colourful tropical fish that multiplies rapidly:—*pl.* **gupp'ies**.

gurgle *gûr'gl*, *v.i.* to flow with, or make, a bubbling sound.—Also *v.t.*:—*pr.p.* **gurg'-ling**.—Also *n.*

Gurkha *gûr'kȧ*, *n.* one of the chief race of Nepal, from whom regiments in the British and Indian armies were formed.

guru *goo'rōō*, *n.* **1** a religious teacher. **2** a respected instructor, an authority.

gush *gush*, *v.i.* **1** to flow out suddenly or violently. **2** to speak too enthusiastically, or to be too friendly and agreeable.—Also *n.*

gush'er *n.* **1** one who gushes. **2** an oil well that flows without pumping.

gush'ing *adj.* **gush'ingly** *adv.*

gusset *gus'it*, *n.* a piece, usu. triangular or diamond-shaped, sewn into a garment to strengthen it or make some part of it larger.

gust *gust*, *n.* **1** a sudden blast of wind. **2** a violent burst (e.g. of rain).

gust'y *adj.*:—*comp.* **gust'ier**; *superl.* **gust'iest**.

gust'ily *adv.* **gust'iness** *n.*

gusto *gus'tō*, *n.* enthusiasm, enjoyment.

gusty. See **gust**.

gut *gut*, *n.* **1** the alimentary canal (see this term). **2** (in *pl.*) bowels, entrails. **3** intestines prepared for violin strings, etc. **4** (in *pl.*; *coll.*) toughness of character.—*v.t.* **1** to take out the guts of. **2** to reduce to a shell (by burning, plundering, etc.):—*pr.p.* **gutt'ing**; *pa.p.* **gutt'ed**.

gut'less (*coll.*) *adj.* cowardly.

gutter *gut'ėr*, *n.* a channel for carrying away water, esp. at a roadside or at the eaves of a roof.—*adj.* low, disreputable: *the gutter press* (the cheap sensational newspapers).—*v.i.* **1** (of a candle) to run down in drops. **2** (of flame) to be blown downwards, threaten to go out.

gutt'ersnipe *n.* a neglected child from a slum, an urchin.

the gutter very poor or disreputable living conditions.

guttural *gut'ůr-ȧl*, *adj.* **1** (of sounds) formed in the throat. **2** using such sounds, harsh.—Also *n.*

gutt'urally *adv.*

guy¹ *gī*, *n.* a rope, rod, etc., to steady anything.

guy² *gī*, *n.* **1** an image of *Guy* Fawkes, made on the anniversary of the Gunpowder Plot (November 5). **2** a person of odd appearance. **3** (*coll.*) a man.—*v.t.* (*coll.*) to make fun of, esp. by imitating:—*pr.p.* **guy'ing**; *pa.p.* **guyed**.

guzzle *guz'l*, *v.t.*, *v.i.* to swallow greedily—*pr.p.* **guzz'ling**.

gymkhana *jim-kä'nȧ*, *n.* a meeting for athletic contests, etc.

gymnasium *jim-nā'zi-ům*, *n.* a hall, building, or school, for gymnastics:—*pl.* **gymnas'iums**, **gymnas'ia**.

gym'nast *n.* one skilled in gymnastics.

gymnas'tic *adj.*

gymnas'tics *n.sing.* or *n.pl.* exercises to strengthen the body and train in agility.

gynaecology *gīn-i-kol'ȯ-ji*, *n.* the branch of medicine that deals with the diseases of women.

gynaecolog'ical *adj.* **gynaecol'ogist** *n.*

gypsum *jip'sům*, *n.* a soft mineral, used to make plaster of Paris, etc.

gypsy. See **gipsy**.

gyrate *jī-rāt'*, *v.i.* to spin, whirl:—*pr.p.* **gyrat'ing**.

gyrā'tion *n.* **gyrā'tory** *adj.*

gyroscope *jī'rō-skōp*, *n* an apparatus in which a heavy wheel rotates at high speed, used e.g. to help to keep a compass needle steady, as a toy, etc.

H

habdabs *hab'dabz*, (*coll.*) *n.pl.* a state of extreme nervousness.

habeas-corpus *hā'bi-ȧs-kör'pus*, *n.* a writ requiring a jailer to produce a prisoner in person, and to state the reasons for his being in prison.

haberdashery *hab'ėr-dash-ėr-i*, *n.* ribbons, needles, thread, buttons and other similar small articles, or a shop which sells them.

habit *hab'it*, *n.* **1** one's ordinary behaviour, practice, custom. **2** a tendency to act in a particular way because one has done so often before. **3** dress, clothes: *a monk's habit.* **4** a woman's dress for riding. **5** addiction to a drug.
habit'ual *adj.* **1** constant. **2** customary. **3** by habit, confirmed: *a habitual drunkard.*
habit'ually *adv.*
habit'uate *v.t.* to accustom (a person to something):—*pr.p.* **habit'uating**.
habitué *hȧ-bit'ū-ā*, *n.* a constant visitor, frequenter: *a habitué of the local inn.*
hab'it-forming *adj.* (of a drug) which a taker will find it difficult or impossible to give up using.

habitable *hab'it-ȧ-bl*, *adj.* fit to be lived in (chiefly of dwellings; see also **inhabitable**).
hab'itat *n.* the natural home of an animal or plant.
habitā'tion *n.* dwelling, residence.

habitual, habituate, etc. See **habit**.

hack[1] *hak*, *v.t.* **1** to cut, chop, clumsily. **2** to notch. **3** to kick.—*n.* **1** a gash. **2** a chap, crack, in the skin. **3** a kick on the shin.
hack'saw *n.* a saw for cutting metal.
hacking cough a rough, dry cough.

hack[2] *hak*, *n.* **1** a horse kept for hire (also **hack'ney**; *pl.* **-neys**). **2** a writer ready to do any kind of literary work for money.—Also *adj.*
hack'neyed *adj.* used too much: *a hackneyed phrase.*
hack'ney cab, carriage one let out for hire.
hack work work done by a hack writer.

hackle *hak'l*, *n.* **1** a comb for flax or hemp. **2** a cock's neck-feather. **3** (in *pl.*) the hair of a dog's neck, which rises in anger.

hackney. See **hack[2]**.

had. See **have**.

haddock *had'ȯk*, *n.* a sea fish of the cod family:—*pl.* **hadd'ock(s)**.

haem(o)-, (esp. *U.S.*) **hem(o)-**, *hēm(o)-*, (as part of a word) blood.
haemoglobin, hem- *hē-mō-glō'bin*, *n.* the red oxygen-carrying pigment in red blood cells.
haemophilia, hem- *hē-mō-fil'i-ȧ*, *n.* a tendency to excessive bleeding when a blood-vessel is injured.
haemophiliac, hem- *n.*
haemorrhage, hem- *hem'ȯr-ij*, *n.* a discharge of blood from damaged blood-vessels.
haemorrhoids, hem- *hem'ȯr-oidz*, *n.pl.* swollen veins about the anus, liable to discharge blood; piles.

haft *häft*, *n.* a handle (e.g. of a knife).

hag *hag*, *n.* an ugly old woman.
hagg'ish *adj.* hag-like.
hag'ridden *adj.* tormented by nightmares, worried.

haggard *hag'ȧrd*, *adj.* wild-looking from suffering, overwork, etc., very thin, hollow-eyed.

haggis *hag'is*, *n.* a food made from the chopped-up heart, lungs and liver of a sheep, mixed with oatmeal and cooked in a sheep's stomach or something similar.

haggish. See **hag**.

haggle *hag'l*, *v.t.* to cut unskilfully.—*v.i.* to argue over a price, etc.:—*pr.p.* **hagg'ling**.

hagridden. See **hag**.

hail[1] *hāl*, *n.* **1** a call from a distance. **2** greeting. **3** earshot: *Keep within hail.*—*v.t.* **1** to call out to. **2** to welcome (as): *to hail as a hero, as saviour of the situation.*
hail'-fell'ow(-well'-met') *adj.* very ready to be friendly and familiar.
hail from to come from, belong to (a place).

hail[2] *hāl*, *n.* **1** particles of ice falling from the clouds. **2** a shower of missiles, abuse, etc.—*v.i.* to shower hail, or as if hail.—Also *v.t.*
hail'stone *n.* a single ball of hail.

hair *hār*, *n.* **1** a thread-like object growing from the skin. **2** a mass of these, e.g. on the human head.
-haired (as part of a word) having hair of a stated kind: *fair-haired.*
hair'y *adj.*:—*comp.* **hair'ier**; *superl.* **hair'iest**.
hair'iness *n.*
hair'breadth, hair's'-breadth *n.* a very tiny distance.—*adj.* (of e.g. an escape) very narrow.

hair'brush *n.* a brush for the hair.
hair'cloth *n.* cloth made partly or wholly of hair.
hair'cut *n.* the act, or style, of cutting hair.
hair'-do (*coll.*) *n.* a woman's haircut, esp. after styling and setting:—*pl.* **hair'-dos.**
hair'dresser *n.* one who cuts, washes, etc., hair.
hair'dressing *n.*
hair'-dryer, -drier *n.* a piece of electrical equipment producing a stream of warm air for drying the hair.
hair'line *adj.* (of a crack) very thin.
hair'pin *n.* a bent wire for fastening hair.—*adj.* (of a bend on a road) U-shaped.
hair'-raising *adj.* terrifying.
hair shirt a penitent's shirt of haircloth.
hair'spray *n.* liquid, sprayed from a can or bottle, used to keep the hair in place.
hair spring a very fine spring coiled up within the balance-wheel of a watch.
hair'style *n.* the way in which a person's hair is cut or shaped.
make someone's hair stand on end to terrify, or horrify.
not turn a hair to remain calm.
split hairs to make small, unnecessary distinctions (*n.* and *adj.* **hair'-splitting**).

hake *hāk n.* an eatable sea-fish like a cod.

halcyon *hal'si-ȯn, n.* the kingfisher.
halcyon days a calm, happy time.

hale[1] *hāl, adj.* healthy, robust: *hale and hearty.*

hale[2] *hāl, v.t.* to drag:—*pr.p.* **hal'ing.**

half *häf, n.* **1** one of two equal parts of a whole. **2** a half-back.—Also *adj.*—*adv.* partly, to some extent: *I half hope he will not come.*
halve *häv, v.t.* **1** to divide into halves. **2** in golf, to draw:—*pr.p.* **halv'ing.**
half'-and-half' *adv.* half one thing, half the other, in equal parts.
half'-back *n.* in football, (a player in) a position directly behind the forwards.
half'-baked' *adj.* **1** foolish. **2** not properly thought out.
half'-breed *n.* a person descended from different races.
half'-broth'er, half'-sis'ter *ns.* a brother or sister by one parent only.
half'-caste *n.* a half-breed.
half'(-)crown' *n.* formerly, a coin worth 2s. 6d. ($12\frac{1}{2}$p).
half'-heart'ed *adj.* lacking in enthusiasm or spirit.
half mast the position of a flag partly lowered in respect for the dead or in signal of distress.
half measures 1 a weak line of action. **2** insufficient effort.
halfpenny *hāp'ni, n.* **1** formerly, a bronze coin worth half a penny. **2** its value ($\frac{1}{2}$d. or $\frac{1}{2}$p):—*pl.* **halfpennies.** (Before the introduction of decimal coinage, **halfpence** *(hā'pėns)* was used as the *pl.* for *def. 2*, but is now rarely if ever heard. Other *coll.* terms heard for $\frac{1}{2}$p were *häf'(-ȧ)-pens'* and *häf'pē'*.)
half-sister. See **half-brother.**
half'-time' *n.* a short break halfway through a game.
half'-truth *n.* a statement conveying only part of the truth, esp. if intended to conceal the rest.
half'way *adv.* to, or at, half the distance.—*adj.* equally distant from two points.
half'wit *n.* an idiot.
half'-witt'ed *adj.*
go halves to share equally with another.

halibut *hal'i-but, n.* the largest of the flatfishes.

halitosis *hal-i-tō'sis, n.* bad breath.

hall *höl, n.* **1** the main room in a great house. **2** a space just inside an entrance door. **3** a large room for public gatherings. **4** a manor-house. **5** a university college or students' residence.
hall'mark *n.* **1** the stamp, indicating purity, impressed on gold or silver articles at Goldsmiths' *Hall* or elsewhere. **2** any mark of high quality. **3** any distinctive mark.—*v.t.* to stamp with a hallmark.

hallelujah, halleluiah *hal-ė-lōō'yȧ, interj.* 'Praise Jehovah'.—*n.* a song of praise to God.

hallo(a). See **hello.**

halloo *hȧ-lōō', n.* a cry to urge on a chase or to draw attention.—Also *v.i.* and *v.t.*

hallow *hal'ō, v.t.* **1** to make holy. **2** to honour as holy.
hall'owed *adj.* made, or honoured as, sacred (in church use sometimes *hal'ō-id*).
hall'owe'en (also *cap.*) *n.* the evening before All-hallows or All Saints' Day.

hallucination *hal-ōō-sin-ā'sh(ȯ)n,* or *-ū-, n.* a vision, sensation, etc., of something that does not really exist.
hallu'cinate *v.i.*:—*pr.p.* **hallu'cinating.**
hallu'cinogen *(-jėn) n.* a drug which causes hallucinations.

halo *hā'lō, n.* a ring of light, esp. one round the sun or moon, or round the head of a saint in a painting:—*pl.* **hā'lo(e)s.**

halt[1] *hölt, v.i.* and *v.t.* to make, or cause, a stop for a time.—*n.* **1** a standstill. **2** a stopping-place.

halt[2] *hölt*, *v.i.* to be lame, to limp.—*adj.* lame.—*n.* a limp.
halt'ingly *adv.*

halter *hölt'ėr*, *n.* **1** a rope for holding and leading a horse, etc. **2** a rope for hanging criminals.

halve, halves. See **half**.

halyard *hal'yȧrd*, *n.* a rope for hoisting or lowering a sail, yard, or flag.

ham[1] *ham*, *n.* **1** the back of the thigh. **2** the thigh of an animal, esp. of a pig.
ham'-fist'ed, ham'-hand'ed *adjs.* clumsy.

ham[2] *ham*, *n.* **1** an actor who overacts. **2** overacting. **3** an amateur: *a radio ham.*

hamburger *ham'bûrg-ėr*, *n.* (a roll containing) a cake of fried or grilled minced beef.

hamlet *ham'lit*, *n.* a small village.

hammer *ham'ėr*, *n.* **1** a tool for beating or breaking hard substances, or driving nails. **2** a striking-piece in a clock, piano, etc. **3** the apparatus that causes explosion of the charge in a firearm. **4** an auctioneer's mallet. **5** (*athletics*) a heavy metal ball with a long handle of steel wire.—*v.t.* **1** to drive, beat, or shape with a hammer. **2** to beat severely.—Also *v.i.*
hammer and tongs violently, fiercely.

hammock *ham'ȯk*, *n.* strong cloth or netting hung by the ends, and used for lying on.

hamper[1] *ham'pėr*, *v.t.* to hinder, obstruct.

hamper[2] *ham'pėr*, *n.* a large basket with a lid.

hamster *ham'stėr*, *n.* a gnawing animal with large cheek pouches.

hamstring *ham'string*, *n.* **1** in humans, a tendon behind the knee. **2** in horses, etc., the great tendon at the back of the hock.—*v.t.* **1** to lame by cutting the hamstring. **2** to make powerless (person, efforts):—*pa.p.* **ham'strung**.

hand *hand*, *n.* **1** the part of the arm below the wrist. **2** a pointer (e.g. on a watch). **3** a workman. **4** a worker, helper. **5** a share (in some action). **6** assistance: *to give a hand with the housework.* **7** pledge. **8** style of handwriting. **9** the cards held by a player at one deal. **10** side of a problem, argument: *on the one hand.* **11** direction: *on all hands, on every hand.* **12** a measurement of horses, 4in. (10.16cm).—*v.t.* **1** to pass with the hand. **2** to give, deliver (with *over*, *out*).
hand- (as part of a word) **1** by hand (as **hand'made, -sewn**). **2** worked by hand (as **hand'-or'gan**). **3** for the hand (as **hand'rail**). **4** held in the hand (as **hand'bag**).
-hand'ed (as part of a word) used with an adj. to show a person's way of acting, e.g. **high-handed, left-handed**, etc.
hand'ful *n.* **1** enough to fill the hand. **2** a small number or quantity. **3** (*coll.*) a person or thing difficult to manage:—*pl.* **hand'fuls**.
hand'less *adj.* **1** without hands. **2** not skilful with the hands.
hand'bag *n.* a woman's small bag for personal belongings.
hand'bill *n.* a small printed notice.
hand'book *n.* a small book of information and directions.
hand'craft *n.* handicraft.
hand'cuff *n.* (usu. in *pl.*) one of a pair of rings joined by a chain for putting on a prisoner's wrists.—*v.t.* to put handcuffs on.
hand-held *adj.* (able to be) held in the hand.
hand'hold *n.* a place or thing for the hand to hold.
hand'made. See **hand-** above.
hand'-out *n.* **1** an official news item given to the press for publication. **2** money, food, or the like, esp. given to the needy.
hand'-picked' *adj.* chosen carefully.
hand'rail. See **hand-** above.
hands'-on *adj.* **1** operated by hands. **2** involving practical experience, knowledge or methods of working.
hand'spring *n.* a cartwheel or similar somersault.
hand's'-turn *n.* a single small act of work.
hand'-to-hand' *adj.* (of fighting) carried on at close quarters.
hand'-to-mouth' *adj.* with barely enough food, money, etc. to survive.
hand'writing *n.* (style of) writing.
at first hand directly from the person concerned.
at hand near in place or time.
hand and (or **in**) **glove** (**with**) very friendly, or working closely (with).
hands down with great ease.
hands up! a call to surrender.
in hand **1** actually in one's possession: *cash in hand.* **2** in preparation.
live from hand to mouth to supply present wants without thought for future needs.—See also **hand-to-mouth**.
out of hand **1** at once. **2** out of control.
take in hand to undertake.
wash one's hands of (**something**) to refuse to take any responsibility in (the matter).
See also **handle, handy**.

handicap *hand'i-kap*, *v.t.* **1** in a race or competition, to make (a good competitor or competitors) start at a disadvantage, so as to make chances of winning more equal. **2** to make something more difficult for (a person):—*pr.p.* **hand'icapping**; *pa.p.* **hand'icapped**.—Also *n.*: *a golf handicap of 10 strokes*; *His lameness is a handicap*.

hand'icapped *adj.* physically or mentally disabled.

handicraft *hand'i-kräft*, *n.* occupation or hobby in which things are made by hand.

handiwork *hand'i-wûrk*, *n.* **1** thing(s) made by hand. **2** work done by, or a result of the action of, a particular person, etc.: *This destruction is the handiwork of a madman*.

handkerchief *hang'kėr-chif*, *n.* a piece of material for wiping the nose.

handle *hand'l*, *v.t.* **1** to touch, hold, with the hand. **2** to use. **3** to manage (a person, animal, or affair). **4** to deal in (goods):—*pr.p.* **hand'ling**.—*n.* **1** part of an object intended to be held in the hand. **2** something that may be used in achieving a purpose.

hand'ler *n.* one who trains and manages a dog, etc., e.g. in the police.

hand'ling *n.*

hand'lebars *n.pl.* the bar at the front of a bicycle with which it is steered.

handmade, **handrail**, etc. See **hand**.

handsel *han'sėl*, *n.* **1** a gift at New Year or at the beginning of something. **2** the first use of anything.—*v.t.* **1** to give a handsel to. **2** to use or experience (something) for the first time:—*pr.p.* **hand'selling**; *pa.p.* **hand'selled**.

handsome *han'sȯm*, *adj.* **1** good-looking. **2** ample. **3** generous.

hand'somely *adv.* **hand'someness** *n.*

handspring, etc. See **hand**.

handy *han'di*, *adj.* **1** skilful in using one's hands. **2** easy to handle or use. **3** ready to use, in a convenient place:—*comp.* **hand'ier**; *superl.* **hand'iest**.

hand'yman *n.* a man for doing odd jobs:—*pl.* **hand'ymen**.

hang *hang*, *v.t.* **1** to support from above, suspend. **2** to put on, e.g. by a hook. **3** to put on (wallpaper). **4** to put to death by suspending by the neck.—*v.i.* **1** to be suspended. **2** to be put to death by suspending by the neck:—*pa.p.* **hanged** (by the neck), or **hung** (in other uses).—*n.* the way in which anything hangs.

hang'er *n.* an object on which something is to be hung.

hang'ing *n.* **1** death by suspension by the neck. **2** (usu. in *pl.*) curtain(s), etc.

hung *adj.* (used only before the noun) esp. of a parliament, with no party having a viable majority.

hang'-dog *adj.* mean, guilty-looking.

hang'er-on' *n.* a follower, one who hangs around hoping for benefits:—*pl.* **hang'ers-on'**.

hang'-glider *n.* a kite-like apparatus from which one hangs in a harness in order to glide from cliff-tops, etc. in the sport of **hang'-gliding**.

hang'over (*coll.*) *n.* **1** uncomfortable after-effects of being drunk. **2** something remaining (from).

hang'-up (*coll.*) *n.* a problem, fear, etc. about which one is obsessed.

get the hang of (*coll.*) to (begin to) understand, learn how to do, use, etc.

hang about to loiter.

hang around 1 to stay near (a person or place) for some purpose. **2** to hang about.

hang back to hesitate.

hang fire 1 to be long in exploding or going off. **2** to delay or be delayed.

hang on 1 to cling (to). **2** to give close admiring attention to: *to hang on his words*. **3** to linger. **4** to wait. **5** to depend upon.

hang together 1 to keep united. **2** to be consistent, agree: *His statements did not hang together*.

hangar *hang'ȧr*, *hang'gȧr*, *n.* a shed for aircraft.

hank *hangk*, *n.* a skein, coil, loop.

hanker *hangk'ėr*, *v.i.* to yearn, have a longing (with *after*, *for*).

hank'ering *n.*

hanky *hang'ki*, (*coll.*) *n.* handkerchief:—*pl.* **han'kies**.

Hansard *han'särd*, *n.* the printed reports of debates in parliament, first published by Luke *Hansard* (1752–1828).

haphazard *hap-haz'ȧrd*, *adj.* **1** chance. **2** without planning or system: *a haphazard arrangement*.

haphaz'ardly *adv.* **haphaz'ardness** *n.*

hapless *hap'lis*, *adj.* unlucky.

happ'en *v.i.* **1** to take place, occur. **2** to occur by chance. **3** to chance (to do).

happ'ening *n.* an event.

happen (up)on to find by chance.

happy *hap'i*, *adj.* **1** lucky. **2** glad, enjoying oneself. **3** pleased. **4** well-chosen: *a happy phrase*:—*comp.* **happ'ier**; *superl.* **happ'iest**.

happ'ily *adv.* **happ'iness** *n.*

happ'y-go-luck'y *adj.* trusting to luck.

hara-kiri *hä'rȧ-ki'ri*, *n.* ceremonious suicide formerly common in Japan.

harangue *hȧ-rang'*, *n.* a loud pompous or wordy speech.—*v.i.* and *v.t.* to deliver, or to address by, a harangue:—*pr.p.* **haranguing** (*-rang'ing*); *pa.p.* **harangued** (*-rangd'*).

harass *har'ȧs*, *v.t.* **1** to worry by making repeated attacks on. **2** to annoy, pester.
har'assment *n.*

harbinger *här'bin-jėr*, *n.* a forerunner.

harbour *här'bȯr*, *n.* **1** any refuge or shelter. **2** a port for ships.—*v.i.* **1** to lodge, shelter. **2** to have (usu. evil, thoughts or feelings): *to harbour a grudge*.
har'bour-mas'ter *n.* the public officer who has charge of a harbour.

hard *härd*, *adj.* **1** firm, solid. **2** stiff. **3** difficult. **4** painful. **5** severe. **6** unfeeling. **7** ungenerous. **8** (of sound) harsh. **9** (of colour) glaring. **10** (of drink) alcoholic. **11** (of *c* or *g*) pronounced as in *cat*, *good*.—*adv.* **1** with vigour. **2** earnestly.
hard'en *v.t.* to make hard, harder or hardy.—*v.i.* to become hard or harder.
hard'ened *adj.* unfeeling.
hard'ly *adv.* **1** scarcely. **2** with difficulty. **3** harshly, severely.
hard'ness *n.*
hard'ship *n.* thing(s) hard to bear (e.g. toil, poverty, etc.).
hard'-and-fast' *adj.* rigid, not to be set aside: *a hard-and-fast rule*.
hard cash ready money.
hard coal anthracite.
hard disk, disc a metal disk used for storing information in a computer.
hard'-earned *adj.* earned with difficulty.
hard'-head'ed *adj.* shrewd, practical.
hard'-heart'ed *adj.* unfeeling, pitiless.
hard shoulder the strip forming the outer edge of a motorway, for stopping on in an emergency.
hard'ware *n.* **1** articles of iron, copper, etc. **2** computer equipment for processing information. **3** mechanical equipment for war, space flights, etc.
hard'-wear'ing *adj.* not quickly showing signs of damage through use.
hard'wood *n.* hard timber obtained from the slow-growing trees (those that shed their leaves).
be hard put to it to be in, or have, great difficulty.
hard at it working hard, very busy.
hard by near.
hard lines bad luck.
hard of hearing partially deaf.
hard up short of money.

hardy *här'di*, *adj.* **1** daring, brave. **2** able to bear cold or fatigue. **3** (of plants) able to grow in the open air throughout the year:—*comp.* **har'dier**; *superl.* **har'diest**.
har'dily *adv.* **har'diness** *n.*
har'dihood *n.* **1** boldness. **2** impudence.

hare *hār*, *n.* a timid, swift rabbit-like animal.
hare'bell *n.* a plant with blue bell-shaped flowers.
hare'-brained *adj.* giddy, very rash.
hare'-lip *n.* a divided upper human lip like the lip of a hare.

harem *hār'ėm*, *hä-rēm'*, *n.* **1** the part of a Muslim house occupied by the women. **2** the women themselves.

haricot *har'i-kō*, *n.* a small white bean.

hark *härk*, *v.i.* to listen (usu. with *to* or *at*).
hark back to return (to a previous subject—e.g. to a grievance).

Harlequin *här'lė-kwin*, (also no *cap.*) *n.* a pantomime character in a brightly coloured, diamond-patterned costume.

harm *härm*, *n.* **1** injury. **2** wrong.—*v.t.* to injure.
harm'ful *adj.* doing harm.
harm'fully *adv.* **harm'fulness** *n.*
harm'less *adj.* **harm'lessly** *adv.*

harmonic, etc. See **harmony**.

harmony *här'mȯ-ni*, *n.* **1** a (usu. pleasing) combination of musical notes, or of colours. **2** a happy, friendly state without disagreements:—*pl.* **har'monies**; *opp.* **dishar'mony**.
harmon'ic *(-mon')* *adj.* of, or concerned with, harmony.—*n.* an overtone.
harmon'ica *(-mon')* *n.* a mouth-organ.
harmon'ious *(-mōn')* *adj.* **1** pleasant sounding. **2** pleasant to the eye. **3** without disagreement or bad feeling:—*opp.* **inharmonious**.
harmon'iously *adv.*
har'monise *v.i.* **1** to be in harmony. **2** to sing in harmony. **3** to agree.—*v.t.* **1** to bring into harmony. **2** (*music*) to add parts to (a melody):—*pr.p.* **har'monising**.
harmon'ium *(-mōn')* *n.* a small organ.

harness *här'nis*, *n.* the equipment (straps, bands, etc.) of a horse.—*v.t.* **1** to put the harness on. **2** to make use of (natural power, as waterfall, etc.).
in harness doing one's daily work, not retired.

harp *härp*, *n.* a musical instrument played by plucking strings stretched from a curved neck to a soundboard.—*v.i.* **1** to play on the harp. **2** to dwell (on a subject) to a boring extent.
harp'er, now usu. **harp'ist,** *ns.*

harpoon *här-pōōn'*, *n.* a barbed dart, esp. one for killing whales.—*v.t.* to strike with the harpoon.
harpoon'er *n.*

harpsichord *härp'si-körd*, *n.* a piano-like musical instrument.

harpy *här'pi*, *n.* **1** (usu. *cap.*) in old story, a monster, half woman, half bird of prey. **2** a grasping, shrewish, woman:—*pl.* **har'pies**.

harridan *har'i-dȧn*, *n.* an ill-tempered old woman.

harrier[1] *har'i-ėr, n.* **1** a small dog for hunting hares. **2** a cross-country runner.

harrier[2]. See **harry**.

harrow *har'ō, n.* a spiked frame for smoothing and breaking up ploughed land, and for covering seeds.—*v.t.* **1** to use a harrow on. **2** to distress deeply.

harr'owing *adj.* extremely distressing: *a harrowing story*.

harry *har'i, v.t.* **1** to plunder. **2** to harass, torment:—*pr.p.* **harr'ying**; *pa.p.* **harr'ied**.

harr'ier *n.* a kind of hawk.

harsh *härsh, adj.* **1** rough. **2** jarring on hearing or sight, etc. **3** very strict or stern. **4** cruel.

harsh'ly *adv.* **harsh'ness** *n.*

hart *härt, n.* a male deer (esp. red deer) from the age of six years:—*fem.* **hind**; *pl.* **hart(s)**.

hartebeest *här'tė-bēst, n.* a South African antelope.

harum-scarum *hā'rum-skā'rum, adj.* reckless, rash.—*n.* a giddy, rash person.

harvest *här'vist, n.* **1** the time of gathering in ripened crops. **2** the crops gathered in. **3** fruits. **4** the product or result of any action.—*v.t., v.i.* to gather (a crop).

har'vester *n.* **1** a reaper. **2** a machine for gathering crops.

harvest home the feast held at the bringing home of the harvest.

harvest moon the full moon nearest September 23.

harvest mouse a very small mouse that builds its nest on stalks of growing corn.

has. See **have**.

hash *hash, v.t.* to mince, chop small.—*n.* a mixed dish of meat and vegetables in small pieces.

make a hash of to spoil completely.

hashish *hash'ish, -ēsh, n.* the leaves, etc., of hemp, intoxicating when smoked, chewed, etc.

hasp *häsp, n.* a hinged piece of metal used to shut and fasten a hut door, suitcase lid, etc.

hassock *has'ȯk, n.* **1** a tuft of grass. **2** a stuffed stool for feet or knees.

hast. See **have**.

haste *hāst, n.* **1** hurry. **2** rash speed.—Also (*poetic*) *v.i.*:—*pr.p.* **hast'ing**.

hasten *hās'ėn, v.i.* **1** to move with speed. **2** to do without delay: *He hastened to add an explanation*.

has'ty *adj.* **1** quick. **2** hurried. **3** too quick, rash: *a hasty temper, hasty words*:—*comp.* **has'tier**; *superl.* **has'tiest**.

has'tily *adv.* **has'tiness** *n.*

make haste to hasten, hurry.

hat *hat, n.* a covering for the head, usu. with crown and brim.

hatt'ed *adj.*

hatt'er *n.* a maker or seller of hats.

hat'-trick *n.* the taking of three wickets by three balls one after another in cricket, the scoring of three goals in one football, etc., game, or three successes in any activity.

keep something under one's hat to keep it secret.

take one's hat off to to express admiration for (a person).

hatch[1] *hach, n.* **1** the covering of an opening in a floor, wall, etc. **2** the opening itself.

hatch'back *n.* (a car with) a sloping rear door which opens upwards.

hatch'way *n.* the opening in a ship's deck into the hold, or from one deck to another.

hatch[2] *hach, v.t.* **1** to produce from the egg. **2** to develop or plan secretly (e.g. a plot).—*v.i.* to come from the egg.—*n.* **1** the act of hatching. **2** the brood hatched.

hatch'ery *n.* a place for the artificial hatching of eggs, esp. those of fish:—*pl.* **hatch'eries**.

hatch[3] *hach, v.t.* to shade by fine lines, in drawing and engraving.

hatch'ing *n.*

hatchback. See **hatch**[1].

hatchery. See **hatch**[2].

hatchet *hach'it, n.* a small axe.

hatch'et-faced *adj.* having a narrow, sharp-featured face.

bury the hatchet to end a quarrel.

hatchway. See **hatch**[1].

hate *hāt, v.t.* to dislike very much:—*pr.p.* **hat'ing**.—*n.* hatred.

hate'ful *adj.* arousing hate, detestable.

hate'fully *adv.* **hate'fulness** *n.*

hat'er *n.*

hat'red *(hāt') n.* extreme dislike, often with longing to injure.

hath. See **have**.

hatted, hatter. See **hat**.

haughty *hö'ti, adj.* proud, arrogant:—*comp.* **haugh'tier**; *superl.* **haugh'tiest**.

haugh'tily *adv.* **haugh'tiness** *n.*

haul *höl, v.t.* **1** to drag. **2** to pull with violence.—Also *v.i.*—*n.* **1** a pull. **2** a quantity obtained at one time, e.g. of fish, stolen goods, or plunder.

haul'age *n.* **1** the act of hauling. **2** the charge for hauling. **3** transport, esp. heavy road transport.

haulier *höl'yėr*, or *-i-ėr, n.* **1** one who takes part in the road haulage business. **2** one who hauls coal to the shaft.—Also **haul'er**.

haunch *hönch, -sh, n.* **1** the hip and buttock. **2** the leg and loin of venison, etc.

haunt *hönt, v.t.* **1** to visit (a place or person) very often. **2** to live in, or visit, as a ghost. **3** to keep coming back to the memory of: *Her look of misery haunts me.*—*n.* a place one visits often.

haun'ted *adj.* visited by ghost(s).

haute couture *ōt kōō-tür'* (the designing and making of) fashionable, expensive clothes.

have *hav, v.t.* **1** to own, possess. **2** to enjoy or suffer: *to have good, bad, weather on holiday.* **3** to hold in the mind: *to have a good idea.* **4** to give birth to (a baby). **5** to cause to be: *Have this picture framed.* **6** to be compelled to: *I have to go now.*—*v.* used to form past tenses of other verbs (e.g. *I have come, I had forgotten*):—*pr.p.* **hav'ing**; *pa.t.* and *pa.p.* **had**; *pr.t. 3rd sing.* **has** *(haz)*; **hast, hath** old forms in the present tense (*thou hast, he hath*).—*n.* a person with money, etc. as opp. to a **have-not**.

have'-not' *n.* a person lacking money or possessions.

had better, best. See **better, best**.

have done with to finish, put an end to, have no further dealings with.

have had it (*slang*) **1** to be done for. **2** not to be going to get it.

have it out to discuss thoroughly a subject of disagreement or ill-feeling.

have up to call before a court of justice, etc.

the ayes (noes) have it the larger number of votes is in favour of (against) the motion.

haven *hā'vn, n.* **1** a harbour or anchorage. **2** any place of safety.

haversack *hav'ėr-sak, n.* a bag for a soldier's or traveller's food, etc.

havoc *hav'ok, n.* very great destruction.

haw *hö, n.* the fruit of the hawthorn.

haw'thorn *n.* a small tree of the rose family with white or pink blossom.

hawk[1]. See **hawker**.

hawk[2] *hök, n.* **1** a bird of prey of the eagle family, esp. one with rounded wings. **2** one who advocates war or confrontation rather than peace and conciliation.—*v.i.* to hunt birds with trained hawks.

hawk'-eyed *adj.* **1** with very keen sight. **2** very observant.

hawker *hök'er, n.* one who goes about offering goods for sale.

hawk *v.t.* to carry round for sale.

hawser *hö'zėr, n.* **1** a small cable. **2** a large rope for towing, etc.

hawthorn. See **haw**.

hay *hā, n.* grass cut down and dried for fodder.

hay'cock *n.* a cone-shaped pile of hay.

hay fever irritation of nose, throat, etc. by pollen.

hay'maker *n.* **1** one who cuts and dries grass for hay. **2** a wild swinging blow. **3** (in *pl.*) a country dance.

hay'rick, hay'stack *ns.* a pile of stacked hay.

hay'wire *adj.* **1** crazy. **2** no longer in working order.

hazard *haz'ärd, n.* **1** chance, risk. **2** a difficulty on a golf course (e.g. a bunker). **3** anything which might cause an accident, create danger, etc.—*v.t.* **1** to risk. **2** to offer with some doubts (e.g. a suggestion).

haz'ardous *adj.* dangerous, perilous.

haz'ardously *adv.* **haz'ardousness** *n.*

haze *hāz, n.* vapour or mist.

hāz'y *adj.* **1** misty. **2** dim. **3** confused in mind:—*comp.* **haz'ier**; *superl.* **haz'iest**.

haz'ily *adv.* **haz'iness** *n.*

hazel *hā'zl, n.* a small tree with a nut (**ha'zelnut**) that can be eaten.—*adj.* of a light-brown colour, like a hazelnut.

H-bomb *āch'-bom, n.* hydrogen bomb.

he *hē, pron.* refers to a male (or thing spoken of as male) already named or understood: *John must go because he can run fastest*:—*objective* **him**; *possessive* **his** (*hiz*; sometimes described as a *possessive adj.*).—*adj.* (usu. as part of a word) male: *a he-goat*.

himself' *pron.* the emphatic or reflexive form of *he, him*: *He himself said so*; *He has hurt himself*.

head *hed, n.* **1** the uppermost or foremost part of an animal's body. **2** a round, solid part: *a head of cabbage.* **3** the brain, the understanding. **4** a chief or leader. **5** a headmaster or headmistress. **6** the front or top of anything. **7** a cape, promontory. **8** a froth on beer, etc. **9** point of suppuration. **10** individual animal or person: *fifty head of cattle.* **11** a chief point of a talk, sermon, etc. **12** the source or spring. **13** a body of water. **14** strength: *to gather head.* **15** the device on a tape-recorder, etc. which converts the recorded form of the information on the tape, etc. into electrical signals, and vice versa.—*v.t.* **1** to lead. **2** to get ahead of and turn (e.g. cattle; often with *off*). **3** to strike (a ball) with the head.—*v.i.* to make straight (for a place).—*adj.* **1** at the head. **2** in the head. **3** chief (e.g. **head waiter**).

head'er *n.* **1** a fall, dive, head foremost. **2** the act of heading a ball.

head'ing *n.* something that is at the head or top.

head'y *adj.* **1** intoxicating. **2** rash, wilful:—*comp.* **head'ier**; *superl.* **head'iest**.
head'ily *adv.* **head'iness** *n.*
head'ship *n.* the position of the person who has chief authority.
head'ache *n.* pain in the head.
head'band *n.* a band worn round the head.
head'board *n.* the panel at the head of a bed.
head'dress *n.* a covering for the head, esp. an ornamental one.
head'hunting *n.* **1** collecting human heads as trophies. **2** trying to attract people away from their present jobs, e.g. by offering them more money.
head'land *n.* a point of land running out into the sea, a cape.
head'light *n.* a light in front of a ship or vehicle.
head'line *n.* **1** a line (title, caption, etc.) at the top of a page, or at the beginning of a newspaper article. **2** (in *pl.*) the chief points of (the news).
head'long *adv.* **1** head first. **2** hastily. **3** without thought, rashly.—*adj.* **1** hasty. **2** rash.
headmas'ter, headmis'tress *ns.* the head teacher in a school.
head'most *adj.* most advanced, farthest forward.
head'-on' *adj.* and *adv.* with the front of one vehicle, etc. hitting the front of another.
head'phones *n.pl.* sound receivers that fix on the head, one at or in each ear, for listening to a radio, CD player, etc.
head'piece *n.* **1** a helmet. **2** a hat. **3** head, intelligence. **4** the top part.
head'quarters (or *-kwör'*) *n.pl.* **1** the residence of a commander-in-chief or general. **2** a central or chief office, etc.
head'room *n.* clearance between the top of something and the lower surface of something else.
head'set *n.* a set of headphones, often with a microphone attached.
head start. See **start**.
head'stone *n.* **1** the principal stone of a building. **2** a gravestone.
head'strong *adj.* self-willed.
head'way *n.* motion forward, esp. of a ship.
head wind a wind blowing in the opposite direction from that in which e.g. a ship is moving, thus slowing it down.
come to a head to reach a climax, or time of urgent need for action.
have a (good) head on one's shoulders to have brains, ability.
head over heels **1** in a somersault. **2** deeply, thoroughly.
heads or tails a phrase used when tossing a coin to see whether the side with the sovereign's head will fall uppermost or the reverse.
keep (lose) one's head to keep (lose) one's presence of mind.
make head against to advance, make progress, against.
make neither head nor tail of to be unable to understand.
off one's head crazy.
over one's head too difficult for one to understand.

heal *hēl*, *v.t.* and *v.i.* **1** to restore, or be restored, to health or normal condition. **2** to mend: *to heal a quarrel*:—*pr.p.* **heal'ing**; *pa.p.* **healed**.
heal'er *n.* **heal'ing** *n.* and *adj.*
health *helth*, *n.* **1** wholeness or soundness, esp. of the body. **2** the state of the body: *in poor health.* **3** a toast, as 'drink someone's health'.
health'y *adj.* **1** in good health. **2** suggesting health. **3** encouraging good health:—*comp.* **health'ier**; *superl.* **health'iest**.
health'ily *adv.* **health'iness** *n.*
health centre a building in which the doctors, nurses, etc. who serve a particular area work.
health visitor a nurse who visits patients at home.

heap *hēp*, *n.* **1** a mass of things resting one above another. **2** a mound. **3** a great quantity (often in *pl.*).—*v.t.* **1** to throw in a heap. **2** to pile (up).

hear *hēr*, *v.t.* **1** to perceive by the ear. **2** to be told: *I hear he is ill.* **3** to listen to. **4** to try (a case in a court of law).—*v.i.* **1** to have the sense of hearing. **2** to listen:—*pa.p.* **heard** *(hûrd)*.
hear'er *n.* **hear'ing** *n.* and *adj.*
hear'say *n.* rumour, report.
give someone a hearing to give him an opportunity to say what he wants to say.
hear, hear! exclamation of approval.
will not hear of will not allow.
within hearing within earshot.

hearken *härk'n*, (*old* or *poetic*) *v.i.* to listen (to), esp. attentively.

hearsay. See **hear**.

hearse *hûrs*, *n.* a vehicle in which a coffin is conveyed.

heart *härt*, *n.* **1** the organ of the body that makes the blood circulate. **2** a core. **3** the most important part. **4** the seat of the affections, etc., esp. love. **5** courage: *His heart failed him*; *His heart failed*—the latter may also mean 'His heart stopped'. **6** vigour. **7** (in *pl.*) a card suit bearing heart-shaped pips.
-hear'ted (as part of a word) having a heart (of a stated kind): *hard-hearted.*
hear'ten *v.t.* **1** to encourage. **2** to

cheer:—*opp.* **dishearten.**
hear'ty *adj.* **1** warm, genuine. **2** strong. **3** healthy. **4** (of a meal) large:—*comp.* **hear'tier**; *superl.* **hear'tiest**.
hear'tily *adv.* **hear'tiness** *n.*
heart'less *adj.* **1** pitiless. **2** cruel.
heart'lessly *adv.* **heart'lessness** *n.*
heart attack a sudden failure of the heart to function correctly.
heart'break *n.* a deep sorrow.
heart'breaking *adj.* crushing one with grief.
heart'broken *adj.* deeply saddened.
heart'burn *n.* a bitter, burning feeling in the throat or chest, caused by indigestion.
heart'burning *n.* discontent, from envy.
heart'felt *adj.* deep, sincere.
heart'-rending *adj.* causing great pain or sadness.
heart'sick *adj.* very depressed or unhappy.
heart'-strings *n.pl.* affections.
heart'warming *adj.* emotionally pleasing.
at heart inwardly, in real character.
break one's heart to feel great grief.
break someone's heart to cause someone great grief.
by heart in, from, memory.
heart to heart frankly (*adj.* **heart'-to-heart'**).
take heart to feel more hope, greater resolve.
take to heart **1** to be upset by. **2** to pay great attention to.

hearth *härth*, *n.* **1** the floor of the fireplace. **2** the fireside. **3** the house itself.

heartily, etc. See **heart**.

heat *hēt*, *n.* **1** the condition of a substance that gives one the sensation of warmth. **2** sensation of warmth, esp. great warmth. **3** a high temperature. **4** the hottest period: *the heat of the day*. **5** passion. **6** the period of sexual excitement in a female animal. **7** a violent or excited stage: *in the heat of the debate.* **8** a preliminary race to eliminate some of the competitors.—*v.t.* **1** to make hot. **2** to agitate.—*v.i.* to become hot.
heat'er *n.* **heat'ing** *n.* and *adj.*
heat barrier difficulty caused by air surrounding aircraft heating at very high speeds.
heat'stroke *n.* exhaustion or illness caused by the heat of the sun.
heat wave (*coll.*) *n.* a spell of very hot weather.
See also **hot**.

heath *hēth*, *n.* **1** barren open country, esp. covered with low shrubs. **2** a hardy evergreen low shrub.

heathen *hē'*TH*n*, *n.* **1** one who believes in a lower form of religion, esp. with many gods. **2** (*coll.*) an uncivilised person:—*pl.* **heath'en** (*the heathen*), **heathens.**—Also *adj.*

heather *he*TH*'ėr*, *n.* kinds of heath (*def. 2*).
heath'ery *adj.* **heath'eriness** *n.*

heave *hēv*, *v.t.* **1** to lift up with great effort. **2** to throw. **3** to haul. **4** to force out (a sigh).—*v.i.* **1** to rise and fall like waves. **2** to retch:—*pr.p.* **heav'ing**; *pa.p.* **heaved** or **hōve.**—Also *n.*
heave in sight to come into view.
heave to to bring a vessel to a standstill.

heaven *hev'n*, *n.* **1** the sky, upper regions of the air (usu. in *pl.*). **2** the dwelling-place of God. **3** (a place or state of) supreme happiness.
heav'enly *adj.* **1** of heaven. **2** in the heavens. **3** divine. **4** beautiful. **5** (*coll.*) very good, delightful.
heav'enliness *n.*
heavenly bodies sun, moon, stars, planets, etc.
heav'en-sent *adj.* **1** sent from heaven. **2** very fortunate or suitable.

heavily, etc. See **heavy**.

heavy *hev'i*, *adj.* **1** difficult to lift or carry. **2** not easy to bear. **3** oppressive. **4** laden (with). **5** clumsy. **6** dull. **7** deep-toned. **8** dark, gloomy: *a heavy sky.* **9** very sad. **10** not easily digested:—*comp.* **heav'ier**; *superl.* **heav'iest.**—*n.* **1** the villain in a play. **2** a large, strong man employed for usu. violent and often criminal purposes:—*pl.* **heav'ies**.
heav'ily *adv.* **heav'iness** *n.*
heav'y-han'ded *adj.* **1** clumsy. **2** inclined to oppress, or to punish too much.
heav'y-hear'ted *adj.* sorrowful.
heavy water a kind of water heavier than ordinary water, used in nuclear reactors.
heav'yweight *n.* a boxer not less than $12\frac{1}{2}$ stone (79.378kg.) or, amateur, not less than 12 stone 10 pounds (80.379kg.).

Hebrew *hē'broo͞*, *n.* **1** a Jew. **2** the language of the Hebrews.—Also *adj.*
Hebraic(al) *hē-brā'ik(ȧl)*, *adjs.*

heckle *hekl*, *v.t.* and *v.i.* to interrupt (a speaker at a meeting) with shouted comments and questions:—*pr.p.* **heck'ling**.
heck'ler *n.* **heck'ling** *n.* and *adj.*

hectare *hek'tār*, *n.* 10000 square metres.

hectic *hek'tik*, *adj.* **1** flushed with fever. **2** excited, intense: *a hectic rush*.
hec'tically *adv.* **hec'ticness** *n.*

hecto- *hek-tō-*, (as part of a word) used to show multiplication by 100, as in **hectogram**, etc.

hector *hek'tȯr*, *v.t.* to bully, annoy.

he'd *hēd*, **1** he had. **2** he would.

hedge *hej*, *n.* **1** a close row of bushes or small trees. **2** a barrier.—*v.t.* **1** to enclose with a hedge. **2** to surround. **3** to hem (in).—*v.i.* **1** to make hedges. **2** to avoid giving a straight answer:—*pr.p.* **hedg'ing**.

hedg'er *n.* one who plants or trims hedges.

hedg'ing *n.* and *adj.*

hedge'hog *n.* a small prickly-backed animal with a snout like a pig.

hedge'hop *v.i.* and *v.t.* to fly (an aeroplane) very close to the ground:—*pr.p.* **hedge'hopping**; *pa.p.* **hedge'hopped**.

hedge'row *n.* a line of hedge, often with trees.

hedge'-sparrow *n.* a sparrow-like bird of the thrush family.

heed *hēd, v.t.* **1** to be attentive to. **2** to concern oneself about.—*n.* notice, attention.

heed'ful *adj.* **heed'less** *adj.*

heed'lessly *adv.* **heed'lessness** *n.*

heel[1] *hēl, n.* **1** the back part part of the foot. **2** the covering or support of the heel in footwear. **3** a thing like a heel in shape.—*v.t.* **1** to strike, or pass back (a ball) with the heel. **2** to put a heel on.

come to heel to obey as a dog does.

down at heel **1** shabby. **2** slovenly.

on a person's heels close behind him.

take to one's heels to flee.

heel[2] *hēl, v.i.* (of e.g. a ship) to lean to one side.

heel over to heel too far to be able to right itself, oneself.

heft *heft, v.t.* **1** to lift. **2** to estimate the weight of by hand.

hefty *hef'ti, adj.* **1** rather heavy. **2** muscular. **3** vigorous:—*comp.* **hef'tier**; *superl.* **hef'tiest**.

heifer *hef'ėr, n.* a young cow.

height *hīt, n.* **1** the state of being high. **2** distance upwards. **3** a hill. **4** utmost degree: *the height of nonsense.*

height'en *v.t.* **1** to make higher. **2** to make greater. **3** to make brighter or more obvious.

heinous *hā'nůs, adj.* very wicked: *a heinous crime.*

heir *ār, n.* **1** one who inherits anything after the death of the owner. **2** a child, esp. a first-born son:—*fem.* **heiress** (*ār'es*; used esp. of a woman who has inherited, or will inherit, wealth).

heir apparent the person acknowledged by law to be heir.

heir'loom *n.* a valued inherited possession.

heir presumptive one who will be heir if no nearer relative should be born.

fall heir to to inherit or receive (something that has belonged to another).

See also **heredity, heritable**.

held. See **hold**.

helical, helices. See **helix**.

helicopter *hel'i-kop-tėr, n.* an aircraft lifted and propelled by blades rotating on a vertical axis.

heliograph *hē'li-ō-gräf, n.* a device for sending messages using the sun's rays.

heliotrope *hel'i-ŏ-trōp, hēl', n.* **1** a plant whose flowers, according to story, always turn towards the sun. **2** a shade of purple.

helium *hēl'i-ům, n.* an element, a very light gas, not inflammable, present in the sun's atmosphere.

helix *hē'liks, n.* a line, thread, or wire curved as if wound regularly round and round along a cylinder:—*pl.* **hē'lixes** or **helices** *(hel'i-sēz).*

helical *hel'i-kål, adj.*

hell *hel, n.* **1** the place or state of punishment of the wicked after death. **2** any place or state of wickedness or misery.

hell'ish *adj.* **hell'ishly** *adv.*

he'll *hēl,* he will.

Hellene *hel'ēn, n.* a Greek.

Hellen'ic (*-ēn'* or *-en'*) *adj.* Greek.

hello, hullo, hallo, halloa *hė-lō', interj.* expressing surprise, etc., calling attention, or as a greeting.

helm *helm, n.* the apparatus by which a ship is steered.

helms'man *n.* one who steers.

helmet *hel'mit, n.* a protective covering (orig. of armour) for the head.

hel'meted *adj.*

help *help, v.t.* **1** to do something necessary or useful for (a person). **2** to aid, to assist. **3** to play a part in the success of: *Henry's good sense helped the negotiations.* **4** to remedy, make less bad: *A hot drink will help your cold.* **5** to prevent oneself from: *I could not help crying out.* **6** to serve food to at table.—Also *v.i.*—*n.* **1** aid, assistance. **2** relief, remedy. **3** one who assists. **4** a hired servant, esp. domestic.

help'er *n.*

help'ful *adj.* **1** useful. **2** willing or able to help.

help'fully *adv.* **help'fulness** *n.*

help'ing *adj.*—*n.* a portion served at a meal.

help'less *adj.* unable (e.g. from weakness) to help oneself.

help'lessly *adv.* **help'lessness** *n.*

help'mate, -meet *ns.* a husband or wife.

help oneself **1** to get out of a difficulty or difficulties by one's own efforts. **2** to take what one wants. **3** to steal.

helter-skelter *hel'tėr-skel'tėr, adv.* in haste and confusion.—*adj.* disorderly.—*n.* a spiral slide in an amusement park.

hem *hem,n.* a border of a garment doubled up and sewn.—*v.t.* **1** to form a hem on. **2** to sew with the stitch usu. used in making a hem:—*pr.p.* **hemm'ing**; *pa.p.* **hemmed**.
hem in to shut in, prevent from moving.

hemi- *hem-i-*, (as part of a word) half.
hemisphere *hem'i-sfēr, n.* **1** a half sphere. **2** half of the globe or a map of it.
hemispher'ical *(-sfer') adj.*

hemlock *hem'lok, n.* **1** a poisonous plant with spotted stem. **2** a poisonous drink made from it. **3** (also **hemlock spruce**) a cone-bearing N. American tree.

hemorrhage, **hemorrhoid**, etc. Same as **haemorrhage**, **haemorrhoid**, etc.

hemp *hemp, n.* **1** a plant from different kinds of which are obtained a coarse fibre, a drug, and an oil. **2** the fibre. **3** the drug (known as hashish, marijuana, etc.).
hemp'en *adj.*

hen *hen, n.* the female of any bird, esp. the domestic fowl.—Also *adj.*
hen'pecked *adj.* (of a man) ruled by his wife.

hence *hens, adv.* **1** from this place. **2** from this time: *a year hence.* **3** for this reason, therefore.—*interj.* away! begone!
hence'forth, **hencefor'ward** *advs.* from this time forth or forward.

henchman *hench'man, -sh', n.* **1** a servant. **2** an active supporter, often political:—*pl.* **hench'men**.

henna *hen'ȧ, n.* **1** a small Eastern shrub. **2** a dye made from its leaves, for nails and hair.

henpecked. See **hen**.

hepatitis *hep-ȧ-tī'tis, n.* inflammation of the liver.

hept(a)- (as part of a word) seven.

her, **hers**, **herself**. See **she**.

herald *her'ȧld, n.* **1** in the past, an officer who made public proclamations, arranged ceremonies, and later kept a register of noble families and their coats of arms, etc. **2** a person, or thing, that goes before, or announces, something else.—*v.t.* to announce or be a sign of (something about to happen).
heral'dic *adj.* of heralds or heraldry.
her'aldry *n.* **1** the science dealing with coats of arms and the persons who have a right to bear them, etc. **2** the pomp and ceremony in which heralds took part.

herb *hûrb, n.* **1** a plant with no woody stem above ground, i.e. not a tree or shrub. **2** a plant used in medicine. **3** a scented plant used in cookery (e.g. sage).
herbaceous *hûr-bā'shus, adj.* **1** herb-like. **2** containing herbs, esp. tall plants that die down in winter: *a herbaceous border or flower bed.*
her'bage *n.* grass for pasture.
her'bal *adj.* of herbs, esp. herbs used for medicine.
her'balist *n.* a person who deals in herbs.
herbiv'orous *adj.* feeding on plants.

herculean *hûr-kū-lē'ȧn*, or *-kū', adj.* having, or requiring, very great strength.

herd[1] *hûrd, n.* a company of animals of one kind that keep, or are kept, together.—*v.i.* and *v.t.* to come, or drive, together.
the (common) herd the mass of ordinary people who accept the same views and act alike.

herd[2] *hûrd, n.* one who looks after a herd of animals.—Also **herds'man**.

here *hēr, adv.* **1** in, or to, this place. **2** in this matter. **3** in the present life or state.
here'about(s) *advs.* near this place.
hereaf'ter *adv.* after this, in some future time or state.—*n.* a future state.
here'by' *adv.* by means of (e.g. a document): *I hereby declare that I will not be responsible for any debts incurred by her.*
here'upon *adv.* immediately after this.
herewith' (or *hēr'*) *adv.* with this (e.g. with this letter).
here and there in, or to, some scattered places.
here's to I drink the health of.
neither here nor there not important or relevant.

heredity *hi-red'i-ti, n.* the passing on of physical and mental characteristics from ancestors to their descendants.
hered'itary *adj.* handed down from ancestors.
See also **heritable**, **inheritance**.

heresy *her'i-si, n.* a belief or opinion different from that held by the majority of people in the (esp. religious) group to which one belongs:—*pl.* **her'esies**.
her'etic *n.* one who upholds a heresy.
heret'ical *adj.* **heret'ically** *adv.*

hereupon, **herewith**. See **here**.

heritable *her'i-tȧ-bl, adj.* that may be inherited.
her'itage *(-tij) n.* something that is inherited.

hermetically sealed *hûr-met'ik-ȧl-i sēld,* closed completely.

hermit *hûr'mit, n.* **1** a person, esp. an early Christian, who went to live by himself in a lonely place. **2** a person who shuns the company of others.
her'mitage *(-ij) n.* the dwelling of a hermit.

hernia *hûr'ni-ȧ, n.* the thrusting out of (part of) a bodily organ through an opening or weak spot in its surrounding walls.

hero *hē'rō*, *n.* **1** a very brave man or boy. **2** one greatly admired for noble qualities, real or imaginary. **3** the principal male character in a book or play:—*pl.* **hē'roes**; *fem.* **heroine** *(her'ō-in)*.
heroic *hė-rō'ik*, *adj.* very brave.
hero'ically *adv.*
her'oism *(her')* *n.* great bravery.
he'ro-wor'ship *n.* very great admiration for, and devotion to, a person regarded as a hero (or heroine).

heroin *her'ō-in*, *n.* a habit-forming drug, obtained from opium.

heroine, **heroism**. See **hero**.

heron *her'ȯn*, *n.* a large wading bird, with long legs and neck.
her'onry *n.* a place where herons breed:—*pl.* **her'onries**.

herring *her'ing*, *n.* a common small sea fish used as food, found moving in great shoals:—*pl.* **herr'ing(s)**.
herr'ing-bone *adj.* applied to masonry, textiles, etc. in which there is a pattern like numbers of herring spines laid side by side, to a stitch of spine-like appearance in sewing, etc.
red herring. See **red**.

hers, **herself**. See **she**.

hertz *hûrts*, *n.* a unit of frequency of radio waves, etc., sometimes known as the **cycle per second**.

he's *hēz*, he is.

hesitate *hez'i-tāt*, *v.i.* **1** to pause. **2** to be unwilling (to): *I hesitate to say he lied, but he certainly misled me.* **3** to stammer:—*pr.p.* **hes'itating**.
hes'itancy, **hesitā'tion** *ns.*
hes'itant *adj.*

hessian *hes'i-ȧn*, *hes'yȧn*, *n.* a coarse cloth made of jute.

hetero- *het-ėr-ō-*, (as part of a word) other, different.
heteroge'neous *(-jē'ni-ŭs)* *adj.* made up of parts or individuals of very different kinds: *a heterogeneous mixture*, *crowd*.
heterosex'ual *adj.* of, having, sexual attraction towards the opposite sex.—Also *n.*

hew *hū*, *v.t.* **1** to cut (away, down, in pieces, etc.) with blows. **2** to shape. **3** to cut (a path): *to hew one's way.*—*pa.t.* **hewed**; *pa.p.* **hewed**, or **hewn**.
hew'er *n.*

hex(a)- *heks(a)-*, (as part of a word) six.
hex'agon *n.* a figure with six sides and six angles.
hexag'onal *adj.*

hey *hā*, *interj.* expressing joy, or a question, or calling attention.

heyday *hā'dā*, *n.* the period of fullest vigour or greatest activity.

hiatus *hī-ā'tŭs*, *n.* **1** a break, gap. **2** a place in a manuscript, etc., where something is missing:—*pl.* **hia'tuses**.

hibernate *hī'bėr-nāt*, *v.i.* **1** to pass the winter in sleep, as some animals do. **2** to remain in an inactive state:—*pr.p.* **hi'bernating**.
hibernā'tion *n.*

Hibernian *hi-bûr'ni-ȧn*, *adj.* of Ireland.

hiccough. A spelling of hiccup.

hiccup *hik'up*, *n.* **1** a sudden spasm of the diaphragm followed immediately by closing of the top of the windpipe. **2** the sound caused by this.—Also *v.i.*—*v.t.* to say with a hiccup:—*pr.p.* **hicc'upping**; *pa.p.* **hicc'uped**.

hickory *hik'ȯr-i*, *n.* any of a number of N. American trees of the walnut family, some having strong wood:—*pl.* **hick'ories**.

hid, **hidden**. See **hide**[1].

hide[1] *hīd*, *v.t.* **1** to put out of sight. **2** to conceal. **3** to keep secret.—*v.i.* to go into, to stay in, a place where one cannot be seen, or easily found:—*pr.p.* **hid'ing**; *pa.t.* **hid**; *pa.p.* **hidd'en**.
hidd'en *adj.* **1** concealed. **2** unknown.
hid'ing *n.* **1** the act or state of concealing. **2** a place of concealment.
hide'-out *n* a place of hiding.

hide[2] *hīd*, *n.* **1** the skin of an animal. **2** (*coll.*) a human skin.
hid'ing *n.* a thrashing.
hide'-bound *adj.* narrow-minded, not ready to accept new ideas or opinions.

hideous *hid'i-ŭs*, *-yŭs*, *adj.* **1** frightful, horrible. **2** extremely ugly.
hid'eously *adv.* **hid'eousness** *n.*

hiding. See **hid**[1,2].

hie *hī*, *v.i.* to hasten:—*pr.p.* **hie'ing**; *pa.p.* **hied** *(hīd)*.

hier(o)- *hī-ėr-(ō-)*, (as part of a word) sacred.
hierarchy *hī'ėr-är-ki*, *n.* **1** an arrangement in grades according to importance (orig. of angels, now of people in power). **2** a controlling group of people:—*pl.* **hi'erarchies**.
hieroglyphics *hī-ėr-ō-glif'iks*, *n.pl.* **1** the pictures used in picture-writing, esp. in that of ancient Egypt. **2** letters or symbols hard to read.

hi-fi *hī'fī*, *n.* **1** high-fidelity sound reproduction. **2** equipment for this. **3** the use of such equipment, esp. as a hobby.—Also *adj.*

higgledy-piggledy *hig'l-di-pig'l-di*, *adv.* and *adj.* in any order, in confusion.

high *hī*, *adj.* **1** tall, lofty. **2** far up from e.g. the ground, sea level, low tide, zero on a scale. **3** great: *high speed*, *price*, *hopes.* **4** of important rank: *a high official.*

5 chief: *High Court*, *the high altar*. **6** noble: *high aims*. **7** (of sound) acute in pitch, shrill. **8** (of meat, etc.) beginning to go bad.—*adv.* **1** far up. **2** to a high degree.—*n.* a high, or the highest, level.
high'ly *adv.* **1** in a high place or rank. **2** very: *highly dangerous*. **3** at a high rate: *highly paid*. **4** with approval: *to think highly of someone*.
high'ness *n.* **1** the quality of being high. **2** (*cap.*) the title of princes, princesses, etc.
high'ball (*U.S.*) *n.* liquor and an effervescent drink (e.g. whisky and soda) with ice in a tall glass.
high'born *adj.* of noble birth.
high'brow *n.* a person with intellectual tastes.—Also *adj.*
High Church a party within the Church of England which attaches importance to ritual and to the authority of the clergy.
High Commissioner the chief representative in a British Commonwealth country of another country that is also a member of the Commonwealth.—See also **Governor-General**.
high explosive a very powerful explosive.
highfalu'tin(g) *(-lōō')* *adj.* pompous, lofty and affected: *a highfalutin style*.
high fidelity good in reproduction of sound.—See also **hi-fi**.
high'flown *adj.* (of style) using words that sound grand, bombastic.
high'-hand'ed *adj.* **1** taking power or authority to oneself. **2** done without considering the views of others: *a high-handed action*.
high jinks boisterous play.
high'lands *n. pl.* a mountainous district, esp. (*cap.*) the north-west of Scotland.
high'land, High'land *adj.*
high'lander, High'lander *n.*
Highland dress kilt, etc., as worn on formal occasions.
high latitudes those far from the equator.
high life life of fashionable society.
high'light *n.* **1** a bright spot in a picture or photograph. **2** (usu. in *pl.*) a patch of hair artificially made lighter than the rest of the hair. **3** a striking or memorable part of an experience.—*v.t.* to draw the attention towards, emphasise.
high living rich, luxurious feeding.
high'ly-col'oured *adj.* exaggerated.
high'ly-strung' *adj.* sensitive and nervous.
high'-mind'ed *adj.* having, or showing, high principles.
high'-octane *adj.* (of petrol) of high octane number and so of high efficiency.
high point the most memorable, enjoyable, etc. moment or occasion.
high'-press'ure *adj.* **1** having or using a pressure above normal. **2** very active.
high'-rise' *adj.* (used only before a noun) with many storeys.
high'road *n.* **1** a highway. **2** an easy way.
high school a secondary school.
high seas the open sea beyond territorial waters.
high'-sound'ing *adj.* sounding, seeming, grand or important.
high'-spir'ited *adj.* **1** bold, daring. **2** showing high spirits.
high spirits (the state of having) a sense of fun.
high summer summer well advanced.
high tea tea with meat, or fish, etc.
high time quite time (that something was done).
high treason. See **treason**.
high water the time at which the tide is highest.
high'way *n.* a public, esp. main, road.
high'wayman *n.* a robber who attacked travellers on the road.
high words angry words.
See also **height**.

hijack *hī'jak*, *v.t.* **1** to steal (a vehicle, aeroplane, etc.) while it is moving. **2** to steal (goods) in transit. **3** to force (an aeroplane, vehicle, etc.) to go to a place of one's choice.—Also *n.*
hi'jacker *n.*

hike *hīk*, *v.i.* to travel on foot esp. with equipment on one's back:—*pr.p.* **hik'ing**.—Also *n.*

hilarious *hi-lā'ri-ůs*, *adj.* very merry or funny.
hila'riously *adv.*
hila'riousness, hilarity *(hi-lar'-)* *ns.*

hill *hil*, *n.* **1** a high mass of land, less than a mountain. **2** an incline on a road. **3** a heap.
hill'ock *n.* a small hill.
hill'y *adj.*:—*comp.* **hill'ier**; *superl.* **hill'iest**.
hill'iness *n.*
hill'top *n.* the top of a hill.

hilt *hilt*, *n.* the handle, esp. of a sword.
(up) to the hilt completely.

him, himself. See **he**.

hind[1] *hīnd*, *n.* a female deer, esp. of the red deer.

hind[2] *hīnd*, **hinder** *hīnd'ėr*, *adjs.* situated at the back:—*superls.* **hind'most, hind'ermost** farthest behind.
hind'leg *n.* a back leg of a four-footed animal.

hind'quarters *n.pl.* the rear parts of an animal.
hind'sight *n.* wisdom or knowledge got only after something (usu. bad) has happened.

hinder[1] *hin'dėr, v.t.* to keep back, to stop, prevent progress of.
hin'drance *n.*

hinder[2], **hindermost**. See **hind**[2].

Hindi *hin'dē, n.* a very important literary language of India, a form of **Hindustani** *(hin'dōō-stän'i)*.
Hindu *hin'dōō, -dōō', n.* an Indian who believes and lives according to the religion of **Hin'duism**.

hindmost, **hindquarters**. See **hind**[2].

hindrance. See **hinder**[1].

hindsight. See **hind**[2].

Hindu. See **Hindi**.

hinge *hinj, n.* the hook or joint on which a door or lid turns.—*v.t.* to add hinges to.—*v.i.* **1** to hang or turn as on a hinge. **2** to depend (on): *Success hinges on what he does next:—pr.p.* **hing'ing** *(hinj')*; *pa.p.* **hinged**.

hint *hint, n.* **1** a statement that passes on information without giving it openly or directly. **2** a helpful suggestion (about, on, how to do something). **3** a very small amount.—Also *v.t.* and *v.i.*

hinterland *hint'ėr-land, n.* a region lying inland from a port.

hip[1] *hip, n.* the projecting part formed by the side of the pelvis and the upper part of the thigh bone.

hip[2] *hip, n.* the fruit of the wild rose.

hippo *hip'ō, n.* a hippopotamus:—*pl.* **hipp'os**.

hippopotamus *hip-ō-pot'ȧ-mus, n.* a large African animal with very thick skin, living in or near water:—*pl.* **hippopot'amuses**, **hippopot'ami** *(-mī)*.

hire *hīr, v.t.* **1** to obtain the use of at a price. **2** (also **hire out**) to give someone the use of (something) for payments. **3** to engage for wages:—*pr.p.* **hir'ing**.—Also *n.*
hire'ling *n.* a hired servant, esp. (usu. slightingly) one who will do anything for money.
hire purchase a system of purchasing by which an article may be taken away by the buyer after payment of a deposit, but becomes his property only after a number of further payments have been made.

hirsute *hûr'sūt, adj.* hairy, shaggy.

his. See **he**.

hiss *his, v.i.* **1** to make a sound like that of the letter *s*, as the goose, serpent, etc. do. **2** to express disapproval, etc., by hissing.—Also *v.t.* and *n.*

history *his'tȯ-ri, n.* **1** an account of events, esp. of those that form the story of a nation. **2** a past of more than common interest:—*pl.* **his'tories**.
histo'rian *(-tō', -tö') n.* **1** a writer of history. **2** one who is learned in history.
histor'ic *(-tor') adj.* **1** famous in history. **2** memorable.
histor'ical *(-tor') adj.* **1** of history. **2** accurate, not fiction or legend.
histor'ically *adv.*

histrionic *his-tri-on'ik, adj.* relating to acting, the stage, or actors.
histrion'ics *n.pl.* an insincere, exaggerated show of emotion.

hit *hit, v.t.* **1** to strike. **2** to reach with a blow or missile. **3** to affect painfully: *The loss hit me hard.* **4** to find or attain by chance.—*v.i.* **1** to come in contact. **2** (with *out*) to (try to) strike:—*pr.p.* **hitt'ing**; *pa.p.* **hit**.—*n.* **1** a lucky chance. **2** a success. **3** a stroke.
hit'-and-run' *adj.* **1** of a driver of a vehicle who does not stop after he has caused an accident, or of his action. **2** of any similar action.
hit below the belt to deal an unfair blow, make an unfair remark about (a person), etc.
hit it off to agree, get on together.
hit off to imitate, or to describe, very well.
hit (up)on to find by chance.

hitch *hich, v.t.* **1** to jerk. **2** to hook. **3** to fasten.—*v.i.* **1** to move jerkily. **2** to travel by getting lifts.—*n.* **1** a jerk. **2** a halt caused by a small difficulty. **3** a knot or noose.
hitch'-hike *v.i.* to hike with the help of lifts in vehicles.

hither *hiTH'ėr, adv.* to this place.
hith'erto *adv.* up to this time.
hither and thither in various directions.

HIV *āch-ī-vē', n.* the *h*uman *i*mmunodeficiency *v*irus, that leads to AIDS.
HIV-pos'itive *adj.* carrying the virus that can lead to AIDS.

hive *hīv, n.* **1** a box or basket in which bees live and store up honey. **2** a place in which people work very busily.
hive off **1** to give (e.g. part of a job) to someone else to do. **2** to make (part of an organisation) independent:—*pr.p.* **hiv'ing off**.

hoar *hōr, hör, (old)* adj. white or greyish-white, esp. with age or frost.—*n.* hoar-frost.
hoar'y *adj.* **1** white or grey with age.

2 old:—*comp.* **hoar'ier**; *superl.* **hoar'iest**.
hoar'iness *n.*
hoar'-frost *n.* the white particles formed by the freezing of dew.

hoard *hōrd, hörd, n.* **1** a store. **2** a hidden stock.—*v.t.* to store, esp. in great quantity or secretly.—Also *v.i.*
hoard'er *n.* **hoard'ing** *n.*

hoarding[1] *hōrd'ing, hörd', n.* a screen of boards round a place where builders are at work, or one used for display of posters.

hoarding[2]. See **hoard**.

hoarier, etc. See **hoar**.

hoarse *hōrs, hörs, adj.* **1** having a rough, husky voice. **2** harsh.
hoarse'ly *adv.* **hoarse'ness** *n.*

hoary. See **hoar**.

hoax *hōks, n.* a trick, a practical joke.—*v.t.* to trick for fun.

hob *hob, n.* **1** a surface beside a fireplace, on which anything may be kept hot. **2** the flat framework on top of a gas, etc. cooker on which pots are placed to be heated.
hob'nail *n.* a nail with a thick head.
hob'nailed *adj.*

hobble *hob'l, v.i.* to walk with difficulty, limp.—*v.t.* to fasten the legs of (horse, etc.) loosely together:—*pr.p.* **hobb'ling**.—Also *n.*

hobby *hob'i, n.* a favourite occupation for one's spare time:—*pl.* **hobb'ies**.
hobb'y-horse *n.* **1** a stick with a horse's head. **2** a horse on a merry-go-round. **3** a favourite topic of conversation.

hobgoblin *hob'gob-lin, n.* a mischievous fairy.

hobnail(ed). See **hob**.

hobnob *hob'nob, v.i.* **1** to drink together. **2** to be friendly (with):—*pr.p.* **hob'nobbing**; *pa.p.* **hob'nobbed**.

hobo *hō'bō, (U.S.) n.* **1** a wandering workman. **2** a tramp:—*pl.* **ho'boes**.

Hobson's choice the choice of taking what one is offered or doing without.

hock[1] *hok, n.* the joint on the hindleg of an animal corresponding to the heel in man.—Also **hough** (*hok*; Scot. *ho*H).

hock[2] *hok, n.* a white Rhine wine.

hockey *hok'i, n.* a game played with a **hockey stick**, a club curved at one end and a ball or (in **ice hockey**, played on ice) a puck.

hocus-pocus *hō'kus-pō'kus, n.* **1** nonsense intended to deceive (orig. the patter of conjurers, etc. at fairs). **2** trickery.
hoc'us *v.t.* to cheat:—*pr.p.* **hoc'us(s)ing**; *pa.p.* **hoc'us(s)ed**.

hod *hod, n.* a small trough on a pole for carrying bricks or mortar on the shoulder.

hodgepodge. Same as **hotchpotch**.

hoe *hō, n.* a tool for scraping up weeds and loosening the earth.—*v.t.* and *v.i.* to scrape or weed with a hoe:—*pr.p.* **hoe'ing**; *pa.p.* **hoed** *(hōd)*.

hog *hog, n.* **1** a pig, sow or boar. **2** a greedy person. **3** a coarse person.—*v.t.* and *v.i.* **1** to eat, or seize, greedily. **2** to take or use selfishly:—*pr.p.* **hogg'ing**; *pa.p.* **hogged**.
hogg'ish *adj.* **hogg'ishness** *n.*
hog'skin *n.* leather made from the skin of swine.
hog'wash *n.* **1** refuse of a kitchen, brewery, etc. used as pig food. **2** insincere nonsense.
go the whole hog to do a thing thoroughly or completely.
road hog a selfish motorist who, by speeding and by cutting in, forces others to give way to him.

hogmanay *hog-mȧ-nā', (Scot.) n.* the last day of the year.

hogshead *hogz'hed, n.* $52\frac{1}{2}$ imperial gallons (238.66 litres), or other large measure.

hoi polloi *hoi pȯ-loi'*, the many, the masses.

hoist *hoist, v.t.* **1** to raise with tackle. **2** to heave up. **3** to raise (as a flag).—*n.* a lift for heavy goods.
hoist with one's own petard caught in one's own trap (a petard being an old explosive device).

hoity-toity *hoi'ti-toi'ti, adj.* **1** huffy. **2** haughty.

hokum *hō'kum, n.* **1** nonsense. **2** insincere sentimental matter in a play, etc.

hold[1] *hōld, v.t.* **1** to keep, or to grasp, in the hand. **2** to have, possess. **3** to keep (in readiness, in reserve). **4** to have (a position). **5** to defend successfully: *He held the castle against all attacks.* **6** to keep in check (e.g. an enemy). **7** to compel to carry out: *We will hold him to his promise.* **8** to (be able to) contain: *The glass holds half a pint.* **9** to think strongly (that): *I hold that this was right.* **10** to regard as: *I hold you responsible for his safety.*—*v.i.* **1** to remain valid or true (also **hold good**). **2** to wait to be connected with a person one wishes to talk to on the telephone.—*n.* **1** an act or manner of grasping. **2** a grip. **3** something to grasp in order to carry, or for support. **4** a means of controlling: *to have a hold on a person.*
hol'der *n.* a person, thing, that holds.
hol'ding *n.* **1** land held from a larger landowner. **2** (often in *pl.*) property, esp. shares, etc.

hold'-all *n.* a canvas bag, or other container, for clothes.
hold forth to talk loud and long.
hold good. See **hold** (*v.i.*, *def. 1*).
hold oneself to have one's body in a good, bad, etc. position: *He holds himself too stiffly*.
hold one's own to stand up successfully against attack.
hold one's tongue to be silent.
hold out 1 to continue to fight, resist, survive, etc. **2** (with *for*) to continue to demand, accept nothing less than.
hold over to postpone.
hold up 1 to attack, stop and rob. **2** to stop or delay:—*n.* **hold'-up**.
hold water (of e.g. an explanation) to be reasonable and convincing.
hold with to approve of.
take, **get**, **hold of** to grasp, grip.

hold[2] *hōld*, *n.* the space below decks in a ship where cargo is stored.

hole *hōl*, *n.* **1** an opening through something. **2** a hollow place (e.g. in the ground). **3** an animal's burrow. **4** a difficulty: *I am in a hole and need your help.* **5** (*slang*) an unattractive place.—*v.t.* **1** to make a hole or holes in. **2** to send into a hole.—Also *v.i.*:—*pr.p.* **hol'ing**.
hole'-and-cor'ner *adj.* secret, underhand.
pick holes in to find faults in.

holiday *hol'i-dā*, *n.* a time of freedom from work.
hol'idaymaker *n.* a person on holiday away from home.

holily, **holiness**. See **holy**.

hollow *hol'ō*, *n.* **1** a place where the surface is lower than it is round about. **2** an empty space inside something.—*adj.* **1** having a space inside, not solid. **2** sunken. **3** (of sound) dull, deep. **4** worth little: *a hollow victory.* **5** insincere.
holl'owness *n.*
hollow out 1 to make a hollow in. **2** to form by taking out inner material.

holly *hol'i*, *n.* an evergreen shrub with prickly leaves and scarlet berries:—*pl.* **holl'ies**.

hollyhock *hol'i-hok*, *n.* a plant with spikes of large flowers, orig. brought from the Holy Land.

holocaust *hol'ȯ-köst*, *n.* a great destruction of life.

holster *hōl'stėr*, *n.* a pistol case, on a saddle or belt.

holt *hōlt*, *n.* an otter's den.

holy *hō'li*, *adj.* **1** pure in heart. **2** religious. **3** set apart for a sacred use:—*comp.* **hol'ier**; *superl.* **hol'iest**.
hō'liness *n.* **1** the state of being holy. **2** religious goodness. **3** (*cap.*) a title of the pope.
Holy Land Palestine.
holy orders (grades in) the Christian ministry: *to take holy orders* (to be ordained a priest).
Holy Week the week before Easter.
Holy Writ the Bible.

homage *hom'ij*, *n.* great respect, esp. shown by outward action: *to pay homage to a great man, to his courage*.

home *hōm*, *n.* **1** the place where one usu. lives, or where one's family lives. **2** one's native country. **3** an institution for e.g. homeless children. **4** a private hospital.—Also *adj.*—*adv.* **1** to home. **2** to the place where a thing belongs. **3** to the point aimed at: *The blow went home.*—*v.i.* to return home:—*pr.p.* **hom'ing**.
home'less *adj.* without a home.
home'ly *adj.* **1** like a home. **2** plain. **3** simple. **4** (*U.S.*; of person) ugly.
home'liness *n.*
hom'er *n.* a pigeon trained to fly home.
hom'ing *n.* returning home.—*adj.* showing a tendency to return home: *homing pigeons*; *the homing instinct*.
home'-bred *adj.* **1** bred at home. **2** native. **3** unpolished.
Home Counties the counties over and into which London has spread.
home economics. See **domestic science**.
home'land *n.* native land.
home'-made *adj.* made at home, sometimes not very skilfully.
Home Secretary the minister in charge of the government department (**Home Office**) concerned with law and order, immigration, etc.
home'sick *adj.* pining for home.
home'stead *n.* a house with outhouses and enclosures.
home truth (a statement of) an unpleasant or an undoubted truth.
home'ward *adj.* and *adv.* in the direction of home (*adv.* also **home'wards**).
at home familiar and at ease (with a person, a subject, etc.; in a subject, etc.).
bring home to 1 to prove to (a person). **2** (of an experience) to make (a person) realise or understand.

homeopathy *hom-i-op'ė-thi*, *n.* the system of treating illness by small quantities of substances that produce symptoms similar to those of the illness.

homicide *hom'i-sīd*, *n.* **1** manslaughter. **2** one who kills another.
homici'dal *adj.*

homily *hom'i-li, n.* a sermon, a moral lecture:—*pl.* **hom'ilies**.

hom(o)- *hom(-ō)-, hōm(-ō)-,* (as part of a word) the same.

homogeneous *hom-ȯ-jē'ni-ùs, adj.* **1** of the same kind. **2** made up of parts that are all the same.

homogenē'ity, homogē'neousness *ns.*

homogenise (*-oj'*, or *hom'*) *v.t.* to break up fat globules, etc. in (milk):—*pr.p.* **homogenising**.

homonym *hom'ȯ-nim, n.* a word having the same sound as another, but a different meaning (e.g. *sea, see*).

homosex'ual *adj.* feeling sexual attraction towards members of one's own sex.—Also *n.*

homosexual'ity *n.*

hone *hōn, n.* a smooth stone used for sharpening, e.g. razors.—*v.t.* to sharpen:—*pr.p.* **hon'ing**.

honest *on'ist, adj.* **1** the opposite of thieving or fraudulent. **2** dealing fairly, upright. **3** sincere, truthful. **4** gained fairly: *an honest living*:—*opp.* **dishonest**.

hon'estly *adv.* **hon'esty** *n.*

honey *hun'i, n* a sweet thick fluid made by bees from the nectar of flowers.

honeyed *hun'id, adj.* sweet.

hon'eycomb *n* **1** a mass consisting of rows of waxy cells formed by bees, in which they store their honey. **2** anything like a honeycomb in shape.—*v.t.* **1** to make many holes in: *a rock honeycombed by the work of underground water.* **2** to spread into all parts of.

hon'eydew *n.* a sweet sticky substance left on leaves by plant lice.

hon'eymoon *n.* (a holiday spent in) the first few weeks after marriage.

hon'eysuckle *n.* a climbing shrub with sweet-scented flowers.

honk *hongk, n.* **1** the cry of the wild goose. **2** the noise of a motor horn.—Also *v.t.* and *v.i.*

honorarium *on-ȯr-ā'ri-ùm, n.* a fee paid, esp. to a professional man, for services for which no fixed price is asked.

honorary. See **honour**.

honour *on'ȯr, n.* **1** fame, glory. **2** the esteem due, or paid, to fine qualities. **3** high principles: *a man of honour.* **4** a rank, title, or other distinction given. **5** a title prefixed to the names of certain officials, e.g. judges. **6** a source of credit. **7** (in a card suit) one of the five highest cards.—*v.t.* **1** to think very highly of. **2** to give a title, etc. to. **3** to accept (e.g. a bill of exchange) and pay when due. **4** to carry out, live up to: *to honour one's obligations*.

honorary *on'ȯr-àr-i, adj.* **1** given as an honour. **2** (of a title or office) either without duties, or without payment: *Honorary President*.

hon'ourable *adj.* **1** worthy of honour. **2** upright and honest. **3** conferring honour. **4** (*cap.*) prefixed as a title to the names of certain persons.

hon'ourably *adv.* **hon'ourableness** *n.*

maid of honour a lady, usu. noble, attending a queen or princess.

hood *hood, n.* **1** a limp covering for the head and neck. **2** a collapsible cover, part of a motor car, etc. **3** (*U.S.*) the bonnet of a car. **4** an ornamental fold worn hanging at the back of an academic gown.—*v.t.* to cover, esp. with a hood.

hood'ed *adj.* **1** wearing a hood. **2** (of a bird, etc.) having a hoodlike part on the head.

hoodwink *hood'wingk, v.t.* to deceive, cause to believe something false.

hoodlum *hōōd'lùm, n.* a criminal, gangster.

hoodwink. See **hood**.

hoof *hōōf, n.* the horny substance on the feet of certain animals, as horses, etc.:—*pl.* **hoofs, hooves**.

hook *hook, n.* **1** a bent object, such as would catch or hold anything. **2** a boxer's blow with bent elbow.—*v.t.* **1** to catch, fasten, hold, as with a hook. **2** (*golf* and *cricket*) to pull sharply. **3** (*Rugby*) to obtain possession of the ball in the scrum.

hooked *adj.* **1** curved like a hook. **2** caught by a hook. **3** (with *on*) addicted to, fascinated by.

hooker *n.* **1** (esp. *Rugby*) a person who hooks **2** (*slang*) a prostitute.

by hook or by crook one way if not another, by some means.

hookah *hook'ȧ, n.* the tobacco pipe of Arabs, Turks, etc., in which the smoke is passed through water.

hooligan *hōōl'i-gàn, n.* a street rough, esp. if he is destructive.

hool'iganism *n.*

hoop¹ *hōōp, n.* **1** a band holding together the staves of casks, etc. **2** a large ring used as a toy, for holding wide a skirt, etc. **3** a ring.—*v.t.* **1** to bind with hoops. **2** to encircle.

hoop², hooping-cough. See **whoop**.

hoorah, hooray *hoo-rä', -rā', interjs.* Same as **hurrah**.

hoot *hōōt, v.i.* **1** to shout in contempt. **2** to cry like an owl. **3** (of a motor horn, siren, etc.) to sound.—Also *v.t.* and *n.*

hoot'er *n.* a siren, steam whistle.

Hoover® *hōō'vėr, n.* (also without *cap.*) a (type of) vacuum-cleaner.—*v.t.* and *v.i.* to clean with a vacuum-cleaner.

hooves. See **hoof**.

hop[1] *hop, v.i.* **1** to leap on one leg. **2** to move in jumps, as some birds. **3** to fly in an aircraft:—*pr.p.* **hopp'ing**; *pa.p.* **hopped**. *n.* **1** a leap on one leg. **2** a jump. **3** (*coll.*) a dance.

hopp'er *n.* **1** one who hops. **2** a funnel, bin, etc. in which something is placed to be passed out later through a hole in the bottom. **3** a barge with an opening in its bottom for discharging refuse.

hop[2] *hop, n.* **1** a climbing plant. **2** (in *pl.*) its fruit clusters used to flavour beer.

hope *hōp, v.t.* to desire and more or less expect: *He is late, but we hope he will still come.*—Also *v.i.* (with *for*): *We hope for peace*:—*pr.p.* **hop'ing**.—*n.* **1** desire with expectation, or an instance of it. **2** confidence in the future.

hope'ful *adj.* **hope'fulness** *n.*

hope'fully *adv.* **1** in a hopeful manner. **2** (*coll.*) it is to be hoped that.

hope'less *adj.* **1** giving no ground to expect good or success: *a hopeless attempt*. **2** despairing. **3** incurable: *a hopeless liar*.

hope against hope to go on hoping when there is no reason, or no longer any reason, for this hope.

hopper. See **hop**[1].

horde *hōrd, hörd, n.* **1** a wandering tribe. **2** a very large number.

horizon *hȯ-rī'z(ȯ)n, n.* **1** the circle in which earth and sky seem to meet. **2** the limit of one's experience, interests, etc.

horizontal *hor-i-zon'tȧl, adj.* **1** of, near, or parallel to, the horizon. **2** at right angles to vertical. **3** flat, level.

horizon'tally *adv.*

hormone *hör'mōn, n.* any of a number of substances produced by certain glands of the body, each of which makes some organ of the body active.

horn *hörn, n.* **1** a hard outgrowth on the head of an animal, e.g. cow, sheep. **2** the material of which this is made. **3** a snail's tentacle. **4** something made of horn, or resembling a horn in shape. **5** a wind instrument orig. made from a horn, now of brass, etc. **6** a hooter, siren.

hor'ny *adj.*:—*comp.* **hor'nier**; *superl.* **hor'niest**.

hor'niness *n.*

horn'beam *n.* a tree like a beech with hard tough wood.

horn'bill *n.* a bird with a horny growth on its bill.

pull, draw, in one's horns to restrain oneself, be more cautious.

hornet *hör'nit, n.* a large kind of wasp.

hornpipe *hörn'pīp, n.* **1** a lively dance, usu. by one person, associated with sailors. **2** a tune for it.

horoscope *hor'ȯ-skōp, n.* an observation of the position of the stars and planets at the hour of a person's birth, from which the events of his life can supposedly be foretold.

horrible, horrid, etc. See **horror**.

horror *hor'ȯr, n.* **1** very great fear or loathing. **2** a cause of such feeling. **3** (*coll.*) a disagreeable person or thing.

horrendous *hȯ-ren'dus, adj.* dreadful or horrifying.

horrible *hor'i-bl, adj.* **1** arousing horror. **2** dreadful. **3** (*coll.*) unpleasant.

horr'ibleness *n.* **horr'ibly** *adv.*

horrid *hor'id, adj.* **1** horrible, shocking. **2** (*coll.*) unpleasant.

horr'idly *adv.* **horr'idness** *n.*

horrify *hor'i-fī, v.t.* to fill with horror:—*pr.p.* **horr'ifying**; *pa.p.* **horr'ified**.

horrif'ic *adj.* frightful.

hors de combat *ör dė köm'bä,* no longer in a state to fight or to take part.

hors-d'œuvre *ör-dûvr'*, a whet for the appetite (olives, sardines, etc.) served before a meal or after soup.

horse *hörs, n.* **1** a solid-hoofed animal used to pull, e.g. vehicles, or carry goods or persons, esp. the male (*fem.* **mare**). **2** (also as *pl.*) cavalry, horsemen: *a regiment of horse*. **3** a horse-like piece of apparatus for gymnastics. **4** a support on which clothes are dried, wood is sawn, etc.

hor'sy *adj.* **1** horse-like. **2** devoted to horse racing or breeding:—*comp.* **hor'sier**; *superl.* **hor'siest**.—See also **equine**.

hor'siness *n.*

horse'back *n.*: **on horseback** on the back of a horse.

horse'-box *n.* a closed trailer for carrying a horse.

horse'-break'er *n.* one who tames and trains horses.

horse chestnut **1** a tree with cone-shaped clusters of white or pink flowers. **2** its bitter, shiny, brown seeds (not related to the **sweet chestnut**; see **chestnut**).

horse'flesh *n.* **1** meat from a horse. **2** horses for riding, racing, etc.

horse'fly *n.* any fly that bites horses:—*pl.* **horse'flies**.

horse'hair *n.* hair from a horse's mane or tail, often used in upholstery.

horse laugh a loud, harsh laugh.
horse'man *n.* **1** a rider. **2** a skilled rider:—*fem.* **horse'woman**.
horse'manship *n.* the art of riding and training and managing horses.
horse'play *n.* rough, boisterous, play.
horse'power *n.* the power a horse can exert—a standard for estimating the power of engines.
horse'-rad'ish *n.* a plant with a sharp-tasting root, used, esp. in a sauce, as a seasoning.
horse sense plain good sense.
horse'shoe *n.* **1** a curved iron shoe for a horse. **2** anything shaped like a horseshoe.
horse'-soldier *n.* a soldier of a mounted regiment.
horse'woman. See **horseman** above.
get on, mount, one's high horse 1 to put on a very superior air. **2** to become huffy or resentful.
straight from the horse's mouth from a very reliable source.

horticulture *hör'ti-kul-chu̇r*, *n.* the art of cultivating gardens.
horticul'tural *adj.* **horticul'turist** *n.*

hosanna *hō-zan'ȧ*, *n.* an exclamation of praise to God.

hose *hōz*, *n.pl.* (*old*) **1** a close-fitting covering for the legs. **2** stockings. **3** socks (*half-hose*).—*n.* (also **hose'pipe**) a flexible pipe for conveying water.—*v.t.* to direct e.g. water at with a hose:—*pr.p.* **hos'ing**.
hosier *hōz'yėr*, *hōzh'*, *n.* a dealer in **hōs'iery**, i.e. knitted goods.

hospice *hos'pis*, *n.* **1** a house for travellers, esp. one kept by monks. **2** a home for the care of people who are seriously ill or dying of e.g. cancer.

hospitable *hos'pit-ȧ-bl*, or *-pit'*, *adj.* giving a generous welcome to guests:—*opp.* **inhospitable**.
hos'pitableness (or *-pit'*) *n.*
hos'pitably (or *-pit'*) *adv.*
hospital *hos'pit-ȧl*, *n.* a building for housing and treating the sick and injured.
hospital'ity *n.* a welcome to and entertainment of guests.

host[1] *hōst*, *n.* **1** a person who entertains someone else in his house or elsewhere (*fem.* **hos'tess**). **2** the compere, etc. of a radio or television programme (*fem.* **hos'tess**). **3** an innkeeper (*fem.* **hos'tess**). **4** an animal or plant on which another lives as a parasite.

host[2] *hōst*, *n.* **1** an army. **2** a very large number.

host[3] *hōst* (*R.C. Church*) *n.* the consecrated wafer of the Eucharist—a thin round wafer of unleavened bread.

hostage *hos'tij*, *n.* one held by an enemy as a guarantee that demands, or the conditions of an agreement, will be carried out.

hostel *hos'tėl*, *n.* **1** an inn. **2** a residence for students or others. **3** temporary accommodation for hikers, etc.
hos'telry (*old*) *n.* an inn:—*pl.* **hos'telries**.

hostile *hos'tīl*, *adj.* **1** of an enemy. **2** warlike. **3** unfriendly.
hostil'ity (*-til'*) *n.* **1** unfriendliness, ill-will. **2** (in *pl.*, **hostil'ities**) acts of warfare.

hot *hot*, *adj.* **1** having a high temperature. **2** very warm. **3** sharp in taste (like pepper). **4** fiery: *a hot temper.* **5** passionate. **6** (*slang*) excitingly good. **7** (*music*; *slang*) with additions to the melody that suggest excitement. **8** radioactive. **9** (*slang*) recently stolen. **10** unsafe or uncomfortable:—*comp.* **hott'er**; *superl.* **hott'est**.
hot'ly *adv.* **hot'ness** *n.*
hot'bed *n.* **1** a bed (usu. glass-covered) heated, e.g. by rotting manure, for making plants grow quickly. **2** a place of rapid growth (of disease or vice).
hot'-blood'ed *adj.* **1** excitable. **2** easily made angry.
hot'-dog' *n.* a hot sausage in a roll.
hot'foot *adv.* in great haste.
hot'head *n.* a hotheaded person.
hot'headed *adj.* **1** easily made angry. **2** inclined to act suddenly and rashly.
hot'house *n.* a greenhouse kept hot for rearing tender plants.
hot line any means of speedy communication ready for an emergency, esp. (and orig.) the one between the U.S. and U.S.S.R. governments.
hot'-plate *n.* a portable heated metal plate, for keeping things hot.
hot seat 1 an uncomfortable or awkward situation. **2** a position of responsibility.
in hot water in trouble, in a scrape.
See also **heat**.

hotchpotch *hoch'poch*, **hotchpot** *hoch'-pot*, **hodge-podge** *hoj'poj*, *ns.* a confused mass of cooking ingredients, or of other things, mixed together.

hotfoot, etc. See **hot**.

hotel *hō-tel'*, *n.* a, usu. large, house run for the purpose of giving travellers food, lodging, etc.

hough. See **hock[1]**.

hound *hownd*, *n.* **1** a dog used, or of a kind orig. used, in hunting. **2** a mean scoundrel.—*v.t.* to pursue or drive: *They hounded the man from place to place.*

hour *owr*, *n.* **1** 60 minutes, the 24th part of a

day. **2** a time or occasion. **3** (in *pl.*) set times of prayers, or services for these. **4** (in *pl.*) set times of business.

hour'ly *adj.* happening or done every hour.—Also *adv.*

hour'-glass *n.* an instrument for measuring the hours by the running of sand through a narrow neck.

after hours after the end of a working day, time of remaining open, etc.

at the eleventh hour at the last possible moment.

in an evil hour unluckily.

the small hours the hours from 1 to 3 or 4 A.M.

house *hows, n.* **1** a building for living in. **2** a building for certain other purposes: *a boiler house*; *a monkey house at the zoo.* **3** an inn. **4** a household. **5** a family. **6** a business firm. **7** a legislative body, or its meeting place. **8** a theatre, etc. **9** an audience. **10** a section of a school:—*pl.* **houses** *(how'ziz).—v.t. (howz)* **1** to shelter. **2** to store. **3** to provide houses for:—*pr.p.* **hous'ing.**

housing *howz'ing, n.* houses, or accommodation, or the act of providing these.

house agent one who arranges the sale or letting of houses.

house'boat *n.* a barge furnished for living in.

house'bound *adj.* unable to leave one's house, e.g. because of illness.

house'hold *n.* those who are living together in the same house.—*adj.* **1** of the household. **2** of the house, domestic.

house'holder *n.* the occupier of a house.

house'keeper *n.* one who has the chief care of a house.

house'keeping *n.* the management of a house or of domestic affairs.

house'master *n.* the head of a school (boarding-)house, esp. at a public school:—*fem.* **house'mistress.**

house'-proud *adj.* taking great care, often too much care, to keep one's house clean and tidy.

house surgeon a resident surgeon in a hospital.

house'-trained *adj.* of an animal, trained to urinate and defecate in the proper place.

house'-warming *n.* an entertainment given after moving into a new house.

housewife *n.* the mistress of a house:—*pl.* **house'wives.**

housewifery *hows-wif'ė-ri, n.* housekeeping.

house'work *n.* the work of keeping a house clean and tidy.

household troops Guards regiments who attend the king or queen.

a household word a familiar saying or name.

hove. See **heave**.

hovel *hov'ėl, huv'ėl, n.* a small or wretched dwelling.

hover *hov'ėr, huv'ėr, v.i.* **1** to remain in the air without forward motion. **2** to remain in an uncertain state, e.g. between two actions. **3** to linger about.

hov'ercraft *n.* a craft able to move a short distance above the surface of water or land by means of a down-driven blast of air.

how *how, adv.* **1** in what manner. **2** to what extent. **3** by what means. **4** in what condition.

howev'er *adv.* and *conj.* **1** in whatever manner or degree. **2** nevertheless.

howsoev'er *adv.* in whatever way.

howdah *how'dȧ, n.* a seat with a canopy fixed on an elephant's back.

however. See **how**.

howitzer *how'it-sėr, n.* a short cannon, used for shelling at a steep angle.

howl *howl, v.i.* to utter or make a long, loud, whining sound.—*v.t.* to utter (words) in this way.—*n.* **1** a loud cry. **2** a loud sound made by the wind.

how'ler (*slang*) *n.* a bad mistake.

howsoever. See **how**.

hub *hub, n.* **1** the centre, e.g. of a wheel. **2** the centre of much traffic, business, etc.

hubbub *hub'ub, n.* a confused sound of many voices, uproar.

huckster *huk'stėr, n.* **1** a hawker or pedlar. **2** a mean fellow. **3** (*U.S.*) an advertising man.

huddle *hud'l, v.t.* **1** to throw or crowd together in disorder. **2** to put hastily or untidily. **3** to crouch, to draw (oneself) together (usu. with *up*). **4** to do hastily and carelessly.—*v.i.* to crowd together in confusion:—*pr.p.* **hudd'ling.**—*n.* a confused mass.

hue[1] *hū, n.* colour, tint.

hue[2] *hū, n.* a shouting, as in *hue and cry*.

hue and cry **1** a loud call to join in chasing a criminal. **2** an outcry.

huff *huf, n.* a fit of anger or sulks.—*v.t.* and *v.i.* **1** to swell. **2** to give or take offence.

huff'y *adj.* **1** inclined to take offence, touchy. **2** in a huff:—*comp.* **huff'ier**; *superl.* **huff'iest.**

huff'ily *adv.* **huff'iness** *n.*

hug *hug, v.t.* **1** to clasp close with the arms. **2** to delight in, cling to (e.g. a thought, an opinion). **3** to keep close to: *to hug the shore*:—*pr.p.* **hugg'ing**; *pa.p.* **hugged.**—

n. a close clasping in the arms.
hug oneself to be very pleased.

huge *hūj*, *n.* very large.
huge'ly *adv.* very greatly.
huge'ness *n.*

hulk *hulk*, *n.* **1** an old ship stripped of its equipment. **2** anything large and difficult to handle.
hulk'ing *adj.* large and clumsy.

hull[1] *hul*, *n.* a husk or outer covering.—*v.t.* to separate from the hull.

hull[2] *hul*, *n.* the frame or body of a ship.—*v.t.* to pierce the hull of.

hullabaloo *hul'ȧ-bȧ-lōō'*, *n.* an uproar.

hullo. See **hello**.

hum *hum*, *v.i.* **1** to make a sound like bees. **2** to sing with closed lips. **3** to pause in speaking and utter an indistinct sound. **4** to be busily active.—*v.t.* to render by humming: *to hum a tune*:—*pr.p.* **humm'ing**; *pa.p.* **hummed**.—*n.* **1** the noise of bees. **2** a murmur.
humm'ing *n.* a low, murmuring sound.
humm'ing-bird *n.* any of various brilliant tropical birds with rapid flight, so called from the humming sound of their wings.
make things hum to cause brisk activity.

human *hū'mȧn*, *adj.* **1** of, belonging to, mankind. **2** having the qualities of man.
humane *hū-mān'*, *adj.* kind, sympathetic, merciful, not cruel:—*opp.* **inhumane**.
humane'ly *adv.* **humane'ness** *n.*
humanise *hū'mȧn-īz*, *v.t.* **1** to make *human* or *humane*. **2** to make gentler:—*pr.p.* **hu'manising**.
hū'manism *n.* seeking, without religion, the best in, and for, human beings.
hū'manist *n.* and *adj.*
humanitā'rian *n.* a person who is anxious to increase the welfare of mankind by reforms, etc.—Also *adj.*
human'ity *n.* **1** the nature of human beings. **2** kindness, generosity (*opp.* **inhumanity**). **3** mankind.
hū'manly *adv.* **1** by man. **2** in keeping with human nature. **3** within human power: *If it is humanly possible, he will do it*.
hū'mankind *n.* thc human race.
human nature the qualities, or conduct, that are common to all mankind (esp. the less admirable).
human rights each person's right to freedom, justice, etc.

humble *hum'bl*, *adj.* **1** low. **2** lowly. **3** modest, meek.—*v.t.* **1** to bring down, defeat completely: *to humble one's enemies*. **2** to make humble or meek:—*pr.p.* **hum'bling**.
hum'bly *adv.* **hum'bleness** *n.*
See also **humility**.

humblebee *hum'bl-bē*, *n.* a bumblebee.

humble pie *hum'bl pī*: **eat humble pie** **1** to be forced to apologise humbly. **2** to suffer humiliation.

humbug *hum'bug*, *n.* **1** a trick, fraud. **2** a person who pretends to be something he is not. **3** nonsense. **4** a peppermint sweet.—*v.t.* to deceive, hoax:—*pr.p.* **hum'bugging**; *pa.p.* **hum'bugged**.

humdrum *hum'drum*, *adj.* dull, without variety: *a humdrum life*.

humerus *hū'mėr-ůs*, *n.* the bone of the upper arm.

humid *hū'mid*, *adj.* moist, damp.
hu'midness, **humid'ity** *ns.*

humiliate *hū-mil'i-āt*, *v.t.* **1** to humble. **2** to wound the dignity of:—*pr.p.* **humil'iating**.
humiliā'tion *n.*
humil'ity *n.* modesty, humbleness.

humming. See **hum**.

hummock *hum'ȯk*, *n.* a small hillock.

humorous, etc. See **humour**.

humour *hū'mȯr*, or *ū'mȯr*, *n.* **1** (also **sense of humour**) ability to see things as amusing or ridiculous. **2** the quality of being funny. **3** temper, mood. **4** fancy, whim.—*v.t.* to please (someone) by agreeing with him or doing as he wishes: *Try to humour the old man*.
hū'morist *n.* one who amuses by pointing out the funny side of life.
hū'morous *adj.* **hūmorously** *adv.*
hū'morousness *n.* **hū'mourless** *adj.*
out of humour irritable, cross.

hump *hump*, *n.* **1** a lump on the back. **2** a knoll. **3** (coll.; with *the*) a fit of depression.—*v.t.* (*Austr.*) to shoulder, to carry on the back.
hump'back(ed) *adj.* **1** having a hump on the back. **2** (of a road, etc.) rising and falling so as to form a hump shape.

humus *hūm'ůs*, *n.* decomposed animal or vegetable matter in the soil.

hunch *hunch*, *-sh*, *n.* **1** a hump. **2** a lump. **3** (*coll.*) a strong feeling (that something will turn out in a certain way).—*v.t.* to hump, bend.
hunch'back *n.* one with a hump on his back.
hunch'backed *adj.*

hundred *hun'drėd*, *n.* **1** ten times ten (100 or C). **2** (chiefly *hist.*) a division of a county in England:—*pl.* **hun'dreds** or (after another number) **hun'dred** (e.g.

two hundred of them).—Also *adj.*
hun'dredth *adj.* **1** next after the ninety-ninth. **2** equal to one of a hundred equal parts.—Also *n.*
hun'dredweight *n.* 112 (orig. 100) pounds:—*abbrev.* **cwt**. (c=100).

hung. See **hang**.

hunger *hung'gėr, n.* **1** desire for, or lack of, food. **2** any strong desire.—*v.i.* **1** to desire food. **2** to long (for).
hungry *hung'gri, adj.* having, or showing eager desire (for food, etc.):—*comp.* **hung'rier**; *superl.* **hung'riest**.
hung'rily *adv.* **hung'riness** *n.*
hunger strike refusal by a prisoner to eat, as a form of protest.

hunt *hunt, v.t.* **1** to chase (animals) for prey or sport. **2** to search for. **3** to hound, drive: *The fugitives were hunted from place to place.*—*v.i.* **1** to go in pursuit of game. **2** to search.—*n.* **1** a chase of wild animals. **2** a search. **3** a body of huntsmen.
hunt'er *n.* **1** one who hunts (*fem.* **hunt'-ress**). **2** a horse used in hunting.
hunts'man *n.* **1** a hunter. **2** a man who manages the hounds during the hunt.
hunt down 1 to search for until found. **2** to hunt for until found and destroyed.

hurdle *hûr'dl, n.* **1** a movable frame of interlaced twigs, etc. **2** a barrier to be jumped in a race. **3** an obstacle, difficulty.—*v.i.* to run in a race in which hurdles are used:—*pr.p.* **hurd'ling**.
hur'dler *n.* **hur'dling** *n.*

hurl *hûrl, v.t.* **1** to throw violently. **2** to utter in uncontrolled anger: *to hurl abuse or threats at someone.*

hurly-burly *hûr'li-bûr'li, n.* **1** tumult. **2** confusion.

hurrah *hu̇r-ä', interj.* a shout of enthusiasm or joy.—Also **hurray'**.

hurricane *hur'i-kȧn, -kān, n.* **1** a violent tropical storm. **2** anything violent.

hurried, etc. See **hurry**.

hurry *hur'i, v.i.* to move or act quickly, often too quickly and in a confused way.—*v.t.* to cause to move or act with speed:—*pr.p.* **hurr'ying**; *pa.p.* **hurr'ied**.—*n.* a (need for) acting with speed.
hurr'ied *adj.* done, carried out, or working, quickly, or too quickly.
hurr'iedly *adv.* **hurr'iedness** *n.*
hurr'y-scurr'y *n.* bustle and confusion.—Also *adv.*
in a hurry 1 in a short time. **2** at a fast rate. **3** eager: *She was in a hurry to open her presents.*

hurt *hûrt, v.t.* **1** to cause pain to. **2** to wound the feelings of. **3** to damage.—Also *v.i.*:—*pa.t.* and *pa.p.* **hurt**.—*n.* **1** pain. **2** injury.
hurt'ful *adj.* causing hurt or loss.
hurt'fully *adv.* **hurt'fulness** *n.*

hurtle *hûrt'l, v.t.* to dash, hurl.—*v.i.* to move rapidly with a whirl or clatter:—*pr.p.* **hurt'ling**.

husband *huz'bȧnd, n.* the man to whom a woman is married—opp. of *fem.* **wife**.—*v.t.* to manage with care, spend or use carefully: *to husband one's resources, one's strength.*
hus'bandman *n.* a working farmer.
hus'bandry *n.* the business of a farmer.

hush *hush, interj.* silence!—*v.t., v.i.* to quieten.—*n.* a silence, esp. after noise.
hush money a bribe to say nothing.
hush up to keep (something) secret by preventing talk about it.

husk *husk, n.* **1** the dry, thin covering of certain fruits and seeds. **2** (in *pl.*) refuse.—*v.t.* to remove the husk from.

husky[1] *hus'ki, adj.* **1** (of a voice) rough in sound. **2** (*U.S.*) big and strong:—*comp.* **hus'kier**; *superl.* **hus'kiest**.
hus'kily *adv.* **hus'kiness** *n.*

husky[2] *hus'ki, n.* a Canadian sledge-dog:—*pl.* **hus'kies**.

hussar *hoo-zär', n.* **1** a light-armed cavalry soldier (orig. Hungarian). **2** a member of a modern regiment with 'Hussars' in its name.

hussy *hus'i, huz'i, n.* **1** a badly behaved or mischievous girl. **2** a woman of low character:—*pl.* **huss'ies**.

hustings *hus'tingz, n. sing.* **1** electioneering platform. **2** (also *n.pl.*) election proceedings.

hustle *hus'l, v.t.* **1** to push (together). **2** to push roughly (into).—*v.i.* to hurry:—*pr.p.* **hus'tling**.—n. great activity.
hus'tler *(-lėr) n.* an energetic person.

hut *hut, n.* **1** a small or mean house. **2** a small temporary building.

hutch *huch, n.* **1** a coop for rabbits, etc. **2** a low wagon in which coal is drawn up out of the pit.

hyacinth *hī'ȧ-sinth, n.* **1** a plant with a bulb, of the lily family, with esp. blue flowers. **2** a red, brown, or orange precious stone.

hyaena. See **hyena**.

hybrid *hī'brid, n.* **1** the offspring of animals, or of plants, of two different breeds, etc. **2** a word formed of parts from different languages (e.g *television*).—Also *adj.*

hydra *hī'drȧ, n.* **1** a water monster in Greek myth with many heads each of which, when cut off, grew again as two. **2** any evil difficult to root out.

hydrangea *hī-drān'j(y)ȧ, n.* a shrubby plant with large heads of flowers.

hydr(o)- *hī-dr(ō)-*, (as part of a word) water.
hydrant *hī'drȧnt, n.* a connection for attaching a hose to a water main.
hydraulic *hī-dröl'ik, adj.* **1** worked by water or other liquid. **2** (of e.g. cement) hardening under water. **3** relating to hydraulics.
hydraul'ics *n.sing.* the study of the behaviour of fluids in motion (e.g. of water in pipes) and of how to deal with them.
hy'drō *n.* a type of hotel (originally with special swimming baths, etc. for health improvement):—*pl.* **hy'dros**.
hydrocarbon *hī-drō-kär'bȯn, n.* a chemical compound containing only hydrogen and carbon.
hydrochloric acid *hī-drō-klor'ik as'id,* or *-klōr'*, a strong acid, compound of hydrogen and chlorine.
hydroelectricity *hī-drō-el-ėk-tris'i-ti, n.* electricity produced by means of water-driven turbines.
hydroelec'tric *adj.*
hy'drofoil *n.* **1** a device on a boat for raising it from the water as its speed increases. **2** a boat with hydrofoils.
hydrogen *hī'drō-jėn, n.* an element, a gas which when combined with oxygen produces water; the lightest of all known substances, and very inflammable.
hydrogen bomb one in which the explosion is caused by turning hydrogen into helium at very high temperature.
hydrophobia *hī-drō-fō'bi-ȧ, n.* **1** horror of water. **2** inability to swallow water (a symptom of rabies). **3** (*old*) rabies.
hydroplane *hī'drō-plān, n.* an aeroplane with floats or a boat-like underpart.

hyena, hyaena *hī-ē'nȧ, n.* a bristly-maned animal, feeding on carrion, with a howl like hysterical laughter.

hygiene *hī'jēn, n.* (the rules of) cleanliness whose aim is to preserve health and prevent spread of disease.
hygien'ic *(-jēn') adj.*
hygien'ically *adv.*

hymn *him, n.* a song of praise.
hym'nal *n.* a book of hymns.—Also **hym'nary** (*pl.* **-ies**).

hyper- *hī'pėr-*, (as part of a word) **1** beyond. **2** over.
hyperac'tive (*medical*) *adj.* abnormally active.
hyperbole *hī-pûr'bȯl-i, n.* exaggeration for sake of effect in speech or writing.
hyperbol'ical *adj.* **hyperbol'ically** *adv.*
hypercrit'ical *adj.* too critical.
hypercrit'ically *adv.*
hypersen'sitive *adj.* too sensitive.
hyperten'sion *n.* high blood pressure.

hyphen *hī'fėn, n.* a short stroke (-) joining two syllables or words (e.g. that in *co-exist, sleeping-bag*).
hy'phenate *v.t.* to put a hyphen in:—*pr.p.* **hy'phenating**.
hyphenā'tion *n.*

hypnosis *hip-nō'sis, n.* a sleeplike state brought on by the action of another person, or operator, who can then influence the sleeper to do many things that he, the operator, wishes.
hypnotic *hip-not'ik, adj.* **1** of hypnosis. **2** of hypnotism. **3** causing sleepiness: *the hypnotic effect of slow regular sound or movement.* **4** causing hypnosis: *a hypnotic stare.*
hyp'notise *v.t.* **1** to put in a state of hypnosis. **2** to fascinate:—*pr.p.* **hyp'notising**.
hyp'notism *n.* **1** the science of hypnosis. **2** the art of producing hypnosis.

hypo- *hī'pō*, **hyp-** (as part of a word) under.

hypochondria *hīp-, hip-ō-kon'dri-ȧ, n.* nervous anxiety about one's health.
hypochon'driac *n.* a person who suffers from hypochondria.—Also *adj.*

hypocrisy *hi-pok'ri-si, n.* pretending to be better than one is, or to have feelings one does not have.
hypocrite *hip'o-krit, n.* one who practises hypocrisy.
hypocrit'ical *adj.* **hypocrit'ically** *adv.*

hypodermic *hīp-ō-dûr'mik, adj.* under the skin, esp. of a method of injecting a drug.—*n.* an injection under the skin or the syringe for giving this.

hypotenuse *hī-pot'ėn-ūz,* or *-ūs, n.* the side of a right-angled triangle opposite to the right angle.

hypothermia *hīp-ȯ-thûr'miȧ, n.* having a dangerously low body temperature.

hypothesis *hī-poth'i-sis, n.* **1** a supposition. **2** something assumed for the sake of argument:—*pl.* **hypoth'eses**.
hypothet'ical *adj.* supposed, assumed.

hysterectomy *his-tėr-ek'tȯ-mi, n* surgical removal of the womb:—*pl.* **hysterec'tomies**.

hysteria *his-tē'ri-ȧ, n.* **1** mental illness causing loss of memory, sleepwalking, etc. **2** wild excitement.
hyster'ics *(-ter') n.pl.* **1** fits of hysteria. **2** fits of laughing and crying.
hyster'ical *adj.* **hyster'ically** *adv.*

I

I *ī, pron.* the word used by a speaker or writer in mentioning himself or herself:—*objective* **me**; *possessive* **my** (*mī*; sometimes described as *possessive adj.*), **mine**: *I hope you will help me by giving me sweets for my stall at the sale; The stall next to the door will be mine.*

myself' *pron.* the emphatic, or reflexive, form of *I, me*: *The majority decided, but I myself disapprove; I blame myself.*

Iberian *ī-bē'ri-ȧn, adj.* of Spain and Portugal.

ibex *ī'beks, n.* a large-horned wild mountain goat.

ibidem *ib'i-dėm, adv.* in the same place, in the place already mentioned:—*abbrev.* **ib'id.**

ibis *ī'bis, n.* a wading bird with curved bill.

ice *īs, n.* **1** water made solid by freezing. **2** an ice-cream.—*v.t.* to cover with ice or icing.—*v.i.* to become covered with ice (with *up* or *over*):—*pr.p.* **ic'ing**; *pa.p.* **iced.**

ic'icle *n.* a long hanging piece of ice formed by freezing of dropping water.

ic'y *adj.* **1** very cold. **2** slippery with ice:—*comp.* **ic'ier**; *superl.* **ic'iest.**

ic'ily *adv.* **ic'iness** *n.*

ic'ing *n.* **1** a mixture of sugar, water, etc. used to cover or decorate cakes, etc. **2** ice formed on a road, vehicle, aircraft, etc.

ice'-age *n.* a time when a great part of the earth's surface was covered with ice.

ice'berg *n.* a huge mass of floating ice.

ice'box (*U.S.*) *n.* a refrigerator.

ice'breaker *n.* a ship for breaking a channel through ice.

ice'-cap *n.* a permanent covering of ice as at the poles.

ice'-cream' *n.* a sweet frozen food containing cream (or a substitute) and flavouring.

ice'-field *n.* a large area covered with ice, esp. floating ice.

ice'-loll'y *n.* a lollipop composed of a piece of flavoured ice on a stick.

ice skate to skate on ice.

icing sugar sugar in a finely powdered form, for icing cakes, etc.

cut no ice to have no influence.

Icelander *īs'lȧn-dėr, n.* a native of Iceland.

Icelan'dic *adj.* of Iceland, its people, or its language.—*n.* **1** the language of Iceland. **2** (also **Old Icelandic**) Icelandic from the 9th to 16th century.

ichneumon *ik-nū'mȯn, n.* **1** a small Egyptian animal once believed to destroy crocodiles' eggs. **2** an insect whose larvae are parasites on other insects.

ichthyology *ik-thi-ol'ȯ-ji, n.* the study of fishes.

ichthyolog'ical *adj.* **ichthyol'ogist** *n.*

icicle, icing, etc. See **ice.**

icon, ikon *ī'kon, n.* **1** an image. **2** in the Orthodox Church, a (esp. ornate) painting, etc. of Christ or a saint.

icon'oclast *n.* **1** orig. a breaker of images. **2** one who attacks old cherished beliefs.

icon'oclasm *n.* **iconoclas'tic** *adj.*

icy. See **ice.**

idea *ī-dē'ȧ, n.* **1** an image in the mind. **2** a project, plan. **3** an impression or opinion.

idē'al *adj.* **1** perfect. **2** existing in the imagination only.—*n.* **1** a person or thing that is looked on as being perfect. **2** a person's standard of behaviour, etc.

idē'alise *v.t.* to regard, treat or represent (a person or thing) as perfect:—*pr.p.* **idē'alising.**

idē'alist *n.* a person who has very high (esp. too high to be realised) standards and aims.

idealis'tic *adj.* of, or suited to, an idealist.

idē'ally *adv.* **1** perfectly: *ideally suited to the job.* **2** in ideal circumstances: *Ideally, all under-fives should attend a playgroup.*

identify *ī-den'ti-fī, v.t.* **1** to (claim to) recognise: *Would you be able to identify the man who robbed you?; He identified the coat as his brother's.* **2** to regard as the same: *He identifies money with happiness:*—*pr.p.* **iden'tifying**; *pa.p.* **iden'tified.**

iden'tifīable *adj.* **identificā'tion** *n.*

iden'tical *adj.* **1** the same in every detail: *identical outfits.* **2** (used only before a noun) the very same. **3** (of twins) produced from one ovum, and very alike.

iden'tically *adv.* **iden'ticalness** *n.*

iden'tikit *(-ti-kit) n.* a device for assembling a portrait from an assortment of features shown on transparent slips.

iden'tity *n.* **1** who or what a person or thing is: *The police have not established the dead man's identity.* **2** the state of being the same:—*pl.* **iden'tities.**

identify oneself, be identified, with to give one's full support or interest to (e.g.

a party, a policy, aims).
identify with to feel as if one is sharing experiences with (esp. a character in a story).

ideology *ī-di-ol'ȯ-ji*, or *id-i-*, *n.* the beliefs, way of thinking, etc. of a large group, esp. of a political party: *Communist ideology*:—*pl.* **ideol'ogies**.

idiocy. See **idiot**.

idiom *id'i-ȯm*, *n.* **1** an expression belonging to a particular language or dialect. **2** an expression that has become fixed in form, often with a meaning that cannot be guessed from the actual words as *fall out*, to quarrel, *not bad*, quite good. **3** expressions generally: *English idiom.* **4** individual style in music, painting, etc.
idiomat'ic *adj.* **idiomat'ically** *adv.*
idiosyncrasy *id-i-ȯ-sing'krȧ-si*, *n.* a characteristic of a person, esp. an eccentricity:—*pl.* **idiosyn'crasies**.
idiosyncrat'ic *adj.* **idiosyncrat'ically** *adv.*

idiot *id'i-ȯt*, *n.* **1** a very feeble-minded person. **2** a foolish or unwise person.
id'iocy *(-si) n.* **1** state of being an idiot. **2** folly, a foolish act (*pl.* **id'iocies**).
idiot'ic *adj.* **idiot'ically** *adv.*

idle *ī'dl*, *adj.* **1** doing nothing. **2** not working. **3** not in use. **4** lazy. **5** pointless, having no effect or result: *idle threats.* **6** groundless: *idle fears.*—*v.t.* to spend in idleness (with *away*).—*v.i.* **1** to be doing nothing. **2** (of an engine) to run gently without doing any work:—*pr.p.* **id'ling**.
id'leness *n.* **id'ler** *n.* **id'ly** *adv.*

idol *ī'dȯl*, *n.* **1** an image worshipped as representing a god. **2** a person or thing too much loved or honoured.
idolater *ī-dol'ȧ-tėr*, *n.* **1** a worshipper of idols. **2** a great admirer:—*fem.* **idol'atress**.
idol'atry *n.* **1** the worship of idols. **2** excessive love.
idol'atrous *adj.* **idol'atrously** *adv.*
i'dolise *v.t.* **1** to make an idol of. **2** to love excessively:—*pr.p.* **i'dolising**.
idolisā'tion *n.*

idyll *id'il*, *n.* **1** a poem describing a simple scene. **2** a story, episode or scene of happy innocence.
idyll'ic *adj.* simple and delightful.
idyll'ically *adv.*

if *if*, *conj.* **1** on condition that. **2** in the case that. **3** whenever. **4** supposing that. **5** whether. **6** though, although: *a kind man, if humourless.*
if only I wish that.

igloo *ig'lōō*, *n.* a snow hut.

igneous *ig'ni-ůs*, *adj.* **1** of, or like, fire. **2** (of rock) produced by action of great heat within the earth.
ignite *ig-nīt'*, *v.t.* to set on fire.—*v.i.* to catch fire:—*pr.p.* **ignit'ing**.
igni'tion *(-ni') n.* **1** the act of igniting. **2** firing of an explosive mixture of gases, etc., e.g. by means of an electric spark. **3** a device for doing this (e.g. in an internal-combustion engine).

ignoble *ig-nō'bl*, *adj.* **1** of low birth. **2** of poor quality. **3** dishonourable.
igno'bleness *n.* **igno'bly** *adv.*

ignominy *ig'nȯ-min-i*, *n.* the loss of one's good name; public disgrace.
ignomin'ious *adj.* (now usu.) humiliating; shameful: *an ignominious retreat*.
ignomin'iously *adv.* **ignomin'iousness** *n.*

ignoramus *ig-nȯ-rā'mus*, *n.* an ignorant person:—*pl.* **ignora'muses**.

ignorant *ig'nȯr-ȧnt*, *adj.* **1** without knowledge or information. **2** resulting from, showing, lack of knowledge: *an ignorant statement.* **3** unaware, uninformed (of).
ig'norance *n.* **ig'norantly** *adv.*
ignore *ig-nōr'*, *-nör'*, *v.t.* to take no notice of:—*pr.p.* **ignor'ing**.

iguana *i-gwä'nȧ*, *n.* a large tree-lizard of tropical America.

ikon. See **icon**.

il- *il-*, *pfx.* See **in**.

ill *il*, *adj.* **1** not well, sick. (Used only before a noun in the following meanings) **2** evil; bad; harmful: *ill effects.* **3** unlucky: *ill omen.* **4** unfriendly: *ill-feeling*:—*comp.* **worse,** *wûrs*; *superl.* **worst,** *wûrst.*—*adv.* badly.—*n.* **1** harm. **2** misfortune. **3** an ailment.
ill'ness *n.* a bad, unhealthy, condition of body or mind.
ill'-advised' *adj.* not wisely cautious, foolish.
ill at ease. See **ease**.
ill'-blood, ill'-feel'ing *ns.* resentment.
ill'-bred' *adj.* rude, ill-mannered.
ill'-disposed *adj.* unfriendly (towards).
ill'-fat'ed *adj.* doomed to end in, or bringing, disaster.
ill'-fa'voured *adj.* ugly.
ill'-gott'en *adj.* obtained by bad, esp. dishonest, means: *ill-gotten gains*.
ill health poor or bad health.
ill humour bad temper.
ill'-hu'moured *adj.*
ill'-mannered *adj.* having, or showing bad manners.
ill'-na'tured *adj.* peevish, cross.
ill'-starred' *adj.* unlucky.
ill'-tem'pered *adj.* **1** having a bad tem-

per. **2** showing bad temper.
ill'-timed' *adj.* **1** done, etc. at an unsuitable time. **2** tactless.
ill-treat' *v.t.* to treat badly, esp. cruelly.
ill-treat'ment *n.*
ill-use *(-ūz')* *v.t.* to ill-treat:—*pr.p.* **illus'ing.**—Also *n.* *(-ūs').*
ill'-will' *n.* unkind feeling (towards someone).
take it ill to be offended.

I'll *īl,* I shall, or I will.

illegal *i-lē'gȧl, adj.* against the law.
illeg'ally *adv.* **illeg'alness** *n.*
illegal'ity *n.* **1** illegalness. **2** an illegal act:—*pl.* **illegal'ities.**

illegible *i-lej'i-bl, adj.* (almost) impossible to read, not legible.
illegibil'ity, illeg'ibleness *ns.*
illeg'ibly *adv.*

illegitimate *i-li-jit'i-mit, adj.* **1** not according to law. **2** born of parents not married to each other. **3** not according to sound reasoning: *That is an illegitimate conclusion from the facts given.*
illegit'imacy *n.* **illegit'imately** *adv.*

illiberal *i-lib'ėr-ȧl, adj.* **1** mean, not generous. **2** narrow-minded.
illiberal'ity, illib'eralness *ns.*
illib'erally *adv.*

illicit *i-lis'it, adj.* **1** unlawful. **2** not permitted.
illic'itly *adv.* **illic'itness** *n.*

illiterate *i-lit'ėr-it, adj.* **1** unable to read and write. **2** uneducated, ignorant.
illit'eracy, illit'erateness *ns.*
illit'erately *adv.*

illness. See **ill.**

illogical *i-loj'i-kl, adj.* not logical, not showing sound reasoning.
illogical'ity, illog'icalness *ns.*
illog'ically *adv.*

illuminate *i-lū'mi-nāt,* or *-lōō', v.t.* **1** to light up. **2** to throw light on (a subject). **3** to decorate (a manuscript) with ornamental lettering or illustrations:—*pr.p.* **illu'minating.**
illuminā'tion *n.* **1** the act of illuminating. **2** (esp. in *pl.*) a decorative display of lights.
illu'minātor *n.*
illu'mine (esp. *poetic*) *v.t.* **1** to illuminate. **2** to enlighten spiritually:—*pr.p.* **illu'mining.**

illusion *i-lōō'zh(ȯ)n,* or *-lū', n.* **1** a false impression, idea, or belief. **2** something that produces a false impression.
illu'sionist *n.* a conjurer.
illu'sory *(-zȯ-)* *adj.* **1** deceptive. **2** unreal.
illu'soriness *n.*

illustrate *il'ȧs-trāt, v.t.* **1** to adorn or explain the text of (e.g. a book) or accompany (e.g. a lecture) with pictures. **2** to make (e.g. a statement) clearer: *This diagram illustrates my meaning; Illustrate your answer with instances from your own experience:*—*pr.p.* **ill'ustrating.**
ill'ustrated *adj.*
illustrā'tion *n.* **1** a picture. **2** an example. **3** the act of adding pictures or giving examples.
ill'ustrātive *adj.* illustrating (with *of*).
ill'ustrātor *n.*

illustrious *i-lus'tri-ȧs, adj.* very distinguished, famous.
illus'triously *adv.* **illus'triousness** *n.*

im- *im-, pfx.* See **in.**

image *im'ij, n.* **1** a likeness or copy of a person, etc. made in wood, stone, etc.: *images of the saints.* **2** a close likeness: *He's the image of his father.* **3** a mental picture. **4** the reputation of a person, company, etc.: *This scandal will harm the firm's image.* **5** the appearance of something in a mirror or through a lens, etc. **6** a metaphor or simile.
im'agery *n.* **1** (making of) mental pictures. **2** (use of) metaphors and similes.

imagine *i-maj'in, v.t.* **1** to form a picture of in the mind. **2** to think, believe (something that has no reality). **3** to suppose: *I imagine you will not want to be out late.*—Also *v.i.*:—*pr.p.* **imag'ining.**
imag'inable *adj.* able to be imagined or thought of: *for no imaginable reason.*
imag'inary *adj.* existing only in the mind or imagination, not real.
imaginā'tion *n.* **1** (the part of the mind that has) the power of imagining. **2** the creative ability of a writer, etc.
imag'inative *adj.* full of, showing, imagination.
imag'inativeness *n.*

imago *i-mā'gō, n.* the perfect, final stage of an insect (see also **larva, pupa**):—*pl.* **ima'gos.**

imam *i-mäm', n.* **1** a leader of prayers in a mosque. **2** a title of any of various Muslim leaders.

imbalance *im-bal'ȧns, n.* a lack of balance or proportion.

imbecile *im'bi-sēl, -sil, n.* a feeble-minded person not capable of managing his own affairs.—Also *adj.*
imbecility *im-bi-sil'i-ti, n.* **1** feebleness of mind. **2** silliness. **3** an instance of either:—*pl.* **imbecil'ities.**

imbibe *im-bīb', v.t.* **1** to drink, drink in. **2** to receive into the mind.—Also *v.i.*:—*pr.p.* **imbib'ing.**

imbroglio *im-brōl'yō*, *n.* a confused situation:—*pl.* **imbrogl'ios.**

imbue *im-bū'*, *v.t.* **1** to saturate (with). **2** to fill, inspire (with feelings, ideas):—*pr.p.* **imbu'ing**; *pa.p.* **imbued'**.

imitate *im'i-tāt*, *v.t.* (to try) to be like (something or someone):—*pr.p.* **im'itating**.
im'itable *adj.*
imitā'tion *n.* **1** the, or an, act of imitating. **2** a copy. **3** something sham, not genuine.—Also *adj.*
im'itātive *adj.* **1** inclined to imitate. **2** used, chosen, to suggest a sound, etc.
im'itātiveness *n.* **im'itātor** *n.*

immaculate *i-mak'ū-lit*, *adj.* **1** spotless; pure; without flaw. **2** very clean and neat.
immac'ulacy, immac'ulateness *ns.*
immac'ulately *adv.*

immaterial *im-ȧ-tēr'i-ȧl*, *adj.* **1** not consisting of matter. **2** not important: *It is immaterial what you do.*
immater'ially *adv.*

immature *im-ȧ-tūr'*, *adj.* not ripe, not fully grown, or fully developed.
immature'ly *adv.*
immatur'ity, immature'ness *ns.*

immeasurable *i-mezh'ủr-ȧ-bl*, *adj.* very great.
immeas'urably *adv.*

immediate *i-mēd'i-it*, *adj.* **1** (used only before a noun) with nothing, no one, coming between: *his immediate successor*; *her immediate* (i.e. nearest) *surroundings.* **2** with no time between, or without delay: *an immediate response.*
immed'iacy *n.*
immed'iately *adv.* at once.—*conj.* as soon as.

immemorial *i-mė-mōr'i-ȧl*, *-mör'*, *adj.* going back beyond memory: *from time immemorial.*

immense *i-mens'*, *adj.* **1** vast. **2** very great.
immense'ly *adv.*
immense'ness, immen'sity *ns.*

immerse *i-mûrs'*, *v.t.* **1** to plunge wholly into a liquid. **2** to involve, engage, absorb fully: *He immersed himself in his work*; *She's immersed in a book*:—*pr.p.* **immers'ing**.
immer'sion *(-sh(ȯ)n)*, *n.*
immersion heater an electrical water-heating device, placed inside the hot water tank.

immigrate *im'i-grāt*, *v.i.* to come into a country to settle:—*pr.p.* **imm'igrating**.
imm'igrant *n.* one who immigrates.—Also *adj.*
immigrā'tion *n.*

imminent *im'i-nėnt*, *adj.* likely to happen very soon.
imm'inence *n.*

immobile *i-mō'bīl*, *-bil*, *adj.* **1** not able to move, or to be moved. **2** motionless.
immo'bilise *(-bil-īz)* *v.t.* to make immobile:—*pr.p.* **immo'bilising**.
immobil'ity *n.*

immoderate *i-mod'ėr-it*, *adj.* going much beyond normal, excessive.
immod'erately *adv.*

immodest *i-mod'ist*, *adj.* **1** not modest. **2** shameless, indecent.
immod'estly *adv.*
immod'estness, immod'esty *ns.*

immo'late *im'ȯ-lāt*, *v.t.* to offer in sacrifice:—*pr.p.* **imm'olating**.
immolā'tion *n.*

immoral *i-mor'ȧl*, *adj.* not moral.
immoral'ity *n.* (*pl.* **-ies**). **immor'ally** *adv.*
See also **amoral**.

immortal *i-mör'tȧl*, *adj.* **1** never dying or ceasing. **2** (of a name, poem, etc.) never to be forgotten.—*n.* **1** (often *cap.*) one (e.g. a god) who lives for ever. **2** a person who will always be remembered.
immor'talise *v.t.* to make famous for ever:—*pr.p.* **immor'talising**.
immortal'ity *n.* **1** the state (usu. of the spirit) of living for ever. **2** lasting fame.

immovable *i-mōō'vȧ-bl*, *adj.* impossible to move, change, or arouse emotion in.
immovabil'ity, immo'vableness *ns.*
immo'vably *adv.*

immune *i-mūn'*, *adj.* **1** exempt (*from*). **2** protected against, or naturally resistant to, infection, influence, attack, etc. (with *to, from, against*).
imm'unise *v.t.* to make immune (esp. against disease, by inoculation, etc.):—*pr.p.* **imm'unising**.
immun'ity *n.*

immure *i-mūr'*, *v.t.* to shut up, imprison:—*pr.p.* **immur'ing**.

immutable *i-mū'tȧ-bl*, *adj.* unchangeable, unalterable.
immutabil'ity, immu'tableness *ns.*
immu'tably *adv.*

imp *imp*, *n.* **1** a mischievous child. **2** a little wicked spirit.
imp'ish *adj.* **imp'ishly** *adv.*

impact *im'pakt*, *n.* **1** the blow of one body in motion striking another. **2** collision. **3** forceful effect, influence.
impac'ted *adj.* (of a tooth) wedged between the jaw and another tooth.

impair *im-pār'*, *v.t.* to make less good, injure, weaken.
impair'ment *n.*

impale *im-pāl'*, *v.t.* to fix on a long pointed object such as a stake:—*pr.p.* **impal'ing**.

impalpable *im-pal'pȧ-bl*, *adj.* **1** not able to be perceived by touch. **2** not easily grasped by the mind.
impalpabil'ity, **impal'pableness** *ns.*
impal'pably *adv.*

impart *im-pärt'*, *v.t.* **1** to give. **2** to make known (e.g. a secret) to someone.

impartial *im-pär'sh(ȧ)l*, *adj.* not favouring one more than another, just.
impartial'ity, **impar'tialness** *ns.*
impar'tially *adv.*

impassable *im-päs'ȧ-bl*, *adj.* (of e.g. a thicket, a road) that cannot be passed through or over.
impassabil'ity, **impass'ableness** *ns.*
impass'ably *adv.*

impasse *am'pas*, *an^{g}'*, *n*, a position from which there is no escape or outlet; a deadlock.

impassioned *im-pash'ȯnd*, *adj.* moved by, or showing, very strong feeling.

impassive *im-pas'iv*, *adj.* not feeling, or not showing, emotion.
impass'iveness, **impassiv'ity** *ns.*
impass'ively *adv.*

impatient *im-pā'shėnt*, *adj.* **1** not patient. **2** irritable. **3** intolerant (of). **4** restlessly eager (for, to do).
impa'tience *n.* **impa'tiently** *adv.*

impeach *im-pēch'*, *v.t.* **1** to accuse, charge with treason, etc. (a person in public office). **2** to find fault with: *to impeach a person's motives.* **3** to question the truthfulness of (a witness).
impeach'able *adj.* **impeach'ment** *n.*

impeccable *im-pek'ȧ-bl*, *adj.* faultless.
impeccabil'ity *n.* **impecc'ably** *adv.*

impecunious *im-pi-kū'ni-ŭs*, *adj.* short of money, poor.

impede *im-pēd'*, *v.t.* to hinder, obstruct:—*pr.p.* **imped'ing**.
impē'dance *n.* the resistance of an electrical apparatus to an alternating current.
imped'iment *(-ped')* *n.* **1** a hindrance. **2** a small defect in speech, esp. a stutter.
impedimen'ta *n.pl.* baggage, orig. military.

impel *im-pel'*, *v.t.* **1** to push forward, propel. **2** to drive to action:—*pr.p.* **impell'ing**; *pa.p.* **impelled'**.
See also **impulse**.

impend *im-pend'*, *v.i.* to be about to happen, to threaten.
impen'ding *adj.*

impenetrable *im-pen'i-trȧ-bl*, *adj.* **1** that cannot be entered or passed through: *an impenetrable jungle*; *a mind impenetrable to new ideas.* **2** impossible to understand: *an impenetrable mystery*.

impenitent *im-pen'i-tėnt*, *adj.* not repenting or sorry.
impen'itence *n.* **impen'itently** *adv.*

imperative *im-per'ȧ-tiv*, *adj.* **1** expressing a command. **2** urgent, or not to be avoided: *It is imperative that you arrive punctually*.
imper'atively *adv.* **imper'ativeness** *n.*

imperceptible *im-pėr-sep'ti-bl*, *adj.* too small to be seen, heard, noticed, etc.
imperceptibil'ity *n.*
impercep'tibly *adv.*

imperfect *im-pûr'fikt*, *adj.* having a fault or defect, not perfect; incomplete.
imperfec'tion *n.* **1** a defect, faulty detail. **2** imperfectness.
imper'fectly *adv.* **imper'fectness** *n.*

imperial *im-pē'ri-ȧl*, *adj.* **1** of, or connected with, empire, emperor, or empress. **2** (of weights and measures) according to the standard legal in Britain.
impe'rialism *n.* (belief in) the policy of having, or extending, an empire or (*loosely*) control over other peoples.
impe'rialist *n.*, *adj.* **imperialis'tic** *adj.*
impe'rious *adj.* haughty, commanding; demanding obedience or attention.
impe'riously *adv.* **impe'riousness** *n.*

imperil *im-per'il*, *v.t.* to put in danger:—*pr.p.* **imper'illing**; *pa.p.* **imper'illed**.

imperious. See **imperial**.

imperishable *im-per'ish-ȧ-bl*, *adj.* **1** not perishable. **2** lasting for ever.
imperishabil'ity *n.* **imper'ishably** *adv.*

impermanent *im-pûr'mȧ-nėnt*, *adj.* not permanent.
imper'manence, **imper'manency** *ns.*

impermeable *im-pûr'mi-ȧ-bl*, *adj.* not allowing fluids to pass through.
impermeabil'ity *n.* **imper'meably** *adv.*

impersonal *im-pûr'sȯn-ȧl*, *adj.* **1** not involving or referring to a person (a verb is impersonal when its subject is 'it'; e.g. *It rained for four days*). **2** not showing, affected by or arising, from personal feeling; formal: *The tone of the letter was impersonal.*
impersonal'ity, **imper'sonalness** *ns.*
imper'sonally *adv.*

impersonate *im-pûr'sȯn-āt*, *v.t.* to act the part of, or pretend to be (another person):—*pr.p.* **imper'sonating**.
impersonā'tion *n.* **imper'sonātor** *n.*

impertinent *im-pûr'ti-nėnt*, *adj.* impudent, rude.
imper'tinence *n.* **imper'tinently** *adv.*

imperturbable *im-pėr-tûr'bȧ-bl*, *adj.* not easily agitated, always calm.

imperturbabil'ity *n.*
impertur'bably *adv.*

impervious *im-pûr'vi-ůs, adj.* not allowing entry or passage (to): *impervious to water.* **2** not affected by (with *to*): *impervious to hints.*

impetigo *im'pi-tī'gō, n.* a contagious skin disease with clusters of sores.

impetuous *im-pet'ū-ůs, adj.* impulsive, acting with, or showing, suddenness and rashness.
impet'uously *adv.* **impet'uousness** *n.*

impetus *im'pi-tůs, n.* **1** the force, or energy with which something moves. **2** stimulus, encouragement: *This discovery gave a fresh impetus to the development of the industry.*

impiety *im-pī'ė-ti, n.* lack of piety.
impious *im'pi-ůs, adj.* not pious, showing lack of reverence for God or for what is sacred.
im'piously *adv.* **im'piousness** *n.*

impinge *im-pinj', v.i.* **1** (of e.g. light, sound; with *on, upon, against*) to strike or fall on. **2** to encroach (on, e.g. another person's rights):—*pr.p.* **impin'ging**.
impinge'ment *n.*
See also **impact**.

impious, etc. See **impiety**.

impish. See **imp**.

implacable *im-plak'å-bl, adj.* not to be appeased, soothed, or satisfied.
implacabil'ity, implac'ableness *ns.*
implac'ably *adv.*

implant *im-plänt', v.t.* **1** to insert, esp. into living tissue. **2** to fix in the mind, e.g. by teaching (an idea, etc.).—*n. (im'plänt)* something implanted, as a graft, etc.
implantā'tion *n.*

implement *im'pli-mėnt, n.* a tool or instrument.—*v.t. (im'pli-ment)* to fulfil, carry out (e.g. a promise).

implicate *im'pli-kāt, v.t.* to involve, or show to have taken part (in a crime, fault, etc.):—*pr.p.* **im'plicating**.
implicā'tion *n.* the act of implicating or state of being implicated (see also **imply**).

implicit *im-plis'it, adj.* **1** meant but not put into actual words: *implicit agreement*:—*opp.* **explicit. 2** (of trust, etc.) unquestioning, complete.
implic'itly *adv.* **implic'itness** *n.*

implied, etc. See **imply**.

implore *im-plōr', -plör', v.t.* **1** to entreat (someone to do something). **2** to ask earnestly for: *She implored his assistance*:—*pr.p.* **implor'ing**.

imply *im-plī', v.t.* **1** to involve, point to, as a necessary circumstance, result, etc.: *A quarrel implies disagreement about something.* **2** to hint at or suggest. **3** (of words) to mean:—*pr.p.* **imply'ing**; *pa.p.* **implied'**.
implication *n.* that which is implied (see also **implicate**).
implied' *adj.* suggested but not actually put into words.

impolite *im-pǒ-līt', adj.* not polite, rude.
impolite'ly *adv.* **impolite'ness** *n.*

impolitic *im-pol'i-tik, adj.* (of an action) not politic or wise.

imponderable *im-pon'dėr-å-bl, adj.* not able to be measured, estimated, etc. because too small, vague, or uncertain.—*n.* an imponderable influence, etc.

import *im-pōrt', -pört', v.t.* **1** to bring in (goods, for sale, etc.) from abroad. **2** to imply, mean.—*n. (im'-)* **1** something imported from abroad. **2** meaning (of words, statements, etc.) **3** importance.
importā'tion *n.* **impor'ter** *n.*

important *im-pōr'tånt, -pör', adj.* **1** having great value, influence, power or effect. **2** pompous.
impor'tance *n.* **impor'tantly** *adv.*

importune *im-pǒr-tūn', v.t.* to urge, beseech, with troublesome persistance:—*pr.p.* **importun'ing**.
import'ūnate *adj.* **importūn'ity** *n.*

impose *im-pōz', v.t.* **1** to make (a duty or burden) compulsory: *to impose a tax, an obligation, a condition, on a person or persons.* **2** to force, inflict. **3** to thrust (oneself) into the company of (with *on*).—*v.i.* (with *on, upon*) to take unfair advantage of (a person, his good nature, etc.), or to deceive, cheat (a person):—*pr.p.* **impos'ing**.
impos'ing *adj.* impressive, stately, large.
imposition *im-pǒ-zish'(ǒ)n. n.* **1** the act of imposing. **2** a burdensome, unjustified demand. **3** a task set as a punishment, esp. at school.
See also **impostor**.

impossible *im-pos'i-bl, adj.* **1** that cannot exist, be true, or be done. **2** hopelessly unsuitable or unacceptable.
impossibil'ity *n.* (*pl.* **-ies**.)
imposs'ibly *adv.*

impostor *im-pos'tǒr, n.* one who pretends to be someone else, or to be something he is not, in order to deceive.
impos'ture *(-chůr) n.* fraud of this kind.

impotent *im'pǒ-tėnt, adj.* **1** without power, strength, or effectiveness. **2** (of men) lacking sexual power.
im'potence *n.* **im'potently** *adv.*

impound *im-pownd', v.t.* **1** to shut in (e.g. a stray animal in a pound). **2** to collect (water) within a reservoir. **3** to take, esp. legal, possession of, to confiscate.

impoverish *im-pov'ėr-ish, v.t.* **1** to make (e.g. a person, a country) poor. **2** to make (e.g. soil) poor in quality.
impov'erished *adj.* **impov'erishment** *n.*

impracticable *im-prak'ti-kȧ-bl, adj.* **1** (of e.g. a plan) not able to be put into practice or used. **2** (of roads) impassable.
impracticabil'ity, imprac'tibleness *ns.*
imprac'ticably *adv.*

impractical *im-prak'ti-kl, adj.* not practical, not able to be done without undue trouble.

imprecation *im-pri-kā'sh(ȯ)n, n.* a curse.

impregnable *im-preg'nȧ-bl, adj.* that cannot be taken by, or overthrown by, attack.

impregnate *im'preg-nāt, v.t.* **1** to saturate. **2** to make pregnant:—*pr.p.* **im'pregnating.**

impresario *im-prė-sä'ri-ō, -zä', n.* **1** the manager of theatre company, etc. **2** one who puts on an entertainment:—*pl.* **impresar'ios.**

impress *im-pres', v.t.* **1** to press (something on something else); to make (a mark) by doing this. **2** to fix (e.g. a fact deeply on someone's mind); to stress, urge: *The scene impressed itself on my memory; I must impress on you the need for hurry.* **3** to arouse feeling, e.g. admiration, interest, in (someone).—Also *v.i.*—*n.* *(im'-pres)* a mark made by, or as if by, pressure.
impression *im-presh'(ȯ)n, n.* **1** the act or a result of impressing; a mark. **2** a single printing of a book. **3** the idea or emotion left in the mind by any experience; a strong effect on the mind. **4** a vague, uncertain memory or notion (that).
impress'ionable *(-presh') adj.* easily impressed or influenced.
impress'ionism *(-presh') n.* (often *cap.*) a style of painting that aims at capturing the effect of light, etc. in a scene rather than at representing the scene in detail.
impress'ive *adj.* making a deep impression on the mind; arousing admiration or awe.
impress'ively *adv.* **impress'iveness** *n.*

imprint *im-print', v.t.* **1** to print, stamp. **2** to fix, mark, deeply (on the mind, memory, etc.).—*n.* *(im'-)* **1** a mark made by pressure. **2** a permanent effect produced on a person by someone else or by an experience. **3** a printer's name and address on a book, etc.

imprison *im-priz'n, v.t.* **1** to put in prison. **2** to shut up.
impris'onment *n.*

improbable *im-prob'ȧ-bl, adj.* not likely to happen or exist; not probable.
improbabil'ity *n.* **1** improbableness. **2** something unlikely (*pl.* **improbabil'-ities.**)
improb'ableness *n.* **improb'ably** *adv.*

impromptu *im-promp'tū, -to͞o, adj.* made or done without preparation beforehand.—Also *adv.* or *n.*

improper *im-prop'ėr, adj.* **1** not suitable. **2** not correct. **3** indecent.
improp'erly *adv.* **improp'erness** *n.*
impropriety *prȯ-prī'ė-ti, n.* **1** improperness. **2** something improper (*pl.* **impropri'eties**).
improper fraction one in which the numerator is larger than the denominator, e.g. $\frac{33}{7}$.

improve *im-pro͞ov', v.t.* and *v.i.* to make, or become, better:—*pr.p.* **improv'ing.**
improve'ment *n.*
improv'ing *adj.* intended to improve morals or mind.
improve on to produce something more useful, or striking, etc., than.

improvident *im-prov'i-dėnt, adj.* not thrifty; not taking thought for the future.
improv'idence *n.*
improv'idently *adv.*

improvise *im'prȯ-vīz, v.t.* **1** to compose and perform without preparation. **2** to make a substitute for from materials at hand: *to improvise a bed.*—Also *v.i.*:—*pr.p.* **im'provising.**
improvisā'tion *n.* **im'proviser** *n.*

imprudent *im-pro͞o'dėnt, adj.* not showing caution or foresight, unwise.
impru'dence *n.* **impru'dently** *adv.*

impudent *im'pū-dėnt, adj.* insolent; shamelessly bold.
im'pudence *n.* **im'pudently** *adv.*

impugn *im-pūn', v.t.* to attack in words or by arguments: *to impugn the truthfulness of an informant.*

impulse *im'puls, n.* **1** a driving or stimulating force, or its effect: *an electrical impulse.* **2** a drive to action caused by a feeling, etc.; a sudden desire (to do something).
impul'sive *adj.* **1** inclined to act suddenly without careful thought. **2** (of action) prompted by impulse.
impul'sively *adv.* **impul'siveness** *n.*

impunity *im-pū'ni-ti, n.* freedom from punishment, injury, or loss: *He had so far ignored the regulation with impunity.*

impure *im-pūr', adj.* **1** mixed with something else; dirty; not pure. **2** not morally pure.

impure'ness, **impur'ity** (*pl.* **-ities**), *ns.* **impure'ly** *adv*.

impute *im-pūt'*, *v.t.* to consider (a happening, action, etc., usu. bad) to be caused, done, etc., by (with *to*): *I impute our failure to lack of preparation*; *No one can impute laziness to me*.

imputā'tion *n.* **1** the act of imputing. **2** suggestion of fault.

in *in*, *prep.* **1** expressing the relation of a thing to what surrounds or includes it (place, time, or circumstances): *in the garden*; *in his youth*; *in daylight*. **2** into: *Throw it in the fire*. **3** within (a particular length of time): *I'll be finished in five minutes*. **4** used in describing manner, method, distribution, etc.: *in a hurry*; *in a loud voice*; *tied in bundles*; *in large numbers*.—*adv.* **1** inside, not out. **2** towards the inside. **3** (*cricket*) at the bat. **4** (of a political party, etc.) in power. **5** fashionable.—*adj.* **1** that is in, inside, or coming in (often as part of a noun, as *in-fighting*, quarrelling within a group; *in-tray*, one for letters, etc. received and awaiting attention). **2** (*coll.*) fashionable.:—*comp.* **inn'er**; *superls.* **inn'ermost**, **in'most**.

inn'er *adj.* (see above; used only before a noun) **1** on the inside; further in. **2** more closely associated, more in the know: *in the inner circle of his helpers*. **3** (of meaning) hidden. **4** of the mind or spirit: *the inner life*.—*n.* (a hit on) the part of the target next to the bull's eye.

inn'ermost *adj.* (see above) **1** furthest from the outside. **2** (also **in'most**) most secret or hidden.

in as much as, **inasmuch as** in consideration of the fact that.

in for **1** about to receive (something unpleasant). **2** trying to get.

in for it in for trouble.

ins and outs **1** windings. **2** details of something complicated (e.g. of long negotiations).

in so far as, **insofar as** to the extent that.

in that because, for the reason that.

in- *in-*, **il-** *il-* (before *l*), **im-** *im-* (before *b*, *m* or *p*), **ir-** *ir-* (before *r*), *pfx.* meaning (1) in (e.g. *include*); into (e.g. *invade*); (2) not (e.g. *insincere*).
See also **in**, *adj.*, above.

inability *in-ȧ-bil'i-ti*, *n.* lack of power, means, etc. (to do something).
See also **unable**.

inaccessible *in-ȧk-ses'i-bl*, *adj.* not to be approached, reached, or obtained.

inaccessibil'ity *n.* **inaccess'ibly** *adv*.

inaccurate *in-ak'ū-rit*, *adj.* not accurate.

inacc'uracy *n.* **1** inaccurateness. **2** a mistake:—*pl.* **inacc'uracies**.

inacc'urately *adv.* **inacc'urateness** *n*.

inactive *in-ak'tiv*, *adj.* **1** not active. **2** making no effort. **3** out of use; not working or functioning.

inac'tion, **inactiv'ity** *ns*.

inadequate *in-ad'i-kwit*, *adj.* **1** not suitable or sufficient. **2** (of person) not able to deal with the situation; not equal (to a task, etc.).

inad'equacy *n.* **1** inadequateness. **2** a defect, shortcoming:—*pl.* **inad'equacies**.

inad'equately *adv.* **inad'equateness** *n*.

inadmissible *in-ȧd-mis'i-bl*, *adj.* not allowable.

inadmissibil'ity *n.* **inadmiss'ibly** *adv*.

inadvertent *in-ȧd-vûr'tėnt*, *adj.* not intentional or deliberate.

inadver'tence, **inadver'tency** *ns*.

inadver'tently *adv*.

inadvisable *in-ȧd-vīz'ȧ-bl*, *adj.* unwise.

inadvisabil'ity *n*.

inalienable *in-āl'yen-ȧ-bl*, *adj.* (of rights) that cannot be taken or given away.

inane *in-ān'*, *adj.* silly; meaningless.

inan'ity *(-an')* *n.* **1** silliness. **2** a silly remark:—*pl.* **inan'ities**.

inanimate *in-an'i-mit*, *adj.* without life.

inapplicable *in-ap'lik-ȧ-bl*, *-ȧ-plik'*, *adj.* not suitable, not applying (to a situation, case under consideration).

inappropriate *in-ȧ-prō'pri-it*, *adj.* not appropriate or suitable.

inappro'priately *adv*.

inappro'priateness *n*.

inapt *in-apt'* *adj.* not apt; unsuitable.

inarticulate *in-är-tik'ū-lit*, *adj.* **1** uttered indistinctly. **2** unable to express oneself clearly and fluently.

inartic'ulately *adv.* **inartic'ulateness** *n*.

inartistic *in-är-tis'tik*, *adj.* not artistic.

inartis'tically *adv*.

inasmuch as. See **in**.

inattentive *in-ȧ-ten'tiv*, *adj.* not paying attention.

inatten'tion, **inatten'tiveness** *ns*.

inatten'tively *adv*.

inaudible *in-ö'di-bl*, *adj.* not able to be heard.

inaudibil'ity, **inau'dibleness** *ns*.

inau'dibly *adv*.

inaugurate *in-ö'gū-rāt*, *v.t.* **1** to make a formal beginning to (something). **2** to open formally to the public. **3** to install (someone) formally in office:—*pr.p.* **inaug'urating**.

inau'gural *adj.* **inaugurā'tion** *n*.

incapacitate *in-kȧ-pas'i-tāt*, *v.t.* to make incapable or unfit (for something):—*pr.p.*

incapac'itating.
incapac'ity *n.* **1** inability (for, to do). **2** lack of physical or mental power. **3** legal disqualification.

incarcerate *in-kär'sėr-āt*, *v.t.* to imprison:—*pr.p* **incar'cerating**.
incarcerā'tion *n.*

incarnate *in-kär'nit*, *-nāt*, *adj.* in bodily human form: *a devil incarnate*.
incarnā'tion *n.* **1** taking of human form by a divine being. **2** a person representing a quality, etc., in a very marked way: *He is the incarnation of selfishness, of reasonableness*.

incautious *in-kö'shus*, *adj.* not cautious.
incau'tiously *adv.* **incau'tiousness** *n.*

incendiary *in-sen'di-ȧ-ri*, *adj.* **1** used for setting on fire: *incendiary bombs*. **2** likely to cause strife: *an incendiary speech*.—*n.* **1** one who sets fire to a building, etc. maliciously. **2** an incendiary bomb:—*pl.* **incen'diaries**.
incen'diarism *n.* the act or practice of an incendiary.

incense[1] *in-sens'*, *v.t.* to make angry:—*pr.p.* **incens'ing**.

incense[2] *in'sens*, *n.* material burned to give fragrant fumes, esp. in religious services.

incentive *in-sen'tiv*, *n.* something that encourages an action: *Hope of promotion was an incentive to hard work*.

inception *in-sep'sh(ȯ)n*, *n.* a beginning.

incessant *in-ses'ȧnt*, *adj.* going on without stopping, continual.
incess'antly *adv.* **incess'antness** *n.*

incest *in'sest*, *n.* sexual intercourse between members of the same family, other than husband and wife.
incest'uous *adj.*

inch *inch*, *n.* a measure of length, $\frac{1}{12}$ of a foot (equal to 2.54 centimetres).—*v.i.* to move little by little.
every inch entirely, thoroughly.
within an inch of dangerously near.

incidence *in'sid-ėns*, *n.* **1** the falling (of e.g. a ray of light on a surface). **2** the range, extent, etc. of occurrence (of e.g. a disease).
in'cident *adj.* **1** (of e.g. a ray) falling or striking (on something). **2** belonging naturally: *dangers incident to the life of an explorer*.—*n.* an event; a happening, e.g. one involving violence.
inciden'tal *adj.* **1** occurring, etc., by chance in connection with something else: *incidental benefits*; *an incidental remark*. **2** additional, but less important: money for fare, hotel bill, and incidental expenses; an event incidental to the main plot. **3** liable to occur: *inconveniences incidental to camping*. **4** (of music) accompanying a play, etc., but not forming part of it.
inciden'tally *adv.* **1** by chance. **2** (as *interj.*) by the way.

incinerate *in-sin'i-rāt*, *v.t.* to burn to ashes:—*pr.p.* **incin'erating**.
incinerā'tion *n.*
incin'erator *n.* a furnace, etc., for incinerating.

incipient *in-sip'i-ėnt*, *adj.* beginning to exist: *an incipient cold*.
incip'ience *n.* **incip'iently** *adv.*
See also **inception**.

incise *in-sīz'*, *v.t.* **1** to cut into. **2** to make (marks, designs) by cutting:—*pr.p.* **incis'ing**.
incision *in-sizh'ȯn*, *n.* **1** the act of cutting into (esp. by a surgeon). **2** a cut made for a surgical or other purpose.
incisive *in-sīs'iv*, *adj.* **1** (of mind) clear and sharp. **2** (of manner, etc.) clear, firm, or sharp, biting.
incis'or *-sīz'*, *n.* a front, cutting tooth.

incite *in-sīt'*, *v.t.* to urge on, encourage (to do something):—*pr.p.* **incit'ing**.
incite'ment *n.*

incivility *in-siv-il'i-ti*, *n.* **1** impoliteness. **2** an impolite act:—*pl.* **incivil'ities**.
See also **uncivil**.

inclement *in-klem'ėnt*, *adj.* (of weather) stormy, very cold.
inclem'ency *n.*

incline *in-klīn'*, *v.i.* **1** to lean (towards); to tend. **2** to slant, slope.—*v.t.* **1** to bow (the head). **2** to cause to lean or tend; to dispose.—*n.* *(in'klīn)* a slope.
inclination *in-kli-nā'sh(ȯ)n*, *n.* **1** act of inclining. **2** a slope. **3** a liking. **4** a tendency or slight desire.
be inclined to 1 to have a tendency to: *She is inclined to make careless mistakes*. **2** to have a slight desire to: *I am inclined to accept their invitation*.

include *in-klo͞od'*, *v.t.* to take in, count:—*pr.p.* **includ'ing**.
includ'ing *prep.* counting also: *the whole family, including the dog*.
inclusion *in-klo͞o'zh(ȯ)n*, *n.* **1** the act of including; being included. **2** something included.
inclusive *in-klo͞o'siv*, *adj.* including everything mentioned or understood: *an inclusive charge*; *7th to 9th May inclusive*—i.e. three days, 7th, 8th, 9th.
inclusive of including.

incognito *in-kȯg-nē'tō*, *adv.*, *adj.* with identity concealed, e.g. under a false name.—*n.* a false name or identity:—*pl.* **incogni'tos**.

incoherent *in-kō-hēr'ėnt, adj.* **1** (of a statement, etc.) loose, rambling, without logical connection. **2** (of a person) expressing himself in a rambling, confused way.
incoher'ence, incoher'ency *ns.*
incoher'ently *adv.*

incombustible *in-kȯm-bus'ti-bl, adj.* that cannot be burnt.

income *in(g)'kum, n.* money that comes in regularly, including salary, etc.
in'coming *adj.* coming in.
income tax a tax paid on income over a certain amount.

incommode *in-kȯ-mōd', v.t.* to cause inconvenience or discomfort to:—*pr.p.* **incommod'ing.**

incommunicable *in-kȯ-mū'ni-kȧ-bl, adj.* that cannot be told or described to others.

incommunicado *in-kȯ-mū-ni-kä'dō, adv., adj.* (of e.g. a prisoner) prevented from communicating with others.

incomparable *in-kom'pȧ-rȧ-bl,* without equal, matchless.
incom'parably *adv.* beyond comparison: *incomparably better than his successor.*

incompatible *in-kȯm-pat'i-bl, adj.* **1** incapable of existing, being used, etc., together. **2** (of statements) contradictory. **3** (of persons) sure, because of their natures, to disagree.
incompatibil'ity *n.* **incompat'ibly** *adv.*

incompetent *in-kom'pė-tėnt, adj.* **1** not legally qualified. **2** (of evidence) not admissible. **3** lacking ability, esp. in one's work.
incom'petence, incom'petency *ns.*
incom'petently *adv.*

incomplete *in-kȯm-plēt', adj.* not complete.
incomplete'ly *adv.* **incomplete'ness** *n.*

incomprehensible *in-kom-pri-hen'si-bl, adj.* impossible to understand.
incomprehensibil'ity *n.*
incomprehen'sion *n.* failure to understand.

inconceivable *in-kȯn-sēv'ȧ-bl, adj.* that cannot be imagined or believed.
inconceiv'ably *adv.*

inconclusive *in-kȯn-kloo͞'siv, adj.* **1** not settling a point that is debated or investigated: *inconclusive evidence.* **2** with no definite result.
inconclu'sively *adv.*

incongruous *in-kong'groo-ůs, adv.* **1** out of keeping, out of place: *Heavy shoes look incongruous with evening dress.* **2** odd, inharmonious: *an incongruous mixture.*
incongru'ity *n.* **1** incongruousness. **2** something incongruous:—*pl.* **incongru'ities.**
incon'gruously *adv.* **incon'gruousness** *n.*

inconsequent *in-kon'sė-kwėnt, adj.* **1** not following logically from what goes before. **2** showing lack of connection in thought, etc.: *inconsequent statements, actions; an inconsequent person.*
incon'sequence *n.*
inconsequen'tial *(-kwen'shȧl) adj.* **1** of no consequence or importance. **2** inconsequent.
incon'sequently *adv.*

inconsiderable *in-kȯn-sid'ėr-ȧ-bl, adj.* **1** not important. **2** small in amount, etc.

inconsiderate *in-kȯn-sid'ėr-it, adj.* not showing thought for the feelings or rights of others; thoughtless.
inconsid'erately *adv.*
inconsid'erateness *n.*

inconsistent *in-kȯn-sis'tėnt, adj.* **1** (of statements, etc.) contradictory in some way: *His conduct on the two occasions was inconsistent.* **2** not in keeping or agreement (with): *Your explanation is inconsistent with the facts; His method of trapping rabbits was inconsistent with his teaching about kindness to animals.* **3** not always speaking or acting according to the same principles or beliefs. **4** not of a steady standard; unreliable.
inconsis'tency *n.* (*pl.* **-ies**).
inconsis'tently *adv.*

inconsolable *in-kȯn-sōl'ȧ-bl, adj.* not to be comforted.
inconsolabil'ity *n.* **inconsol'ably** *adv.*

inconspicuous *in-kȯn-spik'ū-ůs, adj.* not noticeable.
inconspic'uously *adv.*
inconspic'uousness *n.*

inconstant *in-kon'stȧnt, adj.* not constant; changeable, fickle.
incon'stancy *n.*

incontestable *in-kȯn-tes'tȧ-bl, adj.* not to be disputed, undeniable.

incontinent *in-kon'ti-nėnt, adj.* **1** unable to control the passing of urine and faeces. **2** lacking control.
incon'tinence *n.*

incontrovertible *in-kon-trȯ-vûr'ti-bl, adj.* (of e.g. truth, evidence) too clear and certain to be questioned or disputed.
incontrover'tibly *adv.*

inconvenient *in-kȯn-vēn'yėnt, adj.* causing trouble or difficulty; awkward.
inconven'ience *n.* (something that causes) trouble or difficulty.—*v.t.* to cause trouble or difficulty to (someone):—*pr.p.* **inconven'iencing.**
inconven'iently *adv.*

incorporate *in-kör'pō-rāt, v.t.* **1** to contain as part of the whole: *The new proposal incorporates all your suggestions.* **2** to add, put in, so that it forms part of the whole. **3** to merge, blend (with):—*pr.p.* **incor'porating**.
incor'porated *adj.* formed into a corporation (*abbrev.* **Inc.**).

incorrect *in-kō-rekt', adj.* **1** not accurate, wrong. **2** (of e.g. behaviour) not according to best, or accepted, standards.
incorrect'ly *adv.*

incorrigible *in-kor'i-ji-bl, adj.* too bad for correction or reform.
incorrigibil'ity *n.* **incorr'igibly** *adv.*

incorruptible *in-kō-rup'ti-bl, adj.* **1** not capable of decay. **2** always upright and just. **3** not able to be bribed.

increase *in-krēs', v.i., v.t.* to grow, or to make greater, in size or numbers:—*pr.p.* **increas'ing.**—*n.* **1** *(in'krēs)* growth. **2** amount added by growth, etc.
increas'ingly *adv.* to an ever greater degree: *It became increasingly difficult to find helpers.*
in'crement *(-krė-) n.* **1** increase. **2** amount of increase. **3** something added.
on the increase becoming greater or more frequent.

incredible *in-kred'i-bl, adj.* impossible to believe, or seeming so.
incredibil'ity, incred'ibleness *ns.*
incred'ibly *adv.*
incredulous *in-kred'ū-lūs, adj.* **1** not believing. **2** showing disbelief.
incredū'lity, incred'ulousness *ns.*
incred'ulously *adv.*

increment. See **increase**.

incriminate *in-krim'i-nāt, v.t.* to show (someone) to have committed, or taken part in, a crime:—*pr.p.* **incrim'inating.**
incrim'inating *adj.* **incriminā'tion** *n.*

incrust . Same as **encrust**.

incubate *in'kū-bāt, v.t.* **1** to sit on (eggs) in order to hatch them. **2** to cause (eggs, embyros, etc.) to develop, esp. in an incubator.—*v.i.* **1** (of eggs, embryos, etc.) to develop. **2** (of disease germs) to develop until signs of the disease appear:—*pr.p.* **in'cubating.**
incubā'tion *n.*
in'cubātor *n.* a heated box-like apparatus for hatching eggs, growing bacteria, etc., or one for rearing premature babies.
incubation period the period between infection and the appearance of the signs of a disease.

incubus *in'kūbūs, n.* an oppressive person or thing.

inculcate *in'kul-kāt, v.t.* to teach by frequent repetitions: *My father tried to inculcate good principles in us; At school we were inculcated with the rules of grammar*:—*pr.p.* **in'culcating.**
inculcā'tion *n.*

incumbent *in-kum'bėnt, adj.* resting as a duty (on or upon someone): *It is incumbent on us to support our leader now.*—*n.* one who holds some office, esp. in the church.

incur *in-kûr', v.t.* **1** to become liable to pay (a debt). **2** to bring upon oneself by one's actions: *to incur someone's displeasure*:—*pr.p.* **incurr'ing**; *pa.p.* **incurred'**.

incurable *in-kūr'ȧ-bl, adj.* not able to be cured or corrected.—*n.* a person who is incurable.
incur'ably *adv.*

incurious *in-kū'ri-ūs, adj.* lacking curiosity; indifferent.

incurring, etc. See **incur**.

incursion *in-kûr'sh(ō)n, n.* a hostile entry, raid, invasion.

indebted *in-det'id, adj.* **1** being in debt (to). **2** obliged (to) for help or kindness.
indebt'edness *n.*

indecent *in-dē'sėnt, adj.* **1** offending against accepted standards of conduct—immodest, improper. **2** not showing good taste: *indecent haste.*
inde'cency *n.* (*pl.* **-ies**).
indecent assault a sexual assault not involving rape.

indecipherable *in-di-sī'fėr-ȧ-bl, adj.* impossible to read.

indecision *in-di-sizh'(ō)n, n.* inability to decide, hesitation.
indecisive *in-di-sī'siv, adj.* **1** not producing a clear decision or having a definite result. **2** (of a person) wavering, not arriving at firm decisions.
indeci'sively *adv.*
See also **undecided**.

indent *in-dent', v.t.* **1** to make notches, or recesses, in. **2** to begin farther in from the margin (also *v.i.*).—*v.i.* to make out a written order (for).—*n.* *(in'dent)* **1** a written order for equipment, etc. **2** the space left at the beginning of the first line of a paragraph.
indentā'tion *n.* **1** a notch. **2** a recess (e.g. in a coastline). **3** an indent (*def. 2*).
inden'ture *(-chūr) n.* a written agreement, esp. a contract by which an apprentice is bound to work for a master for a given period.

independent *in-di-pen'dėnt, adj.* **1** free from control by others. **2** (of e.g. a country) self-governing. **3** thinking or acting

for oneself; not willing to accept help; self-reliant. **4** not influenced by, or showing influence of, anyone or anything else: *an independent observer*; *He arrived at an independent conclusion*.
indepen'dence *n.* **indepen'dently** *adv.*
independent means an income not dependent on employment by others.
independent of not depending on.

in-depth *in'depth adj.* thorough, detailed.

indescribable *in-di-skrī'bȧ-bl, adj.* that cannot be described, either because vague or because too great: *indescribable horrors*.
indescri'bably *adv.*

indestructible *in-di-struk'ti-bl, adj.* that cannot be destroyed.

indeterminate *in-di-tûr'mi-nit, adj.* **1** not fixed in amount, etc. **2** vague, uncertain.
indeter'minately *adv.*
indeter'minateness *n.*

index *in'deks, n.* **1** an alphabetical list of subjects, names, etc. at the end of a book, or on cards. **2** a sign, indication. **3** a raised figure showing how many times a number is multiplied by itself (e.g. the 3 in the statement 5555). **4** a numerical scale showing changes in the cost of living, in wages, etc.:—*pl.* **in'dexes** or (esp. *def. 3*) **in'dices** *(-di-sēz)*.—*v.t.* to supply with, or enter in, an index.
index finger the forefinger.

Indian *in'di-ȧn, n.* **1** one of the native inhabitants of North, Central or South America. **2** a native or inhabitant of India.—*adj.* of India or Indians.
East Indian, **West Indian** (a native or inhabitant) of the East, or West, Indies.
Indian corn maize.
Indian file. See **file**.
Indian ink a black ink used by artists, etc.
Indian summer a period of warm, dry, calm weather in late autumn.
in'dia-rubb'er *n.* rubber, esp. a piece for rubbing out pencil marks, etc.

indicate *in'di-kāt, v.t.* **1** to point out. **2** to show. **3** to be a sign of. **4** to give some idea of. **5** to point to as the best treatment or remedy:—*pr.p.* **in'dicating**.
indicā'tion *n.*
indic'ative *(-ȧ-tiv) adj.* **1** showing or suggesting the existence (of): *The change in her manner was indicative of a new attitude to us.* **2** denoting those parts of the verb that make statements or ask questions (e.g. I *am speaking*; he *ran*; will he *die*?)
in'dicator *n.* a pointer, e.g. one on a measuring instrument, etc., or the instrument itself.
See also **index**.

indices. See **index**.

indict *in-dīt', v.t.* to accuse, charge, with a crime (formally or in writing): *indicted on a charge of murder*.
indict'able *adj.* (of an offence) for which one can be charged in court.
indict'ment *n.*

indifferent *in-dif'ėr-ėnt, adj.* **1** without interest, not caring. **2** lacking feeling, sympathy, etc. (towards, to). **3** rather poor in quality.
indiff'erence *n.* **indiff'erently** *adv.*

indigence. See **indigent**.

indigenous *in-dij'i-nu̇s, adj.* native; produced naturally in a country or soil: *plants indigenous to northern Europe*.

indigent *in'di-jėnt, adj.* poor, in need.
in'digence *n.* **in'digently** *adv.*

indigestion *in-di-jes'ch(ȯ)n, n.* discomfort caused by imperfectly digested food.
indiges'tible *adj.* not easily digested.
indigestibil'ity *n.* **indiges'tibly** *adv.*

indignant *in-dig'nȧnt, adj.* angry and with a sense of injustice to oneself or other(s).
indig'nantly *adv.* **indignā'tion** *n.*
indig'nity *n.* a hurt to dignity, affront, insult:—*pl.* **indig'nities**.

indigo *in'di-gō, n.* **1** a violet-blue dye. **2** the colour in the rainbow between blue and violet.

indirect *in-di-rekt', -dī-, adj.* **1** not direct. **2** not in a straight line. **3** roundabout; not going straight to the point or subject. **4** not the one directly aimed at or following directly: *an indirect result*.
indirect'ly *adv.* **indirect'ness** *n.*
indirect speech speech as it is reported rather than as the speaker uttered it (e.g. *'I have no time'* reported as *He said he had no time*).
indirect tax a customs and excise duty etc., which is collected indirectly from the customer, who has to pay higher prices for taxed goods.

indiscipline *in-dis'i-plin, n.* lack of discipline.

indiscreet *in-dis-krēt', adj.* **1** not prudent or cautious. **2** giving too much information away.
indiscretion *in-dis-kresh'(ȯ)n, n.* **1** lack of prudence, etc. **2** an indiscreet act.
indiscreet'ly *adv.*

indiscriminate *in-dis-krim'in-it, adj.* not making any distinction as regards merit, worth, etc., between one person, thing, etc. and another: *indiscriminate praise, blame, generosity, slaughter*.
indiscrim'inately *adv.*

indiscrim'ināting *adj.* not making, or able to make, distinctions.

indiscernible *in-dis-ûn'ȧ-bl, adj.* too small to be noticed.
indiscern'ably *adv.*

indispensable *in-dis-pen'sȧ-bl, adj.* that cannot be done without or neglected.
indispensabil'ity *n.*

indisposed *in-dis-pōzd', adj.* (not used before a noun) **1** unwilling (to). **2** slightly ill.
indisposi'tion *(-pȯ-zish'(ȯ)n) n.*

indisputable *in-dis-pū'tȧ-bl, adj.* certainly true.
indispu'tably *adv.*

indissoluble *in-di-sol'ū-bl, adj.* **1** that cannot be dissolved, undone, or broken. **2** binding for ever.
indissolubil'ity *n.*
indissol'ubly (or *-dis'*) adv.

indistinct *in-dis-tingkt', adj.* not clear to eye, ear, or mind; dim.
indistinct'ly *adv.* **indistinct'ness** *n.*

indistinguishable *in-dis-ting'gwish-ȧ-bl, adj.* that cannot be distinguished, i.e. seen, or seen as different or separate.
indistin'guishably *adv.*

individual *in-di-vid'ū-ȧl, adj.* **1** belonging to one only, or to each one separately, of a group. **2** single, separate. **3** having marked special qualities: *He had a very individual style.—n.* a single person or animal.
individ'ualist *n.* one who shows great, or too great, independence in thought and action.
individ'ualism *n.* **individualis'tic** *adj.*
individual'ity *n.* the qualities that distinguish one person from others.
individ'ually *adv.* **1** each separately. **2** personally: *This rule affects me individually.*

indivisible *in-di-viz'i-bl, adj.* not able to be divided, or separated.
indivisibil'ity *n.* **indivis'ibly** *adv.*

indoctrinate *in-dok'trin-āt, v.t.* to fill, inspire (a person, with a doctrine, set of beliefs, etc.)
indoctrinā'tion *n.*

indolent *in'dȯ-lėnt, adj.* lazy, avoiding exertion.
in'dolence *n.* **in'dolently** *adv.*

indomitable *in-dom'i-tȧ-bl, adj.* that cannot be overcome (used e.g. of courage, pride, a very resolute person).
indom'itably *adv.*

indoor *in'dōr, -dör, adj.* used, carried on, etc., inside a building: *indoor games.*
indoors' *adv.*

indubitable *in-dū'bi-tȧ-bl, adj.* that cannot be doubted, certain.
indu'bitably *adv.*
See also **undoubted**.

induce *in-dūs', v.t.* **1** to lead, persuade (a person): *I could not induce her to come.* **2** to bring on or bring about: *The heat induced sleepiness.* **3** (*medical*) to bring on (labour), cause (a female) to begin labour, by means of drugs, etc.:—*pr.p.* **indu'cing**.
induce'ment *n.* **1** something that persuades, an incentive. **2** the act of inducing (*defs. 1,2*).

induct *in-dukt', v.t.* to introduce formally (to, into, a new office, esp. a clergyman).
induc'tion *n.* **1** the act of inducting. **2** the act of inducing (*def. 3*). **3** production by one body of an opposite electrical state in another.

indulge *in-dulj', v.t.* **1** to yield to the wishes of (a person, oneself). **2** not to restrain (a desire, etc.): *indulging his love of practical jokes.—v.i.* **1** (*coll.*) to eat, or esp. drink (too much). **2** (with *in*) to allow oneself to have, do (something): *to indulge in a glass of sherry, a fit of temper.*
indul'gence *n.* **1** the act of gratifying. **2** too great leniency. **3** a privilege granted. **4** something indulged in. **5** a pardon to a repentant sinner.
indul'gent *adj.* **indul'gently** *adv.*

industry *in'dus-tri, n.* **1** steady attention to work. **2** (any branch of) production or trade:—*pl.* **in'dustries**.
indus'trial *adj.* **indus'trially** *adv.*
indus'trialise *v.t.* to give (e.g. a country) industries on a large scale:—*pr.p.* **indus'trialising**.
indus'trialist *n.* one who takes part in running a large industrial organisation.
indus'trialism *n.*
indus'trious *adj.* diligent, hard-working.
indus'triously *adj.*
heavy (light) industry industry making large (small) products.
industrial action action, eg. a strike, taken by workers as a protest.

inebriate *in-ē'bri-āt, v.t.* to make drunk:—*pr.p.* **ine'briating**.—*n.* (*-it*, or *-āt*) a drunk person.
ine'briāted *adj.* **inebriā'tion** *n.*

inedible *in-ed'i-bl, adj.* **1** not fit to be eaten. **2** not suitable as food.

ineducable *in-ed'ū-kȧ-bl, adj.* impossible to educate.

ineffable *in-ef'ȧ-bl, adj.* **1** impossible to describe in words. **2** not to be uttered.

ineffective *in-i-fek'tiv, adj.* **1** not producing the effect desired. **2** not efficient.

ineffec'tively *adv.* **ineffec'tiveness** *n.*
ineffec'tual *(-fek'tū-ȧl) adj.* **1** without effect, useless. **2** powerless.
ineffectual'ity *n.* **ineffec'tually** *adv.*
ineffec'tualness *n.*
ineffica'cious *(-kā'shus) adj.* not able to produce the desired effect.
ineff'icacy *(-i-kȧ-si) n.* lack of power to produce the desired effect.
inefficient *in-i-fish'ėnt, adj.* **1** not efficient. **2** not accomplishing, or able to carry out, in the best way.
ineffic'iency *n.* **ineffic'iently** *adv.*

inelegant *in-el'i-gȧnt, adj.* not graceful; not elegant.
inel'egance, inel'egancy *ns.*
inel'egantly *adv.*

ineligible *in-el'i-ji-bl, adj.* not eligible.
ineligibil'ity *n.*

inept *in-ept', adj.* **1** foolish. **2** tactless. **3** awkward, clumsy.
inep'titude, inept'ness *ns.*
inept'ly *adv.*

inequality *in-i-kwol'i-ti, n.* **1** lack of equality, or an instance of it. **2** unevenness:—*pl.* **inequal'ities.**
See also **unequal.**

inequitable *in-ek'wi-tȧ-bl, adj.* unfair, unjust.
ineq'uitably *adv.* **ineq'uity** *n.*

ineradicable *in-i-rad'i-kȧ-bl, adj.* that cannot be rooted out or removed completely.

inert *in-ûrt', adj.* **1** unable to move of itself. **2** chemically inactive. **3** unwilling to move or act.
inert'ly *adv.* **inert'ness** *n.*
inertia *in-ûr'shi-ȧ, n.* inertness.
iner'tia-reel' *adj.* (of a safety-belt) paid out from a reel and designed to tighten on sudden braking.
inertia selling the practice of sending a householder goods he has not ordered and charging for them if they are not returned.

inescapable *in-is-kā'pȧ-bl, adj.* that cannot be escaped or avoided.

inessential *in-i-sen'sh(ȧ)l, adj.* not necessary.—Also *n.*

inestimable *in-es'ti-mȧ-bl, adj.* too great, of too great value, to be estimated.
ines'timably *adv.*

inevitable *in-ev'i-tȧ-bl, adj.* **1** that cannot be avoided. **2** certain, necessary.
inevitabil'ity, inev'itableness *ns.*
inev'itably *adv.*

inexact *in-ig-zakt', adj.* not exactly correct or true.
inexac'titude, inexact'ness *ns.*
inexact'ly *adv.*

inexcusable *in-iks-kūz'ȧ-bl, adj.* that cannot be excused or justified.
inexcus'ably *adv.*

inexhaustible *in-ig-zös'ti-bl, adj.* **1** that cannot be tired. **2** that cannot be used up.
inexhaustibil'ity *n.* **inexhaus'tibly** *adv.*

inexorable *in-eks'ȯr-ȧ-bl, adj.* **1** impossible to move by entreaty. **2** unalterable.
inexorabil'ity *n.*
inex'orably *adv.* relentlessly.

inexpedient *in-iks-pē'di-ėnt, adj.* not advisable, or suitable, in the circumstances.
inexpe'dience, inexpe'diency *ns.*

inexpensive *in-ik-spen'siv, adj.* not costly.
inexpen'sively *adv.*

inexperience *in-iks-pē'ri-ėns, n.* **1** lack of experience. **2** lack of knowledge or skill.
inexpe'rienced *adj.* lacking experience or skill.

inexpert *in-eks'pûrt, adj.* **1** unskilled. **2** clumsy.

inexplicable *in-eks'pli-kȧ-bl,* or *iks-plik'ȧ-, adj.* impossible to explain or understand.
inex'plicably (or *-plik'*) *adv.*

inexplicit *in-iks-plis'it, adj.* not clearly stated and exact.

inexpressible *in-iks-pres'i-bl, adj.* that cannot be expressed; indescribable.
inexpress'ibly *adv.*
inexpress'ive *adj.* without expression; not expressive.

inextinguishable *in-iks-ting'gwish-ȧ-bl, adj.* (of e.g. enthusiasm, hope) that cannot be put out or suppressed.

inextricable *in-eks'tri-kȧ-bl,* or *-trik', adj.* **1** that cannot be disentangled. **2** from which it is impossible to get free.
inex'tricably (or *-trik'*) adv.

infallible *in-fal'i-bl, adj.* **1** (of person or judgment) never making a mistake. **2** always successful: *an infallible remedy.*
infallibil'ity *n.* **infall'ibly** *adv.*

infamous *in'fȧ-mus, adj.* **1** having an evil reputation. **2** disgraceful.
in'famy *n.* **1** evil reputation. **2** public disgrace. **3** an evil act:—*pl.* **in'famies.**

infant *in'fȧnt, n.* **1** a baby. **2** (*law*) a person under 21 years.—Also *adj.*
in'fancy *n.* **1** state or time of being a baby or (*law*) under 21. **2** earliest stage.
infan'ticide *(-sīd) n.* **1** the murder of a child. **2** one who murders a child.
infantile *in'fȧn-tīl, adj.* **1** (of e.g. conduct) babyish. **2** of babies: *infantile diseases.*

infantry *in'fȧn-tri, n.* foot-soldiers.

infatuated *in-fat'ū-āt-id, adj.* filled with blind foolish love (with *with*): *infatuated* *with the skiing instructor*.

infatuā'tion *n*.

infect *in-fekt'*, *v.t.* **1** to fill with germs that cause disease; to pass on disease to. **2** to give, pass on, a quality, feeling, to: *to infect someone with discontent, enthusiasm*.

infec'tion *n*. **infec'tious** *(-shŭs) adj*.

infer *in-fûr'*, *v.t.* to judge, conclude, from facts or evidence:—*pr.p.* **inferr'ing**; *pa.p.* **inferred'**.

in'ference *n*. **1** something that is deduced or concluded. **2** the act of inferring.

inferior *in-fēr'i-ŏr*, *adj*. **1** lower in place. **2** lower in rank; less important. **3** of poor quality.—Also *n*.

inferior'ity *n*.

inferiority complex a constant feeling that one is not as good as others in some way.

infernal *in-fur'năl*, *adj*. **1** belonging to the lower regions, to hell. **2** devilish. **3** (*coll*; used in mild abuse) annoying.

infer'nally *adv*.

infer'no (from It.) *n*. **1** hell. **2** any place of horror or fire:—*pl*. **infer'nos**.

infertile *in-fûr'tīl*, *adj* **1** (of e.g. soil) not fertile, unproductive. **2** unable to have young.

infertil'ity *(-til') n*.

infest *in-fest'*, *v.t.* to swarm in or over: *Robbers infest the hills*; *a dog infested with fleas*.

infidel *in'fi-dĕl*, *n*. one who does not hold the faith (e.g. Christianity or Islam) of the speaker.—Also *adj*.

infidel'ity *n*. **1** unfaithfulness. **2** adultery:—*pl*. **infidel'ities**.

infield *in'fēld*, *n*. **1** land near the farm buildings. **2** (*cricket*) the field near the wicket, or the fielders there.

infiltrate *in'fil-trāt*, *-fil'*, *v.t.* **1** to filter into or through. **2** (of soldiers) to get through (the enemy lines) a few at a time. **3** (of members of e.g. a political party) to enter (an organisation) gradually with the purpose of influencing its decisions, or (of a spy) to do so in order to obtain secret information.—Also *v.i.* (with *into*, etc.):—*pr.p.* **in'filtrating**.

infiltrā'tion *n*.

infinite *in'fin-it*, *adj*. **1** without end, limit, or bounds. **2** very great.

in'finitely *adv*. **in'finiteness** *n*.

infin'ity *n*. **1** infinite space, time, or quantity. **2** an infinitely distant place.

infinites'imal *(-tes') adj*. infinitely, or (*usu.*) extremely, small.

infinites'imally *adv*.

infinitive *in-fin'i-tiv*, *n*. the part of the verb that expresses the action but has no subject (e.g. *to err*, *to lose*, *stay* in the sentences *To err is human*; *I hated to lose*; *you need not stay*).

infinity. See **infinite**.

infirm *in-fûrm'*, *adj*. **1** feeble, sickly. **2** weak, not resolute.

infir'mary *n*. a hospital:—*pl*. **infirm'aries**.

infir'mity *n*. **1** weakness. **2** a bodily ailment:—*pl*. **infir'mities**.

inflame *in-flām'*, *v.t.* **1** to cause (feelings, etc.) to become violent. **2** to make hot or red. **3** to excite anger, love, etc., in (someone):—*pr.p.* **inflam'ing**.

inflamm'able *(-flam') adj*. **1** easily set on fire (see also **flammable**). **2** easily excited to anger, etc.

inflammabil'ity *n*.

inflammā'tion *n*. **1** heat in a part of the body with pain, redness, and swelling. **2** the process of inflaming.

inflamm'atory *adj*. tending to inflame angry feelings: *inflammatory speeches*.

inflate *in-flāt'*, *v.t.* **1** to expand, blow up, with air or gas. **2** to puff up (with e.g. pride). **3** to increase esp. unduly (e.g. prices, amount of money in circulation, a person's reputation):—*pr.p.* **inflat'ing**.

infla'table *adj*.

inflated *in-flā'tid*, *adj*.

inflation *in-flā'sh(ŏ)n*, *n*. the process of inflating, esp. undue increase of money in circulation.

inflā'tionary *adj*. of or causing inflation.

inflect *in-flekt'*, *v.t.* to vary the pitch of (e.g. the voice).

inflec'tion, **inflex'ion** *(-flek'sh(ŏ)n) n*.

inflexible *in-fleks'i-bl*, *adj*. **1** rigid, unbending. **2** unyielding: *inflexible determination*. **3** unalterable.

inflexibil'ity, **inflex'ibleness** *ns*.

inflex'ibly *adv*.

inflexion. See **inflect**.

inflict *in-flikt'*, *v.t.* **1** to give (e.g. a wound). **2** to impose (punishment, or anything unpleasant; with *on*).

inflic'tion *n*.

inflorescence *in-flŏr-es'ĕns*, *n*. a group of flowers forming one head on a plant.

influence *in'floo-ĕns*, *n*. **1** power to affect people, actions or events through e.g. personality, importance of office, or less obvious means. **2** a person or thing that has this power.—*v.t.* to have and use power to move or sway: *He seems to have been influenced by his father in his decision to leave school*:—*pr.p.* **in'fluencing**.

influential *in-floo-en'shăl*, *adj*. **1** having much influence. **2** playing an important part (in): *influential in getting the plan*

adopted.
influen'tially *adv.*

influenza *in-floo-en'zȧ, n.* an infectious illness, usu. with a headache, fever, cold, etc., caused by any of various viruses.

influx *in'fluks, n.* a flowing in; a coming in or arrival (of something) in large numbers or quantities.

inform *in-förm', v.t.* **1** to tell, impart knowledge to: *I was informed of your absence, that you were absent.* **2** to obtain knowledge for (oneself): *I took care to inform myself of all that happened.—v.i.* to tell facts, e.g. to the police (about a criminal, etc.; with *on* or *against*): *Jones informed against his fellow thieves.*
infor'mant *n.* one who informs.
information technology technology for gathering, storing and communicating information using computers and microelectronics.
informā'tion *n.* **1** facts told; knowledge gained or given. **2** data stored in computer, etc.
infor'mative *adj.* giving useful information.
infor'mer *n.* one who gives information, esp. to the police, etc.

informal *in-för'mȧl, adj.* **1** not formal or official. **2** friendly and relaxed.
informal'ity *n.* (*pl.* **-ies**).
infor'mally *adv.*

infra- *pfx.* below, beneath.
infra-red *in'frȧ-red', adj.* beyond the red end of the visible spectrum (**infra-red rays** have heating and other useful effects).

infra dig *in'frȧ-dig', (coll.)* short for Latin **infra dignitatem** *(dig-ni-tä'tėm)* beneath one's dignity.

infrastructure *in'frȧ-struk-chu̇r, n.* the permanent services and equipment, eg. the communications, factories and schools, needed for a country to run smoothly.

infrequent *in-frē'kwėnt, adj.* not frequent.
infrē'quency *n.*

infringe *in-frinj', v.t.* **1** to break (e.g. a law). **2** to trespass on (another's right): *to infringe a copyright:—pr.p.* **infrin'ging.**
infringe'ment *n.*

infuriate *in-fūr'i-āt, v.t.* to make very angry:*—pr.p.* **infūr'iating.**

infuse *in-fūz', v.t.* **1** to fill, inspire with (a quality, etc): *to infuse some enthusiasm into the players.* **2** to soak (herbs, etc.) in hot water; to prepare (tea, etc.) in this way (also *v.i.*).
infusion *in-fū'zh(ȯ)n, n.* **1** the act of infusing. **2** something infused.

ingenious *in-jē'ni-u̇s, adj.* **1** (of a person) skilful in inventing. **2** (of thing) skilfully designed and made. **3** skilfully planned.
ingē'niously *adv.* **ingē'niousness** *n.*
ingenuity *in-jin-ū'i-ti, n.* ingeniousness (the meaning arose by confusion; this was orig. a noun from **ingenuous**).

ingenuous *in-jen'ū-u̇s, adj.* frank, artless, free from deception.
ingénue *an^g-zhā-nū'* (from Fr.) *n.* an ingenuous girl, esp. as a stage part.
ingen'uously *adv.* **ingen'uousness** *n.*

ingle *ing'gl, (Scot.) n.* a fireplace.
ing'le-nook *n.* a fireside corner.

inglorious *in-glō'ri-u̇s, -glö', adj.* not glorious, shameful.
inglo'riously *adv.*

ingot *ing'got, n.* a mass of metal (e.g. of gold or silver) cast in a mould.

ingrained *in-grānd', adj.* fixed firmly into a surface, or in one's nature: *ingrained selfishness.*

ingratiate *in-grā'shi-āt, v.t.* to get (oneself) into favour (with a person):*—pr.p.* **ingra'tiating.**

ingratitude *in-grat'i-tūd, n.* lack of gratitude or thankfulness.
See also **ungrateful.**

ingredient *in-grē'di-ėnt, n.* one of the things that goes into a mixture.

ingress *in'gres, n.* **1** entrance. **2** right or means of entrance.

ingrowing *in'grō-ing, adj.* growing into the flesh.

inhabit *in-hab'it, v.t.* (of people, animals) to live in (a region, etc.).
inhab'itable *adj.* fit to be lived in (see also **habitable**).
inhab'itant *n.* one who lives permanently in a place.

inhale *in-hāl', v.t.* and *v.i.* to breathe in:*—pr.p.* **inhal'ing.**
inhāl'ant *n.* a drug to be inhaled.
inhalation *in-hȧ-lā'sh(ȯ)n, n.*
inhal'er *n.* a small apparatus by means of which to inhale a drug, etc.

inharmonious *in-här-mō'ni-u̇s, adj.* not harmonious.

inhere *in-hēr', v.i.* to belong as a permanent quality, or as a right (with *in*):*—pr.p.* **inher'ing.**
inher'ent *adj.* **inher'ently** *adv.*
inher'ence, inher'ency *ns.*

inherit *in-her'it, v.t.* **1** to receive (property, etc.) as heir (also *v.i.*). **2** to possess (qualities) as handed down from previous generations.
inher'itance *n.* **1** act of inheriting. **2** any-

thing inherited.

inher'itor *n.*

inhibit *in-hib'it, v.t.* to hold back, check, restrain.

inhib'ited *adj.* suffering from restraint.

inhibi'tion *n.* **1** the act of restraining; a restraint (good or bad) on natural impulses, etc. **2** check to, or stoppage of, an action or function in the body.

inhospitable *in-hos'pi-tȧ-bl*, or *-pit'*, *adj.* **1** not hospitable. **2** (of climate, etc.) harsh, unpleasant.

inhuman *in-hū'mȧn, adj.* **1** barbarous, cruel. **2** not human.

inhuman'ity *n.* **inhu'manly** *adv.*

inhumane *in-hū-mān', adj.* not humane.

inhumane'ly *adv.*

inimical *in-im'i-kȧl, adj.* **1** unfriendly, hostile. **2** unfavourable (to): *conditions inimical to healthy growth.*

inim'ically *adv.*

inimitable *in-im'i-tȧ-bl, adj.* that cannot be imitated; distinctive.

inim'itably *adv.*

iniquity *in-ik'wi-ti, n.* (an act of) wickedness:—*pl.* **iniq'uities**.

iniq'uitous *adj.* **iniq'uitously** *adv.*

initial *in-ish'ȧl, adj.* of, at, the beginning.—*n.* the letter beginning a word, esp. a name.—*v.t.* to put the initials of one's name on:—*pr.p.* **ini'tialling**; *pa.p.* **ini'tialled**.

ini'tially *adv.* at the beginning; at first.

initiate *in-ish'i-āt, v.t.* to start, begin, introduce: *to initiate changes, legislation.* **2** to give primary instruction to: *to initiate him in business methods.* **3** to admit, with ceremonies (into e.g. a secret society):—*pr.p.* **ini'tiating**.—*n.* *(-it)* one who has been initiated.

initiā'tion *n.*

initiative *in-ish'i-ȧ-tiv, n.* **1** the first step, the lead: *Brown took the initiative, the others then joined in.* **2** the right to make the first move. **3** enterprise, ability to take the lead: *He failed because he had no initiative.*

on one's own initiative without prompting, advice, etc. from others.

inject *in-jekt', v.t.* **1** to force (a fluid, etc.) into a vein or muscle with a needle and syringe; to put fluid, etc. into the body of (a person) thus. **2** to introduce: *This injected some life into the dull play.*

injec'tion *n.*

injudicious *in-jo͞o-dish'ȧs, adj.* not wise or prudent; ill-judged.

injudic'iously *adv.*

injunction *in-jung(k)'sh(ȯ)n, n.* **1** a command earnestly expressed. **2** (*law*) an order requiring a person or persons not to do, or to do, something.

injure *in'jȧr, v.t.* **1** to wrong. **2** to harm, damage:—*pr.p.* **in'juring**.

in'jured *adj.* **1** hurt. **2** offended.

in'jury *n.* (*pl.* **-ies**).

inju'rious *(-joo')* *adj.* harmful.

injur'iously *adv.* **inju'riousness** *n.*

injustice *in-jus'tis, n.* **1** quality of being unjust. **2** a wrong.

ink *ingk, n.* **1** a black, or coloured, liquid used in writing, or a thicker, oily fluid used in printing. **2** a dark liquid thrown out by cuttlefish, etc.

ink'y *adj.*:—*comp.* **ink'ier**; *superl.* **ink'iest**.

ink'ily *adv.* **ink'iness** *n.*

ink'well *n.* a container for ink, esp. one set into the surface of a desk.

inkling *ingk'ling, n.* **1** a hint. **2** a suspicion (with *of*).

inky. See **ink**.

inlaid. See **inlay**.

inland *in'lȧnd, adj.* **1** not beside the sea. **2** carried on, etc., within a country: *inland trade.*—*adv.* *(in-land')* in, or towards, parts away from the sea.

inland revenue. See **revenue**.

in-law *in'lö*, (*coll.*) *n.* a relation by marriage.

inlay *in-lā', v.t.* to ornament by inserting pieces of fine material e.g. ivory:—*pr.p.* **inlay'ing**; *pa.p.* **inlaid'**.—Also *n.* *(in'lā)*.

inlet *in'lėt, n.* **1** a small bay, usu. narrow. **2** a way in. **3** a piece inserted.

inmate *in'māt, n.* one of those who live in an institution.

in memoriam *in mė-mō'ri-ȧm, -mö-* to the memory of.

inmost. See **in**.

inn *in, n.* a house providing food, lodging for travellers, a small hotel.

inn'keeper *n.* keeper of an inn.

innards *in'ȧrdz, n.pl.* the entrails; the inner parts.

innate *i-nāt', adj.* inborn, natural: *his innate gentleness.*

innate'ly *adv.* **innate'ness** *n.*

inner, innermost. See **in**.

innings *in'ingz, n.* **1** (*cricket*) a team's turn to bat. **2** a spell of power or opportunity to act.

innocent *in'ȯ-sėnt, adj.* **1** free from, or ignorant of, evil: *an innocent child.* **2** not guilty (of a crime or fault). **3** not having a bad or malicious intention: *an innocent remark.* **4** harmless.

inn'ocence *n.* **inn'ocently** *adv.*

innocent of lacking, without.

innocuous *i-nok'ū-ůs, adj.* harmless.

innovate *in'ȯ-vāt, v.i.* to introduce something new, make changes:—*pr.p.* **inn'ovating.**
innovā'tion *n.* **inn'ovātor** *n.*
inn'ovātive, innovā'tory *adjs.*

innuendo *in-ū-en'dō, n.* **1** a remark containing an underlying accusation or insult. **2** insinuation:—*pl.* **innuen'do(e)s.**

innumerable *i-nū'mėr-ȧ-bl, adj.* that cannot be numbered, countless.
innū'merate *(-it) adj.* not understanding basic mathematics and science.
innū'meracy *n.*

inoculate *in-ok'ū-lāt, v.t.* to introduce a disease in mild form into the body of (a person, animal) through a puncture, etc., so as to safeguard against later infection:—*pr.p.* **inoc'ulating.**
inoculā'tion *n.*

inoffensive *in-ȯ-fen'siv, adj.* **1** not objectionable. **2** harmless.

inoperable *in-op'ėr-ȧ-bl, adj.* not suitable for surgical operation.

inoperative *in-op'ėr-ȧ-tiv, adj.* not working or taking effect.

inopportune *in-op'ȯr-tūn, adj.* ill-timed, inconvenient.

inordinate *in-ör'di-nit, adj.* unreasonably great: *inordinate demands.*
inor'dinately *adv.*

inorganic *in-ör-gan'ik, adj.* **1** not having the special characteristics of living bodies. **2** (*chemistry*) dealing with elements and their compounds excluding many of the carbon compounds.

in-patient *in'pā-shėnt, n.* a patient living, as well as treated, in a hospital.

input *in'poot, n.* something put in, as data fed into a computer.

inquest *in'kwest, n.* a legal enquiry into a case of sudden death.

inquire, enquire *in-kwīr', v.i.* **1** to seek information. **2** to make an investigation (into). **3** to ask (after e.g. a person).—*v.t.* to ask: *She inquired (of me) what time the bus left*:—*pr.p.* **inquir'ing, enquir'ing.**
inquir'er, enquir'er *n.*
inquir'ing, enquir'lng *adj.*
inquir'y, enquir'y *n.* **1** seeking for information. **2** an investigation. **3** a question:—*pl.* **inquir'ies, enquir'ies.**

inquisition *in-kwi-zish'ȯn, n.* **1** searching examination, careful questioning. **2** (*cap.*; *history*) a tribunal in the R.C. church for various purposes including questioning of heretics.
inquisitive *in-kwiz'i-tiv, adj.* **1** eager to know. **2** prying into other people's affairs.
inquis'itively *adv.* **inquis'itiveness** *n.*
inquis'itor *n.*

inroad *in'rōd, n.* **1** a raid. **2** an advance (into).
make inroads on to take away from (e.g. savings, liberty, someone's time) to a serious extent.

insane *in-sān', adj.* **1** mad. **2** very unwise.
insan'ity *(-san') n.*

insanitary *in-san'i-tȧr-i, adj.* not sanitary, dangerous to health.
insan'itariness *n.*

insatiable *in-sā'shȧ-bl, adj.* (of e.g. greed, curiosity) that cannot be satisfied.
insatiabil'ity *n.* **insa'tiably** *adv.*

inscrutable *in-skrōōt'ȧ-bl, adj.* **1** that cannot be searched into and understood. **2** (of e.g. person, smile) mysterious.
inscrutabil'ity *n.* **inscrut'ably** *adv.*

insect *in'sekt, n.* a small animal with body in three parts—head, thorax and abdomen—three pairs of legs, and often two pairs of wings (e.g. bee, beetle); in ordinary use including other small animals such as the spider (see this).
insec'ticide *(-sīd) n.* a substance for killing insects.
insectiv'orous *adj.* living on insects.

insecure *in-si-kūr', adj.* **1** not safe. **2** not firmly fixed, likely to give way, etc. **3** anxious, apprehensive.
insecur'ity, insecure'ness *ns.*
insecure'ly *adv.*

inseminate *in-sem'in-āt, v.t.* to introduce semen into (a female), esp. artificially:—*pr.p.* **insem'inating.**
inseminā'tion *n.*

insensate *in-sen'sāt, -sit, adj.* unthinking; senseless.

insensible *in-sen'si-bl, adj.* **1** unconscious. **2** unaware, without understanding (of): *I am not insensible of your kindness.* **3** not feeling (with *to*): *insensible to fear.* **4** so small or gradual as not to be noticed.
insensibil'ity *n.* **insen'sibly** *adv.*

insensitive *in-sen'si-tiv, adj.* **1** not sensitive. **2** not sympathetic (to).

inseparable *in-sep'ȧ-rȧ-bl, adj.* not to be separated or parted.

insert *in-sûrt', v.t.* to put in.—*n.* *(in'sėrt)* something additional put in (e.g. extra leaf, leaves, in a magazine, etc.).
inser'tion *n.* **1** the act of inserting. **2** something inserted.

in-service *in-sûr'vis, adj.* happening while a person is employed.

inset *in'set, n.* a small picture, photograph, etc., within a larger one.

inshore *in'shōr, -shör, adj.* **1** (of e.g. fishing) carried on near the shore. **2** operating near the shore.—*adv. in-shōr', -shör'* near, or towards, the shore.

inside *in-sīd', in', n.* **1** the side, space, or part within. **2** (often *pl.*) the entrails.—*adj. (in'sīd)* **1** being on, or in, the inside. **2** (*coll.*) coming from, done by, someone within the organisation, etc. mentioned: *inside information.*—*adv. (in-sīd')* **1** to, in or on, the inside. **2** indoors. **3** (*coll.*) in jail.—*prep. (in-sīd')* **1** within; to or on the inside of. **2** within, in less than, a certain time.
inside out **1** with the inner side outside. **2** thoroughly: *I know him inside out.*

insidious *in-sid'i-ůs, adj.* **1** ready to trap or ensnare; treacherous. **2** (of e.g. a disease, a vice) advancing unnoticed or secretly.
insid'iously *adv.* **insid'iousness** *n.*

insight *in'sīt, n.* **1** the power of seeing into and understanding e.g. truths, persons. **2** an imaginative view (into).

insignia *in-sig'ni-ȧ, n.pl.* badges of office or honour, authority, etc.

insignificant *in-sig-nif'i-kȧnt, adj.* unimportant; petty.
insignif'icance *n.*

insincere *in-sin-sēr', adj.* not sincere.
insincer'ity *(-ser') n.* (*pl.* **-ies**).
insincere'ly *adv.*

insinuate *in-sin'ū-āt, v.t.* **1** to introduce, work in, slyly and little by little: *to insinuate doubts into someone's mind*; *She insinuated herself into her boss's favour by tale-bearing.* **2** to hint (that):—*pr.p.* **insin'uating.**
insinuā'tion *n.* **1** the act of insinuating. **2** artful suggestion; a sly hint.

insipid *in-sip'id, adj.* **1** tasteless. **2** dull.
insipid'ity, insip'idness *ns.*

insist *in-sist', v.i.* **1** to put emphasis (on a point in a speech, etc.). **2** to hold firmly to an intention or to something desired: *She insisted on going by bus*; *He insisted on prompt action by the club.*—*v.t.* to go on saying or demanding (that): *He insists that he saw a ghost, that I should be dismissed.*
insis'tence *n.*
insis'tent *adj.* **1** insisting. **2** compelling attention: *an insistent noise.*
insis'tently *adv.*

in situ *in sit'ū, -o͞o,* in (the original) position.

insole *in'sōl n.* a lining for placing over the inner sole of a shoe.

insolent *in'sȯ-lėnt, adj.* (of person, remark, etc.) too bold, impertinent, insulting.
in'solence *n.* **in'solently** *adv.*

insoluble *in-sol'ū-bl, adj.* **1** (of substance) impossible to dissolve. **2** (of problem, difficulty) impossible to solve.
insolubil'ity *n.*

insolvent *in-sol'vėnt, adj.* not able to pay one's debts.
insol'vency *n.*

insomnia *in-som'ni-ȧ,* sleeplessness.
insom'niac *(-ni-ak) n., adj.* (a person) suffering from insomnia.

insouciant *in-so͞o'si-ȧnt, an^{g}-so͞o-si-on^{g}', adj.* carefree, unconcerned.
insou'ciance *(-si-ȧns, si-on^{g}s') n.*

inspect *in-spekt', v.t.* **1** to look at, examine carefully. **2** to look at (e.g. troops) ceremonially.
inspec'tion *n.*
inspec'tor *n.* **1** one who is appointed to inspect. **2** a police officer below a superintendent and above a sergeant.

inspire *in-spīr', v.t.* **1** (of a divine or supernatural power) to teach (a person), or to influence (what he says or writes). **2** (of a person or circumstance) to affect, influence, rouse, impel, prompt: *The leader inspired his followers with confidence*, or *inspired confidence in his followers*; *This small success inspired him to fresh efforts*; *What inspired that remark?*:—*pr.p.* **inspir'ing.**
inspiration *in-spir-ā'sh(ȯ)n, n.* **1** something or someone that inspires. **2** the influence that moves those who create great works of literature or art. **3** an idea, plan, that has fortunate results.
inspired' *(-spīrd') adj.* **1** moved by divine or other influence. **2** brilliantly good.

inspirit *in-spir'it, v.t.* to encourage, put new energy into.

instability *in-stȧ-bil'i-ti, n.* lack of stability or steadiness.
See also **unstable.**

install *in-stöl', v.t.* **1** to introduce formally into an office: *to install a new bishop.* **2** to place: *He installed himself in the best chair.* **3** to fix in position and put in use: *to install a new heating system.*
installā'tion *(-stȧ-) n.* **1** the act of installing. **2** something installed.

instalment *in-stöl'mėnt, n.* **1** one payment out of a number of payments into which a sum owed is divided. **2** one part of a serial story.

instance *in'stȧns, n.* **1** an example; a case. **2** suggestion: *He did it at the instance of his companions.*—*v.t.* to mention as an example:—*pr.p.* **in'stancing.**
in the first instance as the first step in an action, etc.

instant *in'stȧnt, adj.* immediate.—*n.* **1** an extremely small space of time. **2** a moment or point of time.

in'stantly *adv.*
instantaneous *in-stàn-tān'-i-ùs, adj.* done, happening, or acting, in an instant.

instead *in-sted', adv.* in place (of something or someone); as a substitute.

instep *in'step, n.* the arched upper part of the foot.

instigate *in'sti-gāt, v.t.* **1** to urge, spur on (a person). **2** to bring about by spurring person(s) on: *to instigate a plot, a crime:—pr.p.* **in'stigating.**
instigā'tion *n.* **in'stigātor** *n.*

instil *in-stil', v.t.* to put slowly into the mind or feelings: *to instil ideas, good principles, hatred:—pr.p.* **instill'ing;** *pa.p.* **instilled'.**

instinct *in'stingt, n.* **1** esp. in animals, a natural tendency to certain actions and responses not taught by experience or reasoning. **2** an ability to see truth or facts without conscious reasoning. **3** a natural ability (for).
instinc'tive *adj.* arising from instinct or natural impulse.
instinc'tively *adv.*
instinc'tiveness *n.*

institute *in'sti-tūt, v.t.* **1** to set up, establish. **2** to set moving, begin (e.g. an enquiry, a lawsuit):*—pr.p.* **in'stituting.***—n.* a society, organisation, or the building used by it.
in'stitūtor *n.*
institū'tion *n.* **1** a society, organisation, etc. set up for a particular purpose. **2** the building it occupies. **3** a home for e.g. old people, a mental hospital, a prison, etc. **4** an established law; a custom. **5** the act of instituting.
institū'tional *adj.*
institū'tionalise *v.t.* **1** to confine in an institution. **2** (usu. *pass.*) to cause (a person so confined) to become apathetic and dependent on routine:*—pr.p.* **institū'tionalising.**

instruct *in-strukt', v.t.* **1** to teach. **2** to direct, order, command.
instruc'tion *n.* **1** teaching. **2** an order, direction. **3** (*pl.*) (a book giving) directions, e.g. for the use of an apparatus.
instruc'tive *adj.* giving useful knowledge or information.
instruc'tively *adv.* **instruc'tiveness** *n.*
instruc'tor *n.:—fem.* **instruc'tress.**

instrument *in'stroo-mėnt, n.* **1** a tool, implement; a recording or indicating device. **2** something for producing musical sounds, e.g. piano, violin. **3** a formal legal document.
instrumen'tal *adj.* **1** of an instrument. **2** performed on or written for, musical instrument(s). **3** playing the important part: *He was instrumental in getting the law repealed.*
instrumen'talist *n.* one who plays a musical instrument.
instrumental'ity *n.* agency, means.
instrumentā'tion *n.* the arrangement of a musical composition for instruments.

insubordinate *in-sùb-ör'di-nit, adj.* disobedient, rebellious.
insubordinā'tion *n.*

insubstantial *in-sùb-stan'sh(à)l, adj.* **1** lacking solidity. **2** not real.

insufferable *in-suf'ėr-à-bl, adj.* not to be endured, detestable.

insufficient *in-sù-fish'ėnt, adj.* **1** not enough. **2** not of necessary quality, power, etc.
insuffic'iency *(-fish'ėn-) n.*
insuffic'iently *adv.*

insular *in'sū-làr, adj.* **1** of, belonging to, an island or islands. **2** (of e.g. a person's views) narrow, prejudiced.
insular'ity *n.*
in'sulate *v.t.* **1** to cut off, isolate. **2** to cover, protect, separate, with a material that does not let e.g. electrical currents, heat, sound, pass through:*—pr.p.* **in'sulating.**
insulā'tion *n.* **in'sulātor** *n.*

insulin *in'sū-lin, n.* an extract from the pancreas, used in treatment of diabetes, etc.

insult *in-sult', v.t.* to treat with contempt or rudeness.—Also *n. (in'sult).*
insult'ing *adj.* **insult'ingly** *adv.*

insuperable *in-sūp'ėr-à-bl, -sōōp', adj.* that cannot be overcome or got over: *an insuperable difficulty, barrier.*

insupportable *in-sù-pōr'tà-bl,* or *-pör', adj.* unbearable: *The pain, such insolence, is insupportable.*

insure *in-shōōr', v.t.* to arrange for payment of a sum of money in the case of the loss of, or damage to (something), or accident or injury to (someone).—Also *v.i.* (with *against*)*:—pr.p.* **insur'ing.**
insur'ance *n.* **1** (regular payment made for) insuring. **2** a protection, safeguard.

insurgent *in-sûr'jėnt, adj.* rising in revolt.*—n.* a rebel.
insur'gence, insur'gency *ns.*
insurrec'tion *n.* (a) revolt.

insurmountable *in-sùr-mown'tà-bl, adj.* that cannot be overcome or got over, insuperable.

insurrection. See **insurgent.**

intact *in-takt', adj.* undamaged, whole.

intaglio *in-tal'yō n.* a stone or gem in which the design is hollowed out:—*pl.* **intagl'ios**.

intake *in'tāk, n.* **1** the place at which e.g. water is taken into a channel, fuel into an engine, etc. **2** the act of taking in. **3** the amount, quantity (e.g. of new recruits, pupils, etc.) taken in, accepted.

intangible *in-tan'ji-bl, adj.* **1** not able to be felt by touch. **2** not clear and definite to the mind; not possible to define exactly.
intangibil'ity, **intan'gibleness** *ns.*
intan'gibly *adv.*

integer *in'ti-jėr, n.* a whole number.
in'tegral *adj.* essential to the completeness of the whole.
in'tegrate *v.t.* **1** to bring, fit, together to form a whole. **2** to fit (into the main part or group).—*v.t.* and *v.i.* to (cause to) mix freely and on an equal footing with other members of society:—*pr.p.* **in'tegrating**.
integrā'tion *n.*

integrity *in-teg'ri-ti, n.* **1** the state of being whole and not made less in any way. **2** uprightness, honesty.

intellect *in'ti-lekt, n.* the thinking power of the mind.
intellec'tual *(-tū-ål) adj.* of, possessing, showing, appealing to, intellect: *intellectual ability, person, face, interests.*—*n.* a person of high mental ability, esp. whose interests are in literature, art, thinking about life, etc.
intell'igence *in-tel'i-jėns n.* **1** mental ability. **2** information given, news. **3** (usu. *cap.*) department of state or armed service(s) dealing with secret information.
intell'igent *adj.* **1** clever, alert, quick in mind. **2** showing these qualities: *an intelligent question.* **3** capable of performing some of the functions of a computer.
intell'igently *adv.*
intelligible *in-tel'i-ji-bl, adj.* able to be understood: *an intelligible statement.*
intelligibil'ity, **intell'igibleness** *ns.*
intell'igibly *adv.*

intemperate *in-tem'pėr-it, adj.* showing lack of restraint or moderation: *intemperate in his drinking*; *intemperate language.*
intem'perance, **intem'perateness** *ns.*
intem'perately *adv.*

intend *in-tend', v.t.* **1** to plan, resolve: *I intend to go, intend going*; *Do you intend us all to go, that we should all go?* **2** to mean: *What did you intend by that remark?*; *It was intended as an insult*; *Was it intended for me?*
inten'ded *adj.*—*n.* (*coll*; *old*) a fiancé(e).
intent' *n.* purpose: *criminal intent*; *with intent to steal.*—*adj.* **1** bent, determined (on some action). **2** with all one's mind (on): *intent on the job he was doing.* **3** very attentive, earnest: *an intent expression.*
intent'ly *adv.* earnestly, attentively.
intent'ness *n.*
inten'tion *n.* **1** the mental act of intending. **2** a plan, purpose, aim.
inten'tional *adj.* done, etc., on purpose, not by accident: *an intentional snub.*
inten'tionally *adv.*
to all intents and purposes practically, really.

intense *in-tens', adj.* **1** very great: *intense heat, bitterness.* **2** having, or showing, very strong feeling or great earnestness.
intense'ly *adv.* to a great degree.
intense'ness, **inten'sity** *ns.*
inten'sify *(-si-fī) v.t.* and *v.i.* to make, or to become, more intense, greater: *to intensify one's efforts*:—*pr.p.* **inten'sifying**; *pa.p.* **inten'sified**.
inten'sive *(-siv) adj.* **1** very great, very thorough: *intensive efforts, search.* **2** (of land cultivation) using methods intended to get the most out of the soil of a limited area.
inten'sively *adv.* **inten'siveness** *n.*
intensive care a unit in a hospital where a patient's condition is carefully monitored.

intent, **intention**, etc. See **intend**.

inter *in-tûr', v.t.* to bury:—*pr.p.* **interr'ing** *(-tûr')*; *pa.p.* **interred'** *(-tûrd')*.
inter'ment *n.*

inter- *in-tėr-, pfx.* in Eng. and L. words, between, amongst, together.

interact *in-tėr-akt', v.i.* to act on one another.
interac'tion *n.* **interac'tive** *adj.*

intercede *in-tėr-sēd', v.i.* **1** to try to act as peacemaker (between). **2** to plead (with someone for someone else): *to intercede with the king for, on behalf of, the rebels*: —*pr.p.* **interced'ing**.
intercess'ion *(-sesh') n.*
intercess'or *(-ses') n.*

intercept *in-tėr-sept', v.t.* **1** to stop or seize on the way from one place to another. **2** to cut off, interrupt (e.g. a view, light).
intercep'tion *n.* **intercep'tor, -ter** *n.*

intercession, etc. See **intercede**.

interchange *in-tėr-chānj', v.t.* to put each in the place of the other: *Interchange the two pictures.*—*v.t.* and *v.i.* to (cause to) occur in succession: *to interchange work with play*:—*pr.p.* **interchan'ging**.—Also *n.*
interchange'able *adj.*

intercom *in'tėr-kom, n.* a telephone system within a building, aeroplane, etc.

intercontinental *in'tėr-kon-ti-nen'tȧl, adj.* (travelling) between, or connecting, different continents.

intercourse *in'tėr-kōrs, -körs, n.* **1** dealings, communication (between people, etc.). **2** sexual intercourse (see **sex**).

interdependent *in-tėr-di-pen'dėnt, adj.* dependent on each other.
interdepen'dence *n.*

interdict *in'tėr-dikt, n.* an official prohibition.

interdisciplin'ary *in-tėr-dis-i-plin'ȧ-ri, adj.* involving, between, different branches of learning.

interest *in'trist, -tėr-ist, n.* **1** curiosity and attention: *to attract someone's interest.* **2** something that arouses these feelings: *Genealogy is one of his interests.* **3** power to arouse these feelings: *a book of great interest.* **4** concern, importance: *business deals of interest to me.* **5** a share in ownership: *bought an interest in the business.* **6** advantage: *It would be to your interest to keep in touch with him.* **7** a group of people involved in the same sort of e.g. political, business, or industrial activity who are likely to act to their common advantage: *The steel, banking interest.* **8** a sum paid on money lent (**simple interest**, on the borrowed money only; **compound interest**, on the borrowed money plus previous interest).—*v.t.* **1** to hold the attention of. **2** to be of importance to. **3** to rouse keenness in (someone) for some proposition, etc. (with *in*): *Can I interest you in (buying) this dictionary?*
in'terested *adj.* (often with *in*) **1** ready to give one's attention. **2** anxious to apply for a job, offer to buy something, etc. **3** (usu. used before a noun) in a position to gain or lose by some transaction and thus likely to be influenced by selfish motives: *the interested parties.*
in'teresting *adj.* arousing or holding one's curiosity and attention.
in the interest(s) of 1 for the benefit of (e.g. a person). **2** for the encouragement of: *in the interests of public safety.*
See also **disinterested, uninterested.**

interface *in'tėr-fās, (computers) n.* the connection between two systems or two parts of the same system.
in'terfacing *n.* strengthening fabric placed inside a garment.

interfere *in-tėr-fēr', v.i.* **1** to come, get, in the way: *He let nothing interfere with his golf.* **2** to meddle: *Stop interfering with the television, in my affairs:—pr.p.* **interfer'ing.**
interfēr'ence *n.*

interim *in'tėr-im, n.* **1** time between. **2** the meantime.—*adj.* temporary.

interior *in-tē'ri-ȯr, adj.* **1** inner. **2** inside a building. **3** inland.—*n.* **1** the inside. **2** the part away from coast, or frontier. **3** a picture of a scene within a house.

interject *in-tėr-jekt', v.t.* to exclaim, interrupting another speaker or a sentence of one's own.
interjec'tion. *n.*

interlace *in-tėr-lās', v.t., v.i.,* to twist or weave together:—*pr.p.* **interlac'ing.**

interleave *in-tėr-lēv', v.t.* to put blank pages between the pages of (a book), or between (pages):—*pr.p.* **interleav'ing.**

interlock *in-tėr-lok', v.t.* and *v.i.* **1** to fasten firmly together. **2** to fit into each other so as to work together.

interlope *in'tėr-lōp', v.i.* to intrude:—*pr.p.* **in'terloping.**
in'terloper *n.*

interlude *in'tėr-lōōd, -lūd, n.* **1** (a performance during) the break between parts of a play, etc. **2** a period, episode, etc. of a particular character.

intermarry *in-tėr-mar'i, v.i.* (of a race, family, etc.) to form marriages (with another race, family, etc.):—*pr.p.* **intermarr'ying**; *pa.p.* **intermarr'ied.**
intermarr'iage *n.*

intermediate *in-tėr-mē'di-it, adj.* placed or occurring between.
intermē'diary *n.* a go-between, one who acts between persons or parties in a negotiation:—*pl.* **intermē'diaries.**

interment. See **inter.**

interminable *in-tûr'mi-nȧ-bl, adj.* never ending; wearisomely long.

intermission *intėr-mish'(ȯ)n, n.* interval, pause.
intermitt'ent *adj.* stopping at intervals and beginning again.
intermitt'ence, intermitt'ency *ns.*
intermitt'ently *adv.*

intern *in-tûrn', v.t.* **1** to compel (an enemy alien) to live within a certain area. **2** to hold until the end of the war (a ship, plane) of a country that is fighting.—*n. (in'tûrn) (U.S.)* a resident doctor in a hospital.
internee' *(-nē') n.* one who is interned.
intern'ment *n.*

internal *in-tûr'nȧl, adj.* **1** in the interior of the body; in one's mind or soul. **2** within a country, organisation, etc.: *internal affairs.*
inter'nally *adv.*
internal-combustion engine an engine

in which the fuel, such as petrol vapour, is burned within the working cylinder.

international *in-tėr-nash'ȯn-ȧl, adj.* of, between or among, different nations.—*n.* **1** a game or contest between players of different nations. **2** a player who takes part in this (also **internat'ionalist**).
internat'ionally *adv.*

Internationale *in-tėr-nä-syō-näl', n.* an international communist song.

internecine *in-tėr-nē'sīn, adj.* **1** (of e.g. war) destructive to both sides. **2** within a group: *internecine feuds.*

internee, internment. See **intern**.

interplanetary *in-tėr-plan'ė-tȧ-ri, adj.* among the planets.

interplay *in'tėr-plā, n.* action of two things on each other.

interpolate *in-tûr'pȯ-lāt, v.t.* **1** to put in, interject. **2** to alter e.g. a book unfairly by putting in (a word, passage):—*pr.p.* **inter'-polating**.
interpolā'tion *n.*

interpose *in'tėr-pōz, v.t.* **1** to place between. **2** to put in (a remark) interrupting speaker(s).—*v.i.* to come into e.g. a dispute to try to settle it, or to support one party:—*pr.p.* **in'terposing**.

interpret *in-tûr'prit, v.t.* **1** to explain the meaning of, understand in a particular way: *a difficult poem to interpret*; *I interpret your remark as a threat.* **2** to bring out the meaning of (music, a play) by playing, acting. **3** to translate orally, as an interpreter (also *v.i.*).
interpretā'tion *n.*
inter'preter *n.* one who translates a speaker's words, as he speaks, into the language of his hearers.

interred, etc. See **inter**.

interregnum *in-tėr-reg'num, n.* the period between two reigns, or between the end of one government and the beginning of another.

interrelated *in-tė-ri-lā'tid, adj.* mutually connected.

interrogate *in-ter'ȯ-gāt, v.t.* to question thoroughly, esp. formally:—*pr.p.* **interr'-ogating**.
interrogā'tion *n.* **interr'ogātor** *n.*
interrog'ative *(-og'ȧ-tiv) adj.* asking a question.—*n.* an interrogative word (e.g. *why? who? where?*).

interrupt *in-tėr-upt', v.t.* **1** to make a break in (e.g. a speech, work). **2** to stop (a person) in the course of something he is saying or doing (also *v.i.*). **3** to block, cut off (e.g. a view).
interrup'tion *n.*

intersect *in-tėr-sekt', v.t.* to divide by cutting or crossing.—*v.i.* to cross one another.
intersec'tion *n.* **1** act or place of intersecting. **2** a crossroads.

intersperse *in-tėr-spûrs', v.t.* to scatter here and there in: *a serious talk interspersed with jokes*:—*pr.p.* **interspers'ing**.

interstellar *in-tėr-stel'ȧr, adj.* among, between, the stars: *interstellar space.*

interstice *in-tûr'stis, n.* a small space between things, or parts, close together.

intertwine *in-tėr-twīn', v.t., v.i.* to twine or twist together:—*pr.p.* **intertwin'ing**.

interval *in'tėr-vȧl, n.* **1** time or space between: *an interval of ten minutes, fifty years, of twenty feet.* **2** a break between parts of a play, etc. **3** the difference of pitch between two notes in music.
at intervals at times, or places, with time, space, between.

intervene *in-tėr-vēn', v.i.* (with *between, in*) **1** to be between two places. **2** to occur between two points of time. **3** to happen and so alter the course of events: *He planned to travel but death intervened.* **4** to join in a dispute between others in the hope of settling it. **5** to interfere:—*pr.p.* **interven'ing**.
interven'ing *adj.* **interven'tion** *(-ven') n.*

interview *in'tėr-vū, n.* **1** a formal meeting between a candidate for a position and (representative(s) of) those who are trying to fill it. **2** a conversation with someone important or interesting that is broadcast, or reported in e.g. a newspaper.—*v.t.* to see and question (a candidate, etc.).
in'terviewer *n.* one who interviews.

intestate *in-tes'tāt, adj.* without having made a will: *He died intestate.*

intestine *in-tes'tin, n.* (often *pl.*) the part of the alimentary canal between stomach and anus, having a narrow, twisting upper section (**small intestine**) and a wider, thick-walled lower section (**large intestine**).
intes'tinal (or *-tīn'*) *adj.*

intimate *in'tim-it, adj.* **1** close, affectionate: *an intimate friend, friendship, connection*; *an intimate gathering of close friends.* **2** private, personal: *intimate thoughts, affairs.* **3** deep, detailed: *an intimate knowledge of the subject.*—*n.* a familiar friend.—*v.t. (-māt)* **1** to hint, indicate. **2** to announce:—*pr.p.* **in'timating**.
in'timacy *(-mȧ-si) n.* close familiarity.
in'timately *adv.*
intimā'tion *n.* **1** the act of intimating. **2** a hint; an announcement.

intimidate *in-tim'i-dāt, v.t.* to strike fear into (a person) so that he does what one wants him to do:—*pr.p.* **intim'idating.**
intimidā'tion *n.*

into *in'too, prep.* **1** towards the inside of. **2** from one state to (another): *ice into water.* **3** expressing division: *2 into 4 goes twice.*

intolerable *in-tol'ėr-ȧ-bl, adj.* that cannot be endured or borne.
intol'erant *adj.* **1** not able or willing to endure (with *of*). **2** not willing to consider opinions, etc. different from one's own.
intol'erance *n.*

intonation *in-tȯ-nā'sh(ȯ)n, n.* rise and fall of the voice in speech.
intone' *in-tōn', v.t., v.i.* to chant, utter in musical tones:—*pr.p.* **inton'ing.**

in toto *in tō'tō* entirely; as a whole.

intoxicate *in-toks'i-kāt, v.t.* **1** to make drunk. **2** to excite with strong feelings:—*pr.p.* **intox'icating.**
intox'icant *n.* something that intoxicates.
intox'icating *adj.* **intox'icatingly** *adv.*
intoxicā'tion *n.*

intra- *in'trä-, in'trȧ-, pfx.* within.

intractable *in-trak'tȧ-bl, adj.* **1** (of a person, etc.) stubborn. **2** (of a thing) hard to deal with.

intransigent *in-trän'zi-jėnt,* or *-si-, adj.* refusing to compromise or come to an agreement.
intran'sigence, intran'sigency *ns.*

intra-uterine *in-trä-ū'tėr-īn, adj.* within the uterus.

intravenous *in-trȧ-vē'nu̇s, adj.* into, or within, a vein.

intrepid *in-trep'id, adj.* very bold, fearless: *an intrepid explorer; intrepid support of the cause.*
intrepid'ity *n.* **intrep'idly** *adv.*

intricate *in'tri-kit, adj.* tangled, complicated, having many details, difficult to understand or to deal with: *intricate pattern, machinery, arrangements.*
in'tricately *adv.* **in'tricateness** *n.*
in'tricacy *(-kȧ-si) n.* **1** intricateness. **2** something intricate:—*pl.* **in'tricacies.**

intrigue *in-trēg'* or *in', n.* **1** underhand scheming. **2** a plot. **3** an illicit love affair.—*v.i.* to plot, etc.—*v.t.* to puzzle, fascinate:—*pr.p.* **intrig'uing**; *pa.p.* **intrigued** *(-trēgd').*
intrig'uing *adj.* **intrig'uingly** *adv.*

intrinsic *in-trin'sik,* or *-zik, adj.* belonging to a thing as part of its nature: *The ring was set with valuable stones, so it had intrinsic as well as sentimental value.*
intrin'sically *adv.*

intro- *in-trō-, pfx.* inwards.

introduce *in-trȯ-dūs', v.t.* **1** to bring in. **2** to put, insert (into a place). **3** to bring to notice; to bring forward (e.g. a subject, bill, suggestion). **4** to present (a speaker, etc.) formally to an audience. **5** to make acquainted (with *to*): *I introduced him to my mother; She and I were introduced at the party; We were introduced to algebra at primary school:*—*pr.p.* **introdu'cing.**
introduc'tion *n.* **1** the, an, act of introducing. **2** an explanation at the beginning of a book, etc., a preface.
introduc'tory *adj.*

introspection *in-trȯ-spek'sh(ȯ)n, n.* studying one's own mind and thoughts.
introspec'tive *adj.*

in'trovert *in'trō-vûrt, n.* a person much concerned with his own thoughts and feelings.—opp. to *extrovert.*—Also *adj.*

intrude *in-trōōd', v.t.* **1** to force, thrust in. **2** to thrust (oneself) uninvited or unwelcome (also *v.i.*):—*pr.p.* **intrud'ing.**
intrud'er *n.*
intru'sion *in-trōō'zh(ȯ)n, n.*
intru'sive *(-siv) adj.* **intru'siveness** *n.*

intuition *in-tū-ish'(ȯ)n, n.* **1** the power of seeing the truth directly without reasoning. **2** a truth so perceived.
intū'itive *adj.*

inundate *in'un-dāt, v.t.* **1** to flood. **2** to overwhelm (a person) with something in very great quantity: *to inundate someone with circulars, questions:*—*pr.p.* **in'undating.**

inure *in-ūr', v.t.* to make (a person) accustomed, hardened (to):—*pr.p.* **inur'ing.**

invade *in-vād, v.t.* **1** to enter as, or as if as, an enemy. **2** to encroach on (someone else's right):—*pr.p.* **invad'ing.**
invād'er *n.* **invā'sion** *(-zh(ȯ)n) n.*

invalid[1] *in-val'id, adj.* **1** (of reasoning, an argument) not sound. **2** (of a contract, etc.) without legal force, not valid.
invalid'ity *n.*
inval'idate *v.t.* to make invalid:—*pr.p.* **inval'idating.**

invalid[2] *in'vȧ-lid, n.* a person who is ill or disabled.—Also *adj.*—*v.t.* **1** to make an invalid. **2** to discharge as an invalid: *He was invalided out of the army.*

invaluable *in-val'ū-ȧ-bl, adj.* of value too great to be estimated: *invaluable assistance; This information was invaluable to him.*

invariable *in-vār'i-ȧ-bl, adj.* not changing, always the same.
invar'iably *adv.* always: *He invariably arrived as we were about to go out.*

invasion. See **invade**.

invective *in-vek'tiv*, *n.* violent attack in words, violent abuse.
inveigh *in-vā'*, *v.i.* to make an attack in words (against).

inveigle *in-vē'gl*, *-vā'*, *v.t.* to draw, entice, wheedle (into):—*pr.p.* **inveig'ling**.
invei'glement *n.*

invent *in-vent'*, *v.t.* **1** to make, or use, for the first time (e.g. a machine, a method). **2** to make up (e.g. a story, an excuse).
inven'tion *n.* **inven'tor** *n.*
inven'tive *adj.* quick to invent, ingenious: *an inventive mind.*

inventory *in'vėn-tȯr-i*, *tri*, *n.* a formal detailed list of goods (e.g. of house furniture, business stock):—*pl.* **in'ventories**.

inverse. See **invert**.

invert *in-vûrt'*, *v.t.* **1** to turn upside down. **2** to reverse the order of.
inversion *in-vûr'sh(ȯ)n*, *n.*
inverse *in-vûrs'*, *in'*, *adj.* (of e.g. order) opposite, reverse.—*n.* the opposite.
inversely (*-vûrs'*, or *in'*) *adv.*
inverted commas. See **comma**.

invertebrate *in-vûr'ti-brit*, *adj.* (of an animal, e.g. a worm) not having a backbone.—Also *n.*

invest[1] *in-vest'*, *v.t.* **1** to clothe, surround, endow (a person, place, etc. with a quality): *to invest with virtue, interest, mystery.* **2** to place formally in office or authority. **3** to lay siege to.
inves'titure *(-ti-chu̇r)* *n.* (a ceremony of) giving (the robes, etc. of) high rank or office to someone.
invest'ment *n.*

invest[2] *in-vest'*, *v.t.* and *v.i.* (with *in*) **1** to lay out (money) for profit, e.g. by buying shares: *He invested (£10 000) in a building firm.* **2** to spend (money, time, energy) on something: *We should invest (our savings) in a new car.*
invest'ment *n.* **1** placing of money to gain profit. **2** something in which money is invested.
inves'tor *n.*
investment trust an organisation that invests its stockholders' money and distributes the net return among them.

investigate *in-ves'ti-gāt*, *v.t.* to inquire into with care:—*pr.p.* **inves'tigating**.
investigā'tion *n.* **inves'tigātive** *adj.*
inves'tigātor *n.*

investment. See **invest**[1,2].

inveterate *in-vet'ėr-it*, *adj.* **1** firmly fixed in a habit by long practice: *an inveterate liar.* **2** (of a habit, quality, etc.) firmly established.
invet'eracy *(-ȧ-si)* *n.*
invet'erately *adv.*

invidious *in-vid'i-u̇s*, *adj.* likely to cause ill-will or sense of injustice.
invid'iously *adv.* **invid'iousness** *n.*

invigilate *in-vij'i-lāt*, *v.t.* and *v.i.* to supervise (an examination):—*pr.p.* **invig'ilating**.
invigilā'tion *n.* **invig'ilātor** *n.*

invigorate *in-vig'ȯr-āt*, *v.t.* to give vigour, strength, energy, to:—*pr.p.* **invig'orating**.
invig'orating *adj.* **invigorā'tion** *n.*

invincible *in-vin'si-bl*, *adj.* that cannot be overcome, defeated, or surmounted.
invincibil'ity, **invin'cibleness** *ns.*
invin'cibly *adv.*

inviolable *in-vī'ȯ-lȧ-bl*, *adj.* (of e.g. an oath, a right, a person) that must be treated as sacred, not to be broken, infringed, harmed.
inviolabil'ity, **invī'olably** *adv.*
invī'olate *adj.* not violated, disturbed, broken, or infringed.

invisible *in-viz'i-bl*, *adj.* not able to be seen, not visible.
invisibil'ity, **invis'ibleness** *ns.*
invis'ibly *adv.*

invite *in-vīt'*, *v.t.* **1** to ask to come (e.g. to a meeting, to stay). **2** to ask for: *to invite suggestions.* **3** to act in such a way, or be of such a kind, as to encourage: *to invite danger, criticism*:—*pr.p.* **invit'ing**.
invitā'tion *(-vi-)* *n.*
invīt'ing *adj.* attractive, tempting.

invocation. See **invoke**.

invoice *in'vois*, *n.* a list sent with goods giving details of price and quantity.—*v.t.* to make such a list of (goods); to send such a list to (a customer):—*pr.p.* **in'voicing**.

invoke *in-vōk'*, *v.t.* **1** to address (God, etc.) in prayer, asking for help. **2** to ask for (e.g. help). **3** to quote as giving support to what one has said: *to invoke the Bible, the authority of one's party leader.* **4** to call forth (a spirit):—*pr.p.* **invok'ing**.
invocā'tion *n.*

involuntary *in-vol'u̇n-tȧr-i*, *adj.* **1** not under control of the will. **2** not done from choice. **3** unintentional.
invol'untarily *adv.*

involve *in-volv'*, *v.t.* **1** to wrap up, entangle (in). **2** to cause to be associated with or concerned in: *Don't involve me in your intrigues.* **3** to include. **4** to require, or bring as a result: *Automation involves reducing the number of workmen.* **5** to lead into difficulty or disagreement (with another):—*pr.p.* **invol'ving**.
involved' *adj.* **1** (of e.g. a story) complicated. **2** (of affairs) in confusion.
involve'ment *n.*

invulnerable *in-vul'nėr-ȧ-bl, adj.* that cannot be wounded, damaged, successfully attacked.

inward *in'wȧrd, adj.* **1** being on, or moving towards, the inside. **2** in the mind or soul.—*adv.* **1** (also **in'wards**) towards the inside. **2** into the mind or soul.

in'wardly *adv.* **1** within. **2** privately, in the thoughts: *He was inwardly pleased; inwardly laughing.*

iodine *ī'ȯ-dēn, n.* an element that is not a metal which gives a violet-coloured vapour.

ī'odise *v.t.* to treat with iodine:—*pr.p.* **ī'odising.**

ion *ī'ȯn, n.* an electrically charged atom or group of atoms that has become so by losing or gaining electrons.

ī'onise *v.t., v.i.* to convert, or be converted, into ion(s):—*pr.p.* **ī'onising.**

īon'osphere *n.* the regions of the upper atmosphere of the earth that contain ions and reflect radio waves.

iota *ī-ō'tȧ, n.* a very small quantity.

I O U *ī ō ū, n.* a signed acknowledgment of a debt.

ir- *ir-, pfx.* See **in.**

irascible *i-ras'i-bl, adj.* easily angered, irritable.

irascibil'ity *n.* **iras'cibly** *adv.*

ire *īr, n.* anger.

irate *ī-rāt', adj.* angry.

iridescence, etc. See **iris.**

iris *ī'ris, n.* **1** the coloured part of the eye. **2** a brightly-coloured flower with sword-shaped leaves:—*pl.* **ī'rises.**

iridescence *ir-i-des'ėns, n.* display of rainbow colours e.g. on a bubble.

irides'cent *adj.*

Irish *ī'rish, adj.* **1** belonging to Ireland, or its inhabitants or language. **2** (*humorous*) comically illogical.—*n.* the Celtic language of Ireland.

irk *ûrk, v.t.* to weary, annoy: *Letter-writing irks me; It irks me to have to write letters.*

irk'some *adj.*

iron *ī'ėn, n.* **1** an element, a common metal from which steel is made, noted for strength and hardness. **2** a golf-club with an iron head. **3** a flat-bottomed instrument that is heated up and used for smoothing clothes. **4** (in *pl.*) fetters.—Also *adj.*—*v.t.* to smooth with a flat-iron.—Also *v.i.*

Iron Age an early period of history in which cutting tools and weapons were made of iron.

i'ronclad *adj.* covered with iron plates.—*n.* a ship so protected.

Iron Curtain the barrier, considered to exist between Communist and other countries, that prevents free communication and trading.

iron foundry a foundry where cast iron is made.

iron lung an apparatus in which changes of pressure are used to force a patient to breathe in and out.

i'ronmonger *n.* a dealer in **i'ronmongery**, articles of metal, e.g. tools, locks, etc., and other goods.

iron ration a small allowance of nutritious food esp. for use in emergency.

i'ronworks *n.pl.* or *n.sing* works where iron is smelted or made into heavy goods.

iron out to smooth out (difficulties).

several, too many, irons in the fire several, too many, jobs, etc., in hand at once.

strike while the iron is hot to act while the situation is favourable.

ironic(al). See **irony.**

irony *ī'rȯ-ni, n.* **1** a form of deliberate mockery in which one says the opposite of what is obviously true, e.g. 'That's clever!' to someone who has broken something. **2** a result that seems to mock previous thoughts, efforts, etc.: *By an irony of fate, he got what he had struggled for when it was no longer of use to him.* **3** (in plays) words which, unknown to the speaker himself, have reference to unhappy past or future events about which the audience has been told:—*pl.* **i'ronies.**

ironic(al) *ī-ron'ik(ȧl), adjs.*

iron'ically *adv.*

irradiate *i-rā'di-āt, v.t.* **1** to shed light or other rays on. **2** to light up (esp. the face with joy):—*pr.p.* **irrad'iating.**

irrational *i-rash'ȯn-ȧl, adj.* not reasonable, illogical: *irrational fears.*

irrational'ity *n.* **irra'tionally** *adv.*

irreconcilable *i-rek-ȯn-sīl'ȧ-bl, adj.* **1** (of people) who cannot be reconciled or brought (back) to friendship or agreement. **2** (of e.g. statements) that cannot both be true.

irreconcil'ably *adv.*

irrecoverable *ir-i-kuv'ėr-ȧ-bl, adj.* that cannot be recovered or regained.

irredeemable *ir-i-dē'mȧ-bl, adj.* that cannot be redeemed.

irredeem'ably *adv.* hopelessly (bad, lost, etc.)

irreducible *ir-i-dū'si-bl, adj.* that cannot be reduced or made less.

irrefutable *i-ref'ū-tȧ-bl, -ri-fūt', adj.* (of e.g. an argument) that cannot be refuted or proved false.

irregular *i-reg'ū-lȧr, adj.* **1** not regular. **2** uneven, variable. **3** not according to rule or regulation. **4** (of troops) not forming part of the forces trained by the state.
irregular'ity *n.* (*pl.* **-ies**).
irreg'ularly *adv.*

irrelevant *i-rel'ė-vȧnt, adj.* not relevant, not having anything to do with the subject under discussion.
irrel'evance, -cy *n.* **irrel'evantly** *adv.*

irreligious *ir-i-lij'ůs, adj.* not religious, impious.

irremediable *ir-i-mē'di-ȧ-bl, adj.* that cannot be remedied.

irremovable *ir-i-mōō'vȧ-bl, adj.* that cannot be removed.
irremo'vably *adv.*

irreparable *i-rep'ȧ-rȧ-bl, adj.* (of injury, loss, etc.) not reparable, that cannot be undone, remedied, made good.
irrep'arably *adv.* in a way that makes remedy etc. impossible.

irreplaceable *ir-i-plā'sȧ-bl, adj.* not replaceable, because too good, rare, etc.

irrepressible *ir-i-pres'i bl, adj.* (of e.g. person, high spirits) not to be repressed or kept under control.
irrepress'ibly *adv.*

irreproachable *ir-i-prō'chȧ-bl, adj.* **1** that cannot be reproached, free from blame. **2** faultless.

irresistible *ir-i-zis'ti-bl, adj.* **1** that cannot be resisted or withstood. **2** extremely charming.
irresistibil'ity, irresis'tibleness *ns.*
irresis'tibly *adv.*

irresolute *i-rez'ȯ-lōōt, -lūt, adj.* **1** not firm in purpose. **2** hesitating.
irres'oluteness, irresolu'tion *ns.*
irres'olutely *adv.*

irrespective *ir-i-spek'tiv, adj.*: **irrespective of** not taking into account, without regard to: *He chose his staff for their ability irrespective of their race.*

irresponsible *i-ri-spon'si-bl, adj.* not capable of, or showing, reliability or a sense of duty: *an irresponsible person; irresponsible conduct.*
irresponsibil'ity *n.* **irrespon'sibly** *adv.*

irretraceable *ir-i-trā'sȧ-bl, adj.* (of a step) that cannot be retraced.

irretrievable *ir-i-trē'vȧ-bl, adj.* (of e.g. something lost, a mistake, ruin) that cannot be retrieved, recovered, undone, made up for.
irretrie'vably *adv.*

irreverent *i-rev'ėr-ėnt, adj.* **1** not reverent. **2** showing lack of respect.
irrev'erence *n.* **irrev'erently** *adv.*

irreversible *ir-i-vûr'si-bl, adj.* **1** that cannot be reversed. **2** (*medical*) (involving damage to the body that is) permanent.

irrevocable *i-rev'ȯ-kȧ-bl, adj.* that cannot be revoked or taken back: *an irrevocable decision.*
irrevocabil'ity *n.* **irrev'ocably** *adv.*

irrigate *ir'i-gāt, v.t.* **1** (of rivers) to supply (land) with water. **2** to water (land) by means of canals, etc.:—*pr.p.* **irr'igating.**
irrigā'tion *n.*

irritable, irritant. See **irritate.**

irritate *ir'i-tāt, v.t.* **1** to make angry or impatient. **2** to make (the skin, etc.) red, painful, etc., e.g. by rubbing:—*pr.p.* **irr'itating.**
irr'itable *adj.* easily annoyed.
irritabil'ity, irr'itableness *ns.*
irr'itably *adv.*
irr'itant *n.* something that causes irritation.—Also *adj.*
irritā'tion *n.* **irr'itating** *adj.*

irruption *i-rup'sh(ȯ)n, n.* a breaking in, sudden invasion.

is. See **be.**

Islam *iz'läm, -läm', n.* **1** the Muslim religion, founded by Mohammed. **2** the Muslim world.
Islam'ic *adj.*

island *ī'lȧnd, n.* **1** a mass of land surrounded by water. **2** anything isolated, detached, or surrounded by something of a different nature.
islander *ī'lȧnd-ėr, n.*

isle *īl, n.* an island.
islet *ī'lit, n.* a little isle.

iso- *ī-sō-, pfx.* equal.
i'sobar *n.* a line on a map passing through places where atmospheric pressure is equal.
isomer *(-mėr) n.* one of two or more substances that have the same molecules but have them differently arranged.
isosceles *ī-sos'i-lēz, adj.* (of a triangle) having two sides equal.
i'sotherm *n.* a line passing through places that have the same temperature.
isotope *(-tōp) n.* one of two or more kinds of atom of the same element, some being heavier than others (e.g. the atoms of 'heavy hydrogen') and some radioactive (e.g. the atoms of the kind of iodine occurring in fall-out from a nuclear explosion).

isolate *ī'sȯ-lāt, v.t.* **1** to set apart, place alone. **2** to separate (something from something else). **3** to keep (an infected person) away from others to whom he might give the disease:—*pr.p.* **isolating.**
i'solated *adj.* **1** lonely, remote. **2** solitary,

alone. **3** not part of a group or trend: *an isolated case*.

isolā'tion *n*.

isolā'tionist *n*. a person who objects to his country's playing a part in international affairs.

isomer, **isosceles**, **isotherm**, **isotope**. See **iso**.

Israeli *iz-rā'li*, *adj*. of modern Israel.—*n*. a native of Israel.

issue *is'ū*, *ish'ōō*, *n*. **1** a flowing out, or the place of it. **2** the act of sending out. **3** distribution. **4** publication. **5** something that comes out. **6** the quantity distributed or published at one time. **7** a result, outcome. **8** children: *died without issue*. **9** a point, esp. important, under discussion or causing dispute.—*v.i.* **1** to flow, come out or spring (from any source). **2** to result (from).—*v.t.* **1** to send out or distribute. **2** to publish:—*pr.p.* **iss'uing**.

at issue being disputed.

join, **take**, **issue** (**with**) to disagree, argue (with) (on a point, etc.).

isthmus *is(th)'mùs*, *n*. a narrow neck of land joining two larger pieces.

it *it*, *pron*. **1** the thing, animal, or child spoken of: *She took an egg and cracked it*; *Put the baby down if it is heavy*. **2** used in sentences (e.g. about the weather) without a real subject: *It rains continually*. **3** used (with little meaning) as the object of some verbs: *There's no bus—we'll have to walk it*:—*objective* **it**; *possessive* **its** (sometimes described as *possessive adj*.).

itself' *pron*. emphatic, or reflexive, form of *it*: *The house is well-furnished but it itself is rather ugly*; *The cow hurt itself by swallowing a piece of wire*.

Italian *i-tal'yàn*, *adj*. of Italy or its people or language.—*n*. **1** a native of Italy. **2** the language of Italy.

ital'ic *adj*. of a sloping type, orig. introduced in Italy, used esp. for emphasis as in '*very* bad'.—*n*. (in *pl*.) this type.

ital'icise *(-i-sīz)* *v.t.* to put in italics:—*pr.p.* **ital'icising**.

itch *ich*, *n*. **1** an irritating sensation in the skin that makes one want to scratch. **2** a restless desire (to do something).—*v.i.* **1** to have an itch. **2** to desire strongly.

itch'y *adj*.:—*comp* **itch'ier**; *superl*. **itch'iest**.

itch'iness *n*.

item *ī'tèm*, *n*. **1** a separate article, esp. one of a number named in a list. **2** a separate piece of information or news.

i'temise *v.i.* to list item by item:—*pr.p.* **i'temising**.

itinerant *i-tin'èr-ànt*, *adj* making journeys from place to place on business, etc.—*n*. a person who does so, esp. judge, preacher, pedlar.

itin'eracy, **itin'erancy** *ns*.

itin'erary (or *ī*-) *n*. **1** a route. **2** a plan or record of a journey:—*pl*. **itin'eraries**.

its. See **it**.

it's *its* a shortening of **it is** or **it has**.

itself. See **it**.

ivory *ī'vò-ri*, *n*. **1** the hard white substance forming most of the tusk of an elephant, walrus, etc. **2** a carving, etc., in ivory:—*pl*. **i'vories**.—*adj*. made of, or like, ivory.

ivy *ī'vi*, *n*. a creeping evergreen plant on trees and walls.

J

jab *jab*, *v.t.* and *v.i.* to poke, stab:—*pr.p.* **jabb'ing**; *pa.p.* **jabbed**.—*n.* a sudden thrust or stab.

jabber *jab'ėr*, *v.i.* to chatter, talk rapidly.—Also *v.t.*—*n.* rapid confused speaking.
jabb'erer *n.* **jabb'eringly** *adv.*

jabot *zha'bō*, *n.* **1** a frill of lace, etc., formerly worn in front of a woman's dress or on a man's shirt front. **2** a similar one worn with Highland full dress.

jack *jak*, *n.* **1** a worthless fellow. **2** a sailor. **3** any instrument that does the work of a boy or helper, as a *bootjack* for taking off boots, a machine for turning a spit in roasting meat, an instrument for lifting heavy weights. **4** the male of some animals. **5** the knave in a pack of cards. **6** the small white ball which is the mark aimed at in bowls. **7** a small ship's flag, esp. one showing nationality.
jack'-a-lan'tern, jack'-o-lan'tern *n.* **1** a will-o'-the-wisp. **2** (*U.S.*) a lantern carved out of a pumpkin.
jack'boot *n.* **1** a large boot reaching to the knee, formerly worn by cavalry. **2** brutal military rule, oppression.
Jack Frost frost personified.
jack'-in-the-box *n.* a box with a figure in it which springs up when the lid is opened.
jack'-knife *n.* **1** a large clasp knife. **2** a type of fancy dive.—*v.i.* (of e.g. an articulated lorry) to double up through faulty control forming an angle of 90° or less.—*v.t.* to cause to do so:—*pr.p.* **jack'-knifing**.
jack'-of-all'-trades *n.* one who can turn his hand to any job.
jack'pot *n.* a prize-money fund.
jack'-rabbit *n.* a long-eared American hare.
jack'-tar' *n.* a sailor.
every man jack one and all.
hit the jackpot 1 to win a jackpot. **2** to have a big success.
jack up to lift (e.g. a car) by means of a jack.

jackal *jak'öl*, *n.* **1** a wild animal, similar to dog and wolf, that eats carrion. **2** a contemptible person—either one who does the dirty work for others, or one who claims a share of profit without facing the danger of obtaining it.

jackanapes *jak'ȧ-nāps*, *n.* an impudent fellow.

jackass *jak'as*, *n.* **1** a male ass. **2** a blockhead.
laughing jackass a kookaburra, an Australian kingfisher that laughs.

jackboot. See **jack**.

jackdaw *jak'dö*, *n.* a kind of small crow.

jacket *jak'it*, *n.* **1** a short coat. **2** a cover, casing. **3** a loose paper cover for a book.
jack'eted *adj.* wearing, in, a jacket.

jackpot. See **jack**.

Jacobite *jak'ō-bīt*, *n.* a supporter of James II and VII or his descendants.—Also *adj.*

Jacob's ladder *jā'kȯbz lad'ėr* **1** a ladder of ropes with wooden steps, used on a ship. **2** a plant with ladder-like leaves.

Jacuzzi® *jȧ-ko͞o'zi*, *n.* a type of bath or small pool equipped with a mechanism that agitates the water to provide extra invigoration.

jade[1] *jād*, *n.* a gemstone, usu. green.

jade[2] *jād*, *n.* **1** a worn-out horse. **2** a worthless ill-tempered woman.
ja'ded *adj.* **1** worn-out, tired. **2** often used of appetite (for food or pleasure) that has been indulged too much.

jag *jag*, *n.* **1** a notch. **2** a splinter. **3** a prick. **4** (*coll.*) an injection. **5** a sharp point of rock.—*v.t.* **1** to prick. **2** to notch. **3** to tear (cloth, etc.) unevenly:—*pr.p.* **jagg'ing**; *pa.p.* **jagged**.
jagged *jag'id*, *adj.* notched, rough-edged.
jagg'edly *adv.* **jagg'edness** *n.*

jaguar *jag'ū-är*, *jag'wär*, *n.* a South American beast of prey, one of the cat family, resembling the leopard.

jail, gaol *jāl*, *n.* a prison.
jail'er, **jail'or**, **gaol'er** *n.* one who has charge of a jail or of prisoner(s).
jail'-bird, **gaol'-bird** *n.* a person who is or has been in jail.

jalousie *zhal'oo-zē*, or *-zē'*, *n.* an outside shutter with slats.

jam[1] *jam*, *n.* **1** a preserve of fruit boiled with sugar. **2** something pleasant or easy.

jam[2] *jam*, *v.t.* **1** to press or squeeze tight. **2** to crowd full. **3** to wedge. **4** to bring (machinery) to a standstill by causing the parts to stick: *He jammed the wheel.* **5** to interfere with (a wireless signal) by sending out other signals.—*v.i.* **1** to become fixed, immovable: *The door often jams.* **2** in jazz, to play enthusiastically with no set pattern:—*pr.p.* **jamm'ing**; *pa.p.* **jammed**.—Also *n.*

jamb *jam, v.t.* the side post of a door or fireplace, etc.

jamboree *jam-bō-rē', n.* **1** a noisy frolic. **2** a large (international or national) gathering of Scouts.

jangle *jang'gl, v.t.* **1** to sound (bells, etc.) harshly. **2** to cause a feeling of irritation in (one's nerves).—*v.i.* **1** to sound harshly. **2** to quarrel:—*pr.p.* **jang'ling**. —*n.* **1** a harsh, discordant sound. **2** a quarrel.
jang'ler *n.* **jang'ling** *n.*

janitor *jan'i-tor, n.* **1** a doorkeeper. **2** a caretaker:—*fem.* **jan'itress**.

January *jan'ū-ar-i, n.* the first month of the year.

japan *ja-pan', v.t.* to cover with a coat of hard black varnish like that on Japanese lacquered ware:—*pr.p.* **japann'ing**; *pa.p.* **japanned'**.
Japanese *ja-pan-ēz', n.* **1** a native of Japan (*pl.* **Japanese**). **2** the language of Japan.—Also *adj.*

jar[1] *jär, v.i.* **1** to make a harsh or unpleasant sound or vibration. **2** to grate (on): *Her insincere praise jarred on me.*—*v.t.* to cause to vibrate unpleasantly:—*pr.p.* **jarr'ing**; *pa.p.* **jarred**.—*n.* **1** a harsh sudden vibration. **2** a shock to body, nerves, feelings.

jar[2] *jär, n.* an earthen or glass bottle with a wide mouth.

jargon *jär'gon, n.* **1** confused talk difficult to understand. **2** the special vocabulary of a trade, science, art, etc.

jasmine *jas'min, n.* a climbing shrub with, in most kinds, fragrant flowers.

jasper *jas'pėr, n.* a precious stone, a type of quartz of various colours.

jaundice *jön'dis, n.* a disease which causes yellowness of eyes and skin.
jaun'diced *adj.* **1** suffering from jaundice. **2** (of a person or his judgment) affected by envy, disappointment, etc.: *He took a jaundiced view of life.*

jaunt *jönt, v.i.* to go from place to place, journey for pleasure.—*n.* an excursion or trip for pleasure.
jaun'ting *adj.* and *n.*

jaunty *jön'ti, adj.* having a lively, carefree manner:—*comp.* **jaun'tier**; *superl.* **jaun'tiest**.
jaun'tily *adv.* **jaun'tiness** *n.*

Javanese *jä-va-nēz', n.* **1** a native of Java (*pl.* **Javanese**). **2** the language of central Java.—Also *adj.*

javelin *jav'(ė)-lin, n.* a light spear thrown by the hand.

jaw *jö, n.* **1** the bones of the mouth in which the teeth are set. **2** (in *pl.*) a narrow entrance, e.g. of a valley.
jaw'bone *n.*

jay *jā, n.* a noisy bird of the crow family with bright feathers.
jay'walker (*coll.*) *n.* a careless pedestrian who does not obey traffic regulations.

jazz *jaz, n.* music developed from the rhythms of the U.S. Negro folk music, having special features of melody, syncopation, etc., and allowing freedom to improvise.
jazz'y *adj.* **1** loud in colour. **2** suggesting jazz music:—*comp.* **jazz'ier**; *superl.* **jazz'iest**.
jazz band combinations of instruments, such as drums, banjo, trumpet, saxophone, clarinet, and piano, suitable for playing jazz.
jazz up to make more interesting, exciting, etc.

jealous *jel'us, adj.* **1** desiring to have what belongs to another, envious. **2** fearing rivalry. **3** guarding anxiously (with *of*): *jealous of his rights.*
jeal'ously *adv.* **jeal'ousy** *n.* (*pl.* **-ies**).

jean *jēn, n.* **1** a type of cotton cloth. **2** (in *pl.*) clothes of this, esp. trousers of blue jean.

jeep *jēp, n.* a small motor vehicle used by U.S. and other armed forces.

jeer *jēr, v.t.* to make fun of.—*v.i.* to scoff (at).—*n.* a taunting remark.
jeer'ingly *adv.*

Jehovah *ji-hō'vä, n.* the Hebrew God, a name used by Christians since 16th cent.

jelly *jel'i, n.* **1** the juice of a fruit boiled in sugar. **2** anything in a half-solid state:—*pl.* **jell'ies**.
jell *v.i.* **1** to set. **2** (*coll.*) to take shape.
jell'ied *adj.* **1** in the state of jelly. **2** covered with or in jelly.
jelly baby, **jell'ybean** *ns.* a baby-shaped, or bean-shaped, jelly sweet.
jell'yfish *n.* a sea animal with a jelly-like body:—*pl.* **jell'yfish(es)**.

jemmy *jem'i, n.* a burglar's short crowbar:—*pl.* **jemm'ies**.

jeopardy *jep'ard-i, n.* danger, peril.
jeop'ardise *v.t.* to put in danger:—*pr.p.* **jeop'ardising**.

jerboa *jûr-bō'a, n.* a small desert animal that has long hindlegs and jumps like a kangaroo.

jerk *jûrk, n.* a short sudden movement.—*v.t.* to move with a jerk.—Also *v.i.*
jer'ky *adj.*:—*comp.* **jer'kier**; *superl.* **jer'kiest**.
jer'kiness *n.*

jerkin *jûr'kin, n.* a short coat or waistcoat.

jerry-built *jer'i-bilt*, *adj.* flimsy, built hastily and cheaply.

jersey *jûr'zi*, *n.* **1** combed wool. **2** a knitted upper garment or jacket. **3** a fine knitted cotton, nylon, etc. fabric. **4** a cow of Jersey breed.

Jerusalem artichoke. See **artichoke**.

jest *jest*, *n.* a joke; something said in fun; something to be laughed at.—*v.i.* **1** to make a jest. **2** to laugh (at).
jes'ter **1** one who jests. **2** (in olden times) a king's or nobleman's fool, whose job it was to amuse his master.
jes'ting *n.* and *adj.* **jes'tingly** *adj.*
in jest as a joke.

Jesuit *jez'ū-it*, *n.* one of the Society of Jesus, an order of monks founded in 1534.

jet[1] *jet*, *n.* a hard black mineral substance, used for ornaments.
jet'-black' *adj.* very black.

jet[2] *jet*, *n.* **1** a gush of liquid or gas through a narrow opening or nozzle: *He directed a jet of water on the flames.* **2** a jet plane.—*v.t.* and *v.i.* to spout:—*pr.p.* **jett'ing**; *pa.p.* **jett'ed**.
jet'-lag *n.* tiredness, inability to concentrate, etc. caused by a person's normal working and sleeping patterns being upset by his travelling long distances rapidly by air.
jet plane one driven by air which is sucked in, heated, and forced out towards the rear.
jet propulsion a method of producing forward motion by expelling air or liquid (which has been sucked in) at high speed from behind.
jet set rich people who enjoy a life of frequent jet travel and expensive holidays.

jetsam *jet'sàm*, *n.* **1** goods thrown overboard and washed up on the shore. **2** goods from a wreck that (unlike *flotsam*) remain under water.
jett'ison *n.* the act of throwing goods overboard to lighten a ship.—*v.t.* **1** to throw overboard in times of danger. **2** to abandon.

jetty *jet'i*, *n.* a small pier:—*pl.* **jett'ies**.

Jew *jōō*, *n.* a person of Hebrew descent and religion:—*fem.* **Jew'ess** (not now polite).
Jew'ish *adj.* **Jew'ishness** *n.*
Jew's-harp' *n.* a small musical instrument played by holding between the teeth and striking a metal tongue with the finger.

jewel *jōō'ėl*, *n.* **1** a precious stone. **2** anything or anyone highly valued.—*v.t.* to adorn or dress with jewels:—*pr.p.* **jew'elling**; *pa.p.* **jew'elled**.
jew'eller *n.* one who makes or deals in ornaments of precious stones, etc.
jew'ellery, **jew'elry** *jōō'ėl-ri*, *n.* articles made by a jeweller.

jib *jib*, *n.* **1** a three-cornered sail in front of a ship's foremast. **2** the jutting-out arm of a crane.—*v.i.* **1** (of a sail) to shift from one side to the other. **2** (of a horse) to shy or balk. **3** (with *at*) to refuse to do (an action):—*pr.p.* **jibb'ing**; *pa.p.* **jibbed**.

jibe *jīb*, *v.i.* to scoff, jeer (at).—Also *v.t.*:—*pr.p.* **jib'ing**.—*n.* a jeer, a taunt.—Also **gibe**.

jig *jig*, *n.* **1** a lively dance. **2** a pattern used in a machine shop.—*v.t.* and *v.i.* **1** to dance (a jig). **2** to move rapidly and jerkily:—*pr.p.* **jigg'ing**; *pa.p.* **jigged**.
jigg'er *n.* **1** anything that jigs. **2** a warehouse crane. **3** the rest for the cue in billiards. **4** one of the 'iron' golf clubs. **5** (*coll.*) a device, gadget. **6** a small measure for drinks.
jigg'le *v.t.* and *v.i.* to move with wiggles and jerks:—*pr.p.* **jigg'ling**.
jig'saw *n.* **1** a narrow saw (usu. power-driven) used for cutting curved lines. **2** a jigsaw puzzle.
jigsaw puzzle a picture cut into pieces to be fitted together.

jilt *jilt*, *v.t.* to discard (a lover) after encouragement.

jingle *jing'gl*, *n.* **1** a clinking sound, such as that of coins shaken together. **2** verse in short lines with quick rhythm and repeated sounds.—Also *v.i.* and *v.t.*:—*pr.p.* **jin'gling**.

jinricksha(w) *jin-rik'shä*, *-shö*. See **rickshaw**.

jinx *jingks*, (*slang*) *n.* **1** a bringer of bad luck. **2** an evil spell or influence.

jitter *jit'ėr*, (*slang*) *v.i.* to be nervous.
jitt'ery *adj.* **jitt'eriness** *n.*
(the) jitt'ers *n.pl.* a nervous, alarmed state.

jive *jīv*, *n.* (dancing to) a lively type of jazz.—*v.i.* to dance or play jive:—*pr.p.* **jiv'ing**.

job *job*, *n.* **1** a person's daily work, employment. **2** a definite piece of work. **3** any work done for a fixed price. **4** a state of affairs: *This is a bad job.*—*v.i.* to work at jobs.—*v.t.* to buy and sell, as a broker:—*pr.p.* **jobb'ing**; *pa.p.* **jobbed**.
jobb'ing *adj* (used only before a noun) doing odd jobs for payment: *a jobbing gardener.*
jobb'ery *n.* dishonest means used for private gain.
job'less *adj.* having no paid employment.—Also *n.*

job centre, **Job'centre** a government-run office where information about available jobs is shown.
a good luck a lucky circumstance.
a job lot a mixed collection (e.g. of goods), esp. if of poor quality.

jockey *jok'i*, *n.* a man (orig. a boy) who rides in a horse race:—*pl.* **jock'eys.**—*v.t.* **1** to jostle by riding against. **2** to cheat. **3** to trick (into doing something).—*v.i.* **1** to cheat. **2** to try to gain an advantage: *to jockey for position.*

jocose *jo-kōs'*, *adj.* **1** full of jokes. **2** merry.
jocose'ly *adv.* **jocose'ness** *n.*
jocular *jok'ū-lår*, *adj.* **1** full of jokes. **2** intended to be humorous: *a jocular remark.*
jocular'ity *n.* **joc'ularly** *adv.*

jodhpurs *jod'pŭrz*, *n.pl.* **1** riding breeches that fit tightly from the knee to the ankle. **2** short riding boots.

jog *jog*, *v.t.* **1** to shake. **2** to nudge. **3** to push with hand or elbow. **4** to stir: *to jog one's memory.*—*v.i.* **1** to move up and down with unsteady motion. **2** to travel slowly. **3** to run gently. **4** to trudge (on, along):—*pr.p.* **jogg'ing**; *pa.p.* **jogged.**
jogg'er *n.* one who jogs (*def. 3*) for exercise.
jog'-trot' *n.* a slow pace.

joggle *jog'l*, *v.t.* **1** to shake slightly. **2** to jostle.—*v.i.* to shake:—*pr.p.* **jogg'ling.**

John Bull *jon bool*, a name for the traditional, typical Englishman.

join *join*, *v.t.* **1** to connect, fasten (one thing to another). **2** to put together. **3** (*geometry*) to connect by a line. **4** to unite (e.g. in marriage). **5** to become a member of (e.g. a club, team). **6** to go to and remain with: *He joined the group at the fire.*—*v.i.* **1** to come (together). **2** to unite (with). **3** to take part (with).
join'er *n.* **1** one who joins or unites. **2** a skilled worker in wood who finishes buildings (puts in doors, stairs, etc.).
joint *n.* **1** the place where two or more things join. **2** a part of the body where two bones meet but are able to move in the manner of a hinge. **3** a piece of meat for cooking containing a bone. **4** (*slang*) a meeting place, usu. low-class. **5** (*coll.*) a cigarette containing marijuana.—*adj.* **1** united. **2** shared by two or more.—*v.t.* to cut (an animal) into joints.
join'ted *adj.*
joint'ly *adv.* together.
join battle to begin a fight.
joint stock stock or capital held by several people together.—*adj.* **joint'-stock'.**
join up to enlist, e.g. in the armed forces.
out of joint **1** dislocated. **2** in disorder, in a bad state. **3** see also **nose.**
See also **disjoin**, **disjoint**, **junction.**

joist *joist*, *n.* a beam to which the boards of a floor or the laths of a ceiling are fastened.—*v.t.* to fit with joists.

joke *jōk*, *n.* **1** a jest, anything said or done to raise a laugh. **2** something unintentionally amusing. **3** something trifling or silly, not serious.—*v.i.* **1** to make jokes. **2** to speak playfully:—*pr.p.* **jok'ing.**
jok'er *n.* **1** one who jokes. **2** an extra card in a pack used in certain games.
See also **jocose**, **jocular.**

jolly *jol'i*, *adj.* merry, cheerful:—*comp.* **joll'ier**; *superl.* **joll'iest.**—*adv.* (*coll.*) very: *jolly good.*
joll'iness *n.*
jollificā'tion *n.* feasting and merriment.
joll'ity *n.* merrymaking.

jollyboat *jol'i-bōt*, *n.* a small boat belonging to a ship.

jolt *jōlt*, *v.i.* to go forward with jerks, as a car on rough ground.—*v.t.* to shake suddenly.—Also *n.*

jonquil *jon'kwil*, *n.* a flower with rush-like leaves, a kind of narcissus.

joss-stick *jos'-stik*, *n.* a stick of gum which gives off a sweet smell when burned.

jostle *jos'l*, *v.t.* **1** to shake or jar by knocking against. **2** to elbow:—*pr.p.* **jost'ling.**—Also *n.*

jot *jot*, *n.* a very small part or amount.—*v.t.* to write briefly or quickly (usu. **jot down**):—*pr.p.* **jott'ing**; *pa.p.* **jott'ed.**
jott'er *n.* **1** one who jots. **2** a book for notes.
jott'ing *n.* a note to help the memory.

joule *jōōl*, *n.* a unit of energy, work and heat.

journal *jûr'n(å)l*, *n.* **1** a diary. **2** in book-keeping, a book containing an account of each day's business. **3** a newspaper published every day (or less often). **4** a magazine. **5** the accounts kept by a society.
journalese' *n.* the kind of writing found in the poorer newspapers.
jour'nalism *n.* the business of running, or writing for, papers or magazines.
jour'nalist *n.* an editor, manager, of, or writer for, paper(s) or magazine(s).
journalis'tic *adj.*

journey *jûr'ni*, *n.* **1** a distance travelled. **2** a tour:—*pl.* **jour'neys.**—*v.i.* to travel:—*pr.p.* **jour'neying**; *pa.p.* **jour'neyed.**
jour'neyman *n.* **1** a hired workman. **2** one whose apprenticeship is finished.

joust *jowst*, *just*, *n.* in olden times at a tournament, a combat between two knights on horseback.—*v.i.* to fight on horseback in this way.

jovial *jō'vi-ȧl, adj.* **1** joyous. **2** full of good humour.
joviality *(-al'i-ti)*, **jo'vialness** *ns.*
jo'vially *adv.*

jowl *jowl, n.* the jaw or cheek.

joy *joi, n.* **1** gladness. **2** a cause of gladness.
joy'ful *adj.* feeling, showing, or giving joy.
joy'fully *adv.* **joy'fulness** *n.*
joy'less *adj.* without joy, dismal.
joy'ous *adj.* poetical form of **joyful**.
joy'-ride *n.* a trip made for amusement in a motor-car, esp. a reckless one in a stolen car.
joy'-stick *n.* the control-lever of an aeroplane.

jubilant *jōō'bi-lȧnt, adj.* **1** shouting for joy. **2** rejoicing.
ju'bilance, -ancy *ns.* **ju'bilantly** *adv.*
jubilā'tion *n.* **1** jubilance. **2** a celebration.

jubilee *jōō'bi-lē, n.* **1** any season of great joy and feasting. **2** a celebration in memory of an event (e.g. a wedding) that happened 50 (also 25, 60 or 75) years before.

Judaism *jōō'dā-izm, n.* the Jewish religion.

judder *jud'ėr, n.* **1** aircraft vibration. **2** shaking.—Also *v.i.*

judge *juj, v.t.* **1** to try and to decide (questions esp. of law or of guilt). **2** to try (a person). **3** to conclude: *I judge that to be true.*—Also *v.i.*:—*pr.p.* **judg'ing.**—*n.* **1** one who judges. **2** one who has been appointed to try accused persons. **3** one who has the knowledge to decide on the worth of anything: *a judge of good food.*
judg'ment, judge'ment *n.* **1** the act of judging. **2** an opinion or decision given. **3** the working of the mind when it compares facts, weighs evidence, etc., in order to make a decision. **4** doom.
judicature *jōō'di-kȧ-chůr, n.* all the judges of a country considered together.
judicial *jōō-dish'ȧl, adj.* **1** of, belonging to, a judge or a court. **2** ordered by law. **3** critical: *He looked at the picture with a judicial air.*
judic'ially *adv.*
judiciary *jōō-dish'(y)ȧr-i, n.* the judicature, esp. when thought of as one of the three branches of government (*legislature, judiciary, and executive*).—Also *adj.*
judicious *jōō-dish'ůs, adj.* wise, showing, or using, sound judgment: *a judicious man, choice*:—*opp.* **injudicious**.
judgment day the day of God's final judgment on mankind.
See also **jurisdiction**, etc.

judo *jōō'dō, n.* a form of wrestling, orig. from Japan.

jug *jug, n.* a dish with a handle and spout for pouring liquids.—*v.t.* to boil or stew (e.g. a hare), orig. in a jar:—*pr.p.* **jugg'ing**; *pa.p.* **jugged**.

juggernaut *jug'ėr-nöt, n.* **1** a very large lorry. **2** a strong destructive force.

juggle *jug'l, v.i.* **1** to show, entertain by showing, great skill of hands and body in keeping a number of objects in the air at once. **2** to use trickery.—*v.t.* **1** to perform feats of skill with (something). **2** to give a false idea of: *to juggle the facts* (more usu. *to juggle with the facts*):—*pr.p.* **jugg'ling.**—*n.* a piece of deception for purpose of cheating.
jugg'ler *n.*

jugular *jug'ū-lȧr, n.* one of the large veins on either side of the neck bringing the blood back from the head.—Also **jugular vein**.

juice *jōōs, n.* **1** the liquid part of fruits, vegetables, or of animal bodies. **2** (*coll.*) electricity. **3** (*coll.*) petrol.
juicy *adj.*:—*comp.* **juic'ier**; *superl.* **juic'iest**.
juic'iness *n.*

ju-jitsu *jōō-jit'sōō, n.* an earlier form of judo.

jujube *jōō'jōōb, n.* **1** the fruit of a shrub, which is dried as a sweet. **2** a jellied sweet.

juke-box *jook'-boks, n.* an instrument that plays gramophone records automatically —usu. run by inserting a coin in a slot.

July *jōō-lī', jōō'lī, n.* the seventh month.

jumble *jum'bl, v.t.* (often used with *up*) **1** to mix together without order. **2** to muddle.—Also *v.i.*:—*pr.p.* **jumb'ling.**—*n.* a confused mixture.
jumble sale a sale of odds and ends, old clothes, etc.

jumbo jet *jum'bō jet'*, a very large jet plane.

jump *jump, v.i.* **1** to move by leaps, to spring or bound. **2** to move suddenly. **3** to rise suddenly: *News of this scarcity made the price jump.*—*v.t.* **1** to help or cause to leap. **2** to leap over: *to jump a ditch*. **3** to get on board (a train) by jumping.—*n.* **1** the act of jumping. **2** a sudden movement or rise.
jump'y *adj.* nervous, easily startled:—*comp.* **jump'ier**; *superl.* **jump'iest**.
jump suit a one-piece trouser and jacket garment.
jump at to take eagerly: *He jumped at the chance.*
jump (one's) bail to run away, losing the bail that has been paid.

jump the gun to start before the proper time, do something too soon, take an unfair advantage.
jump the queue to get oneself unfairly ahead of people who have been waiting longer.
jump to conclusions to arrive at a conclusion or judgment without waiting to make sure of the facts.
the jumps nervousness.

jumper *jump'ėr, n.* a loose-fitting jersey slipped over the head.

junction *jungk'sh(ȯ)n, n.* **1** a joining or union. **2** a place or point of joining, as a place where railway lines meet.
juncture *jungk'chůr, n.* **1** a joining, connection. **2** an important point of time: *At this juncture, she began to cry.*

June *jōōn, n.* the sixth month.

jungle *jung'gl, n.* a dense growth of trees and plants in tropical areas.

junior *jōōn'yȯr, adj.* **1** younger. **2** in a lower class or rank.—Also *n.*

juniper *jōō'ni-pėr, n.* an evergreen shrub.

junk[1] *jungk, n.* a Chinese boat with a high stern and flat bottom.

junk[2] *jungk, n.* **1** rubbish in general. **2** worthless articles. **3** salt meat. **4** (*slang*) narcotic drugs.—*v.t.* to throw away, discard as worthless.
junk'ie, junky *n.* a narcotics addict: *pl.* **junk'ies.**
junk food food with little nutritional value.

junket *jung'kit, n.* **1** milk thickened by rennet, sweetened and flavoured. **2** a feast or merrymaking. **3** (*U.S.*) an outing at public expense.—*v.i.* **1** to feast. **2** (*U.S.*) to go on an outing at public cost.
junk'eting *n.*

junkie, junky. See **junk**[2].

junta *jun'tȧ,* **junto** *jun'tō, ns.* **1** a number of people joining together for a purpose, a clique, usu. political. **2** a government formed by a, usu. small, group following a coup d'état:—*pl.* **jun'tas, jun'tos.**

Jupiter *jōō'pi-tėr, n.* **1** the chief god of the Romans. **2** the largest, and second brightest, planet.

jurisdiction *jōō-ris-dik'sh(ȯ)n, n.* **1** legal authority or power. **2** the district over which a judge, court, etc., has power.
jurisprudence *jōō-ris-prōō'dėns, n.* **1** the science of law. **2** a branch of law.
jurist *jōō'rist, n.* one who has a skilled knowledge of law.

juror. See **jury**.

jury *jōō'ri, n.* **1** a group of men or women legally selected to hear a case and to decide what are the facts (e.g. whether or not a prisoner accused of crime is guilty). **2** a committee for judging the worth of plays, etc., or for deciding the winner of a competition:—*pl.* **jur'ies.**
ju'ror *n.* a person who serves on a jury.

just *just, adj.* **1** fair, without prejudice, not favouring one more than another. **2** based on rights or on good grounds: *a just claim.* **3** deserved: *his just reward.* **4** exact, accurate.—*adv.* **1** exactly, precisely: *It lay just there.* **2** very lately, not long since. **3** barely, by a small time: *He just managed to reach safety.*
justice *(-is) n.* **1** fairness in making judgments. **2** rightness. **3** the awarding of punishments, or of rewards, that are deserved. **4** a judge. **5** a magistrate:—*opp.* (*defs. 1,2,3*) **injustice.**
jus'tifiable (or *-fī'*) *adj.* that can be justified or defended.
justify *jus'ti-fī, v.t.* **1** to prove or show to be just, right, or desirable: *Can you justify the spending of such a large sum?* **2** to clear from blame. **3** to adjust the spaces in (lines of printing) to make the lines all the same length:—*pr.p.* **jus'tifying;** *pa.p.* **jus'tified.**
justificā'tion *n.* **jus'tifier** *n.*
just'ly *adv.* **just'ness** *n.*
do justice to to treat, appreciate, fully and fairly.
Justice of the Peace (or **J.P.**) a citizen appointed to keep peace in his district, who can act as a judge in some matters.
justifiable homicide the killing of a person in self-defence.
High Court of Justice a part of the English Supreme Court.
High Court of Justiciary the most important criminal court in Scotland.

jut *jut, v.t.* to stick out, to project:—*pr.p.* **jutt'ing;** *pa.p.* **jutt'ed.**

jute *jōōt, n.* the fibre of plants found in Pakistan and India, used for making coarse sacks, etc.

juvenile *jōō'vi-nīl, adj.* **1** young, youthful. **2** concerned with, suited to, young people.—*n.* a young person.
juvenile delinquency law-breaking by a young person (**juvenile delinquent**).

juxtaposition *juks-tȧ-pȯ-zish'(ȯ)n, n.* a placing, or being placed, close together.
juxtapose' (or *juks'*) *v.t.* to place (things) side by side:—*pr.p.* **juxtaposing.**

K

kaftan. See **caftan**.

kail. See **kale**.

kale, kail *kāl, n.* a cabbage with open curled leaves.

kaleidoscope *kȧ-lī'dȯ-skōp, n.* a toy in which loose pieces of coloured glass or the like form changing patterns.

kaleidoscop'ic *adj.* **1** with changing colours. **2** changing quickly: *a kaleidoscopic career.*

kamikaze *kä-mi-kä'zi, n.* **1** in World War II, a suicidal attack made by a Japanese airman deliberately crashing his aeroplane into its target. **2** the airman or aeroplane.—Also *adj.*

kangaroo *kang-gȧ-rōō', n.* a large Australian animal with very long hindlegs and great power of leaping (the female carries her young in a pouch on the front of her body).

kaolin *kā'ō-lin, n.* China clay.

kapok *kāp'ok, kap', n.* very light waterproof oily fibre covering the seeds of a tropical tree, used to stuff pillows, lifebelts, etc.

kaput *kȧ-poot',* (*coll.*) *adj.* broken, ruined, etc.

karaoke *kar-i-ō'kē, n.* a form of entertainment in pubs, etc. in which pop songs are sung live to the accompaniment of recorded music provided by a **karaoke machine**.

karate *kȧ-rä'tā, n.* a Japanese sport and method of defence and attack using blows and kicks.

kart. See **go-kart**.

kayak *kī'ak, n.* an Eskimo sealskin canoe.

kazoo *kȧ-zōō', n.* a musical instrument which makes a buzzing sound when sung or hummed through.

kebab *ki-bab', n.* small pieces of meat, etc., usu. cooked on a skewer.

kedgeree *kej'(ė-)rē, n.* a mixture of rice with butter, spices, etc., or with fish.

keel *kēl, n.* the part of a ship stretching along the middle of the bottom and supporting the whole frame.

keel'haul *v.t.* to punish by hauling under the keel of a ship.

keel over 1 of a ship, to turn keel upwards. **2** to fall over, fall down.

keen *kēn, adj.* **1** sharp: *a keen blade.* **2** very cold, biting: *a keen wind.* **3** eager, enthusiastic: *a keen golfer.* **4** of prices, very low, competitive.

keen'ly *adv.* **keen'ness** *n.*

keen about, on very enthusiastic about, much interested in.

keep *kēp, v.t.* **1** to feed, clothe, and house. **2** to look after (e.g. a garden). **3** to hold, not give or throw away. **4** to have usu. in stock. **5** to hold: *to keep someone in prison, keep someone prisoner, keep someone a prisoner.* **6** to detain, delay: *Sorry to keep you, keep you waiting.* **7** to cause to continue in a certain state: *to keep peace, the peace; to keep the fire burning.* **8** to act in the way laid down by: *to keep the law, a promise.* **9** to note happenings in (e.g. a diary). **10** to celebrate (e.g. Christmas).—*v.i.* **1** to remain in good condition. **2** to continue: *He kept saying so.* **3** to be able to be left (e.g. for action or discussion) till a later time:—*pa.t.* and *pa.p.* **kept.**—*n.* **1** food and other necessaries. **2** the strongest part of a castle.

keep'er *n.* **1** one who, or something that, keeps. **2** a gamekeeper.

keep'ing *n.* care, custody.

keep'sake *n.* something given to be kept for the sake of the giver.

in (out of) keeping suitable (or not suitable) in the circumstances or place.

keep at it to work on and on at anything.

keep from 1 to refrain from. **2** to prevent from.

keep in with to remain in favour with.

keep on at (*coll.*) to nag, badger.

keep one's hand in to retain one's skill by practice.

keep to 1 to confine oneself to. **2** to keep (*def. 8*).

keep up 1 to keep (e.g. prices) from falling. **2** to retain (one's strength or spirit). **3** to keep (e.g. property) in repair. **4** to carry on (e.g. a conversation).

keep up with to keep as far forward (in a race, etc.) as, walk, run, as fast as.

keep up with the Joneses to have everything one's neighbours have.

keg *keg, n.* a small cask.

kelp *kelp, n.* large brown seaweed.

ken *ken*: **beyond one's ken** outside the limits of one's knowledge.

kennel *ken'ėl, n.* **1** a house for a dog. **2** (in *pl.*) a place where dogs can be looked after.

kept. See **keep**.

kerb *kûrb, n.* **1** the edging of a pavement.

2 a fender at a fireside.
kerb'stone *n.*

kerchief *kûr'chif, n.* a square piece of cloth to cover the head, neck, etc.

kerfuffle *kėr-fuf'l, n.* commotion.

kernel *kûr'nėl, n.* **1** the softer substance within the shell of a nut and inside the stone of a pulpy fruit. **2** the important part of anything.

kerosene, -sine *ker'ȯ-sēn, n.* paraffin oil.

kestrel *kes'trėl, n.* a small kind of falcon.

ketch *kech, n.* a two-masted sailing boat.

ketchup *kech'up, n.* a sauce made from tomatoes, etc.

kettle *ket'l, n.* a metal pot for heating liquids, with (usu.) a spout, (usu.) a lid, and a handle.
kett'ledrum *n.* a drum made of a half globe of brass or copper with stretched parchment covering the open end.

key *kē, n.* **1** a device by which something (e.g. a nut, a lock) is screwed or turned. **2** in musical instruments, one of the small parts pressed to sound the notes. **3** a similar part, e.g. in a typewriter or computer. **4** the chief note of a piece of music. **5** pitch, tone of voice, etc. **6** something that explains a mystery. **7** a book containing answers to exercises, etc.:—*pl.* **keys**.—*adj.* (used only before a noun) most important, controlling: *key industries*; *a key man.*—*v.t.* to type on a typewriter or computer.
key'board *n.* **1** the keys in a piano, organ, etc. arranged along a flat board. **2** (usu. in *pl.*) a, usu. electronic, musical instrument with a keyboard. **3** the keys of a typewriter or computer.
key'hole *n.* the hole in which a key of a door, etc. is placed.
key'note *n.* **1** the chief note of a piece of music. **2** the chief point: *The keynote of his speech was 'Let us prepare!'*
key'stone *n.* the stone at the highest point of an arch holding the rest in position.
keyed up 1 tightened up. **2** excited.
key in to put data into a computer by pressing keys.

khaki *kä'ki, adj.* dull brownish or greenish yellow.—*n.* cloth of such colour used for soldiers' uniforms.

kibbutz *ki-boots', n.* a farming settlement in modern Israel in which everyone shares the work:—*pl.* **kibbutzim'** *(-ēm').*

kick *kik, v.t.* to hit, put, or drive, with the foot.—*v.i.* **1** to thrust out the foot with violence. **2** (with *at, against*) to resist, object. **3** (of a gun) to spring back violently when fired.—*n.* **1** a blow with the foot. **2** the spring back of a gun. **3** (*slang*) a pleasant thrill.
kick against the pricks to resist when one can only hurt oneself by doing so (Acts ix. 5, where prick means 'goad').
kick off to start a football game (*n.* **kick'-off**).
kick over the traces to throw off control—see **trace²**.

kid¹ *kid, n.* **1** a young goat. **2** leather from the skin of a kid. **3** (*coll.*) a child.

kid² *kid,* (*coll.*) *v.t.* to deceive, hoax (esp. for amusement):—*pr.p.* **kidd'ing**; *pa.p.* **kidd'ed**.

kidnap *kid'nap, v.t.* to carry off (a human being) by force:—*pr.p.* **kid'napping**; *pa.p.* **kid'napped**.—Also *n.*
kid'napper *n.* one who kidnaps.

kidney *kid'ni, n.* **1** either of a pair of glands in the lower part of the back, one on each side (*pl.* **kid'neys**). **2** sort, kind, character: *His brother was of a different kidney.*
kidney bean a common kidney-shaped bean, or the plant that bears it.
kidney machine. See **dialysis**.

kill *kil, v.t.* **1** to cause the death of. **2** to destroy. **3** to put an end to. **4** to stop (e.g. an engine, a ball in play).—*n.* **1** the act of killing by a hunter. **2** animal(s) so killed. **3** an enemy aeroplane, etc., destroyed.
kill'er *n.*
kill'ing *adj.* **1** causing death. **2** exhausting. **3** (*coll.*) very funny.—Also *n.*
kill-joy *kil'joi, n.* someone who keeps other people from enjoying themselves.
be in at the kill to be there at the most exciting moment.
kill off to destroy completely.
kill time to use up spare time, such as a time of waiting.

kiln *kiln, n.* a large oven in which bricks, hops, etc., are dried.

kilo- *kil-ō-, pfx.* used to show multiplication by 1000.
kilo *kē'lō, n.* a kilogramme:—*pl.* **ki'los**.
kilobyte *kil'ȯ-bīt, n.* (*computers*) a unit of 1024 bytes.
kilogram(me) *kil'ȯ-gram, n.* 1000 grams.
kilometre *kil'* or *-om', n.* 1000 metres.
kilowatt *kil'ō-wot, n.* a measure of power, esp. electrical—1000 watts.

kilt *kilt, n.* a pleated tartan skirt reaching to the knees, part of Highland dress.

kimono *ki-mō'nō, n.* a loose robe, fastened with a sash:—*pl.* **kimo'nos**.

kin *kin, n.* persons of the same family, relatives.
kin'dred *n.* kin.—*adj.* **1** related. **2** of the same or similar nature: *kindred spirits*

(= people having the same nature and tastes).

kins'man, kins'woman, kins'folk *ns.* a man, a woman, people, related to one.

next of kin the nearest relative(s) of a person, esp. of one who has died.

kind *kīnd, n.* **1** sort: *What kind of car is it?* **2** variety, race: *The tiger is an animal of the cat kind.—adj.* **1** ready or anxious to do good to others. **2** friendly, gentle.

kind'ly *adv.* **1** in a kind manner. **2** please: *Would you kindly sit down.*

kind'ly (*comp.* **-ier**; *superl.* **-iest**), **kind-heart'ed** *adjs.* kind.

kind'liness, kind'-heart'edness *ns.*

kind'ness *n.*

in kind 1 (of payment) in goods, not money. **2** in the same way, with the same treatment: *He spoke rudely to her and she replied in kind.*

of a kind 1 of the same sort: *They are two of a kind—both unreliable.* **2** scarcely deserving the name: *hospitality of a kind.*

kindergarten *kin'dėr-gär-t(ė)n, n.* a school for very young children, who learn through games, toys, handicrafts.

kindle *kin'dl, v.t.* **1** to set fire to. **2** to stir up (feelings): *This kindled the anger of the crowd.—v.i.* to catch fire:—*pr.p.* **kind'-ling.**

kind'ling *n.* material for starting a fire.

kindliness, kindly. See **kin**d.

kindred. See **kin**.

kine *kīn, (old) n.pl.* cows.

kinema, kinematograph. Same as **cinema, cinematograph**.

kinetic *kin-et'ik, adj.* having to do with motion.

king *king, n.* **1** a male who succeeds by right of birth as head of nation. **2** a playing-card having the picture of a king. **3** the most important piece in chess:—*fem.* **queen**.

king'dom *n.* **1** a state having a king (or queen) as its head. **2** any of the three great divisions of natural objects—animal, vegetable, or mineral.

king'ly *adj.* **1** of royal rank. **2** suitable for a king. **3** very dignified.

king'liness *n.*

king'cup *n.* **1** a buttercup. **2** a marsh marigold.

king'fisher *n.* a bird with brilliant feathers, which feeds on fish.

King'-of-Arms' (sometimes **-at-Arms'**) *n.* a principal herald.

King's (or **Queen's**) **Bench** a court of justice orig. held in the presence of the sovereign.

King's (or **Queen's**) **Counsel** an honorary rank of barristers and advocates.

king's (queen's) English correct standard speech.

king'-size(d) *adj.* of a large size.

turn King's (Queen's) evidence. See **evident**.

kink *kingk, n.* **1** a twist in a string, rope, etc. **2** a mental twist or oddness.

kink'y *adj.* **1** having kinks. **2** odd. **3** perverted:—*comp.* **kink'ier**; *superl.* **kink'-iest**.

kinsfolk, -man, -woman. See **kin**.

kiosk *ki-osk', kē', n.* **1** a small out-of-doors roofed stall for the sale of papers, sweets, etc. **2** a public telephone box.

kipper *kip'ėr, n.* a herring split down the back and smoked.

kirk *kûrk, (Scot.) n.* church.

kirk session the session at a Scottish Presbyterian church.

kismet *kis'met, kiz', n.* fate, destiny.

kiss *kis, v.t.* **1** to caress or touch with the lips esp. as a sign of affection. **2** to touch gently.—Also *n.*

kiss hands (of e.g. a new prime minister) to kiss the sovereign's hand on accepting office.

kiss of death (*coll.*) something that causes failure, destruction, etc.

kiss of life a mouth-to-mouth method of reviving a person whose breathing has stopped by blowing one's own breath into his lungs.

kiss the dust to be slain or defeated.

kit *kit, n.* **1** a complete outfit needed for some purpose. **2** the materials, instructions, and sometimes tools, needed to make something, packed in a container.

kit'bag *n.* a strong bag for holding one's kit (*def. 1*).

kit out to provide with kit:—*pr.p.* **kitt'-ing out**; *pa.p.* **kitt'ed out**.

kitchen *kich'ėn, n.* a place where food is cooked.

kitchenette' *n.* a small kitchen.

kitch'en-gar'den *n.* a garden where vegetables for the kitchen are grown.

kite *kīt, n.* **1** a bird of prey of the hawk family. **2** a light frame covered with paper or cloth, and with string attached for flying in the air.

fly a kite to give out a hint to test public opinion (as a kite shows the direction and force of the wind) (*n.* **kite'-flying**).

kith *kith, n.* in the phrase **kith and kin**, friends and relatives.

kitten *kit'n, n.* the young of a cat.

kitt'enish *adj.* playful (used slightingly of a woman).

kittiwake *kit'i-wāk, n.* a kind of long-winged gull.

kitty *kit'i, n.* money put aside for a purpose, or the box, etc. containing it:—*pl.* **kitt'ies**.

kiwi *kē'wē, n.* an almost wingless bird of New Zealand.
kiwi fruit an oval fruit with green juicy flesh and hairy brown skin.

Klaxon® *klaks'on, n.* an electric motor-horn.

kleptomania *klep-tō-mā'nyȧ, -ni-ȧ, n.* a violent urge to steal.
kleptomā'niac *n.* one who suffers from kleptomania.

knack *nak, n.* the ability to do a particular thing skilfully.

knacker *nak'ėr, n.* **1** a horse-slaughterer. **2** a worn-out horse. **3** one who buys and breaks up old houses, ships, etc.

knapsack *nap'sak, n.* a bag carried on the back when e.g. hiking.

knave *nāv, n.* **1** a dishonest man, rogue. **2** a playing-card having the picture of a servant or soldier.
knav'ery *n.* dishonesty.
knav'ish *adj.* dishonest, rascally.
knav'ishly *adv.* **knav'ishness** *n.*

knead *nēd, v.t.* **1** to press together into a mass, as damped flour into dough. **2** to massage with a movement like this.

knee *nē, n.* **1** in man, the joint between the thigh and shin bones. **2** a joint in an animal (e.g. a horse) regarded as corresponding to the human knee. **3** the part of a trouser-leg, etc., covering the knee.—*v.t.* to strike with the knee:—*pr.p.* **knee'ing**; *pr.p.* **kneed**.
kneel *nēl, v.i.* to rest or go down on bent knee(s):—*pa.p.* **kneeled, knelt**.
knee breeches breeches coming to just below the knee.
knee'-cap *n.* **1** the patella, a flat, round bone on the front of the knee joint. **2** a warm or protective covering for the knee.—*v.t.* to shoot or otherwise injure in the knee-cap as a punishment:—*pr.p.* **knee'-capping**; *pa.p.* **knee'-capped**.
knee'-jerk *n.* a quick raising of the leg caused by a tap below the knee-cap.
knee'-pan *n.* the knee-cap.

knell *nel, n.* **1** the sound of a bell, esp. at a death or a funeral. **2** a warning of the end or failure of something.

knelt. See **kneel**.

knew. See **know**.

knickerbockers *nik'ėr-bok-ėrz, n.pl.* loose breeches gathered in at the knee.
knick'ers *n.pl.* **1** knickerbockers. **2** a woman's undergarment gathered in at the knee.

knick-knack *nik'nak, n.* a small trifling ornamental article.

knife *nīf, n.* **1** an instrument for cutting. **2** a surgeon's instrument. **3** a weapon with a blade:—*pl.* **knives** *(nīvz).*—*v.t.* to stab with a knife:—*pr.p.* **knif'ing**.

knight *nīt, n.* **1** (*history*) a man-at-arms of gentle birth. **2** a man of rank next below a baronet (not hereditary) with the title 'Sir'. **3** a piece used in chess.—*v.t.* to make (a person) a knight.
knight'hood *n.* **1** the rank or title of knight. **2** knights as a group.
knight'ly *adj.* **1** of a knight. **2** (of conduct) suited to a knight. **3** made up of knights.
knight'liness *n.*
knight'-err'ant *n.* **1** a knight who travelled in search of adventure. **2** a very chivalrous man.
knight'-err'antry *n.* the character or conduct of a knight-errant.

knit *nit, v.t.* **1** to form (material, a garment) from yarn (of wool, etc.) by making and connecting loops, using knitting needles. **2** to cause (e.g. broken bones) to grow together. **3** (of common interests, etc.) to draw (persons) together. **4** to wrinkle (the brows).—Also *v.i.*:—*pr.p.* **knitt'ing**; *pa.p.* **knitt'ed**, or **knit**.
knitt'er *n.*
knitt'ing *n.* **1** the work of a knitter. **2** material made by knitting. **3** joining.
knitting needle a thin rod, e.g. of steel, used in knitting.

knives. See **knife**.

knob *nob, n.* **1** a hard swelling or lump. **2** a more or less round handle (e.g. on a door).
knobbed *adj.*
knobb'y *adj.*:—*comp.* **knobb'ier**; *superl.* **knobb'iest**.
knobb'iness *n.*

knock *nok, v.i.* **1** to rap (on e.g. a door) for admittance. **2** to be driven (against). **3** (of machinery) to make a rattling or clanking noise.—*v.t.* **1** to strike. **2** to send by a blow. **3** to drive (against, on, something). **4** to make by a blow: *He knocked his opponent senseless.*—*n.* **1** a sudden stroke. **2** a rap.
knock'er *n.* a device, e.g. of brass, fixed to a door for knocking.
knock'about *adj.* **1** rough. **2** for rough use.
knock'-kneed' *adj.* having inward-curving legs and knees that touch in walking.
knock'-out *adj.* (used only before a noun; of a competition) eliminating the losers at each round.
knock back (*slang*) to eat or drink, esp. quickly.
knock down **1** to cause to fall by a blow or blows. **2** to give (an article) to

the highest bidder with a tap of the auctioneer's hammer.

knock off **1** to stop e.g. work. **2** to make or carry out hastily. **3** (*slang*) to steal.

knock on the head to bring (e.g. a plan) to a sudden stop.

knock out to strike insensible.

knock up **1** to rouse by knocking. **2** to exhaust. **3** to make hastily. **4** to score (a certain number of runs) in cricket.

knoll *nōl*, *n.* a round hillock.

knot *not*, *n.* **1** a lump or join made in string, rope, etc., by twisting ends together and drawing tight the loops thus formed. **2** a lump or joint in something growing or that was growing, esp. wood. **3** a cluster. **4** a tangle. **5** a difficulty. **6** a nautical mile per hour.—*v.t.* to form a knot or knots in.—*v.i.* to form a knot or knots:—*pr.p.* **knott'ing**; *pr.p.* **knott'ed**.

knott'y *adj.* **1** containing knots. **2** (of e.g. a problem) difficult:—*comp.* **knott'ier**; *superl.* **knott'iest**.

knott'iness *n.*

know *nō*, *v.t.* **1** to be aware of, or have been informed of (a fact). **2** to have learned and remember. **3** to have experience of: *He had known sorrow.* **4** to have as a friend or acquaintance. **5** to recognise: *I know a good car when I see it*:—*pa.t.* **knew** *(nū)*; *pa.p.* **known** *(nōn)*.

know'ing *adj.* **1** shrewd, cunning. **2** expressing secret understanding: *a knowing look*.

know'ingly *adv.* **1** in a knowing manner. **2** intentionally.

knowledge *nol'ij*, *n.* **1** familiarity with the facts, etc. **2** information. **3** learning.

know'ledgeable *adj.* having, or showing, knowledge: *He is knowledgeable about plants*; *a knowledgeable essay*.

know'ledgeably *adv*.

know'-how *n.* the practical knowledge and skill to deal with something.

be in the know to have information possessed by a small group of people and not by those outside it.

know better than to be too wise (to do something).

know on which side one's bread is buttered to know which action will be more profitable to one.

know the ropes to know the detail and methods of something as a sailor knows the rigging on a sailing ship.

to one's knowledge correctly according to the information one has (but with the possibility that one may be wrong).

knowledge, -able. See **know**.

knuckle *nuk'l*, *n.* **1** a joint of a finger, esp. one where the finger joins the hand. **2** a knee-joint of a calf or pig.

knuck'le-duster *n.* a metal covering for the knuckles, for attack or defence.

knuckle down **1** to yield (to someone) (also **knuckle under**). **2** to begin to work hard:—*pr.p.* **knuck'ling down**.

koala *kō-ä'lȧ*, *n.* an Australian pouched animal, like a small bear.

kookaburra *kook'ȧ-bur-ȧ*, or *-bur'*, *n.* the laughing jackass.

kopje *kop'i*, *n.* a low hill.

Koran *kō-rän'*, *kö-*, *n.* the Muslim Scriptures.

kosher *kō'shėr*, *adj.* pure, clean, according to Jewish law (e.g. of meat killed and prepared by Jews).

kowtow *kow'tow'*, *n.* the former Chinese ceremony of touching the ground with the forehead.—*v.i.* **1** to perform that ceremony. **2** to show too much respect for wishes and views of (with *to*): *I hate the way Tom kowtows to the boss.*—Also **kotow** *(kō'tow')*.

kraal *kräl*, *n* **1** a S. African native village. **2** an enclosure for cattle. **3** a native hut with bush stockade round it.

kremlin *krem'lin*, *n.* **1** a citadel, a fortress, esp. that of Moscow. **2** (*cap.*) the government of the former Soviet Union.

krona *kro͞o'nȧ*, *n.* a coin of Sweden:—*pl.* **kro'nor**.

krone *krōn'ė*, *n.* **1** a coin of Denmark. **2** a coin of Norway:—*pl.* **kron'er**.

kudos *kū'dos*, *n.* credit, fame, renown.

kultur *kool-to͞or'*, *n.* **1** culture. **2** civilisation. **3** a type of civilisation (often used mockingly).

kung fu *kung fo͞o*, the art of unarmed combat and self-defence developed in ancient China.

L

lab *lab, n.* short for **laboratory**.

label *lā'b(ė)l, n.* a small slip placed on or near anything to state its nature, ownership, etc.—*v.t.* **1** to attach a label to. **2** to mark, describe (sometimes with *as*):—*pr.p.* **lā'belling**; *pa.t., pa.p.* **lā'belled**.

labial *lā'bi-ȧl, n.* a sound formed by the lips.—Also *adj.*

laboratory *lȧ-bor'ȧ-tȯr-i,* or *lab', n.* **1** a place where scientific experiments are carried on. **2** a place where drugs, etc., are prepared:—*pl.* **laboratories**.

labour *lā'bȯr, n.* **1** hard work. **2** labourers, artisans, etc. **3** the pains or process of childbirth.—*v.i.* **1** to work hard. **2** to take pains. **3** to be oppressed by, suffer through (with *under*): *to labour under a disadvantage, a false belief.* **4** to move slowly. **5** (*naut.*) to pitch and roll heavily. —*v.t.* to elaborate too much upon.

labō'rious *adj.* **1** requiring hard work. **2** wearisome.

labō'riously *adv.* **labō'riousness** *n.*

lā'boured *adj.* **1** showing signs of effort. **2** elaborated too much upon.

lā'bourer *n.* **1** one who does heavy work requiring little skill. **2** one who works hard.

Labour Party **1** a political party formed by trade unions, etc. to represent the working community and its interests **2** its representatives in parliament.

lā'bour-sav'ing *adj.* intended to lessen work.

laburnum *lȧ-bûr'num, n.* a small tree of the pea family with hanging yellow flowers.

labyrinth *lab'i-rinth, n.* a place full of puzzling windings, a maze.

lace *lās, n.* **1** a string for fastening esp. a shoe. **2** an ornamental fabric woven of fine thread.—*v.t.* **1** to fasten with a lace (often with *up*). **2** to add a dash of spirits to (e.g. coffee):—*pr.p.* **lac'ing**.

lac'ing *n.* and *adj.*

lac'y *adj.* like lace:—*comp.* **lac'ier**; *superl.* **lac'iest**.

lacerate *las'ėr-āt, v.t.* **1** to tear, wound. **2** to cause great pain to (feelings, etc.):—*pr.p.* **lac'erating**.

lacerā'tion *n.*

lachrymose *lak'ri-mōs, adj.* **1** shedding tears. **2** given to weeping.

lacing. See **lace**.

lack *lak, n.* absence or insufficiency (of something).—*v.t.* **1** to have too little of. **2** to have none of.—*v.i.* to be absent or too little, or to have none or too little of (usu. in tenses with *pr.p.*): *Funds were lacking; He is lacking in common sense.*

lack'-lus'tre *adj.* without brightness.

lackadaisical *lak-ȧ-dā'zi-kȧl, adj.* **1** sentimental in an affected way. **2** listless. **3** without effort or interest.

lackey, lacquey *lak'i, n.* **1** a footman, manservant. **2** a servile, mean-spirited person:—*pl.* **lack'eys, lac'queys**.

laconic *lȧ-kon'ik, adj.* expressing, or expressed, in few words.

lacon'ically *adv.*

lacquer *lak'ėr, n.* a varnish.—*v.t.* to cover with lacquer.

lacquey. See **lackey**.

lacrosse *lȧ-kros', n.* a game played with a **crosse,** a long stick with a shallow net at one end.

lacy. See **lace**.

lad *lad, n.* **1** a boy. **2** a youth:—*fem.* **lass**.

ladder *lad'ėr, n.* **1** a set of rungs between two supports, for climbing up (or down). **2** a run, e.g. in a stocking, caused by breaking of a thread, the damaged part having the appearance of rungs.—*v.t.* and *v.i.* to cause, or to develop, a ladder, run.

lade *lād, v.t.* to load (a ship), or (something) on to a ship:—*pr.p.* **lad'ing**; *pa.t.* **lad'ed**; *pa.p.* **lad'ed, lad'en**.

la'den *adj.* **1** loaded. **2** burdened (with).

la'ding *n.* **1** loading. **2** cargo, freight.

bill of lading. See **bill[3]**.

ladle *lād'l, n.* **1** a large spoon for lifting out liquid, etc., from a container. **2** a container used for conveying molten metal.—*v.t.* to lift and carry, or deal (out), with, or as if with, a ladle:—*pr.p.* **lad'ling**.

lady *lā'di, n.* **1** the mistress of a house. **2** used as the feminine of **lord**. **3** (*cap.*) a title given to the wife of a lord, a baronet, or a knight and used with the Christian name of daughter of a duke, marquis or earl, etc. **4** a woman of refined manners and instincts:—*pl.* **ladies** *(lā'diz)*.

lā'dylike *adj.* like a lady in manners.

lā'dyship *n.* a word used in speaking to, or about, a woman with the title 'Lady': *Your Ladyship; Her Ladyship.*

lā'dybird *n.* a little round beetle, usu. red with black spots.—Also (esp. *U.S.*) **lā'dybug**.

Lady Day March 25, the day of the Annunciation of the Virgin.
lad'y-in-wait'ing *n.* an attendant of a queen or princess.

lag¹ *lag, n.* the act of falling behind, or amount of that fall.—*v.i.* to move too slowly:—*pr.p.* **lagg'ing**; *pa.p.* **lagged**.
lagg'ard *adj.* **1** slow. **2** backward.
lagg'ard, **lagg'er** *ns.*

lag² *lag, n.* a covering for a boiler, etc. to prevent heat loss.—*v.t.* to cover with this:—*pr.p.* **lagg'ing**; *pa.p.* **lagged**.
lagg'er *n.* **lagg'ing** *n.*

lager¹. See **laager**.

lager² *lä'gėr, n.* a light beer.—Also **lager beer**.

lagoon *là-gōōn', n.* a shallow stretch of water separated from the sea by low sand-banks, rocks, etc.

laid *lād.* See **lay²**.

lain. See **lie²**.

lair *lār, n.* the den of a wild beast.

laird *lārd, (Scot.) n.* a landed proprietor.

laissez-faire *lā'sā-fār', -fûr', n.* **1** not interfering with the free action of the individual. **2** the let-alone principle in government, business, etc.—Also **laiss'-er-faire'**.

laity. See **lay⁴**.

lake¹ *lāk, n.* a large body of water within land.

lake² *lāk, n.* a reddish colouring matter.

Lallans *lal'ànz, n.* broad Scots.

lama *lä'mä, n.* a Buddhist priest in Tibet.
la'masery (or *-mä'*) *n.* a Tibetan monastery:—*pl.* **lamaseries**.

lamb *lam, n.* **1** the young of a sheep. **2** its flesh, or that of a sheep. **3** one gentle as a lamb.
lamb'like *adj.* gentle.
lamb'skin *n.* the skin of a lamb with the wool or as leather.

lambast *lam-bast', v.t.* **1** to thrash. **2** to reprimand severely.

lame *lām, adj.* **1** disabled in a leg. **2** unsatisfactory: *a lame excuse.*—*v.t.* to cripple:—*pr.p.* **lam'ing**.
lame'ly *adv.* **lame'ness** *n.*
lame duck **1** a disabled, helpless, or inefficient person. **2** a bankrupt. **3** an inefficient organisation, esp. if about to collapse.

lamé *lä'mā, n.* a fabric into which metal threads are woven.

lament *là-ment', v.i.* to wail, mourn.—*v.t.* **1** to mourn for. **2** to regret.—*n.* **1** a show of grief. **2** a sorrowful song or poem.
lamentable *lam'ėn-tà-bl, adj.* **1** sad. **2** regrettable. **3** deplorable, pitiful, worthless. **lam'entably** *adv.* **lam'entableness** *n.*
lamentā'tion *n.*

laminated *lam'in-āt-id, adj.* in thin layers.
laminated plastics sheets of paper, linen, etc. soaked in a resin, dried and pressed together.

Lammas *lam'às, n.* the harvest feast, August 1.

lamp *lamp, n.* an apparatus for producing light by means of electricity, burning oil or gas, etc.
lamp'black *n.* **1** soot from the burning of oil, gas, tar, etc. **2** colouring matter made from this.
lamp'post *n.* the post supporting a street lamp.
lamp'shade *n.* a shade over a light bulb to soften the light coming from it.

lampoon *lam-pōōn', n.* a low, abusive satire against a person.—Also *v.t.*

lamprey *lam'pri, n.* a fish that fixes itself to its prey, etc., by its mouth:—*pl.* **lam'-preys**.

lance *läns, n.* **1** a weapon with a long shaft, a spearhead and often a small flag. **2** the bearer of a lance.—*v.t.* to open (e.g. an abscess) with a surgical instrument:—*pr.p.* **lan'cing**.
lan'cer *n.* **1** formerly, a soldier armed with a lance. **2** a soldier of a regiment (formerly cavalry) called Lancers. **3** (in *pl.*) a square dance of a certain arrangement.
lance corporal the rank between private and corporal, or a person of this rank.

lancet *län'sit, n.* a surgical instrument used (esp. formerly) for opening abscesses, etc.

land *land, n.* **1** the solid portion of the surface of the globe. **2** a country. **3** an estate.—*v.t.* **1** to set on land (or water). **2** to bring on to land (e.g. a fish). **3** to succeed in obtaining: *to land a prize, a job.* **4** (*coll.*) to deal (a person e.g. a blow).—*v.i.* **1** to come ashore. **2** to come down on land (or water). **3** to fall. **4** to come by chance (on).
land'ed *adj.* **1** possessing land or estates. **2** (*coll.*) in a difficult situation.
land'ing *n.* **1** a coming to shore or to ground. **2** a place for doing so. **3** the level part of a staircase between flights of steps.
land breeze a breeze blowing from the land towards the sea.
land'fall *n.* **1** an approach to land after a journey by sea or air. **2** the land so approached.
land'ing-craft *n.* a small, low, open vessel for landing troops and military

equipment on beaches:—*pl.* **land'ing-craft**.
land'ing-gear *n.* the parts of an aircraft that carry the load when it alights.
land'ing-stage *n.* a platform, fixed or floating, on which to land passengers or goods.
land'lady *n.* a woman who has tenants or lodgers, or keeps an inn:—*pl.* **land'-ladies**.
land'locked *adj.* enclosed by land.
land'lord *n.* one who has tenants or lodgers, or keeps an inn.
land'lubber *n.* a landsman.
land'mark *n.* **1** an object on land that serves as a guide to seamen or others. **2** an event of great importance.
land mine a mine laid on or near the surface of the ground to be exploded by something passing over it.
land'owner *n.* one who owns land.
land'slide *n.* **1** a portion of land that falls down from the side of a hill. **2** in an election, a great majority of votes for one side.
lands'man *n.* one who lives or serves on land, inexperienced in seafaring.
land'ward, -s *advs.* towards the land.
land'ward *adj.* lying toward the land.
land (someone) with (something) (*coll.*) to give (someone) (something considered unpleasant.).

landau *lan'dö, n.* a carriage with a top that may be opened in the middle and thrown back.

landscape *land'skāp, n.* **1** a portion of land that the eye can take in in a single view. **2** inland scenery. **3** a picture showing this.

lane *lān, n.* **1** a narrow road, street, or passage. **2** a regular course for ships. **3** a division of a road for one line of traffic.

language *lang'gwij, n.* **1** human speech. **2** a distinct variety of speech (as *English, French, Latin,* etc.). **3** any manner of expressing thought: *sign language*. **4** a system of signs and symbols for use e.g. in a computer.
bad language profane oaths, etc.

languid *lang'gwid, adj.* feeble, sluggish, spiritless.
lang'uidly *adv.* **lang'uidness** *n.*
languish *lang'gwish, v.i.* **1** to lose strength. **2** to pine (for). **3** to wear an expression of melancholy tenderness.
lang'uishing *adj.*
languor *lang'gȯr, n.* **1** the state of being languid. **2** listlessness. **3** a soft, tender mood.
lang'uorous *(-gȯr-ůs) adj.*

laniard. See **lanyard**.

lank *langk, adj.* **1** tall and lean. **2** long and limp. **3** straight and limp.
lank'y *adj.* lean, tall, and ungainly:—*comp.* **lank'ier**; *superl.* **lank'iest**.
lank'iness *n.*

lanolin(e) *lan'ō-lin, lēn, n.* fat from wool.

lantern *lan'tėrn, n.* a case for holding or carrying a light.
lan'tern-jawed *adj.* with long thin jaws, hollow-faced.
Chinese lantern a collapsible paper lantern.
magic lantern an instrument by means of which small pictures are thrown in larger form on a screen.

lanyard, laniard *lan'yȧrd, n.* **1** a short rope used on board ship for fastening, etc. **2** a cord for hanging a whistle, etc. round the neck.

lap[1] *lap, v.t.* **1** to lick up with the tongue. **2** to wash or flow against. **3** to drink (up) greedily.—Also *v.i.*:—*pr.p.* **lapp'ing**; *pa.p.* **lapped**.

lap[2] *lap, n.* **1** a fold. **2** the part from waist to knees of a person sitting. **3** a round of a racecourse, etc.—*v.t.* **1** to wrap, surround. **2** to make (something) lie partly (over). **3** in a race, to get a lap ahead of (another competitor):—*pr.p.* **lapp'ing**; *pa.p.* **lapped**.
lap dog a small dog fondled in the lap.
lap'top *n.* a small portable personal computer.
lap of honour a round of the field run, etc. by a team, person, etc. that has won a notable victory.

lapel *lȧ-pel', n.* part of a coat or jacket folded back, continuing the collar.

lapis lazuli *la'pis laz'ū-lī,* a deep blue stone.

Lapp, *lap,* **Laplander** *lap'lan-dėr, ns.* a member of a nomadic people living in the far north of Scandinavia.
Lap'landish, Lapp'ish *adjs.*

lapse *laps, v.i.* **1** to slip, esp. by degrees. **2** to fall away because of lack of effort. **3** to pass into disuse:—*pr.p.* **lap'sing**.—*n.* **1** a slip. **2** passage (of time). **3** a failure (in virtue, memory, etc.).
lapsed *adj.* having fallen into disuse, or into sin or error.

lapwing *lap'wing, n.* a crested kind of plover, the peewit.

larboard *lär'bōrd, -bȯrd, -läb'ȯrd,* (*old*) *n., adj.* (the) port or left (side of a ship).

larceny *lär'sni, -sėn-i, n.* **1** the legal term in England and Ireland for stealing. **2** theft:—*pl.* **lar'cenies**.

larch *lärch, n.* a cone-bearing tree related to the pines and firs.

lard *lärd, n.* the melted fat of the pig.—*v.t.* **1** to smear with lard. **2** to stuff with bacon or pork. **3** to mix freely: *He larded his conversation with Latin tags.*

larder *lär'dėr, n.* a place where food is kept.

large *lärj, adj.* **1** great in size or in quantity. **2** pompous.
large'ly *adv.* **1** mainly, chiefly. **2** to a great extent. **3** pompously.
large'ness *n.*
at large **1** at liberty. **2** in general: *the country at large* (the people of the country as a whole). **3** at considerable length.

largess(e) *lär'jes, n.* money liberally given.

largo *lär'gō,* (*music*) *adj.* slow and dignified.—Also *n.* (*pl.* **-os**) and *adv.*

lariat *lar'i-ȧt, n.* **1** a rope for picketing animals. **2** a lasso.

lark[1] *lärk, n.* a family of singing-birds which includes the skylark.
lark'spur *n.* a flower with calyx suggesting a spur.

lark[2] *lärk, n.* a frolic.—*v.i.* to frolic.

larva *lär'vȧ, n.* an insect in its first stage after leaving the egg, e.g. the caterpillar of a butterfly:—*pl.* **larvae** *(lär'vē).*
lar'val *adj.*
See also **imago, pupa.**

larynx *lar'ingks, n.* the upper end of the windpipe.
laryngitis *lar-in-jī'tis, n.* inflammation of the larynx.

lasagne *lȧ-sän'yė, -zän', n.pl.* flat pieces of pasta.—*n.sing.* a baked dish of this with tomatoes, cheese, and meat.—Also (*sing.*) **lasagna.**

lascar *las'kȧr, n.* an East Indian sailor, etc.

lascivious *lȧ-siv'i-ůs, adj.* lustful.
lasciv'iously *adv.* **lasciv'iousness** *n.*

laser *lā'zėr, n.* a device for producing a narrow and very intense beam of light.

lash *lash, n.* **1** a thong or cord, esp. of a whip. **2** an eyelash. **3** a stroke with a whip, etc.—*v.t.* **1** to strike with a lash. **2** to fasten with a rope. **3** to attack: *He lashed him with his tongue* (he said many harsh and painful things to him). **4** to drive, urge: *He lashed himself into a rage.* **5** to make sudden or restless movement with (a tail).
lash'ing *n.* and *adj.*
lash'ings (*coll.*) *n.pl.* a lot (of).
lash out **1** to kick out. **2** to hit out recklessly. **3** to spend in large amounts.

lass *las, n.* **1** a girl. **2** a sweetheart:—*masc.* **lad.**

lassitude *las'i-tūd, n.* weariness, listlessness.

lasso *las'ō, lȧ-so͞o', n.* a long rope with a running noose for catching wild horses, etc.:—*pl.* **lasso(e)s.**—*v.t.* to catch with a lasso:—*pr.p.* **lass'ōing** (or *-o͞o'*); *pa.p.* **lass'oed** (or *-o͞od'*).

last[1] *läst, n.* a shoemaker's model of a foot.

last[2] *läst, v.i.* **1** to continue in existence. **2** to remain in good state. **3** to suffice for a given time (also *v.t.*).
last'ing *adj.*
last out to last as long as required.

last[3] *läst, adj.* **1** coming at the end of a series. **2** next before the present. **3** coming or remaining after all the others. **4** very late, the latest possible: *at the last moment.* **5** the least likely, suitable, willing, etc.: *He'd be the last person to say a thing like that*; *That's the last thing I would do.*
last, last'ly *advs.*
last'-ditch' *adj.* (used only before a noun) made at the last moment or in the last resort (see **resort**).
Last Supper the last meal taken by Christ with His disciples before His crucifixion.
on one's last legs on the verge of utter failure or exhaustion.
the last post **1** the second of two bugle calls at the hour of retiring for the night. **2** a farewell bugle call at military funerals.
to the last **1** to the end. **2** till death.

latch *lach, n.* a small catch of wood or metal to fasten a door.—*v.t.* to fasten with a latch.
latch'key *n.* a small front-door key.
latch on (to) (*coll.*) to begin to understand.

late *lāt, adj.* **1** after the expected or usual time. **2** far on in day or night. **3** recently past. **4** deceased. **5** out of office:—*comp.* **lat'er**; *superl.* **lat'est.**—Also *adv.*
late'ness *n.*
late'ly (*adv.*), **of late** recently.
later on at a later time.
the latest (*coll.*) the latest news.

latent *lā'tėnt, adj.* **1** hidden: *a latent talent*; *latent hostility.* **2** undeveloped, but capable of development.

lateral *lat'ėr-ȧl, adj.* of, at, to, from, the side.
lat'erally *adv.*

latex *lā'teks, n.* the milky juice of plants.

lath *läth, n.* a thin slip of wood:—*pl.* **laths** *(läTHz, läths).*—*v.t.* to cover with laths.

lathe *lā*TH, *n.* a machine for turning and shaping articles of wood, metal, etc.

lather *lä*TH*'ėr, la*TH*'ėr, n.* **1** a foam made with water and soap. **2** froth from sweat.—*v.t.* to spread over with lather.—*v.i.* to form a lather.

Latin *lat'in, adj.* **1** of ancient Latium, the district round Rome, or its inhabitants, or its language. **2** also of languages descended from Latin or of peoples speaking them.—*n.* **1** the language of ancient Rome. **2** a person belonging to a Latin people.
Lat'in-Amer'ican *adj.* and *n.* (a person) of a country of Central or South America where a language derived from Latin (Spanish, Portuguese, French) is the official language.

latitude *lat'i-tūd, n.* **1** freedom from restraint or control. **2** the angular distance from the equator: *The latitude of London is between 51 and 52 degrees north of the equator.* **3** (in *pl.*) regions: *In these latitudes summer is short.*

latrine *lȧ-trēn', n.* a privy, in barracks, etc.

latter *lat'ėr, adj.* **1** second-mentioned of two. **2** modern, recent.
latt'erly *adv.* **1** of late. **2** in the last part of a period of time.
latt'er-day *adj.* (used only before a noun) recent, modern.
Latter-day Saint a Mormon.

lattice *lat'is, n.* **1** a network of crossed laths or bars (also **latt'ice-work**). **2** a window with small diamond-shaped panes.

laud *lōd, v.t.* to praise highly.
laud'able *adj.* praiseworthy.
laud'ably *adv.* **laud'ableness** *n.*
laud'atory *adj.* expressing praise.

laudanum *lōd'(ȧ)-nŭm, n.* tincture of opium.

laugh *läf, v.i.* to make sounds with the voice expressing amusement, scorn, etc.—*n.* an act or sound of laughing.
laugh'able *adj.* amusing, ridiculous.
laugh'ably *adv.* **laugh'ing** *n.* and *adj.*
laugh'ingly *adv.* **1** with a laugh. **2** jestingly.
laugh'ter *n.* the act or sound of laughing.
laughing jackass. See **jackass**.
laugh'ing-stock *n.* an object of ridicule.
laugh at **1** to make fun of. **2** to treat with scorn.
laugh in, up, one's sleeve to laugh secretly.

launch[1] *lönch, -sh, v.t.* **1** to throw or hurl. **2** to start (a person, an enterprise) on a course. **3** to cause (a boat, ship) to slide into the water. **4** to put (a product) on the market with suitable publicity. **5** to cause a rocket etc. to take off.—*n.* the act or occasion of launching.
launch'ing-pad *n.* a platform from which a rocket can be launched.
launch out, launch oneself into to throw oneself freely into, start off in, some activity (e.g. spending money).

launch[2] *lönch, -sh, n.* **1** the largest boat carried by a warship. **2** a power-driven boat for pleasure or short trips.

launder *lön'dėr, v.t.* and *v.i.* to wash and iron.
launderette' *n.* a shop where customers may wash clothes in washing-machines.
laun'dress *n.* a woman who launders.
laun'dry *n.* **1** a place where clothes etc. are washed. **2** clothes etc. to be washed:—*pl.* **laun'dries**.

laurel *lö'rėl, n.* **1** the bay tree once used for making honorary wreathes. **2** any closely related tree. **3** (in *pl.*) honours gained.
laureate *lö'ri-ėt, adj.* **1** crowned with laurel. **2** given special honour.
poet laureate. See **poem**.
look to one's laurels to be careful not to lose a good position or reputation because of better performances, etc. by others.
rest on one's laurels to be content with one's past successes and the honour they bring, without attempting any further achievements (sometimes said as a criticism).

lava *lä'vȧ, n.* matter thrown out in a molten stream from a volcano.

lavatory *lav'ȧ-tŏr-i, n.* **1** a place for washing. **2** now usu. a water-closet, toilet:—*pl.* **lav'atories**.

lavender *lav'ėn-dėr, n.* a plant, with pale lilac flowers, yielding sweet-scented oil.
lavender water a perfume containing oil of lavender.

lavish *lav'ish, v.t.* to expend, give, very freely.—*adj.* extravagant, unrestrained, very abundant.
lav'ishly *adv.* **lav'ishness** *n.*

law *lö, n.* **1** the rules of a community or state. **2** a statute. **3** a general statement about facts observed: *The second law of heat is that heat can never pass spontaneously from a colder to a hotter body.*
law'ful *adj.* **1** allowed by law. **2** rightful.
law'fully *adv.* **law'fulness** *n.*
law'less *adj.* not controlled by law, unruly, disorderly.
law'lessly *adv.* **law'lessness** *n.*
law'yer *n.* one who practises law.
law'-abid'ing *adj.* obedient to the law.
law'breaker *n.* **law'breaking** *n.*
law centre an office, usu. in a deprived area of a town, where free legal advice and assistance are given.
law court, court of law **1** a place in which persons accused of crimes or other offences are tried. **2** those who try accused persons.
law'suit *n.* a taking of a claim or dispute to a court of law for judgment.

common law the unwritten law (esp. of England) arising from ancient usage.
international law the rules accepted by civilised nations as governing their conduct towards each other.
statute law law depending on Acts of Parliament (opp. to *common law*).
break the law to do something forbidden by the law.
lay down the law to say what should be done in a very positive, rather bullying, way.
See also **legal**.

lawn[1] *lön, n.* a sort of fine linen.

lawn[2] *lön, n.* a space of ground covered with well-kept short grass.
lawn'-mower *n.* a machine for cutting the grass on a lawn.
lawn tennis. See **tennis**.

lax *laks, adj.* **1** slack. **2** not strict in discipline or morals. **3** careless.
lax'ative *n.* a medicine having the power of loosening the bowels.
lax'ity, lax'ness *ns.* **lax'ly** *adv.*

lay[1]. See **lie**[2].

lay[2] *lā, v.t.* **1** to cause to lie. **2** to flatten (e.g. crops). **3** to place. **4** to cause (a ghost) to cease haunting. **5** to wager, bet. **6** to put forward (e.g. a claim). **7** (also *v.i.*) to produce (eggs). **8** to set (a trap):—*pa.p.* **laid.**
lay'er *n.* **1** a thickness, covering, or stratum. **2** a shoot bent down to earth in order to take root.
lay'about *n.* a lazy, idle person.
lay'-by *n.* a place at the side of a road where motor vehicles may stand for a time:—*pl.* **lay'-bys.**
lay'-out *n.* **1** a plan. **2** an arrangement. **3** the way something is displayed, placed, etc.
laid up ill in bed.
lay about one to deal blows on all sides.
lay by to keep for future use.
lay down 1 to set, put, down. **2** to surrender, give up (arms, office). **3** to arrange, establish (e.g. plan, rules). **4** to store (supply of wine). **5** to decree (that).
lay down the law. See **law**.
lay hold of to seize.
lay in to get in a supply of.
lay off 1 to take off. **2** to talk volubly. **3** to dismiss temporarily (*n.* **lay'-off**).
lay on to provide.
lay oneself out to to put forth one's best efforts in order to.
lay out 1 to display. **2** to spend. **3** to dress in grave-clothes. **4** to fell.
lay up 1 to put away, to store, for future use. **2** to prepare future (trouble) for oneself.
lay wait for to lie in wait for.
lay waste to devastate, destroy.

lay[3] *lā, n.* **1** a short poem telling a story. **2** a song.

lay[4] *lā, adj.* **1** of the people. **2** not of the clergy.
lā'ity *n.* lay persons.
lay brother, sister one under religious vows, who serves a religious house, but does not have to take part in studies and certain religious services.
lay'man, -woman, -person *n.* **1** one who is not of the clergy. **2** one who does not belong to the profession mentioned: *Consult a trained lawyer, not a layman, about this.*
lay reader in the Anglican Church, a layman who reads part of the service.

layer. See **lay**[2].

layette *lā-et', n.* a complete outfit for a new-born child.

lazy *lā'zi, adj.* **1** disinclined to work or make any effort. **2** idle:—*comp.* **lā'zier**; *superl.* **lā'ziest**.
laze *v.i.* to lie or sit idly:—*pr.p.* **la'zing.**
lā'zily *adv.* **lā'ziness** *n.*
la'zy-bones *n.* a lazy person.

lea *lē, n.* open country, esp. meadow.

lead[1] *lēd, v.t.* **1** to show the way by going first. **2** to guide by the hand. **3** to take the principal part in: *to lead an orchestra.* **4** to convey: *to lead water to the fields.* **5** to guide, cause: *This leads me to think.* **6** to live: *He leads an idle life.*—*v.i.* **1** to be first. **2** to be guide. **3** to form a way: *This path leads to the pond*:—*pa.p.* **led.**—*n.* **1** the first place. **2** direction, guidance. **3** an electric wire or cable. **4** a leash for a dog, etc. **5** a chief part in a play: *juvenile lead.* **6** a principal or directing role: *He took the lead in this escapade.* **7** a clue, information which could help to solve a crime: *The police are following several leads.*
lead'er *n.* **1** one who leads. **2** a chief. **3** an editorial article in a newspaper (also **leading article**).
lead'ership *n.* **1** the office of leader or conductor. **2** ability to lead. **3** the act of leading.
leading edge the foremost edge of an aeroplane wing or propeller blade (opp. to **trailing edge**).
leading lady, man the actor and actress playing the principal rôles in a play, etc.
leading light a very influential or active member.
leading question a question so put as to suggest the desired answer.
lead on 1 to go forward first. **2** to

deceive by causing to have false hopes.

lead to to tend towards, have as a (probable) result.

lead up to to bring about, prepare for, by steps or stages (*n.* **lead'-up**).

lead[2] *led, n.* **1** an element, a soft heavy bluish-grey metal. **2** a plummet for sounding. **3** a thin plate of lead separating lines of type. **4** (in *pl.*) a flat roof covered with sheets of lead.—*v.t.* **1** to cover or fit with lead. **2** to separate lines of (type) with leads.

lead'en *adj.* **1** made of lead. **2** heavy. **3** dull.

lead'-free *adj.* (of petrol) unleaded.

lead pencil a blacklead (see this word) pencil for writing or drawing.

leaf *lēf, n.* **1** one of the, usu. green, structures of a plant growing from stem, branch, or root. **2** (*rare*) a petal: *a rose leaf.* **3** anything thin like a leaf, e.g. the sheet of paper on which two pages of a book are printed. **4** a part or division, as of folding doors, table tops, etc.:—*pl.* **leaves** *(lēvz).*

leaf'let *n.* **1** a little leaf. **2** a flat or folded sheet of printed political, religious, advertising, etc. matter, or several sheets folded together.—*v.t.* to distribute leaflets to.—Also *v.i.*:—*pr.p.* **leaf'leting**, less correctly **leaf'letting**; *pa.p.* **leaf'leted**, less correctly **leaf'letted**.

leaf'y *adj*:—*comp.* **leaf'ier**; *superl.* **leaf'iest**.

leaf'iness *n.*

leaf through to turn the pages of (a book, etc.).

league[1] *lēg, n.* an old measure of length, varying, but usu. about 3 miles (4.83 km).

league[2] *lēg, n.* **1** a union for advantage of all who belong to it. **2** a group of clubs competing with each other. **3** group or class of the same quality, ability, etc.—*v.t.* and *v.i.* to join in league:—*pr.p.* **leag'uing**; *pa.p.* **leagued**.

leak *lēk, n.* **1** a crack or hole through which liquid etc. may pass. **2** an escape of gas, electric current, secret information, etc.—*v.i.* **1** to have a leak. **2** to pass through a leak.—*v.t.* to cause to leak or to leak out.

leak'age *n.* **1** a leaking. **2** something that enters or escapes by leaking.

leak'y *adj.*:—*comp.* **leak'ier**; *superl.* **leak'iest**.

leak out to come to be known in spite of efforts at concealment.

lean[1] *lēn, v.i.* **1** to be not quite vertical or upright. **2** to rest (against). **3** to bend (over). **4** to rely (on). **5** to have an inclination, preference: *I lean to this view.*—*v.t.* to support, rest:—*pa.p.* **leaned** or **leant** *(lent).*

lean'ing *adj.*—*n.* **1** inclination, preference. **2** the state of being not quite vertical.

lean'-to *n.* a shed whose supports lean upon another building or wall:—*pl.* **lean'-tos**.

lean[2] *lēn, adj.* **1** thin, not fat. **2** lacking in quality or contents: *a lean harvest, purse.*—*n.* flesh without fat.

lean'ness *n.*

leant. See **lean**[1].

leap *lēp, v.i.* **1** to jump. **2** to rush eagerly.—*v.t.* to jump over:—*pa.p.* **leaped** or **leapt** *(lept).*—*n.* **1** the act of leaping. **2** the space passed by leaping.

leap'-frog *n.* a game in which one player vaults over another.—Also *v.t.* and *v.i.*:—*pr.p.* **leap'-frogging**; *pa.p.* **leap'-frogged**.

leap year every fourth year (excluding years divisible by 100 but not those exactly divisible by 400), consisting of 366 days, adding one day in February.

learn *lûrn, v.t.* **1** to get to know. **2** to gain knowledge or skill in. **3** to commit to memory.—*v.i.* to gain knowledge:—*pa.p.* **learned** *(lûrnd)* or **learnt**.

learned *lûr'nid, adj.* **1** having learned. **2** not in ordinary popular use: *learned word(s).*

lear'ner *n.* one who learns or is in the process of learning.

lear'ning *n.* **1** knowledge. **2** scholarship.

lease *lēs, n.* **1** a contract letting a house, etc., for a period. **2** the period for which the contract is made.—*v.t.* to grant or take under lease:—*pr.p.* **leas'ing**.

lessee *les-ē', n.* one to whom a lease is granted.

less'or *n.* one who grants a lease.

lease'hold *n.* **1** property or land held by lease. **2** the holding of it.

a new lease of life a happier, more active, etc. state than before due to a renewed prospect of survival, etc. brought about by the removal of some problem, defect, worry, etc.

leash *lēsh, n.* a line by which a hawk or hound is held.—Also *v.t.*

least. See **little**.

leather *leTH'ėr, n.* **1** the prepared skin of an animal. **2** a cricket ball, football.—*v.t.* to thrash.

leath'ery *adj.* **leath'eriness** *n.*

leath'er-jacket *n.* the grub of a crane-fly.

patent leather leather with a finely varnished surface.

leave[1] *lēv, n.* **1** permission. **2** permission to be absent (also **leave of absence**). **3** the period covered by this. **4** formal parting.

leave'-taking *n.* saying goodbye.

take (one's) leave (of) to say goodbye (to).

leave[2] *lēv*, *v.t.* **1** to allow to remain. **2** to abandon. **3** to depart from. **4** to bequeath. **5** to refer for decision or action: *Leave it to me.* **6** to allow (to do): *Leave me to finish this.*—*v.i.* to depart:—*pr.p.* **leav'-ing**; *pa.p.* **left**.

leav'ings *n.pl.* **1** things left. **2** refuse.

left'-overs *n.pl.* food remaining after a meal.

leave alone not to interfere with.

leave off to stop (doing etc.).

leaven *lev'n*, *n.* **1** the ferment, e.g. yeast, that makes dough rise. **2** anything that brings about a change.—*v.t.* **1** to raise with leaven. **2** to transform.

leaves. See **leaf**.

lecherous *lech'ėr-ŭs*, *adj.* sexually lustful.

lech'er *n.* a lecherous person.

lech'ery *n.*

lectern *lek'tûrn*, *n.* a reading-desk in a church, etc.

lecture *lek'chŭr*, *n.* **1** a formal talk intended to give information. **2** a tiresome speech, warning or scolding.—Also *v.t.* and *v.i.*:—*pr.p.* **lec'turing**.

lec'turer *n.*

lec'tureship *n.* the position of one whose job is lecturing in a college or university.

led. See **lead**[1].

ledge *lej*, *n.* a shelf or shelf-like projection.

ledger *lej'ėr*, *n.* the chief account book in which entries from other books are recorded.

ledger line (*music*) a short line added above or below the stave when required (often **leger line**).

lee *lē*, *n.* the sheltered side.

lee shore a shore on the lee side of a ship.

lee'ward (*lē'wėrd*; by sailors, *lōō'ėrd*) *adj.* in the direction towards which the wind blows.—Also *n.*

lee'way *n.* the distance a ship, aircraft, etc., is driven to leeward of her true course.

make up leeway to make up for lost time, ground, etc.

leech *lēch*, *n.* **1** a blood-sucking worm. **2** a person who sucks profit out of another. **3** a physician.

leek *lēk*, *n.* a vegetable closely related to the onion—national emblem of Wales.

leer *lēr*, *n.* a sly, sidelong, or lecherous look.—Also *v.i.*

leer'y *adj.* **1** wary, suspicious. **2** knowing:—*comp.* **leer'ier**; *superl.* **leer'iest**.

lees *lēz*, *n.pl.* sediment, dregs, of liquor.

leet *lēt*, (*Scot.*) *n.* a selected list of candidates.

left[1]. See **leave**[2].

left[2] *left*, *adj.* **1** on, for, or belonging to, the side that in most people has the less skilful hand (opp. to *right*). **2** (often *cap.*) belonging to the political left.—*n.* **1** the left side. **2** (often *cap.*) the more progressive, liberal, socialist, etc. party or part of a party in politics (in certain legislative assemblies these people sit by custom to the left of the presiding officer).

left'-hand'ed *adj.* **1** having the left hand more skilful than the right. **2** awkward. **3** having a double or an unflattering meaning: *a left-handed compliment*.

left wing **1** the political left. **2** the wing on the left side of an army, football pitch, etc.

left'-wing' *adj.* **left'-wing'er** *n.*

left-hand drive a driving mechanism on the left-hand side of a vehicle.

left-hand side the left side.

leg *leg*, *n.* **1** a limb on which a person or animal walks. **2** the part of a garment which covers this. **3** a long, slender support e.g. of a table. **4** (*cricket*) the part of the field behind and to the right of the batsman. **5** a distinct stage of a course, e.g. of a flight. **6** one event or part in a contest consisting of more than one event or part.

-legged (*-legd*, *-leg'id*; as part of a word) having a stated number or types of legs: *long-legged*; *a three-legged stool*.

legg'ing *n.* an outer covering for the lower leg.

legg'y *adj.* **1** having long and lank legs. **2** have long and shapely legs:—*comp.* **legg'ier**; *superl.* **legg'iest**.

leg'warmers *n.pl.* long socks without feet.

leg before wicket (abbrev. **l.b.w.**; *cricket*) saving the wicket by having the leg in front of the stumps, and therefore out.

a leg up help.

legacy *leg'ȧ-si*, *n.* **1** something left by will. **2** anything handed down by a predecessor:—*pl.* **leg'acies**.

legatee' *n.* one to whom a legacy is left.

legal *lē'găl*, *adj.* **1** of law. **2** lawful:—*opp.* **illegal**.

lēgal'ity *n.* **lē'gally** *adv.*

lē'galise *v.t.* to make legal or lawful:—*pr.p.* **le'galising**.

legate *leg'it*, *-āt*, *n.* an ambassador, esp. from the Pope.

legā'tion *n.* **1** person(s) sent as legate(s) or ambassador(s). **2** the official residence of a legation.

legatee. See **legacy**.

legato *lā-gä'tō*, (*music*) *adj.* and *adv.* smooth(ly).—Also *n.* (*pl.* **-os**).

legend *lej'ėnd*, *n.* **1** a story handed down from one generation to another but not historically accurate. **2** words accompanying an illustration or picture.
leg'endary *adj.*

legerdemain *lej'ėr-dē-mān'*, *n.* sleight of hand.

leger line. Same as **ledger line**.

leggy, etc. See **leg**.

legible *lej'i-bl*, *adj.* clear enough to be read:—*opp.* **illegible**.
leg'ibleness, **legibil'ity** *ns.*
leg'ibly *adv.*

legion *lē'jȯn*, *n.* **1** in ancient Rome, a body of soldiers of from three to six thousand. **2** a military force. **3** a great number. **4** (often *cap.*) a national association of those who have served in war.
lē'gionary *n.* a soldier of a legion:—*pl.* **le'gionaries.**
Legionnaires' disease a severe pneumonia-like disease caused by a bacterium.

legislate *lej'is-lāt*, *v.i.* to make laws:—*pr.p.* **leg'islating.**
legislā'tion *n.*
leg'islātive *adj.* law-making.
leg'islātor *n.* **1** a lawgiver. **2** a member of a legislative body.
leg'islāture *n.* the body of those in a state who have the power of making laws.

legitimate *li-jit'i-mit*, *adj.* **1** lawful. **2** born to parents who are married to each other. **3** (of e.g. argument, deduction) reasonable, logical:—*opp.* **illegitimate.**
legit'imacy *n.* **legit'imately** *adv.*
legit'imise *v.t.* to make legitimate:—*pr.p.* **legit'imising.**

leguminous *le-gū'min-ůs*, *adj.* **1** having a pod splitting along both sides. **2** of peas, beans, etc.

leisure *lezh'ůr*, *n.* **1** time at one's own disposal. **2** freedom from occupation.
leis'ured *adj.* having leisure.
leis'urely *adj.* and *adv.* not hasty or hastily.
leisure centre a centre providing a variety of recreational activities.

lemming *lem'ing*, *n.* a small northern rodent closely related to the voles, noted for occasional mass migrations in which the animals swim out to sea until they die of exhaustion.

lemon *lem'ȯn*, *n.* **1** an oval citrus fruit (see **citrus**) with an acid pulp. **2** the tree bearing it.

lemonade' *n.* **1** a drink made with lemon juice. **2** a similar fizzy drink.

lemon sole *lem'ȯn sōl*, a small kind of sole.

lemur *lē'mūr*, *n.* an animal related to monkeys.

lend *lend*, *v.t.* **1** to give the use of for a time. **2** to give, add (e.g. interest, beauty, courage) to something or someone:—*pa.p.* **lent.**
lend'er *n.*
lend itself to to be suitable for, adapt easily to.
lend oneself to to give one's support or approval to (e.g. a deception).
See also **loan.**

length *length*, *n.* **1** the quality of being long. **2** extent from end to end. **3** the longest measure of anything. **4** a piece (e.g. of cloth).
length'en *v.t.* and *v.i.* to increase in length.
length'ways, **length'wise** *advs.* in the direction of the length.
length'y *adj.* of great or wearisome length:—*comp.* **length'ier**; *superl.* **length'iest.**
length'ily *adv.*
-length (as part of a word) reaching as far as: *a knee-length/ankle-length skirt.*
at length **1** in detail. **2** at last.

lenient *lēn'yėnt*, *lē'ni-ėnt*, *adj.* (of punishment, person) mild, merciful.
lē'nience, **lē'niency** *ns.*
lē'niently *adv.*

lens *lenz*, *n.* **1** a piece of transparent substance (e.g. glass) so shaped as to bring light rays together at a point, or to make them spread out from one, used in spectacles, cameras, etc. **2** a similar structure in the eye:—*pl.* **lens'es.**

lent. See **lend**.

Lent *lent*, *n.* an annual fast of forty days from Ash Wednesday to Easter, in commemoration of Christ's fast in the wilderness.
Lent'en *adj.*

lentil *len'til*, *n.* **1** an annual plant, common near the Mediterranean. **2** its seed used for food.

lento *len'tō*, (*music*) *adj.*, *adv.* slow(ly).—Also *n.* (*pl.* **-tos**, **-ti** *-tē*).

leonine *lē'ȯ-nīn*, *adj.* lionlike.

leopard *lep'ȧrd*, *n.* a large spotted animal of the cat kind.

leotard *lē'ō-tärd*, *n.* a skin-tight garment worn by dancers and acrobats.

leper *lep'ėr*, *n.* **1** one who has leprosy. **2** an outcast.
leprosy *lep'rȯ-si*, *n.* a serious contagious

skin disease.
lep'rous *adj.*

Lepidoptera *lep-i-dop'tėr-ȧ, n.pl.* butterflies and moths.

leprechaun *lep'rė-kön, n.* a small Irish brownie.

leprosy, leprous. See **leper**.

lesbian *lez'bi-ȧn, n.* a female homosexual.—Also *adj.*
les'bianism *n.*

lese-majesty *lēz'-maj'is-ti, n.* treason.

lesion *lē'zhȯn, n.* **1** a wound. **2** a change due to disease.

less *les, adj.* **1** not so much. **2** smaller.—Also *adv.* and *n.*—*prep.* minus.
less'er *adj.* **1** smaller. **2** less important.
less'en *v.t., v.i.* to make, becomes, less.

lessee. See **lease**.

lesson *les'(ȯ)n, n.* **1** a portion of Scripture read in divine service. **2** a thing (to be) learned by a pupil at one time. **3** a class in which this is taught. **4** something of moral importance (to be) learned from a story, experience, etc.

lessor. See **lease**.

lest *lest, conj.* for fear that.

let[1] *let, v.t.* **1** to allow, permit. **2** to grant to a tenant or hirer. **3** to cause (with infinitive without to): *He will let you know*:—*pr.p.* **lett'ing**; *pa.p.* **let**.
let alone **1** not to mention: *I can't even see it, let alone read it!* **2** (also **let be**) not to interfere with: *I think the best thing to do is to let them both alone.*
let down **1** to lower. **2** to disappoint, desert (*n.* **let'-down**).
let go to stop holding.
let in for to involve in: *The trip let me in for more expense than I intended.*
let off **1** to discharge (a gun). **2** to excuse.
let out **1** to release. **2** to hire. **3** to give away (a secret).
let up to become less (*n.* **let'-up**).
to let for letting: *house to let.*

let[2] *let, n.* **1** (*tennis* or *old*) hindrance, obstruction (as in tennis). **2** (*old*) delay.

lethal *lē'thȧl, adj.* causing death.

lethargy *leth'ȧr-ji, n.* **1** heavy unnatural sleep. **2** lack of interest or energy.
lethar'gic, al *(-är'-) adjs.*

letter *let'ėr, n.* **1** a mark expressing a sound. **2** a written or printed message. **3** a printing type. **4** (in *pl.*) learning, literature.
lett'ering *n.* **1** the act of forming letters. **2** the letters formed.
lett'er-bomb *n.* a device inside an envelope which explodes when the envelope is opened.
lett'er-box *n.* a box for receiving letters for or from the post.
lett'er-card *n.* a piece of paper gummed round the edges for use as paper and envelope combined.
lett'erhead *n.* **1** a printed heading on notepaper, etc. **2** a piece of such notepaper.
lett'erpress *n.* the printed matter in an illustrated book.
letter of credit a letter authorising a certain sum to be paid to the bearer.
the letter the strict verbal meaning (e.g. *the letter of the law*—often opp. to *the spirit*, the intention of the framer of the law).

lettuce *let'is, n.* a green plant with large leaves used as a salad.

leukaemia *lōō-kē'mi-ȧ, n.* a sometimes fatal cancerous disease in which too many white blood cells accumulate in the blood.

Levant *li-vant', n.* the Eastern Mediterranean and its shores.
Levan'tine *adj.*

levee[1] *lev'ā, lev'ē, le-vē', n.* **1** a reception of men only by a king, etc.—orig. on his rising from bed. **2** a formal reception of visitors.

levee[2] *lev'ē, le-vē', n.* an embankment, esp. on the lower Mississippi.

level *lev'l, n.* **1** an instrument for testing that a line or surface is horizontal. **2** a flat stretch of country. **3** height, position, strength, etc., in comparison with some standard: *The level of the river rose; a conference at summit level; a high level of intelligence.* **4** appropriate position or rank.—*adj.* **1** horizontal. **2** even, smooth. **3** in the same line or plane. **4** equal in position or dignity.—*v.t.* **1** to make horizontal. **2** to make flat or smooth. **3** to lay flat: *to level to, with, the ground.* **4** to make equal. **5** to aim (gun, etc. at):—*pr.p.* **lev'elling**; *pa.p.* **lev'elled**.
lev'eller *n.* **lev'elling** *n., adj.*
lev'elness *n.* **lev'elly** *adv.*
level crossing a place at which a road crosses a railway at the same level.
lev'el-head'ed *adj.* having sound common sense.
find one's level to find the place or rank to which one naturally belongs.
level with (*slang*) to be honest with, tell the truth to.
on the level (*slang*) honest(ly), playing fair.

lever *lē'vėr, n.* **1** a bar, turning on a support called the prop or fulcrum, for prizing up or moving an object. **2** anything that exerts influence.—*v.t.* to move (as) with a lever.
lē'verage *n.* **1** the power gained by the

use of the lever. **2** power, advantage, that can be used to achieve a purpose.

leveret *lev'ėr-it, n.* a hare in its first year.

leviathan *li-vī'ȧ-thȧn, n.* **1** a huge water animal. **2** anything of huge size.

levitation *lev-i-ta'sh(ȯ)n, n.* the (illusion of) raising a heavy body in the air without support.
lev'itate *v.t.* to cause to float in the air.—Also *v.i.*:—*pr.p.* **lev'itating**.

levity *lev'it-i, n.* **1** thoughtlessness. **2** frivolity.

levy *lev'i, v.t.* **1** to raise, collect, esp. an army or a tax. **2** to make (war):—*pr.p.* **lev'ying**; *pa.p.* **lev'ied** *(lev'id).*—*n.* troops or money collected by authority:—*pl.* **lev'ies**.

lewd *lōōd, lūd, adj.* **1** lustful. **2** indecent.
lewd'ness *n.*

lexicon *leks'i-kȯn, n.* a dictionary.
lexicog'rapher *n.* one who makes a dictionary.
lexicog'raphy *n.*

liable *lī'ȧ-bl, adj.* **1** legally responsible (for): *He is liable for this debt.* **2** under an obligation (to do something). **3** likely, apt (to do, to happen).
liabil'ity *n.* **1** the state of being liable. **2** an obligation, debt, etc. **3** something disadvantageous:—*pl.* **liabil'ities**.

liaison *lē-ā-zon^{g}, li-āz'(ȯ)n, n.* **1** (orig. *military*) contact, communication. **2** illicit union between a man and a woman. **3** in French, the linking of a final consonant to the initial vowel of the next word.
liaise *v.i.* to get or be in contact (with): *The sales manager has to liaise with book-sellers*:—*pr.p.* **liais'ing**.

liana *li-ä'nȧ, n.* a general name for climbing plants in tropical forests.

liar. See **lie**.

libel *lī'bėl, n.* **1** a publication or (*loosely*) statement damaging to a person's reputation. **2** an unflattering portrait.—*v.t.* **1** to damage the reputation of by a libel. **2** to satirise unfairly:—*pr.p.* **lī'belling**; *pa.p.* **lī'belled**.
lī'beller *n.*
lī'bellous *adj.* **lī'bellously** *adv.*

liberal *lib'ėr-ȧl, adj.* **1** generous. **2** ample. **3** broadminded, unprejudiced. **4** (of an education) not specialised or technical, aiming at general culture. **5** (*cap.*) of the Liberal Party:—*opp.* (*defs. 1–3*) **illiberal**.—*n.* **1** (*cap.*) a member or supporter of the Liberal Party. **2** a person of liberal views.
liberal'ity, lib'eralness *ns.*
lib'erally *adv.*
Liberal Democrats **1** a political party formed in 1988 from the Liberal Party and the Social Democratic Party. **2** its representatives in parliament.

liberate *lib'ėr-āt, v.t.* to set free, release:—*pr.p.* **lib'erating**.
liberā'tion *n.* **lib'erator** *n.*
lib'ertine *n.* one who leads a dissolute life, a rake.

liberty *lib'ėr-ti, n.* **1** freedom from captivity or from slavery. **2** freedom to do as one pleases. **3** power of free choice. **4** (in *pl.*) privileges, rights, etc.: *civil liberties.* **5** too great freedom of speech or action, impertinence, abuse of one's freedom (as *to take liberties*):—*pl.* **lib'erties**.—*adj.* of, or having, leave to go ashore (e.g. *liberty man, boat*).
take the liberty to do something esp. without permission: *Since you were not here, I took the liberty of answering that letter for you.*

library *lī'brȧ-ri, n.* **1** a building or room containing a collection of books. **2** a collection of books—also of gramophone records:—*pl.* **lib'raries**.
librā'rian *n.* the keeper of a library.
librā'rianship *n.*

libretto *li-bret'ō, n.* **1** a book of the words of an opera, oratorio, etc. **2** the text itself:—*pl.* **librett'i, librett'os**.

lice. See **louse**.

licence *lī'sėns, n.* **1** permission. **2** the document by which permission is legally given to drive or run a car, keep a dog, etc. **3** legal permission to sell alcoholic liquors, for consumption on the premises (**on'-licence**), or for taking away (**off'-licence**). **4** too great freedom of action.
lī'cense *v.t.* **1** to grant a licence to. **2** to authorise or permit:—*pr.p.* **li'censing**.
licensee' *n.* one to whom a licence is granted.
lī'censer *n.* one who grants a licence.
licen'tiate *n.* **1** the holder of any of certain diplomas or licences. **2** the diploma or licence itself.
licen'tious *adj.* given to indulgence of the animal passions, dissolute.
licen'tiousness *n.*

lichee. See **lychee**.

lichen *lī'kėn, lich'ėn, n.* any of a large group of plants consisting of an alga and a fungus together, growing on stones, trees, etc.

lichgate *lich'gāt, n.* a churchyard gate with a porch under which to rest a bier.

lick *lik, v.t.* **1** to pass the tongue over. **2** to pass lightly over: *Flames licked the walls.* **3** (*coll.*) to beat. **4** (*coll.*) to overcome.—*n.* **1** a passing of the tongue over. **2** a slight smear. **3** a blow. **4** (*coll.*) a fast speed.
lick'ing *n.* a thrashing.
lick into shape to put into more perfect

form, or make more efficient.
lick the dust to be utterly defeated.

lid *lid*, *n.* **1** a cover of a container. **2** the cover of the eye.

lido *lē'dō*, *n.* **1** a bathing beach. **2** an open-air swimming-pool:—*pl.* **li'dos**.

lie[1] *lī*, *v.i.* **1** to make a false statement with the intention of deceiving. **2** to give a false impression:—*pr.p.* **ly'ing**; *pa.p.* **lied**.—Also *n.*
liar *lī'ar*, *n.* one who tells lies, esp. as a habit.
ly'ing *n.* and *adj.*
give the lie to 1 to charge with falsehood. **2** to show (e.g. a statement) to be false.
white lie a lie told from good motives.

lie[2] *lī*, *v.i.* **1** to be in, or take, a more or less horizontal position. **2** to be situated. **3** to extend, stretch. **4** to remain in a certain place: *The book lies on the table.* **5** to remain in a certain state: *to lie hidden idle.* **6** to consist (in): *His charm lies in his high spirits*:—*pr.p.* **ly'ing**; *pa.t.* **lay**; *pa.p.* **lain**.—*n.* **1** slope and direction: *the lie of the land.* **2** (*golf*) the position of the ball.
lie at someone's door (of a crime, error, blame) obviously to have been committed by, or to belong to, one person, not another.
lie down to take a flat or horizontal position, esp. to rest (*n.* **lie-down'**).
lie in to stay in bed longer than usual (*n.* **lie-in'**).
lie in state (of a corpse) to be laid out in a place of honour before being buried.
lie in wait for to be waiting ready to trap or attack.
lie low to keep quiet or hidden.
lie to (of a ship) to lie almost at a stop with head to windward.
lie up (of a ship) to be in dock or beached for the winter.
lie with to rest with, to belong to as a privilege or as an obligation: *The decision lies with you.*
take it lying down to endure tamely.
the lie of the land 1 see **lie** above. **2** the current situation or outlook.

lied *lēt*, *n.* a German song or ballad, not operatic, type:—*pl.* **lieder** *(lē'dėr)*.

liege *lēj*, *n.* **1** a vassal. **2** a loyal vassal. **3** a lord or superior.

lieu *lū*, *lōō*: **in lieu of** in place of, instead of.

lieutenant *lef-ten'ant*, *n.* **1** one representing, or performing the work of, another. **2** a commissioned officer in the army or (pronounced *lė-ten'ant*) navy.—*adj.* (usu. as part of a word) next in rank to a superior named, as **lieuten'ant-comman'der**, **lieuten'ant gen'eral**, an officer next in rank below commander, general.
lieuten'ancy *n.* the office or commission of a lieutenant:—*pl.* **lieuten'ancies**.
Lord Lieutenant a magistrate appointed by the sovereign as the chief executive authority in a country.

life *līf*, *n.* **1** the sum of the activities of plants and animals that distinguish them from dead matter. **2** the period between birth and death. **3** a series of experiences. **4** manner of living. **5** liveliness. **6** living things. **7** the story of a life. **8** a life sentence (see this):—*pl.* **lives** *(līvz)*.—*adj.* (only used before a noun) **1** lasting for life. **2** of life. **3** (*art*) from a living model.
life'less *adj.* **1** dead. **2** without vigour. **3** uninteresting because of this.
life'like *adj.* **1** like a living person. **2** vivid.
life'-and-death' *adj.* **1** critical, crucial: *a life-and-death matter.* **2** desperate, fierce: *a life-and-death struggle.*
life assurance, **insurance** any form of insurance payable at a person's death or at a certain age.
life'belt *n.* a belt either blown up with air, or of cork, etc., for holding a person up in water.
life'-blood *n.* **1** the blood necessary to life. **2** any influence that gives strength and energy.
life'boat *n.* a boat for saving shipwrecked persons.
life'buoy *n.* a buoy intended to support a person in the water till he can be rescued.
life cycle. See **life history**.
life'guard *n.* one employed to rescue bathers in difficulty.
Life Guards a cavalry regiment whose ceremonial dress includes a red jacket and white-plumed helmet.
life history, **life cycle** the various stages through which a living thing passes up to full development and death.
life insurance. See **life assurance**.
life jacket a sleeveless jacket, of material that will float, for holding a person up in water.
life line 1 a rope for support in dangerous operations. **2** a line thrown to rescue a drowning person. **3** an essential line of communication.
life'long *adj.* during the length of a life.
life preserver a cane with a loaded head used as a club.
life sentence 1 a sentence of imprisonment for life (in practice only for a number of years). **2** a lifetime of en-

during something.
life'size(d) *adj.* (of e.g. a picture) of the same size as the thing represented.
life style one's way of living, e.g. one's attitudes, possessions, etc.
life'time *n.* duration of life.
to the life exactly like the original.
See also **live**[1].

lift *lift*, *v.t.* **1** to bring to a higher position. **2** to make higher in rank or condition or the opinion of others. **3** to make (one's spirits) joyful. **4** to make (the voice) audible or loud. **5** to take and carry away.—*v.i.* **1** to rise. **2** (of fog, cloud, etc.) to disappear.—*n.* **1** the act of lifting. **2** upward movement. **3** conveyance in one's car, etc. **4** a small enclosed platform that moves up and down, e.g. between the floors of a building, carrying people and goods. **5** the force on an aircraft acting upwards at right angles to the *drag*.
have one's face lifted to undergo an operation for smoothing out wrinkles.—See also **face-lift**.
lift'-off *n.* the (movement of) take-off of an aircraft or rocket.

ligament *lig'a-mėnt*, *n.* the bundle of fibrous tissue joining the movable bones.
lig'ature *n.* something that binds.

light[1] *līt*, *n.* **1** the agency (electromagnetic radiation) by which objects are made visible. **2** a source of light, as the sun or a lamp. **3** a means of kindling. **4** a bright appearance. **5** mental or spiritual illumination. **6** a distinguished person. **7** a way of viewing, regarding: *to look at his action in a favourable, different, light.*—*adj.* **1** not dark. **2** bright.—*v.t.* **1** to give light to. **2** to set fire to:—*pa.p.* **light'ed**, or **lit**.
lighten *līt'(ė)n*, *v.t.* to make brighter.—*v.i.* to become brighter.
light'er *n.* **1** a device for producing a light. **2** one who lights.
light'ness *n.*
light'house *n.* a building with a light to guide or warn ships or aircraft.
light'ship *n.* a stationary ship carrying a light, serving as a lighthouse.
light wave one of the electromagnetic waves on which our seeing depends.
light'-year *n.* the distance light travels in a year (nearly 6 billion miles)—a unit used to express distances of the stars.
according to one's lights in accordance with one's own standards, knowledge, etc.
bring, come, to light, to discover, reveal, or be revealed.
in the light of taking into consideration (facts learned, etc.).
light up to put on lights (**lighting-up time**) the time when street lights, motorcar lights, etc., must be put on).
see the light 1 to be born. **2** to come to an understanding of a situation, explanation, problem. **3** to be converted.
shed, throw, light on to make (e.g. a reason, motive, situation) more clear.

light[2] *līt*, *adj.* **1** not heavy. **2** not as heavy as it should be. **3** not massive in appearance. **4** easy to endure, to do, or to digest. **5** not heavily armed or burdened: *light infantry, truck.* **6** (of mist, rain, frost) little in quantity, not intense. **7** nimble. **8** cheerful, lively. **9** (of soil) sandy.—*adv.* in phrases such as *to travel light*, i.e. without much luggage.
lighten *līt'(ė)n*, *v.t.* and *v.i.* to make, or become, less heavy.
light'er *n.* a large open boat used in unloading and loading ships.
light'erage *n.* the price paid for unloading ships by lighters.
light'ly *adv.* **1** in a light way. **2** slightly.
light'ness *n.*
lights *n.pl.* the lungs of an animal.
light'-armed' *adj.* with light weapons and equipment.
light engine a locomotive without a train.
light'-fing'ered *adj.* **1** light or active with one's fingers. **2** thievish.
light'-head'ed *adj.* **1** giddy, delirious. **2** thoughtless, unsteady.
light'-heart'ed *adj.* **1** merry of heart. **2** free from anxiety, cheerful.
light industry. See **industry**.
light'-mind'ed *adj.* frivolous.
light'weight *n.* **1** (*boxing*) a man not more than 9st. 9lb. (61.235kg), in amateur boxing 9st. 7lb (60.328kg), or less than 9st (57.153kg). **2** a person of little importance.—Also *adj.*
make light of. See **make**.

light[3] *līt*, *v.i.* to come by chance (on):—*pa.t.* and *pa.p.* **light'ed** or **lit**.

lighten[1,2], **lighter**[1,2]. See **light**[1,2].

lightning *līt'ning*, *n.* the flash (a very large spark) that marks the discharge of an electrified cloud either to earth or to another cloud.—Also *adj.*
lightning conductor a metal rod for protecting buildings from lightning.

lignite *lig'nīt*, *n.* brown coal, coal retaining the texture of wood.

like[1] *līk*, *adj.* **1** identical. **2** similar.—*n.* **1** one of the same kind. **2** the same thing: *to do the like.*
like'ly *adj.* **1** probable. **2** promising:—*comp.* **like'lier**; *superl.* **like'liest**.—*adv.* probably.
like'liness, like'lihood *ns.*

lik'en *v.t.* to represent as like, similar (to).
like'ness *n.* **1** resemblance. **2** one who, or something that, has a resemblance. **3** a portrait.
like'-mind'ed *adj.* having a similar opinion or purpose.
like'wise *adv.* **1** in like manner. **2** also.
feel like to be inclined for (any action or thing).
look like **1** to suggest the effects, symptoms, or likelihood of: *It looks like rain.* **2** to appear similar to.

like² *līk, v.t.* **1** to be pleased with. **2** to enjoy:—*pr.p.* **lik'ing**; *opp.* **dislike'**.—*n.* a liking, in phrase 'likes and dislikes'.
lik(e)'able *adj.* lovable, attractive.
lik'ing *n.* **1** a taste (for). **2** satisfaction or taste: *to my liking.*

lilac *lī'lȧk, n.* a shrub with roughly pyramid-shaped clusters of light-purple or white flowers.—*adj.* having purplish colour of lilac flower.

lilt *lilt, v.i.* or *v.t.* to sing or play merrily.—*n.* **1** a cheerful song. **2** a springy movement.

lily *lil'i, n.* **1** the white madonna lily, the tiger lily, or similar plant with bulb. **2** extended to include other flowers of the same family, as narcissi:—*pl.* **lil'ies**.—*adj.* **1** resembling a lily. **2** white. **3** pure.
lil'y-liv'ered *adj.* cowardly (**liver²**).
lily of the valley a small plant with white bell-shaped flowers.

limb *lim, n.* **1** an arm, leg, or wing. **2** a projecting part. **3** a branch.
out on a limb alone in a dangerous position.

limber *lim'bėr, adj.* supple.
limber up to exercise so as to become supple.

limbo¹ *lim'bō, n.* **1** the borderland of Hell. **2** a place or condition of neglect:—*pl.* **lim'bos**.

limbo² *lim'bō, n.* a West Indian dance in which the dancer bends backwards and passes under a bar which is gradually placed lower and lower:—*pl.* **lim'bos**.

lime¹ *līm, n.* quicklime, the white substance, prepared from limestone, used for cement.—*v.t.* to cover with, or manure with, lime:—*pr.p.* **lim'ing**.
lim'y *adj.* **lim'iness** *n.*
lime'kiln *n.* a furnace in which limestone is burned to lime.
lime'light *n.* a light produced by making quicklime very hot by means of a strong flame.
lime'stone *n.* a rock composed chiefly of calcium carbonate.
in the limelight **1** (on a stage) picked out by a strong light. **2** (in life) conspicuous, attracting public attention.

lime² *līm, n.* **1** a tree closely related to the lemon. **2** its small greenish-yellow fruit.
lim'ey (*U.S. slang*; also with *cap.*) *n.* a British person (from the former use of lime juice on British ships to prevent scurvy):—*pl.* **lim'eys**.—Also *adj.* (used only before a noun).

lime³ *līm, n.* the linden tree.

limerick *lim'ėr-ik, n.* a humorous verse in a five-line stanza, the third and fourth lines being shorter than the others.

limit *lim'it, n.* **1** a boundary. **2** the largest (or smallest) extent, degree, etc. **3** restriction.—*v.t.* to fix, or to keep to, a limit for: *to limit money spent*.
limitā'tion *n.* **1** the act of limiting. **2** the state of being limited. **3** restriction. **4** a shortcoming: *We all have our limitations.*
lim'itless *adj.*
limited liability limitation of the liability or responsibility of individual shareholders of a company by the value of stock each holds in it (abbrev. **Ltd.**).
limited monarchy one in which the monarch shares power with others.
off limits out of bounds.
within limits to a certain extent only.

limousine *lim'oo-zēn, n.* a large closed motor car with a separate compartment for the driver.

limp¹ *limp, adj.* **1** lacking stiffness. **2** drooping.

limp² *limp, v.i.* **1** to walk lamely. **2** (of a damaged ship, aircraft, etc.) to move along with difficulty.—*n.* **1** the act of limping. **2** a limping walk.

limpet *lim'pit, n.* **1** a shellfish, with shell open beneath, that clings to rocks. **2** a person difficult to dislodge, get rid of.

limpid *lim'pid, adj.* (of a stream, the air eyes, etc.) clear.
limpid'ity, lim'pidness *ns.*

linchpin *linch'pin*, or *linsh', n.* a pin used to keep a wheel on its axle-tree.

linctus *lingk'tŭs, n.* a syrup-like medicine.

linden *lin'dėn, n.* a tree with heart-shaped leaves with notched edges, the lime.

line¹ *līn, v.t.* to cover on the inside:—*pr.p.* **lin'ing**.
lin'ing *n.* **1** the action of covering the inside. **2** material on the inner surface of a garment.
line one's pocket(s) to make a profit, esp. dishonestly.

line² *līn, n.* **1** a thread, cord, rope. **2** a long narrow mark or band. **3** (in *pl.*) outline (e.g. of a ship). **4** a wrinkle. **5** a row (e.g. of trees, people, printed words). **6** lineage.

7 a route, system. **8** a railroad. **9** a service of ships or aircraft. **10** a telegraph or telephone wire or section of wires. **11** a system (of pipes) for conveying e.g. oil. **12** a trench. **13** a series or succession. **14** direction: *in the line of fire.* **15** style, method: *on the lines of.* **16** course of conduct: *to take the line of least resistance.* **17** a sphere of activity or interest: *in his own line.* **18** a class of goods. **19** the equator. **20** one row in the pattern of a poem as written, a division of the rhythm pattern. **21** a short letter. **22** the regular army. **23** (in *pl.*) a marriage certificate. **24** (in *pl.*) a certificate of church membership. **25** (in *pl.*) the arrangement of troops for defence or attack. **26** (in *pl.*) a written punishment task.—*v.t.* **1** to mark with lines. **2** to form lines along (a street). **3** to put in line:—*pr.p.* **lin'ing**.

lineage *lin'i-ij, n.* ancestry, race, family.

lineal *lin'i-ȧl, adj.* (of ancestry) in a direct line: *a lineal descendant of the poet.*

lineament *lin'i-ȧ-mėnt, n.* a feature, esp. of the face.

lin'ear *(lin') adj.* involving measurement in one dimension only (measurement of length, or breadth, or height).

lin'er *(līn') n.* a vessel or aircraft of a regular line or company.

line fish fish caught with the line.

line(s)'man *n.* one who attends to railway, telegraph, telephone, etc. lines.—See also **linesman.**

line'-out *n.* in Rugby football, a method of restarting play when the ball has gone into touch, the forwards of each team lining up facing the touch-line and trying to catch the ball when it is thrown in.

lines'man *n.* **1** in football, one who marks the spot at which the ball passes the boundary line. **2** in tennis, one who decides on which side of a line the ball has fallen.—See also **line(s)man.**

line'-up *n.* **1** an arrangement in a line. **2** people appearing on a show, etc.

hard lines bad luck.

line up to form a line.

one's line of country one's field of study or interest.

shoot a line *(slang)* to boast, exaggerate.

linen *lin'ėn, n.* **1** cloth made of flax. **2** underclothing, sheets and tablecloths, etc. of linen, or sometimes other materials.

liner. See **line²**.

ling¹ *ling, n.* a fish resembling the cod.

ling² *ling, n.* heather.

linger *ling'gėr, v.i.* **1** to loiter. **2** to delay. **3** to remain, last, continue, for a long time, or after the expected time.

ling'ering *adj.*

lingerie *lanᵍ-zhė-rē, n.* women's underclothing.

lingo *ling'gō, (humorous* or *in contempt) n.* a language:—*pl.* **lin'goes**.

lingua franca *ling'gwȧ frangk'ȧ,* any language, usu. simplified, used by speakers of different languages, esp. traders, as a means of communication.

lingual *ling'gwȧl, adj.* of the tongue.

ling'uist *n.* **1** one skilled in languages. **2** one who studies linguistics.

linguist'ic, -al *adjs.* of languages or linguistics.

linguist'ics *n. sing.* the scientific study of languages.

liniment *lin'i-mėnt, n.* a kind of thin, usu. oily, ointment for rubbing on the skin.

lining. See **line²**.

link *lingk, n.* **1** a ring of a chain. **2** a single part of a series. **3** anything connecting.—*v.t.* to connect (as) by a link.—*v.i.* to be connected.

link'age *(-ij) n.* the act of linking or state of being linked.

missing link **1** something needed to complete a series. **2** a supposed creature between man and his ape-like ancestors.

lint *lint, n.* **1** linen scraped into a soft woolly substance for dressing wounds. **2** fine pieces of fluff.

lintel *lint'(ė)l, n.* a timber or stone over a doorway or window.

lion *lī'ȯn, n.* **1** a large, tawny, flesh-eating animal of the cat family (*fem.* **lī'oness**). **2** a very brave man. **3** a famous person.

lī'onise *v.t.* to treat (a person) as a celebrity:—*pr.p.* **lī'onising.**

lī'on-hear'ted *adj.* of great courage.

lion's share the largest share.

See also **leonine.**

lip *lip, n.* **1** either of the flaps of flesh in front of the teeth by which things are taken into the mouth. **2** the edge of anything.

lipped *adj.* having lips, or edges like lips.

lip'-reading *n.* understanding what a person says by watching the movement of his lips (*v.i., v.t.* **lip'-read**).

lip service insincere expressions of approval or devotion: *Most of us pay at least lip service to democracy.*

lip'stick *n.* colouring matter in stick form for the lips.

liquefy. See **liquid.**

liqueur *li-kūr',* or *lē-kûr', n.* a strong alcoholic drink, strongly flavoured.

liquid *lik'wid, adj.* **1** able to flow—fluid, but not in gas form. **2** clear in appearance:

liquid eyes. **3** clear in sound. **4** in cash, or convertible into it: *liquid assets.*—*n.* **1** a liquid substance. **2** a flowing consonant sound, as *l, r.*

liquefy *lik'wi-fī, v.t., v.i.* to make, or to become, liquid:—*pr.p.* **liq'uefying**; *pa.p.* **liq'uefied.**

liquefac'tion *n.*

liq'uidate *v.t.* **1** to clear or pay off (a debt). **2** to arrange or wind up (the affairs of a bankrupt). **3** (*coll.*) to do away with, kill:—*pr.p.* **liq'uidating.**

liquidā'tion *n.* **liq'uidātor** *n.*

liq'uidise *v.t.* **1** to make liquid. **2** to puree (food):—*pr.p.* **liq'uidising.**

liq'uidiser *n.* a machine which liquidises food.

liquid'ity *n.* **1** the state of being liquid. **2** the state of having liquid assets.

liquid oxygen, helium, etc. these gases reduced to liquid condition at very low temperatures.

liquid crystal display a means of showing information, e.g. in electronic calculators, based on the changes in light-reflecting properties of certain substances (**liquid crystals**) when affected by an electric current.

liquor *lik'ȯr, n.* **1** strong drink. **2** a strong solution of a substance.

liquorice *lik'ȯr-is, n.* a plant with a sweet root used in medicine and as a sweet.

lira *lē'rȧ, n.* **1** an Italian coin. **2** a Turkish coin:—*pl.* **lire** *(lē'rā),* **lir'as.**

lisp *lisp, v.i.* **1** to speak with the tongue against the upper teeth or gums, as in saying *th* for *s.* **2** to speak as a small child does.—Also *v.t.*—*n.* the act or habit of lisping.

lissome, lissom *lis'ȯm, adj.* **1** nimble. **2** bending easily.

list[1] *list, n.* a series, roll (e.g. of names, articles).—*v.t.* to place in a list, read out a list of, etc.

listed building one officially listed as being of special architectural or historic interest, and which cannot be knocked down or altered without government, or local government, consent.

list[2] *list, v.i.* to heel, lean, over to one side.—*n.* such a heeling over.

listen *lis'n, v.i.* **1** to give attention so as to hear. **2** to follow advice.

list'ener *n.*

listeriosis *lis-tēr-i-ō'sis, n.* a disease affecting the brain, caused by eating food contaminated by **listeria** bacteria.

listless *list'lės, adj.* without energy or interest, weary.

lists *lists, n.pl.* a ground for jousting (see this), scene of fighting.

enter the lists to take part in a contest.

lit. See **light**[1,3].

litany *lit'ȧ-ni, n.* an appointed form of prayer with responses, in public worship:—*pl.* **lit'anies.**

litchi. See **lychee.**

literacy. See **literate.**

literal *lit'ėr-ȧl, adj.* **1** according to the plain, strict meaning with no exaggeration and nothing added by the imagination. **2** following the meaning word for word: *a literal translation.* **3** (of a person) unimaginative.

lit'erally *adv.* **lit'eralness** *n.*

literary *lit'ėr-ȧr-i, adj.* **1** of literature or learning. **2** concerned with the writing of books.

lit'eracy *n.* the state of being literate.

lit'erate *(-it) adj.* able to read and write:—*opp.* **illiterate.**

literature *lit'(ė-)rȧ-chůr, n.* **1** compositions in verse or prose, esp. those of fine quality. **2** the whole body of literary compositions in a language. **3** the whole body of writings on a given subject. **4** the writer's profession.

lithe *līTH, adj.* bending easily, supple.

lithe'ness *n.*

lithium *lith'i-ům, n.* an element, the lightest metal.

lithograph *lith'ȯ-gräf, v.t.* to print from stone, or a substitute, with greasy ink.—*n.* a print so made (*abbrev.* **lī'tho,** *pl.* **-os**).

lithog'rapher *n.* **lithog'raphy** *n.*

lithograph'ic, -al *adjs.*

lithograph'ically *adv.*

litigate *lit'i-gāt, v.i.* to go to law.—*v.t.* to contest at law:—*pr.p.* **lit'igating.**

litigā'tion *n.*

lit'igant *n.* a person engaged in a lawsuit.

litig'ious *adj.* fond of taking cases to court.

litmus *lit'mus, n.* a substance, orig. obtained from certain lichens, turned red by acids, blue by bases.

litre *lē'tėr, n.* a metric unit of capacity, equal to about 1.76 pints.—(as part of a word) denoting the capacity of the cylinders of a motor-vehicle engine: *three-litre.*

litter *lit'ėr, n.* **1** a heap of straw for animals to lie on. **2** objects, esp. of little value, rubbish, etc. lying scattered about. **3** a couch carried by men or animals. **4** a number of animals born at one birth.—*v.t.* to cover (e.g. the ground) with scattered objects.—*v.i.* of animals, to produce a litter of young.

litter bin a container in which small items of rubbish can be put.

little *lit'l, adj.* **1** small in size. **2** small in amount or importance. **3** not much:—*comp.* **less**; *superl.* **least** *(lēst).—n.* **1** a small amount. **2** a short time or distance.—*adv.* **1** not much. **2** to a small degree. **3** not at all: *He little knows what is going to happen* (i.e. he does not know or suspect).

litt'leness *n.*

Little Bear the northern group of stars that contains the pole star.

make, think, little of. See **make, think.**

the little man the underdog.

See also **less, lesser, lessen.**

littoral *lit'ȯr-ȧl, adj.* belonging to the seashore.—*n.* the strip of land along it.

liturgy *lit'ur-ji, n.* the regular form of service of a church:—*pl.* **lit'urgies.**

litur'gic(al) *adjs.* **litur'gically** *adv.*

live[1] *liv, v.i.* **1** to have life. **2** to continue to be alive. **3** to dwell. **4** to keep oneself alive (on): *to live on fish.* **5** to be supported by (with *on*). **6** to get a livelihood (by): *He makes a/his living by buying and selling old books.* **7** to pass one's life: *to live in luxury.* **8** to be lifelike or vivid.—*v.t.* **1** to spend or pass: *to live a life of ease.* **2** to show in one's life: *He really lives his Christian faith*:—*pr.p.* **liv'ing.**

liv'er *n.*

liv'ing *adj.* **1** having life. **2** now alive. **3** active, lively. **4** (of a likeness) exact.—*n.* **1** a means of keeping oneself alive. **2** the benefice of a clergyman.

living language one still spoken and still developing.

living memory the memory of people still alive.

living prefix one that can still be used to form new compound words (e.g. *re-*, again, *un-*, as opposed to *ad-*, *for-*).

liv'ing-room *n.* the room in the house in which people spend most of the day.

living wage a wage on which it is possible for a man and his family to live decently.

live and let live to allow others to live as they please.

live down to undo the effect of (a misdeed, scandal, etc.) by good conduct.

live up to to be as good as (what is expected of one).

See also **life.**

live[2] *līv, adj.* **1** having life, not dead (used before a noun; e.g. *a live mouse*; but *the mouse was alive*). **2** full of life, energy, activity. **3** burning: *a live coal.* **4** capable of exploding: *a live shell.* **5** (of a broadcast, telecast, or performance in the theatre) heard, seen, as the event takes place, not recorded.—Also *adv.*

lively *līv'li, adj.* **1** vigorous, active. **2** sprightly:—*comp.* **live'lier;** *superl.* **live'liest.**

live'liness *n.*

live rail a rail carrying an electric current.

live'stock *n.* domestic animals, esp. horses, cattle, sheep, and pigs.

live wire **1** a wire carrying an electric current. **2** (**live'-wire**) a person of energy and forcefulness.

livelihood *līv'li-hood, n.* a means of living.

livelong *liv'long, adj.* whole: *the livelong day.*

lively, liveliness. See **live**[2].

liver[1]. See **live**[1].

liver[2] *liv'ėr, n.* a large gland carrying out several important functions in the life of the body, formerly thought to be the seat of courage.

liv'erish, liv'ery *adjs.* **1** suffering from disordered liver. **2** irritable.

liver salts substances taken to cure indigestion.

liv'erwort *n.* any of many small plants related to the mosses.

livery[1] *liv'ėr-i, n.* **1** (*orig.*) the distinctive dress provided for his household by a king or nobleman. **2** uniform worn by menservants:—*pl.* **liv'eries.**

liv'eried *adj.* clothed in livery.

livery stable a stable where horses and vehicles are kept for hire.

livery[2]. See **liver**[2].

lives. See **life.**

livid *liv'id, adj.* **1** black and blue. **2** very pale, esp. with emotion, e.g. anger.

liv'idly *adj.* **liv'idness** *n.*

living. See **live**[1].

lizard *liz'ȧrd, n.* a usu. four-footed scaly reptile.

llama *lä'mȧ, n.* a S. American cud-chewing animal of the camel family.

llano *lyä'nō, lä'nō, n.* one of the vast plains in northern South America:—*pl.* **llan'os.**

Lloyd's Register *loidz rej'is-tėr*, a list of ships classified (as A1, etc.) according to type, size, seaworthiness, etc.

lo *lō, interj.* look!, behold!

loach *lōch, n.* a type of small river fish.

load *lōd, n.* **1** a freight or cargo. **2** a burden. **3** a heavy weight or task. **4** the output of an electrical machine, generating station, etc. **5** the power carried by a circuit.—*v.t.* **1** to put a load on, in. **2** to burden. **3** to give in abundance: *to load him with gifts, honours.* **4** to increase weight of by adding something heavy: *to load a stick.* **5** to

weight for the purpose of cheating: *to load dice.* **6** to fill (e.g. a gun, a camera) with something.
load'ed *adj.* rich.
load'ing *n.*
loaded question one meant to force or trap a person into admitting, agreeing to, etc. something unwillingly.
load'line *n.* a line along the ship's side to mark the depth to which her proper cargo causes her to sink.

loadstar. Same as **lodestar**.

loadstone. Same as **lodestone**.

loaf[1] *lōf, n.* a regularly shaped mass of bread:—*pl.* **loaves** *(lōvz)*.
loaf'-sug'ar *n.* sugar in the form of a cone, often later formed into cubes.

loaf[2] *lōf, v.i.* to loiter, pass time idly.
loaf'er *n.*

loam *lōm, n.* a fertile soil containing vegetable matter.

loan *lōn, n.* **1** anything lent. **2** the act of lending.—*v.t.* (chiefly *U.S.*) to lend.

loath, **loth** *lōth, adj.* unwilling (to).
nothing lo(a)th willing, willingly.

loathe *lō*TH, *v.t.* to dislike greatly:—*pr.p.* **loath'ing**.
loath'ing *n.*
loath'some (*-th-* or -TH-) *adj.* arousing loathing, horrible.

loaves. See **loaf**[1].

lob *lob, n.* **1** in cricket, a slow high underhand ball. **2** in tennis, a ball high overhead dropping near the back of the court.—*v.t.* to bowl or strike (a ball) as a lob:—*pr.p.* **lobb'ing**; *pa.p.* **lobbed**.

lobate. See **lobe**.

lobby *lob'i, n.* **1** a hall or passage serving as an entrance usu. to several rooms. **2** a group of people trying to persuade the government or other authority to do, or not to do, something.—*v.t.* to try as a lobby to persuade or dissuade (someone), or to get (support for something).—*v.i.* to act as a lobby, formerly esp. to frequent the lobby of a legislative chamber (e.g. House of Commons) with the intention of influencing members' votes:—*pr.p.* **lobb'ying**; *pa.p.* **lobb'ied**.

lobe *lōb, n.* **1** the soft lower part of the ear. **2** a division of the lungs, brain, etc. **3** a division of a leaf.
lob'āte, **lobed** *adjs.* having or consisting of lobes.
lobot'omy *n.* an operation performed on the frontal lobes of the brain, to cure certain types of mental disorder:—*pl.* **lobot'omies**.

lobster *lob'stėr, n.* a shellfish with large claws, used for food.
lob'ster-pot *n.* a basket for trapping lobsters.

lobworm *lob'wûrm, n.* a lugworm.

local *lō'kȧl, adj.* **1** of a place. **2** confined to a spot or district.—*n.* (*coll.*) the local inn or public house.
locale *(-käl') n.* the scene (of an event).
lō'calise *v.t.* to confine or restrict to a place or area:—*pr.p.* **lo'calising**.
local'ity *n.* **1** a position. **2** a district:—*pl.* **local'ities**.
lō'cally *adv.* **1** near the place mentioned. **2** in (a) certain place(s).
locāte' *v.t.* **1** to set in a particular position. **2** to situate. **3** to find the place of:—*pr.p.* **locat'ing**.
locā'tion *n.* **1** the act of locating. **2** situation.
local authority a body of people elected as local government.
local colour details characteristic of the time or place spoken of.
local government the administration of local affairs of towns, counties, etc., *opp.* to national or central government.
on location (*cinema*) in natural surroundings outside the studio.

loch *lo*H, *n.* **1** a lake. **2** an arm of the sea.

lock[1] *lok, n.* **1** a device for fastening doors, etc. **2** an enclosure in a canal for raising or lowering boats. **3** the part of a firearm by which the charge is exploded. **4** a grapple in wrestling.—*v.t.* **1** to fasten with a lock. **2** to close fast. **3** to make immovable. **4** to embrace closely.—Also *v.i.*
lock'er *n.* a small cupboard, esp. for sports gear.
lock'et *n.* a little ornamental case hung from the neck.
lock'jaw *n.* a form of tetanus affecting the muscles of the jaw.
lock'out *n.* the act of locking out, esp. used of the closing of works by employers during a trade dispute.
lock'smith *n.* a person who makes and mends locks.
lock'-up *n.* a place for locking up prisoners, motor-cars, etc.
lock, stock, and barrel completely.
lock up 1 to lock. **2** to close by locking.
under lock and key locked up, imprisoned.

lock[2] *lok, n.* a tuft or ringlet of hair.

locker, **locket**, etc. See **lock**[1].

locomotive *lō-kȯ-mōt'iv, adj.* **1** capable of, or assisting in, movement from place to place. **2** moving, travelling.—*n.* a railway engine.
locomō'tion *n.*

locum(-tenens) *lō'kum (-tēn'enz, -ten')* *n.* a substitute for an absent doctor, clergyman, etc:—*pl.* **lo'cums**, **lo'cum-tenen'tēs**.

locus *lō'kus*, *n.* the line (or the surface) formed by taking all positions of a point (or of a line) that satisfy a given condition:—*pl.* **loci** *(lō'sī)*.

locust *lō'kust*, *n.* **1** an insect related to grasshoppers, very destructive to crops. **2** a tree whose pods resemble insects, the carob.

locution *lō-kū'sh(o)n*, *n.* **1** a word or phrase. **2** a style of speaking.

lode *lōd*, *n.* a vein in rock containing metal.
lode'star *n.* **1** the star that guides, the pole star. **2** something that guides.
lode'stone *n.* magnetic iron ore in the form in which it not only is attracted but also attracts.

lodge *loj*, *n.* **1** a dwelling at a gate to the grounds of a large house. **2** a house occupied during the shooting or hunting season. **3** a room at a college gate, etc., for the porter. **4** the meeting-place of a branch of some societies. **5** the branch itself. **6** a beaver's dwelling.—*v.t.* **1** to provide (a person) with a place to stay. **2** to deposit. **3** to fix (in) (*opp.* **dislodge**'). **4** to make formally: *to lodge a complaint.*—*v.i.* **1** to reside, on payment for room(s) and attendance, in someone else's house. **2** to become fixed (in):—*pr.p.* **lodg'ing**.
lodg'er *n.* one hiring rooms in another's house.
lodg'ing *n.* a room or rooms hired in the house of another (often in *pl.*).

loess *lûs*, *lō'is*, *n.* a deposit of loam in certain river valleys.

loft *loft*, *n.* **1** a room or space under a roof. **2** a gallery in a hall or church. **3** the slope on the face of a golf club.—*v.t.* to cause to rise into the air.
lof'ty *adj.* **1** very high. **2** high in position, character, etc. **3** high-flown. **4** haughty:—*comp.* **lof'tier**; *superl.* **lof'tiest**.
lof'tily *adv.* **lof'tiness** *n.*

log¹ *log*, *n.* **1** a thick piece of unshaped wood. **2** an apparatus, orig. a block of wood, for finding a ship's speed. **3** a logbook.—*v.t.* to enter in a logbook:—*pr.p.* **logg'ing**; *pa.p.* **logged**.
log'book *n.* **1** an official record of a ship's or aeroplane's progress. **2** a similar record kept by the headmaster of a school, etc. **3** the registration documents of a motor vehicle.
logg'erhead *n.* a blockhead, a dunce.
log'-line *n.* the line fastened to the log and marked for finding the speed of a vessel.
log'rolling *n.* **1** causing log(s) to roll to a desired place. **2** (*in a bad sense*) mutual aid among politicians to further their own ends.
at loggerheads quarrelling.

log² *log*, *n.* abbrev. for **logarithm**.

loganberry *lō'gan-ber-i*, *n.* a fruit usu. considered to be a cross between raspberry and blackberry, obtained by Judge *Logan*:—*pl.* **log'anberries**.

logarithm *log'a-rithm*, *-ri*THm, *n.* the power to which a base (10 in **common logarithms**) must be raised to produce a given number (e.g. 3 is the logarithm of 1000 to the base 10 because 10^3 or $10 \times 10 \times 10 = 1000$).
logarith'mic(al) *adjs.*

loggia *loj'(y)a*, *n.* an open arcade, gallery, or balcony.

logic *loj'ik*, *n.* **1** the science and art of reasoning correctly. **2** correctness of reasoning.
log'ical *adj.* according to the rules of logic:—*opp.* **illogical**.
logical'ity *n.* **log'ically** *adv.*

logistics *lo-jis'tiks*, *n. sing.* **1** the art of transporting, housing, and supplying troops. **2** the handling of the practical details of any large or complex undertaking.
logis'tic *adj.*

logo *log'ō*, *n.* a badge or symbol of an association, business firm, etc., consisting of a simple picture or design and/or letters:—*pl.* **log'os**.

loin *loin*, *n.* **1** the back of a beast cut for food. **2** (in *pl.*) the lower part of the back.
loin'-cloth *n.* a piece of cloth worn round the hips, esp. in India and south-east Asia.
gird up one's loins to prepare for energetic action.

loiter *loi'tėr*, *v.i.* **1** to proceed, work, slowly. **2** to linger, stand around.
loi'terer *n.*

loll *lol*, *v.i.* **1** to lie, etc., lazily about, to lounge. **2** (of the tongue) to hang down or out.

lollipop *lol'i-pop*, *n.* a large sweet on a stick.
lolly (*slang*) *n.* **1** a lollipop (*pl.* **loll'ies**). **2** money.

lone *lōn*, *adj.* (used only before a noun) solitary, companionless (e.g. *a lone figure on the deserted beach*; but *he was alone on the beach)*.
lone'ly *adj.* **1** lacking, or feeling the lack of, companionship. **2** (of a place) isolated, with few people:—*comp.* **lone'lier**; *superl.* **lone'liest**.

lone'liness *n.*
lon'er *n.* a lone wolf (see below).
lone'some *adj.* dismal or depressed because of solitariness.
lone'someness *n.*
lone wolf one who prefers to be by himself without companions.

long *long, adj.* **1** not short—such that there is a considerable distance from one end to the other. **2** of a stated length: *Draw a line three inches long.* **3** (of time) such that there is a considerable interval from the first moment to the last. **4** slow (in coming). **5** tedious. **6** far-reaching:—*comp.* **longer** *(long'gėr)*; superl. **longest** *(long'gėst).*—*adv.* **1** to a great extent of time. **2** through the whole time: *all day long.*—*v.i.* (with *for, to*) to desire earnestly.
long'ing *n.* an eager desire, craving.—*adj.* yearning.
long'ingly *adv.*
long'boat *n.* **1** the largest and strongest boat of a ship. **2** a longship.
long'bow *n.* a large bow drawn by hand (see also **crossbow**).
long'-dis'tance *adj.* covering, travelling, etc. a long distance or time.
long'-drawn(-out') *adjs.* taking a long time, esp. unnecessarily.
long drink a large thirst-quenching drink, sometimes alcoholic, in a tall glass.
long face a dismal expression.
long'hand *n.* writing of the ordinary kind, as opposed to *shorthand.*
long'-head'ed *adj.* **1** far-seeing, shrewd. **2** having a long head.
long johns long-legged underwear.
long leg *(cricket)* a position in leg distant from the wicket.
long'-life *adj.* of food, treated so as to prolong freshness.
long'-lived' *adj.* living, or lasting, a long time.
long'-play'ing *adj.* denoting a record, usu. twelve inches in diameter, which is able to have a relatively large amount of music, etc. recorded on it because of its very fine groove.
long'-range' *adj.* **1** able to reach a long distance. **2** taking into consideration a long period of time.
long'ship *n.* a viking ship.
long'-sight'ed *adj.* **1** able to see far but not close at hand. **2** having foresight.
long stop *(cricket)* one who stands behind the wicket-keeper and tries to stop balls missed by him.
long'-suff'ering *adj.* enduring much and patiently.—*n.* long endurance or patience.
long'-term *adj.* (of a policy) concerned with the future, not just with the present.
long'-tongued' *adj.* talkative.
long'-wind'ed *adj.* **1** having ability to run far without rest. **2** (of a speaker or a speech) tiresomely long.
before long, ere long soon.
draw the longbow, long bow to exaggerate, tell tall stories.
in the long run in the end.
long ago in the far past.
the long and the short of it the matter, story, etc. summed up briefly.
See also **length**.

longevity *lon-jev'i-ti, n.* great length of life.

longitude *lon'ji-tūd, long'gi-, n.* the arc of the equator between the meridian of a place and a standard meridian (usu. that of Greenwich) expressed in degrees E. or W.
longitud'inal *adj.* **longitud'inally** *adv.*

longshoreman *long'shōr-mȧn, -shōr-, n.* **1** a stevedore. **2** a man employed along the shore:—*pl.* **long'shoremen**.

loo *lōō, (coll.) n.* a lavatory.

loofa(h) *lōō'fȧ, n.* the fruit of a tropical plant, the dried fibres of which are used as a sponge or scrubber in the bath.

look *look, v.i.* **1** to direct the eyes with attention. **2** to seem. **3** to face: *The house looks west.*—*v.t.* to express by a look: *She looked daggers at him.*—*n.* **1** the act of looking or seeing. **2** a glance: *a look of scorn.* **3** appearance.—*imper.* or *interj.* see, behold!
look'er-on' *n.* a mere spectator:—*pl.* **look'ers-on'**.
look'-in *(coll.) n.* **1** a chance of success. **2** a share in an activity.
look'ing-glass *n.* a piece of glass, to which a reflecting back has been added, in which one can see oneself.
look'-out *n.* **1** a careful watch. **2** a place from which to observe. **3** a person employed in watching. **4** prospect. **5** concern: *That's your look-out.*
look after to attend to, take care of.
look at to consider: *He would not look at the proposal.*
look down on to despise.
look for 1 to search for. **2** to expect.
look forward to to anticipate with pleasure.
look in to watch television.
look into to inspect closely, to investigate.
look on 1 to be a spectator. **2** to regard, view: *I look on this as a grave mistake.*
look out 1 to watch (**look out!** *interj.* of warning, beware! take care!). **2** to search for or select.
look over to examine, but not with great

care.
look sharp. See **sharp**.
look up **1** to improve, become better. **2** to pay a visit to (a person). **3** to search for in a book of reference.
look up to to respect the conduct, opinions, etc., of.

loom[1] *lōōm*, *n.* a machine in which yarn or thread is woven into a fabric.

loom[2] *lōōm*, *v.i.* to appear indistinctly, often threateningly.

loon *lōōn*, *n.* the diver, a fish-eating diving-bird.

loony *lōō'ni*, (*coll.*) *n.* a madman:—*pl.* **loo'-nies**.—Also *adj.*

loop *lōōp*, *n.* **1** a doubling of a cord, chain, etc., through which another cord, etc., may pass. **2** a U-shaped bend (e.g. in a river). **3** a loop-shaped contraceptive device.—*v.t.* to fasten with, or form into, a loop or loops.
loop the loop esp. of an aeroplane, to move in a complete vertical loop or circle.

loophole *lōōp'hōl*, *n.* **1** a slit in a wall, etc. **2** a means of escape or of getting round, avoiding obeying, e.g. law.

loose *lōōs*, *adj.* **1** slack, not tight. **2** not tied. **3** free. **4** not compact. **5** not strict in form or logic: *a loose statement*, *argument.* **6** licentious: *loose living.*—*v.t.* to unfasten, untie:—*pr.p.* **loos'ing**.
loose'ly *adv.* **loose'ness** *n.*
loos'en *v.t.* **1** to make loose. **2** to relax (e.g. a hold). **3** to open, as the bowels.—*v.i.* to become loose, or less tight.
loose'-box *n.* a part of a stable where a horse is kept untied.
loose'-leaf' *adj.* having a cover which allows one to add or remove pages at will.
at a loose end. See **end**.
break, **let**, **loose** to escape, set free, from restraint or control.
on the loose **1** on holiday, esp. having a spree. **2** free from confinement.

loot *lōōt*, *n.* plunder.—*v.t.* and *v.i.* to plunder, ransack.

lop[1] *lop*, *v.i.* to hand down loosely:—*pr.p.* **lopp'ing**; *pa.p.* **lopped**.
lop'-eared *adj.* having drooping ears.
lop'-sīd'ed *adj.* leaning to one side, not having the two sides the same.

lop[2] *lop*, *v.t.* **1** to cut off the top or ends of (esp. a tree). **2** to cut (off unnecessary parts):—*pr.p.* **lopp'ing**; *pa.p.* **lopped**.

lope *lōp*, *v.i.* to run with a long stride:—*pr.p.* **lop'ing**.

loquacious *lō-kwā'shus*, *adj.* talkative.
loqua'ciousness, **loquac'ity** *(-kwas')*, *ns.*

lord *lörd*, *n.* **1** a master. **2** a superior. **3** a ruler. **4** a peer of the realm. **5** the son of a duke or marquis, or the eldest son of an earl. **6** (*cap.*) used as a part of various official titles, as **Lord Mayor**, **Lord Provost**. **7** (*cap.*) God, Christ.—*v.i.* to act the lord, tyrannise—usu. **lord it over** (someone).
lord'ly *adj.* **1** dignified. **2** haughty. **3** tyrannical. **4** grand:—*comp.* **lord'lier**; *superl.* **lord'liest**.
lord'liness *n.*
lord'ship *n.* **1** a word used in speaking to, or about, a man with the title 'Lord' and also certain judges not having this title (e.g. *Your Lordship*, *His Lordship*). **2** (*history*) the territory belonging to a lord. **3** rule, authority.
Lord's Day Sunday.
lords spiritual the archbishops and bishops in the House of Lords—*opp.* to **lords temporal**, the peers proper.
Lord's Supper the sacrament commemorating the last supper taken by Christ with His disciples before His crucifixion.
House of Lords the upper house in the British parliament.

lore *lōr*, *lör*, *n.* the whole body of knowledge (esp. knowledge handed down by word of mouth) on a subject.

lorgnette *lör-nyet'*, *n.* eyeglasses with a handle.

lorry *lor'i*, *n.* a road wagon without sides, or with low sides:—*pl.* **lorr'ies**.

lose *lōōz*, *v.t.* **1** to have taken away from one (e.g. by death or accident). **2** to cease to have. **3** to mislay. **4** to waste (time). **5** to miss: *to lose one's way.* **6** to cause to perish (usu. in passive): *The ship was lost in the storm.* **7** to fail to gain or win (a game, prize).—*v.i.* **1** to be unsuccessful. **2** to be worse off as the result of some happening:—*pr.p.* **los'ing**; *pa.p.* **lost**.
los'er *n.* **1** one who loses. **2** (*coll.*) an unsuccessful person.
los'ing *adj.* and *n.*
loss *los*, *n.* **1** the act, or fact, of losing. **2** destruction. **3** defeat. **4** something that is lost. **5** the amount taken away or by which something is made less: *It is difficult to estimate the loss.*
lost *lost*, *adj.* **1** parted with: *a long lost friend.* **2** no longer possessed. **3** missing. **4** not won. **5** thrown away: *a lost opportunity.* **6** squandered. **7** ruined. **8** with attention wholly taken up: *lost in thought.* **9** (with *to*) no longer, or not, feeling, etc.: *lost to all sense of shame.* **10** (with *to*) no longer belonging, or (of e.g. an opportunity) open, to (a person).
loss'-leader *n.* a thing sold at a loss to

attract other custom.

a losing fight, **game**, etc., one in which defeat is certain.

a lost cause an aim, object, that cannot be achieved.

at a loss 1 uncertain what to do. **2** at less than its cost or value.

be lost (up)on to be wasted, or have no effect, on (a person).

lose oneself 1 to lose one's way. **2** to have all one's attention taken up by (with *in*): *to lose oneself in a book*.

lot *lot*, *n*. **1** an object drawn from among a number so as to reach a decision by chance. **2** one's fortune in life. **3** a separate portion. **4** (*coll.*, also in *pl.*) a large quantity or number: *a lot of*, *lots of*, *people*.

the lot the entire amount.

loth *lōth*, *adj*. Same as **loath**.

lotion *lō'sh(ȯ)n*, *n*. a liquid applied to the skin, either as medicine or cosmetic.

lottery *lot'ėr-i*, *n*. **1** a distribution of prizes by lot. **2** anything of which the result is a matter of chance:—*pl*. **lott'eries**.

lotus *lō'tus*, *n*. **1** either of two African water-lilies. **2** in Greek legend, a tree of North Africa whose fruit made strangers forget their home.

loud *lowd*, *adj*. **1** making a great sound. **2** noisy. **3** showy and in bad taste.

loud, **loud'ly** *advs*. **loud'ness** *n*.

loud'hail'er *(-hāl')* *n*. a simple type of loudspeaker.

loud'speak'er *n*. an instrument for increasing the loudness of sounds so that they can be heard at a distance.

lough *loH*, *n*. the Irish form of **loch**.

lounge *lownj*, *v.i.* **1** to loll. **2** to move about without energy or purpose:—*pr.p.* **loung'ing**.—*n*. **1** a room where one may lounge, a sitting-room. **2** a waiting-room e.g. at an airport.

loung'er *n*. **1** one who makes a habit of lounging, an idler. **2** a type of chair on which one may stretch out and relax.

lounge suit a man's suit, less formal than morning or evening dress.

lour *lowr*, **lower** *low'ėr*, *v.i.* **1** to look sullen or threatening. **2** to scowl.

lour'ing, **low'ering** *adj*.

louse *lows*, *n*. **1** a wingless insect, a parasite on men and animals. **2** any of various other small parasites on animals or plants. **3** (*coll.*) a contemptible person:—*pl.* (*defs. 1,2*) **lice** *(līs)*, (*def. 3*) **lous'es**.

lousy *low'zi*, *adj*. **1** swarming with lice. **2** (*slang*) of very poor quality, worthy of contempt:—*comp*. **lous'ier**; *superl*. **lous'iest**.

lous'iness *n*.

lout *lowt*, *n*. **1** an awkward fellow. **2** a big ill-mannered fellow, a boor.

lout'ish *adj*.

louvre-door, **-window** *lōō'vėr-dōr*, *-dör*, *-win'dō*, *ns*. a door, window, consisting of sloping slats of wood (**louv'reboards**).—Also **louv'er-door**, etc.

love *luv*, *n*. **1** great fondness, a feeling roused by a person or thing that gives one delight. **2** strong attachment with sexual feeling. **3** the object of affection. **4** (*cap.*) the god of love, Cupid. **5** a score of nothing in tennis, etc.—*v.t.* **1** to be fond of. **2** to delight in.—*v.i.* to have the feeling of love:—*pr.p.* **lov'ing**.

lov'able *adj*. worthy of love.

lov'ably *adv*. **lov'ableness** *n*.

love'less *adj*. without love.

love'ly *adj*. **1** rousing love or admiration. **2** beautiful. **3** delightful in any way:—*comp*. **love'lier**; *superl*. **love'liest**.

love'liness *n*.

lov'er *n*. **1** one who has a strong liking for: *a lover of art*; *a music-lover*. **2** one who has a close sexual relationship with another to whom he or she is not married.

lov'ing *adj.*, *n*. **lov'ingly** *adv*.

love affair love and love-making outside of, or not ending in, marriage.

love'bird *n*. a small parrot, strongly attached to its mate.

love'-letter *n*. a letter expressing love.

love'lorn *adj*. forsaken by one's love.

love'sick *adj*. yearning, melancholy with love.

lov'ing-kind'ness *n*. kindness full of love, tenderness, mercy.

for love or money in any way whatever.

in love (with) feeling love, passion (for).

make love to 1 to try to gain the affections of. **2** to caress, have sexual intercourse with.

low[1] *lō*, *adj*. **1** not high. **2** not lying or reaching far up. **3** not loud. **4** not high in pitch. **5** small in number or amount: *a low price*. **6** feeble, weak. **7** depressed, dejected. **8** vulgar, coarse, indecent. **9** mean, bad, or holding someone to be so: *a low trick*; *a low opinion of someone*. **10** (of latitude) near the equator:—*comp*. **low'er**; *superl*. **low'est**.—*adv*. **1** in, or to, a low position or state. **2** not loudly. **3** cheaply.

low'er *v.t.* **1** to make less high. **2** to let down. **3** to lessen.—*v.i.* to become less high or less.

low'ermost *adj*. lowest.

low'ly *adj*. **1** humble in rank. **2** modest in character or conduct:—*comp*. **low'lier**; *superl*. **low'liest**.

low'liness *n*.

low'brow *n*. and *adj*. (one whose tastes

are) not intellectual.
Low Church (of) a party within the Church of England setting little value on sacraments and ceremonies or the authority of the priesthood.
low'-class *adj.* **1** of lower class. **2** vulgar.
low comedy comedy in which actions and happenings, rather than dialogue, are funny.
Low Countries the Netherlands.
low'-down *adj.* **1** low in position. **2** mean, worthy of contempt.—*n.* (*coll.*) information, esp. damaging (about a person, organisation, activity).
low'er-case' *adj.* of small letters as opp. to capitals.
lower class the least skilled and educated, and usu. poorest, section of a community.—*adj.* **low'er-class'**.
lower deck the (quarters of) petty officers and men.
Lower House the larger and more representative branch of a legislature that has two chambers.
low gear. See **gear**.
low'-key' *adj.* **1** undramatic, restrained. **2** not easily excited, showing no visible reaction.
low'lands *n.pl.* land low in comparison with higher land, esp. (*cap.*) south and east Scotland.
low'land, Low'land *adj.*
low'lander, Low'lander *n.*
low'-press'ure *adj.* **1** employing or exerting little pressure (of steam, steam-engine). **2** at low atmospheric pressure.
low profile a manner or attitude revealing very little of one's feelings, intentions, activities, etc.
low'-spir'ited *adj.* not lively, sad.
Low Sunday the first Sunday after Easter.
low tide, water the lowest point of the tide at ebb.
the Low Countries the Netherlands.

low[2] *lō*, *v.i.* to make the noise of cattle, moo.

lower[1]. See **lour**.

lower[2], **lower**[3]. See **low**[1].

loyal *loi'ȧl*, *adj.* faithful:—*opp.* **disloy'al**.
loy'alist *n.* one who is loyal to his sovereign, etc.—Also *adj.*
loy'ally *adv.* **loy'alty** *n.* (*pl.* **-ies**).

lozenge *loz'inj*, *n.* **1** a diamond-shaped parallelogram. **2** a small sweet.

lubber *lub'ėr*, *n.* a clumsy, or lazy, fellow.

lubricate *lōō'bri-kāt*, *lū'*, *v.t.* to oil:—*pr.p.* **lu'bricating**.
lu'bricant *n.* **lubricā'tion** *n.*
lu'bricator *n.*

lucerne *lōō-sûrn'*, *lū-*, *n.* a valuable plant for feeding horses and cattle, alfalfa.

lucid *lōō'sid*, *lū'*, *adj.* **1** easily understood. **2** clear in mind. **3** sane.
lucid'ity, lu'cidness *ns.* **lu'cidly** *adv.*

luck *luk*, *n.* **1** fortune, good or bad. **2** chance. **3** good fortune.
luck'less *adj.* unfortunate.
luck'y *adj.* **1** having good luck. **2** bringing good fortune:—*comp.* **luck'ier**; *superl.* **luck'iest**.
luck'ily *adv.* **luck'iness** *n.*
be down on one's luck 1 to be experiencing misfortune. **2** to be depressed.

lucre *lōō'kėr*, *lū'*, *n.* **1** sordid gain. **2** riches.
lu'crative *adj.* profitable.
lu'cratively *adv.* **lu'crativeness** *n.*

ludicrous *lōō'di-krŭs*, *lū'*, *adj.* absurd.
lu'dicrously *adv.* **lu'dicrousness** *n.*

ludo *lōō'dō*, *n.* a game played with counters on a board.

luff *luf*, *v.i.* to turn a ship towards the wind.

lug *lug*, *v.t.* to pull or carry (something heavy or bulky):—*pr.p.* **lugg'ing**; *pa.p.* **lugged**.
lugg'age *n.* the baggage of a traveller.

lug(sail) *lug('sāl, -sl)*, *n.* a square sail on a yard that crosses the mast obliquely.
lugg'er *n.* a small vessel with lugsails.

luggage. See **lug**.

lugubrious *lōō-gū'bri-ŭs*, *lū'-*, *adj.* mournful.
lugū'briously *adv.* **lugū'briousness** *n.*

lugworm *lug'wûrm*, *n.* a worm found in sea sand, used for bait.

lukewarm *lōōk'wörm*, *adj.* **1** slightly warm. **2** (of e.g. interest, supporters) indifferent, not enthusiastic.
luke'warmly *adv.* **luke'warmness** *n.*

lull *lul*, *v.t.* to soothe, to quiet.—*n.* an interval of calm.
lull'aby *(-bī)* *n.* a song to lull children to sleep:—*pl.* **lull'abies**.

lumbago *lum-bā'gō*, *n.* a rheumatic pain in the lower part of the back.
lum'bar *adj.* of the lower part of the back.

lumber[1] *lum'bėr*, *n.* **1** anything no longer of use, esp. if bulky. **2** timber sawed or split.
lum'berer, lum'berjack, lum'berman *ns.* one employed in **lum'bering**, the felling, sawing, and removal of timber.

lumber[2] *lum'bėr*, *v.i.* to move heavily and clumsily.

luminary *lōō'min-ȧr-i*, *lū'*, *n.* **1** a source of light, esp. one of the heavenly bodies. **2** a very eminent person:—*pl.* **lu'minaries**.
lumines'cence *(-es'ėns)* *n.* light (e.g. phosphorescence) that is not the result of high temperature.

lumines'cent *adj.*
lu'minous *adj.* **1** giving light. **2** shining. **3** clear. **4** glowing in the dark.
lu'minously *adv.*
lu'minousness, luminos'ity *ns.*

lump *lump, n.* **1** a small shapeless mass. **2** a swelling. **3** the whole together: *considered in the lump.* **4** a heavy, spiritless person.—*v.t.* **1** to treat as all alike (usu. **lump together**). **2** (*coll.*) to put up with: *to lump it.*—*v.i.* to form into lumps.
lump'ish *adj.* **1** like a lump. **2** heavy. **3** dull.
lump'y *adj.*:—*comp.* **lump'ier**; *superl.* **lump'iest**.
lump'iness *n.*
lump sum a sum of money given at one time, not by instalments.

lunacy *lo͞o'nȧ-si, lū', n.* **1** a kind of madness once believed to come with changes of the moon. **2** insanity.
lu'natic *adj.* and *n.*
lunatic fringe the more extreme in views or behaviour among the members of a group.

lunar *lo͞o'nȧr, lū', adj.* of the moon.—Also **lu'nary**.

lunatic. See **lunacy**.

lunch *lunch,* or *-sh, n.* a midday meal.—*v.i.* to take lunch.
luncheon *lunch'ȯn, lunsh', n.* lunch.
lunch'eon-meat *n.* a type of preserved cooked meat.
luncheon voucher a voucher given to an employee to be used as (part) payment for his lunch.

lung *lung, n.* one of the organs of breathing, either of two sacs in the body filled with constantly renewed air.

lunge *lunj, n.* a sudden thrust, as in fencing.—*v.i.* to make such a thrust:—*pr.p.* **lung'ing, lunge'ing**.

lupin *lo͞o'pin, lū', n.* a plant of the pea family, with flowers on long spikes.

lurch[1] *lûrch*: **leave in the lurch** to desert (a person) when he has got into difficulties.

lurch[2] *lûrch, v.i.* to pitch suddenly forward, or roll to one side.—Also *n.*

lurcher *lûr'chėr, n.* a crossbred dog with greyhound characteristics.

lure *lūr, lo͝or, n.* something used to entice, a bait.—*v.t.* to entice, tempt (away):—*pr.p.* **lur'ing**.

lurid *lū'rid, lo͞o', adj.* **1** ghastly pale. **2** gloomily threatening. **3** sensational.
lu'ridly *adv.* **lu'ridness** *n.*

lurk *lûrk, v.i.* **1** to lie in wait. **2** to be concealed.

luscious *lush'ùs, adj.* sweet in a great degree, esp. juicy and delicious.
lus'ciously *adv.* **lus'ciousness** *n.*

lush *lush, adj.* green and luxuriant.
lush'ness *n.*

lust *lust, n.* **1** depraved desire. **2** longing desire (for): *a lust for power.*—*v.i.* **1** to desire eagerly (with *after, for*). **2** to have depraved desires.
lust'ful *adj.* **lust'fully** *adv.*
lust'fulness *n.*
lus'ty *adj.* **1** vigorous. **2** healthy:—*comp.* **lus'tier**; *superl.* **lus'tiest**.
lus'tily *adv.* **lus'tiness** *n.*

lustre *lus'tėr, n.* **1** gloss, brightness. **2** splendour. **3** renown.
lus'trous *adj.* bright, shining.

lusty. See **lust**.

lute *lo͞ot, lūt, n.* an old stringed instrument shaped like a half pear.

luxury *luk'shù-ri, n.* **1** free indulgence in costly pleasures. **2** anything rare and delightful. **3** something pleasant but not necessary:—*pl.* **lux'uries**.
luxū'riant *(lug-zūr') adj.* **1** very free in growth. **2** over-rich in ornament.
luxū'riance, luxū'riancy *ns.*
luxū'riantly *adv.*
luxū'riate *v.i.* **1** to be luxuriant. **2** to live luxuriously. **3** to revel (in):—*pr.p.* **luxur'iating**.
luxū'rious *adj.* supplied with luxuries.
luxū'riously *adv.* **luxū'riousness** *n.*

lychee, litchi, lichee *lī'chē, lē'chē, n.* a Chinese fruit, with edible pulp.

lychgate. Same as **lichgate**.

lying. See **lie**[1,2].

Lyme disease *līme' diz-ēz' n.* a viral disease transmitted by ticks.

lymph *limf, n.* **1** a colourless or yellowish fluid in animal bodies. **2** a vaccine.
lymphat'ic *adj.* **1** of lymph. **2** sluggish. —*n.* a vessel which conveys the lymph.

lynch *linch, -sh, v.t.* to condemn and put to death with the usual forms of law.

lynx *lingks, n.* a catlike animal noted for its sharp sight.
lynx'-eyed *adj.* sharp-sighted.

lyre *līr, n.* musical instrument like harp.
lyric (*lir'*) *n.* **1** a lyric poem. **2** (in *pl.*) the words for song.
lyrical (*lir'*) *adj.* **1** (of poetry: also **lyr'ic**) expressing the individual emotions of the poet. **2** expressing great enthusiasm.
lyre'bird *n.* an Australian bird having the tail-feathers of the male arranged in a form like that of a lyre.

M

ma'am *mam, mäm, n.* a form of **madam**.

mac *mak, n.* short for **mackintosh**.

macabre *mȧ-kä'br', -bėr, adj.* gruesome, horrible.

macadamise *mȧ-kad'ȧm-īz, v.t.* to cover with small broken stones, so as to form a smooth, hard surface:—*pr.p.* **macad'amising**.

macaroni *mak-ȧ-rō'ni, n.* a paste of hard wheat flour, pressed out through small holes to form long tubes, and dried.

macaroon *mak-ȧ-ro͞on', n.* a sweet cake or biscuit made of almonds, etc.

macaw *mȧ-kö', n.* a large, long-tailed, brightly-coloured tropical American parrot.

mace¹ *mās, n.* **1** a metal or metal-headed war club, often spiked. **2** a staff used as a mark of authority.
mac'er *n.* **1** a mace-bearer. **2** in Scotland, an usher in a law court.
mace'-bearer *n.* an official who carries a mace in a procession in front of a person in authority.

mace² *mās, n.* a spice obtained from the same fruit as nutmeg.

macédoine *ma-sā-dwän', n.* a mixture of diced vegetables.

macer. See **mace¹**.

macerate *mas'ėr-āt, v.t.* and *v.i.* to soften by steeping:—*pr.p.* **mac'erating**.
macerā'tion *n.*

Mach. See **Mach number**.

machete *mȧ-chet'i, -shet', n.* a type of heavy knife or sword.

machination *mak-i-nā'sh(ȯ)n, n.* (esp. in *pl.*) a crafty scheme, plot.

machismo. See **macho**.

Mach number *mäH num'bėr,* the ratio of the speed of an aircraft to the velocity of sound (e.g. Mach 5 means 5 times the speed of sound).

macho *mach'ō, adj.* **1** aggressively male. **2** ostentatiously virile.
machismo *mȧ-chiz'mō, -chēz', -kiz', -kēz', n.* (the cult of) virility and masculine pride.

macintosh. See **mackintosh**.

mackerel *mak'(ė-)rėl, n.* a food fish, bluish green with wavy markings.

mac(k)intosh *mak'in-tosh, n.* a waterproof overcoat, orig. of rubber-coated material.

macramé *mȧ-krä'mi, n.* (the craft of making) articles of knotted thread or string.

macro- *mak-rō-,* (as part of a word) **1** large. **2** long. **3** too large, over-developed.

mad *mad, adj.* **1** insane. **2** (of a dog) suffering from rabies. **3** rash, foolish. **4** furious: *a mad bull.* **5** (*coll.*) very angry. **6** frantic (with pain, etc.):—*comp.* **madd'er**; *superl.* **madd'est**.
madd'en *v.t.* to make mad, esp. furiously angry.
madd'ening *adj.* **madd'eningly** *adv.*
mad'ly *adv.* **mad'ness** *n.*
mad'cap *adj.* impulsive, rash.—Also *n.*
mad'house *n.* **1** a lunatic asylum. **2** a place of confusion and noise.
mad'man *n.*
like mad **1** frantically. **2** very energetically.

madam *mad'ȧm, n.* a polite form of address to a lady:—*pl.* **mad'ams** or, in letters, **Mesdames** *(mā-dam').*

madcap, madden, etc. See **mad**.

madder¹ *mad'ėr, n.* a plant whose root gives a red dye.

madder², maddest. See **mad**.

made, etc. See **make**.

Madeira cake *mȧ-dē'rȧ kāk,* a type of sponge cake.

mademoiselle *mad-mwä-zel, mad-(ė-)mȯ-zel', n.* a form of address to a young woman.

madhouse. See **mad**.

Madonna *mȧ-don'ȧ, n.* the Virgin Mary, esp. as seen in works of art.

madrigal *mad'ri-gȧl, n.* a song in several parts sung without accompaniment.

maelstrom *māl'strȯm, n.* **1** a whirlpool, or more correctly current, off the coast of Norway. **2** any whirlpool. **3** any place or state of confusion and struggle.

maestro *mīs'trō, n.* a master, especially a musical composer or conductor:—*pl.* **maes'tros**.

Mae West *mā west,* (*slang*) an inflatable life-saving jacket.

Mafia *mä'fē-ȧ, n.* a secret criminal society, orig. from Sicily and now particularly active in the U.S.A.

magazine *mag-ȧ-zēn',* also *mag'-, n.* **1** a place for military stores. **2** the gunpowder room in a ship. **3** a compartment in a rifle, etc. for holding extra cartridges. **4** a publication issued at intervals, containing articles, stories, etc., by various writers.

magenta *mȧ-jen'tȧ, n.* a reddish-purple colour.—Also *adj.*

maggot *mag'ȯt, n.* **1** a legless grub, esp. of a fly. **2** a fad.
magg'oty *adj.*

Magi. See **Magus**.

magic *maj'ik, n.* **1** any influence that produces results which cannot be explained, or are marvellous or surprising. **2** conjuring tricks.—*adj.* **1** used in magic: *magic wand.* **2** using magic. **3** magical.
mag'ical *adj.* **1** produced by, or as if by, magic. **2** mysterious and beautiful.
mag'ically *adv.*
magician *mȧ-jish'ȧn, n.* one skilled in magic.
black magic magic done with the help of evil spirits.

magisterial *maj-is-tē'ri-ȧl, adj.* in the manner of a teacher or a magistrate.
magistē'rially *adv.*
mag'istracy *n.* the office or dignity of a magistrate.
mag'istrāte *n.* one who has power to put the laws into force, esp. a justice of the peace, or one who sits in a police court.

Magna Carta (**Charta**) *mag'nȧ kär'tȧ,* **1** the 'Great Charter' obtained from King John in 1215. **2** any charter guaranteeing liberty.

magnanimity *mag-nȧ-nim'i-ti, n.* **1** nobleness of nature. **2** generosity.
magnan'imous *adj.*
magnan'imously *adv.*

magnate *mag'nāt, n.* a man of rank or wealth, or of power.

magnesia *mag-nē'zhi-ȧ,* or *-zi-,* or *-s(h)i-, n.* a white magnesium salt used as a medicine.
magnē'sium *n.* an element, a silver-white metal, burning with a dazzling white light.

magnet *mag'nit, n.* **1** a piece of iron, or of certain other materials, that attracts or repels other pieces of iron, etc. **2** any thing, person, having strong attraction.
magnet'ic *adj.* **1** having the powers of a magnet. **2** strongly attractive.
mag'netise *v.t.* **1** to make magnetic. **2** to attract or to influence strongly:—*pr.p.* **mag'netising**.
mag'netism *n.* **1** the magnet's power to attract. **2** the science that deals with magnets. **3** attraction, charm.
magnē'to *n.* a device producing electric sparks, esp. one for lighting the fuel in a motor car engine:—*pl.* **magnē'tos**.
magnetic needle any slender bar of magnetised steel, esp. that in a compass which always points to the **magnetic north**, a direction usu. either east or west of the geographical pole (the true north).
magnetic tape material on which sound, pictures, or material for a computer, can be recorded.

magnificent *mag-nif'i-sėnt, adj.* **1** splendid in appearance. **2** great in deeds. **3** noble.
magnif'icence *n.* **magnif'icently** *adv.*
magnify *mag'ni-fī, v.t.* **1** to make to appear greater. **2** to exaggerate. **3** (*Bible*) to praise highly:—*pr.p.* **mag'nifying**; *pa.p.* **mag'nified**.
magnificā'tion *n.* **mag'nifier** *n.*
mag'nitude *(-tūd) n.* **1** size. **2** greatness. **3** importance.
magnifying glass a glass with curved surfaces which makes an object looked at through it appear larger.

magnolia *mag-nō'li-ȧ, -nōl'yȧ, n.* an American and Asiatic tree with large, usu. scented, flowers.

magnum *mag'nům, n.* a two-quart bottle.

magpie *mag'pī, n.* **1** a black-and-white chattering bird of the crow family, known also for its habit of collecting objects. **2** a chattering person. **3** one who hoards or steals trifles.

Magus *mā'gůs, n.* an ancient Persian astrologer and magician, esp. (in *pl.*) the three who brought gifts to the infant Jesus:—*pl.* **Ma'gi** *(-jī)*.

Magyar *mag'yär, n.* **1** a Hungarian. **2** the Hungarian language.

Maharaja(h) *mä-hä-rä'jä, n.* the title given to a great Indian prince:—*fem.* **Maharani, Maharanee** *(-rä'nē)*.

mahatma *mȧ-hät'mȧ, n.* a wise and holy leader.

mahogany *mȧ-hog'ȧ-ni, n.* **1** a tropical American tree. **2** its wood, valued for furniture making. **3** the colour of this, a dark reddish-brown (also *adj.*).

Mahomedan. Same as **Mohammedan**.

mahout *mä-howt', n.* the keeper and driver of an elephant.

maid *mād, n.* **1** an unmarried woman, esp. a young one (also **maid'en**). **2** a female servant (also **maid'-servant**).
maid'en *n.* a maid.—*adj.* (used only before a noun) **1** unmarried: *a maiden aunt.* **2** first: *maiden speech, voyage.*
maid'enly *adj.* **1** like a maiden. **2** gentle. **3** modest.
maiden name a married woman's surname before her marriage.
maiden over (*cricket*) an over in which no runs are scored.

mail[1] *māl, n.* **1** armour for the body made of steel rings. **2** armour generally.
mailed fist physical force.

mail[2] *māl, n.* letters, parcels, etc. sent by post.—*v.t.* (esp. *U.S.*) to post, send by post.
mail'bag *n.* a bag for letters, etc.
mailing list a list of the names and addresses of those to whom advertising material, etc. is to be posted.
mail order an order for goods to be sent by post.
mail shot unsolicited advertising material sent by post.

maim *mām, v.t.* to cripple, disfigure, damage.

main *mān, adj.* **1** chief, principal, most important. **2** sheer: *by main force.*—*n.* **1** the chief pipe or cable in a branching system of pipes or cables. **2** (in *pl.*) the water, gas, or electricity supply from such a system. **3** the high sea.
main'ly *adv.* chiefly, more (of) the thing mentioned than anything else: *mainly dark grey; a crowd mainly of children.*
main'deck, main'mast, main'sail, etc., *ns.* the principal deck, mast, sail, etc. of a ship.
main'frame *n.* the information-processing and storing unit of a computer.—*adj.* (of a computer) large and powerful.
main'land *n.* a large piece of land as opposed to neighbouring islands.
main'spring *n.* **1** the chief spring, esp. the spring that causes the wheels to move in a watch or clock. **2** the chief motive or cause.
main'stay *n.* **1** a rope (usu. wire) stretching forward from the mainmast. **2** a chief support.
main'stream *adj.* in accordance with what is normal or standard.
in the main for the most part.
with might and main with all one's strength (see derivation).

maintain *mėn-tān',* or *mān-, v.t.* **1** to keep: *to maintain silence.* **2** to continue, keep up: *to maintain an attack, a correspondence.* **3** to keep in good condition: *to maintain a road.* **4** to pay the expenses of, support: *to maintain a family.* **5** to continue to assert (that), to argue (that).
maintenance *mān'tėn-ȧns, n.* **1** support. **2** upkeep. **3** means of support.

maison(n)ette *māz-ȯn-et', n.* a small house or flat.

maize *māz, n.* an important cereal in America, etc., with large ears—called also **(Indian) corn.**

majesty *maj'is-ti, n.* **1** the greatness and glory (of God). **2** impressive dignity. **3** (*cap.*) a title of monarchs:—*pl.* **maj'esties.**
majes'tic(al) *adjs.*

major *mā'jor, adj.* greater, or great, in size, importance, etc.—*n.* **1** a person of full legal age (18 years). **2** a rank in the army, or a person of that rank.
majority *mȧ-jor'i-ti, n.* **1** (the party having) the greater number—opp. to *minority.* **2** the difference between the greater and the smaller number: *Black had 17 votes, White had 11; Black had, therefore, a majority of 6*:—*pl.* **major'ities.**
maj'or-gen'eral *n.* a rank in the army, or a person of that rank.
major scale one in which the third note is a major third above the first.
major third an interval of four semitones (e.g. C to E).—See also **minor third.**

make *māk, v.t.* **1** to construct, form: *to make a chair.* **2** to bring about (a change). **3** to perform (e.g. a journey). **4** to carry out (e.g. an attempt). **5** to compel. **6** to cause (e.g. trouble). **7** to prepare (e.g. tea). **8** to earn (e.g. a living). **9** to approach, reach (e.g. the shore). **10** to amount to:—*pr.p.* **mak'ing;** *pa.p.* **made.**—*n.* **1** form or shape. **2** texture. **3** brand.
mak'er *n.* **mak'ing** *n.*
made'-to-meas'ure *adj.* of clothing, made to fit the measurements of a particular person.
made'-up' *adj.* **1** wearing make-up. **2** (of a garment) fully manufactured. **3** (of e.g. a story) invented, not telling of facts.
make'shift *n.* something, usu. not very satisfactory, used for a time because the proper thing cannot be had.—Also *adj.*
make'-up *n.* **1** powder, lipstick, etc. for the face. **2** an actor's cosmetics, etc.
be made, be a made man to be sure (because of something that has happened) to succeed in life.
be the making of (someone) to result in his becoming a self-reliant person, or in his having a successful career.
in the making in the process of being made.
make away with. See **away.**
make believe to pretend (*n.* **make'-believe**).
make do to use or manage with (something less desirable) because what is wanted is not available.
make for to go towards, try to reach.
make good. See **good.**
make light of to treat as unimportant.
make little of 1 to treat as easy, or as unimportant. **2** to understand hardly at all.
make much of 1 to make a fuss about, treat as important. **2** to treat (a person)

with honour. **3** to understand much of.

make nothing of 1 to be unable to understand, to solve, or to do. **2** to consider of no difficulty or importance.

make off to run away.

make off with to steal.

make out 1 to see, but not very clearly. **2** to say, (try to) prove: *He made out that he had told them he would be late.* **3** to draw up in writing.

make up 1 to put make-up on. **2** to invent (a story). **3** to re-establish friendship after a quarrel.

make up for to atone, compensate for.

mal- *mal, prx.* bad(ly).

maladjusted *mal'ȧ-jus'tid, adj.* unable to be happy and successful in one's home life, work, etc.

maladjust'ment *n.*

maladministration *mal-ȧd-min-is-trā'-sh(ȯ)n, n.* bad management, esp. of public affairs.

See also **mal-**.

maladroit *mal'ȧ-droit*, or *-droit', adj.* clumsy.

malady *mal'ȧ-di, n.* an illness, disease:—*pl.* **mal'adies.**

malaise *mȧ-lāz', n.* a feeling of uneasiness, discomfort or sickness.

malaria *mȧ-lā'ri-ȧ, n.* a fever caused by exceedingly small parasites carried from man to man by certain mosquitos.

Malay *mȧ-lā', adj.* **1** a member of a race living in the Malay Peninsula, etc. **2** their language.—Also *adj.*—Also **Malay'an.**

malcontent *mal'kȯn-tent, n.* a person who is dissatisfied and inclined to rebel.

male *māl, adj.* **1** of the sex that fathers, not bears, young. **2** (*bot.*) having stamens.—Also *n.*

male chauvinist (pig) (*coll.*; *slightingly*) a man who believes in the superiority of men over women, and acts accordingly.

male- *mal-i-*, (as part of word) ill, evil.

malediction *(-dik'sh(ȯ)n) n.* a curse.

mal'efactor *(-i-fak-tȯr) n.* an evil-doer.

malevolent *mal-ev'ȯ-lėnt, adj.* wishing evil to others.

malev'olence *n.* **malev'olently** *adv.*

See also **mal.**

malformation *mal-fȫr-mā'sh(ȯ)n, n.* faulty or bad shape.

malfunction *mal-fungk'sh(ȯ)n, n.* the act or fact of working imperfectly.—Also *v.i.*

malice *mal'is, n.* ill-will, spite.

malicious *mȧ-lish'ȯs, adj.*

malic'iously *adv.*

with malice aforethought with deliberate intention to commit the evil act.

malign *mȧ-līn', v.t.* to speak evil of, esp. falsely.—*adj.* malignant, intending harm.

maligner *(-līn') n.* **malignly** *(-līn') adv.*

malignant *mȧ-lig'nȧnt, adj.* **1** anxious to do harm. **2** (of disease) causing death, or going from bad to worse, esp. cancerous.

malig'nance, -ancy *ns.*

malig'nantly *adv.*

malignity *mȧ-lig'ni-ti, n.* **1** great ill-will, malevolence. **2** deadliness.

malinger *mȧ-ling'gėr, v.i.* to pretend to be sick in order to avoid work.

maling'erer *n.*

mallard *mal'ȧrd, n.* the common wild duck.

malleable *mal'i-ȧ-bl, adj.* **1** (esp. of metal) able to be beaten, rolled, etc., into shape. **2** (of a person) impressionable, easy to influence.

malleabil'ity *n.*

mallet *mal'it, n.* **1** a small wooden hammer. **2** a long-handled hammer for playing croquet or polo.

malnutrition *mal-nū-trish'(ȯ)n, n.* **1** faulty nutrition. **2** underfeeding.

malodorous *mal-ō'dȯr-ȯs, adj.* evil-smelling.

malpractice *mal-prak'tis, n.* **1** evil practice. **2** wrongdoing, esp. improper professional behaviour.

malt *mölt, n.* barley or other grain soaked in water, allowed to sprout, and dried in a kiln.—*v.t.* to make into malt.

mal'ted *adj.*

malt'ster *n.* one whose job is making malt.

malted milk (a drink prepared from) powder made from dried milk and malted cereals.

malt liquor a liquor (e.g. beer) made with malt.

malt whisky whisky made from malted barley.

maltreat *mal-trēt', v.t.* to use roughly, or treat unkindly.

maltreat'ment *n.*

mama. See **mamma.**

mamba *mam'bȧ, n.* a large deadly snake of S. Africa.

mamma, mama *mȧ-mä', n.* mother.

mamm'y *n.* a child's word for mother:—*pl.* **mamm'ies.**

mammal *mam'ȧl, n.* any member of the class of animals in which the females feed the young with their own milk.

mammā'lian *n.*

mammary *mam'ȧr-i, adj* of the breasts or other milk-producing glands.

mammon *mam'ȯn, n.* riches, (the acquiring of) wealth.

mammoth *mam'ȯth*, *n.* a large elephant of a kind no longer found living.—*adj.* very large.

mammy. See **mamma**.

man *man*, *n.* **1** a human being. **2** human beings in general. **3** a grown-up human male. **4** a valet. **5** a member of a team. **6** a husband. **7** a piece used in playing chess or draughts:—*pl.* **men**.—*v.t.* to operate, work on or with (e.g. a ship, a gun):—*pr.p.* **mann'ing**; *pa.p.* **manned**.
man'ful *adj.* **1** manly. **2** courageous.
man'fully *adv.* **man'fulness** *n.*
man'hood *n.* **1** the state of being a man. **2** manly quality.
mankind' *n.* the human race.
man'ly *adj.* **1** having qualities suitable to a man. **2** brave and frank:—*comp.* **man'lier**; *superl.* **man'liest**.
man'liness *n.*
mann'ish *adj.* (of a woman) like a man in manner.
man'-at-arms' *n.* a soldier, esp. mounted and heavily-armed.
man'-eater *n.* an animal, esp. a tiger, who will eat human beings.
man'handle *v.t.* **1** to move by manpower. **2** to handle roughly:—*pr.p.* **man'handling**.
man'hole *n.* a hole large enough for a man to enter e.g. a sewer by it.
man'-hour *n.* an hour's work by one person:—*pl.* **man'-hours**.
man'-made *adj.* of a fibre, made artificially, not occurring naturally.
man'-of-war' *n.* a warship:—*pl.* **men'-of-war**.
man'power *n.* **1** power supplied by the physical effort of man. **2** the number of men available for service in the armed forces, etc.
man'servant *n.* a male servant with domestic duties:—*pl.* **men'servants**.
man'slaughter *n.* unintentional, but blameworthy, killing of a person.
man'trap *n.* **1** a trap to catch trespassers. **2** a source of danger to human being(s).
man about town a fashionable, sophisticated man.
man in the street the ordinary man.
man of letters **1** a scholar. **2** a writer.
man of the world one who knows all about, and does not condemn, the more or less sinful conduct of men and women.
to a man every one, without exception.

manacle *man'ȧ-kl*, *n.* a handcuff.—*v.t.* to handcuff:—*pr.p.* **man'acling**.

manage *man'ij*, *v.t.* **1** to control, to be in charge of. **2** to deal with tactfully. **3** to succeed: *to manage to do something.* —*v.i.* to survive, succeed, cope:—*pr.p.* **man'aging**.
man'ageable *adj.* **1** that can be done. **2** that can be controlled.
man'agement *n.* **1** the act, or the art, of managing. **2** the managers of a firm, etc. as a group.
man'ager *n.*:—*fem.* **man'ageress**.

mañana *män-yä'nä*, *n.* and *adv.* **1** tomorrow. **2** (at) some unstated time in the future.

mandarin *man'dȧ-rin*, *n.* **1** an official of high rank (orig. in the days of the Chinese Empire). **2** a person with position and influence, e.g. in literary circles. **3** the standard national Chinese language. **4** a small orange.

mandate *man'dāt*, *n.* (also *-dit*) **1** a command, esp. one from a higher authority. **2** power given to a nation or person to act in the name of another.—*v.t.* to give (a territory, etc.) into the charge of a nation, etc.:—*pr.p.* **man'dating**.
man'datory *adj.* compulsory.

mandible *man'di-bl*, *n.* **1** a jaw or jawbone, esp. the lower. **2** part of the beak of a bird, esp. the lower.

mandoline, **mandolin** *man'do-lin*, *n.* a round-backed instrument like a guitar.

mandrill *man'dril*, *n.* a large West African baboon.

mane *mān*, *n.* long hair on the back of the neck and neighbouring parts, as in the horse and the lion.

manful, etc. See **man**.

manganese *man'gȧ-nēz*, *n.* an element, a hard brittle greyish-white metal.

mange *mānj*, *n.* inflammation of the skin of animals caused by mites.
man'gy *adj.* **1** suffering from mange. **2** (of outer clothing) having bare spots, very shabby. **3** squalid, mean:—*comp.* **man'gier**; *superl.* **man'giest**.
man'gily *adv.* **man'giness** *n.*

mangel-wurzel *mang'gl-wûr'zl*, *n.* a variety of beet grown as cattle food.

manger *mān'jėr*, *n.* a trough in which food is laid for horses and cattle.
dog in the manger. See **dog**.

mangily, **-iness**. See **mange**.

mangle[1] *mang'gl*, *v.t.* **1** to hack, or crush, to pieces. **2** to spoil (e.g. a piece of music) by bad mistakes:—*pr.p.* **mang'ling**.

mangle[2] *mang'gl*, *n.* a machine with rollers for smoothing linen or squeezing water out of washed articles.—*v.t.* to smooth or dry with a mangle:—*pr.p.* **mang'ling**.

mango *mang'gō*, *n.* a tree of India, etc., or its oblong fruit:—*pl.* **mang'oes**.

mangrove *mang'grōv*, *n.* a tree that grows on a swampy shores, coasts, or river banks in very hot countries.

mangy. See **mange**.

manhandle, -hole, -hood. See **man**.

mania *mā'ni-ȧ*, *n.* **1** madness. **2** very great or unreasonable desire or enthusiasm: *He has a mania for sports cars.*
mā'niac *n.* **1** a madman. **2** a very rash or too enthusiastic person.—Also *adj.*
manī'acal *adj.*
ma'nic *ma'*, *adj.*

manicure *man'i-kūr*, *n.* the care of hands and nails.—Also *v.t.*:—*pr.p.* **man'icuring**.
man'icurist *n.*

manifest *man'i-fest*, *adj.* easily seen by the eye, or understood by the mind.—*v.t.* to show plainly.
manifestā'tion *n.* **1** an act of showing plainly. **2** a revelation, display, expression: *this manifestation of his ignorance.*
man'ifestly *adv.* obviously.

manifesto *man-i-fes'tō*, *n.* a public written declaration of the intentions of a ruler or of a party:—*pl.* **man'ifesto(e)s**.

manifold *man'i-fōld*, *adj.* many and varied.—*v.t.* to make several copies of.—*n.* a pipe, etc. with several inlets or outlets.

manikin *man'i-kin*, *n.* **1** a dwarf. **2** a little fellow.

manila, **manilla** *mȧ-nil'ȧ*, *n.* **1** Manila hemp, a fibre used in making ropes. **2** paper formerly made from Manila hemp.

manipulate *mȧ-nip'ū-lāt*, *v.t.* **1** to handle with skill (e.g. an object, a question). **2** to manage, influence, by unfair means or with cunning (e.g. a person, a committee). **3** to give a false appearance to (e.g. accounts):—*pr.p.* **manip'ulating**.
manipulā'tion *n.* **manip'ulator** *n.*
manip'ulative *adj.* of, using, manipulation: *manipulative skill, practices.*

mankind, manly. See **man**.

manna *man'ȧ*, *n.* **1** the food of the Israelites in the wilderness (Exodus xvi.). **2** delicious food.

mannequin *man'i-kin*, *n.* **1** a person, usu. a woman, employed to wear and display clothes to possible buyers. **2** (*less often*) a dummy for clothes.

manner *man'ėr*, *n.* **1** way (in which anything is done). **2** personal style of speaking or behaving. **3** (in *pl.*) social customs (of a particular time or place). **4** (in *pl.*) social conduct towards others judged as pleasant and tactful, or the reverse. **5** (in *pl.*) polite social conduct.
mann'erism *n.* a noticeable habit in speaking, writing, or behaving—often wearisome to others.
mann'erly *adj.* showing good manners.
mann'erliness *n.*
all manner of all kinds of.

mannish. See **man**.

manoeuvre *mȧ-nōō'vėr*, or *-nū'*, *n.* **1** a clever movement (of troops, ships, or aircraft). **2** a cunning plan. **3** a trick. **4** (in *pl.*) a training-exercise of armed forces.—*v.i.* **1** to carry out a manoeuvre. **2** to scheme.—*v.t.* to move skilfully, to manage, force, or induce cunningly:—*pr.p.* **manoeuv'ring**.
manoeu'vrable *adj.* able to be moved in a small space, etc.

manor *man'ȯr*, *n.* **1** under the feudal system, the land belonging to a nobleman, or as much of it as he kept for his own use. **2** an estate that originated in this way.
manor'ial *(-nōr', -nör') adj.*
man'or-house *n.* the house of a lord of the manor.

manpower. See **man**.

manse *mans*, *n.* (in Scotland) the house of a clergyman.

mansion *man'sh(ȯ)n*, *n.* a large house.
Mansion House the official residence of the Lord Mayor of London.

manslaughter. See **man**.

mantel *man'tl*, *n.* **1** a mantelpiece. **2** a mantelshelf.
man'telpiece *n.* the structure over and around a fireplace.
man'telshelf *n.* a shelf above a fireplace.

mantilla *man-til'ȧ*, *n.* a kind of veil covering the head and falling down on the shoulders.

mantis *man'tis*, *n.* an insect rather like a locust, which bends its front legs as if in prayer.

mantle *man'tl*, *n.* **1** a cloak or loose outer garment. **2** a covering. **3** a network round a gas burner to give a white light.

mantra *man'trȧ*, *n.* **1** a sacred devotional chant. **2** a sacred word used in meditation.

mantrap. See **man**.

manu- *man-ū-*, (as part of a word) hand.
manual *man'ū-ȧl*, *adj.* **1** of the hand. **2** done, worked, or used by the hand. **3** using the hands: *a manual worker.*—*n.* **1** a handbook. **2** the keyboard of an organ, etc.
man'ually *adv.*
manufacture *man-ū-fak'chu̇r*, *v.t.* to make, orig. by hand, now usu. by machinery and on a large scale:—*pr.p.* **manufac'turing**.—*n.* **1** the process of manufacturing. **2** anything manufactured.
manufac'turer *n.* one who owns (in whole or in part), or who is a director of,

a manufacturing firm.
manumit *man-ū-mit'*, *v.t.* to set free (a slave):—*pr.p.* **manumitt'ing**; *pa.p.* **manumitt'ed**.
manumiss'ion *(-mish')* *n.*

manure *mȧ-nūr'*, *v.t.* to add something e.g. animal excrement, dung, to (land) so as to make it more fertile:—*pr.p.* **manur'ing**.—*n.* something that makes the land give better crops.

manuscript *man'ū-skript*, *adj.* written by hand.—*n.* **1** a book or document written by hand. **2** an author's copy of a work in writing or typescript.

Manx *mangks*, *n.* the Celtic language of the Isle of *Man*.—*adj.* of the Isle of Man or its inhabitants.
Manx cat a breed of cat with a tail that has never developed.

many *men'i*, *adj.* a great number of:—*comp.* **more** *(mōr, mör)*; *superl.* **most** *(mōst)*.—Also *n.*
ma'ny-si'ded *adj.* **1** having many sides or aspects. **2** having wide interests or varied talents.
ma'ny-si'dedness *n.*
many a (with *sing.* noun) a large number of: *many a man*; *for many a day*.
more *adj.* a larger number of (see also **much**).—Also *n.*
most *adj.* and *n.* (see also **much**).
most'ly *adv.* **1** for the most part. **2** chiefly.

Maoism *mow'izm*, *n.* the communist doctrines of the Chinese leader *Mao* Tse-Tung (or Zedong).
Mao'ist *n.* and *adj.*

Maori *mow'ri*, *mä'ō-ri*, *n.* **1** a member of the aboriginal Polynesian race of New Zealand. **2** the language of this race:—*pl.* **Maoris**.

map *map*, *n.* **1** a drawing in outline of the surface features of the earth, the moon, etc., or of part of it, usu. on a flat surface. **2** a similar plan of the stars in the sky.—*v.t.* to make a map of:—*pr.p.* **mapp'ing**; *pa.p.* **mapped**.
map out to plan in detail (a route, a course of action).

maple *mā'pl*, *n.* a tree of several kinds, some of which yield sugar.

mar *mär*, *v.t.* to spoil, impair (e.g. enjoyment, beauty):—*pr.p.* **marr'ing**; *pa.p.* **marred**.

maraschino cherry *mar-ȧ-skē'nō, -shē', cher'i*, a type of preserved cherry used e.g. as decoration.

marathon *mar'ȧ-thȯn*, *n.* **1** a long-distance footrace (now usu. about 26 miles, 42.7 km). **2** any contest that requires great endurance.

maraud *mȧ-röd'*, *v.i.* to roam about in search of plunder.—Also *v.t.*
maraud'er *n.* **maraud'ing** *adj.*

marble *mär'bl*, *n.* **1** any kind of limestone taking a high polish. **2** a slab, work of art, or other object made of marble. **3** a little hard ball (orig. of marble) used by children to play the game of **marbles**.—*adj.* **1** composed of marble. **2** hard and cold.
mar'bled *adj.* mottled and streaked, like some types of marble.

marcasite *mär'kȧ-sīt*, *n.* a compound of iron in crystal form used in ornaments.

March *märch*, *n.* the third month of year.

march[1] *märch*, *n.* **1** a boundary. **2** a border district:—used chiefly in *pl.* **march'es**.

march[2] *märch*, *v.i.* **1** to walk in time with regular step. **2** to go on steadily.—*v.t.* to make (someone) march or go.—*n.* **1** a marching movement. **2** the distance covered by marching. **3** a regular forward movement: *the march of events*. **4** a piece of music suitable for marching to.

marchioness. See **marquis**.

mare *mār*, *n.* the female of the horse.
mare's'-nest *n.* **1** a supposed discovery that turns out to be imaginary. **2** a hoax.
mare's'-tail *n.* a tall, erect marsh plant.

margarine *mär'gȧ-rēn, -jȧ-, -rēn'*, *n.* a butter-like substance made chiefly of vegetable fats.
marge *märj*, *n.* short for **margarine**.

margin *mär'jin*, *n.* **1** an edge, border. **2** the blank edge on the page of a book. **3** something extra, beyond what appears to be necessary, to provide for unexpected happenings, errors, etc.: *We should allow a margin of error in case our calculations are wrong*.
mar'ginal *adj.*—*n.* a marginal seat.
mar'ginalise *v.t.* to push (a person) to the edges (of eg. society):— *pr.p.* **mar'ginalising**.
marginal constituency, **seat**, etc. a constituency, seat, etc. that does not provide a safe seat for any of the political parties.
marginal land less fertile land which will be cultivated only in times when there is special need for farm produce.

marguerite *mär'gė-rēt*, *n.* the ox-eye daisy.

marigold *mar'i-gōld*, *n.* a plant of the daisy type, or its yellow flower.

marijuana, **marihuana** *ma-ri(h)wä'nä*, *n.* the dried flowers and leaves of hemp smoked in cigarettes for their temporarily exciting effect.

marine *mȧ-rēn'*, *adj.* **1** having to do with the sea. **2** done, or used, at sea. **3** living in, found in, the sea.—*n.* **1** a soldier serving on board a ship. **2** shipping as a whole: *the mercantile marine.*

marina *mȧ-rē'nȧ*, *n.* a place designed for the mooring of yachts, etc.

mariner *mar'in-ėr*, *n.* a sailor.

mariner's compass a form of compass suitable for use on board ship.

tell that to the marines only the marines would believe that—I don't (from the sailor's contempt for the marine's ignorance of seamanship).

marionette *mar-i-ȯ-net'*, *n.* a puppet moved by strings.

marital *mar'i-tȧl*, *adj.* having to do with a husband or with marriage.

maritime *mar'i-tīm*, *adj.* **1** connected with the sea. **2** relating to seagoing or sea trade. **3** having a navy and sea trade.

marjoram *mär'jȯ-rȧm*, *n.* a scented plant used as a seasoning.

mark^1 *märk*, *n.* **1** a sign that can be seen. **2** a stain. **3** a scar. **4** an object aimed at. **5** a sign used as a guide to position. **6** a cross used instead of a signature. **7** a point or number of points awarded according to the merit of one's work, etc. **8** a distinguishing sign. **9** (usu. with a number) a type or model.—*v.t.* **1** to make a mark on. **2** to correct and value by giving marks (e.g. an examination paper). **3** to show. **4** to note. **5** to watch closely, give attention to. **6** (in football, etc.) to keep close to (an opponent) so as to hinder him if he receives the ball. **7** to be a feature of: *Ancient villages marked the lonely valley.* **8** to be a sign of: *A movement in the crowd marked his approach.*

marked *adj.* **1** having marks. **2** striking, noticeable: *marked signs of improvement.* **3** watched and suspected: *a marked man.*

mark'edly *(-id-) adv.* noticeably.

mark'er *n.* **1** one who marks the score at games, marks examination papers, etc. **2** a counter, etc., for scoring.

marks'man *n.* one who shoots well.

marks'manship *n.* ability to shoot.

beside the mark not connected with what is being spoken about.

make one's mark 1 to sign (e.g. a document) by making e.g. a cross. **2** to gain great influence. **3** to make a notable impression on people.

man of mark one who has become known for his ability.

mark down, **up** to lower, raise, the price of.

mark time 1 to move the feet up and down as if marching but without going forward. **2** to keep things going without making progress.

up to the mark 1 perfect according to a certain standard. **2** in good health.

mark^2 *märk*, *n.* a Deutschmark.

market *mär'kit*, *n.* **1** a public place where people meet to buy and sell. **2** sale: *to put on the market.* **3** demand (for): *There is a market for cotton goods in hot countries.* **4** a place where there is a chance of selling: *Countries that are developing their industries are a market for machinery.*—*v.t.* **1** to put on sale. **2** to sell.

mar'ketable *adj.* **1** fit to be sold. **2** in demand.

mar'keting *n.* the act or practice of (advertising and) selling.

mar'ket-gar'den *n.* a garden where fruit and vegetables are grown for sale.

mar'ket-place *n.* an open space where a market is held.

market price, **value** the price at which a thing is being sold at the time.

market research the investigation of what people like to buy, how many customers there might be for a certain product, etc.

market town a town holding a public market, with fixed market days.

marl *märl*, *n.* lime and clay soil used as fertiliser.

marline *mär'lin*, *n.* a small rope for winding round a larger one to keep it from wearing.

mar'line-spike *n.* a spike for separating the strands of a rope in splicing.

marmalade *mär'mȧ-lād*, *n.* a jam usu. made from oranges—orig. from quinces.

marmoset *mär'mȯ-zet*, *n.* a very small American monkey.

marmot *mär'mȯt*, *n.* a burrowing rodent, also called **wood'chuck**, **ground'hog**.

maroon^1 *mȧ-ro͞on'*, *n.* **1** a dark brownish-red (also *adj.*). **2** a loud warning firework.

maroon^2 *mȧ-ro͞on'*, *v.t.* **1** (as a punishment) to put on shore on a lonely island and leave. **2** to leave in a lonely, helpless, or uncomfortable, position.

marquee *mär-kē'*, *n.* a large tent.

marquess. See **marquis**.

marquetry, **marqueterie** *mär'ki-tri*, *n.* inlaid work, esp. in furniture.

marquis, **marquess** *mär'kwis*, *n.* a title next below that of duke:—*fem.* **mar'chioness** *(mär'shȯn-is, -es)*.

marriage. See **marry**.

marrow *mar'ō*, *n.* **1** the soft substance in the hollow parts of bones. **2** a vegetable marrow (see **vegetable**). **3** the best part of anything.

marry *mar'i, v.t.* **1** to take (a person) as one's husband or wife. **2** to give as husband or wife (e.g. *He married his son to an heiress*). **3** (of a clergyman, etc.) to perform the ceremony of marriage between (two people).—Also *v.i.*:—*pr.p.* **marr'ying**; *pa.p.* **marr'ied**.

marriage *mar'ij, n.* **1** the ceremony by which a man and woman become husband and wife. **2** the state of being married. **3** a close union.
marr'iageable *adj.* suitable, or at a proper age, for marrying.
See also **marital**.

Mars *märz, n.* **1** the Roman god of war. **2** the planet next after the earth in the order of distance from the sun.
See also **martial, Martian**.

Marseillaise *mär-sė-lāz', -sā-āz', -sā-yāz', n.* the French national anthem, first sung in Paris by men from *Marseilles* during the Revolution.

marsh *märsh, n.* a piece of low, wet land.—*adj.* found in marshes.
marsh'y *adj.*:—*comp.* **marsh'ier**; *superl.* **march'iest**.
marsh'iness *n.*
marsh gas fire-damp (see this).
marsh mallow **1** a marsh plant with pink flowers. **2** (**marsh'mall'ow** *n.*) a sweet, orig. made from its root, now of sugar, gelatine, etc.
marsh marigold a marsh plant with golden flowers.

marshal *mär'shål, n.* **1** a high-ranking officer in the army or air force, or the rank itself. **2** an officer arranging ceremonies, etc. **3** (*U.S.*) a civil officer with certain legal duties.—*v.t.* **1** to arrange in order (e.g. troops, or facts, or arguments). **2** to usher:—*pr.p.* **mar'shalling**; *pa.p.* **mar'shalled**.
marshalling yard a place where railway wagons are sorted out and made up into trains.

marsupial *mär-sū'pi-ål, -sōō', n.* an animal that carries its young in a pouch (e.g. a kangaroo).—Also *adj.*

mart *märt, n.* a place of trade, market.

marten *mär'tėn, n.* an animal related to the weasel, valued for its fur.—Also **pine'-marten**.

martial *mär'shål, adj.* **1** warlike. **2** belonging to, suitable for, war: *martial music*.
martial art any of various fighting sports or methods of self-defence, such as karate or kung fu.
martial law military rule in time of war, or in great national emergency, when ordinary law is suspended.

Martian *mär'shån, -shi-ån, adj.* of Mars (god or planet).—*n.* an imagined inhabitant of Mars.

martin *mär'tin, n.* a type of swallow.

martinet *mär-ti-net', or mär', n.* one whose discipline is very strict.

martini *mär-tē'nē, n.* a cocktail of gin, vermouth, etc.

Martinmas *mär'tin-mås, n.* the mass or feast of St *Martin*, Nov. 11.

martyr *mär'tėr, n.* **1** one who suffers death or hardship for what he believes. **2** one who continually suffers from a disease, etc. (with *to*): *She is a martyr to rheumatism*.—*v.t.* **1** to put (person) to death for his belief. **2** to cause to suffer greatly.
mar'tyrdom *n.* the sufferings or death of a martyr.

marvel *mär'vėl, n.* anything astonishing or wonderful.—*v.i.* **1** to wonder (how, why). **2** to feel astonishment (at): *I marvel at his rashness*:—*pr.p.* **mar'velling**; *pa.p.* **mar'velled**.
mar'vellous *adj.* **1** very wonderful. **2** beyond belief.

Marxist *märks'ist, adj.* of the socialist Karl *Marx* or his theories.—*n.* a follower of Marx.
Marx'ism *n.*

marzipan *mär-zi-pan', n.* a sweetmeat of crushed almonds and sugar.

mascara *mas-kä'rå, n.* colouring for the eyelashes.

mascot *mas'kȯt, n.* a person, animal, or thing supposed to bring good luck.

masculine *mäs'kū-lin, mas', adj.* **1** having to do with, or belonging to, the male sex or a man. **2** mannish. **3** (*grammar*) of the gender to which words denoting males belong.
mas'culineness, masculin'ity *ns.*

maser *māz'ėr, n.* a device used to strengthen radar and radio astronomy signals which are very small when not amplified.

mash *mash, n.* **1** crushed malt and hot water. **2** a mixture, e.g. of bran with meal or turnips, used as food for animals. **3** mashed potatoes.—*v.t.* **1** to make into a mash. **2** to crush.

mask *mäsk, n.* **1** something for disguising, hiding, or protecting, esp. the face. **2** a face that expresses nothing. **3** a likeness of a face in clay, etc. **4** a fox's head.—*v.t.* **1** to hide. **2** to disguise.

masochism *maz'ȯ-kizm, n.* pleasure, esp. sexual pleasure, got from one's own suffering, pain, being dominated, etc.
mas'ochist *n.* **masochist'ic** *adj.*

mason *mā'sn*, *n.* **1** a skilled worker or builder in stone. **2** a freemason.

masonic *mȧ-son'ik*, *adj.* of, connected with, freemasonry.

mā'sonry *n.* **1** work done in stone by a mason. **2** freemasonry.

masque *mäsk*, *n.* a kind of dramatic entertainment popular in the 16th and 17th centuries.

masquerade *mäs-kė-rād'*, *n.* **1** a social gathering, usu. a ball, of people wearing masks. **2** acting or living under false pretences.—*v.i.* **1** to join in a masquerade. **2** to pretend to be: *He was masquerading as a policeman*:—*pr.p.* **masquerad'ing**.

mass[1] *mas*, *n.* **1** a lump of matter. **2** a large quantity or number. **3** the bulk, principal part or main body. **4** a measure of quantity of matter in any object.—*v.t.* to bring together in large number or quantity: *to mass troops for an attack.*—Also *v.i.*

massive *mas'iv*, *adj.* **1** bulky and heavy. **2** large and impressive. **3** (of the features) large and bold. **4** very great in number, quantity, or power.

mass'ively *adv.* **mass'iveness** *n.*

mass media the various means of communicating information to a large number of people, e.g. television, newspapers.

mass meeting a large meeting for a public discussion.

mass production production on a huge scale of articles all exactly the same.

mass'-produce' *v.t.*:—*pr.p.* **mass'-produc'ing**.

mass'-produced' *adj.*

the masses the common people, esp. the working class.

mass[2] *mas*, *mäs*, *n.* **1** the celebration of the Lord's Supper in the Roman Catholic church. **2** music to go with this.

High Mass mass celebrated with music and incense; **Low Mass** mass celebrated without.

massacre *mas'ȧ-kėr*, *n.* the killing of a large number of people, esp. with great cruelty.—*v.t.* to kill with violence, slaughter:—*pr.p.* **mass'acring**.

massage *mas'äzh*, *mȧ-säzh'*, *n.* rubbing, kneading, etc., of parts of the body to remove pain or stiffness.—*v.t.* to treat by massage:—*pr.p.* **massaging**.

masseur' *(-ûr) n.* a man who gives massage:—*fem.* **masseuse'** *(-ûz')*.

massif *mas'if*, *ma-sēf'*, *n.* a central mountain mass.

massive. See **mass**[1].

mast[1] *mäst*, *n.* a long upright pole, esp. one for carrying the sails of a ship.

mast'ed *adj.* (usu. as part of a word) having a mast or masts.

mast'head *n.* the top of a mast.

lower mast, **topmast**, **topgallant mast**, **royal mast** the names of the lengths (reckoning from the deck upwards) of which a built-up mast on a large sailing vessel is formed.

mast[2] *mäst*, *n.* the fruit of the oak, beech, chestnut, etc., on which swine feed.

mastectomy *mas-tek'to-mi*, *n.* the surgical removal of a breast.

master *mäs'tėr*, *n.* **1** one who commands or controls. **2** an owner (e.g. of a slave, a dog). **3** a male teacher. **4** an employer. **5** the commander of a merchant ship. **6** one very skilled in an art, science, etc. **7** a painting by a great artist. **8** (a person holding) a certain degree given by universities: *Master of Arts.* **9** an original (film, record, etc.) from which copies are made:—*fem.* (*defs. 1–4*) **mistress**.—*adj.* (usu. used before a noun) **1** chief. **2** controlling, directing. **3** showing the ability of a master. **4** original, for copying. **5** employing others: *a master builder.*—*v.t.* **1** to overcome. **2** to become skilful in: *Will he ever master mathematics?*

mas'terful *adj.* showing power, or determination to be in control.

mas'terfully *adv.* **master'fulness** *n.*

mas'terly *adj.* showing the skill of a master.

mas'terliness *n.*

mas'tery *n.* **1** the power or authority of a master. **2** victory (over). **3** control (of). **4** great skill in or knowledge (of).

master key a key that opens a number of locks.

mas'termind *n.* **1** a person who shows great mental power. **2** the person planning and controlling an undertaking or scheme.—*v.t.* to plan and direct (a scheme, etc.)

mas'terpiece *n.* **1** a piece of work or art worthy of a master. **2** one's greatest achievement.

master stroke a very skilful move.

master switch a switch for controlling a number of other switches.

masticate *mas'ti-kāt*, *v.t.* to chew:—*pr.p.* **mas'ticating**.

masticā'tion *n.*

mastiff *mas'tif*, *n.* a thick-set, powerful dog, formerly used in hunting.

mastoid *mas'toid*, (*loosely*) *n.* an inflammation of the **mastoid process,** a bone projection behind the ear.

masturbate *mas'tur-bāt*, *v.i.* to stimulate the sexual organs by hand:—*pr.p.* **mas'turbating**.

masturbā'tion *n.*

mat¹ *mat, n.* **1** a piece of material (plaited rushes, rubber, wire, carpet, etc.) for wiping shoes on, or for covering a floor, or for sleeping on, or for other purpose. **2** a piece e.g. of linen or cork, put under dishes at table, etc.—*v.t.* and *v.i.* to make, become, thickly tangled:—*pr.p.* **matt'ing**; *pa.p.* **matt'ed**.
matt'ed *adj.* thickly tangled.
matt'ing *n.* material used as mats.

mat², **matt** *mat, adj.* having a dull surface, without gloss or shine.

matador, **matadore** *mat'ȧ-dör, n.* the man who kills the bull in a bullfight.

match¹ *mach, n.* **1** a short stick of wood or other material tipped with a material that catches fire when rubbed. **2** a cord, etc., made to burn at a definite speed.
match'wood *n.* splinters.

match² *mach, n.* **1** a person or thing the same as another in some respect(s). **2** an equal. **3** a person able to cope with another: *In argument Jack is no match for Jim.* **4** a marriage, or a person to be gained in marriage. **5** a contest or game.—*v.i.* **1** to be exactly or nearly alike: *Those earrings match.* **2** to fit in, be suitable (with).—*v.t.* **1** to be equal or similar to (something) in e.g. size, colour, or to (a person) in e.g. skill, courage. **2** to set to compete (against): *to match Roland against Oliver*; *to match his skill against my better tools.* **3** to hold one's own against. **4** to pair. **5** to join in marriage.
match'less *adj.* having no equal.

mate¹ *māt, n.* **1** a companion. **2** a fellow workman. **3** an equal. **4** a husband or wife. **5** an animal with which another is paired for breeding purposes. **6** a merchantship's officer under the master. **7** an assistant workman.—*v.t.* and *v.i.* **1** to marry. **2** to make a pair for breeding purposes:—*pr.p.* **mat'ing**.
māt'ey, **māt'y** (*coll.*) *adj.* friendly:—*comp.* **mat'ier**; *superl.* **mat'iest**.

mate² *māt, v.t.* (*pr.p.* **mat'ing**), *n.* and *interj.* checkmate.

mater *mā'tėr,* (*old-fashioned coll.*) *n.* mother.
maternal *mȧ-tûr'nȧl, adj.* **1** of a mother. **2** suitable to a mother, motherly.
mater'nally *adv.*
mater'nity *n.* the state of being a mother.—*adj.* (used only before a noun) for expectant mother(s).
See also **matriarchy, matricide.**

material *mȧ-tē'ri-ȧl, adj.* **1** consisting of matter. **2** bodily, not spiritual. **3** lacking spirituality: *His outlook and aims were material.* **4** essential or important (*opp.* **immaterial**).—*n.* something out of which anything is, or may be, made, esp. cloth.
mate'rially *adv.* to a considerable or important extent: *Circumstances have altered materially since then.*
mate'rialise *v.i.* **1** to take bodily form. **2** to become actual fact. **3** (of e.g. something promised) to turn up as expected:—*pr.p.* **matē'rialising**.
mate'rialism *n.* **1** the belief that nothing exists but matter, and that there are no spiritual forces. **2** a tendency to attach too great importance to material things (e.g. to bodily comfort, money, success).
mate'rialist *n.* **materialist'ic** *adj.*
raw material. See **raw**.

maternal, etc. See **mater**.

matey. See **mate¹**.

mathematics *math-ė-mat'iks, n. sing.* the science or branch of knowledge dealing with measurements, numbers, quantities, and the relationships between these or operations done on them (*coll.* **maths**, *U.S.* **math**).
mathemat'ical *adj.* **1** of, done by, mathematics. **2** very exact or accurate.
mathematic'ian *(-ish'ȧn) n.* one who knows and can work with mathematics.

matins *mat'inz, n. sing.* or *pl.* (often **matt'-ins**) **1** morning prayers or service. **2** (*poetic*) morning song of birds.

matinee *mat'i-nā, n.* a public entertainment held in the daytime, usu. in the afternoon.

matriarchy *mā'tri-är-ki, n.* **1** government by a woman or by women. **2** a society so governed:—*pl.* **mat'riarchies**.
mā'triarch *n.* a woman who is head and ruler of her family and descendants:—*masc.* **patriarch**.
mātriar'chal *(-kȧl) adj.*

matricide *mat'ri-sīd, n.* **1** the killing of one's own mother. **2** one who kills his, or her, mother.
matricī'dal *adj.*

matrices. See **matrix**.

matriculate *mȧ-trik'ū-lāt, v.t.* to admit (a student) to membership of a college, etc., by entering his name in a register. —*v.i.* to become a member of a university, etc., by being enrolled:—*pr.p.* **matric'-ulating**.
matriculā'tion *n.*

matrimony *mat'ri-mon-i, n.* **1** the state of being married. **2** the act of marrying.
matrimonial *(-mō'ni-ȧl) adj.*

matrix *mā'triks,* or *mat'riks, n.* **1** something in which something else is embedded (e.g.

rock in which a gem, metal, lies). **2** a mould, esp. in which metals, etc., are shaped:—*pls.* **matrices** *(-sēz)*, **-ixes**.

matron *mā'trȯn*, *n.* **1** a married woman. **2** an elderly lady. **3** a woman in charge of nursing and domestic arrangements in a hospital, school, etc.
mā'tronly *adj.* elderly and sedate.

matt. See **mat²**.

matted, etc. See **mat¹**.

matter *mat'ėr*, *n.* **1** something that takes up space, and which we can see, feel, etc. **2** physical substance, not spirit or mind. **3** material: *dead*, *colouring*, *matter.* **4** the subject being written, spoken, or thought, about. **5** the trouble, difficulty, thing wrong: *What is the matter now?* **6** (in *pl.*) affairs: *He is clever in money matters.* **7** pus.—*v.i.* **1** to be of importance: *That matters a great deal to him.* **2** to form or give out pus:—*pr.p.* **matt'ering**; *pa.p.* **matt'ered**.
matt'er-of-fact' *adj.* **1** keeping to the actual fact, not fanciful or imaginative. **2** rather dull.
a matter of used in giving quantity, time, etc. roughly: *It will take a matter of minutes* (i.e. a very short time).
a matter of course a thing to be expected: *His promotion came as a matter of course.*
no matter it makes no difference.

matting. See **mat¹**.

mattins. See **matins**.

mattock *mat'ȯk*, *n.* a kind of pickaxe with a broad end for breaking the soil.

mattress *mat'rės*, *n.* part of a bed consisting usu. of a large flat cloth case or bag stuffed with horsehair, foam rubber, or other material, and often enclosing springs.

mature *mȧ-tūr'*, *adj.* **1** fully grown or developed. **2** ripe. **3** (of a plan) completely worked out. **4** (of e.g. a bill of exchange) due:—*opp.* **immature.**—*v.t.*, *v.i.* to cause to be, or to become, ripe, grown, mature:—*pr.p.* **matur'ing**.
maturā'tion *n.*
mature'ness, **matur'ity** *ns.*

matey. See **mate¹**.

maudlin *mȯd'lin*, *adj.* **1** sickly sentimental. **2** half drunk.

maul *mȯl*, *n.* a heavy wooden hammer.—*v.t.* to hurt badly by rough treatment.

maunder *mȯn'dėr*, *v.i.* **1** to talk in a rambling manner. **2** to move or act without energy.

mausoleum *mȯ-sȯ-lē'ům*, *n.* a very fine tomb or monument.

mauve *mōv*, *n.* a delicate purple colour.—Also *adj.*

maverick *mav'ėr-ik*, *n.* a person who does not conform.

mavis *mā'vis*, (*poetic* or *dial.*) *n.* a type of thrush, the *song-thrush*.

mawkish *mȯ'kish*, *adj.* **1** sickening. **2** (of e.g. a story) weak and sentimental.
maw'kishness *n.*

maxim *maks'im*, *n.* an expression of a truth or rule, esp. one serving as a guide to conduct.

maximum *maks'i-mům*, *adj.* greatest.—*n.* **1** the greatest number or quantity. **2** the highest point or degree:—*pl.* **max'ima**.
max'imise *v.t.* to make as great as possible:—*pr.p.* **max'imising**.

may¹ *mā*, *v.* **1** used with another verb to express permission, possibility, etc.: *That is all—you may go now*; *I may go*, *if the weather is good.* **2** used to express a wish: *May you be successful!*:—*pa.t.* **might** *(mīt)*.

may². See **May**.

May *mā*, *n.* **1** the fifth month of the year. **2** (without *cap.*) may blossom.—*v.i.* to gather may on May Day.
may blossom the hawthorn flower.
May Day the first day of May.
may'fly *n.* a type of small fly which lives only a short time, appearing in May.
may'pole *n.* a pole for dancing round on May Day.
May Queen a girl crowned with flowers as queen on May Day.

maybe *mā'bē*, *adv.* perhaps.

mayday *mā'dā*, *n.* an international distress signal sent out by ships and aircraft.

mayhem *mā'hem*, *n.* violent destruction.

mayonnaise *mā-ȯn-āz'*, *mā'-*, *n.* a thick sauce made of yolk of egg, oil, vinegar or lemon, and seasoning.

mayor *mā'ȯr*, *mār*, *n.* the chief public official (man or woman) of a city, town, or borough.
may'oress *n.* a mayor's wife, or other lady who carries out the social duties of the position.
may'orship *n.* the office of mayor.

maypole. See **May**.

maze *māz*, *n.* **1** a place full of windings. **2** a state of not knowing what to think or do.

mazurka *mȧ-zûr'kȧ*, or *-zo͞or'*, *n.* **1** a lively Polish dance. **2** music for it.

me. See **I**.

mead *mēd*, *n.* an alcoholic drink made from honey and water.

meadow *med'ō*, (*poetic*) **mead** *mēd*, *ns.* **1** a field of grass to be mown. **2** a rich pasture-ground, esp. beside a stream.

meagre *mē'gėr*, *adj.* **1** lean. **2** poor in quality. **3** scanty, not enough.

meal[1] *mēl*, *n.* the food taken at one time.

meal[2] *mēl*, *n.* grain, or seeds such as peas, ground to powder.
meal'y *adj.*:—*comp.* **meal'ier**; *superl.* **meal'iest**.
meal'iness *n.*
meal'y-mouthed' *adj.* unwilling to use plain terms, not frank and sincere.

mean[1] *mēn*, *adj.* **1** low in rank or birth. **2** of little worth. **3** (of e.g. a house) humble, shabby. **4** (of a motive) not noble. **5** selfish, petty. **6** stingy, not generous with money.
mean'ly *adv.* **mean'ness** *n.*
no mean (before a noun) important, good: *This is no mean city*; *He is no mean actor*.

mean[2] *mēn*, *adj.* **1** having the middle position. **2** average.—*n.* something that is midway between two opposite ends or extremes.
means *n. sing.* or *pl.* the instrument, method, etc., by which a thing is, or may be, done or brought about: *It was, these were, the means by which we were saved.*—*n.pl.* money necessary e.g. for a living: *Our means are small.*
mean time time based on the average interval between two appearances of the sun above the meridian (the interval varies a little).
mean'time, mean'while *advs.* in the time between.
golden mean a wise middle course.
man of means a wealthy man.

mean[3] *mēn*, *v.t.* **1** to intend, have in mind as a purpose: *I mean to mend the leak*; *He means mischief.* **2** to have in mind for a special use (e.g. *I meant the box for keeping nails in*). **3** to express, convey, indicate: *'Vacation' means 'holiday'*; *What does his silence mean?* **4** to intend to express: *By 'difficult' I mean 'stubborn'.*—*v.i.* **1** to have importance: *Her gift means much to her grandmother*:—*pr.p.* **mean'ing**; *pa.p.* **meant** *(ment)*.
mean'ing *n.* **1** what one intended to express. **2** the sense in which a statement, etc., is to be understood. **3** purpose: *I now saw the meaning of his action.*—*adj.* showing feelings or conveying a message: *a meaning look*.
mean'ingful *adj.* **mean'ingless** *adj.*
mean well (ill) to have good (bad) intentions.

meander *mē-an'dėr*, *n.* **1** a loop of a river. **2** (in *pl.*) winding course.—*v.i.* **1** to flow in a winding course. **2** to wander about or along aimlessly.

meant. See **mean**[3].

meantime, meanwhile. See **mean**[2].

measles *mē'zlz*, *n. sing.* an infectious fever with red spots on the skin.
mea'sly *adj.* **1** ill with measles. **2** (*coll.*) poor, mean, deserving contempt:—*comp.* **mea'slier**; *superl.* **mea'sliest**.

measure *mezh'ůr*, *n.* **1** the dimensions, size, or amount of a thing as discovered by measuring. **2** an instrument for measuring: *a tape measure.* **3** a system of measuring: *dry, liquid, square measure.* **4** a certain amount: *I feel a measure of sympathy for her.* **5** musical time. **6** a dance, esp. a slow and stately one. **7** (often in *pl.*) a plan of action, steps towards an end: *to take measures to stop vandalism.* **8** a bill brought before parliament. **9** (*pl.*) rock strata: *the coal measures.*—*v.t.* **1** to find the size or amount of. **2** (with *off*, *out*) to mark off, weigh out, etc. in portions. **3** to judge in comparison with: *She measured her skill in cooking against her friend's.*—*v.i.* **1** to be of (a certain size). **2** to take measurements.
meas'urable *adj.* that can be measured:—*opp.* **immeasurable**.
meas'urably *adv.*
meas'ured *adj.* **1** in rhythm, slow and steady: *with measured steps.* **2** slow, carefully considered: *measured speech*.
meas'ureless *adj.* having no limits.
meas'urement *n.* **1** the act of measuring. **2** a dimension found by measuring.
beyond measure very great.
in a, some, measure to some extent.
take someone's measure to judge someone's character, ability, etc.

meat *mēt*, *n.* **1** the flesh of animals used as food. **2** anything eaten as food.
meat'y *adj.* **1** full of meat. **2** full of matter for thought: *a meaty lecture*:—*comp.* **meat'ier**; *superl.* **meat'iest**.

mechanic *mė-kan'ik*, *n.* a skilled worker with tools or machines.
mechan'ical *adj.* **1** having to do with machines. **2** worked or done by machinery. **3** done, etc., without thinking, from force of habit. **4** having a talent and liking for machinery.
mechan'ically *adv.*
mechan'ics *n. sing.* **1** the science of the action of forces on objects. **2** the art of machine building.—*n. sing.* or *pl.* the way in which something works.
mech'anise *v.t.* **1** to make machine-like. **2** to introduce machinery into (an industry).

3 to equip (troops) with armed armoured motor vehicles:—*pr.p.* **mech'anising**.
mechanisā'tion *n.*
mech'anism *n.* 1 the parts of a machine taken as a whole. 2 mechanical working. 3 action by which a result is produced.

medal *med'ȧl, n.* a piece of metal in the form of a coin with a figure or inscription stamped on it, given e.g. as a reward of merit.

medallion *mė-dal'yȯn, n.* a large medal.
med'alist *n.* one who has gained a medal, esp. in sporting or other competitions.

meddle *med'l, v.i.* 1 to interfere, try to play a part (in another's affairs): *She was always trying to meddle in her neighbours' lives; to meddle with things she knew nothing about.* 2 to tamper (with):—*pr.p.* **medd'ling**.
medd'ler *n.* one who meddles.
medd'lesome *adj.* inclined to meddle.
medd'ling *n.* and *adj.*

media. See **medium**.

mediaeval, medieval *me-di-ē'vȧl, mē-, adj.* of, having to do with, the Middle Ages.

medial *mē'di-ȧl, adj.* 1 middle. 2 average.

median *mē'di-ȧn, n.* the value middle in position, not usu. in size.

mediate *mē'di-āt, v.i.* to come between two people or groups who are disagreeing and, as the friend of each, try to settle their dispute.—*v.t.* to bring about (a settlement of a dispute, an agreement) by helping the two sides to arrange it:—*pr.p.* **me'diating**.
mediā'tion *n.* **me'diator** *n.*

medical *med'i-kȧl, adj.* of, having to do with, healing, medicine, or doctors.
med'icate *v.t.* to put a medicine into (something):—*pr.p* **med'icating**.
med'icated *adj.* **medicā'tion** *n.*
medicine *med'sin, n.* 1 any substance (esp. one taken by the mouth) used to treat or keep away disease. 2 the science of curing people who are ill, or making their suffering less (esp. by means other than surgery).
medicinal *me-dis'in-ȧl, adj.* 1 having power to heal. 2 used in medicine.
medic'inally *adv.* for the purpose of (or with the effect of) curing an ailment: *alcohol taken medicinally.*
medicine man among certain peoples, a witch-doctor.

medieval. See **mediaeval**.

mediocre *mē'di-ō-kėr*, or *-ō', adj.* (of e.g. a person, performance, quality) middling, ordinary, not very good or great.
medioc'rity *(-ok'-) n.* 1 mediocre quality. 2 a person of little ability, etc.:—*pl.* **medioc'rities**.

meditate *med'i-tāt, v.i.* 1 to think deeply (with *on, upon*): *meditating on his troubles.* 2 to engage one's mind in some form of deep religious thought.—*v.t.* 1 to think about. 2 to consider, to plan: *I am meditating a campaign to encourage politeness*:—*pr.p.* **med'itating**.
meditā'tion *n.*
med'itative *adj.* thoughtful.
med'itatively *adv.* **med'itativeness** *n.*

Mediterranean *me-di-tė-rā'nyȧn, -ni-ȧn, adj.* of, having to do with, the *Mediterranean Sea* or its shores: *Mediterranean fruits.*
Mediterranean climate a climate like that round the Mediterranean Sea—mild, moderately wet winters and warm dry summers.

medium *mē'di-ŭm, n.* 1 a middle condition, way: *There is a medium between extravagance and meanness.* 2 something through which an effect is produced: *Air is the medium through which sound is carried to a distance.* 3 means, esp. of communication: *TV is a powerful advertising medium* (see also **mass media** under **mass**[1]). 4 a person through whom spirits are said to speak. 5 a substance in which specimens are preserved, or in which bacteria are grown:—*pl.* **mē'dia** (not of persons), **mē'diums**.—*adj.* middle in size, quality, etc.

medlar *med'lȧr, n.* a small tree with sour fruit something like a crab apple.

medley *med'li, n.* 1 a mixture, jumble. 2 a piece of music put together from a number of other pieces:—*pl.* **med'leys**.—Also *adj.*

meek *mēk, adj.* gentle, humble, patient.
meek'ly *adv.* **meek'ness** *n.*

meet[1] *mēt, v.t.* 1 to come face to face with. 2 to come into the company of for discussion, combat, etc. 3 to be introduced to. 4 to join: *This road soon meets another.* 5 to experience: *to meet disapproval.* 6 to come up to (e.g. hopes). 7 to satisfy (e.g. requirements); to answer (e.g. objections). 8 to answer, oppose: *to meet force with greater force.* 9 to pay fully (e.g. debts).—*v.i.* 1 to come together. 2 to assemble:—*pa.p.* **met**.—*n.* a meeting, esp. of huntsmen.
meet'ing *n.* 1 a coming together. 2 an assembly or gathering. 3 a joining (e.g. of rivers).

meet[2] *mēt, (old) adj.* fitting, proper: *It is meet that bravery should be rewarded.*

mega- *meg-ȧ-*, **meg-** *meg-*, (as part of a word) **1** (also **megalo-** *meg'ȧ-lō-*) great, powerful. **2** a million.

megabyte *meg'ȧ-bīt*, *n.* (*computers*) a unit of storage capacity equal to 2^{20} or 1 048 576 bytes.

megalomania *meg-ȧ-lō-mā'ni-ȧ*, *n.* the idea, usu. false, that one is great or powerful.
megalomā'niac *n.* and *adj.*

megaphone *meg'ȧ-fōn*, *n.* a funnel-shaped device for causing sounds to be heard better and at a greater distance.

meg'aton *n.* a unit of explosive power equal to a million tons of TNT: *a five-megaton bomb.*

melamine (resin) *mel'ȧ-mēn (rez'in)*, *n.* a type of plastic.

melancholy *mel'ȧn-kol-i*, *n.* lowness of spirits, sadness.—*adj.* **1** sad, low-spirited. **2** dismal, depressing.

mélange *mā-long̃zh'*, *n.* a mixture.

mêlée *me'lā*, *n.* a confused fight between two groups of people.

meliorate *mē'li-ȯ-rāt*, *v.t.* to make better.—*v.i.* to grow better:—*pr.p.* **me'liorating**.
meliorā'tion *n.*

mellifluous *mė-lif'loo-ůs*, *adj.* (of e.g. voice, words) sweet as honey.—Also **mellif'luent**.
mellif'luence *n.* **mellif'luently** *adv.*

mellow *mel'ō*, *adj.* **1** (of fruit) ripe, juicy, sweet. **2** (of wine) kept till the flavour is fine. **3** (of sound, colour, light) soft, not harsh. **4** (of character) softened by age or experience.—*v.i.* **1** to soften by ripeness or age (also *v.t.*). **2** to become gentler and more tolerant.

melodic, melodious. See **melody**.

melodrama *mel'ō-drä-mȧ*, *n.* sensational drama in which emotions are exaggerated.
melodramatic *(-drȧ-mat'ik) adj.* **1** sensational. **2** expressing more feeling than is suitable in the circumstances.

melody *mel'ȯ-di*, *n.* **1** an air or tune. **2** sweet music:—*pl.* **mel'odies**.
melod'ic *adj.* having to do with melody.
melō'dious *adj.* pleasing to the ear, tuneful.
melo'diously *adv.* **melo'diousness** *n.*

melon *mel'ȯn*, *n.* a large sweet fruit with much juice.

melt *melt v.i.* **1** to become liquid, usu. by heat. **2** to dissolve. **3** to feel very hot. **4** (often with *away*) to disappear almost unnoticed: *The crowd, his money, melted away.* **5** to shade, change (into) gradually without a distinct border line. **6** to soften in feeling, relent, feel sudden affection, etc.—Also *v.t.*
melt'ing *n.* and *adj.* **melt'ingly** *adv.*
mōlten *adj.* (of metal) melted.
melt'down *n.* the overheating of the core of a nuclear reactor.
in the melting-pot in the process of changing and forming something new.

member *mem'bėr*, *n.* **1** a limb of the body. **2** one who belongs to a group of persons, e.g. to a society. **3** one who belongs to a law-making body, e.g. the House of Commons: *a Member of Parliament.* **4** a part of a structure.
mem'bership *n.* **1** the state of being a member. **2** the body of members: *a society with a large membership.*

membrane *mem'brān*, *n.* a thin pliable layer of animal or vegetable tissue that lines parts of the body, forms the outside of cells, etc.

memento *mė-men'tō*, *n.* something kept as a reminder, souvenir, keepsake:—*pl.* **memen'to(e)s**.

memo *mem'ō*, *n.* abbrev. of **memorandum**:—*pl.* **mem'os**.

memoir *mem'wär, -wör*, *n.* **1** (often in *pl.*) a written account of events set down from personal knowledge. **2** (in *pl.*) an autobiography. **3** a biography: *He wrote a memoir of the Duke.* **4** a treatise.

memorandum *mem-ȯ-ran'dům*, *n.* **1** a note to help one to remember. **2** a written statement or summary of a matter being discussed:—*pl.* **memoran'dums, -da**.
memorabil'ia *n.pl.* souvenirs of people or events.
mem'orable *adj.* **1** worthy of being remembered. **2** remarkable.
mem'orableness, memorabil'ity *ns.*
memo'rial (*-mō'* or *-mö'*) adj. honouring the memory of a person or persons.—*n.* **1** something (e.g. a monument) which honours persons, events of the past. **2** a written statement of facts.

mem'orise *v.t.* **1** to learn: *to memorise a poem.* **2** to store in the memory:—*pr.p.* **mem'orising**.
mem'ory *n.* **1** power to remember. **2** an imagined part of the mind where facts and experiences are stored: *a memory filled with stories about interesting people.* **3** something remembered: *I have an early memory of seeing a comet.* **4** what is remembered about a person, his reputation:—*pl.* **mem'ories**.
in memory of as a remembrance of or memorial to.
See also **immemorial**.

men. See **man**.

menace *men'ȧs, n.* **1** a threat: *to utter menaces.* **2** something likely to cause injury or destruction (to).—*v.t.* (of a person, circumstances, etc.) to threaten to harm:—*pr.p.* **men'acing.**

men'acing *adj.*

menial *mē'ni-ȧl, adj.* (of work) mean, humble.—*n.* **1** (*orig.*) a household servant. **2** one doing humble jobs.

meningitis *men-in-jī'tis, n.* inflammation of the membranes round the brain or spinal cord.

meniscus *mėn-is'kus, n.* the curved upper surface of a liquid in a narrow tube.

menopause *men'ō-pöz, n.* **1** the ending of menstruation. **2** the time of life when this occurs.

menses *men'sēz, n.pl.* the monthly flow of blood from the uterus.

men'strual *adj.* of the menses or menstruation.

men'struate *v.i.* to discharge the menses:—*pr.p.* **men'struating.**

menstruā'tion *n.*

mensurable *men'shur-ȧ-bl, adj.* measurable.

mensurā'tion *n.* the act or art of finding the length, area, volume, etc., of objects.

mental *men'tȧl, adj.* **1** of, having to do with, the mind. **2** done, made, happening, in the mind: *mental arithmetic*; *a mental picture.* **3** suffering from an illness of the mind: *a mental patient.* **4** for those who are ill in mind: *a mental hospital.*

mentality *(-tal'i-ti) n.* **1** mental power. **2** way of thinking, outlook.

men'tally *adv.* in the mind.

mental age the age at which an average child would reach the same stage of mental development as the person being considered: *She is only seven, but she has a mental age of twelve* (i.e. she can read, count, etc. as well as an average twelve-year-old).

menthol *men'thol, n.* a sharp-smelling substance got from peppermint oil, etc., which gives relief in colds, etc.

mention *men'sh(ȯ)n, v.t.* **1** to speak of, refer to, briefly: *He mentioned the plan but gave no details.* **2** to remark (that). **3** to name because of bravery, etc.: *a soldier mentioned in dispatches.*—*n.* **1** a passing or brief reference (with *of*). **2** an honourable reference.

men'tionable *adj.* fit to be mentioned.

mentor *men'tȯr, n.* a wise giver of advice.

menu *men'ū, n.* (a card with) a list of dishes to be served, or available to be ordered, at a meal.

mercantile *mûr'kȧn-tīl, adj.* having to do with merchants or trade.

mercantile marine the ships and crews of a country that are employed in trading.

mercenary *mûr'sėn-ȧr-i, adj.* **1** hired for money. **2** too strongly influenced by desire for money.—*n.* a soldier hired into a foreign service:—*pl.* **mer'cenaries.**

merchant *mûr'chȧnt, n.* **1** a trader, esp. wholesale or in a large business. **2** (*U.S.* and *Scot.*) a shopkeeper.—*adj.* (used only before a noun) **1** having to do with trade. **2** used in trade.

mer'chandise *(-dīz) n.* goods bought and sold for gain.

mer'chantman *n.* a trading ship:—*pl.* **-men.**

merchant navy, service the mercantile marine (see this).

merchant ship a merchantman.

merciful, -fully, etc. See **mercy.**

mercury *mûr'kū-ri, n.* **1** an element, a silvery liquid metal, quicksilver. **2** (*cap.*) a Roman god, the messenger of the gods. **3** (*cap.*) the planet nearest to the sun.

mercu'rial *(-kū') adj.* (of a person, temperament) lively, sprightly, showing quick changes of mood.

mercy *mûr'si, n.* **1** willingness not to harm a person, e.g. an enemy, who is in one's power. **2** (esp. of God) an act of kindness or pity. **3** (*coll.*) a piece of good luck:—*pl.* **mer'cies.**

mer'ciful *adj.* **1** willing to forgive or to punish only lightly. **2** (of an event, when something bad is happening or expected) fortunate.

mer'cifully *adv.* **mer'cifulness** *n.*

mer'ciless *adj.* **1** without mercy. **2** cruel.

at the mercy of **1** wholly in the power of. **2** liable to be harmed by: *A camper is at the mercy of the weather.*

mere[1] *mēr, n.* a pool or lake.

mere[2] *mēr, adj.* (used only before a noun) no more or better than: *a mere child*; *a mere nothing*:—*comp.* (none); *superl.* **mer'est** (e.g. *The merest child could do it*).

mere'ly *adv.* simply, only.

meretricious *mer-ė-trish'ụs, adj.* **1** flashy, showily attractive but false, insincere. **2** relating to prostitutes.

merge *mûrj, v.i., v.t.* **1** to be, or cause to be, swallowed up (in something greater). **2** to combine or join:—*pr.p.* **mer'ging.**

mer'ger *n.* a joining together of business firms.

meridian *mė-rid'i-ȧn, n.* **1** the highest point (of the sun's course, of success). **2** an

imaginary circle or half circle on the earth's surface passing through the poles and any given place.
prime meridian the meridian (0) passing through Greenwich, from which longitudes are measured east or west.

meringue *mė-rang'*, *n.* (a cake made of) a crisp cooked mixture of sugar and white of eggs, or a substitute.

merino *mė-rē'nō*, *n.* **1** a sheep of Spanish origin that has very fine wool. **2** a cloth made from the wool:—*pl.* **meri'nos.**—Also *adj.*

merit *mer'it*, *n.* **1** excellence that deserves honour or reward. **2** worth, value. **3** (in *pl.*) rights or wrongs (of a case).—*v.t.* to deserve as reward or punishment:—*pr.p.* **mer'iting**; *pa.p.* **mer'ited.**

merito'rious *(-tōr', -tör') adj.* deserving (usu. moderate) reward or praise.

mermaid *mûr'mād*, *n.* an imaginary sea creature, woman to the waist with a fish's tail:—*masc.* **mer'man.**

merry *mer'i*, *adj.* **1** cheerful, esp. noisily or laughingly so. **2** slightly drunk. **3** (*old*) fair, pleasant, as orig. used e.g. by the poet Spenser: *merry England*:—*comp.* **merr'ier**; *superl.* **merr'iest.**
merr'ily *adv.* **merr'iness** *n.*
merr'iment *n.* fun, gaiety, with laughter and noise.
merr'y-go-round *n.* a kind of roundabout with wooden horses, seats, or the like, for riding on.
merr'ymaking *n.* **1** a merry entertainment. **2** the act of making merry.
merr'ymaker *n.*
merry men (*old*) the followers of a knight or outlaw chief.
merr'ythought *n.* a wishbone.
make merry 1 to be merry. **2** to hold, take part in, a merry entertainment.
See also **mirth.**

Mesdames. See **madam.**

mesembryanthemum *mė-zem-bri-an'-thi-mum*, *n.* any of a number of sun-loving plants most of which are S. African.

mesh *mesh*, *n.* **1** the opening between the threads of a net. **2** (in *pl.*) the threads around the opening. **3** network, net. **4** means of catching.—*v.t.* to catch in a net.—*v.i.* (of teeth on geared wheels) to become engaged with each other.

mesmerise *mez'mėr-īz*, *v.t.* **1** to hypnotise. **2** (*loosely*) to control the will, or fix the attention, of (a person):—*pr.p.* **mes'merising.**
mes'merism *n.*

mess *mes*, *n.* **1** a number of persons who take their meals together, esp. in the armed services. **2** the place where they eat together. **3** a dish of soft, pulpy or liquid stuff. **4** the result of spilling e.g. this. **5** a mixture disagreeable to the sight or taste. **6** disorder, confusion.—*v.t.* (often with *up*) to make a mess of.—*v.i.* to belong to a mess (with), eat one's meals (with).
mess'y *adj.*:—*comp.* **mess'ier**; *superl.* **mess'iest.**
mess'ily *adv.* **mess'iness** *n.*
mess'mate *n.* a member of the same (usu. ship's) mess.
make a mess of 1 to make dirty, untidy, or muddled. **2** to do badly. **3** to spoil, ruin (e.g. one's life).
mess about, around 1 to potter about. **2** to act in a foolish or annoying way.

message *mes'ij*, *n.* **1** any information, spoken or written, passed from one person to another. **2** an official notice from a president, etc., to a law-making body, etc. **3** the teaching of a poet, prophet, or wise man.
mess'enger *n.* one who carries message(s).

Messiah *mė-sī'ȧ*, *n.* **1** Christ. **2** an expected deliverer.

messily, etc. See **mess.**

messrs *mes'ėrz*, *n.pl.* English form of **messieurs** (see **monsieur**).

messy. See **mess.**

met. See **meet.**

metabolism *mė-tab'ŏl-izm*, *n.* the chemical changes in the cells of a living body which provide energy for living processes and activities.

metal *met'l*, *n.* **1** a substance (such as gold, silver, iron) which has a lustre or shine, conducts heat and electricity, can be hammered into shape, or drawn out in threads, etc., or any element that behaves chemically in a similar way. **2** broken stones used for making roads, etc.—Also *adj.*—*v.t.* to cover with metal:—*pr.p.* **met'alling**; *pa.p.* **met'alled.**
metallic *mė-tal'ik*, *adj.* **1** made of metal. **2** like a metal (e.g. in look, sound).
metallurgy *me-tal'ur-ji*, *met'ȧl-*, *n.* the study of metals, or the art of getting metals from ores and preparing them for use.
metall'urgist (or *met'*) *n.*
metallur'gic (-al) (or *met'*) *adjs.*

metamorphosis *met-ȧ-mör'fō-sis*, *n.* **1** change of form, substance, appearance, character, condition, etc., by natural development, or by, or as if by, magic. **2** the marked change that some living creatures undergo during their growth, as caterpillar to butterfly, tadpole to frog, etc.:—*pl.*

metamor'phoses *(-sēz)*.
metamorphose' *v.i.* and *v.t.*:—*pr.p.* **metamorphos'ing.**
metamor'phic *adj.* **metamor'phism** *n.*

metaphor *met'ȧ-fȯr, n.* a way of showing vividly a quality or characteristic of a person or thing by giving the person, thing, the name of something which has that quality in a marked degree (e.g. *He is a tiger when angry,* i.e. he has the fierceness of a tiger...). Similar comparisons can be made by using an adjective, verb, or adverb (e.g. *a violent red colour*; *she sailed into the room*; *the story ended lamely*). 'Like' and 'as' are not used (see **simile**).
metaphor'ical *adj.* expressing, in, metaphor(s), not literal fact.
metaphor'ically *adv.*
mixed metaphor a metaphor that is a confusion of two or more metaphors (e.g. *We are sailing fast towards bankruptcy, we must put the brake on.*)

metaphysics *met-ȧ-fiz'iks, n. sing.* **1** philosophy, esp. the parts which discuss the reality behind physical and natural facts and the nature of knowledge and thought. **2** (*loosely*) anything hard to understand.
metaphys'ical *adj.*

mete *mēt, v.t.* to give out (punishment, reward)—usu. **mete out**:—*pr.p.* **met'ing.**

meteor *mē'tyȯr, n.* **1** any of numberless small bodies travelling through space, seen when they enter the earth's atmosphere as fiery streaks in the sky—'falling', or 'shooting', 'stars'. **2** anything brilliant which does not last long.

meteoric *mē-ti-or'ik, adj.* **1** of, like, consisting of, a meteor or meteors. **2** rapid. **3** bright and successful for a short time: *a meteoric career*.
mē'teorite *n.* a meteor (of stone or metal) which has fallen to earth.
meteorol'ogy *n.* the study of weather and climate.
meteorol'ogist *n.* **meteorolog'ical** *adj.*

meter *mē'tėr, n.* an instrument for measuring, esp. the quantity of electricity, gas, water, etc., used.

method *meth'ȯd, n.* **1** the way in which one does something. **2** an orderly or fixed series of actions for doing something. **3** arrangement according to a plan.
method'ical *adj.* arranged, done, or in the habit of acting, in an orderly manner according to a plan: *a methodical filing system, search, person.*
method'ically *adv.* **method'icalness** *n.*
Meth'odist *n.* one of a denomination of Christians founded by John Wesley.
method acting acting by living a part, not just using stage technique.

meths *meths, n.sing.* short for **methylated spirits**.

methylated spirit(s) *meth'i-lā-tid spir'it(s),* an alcohol made unsuitable for drinking by adding certain substances.

meticulous *mė-tik'ū-lůs, adj.* **1** very careful about small details. **2** too careful.

métier *mā'tyā, n.* **1** one's trade, profession. **2** something in which one is skilled.

metonymy *mi-ton'i-mi, n.* a figure of speech in which the name of one thing is put for that of another related to it (e.g. 'the bottle' for 'alcoholic drink').

metre[1] *mē'tėr, n.* **1** (in English verse) the regular arrangement of syllables that are stressed. **2** the pattern seen in poetry of other kinds. **3** rhythm.
met'rical *adj.* **1** with syllables arranged in regular order. **2** made up of verses.

metre[2] *mē'tėr, n.* the chief unit of length in the metric system (39.37 inches).
met'ricate *(met')* *v.t.* and *v.i.* to change to the metric system:—*pr.p.* **met'ricating.**
metricā'tion *n.*
metric system a system of weights and measures based on tens (e.g. 1 metre = 10 decimetres = 100 centimetres, etc.).

metrical. See **metre**[1].

metronome *met'rȯ-nōm, n.* an instrument that beats to mark musical time.

metropolis *mė-trop'ȯ-lis, n.* **1** the chief city of a country. **2** the chief cathedral city (as Canterbury in England). **3** a chief centre.
metropol'ītan *adj.*

mettle *met'l, n.* spirit, courage, pluck.
mett'led, mett'lesome *adjs.* high-spirited.
put a person on his mettle to rouse him to put forth his best efforts.

mew[1] *mū, n.* a seagull.

mew[2] *mū, v.i.* to cry as a cat.—Also *n.*

mews *mūz, n.* a street or yard with, or orig. with, stables, now often made into houses.

mezzanine *mez'ȧ-nēn, n.* a storey between two floors, esp. the ground floor and first floor.

mezzo-soprano *met'zō-sō-prä'nō, n.* **1** the quality of voice between soprano and alto. **2** a low soprano. **3** a singer with such a voice:—*pl.* **mezz'o-sopra'nos.**—Also **mezz'o** (*pl.* **-os**).—Also *adjs.*

miaow *mi-ow', n.* the cry of a cat.—Also *v.i.*

miasma *mi-az'mȧ, mī-, n.* a poisonous atmosphere or influence.

mica *mī'kȧ*, *n.* a glittering mineral that divides easily into thin plates or layers and can usu. be seen through.

mice. See **mouse**.

Michaelmas *mik'ȧl-mȧs*, *n.* the festival of St. *Michael*, Sept. 29.

Michaelmas daisy a type of aster with clusters of small purple, pink, etc. flowers.

micro- *mī-krō-*, (as part of a word) **1** very small. **2** one millionth part.

microbe *mī'krōb*, *n.* a very tiny living thing, a germ (esp. causing disease).

mi'crobiol'ogy *n.* the study of tiny organisms such as bacteria.

microchip. See **chip**.

mi'crocosm *n.* any structure or system which contains, in miniature, all the features of the larger structure or system that it is part of.

microfilm *mī'krō-film*, *n.* a very small film on which documents, books, etc. are recorded.—Also *v.t.*

microgroove *mī'krō-grōōv*, *n.* the fine groove of a long-playing record.

micrometer *mī-krom'ė-tėr*, *n.* an instrument for measuring very small distances or angles.

microminiaturisā'tion *n.* reduction (e.g. of electronic equipment) to an extremely small size.

micro-organism *mī'krō-ör'gan-izm*, *n.* a very small organism (animal or plant).

microphone *mī'krō-fōn*, *n.* **1** an instrument for making sounds louder. **2** an instrument for picking up sound waves to be broadcast (e.g. in radio or telephone) and turning them into electrical waves.—Also (*coll.*) **mike** *(mīk)*.

micropro'cessor *n.* the part of a computer, comprising one or more microchips, which processes information, controls other parts of the computer system, etc.

microscope *mī'krō-skōp*, *n.* an instrument which makes very small objects able to be seen by means of lenses, or reflecting mirrors, or other methods.

microscop'ic *adj.* **1** having to do with a microscope. **2** seen only by the aid of a microscope. **3** very tiny.

mi'crowave *n.* a wave of a wavelength between those of radio waves and infrared waves.

microwave oven an oven in which food is cooked by the heat produced by microwaves passing through it.

mid *mid*, *adj.* (used only before a noun; of a time, position, etc.) at, in, the middle of: *in mid September*; *in mid ocean*:—*superl.* **mid'most.**—*prep.* amid.

midst *midst*, *n.* middle—as in the phrases **1 in the midst of**: *in the midst of these troubles.* **2 in our**, **your**, **their midst**: *foreigners living in our midst* (i.e. among us, in the same town, etc.).—*prep.* amid.

mid'day *n.* the middle of the day, noon.—Also *adj.*

mid'land *adj.* **1** in the middle of land, distant from the coast. **2** of the Midlands.

Midlands *n.pl.* the counties in the centre of England.

mid'night *n.* the middle of the night, twelve o'clock at night.—*adj.* **1** being at midnight. **2** dark as midnight.

mid-off, **mid-on**. See **mid-wicket**.

mid'ship *adj.* in the middle of a ship.

mid'shipman *n.* a former rank of a young officer on a ship in the navy (orig. serving amidships), now a shore ranking during training.

mid'summer *n.* the middle of summer, the period about June 21.—Also *adj.*

mid-term' *n.* (a holiday at) the middle of a term.

mid'way *adj.* and *adv.* in the middle of the distance, half way.

mid'-wicket *n.* a fielder near the bowler (**mid-off'** or **mid-on'**), or his place.

mid'winter *n.* the middle of winter, the period about Dec. 21 or 22.

in mid air in the air and well above the ground.

midden *mid'ėn*, *n.* **1** a dunghill. **2** a refuse heap.

middle *mid'l*, *adj.* (used only before a noun) **1** equally distant from both ends. **2** coming between.—*n.* **1** the middle point or part. **2** midst. **3** the central portion, waist.

midd'lemost *adj.* nearest the middle.

midd'ling *adj.* **1** of middle size, quality, rate, state. **2** second-rate, moderate.

midd'le-aged *adj.* between youth and old age.

Middle Ages the time between the downfall of the Roman empire and the Renaissance.

middle class the people (including professional people, bankers, shop-owners, etc.) who come between the working class and the aristocratic or the very wealthy.

Middle East an area including the Arabic-speaking countries around the eastern end of the Mediterranean Sea, the Arabian Peninsula, Greece, Turkey, Iran and much of N. Africa.

Middle English. See **English**.

midd'leman *n.* **1** a dealer who comes between the person who makes or grows a product and one who buys it. **2** a go-between or agent.

midd'leweight *n.* (*boxing*) a man weighing not more than 11 st 6 lb (72.574kg) or not less than 10 st 7 lb (66.678kg).

in the middle of **1** engaged in (doing something). **2** during. **3** while.

midge *mij*, *n.* **1** any small gnat or fly. **2** a very small person.

midg'et *n.* **1** a person not grown to ordinary size. **2** anything very small of its kind.—Also *adj.*

midland, **midnight**, etc. See **mid**.

midriff *mid'rif*, *n.* the diaphragm or middle of the body, just above the stomach.

midship, **midst**, **midway**, etc. See **mid**.

midwife *mid'wīf*, *n.* a person who helps at the birth of children:—*pl.* **mid'wives**.

mid'wifery *(-wif-ė-ri) n.* the art or practice of a midwife.

mien *mēn*, *n.* expression of face, manner: *a man of proud mien*.

miffed *mift*, (*coll.*) *adj.* slightly offended.

might[1]. See **may**[1].

might[2] *mīt*, *n.* power, strength.

might'y *adj.* **1** having great power. **2** very large. **3** (*coll.*) very great:—*comp.* **might'ier**; *superl.* **might'iest**.—*adv.* very.

might'ily *adv.* **might'iness** *n.*

migraine *mē'grān*, *n.* a type of headache, usu. on one side of the head only.

migrate *mī-grāt'*, *v.i.* **1** to pass regularly from one region to another, as certain birds and animals do. **2** to change one's home to another country:—*pr.p.* **migrat'ing**.

mī'gratory *(-grȧ-) adj.* **1** migrating. **2** wandering.

mī'grant *adj.* and *n.* **mīgrā'tion** *n.*

mikado *mi-kä'do'*, *n.* a title of the Emperor of Japan:—*pl.* **mika'dos**.

mike. See **microphone**.

milage. See **mile**.

milch. See **milk**.

mild *mīld*, *adj.* **1** gentle in temper or behaviour. **2** not sharp or bitter. **3** (of punishment, etc.) not severe. **4** (of weather) neither cold nor very hot.

mild'ly *adv.* **mild'ness** *n.*

mildew *mil'dū*, *n.* a disease on plants, cloth, etc. caused by the growth and spread of very tiny fungi.

mile *mīl*, *n.* **1** a (measure of) length of 1760 yards (1.61 kilometre). **2** in Roman times, 1000 paces.

mile'age, **mil'age** *n.* **1** length in miles. **2** the number of miles travelled. **3** (also **mil(e)age allowance**) expense of travel reckoned by the mile.

mileom'eter, **mīlom'eter** *n.* an instrument that records the number of miles that a vehicle has travelled.

mile'stone *n.* **1** a stone set up to mark the distance from somewhere in miles. **2** something which marks an important step or point: *Magna Carta was a milestone in British history*.

geographical, or **nautical**, **mile** any of several units used for measurement at sea, in Britain 6080 ft. (1.85km.).

milieu *mēl-yû'*, *n.* **1** setting in place and time. **2** social surroundings:—*pl.* **milieus'** *(-yûz')* or **milieux'** *(-yû')*.

militant *mil'i-tȧnt*, *adj.* **1** fighting. **2** warlike.

mil'itancy *n.* **mil'itantly** *adv.*

mil'itary *adj.* having to do with soldiers or with warfare.—*n.* the army.

mil'itate *v.i.* to work, exert force or influence (against): *These unforeseen events militated against his success*.

militia *mi-lish'ȧ*, *n.* a body of men trained to fight as soldiers, but liable only for home service.

milit'iaman *n.* a militia soldier.

milk *milk*, *v.t.* **1** to squeeze or draw milk, etc., from. **2** to force, take, money, information, etc. from (a person) in order to use it for one's own profit.—*n.* a white liquid produced by female animals as food for their young.

milk'er *n.* **1** a machine for milking cows. **2** a cow that gives milk.

milk'ing *n.* **1** the act of drawing milk from cows, etc. **2** the amount of milk drawn at one time.

milk'y *adj.*:—*comp.* **milk'ier**; *superl.* **milk'iest**.

milk'iness *n.*

milch *milch*, *milsh*, *adj.* giving milk.

milk bar a place where milk drinks, etc., are sold.

milk'maid *n.* a woman who milks cows.

milk'man *n.* a man who sells, or delivers, milk.

milk'sop *n.* a weak, unmanly man or boy.

Milky Way *n.* a band of stars stretching across the sky.

mill *mil*, *n.* **1** a machine for grinding (e.g. corn, coffee) by crushing between hard, rough surfaces. **2** a building where grain is ground. **3** one where manufacture of some kind is carried on: *a steel mill*.—*v.t.* **1** to grind, press, or stamp, in a mill. **2** to put ridges and grooves on the rim of (coins).—*v.i.* **1** (*slang*) to box, fight. **2** to move round and round aimlessly in a confused group.

mill'er *n.* one who works a grain mill.

mill'ing *n.* **1** the act of passing anything through a mill. **2** ridges and grooves on the rim of a coin.

mill'-race *n.* (the channel in which runs)

the current of water that turns a mill-wheel.

mill'stone *n.* **1** one of the two stones used in a mill for grinding grain. **2** a burden.

mill'-wheel *n.* a wheel, esp. a water-wheel, used for driving a mill.

millennium *mi-len'i-ŭm*, *n.* **1** a thousand years. **2** the period during which, it was prophesied (Revelation xx), Christ will live again on earth. **3** a coming golden age.—*pl.* **millenn'ia**, **millenn'iums**.

millepede. See **millipede** (at **milli-**).

millet *mil'it*, *n.* a grain used for food.

milli- *mil-i-*, (as part of a word) **1** thousand. **2** a thousandth part, e.g. **milligram**, **-litre**, **-metre**.

millipede, **millepede** *mil'i-pēd*, *n.* a small many-legged creature with a long round body.

milliner *mil'in-ėr*, *n.* one who makes and sells hats for women.

mill'inery *n.* **1** articles made or sold by milliners. **2** the hat industry.

million *mil'yȯn*, *n.* **1** a thousand thousands (1 000 000). **2** a very great number.—Also *adj.*

millionaire', *n.* a man having a million pounds, dollars, etc., or more:—*fem.* **millionair'ess**.

millionth *n.* and *adj.*

millipede. See **milli**.

mill-race, **millstone**, etc. See **mill**.

milometer. See **mile**.

mime *mīm*, *n.* **1** a play in which no words are spoken and the actions tell the story. **2** an actor in such a play.

mimic *mim'ik*, *n.* one who imitates or copies, esp. in a mocking way.—*v.t.* to imitate, esp. in a mocking way:—*pr.p.* **mim'icking**; *pa.p.* **mim'icked**.—*adj.* mock, sham: *a mimic battle.*

mim'icry *(-kri) n.* **1** the act of mimicking. **2** (in an animal) likeness to another or to some object in its surroundings.

mimosa *mi-mō'zȧ*, *n.* a tree with bunches of yellow, scented flowers.

minaret *min'ȧ-rėt*, *n.* a slender tower on a mosque, from which the call to prayer is sounded.

mince *mins*, *v.t.* to cut into small pieces, to chop fine.—*v.i.* to walk in an affected way with prim steps:—*pr.p.* **min'cing**.—*n.* meat chopped up.

min'cer *n.* a machine for mincing.

min'cing *adj.* **min'cingly** *adv.*

mince'meat *n.* **1** anything cut to pieces. **2** a mixture of raisins, other fruits, etc., usu. with suet (used in pastry to form a **mince'-pie'**).

mince matters, **words** to soften a statement, make it less frank, so as to be polite.

mind *mīnd*, *n.* **1** the power by which we think, etc. **2** intelligence, understanding. **3** a person who has great powers of reasoning, etc. **4** intention: *to change one's mind.* **5** inclination, desire: *I have a mind*, or *a good mind*, or *a great mind, to tell your father.* **6** frank opinion: *to speak one's mind.*—*v.t.* **1** to look after. **2** to pay attention, obey: *You should mind your parents, mind what they say.* **3** to watch out for: *Mind the step!* **4** to be upset by, object to: *I mind your going very much.*

mind'ed *adj.* **1** (combined with other words) having a certain type of mind: *strong-minded, narrow-minded.* **2** inclined (to). **3** determined (to).

mind'ful *adj.* bearing in mind (with *of*): *mindful of the danger.*

mind'less *adj.* **1** without mind. **2** stupid.

mind's eye the part of the imagination that forms pictures.

absence of mind **1** forgetfulness. **2** inattention.

bear, keep, in mind to remember, take into consideration.

in two minds undecided.

lose one's mind to become insane.

make up one's mind to decide.

never mind do not consider, trouble about, be upset by.

of one mind in agreement.

on one's mind troubling one.

out of mind out of one's thoughts.

out of one's mind insane.

presence of mind a state of calmness and readiness for any action required.

put in mind to remind.

mine[1]. See **I**.

mine[2] *mīn*, *n.* **1** a place from which metals, coal, etc., are dug. **2** a rich source (of e.g. information). **3** a heavy charge of explosive material for blowing up (e.g. a ship).—*v.t.* **1** to make passages in or under. **2** to lay mines in. **3** to blow up with mines.—*v.i.* to dig or work a mine:—*pr.p.* **min'ing**.

mī'ner *n.* one who works in a mine.

mine'-field *n.* an area covered with explosive mines.

mine'-layer, **mine'-sweeper** *ns.* ships used for placing, removing, mines in the sea.

mineral *min'ėr-ȧl*, *n.* a substance found naturally in the earth and mined—metal, rock, coal, asphalt.—*adj.* of, having to do with, minerals.

mineral'ogy *n.* the study of minerals.

mineralog'ical *adj.* **mineral'ogist** *n.*

mineral oil an oil, esp. petroleum, obtained from minerals.
mineral water 1 a spring water containing minerals. **2** a fizzy non-alcoholic drink.

minestrone *mi-ni-strōn'i*, *n.* a thick vegetable soup, orig. Italian, with pieces of pasta, etc.

mingle *ming'gl*, *v.t.* to mix.—*v.i.* **1** to mix. **2** to go about among (with *with*): *The thief mingled with the guests*:—*pr.p.* **ming'ling**.
mingled *ming'gld*, *adj.* **ming'ling** *n.*

mini- *mi'ni-*, (as part of a word) small.
min'ibus *n.* a small bus.
min'iskirt *n.* a very short skirt.

miniature *min'yȧ-chủr*, *min'i-(ȧ-)*, *n.* **1** a painting on a very small scale. **2** a small copy of anything.—*adj.* on a small scale.
min'iaturise *(-īz) v.t.* to reduce the size of (esp. electronic equipment) very greatly:—*pr.p.* **min'iaturising**.
miniaturisā'tion *n.*

minim *min'im*, *n.* (*music*) a note equal to two crotchets.

minimum *min'i-mủm*, *adj.* smallest.—*n.* **1** the smallest number or quantity. **2** the lowest point or degree:—*pl.* **min'ima**.
min'imal *adj.* **1** the least possible. **2** very small indeed.
min'imise *v.t.* **1** to make as little as possible: *He took steps to minimise the dangers.* **2** (to try) to make seem little: *He spoke as if he had done it all, minimising help he had received*:—*pr.p.* **min'imising**.

minion *min'yȯn*, *n.* **1** a favourite, esp. of a prince. **2** a follower who will do anything he is told to do.

minister *min'is-tėr*, *n.* **1** a clergyman. **2** the head of one of the divisions or departments of the government. **3** the representative of a government at a foreign court.—*v.i.* to give help (to), supply necessary things (to).
ministē'rial *adj.*
ministrā'tion *n.* (often in *pl.*) the act of giving help, care, etc.
min'istry *n.* **1** the profession, duties, or period of service, of a minister of religion. **2** the ministers of state as a group. **3** a department of government, or the building where it works:—*pl.* **min'istries**.

mink *mingk*, *n.* **1** a small weasel-like animal. **2** its fur. **3** a coat or jacket made of the fur.

minnow *min'ō*, *n.* a very small freshwater fish.

minor *mī'nȯr*, *adj.* **1** less in importance, size, etc. **2** of little importance.—*n.* a person under age (under 18 years).
minor'ity *n.* **1** the state of being under age. **2** (the party having) the smaller number—opp. to *majority*; *pl.* **minor'ities**.
minor interval one that is a semitone less than the major, e.g. **minor third**, e.g. C to E flat (**major**, C to E).
minor scale one in which the third note is a minor third above the first, and which contains other minor intervals.

minstrel *min'strėl*, *n.* **1** a harpist who went about the country in olden days reciting or singing poems. **2** an entertainer, esp. one with blackened face who sings Negro songs.
min'strelsy *n.* **1** a collection of songs. **2** a group of minstrels. **3** music:—*pl.* **min'strelsies**.

mint[1] *mint*, *n.* **1** (usu. *cap.*) the place where money is coined by a government. **2** a large sum (of money).—*v.t.* **1** to coin. **2** to invent.
in mint condition 1 unused. **2** undamaged.

mint[2] *mint*, *n.* a plant, used for flavouring, with sweet-smelling leaves.

minuet *min-ū-et'*, *n.* **1** a slow, graceful dance with short steps. **2** music for it.

minus *mī'nủs*, *prep.* **1** used to show subtraction: *Ten minus two equals eight (10-2=8).* **2** (*coll.*) without.—*n.* and *adj.* **1** (a quantity) less than zero or nought. **2** (the sign) showing subtraction (-).

minute[1] *mī-nūt'*, *mi-*, *adj.* **1** extremely small. **2** paying attention to the smallest details: *minute care*; *a minute examination.*
minute'ly *adv.* **minute'ness** *n.*

minute[2] *min'it*, *n.* **1** the sixtieth part of an hour. **2** (in measuring an angle) the sixtieth part of a degree. **3** a very short time. **4** (in *pl.*) the notes taken at a meeting recording what was said.

minutiae *mī-nū'shi-ē*, *mi-*, *n.pl.* very small details.

minx *mingks*, *n.* a cheeky young girl.

miracle *mir'ȧ-kl*, *n.* **1** an act beyond the power of man, or a fortunate happening that has no natural cause or explanation. **2** a wonder, marvel.
miraculous *mi-rak'ū-lủs*, *adj.*

mirage *mi'räzh*, *-räzh'*, *n.* something not really there that one imagines one sees, esp. the appearance of an expanse of water seen by travellers in a desert.

mire *mīr*, *n.* deep mud.—*v.t.* **1** to cause to stick fast in mire. **2** to stain with mud:—*pr.p.* **mir'ing**.
mir'y *adj.*:—*comp.* **mir'ier**; *superl.*

mir'iest.
mir'iness *n.*

mirror *mir'ȯr, n.* **1** a looking-glass. **2** a surface that reflects. **3** something that gives a true picture or likeness.—*v.t.* to reflect as a mirror does.

mirth *mûrth, n.* **1** merriness. **2** laughter or amusement caused by something funny.
mirth'ful *adj.* **1** merry. **2** funny.
mirth'less *adj.* joyless, cheerless.

miry. See **mire**.

mis- *mis-, pfx.* **1** wrong(ly). **2** bad(ly).

misadventure *mis-ȧd-ven'chu̇r, n.* **1** an unlucky happening. **2** an accident.

misadvise *mis-ȧd-vīz', v.t.* to give bad advice to:—*pr.p.* **misadvis'ing.**

misalliance *mis-ȧ-lī'ȧns, n.* an unsuitable alliance (esp. marriage with one of a lower rank) or combination.
misally *mis-ȧ-lī, v.t.*:—*pr.p.* **misally'ing**; *pa.p.* **misallied'**.

misanthrope *mis'ȧn-thrōp, miz', n.* a hater of mankind.—Also **misan'thropist**.
misanthrop'ic *adj.*
misan'thropy *n.* hatred, distrust, of man.

misapply *mis-ȧ-plī', v.t.* **1** to use for a wrong purpose. **2** to apply to a wrong person or thing:—*pr.p.* **misapply'ing**; *pa.p.* **misapplied'**.
misapplicā'tion *n.*

misapprehend *mis-ap-ri-hend', v.t.* **1** to misunderstand (meaning, person in what he says). **2** to take a wrong meaning from.—Also *v.i.*
misapprehen'sion *n.* misunderstanding of meaning, or false belief as to fact: *to be under a misapprehension.*

misappropriate *mis-ȧ-prō'pri-āt, v.t.* to put to a wrong use, esp. to use (another's money) for oneself:—*pr.p.* **misappro'priating**.
misappropriā'tion *n.*

misbehave *mis-bi-hāv', v.i.* to behave badly:—*pr.p.* **misbehav'ing**.
misbehaviour *(-yėr) n.*

miscalculate *mis-kal'kū-lāt, v.t., v.i.* to calculate, estimate, or judge, wrongly:—*pr.p.* **miscal'culating**.

miscarriage *mis-kar'ij, n.* **1** failure (of a plan). **2** failure to gain the right result: *By a miscarriage of justice the wrong man was condemned.* **3** the act of bringing forth young too early for survival and development.
miscarr'y *v.i.* **1** to be unsuccessful. **2** to have the wrong result. **3** (of e.g. a letter) to go astray. **4** (of a female) to have a miscarriage:—*pr.p.* **miscarr'ying**; *pa.p.* **miscarr'ied** *(-id).*

miscegenation *mis-i-jė-nā'sh(ȯ)n, n.* mixture of races resulting from marriage between people of different races.

miscellaneous *mis-ėl-ān'yu̇s, adj.* mixed, made up of several different kinds.
miscell'any *n.* **1** a mixture of different kinds. **2** a collection of writings on different subjects or by different authors:—*pl.* **miscell'anies**.

mischance *mis-chäns', n.* **1** bad luck. **2** mishap, accident.

mischief *mis'chif, n.* **1** evil, trouble, harm, damage. **2** action or behaviour that causes small troubles or annoyance to others.
mischievous *mis'chi-vu̇s, adj.* **1** harmful. **2** tending, or inclined, to cause trouble or to annoy. **3** (fond of) teasing, etc., in a playful manner.
mis'chief-maker *n.* one who causes bad feeling or trouble, e.g. by carrying tales.

misconceive *mis-kȯn-sēv', v.t.* to form a wrong idea of.—Also *v.i.*:—*pr.p.* **misconceiv'ing**.
misconcep'tion *n.*

misconduct *mis-kon'dukt, n.* bad conduct. —*v.t.* *(-kȯn-dukt')* **1** to misbehave (oneself). **2** to mismanage.

misconstrue *mis-kȯn-stro͞o', v.t.* to misunderstand, take a wrong meaning from: *He misconstrues the men's action; they are not out for gain, they really want to help*:—*pr.p.* **misconstru'ing**.
misconstruc'tion *n.*

miscount *mis-kownt', v.t.* to count wrongly.—*n.* a wrong count.

miscreant *mis'kri-ȧnt, n.* a very wicked person, scoundrel, rascal.

misdeal *mis-dēl', n.* a wrong deal, as at cards.—*v.t., v.i.* to deal wrongly:—*pa.p.* **misdealt'** *(-delt').*

misdeed *mis-dēd', n.* **1** an evil deed. **2** an instance of bad behaviour.

misdemeanour *mis-di-mē'nȯr, n.* **1** bad behaviour. **2** a petty crime.

misdirect *mis-di-rekt', -dī-, v.t.* to direct wrongly.

miser *mī'zėr, n.* a mean, ungenerous person who lives very poorly in order to store up wealth.
mi'serly *adj.* **mi'serliness** *n.*

miserable *miz'ėr-ȧ-bl, adj.* **1** very unhappy. **2** very poor in quantity or quality: *miserable payment; a miserable hovel.* **3** shameful: *his miserable cowardice.*
mis'erableness *n.* **mis'erably** *adv.*
misery *miz'ėr-i, n.* great unhappiness.

misfire *mis-fīr', v.i.* **1** to fail to explode or catch fire. **2** to produce no effect, have no success:—*pr.p.* **misfir'ing**.—Also *n.*

misfit *mis'fit, -fit', n.* **1** a bad fit. **2** a thing that fits badly. **3** a person not able to live or work happily in the society in which he finds himself.

misfortune *mis-för'chun, n.* **1** bad luck. **2** a mishap or calamity.

misgiving *mis-giv'ing, n.* a feeling of fear or doubt e.g. about the result of an action.

misgovern *mis-guv'ėrn, v.t.* to govern or rule badly or unjustly.

misguide *mis-gīd', v.t.* **1** to lead astray. **2** to lead into thinking wrongly.
misguid'ed *adj.* acting from, or showing, mistaken beliefs or motives: *misguided attempts to help.*

mishandle *mis-han'dl, v.t.* **1** to handle without skill. **2** to treat roughly:—*pr.p.* **mishand'ling.**

mishap *mis'hap, -hap', n.* an unlucky accident (often not serious).

mishear *mis-hēr', v.t.* and *v.i.* to hear wrongly:—*pa.p.* **misheard'** *(-hûrd').*

misinform *mis-in-förm', v.t.* to give wrong information to.

misinterpret *mis-in-tûr'prit, v.t.* **1** to take a wrong meaning from. **2** to explain wrongly.

misjudge *mis-juj', v.t., v.i.* **1** to judge wrongly. **2** to have an unjust opinion of (a person):—*pr.p.* **misjudg'ing.**

mislay *mis-lā', v.t.* to lay (something) in a place and forget where it is:—*pa.p.* **mislaid'** *(-lād').*

mislead *mis-lēd', v.t.* **1** (of e.g. a remark) to give a wrong idea to (a person). **2** to cause to make mistakes:—*pa.p.* **misled'.** —Also *v.i.*
mislead'ing *adj.*

mismanage *mis-man'ij, v.t.* to manage badly, without skill:—*pr.p.* **misman'aging.**

misnomer *mis-nō'mėr, n.* **1** a wrong name. **2** an unsuitable name: *'Road' was a misnomer; the way was a rutted track.*

misogynist *mis-oj'i-nist, n.* a hater of women.
misog'yny *n.*

misplace *mis-plās', v.t.* **1** to put in the wrong place. **2** to give (e.g. trust, affection) to an unworthy object:—*pr.p.* **misplac'ing.**

misprint *mis'print, -print', n.* a mistake in printing.—Also *v.t.*

mispronounce *mis-prȯ-nowns', v.t.* to pronounce wrongly:—*pr.p.* **mispronoun'cing.**
mispronunciā'tion *(-nun-) n.*

misquote *mis-kwōt', v.t.* to make a mistake in repeating what someone has written or said:—*pr.p.* **misquot'ing.**

misread *mis-rēd', v.t.* **1** to read wrongly. **2** to take a wrong meaning from reading:—*pa.p.* **misread'** *(-red').*
misread'ing *n.*

misreport *mis-ri-pōrt', -pört', v.t.* to report incorrectly.

misrepresent *mis-rep-ri-zent', v.t.* to give a false idea of (a person, what he does or says).

misrule *mis-ro͞ol', n.* **1** unjust rule. **2** disorder.—*v.t.* to rule badly:—*pr.p.* **misrul'ing.**

miss¹ *mis, n.* **1** (*cap.*, with Christian name or surname) used in addressing formally an unmarried female: *You are Miss Smith, I believe.* **2** a young woman or girl:—*pl.* **miss'es** (on letters put *The Misses Smith*; *The Miss Smiths* is less formal).

miss² *mis, v.t.* **1** to fail to hit, reach, get, find, see, hear, understand. **2** to fail to have, keep: *She missed her French lesson, her appointment.* **3** to avoid: *He just missed being caught.* **4** to fail to take advantage of (an opportunity). **5** to discover the absence of: *He missed his umbrella when he reached home.* **6** to feel the want of: *He misses his friends.* —*v.i.* **1** to fail to hit. **2** to be unsuccessful.—*n.* **1** a failure to hit the mark. **2** a loss.
miss'ing *adj.* **1** not in its place. **2** not found. **3** lacking.
miss out **1** to leave out, not put in. **2** (with *on*) to fail to get, experience, or benefit from.

missal *mis'ȧl, n.* the book that contains the year's mass services for the Roman Catholic Church.

missel thrush *mis'l thrush,* a large thrush fond of mistletoe berries.

misshapen *mis-shāp'ėn, adj.* badly shaped.

missile *mis'īl, -il, n.* a weapon or object for throwing or shooting, now esp. a **guided missile,** a jet- or rocket-propelled missile directed to its target by a built-in device, or by radio waves, etc.

missing. See **miss².**

mission *mish'(ȯ)n, n.* **1** a purpose for which a messenger, delegate, etc. is sent: *His mission was to seek help.* **2** a group of delegates sent to carry out negotiations. **3** persons sent to spread a religion. **4** a station or post where these live. **5** one's chosen purpose or duty: *He regarded it as his mission to get rid of the tyrant.*
miss'ionary *n.* one sent on a mission to spread religion:—*pl.* **miss'ionaries.**

missive *mis'iv, n.* something sent, esp. a letter.

misspell *mis-spel', v.t.* to spell wrongly:—*pa.p.* **misspelt'**, **misspelled'**.

misspend *mis-spend', v.t.* to waste, squander on wrong things (money, one's life):—*pa.p.* **misspent'** (also *adj.*).

misstate *mis-stāt', v.t.* to state wrongly:—*pr.p.* **misstat'ing**.
misstate'ment *n.*

mist *mist, n.* **1** a cloud of moisture in the air, very thin fog, or drizzle. **2** anything that clouds the sight or the judgment.—*v.t.* and *v.i.* to blur, cloud over, as with mist.
mis'ty *adj.—comp.* **mis'tier**; *superl.* **mis'tiest**.
mis'tily *adv.* **mis'tiness** *n.*

mistake *mis-tāk', v.t.* **1** to make an error about. **2** to take (one person or thing for another). **3** to understand wrongly: *You mistake my meaning, my intention.*—Also *v.i.—n.* **1** the act of understanding wrongly. **2** an error, wrong action or statement. **3** an error arising from bad judgment: *It was a mistake to trust him.—pa.t.* **mistook'**; *pa.p.* **mistak'en**.
mistak'en *adj.* **1** in error: *You are mistaken about what happened.* **2** showing bad judgment: *a mistaken attempt to help.*
mistak'enly *adv.*
mistaken identity a mistake in identifying someone, picking out the wrong person.

mister *mis'tėr, n.* used formally before the name of a man (written **Mr**):—for the *pl.*, **Messrs** (see this word) is used.

mistime *mis-tīm', v.t.* **1** to time badly. **2** to do or say at an unsuitable time:—*pr.p.* **mistim'ing**.

mistiness, etc. See **mist**.

mistletoe *mis'l-tō, miz'-, n.* a plant with white berries, growing on trees, used in Christmas decorations.

mistook. See **mistake**.

mistreat *mis-trēt', v.t.* to treat badly.

mistress *mis'tris, n.* **1** a woman who commands or controls. **2** a state, etc. that controls. **3** a female owner (of e.g. a dog) or employer. **4** a woman teacher. **5** a woman very skilled in an art. **6** a woman who has a close and enduring sexual relationship with a man without being his legal wife. **7** used formally before the name of a married woman (written **Mrs**, pronounced *mis'iz*):—*pl.* **mis'tresses**; *masc.* (*defs. 1–5*) **master**.

mistrial *mis-trī'ȧl, n.* a trial declared to have no legal force because of error or fault in the proceedings.

mistrust *mis-trust', n.* lack of trust.—*v.t.* to suspect, distrust.

misty. See **mist**.

misunderstand *mis-un-dėr-stand', v.t.* to take a wrong meaning from (e.g. a statement, or a person or his words or actions):—*pa.p.* **misunderstood'**.
misunderstand'ing *n.* **1** a mistake as to meaning. **2** a slight disagreement.
misunderstood' *adj.* (of a person) not understood or appreciated.

misuse *mis-ūs', n.* **1** wrong use. **2** use for a bad purpose.—*v.t.* *(mis-ūz')* **1** to use wrongly. **2** to treat badly:—*pr.p.* **misus'ing**.

mite[1] *mīt, n.* a very small insect living on other insects, animals, or plants, or in food (such as cheese).

mite[2] *mīt, n.* **1** anything very small. **2** a tiny person.

mitigate *mit'i-gāt, v.t.* **1** to make (e.g. pain, anger) less great. **2** to make (e.g. punishment) less severe. **3** to excuse (a wrong action) to some extent: *The circumstances mitigated his offence*:—*pr.p.* **mit'igating**.
mit'igating *adj.* **mitigā'tion** *n.*

mitre[1] *mī'tėr, n.* a headdress worn by archbishops and bishops.

mitre[2] *mī'tėr, n.* a joint made between two pieces that form an angle, usu. a right angle, the end of each piece being cut on a slant (also **mi'tre-joint**).—*v.t.* to make a mitre in:—*pr.p.* **mi'tring**.

mitten *mit'n*, **mitt** *mit, n.* **1** a kind of glove having one cover for all the four fingers. **2** a glove for the hand and wrist, but not the fingers.

mix *miks, v.t.* **1** to unite or blend several things into one mass (e.g. by stirring). **2** to form by doing this: *to mix cement.* **3** to muddle, confuse (often **mix up**).—*v.i.* **1** to blend: *Oil and water do not mix.* **2** to associate as friends or in society: *He did not mix with his neighbours.—n.* a mixture.
mixed *adj.* **1** jumbled together. **2** confused. **3** including people of both sexes.
mix'er *n.* **1** one who, or a machine which, mixes. **2** (with *good* or *bad*) one who gets on well, or not well, with other people. **3** a soft drink for adding to an alcoholic one.
mix'ture *(-chůr) n.* **1** the act of mixing or state of being mixed. **2** a mass or blend formed by mixing.
mix'-up *n.* a confusion or misunderstanding.
mixed blessing something having both advantages and disadvantages.
mixed marriage one between persons of

different races or religions.
mixed up **1** confused. **2** bewildered, not fitting into the life around one.

mizzen-mast *miz'n-mäst*, *n.* the mast nearest the stern of a two- or three-masted ship.

mnemonic *nē-mon'ik*, *ni-*, *n.* something (often a jingle) that helps the memory (e.g. the spelling rule *'i* before *e* except after *c'.*)

moan *mōn*, *n.* a low sound of grief or pain.—*v.i.* to utter a moan.

moat *mōt*, *n.* a deep trench round a castle, etc., usu. filled with water.

mob *mob*, *n.* **1** the mass of the people. **2** a (noisy or disorderly) crowd of people or animals.—*v.t.* to crowd round, or attack, in a disorderly way:—*pr.p.* **mobb'ing**; *pa.p.* **mobbed**.
mobbed (*coll.*) *adj.* crowded.

mobile *mō'bīl*, *-bil*, *-bēl*, *adj.* **1** able to move (*opp.* **immobile**). **2** easily or quickly moved. **3** (of mind) quick. **4** (of face) changing easily in expression.—*n.* **1** an artistic object hung so that it moves slightly in the air. **2** a mobile phone.
mo'bileness, mobil'ity *ns.*
mōbilise *v.t.* **1** to put in readiness for service. **2** to call (e.g. troops) into active service:—*pr.p.* **mo'bilising**.
mobilisā'tion *n.*

moccasin, **mocassin** *mok'à-sin*, *n.* **1** a shoe of soft leather, worn by American Indians. **2** a shoe or slipper like this.

mocha *mok'à*, *mō'kà*, *n.* a fine coffee, brought from *Mocha* on the Red Sea.

mock *mok*, *v.t.* **1** to laugh at. **2** to mimic in scorn. **3** to disappoint or to bring no success to (e.g. hopes, efforts).—*adj.* sham, not real: *a mock battle*.
mock'ery *n.* **1** the act of making fun of something. **2** a false show. **3** something very far from what it should be: *a mockery of a reward*:—*pl.* **mock'eries**.
mock'ing *adj.* and *n.* **mock'ingly** *adv.*
mock'ing-bird *n.* an American bird of the same family as the thrushes, which copies the notes of other birds.
mock'-up *n.* a full-size dummy model.

mod. con. *mod kon*, abbrev. of *modern convenience*, any item of up-to-date plumbing, heating, etc.; usu. in *pl.* **mod. cons**.

mode *mōd*, *n.* **1** one's manner of acting, doing, etc. **2** fashion.
mo'dish *adj.* fashionable, smart.
modiste *(-dēst')* *n.* **1** a dressmaker. **2** a milliner.

model *mod'l*, *n.* **1** something to be copied. **2** something worth copying: *She is a model of kindness.* **3** a copy of something, usu. made in a smaller size. **4** a person who poses for an artist. **5** one who wears clothes to show them off to possible buyers.—*adj.* **1** acting as a model. **2** fit to be copied, perfect: *model behaviour.*—*v.t.* **1** to make a model or copy of. **2** to shape. **3** to form after a pattern: *He models his conduct on that of his brother.* **4** to wear (clothes) to show them off:—*pr.p.* **mod'elling**; *pa.p.* **mod'elled**.
mod'elling *n.* the art of making models, a branch of sculpture.

modem *mōd'em*, *n.* (*computers*) an electronic device that transmits information from one computer to another along a telephone line.

moderate *mod'ėr-āt*, *v.t.* and *v.i.* to make, or to become, less great or severe: *He was forced to moderate his demands*; *The pain moderated*:—*pr.p.* **mod'erating**.—*adj.* *(-it)* **1** not unreasonably great (*opp.* **immoderate**): The prices were moderate. **2** of medium quality. **3** rather poor: *a man of only moderate ability.*—*n.* a person whose views, aims, are not extreme.
mod'erately *adv.* **mod'erateness** *n.*
moderā'tion *n.* **1** lessening of severity, etc. **2** moderateness.
mod'erātor *n.* a chairman of a meeting, esp. of Presbyterian clergymen.

modern *mod'ėrn*, *adj.* **1** belonging to the present or to time not long past. **2** not ancient.—*n.* **1** one living in modern times. **2** one whose views or tastes are modern.
mod'ernise *v.t.* to bring up to date, adapt to suit present ideas or taste:—*pr.p.* **mod'ernising**.
mod'ernisā'tion *n.*
mod'ernness, **moder'nity** *ns.*

modest *mod'ist*, *adj.* **1** not vain, boastful, or pushing. **2** shy. **3** decent, showing good taste, not shocking (*opp.* **immodest**). **4** not very large, showy, etc.: *a modest income*, *house*.
mod'estly *adv.* **mod'esty** *n.*

modicum *mod'i-kum*, *n.* a small quantity.

modify *mod'i-fī*, *v.t.* to alter, change the form or quality of, add to or alter the sense of, usu. slightly: *to modify a design*, *a plan*, *one's views*; *An adverb modifies a verb*:—*pr.p.* **mod'ifying**; *pa.p.* **mod'ified**.
modificā'tion *n.*

modish, **modiste**. See **mode**.

modulate *mod'ū-lāt*, *v.t.* **1** to vary the tone, pitch, etc. of (e.g. the voice). **2** to soften, tone down. **3** to vary some characteristic of (a radio wave).—*v.i.* **1** to pass from one state to another. **2** (*music*) to pass from one key to another:—*pr.p.* **mod'ulating**.
modular *mod'ū-lȧr*, *n.*

modulā'tion *n.* **mod'ulātor** *n.*
mod'ule *n.* **1** a unit of size for measuring or for regulating proportions. **2** a self-contained unit forming part of a space-craft. **3** a course of teaching material forming a unit of an educational scheme.

mohair *mō'hār, n.* **1** the long silken hair of an Angora goat. **2** cloth made of it.

moist *moist, adj.* **1** damp. **2** rainy. **3** humid.
moisten *mois'n, v.t.* to wet slightly.
mois'ture *(-chůr) n.* enough liquid to make slightly wet.

molar *mō'lår, adj.* used for grinding.—*n.* a back tooth which grinds food.

molasses *mȯ-las'iz, n.sing.* treacle.

mole[1] *mōl, n.* a small usu. dark, spot on the skin.

mole[2] *mōl, n.* **1** a small burrowing animal with very small eyes and soft fur. **2** a spy who infiltrates an organisation.
mole'hill *n.* a little heap of earth cast up by a mole.

mole[3] *mōl, n.* a breakwater, or a stone pier.

molecule *mol'ė-kūl, mōl', n.* the smallest part of a substance that has the properties or qualities of that substance.
molec'ular *adj.*

molehill. See **mole**[2].

molest *mō-lest', mȯ-lest', v.t.* to meddle with, annoy, torment.
molestā'tion *n.*

mollify *mol'i-fī, v.t.* **1** to soften, calm (e.g. a person). **2** to make less (e.g. anger):—*pr.p.* **moll'ifying**; *pa.p.* **moll'ified**.
mollificā'tion *n.*

mollusc, mollusk *mol'usk, n.* a soft animal without backbone and usu. with a hard shell (e.g. a shellfish, snail).

mollycoddle *mol'i-kod-l, n.* a milksop.—*v.t.* to pamper, coddle:—*pr.p.* **moll'y-coddling**.

Molotov cocktail *mol'ȯ-tof kok'tāl,* a missile consisting of a bottle with inflammable liquid and a wick to be ignited just before throwing.

molten. See **melt**.

moment *mō'mėnt, n.* **1** a very short space of time, instant. **2** importance: *Nothing of moment happened.*
mo'mentary *adj.* lasting for a moment, short-lived.
mo'mentarily *adv.* **mo'mentariness** *n.*
momen'tous *adj.* of great importance: *momentous events.*
momen'tously *adv.* **momen'tousness** *n.*
momen'tum *n.* **1** the quantity of motion in a body. **2** force of motion gained by movement: *He tried to stop, but his momentum carried him over the cliff edge.*

mon-. See **mono**.

monarch *mon'årk, n.* a king, queen, emperor, or empress.
monarchic(al) *(-ärk') adjs.*
mon'archist *n.* a believer in monarchic government.
mon'archy *n.* **1** government by a monarch. **2** a kingdom, the territory of a monarch:—*pl.* **mon'archies**.

monastery *mon'ås-tėr-i, n.* the home of a community of monks:—*pl.* **mon'asteries**.
monas'tic(al) *adjs.* having to do with monks, monasteries, nuns: *monastic orders, vows.*
monas'ticism *(-sizm) n.* **1** the way of life in a monastery. **2** the system of monks and monasteries.

monaural *mon-ö'rål, adj.* (of a gramophone record) giving the effect of sound from a single direction.

Monday *mun'di, n.* the second day of the week.

monetary. See **money**.

money *mun'i, n.* **1** coins or notes, used in trading. **2** wealth. **3** (in *pl.*) sums of money:—*pl.* **mon'eys, mon'ies**.
monetary *mun'i-tår-i, mon'-, adj.* **1** having to do with money. **2** consisting of money: *a monetary reward.*
mon'eyed, mon'ied *mun'id, adj.* rich.
mon'eylender *n.* one whose business is lending money.
money order an order for payment of money to a named person at a named post office (the sum concerned being paid in at another post office).
mon'ey-spinner *n.* something that brings in much money.

monger *mung'gėr, n.* a trader, dealer (usu. as part of a word, e.g. *fishmonger*).

Mongol *mong'gȯl, n.* and *adj.* **1** (one) of the people living in *Mongolia.* **2** (*now offensive*) (a person) affected by **Down's syndrome**.

mongoose *mong'gōōs, n.* a small weasel-like animal of India that kills snakes:—*pl.* **mon'gooses**.

mongrel *mung'grėl, n.* an animal, esp. a dog, of a mixed breed.—*adj.* **1** mixed in breed. **2** of no special class or type.

monied, monies. See **money**.

monition *mon-ish'(ȯ)n, n.* a warning.
mon'itor *n.* **1** one who warns or scolds. **2** a senior pupil who helps to see that school rules are kept. **3** a school pupil who has been given any of various duties. **4** a screen in a television studio showing

the picture being transmitted. **5** an arrangement or instrument of different kinds for checking such things as quality of electrical communication, level of radioactivity. **6** a large lizard.—*v.i.* **1** to be, or to use, a monitor. **2** to listen to foreign broadcasts in order to obtain news, code messages, etc. **3** to check, keep a watch on something.—Also *v.t.*

monk *mungk*, *n.* one of a religious group living apart from the world in monastery.
monk'ish *adj.* like a monk.

monkey *mungk'i*, *n.* **1** any member of the most advanced group of animals, except man; used especially for those members of the group that are smaller and have long tails (i.e. leaving out the apes). **2** a mischievous child:—*pl.* **monk'eys**.—*v.i.* to meddle (with something).
monkey nut a peanut, groundnut.
monk'ey-puzz'le (tree) *n.* a kind of pine tree with prickly leaves along its branches.
monkey wrench a wrench with a movable jaw.

mono- *mon-ō-*, **mon-** (as part of a word) one, single.
mon'o *n.* (a record made in) monaural sound:—*pl.* **mon'os**.—Also *adj.*
monochromatic *mon-ȯ-krō-mat'ik*, *adj.* of one colour only.
mon'ochrome *n.* **1** a painting, etc., in a single colour. **2** black and white only, as in a television (also *adj.*).
monocle *mon'ȯ-kl*, *n.* a single eyeglass.
monogamy *mȯ-nog'ȧ-mi*, *n.* marriage to one wife or husband only.
monog'amist *n.* **monog'amous** *adj.*
monogram *mon'ȯ-gram*, *n.* a single design made up of several intertwined letters.
monolith'ic *adj.* (of e.g. a state, business organisation) very large and very much the same throughout.
monologue *mon'ȯ-log*, *n.* a long speech by one person.
monomania *mon-ō-mā'ni-ȧ*, *n.* **1** madness limited to one subject. **2** a too great interest in, or enthusiasm for, one thing.
monoma'niac *n.*
monophon'ic *adj.* (of e.g. a record) monaural.
monoplane *mon'ȯ-plān*, *n.* an aeroplane with one set of wings.
monop'olise *v.t.* **1** to have a monopoly of. **2** to keep complete possession, control, etc. of. **3** to take up completely: *She monopolised their time, attention*:—*pr.p.* **monop'olising**.
monopoly *mȯ-nop'ȯ-li*, *n.* **1** sole right of making or selling something. **2** something thus controlled. **3** sole possession (of): *No race has a monopoly of courage*:—*pl.* **monop'olies**.
monorail *mon'ȯ-rāl*, *n.* a railway with carriages suspended from, or running astride of, one rail.
monosyllab'ic *adj.* **1** having one syllable. **2** (speaking) in one-syllabled words only.
monosyllable *mon-ȯ-sil'ȧ-bl*, *n.* a word of one syllable.
monotheism *mon'ȯ-thē-izm*, *n.* the belief in only one God.
monotone *mon'ȯ-tōn*, *n.* a single unchanging tone of voice.
monot'onous *adj.* **1** in one unchanging tone. **2** lacking in variety, dull.
monot'ony *n.* **1** lack of change. **2** dullness.

Monseigneur *mon*^{g}*-sen-yûr'*, *n.* a title in France given to a person of high rank, a bishop, etc. (written **Mgr**).
monsieur *mė̇s-yû'* **1** sir. **2** (*cap.*) a title (often written *M.*) in France equal to *Mr* in English:—*pl.* **messieurs** *mes-yû'*.

Monsignor *mon-sēn'yȯr*, *n.* a title given to certain R.C. prelates.

monsoon *mon-sōōn'*, *n.* **1** a wind that blows in the Indian Ocean, from the S.W. in summer, from the N.E. in winter. **2** the rainy season caused by the S.W. monsoon.

monster *mon'stėr*, *n.* **1** a plant or animal of unusual form or appearance. **2** a huge creature, causing fear. **3** a horribly wicked person.—*adj.* huge.
monstros'ity *n.* **1** something not natural. **2** the state of being monstrous:—*pl.* **monstros'ities**.
mon'strous *adj.* **1** huge. **2** horrible.

month *munth*, *n.* **1** the time from new moon to new moon, called a *lunar* month. **2** one of twelve divisions of the year (January, etc.), a calendar month.
month'ly *adj.* **1** completed in a month. **2** happening once a month.—*n.* a paper published once in a month:—*pl.* **month'lies**.—*adv.* **1** once a month. **2** in every month.
See also **lunar**.

monument *mon'ū-mė̇nt*, *n.* **1** something put up in memory of a person or event, e.g. a building, tomb, etc. **2** a notable example (of). **3** lasting evidence of (with *to*): *The work, result, is a monument to your industry.*
monument'al *adj.* **1** acting as a monument. **2** of great size or lasting qualities.

moo *mōō*, *v.i.* to low like a cow.—Also *n.*

mooch *mōōch*, *v.i.* to loiter, wander (about).

mood[1] *mōōd*, *n.* any of a number of forms (four in English) of the verb, expressing e.g. fact (*indicative mood*), possibility, etc. (*subjunctive*), command (*imperative*), and an idea without a subject (*infinitive*).

mood[2] *mōōd*, *n.* the state of a person's feelings, temper, mind, at the time in question.
mood'y *adj.* **1** often changing one's mood. **2** gloomy, ill-humoured:—*comp.* **mood'ier**; *superl.* **mood'iest**.
mood'ily *adv.* **mood'iness** *n.*

moon *mōōn*, *n.* **1** the heavenly body that moves round the earth. **2** a satellite of any other planet. **3** a month.—*v.i.* to wander about or gaze absently.
moon'beam *n.* a beam of light from the moon.
moon'light *n.* the light of the moon.—*adj.* **1** lighted by the moon. **2** happening in moonlight or at night.
moon'lighter *n.* a person who takes work in the evening in addition to his normal day's work.
moon'lit *adj.* lit by the moon.
moon'shine *n.* **1** the shining of the moon. **2** false show, nonsense. **3** illegally distilled or smuggled spirits.
moon'stone *n.* a gemstone with a pearly shine.
moon'struck *adj.* crazed, lunatic.

moor[1] *mōōr*, *n.* a large stretch of open land with poor soil often covered with heath.
moor'cock, **moor'fowl** *n.* a red grouse.
moor'hen *n.* **1** a coot. **2** a female moorfowl.
moor'land *n.* a stretch of moor.

moor[2] *mōōr*, *v.t.* to fasten, secure (a ship, etc.) by cable or anchor.—Also *v.i.*
moor'ing *n.* **1** the act or means of fastening a ship. **2** (in *pl.*) the place where a ship is fastened.

Moor *mōōr*, *n.* a member of a Muslim people from North Africa.
Moor'ish *adj.*

moorcock, etc. See **moor**[1].

mooring. See **moor**[2].

moose *mōōs*, *n.* the largest deer of America, rather like the European elk.

moot *mōōt*: **moot point** an undecided point, one to be argued about.

mop *mop*, *n.* **1** a bunch of rags or coarse yarn, or other absorbent material, fixed on a handle, for washing floors, dishes, etc. **2** a thick mass of hair like a mop.—*v.t.* **1** to rub or wipe with a mop. **2** to wipe away tears, sweat, etc. from:—*pr.p.* **mopp'ing**; *pa.p.* **mopped**.
mop up 1 to clean up or clear away. **2** to kill or capture remnants of a defeated enemy force in an area.

mope *mōp*, *v.i.* to give way to low spirits, or sadness:—*pr.p.* **mop'ing**.

moped *mō'ped*, *n.* a *mo*tor-assisted *ped*al bicycle.

moraine *mo̊-rān'*, *n.* a line of rocks and gravel carried by, left by, a glacier.

moral *mor'ȧl*, *adj.* **1** having to do with character or behaviour, esp. with right; virtuous in matters of sex (*opp.* **immoral**): *a moral life.* **2** capable of knowing right and wrong: *Man is a moral being.*—*n.* **1** (in *pl.*) one's principles and conduct. **2** the lesson to be learned from something that happens, or from a story.
mor'alise *v.t.* to make (more) moral.—*v.i.* to talk or write about morals or about lessons to be learned from events:—*pr.p.* **mor'alising**.
mor'alist *n.* one who studies or teaches moral behaviour.
moral'ity *n.* **1** the quality of being morally right or wrong. **2** virtuous conduct. **3** (also **morality play**) a mediaeval drama in which vices and virtues are characters:—*pl.* **moral'ities**.
mor'ally *adv.* **1** in a moral manner. **2** from the point of view of morals. **3** practically: *morally certain.*
moral certainty a probability of which one is convinced.
moral courage courage to face disapproval and ridicule in support of what one believes right.
moral obligation, **responsibility** one arising from sense of duty.
moral sense (ability to have) the feeling that some actions are right, others wrong.
moral support encouragement, approval, but not physical help.
moral victory a defeat which is nonetheless in some important sense a victory.

morale *mo̊r-äl'*, *n.* mood as regards courage and confidence or the reverse in e.g. an army: *In spite of reverses, morale was still high.*

moralise, **moralist**. See **moral**.

morass *mo̊-ras'*, *n.* **1** a stretch of soft, wet ground. **2** a marsh.

moratorium *mor-ȧ-tō'ri-um*, *-tö'*, *n.* a temporary ban on, or stopping of, an activity:—*pl.* **morato'riums**, **-ia**.

morbid *mör'bid*, *adj.* **1** diseased (mentally or physically). **2** (of mind, thoughts, person) not healthy, dwelling too much on gruesome and gloomy things.
morbid'ity, **mor'bidness** *ns.*
mor'bidly *adv.*

mordant *mör'dȧnt, adj.* **1** (of wit) biting, sarcastic. **2** fixing colours.—*n.* **1** a substance used in dyeing to fix colour. **2** acid, etc., used in etching.
mor'dancy *n.* **mor'dantly** *adv.*

more. See **many** and **much**.

moreover *mōr-ō'vėr, mör-, adv.* besides, also.

morgue *mörg, n.* a place where dead bodies are laid for identification.

moribund *mor'i-bund, adj.* **1** about to die. **2** in a dying state.

Mormon *mör'mon, n.* one of a religious group founded in 1830 by Joseph Smith, with headquarters in Utah, U.S.

morn *mörn,* (*poetic* or *dial.*) *n.* morning.
morning *mörn'ing, n.* **1** the first part of the day. **2** the early part of anything.—Also *adj.*
morning dress a man's formal clothes worn esp. during the early part of the day: *Some men wear morning dress at weddings.*
morning star a planet, esp. Venus, when it rises before the sun.

morocco *mȯ-rok'ō, n.* fine goat- or sheepskin leather, first brought from Morocco.

moron *mōr'on, mör', n.* **1** a person of low mental ability. **2** (*coll.*) a foolish person.
moron'ic *adj.*

morose *mȯ-rōs', adj.* sullen, gloomy.
morose'ly *adv.* **morose'ness** *n.*

morphia *mör'fi-ȧ, n.* a habit-forming drug that causes sleep or deadens pain.—Also **mor'phine** *(mör'fēn).*

morris-dance *mor'is-däns, n.* any of various types of traditional English dance.

morrow *mor'ō, n.* **1** the day following the present. **2** the time just after any event.

Morse *mörs, n.* a code for signalling and telegraphy in which each letter is made up of dots and/or dashes (short and long sounds, flashes of light, etc.); invented by Samuel F. B. *Morse*.

morsel *mör'sėl, n.* **1** a small piece of food. **2** a small piece of anything.

mortal *mör't(ȧ)l, adj.* **1** liable to death (*opp.* **immortal**). **2** human. **3** causing death. **4** punishable by death. **5** (of enemy, fight) bitter, deadly. **6** very great: *mortal fear.*—*n.* a human being.
mortal'ity *n.* **1** the state of being mortal. **2** number of deaths. **3** deaths in proportion to the population, death rate:—*pl.* **mortal'ities**.
mor'tally *adv.*
mortal sin a wicked act done deliberately in the full knowledge that one is disobeying God.

mortar *mör'tȧr, n.* **1** a basin in which substances are ground with a pestle. **2** a short gun for throwing shells. **3** a mixture of lime, sand, water, etc., used in building.
mor'tar-board *n.* a cap with a square flat top, formerly worn on formal occasions at universities and schools.

mortgage *mör'gij, n.* (a document containing) a legal agreement by which a sum of money is lent on the security of buildings, land, etc. (the borrower promises to give up the buildings to the lender if he fails to repay the loan according to the conditions).—*v.t.* **1** to pledge (buildings, etc.) as security for a debt. **2** to pledge, and so risk losing control over:—*pr.p.* **mort'gaging**.
mortgagor *(mör'gi-jör), n.* one who borrows money on mortgage from a **mortgagee** *(mör'gi-jē')* or lender.

mortice. See **mortise**.

mortify *mör'ti-fī, v.t.* **1** to make someone feel ashamed or hurt by wounding his pride. **2** to bring (one's desires, the body) under control by fasting, inflicting pain on oneself, etc. **3** to destroy the life in (a part of the body).—*v.i.* (of a part of the body) to die, become gangrenous:—*pr.p.* **mor'tifying**; *pa.p.* **mor'tified**.
mortificā'tion *n.*

mortise *mör'tis, n.* a hole cut into a piece of wood, etc. to receive a tenon, a part shaped to fit the hole, on another piece.—Also **mor'tice**.
mor'tise-lock *n.* a lock sunk into the edge of a door.

mortuary *mör'tū-ȧ-ri, n.* a place where bodies are kept before burial:—*pl.* **mor'tuaries**.

mosaic *mō-zā'ik, n.* **1** a design formed by arranging small pieces of coloured marble, glass, etc. **2** anything made by piecing different things together.

Moslem *moz'lėm, n.* and *adj.* Muslim.

mosque *mosk, n.* a Muslim place of worship.

mosquito *mos-kē'tō, n.* any of numbers of insects, the females of which pierce the skin of animals and suck blood:—*pl.* **mosqui'to(e)s**.

moss *mos, n.* **1** a small flowerless plant, found in moist places, on tree trunks, etc. **2** a clump of these plants. **3** a bog.
moss'y *adj.*:—*comp.* **moss'ier**; *superl.* **moss'iest**.
moss'iness *n.*
moss'-grown *adj.* covered with moss.

most, mostly. See **many** and **much**.

MOT (test) *em-ō-tē' (test), n.* a compulsory annual check made by order of the Department of Transport (formerly the *M*inistry of Transport) on vehicles of more than a certain age.

mote *mōt*, *n.* a speck, e.g. of dust.

motel *mō-tel'*, *n.* a *mo*tor ho*tel*, orig. one made up of units, each unit for a car and occupants, now any hotel catering especially for motorists.

moth *moth*, *n.* **1** any of a large number of insects, rather like butterflies, seen mostly at night, and attracted by light. **2** the larva of the **clothes moth**, which eats cloth.

moth'ball *n.* a ball of a chemical used to protect clothes from moths.

moth'-eaten *adj.* **1** eaten or cut by moths. **2** old and worn. **3** (of an idea, person, etc.) behind the times and dull.

mother *mu*TH*'ėr*, *n.* **1** a female parent, esp. a human one. **2** the female head of a religious group, e.g. a convent. **3** something that was the origin or the first example: *The English parliament is sometimes called the mother of parliaments.*—*adj.* acting the part of, or belonging to, a mother.—*v.t.* to care for as a mother does.

moth'erhood *n.* the state of being a mother.

moth'erless *adj.* without a mother.

moth'erly *adj.* **1** like a mother. **2** suitable to a mother: *motherly love*.

moth'erliness *n.*

moth'er-coun'try, **-land** *ns.* **1** the country of one's birth. **2** the country that has founded a colony.

moth'er-in-law *n.* the mother of one's husband or wife:—*pl.* **moth'ers-in-law**.

moth'er-of-pearl *n.* a shining, hard, smooth substance on the inside of certain shells, esp. that of the pearl oyster.

mother tongue a person's native language.

motif *mō-tēf'*, *n.* a theme or important feature in a play or musical work.

motion *mō'sh(ȯ)n*, *n.* **1** the act, state, power, or manner, of moving. **2** a single movement. **3** a piece of mechanism. **4** a proposal put before a meeting.—*v.t.*, *v.i.* to make a movement or sign which tells (a person) to do something: *Motion (to) him to come here*.

mo'tionless *adj.* without motion.

motion (or **moving**) **picture** a picture showing action and movement, produced by running a series of photographs very rapidly across the screen.

mo'tivate *v.t.* **1** to be the thing that causes (a person) to act in a certain way: *Jealousy motivated him.* **2** to be a motive, reason, inducement, for an action:—*pr.p.* **mo'tivating**.

motive *mō'tiv*, *adj.* causing motion.—*n.* something that makes a person choose to act in a particular way: *His motive for asking me was not clear*.

in motion moving.

motley *mot'li*, *adj.* **1** of many different colours. **2** made up of many different kinds: *a motley crowd.*—*n.* the dress of a jester.

motor *mō'tȯr*, *n.* **1** a machine (usu. a petrol engine) which gives motion or does work. **2** a motor-car.—*adj.* **1** giving or transmitting (passing on) motion. **2** driven by a motor.—*v.t.* and *v.i.* to carry (something), or to travel, by motor vehicle.

mo'torise *v.t.* **1** to supply (e.g. troops) with motor vehicles: *a motorised unit.* **2** to adapt to motor power:—*pr.p.* **mo'torising**.

mo'torist *n.* one who drives, and travels by, a motor-car.

mo'torbike, **-boat**, **-car**, etc., *ns.* a bicycle, boat, car, etc. powered or moved by a motor.

mo'torway *n.* a road for fast traffic, with no crossings on the same level.

mottled *mot'ld*, *adj.* marked with spots of many colours or shades.

motto *mot'ō*, *n.* a short sentence or phrase which expresses a guiding principle: *'Honesty is the best policy' is my motto*:—*pl.* **mott'oes**.

mould[1] *mōld*, *n.* **1** loose or crumbling earth. **2** soil rich in rotted leaves.

moul'der *v.i.*, *v.t.* **1** to crumble to dust. **2** to waste away gradually.

mould[2] *mōld*, *n.* a woolly or fluffy growth on bread, cheese, etc.

moul'dy *adj.* **1** overgrown or covered with mould. **2** like mould. **3** (*slang*) old and stale, or depressing:—*comp.* **moul'dier**; *superl.* **moul'diest**.

moul'diness *n.*

mould[3] *mōld*, *n.* **1** a shape into which a substance in liquid form is poured so that it may take on that shape when it cools. **2** a thing formed in a mould.—*v.t.* **1** to form in a mould. **2** to work into a shape. **3** to give particular qualities to (e.g. character, opinions).

moul'der *n.*

moul'ding *n.* a decorated border, e.g. on a picture frame, wall, etc.

moulder. See **mould**[1,3].

mouldiness, **mouldy**. See **mould**[2].

moult *mōlt*, *v.i.* to shed feathers or a skin.—Also *v.t.*

mound *mownd*, *n.* **1** a bank of earth or stones raised as a protection. **2** a hill. **3** a heap.

mount[1] *mownt*, *v.i.* **1** to go up, climb. **2** (often **mount up**) to rise in level or in amount.—*v.t.* **1** to go up. **2** to get up upon. **3** to place on horseback. **4** to fix (e.g. a jewel) in a holder that shows it off, or (e.g. a photograph) on a backing. **5** to put, have (guns) in position for use.—*n.* **1** a riding animal or bicycle. **2** a support or backing on which anything is placed for display.

moun'ted *adj.* **1** on horseback. **2** provided with horses or other means of transport. **3** set in position for use, or on support, background.

Moun'ties *n.pl.* the Canadian mounted police.

moun'ting *n.* something in or on which a thing is mounted, placed, etc. for some purpose.

mount an attack, **offensive**, etc., to prepare and carry it out.

mount guard. See **guard**.

See also **dismount**.

mount[2] *mownt*, *n.* (*old* except in names) a mountain.

mountain *mown'tin*, *n.* **1** a high hill. **2** anything very large.—*adj.* (used only before a noun) **1** of a mountain. **2** growing or living on a mountain.

mountaineer' *n.* a climber of mountains.

moun'tainous *adj.* **1** full of mountains. **2** large as a mountain, huge.

mountain ash the rowan (not an ash).

mountain bike a strong bicycle with wide tyres and many gears designed for use on rough terrain.

mountebank *mown'ti-bangk*, *n.* **1** a quack, seller of sham remedies, who draws a crowd by means of jokes, etc. **2** a buffoon.

mourn *mōrn*, *mörn*, *v.i.* to grieve for (a person, a loss).

mourn'er *n.*

mourn'ful *adj.* causing, feeling, or showing, sorrow.

mourn'ing *n.* **1** the act of showing grief. **2** the formal dress of mourners.—Also *adj.*

mouse *mows*, *n.* **1** a small gnawing animal of several kinds found in houses (**house mouse**) and in fields (**field-mouse**; see also **harvest mouse**). **2** a timid, shy, colourless person. **3** (*computers*) a device which when moved by hand causes the cursor to move on a screen:—*pl.* **mice** *(mīs)*.

mous'y *adj.* like a mouse, esp. in colour:—*comp.* **mous'ier**; *superl.* **mous'iest**.

mousse *mōōs*, *n.* a whipped-up mixture of cream, etc. sometimes frozen.

moustache *mus-täsh'*, *n.* hair on the upper lip of a man.

mousy. See **mouse**.

mouth *mowth*, *n.* **1** the opening in the head of a person or animal by which it eats and utters sounds. **2** the opening or entrance, e.g. of a bottle, river, etc.:—*pl.* **mouths** *(-*THz*)*.—*v.t.* and *v.i.* *(mow*TH*)* to say in a pompous way, or with exaggerated mouth movements.

mouth'ful *n.* **1** as much as fills the mouth. **2** a small quantity:—*pl.* **mouth'fuls**.

mouth'-organ *n.* a small musical instrument played by holding it to the lips and blowing or sucking air through it.

mouth'piece *n.* **1** the piece of a musical instrument, or tobacco-pipe, held in the mouth. **2** one who speaks for others.

down in the mouth out of spirits, sad.

See also **oral**.

move *mōōv*, *v.t.* **1** to cause to change place or position. **2** to set in motion. **3** to excite or stir (to action or to emotion); to touch the feelings of: *The scene moved him to take up the cause of the refugees*; *It moved him to tears*; *The book moved him deeply.* **4** to propose: *I move the adoption of the minutes, that the meeting should now adjourn.*—*v.i.* **1** to go from one place to another. **2** to change homes. **3** to carry oneself in walking, etc. **4** to change position:—*pr.p.* **mov'ing.**—*n.* **1** the act of moving. **2** a movement, esp. at chess. **3** a step taken: *He now made his first move towards gaining control.*

movable *mōōv'ȧ-bl*, *adj.* that may be moved; not fixed:—*opp.* **immovable.**—*n.* (esp. in *pl.*) movable furnishing.—Also **move'able**.

move'ment *n.* **1** the act or manner of moving. **2** a change of position. **3** the moving part of a mechanism. **4** a main division of a long piece of music. **5** actions intended to bring about a change or improvement: *a movement to reform the law.* **6** a group of people united to achieve some aim. **7** change.

mov'ie (*coll.* esp. *U.S.*) *n.* a motion picture.

mov'ing *adj.* **1** causing motion. **2** changing position. **3** causing emotion, esp. pity.

moving picture. See **motion**.

See also **motion, mobile**.

mow *mō*, *v.t.* **1** to cut (grass), or to cut grass on (e.g. a lawn), with a scythe or machine. **2** to cut (down) in great numbers: *Tanks mowed down the enemy*:—*pa.t.* **mowed**; *pa.p.* **mowed** or **mown**.

mow'er *n.* **1** one who mows. **2** a machine with turning blades for cutting grass.

Mr. See **mister**.

Mrs. See **mistress**.

Ms *miz, n.* a title sometimes used before the names of married or unmarried women.

much *much, adj.* a great quantity of:—*comp.* **more** *(mōr, mör)*; *superl.* **most** *(mōst).—adv.* **1** to a great degree: *much brighter, much loved, much to be pitied.* **2** often: *He spoke much of his childhood.* **3** nearly: *much the same.—n.* **1** a great deal. **2** something important.
more *adj.* a larger quantity of (see also **many**).—*adv.* to a greater degree: *more foolish.*—Also *n.*: *It costs a little more.*
most *adj.* and *n.* the greatest quantity (of).—Also *adv.*
as much as to say as if to say, the same as saying.
be too much (for one) to be more than one can bear, believe, etc.
make much of. See **make**.

mucilage. See **mucus**.

muck *muk, n.* **1** dung. **2** anything filthy.
muck'y *adj.*:—*comp.* **muck'ier**; *superl.* **muck'iest**.
muck'iness *n.*
muck'-raking *n.* the seeking out and exposing of scandals, esp. if from bad motives.
muck about, around (*coll.*) to mess about.
muck in (*coll.*) **1** to help, participate. **2** to share (with).
muck up (*coll.*) to make a mess of, do badly.

mucus *mū'kŭs, n.* the slimy fluid from the nose, etc. (produced by cells in the mucous membrane).
mucilage *mū'sil-ij, n.* **1** a gluey substance found in some plants. **2** gum.
mu'cous *adj.* **1** like mucus. **2** slimy.
mucous membrane a membrane (thin layer of tissue) lining those passages of the body (e.g. the nose) that communicate with the outside.

mud *mud, n.* wet soft earth.
muddy *adj.* **1** covered with, or containing, mud. **2** not clear or pure:—*comp.* **mudd'ier**; *superl.* **mudd'iest**.—*v.t., v.i.* to make, or become, muddy:—*pr.p.* **mudd'ying**; *pa.p.* **mudd'ied**.
mud'guard *n.* a screen to catch mud splashes from wheels.
mud'-slinging *n.* saying bad things about someone.

muddle *mud'l, v.t.* **1** to bungle, make a mess of. **2** to confuse, make stupid:—*pr.p.* **mudd'ling**.—*n.* **1** confusion, a mess. **2** bewilderment.

muesli *mū'zli, n.* a dish of oats, nuts, fruit, etc. eaten with milk esp. as a breakfast cereal.

muff[1] *muf, n.* a tube-shaped cover e.g. of fur for keeping the hands warm.

muff[2] *muf, n.* a stupid or clumsy fellow, esp. in sport.—*v.t.* **1** to fail to hold (a catch, ball). **2** to do badly.—Also *v.i.*

muffin *muf'in, n.* a soft cake, eaten hot with butter.

muffle *muf'l, v.t.* **1** to wrap up for warmth or in order to hide the face. **2** to deaden the sound of: *to muffle his cries*:—*pr.p.* **muff'ling**.
muff'ler *n.* a scarf for the throat.

mufti *muf'ti, n.* clothes worn when off duty by someone who is usu. in uniform.

mug[1] *mug, n.* **1** a cup with more or less straight sides. **2** its contents.

mug[2] *mug,* (*coll.*) *n.* the face.

mug[3] *mug,* (*coll.*) *n.* a fool, dupe.

mug[4] *mug*: **mug up** (*coll.*) *v.t.* and *v.i.* to study hard, learn:—*pr.p.* **mugg'ing up**; *pa.p.* **mugged up**.

mug[5] *mug,* (*coll.*) *v.t.* to attack suddenly with the intention of robbing:—*pr.p.* **mugg'ing**; *pa.p.* **mugged**.
mugg'er *n.*

muggy *mug'i, adj.* (of weather) close and damp:—*comp.* **mugg'ier**; *superl.* **mugg'iest**.

mulatto *mū-lat'ō, n.* the child of a black and a white parent:—*pl.* **mulatt'os**.

mulberry *mul'bĕr-i, n.* **1** a type of tree on whose leaves silkworms feed. **2** the fruit of this tree, usu. purple:—*pl.* **mul'berries**.

mulch *mulch, -sh, n.* loose straw, etc., laid down to protect the roots of plants.—*v.t.* to cover with mulch.

mulct *mulkt, n.* a fine.—*v.t.* **1** to fine. **2** to deprive, swindle (of).

mule[1] *mūl, n.* a kind of slipper usu. without a heel.

mule[2] *mūl, n.* **1** an animal whose parents are a horse and an ass. **2** a cross between a canary and another finch. **3** an instrument for cotton spinning. **4** a stubborn person.
muleteer' *n.* one who drives mules.
mul'ish *adj.* **1** like a mule. **2** stubborn.

mull[1] *mul, v.t.* (with *over*) to think or ponder over.

mull[2] *mul, v.t.* to warm, spice, and sweeten (wine, ale, etc.).
mulled *adj.*

mullah *mul'ȧ, mool'ȧ, n.* a Muslim learned in theology and law.

mullet *mul'it, n.* a type of small sea fish.

mulligatawny *mul-i-gȧ-tö'ni, n.* an E. Indian soup containing curry.

mullion *mul'yȯn, n.* an upright division between the lights of windows, etc.

multi- *mul-ti-*, (as part of a word) many, much.
mul'ticoloured *adj.* many-coloured.
multifarious *mul-ti-fā'ri-ůs, adj.* of many kinds: *multifarious activities*.
multilateral *mul-ti-lat'ėr-ȧl, adj.* **1** many-sided. **2** involving several parties, states, etc.: *a multilateral treaty, multilateral disarmament*.
multilingual *mul-ti-ling'gwȧl, adj.* **1** in many languages. **2** speaking many languages.
multimillionaire' *n.* one having property worth several millions of pounds.
multina'tional *adj.* and *n.* (of) a company which has branches in several different countries.
multiracial *mul-ti-rā'sh(i-ȧ)l, adj.* **1** of many races. **2** including (people of) many races: *a multiracial population*.

multiple *mul'ti-pl, adj.* **1** having many parts, esp. of the same kind. **2** repeated many times.—*n.* a number that contains another an exact number of times: 65 *is a multiple of* 5.
multiple sclerosis *(sklė-rō'sis)* a progressive disease resulting in various forms of paralysis.

multiply *mul'ti-plī, v.t.* **1** to increase the number, quantity, of. **2** to take a number a given number of times and find the total (e.g. 4 taken 3 times, or 4+4+4, or 4 *multiplied by* 3, or 4 × 3, = 12).—*v.i.* to become greater in number:—*pr.p.* **mul'tiplying**; *pa.p.* **mul'tiplied**.
multiplicā'tion *n.*
multiplic'ity *n.* **1** a great number. **2** the state of being many and varied.
mul'tiplier *n.* the number by which another is to be multiplied.

multiracial. See **multi**.

multitude *mul'ti-tūd, n.* **1** a great number. **2** a crowd. **3** the mob. **4** the state of being many: *the multitude of his difficulties*.
multitud'inous *adj.* **1** very many. **2** looking like a multitude.

mum[1] *mum, adj.* silent, not speaking.—*v.i.* **1** to act in dumb show. **2** to wear a mask, etc. at a festival. **3** to act in a type of traditional play:—*pr.p.* **mumm'ing**; *pa.p.* **mummed**.
mumm'er *n.*
mumm'ery *n.* **1** mumming. **2** meaningless ceremonial:—*pl.* **mumm'eries**.

mum[2]. See **mummy**[2].

mumble *mum'bl, v.t.* and *v.i.* to utter, or speak, indistinctly:—*pr.p.* **mum'bling**.—Also *n.*

mummer, etc. See **mum**[1].

mummie. See **mummy**[2].

mummy[1] *mum'i, n.* a human body preserved by the Egyptians, etc., in past times, using wrappings, spice, wax, etc.:—*pl.* **mumm'ies**.
mumm'ify *v.t.* to make into a mummy:—*pr.p.* **mumm'ifying**; *pa.p.* **mumm'ified**.
mummificā'tion *n.*

mummy[2], **mummie** *mum'i, n.* an affectionate name for mother:—*pl.* **mumm'ies**.—Also **mum**.

mump *mump, v.i.* to be sulky.
mumps *n. sing.* a disease of the glands of the neck, causing swelling.

munch *munch, -sh, v.t., v.i.* to chew with a crunching sound.

mundane *mun-dān', adj.* **1** belonging to the world. **2** everyday, dull.

municipal *mū-nis'i-pȧl, adj.* **1** having to do with the government of a city or town. **2** carried on by a city or town.
municipal'ity *n.* a self-governing city or town:—*pl.* **municipal'ities**.
munic'ipally *adv.*

munificence *mū-nif'i-sėns, n.* **1** fondness for giving gifts. **2** generous quality.
munif'icent *adj.* **munif'icently** *adv.*

munition *mū-nish'(ȯ)n,* (usu. in *pl.*) *n.* **1** weapons and ammunition used in war. **2** necessary equipment for any campaign.

mural *mū'rȧl, adj.* having to do with a wall.—*n.* a painting on a wall.

murder *mûr'dėr, n.* the act of putting a person to death on purpose and unlawfully.—*v.t.* **1** to kill on purpose and unlawfully. **2** to ruin by saying, etc., very badly: *to murder a poem*. **3** (*coll.*) to defeat utterly.
mur'derer *n.* **mur'deress** *fem. n.*
mur'derous *adj.* **1** deadly. **2** capable of, or guilty of, murder. **3** very cruel: *a murderous light in his eye*.
mur'derously *adv.*

murky *mûr'ki, adj.* **1** dark, gloomy. **2** (of darkness) thick:—*comp.* **mur'kier**; *superl.* **mur'kiest**.
mur'kily *adv.* **mur'kiness** *n.*

murmur *mûr'mủr, n.* **1** a low, confused sound, e.g. that of running water or low voices. **2** a complaint, uttered in a low voice.—*v.i.* **1** to grumble. **2** to make a murmur.

muscle *mus'l, n.* a bundle of fibres in the body which, by drawing together or stretching out, causes movements of the body.
muscular *mus'kū-lȧr, adj.* **1** having to do with muscle(s). **2** strong.
muscular'ity *n.* state of being strong.

muscular dystrophy *(dis'trȯ-fi)* a hereditary disease in which muscles deteriorate.

muse[1] *mūz, v.i.* **1** to think over a matter quietly. **2** to be absent-minded:—*pr.p.* **mus'ing**.

muse[2] *mūz*, (usu. *cap.*) *n.* one of the nine goddesses of poetry, music, and arts.

museum *mū-zē'ụm, n.* a place where collections of things of artistic, scientific, or historic interest are set out for show.

mush *mush, n.* **1** meal boiled in water, esp. Indian meal. **2** anything pulpy. **3** anything too sentimental.
mush'y *adj* like mush:—*comp.* **mush'ier**; *superl.* **mush'iest**.

mushroom *mush'room, n.* **1** a type of fungus, usually umbrella-shaped, esp. one that can be eaten. **2** anything springing up very quickly and usu. dying rapidly: *a mushroom town, firm.*—*v.i.* to grow very quickly: *New buildings mushroomed all over the town.*
mushroom cloud a mushroom-shaped cloud, esp. one resulting from a nuclear explosion.

music *mū'zik, n.* **1** an arrangement of, or the art of combining or putting together, sounds that please the ear. **2** the score of a musical composition. **3** any pleasant sound.
mū'sical *adj.*—*n.* a theatrical performance or film in which singing and usu. dancing play an important part.
mu'sically *adv.*
musi'cian *(-shȧn) n.* **1** one skilled in music. **2** a performer of music.
music centre apparatus consisting of a record-player, tape-recorder, and radio, with loudspeakers.
music hall 1 (*orig.*) a hall for concerts. **2** (a theatre for) variety entertainment.

musk *musk, n.* **1** a substance with a strong scent, obtained from the male musk deer. **2** the musk deer.
mus'ky *adj.*:—*comp.* **musk'ier**; *superl.* **musk'iest**.
mus'kiness *n.*
musk deer a small hornless deer, found in mountains of Central Asia.
musk melon the common melon.
musk'-rat *n.* a musky-scented N. American water animal with valuable fur.
musk rose a fragrant type of rose.

musket *mus'kit, n.* a gun once carried by foot soldiers.
musketeer' *n.* a soldier armed with a musket.
mus'ketry *n.* the art of firing on the enemy with rifles.

Muslim *muz'lim, mooz', mus', n.* a follower of or believer in Islam.—*adj.* pertaining to Muslims or Islam.

muslin *muz'lin, n.* fine soft cotton cloth looking like gauze.—Also *adj.*

musquash *mus'kwosh, n.* **1** the musk-rat. **2** its fur.

mussel *mus'l, n.* a shellfish enclosed within a shell in two parts, used for food.

must[1] *must, v.* generally used with another verb to express a necessity or requirement: *I must have more time if I am to finish it.*—*n.* **1** an essential, a necessity. **2** a thing that should not be missed or neglected.

must[2] *must, n.* grape juice not fully fermented.

mustang *mus'tang, n.* the wild horse of the American prairies.

mustard *mus'tȧrd, n.* a hot seasoning made from the seeds of the mustard plant.

muster *mus'tėr, v.t.* **1** to gather together (esp. troops for duty or inspection). **2** to gather. **3** (also **muster up**) to summon up and show (e.g. courage).—Also *v.i.*—*n.* **1** a gathering of troops, etc. **2** an assembly.
pass muster to be accepted as satisfactory.

musty *must'i, adj.* **1** mouldy, spoiled by damp. **2** stale in smell or taste:—*comp.* **must'ier**; *superl.* **must'iest**.
must'iness *n.*

mutation *mū-tā'sh(ȯ)n, n.* **1** the act or process of changing. **2** (a plant or animal showing) a characteristic not found in its parents which can yet be passed on to later generations.
mū'tant *n.* a form arising by mutation.
See also **immutable**.

mute *mūt, adj.* **1** dumb. **2** silent. **3** not sounded.—*n.* **1** a dumb person. **2** a silent person.—*v.t.* to deaden the sound of:—*pr.p.* **mut'ing**.
mut'ed *pa.p.* and *adj.* **mute'ly** *adv.*

mutilate *mū'ti-lāt, v.t.* **1** to cut off a limb, etc. from. **2** to remove an important part of, damage badly:—*pr.p.* **mut'ilating**.
mutilā'tion *n.* **mu'tilator** *n.*

mutiny *mū'ti-ni, v.i.* **1** to rise against those in authority in the army, navy, or air force. **2** to refuse to obey any rightful authority:—*pr.p.* **mu'tinying**; *pa.p.* **mu'tinied**. —*n.* **1** refusal to obey. **2** a revolt:—*pl.* **mu'tinies**.
mutineer' *n.* one who mutinies.
mū'tinous *adj.* rebellious, unruly.

mutter *mut'ėr, v.i.* **1** to utter words in a low voice. **2** to murmur, grumble. **3** to make a low, rumbling noise.—Also *v.t.* and *n.*
mutt'ering *n.* and *adj.*

mutton *mut'n, n.* flesh of sheep as food.

mutual *mū'tū-ȧl, adj.* **1** given, etc., by each to the other(s): *mutual help, mutual dislike.* **2** common to two or more, shared: *a mutual friend.*

mu'tually *adv.*

muzzle *muz'l, n.* **1** the jaws and nose of an animal such as a dog. **2** an arrangement e.g. of straps round the muzzle of an animal to prevent it from biting. **3** the open end of a gun, etc.—*v.t.* **1** to put a muzzle on. **2** to gag or silence:—*pr.p.* **muzz'ling**.

muzzy *muz'i, adj.* dazed, muddled:—*comp.* **muzz'ier**; *superl.* **muzz'iest**.

muzz'iness *n.*

my. See **I**.

myopia *mī-ō'pi-ȧ, n.* short-sightedness.

myop'ic *(-op') adj.*

myriad *mir'i-ȧd, n.* any very great number.—*adj.* numberless.

myrrh *mûr, n.* a gum with a bitter taste, used in medicines, perfumes, etc.

myrtle *mûr'tl, n.* an evergreen shrub with beautiful sweet-smelling leaves.

myself. See **I**.

mystery *mis'tėr-i, n.* **1** something that cannot be, or has not been, explained. **2** a deep secret. **3** a puzzle or riddle. **4** a puzzling quality:—*pl.* **mys'teries**.

mystē'rious *adj.* **1** difficult to understand. **2** secret. **3** hidden. **4** suggesting mystery.

mystic(al) *mis'tik(ȧl), adjs.* **1** mysterious and holy. **2** having a sacred or secret meaning which can usu. be understood only by a mind that is spiritually in touch with God.

mys'tic *n.* one who has or seeks direct experience of or communion with God, or direct knowledge of truth by spiritual means higher than that of the intellect.

mys'tically *adv.* **mys'ticism** *n.*

mys'tify *v.t.* **1** to puzzle greatly. **2** to bewilder, confuse purposely:—*pr.p.* **mys'tifying**; *pa.p.* **mys'tified**.

mystique *mis-tēk', n.* a sense of mystery, impression of something mysterious or out of the ordinary.

myth *mith, n.* **1** an old story, long handed down, about gods or heroes, giving an explanation of some fact of nature. **2** a fable. **3** a person or thing imagined.

myth'ical *adj.* **1** having to do with myths. **2** told of in a myth. **3** imaginary.

mythol'ogy *n.* **1** a collection of myths. **2** the study of myths:—*pl.* **mythol'ogies**.

mythol'ogist *n.* **mytholog'ical** *adj.*

myxomatosis *miks-ō-mȧ-tō'sis, n.* a contagious disease of rabbits.

N

nab *nab, (coll.) v.t.* **1** to catch, waylay. **2** to arrest:—*pr.p.* **nabb'ing**; *pa.p.* **nabbed**.

nacelle *nȧ-sel', n.* an enclosed part of an aircraft, esp. one for housing the engine.

nacre *nā'kėr, n.* mother-of-pearl.

nadir *nā'dėr, -dėr, n.* **1** the point in the heavens opposite to the zenith. **2** the lowest point.

nag[1] *nag, n.* a horse, esp. a small one.

nag[2] *nag, v.t.* to find fault with constantly.—*v.i.* to cause constant discomfort: *a pain that nags all the time*:—*pr.p.* **nagg'ing**; *pa.p.* **nagged**.

nail *nāl, n.* **1** a horny plate at the end of a finger or toe. **2** a thin pointed piece of metal for fastening wood, etc.—*v.t.* **1** to fasten with nail(s). **2** *(coll.)* to catch or trap.

naïve, naive *nä-ēv', adj.* simple in thought, speech or manners.

naïveté *nä-ēv'tā, n.*

naked *nā'kid, adj.* **1** without clothes. **2** without covering, protection or disguise. **3** (of the eye) not assisted by a telescope, microscope, etc.

na'kedly *adv.* **na'kedness** *n.*

namby-pamby *nam'bi-pam'bi, adj.* childish, not manly.

name *nām, n.* **1** the word or words by which a person, place, thing, etc., is known or called. **2** reputation: *to have a name for honesty.* **3** a celebrity. **4** authority: *I arrest you in the name of the Queen.*—*v.t.* **1** to give a name to. **2** to speak of by name, mention. **3** to state: *Name your price*:—*pr.p.* **nam'ing**.

name'less *adj.* **1** without a name; indefinable, obscure. **2** not named.

name'ly *adv.* that is to say.

name'-dropping *n.* the mentioning of famous people's names as though they were one's friends.

name'plate *n.* a piece of metal having on it a person's name.

name'sake *n.* someone having the same name as oneself.

name after to give (esp. a child) the same name as.

nan *nän, n.* a type of slightly leavened bread similar to pitta.

nanny *nan'i, n.* **1** a children's nurse. **2** (also **nann'y-goat**) a female goat:—*pl.* **nann'ies**.

nano- *nan'ō-, nā', as part of a word,* one thousand millionth.

nap[1] *nap, n.* a short sleep.

catch napping to catch (someone) when he is unprepared or inattentive.

nap[2] *nap, n.* a woolly surface on cloth (see **pile**[3]).

nap[3] *nap, n.* a game of cards.

napalm *nā'päm, n.* a jelly that catches fire very readily, used in bombs.

nape *nāp, n.* the back of the neck.

naphtha *naf'thȧ, n.* liquids that catch fire readily, obtained from coal tar, wood, etc.

napkin *nap'kin, n.* **1** a small square of linen, paper, etc., used at table for protecting the clothes, wiping the hands, etc. **2** a thick piece of cloth, or disposable material, secured between a baby's legs to absorb urine, etc. (usu. shortened to **napp'y**:—*pl.* **napp'ies**).

narcissus *när-sis'us, n.* any of various plants of the daffodil type, grown from bulbs:—*pl.* **narciss'uses, narciss'ī**.

narcotic *när-kot'ik, n.* a drug that eases pain or makes one sleep.—Also *adj.*

narked *närkt, (coll.) adj.* annoyed.

nar'ky *(coll.) adj.* irritable:—*comp.* **nark'ier**; *superl.* **nark'iest**.

narrate *nȧ-rāt', v.t.* to tell the story of: *He narrated his adventures.*—Also *v.i.*:—*pr.p.* **narrat'ing**.

narrā'tion *n.* **narrā'tor** *n.*

narrative *nar'ȧ-tiv, n.* a story.—*adj.* telling a story.

narrow *nar'ō, adj.* **1** having little breadth, not wide. **2** only just successful, with little to spare: *a narrow escape, a narrow majority.* **3** narrow-minded (see below).—*v.t.* and *v.i.* to make or become narrow.

narr'ows *n.pl.* a sea passage of little width.

narr'ow-gauge' *adj.* (of a railway) with a distance between the rails less than 4 ft. 8 in. (about 1.4 m.).

narr'ow-mind'ed having opinions already formed and being unsympathetic towards other people's ideas.

narwhal *när'wȧl, n.* a kind of whale, the male of which has a large tusk.

nasal *nā'zȧl, adj.* **1** of the nose. **2** sounded through the nose.

nascent *nas'ėnt, nā', adj.* coming into existence, beginning to develop.

nasturtium *nȧ-stûr'shum, n.* a climbing plant with round flat leaves and orange, yellow or red flowers.

nasty *näs'ti, adj.* **1** dirty. **2** very disagreeable. **3** difficult; dangerous. **4** obscene. —*comp.* **nas'tier**; *superl.* **nas'tiest**.
nas'tily *adv.* **nas'tiness** *n.*

natal *nā'tȧl, adj.* of, relating to, birth.

nation *nā'sh(ȯ)n, n.* **1** a people with a common history living in the same country, usu. under the same government. **2** a race of people: *the Jewish nation.*
national *nash'ȯn-ȧl, adj.* **1** belonging to a nation. **2** concerning all the people of a country.—*n.* a person belonging to a particular nation: *The missing man was a British national.*
na'tionalise *v.t.* to make (something) the property of the nation: *Coalmining is a nationalised industry.*:—*pr.p.* **na'tionalising**.
nationalisā'tion *n.*
na'tionalism *n.* the desire to unite people of a nation under their own independent government.
na'tionalist *n.* **nationalis'tic** *adj.*
national'ity *n.* **1** membership of a particular nation. **2** a people or nation:—*pl.* **national'ities**.
na'tionally *adv.* by, to, etc. the nation as a whole.
national anthem the special song or hymn of a country, e.g. in Britain 'God Save the Queen'.
national debt money borrowed by the Government and not yet paid back.
national park land, usually in the country, owned by or for the nation.
national service in some countries, a period of compulsory service in the armed forces.
National Trust a society that looks after places, esp. buildings, of interest and beauty.
na'tion-wide *adj.* taking place, acting, etc. throughout the nation.

native *nā'tiv, adj.* **1** born in a person: *native intelligence.* **2** being, relating to, place of birth or origin: *my native land*; *Is English your native tongue?*—*n.* **1** a person born in a place named: *a native of Switzerland, of Leeds.* **2** one of the inhabitants of a country before the arrival of explorers, immigrants, etc.
the Nativ'ity *(nȧ-)* the birth of Christ.
native to (of plants, animals, etc.) belonging to the place mentioned: *The coyote is native to North America.*

natter *nat'ėr, v.i.* to chatter.—Also *n.*

natty *nat'i, adj.* trim, tidy, smart:—*comp.* **natt'ier**; *superl.* **natt'iest**.
natt'ily *adv.* **natt'iness** *n.*

nature *nā'chur, n.* **1** the world around us (animals, plants, streams, mountains, etc.). **2** the quality, or qualities, that make a person or thing, what he, or it, is: *He has a gentle nature.* **3** what something consists of: *What is the nature of your work?* **4** type, sort: *bankers and people of that nature.*
natural *nach'ur-ȧl, adj.* **1** produced by nature, not made or worked on by man. **2** of, relating to, nature. **3** (of a quality) born in a person. **4** (of manner) simple, unaffected. **5** (of e.g. a result) normal, expected. **6** (*music*) not sharp or flat.—*n.* **1** one having a natural ability. **2** in music (a sign (♮) indicating) a note that is not to be played sharp or flat.
nat'uralise *v.t.* **1** to give a citizen's rights to (someone born in another country). **2** to cause (a plant, etc.) to adapt to a new environment.
nat'uralist *n.* one who studies animal and plant life.
naturalis'tic *adj.* (of e.g. a picture) very like the natural thing, etc.
nat'urally *adv.* **1** by nature. **2** simply; unaffectedly. **3** of course.
-nā'tured (as part of a word) having a certain disposition: *good-natured.*
nā'turism *n.* nudism.
natural gas gas suitable for burning found underground or under the sea.
natural history the study of plants, animals and (formerly) rocks.
natural philosophy (*old*) physics.
natural resources naturally occurring sources of energy and wealth, e.g. timber, minerals, water for power, etc.
natural selection in evolution, the process by which the plants and animals best adapted to their environment are the ones to survive, while others die out.
in, of, the nature of having the qualities of: *His remark was in the nature of a threat.*

naught *nöt, n.* nothing. The name of the figure 0 is usu. spelt **nought**.

naughty *nö'ti, adj.* **1** badly behaved; disobedient. **2** indecent.:—*comp.* **naugh'tier**; *superl.* **naugh'tiest**.
naugh'tily *adv.* **naugh'tiness** *n.*

nausea *nö'si-ȧ, n.* a feeling of sickness.
nau'seate *v.t.* to fill with disgust, to make sick:—*pr.p.* **nau'seating**.
nau'seating, **nau'seous** *adjs.* sickening.

nautical *nö'ti-kȧl, adj.* of, relating to, ships or sailors.
nautical mile. See **mile**.

nautilus *nö'ti-lus, n.* **1** a small sea-creature related to the octopus (**paper nautilus**). **2** a shellfish of the Indian ocean, etc. (**pearly nautilus**).

naval. See **navy** under **navigate**.
nave[1] *nāv*, *n.* the main part of a church.
nave[2] *nāv*, *n.* the hub or central part of a wheel, through which the axle passes.
navel *nā'vėl*, *n.* the small hollow in the centre of the front of the body.
navigate *nav'i-gāt*, *v.t.* to manage, direct on its course (a ship, aircraft, etc.).—*v.i.* to find one's way and keep one's course:—*pr.p.* **nav'igating**.
nav'igable *adj.* (of a channel, etc.) able to be used by ships.
navigā'tion *n.* art of directing ships, etc.
nav'igātor *n.* one who sails or steers a ship, etc.
navvy (short for **navigator**) *nav'i*, *n.* **1** a labourer working on roads, etc. **2** a digging machine.
navy *nā'vi*, *n.* **1** a nation's fighting ships. **2** the men who belong to these.—See also **merchant navy**.—*adj.* navy blue.
nāv'al *adj.* of, relating to, the navy.
navy blue *adj.* dark blue.
nay *nā*, (*old*) *interj.* **1** no. **2** indeed.
Nazi *nä'tsē*, *n.* and *adj.* for *Nationalsozialist*, National Socialist, (member) of a party headed by Hitler.
neap *nēp*, *adj.* (of a tide) of smallest range, less high, and also less low, than a spring tide (see this).
Neapolitan *nē-ȧ-pol'i-tȧn*, *adj.* belonging to the city of Naples or its inhabitants.
near *nēr*, *adv.* to or at a little distance.—*prep.* close to.—*adj.* **1** not far away in place or time. **2** close in relationship, friendship, etc. **3** barely avoiding, or almost reaching, something. **4** mean, stingy. **5** (of the side, etc., of a horse or vehicle) left: *the near foreleg*.—*v.t.* and *v.i.* to approach, come nearer.
near'ly *adv.* **1** closely. **2** almost.
near'ness *n.*
nearby *nēr-bī'*, *adj.* and *adv.* a short distance away.
Near East the Middle East.
near'side *adj.* (of the side, etc. of a vehicle) left: *the nearside headlight*.
near'-sight'ed *adj.* short-sighted.
near'-sight'edness *n.*
a near miss a miss that is almost a hit.
a near thing a narrow escape.
neat *nēt. adj.* **1** trim, tidy. **2** skilful; skilfully made, done or said. **3** (of liquor) not weakened by adding e.g. water.
neat'ly *adv.* **neat'ness** *n.*
nebula *neb'ū-lȧ*, *n.* a faintly shining appearance in the night sky, produced by a great mass of gas, etc., or by a distant cluster of stars:—*pl.* **neb'ulae** *(-lē)*.
neb'ulous *adj.* misty, vague.
necessary *nes'i-sȧr-i*, *adj.* not able to be done without, or to be avoided.—*n.* **1** something that cannot be done without. **2** (in *pl.*) food, clothing:—*pl.* **nec'essaries**.
nec'essarily *adv.*
necess'itate *v.t.* to make necessary: *Icy roads necessitate cautious driving*:—*pr.p.* **necess'itating**.
necessity *ni-ses'i-ti*, *n.* **1** something that cannot be done without. **2** state of things by which one is compelled to do something. **3** great need; poverty:—*pl.* **necess'ities**.
necess'itous *adj.* very poor, in want.
of necessity necessarily, unavoidably.
neck *nek*, *n.* **1** the part between head and body. **2** the part of a garment that covers this. **3** anything like a neck, esp. a narrow connecting part: *the neck of a bottle*.—*v.i.* (*slang*) to hug and kiss.
neck'lace *n.* a string of precious stones, beads, etc. worn round the neck.
neck'tie *n.* a scarf or tie for the neck.
neck and neck (of competitors) abreast; exactly equal.
neck or nothing risking everything.
necr(o)- *nek-r(ō)-* (as part of word) dead (body).
necromancer *nek'rō-man-sėr*, *n.* one who practises magic (e.g. by communicating with the dead).
nec'romancy *n.*
nectar *nek'tȧr*, *n.* **1** the drink of the ancient Greek gods. **2** a delicious drink. **3** a sweet liquid from flowers, used by bees to make honey.
nectarine *nek'tȧr-in*, or *-ēn*, *n.* a kind of peach.
née *nā*, *adj.* born, used of married women (e.g. *Mrs White*, *née Black*, means that Mrs White was Miss Black before marriage).
need *nēd*, *n.* **1** necessity. **2** difficulty, want, poverty.—*v.t.* **1** to be in want of. **2** to require: *I need to rest*; *your hair needs washing*.
need'ful *adj.* necessary, required.
need'less *adj.* unnecessary.
need'y *adj.* poor:—*comp.* **need'ier**; *superl.* **need'iest**.
need'iness *n.*
if need be if necessary.
needs must 1 it has, had, to be. **2** (also **must needs**) must inevitably.
needle *nēd'l*, *n.* **1** a small, slender, pointed piece, e.g. of steel, with an eye, used in sewing. **2** any of various similar implements (without an eye) used in e.g. knitting, giving injections, playing gramophone records. **3** a pointer (e.g. in a

compass). **4** the long, pointed leaf of a pine, fir, etc.—*adj.* (of a match) very important and keenly played.—*v.t.* **1** to irritate. **2** to goad:—*pr.p.* **need'ling.**
need'lewoman *n.* a woman that sews.
need'lework *n.* work done with a needle, i.e. sewing, embroidery, etc.
like looking for a needle in a haystack (of a search) hopeless.

needless, **needy**, etc. See **need**.

ne'er *nār, adv.* never.
ne'er-do-well' (*Scot.* **-weel'** *-wēl'*) *n.* a good-for-nothing person.

nefarious *ni-fā'ri-ůs, adj.* extremely wicked.
nefa'riously *adv.* **nefa'riousness** *n.*

negate, etc. See **negative**.

negative *neg'ȧ-tiv, adj.* **1** meaning or saying 'no': *a negative answer.* **2** (of an attitude, etc.) pessimistic. **3** (of a person) dull. **4** (of the result of a test, etc.) showing the absence of whatever was being looked for. **5** less than zero: *-4 is a negative or minus value.* **6** of the kind of electricity developed on resin when rubbed with wool; having more electrons than normal (the **negative terminal** is the one from which electrons flow).—*n.* **1** a word or form of words by which something is denied: *The answer is in the negative.* **2** (*photography*) an image in which the lights and shades are the opposite of those in nature.—*v.t.* **1** to prove the opposite of. **2** to refuse to adopt: *The Committee negatived the proposal*:—*pr.p.* **neg'ativing**.
negate *ni-gāt' v.t.* **1** to nullify. **2** to deny:—*pr.p.* **negat'ing**.
negātion *n.*

neglect *ni-glekt', v.t.* **1** to treat carelessly. **2** to fail to give proper attention to. **3** to fail (to do something).—*n.* want of care or attention.
neglect'ful *adj.* **neglect'fully** *adv.*
See also **negligence**.

négligé(e) *neg'li-zhā, n.* a thin dressing-gown or similar wrap.

negligence *neg'li-jėns, n.* carelessness.
neg'ligent *adj.* **neg'ligently** *adv.*
neg'ligible *adj.* not worth considering, very small.

negotiate *ni-gō'shi-āt, v.i.* to bargain (with), discuss a subject (with), in order to reach agreement.—*v.t.* **1** to arrange (e.g. a treaty or a loan). **2** to get past (an obstacle or difficulty):—*pr.p.* **nego'tiating**.
nego'tiable *adj.* **1** that can be negotiated. **2** (of a paper concerned with payment of money) that can be transferred from one person to another.
negotiation *ni-gō-shi-ā'sh(ȯ)n, n.* **1** the act of negotiating. **2** discussion aimed at reaching an agreement: *The dispute was settled by negotiation.*
nego'tiātor *n.*

Negro *nē'grō, n.* (*often offensive*) a member of any of the dark-skinned peoples of Africa or a person racially descended from one of these:—*pl.* **Ne'groes**.—Also *adj.*
Ne'gress *n.* (*often offensive*) a female Negro.
ne'groid *adj.* of Negro type.

neigh *nā, v.i.* to whinny, utter the cry of a horse.—*n.* the cry of a horse.

neighbour *nā'bȯr, n.* a person who lives near one.
neigh'bourhood *n.* **1** the district surrounding the place mentioned: *in the neighbourhood of Paris.* **2** a district: *a poor neighbourhood.*
neigh'bouring *adj.* near or next in place: *France and Belgium are neighbouring countries.*
neigh'bourly *adj.* of, behaving as, a good neighbour.
neigh'bourliness *n.*

neither *nī'THer,* or *nē', adj., pron.,* not one nor the other: *Neither twin is married; Neither of the twins is married.*—*conj.* (*rather poetical*) and not: *They toil not, neither do they spin.*
neither... nor not... and not: *Neither George nor Mary is at home; He neither wrote nor telephoned.*

nemesis *nem'i-sis, n.* punishment that is bound to follow wrongdoing.

neo- *nē-ō-* (as part of a word) new.
neolithic *(-lith'ik) adj.* belonging to the later Stone Age.
neologism *ni-ol'ȯj-izm, n.* a new word or expression.

neon *nē'on, n.* a colourless gas, used with other gases very like it, in **neon lighting**. When an electric current is passed through a very small quantity of any of these gases in a tube a coloured light appears.

nephew *nef'ū, n.* the son of a brother or sister.

nepotism *nep'ȯ-tizm, n.* the practice of appointing one's own relations to good positions.

Neptune *nep'tūn, n.* **1** the Roman god of the sea. **2** a distant planet.

nerve *nûrv, n.* **1** a bundle of fibres that carries messages between the brain or spinal cord and other parts of the body. **2** (*old*) a sinew. **3** courage, coolness: *Don't lose your nerve.* **4** (*coll.*) impudence. **5** (in *pl.*) the condition of being too easily upset: *She suffers from nerves.*—*v.t.* to give courage to: *He nerved himself to face the danger*:—*pr.p.* **nerv'ing**.

nerve'less *adj.* without strength.

ner'vous *adj.* **1** of, relating to, the nerves: *nervous tension, energy.* **2** excitable. **3** agitated, anxious.

ner'vously *adv.* **ner'vousness** *n.*

ner'vy *adj.* excitable:—*comp.* **ner'vier**; *superl.* **ner'viest**.

nerve'-racking *adj.* causing anxiety.

nervous breakdown. See **breakdown** under **break**.

nervous system the brain, spinal cord, nerves, of an animal or human being.

get on someone's nerves to irritate someone.

nest *nest, n.* **1** a place or structure in which birds, certain animals (e.g. mice), certain insects (e.g. wasps) live and bring up their young. **2** a set of things fitting one inside another: *a nest of tables.*—*v.i.* to build or occupy a nest.

nestle *nes'l, v.i.* to lie close as in a nest; to settle comfortably:—*pr.p.* **nest'ling**.

nestling *nes'ling, n.* a young bird in the nest.

nest'-egg *n.* something (usu. money) saved or stored.

net[1] *net, n.* (any of various articles for e.g. catching fish, birds, etc., for dividing a tennis-court, etc., for keeping the hair in place, made of) cord, thread, etc. knotted so as to form a loose arrangement of crossing lines and spaces.—Also *adj.*—*v.t.* to catch as in a net:—*pr.p.* **nett'ing**; *pa.p.* **nett'ed**.

nett'ing *n.* a net material: *wire-netting.*

net'ball *n.* a game in which a ball is thrown into a net hanging from a pole.

net'work *n.* **1** anything showing many lines crossing one another: *A network of roads covered the countryside.* **2** a widespread organisation: *a radio network.*—*v.t.* to broadcast throughout the country.

net[2], nett *net, adj.* remaining after expenses or other charges have been paid: *Our net profit*; *We made £100 net.*—*v.t.* to gain as profit:—*pr.p.* **nett'ing**; *pa.p.* **nett'ed**.

netball. See **net[1]**.

nether *neTH'ėr, adj.* lower.

neth'ermost *adj.* lowest.

the Netherlands *n. pl.* the country inhabited by the Dutch (the Low Countries or Holland).

nett. See **net[2]**.

netting. See **net[1,2]**.

nettle *net'l, n.* a wild plant with stinging hairs.—*v.t.* to annoy, offend:—*pr.p.* **nett'ling**.

nett'le-rash *n.* a skin rash that looks like the effect of nettle stings.

network. See **net[1]**.

neur(o)- *nūr(-ō)-* (as part of a word) nerve(s).

neuralgia *nū-ral'jȧ, n.* pain in the nerves usu. in the head or face.

neuritis *nū-rī'tis, n.* inflammation of a nerve.

neurol'ogy *nū-rol'ȯ-ji, n.* the study of the nervous system.

neurol'ogist *n.* **neurolog'ical** *adj.*

neurosis *nū-rō'sis, n.* an emotional and mental illness with symptoms such as unreasonable anxiety:—*pl.* **neuro'ses** *(-sēz)*.

neurotic *nū-rot'ik, adj.* in a bad nervous state, having a neurosis.—*n.* a person with a neurosis.

neuter *nū'tėr, adj.* **1** (in grammar) neither masculine nor feminine. **2** without sex (as e.g. worker bees).—Also *n.*—*v.t.* to deprive (an animal) of the power to reproduce young.

neutral *nū'trȧl, adj.* **1** not taking sides: *Sweden was neutral in the war.* **2** (of a colour, etc.) not definite or strong: *Grey is a neutral colour.* **3** (*chemistry*) being neither acid nor base.—*n.* **1** a person or country not taking part in a war or quarrel. **2** a position of gear (e.g. in a car) where no power passes.

neutral'ity *n.* the state of being neutral.

neu'tralise *v.t.* **1** to make neutral. **2** to undo the effect of, counteract. **3** to put out of action (e.g. an enemy force):—*pr.p.* **neu'tralising**.

neu'tralism *n.* neutrality as a policy.

neu'tralist *n.*

neutron *nū'tron, n.* one of the particles (without electrical charge) which, with protons, make up the nucleus of the atom.

never *nev'ėr, adv.* **1** not ever; at no time. **2** not at all.—*interj.* surely not.

nevermore' *adv.* never again.

nevertheless' *adv.* in spite of that.

the never-never (*humorous*) hire purchase.

well I never! an expression of surprise.

new *nū, adj.* **1** recently introduced, discovered, bought, etc. **2** not before seen or known. **3** changed, improved: *He's a new man since his operation.* **4** just arrived: *a new pupil.*—*adv.* (as part of a word) recently: *new-laid*; *newborn.*

new'ly *adv.* **new'ness** *n.*

new'comer *n.* one who has lately come.

new moon the moon when seen as a narrow waxing crescent.

New World North and South America.

New Year the first few days of a fresh year.

newel *nū'ėl n.* **1** the central column in a spiral staircase. **2** the post at the bottom or top of a stair, supporting the banister.

newfangled *nū-fan'gld, adj.* (of things, ideas) new but not very good.

news *nūz, n. sing.* a report of recent events; new information: *Have you any news of your friend?*

new'sy *adj.* full of news:—*comp.* **new'sier**; *superl.* **new'siest**.

news'agent *n.* one who sells newspapers and usu. other goods.

news'cast *n.* broadcast of news in a radio or television programme.—Also *v.i.*

news'caster *n.*

news'paper *(nūs') n.* a paper printed each day, or week, and containing news.

news'print *n.* cheap paper on which newspapers are printed.

news'reel *n.* a cinema or television film showing, or a radio programme telling about, recent events.

newt *nūt, n.* a small amphibious animal rather like a lizard.

next *nekst, adj.* nearest, closest, in place, time, etc.: *the next chapter*; *the next street to this one*; *I'll see you Sunday next*; *the next best solution.*—Also *pron.*: *I can do this sum but not the next.*—*adv.* immediately after in place or time: *Alice led, Jane came next*; *Do that sum next*.

next door in the next house.

next to 1 alongside: *The house is next to the school.* **2** almost: *It cost next to nothing*.

nib *nib, n.* a writing point for a pen that is not a ball-point.

nibble *nib'l, v.t.* or *v.i.* (with *at*) to take very small bites of (something).—*v.i.* (often with *at*) to begin to show interest in a bargain, etc.:—*pr.p.* **nibb'ling**.—*n.* a small bite.

nice *nīs, adj.* **1** agreeable, pleasant. **2** careful, exact: *a nice sense of timing*.

nice'ly *adv.* **1** pleasantly. **2** very well: *It will do nicely*.

nice'ness *n.* **1** exactness. **2** agreeableness.

nicety *nis'i-ti, n.* a delicate or exact detail:—*pl.* **nic'eties**.

to a nicety with great exactness.

niche *nich, n.* **1** a hollow in a wall for a statue or ornament. **2** a suitable place in life: *He found his niche in engineering*.

nick *nik, n.* **1** a notch, a small cut. **2** (*slang*) a prison or police-station.—*v.t.* **1** to make a small cut in. **2** (*slang*) to steal. **3** (*slang*) to arrest (a criminal).

in good nick (*slang*) in good condition.

in the nick of time at the last possible moment.

nickel *nik'ėl, n.* **1** an element, a greyish-white metal used esp. for mixing with other metals, and for plating. **2** (*U.S.*) a 5-cent coin.

nick'el-sil'ver *n.* a mixture of copper, zinc and nickel.

See also **cupro-nickel**.

nickname *nik'nām, n.* an added name, given in fun, or contempt, or admiration: *Wellington's nickname was 'the Iron Duke'.*—*v.t.* to give a nickname to:—*pr.p.* **nick'naming**.

nicotine *nik'ō-tēn, n.* a poisonous substance present in tobacco.

niece *nēs, n.* the daughter of a brother or sister.

nifty *nif'ti,* (*coll.*) *adj.* clever, smart:—*comp.* **nif'tier**; *superl.* **nif'tiest**.

niggard *nig'ard, n.* one who dislikes spending or giving.

nigg'ardly *adj.* mean, not generous: *a niggardly man*; *a niggardly gift*.

nigg'ardliness *n.*

nigger *nig'ėr, n.* (*offensive*) a person of black African origin or race.

niggle *nig'l, v.i.* **1** to spend time on, or complain about, small details. **2** to be a slight annoyance:—*pr.p.* **nigg'ling**.

nigg'ling *adj.* **1** unimportant. **2** slightly troublesome.

nigh *nī,* (*old*) *adj.* and *prep.* near.

night *nīt, n.* **1** the time between sunset and sunrise. **2** darkness.—*adj.* **1** of, for, night. **2** happening, active, used, etc. at night.

night'ly *adj.* happening, etc. by night or every night.—*adv.* every night.

night'cap *n.* **1** a drink taken before going to bed. **2** a cap worn in bed.

night club a club open during the night for dancing or other entertainment.

night'dress, night'gown, night'shirt *ns.* garments worn in bed.

night'fall *n.* the beginning of the night.

night'long *adj.* and *adv.* (lasting) all night.

night'mare *n.* a frightening dream.

night safe a safe built into the outer wall of a bank, in which to deposit money when the bank is closed.

night school (a place providing) evening educational classes for people who work during the day.

night'shade *n.* any of various poisonous plants.

night shift a turn of duty during the night.

night'-watch'man *n.* one who looks after a building during the night.

nightingale *nīt'ing-gāl, n.* a small bird with a beautiful song, which it sings at night as well as by day.

nightmare, nightshade. See **night**.

nil *nil, n.* nothing.

nimble *nim'bl, adj.* **1** quick in movement. **2** clever: *a nimble wit*.

nim'bleness *n.* **nim'bly,** *adv.*

nimbus *nim'bus, n.* **1** a bright disc, ring, etc., representing light round a person's head in a picture. **2** a dark, rain-filled cloud.

nincompoop *ning'kom-pōōp, n.* a fool.

nine *nīn, adj.* and *n.* **1** the number next above eight (9 or IX). **2** a set of nine things or persons. **3** the ninth hour after midday or midnight. **4** the age of nine years. **5** any thing (e.g. a shoe, a playing-card) denoted by nine.—*adj.* **1** 9 in number. **2** nine years old.

ninth *nīnth, adj.* **1** next after the eighth. **2** equal to one of nine equal parts.—Also *n.*

nine'teen (also *-tēn'*) *n.* and *adj.* nine and ten (19 or XIX).

nine'teenth (also *-tēnth'*) *adj.* **1** next after the eighteenth. **2** equal to one of nineteen equal parts.—Also *n.*

nine'ty *n.* and *adj.* nine times ten (90 or XC).

nine'ties *n.pl.* the numbers ninety to ninety-nine.

nine'tieth *adj.* **1** next after the eighty-ninth. **2** equal to one of ninety equal parts.—Also *n.*

nine'pins, *n. sing.* a game in which nine bottle-shaped objects have to be knocked down by a ball.

nine days' wonder something that attracts attention for a short time and is then forgotten.

ninny *nin'i, n.* a foolish person:—*pl.* **ninn'ies**.

nip *nip, v.t.* **1** to pinch. **2** to cut, bite, etc. **3** to hinder growth of, damage: *The frost nips the dahlias.* **4** (of e.g. cold) to cause pain in (also *v.i.*).—*v.i.* to move quickly:—*pr.p.* **nipp'ing**; *pa.p.* **nipped**. —*n.* **1** a pinch. **2** a small quantity esp. of spirits. **3** sharp coldness: *a nip in the air*.

nipp'er *n.* **1** something that nips, such as a crab's claw. **2** (*coll.*) a young child, esp. a boy. **3** (in *pl.*) pincers or pliers.

nipple *nip'l, n.* **1** the part of the breast through which a baby sucks milk. **2** a teat of a baby's bottle. **3** anything like this, e.g. a small projection through which oil or grease is put into machinery.

nisi *nī'sī, nis'i, conj.* unless.

decree nisi. See **decree**.

nit *nit, n.* the egg or young of a louse or other small insect.

nit'-picking (*coll.*) *n.* petty criticism.

nit'wit (*slang*) *n.* a very foolish person.

nitrate, nitre, etc. See **nitrogen**.

nitrogen *nī'trō-jen, n.* an element, a colourless gas with no taste or smell, forming nearly four-fifths of the air.

ni'trate *n.* any of a number of salts formed from nitric acid esp. one used as a fertiliser.

nitre *nī'tėr, n.* saltpetre.

ni'tric, ni'trous *adjs.* (*chemistry*) containing nitrogen in fixed proportions.

nitrogenous *nī-troj'in-us, adj.* containing nitrogen: *a nitrogenous fertiliser*.

nitric acid a strong acid of which nitrogen is a component.

ni'tro-glyc'erine *n.* a powerful explosive.

nitty-gritty *nit'i-grit'i,* (*coll.*) *n.* the basic details, work, etc.

nitwit. See **nit**.

no *nō, adj.* **1** not any: *We have no coal*; *Call no man happy.* **2** not a: *He is no singer, no beauty.*—*adv.* not at all: *The patient is no better.*—*interj.* indicating refusal, denial, disagreement, etc.—*n.* **1** a refusal. **2** a vote against:—*pl.* **noes**: *The noes have won*.

no'body *(-bo-di) pron.* not any person.—*n.* a person of no importance:—*pl.* **no'bodies**.

no'-go' (*coll.*) *adj.* (of a district, etc.) that cannot be entered.

no'-man's-land *n.* land that no-one controls or owns, esp. between opposing armies.

no'-one *pron.* not any person, nobody.

no-win' *adj.* (of a situation etc.) that cannot turn out well.

nob *nob,* (*slang*) *n.* a superior person.

nobble *nob'l,* (*coll.*) *v.t.* **1** to waylay, esp. in order to bribe or persuade. **2** to drug or injure (a horse) to prevent it winning:—*pr.p.* **nobb'ling**.

nobility. See **noble**.

noble *nō'bl, adj.* **1** great in character or of fine moral quality: *a noble mind, deed.* **2** of high birth or rank:—*opp.* **ignoble**.—*n.* **1** a gold coin, no longer used. **2** a man of high rank (also **no'bleman**).

nobility *nōbil'i-ti, n.* **1** nobleness. **2** nobles (dukes, earls, etc.) considered together.

no'bly *adv.* **no'bleness** *n.*

nobody. See **no**.

nocturnal *nok-tûr'nal, adj.* **1** happening at night: *a nocturnal alarm.* **2** active at night:

Though sometimes seen by day, the hedgehog is really a nocturnal animal.
nocturne *nok'tû'rn, n.* **1** a piece of music describing a night scene. **2** a painting of a night scene.

nod *nod, v.i.* and *v.t.* to give a quick forward shake of (the head), often showing agreement.—*v.i.* **1** to let the head droop in weariness. **2** to make a careless mistake:—*pr.p.* **nodding**; *pa.p.* **nodd'ed**.—*n.* a quick forward movement of the head.

noddle *nod'l, n.* head.

node *nōd, n.* a knob, joint, e.g. where a leaf stalk joins a branch.
nō'dal *adj.*
nodule *nod'ūl, n.* a little rounded lump.
nod'ular *adj.*

Noël also **Nowel(l)** *nō-el', n.* Christmas.

noggin *nog'in, n.* a small mug or cup.

no-go. See **no**.

noise *noiz, n.* **1** a sound of any kind. **2** a loud or disturbing sound. **3** interference, intrusions, on radio, television, in a computer, etc.—*v.t.* to spread by talk: *The story was noised abroad*:—*pr.p.* **nois'ing**.
noise'less *adj.* silent, without sound.
noise'lessly *adv.* **noise'lessness** *n.*
nois'y *adj.* making a loud sound:—*comp.* **nois'ier**; *superl.* **nois'iest**.
nois'ily *adv.* **nois'iness** *n.*

noisome *noi'sum, adj.* **1** harmful to health. **2** disgusting.

nomad *nō'mad, n.* **1** one of a group of people without fixed home who wander with flocks searching for pasture. **2** a wanderer.
nomadic *nō-mad'ik, adj.*
nomad'ically *adv.*

no-man's-land. See **no**.

nom de plume *nom'dė-plōōm, n.* a name taken by a writer who wishes to conceal his own name.

nomenclature *nȯ-men'klȧ-chür, n.* a system, or set, of (esp. scientific or technical) names for things.

nominal *nom'in-ȧl, adj.* **1** in name only, not real: *the nominal head of the firm.* **2** trifling, not important: *a nominal fine*.
nom'inally *adv.*
nominate *nom'in-āt, v.t.* **1** (*old*) to specify, name. **2** to appoint: *The bishops are nominated by the king.* **3** to propose for election or for approval: *Four candidates were nominated for the post*: *pr.p.* **nom'inating**.
nominā'tion *n.*
nominative *nom'in-ȧ-tiv, adj.* and *n.* (in grammar) (the case) showing the subject of the verb.
nominee *nom-in-ē', n.* one who is proposed for a position or duty.

non- *non-, pfx.* used to change the meaning of a word to its opposite.
non-appear'ance *n.* failure to appear.
non-attend'ance *n.* absence.
non-com'batant *n.* someone connected with the armed forces who does not fight, e.g. a doctor.—Also *adj.*
non-commiss'ioned *adj.* (of officer in army) below rank of second-lieutenant.
non-committ'al *adj.* unwilling to express, or not expressing, an opinion: *When questioned, he was non-committal*; *a non-committal answer*.
non-conduct'ing *adj.* not readily transmitting heat, electricity, etc.
non-conduct'or *n.*
non-conform'ist *n.* **1** one who does not agree with those in authority. **2** (*cap*) a Protestant separated from the Church of England. **3** one who behaves, etc. unconventionally.—Also *adj.*
non-conform'ity *n.*
non-event' (*coll.*) *n.* an event that fails to live up to expectations.
non-exist'ent *adj.* not existing, not real: *Many people think the Loch Ness monster is non-existent.*
non-exist'ence *n.*
non-ferr'ous *adj.* containing no iron: *non-ferrous metals* (i.e. all the metals except iron).
non-flamm'able *adj.* not able to be set on fire.
non-interven'tion *n.* not interfering in the affairs, esp. quarrels, of e.g. another country.
non-pay'ment *n.* failure to pay money that is owed.
non-res'ident *adj.* not living in the place mentioned: *In this boarding school, some of the teachers are non-resident.*—Also *n.*
non-smo'ker *n.* **1** one who does not smoke. **2** a railway compartment in which smoking is forbidden.
non-star'ter *n.* **1** a horse, etc., that, though entered for a race, does not compete. **2** a person, idea, etc. with no chance of success.
non-stick' *adj.* (of a pan, etc. or its surface) to which food will not stick in cooking.
non'-stop' *adj.* going on without a stop.

nonagenarian *nōn-ȧ-ji-nā'ri-ȧn, n.* someone who is ninety years old.

nonchalance *non'shȧ-lȧns, n.* coolness, lack of worry or excitement.
non'chalant *adj.* **non'chalantly** *adv.*

nondescript *non'di-skript*, *adj.* not distinctive enough to be described: *a nondescript appearance.*—Also *n.*

none *nun, pron.* not one; not any: *Lend me some eggs, sugar—I've none left*; *None of us is* (or *are*) *going.*—*adv.* not at all: *none the worse.*

nonetheless', **none the less** nevertheless, in spite of this.

nonentity *non-en'ti-ti*, *n.* a person of no importance:—*pl.* **nonen'tities**.

nonplus *non-plus'*, *v.t.* to puzzle completely, bewilder: *The boy was nonplussed by the unexpected question*:—*pr.p.* **nonpluss'ing**; *pa.p.* **nonplussed'**.

nonsense *non'sėns*, *n.* foolish or absurd words or actions.

non-sequitur *nōn-sek'wi-tėr*, *n.* something that does not follow logically from what has just been said, etc.

noodle[1], *nōōd'l*, (*coll.*) *n.* a foolish person.

noodle[2] *nōōd'l*, *n.* a strip of pasta sometimes put in soup.

nook *nook*, *n.* a corner, recess.

noon *nōōn*, *n.* twelve o'clock, midday.

noon'day, **noon'tide** *ns.* and *adjs.* midday.

no-one. See **no**.

noose *nōōs*, *n.* **1** a loop in rope or cord which tightens when pulled. **2** a snare.

nor *nör*, *conj.* and not (with order of subject and verb reversed): *He did not know why then, nor did he ever find out.*

See also **neither**.

Nordic *nör'dik adj.* of, relating to, the Germanic or Scandinavian peoples of Northern Europe.

norm *nörm*, *n.* an expected pattern or standard by which to judge.

nor'mal *adj.* ordinary, usual.

nor'mally *adv.* **1** in an ordinary way. **2** usually, as a rule.

normal'ity, **nor'malness**, *ns.*

See also **abnormal**.

Norman *nör'man*, *n.* a native of Normandy, the part of France conquered by Norsemen in 10th century.—Also *adj.*

Norse *nörs*, *adj.* of, relating to, ancient Scandinavia or its language.

Norse'man *n.* a Scandinavian of earlier times, one of those who made settlements in Britain, etc.

Old Norse Norwegian and Icelandic as spoken and written before the mid 14th century.

north *nörth*, *n.* **1** the direction to the left of a person facing the rising sun. **2** a region, etc. in this direction.—Also *adj.*, *adv.*

nor'therly (-TH-) *adj.* of, from, or looking towards, the north.—Also *adv.*

nor'thern (-TH-) *adj.* of, or towards the north.

nor'therner (-TH-) *n.* one who belongs to the north.

nor'thernmost (-TH-) *adj.* farthest north.

north'ward *adj.* and (also **north'wards**) *adv.* towards the north.

north-east', **-west'** *ns.* **1** the direction midway between north and east, north and west. **2** a region, etc. in that direction.—Also *adjs.* and *advs.*

north-eas'ter, **-wes'ter** *ns.* a wind blowing from north-east, north-west.

northern lights greenish lights sometimes seen in the northern sky at night.

north pole **1** the end of the earth's axis in the ice-covered Arctic Ocean. **2** the highest point of the heavens as seen from there.

North Star the Pole Star, a star which is very near the north pole of the heavens.

north wind a wind from the north.

Norwegian *nör-wē'jȧn*, *adj.* belonging to Norway or its inhabitants or language.—*n.* **1** a native of Norway. **2** the language of Norway.

nose *nōz*, *n.* **1** the part of the face through which we breathe and smell. **2** the jutting-forward part: *the nose of an aeroplane, car*:—*v.i.* to search (about, around) (as if) by smelling.—*v.t.* **1** (with *out*) to track by smelling: *The dog nosed out the bone.* **2** to make (one's way) by feeling or pushing: *The ice-breaker nosed its way through the ice*:—*pr.p.* **nos'ing**.

nos'y (sometimes **nos'ey**) *adj.* fond of prying:—*comp.* **nos'ier**; *superl.* **nos'iest**.

nos'ily *adv.* **nos'iness** *n.*

nose'bag *n.* a bag for food, hung on a horse's head.

nose'-dive *n.* a fall head or front first: *The aeroplane did a nose-dive into the sea.*—Also *v.i.*

blow one's nose to clear the nose by breathing sharply through it into a handkerchief.

follow one's nose to go straight forward.

pay through the nose to pay heavily or too much for something.

put someone's nose out of joint to make someone feel disappointed and annoyed by taking his place, or spoiling his plans.

poke one's nose into to meddle in (someone else's business).

turn up one's nose at **1** to refuse with contempt. **2** (also **look down one's nose at**) to treat with contempt.

nosegay *nōz'gā*, *n.* a bunch of sweet-smelling flowers.

nosey. See **nose**.

nostalgia *nos-tal'ji-ȧ, -jȧ*, *n.* **1** homesickness **2** longing for past times.
nostal'gic *adj.*

nostril *nos'tril*, *n.* one of the openings of the nose.

nostrum *nos'trum*, *n.* a person's favourite medicine, remedy, scheme for reform.

nosy. See **nose**.

not *not*, *adv.* expressing refusal or denial, shortened to **n't** when used after certain verbs, e.g. **have**, **be**.
not at all absolutely not.
not on (*coll.*) **1** not possible. **2** not acceptable.
not that although it is not true that.

notable, etc. See **note**.

notary *nō'tȧ-ri*, *n.* an official whose duties are concerned with formal documents and statements, e.g. who gives a certificate of the making of a contract.—Also **no'tary pub'lic**:—*pl.* **no'taries (pub'lic)**.

notation *nō-tā'sh(ȯ)n*, *n.* a system of signs, symbols, etc. for a special use: *Sol-fa notation is a way of writing music.*

notch *noch*, *n.* a nick, a small v-shaped cut.—*v.t.* to make a nick in.

note *nōt*, *n.* **1** a sign or piece of writing to draw attention to, or to remind of, something. **2** (in *pl.*) ideas set down in short form (for e.g. a speech). **3** a short explanation: *There is a note in your textbook about that difficult word.* **4** a short letter. **5** a letter from the representative of one government to that of another: *A note has been sent by the Prime Minister to the President.* **6** a piece of paper used as money: *a five-pound note.* **7** a mark standing for a sound in music. **8** the sound itself: *The song ended on a high note.*—*v.t.* **1** to write (down), make a note of. **2** to notice:—*pr.p.* **not'ing**.
notable *nō'tȧ-bl*, *adj.* **1** worthy of being noted, memorable. **2** important.—*n.* an important person: *The Prime Minister and other notables were present.*
no'tableness *n.*
notabil'ity *n.* **1** notableness. **2** a notable person:—*pl.* **notabil'ities**.
no'tably *adv.* **1** in a notable way. **2** noticeably. **3** particularly: *Some of them looked alarmed, notably Mr Brown.*
no'ted *adj.* well-known.
note'let *n.* a folded, decorated sheet of notepaper for brief letters.
note'book *n.* a small book in which to make notes.
note'case *n.* a wallet for banknotes.
note'pad *n.* a pad of paper for writing notes on.
note'paper *n.* paper for writing letters on.
note'worthy *adj.* notable, remarkable: *Nothing noteworthy happened.*
of note distinguished.
take note of to notice and remember.
worthy of note noteworthy.

nothing *nuth'ing*, *pron.* **1** no thing. **2** not anything.—*n.* **1** (*arithmetic*) a nought. **2** a trivial thing or (esp. in *pl.*) remark.—Also *adv.* not at all: *It was nothing like what I had said.*
noth'ingness *n.* state of being nothing.
come to nothing to fail, have no result.

notice *nō'tis*, *n.* **1** an announcement made, or shown, publicly. **2** warning: *We hereby give notice that late arrivals will not be admitted*; *I had only two days' notice of the meeting.* **3** warning that an agreement is ending, given esp. when leaving a job or dismissing someone: *His employer gave the boy a week's notice.* **4** attention: *His strange hat, his skill, attracted notice.*—*v.t.* to see, observe, take note of:—*pr.p.* **not'icing**.
no'ticeable *adj.* likely to be, easily, seen, heard, felt, etc.: *a noticeable difference.*
no'ticeably *adv.* **no'ticeableness** *n.*
take notice to observe, pay attention (often with *of*).
See also **notify**.

notify *nō'ti-fī*, *v.t.* **1** to inform: *He notified the milkman that he would be away for three days*; *He notified me of his intentions.* **2** to report officially (e.g. a theft to the police):—*pr.p.* **no'tifying**; *pa.p.* **no'tified**.
no'tifiable *adj.* (of diseases) that must be reported to public health authorities.
notificā'tion *n.*

notion *nō'sh(ȯ)n*, *n.* **1** an idea. **2** a fancy or vague belief.

notoriety. See **notorious**.

notorious *nō-tō'ri-us, -tö'*, *adj.* well known in a bad way: *He is a notorious thief.*
notori'ety (*-rī'*), **noto'riousness** *ns.*
noto'riously *adv.* in a way, to a degree, that is very well known: *It is notoriously difficult to get giant pandas to mate in captivity.*

notwithstanding *not-with-stand'ing*, *prep.* in spite of: *Notwithstanding the bad weather, all the children reached school.*—*adv.* nevertheless.

nougat *nōō'gä*, *n.* a sticky kind of sweet containing chopped nuts.

nought. See **naught**.

noun *nown, n.* (*grammar*) a word used as a name of a person, thing, etc.: *The words 'boy', 'James', and 'brevity' are all nouns.*

nourish *nur'ish, v.t.* **1** to feed. **2** to encourage growth of. **3** to have, cherish: *He nourished feelings of envy towards his rival.*

nour'ishing *adj.* (of food) giving the body what is necessary for health and growth.

nour'ishment *n.* something that nourishes: *Plants draw nourishment from the earth.*

See also **nutrient**, etc.

nous *nows, (coll.) n.* common sense.

nova *nō'vȧ, n.* a star that flares into brightness and then fades.

novel *nov'l, adj.* new and strange: *Space travel was a novel idea to most people in 1957.*—*n.* a long story in prose.

nov'elist *n.* the writer of a novel.

nov'elty *n.* **1** newness. **2** something new or strange. **3** a small cheap toy, souvenir, etc.:—*pl.* **nov'elties**.

November *nō-vem'bėr, n.* the eleventh month (ninth of the Roman year).

novice *nov'is, n.* **1** a beginner. **2** a nun or monk who has not yet taken all the vows.

novitiate, noviciate *no-vish'i-it, n.* the period of being a novice.

now *now, adv.* **1** at the present time. **2** as things are: *You see why I cannot now go.*—*conj.* (often with *that*) since, because: *I can go now (that) you have come.*—*interj.* used in warning, reassurance, etc.: *Now, don't cry.*

nowadays *now'ȧ-dāz, adv.* at the present time.

now and then, now and again sometimes, from time to time.

Nowel(l). See **Noël**.

nowhere *nō'(h)wār, adv.* in or to no place.

no-win. See **no**.

noxious *nok'shus, adj.* **1** harmful to man or other living things: *noxious fumes.* **2** harmful to morals or mind: *a noxious influence.*

nozzle *noz'l, n.* a spout fitted to the end of a pipe, etc., through which liquid or gas can come out.

nuance *nū'on^{g}s, n.* a slight shade of difference in meaning, colour, etc.

nub *nub, n.* the point or gist.

nubile *nū'bīl, adj.* marriageable; sexually attractive.

nucleus *nū'kli-ůs, n.* **1** a central point or mass around which something collects, or from which something grows: *The Greek vases formed the nucleus of the museum's collection.* **2** the part of a plant cell or animal cell that controls its development. **3** the central part of an atom, consisting of two kinds of particle known as protons and neutrons (except in the case of hydrogen where the nucleus is one proton):—*pl.* **nuclei** *(nū'kli-ī)*.

nu'clear *(-kli-ȧr) adj.* **1** of, relating to, a nucleus. **2** of, relating to, atomic energy or the atomic bomb.

nuclear energy the energy released by splitting the nuclei of atoms.

nuclear fission. Same as **fission** (*def. 2*).

nuclear reactor an apparatus for splitting the nuclei of atoms.

nude *nūd, adj.* naked, without clothes.—*n.* an unclothed human figure or statue.

nū'dist *n.* one who advises (and follows) the practice of going without clothes.

nū'dism *n.*

nū'dity *n.* the state of being nude.

in the nude naked.

nudge *nuj. n.* a gentle poke, e.g. with the elbow.—*v.t.* to poke gently:—*pr.p.* **nud'ging**.

nugatory *nū'gȧ-tȯ-ri, adj.* trifling.

nugget *nug'it, n.* a lump, esp. of gold.

nuisance *nū'sȧns, n.* a person or thing that is annoying, troublesome, or (*law*) that harms, inconveniences, or is offensive.

null *nul, adj.* of no value or effect.

nullify *nul'i-fī, v.t.* **1** to undo the effect of. **2** to make (e.g. a contract) without legal force, or to declare it to be so:—*pr.p.* **null'ifying**; *pa.p.* **null'ified**.

null'ity *n.* the state of being null.

null and void having no legal force, no longer binding or controlling.

numb *num, adj.* having lost the power to feel or move.—*v.t.* to make numb, to deaden.

numb'ly *adv.* **numb'ness** *n.*

number *num'bėr, n.* **1** a numeral. **2** a thing named by its place in a series: *He lives at Number 7.* **3** a collection of things, persons, etc.: *You may have a number of hobbies.* **4** one issue of a newspaper or magazine: *Some magazines publish a Christmas number.* **5** a song or piece of music: *His latest musical includes many popular numbers.*—*v.t.* **1** to count. **2** to give numbers to. **3** to amount to in number: *His party numbers ten.* **4** to include, reckon (among, with, etc.) (also *v.i.*): *He numbers me among his friends.*

num'berless *adj.* more than can be counted.

number one (*coll.*) oneself.

num'ber-plate *n.* a plate at the front and

rear of a vehicle showing its official number.
his, etc. **days are numbered** he, etc. cannot survive much longer.

numeral *nū'mėr-ȧl, n.* a figure (e.g. 1, 2, etc.) used to express a number.
nū'merate *(-it) adj.* able to understand basic mathematics and science:—*opp.* **innumerate.**
nū'meracy *n.*
nū'merātor *n.* (in fractions) the number above the line.
numerical *nū-mer'ik-ȧl, adj.* **1** using or consisting of numbers: *The secret messages were written in a numerical code.* **2** in numbers: *the great numerical strength of the enemy.*
numer'ically *adv.*
nū'merous *adj.* very many.
numerical order the order in which we normally count (e.g. 1, 2, 3, 4; or 20, 21, 22, 23, etc.).
See also **innumerable.**

numismatic *nū-miz-mat'ik, adj.* of, relating to, coins and medals.
numismat'ics *n.sing.* the study of these.
numis'matist *n.*

numskull *num'skul, n.* a blockhead.

nun *nun, n.* a woman who has taken vows to live in a convent and devote herself to religion.
nunn'ery *n.* a house for nuns:—*pl.* **nunn'eries.**

nuptial *nup'shȧl, adj.* of, relating to, marriage.
nup'tials *n.pl.* a wedding ceremony.

nurse *nûrs, n.* one who is trained to look after sick or injured people, or (esp. a woman) after small children.—*v.t.* **1** to look after (invalids) esp. in hospital. **2** to suckle (see this word). **3** to hold in the arms with care. **4** to take care of: *This plant is delicate and must be nursed.* **5** to manage with care: *You must nurse your resources.* **6** to encourage (anger, hatred, etc.) in oneself:—*pr.p.* **nur'sing.**
nur'sery *n.* **1** a room, place, for young children. **2** a piece of ground where young plants and trees are grown:—*pl.* **nur'series.**
nurse'maid *n.* a maid who looks after young children.
nur'sery-man *n.* a man who works in a nursery (*def.* 2).
nursery rhyme a traditional rhyme repeated to and by children.
nursery school a school for children under five.
nursing home a private hospital.

nurture *nûr'chůr, v.t.* **1** to bring up. **2** to cause to develop. **3** to feed:—*pr.p.* **nur'turing.**—*n.* **1** upbringing, training. **2** food, nourishment.

nut *nut, n.* **1** a fruit with one seed (kernel) in a hard shell. **2** a small block with a hole, usu. of metal, for screwing on the end of a bolt. **3** a small lump, e.g. of coal. **4** (*coll.*) a head. **5** (*slang*) a crazy person.
nuts *nuts,* (*slang*) *adj.* crazy.
nutt'ing *n.* gathering nuts.
nutt'y *adj.* **1** containing nuts; having the flavour of nuts. **2** (*coll.*) crazy:—*comp.* **nutt'ier**; *superl.* **nutt'iest.**
nut'-brown *adj.* brown like a ripe nut.
nut'-case (*coll.*) *n.* a crazy person.
nut'crackers *n. pl.* a pair of hinged metal arms used for cracking nuts.
nut'hatch *n.* a small climbing bird that lives on nuts and insects.
a hard nut to crack someone or something difficult to deal with.
in a nutshell expressed very briefly.

nutmeg *nut'meg, n.* the hard kernel or seed of the fruit of an East Indian tree, used as a spice in food.

nutria *nū'tri-ȧ, n.* **1** the coypu. **2** its fur.

nutrient *nū'tri-ėnt, adj.* and *n.* (a substance) giving nourishment.
nutriment *nū'tri-ment, n.* nourishment, food.
nutrition *nu-tri'sh(ȯ)n, n.* **1** the act or process of nourishing. **2** food.
nutri'tional *adj.*
nutri'tionist *n.* an expert on nutrition.
nutri'tious *(-shůs) adj.* nourishing.
nu'tritive *adj.* of, relating to, providing, nutrition.

nuzzle *nuz'l, v.t.* and *v.i.* to press, rub, or caress with the nose: *The dog nuzzled my hand*:—*pr.p.* **nuzz'ling.**

nylon *nī'lon, n.* **1** a fibre, or a material, made from chemicals, used for clothes, ropes, bristles, etc. **2** (in *pl.*) stockings made of this material.

nymph *nimf, n.* **1** a Greek goddess of lower rank living in the sea, a river, tree, or hill, etc. **2** a beautiful girl. **3** a young insect that is of the same form as the adult.
nymphoma'nia *(-ȯ-mā'ni-ȧ) n.* overpowering sexual desire in women.
nymphoma'niac *adj., n.*

O

O, oh *ō, interj.* an exclamation expressing surprise, admiration, pain, longing, etc.
O, oh that I wish that.

oaf *ōf, n.* **1** a stupid fellow. **2** a lout, awkward person:—*pl.* **oafs.**
oaf'ish *adj.*

oak *ōk, n.* **1** a tree related to the beech, having acorns as fruit. **2** its hard wood.
oak'en (*old*) *adj.* made of oak.

oakum *ō'kum, n.* tarry ropes untwisted, used for stopping up the seams of wooden parts of ships.

oar *ōr, ör, n.* **1** a light pole with flat end (the blade) for rowing a boat. **2** an oarsman.
oars'man *n.* one who rows with an oar.
put one's oar in to interfere, meddle.

oasis *ō-ā'sis, n.* a fertile green spot in a sandy desert:—*pl.* **oases** *(-sēz).*

oast *ōst, n.* a large oven to dry hops.
oast'house *n.* a building containing this.

oatcake, oatmeal. See **oats.**

oath *ōth, n.* **1** a solemn promise (calling on God or something holy as witness) to speak the truth, to keep one's word, to be loyal, etc. **2** a swear-word:—*pl.* **oaths** *ōTHz, ōths.*

oats *ōts, n.pl.* or *n.sing.* **1** a cereal, a type of grass whose seeds are used as food. **2** the seeds.
oat'cake *n.* a thin hard cake of oatmeal.
oat'meal *n.* meal made by grinding oat grains.

obbligato *ob-li-gä'tō, n.* (*music*) an accompaniment forming an essential part of a composition:—*pl.* **obbliga'tos.**

obdurate *ob'dū-rit, adj.* stubborn; impossible to persuade to change, yield, etc.
ob'duracy, ob'durateness *ns.*

obedience, obedient. See **obey.**

obeisance *ō-bā'sȧns, n.* a bow or curtsy showing respect.

obelisk *ob'i-lisk, n.* **1** a tall, four-sided pillar with a pointed top. **2** a dagger (*def. 2*).

obese *ō-bēs', adj.* very fat, fleshy.
obes'ity *(-bēs)*, **obese'ness** *ns.*

obey *ō-bā', v.i.* to do what one is told to do.—*v.t.* **1** to do as one is told to by (a person, or in (a command): *Obey your father!*; *They refused to obey the order to surrender.* **2** to follow the guidance of (e.g. one's conscience, an impulse).
obedience *ō-bē'di-ėns, n.*
obe'dient *adj.* **obe'diently** *adv.*
See also **disobey.**

obituary *ō-bit'ū-ȧr-i, n.* a notice (e.g. in a newspaper) of a person's death, esp. an account of his career:—*pl.* **obit'uaries.**—Also *adj.*

object *ob'jikt, n.* **1** a thing able to be seen or felt, a material thing: *Name all the objects in the shop window.* **2** something to which attention is given: *The life of Nelson was the object of his study.* **3** aim, purpose: *His object was to make money so that he could travel abroad.* **4** a person or thing whose appearance causes scorn, amusement, pity, etc.: *a pitiful object with tear-stained face and ragged clothes.* **5** (*grammar*) the word(s) in a sentence standing for the person or thing on which the action of the verb is done: *In 'He hit me', 'me' is the object of the verb 'hit'*; also the word(s) following a preposition: *In 'under the table', '(the) table' is the object of 'under'.*—*v.i.* *(ob-jekt')* to feel, or express, disapproval of something (with *to*): *I object to smoking in theatres.*—*v.t.* to protest: *He objected that the instructions were not clear.*
objec'tion *n.* **1** the, an act of objecting. **2** a reason for disapproving.
objec'tionable *adj.* disagreeable, nasty.
objec'tive *adj.* **1** of, relating to, an object. **2** not involving, or not influenced by, personal feeling or consideration: *He tried to forget his own feelings and to take an objective view of the problem.* —*n.* an aim, goal: *The enemy objective was a fort on the other side of the valley.*
objec'tively *adv.* impartially.
objec'tiveness, objectiv'ity *ns.*
objec'tor *n.*
object lesson an example that should act as a warning.
no object not a problem: *Cost is no object.*

oblige *ō-blīj', v.t.* **1** to force, compel: *The police obliged him to leave*; *His work was so poor that I was obliged to dismiss him.* **2** (also *v.i.*) to do a favour or service for: *Could you oblige me by telling me what happened?*; *She obliged me with an account of the accident*:—*pr.p.* **oblig'ing.**
obligā'tion *(ob-li-gā')* *n.* **1** a promise, or duty, by which one is bound: *I am under an obligation to care for him.* **2** a debt of gratitude for a favour received: *I am under an obligation to you for your kindness*

to my son.

obligatory *ȯ-blig'ȧ-tȯ-ri, adj.* required by law, rule, custom, duty, etc. (with *on*): *Military service is obligatory in some countries*; *It is obligatory on us to leave the picnic area tidy.*

oblig'ing *(-līj') adj.* ready to help.

be obliged to be grateful: *I'm much obliged to you for your kindness*; *I'd be obliged if you'd make less noise.*

oblique *ȯ-blēk', adj.* **1** slanting, not vertical or horizontal. **2** not straight or direct: *He steered an oblique course*; *oblique references, hints, sneers.*

oblique'ly *adv.*

oblique'ness, **obli'quity** *(-bli'), ns.*

obliterate *ȯ-blit'ėr-āt, v.t.* **1** to blot out. **2** to destroy completely:—*pr.p.* **oblit'erating**.

obliterā'tion *n.*

oblivion *ȯ-bliv'i-ȯn, n.* **1** forgetfulness. **2** the state of being forgotten.

obliv'ious *adj.* not conscious, unaware (with *of* or *to*): *Deep in thought, he was oblivious of the crowds*; *He was so full of his plan that he was oblivious to our warnings.*

oblong *ob'long, adj.* long in one direction, longer than broad, esp. rectangular.—*n.* a figure longer than broad, esp. a rectangle.

obnoxious *ȯb-nok'shu̇s, adj.* objectionable, causing dislike or offence.

obnox'iously *adv.* **obnox'iousness** *n.*

oboe *ō'bō, n.* a high-pitched wooden wind instrument.

obscene *ȯb-sēn', adj.* **1** indecent, very coarse. **2** (*law*; of a book, etc.) tending to deprave.

obscene'ly *adv.* **obscene'ness** *n.*

obscen'ity *(-sen'i-ti) n.* **1** obsceneness. **2** an obscene remark, etc.:—*pl.* **obscen'ities**.

obscure *ȯb-skūr', adj.* **1** dark; not distinct; difficult to see. **2** not clear or easily understood. **3** unknown, not famous; humble: *an obscure painter.*—*v.t.* to make obscure; to hide: *A cloud obscured the sun*:—*pr.p.* **obscur'ing**.

obscure'ly *adv.* **obscure'ness** *n.*

obscur'ity *n.* **1** obscureness. **2** an instance of uncertain meaning:—*pl.* **obscur'ities**.

obsequies *ob'sė-kwiz, n.pl.* funeral rites.

obsequious *ȯb-sē'kwi-u̇s, adj.* trying to win favour by being too humble and ready to agree.

obse'quiously *adv.* **obse'quiousness** *n.*

observe *ȯb-zûrv', v.t.* **1** to notice. **2** to watch with attention. **3** to obey: *to observe the rules.* **4** to keep, or carry out, duly: *Please observe silence in the library*; *Few families observe Sunday in the traditional way.* **5** to say in passing (that).—*v.i.* **1** to take notice. **2** to remark (on):—*pr.p.* **obser'ving**.

obser'vance *n.* **1** the keeping of (a law, a special day, etc.). **2** a usual ceremony, practice, etc.: *Fasting is an observance required by several religions.*

obser'vant *adj.* (with *of*) **1** quick to notice: *A scientist must be observant.* **2** careful to conform to: *always observant of the law.*

observā'tion *n.* **1** the act, or power, of noticing. **2** watching or being watched: *She's in hospital for observation*; *The police kept him under observation.* **3** a remark.

observā'tional *adj.* found by, based on, observation.

obser'vatory *n.* a place for making observations of the stars, weather, etc.:—*pl.* **obser'vatories**.

obser'ver *n.* **1** one who observes. **2** one who is sent to listen to, but not take part in, discussions.

obsess *ȯb-ses', v.t.* to fill the mind of, worry continually: *The thought of the starving millions obsesses him.*

obsession *(-sesh'-) n.* **1** an idea or emotion from which one cannot free oneself. **2** the state of being obsessed.

obsess'ive *adj.* relating to (an) obsession.

obsess'ively *adv.*

obsolescent *ob-sȯ-les'ėnt, adj.* going out of use.

obsoles'cence *n.*

ob'solete *(-lēt) adj.* gone out of use.

obstacle *ob'stȧ-kl, n.* anything that stands in one's path or hinders progress.

obstacle race a race in which obstacles are laid in the course.

obstetrics *ȯb-stet'riks, n.sing.* midwifery, the science of helping women before, in, and after the birth of children.

obstetric'ian *(-trish'ȧn) n.* one skilled in obstetrics.

obstinate *ob'sti-nit, adj.* **1** stubborn and unreasonable. **2** stubborn, unyielding: *obstinate resistance.*

ob'stinately *adv.* **ob'stinacy** *n.*

obstreperous *ȯb-strep'ėr-u̇s, adj.* noisy; uncontrolled, unruly.

obstruct *ȯb-strukt', v.t.* **1** to block, close (e.g. a road, an artery). **2** to keep from passing or progressing, hold back (e.g. a person). **3** to shut off (e.g. a light, view).

obstruc'tion *n.* **1** the act of obstructing. **2** something that hinders progress or action.

obstruc'tive *adj.* tending to obstruct or hinder.

obtain *ob-tān'*, *v.t.* to get, gain possession of by effort.—*v.i.* to be in general use, to exist: *The custom of having several wives no longer obtains in Turkey*.

obtain'able *adj.* **obtain'ment** *n.*

obtrude *ob-trōōd'*, *v.t.* **1** to thrust (something unwanted on someone). **2** to push out.—*v.i.* to push oneself forward when not welcome:—*pr.p.* **obtrud'ing**.

obtru'sion *n.*

obtrusive *ob-trōō'siv*, *adj.* **1** pushing, impudent. **2** very noticeable.

obtuse *ob-tūs'*, *adj.* **1** blunt, not pointed. **2** stupid. **3** not very sensitive.

obtuse'ly *adv.* **obtuse'ness** *n.*

obtuse angle an angle greater than a right angle.

obverse *ob'vûrs*, *n.* **1** the side of a coin bearing the head or chief design. **2** the front.

obviate *ob'vi-āt*, *v.t.* to prevent, or get round, or remove (e.g. a necessity, a difficulty, a danger):—*pr.p.* **ob'viating**.

obvious *ob'vi-us*, *adj.* easily seen or understood, plain, evident.

ob'viously *adv.* **ob'viousness** *n.*

occasion *o-kā'zh(o)n*, *n.* **1** a time, an instance: *I'll forgive you on this occasion.* **2** a special event, function: *a great occasion.* **3** an opportunity: *I'll mention it if the occasion arises.* **4** a cause, reason: *What was the occasion of their quarrel?*; *I had no occasion to complain.*—*v.t.* to cause: *The quarrel was occasioned by a chance remark.*

occā'sional *adj.* **1** happening now and then. **2** for use when needed: *an occasional table.*

occā'sionally *adv.* now and then, not often.

occident *ok'si-dent*, *n.* (often *cap.*) the West.

occiden'tal *adj.*

occluded *o-klōō'did*, *adj.* (*weather*; of a front) composed of advancing cold air into which warm air has been driven.

occult *o-kult'*, *ok'ult*, *adj.* mysterious, magical, supernatural.

the occult things, or practices, of this nature.

occupy *ok'ū-pī*, *v.t.* **1** to take, seize (e.g. an enemy town). **2** to live in (e.g. a house). **3** to hold, fill (e.g. a position): *to occupy the post of mayor.* **4** to take up (time or space). **5** to employ, use the energies of: *to occupy oneself in gardening*; *to occupy one's mind with money problems*:—*pr.p.* **occ'upying**; *pa.p.* **occ'upied**.

occ'upancy *n.* act, or fact, or period, of occupying:—*pl.* **occ'upancies**.

occ'upant *n.* one who occupies.

occupā'tion *n.* **1** the state of being occupied or act of occupying. **2** possession (of a place). **3** work that takes up one's attentions for a time. **4** one's trade or job.

occupā'tional *adj.*

occ'upīer *n.* one who occupies a house, etc.

occupational disease, **hazard** a disease, injury, etc. associated with a particular job: *Lumbago is an occupational disease of gardeners.*

occupational therapy treatment of a disease or injury by work that helps recovery.

occur *o-kûr'*, *v.i.* **1** to happen. **2** to appear, be found: *Gold occurs in these rocks.* **3** to come into the mind (with *to*): *It suddenly occurred to me that you wouldn't know*; *Did it never occur to you to warn me?*; *An idea occurs to me*:—*pr.p.* **occurr'ing**; *pa.p.* **occurred'**.

occurr'ence *n.* **1** a happening, incident. **2** the act or fact of happening or being found: *the frequent occurrence of this species of animal in desert areas.*

ocean *ō'shan*, *n.* **1** the large stretch of salt water covering the greater part of the surface of the earth. **2** any of its five divisions (Atlantic, Pacific, Indian, Arctic, Antarctic). **3** a huge expanse or large quantity.

oceanic *ō-shi-an'ik*, *adj.* of, relating to, found in, the ocean.

oceanog'raphy *n.* the study of the oceans.

oceanog'rapher *n.* **oceanograph'ic** *adj.*

ocelot *os'i-lot*, *n.* an American animal resembling a small leopard.

och *oH*, *interj.* (*Scot.*) an exclamation expressing surprise, impatience, regret etc.

ochre *ō'kėr*, *n.* a fine yellow or red clay.

o'clock *ō-klok'*, *adv.* used in stating the time: *It was five o'clock (in the morning, afternoon).*

oct- *okt-*, **octa-** *-ta-*, *-ta-*, **octo-** *-tō-*, *-to-*, *-to-*, (as part of a word) eight.

oc'tagon *n.* a figure with eight sides and eight angles.

octag'onal *adj.*

octahē'dron *n.* a solid figure with eight faces.

oc'tane *n.* a chemical put in measured quantities into chemical mixtures; with these motor fuel is compared in order to give it an **octane number** (high numbers showing that the fuel is of high quality).

octave *ok'tiv, n.* (*music*) **1** a series of eight notes in a major or minor scale (e.g. from C to the C above). **2** the next note of the same name above or below a given note.

octavo *ȯk-tā'vō, n.* **1** the page size resulting when a sheet is folded into eight leaves. **2** a book having such a page size:—*abbrev.* **8vo**:—*pl.* **octā'vos**.

octet, **octette** *ok-tet', n.* **1** a group of eight (lines of poetry, singers, etc.). **2** a musical composition for eight instruments.

October *ȯk-tō'bėr, n.* the eighth month of the Roman year (which began in March), tenth in our calendar.

octogenarian *ok-tȯ-ji-nā'ri-ȧn, n.* one who is eighty years old.

octopus *ok'tȯ-pu̇s, n.* a sea creature with eight arms:—*pl.* **oc'topuses**.

ocular *ok'ū-lȧr, adj.* of, relating to, the eye.

oc'ulist *n.* a doctor skilled in diseases of the eye.

odd *od, adj.* **1** (of a number) leaving a remainder of one when divided by two. **2** remaining from a pair: *an odd glove.* **3** not one of a set or group. **4** left over, or extra. **5** (after a number) or more: *a hundred odd.* **6** unusual, queer, strange.

odd'ity *n.* **1** oddness, strangeness. **2** a queer person or thing:—*pl.* **odd'ities**.

odd'ly *adv.*

odd'ments *n.pl.* scraps, remnants.

odd'ness *n.*

odds *n.pl.* **1** chances, probability: *The odds are that he will succeed.* **2** (sometimes treated as *sing.*) difference; difference in favour of one side: *It makes no odds*; *They fought against heavy odds.* **3** in betting, the number of times greater the amount of money a person wins will be than the amount he bets.

odd'ball *n.* an eccentric person.

odd jobs jobs of different kinds, not part of regular work or employment.

at odds (**with**) quarrelling (with).

odds and ends objects, scraps, etc., of different kinds.

ode *ōd, n.* a poem written to a person or thing.

odium *ō'di-u̇m, n.* hatred; dislike aroused by a bad, or an unpopular, action: *He suffered the odium of having betrayed his leader.*

o'dious *adj.* hateful, disgusting.

o'diously *adv.* **o'diousness** *n.*

odour *ō'dȯr, n.* smell.

o'dorous *adj.* (sweet-) smelling.

o'dourless *adj.* without odour.

in bad, ill (or **good**) **odour** having a bad (or good) reputation (with a person or persons); out of (or in) favour.

Odyssey *od'is-i, n.* **1** a Greek poem by Homer telling of the ten years' wanderings of *Odysseus* (L. *Ulysses*). **2** (usu. without *cap.*) a long, wandering journey.

oesophagus *ē-sof'ȧ-gu̇s, n.* the gullet.

of *ov, ȯv, adv.* **1** from: *wide of the mark*; *within a week of his death.* **2** coming from (a group, etc.): *one of my hats, of my friends.* **3** showing material from which a thing is made: *a house of bricks.* **4** with, containing: *a book of poetry*; *a cup of water.* **5** showing part, amount, etc.: *two litres of milk.* **6** showing cause: *to die of hunger.* **7** showing some kind of losing or lack: *to get rid of*; *a land bare of trees.* **8** showing possession; belonging to: *This cup is the property of British Rail*; *the land of the Sioux tribe.* **9** showing quality possessed: *a man of courage.* **10** about, concerning: *to talk of many things.* **11** showing, depicting: *a picture of my father.* **12** indicating the connection between an action and its object: *the smoking of one cigarette.*

off *of, adv.* **1** away from the place or position mentioned: *He went off without saying goodbye*; *He took off his coat*; *She cut her hair off*; *He got off at Bayswater.* **2** away from a usual state: *His profits fell off*; *The milk has gone off.* **3** away from the usual working condition: *He shut the engine off*; *He took a day off.* **4** away: *The picnic is only a week off*; *The village is a mile off.* **5** completely: *Finish off your work.*—*adj.* **1** not to take place or continue; no longer available: *The engagement is off*; *Steak is off, sir.* **2** more distant; (in speaking of the side of a horse, vehicle) right. **3** remote, slight: *an off chance.* **4** not given to usual business: *the off season.* **5** not up to usual standard of health, work, etc.: *I'm having an off day.* **6** indicating the condition of not working: *The switch was in the off position.*—*prep.* **1** not on, away or down from: *It fell off the table*; *10% off the normal price.* **2** no longer wanting or in favour of: *I've gone off discos*; *He's off his food.*—*n.* (*cricket*) the off side of the wicket.

off'ing *n.* **1** the part of the sea some distance from the shore, but still in sight of it. **2** a place, or time, a short way off: *A policeman, a new job, is in the offing.*

off'-beat *adj.* unusual; eccentric.

off'-col'our *adj.* unwell.

offhand' *adv.* without preparing or investigating beforehand.—*adj.* (**off'-hand**) free and easy, casual, often lacking in politeness: *an offhand manner.*

off'-li'cence *n.* a licence to sell alcoholic liquors for drinking away from, not on, the premises.
off'-line *adj.* (*computers*) not under the direct control of the central unit.
off'-load *v.t.* to unload.
off'peak *adj.* relating to periods when demand, use, etc. are low.
off'print *n.* a reprint of a single article from a publication.
off'-putting *adj.* disconcerting.
off'set *v.t.* to counterbalance, make up for: *This gain offset some of his losses*:—*pr.p.* **off'setting**; *pa.p.* **off'set**.
off'shoot *n.* **1** a shoot that goes off from the main stem. **2** anything of smaller importance growing out of, or starting or arising from, something else.
off'shore *adj.* **1** in or on the sea close to the coast. **2** (of winds) blowing out to sea.
off'side *adj.* (of the side, etc. of a vehicle) right: *the offside headlight.*—*adv.*, *adj.* (*football*, etc.) in a position (not allowed) between the ball and the opponents' goal.—*n.* (*cricket*; usu. **off side**) the side of the field opposite to that on which the batsman stands.
off'spring *n.* child(ren), descendant(s).
off'-white' *adj.* not absolutely white.
badly, ill, off 1 poor. **2** (with *for*) not well supplied with.
be off to go away quickly.
off and on, on and off intermittently.
well off 1 rich. **2** (with *for*) well supplied with.

offal *of'ȧl*, *n.* **1** parts of an animal unfit to use as food. **2** entrails eaten as food (e.g. heart, liver). **3** anything worthless.

offend *ȯ-fend'*, *v.t.* **1** to displease, make angry. **2** to hurt the feelings of. **3** to be disagreeable to: *Cigarette smoke offends me.*—*v.i.* **1** to sin. **2** to act wrongly in face of a law, usual custom, etc.: *to offend against good manners*.
offence' *n.* **1** (any cause of) anger, displeasure, or hurt feelings. **2** a crime. **3** a sin.
offen'der *n.* one who offends.
offen'sive *adj.* **1** causing displeasure or hurt. **2** insulting. **3** disgusting. **4** used in attack: *an offensive weapon.*—*n.* **1** an act of attacking. **2** position of attack.
on the offensive attacking, or ready to attack.
give offence to cause displeasure.
take offence at to be made angry, or hurt, by.
take the offensive to attack first.

offer *of'ėr*, *v.t.* **1** to hold out, or put forward, for acceptance or refusal (e.g. a gift, goods for sale, payment, a suggestion). **2** to say that one is willing (to do something): *to offer to help.* **3** to give, put before someone (a choice, a chance, etc.) **4** to attempt (resistance).—*v.i.* to present itself, occur: *if the opportunity offers.*—*n.* **1** an act of offering; something offered (e.g. as a bargain). **2** a bid. **3** a proposal, something proposed.
off'ering *n.* **1** a gift. **2** a church collection.
off'ertory *n.* **1** the verses or anthem said or sung while the offerings of the congregation are being collected. **2** the money collected at a religious service:—*pl.* **off'ertories**.
on offer for sale, usu. cheaply.

offhand. See **off**.

office *of'is*, *n.* **1** a place where business, esp. clerical or administrative, is carried on. **2** such a place offering a particular service: *a booking-office, ticket-office.* **3** a room occupied by a particular member of a firm, etc.: *the manager's office.* **4** (in *pl.*) the rooms of a house where domestic, etc. work is done. **5** a duty, job. **6** a position of authority, esp. in the government. **7** (in *pl.*) act(s) of help or service: *We found a flat through the good/kind offices of a friend.*
off'icer *n.* **1** a person who carries out a public duty: *an officer of the law.* **2** a person holding a commission in the army, navy, or air force. **3** an office-bearer.
official *ȯ-fish'ȧl*, *adj.* **1** of, relating to, a position of authority: *official powers.* **2** publicly appointed or arranged. **3** done by, or given out by, those in power, or having the proper authority: *an official action, announcement.*—*n.* **1** one who holds an office. **2** a public officer, esp. one in a not very important position.
offic'ially *adv.* **1** as, because of being, an official: *He attended the ceremony officially.* **2** formally: *The key was officially handed over.* **3** according to what is said or professed: *Officially he is helping Smith; actually he is helping Lee.*
offic'iate *v.i.* to carry out the duties of an office on a particular occasion: *The Rev. John White will officiate at the funeral*:—*pr.p.* **offic'iating**.
off'ice-bear'er *n.* one who has a special duty to perform in a society, church, etc.
hold office to have a position in the government, etc.
in office in power, e.g. as the governing party.

officious *ȯ-fish'ủs*, *adj.* offering help, etc., where it is not wanted, interfering.

offing, offpeak, offspring, etc. See **off**.

oft (*poetic*) *oft,* **often** *of'n*, also *-tėn, advs.* many times, frequently.

ogle *ō'gl, v.t.* to eye (someone) impudently, by way of admiration.—Also *v.i.*:—*pr.p.* **o'gling**.

ogre *ō'gėr, n.* **1** a man-eating giant or monster of fairy tales. **2** a fierce, frightening person:—*fem.* **ō'gress**.

oh. See **O**.

oil *oil, n.* **1** a greasy liquid (of animal, vegetable, or mineral origin) which will dissolve in ether or alcohol but not in water. **2** (in *pl.*) oil-paint.—*v.t.* to smear, or supply, with oil.

oil'y *adj.* **1** of or like oil. **2** greasy. **3** (of a person, manner) too polite and agreeable:—*comp.* **oil'ier**; *superl.* **oil'iest**.

oil'ily *adv.* **oil'iness** *n.*

oil'cake *n.* cattle food made of linseed, etc., when most of the oil has been pressed out.

oil'cloth *n.* canvas made waterproof with linseed-oil paint, used as a covering.

oil'-colour *n.* a colouring substance mixed with oil.

oil'-field *n.* a district where mineral oil is found underground.

oil'-fired *adj.* burning oil as fuel.

oil'-paint *n.* oil-colour.

oil'-painting *n.* a picture painted in oil-colours.

oil'-rig. See **rig**.

oil'skin *n.* **1** cloth made waterproof by means of oil. **2** a garment of this.

oil'-well *n.* a hole drilled to obtain petroleum.

ointment *oint'mėnt, n.* any greasy substance put on the skin to heal injuries, etc.

O.K., **okay** *ō-kā', interj.* all right, agreed.—*v.t.* to pass as all right:—*pr.p.* **OK'ing**, **OKing**, **okay'ing**; *pa.p.* **OK'd**, **OKed**, **okayed'**.—Also *n.*, *adj.*, *adv.*

old *ōld, adj.* **1** advanced in age. **2** having a certain age: *He is ten years old.* **3** not new—having been long in existence, worn or worn out, out-of-date, old-fashioned. **4** belonging to the past; previous, former. **5** of long standing or experience.

olden *ōl'dėn,* (*poetic*) *adj.* of long ago.

old age the later part of life (**old age pension**, **pensioner** see **pension**).

old boy, **old girl** former pupil of a school.

old-fash'ioned *adj.* **1** in a style common in the past. **2** out-of-date.

old hand an experienced, practised person.

old'-hat' (*coll.*) *adj.* out-of-date.

Old English. See **English**.

old maid (*offensive*) an oldish woman unlikely ever to marry.

old master (a painting by) a great painter of the past.

Old Norse, **Old Testament**, **Old World**. See **Norse**, **testament**, **world**.

old'-ti'mer (*coll.*) *n.* an old man.

of old (from) long ago.

See also **elder**, **eldest**.

oleaginous *ō-li-aj'in-ůs, adj.* oily.

olfactory *ol-fak'tȯr-i, adj.* of, relating to, or used in, smelling.

oligarchy *ol'i-gär-ki, n.* government by a few people in power:—*pl.* **ol'igarchies**.

olive *ol'iv, n.* **1** a tree grown round the Mediterranean for its oily fruit. **2** its fruit. **3** a brownish-green colour like the unripe olive.

olive oil oil pressed from the fruit of the olive tree.

olive branch a symbol of peace.

Olympus *ō-lim'pus, n.* a mountain in Greece where the gods were thought to live.

Olym'piad (*-pi-ad*) *n.* **1** the period between celebrations of the ancient Olympic Games. **2** a celebration of the modern Olympic games.

Olym'pian *adj.* **1** god-like. **2** great, splendid.

Olym'pic *adj.*

Olympic games athletic contests held every four years at different centres since 1896, named after games held every four years in ancient Greece.

ombudsman *om'boodz-mån, n.* an official who investigates complaints by individuals against the government or public authorities:—*pl.* **om'budsmen**.

omega *ō'mi-gå, n.* **1** the last letter of the Greek alphabet. **2** the end.

omelet(te) *om'(i-)lit, n.* a dish made of beaten eggs, herbs, etc. cooked in a frying pan.

omen *ō'mėn, n.* a sign of a future event.

om'inous (*om'*) *adj.* suggesting future trouble.

om'inously *adv.* **om'inousness** *n.*

ill'-o'mened *adj.* unlucky.

of good (**ill**) **omen** telling beforehand of good (or bad) luck.

omit *ō-mit', v.t.* **1** to leave out. **2** to fail to do, etc.):—*pr.p.* **omitt'ing**; *pa.p.* **omitt'ed**.

omiss'ion *n.* **1** the act of omitting. **2** a thing omitted.

omni- *om-ni-,* (as part of a word) all.

omnibus *om'ni-bůs, n.* the orig. form of **bus**:—*pl.* **om'nibuses**.—*adj.* containing, or dealing with, many things: *an omnibus edition containing four novels.*

omnipotent *om-nip'ȯ-tėnt, adj.* having

unlimited, complete, power or authority.
omnip'otence *n.* **omnip'otently** *adv.*
omnipresent *om-ni-prez'ėnt, adj.* present everywhere.
omnipres'ence *n.*
omniscient *om-nis'i-ėnt, adj.* knowing everything.
omnis'cience *n.* **omnis'ciently** *adv.*
omnivorous *om-niv'ȯr-ůs, adj.* feeding on both plant and animal food.

on *on, prep.* **1** touching, fixed to, covering, etc., the upper or outer side of: *on the table; the ring on his finger.* **2** at or in: *on the left; on the continent.* **3** in, into (a boat, bus, train, etc.). **4** at, during (a particular time): *on August 30; on Monday.* **5** towards: *The army advanced on the town.* **6** for (a particular object): *Spend the money on clothes; Have pity on me.* **7** about: *a book on rats.* **8** in, into (a state, situation): *on sale; on guard.* **9** by (a means or medium): *a tune played on the violin, a play on television.* **10** after, at the point of: *On arriving, he rang his son.—adv.* **1** in, into, position for being worn: *Put on your gloves.* **2** further, forwards: *They walked on; Read on; from then on.* **3** into the working position: *Turn on the light.* **4** into a bus, boat, train, etc.: *Get on at Crewe Road.—adj.* **1** in progress; going ahead as planned; possible: *Is the match on?* **2** in the state of working: *Is the television on?—n.* (*cricket*) the on side.
onward *on'wȧrd, adj.* going forward: *the onward march, path.—adv.* (also **on'-wards**) towards a point ahead, forward.
on'-li'cence *n.* a licence to sell alcoholic drinks for drinking in the building where they are sold.
on'-line *adj.* (*computers*) under the direct control of the central unit.
on side (*cricket*) the side of the field on which the batsman stands.
on and off. See **off**.
on and on ever further or more.
on to, on'to 1 to a position on. **2** in, into, a position of knowing the truth about.

once *wuns, adv.* **1** a single time. **2** at a time in the past. **3** at all, at any time: *If he once slipped, he would be killed.—conj.* as soon as: *Once (it had been) oiled, the lock worked easily.*
once'-over *n.* a quick appraisal.
at once without delay.
for once as an exception.
once (and) for all once only and finally.
once in a while occasionally, rarely.
once upon a time at a time in the past.

oncoming *on'kum-ing, adj.* advancing, approaching.

one *wun, adj.* **1** a single. **2** united; having the same opinion, qualities, etc.—*n.* **1** the number showing unity (1 or I). **2** a single person or thing: *Which one(s) do you like?* **3** the age of one year.—*pron.* any person, esp. the person speaking: *If a stranger asks one one's name, one need not answer.*
one another each other.
one'-off' (*coll.*) *adj.* made, intended, etc. for one occasion only.
oneself' *pron.* emphatic or reflexive form of *one*: *One should avoid telling lies oneself; One generally enjoys talking about oneself.*
one'-sid'ed *adj.* **1** larger, etc., on one side than on the other. **2** unfair, unjust: *a one-sided view of the subject.*
one'-time *adj.* former.
one'-way *adj.* proceeding, or permitting, movement in one direction only.
all one just the same, making no difference.
at one in agreement.
one by one singly, in order.
one up on (*coll.*) in a position of advantage over.

onerous. See **onus**.

ongoing *on'gō-ing, adj.* ever-continuing.

onion *un'yȯn, n.* (a bulb that can be eaten of) a plant of the lily family.

onlooker *on'look-ėr, n.* a spectator, esp. by chance.

only *ōn'li, adj.* (used before a noun) **1** without others of the kind: *an only son, child; We were the only ones to say thank you.* **2** without others worthy to be counted, the best: *This is the only way to make bread.—adv.* **1** not more than: *only two cups; only six yards.* **2** alone, solely: *I can tell it to you only.* **3** no longer ago than: *only yesterday.* **4** showing the sole or most important result: *You will only annoy him; Practice can only improve you.* **5** merely: *I only wanted to help.—conj.* except that; but: *He would come, only he is being sent abroad.*
only too very: *only too glad.*

onomatopoeia *on-ȯ-mat-ȯ-pē'ȧ, n.* the formation of words in imitation of the sound of the object or action to be named.
onomatopoe'ic *adj.*

onrush *on'rush, n.* a rush forward.

onset *on'set, n.* **1** fierce attack. **2** a beginning: *the onset of a cold.*

onslaught *on'slöt, n.* an attack, onset.

onto. See **on**.

onus *ō'nůs, n.* **1** responsibility. **2** blame.
on'erous *(on', ōn') adj.* requiring much work or effort: *an onerous task.*

onward(s). See **on**.

onyx *on'iks, n.* a precious stone with layers of different colours.

oodles *o͞o'dlz,* (*coll.*) *n.pl.* or *n.sing.* an abundance.

ooze *o͞oz, n.* **1** slimy mud. **2** a gentle flow.—*v.i.* **1** to flow gently. **2** to leak out very slowly.—Also *v.t.*: *His knee oozed blood*:—*pa.p.* **ooz'ing**.
ooz'y *adj.*:—*comp.* **ooz'ier**; *superl.* **ooz'iest**.
ooz'iness *n.*

opacity. See **opaque**.

opal *ō'pȧl, n.* a precious stone, milky white with changing rainbow colours.
opales'cent *adj.* iridescent like an opal.
opales'cence *n.*

opaque *ō-pāk', adj.* **1** not allowing light to pass through. **2** not able to be seen through. **3** obscure, not clear.
opacity *ō-pas'i-ti,* **opaque'ness** *ns.*

open *ō'p(ė)n, adj.* **1** not shut; not closed, fastened or covered. **2** free to be entered, etc.: *open to the public.* **3** not enclosed. **4** free from obstruction; free from ice or frost. **5** widely spaced. **6** not kept secret or concealed. **7** frank, candid.—*v.t.* **1** to make open. **2** to begin: *He opened the meeting.*—Also *v.i.*—*n.* clear space.
o'penly *adv.* **o'penness** *n.*
o'pening *n.* **1** an open place, gap, break. **2** a beginning. **3** a chance or opportunity (for).
o'pener *n.* something, esp. a tool, that opens.
open air places out of doors.
o'pencast *adj.* (of mining) on the surface, not underground.
open-end'ed *adj.* with no limits or restrictions.
o'pen-hand'ed *adv.* giving freely, generous.
o'pen-heart'ed *adj.* frank and kindly.
o'pen-mind'ed *adj.* willing to consider new ideas.
o'pen-plan' *adj.* having few, or no, internal walls, partitions, etc.
open question a matter not decided, still unsettled.
open sandwich a single slice of bread with food placed on top of it.
open verdict a verdict saying that a crime has been committed but not naming a criminal.
Open University a British university for students at home, with no fixed entry qualifications, whose teaching is done by correspondence, radio, television and telephone.
o'penwork *n.* ornamental work, in any material having openings through it.—Also *adj.*
open to 1 likely to receive or undergo: *open to attack, criticism.* **2** ready to be influenced by: *open to suggestions.*
with open arms cordially.

opera[1] *op'ėr-ȧ, n.* a musical drama in which the dialogue is sung.
operat'ic *adj.* **operat'ically** *adv.*
operett'a *n.* a short, light musical drama.
opera glasses binoculars for use in the theatre.

opera[2]. See **opus**.

operate *op'ėr-āt, v.i.* **1** to act, work. **2** to bring about an effect. **3** to exert influence (on, upon). **4** to carry out military acts. **5** (*surgery*) to cut a part of the body in order to undo the effect of disease, injury, deformity (with *on, upon*).—*v.t.* **1** to work (e.g. a machine). **2** to direct, conduct, run:—*pr.p.* **op'erating**.
op'erable *adj.* (*surgery*) that can be operated on:—*opp.* **inoperable**.
operā'tion *n.* **1** an action, esp. planned. **2** the process, or way of working. **3** a military, etc. campaign. **4** (*surgery*) a cutting of a part of the body in order to restore health or normal condition.
operā'tional *adj.* **1** of, relating to, operations. **2** working in, or forming part of, an operation of war. **3** ready for action.
op'erative *adj.* **1** working, in action. **2** (of rule, law) in force, having effect:—*opp.* **inoperative**.—*n.* a workman in a factory.
op'erator *n.* one who operates (esp. the connecting equipment in a telephone exchange).
in operation in force, in action, operative.

operetta. See **opera**[1].

ophthal'mic *of-thal'mik, adj.* of, relating to, the eye.
ophthalmol'ogy *n.* the study of the eye.
ophthalmol'ogist *n.*

opiate. See **opium**.

opinion *ȯ-pin'yȯn, n.* **1** what a person thinks or believes on a matter. **2** a professional judgment given formally by a lawyer, doctor, etc. **3** what one thinks of the value (of someone or something): *I have a high,* or *low, opinion of Jack's work.*
opin'ionated *adj.* having strong opinions and refusing to give them up.
a matter of opinion a question on which different views are held.
be of the opinion that to think that.
have no opinion of to have a very low opinion of, think very little of.

opium *ō'pi-ūm, n.* the dried juice of a type of poppy, containing materials used as drugs.

opiate *ō'pi-it*, *n.* **1** a medicine containing opium used to make one sleep. **2** anything that dulls mind or feelings.

opossum *ȯ-pos'ùm*, *n.* one of the marsupials, a small animal of America or Australia.

opponent. See **oppose**.

opportune *op'ȯr-tūn*, *adj.* **1** coming at the right moment: *Without this opportune help, we should have had to give up.* **2** convenient: *an opportune moment*:—*opp.* **inopportune**.

opp'ortunely *adv.* **opp'ortuneness** *n.*

opportunism (*op'*, or *-tūn'*) *n.* the practice of acting, etc. so as to take best advantage of the current circumstances, rather than according to a consistent policy.

opportunist (*op'*, or *-tūn'*) *n.* and *adj.*

opportun'ity *n.* a chance (to do something):—*pl.* **opportun'ities**.

oppose *ȯ-pōz'*, *v.t.* **1** to resist, fight against, by force or argument. **2** to act, or compete, against: *Who is opposing him in the election?* **3** to set (one force) against another: *He opposed his wits to his enemy's strength.*—*v.i.* to be, or act, on the opposing side:—*pr.p.* **oppos'ing**.

opponent *ȯ-pō'nėnt*, *n.* one who fights or strives against a person or course of action.

oppos'er *n.*

opposite *op'ȯ-zit*, *adj.* (often with *to*) **1** in a position facing, face to face, or on the other side: *the opposite house to ours.* **2** opposed: *the opposite side in a fight.* **3** as different as possible: *in opposite directions*; *the opposite effect.*—*prep.* facing: *the house opposite mine*; *They sat opposite each other.*—*adv.* in a position facing: *He sat opposite.*—*n.* something that is as different as possible: *Hate is the opposite of love.*

opposition *op-ȯ-zish'(ȯ)n*, *n.* **1** the act of opposing. **2** contrast. **3** those who resist or oppose. **4** (*cap.*) the political party opposed to the party in power.

opposite number the person corresponding to oneself in a different group.

as opposed to as distinct, separate, different, from.

be opposed to to disapprove of.

opposite to used similarly to **opposite**, *prep.*

oppress *ȯ-pres'*, *v.t.* **1** to weigh down; to depress: *The thought of his danger constantly oppresses me.* **2** to treat cruelly, govern harshly.

oppress'or *n.*

oppress'ive *adj.* **1** harsh, heavy, unjust. **2** (of weather) heavy, tiring.

oppress'ively *adv.* **oppress'iveness** *n.*

oppress'ion *(-presh'(ȯ)n)* *n.* **1** the act of oppressing. **2** the state or feeling of being oppressed.

opprobrium *ȯ-prō'bri-ùm*, *n.* **1** the disgrace following shameful behaviour. **2** contempt aroused by some action.

oppro'brious *adj.* expressing scorn: *opprobrious names, remarks.*

opt. See **option**.

optic, **-al** *op'tik*, *-ȧl*, *adjs.* of, relating to, sight or optics.

optician *op-tish'ȧn*, *n.* one who makes or sells spectacles, etc.

op'tics *n.sing.* the science of light.

optimism *op'ti-mizm*, *n.* the habit of taking a hopeful view of things; hopefulness:—*opp.* **pessimism**.

op'timist *n.* one who is always hopeful.

optimis'tic *adj.* **optimis'tically** *adv.*

op'timum *adj.* best: *optimum conditions for growth.*—Also *n.*

option *op'sh(ȯ)n*, *n.* **1** act of choosing. **2** power of choosing. **3** choice; something that may be chosen. **4** a right of buying or selling at a fixed price, to be exercised within a time-limit.

opt *opt*, *v.i.* to choose, decide (to do, for).

op'tional *adj.* left to choice; not compulsory.

op'tionally *adv.*

opt out (with *of*) to decide not to do something or take part in something.

opulent *op'ū-lėnt*, *adj.* **1** wealthy. **2** luxurious, costly looking. **3** luxuriant.

op'ulence *n.* **op'ulently** *adv.*

opus *ō'pùs*, *op'*, *n.* a work, esp. a musical composition:—*pl.* **op'era**.

or *ör*, *conj.* **1** used in expressing alternatives, the one excluding the other: *Are you going or aren't you?* **2** and not: *I don't ski or skate.* **3** introducing a choice: *I'd like a sandwich or bun or something.*

oracle *or'ȧ-kl*, *n.* **1** in ancient times, an answer (usu. puzzling), supposed to come from a god, given by a priest or priestess in response to a question esp. about the future. **2** a special place where such answers were given. **3** a person of great wisdom. **4** a wise saying. **5** (*cap.*) the teletext service of the Independent Broadcasting Service.

oracular *ȯ-rak'ū-lȧr*, *adj.*

oral *ō'rȧl*, *ö'*, *adj.* **1** of, relating to, the mouth. **2** spoken, not written.

o'rally *adv.*

orange *or'inj*, *n.* **1** a juicy gold-coloured fruit. **2** the tree on which it grows. **3** a reddish-yellow colour.—Also *adj.*

orangeade *or-in-jād'*, *n.* a drink made with oranges.

orang-utan *o-rang'-ōō-tan'*, *ö'rang-ōō'tan*, *n.* a large man-like ape, reddish brown in colour, living in trees in Sumatra and Borneo.

oration. See **orator**.

orator *or'ȧ-tȯr*, *n.* a public speaker, esp. one with power to touch the feelings and persuade.
or'atory *n.* **1** the art of public speaking. **2** eloquent public speaking. **3** a small chapel, etc. for private prayer:—*pl.* **or'-atories**.
orator'ical *adj.* **orator'ically** *adv.*
oration *ö-rā'sh(ȯ)n*, *n.* a formal speech, esp. one in fine language.
orate' (*humorous*) *v.i.* to make an oration:—*pr.p.* **orat'ing**.

oratorio *or-ȧ-tō'ri-ō*, *-tö'*, *n.* a sacred, usu. biblical, story set to music:—*pl.* **orato'-rios**.

orb *örb*, *n.* **1** a heavenly body (e.g. moon, star). **2** a globe carried as part of a monarch's regalia. **3** (*poetic*) the eye.

orbit *ör'bit*, *n.* **1** the path in which a heavenly body moves round another (e.g. the path of the earth round the sun). **2** the path in which a satellite, etc., goes round the earth, etc.—*v.t.* and *v.i.* **1** to go round in orbit. **2** to circle.
or'bital *adj.*

Orcadian *ör-kā'di-ȧn*, *adj.*, *n.* (an inhabitant or native) of Orkney.

orchard *ör'chȧrd*, *n.* a garden of fruit trees.

orchestra *ör'kės-trȧ*, *n.* **1** the part of a theatre in which the musicians are placed. **2** a company or group of musicians playing together under a conductor.
orches'tral *adj.* (of music) for, or performed by, an orchestra.
or'chestrate *v.t.* **1** to arrange (a piece of music) for performance by an orchestra. **2** to organise so as to achieve the best effect:—*pr.p.* **or'chestrating**.

orchid *ör'kid*, *n.* a plant with a rich, showy flower.

ordain *ör-dān'*, *v.t.* **1** to make a law, rule, or decision (that). **2** (of God, fate) to destine. **3** to appoint a (person) by means of a church ceremony to be priest, minister, or elder.
or'dinance *n.* something ordered by person(s) in authority; a law.
ordinā'tion *n.* receiving into the Christian ministry or the post of elder.

ordeal *ör'dēl*, *ör-dēl'*, *n.* a hard trial or test, painful experience.

order *ör'dėr*, *n.* **1** arrangement in space or time: *Write the names in any order; alphabetical order; the order of events.* **2** normal, fixed, tidy or efficient arrangement or condition: *Have you left your room in order?* (*opp.* **disorder**). **3** system, method. **4** peaceful condition: *The police keep law and order.* **5** a rule. **6** a command. **7** a direction to make or supply goods, or the goods supplied. **8** a written instruction to pay money: *a postal order.* **9** a group, grade, class, or kind: *the lower orders of animals; courage of a high order.* **10** a body of persons of the same profession, etc. **11** a monastic society: *the Franciscan order of monks.* **12** (in *pl.*) the office and dignity of a priest or clergyman. **13** an honour given by a monarch, etc.: *the Order of the Garter.*—*v.t.* **1** to arrange. **2** to give an order for. **3** to command.
or'derly *adj.* **1** in good order. **2** well behaved, quiet: *an orderly crowd:*—*opp.* **disorderly**.—*n.* **1** a soldier who carries official messages and orders for his superior officer. **2** an attendant (e.g. in a hospital):—*pl.* **or'derlies**.
or'derliness *n.*
holy orders. See **holy**.
working order. See **work**.
in order **1** correct according to what is regularly done: *It is in order to end the meeting now.* **2** (with *to*, *that*) for the purpose mentioned: *Arrive early in order that we can start promptly*; *He arrived early in order to start promptly*.
on order having been ordered but not yet supplied.
out of order **1** not following correct procedure. **2** not working; not working properly.
take orders to be ordained as a priest or minister.

ordinal *ör'din-ȧl*, *adj.* showing order in a series.—*n.* an ordinal number (e.g. first, second, third, etc.).

ordinance, **ordination**. See **ordain**.

ordinary *ör'di-nȧ-ri*, *adj.* **1** usual, common, normal. **2** not specially good.
or'dinarily normally, as a rule.
in ordinary (of e.g. a king's doctor) in regular and usual service.
out of the ordinary unusual.
See also **extraordinary**.

ordnance *örd'nȧns*, *n.* military supplies—ammunition, cannon, etc.
Ordnance Survey (a government department, orig. under military supervision, concerned with) the production of official detailed maps of Great Britain and N. Ireland.

ore *ōr*, *ör*, *n.* naturally occurring rock or mineral from which metal(s), etc. can be obtained.

oregano *or-i-gä'nō, n.* a type of wild marjoram, used as seasoning.

organ *ör'gȧn, n.* **1** (in an animal or plant) a part that does a special job (e.g. heart, lung, leaf). **2** a means of spreading information or opinions (e.g. newspaper). **3** a large musical instrument similar to a piano in which sound is produced by air forced through pipes; a similar instrument without pipes.

organ'ic *adj.* **1** of, relating to organ(s) of animal or plant. **2** originating from living creatures: *organic remains from past ages.* **3** (*chemistry*) containing carbon. **4** (of food) grown without the use of artificial fertilizers. **5** consisting of parts all having their own function.

or'ganise *v.t.* **1** to form into a whole where each part has its own function. **2** to form a trade union, party, etc. among (a group of people). **3** to arrange: *to organise a jumble sale*:—*pr.p.* **or'ganising**.

or'ganised *adj.*

organisā'tion *n.* **1** the act of organising. **2** a body of people working together for a purpose: *a business organisation.*

or'ganism *n.* a living animal or plant.

or'ganist *n.* one who plays an organ.

organ grinder a street musician who plays an organ by turning a crank.

organic chemistry chemistry of compounds containing carbon.

See also **disorganise**, **inorganic**.

organdie *ör'gȧn-di, n.* a fine thin stiff muslin.

organic, organism, etc. See **organ**.

orgasm *ör'gazm, n.* the climax of sexual excitement.

orgy *ör'ji, n.* **1** a wild party or other unrestrained celebration. **2** a bout of indulgence in something: *an orgy of buying*:—*pl.* **or'gies**.

oriel *ō'r'i-ėl, ör', n.* a window in a recess built out from a wall.—Also *adj.*

orient *ōr'i-ėnt, ör', n.* (*cap.*) (the countries of) the East.—*v.t.* **1** to set (e.g. oneself, a building) facing (to, or towards, the east or other direction). **2** (with *oneself*) to find the direction in which one is facing, one's position. **3** (with *oneself*) to come to understand new, at first bewildering, surroundings and way of life.

orien'tal *adj.* (often *cap.*) in or from the East.—*n.* (*cap.*) a native of the East (usu. the Far East).

or'ientate *v.t.* to orient:—*pr.p.* **or'ientating**.

orientā'tion *n.* **1** position with regard to the points of the compass. **2** the act or process of finding one's position in a place, or in a society.

orienteer'ing *n.* the sport of making one's way across country with the help of map and compass.

orifice *or'i-fis, n.* a mouth-like opening.

origami *or-i-gä'mi, n.* the Japanese art of folding paper into decorative shapes.

origin *or'i-jin, n.* **1** beginning. **2** the source from which anything first comes. **3** parentage.

orig'inal *adj.* **1** existing from, or at, the beginning: *This part is the original building.* **2** able to have new ideas: *an original mind.* **3** new and different.—*n.* **1** the actual painting, etc., made by an artist, etc., not a copy. **2** the real person, place, etc., on whom, which, a picture, description, is based. **3** a person with original mind. **4** an odd person.

orig'inally *adv.*

original'ity *n.* **1** ability to think, or to do things, without copying others. **2** newness, freshness.

orig'ināte *v.t.* to bring into being; to begin.—*v.i.* to begin:—*pr.p.* **orig'inating**.

original sin. See **sin**.

oriole *ōr'i-ōl, ör', n.* a golden-yellow bird.

ornament *ör'nȧ-mėnt, n.* **1** anything that adds, or is intended to add, beauty. **2** a decorative object for display rather than use.—*v.t.* (*-ment'*) to adorn, decorate.

ornament'al *adj.* intended as, used for, ornament; decorative.

ornamentā'tion *n.*

ornate *ör-nāt', adj.* much decorated or ornamented.

ornithology *ör-ni-thol'ȯ-ji, n.* the science and study of birds.

ornitholog'ical *adj.*

ornithol'ogist *n.* one who makes a special study of birds.

orography *ȯr-og'rȧ-fi, adj.* the scientific study of mountains.

orphan *ör'fȧn, n.* a child (or a young animal) that has lost mother and father (or sometimes one parent only).—Also *adj.*

or'phanage (*-nij.*) *n.* a home for orphans.

orth(o)- *ör-th(ō)-*, (as part of word) right, straight, correct.

orthodontics *ör-thō-don'tiks, n.sing.* the correction of abnormalities in the teeth or jaw.

orthodon'tist *n.*

orthodox *ör'thȯ-doks, adj.* **1** holding views and beliefs (esp. in religion) that are the same as those generally held in one's country, etc. (**Orthodox Church** an esp. east European branch of the Christian church, that rejects papal supremacy). **2** (of views) usual, accepted. **3** (of behaviour) conventional, proper.

or'thodoxy *n.* holding of the commonly accepted opinions, esp. in religion.

orthography *ör-thog'rȧ-fi, n.* the art or practice of spelling words correctly.

orthopaedics *ör-thō-pē'diks, n.sing.* the branch of medicine dealing with diseases of, and injuries to, the bones, orig. esp. in children.

orthopae'dic *adj.*

oscillate *os'i-lāt, v.i.* **1** to swing to and fro, as the pendulum of a clock does. **2** to go back and forth between two limits. **3** to vibrate. **4** (of an alternating current) to undergo frequent, regular reverses of direction. **5** to vary, fluctuate, be undecided:—*pr.p.* **os'cillating.**

oscillā'tion *n.*

oscill'oscope *n.* an instrument that records electrical oscillations on a screen.

osculation *os-kū-lā'sh(ȯ)n, n.* kissing.

osier *ōz'i-ėr, n.* willow twigs used in making baskets.

osmosis *oz-mō'sis, n.* the passing of a less concentrated solution into one more so, through a porous barrier.

osprey *os'prā, n.* a hawk that feeds on fish.

ossify *os'i-fī, v.t.* to make into bone or harden into bone-like substance.—Also *v.i.*:—*pr.p.* **oss'ifying**; *pa.p.* **oss'ified.**

ossificā'tion *n.*

ostensible *ȯs-ten'si-bl, adj.* (of e.g. a reason) pretended, claimed: *Illness was the ostensible reason for his absence, laziness the real one.*

osten'sibly *adv.* according to the impression deliberately given.

ostentatious *os-tėn-tā'shus, adj.* making a great show intended to impress or attract notice: *his ostentatious spending and style of living; his ostentatious refusal of a reward.*

ostentā'tion, ostentā'tiousness *ns.*

ostantā'tiously *adv.*

osteo- *os-ti-ō-,* (as part of a word) bone.

os'teopath *n.* a person who practises **osteop'athy** *(-op'-)*, a method of treating pain, etc. using manipulation to ensure that all bones and parts of the body are in the correct position.

ostracise *os'trȧ-sīz, v.t.* to refuse to accept (someone) in society or a group: *His class ostracised him after he betrayed his friend to the teacher*:—*pr.p.* **os'tracising.**

os'tracism *(-sizm) n.*

ostrich *os'trich, n.* a large, swift-running bird, whose feathers are valuable.

other *u*TH*'ėr, adj.* **1** the second of two: *Give me my other glove.* **2** the remaining: *I'll take the baby: you take the other children.* **3** different: *He was not ill: he stayed away for some other reason.* **4** additional, more.—Also *pron.*: *one twin but not the other; two scientific subjects and one other; these ones and (some/any) others.*

oth'erwise *adv.* **1** in another, different way: *I agree, but he thinks otherwise.* **2** in other respects: *He's bald but otherwise good-looking.* **3** under other conditions: *I'm engaged—I would have helped otherwise.*—*conj.* or else: *Go now, otherwise you'll miss the bus.*

every other each alternate or second.

other than except: *I know of no reason for his failure other than bad luck.*

no, none, other than the very (person, thing) mentioned.

the other day, week, etc. **1** a day, week, etc., or two ago. **2** not long ago.

otter *ot'ėr, n.* a water animal living on fish, of the weasel family.

ottoman *ot'ȯ-mȧn, n.* a low stuffed seat, or couch, usu. without a back.

ought *öt, v.* (used with other verbs) **1** indicating duty or need: *We ought to visit them; I ought to wash my hair, oughtn't I?* **2** indicating probability, likelihood, etc.: *The total ought to be more than that; He ought to arrive by 6.00 p.m.*

ounce *owns, n.* **1** a weight—one-sixteenth of a pound (28.35 grammes). **2** a small quantity.

our, ours, ourselves. See **we.**

oust *owst, v.t.* **1** to drive out (from position or possession). **2** to take the place of.

out *owt, adv.* **1** not within or inside. **2** not at home. **3** from inside; in or into the open air. **4** away from one's home, etc.: *to set out for the office.* **5** no longer in office, in the game, etc. **6** no longer in fashion. **7** no longer hidden; available, published: *The secret is out; The book will be out next week.* **8** as fully as possible; completely: *They talked the matter out; tired out.* **9** not burning: *The fire is out.* **10** loudly and clearly: *to shout out.* **11** on strike. **12** inaccurate, incorrect: *Our calculations are out.*—*adj.* that is out, outside, or coming out (often as part of a noun; see **out-**):—*comp.* **out'er**; *superl.* **out'ermost, out'most.**

out'er *adj.* (see above; used only before a noun) on the outside; further out.

out'ermost, out'most *adjs.* (see above) **1** furthest from the inside. **2** most distant.

out'ing *n.* a trip, walk, etc., out of doors.

out'ward *owt'wȧrd, adj.* **1** on the outside or surface. **2** away from a place.—*adv.* (also **out'wards**) toward the outside.

out'wardly *adv.* **1** on the outside. **2** in

appearance: *He is sad at heart, but outwardly he is cheerful.*

out-and-out *adj.* thorough, complete: *an out-and-out rogue.*

out of 1 from something that contains; from the inside of: *out of the box, room, house, country,* etc. **2** from a larger quantity, etc.: *four out of five.* **3** not in. **4** completely lacking: *We are out of coal.* **5** foaled by. **6** indicating material used: *He made it out of paper.* **7** because of: *I asked out of curiosity.*

out(-)of(-)date. See **date**[1].

out of doors 1 outside the house. **2** in the open air.—*adj.* **out'-of-door(s)'**.

out of the way unusual.—*adj.* **out'-of-the-way'** remote.

out- *owt-, pfx.* (1) before nouns and adjectives, meaning away from, not inside, the place, thing, mentioned or understood: *outhouse, outboard, outlying*; (2) showing some kind of outward movement: *outburst, outlet*; (3) before some verbs showing that the action goes beyond a previous or a normal action: *outbid, outshine.*

outback *owt'bak, n.* in Australia, country or settlements far away from the towns on the coast.

outbid *owt-bid', v.t.* to offer a higher price than:—*pr.p.* **outbidd'ing**; *pa.t* and *pa.p.* **outbid'**.

outboard *owt'bōrd, -börd, adj.*: **outboard motor** one fixed to the outside of a boat.

outbreak *owt'brāk, n.* the breaking out or beginning (of e.g. anger, disease, war).

outbuilding *owt'bil-ding, n.* a building attached to, or near, a main building.

outburst *owt'bûrst, n.* a bursting out (of e.g. cheering, anger).

outcast *owt'käst, n.* one who is driven away from society or home.

outclass *owt-kläs', v.t.* to be so much better than (someone, something) as to seem in a different class.

outcome *owt'kum, n.* the result (of e.g. efforts, discussion).

outcrop *owt'krop, n.* **1** part of a rock that can be seen at the surface of the ground. **2** an outbreak.

outcry *owt'krī, n.* a loud cry of anger, distress, protest, etc.

outdated *owt-dā'tid, adj.* out-of-date.

outdistance *owt-dis'tans, v.t.* to leave far behind (e.g. in race):—*pr.p.* **outdis'tancing**.

outdo *owt-dōō', v.t.* to do better than:—*pr.t. 3rd pers. sing.* **outdoes'** *(-duz')*; *pa.t.* **outdid'**; *pa.p.* **outdone'**.

outdoor *owt'dōr, -dör, adj.* outside the house; in the open air.

outdoors' *adv.*

outer, outermost. See **out**.

outface *owt-fās', v.t.* to confront or defy successfully:—*pr.p.* **outfac'ing**.

outfall *owt'föl, n.* the place where water from a river, sewer, etc., comes out.

outfield *owt'fēld, n.* **1** any open field at a distance from the farm buildings. **2** in cricket or baseball, the outer part of the field.

outfit *owt'fit, n.* **1** a set of (esp. selected and matching) clothes. **2** the equipment and clothes needed for a purpose. **3** (*coll.*) a firm, company; a group, gang.

out'fitter *n.* one who sells outfits, esp. clothing.

outflank *owt-flangk', v.t.* to pass round the side of and get behind or beyond (an enemy force, etc.).

outgoing *owt'gō-ing, n.* (in *pl.*) expenditure.—*adj.* **1** leaving. **2** retiring from office. **3** friendly, sociable.

outgrow *owt-grō', v.t.* **1** to grow larger than. **2** to grow too big for (e.g. one's clothes). **3** to lose (e.g. a habit) as one grows older.

out'growth *n.* **1** something that grows out. **2** a natural result.

outhouse *owt'hows, n.* an outbuilding (see this).

outing. See **out**.

outlandish *owt-land'ish, adj.* **1** foreign. **2** strange; odd, fantastic.

outlast *owt-läst', v.t.* to last longer than.

outlaw *owt'lö, n.* **1** someone put outside the protection of the law. **2** a lawless person, bandit.—*v.t.* **1** to place (someone) beyond the protection of the law. **2** to ban, prohibit.

out'lawry *n.* **1** the act of outlawing. **2** the state of being outlawed.

outlay *owt'lā, n.* money paid out.

outlet *owt'let, n.* **1** a way, passage, outwards. **2** a means of letting something out: *Sports are an outlet for energy.* **3** an opportunity for selling a particular product.

outline *owt'līn, n.* **1** a line showing or forming the outer edge of a drawn figure, etc. **2** a brief explanation (of e.g. the main ideas of e.g. a plan, book, talk).—*v.t.* **1** to draw the outer line of. **2** to tell the main points of:—*pr.p.* **out'lining**.

outlive *owt-liv', v.t.* **1** to live longer than. **2** to live or last through (e.g. a time of danger):—*pr.p.* **outliv'ing**.

outlook *owt'look, n.* **1** a view: *the outlook from my window.* **2** mental view: *He has a gloomy outlook on life.* **3** what is likely to happen in the future: *The weather outlook is good.*

outlying *owt'lī-ing, adj.* lying away from the centre, distant: *outlying villages.*

outmanoeuvre *owt-mȧ-nōō'vėr, v.t.* to surpass in, or by, manoeuvring:—*pr.p.* **outmanoeu'vring.**

outmatch *owt-mach', v.t.* to surpass.

outmoded *owt-mō'did, adj.* **1** no longer in fashion. **2** no longer accepted: *outmoded beliefs.*

outnumber *owt-num'bėr, v.t.* to be greater in number than.

out(-)of(-)date. See **date**[1].

out'-patient *owt'-pā-shėnt, n.* a patient who visits hospital for treatment without staying overnight.

outpost *owt'pōst, n.* a post or station in front of the main body of an army, etc., or in the wilds.

outpour *owt-pōr', -pör', v.t.* to pour out.
out'pouring *n.* a pouring out (e.g. of emotion).

output *owt'poot, n.* quantity of goods produced by a machine, factory, etc.

outrage *owt'rāj, n.* **1** a wicked and violent act. **2** an act that is an offence (e.g. to someone's feelings, against justice), etc.—*v.t.* to hurt, insult, shock: —*pr.p.* **out'raging.**
outrā'geous *adj.* **1** very wrong. **2** shocking, offensive.
outrā'geously *adv.* **outrā'geousness** *n.*

outright *owt'rīt, adj.* absolute; direct.—*adv.* *(owt-rīt')* **1** directly, truthfully. **2** at once: *killed outright.* **3** in a single transaction: *to sell outright.*

outrun *owt-run', v.t.* **1** to run faster than. **2** to go beyond, become greater than, etc.:—*pr.p.* **outrunn'ing**; *pa.t.* **outran'**; *pa.p.* **outrun'.**

outset *owt'set, n.* beginning.

outshine *owt-shīn', v.t.* to shine brighter than, be cleverer than, more successful than, etc.:—*pr.p.* **outshin'ing.**

outside *owt'sīd', n.* **1** the outer side. **2** the surface.—*adj.* **1** on the outside. **2** not done, belonging, etc., within the group, concern, etc. mentioned. **3** remote: *an outside chance.* **4** the greatest or most possible.—*adv.* on or to the outside; not within.—*prep.* **1** not in. **2** beyond.
out'sid'er *n.* **1** one not included in a social group, profession, etc. **2** a contestant unlikely to win.
at the outside and no more; at the most.

outsize *owt'sīz, adj.* over normal size.—*n.* a very large size.

outskirts *owt'skûrtz, n.pl.* the outer border: *on the outskirts of the town.*

outsmart *owt-smärt', (coll.) v.t.* to outwit.

outspoken *owt-spō'kėn, adj.* (of person, thing said) expressing thoughts frankly or boldly.

outstanding *owt-stand'ing, adj.* **1** striking, great, excellent. **2** (of e.g. debts) unpaid. **3** still to be done.

outstay *owt-stā', v.t.* to stay longer than.

outstretched *owt'strecht, adj.* reaching out.

outstrip *owt-strip', v.t.* to leave behind in running, etc.:—*pr.p.* **outstripp'ing**; *pa.p.* **outstripped'.**

out'-tray *owt'-trā, n.* a container for letters, etc. waiting to be dispatched.

outvote *owt-vōt', v.t.* to defeat by casting more votes: *The supporters of the plan were outvoted by its opponents.*

outward(s). See **out**.

outweigh *owt-wā', v.t.* to be heavier, or more important, than.

outwit *owt-wit', v.t.* to be too clever for, defeat by greater cunning:—*pr.p.* **outwitt'ing**; *pa.p.* **outwitt'ed.**

outwork *owt'wûrk, n.* a fortified position outside main defences.

outworn *owt-wōrn', -wörn', owt', adj.* **1** worn out. **2** out of date, no longer in use.

ova, oval, ovary. See **ovum**.

ovation *ō-vā'sh(ȯ)n, n.* an outburst of cheering and applause.

oven *uv'n, n.* **1** a closed space for baking, heating, or drying. **2** a small furnace.

over *ō'vėr, prep.* **1** higher than, above—in place, rank, value, number, etc. **2** across; from one side to the other of: *to jump over the hole; to walk over the bridge.* **3** on the far side of: *the town over the river.* **4** on; here and there on; on all parts of: *He threw his coat over a chair; little towns dotted over the plain; He stuck paper over the stain.* **5** about, concerning: *They talked over the problem.* **6** about, on account of: *They quarrelled over the money.* **7** in the course of; during: *over the last few weeks.*—*adv.* **1** expressing movement above: *A plane flew over.* **2** above in number or quantity; higher: *nine and over.* **3** across: *He came over to see me.* **4** outward, downward; so as to be no longer upright, etc.: *to knock over the vase.* **5** expressing turning, rotation, etc.: *The dog rolled over.* **6** in addition, as remainder: *three left over.* **7** through (again) from beginning to end; completely, carefully: *to talk it over.*—*adj.* **1** often as part of a

noun—see **over**. **2** finished, at an end: *The war is over.—n.* (*cricket*) a fixed number of balls bowled at one end before change to the other end.
o'verly *adv.* too; excessively.
over again once more, afresh.
over and above in addition to.
over and over again and again.
all over 1 completely. **2** at an end.

over- *ō-vėr-*, *pfx.* (1) above: *overhead*; across, from a higher position: *overlook*; across a surface: *overrun*; beyond: *overseas*; beyond a barrier; *overflow*, *overstep*; away from the upright position: *overturn*. (2) upper: *overcoat*; higher in authority: *overlord*. (3) beyond the usual: *overtime*; too great, too much: *overweight*, *overeat*. (4) completely: *overawe*, *overwhelm*.

overact *ō'vėr-akt'*, *v.t.*, *v.i.*, to overdo, exaggerate (a part).
overac'ting *n.*

overactive *ō'vėr-ak'tiv*, *adj.* acting, working, too quickly or too hard.
o'veractiv'ity *n.*

overall *ō'vėr-öl*, *n.* a garment worn over ordinary clothes to keep them clean.—*adj.* including the whole or everything.—*adv.* considering everything.

over-anxious *ō'vėr-angk'shus*, *adj.* too anxious or worried.

overarm *ō'vėr-ärm'*, *adj.*, *adv.* with the arm raised above the shoulder.

overawe *ō-vėr-ö'*, *v.t.* to make silent by fear or wonder:—*pr.p.* **overaw'ing**.

overbalance *ō-vėr-bal'ȧns*, *v.t.* to cause to lose balance.—*v.i.* to lose balance and fall:—*pr.p.* **overbal'ancing**.

overbear'ing *ō-vėr-bār'ing*, *adj.* haughty, domineering, too certain that one is right.

overboard *ō'vėr-bōrd*, *-börd*, *adv.* over the side of a ship.
go overboard (*coll.*) to feel extreme enthusiasm (for, about).
throw overboard to discard.

overburden *ō-vėr-bûr'dn*, *v.t.* to load with too much weight, work, etc.

overcast *ō-vėr-käst'*, *v.t.* to sew over the edges of (cloth) to reinforce them.—*adj.* (of the sky) cloudy.

overcharge *ō'vėr-chärj'*, *v.t.* **1** to charge (a person) too great a price. **2** to charge (an amount) beyond the fair price (also *v.i.*). **3** to load too heavily, fill too full:—*pr.p.* **o'verchar'ging**.—Also *n.* *(ō'vėr-chärj)*.

overcoat *ō'vėr-kōt*, *n.* an outdoor coat worn over all other clothes.

overcome *ō-vėr-kum'*, *v.t.* to get the better of, defeat (as *pa.p.*, means 'helpless because of exhaustion or emotion'):—*pr.p.* **overcom'ing**; *pa.t.* **overcame'**; *pa.p.* **overcome'**.

over-confident *ō-vėr-kon'fi-dėnt*, *adj.* too sure of oneself, or too hopeful.

overcrowd *ō-vėr-krowd'*, *v.t.* to fill with too many people or things.

overdo *ō-vėr-dōō'*, *v.t.* to do, use, etc., too much: *to overdo physical exercise*, *exclamation marks*:—*pa.t.* **overdid'**; *pa.p.* **overdone'**.
overdone' *(-dun')* *adj.* cooked too long.

overdose *ō'vėr-dōs*, *n.* too great an amount of medicine, a drug, etc.—Also *v.t.* *(ō-vėr-dōs')*:—*pr.p.* **overdos'ing**.

overdraw *ō-vėr-drö'*, *v.t.* to draw more money from (one's account at the bank) than one has in it:—*pa.t.* **overdrew'**; *pa.p.* **overdrawn'**.
o'verdraft *n.* money drawn from the bank beyond the sum that one has put in.

overdress *ō-vėr-dres'*, *v.t.* to dress too showily, or more formally than is suitable for the occasion.

overdrive *ō'vėr-drīv*, *n.* a device for providing a motor vehicle with a gear higher than its normal top gear.

overdue *ō'vėr-dū'*, *adj.* not paid, not done, etc., although the time for paying, doing, is past: *an overdue bill*; *The train is overdue*.

overeat *ō-vėr-ēt'*, *v.i.* to eat too much.

overestimate *ō-vėr-es'ti-māt*, *v.t.* **1** to estimate, judge (the number, quantity, value, worth) to be greater than it really is. **2** to think too highly of (a person):—*pr.p.* **overest'imating**.—Also *n.* *(-mit)*.

overexpose *ō-vėr-iks-pōz'*, *v.t.* to expose too much, esp. to light:—*pr.p.* **overexpos'ing**.

overflow *ō-vėr-flō'*, *v.t.* and *v.i.* to flow over, extend beyond (a barrier, limit, etc.)—*v.i.* (of one's heart) to be filled (with happiness, etc.).—*n.* *(ō'vėr-)* **1** a flowing over. **2** the amount overflowing. **3** a pipe or channel for excess water, etc.

overgrown *ō-vėr-grōn'*, *adj.* **1** grown too large. **2** covered or choked with spreading plants.

overhand *ō'vėr-hand*, *adj.*, *adv.* **1** overarm. **2** with the palm of the hand turned downwards.

overhang *ō-vėr-hang'*, *v.t.*, *v.i.* to hang, or jut out, over:—*pa.t.* and *pa.p.* **overhung'**.

overhaul *ō-vėr-höl'*, *v.t.* **1** to examine, and repair, thoroughly. **2** (esp. of ship) to catch up with, overtake (another).—*n.* *(ō'vėr-)*.

overhead *ō'vėr-hed'*, *adv.*, *adj.* above head-level.—*adj.* (of expenses) connected e.g. with the premises of a business, e.g. for heating, lighting, rent, etc.—*n.* (in *pl.*) overhead expenses.

overhear *ō-vėr-hēr'*, *v.t.* to hear, by accident or intention, what was not meant to be heard.

overjoyed' *ō-vėr-joid'*, *adj.* very glad.

overlaid. See **overlay**.

overland *ō'vėr-land*, *adj.* entirely across land: *an overland journey.—adv. (-land')* by land rather than sea or air.

overlap *ō-vėr-lap'*, *v.t.* to extend over the edge of and partly cover.—Also *v.i.*:—*pr.p.* **overlapp'ing**; *pa.p.* **overlapped'**. —*n.* *(ō'vėr-)* the amount by which something overlaps.

overlay *ō-vėr-lā'*, *v.t.* (with *with*) to cover by spreading something over:—*pa.p.* **overlaid'**.—*n.* *(ō'vėr-)* that with which something is overlaid.

overleaf *ō-vėr-lēf'*,*adv.* on the other side of the page.

overload *ō-vėr-lōd'*, *v.t.* to load or fill too much.

overlook *ō-vėr-look'*, *v.t.* **1** to look across, or down upon, from a higher position. **2** to fail to notice. **3** to allow to go without punishment: *We'll overlook your lateness this time.*

overlord *ō'vėr-lörd*, *n.* **1** (under feudal system) a lord who was over another lord. **2** one who has power or control.

overly. See **over**.

overmuch *ō-vėr-much'*, *adj.* and *adv.* too much.

overnight *ō'vėr-nīt'*, *adv.* during, or throughout, the night: *He travelled overnight.—adj.* **1** done, made, during the night: *an overnight journey*; *an overnight decision.* **2** lasting, staying, etc. for one night.

overpass *ō'vėr-päs*, *n.* a road going over above another road, railway, canal, etc.

overpower *ō-vėr-pow'ėr*, *v.t.* **1** to overcome by greater strength. **2** (of strong emotion or bodily feeling—e.g. sleepiness) to make helpless.

overrate *ō-vėr-rāt'*, *v.t.* to rate or value too highly:—*pr.p.* **overrat'ing**.

overreach *ō-vėr-rēch'*, *v.t.* (with *oneself*) to fail by being too ambitious or greedy.

overreact *ō-vėr-ri-akt'*, *v.i.* to react too much, esp. too emotionally.

override *ō-vėr-rīd'*, *v.t.* **1** to trample down (opposition, advisers), firmly doing as one wishes. **2** to set aside (a decision, law):—*pr.p.* **overrid'ing**.

overrule *ō-vėr-rōōl'*, *v.t.* **1** to rule against, set aside, the arguments of (a person). **2** to declare (a law) is not valid, (a decision) is not to stand:—*pr.p.* **overrul'ing**.

overrun *ō-vėr-run'*, *v.t.* **1** to run beyond; to exceed (a limit). **2** to swarm, or to grow, over. **3** to spread over (country) and take possession of it:—*pr.p.* **overrunn'ing**; *pa.t.* **overran'**; *pa.p.* **overrun'**.

overseas *ō-vėr-sēz'*, *adj.*, *adv.* across the sea; abroad.

oversee *ō-vėr-sē'*, *v.t.* to be in charge of, to supervise:—*pa.t.* **oversaw'**; *pa.p.* **overseen'**.

o'verseer *(-sē-ėr) n.*

overshadow *ō-vėr-shad'ō*, *v.t.* **1** to throw a shadow over. **2** to make seem less important by being better, greater, than.

overshoe *ō'vėr-shōō*, *n.* a shoe, esp. waterproof, worn over another.

overshoot *ō-vėr-shōōt'*, *v.t.* to shoot over or beyond (a mark).

oversight *ō'vėr-sīt*, *n.* **1** failure to notice. **2** a mistake due to overlooking, or leaving out, something.

oversleep *ō-vėr-slēp'*, *v.i.* to sleep beyond one's usual time.

overspend *ō-vėr-spend'*, *v.t.* to spend more than (one's income or allowance).—Also *v.i.*

overspill *ō'vėr-spil*, *n.* excess, or displaced, population of a town, etc.

overstate *ō-vėr-stāt'*, *v.t.* to state too strongly, exaggerate:—*pr.p.* **overstat'ing**.

overstate'ment *n.*

overstep *ō-vėr-step'*, *v.t.* to go further than (the proper limit):—*pr.p.* **overstepp'ing**; *pa.p.* **overstepped'**.

overt *ō-vûrt'*, *adj.* **1** openly done. **2** not hidden or secret.

overtake *ō-vėr-tāk'*, *v.t.* **1** to catch up with. **2** to pass (someone or something) moving in the same direction. **3** to come suddenly upon: *A storm overtook him*:—*pr.p.* **overtak'ing**.

overtax *ō-vėr-taks'*, *v.t.* **1** to tax too highly. **2** to put too great a strain on: *to overtax one's strength.*

overthrow *ō-vėr-thrō'*, *v.t.* to defeat completely.—Also *n. (ō'vėr-)*.

overtime *ō'vėr-tīm*, *n.* **1** time spent in working beyond usual hours. **2** payment, usu. at special rate, for this.—*adv.* beyond normal working-hours.

overtones *ō'vėr-tōnz*, *n. pl.* an extra impression conveyed: *His speech had revolutionary overtones*; *clothes with overtones of 1950.*

overture *ō'vėr-tūr*, *n.* **1** an act or proposal intended to open discussions or negotiations: *overtures, an overture, of peace.* **2** a piece of music played as introduction to opera, etc.

overturn *ō-vėr-tûrn'*, *v.t.* **1** to throw down or over, upset (also *v.i.*). **2** to destroy the power of.

overview *ō'vėr-vū*, *n.* a general survey.

overweening *ō-vėr-wē'ning*, *adj.* very arrogant.

overweight *ō-vėr-wāt'*, *adj.* too fat; too heavy.—*n.* *(ō'vėr-)* excess weight.

overwhelm *ō-vėr-(h)welm'*, *v.t.* **1** (of e.g. the sea) to cover completely. **2** to defeat utterly. **3** (of emotion) to overcome, make helpless.

overwhelm'ing *adj.* very great.

overwork *ō-vėr-wûrk'*, *v.t.*, *v.i.* to (force to) work too much.—*v.t.* to use (e.g. an excuse) too often.—Also *n.*

overwrought *ō-vėr-röt'*, *adj.* in a highly nervous or anxious state.

oviparous, ovoid, ovule. See **ovum**.

ovum *ō'vum*, *n.* **1** a cell produced in an ovary. **2** an egg:—*pl.* **o'va**.

o'val, o'void *adjs.* egg-shaped (**oval** usu. of an outline, not a solid).—Also *ns.*

o'vary *n.* **1** the organ in a female that produces egg cells. **2** the part of a plant that produces ovules:—*pl.* **o'varies**.

ovulate *ov'ūl-āt*, *v.i.* to release an egg cell from the ovary:—*pr.p.* **ov'ulating**.

ovule *ov'ūl*, *n.* (in flowering plants) the part that becomes the seed.

owe *ō*, *v.t.* **1** to be in debt to, or under an obligation to: *I owe you sixpence*; *I owe you for my lunch.* **2** to attribute (something that has happened to one to): *I owe my success to you.* **3** to give as a duty: *We owe allegiance to the king*:—*pr.p.* **ow'ing**.

owing *ō'ing*, *adj.* due, to be paid.

owing to because of.

owl *owl*, *n.* a nocturnal bird of prey, with disc-shaped markings round its eyes and a loud cry.

owl'ish *adj.*

own *ōn*, *v.t.* **1** to possess, have. **2** to admit that (something) is one's own. **3** to admit, confess.—*v.i.* to confess (to).—*adj.*, *pron.* used for emphasis with possessive adjs., etc.: *my own*; *John's own pen.*

own'er *n.* a legal possessor.

own'ership *n.* legal possession.

get one's own back to get even, revenge oneself.

hold one's own. See **hold**.

on one's own **1** by one's own efforts. **2** without control or help, independent(ly).

own up to admit one's guilt.

See also **disown**.

ox *oks*, *n.* the male of the cow used for drawing loads:—*pl.* **ox'en** (used for both male and female).

oxide *oks'īd*, *n.* a compound of oxygen and another element.

ox'idise *(-id-)* *v.i.*, *v.t.* **1** to combine with oxygen. **2** to rust:—*pr.p.* **ox'idising**.

oxygen *oks'i-jėn*, *n.* a gas without taste, colour, or smell, forming part of air, water, etc. and necessary for life and burning.

oxygen mask a device for supplying oxygen, fitted over the nose and mouth.

oxygen tent an oxygen-filled tent put round a patient to aid breathing.

oyster *ois'tėr*, *n.* a shellfish with shell in two parts, used as food.

ozone *ō'zōn*, *n.* **1** (usu. *humorous*) fresh sea air. **2** a form of oxygen.

ozone layer a layer of the upper atmosphere which protects the earth from the sun's ultraviolet rays.

P

pace *pās, n.* **1** a step. **2** rate of motion (of a man or a beast).—*v.t.* **1** to measure by steps. **2** to walk backwards and forwards over. **3** to set the rate of movement for (a fellow competitor in a race) by one's example.—*v.i.* to walk slowly:—*pr.p.* **pac'ing.**

pace'maker *n.* **1** one who sets the pace in a race, or acts as an example in some other activity. **2** a device used to correct weak or irregular heart rhythms.

pachyderm *pak'i-dûrm, n.* a thick-skinned animal, such as an elephant.

pacify *pas'i-fī, v.t.* **1** to calm, sooth: *to pacify the angry victim of the trick.* **2** to make peaceful: *to pacify warring tribesmen*:—*pr.p.* **pac'ifying**; *pa.p.* **pac'ified.**

pacif'ic *adj.* **1** peace-making. **2** peaceful. **3** peaceable: *He has a pacific disposition.*

pacificā'tion *n.*

pac'ifist *n.* one who is against war, or believes all war to be wrong and unnecessary.

pac'ifism *n.*

Pacific (Ocean) the ocean between America and Asia, so named because Magellan, the first European to sail on it, found it in calm weather.

pack *pak, n.* **1** a bundle to be carried on the back, as a soldier's. **2** something put into a container or wrapped in some way; the type of container or method of wrapping: *a vacuum pack.* **3** a complete set of cards. **4** a number of animals of the same kind kept, or keeping, together: *a pack of hounds for hunting*; *a pack of wolves.* **5** the forwards in a rugby football team. **6** a mass of large pieces of floating ice (**pack'-ice**). **7** a group of Cubs or Brownies. **8** (*abusively*) a group or number: *a pack of thieves*; *a pack of lies.*—*v.t.* **1** to put (clothes, etc.) into a bag or other luggage, or (goods) into a container. **2** to press together closely. **3** to crowd, to cram.—*v.i.* **1** to gather into packs or crowd together. **2** to form a scrum. **3** to put one's belongings into bags, cases, etc. before leaving.—*adj.* used for carrying goods: *a pack horse.*

pack'age *n.* **1** a bundle, packet, parcel. **2** all the items or elements in a package deal.—*v.t.* to make up in a parcel:—*pr.p.* **pack'aging.**

pack'aging *n.* the presentation of a product for sale, e.g. its design, wrapping, etc.

pack'et *n.* **1** a small package. **2** a ship that carries letters, passengers, etc., on a regular run between two ports (also **pack'et-boat, -ship**). **3** (*coll.*) a large amount of money.

pack'ing *n.* **1** the act of putting into packs. **2** material for wrapping goods to pack. **3** anything used to fill an empty space, or to make a joint close.

package deal a deal which includes a number of matters and which has to be accepted as a whole.

package holiday, tour one completely arranged by the organiser before it is advertised, and for which he is paid a fixed price which covers all costs.

pack-ice. See **pack** (*def.* 6) above.

pack'ing-case *n.* a large wooden box in which goods are transported.

pack'man *n.* a pedlar.

pack'saddle *n.* a saddle for a pack horse, etc.

pack a jury, meeting, etc., to fill it with people who will be sure to give the verdict or decision one wants.

pack up **1** to put one's belongings in boxes, bags, etc., before leaving. **2** (*coll.*; also **pack in**) to stop working or operating: *The engine has packed up.*

send someone packing to send someone away roughly.

pact *pakt, n.* **1** an agreement or compact. **2** a treaty.

pad[1] *pad, v.i.* **1** to trudge (along). **2** to walk making a dull, soft, noise:—*pr.p.* **padd'ing**; *pa.p.* **padd'ed.**

pad[2] *pad, n.* **1** a soft cushion-like mass to prevent jarring or rubbing. **2** a firm cushion-shaped mass. **3** sheets of paper fastened together in a block. **4** a rocket-launching platform. **5** the paw of the fox, hare, etc. **6** (*slang*) a bed, room, or home, esp. one's own.—*v.t.* **1** to stuff with anything soft. **2** (also **pad out**) to fill out (a book or paper) to greater length with material that really adds nothing to the meaning:—*pr.p.* **padd'ing**; *pa.p.* **padd'ed.**

padd'ing *n.* **1** stuffing. **2** useless matter put into a book to make it longer.

paddle[1] *pad'l, v.i.* **1** to wade about in shallow water. **2** to walk unsteadily, toddle. **3** to dabble, play with the fingers (with *in, on, about*):—*pr.p.* **padd'ling.**

paddle[2] *pad'l, n.* **1** a short oar with broad blade, used for moving canoes. **2** the blade of an oar. **3** one of the boards of a paddle-wheel.—*v.i.* **1** to move forward by the use of paddles. **2** to row gently.—*v.t.* to move (a canoe), or to convey (something), by paddling:—*pr.p.* **padd'ling.**

padd'le-steamer *n.* a boat run by means of one or more paddle-wheels.

padd'le-wheel *n.* a wheel with boards on its outer edge which, as the wheel turns, act as paddles.

paddock *pad'ȯk, n.* **1** a small closed-in field, usu. near a house or stable and used for pasture. **2** an area enclosed by a fence at a racecourse for saddling the horses.

paddy *pad'i, n.* **1** growing rice. **2** rice in the husk.

paddy field a muddy field in which rice is grown.

padlock *pad'lok, n.* a removable lock which has a metal link which can be passed through a staple or chain and then fastened firmly.—*v.t.* to fasten a padlock.

padre *pä'drā, n.* **1** father, a title given to priest. **2** a chaplain.

paean *pē'ȧn, n.* a song of triumph or joy.

paediatrics *pē-di-at'riks, n.sing.* the treatment of children's diseases.

paediat'ric *adj.* **paediatri'cian** *n.*

paella *pī-el'ȧ, pä-el'yȧ, n.* a dish containing chicken, rice, vegetables, etc.

pagan *pā'gȧn, n.* **1** a civilised heathen. **2** later, one who was not Christian, Jew, or Muslim. **3** now often used to describe someone who does not believe in any religion.

pa'ganism *n.*

page[1] *pāj, n.* **1** a young boy serving a person of high degree. **2** (also **page'-boy**) a boy who does errands and carries messages.—*v.t.* to seek (a person) by calling out his name or by using a **pag'er**, an electronic device which is carried around by the person and which can be made to bleep when the person is required:—*pr.p.* **pag'-ing.**

page[2] *pāj, n.* **1** one side of the blank, printed or written leaf of a book, letter, etc. **2** the leaf thought of as a single item.—*v.t.* (also **pag'inate** *paj'in-āt*) to number the pages of:—*pr.ps.* **pag'ing, pag'inating.**

paginā'tion *n.*

pageant *paj'ėnt, n.* **1** spectacle or display, esp. one on a moving vehicle in a parade. **2** a series of dramatic scenes to show the history e.g. of a place.

page'antry *n.* **1** splendid show or display. **2** a show of magnificence.

paginate. See **page[2]**.

pagoda *pȧ-gō'dȧ, n.* a temple of China, India, etc., esp. in the form of a tower of many storeys narrowing upwards.

paid. See **pay**.

pail *pāl, n.* a deep rounded container with an arched handle, used for carrying liquids; a bucket.

paillasse, palliasse *pal-yas', pal'i-as, n.* a straw mattress.

pain *pān, n.* **1** suffering, hurt to body or mind. **2** threat of punishment: *under pain of death.* **3** (in *pl.*) care: *He takes pains with his work.*—*v.t.* to cause suffering to, to distress (someone).

pained *adj.* showing pain: *He had a pained expression.*

pain'ful *adj.* **1** causing pain. **2** full of pain. **3** requiring much work.

pain'less *adj.* without pain.

pain'-killer *n.* a drug which stops pain.

pains'taking *adj.* **1** taking great care. **2** done with careful attention.

paint *pānt, v.t.* **1** to put colour on. **2** to make (a picture) with colours. **3** to describe in words.—*v.i.* to practise the art of painting.—*n.* a colouring substance.

paint'er *n.* **1** an artist in paint. **2** a house-decorator.

paint'ing *n.* **1** the act of covering with colour or making a picture. **2** a painted picture. **3** a clear description in words.

paint'-brush *n.* a brush for putting on paint.

painter[1]. See **paint**.

painter[2] *pānt'ėr, n.* a rope used to fasten a boat.

pair *pār, n.* **1** two of a kind: *a pair of shoes.* **2** a set of two similar things which form one article: *a pair of scissors.* **3** a husband and wife. **4** two together, a couple.—*v.t.* **1** to join to form a pair. **2** to sort out in pairs.—*v.i.* **1** to mate. **2** to go two and two.

pair off to (cause to) go off in pairs.

Pakistani *pä-ki-stän'i, adj.* of or having to do with Pakistan.—*n.* **1** a native or citizen of Pakistan. **2** a person whose ancestors were born in Pakistan.

pal *pal, n.* a partner, mate, chum.

palace *pal'ȧs, n.* **1** a royal house. **2** any splendid house. **3** the official home of a bishop.

palatial *pȧ-lā'sh(ȧ)l, adj.* like a palace, large, spacious.

palace revolution a revolution within the government itself.

palae(o)-, pale(o), *pal-i-ō-*, or *pāl-i-ō-*, (as part of a word) old.

palaeolithic *(-lith'ik) adj.* belonging to the early Stone Age (i.e. when people used primitive stone tools).

palais de danse *pa-lā dė dong̃s, n.* a public dance-hall.

palate *pal'ȧt, n.* **1** the roof of the mouth, consisting of the *hard palate* in front and the *soft palate* behind. **2** taste. **3** liking: *He had no palate for sermons.*

palatable *pal'ȧt-ȧ-bl, adj.* **1** pleasant to the taste. **2** (of advice, truth, etc.) pleasing, acceptable: *He did not find this advice palatable.*

pal'atal *adj.* having to do with the palate.

palatial. See **palace**.

palaver *pȧ-läv'ėr, n.* **1** unnecessary fuss. **2** a conference, esp. (19th cent.) with African tribesmen. **3** idle talk. **4** talk intended to deceive or flatter.

pale¹ *pāl, n.* **1** a piece of wood, a stake, driven into the ground for a fence. **2** a fence. **3** an enclosed space. **4** limits.

pal'ing *n.* **1** wood or stakes for fencing. **2** a fence. **3** one upright board or stake of a fence.

beyond the pale **1** (of a person) given to behaving in a way of which the person speaking strongly disapproves. **2** (of conduct) socially or morally very bad, unacceptable.

pale² *pāl, adj.* **1** whitish in colour. **2** wan. **3** dim, not bright.—*v.t.* to make pale.—*v.i.* to turn pale, to lose colour:—*pr.p.* **pal'ing**.

pale(o)-. See **palae(o)-**.

palette *pal'it, n.* a little board on which a painter mixes his colours.

palindrome *pal'in-drōm, n.* a word, phrase, etc. that reads the same backwards or forwards (e.g. *Able was I ere I saw Elba*; *So patient a doctor to doctor a patient so*).

paling. See **pale¹,²**.

palisade *pal-i-sād', n.* a fence of stakes.

pall¹ *pöl, n.* **1** a cloth which covers the coffin at a funeral. **2** a cloak. **3** a curtain or haze, e.g. of smoke, darkness.

pall'-bear'er *n.* one of those mourners at a funeral who used to hold the corners of the pall but now attend the coffin.

pall² *pöl, v.i.* to become uninteresting or boring—often *pall on*: *Too much soft music palls on one*; *It palls after a while*.

pallet¹ *pal'it, n.* **1** a flat wooden tool with a handle, as that used in making pottery. **2** a board for carrying newly made bricks. **3** a platform or tray used for lifting and stacking goods, used with a fork-lift truck.

pallet² *pal'it, n.* a mattress or couch.

palliasse. Same as **paillasse**.

palliate *pal'i-āt, v.t.* **1** to make seem less grave: *to palliate one's faults.* **2** to lessen, ease, without curing: *to palliate a disease*:—*pr.p.* **pall'iating**.

palliā'tion *n.*

pall'iative *(-ȧt-) adj.* making less severe or harsh.—*n.* something that lessens pain, as a drug or treatment.

pallid *pal'id, adj.* **1** pale. **2** wan, sickly.

pallor *pal'ȯr, n.* unnatural paleness.

palm¹ *päm, n.* the surface of the inside of the hand, between the wrist and the fingers.—*v.t.* to conceal in the hand, as in a magician's act.

palmist *päm'ist, n.* a person who tells fortunes by reading the lines of the palm.

palm'istry *n.* the telling of fortunes in this way.

palm off (with *on* or *upon*) to pass off, give with intention of cheating: *He palmed off a faulty set on me.*

palm² *päm, n.* **1** a tall tree with large fan-shaped leaves at the top, growing mainly in hot countries. **2** a leaf of the palm tree carried as a sign of victory or rejoicing. **3** a token of success.

palm oil an oil or fat obtained from the pulp of the fruit of palm trees.

palm sugar sugar obtained from certain palms.

Palm Sunday the Sunday before Easter, celebrated in memory of the strewing of palm branches when Christ entered Jerusalem.

palmist, palmistry. See **palm¹**.

palomino *pal-ō-mēn'ō, n.* a tan, yellow, or gold horse with white or silver mane or tail:—*pl.* **palomin'os**.

palpable *pal'pȧ-bl, adj.* **1** able to be touched or felt. **2** easily noticed by the senses (e.g. easily seen, heard, etc.). **3** easily noticed by the mind, obvious: *palpable errors, lies*:—*opp.* **impalpable**.

palpabil'ity, pal'pableness *ns.*

palpitate *pal'pi-tāt, v.i.* **1** (of the heart) to throb, beat rapidly. **2** to tremble:—*pr.p.* **pal'pitating**.

palpitā'tion *n.* rapid beating of the heart due to disease.

palsy *pöl'zi, n.* paralysis.—*v.t.* **1** to affect with palsy. **2** to destroy power of action or energy in (someone):—*pr.p.* **pal'sying**; *pa.p.* **pal'sied**.

paltry *pöl'tri, adj.* **1** trashy, worthless. **2** mean. **3** not worth considering:—*comp.* **pal'trier**; *superl.* **pal'triest**.

pal'trily *adv.* **pal'triness** *n.*

pampas *pam'pȧz, -pȧs, n.pl.* or *sing.* a name for the vast treeless plains of South America.—Also *adj. (pam'pȧs)*.

pamper *pam'pėr, v.t.* **1** to indulge too much, spoil (e.g. a child, oneself, a taste, etc.). **2** to feed to the full.

pamphlet *pam'flit, n.* **1** a small book, stitched together but not bound. **2** a tract or a small treatise, on some subject being discussed at the time.

pamphleteer' *n.* a writer of pamphlets. —Also *v.i.*

pan[1] *pan, n.* **1** an esp. metal container used in cooking. **2** a broad, shallow container of larger size used in industry. **3** anything of a similar shape, as the upper part of the skull (*brain-pan*). **4** the part of the lock of old guns that holds the priming.—*v.t.* to wash (gold-containing sand, etc.) with water in a pan.—*v.i.* to yield gold:—*pr.p.* **pann'ing**; *pa.p.* **panned**.

pan'cake *n.* **1** a thin cake of batter fried in a pan. **2** a landing in which an aircraft with stalled engine drops almost straight to the ground.

pan out to turn out (well, badly).

pan[2] *pan, v i* to move a cinema or television camera so as to follow an object or produce a wide view (also *v.t.*):—*pr.p.* **pann'ing**; *pa.p.* **panned**.

Pan-, **pan-** *pan-* (placed before a word or part of a word) all, every, as in **panacea**, **panorama**.

Pan-Amer'ican, including all of America, North and South.

panacea *pan-ȧ-sē'ȧ, n.* a cure for all things.

panache *pȧ-nash', n.* (a sense of) style, display.

panama *pan-ȧ-mä', n.* a hat made of braided leaves of a South American plant, or an imitation of it.

panatella *pan-ȧ-tel'ȧ, n.* a long thin cigar.

pancake. See **pan**[1].

panchromatic *pan-krō-mat'ik, adj.* sensitive to light of all colours, as in *panchromatic film* used in photography.

pancreas *pan(g)'kri-ȧs, n.* a large gland of the body under and behind the stomach that gives off a fluid which aids digestion in the intestines.

panda *pan'dȧ, n.* **1** a flesh-eating animal of the Himalayas. **2** (**giant panda**) a larger black-and-white animal of Tibet.

pandemic *pan-dem'ik, adj.* (of a disease) occurring over a wide area and affecting many people.

pandemonium *pan-di-mō'ni-ŭm, n.* **1** a noisy meeting. **2** an uproar.

pander *pan'dėr, v.i.* **1** deliberately to provide something that is pleasing to low morals or taste: *Some newspapers pander to the public's taste for scandal.* **2** to give way (to other's wishes) when one should not.

pane *pān, n.* a plate or sheet of glass.

panegyric *pan-i-jir'ik, n.* (with *on, upon*) a speech praising highly some person or event.

panel *pan'(ė)l, n.* **1** a rectangular area bordered by a frame of some sort, e.g. a part of a door lower than the general surface. **2** a list of names, esp. of a jury. **3** a group of persons chosen for a purpose, e.g. to judge a contest, be the guessers in radio and television games, etc.—*v.t.* to put panels on or in:—*pr.p.* **pan'elling**; *pa.p.* **pan'elled**.

pan'elling *n.* (material for) panels.

control panel a board of dials, switches, etc. controlling or monitoring apparatus, etc.

pang *pang, n.* a sudden, brief, sharp pain in body or emotions.

panic *pan'ik, n.* **1** sudden or frantic fright. **2** fear that spreads from person to person.—Also *adj.*—*v.i.* to lose through fear one's power to act sensibly.—*v.t.* to cause panic in:—*pr.p.* **pan'icking**; *pa.p.* **pan'icked.**

pan'icky (*coll.*), *adj.* **1** inclined to panic. **2** moved by panic. **3** caused by panic.

pan'ic-buy'ing *n.* the buying of unnecessarily large quantities of something of which there might be a shortage later, thereby often causing or worsening the shortage.

pan'ic-strick'en *adj.* overcome by fear.

pannier *pan'i-ėr, yėr, n.* a basket, usu. one of a pair thrown over the back of a pack animal.

panoply *pan'ȯ-pli, n.* **1** a full suit of armour. **2** full dress or brilliant covering:—*pl.* **pan'oplies**.

panorama *pan-ȯ-rä'mȧ, n.* **1** a wide or complete view. **2** a picture seen a part at a time as it is unrolled.

panoramic *(-ram'ik) adj.*

pansy *pan'zi, n.* **1** a type of flower like the violet, usu. larger. **2** (*offensive*) an effeminate man:—*pl.* **pan'sies**.

pant[1] *pant, v.i.* **1** to gasp for breath, be out of breath. **2** to move (along), breathing with difficulty. **3** to wish eagerly (*for* or *after* something).—*v.t.* to utter with gasps.—Also *n.*

pant[2]. See **pants**.

pantaloons *pan-tȧ-lo͞onz', n.pl.* a kind of wide trousers gathered at the ankles.

pantechnicon *pan-tek'ni-kȯn, n.* a furniture van.

pantheism *pan'thē-izm, n.* the belief or teaching that everything is God.

pan'theist *n.*

pantheon *pan'thē-ȯn, n.* **1** a temple of all the gods, esp. (*cap.*) a round temple in Rome. **2** a building containing the tombs of many of a country's famous men.

panther *pan'thėr*, *n.* a large leopard.

pantihose. See **panty hose**.

pantile *pan'tīl*, *n.* a curving roof-tile.

pantomime *pan'tō-mīm*, *n.* **1** dumb show. **2** a dramatic show, usu. about Christmas, in which a fairy story is acted with songs, dancing, topical jokes, etc.

pantry *pan'tri*, *n.* a room for storing food, or for dishes and silver:—*pl.* **pantries**.

pants *pants*, *n.pl.* **1** drawers. **2** (esp. *U.S.*) trousers.

panty hose, **pantihose** *pan'ti-hōz*, *ns.* women's tights.

pap *pap*, *n.* **1** soft, mushy food. **2** trivial ideas, etc.

papa *pȧ-pä'* (*old-fashioned*) *n.* father.

papacy *pā'pȧ-si*, *n.* **1** the office of pope. **2** a pope's term of office. **3** the papal system of government.—*pl.* **pa'pacies**.

papal *pā'pȧl*, *adj.* having to do with the pope or the papacy.

papist *pā'pist*, *n.* **1** a follower of the pope. **2** (*slightingly or abusively*) a Roman Catholic.

pa'pistry *n.* popery.

papaw *pȧ-pö'*, *pö'pö*, *n.* **1** a (small S. American tree with) yellow fruit which contains a substance that aids digestion. **2** also a N. American tree.—Also **paw'paw**, **papaya** *(pȧ-pä'yȧ)*.

paper *pā'pėr*, *n.* **1** the material on which we commonly write and print, made from wood pulp, esparto grass, or rags, etc. **2** similar material for wrapping, etc. **3** a document or official writing. **4** a newspaper. **5** an essay written to be read to e.g. a society. **6** a material used to cover walls. **7** (in *pl.*) documents proving identity, rights, etc. **8** a set of examination questions.—*adj.* consisting, or made, of paper.—*v.t.* to cover with paper.

pa'perback *n.* a book with a limp paper cover.—Also *adj.*

pa'per-knife *n.* a thin, flat blade for cutting the leaves of books, letters, etc.

paper money pieces of paper stamped by a bank or government as having a certain value in money.

pa'perweight *n.* a heavy glass, metal, etc. object used to keep a pile of loose papers in place, or as an ornament.

pa'perwork *n.* the keeping of written records, writing of letters, etc.

on paper in theory, though perhaps not in practice: *The scheme seemed all right on paper*.

papier-mâché *pap'yā-mä'shā*, *n.* a substance made of paper pulp, or of sheets of paper pasted together, that can be moulded into shapes.

papist, **papistry**. See **papacy**.

papoose *pȧ-po͞os'*, *n.* a Native American Indian baby or young child.

paprika *pap'ri-kȧ*, *pȧ-prēk'ȧ*, *n.* (a powder of) a type of red pepper.

papyrus *pȧpi'rus*, *n.* **1** a reed from the pith of which people (esp. of Egypt) in olden times made material for writing on. **2** material thus prepared. **3** a manuscript on papyrus:—*pl.* **papy'ri** *(-rī)*, **-ruses**.

par *pär*, *n.* **1** the normal level, the standard. **2** equality in value. **3** (in golf) the number of strokes allowed for each hole if the play is perfect.

above par higher than face value or normal level.

at par at the exact face value (used in speaking of stocks and shares).

below par **1** less than face value. **2** (*coll.*) not up to normal, esp. in health: *He felt below par that morning*.

on a par with equal to in kind: *Throwing up his job was on a par with his other follies*.

par(a)- *par(-a, -ȧ)-*, (as part of a word) **1** beside, alongside of. **2** beyond. **3** abnormal. **4** out of order.

para-mil'itary *adj.* used as an addition to the regular military.—Also *n.*:—*pl.* **para-mil'itaries**.

parable *par'ȧ-bl*, *n.* a fable or fairy story told to teach a lesson.

parabola *pȧr-ab'ȯ-lȧ*, *n.* a type of regular curve—the cables of a suspension bridge, and the path of a ball thrown, both form arcs of parabolas.

parabolic *par-ȧ-bol'ik*, *adj.* like a parabola.

paracetamol *pa-rȧ-set'ȧ-mol*, *n.* a mild pain-killing drug.

parachute *par'ȧ-sho͞ot*, *n.* a contrivance opening like an umbrella for helping a person or object to come down to earth safely from an aeroplane, etc.—*v.i.* to descend by parachute.—*v.t.* to drop (something) by means of a parachute:—*pr.p.* **par'achuting**.

par'achutist *n.*

parade *pȧ-rād'*, *n.* **1** show, display. **2** an orderly arrangement of troops for inspection or exercise. **3** the ground on which troops assemble for this. **4** a procession. **5** a public promenade, esp. at the seaside.—*v.t.* to show off.—*v.i.* **1** to march up and down as if for show. **2** to march in a procession:—*pr.p.* **parad'ing**.

paradigm *par'ȧ-dīm, n.* an example showing a certain pattern.
paradigmat'ic *(-dig-mat') adj.*

paradise *par'ȧ-dīs, n.* **1** the garden of Eden. **2** Heaven. **3** any place of great happiness.

paradox *par'ȧ-doks, n.* **1** a statement which seems absurd and self-contradictory, but may actually be true (e.g. *The summary of the book takes ten times longer to read than the full version*). **2** a statement that really contradicts itself and is, in fact, false.
paradox'ical *adj.* **paradox'ically** *adv.*

paraffin *par'ȧ-fin, n.* **1** (also **paraffin oil**) an oil used for burning, etc., obtained from petroleum, etc. **2** paraffin wax.
paraffin wax a white substance obtained from petroleum, coal, etc.

paragon *par'ȧ-gon, n.* a model of perfection or excellence: *He was a paragon of good manners.*

paragraph *par'ȧ-gräf, n.* **1** a division of a piece of writing in which the sentences are concerned with one general thought. **2** a short news item or comment in a newspaper. **3** a sign (usu. ¶) marking off a section of a book.—Also *v.t.*

parakeet *par'ȧ-kēt, n.* a small type of parrot.

parallel *par'ȧ-lel, adj.* **1** (of lines) going in the same direction and never meeting, remaining the same distance apart. **2** alike in an important respect, similar: *There are parallel passages in the two books.—n.* **1** a parallel line. **2** a line of latitude. **3** a similarity in the main points: *Is there a parallel between the Roman Empire and the British Empire?* **4** a person or thing similar in important points to another.—*v.t.* **1** to mention (something) as similar to (with *with*). **2** to match (often in passive): *His folly cannot be paralleled.* **3** to correspond to:—*pr.p.* **par'alleling**; *pa.p.* **par'alleled.**
parallelogram *par-ȧ-lel'ȯ-gram, n.* a four-sided figure in which the opposite sides are equal and parallel.

paralysis *pȧ-ral'i-sis, n.* palsy, a loss of power of motion or feeling in any part of the body.
par'alyse *(-līz), v.t.* **1** to strike with paralysis. **2** to make unable to move or act: *to paralyse with fear:—pr.p.* **par'alysing**.
paralytic *par-ȧ-lit'ik, adj.* and *n.* (a person) afflicted with paralysis.

paramed'ic *n.* a person trained in emergency medical procedures.

parameter *pȧ-ram'i-tėr, n.* **1** a variable quantity. **2** a limit.

para-military. See **para**.

paramount *par'ȧ-mownt, adj.* **1** above all others in rank or power. **2** the very greatest: *It was of paramount importance.*

paramour *par'ȧ-mōōr, n.* a lover, esp. of a married person.

paranoia *par-ȧ-noi'ȧ, n.* **1** a mental disorder characterised by delusions that one is very important, that one is being persecuted, etc. **2** great irrational fear of suspicion.
par'anoid *adj.*

paranormal *par-ȧ-nör'mȧl, adj.* not explicable by generally accepted facts or hypotheses.—Also *n.*

parapet *par'ȧ-pet, n.* **1** a bank or wall to protect soldiers from the fire of an enemy in front. **2** a low wall along the side of a bridge, etc.

paraphernalia *par-ȧ-fėr-nāl'i-ȧ, -yȧ, n. sing.* **1** belongings. **2** equipment.—*n.pl.* formerly, all the belongings of a woman who married other than the dowry (which went to her husband).

paraphrase *par'ȧ-frāz, n.* **1** the expression of the same thing in other words. **2** a rhymed version of a biblical passage.—*v.t.* to put into other words.—*v.i.* to make a paraphrase:—*pr.p.* **par'aphrasing**.

paraplegia *par-ȧ-plē'j(y)ȧ, n.* paralysis of the lower part of the body.
paraplē'gic *n.* and *adj.*

parasite *par'ȧ-sīt, n.* **1** an animal or plant that lives on another without giving it any benefit in return, as the flea, mistletoe, etc. **2** one who lives at the expense of someone else or of society.
parasitic *(-sit'ik) adj.*

parasol *par'ȧ-sol, n.* a sunshade.

paratroops *par'ȧtrōōps, n.pl.* troops carried by air to be dropped by a parachute.
par'atrooper *n.* a member of a group trained for this purpose.

par avion *pär av-yon*[g], by air mail.

parboil *pär'boil, v.t.* to boil slightly.

parcel *pär'sl, n.* **1** a package, esp. one wrapped in paper. **2** a part. **3** (*slightingly*) a set, pack: *a parcel of fools.—v.t.* **1** to divide (out) into portions. **2** to make into a parcel:—*pr.p.* **par'celling**; *pa.p.* **par'celled.**
part and parcel an essential or inseparable part.

parch *pärch, v.t.* (of the sun, fever, etc.) **1** to make hot and very dry. **2** to make thirsty.
parched *adj.*

parchment *pärch'mėnt, n.* **1** the skin of a goat, sheep or other animal cleaned, scraped, etc. for writing on. **2** paper resembling this. **3** a document on parchment.

pardon *pär'd(o̊)n, v.t.* **1** to forgive (a person, or a sin, etc.). **2** to free from punishment. **3** to excuse.—*n.* **1** forgiveness. **2** a freeing from punishment, or the document declaring it.
par'donable *adj.* **1** excusable. **2** able to be forgiven.
par'doner *n.* formerly, one who sold pardons from the pope.

pare *pār, v.t.* **1** to cut off the outer surface or edge. **2** to peel (e.g. an apple). **3** to make smaller little by little:—*pr.p.* **par'ing.**
par'ing *n.* **1** the act of shaving off or peeling. **2** what is removed thus.

parent *pār'ėnt, n.* **1** a father or mother. **2** a forefather. **3** a plant or animal which produces others. **4** an author, source: *He was the parent of the new philosophy*.
par'entage *n.* origin, lineage, family: *He was of noble parentage*.
parental *pȧ-ren'tȧl, adj.*
par'enthood *n.* the state of being a parent.

parenthesis *pȧ-ren'thė-sis, n.* **1** a word or group of words that interrupts a sentence giving an explanation, comment, etc. (e.g. *I have asked Smith—John Smith, I mean—to come to tea*; the words between dashes are the parenthesis). **2** (usu. in *pl.*) a round bracket (), one of the means used to mark off a parenthesis:—*pl.* **paren'-theses.**
parenthetic(al) *par-ėn-thet'ik(-ȧl), adjs.*

par excellence *pär ek-sė-lon^g s*, above all others: *Shakespeare is the writer of tragedy par excellence*.

pariah *par'i-ȧ, pȧ-rī'ȧ, n.* **1** a social outcast. **2** a wandering dog (**pariah dog**).

paring. See **pare**.

parish *par'ish, n.* **1** a district having its own church and clergyman. **2** a division of a county for local government purposes (not in Scotland). **3** the people of a parish.—*adj.* belonging to a parish.
parishioner *pȧ-rish'ȯn-ėr, n.* one who belongs to a church parish.
parish pump (often used as *adj.*) minor local affairs: *parish-pump politics*.
parish register a book in which the baptisms, marriages, and burials of a parish are recorded.
See also **parochial.**

Parisian *pȧ-riz'yȧn, -rizh'(y)ȧn, adj.* having to do with *Paris*.—*n.* a person born or living in Paris.

parity *par'i-ti, n.* the state of being equal:—*opp.* **dispar'ity.**

park *pärk, n.* **1** a piece of land surrounding a mansion. **2** a piece of ground for public recreation. **3** a piece of country kept in its natural condition, as a nature reserve. **4** a piece of ground where motor-cars or other vehicles may be left for a time.—*v.t.* **1** to stop and (usu.) leave (a car, etc.) (also *v.i.*). **2** (*coll.*) to place and leave.
parking meter a coin-operated meter which charges for car-parking time.
park'ing-ticket *n.* notice of a fine, or a summons to appear in court, for a parking offence.

parka *pär'kȧ, n.* a type of warm hooded jacket.

parky *pär'ki, (slang) adj.* chilly:—*comp.* **par'kier**; *superl.* **par'kiest.**

parlance *pär'lȧns, n.* a way of speaking, language: *in legal parlance*.
par'ley *v.i.* to discuss, hold a conference, esp. with an enemy.—*n.* a conference, esp. with an enemy.

parliament *pär'lȧ-mėnt, n.* (often with *cap.*) a law-making body, esp. the legislature of Great Britain (consisting of House of Commons and House of Lords) and of certain other countries in the Commonwealth.
parliamentā'rian *n.* one skilled in the ways and rules of parliament.
parliament'ary *adj.* **1** connected with parliament. **2** done by parliament. **3** according to the rules of law-making bodies.

parlour *pär'lȯr, n.* **1** the room used for entertaining guests. **2** (*U.S.*) the business rooms of a firm providing services: *beauty parlour*.
par'lour-maid *n.* a female servant who waits at table.

parlous *pär'lus, (coll.) adj.* full of danger.

Parmesan *pär-mi-zan', or pär', adj.* of *Parma*, in Italy.—*n.* Parmesan cheese.
Parmesan cheese a hard, dry, skim-milk cheese.

parochial *pȧr-ō'ki-ȧl, adj.* **1** of or relating to a parish. **2** interested only in local affairs. **3** not broad-minded, narrow in outlook.
parō'chialism *n.* narrowness of interests.

parody *par'ȯ-di, n.* writing in which words and style of a serious author are imitated so as to produce an amusing effect:—*pl.* **par'-odies.**—*v.t.* to make a parody of:—*pr.p.* **par'odying**; *pa.p.* **par'odied.**
par'odist *n.* one who writes a parody.

parole *pȧ-rōl', n.* **1** word of honour (esp. given by a prisoner of war that he will not escape). **2** release of a prisoner, etc. with the condition that he will have to return to prison if his conduct is bad.—*v.t.* to release on parole:—*pr.p* **parol'ing.**

paroxysm *par'oks-izm, n.* **1** a fit of acute pain. **2** a fit of laughter, rage, etc.

parquet *pär'kā, n.* a floor covering of wood blocks set in a pattern.
par'quetry, *pär'kit-ri, n.*

parr *pär, n.* a young salmon before it descends to the sea.

parricide *par'i-sīd, n.* **1** the murder of a parent or near relative. **2** a person who commits this crime.
parricid'al *adj.*

parrot *par'ot, n.* **1** a bird of warm regions, with bright feathers and hooked bill, a good imitator of human speech. **2** a person who repeats words or ideas without understanding them (also *v.t.:—pr.p.* **parr'oting**; *pa.p.* **parr'oted**.)

parry *par'i, v.t.* to keep off, turn aside (blow, question, etc.):—*pr.p.* **parry'ing**; *pa.p.* **parried**.

parse *pärz, v.t.* to name the parts of speech of (words in a sentence) and say how the words are connected with each other:—*pr.p.* **pars'ing**.
pars'ing *n.*

parsimony *pär'si-mon-i, n.* **1** great care in spending money, etc. **2** stinginess.
parsimo'nious *(-mō'ni-us) adj.*

parsley *pärs'li, n.* a bright-green leafy herb, used in cookery.

parsnip *pärs'nip, n.* (a plant with) a yellowish root used as a vegetable.

parson *pär's(o)n, n.* **1** the clergyman of a parish. **2** (*coll.*) any minister of religion.
par'sonage *n.* the home set aside for the parson.

part *pärt, n.* **1** something less than the whole—a portion (of a thing), some (of a number of things). **2** a section. **3** a separate piece or member (e.g. of a body, of a machine). **4** an equal division of a whole: *a fourth part*, i.e. a quarter. **5** a character in a play. **6** his words and actions. **7** a copy of the actor's words. **8** a melody given to one instrument or voice performing with others.—*v.t.* and *v.i.* **1** to divide into parts, break apart. **2** to separate, send or go different ways.
part'ing *n.* **1** the act of separating, etc. **2** a place of separation: *the parting of the ways.* **3** a leave-taking.
part'ly *adv.* so far as a part is concerned; to a certain extent.
part-exchange' *n.* a transaction in which an article is handed over as part of the payment for another article.
part-time' *adj.* involving, working only part of the normal working day or working week.—Also *adv.*
part-tim'er *n.*
a man of parts a talented man.
do one's part to do one's share.
for my part as far as concerns me.
for the most part in most cases.
in good part without taking offence: *He took my refusal in good part.*
in part partly.
part and parcel. See **parcel**.
part of speech one of the classes (e.g. noun, verb) into which words are divided in grammar.
part with to give up, let go.
take part to have an active part or share (in e.g. a play, a battle).
take someone's part to side with him, support him.
See also **partial**.

partake *pär-tāk', v.i.* **1** (with *of*) to eat or take some (food, drink). **2** (with *in*) to take part (in): *He will partake in the festivities*:—*pr.p.* **partak'ing**; *pa.t.* **partook'**; *pa.p.* **partak'en**.

partial *pär'sh(a)l, adj.* **1** in part only, not total or complete: *The attempt was a partial failure.* **2** tending to favour one person or side, biassed, unfair (*opp.* **impar'tial**). **3** (with *to*) fond of: *He was partial to tripe, to long walks.*
partiality *(-shi-al'i-ti) n.* **par'tially** *adv.*

participate *pär-tis'i-pāt, v.i.* to take a share or part (in e.g. a discussion, sports):—*pr.p.* **parti'cipating**. (Often used as **partake**, but not of material things such as food.)
participā'tion *n.*
partic'ipant, partic'ipator *ns.*

participle *pär'ti-si-pl, n.* an adjective formed from a verb, ending in *-ing* or *-ed* (e.g. the verb *to act* forms the adjectives *acting* and *acted*, as in *acting manager*, *an acted story*).
particip'ial *adj.*

particle *pär'ti-kl, n.* **1** a tiny piece (of matter, e.g. of dust). **2** any of the parts of an atom. **3** a tiny amount: *a particle of truth.*
particular *par-tik'ū-lar, adj.* **1** pointing out specially a single person or thing: *this particular waiter*; *in this particular race.* **2** personal: *my particular dislikes.* **3** special: *to take particular care.* **4** very careful, exact: *particular in her dress.*—*n.* a single point, a detail.
partic'ularise *v.i.* to mention the details.—Also *v.t.:—pr.p.* **particularising**.
partic'ularly *adv.* in a very high degree, especially: *He was particularly glad.*
in particular especially.

parti-coloured *pär'ti-kul-erd, adj.* with different colours in different parts.

particular. See **particle**.

partisan *pär-ti-zan'*, *pär'*, *n.* **1** a devoted follower, or member of a party or side. **2** a light soldier who scours the country and raids the enemy, a guerilla.

par'tisanship (or *-zan'*) *n.*

partition *pȧr-tish'(ȯ)n*, *n.* **1** the act of dividing. **2** the state of being divided. **3** something that divides, as a wall between rooms.

partly. See **part**.

partner *pärt'nėr*, *n.* **1** one who shares with another the ownership of a business. **2** one who plays or works on the same side as another. **3** one who dances with another. **4** a husband or wife.—*v.t.* to act as a partner to.

part'nership *n.* **1** the state of working together for some end. **2** an association of persons as partners.

partook. See **partake**.

partridge *pär'trij*, *n.* a bird of the pheasant family, shot for sport.

party *pär'ti*, *n.* **1** a large group of persons united for special or other action: *the Conservative or Labour party.* **2** a smaller group formed for a purpose: *a raiding party.* **3** a meeting, esp. of guests. **4** an entertainment, celebration. **5** a person taking part in, or approving of, an affair: *He was a party to the crime.* **6** either of the persons or groups concerned in a contract, or in a lawsuit:—*pl.* **part'ies**.—*adj.* (used only before a noun) having to do with a party.

party line **1** a telephone line used by several subscribers. **2** a boundary between properties. **3** a policy strictly laid down for a political party by its leaders.

parvenu *pär'vė-nū*, *n.* a person who has risen in society, an upstart.

pass *päs*, *v.t.* **1** to go alongside, over, through, and then beyond: *to pass another car, to pass a large stream.* **2** to go, be, beyond: *This passes my comprehension.* **3** to cause to go: *Pass the rope through the ring.* **4** to send from person to person, place to place, etc. **5** to be successful in (an examination). **6** to approve (e.g. an examination candidate, a resolution); to accept as being of the required standard. **7** to make (a law). **8** to pronounce (judgment). **9** to spend (time). **10** to produce and remove from the body: *to pass urine.* **11** to utter (a remark).—*v.i.* **1** to go past or by, and away. **2** to go (through, over, etc.). **3** to go (from one place, person, state, etc., to another): *to pass from Athens to Rome, from mother to daughter, from joy to despair.* **4** (with *as*, *for*) to be regarded, accepted as: *dyed rabbit passing as an expensive fur; rudeness passing for wit.* **5** to be successful in an examination, up to a required standard, etc.:—*pa.t.* and *pa.p.* **passed** (see also **past**).—*n.* **1** a narrow way through mountains. **2** a ticket for free travel or admission. **3** giving of the ball from one member of a team to another. **4** a thrust, threatening move, or unwanted amorous approach. **5** success in an examination, without honours.

pass'able *adj.* **1** that may be travelled over or through (*opp.* **impass'able**). **2** moderately good.

passage *pas'ij*, *n.* **1** the act of passing. **2** a crossing. **3** a voyage. **4** a sum paid for a voyage. **5** the making (of a law). **6** a long narrow way, as a corridor, or a channel. **7** a portion of a book, etc. or piece of music.

pass'er, **pass'er-by'** *ns.* one who passes near:—*pl.* **pass'ers(-by')**.

passing *pä'sing*, *adj.* **1** going by. **2** not lasting long. **3** (used only before a noun) made in passing, casual: *a passing remark.*—*adv.* (*old-fashioned*) very: *She was passing fair.*—*n.* **1** the act of one who, that, passes. **2** death.

pass'book *n.* a book in which records of money put into or taken out of a bank, etc. account are written.

passer-by. See **passer**.

pass'key *n.* **1** a latchkey. **2** a key for opening several locks.

pass'word (*military*) *n.* a secret word by which a friend can be recognised and allowed to pass or to enter camp, etc.

bring to pass to cause to happen.

come to pass to happen.

in passing in the course of doing or saying something else.

pass off **1** (of e.g. sickness) to go away gradually. **2** to be carried through (successfully). **3** to palm off. **4** to turn attention away from (something awkward, etc.).

pass out to faint.

pass over **1** to overlook, ignore. **2** to say nothing about.

pass the buck (*coll.*) to shift the responsibility or blame (to someone else).

passé *pas'ā*, *pas-ā'*, *adj.* **1** past one's best. **2** out of date:—*fem.* **passée**: *Last year's styles are now passé.*

passenger *pas'in-jėr*, *n.* **1** one who travels, esp. one who travels by public transport (train, bus, ship, etc.) or in another's car. **2** one of a group or team who does not or cannot do his share of the work.

passenger seat the seat in the front of a vehicle beside the driver's seat.

passion *pash'(ȯ)n, n.* **1** strong feeling, esp. anger. **2** strong love. **3** great liking. **4** something one has a great liking for. **5** (with *cap.*) the sufferings and death of Christ.
pass'ionate *adj.* **1** easily moved to anger or other strong feeling esp. love or desire. **2** intense, very great: *a passionate loyalty:—opp.* **dispassionate**.
passion play a religious drama showing the sufferings and death of Christ.
Passion Week the week before Easter.

passive *pas'iv, adj.* **1** not resisting. **2** not showing energy or movement. **3** not active, but acted upon. **4** (*grammar*) of a form of the verb used when the subject is acted upon (also *n.*) (e.g. *The boy was bitten by a dog*).
passive resistance refusing to obey the law when it goes against one's conscience and submitting to punishment rather than have any violence.
passive smoking the involuntary inhaling of smoke from tobacco smoked by others.

Passover *päs'ō-vėr, n.* an annual feast of the Jews in memory of the Israelites' escape from captivity in Egypt, so named from the fact that the angel *passed over* their doors though he killed the first-born sons of the Egyptians (Exodus 12).

passport *päs'pōrt, -pört, n.* a document giving permission to travel abroad.

past *päst, adj.* **1** having happened in a time gone by: *He thanked me for past kindnesses.* **2** ended.—*prep.* beyond, farther than: *He ran past the house.*—*n.* **1** something that has passed, esp. time. **2** a past history, career, esp. a scandalous one.
past'mast'er *n.* one who has great experience or skill: *a pastmaster in the art of deceit.*

pasta *päs'tȧ, pas', n.* (dough used in making) spaghetti, macaroni, etc.

paste *pāst, n.* **1** a soft damp mixture. **2** dough for pies, etc. **3** a smooth food mixture made by grinding: *almond paste.* **4** a mixture used for sticking paper, etc. on or together. **5** a clay mixture for making china. **6** glass for making artificial jewels.—*v.t.* to fasten with paste:—*pr.p.* **past'ing**.
pās'ty[1] *adj.* like paste:—*comp.* **pās'tier**; *superl.* **pās'tiest**.
pās'tiness *n.*
pasty[2] *pas'ti, n.* a pie baked without a dish:—*pl.* **pas'ties**.
pastry *pās'tri, n.* **1** articles of food made of paste or dough. **2** crust of pies, etc.:—*pl.* **pas'tries**.
paste'board *n.* a stiff board made of sheets of paper pasted together.

pastel *pas'tėl, n.* **1** chalk mixed with other materials, used for crayons. **2** a drawing made with these crayons.
pastel shades pale, soft colours.

pasteurise *pas'tėr-īz, -chėr-, v.t.* to make (milk, etc.) free from certain germs, and less apt to sour, by heating to a given temperature for a given time:—*pr.p.* **pas'teurising**.
pasteurisā'tion *n.*

pastiche *pas-tēsh', n.* a musical or literary composition made up of parts from, or imitations of, other compositions.

pastille *pas-tēl', pas'til, n.* a small sweet, often medicated for coughs, etc.

pastime *päs'tīm, n.* something that serves to pass the time, a recreation.

pastor *päs'tȯr, n.* a clergyman (orig. a shepherd).
pas'toral *adj.* **1** having to do with shepherds, or their life, or country life in general. **2** having to do with a pastor.—*n.* a poem, etc. that claims to show shepherd or country life.
pas'torate, pas'torship *ns.* the office of a pastor.
pasture *päs'chur̊, -tyur̊, n.* growing grass for grazing animals.—*v.t.* to graze (cattle).—Also *v.i.*:—*pr.p.* **pas'turing**.
pas'turage *n.* grazing land.

pastrami *pas-trä'mi, n.* strongly spiced smoked beef.

pastry. See **paste**.

pasture. See **pastor**.

pasty[1,2]. See **paste**.

pat *pat, n.* **1** a gentle tap, as with the palm of the hand. **2** a small lump of butter. **3** a light sound.—*v.t.* **1** to strike gently. **2** to tap:—*pr.p.* **patt'ing**; *pa.p.* **patt'ed**.—*adj.* **1** hitting the point exactly. **2** thoroughly memorised. **3** ready to be given easily: *He had his answer pat.*
a pat on the back a mark of approval.

patch *pach, n.* **1** a piece put on to mend or cover a hole, etc. **2** a scrap of material. **3** a small piece of ground.—*v.t.* **1** to mend with a patch. **2** (usu. *patch up*) to mend clumsily or in a hurry (e.g. a building, quarrel).
patch'y *adj.* uneven, mixed in quality:—*comp.* **patch'ier**; *superl.* **patch'iest**.
patch'ily *adv.* **patch'iness** *n.*
patch'work *n.* **1** work formed of pieces sewed or put together. **2** work clumsily done. **3** something made up of pieces of various colours, shapes, etc.
not a patch on not fit to be compared with.

pate *pāt*, *n.* (the top of) the head.

pâté *pat'ā*, *n.* **1** (*orig.*) a pie, patty. **2** a paste made of finely minced meat or fish, flavoured with herbs, spices, etc.
pâté de foie gras *(dė fwä grä)* pâté of fat goose liver.

patella *pȧ-tel'ȧ*, *n.* the knee-cap, knee-pan.

patent *pā'tėnt*, sometimes *pat'*, *adj.* **1** lying open, obvious. **2** (usu. *pat'ėnt*) protected by patent.—*n.* an official document, open, and having the Great Seal of the government attached, giving a right or privilege, such as a title of nobility, or the right to all the profits from an invention for a number of years.—*v.t.* to obtain a patent for.
patentee' *n.* one who holds a patent.
pā'tently *adv.* openly, clearly.
patent leather varnished leather.

pater *pā'tėr*, (*old-fashioned coll.*; esp. with *my*, *his*, etc.) *n.* father.
paternal *pȧ-tûr'nȧl*, *adj.* **1** fatherly. **2** on father's side of family: *paternal grandmother* (= one's father's mother).
pater'nally *adv.*
pater'nity *n.* the state of being a father.
patricide *pat'ri-sīd*, *n.* **1** the murder of father by his son or daughter. **2** a person who commits this crime.
paternoster *pat'ėr-nos'tėr*, or *pāt'*, *n.* the Lord's Prayer.

path *päth*, *n.* **1** a way made by, or for, people or animals walking on it, a track. **2** a route taken. **3** a course of action or conduct:—*pl.* **paths** *(päTHz)*.
path'less *adj.* without paths, untrodden.
path'finder *n.* one who explores the route, a pioneer.
path'way *n.* a path.

pathetic *pȧ-thet'ik*, *adj.* **1** touching, causing pity or sorrow. **2** (*coll.*) very poor, inadequate.
pathet'ically *adv.*
pathos *pā'thos*, *n.* the quality that arouses pity: *He told the story with pathos, and tears filled my eyes.*

pathology *pȧ-thol'ȯ-ji*, *n.* the study of diseases.
pathol'ogist *n.* **1** a specialist in the causes and effects of disease. **2** one who makes post-mortem examinations.

pathos. See **pathetic**.

patience *pā'shėns*, *n.* **1** the ability to wait quietly. **2** the ability to suffer annoyance, pain, etc. calmly. **3** perseverance. **4** a card game, usu. for one person:—*opp.* (*defs. 1, 2*) **impatience**.
pā'tient *(-shėnt) adj.* **1** enduring delay, etc. without complaining. **2** not easily angered.—*n.* a person under medical treatment.
pā'tiently *adv.*

patio *pat'i-ō*, *n.* **1** a courtyard conn. with a house, esp. an inner court open to the sky. **2** a paved area usu. adjoining a house, where outdoor meals can be served, etc.:—*pl.* **pat'ios**.

pâtisserie *pa-tēs'rē*, *n.* **1** a pastry or cake shop. **2** pastries and other fancy cakes.

patois *pat'wä*, *n.* a regional dialect used in informal everyday situations:—*pl.* **pat'ois** *(pat'wäz)*.

patriarch *pā'tri-ärk*, *n.* **1** one who governs his family by right as father, or as head of the tribe (*fem.* **matriarch**). **2** the head of various African, Asian and eastern European Christian churches.

patrician *pȧ-trish'ȧn*, *n.* an aristocrat.—Also *adj.*
patrimony *pat'ri-mȯn-i. n.* property handed down from one's father or ancestors.

patricide. See **pater**.

patrimony. See **patrician**.

patriot *pā'tri-ȯt*, *pat'*, *n.* one who truly loves and serves his country.
patriotic *pat-ri-ot'ik*, *pāt-*, *adj.* **1** like a patriot. **2** inspired by love of, or duty towards, one's country.
patriot'ically *adv.*
pa'triotism *n.* love of one's country.

patrol *pȧ-trōl*, *v.t.* to go the rounds of (camp, town), walk through (streets), sail (an area of sea, etc.), in order to watch or protect.—Also *v.i.*:—*pr.p.* **patroll'ing**; *pa.p.* **patrolled'**.—*n.* **1** the act of keeping watch in this way. **2** a body of men, etc. who do so. **3** a small group of Scouts or of Girl Guides.
patrol car a car used by police patrolling an area.

patron *pā'trȯn*, *n.* **1** a protector. **2** one who encourages, supports, another. **3** one who has the right to appoint to an office.
patronage *(pat', pāt') n.* **1** support given by a patron. **2** the right of giving offices or church appointments.
pat'ronise *(pat') v.t.* **1** to act as a patron towards (someone). **2** to encourage. **3** to treat (person) as if one is better than he is:—*pr.p.* **pat'ronising**.
patron saint a saint considered or chosen as a protector.

patter[1] *pat'ėr*, *v.i.* to strike against something with quick taps.—*n.* the sound so made: *a patter of rain on the roof.*

patter[2] *pat'ėr*, *v.i.* and *v.t.* **1** to mumble. **2** to talk, or say, rapidly.—*n.* **1** chatter. **2** many words sung or spoken very rapidly.

3 the words used for comic, etc. effect by a stage comedian or conjuror.

pattern *pat'ėrn, n.* **1** a person or thing suitable to copy. **2** an example of excellence. **3** a model or guide for making something. **4** a decorative design (e.g. on cloth, wallpaper). **5** a sample: *a book of tweed patterns*.

patt'ern-maker *n.* one who makes patterns, esp. in wood or metal, for use in a foundry.

patty *pat'i, n.* a little pie:—*pl.* **patt'ies**.

paucity *pö'sit-i, n.* smallness of number or quantity: *a paucity of supporters*; *paucity of evidence*.

paunch *pönch, pönsh, n.* **1** the belly. **2** a potbelly.

pauper *pö'pėr, n.* **1** a very poor person. **2** one who lives on charity, esp. public.

pau'perise *v.t.* to make a pauper of:—*pr.p.* **pau'perising**.

pause *pöz, n.* **1** a stop for a time. **2** hesitation caused by doubt. **3** (*music*) (a mark showing) the holding of a note or rest.—Also *v.i.*:—*pr.p.* **pau'sing**.

pavan(e) *pav'ȧn,* or *-än', n.* **1** a slow stately dance. **2** the music for it.

pave *pāv, v.t.* to cover with flat stones, etc. so as to form a level surface for walking on:—*pr.p.* **pav'ing**.

pave'ment *n.* **1** a paved surface. **2** a footpath beside a road.

pav'ing-stone *n.* a piece of stone prepared for paving.

pave the way for, to to make an easy way for (something to happen).

pavilion *pȧ-vil'yȯn, n.* **1** a large tent. **2** an ornamental building. **3** a clubhouse for changing on a games field.

paw *pö, n.* **1** a foot with claws. **2** (*scornfully*) the hand.—*v.i.* to draw the forefoot along the ground.—*v.t.* **1** to scrape with the forefoot. **2** to handle roughly or clumsily. **3** to strike wildly with the hands: *to paw the air*.

pawky *pök'i,* (*Scot.*) *adj.* sly, shrewd, cunning:—*comp.* **pawk'ier**; *superl.* **pawk'iest**.

pawl *pöl, n.* a short bar falling between teeth of a notched wheel to prevent it from running back.

pawn[1] *pön, v.t.* to give over (an article of value) in return for a loan of money on the understanding that when the money is returned, with interest, the article will be given back.—*n.* the state of being pawned: *His watch is in pawn*.

pawn'broker *n.* one who lends money on pawns or pledges placed at a **pawn'shop**.

pawn[2] *pön, n.* **1** a small piece of lowest rank in chess. **2** a person who is considered unimportant and is used for a purpose by someone else.

pawpaw. See **papaw**.

pay *pā, v.t.* **1** to rid oneself of (a debt), esp. by returning money owed. **2** to give (money), or to give money to (a person), for goods or services. **3** to reward, or punish. **4** to give (attention, homage).—*v.i.* **1** to hand over money. **2** to be profitable, worth the effort: *It pays to be careful*. **3** to be punished (for): *He will pay for his crime*:—*pr.p.* **pay'ing**; *pa.p.* **paid**.—*n.* money given for service, wages, salary.

pay'able *adj.* **1** that should be paid. **2** due.

payee' *n.* one to whom money is paid.

pay'ment *n.* **1** the act of paying. **2** money paid. **3** reward. **4** punishment.

payō'la *n.* (the paying of) a bribe to secure a favour.

pay'-as-you-earn' *n.* a method of income-tax collection in which the taxes are taken out of the pay before it is given to the worker (often **P.A.Y.E.**).

pay'-load *n.* **1** the part of the cargo of an aeroplane, etc. for which money is obtained. **2** the part of a rocket used as warhead, or for obtaining information.

pay'phone *n.* a coin- or card-operated public telephone.

pay'roll *n.* **1** a list of employees to be paid, with amounts due to them. **2** the money for paying wages.

pay off 1 to pay in full and discharge from work. **2** to give good results.—*n.* **pay'off**.

pay out 1 to cause to run out, as rope. **2** to punish.

put paid to to stop, ruin, etc.

pea *pē, n.* a climbing plant bearing in pods round seeds used as food.—Older sing. **pease**. (pl. *peasen*).

peace *pēs, n.* **1** a state of quiet. **2** freedom from war or disturbance. **3** a treaty that ends a war. **4** ease (of mind, conscience).

peace'able *adj.* **1** inclined to peace: *She has a peaceable nature*. **2** peaceful.

peace'ful *adj.* **1** quiet. **2** not intended or likely to cause war or disturbance.

peace'fully *adv.*

peace'maker *n.* **1** one who makes peace. **2** one who helps to make enemies friendly.

hold one's peace to be silent.

peace-keeping force a military force sent into an area with the task of preventing fighting between opposing factions.

peach *pēch, n.* a juicy, velvety-skinned fruit with a stone in the centre.

peacock *pē'kok, n.* a large bird noted for gay coloured feathers, esp. in the tail:—*fem.* **pea'hen.**

peacock blue a deep greenish blue.

pea-jacket *pē'jak'it, n.* a coarse thick jacket worn by seamen.

peak[1] *pēk, n.* **1** a point. **2** the top of a mountain. **3** the highest point: *at the peak of his career.* **4** the brim of a hat that juts out.—*adj.* (used only before a noun) maximum, greatest: *peak viewing hours.*—*v.i.* to reach the maximum point: *The rate of inflation has peaked and should start falling soon.*

peaked *adj.* pointed.

peak[2] *pēk, v.i.* to look thin and sickly.

peak'y *adj.* having a sickly look:—*comp.* **peak'ier**; *superl.* **peak'iest.**

peal *pēl, n.* **1** a loud sound. **2** a set of bells tuned to each other. **3** the changes rung on such bells.—*v.i.* to sound loudly.

peanut *pē'nut, n.* a groundnut, monkey nut.

pear *pār, n.* **1** a fruit narrowing towards the stem and bulging at the end. **2** the tree which bears this, of the apple family.

pearl *pûrl, n.* **1** a round growth found in the shells of oysters and other shellfish which is used as a gem. **2** something resembling a pearl in shape, size, colour, or value.—*adj.* **1** of, or like, a pearl. **2** (of barley, tapioca, etc.) having grains of medium size.—*v.i.* to fish or dive for pearls.

pear'ly *adj.* **1** like pearl. **2** rich in pearls:—*comp.* **pear'lier**; *superl.* **pear'liest.**

pearl'-diver, -fisher *ns.*

peasant *pez'ȧnt, n.* in poor agricultural societies, a farm worker or small farmer. —Also *adj.*

peas'antry *n.* the body of peasants.

pease. See **pea**.

peat *pēt, n.* **1** a piece of material cut from a bog, dried for fuel. **2** the decayed vegetable matter from which this is cut.

peat'y *adj:*—*comp.* **peat'ier**; *superl.* **peat'iest.**

peat'iness *n.*

pebble *peb'l, n.* **1** a small roundish stone, usu. worn by water. **2** colourless quartz.

pebb'ly *adj:*—*comp.* **pebb'lier**; *superl.* **pebb'liest.**

pebb'liness *n.*

pebble dash small stones set in mortar as a covering for walls.

pecan *pi-kan', n.* **1** a North American hickory. **2** its thin-shelled nut.

peccadillo *pek-ȧ-dil'ō, n.* a slight misdemeanour:—*pl.* **peccadill'os, -oes.**

peck[1] *pek, n.* a measure for dry goods, one-fourth of a bushel.

peck[2] *pek, v.t.* **1** to strike, or to pick up, with the beak. **2** to strike repeatedly with anything pointed. **3** to kiss with a dabbing movement. **4** to eat little of.—Also *v.i.* and *n.*

peck'ish *adj.* rather hungry.

pectin *pek'tin, n.* a substance found in fruit, which makes jam set.

pectoral *pek'tȯ-rȧl, adj.* of or on the breast or chest.

peculiar *pi-kūl'yȧr, adj.* **1** belonging to, characteristic of, only one (country, person, etc.): *a custom peculiar to England.* **2** odd, strange.

peculiarity *pi-kū-li-ar'i-ti, n.* **1** something that is found in one only. **2** an odd trait. **3** oddity:—*pl.* **peculiar'ities.**

pecuniary *pi-kūn'yȧr-i, -i-ȧr-i, adj.* **1** consisting of money: *a pecuniary reward.* **2** having to do with money.

pedagogue *ped'ȧ-gog, n.* a teacher.

pedagogy *(-goj'i) n.* the science of teaching.

pedal *ped'ȧl, adj.* having to do with the foot.—*n.* a lever pressed by the foot (e.g. in a cycle, piano).—*v.t.* to work the pedals of:—*pr.p.* **ped'alling**; *pa.p.* **ped'alled.**

pedant *ped'ȧnt, n.* **1** one who makes a great display of learning. **2** one who attaches great importance to tiny details.

pedant'ic *adj.*

ped'antry *n.* **1** display of knowledge. **2** too great concern with tiny details.

peddle *ped'l, v.i.* **1** to travel from door to door selling small objects. **2** to trifle.—*v.t.* to sell as a pedlar: *to peddle brushes:*—*pr.p.* **pedd'ling.**

pedd'ler (esp. *U.S.*) *n.* a pedlar.

pedd'ling *adj.* unimportant.—*n.* the trade of a pedlar.

pedestal *ped'is-tȧl, n.* the foot or support of a column, statue, vase, etc.

pedestrian *pi-des'tri-ȧn, adj.* **1** going on foot. **2** dull, common.—*n.* one who goes on foot.

pedestrian crossing a part of a road marked for the use of pedestrians who wish to cross.

pedicure *ped'i-kūr, n.* **1** the treatment of corns, bunions, etc. **2** a chiropodist.

pedigree *ped'i-grē, n.* **1** a list of the ancestors from whom one has descended. **2** old or distinguished lineage.

ped'igree(d) *adjs.* **1** having known ancestry. **2** pure-bred.

pedlar *ped'lȧr, n.* one who goes about with a pack of goods for sale.

ped'lary *n.* the wares or trade of a pedlar.

peek *pēk, v.i.* to look quickly or slyly.—Also *n.*

peel *pēl, v.t.* **1** to strip off skin or bark from. **2** to strip off (skin etc.).—*v.i.* to come off, as skin, rind.—*n.* rind, esp. that of oranges, lemons, etc.

peep[1] *pēp, v.i.* to cheep, as a baby bird.

peep[2] *pēp, v.i.* **1** to look through a narrow opening. **2** to look slyly or carefully. **3** (to begin) to appear: *violets peeping through the grass.*—*n.* **1** a sly look. **2** a glimpse. **3** a first appearance.

peep'er *n.* **1** one that peeps. **2** a prying person.

Peeping Tom someone who peeps in at people's windows.

peep'-show *n.* a series of pictures looked at through a small hole.

peer[1] *pēr, n.* **1** an equal in rank, age, or merit. **2** a nobleman of the rank of baron upwards. **3** a member of the House of Lords:—*fem.* (*defs. 2, 3*) **peer'ess**.

peer'age *n.* **1** a peer's title. **2** all the peers taken together, or a book listing them.

peer'less *adj.* unequalled, matchless.

peer group one's peers or companions as a group, esp. as an influence on one's attitudes.

peer[2] *pēr, v.i.* to look closely, searchingly, or with difficulty: *to peer into the dark.*

peevish *pēv'ish, adj.* ill-natured, cross, fretful.

peeved (*coll.*) *adj.* annoyed.

peev'ishly *adv.* **peev'ishness** *n.*

peewit *pē'wit, pū'it, n.* the lapwing, so named from its cry.

peg *peg, n.* a pin (esp. of wood) for hanging up, fastening, tightening, or for marking a position or point.—*v.t.* **1** to fasten or mark with a peg. **2** to hold (prices, etc.) at a fixed level or at a level proportionate to something else.—*v.i.* (with *away*) to work very hard: *He pegged away at his chores*:—*pr.p.* **pegg'ing**; *pa.p.* **pegged**.

off the peg (bought) ready to wear, from an already-existing stock.

take down a peg to humble.

pejorative *pi-jor'ȧ-tiv, pē', adj.* showing disapproval, dislike, scorn, etc.

Pekin(g)ese *pē-king(g)-ēz', n.* a small pug-nosed dog of orig. Chinese breed.—Also (*coll.*) **Peke**.

pelican *pel'i-kȧn, n.* a type of water bird with an enormous pouched bill.

pellet *pel'it, n.* **1** a little ball. **2** a small pill. **3** a ball of shot.

pell-mell *pel'-mel', adv.* **1** in great disorder. **2** helter-skelter: *The children rushed pell-mell into the room.*

pellucid *pe-lū'sid, -lōō', adj.* perfectly clear.

pel'met *n.* a strip of fabric or a narrow board fitted along the top of a window to conceal the curtain rail.

pelt[1] *pelt, n.* a raw skin or hide.

pelt'ry *n.* **1** pelts. **2** furs.

pelt[2] *pelt, v.t.* **1** to strike repeatedly with blows or objects, e.g. stones. **2** to throw (things, at):—*v.i.* **1** (of rain, etc.) to fall heavily. **2** to rush, speed.

(at) full pelt very quickly.

pelvis *pel'vis, n.* (the frame of bones forming) the lower part of the abdomen.

pel'vic *adj.*

pen[1] *pen, n.* a small enclosure, esp. for animals.—*v.t.* to put or keep in a pen:—*pr.p.* **penn'ing**; *pa.p.* **penned**.

pen[2] *pen, n.* an instrument used for writing in ink.—*v.t.* to write:—*pr.p.* **penn'ing**; *pa.p.* **penned**.

pen'-friend, (*coll.*) **pen'-pal** *ns.* a person, usu. living abroad, with whom one exchanges letters but whom one has never met.

pen'knife *n.* a small pocket knife, orig. for mending pens made from quills.

pen'manship *n.* (the art of) handwriting.

pen'-name *n.* a name assumed by an author.

penal *pē'nȧl, adj.* having to do with punishment.

pe'nalise *v.t.* **1** to punish. **2** to attach a penalty or disadvantage to (e.g. breaking of rule in a game):—*pr.p.* **pe'nalising**.

penalty *pen'ȧl-ti, n.* **1** punishment. **2** a fine. **3** a loss, etc. that must be suffered e.g. for breaking the rules. **4** a penalty kick, goal:—*pl.* **pen'alties**.

penal servitude hard labour in prison as punishment for a crime.

penalty goal a goal scored from a **penalty kick**, a free kick at goal awarded because a player on the opposite side has broken a rule.

penance *pen'ȧns, n.* punishment a person undergoes willingly because they are sorry for wrongdoing.

pence. See **penny**.

penchant *pong'shong, n.* a liking (for).

pencil *pen'sl, n.* **1** an instrument containing graphite or coloured material for writing, drawing, etc. **2** any stick of coloured material of similar shape: *an eyebrow pencil.* **3** a number of rays coming to a point.—*v.t.* to write or draw with a pencil:—*pr.p.* **pen'cilling**; *pa.p.* **pen'cilled**.

pendant *pen'dȧnt*, *n.* anything that hangs, esp. an ornament on a chain.
pen'dent *adj.* **1** hanging. **2** not yet decided.
pen'ding *adj.* awaiting a decision.—*prep.* awaiting, until: *They held him in prison pending trial.*
pen'dulous *adj.* **1** hanging loosely. **2** swinging freely.
pendulum *pen'dū-lu̇m*, *n.* a weight hung from a fixed point and swinging freely to and fro, as in a clock.

penetrate *pen'i-trāt*, *v.t.* **1** to force a way into. **2** to pierce. **3** to reach the mind or feelings of. **4** to see into, understand:—*pr.p.* **pen'etrating**.
pen'etrable *adj.* able to be penetrated:—*opp.* **impen'etrable**.
pen'etrating *adj.* **1** piercing. **2** keen, understanding: *a penetrating look*; *a penetrating mind.*
penetrā'tion *n.* **1** the act of entering into. **2** cleverness in understanding.

penguin *peng'gwin* or *pen'*, *n.* a large, black-and-white, flightless sea-bird of the Antarctic and other southern regions.

penicillin *pen-i-sil'in*, *n.* a substance, obtained from mould, which stops the growth of many disease bacteria.

peninsula *pen-in'sū-lȧ*, *n.* a piece of land that is almost surrounded by water.
penin'sular *adj.* **1** in the form of a peninsula. **2** living on a peninsula.

penis *pē'nis*, *n.* the part of the body of a male human or animal used in sexual intercourse and for urinating.

penitent *pen'i-tėnt*, *adj.* sorry for sin, repentant:—*opp.* **impenitent**.—*n.* one who is sorry for his sins.
pen'itence *n.* the state of being sorry.
penitentiary *pen-i-ten'shȧr-i*, (*U.S.*) *n.* a state or federal prison:—*pl.* **peniten'tiaries**.

penknife, penmanship. See **pen²**.

pennant *pen'ȧnt*, *n.* **1** a long tapering flag, at the masthead of warship or for signalling. **2** a small, usu. triangular, flag for decoration or awarded as a prize.

pennon *pen'ȯn*, *n.* a flag of various shapes.

penny *pen'i*, *n.* a coin (orig. silver, later copper, then bronze) orig. equal to 1/12 of a shilling (abbrev. *d.*), now equal to one hundredth of a pound (abbrev. *p*):—*pl.* **pennies** (*pen'iz*; used in giving the number of coins: *I have six pennies*), or **pence** (*pens*; used in giving a value: *The chocolate costs twenty pence*); **pence** and **p** (*pē*) are also used *coll.* for 1p: *a one-pence coin.*
penn'iless *adj.* **1** without money. **2** poor.
penn'yworth *n.* **1** a penny's worth. **2** a bargain: *a good, bad, pennyworth.*
a pretty penny a large sum of money.
penny-wise but pound-foolish saving small sums but not caring about large.

pension *pen'shȯn*, *n.* **1** a sum of money given regularly to a person because of past services or old age. **2** a boarding school or boarding house on the Continent.—*v.t.* to grant a pension to (someone).
pen'sionable *adj.* (of a person) entitled to, (of service) entitling to, a pension.
pen'sioner *n.* **1** one who receives a pension. **2** a dependant, hireling.
pension off to dismiss, or allow to retire, with a pension.

pensive *pen'siv*, *adj.* **1** dreamily thoughtful. **2** suggesting sad thought.

pent *pent*: **pent in, up** shut in or up.

pent(a)- *pent(ȧ)-*, (as part of a word) five.
pentagon *pen'tȧ-gon*, *n.* **1** (*geometry*) a figure with five sides and five angles. **2** (*cap.*) the headquarters of the U.S. armed forces in Washington (from the shape of the building).
pentag'onal *adj.*
pentameter *pen-tam'i-tėr*, *n.* a line in poetry with five stresses.
pentathlon *pen-tath'lon*, *n.* **1** in ancient Greek games, a contest in five events. **2** a five-event Olympic games contest for women. **3** (**modern pentathlon**) an Olympic games contest in swimming, cross-country riding and running, fencing and revolver-shooting.
pentath'lete *n.*

Pentecost *pent'i-kost*, *n.* **1** a Jewish festival held on the fiftieth day after the Passover. **2** Whitsun.
Pentecost'al *adj.* **1** relating to Pentecost. **2** relating to any of several Christian groups placing great emphasis on the spiritual powers of The Holy Spirit (also *n.*).
Pentecost'alist *n.*

penthouse *pent'hows*, *n.* **1** a shed or lean-to joined to a main building. **2** a (luxurious) apartment or dwelling at the top of a building:—*pl.* **penthouses** *(-ziz)*.

penultimate *pe-nult'i-mit*, *adj.* last but one.

penury *pen'ū-ri*, *n.* great poverty, want.
penū'rious *adj.* **1** needy. **2** stingy, mean.

peon *pē'on*, *n.* in Spanish-speaking America, a member of the labouring class.

peony *pē'ȯ-ni*, *n.* a garden plant with large red, pink, or white flowers:—*pl.* **pe'onies**.

people *pē'pl*, *n. pl.* (except *def. 1.*) **1** a nation, a community, or a race (in these senses treated as *sing.*, with *pl.* **peoples**;

e.g. *the peoples of the world*). **2** the mass of the nation. **3** human beings. **4** persons generally: *So people say.* **5** near relatives: *His people came from France.* **6** followers. **7** servants.—*v.t.* **1** to fill with inhabitants, people, animals. **2** (of persons, etc.) to inhabit, fill:—*pr.p.* **peop'ling.**
See also **populace, popular.**

pep *pep*, (*coll.*) *n.* energy, vigour.
pep pill a pill containing a stimulant drug.
pep talk a talk intended to increase the listener's enthusiasm, effort, etc.

pepper *pep'ėr*, *n.* a seasoning made from the dried berries of a **pepper plant.**—*v.t.* **1** to sprinkle with pepper. **2** to hit or pelt, e.g. with shot.
pepp'ery *adj.* **1** like pepper. **2** hot-tempered. **3** fiery: *peppery words.*
pepp'eriness *n.*
pepp'er-and-salt' *adj.* mixed black and white.
pepp'ercorn *n.* **1** the berry of the pepper plant. **2** something of little value.
pepp'ermint *n.* **1** a type of mint. **2** a usu. round, white sweet with a flavouring got from the peppermint.
cayenne pepper, chilli pepper. See **cayenne, chilli.**
green, red pepper. See **capsicum.**

peptic *pep'tik:* **peptic ulcer** an ulcer of the stomach or duodenum.

per *pûr*, *prep.* **1** for each: *eighty pence per dozen.* **2** by: *per parcel post.*
per annum for each year.
per cent *pėr sent'*, in or for every hundred (pounds, etc.); symbol (%).
percent'age *n.* **1** the rate or amount in a hundred. **2** a proportion.

per- *pėr-*, *per-*, *pûr-*, *pfx.* through, thoroughly, very.

perambulate *pėr-am'bū-lāt*, *v.t.* to walk about, through, over.—*v.i.* to stroll:—*pr.p.* **peram'bulating.**
peram'bulātor *n.* **1** one who walks. **2** a pram.

perceive *pėr-sēv'*, *v.t.* **1** to become aware of (something) through the senses. **2** to see. **3** to understand:—*pr.p.* **perceiv'ing.**
percep'tible *adj.* **1** able to be seen, heard, etc. **2** enough to be noticed: *a perceptible delay*:—*opp.* **imperceptible.**
percep'tibly *adv.*
percep'tion *n.* **1** the act of perceiving. **2** awareness of objects. **3** ability to recognise objects or feelings.
percep'tive *adj.* able, or quick, to perceive or understand.
percip'ient *pėr-sip'i-ėnt*, *adj.* perceptive.

per cent, percentage. See **per.**

perceptible, etc. See **perceive.**

perch¹ *pûrch*, *n.* a type of freshwater fish.

perch² *pûrch*, *n.* **1** a rod on which birds sit or roost. **2** any high seat.—*v.i.* and *v.t.* to alight or rest on a perch or high place, or to cause to do so.

perchance *pėr-chäns'*, (*old*) *adv.* **1** by chance. **2** perhaps.

percipient. See **perceive.**

percolate *pûr'kȯ-lāt*, *v.t.*, *v.i.* to pass through holes, filter:—*pr.p.* **per'colating.**
per'colator *n.* a device for percolating, esp. for making coffee by allowing water to percolate through ground coffee.

percussion *pėr-kush'(ȯ)n*, *n.* **1** the striking of one body against another, impact. **2** in medicine, tapping the body to find by the sound the condition of the organ underneath. **3** musical instruments played by striking, as drums, cymbals, etc.
percuss'ionist *n.* a musician who plays percussion instruments.

perdition *pėr-dish'(ȯ)n*, *n.* **1** utter ruin. **2** damnation, lasting punishment.

peregrinate *per'i-gri-nāt*, *v.i.* to travel about:—*pr.p.* **per'egrinating.**
peregrinā'tion *n.*

peremptory *pėr-em(p)'tȯr-i*, *adj.* **1** (of a command, etc.) to be obeyed at once. **2** (of manner) commanding, dictatorial.
peremp'torily *adv.* **peremp'toriness** *n.*

perennial *pėr-en'yȧl*, *adj.* **1** (of plants) coming up again year after year. **2** (of e.g. a stream) never drying up. **3** continual.—*n.* a perennial plant.

perestroika *per-ė-stroi'ka*, *n.* in Russia, reconstruction, restructuring (of the state, etc.).

perfect *pûr'fikt*, *adj.* **1** complete, accurate, exact. **2** faultless. **3** completely skilled:—*opp.* **imperfect.**—*v.t.* (*pėr-fekt'*) **1** to make perfect. **2** to finish. **3** to improve.
perfect'ible *adj.* capable of being made perfect.
perfec'tion *n.* **1** the state of being perfect. **2** the highest state or degree.
perfec'tionist *n.* **1** one who believes that perfection is possible. **2** one who is not content with less than perfection.

perfidious *pėr-fid'i-ůs*, *adj.* treacherous, untrustworthy, false.
perfid'iousness, per'fidy (*pl.* **-ies**), *ns.*

perforate *pûr'fȯ-rāt*, *v.t.* **1** to make a hole or holes through. **2** to pierce:—*pr.p.* **per'-forating.**
perforā'tion *n.* **1** the act of perforating. **2** a hole, or row of holes, made by boring.

perform *pėr-förm'*, *v.t.* **1** to do. **2** to carry out (duties, etc.). **3** to carry out, fulfil (e.g.

a promise, a command). **4** to act.—*v.i.* **1** to act a part on stage. **2** to play e.g. on a musical instrument.
perform'ance *n.* **1** the carrying out (of a task, etc.). **2** success in working: *good performance of the car's engine.* **3** an entertainment on stage. **4** an act or action. **5** (*coll.*) an instance of awkward, aggressive, embarrassing, etc. behaviour.
perform'er *n.*

perfume *pûr'fūm*, *n.* **1** a sweet scent, fragrance. **2** a liquid containing fragrant oil, scent.—*v.t.* (also *pėr-fūm'*) to scent:—*pr.p.* **perfuming**.
perfūm'ery *n.* **1** perfumes in general. **2** a shop, or part of a shop, where perfumes are sold:—*pl.* **perfūm'eries**.

perfunctory *pėr-fungk'tȯ-ri, adj.* **1** done merely as a duty. **2** done hurriedly, mechanically. **3** acting without interest.
perfun'ctorily *adv.*

pergola *pûr'gȯ-lȧ, n.* a framework constructed from slender branches, for plants to climb up.

perhaps *pėr-haps'*, *adv.* it may be, possibly.

peri- *per-i-*, (as part of a word) around.
perinatal *(-nā'tȧl) adj.* relating to the period of time just before and after birth.

peril *per'il*, *n.* great danger.
per'ilous *adj.* very dangerous.
per'ilously *adv.* **per'ilousness** *n.*

perimeter *pėr-im'i-tėr*, *n.* **1** (*geometry*) the outside boundary of a figure. **2** (*geometry*) the sum of the sides of a figure. **3** the outer edge of any area.

perinatal. See **peri-**.

period *pē'ri-ȯd*, *n.* **1** a division of time. **2** a stage of history. **3** the time a planet, etc. takes to move round its orbit. **4** the time taken for one complete movement of something (e.g. a pendulum) that goes on repeating the same movement. **5** a sentence. **6** a full stop, the mark (.) to end a sentence. **7** a conclusion, end. **8** a part of the school day, the time of one lesson or class. **9** the time of menstruation.
periodic *pēr-i-od'ik*, *adj.* happening again and again at regular intervals, or (loosely) from time to time.
period'ical *n.* a magazine that appears at regular intervals.—*adj.* issued, done, etc. at intervals.
period'ically *adv.*

peripatetic *per-i-pȧ-tet'ik*, *adj.* **1** walking about. **2** going from place to place.

periphery *pėr-if'ėr-i*, *n.* the outer or bounding line or surface:—*pl.* **periph'eries**.
periph'eral *adj.* **1** relating to the periphery. **2** not especially important, minor.

periscope *per'i-skōp*, *n.* a tube with mirrors by which an observer in a trench, submarine, etc. can see what is going on above.

perish *per'ish*, *v.i.* **1** to decay, rot. **2** to die. **3** to be destroyed.
per'ishable *adj.* **1** that may perish. **2** liable to go bad quickly, as food:—*opp.* **imperishable.**—*n.* (in *pl.*) food, etc. liable to perish.
per'ished *adj.* suffering because of cold; very cold.
per'isher (*coll.*) *n.* a bad or annoying person.
per'ishing *adj.* **1** extremely cold. **2** (*coll.*) irritating, etc.

periwinkle[1] *per'i-wingk-l*, *n.* a creeping evergreen plant usu. with blue flowers.

periwinkle[2] *per'i-wingk-l*, *n.* a small shellfish, a sea snail, eaten as food.

perjure *pûr'jūr*, *v.t.* (with *oneself*) to tell a lie when one has sworn to tell the truth:—*pr.p.* **per'juring**.
per'jury *n.* **1** false swearing. **2** (*law*) the crime of knowingly giving false evidence on oath:—*pl.* **per'juries**.

perk[1] *pûrk:* **perk up** to (cause to) recover energy, become lively.
perk'y *adj.* lively, spry, jaunty:—*comp.* **perk'ier**; *superl.* **perk'iest**.
perk'ily *adv.* **perk'iness** *n.*

perk[2] *pûrk*, (*coll.*) *n.* short for **perquisite**.

perk[3] *pûrk*, *v.t.*, *n.* short for **percolate**, **percolator**.

perm[1] *pûrm*, *n.* short for **permanent wave**.—*v.t.* to put a perm in (hair).

perm[2] *pûrm*, (*coll.*) *n.* short for **permutation**.—*v.t.* (esp. football pools) to select by some permutation or combination.

permanent *pûr'mȧ-nėnt*, *adj.* **1** lasting indefinitely. **2** not temporary:—*opp.* **impermanent**.
per'manence, **per'manency** *ns.* **1** the fact or state of being permanent. **2** (**permanency**) a person, thing, or position that is permanent:—*pl.* **per'manenc(i)es**.
permanent wave an artificial wave in the hair, usu. lasting some months.

permeate *pûr'mi-āt*, *v.t.* **1** to pass through the pores of. **2** to soak into, pervade:—*pr.p.* **per'meating**.
permeabil'ity *n.*
per'meable *adj.*:—*opp.* **impermeable**.

permit *pėr-mit'*, *v.t.* **1** to allow. **2** to give consent to. **3** to make possible:—*pr.p.* **permitting**; *pa.p.* **permitt'ed**.—*n.* *(pûr'mit)* permission, esp. in writing.
permiss'ible *adj.* allowable.
permiss'ion *(-mish'(ȯ)n) n.* **1** the act of permitting. **2** freedom given to do some-

thing.

permiss'ive *adj.* allowing (too much) freedom (of e.g. choice), permitting (too) much.

permutable *pėr-mūt'ȧ-bl*, *adj.* capable of being changed or interchanged.

permute', **per'mutate** *vs.t.*:—*pr.p.* **-ting.**

permutā'tion *n.*

pernicious *pėr-nish'ús*, *adj.* very harmful or bad.

pernic'iously *adv.* **pernic'iousness** *n.*

pernickety *pėr-nik'ė-ti*, *adj.* **1** fussy, hard to please. **2** requiring great care.

peroration *per-ȯ-rā'sh(ȯ)n*, *n.* the closing part of a speech, summing up of an argument.

peroxide *pėr-oks'īd*, *n.* **1** an oxide with a large amount of oxygen. **2** (*coll.*) hydrogen peroxide, a colourless oily liquid used e.g. for bleaching har.

perpendicular *pûr-pėn-dik'ū-lȧr*, *adj.* **1** standing upright. **2** vertical. **3** (*geometry*) at right angles (to a line or surface).—*n.* a line at right angles to another.

perpendicular'ity *n.*

perpendic'ularly *adv.*

perpetrate *pûr'pi-trāt*, *v.t.* to commit (e.g. an offence, sin, error):—*pr.p.* **per'petrating.**

perpetrā'tion *n.* **per'petrator** *n.*

perpetual *pėr-pet'ū-ȧl*, *adj.* **1** never ceasing. **2** lasting for ever. **3** very frequent.

perpet'ually *adv.*

perpetuate *pėr-pet'ū-āt*, *v.t.* to cause to last, go on existing, for a long time:—*pr.p.* **perpet'uating.**

perpetuā'tion *n.* continuation or preservation for a very long time.

perpetū'ity *n.* endless time or duration.

in perpetuity for ever.

perplex *pėr-pleks'*, *v.t.* **1** to puzzle, bewilder. **2** to make complicated (e.g. a problem, situation).

perplex'ity *n.* **1** the state of being perplexed. **2** something that perplexes:—*pl.* **perplex'ities.**

perquisite *pûr'kwi-zit*, *n.* something of value that one is allowed by employers over and above salary or wages, a perk.

perruque. See **peruke.**

persecute *pûr'si-kūt*, *v.t.* **1** to cause to suffer or die, esp. for religious beliefs or political opinions. **2** to harass, worry, continually:—*pr.p.* **per'secuting.**

persecū'tion *n.* **per'secutor** *n.*

persevere *pûr-si-vēr'*, *v.i.* to continue steadily to try to do a thing, even though difficulties arise:—*pr.p.* **persever'ing.**

persevēr'ance *n.* **persevēr'ing** *adj.*

Persian *pûr'sh(y)ȧn*, *-zh(y)ȧn*, *adj.* of from, or relating to Persia (Iran).—*n.* **1** a native of Persia. **2** the language of Persia.

persist *pėr-sist'*, *v.i.* **1** to continue to try or do in spite of opposition or difficulty, to persevere. **2** to be insistent in repeating e.g. a question. **3** to continue to exist: *The belief persists that killing spiders brings rain.*

persis'tence *n.* **1** doggedness, perseverance. **2** continued existence.

persis'tent *adj.* **1** constantly coming again (e.g. rumours) or long-continued (e.g. efforts). **2** obstinate.

person *pûr'sȯn*, *n.* **1** an individual human being. **2** one's outward body. **3** (*cap.*) any of the three aspects or parts of the Trinity. **4** (as part of a word) used instead of *-man* to avoid discrimination with regard to sex, as *chairperson*:—*pl.* (*def. 1*) usu. **people**, otherwise **persons.**

personable *pûr'sȯn-ȧ-bl*, *adj.* of good appearance.

per'sonage *n.* a person, esp. of rank, importance, or character.

per'sonal *adj.* **1** relating, belonging, to an individual: *his personal luggage.* **2** private: *for personal reasons.* **3** for one particular person (*opp.* **impersonal**): a personal favour. **4** carried out, done, in person (e.g. interview, service) (*opp.* **impersonal**). **5** having to do with the body: *personal charms, injury.* **6** aimed in an unkind manner at a particular person (*opp.* **impersonal**): *personal remarks.*

per'sonalise *v.t.* **1** to mark with a person's name, initials, etc.: *personalised notepaper.* **2** to apply (a remark) to a particular person, esp. in an unpleasant way:—*pr.p.* **per'sonalising.**

personal'ity *n.* **1** all of an individual's characteristics (emotional, physical, intellectual, etc.) as they appear to other people. **2** notable character. **3** a person of distinctive character. **4** a well-known person: *a TV personality.* **5** (in *pl.*) remarks (esp. nasty ones) made about other people:—*pl.* **personal'ities.**

per'sonally *adv.* **1** in person. **2** as a person. **3** as far as I (etc.) am concerned: *Personally I prefer the black one.*

per'sonate *v.t.* **1** to pretend to be (someone else), esp. for the purpose of fraud. **2** to play the part of:—*pr.p.* **per'sonating.**

personify *pėr-son'i-fī*, *v.t.* **1** to speak of, represent (something not material) as a person: *We personify Justice as a blind woman holding scales.* **2** to be typical, a perfect example, of: *Mary is pride personified*:—*pr.p.* **person'ifying**; *pa.p.* **per-**

son'ified.
personificā'tion *n.*
personnel' *n. pl.* or *n. sing.* the persons employed in any service.
first person the person or persons speaking (with or without others) (I, etc.).
second person the person or persons spoken to (with or without others) (you).
third person the person or persons spoken about (he, etc.).
in person 1 by one's own act, not through someone else. **2** in bodily presence: *He was there in person.*
to be(come) personal to make personal (usu. offensive) remarks.

persona grata *pėr-sō'nȧ grä'tȧ*, a person welcomed or regarded with pleasure.
persona non grata an unwelcome or unacceptable person.

perspective *pėr-spek'tiv, n.* the art of drawing or otherwise showing solid objects, a scene, etc., on a flat surface so as to give the correct appearance of solidity, shape and distance.
in (or **out of**) **perspective 1** having (or not having) the appearance of correct size, position, etc.: *In this photograph his feet are out of perspective.* **2** (of an event, subject) in (or not in) its true importance when other things are considered with it.

Perspex® *pûr'speks, n.* a transparent plastic which looks like glass.

perspicacious *pûr-spi-kā'shu̇s, adj.* having a keen mind that notices and understands much.
perspicacity *(-kas'i-ti) n.*

perspicuity *pûr-spik-ū'it-i, n.* clearness in expressing one's thoughts.

perspire *pėr-spīr', v.i.* to give off fluid through the pores of the skin, to sweat:—*pr.p.* **perspir'ing**.
perspiration *pûr-spir-ā'sh(ȯ)n, n.*

persuade *pėr-swād', v.t.* **1** to cause (someone to do something) by arguing or advising (*opp.* **dissuade**). **2** to convince: *We persuaded him that it was best to go by air*:—*pr.p.* **persuad'ing**.
persuasion *pėr-swā'zh(ȯ)n, n.* **1** an act of persuading. **2** settled opinion, beliefs: *It is my persuasion that any change would be for the better.* **3** a group of people with the same religious, political, etc., beliefs: *of the Catholic persuasion.*
persuas'ive *(-swās'* or *-swāz') adj.* having power to win over or influence: *He is a persuasive speaker.*

pert *pûrt, adj.* saucy, free in speech, cheeky.
pert'ly *adv.* **pert'ness** *n.*

pertain *pėr-tān', v.i.* **1** to belong (to) as a necessary or characteristic part: *all the duties pertaining to nursing.* **2** to have to do with, have reference (to): *the documents pertaining to the case.*
per'tinent *adj.* having close connection with the subject spoken about, to the point, relevant.
per'tinence, per'tinency *ns.*

pertinacious *pûr-ti-nā'shu̇s, adj.* **1** (often as a bad quality) holding firmly to an opinion or purpose. **2** persistent.
pertinacity *(-nas'i-ti) n.*

pertinent. See **pertain**.

perturb *pėr-tûrb', v.t.* **1** to disturb greatly. **2** to trouble, make anxious.
perturb'able *adj.*:—*opp.* **imperturbable**.
perturbā'tion *n.* uneasiness of mind.

peruke, perruque *pėr-o͞ok', n.* a wig.

peruse *pėr-o͞oz', v.t.* to read, esp. carefully:—*pr.p.* **perus'ing**.
perus'al *n.*

Peruvian *pėr-o͞o'vi-ȧn, adj.* having to do with Peru, in South America.—*n.* a native of Peru.

pervade *pėr-vād', v.t.* to pass or spread through the whole of: *A smell of burning pervaded the house*:—*pr.p.* **pervad'ing**.
pervās'ive *adj.* tending to pervade.

perverse *pėr-vûrs', adj.* **1** turned aside from right or truth. **2** obstinate in doing the wrong thing. **3** wilful, unreasonable.
perversion *pėr-vûr'sh(ȯ)n, n.* **1** turning away from what is normal. **2** a wrong or corrupted form of anything: *This statement is a perversion of the truth.*
pervers'ity (*pl.* **-ies**), **perverse'ness**, *ns.*
pervert *v.t.* **1** to turn away from what is normal or right: *to pervert the course of justice.* **2** to distort, give a wrong meaning to: *You have perverted my statement.* **3** to lead (a person) astray, into sin, error, or abnormality.—*n.* (**per'vert**) one who has been perverted, who is abnormal, unnatural (esp. in sexual matters).

peseta *pe-sā'tȧ, n.* the standard unit of Spanish currency.

pessimism *pes'i-mizm, n.* **1** the belief that the world is bad rather than good. **2** a state of mind that thinks everything will turn out badly, hopelessness:—*opp.* **optimism**.
pess'imist *n.* one who looks too much on the dark side of things.
pessimis'tic *adj.* **pessimis'tically** *adv.*

pest *pest, n.* **1** anything (e.g. an insect, animal) destructive to food or material. **2** a troublesome person.
pest'icide *n.* a pest killer.

pest'ilence *n.* any deadly disease that spreads from person to person.
pes'tilent *adj.* **1** very unhealthy. **2** endangering morals, peace, etc. **3** annoying.—Also **pestilen'tial** *(-sh(ȧ)l)*.

pester *pes'tėr, v.t.* to annoy (someone) continually: *pestering him for help*.

pesticide, **pestilence**, etc. See **pest**.

pestle *pes'l, pest'l, n.* a chemist's tool for grinding things to powder.

pet[1] *pet, n.* **1** a much loved tame animal. **2** a favourite person esp. one who is given too much.—*adj.* (used only before a noun) **1** kept as a pet. **2** favourite.—*v.t.* **1** to treat as a pet. **2** to fondle:—*pr.p.* **pett'ing**; *pa.p.* **pett'ed**.
pet aversion, **hate** one's chief object of dislike.
pet name a name used in affection.

pet[2] *pet, n.* a fit of sulks.
pett'ish *adj.* peevish, sulky.

petal *pet'ȧl, n.* one of the leaf-like parts forming a flower.

peter *pē'tėr*: **peter out** to dwindle away to nothing.

petite *pė-tēt', adj. (fem.)* small and neat in figure.

petition *pė-tish'(ȯ)n, n.* **1** a formal request to an authority (parliament, court of law) asking a favour of some sort. **2** a written request signed by several persons. **3** a prayer.—*v.t.* **1** to send a petition to. **2** to ask (someone) for something, or to do something).

petrel *pet'rėl, n.* a dark-coloured, small, long-winged sea bird.

petrify *pet'ri-fi, v.t.* **1** to turn into stone. **2** to make stiff with fear or horror.—*v.i.* to become stone or hard like stone:—*pr.p.* **pet'rifying**; *pa.p.* **pet'rified**.
petrifac'tion *n.* **1** turning to stone. **2** turning stiff. **3** a petrified object.

petro- *pet-rō-*, (as part of a word) **1** stone. **2** petroleum.
petrochemical *pet-rō-kem'i-kȧl, n.* any chemical obtained from petroleum.—Also *adj.*
petrol *pet'rol, -rȯl, n.* purified petroleum for cars, aeroplanes, etc.
petroleum *pi-trō'li-ȯm, -trōl'yȯm, n.* a mixture of fuel oils got from oil wells.

petticoat *pet'i-kōt, n.* orig. a skirt, now a woman's light undergarment hanging from the shoulders or waist.

pettifogger *pet'i-fog-ėr, n.* **1** a lawyer who practises only in trifling cases, esp. one who uses mean and crooked methods. **2** any similar person.
pett'ifogging *n.* and *adj.* (behaviour which is) paltry, cavilling, showing too much concern with trivial points.

petty *pet'i, adj.* **1** of small importance. **2** trivial. **3** small-minded, narrow. **4** mean:—*comp.* **pett'ier**; *superl.* **pett'iest**.
pett'ily *adv.* **pett'iness** *n.*
petty cash small sums of money paid or received, or money kept for minor expenses.
petty larcency theft of money or articles of little value.
petty officer a naval officer ranking with an army non-commissioned officer, or his rank.

petulant *pet'ū-lȧnt, adj.* showing peevish impatience or irritation.
pet'ulance *n.* **pet'ulantly** *adv.*

petunia *pi-tū'ni-ȧ, n.* a type of tropical S. American plant with funnel-shaped flowers, related to tobacco.

pew *pū, n.* an enclosed compartment or fixed bench with back in a church.

pewter *pūtėr, n.* **1** an alloy or mixture of tin with e.g. lead. **2** utensils or dishes made of pewter.—Also *adj.*

phalanges. See **phalanx**.

phalanx *fal'angks, fāl', n.* **1** a body of troops, etc. in close formation. **2** a solid body of supporters (in these two senses, *pl.* **phal'anxes**). **3** a bone of a finger or toe (*pl.* **phalanges**, *fȧ-lan'jēz*).

phallus *fal'ȯs, n.* a penis.
phallic *adj.*

phantasy *fan'tȧ-si, -zi,* fantasy:—*pl.* **phan'tasies**.
phan'tom *n.* **1** a ghost, apparition. **2** a vision. **3** appearance without reality.

Pharaoh *fā'rō, n,* (the title of) the king in ancient Egypt.

Pharisee *far'i-sē, n.* **1** one of a religious group among the Jews who held strictly to the old laws. **2** anyone who is more concerned with the forms of religion than with the spirit.
pharisā'ic(al) *adjs.*

pharmaceutical *fär-mȧ-sū'tik-ȧl, adj.* having to do with the knowledge of art or preparing medicines or drugs.—*n.* a chemical used in medicine.
pharmaceu'tics *n. sing.* the science of making medicines.
pharmacy *fär'mȧ-si, n.* **1** the art of preparing medicines. **2** a chemist's shop: —*pl.* **phar'macies**.
phar'macist *n.* one who sells medicines.

pharyngitis *far-in-jī'tis, n.* inflammation of the **pharynx** *(far'ingks)*, the tube that connects the mouth with the tube leading to the stomach.

phase *fāz*, *n.* **1** any of the appearances or stages of a thing that goes through a series of changes again and again: *the phases of the moon* (full moon, half moon, etc.). **2** a stage of development: *a phase of a person's career*; *a new phase in the war.* **3** a side, aspect, of a situation or question:—*v.t.* to do by phases or stages:—*pr.p.* **phas'ing.**

phase in, out to begin, cease, gradually to use, make, etc.

pheasant *fez'(ȧ)nt*, *n.* **1** a type of long-tailed richly coloured half-wild game bird in Britain. **2** the bird as food.

phenomenon *fė-nom'i-non*, *n.* **1** anything (a fact, occurrence) observed by the senses or by one of them: *the phenomenon of rust eating away iron.* **2** anything (an occurrence, person, thing, appearance) remarkable:—*pl.* **phenom'ena.**

phenom'enal *adj.* **1** very unusual or remarkable. **2** (*coll.*) very good, great, etc. **3** known by the senses.

phew *fū*, *interj.* an exclamation of relief or disgust.

phial *fī'ȧl*, *n.* a small glass bottle, esp. for holding medicines.

phil(o)- *fil(-ȯ)-*, (as part of a word) loving, friend.

philander *fil-an'dėr*, *v.i.* to make love, esp. in a trifling manner.

philan'derer *n.*

philanthropy *fil-an'thrȯ-pi*, *n.* love of people, esp. as shown by work done, or money given for the welfare of large numbers of people.

philanthrop'ic *adj.*

philanthrop'ically *adv.*

philan'thropist *n*, one who tries to do good to others.

philately *fil-at'ė-li*, *n.* the study and collection of postage stamps.

-phile *-fīl*, *sfx.* lover—e.g. **Anglophile.**

philharmonic *fil-här-mon'ik*, *adj.* loving music (used in names of societies, etc.).

-philia *-fil-i-ȧ*, *sfx.* love.

philology *fil-ol'ȯ-ji*, *n.* **1** the science which deals with words and their history. **2** the study of old literature.

philol'ogist *n.* one who is skilled in philology.

philosopher *fil-os'ȯ-fėr*, *n.* **1** a lover of wisdom. **2** one who studies philosophy. **3** one who practises the principles of philosophy by acting calmly and reasonably in the affairs of life.

philosoph'ic *-sof'*, or *-zof'*, *adj.* **1** having to do with philosophy. **2** calm, not easily upset or disturbed.

philos'ophise *v.i.* **1** to form theories about the reason and nature of things. **2** to moralise:—*pr.p.* **philos'ophising.**

philos'ophy *n.* **1** the study of the principles of human behaviour and reasoning about what we really know of ourselves and the universe, as opp. to what we seem to know. **2** a person's view of life and principles of conduct. **3** calmness of temper:—*pl.* **philos'ophies.**

Philistine *fil'is-tīn*, *n.* **1** an individual of one of the ancient peoples of Palestine. **2** (also no *cap.*) a person who cares nothing for literature, art, etc., whose interests are in material things, and whose ideas are ordinary.

philology, philosophy, etc. See **phil(o).**

phlebitis *fli-bī'tis*, *n.* inflammation of a vein.

phlegm *flem*, *n.* **1** the thick slimy matter brought up from the throat by coughing. **2** coolness of temper, calmness.

phlegmatic *fleg-mat'ik*, *adj.* not easily excited, calm.

phlox *floks*, *n.* a garden plant with flat-shaped flowers, often bluish-red.

phobia *fō'bi-ȧ*, *n.* a fear, dislike, or hatred, esp. without reason (orig. used only as part of a word—e.g. **Anglophobia**).

phō'bic *adj.*

phoenix *fē'niks*, *n.* in old stories, a miraculous bird, the only one of its kind, which burned itself every 500 or 600 years and then rose again from its ashes as a young bird—hence an emblem of everlasting life.

phon(o)-, *fōn(-o)-*, (as part of a word) sound.

phonic *fōn'ik*, *fon'*, *adj.* of speech sounds.

phon'ics *n. sing.* a method of teaching reading by means of the sounds of the letters.

phone *fōn* (*coll.*) *n.*, *v.i.*, *v.t.* short for **telephone.**

phone'card *n.* a card that can be used instead of cash to operate certain public telephones.

phone'-in *n.* a radio programme which mainly consists of telephone calls from listeners on selected topics.

phonetic *fō-net'ik*, *fȯ-*, *adj.* **1** having to do with the sounds of language. **2** spelled according to sound: *'Sivik' is a phonetic spelling of 'civic'.*

phonet'ics *n. sing.* the science that deals with pronunciation, speech production, etc.—*n. pl.* phonetic representations of the pronunciation of words.

phosphorus *fos'fȯr-ůs*, *n.* an element, a waxy, poisonous, inflammable substance which gives out light in the dark.

phosphate *fos'fāt*, *n.* a salt or salts con-

taining phosphorus, used e.g. as fertilizer.
phosphoresce' *(-es')* *v.i.* to shine in the dark, as phosphorus does:—*pr.p.* **phosphoresc'ing.**
phosphores'cence *n.* **phosphores'cent** *adj.*
phosphor'ic, **phos'phorous** *adjs.* having to do with, or containing, phosphorus.

photo- *fōt-ō-*, (as part of a word) light.—See also next article.
photo-electric'ity *n.* electricity produced by the action of light.
photo-sen'sitive *adj.* affected by light, either visible or invisible.
photosynthesis *fō-tō-sin'thi-sis*, *n.* (in plants) the process of building up food which takes place in the presence of light.

photo *fō'tō*, *n.*, *v.t.*, *adj.* a shortening of **photograph**:—*pl.* **phō'tos.**—Also, as part of a word, **photo.**—See also article above.
pho'tocopier *n.* a machine that makes photocopies.
pho'tocopy *n.* a photographic reproduction of written, etc. material:—*pl.* **pho'tocopies.**—Also *v.t.*:—*pr.p.* **pho'tocopying**; *pa.p.* **pho'tocopied.**
pho'to-fin'ish *n.* a finish of a race so close that a special type of photography is used to show the winner.
Photo-fit® or **photophit**, *fō'tō-fit* *n.* a method of making identification pictures by combining photographs of individual features.
photogenic *fō-tō-jen'ik*, *-jēn'*, *adj.* photographing well, making a good subject for a picture.
photography *fō-tog'rȧ-fi*, *n.* the art of taking pictures by means of a camera, making use of the action of light on chemically prepared films and plates.
pho'tograph *n.* an image so produced.—*v.t.* to take a photograph of (also *v.i.*).—*v.i.* to come out (well, badly) in photographs.
photog'rapher *n.* **photograph'ic** *adj.*
Photostat® *fō'tō-stat*, *n.* **1** a device for making copies of drawings, maps, etc. directly on prepared paper, without a reversed image. **2** a copy so made.

photosynthesis. See **phot(o)**.

phrase *frāz*, *n.* **1** a group of words expressing a single idea (e.g. *after dinner*; *on the water*). **2** a short saying. **3** (*music*) a short group of notes.—*v.t.* to express in words:—*pr.p.* **phras'ing.**
phraseol'ogy *(frāz-i-ol')* *n.* manner of putting phrases together, style.
phras'ing *n.* **1** the wording of a speech or written passage. **2** (*music*) the grouping of notes to form musical phrases.
turn of phrase 1 an expression. **2** manner of expression.

phrenology *frin-ol'ȯ-ji*, *n.* the study of the shape of the skull, supposed to show a person's mental powers.

phut *fut*: **go phut** (*coll.*) to break, burst, cease to work properly.

physi(o)- *fiz-i(-ō)-*, (as part of a word) **1** nature, natural. **2** having to do with the body.
phys'ical *adj.* **1** having to do with the body: *physical strength*, *physical exercises.* **2** having to do with physics. **3** having to do with the study of the earth's natural features (e.g. mountains, rivers, etc.): *physical geography*.
phys'ically *adv.*

physician *fi-zish'ȧn*, *n.* **1** a doctor, one who decides on treatment and medicine but does not perform operations. **2** a healer or healing influence.
phys'icist *(-i-sist)* *n.* a specialist in physics.
phys'ics *n. sing.* a branch of science studying the facts and laws of mechanics, heat, sound, light, magnetism, electricity, and the structure of the atom (but not concerned with purely chemical changes or living processes).
physiognomy *fiz-i-on'ȯ-mi*, *-og'nȯ-mi*, *n.* **1** the face, esp. with its characteristic expression. **2** the art of judging character from the face.
physiography *fiz-i-og'rȧ-fi*, *n.* **1** the description and history of the earth's surface. **2** physical geography.
physiology *fiz-i-ol'ȯ-ji*, *n.* the science dealing with living processes in animals and plants (e.g. blood circulation, photosynthesis in plants, etc.).
physiolog'ical *(-log')* *adj.*
physiolog'ically *adv.* **physiol'ogist** *n.*
physiotherapy *fiz-i-ō-ther'ȧ-pi*, *n.* treatment of disease without drugs, using fresh air, massage, etc.
physiother'apist *n.*
physique *fiz-ēk'*, *n.* the build or structure of one's body: *He has a poor, a powerful physique.*

pi *pī*, *n.* the Greek letter which is used to stand for the number by which the diameter of a circle must be multiplied in order to find the circumference (approximately 3.14).

pianoforte *pya'nō-fōr'tā*, or *pē-a'*, or *-ä'* usu. shortened to **piano**, *pya'nō*, or *pē-a'*, or *-ä'*, *ns.* a musical instrument played by touching keys and so causing hammers to strike wires stretched across a soundboard:—*pls.* **pia'nofortes, pia'nos.**

pianissimo *pya-nis'si-mō, adj.* and *adv.* very soft(ly).

pianist *n.* one who plays the piano, esp. with skill.

piazza *pē-ät'sä, -az'ȧ, n.* **1** a market place or square in a town. **2** (*U.S.*) a veranda.

pibroch *pē'bro*H, *n.* a type of bagpipe music, comprising a theme and variations on the theme.

picador *pik'ȧ-dör, n.* a mounted bull-fighter, with a lance.

piccaninny, pickaninny *pik-ȧ-nin'i, n.* (*offensive*) an African-American or Australian Aboriginal child:—*pl.* **piccaninn'ies, pick-.**

piccolo *pik'ȯ-lō, n.* a small flute, pitched an octave higher than an ordinary flute:—*pl.* **picc'olos.**

pick *pik, n.* **1** a tool for breaking ground, rock, etc., with head pointed at one end or both ends and fixed to a handle in the middle. **2** any instrument for picking (as in *toothpick*). **3** the act of choosing. **4** a portion or amount picked. **5** the best, best part (of something).—*v.t.* **1** to pull apart. **2** to gather (flowers). **3** to peck, bite, or nibble. **4** to remove something from (something) with a pointed instrument. **5** to open (e.g. a lock) with a sharp instrument. **6** to rob: *to pick pockets.* **7** to choose. **8** to seek and start: *to pick a quarrel.*

pick'ing *n.* **1** the act of one that picks. **2** something picked or picked up. **3** (in *pl.*) something gained.

pick'pocket *n.* a thief who steals from people's pockets.

pick'-up *n.* **1** a thing or person picked up. **2** a device for picking up an electric current. **3** a device holding the needle which follows the track on a gramophone record. **4** a device enabling gramophone records to be reproduced through a radio loud-speaker. **5** a vehicle like a car in front and a lorry at the rear. **6** the accelerating power (of a vehicle).

pick at **1** to find fault with. **2** to eat little of, without enthusiasm.

pick holes in to point out faults in.

pick off to kill or wound one by one.

pick on **1** to select, usu. for something unpleasant. **2** to criticize, nag at.

pick one's way to choose carefully where to put one's feet.

pick out **1** to select. **2** to see, recognise.

pick to pieces **1** to take apart. **2** to criticise, tell the faults of, in detail.

pick up **1** to lift from the ground. **2** to take into a vehicle: *On the way there in my car I picked up Jack.* **3** to make the acquaintance of informally. **4** to get by chance. **5** to get, esp. little by little: *to pick up a language, a habit.* **6** to come upon, make out: *to pick up signals, the track over the hill.* **7** to improve, gain strength: *He picked up slowly after his illness*; *Business is picking up.* **8** to increase (speed).

pickaback. See **piggyback**.

pickaninny. See **piccaninny**.

pickaxe *pik'aks, n.* a tool used in digging, a pick.

picket *pik'it, n.* **1** a pointed stake driven into the ground, used for fences, tethering a horse, surveying, etc. **2** a small patrol or group of men for guarding or special duty. **3** a group of people on strike stationed in a **pick'et-line** at place of employment to keep others from going to work.—*v.t.* **1** to tether or tie to a stake. **2** to set guard of soldiers, strikers, at (a place).

pickle *pik'l, n.* **1** a liquid in which food is preserved. **2** vegetables preserved in vinegar. **3** a difficult situation.—*v.t.* to preserve in salt liquid or vinegar:—*pr.p.* **pick'ling.**

pick'led (*coll.*) *adj.* drunk.

picnic *pik'nik, n.* **1** an informal outing on which food is eaten in the open air. **2** a very informal meal. **3** an easy or pleas-ant experience.—Also *adj.* (used only before a noun): *a picnic lunch.*—*v.i.* to have a picnic:—*pr.p.* **pic'nicking**; *pa.p.* **pic'nicked.**

pico- *pī'kō-* (as part of a word) a millionth of a millionth, as in *picosecond.*

pictorial *pik-tō'ri-ȧl, -tö', adj.* **1** having to do with painting or drawing. **2** filled with pictures: *a pictorial magazine.* **3** expressed in pictures. **4** calling up pictures in the mind.

picture *pik'chur, n.* **1** an image, representation, of an object or scene by painting, drawing, or photography. **2** a portrait. **3** a symbol or type: *a picture of health.* **4** a description so clear as to form in the mind an image of the thing described. **5** a film show. **6** (in *pl.*) the cinema.—*v.t.* **1** to represent in a picture. **2** to form a likeness of in the mind. **3** to describe clearly:—*pr.p.* **pic'turing.**

picturesque *pik-chur-esk', adj.* **1** such as would make a good or striking picture, usu. suggesting beauty or quaintness. **2** (of language) colourful rather than matter-of-fact.

picture gallery a hall or gallery where pictures are shown to the public.

picture window a usu. large window which looks out on to a particularly attractive view.

in the picture **1** having a share of attention. **2** being informed and therefore able to understand the situation.

piddle *pid'l, v.i.* **1** to deal in trifles. **2** (*coll.*) to urinate:—*pr.p.* **pidd'ling**.

pidgin English *pij'in ing'glish*, a language with mainly English words (often simplified or modified in form) but its own grammar and constructions; *orig.* one used to talk to the Chinese.

pie[1] *pī, n.* **1** a magpie. **2** a chatterer.

pie[2] *pī, n.* meat, vegetables or fruit baked within a pastry crust.

piebald, pyebald *pī'böld, adj.* black and white (or, *loosely*, other colours) in patches.

piece *pēs, n.* **1** a part or portion. **2** a single article. **3** a definite length, as of cloth or paper. **4** a composition in writing, music, drama, painting. **5** a coin. **6** a token in chess, draughts, etc.—*v.t.* **1** to make larger by adding a piece. **2** to patch. **3** to put (together):—*pr.p.* **piec'ing**.
piece goods textile fabrics made in definite lengths.
piece'meal *adv.* **1** in pieces. **2** bit by bit.—*adj.* **1** done bit by bit. **2** in pieces.
piece'work *n.* work paid for by the number of pieces or quantity done, not by time.
a piece of cake easy, simple.
a piece of one's mind a frank outspoken scolding or opinion.
go to pieces **1** to break into parts. **2** to break down nervously or physically.
of a piece of the same kind: *This deceit was of a piece with his usual conduct.*

pièce de résistance *pyes dė rā-zēs-tong̃s*, **1** the main dish of a meal. **2** the best, most important article, incident, event.

piecemeal, piecework. See **piece**.

pied *pīd, adj.* with two or more colours in patches.

pier *pēr, n.* **1** a pillar, the support of an arch, bridge, etc. **2** a stone, wooden, etc. platform stretching from the shore into the sea or other water for use as a landing place, etc.
pier'-head the seaward end of a pier.

pierce *pērs, v.t.* **1** to thrust a hole through. **2** to force a way into. **3** to touch the emotions of, move deeply. **4** to see right through (e.g. a mystery):—*pr.p.* **pier'cing**.
pierc'ing *adj.* **1** loud and shrill. **2** sharp, biting (e.g. cold). **3** seeing very clearly.

pierrot *pē'ėr-ō, n.* a comic entertainer with white face and loose white clothes.

piety *pī'ė-ti, n.* **1** devoutness, reverence for God. **2** dutiful carrying out of one's religious duties. **3** a religious act (*pl.* **pi'eties**):—*opp.* **impiety**.

pious *pī'ůs, adj.* **1** showing piety, real or sham. **2** sacred. **3** done with a good motive: *a pious deception*:—*opp.* **impious** (*im'pi-ůs*).

piffle *pif'l, n.* nonsense, worthless talk.

pig *pig, n.* **1** a swine, a farm animal from which we get bacon, pork, etc. **2** (*scornfully*) a dirty, greedy, etc. person. **3** (an oblong piece of) metal (e.g. *pig-iron*) run while molten into a mould:—*v.i.* **1** to live in dirt or muddle. **2** to feed like a pig:—*pr.p.* **pigg'ing**; *pa.p.* **pigged**.
pigg'ery *n.* a place where pigs are kept:—*pl.* **pigg'eries**.
pigg'ish *adj.* **1** greedy. **2** dirty.
piglet *pig'lėt, n.* a young pig.
pigg'y-bank *n.* a child's usu. pig-shaped money-box.
pig'head'ed *adj.* stubborn.
pig'skin *n.* pig's leather.
pig'sty *n.* **1** a pen for keeping pigs. **2** a dirty or untidy place:—*pl.* **pig'sties**.
pig'tail *n.* the hair of the head plaited behind in a braid.

pigeon[1] *pij'in, n.* a heavy-bodied, long-winged bird, often domesticated.
pig'eon-heart'ed *adj.* timid, meek.
pig'eon-hole *n.* a compartment, e.g. in a desk, for storing papers, etc.—*v.t.* **1** to arrange, classify. **2** to file. **3** to put aside to be dealt with later, if ever:—*pr.p.* **pig'eon-holing**.
clay pigeon *n.* a disc, etc., thrown up by a special device and shot at for shooting practice or sport.

pigeon[2] *pij'in, n.* a spelling of *pidgin* (see **pidgin English** for the derivation of this).
that's (not) my pigeon that is (not) my affair.

piggery, piggish. See **pig**.

piggyback *pig'i-bak*, **pickaback** *pik'ȧ-bak, adv.* and *adj.* on the back like a pack: *a piggyback ride*; *to carry someone piggy-back.*—Also *n.*

piggy-bank. See **pig**.

piglet. See **pig**.

pigment *pig'mėnt, n.* **1** paint. **2** any substance used for colouring. **3** a substance in plants or animals that gives colour to skin.
pigmentā'tion *n.* coloration by pigments in the tissues.

pigmy. See **pygmy**.

pigskin, pigsty, pigtail. See **pig**.

pike, *pīk, n.* **1** a weapon with a long shaft and a sharp head like a spear. **2** a sharp-pointed hill. **3** a freshwater fish with a pointed snout.

pilaff *pil-af', pil'*, **pilau** *pil-ow', ns.* a spiced dish of rice, meat, etc.

pilaster *pil-as'tėr*, *n.* a rectangular column standing out in relief from the side of a building as a decorative feature.

pilchard *pil'chȧrd*, *n.* a small sea-fish like the herring, often called *sardine*.

pile[1] *pīl*, *n.* **1** a number of things lying one on top of another. **2** a tall or large building. **3** (*coll.*) a large amount of money, fortune: *He has made his pile.* **4** (often in *pl.*) a large amount.—*v.t.* **1** to heap (often *up* or *on*). **2** to cover with something in piles: *to pile a table with books.*—*v.i.* **1** to become piled up. **2** to gather. **3** to crowd: *to pile into a bus*:—*pr.p.* **pil'ing.**

pile'-up *n.* a collision involving several motor vehicles.

atomic pile a device using uranium rods, embedded in graphite to obtain a slow regular amount of nuclear energy.

pile[2] *pīl*, *n.* a large stake or pillar driven into the ground as a foundation for a building, etc.

pile'-driver *n.* a machine for driving in piles.

pile[3] *pīl*, *n.* a raised surface on certain cloths, e.g. velvet (produced in a different way from *nap*).

pile[4] *pīl*, *n.* (usu. in *pl.*) a haemorrhoid (see this word).

pilfer *pil'fėr*, *v.i.* and *v.t.* to steal, esp. in small quantities.

pilgrim *pil'grim*, *n.* one who travels a distance to visit a holy place.

pil'grimage *n.* **1** a journey to a shrine or holy place. **2** any long journey.

Pilgrim Fathers the Puritans who sailed in the *Mayflower* and founded Plymouth, Massachusetts, in 1620.

pill *pil*, *n.* **1** a little ball of medicine. **2** anything unpleasant which must be accepted or endured.

the pill any of various contraceptive pills.

pillage *pil'ij*, *n.* **1** the act of plundering. **2** booty.—*v.t.* to plunder, loot, take money and goods from.—Also *v.i.*:—*pr.p.* **pill'aging.**

pillar *pil'ȧr*, *n.* **1** an upright support for a roof, arch, etc., a column. **2** a shaft like this as a monument. **3** anything that supports: *He is a pillar of the church.*

pill'ar-box a short hollow pillar, usu. red, in which to post letters.

from pillar to post **1** from one place to another. **2** from one difficulty to another.

pillion *pil'yȯn*, *n.* a seat for a passenger on a motorcycle or horse, behind the driver or rider.

pillory *pil'ȯr-i*, *n.* a wooden frame on a post, with holes to hold firmly the head and hands of prisoners:—*pl.* **pill'ories.**—*v.t.* to hold up to ridicule, mock, laugh at publicly:—*pr.p.* **pill'orying**; *pa.p.* **pill'oried.**

pillow *pil'ō*, *n.* **1** a cushion for a sleeper's head. **2** any support used for a similar purpose.—*v.t.* to rest on, or as on, a pillow.

pill'owcase, -slip *ns.* a cover for a pillow.

pilot *pī'lȯt*, *n.* **1** one who steers ships in and out of a harbour, along a dangerous coast, etc. **2** one who actually operates the flying controls of an aircraft. **3** a mechanism that regulates another. **4** (**automatic pilot**) a device for directing an aeroplane, ship. **5** a guide, leader. **6** a pilot broadcast or film.—*v.t.* to act as pilot or guide to.

pi'lot-balloon' *n.* a small balloon sent up to find how the wind blows.

pi'lot-boat *n.* a boat used by pilots for meeting and leaving ships.

pilot broadcast, film one intended to test the popularity of a proposed radio or television service.

pi'lot-light *n.* **1** a small electric light used to show e.g. that power is switched on. **2** a small gas light kept burning to light a larger jet, e.g. on a cooker.

pilot officer an Air Force rank, or a person of this rank.

pilot plant trial machinery set up to test a new process before it becomes full-scale.

pilot scheme a small-scale scheme serving as a guide or test for a proposed full-scale scheme.

pimento *pi-men'tō*, *n.* **1** allspice or Jamaica pepper. **2** the tree producing it:—*pl.* **pimen'tos.**

pimiento *pi-mien'tō*, *n.* a variety of sweet pepper, widely cultivated for its mild-flavoured red fruit, eaten raw or cooked.

pimp *pimp*, *n.* **1** one who procures gratifications for the lusts of others. **2** someone who lives off prostitutes' earnings, and often also attempts to get clients for them.

pimple *pim'pl*, *n.* a small pointed swelling on the skin.

pim'pled, pim'ply (*comp.* **-ier**; *superl.* **-iest**), *adjs.* having pimples.

PIN *pin*, *n.* *p*ersonal *i*dentification *n*umber, a unique multi-digit number allocated to cards used in computerised transactions.

pin *pin*, *n.* **1** a pointed instrument of wood or metal used to fasten things together. **2** a peg. **3** anything of little value. **4** (*coll.*) a leg: *to knock him off his pins.*—*v.t.* **1** to fasten with a pin. **2** to hold fast, pressed against something: *The heavy log pinned him to the ground*:—*pr.p.* **pinn'ing**; *pa.p.*

pinned.
pin'ball *n.* a form of bagatelle, often played on slot-machines.
pin cushion a padded object of some sort for holding pins.
pin money (*old fashioned*) money given to or earned by a wife for private expenses.
pin'point *n.* anything very sharp and tiny.—*v.t.* to place, or show the place of, very exactly.—*adj.* very accurate.
pin'prick *n.* a very small irritation, worry, or pain.
pin'-stripe *n.* a very narrow stripe in cloth.
pin'-up *n.* **1** a picture of an attractive person, often pinned on a wall. **2** this person.
pin it on (someone) to prove, or make it seem, that he did it.
pin one's faith, hopes, etc. **on 1** to put entire trust in. **2** to rely on.
pins and needles a tingling feeling in one's arm, foot, etc.
pin someone (down) to make someone commit themselves, express a definite opinion, etc.

pinafore *pin'ȧ-fōr, -fŏr, n.* **1** an apron covering the whole front. **2** (also **pinafore dress**) a kind of sleeveless dress designed to be worn over a blouse, sweater, etc.

pince-nez *pan^{g}s'-nā, n.* a pair of eyeglasses with a spring for catching the nose:—*pl.* **pince'-nez** *(-nāz)*.

pincers *pin'sėrz, n. pl.* **1** a gripping tool, used for drawing out nails, etc. **2** a crab's, lobster's, etc. claws.

pinch *pinch* or *-sh, v.t.* **1** to squeeze between the thumb and finger or between any two surfaces, as the jaws of a tool. **2** to nip. **3** to nip (off). **4** to hurt by tightness. **5** (of hunger or cold) to give pain. **6** to limit too much, stint: *to pinch oneself for food.* **7** to make (a face) look thin and haggard. **8** (*slang*) to steal. **9** (*slang*) to catch or arrest.—Also *v.i.*—*n.* **1** an act of pinching. **2** a very small amount: *a pinch of salt.* **3** pressure, distress: *the pinch of poverty.* **4** an emergency.
pinched *adj.*
at a pinch in a case of emergency.

pine¹ *pīn, n.* a cone-bearing evergreen tree with needle-shaped leaves.
pine'apple *n.* a fruit growing in hot countries shaped like a large pine-cone.
pine-cone the egg-shaped woody fruit of the pine tree.
pine-marten. See **marten**.
pine'-needle *n.* the needle-shaped leaf of the pine tree.

pine² *pīn, v.i.* **1** to waste away, esp. with pain, grief. **2** to long (for, to do):—*pr.p.* **pin'ing**.

ping *ping, n.* a whistling or ringing sound such as that of a bullet.—Also *v.i.* and *v.t.*
ping'-pong' (®; should have *cap.*) *n.* table-tennis.

pinion¹ *pin'yȯn, n.* **1** a bird's wing. **2** a feather.—*v.t.* **1** to cut the wings or feathers of (a bird) so that it is unable to fly. **2** hold (a person) by the arms, or hold (the arms) tightly.

pinion² *pin'yȯn, n.* a small toothed wheel fitting into notches e.g. on another wheel.

pink¹ *pingk, v.t.* **1** to wound, esp. slightly, e.g. with rapier. **2** to decorate (cloth, etc.) by cutting small holes or scallops. **3** to make a serrated edge on.

pink² *pingk, n.* **1** a scented garden flower (when double, known as 'carnation'). **2** a light red colour. **3** a scarlet hunting-coat. **4** the person wearing it. **5** perfect condition: *in the pink* (*of health*).

pink³ *pink, v.i.* to make a tinkling or pinging noise.

pinnace *pin'is, n.* **1** a light sailing ship. **2** a warship's small boat.

pinnacle *pin'ȧ-kl, n.* **1** a slender turret. **2** a high pointed rock or mountain. **3** the highest point.

pint *pīnt, n.* **1** a measure of capacity, one-eighth of a gallon (0.57 litre, 20 fluid ounces). **2** a pint of beer.

pioneer *pī-ȯn-ēr', n.* **1** a soldier who builds roads, etc. **2** one who goes before to clear the way for others. **3** one of the first to do, study, etc., something: *pioneers in the field of science.*—*v.i.* to act as a pioneer.—*v.t.* to take the first steps in (a new development).

pious. See **piety**.

pip¹ *pip, n.* a seed of fruit.

pip² *pip, n.* **1** a spot on dice, cards, etc. **2** a star as a mark of rank.

pip³ *pip, n.* a short note given on the radio and by telephone as a time signal.

pip⁴ *pip*: **give someone the pip** (*coll.*) to annoy, offend someone.

pip⁵ *pip*: **pip someone at the post** to defeat someone just at the point when their success seemed certain:—*pr.p.* **pipp'ing**; *pa.p.* **pipped**.

pipe *pīp, n.* **1** a musical instrument in which the sound is made by blowing in a tube. **2** any tube, esp. one of earthenware, metal, etc. for carrying water, gas, etc. **3** a tube with a bowl at the end, for smoking. **4** a voice, esp. a high voice. **5** the note of a bird.—*v.i.* to play a pipe.—*v.t.* **1** to play (a tune) on a pipe. **2** to utter shrilly. **3** to convey by pipe:—*pr.p.* **pip'ing**.

pip'er *n.* a player on a pipe or bagpipe.

pip'ing *adj.* **1** playing a pipe. **2** thin and high-pitched.—*n.* **1** the singing (of birds). **2** a system of pipes. **3** small cord used as a trimming for clothes, or sugar trimming a cake.

pipe'clay *n.* a kind of fine white clay used to whiten leather, etc. and to make clay pipes for smoking.

piped music continuous background music conveyed from a central studio to various loud-speakers, often in several buildings.

pipe'dream *n.* a futile or unreal hope or dream.

pipe'line *n.* **1** a long line of pipes to carry oil from an oil field, etc. **2** a direct course along which information, etc., is passed.

pipe organ an organ with pipes.

in the pipeline soon to become available, in preparation.

piping hot very hot.

pipe down (*coll.*) to become quiet, stop talking.

pipe up (*coll.*) **1** to say. **2** to begin to speak.

pipette *pip-et'*, *n.* a small glass tube for measuring liquid and conveying it from one vessel to another.

pipit *pip'it*, *n.* a small bird, rather like a lark.

pippin *pip'in*, *n.* a kind of apple.

piquant *pē'kȧnt*, *adj.* **1** sharp. **2** arousing the interest: *a piquant face*, *situation*.

pi'quancy *n.* **pi'quantly** *adv.*

pique *pēk*, *n.* anger caused by wounded pride, resentment.—*v.t.* **1** to wound the pride of. **2** to arouse (curiosity). **3** to pride (*oneself on* or *upon*):—*pr.p.* **pi'quing**.

piranha *pē-rän'yȧ*, *n.* a ferocious South American river fish.

pirate *pī'rit*, *n.* **1** one who robs ships at sea. **2** one who seizes rights of another (e.g. one who publishes something without permission from the owner of the copyright).—*v.t.* to take, or publish, without permission:—*pr.p.* **pir'ating**.

piracy *pī'rȧ-si*, *n.* **pīra'tical** *adj.*

pirouette *pir-ōō-et'*, *n.* a spinning round on tiptoe in dancing.—Also *v.i.*:—*pr.p.* **pirouett'ing**.

piss *pis*, (*vulg.*) n. **1** the act of urinating. **2** urine.—Also *v.i.*

pistachio *pis-ta'shi-ō*, *-tä'*, *n.* a greenish seed or nut:—*pl.* **pista'chios**.

pistil *pis'til*, *-tl*, *n.* the seed-bearing part of a flower.

pistol *pis'tl*, *n.* a small hand-gun.

piston *pis'tȯn*, *n.* a sliding piece, usu. of metal, which moves up and down a hollow cylinder in engines, pumps, etc.

pit[1] *pit*, *n.* **1** a hole in the earth. **2** a mine shaft. **3** a covered heap (of potatoes, etc.). **4** a hole used as a trap for wild beasts. **5** a hole in the ground or floor made to allow underparts of cars to be repaired easily. **6** the place beside the course for refuelling and repairing racing cars. **7** the hole or scar left by smallpox. **8** the ground floor of a theatre behind the stalls.—*v.t.* **1** to lay or store in a pit. **2** to set (against) in a contest: *to pit John against James*:—*pr.p.* **pitt'ing**; *pa.p.* **pitt'ed**.

pit'fall *n.* **1** a trap for beasts. **2** a danger, usu. hidden.

pit'-prop *n.* a timber or metal upright support used to hold up the roof in a coal mine.

pit of the stomach the depression of the body below the breastbone.

pit[2] *pit*, *n.* a fruit-stone.

pita. See **pitta**.

pitch[1] *pich*, *n.* a black shining substance obtained by distilling coal tar or wood.—*v.t.* to cover with pitch.

pitch'-black *adj.* black as pitch.

pitch'-dark *adj.* completely dark.

pitch'-pine *n.* a North American tree from which pitch is obtained.

pitch[2] *pich*, *v.t.* **1** to set up, fix firmly in position (e.g. camp, a tent). **2** to throw, toss, or hurl. **3** (*music*) to set at a particular level, set the keynote: *to pitch one's voice too high*. **4** (*baseball*) to deliver (the ball) to the batsman.—*v.i.* **1** to fall forward. **2** (of a ship) to rise and fall with the waves so that the bow and stern lurch up and down. **3** to slope down. **4** to let one's choice fall (on).—*n.* **1** a throw. **2** the field for certain games. **3** (*cricket*) the ground between the wickets. **4** the place at which e.g. a street trader is stationed. **5** the height or depth of a note. **6** slope or the amount of slope: *the pitch of the roof*. **7** distance between similar points, e.g. on the thread of a screw. **8** a point, peak, extreme.

pitch'er *n.*

pitched battle a battle on chosen ground between sides which have been arranged in position beforehand.

pitched roof a sloping roof as distinct from a flat one.

pitch'fork *n.* **1** a fork for pitching hay, etc. **2** a tuning-fork.—*v.t.* **1** to throw with a pitchfork. **2** to thrust suddenly (into): *This accident pitchforked him into the position of leader*.

pitch'pipe *n.* the small pipe used to set the pitch for singers or for tuning instru-

ments.
pitch in 1 to join in. **2** to set to work briskly.
pitch into to attack violently.

pitcher[1]. See **pitch**[2].

pitcher[2] *pich'ėr, n.* a large jug for holding or pouring liquids.

piteous. See **pity**.

pitfall. See **pit**.

pith *pith, n.* **1** a soft spongy substance inside something, e.g. that in the centre of the stems of plants. **2** the important part: *the pith of the matter under discussion*.
pith'y *adj.* **1** full of pith. **2** full of meaning: *a pithy saying*:—*comp.* **pith'ier**; *superl.* **pith'iest**.

pitiable, **pitiful**, etc. See **pity**.

piton *pē'ton*[g], *-ton, n.* a steel peg to be driven into rock or ice, used in climbing.

pit(t)a (bread) *pit'ȧ (bred), n.* a type of slightly leavened bread, orig. from the Middle East, in the form of a hollow flat cake.

pittance *pit'ȧns, n.* **1** a very small allowance, a dole. **2** a very small income.

pity *pit'i, n.* **1** feeling for the sufferings of others, sympathy, compassion. **2** a cause of grief. **3** a regrettable fact.—*v.t.* to feel pity for:—*pr.p.* **pit'ying**; *pa.p.* **pit'ied**.
piteous *pit'i-ůs, adj.* arousing pity.
pit'iable *adj.* **1** to be pitied. **2** contemptible.
pit'iful *adj.* **1** sad. **2** contemptible.
pit'iless *adj.* **1** without pity. **2** cruel.
take pity on to show pity or mercy to.

pivot *piv'ȯt, n.* **1** the pin or centre on which anything turns. **2** that on which anything depends (e.g. a key person, most important fact, etc.).—*v.i.* and *v.t.* (to cause) to turn on, or as if on, a pivot:—*pr.p.* **piv'oting**; *pa.p.* **piv'oted**.
piv'otal *adj.*

pixy, **pixie** *pik'si, n.* a small fairy:—*pl.* **pix'ies**.

pizza *pēt'sȧ, n.* a large flat tart of dough spread with tomato, etc. and baked in a hot oven.

pizzicato *pit-si-kä'tō, (music) adj.* played, not with the bow, but by plucking the strings.—Also *adv.*

placable *plak'ȧ-bl, adj.* willing to forgive:—*opp.* **implacable**.
placate *plȧk-āt', plāk-, v.t.* to pacify, soothe, appease (an angry person):—*pr.p.* **placat'ing**.

placard *plak'ärd, n.* **1** a written or printed paper or poster placed on a wall, etc. (e.g. as an advertisement). **2** a notice written or printed on wood, cardboard or other stiff material, and carried, hung, etc. in a public place.—*v.t.* to stick placards on.

place *plās, n.* **1** an open space in a town. **2** a village, town, or city: *in my native place*. **3** a dwelling or home. **4** a building or room with a special purpose: *one's place of business*. **5** a seat or accommodation in a theatre, a train, at table, etc. **6** position. **7** a particular spot. **8** one's proper position or dignity. **9** rank. **10** office or employment, esp. in the government. **11** a position won in a competition. **12** (*racing*) a position in the first three. **13** the position of a number in a row or series: *in the first decimal place*.—*v.t.* **1** to put in any place. **2** to find a place for. **3** to remember who (a person) is:—*pr.p.* **plac'ing**.
placed *adj.* **1** having a place. **2** among the first three in a race or contest.
place setting a person's set of crockery, cutlery and glasses at a dining table.
be one's place to be one's duty.
give place. See **give**.
in place 1 in proper position. **2** suitable in the circumstances.
in place of instead of.
in the first, **second**, etc. **place** firstly, secondly, etc. (when listing points in a discussion, etc.).
out of place 1 not in position. **2** not suitable in the circumstances.
take place. See **take**.

placebo *plȧ-sē'bō, n.* a substance with no curative effect given as a medicine to one who imagines himself to be ill:—*pl.* **placē'bos**.

placenta *plȧ-sen'tȧ, n.* the structure that joins an unborn mammal to the womb of its mother, and through which the foetus is fed.

placid *plas'id, adj.* **1** calm, not easily disturbed. **2** peaceful.

plagiarise *plā'jėr-īz, v.t.* to steal from (the writings or ideas of someone else):—*pr.p.* **pla'giarising**.
pla'giarism *n.* an act, or the practice, of plagiarising.
pla'giarist *n.*

plague *plāg, n.* **1** a deadly epidemic or spreading disease, esp. a fever carried by rat fleas. **2** a great and troublesome quantity: *a plague of flies*. **3** a nuisance.—*v.t.* to pester or annoy:—*pr.p.* **plag'uing**; *pa.p.* **plagued**.

plaice *plās, n.* a yellow-spotted broad flatfish like the flounder.

plaid *plād, plad, n.* a long piece of cloth worn over the shoulder, usu. in tartan (as part of Highland dress).

plain *plān*, *adj.* **1** flat, level. **2** clear (e.g. view). **3** clear to the mind, obvious. **4** easily understood: *plain words.* **5** often unkindly frank. **6** outspoken. **7** simple, without ornament, not luxurious: *plain living.* **8** not coloured. **9** not highly born or gifted. **10** without beauty. **11** in knitting, denoting an ordinary stitch with the wool passed round the front of the needle (*opp.* **purl**).—*n.* a level stretch of land.

plain chocolate dark chocolate, made with some sugar added, but no milk.

plain'-clothes' *adj.* wearing ordinary clothes, not uniform, as a policeman on detective work.

plain sailing 1 plane sailing. **2** sailing on an easy course. **3** easy progress.

plains'man *n.* one who lives in a plain.

plain'-spok'en *adj.* speaking one's thoughts openly and honestly, or bluntly.

plaint *plānt*, *n.* **1** a complaint. **2** a mournful song.

plaint'iff (*Eng. law*) *n.* one who begins a suit against another.

plaint'ive *adj.* mournful, sorrowful.

plaint'ively *adv.* **plaint'iveness** *n.*

plait *plat*, sometimes *plāt*, *n.* **1** twined hair, etc. **2** a pigtail or braid. **3** a pleat:—*v.t.* to braid (hair).

plan *plan*, *n.* **1** a drawing of a building showing the shape it makes on the ground or parallel to the ground. **2** a detailed map of an area. **3** a scheme, arrangement to do something. **4** the way of doing it.—*v.t.* **1** to make a plan of. **2** to decide on (a course of action):—*pr.p.* **plann'ing**; *pa.p.* **planned**.

plane[1] *plān*, *n.* **1** any flat or level surface. **2** one of the surfaces such as wings and tail which support an aeroplane in flight. **3** short for **aeroplane**. **4** any grade or level of life, development, or thought: *Human beings are on a higher plane than the apes.*—*adj.* **1** perfectly level. **2** lying within a plane.—*v.t.* to make smooth.—*v.i.* (of a boat) to lift out of the water while in motion and skim across the surface:—*pr.p.* **plan'ing.**

plane figure a figure all of whose points lie in one plane or surface.

plane sailing calculating a ship's position as if the earth were flat.

plane[2] *plān*, *n.* a carpenter's tool for making a smooth surface.—*v.t.* to make (a surface) level by using a plane:—*pr.p.* **plan'ing**.

plane[3], **plane tree** *plān' trē*, *n.* a type of tree with broad leaves.

planet *plan'it*, *n.* any body (except a comet or meteor) that revolves about the sun or other fixed star.

plan'etary *adj.*

planetār'ium *n.* a building that houses a special projector for showing the position of planets and stars.

plan'etoid *n.* a minor planet.

plank *plangk*, *n.* **1** a long piece of timber, thicker than a board. **2** one of the aims that forms the 'platform' or programme of a political party.—*v.t.* **1** to cover with planks. **2** (*coll.*) to lay (down, e.g. money).

plank'ing *n.* planks.

plankton *plangk'tȯn*, *n.* the floating organisms in seas, lakes, etc.

plant *plänt*, *n.* **1** any member of the vegetable kingdom, having stem, root, and leaves. **2** machinery used in a factory. **3** a factory. **4** (*slang*) a person put into an organisation secretly, e.g. as a spy. **5** (*slang*) something placed as false evidence. **6** (*slang*) a swindle, a put-up job.—*v.t.* **1** to put into the ground for growth. **2** to set down firmly. **3** to implant, to cause (e.g. an idea) to take hold. **4** to found, settle (e.g. a colony). **5** (*slang*) to deliver (a blow in a particular place). **6** (*slang*) to place (something) as false evidence or a false clue, or to place (a spy).

plantā'tion *n.* **1** a place planted, esp. with trees. **2** a large estate used for growing cotton, rubber, tea, etc. in southern U.S. or other warm countries. **3** a colony.

plant'er *n.* **1** one who plants. **2** the owner of a plantation.

plantain *plan'tin*, *n.* a plant with leaves pressed flat on the ground.

plantation. See **plant**.

plaque *pläk*, *plak*, *n.* **1** a thin piece or tablet of metal, etc. used for ornament (e.g. on a wall), or with an inscription, to commemorate something. **2** a film of saliva and bacteria formed on teeth.

plasma *plaz'mȧ*, *n.* **1** the liquid part of blood, lymph, and milk. **2** a very hot gas.

plaster *pläs'tėr*, *n.* **1** a sticky substance spread on a cloth, applied to the body to cure an ailment: *a mustard plaster.* **2** a sticky material, often in strips, used e.g. to hold in place dressings on wounds. **3** a mixture of lime, water, and sand which sets hard and is used to coat walls, ceilings, etc. **4** plaster of Paris.—*adj.* made of plaster.—*v.t.* **1** to apply plaster to. **2** to smear. **3** to cover too thickly (with).

plas'terer *n.* one who plasters.

plaster cast 1 a copy got by pouring a mixture of plaster of Paris and water into a mould of the object. **2** a cast (*def.* 6).

plaster of Paris a quick-hardening plaster.

plastic *plas'tik*, *adj.* **1** easily moulded or shaped, as clay or wax. **2** concerned with modelling objects. **3** easily influenced. **4** made of plastic.—*n.* **1** a substance that can be moulded. **2** any of various chemical compounds made artifically (not found in nature) that can be used to form materials of many kinds.

Plasticine® *plas'ti-sēn, n.* a soft, clay-like substance used for modelling.

plasticity *(-tis'i-ti) n.* the state or quality of being plastic or easily moulded.

plastic explosive mouldable explosive materials.

plastic surgery surgery which repairs damaged (esp. deformed or disfigured) parts of the body.

plate *plāt, n.* **1** a flat sheet of metal. **2** an engraved piece of metal, often one used for printing. **3** a whole page illustration on different paper inserted in a book. **4** a sheet, usu. of glass, coated with a substance sensitive to light and used in photography. **5** the part of false teeth that fits to the mouth. **6** gold and silver articles. **7** a shallow dish for holding food. **8** a helping (of food), a plateful. **9** a plate-like dish used for a church collection.—*v.t.* to cover (a metal) with a thin coating of nickel, silver, gold, etc.:—*pr.p.* **plat'ing.**

plate armour armour of metal plates.

plate'-glass' *n.* a fine kind of glass cast in thick sheets, used for windows, etc.

plate'layer *n.* one who lays and fixes the rails of a railway.

on one's plate awaiting or requiring one's attention.

plateau *pla'tō, pla-tō', n.* a broad level stretch of high land, a tableland:—*pl.* **plateaux, plateaus** *(-ōz).*

platen *plat'n, n.* **1** in printing, a plate or roller that presses paper against inked type. **2** the roller of a typewriter.

platform *plat'förm, n.* **1** a raised level surface, as that in a railway station. **2** a raised floor for speakers, entertainers, etc. **3** a position for mounting a gun. **4** a piece of flooring at the entrance to a bus, etc. **5** the plan or policy made public by a political party. **6** a floating installation, usu. moored to the sea-bed, for drilling for oil, etc.

platinum *plat'in-um, n.* an element, a valuable heavy steel-grey metal used in electrical and electronic apparatus, jewellery, etc.

platitude *plat'i-tūd, n.* a dull, ordinary remark made as if it were important.

platitud'inous *adj.*

Platonic *pla-ton'ik, adj.* **1** having to do with the Greek philosopher Plato or his teaching. **2** (of love; also no *cap.*) on a spiritual level, without physical passion.

platon'ically *adv.*

platoon *pla-tōōn', n.* a part, subdivision, of a company of soldiers.

platter *plat'ėr, n.* a large flat plate.

platypus *plat'i-pus, n.* a small water animal of Australia and Tasmania, with webbed feet and a muzzle like a duck's bill, that lays eggs.

plaudit *plöd'it, n.* (usu. in *pl.* **plaudits**) **1** a round of applause. **2** praise.

plausible *plöz'i-bl, adj.* **1** seeming to be worthy of (orig.) praise, (now) belief. **2** (of e.g. an explanation) reasonable:—*opp.* **implaus'ible**.

play *plā, v.i.* **1** to gambol, frisk, as a young animal does. **2** to take part in games or amusements. **3** to amuse oneself (with). **4** to trifle (with): *He is playing with her affection.* **5** (with *with*) to handle, waste time with, push around, etc. (one's food) in a silly or unenthusiastic way: *If he plays with his food, he probably is not hungry.* **6** to gamble. **7** to act on a stage. **8** to perform on an instrument. **9** to move to and fro, to flicker. **10** to move freely as part of a mechanism.—*v.t.* **1** to act (a part). **2** to (know how to) take part in (a game). **3** to compete against in a game. **4** to perform music on. **5** to carry out (a trick). **6** to bring about: *to play havoc.* **7** to direct on: *They played hoses on the fire.* **8** to put down (a card) in a game. **9** to give a certain freedom of action or movement to: *to play a fish after hooking it.*—*n.* **1** recreation. **2** amusement. **3** the playing of a game. **4** gambling. **5** a drama, acted story. **6** manner of dealing: *fair play.* **7** freedom of movement: *to give full play to.*

play'er *n.*

play'ful *adj.* **1** (of e.g. a kitten) full of desire to play. **2** joking, not serious.

play'boy *n.* a light-hearted, irresponsible man, esp. rich and leisured.

play'fellow, play'mate *ns.* a friend with whom one plays.

play'ground *n.* an area, esp. outside a school, for children's play.

play'group *n.* an informal group, usu. run by volunteers, attended by preschool children and their carers for creative and co-operative play.

play'house *n.* a theatre.

play'ing-card *n.* one of a pack of usu. 52 cards used in playing games.

play'-off *n.* a game to decide a tie, or between the winners of other games or competitions.

play'school *n.* a nursery school or playgroup.

play'thing *n.* **1** a toy. **2** someone, etc. treated as if a toy.

play'wright *n.* a dramatist.

bring, come, into play to bring, come, into use, operation, etc.
hold in play to keep (a person) busy, esp. in order to gain time.
in play (of a ball in a game) in a position in which the rules allow it to be hit or kicked.
out of play not in play.
play along (with) to co-operate, agree (with), usu. temporarily.
play ball to co-operate (with).
play down to treat (something) as less important than it is.
played out 1 exhausted. **2** used up.
play fair (*arch.* **false**) to act, or act towards, in a fair and honest (dishonest) way.
play for time to act so as to gain time and better opportunity.
play into a person's hands to act so as to give him the advantage.
play off 1 to pass (a thing) off (as something else). **2** to set (one person) against (another). **3** to have a play-off.
play on to work upon and make use of: *to play on a person's fears.*
play on words a pun, etc.
play out to play to the end, finish.
play safe to take no risks.
play the game to act fairly and honestly.
play up to (*coll.*) to flatter.

plea *plē*, *n.* **1** an excuse. **2** a prisoner's answer to a charge. **3** an urgent request.
plead *plēd*, *v.i.* **1** to carry on a lawsuit. **2** to argue in favour of a cause in court, or to give an answer in defence. **3** to beg earnestly (with *with*): *You must plead with Mary not to go.*—*v.t.* **1** to support (a cause) by argument. **2** to give as an excuse: *to plead ignorance*:—*pa.t.* and *pa.p.* **plead'ed**, or **pled**.
plead'ings *n. pl.* the statements of the two sides in a lawsuit.
plead guilty, or **not guilty** to admit, or deny, guilt.
special pleading unfair argument aiming at winning rather than at truth.

please *plēz*, *v.t.* **1** to give pleasure to. **2** to delight. **3** to satisfy:—*opp.* **displease.**—*v.i.* **1** to give pleasure. **2** to choose: *He does as he pleases*:—*pr.p.* **pleas'ing.**—*interj.* if you please.
pleas'ant *plez'ȧnt*, *adj.* **1** agreeable. **2** cheerful.
pleas'antly *adv.* **pleas'antness** *n.*
pleas'antry *n.* good-humoured joking:—*pl.* **pleas'antries.**
pleas'ing *adj.* attractive, charming.
pleas'urable *plezh'ůr-ȧbl*, *adj.* delightful.
pleasure *plezh'ůr*, *n.* **1** a state of enjoyment or joy. **2** delight. **3** frivolous enjoyment as one's chief aim: *to live a life of pleasure.* **4** what one wishes: *What is your pleasure?*
pleas'ure-boat *n.* a boat used for amusement.
at pleasure when or if one pleases.
(if you) please if you are willing (added for politeness to a command or request).

pleat *plēt*, *n.* a fold sewn or pressed into cloth.—*v.t.* to make a pleat or pleats in.

plebeian *plė-bē'ȧn*, *adj.* **1** of the common people. **2** common, vulgar.—Also *n.* (also **pleb** *pleb*).
plebiscite *pleb'i-sit*, *sīt*, *n.* a direct vote of the whole nation or region on a special point.

plectrum *plek'trům*, *n.* a small piece of horn, metal, etc. used for plucking the strings of a guitar, etc.

pledge *plej*, *n.* **1** something handed over by a person who borrows money, etc., which will not be returned to them if they do not repay, etc. **2** a solemn promise.—*v.t.* **1** to give as security, to pawn. **2** to promise. **3** to drink to the health of:—*pr.p.* **pledg'ing.**

plenary *plē'nȧr-i*, *adj.* **1** full, complete. **2** fully attended (e.g. an assembly).
plenipotentiary *plen-i-pō-ten'shȧr-i*, *adj.* having full powers.—*n.* a person with full powers, as an ambassador:—*pl.* **plenipoten'tiaries.**
plenitude *plen'i-tūd*, *n.* **1** fullness. **2** abundance.
plenary powers full powers to carry out some business.

plenty *plen'ti*, *n.* **1** a full or sufficient supply. **2** abundance (of food, money, etc.).—*adj.* (*coll.*) plenty of.
plenteous (*poetic*) *plen'tyůs*, **plen'tiful**, *adjs.* generously sufficient, abundant.

plethora *pleth'ȯr-ȧ*, *n.* **1** the state of having too much e.g. blood. **2** a too large quantity (of).
plethoric *(-thor'ik) adj.*

pleurisy *plōō'ri-si*, *n.* inflammation of the membrane covering the lung.

pliable, plied, pliers. See **ply**[1].

plight[1] *plīt*, *v.t.* to pledge (e.g. one's word, troth—see this):—*pa.p.* **plight'ed.**

plight[2] *plīt*, *n.* state, situation (usu. bad): *a hopeless plight, sad plight.*

plimsoll *plim'sȯl*, *-sol*, *-sōl*, *n.* a rubber-soled canvas shoe.—**Plimsoll('s) line** or **mark** *(-sȯl, -sol)* a ship's loadline (see this word), introduced by the English M.P. Samuel *Plimsoll.*

plinth *plinth*, *n.* **1** the square slab at the foot of a column. **2** the base or pedestal of a statue, vase, etc.

plod *plod*, *v.i.* **1** to walk heavily and slowly. **2** to work or study steadily, toil:—*pr.p.* **plodd'ing**; *pa.p.* **plodd'ed**.
plodd'er *n.* a dull or slow but hard-working person.

plop *plop*, *n.* the sound of a small object falling into water.—*v.i.* to make the sound of a plop:—*pr.p.* **plopp'ing**; *pa.p.* **plopped**.

plot *plot*, *n.* **1** a small piece of ground. **2** the main story told in a play, novel, etc. **3** a secret plan or scheme, esp. for doing evil.—*v.t.* **1** to make a plan of, show by a graph. **2** to mark (points) on a graph. **3** to work out secret plans for (something evil), plan (to do).—*v.i.* to form a plot:—*pr.p.* **plott'ing**; *pa.p.* **plott'ed**.
plott'er *n.*

plough *plow*, *n.* a tool for turning up the soil.—*v.t.* **1** to turn up (the ground) in furrows. **2** (of a ship) to make a way through (e.g. the sea).—*v.i.* **1** to tear or force a way (through): *The car ploughed through the crowd.* **2** to progress with difficulty (through): *He ploughed through his homework.*—*v.t.* and *v.i.* (*coll.*) to fail in (an examination).
ploughshare *plow'shār*, *n.* the blade of the plough, which cuts the slice of earth.
plough back to put (profits of a business) back into the business.
ploughman's lunch a meal of bread, cheese, cold meat, pickle, etc.
put one's hand to the plough to begin a project or business.
the Plough a group of stars forming a shape like a plough, containing the Pointers (two stars in line with the North Star).

plover *pluv'ėr*, *n.* the lapwing or related bird.

plow (*chiefly U.S.*). Same as **plough**.

ploy *ploi*, *n.* **1** something one is doing or involved in. **2** something done, esp. if rather underhand, to achieve a certain result.

pluck *pluk*, *v.t.* **1** to pull off or out. **2** to strip the feathers off (a fowl). **3** to pull (a string of a musical instrument).—*v.i.* to tug (at).—*n.* **1** the heart, liver, and lungs of an animal—whence used for courage, spirit. **2** an act of plucking.
pluck'y *adj.* brave, resolute:—*comp.* **pluck'ier**; *superl.* **pluck'iest**.
pluck'ily *adv.* **pluck'iness** *n.*
pluck up 1 to pull out by the roots. **2** to rouse up in oneself (e.g. courage).

plug *plug*, *n.* **1** a block, peg, or wad of material, used to stop a hole. **2** a fitting put into a socket to get electric current. **3** a connection in a water main for a hose. **4** a device releasing a flow of water. **5** a cake of tobacco. **6** a sparking-plug. **7** (*coll.*) a piece of favourable publicity inserted somewhere.—*v.t.* **1** to stop with a plug. **2** (*slang*) to shoot, or to hit with the fist. **3** (*coll.*) to advertise or publicise, esp. by repeating or mentioning often.—*v.i.* (*coll.*) to plod, keep working (at a dull or difficult task):—*pr.p.* **plugg'ing**; *pa.p.* **plugged**.

plum *plum*, *n.* **1** a fruit of blue-red colour with a stone in the centre. **2** the tree bearing it. **3** a raisin when used in cake or pudding. **4** a good thing (also *adj.*): *a plum of a job*.
plum'-pudd'ing *n.* a pudding of flour, suet, raisins, currants, etc.

plumage. See **plume**.

plumb *plum*, *n.* a lead weight hung on a string (or **plumb'-line**), used to tell a straight up and down position by builders, etc., a plummet.—*adj.* straight up and down, vertical.—*adv.* **1** vertically. **2** exactly. **3** (*coll.* esp. *U.S.*) downright: *That is plumb stupid.*—*v.t.* **1** to test by a plumb-line: *to plumb a wall.* **2** to test the depth of (the sea, etc.). **3** to reach the bottom of: *to plumb the depths of misery*.
plumber *plum'ėr*, *n.* a person who fits and mends water and sewage fittings, gas pipes, etc.
plumbing *plum'ing*, *n.* **1** the craft of a plumber. **2** the water and sewage pipes, sinks, water-closets, etc. fitted by a plumber.
plumb bob the weight at the end of a plumb-line.

plume *plōōm*, *n.* **1** a feather, esp. a large showy one. **2** a bird's crest. **3** something looking like a feather: *a plume of smoke.* **4** a tuft of feathers used as an ornament, as on a helmet.—*v.t.* to pride (oneself): *He plumed himself on his success*:—*pr.p.* **plum'ing**.
plumage *plōōm'ij*, *n.* feathers.
borrowed plumes finery, or honour, that does not really belong to one.

plummet *plum'it*, *n.* a plumb bob on a plumb-line for measuring depths.—*v.i.* to plunge:—*pr.p.* **plumm'eting**; *pa.p.* **plumm'eted**.

plump[1] *plump*, *v.i.* **1** to drop or fall suddenly (into a liquid). **2** to flop down. **3** to decide on, choose, decisively or abruptly (with *for*). **4** to give all one's votes to one candidate: *to plump for Jones.*—*v.t.* to fling down or let fall flat or heavily.—*n.* the sound or act of plumping.—*adv.* **1** with a plump. **2** in plain language, bluntly. **3** directly, without a pause.—*adj.* blunt, direct.

plump[2] *plump, adj.* pleasantly fat and rounded, well filled out.—Also *v.t., v.i.*
plump'ness *n.*

plunder *plun'dėr, v.t.* **1** to carry off the goods of (another) by force. **2** to loot, rob (a place).—Also *v.i.*—*n.* booty.

plunge *plunj, v.t.* **1** to thrust suddenly (into water, other liquid, a hole). **2** to push deep into: *to plunge a person into gloom, a nation into war.*—*v.i.* **1** to throw oneself (e.g. into water). **2** to rush (e.g. into danger). **3** to pitch forward suddenly, as a ship or horse. **4** to gamble recklessly:—*pr.p.* **plung'ing.**—*n.* **1** the act of plunging. **2** a dive.
plung'er *n.* **1** one who plunges. **2** a piston used as a forcer in pumps, etc. **3** an instrument for clearing blocked pipes by suction.

plush *plush, n.* a cloth of cotton, silk, etc. with long pile.—*adj.* luxurious: *plush apartments.*
plush'y, *adj.*:—*comp.* **plush'ier**; *superl.* **plush'iest.**
plush'iness *n.*

Pluto *plōō'tō, n.* **1** the Greek god of the underworld. **2** the planet furthest from the sun.
plutō'nium *n.* a radioactive element used in nuclear reactors and nuclear weapons.

plutocracy *plōō-tok'rȧ-si, n.* **1** government by the rich. **2** a ruling body of rich men:—*pl.* **plutoc'racies.**
plutocrat *plōō'tō-krat, n.* one who is powerful because of his money.

plutonium. See **Pluto**.

ply[1] *plī, n.* **1** a fold, layer. **2** a strand of rope, etc.:—*pl.* **plies.**—*v.t.* and *v.i.* to bend, fold:—*pr.p.* **ply'ing**; *pa.p.* **plied.**
pliable *plī'ȧ-bl, adj.* **1** easily bent or folded, flexible. **2** easily persuaded.—Also **plī'ant.**
pliabil'ity, pli'ancy *ns.*
pli'er *n.* **1** one who plies. **2** (in *pl.*) small pincers for bending or cutting wire, etc.
ply'wood boarding made of thin layers of wood glued together.

ply[2] *plī, v.t.* **1** to work at steadily. **2** to use with vigour: *to ply an axe.* **3** to keep supplying: *to ply the guests with food.* **4** to address continually: *to ply someone with questions.*—*v.i.* to make regular journeys over a route: *The ship plies between London and Glasgow*:—*pr.p.* **ply'ing**; *pa.p.* **plied.**

pneumatic *nū-mat'ik, adj.* **1** filled with air. **2** operated or moved by air.
pneumat'ically *adv.*

pneumonia *nū-mō'ni-ȧ, n.* a disease in which the lungs become inflamed.

poach[1] *pōch, v.t.* to cook (eggs without their shells, etc.) in very hot liquid, e.g. water.

poach[2] *pōch, v.i.* **1** to intrude on another's ground in order to hunt game or catch fish illegally. **2** to encroach on another's rights, area of influence. **3** to try to play a ball one's partner should play.—Also *v.t.*
poach'er *n.*

pock *pok, n.* a small blister on the skin, as in smallpox.
pock'mark *n.* the pit or scar left by a pock.—Also *v.t.*
See also **pox**.

pocket *pok'it, n.* **1** a little pouch or bag, esp. in a garment or a billiard table. **2** (one's) money or resources. **3** (**air pocket**) an area of different pressure. **4** a small isolated area or patch: *a pocket of unemployment.*—*v.t.* **1** to put in the pocket. **2** to steal.
pock'et-book *n.* a wallet for papers or money carried in the pocket.
pocket money **1** money for personal expenses. **2** an allowance, esp. to a child.
in, out of, pocket **1** with, or without, money. **2** richer, or poorer, after a deal.
line one's pockets to make money dishonestly or immorally from business, etc. entrusted to one.

pockmark. See **pock**.

pod *pod, n.* the long seed-case or shell in peas, beans, etc.—*v.i.* to form pods.—*v.t.* to remove the pod from:—*pr.p.* **podd'ing**; *pa.p.* **podd'ed.**

podgy *poj'i, adj.* short and fat:—*comp.* **podg'ier**; *superl.* **podg'iest.**

podium *pō'di-ŭm, n.* a platform or rostrum:—*pl.* **pō'dia.**

poem *pō'im, n.* **1** a piece of writing in lines which usu. have a regular beat and often rhyme. **2** a piece of writing in striking language or showing imagination or beauty of thought, which may or may not be in metre.

poet *pō'it, n.* **1** the author of a poem. **2** one with a great imagination and the ability to express this in striking language:—*fem.* (*old*) **po'etess.**
poetic *pō-et'ik, adj.* **1** having to do with poetry, like poetry. **2** in the language of poetry. **3** imaginative.—Also **poet'ical.**
po'etry *n.* **1** the art of the poet. **2** the special quality of poems. **3** poems as a whole.
poetic justice ideal justice, giving out of rewards and punishments as deserved.

Poet Laureate an official poet attached to the royal household.

poignant *poin'ănt, -yănt, adj.* **1** sharp, very painful: *poignant regret.* **2** very sad: *a poignant scene.* **3** (of interest) very keen.

point *point, n.* **1** a dot. **2** a mark of punctuation, esp. the full stop. **3** the dot used in writing decimals (e.g. 4.2, *four point two*). **4** an exact place, spot. **5** a moment in time: *at the point of death.* **6** a place in a scale: *boiling point.* **7** a division on a compass. **8** a mark in scoring a competition, game, or test. **9** a sharp end of anything. **10** a cape or headland. **11** (in *pl.*) a movable rail for passing (e.g. a locomotive) from one track to another. **12** a detail to be taken into account. **13** the main question in an argument or discussion. **14** the meaning or force of a story or joke. **15** an aim: *He gained his point.* **16** a trait, quality: *I do not like him, but he has his good points.* **17** in various games, (the position of) a certain player, e.g. in cricket (that of) a fielder near the batsman on the off side.—*v.t.* **1** to give a point to. **2** to aim or direct (at). **3** to fill the joints of (stone- or brick-work) with mortar. **4** to give force or special meaning to (a remark).—*v.i.* **1** to direct the finger or eye towards an object. **2** to show game by looking, as a dog does.

point'ed *adj.* **1** having a sharp point. **2** sharp. **3** having force or meaning. **4** (of a remark) obviously aimed at someone.

point'er *n.* **1** a rod for pointing. **2** a breed of dog trained to look for game. **3** a hint, suggestion.

point'less *adj.* **1** having no meaning. **2** senseless.

point duty the duty e.g. of a policeman stationed at a particular point to regulate traffic.

a case in point an example illustrating the matter being discussed.

beside the point not to the point.

in point of fact in fact.

make a point of **1** to treat as important. **2** to insist upon (doing something, or having something done).

on the point of (doing something), just going to (do it).

point of order a question raised in a meeting as to whether the business is being done according to the rules.

point of view the way in which one looks at things.

point out to indicate, draw attention to.

to the point connected with the matter being discussed.

point-blank *point'-blangk', adj.* **1** (of a shot) fired levelly, from close range. **2** direct, plain: *a point-blank question.*—Also *adv.*

poise *poiz, v.t.* **1** to balance evenly. **2** to hold ready to throw or drop.—Also *v.i.*:—*pr.p.* **pois'ing.**—*n.* **1** a state of balance. **2** dignity and self-confidence. **3** carriage (of body, head).

poison *poi'zn, n.* **1** any substance which, when taken into the body, kills, or harms health. **2** anything harmful.—*v.t.* **1** to injure or kill, or to make harmful, with poison. **2** to corrupt, or cause to think evil (e.g. a person, his mind).

pois'oner *n.* **pois'onous** *adj.*

poke[1] *pōk, (dial.) n.* a bag, sack.

poke[2] *pōk, v.t.* **1** to push the end of (something into or against something). **2** to thrust at. **3** to stir up (a fire).—*v.i.* **1** to grope or feel (about). **2** to go prying or searching (into). **3** to stick out:—*pr.p.* **po'king.**—*n.* **1** a prod, nudge. **2** a look, search.

po'ker *n.* a rod for stirring a fire.

pō'ky *adj.* **1** small, cramped, and shabby. **2** (of e.g. a job) pottering, dull:—*comp.* **po'kier**; superl. **po'kiest**.

poke one's nose into to pry into (other people's concerns).

poker[1]. See **poke**[2].

poker[2] *pō'kėr, n.* a gambling card game.

poker face a blank face or expression telling nothing of the emotions behind it, useful to a poker player.

poky. See **poke**[2].

polar, polarise. See **pole**[1].

polder *pōl'dėr, pol', n.* land below sea level reclaimed for use.

pole[1] *pōl, n.* **1** the north or the south end of the earth's axis. **2** either of the two points in the heavens (north and south) to which the earth's axis points and around which the stars appear to turn. **3** either of the opposite points of a magnet. **4** an electrical terminal.

polar *adj.* **1** having to do with a pole. **2** near, or living near, a pole: *polar regions, polar bear.*

pol'arise *v.t.* and *v.i.* (to cause people, etc.) to adopt extremely opposing views, or (differences of opinion) to become increased:—*pr.p.* **pol'arising**.

Pole star. See **North Star**.

pole[2] *pōl, n.* **1** a long rounded rod or post, usu. of wood. **2** an old measure of length, or of area.—*v.t.* to push (e.g. a boat) with a pole:—*pr.p.* **pol'ing**.

Pole *pōl, n.* a native or citizen of Poland.

Pol'ish *adj.* of Poland or its people.—*n.* the language of Poland.

pole-axe *pōl'aks, n.* a battleaxe having a long handle.

polecat *pōl'kat*, *n.* **1** an animal like a weasel which gives off a strong smell. **2** (*U.S.*) a skunk.

polemic(al) *po-lem'ik(-ȧl)*, *adjs.* having to do with controversy or dispute.—*n.* (**polem'ic**) a polemical writing.

police *pȯl-ēs'*, *n.* the body of men and women employed to keep order, enforce laws, etc. in a country.—*v.t.* to control (as if) by means of police:—*pr.p.* **polic'ing.**
police'man, -woman *ns.*
police state a country in which secret police keep down all opposition to the government.
police station the headquarters of the police in a district.
secret police a police force which operates in secret, usu. dealing with matters of politics, national security, etc.

policy[1] *pol'i-si*, *n.* **1** a course of action decided on by a government, political party, person, etc. **2** wisdom in managing affairs:—*pl.* **pol'icies.**
See also **politic.**

policy[2] *pol'i-si*, *n.* a writing containing an insurance agreement with an insurance company:—*pl.* **pol'icies.**

polio *pōl'i-ō*, *n.* short for **poliomyelitis** *(pōl-i-ō-mī-ė-lī'tis)*, inflammation of the grey matter of the spinal cord, a disease also called 'infantile paralysis'.

Polish. See **Pole.**

polish *pol'ish*, *v.t.* **1** to make smooth and shiny by rubbing. **2** to improve, make polite and refined (manners, literary style, etc.).—*v.i.* to take a polish.—*n.* **1** gloss. **2** a substance used to produce a smooth and shiny surface. **3** refinement.

polite *pȯ-līt'*, *adj.* having or showing good manners, courteous:—*opp.* **impolite.**

politic *pol'i-tik*, *adj.* **1** (of actions) wise, following a good policy, leading to one's advantage. **2** (of persons) shrewd:—*opp.* **impolitic.**
polit'cal *adj.* **1** having to do with government. **2** having to do with parties that have different views of government.
polit'ically *adv.*
politician (*-tish'ȧn*) *n.* **1** one whose business is politics. **2** one skilled in the ways of party politics (often used in a bad sense).
pol'itics *n.* **1** (*sing.* or *pl.*) political affairs, or methods, or principles. **2** (*sing.*) the art or science of government.
political economy economics.
political prisoner one imprisoned for his or her political beliefs, activities, etc.

polka *pol'kȧ, pōl'*, *n.* a lively type of dance.
pol'ka-dot *n.* one of a number of dots forming a pattern on a fabric.

poll *pōl*, *n.* **1** the head. **2** an individual. **3** a counting of voters. **4** (usu. in *pl.*) a place of voting. **5** a total number of votes. **6** (also **opinion poll**) the taking of public opinion by means of questioning.—*v.t.* **1** to cut the hair or horns from, or to cut the top off. **2** to receive (a number of votes).
polled *adj.* hornless.
polling booth the place in a **polling station** where people vote.
poll tax formerly, a community charge.

pollard *pol'ȧrd*, *n.* **1** a tree having the top cut off. **2** an animal which has had its horns removed.

pollen *pol'ėn*, *n.* the fertilising powder in flowers.
pollinā'tion *n.* the carrying of pollen to the stigma of a flower by insects, etc.

pollute *pol-ōōt', -ūt'*, *v.t.* **1** to make filthy, contaminate. **2** to use (something sacred) without respect. **3** to make any feature of the environment harmful to life:—*pr.p.* **pollut'ing.**
pollu'tant *n.* something, e.g. chemical or industrial waste, that pollutes the environment.
pollu'tion *n.*

polo *pō'lō*, *n.* **1** a game like hockey played on horseback. **2** any of various similar games played in water (**water polo**), on bicycles or skates, etc.
polo neck on a garment, a close-fitting neck with a part turned over at the top.

poltergeist *pol'tėr-gīst*, *n.* a noisy ghost, said to move furniture, etc.

poly- *pol-i-*, (as part of a word) much, many.
polyest'er *n.* any of a number of plastics formed by polymerisation of chemicals known as *esters*.
polyethylene. See **polythene.**
polygamy *pȯl-ig'ȧ-mi*, *n.* the custom of having more than one husband or wife at the same time.
polyg'amist *n.* **polyg'amous** *adj.*
polyglot *pol'i-glot*, *adj.* using many languages.—*n.* one who speaks or writes many languages.
polygon *pol'i-gon*, *n.* a figure of many angles and sides.
pol'ymer *pol'i-mėr*, *n.* a substance produced by **polymerisā'tion**, the combining of several molecules of a substance to form one large molecule of a new substance, a process by which many plastics are obtained.
polyp *pol'ip*, *n.* **1** an animal with many

arms or tentacles (either an animal more or less fixed to the place where it lives or one joined to others). **2** (also **pol'ypus** *-i-pŭs*) a tumour growing from the mucous membrane.

polystyrene *pol-i-stī'rēn*, *n.* a plastic, a polymer of a chemical *styrene*.

polysyllable *pol'i-sil-ȧ-bl*, *n.* a word of three or more syllables.

polysyllab'ic *adj.*

polytechnic *(-tek'nik)* *n.* formerly, in Britain, a college in which various technical subjects were taught.

pol'ytheism *(-thē-izm)* *n.* belief in many gods.

pol'ythene, **polyeth'ylene** *ns.* the name for several types of plastics which can be moulded when hot, polymers of the chemical *ethylene*.

polyurethane *pol-i-ūr'ė-thān*, *n.* any of a number of plastics produced by polymerisation.

polyvinyl chloride *(pol-i-vī'nil)* a plastic formed by polymerisation of the chemical *vinyl chloride* (*abbrev.* **PVC**).

polyp. See **poly**.

pomander *pȯ-man'dėr*, *n.* a box, etc. with holes in it, filled with sweet-smelling substances.

pomegranate *pom'i-gran-it*, *n.* a large Oriental fruit with a very thick rind and many seeds.

pommel *pum'ėl*, *pom'*, *n.* **1** the knob on a sword-hilt. **2** the high part in front of a saddle.—*v.t.* to pummel:—*pr.p.* **pomm'elling**; *pa.p.* **pomm'elled**.

pomp *pomp*, *n.* splendid display, great ceremony.

pomp'ous *adj.* grand and self-important in manner.

pomp'ousness, **pompos'ity** *ns.*

pompom *pom'pom*, *n.* a fluffy or woolly ball, tuft or tassel on a hat, etc.

poncho *pon'chō*, *n.* **1** a South American cloak, a blanket with a hole in the middle for the head. **2** any similar garment:—*pl.* **pon'chos**.

pond *pond*, *n.* a small lake, usu. artificial.

ponder *pon'dėr*, *v.t.* to think over, consider.—*v.i.* to think (about, over).

pon'derous *adj.* **1** weighty, clumsy, difficult to handle. **2** (of manner, style) solemn and dull.

pon'derously *adv.* **pon'derousness** *n.*

See also **imponderable**.

pong *pong*, (*coll.*) *n.* a bad smell—Also *v.i.* and *v.t.*

poniard *pon'yȧrd*, *n.* a small dagger.

pontiff *pon'tif*, (*Roman Catholic*) *n.* a bishop, esp. the pope.

pontif'ical *adj.* **1** belonging to a pontiff. **2** speaking, or spoken, pompously, as if with authority.

pontif'icals *n.pl.* the dress or robes of a bishop or pope.

pontif'icate *(-i-kit, -kāt)* *n.* the office and dignity or reign of a pope.—*v.i.* *(-i-kāt)* to speak in a pompous manner:—*pr.p.* **pontif'icating**.

pontoon[1] *pon-tōōn'*, *n.* **1** a flat-bottomed boat. **2** a float. **3** such a boat or float used to support a bridge.

pontoon[2] *pon-tōōn'*, *n.* a card game.

pony *pō'ni*, *n.* a small horse:—*pl.* **pon'ies**.

po'ny-tail *n.* a hairstyle with the hair tied together at the back of the head, looking like a horse's tail.

po'ny-trekking *n.* the pastime of cross-country riding in small parties.

poodle *pōō'dl*, *n.* a curly-haired dog, fond of water, often clipped in a fancy manner.

poof *poof*, *pŏŏf*, *n.* (*offensive slang*) a male homosexual.

pooh *pōō*, *interj.* a sound of scorn.

pooh-pooh' *v.t.* to make light of.

pool[1] *pōōl*, *n.* **1** a small body of still water. **2** a deep part of a stream.

pool[2] *pōōl*, *n.* **1** the stakes or amount of money played for in certain games and contests. **2** a game in which the winner takes the pool or part of it. **3** a variety of billiards. **4** a common or joint stock or fund. **5** a combination, e.g. of firms to gain control of the market.—*v.t.* to put into a joint fund or stock.

football pool a form of gambling in which people predict the results of certain football games, the ones who are right winning a part of the money paid to enter the gamble.

poop *pōōp*, *n.* **1** the back part or stern of a ship. **2** a high deck in the stern.

poor *pōōr*, *pör*, *adj.* **1** having little money or few possessions. **2** not good, inferior, unsatisfactory: *goods of poor quality.* **3** lacking (in). **4** to be pitied: *Poor Tom has had many troubles.*—*n.* (**the poor**) those with little money.

poor'ly *adv.* **poor'ness** *n.*

poor'ly *adj.* not in good health.

poor'house *n.* (*old*) a house paid for by public money for sheltering the very poor.

See also **poverty**.

pop[1] *pop*, *n.* **1** a sharp, quick sound, as of drawing a cork. **2** a shot. **3** a fizzy drink.—*v.i.* **1** to make a pop, burst with a pop. **2** to shoot. **3** to come or go suddenly: *to pop in, out*, etc.—*v.t.* **1** to cause to make a pop. **2** (*slang*) to pawn:—*pr.p.* **popp'ing**; *pa.p.*

popped.

pop'corn *n.* kind of maize which bursts open when heated.

pop'-eyed *adj.* with eyes wide with excitement, surprise, etc.

pop'gun *n.* a tube and rammer for shooting pellets by compressed air.

pop off (*slang*) **1** to die. **2** to fall asleep.

pop[2] *pop*, (*coll.*) *adj.* short for **popular**, esp. relating to modern popular music played with electric guitars, etc.: *pop music: pop group.*—*n.* pop music.

pop art art showing commonplace subjects of modern urban life.

pop[3] *pop*, (*slang*) *n.* father.

pope *pōp*, *n.* (often with *cap.*) the bishop of Rome, head of the Roman Catholic Church.

pope'dom *n.* office, dignity, or authority of the pope.

pop'ery *n.* a hostile term for Roman Catholicism.

See also **papacy**.

popinjay *pop'in-jā*, *n.* **1** a parrot. **2** a target shaped like one. **3** a fop or dandy.

poplar *pop'lȧr*, *n.* a spire-shaped tree, tall and quick-growing.

poplin *pop'lin*, *n.* a strong dress material ribbed crosswise.

poppy *pop'i*, *n.* **1** a cornfield flower of showy colours, usu. red. **2** a related plant from which opium is obtained.—*pl.* **popp'ies**.

poppycock *pop'i-kok*, *n.* nonsense.

populace *pop'ū-lȧs*, *n.* the common people.

pop'ulāte, *v.t.* to fill with people:—*pr.p.* **pop'ulating**.

populā'tion *n.* the people, or number of people, living in any place.

pop'ulous *adj.* (of a country, region) full of people.

popular *pop'ū-lȧr*, *adj.* **1** pleasing to most people. **2** widely held: *a popular belief.* **3** easily understood by most people: *a popular account of modern science.* **4** of the people: *chosen by popular vote.*

pop'ularise *v.t.* **1** to make generally known or widely liked. **2** to simplify so as to make easily understood by ordinary people:—*pr.p.* **pop'ularising**.

popular'ity *n.* **pop'ularly** *adv.*

popular front an alliance of those parties in a country that want to make the greatest changes (e.g. of Communists with Socialists).

populate, populous, etc. See **populace**.

porcelain *pōrs'lin*, *pōrs'*, *n.* a fine thin white china.

porch *pōrch*, *pörch*, *n.* **1** a part of a building forming an enclosure or covering for a doorway. **2** (*U.S.*) a veranda.

porcupine *pör'kū-pīn*, *n.* a gnawing animal with bristling quills or spines in its hair.

pore[1] *pōr*, *pör*, *n.* a tiny opening esp. that of a sweat gland in the skin.

por'ous *adj.* **1** having pores. **2** (of a material) through which fluid will pass.

pore[2] *pōr*, *pör*, *v.i.* to look with great attention: *He pores over his books:*—*pr.p.* **por'ing**.

pork *pörk*, *pōrk*, *n.* the flesh of the pig.

pork'er *n.* a young pig.

pork chop a slice from a pig's rib.

pork-pie hat a soft felt hat with a round flat crown and turned-up brim.

pornography *pör-nog'rȧ-fi*, *n.* sexually arousing literature or art, often of an explicit nature.

pornographic *adj.* **pornog'rapher** *n.*

porous. See **pore**[1].

porpoise *pör'pus*, *n.* a blunt-nosed sea animal like the dolphin.

porridge *por'ij*, *n.* a food made from oatmeal in boiling water or milk.

porringer *por'in-jėr*, *n.* a small dish.

port[1] *pōrt*, *pört*, *n.* the left side of a ship.

port[2] *pōrt*, *pört*, *v.t.* to hold (a rifle) in a slanting position across the body.

port'able *adj.* easily carried or moved.

port'age *n.* **1** the act, or cost, of carrying. **2** the route over which boats, goods, have to be carried overland between waterways.

port[3] *pōrt*, *pört*, *n.* **1** a harbour. **2** a town with a harbour.

port of call a port where vessels can call for stores or repairs.

port of entry a port where goods are allowed by law to enter.

port[4] *pōrt*, *pört*, *n.* a dark-red wine.

portable, portage. See **port**[2].

portal *pōr'tȧl*, *pör'*, *n.* a doorway or entrance, esp. a magnificent one.

portcullis *pōrt-kul'is*, *pört-*, *n.* a grating that can be let down to close a gateway.

portend *pör-tend'*, *pōr-*, *v.t.* (of an omen) to give warning of, foretell.

portent *pōr'tent*, *pör'*, *n.* a forewarning, sign of what is to come.

portent'ous *adj.* **1** like a warning. **2** very great. **3** dreadful. **4** impressive: *She had a portentous manner.*

porter[1] *pōrt'ėr*, *pört'*, *n.* a doorkeeper or gatekeeper.

porter[2] *pōrt'ėr*, *pört'*, *n.* **1** one employed to carry luggage, etc. **2** a dark brown beer.

portfolio *pōrt-fō'li-ō*, *pört-*, *n.* **1** a portable case for loose papers, drawings, etc. **2** a collection of such papers. **3** a list of investments held. **4** the post or responsibilities of a government minister.—*pl.* **portfo'lios.**

porthole *pōrt'hōl, pört'*, *n.* an opening in a ship's side for light and air.

portico *pōr'ti-kō, pör'*, (*architecture*) *n.* a porch, or a covered walk, consisting of a row of columns supporting a roof:—*pl.* **por'ticos, -coes.**

portion *pōr'sh(ȯ)n, pör'*, *n.* **1** a part. **2** a helping. **3** a share (of an estate) inherited. **4** a dowry. **5** one's destiny or fate.—*v.t.* to divide (out) in portions.

por'tionless *adj.* having no dowry or property.

portly *pōrt'li, pört'li*, *adj.* **1** dignified in manner, stately. **2** bulky, stout:—*comp.* **port'lier**; *superl.* **port'liest.**

port'liness *n.*

portmanteau *pōrt-man'tō, pört-*, *n.* a large leather travelling-bag:—*pl.* **portman'teaus** or **-teaux** (*-tōz*).

portrait *pōr'trit, pör'*, *n.* **1** the likeness of a real person drawn, painted, or photographed. **2** a description in words of a person or place.

por'traiture (*-chůr, -tūr*) *n.* the art or act of making portraits.

portray' *-trā'*, *v.t.* **1** to paint or draw the likeness of. **2** to describe in words:—*pr.p.* **portray'ing**; *pa.p.* **portrayed'** (*-trād*).

portray'al *n.* the act of portraying.

Portuguese *pōr-tū-gēz', pör-*, *adj.* having to do with Portugal.—*n.* **1** a native of Portugal (*pl.* **Portuguese**). **2** the language of Portugal.

pose[1] *pōz*, *n.* **1** a position or attitude. **2** a character, attitude, or manner, put on to impress others, a pretence: *His dislike of praise was only a pose.*—*v.i.* **1** to take a position, esp. for effect: *to pose for a picture.* **2** to claim to be what one is not: *He posed as a doctor.*—*v.t.* **1** to put forward (a problem or question). **2** to arrange (e.g. a model) in a pose:—*pr.p.* **pos'ing.**

pos'er *n.* one who poses.

pose[2] *pōz*, *v.t.* (of a question, problem, or questioner) to puzzle (a person), put (them) in a difficulty:—*pr.p.* **pos'ing.**

pos'er *n.* a difficult question or problem.

poser[1,2]. See **pose**[1,2].

posh *posh*, *adj.* smart, superb, high-class.

posit *poz'it*, *v.t.* to assume (something) to be true:—*pr.p.* **pos'iting**; *pa.p.* **pos'ited.**

position *poz-ish'(ȯ)n*, *n.* **1** situation: *the position of the house.* **2** place: *a fortified position.* **3** posture: *with head bent, in a cramped position.* **4** one's way of looking at a subject, one's side in an argument or dispute: *to explain one's position about disarmament.* **5** one's place in society. **6** official employment, job.—*v.t.* to put, place.

in, out of, position in, not in, the correct place.

positive *poz'i-tiv*, *adj.* **1** definite: *a positive statement.* **2** that cannot be doubted: *positive proof.* **3** certain, convinced: *I am positive she did it.* **4** confident in one's opinion: *Don't be so positive; you don't really know.* **5** meaning or saying 'yes': *a positive answer.* **6** (*coll.*) downright, out-and-out: *The state of the garden was a positive disgrace.* **7** (of e.g. a test) showing that what was tested for is in fact present. **8** greater than zero: *+4 is a positive or plus value.* **9** having fewer electrons than normal (the **positive terminal** is the one to which electrons flow through a circuit). **10** (*grammar*) of the first degree of comparison of adjectives or adverbs: *positive 'tall', as opp. to comparative 'taller', superlative 'tallest'.*—*n.* **1** something that is positive. **2** (*photography*) a print from a negative, having the lights and shades as in the original.

positive discrimination **1** deliberately liberal provision of social and educational facilities, etc. in deprived areas. **2** steps taken to ensure that minority groups, etc. are not discriminated against, e.g. in employment.

positive pole of a magnet, the end (or pole) which turns to the north when the magnet swings freely.

posse *pos'ė*, *n.* a force or group (e.g. of police).

possess *poz-es'*, *v.t.* **1** to have, to own. **2** to have (a quality): *He possesses courage.* **3** to have control of the mind of (someone): *Fear, anger, possessed me.*

possessed' *adj.* **1** in the power of an evil spirit. **2** self-possessed, calm.

possession *pȯz-esh'(ȯ)n*, *n.* **1** the state of possessing or being possessed. **2** a thing owned. **3** a territory governed or controlled: *foreign possessions.*

possess'ive *adj.* **1** showing possession (esp. in grammar, as: *John's* book, *badgers'* habits, *my*, *mine*, *his*, *her*, etc.). **2** showing origin, measure, etc. (as the *sun's* light, two *days'* rest). **3** tending to treat person(s) or thing(s) as a possession, esp. to try to control person(s) emotionally: *They were children of a possessive mother.*—*n.* **1** a possessive word. **2** the state of being possessive (*defs. 1,2*).

possess'iveness *n.*

possible *pos'i-bl*, *adj.* **1** not unlikely. **2** able to happen or to be done, etc. **3** able, as far as one knows, to be true or correct: *a pos-*

sible explanation:—*opp.* **impossible**.
possibil'ity *n.* **1** the state of being possible. **2** something that may happen or be done:—*pl.* **possibil'ities**.
poss'ibly *adv.*

post[1] *pōst*, *n.* a stake or pole of wood or other material, usu. fixed upright.—*v.t.* **1** to fix (e.g. a notice) on a post, board, etc. **2** to give information to the public by naming in a list, etc.: *to post a soldier*, *a ship*, *as missing*.
post'er *n.* a large bill or placard.

post[2] *pōst*, *n.* **1** a fixed place or position, esp. one where a soldier is stationed. **2** any place of duty. **3** an office, job, or appointment. **4** a store, settlement, or camp in thinly inhabited country: *a trading post*, *military post*. **5** a system of carrying mail.—*v.t.* **1** to station. **2** to give over (a letter, etc.) to the post office for carrying. **3** (*bookkeeping*) to transfer (an entry) to the ledger. **4** (*coll.*; often **keep posted**) to supply with necessary information.—*v.i.* to travel with speed.
post'age *n.* money paid for sending a letter by public post.
post'al *adj.* having to do with the mail service.
postage stamp a small printed label or design to show that postage has been paid.
postal order an order bought at a post office to serve as a cheque for the amount printed on it.
postcard (or **post card**) *n.* a card on which a message may be sent by post.
postcode, postal code a series of letters and numbers denoting a small district, used for sorting mail by machine.
post'-free *adj.*, *adv.* **1** without charge for postage. **2** postage prepaid.
post haste, post'-haste' *adv.* with great speed.
post'man *n.* one who collects or delivers mail.
post'mark *n.* a mark put on a letter at the post office cancelling the stamp and showing the date of sending.
post'master *n.* the manager of a post office:—*fem.* **post'mistress**.
post'(-)office **1** an office for receiving and sending off letters by post, etc. **2** (*cap.*) the public corporation concerned with sending mail, etc.
last post a bugle call played at a military funeral.

post- *pōst-*, (as part of a word) after, behind.
post'date' *v.t.* **1** to date after the real time. **2** to mark with a date later than the time of signing:—*pr.p.* **post'dat'ing**.
post'-grad'uate *adj.* (of studies) continued after graduation.—*n.* a student carrying on such studies.

postage, etc. See **post**[2].

postdate. See **post**.

poster. See **post**[1].

poste restante *pōst res-tong̃t'*, *n.* (used in addressing letters) the department of a post office where letters are kept till called for.

posterior *pos-tē'ri-ȯr*, *adj.* **1** coming after. **2** situated behind.—*n.* the hinder part of the body, buttocks.
posterity *(-ter'i-ti)*, *n.* descendants, following generations.

posthumous *post'ū-mŭs*, *adj.* **1** born after the father's death. **2** published after the author's or composer's death.
post'humously *adv.*

postilion *pȯs-til'yȯn*, *n.* one who guides the horses of a carriage and rides one of them.—Also **postill'ion**.

postman, etc. See **post**[2].

post-mortem *pōst-mör'tėm*, *adj.* after death.—*n.* (often without *hyphen*) an examination of a dead body to find out the cause of death.

post-natal *pōst'-nā'tȧl*, *adj.* after the birth of a baby.

postpone *pōs(t)-pōn'*, *v.t.* to put off to a future time, to delay:—*pr.p.* **postpon'ing**.
postpone'ment *n.*

postscript *pōs(t)'skript*, *n.* a part added to a letter or a book after it is signed or finished.

postulate *pos'tū-lāt*, *v.t.* **1** to assume or take for granted. **2** to assume as true (that):—*pr.p.* **pos'tulating**.—*n.* *(-lȧt)* something postulated.

posture *pos'chŭr*, *-tūr*, *n.* **1** the position and carriage of the body as a whole. **2** pose.—*v.i.* to assume postures for effect:—*pr.p.* **pos'turing**.

posy *pō'zi*, *n.* **1** a bunch of flowers. **2** a motto, as on a ring:—*pl.* **pos'ies**.

pot *pot*, *n.* **1** a deep bowl or jar, esp. one used for cooking. **2** a drinking vessel. **3** a vessel for plants. **4** a receptacle for urine, etc., a potty. **5** (*coll.*; usu. in *pl.*) a large sum (of money). **6** (*coll.*) an important person (usu. *big pot*). **7** (*coll.*) marijuana. **8** (*coll.*) a fat belly.—*v.t.* **1** to plant in a pot. **2** to put in a pot in order to preserve. **3** to kill by a pot-shot. **4** to pocket (as a billiard ball). **5** to make a short version of (e.g. a book).—*v.i.* to shoot (usu. *pot at*):—*pr.p.* **pott'ing**; *pa.p.* **pott'ed**.
pot'belly *n.* a large round belly:—*pl.* **pot'bellies**.
pot'bellied *adj.*
pot'boiler *n.* a work of art or writing

produced only for the money it brings in.

pot'hole *n.* **1** an, esp. underground, hole made in rock by swirling water. **2** a round hole in a road surface.

pot'holing *n.* exploring potholes in limestone rock.

pot'house *n.* an alehouse.

pot'-luck' *n.* what may happen to be in the pot for a meal without special preparation for guests.

pot'-shot *n.* **1** a shot for the sake of food rather than sport. **2** a shot within easy range. **3** a random shot.

go to pot (*coll.*) to be ruined, wasted.

potash *pot'ash, n.* **1** potassium carbonate, a substance orig. got from the ashes of wood, used in making glass, soap, etc. **2** other potassium salts used as fertilisers.

potass'ium *n.* an element, a silvery white metal.

potation *pō-tā'sh(ȯ)n, n.* **1** drinking. **2** a drink.

potato *pȯ-tā'tō, n.* a plant, orig. South American, whose tubers are used as food:—*pl.* **pota'toes**.

potbelly, etc. See **pot**.

potent *pō'tėnt, adj.* powerful, strong (used of people, drugs, motives, reasons, influence, etc.):—*opp.* **im'potent**.

po'tency *n.* **1** power. **2** strength:—*pl.* **pot'encies**.

po'tentate *n.* one with power, a prince.

potential *(-ten'shl) adj.* possible, in the making: *a potential danger.*—*n.* **1** the power to produce, develop, act. **2** possible resources.

potential'ity *n.* **1** possibility. **2** something that may develop:—*pl.* **potential'ities**.

poten'tially *adv.*

pothole, etc. See **pot**.

potion *pō'sh(ȯ)n, n.* **1** a drink. **2** a dose of medicine or poison.

pot-luck. See **pot**.

pot-pourri *pō-pōō'rē, n.* **1** a mixed dish. **2** a mixture of dried petals, of tunes, etc.

potsherd *pot'shûrd, (archaeology, etc.) n.* a piece of broken pottery.

pot-shot. See **pot**.

pottage *pot'ij, n.* a thick soup of meat and vegetables.

potter¹ *pot'ėr, n.* one who makes articles of baked clay.

pott'ery *n.* **1** vessels of baked clay. **2** a place where these are made:—*pl.* **pott'eries**.

potter² *pot'ėr, v.i.* **1** to busy oneself with small jobs. **2** to dawdle.

potty¹ *pot'i, (coll.) adj.* silly, foolish, crazy:—*comp.* **pott'ier**; *superl.* **pott'iest**.

potty² *pot'i, (coll.)* n. a specially-designed pot intended for use by children too young to use a normal toilet:—*pl.* **pott'ies**.

pouch *powch, n.* **1** a pocket or bag. **2** anything like a pocket, as a kangaroo's sac for carrying its young.—*v.t.* to pocket.—*v.i.* to form a pouch.

pouf, **pouffe** *pōōf, n.* a large hassock or cushioned seat.

poulterer *pōl'tėr-ėr, n.* one who sells poultry and game for food.

poult'ry *n.* domestic or farmyard fowls as a whole.

poultice *pōl'tis, n.* a soft, usu. hot, mixture spread on a cloth and put on sores, etc.—*v.t.* to put a poultice on:—*pr.p.* **poulticfiing**.

pounce *powns, n.* **1** the claw of a bird (e.g. hawk). **2** a sudden spring or swoop.—*v.i.* **1** to sweep down suddenly, attack. **2** to spring, dash. **3** to seize (upon, e.g. an idea, statement):—*pr.p.* **pounc'ing**.

pound¹ *pownd, n.* **1** a unit of weight=16 ounces or approx. 0.454 kilograms (abbrev. *lb.*). **2** a unit of money, orig. the value of a pound weight of silver, since 1971, 100 new pence (the *pound sterling*, written £ for L. *libra*), orig. 20 shillings. **3** a note or coin of this value.

pound'age *n.* a charge or tax, of so much per pound, on a money transaction.

pound'er (as part of a word) one who has, or thing that weighs, a certain number of pounds: *a 12-pounder*.

pound² *pownd, n.* a pen in which stray animals are put.—*v.t.* to put in a pound.

pound³ *pownd, v.t.* **1** to beat into small pieces. **2** to beat or bruise.—*v.i.* to walk, run, with heavy steps.

pour *pōr, pör, v.t.* **1** to make flow in a stream. **2** to send forth like a stream: *He poured forth his troubles.* **3** (*Scot.*) to drain water from (cooked vegetables).—*v.i.* **1** to stream. **2** to rain heavily.

pout *powt, v.i.* **1** to push out the lips crossly in displeasure. **2** (of lips) to stick out.—*n.* a pushing out of the lips.

poverty *pov'ėr-ti, n.* **1** poorness, the state of lacking money, etc., or good qualities. **2** lack, scarcity (of e.g. ideas).

pov'erty-stricken *adj.* suffering from poverty.

See also **poor**.

powder *pow'dėr, n.* **1** dust. **2** any substance in fine particles. **3** gunpowder. **4** cosmetic powder for the face.—*v.t.* **1** to make into powder. **2** to sprinkle or cover with powder. **3** to salt by sprinkling.—*v.i.* **1** to crumble into powder. **2** to use powder on the face, etc.

pow'dered *adj.* **1** in the form of fine dust. **2** sprinkled with powder. **3** salted.

pow'dery *adj.* **1** like powder. **2** covered with powder.

powder magazine a place where gunpowder is stored.

powder puff a soft pad for dusting powder on the skin.

power *pow'ėr*, *n.* **1** strength, might. **2** force. **3** ability to do anything—physical or mental. **4** authority. **5** someone who has authority or strong influence. **6** a nation with much influence in international affairs: *the big powers.* **7** legal right. **8** legal permission to act. **9** (*coll.*) a great deal or great many. **10** the product obtained by multiplying a number by itself a given number of times: 2×2×2, or 2^3, is the third power of 2. **11** (*physics*) the rate of doing work.—*adj.* **1** concerned with power. **2** worked by steam or oil, or electricity, etc.—*v.t.* to cause to move or work (by fuel, engine, etc.).

pow'erful *adj.* **pow'erfully** *adv.*

pow'erfulness *n.*

pow'erless *adj.* without power or ability.

pow'er-cut *n.* a stopping, or sometimes a lessening, of the electricity supply to an area.

pow'er-driven *adj.* worked by electricity, etc., not by hand.

pow'er-house, -station *n.* a place where electricity is generated or produced.

pow'er-point *n.* a socket into which an electric plug may be inserted.

power politics international politics where the actions of nations are based on the amount of armed strength they can use to back their opinions.

in one's power **1** at one's mercy. **2** within the limits of what one can do.

in power (esp. of political party) in office, having control.

the powers that be the ruling authorities at the moment.

See also **potent.**

powwow *pow'wow*, *n.* **1** a meeting for discussion held by, or with, Native Americans. **2** any conference.

pox *poks*, *n.* a disease with eruptions or pimples on the skin: *smallpox*, *chickenpox.*

practicable, etc. See **practice.**

practice *prak'tis*, *n.* **1** actual doing: *In practice, the longer method is better.* **2** habit, usual action. **3** repeated performance to gain skill: *practice for a race*; *practice on the piano.* **4** a professional man's business: *a doctor's practice.*

prac'ticable *adj.* capable of being used or done:—*opp.* **imprac'ticable.**

prac'ticableness, practicabil'ity *ns.*

prac'tical *adj.* **1** having to do with practice or action. **2** efficient when put to use. **3** taught by practice: *a practical knowledge of carpentry.* **4** inclined by nature to act and to act capably:—*opp.* **imprac'tical** (*defs. 2,4*).

prac'tically *adv.* **1** in a practical way. **2** in effect or reality: *He said nothing but practically his silence was an admission of guilt.* **3** (*coll.*) almost.

practise *prak'tis*, *v.t.* **1** to put, make a habit of putting, into practice or action. **2** to do exercises in, train in, so as to get and keep a skill: *to practise judo.* **3** to follow (a profession): *to practise law.*—Also *v.i.*:—*pr.p.* **prac'tising.**

prac'tising *adj.* holding the beliefs and regularly performing the required practices of a particular religion: *a practising Christian.*

practitioner (*-tish'ȯn-ėr*) *n.* one who is in practice, or who practises.

practical joke a joke consisting of action, not words, usu. an annoying trick.

general practitioner. See **general.**

out of practice having lost one's former skill through lack of practice: *I used to be able to skip quite well, but now I'm out of practice.*

pragmatic *prag-mat'ik*, *adj.* **1** practical. **2** matter-of-fact. **3** more interested in facts and feasible actions than in theories.

pragmat'ical *adj.* **1** pragmatic. **2** too busy interfering in the affairs of others, meddlesome.

prag'matist *n.*

prairie *prā'ri*, *n.* a treeless plain, covered naturally with grass.

prairie dog a burrowing, gnawing, barking, North American animal.

praise *prāz*, *v.t.* **1** to speak highly of (a person or thing). **2** to extol (God) with gratitude and reverence:—*pr.p.* **prais'-ing.**—*n.* **1** an expression of approval or honour. **2** the singing part of church service.

praise'worthy *adj.* worthy of praise.

praline *prä'lēn*, *n.* a sweet with a nutty centre and a brown coating of sugar or a similar sweet with crushed nuts, etc.

pram *pram*, *n.* a kind of small carriage on wheels for carrying a baby.

prance *präns*, *v.i.* **1** (of a horse) to spring from the hind legs. **2** to go with a dancing movement. **3** to swagger, strut:—*pr.p.* **pranc'ing.**

prank *prangk*, *n.* a mischievous trick.

prate *prāt*, *v.i.* **1** to talk foolishly. **2** to talk too much.—Also *v.t.*:—*pr.p.* **prat'ing.**

prat'ing *n.* and *adj.*
prattle *prat'l*, *v.i.* to talk much and idly, or as a child does:—*pr.p.* **pratt'ling.**—*n.* empty talk.

prawn *prön*, *n.* a small shellfish like the shrimp.—*v.i.* to fish for prawns.

pray *prā*, *v.i.* **1** to ask earnestly: *to pray to someone, for something.* **2** to speak and tell one's desires to God.—*v.t.* to beg earnestly or reverently:—*pr.p.* **pray'ing**; *pa.p.* **prayed**.
pray'er *n.* **1** the act of praying. **2** a request. **3** a solemn request and giving of thanks to God. **4** (in *pl.*) divine service, worship.
prayer book a book containing prayers or forms of devotion.

pre- *prē-*, *pfx.* **1** before: *predecease*, *prearrangement.* **2** happening before: *prewar.*

preach *prēch*, *v.t.* **1** to give (a sermon). **2** to teach, talk in favour of: *to preach patience.*—*v.i.* **1** to give a public speech on sacred subjects. **2** to give advice in an offensive or tedious manner.
preach'er *n.*

preamble *prē-am'bl*, *n.* a preface, introduction (e.g. to an Act of Parliament).

prearrange *prē-ȧ-ranj'*, *v.t.* to arrange beforehand:—*pr.p.* **prearrang'ing.**
prearrange'ment *n.*

precarious *pri-kā'ri-ŭs*, *adj.* **1** depending on chance, or on the will of another. **2** uncertain, risky. **3** insecure: *precarious situation.*
preca'riously *adv.* **preca'riousness** *n.*

precast *prē'käst*, *adj.* of concrete blocks, cast before being put in position.

precaution *pri-kö'sh(ȯ)n*, *n.* care, or an action taken beforehand, to prevent or avoid disease, accident, etc.
precau'tionary *adj.* **1** using precaution: *to take precautionary measures.* **2** (of speech, words) advising precaution.

precede *prē-sēd'*, *v.t.* to go before in time, rank, or importance.—Also *v.i.*:—*pr.p.* **preced'ing.**
precedent *pres'i-dėnt*, *prēs'*, *n.* a past happening which may serve as an example to be followed in the future.
prec'edented *adj.* **1** having been done before. **2** justified by an example.
precē'ding *adj.* **1** going before. **2** previous.
take precedence to precede in importance.

precentor *pri-*, *prē-sen'tȯr*, *n.* the person in charge of, or leader of, the singing in a church.

precept *prē'sept*, *n.* **1** a rule to guide one's action. **2** a commandment.
precep'tor *n.* a teacher.

precinct *prē'singkt*, *n.* **1** (in *pl.*) the parts immediately round any place. **2** a space, esp. an enclosure, round a building (e.g. a church). **3** a district, or subdivision of one: *a police precinct.*
pedestrian precinct a traffic-free area of town, esp. a shopping centre.
shopping precinct a shopping centre, esp. if traffic-free.

precious *presh'ŭs*, *adj.* **1** of great price or worth. **2** highly valued by (with *to*).—*adv.* (*coll.*) very, extremely: *precious little.*

precipice *pres'i-pis*, *n.* a steep cliff.
precip'itance, **precip'itancy** *ns.* headlong haste, rashness.
precip'itāte *v.t.* **1** to throw headlong. **2** to force (into hasty action). **3** to bring on suddenly: *to precipitate a quarrel.* **4** (*chemistry*) to bring (a substance) into solid form out of a state of solution.—*v.i.* **1** (of vapour) to turn into, fall as, rain, hail, etc. **2** (*chemistry*) of a substance, to come into solid form from a solution:—*pr.p.* **precip'itating.**—*adj.* (*-tit*) **1** headlong. **2** hasty.—*n.* a substance separated from solution.
precip'itately *adv.*
precipitā'tion *n.* **1** the act of precipitating. **2** great hurry. **3** rash haste. **4** rain, etc., or the amount of it.
precip'itous *adj.* like a precipice, steep.

précis *prā'sē*, *n.* a summary of a writing:—*pl.* **précis** *(-sēz)*.

precise *pri-sīs'*, *adj.* **1** very definite: *precise instructions.* **2** exact: *his precise words.* **3** very accurate. **4** particular, prim in manner.
precise'ly *adv.* **precise'ness** *n.*
preci'sion *(-sizh'(ȯ)n)* *n.* **1** preciseness. **2** exactness.—*adj.* (used only before a noun) used to produce very accurate results: *precision instruments.*

preclude *pri-klōōd'*, *v.t.* **1** to prevent (a person from). **2** to make impossible by some action: *to preclude mistakes, doubt*:—*pr.p.* **preclud'ing.**
preclusion *pri-klōō'zh(ȯ)n*, *n.*

precocious *pri-kō'shŭs*, *adj.* early in reaching a stage of development, esp. mental maturity.
preco'ciousness, **precoc'ity** *(-kos')*, *ns.*

preconceive *prē-kȯn-sēv'*, *v.t.* to form (a notion or idea about something) before having actual knowledge:—*pr.p.* **preconceiv'ing.**

preconcep'tion *n.* an opinion formed without actual knowledge.

precondition *prē-kȯn-di'sh(ȯ)n, n.* a condition that must be satisfied beforehand.

precursor *prē-kûr'sȯr, n.* **1** a forerunner. **2** a predecessor. **3** a person or thing that is a sign of a coming event: *A too dry summer is a precursor of a poor harvest.*

predate *prē-dāt', v.t.* **1** to date before the true date. **2** to be earlier than:—*pr.p.* **predat'ing**.

predator *pred'ȧ-tȯr, n.* **1** a bird or animal (e.g. hawk) living on prey. **2** a creature that plunders (e.g. crops).
pred'atory *adj.* **1** plundering. **2** living by plunder or on prey: *a predatory bird.*

predecease *prē-di-sēs, v.t.* to die before:—*pr.p.* **predeceas'ing.**—Also *n.*

predecessor *prē-di-ses'ȯr, n.* **1** one who has held an office or position before another: *Jones was my predecessor as chairman.* **2** an ancestor.

predestine *prē-, pri-des'tin, v.t.* **1** (of fate, God) to decide, decree beforehand: *Fate predestined this loss: His success was predestined.* **2** to appoint, choose: *Fate predestined him to suffer:*—*pr.p.* **predes'tining**.
predestinā'tion (*theology*) *n.* God's decree fixing what is to happen for all eternity, esp. whether individuals are to be saved or damned.

predetermine *prē-di-tûr'min, v.t.* to determine or settle beforehand:—*pr.p.* **predeter'mining**.

predicament *pri-dik'ȧ-mėnt, n.* an unfortunate or difficult position.

predicate *pred'i-kit, (grammar) n.* what is stated about the subject of a sentence (e.g. Jack *is a foolish boy*; The chains *clanked*; The bullet *hit the roof*).

predict *pri-dikt', v.t.* to foretell (esp. after a study of the facts).
predic'table *adj.*
predic'tion *n.* **1** the act of predicting. **2** something that is foretold.
predic'tor *n.* **1** one who predicts. **2** a device used in anti-aircraft defence which tells the gun crew the exact position of an aircraft.

predilection *prē-di-lek'sh(ȯ)n, n.* a preference or special liking (for).

predispose *prē-dis-pōz', v.t.* **1** to incline (a person) beforehand: *The stranger's friendly manner predisposed us to trust him.* **2** to make liable: *Too little to eat predisposed him to infection:*—*pr.p.* **predispos'ing.**
predisposi'tion *n.*

predominate *pri-dom'in-āt, v.i.* **1** to be the stronger, or have the greater authority. **2** to have control (over). **3** to exist in the greater or greatest quantity:—*pr.p.* **predom'inating.**
predom'inant *adj.* **1** ruling. **2** superior in position. **3** more, most, noticeable.
predom'inance *n.* **predom'inantly** *adv.*

pre-eminent *prē-em'in-ėnt, adj.* **1** standing above all others in good, or bad, qualities. **2** outstanding. **3** more important or influential than others.
pre-em'inence *n.* **pre-em'inently** *adv.*

pre-emption *prē-em(p)'sh(ȯ)n. n.* the act or right of buying in preference to others.
pre-empt' *v.t.* to forestall.
pre-empt'ive *adj.* **1** of pre-emption. **2** intended to forestall: *a pre-emptive attack.*

preen *prēn, v.t.* **1** to arrange (feathers), as birds do. **2** to pride (oneself).

pre-establish *prē-is-tab'lish, v.t.* to establish, decide, prove, beforehand.

pre-exist *prē-ig-zist', v.i.* to exist beforehand or previously.
pre-exist'ence *n.*

prefab *prē'fab, n.* a *prefab*ricated house.

prefabricated *prē-fab'ri-kā-tid, adj.* made of parts manufactured beforehand and ready to be fitted together.

preface *pref'is, n.* **1** something said, written, or done, by way of introduction in the beginning. **2** a foreword.—*v.t.* to introduce by a preface: *He prefaced his remarks with an appeal for silence:*—*pr.p.* **pre'facing.**

prefect *prē'fekt, n.* **1** one set in authority over others. **2** in a school, a senior pupil with certain powers. **3** the governor of a department in France, of a province in Italy, etc.

prefer *pri-fûr', v.t.* to regard with greater favour, like better (sometimes with *to*): *I prefer this one (to that one); I prefer to walk; I prefer walking to cycling:*—*pr.p.* **preferr'ing**; *pa.p.* **preferred'**.
pref'erable *(pref'-) adj.* to be preferred, more desirable.
pref'erably *adv.*
pref'erence *n.* **1** the act of choosing. **2** greater liking. **3** a thing that is preferred.
preferential *pref-ėr-en'shl, adj.* showing, having the benefits arising from, a preference: *preferential treatment.*
prefer'ment *n.* promotion.
preference shares, or **stock**, shares on which the dividends must be paid before those on ordinary shares are paid.

prefix *prē-fiks', v.t.* to put before or at the beginning.—*n.* *(prē')* a syllable or word put before another word to alter its meaning in some way (e.g. *dis*like, *un*tie, *re*write, *super*natural, *semi*circle).

pregnant *preg'nȧnt, adj.* **1** having a child or young in the womb. **2** full of meaning.
preg'nancy *n.* (*pl.* **-cies**).

prehensile *pri-hen'sīl, adj.* able to grasp or hold on to something.

prehistoric, al *prē-his-tor'ik, -ȧl, adjs.* belonging to a time before written history.

prejudge *prē-juj', v.t.* to judge before hearing the whole case, condemn before knowing the facts:—*pr.p.* **prejudg'ing.**

prejudice *prej'oo-dis, n.* **1** an opinion formed without careful thought. **2** an unreasonable or unfair feeling (in favour of, or against, something). **3** injury, harm: *to the prejudice of his own interests.*—*v.t.* **1** to bias the mind of. **2** to damage, spoil: *This rash act prejudiced his chances of success*:—*pr.p.* **prej'udicing.**
prej'udiced *adj.* having, or showing, prejudice.
prejudicial *prej-oo-dish'l, adj.* damaging, disadvantageous (to).

prelate *prel'it, n.* a churchman of high rank, as a bishop or archbishop.
prel'acy *n.* the office of a prelate.

preliminary *pri-lim'in-ȧr-i, adj.* introductory, preparing the way.—*n.* something that goes before or prepares the way:—*pl.* **prelim'inaries.**

prelude *prel'ūd, n.* **1** an introductory event, often leading up to another of greater importance. **2** (*music*) an introductory passage or movement. **3** a short piece e.g. for piano.

pre-marital *prē-mar'i-tȧl, adj.* before marriage.

premature *prem'ȧ-tūr, -tūr',* or *prēm', adj.* coming, born, etc., before the right time.
prematurely *adv.* **prematureness** *n.*

premeditate *prē-med'i-tāt, v.t.* **1** to think out beforehand. **2** to plan, intend: *a premeditated murder*:—*pr.p.* **premed'itating.**
premeditā'tion *n.*

premier *prem'i-ėr, -yėr, adj.* first, chief, leading.—*n.* the prime minister.
première *prem'yėr, n.* the first performance, e.g. of a play.

premise *prem'is, n.* **1** something assumed from which a conclusion is drawn (also **prem'iss**). **2** (in a legal document, in *pl.*) the house, etc., mentioned above. **3** (in *pl.*) a building and its grounds.

premium *prē'mi-ŭm, n.* **1** a reward, prize. **2** money paid, usu. yearly, for insurance. **3** the fee paid for training in a trade or profession. **4** a sum above the original price or par, e.g. of stock.
Premium (Savings) Bond a bond issued by the Government, the holder of which receives no interest but may win a cash prize.
at a premium 1 above par. **2** in demand.

premolar *prē-mō'lȧr, n.* a tooth between the canine and the molars, a bicuspid.

premonition *prē-mȯn-ish'(ȯ)n, n.* **1** a forewarning. **2** a feeling (that something is going to happen).
premon'itory *adj.* giving warning.

pre-natal *prē-nā'tl, adj.* before birth.

preoccupy *prē-ok'ū-pī, v.t.* to fill the mind of, take up the attention of:—*pr.p.* **preocc'upying;** *pa.p.* **preocc'upied.**
preoccupā'tion *n.*
preocc'upied *adj.* lost in thought.

prep, prep school. See under **prepare.**

prepacked *prē'pakt', adj.* packed before being offered for sale.

prepaid. See **prepay.**

prepare *pri-pār', v.t.* **1** to make ready. **2** to train, equip (for). **3** to make (someone) ready, fit, to bear a shock.—Also *v.i.*:—*pr.p.* **prepar'ing.**
preparation *prep-ȧ-rā'sh(ȯ)n, n.* **1** the act of preparing. **2** study or work for a lesson in class (often shortened to **prep**). **3** the state of being prepared. **4** something mixed and prepared for use (e.g. face cream).
prepar'ative *(-par') adj.*
prepar'atory *adj.*
prepared' *adj.* **1** ready. **2** willing.
preparatory school (often shortened to **prep school**) one which prepares pupils for a public school (*def. 2*).
preparatory to before (doing something).

prepay *prē'pā', v.t.* to pay in advance:—*pa.t.* and *pa.p.* **pre'paid'.**

preponderate *pri-pon'dėr-āt, v.i.* to be greater in weight, number, power:—*pr.p.* **prepon'derating.**
prepon'derance *n.* **prepon'derant** *adj.*

preposition *prep-ȯ-zish'(ȯ)n, n.* a word placed before a noun or pronoun to show its relation to another word (e.g. a sum *of* money; lost *by* Mary; dropped *under* the table; a prize *for* you).
preposi'tional *adj.*

prepossess *prē-pŏz-es', v.t.* **1** to fill the mind beforehand with a feeling or opinion. **2** to prejudice, esp. favourably: *I was prepossessed by, with, her.*
prepossess'ing *adj.* attractive.

preposterous *pri-pos'tėr-ŭs, adj.* against reason or common sense, utterly absurd.

prerequisite *prē-rek'wi-zit, n.* something that must be done, a condition that must be fulfilled, before something else can happen.—Also *adj.*

prerogative *pri-rog'ȧ-tiv, n.* a special right or privilege belonging to a person because of his rank, etc.

presage *pres'ij, n.* **1** a sign of the future, omen. **2** a feeling of what is going to happen.—*v.t.* (also *pri-sāj'*) to foretell, portend:—*pr.p.* **presaging**.

presbyter *prez'bi-tėr, n.* **1** one who managed the affairs of an early Christian church. **2** a clergyman ranking below a bishop. **3** a church elder.

Presbytē'rian *adj.* having to do with a form of church government in which there is no higher office than the presbyter or elder (clergymen being considered as 'ruling and teaching elders').—*n.* a member of a church governed in this way.

Presbyte'rianism *n.*

pres'bytery *n.* **1** a group of ministers and elders forming the church court of a district. **2** (*R.C.*) a priest's house:—*pl.* **pres'byteries**.

preschool *prē'skōōl, adj.* **1** before school. **2** not yet at school.

prescribe *pri-skrīb', v.t.* **1** to lay down as a rule to be followed. **2** to order the use of (a medicine):—*pr.p.* **prescrib'ing**.

prescrip'tion *n.* **1** something prescribed. **2** a written direction for preparing a medicine.

prescrip'tive *adj.*

presence *prez'ėns, n.* **1** the fact or state of being present. **2** personal appearance and manner: *He has a good presence.*

present *prez'ėnt, adj.* **1** in the place thought, spoken, etc. of. **2** (used only before a noun) belonging to the time in which we are, not past or future: *the present premier.* **3** now being considered: *It has nothing to do with the present subject.* **4** (*grammar*) of a tense of a verb, showing time just now, or making a general statement (e.g. I *approve* of this; She *is coming* towards us; She *comes* on Mondays).—*n.* the time we are now at: *At present, there are only four of us.*

pres'ently *adv.* **1** soon. **2** now, at present.

presence of mind coolness and readiness in any emergency or surprise.

in the presence of while in the same place as and very near: *He said it in the presence of his family.*

present[1]. See **presence**.

present[2] *pri-zent', v.t.* **1** to introduce (a person) to another or others. **2** to introduce at court. **3** to show to the public. **4** to put on the stage. **5** to give, esp. formally: *He presented a rose to her; They presented her with a silver teapot.* **6** to put something before the mind of (a person): *John's refusal to help presented her with a problem about what to do next.* **7** to appoint to a church living. **8** to point (a gun) before firing.

present'able *adj.* fit to be given or seen.

presentation *prez-ėn-tā'sh(ȯ)n, n.* **1** the act of presenting. **2** a showing (e.g. of a play). **3** a setting forth (e.g. of ideas). **4** a formal giving of a gift to mark an occasion such as retirement from office. **5** the gift itself.

present arms to bring a rifle to the saluting position, held perpendicularly in front of the centre of the body.

present itself **1** to appear, arise, turn up. **2** to suggest itself (to one's mind).

present oneself **1** to introduce oneself. **2** to arrive, appear.

present[3] *prez'ėnt, n.* a gift, something given.

presentiment *pri-zent'i-mėnt, or -sent' n.* a vague feeling that something unpleasant is about to happen, foreboding.

presently. See **presence**.

preserve *pri-zûrv', v.t.* **1** to keep alive, or safe from harm. **2** to keep in existence. **3** to keep up, continue: *to preserve silence.* **4** to keep from decay. **5** to cook (fruit, etc.) with sugar:—*pr.p.* **preserv'ing**.—*n.* **1** something preserved, e.g. fruit. **2** a place of protection for e.g. game (**game preserve**). **3** a sphere into which others, regarded as outsiders, are not allowed to enter: *Is the diplomatic service a preserve of boys who have been to public schools?*

preservā'tion *n.* **1** the act of preserving. **2** the state of being preserved.

preserv'ative *n.* and *adj.* (something) that preserves.

preside *pri-zīd', v.i.* **1** to sit in the chair or chief seat (e.g. at a meeting). **2** to exercise authority or control (over):—*pr.p.* **presid'ing**.

pres'idency *prez'i-dėn-si, n.* **1** the office of a president. **2** his term of office:—*pl.* **pres'idencies**.

pres'ident *n.* **1** the head of a college, council, board, etc. **2** the head executive officer of a republic.

presidential *pre-zi-den'sh(ȧ)l, adj.* having to do with a president.

preside at the piano, organ to act as pianist, organist (orig. also as a conductor).

press[1] *pres, v.t.* **1** to push against. **2** to weigh down. **3** to squeeze. **4** to thrust. **5** to urge strongly (to do). **6** to offer urgently (with *on*). **7** to harass with difficulties or dangers: *He was now hard pressed.* **8** to insist on: *to press a point.* **9** to smooth out, iron (e.g. clothes).—*v.i.* **1** to push with force. **2** to crowd. **3** to make haste necessary: *Time presses.*—*n.* **1** an act of pressing. **2** a crowd. **3** stress. **4** a printing machine. **5** newspapers and magazines as a whole. **6** the journalistic profession.

press'ing *adj.* **1** requiring action at once. **2** earnest: *a pressing invitation.*

pressure *presh'ůr, n.* **1** the act of pressing. **2** the state of being pressed. **3** force on a surface. **4** strong persuasion. **5** difficulties, trouble. **6** urgency.

press'urise *(presh') v.t.* **1** to fit (an aeroplane cabin, etc.) with a device that keeps the air pressure in it nearly normal. **2** to force by pressure into doing something:—*pr.p.* **press'urising.**

press conference a meeting of a person in the news with the press to make an announcement or answer questions.

press release an official statement or report supplied to the press.

press'-up *n.* an exercise in which the prone body is kept rigid while being raised and lowered by straightening and bending the arms.

pressure cooker a special type of pot in which food is cooked quickly by steam under great pressure.

pressure group a group of people who put pressure on e.g. the government to gain a certain result.

in the press about to be published.

press on to continue, esp. energetically, often in spite of difficulties or opposition.

press[2] *pres, v.t.* **1** *(formerly)* to carry off (a person) and force him into service, usu. in the navy. **2** to take (into use, service) in an emergency for want of something, someone, more suitable.

press'-gang *n.* a group of men hired to seize others for the navy.—*v.t.* *(coll.)* to force (someone) into doing something.

prestige *pres-tēzh', n.* reputation or influence of a person due to rank, success, etc.—*adj.* (used only before a noun) showing or bringing prestige, superior in quality, etc.

prestig'ious *(-tij'ůs) adj.* having or bringing prestige.

presto *pres'tō, adv.* **1** quickly. **2** at once.

prestressed *prē'strest', adj.* (of concrete) with stretched wires or rods inserted to strengthen it.

presume *pri-zūm', v.t.* **1** to take for granted. **2** to take as true without proof.—*v.i.* **1** to venture without right (to). **2** to take too much liberty, act impertinently. **3** (with *on*) to take advantage of: *You presume on his good-nature:*—*pr.p.* **presum'ing.**

presum'ably *adv.* probably, it may be supposed.

presum'ing *adj.* acting without permission, unsuitably bold.—*conj.* (often with *that*) making the presumption that.

presumption *pri-zum(p)'sh(ȯ)n, n.* **1** something supposed. **2** a strong likelihood. **3** behaviour going beyond proper bounds, impertinence.

presumptuous *(-zump'tū-ůs) adj.* presuming.

presuppose *prē-sů-pōz', v.t.* **1** to take for granted. **2** to require as necessity: *True kindness presupposes sympathy:*—*pr.p.* **presuppos'ing.**

presupposi'tion *n.*

pretend *pri-tend', v.t.* **1** to make a false show of, of being: *to pretend friendship, to be friendly.* **2** to feign (that).—*v.i.* **1** to make believe. **2** to lay claim (to e.g. the crown). **3** to claim to have (a quality): *He pretended to genius.*

pretence' *n.* **1** the act of pretending. **2** make-believe. **3** a claim. **4** a false reason given.

preten'sion *n.* **1** a claim. **2** too great show. **3** self-importance.

preten'tious *(-shůs) adj.* **1** claiming more than is right. **2** showy. **3** self-important.

preten'tiousness *n.*

preternatural *prē-tėr-na'chůr-ȧl, adj.* beyond what is natural, abnormal.

preterna'turally *adv.*

pretext *prē'tekst, n.* **1** a reason given to hide the real motive. **2** an excuse.

pretty *prit'i, adj.* **1** pleasing or attractive to eye, ear, or mind, but not grand or beautiful. **2** *(coll.)* fairly large: *a pretty sum of money.* **3** fine (usu. said of something bad): *a pretty mess:*—*comp.* **prett'ier**; *superl.* **prett'iest.**—*adv.* **1** moderately. **2** very.

prett'ily *adv.* **prett'iness** *n.*

pretty much very nearly.

prevail *pri-vāl', v.i.* **1** to gain control or victory (with *over, against*). **2** to succeed. **3** to persuade (with *on*): *She prevailed on him to stay.* **4** to be usual, common. **5** to be in the largest number: *Chinese prevail in this area.*

prevail'ing *adj.* **1** controlling. **2** most common.

prev'alent *adj.* widespread, common.

prev'alence *n.*

prevaricate *pri-var'i-kāt, v.t.* to avoid telling the truth, to quibble:—*pr.p.* **prevar'icating**.
prevaricā'tion *n.* **prevar'icātor** *n.*

prevent *pri-vent', v.t.* **1** to hinder. **2** to keep from happening or occurring, make impossible.
preven'tion *n.* the act of preventing.
preven'tive *adj.* and *n.* (something) tending to hinder, keep away, or prevent (e.g. disease).—Also **preven'tative**.

preview *prē'vū, n.* a view of a performance, exhibition, excerpts from a film, etc., before it is open to the public.—*v.t.* **1** *(prē-vū')* to see at a preview. **2** *(prē'vū)* to give a preview of.

previous *pre'vi-ūs, adj.* **1** before in time. **2** former. **3** coming too soon, premature.
pre'viously *adv.* **pre'viousness** *n.*

prey *prā, n.* **1** an animal that is, or may be, killed and eaten by another. **2** a victim.—*v.i.* **1** to make raids (on, upon). **2** to seize and eat other animals. **3** to live (on a victim). **4** to waste or worry (with *on*): *Cares prey on his mind.*
bird, beast, of prey one that lives on other animals.

price *prīs, n.* **1** the amount, usu. in money, for which a thing is sold, cost. **2** what one gives up or suffers in order to gain something: *The price of freedom is often great.*—*v.t.* **1** to fix the price of. **2** (*coll.*) to ask the price of:—*pr.p.* **pric'ing**.
price'less *adj.* **1** of very great value. **2** (*coll.*) absurd, amusing.
prīc'ey, prīc'y (*coll.*) *adj.* somewhat expensive:—*comp.* **pric'ier**; *superl.* **pric'iest**.
a price on one's head a reward offered for one's capture or slaughter.
at a price at a rather high price.
at any price 1 no matter what the price. **2** (not) at all.
beyond, without, price priceless.
one's price the terms on which one will agree to do something, or the amount needed to bribe one.

prick *prik, n.* the act, or sensation, of piercing with a small sharp point, e.g. of a needle.—*v.t.* **1** to pierce slightly with a sharp point. **2** to pain sharply. **3** to stick up (the ears). **4** to mark with prick(s) or dot(s).
prickle *prik'l, n.* **1** a little prick. **2** a sharp point growing on a plant or animal.
prick'ly *adj.* **1** covered in prickles: *a prickly plant.* **2** tingling, as if touching prickles:—*comp.* **prick'lier**; *superl.* **prick'liest**.
prick'liness *n.*
kick against the pricks. See **kick**.
prick up one's ears to begin to listen with interest.
the prick(s) of conscience painful awareness that one has done wrong.

pride *prīd, n.* **1** the state of feeling proud. **2** too great an opinion of oneself. **3** proper self-respect. **4** a feeling of pleasure in having done something. **5** something of which one is proud: *His son was his pride and joy.*—*v.t.* (with *oneself*) to allow oneself to feel pride (with *on*): *He prides himself on his good French:*—*pr.p.* **prid'ing**.
proud *prowd, adj.* **1** thinking too highly of oneself. **2** haughty. **3** having proper self-respect. **4** being highly pleased. **5** giving reason for pride: *It was a proud moment for him.*
do someone proud to honour someone, give generous entertainment or treatment to someone.
give pride of place to to give the most important place to.

priest *prēst, n.* **1** one who performs sacrifices or sacred rites (*fem.* **priest'ess**). **2** a clergyman, minister.
priest'hood *n.* **1** the office of a priest. **2** those who are priests.

prig *prig, n.* a smug, self-righteous person.
prigg'ish *adj.*

prim *prim, adj.* (of a person, manner) exact and correct, prudishly proper, formal:—*comp.* **primm'er**; *superl.* **primm'est**.

prima ballerina *prē'mä bal-ē-rē'nä,* the leading lady in a ballet company.
prima donna *prē'mä don'ä,* **1** the leading lady in opera. **2** one, esp. a woman, who is temperamental and hard to please.

primacy, primary, etc. See **prime[1]**.

prime[1] *prīm, adj.* **1** first in order of time, rank, or importance. **2** chief. **3** of the highest quality: *prime meat.*—*n.* the time of full health and strength: *in the prime of life.*
primacy *prī'mȧ-si, n.* **1** the state of being first. **2** the office of an archbishop.
pri'mal *adj.* **1** first. **2** original. **3** most important.
primary *prī'mȧr-i, adj.* **1** first. **2** original. **3** chief. **4** of the first stage, elementary: *primary schools.*—*n.* **1** (*U.S.*) a preliminary election in which voters of each party nominate candidates. **2** a primary school:—*pl.* **prī'maries**.
primate *prī'mit, -māt, n.* **1** an archbishop. **2** *(-māt)* a member of the highest order of mammals—human beings, monkeys, lemurs.
primary colours 1 those from which all others can be made—red, blue, yellow. **2** also the seven colours of the rainbow.

prime minister the chief minister of a government.
prime number a number divisible only by itself and 1 (e.g. 3, 5, 7, 11, etc.).
See also **primer**, etc.

prime[2] *prīm, v.t.* **1** to supply (a firearm) with powder. **2** to prepare for painting by laying on a first coat of paint or oil. **3** to fill (a person) with liquor. **4** to bring into working order by putting in water, gas, or oil: *to prime a pump by putting in water to swell the sucker.* **5** to prepare with full information: *to prime someone with the facts*; *to prime oneself about something*:—*pr.p.* **prim'ing.**

primer *prī'mėr, prim'ėr, n.* **1** a first reading-book. **2** a simple introduction to any subject.

primeval *prī-mē'väl, adj.* belonging to the first ages of the world.

primitive *prim'i-tiv, adj.* **1** belonging to the beginning, or to earliest times. **2** old-fashioned, out-of-date. **3** crude, clumsy. **4** (of a people or their culture) having only fairly simple technical skills.
See also **prime**[1].

primordial *prī-mör'di-äl, adj.* existing from the beginning.

primrose *prim'rōz, n.* a pale yellow spring flower of woods and meadows.—*adj.* pale yellow.

prince *prins, n.* **1** a son of a king, etc. **2** a noble ruler. **3** one of the most important or greatest members of a group or class: *a merchant prince*; *a prince of poets*:—*fem.* **prin'cess** (also *prin-ses'*).
prince'ly *adj.* **1** suited to a prince. **2** splendid.
prince'liness *n.*
principal *prin'si-pl, adj.* **1** highest in rank, character, or importance. **2** chief. —*n.* **1** a chief person. **2** the head of a school, college, or university. **3** one who takes a leading part, esp. in a transaction. **4** money on which interest is paid.
principal'ity *n.* the territory of a prince:—*pl.* **principal'ities.**
prin'cipally *adv.* chiefly, for the most part.

principle *prin'si-pl, n.* **1** an important general truth or law. **2** (in *pl.*) rules to guide one's actions. **3** a sense of what is right in conduct. **4** the manner of working: *the principle of a jet engine*.
prin'cipled *adj.* having, showing, good principles.
in principle so far as the general idea is concerned, without taking details into account.
on principle for the sake of obeying a principle.

print *print, n.* **1** a mark made by pressure. **2** printed lettering. **3** an engraving. **4** a printed cotton cloth. **5** a photograph made from a negative. **6** a printed reproduction of a painting or drawing. **7** a fingerprint.—*v.t.* **1** to mark. **2** to stamp a pattern on. **3** to mark letters on paper with type. **4** to publish. **5** to produce as a finished photograph.—Also *v.i.*
print'er *n.* **1** one who prints books, newspapers, etc. **2** a machine that prints.
printed circuit a circuit formed by printing the design of the wiring on copper foil fixed to a flat base and etching away the unprinted foil.
print'ing-press *n.* a machine by which ink, etc. impressions are put on paper.
print'-out *n.* the printed information given out by a computer, etc.
in print having been printed and available from a publisher.
out of print sold out and unable to be obtained from the publisher.

prior *prī'ör, adj.* **1** earlier. **2** previous (to).—*n.* the head of a priory:—*fem.* **pri'-oress.**
prior'ity *n.* **1** the state of being first in time, position, or importance. **2** the right to be, go, first: *A fire engine has priority in traffic.* **3** a thing having, requiring, this:—*pl.* **prior'ities.**
pri'ory *n.* a convent of monks or nuns, next in rank below an abbey:—*pl.* **pri'-ories.**

prise. See **prize**[1].

prism *prizm, n.* **1** (*geometry*) a solid whose ends are two figures equal in all respects and parallel to each other, and whose sides are parallelograms. **2** a prism-shaped piece of glass, etc., used to divide light into separate colours, or for other purposes in optical instruments.

prison *priz'n, n.* **1** a building for the holding of criminals, etc., a jail. **2** any place of confinement.
pris'oner *n.* **1** one under arrest or locked up in a prison. **2** a captive.
prisoner of conscience a person imprisoned because of his or her political beliefs.
prisoner of war a soldier, etc. captured during a war.

pristine *pris'tīn, -tēn, adj.* (used mainly before a noun) in its original unspoilt condition.

privacy *prīv'ä-si, priv', n.* **1** the state of being away from company. **2** secrecy.
private *prī'vit, adj.* **1** having to do with a person or a group, not with the general

public. **2** personal: *my private views.* **3** hidden from view. **4** secret, not made generally known. **5** (of a soldier) not an officer or non-commissioned officer. **6** (of a member of parliament) not in the cabinet. **7** (of a person) not in public office. **8** not run by the state.—*n.* a common soldier.

private detective a person paid to carry out investigations.

private enterprise the financing and management of business by individuals or companies, not the state.

in private privately, in secret.

See also **privilege**, **privy**.

privateer *prī-vȧ-tēr'*, *n.* (the captain, or a member of the crew, of) a privately-owned ship commissioned by a government to attack and plunder enemy ships.

privation *prī-vā'sh(ȯ)n*, *n.* **1** the state of being in want, poverty, hardship. **2** the act of taking away.

privet *priv'it*, *n.* a shrub used for hedges.

privilege *priv'i-lij*, *n.* an advantage or favour granted to, or enjoyed by, only one person or a few.—*v.t.* to grant a privilege to:—*pr.p.* **priv'ileging**.

privy *priv'i*, *adj.* **1** private. **2** belonging to a person, esp. to the king or queen.—*n.* (*old-fashioned*) a room or small building used as a toilet:—*pl.* **priv'ies**.

privy council a body of persons appointed as advisers to the monarch in affairs of state, their duties now being mainly formal.

privy councillor, **counsellor** (also with *caps.)*

privy to knowing about (e.g. a secret plan).

prize[1], **prise** *prīz*, *v.t.* to force (esp. *up* or *open)* with a lever or tool:—*pr.p.* **prizfing**, **pris'ing**.

prize[2] *prīz*, *n.* anything taken from an enemy in war, esp. a ship.

prize[3] *prīz*, *n.* **1** a reward, or a symbol of success, won in competition or by chance. **2** anything well worth working for. **3** a valued possession.—*adj.* very fine, that has won a prize: *a prize pig.*—*v.t.* to value highly: *He prized my friendship*:—*pr.p.* **priz'ing**.

prize'(-)fight *n.* a public boxing-match for money.

prize'-fighter *n.* **prize'-fighting** *n.*

pro[1] *prō*, *n.* short for **professional**:—*pl.* **pros**.

pro[2]. See under **pro-**.

pro- *prō-*, *pfx.* **1** (as part of a word) before (e.g. *prologue*). **2** (before a word) in place of (e.g. **pro-cathe'dral**, a church used for a time as a cathedral). **3** (before a noun) in favour of (e.g. **pro-Chinese'** favouring the Chinese).

pro and con for and against (L. *prō et contrā)*.

pros and cons arguments for and against an opinion, plan, etc.

probable *prob'ȧ-bl*, *adj.* **1** that may be expected to happen. **2** that is likely to be true:—*opp.* **improbable**.

probabil'ity *n.* **1** likeliness. **2** appearance of truth. **3** a probable event, etc.:—*pl.* **probabil'ities**.

prob'ably *adv*.

probate *prō'bāt*, *-bit*, *n.* the official copy of a will, or the proof before a court that it is a lawful one.

probation *prō-bā'sh(ȯ)n*, *n.* **1** testing. **2** a time of testing. **3** the suspending of a sentence (depending on good behaviour) requiring the offender who is allowed free to report to a **probation officer** at certain times.

probā'tionary *adj.* on probation.

probā'tioner *n.* **1** one who is undergoing a time of testing before e.g. becoming a full member of a profession. **2** an offender on probation.

probe *prōb*, *n.* **1** a long thin instrument used to explore a wound, etc. **2** an investigation **3** a spacecraft for exploring space:—*v.t.* **1** to examine with a probe. **2** to examine searchingly:—*pr.p.* **prob'ing**.

probity *prōb'i-ti*, *prob'*, *n.* honesty, uprightness.

problem *prob'lėm*, *n.* **1** a matter in which it is difficult to decide the best course of action. **2** a person difficult to deal with. **3** a question to be solved.

problemat'ic(al) *adjs.* doubtful, uncertain: *His future is problematical*.

proboscis *prō-bos'is*, *n.* the snout or trunk of some animals, as the elephant.

proceed *prō-sēd'*, *v.i.* **1** to go on. **2** to go on (to do something). **3** to continue (with). **4** to come, arise (from). **5** to take legal action (against).—*v.t.* to say in continuation of what one has said.—*n.* (in *pl.*; *prō'*) money taken at a sale or made by some action.

procē'dure *n.* **1** the method or order of conducting business, esp. in a law case or in a meeting. **2** a course of action. **3** a step taken.

procē'dural *adj.*

proceed'ing *n.* **1** an action. **2** a going forward. **3** (in *pl.*) (steps in) a legal action. **4** (in *pl.*) a record of the business of a society.

process *prō'ses*, *pros'*, *n.* **1** a continued

series of actions, events, etc. causing change. **2** course: *in the process of time.* **3** an operation, method, used in manufacturing, preparing, etc. **4** a legal action. **5** a projecting part in a body, esp. a bone.—*v.t.* **1** to prepare by some process. **2** to handle, deal with.

procession *prō-sesh'(ȯ)n*, *n.* a large company (people or vehicles) moving forward in order.

process'ional *adj.* having to do with a procession.—*n.* a hymn sung during a procession.

prō'cessor *n.* a device, e.g. in a computer, which processes data.

in the process of in the middle, course, of (doing or being done, etc.)

proclaim *prō-klām'*, *v.t.* **1** to make known, cry aloud. **2** to announce or declare officially.

proclamation *prok-lȧ-mā'sh(ȯ)n*, *n.* an official notice given to the public.

proclivity *prō-kliv'i-ti*, *n.* a leaning, inclination: *a proclivity towards gambling*:—*pl.* **procliv'ities**.

procrastinate *prō-kras'ti-nāt*, *v.i.* to put off action, be very slow to act:—*pr.p.* **procras'tinating**.

procrastinā'tion *n.*

procreate *prō'krē-āt*, *v.t.* **1** to bring (offspring) into being. **2** to produce.—Also *v.i.*:—*pr.p.* **pro'creating**.

procure *prō-kūr'*, *v.t.* **1** to get, obtain. **2** to bring about: *steps to procure his appointment*:—*pr.p.* **procur'ing**.

procure'ment *n.*

procurator-fiscal. See **fiscal**.

prod *prod*, *v.t.* **1** to poke. **2** urge into action:—*pr.p.* **prodd'ing**; *pa.p.* **prodd'ed**.—*n.* **1** an act of prodding. **2** a sharp instrument.

prodigal *prod'i-g(ȧ)l*, *adj.* **1** wastefully, recklessly, extravagant. **2** giving very freely: *He was prodigal of promises.* **3** very plentiful.—*n.* **1** a waster. **2** a spendthrift.

prodigal'ity *n.* **prod'igally** *adv.*

prodigy *prod'i-ji*, *n.* **1** a wonder. **2** a person of unusual genius or cleverness (esp. a **child prodigy**). **3** a monster:—*pl.* **prod'igies**.

prodig'ious *(-dij'ŭs) adj.* **1** astonishing. **2** huge, enormous. **3** monstrous.

prodig'iously *adv.* **prodig'iousness** *n.*

produce *prȯ-dūs'*, *v.t.* **1** to bring forward or out. **2** to bring into being, yield. **3** to bring about, cause. **4** to make, manufacture. **5** to be the producer of (a play, film). **6** (*geometry*) to make (a line) longer:—*pr.p.* **produc'ing**.—*n.* *(prod'ūs)* something that is produced, esp. crops, etc., from a farm, etc.

produc'er *n.* **1** one who produces. **2** a farmer or manufacturer. **3** one who is in general charge of the preparation of a play or a motion picture.

product *prod'ukt*, *n.* **1** a thing produced. **2** a result. **3** a work. **4** (*arithmetic*) the result of multiplication. **5** (in *pl.*) the crops, manufactured goods, etc., that a country yields.

produc'tion *n.* **1** the act or process of producing. **2** something that is produced. **3** a work of art or literature.

produc'tive *adj.* **1** having the power to produce. **2** fruitful. **3** bringing results.

produc'tiveness *n.*

productiv'ity *n.* productiveness, esp. the rate or efficiency of work done e.g. in industrial production.

producer(s') goods goods, such as tools and raw materials, used in the making of *consumer(s') goods* (see this).

profane *prȯ-fān'*, *adj.* **1** not sacred. **2** showing contempt for holy things.—*v.t.* **1** to violate, treat with no reverence. **2** to put to an unworthy use:—*pr.p.* **profan'ing**.

profan'ity *n.* **1** lack of respect for sacred things. **2** bad language, swearing.

profess *prȯ-fes'*, *v.t.* **1** to make an open declaration of. **2** to pretend: *He professes to be a friend.* **3** to claim knowledge of or skill in.

professed' *adj.* **1** declared. **2** pretended.

profession *prȯ-fesh'(ȯ)n*, *n.* **1** the act of professing. **2** a declaration of religious belief. **3** a pretence. **4** an employment requiring some thought, skill and special knowledge. **5** (often *n.pl.*) the people engaged in such an employment: *The medical profession believe this.*

profess'ional *adj.* **1** having to do with a profession. **2** making one's living by an art, game, etc.: *a professional actor, golfer.* **3** showing the skill, etc., of one who is trained.—Also *n.*

profess'ionally *adv.*

profess'or *n.* a teacher of the highest grade (or, in the U.S., of any grade, as *associate professor*, *assistant professor*) in a university.

professō'rial *adj.* **profess'orship** *n.*

proffer *prof'ėr*, *v.t.* to offer for acceptance:—*pr.p.* **proff'ering**; *pa.p* **proff'ered**.—Also *n.*

proficient *prȯ-fish'ėnt*, *adj.* **1** skilled, expert. **2** qualified (in, at).—*n.* an expert.

profi'ciency *n.* **profi'ciently** *adv.*

profile *prō'fīl*, *n.* **1** a head, face, etc., seen from the side. **2** the outline of an object.

3 (*orig. U.S.*) a short sketch of character and career.
a low profile behaviour or attitude intended to attract little attention to oneself or to reveal little of one's feelings, intentions, etc.

profit *prof'it*, *n.* **1** gain. **2** benefit. **3** the amount by which the selling price exceeds the cost of an article, etc.—*v.t.* to bring gain or advantage to.—*v.i.* to gain, or receive benefit: *to profit from mistakes*:—*pr.p.* **prof'iting**; *pa.p.* **prof'ited**.
prof'itable *adj.* bringing profit or gain.
profiteer' *n.* one who makes large profits unfairly.—Also *v.i.*
profit sharing an agreement by which workers receive a fixed share of the profits of a business.

profligate *prof'li-git*, *adj.* **1** living in an immoral, dissipated way. **2** extravagant.—*n.* one leading a profligate life.
prof'ligacy *(-ȧs-i) n.*

profound *prō-fownd'*, *adj.* **1** very deep. **2** deeply felt: *profound sympathy.* **3** difficult to understand or solve: *profound problem.* **4** showing great knowledge and understanding: *a profound comment*; *a profound thinker*.
profound'ly *adv.*
profound'ness, **profund'ity** *(-fund') ns.* **1** the state or quality of being profound. **2** great depth (of e.g. ocean, knowledge).

profuse *prȯ-fūs'*, *adj.* abundant, excessive, extravagant: *profuse thanks*; *profuse in his apologies*.
profusion *prȯ-fū'zh(ȯ)n*, *n.* **1** great abundance. **2** extravagance, wastefulness.

progenitor *prō-jen'i-tȯr*, *n.* a forefather, an ancestor.
prog'eny *(proj') n.* descendants, children, offspring.

prognosis *prog-nō'sis*, *n.* a forecast of the expected course of a disease:—*pl.* **prog-no'sēs**.
prognosticate *prog-nos'ti-kāt*, *v.t.* to foretell, forecast:—*pr.p.* **prognos'ticating**.
prognosticā'tion *n.* **prognos'ticator** *n.*

programme, (*U.S.* and *computers*) **program** *prō'gram*, *n.* **1** a sheet or booklet giving details of proceedings at a ceremony. **2** the items of an entertainment, etc. **3** a scheme or plan. **4** the actions to be carried out by a computer in dealing with certain facts.—*v.t.* **1** to prepare a program for (a computer). **2** to prepare, or put (something) on, a programme or schedule:—*pr.p.* **pro'gram-ming**; *pa.p.* **pro'grammed**.
pro'grammable *adj.* **pro'grammer** *n.*

progress *prō'gres*, *prog'res*, *n.* **1** forward movement. **2** advance. **3** improvement, a gradual becoming better, or becoming more skilful. **4** the course (of a story, an event).—*v.i.* *(prȯ-gres')* **1** to go forward. **2** to continue. **3** to advance. **4** to improve.
progression *prȯ-gresh'(ȯ)n*, *n.* **1** motion onward. **2** advance. **3** a connected series.
progress'ive *adj.* **1** moving forward, advancing by stages. **2** favouring reforms, keen to adopt new methods. **3** of a disease, which becomes more and more serious.
progress'ively *adv.* **progress'iveness** *n.*
in progress going on, taking place.

prohibit *prō-hib'it*, *v.t.* **1** to forbid. **2** to prevent.
prohibition *prō-(h)i-bi'sh(ȯ)n*, *n.* **1** the act of forbidding. **2** the forbidding by law of the making and selling of alcoholic drinks.
prohibitive *(-hib')*, **prohib'itory** *adjs.* tending to prohibit (as high prices that make it nearly impossible to buy).

project *proj'ekt*, *n.* **1** a scheme, plan. **2** a task, or piece of research.—*v.t.* *(pro-jekt')* **1** to throw out, forward, or up. **2** to propose, plan. **3** to plan for, expect, in the future on the basis of past results. **4** to cast (e.g. a light, image) on a surface or into space:—*v.i.* to jut out.
projec'tile *n.* a missile.
projec'tion *n.* **1** an act or method of projecting. **2** something that is projected. **3** a planning. **4** something which juts out. **5** a method of making maps showing the earth's surface on a plane.
projec'tionist *n.* one who operates a projector.
projec'tor *n.* a machine for projecting, esp. a beam of light, or an image (as in motion pictures).

prolapse *prō'laps*, (*medical*) *n.* a falling out of place, esp. of the womb or the rectum.

proletarian *prō-li-tā'ri-ȧn*, *adj.* and *n.* (a member) of the proletariat.
proletā'riat *(-ȧt) n.* the wage-earning class with little or no property.

proliferate *prō-lif'ėr-āt*, *v.i.* **1** (of plant or animal tissue) to grow rapidly by producing new parts. **2** to increase much and rapidly.—Also *v.t.*:—*pr.p.* **prolif'erating**.
proliferā'tion *n.*

prolific *prō-lif'ik*, *adj.* **1** bringing forth many offspring, much fruit, much literary work, etc. **2** abounding (with *in* or *of*).

prolix *prō'liks*, *prō-liks'*, *adj.* **1** long, wordy, and dull. **2** speaking or writing thus.
prolix'ity, **prolix'ness** *ns.*

prologue *prō'log*, *n.* **1** an introduction to a poem, play, etc. **2** any introductory event or action.

prolong *prō-long'*, *v.t.* to make longer: *to prolong a discussion.*
prolongation *prō-long-gā'sh(ȯ)n*, *n.* **1** a lengthening, in time or space. **2** a piece added.

prom (concert) *prom (kon'sėrt)* a promenade concert.

promenade *prom-ė-näd'*, *prom'*, *n.* **1** a walk, etc., in a public place for pleasure or to be seen. **2** an esplanade, public walk.—*v.i.* and *v.t.* to walk, etc. publicly in a leisurely way:—*pr.p.* **promenading**.
promenade concert one in which some of the audience are not seated.

prominent *prom'i-nėnt*, *adj.* **1** standing out. **2** projecting. **3** easily seen. **4** famous, distinguished: *a prominent citizen.*
prom'inence *n.* **prom'inently** *adv.*

promiscuous *prȯ-mis'kū-ůs*, *adj.* **1** mixed in kind. **2** not making a distinction between one thing, or person, and another: promiscuous in his choice of friends. **3** (*coll.*) casual, random, without plan. **4** having many casual sexual relationships.
promiscu'ity, **promis'cuousness** *ns.*
promis'cuously *adv.*

promise *prom'is*, *n.* **1** a statement to another that one will do, or not do, something. **2** a sign (of what may be expected in the future): *a promise of success, of storms.* **3** an indication of future excellence: *a writer who shows promise*; *a child of promise.*—*v.t.* **1** to give one's word (to do, not to do, something). **2** to say that one will give (e.g. gift, help). **3** to assure: *She will be there, I promise you.* **4** to show signs of (something to come): *The sky promises a fine day.*—*v.i.* to make a promise:—*pr.p.* **prom'ising**.
prom'ising *adj.* full of promise.
prom'isingly *adv.* **prom'isingness** *n.*
promissory note a written promise to pay a sum of money to another at a certain date or on demand.

promontory *prom'ȯn-tȯr-i* or *-tri*, *n.* a headland or high cape jutting into the sea:—*pl.* **prom'ontories**.

promote *prȯ-mōt'*, *v.t.* **1** to raise to a higher rank or position. **2** to help the growth of, encourage: *to promote the cause of peace.* **3** to help to arrange (a business enterprise, the passing of a law, etc.):—*pr.p.* **promot'ing**.
promō'ter *n.* **promō'tion** *n.*

prompt *prom(p)t*, *adj.* **1** ready in action. **2** done, sent, etc. without delay.—*v.t.* **1** to move to action: *Mary prompted the other children to ask for more.* **2** to inspire: *Fear prompted this reply.* **3** to give forgotten words or a cue to (e.g. an actor).
prompt'er *n.* one who prompts, esp. actors.
prompt'ing *n.* **prompt'ly** *adv.*
prompt'ness, **prompt'itude** *(-tūd)*, *ns.* quickness, readiness.

promulgate *prom'ůl-gāt*, *v.t.* to proclaim, make widely known (a law, a doctrine):—*pr.p.* **prom'ulgating**.
promulgā'tion *n.*

prone *prōn*, *adj.* **1** lying face downward, or flat. **2** inclined (to): *prone to laziness*; *prone to accidents, accident-prone.*

prong *prong*, *n.* the spike of a fork.
pronged *adj.* having prongs.

pronoun *prō'nown*, *n.* a word used instead of a noun (e.g. *he, she, it, you, who*).

pronounce *prȯ-nowns'*, *v.t.* **1** to speak, utter (words, sounds) **2** to give (judgment) officially or formally. **3** to declare: *He pronounced the vase to be an imitation*:—*pr.p.* **pronoun'cing**.
pronounced' *adj.* noticeable, decided: *a pronounced squint.*
pronounce'ment *n.* an announcement or statement.
pronunciation *prȯ-nun-si-ā'sh(ȯ)n*, *n.* the act, or way, of saying a word.

proof. See **prove**.

prop[1] *prop*, *n.* **1** a support. **2** a supporter on whom one depends.—*v.t.* to hold (up) by placing something under or against:—*pr.p.* **propp'ing**; *pa.p.* **propped**.

prop[2] *prop*, *n.* short for **propeller**, **property**.

propagate *prop'ȧ-gāt*, *v.t.* **1** to cause (plants or animals) to produce offspring. **2** to spread from one to another: *to propagate a rumour, belief, knowledge.* **3** to transmit, pass on (sound).—*v.i.* to breed, produce young, multiply:—*pr.p.* **prop'agating**.
propagan'da *n.* **1** action for the spread of particular ideas or opinions. **2** the material used, e.g. film, posters, leaflets.
propagand'ist *n.* one who works to spread political or other ideas.
propagā'tion *n.* **1** the spreading of anything. **2** the producing of young. **3** the increasing of the number of plants by growing more from seed, cuttings, etc.

propel *prȯ-pel'*, *v.t.* to drive forward:—*pr.p.* **propell'ing**; *pa.p.* **propelled'**.
propell'er *n.* a shaft with blades for driving a ship, aeroplane, etc.
propulsion *prȯ-pul'sh(ȯ)n*, *n.* the act of driving forward.

propensity *prȯ-pens'i-ti*, *n.* a natural leaning, tendency, towards: *a propensity to contradict, for writing poetry*:—*pl.* **propen'sities**.

proper *prop'ėr*, *adj.* **1** fitting, right. **2** correct. **3** prim, well-behaved. **4** suitable. **5** belonging (to). **6** strictly so-called: *London proper, not including Greater London.* **7** (*coll.*) thorough:—*opp.* **improper** (*defs. 1–4*).

prop'erly *adv.* **1** in the right way. **2** (*coll.*) thoroughly.

proper noun, name a noun, name, with *cap.*, naming a particular person, thing, place (e.g. *John*; *the Pole Star*; *the ship called the Revenge*; *New York*).

property *prop'ėr-ti*, *n.* **1** a quality of a thing: *Hardness is a property of the diamond.* **2** something that is one's own. **3** land or buildings. **4** (in *pl.*) small articles or furniture used by actors in a play (**props**):—*pl.* **prop'erties**.

prophecy *prof'i-si*, *n.* **1** a prediction, foretelling the future. **2** a thing foretold:—*pl.* **proph'ecies**.

prophesy *prof'i-sī*, *v.i.* to foretell the future.—Also *v.t.*: to prophesy disaster; *to prophesy that it will rain*:—*pr.p.* **proph'esying**; *pa.p.* **proph'esied**.

proph'et *n.* **1** one who tells beforehand of things to come. **2** one who tells the will of God:—*fem.* (*rare*) **proph'etess**.

prophet'ic(al) *adjs.* foreseeing or foretelling events.

prophet'ically *adv.*

propinquity *prȯ-ping'kwi-ti*, *n.* nearness in place, time, blood relationship.

propitiate *prȯ-pish'i-āt*, *v.t.* **1** to calm the anger of. **2** to gain the favour of:—*pr.p.* **propi'tiating**.

propitiā'tion *n.*

propi'tious *adj.* favourable: *The time seemed propitious for the rebellion*; *The weather proved propitious to the attempt*.

proportion *prȯ-pōr'sh(ȯ)n*, or *-pör'*, *n.* **1** the ratio or comparative size, number, quantity, of one thing considered alongside another: *the proportion of women to men at the concert*; *in the proportion of three ounces of butter to four of flour.* **2** a part, esp. considered alongside the whole: *A small proportion of the class failed.* **3** balance, appropriateness, or suitability in size of different parts: *Her feet are out of proportion to her body.* **4** balance or appropriateness in importance, strength, etc.: *His anger was out of proportion to the harm done.* **5** (in *pl.*) dimensions: *a giant of vast proportions.*—*v.t.* to make in correct proportion (to).

propor'tional, propor'tionate *adjs.* in proportion.

in (out of) proportion correct (or not correct), suitable (or not suitable), in size, etc. when compared with something else.

propose *prȯ-pōz'*, *v.t.* **1** to put forward for consideration, to suggest (e.g. a plan, a candidate). **2** to intend: *He proposes to build a new house.*—*v.i.* to make an offer, especially of marriage:—*pr.p.* **propos'ing**.

propōs'al *n.* **1** the act of proposing. **2** anything proposed. **3** an offer of marriage.

proposition *prop-ȯ-zish'(ȯ)n*, *n.* **1** a proposal, suggestion. **2** a statement. **3** (*slang*, orig. *U.S.*) any situation, thing, or person considered as something to be coped or dealt with.

propound *prȯ-pownd'*, *v.t.* to offer for consideration, state (e.g. a problem).

proprietor *prȯ-prī'ė-tȯr*, *n.* an owner:—*fem.* **proprī'etress, proprī'etrix**.

proprī'etary *adj.* **1** owning property. **2** legally made by a firm having sole right to do so: *a proprietary drug*.

proprietary name a trademark.

propriety *prȯ-prī'ė-ti*, *n.* **1** fitness, suitability, rightness. **2** the standard of behaviour and morals accepted in society as correct or proper. **3** (in *pl.*, **propri'eties**) the details of this.

props. See **property**.

propulsion. See **propel**.

prorogue *prō-rōg'*, *v.t.* to bring the meetings of (parliament) to an end for a time:—*pr.p.* **prorog'uing**; *pa.p.* **prorogued'**.

prosaic *prō-zā'ik*, *adj.* **1** dull, uninteresting. **2** matter-of-fact.

prosa'ically *adv.*

proscenium *prō-sē'ni-ŭm*, *n.* the front part of the stage.

proscribe *prō-skrīb'*, *v.t.* **1** to outlaw. **2** to prohibit or refuse to tolerate:—*pr.p.* **proscrib'ing**.

prose *prōz*, *n.* **1** writing that is not in verse. **2** ordinary spoken and written language.—*adj.* (used only before a noun) **1** of, in, prose. **2** dull.

pros'y *adj.* dull, tiresome:—*comp.* **pros'ier**; *superl.* **pros'iest**.

pros'ily *adv.* **pros'iness** *n.*

See also **prosaic**.

prosecute *pros'i-kūt*, *v.t.* **1** to bring a legal action against. **2** to follow up (e.g. an enquiry). **3** to carry on: *He prosecutes his studies*:—*pr.p.* **pros'ecuting**.

prosecū'tion *n.* **1** the act of bringing a court case against another. **2** the party bringing a court action. **3** the carrying on,

continuity (of e.g. an enquiry, a task).
pros'ecūtor *n.* the law officer who leads a case against a prisoner.

prospect *pros'pekt, n.* **1** a wide view. **2** a scene. **3** outlook for the future, likely result: *faced with the prospect of defeat.* **4** (in *pl.*) measure of success to be expected: *He has good prospects in his present job.*—*v.i.* *(pros-pekt')* to make a search (for e.g. gold).
prospec'tive *adj.* expected, likely to be or happen, future.
prospec'tus *n.* a small book giving information about a business, school, literary work, etc.

prosper *pros'pėr, v.i.* to succeed, turn out well.—*v.t.* to cause to thrive.
prosper'ity *n.* success, good fortune.
pros'perous *adj.* **pros'perously** *adv.*

prostitute *pros'ti-tūt, v.t.* to offer or sell for evil or unworthy use:—*pr.p.* **pros'tituting.**—*n.* a person who offers sexual intercourse for money.
prostitū'tion *n.*

prostrate *pros'trāt, -trit, adj.* **1** lying with one's face on the ground. **2** reduced to helplessness. **3** worn out, exhausted.—*v.t.* *(pros-trāt', pros')* **1** to throw forwards on the ground. **2** to defeat utterly. **3** to exhaust. **4** to bow (oneself) in reverence: *He prostrated himself before the king:*—*pr.p.* **prostrating.**
prostrātion *n.*

prosy. See **prose**.

protagonist *prō-tag'ȯn-ist, n.* **1** the chief actor or character. **2** a champion (of a cause).

protect *prō-tekt', v.t.* **1** to guard, defend (e.g. *from, against, danger, injury, loss, change*). **2** to put safety devices on. **3** to aid (an industry) by putting a tax on goods of rival foreign firms.
protec'tion *n.*
protec'tive *adj.* giving protection, intended to protect.
protec'tor *n.* **1** a guardian. **2** one who shields from harm or injury.
protec'torate *n.* a country that is partly governed and defended by a stronger country.

protégé *prō'tė-zhā, prot', n.* one having help from an important person in making his career, etc.: *He was a protégé of a cabinet minister:*—*pl.* **protégés**; *fem.* **protégée** (*pl.* **protégées**).

protein *prō'tēn, n.* any of a large number of substances (present in milk, eggs, meat, etc.) essential as part of the diet of human beings and animals.

pro tempore *prō tem'pȯ-rē*, for the time being, temporarily—Abbrev. **pro tem**.

protest *prȯ-test', v.i.* to express an objection (with *at, against*).—*v.t.* to make a solemn declaration of: *He protested his innocence.*—*n.* *(prō'test)* a strong statement of objection or disapproval.
Prot'estant *(prot')* *n.* a member of one of the western Christian churches founded at the Reformation (by breaking away from the Roman Catholic Church) or later.—Also *adj.*
Prot'estantism *n.* the Protestant religion.
protestation *prō-tes-tā'sh(ȯ)n, prot-, n.* **1** a solemn declaration (with *of*): his protestation of loyalty. **2** a protest (against).

proto- *prō-tō, -to, -tȯ,* (as part of a word) first in time, earliest.

protocol *prō-tȯ-kol, n.* **1** a draft of a treaty. **2** a body of rules, etiquette, for diplomatic ceremonies.

proton *prō'ton, n.* a particle with positive charge forming the nucleus of the hydrogen atom and part of the nucleus of all other atoms.

protoplasm *prō'tō-plazm, n.* the half-liquid substance which is the chief material found in all living cells.

prototype *prō'tō-tīp, n.* the first model from which anything is copied.

protract *prȯ-trakt', v.t.* to draw out or lengthen in time: *Let us not protract the discussion.*
protrac'tor *n.* an instrument for drawing angles on paper.

protrude *prȯ-trōōd', v.t.* and *v.i.* to stick, thrust, out or forward:—*pr.p.* **protrud'ing.**
protrusion *prȯ-trōō'zh(ȯ)n, n.* **1** the act or state of sticking out. **2** something that sticks out.

protuberance *prȯ-tūb'ėr-ȧns, n.* a bulging out, a swelling.
protu'berant *adj.* swelling.

proud. See **pride**.

prove *prōōv, v.t.* **1** to test. **2** to show to be true. **3** to show the correctness of (a result).—*v.i.* to turn out to be: *The report proved to be true:*—*pa.p.* (*usu.*) **proved**.
proven *prōōv'n* (Scots law, *prōv'n*), *pa.p.* (chiefly *U.S.*) and *adj.* proved.
proof *prōōf, n.* **1** evidence that convinces. **2** a test making something clear beyond doubt. **3** the act of showing to be true. **4** a copy taken from printing type for correction before printing. **5** (*photography*) the first print from a negative. **6** the standard of strength of whisky, etc.—*adj.* (not usu. before a noun) firm (against), able to withstand: *proof against the arguments of the rebels*; often used as part of

a word, e.g. in **bullet-proof**, **fireproof**.

proof'ing *n.* **1** the process of making waterproof, fireproof, etc. **2** material used for this.

provender *prov'in-dėr*, *n.* food, esp. a dry meal for horses and cattle.

proverb *prov'ûrb*, *n.* a short familiar sentence expressing a moral lesson or something supposed to be true (e.g. 'A penny saved is a penny earned').

prover'bial *adj.* **1** like a proverb. **2** widely known, or spoken of by everyone: *the cat's proverbial nine lives.*

provide *prȯ-vīd'*, *v.t.* **1** to make ready beforehand. **2** to supply. **3** to supply (a person with).—*v.i.* **1** to get what is necessary ready (for): *to provide for, against, a hard winter.* **2** to allow (for):—*pr.p.* **provid'ing.**

provid'ed (often **provided that**), **provid'ing** *conjs.* on condition (that), if.

provision *prȯ-vizh'(ȯ)n*, *n.* **1** the act of providing (for, against). **2** an agreement or arrangement made earlier. **3** a clause in a law or a deed. **4** a store or stock. **5** (in *pl.*) (a store of) food-—*v.t.* to supply with food.

provis'ional *(-vizh') adj.* temporary, not final, with the possibility of change: *a provisional government*.

proviso *prō-vī'zō*, *n.* a condition made, esp. in a document: *He agreed to come, with the proviso that he must not be asked to sing*:—*pl.* **provī'so(e)s**.

provī'sory *adj.* **1** provisional. **2** having to do with a proviso.

providence *prov'i-dėns*, *n.* **1** foresight. **2** thrift. **3** the care of God for all creatures. **4** an event showing God's care. **5** (*cap.*) God.

prov'ident *adj.* **1** seeing beforehand, and providing for the future. **2** thrifty:—*opp.* **improv'ident**.

providential *prov-i-den'sh(ȧ)l*, *adj.* **1** coming from divine will or God's care. **2** fortunate: *the providential arrival of help.*

province *prov'ins*, *n.* **1** a division of a country or party of an empire. **2** the extent or limits of one's duty, knowledge, etc.: *Keeping the garden is outside my province.* **3** (in *pl.*) all parts of the country outside the capital.

provincial *prȯ-vin'sh(ȧ)l*, *adj.* **1** having to do with a province. **2** unpolished in manners, or narrow in interests.

provin'cialism *n.* **1** a manner, custom, or way of speaking found in country districts. **2** interest in area where one lives and not in one's country as whole.

provision, **proviso**, etc. See **provide**.

provocation, etc. See **provoke**.

provoke *prȯ-vōk'*, *v.t.* **1** to rouse to anger, annoy. **2** to stir up (a person, etc. to action). **3** to give rise to, result in (e.g. laughter, trouble):—*pr.p.* **provok'ing.**

provocā'tion *n.* **1** the act of provoking. **2** something that rouses anger.

provoc'ative *adj.* **1** tending to provoke or excite. **2** encouraging one to think or react.

provost *prov'ȯst*, *n.* **1** the head of a cathedral. **2** the head of a college. **3** (*Scotland*) the mayor, or chief magistrate, of a burgh.

Lord Provost the mayor or chief magistrate of each of five large Scottish cities.

prow *prow*, *n.* the front part of a ship.

prowess *prow'es*, *n.* **1** bravery, esp. in war. **2** great skill, ability, etc.

prowl *prowl*, *v.i.* to move about stealthily, or quietly, esp. seeking to rob or attack someone.

proximity *proks-im'i-ti*, *n.* the state of being very near in place, time, etc.

proxy *prok'si*, *n.* **1** one who acts or votes for another. **2** the writing by which he is allowed to do so:—*pl.* **prox'ies.**

prude *prōōd*, *n.* a person who prides himself on modesty and correct behaviour, or who is priggish and over-modest.

pru'dery *n.* **1** the state of being like a prude. **2** prudish actions, speeches:—*pl.* **prud'eries**.

prud'ish *adj.*

prudent *prōō'dėnt*, *adj.* cautious and wise:—*opp.* **imprudent.**

pru'dence *n.* **1** wisdom in managing practical affairs. **2** caution.

pruden'tial *adj.* using caution.

prudery, **prudish**. See **prude**.

prune[1] *prōōn*, *v.t.* **1** to trim (a tree, etc.) by cutting off unnecessary parts. **2** to cut off (e.g. twigs). **3** to delete parts of (e.g. a story). **4** to take out (unnecessary details):—*pr.p.* **prun'ing.**

prune[2] *prōōn*, *n.* a dried plum.

prurient *prōō'ri-ėnt*, *adj.* excessively interested in sexual matters.

pry[1] *prī*, *v.i.* **1** to peer or peep (into what is closed, or into what is not told). **2** to try to find out about other people's affairs:—*pr.p.* **pry'ing**; *pa.p.* **pried.**

pry'ing *adj.* **1** curious. **2** peering.

pry[2]. Same as **prize**[1]:—*pr.p.* **pry'ing**; *pa.p.* **pried.**

psalm *säm*, *n.* a sacred song or hymn, esp. one from the Book of Psalms in the Bible.

psalmist *säm'ist*, *n.* a writer of psalms.

psalter *söl'tėr, n.* a book of psalms.
psal'tery *n.* an ancient stringed instrument:—*pl.* **psal'teries**.

pseud(o)- *sūd(-ō, -o, -ȯ)-*, (as part of a word) false, sham, fake, e.g. **pseu'do-antique'**: *He bought a pseudo-antique vase.*
pseud'ō *adj.* sham: *His foreign accent is pseudo.*
pseudonym *sū'dȯ-nim, n.* a false name assumed by an author: *Mark Twain was the pseudonym of Samuel Clemens.*
pseudon'ymous *adj.*

psyche *sī'kē, n.* soul, spirit, mind.
psych(o)- *sīk(-ō, -o, -ȯ)-*, (as part of a word) **1** of the psyche. **2** of psychology.
psychedelic, **psychodelic** *sī-ki-del'ik, -kȯ-, dēl', adjs.* **1** (of a drug) producing pleasant physical sensations and a feeling of exultation and self-confidence. **2** (of art, colour patterns, shifting lights, etc.) causing sensations in some way like those produced by a psychedelic drug.
psychī'atrist *n.* one who treats diseases of the mind.
psychī'atry *n.* the treatment of mental diseases.
psychiat'ric *adj.*
psy'chic *adj.* **1** having to do with soul or mind. **2** sensitive to forces that have no physical cause. **3** connected with such forces.—Also **psy'chical**.
psychoanal'ysis *n.* a method of treating nervous diseases by tracing forgotten events or thoughts in the patient's mind and bringing them to light.
psychoan'alyse *v.t.*:—*pr.p.* **psychoan'alysing**.
psychoan'alyst *n.*
psychodel'ic. See **psychedelic**.
psychol'ogy *n.* the science that studies the human mind and mental life.
psycholog'ical *adj.* **psycholog'ically** *adv.*
psychol'ogist *n.*
psy'chopath *n.* a very ill-balanced person who is not morally responsible, e.g. for crimes he may commit.
psychopath'ic *adj.*
psychō'sis *n.* any grave illness of the mind:—*pl.* **psychō'sēs**.
psychosomat'ic *adj.* having to do with the relationship of mind and body, as with physical diseases coming from a mental disturbance.
psychother'apy *n.* the treatment of disease by hypnosis, psychoanalysis, etc.
psychot'ic *n.* and *adj.* (a person) suffering from a psychosis.
psychological moment the best moment.
psychological warfare the use of propaganda to influence enemy opinion or state of mind.

ptarmigan *tär'mi-gȧn, n.* a type of grouse.

pub *pub, (coll.) n.* short for **public house**.

puberty *pū'bėr-ti, n.* the beginning of sexual maturity.

public *pub'lik, adj.* **1** of, or concerning, the people in general. **2** having to do with a community or nation. **3** common, or shared in by all. **4** generally known. **5** not private: *a public park*; *public transport* (buses, trains, etc.).—*n.* **1** the people in general. **2** a certain section of people: *an author's public*; *the reading public*.
pub'lican *n.* **1** the keeper of an inn or public house. **2** in Roman times, a tax-collector.
publicā'tion *n.* **1** the act of making public, or of putting a book, etc. on sale. **2** something published, as a book.
publicity *pub-lis'i-ti, n.* **1** the state of being public or open to the knowledge of all. **2** advertising.
pub'licise *v.t.* to advertise, make known to the public:—*pr.p.* **pub'licising**.
pub'licly *adv.*
publish *pub'lish, v.t.* **1** to make public. **2** to announce formally. **3** to put out (e.g. a book) for sale.
pub'lisher *n.*
public address system a system of devices (e.g. microphones, amplifiers, loudspeakers) used to enable (large) groups of people to hear voices, music, etc.
public holiday a day on which all (or most) offices, shops, factories, etc. are closed for a holiday.
public house *n.* an establishment where alcoholic liquors are sold to the public, an inn or tavern.
public opinion poll testing of public opinion by questioning certain people (taken as samples) in a community.
public relations the activities of a firm, government, person, to keep on good terms with the public.
public school **1** a school maintained by a local education authority. **2** a fee-paying school run partly on money given to it in the past.
public servant. See **servant** (*def.* 3).
public spirit an unselfish desire, shown in one's actions, for the welfare of one's fellow citizens.
pub'lic-spir'ited *adj.*
in public in open view, among people: *They quarrelled in public.*

puce *pūs, n.* a brownish-purple.—Also *adj.*

puck *puk*, *n.* a rubber disc used instead of a ball in ice-hockey.

pucker *puk'ėr*, *v.t.* and *v.i.* to wrinkle.—*n.* a fold or wrinkle.

pudding *pood'ing*, *n.* **1** a type of sausage: *black pudding.* **2** a soft food made of sugar, milk, eggs, etc. **3** a sweet.

puddle *pud'l*, *n.* a small muddy pool.—*v.t.* to cause (molten pig iron) to undergo the process of **puddling**, which turns it into wrought iron.—*v.i.* to dabble:—*pr.p.* **pudd'ling**.

puerile *pū'ėr-īl*, *adj.* childish, silly.
pu'erileness, **pueril'ity** *ns*.

puff *puf*, *v.i.* **1** to blow out in small gusts. **2** to breathe heavily (as after running). **3** to swell (up, out).—*v.t.* **1** to drive with a puff. **2** to blow up, inflate. **3** to praise, esp. by way of advertisement.—*n.* **1** a sudden gust of wind. **2** a cake of light pastry. **3** a powder puff. **4** praise, esp. as an advertisement.
puff'y *adj.* **1** breathing heavily. **2** puffed out with air. **3** flabby:—*comp.* **puff'ier**; *superl.* **puff'iest**.
puff'iness *n.*
puff'ball *n.* a type of round fungus.
puffed up swollen with pride.
puff pastry a light, flaky type of pastry.

puffin *puf'in*, *n.* a type of sea-bird with a short, thick, brightly-coloured beak.

puffy. See **puff**.

pug *pug*, *n.* a type of small dog.
pug'-nose *n.* a short thick nose with the tip turned up.
pug'-nosed *adj.*

pugilism *pū'jil-izm*, *n.* **1** the art of boxing. **2** prize-fighting.
pu'gilist *n.*

pugnacious *pug-nā'shu̇s*, *adj.* fond of fighting, quarrelsome.
pugnac'ity *n.* readiness to fight.

puissant *pū'is-ȧnt*, *pwis'*, *adj.* powerful.

pukka *puk'ȧ*, *adj.* **1** good. **2** genuine, real.

puke *pūk*, *v.i.* to vomit:—*pr.p.* **puk'ing**.

pule *pūl*, *v.i.* to whimper or whine:—*pr.p.* **pul'ing**.

pull *pool*, *v.t.* **1** to pluck (e.g. flowers). **2** to move, or try to move, towards oneself, drag, draw, tug. **3** to row (a boat). **4** to draw out: *to pull a tooth.* **5** to stretch, or strain. **6** to hold back (esp. a horse in racing). **7** to draw out (a knife, gun). **8** to send (a ball) to the left (in case of left-handed players, to the right) of the direction intended.—*v.i.* to do an action of pulling.—*n.* **1** the act of pulling. **2** a pulling force. **3** a draught of liquor. **4** an advantage (in a contest—as in weight, quickness, etc). **5** influence.
pull'over *n.* a jersey.
pull in to steer a vehicle to the side of a road, into a car-park, etc., and stop.
pull off to gain, or to succeed in, by effort.
pull oneself together to regain self-control.
pull one's weight to take one's full share in an undertaking.
pull out **1** to steer a vehicle out from the side of a road. **2** to withdraw from an undertaking, etc.
pull round to bring, or come, back to good health.
pull through to get safely to the end of a difficult or dangerous experience.
pull up to stop, halt.

pullet *pool'it*, *n.* a young hen.

pulley *pool'i*, *n.* a wheel with a grooved rim in which fits a cord, chain, etc., used for lifting weights, changing direction of pull, etc.:—*pl.* **pull'eys**.

Pullman (car) *pool'mȧn (kär)*, *n.* a railway saloon or sleeping-car, first made by G. M. *Pullman* in America.

pullover. See **pull**.

pulmonary *pul'mȯn-ȧr-i*, *adj.* having to do with, or affecting, the lungs.

pulp *pulp*, *n.* **1** the soft fleshy part of a fruit. **2** any soft mass, as the tissue in the cavity of a tooth. **3** the soft mass (made from e.g. wood) which is made into paper.—*v.t.* to reduce to pulp.

pulpit *pool'pit*, *n.* a raised structure, esp. in a church, occupied by a preacher.

pulsate *pul'sāt*, *v.i.* **1** to beat, throb. **2** to be vibrant with energy, emotion, etc.:—*pr.p.* **pulsat'ing**.
pulsā'tion *n.* a beating or throbbing.
pulse *puls*, *n.* **1** a regular beat or throb. **2** the beating of heart and arteries:—*v.i.* to pulsate:—*pr.p.* **puls'ing**.

pulse¹. See **pulsate**.

pulse² *puls*, *n.* the edible seeds of beans, peas, etc.

pulverise *pul'vėr-īz*, *v.t.* **1** to make or crush into dust or fine powder. **2** to beat thoroughly:—*pr.p.* **pul'verising**.
pulverisā'tion *n.* **pul'veriser** *n.*

puma *pū'mȧ*, *n.* a wild cat found in America.

pumice (stone) *pu'mis (stōn)*, *n.* a piece of light, hardened, glassy lava, used for smoothing or cleaning.

pummel *pum'l*, *v.t.* to beat with the fists: —*pr.p.* **pumm'elling**; *pa.p.* **pumm'elled**.

pump¹ *pump*, *n.* a machine for raising water, etc. or for compressing or moving gases.—

v.t. **1** to raise or force with a pump. **2** to draw out information from (a person) by cunning questions.

pump² *pump, n.* a light dancing shoe.

pumpkin *pum(p)'kin, n.* a large, roundish, thick-skinned, yellow or orange fruit of the gourd family.

pun *pun, v.i.* to play upon words alike in sound but different in meaning, as in *They went and told the sexton, and the sexton tolled the bell:—pr.p.* **punn'ing**; *pa.p.* **punned**.—*n.* a play upon words.
  pun'ster *n.* one who makes puns.

punch¹ *punch* or *-sh, n.* a drink of spirits, water, sugar, juices and spice.

punch² *punch* or *-sh, v.t.* **1** to strike, esp. with the fists. **2** to stamp or pierce by a thrust of a tool or machine.—*n.* **1** a thrust, blow. **2** striking power, vigour. **3** a tool for punching holes.
  punch'-drunk' *adj.* (of a boxer) dizzy, having a brain injury, through blows.
  punch line the last line of a story or joke which gives meaning or an unexpected twist.

puncheon *pun'ch(o̊)n, n.* a tool for piercing or stamping metal plates.

punctilious *pungk-til'i-ůs, adj.* giving great care to small points, esp. in behaviour or ceremony.

punctual *pungk'tū-ål, adj.* **1** strict in being on time for appointments. **2** up to time, not late. **3** prompt.
  punc'tually *adv.* **punctual'ity** *n.*

punctuate *pungk'tū-āt, v.t.* **1** to divide into sentences, etc. by commas, full stops, etc. **2** to interrupt at intervals: *silence punctuated by*, or *with, bird cries:—pr.p.* **punc'tuating**.
  punctuā'tion *n.*
  punctuation marks the comma, semicolon, colon, period, etc.

puncture *punk'chůr, n.* **1** the act of pricking, piercing. **2** a small hole made with a sharp point. **3** a hole in a tyre.—*v.t.* **1** to prick. **2** to pierce with a sharp point:—*pr.p.* **punc'turing**.

pundit *pun'dit, n.* **1** a Hindu scholar. **2** any learned person, esp. one who is considered, or considers himself to be, an authority on something.

pungent *pun'jėnt, adj.* **1** sharp in taste or smell. **2** painful. **3** biting, sarcastic: *a pungent remark.*

punish *pun'ish, v.t.* **1** to cause (a person) to suffer for a fault or crime. **2** to make person(s) suffer for (an offence): *to punish carelessness.* **3** (*coll.*) to handle roughly.
  pun'ishable *adj.* (of persons or crimes) that may be punished: *punishable by death.*
  pun'ishment *n.* **1** the act or method of punishing. **2** the penalty imposed for an offence.
  punitive *pū'ni-tiv, adj.* **1** inflicting punishment. **2** aiming at punishment.

punnet *pun'it, n.* a small basket for fruit.

punster. See **pun**.

punt¹ *punt, n.* a flat-bottomed boat with square ends.—*v.t.* to move (a punt, etc.) by pushing a pole against the bottom of a river, etc.

punt² *punt, n.* the act of kicking a dropped football before it touches the ground.—*v.t.* to kick in this manner.

punt³ *punt, v.i.* to bet on a horse.
  punt'er *n.* a habitual gambler.

puny *pū'ni, adj.* **1** little and weak. **2** feeble:—*comp.* **pu'nier**; *superl.* **pu'niest**.

pup *pup, n.* a young dog, seal, etc.

pupa *pū'på, n.* a stage (often passed in a cocoon) in the growth of an insect between the larva (e.g. caterpillar) and the perfect form or *imago* (e.g. butterfly).

pupil¹ *pū'pil, n.* one who is being taught by a teacher or tutor.

pupil² *pū'pil, n.* the round opening in the middle of the eye through which the light passes.

puppet *pup'it, n.* **1** a doll moved by wires or hands. **2** one who acts just as another tells him.
  pupp'etry *n.* the art of producing puppet-shows.
  pupp'et-show *n.* a drama performed by puppets on a small stage.

puppy *pup'i, n.* **1** a young dog. **2** a conceited young man:—*pl.* **pupp'ies**.

purchase *pûr'chås, v.t.* **1** to buy. **2** to obtain by work, effort, etc.:—*pr.p.* **pur'chasing**.—*n.* **1** anything that is bought. **2** the act of buying: *money for the pur·chase of books.* **3** any extra power, or advantage, in raising or moving things, obtained by using e.g. a lever, a capstan. **4** a means of exerting force.
  pur'chaser *n.*
  purchase tax formerly, a tax on certain goods sold within the country.

pure *pūr, adj.* **1** clean, spotless. **2** free from dirt or infection: *pure milk.* **3** not mixed with anything less valuable: *pure gold.* **4** free from faults: *Though a German, he spoke very pure Russian.* **5** innocent. **6** (only used before a noun) that and that only: *a pure accident.* **7** (only used before a noun) utter: *That is pure nonsense.* **8** (*music*) clear and smooth in tone. **9** perfectly in tune:—*opp.* **impure**.

pure'ly *adv.* **1** in a pure manner. **2** wholly, entirely. **3** solely, merely.
pure'ness, **pur'ity** *ns.*
purificā'tion *n.* the act of purifying.
purify *pū'ri-fī*, *v.t.* to make pure:—*pr.p.* **pu'rifying**; *pa.p.* **pu'rified**.
pur'ist *n.* one who insists on absolute correctness.
pure'-blood'ed *adj.* whose ancestors are all of the same race.
pure'-bred' *adj.* (of an animal) whose ancestors are all of the same breed.
pure mathematics, **science** mathematics or science in the theory, apart from practical uses.

puree, **purée** *pū'rā*, *n.* food material reduced to a pulp and passed through a sieve, or pulped in a liquidiser.—*v.t.* to make a puree of:—*pr.p.* **pur'eeing**, **pur'-éeing**; *pa.p.* **pur'eed**, **puréed**.

purgatory, etc. See **purge**.

purge *pûrj*, *v.t.* **1** to purify, clean. **2** to clear (something) of unwanted things, or (e.g. a political party) of people who are thought not to be loyal to it. **3** to empty (the bowels).—Also *v.i.*:—*pr.p.* **purg'ing**.—*n.* **1** the act of purging. **2** a medicine that purges.
purgation *pûr-gā'sh(ȯ)n*, *n.*
purgative *pûr'gȧ-tiv*, *adj.* and *n.* (something) that purges.
pur'gatory *(-gȧ-)* *n.* **1** (*R.C.*) a place or state in which the soul is made clean of sins before entering heaven. **2** any state of suffering for a time:—*pl.* **pur'gatories**.

purification, **purify**, **purist**. See **pure**.

Puritan *pūr'i-tȧn*, *n.* **1** one of a religious group which desired to keep religion pure in belief and simple in ceremony. **2** (often without *cap.*) a person who believes in strict (often narrow) morals and self-restraint and seriousness.
puritan'ical *adj.*
pur'itanism *n.* the principles and ways of Puritans.

purity. See **pure**.

purl[1] *pûrl*, *v.i.* to flow with a murmuring or rippling sound.—Also *n.*

purl[2] *pûrl*, *v.t.* **1** to fringe with a wavy edging, as in lace. **2** to knit in stitches made with the wool, etc., passed behind the needle.—Also *n.* and *adj.*

purlieus *pûr'lūz*, *n. pl.* **1** borders or outskirts. **2** neighbourhood.

purloin *pûr-loin'*, *v.t.* to filch, steal.

purple *pûr'pl*, *n.* **1** a colour formed by mixture of blue and red. **2** a purple dress or robe, orig. worn by royalty. **3** royal rank or any high position.—Also *adj.*

purport *pûr'pōrt*, *-pört*, *n.* **1** meaning. **2** substance, gist.—*v.t.* *(-pōrt', -pört')* **1** to mean. **2** to seem, be given appearance of: *It was a letter purporting to come from you.*

purpose *pûr'pu̇s*, *n.* **1** the aim towards which an effort or action is directed. **2** the use, function (of e.g. a tool). **3** constancy of aim: *a man of purpose.*—*v.t.* to intend:—*pr.p.* **pur'posing**.
pur'poseful *adj.* **1** knowing what one wants to do. **2** serving a purpose.
pur'posely *adv.* intentionally.
pur'pose-built' *adj.* specially made to meet particular needs.
on purpose purposely.
to good, little, no, some, purpose with good, few, no, some, results.
to the purpose to the point, relevant.

purr *pûr*, *v.i.* to utter a low, murmuring sound, as a cat when pleased.—Also *n.*

purse *pûrs*, *n.* **1** a small bag for carrying money. **2** a sum of money (often given as a prize).—*v.t.* **1** to draw (esp. the lips) together as the mouth of a purse that is closed by strings. **2** to wrinkle:—*pr.p.* **purs'ing**.
purs'er *n.* the officer in charge of a ship's accounts, cabins, stewards, etc.

pursue *pûr-sū'*, *-so͞o'*, *v.t.* **1** to follow, esp. in order to overtake and capture. **2** to seek to gain: *to pursue pleasure.* **3** to follow (a path, course of action). **4** to carry on, continue. **5** to be engaged in (e.g. enquiries, studies). **6** to persecute, annoy.—*v.i.* to go in pursuit:—*pr.p.* **pursu'ing**.
pursū'ance (or *-so͞o'*) *n.* the act of carrying out.
pursū'er *n.* **1** one who pursues. **2** (*Scots law*) one who brings another to court, a plaintiff.
pursuit *(-sūt', so͞ot')*, *n.* **1** the act of pursuing. **2** what one pursues or is engaged in—occupation, employment, hobby.

purulent. See **pus**.

purvey *pûr-vā'*, *v.t.* to provide, supply.—*v.i.* to supply provisions or meals as one's business.
purvey'ance *n.*
purvey'or *n.* one whose business is to provide food.

pus *pus*, *n.* a thick yellowish fluid produced in wounds, abscesses, etc.
purulent *pūr'yė-lėnt*, *adj.* full of, forming, etc. pus.

push *poosh*, *v.t.* **1** to press against with force. **2** to drive, move thus. **3** to thrust (out). **4** to advance, carry to a further point. **5** to urge (to): *They pushed him to accept the post.* **6** to recommend vigorously: *to* *push a product by advertising on television.* **7** to peddle (drugs).—*v.i.* **1** to make a thrust. **2** to make an effort. **3** to press (on, forward).—*n.* **1** a thrust. **2** effort. **3** energy and forcefulness: *He has push and will get on in his profession.*

push'er *n.* **1** one who pushes. **2** (*coll.*) an ambitious and forceful person.

push'ing *adj.* **1** pressing forward in business. **2** too sure of oneself, presuming.

push'y *adj.* aggressive, tending to assert oneself too much:—*comp.* **push'ier**; *superl.* **push'iest**.

push button a small knob pressed to close an electric circuit, so operating, or stopping, some device.

push'-chair *n.* a folding chair with wheels, for a child.

push'-over *n.* **1** something easy to do. **2** a person or thing easily overcome.

pusillanimous *pū-si-lan'i-mŭs*, *adj.* **1** lacking firmness of mind. **2** cowardly.

puss *poos*, *n.* a cat.—Also **puss'y** (*pl.* **-ies**).

pustule *pus'tūl*, *n.* a small pimple containing pus.

put[1] *poot*, *v.t.* **1** to move or push (into). **2** to lay, set: *to put books on a table.* **3** to bring into a position or state: *to put oneself in the hands of a doctor*; *to put John in a temper.* **4** to apply (to): *to put to a new use.* **5** to give, attribute: *He put the wrong meaning on what I said.* **6** to pose (a question). **7** to express in a particular way:—*pr.p.* **putt'ing**; *pr.p.* **put**.

a put-up job something arranged to give a false impression.

hard put (to it) **1** hard pressed. **2** having great difficulty in: *hard put (to it) to find any money.*

put about **1** to change course, or course of, at sea. **2** to publish (e.g. news). **3** to upset.

put by to save up, put in store.

put down **1** to crush (a rebellion). **2** to kill (esp. an old or ill animal). **3** to snub, humiliate (*n.* **put'-down**). **4** to pay (a deposit).

put in for to make a claim or application for.

put off **1** to take off. **2** to delay, postpone. **3** (*coll.*) to turn (a person) away from his purpose or inclination. **4** to extinguish (a light, etc.).

put on **1** to switch on (a light, etc). **2** to assume (a pose, etc.). **3** to dress oneself in.

put out **1** to extinguish, as a fire. **2** to annoy or embarrass. **3** to head (for), at sea.

put through to bring to an end, accomplish.

put two and two together to draw a conclusion from certain circumstances.

put upon to impose on.

put (a person) up to (an action) to suggest it and encourage (him) to carry it out.

put up with to endure, bear patiently.

put[2]. See **putt**.

putative *pū'tà-tiv*, *adj.* supposed, commonly regarded as such.

putrefy *pū'tri-fī*, *v.t.* and *v.i.* to rot:—*pr.p.* **pu'trefying**; *pa.p.* **pu'trefied**.

putrefac'tion *n.*

pu'trid *adj.* **1** rotten. **2** stinking. **3** (*slang*) wretchedly bad.

putsch *pooch*, *n.* a sudden revolutionary outbreak.

putt also **put** *put*, *v.t.* **1** (*Scot.*) to hurl (as a weight). **2** (*golf*) to send a ball forward lightly on the green:—*pr.p.* **putt'ing**; *pa.p.* **putt'ed**.—Also *n.*

putt'er *n.* a club used for putting.

putt'ing-green *n.* **1** the smooth grass round any of the holes on a golf course. **2** an area of smooth grass with holes, for putting as a game.

putty *put'i*, *n.* **1** a cement of whiting and oil. **2** a powder for polishing glass, etc.—*v.t.* to fix or fill with putty:—*pr.p.* **putt'ying**; *pa.p.* **putt'ied**.

puzzle *puz'l*, *v.t.* **1** to be difficult for (someone) to understand: *The girl, the situation, puzzles me.* **2** to worry with a difficult question: *to puzzle one's brains about what to do.*—*v.i.* **1** to be bewildered. **2** to work long and carefully (over a problem):—*pr.p.* **puzz'ling**.—*n.* **1** a difficulty that causes much thought. **2** a riddle or game which tests one's thinking.

puzz'lement *n.*

puzz'ling *adj.* baffling, difficult.

puzzle out to discover the solution of by hard mental effort: *to puzzle out a mystery.*

pyebald. See **piebald**.

pygmy, pigmy *pig'mi*, *n.* **1** one of a race of very small human beings. **2** a dwarf:—*pl.* **pyg'mies**, **pig'mies**.—Also *adj.* very small.

pyjamas *pi-jä'màz*, *n.pl.* clothes for sleeping in.

pyja'ma *adj.* e.g. in **pyjama jacket, trousers**.

pylon *pī'lon*, *n.* **1** a guiding mark at an air field. **2** a high structure supporting electric power-cables.

pyramid *pir'à-mid*, *n.* **1** a solid shape with a base and triangle-shaped sides meeting in a point. **2** a structure like this, esp. one of those used as tombs in ancient Egypt.

pyre *pīr*, *n.* a pile of wood, etc., for burning a dead body.

Pyrex® *pi'reks*, *n.* a type of glassware for cooking that will stand heat.

pyro- *pir-o-*, (as part of a word) fire.

pyrotechnics *pī-rō-tek'niks* **1** (*n.sing.*) the art of making fireworks. **2** (*n.sing.* or *n.pl.*) a firework display. **3** (*n.sing.* or *n.pl.*) a showy display (e.g. in a speech, a musical performance).

python *pī'thòn*, *n.* a type of snake that crushes its victim.

pyx *piks*, *n.* **1** (*R.C.*) a vessel in which the host is kept, or carried to the sick. **2** a box at the Mint with sample coins for testing.

Q

qua *kwā, kwä, conj.* in the character or capacity of; as.

quack[1] *kwak, n.* the cry of a duck.—*v.i.* to make such a sound.

quack[2] *kwak, n.* one who pretends that he has skill and knowledge (esp. in medicine) that he does not really possess.—Also *adj.*
quack'ery *n.* the pretences or methods of a quack:—*pl.* **quack'eries**.

quadr(i)- *kwod-r(i)-*, (as part of a word) four.
quadrangle *kwod-rang'gl,* or *kwod', n.* **1** (*geometry*) a figure with four angles (and therefore four sides). **2** a four-sided open space enclosed by buildings (e.g. in a college):—*abbrev.* **quad**.
quadrang'ular *(-rang'gū-) adj.*
quadrant *kwod'rȧnt, n.* **1** a quarter of a circle, i.e. a sector with a 90° angle. **2** an instrument used in navigation, astronomy, etc., for measuring the angular height above the horizon e.g. of the sun.
quadraphonic *kwod'rȧ-fon'ik, adj.* (of sound transmission) using four separate signals or channels.
quadrennial *kwod-ren'i-ȧl, adj.* **1** happening, etc. every four years. **2** lasting four years.
quadrilateral *kwod-ri-lat'ėr-ȧl, n.* (*geometry*) a four-sided figure or area.—Also *adj.*
quadruped *kwod'roo-ped, n.* a four-footed animal.
quadruple *kwod-roo'pl, adj.* **1** consisting of four parts. **2** four times as much or many.—*v.t.* and *v.i.* to make, or to become, four times as great:—*pr.p.* **quadru'pling**.
quadruplet *kwod'roo-plit,* or *-rōō', n.* one of four children born at the same time to one mother:—*abbrev.* **quad**.

quadrille *kwȯ-dril', n.* **1** square dance for four couples. **2** music for such a dance.

quadruped, quadruple, etc. See **quadr(i)**.

quaff *kwof, v.t.* and *v.i.* to drink in large draughts.

quagmire *kwag'mīr, n.* boggy ground into which one may sink.

quail[1] *kwāl, v.i.* to shrink with fear, flinch.

quail[2] *kwāl, n.* a small bird of the partridge family.

quaint *kwānt, adj.* pleasantly odd or strange, esp. because old-fashioned.
quaint'ly *adv.* **quaint'ness** *n.*

quake *kwāk, v.i.* to shake or tremble, esp. with fear:—*pr.p.* **qua'king**.—*n.* **1** a shudder. **2** an earthquake.

Quaker *kwā'kėr, n.* one of the Religious Society of Friends, a sect founded by George Fox:—*fem.* (*old*) **Qua'keress**.

qualify *kwol'i-fī, v.i.* (with *as*) to reach the required standard for a profession, etc.: *to qualify as a doctor*; to fulfil a requirement.—*v.t.* and *v.i.* to make or prove oneself fit (for an activity, etc.).—*v.t.* **1** to mention a quality of: *An adjective qualifies a noun*; *In the phrase 'the red book', 'red' qualifies 'book'.* **2** to make (a statement) less strong: *He said he was never late, but qualified that by adding 'Well, almost never'*:—*pr.p.* **qual'ifying**; *pa.p.* **qual'ified**.
qualificā'tion *n.* **1** the act of making fit for an activity or position. **2** a quality or attainment that makes one fit or suitable. **3** making, or something that makes, a statement less strong.
qual'ified *adj.* **qual'ifier** *n.*
See also **disqualify**.

quality *kwol'i-ti, n.* **1** nature. **2** the degree of goodness or badness of something. **3** characteristic: *She may be bad-tempered, but she has one good quality—fairness*:—*pl.* **qual'ities**.
qual'itātive *adj.* of, relating to, quality.

qualm *kwäm, n.* a sudden feeling of nervousness or uneasiness.

quandary *kwon'dȧ-ri, n.* a state of perplexity about what to do; a plight:—*pl.* **quan'daries**.

quango *kwang'gō, n.* an official body that supervises some part of national activity, culture, etc.:—*pl.* **quan'gos**.

quantity *kwon'ti-ti, n.* **1** amount, number. **2** a large amount.—*pl.* **quan'tities**.
quan'tify *(-ti-fī) v.t.* to express in terms of quantity:—*pr.p.* **quan'tifying**; *pa.p.* **quan'tified**.
quan'titātive *adj.* of, relating to, quantity.
quantity surveyor one whose job is to estimate the quantity and cost of materials needed for constructing something.

quantum *kwon'tum, n.* **1** an amount. **2** a unit of energy in atomic physics.

quarantine *kwor'ȧn-tēn, n.* (a period of) compulsory isolation (orig. forty days for a ship) to prevent spread of disease.—*v.t. to put in quarantine*:—*pr.p.* **quar'antining**.

quark *kwärk, n.* any of three particles imagined as the smallest constituents of an atom.

quarrel *kwor'ėl, n.* **1** an angry dispute. **2** a disagreement. **3** a break in friendship.—*v.i.* **1** to disagree, dispute angrily. **2** to object to, find fault (with something):—*pr.p.* **quarr'elling**; *pa.p.* **quarr'elled**.

quarr'elsome *adj.* inclined to quarrel.

quarr'elsomeness *n.*

quarry[1] *kwor'i, n.* an excavation from which stone is cut or blasted:—*pl.* **quarr'ies**.—*v.t.* to dig (stone) from a quarry.—*v.i.* to make, or dig in, a quarry:—*pr.p.* **quarr'ying**; *pa.p.* **quarr'ied**.

quarr'yman *n.* a man who works in a quarry.

quarry[2] *kwor'i, n.* **1** a hunted animal. **2** a prey, victim:—*pl.* **quarr'ies**.

quart- *kwört-*, (as part of a word) fourth, four.

quart *n.* the fourth part of a gallon.

quarter *kwör'tėr, n.* **1** a fourth part. **2** the fourth of an hour, a year, or of the moon's period. **3** a measure of weight, a quarter of a hundredweight (28 lbs or 12.7 kg.). **4** the leg of a usu. large animal. **5** a direction. **6** a district. **7** (in *pl.*) lodgings for soldiers, staff, etc. **8** mercy granted to an enemy in return for his surrender.—*v.t.* **1** to divide in four equal parts; to divide by four. **2** to lodge in quarters. **3** (*history*) to cut (a criminal's body) into four parts.

quar'terly *adj.* happening, published, etc. once every three months.—*adv.* once every three months.—*n.* a magazine, etc., published every three months:—*pl.* **quar'terlies**.

quartet, **quartette** *kwör-tet', n.* **1** a set of four. **2** a piece of music for four voices or instruments. **3** a set of performers for such pieces.

quarto *kwör'tō, n.* **1** the page size resulting when a sheet is folded into four leaves. **2** a book of sheets so folded:—*pl.* **quar'tos**:—*abbrev.* **4to**.

quarter day the first or last day of a quarter, on which payments are made.

quar'ter-deck *n.* the after part (i.e. that at the stern) of the upper deck.

quar'ter-fi'nal *n.* a match, etc. in a competition immediately before the semi-final.—Also *adj.*

quar'termaster *n.* (*army*) an officer whose job is to provide rations, lodgings, etc.

quarter sessions (formerly) a court held quarterly.

at close quarters very near.

quartz *kwörts, n.* the commonest rock-forming mineral, silica, occurring in many varieties.

quasar *kwā'sär, n.* a star-like object outside our galaxy, that produces very strong radio waves.

quash *kwosh, v.t.* to annul, cancel: *He was convicted of theft, but the conviction was later quashed.*

quasi- *kwā'sī-, kwä'zi-,* (put before a word) **1** in appearance only, not reality: *quasi-historical.* **2** almost.

quater- *kwat-ėr-,* (as part of a word) four times.

quatercentenary *kwat-ėr-sen-tēn'-ȧ-ri, n.* a 400th anniversary:—*pl.* **quatercenten'aries**.

quatrain *kwot'rān, n.* a stanza of four lines of verse.

quaver *kwā'vėr, v.i.* **1** to tremble, quiver. **2** to speak or sing in a shaky voice.—Also *v.t.*—*n.* **1** a trembling, esp. of the voice. **2** (*music*) half a crotchet.

qua'very *adj.* trembling.

quay *kē, n.* a landing place, wharf.

quay'side *adj.* and *n.*

queasy *kwē'zi, adj.* **1** sick. **2** squeamish:—*comp.* **quea'sier**; *superl.* **quea'siest**.

quea'siness *n.*

queen *kwēn, n.* **1** the wife of a king. **2** a female monarch. **3** the egg-laying female of bees and other insects that live together in communities. **4** a playing-card bearing a picture of a queen. **5** the most important piece in chess. **6** (*offensive slang*) a male homosexual.

queen'ly *adj.* of, like, or suitable for, a queen:—*comp.* **queen'lier**; *superl.* **queen'liest**.

queen mother the mother of the reigning king or queen.

Queen's Bench, Counsel, queen's evidence, etc. (used during the reign of a queen). See **king**.

queen it (*coll.*) to act like a queen, behave imperiously.

queer *kwēr, adj.* **1** odd, strange. **2** sick or faint. **3** (*offensive slang*; of a man) homosexual (also *n.*).—*v.t.* (*slang*) to spoil, ruin.

queer'ly *adv.* **queer'ness** *n.*

Queer Street trouble, esp. money difficulties.

queer someone's pitch to spoil someone's plans.

quell *kwel, v.t.* **1** to crush (e.g. a rebellion). **2** to subdue (a person). **3** to quiet (e.g. uproar, fears).

quell'er *n.*

quench *kwench,* or *-sh, v.t.* **1** to put out (e.g. flame, enthusiasm). **2** to slake (thirst).

quern *kwûrn*, *n.* (*history*) a stone implement for grinding grain.

querulous *kwer'oo-lůs*, or *-ū-*, *adj.* complaining, peevish.
quer'ulously *adv.* **quer'ulousness** *n.*

query *kwē'ri*, *n.* **1** a question. **2** a question-mark:—*pl.* **que'ries**.—*v.t.* **1** to question, doubt (a statement). **2** to mark with a query:—*pr.p.* **que'rying**; *pa.p.* **que'ried**.

quest *kwest*, *n.* search, pursuit.—*v.i.* to go searching (for).

question *kwes'ch(ȯ)n*, *n.* **1** a sentence requiring an answer, an inquiry. **2** a problem. **3** a matter about which there is doubt. **4** room for discussion, doubt, etc.: *There was no question of dismissing him, no question about his honesty.* **5** a separate item in a test or examination, to be answered or discussed.—*v.t.* **1** to put questions to (a person). **2** to regard as doubtful: *Are you questioning my ability?*; *I question whether it's possible.*
ques'tionable *adj.* **1** able to be doubted. **2** prob. not true, honest, respectable, etc.
ques'tionableness *n.*
ques'tionably *adv.*
questionnaire *kwes-ti-ȯ-nār'*, or *-tyȯn-*, also *-kes-*, *n.* a set of written questions to obtain information on which to base a report (e.g. a report on industrial conditions).
ques'tion-mark *n.* a mark showing and following a question (?).
ques'tion-mas'ter *n.* the person who asks the questions in a quiz, etc.
in question **1** under consideration. **2** being disputed.
out of the question not to be considered as possible.

queue *kū*, *n.* **1** a pigtail at the back of the head. **2** a line of people waiting their turn.—*v.i.* to stand in a queue:—*pr.p.* **queu'ing**, **queue'ing**.
queue'-jumping *n.* the practice of jumping the queue (see **jump**).

quibble *kwib'l*, *v.i.* **1** to argue about trivial details instead of discussing the main point. **2** to object to (with *at*, *about*): *He quibbled at the price*:—*pr.p.* **quibb'ling**; *pa.p.* **quibb'led**.—Also *n.*

quick *kwik*, *adj.* **1** done or happening in a short time. **2** speedy, rapid. **3** acting or responding at once: *a quick brain*; *quick sympathy*; *a quick temper.* **4** (*old*) alive.—*adv.* (*coll.*) without delay; rapidly.—*n.* a sensitive part, esp. under one's nails.
quick'ly *adv.* **quick'ness** *n.*
quick'en *v.t.* and *v.i.* **1** to make or become faster. **2** to make or become alive.
quick'ening *n.*
quick'lime *n.* lime when recently burnt but not treated with water.
quick'sand *n.* loose, wet sand that sucks in anyone who stands on it.
quick'silver (*old*) *n.* mercury (so called because it is quick-moving and silvery in colour).
quick'step *n.* a dance performed in couples, to a fast walking rhythm.
quick'-tem'pered *adj.* easily made angry.
quick'-witt'ed *adj.* alert, sharp, thinking quickly.

quid *kwid*, *n.* (*slang*) a pound (100 pence):—*pl.* **quid**.

quid pro quo *kwid prō kwō,* something given or taken in fair exchange.

quiescent *kwī-es'ėnt*, *adj.* still; not in an active state.
quies'cence *n.* **quies'cently** *adv.*

quiet *kwī'ėt*, *adj.* **1** at rest. **2** calm. **3** gentle. **4** silent.—*n.* rest, peace.—*v.t.* and *v.i.* to quieten.
qui'eten *v.t.* and *v.i.* to make or become quiet.
qui'etly *adv.*
qui'etness, qui'etude *(-tūd)*, *ns.*
quietus *kwī-ē'tůs*, *n.* death or a death-blow.
on the quiet secretly.
See also **disquiet**.

quiff *kwif*, *n.* a tuft of hair sticking up above the forehead.

quill *kwil*, *n.* **1** the hollow part at the foot of a large feather. **2** a large feather, esp. (*hist.*) that of a goose made into a pen. **3** a spine of e.g. a porcupine.

quilt *kwilt*, *n.* a bed cover filled with down, etc., stitched to keep the filling in place.

quin-, quinqu(e)- *kwin-*, *kwing-kw(i)-*, (as part of a word) five.
quincentenary *kwin-sen-tēn'ȧ-ri*, *n.* a 500th anniversary.—Also *adj.*
quinquenn'ial *kwin-*, *kwing-kwen'i-ȧl*, *adj.* **1** happening, etc. every five years. **2** lasting five years.
quinquereme *kwing'kwi-rēm*, *n.* an ancient ship with five 'banks', or rows, of oars. See also **quint**.

quince *kwins*, *n.* a fruit with an acid taste, used in making jam, etc.

quinine *kwin'ēn*, *n.* a bitter substance got from the bark of the cinchona (*sing-kō'nȧ*) tree, native of the Andes region, used in medicine.

quinqu(e)- . See **quin**.

quint- *kwint-*, (as part of a word) fifth, five.
quintessence *kwint-es'ėns*, *n.* the absolute essence or embodiment of something.
quintet, quintette *kwin-tet'*, *n.* **1** a set of

five. **2** a piece of music for five voices or instruments. **3** a set of performers for such pieces.

quintuplet *kwin'tū-plit*, or *-tū'*, *n.* one of five children born to one mother at the same time.

See also **quin**.

quip *kwip*, *n.* a quick, witty reply.—*v.i.* to make quips:—*pr.p.* **quipp'ing**; *pa.p.* **quipped**.

quire *kwīr*, *n.* a twentieth of a ream.

quirk *kwûrk*, *n.* **1** a twist, turn; a trick. **2** an oddity (e.g. of character).

quirk'y *adj.* having quirks; eccentric:—*comp.* **quirk'ier**; *superl.* **quirk'iest**.

quirk'iness *n.*

quisling *kwiz'ling*, *n.* a traitor who takes office in a government formed by an enemy occupying his country.

quit *kwit*, *v.t.* **1** to depart from, leave. **2** (*U.S.*) to leave off, stop.—*v.i.* **1** to leave, vacate a house, etc. **2** (*coll.*) to desert one's job or task:—*pr.p.* **quitt'ing**; *pa.p.* **quitt'ed**.

quits *adj.* (not used before a noun) even (with), neither owing nor owed.

quitt'ance *n.* release.

be, get, quit of to be, get, rid of.

quite *kwīt*, *adv.* **1** completely. **2** exactly. **3** fairly; rather.—*interj.* indeed; yes.

quiver¹ *kwiv'ėr*, *n.* a case for arrows.

quiver² *kwiv'ėr*, *v.i.* to tremble, shiver.—*n.* a trembling motion.

quixotic *kwiks-ot'ik*, *adj.* ridiculously and impractically idealistic and generous, like the hero, Don *Quixote,* of Cervantes's book.

quixot'ically *adv.* **quix'otry** *n.*

quiz *kwiz*, *n.* a competition to test knowledge, esp. for the amusement of an audience:—*pl.* **quizz'es**.—*v.t.* to question:—*pr.p.* **quizz'ing**; *pa.p.* **quizzed**.

quizz'ical *adj.* (of e.g. a look) humorously questioning or gently mocking.

quoit *koit*, *n.* a ring of metal, rope, or rubber.

quoits *n. sing.* a game in which such a ring is to be thrown over a peg.

Quorn® *kwörn*, *n.* a vegetable protein used as a meat substitute.

quorum *kwō'rum*, *kwö'*, *n.* the smallest number of members necessary at a meeting before business can proceed.

quota *kwō'tȧ*, *n.* the share that one must receive or contribute.

quote *kwōt*, *v.t.* **1** to refer to. **2** to give the actual words of. **3** to name (a price):—*pr.p.* **quot'ing**.

quotā'tion *n.* **1** the act of quoting. **2** something quoted. **3** an estimate of price.

quota'tion-marks *n.pl.* marks used at the beginning and end of a written or printed quotation (" ", or ' ').

quoth *kwōth*, (*old*) *v.t.*, *pa.t.* (with subject *I*, *he*, *she*, usu. following verb) said.

quotient *kwō'shėnt*, *n.* the number of times one quantity is contained in another: *In* $12 \div 3 = 4$, *4 is the quotient.*

R

rabbi *rab'ī*, *n.* a Jewish priest or teacher of the Jewish law:—*pl.* **rabb'īs**.
rabbin'ical *(-bin') adj.*

rabbit *rab'it*, *n.* **1** a small burrowing animal with long ears and short tail. **2** (*slang*) a timid or unathletic person.
rabb'it-punch *n.* a blow on the back of the neck.
rabbit on (*coll.*) to talk long and ineffectually.

rabble *rab'l*, (*abusively*) *n.* **1** a noisy crowd. **2** the socially lowest class of people.

rabid *rab'id*, or *rā'*, *adj.* **1** mad; suffering from rabies. **2** violent, extreme: *a rabid supporter of the local team*.
rabies *rā'bēz*, *n.* a disease that causes madness in dogs and other animals, also formerly called hydrophobia (see this).

raccoon, **racoon** *rȧ-kōōn'*, *n.* a small animal related to bears.

race[1] *rās*, *n.* **1** a distinct group amongst living beings: *the human race*. **2** a section of mankind with distinct physical characteristics or a distinct culture, language, etc.: *the white*, *Negro*, *races*; *the Anglo-Saxon race*. **3** (*old*) family, ancestry.
racial *rā'sh(ȧ)l*, *adj.* of, having to do with, race.
ra'cialism *n.* **1** belief that some races of men are better than others. **2** policy based on this belief. **3** hatred between races.—Also **ra'cism** *(-sizm)*.
ra'cialist, **ra'cist** *ns.*, *adjs*.

race[2] *rās*, *n.* **1** a competition between persons, animals or vehicles to see which can move most quickly: *a horse-race*. **2** a competition in getting ahead of others: *The accumulation of ever more deadly weapons by opposing nations is known as the arms race*. **3** a rush: *a race for a train*. **4** a rapid current. **5** a channel taking water to a mill-wheel: *a mill-race*.—*v.i.* **1** to run or move swiftly. **2** to take part in a race.—*v.t.* **1** to run (e.g. car engine) wildly. **2** to enter (a horse, etc.) for a race:—*pr.p.* **ra'cing**.
ra'cer *n.* person, animal, or vehicle taking part in racing.
race card a programme of races.
race'course, **-track** *n.* a course over which races are run.
race'horse *n.* a horse bred for racing.
race meeting a gathering for fixed series of horse, or dog, etc., races.
the races a (horse-) race meeting.

racial, **racialism**, **racism**. See **race**[1].

rack[1] *rak*, *n.* **1** a framework in or on which things are arranged for tidy storage, etc. **2** a shelf for luggage in e.g. a railway carriage. **3** a bar with teeth to fit into and move a toothed wheel, etc. **4** an instrument to torture people by stretching them.—*v.t.* **1** to torture. **2** to strain: *He racked his brains for the answer*.

rack[2] *rak*, *n.*: **rack and ruin** a state of neglect and decay.

racket[1], **racquet** *rak'it*, *n.* a bat with a wooden or metal frame strung with catgut or nylon etc., used in tennis and other games.
rackets, **racquets** *n. sing.* a game in which rackets and a hard ball are used, played in a four walled court.

racket[2] *rak'it*, *n.* **1** a din, a great noise. **2** a dishonest way of making money.
racketeer' *n.* one who makes money by dishonest means.

racoon. See **raccoon**.

raconteur *rak-on^{g}-tûr'*, *n.* one who tells stories and anecdotes.

racquet(s). See **racket(s)**.

racy *rā'si*, *adj.* lively, spirited: *He has a racy style of writing*:—*comp.* **ra'cier**; *superl.* **ra'ciest**.
ra'cily *adv.* **ra'ciness** *n.*

radar *rā'där*, *n.* a method of showing the direction and distance of an object by means of radio waves which bounce off the object and return to their source.

radial *rā'di-ȧl*, *adj.* **1** arranged like the spokes of a wheel. **2** having to do with a radius.
ra'dially *adv.*
radial(-ply) tyre one whose tread is scored from side to side rather than lengthwise.

radiant *rā'di-ȧnt*, *adj.* **1** sending out rays of light or heat. **2** transmitted by radiation. **3** glowing. **4** beaming with joy: *She has a radiant smile*.
ra'diance, **ra'diancy** *ns.*
ra'diantly *adv.*
See also **radiate**, **radio**.

radiate *rā'di-āt*, *v.i.* **1** to send out rays of e.g. heat or light. **2** to spread out in many directions: *All the roads radiate from the town centre*.—*v.t.* to send out in rays, or as if in rays: *His face radiated kindness*:—*pr.p.* **ra'diating**.
radiā'tion *n.* **1** the act of radiating. **2** the act of sending out rays. **3** that which is

sent out in waves or rays, e.g. by a radioactive material.

ra'diātor *n.* **1** an apparatus for heating a room by hot water, gas, electricity, etc. **2** an apparatus in a car, etc., which cools the engine.

radiation sickness illness caused by exposure to dangerous rays.

radical *rad'i-kl, adj.* **1** of, relating to, the root or basic character: *The machine has radical faults, and should be scrapped.* **2** thorough: *The arrangements are not efficient and need a radical overhaul.* **3** (*botany*) coming from near the root. **4** (*politics*; usu. with *cap.*) bent on thorough reform.—*n.* **1** a root. **2** (often with *cap.*) one who wants great changes, esp. political. **3** a group of atoms behaving like a single atom and passing unchanged from one compound to another.

rad'icalism *n.* the beliefs or spirit of a radical.

rad'ically *adv.* **rad'icalness** *n.*

radicle *rad'i-kl, n.* the part of a seed that becomes a root.

radii. See **radius**.

radio- *rā-di-ō-*, (as part of a word) **1** rays, radiation. **2** radioactive. **3** radium. **4** radio.

ra'dio *n.* **1** communication or signalling through space without connecting wires, by means of electromagnetic waves. **2** an apparatus for receiving such signals (*pl.* **-os**). **3** (usu. sound) broadcasting. —*v.t.* **1** to send out (a message) by radio. **2** to send a message to (a person, etc.) by radio.—*pr.p.* **ra'dioing**; *pa.p.* **ra'dioed**.

ra'dioac'tive *adj.* giving off rays that can harm living matter, and result from the disintegration of atomic nuclei.

ra'dioactiv'ity *n.*

ra'diocar'bon (*archaeology*) *n.* a radioactive isotope of carbon that can be measured in organic materials to establish their age.

ra'diogram *n.* a combined radio receiver and record-player.

ra'diograph *n.* an X-ray (or other radiation) photograph.

radiog'rapher *n.* one who makes these.

radiog'raphy *n.* making of radiographs.

radiol'ogist *n.* one who studies or practises radiology.

radiol'ogy *n.* **1** the study of radiation and radioactivity. **2** their use in medicine.

ra'diother'apy *n.* treatment of disease by radiation, e.g. by X-rays.

radish *rad'ish, n.* a plant with a red or white root eaten raw in salads.

radium *rā'di-ům, n.* an element, a rare, radioactive metal whose rays are used in treating certain diseases; used also in making luminous paints, etc.

radius *rā'di-ůs, n.* **1** (*geometry*) a straight line from the centre of a circle to its circumference. **2** the bone on the thumb side of the forearm. **3** the area within a given distance from a central point: *They searched within a radius of one mile from the school*:—*pl.* **ra'dii** (*-di-ī*), **ra'diuses**.

raffia *raf'i-å, n.* strips of fibre from the raffia palm, used for making mats, etc.

raffish *raf'ish, adj.* rather disreputable-looking.

raffle *raf'l, n.* a way of raising money by selling marked or numbered tickets, some of which win a prize.—*v.t.* to dispose of by using as prize in raffle:—*pr.p.* **raff'ling**.

raft *räft, n.* a platform of logs or planks made to float on water.

rafter *raf'tėr, n.* a sloping beam supporting the roof of a house.

rag[1] *rag, n.* **1** a small piece of worn or torn cloth. **2** (in *pl.*) shabby or torn clothes: *Cinderella was dressed in rags.*—*adj.* made of rags or cloth: *a rag doll*; *a rag book*.

ragged *rag'id, adj.* **1** in rags. **2** torn. **3** uneven: *The wind blew the ragged clouds across the sky*.

ragg'edly *adv.* **ragg'edness** *n.*

rag'time *n.* a type of lightly-syncopated music of American Negro origin, developed in the 1920s.

rag trade (*coll.*) the clothes-making industry.

rag[2] *rag, v.t.* to tease, or play tricks on (someone):—*pr.p.* **ragg'ing**; *pa.p.* **ragged**.—*n.* **1** (sometimes with *cap.*) (a period of) jokes and foolery to raise money for charity. **2** a trick or practical joke.

lose one's rag (*slang*) to lose one's temper.

ragamuffin *rag'å-muf-in, n.* a ragged, dirty person.

rage *rāj, n.* (a fit of) violent anger.—*v.i.* **1** to be very angry; to act or shout very angrily. **2** (of e.g. the wind) to be violent. **3** (of e.g. battle, argument) to continue violently:—*pr.p.* **rag'ing**.

rag'ing *adj.* and *n.*

be (all) the rage to be very fashionable or popular.

raglan *rag'lån, adj.* (of a sleeve) made to cover arm and shoulder, attached by a seam running from neck to armpit.

ragout *ra-gōō', n.* a highly-seasoned stew of meat and vegetables.

ragwort *rag'wûrt, n.* a large coarse weed with a yellow flower.

raid *rād, n.* a quick, short, (usu.) surprise attack in order to damage or to seize something: *The enemy made a raid on the docks.*—*v.t.* **1** to make a raid on: *The police raided the gambling club.* **2** to help oneself to things from: *to raid the larder.*—Also *v.i.*

rai'der *n.* **1** one who makes a raid. **2** a raiding plane or ship.

rail[1] *rāl, n.* a horizontal bar forming part of a protective barrier, or for any of various purposes. **2** a steel bar, usu. one of a pair of parallel ones, that forms the track for trains, etc. **3** the railway: *Some goods are sent by rail.*—*v.t.* to enclose with rails or railings (with *off* or *in*): *The playground has been railed off.*

rail'ing *n.* (often in *pl.*) a fence of posts and rails.

rail'card *n.* a card entitling its holder to reduced train fares.

rail'head *n.* the farthest point reached by a railway.

rail'road (chiefly *U.S.*) *n.* a railway.—*v.t.* (*coll.*) to force (e.g. a person into doing something, a bill through parliament).

rail'way *n.* a track laid with rails on which trains, etc. run.

off the rails (*coll.*) slightly mad.

rail[2] *rāl,* (*old*) *v.i.* to speak angrily and bitterly (with *at, against*): *The rivals railed at each other.*

raillery *rā'lė-ri, n.* good-tempered mockery.

raiment *rā'mėnt, n.* (old) clothing.

rain *rān, n.* **1** water from the clouds in drops. **2** anything falling like rain: *The wind brought down a rain of nuts from the tree.*—*v.i.* (used impersonally of the weather) to send down rain: *It is raining.*—*v.i.* and *v.t.* to fall, or send down, like rain.

rain'y *adj.* having, producing, showers of rain:—*comp.* **rain'ier**; *superl.* **rain'iest**.

rain'bow *n.* the coloured bow or arch seen opposite the sun when the sun's rays strike raindrops.

rain'coat *n.* a light coat to keep out rain.

rain'fall *n.* the amount of rain that falls in a certain time in a certain area: *the annual rainfall in East Anglia.*

rain'forest *n.* tropical forest with very heavy rainfall.

rain gauge (*gāj*) an instrument for measuring rainfall.

a rainy day hard times; a time of need: *to save up for a rainy day.*

rain cats and dogs to rain very hard.

raise *rāz, v.t.* **1** to cause to rise: *to raise prices.* **2** to lift up. **3** to set up: *to raise a statue to someone.* **4** to make higher: *to raise the wall by twenty centimetres.* **5** to grow or breed: *to raise crops, pigs.* **6** to bring up: *to raise a family.* **7** to cause, give rise to: *to raise a laugh, an outcry.* **8** to put forward, suggest: *to raise an objection.* **9** to collect together: *to raise money; to raise an army.* **10** (*coll.*) to make contact with, by radio: *I can't raise the mainland*:—*pr.p.* **rais'ing**.

raising agent a substance, e.g. baking powder, that causes a cake, etc. to rise.

raise a siege. See **siege**.

raise Cain, hell (*coll.*) to make a lot of noise, esp. in anger.

raise the roof (*coll.*) to make or cause a great noise, esp. laughter or applause.

raisin *rā'z(i)n, n.* a dried grape.

raj *räj, n.* rule, government, esp. that of the British in India, 1858–1947.

raja(h) *rä'jȧ n.* an Indian king or prince:—*fem.* **ra'ni**, **ra'nee** (*-nē*).

rake[1] *rāk, n.* a tool having a bar with teeth on the end of a long handle, used, esp. in gardening, etc., for smoothing, gathering together, etc.—*v.t.* **1** to draw a rake over. **2** to scrape (up, together). **3** to sweep with gunfire from end to end: *The destroyer raked the enemy ship with all her guns.* **4** to search closely.—*v.i.* **1** to work with a rake. **2** to make a search (through):—*pr.p.* **ra'king**.

rake'-off (*coll.*) *n.* a share of profits, generally illegal.

rake up to bring to light (an old story, generally unpleasant).

rake[2] *rāk, n.* a slope or slant in a ship or building: *The rake of the floor in a theatre enables everyone to see the stage.*—*v.t.* and *v.i.* to (cause to) slope:—*pr.p.* **rak'ing**.

ra'kish *adj.* slanting, jaunty: *She wore her hat at a rakish angle.*

ra'kishly *adv.* **ra'kishness** *n.*

rake[3] *rāk, n.* a man who lives an immoral life.

rallentando *ral-ėn-tan'dō, adj.* and *adv.* becoming slower.—*n.* a passage of music so played:—*pl.* **rallentan'dos**.

rally[1] *ral'i, v.t.* **1** to gather together again: *The Colonel tried to rally his men.* **2** to make an effort to revive and use to the full: *You must rally your wits, all your powers, to deal with the difficult situation.*— *v.i.* **1** to come together for joint action or effort (esp. with *round*): *All supporters of the football club must rally (round) to save its existence.* **2** to recover in health: *She rallied from her severe illness*:—*pr.p.* **rall'ying**; *pa.p.* **rallied** (*ral'id*).—*n.* **1** act of rallying. **2** a gathering: *a Scouts' rally.* **3** a meeting for a competition or other event: *a car rally.* **4** a recovery from illness, not always complete. **5** a series of shots in tennis, etc., before the point is won or lost. **6** a competition to test driving skills and vehicles over an unknown route:—*pl.* **rall'ies.**

rallying *n.* long-distance motor-racing over public roads.

rally[2] *ral'i, v.t.* to tease:—*pr.p.* **rall'ying**; *pa.p.* **rall'ied.**

ram *ram, n.* **1** a male sheep. **2** a battering ram (see this). **3** something heavy, or a part of a machine, for forcing by pressure.—*v.t.* **1** to make (e.g. earth) firm by pounding. **2** to drive by heavy blows. **3** to thrust tightly (into). **4** to drive against, crash hard into (a ship, a vehicle, etc.):—*pr.p.* **ramm'ing**; *pa.p.* **rammed.**

ram'rod (*hist.*) *n.* a rod for ramming down the charge in a gun loaded through the muzzle; used as an image of straightness, stiffness and so strictness.

ram down someone's throat to try to force someone to believe, accept, etc. (a statement, idea).

Ramadan *ram'ȧ-dan, n.* in the Muslim year, the month when Muslims must fast by day.

ramble *ram'bl, v.i.* **1** to walk about for pleasure. **2** to wander. **3** to talk in an aimless or confused way esp. as a symptom of old age or illness:—*pr.p.* **ram'bling.**—*n.* **1** a long country walk. **2** a walk with no fixed aim.

ram'bler *n.* **1** one who walks in the countryside for pleasure. **2** a trailing climbing rose or other plant.

ram'bling *adj.* wandering; confused.

ramekin *ram'ė-kin, n.* a small round baking dish with straight sides.

ramification *ram-i-fi-kā'sh(ȯ)n, n.* **1** division into branches, sections, topics, etc. **2** such a branch, section, etc. **3** a complication or indirect consequence, esp. one of many.

rammer. See **ram**.

ramp *ramp, n.* **1** a slightly sloping surface or way. **2** (*slang*) a swindle.

ram'pant *adj.* **1** fearsomely widespread and out of control: *Forest fires were rampant.* **2** (*heraldry*) standing on the left hindleg: *The Scottish standard has a lion rampant in red on a yellow ground.*

ram'pancy *n.* **ram'pantly** *adv.*

rampage *ram-pāj', v.i.* to rush about wildly or angrily:—*pr.p.* **rampag'ing.**

rampā'geous *adj.* wild, out of control.

on the rampage rampaging.

rampant, etc. See **ramp**.

rampart *ram'pärt, n.* (often in *pl.*) a flat-topped mound or wall for defence.

ramrod. See **ram**.

ramshackle *ram'shak-l, adj.* shaky, badly made.

ran. See **run**.

ranch *rănch*, or *-sh, n.* a farm, esp. one consisting of grassland used for raising cattle or horses.—*v.i.* to manage or work on a ranch.

ran'cher *n.* one employed in ranching.

rancid *ran'sid, adj.* tasting or smelling stale: *In hot weather, butter soon becomes rancid.*

rancid'ity, **ran'cidness** *ns.*

rancour *rang'kŭr, n.* bitter feeling, hatred and ill-will.

ran'corous *adj.* **ran'corously** *adv.*

rand *rand, n.* the standard coin of South Africa, worth 100 cents.

random *ran'dȯm, adj.* chance, haphazard: *They interviewed a random sample of teenagers.*

at random without any particular plan or system: *Choose any number at random.*

random access memory a computer memory in which data can be directly located.

randy *ran'di,* (*coll.*) *adj.* full of sexual desire:—*comp.* **ran'dier**; *superl.* **ran'diest.**

ran'diness *n.*

ranee. See **raj**.

rang. See **ring**[2].

range *rānj, v.t.* **1** to set in a row; to place (troops, etc.) in order. **2** to wander over: *The shepherd ranged the hills.*—*v.i.* **1** to extend: *His research ranges over a vast number of topics.* **2** to vary: *Your marks range from 10 to 90.* **3** to wander: *to range over the moors*:—*pr.p.* **ran'ging.**—*n.* **1** a line, series, group, esp. of mountains. **2** a variety: *the range of goods for sale.* **3** the distance over which an object can be sent or thrown, a sound can be heard, etc.: *What is the range of this missile?*; *Are we out of hearing-range of the house?* **4** a place where shooting, etc. is practised. **5** a kitchen stove with broad flat top.

ran'ger *n.* a keeper who looks after a forest or park.

ran'gy *adj.* long-legged and thin:—*comp.* **ran'gier**; *superl.* **ran'giest.**

range'-finder *n.* **1** an instrument for finding the range of a target. **2** a similar fitting attached to a camera.

rani. See **raj**.

rank[1] *rangk, n.* **1** a line or row: *The officer ordered the front rank to fire*; *the ranks of the unemployed*; *a taxi-rank.* **2** position, level: *He rose to the rank of General.* **3** (in *pl.*) private soldiers, or ordinary people.

4 (high) class or station in society.—*v.t.* **1** to put in order of importance: *Horses are usually ranked higher than donkeys.*—*v.i.* to have a place in a scale of importance: *Apes rank above dogs in intelligence.*

ran'ker *n.* a private soldier.

rank and file 1 private soldiers. **2** ordinary people.

rank² *rangk, adj.* **1** growing freely, coarsely: *rank weeds.* **2** (of a smell, etc.) stale or unpleasantly strong. **3** (used only before a noun) absolute; utter, extreme: *The race was won by a rank outsider; rank stupidity.*

rank'ly *adv.* **rank'ness** *n.*

rankle *rangk'l, v.i.* to cause annoyance or bitterness: *The unkind remark rankled in Mary's mind for days*:—*pr.p.* **rank'ling.**

ransack *ran'sak, v.t.* **1** to search thoroughly. **2** to plunder: *The army ransacked the conquered city.*

ransom *ran'som, n.* sum of money paid so that a captive may be set free.—*v.t.* to pay, demand, or accept ransom for.

hold to ransom to keep (someone) prisoner until money is paid for his release.

rant *rant, v.i.* **1** to talk long, angrily, and foolishly (about). **2** (of an actor) to speak a part too loudly and dramatically.

ran'ter *n.* **rant'ing** *n.* and *adj.*

rap¹ *rap, n.* **1** a sharp blow. **2** a sound made by knocking.—*v.t.* **1** to hit sharply. **2** (with *out*) to speak, utter, peremptorily.—*v.i.* to knock or tap:—*pr.p.* **rapp'ing**; *pa.p.* **rapped.**

rap² *rap, n.* a whit; the least bit: *It's not worth a rap.*

rapacious *ra-pā'shus, adj.* **1** greedy. **2** eager to seize as much as possible.

rapa'ciously *adv.*

rapa'ciousness, rapa'city *(-pa'si-ti), ns.*

rape¹ *rāp, v.t.* **1** to force (esp. a woman) to have sexual intercourse against her will. **2** to destroy, devastate (the countryside, etc.). **3** (*poetic*) to carry off by force:—*pr.p.* **rap'ing.**—*n.* the act of raping.

rap'ist *n.* a person who commits the crime of rape (*def. 1*).

rape² *rāp, n.* a plant like the turnip, with seeds yielding oil.

rapid *rap'id, adj.* quick, fast.

rapid'ity, rap'idness *ns.* **rap'idly** *adv.*

rap'ids *n.pl.* a part in a river where the current flows swiftly over sloping ground.

rapier *rā'pi-ėr, n.* a long thin sword for fencing.

rapine *rap'īn, n.* plunder.

rapport *ra-pör', n.* understanding and sympathy in a relationship.

rapscallion *rap-skal'yon, n.* a rascal.

rapt *rapt, adj.* lost in thought or wonder: *The children watched the puppets with rapt attention.*

rapture *rap'chur, n.* great delight.

rap'turous *adj.* **rap'turously** *adv.*

rare¹ *rār, adj.* (of meat) undercooked.

rare² *rār, adj.* **1** uncommon. **2** unusually good.

rarefied *rār'i-fīd, adj.* (of atmosphere, etc.) thin, sparse; refined.

rare'ly *adv.* **rare'ness** *n.*

rarity *rār'i-ti, n.* **1** the quality of being uncommon. **2** a rare, uncommon object:—*pl.* **rar'ities.**

Welsh rare'bit. See **Welsh.**

raring *rār'ing, adj.* very eager (for something, or to do something).

rarity. See **rare².**

rascal *räs'kal, n.* a rogue, scamp.

ras'cally *adj.* wicked, dishonest.

rase. See **raze.**

rash¹ *rash, adj.* **1** acting without thought. **2** too hasty, reckless: *That rash move will lose you the game.*

rash'ness *n.* **rash'ly** *adv.*

rash² *rash, n.* a redness, or outbreak of spots, on the skin.

rasher *rash'ėr, n.* a thin slice (of bacon).

rasp *räsp, n.* **1** a coarse file. **2** a grating sound.—*v.t.* **1** to scrape with a rasp. **2** to say in a grating voice.—*v.i.* to make a grating sound.

ras'ping *adj.* **ras'piness** *n.*

raspberry *räz'bėr-i, räs', n.* a red, juicy fruit, rather like a blackberry in shape:—*pl.* **rasp'berries.**

rasping. See **rasp.**

rat *rat, n.* a gnawing animal like the mouse, but larger.—*v.i.* **1** to hunt or catch rats. **2** (*coll.*; with *on*) to desert one's friends or fellow members of a group: *A good union member will not rat (on his fellow-strikers) during a strike*:—*pr.p.* **ratt'ing**; *pa.p.* **ratt'ed.**

ratt'er *n.* killer of rats: *This terrier is a good ratter.*

ratt'y *adj.* **1** of, or like, a rat. **2** (*slang*) angry:—*comp.* **ratt'ier**; *superl.* **ratt'iest.**

ratt'iness *n.*

rat race the fierce, never-ending struggle for success, wealth, etc.

smell a rat to suspect something.

ratable. See **rate.**

ratafia *rat-a-fē'a, n.* **1** a liqueur flavoured with almonds or fruit-kernels. **2** a biscuit or cake with this flavour.

ratan. See **rattan.**

ratatouille *rat-ȧ-tōō'i, n.* a stew of tomatoes, aubergines, peppers, etc.

ratchet *rach'it, n.* **1** a pawl (see this) and/or a ratchet-wheel. **2** a toothed bar.
rat'chet-wheel *n.* a toothed wheel used with a ratchet or catch which allows turning in one direction only.

rate[1] *rāt, n.* **1** standard of payment: *Some men are paid at a higher rate than others.* **2** speed: *Your rate of work is too slow.* **3** the number of occurrences of something over a given period; frequency: *What is the yearly accident rate in this factory?* **4** proportion, ratio: *There was a failure rate of one pupil in ten in the exam.* **5** (usu. in *pl.*) a tax paid yearly by owners of property to provide money for local public services: *the water rate.* **6** (as part of a word) class, quality: *a first- (second-, third-) rate film.*—*v.t.* **1** to put a value on for purposes of such taxation. **2** to value: *I rate this book highly.*—*v.i.* **1** to be classed (as). **2** to rank: *How does a physiotherapist rate compared with a nurse?*:—*pr.p.* **rat'ing.**
rat(e)'able *adj.*: **rat(e)able value** a value placed on a property and used to assess the amount of rates payable to the local government each year.
rat'ing *n.* **1** fixing of rates. **2** grade or position. **3** a sailor below the rank of commissioned officer. **4** (usu. in *pl.*) an estimate of the size of the audience for a television or radio programme, as an indicator of its popularity.
rate'-capping *n.* the upper limit on the rates that can be levied by a local authority.
rate'payer *n.* one who pays rates.
at any rate at least; in spite of that.

rate[2] *rāt, (old) v.t.* to scold:—*pr.p.* **rat'ing.**
rat'ing *n.* a scolding.

rather *rä'THėr, adv.* **1** (esp. with *than*) more willingly; preferably; in preference to: *I would rather walk than cycle*; *I'll have tea rather than coffee*; *Rather than wait, go now*; *I would/had rather you didn't make that noise*; *'Are you coming?' 'I'd rather not'.* **2** (sometimes with *than*) more correctly speaking: *He agreed, or rather he did not say 'No'*; *It's a pamphlet rather than a book.* **3** to some extent; fairly, quite: *He looks rather nice.*—*interj. (rä-THûr')* certainly: *Would you like to go to the match? Rather!*

ratify *rat'i-fī, v.t.* to agree to, to approve: *Parliament ratified the treaty*:—*pr.p.* **rat'ifying;** *pa.p.* **rat'ified.**
ratificā'tion *n.*

rating. See **rate**[1,2].

ratio *rā'shi-ō, n.* the proportion of one thing to another: *There is a ratio of 10 girls to 11 boys in the school*:—*pl.* **ra'tios.**
ration *ra'sh(ȯ)n, n.* **1** a fixed allowance or portion: *In wartime each person had a ration of butter.* **2** (in *pl.*) food for the day, esp. of soldiers.—*v.t.* to share (out) in fair portions.

rational *ra'shȯn-ȧl, adj.* **1** having or using reason: *Man is a rational animal.* **2** reasonable, logical: *That is a rational idea, explanation*:—*opp.* **irra'tional.**
rationale *ra-shȯn-äl', n.* the principle that explains a particular policy, series of actions, etc.
ra'tionalise *v.t.* **1** to invent a reasonable and creditable explanation of (a feeling or action) so as not to feel guilty about it. **2** to interpret in a way that seems to oneself reasonable, acceptable, etc. **3** to organise work in (e.g. an industry, a department) so as to make it efficient and economical.—Also *v.i.*:—*pr.p.* **ra'tionalising.**
rationalisā'tion *n.*
ra'tionalist *n.* a person who thinks that human reason is the only guide to truth.
ra'tionalism *n.*
rational'ity *n.*
ra'tionally *adv.* **ra'tionalness** *n.*

ratlin(e), ratling *rat'lin, n.* one of the small lines or ropes forming steps in the rigging of ships.

rattan, ratan *ra-tan', n.* **1** a tall thin palm tree. **2** a cane made from this.

rat-tat *rat'tat', n.* a knocking sound.

rattle *rat'l, v.i.* **1** to make a series of short sharp noises by knocking together; to clatter. **2** to move quickly (and noisily). **3** to chatter (with *away, on*).—*v.t.* **1** to cause to rattle. **2** (*coll.*) to confuse, upset: *Don't let his aggressive manner rattle you*:—*pr.p.* **ratt'ling.**—*n.* **1** the sound made by things knocking together: *the rattle of cups.* **2** a child's toy, or a percussion instrument, that makes this noise when shaken. **3** (usu. **death'-rattle**) a sound in the throat of a dying person. **4** the bony rings of a rattlesnake's tail.
ratt'ling *adj.* **1** lively, vigorous. **2** that rattles.—*adv.* (*coll.*; *old*) really, very: *a rattling good story.*
ratt'lesnake *n.* a poisonous American snake with rattling bony rings on the tail (also **ratt'ler**).
rattle off to recite, perform, enumerate, etc. at great speed.

ratty. See **rat.**

raucous *rö'kus, adj.* hoarse, harsh: *the raucous cry of the crow.*
rau'cously *adv.* **rau'cousness** *n.*

ravage *rav'ij, v.t.* to lay waste, plunder: *The enemy ravaged the country:—pr.p.* **rav'-aging**.
rav'ager *n.* **rav'aging** *n.* and *adj.*
rav'ages *n.pl.* damaging effects, of e.g. war, time.

rave *rāv, v.i.* **1** to rage. **2** to talk as if mad or over-excited. **3** (*coll.*) to talk enthusiastically: *His fans are raving over his latest album:—pr.p.* **rav'ing.**—*adj.* (*coll.*; of a review, etc.) highly enthusiastic.
rav'ing *n.* wild talk.—*adj.* inclined to, or causing others to, rave: *a raving lunatic*; *a raving beauty.*—Also *adv.*: *He's raving mad.*
rave'-up (*slang*) *n.* a wildly successful party, etc.

ravel *rav'l, v.t.* and *v.i.* to tangle:—*pr.p.* **rav'elling**; *pa.p.* **rav'elled**.
See also **unravel**.

raven *rā'vn, n.* a large black glossy bird related to the crows.—*adj.* (of hair) glossy black.

rav'enous *rav'i-nus, adj.* very hungry.
rav'ening (*poetic*) *adj.* seeking for prey.
rav'enously *adv.* **rav'enousness** *n.*

ravine *rȧv-ēn', n.* a deep, narrow valley.

raving. See **rave**.

ravioli *rav'i-ō'li, n.* small envelopes of pasta containing minced meat.

ravish *rav'ish, v.t.* **1** to rape. **2** to plunder (e.g. country). **3** to delight, enrapture.
rav'isher *n.*
rav'ishing *adj.* very beautiful.

raw *rö, adj.* **1** not cooked or prepared. **2** in the natural state: *raw cotton.* **3** having the skin rubbed and sore: *These new shoes have made my heels raw.* **4** untrained, inexperienced: *raw recruits.* **5** (of weather) chilly and damp.
raw'ness *n.*
raw'boned *adj.* thin, gaunt.
raw'hide *adj.* of untanned leather.
raw material material, esp. in its natural state, from which something is manufactured or developed.
a raw deal harsh or unfair treatment.
in the raw in its natural state; naked.

ray[1] *rā, n.* **1** a narrow beam of light, heat, etc. or a stream of subatomic particles. **2** a gleam (of hope, etc.). **3** one of a group of lines going outwards from a centre. **4** fringed outer part of a flower cluster.
See also **radial**.

ray[2] *rā, n.* a type of flat-bodied fish, often with whiplike stinging tail.

rayon *rā'on, n.* artificial silk.

raze, rase *rāz, v.t.* to demolish, knock down, lay flat: *The old factory has been razed to the ground:—pr.p.* **raz'ing, ras'ing**.

razor *rā'zȯr, n.* a sharp-edged instrument for shaving esp. the face.
ra'zorbill *n.* a bird, a kind of auk, with a sharp-edged bill.
ra'zor-blade *n.* sharp blade for shaving.
ra'zor-edge *n.* **1** a very fine sharp edge. **2** a critically-balanced situation.
ra'zor-sharp' *adj.* **1** very sharp. **2** incisive.

razzle *raz'l, n.*: **on the razzle** having a spree.

razzmatazz *raz'mȧ-taz',* **razzamatazz** *raz'ȧ-,* (*coll.*) *ns.* flamboyant bustle or activity.

re *rē, prep.* in the matter of.

re- *rē-, pfx.* again.

reach[1] *rēch, v.t.* **1** to arrive at. **2** to stretch, extend, or go, as far as: *The noise reached our ears.* **3** to touch or get hold of (something) by stretching: *Can you reach the switch?* **4** to manage to contact: *You could reach me by phoning my neighbour.*—*v.i.* **1** to stretch out the hand (for something). **2** to stretch, extend.—*n.* **1** extent of stretch: *He has a long reach*; *out of the children's reach.* **2** distance that can be covered easily: *within reach of home.* **3** part of a stream, etc. between bends.

react *ri-akt', v.i.* **1** to act, behave, feel, think, etc. in response to something. **2** to undergo chemical change by action with another substance: *Iron reacts with acid.* **3** (with *against*) to show resistance to: *Children react against parental discipline as they get older.*
reac'tion *n.* **1** behaviour as the result of an action or a stimulus. **2** a (usu. adverse) response to a drug, etc.: *an allergic reaction.* **3** a (desire for a) return towards a former state, esp. to less free political conditions. **4** a reversal of (esp. public) opinion. **5** a chemical change. **6** a change within the nucleus of an atom.
reac'tionary *adj., n.* (in politics, etc., a person) favouring a return to things as they were, or opposed to change and progress:—*pl.* **reac'tionaries**.
reagent *rē-ā'jėnt, n.* a substance with characteristic reactions, used in chemical tests.
nuclear reactor. See **nucleus**.

read *rēd, v.t.* **1** to look over and understand, in silence or speaking aloud, (written or printed words, books, letters, etc.). **2** to look at and understand or interpret (signs, or signs on): *to read music, a thermometer.* **3** to show, record: *The thermometer reads 38°.* **4** to study (a subject) at university: *She's reading biology at Cambridge.* **5** (*computers*) to take in and process (data) as required.—*v.i.* **1** to pass one's time in reading. **2** to be written or worded in a particular way: *His letter reads as follows*:—*pa.t.* and *pa.p.* **read** *(red).*—*n.* an act of reading.

read'able *(rēd') adj.* **1** distinct enough to be read. **2** quite interesting to read.

readabil'ity, **read'ableness** *ns.*

read'er *n.* **1** one who reads. **2** a higher grade of university lecturer. **3** a proof corrector. **4** one who reads and reports on manuscripts for a publisher. **5** one who reads the particular newspaper, magazine, author, etc. already mentioned. **6** a reading-book (usu. for schools). **7** a machine for producing an enlarged image of a microfilm, etc., readable by the naked eye.

read'ership *n.* **1** the (number of) readers of a magazine, newspaper, etc. **2** the position of reader at a university.

read'ing *adj.* **1** interested in reading. **2** (as part of a word) used for reading: *reading-desk*, *lamp*; or for learning to read: *reading-book*.—*n.* **1** the action of the verb **read**. **2** literary study. **3** a public recital: *a poetry reading*. **4** an interpretation, meaning, given to something: *an actor's reading of a part*. **5** a version of part of a text, etc.: *There are three different readings for this passage*. **6** the figure indicated on an instrument such as a thermometer. **7** any of the three stages through which a bill must pass in Parliament before it is accepted.

read between the lines to see a hidden meaning.

read only memory (*computers*) a memory device that can only be read, not written to.

take as read to assume (something) without checking.

See also **misread**.

readdress *rē-ȧ-dres'*, *v.t.* to change the address on.

readily, **readiness**. See **ready**.

reading. See **read**.

readjust *rē-ȧ-just'*, *v.t.* to put in order again, or arrange in a new way.

readjust'ment *n.*

readmit *rē-ȧd-mit'*, *v.t.* to admit again:—*pr.p.* **readmitt'ing**; *pa.p.* **readmitt'ed**.

readmiss'ion, **readmitt'ance** *ns.*

ready *red'i*, *adj.* **1** prepared. **2** at hand. **3** willing. **4** quick to act:—*comp.* **read'ier**; *superl.* **read'iest**.

read'ily *adv.* **read'iness** *n.*

read'y-made' *adj.* **1** (of e.g. clothes) made for anyone who will buy, not made to order to a particular person. **2** not original.

ready money money at hand, cash.

ready reckoner a book of tables giving answers to calculations required in ordinary business.

at the ready ready for action or use.

in readiness **1** ready, prepared. **2** as a preparation (for).

reagent. See **react**.

real *rē'ȧl*, *adj.* **1** actually existing. **2** sincere; genuine: *a real love of literature*. **3** not imitation: *real leather*. **4** true, actual: *He may own the business, but his wife is the real boss*. **5** undoubted: *a real help*.

rē'alise *v.t.* **1** to come to understand: *I realise you did not mean it*. **2** (used in *pass.*) to make real: *His fears* (i.e. the things he feared) *were realised*. **3** to achieve: *He realised his ambition*. **4** to turn (shares, assets) into actual money. **5** to make, obtain: *He realised £20 000 on the sale of his house*:—*pr.p.* **rē'alising**.

realisā'tion *n.*

rē'alism *n.* **1** the habit of taking a practical view of life. **2** (in art or literature) the representation of life, etc., as it is in reality.

rē'alist *n.* one who believes in realism.

realis'tic *adj.* **1** showing, dealing with, things as they are in reality. **2** taking a practical view.

realis'tically *adv.*

reality *rē-al'i-ti*, *n.* **1** the state of actually existing. **2** the actual state of things: *He says he's ill—in reality he's just lazy*. **3** what actually exists. **4** that which is true, a fact:—*pl.* **real'ities**.

re'ally *adv.* **1** in reality. **2** very.—*interj.* expressing surprise, protest, doubt, etc.

real'ness *n.*

Realtor®, **realtor** *rē'ȧl-tör*, (*U.S.*) *n.* an estate agent.

real estate (the buying and selling of) land and houses.

realign *rē-ȧ-līn'*, *v.t.* **1** to put back in line, straighten. **2** to group together (political parties, etc.) differently (also *v.i.*).

realise, **reality**, etc. See **real**.

realm *relm*, *n.* **1** a kingdom. **2** a part of life or action: *the realm of sport*.

realtor. See **real**.

ream *rēm*, *n.* **1** 20 quires (usu. 480 sheets; also 500 sheets, or 516 sheets). **2** (in *pl.*; *coll.*) large quantities.

reanimate *rē-an'i-māt*, *v.t.* **1** to restore to life. **2** to put new life or spirit into:—*pr.p.* **rean'imating**.

reanimā'tion *n.*

reap *v.t.* **1** to cut down (crops). **2** to obtain (an advantage or reward).

reap'er *n.* a person or machine that reaps.

reappear *rē-ȧ-pēr'*, *v.i.* to appear again.
reappear'ance *n.*

rear[1] *rēr*, *n.* **1** the back part. **2** a position behind. **3** (*coll.*) the buttocks.
rear'most *adj.* last.
rear'ward *adj.*, *adv.* towards, or in, the rear.
rear'wards *adv.*
rear admiral (a person of) a high rank in the navy.
rear'guard *n.* troops protecting the rear of the main army.
rear-view mirror a mirror which reflects the vehicles behind (a car or motorbike).
bring up the rear to come last.

rear[2] *rēr*, *v.t.* **1** to raise. **2** to set up. **3** to bring up (e.g. a child).—*v.i.* to rise on the hindlegs.

rearm *rē'ärm'*, *v.t.* to arm again, esp. with modern weapons.—Also *v.i.*
rearm'ament *n.*

rearrange *rē-ȧ-rānj*, *v.t.* to arrange differently, adjust:—*pr.p.* **rearran'ging**.

reason *rē'zn*, *n.* **1** cause. **2** excuse or explanation. **3** the mind's power to think and to form opinions and judgements. **4** common sense.—*v.i.* **1** to use one's reason. **2** to argue (also *v.t.*).—*v.t.* (usu. with *out*) to think out clearly.
rea'sonable *adj.* **1** sensible. **2** moderate. **3** fair. **4** not expensive.
rea'sonably *adv.* **rea'sonableness** *n.*
rea'soning *n.* **1** the act of using the reason, of thinking things out. **2** argument, line of thought.
by reason of because of.
listen to reason to allow oneself to be persuaded to take a sensible view.
lose one's reason to go mad.
see reason to change to more sensible view.
within reason within limits of common sense.

reassemble *rē-ȧ-sem'bl*, *v.t.* and *v.i.* to put, or come, together again:—*pr.p.* **reassemb'ling**.

reassure *rē-ȧ-shoo͞r'*, *v.t.* to take away doubts or fears from (a person):—*pr.p.* **reassur'ing**.
reassur'ance *n.* **reassur'ing** *adj.*

rebate *rē'bāt*, *n.* discount; money repaid to the payer (esp. of a tax).

rebel *reb'(ė)l*, *n.* one who rebels.—*v.i.* (*ri-bel'*) to oppose someone in authority (esp. to oppose a government with force):—*pr.p.* **rebell'ing**; *pa.p.* **rebelled'**.
rebell'ion (*-bel'yȯn*) *n.* **1** revolt on a large scale, uprising against authority. **2** refusal to obey.
rebell'ious (*-bel'yůs*) *adj.* **1** rebelling or inclined to rebel. **2** like that of a rebel: *in a rebellious mood.*
rebell'iously *adv.* **rebell'iousness** *n.*

rebind *rē'bīnd'*, *v.t.* to put new binding on:—*pa.t.* and *pa.p.* **re'bound'**.

rebound[1] *ri-bownd'*, *v.i.* to bounce or spring back.—*n.* (*rē'*) act of rebounding: *to catch a ball on the rebound.*

rebound[2]. See **rebind**.

rebuff *ri-buf'*, *n.* **1** a refusal. **2** a snub.—*v.t.* **1** to snub. **2** to refuse, reject.

rebuke *ri-būk'*, *v.t.* to scold, reprove sternly:—*pr.p.* **rebuk'ing**.—*n.* a reproach, scolding.

rebut *ri-but'*, *v.t.* to produce evidence, or arguments, showing the falseness of (something said): *to rebut an accusation*:—*pr.p.* **rebutt'ing**; *pa.p.* **rebutt'ed**.
rebutt'al *n.*

recalcitrant *ri-kal'si-trȧnt*, *adj.*, *n.* (a person who is) obstinate, or disobedient to authority.
recal'citrance *n.*

recall *ri-köl'*, *v.t.* **1** to call back. **2** to remember.—*n.* (*rē'*) the act of recalling.

recant *ri-kant'*, *v.i.* **1** to take back what one has said. **2** to renounce publicly one's former religious or political beliefs.—Also *v.t.*
recantā'tion *n.* act of recanting.

recapitulate *rē-kȧ-pit'ū-lāt*, *v.t.* to go over again the chief points of (e.g. a statement, an argument).—Also *v.i.*:—*pr.p.* **recapit'ulating**:—*abbrev.* **re'cap**:—*pr.p.* **re'capping**; *pa.p.* **re'capped**.
recapitula'tion *n.*:—*abbrev.* **re'cap**.

recapture *rē-kap'chůr*, *v.t.* to capture back, retake, regain:—*pr.p.* **recap'turing**.—*n.* act of retaking.

recast *rē'käst'*, *v.t.* to cast or shape anew:—*pa.t.* and *pa.p.* **recast'**.

recce *rek'i*, *n.*, *v.i.*, coll. abbrev. for **reconnaissance**, and **reconnoitre**:—*pr.p.* **recc'ēing**; *pa.p.* **recc'ēd**.

recede *ri-sēd'*, *v.i.* to go or move back: *When the rain stopped, the floods receded*: *pr.p.* **reced'ing**.
reced'ing *adj.* sloping backwards: *a receding chin.*
See also **recess**, **recession**.

receipt. See **receive**.

receive *ri-sēv'*, *v.t.* **1** to get or be given: *to receive a present, a letter, thanks, praise, a shock.* **2** to meet or welcome (e.g. guests), or to give a formal audience to: *The Pope received the pilgrims.* **3** to accept and pay for (stolen goods), esp. with the intention of reselling them. **4** to be acted upon by, and transform (electrical signals) (also *v.i.*):—*pr.p.* **receiv'ing**.

received' *adj.* (of e.g. an opinion) generally accepted.

receiv'er *n.* **1** a person or thing that receives. **2** one who accepts goods knowing them to be stolen. **3** an apparatus for receiving radio or television signals. **4** the part of a telephone through which messages are received.

receipt *ri-sēt'*, *n.* **1** act of receiving. **2** a written acknowledgment of anything received. **3** (*old*) a recipe. **4** (in *pl.*) amount of money received, esp. in business: *Our receipts are higher this year.*—*v.t.* to mark as paid: *to receipt a bill.*

See also **recipient**, **receptacle**.

recent *rē'sėnt*, *adj.* happening, done, made, etc., a short time ago.

re'cency, **re'centness** *ns.*

re'cently *adv.*

receptacle *ri-sep'tȧ-kl*, *n.* an object in which anything may be received or contained: *a receptacle for rubbish.*

reception *ri-sep'sh(ȯ)n*, *n.* **1** the act of receiving or being received. **2** a welcome: *a warm reception.* **3** a party where guests are received formally: *a wedding reception.* **4** the part of a hotel, hospital, office, etc., where callers are received. **5** (*radio*) the quality of signals: *The reception seems poor tonight.*

recep'tionist *n.* a person employed, in an office, hotel, hospital, etc. to receive callers, guests, patients, etc.

recep'tive *adj.* (of person, mind) quick to take in and accept ideas, etc.

recep'tiveness, **receptiv'ity** *ns.*

recess *ri-ses'*, or *rē'ses*, *n.* **1** a place set back in a wall, an alcove. **2** a short stop in work (e.g. of law court, school). **3** a holiday (esp. of Parliament). **4** (in *pl.*) inner parts.

recession *ri-sesh'(ȯ)n*, *n.* **1** act of receding or going back. **2** a temporary decline in trade, etc.

recess'ive *adj.* (of genes) not dominant; less likely to be passed on to a child.

in recess (of Parliament) on holiday.

recherché *rė-sher'shā*, *adj.* rare; exotic; obscure.

recidivism *ri-sid'i-vizm*, *n.* the habit of relapsing into crime.

recid'ivist *n.* one who does this.

recipe *res'i-pi*, *n.* **1** a set of directions for making something to be cooked. **2** (*humorous*) a formula (for success, etc.).

recipient *ri-sip'i-ėnt*, *n.* one who receives.

reciprocal *ri-sip'rȯ-k(ȧ)l*, *adj.* given and received, shared, mutual: *reciprocal affection*; *reciprocal aid.*—*n.* (*mathematics*) the number by which another must be multiplied to produce 1.

recip'rocally *adv.*

reciprocity *res-i-pros'i-ti*, *n.* state of being reciprocal or mutual.

reciprocate *ri-sip'rȯ-kāt*, *v.t.* **1** to feel in return: *Jones reciprocates Lewis's dislike of him.* **2** to repay in the same way: *A good turn deserves to be reciprocated.*—*v.i.* **1** to make a return for something done, given, etc. **2** (of part of a machine) to move backwards and forwards in a straight line:—*pr.p.* **recip'rocating**.

reciprocā'tion *n.* act of reciprocating.

recite *ri-sīt'*, *v.t.* **1** to repeat from memory. **2** to list tediously and repetitiously: *He loved to recite his grievances*:—*pr.p.* **recit'ing**.

recīt'al *n.* **1** act of reciting. **2** a public performance, e.g. of music.

recitation *res-i-tā'sh(ȯ)n*, *n.* **1** a poem, etc. for repeating from memory. **2** the act of repeating it.

recitative *res-i-tȧ-tēv'*, *n.* a style of song resembling speech (from It. *recitativo*).

reckless *rek'lės*, *adj.* careless, very rash.

reck'lessly *adv.* **reck'lessness** *n.*

reckon *rek'(ȯ)n*, *v.t.* **1** to count. **2** to consider; to think, believe.—*v.i.* to calculate.

reck'oner *n.*

reck'oning *n.* **1** calculation. **2** a bill.

day of reckoning the day for settling accounts, or for paying for one's sins or mistakes.

reckon on to rely on, base one's plans on.

reckon with to allow for, take into consideration (a person, his actions, a possibility or probability, etc.).

reclaim *ri-klām'*, *v.t.* **1** to win (someone) back from wrong behaviour, beliefs, etc. **2** to make (land) fit for use, or to recover (land) from under water by draining it. **3** to obtain from waste material. **4** *(rē-klām')* to claim back.

reclaim'able *adj.*

reclamation *rek-lȧ-mā'sh(ȯ)n*, *n.*

recline *ri-klīn'*, *v.i.* to lean or lie on back or side:—*pr.p.* **reclin'ing**.

reclin'ing *adj.* **1** leaning or lying back. **2** (of a chair) that can be lowered towards a horizontal position.

recluse *ri-kloo͞s'*, *n.* one who lives alone and shuns company e.g. for religious reasons.

recognise *rek'ȯg-nīz*, *v.t.* **1** to know again. **2** to acknowledge, admit: *All recognised his skill.* **3** to show appreciation of: *They* *recognised the boy's courage by presenting him with a suitable gift*:—*pr.p.* **rec'ognising.**

recognis'able *adj.*

recognisance *ri-kog'ni-zȧns, n.* a legal promise to do something, made before a magistrate, or the sum pledged as surety for this.

recognition *rek-ȯg-nish'(ȯ)n, n.* **1** act or sign of recognising. **2** acknowledgment.

recoil *ri-koil', v.i.* **1** to shrink back. **2** (of a gun when fired) to jump back.—*n.* (or *rē'koil*) a rebound, sudden jumping back.

recollect *rek-ȯl-ekt', v.t.* **1** to remember. **2** (with *oneself*) to recover composure, collect one's thoughts.

recollec'tion *n.* **1** the act or power of recollecting. **2** a thing remembered.

recommend *rek-ȯ-mend', v.t.* **1** to advise. **2** to praise as being worth having, eating, etc.: *I can recommend these cakes.* **3** to render acceptable or desirable: *The job has a lot to recommend it.*

recommend'able *adj.*

recommendā'tion *n.*

recompense *rek'ȯm-pens, v.t.* to repay or reward (a person), or to make up to (him) for loss:—*pr.p.* **rec'ompensing.**—*n.* **1** reward. **2** something to make up for injury or loss.

reconcile *rek'ȯn-sīl, v.t.* **1** to bring or restore (enemies) to friendship. **2** to make (someone) accept a situation, etc. patiently (with *to*): *This reconciled me, I reconciled myself, to the loss.* **3** to bring (e.g. different aims, points of view) into agreement: *How do you reconcile the charging of such high rents with your social principles?* **4** to show that (e.g. two statements) are not contradictory. **5** to settle (e.g. a quarrel):—*pr.p.* **rec'onciling.**

reconciliā'tion *(-sil-) n.*

See also **irreconcilable.**

recondite *rė-kon'dīt, adj.* obscure.

recondition *rē-kȯn-dish'(ȯ)n, v.t.* to restore to good condition.

reconnaissance *ri-kon'i-sȧns, n.* a cautious exploring to obtain information before e.g. a battle.

reconnoitre *rek-ȯ-noi'tėr, v.t.* and *v.i.* to explore or examine before a battle or similar action:—*pr.p.* **reconnoi'tring** *(-tėr-)*; *pa.p., pa.t.* **reconnoi'tred** *(-tėrd)*.

reconsider *rē-kȯn-sid'ėr, v.t.* **1** to consider again with a view to altering: *Will you not reconsider your decision to go?* **2** to alter (a decision).

reconsiderā'tion *n.*

reconstitute *rē-kon'sti-tūt, v.t.* **1** to restore to its original form: *The dried milk must be reconstituted before use.* **2** to form, make up, in a different way:—*pr.p.* **recon'stituting.**

reconstitu'tion *n.*

reconstruct *rē-kȯn-strukt', v.t.* **1** to rebuild. **2** to piece together in imagination: *Let us try to reconstruct the crime.*

reconstruc'tion *n.*

record *ri-körd', v.t.* **1** to set down in writing for future use. **2** (of instrument) to show as reading: *Yesterday the thermometer recorded 30°C., 86°F.* **3** to register, show in required form: *You will be issued with a ballot-paper on which to record your vote.* **4** to put (sounds or images) on to a disc or tape from which they can later be reproduced (also *v.i.*). **5** to perform (a song, etc.) before a recording instrument.—*n. (rek'örd).* **1** (often in *pl.*) a written report of facts or events: *The records of a society.* **2** an event or performance that has never been equalled: *John holds the school record for the mile.* **3** a reputation based on past evidence: *The school has a good academic record*; *The thief already had a criminal record.* **4** a disc on which sounds are recorded.

record'er *n.* **1** one who records. **2** a judge in certain courts. **3** a musical instrument, a wooden or plastic pipe blown through a hole at one end.

record'ing *n.* (the process of making) a copy of sounds or images on disc or tape for future reproduction.

recorded delivery a service of the Post Office by which a record is kept of the collection and delivery of a letter, etc.

record office a place where public records (i.e. documents dealing with births, marriages, deaths, etc.) are kept.

rec'ord-player *n.* a gramophone worked by electricity, not an earlier type, usu. portable.

beat, break, the record to do better than any previous performance.

for the record so as to get the facts straight.

off the record (of information given) not to be published.

recount[1] *rē'kownt', v.t.* to count over again.—*n. (rē'kownt)* a second count: *Sometimes in an election there has to be a recount of votes.*

recount[2] *ri-kownt', v.t.* to tell, narrate, in detail: *He recounted his adventures.*

recoup *ri-ko͞op', v.t.* to make good (losses), recover (expenses).

recourse *ri-kōrs', -körs', n.*: **have recourse to** to turn to for help in emergency.

recover[1], **re-cover** *rē'kuv'ėr*, *v.t.* to cover again.

recover[2] *ri-kuv'ėr*, *v.t.* **1** to get or find again. **2** to regain control of (oneself): *The actor forgot a line, but quickly recovered himself.* **3** to obtain as compensation: *He recovered the cost of the repairs from the insurance company.*—*v.i.* to regain health or position.
recov'erable *adj.* able to be regained: —*opp.* **irrecov'erable.**
recov'ery *n.* **1** act of recovering. **2** a return to former state e.g. of health:—*pl.* **recov'eries.**

recreate *rē'krė-āt'*, *v.t.* to create again, esp. in the mind: *Try to recreate the scene*:—*pr.p.* **recreat'ing.**
recreā'tion *n.*

recreation[1] *rek-ri-ā'sh(ȯ)n*, *n.* a pleasant activity, sport, amusement, etc., pursued out of working hours.
recreā'tional *adj.*

recreation[2]. See **recreate.**

recriminā'tion *ri-krim'i-nā'sh(ȯ)n*, *n.* (usu. in *pl.*) blaming and accusing of one another.
recrim'inatory *adj.*

recrudescence *rēk-rōōd-es'ns*, *n.* breaking out afresh into activity, etc.: *a recrudescence of violence.*

recruit *ri-krōōt'*, *n.* a newly enlisted soldier or member.—*v.t.* **1** to enlist (new soldiers, members, etc) (also *v.i.*). **2** to renew or restore (strength, etc.).
recruit'er *n.* **recruit'ment** *n.*

rect(i)- *rek-t(i)-*, (as part of a word) right, straight.
rectangle *rek'tang-gl*, *-tang'*, *n.* a four-sided figure with opposite sides equal and all angles right angles.
rectang'ular *adj.* **1** of the form of a rectangle. **2** having right angles or a right angle.
rectify *rek'ti-fī*, *v.t.* **1** to put right. **2** (*chemistry*) to purify (a liquid) by distilling. **3** to change (an electric current) from alternating to direct:—*pr.p.* **rec'tifying**; *pa.p.* **rec'tified.**
rec'tifiable *adj.* **rectificā'tion** *(-fi-) n.*
rec'tifier *n.* an apparatus that changes an alternating current into a direct current.
rectilinear *rek-ti-lin'i-ȧr*, *adj.* made up of, having, straight lines.
rectitude *rek'ti-tūd*, *n.* honesty of character; uprightness.

rector *rek'tȯr*, *n.* **1** (Church of England, etc.) a clergyman in charge of a parish. **2** (esp. in Scotland) the headmaster of some secondary schools. **3** the head of some colleges. **4** the elected honorary head of a Scottish university.
rector'ial *(-tōr'*, *-tör') adj.* of a rector.—*n.* an election of a university rector.
rec'tory *n.* the house in which a Church of English, etc. rector lives:—*pl.* **rec'tories.**

rectum *rek'tu̇m*, *n.* the lowest part of the alimentary canal, ending in the anus.

recumbent *ri-kum'bėnt*, *adj.* lying down.

recuperate *ri-kū'pėr-at*, *v.t.*, *v.i.*, to recover:—*pr.p.* **recu'perating.**
recuperā'tion *n.*
recu'perative *adj.* helping recovery.

recur *ri-kûr'*, *v.i.* **1** to occur again, to come back. **2** (*mathematics*; of a decimal figure) to be repeated indefinitely:—*pr.p.* **recurr'ing**; *pa.p.* **recurred'.**
recurr'ence *n.* another occurence, a happening again: *He had a recurrence of his illness.*
recurr'ent *adj.* returning at intervals.

recycle *rē-sī'kl*, *v.t.* to put (waste materials) through a manufacturing process by which they can be reused:—*pr.p.* **recyc'ling.**

red *red*, *adj.* **1** of a colour like blood. **2** (of hair) of a colour varying from golden-brown to reddish-brown. **3** revolutionary. **4** communist:—*comp.* **redd'er**; *superl.* **redd'est.**—Also *n.*
redd'en *v.t.*, *v.i.* to make, or grow, red.
redd'ish *adj.* like, or tinged with, red.
red'ness *n.*
red admiral a common butterfly with an orange-red band across each forewing.
red'-blood'ed *adj.* strong, lusty, virile.
red'breast *n.* the robin.
red'brick' *adj.* applied to the more recent type of English university as opp. to Oxford and Cambridge.
red carpet that laid down for royal personages to tread on, hence a symbol of lavish ceremonial treatment.
red'coat (*history*) *n.* a British soldier.
red'curr'ant *n.* a shrub related to the gooseberry, with a small red berry.
red flag **1** a danger signal. **2** (*caps.*) a communist and socialist song.
red'-hand'ed *adv.* in the act of doing wrong: *The police caught the thief red-handed.*
red'head *n.* a person with red hair.
red herring **1** a cured herring. **2** in a discussion, something mentioned to take attention off the subject (as a herring would put hounds off the scent they were following). **3** a false clue.
red'-hot' *adj.* **1** heated so as to glow red. **2** very keen, enthusiastic.
Red Indian (*usu. offensive*) a Native American, *esp.* of N. America.
red lead an oxide of lead used in paint-

making.

red-lett'er day a happy, memorable day, from the old custom of marking holidays etc. in red in calendars.

red light 1 a signal to stop. **2** a danger signal.

red'skin *n.* (*offensive*) a Native American.

red tape 1 the tape (usu. of a dark pink colour) used in legal or government offices to secure bundles of documents. **2** unnecessary rules about how things should be done, obstructive bureaucracy.

red'wood *n.* an American timber tree of great height.

in the red in debt.

see red to become very angry.

the Red Army the army of the former USSR.

the Red Cross a world-wide organisation that helps people wounded, homeless, etc. in time of war or disaster.

redeem *ri-dēm'*, *v.t.* **1** to buy back (something that has been pawned). **2** to rescue, get back, by paying a ransom. **3** (of Jesus Christ) to save (sinners) from punishment through the sacrifice of his own life. **4** to fulfil (a promise). **5** to make up for: *He redeemed his lateness by hard work.*

redeem'able *adj.*:—*opp.* **irredeemable**.

redeem'er *n.*

redeem'ing *adj.* making up for bad qualities: *The house is ugly, but its position on the hill is a redeeming feature.*

redemption *ri-dem(p)'sh(ȯ)n*, *n.* **1** act of redeeming. **2** salvation. **3** improvement. **4** atonement.

redeploy *rē-di-ploi'*, *v.t.* to move (soldiers, staff, etc.) to another area where they will be more effective.

redeploy'ment *n.*

red-handed, **redhead**. See **red**.

redirect *rē-di-rekt'*, *dī-*, *v.t.* to direct again, esp. to put a new address on (a letter).

redolent *red'ȯ-lėnt*, *adj.* **1** fragrant. **2** smelling (of): *The room was redolent of tobacco.*

red'olence *n.*

redouble *ri-dub'l*, *v.t.* and *v.i.* **1** to make twice as great, increase: *He redoubled his efforts.* **2** (*bridge*; *rē'dub'l*) to double (a bid already doubled):—*pr.p.* **redoubling**.

redoubt *ri-dowt'*, *n.* an outlying fortification, e.g. on a hill, or one built within a stronghold for use as a last retreat.

redoubtable *re-dowt'ȧ-bl*, *adj.* (of person) bold, arousing fear, awe, or respect.

redound *ri-downd'*, *v.i.* to have the result of adding (to): *This action will redound to his credit, advantage.*

redraft *rē'dräft'*, *n.* a new draft or copy.—Also *v.t.*

redress *ri-dres'*, *v.t.* to set right, or make up for (e.g. a wrong).—*n.* **1** the act of redressing; corrective measures. **2** compensation: *He is seeking redress for his abrupt dismissal from the company.*

redress the balance to make things more equal again.

redskin. See **red**.

reduce *ri-dūs'*, *v.t.* **1** to make smaller or less: *The train reduced speed*; *The strikers reduced their demands.* **2** to bring (someone or something) down (to a lesser, or worse, state): *Reduce your ideas to some kind of order*; *The bombs reduced the town to ruins*; *She was reduced to tears*; *The officer was reduced* (*i.e.* demoted) *to the ranks.* **3** to weaken.—*v.i.* to slim:—*pr.p.* **reduc'ing**.

reduced' *adj.* **1** made less. **2** weakened. **3** poor: *In reduced circumstances.*

reduc'ible *adj.* able to be reduced:—*opp.* **irreduc'ible**.

reduction *ri-duk'sh(ȯ)n*, *n.* **1** act of reducing or state of being reduced. **2** amount by which a thing is reduced: *great reductions in price this week.*

redundant *ri-dun'dȧnt*, *adj.* **1** beyond what is necessary. **2** expressing an idea already satisfactorily conveyed by (an)other word(s) in the sentence, etc.: *In "in the end, they finally decided", 'finally' is redundant.* **3** (of a worker) dismissed because no longer required.

redun'dancy *n.*:—*pl.* **redun'dancies**.

reduplicate *ri-dū'pli-kāt*, *v.t.* to repeat, copy (e.g. an action, sound, object, machine):—*pr.p.* **redup'licating**.

reduplicā'tion *n.*

redwood. See **red**.

re-echo *rē-ek'ō*, *v.t.* **1** to echo back. **2** to repeat like an echo.—*v.i.* to resound: *The boys cheered until the hall re-echoed.*

reed *rēd*, *n.* **1** a tall stiff grass growing near water. **2** a vibrating part of a musical wind instrument.

reed'y *adj.* **1** full of reeds. **2** like a reed. **3** (of a voice, etc.) having the thin, high sound of a reed instrument:—*comp.* **reed'ier**; *superl.* **reed'iest**.

reed'iness *n.*

reef[1] *rēf*, *n.* a chain of rocks near the surface of water.

reef[2] *rēf*, *n.* part of a ship's sail that may be rolled up to reduce the area acted on by the wind.—*v.t.* to gather up (a sail) in this way.

reef'er *n.* **1** a short jacket worn by sailors, or similar coat. **2** (*slang*) a marijuana cigarette.

reef knot a flat knot having two loops passing symmetrically through each other.

reek *rēk*, *n.* a strong, unpleasant smell: *the reek of tobacco smoke.*—*v.i.* to smell strongly (of): *His clothes reek of mothballs.*

reel *rēl*, *n.* **1** a bobbin or cylinder of wood, metal, or plastic on which thread, cable, film, fishing line, etc., may be wound. **2** a dance of quick tempo, esp. Highland or Irish, or the music for it. **3** a length of cinematograph film.—*v.t.* **1** to wind on a reel. **2** (with *in*) to draw in (fish) by winding the line on the reel.—*v.i.* **1** to sway, stagger. **2** to seem (to someone dizzy or confused) to go round and round: *The numbers made his head reel; The room reeled.*

reel off to repeat quickly and easily.

re-elect *rē-i-lekt'*, *v.t.* to elect again.

re-elec'tion *n.*

re-embark *rē-im-bärk'*, *v.t.* and *v.i.* to go, or put, on board again.

re-embarkā'tion *(-em-) n.*

re-enter *rē-en'tėr*, *v.t.*, *v.i.* to enter again.

re-en'trant *n.* an inward-pointing angle.

re-en'try *n.* the act of re-entering, e.g., in space-travel, the earth's atmosphere:—*pl.* **re-en'tries**.

re-establish *re-is-tab'lish*, *v.t.* to establish again, to restore.

re-estab'lishment *n.*

re-examine *rē-ig-zam'in*, *v.t.* to examine again:—*pr.p.* **re-exam'ining**.

re-examinā'tion *n.*

refectory *ri-fek'tȯ-ri*, *n.* a dining hall, for monks, students etc.:—*pl.* **refec'tories**.

refer *ri-fûr'*, *v.t.* **1** to hand over for consideration: *The patient, the case, was referred to a skin specialist.* **2** to direct for information: *For the historical facts, I refer you to the encyclopaedia.*—*v.i.* **1** to turn (to) for information. **2** to relate or apply (to): *This remark refers to something I told him in my letter.* **3** (with *to*) to mention: *Do not refer to John's illness*:—*pr.p.* **referr'ing**; *pa.p.* **referred'**.

referee *ref-ė-rē'*, *n.* **1** an umpire or judge. **2** a person willing to provide a potential employer, etc. with a note of one's character and abilities.

ref'erence *n.* **1** the act of referring. **2** a mention. **3** a note (from a referee) about a person's character, work, etc. **4** an indication in a book, report, etc., of the source of information for any particular statement.

referen'dum *n.* the practice of, or the action of, giving to all the people (of e.g. a country) an opportunity to vote on an important question: *Should there be a referendum on the restoration of the death penalty?*:—*pl.* **referen'da** or **referen'-dums**.

referr'al *(-fûr') n.* the act of referring, esp. a patient to a specialist.

reference book a book to be consulted occasionally for information, e.g. an encyclopaedia or dictionary.

reference library a library of books to be looked at but not taken away.

terms of reference (a guiding statement laying down) the exact work or enquiries to be carried out by e.g. a committee.

without reference to without taking into consideration.

with reference to in connection with, referring to: *With reference to your caravan holiday, I have some advice to give you.*

refill *rē-fil'*, *v.t.* to fill again.—*n.* *(rē'fil)* a fresh fill.

refine *ri-fīn'*, *v.t.* **1** to purify. **2** to free from coarseness. **3** to improve, make more exact, delicate, or elegant:—*pr.p.* **refin'ing**.

refined' *adj.* **1** freed from impurities. **2** polished, well-mannered.

refine'ment *n.* **1** good manners; good taste. **2** an improvement; a perfected feature or method.

refin'ery *n.* a place for refining sugar, oil, whisky, etc.:—*pl.* **refin'eries**.

refit *rē'fit'*, *v.t.*, *v.i.* to fit out, or be fitted out, again:—*pr.p.* **refitt'ing**; *pa.p.* **refitt'ed**.—Also *n.* *(rē'fit)*.

reflation *rē-flā'sh(ȯ)n*, *n.* an increase in available money after deflation.

reflect *ri-flekt'*, *v.t.* **1** to throw back (light, heat, etc.). **2** to mirror, give an image of: *The still water reflects the swan.* **3** to cast blame, credit: *His refusal to yield reflects credit on him.* **4** to realise while thinking: *He reflected that this was his last chance.* **5** to be an indication of: *His high mark reflects his talent for the subject.*—*v.i.* **1** to throw back. **2** to mirror. **3** to think carefully. **4** (with *on*) to show up (well or badly): *Her behaviour reflects badly on her parents.*

reflec'ted *adj.* **reflec'ting** *adj.*

reflection, **reflexion** *ri-flek'sh(ȯ)n*, *n.* **1** the act of throwing back (e.g. a ray of light). **2** an image in a mirror, etc. **3** careful thought. **4** a thought or remark. **5** something that casts credit or (esp.) blame: *Your bad behaviour is a reflection on me.*

reflec'tive *adj.* thoughtful.

reflec'tively *adv.*

reflec'tor *n.* a reflecting surface.

reflex *rē'fleks, adj.* **1** bent or turned back; (of an angle) greater than 180°. **2** happening involuntarily or automatically, without being intended: *The knee-jerk is a reflex action.*—*n.* a reflex action.

reflexion. See **reflect**.

reflex'ive *adj.* referring back, as in **reflexive pronoun**, a pronoun which shows that the object of an action is the same as the subject (or doer) of the action just mentioned (e.g. in *He cut himself badly*, 'himself' refers back to 'he' and is a reflexive pronoun).

reflexol'ogy *n.* therapy in which the soles of the feet are massaged.

reflexol'ogist *n.*

reform[1], **re-form** *rē'fŏrm', v.t.* and *v.i.* to form again or anew.

re'(-)formā'tion *n.* **re'(-)formed'** *adj.*

reform[2] *ri-fŏrm', v.t.* **1** to improve, remove faults from (a person, conduct, organisation, etc.). **2** to put an end to (abuses, i.e. bad customs).—*v.i.* to give up evil or foolish ways.—*n.* improvement; a change for the better.

reformā'tion *(ref-) n.*

refor'matory (*old*) *n.* a school for reforming young wrongdoers:—*pl.* **refor'matories.**—*adj.* having the effect of reforming.

reformed' *adj.* improved, esp. in conduct.

reform'er *n.* **1** one who wishes to bring about improvements. **2** (with *cap.*) one of the leaders of the Reformation.

the Reformation the 16th-century religious movement which led to the forming of the Protestant churches.

refract *ri-frakt', v.t.* to change the direction of (a ray, e.g. of light), as when a slanting ray is bent by passing from air into water.

refrac'tion *n.*

refractory *ri-frak'tŏ-ri, adj.* **1** (of person, etc.) stubborn, unruly. **2** (of a substance) difficult to work, melt, etc.; able to stand great heat.

refrac'toriness *n.*

refrain[1] *ri-frān', n.* a line of words or music repeated regularly in a song, etc.

refrain[2] *ri-frān', v.i.* to keep oneself (from some action): *You are asked to refrain from smoking.*

refresh *ri-fresh', v.t.* **1** to make fresh again. **2** to give new strength and energy or spirit to. **3** to make (memory) more clear by reminding, studying again, etc.

refresh'ing *adj.* **refresh'ingly** *adv.*

refresh'ment *n.* **1** the act of refreshing or the state of being refreshed. **2** something that refreshes, e.g. food or drink.

refresh'er course a course of study or training intended to keep up the knowledge or skill one already has.

refrigerate *ri-frij'ėr-āt, v.t.* **1** to make cold. **2** to preserve (e.g. food) by exposing to great cold:—*pr.p.* **refrig'erating.**

refrigerā'tion *n.*

refrigerator *ri-frij'ėr-ā-tŏr, n.* a storage machine which preserves food by keeping it cold.

refuel *rē'fū'ėl, v.t., v.i.* to supply with, or take in, fresh fuel:—*pr.p.* **refu'elling**; *pa.p.* **refu'elled.**

refuge *ref'ūj, n.* **1** a place of shelter (from danger or trouble). **2** a street island for pedestrians.

refugee' *(-jē') n.* one who seeks shelter in another country e.g. from religious or political persecution or from devastation caused by war or natural disaster.

refund *ri-fund', v.t.* to repay.—*n.* *(rē'fund)* repayment.

refurbish *ri-fûr'bish, v.t.* to redecorate.

refur'bishment *n.*

refuse[1] *ri-fūz', v.t.* **1** to say that one will not, to decline (to do, etc., something). **2** not to accept, to decline (something offered). **3** not to grant (permission, etc.). **4** (of a horse) to be unwilling to jump (a fence, etc.).—Also *v.i.*:—*pr.p.* **refus'ing.**

refus'al *n.*

refuse[2] *ref'ūs, n.* rubbish.

refute *ri-fūt', v.t.* to prove (an argument, or the person making it) wrong:—*pr.p.* **refut'ing.**

See also **irrefutable.**

regain *ri-gān',* or *rē-, v.t.* **1** to gain back. **2** to get back to: *to regain the shore.*

regal *rē'gål, adj.* royal, kingly.

regal'ity, re'galness *ns.*

re'gally *adv.*

regale *ri-gāl', v.t.* to entertain with food, or with conversation.—*v.i.* to feast:—*pr.p.* **regal'ing.**

regalia *ri-gā'li-å, n.pl.* **1** marks or signs of royalty (e.g. crown and sceptre). **2** any ornaments to show a person's position of authority.

regard *ri-gärd', v.t.* **1** to look at. **2** to view in a particular way: *to regard with amusement.* **3** to consider (as): *I regard you as a nuisance.* **4** to pay heed to.—*n.* **1** attentive look. **2** concern (for); affection; respect. **3** (in *pl.*) good wishes.

regard'ing *prep.* concerning.

regard'less *adj., adv.* not considering or caring; heedless (of): *He was asked to stop talking in the lesson, but he carried on regardless; We shall continue regardless of the cost, consequences.*

as regards, **with regard to** (something), as far as (it) is concerned.

regatta *ri-gat'ȧ, n.* a meeting for yacht or boat races.

regency. See **regent**.

regenerate *ri-jen'ėr-āt, v.t.* **1** to produce, or to make, anew. **2** to reform morally, uplift spiritually.—*v.i.* to grow again:—*pr.p.* **regen'erating.**—*adj. (-it)* remade in better form, esp. spiritually.

regen'eracy *n.* regenerate state.

regenerā'tion *n.* **1** the act of regenerating. **2** regeneracy.

regent *rē'jėnt, n.* one who governs in place of a king or queen.

re'gency *n.* **1** position of a regent. **2** (a period of) rule by a regent:—*pl.* **re'gencies**.

reggae *reg'ā, n.* a strongly rhythmic type of West Indian music.

regicide *rej'i-sīd, n.* the killing, or killer, of a king.

régime *rā-zhēm', n.* a system of rule, government: *under the Communist régime.*

regimen *rej'i-mėn, n.* a set of rules for following with regard to health, diet, exercise, etc.

regiment *rej'i-mėnt, n.* a body of soldiers commanded by a colonel.—*v.t.* to organise, control, too strictly.

regimentā'tion *n.* too severe control.

regiment'al *adj.* of a regiment: *the regimental mascot.*—*n.* (in *pl.*) uniform of a regiment.

region *rē'jȯn, n.* **1** a district. **2** a part of the earth's surface or of the universe. **3** a part, division, e.g. of the body: *Many people suffer from pain in the lumbar region.* **4** (esp. with *cap.*) an administrative division of Scotland.

re'gional *adj.* **re'gionally** *adv.*

in the region of approximately.

register *rej'is-tėr, n.* **1** a written record or list; a book containing such records: *an attendance register*; *marriage register.* **2** a part of the range of a voice or musical instrument: *the upper register of the voice.*—*v.t.* **1** to enter in a register. **2** (of an instrument, e.g. a thermometer) to record, show. **3** (*coll.*) to show in one's appearance: *to register amusement.* **4** to pay a fee so that (a letter, etc.) may have special care.—*v.i.* to enter one's name (e.g. at a hotel).

reg'istered *adj.* **registrā'tion** *n.*

reg'istrar (or *-trär'*) *n.* one who keeps official records.

reg'istry *n.* an office or place where registers are kept:—*pl.* **reg'istries.**

register office, registry office an office where records of births, marriages, etc. are kept, and where marriages are performed.

registration number the sequence of letters and numbers by which a vehicle is registered, displayed on its number plate.

Regius *rē'ji-ůs, adj.*: **Regius professor** the holder of a university chair founded by a king.

regress *ri-gres', v.i.* to go back to a lower, less advanced or less perfect state.

regression *ri-gresh'(ȯ)n, n.*

regret *ri-gret', v.t.* **1** to feel sorry about (something). **2** to be sorry (to say, etc.):—*pr.p.* **regrett'ing**; *pa.p.* **regrett'ed.**—*n.* **1** a sorrowful wish that something had happened differently. **2** sorrow felt at loss or death.

regret'ful *adj.* feeling regret.

regret'fully *adv.*

regrett'able *adj.* that should be regretted.

regrett'ably *adv.*

regroup *rē'grōōp', v.i.* and *v.t.* to form (into) new groups.

regular *reg'ū-lȧr, adj.* **1** according to rule, or to habit. **2** usual, normal. **3** happening at fixed times or intervals. **4** habitual, frequent: *a regular customer, visitor.* **5** even: *regular teeth.* **6** symmetrical: *A square is a regular figure*; *regular features.* **7** (of soldiers) belonging to the regular (i.e. permanent) army:—*opp.* **irregular.**—*n.* **1** a soldier of the regular army. **2** a member of a religious order. **3** a frequent visitor, etc.

reg'ularise *v.t.* to make regular, esp. according to law, custom, rule:—*pr.p.* **reg'ularising.**

regular'ity *n.* **reg'ularly** *adv.*

reg'ulāte *v.t.* **1** to control by rules. **2** to keep in order. **3** to adjust (a watch, etc.) so that it works accurately:—*pr.p.* **reg'ulating.**

regulā'tion *n.* **1** the act of regulating. **2** a rule or order.—*adj.* as required by rules.

reg'ulātor *n.* **1** a person, or a device, that regulates. **2** a controlling lever esp. for the speed of a watch.

regurgitate *ri-gûr'ji-tāt, v.t.* to bring back into the mouth after swallowing:—*pr.p.* **regur'gitating.**

rehabilitate *rē-(h)ȧ-bil'i-tāt, v.t.* **1** to give back rights or powers that have been lost. **2** to restore to health. **3** to clear the character of:—*pr.p.* **rehabil'itating.**

rehabilitā'tion *n.*

rehash *rē'hash', n.* something (esp. a book, speech etc.) made of materials previously used.—Also *v.t.*

rehearse *ri-hûrs'*, *v.t.* **1** to practise beforehand. **2** to relate, go over: *He rehearsed the whole incident in his mind.—v.i.* to take part in a rehearsal or practice:—*pr.p.* **rehears'ing.**
rehear'sal *n.*
dress rehearsal (*theatre*) final rehearsal with costumes, etc.

rehouse *rē'howz'*, *v.t.* to provide with a new or different house or houses:—*pr.p.* **rehous'ing.**
rehous'ing *n.*

reign *rān*, *n.* **1** the rule of a king or queen. **2** the time of this. **3** a period of domination by some influence, etc.: *a reign of terror.—v.i.* **1** to be ruler. **2** to prevail: *Confusion reigned.*

reimburse *rē-im-bûrs'*, *v.t.* to repay:—*pr.p.* **reimburs'ing.**
reimburse'ment *n.*

rein *rān*, *n.* one of two straps for guiding a horse.—*v.t.* (with *in* or *back*) **1** to control with reins. **2** to check.
draw rein to stop.
give rein to to allow (e.g. one's imagination, passion) to act unchecked.

reincarnation *rē'in-kär-nā'sh(ȯ)n.* **1** rebirth of the soul in another body after death. **2** an instance of this.

reindeer *rān'dēr*, *n.* a kind of deer found in the far North.

reinforce *rē-in-fōrs',-förs'*, *v.t.* to strengthen with new forces or material: *to reinforce an army*; *to reinforce the elbows of a jacket*:—*pr.p.* **reinfor'cing.**
reinforce'ment *n.* **1** strengthening. **2** (in *pl.*) extra troops or help.
reinforced concrete concrete that has steel bars or mesh embedded in it.

reinstate *rē-in-stāt'*, *v.t.* to put back in a former position, restore to previous status:—*pr.p.* **reinstat'ing.**
reinstate'ment *n.*

reinvigorate *rē-in-vig'ȯr-āt*, *v.t.* to put new vigour into:—*pr.p.* **reinvig'orating.**

reissue *rē-is'ū*, *-ish'ōō*, *v.t.* to issue again:—*pr.p.* **reiss'uing.**—*n.* a second or later issue (e.g. of stamps.)

reiterate *rē-it'ė-rāt*, *v.t.* to repeat, esp. again and again:—*pr.p.* **reit'erating.**
reiterā'tion *n.* repetition.

reject *ri-jekt'*, *v.t.* **1** to throw out or away. **2** to refuse to take or to grant.—*n.* *(rē'jekt)* a person or thing put aside as unsatisfactory.
rejec'tion *n.*

rejoice *ri-jois'*, *v.t.* (*old*) to make joyful.—*v.i.* to feel joy:—*pr.p.* **rejoic'ing.**
rejoic'ing *n.* **1** the feeling or expressing of joy. **2** (in *pl.*) celebrations.
rejoice in to be glad to have (something).

rejoin[1] *rē'join'*, *v.t.*, *v.i.* to join again.

rejoin[2] *ri-join'*, *v.t.* to say in answer.
rejoin'der *n.* an answer, esp. to a reply.

rejuvenate *ri-jōō'vi-nāt*, *v.t.* to make young again:—*pr.p.* **rejuv'enating.**
rejuvenā'tion *n.*

rekindle *rē'kin'dl*, *v.t.* to set on fire, or to arouse, anew:—*pr.p.* **re'kind'ling.**

relapse *ri-laps'*, *v.i.* to slide back, revert, to a worse state after improving:—*pr.p.* **relap'sing.**—*n.* **1** an act of relapsing. **2** a return of illness after partial recovery.

relate *ri-lāt'*, *v.t.* **1** to tell, narrate. **2** to link up in the mind, associate (facts, circumstances, etc.): *Sociologists tend to relate poor housing and crime, poor housing with* (or *to*) *crime.—v.i.* **1** to have reference (to). **2** (often with *to*) to form a relationship with, communicate with, etc.:—*pr.p.* **relat'ing.**
relā'ted *adj.* **1** connected. **2** akin by birth or marriage.
relā'tion *n.* **1** act of telling. **2** way of being connected. **3** a person connected with one by birth or marriage. **4** (in *pl.*) behaviour or feeling between people: *to establish good relations with someone.*
relā'tionship *n.* state, or way, of being related, or of being friendly, etc.
relative *rel'ȧ-tiv*, *adj.* **1** comparative: *the relative speeds of car and train*; *She lives in relative poverty* (i.e. compared to others). **2** connected with, referring (to): *the papers relative to his case.—n.* a relation (*def.* 3).
rel'atively *adv.* **1** in comparison with other things or people. **2** fairly, quite.
relativ'ity *n.* **1** the fact or state of being relative. **2** a scientific theory about motion and position in space.
relative to 1 in comparison with. **2** with reference to.

relax *ri-laks'*, *v.t.* **1** to loosen (e.g. one's hold). **2** to make less strict or severe: *Rules were relaxed on Speech Day.—v.i.* **1** to become less tense, rest completely. **2** to take recreation. **3** to become less strict.
relaxāt'ion *(rē-) n.*

relay[1] *rē'lā'*, *v.t.* to lay again.

relay[2] *rē'lā*, *n.* **1** a fresh set of men or animals to relieve others. **2** the sending out of a broadcast received from another station. **3** an electrically-operated device for controlling an independent circuit.—*v.t.* *(ri-lā')* to send on or out (a broadcast, or news, etc.):—*pr.p.* **relay'ing**; *pa.p.* **relayed'.**

relay *(rē'lā)* **race** a race in which members of a team take over from each other, each individual competitor running, etc., an arranged distance.

release *ri-lēs'*, *v.t.* **1** to let go. **2** to set free. **3** to permit to be made public (e.g. news or a film):—*pr.p.* **releas'ing.**—*n.* **1** a setting free. **2** permitting to make publicly known, or available. **3** something that is made public or available: *a press release* (i.e. a report issued to the press).

relegate *rel'i-gāt*, *v.t.* to put down (to a lower grade, position, etc.):—*pr.p.* **rel'-egating.**
relegā'tion *n.*

relent *ri-lent'*, *v.i.* to become less severe, more forgiving.
relent'less *adj.* **1** without pity. **2** not turned aside from one's aim by anything.
relent'lessly *adv.* **relent'lessness** *n.*

relevant *rel'ė-vȧnt*, having to do with the matter being spoken of or considered:—*opp.* **irrelevant.**
rel'evance *n.*

reliable, **reliance**, etc. See **rely**.

relic *rel'ik*, *n.* **1** (in *pl.*) a dead body. **2** something left from a past time or age. **3** something, esp. a bone, from the body of a saint, etc.
relict *rel'ikt*, (*old*) *n.* a widow.
reliquary *rel'i-kwȧr-i*, *n.* a receptacle for a saint's, etc. relics:—*pl.* **rel'iquaries.**

relief *ri-lēf'*, *n.* **1** a lessening of pain or anxiety, or of boredom, etc.; something that allows this. **2** release from a post or duty. **3** the person(s) taking the duty over. **4** help given to people in need: *famine relief.* **5** the act of freeing a town, etc. from siege. **6** a way of carving, etc. in which the design is raised above the level of its background.
relieve *ri-lēv'*, *v.t.* **1** to give relief to; to ease (pain, worry, boredom, etc.). **2** to give help to (people in distress). **3** to raise the siege of. **4** to take over a duty from (someone). **5** to introduce variety into. **6** (with *of*) to take (something, esp. a burden) from (somebody): *He kindly relieved me of my suitcase*; *He was relieved of* (i.e. dismissed from) *his duties*:—*pr.p.* **reliev'ing.**
relieved' *adj.* no longer anxious or worried.
relief map a map which shows, by colouring or other means, the highlands and lowlands of a country.
relieve oneself to urinate or defecate.

religion *ri-lij'ȯn*, *n.* belief in, or worship of, a God or gods.
relig'ious *adj.* **1** concerned with religion. **2** devoted to religion, pious (*opp.* **irreligious**). **3** faithful, conscientious: *He was religious in his efforts*; *with religious care.*
relig'iously *adv.* **relig'iousness** *n.*

relinquish *ri-ling'kwish*, *v.t.* **1** to give up. **2** to let go.
relin'quishment *(-ling') n.*

reliquary. See **relic**.

relish *rel'ish*, *n.* **1** a flavour. **2** something (e.g. a sauce or pickles) to give a flavour. **3** liking (for). **4** enjoyment.—*v.t.* **1** to like the taste of. **2** to enjoy.

reluctance *ri-luk'tȧns*, *n.* unwillingness.
reluc'tant *adj.* **reluc'tantly** *adv.*

rely *ri-lī'*, *v.i.* to trust confidently, depend (on e.g. person, person's help, a happening):—*pr.p.* **rely'ing**; *pa.p.* **relied'.**
relīabil'ity *n.* the quality of being reliable.
relī'able *adj.* trustworthy.
relī'ableness *n.* **relī'ably** *adv.*
relī'ance *n.* trust; dependence.
relī'ant *adj.* depending (on).

remain *ri-mān'*, *v.i.* **1** to stay or be left behind. **2** to go on unchanged: *He remained obstinate.*
remain'der *n.* **1** an amount, quantity left after the removal of the rest. **2** (*arithmetic*) a number left over when one quantity cannot be exactly divided by another.—*v.t.* to sell off (surplus books) at a reduced price.
remains' *n.pl.* **1** what is left, e.g. after a meal. **2** a dead body.
See also **remnant**.

remake *rē'māk'*, *v.t.* to make again:—*pr.p.* **re'mak'ing.**—Also *n.* *(rē'māk)*.

remand *ri-mänd'*, *v.t.* to send back (esp. a prisoner to await further evidence).
remand home a home to which a child or young person may be sent by a magistrate.
on remand having been remanded.

remark *ri-märk'*, *v.t.* **1** to notice. **2** to comment, say.—*v.i.* to comment (on).—*n.* a comment, something said.
remark'able *adj.* **1** unusual. **2** worth mentioning.
remark'ableness *n.* **remark'ably** *adv.*

remedy *rem'i-di*, *n.* a cure for an illness or evil:—*pl.* **rem'edies.**—*v.t.* to correct; to put right:—*pr.p.* **rem'edying**; *pa.p.* **rem'-edied** *(-did)*.
remē'diable *adj.* that may be put right:—*opp.* **irremediable.**
remē'dial *adj.* **1** able, or intended, to cure. **2** (of teaching, etc.) providing special help for slow-learning children.

remember *ri-mem'bėr, v.t.* **1** to keep in the mind, or to bring back into the mind after forgetting for a time. **2** to reward, make a present to, or tip. **3** to pass on greetings from (someone to someone else).
remem'brance *n.* **1** memory. **2** a keepsake. **3** (in *pl.*) friendly greetings.

remind *ri-mīnd', v.t.* **1** to cause to remember: *Remind me to post the letter*; *She reminded me of my promise.* **2** to make (one) think (of): *The hat reminds me of a beehive.*
remin'der *n.* something that reminds.

reminisce *rem-in-is', v.i.* to talk about things remembered:—*pr.p.* **reminis'cing**.
reminiscence *rem-in-is'ėns, n.* **1** something remembered. **2** (usu. in *pl.*) an account of remembered past events.
reminis'cent *adj.* reminding one (of).

remiss *ri-mis', adj.* (not used before a noun) careless, slack (in carrying out duties, etc.)
remiss'ness *n.*

remission. See **remit**.

remit *ri-mit', v.t.* **1** to cancel (a debt, punishment, etc.). **2** to send (money) usu. in payment for something. **3** to hand over, refer (esp. a case to a lower court):—*pr.p.* **remitt'ing**; *pa.p.* **remitt'ed**.
remission *ri-mish'(ȯ)n, n.* **1** forgiveness. **2** cancellation (of a punishment, etc.): *He earned remission of part of his sentence.* **3** the act of remitting.
remitt'ance *n.* **1** the sending of money, esp. by post, in payment for something. **2** the money, payment, thus sent.
See also **unremitting**.

remnant *rem'nȧnt, n.* a small piece or number left over from a larger piece or number.

remodel *rē'mod'l, v.t.* to model again, esp. so as to change the shape:—*pr.p.* **re'mod'elling**; *pa.p.* **re'mod'elled**.

remonstrance *ri-mon'strȧns, n.* a strong protest.
rem'onstrāte *v.i.* to make a protest: *I remonstrated with him about his treatment of his friend*:—*pr.p.* **rem'onstrāting**.

remorse *ri-mörs', n.* sorrow for a fault or sin.
remorse'ful *adj.* **remorse'fully** *adv.*
remorse'less *adj.* cruel; relentless.
remorse'lessly *adv.* **remorse'lessness** *n.*

remote *ri-mōt', adj.* **1** distant in time or place. **2** out of the way: *a remote village.* **3** slight: *a remote chance.*
remote'ly *adv.* **remote'ness** *n.*
remote control control of apparatus by means of distant electric switches, or by radio waves.

remould *rē'mōld', v.t.* to mould anew.—*n.* *(rē'mōld)* a tyre on which the tread has been renewed.

remount *rē'mount', v.t.* and *v.i.* to mount again.

remove *ri-mōōv', v.t.* **1** to take off. **2** to take away. **3** to dismiss, put out (e.g. a person from a post).—*v.i.* to change one's dwelling place:—*pr.p.* **remov'ing.**—*n.* **1** a stage, step away: *This harsh treatment is only one remove from bullying.* **2** in some schools, an intermediate class.
remov'able *adj.* that can be removed:—*opp.* **irremovable**.
remov'al *n.* **1** the act of taking, or of going, away. **2** change of home. **3** the transfer of furniture, etc. during such a change.
removed' *adj.* **1** separated: *a house (well-)removed from the main road.* **2** used in indicating the number of generations between cousins: *My mother's cousin is my first cousin once removed.*

remunerate *ri-mū'nė-rāt, v.t.* to pay (a person) for a service:—*pr.p.* **remu'nerating**.
remunerā'tion *n.* payment.
remun'erative *adj.* profitable.

renaissance *ri-nā'sȧns, n.* **1** a new birth or revival. **2** (*cap.*) revival of arts and literature in Europe in the 14th to 16th centuries.—Also *adj.* (with *cap.*).

renal *rē'n(ȧ)l, adj.* of the kidneys.

rend *rend,* (*poetic*) *v.t., v.i.* **1** to tear apart, split. **2** to pull or tear roughly:—*pa.p.* **rent.**
rent *n.* a tear, split.

render *ren'dėr, v.t.* **1** (*old*) to give (back). **2** to give (e.g. aid, thanks). **3** to present (e.g. a bill). **4** to translate: *to render Latin into English.* **5** to represent, e.g. in a painting. **6** to perform (e.g. music). **7** to cause to be: *This rendered me speechless.* **8** to melt and purify (fat).
ren'dering *n.*
rendi'tion *n.* **1** interpretation, manner of performance of a dramatic part or piece of music. **2** translation.

rendezvous *ron'di-vōō, rong'dā-, n.* **1** a meeting place. **2** a meeting by appointment:—*pl.* **ren'dezvous** *(-vōōz).*—*v.i.* to meet at an appointed place: —*pr.p.* **ren'dezvousing** *(-vōō-ing)*; *pa.p.* **ren'dezvoused** *(-vōōd).*

rendition. See **render**.

renege *ri-nāg', v.t.* and *v.i.* (often with *on*) to go back on (a promise or agreement etc.):—*pr.p.* **reneg'ing**.

renegade *ren'i-gād, n., adj.* (one) faithless to party or principles.

renew *ri-nū', v.t.* **1** to begin again (e.g. an attempt). **2** to make as if new. **3** to put in a fresh store of: *to renew the water in the fish-tank.* **4** to recover (youth, energy, etc.). **5** to continue for a longer period (e.g. membership, a licence).
renew'able *adj.* able to be renewed.
renew'al *n.*

rennet *ren'it, n.* a substance used for curdling milk to make junket, etc.

renounce *ri-nowns', v.t.* **1** to give up, esp. formally (a title, claim, etc.). **2** to reject, give up, dissociate oneself from, formally: *He renounced his religion, his family, alcohol.*—*v.i.* to play a card not of the suit led:—*pr.p.* **renoun'cing**.
renunciation *ri-nun-si-ā'sh(ȯ)n, n.* **1** the act of giving up. **2** self-denial.

renovate *ren'ȯ-vāt, v.t.* to make new, or as if new, again; to mend, repair:—*pr.p.* **ren'ovating**.
renovā'tion *n.* **ren'ovātor** *n.*

renown *ri-nown', n.* fame, high repute.
renowned' *adj.* famous.

rent[1]. See **rend**.

rent[2] *rent, n.* payment for use of someone else's property, esp. houses and lands.—*v.t.* **1** to hold or use by paying rent. **2** to let or hire out for rent.
ren'tal *n.* **1** rent. **2** income from rents. **3** the act of renting.

renunciation. See **renounce**.

rep[1], **repp** *rep, n.* a corded cloth.

rep[2] *rep, n.* abbrev. for **repertory**, **representative** (esp. a commercial traveller).

repaid. See **repay**.

repair[1] *ri-pār', v.i.* to go: *He repaired to his house.*

repair[2] *ri-pār', v.t.* **1** to mend. **2** to put right. **3** to make up for (a wrong).—*n.* **1** (often in *pl.*) mending. **2** soundness of condition: *in a poor state of repair; in good repair.*
repair'er *n.* one who repairs.
reparable *rep'ār-ȧ-bl, adj.* able to be mended, or put right:—*opp.* **irreparable**.
reparā'tion *n.* **1** putting right a wrong. **2** compensation.
See also **disrepair**.

repartee *rep-ār-tē', n.* **1** (the making of) quick, witty replies. **2** conversation consisting of witty remarks and retorts.

repast *ri-päst', n.* a meal.

repatriate *rē-pat'ri-āt,* or *ri-,* or *-pā'tri-, v.t.* to send (someone) back to his own country:—*pr.p.* **repat'riating**.
repatriā'tion *n.*

repay *rē-pā', v.t.* **1** to pay back. **2** to do something in return for:—*pr.p.* **repay'ing**; *pa.p.* **repaid'**.
repay'able *adj.* that must be repaid: *money repayable within ten years.*
repay'ment *n.*

repeal *ri-pēl', v.t.* to cancel (e.g. a law).—Also *n.*

repeat *ri-pēt', v.t.* **1** to say or do again. **2** to say from memory. **3** to tell (something heard) esp. when one ought not to.—*v.i.* **1** to happen again, recur. **2** (of an instrument) to perform a function over again. **3** (of guns) to fire several shots without reloading.—*n.* **1** (*music*) a passage to be repeated. **2** a second, or later, performance.—Also *adj.*
repeat'able *adj.* **1** fit to be repeated. **2** that can be repeated.
repeat'ed *adj.* occurring many times.
repeat'edly *adv.* many times.
repeat'er *n.* **1** a gun or other device that repeats. **2** a recurring decimal figure.
repeat'ing *n.* and *adj.*
repetition *rep-i-tish'(ȯ)n, n.* **1** act of repeating. **2** recital from memory. **3** a repeat performance or occurrence.
repeti'tious *(-tish'ŭs),* **repetitive** *ri-pet'i-tiv, adjs.* repeating something too often.
repeat oneself to say the same thing more than once.

repel *ri-pel', v.t.* **1** to drive back or away. **2** to be distasteful to, to disgust:—*pr.p.* **repell'ing**; *pa.p.* **repelled'**.
repell'ent *adj.* disgusting.—*n.* an ointment, spray, etc. that repels (insects, etc.). See also **repulse**.

repent *ri-pent', v.t.* and *v.i.* (with *of*) **1** to be sorry for what one has done or left undone: *He repented (of) his cruel act.* **2** to regret: *He repented (of) his generosity to the ungrateful boy.*
repent'ance *n.* **repent'ant** *adj.*

repercussion *rē-pėr-kush'(ȯ)n, n.* **1** a reverberation. **2** a rebound. **3** an after-effect of an action or event (esp. if bad).

repertoire. See **repertory**.

repertory *rep'ėr-tȯr-i, n.* **1** the work of a repertory theatre. **2** a stock of pieces that a person or group can perform, or plays that a company can perform:—*pl.* **rep'ertories**.
repertoire *rep'ėr-twär, n.* (from Fr. *répertoire*) the repertory of a performer or group of performers.
repertory theatre a theatre with a more or less permanent company acting a series of plays.

repetition, **repetitive**, etc. See **repeat**.

rephrase *rē-frāz'*, *v.t.* to express (something) in different words:— *pr.p.* **rephras'ing**.

repine *ri-pīn'*, *v.i.* to fret; to feel discontent:—*pr.p.* **repin'ing**.

replace *ri-plās'*, *rē-*, *v.t.* **1** to put back in the correct place. **2** to put something new or something else in place of: *We should replace that broken lock*; *We replaced it with a new one.* **3** to be put in place of: *He replaced his brother as managing director*:—*pr.p.* **replac'ing**.
replace'able *adj.* that can be replaced:—*opp.* **irreplace'able**.
replace'ment *n.* **1** the act of replacing. **2** a substitute.

replay *rē'plā'*, *v.t.* to play (a football match, etc.) again.—*n.* *(rē'plā)* **1** a replayed match. **2** part of a recording, esp. of a match, played again.

replenish *ri-plen'ish*, *v.t.* **1** to fill again. **2** to stock up.
replen'ishment *n.*

replete *ri-plēt'*, *adj.* **1** full. **2** well stocked (with).
replete'ness, **replē'tion** *ns.* fullness almost to excess.

replica *rep'lik-ȧ*, *n.* an exact copy, esp. of a work of art.
rep'licāte *v.t.* to make a replica of:—*pr.p.* **rep'licating**.

reply *ri-plī'*, *v.i.*, *v.t.* to answer, respond, in words or by an action:—*pr.p.* **reply'ing**; *pa.p.* **replied'** *(-plīd')*.—Also *n.*

report *ri-pōrt'*, *-pört'*, *v.t.* **1** to pass on news (that something has happened). **2** to give news, or an account, of. **3** to take notes of (e.g. a speech), esp. for a newspaper. **4** to make a formal complaint against (a person).—*v.i.* **1** to make a statement. **2** to present oneself for duty, etc.—*n.* **1** a statement of facts. **2** an account in a newspaper, on television, etc. **3** a rumour. **4** a written statement on e.g. a pupil's work. **5** a loud noise.
report'er *n.* one who reports, esp. for a newspaper.
report'ing *n.* and *adj.*

repose[1] *ri-pōz'*, *v.t.*, *v.i.* to rest:—*pr.p* **reposing**.—*n.* rest; calm.

repose[2] *ri-pōz'*, *v.t.* to place (trust, etc., in a person or thing):—*pr.p.* **repos'ing**.
repository *ri-poz'i-tȯr-i*, *n.* a place where something is stored:—*pl.* **repos'-itories**.

repossess *rē'pȯz-es'*, *v.t.* to regain possession of.
repossession *rē-pȯz-esh'(ȯ)n*, *n.*

repp. See **rep**[1].

reprehend *rep-ri-hend'*, *v.t.* to find fault with, reprove.
reprehens'ible *adj.* blameworthy.
reprehens'ibly *adv.* in a manner deserving blame.

represent *rep-ri-zent'*, *v.t.* to point out, explain: *He represented the difficulties to the rest of the committee.* **2** to claim to be (with *as*): *She represents herself as an expert.* **3** to speak or act for someone or something else: *Will you represent the school at the Sports Meeting?* **4** to act the part of (a character in e.g. a play). **5** to symbolise, stand for. **6** (of e.g. a picture) to show. **7** to correspond to or imply: *This rise represents an increase of 5.* **8** to reflect, give a fair idea of: *His words represented the general feeling*.
representation *rep-ri-zen-tā'sh(ȯ)n*, *n.* **1** act of representing or being represented. **2** an image or picture. **3** a dramatic rendering. **4** a strong statement or appeal.
representā'tional *adj.* (of art, etc.) realistic.
representative *rep-ri-zen'tȧ-tiv*, *adj.* **1** typical. **2** carried on by elected persons: *representative government.*—*n.* **1** one who represents another, e.g. in business or government. **2** a commercial traveller.
House of Representatives lower house of U.S. Congress, etc.

repress *ri-pres'*, *v.t.* **1** to put down by force, quell, suppress. **2** to keep under control, check (e.g. a desire, action). **3** to keep under too severe control.
repressed' *adj.*
repress'ible *adj.*:—*opp.* **irrepress'ible**.
repression *ri-presh'(ȯ)n*, *n.*
repress'ive *adj.* severe, harsh.

reprieve *ri-prēv'*, *v.t.* **1** to delay execution of (someone). **2** to give an interval of ease or freedom to:—*pr.p.* **repriev'ing**.—*n.* **1** a delay of execution. **2** an interval of rest or relief.

reprimand *rep'ri-mänd*, *n.* a severe scolding.—*v.t.* to reprove severely.

reprint *rē'print'*, *v.t.* **1** to print again. **2** to print more copies of.—*n.* *(rē'print)* a new printing.

reprisal *ri-prīz'ȧl*, *n.* an act of returning like for like: *The raid was a reprisal for an earlier attack by the other side*.

reprise *rė-prēz'*, *n.* a repeated passage of music, etc.

reproach *ri-prōch'*, *v.t.* **1** to scold, chide: *She reproached me for not telling her.* **2** to blame for (with *with*): *She reproached me with the failure of her plan.*—*n.* **1** blame. **2** reproof. **3** something that brings disgrace: *The state of the roads is a reproach*

to the local authorities.
reproach'ful *adj.* full of, or expressing, disappointment and blame.
reproach'fully *adv.* **reproach'fulness** *n.*
above, beyond, reproach faultless.
See also **irreproachable.**

reprobate *rep'rȯ-bāt,n.* a person who leads a life of wickedness or immorality.—Also *adj.*

reproduce *rē-prȯ-dūs', v.t.* **1** to produce a copy of. **2** to imitate.—*v.i.* to produce young:—*pr.p.* **reproduc'ing.**
reproduction *rē-prȯ-duk'sh(ȯ)n, n.* **1** the act of reproducing. **2** a copy, e.g. of a painting.—*adj.* (of furniture) made in imitation of a past style.
reproduc'tive *adj.*

reproof[1] *rē'prōōf', v.t.* to make waterproof again.

reproof[2] *ri-prōōf', n.* scolding; a mild rebuke.
reprove' *ri-prōōv', v.t.* to blame, rebuke, find fault with:—*pr.p.* **reprov'ing.**
reprov'ing *adj.* **reprov'ingly** *adv.*

reptile *rep'tīl, n.* a crawling or creeping animal, cold-blooded and scaly, e.g. a snake, crocodile.
reptilian *rep-til'i-ȧn, adj.* belonging to, or resembling, these animals.

republic *ri-pub'lik,n.* a form of government without a king or queen, the country being ruled by an elected representative of the people.
repub'lican *adj.*
Republican *n.* and *adj.* (a member) of the **Republican Party,** one of the two great political parties in U.S.A.

republish *rē-pub'lish, v.t.* to publish again.
republicā'tion *n.*

repudiate *ri-pū'di-āt, v.t.* **1** to disown (e.g. a son). **2** to reject; to refuse to recognise (e.g. authority), accept (an idea), acknowledge (e.g. a debt, obligation, or claim), admit (a charge):—*pr.p.* **repud'iating.**
repudiā'tion *n.*

repugnance *ri-pug'nȧns, n.* **1** strong dislike, disgust. **2** unpleasantness.
repug'nant *adj.* **1** unpleasant. **2** distasteful (to).

repulse *ri-puls', v.t.* **1** to drive back (an enemy). **2** to snub:—*pr.p.* **repul'sing.** —*n.* **1** a defeat. **2** a snub.
repulsion *ri-pul'sh(ȯ)n, n.* **1** disgust. **2** the act of driving back an enemy, etc.
repul'sive *adj.* that disgusts.
repul'sively *adv.* **repul'siveness** *n.*

reputation *rep-ū-tā'sh(ȯ)n, n.* **1** opinion generally held of a person or thing. **2** good opinion, respect. **3** good name.
reputable *rep'ūt-ȧ-bl, adj.* respectable, well thought of.
repute *ri-pūt', n.* reputation; fame.
reputed *ri-pūt'id, adj.* **1** (used before a noun) supposed: *the reputed author of the article.* **2** believed (to be): *He is reputed to be wealthy.*
reput'edly *adv.* in common opinion.
by repute reputedly.
of repute well thought of by many people.
See also **disrepute, disreputable.**

request *ri-kwest', n.* **1** something asked for. **2** an act of asking for something.—*v.t.* to ask, or ask for, politely or as a favour.
by, on, request when asked: *Buses stop on request.*

requiem *rek'wi-ėm, n.* **1** mass for the souls of the dead. **2** music for this mass.

require *ri-kwīr', v.t.* **1** to need. **2** to demand, order, esp. by law:—*pr.p.* **requir'ing.**
require'ment *n.* **1** something needed. **2** something with which one must comply.
requisite *rek'wi-zit, adj.* **1** required. **2** necessary.—*n.* something necessary: *toilet requisites.*
requisi'tion *n.* a formal demand or request, e.g. for military or other supplies.—*v.t.* to demand or take in this way.

requite *ri-kwīt', v.t.* **1** to repay or avenge (one action) by another. **2** to repay (a person):—*pr.p.* **requit'ing.**
requit'al *n.*

reredos *rēr'dos, n.* in a church, an ornamental screen behind the altar, or separating the choir from the nave.

rerun *rē'run', v.t.* to show (a film), broadcast (a television series, etc.), again.

rescind *ri-sind', v.t.* to annul, cancel (a decision, an order, a law).

rescue *res'kū, v.t.* to free from danger, harm, or captivity:—*pr.p.* **res'cūing;** *pa.p.* **res'cued** *(-kūd).*—*n.* act of saving from danger, etc.
res'cuer *n.* one who rescues.

research *ri-sûrch', n.* careful search or study to find out new facts: *cancer research.*—*v.i.* to do research (into).—*v.t.* to investigate (a subject).
research'er *n.* one who does research.

resemble *ri-zem'bl, v.t.* to be like:—*pr.p.* **resemb'ling.**
resem'blance *n.*

resent *ri-zent', v.t.* to feel injured or insulted and annoyed by.
resent'ful *adj.* **resent'fully** *adv.*
resent'ment *n.* the state of feeling badly treated and annoyed.

reserve *ri-zûrv', v.t.* **1** to keep back for later use, or for a special use. **2** to book: *Have* *you reserved a seat?*:—*pr.p.* **reserv'ing.**—*n.* **1** a supply of something kept for later. **2** shyness, habit of not speaking thoughts freely. **3** (esp. in *pl.*) extra troops kept until wanted. **4** a piece of public land kept e.g. for protection of wild animals (**game reserve**) or natural plant life.

reservā'tion *(rez-) n.* **1** the act of reserving. **2** the act of booking seats, rooms etc. **3** a room, seat, etc., so booked. **4** an exception or condition made openly or mentally: *He agreed to the plan with one reservation.* **5** a land reserve.

reserved' *adj.* **1** not showing thoughts or feelings. **2** booked in advance.

reserv'ist *n.* a member of a reserve force, not in regular army, navy, or air force.

reservoir *rez'ėr-vwär, n.* **1** a store. **2** a lake where water for drinking, etc., is stored.

reset *rē'set', v.t.* **1** to set again. **2** (*printing*) to set up in type again:—*pr.p.* **re'sett'ing;** *pa.p.* **re'set'.**

reshuffle *rē-shuf'l, v.t.* **1** to shuffle again. **2** to rearrange (government posts, etc.).—Also *n.*

reside *ri-zīd', v.i.* **1** to live (in, at, abroad). **2** (of powers, rights; with *in*) to belong to. **3** (of a quality, etc.; with *in*) to be present in, be a part of:—*pr.p.* **resid'ing.**

residence *rez'i-dėns, n.* **1** a grand house. **2** the act, or period, of dwelling in a place: *during his residence in Spain.*

res'idency *n.* the official home of a governor, etc., in a colony, etc.:—*pl.* **res'idencies.**

res'ident *n.* **1** one who lives permanently in a particular place. **2** one who is staying at a hotel, as opposed to someone merely eating or drinking there.—*adj.* **1** dwelling or staying (in a place). **2** (of a job or post) requiring one to live on the premises.

residential *rez-i-den'sh(ȧ)l, adj.* **1** for (esp. good) houses. **2** connected with residence. **3** (of a job or post) resident.

in residence staying in a place esp. to carry out duties there.

residue *rez'i-dū, n.* what is left over; remainder.

resid'ūal *adj.* (used only before a noun) remaining.

resid'ūum *n.* a residue:—*pl.* **resid'ūa.**

resign *ri-zīn', v.t.* **1** to give up (e.g. a position). **2** to give (something) over (to someone). **3** (with *oneself*) to submit quietly: *to resign oneself to one's fate.*—*v.i.* to give up office, etc.

resignation *rez-ig-nā'sh(ȯ)n, n.* **1** act of giving up. **2** the state of being resigned; quiet acceptance of the situation or events.

resigned *ri-zīnd', adj.* not complaining.

resilient *ri-zil'i-ėnt, adj.* **1** springing back, elastic. **2** coming back quickly from depression to good spirits, or illness to health.

resil'ience, resil'iency *ns.*

resin *rez'in, n.* **1** a sticky substance that oozes out of certain trees and other plants. **2** a synthetic substance with similar properties, used in plastics.

res'inous *adj.* like or containing resin.

resist *ri-zist', v.t.* **1** to struggle against, esp. successfully. **2** to refrain from: *I could not resist saying so.* **3** to be little affected by: *a metal that resists rust.*

resis'tance *n.* **1** the act or power of resisting. **2** the body's ability to resist disease. **3** (a secret organisation offering) opposition in a country to forces of another country that has conquered and occupied it. **4** the ability of a substance to oppose an electric current, turning its energy into heat.

resis'tant *adj.* (with *to*) not affected by.

resis'tible *adj.* able to be resisted:—*opp.* **irresistible.**

resis'tor *n.* a piece of apparatus used to offer electrical resistance.

resolute *rez'ȯl-ōōt, -ūt, adj.* firm, determined:—*opp.* **irresolute.**

res'olutely *adv.* **res'oluteness** *n.*

resolution *rez-ȯl-ōō'sh(ȯ)n, -ū', n.* **1** resoluteness, firmness of mind or purpose. **2** a proposal put before a public meeting. **3** a firm decision: *a New Year resolution.* **4** solution (of a difficulty).

resolve *ri-zolv', v.t.* **1** to decide. **2** to pass as a resolution. **3** to solve. **4** to take away (doubt). **5** to break up, or transform (into): *to resolve (something) into the parts of which it is made up*:—*pr.p.* **resol'ving.**—*n.* **1** purpose, decision. **2** firmness of purpose.

resolved' *adj.* fixed in purpose, determined.

resonance *rez'ȯn-ȧns, n.* increase of intensity of sound, by echoing, vibrating, etc.

res'onant *adj.* **1** echoing, resounding. **2** loud ringing. **3** prolonging or increasing sound by vibrating.

res'onāte *v.i.* to have or produce resonance:—*pr.p.* **res'onating.**

res'onator *n.* a device, etc. that resonates.

resort *ri-zört', v.i.* **1** to go, e.g. in a group (to). **2** to turn (to) in difficulty.—*n.* **1** act of resorting, or something resorted to. **2** a popular place, e.g. for holidays.

as a, in the, last resort when all else fails.

resound *ri-zownd'*, *v.i.* **1** to sound loudly. **2** to echo. **3** to be much repeated or mentioned. **4** to be filled with sound.
resound'ing *adj.* **1** loud; echoing. **2** emphatic.
resource *ri-sōrs'*, *-sörs'*, *n.* **1** a source of help. **2** (in *pl.*) money or other property, or means of raising money. **3** (in *pl.*) means of helping or entertaining oneself. **4** resourcefulness.
resource'ful *adj.* quick-witted, good at finding ways out of difficulties.
resource'fully *adv.* **resource'fulness** *n.*
respect *ri-spekt'*, *v.t.* **1** to show or feel esteem for, regard highly. **2** to treat with care or consideration: *to respect other people's property.*—*n.* **1** high opinion, esteem. **2** consideration, thoughtfulness. **3** (in *pl.*) greetings, good wishes. **4** a detail, point: *in this respect*.
respec'table *adj.* **1** worthy of respect or notice. **2** fairly good; fairly large. **3** decent, proper.
respectabil'ity, respec'tableness *ns.*
respec'tably *adv.*
respect'ful *adj.* showing or feeling respect.
respect'fully *adv.* **respect'fulness** *n.*
respec'ting *prep.* concerning.
respec'tive *adj.* belonging to each separately: *The boys went to their respective homes*.
respec'tively *adv.* in the order given: *Give the large, medium, and small bed to the father, mother, and baby bear respectively*.
in respect of as regards, as far as concerns.
with respect to with reference to.
See also **disrespect, irrespective**.
respire *ri-spīr'*, *v.i.* to breathe:—*pr.p.* **respir'ing**.
respiration *res-pir-ā'sh(ȯ)n*, *n.* breathing.
res'pirātor *n.* a mask worn over mouth and nose to purify the air breathed in.
respiratory (*res'pir-*, or *ri-spīr'*) *adj.* connected with breathing.
artificial respiration a method of forcing air into the lungs of an unconscious person.
respite *res'pīt*, *-pit*, *n.* **1** a pause. **2** a rest (from).
resplendent *ri-splen'dėnt*, *adj.* very splendid; brilliant.
resplen'dence *n.* **resplen'dently** *adv.*
respond *ri-spond'*, *v.i.* **1** to answer; to act by way of reply (to). **2** to react satisfactorily (to something done, etc.): *The illness responded to treatment*; *The plane did not seem to respond to the controls.*—*v.t.* to say, in answer.
respon'dent *n.* a defendant, e.g. in a divorce case.
response' *n.* **1** an answer. **2** the answer made by the people to the priest during a church service. **3** action or feeling in reply to a request, speech, action, etc.
respon'sible *adj.* **1** trustworthy, sensible: *a responsible person:*—*opp.* **irresponsible**. **2** involving care of people or affairs: *a responsible post.* **3** having a particular duty or charge (with *for*): *I'll be responsible for buying the wine for the party.* **4** obliged to give a satisfactory account of one's conduct, management, etc.: *I am responsible to my employer for the care of the petty cash.* **5** being the cause of, or to blame for, something (with *for*).
responsibil'ity *n.* **1** the stake of being responsible. **2** something for which one is responsible:—*pl.* **responsibil'ities**.
respon'sibleness *n.*
respon'sibly *adv.* in a trustworthy or serious way.
respon'sive *adj.* **1** quick to respond, e.g. by giving interest, sympathy. **2** quick to react.
respon'sively *adv.* **respon'siveness** *n.*
rest[1] *rest*, *n.* **1** state of being still, not working. **2** peace. **3** sleep. **4** a support or prop: *a book-rest.* **5** (*music*) a pause, or the mark showing it.—*v.i.* **1** to stop work. **2** to be still, relax. **3** to lean (on). **4** to depend (on), be based (on): *The conclusion rests on good evidence.*—*v.t.* **1** to give rest to: *Rest your back.* **2** to place, lean (something; with *on*, *against*). **3** to base (something; with *on*).
rest'ful *adj.* bringing rest; peaceful, calm.
rest'fully *adv.* **rest'fulness** *n.*
rest'less *adj.* **1** unable to rest. **2** uneasy; fidgeting.
rest'lessly *adv.* **rest'lessness** *n.*
rest cure treatment by rest.
rest'ing-place *n.* a place for rest, esp. the grave.
at rest **1** free from pain, worry, etc. **2** not moving.
come to rest to stop moving.
rest[2] *rest*, *n.* (with *the*) **1** what is left, remainder. **2** all the others.—*v.i.* to remain, be: *Rest assured that* ..., i.e. you may be sure that....
rest with to be the duty or right of: *The choice rests with you*; *It rests with you to decide*.
restaurant *res'tė-ron*[g], *n.* a place where meals are served to customers.
restaurateur *res-tȯr-ȧ-tûr'*, *n.* the keeper of a restaurant.

restitution *res-ti-tū'sh(ȯ)n, n.* **1** the act of giving back what was lost or taken away. **2** compensation for harm done.

restive *res'tiv, adj.* impatient of delay, or control, etc.

restore *ri-stōr', -stör', v.t.* **1** to bring, put, or give back. **2** to repair (e.g. a picture). **3** to cure (a person):—*pr.p.* **restor'ing**.
restoration *res-tȯ-rā'sh(ȯ)n, n.* **1** act of restoring. **2** repair. **3** (with *cap.*) the return of Charles II as King in 1660.
restorative *ris-tōr'ȧ-tiv, -tör', adj.* restoring, able to restore.—*n.* a substance that restores.
restor'er *n.*

restrain *ri-strān', v.t.* **1** to hold back (from). **2** to check. **3** to keep in prison, etc.
restrained' *adj.* **1** kept under control. **2** not showing excess (e.g. of emotion).
restraint' *n.* **1** the act of restraining. **2** the state of being restrained. **3** self-control. **4** a check or impediment to progress. **5** confinement, esp. because of insanity. **6** moderation or understatement in description, etc.

restrict *ri-strikt', v.t.* to limit, keep within bounds of e.g. space, time, quantity.
restric'ted *adj.*
restric'tion *n.* **1** the act of restricting. **2** something (e.g. a rule) which limits freedom.
restric'tive *adj.* limiting.
restrictive practice an agreement between manufacturers, companies, etc. that keeps prices high, prevents the most efficient use of men and machinery, etc.

restruc'turing *n.* the reorganisation of a business, often involving redundancies.

result *ri-zult', v.i.* **1** to end (in). **2** to follow as a consequence (from).—*n.* **1** outcome, effect, consequence. **2** the number, etc. obtained by working out a sum, etc.
resul'tant *adj.* resulting.

resume *ri-zūm', -zōōm', v.t.* **1** to take up, begin, again: *to resume work.* **2** to take again; to take back.—*v.i.* to begin again: *After tea the meeting resumed.*:—*pr.p.* **resum'ing**.
resumption *(-zump'sh(ȯ)n, -zum'sh(ȯ)n) n.*

résumé *rā'zü-mā, n.* a summary.

resurgent *ri-sûr'jėnt, adj.* rising again.
resur'gence *n.*

resurrect *rez-ůr-ekt', v.t.* **1** to restore to life. **2** to bring back into use.
resurrec'tion *n.* **1** the act of resurrecting. **2** rising from the dead, esp. (*cap.*) of Christ.

resuscitate *ri-sus'i-tāt, v.t.* to revive, e.g. from unconsciousness:—*pr.p.* **resus'citating**.
resuscitā'tion *n.*

retail *rē'tāl, n.* sale of goods to consumer, or in small quantities.—*adj.* concerned, connected, with such sale.—*v.t.* *(ri-tāl')* **1** to sell in this way. **2** to repeat in detail (e.g. a story).
retail'er *n.* a shopkeeper.

retain *ri-tān', v.t.* **1** to keep in one's possession. **2** to continue to have. **3** to hold back or in place. **4** to reserve the services of (someone) by paying a fee.
retain'er *n.* **1** a servant, esp. to a family. **2** a fee paid (e.g. to a lawyer) to retain his services.
reten'tion *n.*
reten'tive *adj.* having the power of retaining, keeping: *a soil retentive of moisture*; *a retentive memory*.
retaining wall a wall to prevent a ridge of earth from slipping down.

retake *rē-tāk', v.t.* **1** to take again. **2** to recapture. **3** to film again:—*pa.t.* **retook'**; *pa.p.* **retak'en**.—*n.* *(rē'tāk)* part of a motion picture filmed again.

retaliate *ri-tal'i-āt, v.i.* to strike back when struck, to return like for like (esp. evil):—*pr.p.* **retal'iating**.
retaliā'tion *n.* **retal'iatory** *adj.*

retina *ret'i-nȧ, n.* the layer at the back of the eye that receives the picture of anything seen.

retinue *ret'i-nū, n.* those who attend on a person of high rank or importance.

retire *ri-tīr', v.i.* **1** to withdraw (from). **2** to go back. **3** to go to bed. **4** to give up employment permanently.—*v.t.* to compel to give up employment:—*pr.p.* **reti'ring**.
reti'ral, retire'ment *ns.*
retired' *adj.* **1** having given up work. **2** (of a place) quiet, secluded.
reti'ring *adj.* avoiding notice, shy.

retort[1] *ri-tört', v.i.* to make a quick, and sharp or witty, reply.—Also *v.t.*—Also *n.*

retort[2] *ri-tört', n.* **1** a glass flask, esp. one with its neck bent down, for distilling liquids. **2** (*industrial use*) a closed oven, e.g. for heating coke.

retouch *rē'tuch', v.t.* to touch up in order to improve.

retrace *rē-trās', rē', v.t.* to trace, go over, again:—*pr.p.* **retracing**.
See also **irretraceable**.

retract *ri-trakt', v.t.* **1** to take back (something said or given). **2** to draw back: *A cat retracts its claws.*—Also *v.i.*
retract'able *adj.* able to be drawn back or up.
retract'ile *(-īl) adj.* (e.g. of a cat's claws)

retractable.
retrac'tion *n.*

retread[1] *rē-tred'*, *v.t.* to tread again:—*pa.t.* **retrod'**; *pa.p.* **retrodd'en.**

retread[2] *rē-tred'*, *v.t.* to make a new tread on (a tyre):—*pa.t., pa.p.* **retread'ed.** —*n.* *(rē'tred)* a retreaded tyre.

retreat *ri-trēt'*, *n.* **1** a movement backward, e.g. from danger. **2** a withdrawal. **3** a quiet place. **4** a refuge.—*v.i.* **1** to draw back, retire. **2** to go away.

retrench *rē-trench'*, *-sh*, *v.i.* and *v.t.* to cut down (expenses).
retrench'ment *n.*

retrial. See **retry**.

retribution *ret-ri-bū'sh(ȯ)n*, *n.* deserved punishment.

retrieve *ri-trēv'*, *v.t.* **1** to search for and fetch, as a dog does. **2** to recover or rescue. **3** to restore. **4** to make amends for:—*pr.p.* **retriev'ing.**
retriev'al *n.* **1** the act of retrieving. **2** (*computers*) the extracting of stored data from a system.
retriev'er *n.* a dog trained to find and fetch game that has been shot.
See also **irretrievable.**

retro- *ret-rō-*, (as part of a word) backwards.
retroactive *ret-rō-ak'tiv*, *adj.* (of a law, decision, etc.) retrospective.
retrograde *ret'rō-grād*, *adj.* **1** going backward. **2** falling from better to worse.
retrogress *ret-rō-gres'*, *v.i.* to go backwards, deteriorate.
retrogression *ret-rō-gresh'(ȯ)n*, *n.*
retro-rocket *ret'rō-rok-it*, *n.* a rocket for slowing down a spacecraft, etc., fired in the opposite direction to that in which it is travelling.
retrospect *ret'rō-spekt*, *rē'trō-*, *n.* a view of, or thought about, the past.
retrospec'tion *n.* looking back on the past.
retrospec'tive *adj.* **1** looking back. **2** going back to a date in the past. **3** (of e.g. a law) applying to past as well as present and future.
retroverted *ret'rō-vûr-tid*, *adj.* turned backwards.

retry *rē-trī'*, *v.t.* to try again (in a court of justice):—*pr.p.* **retry'ing**; *pa.p.* **retried'.**
retrī'al *n.* a second trial.

return *ri-tûrn'*, *v.i.* to come or go back.—*v.t.* **1** to give, throw, send, pay, back. **2** to retort, reply. **3** to elect (to parliament). **4** (of a jury) to give (a verdict).—*n.* **1** act of returning. **2** a repetition, recurrence. **3** something returned. **4** (often in *pl.*) proceeds, profit. **5** a return ticket. **6** an official statement, e.g. of one's taxable income.
return'able *adj.* that may be, or must be, returned.
returning officer an officer in charge at an election.
return match a second match played by the same set of players.
return ticket a ticket entitling a passenger to travel to a place and back again to the starting-point.
by return by the next post back.
in return for as an exchange for.
many happy returns (of the day) a wish expressed to someone on his birthday.

reunion *rē-ūn'yȯn*, *n.* a meeting of people who have not met for some time.
reunite *rē-ū-nīt'*, *v.t., v.i.* to join after separation:—*pr.p.* **reunit'ing.**

reuse *rē-ūz'*, *v.t.* to use again:—*pr.p.* **reus'ing.**
reus'able *adj.*

rev *rev*, *v.t.* to increase the speed of revolution in (an engine; often with *up*).—Also *v.i.*:—*pr.p.* **revv'ing**; *pa.p.* **revved.**
revs *n.pl.* revolutions.

revamp *rē-vamp'*, *v.t.* to renovate, give a new appearance to.

reveal *ri-vēl'*, *v.t.* **1** to make known. **2** to show.
reveal'ing *adj.*
revelation *rev-ė-lā'sh(ȯ)n*, *n.* **1** the act of revealing. **2** something, esp. unsuspected, that is made known or shown. **3** (*cap.*) the last book of the New Testament (also **Revelations** *n.sing.*).

reveille *ri-val'i*, *n.* a bugle call at daybreak to awaken soldiers.

revel *rev'l*, *v.i.* **1** to make merry. **2** to find great enjoyment (in):—*pr.p.* **rev'elling**; *pa.p.* **rev'elled.**—*n.* (usu. in *pl.*) merrymaking.
rev'eller *n.*
rev'elry *n.* revelling.

revelation. See **reveal.**

revenge *ri-venj'*, *v.t.* **1** to seek satisfaction for (an injury done) by injuring in return: *He revenged his father's death by killing the assassin.* **2** to avenge (oneself, e.g. on one's enemies).—*n.* **1** an injury in return for an injury. **2** desire for this:—*pr.p.* **reven'ging.**
revenge'ful *adj.* anxious for revenge.
revenge'fully *adv.* **reveng'er** *n.*

revenue *rev'ėn-ū*, *n.* **1** income, esp. income of a country from all sources. **2** the department of civil service dealing with this.
inland revenue **1** income from taxes and duties within the country. **2** the department dealing with this.

reverberate *ri-vûr'bėr-āt*, *v.i.* **1** to echo and re-echo, resound. **2** to be reflected:—*pr.p.* **rever'berating**.
reverberā'tion *n.*

revere *ri-vēr'*, *v.t.* to respect greatly:—*pr.p.* **rever'ing**.
reverence *rev'ėr-ėns*, *n.* **1** deep respect; veneration. **2** (*old*, or *Ir.*; *cap.*, with *His*, *Your*, etc.) used in addressing a clergyman.—*v.t.* to revere:—*pr.p.* **rev'erencing**.
rev'erend *adj.* **1** worthy of respect. **2** (with *cap.*; usu. written **Rev.**) a title put before the names of a clergyman: *The Rev. John Brown*.
rev'erent *adj.*:—*opp.* **irreverent**.
rev'erently *adv.*
reverential *rev-ėr-en'sh(ȧ)l*, *adj.* showing great respect.

reverie *rev'ė-ri*, *n.* **1** a state of dreamy thought. **2** a day-dream.

reverse *ri-vûrs'*, *v.t.* **1** to turn the other way, e.g. upside down. **2** to set moving backwards. **3** to undo: *to reverse a decision*.—*v.i.* to move backwards:—*pr.p.* **rever'sing**.—*n.* **1** the opposite (of). **2** the back (of e.g. a coin). **3** a defeat. **4** in motor car, reversing gear.
rever'sal *n.* act of reversing or process of being reversed.
rever'sible *adj.* **1** able to be reversed (*opp.* **Irreversible**). **2** (of clothes) able to be worn with either side out.
reversion *ri-vûr'sh(ȯ)n*, *n.* **1** the act of reverting. **2** (the right to) the future possession (of something in the hands of another).
revert *ri-vûrt'*, *v.i.* to return to a former state, subject, or owner.
reverse the charges (of a telephone caller) to ask for the call to be paid for by the person receiving it.

review *ri-vū'*, *n.* **1** a (second or additional) study or consideration of a matter: *a review of the subject of parking in cities*. **2** an inspection (of troops). **3** a critical essay on a book, play, etc., or a magazine devoted to such essays.—*v.t.* **1** to examine again; to go over the whole of: *to review the facts, the situation*. **2** to write a review of. **3** to inspect (usu. troops).
review'er *n.*

revile *ri-vīl'*, *v.t.* to say harsh things about:—*pr.p.* **revil'ing**.

revise *ri-vīz'*, *v.t.* **1** to examine and correct. **2** to change: *to revise one's opinion*.—*v.i.* and *v.t.* to study one's previous notes, etc. on (a subject) in preparation for an examination, etc.:—*pr.p.* **revis'ing**.
revis'er *n.* **revision** *ri-vizh'(ȯ)n*, *n.*
revis'ory *adj.*

revitalise *ri-vīt'ȧl-īz*, *v.t.* to give (someone) new life or energy:—*pr.p.* **revit'alising**.

revive *ri-vīv'*, *v.t* and *v.i.* to bring, or come, back to life, strength, active state, use, etc.:—*pr.p.* **reviv'ing**.
reviv'er *n.*
reviv'al *n.* **1** return to life or strength. **2** bringing back to use, or (of a play) to the stage. **3** (a time of) new interest, in e.g. religion, learning.
reviv'alist *n.* one who helps to promote a religious revival.
revivify *rē-viv'i-fī*, *v.t.* to give new life to:—*pr.p.* **reviv'ifying**; *pa.p.* **reviv'ified**.

revoke *ri-vōk'*, *v.t.* to cancel (e.g. a decision).—*v.i.* to fail to follow suit at cards when one can do so:—*pr.p.* **revok'ing**.
rev'ocable *adj.*:—*opp.* **irrev'ocable**.
revocā'tion *n.*

revolt *ri-vōlt'*, *v.i.* **1** to rebel. **2** to rise up (against). **3** (of the mind, senses, etc.) to feel disgust (at).—*v.t.* to disgust.—*n.* rebellion.
revol'ting *adj.* disgusting.
revol'tingly *adv.* **revol'tingness** *n.*

revolution *rev-ȯl-ōō'sh(ȯ)n*, or *-ū'*, *n.* **1** turning round a centre. **2** a complete turn. **3** a great change. **4** the complete overthrowing of a government.
revolu'tionary *adj.* **1** (aimed at) bringing about great changes (or tending to do so). **2** of political revolution.—*n.* one who participates in, or is in favour of, revolution:—*pl.* **revolu'tionaries**.
revolu'tionise *v.t.* to cause great changes in:—*pr.p.* **revolu'tionising**.
revolve *ri-volv'*, *v.t* and *v.i* to roll or turn around.—*v.i.* to move in a circle (round, about).—*v.t.* to turn over (in the mind):—*pr.p.* **revolv'ing**.
revol'ver *n.* a pistol with a revolving magazine.

revue *ri-vū'*, *n.* a light theatre show, consisting usu. of sketches satirising recent events.

revulsion *ri-vul'sh(ȯ)n*, *n.* **1** disgust. **2** a recoil (from). **3** a sudden change of feeling, e.g. from love to hate.

revved, revving. See **rev**.

reward *ri-wörd'*, *n.* something given in return for good (or sometimes evil) behaviour or work or service.—*v.t.* **1** to give a reward to. **2** to repay (e.g. a service).
reward'ing *adj.* giving pleasure or profit.

reword *rē'wûrd'*, *v.t.* to put into different words.

rewrite *ri-rīt'*, *v.t.* to write (something) again in different words:—*pr.p.* **rewrit'ing**.—Also *n.* (*rē'rīt*).

rhapsody *rap'sȯ-di, n.* an emotional, excited piece of music, poetry, prose, etc.:—*pl.* **rhap'sodies**.
rhap'sodise *v.i.* to write or talk with great enthusiasm:—*pr.p.* **rhap'sodising**.

rhea *rē'ȧ, n.* a South American ostrich.

rheostat *rē'ȯ-stat, n.* an instrument for varying electrical resistance.

rhesus *rē'sȯs, n.* a small Indian monkey, whose red blood cells, like those of most humans, contain the **Rhesus factor**. Human blood with the factor is **Rhe'sus-pos'itive**, without it, **Rhe'sus-neg'ative**.

rhetoric *ret'ȯr-ik, n.* **1** the art of good speaking or writing. **2** showy, insincere expressions.
rhetor'ical *adj.* showy in style.
rhetorical question one that the speaker answers himself, or that does not need an answer.

rheumatism *rōō'mȧ-tizm, n.* a disease causing pain and stiffness in the joints.
rheumat'ic *adj.* caused by, connected with, having, rheumatism.—*n.* **1** one who suffers from rheumatism. **2** (in *pl.*) rheumatic pains.
rheu'matoid *adj.* resembling rheumatism.

rhinoceros *rī-nos'ėr-ōs, n.* a large thick-skinned animal with one, or two, horns on its nose:—*pl.* **rhinoc'eros(es)**:—*abbrev.* **rhi'no** *(rī'nō)*:—*pl.* **rhi'nos**.

rhizome *rī'zōm, n.* an underground stem producing roots and shoots.

rhododendron *rō-dȯ-den'drȯn, n.* a shrub with large showy flowers.

rhombus *rom'bȯs, n.* an equal-sided parallelogram, other than a square.

rhubarb *rōō'bärb, n.* a plant whose stalks are used in cooking and roots in medicine.

rhyme *rīm, n.* **1** a word like another in its final sound or sounds (e.g. *beef* is a rhyme for *leaf* and *belief*; *sensible* and *reprehensible* are rhymes). **2** likeness of this kind in sound of words. **3** poetry. **4** a short poem.—*v.i.* **1** (of words) to be rhymes. **2** to write verses:—*pr.p.* **rhym'ing**.
rhy'mer *n.* one who writes verses.

rhythm *riTHm, n.* **1** a regular repeated pattern of stresses, beats or sounds in music or verse. **2** a regularly repeated pattern of movements. **3** an ability to sing, move, etc. with rhythm.
rhyth'mic(al) *adjs.* **rhyth'mically** *adv.*

rib *rib, n.* **1** one of the bones that curve round and forward from the backbone. **2** one of the members of the frame of a ship, curving upwards from the keel. **3** a support for the fabric of an aeroplane wing or an umbrella. **4** a ridge. **5** in knitting, a pattern giving regular ridges and added elasticity.—*v.t.* to form ribs in, or provide with ribs:—*pr.p.* **ribb'ing**; *pa.p.* **ribbed**.
ribb'ing *n.* **1** an arrangement of ribs. **2** a rib in knitting.
rib'cage *n.* the protective framework formed by the ribs around the lungs.

ribald *rib'ȧld, adj.* (of humour) coarse, obscene.
rib'aldry *n.*

riband *rib'ȧnd, n.* an older variant of **ribbon**.

ribbon *rib'on, n.* a long narrow strip of material.
ribbon development growth of towns in long strips along the main roads.

rice *rīs, n.* a grass grown in tropical countries, the seed of which is used for food.
rice paper paper made from straw of rice, or from the pith of a tree.

rich *rich, adj.* **1** wealthy. **2** costly, valuable: *rich materials*; *a rich reward.* **3** having plenty of (with *in*): *a district rich in coal.* **4** plentiful, abundant. **5** (of colour) deep, strong. **6** (of food) containing much fat, egg, sugar, etc.
riches *rich'iz, n.pl.* wealth.
rich'ly *adv.* **rich'ness** *n.*

rick[1] *rik, n.* a stack (of hay, etc.).

rick[2] *rik, v.t.* to sprain or strain.

rickets *rik'its, n.sing.* a disease of children, causing softening and bending of the bones.
rick'ety *adj.* unsteady: *a rickety table.*

rickshaw, ricksha *rik'shö, -shä, n.* abbrev. of **jinrick'sha(w)**, a small two-wheeled carriage drawn by a man.

ricochet *rik'ȯ-shā,* or *-shet, n.* a glancing, rebound, e.g. of a bullet.—*v.i.* to glance (off):—*pr.p.* **ric'ochet(t)ing** *(-shā-ing, -shet-ing)*; *pa.p.* **ric'ochet(t)ed** *(-shād, -shet-id)*.

rid *rid, v.t.* to free from, to clear (of):—*pr.p.* **ridd'ing**; *pa.t.* **rid** or **ridd'ed**; *pa.p.* **rid**.
ridd'ance *n.* **1** clearance. **2** deliverance.
a good riddance a welcome relief from something.
get rid of to free oneself from.

ridden. See **ride**.

riddle[1] *rid'l, n.* **1** a question intended to puzzle, a conundrum. **2** a person, happening, etc. difficult to understand.

riddle[2] *rid'l, n.* a large coarse sieve.—*v.t.* **1** to sift with a riddle. **2** to make full of holes: *to riddle with bullets*:—*pr.p.* **ridd'ling**.

ride *rīd, v.i.* **1** to travel, be carried, on a horse, bicycle, etc. or in a car, etc. **2** to lie at anchor. **3** (with *up*) to work up out of position.—*v.t.* **1** to travel on (a horse, etc.) **2** to take part in (a horse race). **3** to control (a person) in a tyrannical way. **4** (with *out*) to keep afloat throughout (a storm); to survive, keep going through (a crisis, etc.):—*pr.p.* **rid'ing**; *pa.t.* **rode** *(rōd)*; *pa.p.* **ridd'en**.—*n.* **1** a journey on horseback, in a vehicle, etc. **2** a road for riding on on horseback.

rid'er *n.* **1** one who rides. **2** something added to what has been said, e.g. in a document.

ri'ding-school *n.* a place where one is taught to ride a horse.

take someone for a ride (*coll.*) to cheat or trick someone.

ridge *rij, n.* **1** a raised part between furrows. **2** a long narrow top or crest, e.g. of hills; something similar to this: *The weather-chart showed a ridge of high pressure.*—*v.t.* and *v.i.* **1** to form into ridges. **2** to wrinkle:—*pr.p.* **ridg'ing**.

ridg'y *adj.*:—*comp.* **ridg'ier**; *superl.* **ridg'iest**.

ridg'iness *n.*

ridicule *rid'i-kūl, n.* mockery.—*v.t.* to laugh at, to mock:—*pr.p.* **rid'iculing**.

ridic'ūlous *adj.* absurd, deserving to be laughed at.

ridic'ulously *adv.* **ridic'ūlousness** *n.*

riding. See **ride**.

rife *rīf, adj.* very common: *Disease and hunger were rife in that country.*

rife with very full of.

riff-raff *rif'-raf, n.* worthless things or people.

rifle[1] *rī'fl, v.t.* **1** to search thoroughly and rob (e.g. a desk, till; also *v.i.* with *through*). **2** to steal:—*pr.p.* **ri'fling**.

rifle[2] *rī'fl, n.* a gun fired from the shoulder with spiral grooves in its barrel.—*v.t.* to cut spiral grooves inside (a gun barrel):—*pr.p.* **ri'fling**.

ri'fling *n.* the spiral grooves in a gun barrel.

rifle range a place for rifle practice.

rift *rift, n.* **1** a split or crack. **2** a disagreement between friends.

rift valley a valley formed by the fall of part of the earth's crust between faults in the rock.

rig *rig, v.t.* **1** to fit (a ship) with sails and tackle. **2** to fit (up): *to rig up a rough shelter.* **3** to fit (out, e.g. with clothes). **4** to arrange (e.g. an election, a trial) dishonestly so as to ensure a particular result:—*pr.p.* **rigg'ing**; *pa.p.* **rigged**. —*n.* **1** the arrangement of sails etc. of a sailing ship. **2** the equipment for drilling an oil-well (also **oil'rig**). **3** (*coll.*) an outfit, clothing.

rigg'ing *n.* the system of ropes, etc. which works a ship's masts and sails.

rig'-out (*slang*) *n.* an outfit.

right *rīt, adj.* **1** opp. to *left*. **2** correct. **3** true. **4** just, good, proper.—*adv.* **1** to or on the right side. **2** correctly. **3** straight; immediately. **4** all the way; completely. **5** exactly.—*n.* **1** the right side. **2** justice. **3** the thing(s) one ought to do. **4** legal or just claim: *to have a right to something.* **5** (often *cap.*) the more conservative party or part of a party in politics (in certain legislative assemblies, these people sit by custom to the right of the presiding officer).—*v.t.* **1** to correct, set right. **2** (with *oneself, itself*) to recover upright position.

right'ful *adj.* by right: *the rightful heir to the throne.*

right'fully *adv.* according to right: *It rightfully belongs to me.*

right'ly *adv.* correctly.

right'ness *n.* **1** correctness. **2** justice.

right angle an angle of 90 degrees, one quarter of a complete revolution.

right'-hand'ed *adj.* having the right hand more skilful than the left.

right wing **1** the political right. **2** the wing on the right side of an army, football pitch, etc.

right'-wing' *adj.* **right'-wing'er** *n.*

by rights rightfully.

in one's own right not through someone else: *a peeress in her own right* (i.e. not because wife of a peer).

in the right having justice or truth to support one.

right away immediately.

right-hand man one's most useful helper.

right-hand side the right side.

Right Honourable a courtesy title, given e.g. to Cabinet ministers.

right of entry legal right to enter.

right of way **1** the public right to use a path over private ground. **2** (**right'-of-way'** *n., pl.* **right'-of-ways'**, **rights'-of-way'**) a path to which this right applies. **3** right to move first in traffic, e.g. at a crossroads.

set, put to rights to put in good order, or satisfactory state.

See also **righteous**.

righteous *rī'chùs, adj.* **1** living a good life. **2** just; morally right.

right'eously *adv.* **right'eousness** *n.*

rightful, rightly. See **right**.

rigid *rij'id, adj.* **1** completely stiff; not bending. **2** very strict.

rigid'ity, rig'idness *ns.*

rig'idly *adv.*

rigmarole *rig'må-rōl*, *n.* a long rambling speech.

rigor mortis *rī'gȯr mŏr'tis*, *rig'*, the temporary stiffening of the body after death.

rigour *rig'ȯr*, *n.* **1** strictness. **2** harshness. **3** (of weather, etc.) severity.
rig'orous *adj.* very strict.
rig'orously *adv.* **rig'orousness** *n.*

rill *ril*, *n.* a very small brook.

rim *rim*, *n.* an edge, border, brim:—*v.t.* to form a rim to:—*pr.p.* **rimm'ing**; *pa.p.* **rimmed**.
rim'less *adj.* without rim or border.

rime[1] *rīm*, *n.* ice formed from frozen fog.

rime[2]. Another spelling of **rhyme**.

rimmed, **rimless**. See **rim**.

rind *rīnd*, *n.* peel, skin, firm covering.

ring[1] *ring*, *n.* **1** a hoop or circular band of metal, etc. as an ornament for the finger, ear, etc., or for another purpose. **2** a hollow circle or something resembling this. **3** a group of people in control of a business or a criminal enterprise. **4** an enclosed space for circus performances, boxing-matches, etc.—*v.t.* **1** to encircle, go round. **2** to mark by putting a ring on (e.g. a bird).
ringed *adj.* marked with ring(s).
ring'let *n.* a long curl of hair.
ring finger the finger on which the wedding ring is worn (usu. third on left hand).
ring'leader *n.* one who takes the lead in mischief, etc.
ring'master *n.* one who is in charge of performances in a circus ring.
ring road, **route** a road that circles a town or a town centre.
ring'side *adj.* (of a view) very clear, as from the front row of seats at a boxing match.
ring'worm *n.* a skin disease causing ring-shaped patches.

ring[2] *ring*, *v.i.* **1** (of a bell) to sound. **2** to give a clear bell-like sound. **3** to be filled (e.g. with sound). **4** to sound, seem to be: *His words ring true.* **5** to call (for) by means of a bell.—*v.t.* **1** to cause (bell, etc.) to sound. **2** to telephone (often with *up*):—*pa.t.* **rang**; *pa.p.* **rung**.—*n.* **1** the sound of a bell. **2** a clear sound. **3** (*coll.*) a telephone call.
ring'ing *n.* and *adj.*
ring a bell to stir one's memory.
ring down, or **up**, **the curtain** to give the signal for lowering or raising the curtain in a theatre.
ring off to end a telephone conversation and connection.
ring the changes **1** to go through all possible arrangements with a chime of bells. **2** to use a small number of things in a variety of ways.

rink *ringk*, *n.* **1** a sheet of ice, often artificial, for skating. **2** an area of ice for curling. **3** part of a bowling green used by one set of players. **4** a team of curlers.

rinse *rins*, *v.t.* **1** to wash lightly to remove soap, etc. **2** to pour, or take, liquid into and let it out of: *Rinse your cup, your mouth*:—*pr.p.* **rins'ing**.—*n.* **1** an act of rinsing. **2** a liquid for rinsing. **3** a liquid for tinting the hair.

riot *rī'ȯt*, *n.* **1** a noisy disturbance by a crowd. **2** wild disorder. **3** brilliance (of colour).—*v.i.* **1** to take part in a riot. **2** to grow, or to behave, in an uncontrolled way.
ri'oter *n.* **ri'oting** *n.* and *adj.*
ri'otous *adj.* uncontrolled.
ri'otously *adv.*
run riot to act, or (of plants) grow, without control.

rip *rip*, *v.t.* and *v.i.* to tear (off, open, etc.).—*v.i.* (*coll.*) to move very fast:—*pr.p.* **ripp'ing**; *pa.p.* **ripped**.—*n.* a tear, rent.
rip'-cord *n.* a cord for opening a parachute.
rip off (*slang*) to cheat, overcharge (*n.* **rip'-off**).

ripe *rīp*, *adj.* **1** ready for harvest. **2** fully developed. **3** ready (for): *ripe for mischief.*
ri'pen *v.t.*, *v.i.* to make, grow, ripe or riper.
ripe'ness *n.*

riposte *ri-post'*, *n.* a quick reply or retort in an argument.

ripple *rip'l*, *n.* **1** a little wave or movement on water. **2** a sound like rippling water.—Also *v.t.* and *v.i.*: —*pr.p.* **ripp'ling**.

rise *rīz*, *v.i.* **1** to get up from bed. **2** to stand up. **3** to go up higher: *The smoke is rising.* **4** (e.g. of cakes, dough) to swell. **5** to become higher. **6** to come into being, to begin: *The river rises in the hills.* **7** to be promoted. **8** to come (into view or notice). **9** to respond (to a challenge, a taunt). **10** to rebel. **11** to come back to life:—*pr.p.* **rīs'ing**; *pa.t.* **rose** (*rōz*); *pa.p.* **risen** (*riz'n*)—*n.* **1** progress upwards. **2** a slope upwards. **3** increase. **4** beginning.
ris'er *n.* **1** one who rises, esp. from bed. **2** the front upright part of a step.
ris'ing *n.* a revolt.
give rise to to cause.
take a rise out of to tease, provoke.

risk *risk*, *n.* **1** chance of loss or injury. **2** a person or thing that represents this.—*v.t.* **1** to take a chance of losing, damaging, etc. (e.g. onc's life, something breakable). **2** to take a chance of experiencing: *to risk* *disaster*.

ris'ky *adj.* that may result in loss or injury:—*comp.* **ris'kier**; *superl.* **ris'kiest**.

ris'kiness *n.*

at risk in danger.

run, take, risks, a risk to act in a way that might cause loss, injury, etc.

risotto *ri-zot'o*, *n.* a savoury rice dish:—*pl.* **risott'os**.

risqué *rēs'kā*, *adj.* (of humour) daring; bordering on the indecent.

rissole *ris'ōl*, *n.* a fried cake or ball of minced food.

rite *rīt*, *n.* a ceremony, esp. religious.

ritual *rit'ū-ȧl*, *n.* a set way of carrying out religious worship, etc.—*adj.* **1** concerned with rites: *ritual laws.* **2** forming a rite or ceremony: *a ritual dance*.

rival *rī'vȧl*, *n.* a person who, or thing that, attempts to equal or beat another.— *v.t.* to equal (someone or something): *He rivals his brother in medical skill, as a surgeon*; *For stupidity, nothing rivals this programme*:—*pr.p.* **ri'valling**; *pa.p.* **ri'valled**.

ri'valry *n.*:—*pl.* **ri'valries**.

riven *riv'n*, (*old*) *adj.* split, torn.

river *riv'ėr*, *n.* a large stream of water flowing across country.

rivet *riv'it*, *n.* a bolt for fastening plates of metal together.—*v.t.* **1** to fasten with rivets. **2** to fix firmly: *The sight riveted him to the spot*:—*pr.p.* **riv'eting**; *pa.p.* **riv'eted**.

riv'eter *n.* one whose work is to rivet.

rivulet *riv'ū-lit*, *n.* a small stream.

road *rōd*, *n.* **1** a way for vehicles and people; a highway. **2** a path, course: *the road to ruin.* **3** (in *pl.*) a roadstead.

road'block *n.* an obstruction placed across a road, e.g. by police, to stop traffic.

road hog. See **hog**.

road'house *n.* an inn beside a main road.

road'-sense *n.* skill in knowing how to drive etc. on roads.

road'show *n.* a touring group of theatrical or musical performers.

road'stead *n.* a place near shore where ships may lie at anchor.

road'way *n.* the part of a road used by cars, etc.

road'works *n.pl.* the excavations, etc., involved in the building or repair of roads.

road'worthy *adj.* fit to be used on the road.

road'worthiness *n.*

roam *rōm*, *v.i.* to walk without fixed purpose, wander about.—*v.t.* to wander over.

roam'er *n.*

roan *rōn*, *adj.* and *n.* (a horse, etc.) with spots of grey or white on darker, esp. red-brown, background.

roar *rōr*, *rȯr*, *v.i.* **1** to give or utter a loud, deep sound. **2** to laugh loudly.—*v.t.* to say very loudly.—Also *n.*

roar'ing *adj.*, *n.*

do a roaring trade to make very brisk sales.

roast *rōst*, *v.t.* **1** to cook before a fire, or (uncovered) in an oven. **2** to heat strongly.—Also *v.i.*—*adj.* roasted: *roast beef*.—*n.* a joint for roasting.

rob *rob*, *v.t.* **1** to steal from (a person, place). **2** to cheat, deprive (of):—*pr.p.* **robb'ing**; *pa.p.* **robbed**.

robb'er *n.*

robb'ery *n.* act of stealing:—*pl.* **robb'eries**.

robe *rōb*, *n.* **1** a long loose garment. **2** (often in *pl.*) dress showing certain ranks or positions. **3** a dressing-gown or other loose covering garment.—*v.t.*, *v.i.* to dress, esp. in official dress:—*pr.p.* **rob'ing**.

robin *rob'in*, *n.* the **robin redbreast**, a small bird known by its red breast.

robot *rō'bot*, *n.* **1** a mechanical man. **2** a person who behaves like a machine.

robust *rō-bust'*, *rō'*, *adj.* **1** strong, healthy. **2** rough, vigorous: *a robust style*.

robustly *adv.* **robustness** *n.*

rock[1] *rok*, *n.* **1** a large lump or mass of stone. **2** a hard sweetmeat made in sticks.

rock'ery *n.* a garden plot composed of rocks and stones among which grow **rock plants**, plants naturally growing in a rocky, esp. alpine, environment:—*pl.* **rock'eries**.

rock'y *adj.* **1** full of rocks. **2** like rock:—*comp.* **rock'ier**; *superl.* **rock'iest**.

rock'iness *n.*

rock'-bott'om *n.* the lowest level or depth.—Also *adj.*

rock crystal colourless quartz.

rock'-garden *n.* a rockery.

rock'-salt *n.* salt as a mineral.

on the rocks 1 penniless. **2** (of a drink) on ice.

rock[2] *rok*, *v.t.* and *v.i.* to sway backwards and forwards, or from side to side.—*n.* **1** a rocking movement. **2** (also **rock music**) music or songs with a strong, heavy beat and simple melody.

rock'er *n.* **1** a curved support, usu. one of two, on which a chair, cradle, etc. rocks. **2** a rocking-chair.

rock'ing *n.* and *adj.*

rock'y *adj.* **1** inclined to rock. **2** shaky:—*comp.* **rock'ier**; *superl.* **rock'iest**.
rock'iness *n.*
rock'ing-chair *n.* a chair on rockers.
rock'ing-horse *n.* a toy horse for sitting astride, on rockers.
off one's rocker (*coll.*) mad; crazy.

rockery. See **rock**[1].

rocket *rok'it*, *n.* **1** a metal cylinder shot through the air by means of an exhaust of hot gas (a rocket carries its own oxygen and does not suck in air as a jet plane does), used, e.g. for space exploration or for powering or launching spacecraft, aircraft, etc. **2** a firework, signal light etc., moved in a similar way. **3** a bomb or missile thus propelled.—*v.i.* to rise or increase very rapidly: *Prices rocketed.*
rock'etry *n.* skill in making and using rockets.

rockier, etc., **rocky**. See **rock**[1,2].

rod *rod*, *n.* **1** a long thin stick or bar. **2** a fishing-rod. **3** an old measure of length equal to $5\frac{1}{2}$ yards or about 5 metres.

rode. See **ride**.

rodent *rō'dėnt*, *n.* a gnawing animal, e.g. rabbit, mouse, squirrel.

rodeo *rō-dā'ō*, *rō'di-ō*, *n.* **1** a round-up of cattle. **2** a show of skill in riding, etc. by cowboys:—*pl.* **rodeos**.

roe[1] *rō*, *n.* the mass of eggs in a female fish (**hard roe**) or of seeds in a male fish (**soft roe**).

roe[2] *rō*, *n.* (also **roe deer**) a small deer found in Europe and Asia.
roe'buck *n.* the male roe deer.

rogue *rōg*, *n.* **1** a rascal, dishonest person. **2** one who is playfully mischievous. **3** a plant, etc. different from the normal.
roguery *rō'gėr-i*, *n.* **1** dishonesty. **2** innocent mischief. **3** a dishonest action:—*pl.* **ro'gueries**.
roguish *rō'gish*, *adj.* **rō'guishly** *adv.*
rogue elephant a savage elephant cast out of the herd.
rogues' gallery a police collection of photographs of criminals.

roister *roi'stėr*, *v.i.* to revel noisily.

role, **rôle** *rōl*, *n.* a part played, esp. by an actor or actress.

roll *rōl*, *n.* **1** anything flat (e.g. a sheet of paper, a carpet) wound into the shape of a tube or cylinder. **2** a list, esp. of names. **3** a small, individually-baked portion of bread. **4** an act of rolling. **5** a side to side rocking movement, e.g. of ship or aircraft. **6** a long, rumbling sound.—*v.t.* and *v.i.* **1** to move as if a ball. **2** to turn like a wheel. **3** (of a person, animal, etc. lying down) to turn (over). **4** to rock from side to side. **5** to sound as if a drum.—*v.t.* **1** to wrap round and round. **2** to flatten with a roller. **3** to move (one's eyes) around in a circle.—*v.i.* **1** to move as a great river or the sea. **2** to move on wheels, or (of a person) in a vehicle.
roll'er *n.* **1** something cylinder-shaped for flattening, etc. **2** a long heavy wave. **3** a small cylindrical object round which the hair is wound to curl it.
roll'-call *n.* the calling of names from a list.
roll'er-coaster *n.* a very fast switchback railway at a fair, etc.
roll'er-skate *n.* a skate with wheels instead of a blade.—*v.i.* to move on such skates:—*pr.p.* **roll'er-skating**.
roll'er-towel *n.* a towel with joined ends hung over a roller.
roll'ing-pin *n.* a wooden, glass, etc., roller for flattening out dough.
roll'ing-stock *n.* the stock of engines, wagons etc. that run on a railway.
rolled gold metal coated with thinly-rolled gold.
be rolling in (*coll.*) to have plenty of (esp. money).

rollicking *rol'ik-ing*, *adj.* noisily merry.

roly-poly *rō'li-pō'li*, *n.* **1** a roll-shaped jam or fruit pudding. **2** short plump person:—*pl.* **rol'y-pol'ies**.

Roman *rō'mȧn*, *adj.* **1** connected with Rome or with Roman Catholic Church. **2** (of printing type; usu. without *cap.*) of the ordinary upright kind. **3** (of numbers) written in letters, e.g. I, II, III, IV, V (for 1, 2, 3, 4, 5).—*n.* a native of Rome.
Roman alphabet the alphabet in which Western European languages such as English are written.
Roman Catholic (a member) of the Christian church recognising the Pope as head of the Church.—Also **Catholic**.
Roman Catholicism the beliefs, governments, etc. of the Roman Catholic Church.

romance *rō-mans'*, *n.* **1** a tale of events not likely to happen in real life at the present time. **2** a love story. **3** the excitement, adventure, love, etc. typically found in such tales.—*v.i.* **1** to write or tell fanciful tales. **2** to lie:—*pr.p.* **romanc'ing**.—Also *adj.*
romanc'er *n.*
romantic *rō-man'tik*, *adj.* **1** full of romance. **2** fanciful. **3** dealing with love.
roman'ticise *v.t.* to make (one's own dull life, etc.) sound or seem romantic.—Also *v.i.*:—*pr.p.* **roman'ticising**.
Romance language one (French, Italian, Spanish, etc.) developed from Latin.

Romany *rō'mȧ-ni, n.* **1** a gipsy. **2** the language of gipsies:—*pl.* **Ro'manies**.—Also *adj.*

romp *romp, v.i.* **1** to play in a boisterous way. **2** to move (along, home, etc.) easily and quickly.—*n.* **1** one who romps. **2** a lively game. **3** a quick, easy run.
rom'per *n.* **1** one who romps. **2** (usu. in *pl.*) a short suit for a baby.

rood *ro͞od, n.* **1** a crucifix esp. in a church, sometimes surmounting a **rood'screen**, a partition between choir and nave. **2** an old measure of area, usu. $\frac{1}{4}$ acre.

roof *ro͞of, n.* **1** the top covering of a building, car, etc. **2** the upper part of the mouth:—*pl.* **roofs**.—*v.t.* to cover with a roof.
roof'ing *n.* **1** a roof. **2** materials for a roof.—*adj.* used for making a roof.
roof'less *adj.* **1** having no roof. **2** having no house.
roof'-rack *n.* a frame to which luggage can be secured, fitted to the roof of a car, etc.
roof'tree *n.* the beam at the highest part of a roof.

rook[1] *rook, n.* a kind of crow.—*v.t.* **1** to cheat. **2** to overcharge.
rook'ery *n.* a nesting-place of rooks, penguins, or seals:—*pl.* **rook'eries**.

rook[2] *rook, n.* a castle in chess.

room *ro͞om, room, n.* **1** space. **2** opportunity or scope: *There is room for improvement.* **3** a compartment in a house. **4** (in *pl.*) lodgings.
room'y *adj.* spacious, having plenty of room:—*comp.* **room'ier**; *superl.* **room'iest**.
room'iness *n.*

roost *ro͞ost, n.* a perch on which a bird rests at night.—*v.i.* to settle or sleep on a perch.
roost'er *n.* a domestic cock.
come home to roost (of one's failings, etc.) to come back on oneself: *His unfriendliness to his neighbours has come home to roost.*

root[1] *ro͞ot, n.* **1** the underground part of a plant, which draws up food from the soil, esp. a part that never bears leaves, etc. **2** the base of anything, e.g. a tooth. **3** a source, cause: *Money is the root of evil.* **4** a word, or part of one, from which other words have been built up. **5** (in *pl.*) one's geographical or family origins.—*v.i.* and *v.t.* to (cause to) form roots and begin to grow.—*v.t.* to fix firmly.
root'ed *adj.* **1** firmly planted. **2** firmly established, deep-seated: *a rooted dislike.*
root'less *adj.*
root'let *n.* a little root.
root'stock *n.* a rhizome.
root and branch leaving nothing behind; completely.
root up, out 1 to tear out by the roots. **2** to get rid of completely.
square, cube, root. See **square, cube.**
take root to grow firmly.

root[2] *ro͞ot, v.i.* **1** (of e.g. pigs) to turn up soil with the snout. **2** to poke, search about.

rope *rōp, n.* **1** a thick twisted cord. **2** a string (of pearls, etc.).—*v.t.* **1** to fasten with a rope. **2** to lasso. **3** to enclose, mark (off), with a rope:—*pr.p.* **rop'ing**.
ro'pery *n.* works where ropes are made:—*pl.* **ro'peries**.
rō'py *adj.* of poor quality; in poor condition:—*comp.* **rō'pier**; *superl.* **rō'piest**.
rō'piness *n.*
rope-ladd'er *n.* a ladder made of rope, usu. with wooden rungs.
give a person rope to give him freedom to ruin himself, etc.
know the ropes. See **know.**
rope in to bring in (an unwilling helper).

rosary. See **rose**[2].

rose[1]. See **rise.**

rose[2] *rōz, n.* **1** a flower, often scented, growing on a usu. prickly bush. **2** a deepish pink colour. **3** a spray, nozzle with holes, e.g. on a watering-can. **4** a circular fitting in a ceiling for the cord of an electric light.
rosary *rō'zȧ-ri, n.* **1** a series of prayers. **2** a string of beads used as a guide in saying prayers:—*pl.* **ro'saries**.
roseate *rō'zi-it, adj.* rosy.
rosette *rō-zet', n.* a rose-shaped arrangement of ribbon, etc.
ro'sy *adj.* **1** rose-coloured. **2** bright, hopeful:—*comp.* **ro'sier**; *superl.* **ro'siest**.
ro'sily *adv.* **ro'siness** *n.*
rose window a circular window with delicate ornamentation.
rose'wood *n.* the valuable dark wood of certain foreign trees used for furniture.
see, look at, through rose-coloured spectacles to assess too favourably.

rosé *rō-zā', n.* a pinkish, light, wine.

roseate. See **rose**[2].

rosemary *rōz'mȧ-ri, n.* a small sweet-scented evergreen shrub.

rosette, rosily, etc. See **rose**[2].

rosin *roz'in, n.* the sticky sap of some trees in hard form.

rosiness. See **rose**[2].

roster *ros'tėr, n.* a list showing order of rotation of duties.

rostrum *ros'trum, n.* a platform for public speaking.

rosy. See **rose**[2].

rot *rot, v.i.* and *v.t.* to go bad, or cause to go bad, decay:—*pr.p.* **rott'ing**; *pa.p.* **rott'ed.**—*n.* **1** decay. **2** applied to some diseases (e.g. *foot rot* of sheep, *dry rot* of timber). **3** (*coll.*) nonsense.
rott'en *adj.* **1** decayed; going bad. **2** very bad; deserving contempt.
rott'enness *n.*
rott'er *n.* a worthless person.

rota *rō'tȧ, n.* a roster, list showing a repeating order of duties.
rotary *rō'tȧ-ri, adj.* **1** turning like a wheel. **2** working by the rotation of a part.
rotate' *v.t., v.i.* **1** to turn like a wheel. **2** to go, or make go, through a series of changes repeated again and again:—*pr.p.* **rotat'ing.**
rotā'tion *n.* **rotā'tor** *n.*
rotatory *rō'tȧ-tȯ-ri,* or *-tā', adj.*
Rotavator® *rō'tȧ-vā-tȯr, n.* a hand-operated, motor-driven, soil-tilling machine (*rotary* culti*vator*).
rotation of crops a regular order in which one kind, etc., follows another on the same piece of land.

rote *rōt, n.*: **by rote** by heart, without thinking of the meaning.

rotisserie *rō-tis'ė-ri, n.* an apparatus in which meat, etc. is roasted on a revolving spit.

rotor *rō'tȯr, n.* a rotating part of a dynamo, motor, etc., or a system of rotating aerofoils as in a helicopter.

rotten, rotter. See **rot**.

rotund *rō-tund', adj.* **1** round. **2** plump.
rotun'dity, rotund'ness *ns.*

rouble *roo'bl, n.* the standard coin of Russia.

roué *roo'ā, n.* a dissolute man.

rouge *roozh, n.* **1** a powder or cream used for reddening the checks. **2** a powder for polishing metal, etc.—*v.t.* and *v.i.* to colour with, or use, rouge:—*pr.p.* **roug'ing.**

rough *ruf, adj.* **1** not smooth. **2** uneven. **3** unpolished. **4** coarse. **5** harsh, unpleasant. **6** noisy, violent. **7** not exact: *a rough estimate.* **8** stormy.—*n.* **1** a noisy, violent person. **2** waste or, e.g. on a golf-course, untended ground. **3** a drawing, etc., in an unfinished state.
rough'age *n.* bran or fibre in food.
rough'en *v.t., v.i.* to make, or become, rough.
rough'ly *adv.* **1** in a rough manner. **2** approximately.
rough'ness *n.*
rough'-and-read'y *adj.* **1** not carefully done, but good enough for the purpose. **2** vigorous but unpolished.
rough'-and-tum'ble *n.* **1** a scuffle. **2** disorderly struggling.—Also *adj.*
rough'cast *n.* plaster mixed with small stones, used on outside walls.—*v.t.* to cover with roughcast.—Also *adj.*
rough'-house *n.* a free fight.
rough'neck *n.* **1** (*U.S.*) a hooligan, a bully. **2** a labourer on an oil-rig.
rough'-rider *n.* a rider of untrained horses.
rough'-shod *adj.* (of horses) shod with shoes with nails sticking out to prevent slipping.
be rough on to be hard luck for.
ride rough-shod over to treat (a person) with no regard for his feelings.
rough it to live without ordinary comforts.
rough out to sketch, shape, roughly.
cut up rough. See **cut**.

roulette *roo-let', n.* a gambling game in which a ball is spun on a wheel on a table.

round *rownd, adj.* **1** having a curved outline. **2** shaped like a ring, circle, cylinder, or globe. **3** plump. **4** with movement in a circle: *a round trip.* **5** (of numbers) complete, without fractions. **6** (of numbers) correct to the nearest ten, hundred, etc.: *Give me the amounts in round figures.*—*adv.* **1** about. **2** on all sides, around. **3** in a circle. **4** from one to another. **5** in circumference: *measuring 2 metres round.* **6** to a house, etc. in the neighbourhood: *Come round this evening.*—*prep.* **1** on, passing, all side of. **2** all over. **3** moving with a curve past.—*n.* **1** something round in shape. **2** a burst (of firing, applause). **3** a single bullet or shell, or a number of these all fired at one time. **4** a full slice (of bread). **5** things happening in order: *a round of duties.* **6** (sometimes in *pl.*) a usual route (e.g. of a postman). **7** a full circuit. **8** a song in which different singers take up the tune in turn. **9** each stage in a competition. **10** a bout in a contest (e.g. boxing). **11** (*golf*) play over the whole course.—*v.t.* **1** to make round. **2** to go round: *to round the Cape.*—*v.i.* to become round.
round'ed *adj.* **1** curved. **2** plump.
round'ers *n.sing.* a game with bat and ball.
round'ly *adv.* plainly, frankly.
round'ness *n.*
round'about *adj.* not direct.—*n.* **1** a revolving apparatus on which to ride in a playground; a merry-go-round. **2** an arrangement at a road junction where vehicles must go round part of a circle so as not to cross each other's paths.
round'-eyed' *adj.* with eyes wide (in surprise, etc.).

Round'head (*hist.*) *n.* a member of the parliamentary party at the time of Charles I.
round-shoul'dered *adj.* having stooping shoulders.
rounds'man *n.* man who goes round for a shopkeeper, e.g. delivering milk.
round'-ta'ble *adj.* (of a conference, etc.) taking place at a round table, at which all are of equal importance.
round off to finish off neatly.
round the clock throughout the day and night (*adj.* **round'-the-clock'**).
round up to drive together, gather (cattle, people e.g. helpers) (*n.* **round'-up**).

rouse *rowz*, *v.t.* **1** to awaken. **2** to stir up. **3** to excite.—*v.i.* to awake:—*pr.p.* **rous'-ing**.
rous'ing *adj.* stirring; exciting.

rout[1] *rowt*, *n.* **1** (*old*) a noisy crowd or party. **2** a complete defeat. **3** disorderly flight.—*v.t.* to defeat completely.

rout[2] *rowt*, *v.t.*: **rout out 1** to get by searching. **2** to force up or out.

route *rōōt n.* a course to be followed, a road.—*v.t.* to fix the route of; to send (by a chosen route):—*pr.p.* **rout'ing**.
route march a long march of troops in training.

routine *rōō-tēn'*, *n.* a regular, fixed order of doing things.—*adj.* regular, ordinary.

rove *rōv*, *v.t.* to wander over or through.—*v.i.* to wander about:—*pr.p.* **ro'ving**.
ro'ver *n.* **1** a wanderer; an unsettled person. **2** (*old*) a pirate; a robber.
ro'ving *adj.* and *n.*

row[1] *rō*, *n.* a line of persons or things.

row[2] *rō*, *v.t.* to propel (a boat) by oars.—Also *v.i.*—*n.* a trip in a rowing-boat.
row'er *n.* one who rows.
row'boat, **row'ing-boat** *ns.* a boat moved by oars.

row[3] *row*, *n.* **1** a noisy quarrel. **2** a noise. **3** a scolding.

rowan *row'ǎn*, *n.* **1** a tree with clusters of small red fruit. **2** the fruit.

rowdy *row'di*, *n.* a rough, quarrelsome, noisy person:—*pl.* **row'dies**.—*adj.* disorderly and noisy:—*comp.* **row'dier**; *superl.* **row'diest**.
row'dily *adv.* **row'diness** *n.*
row'dyism *n.* behaviour of a rowdy.

rowlock *rol'ok*, *n.* the rest for the oar on the side of a rowing boat.

royal *roi'ǎl*, *adj.* **1** of, having to do with, given by, a king or queen: *royal family*; *royal charter.* **2** magnificent, splendid.
roy'ally *adv.* **roy'alness** *n.*
roy'alty *n.* **1** the state of being royal. **2** royal person. **3** money paid to the author of a book etc. for each copy sold, and to landowners for use of minerals found in their land:—*pl.* **roy'alties**.
roy'alist *n.* a supporter of the monarch or of monarchy.
royal blue a bright deep blue.
royal mast. See **mast**[1].

rub *rub*, *v.t.* **1** to move (one thing on, against, the surface of another). **2** (with *out, away*) to remove (a mark) by such action. **3** (sometimes with *up*) to wipe, clean, polish. **4** (with *in*) to work (e.g. ointment) into skin, etc. **5** (with *down*) to clean or make smooth.—Also *v.i.*:—*pr.p.* **rubb'ing**; *pa.p.* **rubbed**.—*n.* **1** an act of rubbing. **2** (*old*) a difficulty.
rubb'er *n.* **1** an elastic material made from juice (latex) of certain plants, or an artificial substitute for it. **2** a piece of such material for rubbing out pencil-marks, etc.
rubb'ery *adj.* **rubb'eriness** *n.*
rubb'ing *n.* and *adj.*
rubber band a thin loop of rubber used to hold things together (also **elastic band**).
rubb'er-stamp' *n.* an instrument with rubber letters or figures for stamping e.g. names, dates, a signature, etc., on documents, books, etc.—*v.t.* **1** to imprint with a rubber-stamp. **2** to approve without due consideration.
rub along to get along fairly well.
rub it in to go on repeating to a person something he finds unpleasant.
rub shoulders with to meet, mix with.
rub up the wrong way to annoy, esp. by tactlessness.

rubber[1]. See **rub**.

rubber[2] *rub'ėr*, *n.* (in cards, etc.) an odd number of games (three, five) the winner being the side that first takes two, three, games.

rubbish *rub'ish*, *n.* **1** waste material; litter. **2** nonsense.
rubb'ishy *adj.* **rubb'ishiness** *n.*

rubble *rub'l*, *n.* **1** broken stone from ruined buildings. **2** small rough stones used in building.

rubicund *rōō'bi-kŭnd*, *adj.* reddish-faced.

ruby *rōō'bi*, *n.* **1** a red gem. **2** its colour:—*pl.* **ru'bies**.—*adj.* red.

ruched *rōōsht*, *adj.* gathered, frilled.

ruck[1] *ruk*, *n.* a wrinkle or fold.—*v.t.* and *v.i.* **1** to wrinkle. **2** to (cause to) become caught (up).

ruck[2] *ruk*, *n.* **1** a crowd. **2** ordinary people.

rucksack *ruk'sak*, *n.* a bag carried on the back by hikers, etc.

ruction *ruk'sh(ȯ)n, n.* (often in *pl.*) a disturbance; a quarrel.

rudder *rud'ėr, n.* **1** flat piece of wood or metal hinged at the stern of a boat for steering. **2** a similar device for steering an aeroplane.

ruddy *rud'i, adj.* **1** red. **2** rosy, as in good health:—*comp.* **rudd'ier**; *superl.* **rudd'iest**.
rudd'iness *n.*

rude *rōōd, adj.* **1** not polite, showing bad manners. **2** roughly made: *a rude shelter.* **3** rough, not refined.
rude'ly *adv.* **rude'ness** *n.*

rudiment *rōō'di-mėnt, n.* (usu. in *pl.*) one of the first simple rules or facts of anything: *the rudiments of cookery*.
rudimen'tary *adj.* in an early stage of development.
rudimen'tariness *n.*

rue[1] *rōō, n.* a strong-smelling shrub with bitter leaves.

rue[2] *rōō, v.t.* to regret:—*pr.p.* **ru(e)'ing**; *pa.p.* **rued** *(rōōd)*.
rue'ful *adj.* sorrowful.
rue'fully *adv.* **rue'fulness** *n.*

ruff *ruf, n.* **1** a frill, usu. starched and pleated, worn round the neck in the reigns of Elizabeth I and James I. **2** frilled appearance on neck of bird or animal.

ruffian *ruf'i-ȧn, -yȧn, n.* a brutal, violent person.
ruff'ianly *adj.* **ruff'ianliness** *n.*

ruffle *ruf'l, v.t.* **1** to make (something) wrinkled, not smooth. **2** (of a bird) to put up (its feathers) in anger. **3** to annoy, agitate, disturb.—*v.i.* **1** to become not smooth. **2** to become agitated, annoyed:—*pr.p.* **ruff'ling**.—*n.* a frill, esp. at neck or wrist.

rug *rug, n.* **1** a mat for the floor. **2** a thick blanket, for use when travelling, etc.

Rugby, rugby *rug'bi, n.* a form of football using an oval ball that may be carried.—*coll. abbrev.* **rugg'er**.

rugged *rug'id, adj.* **1** rough. **2** uneven. **3** strong, stern: *a rugged character*.
rugg'edly *adv.* **rugg'edness** *n.*

rugger. See **Rugby**.

ruin *roo'in, n.* **1** downfall. **2** complete loss of money, etc. **3** wrecked or decayed state. **4** a cause of downfall: *Drink was his ruin.* **5** (often in *pl.*) broken-down remains, e.g. of buildings.—*v.t.* **1** to cause decay or ruin to. **2** to spoil completely.
ruina'tion *n.* **1** the act of ruining. **2** the state of being ruined. **3** something that ruins.
ru'inous *adj.* **1** ruined. **2** leading to disaster or ruin.

ruing. See **rue**[2].

rule *rōōl, n.* **1** a strip of wood or metal used for measuring. **2** government: *a country under foreign rule.* **3** a regulation, order. **4** a principle on which one acts. **5** what usually happens, is done, etc.: *Dick was an exception to the rule that poor people are generous.*—*v.t.* **1** to draw (a straight line) with the help of a ruler, etc. **2** to draw usu. parallel lines in this way on (paper, etc.) **3** to govern. **4** to decide (that).—*v.i.* to be in power:—*pr.p.* **ru'ling**.
ru'ler *n.* **1** one who rules. **2** a narrow, straight-edged strip of wood, metal or plastic for guiding the pencil, etc. in drawing straight lines.
ru'ling *adj.* **1** reigning. **2** most important.—*n.* a decision.
as a rule usually.
rule of thumb a rough-and-ready method (also as *adj.* **rule'-of-thumb'**).
rule out deliberately to leave out, not take into consideration.

rum[1] *rum, n.* a spirit made from sugar-cane.

rum[2] *rum, adj.* odd, queer:—*comp.* **rumm'er**; *superl.* **rumm'est**.

rumba *rum'bȧ, n.* S. American dance.

rumble[1] *rum'bl, v.i.* to make a low grumbling or rolling sound:—*pr.p.* **rum'bling**.—Also *n.*
rum'bling *n.* and *adj.*

rumble[2] *rumb'l, (coll.) v.t.* to detect:—*pr.p.* **rum'bling**.

rumbustious *rum-bus'chu̇s, (coll.) adj.* boisterous.

ruminant *rōō'mi-nȧnt, n.* an animal (e.g. cow) that chews the cud.—Also *adj.*
ru'mināte *v.i.* **1** to chew the cud. **2** to be deep in thought.—Also *v.t.*:—*pr.p.* **ru'minating**.
ruminā'tion *n.* deep thought.
ru'minative *adj.* meditative.

rummage *rum'ij, n.* a thorough search.—*v.i.* to search:—*pr.p.* **rumm'aging**.
rummage sale a jumble sale.

rummy *rum'i, n.* a card game for two or more.

rumour *rōō'mȯr, n.* **1** a story, piece of news, etc., that may not be true. **2** general talk.—*v.t.* (usu. in *pass.*) to report by way of hearsay: *His death is rumoured*; *It is rumoured that he is dead.*

rump *rump, n.* the hind part of an animal.
rump steak meat from this part of an ox.

rumple *rum'pl, n.* a fold or wrinkle.—*v.t.* to crease, make untidy:—*pr.p.* **rump'ling**.

rumpus *rum'pu̇s, n.* **1** an uproar. **2** a disturbance.

run *run, v.i.* **1** to move swiftly. **2** to hurry. **3** to race. **4** (of trains, etc.) to travel. **5** (of water, etc.) to flow. **6** (of a machine) to work. **7** to spread: *This colour runs.* **8** to reach, stretch (to). **9** to go on being repeated: *This play runs for two weeks.* **10** to continue.—*v.t.* **1** to cause to run. **2** to keep and use (a motor-car). **3** to organise, conduct (e.g. a business). **4** to get through (a blockade). **5** to smuggle (guns):—*pr.p.* **runn'ing**; *pa.t.* **ran**; *pa.p.* **run**.—*n.* **1** an act of running. **2** a trip. **3** distance or time of running. **4** a spell or period: *a run of bad luck.* **5** a rush to obtain (with *on*): *a run on tickets for the show.* **6** a rush to obtain something (e.g. money) from: *a run on the bank.* **7** a ladder e.g. in a stocking. **8** a single score (e.g. in cricket). **9** the free use (of a place). **10** a pen for fowls.

runn'el *n.* a little river or stream.

runn'er *n.* **1** one who runs. **2** a messenger. **3** a rooting stem of a plant. **4** a blade of a skate or sledge.

runn'ing *n.* **1** the act of moving fast, flowing, etc. **2** management, control.—*adj.* **1** kept for use when running: *running shoes.* **2** oozing fluid: *a running sore.* **3** continuous.—*adv.* one after another: *three days running.*

runn'y *adj.* liquid, watery:—*comp.* **runn'ier**; *superl.* **runn'iest**.

run'about *n.* a small light car, etc.

run'away *n.* a person or animal that runs away, escapes.—Also *adj.*

run'-down' *adj.* in poor health.

runn'er-up' *n.* one who is second in a race or competition.

running commentary a description (esp. broadcast) of a game or event while it is happening.

running knot one that slips along the string to alter the size of the loop.

runn'ing-lights *n.pl.* lights shown by ships after sunset.

running water water available from taps.

run-of-the-mill' *adj.* ordinary.

run'way *n.* a path for aircraft to take off from or land on.

a (good) run for one's money a spell of fun or success in return for effort.

in (or **out of**) **the running** having (or not having) a chance of success.

on the run escaping.

run across, into to meet.

run down 1 (of a vehicle or driver) to knock down. **2** to speak ill of. **3** to catch by chasing.

run for to stand for election for.

run in 1 to arrest. **2** to start (a new machine) working properly.

run it fine to leave it nearly too late.

run out 1 to leak. **2** to become short (of). **3** to put (a batsman) out while he is running.

run over 1 to overflow. **2** to knock down or pass over with a car or other vehicle. **3** to practise.

run to earth, ground. See **ground**.

run to seed to decay, go to waste.

run up to make or build hastily.

rune *ro͞on, n.* a letter from any of several ancient N. European alphabets.

rung[1] *rung, n.* a step of a ladder.

rung[2]. See **ring**[2].

runnel, runner, running. See **run**.

runt *runt, n.* a small stunted animal or person.

rupee *ro͞o-pē', n.* the standard coin of India, Pakistan, Sri Lanka, Nepal and other countries.

rupture *rup'chůr, n.* **1** a breaking (e.g. of friendship. **2** a hernia (see this).—*v.t., v.i.* to break, burst:—*pr.p.* **rup'turing**.

rural *ro͞o'răl, adj.* of or connected with the country.

ruse *ro͞oz, n.* **1** a trick. **2** a cunning scheme.

rush[1] *rush, v.i.* to move quickly, hurry.—*v.t.* to hurry (someone).—*n.* **1** a quick movement forward. **2** a hurry.

rush hour the period in the morning or evening when most people are travelling.

rush[2] *rush, n.* a tall grass-like plant growing in or near water, used for basketwork, etc.

rush'y *adj.*:—*comp.* **rush'ier**; *superl.* **rush'iest**.

rush'iness *n.*

rusk *rusk, n.* a kind of biscuit like very hard toast.

russet *rus'it, n.* **1** a reddish-brown colour. **2** a rough-skinned type of apple.

Russian *rush'ăn, n.* **1** a native of Russia. **2** the language of Russia.—*adj.* of, or connected with, Russia.

Russo- *rus-ō,* (as part of a word) Russian.

Russian roulette foolhardy or risky action, orig. the exploit of loading a revolver with one bullet, spinning the cylinder, and firing at one's own head.

rust *rust, n.* **1** the reddish-brown coating formed on iron and its alloys by air and moisture. **2** a plant disease causing a rusty appearance. **3** the colour of rust.—*v.i., v.t.* to form rust, cause rust on.

rus'ty *adj.* **1** covered with rust. **2** looking like rust. **3** showing lack of recent practice: *My French is rusty; I haven't played for so long that I'm rusty*:—*comp.* **rus'tier**; *superl.* **rus'tiest**.

rus'tiness *n.*

rust'less, rust'proof *adjs.* not rusting.

rustic *rus'tik*, *adj.* **1** having to do with the country. **2** simple, not refined. **3** (of a fence, etc.) simply made of rough timber.—*n.* a country dweller, usu. a simple, uneducated one.

rus'ticate *v.i.* to live in the country.—*v.t.* to dismiss (a student) temporarily from a university:—*pr.p.* **rus'ticating**.

rustiness. See **rust**.

rustle *rus'l*, *v.i.* to make a soft, whispering sound.—*v.t.* to steal (cattle, etc.):—*pr.p.* **rust'ling**.

rus'tler *n.* a cattle thief.

rustle up to get together, prepare hastily.

rustless, **rusty**, etc. See **rust**.

rut¹ *rut*, *n.* **1** a deep track made by wheels. **2** a fixed way of behaving, dull routine: *to get into a rut*.—*v.t.* to mark with ruts:—*pr.p.* **rutt'ing**; *pa.p.* **rutt'ed**.

rut² *rut*, *n.* the period of sexual excitement in a male animal, esp. a stag.

ruthless *rōōth'lis*, *adj.* cruel, without pity.

ruth'lessly *adv.* **ruth'lessness** *n.*

rye *rī*, *n.* **1** a grass-like cultivated plant. **2** its grain, used for making break, etc. **3** whisky make from rye.

rye'-grass *n.* a kind of grass grown for hay and as cattle feed.

S

Sabbath *sab'ath, n.* a day of the week regularly set aside for religious services and rest—e.g. among the Jews, Saturday, among most Christians, Sunday.

sabbat'ical *adj.* **1** of the Sabbath. **2** pertaining to a sabbatical.—*n.* a period of time off from one's work, esp. for teachers and lecturers to study, carry out research, etc.

sable[1] *sā'bl, n.* **1** a marten found in arctic regions, valued for its glossy fur. **2** its fur.

sable[2] *sā'bl, adj.* **1** black. **2** dark.

sabot *sab'ō, n.* a wooden shoe worn by the peasants of several countries.

sab'otage *(-täzh) n.* **1** deliberate destruction of machinery, etc., during labour troubles, or in war. **2** anything done to hinder effort, spoil a plan, etc.—*v.t.* to destroy, damage, cause to fail, by sabotage.—Also *v.i.*:—*pr.p.* **sab'otaging.**

saboteur' *(-tûr') n.* one who sabotages.

sabre *sā'bėr, n.* a one-edged sword, slightly curved towards the point, used by cavalry.

sac *sak, n.* (in a plant or animal body) a bag, often containing a liquid.

saccharine *sak'ȧ-rēn, -rīn, adj.* **1** having to do with, or like, sugar. **2** sickly-sweet: *a saccharine smile.*

sacch'arin(e) *(-rin, -rēn) n.* a very sweet substance, used as a substitute for sugar.

sachet *sa'shā, n.* **1** a small bag, usu. containing scented powder, etc. **2** a small sealed envelope containing a liquid such as shampoo.

sack[1] *sak, n.* **1** a large bag of coarse material for holding grain, flour, etc. **2** the amount a sack will hold.—*v.t.* **1** to put into a sack. **2** (*coll.*) to dismiss from one's job.

sack'ing *n.* coarse cloth or canvas for sacks, etc.

sack'cloth *n.* **1** cloth for sacks. **2** coarse cloth formerly worn as a sign of mourning or of sorrow for sin.

get the sack to be dismissed.

give the sack to sack, dismiss.

sack[2] *sak, n.* plundering (of a captured town).—*v.t.* to plunder, take everything valuable from.

sacrament *sak'rȧ-mėnt, n.* a religious ceremony such as the Lord's Supper and baptism.

sacramen'tal *adj.* belonging to or being a sacrament.

sacred *sā'krid, adj.* **1** dedicated, esp. to God, holy. **2** to be treated with reverence. **3** connected with religion: *sacred music.*

sa'credly *adv.* **sa'credness** *n.*

sacred cow a person, institution, etc. so revered as to be above criticism.

See also the following words.

sacrifice *sak'ri-fīs, n.* **1** the act of offering something, esp. a victim on an altar, to a god. **2** the thing so offered. **3** something given up in order to benefit another person, or to gain a more important end. **4** the act of giving up in this way. **5** loss of profit.—*v.t.* **1** to make a sacrifice of. **2** to give up something better or thought to be more important: *He sacrificed his life to save the child, for the good cause*; *He sacrificed his happiness to his ambition*:—*pr.p.* **sac'rificing.**

sacrificial *(-fish'ȧl) adj.* having to do with sacrifice.

sacrilege *sak'ri-lij, n.* the using of a holy thing or place in an evil way.

sacrilegious *sak-ri-lij'ŭs, adj.*

sacristan *sak'ris-tȧn, n.* an official with certain duties in a church.

sacrosanct *sak'rō-sang(k)t, adj.* **1** holy and worthy of reverence. **2** not to be harmed.

sad *sad, adj.* **1** sorrowful, unhappy. **2** showing grief. **3** (often used playfully) terrible, shocking. **4** (of e.g. colour) dull. **5** (of e.g. bread) not properly risen, damp and heavy:—*comp.* **sadd'er**; *superl.* **sadd'est.**

sadd'en *v.t.* and *v.i.* to make, or grow, sad.

sad'ly *adv.* **1** in a sad manner. **2** unfortunately, it is sad to say. **3** quite: *sadly mistaken.*

sad'ness *n.*

saddle *sad'l, n.* **1** a seat for a rider used on a horse, etc. or on a bicycle, etc. **2** anything of a similar shape. **3** a type of cut from the back of an animal used for food.—*v.t.* **1** to put a saddle on. **2** to put a burden, or a responsibility on (with *with*): *He saddled his parents with his debts, with the boring visitor, with the care of his children*:—*pr.p.* **sadd'ling.**

sadd'ler *n.* a maker of saddles and harness.

sadism *sad', sād', or säd'izm, n.* sexual pleasure in torturing, or in watching cruelty to, someone.

sad'ist *n.* one who takes such pleasure.

sadis'tic *adj.*

sadis'tically *adv.*

safari *sa-fä'ri*, *n.* **1** an expedition, esp. for hunting. **2** the persons, animals, etc. forming this.
safari park an enclosed park where wild animals are kept in the open, not in cages, on view to the public.

safe *sāf*, *adj.* **1** unharmed. **2** free from danger. **3** free, secure (from). **4** not risky. **5** reliable, trustworthy. **6** cautious: *a safe driver.*—*n.* **1** a steel or iron chest, etc., for money, valuables, etc. **2** a cupboard, cabinet, for meats, etc.
safe'ly *adv.* **safe'ty**, **safe'ness** *ns.*
safe'-con'duct *n.* (a document, passport, etc., attesting) permission given to a person to travel without arrest, etc., esp. in time of war.
safe'guard *n.* anything that prevents danger or gives security or protection.—*v.t.* to protect, make secure.
safe keeping 1 protection. **2** custody.
safe seat a seat that the political party spoken, thought, of will certainly win.
safety belt a belt fixed to a seat in a car or aircraft used to keep a passenger from being jolted out of the seat (also **seat'belt**).
safety lamp a lamp used in mines which does not set fire to the gases found there.
safe'ty-pin *n.* a pin that has a cover over its point when it is closed.
safety valve 1 a valve that opens when pressure becomes too great. **2** a harmless outlet for emotion, etc.
safe and sound unharmed.
to be on the safe side so as not to run much risk: *Take a waterproof to be on the safe side.*

saf'flower *n.* a plant with seeds that yield safflower oil, used in cooking, medicines and paints.

saffron *saf'ron*, *n.* a type of crocus with deep yellow flowers, or a colouring substance prepared from it.

sag *sag*, *v.i.* to bend, sink, or droop, esp. in the middle:—*pr.p.* **sagg'ing**; *pa.p.* **sagged**.

saga *sä'ga*, *n.* **1** a story of a hero, or a family, composed very long ago in Norway or Iceland. **2** a novel about several generations of a family. **3** a long detailed story.

sagacious *sa-gā'shus*, *adj.* **1** having, or showing, good judgment, shrewd and practical. **2** (of animals) intelligent.
saga'ciously *adv.*
saga'ciousness, **sagac'ity** *(-gas'i-ti) ns.*

sage[1] *sāj*, *n.* **1** a plant whose leaves are used for flavouring and stuffings. **2** (also **sage green**) a greyish green.
sage'brush *n.* a growth of shrubs, with scent like sage, on dry American plains.

sage[2] *sāj*, *adj.* wise.—*n.* a person of great wisdom.

sago *sā'gō*, *n.* a starchy substance obtained from inside the trunk of E. Indian palms, used in e.g. puddings.

sahib *sä'ib*, *n.* a term of respect given in India to persons of rank or to Europeans.

said *sed*, *pa.p.* of **say**.—*adj.* previously mentioned: *the said witness.*

sail *sāl*, *n.* **1** a sheet of canvas, etc., spread to catch the wind, by which a ship is driven forward. **2** a ship or ships: *a fleet of forty sail.* **3** a journey in a ship. **4** an arm of a windmill.—*v.i.* **1** to be moved by sails. **2** to go by water in a ship (with, or without, sails). **3** to begin a voyage. **4** to glide easily (along) on water or in air. **5** (*coll.*) to go easily and successfully: *He sailed through his exams.*—*v.t.* **1** to navigate or steer. **2** to move upon in a ship: *to sail the sea.*
sail'ing *n.* and *adj.*
sail'or *n.* **1** one whose job is helping to sail a ship, esp. a common seaman. **2** one who is, or is not, easily made seasick: *a bad, good, sailor.*
sail'cloth *n.* strong cloth for sails.
set sail to set out on a voyage.

saint *sānt*, (before a name) *s(i)nt*, *n.* a very good or holy person, esp. one canonised (formally recognised after death) by the R.C. or other Church.
saint'ed *adj.* **1** holy, saintly. **2** gone to heaven.
saint'ly *adj.*:—*comp.* **saint'lier**; *superl.* **saint'liest**.
saint'liness *n.*
saint's day a day set apart for remembering a particular saint.
Latter-day saints the Mormons' name for themselves.

sake[1] *sāk*, *n.* **1** cause, purpose: *for the sake of peace.* **2** benefit, advantage: *for my sake.*

sake[2] *sä'ki*, *n.* a kind of Japanese alcoholic drink made from rice.

salaam *sa-läm'*, *n.* **1** an Eastern greeting. **2** a deep bow with palm of right hand on forehead.—Also *v.i.* and *v.t.*

salacious *sa-lā'shus*, *adj.* **1** lustful. **2** causing lustful feelings.

salad *sal'ad*, *n.* a mixture or raw or cooked vegetables, etc. cut up and seasoned.
salad dressing a sauce of olive oil, etc. put on salads.

salamander *sal'a-man-dėr*, or *-man'*, *n.* a small lizard-like animal, once believed to be able to live in fire.

salami *sȧ-lä'mi, n.* a highly seasoned Italian sausage.

salary *sal'ȧ-ri, n.* fixed sums of money regularly paid for, usu. professional, services (e.g. to managers rather than to labourers; compare **wages**):—*pl.* **sal'aries.**

sal'aried *adj.* receiving a salary.

sale *sāl, n.* **1** the exchange of anything for money. **2** demand, market: *There is no sale for fur coats in the jungle.* **3** a public offer of goods to be sold, esp. at reduced prices or by auction.

sal(e)'able *adj.* **1** fit to be sold. **2** easy to sell.

sale'room *n.* an auction room.

sales'man, -woman *ns.* a person who sells, or shows, goods to customers.

sales'manship *n.* the art of persuading people to buy.

sale of work a sale of needlework and other articles to raise money for charity, etc.

for, on, sale being offered to people to buy.

See also **sell.**

salient *sā'li-ėnt, adj.* **1** (of e.g. an angle) pointing outwards. **2** outstanding, chief: *the salient points of a speech.*—*n.* an outward pointing angle, esp. in a line of defences.

saline *sā'līn, sa'līn', sȧ-līn', adj.* **1** containing salt. **2** salty.

salin'ity *(sȧ-lin') n.* saltness.

saliva *sȧ-lī'vȧ, n.* spittle, the liquid from the glands of the mouth, a digestive fluid.

salivary (*sa'li-*, or *sȧ-lī'-*) *adj.* having to do with saliva.

sal'ivāte *v.i.* to produce saliva, esp. too much:—*pr.p.* **sal'ivating.**

sallow[1] *sal'ō, n.* a type of willow.

sallow[2] *sal'ō, adj.* (of complexion) pale, yellowish, rather sickly-looking.

sally *sal'i, n.* **1** a sudden rush forth (e.g. from a fort) to attack attackers. **2** an excursion, jaunt. **3** outburst of e.g. wit, anger:—*pl.* **sall'ies.**—*v.i.* to rush out suddenly:—*pr.p.* **sall'ying;** *pa.p.* **sall'ied.**

sally forth (esp. *humorous*) to go out, e.g. for a walk.

salmon *sam'ȯn, n.* **1** a large fish, with silvery sides and orange-pink flesh, that swims up rivers to spawn. **2** the colour of its flesh (also **salmon pink**).

salmon leap a waterfall which salmon leap over in going upstream.

salmonella *sal-mȯn-el'ȧ, n.* a bacterium which causes food poisoning.

salon *sal'on^g, n.* **1** a drawing-room. **2** a gathering of notable people at the house of a well-known hostess. **3** (a large hall, etc., used for) an exhibition of pictures (or other purpose).

saloon *sȧ-lo͞on', n.* **1** a large public room. **2** a dining-room for ship's passengers. **3** a railway carriage not divided into compartments. **4** a motor car with a closed-in body of one compartment. **5** (*U.S.*) a drinking bar.

salt *sölt, n.* **1** common salt, a substance used for seasoning, either mined from the earth (**rock salt**) or obtained from brine, etc. **2** any other substance, formed, as common salt is, from a metal and an acid. **3** (in *pl.*) a mixture of salts used as a medicine. **4** (*coll.*) a sailor, esp. an old sailor. **5** something that gives liveliness, interest, etc.—*adj.* **1** containing salt. **2** seasoned or cured with salt. **3** growing in, or covered with, salt water.—*v.t.* **1** to sprinkle, cure, with salt. **2** to overcharge (a person for goods).

salt'ness *n.*

sal'ty *adj.*:—*comp.* **sal'tier;** *superl.* **sal'tiest.**

sal'tiness *n.*

salt'-lick *n.* a place where salt is found or is placed for animals.

salt marsh a marsh flooded at times by the sea.

above (or **below**) **the salt** among those of high (or low) social rank.

take with a pinch or **grain of salt** to hear, receive, with slight feeling of disbelief.

worth one's salt worth at least the value of the salt one eats.

saltcellar *sölt'sel-ȧr, solt', n.* a small table dish for holding salt.

saltpetre *sölt-pē'tėr, n.* nitre, a nitrogen salt used in gunpowder, etc.

salubrious *sȧ-lo͞o'bri-ŭs,* or *-lū', adj.* (of the air, a place, etc.) health-giving.

salu'briousness, salū'brity *ns.*

salutary *sal'ū-tȧr-i, adj.* **1** giving health or safety. **2** wholesome. **3** having a good effect.

sal'utariness *n.*

salute *sȧ-lo͞ot', -lūt', v.t.* **1** to greet with words, a kiss, a gesture (e.g. of the hand), or show respect to by a formal gesture. **2** to honour (person) by firing guns, striking the flag, etc.—*v.i.* to make a formal gesture of greeting or respect:—*pr.p.* **salut'ing.**—Also *n.*

salutā'tion *n.* **1** the act, or words, of greeting. **2** the introductory words of a letter.

salvage *sal'vij, n.* **1** the act of saving a ship or cargo, or of saving goods from a fire, etc. **2** a reward paid for this. **3** goods saved from waste.—*v.t.* to save from loss and ruin:—*pr.p.* **sal'vaging**.

salve *v.t.* to salvage:—*pr.p.* **sal'ving**.

salvation *sal-vā'sh(ȯ)n, n.* **1** the act of saving. **2** the means or cause of saving: *This deep sleep was the patient's salvation.* **3** the saving of man from sin and its consequences.

salve¹. See **salvage**.

salve² *säv*, also *salv, n.* **1** an ointment to heal or sooth. **2** anything to soothe the feelings or conscience.—*v.t.* to soothe:—*pr.p.* **sal'ving**.

salver *sal'vėr, n.* a tray for presenting things.

salvo *sal'vō, n.* **1** a burst of gunfire, in salute, etc., or a discharge of bombs, etc. **2** a round of applause:—*pl.* **salvo(e)s**.

Samaritan *sȧ-mar'i-tȧn, n.* **1** an inhabitant of *Samaria* (in Palestine). **2** a member of an organisation formed to help people in despair, esp. by talking to them on the telephone.

good Samaritan. See **good**.

same *sām, adj.* **1** exactly alike, identical. **2** not different. **3** unchanged. **4** mentioned before.—*pron.* the thing just mentioned.

same'ness *n.* tiresome lack of variety.

sā'mey (*coll.*) *adj.* **1** (boringly) similar. **2** monotonous.

all, just, the same for all that.

at the same time still, nevertheless.

samosa *sȧ-mō'zȧ, n.* a small deep-fried triangular spicy meat or vegetable pasty of Indian origin.

samovar *sam'ȯ-vär, -vär', n.* a Russian tea urn.

sampan *sam'pan, n.* a Chinese boat.

sample *säm'pl, n.* a small portion to show the quality of the whole, a specimen, example.—Also *adj.*—*v.t.* to test a sample of:—*pr.p.* **sam'pling**.

sam'pler *n.* **1** one who samples. **2** a piece of embroidery, etc. to show one's skill.

sanatorium *san-ȧ-tō'ri-ùm, -tö', n.* a hospital, esp. for people with diseases of the lungs:—*pl.* **sanator'iums, -ia**.

sanctify, etc. See **sanctity**.

sanction *sang(k)'sh(ȯ)n, n.* **1** permission, approval, support (given e.g. by a person in authority, by custom): *I can do nothing without the sanction of the headmistress.* **2** (in *pl.*) a measure applied, e.g. to a nation, to force it to stop a course of action.—*v.t.* to permit, give sanction for: *she will not sanction the girls' use of lipstick.*

sanctity *sang(k)'ti-ti, n.* **1** purity, holiness. **2** sacredness. **3** (of an oath, custom, etc.) quality that should make it unbreakable or impossible to change.

sanc'tify *(-fī) v.t.* **1** to make sacred or holy. **2** to free from sin:—*pr.p.* **sanc'tifying**; *pa.p.* **sanc'tified** *(-fīd)*.

sanctificā'tion *n.*

sanctimō'nious *adj.* pretending, or making a show of, holiness.

sanctimō'niously *adv.*

sanctimō'niousness *n.*

sanc'tuary *n.* **1** a sacred place. **2** (the most sacred part of) a temple or church. **3** a place where one can be safe from arrest or violence. **4** an animal or plant reserve:—*pl.* **sanc'tuaries**.

sanc'tum *n.* a private room.

sand *sand, n.* **1** a mass of fine particles of crushed or worn rock, esp. quartz. **2** (often in *pl.*) land covered with sand, esp. the seashore.—*v.t.* **1** to sprinkle with sand. **2** to add sand to. **3** to smooth with sand or sandpaper.

san'dy *adj.*:—*comp.* **san'dier**; *superl.* **san'diest**.

san'diness *n.*

sand'bag *n.* a bag filled with sand.—*v.t.* **1** to protect with sandbags. **2** to hit or stun with one:—*pr.p.* **sand'bagging**; *pa.p.* **sand'bagged**.

sand'bank *n.* a bank of sand formed by tides and currents.

sand dune. Same as **dune**.

sand'-glass *n.* an hour-glass, or a similar device for measuring shorter periods of time.

sand martin a martin that nests in sandy banks.

sand'paper *n.* paper covered with sand for smoothing and polishing.—*v.t.* to use sandpaper on.

sand'piper *n.* a type of wading bird.

sand'shoe *n.* a light shoe with a canvas upper and rubber sole.

sand'stone *n.* a soft rock made of layers of sand pressed together.

sandal *san'd(ȧ)l, n.* **1** a sole bound to the foot with straps. **2** a light, low shoe or slipper.

san'dalled *adj.* wearing sandals.

sandalwood *san'd(ȧ)l-wood, n.* a wood from Asia noted for its fragrance.

sandwich *san(d)'wij, -wich, n.* **1** two slices of bread with any kind of food between. **2** anything like this in arrangement.—*v.t.* to place (something, between two layers or between two objects).

sandwich course a course of education consisting of alternating periods of college and industrial work.

sandy. See **sand**.

sane *sān, adj.* **1** sound in mind, not mad. **2** sensible: *It is the sane thing to do*:—*opp.* **insane.**
sane'ly *adv.*
sane'ness, san'ity *(san') ns.*

sang. See **sing**.

sangfroid, sang-froid *song-frwä', n.* coolness, self-possession, in danger, etc.

sanguinary *sang'gwin-ȧr-i, adj.* **1** bloodthirsty. **2** (of e.g. a battle) with much bloodshed.

sanguine *sang'gwin, adj.* **1** (of complexion) ruddy. **2** cheerful, hopeful.
san'guinely *adv.* **san'guineness** *n.*

sanitary *san'i-tȧr-i, adj.* **1** having to do with conditions or arrangements that encourage health, esp. good drainage, etc. **2** free from dirt, etc. (*opp.* **insanitary**).
sanitā'rium (*U.S.*) *n.* a sanatorium.
sanitā'tion *n.* sanitary, healthy, condition, or arrangements for bringing this about.
sanitary towel a pad of absorbent material for wearing during menstruation, etc.

sanity. See **sane**.

sank. See **sink**.

Sanskrit *san'skrit, n.* the ancient literary language of India.

Santa Claus *san'tȧ klöz, n.* in folklore, Father Christmas, who brings children Christmas presents.

sap¹ *sap, n.* **1** juice, esp. the liquid that flows in plants. **2** a weakling or fool.
sap'ling *n.* a young tree.
sapp'y *adj.*:—*comp.* **sapp'ier**; *superl.* **sapp'iest**.
sapp'iness *n.*

sap² *sap, n.* (the building of) a trench or tunnel leading towards the enemy's position.—*v.t.* **1** to approach, or weaken, destroy, by digging beneath. **2** (partly from **sap¹**) to weaken, exhaust: *to sap one's strength.*—Also *v.i.*:—*pr.p.* **sapp'ing**; *pa.p.* **sapped**.
sapp'er *n.* one, esp. a soldier, who saps, esp. a private in the Royal Engineers.

sapience *sā'pi-ėns, n.* judgment, wisdom (often used in irony).
sa'pient *adj.* wise.

sapling. See **sap¹**.

sapper. See **sap²**.

sapphire *saf'īr, n.* (a precious stone of) a beautiful blue colour.—Also *adj.*

sappy. See **sap¹**.

sarcasm *sär'kaz-ėm, n.* **1** a cutting or biting remark in scorn or contempt, esp. one in ironical wording. **2** the use of such remarks.
sarcas'tic *adj.* **1** containing sarcasm. **2** often using sarcasm.
sarcas'tically *adv.*

sarcophagus *sär-kof'ȧ-gus, n.* **1** a stone coffin. **2** a tomb.

sardine *sär-dēn', sär', n.* a young pilchard or other fish tinned in oil.

sardonic *sär-don'ik, adj.* (of smile, person, etc.) bitterly scornful.
sardon'ically *adv.*

sargasso *sär-gas'ō, n.* a type of seaweed.

sari *sä'rē, n.* a Hindu woman's outer garment, wrapped round the waist and passed over the shoulder.

sarong *sä-rong', n.* a type of skirt worn by women and men in Malaysia.

sarsaparilla *sär-sȧ-pȧ-ril'ȧ, n.* **1** a trailing plant. **2** a flavouring made from its root. **3** a soft drink made with this flavouring.

sartorial *sär-tōr'i-ȧl, -tör', adj.* having to do with dress, or with tailor-made clothes: *The tramp cared nothing about sartorial elegance.*

sash¹ *sash, n.* a band or scarf worn round the waist or over the shoulder.

sash² *sash, n.* a frame, esp. a sliding frame, for panes of glass.

sassafras *sas'ȧ-fras, n.* **1** a type of laurel tree of N. America. **2** the dried bark, esp. of its root, used in medicine and for flavouring.

Sassenach *sas'ė-naH, n.* **1** an Englishman. **2** (*wrongly; Scot.*, etc.) a Lowlander.

sat. See **sit**.

Satan *sā'tȧn, n.* the Devil, the chief of the fallen angels.
Satan'ic *(sȧ-tan') adj.*

satchel *sach'ėl, n.* a small bag, esp. for schoolbooks.

sate *sāt, v.t.* to make (a person) feel he has had more than enough: *to sate a person with food, advice*:—*pr.p.* **sat'ing**.
sat'ed *adj.*

sateen *sȧ-tēn', n.* a glossy-looking cotton or woollen cloth.

satellite *sat'ė-līt, n.* **1** a follower who attaches himself to a more powerful person. **2** a planet that revolves around a larger planet, or a man-made object launched into orbit round a planet. **3** a town, nation, etc., controlled by, or in some way dependent on, a more powerful neighbour.
satellite dish a saucer-shaped aerial for receiving television signals broadcast by satellite.

satiate *sā'shi-āt, v.t.* to give more than enough to, sate utterly, and so sicken:—*pr.p.* **sā'tiating**.
satiā'tion *n.* **sā'tiable** *adj.* (*opp.* **insatiable**).

satiety *sȧ-tī'ė-ti, n.* **1** satiation. **2** an excessive amount.

satin *sat'in, n.* a closely woven silk with a glossy surface.—Also *adj.*
sat'iny *adj.* **sat'ininess** *n.*
sat'inwood *n.* a beautiful smooth wood from East Indies.

satire *sat'īr, n.* **1** a piece of writing making fun of people esp. of their vices, foolish actions and beliefs, etc. **2** ridicule, cutting comment.
satir'ic(al) *(-ir') adjs.* **satir'ically** *adv.*
sat'irise *v.t.* to ridicule, compose a satire on (persons or their ways):—*pr.p.* **sat'irising**.
sat'irist *n.* a writer of satire.

satisfy *sat'is-fī, v.t.* **1** to give enough to (a person). **2** to please, make content. **3** to pay (a creditor). **4** to give enough to quiet, get rid of: *to satisfy hunger, curiosity, a desire.* **5** to fulfil (requirements, conditions laid down). **6** to convince: *His explanation should satisfy them that he is innocent.* **7** to lay one's doubts to rest by investigation: *I must go out and satisfy myself that the loafer has moved away.*—Also *v.i.*:—*pr.p.* **sat'isfying**; *pa.p.* **sat'isfied** *(-fīd)*.
satisfac'tion *n.* **1** the act of satisfying. **2** the state of being satisfied. **3** a feeling of comfort and pleasure. **4** something that satisfies. **5** payment. **6** amends, compensation:—*opp.* (*defs. 1–3*) **dissatisfaction**.
satisfac'tory *adj.* **1** satisfying, meeting requirements: *a satisfactory report, response.* **2** convincing; *a satisfactory explanation.*
satisfac'torily *adv.* **satisfac'toriness** *n.*

satsuma *sat-sōō'mȧ, n.* a type of mandarin orange.

saturate *sat'ū-rāt, v.t.* **1** to soak, or to fill, completely (with e.g. water, dirt, a smell, a crowd). **2** to cover (a target) completely with bombs, etc.:—*pr.p.* **sat'urating**.
sat'urated *adj.*
saturā'tion *n.* **1** the act of saturating. **2** the state of being saturated. **3** (of colour) freedom from white.

Saturday *sat'ůr-di, n.* the seventh day of the week.

Saturn *sat'ůrn, n.* **1** a Roman god. **2** the sixth planet in order of distance from the sun.
saturnine *sat'ůr-nīn, adj.* **1** gloomy, given to saying little, as those born under the planet *Saturn* were supposed to be. **2** sardonic.

satyr *sat'ėr, n.* a god of the woods supposed to be half man, half goat, and very wanton.

sauce *sös, n.* **1** a dressing poured over food to give flavour: *tomato sauce.* **2** (*coll.*) impudence, cheek.
saucy *sö'si, adj.* **1** bold, forward, cheeky. **2** smart and trim:—*comp.* **sau'cier**; *superl.* **sau'ciest**.
sau'cily *adv.* **sau'ciness** *n.*
sauce'pan *n.* a rather deep pan for boiling, stewing, etc. in.

saucer *sö'sėr, n.* **1** a shallow dish placed under a cup. **2** anything of that shape.

saucy. See **sauce**.

sauerkraut *sowr'krowt, n.* a German dish of cabbage cut fine and pickled in salt.

sauna *sö'nȧ, n.* (a building, etc. equipped for) an orig. Finnish form of steam bath.

saunter *sön'tėr, v.t.* to wander about without hurry, stroll.—Also *n.*

sausage *sos'ij, n.* chopped meat, etc. seasoned and stuffed into a tube of e.g. animal gut.
sau'sage-roll' *n.* minced meat, etc. cooked in a roll of pastry.

sauté *sō'tā, adj.* fried lightly and quickly.—*v.t* to fry lightly and quickly:—*pr.p.* **sau'téing**; *pa.p.* **sau'té(e)d**.

sauterne(s) *sō-tûrn', n.* a sweet white wine made at *Sauternes*, in France.

savage *sav'ij, adj.* **1** in a state of nature, primitive. **2** (of an animal) wild. **3** fierce and cruel. **4** very angry.—*n.* **1** a human being in an uncivilised state. **2** a cruel or fierce person.
sav'agely *adv.* **sav'ageness** *n.*
sav'agery *n.* **1** savageness, the state of being savage. **2** a savage deed:—*pl.* **sav'ageries**.

savanna, **savannah** *sȧ-van'ȧ, n.* a grassy plain with few trees.

savant *sa'vonᵍ, sa'vȧnt, n.* a learned man.

save *sāv, v.t.* **1** to rescue, bring out of danger. **2** to prevent the loss of, or damage to. **3** to keep or preserve (from). **4** to keep from spending, using, wasting (e.g. money, time, energy). **5** to rescue (from evil or sin).—*v.i.* **1** to put money aside for future use. **2** to rescue from evil or sin:—*pr.p.* **sav'ing**.—*prep.* except: *All, save one, were there.*
sa'ver *n.* a person or thing that keeps from spending, using, wasting.
sa'ving *adj.* **1** thrifty. **2** (used only before a noun) making an exception: *a saving clause in an agreement.* **3** (used only before a noun) making up for bad qualities: *She has the saving grace—or good quality—of honesty.*—*n.* **1** (in *pl*) money put aside for the future. **2** a lessening (of expense, etc.).

saviour *sā'vyȯr, n.* **1** one who saves from

evil, sin, or danger. **2** (*cap.*) Jesus Christ.
savings bank a bank which receives small deposits and gives interest.
save up to put aside money gradually for future use.
See also **safe, salvation**.

savoir-faire *sav'wär-fer'*, *n.* the ability to act in any social situation with self-confidence, skill and tact.

savour *sā'vȯr*, *n.* **1** taste. **2** a characteristic flavour or quality. **3** a quality that pleases or interests: *a book, an occupation, without savour.*—*v.i.* to have the taste, smell, or quality (of): *This action savours of rebellion.*—*v.t.* **1** to recognise and appreciate the special quality of: *to savour delicious food, a witty book.* **2** to taste, or to have experience of.
sā'voury *adj.* having an attractive taste or smell (salt or sharp, not sweet): (of news, etc.) appealing to one's appetite for scandal, etc.—*n.* a savoury course or dish:—*pl.* **sā'vouries**.
sa'vouriness *n.*

savoy *sȧ-voi'*, *n.* a type of winter cabbage.

saw[1]. See **see**[2].

saw[2] *sö*, *n.* an instrument for cutting, having a blade, band, or disc of thin steel with a toothed edge.—*v.t.* to cut with a saw.—*v.i.* to use a saw:—*pa.t.* **sawed**; *pa.p.* **sawed** or **sawn**.
saw'yer *n.* one whose job is to saw.
saw'dust *n.* dust or small pieces of wood, etc., made in sawing.
saw'horse *n.* a support for wood while it is being sawn.
saw'mill *n.* a mill for sawing timber.

saw[3] *sö*, *n.* an old wise saying, proverb.

saxifrage *sak'si-frij*, *n.* a type of rock plant.

Saxon *sak'sȯn*, *n.* one of a North German people who conquered part of Britain in the 5th and 6th centuries.

saxophone *sak'sȯ-fōn*, *n.* a wind instrument with a curved, usu. metal, tube and finger keys.
saxoph'onist *(-of')* *n.*

say *sā*, *v.t.* **1** to utter (a word, etc.): *to say Yes.* **2** to express, state, in words. **3** to assert, declare: *I say it is so.* **4** to repeat (prayers). **5** to tell: *to say one's mind*:—*pr.p.* **say'ing**; *pa.t., pa.p.* **said** *(sed)*; *pr.t. 3rd person sing.* **says** *(sez).*—*n.* **1** what one wants to say: *to say one's say.* **2** the right to speak, or influence on what is decided: *I have no say in the matter.* **3** opportunity of speaking: *to have one's say.*
say'ing *n.* something often said, esp. a proverb, etc.
have the say to be the one in authority.
I say! *interj.* expressing surprise or protest, or trying to attract someone's attention.
that is to say in other words.

scab *skab*, *n.* **1** a crust formed over a sore. **2** any of several diseases of animals, or of plants: *potato scab.* **3** a scoundrel. **4** a blackleg.
scabbed, **scabb'y** (*comp.* **-ier**; *superl.* **-iest**) *adjs.*
scabb'iness *n.*

scabbard *skab'ȧrd*, *n.* a sheath, case in which the blade of a sword is kept.

scabby, etc. See **scab**.

scabies *skā'bi-ēz*, *-bēz*, *n.* a skin disease, also called *'the itch'*, caused by a mite.

scabious *skā'bi-u̇s*, *n.* a plant with heads of often blue flowers.

scaffold *skaf'ȯld*, *-ōld*, *n.* **1** a system of platforms for men at work on a building. **2** a raised platform, esp. for use when putting a criminal, etc., to death.
scaff'olding *n.* **1** scaffold(s) for workmen. **2** materials for scaffolds. **3** a framework.

scalable, **scalar**. See **scale**.

scald *sköld*, *v.t.* **1** to burn with hot liquid. **2** to cook or heat just short of boiling.—Also *n.*

scale[1] *skāl*, *n.* **1** something with marks made at regular distances, for use as a measure: *the scale on a thermometer.* **2** a system of numbers. **3** a system of increasing values: *a wage scale.* **4** (*music*) group of notes going up or down in order of pitch with a regular (not necessarily equal) space between them. **5** dimensions of one thing as compared with another (e.g. of a map as compared with the actual country it shows): *a map drawn to a scale of one inch to the mile.* **6** the size of an activity, of production, etc.: *manufacture on a large, small, scale.*—*v.t.* **1** to climb up (e.g. a ladder, a mountain). **2** (usu. with *up* or *down*) to change something, make it larger or smaller, etc., according to a fixed scale:—*pr.p.* **scal'ing**.—*adj.* made to scale.
scā'lable *adj.* that can be climbed.
sca'lar *adj.* **1** arranged like a ladder or measuring scale. **2** (*mathematics*; of a quantity) having size but not direction.
to scale in proportion to the actual dimensions.

scale[2] *skāl*, *n.* a small thin plate or flake on the skin of a fish, snake, plant leaf bud, etc.—*v.t.* **1** to clear of scales. **2** to remove in thin layers.—*v.i.* to come (off) in flakes:—*pr.p.* **scal'ing**.
sca'ly *adj.*:—*comp.* **sca'lier**; *superl.*

sca'liest.
sca'liness *n.*

scale[3] *skāl*, *n.* **1** the dish of a balance. **2** (usu. in *pl.*) a weighing machine.

scalene *skā'lēn*, *-lēn'*, *adj.* (of a triangle) having three unequal sides.

scaliness, etc. See **scale**[2].

scallop *skol'op*, *skal'*, *n.* **1** a type of shell-fish, with hinged, more or less fan-shaped, shells. **2** a wave in the edge of anything.—*v.t.* **1** to cut into curves. **2** to cook (esp. oysters) by baking, e.g. in a scallop shell, with breadcrumbs.:—*pr.p.* **scall'oping**; *pa.p.* **scall'oped**.

scallywag *skal'i-wag*, *n.* a good-for-nothing, a scamp.

scalp *skalp*, *n.* **1** the outer covering of the skull. **2** the skin and hair of the top of the head, once cut off a defeated enemy by N. American Indians.—*v.t.* to cut the scalp from.

scalpel *skal'pėl*, *n.* a small knife with a thin blade used in surgical operations.

scaly. See **scale**[2].

scamp[1] *skamp*, *n.* **1** a rascal. **2** a lively tricky fellow.
scam'pish *adj.*
scam'per *v.i.* **1** to run away in haste. **2** to run about gaily.—*n.* **1** a hurried flight. **2** a romp.

scamp[2] *skamp*, *v.t.* to do (work) carelessly and hastily.

scampi *skam'pē*, *n.pl.* Norway lobsters (small, slender lobsters of European seas) when considered as food (often *n.sing.* when considered as a dish).

scan *skan*, *v.t.* **1** to examine the metre or rhythm of (a line of verse; in English verse, to find or mark accented syllables, etc.). **2** to examine carefully. **3** to cast an eye quickly over: *to scan a newspaper.* **4** (*television*, etc.) to pass a beam of light, electrons, radar, etc., over every part of.—*v.i.* (of English verse) to have accented syllables in the correct places:—*pr.p.* **scann'ing**; *pa.p.* **scanned**.
scann'er *n.* **scann'ing** *n.*
scan'sion *n.* scanning of verse.

scandal *skan'd(ȧ)l*, *n.* **1** a disgraceful action, circumstance, or person, arousing the strong disapproval of people in general. **2** the disapproval aroused. **3** damage to reputation, disgrace. **4** gossip about people's misdeeds, real or invented: *ladies talking scandal about their neighbours.*
scan'dalise *v.t.* **1** to shock, horrify. **2** to slander.—*v.i.* to talk scandal:—*pr.p.* **scan'dalising**.
scan'dalous *adj.* **1** shocking, disgraceful. **2** slanderous: *C spread scandalous stories about B.* **3** loving scandal.
scan'dalmonger *n.* one who spreads gossip or scandal.

Scandinavian *skan-di-nā'vi-ȧn*, *adj.* of *Scandinavia* (Norway, Sweden, Denmark and Iceland).—Also *n.*

scanning, **scansion**, etc. See **scan**.

scant *skant*, *adj.* barely, sufficient, cut down or reduced much: *a scant allowance*; *scant attention*; *scant justice.*—*v.t.* to give too little of.
scant'ly *adv.* **scant'ness** *n.*
scan'ty *adj.* little or not enough in amount: *scanty clothing*, *vegetation*:—*comp.* **scan'tier**; *superl.* **scan'tiest**.
scan'tily *adv.* **scan'tiness** *n.*
scant of having too small a supply of.

scapegoat *skāp'gōt*, *n.* one who bears the blame for wrongdoing of others.

scapegrace *skāp'grās*, *n.* a good-for-nothing, a scamp.

scapula *skap'ū-lȧ*, *n.* the shoulder-blade.
scap'ular *adj.*

scar[1] *skär*, *n.* **1** the mark left by a wound or sore. **2** any mark or blemish. **3** the damage done by any mental or psychological upset.—*v.t.* to cause, leave, mark with a scar:—*pr.p.* **scarr'ing**; *pr.p.* **scarr'ing**; *pr.p.* **scarred**

scar[2] *skär*, *n.* **1** a bare rocky place on the side of a hill. **2** a steep rock.

scarab *skar'ȧb*, *n.* **1** a type of beetle. **2** a gem cut in the form of a beetle.

scarce *skārs*, *adj.* **1** not plentiful, not enough to meet the demand. **2** rare, seldom found.
scarce'ly *adv.* **1** barely, not quite. **2** probably, or definitely, not: *You could scarcely expect her to cross the swollen stream.*
scarce'ness, **scar'city** (*pl.* **-ies**) *ns.*
make onself scarce to go, run away.

scare *skār*, *v.t.* **1** to startle, frighten. **2** to drive (away, off) by frightening—*v.i.* to become frightened:—*pr.p.* **scar'ing.**—*n.* a sudden, usu. unnecessary, fright or alarm.
scā'ry, **scār'ey** *adj.* frightening:—*comp.* **scar'ier**; *superl.* **scar'iest**.
scare'crow *n.* **1** a figure set up to scare away birds. **2** a cause of a needless fear. **3** a person in rags, or very thin or odd-looking.
scare'monger *n.* one who spreads alarming rumours.

scarf[1] *skärf*, *n.* a piece of material worn loosely on the shoulders or round the neck or head:—*pl.* **scarves**, **scarfs**.

scarf[2] *skärf*, *v.t.* to join (two pieces of timber) by a **scarf joint**, part of each piece being cut away so that one fits over the other.—*n.* a scarf joint.

scarify *skar'i-fī*, *v.t.* to make slight cuts or scratches in (e.g. the skin): to pain by criticising very severely:—*pr.p.* **scar'ifying**; *pa.p.* **scar'ified**.
scarificā'tion *n.*

scarlatina *skär-lȧ-tē'nȧ*, *n.* scarlet fever, esp. when mild.

scarlet *skär'lit*, *n.* **1** a bright red colour. **2** red cloth or clothes.—Also *adj.*
scarlet fever an infectious fever usu. with sore throat and rash.

scarp *skärp*, *n.* a steep slope.

scarves. See **scarf**[1].

scary. See **scare**.

scathe *skāTH*, *n.* damage, injury.—*v.t.* to injure:—*pr.p.* **scath'ing**.
scāth'ing *adj.* **1** damaging. **2** (of e.g. remarks, criticism) bitter, cruel.
scathe'less *adj.* unharmed.

scatter *skat'ėr*, *v.t.* **1** to spread widely, send in all directions. **2** to throw loosely about, sprinkle.—*v.i.* to go away in all directions.—*n.* a sprinkling, scattering.
scatt'ered *adj.* thrown, sent, or placed, widely here and there.
scatt'ering *n.* **1** the act of spreading, or being spread, widely. **2** a small number here and there.
scatt'erbrain *n.* **1** a forgetful, unreliable person. **2** one unable to keep his attention fixed.
scatt'erbrained *adj.*

scatty *skat'i*, (*coll.*) *adj.* **1** slightly crazy, unpredictable. **2** scatterbrained:—*comp.* **scatt'ier**; *superl.* **scatt'iest**.

scavenger *skav'in-jėr*, *n.* **1** one who cleans the streets or picks up refuse. **2** one who scavenges for food, usable items, etc. in rubbish.
scav'enge *v.i.* **1** to act as a scavenger. **2** to search (for food, etc.) in rubbish:—*pr.p.* **scav'enging**.

scenario *si-nä'ri-ō*, *n.* **1** an outline of a film, play, etc. scene by scene. **2** an outline of an expected sequence of events, plan, etc.:—*pl.* **scenar'ios**.

scene *sēn*, *n.* **1** (*orig.*) a stage (this explains such phrases as *to come on the scene*, to appear and take part in some action). **2** the place where something, real or imaginary, happens. **3** one part of, or episode in, a play, shorter than an act. **4** a particular area of activity: *There have been changes on the business scene.* **5** stage scenery (also in *pl.*). **6** a landscape, view. **7** an embarrassing show of strong feeling, esp. of bad temper. **8** (*coll.*) area of interest or activity.
sce'nery *n.* **1** painted background of hangings, movable structures, etc., used on a stage. **2** the general appearance of a stretch of country.
scenic *sē'nik*, *sen'*, *adj.* **1** having to do with scenery, real or theatrical: *The stage was small but the scenic effect was good.* **2** having beautiful scenery: *a scenic route*.

scent *sent*, *v.t.* **1** to discover by the sense of smell. **2** to have some suspicion of: *I scent a mystery here.* **3** to cause to smell pleasantly: *Hawthorn scents the air.*—*n.* **1** a perfume. **2** odour. **3** the trail of smell by which an animal or person may be tracked.
scen'ted *adj.* **scent'less** *adj.*
on the scent on the trail that will lead to the hunted animal or to the information wanted.
off the scent on the wrong track.

sceptic *skep'tik*, *n.* **1** one who questions commonly held opinions, or doubts common beliefs. **2** one who is always ready to doubt what he is told, etc.
scep'tical *adj.* **1** unwilling to believe without absolute evidence. **2** showing, or feeling, doubt: *a sceptical glance*; *I am sceptical about his ability to keep his promise*.
scep'tically *adv.* **scep'ticalness** *n.*
scep'ticism *(-ti-sizm)*, *n.* an attitude of doubt.

sceptre *sep'tėr*, *n.* **1** a rod or staff carried on certain formal occasions by monarchs. **2** royal power.

schedule *shed'ūl*, (*U.S.*) *sked'ūl*, *n.* **1** a list of articles. **2** a statement of details (added to a document). **3** a form for filling in information. **4** a timetable, programme.—*v.t.* **1** to form into a schedule or list. **2** to plan, arrange: *to schedule a meeting*:—*pr.p.* **sched'uling**.
sched'uled *adj.* planned, arranged: *scheduled for, to happen at, 7 p.m.*

scheme *skēm*, *n.* **1** a diagram. **2** a system. **3** an arrangement: *a colour scheme.* **4** a plan for building operations of several kinds, or the buildings, etc., put up: *a housing scheme.* **5** a plan of action. **6** a crafty or dishonest plan.—*v.i.* to plan craftily, lay schemes (for).—Also *v.t.*:—*pr.p.* **sche'ming**.
schē'mer *n.* **schē'ming** *n.* and *adj.*

scherzo *skûrt'sō*, *n.* (*music*) a lively movement e.g. in a sonata:—*pl.* **scher'zos**.

schism *sizm*, *skizm*, *n.* **1** a breaking away, division. **2** a group of persons breaking away from a main group (e.g. in a church).

schist *shist*, *n.* a type of rock easily split into layers.

schizophrenia *skit-sō-frē'ni-ȧ, skid-zō-, n.* **1** a form of insanity. **2** split personality.
schizophren'ic *(-fren') n.* and *adj.*

schnap(p)s *shnaps, n.* a type of gin.

schnitzel *schnit'sėl, n.* a veal cutlet.

schnorkel *shnör'kėl.* Same as *snorkel.*

scholar *skol'ȧr, n.* **1** a pupil, student. **2** the holder of a scholarship. **3** a person of great learning.
schol'arly *adj.* having, showing, the knowledge and love of accuracy of a truly learned person.
schol'arliness *n.*
schol'arship *n.* **1** scholarliness. **2** learning. **3** money awarded to a good student to enable him to go on with further studies.
scholastic *skȯl-as'tik, adj.* having to do with schools or with education.
school *skōōl, n.* **1** a place for teaching, esp. children. **2** the pupils of a school. **3** a series of meetings for instruction: *a music summer school.* **4** a group of people with the same opinions, ideas, or methods of working: *a philosopher of the school of Plato*; *an artist of the school of Raphael.* **5** students and instructors in a branch of learning, in e.g. a university: *the mathematical school at Cambridge.*—*v.t.* **1** to send to, or educate in, a school. **2** to train by practice: *We must school ourselves in patience, to be patient.*
school'ing *n.* **1** instruction in school. **2** training.
school'book *n.* a book for use in school.
school'boy *n.* **school'girl** *n.*
school'child *n.*:—*pl.* **school'children**.
school'fellow *n.* one taught at the same school, esp. in the same class.
school'marm *n.* a schoolmistress, esp. one who is prim and too particular about trifles.
school'master *n.* a master or teacher in a school:—*fem.* **school'mistress**.
school'mate a schoolfellow, esp. a friend.

school[1]. See **scholar**.

school[2] *skōōl, n.* a number of fish, whales, or other water animals of one kind, swimming about together.

schooner *skōōn'ėr, n.* **1** a swift-sailing ship, with two or more masts. **2** a large beer or sherry glass.

schottische *sho-tēsh', n.* a dance or dance tune like the polka.

sciatic *sī-at'ik, adj.* in the region of the hip.
sciat'ica *n.* a severe pain in the upper part of the leg.

science *sī'ėns, n.* **1** knowledge gained by observation and experiment, carefully arranged so that it can be studied as a whole. **2** a branch of such knowledge (e.g. the facts learned about heat, or light, electricity, chemistry, biology, etc.). **3** trained skill (e.g. in games).
scientif'ic *adj.* **1** having to do with science. **2** careful, thorough: *They made a scientific search for the document.*
scientif'ically *adv.*
sci'entist *n.* one who studies science.
Scientology *n.* a religious system which, it is claimed, improves the mental and physical well-being of its adherents by scientific means.
science fiction stories dealing with future times on earth or in space.

scimitar *sim'i-tȧr, n.* a short, single-edged, curved sword, used by Turks.

scintillate *sin'ti-lāt, v.i.* to sparkle, twinkle (also used of e.g. eyes, wit, a person):—*pr.p.* **scin'tillating**.
scintillā'tion *n.*

scion *sī'ȯn, n.* **1** a cutting or twig for grafting on another plant. **2** a young member of a family (esp. noble or wealthy). **3** a descendant.

scissors *siz'ȯrz, n.pl.* a cutting instrument with two blades.

sclerosis *sklėr-ō'sis, n.* hardening, e.g. of arteries or nerve tissue.
multiple sclerosis. See **multiple**.

scoff[1] *skof, v.i.* **1** to mock, jeer (at). **2** to express scorn.—*n.* **1** an expression of scorn. **2** an object of scorn.

scoff[2] *skof, (slang) v.t.* to eat.

scold *skōld, n.* a rude, bad-tempered person, esp. a woman.—*v.t.* to find fault with (someone) angrily or sternly.—Also *v.i.*
scold'ing *n.* and *adj.*

scone *skon*, in England often *skōn, (Scot.) n.* a flat plain cake baked on a girdle (griddle) or in an oven.

scoop *skōōp, n.* **1** a ladle or deep shovel in which water or loose material can be taken up and carried. **2** an unexpected gain, large haul of e.g. money. **3** a piece of news which one newspaper prints before others have heard about it.—*v.t.* **1** to lift (up) with a scoop. **2** to dig (out, a hole). **3** to get (news) before a rival.

scoot *skōōt, (coll.) v.i.* to move or go swiftly, dart.
scoot'er *n.* **1** a two-wheeled child's toy driven by the foot. **2** a type of light motor-cycle.

scope *skōp, n.* **1** the area (of e.g. a subject) covered, included: *The enquiry is concerned with large businesses*; *small firms* *are outside its scope.* **2** room or opportunity: *His job, instructions, gave no scope for orginality.*

scorch *skörch, v.t.* **1** to burn slightly, singe. **2** to dry up with heat. **3** to subject (e.g. a person) to bitter criticism.—*v.i.* **1** to be burned on the surface. **2** to be dried up. **3** to drive at very high speed.—Also *n.*

scorch'er (*coll.*) *n.* a very hot day.

scorch'ing *adj.* **1** very hot. **2** (of criticism) bitterly scornful.

scorched earth complete destruction in a region to hinder the advance of an enemy.

score *skōr, skör, n.* **1** a notch. **2** a line. **3** an arrangement of music on a number of staves (see this word). **4** the total of points gained in a game or an examination. **5** a point gained. **6** an amount owed. **7** a set of twenty. **8** (in *pl.*) a great many. **9** reason: *He declined on the score of lack of practice.* **10** account, matter: *Don't worry on that score.*—*v.t.* **1** to mark with notches or lines. **2** to gain or record (points) in a game.—*v.i.* to gain a point, or a success:—*pr.p.* **scor'ing.**

scor'er *n.*

know the score to be aware of and understand the hard realities of a situation.

score out to delete by putting one or more lines through.

settle old scores to have revenge for an old wrong or grudge.

scorn *skörn, n.* **1** extreme disapproval, contempt, angry disgust. **2** the object of contempt.—*v.t.* **1** to look down on, despise. **2** to refuse, esp. proudly: *He scorns to ask for help.*

scorn'ful *adj.* **scorn'fully** *adv.*

scorpion *skör'pi-ȯn, n.* an animal of the same class as spiders, with a tail with a sting.

scot *skot,* (*old*) *n.* **1** a payment. **2** a tax.

scot'-free *adj.* **1** without payment or loss. **2** unhurt, unpunished.

Scot *skot, n.* **1** a native of Scotland. **2** one of a Gaelic-speaking people of Ireland who settled in Scotland in about the 5th century.

Scotch *skoch, adj.* form of **Scottish,** correctly applied to certain products (e.g. *Scotch whisky, Scotch terrier*).—*n.* Scotch whisky.

Scots *skots, adj.* Scottish (used of law, language).—*n.* a form of English spoken, esp. long ago, in the Lowlands of Scotland—as spoken in later times, called also **Broad Scots.**

Scott'icism *n.* a Scottish word, phrase, or idiom.

Scott'ish *adj.* of Scotland, its people, or its form of English.

Scotch broth a soup made with barley and chopped vegetables.

Scotch mist a fine rain.

Scots pine the only native British pine.

scotch *skoch, v.i.* **1** to cut or wound slightly. **2** to stamp out (e.g. a rumour).

Scotch. See **Scot.**

scot-free. See **scot.**

Scotland Yard *skot'lȧnd yärd, n.* the Criminal Investigation Department of the London Metropolitan Police.

Scots, Scotticism, Scottish. See **Scot.**

scoundrel *skown'drėl, n.* a low, mean, unscrupulous person, utter rascal.

scoun'drelly *adj.*

scour[1] *skowr, v.t.* **1** to clean by hard rubbing, scrub. **2** to clear out (e.g. a pipe) by a current of water.—Also *n.*

scour[2] *skowr, v.i.* **1** to rush along. **2** to move (about, over) quickly, esp. in search of something.—*v.t.* to pass over or along in search: *They scoured the neighbourhood for the child.*

scourge *skûrj, n.* **1** a whip made of leather thongs. **2** a means of punishment, or conqueror, etc. who punishes. **3** a cause of calamity, esp. widespread.—*v.t.* **1** to whip. **2** to punish severely:—*pr.p.* **scourg'ing.**

scout[1] *scowt, n.* **1** one sent out to bring in information, observe the enemy, etc. **2** a member of the **Scout Association,** a young people's organisation formed to develop alertness, character, sense of responsibility, etc. **3** a road patrolman to help motorists.—*v.i.* to act as a scout.

scout[2] *skowt, v.t.* to reject (an idea, suggestion) with scorn.

scowl *skowl, v.i.* **1** to wrinkle the brow in displeasure or anger. **2** (of e.g. a mountain) to look gloomy or threatening.—Also *n.*

scrabble *skrab'l, v.t.* and *v.i.* **1** to scratch, scrape. **2** to scribble, scrawl:—*pr.p.* **scrabb'ling.**—*n.* (®; *cap.*) a word-building game.

scrag *skrag, n.* **1** anything thin, or lean, and rough. **2** the bony part of the neck.

scragg'y *adj.* **1** lean, gaunt. **2** rugged:—*comp.* **scragg'ier**; *superl.* **scragg'iest.**

scragg'iness *n.*

scramble *skram'bl, v.i.* **1** to climb (up, along) on hands and knees or with difficulty. **2** to dash or struggle (for something one wants). **3** (of an aircraft or its crew) to take off immediately, as in an emergency—*v.t.* **1** to toss or mix together. **2** to jumble up (a message) so that it has to be decoded before it can be understood, or the sound of (a telephone conversation) so that it becomes clear only in a special receiver:—*pr.p.* **scram'bling.**—*n.* **1** the act of scrambling. **2** a struggle for what can be had. **3** a motor-cycle trial over rough country.

scram'bler *n.* **scram'bling** *n.*

scrambled eggs eggs beaten up with milk, butter, etc., heated until thick.

scrap[1] *skrap, n.* **1** a small piece, fragment: *a scrap of paper.* **2** a piece left over. **3** a picture to be kept in a scrapbook. **4** parts or articles no longer required for orig. purpose: *metal scrap* (also *adj.*: *scrap metal*).—*v.t.* **1** to throw away as useless. **2** to abandon (e.g. a plan).—*pr.p.* **scrapp'ing**; *pa.p.* **scrapped**.

scrapp'y *adj.* **1** in small pieces, portions: *a scrappy meal.* **2** not connected so as to make a satisfactory whole: *a scrappy essay*:—*comp.* **scrapp'ier**; *superl.* **scrapp'iest**.

scrapp'ily *adv.* **scrapp'iness** *n.*

scrap'book *n.* a blank book in which to stick pictures, etc.

scrap'-heap *n.* **1** a heap of e.g. old metal. **2** a rubbish-heap.

scrap iron, metal iron, metal, for remelting and using again.

scrap[2] *skrap, (slang) n.* a fight.—Also *v.i.*:—*pr.p.* **scrapp'ing**; *pa.p.* **scrapped**.

scrape *skrāp, v.t.* **1** to rub, and (usu.) mark, with something sharp. **2** to grate against with a harsh noise. **3** (with *off*) to remove by drawing a sharp edge over: *to scrape off skin.* **4** to gain (e.g. a living), collect (e.g. money), with great effort or in small quantities (often with *up, together*).—Also *v.i.*:—*pr.p.* **scrap'ing.**—*n.* **1** an act of scraping. **2** a mark, or sound, made by scraping. **3** a difficulty that may lead to disgrace or punishment.

scrap'er *n.* **scrap'ing** *n.* and *adj.*

scrape through only just to avoid failure.

scrapping, etc. See **scrap**[1] or **scrap**[2].

scratch *skrach, v.t.* **1** to draw a sharp point over the surface of. **2** to mark by so doing. **3** to tear or dig with nails or claws: *to scratch a hole.* **4** to rub with the nails to relieve itching. **5** to write in a hurry. **6** to rub (out) by scratching. **7** to withdraw (e.g. a horse) from a race or competition.—Also *v.i.*—*n.* **1** a mark, or sound, made by scratching. **2** a slight wound.—*adj.* **1** made up of people hurriedly got together: *a scratch team.* **2** receiving no handicap.

scratch'y *adj.* **1** likely to scratch. **2** harsh or grating. **3** uneven in quality:—*comp.* **scratch'ier**; *superl.* **scratch'iest**.

scratch'ily *adv.* **scratch'iness** *n.*

come up to scratch **1** (formerly, of a boxer) to come up to the starting line drawn across the ring. **2** (also **be up to scratch**) to be of satisfactory quality, or in satisfactory condition.

start from scratch **1** to start from the line marked, or at the time chosen, for competitors who are given no handicap. **2** to start from nothing: *He now has a large business but he started from scratch.*

scrawl *skröl, v.t. v.i.* to mark or write hastily or untidily.—*n.* untidy, hasty, or bad writing.

scrawny *skrö'ni, adj.* thin and tough-looking:—*comp.* **scraw'nier**; *superl.* **scraw'niest**.

scraw'niness *n.*

scream *skrēm, v.i., v.t.* to cry out in a loud shrill voice, as in fear, pain, mirth.—*v.i.* (of colours) to have a startling unpleasant effect together.—Also *n.*

scree *skrē, n.* loose stones lying on a rocky slope.

screech *skrēch, v.i.* to utter a harsh, or shrill, cry.—Also *v.t.* and *n.*

screech'-owl *n.* an owl with a harsh cry, esp. the barn owl.

screed *skrēd, n.* **1** a piece torn off. **2** a long tiresome speech, letter, etc.

screen *skrēn, n.* **1** something that shuts off from view, or that protects from danger, heat, wind, etc. **2** a decorated partition in a church. **3** the sheet or surface on which motion pictures are shown. **4** the motion picture business. **5** the surface on which a television picture appears.—*v.t.* **1** to shelter, or hide. **2** to make a motion picture of. **3** to show on a screen. **4** to put through a coarse sieve. **5** to test (people) to find out which kind of work they can best do. **6** to examine closely the record, esp. political, of (a person) to find out whether it is safe to employ him where loyalty matters. **7** to test for the presence of a disease.

screen'play *n.* the written text of a film, with descriptions of characters, etc.

screw *skrōō, n.* **1** a kind of nail with slotted head and a winding groove or ridge (called the thread) on its surface. **2** a turn or twist e.g. of a screw. **3** spin given to a ball. **4** a **screw-propeller** (with spiral blades, used in steamships and aircraft). **5** a twisted cone of paper. **6** (*slang*) a prison officer. **7** a stingy fellow.—*v.t.* **1** to fasten, tighten, force, or force (out or in) by a screw or a screwing motion. **2** to turn (round, e.g. one's head). **3** to pucker (up, e.g. one's face).

screw'y (*coll.*) *adj.* crazy:—*comp.*

screw'ier; *superl.* **screw'iest**.
screw'-driv'er *n.* an instrument for putting in, or taking out, screws.
a screw loose something not right, e.g. in a person's character or mind.
screw up courage, etc. to manage to make onself brave, etc., enough (to do something).

scribble *skrib'l, v.t.* **1** to write badly or carelessly. **2** to fill with worthless writing.—Also *v.i.*:—*pr.p.* **scribb'ling**.—*n.* **1** careless writing. **2** meaningless marks. **3** a hastily written letter, etc.

scribe *skrīb, n.* **1** a public or official writer. **2** a writer. **3** (*history*) a teacher of the law among the Jews.

scrimmage *skrim'ij*, **scrummage**, *skrum'ij, ns.* **1** a tussle, rough, struggle. **2** (*rugby*) see **scrum**.—*vs.i.* to take part in a scrimmage:—*pr.ps.* **scrimm'aging**, **scrumm'aging**.

scrimp *skrimp, v.i.* to be sparing or stingy with money: *She scrimps and saves for her sons' education.*—*v.t.* to keep to a very small amount: *He scrimps his wife for money; to scrimp food.*
scrim'py *adj.* too small or little:—*comp.* **scrim'pier**; *superl.* **scrim'piest**.
scrim'pily *adv.* **scrim'piness** *n.*

scrip[1] *skrip, n.* **1** a writing. **2** a preliminary certificate for shares allotted. **3** a share certificate.
scrip issue shares given to shareholders without payment as a bonus.

scrip[2] *skrip, n.* small bag or pouch.

script *skript, n.* **1** a manuscript. **2** the text of a talk, play, etc. **3** handwriting like print, or print like handwriting.

scripture *skrip'chůr, n.* the sacred writings of a religion, esp. (**Scripture, the Scriptures**) the Bible.
scrip'tural *adj.* of, in, according to, scripture.

scrivener *skriv'nėr*, (*old*) *n.* **1** a scribe. **2** one who draws up contracts.

scroll *skrōl, n.* **1** a roll of paper, parchment, etc. **2** a schedule or list. **3** an ornament shaped like a partly opened scroll.

scrotum *skrō'tům, n.* the bag of skin enclosing the testicles.

scrounge *skrownj, v.t.* and *v.i.* to cadge, (try to) get by begging:—*pr.p.* **scroung'ing**.
scroung'er *n.*

scrub[1] *skrub, v.t.* and *v.i.* **1** to rub hard in order to clean. **2** (*coll.*) to cancel, call off (e.g. an arrangement):—*pr.p.* **scrubb'ing**; *pa.p.* **scrubbed**.—Also *n.*

scrub[2] *skrub, n.* **1** a stunted tree or bush. **2** (country covered with) low trees and bushes. **3** an undersized animal. **4** an unimportant person.
scrubb'y *adj.* **1** stunted. **2** covered with scrub. **3** mean, shabby:—*comp.* **scrubb'ier**; *superl.* **scrubb'iest**.
scrubb'iness *n.*

scruff[1] *skruf, n.* the back of the neck.

scruff[2] *skruf*, (*coll.*) *n.* a dirty, untidy person.
scruff'y (*coll.*) *adj.*:—*comp.* **scruff'ier**; *superl.* **scruff'iest**.

scrum *skrum, n.* **1** a scrimmage. **2** (*rugby*) a struggle for the ball by the rival forwards bunched tightly round it.

scrummage. See **scrimmage**.

scruple *skrōō'pl, n.* **1** a small weight. **2** a difficulty or hestitation over what is right or wrong which keeps one from action: *I have scruples, no scruples, about accepting the money.*—*v.t.* to hesitate (to do something) because of a scruple:—*pr.p.* **scrup'ling**.
scrup'ūlous *adj.* **1** having scruples, very upright in conduct. **2** careful, exact in the smallest details: *scrupulous honesty, cleanliness.*
scrup'ulously *adv.*
scrup'ulousness, scrupulos'ity *ns.*

scrutiny *skrōō'ti-ni, n.* **1** a close or careful examination. **2** a searching look:—*pl.* **scrut'inies**.
scru'tinise *v.t.* to examine carefully:—*pr.p.* **scru'tinising**.

scud *skud, v.i.* **1** to move or run swiftly. **2** to run before a gale:—*pr.p.* **scudd'ing**; *pa.p.* **scudd'ed**.—*n.* **1** the act of moving quickly. **2** cloud, shower, spray, driven by the wind.

scuff *skuf, v.t.* to scrape (esp. shoes) while walking etc.

scuffle *skuf'l, v.i.* **1** to struggle, fight, confusedly. **2** to shuffle (along):—*pr.p.* **scuff'ling**.—*n.* a confused fight at close quarters.

scull *skul, n.* a short, light oar.—*v.t., v.i.* to move (a boat) with a pair of these, or with one oar worked at the stern of the boat.

scullery *skul'ėr-i, n.* a room for rough kitchen work, e.g. cleaning utensils:—*pl.* **scull'eries**.

sculptor *skulp'tǫr, n.* an artist who carves or models figures or designs in marble, clay, etc.:—*fem.* **sculp'tress**.
sculp'ture *(-chůr) n.* the art of, or the work done by, a sculptor.—*v.t.* **1** to carve. **2** to give the appearance of sculpture to:—*pr.p.* **sculp'turing**.

scum *skum, n.* **1** unclean foam or skin on the surface of a liquid. **2** anything worthless: *the scum of the earth* (=people of very low character).

scupper[1] *skup'ėr*, *n.* a hole in a ship's side to drain the deck.

scupper[2] *skup'ėr*, (*slang*) *v.t.* **1** to ruin. **2** to slaughter. **3** to sink (a ship).

scurf *skûrf*, *n.* a crust of flaky scales.
scur'fy *adj.*:—*comp.* **scurf'ier**; *superl.* **scurf'iest**.
scur'finess *n.*

scurrilous *skur'i-lus*, *adj.* **1** (of a joke, etc.) coarse, indecent. **2** abusive, very insulting: *a scurrilous attack on his rival.*
scurr'ilously *adv.* **scurr'ilousness** *n.*
scurril'ity *n.* **1** scurrilousness. **2** an instance of this:—*pl.* **scurril'ities**.

scurry *skur'i*, *v.i.* to hurry along, scamper: *pr.p.* **scurry'ing**; *pa.p.* **scurr'ied**.—Also *n.*

scurvy *skûr'vi*, *adj.* mean, low-down: *a scurvy fellow*, *trick*:—*comp.* **scur'vier**; *superl.* **scur'viest**.—*n.* a disease due to lack of fresh fruit and vegetables.
scur'vily *adv.* **scur'viness** *n.*

scut *skut*, *n.* the short tail of a hare, etc.

scuttle[1] *skut'l*, *n.* (also **coal'-scuttle**) a box for holding coal.

scuttle[2] *skut'l*, *v.i.* to hurry, or hurry away:—*pr.p.*—**scutt'ling**.—Also *n.*

scuttle[3] *skut'l*, *n.* an opening with a lid in a ship's deck or side.—*v.t.* to make a hole in (a ship) in order to sink it:—*pr.p.* **scutt'-ling**.

scythe *sīTH*, *n.* a large curved blade, on a handle, for cutting grass, etc.—*v.t.* to cut with a scythe.—Also *v.i.*:—*pr.p.* **scyth'-ing**.

sea *sē*, *n.* **1** the mass of salt water covering the greater part of the earth's surface. **2** a great stretch water (salt or fresh) less than an ocean. **3** a swell or a wave: *The ship was lost in a heavy sea, or heavy seas.* **4** the tide. **5** a quantity or number felt to be like the sea in extent, etc.: *a sea of faces, of sand, of passion.*
sea'ward *adj.* towards the sea.—Also *adv.* (also **sea'wards**).
sea anemone a small plant-like animal found on rocks on the seashore.
sea'board *n.* a seacoast.—Also *adj.*
sea breeze a breeze blowing from the sea towards the land.
sea'-captain *n.* the captain of a merchant ship.
sea'coast *n.* the land next to the sea.
sea'-dog *n.* **1** the common seal. **2** the dogfish. **3** an old sailor. **4** a pirate.
sea'farer (*-fār-*) *n.* a traveller by sea, usu. a sailor.
sea'faring *n.* travelling by sea, esp. if working as a sailor.—Also *adj.*
sea fight a battle between ships.
sea'-food *n.* food got from the sea, esp. shellfish.
sea'front *n.* a promenade with its buildings facing the sea.
sea'going *adj.* (of a ship) sailing on the ocean, not a coast or river vessel.
sea'gull *n.* a gull (see this word).
sea'horse *n.* **1** a type of small fish looking a little like a horse. **2** (**sea'-horse**) a walrus.
sea'-kale *n.* a cabbage-like seaside plant.
sea legs *n.* **1** ability to walk on a ship's deck when it is rolling. **2** resistance to seasickness.
sea'-level *n.* the level of the surface of the sea.
sea'-lion *n.* a large seal found in the Pacific Ocean (it roars and the male has a mane).
sea'man *n.* **1** a sailor. **2** one of a ship's crew other than an officer.
sea'manship *n.* the art of handling ships at sea.
sea'-mew *n.* a seagull.
sea'plane *n.* an aeroplane that can land on or take off from the sea.
sea'port *n.* a port on the seashore.
sea power **1** a nation with a strong navy. **2** naval power, control of the sea.
sea'-ro'ver *n.* **1** a pirate. **2** a pirate ship.
sea'scape *n.* a picture of a scene at sea.
sea serpent an imaginary sea monster.
sea'shell *n.* empty shell of a sea creature.
sea'-shanty. Same as **shanty**.
sea'shore *n.* the land close to the sea.
sea'sick *adj.* ill because of the motion of a ship at sea.
sea'sickness *n.*
sea'side *n.* the land beside the sea.—Also *adj.*
sea trout any of a number of trout living in the sea, but spawning in rivers.
sea'-urchin *n.* a small creature with a shell that bears spines.
sea wall a wall to keep out the sea.
sea'weed *n.* plant(s) growing in the sea.
sea'worthy *adj.* suitably built and in sufficiently good condition to sail at sea.
sea'worthiness *n.*
sea'wrack *n.* (coarse) seaweed, esp. if cast up on the shore.
all at sea at a loss, bewildered.
at sea **1** away from land. **2** lost, puzzled.
go to sea to become a sailor.
heavy sea a sea in which the waves have great force.

ship a sea (of a ship, boat) to have a wave wash over the side.

seal[1] *sēl*, *n.* **1** a piece of wax or other material bearing a design, attached to a document to show that it is genuine and legal: *Four of the copies of Magna Carta have the Great Seal of King John attached.* **2** (in *pl.*) a mark or sign (of office). **3** a stamp, object with a raised design, for marking wax, etc. **4** a piece of wax used to keep closed (e.g. a letter). **5** (something that makes) a tight join or complete closure. **6** an adhesive piece of paper with a design: *Christmas seals for parcels.*—*v.t.* **1** to mark or fasten with a seal. **2** to close completely: *He must seal the windows to keep all air out.* **3** to decide, make certain: *This mistake sealed his fate.* **4** to make legal and binding: *to seal a bargain.*

seal'ant *n.* something that seals a place where there is a leak.

seal'ing-wax *n.* wax for sealing letters.

seal off to cut off approach to, isolate completely.

set one's seal on to give recognition, one's approval, to.

set one's seal to to give one's authority or agreement to.

under seal of secrecy, **silence**, etc., under promise of keeping secret, etc.

seal[2] *sēl*, *n.* any of various sea animals valuable for skin and oil.—*v.i.* to hunt seals.

seal'er *n.* a man or ship engaged in seal-hunting.

seal'skin *n.* **1** the fur esp. of the 'fur seal'. **2** a garment made of this.

sealant. See **seal**[1].

seam *sēm*, *n.* **1** the line formed by the sewing together of two pieces of cloth, etc. **2** a line of meeting. **3** a crack. **4** a wrinkle. **5** a thin layer of coal, etc. in the earth.—*v.t.* **1** to make a seam in. **2** to sew.

seamstress *sem'strės*, *sēm'*, *n.* one who sews, esp. for a living.

sea'my *(sē')* *adj.* disreputable, sordid:—*comp.* **sea'mier**; *superl.* **sea'miest**.

the seamy side 1 (*orig.*) the inner side of a garment. **2** the more unpleasant or disreputable side (e.g. of life).

seance *sā'on^gs* *n.* a meeting at which people, e.g. Spiritualists, seek to obtain messages from the dead.

sear *sēr*, *v.t.* **1** to burn the surface of. **2** to dry up or wither. **3** to injure or pain as if with fire.—Also *v.i.*—*adj.* usu. spelt **sere** (see this).

search *sûrch*, *v.t.* **1** to look over (a place) carefully in order to find something. **2** to examine (a person, his pockets, etc.) closely.—Also *v.i.*—*n.* **1** the act of searching. **2** a careful examination. **3** an attempt to find (with *for*).

search'ing *adj.* **1** (of eyes, a look, etc.) very observant, penetrating. **2** (of e.g. an enquiry, investigation) very thorough. **3** (of a question) likely to get right at the truth. **4** (of e.g. the wind) piercing.

search'light *n.* (a lamp producing) a strong beam of light for picking out objects by night.

search party a group of people participating in an organised search for a missing person.

search warrant legal permission given to the police to search a house, etc., e.g. for stolen goods.

search out to find by searching.

seashore, **seasick**, **seaside**, etc. See **sea**.

season *sē'z(ȯ)n*, *n.* **1** one of the four divisions of the year. **2** the usual, proper, or suitable, time (for anything). **3** a short time.—*v.t.* **1** to add, e.g. salt, in order to improve the flavour of (food). **2** to make more enjoyable, add zest to. **3** to dry (timber) until it is ready for use. **4** to accustom (to): *troops seasoned to battle*; *seasoned troops*.

sea'sonable *adj.* happening at the right time: (of weather) suited to the season.

sea'sonably *adv.* **sea'sonableness** *n.*

sea'sonal *adj.* (of work, games) taking place at a particular season only.

sea'soning *n.* something added to food to give it more taste.

season ticket a ticket which can be used repeatedly during a certain period.

in season 1 fit and ready for eating, hunting, etc. **2** at a suitable time.

out of season not in season.

seat *sēt*, *n.* **1** a chair, bench, etc. **2** the part of a chair on which the body rests, or of the body or a garment on which one sits. **3** the manner in which one sits (esp. on a horse). **4** a place from, or in, which something is carried on or happens: *the seat of government*; *a seat of learning*; *the seat of the disease.* **5** a (country) mansion. **6** a right to sit and e.g. take part, express one's opinion, etc.: *to have a seat in Parliament.*—*v.t.* **1** to cause to sit down. **2** to have seats for (a certain number). **3** to put a seat on (a garment).

seat'ed *adj.*

seat'ing *n.* the supply, or arrangement, of seats.

seat'-belt *n.* a safety belt (see this).

take a seat to sit down.

secateurs *sek'ȧ-tûrz*, *-tûrz'*, *n.pl.* a tool like scissors, used for pruning plants, etc.

secede *si-sēd'*, *v.i.* to withdraw, break away from, a group, society, etc.:—*pr.p.* **seced'ing.**

secē'der *n.* **secess'ion** *(-sesh') n.*

seclude *si-klōōd*, *v.i.* to shut off, keep away (from company of others, or from sight):—*pr.p.* **seclud'ing.**

seclu'ded *adj.* private, remote: *a secluded spot.*

seclusion *si-klōō'zh(ȯ)n*, *n.* **1** privacy, solitude. **2** a secluded place.

second *sek'ȯnd*, *adj.* **1** next after, or following, the first in time, place, etc. **2** other, alternate: *every second day.* **3** of the same kind as: *The admiral was not a second Nelson.*—*n.* **1** a person, thing, that is second. **2** a supporter. **3** one who helps, backs, a person who is e.g. fighting. **4** a 60th part of a minute of time, or (in measuring angles) of a degree. **5** (in *pl.*) articles not quite perfectly made.—*v.t.* **1** to support, back up. **2** to make the second speech in support of (a motion). **3** *(si-kond')* to transfer temporarily to a special job.

sec'ondary *adj.* **1** second in importance. **2** (of education) between primary and university, etc.

sec'onder *n.* one who seconds e.g. a motion.

sec'ondly *adv.* in the second place (see example at **firstly**).

second'ment *n.* **1** the act of seconding (*def. 3*). **2** the state of being seconded.

sec'ond-best', *adj.* **1** next to the best. **2** not the best.

sec'ond-class' *adj.* **1** of the class next to the highest. **2** second-rate. **3** (of a citizen) not having a citizen's full privileges.

second cousin the child of a cousin of a person's parent.

sec'ond-hand' *adj.* **1** not new. **2** that has been used by, or has come from, another. **3** dealing in second-hand goods.

second lieutenant a rank in the army, or a person of this rank.

second nature a firmly fixed habit: *It was second nature to, or with, him to think carefully before spending.*

sec'ond-rate' *adj.* inferior, not of the best quality.

sec'ond-rat'er *n.*

second thoughts a change of opinion after further thought.

at second hand through, from, another.

come off second best to get the worst in a contest, receive the least attention, etc.

secret *sē'krit*, *adj.* **1** hidden from, not known to or told to, others. **2** secretive (see below).—*n.* **1** a fact, purpose, method, etc., that is not told, or not known. **2** the explanation: *the secret of his success.* **3** the best method of achieving: *the secret of good health.*

se'crecy *n.* **1** secretness. **2** mystery: *an air of secrecy.*

secrete *si-krēt'*, *v.t.* **1** to hide in a secret place. **2** (of a gland or similar organ of the body) to produce, e.g. by separating from the blood, store, and pass out: *The liver secretes bile:*—*pr.p.* **secret'ing.**

secrē'tion *n.* **1** the act of secreting. **2** a fluid secreted.

sē'cretive *adj.* inclined to conceal one's activities, thoughts, etc.

se'cretly *adv.* **se'cretness** *n.*

secret police. See **police**.

Secret Service the government department dealing with spying, etc.

in secret **1** secretly. **2** as a secret.

secretary *sek'ri-t(ȧ-)ri*, *n.* one employed to write letters and carry out business for another, or for a society:—*pl.* **sec'retaries.**

secretā'rial *adj.* having to do with a secretary, or with his, her, duties.

secretā'riat *n.* the administrative department of a large organisation.

Secretary of State **1** a cabinet minister holding one of the more important positions. **2** (*U.S.*) the American equivalent of the British Foreign Secretary.

secrete, etc. See **secret**.

sect *sekt*, *n.* a group of people united by holding certain views, esp. in religion—usu. not the views of the majority of believers in that religion.

sectā'rian *adj.* **1** having to do with a sect. **2** devoted, or loyal, to a sect. **3** (esp. of views) narrow.—*n.* a member of a sect.

section *sek'sh(ȯ)n*, *n.* **1** a part or division. **2** a thin slice for examination under microscope. **3** the view of the inside of anything when it is cut through from top to bottom. **4** a small military unit. **5** a district or a community having separate interests or characteristics.

sec'tional *adj.* **1** built up by sections. **2** local, having to do with a part of the community: *It was in the general interest to bypass the town, but sectional interests were against it.*

sector *sek'tȯr*, *n.* **1** part of a circle bounded by an arc and two radii. **2** a division of an army front. **3** a section, e.g. of occupied territory.

secular *sek'ū-lȧr*, *adj.* **1** having to do with the things of the world, not spiritual. **2** not under church control: *secular courts.* **3** not sacred: *secular music.* **4** (of clergy) not belonging to a religious order.

sec'ularise *v.t.* to turn (something) from sacred to common use:—*pr.p.* **sec'ularising**.

sec'ularism *n.* the belief that politics, morals, education, etc. should be independent of religion.

secure *si-kūr'*,*adj.* **1** free from danger, safe. **2** firmly fixed, not likely to fall, etc. **3** without fears, confident: *secure in the knowledge that he had prepared most carefully.* **4** sure, certain: *a secure victory*: —*opp.* **insecure**.—*v.t.* **1** to make safe (from against). **2** to make firm. **3** to fasten. **4** to seize, take possession of. **5** to obtain: *to secure a good job.* **6** to ensure, make it certain (that such-and-such will happen). **7** to guarantee (against):—*pr.p.* **secur'ing**.

secure'ly *adv.* **secure'ness** *n.*

secur'ity *n.* **1** secureness. **2** a pledge, something given or promised as guarantee of payment, etc.: *He borrowed the money on the security of his house.* **3** someone who gives a pledge on behalf of another. **4** (in *pl.*) certificates or other evidence of ownership or of money lent:—*pl.* **secur'ities**.

security measures measures to prevent spying or leakage of information.

security risk a person considered unsafe for state service, etc. because likely to be disloyal.

sedan *si-dan'*, *n.* (also **sedan chair**) a covered chair for one carried on two poles.

sedate *si-dāt'*, *adj.* (of person, manner) calm, serious.

sedate'ly *adv.* **sedate'ness** *n.*

sed'ative *adj.* tending to calm, soothe.—*n.* a soothing medicine.

sedā'tion *n.* use of sedatives to calm a patient.

sedentary *sed'(ė)n-tȧ-ri*, *adj.* **1** (of an occupation, e.g. in an office) requiring much sitting. **2** taking little exercise.

sed'entariness *n.*

sedge *sej*, *n.* a coarse grass growing in swamps and rivers.

sedg'y *adj.* overgrown with sedge:—*comp.* **sedg'ier**; *superl.* **sedg'iest**.

sedg'iness *n.*

sediment *sed'i-mėnt*, *n.* what settles at the bottom of a liquid, dregs: matter deposited on the land by water or ice.

sedimen'tary *adj.*

sedimenary rocks rocks formed from layers of sediment.

sedition *si-dish'(ȯ)n*, *n.* **1** the stirring up of rebellion against the government. **2** action or language intended to do this.

sedi'tious *(-shus) adj.* (of a speech, action, person) encouraging rebellion.

seduce *si-dūs'*, *v.t.* **1** to lead astray from right conduct or belief, e.g. from loyalty, chastity, faith. **2** to attract:—*pr.p.* **seduc'ing**.

seduc'tion *n.* **1** the act of seducing. **2** attraction.

seduc'tive *adj.* attractive, tempting.

sedulous *sed'ū-lus*, *adj.* working steadily and hard: *a sedulous student*; *sedulous attempts*.

see^1 *sē*, *n*, the district over which a bishop or archbishop has authority.

see^2 *sē*, *v.t.* **1** to perceive, be aware of, by means of the eye. **2** to have a picture of in the mind. **3** to understand: *I see what you mean.* **4** to find out: *I'll see what is happening.* **5** to make sure: *See that he does what he promised.* **6** to look at, visit (e.g. a play, sights). **7** to accompany: *I'll see you home.* **8** to meet. **9** to consult (e.g. a lawyer). **10** to experience (e.g. trouble).—*v.i.* **1** to have the power of vision. **2** to look (into). **3** to consider: *Let me see—what should we do next?*:—*pa.t.* **saw**; *pa.p.* **seen**.

seer *sē'ėr*, *n.* **1** one who sees. **2** *(sēr)* one who sees into the future, a prophet.

see'ing *n.* sight, vision.—*adj.* having sight, or power of noticing.—*conj.* (also **seeing that**) since, because, considering.

see'-through *adj.* transparent.

see about 1 to deal with, attend to. **2** to consider, think about.

see fit to think suitable (to do), decide (to do).

see off 1 to accompany to one's point of departure. **2** (*coll.*) to chase away.

see over, round to be taken, or go, all through (a place of interest, etc.).

see through 1 to take part in, or support, to the end. **2** to see the reality behind (a pretence, etc.).

see to to deal with, make sure that (something) is done.

see to it that to make sure that (something is done).

See also **sight**.

seed *sēd*, *n.* **1** the part of a flowering plant that develops after the flower withers, from which a new plant may be grown. **2** a seed-like part such as a grain of wheat. **3** a quantity of seeds or of grains for sowing. **4** children, descendants. **5** the beginning from which anything grows: *a seed of doubt*; *seeds of rebellion.* **6** a seeded player.—*v.i.* to produce seed.—*v.t.* **1** to sow. **2** to remove the seeds from. **3** to arrange (the draw for a tournament) in such a way that the best players will not meet in the early rounds. **4** to deal with

(good competitors) in this way.
seed'ling *n.* a young plant just sprung from a seed.
seed'y *adj.* **1** full of seeds. **2** shabby, uncared-for. **3** not very well:—*comp.* **seed'ier**; *superl.* **seed'iest**.
seed'iness *n.* **seed'ily** *adv.*
seed'bed *n.* ground prepared for growing seeds.
seed'-coat *n.* the outer covering of a seed.
seed potato one for planting rather than eating.
seeds'man *n.* a seller of seeds.
seed'-vessel *n.* the container of a plant seed or seeds, consisting of a single part (**seed'-case** or **pod**) or of two or more parts (**seed'box**).
go, run, to seed 1 to develop flowers and seeds rather than the growth desired by the grower: *The turnips have gone to seed, they're not fit to eat now.* **2** to deteriorate, become shabby, etc.: *This part of the town is going to seed.*

seek *sēk*, *v.t.* **1** to look for. **2** to try to get (e.g. fame, advice). **3** to try (to do). **4** to go to: *to seek the shade.*—*v.i.* to search (for):—*pa.t.* and *pa.p.* **sought** *(söt)*.
(much) sought after (of a person, thing) in great demand, much desired.
seek after to go in search of.
seek out to look for and find.

seem *sēm*, *v.i.* **1** to appear to be: *He seems kind.* **2** to appear (to be, to do): *He seems to be reading.* **3** (used impersonally with *it*) the evidence shows or suggests: *It seems to me that you were very foolish.* **4** (used impersonally with *it*) it is said that: *It seems he had no money at all.*
seem'ing *adj.* (used only before a noun) having the appearance, but usu. not the reality: *a seeming success.*
seem'ly *adj.* **1** fitting, suitable. **2** (of behaviour) decent, proper. **3** handsome:—*comp.* **seem'lier**; *superl.* **seem'liest**.
seem'liness *n.*

seen. See **see**^{2}.

seep *sēp*, *v.i.* to ooze gently, leak (away, through, out of, into).
seep'age *n.* **1** the act of seeping. **2** fluid that has seeped out.

seer. See **see**^{2}.

seesaw *sē'sö*, or *-sö'*, *n.* **1** a plank balanced so that its ends may move up and down. **2** an up-and-down, or sometimes, back-and-forth, motion. **3** a movement from success to failure and back again.—*v.i.*, *v.t.* to move, or make move, in a seesaw manner.

seethe *sē*TH, *v.t.* **1** to boil. **2** to soak.—*v.i.* **1** to be very angry or excited. **2** to surge:—*pr.p.* **seeth'ing**; *pa.p.* **seethed**.
sodd'en *adj.* (old *pa.p.*) **1** completely soaked. **2** (of food) heavy, not well baked.

segment *seg'mėnt*, *n.* **1** a part cut off. **2** part of a circle cut off by a straight line. **3** any of the parts into which e.g. an insect body is naturally divided.—*v.t.*, *v.i.* (also *seg-ment'*) to divide into segments.
segmentā'tion *n.*

segregate *seg'ri-gāt*, *v.t.* **1** to separate from others: *to segregate the infected sheep.* **2** to keep in separate groups: *to segregate the sexes; to segregate one race of people from another*:—*pr.p.* **seg'regating**.
segregā'tion *n.*

seine *sān*, *n.* a large fishing-net with floats on one edge, sinkers on the other.

seismograph *sīz'mō-gräf*, *n.* an instrument that records earthquake shocks.
seis'mic *adj.* having to do with an earthquake.

seize *sēz*, *v.t.* **1** to take suddenly, esp. by force. **2** to snatch, grasp. **3** to take prisoner. **4** to overcome: *Faintness, fury seized him.*—*v.i.* (of machinery) to become stuck, jam (also **seize up**):—*pr.p.* **seiz'ing**.
sei'zure *n.* **1** the act of seizing. **2** capture. **3** grasp. **4** a sudden attack (e.g. of illness).

seldom *sel'dȯm*, *adv.* rarely, not often.

select *si-lekt'*, *v.t.* to pick out from a number according to preference, choose.—*adj.* **1** picked out. **2** very good. **3** (of a society) exclusive, admitting only certain people.
selec'tion *n.* **1** the act of selecting. **2** thing(s) chosen. **3** a number of things from which to choose.
selec'tive *adj.* **1** using power of selection. **2** (of a radio set) able to receive any station without interference from others. **3** choosing, involving, etc. only certain people or things. **4** of a weed killer, destroying only weeds, not grass, vegetables, or whatever.
selec'tiveness, **selectiv'ity** *ns.*
selec'tor *n.*
select committee a group from parliament chosen to report and advise on some matter.

self *self*, *n.* **1** one's own person. **2** one's personality, nature. **3** personal advantage: *He always thinks first of self*:—*pl.* **selves** *(selvz)*.
self'ish *adj.* thinking of one's own pleasure or good, not caring much about others.
self'less *adj.* utterly unselfish, thinking of others before oneself.

self- *self-*, (as part of a word) **1** showing that the person or thing acting is acting upon himself or itself: *self-torture.* **2** showing that the thing is acting automatically, without outside aid: *a self-adjusting machine*; *self-closing doors.* **3** by oneself: *self-imposed*; *self-made* (see below). **4** in, within, etc., oneself or itself: *self-centred*; *self-contained* (see below).
Examples include the following:—
self'-addressed' *adj.* addressed to oneself.
self'-advert'isement *n.* calling public attention to oneself.
self-appoint'ed *adj* acting on one's own authority.
self'-assert'ing, self'-assert'ive *adjs.* in the habit of putting forward oneself, one's claims, one's opinions.
self'-assur'ance *n.* self-confidence.
self'-assur'ed *adj.*
self'-cat'ering *adj.* of a holiday, accommodation, etc., in which one cooks for oneself.
self'-cen'tred *adj.* with one's thoughts centred in oneself and one's affairs.
self'-col'oured *adj.* **1** of one colour. **2** of the natural colour.
self'-conceit' *n.* too high an opinion of one's abilities, etc., vanity.
self'-confessed' *adj.* admitted, openly acknowledged, by oneself.
self'-con'fidence *n.* belief or trust in one's own powers.
self'-con'fident *adj.*
self'-con'scious *adj.* too conscious of oneself when in the presence of others, embarrassed by a sense of inferiority or awkwardness.
self'-con'sciousness *n.*
self'-contained' *adj.* **1** hiding one's feelings within oneself, reserved. **2** complete in itself. **3** (of a house) intended for use of one family and not sharing entry, etc., with others.
self'-control' *n.* control of oneself, esp. of one's emotions, passions, etc.
self'-defence' *n.* the act of defending one's own person, property, etc.
self'-denī'al *n.* **1** refusal to yield to natural desires. **2** doing without something in order to give to others.
self'-determinā'tion *n.* the power of a community or country to decide its own form of government.
self'-dis'cipline *n.* control of oneself, esp. with regard to one's behaviour, diligence, etc.
self'-drive' *adj.* of a vehicle, to be driven by the person who hires it.
self'-ed'ucated *adj.* **1** educated by one's own efforts, without help in money from others. **2** self-taught.
self'-effac'ing *adj.* **1** keeping oneself in the background, modest. **2** not claiming rights or reward.
self'-efface'ment *n.*
self'-employed' *adj.* working in one's own business, on one's own.
self'-esteem' *n.* **1** self-respect. **2** conceit.
self'-ev'ident *adj.* clear enough to need no proof.
self'-explan'atory *adj.* needing no explanation.
self'-express'ion *n.* giving expression to one's personality, e.g. in art, poetry.
self'-gov'ernment *n.* **1** self-control. **2** government by the people of the country without outside control.
self'-impor'tance *n.* an absurdly high sense of one's own importance.
self'-impor'tant *adj.*
self'-imposed' *adj.* (of e.g. a task) imposed on one, laid on one, by oneself.
self'-indul'gence *n.* gratifying too much one's appetites or desires.
self'-indul'gent *adj.*
self'-in'terest *n.* selfish desire to work for one's private aims or advantage.
self'-made' *adj.* **1** made by oneself. **2** owing wealth or important position to one's efforts, not to birth, education, etc.
self'-opin'ionated *adj.* obstinately adhering to one's own opinion(s).
self'-por'trait *n.* an artist's (or other's) portrait (or description) of himself.
self'-possessed' *adj.* calm in manner.
self'-possess'ion *n.* **1** calmness, composure. **2** the ability to act calmly in an emergency.
self'-preservā'tion *n.* (a natural tendency towards) trying to keep oneself safe from destruction or harm.
self'-protec'tion *n.*
self'-propelled' *adj.* moved by its own motor, etc., not pulled or pushed.
self'-rais'ing *adj.* (of flour) so prepared that it rises without the addition of baking powder or similar ingredient.
self'-relī'ance *n.* healthy confidence in one's own abilities.
self'-relī'ant *adj.*
self'-respect' *n.* respect for oneself and concern for one's character and reputation.
self'-respec'ting *adj.*
self'-righ'teous *adj.* thinking highly of one's own goodness.
self'-righ'teousness *n.*
self'-sac'rifice *n.* the act of giving up one's own life, possessions or advantage, etc. in order to help others.
self'same *adj.* the very same.
self'-sat'isfied *adj.* too pleased with

oneself, one's achievements, etc.
self'-seek'er *n.* one who has only selfish aims.
self'-ser'vice *adj.* **1** (of a restaurant, shop) in which customers are not waited on but serve themselves. **2** (of a meal), collected and taken to the table by the purchaser.
self'-star'ter *n.* **1** a small electric motor or other device for starting an engine. **2** a person with initiative.
self'-styled' *adj.* so called by oneself, usu. wrongly so.
self'-suffi'cient *adj.* **1** needing no help from outside. **2** not dependent on imports from other countries. **3** having too great confidence in oneself.
self'-suffi'ciency *n.*
self'-suppor'ting *adj.* supporting oneself or itself (esp. providing enough for one's living).
self'-taught' *adj.* taught by oneself without help from others.
self'-willed' *adj.* determined to have one's own way.

selfish, selfless. See **self.**

sell *sel, v.t.* **1** to give or hand over for money. **2** to have, keep, for sale. **3** to betray in return for e.g. money.—*v.i.* **1** to make sales. **2** to be sold: *It sells for tenpence a pound:—pa.t., pa.p.* **sold** *(sōld).*—*n.* a fraud or disappointment.
sell'er *n.* **sell'ing** *n.* and *adj.*
sell-by date a date on a label to show the shelf-life of a product.
sell off to sell quickly and cheaply.
sell out 1 to sell the whole stock. **2** to betray (friends or companions) by secret agreement.—*n.* **sell'-out.**
See also **sale.**

Sellotape® *sel'ȯ-tāp, n.* a brand of transparent adhesive tape.

seltzer *selt'zėr, n.* a mineral water.

selvage, selvedge *sel'vij, n.* **1** the firm edge of a piece of cloth. **2** a border.

selves. See **self.**

semantics *si-man'tiks, n.sing.* the science of the meanings of words, etc.—*n.pl.* differences in, shades of, meaning.
seman'tic *adj.*

semaphore *sem'ȧ-fōr, -för, n.* **1** an apparatus for signalling by means of movable arms. **2** signalling by means of a flag held in each hand.

semblance *sem'blȧns, n.* appearance, often with little or no reality behind: *He gave the speaker a semblance of attention.*

semen *sē'mėn, n.* the liquid produced by males in sexual intercourse.

semester *si-mes'tėr, n.* a half-year at university.

semi- *sem'i-,* (as part of a word) **1** half. **2** (*loosely*) partly.
sem'i-ann'ual *adj.* half-yearly.
sem'ibreve *(-brēv) n.* a half *breve* (old note in music), equal to four crotchets.
sem'icircle *n.* a half circle.
sem'icir'cular *adj.*
sem'icōlon *n.* the point (;) which marks a more distinct division of a sentence than a comma does.
sem'i-detached' *adj.* **1** partly separated. **2** (of a house) joined to another house on one side by separate on the other.
sem'i-fīn'al *n.* a stage, match, etc. immediately before a final.—Also *adj.*
sem'i-fin'alist *n.*
sem'i-offic'ial *adj.* **1** partly official. **2** having some official authority.
sem'i-pre'cious *adj.* (of a gemstone) valuable, but not of the highest value.
sem'iquaver *n.* a note half the length of a quaver.
sem'itone *n.* half a tone in the musical scale.

seminar *sem'i-när, n.* **1** a group of advanced students working under a teacher in a branch of study. **2** a discussion group, of students and a tutor or others, on some topic.
sem'inary *n.* **1** (*formerly*) a school. **2** a college educating for priesthood or ministry:—*pl.* **sem'inaries.**

semiquaver. See **semi.**

Semitic *sė-mit'ik, adj.* **1** having to do with Hebrew, Arabic, and related languages. **2** Jewish.

semitone. See **semi.**

semolina *sem-ȯ-lē'nȧ, -lī'nȧ, n.* hard particles of wheat sifted from flour.

senate *sen'it, n.* **1** the governing body of ancient Rome. **2** a lawmaking body, esp. the upper house of the parliament in some countries (e.g. U.S., Australia, etc.). **3** the governing council in some British universities.
sen'ator *n.* a member of a senate.

send *send, v.t.* **1** to cause (a person) to go, or (something) to be carried (to a place). **2** to cause (e.g. a ball) to go with speed or force. **3** to give (out, e.g. a smell).—Also *v.i.:—pa.t., pa.p.* **sent.**
sen'der *n.*
send'-off *n.* **1** a start. **2** a farewell party, etc., to show good wishes for a person setting out on a journey, career, etc.
send down to expel, or to banish for a time, from a university.
send for to summon (a person), order (a

thing) to be brought or posted to one.

send up (*coll.*) to make fun of (*n.* **send'-up**).

senile *sē'nīl, adj.* showing the feebleness or childishness of old age.

senility *sė-nil'i-ti, n.*

senior *sēn'yȯr, adj.* **1** older in age. **2** higher in rank or standing: *senior officials.* **3** more advanced: *senior pupils.*—Also *n.*

seniority *sē-ni-or'i-ti, n.* the state of being senior.

senior citizen an elderly person.

senna *sen'ȧ, n.* the dried leaves of certain plants, used as a laxative.

señor *se-nyor', n.* **1** a gentleman. **2** (*cap.*) the Spanish word for Mr.:—*pl.* **señor'es** *(-ės)*.

señor'a *n.* **1** a lady. **2** (*cap.*) Mrs.

señori'ta *(-ē'ta) n.* **1** a young lady. **2** (*cap.*) Miss.

sensation *sen-sā'sh(ȯ)n, n.* **1** feeling, knowledge of physical experience gained through the senses. **2** a vague effect on the senses: *a sensation of faintness, of floating.* **3** a state of excitement or interest: *The elopement created a sensation.* **4** something that causes this.

sensā'tional *adj.* **1** causing great excitement. **2** aiming, or aimed, at doing this.

sensā'tionally *adv.*

sensā'tionalism *n.* **1** sensational facts, language, etc. **2** an attempt, tendency, to be sensational.

sense *sens, n.* **1** a power by which we notice or feel objects (sight, hearing, smell, taste, and touch). **2** a sensation, feeling, vague impression: *a sense of chill, of strangeness.* **3** a special ability to appreciate something: *a sense of humour*; *a musical sense.* **4** a moral feeling: *a sense of duty, of shame.* **5** (in *pl.*) one's right mind: *Is he out of his senses?* **6** practical wisdom: *She has no sense.* **7** what is sensible or reasonable: *It would be sense to tell her so*; *It does not make sense.* **8** meaning: *What is the sense of the word in this phrase?* **9** general opinion: *the sense of the meeting.*—*v.t.* to feel, realise: *I sensed his disapproval*, or *that he disapproved*:—*pr.p.* **sens'ing**.

sense'less *adj.* **1** stunned, unconscious. **2** foolish, lacking good sense.

sense'lessly *adv.* **sense'lessness** *n.*

sen'sible *adj.* **1** wise, reasonable. **2** able to be felt or noticed, esp. by one of the senses. **3** aware: *I am sensible of the danger*, or *that there is danger.*—See also **insensible**.

sen'sibleness *n.* **sen'sibly** *adv.*

sensibil'ity *n.* **1** ability to feel, or to appreciate. **2** sensitiveness, tendency to feel esp. pain (*pl.* **sensibil'ities**): *We must not wound his sensibilities.*

sen'sitise *(-īz), v.t.* to make sensitive, esp. to rays of light:—*pr.p.* **sen'sitising**.

sen'sitive *adj.* **1** feeling, esp. readily, strongly, or painfully; easily hurt or offended. **2** strongly affected by light, etc. **3** showing or measuring small amounts or changes:—*opp.* **insensitive**.

sen'sitiveness, sensitiv'ity *ns.*

sen'sory *adj.* **1** of the senses. **2** (of a nerve) bringing impulses to the brain that result in a sensation.

sensual *sen'sū-ȧl, sen'shoo-ȧl, adj.* **1** having to do with the senses and not the mind. **2** (of a person) indulging too much in coarser pleasures of the senses. **3** (of pleasures) bodily, fleshly.—Compare **sensuous**.

sen'sually *adv.*

sensual'ity, sen'sualness *ns.*

sen'suous *adj.* **1** of, having a pleasant effect on, the senses. **2** easily affected through the senses. (*Sensual* implies excess of which one disapproves; *sensuous* does not).

sensitive plant a plant that closes its leaves, etc., when touched.

sent. See **send**.

sentence *sen'tėns, n.* **1** a judgment. **2** a punishment decreed by a court or a judge. **3** a number of words which together make a complete statement, command, or question *I saw her on Monday*; *Go away!*; *What do you mean by that?*— *v.t.* to condemn (a person, to a stated punishment): *The judge sentenced him to four months in prison*:—*pr.p.* **sen'tencing**.

senten'tious *(-shùs) adj.* (of a person, style) full, or too full, of wise sayings or moralising.

sentient *sen'shėnt, adj.* that has feeling or consciousness: *a sentient being.*

sentiment *sen'ti-mėnt, n.* **1** (a show of) the softer emotions, sometimes partly insincere. **2** a feeling, emotion: *a sentiment of pity*; *patriotic sentiment.* **3** feeling as opposed to reason. **4** a thought, opinion.

sentimen'tal *adj.* having, or expressing, too much emotion or feeling (usu. worked up or partly insincere).

sentimen'tally *adv.*

sentimental'ity, sentimen'talness *ns.*

sentimen'talise *v.t.* to be sentimental about (a person, event, etc.) overlooking what is unpleasant or cruel.—Also *v.i.* (with *over, about*):—*pr.p.* **sentimen'talising**.

sentimen'talist *n.* one who delights in sentiment or sentimentality.

sentinel *sen'ti-nėl*, *n.* one posted on guard, a sentry.

stand sentinel to keep watch.

sentry *sen'tri*, *n.* a soldier on guard to stop anyone who has not a right to pass:—*pl.* **sen'tries**.

sen'try-box *n.* a small shelter for a sentry.

sepal *sep'ȧl*, *sē'pȧl*, *n.* one of the leaves forming the calyx outside the petals of a flower.

separate *sep'ȧ-rāt*, *v.t.* **1** to disconnect. **2** to take, set, force, apart. **3** to keep apart, divide.—*v.i.* **1** to come apart. **2** to go different ways. **3** (of a husband and wife) to live apart by choice:—*pr.p.* **sep'arating**.—*adj.* *(sep'ȧ-rit)* **1** existing, placed, etc., apart. **2** not connected: *two separate problems.* **3** distinct, different: *on two separate occasions*.

sep'arable *adj.* (*opp.* **inseparable**).

separā'tion *n.*

sep'aratist *n.* one who withdraws, or urges separation, from an established church, state, etc.

sep'arator *n.* a machine for dividing milk from cream.

sepia *sē'pi-ȧ*, *n.* **1** the ink of a cuttlefish. **2** a brown paint or colour (also *adj.*).

sepsis *sep'sis*, *n.* a poisoned condition of the blood caused by bacteria in e.g. a wound.

sep'tic *adj.* **1** having to do with, or causing, sepsis. **2** suppurating.

septicae'mia *(-sē'mi-ȧ)* *n.* serious general blood-poisoning.

septic tank a tank in which sewage is partly made pure by action of bacteria.

sept *sept*, *n.* a division of a tribe, or of a clan.

sept- *sept-*, (as part of a word) seven.

septuagenarian *sep-tū-ȧ-ji-nā'ri-ȧn*, *n.* a person from seventy to seventy-nine years old.—Also *adj.*

September *sep-tem'bėr*, *n.* the ninth (Roman seventh) month.

septic, **septicaemia**. See **sepsis**.

septuagenarian. See **sept**.

sepulchre *sep'ul-kėr*, *n.* a tomb.

sepulchral *si-pul'krȧl*, *adj.* **1** having to do with a tomb or with burials. **2** dismal, gloomy. **3** (of a voice) deep, hollow in tone.

sepul'chrally *adv.*

sequel *sēkwėl*, *n.* **1** outcome. **2** result, consequence. **3** a story which is a continuation of an earlier story.

sequence *sē'kwėns*, *n.* **1** the order (of events) in time. **2** a number (of things) following in order. **3** a connected series. **4** a part of a film showing one incident without breaks or change of scene.

sequester *si-kwes'tėr*, *v.t.* **1** to withdraw: *to sequester oneself from society.* **2** (*law*) to take (property) from the owner until e.g. debts are paid.

seques'tered *adj.* lonely, secluded.

sequin *sē'kwin*, *n.* a small round shining ornament, one of a number sewn on e.g. a dress.

sequoia *si-kwoi'ȧ*, *n.* a giant tree growing in California, also called 'redwood'.

seraglio *si-räl'yō*, *n.* a harem:—*pl.* **seragl'ios**.

seraph *ser'ȧf*, *n.* an angel of the highest rank:—*pl.* **ser'aphs**, **ser'aphim**.

seraph'ic *adj.* like, befitting, an angel.

sere *sēr*, *adj.* dry and withered.

serenade *ser-ė-nād'*, *n.* music sung or played in open air at night (esp. by a lover under a lady's window), or suitable for this purpose.—*v.t.* to entertain (a person) with a serenade.—Also *v.i.*:—*pr.p.* **serenad'ing**.

serene *si-rēn'*, *adj.* **1** (of e.g. the sea) calm. **2** (of e.g. the sky) clear, unclouded. **3** not worried, quietly happy.

serene'ly *adv.*

serene'ness, **seren'ity** *(-ren')* *ns.*

serf *sûrf*, (*hist.*) *n.* a person who was bought and sold with the land on which he worked:—*pl.* **serfs**.

serf'dom *n.* the state of a serf.

serge *sûrj*, *n.* a strong cloth, now usu. made of wool.—Also *adj.*

sergeant *sär'jȧnt*, *n.* **1** a rank in the armed forces, or a person of this rank. **2** an officer of the police force.

Ser'geant-at-arms' *n.* an officer of a law-making body, e.g. parliament, whose duty is to make arrests, etc. (also **Ser'jeant-at-arms'**).

serial. See **series**.

series *sē'rēz*, *n.* **1** a set of things in line or following one another in some kind of order. **2** a group of things with something in common: *It was published in the Peewit series of children's books*:—*pl.* **sē'ries**.

sē'rial *(-ri-ȧl)* *adj.* **1** in a series. **2** in a row. **3** (of a story, etc.) published, broadcast, etc., in instalments.—*n.* a serial story, etc.

se'rially *adv.*

sē'rialise *v.t.* to publish, etc., as a serial:—*pr.p.* **sē'rialising**.

serious *sē'ri-us*, *adj.* **1** grave, thoughtful. **2** in earnest: *I am not joking*; *I am serious about this.* **3** requiring deep thought, or causing anxiety: *a serious matter*, *injury*, *situation*.

sē'riously *adv.* **sē'riousness** *n.*

Serjeant. See **sergeant**.

sermon *sûr'mȯn, n.* **1** a serious talk, esp. one given from the pulpit and based on a verse from the Bible. **2** a lecture on one's behaviour or duty.

serpent *sûr'pėnt, n.* a snake.

ser'pentine *adj.* **1** like a serpent. **2** winding, full of twists.

serrated *sė-rā'tid, adj.* notched as a saw edge is.

serrā'tion *n.* **1** the state of being notched. **2** a notched edge. **3** a tooth or notch.

serried *ser'id, adj.* crowded, set close together: *serried ranks*.

serum *sē'rŭm, n.* **1** a watery fluid from the body, esp. the fluid that separates from blood when it clots. **2** this fluid taken from an animal that has been made immune to a disease, or from a human being, and injected into a human being to help him to fight the disease.

servant *sûr'vȧnt, n.* **1** one hired to work for another. **2** a domestic. **3** one in the service of the state, etc.: *a public servant*; *a civil servant*.

serve *v.t.* **1** to work for. **2** to wait upon, help to food. **3** to hand out (food) at table (also with *out*, *up*). **4** to wait on (a customer). **5** to be of use, suitable, adequate, to or for: *That will serve me*, *will serve my purpose*. **6** to undergo (e.g. a prison sentence). **7** to present formally (a writ). **8** to strike (a ball) to begin a rally in tennis.—*v.i.* **1** to act as a servant. **2** to portion out food at table. **3** to carry out duties (e.g. in the armed forces). **4** to be used, be suitable to use: *The box serves as a chair*; *It will serve to hold the door shut*. **5** (*tennis*) to put the ball in play:—*pr.p.* **ser'ving**.

ser'ver *n.*

service *sûr'vis, n.* **1** the act of serving. **2** employment in one of the armed forces, etc. **3** duty required of an employee. **4** (in *pl.*) the armed forces. **5** a public department, or the people in it: *the civil service*. **6** help: *This was a service to mankind*; often in *pl.*, e.g. *He gave his services to the society without charge*. **7** use: *We must now bring the new machine into service*. **8** a supply of something provided according to a regular arrangement: *The bus service is poor*. **9** a performance of public worship, or of a religious ceremony: *a marriage service*. **10** a set of dishes: *a dinner service*.—*v.t.* **1** to keep (a machine, e.g. a car) in good running order, by regular repairs, etc. **2** to send out supplies to regularly: *One firm services the entire area*:—*pr.p.* **ser'vicing**.

ser'viceable *adj.* **1** useful; capable of being used. **2** designed for some practical purpose rather than for decoration; hard-wearing: *serviceable clothes*.

ser'vile *(-vīl) adj.* **1** having to do with slaves or servants. **2** (of a person or conduct) cringing, showing lack of spirit.

ser'vileness, servil'ity *(-vil') ns.*

ser'vitor *n.* a male servant.

servitude *sûr'vi-tūd, n.* the state of being a slave, or a servant, or other person very strictly controlled.

service charge a charge added to a bill, e.g. in a restaurant, for service provided.

service industry an industry which provides a service rather than a product, e.g. transport, entertainment.

ser'viceman *n.* a man in one of the armed services:—*fem.* **ser'vicewoman**.

active service service in battle.

at one's service (of helpful person or thing) ready if one wants to use him, it.

be of service to to be useful to.

have seen service 1 to have been in active military service. **2** to have been put to hard use.

penal servitude. See **penal**.

serve someone right to be no worse than someone deserves.

serviette *sûr-vi-et', n.* a table napkin.

servile, servitude, etc. See **servant**.

session *sesh'(ȯ)n, n.* **1** a sitting of a court, council parliament, etc. or the time during which this takes place. **2** a kirk session. **3** a series of sittings. **4** the period of the year during which classes are held in a school, etc. **5** a period of time spent engaged in some activity.

set *set, v.t.* **1** to place, put. **2** to fix in proper place (e.g. broken bones). **3** to put together (type for printing). **4** to put into type (e.g. a book). **5** to arrange (a table) for a meal. **6** to put (a hen) on eggs, or (eggs) under a hen. **7** to plant (seedlings). **8** to mount (e.g. gems) in a frame of metal. **9** to adorn, scatter (with gems, etc.). **10** to put (a clock) to the correct time, or to fix (an instrument) so that it will give a desired signal, make a desired record, etc. **11** to cause (e.g. jelly, mortar) to become firm, solid. **12** to fix (hair) in a particular style when wet so that it will remain in it when dry. **13** to prepare (the scene) for action, in theatre, etc. **14** to put in a certain state: *to set on fire*; *to set free*. **15** to start: *to set people talking, complaining*. **16** to pitch: *The song is set too high for me*. **17** to compose music for (words): *to set, set to music*. **18** to fix, arrange (date, limit, price, value, etc.). **19** to put before one to be done, solved, followed, etc. (e.g. a task, examination, problem, or an example). **20** to prepare (an examination).—*v.i.* **1** to go out of sight below the horizon. **2** to become firm or solid. **3** (of bone) to knit. **4** (of fruit) to begin to develop. **5** to have or take a direction: *The stream sets to the north.* **6** (of a dog) to point out game:—*pr.p.* **sett'ing**; *pa.p.* **set.**—*adj.* **1** fixed, arranged beforehand. **2** carefully composed beforehand: *a set speech.* **3** deliberate: *with the set intention of doing so.* **4** ready: *all set to leave home.* **5** stiff: *with a set face.*—*n.* **1** a group of persons in the habit of meeting or associating. **2** a group of things used together or associated in some way. **3** a series (e.g. of stamps). **4** an apparatus, e.g. for receiving radio or television signals or programmes. **5** scenery made ready for a scene in a play or motion picture. **6** a fixing of hair in some style. **7** the direction, e.g. of a current. **8** bent, inclination of mind. **9** carriage, pose: *the set of his head.* **10** a number of games in tennis. **11** a street paving block (also **sett**). **12** a badger's burrow (usu. **sett**).

sett'er *n.* a dog of certain breeds that can be trained to point out game.

sett'ing *n.* **1** the act of one who, thing that, sets. **2** the frame in which gems are set. **3** an arrangement of a piece of music. **4** scene. **5** background.

set'back *n.* a movement in the wrong direction, check, reverse, relapse: *His plans for the sports complex suffered a setback when he was unable to buy all the ground.*

set piece 1 a carefully prepared performance. **2** a picture in fireworks.

set square a triangular drawing instrument with one right angle.

set'-to' *n.* a hot argument or fight:—*pl.* **set'-tos'**, **set'-to's'**.

set'-up *n.* an arrangement.

set about 1 to begin (doing something). **2** to attack (a person).

set against to make (a person) feel unfriendly towards (someone else).

set alight. See **set fire to** below.

set apart 1 to put at some distance (from). **2** to separate. **3** to keep for special use or purpose.

set back 1 to delay the progress of. **2** to cost: *That set me back £100.*

set fair (of weather) steadily fair.

set fire, light, to, or **set on fire**, **set alight** to cause to begin to burn.

set forth 1 to put out on show. **2** to express in words: *to set forth arguments.* **3** to start (for a place, on a journey to a place).

set in to begin: *Winter set in.*

set off 1 to cause to explode. **2** to start (a person) off (doing something). **3** to show to advantage. **4** to begin a journey.

set on, upon 1 to attack. **2** to urge (e.g. a person, dog) to attack.

set oneself to try in a determined manner (to do something).

set one's teeth 1 to clench one's teeth. **2** to face resolutely something unpleasant to be done or suffered.

set on fire. See **set fire to** above.

set out 1 to begin a journey. **2** to begin with an intention: *to set out to win.*

set up 1 to put upright. **2** to build. **3** to raise: *to set up a howl.* **4** to help to begin: *to set one's son up in business.* **5** (*printing*) to put in type.

sett. See **set** (*n*).

settee *sė-tē'*, *n.* a long seat with a back.

setter, **setting**, etc. See **set**.

settle *set'l*, *n.* a long high-backed bench.—*v.t.* **1** to place at rest or in comfort: *to settle oneself in a chair.* **2** to go in numbers, or cause others to go, to live in (empty country). **3** to establish (someone, e.g. in a job). **4** to quiet (e.g. nerves, stomach). **5** to decide. **6** to agree upon (e.g. a price, date). **7** to bring to an end (e.g. a dispute). **8** to pay (a bill) completely.—*v.i.* **1** to come to rest. **2** to sink to the bottom. **3** to make one's home (in a place) permanently. **4** to grow calm or clear. **5** to decide (on). **6** to come to an agreement (with). **7** (also with *up*) to pay debts: *to settle with one's creditors*:—*pr.p.* **sett'ling**.

settle'ment 1 the act of settling. **2** payment. **3** arrangement. **4** a small community. **5** a colony newly established. **6** money given to a woman on her marriage.

sett'ler *n.* one who, or that which, settles, esp. one who goes to live in a new, usu. previously uninhabited, country.

settle down 1 to (cause to) become, quiet, calm and peaceful. **2** to begin to work, live, etc. in a quiet, calm, etc. way.

seven *sev'n*, *n.* **1** the number next above six (7 or VII). **2** a set of seven things or persons. **3** the seventh hour after midday or midnight. **4** the age of seven years. **5** any thing (e.g. a shoe, a playing-card) denoted by seven.—*adj.* **1** 7 in number. **2** seven years old.

sev'enth *adj.* **1** next after the sixth. **2** equal to one of seven equal parts.—Also *n.*

seventeen (*sev'*, or *-tēn*) *adj.* and *n.* seven and ten (17 or XVII).

seventeenth (*sev'*, or *-tēnth'*) *adj.* **1** next after the sixteenth. **2** equal to one of seventeen equal parts.—Also *n.*

sev'enty *adj.* and *n.* seven times ten (70

or LXX).

sev'enties *n.pl.* the numbers seventy to seventy-nine.

sev'entieth *adj.* **1** next after the sixty-ninth. **2** equal to one of seventy equal parts.—Also *n.*

sever *sev'ėr, v.t.* **1** to separate, part (also *v.i.*): *This severed him from his family.* **2** to cut or to break, or to be broken, off (also *v.i.*): *He severed an arm with his sword; The branch severed from the tree.* **3** to cut in two. **4** to break off (relations, ties).

sev'erance *n.*

several *sev'ėr-ȧl, adj.* **1** more than one (usu. more than three) but not very many. **2** various. **3** separate, respective: *The boys went their several ways.*

sev'erally *adv.* separately, singly.

severe *sė-vēr', adj.* **1** serious: *a severe illness.* **2** very strict: *a severe master.* **3** (of criticism, rebuke, etc.) harsh. **4** (of weather) very cold. **5** very plain: *a severe style.*

severe'ly *adv*

severe'ness, sever'ity *(-ver') ns.*

sew *sō, v.t.* **1** to fasten together with a needle and thread. **2** to make or mend in this way.—Also *v.i.*:—*pa.t.* **sewed**; *pa.p.* **sewn**, or **sewed**.

sew'er *n.* **sew'ing** *n.* and *adj.*

sewer[1]. See **sew**.

sewer[2] *sū'ėr, n.* a channel for receiving water and waste matter from drains of buildings and streets.

sew'age *n.* matter carried off by sewers.

sew'erage *n.* the system of sewers in a town, etc.

sewn. See **sew**.

sex *seks, n.* **1** either of the two classes into which animals are divided according to the part they play in reproduction: *male sex, female sex.* **2** characteristics, instincts, etc., connected with this division. **3** sexual relations or intercourse.

sexed *adj.* (often as part of a word) having sex or sexual feeling.

sex'ism *n.* discrimination against, or the assigning of stereotyped roles to, a person on the grounds of sex.

sex'ist *n.* and *adj.*

sex'ual *adj.* having to do with sex.

sexual'ity *n.* **sex'ually** *adv.*

sex'y *adj.* **1** very attractive to the opposite sex. **2** arousing sexual desires, etc.:—*comp.* **sex'ier**; *superl.* **sex'iest**.

sex appeal attractiveness to, ability to arouse sexual desires in, members of the opposite sex.

sexual intercourse the activity between a man and a woman which involves the insertion of the man's penis into the woman's vagina.

sexual relations sexual intercourse and kindred activities.

sex- *seks-*, (as part of a word) six.

sexagenarian *seks-ȧ-ji-nā'ri-ȧn, n.* a person from sixty to sixty-nine years old.—Also *adj.*

sextant *seks'tȧnt, n.* an instrument for finding distances (measured by angle), e.g. the distance between two stars, or the height of the sun above the horizon.

sextet *seks-tet', n.* a group of six musicians or singers.

sexton *seks'tȯn, n.* an officer who rings a church bell, attends the clergyman, sees to the digging of graves, etc.

sexual, etc. See **sex**.

shabby *shab'i, adj.* **1** (of clothes, etc.) worn-looking. **2** poorly dressed. **3** (of action, person, etc.) mean, unfair, not generous:—*comp.* **shabb'ier**; *superl.* **shabb'iest**.

shabb'ily *adv.* **shabb'iness** *n.*

shack *shak, n.* a roughly built hut.

shackle *shak'l, n.* (often in *pl.*) **1** a ring or other device that clasps a prisoner's or slave's wrist or ankle and is fastened to another on the other arm or leg, or to something else. **2** a hobble for a horse, etc. **3** anything that checks one's freedom.—*v.t.* to put shackles, or a check, on:—*pr.p.* **shack'ling**.

shade *shād, n.* **1** slight darkness caused by cutting off some light. **2** a place not in full sunlight. **3** (in *pl.*) darkness: *the shades of night.* **4** darker parts in a picture, etc.: *a portrait with no light and shade.* **5** a screen, etc., to shelter from light, heat, or dust. **6** degree of colour: *a deep, dark, shade of green.* **7** a very small amount: *a shade of difference; a shade too big.* **8** a ghost.—*v.t.* **1** to screen, shelter. **2** to mark with different tones of colour or shadow. **3** to darken.—*v.i.* to change gradually e.g. from one colour (into another):—*pr.p.* **shad'ing**.—See also **shadow**.

shā'ding *n.* **1** the act of making a shade, or of marking shadows. **2** the marking that shows darker places in a picture. **3** gradual change.

shadow *shad'ō, n.* **1** shade caused by an object coming in the way of a light. **2** the dark shape of that object on e.g. the ground. **3** (in *pl.*) darkness. **4** a dark part, in e.g. a picture. **5** unhappiness, trouble, etc.: *A shadow fell on his life, friendship, reputation.* **6** an appearance without reality. **7** a very small amount (of e.g. doubt, suspicion, evidence). **8** a very close companion.—*v.i.* **1** to shade, darken. **2** to hide. **3** to follow (a person) about and watch him closely.—*adj.* (used only before a noun) **1** unreal. **2** ready to come into operation when required.—See also **shade** above.

shad'owy *adj.* **1** full of shadows. **2** faint, slight. **3** not real, fanciful.

shad'owiness *n.*

shā'dy *adj.* **1** sheltered from light or heat. **2** (*coll.*) dishonest, etc.: *a shady business, person*:—*comp.* **shā'dier**; *superl.* **shā'diest**.

shā'diness *n.*

shadow cabinet leaders of the opposition in parliament, each chosen to take a particular office when there is a change of government.

in the shade 1 in a place screened from light. **2** in an unimportant position where no notice is taken of one.

shade off to lessen gradually to little or nothing.

shaft *shäft*, *n.* **1** anything long and straight. **2** the main upright part (of e.g. a pillar). **3** the long rod on which the head of a spear, golf club, etc. is fixed. **4** an arrow. **5** something sharp thought of as like an arrow: *shafts of love, ridicule.* **6** a pole e.g. of a carriage. **7** a long revolving bar transmitting motion in an engine. **8** a ray or beam (of light). **9** a well-like space: *a lift shaft.* **10** a passage in a mine.

shag *shag*, *n.* **1** a rough mass of hair or wool. **2** a kind of tobacco cut into shreds. **3** a diving bird, the cormorant.

shagg'y *adj.* **1** covered with rough hair, wool, or other growth. **2** untidy:—*comp.* **shagg'ier**; *superl.* **shagg'iest**.

shagg'ily *adv.* **shagg'iness** *n.*

shagreen *shȧ-grēn'*, *n.* dyed leather with rough surface made from the skin of a horse, seal, shark, etc.

Shah *shä*, *n.* the king of Iran (formerly Persia).

shake *shāk*, *v.t.* and *v.i.* **1** to move, or be moved, esp. to and fro, with quick, short movements. **2** to make, or to be made, unsteady. **3** to (cause to) tremble:—*pr.p.* **shā'king**; *pa.t.* **shook**; *pa.p.* **shā'ken**. —*n.* **1** a shaking or trembling. **2** a shock. **3** a drink made by shaking the ingredients together.

sha'ker *n.* a container with holes from which something, e.g. sugar, may be shaken.

sha'ky *adj.* **1** (of a person, voice, etc.) trembling through age, illness, etc. **2** (of writing, etc.) (as if) produced by a shaky person. **3** likely to collapse. **4** not steady. **5** not to be relied on: *a shaky supporter*:—*comp.* **shā'kier**; *superl.* **shā'kiest**.

shā'kily *adv.* **shā'kiness** *n.*

shake'-down *n.* a makeshift bed, e.g. of straw, or a mattress on the floor.

no great shakes (*coll.*) not very important, or not very good.

shake hands to greet someone by clasping his or her hand and moving it up and down.

Shakespearian *shāk-spē'ri-ȧn*, *adj.* having to do with *Shakespeare* or his work.

shaky. See **shake**.

shale *shāl*, *n.* a clay rock that splits into layers, from which oil is sometimes obtained.

shall *shal*, *sh(ȧ)l*, *v.* **1** used to form future tenses of other verbs when the subject is *I* or *we*: *I, we, shall never forget.* **2** expresses a command or a promise when the subject is *he, she, it, you,* or *they*: *You shall go, whether you want to or not*; *He shall have it, if I can find it*:—*pr.t. 2nd person sing.* (*thou*) **shalt**.

should *shood*, *shd*, *shd*, *v.* **1** used in conditional sentences: *I, we, should go, if they would let me, us.* **2** ought to: *I, he, should have gone, but I, he, did not*.

See also **will** and **would**.

shallot *shȧ-lot'*, *n.* a kind of onion.

shallow *shal'ō*, *adj.* **1** not deep. **2** (of a mind or nature) that does not think, or feel, deeply.—*n.* (often in *pl.*) a place where the water is not deep.

shalt. See **shall**.

sham *sham*, *adj.* not real, pretended, imitation: *a sham fight, lord*; *sham jewellery.*—*n.* **1** something which is not what it is supposed to be. **2** pretence.—*v.t.* to pretend, or pretend to be: *to sham illness*; *to sham dead.*—Also *v.i.*:—*pr.p.* **shamm'ing**; *pa.p.* **shammed**.

shamble *sham'bl*, *v.i.* to walk in a shuffling or awkward way:—*pr.p.* **sham'bling**.—Also *n.*

shambles *sham'blz*, *n.pl.* or *sing.* a slaughterhouse.—*n. sing.* a scene of blood and slaughter, or of destruction: *After the raid the streets were a shambles*.

shame *shām*, *n.* **1** a painful feeling caused by awareness of guilt, fault, or failure. **2** dishonour, disgrace. **3** a cause of disgrace. **4** (*coll.*) hard luck, a pity.—*v.t.* **1** to make feel shame. **2** to do so by one's greater excellence. **3** to drive by shame (into): *This shamed him into paying his share*:—*pr.p.* **sham'ing**.

shame'ful *adj.* disgraceful.

shame'fully *adv.* **shame'fulness** *n.*

shame'less *adj.* **1** feeling, showing, no shame. **2** impudent, unscrupulous.

shame'faced *adj.* **1** very bashful. **2** (of e.g. a confession) showing shame.
for shame! you should be ashamed.
have no shame to be shameless.
put to shame to make (someone) feel shame (e.g. by greater excellence).
think shame to be ashamed (to).

shammed, shamming. See **sham**.

shammy. See **chamois**.

shampoo *sham'pōō'*, *v.t.* to wash (the scalp and hair):—*pr.p.* **shampoo'ing**; *pa.p.* **shampooed'** *(-pōōd')*.—*n.* **1** the act of shampooing. **2** soap, etc., used for this purpose.

shamrock *sham'rok*, *n.* a plant with leaves divided in three, a type of clover—the national plant of Ireland.

shanghai *shang-hī'*, *v.t.* **1** to drug or make drunk and carry off as a sailor. **2** to compel (into doing something):—*pr.p.* **shanghai'-ing**; *pa.p.* **shanghaied'** *(-hīd')*.

shank *shangk*, *n.* **1** the part of the leg between the knee and the foot. **2** a straight or long part, shaft.

shan't *shänt*, abbrev. of **shall not**.

shanty[1] *shan'ti*, *n.* a roughly built hut, etc.—*pl.* **shan'ties**.
shanty town a town, or part of one, consisting of shanties.

shanty[2] *shan'ti*, *n.* a sailors' song with chorus:—*pl.* **shan'ties**.—Also **chan'ty** *(shan')*.

shape *shāp*, *v.t.* **1** to make (into a certain form): *to shape dough into little cakes.* **2** to model, mould. **3** to settle the nature or direction of: *This event shaped his life.*—*v.i.* **1** to take shape, develop. **2** to show promise of doing (often with *up*): *He is shaping (up) well at football*:—*pr.p.* **shap'ing**.—*n.* **1** form or figure. **2** condition: *in good shape.* **3** a jelly, etc., turned out of a mould.
shape'less *adj.* having no shape or regular form.
shape'ly *adj.* well-proportioned, of attractive shape:—*comp.* **shape'lier**; *superl.* **shape'liest**.
shape'liness *n.*
take shape to take definite form: *The book, plan, is taking shape.*

shard *shärd*, *n.* a broken piece of earthenware.

share[1] *shār*, *n.* **1** one of the parts of something that is divided among several people, etc. **2** one of the parts into which the capital of a business firm is divided.—*v.t.* **1** to divide among a number of people (often with *out*). **2** to have in common: *They share a liking for sport.*—*v.i.* to receive, to take, a share (in):—*pr.p.* **shar'ing**.
share'holder *n.* one who owns shares in a business company.

share[2] *shār*, *n.* the iron blade of a plough which cuts the ground.

shark *shärk*, *n.* **1** a large, fierce, flesh-eating fish. **2** a swindler, or a greedy unscrupulous person.

sharp *shärp*, *adj.* **1** cutting, piercing. **2** having a thin edge or fine point. **3** stinging, hurting: *a sharp wind*; *sharp words.* **4** (of pain, etc.) keen, intense. **5** alert: *a sharp lookout.* **6** perceptive, clever. **7** raised a semitone. **8** too high in pitch. **9** shrill. **10** quick to see, hear, or understand. **11** clear-cut: *a sharp outline.*—*adv.* **1** with pitch too high. **2** briskly. **3** abruptly. **4** punctually: *at 10 a.m. sharp.*—*n.* **1** a sign (♯) in music to show that a note is to be raised a semitone. **2** the note so raised. **3** a cheat.
shar'pen *v.t.*, *v.i.* to make, grow, sharp.
sharp'ener *n.* an instrument for sharpening, esp. pencils.
shar'per *n.* a cheat, esp. at cards.
sharp'ly *adv.* **sharp'ness** *n.*
sharp practice **1** cunning, barely honest, dealing. **2** an instance of this.
sharp'-shoot'er *n.* a good marksman, esp. a soldier given duties that need skilled shooting.
sharp'-sight'ed *adj.* having keen sight.
sharp'-witt'ed *adj.* having quick wit.
look sharp to be quick.

shatter *shat'ėr*, *v.t.* **1** to break in pieces (also *v.i.*). **2** to upset completely, ruin (e.g. health, nerves, hopes).

shave *shāv*, *v.t.* **1** to scrape, cut off the surface of. **2** to cut (off) closely (e.g. hair from the face). **3** to graze, touch lightly, the surface of in passing.—*v.i.* to use a razor in removing hair:—*pr.p.* **shav'-ing**.—*n.* **1** the act of shaving. **2** a narrow miss or escape: *a close shave.*
shā'ven *adj.* shaved.
shā'ver *n.* an electric razor.
shā'ving *n.* **1** the act of scraping off. **2** a thin slice, esp. of wood planed off.

Shavian *shā'vi-ȧn*, *adj.* having to do with the playwright George Bernard *Shaw*.

shawl *shöl*, *n.* a wrap or loose covering for the shoulders.

she *shē*, *pron.* *(fem.)* refers to the female (or thing spoken of as female) already named: *When they noticed the girl, the ship, she was already near*:—*objective* **her**; *possessive* **her** (sometimes described as *possessive adj.*), **hers**: *Give Mary her book*; *you know it is hers.*—*adj.* (often as part of a word) female: *a she-devil.*

herself' *pron.* the emphatic or reflexive form of *she, her*: *She herself told me*; *She has made herself look a fright*.

sheaf *shēf, n.* a bundle (of e.g. corn, papers) bound or tied together:—*pl.* **sheaves** *(shēvz)*.

shear *shēr, v.t.* to clip, cut the wool from (a sheep):—*pa.t.* **sheared**; *pa.p.* **sheared** or **shorn**.
shears *n. pl.* **1** large scissors. **2** a larger scissors-like cutting implement.

sheath *shēth, n.* **1** a case for a sword or blade. **2** a long close-fitting covering. **3** a condom:—*pl.* **sheaths** *(shēTHz)*.
sheathe *shēTH, v.t.* to put into, or cover with, a sheath or case:—*pr.p.* **sheath'ing**.
sheath'-knife *n.* a knife carried in a sheath.

sheave *shēv, n.* a grooved pulley over which a rope, belt, runs:—*pl.* **sheaves** (also *pl.* of **sheaf**).

shed[1] *shed, v.t.* **1** to throw or cast off (e.g. clothing, skin, leaves). **2** to pour out (e.g. tears). **3** to send forth, throw: *to shed light on, a gloom over*:—*pr.p.* **shedd'ing**; *pa.p.* **shed**.

shed[2] *shed, n.* **1** a building for storage or shelter. **2** an outhouse.

she'd *shēd*, **1** she had. **2** she would.

sheen *shēn, n.* shine, brightness, gloss.

sheep *shēp, n.* **1** an animal raised for its wool, flesh, etc. **2** a silly, helpless creature:—*pl.* **sheep**.
sheep'ish *adj.* bashful, foolishly shy.
sheep'-dip *n.* **1** a liquid for disinfecting sheep. **2** the place where sheep are disinfected by dipping in such a liquid.
sheep dog a dog trained to watch sheep, or of a breed used for this work.
sheep'shank *n.* a knot for shortening a rope.
sheep'skin *n.* **1** the skin of a sheep. **2** leather prepared from it.

sheer[1] *shēr, adj.* **1** pure: *sheer delight*. **2** downright: *sheer foolishness*. **3** very steep, vertical. **4** (of a cloth) very thin.—*adv.* straight up or down, very steeply.

sheer[2] *shēr, v.i., v.t.* to turn aside from a straight line, swerve.
sheer off **1** to turn aside. **2** to move away.

sheet[1] *shēt, n.* **1** a large, thin piece (of ice, glass, metal, etc.). **2** a broad piece of linen, etc. for a bed. **3** a piece of paper. **4** a sail.
sheet'ing *n.* **1** cloth for sheets. **2** a lining or covering of wood or metal.
sheet lightning lightning which appears to be in great sheets because of the reflection and spreading of flashes by the cloud.

sheet[2] *shēt, n.* a rope attached to the lower corner of a sail.

sheet-anchor *shēt-ang'kȯr, n.* **1** a large anchor for use in emergency. **2** a thing or person one counts on in danger, or when all else has failed.

sheik(h) *shāk, shēk, n.* an Arab chief.

shekel *shek'l, n.* **1** a Jewish weight and coin. **2** the unit of currency of Israel. **3** (in *pl.*; *slang*) money.

shelf *shelf, n.* **1** a board for laying things on, fixed in a cupboard or on a wall. **2** a flat layer of rock, a ledge. **3** a flat bank of sand:—*pl.* **shelves**.
shelve *v.t.* **1** to put up shelves in (e.g. a library). **2** to put on a shelf. **3** to put (e.g. a problem) aside for consideration later. **4** to dismiss, retire (a person).—*v.i.* to slope in a way that suggests a shelf: *The land shelves towards the sea*:—*pr.p.* **shelv'ing**.
shelv'ing *n.* (material for) shelves.
shelf'-life *n.* the length of time that a product remains usable, edible etc.
on the shelf no longer in use, at work, or having prospects (esp. of marriage).

shell *shel, n.* **1** a hard outer covering of a shellfish, egg, nut, etc. **2** a husk or pod. **3** any framework, as of a building not completed or burnt out. **4** a frail boat. **5** a metal case, filled with explosive material, fired from a gun.—*v.t.* **1** to separate from the shell. **2** to fire shells at.
shell'y *adj.* covered with shells.
shell'iness *n.*
shellac (*-lak'*, or *she'*) *n.* a resin in thin sheets, used for making varnish.
shell'fish *n.* a sea animal covered with a shell (e.g. oyster, crab).
shell'proof *adj.* able to resist shells or bombs.
shell'shock *n.* mental disturbance due to war experiences, once thought to be due to the bursting of shells.

she'll *shēl*, she will.

shellac, shelly. See **shell**.

shelter *shel'tėr, n.* **1** a building or structure that protects against wind, rain, attack, etc. **2** protection from harm.—*v.t.* **1** to give protection to. **2** to hide.—*v.i.* to take shelter.

shelve, shelves, shelving. See **shelf**.

shepherd *shep'ėrd, n.* one who looks after sheep:—*old fem.* **shep'herdess**.—*v.t.* **1** to watch over carefully. **2** to guide.
shepherd's pie a dish of minced meat with potatoes on the top.

sherbet *shûr'bėt, n.* a fizzy drink, or the powder for making it.

sheriff *sher'if, n.* **1** the chief representative of the crown in a county, whose duties include keeping the peace, presiding at elections, etc. **2** (in Scotland) the chief judge of the county. **3** in the United States, the chief law-enforcement officer of a county.

sherry *sher'i, n.* a fortified wine which gets its name from the town of *Jerez* in Spain:—*pl.* **sherr'ies**.

shied, shier, etc. See **shy**.

shield *shēld, n.* **1** a broad piece of metal, etc., carried for defence against weapons. **2** anything that protects. **3** a person who protects. **4** a trophy shaped like a shield.—*v.t.* to protect by sheltering.

shift *shift, v.i.* **1** to manage, get on, do as one can: *He must shift for himself.* **2** to change position or direction: *The huge mass, the wind, shifted.*—*v.t.* **1** to change (e.g. the scene on stage). **2** to change the position of. **3** to transfer (to, upon): *He tried to shift the burden, blame, to his brother.* **4** to dislodge, get rid of.—*n.* **1** a change. **2** a change of position, a transfer. **3** a set of persons taking turns with another set: *The night shift now came on duty.* **4** the time worked by such a set. **5** a means used, measure taken, in an emergency. **6** a dodge, trick.
shif'ter *n.* **1** one who shifts. **2** a trickster.
shift'less *adj.* inefficient, lazy, without steady purpose.
shif'ty *adj.* **1** tricky, not trustworthy. **2** (of eyes, looks) not frank and honest:—*comp.* **shif'tier**; *superl.* **shif'tiest**.
shif'tily *adv.* **shif'tiness** *n.*
make shift to manage somehow.
shift for oneself to manage by one's own efforts.

shilling *shil'ing, n.* a coin, formerly silver, later cupro-nickel, worth orig. 12 pence, now 5 (new) pence.

shilly-shally *shil'i-shal'i, n.* hesitation, indecision.—*v.i.* to hesitate in making up one's mind, waver:—*pr.p.* **shill'y-shall'ying**; *pa.p.* **shill'y-shall'ied**.

shimmer *shim'ėr, v.i.* to shine with a quivering light, glisten.—*n.* a trembling light, glimmer.

shin *shin, n.* the front part of the leg below the knee.—*v.i.* (with *up*) to climb by gripping with hands and legs:—*pr.p.* **shinn'ing**; *pa.p.* **shinned**.
shin'bone *n.* the tibia (see this).

shindy *shin'di, (slang) n.* an uproar:—*pl.* **shin'dies**.

shine *shin, v.i.* **1** to give out or reflect light. **2** to be bright. **3** to be very good (at): *He shines at games.*—*v.t.* to cause to shine:—*pr.p.* **shin'ing**; *pa.t., pa.p.* (*v.i.*) **shone** *(shon)*, (*v.t.*) **shone** or **shined**.—*n.* **1** brightness. **2** an act of polishing.
shin'ing *adj.* **1** very bright and clear. **2** (usu. used before a noun) greatly to be admired: *shining courage, a shining example.*
shī'ny *adj.* glossy, polished:—*comp.* **shī'nier**; *superl.* **shī'niest**.
shī'nily *adv.* **shī'niness** *n.*

shingle[1] *shing'gl, n.* **1** a slab of wood, etc. used in the same way as a roofing slate. **2** a woman's haircut showing the shape of the head at the back.—*v.t.* **1** to cover (e.g. a roof) with shingles. **2** to cut in the manner of a shingle:—*pr.p.* **shing'ling**.

shingle[2] *shing'gl, n.* coarse gravel consisting of rounded stones, esp. on the seashore.

shingles *shing'glz, n. pl.* a disease with firm blister-like swellings along nerves, sometimes spreading round the body.

shinier, shiny, etc. See **shine**.

shin'ty *n.* a game, originally Scottish, similar to hockey, played by two teams of 12.

ship *ship, n.* **1** a large vessel for journeys on sea, lake, or river. **2** a spaceship.—*v.t.* **1** to take on to a ship. **2** to send by ship. **3** to engage for work on a ship.—*v.i.* **1** to embark. **2** to hire oneself for work on a ship:—*pr.p.* **shipp'ing**; *pa.p.* **shipped**.
ship'ment *n.* **1** the act of putting on board ship. **2** goods sent by ship or (now) other means of transport.
shipp'ing *n.* **1** ships as a whole. **2** transport by ship.
ship'board *n.* **1** a ship's side. **2** a ship.
ship canal a canal deep enough for seagoing vessels.
ship'master *n.* the captain of a ship.
ship'mate *n.* a fellow sailor.
ship'shape *adj.* in good order, neat, trim.
ship'wreck *n.* **1** the wreck (esp. by accident) of a ship. **2** ruin, disaster.
ship'wright *n.* one employed in building or repairing ships.
ship'yard *n.* a yard where ships are built or repaired.

shire *shīr*, (as part of a word, *-shėr*), *n.* **1** a county. **2** also applied to some smaller districts.

shirk *shûrk, v.t.* to slink out of facing or doing (something one ought to).—Also *v.i.*
shir'ker *n.*

shirt *shûrt*, *n.* **1** a man's garment with sleeves, worn on the upper part of the body. **2** a woman's tailored blouse.

shirt'ing *n.* cloth for shirts.

shirt'y *adj.* (*coll.*) ill-tempered.

shirt'waist (*U.S.*) *n.* a tailored blouse with ends for tucking under the skirt.

shirt'waister *n.* a tailored dress with top like a shirtwaist.

shit *shit*, (*vulg.*) *n.* **1** excrement, waste matter from the bowels. **2** an unpleasant or worthless person or thing.—*v.i.* to empty the bowels: *pr.p.* **shitting**; *pa.t.*, *pa.p.* **shit**, **shitted** or **shat**.—*interj.* expressing anger, annoyance, displeasure, etc.

shiver[1] *shiv'ėr*, *n.* a small chip, splinter.—*v.t.*, *v.i.* to break into fragments.

shiver[2] *shiv'ėr*, *v.i.* to quiver, tremble (with e.g. cold or fear).—Also *n.*

shiv'ery *adj.* inclined to shiver.

shiv'eriness *n.*

shoal[1] *shōl*, *n.* a great number, esp. of fishes together in one place.

shoal[2] *shōl*, *n.* a shallow place, sandbank.

shock[1] *shok*, *n.* **1** a violent blow coming suddenly. **2** a jarring or shaking as if by a blow. **3** unexpected bad news or experience. **4** an earthquake. **5** the usu. painful and sometimes harmful effect on the body of an electric current (also **electric shock**). **6** the state of exhaustion, depression, etc., caused by being injured, etc. **7** (*coll.*) a stroke of paralysis.—*v.t.* **1** to give a shock to. **2** to upset or horrify.—*v.i.* to be horrified.

shock'er (*coll.*) *n.* a person or thing that shocks.

shock'ing *adj.* causing horror or dismay, disgusting.

shock'-absorber *n.* a device for reducing shock in an aeroplane or motor car.

shock action, tactics action in which suddenness and force are used to achieve a purpose.

shock troops soldiers specially trained for attack and hard fighting.

shock[2] *shok*, *n.* a number of sheaves of corn placed together on end.

shock[3] *shok*, *n.* a bushy mass (of hair).

shock'headed *adj.* having such hair.

shocking, etc. See **shock**[1].

shod. See **shoe**.

shoddy *shod'i*, *n.* wool or cloth made from old wool and cloth pulled to pieces.—*adj.* **1** made of shoddy. **2** of poor material or quality but pretending to be good: *shoddy furniture, person, excuse*:—*comp.* **shodd'ier**; *superl.* **shodd'iest**.

shodd'iness *n.*

shoe *shōō*, *n.* **1** a stiff outer covering for the foot, not coming above the ankle. **2** a rim or iron nailed to the hoof of an animal. **3** a metal tip. **4** a piece attached where there is friction, the touching part of a brake:—*pl.* **shoes**.—*v.t.* to put shoe(s) on:—*pr.p.* **shoe'ing**; *pa.p.* **shod**.

shoe'horn *n.* a curved piece of horn, metal, etc. used for making one's shoe slip easily over one's heel.

shoe'lace, shoe'string *ns.* a string for fastening a shoe.

shoe'maker *n.* one who makes, repairs, or sells, shoes.

shoe'-tree *n.* a wooden, metal or plastic support inserted in a shoe when it is not being used in order to preserve the shoe's shape.

in someone's shoes in his place.

on a shoestring with very little money.

shone. See **shine**.

shook. See **shake**.

shoot *shōōt*, *v.t.* **1** to send, fire (an arrow, bullet, etc.) from a bow, gun, etc. **2** to send, let fly (e.g. a ball) swiftly and with force. **3** to throw out suddenly (e.g. rubbish). **4** to slide (a bolt). **5** to ask or say suddenly: *Don't shoot questions at me.* **6** to hit or kill with an arrow, bullet, etc. **7** to score (a goal). **8** to pass swiftly over (rapids), under (a bridge). **9** to pass over (country) shooting game. **10** to put forth (buds, etc.). **11** to photograph, esp. for motion pictures.—*v.i.* **1** to fire a weapon. **2** to kick a ball. **3** to kill e.g. game birds for sport. **4** to move suddenly or quickly. **5** to grow, increase (also with *up*). **6** to put out buds, etc., esp. of plants such as rhubarb and vegetables where this is not wanted. **7** to photograph or film:—*pa.t.*, *pa.p.* **shot**.—*n.* **1** the act of shooting. **2** a shooting party. **3** a new growth, sprout. **4** a chute.

shoot'ing *n.* and *adj.*

shot *adj.* **1** hit or killed by shooting. **2** (of silk) showing changing colours. **3** streaked (with colour). **4** mixed (with).

shoot'ing-star *n.* a meteor (see this). See also **shot**[1].

shop *shop*, *n.* **1** a place where goods are sold. **2** a workshop, or a place where any kind of industry is carried on. **3** details of, or talk about, one's own work. **4** (*slang*) an institution.—*v.i.* to visit shops for the purpose of buying.—*v.t.* (*slang*) to betray, inform against:—*pr.p.* **shopp'ing**; *pa.p.* **shopped**.

shopp'er *n.* **1** one who shops. **2** a large bag for carrying purchased articles in.

shopp'ing *n.* **1** the act of buying goods in shops. **2** the goods bought.

shop assistant someone serving customers in a shop.

shop'-floor' *n.* (the people who work in) that part of the factory, etc. containing the production machinery and the main part of the workforce.

shop'keeper *n.* one who keeps a shop of his own.

shop'lifter *n.* one who steals goods from a shop.

shop'lifting *n.*

shopping centre a place, completely or partly roofed, with a large number of shops of different kinds.

shop'-soiled' *adj.* having been made slightly dirty while on display in a shop.

shop steward a representative of factory or workshop employees elected from their own number.

talk shop (*coll.*) to talk about one's work when one is off duty.

shore[1] *shōr, shör, n.* a prop, beam, to support a building or to keep a ship in dock steady.—*v.t.* to prop (up), support:—*pr.p.* **shor'ing.**

shore[2] *shōr, shör, n.* land bordering on the sea or on any expanse of water.

shorn. See **shear.**

short *shört, adj.* **1** not long. **2** not tall. **3** brief, not lasting long. **4** not as much as it should be, not enough: *My change is short; short rations.* **5** having too little (of): *I am short of money.* **6** (of one's manner of speaking) rude, sharp. **7** (of e.g. pastry) crumbling easily.—*adv.* **1** suddenly, abruptly: *He stopped short when he saw me.* **2** in a place not as far as intended: *The shot fell short.*—*n.* a short-circuit.—*v.t.* and *v.i.* to short-circuit.

shor'tage *n.* a lack or deficiency, not enough (of).

shor'ten *v.t.* to make shorter.

shortening *shört'ning, n.* **1** the act of making, or becoming, shorter. **2** fat suitable for making pastry.

short'ly *adv.* **1** in a short time, soon. **2** briefly. **3** abruptly, curtly.

shorts *n.pl.* short trousers.

short'bread *n.* a crisp, brittle cake of flour and butter.

short-change' *v.t.* to give (a customer) less than the correct amount of change.

short'-cir'cuit *n.* a short cut in an electric circuit, usu. made accidentally and causing sparking and fire.—*v.t., v.i.* to have or cause a short-circuit.—*v.t.* to get over or round (a difficulty or hindrance).

short'coming *n.* **1** the act of falling short. **2** a fault or lack.

short cut. See **cut.**

short'fall *n.* the amount by which something is deficient.

short'hand *n.* a method of swift writing using strokes, etc., for speech sounds and groups of sounds.

short'-hand'ed *adj.* having fewer workers, helpers, than are necessary.

short'-list *n.* a list of candidates selected from the total number of applicants.—Also *v.t.*

short'-lived' *(-livd') adj.* **1** living only for a short time. **2** not lasting long.

short'-sight'ed *adj.* **1** seeing clearly only things that are near. **2** (of a person, action) foolishly ignoring what is likely to happen in the future.

short'-sight'edness *n.*

short'-tem'pered *adj.* easily made angry.

short'-term' *adj.* **1** (of an arrangement, esp. money) lasting a short time. **2** (of a plan, policy) concerned only with the near future.

in short in a few words.

short for a shortened form of.

short of 1 less than. **2** without going so far as: *They will use any means short of war.*

make short work of to do, deal with, settle, very quickly.

shot[1] *shot, n.* **1** a single act or sound of shooting. **2** something that is shot, e.g. a bullet, projectile. **3** a number of bullets together. **4** a marksman. **5** the distance covered by a bullet, etc. **6** a throw, stroke, in a game. **7** an attempt (at doing something, at guessing, etc.) **8** a photograph, a scene in a motion picture. **9** the act of making this. **10** an injection: *a shot of cocaine.*

shot'gun *n.* a smooth-bore gun for small shot.

shot'-put *n.* the athletic event of putting the shot.

big shot (*coll.*) an important person.

shotgun wedding one forced on one or both partners.

shot in the dark a guess.

shot[2]. See **shoot.**

should. See **shall.**

shoulder *shōl'dėr, n.* **1** the part of the body between the neck and the upper arm. **2** the upper joint of a foreleg of an animal cut for the table. **3** something that sticks out or curves gently.—*v.t.* **1** to push with the shoulder. **2** to carry on the shoulder. **3** to bear the full weight of.

shoul'der-blade *n.* the broad flat bone of the shoulder.

cold-shoulder, give the cold shoulder. See **cold.**

shout *showt, n.* **1** a loud call. **2** a loud burst (of e.g. laughter, applause).—*v.i., v.t.* to utter, or utter with, a shout.
shout down to make it impossible to hear (a speaker) by shouting.

shove *shuv, v.t., v.i.* **1** to thrust. **2** to push along. **3** to push aside rudely:—*pr.p.* **shov'ing.**—Also *n.*
shove off 1 to push a boat from the shore. **2** (*coll.*) to go away.

shovel *shuv'l, n.* **1** a broad spade-like tool, scoop. **2** a machine for scooping up.—*v.t.* to move with, or as if with, a shovel:—*pr.p.* **shov'elling**; *pa.p.* **shov'elled.**

show *shō, v.t.* **1** to allow, or cause, to be seen. **2** to exhibit, display (e.g. an art collection). **3** to point out (e.g. the way). **4** to guide or conduct: *Show her to a seat.* **5** to demonstrate or prove: *to show the truth of his story.*—*v.i.* to be able to be seen:—*pa.t.* **showed** *(shōd)*; *pa.p.* **shown** or **showed.**—*n.* **1** the act of showing. **2** a display. **3** an entertainment. **4** (*coll.*) a theatrical performance. **5** a false appearance: *a show of penitence.*
showy *shō'i, adj.* **1** making a striking show. **2** gaudy, bright and cheap:—*comp.* **show'ier**; *superl.* **show'iest.**
show'ily *adv.* **show'iness** *n.*
show business the branch of the theatrical profession concerned with variety entertainments.
show'down *n.* **1** a showing of one's cards, resources, plans. **2** a final, decisive struggle or argument after a period of conflict.
show'jumping *n.* a competition in which horses and riders have to jump a succession of obstacles.
show'man *n.* **1** a person who owns a show. **2** one who is skilled in displaying things (e.g. his own merits) so as to arouse public interest.
show'manship *n.*
show'room *n.* a room where goods are displayed for people to see.
a show of hands a vote by raising hands.
show off 1 to show, display, to advantage. **2** to try to make an impression by one's possessions or talents.
show up 1 to stand out clearly. **2** to expose (e.g. faults). **3** to come, turn up.

shower *show'ėr, showr, n.* **1** a short fall, of e.g. rain, or of tears, bullets, etc. **2** a large quantity (of e.g. presents, questions). **3** a shower-bath.—*v.t.* **1** to pour down: *They showered confetti on the bride.* **2** to give in great quantity (e.g. kindnesses, invitations).—*v.i.* **1** to pour down. **2** to come in great quantity. **3** to have a shower-bath.

showery *show'ėr-i, showr'i, adj.* raining now and then:—*comp.* **showerier**; *superl.* **showeriest.**
showeriness *n.*
shower-bath *n.* a bath in which water is sprayed from above.

showing, shown, etc. See **show.**

shrank. See **shrink.**

shrapnel *shrap'n(ė)l, n.* **1** a shell holding e.g. bullets, which scatter after explosion. **2** shell, bomb, or mine, fragments.

shred *shred, n.* **1** a fragment, esp. strip, torn or cut off. **2** a scrap (e.g. *not a shred of evidence*).—*v.t.* to cut or tear into shreds:—*pr.p.* **shredd'ing**; *pa.p.* **shredd'ed.**

shrew *shrōō, n.* **1** a small mouse-like animal with a sharp nose. **2** a quarrelsome or scolding woman.
shrewd *adj.* showing keen judgment.
shrewd'ly *adv.* **shrewd'ness** *n.*
shrew'ish *adj.* **shrew'ishness** *n.*

shriek *shrēk, v.i., v.t.* to utter, or utter with, a shrill scream or laugh.—Also *n.*

shrift. See **shrive.**

shrill *shril, adj.* **1** high in tone and piercing. **2** sharp sounding through impatience.
shrill'ness *n.* **shril'ly** *adv.*

shrimp *shrimp, n.* **1** a small long-tailed shellfish. **2** a small person.—*v.i.* to catch shrimps.

shrine *shrīn, n.* **1** a case for holding holy objects. **2** a holy or sacred place.

shrink *shringk, v.i.* **1** to grow smaller. **2** to draw back in fear or disgust (from).—*v.t.* to cause to become smaller:—*pa.t.* **shrank**; *pa.p.* **shrunk.**
shrink'age *n.* the amount by which a thing grows smaller.
shrunk'en *adj.* **1** grown smaller. **2** shrivelled.—Also **shrunk.**

shrive *shrīv, v.t.* to hear the confession of and give pardon to (a person):—*pr.p.* **shriv'ing**; *pa.t.* **shrove** or **shrived**; *pa.p.* **shriv'en** *(shriv')* or **shrīved.**
shrift *n.* the act of shriving.
give short shrift to to waste little time or consideration on.
Shrove Sunday, Monday, Tuesday days immediately before Ash Wednesday.

shrivel *shriv'l, v.i., v.t.* to dry up, wrinkle, wither:—*pr.p.* **shriv'elling**; *pa.p.* **shriv'elled.**

shroud *shrowd, n.* **1** cloth around a dead body. **2** anything that covers. **3** (in *pl.*) ropes from the masthead to a ship's sides.—*v.t.* **1** to cover with a shroud. **2** to hide.

shrove. See **shrive.**

shrub *shrub, n.* a low woody plant, bush.
shrubb'ery *n.* a place where shrubs grow:—*pl.* **shrubb'eries**.
shrubb'y *adj.* **shrubb'iness** *n.*

shrug *shrug, v.i.* to draw up the shoulders to show doubt, lack of interest, etc.:—*pr.p.* **shrugg'ing**; *pa.p.* **shrugged**.—Also *n.*
shrug off to treat as unimportant.

shrunk, shrunken. See **shrink**.

shudder *shud'ėr, v.i.* to shiver, tremble, from cold, fear, disgust.—Also *n.*

shuffle *shuf'l, v.t.* **1** to mix (e.g. playing cards). **2** to shove (the feet) along without lifting them. **3** to move (something) quietly and hastily.—*v.i.* **1** to mix cards. **2** to move without lifting the feet. **3** to avoid answering question(s) honestly and directly:—*pr.p.* **shuff'ling**.—Also *n.*
shuff'ler *n.* **shuff'ling** *n.* and *adj.*

shun *shun, v.t.* to avoid, keep clear of:—*pr.p.* **shunn'ing**; *pa.p.* **shunned**.

shunt *shunt, v.t., v.i.* to turn aside, on to a side track (e.g. an engine, train, electric current).—*n.* **1** an act of moving out of the way. **2** a switch.
shun'ter *n.* a small locomotive used for shunting.

shut *shut, v.t.* **1** to close the opening of. **2** to lock, fasten. **3** to confine: *Shut him in his kennel.*—*v.i.* to become closed:—*pr.p.* **shutt'ing**; *pa.t., pa.p.* **shut**.
shutt'er *n.* a cover over a window or opening e.g. in a camera.
shut down to close (works), or (of works) to be closed, for a time or permanently.
shut up **1** to close completely. **2** (*coll.*) to stop speaking. **3** (*coll.*) to silence.

shuttle *shut'l, n.* **1** in weaving, the device that carries the weft threat from side to side through the warp threads. **2** a similar device in a sewing-machine. **3** a shuttle service, or the vehicle, aeroplane, etc. used for this.—*adj.* running backwards and forwards: *a shuttle bus service.*—*v.t., v.i.* to carry, move, regularly between two points:—*pr.p.* **shutt'ling**.
shutt'lecock *n.* a cork, etc., struck with feathers, used in badminton, etc.

shy[1] *shī, adj.* **1** (of e.g. a wild animal) easily frightened, timid. **2** bashful, anxious not to attract attention to oneself. **3** not very willing to (with *of*): *He is shy of giving his opinion.* **4** suspicious (of):—*comp.* **shy'er, shī'er**; *superl.* **shy'est, shī'est**.—*v.i.* **1** (of e.g. a horse) to start aside from fear. **2** to take alarm, hesitate (at): *I shy at the thought of tackling him*:—*pr.p.* **shy'ing**; *pa.p.* **shied** *(shīd)*.
shy'ly *adv.* **shy'ness** *n.*
shy'ster *n.* a person who is unscrupulous or dishonest in his professional conduct.
fight shy of to avoid, shrink from, not go near.

shy[2] *shī, v.t.* to toss, throw.—*n.* a try, attempt:—*pl.* **shies**.

Siamese *sī-ȧm-ēz', adj.* of *Siam*, now Thailand.—Also *n.*
Siamese cat a type of domestic cat, with fawn coat, dark legs, ears and tail, and blue eyes.
Siamese twins twins whose bodies are joined together at some place.

sibilant *sib'i-lȧnt, n.* a hissing sound.—Also *adj.*

sibling *sib'ling, n.* a brother or sister.

sic *sik, adv.* so, thus. (This word is put into a quotation after something that is, or seems to be, an error to show that the passage is given exactly as in the original: *Cockroaches were brought to this country by sea; the writer says: 'We were much troubled on the ship by what the Spaniards call cacarootches* [*sic*]'.)

sick *sik, adj.* **1** not well, ill. **2** vomiting or inclined to vomit. **3** thoroughly tired (of). **4** disgusted. **5** (of humour) joking about things not normally considered amusing, e.g. death, physical or mental handicaps.
sick'en *v.t., v.i.* to make, or become, sick.
sick'ening *adj.* making sick, disgusted, or tired and bored.
sick'ly *adj.* **1** ailing, not healthy. **2** causing sickness. **3** suggesting sickness, pale, feeble: *a sickly complexion, smile*:—*comp.* **sick'lier**; *superl.* **sick'liest**.
sick'liness *n.*
sick'ness *n.*
sick bay. See **bay**[1].
sick'-leave *n.* leave of absence because of sickness.
sick pay the payments made to a worker while off sick.
sick'-room *n.* a room in which a sick person is living.
sicken for to show early symptoms of (a disease).

sickle *sik'l, n.* a tool with a curved blade for cutting grain, etc.

side *sīd, n.* **1** a bounding line, or a surface or surface part, esp. one that is not top, bottom, front, or back. **2** either surface of paper, etc. **3** the right or left part of the body, esp. between armpit and hip. **4** a region, division: *the north side of the town.* **5** a slope (of a hill). **6** aspect: *We must look at all sides of the problem.* **7** a party, team, etc., opposed to, fighting against, another. **8** an air of superiority: *After he* *became rich, he put on side.*—*adj.* (only used before a noun) **1** at, towards, or from, one side. **2** indirect, additional, but less important, etc. (see **side effect, issue**).

sid'ing *n.* a short line of rails on which wagons, etc., are shunted from the main line.

side'board *n.* **1** a piece of dining-room furniture for holding dishes, etc. **2** (in *pl.*) whiskers on the side of the face.

side'burns *n.pl.* short sideboards.

side'car *n.* a small car for passenger(s), attached to a motor-cycle.

side effect an effect (usu. bad) of a drug, etc., in addition to its good effect on the ailment for which it is given.

side issue a matter that is not the main problem under consideration though to some extent connected with it.

side'light *n.* **1** light coming from the side. **2** a light carried on the side of a vehicle. **3** information that throws light (on a puzzling subject).

side line **1** a branch route or track. **2** (**side'line**) a business carried on outside one's regular job or activity.

side'long *adj.* from or to the side, not direct: *a sidelong glance.*—Also *adv.*

side'show *n.* a less important show, or a show that is part of a larger one.

side'slip *v.i.* to skid, slide sideways:—*pr.p.* **side'slipping**: *pa.p.* **side'slipped**.—Also *n.*

side'splitting *adj.* causing one to hurt one's side with laughter.

side'step *v.t.* **1** to avoid by stepping to one side. **2** to avoid having to tackle (e.g. a problem):—*pr.p.* **side'stepping**; *pa.p.* **side'stepped**.

side street a minor street opening off a more important one.

side'track *v.t.* **1** a turn into a siding. **2** to turn (a person) from his purpose. **3** to turn (a subject) away from discussion.

side'walk (*U.S.*) *n.* a pavement or footpath.

side'ways, **side'wise** *adv.* with the side facing to the front: *to move sideways.*

on the side (*coll.*) **1** by means, sometimes unworthy, other than one's regular job: *to earn more money on the side.* **2** in addition.

side with to give one's support to (one party in a disagreement, etc):—*pr.p.* **sid'ing with.**

take sides to choose to support a party, opinion, etc.

sidle *sīd'l*, *v.i.* **1** to go or move sideways. **2** to edge along in a stealthy manner:—*pr.p.* **sid'ling**.

siege *sēj*, *n.* **1** an attempt to take a fort or town by keeping it surrounded by an armed force. **2** a constant attempt to gain possession or control (of).

lay siege to to besiege.

raise a siege to bring it to an end.

sienna *si-en'ȧ*, *n.* a material used for colouring, brownish-yellow (**raw sienna**), or (when roasted) reddish-brown (**burnt sienna**).

sierra *si-er'ȧ*, *n.* a range of mountains with jagged peaks.

siesta *si-es'tȧ*, *n.* a short sleep or rest, esp. one taken in the afternoon.

sieve *siv*, *n.* a vessel with a bottom containing very small holes, used to separate liquids or fine grains from coarser solids.—*v.t.* to put through a sieve:—*pr.p.* **siev'ing**.

sift *sift*, *v.t.* **1** to separate by passing through a sieve. **2** to examine closely: *to sift the evidence.*

sigh *sī*, *v.i.* **1** to take a long, deep-sounding breath showing tiredness, sadness, or longing. **2** (of wind) to make a sound like this. **3** to long (for). **4** to grieve.—*v.t.* to express by sighs.—Also *n.*

sight *sīt*, *n.* **1** the ability to see. **2** the act of seeing. **3** a view, glimpse. **4** something unusual that is seen (e.g. something worth seeing, ridiculous, terrible). **5** a device in a gun or other instrument to guide the eye in aiming, etc.—*v.t.* **1** to get a view of, see suddenly. **2** to look at through a sight.

sight'ed *adj.* having sight, or (as part of a word) a certain type of sight (e.g. *short-sighted*).

sight'ly *adj.* pleasing to the eye:—*comp.* **sight'lier**; *superl.* **sight'liest**.

sight'liness *n.*

sight'-read'ing *n.* reading or playing music at first sight of the notes.

sight'-see'ing *n.* visiting scenes or objects of interest.

sight'-seer *n.*

at sight **1** as soon as seen: *a bill payable at sight.* **2** without previous study or practice.

at thirty (etc.) days' sight (of a bill of exchange) (payable) thirty (etc.) days after it is presented.

in (or **out of**) **sight** where it, etc., can (or cannot) be seen.

on sight as soon as seen.

sign *sīn*, *n.* **1** a movement (e.g. a wave of the hand, nod of the head) by which one can show one's meaning. **2** a mark with a meaning. **3** proof or evidence of something present or to come: *signs of life*; *A red sunset is a sign of good weather.* **4** (*mathematics*) a mark to show what is to be done: + *is a sign of addition.* **5** a notice displayed publicly showing an inn, etc., or giving a shopkeeper's name or trade.—*v.t.* **1** to show (one's meaning), or to give a message to (a person), by means of a sign: *He signed approval, signed the other to go ahead.* **2** to write (one's name) on a document. **3** to put one's signature on (a document).—Also *v.i.*

signal *sig'n(ȧ)l*, *n.* **1** a sign (e.g. gesture, light, sound) arranged beforehand giving command, warning, etc., or showing moment to begin some action. **2** a wave, sound, sent out by, or received by, a wireless set, etc.—*adj.* notable: *a signal success.*—*v.t.* **1** to make signals to (a person). **2** to send (information) by signals:—*pr.p.* **sig'nalling**; *pa.p.* **sig'nalled**.

sig'nally *adv.* notably, extremely.

sig'natory *n.* one who has signed an agreement to do something:—*pl.* **sig'natories**.

signature *sig'nȧ-chůr*, *n.* **1** a signing. **2** a signed name. **3** (*music*) flats and sharps, etc., that show the key, or a sign showing the time.

signet *(sig')* *n.* a small seal, e.g. on a ring (**sig'net-ring**).

signif'icant *adj.* having meaning or importance, esp. much meaning: *significant facts*; *a significant glance*:—*opp.* **insignificant**.

signif'icantly *adv.* **1** in a significant manner. **2** to an important degree: *The sales were significantly smaller*.

signif'icance *n.* **1** meaning. **2** importance.

significā'tion *n.* **1** the act of signifying. **2** significance.

signify *sig'ni-fī*, *v.t.* **1** to be a sign of. **2** to mean. **3** to make known: *to signify one's approval.*—*v.i.* to have meaning or importance;—*pr.p.* **sig'nifying**; *pa.p.* **sig'nified** *(-fīd)*.

sig'nalman *n.* **1** one who sends signals. **2** one who works railway signals.

signature tune a tune used to introduce, and hence associated with, a particular radio or television programme, performer, etc.

sign'board *n.* a board with a notice, etc.

sign'post *n.* a post on which a sign (esp. one showing direction) is hung.

sign away to transfer (esp. property, rights) to another person by signing.

sign off **1** to stop work. **2** to stop broadcasting.

sign on to engage oneself for work by signing.

Signor *sē'nyor*, *n.* Italian word for Mr (**signore** *-nyō'rā*, a gentleman).

signo'ra *n.* **1** a lady. **2** (*cap.*) Mrs.

signori'na *(-ē')* *n.* **1** a young lady. **2** (*cap.*) Miss.

silage. See **silo**.

silence *sī'lėns*, *n.* **1** absence of sound or of speech, or a time of this. **2** failure to mention or tell something.—*v.t.* to cause to be silent:—*pr.p.* **sil'encing**.—*interj.* be silent!

sī'lencer *n.* a device (e.g. on gun, in engine) for making noise less.

sī'lent *adj.* **sī'lently** *adv.*

silhouette *sil-oo-et'*, *n.* **1** an outline drawing filled in with black. **2** the profile of a person.—*v.t.* to show like a silhouette against a background:—*pr.p.* **silhouett'ing**.

silica *sil'i-kȧ*, *n.* a very common whitish substance, a compound of silicon and oxygen, found in the form of quartz, sandstone, flint, etc.

sil'icon *n.* an element, the second most abundant of all elements, found in many rocks as e.g. silica.

sil'icone *n.* any of a number of substances containing silicon, used e.g. in polishes.

silicon chip. See **chip** (*def. 4*).

silk *silk*, *n.* **1** the very fine, soft, fibres spun by silkworms to form cocoons. **2** thread, cloth, made from the fibres.—Also *adj.*

sil'ken *adj.* **1** made of silk. **2** silky.

sil'ky *adj.* like silk, soft, smooth:—*comp.* **sil'kier**; *superl.* **sil'kiest**.

sil'kiness *n.*

silk'worm *n.* the caterpillar of certain moths which spins silk.

sill *sil*, *n.* the wood or stone at the foot of an opening, as the ledge under a door or window.

sillabub. See **syllabub**.

silly *sil'i*, *adj.* foolish, not sensible:—*comp.* **sill'ier**; *superl.* **sill'iest**.—*n.* a silly person:—*pl.* **sill'ies**.

sill'iness *n.*

silo *sī'lō*, *n.* **1** a tower-like building for storing grain. **2** a pit or building for preparing silage. **3** an underground chamber containing a guided missile;—*pl.* **si'los**.

si'lage *sī'lij*, *n.* green fodder preserved in silos.

silt *silt*, *n.* fine sand and mud carried and left behind by flowing water.—*v.t.*, *v.i.* (with *up*) to fill, block, with mud.

silvan, sylvan *sil'vȧn*, *adj.* **1** wooded. **2** living in woods. **3** located in woods.

silver *sil'vėr*, *n.* **1** an element, a soft white metal able to take on a high polish. **2** money made of silver or a substitute. **3** anything looking like silver.—*adj.* **1** made of, or looking like, silver. **2** (of a sound) silvery.—*v.t.*, *v.i.* to cover with, or to become like, silver.
sil'vering *n.* **1** covering with silver. **2** coating of (or like) silver on an object.
sil'very *adj.* **1** like silver. **2** (of sound) clear and musical.
sil'veriness *n.*
sil'verfish *n.* **1** a whitish goldfish. **2** a wingless silvery insect sometimes found in houses.
silver paper a wrapping material made of metal and having a silvery appearance.
sil'ver-plate' *n.* dishes, spoons, etc. silver, or plated with silver.
sil'versmith *n.* one who makes or sells articles of silver.
sil'ver-tongued *adj.* eloquent, pleasing in speech.
silver wedding, jubilee the twenty-fifth anniversary of a marriage, or other important event.

similar *sim'i-lår*, *adj.* **1** like, alike, in most ways. **2** having a resemblance (to):—*opp.* **dissim'ilar.**
similar'ity, sim'ilarness *ns.*
sim'ilarly *adv.* **1** in the same, or a similar, way. **2** likewise, also.
simile *sim'i-li*, *n.* an expression, figure of speech, in which one thing is compared to another unlike it in all but one way, or certain ways (e.g. *a wind like a knife*; *a mind sharp as a needle*); a simile always uses 'like' or 'as' (compare **metaphor**).
simil'itude *n.* likeness.

simmer *sim'ėr*, *v.i.* **1** to be, remain, on the point of boiling, esp. if making a gentle hissing sound. **2** (of e.g. anger, excitement, revolt) to be ready to burst out. **3** (of person) to go on feeling annoyance without saying much.—Also *v.t.*
simmer down to calm down.

simper *sim'pėr*, *v.i.* to smile in a silly manner.—Also *n.*

simple *sim'pl*, *adj.* **1** easy: *a simple problem.* **2** plain: *a simple dress.* **3** mere, bare: *the simple facts.* **4** ordinary. **5** of humble rank. **6** too trusting, easily cheated. **7** foolish, silly.—*n.* **1** a simple person. **2** a healing plant.
sim'pleton *n.* a simple, foolish, person.
simplic'ity *(-plis')*, **sim'pleness** *ns.*
simplificā'tion *n.* **1** the act of making simpler **2** a simpler form.
sim'plify *v.t.* to make simpler:—*pr.p.* **sim'plifying**; *pa.p.* **sim'plified.**
sim'ply *adv.* **1** in a simple manner. **2** merely. **3** absolutely: *simply lovely*.
simple interest. See **interest** (*def.* 8).
sim'ple-min'ded *adj.* **1** lacking intelligence. **2** foolish.

simulate *sim'ū-lāt*, *v.t.* **1** to make a pretence of: *to simulate illness, unwillingness.* **2** to have the appearance of:—*pr.p.* **sim'ulating.**
simulā'tion *n.*

simultaneous *sim-ul-tā'nyus*, *adj.* happening, done, at the same time: *He received a simultaneous protest from all his listeners.*
simultā'neously *adv.*
simultaneous translation translation of a speaker's words into other languages at the same time as he is speaking.

sin *sin*, *n.* **1** a wicked act, esp. one that breaks a law of one's religion. **2** wrongdoing. **3** a shortcoming. **4** (*coll.*) shame, pity: *It is a sin to spoil the beautiful old town.*—*v.i.* to do wrong, commit sin:—*pr.p.* **sinn'ing**; *pa.p.* **sinned.**
sin'ful *adj.* **sinn'er** *n.*
sin'fully *adv.* **sin'fulness** *n.*
live in sin to cohabit with someone to whom one is not married.
original sin the supposed sinfulness of all human beings, held to be due to the sin of Adam.

since *sins*, *adv.* **1** (often **ever since**) from then till now: *We fought, and I have avoided him ever since.* **2** at a later time: *We fought, but we have since become friends.* **3** ago: *It happened long since.*—*prep.* from the time of: *since his arrival.*—*conj.* **1** after, or from the time in the past when: *Since he agreed to come he has taken ill*; *I have been at home since I returned from Italy.* **2** because: *Since you are going, I will go too*.

sincere *sin-sēr'*, *adj.* **1** honest in word and deed, **2** true, genuine: *a sincere desire*; *sincere friends*:—*opp.* **insincere.**
sincerity *(-ser')*, **sincere'ness** *ns.*
sincere'ly *adv*.

sinecure *sī'nė-kūr*, *sin'*, *n.* a job with a salary but little or no work.

sine die *sī'ni dī'ē*, *sin'e dē'ā* without a fixed date for resumption, indefinitely (used in speaking e.g. of the adjournment of a meeting).

sine qua non *sī-ni kwā non*, *sin'e kwä nōn* a necessity, necessary condition.

sinew *sin'ū*, *n.* **1** a tendon (see this word). **2** strength. **3** (in *pl.*) equipment, resources (esp. financial) for: *lacking the sinews of war*.
sin'ewy *adj.* **1** having sinews, esp. well-

developed ones. **2** strong, tough, vigorous.

sinful, etc. See **sin**.

sing *sing, v.i.* **1** to make musical sounds with one's voice. **2** to ring, hum, murmur, etc.—*v.t.* **1** to utter musically. **2** to utter with enthusiasm: *to sing her praises*:—*pa.t.* **sang**; *pa.p.* **sung**.
sing'er *n.* **sing'ing** *n.* and *adj.*
sing'song *n.* **1** a boring up-and-down tone of voice (also *adj.*). **2** jingly verse. **3** (*coll.*) a meeting where everyone should sing.
sing another song or **tune** to change one's attitude, esp. behave more humbly.
sing out to shout, call out.
See also **song**.

singe *sinj, v.t., v.i.* to burn on the surface, scorch:—*pr.p.* **singe'ing**; *pa.p.* **singed**.—Also *n.*

Singhalese. Same as **Sinhalese**.

single *sing'gl, adj.* **1** one only. **2** not double. **3** unmarried. **4** for one person. **5** between two, man to man: *single combat*. **6** for one direction of a journey: *a single ticket*.—*v.t.* to choose, pick (out):—*pr.p.* **sing'ling**.—*n.* **1** a small gramophone record with usu. only one tune or other short recording on each side. **2** (in *pl.*) in tennis, etc., a game between two players.
sin'gleness *n.* **1** thc state of being single. **2** the state of having one only: *singleness of aim, purpose*.
sin'gly *adv.* **1** one by one. **2** separately. **3** single-handed.
singular *sing'gū-lȧr, adj.* **1** (*grammar*) showing one person or thing. **2** exceptional, unusual, strange.—*n.* (*grammar*) **1** the state of being singular: *All these words are in the singular.* **2** the form of a word in the singular.
singular'ity (*pl.* **-ies**), **sin'gularness** *ns.*
sin'gularly *adv.* **1** unusually. **2** strangely.
single cream cream with little fat, which will not thicken when beaten.
sin'gle-han'ded *adj.* by oneself, with no help.
sin'gle-hear'ted *adj.* sincere.
sin'gle-min'ded *adj.* **1** bent on one purpose only. **2** sincere.
in single file one behind another.

singsong. See **sing**.

Sinhalese *sing-hȧ-lēz', sin-*, **Singhalese**, *sing-hȧ-, sing-gȧ-, adj.* of Sri Lanka, or of one (the most numerous) of the peoples of Sri Lanka or their language.—Also *n.*—Also **Cing'alese**.

sinister *sin'is-tėr, adj.* **1** of, on, the left side. **2** suggesting evil, present or to come: *sinister happenings*; *a sinister look*.
sin'isterly *adv.* **sin'isterness** *n.*

sink *singk, v.i.* **1** to go down, wholly or partly, below the surface of e.g. water. **2** to pass slowly to a lower position or level, or a less active state: *The sun, a fire, a voice sinks*; *hopes sink*. **3** to slope downwards. **4** (of a dying person) to become weaker. **5** to lower oneself (into e.g. a chair). **6** to pass (into e.g. silence, sleep).—*v.t.* **1** to cause to go below the surface, or to a lower position, level or state. **2** to make by digging (e.g. a well). **3** to drive (e.g. a knife, teeth, into something). **4** to invest, usu. at a loss: *to sink money in a business.* **5** to avoid bringing (e.g. one's own desires, unpleasant facts) into consideration, etc.:—*pa.t.* **sank**; *pa.p.* **sunk**.—*n.* **1** a drain to carry off dirty water. **2** a kitchen or scullery basin with a drain. **3** a hollow in a land surface. **4** a place where evil and vice live and thrive.
sink'er *n.* anything that causes sinking, esp. a weight on a fishing-line.
sunk *adj.* **1** on a lower level than the surroundings. **2** sunken. **3** (*coll.*) done for, unable to carry on.
sunk'en *adj.* **1** hollowed (esp. of cheeks). **2** sunk.
Sunk and *sunken* are used in much the same way, except that *sunk* is the usual *adj.* for something that has been made or placed at a lower level, esp. in certain technical senses, e.g. *a sunk fence*.
sinking feeling an unpleasant feeling in one's stomach caused by one's awareness of impending and unavoidable trouble.
sinking fund money put aside every year for paying off debts.
sink in **1** to be absorbed. **2** to be understood.

sinner. See **sin**.

sinuous *sin'ū-ůs, adj.* **1** bending in and out. **2** (of a person) making strong, smooth movements (also used of movement, grace).
sinuos'ity *n.* **1** sinuousness. **2** a bend.
sin'uously *adv.* **sin'uousness** *n.*

sinus *sī'nůs, n.* a cavity, hollow, as an air cavity in the head connected with the nose:—*pl.* **sī'nuses**.
sinusī'tis *n.* inflammation of one of the sinuses of the nose.

sip *sip, v.t.* to drink in very small quantities:—*pr.p.* **sipp'ing**; *pa.p.* **sipped**.—Also *n.*

siphon *sī'fȯn, n.* **1** a pipe or tube with a bend through which liquid can be drawn off from one container to another at a lower level. **2** (also **siphon bottle**) a glass bottle with bent tube for soda water, etc.—*v.t.* to draw (off) by means of, or as if by means of, a siphon.

sirloin *sûr'loin, n.* the upper part of the loin of beef.

sisal *sīs'(ȧ)l, sīz', n.* fibre from a West Indian plant, used in making ropes.

sissy, cissy *sis'i, n.* an effeminate man or boy:—*pl.* **siss'ies, ciss'ies.**

sister *sis'tėr, n.* **1** the name given to a female by other children of the same parents. **2** a member of a sisterhood. **3** a senior nurse in a hospital, one in charge of a ward. **4** a female of the same kind or class.—*adj.* (used only before a noun) **1** closely related. **2** alike, e.g. in design: *sister ships.*

sis'terhood *n.* **1** the state of being a sister. **2** a group of women formed for purposes of religion, good works, etc.

sis'terly *adj.* like a sister, kind, loving.

sis'terliness *n.*

sis'ter-in-law *n.* **1** a husband's or wife's sister, or a brother's wife. **2** a husband or wife's brother's wife:—*pl.* **sis'ters-in-law.**

sit *sit, v.i.* **1** to rest on the lower part of the body, be seated. **2** (of birds) to perch. **3** to rest on eggs in order to hatch them. **4** to be an official member: *to sit in Parliament; to sit on a committee.* **5** (of Parliament, etc.) to be in session. **6** to be located: *The wind sits in the west.* **7** to pose, be a model. **8** to hang, fit: *The coat sits well.*—*v.t.* **1** to seat. **2** to have a seat on, ride. **3** to take (an examination):—*pr.p.* **sitt'ing**; *pa.p.* **sat.**

sitt'er *n.* **1** one who poses. **2** a sitting bird. **3** an easy target. **4** a baby-sitter.

sitt'ing *n.* **1** the state of resting on a seat. **2** a seat in a church pew. **3** brooding on eggs. **4** a meeting of a court, etc. **5** a time of posing for an artist or photographer.—*adj.* **1** seated. **2** brooding. **3** meeting, in session. **4** actually in office or possession: *the sitting member of parliament for Bath; the sitting tenant.*

sit'-in *n.* the occupying of a building, etc. as an organised protest against some (supposed) injustice, etc. (also *adj.*)

sitt'ing-room *n.* a room chiefly for sitting in.

sit back **1** to rest. **2** to take no part in an activity.

sit down to move to a sitting position, e.g. on a seat.

sit-down strike a strike in which workers stay in the factory but refuse to work.

sit in **1** to be present, and often actively involved, (at a conference or meeting) without being an actual member. **2** to take part in a sit-in.

sit out **1** to remain seated during (a dance) **2** to sit to the end of.

sit tight to refuse to move or act.

sit up **1** to sit with one's back straight. **2** to move to a sitting from a lying position. **3** to keep watch during the night.

site *sīt, n.* the ground on which e.g. a building is, was, or is to be, put up or placed.—*v.t.* to locate, place (building, etc.):—*pr.p* **sit'ing.**

situate *sit'ū-āt, v.t.* **1** to locate, place. **2** to place with regard to problems, etc. (usu. in *pa.p.*): *Having inherited money, he was now more happily situated:*—*pr.p.* **sit'uating.**

situā'tion *n.* **1** position. **2** circumstances, state of affairs, esp. difficult: *In this situation, help was necessary.* **3** employment, job (esp. unimportant).

six *siks, n.* **1** the number next above five (6 or VI). **2** a set of six things or persons. **3** the sixth hour after midday or midnight. **4** the age of six years. **5** anything (e.g. a shoe, a playing-card) denoted by six.—*adj.* **1** 6 in number. **2** six years old.

sixth *adj.* **1** next after the fifth. **2** equal to one of six equal parts.—Also *n.*

sixteen *siks'tēn, siks-tēn', adj.* and *n.* six and ten (16 or XVI).

sixteenth *adj.* **1** next after the fifteenth. **2** equal to one of sixteen equal parts.—Also *n.*

sixty *siks'ti, adj.* and *n.* six times ten (60 or LX).

sixties *n.pl.* the numbers sixty to sixty-nine.

six'tieth *adj.* **1** next after the fifty-ninth. **2** equal to one of sixty equal parts.—Also *n.*

six'pence *n.* formerly, a coin, orig. silver, later cupro-nickel, worth six (old) pennies.

six'penny *adj.* **1** worth or costing sixpence. **2** of little value.

sixth sense an ability to perceive things beyond the powers of the five basic senses.

at sixes and sevens in a muddle.

sixth form college a school which provides the sixth form education for the pupils of an area.

sixty-four (thousand) dollar question the most difficult question (*orig.* in a quiz).

size[1] *sīz, n.* **1** the space taken up by anything. **2** measurements, dimensions. **3** largeness. **4** one of a number of classes in which shoes, dresses, etc. are grouped according to measurements: *I take size 5* *in shoes.*

sīz'able, **size'able** *adj.* fairly large.

sized (as part of a word) having a certain kind of size: *middle-sized.*

size up to form an opinion about the worth, nature, etc. of (a person, situation):—*pr.p.* **siz'ing up'**.

size[2] *sīz*, *n.* (also **sizing** *sī'zing*) weak glue, or other material for glazing.—*v.t.* to cover with size:—*pr.p.* **siz'ing**.

sizzle *siz'l*, *v.i.* to make a hissing sound.—*v.t.*, *v.i.* to fry or scorch:—*pr.p.* **sizz'ling**.

skate[1] *skāt*, *n.* a steel blade (**ice'-skate**) or rollers (**roll'er-skate**) which can be fixed to a shoe for gliding on ice, etc.—*v.i.* to move on skates:—*pr.p.* **skā'ting**.

skā'ter *n.* **skā'ting** *n.*

skate'board *n.* a narrow board on roller-skate wheels, on which one balances to ride.

skate[2] *skāt*, *n.* a type of large flatfish.

skean-dhu *skēn'dōō*, *skē'ȧn-*, *n.* a Highlander's dagger, worn in the stocking.

skedaddle *ski-dad'l*, (*coll.*) *v.i.* to rush off:—*pr.p.* **skedadd'ling**.

skein *skān*, *n.* a length of thread or yarn, loosely coiled.

skeleton *skel'i-t(ȯ)n*, *n.* **1** the bony framework of an animal. **2** any framework or outline. **3** a very thin person.—*adj.* (of e.g. a staff, crew) reduced to very small number.

skeleton key a key with parts filed away, that can open different locks.

a skeleton in the cupboard a closely kept secret, hidden shame.

sketch *skech*, *n.* **1** a rough plan, or drawing or painting. **2** an outline or short account. **3** a short slight play, dramatic scene, etc.— *v.t.* **1** to draw, describe, or plan, roughly. **2** to give the chief points of.—Also (in art sense) *v.i.*

sketch'y *adj.* **1** roughly done or carried out. **2** slight, incomplete: *a sketchy knowledge*:—*comp.* **sketch'ier**; *superl.* **sketch'iest**.

sketch'ily *adv.* **sketch'iness** *n.*

skew *skū*, *adj.*, *adv.* off the straight, slanting.—*v.t.*, *v.i.* to set, be set, at a slant.

skewer *skū'ėr*, *n.* a long pin of wood or metal for keeping meat together while roasting.—*v.t.* to fasten, fix, with a skewer, or with something sharp.

ski *skē*, *n.* one of a pair of long narrow strips of wood, etc. for gliding over snow:—*pl.* **ski**, **skis**.—*v.i.* to travel on, use, skis:—*pr.p.* **ski'ing**; *pa.p.* **skied** (*skēd*).

ski'er *n.* **ski'ing** *n.* and *adj.*

skid *skid*, *n.* **1** a wedge, etc., put under a wheel to check it on a steep place. **2** one or more planks, logs, etc., on which things can be moved by sliding. **3** a slide sideways: *The road was wet and my car went into a skid.*—*v.t.* to cause to slide sideways.—*v.i.* **1** (of wheels) to slide along without turning. **2** to slip, esp. sideways:—*pr.p.* **skidd'ing**; *pa.p.* **skidd'ed**.

skid row a squalid place where vagrants, chronic drunks, etc. live.

skied[1]. See **sky**.

skied[2], **skier**. See **ski**.

skiff *skif*, *n.* a small light boat.

skill *skil*, *n.* **1** cleverness at doing something—either from practice or from natural gift. **2** an ability required for a craft: *a manual skill.*

skil'ful *adj.* having, or showing, skill.

skil'fully *adv.* **skil'fulness** *n.*

skilled *adj.* **1** skilful. **2** requiring skill, esp. skill gained by training: *a skilled job.*

skillet *skil'it*, *n.* a small metal dish with a long handle used in cooking.

skim *skim*, *v.t.* **1** to remove floating matter from the surface of: *to skim soup.* **2** to take (e.g. cream) from the surface of liquid. **3** to glide lightly over. **4** to read hurriedly, skipping parts.—*v.i.* to glide along near the surface, or lightly:—*pr.p.* **skimm'ing**; *pa.p.* **skimmed**.

skim milk milk from which the cream has been skimmed.

skimp *skimp*, *v.t.* **1** to give (a person) hardly enough. **2** to do (a job) imperfectly.—*v.i.* to give, spend, etc. too little.

skim'py *adj.* **1** (of quantity) too small. **2** (of e.g. dress) not long, full, enough. **3** stingy:—*comp.* **skimp'ier**; *superl.* **skimp'iest**.

skim'pily *adv.* **skim'piness** *n.*

skin *skin*, *n.* **1** the natural outer covering of an animal. **2** a thin outer layer, as on a fruit. **3** a film on liquid. **4** a container of animal skin, etc., for e.g. liquids.—*v.t.* **1** to strip the skin from. **2** (*slang*) to strip of money, to fleece:—*pr.p* **skinn'ing**; *pa.p.* **skinned**.

skinn'y *adj.* very thin:—*comp.* **skinn'ier**; *superl.* **skinn'iest**.

skinn'iness *n.*

skin'-deep' *adj.* no deeper than the skin: *The cut, his sorrow, was skin-deep.*

skin'-diver *n.* **1** originally, one who dives naked for pearls. **2** a diver wearing simple equipment and not connected to a boat.

skin'flint *n.* a mean, grasping person.

skin'-tight' *adj.* fitting as tightly as the skin.

by the skin of one's teeth very narrowly, only just: *We escaped by the skin of our teeth.*

get under someone's skin 1 to annoy someone greatly. **2** to fill someone's thoughts.

save one's skin to escape without injury, esp. in a cowardly way.

skint *skint*, (*slang*) *adj.* having no money.

skip[1] *skip*, *v.i.* **1** to spring or hop over a turning rope. **2** to leap, esp. lightly or joyfully. **3** to leave out parts of e.g. a book.—*v.t.* **1** to leave out. **2** not to got to (e.g. a class):—*pr.p.* **skipp'ing**; *pa.p.* **skipped**.—Also *n.*

skipp'ing-rope *n.* a piece of rope used in skipping.

skip[2] *skip*, *n.* a large container for rubbish, etc.

skipper *skip'ėr*, *n.* the captain of a merchant or small ship, aircraft (*coll.*), or team.—*v.t.* to act as skipper of.

skirmish *skûr'mish*, *n.* **1** a fight between small parties of soldiers. **2** a short, sharp contest or disagreement.—Also *v.i.*

skirt *skûrt*, *n.* **1** a woman's garment that hangs from the waist. **2** the lower part of a dress, etc. **3** (in *pl.*) the outer edge or border.—*v.t.* to lie on, or pass along, the edge of.

skir'ting (board) *n.* the narrow board next to the floor round the walls of a room.

skit *skit*, *n.* a short piece of writing or a dramatic scene making fun of person(s), etc: *a skit on opera singers.*

skittish *skit'ish*, *adj.* **1** (of a horse) easily frightened. **2** too frisky or lively.

skittle *skit'l*, *n.* a pin for the game of skittles.

skittles *n. sing.* a form of ninepins in which a ball or cheese-shaped missile is used.

skive *skīv*, *v.i.* (often with *off*) to avoid doing a duty.—Also *n.*

skulduggery *skul-dug'ėr-i*, *n.* underhanded actions.

skulk *skulk*, *v.i.* **1** to lie hidden for a bad purpose. **2** to move in a sneaking way. **3** to avoid doing one's job.

skull *skul*, *n.* **1** the bony case that encloses the brain. **2** the head.

skull'cap *n.* a cap that fits closely to the head.

skull and cross-bones a design on a pirate's flag, etc.

skunk *skungk*, *n.* **1** a small American animal which defends itself by squirting out an evil-smelling liquid. **2** a mean, low fellow.

sky *skī*, *n.* (often in *pl.* **skies**) **1** the upper atmosphere, the heavens. **2** weather or climate: *stormy skies*; *Arctic skies.*—*v.t.* **1** to raise, or hit, high into the air. **2** to hang (e.g. a picture) above line of sight:—*pr.p.* **sky'ing**; *pa.p.* **skied** *(skīd)*.

sky'-blue *adj.* blue like the sky.

sky'-div'ing, jump'ing *ns.* the sport of jumping from aircraft with delayed opening of parachute.

sky'-high *adj.* very high.

sky'lark *n.* the common lark, which sings while hovering overhead.—*v.i.* to be merry in a rough, mischievous way.

sky'larking *n.* and *adj.*

sky'light *n.* a window in a roof or ceiling.

sky'line *n.* the horizon.

sky'scrāper *n.* a high building of many storeys.

slab *slab*, *n.* a thick plate or slice of e.g. stone, cake.

slabber. Same as **slobber**.

slack *slak*, *adj.* **1** not firmly stretched. **2** not firmly in position. **3** not holding fast. **4** not strict. **5** lazy and careless. **6** not busy: *the slack season.* **7** (of tide, etc.) moving slowly.—*n.* **1** the loose part of a rope. **2** (in *pl.*) a type of trousers for informal wear.—*v.i.* **1** to do less work than one should. **2** to slacken.

slacken *v.t.*, *v.i.* to make, or become, looser, or less active, less tense, etc.

slack'er *n.* one who slacks.

slack water turn of the tide.

slag *slag*, *n.* refuse from metal-smelting.

slain. See **slay**.

slake *slāk*, *v.t.* **1** to quench, satisfy (e.g. thirst, anger). **2** to put out (fire). **3** to mix (lime) with water:—*pr.p.* **slak'ing**.

slalom *slä'lȯm*, *n.* **1** a downhill or zigzag ski run among posts or trees. **2** an obstacle race in canoes.

slam[1] *slam*, *v.t.*, *v.i.* **1** to shut with noise, bang. **2** to put, come, noisily, hurriedly (down, against, etc.):—*pr.p.* **slamm'ing**; *pa.p.* **slammed**.

slam[2] *slam*, *n.* (in cards) the winning of every trick.

grand slam 1 in cards, a slam. **2** the winning of every competition, contest, etc. in a sport, etc.

little slam the winning of every trick but one.

slander *slän'dėr*, *slan'*, *n.* false statement(s) made with the desire to harm a person's reputation (in English law, the term applies to spoken words only; compare **libel**).—*v.t.* to speak slander against.

slan'derous *adj.* **slan'derously** *adv.*

slang *slang*, *n.* **1** words or phrases in everyday speech coined in an attempt to be new, different, and striking, usu. lasting only a short time, but sometimes later accepted for general or dignified use (see **donkey**). **2** the special language of a group (compare, **argot**, **cant**, **jargon**).—*v.t.* to scold, abuse.
slang'y *adj.*:—*comp.* **slang'ier**; *superl.* **slang'iest**.
slang'iness *n.*

slant *slänt*, *slant*, *v.t.*, *v.i.* **1** to slope. **2** to place, lie, move, diagonally: *Cross straight; do not slant across the street.* **3** to give (facts) in a way that makes them seem to mean what one wishes them to mean.—*n.* **1** a turning away from a straight line **2** a way of looking at (with *on*): *a new slant on the question.*
slan'ting *adj.* and *n.*

slap *slap*, *n.* **1** a blow with the hand or anything flat. **2** a snub.—*v.t.* to give a slap to:—*pr.p* **slapp'ing**; *pa.p* **slapped**.
slap'dash *adv.* in a bold, careless way.—*adj.* off-hand, hasty.
slap'stick comedy knockabout comedy or farce.

slash *slash*, *v.t.* **1** to make long cuts in. **2** to strike violently. **3** to criticise harshly. **4** (*coll.*) to reduce greatly.—Also *v.i.*—*n.* **1** a long cut. **2** a sweeping blow.

slat *slat*, *n.* a thin strip of wood.
slatt'ed *adj.* having slats.

slate[1] *slāt*, *n.* an easily split rock of dull blue, grey, etc., used for roofing, etc. or writing upon.—*adj.* **1** made of slate. **2** slate-coloured.—*v.t.* to cover with slate:—*pr.p.* **slat'ing**.
slā'ty *adj.*:—*comp.* **sla'tier**; *superl.* **sla'tiest**.
slā'tiness *n.*

slate[2] *slāt*, *v.t.* to say harsh things to or about:—*pr.p.* **slat'ing**.
slā'ting *n.* a harsh scolding.

slatted. See **slat**.

slattern *slat'ėrn*, *n.* a slut, dirty woman.
slatt'ernly *adj.* **slatt'ernliness** *n.*

slaughter *slö'tėr*, *n.* **1** killing of animals, esp. for food. **2** brutal killing. **3** killing of great numbers of people.—Also *v.t.*
slaugh'ter-house *n.* a place where animals are killed for the market.

Slav *släv*, *n.* a person whose language is **Slav(onic)** (Russian, Polish, Czech, etc.).

slave *slāv*, *n.* **1** one who is forced to work for a master to whom he belongs. **2** one who is completely devoted (to another whom he serves). **3** one who has lost power to resist: *He is a slave to drink.* **4** one who works very hard.—*v.i.* to work like a slave:—*pr.p.* **sla'ving**.
slā'ver *n.* **1** a dealer in slaves. **2** a ship used to carry slaves.
slā'very *n.* **1** the state of being a slave. **2** the system of ownership of slaves.
slā'vish *adj.* **1** slave-like. **2** (acting or thinking) exactly according to instructions or to rules. **3** (of e.g. imitation) too close.
slā'vishly *adj.* **slā'vishness** *n.*
slave driver **1** an overseer of slaves. **2** a hard master.

slaver[1] *slav'ėr*, or *slāv'ėr*, *n.* saliva running from the mouth.—*v.t.* to let the saliva run out of the mouth.

slaver[2], **slavery**, **slavish**. See **slave**.

Slavonic. See **Slav**.

slay *slā*, *v.t.* to kill:—*pr.p.* **slay'ing**; *pa.t.* **slew**; *pa.p.* **slain**.

sleazy *slē'zi*, (*coll.*) *adj.* squalid:—*comp.* **sleaz'ier**; *superl.* **sleaz'iest**.

sled *sled*, *n.* a vehicle with runners made for sliding on snow.—*v.t.* to travel in a sled: *pr.p.* **sledd'ing**; *pa.p.* **sledd'ed**.

sledge[1] *slej*, *n.*, *v.i.* (*pr.p.* **sledg'ing**). Same as **sled**.
sledge'-dog *n.* a dog trained to pull a sledge.

sledge[2] *slej*, *n.* a large heavy hammer.—Also **sledge'-hammer**.

sleek *slēk*, *adj.* **1** smooth and glossy. **2** well fed and cared for. **3** smoothly polite.—*v.t.* to make sleek.
sleek'ly *adv.* **sleek'ness** *n.*

sleep *slēp*, *v.t.* **1** to take rest in a state of unconsciousness. **2** to be motionless. **3** to be dead. **4** (of limbs) to be numb. **5** (of a top) to spin so steadily that it looks as if it were standing still:—*pa.t.* and *pa.p.* **slept**.—Also *n.*
slee'per *n.* **1** one who sleeps. **2** a wooden or steel beam supporting railway lines. **3** a sleeping-car, or berth, on a railway train.
sleep'less *adj.* **1** unable to sleep. **2** always watchful, alert, active.
slee'py *adj.* **1** drowsy, inclined to sleep. **2** not alert, or seeming not to be: *a sleepy manner.* **3** very quiet: *a sleepy town*:—*comp.* **slee'pier**; *superl.* **slee'piest**.
slee'pily *adv.* **slee'piness** *n.*
slee'ping-bag *n.* a bag for sleeping in, used by campers, etc.
slee'ping-car *n.* a railway coach with berths or beds.
sleeping partner a partner who has money invested in a business but takes no part in its management.
sleeping policeman a low hump across a road intended to slow traffic down.
slee'ping-sickness *n.* a serious disease

of tropical Africa, causing drowsiness and exhaustion.

sleep'walker *n.* one who walks while asleep.

slee'pyhead *n.* a lazy person.

go to sleep 1 to become asleep. **2** (of a limb) to become numb.

put to sleep 1 to make unconscious. **2** to kill (an animal) painlessly, usu. by injection of a drug.

sleet *slēt*, *n.* rain mixed with snow or hail.—*v.i.* to shower sleet.

sleeve *slēv*, *n.* **1** the part of a garment that covers the arm. **2** a container for a gramophone record. **3** (in machinery) something that covers as a sleeve does.

sleeve'less *adj.* without sleeves.

have up one's sleeve to keep hidden for use if the need arises.

sleigh *slā*, *n.* a sledge, esp. a large horse-drawn one.

sleight *slīt*, *n.* cunning.

sleight'-of-hand' *n.* (skill in) tricks depending on quickness of hand.

slender *slen'dėr*, *adj.* **1** thin or narrow. **2** slim. **3** slight: *a slender chance.* **4** small in amount: *a slender income*.

slept. See **sleep**.

sleuth *slōōth*, *n.* a tracker or detective.

sleuth'-hound *n.* a bloodhound.

slew[1] *slōō*, *v.t.* to turn, swing (a ship, boat) round.—Also *v.i.*

slew[2]. See **slay**.

slice *slīs*, *n.* **1** a thin broad piece. **2** a broad-bladed implement, esp. for serving fish. **3** a slash. **4** (*golf*) a sliced stroke.—*v.t.* **1** to cut in slices. **2** to cut through. **3** to cut (off, from, etc.) **4** to hit (a ball) in such a way that it curves away to the right (in the case of left-handed player, to the left):—*pr.p.* **sli'cing**.

slī'cing *n.* and *adj.*

slick *slik*, *adj.* **1** sleek, smooth. **2** smooth in speech and manner. **3** skilful, often in a sly way.—*v.t.* **1** to polish. **2** to tidy up.—*n.* a thin layer of spilt oil, esp. on the sea (also **oil-slick**).

slick'ly *adv.* **slick'ness** *n.*

slide *slīd*, *v.i.* **1** to slip or glide. **2** to pass along smoothly. **3** to pass quietly or secretely. **4** to take its course: *Do nothing*; *just let the matter slide.*—*v.t.* **1** to push smoothly along. **2** to slip:—*pr.p.* **sli'ding**; *pa.t.* and *pa.p.* **slid** *(slid)*.—*n.* **1** a slip, act of sliding. **2** a slippery track. **3** a chute. **4** a groove or rail on which a thing slides. **5** a slippery sloping surface in a park, etc. for children to slide down. **6** a sliding part, e.g. of a trombone. **7** a piece of glass, etc., on which to place objects to be looked at through a microscope. **8** a picture for showing on a screen.

slī'der *n.* one who, or something that, slides.

slide'-rule *n.* an instrument for multiplying, dividing, etc. made of rulers sliding against each other.

sliding scale a scale of wages, charges, etc. which can be changed as conditions change.

slier, **sliest**. See **sly**.

slight *slīt*, *adj.* **1** small in amount: *a slight breeze, improvement.* **2** (of a person) slender in build. **3** of little importance.—*v.t.* to treat as unimportant, insult by ignoring.—*n.* an insult by showing no interest in or respect for.

slight'ing *adj.* insulting or discourteous.

slight'ingly *adv.*

slight'ly *adv.* **1** in a small degree. **2** slenderly.

slily. See **sly**.

slim *slim*, *adj.* **1** slender, slight. **2** poor: *a slim chance*:—*comp.* **slimm'er**; *superl.* **slimm'est**—*v.t.* to use certain means (e.g. eating less) to make the figure more slender:—*pr.p.* **slimm'ing**; *pa.p.* **slimmed**.

slimm'ing *n.* **slim'ness** *n.*

slime *slīm*, *n.* **1** fine, thin, slippery mud. **2** wet filth. **3** a secretion (e.g. mucus).

slī'my *adj.* **1** covered with slime. **2** disgustingly meek or flattering:—*comp.* **sli'mier**; *superl.* **sli'miest**.

slī'miness *n.*

sling *sling*, *n.* **1** a strap with a string attached to each end for hurling e.g. a stone. **2** a hanging bandage to support an injured limb. **3** a band, rope net, etc., used in hoisting and lowering or carrying to weight.—*v.t.* **1** to throw with a sling. **2** to move or swing by means of a rope, rope net, etc. **3** (*coll.*) to throw:—*pa.t.*, *pa.p.* **slung**.

sling'-back *n.* a shoe with only a strap at the back.

slink *slingk*, *v.i.* to sneak (away):—*pa.t.*, *pa.p.* **slunk**.

slink'y *adj.* **1** sneaky. **2** close-fitting:—*comp.* **slink'ier**; *superl.* **slink'iest**.

slip[1] *slip*, *v.i.* **1** to slide or glide. **2** to move quietly or secretly. **3** to move out of place, or out of one's grasp: *I let the hammer slip.* **4** to lose one's footing. **5** to make a mistake (often with *up*).—*v.t.* **1** to cause to slide or pass, or to give, quietly or secretly: *to slip on a ring*; *to slip a letter into his hand*; *to slip him money.* **2** to escape (e.g. one's memory, attention):—*pr.p.* **slipp'-ing**; *pa.p.* **slipped**. —*n.* **1** the act of

slipping. **2** a slight error. **3** a garment easily slipped on, esp. under a dress. **4** a pillow cover. **5** (*cricket*) a fielder, or (often in *pl.*) his position, on the offside, somewhat behind the batsman. **6** an artificial slope leading down to water, on which ships are built or repaired (also **slip'way**).
slipp'er *n.* a loose indoor shoe.
slipp'ery *adj.* **1** so smooth as to cause slipping. **2** not to be trusted, shifty.
slipp'eriness *n.*
slip'-knot *n.* a knot that slips along rope or string.
slip road **1** a local bypass. **2** a road by which vehicles come off or on to a motorway.
slip'shod *adj.* **1** having shoes worn away at the heel. **2** (of work, etc.) careless.
slip'stream *n.* the stream of air driven back by an aircraft propeller.
slip'-up (*coll.*) *n.* a mistake or failure.
slipway. See **slip** (*n.*) above.
give someone the slip to escape from (someone) secretly.
let slip to reveal (information) accidentally.
slip off **1** to take off. **2** to move off noiselessly or hastily.
slip on to put on in a hurry.

slip² *slip*, *n.* **1** a cutting from a plant. **2** a young shoot or person. **3** a strip or narrow piece of e.g. paper.

slit *slit*, *v.t.* **1** to make a long cut in. **2** to cut into strips:—*pr.p.* **slitt'ing**; *pa.p.* **slit**.—*n.* a long cut, or narrow opening.

slither *sli*TH'*ėr*, *v.i.* **1** to slide, slip about, as on mud. **2** to walk, move, with gliding motion.

sliver *sliv'ėr*, *slī'*, *n.* a long thin piece cut off.—*v.t.*, *v.i.* to split.

slobber *slob'ėr*, *v.i.* **1** to slaver. **2** to be sentimental.—Also *v.t.* and *n.*
slobb'ery *adj.* unpleasantly moist.

sloe *slō*, *n.* **1** a small sour plum, the fruit of the blackthorn. **2** the blackthorn.

slog *slog*, *v.i.* **1** to hit, or work, hard. **2** to walk on steadily.—*v.t.* **1** to hit hard. **2** to make (one's way) with difficulty:—*pr.p.* **slogg'ing**; *pa.p.* **slogged**.—*n.* **1** a hard blow. **2** (something requiring) a hard spell of work.
slogg'er *n.*

slogan *slō'gȧn*, *n.* **1** a war cry among ancient Highlanders. **2** a catchword, or phrase expressing the view, aim, etc., of e.g. a political party, or one used in advertising.

slogging, etc. See **slog**.

sloop *sloo͞p*, *n.* **1** a light boat. **2** a one-masted sailing-vessel.

slop *slop*, *n.* **1** spilled liquid. **2** (in *pl.*) dirty water. **3** (in *pl.*) thin, tasteless food. **4** gush, sentimentality.—*v.t.*, *v.i.* **1** to spill. **2** to gush.—*v.i.* to walk (through slush, water, etc.):—*pr.p.* **slopp'ing**; *pa.p.* **slopped**.
slopp'y *adj.* **1** wet. **2** muddy. **3** careless, slovenly. **4** very sentimental:—*comp.* **slopp'ier**; *superl.* **slopp'iest**.
slopp'ily *adv.* **slopp'iness** *n.*

slope *slōp*, *n.* **1** an upward or downward slant. **2** a surface with one end higher than the other.—*v.t.* **1** to make with a surface that is not level, not horizontal. **2** to put in a sloping position or direction:—*pr.p.* **slop'ing**.

slopping, **sloppy**, etc. See **slop**.

slosh *slosh*, *v.t.* **1** to splash. **2** (*coll.*) to hit.

slot *slot*, *n.* **1** a narrow opening to receive a coin, or to receive part of a machine, etc. **2** a place or position in a programme, organisation, etc.—*v.t.* **1** to cut a slot in. **2** to fit (in) in a programme, organisation, etc. or in a small space.—Also *v.i.*:—*pr.p.* **slott'ing**; *pa.p.* **slott'ed**.
slot'-machine *n.* a machine, e.g. one containing small articles for sale, worked by putting a coin in a slot.

sloth *slōth*, rarely *sloth*, *n.* **1** laziness, esp. as a habit. **2** a slow-moving animal that lives in trees in South America.
sloth'ful *adj.* **sloth'fully** *adv.*
sloth'fulness *n.*

slouch *slowch*, *n.* a hunched-up loose position of the body in walking.—*v.t.* to move or walk with a slouch.

slough¹ *slow*, *n.* a bog, swamp, marsh.

slough² *sluf*, *n.* the cast-off skin of a snake.—*v.i.* **1** to cast the skin. **2** to come (off).—*v.t.* to cast off.

sloven *sluv'n*, *n.* a person carelessly or dirtily dressed, or slipshod in work.
slov'enly *adj.* **slov'enliness** *n.*

slow *slō*, *adj.* **1** not fast. **2** leisurely. **3** not hasty. **4** (of e.g. a clock) behind in time. **5** not quick at learning. **6** dull, not lively or interesting.—*adv.* slowly.—*v.t.*, *v.i.* (often with *down*, *up*) to make, or become, slower.
slow'ly *adv.* **slow'ness** *n.*
slow'coach *n.* a slow person.
slow'-mo'tion *n.*, *adj.*, *adv.* (speed) much slower than normal, or (in motion-pictures) actual, movement.
go slow deliberately to work more slowly than necessary, as a form of protest (*n.* **go'-slow'**).

sludge *sluj*, *n.* **1** soft mud. **2** slimy sediment.

slug[1] *slug, n.* **1** a heavy, lazy fellow. **2** an animal related to snails but with no shell.
slugg'ard *n.* one who is slow and lazy in habits.
slugg'ish *adj.* **1** lazy, without energy. **2** having little motion or power.

slug[2] *slug, n.* **1** a lump of metal, esp. one for firing from a gun. **2** a bullet. **3** a heavy blow.

sluice *slōōs, n.* **1** an artificial channel for water, provided with a **sluice'gate** (a sliding gate) or other device for controlling the flow. **2** the gate. **3** the water in the channel.—*v.t.* to flood, or clean out, with a flow of water.—*v.i.* to pour:—*pr.p.* **sluic'ing**.

slum *slum, n.* an overcrowded part of a town where living conditions are dirty and unhealthy.

slumber *slum'bėr, v.i.* **1** to sleep, esp. lightly. **2** to be careless or idle.—*n.* light sleep.

slump *slump, v.i.* **1** to fall or sink suddenly into water or mud. **2** to drop limply and heavily. **3** (of stocks, trade, etc.) to lose value suddenly.—*n.* a serious fall of prices, business, etc.

slung. See **sling**.

slunk. See **slink**.

slur *slûr, v.t.* **1** to run down, speak evil of. **2** to pass over lightly so as not to attract attention to: *to slur, or slur over, one's mistakes, the help one has received.* **3** to sound indistinctly: *He slurs his words*:—*pr.p.* **slurr'ing**; *pa.p.* **slurred**.—*n.* **1** a blot or stain (on one's reputation). **2** a remark suggesting that one has this. **3** (*music*) a mark showing that notes are to be sung to the same syllable or played with a smooth gliding effect. **4** a running together of sounds.

slurp *slûrp, v.t.* to drink noisily—Also *v.i.* and *n.*

slush *slush, n.* **1** liquid mud. **2** melting snow. **3** (something said or written showing) weak sentimentality.—*v.t.* to wash by throwing water on.
slush'y *adj.*:—*comp.* **slush'ier**; *superl.* **slush'iest**.
slush'iness *n.*
slush fund, money (*slang*, orig. *U.S.*) a fund of money used secretly, and usu. corruptly, in political campaigning, for bribery, etc.

slut *slut, n.* a dirty, untidy woman.
slutt'ish *adj.*

sly *slī, adj.* **1** (of a person, action, manner, etc.) cunning, crafty, deceitful. **2** playfully mischievous: *a sly reference to his friend's mistake*:—*comp.* **sly'er**, **slī'er**; *superl.* **sly'est**, **slī'est**.
sly'ly *adv.* **sly'ness** *n.*
on the sly secretly.

smack[1] *smak, n.* **1** taste or flavour. **2** a trace.—*v.i.* to have a taste, suggestion (of): *This smacks of treason.*

smack[2] *smak, n.* a small fishing vessel.

smack[3] *smak, v.t.* **1** to strike smartly, slap. **2** to put, etc., with speed and noise. **3** to kiss noisily. **4** to make a noise with (the lips), expressing enjoyment.—Also *n.*—*adv.* with sudden violence: *to run smack into a door.*

small *smöl, adj.* **1** little, not big or much. **2** of little importance: *a small point in an argument.* **3** working, or doing business, etc., with little material, or with little success or influence: *a small tradesman, thief, poet.* **4** (of rain) in fine drops. **5** (of voice) soft. **6** mean, petty: *It was small of him to do that.*—*adv.* into small pieces.—*n.* the slenderest part, esp. of the back.
small arms weapons, esp. firearms, that can be carried by a man.
small beer **1** a weak kind of beer. **2** people of little importance (also **small fry**).
small change coins of little value.
small'-holding *n.* a small farm.
small hours the hours immediately after midnight.
small'-min'ded *adj.* having, or showing, an ungenerous mind with narrow interests and sympathies.
small'pox *n.* a serious disease causing *pocks* or blisters, usu. leaving marks on skin.
small talk light conversation.
small'-time (*slang*) *adj.* unimportant.
feel small to feel that one has made a fool of oneself, or has appeared mean or dishonourable.
in a small way **1** to a small extent. **2** with little money or stock.
look small to appear foolish, or mean or dishonourable.
small wonder (it is) a matter little to be wondered at.
the small print (the part of e.g. an agreement or contract containing) important information printed in small letters so as not to attract attention.

smarmy *smär'mi, (coll.) adj.* obsequious, flattering:—*comp.* **smar'mier**; *superl.* **smar'miest**.

smart *smärt, n.* quick stinging pain.—*v.i.* **1** to feel such a pain. **2** to be punished.—*adj.* **1** sharp and stinging. **2** brisk: *a smart walk.* **3** quick in learning. **4** quick and efficient. **5** witty. **6** trim. **7** well-dressed, fashionable.

smart'ly *adv.* **smart'ness** *n.*
smart'en *v.t.* to make smart(er) (often with *up*; with *up*, also *v.i.*).

smash *smash, v.t.* **1** to shatter, break in pieces. **2** to strike with great force. **3** to ruin.—*v.i.* **1** to fly into pieces. **2** to be ruined. **3** to dash violently (into, against, etc.)—Also *n., adv*.
smash'ing (*coll.*) *adj.* very good.
smash'-and-grab' *adj.* of a theft, involving smashing a shop window and grabbing goods out of it.

smattering *smat'ėr-ing, n.* a very slight knowledge (of a subject).

smear *smēr, v.t.* **1** to spread (something sticky or oily). **2** to spread or smudge (a surface with). **3** to slander (a person or reputation).—*v.i.* to become smeared.—Also *n.*

smell *smel, n.* **1** the sense, located in the nose, that makes us aware of vapours or fine particles arising from substances. **2** an act of using this sense. **3** odour, perfume, scent, fragrance, stink, stench, etc. **4** a suggestion, trace—*v.t.* **1** to notice by using the sense of smell. **2** to use this sense on: *Smell this egg.*—*v.i.* to have an odour:—*pa.t., pa.p.* **smelled, smelt**.
smell'y *adj.* having a bad smell:—*comp.* **smell'ier**; *superl.* **smell'iest**.
smell'iness *n.*
smell'ing-salts *n.pl.* chemicals in a bottle used to revive fainting persons.
smell out to find out by prying.

smelt[1]. See **smell**.

smelt[2] *smelt, n.* a fish of the salmon kind.

smelt[3] *smelt, v.t.* to melt (ore) in order to separate metal from other material.

smile *smīl, v.i.* **1** to express pleasure, amusement, etc., by drawing up the corners of the lips. **2** to look happy. **3** to be favourable: *Fortune smiled on him.*—*v.t.* **1** to express (e.g. approval) by smiling. **2** to give (a smile):—*pr.p.* **smil'ing**.—Also *n.*
smil'ing *adj., n.* **smil'ingly** *adv.*

smirch *smûrch, v.t.* to stain, soil.

smirk *smûrk, v.i.* to put on a conceited or foolish smile.—Also *n.*

smite *smīt, v.t.* to strike, hit hard:—*pr.p.* **smit'ing**; *pa.t.* **smote**; *pa.p.* **smitt'en**.

smith *smith, n.* **1** one who forges with the hammer. **2** a worker in metals.
smith'y (-TH-, *-th-*) *n.* the workshop of a smith:—*pl.* **smith'ies**.

smithereens *smi*TH-*ėr-ēnz'*, (*coll.*) *n.pl.* small fragments, pieces.

smitten. See **smite**.

smock *smok, n.* a shirt-like garment worn over the clothes to protect them.

smog *smog, n. smo*ky f*og*.

smoke *smōk, n.* **1** the cloudlike gases and particles of soot that come off something burning. **2** (*coll.*) a cigar or cigarette. **3** an act of smoking.—*v.i.* **1** to send up, give off, smoke or vapour. **2** to draw in and puff out the smoke of tobacco, etc.—*v.t.* **1** to dry, cure (e.g. ham), darken (e.g. glass), etc., by smoke. **2** to draw in and puff out the smoke from:—*pr.p.* **smo'king**.
smoke'less *adj.* having no smoke.
smo'ker *n.* **1** one who smokes tobacco. **2** a railway carriage, or a concert, etc., in which smoking is allowed.
smo'king *adj.* and *n.*
smo'ky *adj.* **1** giving out smoke. **2** like smoke, e.g. in colour. **3** filled with smoke:—*comp.* **smo'kier**; *superl.* **smo'kiest**.
smo'kily *adv.* **smo'kiness** *n.*
smoke screen **1** a dense cloud of smoke to hide movements or objects from the enemy. **2** anything meant to confuse or conceal.
smoke'stack *n.* a ship's or train's funnel or a factory chimney.
smoke out **1** to drive out by smoke. **2** to force into the open.

smolt *smōlt, n.* a young salmon at the stage when it goes to sea.

smooth *smōō*TH, *adj.* **1** having an even surface. **2** not rough. **3** hairless. **4** without lumps. **5** (of movement—e.g. flow—, speech, etc.) easy, even, without breaks or stops. **6** (of a person, machine, etc.) moving in such a way. **7** deceiving by agreeable manner and speech (also **smooth'-spoken, smooth'-tongued**).—*v.t.* **1** to make smooth. **2** to free from difficulty. **3** to calm, soothe (a person, feelings). **4** to pass (over) quickly: *He smoothed over his own guilt.* **5** (with *over*) to make (difficulties) seem less serious.—*v.i.* to become smooth.—*n.* a smooth part.
smooth'-bore *adj.* (of a firearm) having the bore or inner tube smooth, not rifled.

smote. See **smite**.

smother *smu*TH'*ėr, v.t.* **1** to kill by keeping the air from, esp. by means of a thick covering. **2** to cause to die down or be hidden (e.g. rebellion, grief).—*n.* **1** smoke. **2** thick floating dust.

smoulder *smōl'dėr, v.i.* **1** to burn slowly or without flame. **2** to continue in a hidden state: *The rivalry between them smouldered.* **3** to show suppressed anger, jealousy, etc.: *His eyes smouldered.*

smudge *smuj, n.* a smear.—*v.t.* and *v.i.* to soil with spots or stains:—*pr.p.* **smudg'ing**.
smudg'y *adj.*:—*comp.* **smudg'ier**;

superl. **smudg'iest**.
smudg'ily *adv.* **smudg'iness** *n.*

smug *smug*, *adj.* well satisfied, openly pleased, with oneself:—*comp.* **smugg'er**; *superl.* **smugg'est**.

smuggle *smug'l*, *v.t.* **1** to bring into, or send out from, a country without paying duty. **2** to send or take secretly.—Also *v.i.*:—*pr.p.* **smugg'ling**.
smugg'ler *n.* **1** a person who smuggles. **2** a vessel used in smuggling.
smugg'ling *n.* and *adj.*

smut *smut*, *n.* **1** soot. **2** a spot of dirt. **3** a disease that blackens plants, esp. grasses. **4** obscene jokes or stories, indecent language.—*v.t.* to soil, spot, or blacken with smut:—*pr.p.* **smutt'ing**; *pa.p.* **smutt'ed**.
smutt'y *adj.*:—*comp.* **smutt'ier**; *superl.* **smutt'iest**.
smutt'iness *n.*

snack *snak*, *n.* a light, hasty meal.
snack'-bar *n.* a place where snacks can be bought.

snaffle *snaf'l*, (*coll.*) *v.t.* to take, steal:—*pr.p.* **snaff'ling**.

snag *snag*, *n.* **1** a sharp part left when a branch is broken off. **2** a tree hidden in water, dangerous to boats. **3** a thread on a garment that has caught on something and pulled to form a loop or hole. **4** a difficulty or drawback.—*v.t.*, *v.i.* to catch, or tear, on a snag:—*pr.p.* **snagg'ing**; *pa.p.* **snagged**.

snail *snāl*, *n.* a soft-bodied small crawling animal with a coiled shell.
a snail's pace a very slow speed.

snake *snāk*, *n.* **1** a legless reptile with a long body. **2** anything snake-like in form or movement. **3** a cunning, deceitful person.

snap *snap*, *v.t.* **1** to bite suddenly. **2** to seize (usu. with *up*): *He snapped up the purse, bargains.* **3** to shut, break suddenly, etc., with a sharp sound. **4** to cause (fingers) to make a sharp sound. **5** to bark out, make angrily (a remark, answer). **6** to take a photograph of, esp. with a hand camera.—*v.i.* **1** to make a bite (often with *at*). **2** to grasp (at). **3** to shut, etc., with a sharp noise. **4** to speak sharply.—*n.* **1** the act of snapping, or the noise made by it. **2** a small catch or lock. **3** a sudden spell of cold weather. **4** liveliness, energy. **5** a snapshot:—*pr.p.* **snapp'ing**; *pa.p.* **snapped**.
snapp'ish *adj.* apt to snap or bite, or to speak sharply and irritably.
snapp'y *adj.* **1** snappish. **2** quick or sudden. **3** (*coll.*) smart:—*comp.* **snapp'ier**; *superl.* **snapp'iest**.
snapp'ily *adv.* **snapp'iness** *n.*
snap'dragon *n.* a garden plant whose flower when pinched open and then let go closes up again like a mouth.
snap'shot *n.* a quickly taken photograph.
snap out of it (*coll.*) to improve one's mood, attitude, etc. at once.

snare *snār*, *n.* **1** a running noose of string, etc., for catching an animal. **2** a trap. **3** a trick to catch. **4** a danger or temptation.—*v.t.* to catch in a snare:—*pr.p.* **snar'ing**.

snarl[1] *snärl*, *v.i.* **1** to make an angry noise with show of teeth. **2** to speak in a sharp quarrelsome manner.—Also *v.t.* and *n.*

snarl[2] *snärl*, *v.t.*, *v.i.* to tangle.—*n.* **1** a knot. **2** a difficult state, condition.

snatch *snach*, *v.t.* **1** to seize suddenly. **2** to pull away quickly (from). **3** to take as the opportunity occurs: *He managed to snatch an hour's sleep.*—*v.i.* to try suddenly or eagerly to take (with *at*): *He snatched at the rope, the offered help.*—*n.* **1** an attempt to seize. **2** a small piece (e.g. of music), or small quantity.

sneak *snēk*, *v.i.* **1** to creep or steal (off, away, about, etc.) meanly. **2** to behave meanly. **3** to tell tales, inform.—*v.t.* **1** to take or give secretly. **2** to steal.—*n.* **1** a deceitful, underhand person. **2** a telltale.
sneak'ers *n.pl.* soft-soled shoes.
sneak'ing *adj.* **1** mean, underhand. **2** not told openly: *I have a sneaking hope, sympathy*, etc. **3** which one is aware of in a corner of one's mind: *a sneaking feeling, suspicion.*
sneak'y **1** mean, underhand. **2** (*coll.*) cunning, clever: — *comp.* **sneak'ier**; *superl.* **sneak'iest**.
sneak'iness *n.*
sneak thief a thief who gets in through an unlocked door, open window, etc.

sneer *snēr*, *v.i.* to show contempt by scornful expression of the face, jeering tone of voice, or harsh words.—Also *n.*

sneeze *snēz*, *v.i.* to blow out air suddenly, involuntarily, and violently through the nose:—*pr.p.* **sneez'ing**.—Also *n.*
not to be sneezed at not to be treated as unimportant.

snick *snik*, *v.t.* to cut, snip, nick.—*n.* a small cut or nick.

snicker. Same as **snigger**.

snide *snīd*, *adj.* **1** not sincere. **2** superior in attitude. **3** sneering: *a snide remark.* **4** mean: *a snide trick.*

sniff *snif*, *v.i.* **1** to draw in air through the nose with a slight noise. **2** to smell a scent. **3** (with *at*) to treat with suspicion or scorn.—Also *v.t.* and *n.*
sniff'le *v.i.* to give frequent little sniffs,

as when one is crying or has a cold:—*pr.p.* **sniff'ling**.—Also *n.*

snigger *snig'ėr*, *v.i.* to laugh in a half-hidden sly way, e.g. at someone's embarrassment or pain.—Also *n.*

snip *snip*, *v.t.* to cut off sharply, esp. with a single cut of the scissors:—*pr.p.* **snipp'ing**; *pa.p.* **snipped**.—*n.* **1** a cut with scissors. **2** a small shred. **3** a certainty.
snipp'et *n.* a little piece.

snipe *snīp*, *n.* a bird with a long straight bill, found in marshy places.—*v.i.* to shoot from a place of hiding (at single enemies):—*pr.p.* **snip'ing**.
snip'er *n.* **snip'ing** *n.*

snippet, etc. See **snip**.

snivel *sniv'l*, *v.i.* **1** to run at the nose. **2** to whine, complain, tearfully:—*pr.p.* **sniv'elling**; *pa.p.* **sniv'elled**.—*n.* **1** cowardly, or pretended, weeping. **2** a sniff. **3** mucus of the nose.

snob *snob*, *n.* one who admires people of high rank, social class, etc. and looks down on those he considers inferior.
snobb'ish *adj.* **snobb'ishly** *adv.*
snobb'ishness, **snobb'ery** *ns.*

snooker *snōō'kėr*, *n.* a game played on a billiard table, in which coloured balls are knocked into pockets round the table.

snoop *snōōp*, *v.i.* to spy or pry in a sneaking manner.

snooty *snōōt'i*, *adj.* haughty and supercilious:—*comp.* **snoot'ier**; *superl.* **snoot'iest**.

snooze *snōōz*, *v.i.* to doze, sleep lightly:—*pr.p.* **snooz'ing**.—*n.* a nap.

snore *snōr*, *snör*, *v.i.* to breathe roughly and hoarsely in sleep:—*pr.p.* **snor'ing**.—Also *n.*

snorkel *snör'kėl*, *n.* tube(s) with end(s) above water for bringing air to underwater swimmer or submarine.—Also **snort**, **schnorkel**.

snort[1] *snört*, *v.i.* **1** to force air noisily through the nostrils, as horses do. **2** to make a similar noise, esp. to show disapproval.—*v.t.* to utter with a snort.—Also *n.*

snort[2]. See **snorkel**.

snot *snot*, *n.* mucus of the nose.
snott'y *adj.* **1** stand-offish, with nose in the air. **2** dirty with snot:—*comp.* **snott'ier**; *superl.* **snott'iest**.

snout *snowt*, *n.* the sticking-out nose part of an animal, esp. of a pig.

snow *snō*, *n.* **1** frozen water vapour which falls in light, white crystals or flakes. **2** a fall, or a layer, of these flakes.—*v.i.*, *v.t.* to shower down in, or like, flakes of snow.
snow'y *adj.* **1** covered with snow. **2** white like snow. **3** pure:—*comp.* **snow'ier**; *superl.* **snow'iest**.
snow'iness *n.*
snow'ball *n.* **1** a ball made of snow pressed hard together. **2** something that grows rapidly as does a snowball rolled in snow.—*v.t.* to pelt with snowballs.—*v.i.* **1** to throw snowballs. **2** to grow greater more and more quickly.
snow'bound *adj.* kept in one place by heavy snow.
snow'-capped *adj.* with tops covered in snow.
snow'drift *n.* a bank of snow blown together by the wind.
snow'drop *n.* a small white flower growing from a bulb in early spring.
snow'fall *n.* a fall of snow.
snow'flake *n.* a flake of snow.
snow'line *n.* the line on a mountain above which there is always snow.
snow'man *n.* a human figure made out of snow.
snow'-plough *n.* a machine for clearing snow from roads and railways.
snow'shoe *n.* a strung frame, one of a pair put on the feet to allow one to walk on snow without sinking.
snow'storm *n.* a storm with falling snow.
snowed up blocked by, or cut off by, snow.
snow under to cover, bury, as if with snow: *We are absolutely snowed under with work*.

snub *snub*, *v.t.* **1** to check or stop, esp. by a cutting remark. **2** to insult, treat scornfully.—*pr.p.* **snubb'ing**; *pa.p.* **snubbed**.—*n.* an act of snubbing.—*adj.* (of a nose) short and slightly turned up at the end.

snuff[1] *snuf*, *v.i.* **1** to sniff. **2** to use snuff.—*v.t.* to discover by smelling.—*n.* **1** powdered tobacco to be taken up into the nose. **2** a pinch of this. **3** a sniff.
snuff'box *n.* a box for holding snuff.

snuff[2] *snuf*, *n.* the burnt portion of a wick of a candle or lamp.—*v.t.* to nip off the burnt portion of a wick.
snuff it (*slang*) to die.
snuff out **1** to put, or go, out. **2** to put a sudden end to, or come to a sudden end: *The rebellion was snuffed out*.

snuffle *snuf'l*, *v.i.* to breathe heavily, or to speak, through the nose:—*pr.p.* **snuff'ling**.—*n.* **1** an act or sound of snuffling. **2** (in *pl.*) a blocked-up state of the nose.

snug *snug*, *adj.* **1** lying close and warm. **2** in hiding. **3** (of a house, room, etc.) cosy, comfortable. **4** neat and trim. **5** comfortably large: *a snug income*:—*comp.*

snugg'er; *superl.* **snugg'est.**
snug'ly *adv.* **snug'ness** *n.*
snugg'le *v.i.* to nestle:—*pr.p.* **snugg'-ling.**

so *sō*, *adv.* **1** in this or that way: *You must do it so.* **2** as stated: *Is it really so?* **3** as shown: *He held his hands about two feet apart, saying 'It is so big'.* **4** to a great, or too great, extent or degree: *It is so heavy that I cannot lift it.*—*conj.* therefore: *He did not come back, so I left.*
so'-and-so *n.* **1** this or that person or thing. **2** a person or thing one despises or is annoyed by:—*pl.* **so'-and-sos.**
so'-called *adj.* named or described thus, usu. in the speaker's opinion wrongly: *a so-called artist, bargain.*
so'-so' *adj.* neither very good nor very bad.—Also *adv.*
just so in order: *He liked everything to be just so.*
or so or about that number or amount: *six or so.*
so as in order (to).
so far to a certain degree, point, or time: *The result is so far satisfactory, satisfactory so far.*
so forth more of the same.
so much for that is the end of.
so that **1** with the purpose that. **2** with the result that.
so to speak if one may use that expression.
so what? does it matter?

soak *sōk*, *v.t.* **1** to let stand in a liquid until wet through and through. **2** to drench (with). **3** to draw in through pores, suck (up). **4** (*slang*) to beat. **5** (*slang*) to overcharge.
soak'ing *n.* and *adj.*—Also *adv.*: *soaking wet.*

so-and-so. See **so**.

soap *sōp*, *n.* a mixture containing oils, fats, and salts, used in washing.—*v.t.* to rub with soap.
soap'y *adj.* **1** like soap. **2** covered with soap. **3** too fond of flattering:—*comp.* **soap'ier**; *superl.* **soap'iest.**
soap'iness *n.*
soap'box *n.* **1** a box for packing soap. **2** a makeshift platform for a person addressing a crowd out of doors.
soap opera a sentimental, melodramatic radio or television serial.
soap'stone *n.* See **French chalk**.
soap'-suds *n. pl.* soapy water, esp. when worked into a froth.

soar *sōr*, *sör*, *v.i.* **1** to fly high into the air. **2** to rise high: *Prices, hopes, soared.*

sob *sob*, *v.i.* **1** to catch the breadth in distress, weep noisily. **2** (of e.g. the wind) to make a noise like this.—*v.t.* to utter with sobs:—*pr.p.* **sobb'ing**; *pa.p.* **sobbed.**—Also *n.*
sob'-story *n.* a story intended to arouse sympathy:—*pl.* **sob'-stories.**
sob'-stuff *n.* a story, scenes in a play, etc., intended to draw tears.

sober *sō'bėr*, *adj.* **1** not drunk. **2** not overdone, excessive, or too emotional: *a sober description, estimate.* **3** serious in mind. **4** quiet in colour.—*v.t.*, *v.i.* (also with *up*) to make, or become, sober.
so'berness, sobrī'ety *ns.*

so-called. See **so**.

soccer. See **association**.

sociable *sō'shȧ-bl*, *adj.* **1** fond of, and friendly in, the company of others. **2** (of an action, etc.) showing this spirit.
sociabil'ity, so'ciableness *ns.*
so'ciably *adv.*
social *sō'sh(ȧ)l*, *adj.* **1** having to do with society in any sense. **2** having to do with the rules, arrangements, and habits of a community or group: *the social life of a savage tribe, or bees.* **3** having to do with the welfare of people in a community: *She did social work in the slums.* **4** having to do with rank or class: *They were not social equals.* **5** growing or living in societies: *social insects.* **6** having to do with friendly companionship: *He spent a social evening with his family.* **7** sociable.—*n.* a gathering of members of a group for entertainment, etc.
so'cially *adv.*
so'cialise *v.i.* to talk sociably to people at a gathering:—*pr.p.* **so'cialising.**
so'cialism *n.* **1** the belief that a country's wealth (its land, mines, industries, railways, etc.) should belong to the people as a whole, not to private owners. **2** a system in which the state controls the country's wealth.
so'cialist *n.* a believer in socialism.
society *sȯ-sī'i-ti*, *n.* **1** the system of living together as a group, not as separate individuals. **2** a body of people who live in this way—mankind as a whole, or a smaller community. **3** (also **high society**) the class of people who have rank and/or wealth. **4** a group of people joined for a purpose: *a dramatic society.* **5** companionship: *I enjoy the society of young people.*—*pl.* **soci'eties.**
sociology *sō-si-ol'ȯ-ji*, *n.* the science which studies man as a member of human groups, the everyday life of people, and their culture.
sociol'ogist *n.*
social democracy the practices and policies of socialists who believe that

socialism can and should be achieved by democratic means.

social insurance insurance against unemployment, etc., in which the government plays a part.

social security the principle or practice of providing social insurance.

social service **1** welfare work (also in *pl.*). **2** (in *pl.*) the public bodies carrying out such work.

social worker one whose job involves social work (see **social** *def.* 3).

sock[1] *sok, n.* a short stocking.

sock[2] *sok, (coll.) v.t.* to hit hard.—Also *n.*

socket *sok'it, n.* a hollow or hole(s) into which something is fitted.

sod *sod, n.* a piece of earth with grass growing on it, a turf.

soda *sō'dȧ, n.* **1** washing soda (**sodium carbonate**, a salt, in crystal form, of sodium). **2** baking soda (**sodium bicarbonate**). **3** soda water. **4** a drink containing soda water, flavouring, etc.

sodium *sō'di-ŭm, n.* an element, a soft silvery metal that forms compounds such as salt (*sodium chloride*), washing soda, and baking soda.

soda fountain a counter where soda water and iced drinks are sold.

soda water a fizzing liquid containing carbon dioxide gas under pressure (formerly made with baking soda).

caustic soda a compound of sodium, oxygen and hydrogen, a powerful cleaning agent.

sodden. See **seethe**.

sodium. See **soda**.

sofa *sō'fȧ, n.* a long seat with stuffed bottom, and with back and end(s).

soft *soft, adj.* **1** not hard or firm. **2** easily put out of shape when pressed. **3** not strict enough. **4** weak in mind. **5** weak in muscle. **6** pleasing to the touch. **7** not loud: *a soft voice.* **8** (of colour) not glaring. **9** not hard in outline. **10** (of a drink) not alcoholic. **11** (of water) free from certain salts. **12** (of *c* or *g*) pronounced as in *city, gentle.*—*adv.* gently, quietly.

soften *sof'n, v.t., v.i.* to make, or become, soft or softer, or less hardy or strong.—*v.t.* to make less painful: *to soften the blow.*

soft'ly *adv.* **soft'ness** *n.*

soft'ball *n.* a game similar to baseball, played with a larger, softer ball which is pitched underarm.

soft'-boiled *adj.* of an egg, not boiled long enough to be completely hard.

soft furnishings curtains, rugs, etc.

soft goods cloth, cloth articles, etc.

soft'-heart'ed *adj.* kind-hearted, generous, sympathetic.

soft option an easier, less demanding, alternative.

soft'-soap' *v.t.* to speak flatteringly and persuasively to (someone).

soft'-spoken *adj.* having, or in, a gentle voice or manner.

soft spot an affection (for).

soft'ware *n.* in computers, programmes, etc.

soft'wood *n.* the soft timber of a cone-bearing, quick-growing tree (e.g. fir).

soggy *sog'i, adj.* **1** very wet. **2** damp and heavy:—*comp.* **sogg'ier**; *superl.* **sogg'iest**.

soigné, soignée (*fem.*), *swä-nyā, adj.* very well groomed, carefully dressed.

soil[1] *soil, n.* **1** the upper layer of the earth in which plants grow. **2** loose earth. **3** the earth of a country: *on Irish soil.*

soil[2] *soil, n.* **1** dirt. **2** sewage. **3** a spot or stain.—*v.t., v.i.* **1** to dirty. **2** to stain.

soirée *swär'ā, swor'ā, n.* an evening social meeting with tea, etc.

sojourn *so', sō'jŭrn, v.i.* to stay for a time.—*n.* a temporary stay.

solace *sol'ȧs, n.* **1** something that makes pain or sorrow easier to bear. **2** comfort in distress.—*v.t.* **1** to comfort. **2** to amuse (oneself). **3** to soothe: *to solace grief*:—*pr.p.* **sol'acing**.

solan (goose) *sō'lȧn (gōōs), n.* the gannet.

solar *sō'lȧr, adj.* **1** having to do with the sun. **2** influenced by the sun.

solar energy energy got from the sun's rays, e.g. by means of **solar panels** comprising a number of **solar cells** which convert the energy of sunlight into electricity.

solar plexus *(plek'sŭs)* an area in the abdomen.

solar system the sun with the planets (earth, etc.) moving round it.

sold. See **sell**.

solder *sol'dėr, sōl'dėr, n.* **1** a metal or alloy which can be melted and used to join metal surfaces. **2** something that unites.—*v.t.* **1** to join (esp. two metals) with solder, etc. **2** to mend, patch (up).

sol'dering-iron *n.* a tool which when heated is used to melt and apply solder.

soldier *sōl'jėr, n.* **1** a man or woman in military service. **2** a private, not an officer.—*v.i.* to serve as a soldier.

sol'dierly *adj.* like a soldier.

soldier of fortune one ready to serve under any flag if there is a good chance of pay or advancement.

soldier on to continue doggedly despite difficulties.

sole[1] *sōl*, *n.* **1** the underside of the foot. **2** the bottom of a boot or shoe. **3** the bottom, under surface, of anything.—*v.t.* to put a sole on (e.g. a shoe):—*pr.p.* **sol'ing**.

sole[2] *sōl*, *n.* a small flat fish with small twisted mouth.

sole[3] *sōl*, *adj.* (used only before a noun). **1** only: *the sole heir.* **2** acting without another: *the sole author of the plot.* **3** not shared, belonging to one person or group only: *the sole right to decide.*

sole'ly *adv.* **1** only. **2** merely.

solecism *sol'ė-sizm*, *n.* a bad mistake (in writing, speaking, manners).

solely. See **sole**[3].

solemn *sol'ėm*, *adj.* **1** carried out with special (esp. religious) ceremonies. **2** (of an oath) made with an appeal to God. **3** serious and earnest. **4** awed. **5** awe-inspiring, wonderful. **6** gloomy, sombre: *Black is a solemn colour.* **7** stately.

solem'nity *n.* **1** solemnness. **2** a solemn ceremony or rite:—*pl.* **solem'nities**.

sol'emnise *v.t.* to perform with religious ceremonies (e.g. a marriage):—*pr.p.* **sol'emnising**.

sol'emnly *adv.* **sol'emnness** *n.*

sol-fa *sol'fä'*, *n.* (*music*) a system of syllables to be sung to the notes of the major scale (*do, re, me, fa, so (l), la, ti, do*).

solicit *sȯ-lis'it*, *v.t.* **1** to ask earnestly for (something): *to solicit a favour.* **2** to ask (a person for something).—Also *v.i.* (esp. of prostitutes).

solicitā'tion *n.*

solic'itor *n.* **1** one who asks earnestly. **2** one who is legally qualified to act for another in a court of law—a lawyer who prepares deeds, manages cases, etc.

solic'itous *adj.* **1** asking earnestly. **2** very anxious (about, for).

solic'itude *n.* anxiety or uneasiness of mind esp. if more than necessary: *her solicitude about my health.*

solid *sol'id*, *adj.* **1** not easily changing shape, not in the form of a liquid or gas. **2** having length, breadth, and height. **3** full of matter, not hollow. **4** hard, firm, or strongly made. **5** dense-looking. **6** completely of one substance: *solid silver.* **7** real, geninue, good: *solid arguments.* **8** sound in finances: *a solid business man.* **9** reliable. **10** without any variation or break, esp. if providing much information: *a pretty solid book.* **11** (*coll.*) without a break in time: *five solid hours.*—*n.* **1** a substance that is solid. **2** a figure that has three dimensions.

solidar'ity *n.* a firm union of interests, feelings, actions (of e.g. a group).

solid'ify *v.t.*, *v.i.* **1** to make, or become, solid. **2** to harden:—*pr.p.* **solid'ifying**; *pa.p.* **solid'ified**.

solidificā'tion *n.*

solidity, sol'idness *ns.*

soliloquy *so-*, *sȯ-lil'ȯ-kwi*, *n.* **1** talking to oneself. **2** a speech to oneself, esp. on the stage:—*pl.* **solil'oquies**.

solil'oquise *v.i.* to speak to oneself:—*pr.p.* **solil'oquising**.

solitaire *sol-i-tār'*, *n.* **1** a gem, esp. a diamond, set by itself. **2** a game one person can play, esp. with balls or pegs on a board.

solitary *sol'i-tȧr-i*, *adj.* **1** alone, without companions. **2** living, or growing, alone. **3** (of a place) remote, lonely. **4** single: *not a solitary example.*—*n.* **1** one who lives alone. **2** a hermit:—*pl.* **sol'itaries**.

solitude *sol'i-tūd*, *n.* **1** the state of being alone. **2** lack of company. **3** a lonely place.

solitary confinement confinement of a prisoner alone in a cell.

solo *sō'lō*, *n.* **1** a musical piece for one voice or instrument. **2** anything (e.g. a song, aeroplane flight) in which only one takes part:—*pl.* **so'los**.—*adj.* **1** performed as a solo. **2** for one.—*v.i.* to fly alone.

so'loist *n.* one who plays or sings a solo.

solstice *sol'stis*, *n.* the time of longest daylight (*summer solstice*, about June 21) or longest darkness (*winter solstice*, about December 21).

soluble *sol'ū-bl*, *adj.* **1** able to be dissolved or made liquid. **2** (of a problem, difficulty) solvable:—*opp.* **insoluble**.

solubil'ity *n.*

solu'tion *-ōō'* or *-ū'*, *n.* **1** the act of dissolving. **2** a liquid with something dissolved in it. **3** an act of discovering an answer to a problem or difficulty. **4** the answer found.

solve *solv*, *v.t.* **1** to discover the answer to. **2** to clear up, explain (a mystery). **3** to find a way round, out of (a difficulty):—*pr.p.* **sol'ving**.

sol'vable *adj.* able to be solved.

sol'vency *n.* the state of being solvent or able to pay all debts.

sol'vent *adj.* able to pay all debts:—*opp.* **insolvent**.—*n.* anything that dissolves another substance.

solvent abuse the inhaling of the fumes given off by glue, etc. for their intoxicating effect.

solve, solvent, etc. See **soluble**.

sombre *som'bėr*, *adj.* **1** dark. **2** gloomy, dismal.
som'brely *(-bėr-) adv.* **som'breness** *n.*

sombrero *som-brā'rō*, *n.* a broad-brimmed hat, usu. of felt:—*pl.* **sombre'ros**.

some *sum*, *sủm*, *adj.* **1** several. **2** a few. **3** a little. **4** certain: *Some people are superstitious.* **5** (*coll.*, esp. *U.S.*) excellent.—*pron.* **1** a number or part out of a larger number or quantity: *The sweets are*, or *the cake is*, *good*; *do take some.* **2** certain people: *Some believed him.*
some'body *pron.* someone.
some'how *adv.* in some way or other.
some'one *pron.* **1** some person. **2** a person of importance.
some'thing *pron.* **1** a thing not known, or not stated: *He had left something behind.* **2** a thing of importance. **3** (referring to character or quality) a suggestion, small degree (of): *There is something of his father in him*; *He is something of a poet.*
some'time *adv.* at a time not definitely known or stated: *He went*, or *will go*, *sometime in the spring.*
some'times *adv.* on some occasions.
some'what *pron.* something: *He is somewhat of a bore.*—*adv.* rather, a little: *He is somewhat sad.*
some'where *adv.* in some place.

somersault *sum'ėr-sölt*, *n.* a leap in which a person turns with his heels over his head.—Also *v.i.*

somnambulist *som-nam'bū-list*, *n.* a sleepwalker.
somnolence *som'nọ-lėns*, *n.* sleepiness.
som'nolent *adj.* **1** sleepy. **2** drowsy.

son *sun*, *n.* **1** a male child. **2** a native or inhabitant: *a son of Italy.*
son'-in-law *n.* one's daughter's husband:—*pl.* **sons'-in-law**.

sonata *sọ-nä'tȧ*, *n.* a piece of music with three or more movements, usu. for one instrument.

son et lumiere *son ā loom'yėr*, a dramatic show, with lighting effects, music, etc., given after dark with e.g. a famous building as scene.

song *song*, *n.* **1** something (to be) sung. **2** singing. **3** the notes of a bird. **4** a poem or poetry in general. **5** a mere trifle: *He bought the lamp for a song.*
song'ster *n.* a singer:—*fem.* **song'stress**.
song'bird *n.* a bird that sings.

sonic *son'ik*, *adj.* having to do with, or using, sound waves.
sonic bang, boom (*flying*) a loud noise caused by shock waves from an aeroplane flying faster than the speed of sound.

sonnet *son'it*, *n.* a poem of fourteen lines with rhymes arranged in a particular way (e.g. *abbaabba cdcdcd*).

sonorous *sọ-nō'rủs*, *-nö'*, *adj.* **1** giving out a deep sound when struck. **2** (of sound, voice) deep, resonant. **3** high-sounding: *sonorous phrases.*
son'orousness, sonor'ity *ns.*

soon *so͞on*, *adv.* **1** immediately or in a short time. **2** early: *Can you come as soon as that?* **3** willingly: *I would as soon go as stay, sooner go than stay.*
sooner or later eventually, at some time.

soot *soot*, *n.* the black powder left by smoke from burning coal, etc.
soot'y *adj.*:—*comp.* **soot'ier**; *superl.* **soot'iest**.
soot'iness *n.*

soothe *so͞oTH*, *v.t.* **1** to calm, comfort, quiet (a person, feelings). **2** to ease (pain):—*pr.p.* **sooth'ing**.
sooth'ing *adj.* **sooth'ingly** *adv.*

soothsayer *so͞oth'sā-ėr*, *n.* one who can, or pretends to, tell the future.

sop *sop*, *n.* **1** bread or other food dipped in liquid. **2** something given to quiet or bribe.—*v.t.* **1** to dip in liquid. **2** to suck or mop (up):—*pr.p.* **sopp'ing**; *pa.p.* **sopped**.
sopp'ing *adj.* soaking wet.—Also *adv.*
sopp'y *adj.* **1** very wet. **2** foolishly sentimental:—*comp.* **sopp'ier**; *superl.* **sopp'iest**.

sophisticate *sọ-fis'ti-kāt*, *v.t.* **1** to take away the simple and natural qualities of. **2** to make worldly-wise by education or experience. **3** to make (e.g. one's tastes) those of a person of worldly experience. **4** to adulterate (e.g. wine). **5** to make (e.g. a machine, machinery) more elaborate and efficient or (a car) more luxurious:—*pr.p.* **sophis'ticating**.
sophis'ticated *adj.* **sophisticā'tion** *n.*

soporific *sō-pọr-if'ik*, *sop-*, *adj.* causing sleep.—*n.* something that causes sleep.

sopping, etc. See **sop**.

soprano *sọ-prä'nō*, *n.* **1** a singing voice of the highest pitch. **2** a singer with such a voice:—*pl.* **sopra'nos**:—Also *adj.*

sorbet *sör'bėt*, *-bā*, *n.* **1** sherbet. **2** water-ice.

sorcery *sör'sėr-i*, *n.* **1** the use of power gained from evil spirits. **2** magic.
sor'cerer *n.*:—*fem.* **sor'ceress**.

sordid *sör'did*, *adj.* **1** (of a place, etc.) dirty, mean, poor. **2** (of actions, etc.) showing low standards or ideals. **3** (of e.g. motives) selfish, mercenary.

sore *sōr*, *sör*, *n.* **1** a painful injured or diseased spot. **2** an ulcer or boil. **3** a cause of pain or grief.—*adj.* **1** painful. **2** suffering pain. **3** irritated or offended. **4** causing irritation or pain of mind.

sore'ly *adv.* **1** painfully. **2** very greatly: *sorely in need of new shoes.*

sore'ness *n.*

sorrel[1] *sor'ėl*, *n.* a plant with sour-tasting leaves.

sorrel[2] *sor'ėl*, *adj.* reddish-brown.—*n.* **1** a reddish-brown colour. **2** a sorrel horse.

sorrow *sor'ō*, *n.* **1** pain of mind, grief. **2** a trouble, misfortune.—*v.i.* to feel sorrow, grieve, mourn (for).

sorr'owful *adj.* **sorr'owfully** *adv.*

sorr'owfulness *n.*

See also **sorry**.

sorry *sor'i*, *adj.* **1** feeling sorrow (much or little) because of some action or happening: *sorry for my sins, that I mislaid the book.* **2** feeling pity or sympathy (for): *sorry for her, for his loss.* **3** poor, worthless: *He proved to be a sorry friend.* **4** miserable, unhappy: *a sorry state of affairs*:—*comp.* **sorr'ier**; *superl.* **sorr'iest**.

sorr'iness *n.*

See also **sorrow**.

sort *sört*, *n.* **1** a class or kind: *people of this sort.* **2** something like but not exactly: *wearing a sort of crown.*—*v.t.* **1** to separate into classes or groups. **2** to pick (out), choose. **3** (*coll.*; usu. with *out*) to deal with, punish.

sor'ter *n.* one who separates and arranges, esp. letters.

in some sort **1** in a way. **2** to some extent.

of a sort, of sorts of a rather poor kind.

out of sorts **1** slightly unwell. **2** not in good spirits or temper.

sortie *sör'tē*, *n.* a sudden attack by the defenders of a place against those who are trying to take it.

SOS *es'ō'es'*, a code signal calling for help (in Morse . . . — — — . . .).—*n.* any signal of distress or call for help.—Also *v.t., v.i.*

so-so. See **so**.

sot *sot*, *n.* a man continually drunk.

sott'ish *adj.* **1** foolish. **2** stupid with drink.

sotto voce *sot'ō vō'chi*, *adv.* in a low voice, so as not to be heard.

soufflé *sōō'flā*, *n.* a light dish, made with white of egg whisked into a froth.

sought. See **seek**.

soul *sōl*, *n.* **1** the innermost being of a person, the part which thinks, feels, desires, etc. **2** nobleness of mind. **3** the moving spirit or leader. **4** a person: *a wonderful old soul.* **5** a perfect example (of): *He is the soul of honour.* **5** (also **soul music**) a type of music that has its roots in Black urban rhythm and blues.

soul'ful *adj.* full of feeling.

soul'less *adj.* **1** without fine feeling or nobleness. **2** (of life, a task) dull, petty.

soul'-destroying *adj.* (of a job, etc.) very monotonous, giving little pleasure or profit, etc.

soul mate a person who shares the same feelings, tastes etc. as someone else.

soul'-searching *n.* a critical examination of one's own conscience, motives, etc.

sound[1] *sownd*, *adj.* **1** healthy. **2** in good condition. **3** (of sleep) deep. **4** (of e.g. a thrashing) thorough. **5** (of reasoning) free from mistake. **6** trustworthy. **7** good in quality. **8** showing good sense: *sound advice.*—*adv.* soundly (only in *to sleep sound* and *sound asleep*).

sound'ly *adv.* **sound'ness** *n.*

sound[2] *sownd*, *n.* a narrow passage of water connecting e.g. two seas.

sound[3] *sownd*, *n.* **1** the sensation of hearing. **2** something that is heard, esp. a musical tone or an element of speech. **3** mere noise. **4** hearing distance: *within sound of Bow Bells.*—*v.i.* **1** to give out a sound. **2** to be able to be heard. **3** to seem to be: *That sounds like a train*; *It sounds like an attempt at blackmail.*—*v.t.* **1** to cause to make a sound. **2** to make the sound of: *Sound the letter h.* **3** to express loudly: *to sound his praises.* **4** to examine by listening carefully: *to sound the patient's chest.*

sound'ing *adj.* **1** giving a sound, esp. a deep one. **2** (as part of a word) having a sound, or giving an impression, of a particular kind (see **high-sounding**).

sound barrier difficulty in increasing speed which an aeroplane meets when flying near the speed of sound.

sound'board *n.* a thin plate of wood that increases sound in a musical instrument.

sound effects sounds other than words or music in plays, etc., e.g. wind, footsteps.

sound'proof *adj.* not allowing sound to pass in, out, through.—*v.t.* to make soundproof.

sound'-track *n.* **1** the strip on which the sounds for a motion picture are recorded. **2** a recording of the sound accompaniment, esp. the music, of a film.

sound[4] *sownd*, *v.t.* **1** to measure the depth of (water, etc.). **2** to measure (the depth). **3** (often with *out*) to try to find out the thoughts and plans of (a person). **4** (often with *out*) to try to find out (views, opinions).—*v.i.* **1** to take soundings. **2** (of a whale) to dive deep.

sound'ing *n.* **1** the act of measuring depth, finding out views, etc. **2** a measured depth.

sound'ing-line *n.* a line with a weight (lead, plummet) at the end for measuring depth.

sound the depth of to experience the greatest degree of (e.g. misery).

sounding[1,2]. See **sound**[3,4].

soup *sōōp*, *n.* a liquid food, made by boiling meat, vegetables, etc., together.

in the soup (*coll.*) in trouble.

sour *sowr*, *adj.* **1** having an acid taste or smell, sometimes as a stage in going bad. **2** peevish, discontented, bitter. **3** (of soil) cold and wet.—*v.t.*, *v.i.* to make, or become, sour.

source *sōrs*, *sörs*, *n.* **1** a spring of water, esp. the beginning of a stream. **2** a place, circumstance, thing, person, etc., from which anything begins or comes: *the source of our meat supply*, *of the trouble*, *of the story*.

souse *sows*, *v.t.* **1** to plunge into water or other liquid. **2** to steep in pickle:—*pr.p.* **sous'ing**.

south *sowth*, *n.* **1** the part of the heavens in which the sun is seen at noon in Britain, etc. **2** a territory in that direction.—Also *adj.* and *adv*.

southerly *su*TH*'ėr-li*, *adj.* **1** towards the south: *in a southerly direction*. **2** (of wind) south.

south'ern *(su*TH*')*, *adj.* of, or towards, the south.

south'erner *(su*TH*')*, *n.* a person living in the south.

south'ward *adv.* towards the south.—Also *adj.*

south'-east' (**south'-west'**) *n.* the direction halfway between south and east (south and west).—Also *adj.*

south-east'er (**south'-west'er**) *n.* a wind blowing from south-east (south-west).

south pole **1** the end of the earth's axis in Antarctica. **2** the south-seeking pole of a magnet.

south wind wind from the south.

sou'west'er *n.* **1** a south-wester. **2** a waterproof hat with a flap at the back of the neck.

souvenir *sōō'vė-nēr*, *-nēr'*, *n.* an object kept to help in remembering a place, person, occasion.

sou'wester. See under **south**.

sovereign *sov'rin*, *adj.* supreme, absolute: *our sovereign lord, the King*; *sovereign power.* **2** (of a state) self-governing. **3** (of a remedy) very effective. **4** extreme: *sovereign contempt*.—*n.* **1** a king or queen. **2** a former gold coin worth £1.

sov'ereignty *n.* highest power.

soviet *sō'vi-et*, *-et'* or *sov'*, *n.* a council, esp. a governing one in the former Soviet Union.—*adj.* (*cap.*) of the former Soviet Union.

sow[1] *sow*, *n.* a female pig.

sow[2] *sō*, *v.t.* **1** to scatter (seed) over, or put (seed) in, the ground. **2** to plant seed over (land). **3** to spread (e.g. trouble).—Also *v.i.*:—*pa.t.* **sowed**; *pa.p.* **sown** or **sowed**.

soya bean, **soy bean** *soi' (ȧ) bēn*, a type of bean grown in Japan, China, etc.

soy(a) sauce a sauce made from fermented soya beans and flour.

spa *spä*, *n.* a place where there is a mineral spring.

space *spās*, *n.* **1** the boundless region about the earth containing all heavenly bodies and all material objects. **2** a part of this, esp. (**outer space**) the part far distant from the earth. **3** room. **4** an open or empty place. **5** a distance between objects. **6** a length of time: *in the space of a day*.—*v.t.* to set (things) apart from each other (also **space out**):—*pr.p.* **spa'cing**.

spa'cing *n.*

spa'cious *(-shůs) adj.* with plenty of room.

spa'ciously *adv.* **spa'ciousness** *n.*

spatial *spā'sh(ȧ)l*, *adj.* having to do with space.

space capsule a self-contained (part of a) spacecraft.

space'craft *n.* a device, manned or unmanned, for journeying in space.

Space Invaders® a game played on an electronic machine with a screen, involving, 'shooting' at figures representing supposed invaders from outer space.

space'man *n.* a traveller in space.

space probe an unmanned spacecraft that is designed to study conditions in space and to transmit the information it gathers back to Earth.

space'ship *n.* a manned spacecraft.

space'-shuttle *n.* a spacecraft designed to transport men and materials to and from space-stations.

space'-station *n.* a satellite to be used as a landing-stage in space travel.

space travel travel in space far from the earth's surface.

spade[1] *spād*, *n.* a tool with a broad blade and handle, used for digging.

spade'work *n.* hard work, esp. in getting a plan ready to be carried out.
call a spade a spade to speak plainly, not softening anything by using vague or inoffensive words.

spade[2] *spād, n.* a playing-card of one of the four suits, distinguished by a black leaf-shaped mark.

spaghetti *spȧ-get'i, n.* an Italian food paste in long solid cords.

span[1] *span, n.* **1** the space from the tip of the thumb to the tip of the little finger when the hand is spread out. **2** nine inches. **3** the distance from wing-tip to wing-tip in an aeroplane. **4** an arch of a bridge between supports. **5** the full time anything lasts.—*v.t.* **1** to measure by spans, etc. **2** to stretch across: *A bridge spans the river*:—*pr.p.* **spann'ing**; *pa.p.* **spanned.**

span[2] *span, n.* a pair of horses or a team of oxen.—*v.t.* to yoke:—*pr.p.* **spann'ing**; *pa.p.* **spanned.**

spangle *spang'gl, n.* a thin glittering piece of metal used as an ornament on a garment.—*v.i.* to glitter.—*v.t.* to sprinkle with spangles, or with small bright objects:—*pr.p.* **spang'ling.**

Spaniard *span'yȧrd, n.* a native of *Spain.*
Span'ish *adj.* having to do with Spain.—*n.* the people or language of Spain.

spaniel *span'yėl, n.* a kind of dog of Spanish origin, with large hanging ears.

Spanish. See **Spaniard.**

spank[1] *spangk, v.i., v.t.* to move, walk, or drive (along) with speed.

spank[2] *spangk, v.t.* to strike with the flat of the hand, to smack.—*n.* a loud slap, esp. on the buttocks.
spank'ing *n.* a series of spanks.

spanner *span'ėr, n.* the tool for tightening or loosening nuts, screws, etc.
a spanner in the works something intended to cause difficulties, stop something happening, etc.

spar[1] *spär, n.* **1** a rafter. **2** a pole. **3** a ship's mast, yard, etc.

spar[2] *spär, v.i.* **1** to fight with the fists. **2** to argue, dispute:—*pr.p.* **sparr'ing**; *pa.p.* **sparred.**

spare *spār, v.t.* **1** to use in small amounts, or little, or not at all: *In trying to reach this result, spare no effort, expense, etc.*; *'Spare the rod and spoil the child' is an old proverb.* **2** to do without: *I cannot spare her today.* **3** to afford: *Try to spare time for it.* **4** to treat with mercy. **5** to refrain from putting to death, injuring, etc. **6** to avoid causing (trouble, etc.) to (a person):—*pr.p.* **spar'ing.**—*adj.* **1** scanty: *a spare allowance of food.* **2** thin: *a spare man.* **3** extra, not actually being used.—*n.* **1** a spare part. **2** another of the same kind kept for emergencies.
spare'ly *adv.* **spare'ness** *n.*
spar'ing *adj.* careful, economical: *Be sparing in your use of pepper.*
spar'ingly *adv.*
spare part a duplicate part of a machine kept for emergencies.
spare time time when one is free to do as one pleases.
to spare over and above what is needed: *He has money and to spare.*

spark *spärk, n.* **1** a small red-hot particle thrown off by something burning. **2** an electric flash across a gap. **3** a trace (e.g. of life, humour). **4** a lively fellow.—*v.i.* to throw off sparks.
spark'ing-plug, spark'-plug *ns.* a device in a motor-car engine that produces a spark to set on fire the explosive gases.
sparkle *spärk'l, n.* **1** a little spark. **2** liveliness or brightness. **3** bubbling, as in wines.—*v.i.* **1** to shine, glitter. **2** to bubble. **3** to be lively or witty:—*pr.p.* **spark'ling.**
spark off to cause to begin: *His casual remark sparked off a bitter row.*

sparrow *spar'ō, n.* a small dull-coloured bird.
sparr'owhawk *n.* a short-winged hawk.

sparse *spärs, adj.* **1** thinly scattered. **2** scanty.

Spartan *spär'tȧn, adj.* (also no *cap.*) **1** (of a person) enduring bravely. **2** (of conditions of life) hard, without luxury.

spasm *spazm, n.* **1** a sudden jerk of the muscles which one cannot prevent. **2** a strong short burst (of e.g. anger, work).
spasmod'ic *adj.* that comes in bursts, stops and starts again: *He made a spasmodic attempt, spasmodic efforts.*
spasmod'ically *adv.*
spastic *(spas') adj.* having to do with a spasm.—*n.* one suffering from spastic paralysis.
spastic paralysis a form of paralysis resulting from an injury to the part of the brain that controls the muscles.

spat. See **spit.**

spate *spāt,* (orig. *Scot.*) *n.* a flood.

spatial. See **space.**

spatter *spat'ėr, v.t.* **1** to scatter, sprinkle (e.g. mud). **2** to splash (something) with mud, liquid, etc.—*n.* **1** the act of spattering. **2** what is spattered.

spatula *spat'ū-lȧ, n.* an implement with broad blunt blade.

spawn *spön, n.* **1** a mass of eggs of fishes, frogs, etc. **2** brood, offspring. **3** material from which mushrooms are grown.—*v.i.* to produce spawn.—*v.t.* **1** to produce (something worthless) in large quantities. **2** to give rise to.

spay *spā*, *v.t.* to remove or destroy the ovaries of: *Has your cat been spayed?*

speak *spēk*, *v.i.* **1** to utter words. **2** to talk. **3** to hold a conversation (with). **4** to make a speech. **5** to be evidence (of): *His success speaks of careful planning.*—*v.t.* **1** to be able to talk in: *He speaks Russian.* **2** to tell, make known: *to speak one's thoughts, the truth.* **3** to utter: *You speak sense.* **4** (of a ship) to hail (another):—*pa.t.* **spoke** *(spōk)*; *pa.p.* **spo'ken**.

speak'er *n.* **1** one who speaks. **2** (*cap.*) the person who presides over meetings of the House of Commons, etc.

speak'ing *n.* and *adj.*

spokes'man *n.* one who speaks for another or others.

so to speak if one might express it this way.

speak out, up **1** to speak clearly and sufficiently loudly. **2** to say boldly what one thinks.

speak to **1** to talk with. **2** to scold. **3** to discuss, explain, talk in support of (a proposal).

speak well for **1** to be a credit to: *The exhibition speaks well for the city.* **2** to lead one to expect good from (the future).

to speak of worth mentioning.

See also **speech**.

spear *spēr*, *n.* **1** a long weapon used in war and hunting, with a point on the end. **2** a barbed implement for catching fish. **3** a shoot (e.g. of grass).—*v.t.* to pierce or kill with a spear.

spear'head *n.* the foremost part of an attacking force.

spec *spek*: **on spec** on the chance, but without any certainty, of achieving or gaining anything.

special *spesh'(ȧ)l*, *adj.* **1** out of the ordinary, exceptional: *a special occasion.* **2** greater than ordinary: *with special care*; *a special friend.* **3** belonging to, or limited to, one person or thing: *The party needs his special talents*; *my own special chair*; *a newspaper's special correspondent.* **4** appointed, put on, etc. for a particular purpose: *a special messenger, train.* **5** additional to the ordinary: *a special edition of a newspaper.* (*Special* is now more common than *especial*; for cases in which *especial* can still be used, see this word.) —*n.* a special train, etc.

spec'ialise *v.i.* to give one's attention to, work in, a single branch of study or business:—*pr.p.* **spec'ialising**.

specialisā'tion *n.*

spec'ialised *adj.* (of knowledge) of the accurate, detailed kind obtained by specialising.

spec'ialist *n.* one who specialises.

speciality *spesh-i-al'i-ti*, **specialty** *spesh'ȧl-ti*, *ns.* **1** a special activity, or subject about which one has special knowledge. **2** a special product: *Brown bread is this baker's speciality, specialty*:—*pls.* **-ies**.

spec'ially *adv.*

Special Branch a British police department which deals with political security.

specie *spē'shi*, *n.* coin, as opposed to paper money.

species *spē'shēz*, *spē'shiz*, *n.* **1** a group of plants, or of animals, alike in certain ways. **2** a kind or sort.

specify *spes'i-fī*, *v.t.* **1** to make particular, definite, mention of. **2** to name in an agreement as a necessary condition or a thing required:—*pr.p.* **spec'ifying**; *pa.p.* **spec'ified**.

specif'ic *adj.* definite, explicit.

specif'ically *adv.*

specificā'tion *n.* **1** the act of specifying. **2** a thing specified. **3** a statement containing all the details of e.g. a building plan or a contract.

specimen *spes'i-mėn*, *n.* something used as a sample of a whole or group, esp. an object to be studied or to be put in a collection: *to look at specimens under the microscope.*

specious *spē'shus*, *adj.* **1** looking well at first sight or on the surface but really not good: *a specious claim, argument.* **2** false.

speck *spek*, *n.* **1** a small spot. **2** a tiny piece (e.g. of dust).

speckle *spek'l*, *n.* a little spot.

speck'led *adj.* marked with speckles.

specs. See **spectacle**.

spectacle *spek'tȧ-kl*, *n.* **1** a sight, esp. one that is very striking. **2** a play, etc., with scenery, dressing, etc., on a grand scale. **3** (in *pl.*) glasses worn to help the eyesight (*coll.* short form **specs**).

spectacular *(-tak'ū-lȧr)* *adj.* **1** making a great show. **2** dramatic.

spectator *(-tā'tȯr)* *n.* one who looks on.

spectra. See **spectrum**.

spectre *spek'tėr*, *n.* a ghost.

spec'tral *adj.* ghostly, like a ghost.

spectroscope. See **spectrum**.

spectrum *spek'trum*, *n.* **1** the band of colours as seen in the rainbow, produced when white light is split up by going through a prism (see this word), etc. **2** a

wide range, variety:—*pls.* **spectra**, **-ums**.
spec'troscope *n.* an instrument for forming and viewing spectra.

speculate *spek'ū-lāt*, *v.i.* **1** to think, make guesses, about (with *about*, *on*). **2** to buy and sell shares etc., with hope of a profit and risk of a loss:—*pr.p.* **spec'-ulating**.
speculā'tion *n.* **1** the act of speculating. **2** a conclusion, guess. **3** a risky investment of money for the sake of profits.
spec'ulative *adj.* **1** having to do with speculation. **2** inclined to indulge in speculation.
spec'ulator *n.*

sped. See **speed**.

speech *spēch*, *n.* **1** the power of speaking. **2** language. **3** a way of speaking. **4** words spoken. **5** a formal talk given to a meeting, etc.
speech'less *adj.* unable to speak, often because of surprise.
speech day a day at the end of a school year when speeches are made and prizes are given out.
speech therapy the treatment of speech and language defects caused by illness, etc.

speed *spēd*, *n.* **1** quickness of moving. **2** rate of motion.—*v.i.* **1** to move quickly, hurry. **2** to drive at high, or too high, speed.—*v.t.* **1** to cause to go with speed. **2** to help the success of (an undertaking). **3** to send (a person on his way) with good wishes:—*pa.p.* **sped**, (chiefly *v.i.*, *def. 2*) **speed'ed**.
speed'ing *n.* driving at high, or dangerously or illegally high, speed.
speedom'eter *n.* an instrument for measuring speed.
speed'y *adj.* **1** swift. **2** prompt:—*comp.* **speed'ier**; *superl.* **speed'iest**.
speed'ily *adv.* **speed'iness** *n.*
speed'-boat *n.* a very fast motor-boat.
speed limit the greatest speed permitted on a particular road.
speed trap a stretch of road where police measure the speed of vehicles.
speed'way *n.* **1** a road for fast traffic. **2** a motor-cycle racing track. **3** the sport of motor-cycle racing.
speed'well *n.* a small plant with blue flowers.
speed up **1** to become quicker. **2** to quicken the rate of:—*pa.t.* **speeded up** (*n.* **speed'-up**).

spell[1] *spel*, *n.* **1** a charm, words that are supposed to have magic power. **2** the influence of magic or other strong influence: *The witch cast a spell, put a spell on him.*
spell'-bound *adj.* fascinated, charmed, held in wonder.

spell[2] *spel*, *v.t.* **1** to name or give in order the letters of (a word). **2** (of letters) to form (a word). **3** to mean, amount to: *This spells disaster.* **4** to read slowly, letter by letter.—*v.i.* to spell words, esp. correctly:—*pr.p.* **spell'ing**; *pa.p.* **spelled**, **spelt**.
spell out **1** to spell (a word). **2** to be very specific in explaining something.

spell[3] *spel*, *n.* **1** a turn at work. **2** a short time. **3** a stretch of time.

spelt. See **spell**[2].

spencer *spens'ėr*, *n.* a short jacket reaching to the waist.

spend *spend*, *v.t.* **1** to pay out (money). **2** to give (e.g. energy, thought) to any purpose (with *on*). **3** to use up, wear out: *The storm will spend itself, its force.* **4** to pass (time): *He will spend a week in Spain.*—*v.i.* to use up or pay out money:—*pa.t.* and *pa.p.* **spent**.
spent *adj.* **1** exhausted. **2** with power gone: *a spent bullet*.
spendthrift *spend'thrift*, *n.* one who spends money freely and carelessly.

sperm *spûrm*, *n.* **1** semen. **2** one of the male seed-cells in semen:—*pl.* **sperms**, **sperm**.

spew *spū*, *v.t.*, *v.i.* to vomit.

sphere *sfēr*, *n.* **1** a solid body with a surface on which all points are an equal distance from the centre; a globe; a ball. **2** a star or planet. **3** (**celestial sphere**) what looks like the hollow sphere of the heavens in the inside of which the stars seem to be placed. **4** a group in society: *He moves in the highest spheres.* **5** range of activity or influence: *the western sphere of influence.*
spherical *sfer'i-kȧl*, *adj.*

Sphinx *sfingks*, *n.* **1** a monster of old Egyptian and Greek story that asked travellers riddles and strangled those who could not solve them. **2** (without *cap.*) a puzzling person whose thoughts one cannot guess.

spice *spīs*, *n.* **1** a strong-smelling, sharp-tasting vegetable substance used to season food (e.g. pepper, nutmeg). **2** anything that adds liveliness or interest. **3** a smack, flavour: *a remark with a spice of malice.*—*v.t.* **1** to season with spice. **2** to give variety or liveliness to (often with *up*):—*pr.p.* **spic'ing**.
spicy *spī'si*, *adj.* **1** tasting or smelling of spices. **2** lively, sometimes with a touch of indecency:—*comp.* **spi'cier**; *superl.* **spi'-ciest**.
spi'ciness *n.*

spick and span *spik' and span'*, neat and trim and spotless.

spicy. See **spice**.

spider *spī'dėr*, *n.* a small creature with body in two sections, eight legs, and no wings, which spins a web to catch flies.
spi'dery *adj.* **1** spider-like. **2** sprawling and thin: *spidery handwriting*.
spi'deriness *n.*

spiel *spēl*, *shpēl*, *n.* a long story, esp. to persuade e.g. to buy.

spigot *spig'ȯt*, *n.* **1** a small pointed peg or plug, esp. for a cask. **2** (*U.S.*) a tap, faucet.

spike[1] *spīk*, *n.* **1** an ear of corn. **2** a head of flowers.

spike[2] *spīk*, *n.* **1** a hard, thin, pointed object. **2** a large nail. **3** a pointed piece of metal e.g. on the sole of a shoe to prevent slipping.—*v.t.* **1** to fasten, set, or pierce, with a spike or spikes. **2** to make (a gun) useless, formerly by driving a spike into the opening through which fire was passed to the explosive:—*pr.p.* **spik'ing**.
spiked *adj.* having spikes.
spik'y *adj.*:—*comp.* **spik'ier**; *superl.* **spik'iest**.
spik'iness *n.*

spill[1] *spil*, *n.* a thin strip of wood or twisted paper for lighting a pipe, etc.

spill[2] *spil*, *v.t.* **1** to allow (liquid, etc.) to run out or overflow. **2** to shed (blood). **3** to cause or allow to fall to the ground.—Also *v.i.*:—*pa.t.* and *pa.p.* **spilled**, **spilt**.—*n.* a fall, tumble.
spill the beans (*coll.*) to give information, esp. without meaning to.

spin *spin*, *v.t.* **1** to draw out (wool, etc.) and twist into thread. **2** to shape (e.g. glass) into threadlike form. **3** to make by spinning. **4** to draw out as a thread, as spiders do. **5** to twirl rapidly. **6** to hurl.—*v.i.* **1** to work at the trade of, or perform the act of, spinning. **2** to whirl. **3** to go swiftly, esp. on wheels:—*pr.p.* **spinn'ing**; *pa.t.*, *pa.p.* **spun**.—*n.* **1** a whirling or turning motion. **2** a cycle ride or short trip in a car. **3** a spurt at high speed. **4** the movement of an aircraft in a steep turning dive.
spinn'er *n.* **spinn'ing** *n.*, *adj.*
spin'-dri'er, **-dry'er** *n.* a machine which takes water out of washed articles by whirling them round.
spinn'ing-wheel *n.* a machine for spinning yarn, a wheel moved by hand, or by a foot treadle, which drives spindle(s).
spin'-off *n.* a by-product, something deriving from (the production of) something else.
spin a yarn to tell a long story, esp. one that is not true.
spin out to make last a long time.

spina bifida *spī'nȧ bif'i-dȧ* a congenital defect in which the two parts of the spinal column have not united along the middle vertical line.

spinach *spin'ij*, *-ich*, *n.* a plant whose young leaves are boiled as a vegetable.

spinal. See **spine**.

spindle *spin'dl*, *n.* **1** the pin by which thread is twisted in spinning. **2** a pin on which anything turns. **3** anything very slender.
spin'dly *adj.* very long and slender, esp. if lacking strength:—*comp.* **spin'dlier**; *superl.* **spin'dliest**.
spin'dliness *n.*

spindrift *spin'drift*, *n.* the spray blown from the crests of waves.

spine *spīn*, *n.* **1** a thorn. **2** a thin, stiff, pointed part growing on an animal. **3** the backbone of an animal. **4** a ridge. **5** the edge of a book opposite the open edge, joining the front and back covers.
spin'al *adj.* of the backbone.
spine'less *adj.* **1** having no spine. **2** weak, not able to make a firm stand.
spī'ny *adj.* **1** full of spines. **2** thorny:—*comp.* **spi'nier**; *superl.* **spi'niest**.
spinal cord a cord of nerve tissue running up through the backbone, and forming the most important part of the central nervous system.
spine'-chilling *adj.* frightening.

spinet *spin'et*, *n.* a small harpsichord.

spinner. See **spin**.

spinney *spin'i*, *n.* a small clump of trees:—*pl.* **spinn'eys**.

spinning. See **spin**.

spinster *spin'stėr*, *n.* **1** an unmarried woman. **2** an old maid.

spiral *spī'rȧl*, *adj.* **1** winding round and round, getting always farther and farther away from a centre. **2** helical (see this word), like the thread of a screw.—*n.* **1** a spiral line or object. **2** a spiral course. **3** an increase or decrease, rise or fall, getting ever more and more rapid (e.g. in prices or in the value of money).—*v.i.* to go or move in a spiral:—*pr.p.* **spi'ralling**; *pa.p.* **spi'ralled**.
spir'ally *adv.*

spire *spīr*, *n.* **1** an object (e.g. a treetop) which tapers to a point. **2** a tapering structure on a roof or steeple, esp. of a church. **3** a steeple.

spirit *spir'it*, *n.* **1** the soul. **2** a being without body. **3** a ghost. **4** a principle or emotion that makes a person act: *the spirit of reform*, *of rivalry*. **5** (usu. in *pl.*) mood: *in good*, *low*, *spirits*. **6** liveliness. **7** courage, boldness: *He acted with spirit.* **8** a lively or courageous person. **9** the real meaning: *the spirit of the law.* **10** a liquid obtained by distillation or cracking. **11** a strong distilled alcoholic drink (esp. whisky or brandy).—*v.t.* to carry secretly, as if by magic.

spir'ited *adj.* full of courage or liveliness: *a spirited attack, description.*

spir'itless *adj.* without liveliness, courage, etc.

spir'itual *adj.* **1** having to do with the spirit or soul. **2** having to do with the church.—*n.* an American Negro hymn with a strong rhythm.

spir'itually *adv.* **spiritual'ity** *n.*

spir'itualism *n.* the belief that the spirits of the dead can talk to living people esp. through certain other people (mediums) who are specially sensitive.

spir'itualist *n.* one who believes in spiritualism.

in (or **out of**) **spirits** feeling cheerful (or the reverse).

spirt. Same as **spurt**.

spit¹ *spit, n.* **1** an iron bar on which meat is roasted. **2** a long narrow strip of land or sand jutting into the sea.—*v.t.* to stab with something sharp:—*pr.p.* **spitt'ing**; *pa.p.* **spitt'ed**.

spit² *spit, v.t.* **1** to throw out from the mouth. **2** to send out with force.—*v.i.* **1** to throw out saliva from the mouth. **2** to rain in scattered drops. **3** to make a spitting sound, as an angry cat does:—*pr.p.* **spitt'ing**; *pa.p.* **spat**.—*n.* **1** spittle. **2** a light fall of rain or snow. **3** (*coll.*) exact likeness: *the very spit of him.*

spitt'le *n.* spit, saliva, the liquid that forms in the mouth.

spit'fire *n.* a hot-tempered person.

spite *spīt, n.* grudge, ill-will, desire to hurt.—*v.t.* to annoy, thwart, out of spite:—*pr.p.* **spīt'ing**.

spite'ful *adj.* showing spite or desire to hurt.

spite'fully *adv.* **spite'fulness** *n.*

in spite of 1 in defiance of: *He went in spite of his father's orders.* **2** although such-and-such had occurred, or is or was fact, etc.: *In spite of the rain that had fallen, the ground was still dry.*

spitfire, spittle. See **spit²**.

spitting. See **spit¹,²**.

splash *splash, v.t.* **1** to spatter with liquid or mud. **2** to throw (about, e.g. liquid). **3** to display, or print, in a place, or in type, that will be noticed.—*v.t.* **1** to dash liquid about. **2** to fall, or move, with splash(es).—*n.* **1** a scattering of liquid, or the noise of this. **2** a wet or dirty mark. **3** a bright patch: *a splash of colour.* **4** display, publicity. **5** a sensation.

splash'y wet and muddy:—*comp.* **splash'ier**; *superl.* **splash'iest**.

splash'down *n.* the landing of a spacecraft in the sea.

splatter. Same as **spatter**.

splay *splā, v.t.* to turn out at an angle.—*n.* a slant of the side of a doorway or window.

spleen *splēn, n.* **1** a spongy organ of the body, close to the stomach. **2** ill-humour, bad-temper.

splenet'ic *(spli-) adj.* irritable, sullen, spiteful.

splendid *splen'did, adj.* **1** brilliant, magnificent, very rich and grand. **2** (*coll.*) very good or fine.

splen'didly *adv.*

splen'dour, splen'didness *ns.*

splenetic. See **spleen**.

splice *splīs, v.t.* **1** to join (two ends of a rope) by weaving the threads together. **2** to join together (two pieces of timber) by overlapping:—*pr.p.* **splic'ing**.—Also *n.*

splint *splint, n.* a piece of wood, etc., used to keep a broken arm or leg in its proper position.

splint'er *n.* a small sharp piece of wood, etc., broken off.—*v.t., v.i.* to split into splinters.

splinter group a group formed by breaking away from a larger group.

split *split, v.t.* **1** to cut or break lengthwise. **2** to break in pieces. **3** to divide into parts. **4** (of a disagreement) to divide, disunite (people).—*v.i.* **1** to be broken apart, or in pieces. **2** to be divided or separated. **3** (*coll.*) to let out secret(s):—*pr.p.* **splitt'ing**; *pa.p.* **split**.—*n.* **1** a crack, break, rent, division, separation. **2** (usu. in *pl.*) the feat of going down to the floor with one leg forward and the other back.

splitt'ing *adj.* **1** cutting. **2** very bad: *a splitting headache.*

split hairs. See **hair**.

split infinitive an infinitive with an adverb between 'to' and the verb (e.g. *Be sure to carefully dry it*).

split personality a mental disease in which the sufferer has two or more personalities, with different attitudes and types of conduct.

split second a fraction of a second.

split one's sides to shake violently with laughter.

split up 1 to split, divide. **2** to part from one another, break off a relationship.

splurge *splûrj, v.i.* (often with *out*) to spend a lot of money (on):—*pr.p.* **splur'ging**.

splutter *splut'ėr*, *v.i.* **1** to scatter liquid with spitting noises. **2** to speak quickly and in a confused way because of excitement, anger, etc.—Also *v.t.*

spoil *spoil*, *v.t.* **1** to take valuables away from by force, plunder. **2** to damage or ruin. **3** to give (esp. a child) too much of what he or she wants, or to make his, her, character, behaviour, worse by doing so.—*v.i.* to decay, become bad:—*pa.t.*, *pa.p.* **spoiled**, (not *v.t. def. 1*) **spoilt**.—*n.* **1** plunder. **2** (in *pl.*) profits.
spoliation *spō-li-ā'sh(ȯ)n*, *n.* plundering.
spoil'sport *n.* someone who prevents others enjoying themselves.
spoiling for eager for: *He was spoiling for a fight.*

spoke[1] *spōk*, *n.* one of the ribs or bars from the centre to the rim of a wheel, etc.
put a spoke in someone's wheel to put a difficulty in someone's way.

spoke[2], **spoken**, **spokesman**. See **speak**.

spoliation. See **spoil**.

sponge *spunj*, *n.* **1** a sea animal, or its soft skeleton which has many pores and is able to suck up and hold water. **2** a piece of such a skeleton, or a substitute, used for washing, etc. **3** a sponge pudding or cake. **4** one who lives at the expense of others, a parasite. **5** a drunkard.—*v.t.* to wipe, soak (up), remove, with sponge.—*v.i.* to get a living, things one wants, from others (with *off*, *on*):—*pr.p.* **spon'ging**.
spong'er *n.* one who lives on others.
spongy *spun'ji*, *adj.* **1** like a sponge. **2** porous, with holes. **3** wet and soft:—*comp.* **spon'gier**; *superl.* **spon'giest**.
spon'giness *n.*
sponge cake, pudding a very light one of flour, eggs, and sugar, etc.
throw up, in, the sponge to give up the fight, admit defeat.

sponsor *spon'sȯr*, *n.* **1** one who gives his word that another will do something, act in a certain way. **2** a godfather or godmother. **3** one who makes himself responsible for e.g. the introduction of a law. **4** (*U.S.*) a business firm that pays for a radio or television programme and is allowed time to advertise. **5** one who agrees to contribute towards the costs of an event, etc., or to a charity if someone else performs some task.—Also *v.t.*

spontaneous *spon-tā'ni-ȯs*, *-tān'yȯs*, *adj.* **1** said, done, etc., of one's free-will. **2** natural, impulsive: *She has a spontaneous manner.* **3** occurring naturally: *a spontaneous growth of trees.*
sponta'neously *adv.*
sponta'neousness, **spontane'ity** *(-nē')*, *ns.*

spoof *spōōf*, (*slang*) *n.* a trick, hoax.—Also *v.t.*, *v.i.* and *adj.*

spook *spōōk*, *n.* a ghost.
spook'y *adj.*:—*comp.* **spook'ier**; *superl.* **spook'iest**.
spook'iness *n.*

spool *spōōl*, *n.* a bobbin, reel, holder, on which thread, photograph film, etc. is wound.

spoon *spōōn*, *n.* **1** an instrument, with a shallow bowl and a handle, for lifting food to the mouth. **2** a wooden-headed golf club.—*v.t.* **1** to lift with a spoon. **2** to scoop (up).—*v.i.* to make love in a sentimental way.
spoon'ful *n.* **1** as much as fills a spoon. **2** a small amount:—*pl.* **spoon'fuls**.
spoon'-feed *v.t.* **1** to feed with a spoon. **2** to pamper. **3** to teach (a person) in a way that does not allow or require him to think for himself.
spoon'-feed'ing *n.* **spoon'-fed'** *adj.*

spoonerism *spōō'nė-rizm*, *n.* a slip that changes the position of first sounds of words (e.g. 'shoving leopard' for 'loving shepherd').

spoor *spōōr*, *n.* footprints or tracks, esp. of a hunted animal.

sporadic *spȯ-rad'ik*, *adj.* happening here and there, or now and again.
sporad'ically *adv.*

spore *spōr*, *spör*, *n.* the tiny seedlike body from which ferns, etc., grow.

sporran *spor'ȧn*, *n.* a pouch worn in front of the kilt.

sport *spōrt*, *spört*, *v.i.* **1** to play, gambol. **2** to make merry. **3** to trifle (with).—*v.t.* to wear in public: *to sport a new tie.*—*n.* **1** a pastime, amusement. **2** a game, or games, or a contest, in which the body is exercised (e.g. football, athletics). **3** fishing, hunting, etc. **4** a person who has sportsmanlike qualities. **5** jest: *I said it in sport.* **6** one who is laughed at. **7** one who is tossed about like a plaything: *the sport of the wind, of Fortune.*
sport'ing *adj.* having to do with, or taking part in, sports, or in sports involving betting.
sport'ive *adj.* playful, merry.
sport'y *adj.* **1** particularly good at or fond of sport. **2** (of clothes) casual. **3** (of a car) like a sports car.
sports car a car, usu. for two, designed to run at high speeds on roads.
sports jacket a man's jacket, usu. of tweed, for casual wear.
sports'man *n.* **1** one who hunts, fishes, etc. **2** one who takes part in athletic sports. **3** one who shows a good spirit in

sport. **4** one ready to win or lose with good grace:—*fem.* **sports'woman.**
sports'manlike *adj.* **sports'manship** *n.*
sporting chance as good a chance of success as of failure.

spot *spot, n.* **1** a mark made by a drop of grease, paint, etc. **2** a stain. **3** a small, usu. round, part of a different colour. **4** a pimple. **5** a place, small area: *a shady spot.* **6** the exact place: *the spot where the bomb fell.* **7** a spotlight.—*v.t.* **1** to mark with spots. **2** to stain (a reputation). **3** (*coll.*) to catch sight of, see, recognise.—*v.i.* to become marked with spots:—*pr.p.* **spott'ing**; *pa.p.* **spott'ed.**
spot'less *adj.* **1** without a spot. **2** pure.
spott'ed, spott'y (*comp.* **-ier**; *superl.* **-iest**), *adjs.* marked, covered, etc., with spots.
spott'iness *n.*
spott'er *n.* one who keeps on the watch for something.
spot check 1 a check done without warning. **2** a check done on samples taken at random.
spot'light *n.* a circle of light that is thrown on an actor or on a small part of the stage.—*v.t.* **1** to show up with (*pa.p.* **spot'lit**). **2** to draw attention to (*pa.p.* **spot'lighted**).
in a spot in trouble.
on the spot 1 at once. **2** in the very place referred to or required. **3** (*slang*) in a dangerous, difficult, or embarrassing, position. **4** alert, ready to act.
spot on (*coll.*) exactly right.

spouse *spowz, spows, n.* a husband or wife.

spout *spowt, v.i., v.t.* **1** to throw out e.g. water in a jet. **2** to blow, as a whale. **3** to talk, or utter, a lot, or loudly and dramatically.—*n.* **1** a mouth such as that of a kettle or teapot. **2** a jet or strong flow of e.g. water. **3** the blowhole of a whale.

sprain *sprān, v.t.* to wrench (a joint, e.g. the ankle) tearing or stretching ligaments.—Also *n.*

sprang. See **spring**.

sprat *sprat, n.* a small fish somewhat like the herring.

sprawl *spröl, v.i.* **1** to stretch the body carelessly, when sitting or lying. **2** (of e.g. writing, vines, buildings) to spread widely in an irregular way.—Also *v.t.* and *n.*

spray[1] *sprā, n.* **1** a cloud of small flying drops. **2** an instrument for sending it out.—*v.t.* to sprinkle with, or to squirt in, mist-like jets.

spray[2] *sprā, n.* **1** a shoot or twig spreading out in branches or flowers. **2** flowers or other ornament in a similar form.

spread *spred, v.t.* **1** to cause to go more widely or more thinly over a surface: *to spread jam.* **2** to open out (e.g. one's arms, a map). **3** to scatter, distribute over a region, time, etc.: *to spread the population*; *to spread the meetings over several days.* **4** to send about, give to others (news, disease, etc.). **5** to coat, cover (a surface with something).—*v.i.* to run, scatter, be distributed, etc.:—*pa.t., pa.p.* **spread** *(spred).*—*n.* **1** the act of spreading. **2** the space covered, extent of spreading. **3** a meal (esp. large) laid out. **4** a cover for a bed or a table. **5** anything for spreading on bread.
spread'-eagled *adj.* with arms and legs spread out.

spree *sprē, n.* a reckless bout of merrymaking, drinking, or spending.

sprig *sprig, n.* **1** a small shoot or twig. **2** a young person.
sprigged *adj.* with a design of sprigs.

sprightly *sprīt'li, adj.* lively, brisk, gay:—*comp.* **spright'lier**; *superl.* **spright'liest.**
spright'liness *n.*

spring *spring, v.i.* **1** to move, start up, suddenly. **2** to leap, jump. **3** to fly (back) as a piece of stretched elastic when let go. **4** to appear, arise: *Water springs from the ground*; *Industries spring up.* **5** to come, result, from: *His energy springs from good health.*—*v.t.* **1** to leap over. **2** to cause (a mine, trap) to go off. **3** to produce suddenly (with *on*): *to spring a surprise on someone.* **4** to put springs in:—*pa.t.* **sprang**; *pa.p.* **sprung.**—*n.* **1** a leap. **2** a sudden movement. **3** the ability to stretch and fly back again. **4** bounce, energy: *He has a spring in his step.* **5** a coil of e.g. wire for setting in motion or reducing shocks: *a watch spring*; *car springs.* **6** a source, cause (of life or action). **7** a small stream flowing out from the ground. **8** (often *cap.*) the season when plants begin to grow.—*adj.* **1** having, or run by, spring(s). **2** (often *cap.*) of, appearing in, or used in, the season of Spring.
spring'er *n.* a kind of spaniel.
spring'y *adj.* having spring, elastic, bounding:—*comp.* **spring'ier**; *superl.* **spring'iest.**
spring'iness *n.*
sprung *adj.* **1** (of wood) split, cracked. **2** (of e.g. sinew) strained.
spring'board *n.* a board from which to take off in vaulting, etc., or in diving.
spring'bok *n.* **1** a South African antelope. **2** (*cap.*) a South African, esp. in sport.
spring cleaning a thorough house-cleaning, esp. in Spring.

spring onion a type of onion whose small bulb and long leaves are eaten raw in salads.
spring tide the very high tide when the moon is full or new.
spring'time (or *cap.*) *n.* the season of Spring.
spring a leak to begin to leak.

sprinkle *spring'kl, v.t.* **1** to scatter in small drops or pieces. **2** to put here and there. **3** to scatter (with):—*pr.p.* **sprink'ling.**—Also *v.i.* and *n.*
sprink'ler *n.*
sprink'ling *n.* **1** a small quantity sprinkled. **2** a small number: *a sprinkling of people.*

sprint *sprint, n.* a short run, row, or race at full speed.—Also *v.i.*
sprin'ter *n.*

sprite *sprīt, n.* an elf, fairy, or impish person.

sprocket *sprok'it, n.* one of a set of teeth on the rim of a wheel that fit into the links of a chain.

sprout *sprowt, n.* **1** a young shoot or bud. **2** a Brussels sprout.—*v.i.* **1** to push out new shoots. **2** to begin to grow.—Also *v.t.*

spruce[1] *sprōōs, adj.* neat, smart.—*v.t., v.i.* (with *up*) to make, become, smarter:—*pr.p.* **spruc'ing.**

spruce[2] *sprōōs, n.* **1** a kind of fir tree, an evergreen with hanging cones. **2** the wood from the spruce fir.

sprung. See **spring**.

spry *sprī, adj.* lively, active, nimble:—*comp.* **spry'er**; *superl.* **spry'est.**
spry'ly *adv.* **spry'ness** *n.*

spume *spūm, n.* **1** foam, froth. **2** scum.—*v.i.* to foam:—*pr.p.* **spum'ing.**

spun. See **spin**.

spunk *spungk, (coll.) n.* spirit, pluck.
spunk'y *adj.*:—*comp.* **spunk'ier**; *superl.* **spunk'iest**.

spur *spûr, n.* **1** an instrument with sharp point(s) worn on a rider's heel and used to drive on his horse. **2** anything that urges a person on to do something. **3** a claw-like point at the back of a bird's (e.g. a cock's) leg. **4** a sticking-out branch or root. **5** a small range of mountains running off from a larger range.—*v.t.* **1** to use spurs on. **2** to urge on.—*v.i.* **1** to press forward with the spur. **2** to hasten:—*pr.p.* **spurr'ing**; *pa.p.* **spurred.**
on the spur of the moment suddenly, without planning beforehand.

spurious *spūr'i-ůs, adj.* not genuine or real, false.

spurn *spûrn, v.t.* to refuse, cast aside, with scorn.

spurred, spurring. See **spur**.

spurt *spûrt, v.t., v.i.* to spout, gush.—*v.i.* to make a great effort suddenly and for a short time, esp. in running.—*n.* **1** a sudden gush. **2** a great but short effort, esp. in running.

sputter *sput'ėr, v.i.* **1** to make a noise as of spitting and throw out moisture in scattered drops. **2** to speak in a hurried confused way because of rage or excitement.—Also *v.t.* and *n.*

sputum *spū'tům, n.* spittle with mucus from the nose, throat, etc.

spy *spī, n.* **1** a secret agent employed to gather information, esp. military. **2** one who watches others secretly. **3** the act of spying:—*pl.* **spies.**—*v.t., v.i.* to watch secretly.—*v.t.* **1** to find (out) by close search. **2** to catch sight of:—*pr.p.* **spy'ing**; *pa.p.* **spied**.
spy'glass *n.* a small telescope.
See also **espionage**.

squabble *skwob'l, v.i.* to quarrel noisily about very little:—*pr.p.* **squabb'ling**.
squabb'ling *n.* and *adj.*

squad *skwod, n.* **1** a small group of soldiers drilled or working together. **2** any working party. **3** a group.

squadron *skwod'rȯn, n.* a division of a regiment, section of a fleet, or group of aeroplanes.
squad'ron-lead'er *n.* a rank in the R.A.F. or an officer of that rank.

squalid *skwol'id, adj.* **1** dirty, uncared-for. **2** poor, mean, miserable.
squal'idness, squal'or *ns.*

squall *skwöl, v.i., v.t.* to cry out loudly.—*n.* **1** a loud cry. **2** a strong and sudden gust of wind.
squall'y *adj.* with many squalls or gusts of wind:—*comp.* **squall'ier**; *superl.* **squall'iest**.
squall'iness *n.*

squander *skwon'dėr, v.t.* to spend or expend (e.g. money, strength, time) wastefully.

square *skwār, n.* **1** a four-sided figure with all sides equal in length and all angles right angles. **2** an open place in a town, with thc buildings round it. **3** the product when a number is multiplied by itself ($9=3 \times 3$, *or* 3^2, i.e. *is the square of* 3). **4** (*coll.*) a person who is not modern in ideas.—*adj.* **1** shaped like a square or a right angle. **2** (of a person's build) broad, thick-set. **3** fair, honest: *a square deal.* **4** (of an account) settled. **5** even, quits. **6** equal in score. **7** solid, satisfying: *a square meal.*

8 (*coll.*) not modern in ideas.—*v.t.* **1** to make square. **2** to straighten (the shoulders). **3** to multiply (a number) by itself. **4** to settle (e.g. a debt). **5** (*coll.*) to bribe, or to arrange a matter with.—*v.i.* to fit, agree: *to square with requirements, with previous statements*:—*pr.p.* **squar'ing**.—*adv.* **1** at right angles. **2** solidly. **3** fairly, honestly. **4** directly.

square dance a dance done by a group of couples in a square formation.

square foot, **inch**, etc. an area equal to a square in which each side is one foot, inch, etc.

square root the number which, multiplied by itself, gives the number being considered (3 is the square root of $\sqrt{}9$, or 9, because $3 \times 3 = 9$).

square sail a four-sided sail.

back at, to, square one back at, or to, one's original state or position with regard to a problem, etc., having made no progress, or no lasting progress.

on the square honestly.

square up to settle accounts.

square up to to face up to, defy.

squash[1] *skwosh*, *v.t.* **1** to press or crush into pulp. **2** to crush flat. **3** to put down: *to squash a revolt*. **4** to snub.—*v.i.* **1** to become crushed or pulpy. **2** to crowd.—*n.* **1** anything soft and easily crushed, or the sound of its fall. **2** a mass of people crowded together. **3** a drink containing the juice of crushed fruits.

squash'y *adj.* **1** pulpy. **2** soft and wet:—*comp.* **squash'ier**; *superl.* **squash'iest**.

squash (**rackets**, **racquets**) a game played in a walled court with a soft ball, the ball being hit against the walls of the court.

squash[2] *skwosh*, *n.* a gourd used as a vegetable.

squat *skwot*, *v.i.* **1** to sit down on the heels or in a crouching position. **2** to settle on land or in property without a right:—*pr.p.* **squatt'ing**; *pa.p.* **squatt'ed**.—*adj.* dumpy:—*comp.* **squatt'er**; *superl.* **squatt'est**.

squatt'er *n.*

squaw *skwö*, *n.* an American Indian woman, esp. a wife.

squawk *skwok*, *n.* a harsh croaky call.—*v.i.* to give such a sound.

squawk'y *adj.*:—*comp.* **squawk'ier**; *superl.* **squawk'iest**.

squeak *skwēk*, *v.i.* **1** to give a shrill cry or sound. **2** (*slang*) to be an informer, or to confess.—*n.* **1** a thin high sound. **2** a narrow escape (also **narrow squeak**). **3** a bare chance.

squeak'y *adj.*:—*comp.* **squeak'ier**; *superl.* **squeak'iest**.

squeak'ily *adv.* **squeak'iness** *n.*

squeal *skwēl*, *v.i.* **1** to give a longish shrill cry. **2** (*coll.*) to be an informer.—Also *n.*

squeamish *skwē'mish*, *adj.* **1** a little bit sick. **2** easily shocked or disgusted. **3** very scrupulous and particular in conduct.

squeeze *skwēz*, *v.t.* **1** to crush, press hard, press together tightly. **2** to grasp tightly. **3** to force (through, into) by pressing. **4** to force out liquid from.—*v.i.* **1** to press. **2** to force a way:—*pr.p.* **squeez'ing**.—*n.* **1** the act of squeezing. **2** pressure. **3** an embrace. **4** a few drops got by squeezing.

squelch *skwelch*, *-sh*, *n.* **1** the sound made by walking through mud, or by a soft wet object falling. **2** a pulpy mass.—*v.i.* to take heavy steps in water, etc.

squib *skwib*, *n.* a firework which explodes with a bang.

squid *skwid*, *n.* a sea creature with ten arms, esp. one of the smaller ones, which are used for bait.

squiggle *skwig'l*, *n.* a wiggly, curly line.

squigg'ly *adj.*:—*comp.* **squigg'lier**; *superl.* **squigg'liest**.

squint *skwint*, *adj.* off the straight.—*v.i.* **1** to look to the side. **2** to have the eyes looking different ways. **3** to screw up the eyes in looking at something.—*v.t.* to cause to squint.—*n.* **1** the act of squinting. **2** a quick look.

squire *skwīr*, *n.* **1** in the Middle Ages, a lad who served a knight in preparation for becoming one himself. **2** one who escorts a lady. **3** an English gentleman, esp. of an old family, who owns land.

squirm *skwûrm*, *v.i.* **1** to wriggle, twist the body. **2** to feel ashamed.

squirrel *skwir'ėl*, *n.* a gnawing animal with a bushy tail, living in trees.

squirt *skwûrt*, *v.t.* **1** to shoot out (liquid) in a jet. **2** to wet (something) in this way.—Also *v.i.*—*n.* **1** an instrument for squirting. **2** (*coll.*) an unimportant but irritating or contemptible person.

stab *stab*, *v.t.* **1** to wound or pierce with a pointed weapon. **2** to pain suddenly and deeply. **3** to aim (at).—*n.* **1** the act of stabbing. **2** a wound made by a sharp point. **3** (*slang*) an attempt (at something):—*pr.p.* **stabb'ing**; *pa.p.* **stabbed**.

stable[1] *stā'bl*, *adj.* **1** standing firm. **2** likely to last: *a stable government*. **3** (of a person, character, etc.) steady in purpose, not likely to be changed by stress of circumstances. **4** (*chemistry*) not easily decomposed or broken down.

stab'ilise (*stāb'*, *stab'*) *v.t.* **1** to make

steady. **2** to fit (an aeroplane, ship) with a device that keeps it steady. **3** to fix the value of (a country's currency).—Also *v.i.*:—*pr.p.* **stab'ilising**.

stab'iliser *n.*

stabil'ity (*stȧ-*; *opp.* **instability**), **sta'bleness** *ns.*

stable² *stā'bl*, *n.* **1** a building for keeping animals, usu. horses. **2** horses under one ownership.—*v.t.* to put or keep in a stable:—*pr.p.* **sta'bling**.

staccato *stȧ-kä'tō*, *adv.* (*music*) **1** with each note sounded separately and clearly. **2** (of speaking) in a jerky manner.—Also *adj.*

stack *stak*, *n.* **1** a large pile of hay, wood, etc. **2** a group of things (e.g. chimneys, rifles) standing together. **3** the funnel of a steamer, etc. **4** (*coll.*; often in *pl.*) a large quantity.—*v.t.* to pile into a stack.

stadium *stā'di-ụm*, *n.* a large sports-ground or racecourse.

staff *stäf*, *n.* **1** a stick carried in the hand. **2** a pole. **3** a stick or sign of authority. **4** lines and spaces on which music is written or printed. **5** a group of officers helping a commanding officer. **6** the people employed in a business, school, etc.:—*pl.* **staffs** (also **staves**, *defs. 1–4*; see also **stave**).—*v.t.* to supply with a staff.

staff nurse a qualified nurse ranking below a sister.

staff officer an officer serving as member of a staff.

staff'room *n.* a room in which the staff, esp. of a school, may relax, prepare lessons, etc.

the staff of life bread.

stag *stag*, *n.* a male deer, esp. a red deer.

stag party a party without women, esp. one held for a man about to be married.

stage *stāj*, *n.* **1** a shelf, floor, storey. **2** a raised platform, esp. for acting on. **3** the theatre, or the job of working in it. **4** a place of rest on a journey or road. **5** the part of a journey between two such places. **6** a period, step, in development: *the first stage of the war*; *at that stage in her life*. **7** a stage-coach.—*v.t.* **1** to put (a play) on the stage. **2** to organise. **3** to carry out publicly: *to stage a demonstration*:—*pr.p.* **stag'ing**.

stage'-coach (*history*) *n.* a horse-drawn public coach that runs regularly from stage to stage.

stage direction an order to an actor playing a part to do this or that.

stage fright nervousness before an audience, esp. the first time.

stage'-hand *n.* a workman employed about the stage.

stage'-man'age *v.t.* **1** to act as stage manager of. **2** to arrange (an event). **3** to do so for a bad purpose:—*pr.p.* **stage'-man'aging**.

stage manager one who has general charge of scenery, properties, etc.

old stager one who has worked long in one job, profession, etc.

stagger *stag'ėr*, *v.i.* to sway from side to side, reel, totter.—*v.t.* **1** to cause to reel. **2** to give a shock to. **3** to arrange (hours of work, etc.) so that some are working while others are free.—Also *n.*

stagg'ering *adj.* overpowering: *a staggering blow*.

stagnant *stag'nȧnt*, *adj.* **1** (of water) standing still, not flowing and thus impure. **2** not active, dull.

stag'nantly *adv.*

stagnate' *v.i.* **1** to be, or become, stagnant. **2** to pass time in a dull state without change or development:—*pr.p.* **stagnat'ing**.

stagnā'tion *n.*

staid *stād*, *adj.* serious in manner.

stain *stān*, *v.t.* **1** to give a different colour to. **2** to spot, mark. **3** to be a cause of shame or reproach (on a character, reputation, etc.).—*v.i.* to take a stain.—*n.* **1** a dye or colouring matter. **2** a spot, mark. **3** a cause of shame.

stain'less *adj.* **1** free from stain. **2** not easily stained or rusted.

stained glass glass painted with certain colours fixed into the surface.

stainless steel an alloy, mixture of steel and chromium, which does not rust.

stair *stār*, *n.* **1** a number of steps from landing to landing (usu. in *pl.*). **2** one of these steps.

stair'case, **stair'way** *ns.* a stretch of stairs with rails on one or both sides.

stake *stāk*, *n.* **1** a strong stick pointed at one end. **2** a post to which a person sentenced to be burned was tied. **3** (**the stake**) death by burning. **4** money put down as a bet. **5** something to gain or lose.—*v.t.* **1** to fasten with, support with, a stake. **2** to pierce with a stake. **3** to mark the bounds of with stakes: *to stake off, out, ground for a pitch*. **4** to put down (money) as a bet. **5** to risk: *He staked everything on the success of this attack*:—*pr.p.* **stak'ing**.

at stake 1 to be won or lost. **2** in danger: *His life is at stake*.

stake a claim to assert a right (to something).

stalactite *stal'ȧk-tīt*, *stȧ-lak'*, *n.* an icicle-shaped piece usu. of calcium carbonate (see this) hanging from the roof of a cave, formed by dripping water containing the carbonate.

stalagmite *stal'ag-mīt, stȧ-lag', n.* a piece of the same substance and similar shape coming up from the floor of a cave.

stale *stāl, adj.* **1** not fresh. **2** dry, flat, tasteless from keeping too long. **3** no longer interesting because heard, done, etc., too often. **4** not able to do one's best because of too much training, study, etc.

stalemate *stāl'māt, n.* (*chess*) **1** a position in which a player cannot move without putting his king into check. **2** (in a contest) a position in which neither side can win, a deadlock, draw.

stalk[1] *stök, n.* **1** the main stem of a plant. **2** a stem on which a flower, etc. grows. **3** a tall chimney.

stalk[2] *stök, v.i., v.t.* **1** to walk stiffly or proudly. **2** to go after (game, etc.) keeping under cover.—*n.* **1** the act of stalking. **2** a stalking walk.

stall[1] *stöl, n.* **1** (a division for one animal in) a stable, cowshed, etc. **2** a table, booth, or stand where articles are laid out for sale. **3** a seat in church esp. for choir or clergy. **4** (usu. in *pl.*) one of the seats in a theatre in the front section of the ground floor. **5** loss of flying speed in an aircraft. **6** a standstill.—*v.t.* **1** to put or keep in a stall. **2** to bring to a standstill.—*v.i.* **1** (of an aircraft) to lose flying speed and so fall out of control for a time. **2** (of a car engine) to stop because of too great load or because of too sudden braking.

stall[2] *stöl,* (*slang*) *v.i.* to avoid for the time being action or decision, play for time.—*v.t.* **1** (usu. with *off*) to put off, keep at a distance: *Stall off that question by changing the subject.* **2** to delay, play for time with (someone).

stallion *stal'yȯn, n.* a male horse, esp. one kept for breeding.

stalwart *stöl'wȧrt, adj.* **1** strong, sturdy. **2** brave, resolute.—*n.* a bold person.

stamen *stā'mėn, n.* a fine stalk in the middle of a flower together with the sac on the end of it that holds pollen:—*pl.* **sta'mens**.

stam'ina *(stam'-) n.* strength, power to endure fatigue, etc.

stammer *stam'ėr, v.i.* **1** to stumble in speaking. **2** to stutter.—Also *v.t.* and *n.*

stamp *stamp, v.t.* **1** to bring (the foot) down heavily. **2** to bring the foot, etc., down heavily on. **3** to fix a mark on by pressing, or by cutting with a downward blow. **4** to stick a postage stamp on. **5** to fix or mark deeply: *His experiences had stamped certain ideas on his mind and a sad expression on his face.* **6** to mark (as), prove to be: *By doing this he stamped himself as untrustworthy.*—*v.i.* to step, or to set down the foot, with force.—*n.* **1** the act of stamping. **2** a mark or design made by stamping. **3** a postage stamp (see **post**). **4** a clear mark: *His story had the stamp of truth.* **5** kind, sort: *a man of a different stamp.* **6** an instrument or machine for stamping.

stamp duty a tax on e.g. legal papers, paid by using specially stamped paper or by putting on a stamp.

stamp out **1** to put out by trampling or other force (e.g. a fire, rebellion). **2** to make by stamping from a sheet of e.g. metal with a cutter.

stampede *stam-pēd', n.* a sudden wild rush of frightened animals, or of a large number of people.—*v.i., v.t.* to rush, or send rushing, in a stampede:—*pr.p.* **stamped'ing.**

stance *stans, n.* a manner of standing e.g. in playing golf, cricket.

stanch *stän(t)sh,* **staunch** *stön(t)sh, v.t.* to stop the flow of (e.g. blood).

stanchion *stan'sh(ȯ)n, n.* an upright bar, post, etc., in a window, screen, or ship.

stand *stand, v.i.* **1** to be in an upright position, not lying or sitting down. **2** (also **stand up**) to rise to one's feet. **3** to resist, fight (against). **4** to hold a place: *The chest stands in the hall.* **5** to be: *to stand firm, along.* **6** to be at the moment: *as the matter, the account, stands.* **7** to remain in force: *This law still stands.* **8** to act as (e.g. sponsor). **9** to be a candidate.—*v.t.* **1** to set upright or on end. **2** to undergo (trial for a crime). **3** to bear: *Can you stand the cold?* **4** to bear the presence of (someone). **5** to pay for (something) for someone: *Let me stand you tea:*—*pa.t., pa.p.* **stood** *(stood).*—*n.* **1** an act, or place, of standing. **2** a post, station. **3** a halt, standstill. **4** a place for vehicles waiting to be hired. **5** rows of raised seats for spectators. **6** (*U.S.*) a witness box. **7** something for putting things on. **8** a piece of furniture for hanging things from. **9** a great effort (*for* or *against*): *to make a stand for freedom.*

stan'ding *adj.* **1** upright on feet or on end. **2** remaining in force, use, or readiness: *a standing army.* **3** not moving: *a standing start.*—*n.* **1** the action of verb 'to stand': *Standing is not allowed.* **2** position, rank, among others. **3** time of lasting: *an agreement of long standing.*

stand'-alone *n., adj.* (*computers*) (of) a system, device, etc. that can operate unconnected to any other.

stand'-by *n.* **1** someone or something

ready when he, it, is needed. **2** the state of being ready in case one is needed: *The helicopter crew was on stand-by*:—*pl.* **stand'-bys**.

stand'-in' *n.* one who takes the place of another for a time.

standing joke a subject which makes people laugh whenever it is mentioned.

standing order 1 an instruction from a customer to his bank to make regular payments from his account. **2** (in *pl.*) regulations about correct procedures at meetings, etc.

stand'ing-room *n.* room for standing, without a seat.

stand'-off'ish *adj.* distant, not friendly, in manner.

stand'point *n.* the position from which one looks at something: *He thought only of his profits, so from his standpoint the new law was bad.*

stand'still *n.* a complete stop.

stand'-up *adj.* (used only before a noun) **1** done in a standing position. **2** (of a fight) in earnest.

stand by 1 to stand close to. **2** to remain faithful to. **3** to accept and act according to (a decision). **4** to be waiting ready to act, help, etc.

stand down 1 to leave the witness box. **2** to withdraw from a contest.

stand fast to refuse to give in.

stand for 1 to be a candidate for. **2** to be a symbol of: *John Bull stands for England.* **3** to approve of or allow to happen.

stand in to be a stand-in (for).

stand off to remain at a distance.

stand on ceremony to insist on, or consider very important, (strict adherence to) the rules of polite behaviour.

stand one's ground to refuse to move or give in.

stand out 1 to stick out. **2** to be noticeable: *She stands out in a crowd.* **3** to continue to fight or urge (for, against).

stand to 1 to set to work. **2** to be likely to: *She stands to win the contest.*

stand to reason that to be reasonable or likely that.

stand up for to support or try to defend.

stand up to 1 to face boldly. **2** to bear (e.g. pain), carry out (e.g. a task), bravely.

stand well to be in favour (with).

standard *stan'dȧrd, n.* **1** a flag or figure on a pole, esp. one carried, etc., by an armed force. **2** a shrub or tree not trained against a support. **3** a weight, measure, etc., used in expressing other weights, etc.: *The pound is the standard of weight.* **4** a model by which things are judged. **5** a level of excellence aimed at: *These people have high, low, standards of cleanliness and morals.* **6** a grade, level: *The standard of work done in this school is high, low.*—*adj.* **1** accepted as a standard or model. **2** usual. **3** (of a type of goods) widely available because of a normal, not special, type.

stan'dardise *v.t.* to make or keep of one size, shape, etc.: *to standardise each part of a machine so that it is easy to obtain a new part to replace it*:—*pr.p.* **stan'dardising**.

standardisā'tion *n.*

stan'dard-bear'er *n.* one who carries a standard or banner.

standard lamp a lamp on a tall support which stands on the floor of a room, etc.

standard of living the amount of possessions, food, etc. which a person has available to him for his comfort and pleasure.

stand-by, etc. See **stand**.

stank. See **stink**.

stanza *stan'zȧ, n.* a group of lines making up a part of a poem, usu. with a special rhyme scheme and length of line.

staple[1] *stā'pl, n.* **1** a chief product of trade or industry. **2** a main item (of diet, reading, etc). **3** a fibre of raw cotton, etc., or its length or fineness.—*adj.* leading, main.

staple[2] *stā'pl, n.* a bent rod or wire, both ends of which are driven through sheets of paper to fasten them together, or into a wall, etc.—*v.t.* to fasten with a staple:—*pr.p.* **stap'ling**.

star *stär, n.* **1** any of the bright heavenly bodies, esp. those whose places appear to be fixed and which shine with their own light. **2** an object or figure with pointed rays, usu. five. **3** a very brilliant person. **4** a leading actor or actress in films or plays, or other leading or popular entertainer.—Also *adj.*—*v.t.* **1** to mark with a star. **2** to have (a certain person) as a star performer.—*v.i.* to act a chief part:—*pr.p.* **starr'ing**; *pa.p.* **starred**.

star'dom *n.* the state of being a leading performer.

starred *adj.* **1** covered with stars. **2** marked with a star, to show excellence, etc.

starr'y *adj.* **1** full of stars. **2** like, or shining like, stars:—*comp.* **starr'ier**; *superl.* **starr'iest**.

starr'iness *n.*

star'fish *n.* a small sea creature with five points or arms.

star'light *n.* light from the stars.

Stars and Stripes the flag of the United States of America.
See also **stellar**, **interstellar**.

starboard *stär'bo(r)d, -bōrd, -börd, n.* the right-hand side of a ship, when one is looking towards the bow.—Also *adj.*

starch *stärch, n.* **1** a white food substance found esp. in flour, potatoes, etc. **2** a preparation of this used for stiffening clothes. **3** stiffness, formal manner.—*v.t.* to stiffen with starch.
star'chy *adj.* **1** like, or containing, starch. **2** stiff, formal, in manner:—*comp.* **star'chier**; *superl.* **star'chiest**.
star'chiness *n.*

stardom. See **star**.

stare *stār, v.i.* to look in a fixed way through wonder, horror, rudeness, etc.:—*pr.p.* **star'ing**.—Also *n.*
be staring one in the face **1** to be obvious. **2** (of something unpleasant) to be, seem to be, waiting for one in near future.

starfish. See **star**.

stark[1] *stärk, adj.* **1** stiff. **2** sheer, out-and-out: *stark foolishness.* **3** (of style) unadorned, simple.—*adv.* completely: *stark mad.*

stark[2] **(-naked)** *stärk'(-nā'kid), adj.* completely naked, quite bare.

starlight. See **star**.

starling *stär'ling, n.* a small bird with glossy dark feathers.

starred, starry. See **star**.

start *stärt, v.i.* **1** to dart or move suddenly out, forward, or up. **2** to jump or jerk suddenly, e.g. in surprise. **3** to begin. **4** (of a car, engine, etc.) to begin to work. **5** to set forth on a journey, etc.—*v.t.* **1** to drive from a hiding place. **2** to begin. **3** to set going. **4** to set up (e.g. in business).—*n.* **1** a sudden movement of the body. **2** a surprised or frightened feeling. **3** a beginning. **4** a setting in motion. **5** the advantage of beginning before, or farther forward than, rivals, or the amount of this (also **head start**).
star'ter *n.* **1** one who starts a race, or starts off in a race. **2** something which starts off a process, starts an engine, etc. **3** (also in *pl.*) the first course of a meal.
star'ting *adj., n.*
star'ting-point *n.* the point from which motion or action begins.
start off **1** to (cause to) begin. **2** (also **start out**) to set forth on a journey.
start up **1** to rise suddenly. **2** to set in motion.

startle *stär'tl, v.i., v.t.* to feel, or cause, a sudden surprise or alarm:—*pr.p.* **start'ling**.
start'ling *adj.* **start'lingly** *adv.*

starve *stärv, v.i.* **1** to die of, or suffer greatly from, hunger. **2** to be in want of, feel a great longing (for): *I starved for company.*—*v.t.* to cause to starve:—*pr.p.* **star'ving**.
starvā'tion *n.*
starve'ling *n.* a starved creature.—Also *adj.*

state *stāt, n.* **1** condition: *The road is in a bad state.* **2** (*coll.*) a bad, disturbed condition: *The house is in a bit of a state at the moment, I'm afraid.* **3** ceremonial pomp: *The king drove there in state.* **4** a group of people under one government, or their territory, either a separate country, or (as in the United States) a division of a federation. **5** the government. —*adj.* **1** ceremonial. **2** having to do with a state, or with the government.—*v.t.* **1** to set out, tell, definitely and in detail, or formally. **2** to assert. **3** to say:—*pr.p.* **stat'ing**.
stat'ed *adj.* fixed, regular: *at stated times.*
state'ly *adj.* noble-looking, dignified, impressive:—*comp.* **state'lier**; *superl.* **state'liest**.
state'liness *n.*
state'ment *n.* **1** the act of stating. **2** something that is stated. **3** a financial record.
state'-aid'ed *adj.* receiving money from the state.
state'room *n.* a large cabin in a ship.
states'man *n.* one skilled in government esp. one who manages affairs with wisdom and foresight:—*pl.* **-men**.
states'manship *n.*
states'manlike, states'manly *adjs.*
lie in state. See **lie**[2].
state of affairs situation, condition of things.

static *stat'ik, adj.* **1** standing still. **2** stable.—*n.* disturbances, noises, in wireless reception.

station *stā'sh(o)n, n.* **1** a fixed stopping-place, esp. for a railway or bus line, with its buildings. **2** a local office, headquarters: *a police station, wireless station.* **3** a fixed place or post, esp. military. **4** a position. **5** position in life, or in the scale of nature: *a lowly station.*—Also *adj.*—*v.t.* to appoint to a post, or put in position (at, in, a particular place).
stā'tionary *adj.* **1** standing, not moving. **2** not changing place.
stā'tioner *n.* one who sells paper and other articles used in writing.

stā'tionery *n.* goods sold by a stationer, paper, envelopes, etc.
sta'tion-master *n.* a person in charge of a railway station.

statistics *stȧ-tis'tiks, n. pl.* figures and facts set out in order: *the statistics of road accidents* (in *sing.*, one such fact or figure).—*n. sing.* the study of such facts.
statis'tical *adj.* **statis'tically** *adv.*
statisti'cian *n.*

statue *stat'ū, n.* a likeness of a person or animal in wood, stone, etc.
stat'uary *n.* statues.
statuesque *stat-ū-esk', adj.* like a statue in dignity, etc.
statuette' *n.* a small statue.

stature *stach'ůr, n.* **1** height of body. **2** importance, eminence.

status *stā'tůs, n.* **1** social position, or rank in a group. **2** position of affairs.
status quo the state of affairs at or before a certain event, date, esp. the present situation.
status symbol a possession supposed to show high social position (e.g. a large car).

statute *stat'ūt, n.* a written law of a country.
stat'utory *adj.* **1** required by statute. **2** that may be punished by law: *a statutory offence*.

staunch[1] *stönch, -sh, adj.* firm, trusty, steadfast: *a staunch believer, supporter*.
staunch'ly *adv.* **staunch'ness** *n.*

staunch[2]. See **stanch**.

stave *stāv, n.* **1** one of the side pieces of a cask or tub. **2** a stick, rod. **3** (*music*) a staff. **4** a stanza, verse, of a poem, song.—*v.t.* **1** (with *in*) to crush in, make hole in. **2** (with *off*) to keep away, delay: *to stave off a cold*; *to stave off the evil day*:—*pr.p.* **stav'ing**; *pa.t., pa.p.* **stāved** or **stōve**.

stay[1] *stā, n.* **1** a rope supporting a mast. **2** a prop, support.—*v.t.* to support:—*pa.t., pa.p.* **stayed**.

stay[2] *stā, v.i.* **1** to spend time in a place, etc. **2** to remain, continue to be: *to stay quiet.* **3** to stop. **4** to pause. **5** to wait (for).—*v.t.* **1** to stop. **2** to hold back. **3** to continue running for the whole of: *to stay the course*:—*pa.t., pa.p.* **stayed**.—*n.* **1** a stop or halt. **2** a living for a time.
stay'ing-power *n.* the ability to go on long without giving up.
stay put (*coll.*) to remain in the same place or position.

stead *sted, n.* place.
in one's stead in place of one: *I could not go, and she went in my stead.*
stand one in good stead to prove of service, help, to one in time in need.

steadfast. See **steady**.

steady *sted'i, adj.* **1** standing, or fixed, firmly. **2** (of e.g. nerve) not easily upset. **3** not changing in views, habits, etc.: *a steady supporter.* **4** hard-working and sensible. **5** (of movement, activity) regular, constant: *a steady beat, flow*; *steady work*:—*comp.* **stead'ier**; *superl.* **stead'iest**.—*v.t., v.i.*, to make, or become, steady:—*pr.p.* **stead'ying** *(-i-ing)*; *pa.p.* **stead'ied**.
stead'fast *adj.* **1** steady, fixed: *a steadfast look.* **2** firm, resolute. **3** faithful.
stead'y-go'ing *adj.* of steady habits or action.

steak *stāk, n.* **1** a slice of meat (esp. hindquarters of beef) or fish. **2** any of several cuts of beef for frying, stewing, etc.
steak'house *n.* a restaurant specialising in fried or grilled steaks of beef.

steal *stēl, v.t.* **1** to take (what does not belong to one), esp. secretly. **2** to take quickly and secretly: *to steal a look, a nap.*—*v.i.* **1** to be a thief. **2** to move, pass, quietly so as not to be seen, heard, noticed:—*pa.t.* **stōle**; *pa.p.* **stōl'en**.
steal'ing *n.* and *adj.*
stealth *stelth, n.* secret manner of acting.
steal'thy *(stel') adj.* acting, or done, with stealth, in a secret manner:—*comp.* **steal'thier**; *superl.* **steal'thiest**.
steal'thily *adv.* **steal'thiness** *n.*

steam *stēm, n.* **1** the invisible gas or vapour that rises from boiling water. **2** (*loosely*) the moist cloud seen when this vapour condenses as it touches cold air. **3** a mist or film of liquid drops. **4** steam power. **5** energy, vigour: *I can't run any more—I've just run out of steam.*—*v.i.* **1** to give off steam. **2** (often with *up*) to become dimmed with steam, etc.: *The windows steamed*, or *steamed up.* **3** to move, travel, by means of steam.—*v.t.* **1** to cook by steam. **2** to put into steam.—*adj.* using, or driven by, steam.
steam'er *n.* **1** a steamboat, steamship. **2** a container in which food, etc., is steamed.
steam'y *adj.*:—*comp.* **steam'ier**; *superl.* **steam'iest**.
steam'iness *n.*
steam'boat, **steam'ship** *ns.* a ship driven by steam.
steam power the force of steam used to work machinery.
steam'-roller *n.* **1** a locomotive engine driven by steam with large heavy roller(s), used, esp. formerly, to flatten material in making roads. **2** any power

that crushes or compels without mercy.—*v.t.* to crush or force as if with a steam-roller.

full steam ahead 1 at the greatest speed possible. **2** with the greatest amount of effort.

let off steam 1 to let steam into the air. **2** to work off energy or anger.

steam open to open (e.g. an envelope) by using steam to soften the sticky part.

under one's own steam by one's own efforts without help.

steed *stēd, n.* a horse for riding.

steel *stēl, n.* **1** iron hardened by treatment, containing some carbon, etc. **2** a cutting tool or weapon. **3** an object for some other use made of steel. **4** a quality of steel, as strength, coldness: *a grip of steel*; *eyes of steel.*—*v.t.* **1** to harden: *He steeled his heart.* **2** to gather courage in oneself: *He steeled himself to meet the attack.*

steel'y *adj.*:—*comp.* **steel'ier**; *superl.* **steel'iest**.

steel'iness *n.*

steel band a band of musicians playing **steel drums**, percussion instruments made from the tops of oil-drums or the like.

steep¹ *stēp, adj.* **1** (of a hill, stairs, etc.) rising nearly straight, not sloping gradually. **2** (*coll.*; of e.g. a price, something one is asked to do or believe) too great or much.

steep'ly *adv.* **steep'ness** *n.*

steep² *stēp, v.t.* **1** to wet thoroughly (and usu. for a period of time) in liquid in order to take out dirt, soften, etc. **2** to give (oneself, a person) the fullest knowledge of a subject: *He steeped himself in Russian literature.*—Also *v.i.* and *n.*

steeple *stēp'l, n.* **1** a high tower of a church, etc., usu. rising to a point. **2** a spire.

steep'lechase *n.* **1** a race, on foot or horse, across country (perh. orig. with a church steeple as goal). **2** a race over a course on which obstacles have been made.—Also *v.i.*:—*pr.p.* **steep'lechasing**.

steep'lejack *n.* one who climbs steeples, tall chimneys, etc., to make repairs.

steer¹ *stēr, n.* a young ox raised solely to produce beef.

steer² *stēr, v.t.* **1** to guide, control the course of (e.g. a ship, car, bill in parliament, discussion). **2** to follow (a course).—Also *v.i.*

steer'age *n.* **1** the act of steering. **2** the part of a ship set aside for passengers who pay the lowest fares.

steer'ing *n.* **1** the act of one who steers. **2** the steering-gear.

steer'ing-gear *n.* the mechanism for steering a ship, car, etc.

steer'ing-wheel *n.* wheel turned in steering a ship, etc.

steers'man *n.* one who steers a ship.

steer clear of to avoid.

stellar *stel'ăr, adj.* having to do with the stars.

stem¹ *stem, n.* **1** a stalk—either the slender centre part of a plant which grows upward from the root, or a part on which leaf, flower, or fruit, grows. **2** a tree trunk. **3** anything stalk-likc, e.g. the slender part of a wineglass. **4** the front part of a ship.—*v.t.* to make way, progress, against (the tide, opposition, etc.).—*v.i.* to spring (from): *a feeling of hate that stems from envy*:—*pr.p.* **stemm'ing**; *pa.p.* **stemmed**.

stemmed *adj.* having a stem.

from stem to stern 1 from one end of a vessel to the other. **2** completely.

stem² *stem, v.t.* to stop the flow of (e.g. blood):—*pr.p.* **stemm'ing**; *pa.p.* **stemmed**.

stench *stench, -sh, n.* a strong, bad smell.

stencil *sten's(i)l, v.t.* **1** to paint (design) by brushing over a plate or sheet on which a pattern is cut out. **2** to decorate, stamp (material, object) thus. **3** to cut a stencil for making copies of (typewriting, writing):—*pr.p.* **sten'cilling**; *pa.p.* **sten'cilled**.—*n.* **1** a plate or card prepared for stencilling. **2** stencilled lettering or design. **3** a piece of waxed paper on which letters are cut by means of a typewriter or a pointed tool.

stenography *sten-og'ră-fi, n.* the art, or any method, of writing in shorthand.

stenog'rapher *n.*

stentorian *sten-tō'ri-ăn, -tö', adj.* (of a voice) very loud or powerful.

step *step, n.* **1** one movement of the leg in walking, running, dancing. **2** the distance passed over by this. **3** the sound made. **4** a footprint. **5** (*dancing*) a pattern of movement that is repeated. **6** a short journey. **7** manner of walking: *with a proud step.* **8** one of the parts of a stair or ladder on which one stands. **9** a doorstep. **10** (*in pl.*) a stepladder. **11** a stage upward or downward: *His new job was a step up.* **12** (in *pl.*) a flight of stairs. **13** a move towards an end: *the first step in carrying out our plan.* **14** a move, action.—*v.i.* **1** to take a step. **2** to walk.—*v.t.* to measure by taking steps:—*pr.p.* **stepp'ing**; *pa.p.* **stepped**.

step'ladder *n.* a ladder with a support on which it rests.

stepp'ing-stone *n.* **1** a stone rising

above water or mud, used to cross on. **2** anything that helps one to advance or rise.

step'-rocket *n.* a rocket with sections which work one after another.

break step to get out of step.

in step 1 with the same feet going forward at the same time, as in marching. **2** changing, acting, etc. in agreement (with).

keep step to continue in step.

out of step not in step.

step down to retire, resign, etc.

step into to come into without effort.

step out 1 to go out a little way. **2** to begin to walk more quickly.

step up 1 to come forward. **2** to increase (e.g. production).

take steps to do something for a purpose: *I shall take steps to make sure that your father hears this.*

step- *step-*, (as part of a word) showing a relationship arising from a second (or later) marriage, not a blood relationship, e.g.:—

step'father *n.* one's mother's husband, but not one's own father.

step'sister *n.* a daughter of a step-parent by another marriage.

Also **step'mother**, **step'brother**, **step'child**, **step'son**, **step'daughter**, etc.

steppe *step*, *n.* a dry, grassy, esp. treeless, plain, as in the south-east of Europe and in Asia.

stereo- *stē-ri-ō-*, *ster-i-ō-*, (as part of a word) having to do with the three dimensions of space.

ste'reo *n.* short for various nouns beginning *stereo-*, esp. a piece of stereophonic equipment such as a record-player or tape-recorder, or a combination of such pieces:—*pl.* **ste'reos**.

stereophonic *stē-ri-ȯ-fon'ik*, *ster-*, *adj.* (of sound, a recording, equipment, etc.) giving out the sounds of different voices, instruments, etc. from different directions, by means of two or more loud-speakers.

ste'reoscope *n.* an instrument which gives the effect of solidity to a picture by showing two images (taken from slightly different points of view) of the same object or scene in such a way that they appear to be one.

stereoscop'ic *adj.*

ste'reotype *n.* **1** a metal plate having on its surface matter for printing e.g. a page of a book. **2** an image or representation, e.g. of a character, type of person, that has become fixed and conventional.—*v.t.* **1** to make a stereotype of. **2** to make in one fixed, monotonous form:—*pr.p.* **ste'reotyping**.

ste'reotyped *adj.* (of e.g. opinions, phrases) fixed, not changing.

sterile *ster'īl*, *adj.* **1** not bringing forth, or unable to produce, offspring, fruit, seeds, results, ideas, etc. **2** free from germs.

ster'ileness, **steril'ity** *(-il')*, *ns.*

ster'ilise *(-il-īz)* *v.t.* **1** to cause to be sterile. **2** to kill germs in (e.g. milk) by boiling or other means:—*pr.p.* **ster'ilising**.

sterilisā'tion *n.*

ster'iliser *n.* an apparatus for sterilising.

sterling *stûr'ling*, *n.* British money of standard value: *payable in sterling.*—*adj.* **1** of, in, etc., sterling: *sterling prices, payments*, but *the pound, £100, sterling.* **2** (of silver) of standard quality, containing at least 92.5 per cent silver. **3** of very high worth: *a man of sterling character*.

sterling area a group of countries whose currencies have close connections with the pound sterling, not gold or dollars.

stern[1] *stûrn*, *adj.* **1** (of look, manner, voice) grim, hard, showing displeasure. **2** firm, strict. **3** hard to endure.

stern'ly *adv.* **stern'ness** *n.*

stern[2] *stûrn*, *n.* **1** the back part of a ship. **2** the rump or tail.

steroid *stē'roid*, *ster'*, *n.* any of a number of substances including certain hormones.

stertorous *stûr'tȯ-rus*, *adj.* with a snoring sound.

stethoscope *steth'ȯ-skōp*, *n.* an instrument by which a doctor can listen to the beats of the heart, etc.

stevedore *stē'vė-dōr*, *-dör*, *n.* one who loads and unloads ships.

stew *stū*, *n.* **1** a dish of stewed food, esp. meat with vegetables. **2** a state of great worry and agitation. **3** (*slang*) one who studies hard, esp. unintelligently.—*v.t.* **1** to simmer or boil slowly with some moisture. **2** to steep (tea) too much. **3** to make (a person) very hot.—Also *v.i.*

steward *stū'ȧrd*, *n.* **1** one who manages an estate or farm for someone else. **2** one who helps to arrange, and is an official at, races, a dance, entertainment, etc. **3** one who sees to stores and serving of meals in a ship, etc. **4** a passengers' attendant on a ship or aeroplane. **5** an overseer, foreman:—*fem.* **stew'ardess** (esp. *def. 4*).

stew'ardship *n.* in the Christian church, the individual's duty to give a share of his time and goods to others.

stick[1] *stik*, *v.t.* **1** to pierce with something sharp. **2** to thrust (into, through, out, etc.). **3** to fix by means of a pointed end, or by gum, etc. **4** (*coll.*) to put: *Stick it there.*

5 to set, decorate (with). **6** (*coll.*) to puzzle, or to bring to a stop: *That problem will stick him.*—*v.i.* **1** to be, become, or remain, fixed. **2** to be caught, held back: *He will stick in the mud.* **3** (of e.g. a door, lid) to jam. **4** to fail to go on (in something one is doing). **5** to hold fast (to a decision). **6** to keep working at: *Stick to your job*:—*pa.p.* **stuck**.

stick'y *adj.* **1** (of e.g. treacle, fly-paper) able to adhere or cling closely. **2** (*coll.*; of weather) hot and damp. **3** apt to become jammed. **4** difficult to deal with: *a sticky problem*:—*comp.* **stick'ier**; *superl.* **stick'iest**.

stick'ily *adv.* **stick'iness** *n.*

stick'-in-the-mud *n.* a person who never makes any advance or does anything new.

sticky end an unpleasant end, disaster, ruin.

be stuck with (*coll.*) to be unable to get rid of.

stick at nothing to be willing to do anything (to achieve some goal).

stick by to support (a friend).

stick out **1** to jut out. **2** to be obvious.

stick up for to speak in defence of.

stick[2] *stik*, *n.* **1** a small shoot or branch from a tree or shrub. **2** a piece of wood cut for burning, etc. **3** a piece of wood shaped for playing hockey, beating a drum, or other purpose. **4** a holder for a candle. **5** something in the form of a stick or rod: *a stick of sealing wax*.

the wrong end of the stick a mistaken understanding of the situation.

stickleback *stik'l-bak*, *n.* a small river-fish with prickles or spines on its back.

stickler *stik'lėr*, *n.* one who is determined to be very exact, accurate, correct: *a stickler for the truth, for convention.*

sticky. See **stick**[1].

stiff *stif*, *adj.* **1** not easily bent. **2** rigid. **3** moving, or moved, with difficulty: *stiff fingers*; *a stiff lock.* **4** thick, not tending to flow: *a stiff dough.* **5** firm. **6** hard: *a stiff examination.* **7** strong: *a stiff breeze*; *a stiff dose.* **8** (*coll.*) too high: *a stiff price.* **9** not natural and easy, cold in manner.—*n.* (*slang*) **1** a corpse. **2** a dull, formal person.

stiff'en *v.t.*, *v.i.* **1** to make, or become, stiff. **2** to make, or become, more stubborn: *to stiffen resistance*; *Resistance stiffened.*

stifle *stī'fl*, *v.t.* **1** to stop the breath of completely. **2** to make breathing difficult for. **3** to put out (e.g. flames). **4** to hold back (e.g. a yawn, sobs).—*v.i.* to die, or to suffer, through lack of air:—*pr.p.* **sti'fling**.

sti'fling *adj.* very hot and stuffy.

stigma *stig'mȧ*, *n.* **1** a mark of disgrace. **2** (in a flower) the top of the pistil which receives the pollen.

stig'matise *v.t.* to mark, describe (as usu. something bad): *to stigmatise a man as ignorant because he knows no Greek*:—*pr.p.* **stig'matising**.

stile *stīl*, *n.* a step, or set of steps, for climbing over a wall or fence.

stiletto *sti-let'ō*, *n.* a dagger, or a pointed instrument, with narrow but thick blade:—*pl.* **stilett'os, -oes**.

still[1] *stil*, *n.* an apparatus, or place, in which something (e.g. whisky) is distilled.

still'room *n.* a pantry where drinks and certain foods are kept.

still[2] *stil*, *adj.* **1** without movement. **2** calm. **3** silent. **4** (of a drink) not effervescing.—*v.t.* **1** to silence. **2** to calm.—*adv.* **1** up to the present time, or to the time spoken of: *Hair was still worn long.* **2** for all that, nevertheless: *He saw the bus start but he still ran on.* **3** even: *still more, worse.*—*n.* **1** stillness, calmness. **2** an ordinary photograph as opposed to a motion picture, esp. one taken from a motion picture.

still'ness *n.*

still'born *adj.* dead when born.

still life a picture of something that is not living (e.g. a table with fruit, etc.):—*pl.* **still lifes**.

still and all (*coll.*) nevertheless.

stilt *stilt*, *n.* one of a pair of poles with foot rests on which a person may stand and thus walk raised off the ground.

stilt'ed *adj.* stiff, not natural in manner, pompous.

stimulant *stim'ū-lȧnt*, *n.* **1** something that makes a part of the body more active for a time: *a heart stimulant.* **2** a happening that makes one feel livelier. **3** a stimulating drug. **4** an alcoholic drink.—Also *adj.*

stim'ūlate *v.t.* **1** to act as a stimulant to, make more active. **2** to incite, move (to do something):—*pr.p.* **stim'ulating**.

stimulā'tion *n.* **stim'ulative** *adj.*

stim'ūlus *n.* **1** something that rouses (e.g. a person, the mind) to action or greater effort. **2** any action of influence that causes a reaction in a living thing: *The stimulus of light causes the flower to open*:—*pl.* **stim'uli** (*-lī*).

sting *sting*, *n.* **1** a part of some plants and animals (e.g. a nettle, a wasp) used to prick and to introduce an irritating or poisonous fluid into the wound. **2** the act of piercing with a sting. **3** the wound or pain caused by a sting. **4** any sharp pain: *the sting of a* *whip, the wind, a friend's unkindness.* **5** the power to hurt. **6** stimulus.—*v.t.* **1** to wound or hurt by means of a sting, etc. **2** to goad, stir up (to action, feeling).—*v.i.* **1** to have a sting. **2** to give pain. **3** to smart, feel painful:—*pa.p.* **stung**.

sting'y *sting'i, adj.* that stings:—*comp.* **sting'ier**; *superl.* **sting'iest**.

stingy[1] *stin'ji, adj.* **1** mean, not generous, in spending or giving. **2** scanty:—*comp.* **stin'gier**; *superl.* **stin'giest**.

stin'gily *adv.* **stin'giness** *n.*

stingy[2]. See **sting**.

stink *stingk, v.i., v.t.* to give out, or to fill with, a strong bad smell:—*pa.t.* **stank**; *pa.p.* **stunk**.—Also *n.*

stint *stint, v.t.* **1** to give (a person) a very small allowance: *to stint oneself in food.* **2** to supply (something) in a stingy way.—Also *v.i.*—*n.* **1** limit or restriction: *He praised him, gave to him, without stint.* **2** a set task, share of piece of work.

stipend *stī'pend, n.* a salary paid for services (esp. to a clergyman in Scotland).

stipend'iary *n.* a paid magistrate:—*pl.* **stipend'iaries**.

stipple *stip'l, v.t.* **1** to engrave, paint, draw, etc., in dots or separate touches. **2** to produce an effect that suggests stippled work:—*pr.p.* **stipp'ling**.—*n.* **1** stippled work. **2** an effect of stippling.

stipulate *stip'ū-lāt, v.t.* and *v.i.* to state as a necessary condition for an agreement: *I stipulated that, if I did the job, I must be paid immediately*; *I stipulated for immediate payment*.

stipulā'tion *n.* something stipulated.

stir *stûr, v.t.* **1** to set (liquid, etc.) in a swirling motion. **2** to move slightly. **3** to arouse emotion in: *The story of such courage stirred him.* **4** to rouse, move to activity.—*v.i.* **1** to move. **2** to be active:—*pr.p.* **stirr'ing**; *pa.p.* **stirred**.—*n.* **1** disturbance, bustle, excitement. **2** an act of stirring.

stirr'ing *adj.* **1** putting in motion. **2** active. **3** exciting.

stir up **1** to mix by stirring. **2** to rouse, cause: *to stir up trouble.* **3** to move to action. **4** to excite, make angry, etc.

stirrup *stir'up, n.* a metal ring or loop hung from the saddle, for a horseman's foot while mounting or riding.

stirrup cup a drink given to a guest who is leaving (orig. on horseback).

stitch *stich, n.* **1** a loop made by drawing a thread, etc. through cloth, etc. by means of a needle. **2** a loop made in knitting. **3** a sharp pain in one's side. **4** a bit of clothing: *He had not a stitch on.*—*v.t.* to sew with a regular line of stitches.

in stitches very amused, laughing uncontrollably.

stoat *stōt, n.* a type of weasel, called the ermine when in white winter fur.

stock[1] *stok, n.* **1** a post, log, block of wood. **2** the trunk or main stem of a plant. **3** the handle of a whip, rifle, etc. **4** family, race: *He is of good stock.* **5** a store or supply (of e.g. goods). **6** the cattle, horses, etc. kept on a farm. **7** the liquid obtained by boiling meat or bones to make soup. **8** money lent to the government at fixed interest. **9** (often in *pl.*) a corporation's or company's capital divided into shares. **10** (in *pl.*) the frame holding a ship while it is building. **11** (in *pl.*) a wooden frame, with holes for the ankles, and sometimes, wrists, to which law-breakers were fastened as a punishment.—*v.t.* **1** to store. **2** to keep for sale: *He stocks lemons.* **3** to fill (with). **4** to supply with farm animals.—*adj.* (usu. used before a noun) **1** kept in stock. **2** usual, widely known and used: *He made the stock joke*.

stock'ist *n.* one who stocks a commodity.

stock'y *adj.* **1** having a strong stem. **2** short and rather stout:—*comp.* **stock'ier**; *superl.* **stock'iest**.

stock'ily *adv.* **stock'iness** *n.*

stock'breeder *n.* one who raises livestock.

stock'broker *n.* a person who buys and sells stocks and shares for others.

stock'-car *n.* a modified model of an ordinary car, as opposed to a specially-built racer, used in **stock-car racing**.

stock exchange **1** a place where stocks, etc., are bought and sold. **2** the brokers and dealers who work there.

stock'holder *n.* one who holds stocks in a public fund, or in a company.

stock'-in-trade' *n.* **1** the whole of the goods a shopkeeper keeps for sale. **2** equipment for business, or for some enterprise: *His stock-in-trade as a political speaker included certain high-sounding phrases which he always used.*

stock'man *n.* one who looks after livestock, esp. in Australia.

stock market a market for the sale of stocks, the stock exchange.

stock'pile *n.* a store, reserve supply.—*v.i.* to build up a reserve supply:—*pr.p.* **stock'piling**.

stock'room *n.* a room where goods are stored or kept in reserve.

stock'-still' *adj.* motionless.

stock'-taking *n.* a regular check of the goods in a shop or warehouse.

stock'yard *n.* a large yard with pens, stables, etc. where cattle are kept for market or slaughter.
on the stocks 1 (of a ship) being built. **2** being prepared.
stock up to give or get a supply or stock of.
take stock 1 to make a list of goods on hand. **2** (with *of*) to look at carefully to try and decide worth, importance.
take no stock in not to have confidence in.

stock[2] *stok, n.* a scented garden flower on a shrubby plant.

stockade *sto-kād', n.* a fence of strong posts put up round an area for defence.—*v.t.* to fortify with such:—*pr.p.* **stockad'-ing**.

stockbreeder, etc. See **stock**[1].

stocking *stok'ing, n.* a close covering for the foot and lower leg.

stock-in-trade, stockist, stocky, etc. See **stock**[1].

stodgy *stoj'i, adj.* **1** (of food) heavy and not easily digested. **2** (of people, writing) heavy and dull:—*comp.* **stodg'ier**; *superl.* **stodg'iest**.
stodge *n.* **1** heavy food, not easy to digest. **2** something that is dull, boring, hard to read.
stodg'ily *adv.* **stodg'iness** *n.*

stoic *stō'ik, n.* one who bears pain or misfortune without showing any sign of feeling it.—Also *adj.*
stō'ical *adj.* **stō'ically** *adv.*
stō'icism *(-is-izm)*, **stō'icalness** *ns.*

stoke *stōk, v.t.* to feed with fuel:—*pr.p.* **stok'ing**.
stok'er *n.* one who, or something that, feeds a furnace with fuel.
stoke'hole *n.* **1** the space where a ship's stokers work. **2** a hole through which a furnace is stoked.

stole[1] *stōl, n.* **1** a narrow strip of e.g. silk round the neck and hanging down in front worn by clergymen. **2** a woman's garment of similar shape of e.g. fur.

stole[2], **stolen**. See **steal**.

stolid *stol'id, adj.* (of a person or his manner) dull, heavy, not emotional.
stolid'ity, -idness *ns.* **stol'idly** *adv.*

stomach *stum'ȧk, n.* **1** the bag-like part of the body into which the food passes when swallowed, and where most of it is digested. **2** (*loosely*) the belly. **3** appetite or desire: *I have no stomach for the job.*—*v.t.* to bear, put up with: *He could not stomach them, their conduct.*

stone *stōn, n.* **1** a, usu. small, piece of loose rock. **2** a piece of this shaped for a purpose: *grindstone, tombstone.* **3** a precious stone or gem. **4** the hard shell round the seed of some fruits (e.g. the cherry). **5** the seed of a grape. **6** a standard weight of 14lb. (6.35kg) (in *pl.* often **stone**). **7** a piece of hard material formed in the bladder.—*adj.* **1** made of stone. **2** made of stoneware.—*v.t.* **1** to throw stones at. **2** to rub, etc., with a stone. **3** to take stones out of:—*pr.p.* **sto'ning**.
stoned (*slang*) *adj.* **1** very drunk. **2** intoxicated by drugs.
stō'nily *adv.* in a cold, hard manner.
stō'ny *adj.* **1** made of, or like, stone. **2** covered with stones. **3** hard, cold: *a stony stare.* **4** (*coll.*) stony-broke:—*comp.* **stō'nier**; *superl.* **stō'niest**.
stō'niness *n.*
Stone Age an early period in history when tools, weapons, were made of stone.
stone'-blind', -cold', -dead', -deaf' *adjs.* completely blind, cold, dead, deaf.
stone fruit a fruit whose seeds are covered with a hard shell (e.g. the cherry, peach, plum).
stone'wall' *v.i.* **1** to bat in cricket so as to stay in rather than to score. **2** to hold up the business of e.g. parliament by talking, etc.
stone'ware *n.* a hard kind of pottery.
stone'work *n.* a structure, or part of it, made of stone.
sto'ny-broke' (*coll.*) *adj.* penniless.
a rolling stone a person who does not settle in any place or job.
a stone's throw a very short distance.
leave no stone unturned to try every means possible.

stood. See **stand**.

stooge *stōōj, n.* **1** a comedian's assistant. **2** a person used by another (e.g. by a gangster) in carrying out his plans.—*v.i.* to act as a stooge:—*pr.p.* **stoog'ing**.

stool *stōōl, n.* **1** a low seat without a back. **2** a low support for the feet, or knees, when sitting or kneeling. **3** evacuation of the bowels, or matter evacuated. **4** a piece of wood to which a pigeon is fastened as a decoy for wild birds.
stool'-pigeon *n.* **1** a decoy pigeon. **2** a decoy. **3** an informer or spy esp. for the police.

stoop *stōōp, v.i.* **1** to bend the body forward and downwards. **2** to lower oneself from dignity (to do something): *He would not stoop to ask for help, stoop to cheating.*—*v.t.* to cause to stoop.—Also *n.*
stooped *adj.* having a stoop.

stop *stop, v.t.* **1** to stuff up and thus close (a hole; also **stop up**). **2** to block. **3** (*music*) to close (a hole), or press down (a string), so as to alter pitch. **4** to bring to a standstill, prevent from moving. **5** to prevent (a person, etc.) from doing something. **6** to put an end to: *Stop this nonsense!* **7** to keep back: *to stop (payment of) a cheque.*—*v.t.* **1** to cease going forward, working, etc. **2** to come to an end. **3** (*coll.*) to stay:—*pr.p.* **stopp'ing**; *pa.p.* **stopped.**—*n.* **1** the act of stopping. **2** the state of being stopped. **3** a halt. **4** a pause. **5** a stopping-place. **6** (*coll.*) a stay. **7** a device for bringing motion to a standstill or limiting action. **8** a means of altering musical pitch, such as a fret or hole. **9** a set of pipes in an organ, or a knob, etc. for bringing them into use. **10** a mark of punctuation. **11** a full stop (.).

stopp'age *(-ij) n.* **1** the act of stopping, or state of being stopped. **2** the obstruction of a passage in the body. **3** money kept back.

stopp'er *n.* **1** one who stops. **2** something that closes a hole or the neck of a bottle.

stopp'ing *n.* and *adj.*

stop'cock *n.* a tap and valve for controlling flow of liquid.

stop'gap *n.* a person or thing that fills a gap in an emergency.

stopp'ing-place *n.* a place where a bus, etc., regularly stops.

stop press a space in a newspaper for last-minute news.

stop'watch *n.* a watch with a hand that can be stopped and started, used in timing a race, etc.

pull out all the stops to act with the greatest possible energy.

storage. See **store**.

store *stōr, stör, n.* **1** a large amount, number. **2** (in *pl.*) supplies of food, ammunition, etc. **3** (in *pl.*) goods gathered for later use. **4** a storehouse. **5** a shop, esp. one with many departments or branches.—*v.t.* **1** to gather and put in a place for keeping. **2** to furnish (a place, with supplies, etc.):—*pr.p.* **stor'ing.**

stor'age *(-ij) n.* **1** the act of storing, or state of being stored. **2** the price charged for keeping goods.

storage heater an electric heater containing a mass of brick which is heated up at times when electricity is relatively cheap and gives off heat at other times.

store'house, store'room *ns.* a place, room, in which things are stored.

in store prepared or destined (for a person): *There was a scolding, a surprise, in store for me.*

set (great) store by to value highly (e.g. a person's approval, opinion).

store up to collect and keep for future use.

storey *stō'ri, stō', n.* all the rooms, flats, etc. at one level in e.g. a block of flats; the space between one floor and the next:—*pl.* **sto'reys.**

sto'reyed *adj.* (esp. as part of a word) having storeys.

storied. See **story**.

stork *störk, n.* a wading bird with long bill, neck, and legs.

storm *störm, n.* **1** a violent disturbance in the air producing wind, rain, etc. **2** a violent outbreak (of e.g. anger, applause). **3** a heavy shower (of): *a storm of bullets.*—*v.i.* **1** to blow, rain, etc. with violence. **2** to show, express, great anger. **3** to rage (at).—*v.t.* to attack and take by force (also **take by storm**).

stor'my *adj.* **1** having many storms. **2** blowing furiously. **3** violent. **4** noisy:—*comp.* **stor'mier**; *superl.* **stor'miest.**

stor'mily *adv.* **stor'miness** *n.*

storm'-beaten *adj.* beaten or injured by storms.

storm'bound *adj.* prevented by storm from getting in touch with the outside.

storm signal a signal shown to warn of a coming storm.

storm'-tossed *adj.* tossed about by storms.

storm troops shock troops (see this).

story *stō'ri, stö', n.* **1** an account of an event, a series of events, real or imaginary. **2** a brief tale leading up to a conclusion that is amusing, or supposed to be so. **3** an untruth.

stō'ried *adj.* having a history, having many stories told about it.

stoup *stoōp, n.* a basin for holy water.

stout *stowt, adj.* **1** strong in body or material: *stout fellows; a stout stick.* **2** brave, forceful, resolute: *They put up a stout resistance.* **3** (of a person) fat and solid.—*n.* a strong dark beer.

stout'-heart'ed *adj.* having a brave heart.

stove[1] *stōv, n.* **1** a closed device for heating a room or for cooking. **2** a kiln.

stove[2]. See **stave.**

stow *stō, v.t.* **1** to place or pack out of the way or in a suitable place. **2** to fill, pack: *to stow the case with boxes.*

stow'age *(-ij) n.* **1** the act of stowing, or state of being stowed. **2** a room for articles to be laid away.

stow'away *n.* one who **stows away**, i.e. hides himself in a ship so that he may get a passage for nothing.

straddle *strad'l, v.i.* **1** to stand or walk with legs far apart. **2** (of legs) to spread wide apart.—*v.t.* **1** to stand or sit with legs on either side of (e.g. a chair, horse). **2** to cover the area containing (a target) with bombs:—*pr.p.* **stradd'ling.**—Also *n.*

straggle *strag'l, v.i.* **1** to stray from the course or line of march. **2** (of e.g. a trailing plant) to wander beyond proper limits. **3** to scatter irregularly: *The crowd straggled over the park*:—*pr.p.* **stragg'ling.**

stragg'ler *n.* **1** one who straggles, esp. who is left behind. **2** a plant that straggles.

stragg'ly *adj.* spread out thinly, untidily: —*comp.* **stragg'lier**; *superl.* **stragg'liest.**

stragg'liness *n.*

straight *strāt, adj.* **1** not bent or curved. **2** direct: *the straight way to the church.* **3** direct, frank, to the point: *a straight answer.* **4** honest, fair: *straight dealings.* **5** placed levelly: *The pictures are not straight.* **6** in order: *Try to get your accounts straight.* **7** unmixed: *a straight whisky.* **8** one after another: *He won the tennis match in three straight sets.*—*adv.* **1** in the shortest way. **2** honestly, fairly. **3** plainly.

straight'en *v.t.* to make straight (also with *up*).—*v.i.* (with *up*) to become straight.

straight'ness *n.*

straight face an unsmiling expression.

straightfor'ward *adj.* **1** going forward in a straight course. **2** honest, frank. **3** simple, without difficulties.

straightfor'wardly *adv.*

straightfor'wardness *n.*

straight'way (*old*) *adv.* at once.

straight thinking clear logical thinking, not affected by feelings, etc.

a straight fight election contest involving two candidates only.

a straight talk a frank talk, esp. one expressing disapproval.

go straight to be, become, honest after a time of dishonesty or criminal activity.

in the straight on the straight part esp. of a racecourse.

keep a straight face to refrain from smiling or laughing.

straight away at once.

straight off without hesitation.

strain[1] *strān, v.t.* **1** to stretch, draw tightly. **2** to work, exert, to the fullest: *to strain every nerve, one's ears, eyes.* **3** to injure by overworking, or using wrongly. **4** to stretch too far (the meaning, the law, one's patience, resources). **5** to separate solid from liquid by passing through a sieve, colander, etc.—*v.i.* to make violent efforts.—*n.* **1** the act of straining. **2** a great effort. **3** an injury cause by straining, esp. to the muscles. **4** (the effect of) too much work, worry, etc.: *suffering from strain*; *the strain of nursing.* **5** too great a demand: *a strain on my purse, patience.*

strained *adj.* showing effort, not easy and natural.

strain'er *n.* something that strains, esp. a screen or sieve for separating solids from liquids.

strained relations a state of unfriendly feeling because of something that has happened.

strain a point to make a special effort, or go beyond the usual limit.

strain at **1** to pull on. **2** to try to get free of, to resist: *to strain at the lead.* **3** to balk at.

strain[2] *strān, n.* **1** race, stock, family. **2** (of plants, animals) a variety with certain characteristics. **3** a tendency, streak, in character: *a strain of recklessness.* **4** (often in *pl.*) a passage of a song or poem. **5** mood, tone, style: *He said he hated me—and more in the same strain.*

strait *strāt, n.* **1** (often in *pl.*) a narrow strip of sea between two pieces of land. **2** (usu. in *pl.*) difficulties, need: *When this happened, he was in great straits.*

strait'ened *adj.*: **in straitened circumstances** in need, having little money.

strait'-jacket *n.* a jacket with long sleeves tied behind to hold back the arms of someone who is being restrained.

strait'-laced' *adj.* **1** (*orig.*) in tightly laced stays. **2** strict and prudish in words and behaviour.

strand[1] *strand, n.* the shore or beach of a sea or lake.—*v.t., v.i.* **1** to run aground on the shore. **2** to put into, arrive in, a helpless, friendless position.

strand'ed *adj.*

strand[2] *strand, n.* **1** one of the threads that make up a rope, etc. **2** a long lock of hair.

strange *strānj, adj.* **1** not known, seen, or heard, before. **2** not one's own: *a strange dog in our garden.* **3** new, unfamiliar: *This method was strange to me.* **4** foreign: *in a strange land.* **5** unusual, odd, queer.

strange'ly *adv.* **strange'ness** *n.*

stranger *strān'jėr, n.* **1** a person one does not know. **2** a guest or visitor. **3** one who does not live locally. **4** one who has had no experience of (with *to*): *He was a stranger to fear.*

strangle *strang'gl, v.t.* **1** to kill by tightening a cord round the throat, or by stopping the breath by any means. **2** to stop the growth of. **3** to suppress: *to strangle a* *sob.*—Also *v.i.*:—*pr.p.* **strang'ling.**

stran'glehold *n.* **1** a choking hold in wrestling. **2** any force that prevents freedom of action, expression, or growth.

strangulate *strang'gū-lāt*, *v.t.* to compress, constrict (a passage in the body) so as to stop circulation, etc.:—*pr.p.* **stran'gulating.**

strangulā'tion *n.* **1** the action of strangling or strangulating. **2** the state of being strangled or strangulated.

strap *strap*, *n.* **1** a narrow strip of leather or cloth, esp. one with a buckle. **2** a razor strop. **3** a loop of e.g. leather for taking hold of.—*v.t.* **1** to beat with a strap. **2** to fasten or bind with a strap:—*pr.p.* **strapp'ing**; *pa.p.* **strapped.**

strapp'ing *adj.* tall and strong.

strata. See **stratum.**

stratagem *strat'ȧ-jėm*, *n.* **1** action planned to deceive and outwit an enemy. **2** a cunning or careful plan.

strategic *strȧ-tē'jik*, *adj.* **1** having to do with strategy. **2** done as part of a strategy or plan: *a strategic retreat.* **3** important to the success of a plan: *a strategic position* (=one which gives the holder an advantage over his enemy).

strat'egy *n.* **1** the art of planning a campaign or large military operation. **2** the art of carrying out a plan skilfully. **3** a stratagem:—*pl.* **strat'egies.**

stratify, etc. See **stratum.**

stratum *strā'tum*, *n.* **1** a bed of earth or rock, made up usually of a series of layers. **2** any layer. **3** a level (of society):—*pl.* **stra'ta.**

stratify *strat'i-fī*, *v.t.*, *v.i.* to form in layers:—*pr.p.* **strat'ifying**; *pa.p.* **strat'ified.**

stratificā'tion *n.*

stratosphere *strat'ō-sfēr*, *n.* a layer of the earth's atmosphere, some miles above the earth.

straw *strö*, *n.* **1** the stalk on which grain grows. **2** a number of dried stalks of corn, etc. **3** a tube for sucking up a drink. **4** a straw hat. **5** a trifle, anything worthless.

straw'berry *n.* **1** the red fruit of a plant of the rose family, with long creeping shoots. **2** the plant itself:—*pl.* **straw'berries.**

straw hat a hat made of straw, etc.

straw vote, poll a vote taken unofficially to get some idea of the general opinion.

clutch, grasp, at straws when in a difficult or dangerous situation, to hope that something will happen which will be of assistance, or to do or use anything that might be of assistance, even though it is very unlikely that it will happen or that it will be of help.

the last straw yet one more unpleasant aspect or occurrence in a situation which makes one unwilling to put up with the situation any more: *The knives and forks were dirty, the food was cold, and the last straw was when the waiter poured wine all over me—we just walked out the restaurant.*

stray *strā*, *v.i.* **1** to wander. **2** to wander (from e.g. the proper place or company). **3** to turn away from duty or virtue.—*n.* **1** a domestic animal, etc., that has strayed. **2** a wandering or homeless person.—*adj.* **1** wandering, lost. **2** casual, isolated, single: *a stray remark*; *a stray example.*

streak *strēk*, *n.* **1** a line or long mark different in colour from the surface that surrounds it. **2** a stripe. **3** a flash. **4** a trace in one's character (of e.g. humour, meanness).—*v.t.* to mark with streaks.— *v.i.* (*coll.*) **1** to run swiftly. **2** to run naked, or in a state of indecent undress, in public.

streak'er *n.*

streak'y *adj.* **1** marked with streaks. **2** (of bacon) fat and lean in layers. **3** varying good and bad: *a streaky performance*:—*comp.* **streak'ier**; *superl.* **streak'iest.**

streak'ily *adv.* **streak'iness** *n.*

stream *strēm*, *n.* **1** a flow of (water, blood, air, light, etc.). **2** a river, brook, etc. **3** anything flowing or moving without a break: *a stream of people, cars, tears, abuse.* **4** a group or section (esp. of the pupils in a school) made on the basis of ability, etc.—*v.t.*, *v.i.* **1** to flow, or cause to flow. **2** to stretch, move, etc. in a long line. **3** to divide into streams.

stream'er *n.* **1** a flag streaming in the wind. **2** a long ribbon, etc., esp. for decoration.

stream'lined *adj.* **1** shaped so as to go most easily through air or water. **2** simplified so as to be as efficient as possible. **3** very up-to-date.

street *strēt*, *n.* a road lined with houses, etc., broader than a lane.

not in the same street of a completely different quality, usu. worse.

streets ahead of very much better than.

up someone's street having to do with some area of life in which a person's knowledge, abilities, etc. lie.

strength, strengthen. See **strong.**

strenuous *stren'ū-us*, *adj.* **1** vigorous, energetic: *a strenuous person, resistance.* **2** (of e.g. task) requiring much effort.

streptococcus *strep-tō-kok'us*, *n.* any of a group of bacteria that cause diseases e.g.

pneumonia:—*pl.* **streptococci** *(-kok'ī, -kok'sī)*.

stress *stres, n.* **1** force, pressure, pull, etc. of one thing on another. **2** influence or effect acting in a bad direction: *Under stress of circumstances he took to theft.* **3** physical or nervous strain. **4** emphasis, importance: *He laid stress on the fact that it was urgent to do something.* **5** force, loudness, etc. given to one part of a word: *In 'widow' the stress is on wid.—v.t.* to put stress, pressure, emphasis, or a physical or nervous strain, on.

stressed-out' *adj.* suffering from nervous or mental tension.

stretch *strech, v.t.* **1** to draw out to greater length, or too far, or more tightly, or from one point to another: *to stretch a piece of elastic, a muscle, a violin string, a rope from post to post.* **2** (usu. with *out*) to lay (oneself) at full length. **3** to straighten or extend (e.g. oneself, wings). **4** to hold (out, etc. e.g. the hand). **5** to make cover more than is right: *to stretch the truth, law, meaning.—v.i.* **1** to be able to be drawn out to greater length, etc. **2** (usu. with *out*) to lay oneself at full length. **3** to reach (out, for something). **4** to extend (from one point to another, or for a stated distance).—*n.* **1** the act of stretching. **2** the state of being stretched. **3** reach, utmost extent. **4** an unbroken length of space or time: *a stretch of grass, of two years.* **5** a straight part of a racecourse.

stretch'er *n.* **1** anything for stretching. **2** a frame for carrying sick or wounded.

stretch'er-bear'er *n.* one who carries a stretcher.

at a stretch **1** continuously: *to work four hours at a stretch.* **2** with difficulty.

stretch a point to do, allow, more than one is bound, or entitled, to do, allow.

stretch one's legs to go for a walk.

strew *stro͞o, v.t.* **1** to scatter loosely. **2** to cover by scattering (with):—*pa.t.* **strewed**; *pa.p.* **strewed** or **strewn**.

stricken *strik'ėn, adj.* **1** struck. **2** wounded. **3** deeply affected (by illness, etc.).— See also **grief-stricken**, **panic-stricken**.

strict *strikt, adj.* **1** exact: *in the strict meaning of the term.* **2** allowing no exception: *strict orders, honesty.* **3** severe, harsh: *strict laws.* **4** (of a person) compelling exact obedience to rules: *Their father was very strict.*

strict'ly *adv.* **strict'ness** *n.*

stricture *strik'chụr, n.* an unfavourable remark, criticism (on).

stride *strīd, v.i.* **1** to walk with long steps. **2** to take a long step.—*v.t.* to walk along, step over, or straddle:—*pr.p.* **strid'ing**; *pa.t.* **strōde**; *pa.p.* **stridd'en**.—*n.* **1** a long step. **2** the space stepped over. **3** a step forward, progress: *great strides toward independence.*

take something in one's stride to do, cope with, something without worry or difficulty.

strident *strī'dėnt, adj.* (of e.g. a voice) loud and grating or harsh-sounding.

strī'dently *adv.* **strī'dency** *n.*

strife *strīf, n.* conflict, fighting, quarrelling.

strike *strīk, v.t.* **1** to hit with force. **2** to attack. **3** to stab, pierce (e.g. to the heart). **4** to dash (against, on): *to strike one's head on a beam.* **5** to knock against, collide with. **6** to give (a blow). **7** to light (a match), or to produce (a light, sparks), by rubbing. **8** to touch (a note, string), or to make (a musical note) sound. **9** (of a clock) to sound (the hour): *The clock struck ten.* **10** to cancel, mark out (with *out, off, from*): *to strike from the record.* **11** (of a tree) to thrust (roots) down in the earth. **12** to lower, let down (flag, tent, sail). **13** to come across suddenly or unexpectedly: *to strike oil.* **14** to come to (one) suddenly or with force, or to affect, impress (one): *A thought strikes me; I am struck by the resemblance; It strikes me with surprise; How does it strike you?* **15** to catch (the eye). **16** to make by, or as if by, a blow: *to strike dead, blind, deaf, dumb*, etc. **17** to make (a bargain, agreement).—*v.i.* **1** to give a quick blow. **2** to attack. **3** to knock (against). **4** (of a clock) to sound a time. **5** to fall (on, across): *The sunlight strikes across the treetops.* **6** to take a course: *To get there, you strike across this field.* **7** to stop work in support of a claim, or as a protest:—*pr.p.* **strik'ing**; *pa.t.*, *pa.p.* **struck** (older *pa.p.* **strick'en**; see this word).—*n.* **1** the act of striking for higher wages, etc.: *The men have come out, are, on strike.* **2** a find (of e.g. oil).

strik'er *n.* **1** one who is on strike. **2** (*football*) an attacking forward.

strik'ing *adj.* **1** that strikes, or is intended to do so. **2** very noticeable: *a striking likeness.* **3** impressive.

strik'ingly *adv.* **strik'ingness** *n.*

strike'-breaker *n.* one who works during a strike, or who does the work of a striker.

striking distance a distance short enough for a blow, attack, etc. to be delivered, carried out, successfully.

strike a balance **1** to find the difference between the debit and credit side of an account. **2** to find a fair middle course.

strike an attitude. See **attitude**.

strike an average 1 to estimate, or to calculate, an average. **2** to arrive at a statement expressing something between two contradictory or extreme statements.
strike camp to take down tents, etc., and move on.
strike home (of a blow, remark, etc.) to strike to the point aimed at, or to the point where it will be felt most.
strike fear, terror, into to frighten, terrify.
strike up 1 to begin to play, sing (a tune). **2** (*coll.*) to form suddenly (e.g. a friendship, acquaintance).
struck on keen on, appreciative of, liking.
See also **stroke¹**.

string *string*, *n.* **1** a long narrow cord, made by twisting threads, used for tying, fastening, etc. **2** a nerve, tendon, fibre. **3** a stretched piece of catgut, silk, wire, etc., in a musical instrument. **4** (in *pl.*) the stringed instruments played by a bow in an orchestra. **5** a group of things threaded on a cord, e.g. beads, onions. **6** a number of things coming one after the other: *a string of cars, of curses.*—*v.t.* **1** to put on a string. **2** to tie with string. **3** to remove the strings from (e.g. beans). **4** to stretch out in a long line.—*v.i.* to move in or into a long line:—*pa.p.* **strung**.
stringed *adj.* having strings.
string'er *n.* a person supplying news information to a newspaper, etc. but who is not on its staff.
string'y *adj.* **1** made up of small threads, strings, or fibres. **2** long, thin, and wiry: —*comp.* **string'ier**; *superl.* **string'iest**.
string'iness *n.*
have strings attached (*coll.*; of a gift, service, etc.) to be given, done, with the understanding that the person who receives it will act in a certain way.
pull strings to use one's influence, or that of others, to gain an advantage.
pull the strings to control the actions of others, be the real mover in something that is done.

stringent *strin'jent*, *adj.* **1** binding strongly, strictly enforced: *stringent rules.* **2** compelling: *stringent necessity.*
strin'gently *adv.* **strin'gency** *n.*

stringy. See **string**.

strip *strip*, *v.t.* **1** to pull (off), remove. **2** to skin, peel, or remove fruit or leaves from. **3** to make bare or empty. **4** to undress. **5** to deprive (of).—*v.i.* to undress:—*pr.p.* **stripp'ing**; *pa.p.* **stripped**.—*n.* a long narrow piece.
stripp'er *n.* **1** something that strips off (paint, etc.). **2** one who removes his or her clothes as an entertainment for others.
comic strip. See **comic**.

stripe *strīp*, *n.* **1** a band of different colour, etc., from the background on which it lies. **2** a blow with a whip or rod. **3** a decoration on a uniform sleeve showing rank, etc.—*v.t.* **1** to make stripes on. **2** to form with lines of different colours, etc.:—*pr.p.* **strīp'ing**.
strip'y, strip'ey *adj.* having stripes:—*comp.* **strip'ier**; *superl.* **strip'iest**.

stripling *strip'ling*, *n.* a lad who has not reached full growth.

stripy. See **stripe**.

strive *strīv*, *v.i.* **1** to try or work hard (to do, or for, something). **2** (*old-fashioned*) to struggle, fight (with, against):—*pr.p.* **striv'ing**; *pa.t.* **strōve**; *pa.p.* **striv'en** *(striv')*.
striv'ing *n.*
See also **strife**.

strode. See **stride**.

stroganoff *strog'ȧ-nof*: **beef stroganoff** a dish of thinly-cut beef cooked with onions, mushrooms and seasoning in a sour-cream sauce.

stroke¹ *strōk*, *n.* **1** an act of striking. **2** a blow. **3** a sudden attack of apoplexy or paralysis. **4** a sudden happening or experience: *a stroke of lightning, of good luck.* **5** the sound of a clock. **6** a dash in writing. **7** the sweep of an oar in rowing. **8** one complete movement, e.g. of the piston of a steam engine. **9** a movement in one direction of a pen, pencil, or paintbrush. **10** a method of striking in games, swimming, etc. **11** a single effort or action. **12** an achievement, feat. **13** the rower of the stroke oar.—*v.t., v.i.* to row the stroke oar of (a boat):—*pr.p.* **strok'ing**.
stroke oar 1 the oar nearest the stern in a rowing boat. **2** its rower.

stroke² *strōk*, *v.t.* to rub gently in one direction, esp. as a sign of affection:—*pr.p.* **strok'ing**.

stroll *strōl*, *v.i.* **1** to wander, roam. **2** to walk about idly.—Also *n.*
strolling player, actor one who wandered round the country giving performances.

strong *strong*, *adj.* **1** able to withstand attack of any kind—firm, solid, hard-wearing, well-fortified, etc. **2** powerful in attack: *a strong wind.* **3** (of a person, etc.) having great physical power. **4** healthy. **5** (of e.g. a person, character) forceful, able to command respect or obedience. **6** having a quality in a great degree: *a strong smell, colour; a strong dislike.* **7** having much of the important ingredient:

strong tea; *a strong whisky.* **8** of the stated number of persons: *a force 30 000 strong* ('strong' always follows the number).

strong'ly *adv.* **strength** *streng(k)th*, *n.*

strength'en *v.t.*, *v.i.* to make, or become, strong or stronger.

strong'-box *n.* a safe or strongly-made box for valuables.

strong drink alcoholic liquor.

strong'hold *n.* **1** a place built to stand against attack, a fortress. **2** a place where a belief or view is strongly held: *a stronghold of conservatism.*

strong language **1** forceful emphatic language. **2** swearing.

strong'-mind'ed *adj.* **1** having strong powers of reasoning. **2** determined to have one's views known and considered.

strong point something one is particularly good at.

strong'-room *n.* a room constructed for the safe storage of valuables.

go from strength to strength to progress from success to greater success.

on the strength a permanent member of the unit, organisation, etc.

on the strength of encouraged by or counting on: *On the strength of this offer of help, he went ahead with the plan.*

strop *strop*, *n.* a strip of e.g. leather on which a razor is sharpened.—*v.t.* to sharpen on a strop:—*pr.p.* **stropp'ing**; *pa.p.* **stropped**.

strontium *stron'shi-ŭm*, *n.* an element, a metal occurring in radioactive form in fall-out (see this).

stroppy *strop'i*, (*coll.*) *adj.* quarrelsome, bad-tempered, angry:—*comp.* **stropp'ier**; *superl.* **stropp'iest**.

strove. See **strive**.

struck. See **strike**.

structure *struk'chŭr*, *n.* **1** a building, esp. a large one. **2** the way the parts of anything are arranged: *the structure of a flower*, *of a novel.* **3** the manner in which something is organised: *the structure of society.*—*v.t.* to organise, give some system or structure to:—*pr.p.* **struc'turing**.

struc'tural *adj.* **struc'turally** *adv.*

strudel *strōō'dl*, *n.* a cake of very thin pastry enclosing fruit, etc.

struggle *strug'l*, *v.i.* **1** to make great effort by twisting about, etc.: *Joe struggled in Jim's grasp.* **2** to fight (with, against, for). **3** to try or work hard (to). **4** to make one's way with difficulty: *to struggle through the mud*, *struggle along with little money*:—*pr.p.* **strugg'ling**.—*n.* **1** a hard effort. **2** a fight.

strum *strum*, *v.t.* **1** to play on (a musical instrument), or to play (a tune) in an unskilful, noisy way. **2** to sound the strings of (a guitar, etc.) with a sweep of the hand (as opposed to plucking single strings).—Also *v.i.*:—*pr.p.* **strumm'ing**; *pa.p.* **strummed**.

strung. See **string**.

strut[1] *strut*, *v.i.* to walk about in a stiff, vain, self-important manner:—*pr.p.* **strutt'ing**; *pa.p.* **strutt'ed**.—Also *n.*

strut[2] *strut*, *n.* a bar, column, taking pressure or supporting weight in the direction of its length.

strychnine *strik'nēn*, *-nin*, *n.* a poison, used in small quantities as a medicine.

stub *stub*, *n.* **1** the stump left after a tree is cut down. **2** a short end (e.g. of a pencil, cigarette).—*v.t.* **1** to put (out, e.g. a cigarette) by pressing the end against something. **2** to strike (e.g. the toe) against anything hard:—*pr.p.* **stubb'ing**; *pa.p.* **stubbed**.

stubb'y *adj.* short, thick, and strong:—*comp.* **stubb'ier**; *superl.* **stubb'iest**.

stubble *stub'l*, *n.* **1** the stubs, ends, of corn left in the ground when the stalks are cut. **2** a short rough growth (e.g. of beard).

stubborn *stub'ŏrn*, *adj.* **1** (of persons) unwilling to give way, obstinate. **2** (of resistance, an attempt, etc.) carried on with great determination. **3** difficult to move, work or deal with, or manage.

stubby. See **stub**.

stucco *stuk'ō*, *n.* **1** a plaster of lime and fine sand, etc., used for covering, or decorating, walls, etc. **2** work done in stucco:—*pl.* **stucc'os**.—*v.t.* to cover with stucco:—*pa.p.* **stucc'oed**, **stucc'o'd**.

stuck. See **stick**[1].

stuck'-up' *adj.* self-important, snobbish, haughty in manner.

stud[1] *stud*, *n.* a collection of horses and mares kept for breeding, or for racing or hunting.

stud[2] *stud*, *n.* **1** a nail with a large head. **2** a knob for ornament. **3** any of various round, tapering, or pointed nails or knobs on or fixed to the sole of a shoe or boot. **4** a double-headed button used for fastening a collar.—*v.t.* **1** to cover with studs. **2** to sprinkle, or be sprinkled over, thickly: *a lake studded with islands*; *Flowers studded the grass.*

student, **studied**, etc. See **study**.

studio *stū'di-ō*, *n.* **1** the workshop of an artist, etc. **2** a building or place where motion pictures are made. **3** a room from which radio or television programmes are broadcast:—*pl.* **stu'dios**.

studious. See **study**.

study *stud'i*, *v.t.* **1** to give time and attention to gaining knowledge of: *to study mathematics.* **2** to memorise (a part in a play). **3** to observe closely: *to study the habits of bees, the face of the accused.* **4** to look at carefully so as to understand (e.g. a problem, situation). **5** to consider, try to act so as to satisfy, etc.: *to study a person's feelings, wishes, needs, convenience.*—Also *v.i.*:—*pr.p.* **stud'ying**; *pa.p.* **stud'ied**.—*n.* **1** applying the mind to a subject so as to gain information or understanding. **2** a written report on the result of such work: *We have just published a study on Shakespeare's works.* **3** (the object of) earnest effort: *He made it his study to please his employer.* **4** a room where one studies. **5** a piece of work in art, music, or literature intended as a preliminary sketch, trial, or outline, or as an exercise in technique:—*pl.* **stud'ies**.

student *stū'dėnt*, *n.* **1** one who studies, esp. at a university, etc. **2** one who is fond of study.—*adj.* (used only before a noun) in training, learning a profession.

stud'entship *n.* the granting of money to a person so that he may study at a university, etc.

stud'ied *adj.* **1** planned, intentional: *a studied insult.* **2** too careful, not natural: *studied politeness.*

studious *stū'di-ŭs*, *adj.* **1** fond of study. **2** studying carefully and much. **3** careful (to do, of). **4** studied, careful: *studious avoidance of subjects about which they disagreed.*

stū'diously *adv.* **stū'diousness** *n.*

make a study of to study in detail.

stuff *stuf*, *n.* **1** the material of which anything is made. **2** fabrics, cloth, esp. woollen. **3** worthless matter. **4** things. **5** possessions, esp. household goods. **6** (*slang*) way of behaving or talking: *rough stuff.*—*v.t.* **1** to fill by crowding. **2** to cram (into). **3** to fill with seasoning: *to stuff a turkey.* **4** to fill the skin of (a dead animal) so that it may be kept.—*v.i.* to cram in food (also **stuff oneself**).

stuff'ing *n.* material used to stuff.

stuffy *stuf'i*, *adj.* **1** (of a room, etc.) close, badly ventilated. **2** (*coll.*) angry, sulky. **3** (*coll.*) dull, old-fashioned and prim:—*comp.* **stuff'ier**; *superl.* **stuff'iest**.

stuff'ily *adv.* **stuff'iness** *n.*

that's the stuff! that's what is wanted!

stultify *stul'ti-fī*, *v.t.* **1** to make futile, of no value: *to stultify all he had done by one wrong step.* **2** to cause to look foolish:—*pr.p.* **stul'tifying**; *pa.p.* **stul'tified**.

stumble *stum'bl*, *v.i.* **1** to strike the feet against something and trip or lose balance. **2** to falter. **3** to light (on), find by chance. **4** to slide into wrongdoing or mistake:—*pr.p.* **stum'bling**.—Also *n.*

stum'bling-block *n.* **1** difficulty in the way of a plan, etc. **2** a cause of error or hesitation.

stump *stump*, *n.* **1** the part of a tree left in the ground after the trunk is cut down. **2** the piece of a limb, tooth, pencil, etc. remaining after a part is cut or worn away. **3** (*cricket*) one of the three sticks forming a wicket.—*v.t.* **1** to put out (a batsman who is not in his ground) by striking the stumps with the ball. **2** to puzzle completely, or make helpless to act: *The problem stumped her.* **3** (*slang*) to pay (up) (also *v.i.*).—*v.i.* to walk along heavily.

stum'py *adj.* short and thick:—*comp.* **stum'pier**; *superl.* **stum'piest**.

stun *stun*, *v.t.* **1** (of a loud noise, blow, bad news, etc.) to daze, knock senseless, bewilder. **2** to surprise greatly, amaze:—*pr.p.* **stunn'ing**; *pa.p.* **stunned**.

stunn'ing *adj.*

stung. See **sting**.

stunk. See **stink**.

stunt[1] *stunt*, *v.t.* **1** to stop the growth of. **2** to check (growth, etc.).

stunt'ed *adj.*

stunt[2] *stunt*, *n.* **1** a daring feat. **2** something done to attract notice.

stunt'man *n.* one who is paid to perform dangerous or difficult stunts e.g. in films.

stupefy *stūp'i-fī*, *v.t.* **1** (of drink, sorrow, etc.) to make stupid, deaden the senses or feelings of. **2** to arouse amazement (usu. disapproving) in (a person).—Also *v.i.*:—*pr.p.* **stup'efying**; *pa.p.* **stup'efied**.

stupefac'tion *n.*

stupendous *stū-pen'dŭs*, *adj.* amazing, wonderful, because of size or power.

stupid *stū'pid*, *adj.* **1** dull in understanding, slow at learning. **2** foolish, not sensible: *It was a stupid thing to do.* **3** stupified: *He is stupid with lack of sleep.*—*n.* a stupid person.

stupid'ity *n.* **1** stupidness. **2** a stupid act:—*pl.* **stupid'ities**.

stu'pidly *adv.* **stu'pidness** *n.*

stu'por *n.* **1** a state (caused e.g. by drugs) in which one is not, or is not wholly, conscious. **2** a dazed condition from amazement, etc.

sturdy *stûr'di*, *adj.* **1** strong, healthy. **2** of strong material. **3** firm, resolute: *sturdy resistance, defenders, independence*:—*comp.* **stur'dier**; *superl.* **stur'diest**.

stur'dily *adv.* **stur'diness** *n.*

sturgeon *stûr'jȯn, n.* a large fish which is the source of true caviare.

stutter *stut'ėr, v.i.* to utter one's words in a jerky way, pausing and repeating parts of them.—Also *n.*
stutt'erer *n.* one who stutters.

sty[1] *stī, n.* **1** a pigsty, pen for pigs. **2** any very dirty place:—*pl.* **sties**.

sty[2] *stī, n.* a small inflamed swelling on the eyelid:—*pl.* **sties**.—Also **stye** (*pl.* **styes**).

stye. See **sty[2]**.

style *stīl, n.* **1** an ancient pointed tool for writing. **2** the pin of a sundial. **3** the middle part of the pistil of a flower. **4** a way of expressing thought in language, or ideas in music, art, etc.: *She has an easy, flowing style.* **5** a way of moving, etc., in doing something, e.g. in playing a game. **6** a skilful way or manner of doing something. **7** fashion, manner: *in the style of 1850.* **8** an air of fashion or elegance. **9** a title or name.—*v.t.* **1** to name, call: *He styled himself 'Lord John' and his house 'castle'.* **2** to arrange (hair, etc.) in a style:—*pr.p.* **styl'ing**.
styl'ish *adj.* smart, in fashion, showy.
styl'ishly *adv.* **styl'ishness** *n.*
styl'ist *n.* **1** one who has a fine and distinctive style of writing, etc. **2** one who cuts and arranges hair.
stylis'tic *adj.* concerning style: *a few stylistic differences between the two versions.*
styl'us *n.* **1** a style (writing tool or sundial pin). **2** a cutting tool used in making gramophone records. **3** a gramophone needle.
in style **1** fashionable, fashionably. **2** with no expense or effort spared.

stymie *stī'mi, (coll.) v.t.* to frustrate, stop, prevent, thwart:—*pr.p.* **sty'mying**.

styptic *stip'tik, n.* something which stops bleeding.—Also *adj.*

suave *swäv, adj.* (of a person, manner) polite, agreeable (esp. on the surface).
suave'ness, **suav'ity** *(swav'), ns.*

sub- *sub-, pfx.* under.
In Latin, and in English words from Latin, this appears before *c, f, g, m, p, r, s* as **suc-** (e.g. *suc*ceed), **suf-** (e.g. *suf*fer), **sug-** (e.g. *sug*gest), **sum-** (e.g. *sum*mon), **sup-** (e.g. *sup*port), **sur-** (e.g. *sur*prise), and **sus-** (e.g. *sus*pend).
Shades of meaning in modern words include:—
1 (from) below (e.g. *subway*). **2** less in rank or importance, or under a superior (e.g. *sublibrarian*). **3** less than (e.g. *subnormal intelligence*), or slightly less than (e.g. *a subtropical climate*). **4** formed by dividing into smaller groups or sections (e.g. *a subdivision, subsection)*.

sub *sub, (coll.) n.* short for **subordinate**, **subaltern**, **submarine**, **subscription**, etc.

subacute *sub-ȧ-kūt', adj.* (of a disease) moderately acute.

subaltern *sub'l-tėrn, (U.S.) sub-öl'tėrn, n.* an officer in the army under the rank of captain.

subaqua *sub-ak'wȧ, adj.* and *n.* (pertaining to) underwater sport.

subatomic *sub-ȧ-tom'ik, adj.* **1** smaller than an atom. **2** happening within an atom.

subcommittee *sub'kȯ-mit'i, n.* a committee having powers given to it by a larger committee.

subconscious *sub-kon'shus, adj.* having to do with workings of the mind of which a person himself is not aware: *His generosity really arose from a subconscious desire for praise.*—*n.* a person's subconscious mind.
subcon'sciously *adv.*

subcontinent *sub-kon'tin-ėnt, n.* a large section of a continent, with certain physical, etc. features which separate it from the rest of the continent.

subcontractor *sub'kȯn-trak'tȯr, n.* one who undertakes work for a contractor (i.e. is not directly employed by the person who wants the work done).
subcon'tract *n.* **subcontract'** *v.t., v.i.*

subcutaneous *sub-kū-tā'ni-ůs, adj.* under the skin.

subdivide *sub-di-vīd', v.t., v.i.* to divide into smaller parts or divisions:—*pr.p.* **subdivid'ing**.
subdivi'sion *n.*

subdue *sub-dū', v.t.* **1** to conquer. **2** to make tame, obedient. **3** to overcome (e.g. a desire). **4** to soften, make less bright (e.g. colour, light), make quieter (e.g. sound, manner):—*pr.p.* **subdu'ing**.
subdued' *adj.* **subdū'al** *n.*

subeditor *sub-ed'it-ȯr, n.* one who assists an editor by checking and editing material, esp. for a newspaper.

subject *sub'jikt, adj.* **1** under the power of another, not independent: *a subject nation.* **2** apt to suffer from (with *to*): *subject to hay fever, to sand storms.* **3** depending on (a condition) for being carried out, etc.: *This plan is subject to your approval, to our obtaining funds.*—*n.* **1** one under the power of another. **2** one who is ruled over (in reality or in theory) by a king, etc. **3** a person or thing on which work is done: *the subject of the biography, of the experi-*

ment. **4** a person or thing about which something is said: *I see the subject of our talk making his way towards us.* **5** the idea, theme, topic of a work of literature, art, music, etc. **6** material, circumstances, etc., suitable for certain treatment: *The hydrogen bomb is not a subject for laughter.* **7** a branch of learning: *He studied two subjects—history and Italian.* **8** a person (*rare*; in certain phrases only): *She is a nervous subject.* **9** (*grammar*) the word(s) in a sentence standing for the person or thing that does the action of the verb: *In 'He hit me', 'he' is the subject of the verb 'hit'.—v.t. (sub-jekt')* **1** to bring under, or under the power of (with *to*): *to subject to control, to a conqueror.* **2** to make liable (to), cause to suffer from: *Such an action would subject you to much criticism.* **3** to cause to undergo: *to subject to heavy rain, pressure, questioning*.

subjec'tion *n.* **1** the act of subjecting. **2** the state of being subjected.

subjec'tive *adj.* **1** having to do with the subject of a verb. **2** arising from, influenced by, one's own mind and emotions: *He took a subjective, not an objective or impartial, view of the problem.*

subjoin *sub-join', v.t.* to add at the end.

sub judice *sub jōō'di-sē* under consideration by the law-courts.

subjugate *sub'joo-gāt, v.t.* **1** to conquer. **2** to make unresisting, obedient:—*pr.p.* **sub'jugating**.

subjunctive *sub-jungk'tiv, adj.* and *n.* (having to do with) a mood of the verb chiefly concerned with something that may happen or have happened, etc.; it is now hardly ever used in English, but survivals include the following:—*if it be so* (indicative mood, *if it is so*); *if it were known that he has been in prison*; *I propose, insist, that he be dismissed.*

sublease, **sublet** *sub'lēs', sub'let', ns.* a lease, let, to another person by one who is himself a tenant of the property.—Also *vs.t.*:—*pr.ps.* **sub'leas'ing**, **sub'lett'ing**; *pa.ps.* **sub'leased'**, **sub'let'**.

sublieutenant *sub-lė(f)-ten'ȧnt,* (*navy*) *n.* a junior officer next below a lieutenant.

sublimate *sub'lim-āt, v.t.* **1** to purify (a solid substance) by turning it into vapour by means of heat and then allowing the vapour to become solid again. **2** to turn (an emotion, impulse) into one of higher or nobler quality:—*pr.p.* **sub'limating**.

sublime *sub-līm', adj.* **1** lofty, noble, causing feelings of awe or deep respect: *a sublime scene*; *sublime truths.* **2** (of an unworthy feeling) very great: *sublime indifference.—v.t.* to sublimate:—*pr.p.* **sublim'ing**.

sublime'ly *adv.*

sublime'ness, **sublim'ity** *(-lim') ns.*

subliminal *sub-lim'i-nȧl, adj.* (producing sensations) so small as to be below the level of conscious thought or feeling.

submachine-gun *sub-mȧ-shēn'gun, n.* a light machine-gun designed to be fired from the shoulder or hip.

submarine *sub-mȧ-rēn', adj.* under, or in, the sea.—*n. (sub')* a ship which can travel under water.

submerge *sub-mûrj',* **submerse**, *sub-mûrs', v.t.* **1** to plunge under water. **2** to flood with water. **3** (**submerge**) to conceal, cover up, overwhelm.—*v.i.* to sink under water:—*pr.ps.* **submerg'ing, submers'ing**.

submerg'ence, **submer'sion** *ns.*

submer'sible *adj.* that can be submerged.

submit *sub-mit', v.t.* **1** to yield (e.g. oneself, one's will, to another, his will, his wishes). **2** to yield, subject (to treatment, conditions, influence): *to submit oneself to the influence of one's elders, one's possessions to rough usage.* **3** to offer to another for acceptance or an opinion: *I submitted my story to a magazine editor.* **4** to offer (a thought) for consideration: *I submit that the other plan was a better one.—v.i.* to yield, give in:—*pr.p.* **submitt'ing**; *pa.p.* **submitt'ed**.

submission *sub-mish'(ȯ)n, n.* **1** the act of submitting. **2** something (e.g. an idea) that is submitted. **3** humble behaviour, obedience.

submiss'ive *adj.* **1** willing or ready to submit. **2** humble, obedient.

submiss'ively *adv.* **submiss'iveness** *n.*

subnormal *sub-nör'mȧl, n.* less than normal or average, esp. in mental ability.

subordinate *sȯ-bör'd(i-)nit, adj.* **1** lower in order, rank, nature, power, etc. **2** under the authority of, subject (to another person). **3** of little or less importance: *The aim of actually bringing about improvements was subordinate to a desire to have people think him a reformer.* **4** (*grammar*) of a clause which cannot act as a separate sentence, but which acts as an adjective, adverb, etc.—*n.* a person who is subordinate.—*v.t. (-āt)* to look upon or treat as of less importance than (with *to*):—*pr.p.* **subor'dinating**.

subordinā'tion *n.* **1** the state of being subordinate. **2** the act of subordinating.

suborn *sūb-örn', v.t.* to persuade (a person) to do an unlawful act, esp. by bribery.

subpoena *sė-pē'nȧ*, *n.* a writ commanding a person to appear in court under threat of penalty if he does not obey.—*v.t.* to summon (a person) by subpoena:—*pr.p.* **subpoe'naing**; *pa.p.* **subpoe'na'd**, **subpoe'naed** *(-nȧd)*.

subscribe *sub-skrīb'*, *v.t.* **1** to write (usu. one's name) at the end of e.g. a statement or document. **2** to give consent or agreement to (something written) by signing one's name underneath. **3** to give (money to): *to subscribe £1 to charity.*—*v.i.* **1** to contribute (to, for). **2** (with *for*) to promise to buy (a book, series of magazines, newspaper for a certain time). **3** to show one's agreement with (with *to*): *I subscribe to that statement*:—*pr.p.* **subscrib'ing**.
subscrip'tion *n.* **1** the act of subscribing. **2** a name subscribed. **3** money subscribed.
subscriber trunk dialling a telephone dialling system in which people in many countries can dial each other directly, without the aid of the operator.

subsequent *sub'sė-kwėnt*, *adj.* following or coming after: *his subsequent repentance.*
sub'sequently *adv.*

subserve *sub-sėrv'*, *v.t.* to help forward: *to subserve a plan, purpose*:—*pr.p.* **subserv'ing**.
subser'vient *adj.* **1** serving as a means (to an end). **2** too ready to do as one is told.
subser'vience *n.*

subside *sub-sīd'*, *v.i.* **1** (of e.g. flood water) to sink in level. **2** to settle down into the ground. **3** (*coll.*) to fall (into a chair). **4** (of a storm, fever, noise, etc.) to become less and less:—*pr.p.* **subsid'ing**.
subsi'dence (or *sub'si-*) *n.*

subsidy *sub'si-di*, *n.* **1** money given by one state to another in payment for help of some kind. **2** money granted by the government to a service (e.g. a form of transport) which is important to the public, or to growers of an important crop (e.g. wheat) to help keep its price down:—*pl.* **sub'sidies**.
subsid'iary *adj.* **1** giving help or additional supplies. **2** contributing, but of less importance: *a subsidiary stream.* **3** (of a company, firm) controlled by another company.—Also *n.* (*pl.* **subsid'iaries**).
sub'sidise *v.t.* to give a subsidy to:—*pr.p.* **sub'sidising**.

subsist *sub-sist'*, *v.i.* **1** to have existence or reality. **2** to keep oneself alive (on): *He subsists on eggs, milk, and bread.*
subsis'tence *n.* **1** the state of existing. **2** the means of keeping alive, livelihood. **3** (the state of having) the barest necessities of life.

subsoil *sub'soil*, *n.* the layer of earth beneath the surface soil.

substance *sub'stȧns*, *n.* **1** a material object that can be seen and felt: *a sticky substance.* **2** (*chemistry*) an element, compound or mixture. **3** material. **4** solidity, worth: *This cloth has no substance.* **5** property, wealth: *a man of substance.* **6** general meaning, gist: *He spoke for an hour, but the substance of his talk could have been given in five minutes.* **7** basis, grounds, value, truth: *There is no substance to his allegations.*
substantial *sub-stan'sh(ȧ)l*, *adj.* **1** solid, strong (*opp.* **insubstan'tial**): *a substantial building, table.* **2** important in amount, size, etc.: *a substantial sum of money.* **3** having property or wealth. **4** in the main though not in all details: *This was the substantial truth*; *They were in substantial agreement.*—*n.* (in *pl.*) essential details.
substan'tially *adv.* in total effect though not necessarily in every detail: *This statement is substantially true.*
substantiate *(-stan'shi-āt) v.t.* to show the truth, of, or grounds for (e.g. a statement, a charge):—*pr.p.* **substan'tiating**.
sub'stantive (*grammar*) *n.* a noun.

substitute *sub'sti-tūt*, *v.t.* to put in place of another person or thing (with *for*):—*v.i.* to act as a substitute:—*pr.p.* **sub'stituting**.—*n.* **1** one who, or something that, is put in place of, or used instead of or for want of, another. **2** a deputy.—Also *adj.*
substitū'tion *n.*

subsume *sub-sūm'*, *v.t.* to include in a larger category, etc.:—*pr.p.* **subsum'ing**.

subterfuge *sub'tėr-fūj*, *n.* a trick or plan for avoiding a difficulty, etc.

subterranean *sub-tė-rān'yȧn*, *-rā'ni-ȧn*, *adj.* **1** under the ground. **2** hidden, secret.

subtitle *sub'tī-tl*, *n.* **1** a second or explanatory title to a book. **2** (usu. in *pl.*) a printed translation at the foot of the screen of the dialogue of a foreign-language film.—Also *v.t.*:—*pr.p.* **sub'titling**.

subtle *sut'l*, *adj.* **1** faint, delicate, difficult to describe: *a subtle perfume*; *a subtle feeling of horror.* **2** not easily grasped by the mind, difficult to put into words: *a subtle difference.* **3** (of a mind) able to grasp difficult points, esp. small differences of e.g. meaning. **4** sly, cunning.
subt'leness *n.* **subtly** *(sut'li) adv.*
subt'lety *n.* **1** subtleness. **2** something subtle. **3** the power of seeing and under-

standing small differences in e.g. meaning:—*pl.* **subt'leties**.

subtract *sŭb-trakt'*, *v.t.* **1** to take away (a part from). **2** to take (one number or quantity from another) in order to find the difference.—Also *v.i.*

subtrac'tion *n.*

subtropical *sub-trop'i-kȧl*, *adj.* (pertaining to a region beside the tropics where the weather is) more temperate than in the tropics.

suburb *sub'ûrb*, *n.* an area of houses in the outskirts of a large town.

subur'ban *adj.* **1** having to do with the suburbs. **2** narrow in outlook.

subur'bia *n.* (the people who live in) suburbs as a whole.

subvert *sub-vûrt'*, *v.t.* to overthrow, ruin completely (e.g. a person's morals, loyalty, arguments, a government).

subver'sion *n.*

subver'sive *adj.* likely to destroy (e.g. government) or to corrupt: *subversive influence*; *subversive of morality.*—Also *n.*

subway *sub'way*, *n.* an underground way for traffic, pedestrians, or electric trains.

succeed *suk-sēd'*, *v.t.* **1** to come after, follow in order: *Spring succeeds winter.* **2** to follow, take the place of: *He succeeded his brother in office.*—*v.i.* **1** to follow in order. **2** to manage to do what one has aimed at (with *in*). **3** to get on well.

success' *n.* **1** favourable result: *the success of our efforts.* **2** a person or thing that turns out well.

success'ful *adj.* **1** turning out as one had planned. **2** having gained wealth or position.

success'fully *adv.* **success'fulness** *n.*

success'ion *n.* **1** the act of following after. **2** a number (of persons or things) following each other in time or place: *a succession of visitors, victories.* **3** the right of becoming the next holder: *the succession to the throne.* **4** the order of succeeding.

success'ive *adj.* following in order.

success'or *n.* one who succeeds or comes after, or follows in office, etc.

in succession one after another.

succinct *suk-singkt'*, *adj.* short, in few words.

succinct'ly *adv.* **succinct'ness** *n.*

succour *suk'ȯr*, *v.t.* to help in time of need.—*n.* **1** aid. **2** one who gives help.

succulent *suk'ū-lėnt*, *adj.* **1** (of fruit, etc.) full of juice or moisture. **2** (of a plant) with thick, fleshy leaves, etc. (also *n.*).

succ'ulence *n.*

succumb *sŭ-kum'*, *v.i.* **1** to yield (with *to*): *to succumb to temptation.* **2** to die.

such *such*, *adj.* **1** of the kind mentioned or thought of: *Such people are not to be trusted.* **2** similar: *silk, rayon and such materials.* **3** of the kind (that, as): *His anger was such that he lost control of himself,* or *such as to make him lose all control.* **4** used to give importance or emphasis: *This is such a fine day.*—Also *pron.*

as such considered as what one would expect from the name: *The music is of no worth as such*—i.e. as music—*but it provides a friendly background noise.*

such and such referring to a person or thing not named: *Such and such a person may stay.*

such as 1 of the same kind, in the same class: *game birds such as grouse.* **2** for example.

suck *suk*, *v.t.* **1** to draw into the mouth. **2** to draw milk from with the mouth. **3** to lick and roll about in the mouth. **4** (often with *in*, *up*, etc.) to draw in, take up: *Plants suck*, or *suck up*, *water from the ground* (see also **suck up to** below).—Also *v.i.*—*n.* a sucking movement, sound, or force.

suck'er *n.* **1** one who sucks. **2** an organ on an animal by which it sticks to objects. **3** something like this. **4** a side shoot from the underground stem of a plant. **5** a person who is easily fooled.

suckle *suk'l*, *v.t.* **1** (of a woman, female animal) to nurse at the breast, give her milk to. **2** to rear, bring up:—*pr.p.* **suck'ling**.

suck'ling *n.* a child or animal still being fed on its mother's milk.

suck dry to drain all the liquid, or money or resources, or strength, etc., from.

suck up to to toady to.

suction *suk'sh(ȯ)n*, *n.* **1** the act of sucking. **2** the act or process of reducing the air pressure on part of the surface of a substance (e.g. a liquid) and thus causing it to be drawn up into e.g. a tube.

sudden *sud'ėn*, *adj.* **1** unexpected, unprepared for: *a sudden attack.* **2** happening, etc. all at once: *a sudden departure, realisation.* **3** sharp, abrupt: *a sudden turn in the road.*

sudd'enly *adv.* **sudd'enness** *n.*

all of a sudden suddenly.

suds *sudz*, *n.pl.* soap-suds.

sue *sū* or *so͞o*, *v.t.* to start a law case against.—*v.i.* **1** to make a legal claim. **2** to beg (for):—*pr.p.* **su'ing**.

See also **suit**.

suede, **suède** *swād*, *swed*, *n.* leather made from sheep or lamb skins with a soft, dull surface.—Also *adj.*

suet *sū'it*, *sōō'*, *n.* a hard animal fat.

suffer *suf'ėr*, *v.t.* **1** to undergo, now esp. something bad: *to suffer a change.* **2** to endure or bear (e.g. pain). **3** to allow (person, thing, to do something). **4** to put up with, tolerate: *He would not suffer any interference with his plan.*—*v.i.* **1** to feel pain. **2** to undergo loss or injury. **3** to be punished (for).
suff'erable *adj.* **1** bearable. **2** allowable:—*opp.* **insufferable**.
suff'erance: **on sufferance** being tolerated rather than wanted: *He was there on sufferance* (i.e. he was suffered or allowed to be there but no one really wanted him, or he was there for as long as he behaved well).
suff'ering *n.* and *adj.*

suffice *su̇-fīs'*, *v.i.* to be enough, sufficient, or good enough: *The meat we have will suffice for lunch*; *The netting will suffice to mend the fence.*—*v.t.* to be sufficient for (a person): *Will that suffice you?*:—*pr.p.* **suffic'ing**.
sufficient *su̇-fish'ėnt*, *adj.* **1** enough in quantity. **2** effective enough (to):—*opp.* **insufficient**.
sufficiency *su̇-fi'shėn-si*, *n.* **1** a large enough quantity to meet one's needs. **2** ability. **3** self-confidence:—*pl.* **suffic'-iencies**.

suffix *suf'iks*, *n.* a small part of a word placed after the root (e.g. *-ly* in 'quickly', *-ness* in 'kindness').

suffocate *suf'ō-kāt*, *v.t.* **1** to kill by stopping the breath. **2** (and *v.i.*) (to cause) to feel or be unable to breathe freely. **3** to destroy or take away conditions necessary for growth or expression: *to suffocate his poetic talent*:—*pr.p.* **suff'ocating**.
suff'ocating *adj.* **suffocā'tion** *n.*

suffrage *suf'rij*, *n.* **1** a vote. **2** the right to vote.
suffragette *suf-rȧ-jet'*, *n.* a woman seeking by sometimes violent methods to obtain the right to vote for women.

suffuse *su-fūz'*, *v.t.* to spread over or cover (with a liquid, colour, or light): *The story suffused her eyes with tears*:—*pr.p.* **suffus'ing**.
suffū'sion *n.*

sugar *shoog'ȧr*, *n.* **1** a sweet substance obtained from the sugar cane and sugar beet, also from maple, palm trees, etc. **2** too much flattery or compliment.—*v.t.* to sprinkle or mix with sugar.
sug'ared *adj.* **1** sweetened or coated with sugar. **2** charming. **3** too sweet.
sug'ary *adj.* **1** tasting of, or like, sugar. **2** sickly sweet.
sug'ariness *n.*
sug'ar-beet *n.* a type of beet from which sugar is obtained.
sugar-candy. See **candy**.
sug'ar-cane *n.* a tall grass that grows in hot countries, from which sugar is obtained.
sugar soap a strong alkaline substance used in solution to clean or strip off paint.

suggest *su̇-jest'*, *v.t.* **1** to propose: *to suggest a plan of action, a person to fill a post.* **2** to put into someone's mind.
sugges'tible *adj.* easily influenced by suggestion.
suggestion *su̇-jes'ch(ȯ)n*, *n.* **1** the act of suggesting. **2** a proposal, idea brought forward. **3** the process by which a person accepts without thought an idea put into his mind by someone else, e.g. under hypnotism. **4** a slight trace: *a suggestion of a cold.*
sugges'tive *adj.* **1** that suggests. **2** that suggests something rather improper. **3** bringing to one's mind the idea or picture (of): *a hat suggestive of a bowl.*

suicide *sū'i-sīd*, *sōō'*, *n.* **1** one who kills himself. **2** the taking of one's own life: *He committed suicide last year.* **3** something very harmful to oneself.
suicī'dal *adj.* **1** having to do with suicide. **2** certain to ruin e.g. one's career: *This action was suicidal*; *he now had no chance of success.*

suit *sūt*, *sōōt*, *n.* **1** the act of suing. **2** an action at law. **3** courtship of a particular woman. **4** one of the four sets of cards of one kind (e.g. of hearts) in a pack. **5** a number of things made to be worn together, as e.g. pieces of clothing.—*v.t.* **1** to fit, make suitable (to): *He suited his speech to his audience.* **2** to look well on: *The hat suits her.* **3** to please: *Suit yourself.* **4** to be convenient to: *The time chosen did not suit him.* **5** to agree with: *The heat did not suit me.*—*v.i.* **1** to go well (with). **2** to be suitable.
suit'able *adj.* **1** fitting, meeting requirements: *a suitable place and time.* **2** convenient, etc. (to a person).
suitabil'ity, suit'ableness *ns.*
suit'ably *adv.*
suit'ed *adj.* **1** fitted, suitable (to, for). **2** (usu. as part of a word) dressed in a suit or clothes: *velvet-suited*, *sober-suited.*
suit'or *n.* one who tries to gain the love of a woman.

suit'case *n.* a travelling-case for carrying clothes, etc.

follow suit to do as someone else has just done.

suite *swēt*, *n.* **1** a body of followers or attendants who go with an important person. **2** a number of things in a set, as rooms, furniture, or pieces of music.

sulky *sulk'i*, *adj.* silent and angry, sullen, because of something (usu. small) that one resents:—*comp.* **sulk'ier**; *superl.* **sulk'iest**.

sulk'ily *adv.* **sulk'iness** *n.*

sulk *v.i.* to be sulky.

sulks *n.pl.* a fit of sulkiness.

sullen *sul'ėn*, *adj.* **1** gloomily angry and silent. **2** dark, dull: *a sullen sky*.

sull'enly *adv.* **sull'enness** *n.*

sully *sul'i*, *v.t.*, *v.i.* **1** to dirty. **2** to make, or become, less pure or bright:—*pr.p.* **sull'ying**; *pa.p.* **sull'ied**.

sulphur *sul'fůr*, *n.* an element, a yellow substance found in the earth which burns with a blue flame giving off a choking smell, used in matches, gunpowder, etc.

sul'phate *n.* a salt containing sulphur, oxygen and a metal.

sul'phide *n.* a compound of sulphur and another element.

sulpha drugs or **sulphon'amides** a group of drugs with a powerful action against certain bacteria.

sulphuric acid *(sul-fūr'ik a'sid)* a powerful acid much used in industry.

sultan *sul'tȧn*, *n.* the king or ruler of some Muslim countries (e.g. long ago of Turkey).

sultana *sul-tä'nȧ*, **1** the mother, wife, or daughter of a sultan. **2** a small kind of raisin.

sultry *sul'tri*, *adj.* **1** hot and moist, close. **2** hot with anger. **3** passionate:—*comp.* **sul'trier**; *superl.* **sul'triest**.

sul'triness *n.*

sum *sum*, *n.* **1** the amount of two or more things taken together. **2** total. **3** a quantity of money. **4** a problem in arithmetic or algebra. **5** the general meaning, gist, of something said or written (also **sum and substance**).—*v.t.* to add together:—*pr.p.* **summ'ing**; *pa.p.* **summed**.

summ'arise *v.t.* **1** to state briefly, make a summary of. **2** to be a summary of:—*pr.p.* **summ'arising**.

summary *sum'ȧ-ri*, *n.* a shortened form (of a statement, story, etc.) giving only the main points:—*pl.* **summ'aries**.—*adj.* **1** short, brief. **2** without waste of time or words: *a summary dismissal.* **3** (of a method of trial) without formalities, speedy.

summ'arily *adv.*

summation *sum-ā'sh(ȯ)n*, *n.* the act of forming a total or sum.

summ'ing-up', *n.* **1** the act of one who sums up. **2** a summary.

sum total **1** the sum of several smaller sums. **2** the main point, total effect.

in sum in short.

sum up to give again the important points of: *The chairman will now sum up the discussion*.

summer *sum'ėr*, *n.* the warmest season of the year—in cooler northern regions May or June to July or August.—Also *adj.*—*v.i.* to pass the summer.

summ'erhouse *n.* a small building for sitting in a garden.

summ'ertime *n.* **1** the summer season. **2** (**summer time**) time one hour ahead of time as reckoned by the position of the sun, adopted in Britain in 1916 for summer months, for a short period (1968–71) used in winter also.

summit *sum'it*, *n.* the highest point.

summit conference a meeting between heads of states, etc.

summon *sum'ȯn*, *v.t.* **1** to order to appear, esp. in court. **2** to call (to do something), expecting to be obeyed: *She summoned me to put coal on the fire.* **3** (also **summon up**) to rouse, call into action: *to summon up courage, energy*.

summ'ons *n.* **1** a call to appear, esp. in court. **2** a call (to surrender, etc.):—*pl.* **summ'onses**.—*v.t.* to give a summons to to appear in court.

sump *sump*, *n.* **1** a small pit into which water drains and out of which it can be pumped. **2** the oil container in a motor vehicle.

sumptuous *sump'tū-ůs*, *adj.* costly, splendid (of e.g. clothes, furnishings, food).

sun *sun*, *n.* **1** the large sphere which gives light and heat to the earth and other planets revolving round it. **2** sunshine. **3** anything like the sun in position of importance or brightness.—*v.t.* **1** to expose (oneself) to the sun's rays. **2** to enjoy (oneself in a person's company, etc.) as if in warmth and brightness:—*pr.p.* **sunn'ing**; *pa.p.* **sunned**.

sun'less *adj.* **1** without sun. **2** without happiness or cheerfulness.

sunn'y *adj.* **1** filled with sunshine. **2** cheerful:—*comp.* **sunn'ier**; *superl.* **sunn'iest**.

sunn'iness *n.*

sun'bathing *(-bāTH-)* *n.* sunning oneself, esp. with little clothing on.

sun'beam *n.* a ray of the sun.

sun'bed *n.* a sun-lamp in the form of a bed, on which one lies in order to get an artificial suntan.
sun'burn *n.* a burning or browning, esp. of the skin, by the sun.
sun'burned, **sun'burnt** *adjs.*
sun'dial *(-dī-ȧl) n.* an instrument for telling time from the shadow of a rod or plate on its surface cast by the sun.
sun'dress *n.* a light dress of a style which leaves the arms, shoulders, and back exposed to the sun.
sun'flower *n.* a large yellow flower with petals like rays of the sun, from whose seeds we get oil.
sun'glasses *n.pl.* spectacles with dark lenses worn when in bright sunshine.
sun'-lamp *n.* a lamp which gives out ultraviolet rays, used e.g. to produce a suntan artificially.
sun'light *n.* the light of the sun.
sun'lit *adj.* lighted up by the sun.
sun'rise *n.* **1** the rising of the sun in the morning, or the time of this. **2** the east.
sun'-roof *n.* a car roof that can be slid open in good weather.
sun'set *n.* **1** the setting of the sun, or the time of this. **2** the west.
sun'shine *n.* **1** bright sunlight. **2** warmth and brightness.
sun'stroke *n.* a serious illness caused by being in blazing sunshine for too long.
sun'tan *n.* a browning of the skin as a result of exposure to the sun.
under the sun in the world, on earth.

sundae *sun'dā*, *n.* an ice cream with fruits in syrup, etc.

Sunday *sun'di*, *n.* **1** the first day of the week, called this because in ancient times it was a day for worship of the sun. **2** a Sunday paper (usu. in *pl.—the Sundays*).
Sunday school a school for learning about religion held on Sunday.
a month of Sundays a very long time.

sunder *sun'dėr*, *v.t.*, *v.i.* to sever.

sundial, etc. See **sun**.

sundry *sun'dri*, *adj.* (used only before a noun) **1** several, more than one or two. **2** various.
sun'dries *n.pl.* various small things, odds and ends.
all and sundry everybody of all kinds.

sung. See **sing**.

sunk, **sunken**. See **sink**.

sunlight, etc. See **sun**.

sup *sup*, *v.t.* to take into the mouth in small amounts, esp. from a spoon.—*v.i.* to eat supper:—*pr.p.* **supp'ing**; *pa.p.* **supped**.—*n.* a small mouthful.
supp'er *n.* a meal taken at the end of the day.

super *sū'pėr*, *sōō'*, *n.* short for **superintendent**, **supervisor**, etc.—*adj.* (*coll.*) extremely good.

super- *sū'pėr-*, *sōō'*, *pfx.* has meanings such as the following:—
1 above, on the top of (e.g. *superstructure*). **2** in addition (e.g. *supertax*). **3** beyond, beyond the normal (e.g. *supernatural*). **4** of higher quality than (e.g. *superman*). **5** excessively (e.g. *supersensitive*).

superabundant *sū'pėr-ȧ-bun'dȧnt*, *sōō'*, *adj.* very abundant or more than enough: *superabundant rainfall, enthusiasm.*
superabound' *v.i.*
superabun'dance *n.*
superabun'dantly *adv.*

superannuate *sū-pėr-an'ū-āt*, *sōō-*, *v.t.* **1** to retire a person from employment because of old age, esp. on pension. **2** to discard, put out of use:—*pr.p.* **superann'-uating**.
superannuā'tion *n.* **1** putting out of employment or use. **2** a pension, retirement allowance.

superb *sū-pûrb'*, *sōō-*, *adj.* **1** grand, stately, magnificent. **2** very fine: *a superb diamond, method.*

supercharger *sū'pėr-chär-jėr*, *sōō'*, *n.* a device for supplying more air to the cylinders of an internal-combustion engine so as to increase power.

supercilious *sū-pėr-sil'i-ůs*, *sōō-*, *adj.* tending to look down on others, haughty.
supercil'iously *adv.*
supercil'iousness *n.*

superconductor *sū'pėr-kȯn-duk'tȯr*, *sōō'*, *n.* a metal which offers little or no resistance to the passage of electricity at very low temperatures.

supereminent *sū-pėr-em'i-nėnt*, *sōō-*, *adj.* very distinguished.

superficial *sū-pėr-fish'(ȧ)l*, *sōō-*, *adj.* **1** of, or near, the surface. **2** (of e.g. a wound) not going deep. **3** not thorough: *a superficial examination of the material.* **4** outward, but not real or in detail: *The flower has a superficial likeness to a violet*; *His interest is superficial.* **5** (of a person) shallow in nature or in knowledge.
superficially *(-fish'ȧ-li) adv.*
superfic'ialness *n.*
superficial'ity *n.* **1** superficialness. **2** (in *pl.*) superficial qualities or characteristics:—*pl.* **superficial'ities**.

superfine *sū'pėr-fīn*, *sōō'*, *adj.* extremely, unusually, or excessively, fine.

superfluous *sū-pûr'flōō-ůs, sōō-, adj.* **1** beyond what is enough or is needed. **2** unnecessary.
super'fluously *adv.* **super'fluousness** *n.*
superflu'ity *n.* **1** a quantity more than enough. **2** an unnecessary thing:—*pl.* **superflu'ities.**

supergrass *sū'per-gräs, sōō', (slang) n.* a police informer who has given information leading to the arrest of a great number of criminals.

superhuman *sū-pėr-hū'mȧn, sōō-, adj.* **1** beyond what is human. **2** divine. **3** greater than would be expected of an ordinary man: *to make a superhuman effort.*

superimpose *sū-pėr-im-pōz', sōō-, v.t.* to lay or impose (one thing on another thing, usu. unlike it): *to superimpose a modern roof on an ancient cottage, new customs on old, one photo over another:—pr.p.* **superimpos'ing.**

superintend *sū-pėr-in-tend', sōō-, v.t.* to have charge of, to control, manage.—Also *v.i.*
superinten'dent *n.* **1** one who has charge of a building, department of work, institution, etc. **2** a police officer above a chief inspector.

superior *sū-pē'ri-ȯr, sōō-, adj.* **1** higher in rank. **2** higher in excellence. **3** greater in number or power: *superior forces.* **4** above the common in quality: *a superior article.* **5** showing that one has a feeling of greater knowledge or importance: *a superior smile, air.* **6** too courageous or self-controlled to yield (to): *He was superior to temptation.*—*n.* a person who is better than, or higher in rank than, others.
superior'ity *n.:—pl.* **superior'ities.**

superlative *sū-pûr'lȧ-tiv,* or *sōō-, adj.* **1** of the highest degree or quality: *a superlative example; superlative skill.* **2** (*grammar*) pertaining to the superlative.—*n.* (*grammar*) (a word expressing) the highest degree of adjectives or adverbs (e.g. *shortest, silliest, best, farthest; most beautiful, most clumsily*).

superman *sū'pėr-man, sōō', n.* **1** a man of amazing powers. **2** an imagined man of the future who will be more powerful than men of today.

supermarket *sū'pėr-mär-kit, sōō', n.* a large, usu. self-service, store selling food and other goods.

supernatural *sū-pėr-nach'ůr-ȧl, sōō-, adj.* **1** not happening as in the course of nature, miraculous. **2** spiritual.—*n.* that which is supernatural.

supernumerary *sū-pėr-nūm'ėr-ȧr-i,* or *sōō-, adj.* over and above the number stated, usual, or necessary.—*n.* a person or thing that is surplus to requirements.—*pl.* **supernum'eraries.**

superpower *sū'pėr-pow-ėr, sōō', n.* a very powerful state, esp. the U.S.A or the former U.S.S.R.

superscribe *sū-pėr-skrīb', sōō-, v.t.* **1** to write or engrave (an inscription) on the outside or top. **2** to write the name on the outside or cover of (something):—*pr.p.* **superscrib'ing.**
superscrip'tion *n.*

supersede *sū-pėr-sēd', sōō-, v.t.* **1** to take the place of: *A new leader superseded the old; Transport by road is superseding transport by rail.* **2** to replace (by): *We must supersede our present arrangements by more efficient ones:—pr.p.* **supersed'ing.**

supersensitive *sū-pėr-sen'si-tiv, sōō-, adj.* extremely sensitive, or too sensitive.

supersonic *sū-pėr-son'ik, sōō-, adj.* **1** (of vibrations and waves) of a frequency higher than that of sound that can be heard by man. **2** faster than sound. **3** (*aircraft*) able to fly faster than sound travels through air.

superstar *sū'pėr-stär, sōō', n.* an extremely popular and successful cinema, popular music, etc. star.

superstition *sū-pėr-stish'(ȯ)n, sōō-, n.* **1** belief in magic and things that cannot be explained by reason. **2** an instance of this. **3** worship, or fear, arising from this.
superstitious *sū-pėr-stish'ůs, sōō-, adj.*
supersti'tiously *adv.*
supersti'tiousness *n.*

superstore *sū'pėr-stōr, -stör, sōō', n.* a large supermarket.

superstructure *sū'pėr-struk-chůr, sōō', n.* a structure above or on something else.

supertanker *sū'pėr-tang-kėr, sōō', n.* a very large tanker holding at least 75000 tons.

supertax *sū'pėr-taks, sōō', n.* an extra tax on large incomes.

supervise *sū'pėr-vīz, sōō', -vīz', v.t.* to superintend, be in charge of (work, workers):—*pr.p.* **su'pervising.**
supervision *(-vizh'ȯn) n.* **1** the act of supervising. **2** inspection, control.
su'pervīsor (or *vīz'*) *n.*

supine *sū'pīn, sōō',* or *-pīn', adj.* **1** lying on the back. **2** not acting because lazy or indifferent. **3** lacking energy.

supper. See **sup**.

supplant *sū-plänt', v.t.* to take the place of (someone), esp. by unfair or cunning

means, or of (something).
supplan'ter *n.*

supple *sup'l, adj.* **1** bending easily without breaking, etc. **2** (of body movement) easy, graceful, agile. **3** (of a person) moving, bending, etc., easily.—*v.t., v.i.* to make, become, supple:—*pr.p.* **supp'ling.**
supp'leness *n.* **supp'ly** *adv.*

supplement *sup'li-mėnt, n.* **1** an addition made to supply something lacking, correct errors, etc. **2** a special part of a magazine or newspaper added to the ordinary part.—*v.t.* **1** (*sup-li-ment',* or *sup'*) to add to (with *with*): *We can supplement the meal provided with fruit and sweets.* **2** to be an addition to.
supplement'ary *adj.* **1** added to supply what is lacking. **2** additional.—Also *n.* (*pl.* **supplement'aries**).
supplementary benefit money paid each week by the state to those with low incomes in order to bring the incomes up to a certain level.

suppliant *sup'li-ȧnt, adj.* asking earnestly, begging humbly.—*n.* one who asks humbly.
supplicā'tion *n.* earnest prayer or entreaty.

supply¹. See **supple**.

supply² *sù-plī', v.t.* **1** to provide (what is wanted): *to supply water to the town.* **2** to meet (a need, lack). **3** to fill (a vacant place). **4** to provide (with): *to supply me, a hotel, with vegetables*:—*pr.p.* **supply'ing;** *pa.p.* **supplied'**.—*n.* **1** the act of supplying. **2** something supplied. **3** something that fills a want: *Get me a supply of paper.* **4** (usu. in *pl.*) the amount of food, money, etc., available. **5** (in *pl.*) stores for e.g. army. **6** a grant by parliament for expenses of government. **7** a person who fills another's place for a time:—*pl.* **supplies'**.

support *sù-pōrt', -pört', v.t.* **1** to hold up, bear part of the weight of. **2** to bear, tolerate: *I cannot support his impudence.* **3** to take the side of, back, or help (a person): *I support him against those who are finding fault with him; I support him in his efforts to raise money.* **4** to give approval or aid to (a cause, course of action, etc.): *Do you support this campaign, plan?* **5** to speak in favour of (a theory, belief, motion). **6** to say that (a statement) is true. **7** to supply with means of living: *He supports his father and mother.* **8** to play (a part, role). **9** to act with (a more important actor).—*n.* **1** the act of supporting. **2** something that supports.
support'able *adj.* (*opp.* **insupportable**).
support'er *n.*

suppose *sù-pōs', v.t.* **1** to take as true for the sake of argument or discussion: *Let us suppose I win £100 in the competition. What shall I do with it?* **2** to think, believe, or to think probable. **3** to presuppose, involve: *The second stage of the plan supposes the success of the first.* **4** used in the imperative to suggest or command in an indirect way: *Suppose we give the prize to Mary; Suppose you go now*:—*pr.p.* **suppos'ing.**
supposed' (also *pō'zid*) *adj.* **1** believed on too slight evidence to exist or to be so: *the once supposed phoenix; the supposed impossibility of splitting the atom.* **2** wrongly believed to be such: *his supposed wife.*
suppos'edly *(-id-li) adv.* according to what is, was, supposed: *The supposedly safe bridge collapsed.*
supposi'tion *n.* **1** the act of supposing. **2** something that is supposed.
suppos'itory *(-poz') n.* a pellet of medicine to be inserted in the rectum or vagina rather than taken orally:—*pl.* **suppos'itories.**

suppress *sù-pres', v.t.* **1** to crush, put down (e.g. rebellion, rebels). **2** to stop, abolish (e.g. parking in narrow streets, freedom of speech). **3** to keep in (e.g. a sigh, an angry retort). **4** to keep from being published or being known (e.g. a book, a name, evidence, the truth).
suppre'ssion *n.* **suppress'or** *n.*

suppurate *sup'ū-rāt, v.t.* (of e.g. a wound) to gather pus or matter, fester:—*pr.p.* **supp'urating.**
suppura'tion *n.*

supra- *sū'pra-, sōō', pfx.* above.
suprana'tional *adj.* **1** in, of, relating to, more that one nation. **2** having powers higher than any one nation: *a supranational authority.*

supreme *sū-prēm', sōō-, adj.* highest, greatest, utmost: *the supreme ruler; supreme courage, contempt.*
suprem'acy *(-prem') n.* **1** the state of being supreme. **2** the highest authority or power: *papal supremacy.* **3** the highest position through achievements: *his supremacy as a painter.*
supreme'ly *adv.*

supremo *sū-prē'mō, sōō-, n.* a chief, head, person in charge:—*pl.* **supre'mos.**

surcharge *sûr-chärj', v.t.* **1** to overcharge. **2** to charge in addition. **3** to mark (a postage stamp) with a surcharge:—*pr.p* **surcharg'ing.**—*n.* *(sûr')* **1** an additional tax or charge. **2** something printed on a postage stamp to alter its value.

sure *shōōr*, *shör*, *adj.* **1** firm, strong: *a sure foundation.* **2** to be depended on, trustworthy: *a sure friend.* **3** never missing, slipping, failing, etc.: *a sure aim*; *a sure foot*; *a sure method.* **4** certain (to do, happen, etc.). **5** having no doubt, or having good reason to believe: *He is quite sure*, *sure of this fact*, *sure that he can do it.* **6** sometimes suggesting hope or a little doubt: *I am sure you will do as I ask.*—Also *adv.*

sure'ly *adv.* **1** firmly. **2** without missing, slipping, failing, etc. **3** certainly, without doubt; sometimes expressing hope or a little doubt: *Surely you will try*; *Surely you will not go*.

sure'ness *n.*

sure'-fire' (*coll.*) *adj.* certain to succeed.

sure'-foot'ed *adj.* not likely to slip or stumble.

be sure see to it that: *Be sure you do it*.

make sure 1 to act so that something is sure, done, etc. **2** to check to see that something has already been done, etc.

sure enough in very fact: *Sure enough, he was late, as I said he would be*.

sure of oneself confident.

to be sure! 1 certainly. **2** I admit: *To be sure, I could buy a new one*.

surety *shōōr'ti*, *shör'*, *n.* **1** one who promises to take responsibility if another person fails to do something, e.g. to appear in court. **2** pledge, guarantee:—*pl.* **sure'ties**.

surf *sûrf*, *n.* the foam made by the dashing of waves.

surf'ing, **surf'-riding** *ns.* the sport of riding on a surfboard.

surf'board *n.* a board on which a bather rides towards shore on the surf.

surface *sûr'fis*, *n.* the outside part or face: *the surface of the earth.*—*v.t.* **1** to put a (usu. smooth) surface on. **2** to bring to the surface of e.g. the sea.—*v.i.* **1** to come to the surface. **2** to appear:—*pr.p.* **sur'facing**.—*adj.* **1** being on the surface only. **2** travelling on the surface.

surface mail mail sent otherwise than by air.

surfboard. See **surf**.

surfeit *sûr'fit*, *n.* **1** too much of anything. **2** too much eating and drinking. **3** sickness or disgust caused by this.—*v.t.* to fill with, or give, too much of anything.

surfing, etc. See **surf**.

surge *sûrj*, *n.* **1** the rising or swelling of a large wave. **2** a movement like this of e.g. a crowd. **3** a sudden rise or increase (of e.g. emotion, pain, sound).—*v.i.* **1** to rise high. **2** to move (forward) like a wave:—*pr.p* **surg'ing**.

surgeon *sûr'jȯn*, *n.* **1** one who treats injuries or diseases by operations on the living body, e.g. by cutting out diseased parts. **2** an army, navy, or ship's doctor.

sur'gery *n.* **1** the act or art of treating diseases, injuries, by operation. **2** a doctor's or dentist's consulting room, or the time of his consultation. **3** a set time when e.g. a member of parliament is available for consultation by the public in his constituency:—*pl.* **sur'geries**.

sur'gical *adj.* **sur'gically** *adv.*

surly *sûr'li*, *adj.* **1** gruff, ill-natured, rude. **2** (of a dog) very unfriendly. **3** (of the sky) dark and threatening:—*comp.* **sur'lier**; *superl.* **sur'liest**.

sur'liness *n.*

surmise *sûr'mīz*, *-mīz'*, *n.* **1** guessing, supposing, conjecturing. **2** something that is supposed or guessed.—*v.t.* (*-mīz'*) **1** to imagine to be, infer, from slight evidence: *I surmise a party from the blaze of lights in the house.* **2** to guess, suppose (that):—*pr.p.* **surmis'ing**.

surmount *sür-mownt'*, *v.t.* **1** to be the top, or on the top, of: *A spire surmounts the tower.* **2** to climb, get, over. **3** to get the better of, overcome (e.g. a difficulty).

surmount'able *adj.* (*opp.* **insurmount'able**).

surname *sûr'nām*, *n.* a person's last name, the family name.

surpass *sür-päs'*, *v.t.* **1** to go beyond, exceed. **2** to be better than. **3** to be beyond the reach or powers of: *to surpass description, my understanding*.

surpass'ingly *adv.* extremely.

surplice *sûr'plis*, *n.* a loose white garment worn by clergymen and members of a choir.

surplus *sûr'plus*, *n.* **1** the amount left over when what is required is taken away. **2** excess. **3** amount by which assets are greater than liabilities.

surprise *sûr-prīz'*, *n.* **1** the act of coming upon without warning: *to take by surprise*. **2** the emotion caused by an unexpected or sudden happening—a less strong word than *astonishment* or *amazement*. **3** an unexpected happening, etc.—*v.t.* **1** to come upon suddenly or unawares. **2** to lead by means of surprise (into): *to surprise him into an admission of guilt*; *to surprise an admission from, out of, him.* **3** to cause some wonder, surprise, to:—*pr.p.* **surpris'ing**.

surrealism *su-rē'ȧl-izm*, *n.* a modern form of art claiming to show the activities of the unconscious mind, not controlled by

reason or preconceptions.
surrealist'ic *adj.*

surrender *sù-ren'dėr, v.t.* **1** to hand over, yield (to another). **2** to give up (e.g. a right, a claim). **3** to abandon (oneself to e.g. grief).—*v.i.* to give oneself up to another.—*n.* the act of surrendering.

surreptitious *sur-ėp-ti'shùs, adj.* **1** done in a secret, underhand way. **2** enjoyed secretly.

surrogate *sur'ō-gāt, -git, n.* a substitute.—Also *adj.*

surround *sù-rownd', v.t.* **1** to come round about, esp. so as to cut off ways of escape. **2** to enclose: *to surround the town with a wall.* **3** to lie, be, all round: *The sea surrounds Britain*; *Mystery surrounds his death.*—*n.* **1** a border. **2** (often in *pl.*) an area of uncovered floor around a carpet.
surroun'ding *adj.* lying round.—*n.* **1** the act of coming, or of putting, round about. **2** (in *pl.*) region, type of country, round. **3** (in *pl.*) people among whom, or conditions in which, one lives.

surtax *sûr'taks, n.* **1** an additional tax on certain goods. **2** tax payable on incomes above a certain high level (term not in official use).

surveillance *sùr-vāl'àns, n.* a close watch or constant guard: *Keep the prisoner under surveillance.* **2** supervision.

survey *sùr-vā', v.t.* **1** to look over (e.g. a scene before one). **2** to get a general view of (e.g. a mass of information, one's prospects) by examining carefully. **3** to measure and estimate the position, shape, etc. of (a piece of land). **4** to supervise.—*n. (sûr'vā)* **1** an examination in detail, in order to come to general conclusions, estimate value, etc. **2** a writing giving the results of this. **3** a measuring, etc., of land, or of a country. **4** a map made using measurements, etc., obtained.
survey'or *n.* one who surveys, esp. officially, examines and supervises roadmaking, building work, etc.

survive *sùr-vīv', v.t.* **1** to live longer than, outlive. **2** to come through alive: *He survived the accident.* **3** to continue to exist after, in spite of.—*v.i.* to remain alive or in existence:—*pr.p.* **surviv'ing**.
survī'val *n.* **1** the state of surviving. **2** anything (e.g. a custom, belief) that survives from earlier times. **3** a relic.
survī'vor *n.*

susceptible *sù-sep'ti-bl, adj.* **1** liable to be affected by: *susceptible to colds, flattery.* **2** easily affected, impressionable: *They are susceptible children.* **3** capable (of): *This theory is not susceptible of proof.*
susceptibil'ity *n.* **1** state of being susceptible. **2** (in *pl.*) feelings:—*pl.* **susceptibil'ities**.

suspect *sùs-pekt', v.t.* **1** to have doubts about, distrust: *to suspect a person's motives.* **2** to imagine (a person, etc.) to be guilty. **3** to be inclined to think (that): *I suspect that we have lost the ball.*—*n. (sus'pekt)* a person, etc., thought to be guilty.—*adj.* suspected, arousing doubt.
suspicion *sùs-pi'sh(ȯ)n, n.* **1** the act of suspecting. **2** mistrust, feeling of doubt. **3** an opinion formed on little evidence: *I have a suspicion that he took my book.* **4** a very slight amount: *Add a suspicion of garlic.*
suspi'cious *adj.* suspecting, or inclined to suspect: *I am suspicious of the tramp*; *I have a suspicious nature.* **2** showing suspicion: *He gave a suspicious glance.* **3** (of an action, etc.) causing suspicion.
suspi'ciously *adv.* **suspi'ciousness** *n.*

suspend *sùs-pend', v.t.* **1** to hang: *to suspend a weight on a string.* **2** to keep from falling or sinking: *dust suspended in the air*; *particles suspended in a liquid.* **3** to stop, or discontinue, usu. for a time: *to suspend business for a week.* **4** to take away a privilege, etc., from, esp. for a time: *to suspend a student* (i.e. not to allow him to attend classes, etc.). **5** to postpone: *to suspend sentence.*
suspen'der *n.* **1** something that suspends. **2** one of a pair of straps to support socks, (*U.S.*) trousers, etc.
suspense' *n.* **1** the state of being undecided: *The matter is in suspense.* **2** a state of uncertainty and worry: *He was in suspense until the winner was announced.*
suspen'sion *n.* **1** the act of suspending. **2** a state of being suspended. **3** a taking away of an office or privilege for a time. **4** the state of a solid which is mixed with a liquid or gas and does not sink or dissolve in it. **5** in a car, etc., the system of springs, etc. which support the chassis on the axles.
suspended sentence a legal sentence which one does not have to serve unless one commits another crime.
suspension bridge a bridge which has its roadway suspended from cables hanging from towers.
suspend judgment to wait for more information before making up one's mind.
suspend payment to stop payments owed to creditors and thus become bankrupt.

suspicion, **suspicious**, etc. See **suspect**.

sustain *sŭs-tān'*, *v.t.* **1** to hold up, bear the weight of. **2** to support, back up. **3** to show to be true (a statement) or just, legal (a claim). **4** to give strength to: *You have eaten too little to sustain you on the journey*; *This belief sustained him.* **5** to bear (e.g. attack) without giving way. **6** to suffer, undergo (defeat, injury, loss, etc.). **7** to act (a role, character). **8** to keep up: *He sustained the conversation with difficulty.* **9** to keep (a note) sounding on evenly.
sustained' *adj.* (of a musical note, effort, etc.) continued without a break.
sustain'er *n.* the main motor in a rocket, continuing with it throughout its flight.
sus'tenance *(-tin-ăns, -tnăns)* *n.* nourishment for the body (food or drink) or for the mind.

suture *sū'chŭr, sōō'*, *n.* **1** a stitching of a wound. **2** a surgical stitch.

svelte *svelt*, *adj.* slender, graceful.

swab *swob*, *n.* **1** a mop for cleaning or drying decks or floors. **2** a piece of cotton wool, etc., used by doctors for several purposes. **3** a specimen of mucus, etc., to be examined for bacteria, taken with a swab.—*v.t.* to clean or wipe with a swab:—*pr.p.* **swabb'ing**; *pa.p.* **swabbed**.

swaddle *swod'l*, *v.t.* **1** to bind (a baby) tightly round with strips of cloth (as used to be done). **2** to wrap up (usu. a person) almost completely:—*pr.p.* **swadd'ling**.
swaddling clothes bands of cloth, or clothes, for a baby.

swag *swag*, *n.* **1** a bundle of belongings. **2** plunder, things stolen.
swag'man *n.* esp. in Australia, a man who carries his swag (*def. 1*) around with him while searching for work.

swagger *swag'ĕr*, *v.i.* **1** to swing the body proudly. **2** to brag noisily.—*n.* **1** a self-confident swinging manner of walking. **2** boastfulness. **3** a conceited attitude.

swain *swān*, *n.* **1** a young peasant. **2** an admirer, suitor.

swallow[1] *swol'ō*, *v.t.* **1** to take (e.g. food) through the throat into the stomach. **2** (of e.g. mud; often with *up*) to take in and hide completely. **3** to use up quickly (e.g. money). **4** to accept meekly (e.g. an insult). **5** to accept as true (something untrue that one is told). **6** to keep back (e.g. tears, a laugh, an angry reply).
swallow one's pride to humble oneself.
swallow up to take in, use up, completely or quickly.

swallow[2] *swol'ō*, *n.* an insect-eating bird with long wings and a forked tail, which goes to warmer climates in winter.
swall'owtail *n.* a type of butterfly.

swam. See **swim**.

swamp *swomp*, *n.* wet, spongy ground, esp. with growth of trees or shrubs.—*v.t.* **1** to cause (e.g. a boat) to fill with water. **2** to overwhelm through, because of, quantity: *They swamped me with work*; *The work swamped me.*
swam'py *adj.*:—*comp.* **swam'pier**; *superl.* **swam'piest**.
swam'piness *n.*

swan *swon*, *n.* a large, stately bird, usu. white, with a long graceful neck, of the duck family.—*v.i.* (with *around*, *about*, etc.) to come or go aimlessly, or as one pleases:—*pr.p.* **swann'ing**; *pa.p.* **swanned**.
swan song the last work, utterance, of a poet, musician, etc. (swans were once said to sing just before death).

swank *swangk*, (*slang*) *n.* bragging, showing off.—Also *v.i.*
swan'ky *adj.* **1** boastful. **2** stylish:—*comp.* **swan'kier**; *superl.* **swan'kiest**.
swan'kiness *n.*

swap *swop*. Same as **swop**.

sward *swörd*, *n.* **1** the grassy surface of land. **2** green turf.

swarm[1] *swörm*, *n.* **1** a large number of small animals in movement together, esp. a number of bees following a queen to form a new colony. **2** a great number, crowd.—*v.i.* **1** to gather as bees do. **2** to appear in large numbers. **3** to be crowded (with): *The street was swarming with tourists.*

swarm[2] *swörm*, *v.t.*, *v.i.* to climb by clinging to with arms and legs and drawing oneself up: *They swarmed,* or *swarmed up*, *the wall*; *They swarmed up*.

swarthy *swör*TH*'i*, *adj.* having a dark complexion:—*comp.* **swarth'ier**; *superl.* **swarth'iest**.

swash *swosh*, *v.t.*, *v.i.* to dash, clash, or splash.
swash'buckler *n.* a bragging, swaggering adventurer (*orig.*, one who clashes his sword against a *buckler* or small shield).
swash'buckling *adj.* having to do with a swashbuckler, exciting, adventurous.

swastika *swos'ti-kă*, *n.* a cross with the ends bent at right angles, adopted as the badge of the Nazi party in Germany before the Second World War.

swat *swot*, *v.t.* to hit (esp. an insect):—*pr.p.* **swatt'ing**; *pa.p.* **swatt'ed**.—Also *n.*

swatch *swoch*, *n.* a sample, or bundle of samples, of material.

swath *swöth*, *n.* **1** a line of grass or corn cut by a scythe or mowing machine. **2** a strip.

swathe *swāTH*, *v.t.* to bind, wrap round, with a band or with loose material:—*pr.p.* **swath'ing**.

sway *swā*, *v.t.*, *v.i.* **1** to swing, move, to and fro: *Wind sways trees*; *Trees sway in the wind.* **2** (to cause) to bend or move to one side, or in a particular direction. **3** to influence, or have influence: *The speaker knew how to sway his audience, their opinions.* **4** to govern.—*n.* **1** motion of swaying. **2** rule, control, or influence: *to hold, have, sway over*.

swear *swār*, *v.i.* **1** to make a solemn promise (e.g. to tell the truth) calling God to witness. **2** to vow. **3** to curse, or to utter the name of God or of sacred things irreverently.—*v.t.* **1** to put on oath to act in a certain way: *Swear her to secrecy* (i.e. make her swear not to tell). **2** to declare on oath (that). **3** to take (an oath):—*pa.t.* **swore** (-*ō*- or -*ö*-); *pa.p.* **sworn** (-*ō*- or -*ö*-).

sworn *adj.* keeping steadily, as if bound by oath, to a certain attitude or way of behaving: *a sworn opponent of higher taxes*; *sworn friends, enemies*.

swear'-word *n.* an obscene word or a sacred word used irreverently, used in anger, etc.

swear by to put complete trust in, reliance on.

swear in to introduce into an office by making swear an oath.

swear off to promise to give up: *to swear off drinking, cigarettes*.

swear to to make a solemn statement on oath, or as if on oath, about (something): *I swear to the truth of this statement, to his having said this, to the identity of this man.*

sweat *swet*, *n.* **1** the moisture from the skin, perspiration. **2** moisture in drops on any surface. **3** the state of one who sweats. **4** (*coll.*) hard work. **5** a state of great nervousness and worry.—*v.i.* **1** to give out sweat or other moisture. **2** to toil, work hard. **3** to suffer (for something one has done). **4** to be anxious.—*v.t.* **1** to cause to sweat. **2** to get rid of by sweating: *to sweat away fat.* **3** to make work hard for very little pay. **4** to squeeze money from.

sweat'er *n.* a heavy jersey used e.g. by athletes.

sweat'y *adj.* wet or stained with sweat: —*comp.* **sweat'ier**; *superl.* **sweat'iest**.

sweat'iness *n.*

sweated labour **1** hard work paid at too low a rate. **2** the workers employed on such work.

sweat'-shirt *n.* a long-sleeved or short-sleeved knitted cotton sweater.

sweat'shop *n.* a workshop or factory in which sweated labour is used.

sweat blood to work very hard or worry very much.

Swede *swēd*, *n.* **1** a native of Sweden. **2** (without *cap.*) a large yellow turnip.

Swēd'ish *adj.* having to do with Sweden.—*n.* **1** the language of Sweden. **2** (*pl.*) the people of Sweden.

sweep *swēp*, *v.t.* **1** to clean by using a brush or broom. **2** to gather (together) by sweeping. **3** to move, carry (away, along, off, etc.) with a long brushing movement, or without caring what anyone else wants: *He sweeps the things off the table and into his case*; *He sweeps his guest away to another room.* **4** to clear, to rid of: *He sweeps the seas (of enemy ships).* **5** to pass over lightly or rapidly: *His fingers sweep the strings*; *His eyes sweep the horizon.*—*v.i.* **1** to use a broom on floor(s), etc. **2** to move quickly in a proud manner: *She sweeps from the room.* **3** to move quickly with force: *The wind sweeps over the plain.* **4** to curve widely or stretch far: *The hills sweep down to the sea*:—*pa.p.* **swept**.—*n.* **1** the act of sweeping. **2** a sweeping movement. **3** the movement, or range, of something turning: *the sweep of the oars.* **4** a curve. **5** a stretch. **6** a chimney sweeper. **7** (*coll.*) a sweepstake.

sweep'er *n.* **1** one who, or that which, sweeps. **2** in football, a player in front of the goal-keeper who helps to defend the goal.

sweep'ing *adj.* **1** that sweeps. **2** (of e.g. victory, changes) very great. **3** not taking into account the exceptions or all the factors or evidence: *All men are liars is a sweeping statement*; *Don't make sweeping charges against me* (i.e. don't make accusations against me without looking properly at the facts).—*n.* (in *pl.*) rubbish, dust, etc. collected by sweeping.

sweep'stake(s) *n.sing.* or *pl.* a prize for, or a gamble on, a race, etc., entrants staking money which goes to the winner(s).

at one sweep by one action, at one time.

make a clean sweep to get rid of everything that may be considered rubbish, e.g. to turn all those of a different party, or those who are inefficient, out of office.

sweet *swēt*, *adj.* **1** tasting like sugar. **2** not sour or salt. **3** pleasant to the taste. **4** pleasant to smell or hearing—fragrant, melodious. **5** (of a person, someone's nature, an action) agreeable, kindly. **6** very pleasing. **7** delightful. **8** (with *on*) in love.—*n.* **1** a small piece of a sweet substance, e.g. of chocolate, candy (also **sweet'ie**). **2** something sweet served towards the end of a meal, a pudding. **3** a term of endearment. **4** (in *pl.*) enjoyable things: *the sweets of victory*.

sweet'en *v.t.*, *v.i.* to make, or become, sweet or sweeter.—*v.t.* **1** to make less unpleasant. **2** (often with *up*) to make less hostile, more agreeable.

sweet'ener *n.* **1** a substance that sweetens, esp. one not containing sugar. **2** (*coll.*) a bribe.

sweet'ening *n.*

sweet'ie *n.* a sweet (*def. 1*).

sweet'ly *adv.* **1** in an agreeable manner. **2** easily, without jarring: *The machinery moves sweetly*.

sweet'ness *n.*

sweet'-and sour' *adj.* with a seasoning of sugar, vinegar, soy sauce, etc.

sweet'bread *n.* the pancreas or thymus of animals, esp. as food.

sweet'corn *n.* a variety of maize.

sweet'heart *n.* a person loved and loving, darling.

sweet'meat *n.* (*old*) a confection, dainty, made wholly or chiefly of sugar.

sweet pea a climbing annual garden plant with sweet-scented flowers.

sweet potato a plant in tropical countries whose tuber-like roots are eaten as a vegetable.

sweet talk flattery, persuasive words.—*v.t.* **sweet'-talk**.

a sweet tooth a fondness for sweet things.

swell *swel*, *v.i.* **1** to grow larger or greater. **2** (of the sea) to rise into waves. **3** to bulge out. **4** to become as if puffed out with excitement, pride, or anger. **5** to grow louder.—*v.t.* **1** to increase the size of, or number of. **2** to increase the sound of:—*pa.t.* **swelled**; *pa.p.* **swollen** (*swō'lėn*), (*rare*) **swelled.**—*n.* **1** the act of swelling. **2** a bulge. **3** an increase in size. **4** a gradual rise in the height of the ground. **5** waves rolling in one direction as after a storm. **6** (*slang*) a dandy, or one fashionably and showily dressed, or an important person.—*adj.* **1** (*slang*) fashionable, showy. **2** very fine, just what is wanted.

swell'ing *n.* **1** the action of the verb to swell. **2** an enlarged part of the body.

swoll'en *adj.* **1** that has swollen. **2** become too great.

swoll'en-head'ed *adj.* conceited.

swelter *swelt'ėr*, *v.i.* to be faint or limp from heat.—*n.* intense heat.

swelt'ering *adj.* very hot.

swept. See **sweep**.

swerve *swûrv*, *v.i.* **1** to turn (from a line or course), esp. quickly. **2** to turn aside (from the right course of action):—*pr.p.* **swer'ving.**—*n.* the act of swerving.

swift *swift*, *adj.* **1** moving, or able to move, very fast. **2** happening or done quickly: *a swift change.* **3** quick, ready (to do something): *swift to take offence.*—*n.* a bird that flies very rapidly and is something like the swallow, though not related.

swift'ly *adv.* **swift'ness** *n.*

swig *swig*, (*coll.*) *n.* a large drink or mouthful.—*v.t.* to gulp down:—*pr.p.* **swigg'ing**; *pa.p.* **swigged**.

swill *swil*, *v.t.* or *v.i.* **1** to drink in quantity or greedily. **2** to wash (out), rinse.—*n.* **1** a large drink of liquor. **2** (partly) liquid food or kitchen waste given to pigs.

swim *swim*, *v.i.* **1** to move on or in water by using hands and feet, fins, etc. **2** to float, not to sink. **3** to move with a gliding motion. **4** to be dizzy; (of one's head) to seem to spin. **5** (with *in*) to be covered or filled with: *greasy food that swims in fat.*—*v.t.* **1** to cross by swimming: *to swim the river.* **2** to make (animals) swim (across water):—*pr.p.* **swimm'ing**; *pa.t.* **swam**; *pa.p.* **swum.**—*n.* **1** the act of swimming. **2** any motion like swimming. **3** dizziness.

swimm'er *n.* **swimm'ing** *n.*, *adj*.

swimm'ingly *adv.* **1** in a gliding manner. **2** smoothly, easily, with success.

swimm'ing-bath (often in *pl.*), **-pool** *ns.* an indoor or outdoor pool large enough for swimming in.

swimm'ing-cos'tume, **swim'suit** *ns.* a garment for swimming and bathing in.

in the swim in the main stream of affairs, business, fashion, etc.

swim with, or **against**, **the stream** or **tide** to conform to, or go against, normal behaviour, opinions, etc.

swindle *swin'dl*, *v.t.* **1** to cheat (a person). **2** to get (money out of a person) by cheating:—*pr.p.* **swin'dling.**—*n.* **1** a fraud. **2** anything not what it appears to be.

swin'dler *n.*

swine *swīn*, *n.* **1** a pig. **2** (*coll.*) a despicable person:—*pl.* **swine.**

swi'nish (*swī'*) *adj.* low, gross, beastly.

swing *swing*, *v.i.* **1** to sway or wave to and fro, as an object hanging in air. **2** to be hanged. **3** to move back and forward on a swinging seat. **4** to hang (from). **5** to turn round a fixed point, as a ship at anchor, a door on its hinges. **6** to turn quickly. **7** to turn (from one opinion, etc., to another). **8** to move forward with a steady swaying movement: *soldiers swinging along.* **9** (*coll.*) to be lively, up-to-date.—*v.t.* **1** to cause to move or sway to and fro (e.g. a golf club), or round. **2** to cause to turn about a point. **3** to cause (people) to come round (to e.g. an opinion). **4** to influence the result of: *to swing the election*:—*pa.p.* **swung**.—*n.* **1** the act of swinging. **2** motion to and fro, or the distance covered by it. **3** steady, swaying or marked movement. **4** a seat hanging from a frame, a branch, etc. for usu. children to swing on.

swing'ing *n.* and *adj.*

swing'-bridge *n.* a bridge that may be opened to let e.g. boats past, by swinging it to one side.

swing'-door' *n.* a door (usu. one of a pair) that can open either way and which swings shut by itself.

in full swing going on energetically: *Work, the party, was in full swing.*

swing'-wing aircraft an aircraft whose wings may be swung backwards or forwards, being set at right angles to the aeroplane for take-off and landing and swung back during flight.

swingeing *swin'jing*, *adj.* very great: *swingeing increases in taxation.*

swinish. See **swine**.

swipe *swīp*, *n.* a blow aimed wildly.—*v.t.* to hit hard and rather wildly.—*v.i.* (with *at*) to aim a blow at, try to hit:—*pr.p.* **swip'ing**.

swirl *swûrl*, *v.t.*, *v.i.* to sweep along with a whirling motion.—*n.* a whirling motion, as of wind or water.

swish *swish*, *v.t.* **1** to strike (something), or to cut the air with (a thin rod), making a whistling, hissing or rustling sound. **2** to cause to swish.—*v.i.* to move with a whistling, hissing or rustling sound.—Also *n.*

Swiss *swis*, *adj.* having to do with Switzerland or its people.—*n.* **1** a native of Switzerland (*pl.* **Swiss**). **2** a type of German spoken there.

Swiss roll a thin sponge cake spread with e.g. jam and rolled up.

switch *swich*, *n.* **1** a small twig, etc., that bends easily, used e.g. in whipping. **2** a device (usu. movable rails) used to change trains from one track to another. **3** a small lever or handle for turning an electric current on or off. **4** an act of switching. **5** a change: *a switch of attention, support, to another person.*—*v.t.* **1** to strike with a switch. **2** to change from one line of rails to another. **3** to turn (off, on, e.g. current, light) by means of a switch. **4** to change over: *to switch the men to more urgent work.* **5** to turn (the conversation) quickly (from one matter to another).—*v.i.* to change over (from, to).

switch'back *n.* **1** (*orig.*) a zigzag railway, for climbing steep hills. **2** a steeply up-and-down railway or road.

switch'board *n.* a board with arrangements for switching electrical currents or making connections between telephones, etc.

swivel *swiv'l*, *n.* **1** a support or base for e.g. a gun which allows it to be turned round. **2** a connecting part between e.g. two parts of a chain which allows each part to move round separately.—*v.i.* to turn on, or as if on, a swivel:—*pr.p.* **swiv'elling**; *pa.p.* **swiv'elled**.

swiv'el-chair *n.* a chair with a seat that swivels round.

swiz *swiz*, **swizzle** *swiz'l*, (*coll.*) *ns.* **1** a great disappointment. **2** a fraud.

swollen. See **swell**.

swoon *swōōn*, *v.i.* to faint.—Also *n.*

swoop *swōōp*, *v.i.* to come down with a sweep (as a hawk on its prey).—*n.* a sudden downward rush.

at one fell swoop all at one time, at one stroke.

swop *swop*, *v.t.* to give (one thing) for another, exchange:—*pr.p.* **swopp'ing**; *pa.p.* **swopped**.—*n.* an exchange.—Also **swap** *(swop)*.

sword *sörd*, *n.* **1** a weapon with a long blade, sharp on one or both edges. **2** this weapon taken as a symbol of authority or war. **3** death by the sword: *The prisoners were put to the sword.* **4** military power.

sword dance a dance over and between swords crossed on the ground, or in which swords are drawn.

sword'fish *n.* a large fish with a long pointed upper jaw like a sword.

sword'-play *n.* **1** fencing. **2** skilful argument.

swords'man *n.* a man skilled in the use of a sword.

the sword of justice the power of the law to compel people.

cross swords **1** to fight. **2** to disagree, or argue, fiercely.

swore, **sworn**. See **swear**.

swot *swot*, *v.t.*, *v.i.* (*coll.*) to study hard, esp. by memorising, for an examination:—*pr.p.* **swott'ing**; *pa.p.* **swott'ed**.—*n.* **1** one who does this. **2** an act of swotting.

swum. See **swim**.

swung. See **swing**.

sycamore *sik'ȧ-mōr*, *-mör*, *n.* the name given to several different trees—in England, a maple (in Scotland called a plane tree), in America, a plane tree.

sycophant *sik'ȯ-fănt*, *n.* a flatterer who seeks to gain by pleasing.

sycophan'tic *adj.*

syl-. See **syn**.

syllable *sil'ȧ-bl, n.* a word or part of a word uttered by only one effort of the voice (e.g. *man, thirst*, or the parts of *kind-ness, faith-ful-ness, con-ser-va-tive*).
syllab'ic *adj.*

syllabub, **sillabub** *sil'ā-bub, n.* a dish of cream curdled with e.g. wine, flavoured and frothed up.

syllabus *sil'ȧ-bu̇s, n.* a programme, e.g. of a course of lectures, or courses of study:—*pl.* **syll'abuses**, **syll'abī**.

syllogism *sil'ȯ-jizm, n.* a logical argument in which a conclusion is derived from two premises.

sylph *silf, n.* **1** a spirit of the air. **2** a slender, graceful woman.

sylvan. Same as **silvan**.

sym- See **syn**.

symbol *sim'bȯl, n.* **1** a thing accepted as standing for another because it suggests the most important quality of the other in some way: *The cross is the symbol of Christianity*; *White is the symbol of purity*; *The dove is the symbol of peace.* **2** a sign used as a short way of stating something, esp. in algebra or chemistry: *x is a symbol used for an unknown quantity*; *O is the symbol for oxygen*.
symbol'ic(al) *adjs.* **1** having to do with symbol(s). **2** (of language, or of a mathematical, etc., statements) using symbols. **3** being a symbol (of).
sym'bolise *v.t.* to be a symbol of: *A ring symbolises love that never ends*:—*pr.p.* **sym'bolising**.
sym'bolism *n.* the practice of expressing or representing by symbols.

symmetry *sim'i-tri, n.* the state in which two parts, on either side of a dividing line, are equal in size, shape, and position: *A larger window to the left of the door spoiled the symmetry of the front of the building*.
symmet'ric(al) *adjs.* having symmetry, not lop-sided:—*opp.* **āsymmet'ric(al)**.
symmet'rically *adv*.

sympathetic, etc. See **sympathy**.

sympathy *sim'pȧ-thi, n.* **1** the state of having the same feelings or outlook: *In this family parents and children are not in sympathy.* **2** ability to understand the feelings of others. **3** pity, sorrow for another, or an expression of this:—*pl.* **sym'pathies**.
sympathet'ic *adj.* **1** showing or feeling sympathy. **2** inclined to be in favour of (with *to, towards*): *I am sympathetic to the scheme*.
sym'pathise *v.i.* **1** to feel with or for another. **2** to express sympathy (with). **3** to understand and approve of (with *with*): *I sympathise with your aims*:—*pr.p.* **sym'pathising**.
in sympathy with 1 in agreement with. **2** in support of.

symphony *sim'fȯ-ni, n.* **1** a long serious piece of music for an orchestra of many instruments, usu. in four, or three, movements. **2** something harmonious and pleasant to the eye: *The scene was a symphony in green and gold*:—*pl.* **sym'phonies**.
symphon'ic *adj.* of, or like, a symphony.

symposium *sim-pō'zi-u̇m, n.* a collection of essays on a single subject by different writers, or a conference where opinions on a subject are gathered:—*pl.* **sympō'sia**.

symptom *sim(p)'tȯm, n.* **1** something that is a usual sign (of a disease): *Spots are one symptom of measles.* **2** a sign (of a state, usu. bad): *Small outbreaks of violence were symptoms of general unrest*.
symptomat'ic *adj.* being a sign or symptom (of).

syn- *sin-, pfx.* together, with.
Before *l*, **syn-** becomes **syl-**; before *b, m, p*, **sym-**; before *s*, **sy-**.

synagogue *sin'ȧ-gog, n.* **1** a Jewish place of worship. **2** a group of Jews gathered to worship.

synch, **sync** *singk.* Short for **synchronise**, **synchronisation**.

synchronise *sing'krȯ-nīz, v.i.* **1** to take place at the same time. **2** to agree in time: *In the film, the movements of the hero's lips did not synchronise with the sounds supposed to come from them.*—*v.t.* **1** to cause to happen at the same time. **2** to cause (clocks, watches) to agree in time:—*pr.p.* **syn'chronising**.

syncopate *sing'kȯ-pāt, v.t.* to change the rhythm of (music) by putting the accent on beats usu. not accented:—*pr.p.* **syn'copating**.
syn'copated *adj.* **syncopā'tion** *n.*

syncretism *sing'kri-tizm, n.* the (attempted) reconciliation of different systems of belief.

syndicate *sin'di-kit, n.* **1** a council or number of persons who join together to manage an important piece of business. **2** a number of people combined for some common purpose or interest. **3** a group of newspapers under the same management. **4** an agency that supplies articles, photographs, etc., for publication at the same time in newspapers, etc., in different places.—*v.t.* *(-kāt)* to sell, use, for publication in a number of newspapers:—*pr.p.* **syn'dicating**.

syndrome *sin'drōm, n.* a characteristic pattern or group of symptoms.

synod *sin'od, n.* **1** a council of clergymen. **2** among Presbyterians, a church court made up of several presbyteries.

synonym, *sin'o-nim, n.* a word having the same, or very nearly the same, meaning as another.

synon'ymous *adj.* having the same meaning as (with *with*).

synon'ymy *n.*

synopsis *si-nop'sis, n.* **1** a short statement giving the main points (of a book, etc.). **2** a general view of a subject: *a synopsis of the political situation*:—*pl.* **synop'sēs**.

syntax *sin'taks, n.* **1** the correct arrangement of words in a sentence. **2** the rules governing this.

syntac'tic *adj.*

synthesis *sin'the-sis, n.* **1** the act of making a whole by putting together its separate parts. **2** the whole so formed:—*pl.* **syn'thesēs**.

syn'thesise *v.t.* to make by synthesis:—*pr.p.* **syn'thesising**.

syn'thesiser *n.* **1** one who, or that which, synthesises. **2** a computerised instrument for producing sounds, used esp. in making electronic music.

synthet'ic *adj.* **1** formed by synthesis. **2** made artificially by putting different substances together—usu. like, but not the same as, the natural product: *synthetic rubber.* **3** not natural: *a synthetic fine accent*; *synthetic charm.*

synthet'ically *adv.*

syphilis *sif'il-is, n.* a type of venereal disease.

syringe *sir'inj, -inj', n.* **1** a tube with a piston or a rubber bulb, by which liquids are sucked up and squirted out. **2** a tube used by doctors, etc. for injecting, etc.—*v.t.* to inject, or to clean, with a syringe:—*pr.p.* **syringing**.

syrup *sir'up, n.* **1** water or the juice of fruits boiled with sugar and made thick and sticky. **2** treacle, molasses, esp. when made pure for table use. **3** a sugar-flavoured liquid medicine.

syr'upy *adj.* **1** like syrup. **2** excessively sweet or sentimental.

golden syrup a light-coloured treacle produced in the manufacture of sugar.

system *sis'tem, n.* **1** an arrangement of many parts which work together: *a system of railways*; *the solar system*; *a spy system.* **2** the body thought of as working as a whole. **3** a set of organs in the body that work together for one purpose: *the digestive system.* **4** a way of organising: *a system of government*; *the feudal system.* **5** a method of working regularly followed. **6** orderliness: *There is no system in his work.* **7** a way of classifying (e.g. plants), of numbering, etc.: *the decimal system.* **8** (with *the*) society seen as something which oppresses the individual and thwarts his efforts.

systemat'ic *adj.* **1** having to do with classification. **2** showing system. **3** methodical, thorough.

systemat'ically *adv.*

sys'tematise *(-tīz) v.t.* **1** to make into a system. **2** to make orderly and methodical:—*pr.p.* **sys'tematising**.

systē'mic *adj.* **1** affecting the body as a whole. **2** spreading throughout the tissues of a plant.

systems analyst one who analyses the operation of a scientific, industrial, etc. procedure, usu. with a computer, in order to plan more efficient methods and use of equipment.

T

T *tē*, letter of alphabet: **to a T** exactly, perfectly.

tab *tab*, *n.* a small tag, flap, or strap.
keep tabs on to keep checking, keep under supervision.

tabard *tab'ȧrd*, *n.* a short, sleeveless or short-sleeved tunic, esp. that with a coat-of-arms on it worn by heralds.

tabby *tab'i*, *n.* (also **tabb'y-cat**) a striped cat, esp. female:—*pl.* **tabb'ies**.—*adj.* striped, or of mixed colouring.

tabernacle *tab'ėr-na-kl*, *n.* **1** (*Bible*; *cap.*) a tent used by the Jews as a temple in the desert. **2** a small church.

table *tā'bl*, *n.* **1** a piece of furniture with a flat top standing on legs. **2** food, supply of food on table: *the pleasures of the table.* **3** a board on which a game (e.g. billiards) is played. **4** a set of facts or figures set out in columns: *timetable.*—*v.t.* **1** to make into a list or table. **2** to put forward (a motion) for discussion:—*pr.p.* **ta'bling**.
ta'blecloth *n.* a cloth for covering a table.
ta'bleland *n.* a stretch of high land with a level surface.
ta'ble-linen *n.* tablecloths, napkins, etc.
ta'blespoon *n.* a large size of spoon.
ta'blespoonful *n.* as much as will fill a tablespoon:—*pl.* **ta'blespoonfuls**.
ta'ble-tennis *n.* a game played on a table with small bats and light balls.
turn the tables on (someone) to put (someone) in the unfavourable position or state in which one has just been oneself.
See also **tabular**.

tableau *tab'lō*, *n.* a striking group or scene:—*pl.* **tableaux** *(tab'lōz)*.

table d'hôte *täb'l dōt'*, a meal of several courses at a fixed price.

tablet *tab'lit*, *n.* **1** a small flat piece of stone, etc. on which to write or cut words, or paint. **2** a small flat cake or piece of e.g. a drug in solid form, soap, chocolate. **3** (*Scot.*) a brittle sweet of sugar and condensed milk, made in slabs.
tabloid *tab'loid*, *n.* a small-sized newspaper, informal in style, with many pictures.—*adj.* small and compressed.

taboo *tȧ-boo͞'*, *adj. n.* (something) forbidden for religious reasons or not approved by social custom, etc.: *Wine-drinking is (a) taboo among Muslims.*

tabor *tā'bȯr*, *n.* a small drum.

tabu. Same as **taboo**.

tabular *tab'ū-lȧr*, *adj.* **1** having a flat top like a table. **2** arranged in a table or column: *He gave the results in tabular form.*
tab'ulāte *v.t.* to arrange (information) in lists or columns:—*pr.p.* **tab'ulating**.
tabulā'tion *n.*
tab'ulātor *n.* a tabulating device on a typewriter.

tachograph *tak'ȯ-gräf*, *n.* a device fitted to a lorry, etc., recording mileage, speed, etc.

tacit *tas'it*, *adj.* understood but not spoken, silent: *tacit agreement*.
tac'itly *adv.*
tac'iturn *adj.* not inclined to talk.
taciturn'ity, **tac'iturnness** *ns.*
tac'iturnly *adv.* silently, as if unwilling to speak.

tack[1] *tak*, *n.* **1** a short pointed nail with a flat head. **2** in sewing, a long stitch that will later be taken out again. **3** the direction or course of a ship moving against the wind and at an angle to it. **4** a change of this. **5** the run on this temporary course. **6** one of the parts of a zigzag course on land. **7** a course, or change of course, of action. **8** adhesiveness, sticky condition.—*v.t.* **1** to fasten with tacks. **2** to attach, add (something extra on, on to).—*v.t.* and *v.i.* **1** to sew with tacks. **2** to change (a ship) to the opposite tack. **3** to sail a ship by a series of tacks.
tacky *adj.* sticky:—*comp.* **tack'ier**; *superl.* **tack'iest**.
tack'iness *n.*

tack[2] *tak*, *n.* harness, saddles, bridles, etc.

tackle *tak'l*, *n.* **1** ropes, rigging, etc., of a ship. **2** tools, gear: *fishing tackle.* **3** ropes, etc., for raising weights. **4** (in football, etc.) an act of tackling.—*v.t.* **1** (*Rugby*) to seize (a player with the ball) in order to bring him down, or (*football*) to obstruct (him) in order to take the ball from him. **2** to grapple with, try to get the better of (e.g. a heavier man, problem).—Also *v.i.*:—*pr.p.* **tack'ling**.

tacky. See **tack**[1].

tact *takt*, *n.* skill and care in dealing with people, so as to avoid hurting or offending.
tact'ful *adj.* **tact'less** *adj.*
tact'fully *adv.* **tact'lessly** *adv.*
tact'fulness *n.* **tact'lessness** *n.*

tactics *tak'tiks*, *n. sing.* the art of moving troops, ships, etc. successfully for, or in, a

battle.—*n. pl.* way of acting in order to gain advantage.
tac'tical *adj.* **1** concerned with tactics. **2** connected with successful planning.
tac'tically *adv.*
tactician *tak-tish'ȧn, n.* one good at planning in difficult circumstances.

tadpole *tad'pōl, n.* a young frog or toad in its first state.

taffeta *taf'i-tȧ, n.* a thin, shiny silk cloth.

taffrail *taf'rāl, n.* the rail round the stern of a ship.

tag *tag, n.* **1** a metal point at the end of a shoelace. **2** a label. **3** a tab, flap. **4** a well-known quotation, e.g. a line of verse.—*v.t.* to put tag(s) or point(s) on.—*v.i.* (with *on to, after*) to attach oneself to (a person):—*pr.p.* **tagg'ing**; *pa.p.* **tagged**.

tagliatelle *tal'yȧ-tel'i, n.* pasta in the form of flat strips.

tail *tāl, n.* **1** the part of an animal, bird, or fish that sticks out behind the rest of the body. **2** anything like a tail in shape or position: *the tail of a kite.* **3** the rear or end of anything: *the tail of the queue.* **4** (in *pl.*) the side of a coin that does not bear the head. **5** (in *pl.*) a tail coat.—*v.t.* **1** (*slang*) to follow closely, shadow. **2** to take the tails off (e.g. gooseberries).
tailed *adj.* **tail'less** *adj.*
tail'-coat *n.* a coat that is short in front and long and divided at the back, part of full evening dress for a man.
tail'gate *n.* the rear door of a hatchback vehicle.
tail'-light *n.* the light at the back of a car, etc.
tail'plane *n.* a horizontal aerofoil on the tail of an aircraft.
tail'-spin *n.* a steep, spinning dive downwards by an aircraft.
tail wind a wind from behind.
tail off to become fewer or worse towards the end.
turn tail to run away.
twist someone's tail deliberately to annoy someone.

tailor *tā'lor, n.* one who cuts out and makes suits, overcoats, etc.—*v.t.* **1** to make (outer clothes, etc.). **2** to fit, adapt (to a particular shape or purpose).—Also *v.i.*
tail'ored *adj.* tailor-made.
tail'oring *n.* the work of a tailor
tail'or-made *adj.* **1** made by a tailor. **2** highly suitable or appropriate (for a person, purpose, etc.).

taint *tānt, v.t.* **1** to spoil by touching with or putting near, something bad. **2** to infect.—*n.* **1** a trace of decay or infection. **2** a touch of evil in character or nature.

take *tāk, v.t.* **1** to get hold of, grasp. **2** to choose: *Take a card.* **3** to accept (something offered). **4** to receive, undergo (e.g. blows, criticism). **5** to do so without complaint. **6** to assume: *to take responsibility, charge.* **7** to have room for. **8** to swallow (food, drink). **9** to use, etc., regularly: *to take sugar, a morning paper.* **10** to capture. **11** to carry away. **12** to subtract: *Take 2 from 4.* **13** to steal. **14** to succeed in getting (e.g. a prize). **15** to lead, drive, or carry: *to take pigs to market, an umbrella to church.* **16** to employ, use: *to take a knife, care, strong measures.* **17** to require: *This takes courage; The journey takes (me) ten minutes.* **18** to travel by. **19** to perform (an action): *Take a look, rest, bath.* **20** to feel (e.g. pride, pleasure). **21** to begin to feel, show (e.g. courage, comfort). **22** to be affected by: *to take a liking, fancy, to someone.* **23** to go to a place of (shelter, refuge). **24** to study, follow a course in or of: *to take French.* **25** to do, write (an examination). **26** to record: *to take notes, a temperature.* **27** to understand (meaning, person in what he says).—*v.i.* **1** to root. **2** (of e.g. an inoculation) to be effective. **3** to please, win approval:—*pr.p.* **tak'ing**; *pa.t.* **took** (*took*); *pa.p.* **tā'ken**.—*n.* **1** quantity (of e.g. fish) taken at one time. **2** the filming of a scene in a cinema film.
tā'ker *n.*
tā'king *adj.* **1** pleasing, attractive.—*n.* (in *pl.*) total money taken (e.g. at a concert).
take'-away *n.* **1** a meal prepared and bought in a restaurant but taken away and eaten somewhere else. **2** a restaurant providing such meals.
have (got) what it takes to have the qualities necessary for success.
(not) take kindly to to be (un)willing to accept (treatment, a routine, etc.).
take after to be like in appearance or ways.
take a joke to be amused, not hurt, by a joke made about oneself.
take down 1 to write down. **2** to dismantle.
take for 1 to believe to be. **2** to mistake for.
take heed 1 to pay attention. **2** to be careful.
take, be taken, ill to become ill.
take in 1 to include. **2** to receive. **3** to understand: *I did not take in what he said.* **4** to make smaller. **5** to cheat.
take it 1 to endure calmly, to bear it. **2** to understand from something said, etc. (that).
take it from me you can believe me.
take (it) into one's head to have a sudden idea (that), a sudden resolve (to

do something).

take it out of 1 to treat (a person) harshly, esp. because of something he has done. **2** (of work, heat, etc) to exhaust.

take it out on to treat unpleasantly because of one's own frustration, etc.

take (it) upon oneself to do something to do something without any particular instruction to do it.

taken up with preoccupied with.

taken with attracted by, pleased with.

take off 1 to remove (clothes, etc.) **2** to imitate unkindly. **3** (*flying*) to leave the ground (*n.* **take'-off**).

take on 1 to undertake (a task). **2** to employ. **3** to accept as an opponent. **4** to take aboard. **5** to assume, have (e.g. a new meaning). **6** (*coll.*) to be upset.

take over 1 to take control of (e.g. a business; *n.* and *adj.* **take'-over**). **2** (with *from*) to do the work previously done by, to succeed.

take place to happen

take (someone's) life to kill (someone).

take to 1 to go, turn, to (e.g. the hills, flight) in an emergency. **2** to begin to do, use, regularly: *to take to playing the harp*, *to drink.* **3** to be attracted by.

take up 1 to lift, raise. **2** to shorten (a garment). **3** to receive for carrying (goods), admit (passengers). **4** to occupy (space, time, energy). **5** to begin to learn, practise, show interest in, support.

take up on 1 to challenge (someone) on (a subject). **2** to ask (someone) to fulfil (a promise).

take up with 1 to discuss (a subject) with (someone). **2** to become friendly with.

talc *talk*, *n.* a soft mineral, soapy to the touch.

tal'cum (pow'der), *n.* a powder, usu. scented, made from talc, applied to the skin to absorb moisture.

tale *tāl*, *n.* **1** a story. **2** an untrue story, lie.

tale'-bear'er *n.* someone who gives information about others that is likely to cause trouble.

tale'-bear'ing *n.* and *adj.*

tell tales to be a tale-bearer.

talent *tal'ėnt*, *n.* **1** a special skill: *a talent for drawing.* **2** (in ancient times) a measure of weight, or the value of this weight of gold or silver.

tal'ented *adj.* skilled, gifted.

talisman, *tal'iz-mȧn n.* a charm supposed to protect the owner:—*pl.* **tal'ismans**.

talk *tök*, *v.i.* **1** to speak. **2** to gossip. **3** to give information.—*v.t.* **1** to utter (e.g. sense, rubbish). **2** to speak about (e.g. politics). **3** to speak in (e.g. French).—*n.* **1** conversation. **2** a discussion. **3** a lecture. **4** the subject of conversation. **5** gossip.

talk'ing *adj.* and *n.* **talk'er** *n.*

talk'ative *adj.* in the habit of talking a lot.

talk'ativeness *n.*

talk'ie *n.* (*coll.*) an early name for a cinema film with sound.

talk'ing-to *n.* a scolding.

talk big to boast.

talk down 1 to silence (another) by talking much oneself. **2** (with *to*) to talk to as if to an inferior.

talk into, out of to persuade (someone) into, out of (a course of action, etc.).

talk over 1 to discuss. **2** to persuade.

talk round 1 to discuss without coming to the point. **2** to persuade.

talk shop see **shop**.

tall *töl*, *adj.* **1** high. **2** higher than usual. **3** hard to believe: *a tall story*, *tale*.

tall'ness *n.*

tall'boy *n.* a high chest of drawers.

a tall order (instructions to do, etc.) something unreasonably difficult or much.

tallow *tal'ō*, *n.* hard fat of animals, melted and used to make candles and soap.

tally *tal'i*, *n.* **1** (old-fashioned) a stick with notches cut in it to keep a score or account. **2** an account:—*pl.* **tall'ies**.—*v.i.* to agree (with), match: *His story tallies with yours*; *The stories tally*:—*pr.p.* **tall'ying**; *pa.p.* **tall'ied**.

tally-ho *tal-i-hō'*, *interj.* a cry used by huntsmen:—*pl.* **tally-hos'**.

talon *tal'ȯn*, *n.* the claw of a bird of prey, e.g. hawk.

tamable. See **tame**.

tambourine *tam-boo-rēn'*, *n.* a small one-sided drum with bells or clinking metal discs, played with the hand.

tame *tām*, *adj.* **1** not wild; used to living with human beings. **2** dull, not exciting.—*v.t.* **1** to make tame. **2** to subdue, humble (spirit, pride):—*pr.p.* **ta'ming**.

tame'ly *adv.* **tame'ness** *n.*

ta'mer *n.* one who tames.

ta'mable, **tame'able** *adjs.*

Tamil *tam'il*, *n.* a language of south-east India and north, east, and central Sri Lanka.

tammy *tam'i*, *n.* a shortening of **tam-o'-shanter**:—*pl.* **tamm'ies**.

tam-o'-shanter *tam-ō-shan'tėr*, *n.* a round flat woollen cap.

tamper *tam'pėr*, *v.i.* **1** to meddle (with) so as to damage, alter, etc. **2** to influence secretly, unfairly (with *with*): *to tamper with a witness*.

tampon *tam'pon*, *n.* a plug of cotton wool, etc. used to absorb blood, esp. inserted into the vagina during menstruation.

tan *tan*, *v.t.* **1** to turn (an animal's skin) into leather by treating it e.g. with bark containing tannin. **2** to make brown, to sunburn. **3** (*coll.*) to beat.—*v.i.* to become brown, tanned:—*pr.p.* **tann'ing**; *pa.p.* **tanned**.—*n.* **1** yellowish-brown colour (also *adj.*). **2** sunburn.

tann'er *n.* one whose work is tanning.

tann'ery *n.* a place where leather is made:—*pl.* **tann'eries**.

tann'in *n.* **1** any of a number of related substances obtained from plants, used in tanning, dyeing, etc. **2** one of these, present in tea.

tann'ing *n.* and *adj.*

tandem *tan'dėm*, *n.* a long bicycle with two seats and two sets of pedals, arranged one behind the other.—*adv.* with one behind the other.

tang *tang*, *n.* **1** a prong or tapering part of a knife or tool that fits into the handle. **2** a strong taste, flavour, or smell: *a tang of the sea*.

tang'y *adj.*:—*comp.* **tang'ier**; *superl.* **tang'iest**.

tang'iness *n.*

tangent *tan'jėnt*, *n.* a line which touches a curve but does not cut it.

go off at a tangent to go off suddenly in another direction, or on a different line of thought.

tangerine *tan-jė-rēn'*, *tan'*, *n.* a small orange, orig. from *Tangier* (Morocco).

tangible *tan'ji-bl*, *adj.* **1** able to be felt by touch. **2** real, definite: *tangible gains*:—*opp.* **intangible**.

tangle *tang'gl*, *n.* an untidy, confused knot or state.—*v.t.*, *v.i.* to twist, knot, together.—*v.i.* to become involved in a struggle, etc. (with):—*pr.p.* **tang'ling**.

tango *tang'gō*, *n.* a dance of S. American origin:—*pl.* **tan'gos**.—*v.i.* to perform this dance:—*3rd person*, *pr.t.* **tan'goes**; *pr.p.* **tan'going**; *pa.p.* **tan'goed**.

tangy. See **tang**.

tank *tangk*, *n.* **1** a large container for liquids or gas. **2** a large armoured car on caterpillar wheels, mounted with guns.

tank'er *n.* **1** a ship or large lorry for carrying liquids, esp. oil. **2** an aircraft used to transport fuel.

tank top a sleeveless pullover.

tankard *tangk'ȧrd*, *n.* a large drinking-mug of metal, glass, etc.

tanker. See **tank**.

tanner[1] *tan'ėr*, *n.* (*old slang*) a sixpence.

tanner[2], **tannin**, etc. See **tan**.

Tannoy ® *tan'oi*, *n.* a communication system with loud-speakers, for making announcement at airports, etc.

tansy *tan'zi*, *n.* a plant with small yellow flowers:—*pl.* **tan'sies**.

tantalise *tan'tȧ-līz*, *v.t.* to tease, torment, by offering something and keeping it just out of reach:—*pr.p.* **tan'talising**.

tantalis'ing *adj*.

tantamount *tan'tȧ-mownt*, *adj.* (with *to*) the same as in effect, meaning, etc.: *This humbler speech was tantamount to an admission that he had been wrong*.

tantrum *tan'trům*, *n.* a fit, outburst, of bad temper.

tap[1] *tap*, *n.* a light knock or touch.—*v.t.* to strike lightly.—*v.i.* to give a gentle knock:—*pr.p.* **tapp'ing**; *pa.p.* **tapped**.

tap'-dance *n.* a dance done with special shoes that make a tapping noise.

tap[2] *tap*, *n.* a stopper or screw to control the flow of liquid or gas.—*v.t.* **1** to draw off (liquid) by opening a tap. **2** to get liquid from (a container) by piercing it or by opening a tap. **3** to draw from (any rich source, e.g. a region of the country). **4** (*slang*) to get money from (a person) as a loan or gift. **5** to take off a message secretly from (telephone wires):—*pr.p.* **tapp'ing**; *pa.p.* **tapped**.

tapp'ing *n.*, *adj.*

tap'room *n.* room where beer is served from the cask.

tap'root *n.* a strong main root growing vertically downwards.

tap'ster *n.* a barman.

on tap ready to be drawn off from the cask; ready for immediate use.

tape *tāp*, *n.* **1** a narrow strip of cloth used for tying, binding, etc. **2** a piece of this stretched above the finishing line on a race track. **3** a narrow strip of paper, plastic, or metal, as *ticker-tape* (see this), *adhesive tape*, *videotape* (see this).—*v.t.* **1** to fasten or seal with tape. **2** to record on tape:—*pr.p.* **tap'ing**.

taped *adj.* recorded on magnetic tape.

tape'-measure *n.* a tape, marked with centimetres, etc., for measuring.—Also **tape'line**.

tape'-recorder *n.* a machine which records sounds on magnetised tape, so that they can be played back later.

tape'worm *n.* a worm, often very long, found in intestines of men and animals.

have (got) something taped 1 to understand fully. **2** to have something

arranged to one's satisfaction.
red tape. See **red**.

taper *tā'pėr*, *n.* a long, thin wax candle or light.—*v.t.*, *v.i.* to make, or to become, thinner towards the end.
tā'pering *adj.* growing gradually thinner.—Also *n.*

tapestry *tap'is-tri*, *n.* a cloth with a picture woven into it, hung on wall or used to cover funiture:—*pl.* **tap'estries**.

tapeworm. See **tape**.

tapioca *tap-i-ō'kȧ*, *n.* a white starchy food obtained from the underground part of the cassava plant.

tapir *tā'pėr*, *n.* wild animal of S. America rather like a pig.

tapped, etc. See **tap**^{2}.

taproom, **taproot**, **tapster**. See **tap**^{2}.

tar *tär*, *n.* **1** any of a number of thick, dark, sticky mixtures obtained from wood, coal, etc. **2** (*old slang*) a sailor.—*v.t.* to smear with tar:—*pr.p.* **tarr'ing**; *pa.p.* **tarred**.
tarr'y *adj.*:—*comp.* **tarr'ier**; *superl.* **tarr'iest**.
tarr'iness *n.*
be tarred with the same brush to have the same faults as someone else.
tar and feather to punish by smearing with tar and covering with feathers.

tarantula *tȧ-ran'tū-lȧ*, *n.* a poisonous spider found in S. Italy.

tardy *tär'di*, *adj.* **1** slow. **2** late:—*comp.* **tar'dier**; *superl.* **tar'diest**.
tar'dily *adv.* **tardiness** *n.*

tare^1 *tār*, *n.* **1** (*Bible*) a weed growing among corn. **2** a vetch.

tare^2 *tār*, *n.* **1** the weight of a container (e.g. truck) when empty. **2** deduction for this.

target *tär'git*, *n.* **1** orig. a small shield. **2** a mark, or position, to be shot, or aimed, at. **3** a result, etc., aimed at. **4** a person, etc., made the object of unfriendly remarks or conduct: *He had always been a target for her scorn.*—*adj.* aimed at.—*v.t.* **1** to aim. **2** to aim at:—*pr.p.* **tar'geting**; *pa.t.* **tar'geted**.
on target on the correct course; proceeding as planned.

tariff *tar'if*, *n.* **1** a list of charges or prices. **2** a list of taxes to be paid on goods.

tarmacadam *tär-mȧ-kad'ȧm*, *n.* a *macadamised* surface bound with *tar*.
tar'mac *(-mak)* *n.* **1** tarmacadam. **2** an area covered with this, esp. the runways at an airport:—*v.t.* to surface with tarmac:—*pr.p.* **tar'macking**; *pa.p.* **tar'macked**.

tarn *tärn*, *n.* a small mountain lake.

tarnish *tär'nish*, *v.t.* **1** to make (metal) dull or discoloured. **2** to stain (e.g. someone's reputation).—*v.i.* to become dull or stained.—*n.* **1** discolouration on metal. **2** staining.

tarot *tar'ō*, *n.* any of a pack of 78 playing-cards used esp. for fortune-telling.

tarpaulin *tär-pö'lin*, *n.* a strong cloth made waterproof e.g. by coating with tar.

tarry^1. See **tar**.

tarry^2 *tar'i*, *v.i.* **1** to be slow. **2** (*old*) to wait (for). **3** to stay:—*pr.p.* **tarr'ying**; *pa.p.* **tarr'ied**.

tart^1 *tärt*, *adj.* **1** sharp or sour. **2** sharp in spirit: *a tart reply.*
tart'ly *adv.* **tart'ness** *n.*

tart^2 *tärt*, *n.* **1** a pie containing fruit or jam. **2** (*slang*) a prostitute. **3** (*offensive*) a girl, woman.
tart'let *n.* a small tart.

tartan *tär'tȧn*, *n.* **1** a woollen cloth with any of many checked patterns in different colours, as orig. worn by the clans of the Scottish Highlands. **2** (any cloth with) such a pattern.—Also *adj.*

Tartar *tär'tȧr*, *n.* **1** (more correctly **Tatar** *tä'tȧr*) in old times a native of *Ta(r)tary* in Central Asia, noted for fierceness. **2** now, a difficult, fierce, irritable person.

tartar *tä'tȧr*, *n.* **1** a substance that forms inside wine casks. **2** a hard substance that gathers on the teeth.
tartar'ic *adj.* obtained from tartar.
cream of tartar. See **cream**.

task *täsk*, *n.* **1** a set amount of work. **2** a duty. **3** any work, esp. hard.
task'master *n.* one who sets a task.
task force **1** a combined land, sea and air force under one commander, with one special task to carry out. **2** a group (e.g. of police) organised for a special project.
take to task to find fault with.

tassel *tas'l*, *n.* **1** an ornament made from a bunch of silk or other threads tied together at one end. **2** flower group like this e.g. a larch, hazel, catkin.
tass'elled *adj.* hung with tassels.

taste *tāst*, *v.t.* **1** to try by eating or drinking a little. **2** to recognise (a flavour): *I can taste ginger in this cake.* **3** to eat or drink a little of. **4** to experience: *He has tasted success.*—*v.i.* **1** to have a flavour (of): *This tastes of onion.* **2** to have a certain kind of flavour: *to taste sour.* **3** (*old*) to try a little (of). **4** to distinguish flavours:—*pr.p.* **tast'ing**.—*n.* **1** the ability to distinguish flavours; the sense of tasting. **2** an act of tasting. **3** a flavour. **4** a small quantity. **5** a liking, preference: *a taste for music.* **6** judgment, sense of what is

beautiful, socially right, etc.: *good taste in dress*.
taste'ful *adj.* showing good taste.
taste'fully *adv.* **taste'fulness** *n.*
taste'less *adj.* **1** without flavour. **2** showing poor judgment, bad taste.
taste'lessly *adv.* **taste'lessness** *n.*
tas'ter *n.* one whose work is to taste and judge tea or wine.
tas'ty *adj.* savoury; having a good taste:—*comp.* **tas'tier**; *superl.* **tas'tiest**.
tas'tiness *n.*
taste'-bud *n.* a group of cells on the tongue, sensitive to taste.
to one's taste (arranged, etc.) according to one's liking.

tat *tat*, *v.i.* to do tatting.—*v.t.* to make in tatting:—*pr.p.* **tatt'ing**; *pa.p.* **tatt'ed**.
tatt'ing *n.* (the art of making) knotted thread work or lace.

Tatar. See **Tartar**.

tatter *tat'ėr*, *n.* (usu. in *pl.*) a torn piece; a rag.
tatt'ered *adj.* in a torn, ragged state.
tatt'y *adj.* untidy, ragged; shabby:—*comp.* **tatt'ier**; *superl.* **tatt'iest**.

tatting. See **tat**.

tattle *tat'l*, *n.* idle chatter.—*v.i.* **1** to gossip. **2** to let out secrets:—*pr.p.* **tatt'ling**.
tatt'ler *n.*

tattoo[1] *tȧ-tōō'*, *n.* **1** a signal at night by drum and bugle to call soldiers to quarters. **2** an outdoor military entertainment with displays of marching and other events:—*pl.* **tattoos'**.
the devil's tattoo drumming the fingers e.g. on a table.

tattoo[2] *tȧ-tōō'*, *v.t.* **1** to make a pattern on the skin of (e.g. person, arm) by pricking it and putting in colouring. **2** to make (a pattern) in this way:—*pr.p.* **tatoo'ing**; *pa.p.* **tattooed'** (*-tōōd'*; also *adj.*).

tatty. See **tatter**.

taught. See **teach**.

taunt *tönt*, *v.t.* to tease, jeer at, unkindly.—*n.* a jeering remark.
taun'ter *n.* **taun'tingly** *adv.*

taut *töt*, *adj.* **1** drawn tight. **2** (of e.g. nerves) in a state of strain.
taut'en *v.t.*, *v.i.* to make, or become, taut.

tautology *tö-tol'o-ji*, *n.* use of words that (esp. needlessly) say the same thing.

tavern *tav'ėrn*, *n.* **1** a place where wines and spirits are sold and drunk. **2** an inn.

tawdry *tö'dri*, *adj.* showy, cheap, flashy:—*comp.* **taw'drier**; *superl.* **taw'driest**.
taw'drily *adv.* **taw'driness** *n.*

tawny *tö'ni*, *adj.* yellowish-brown:—*comp.* **taw'nier**; *superl.* **taw'niest**.
taw'niness *n.*

tax *taks*, *n.* **1** a government charge on certain things to provide money for the state. **2** a strain, burden: *Delay is a tax on my patience.*—*v.t.* **1** to lay a tax on. **2** to put a strain on: *to tax one's strength.* **3** (with *with*) to accuse of, reproach with: *She taxed him with having spilt the ink*.
tax'able *adj.* liable to be taxed.
taxā'tion *n.* act or system of taxing.
tax disc a paper disc displayed on a vehicle to show that it has been taxed.
tax'-free *adj.*, *adv.* without payment of tax.
tax'payer *n.* one who pays taxes.
tax return a yearly statement of one's income, from which the amount due in tax is calculated.

taxi *tak'si*, *n.* a car which may be hired with driver (also **tax'i-cab**):—*pl.* **tax'is**, **tax'-ies**.—*v.i.* **1** to go by taxi. **2** (of aircraft) to run along the ground:—*3rd person*, *pr.t.* **tax'is**, **tax'ies**; *pr.p.* **tax'iing**, **tax'ying**; *pa.p.* **tax'ied**.

taxidermy *tak'si-dûr-mi*, *n.* the process of preparing and stuffing skins of animals, etc.
tax'idermist *n.* one who does this work.

tea *tē*, *n.* **1** a shrub grown in parts of Asia, esp. India, Sri Lanka, and China. **2** its dried and prepared leaves. **3** a drink made by adding boiling water to the dried leaves. **4** a drink like tea in appearance (e.g. *beef tea*) or made in the same way (e.g. *camomile tea*). **5** an afternoon or evening meal at which tea is often drunk.
tea'-bag *n.* a sachet of tea-leaves for easy tea-making.
tea'-caddy *n.* a caddy (see this).
tea'cake *n.* a bun containing currants, etc.
tea'-cosy *n.* a cosy (see this).
tea'cup *n.* a cup of moderate size from which tea is drunk.
tea'cupful *n.* as much as fills a tea-cup:—*pl.* **tea'cupfuls**.
tea'leaf *n.*:—*pl.* **tea'leaves**.
tea'-party *n.* an afternoon party at which tea is served:—*pl.* **tea'-parties**.
tea'pot *n.* a pot with a spout, used for making and pouring out tea.
tea'room *n.* restaurant where tea, etc., may be had.
tea'-rose *n.* a rose that smells like tea.
tea'-service, **-set** *ns.* articles (teapot, cups, etc.; not cutlery) used at tea.
tea'spoon *n.* a small spoon used with a teacup.
tea'spoonful *n.* as much as fills a tea-spoon:—*pl.* **tea'spoonfuls**.
tea'-towel *n.* a cloth for drying dishes.
tea'-urn *n.* an urn for making tea.

(not) one's cup of tea giving one (no) special enjoyment.

teach *tēch, v.t.* **1** to give (a person) knowledge or skill. **2** to give knowledge of: *to teach French.* **3** to explain, show (that, how to). **4** to train in: *Life teaches us patience.—v.i.* to be a teacher:—*pa.p.* **taught** *(töt)*.
teach'able *adj.* able or willing to learn.
teach'er *n.* one whose profession, or talent, is to give knowledge or skill.
teach'ing *adj.—n.* **1** the work of a teacher. **2** (often in *pl.*) beliefs, rules of conduct, etc., preached or taught.

teacup. See **tea**.

teak *tēk, n.* **1** an East Indian tree. **2** its very hard wood. **3** an African tree.

team *tēm, n.* **1** a group of people acting together. **2** a side in a game: *a football team.* **3** two or more animals working together: *a team of horses*.
team'ster *n.* one who drives a team.
team spirit willingness to work loyally as a team, or as a member of a team.
team'work *n.* **1** work for which a team is required. **2** working together, co-operation in achieving an aim.
team (up) with to come, bring, together for co-operation.

teapot. See **tea**.

tear[1] *tēr, n.* **1** a drop of liquid coming from the eye. **2** (in *pl.*) grief.
tear'ful *adj.* inclined to weep, or to cause tears.
tear'fully *adv.* **tear'fulness** *n.*
tear'less *adj.* shedding, or causing, no tears.
tear'-gas *n.* a gas causing blinding tears, used against e.g. rioters.
tear'-jerker *n.* a sentimental play, film, story, etc.
tear'stained marked with tears.
in tears weeping.

tear[2] *tār, v.t.* **1** to pull with force (apart, away, down, etc.). **2** to make a rent in. **3** to make (a hole, gash). **4** to wound. **5** to cause to suffer: *The story tore her heart.—v.i.* **1** to have rent(s) made in it. **2** (*coll.*) to move or act with great speed or force:—*pa.t.* **tore** *(tōr, tör)*; *pa.p.* **torn** *(tōrn, törn).—n.* a rent.
tear'away (*coll.*) *n.* a rough, disorderly youngster.

tearoom. See **tea**.

tease *tēz, v.t.* **1** to pull out (wool) with a comb. **2** to sort (out, e.g. a tangle). **3** to annoy, irritate on purpose. **4** to pretend playfully to do so.—Also *v.i.*:—*pr.p.* **teas'ing**.—*n.* one who teases.
teas'er *n.* a puzzle; a difficult problem.

teasel, **teazle** *tēz'l, n.* a plant with large prickly heads.

teaspoon, etc. See **tea**.

teat *tēt, n.* **1** the part of a female animal's breast or udder through which the young suck milk, the nipple. **2** the rubber end of a baby's feeding-bottle.

teazle. See **teasel**.

technical *tek'ni-kȧl, adj.* **1** belonging to a particular art, skill, science, etc.: *the technical terms used by artists, by civil engineers.* **2** of, relating to, the practical (esp. mechanical and industrial) sciences: *technical skills.* **3** judged by strict laws or rules: *This was a technical assault, defeat*.
technical'ity *n.* a technical detail, or term:—*pl.* **technical'ities**.
tech'nically *adv.*
technician *tek-nish'ȧn, n.* one having trained skill in the practical side of an art.
technique *tek-nēk', n.* the way in which a skilled process is carried out: *His technique as a pianist is faultless*.
technoc'racy *n.* (a state having) government by technical experts:—*pl.* **technoc'racies**.
technol'ogy *n.* **1** (the study of) science applied to practical purposes. **2** the technical achievement of a particular civilisation, etc.:—*pl.* **technol'ogies**.
technolog'ical *adj.* **technol'ogist** *n.*
technical college one teaching technical subjects.—*Coll. abbrev.* **tech** *(tek)*.

teddy *ted'i, n.* a stuffed toy bear:—*pl.* **tedd'ies**.—Also **tedd'y-bear** *(-bār)*.

tedious *tē'di-us, adj.* tiresome, long-lasting and slow.
te'diously *adv.* **te'diousness** *n.*
te'dium *n.* tediousness.

tee *tē, n.* (*golf*) **1** the peg or heap of sand on which the ball is placed for the first stroke at each hole. **2** the level ground where this is used.—*v.t.* to place (ball) on the tee:—*pr.p.* **tee'ing**; *pa.p.* **teed**.
tee off to make the first stroke in golf.

teem[1] *tēm, v.i.* to be full of, swarm (with).

teem[2] *tēm, v.i.* (*dial.*) to rain heavily.

teens *tēnz, n.pl.* the years of one's age from thir*teen* to nine*teen*.
teen'āge *adj.* suitable for, or characteristic of persons between these ages.
teen'āger *n.* a person in the teens.

tee-shirt *tē'shûrt, n.* a short-sleeved shirt in a light knitted fabric, pulled on over the head.

teeth, **teethe**, **teething**. See **tooth**.

teetotal(l)er *tē-tō'tȧl-ėr, n.* one who never takes an alcoholic drink.
teetō'tal *adj.* never taking alcohol.

tele- *tel-i-*, (as part of a word) **1** at a distance. **2** television.

telecommunicā'tions *n.pl.* or *n. sing* the science of sending messages, information, etc. by telephone, telegraph, radio, television, etc.

telegram *tel'i-gram*, *n.* a message sent by telegraph.

telegraph *tel'i-gräf*, *n.* an instrument or system for sending messages to a distance, esp. using wires and electricity.—*v.t.* **1** to send (a message) by telegraph. **2** to inform by telegraph (that).

telegraph'ic *adj.* **1** of telegraphs or telegraphy. **2** (of style) as brief as possible.

teleg'raphist, **teleg'rapher** *ns.* one who works a telegraph.

teleg'raphy *n.* the art of making or using telegraphs.

telemessage *tel'i-mes-ij*, *n.* a message sent by telex or telephone.

telemeter *ti-lem'i-tėr*, *n.* an instrument for measuring quantities and signalling them to a distant point.

telepathy *ti-lep'ȧ-thi*, *n.* passage of thought from one person to another without the help of hearing, sight, or other physical sense.

telepath'ic *adj.*

telephone *tel'i-fōn*, *n.* instrument for speaking to a person at a distance by sending an electric current along a wire, or by sending out radio waves.—*v.i.*, *v.t.*, to send (a message) by telephone:—*pr.p* **tel'ephoning**.

telephon'ic *(-fon') adj.*

telephonist *ti-lef'ȯn-ist*, *n.* one whose work is operating a telephone switchboard.

teleph'ony *n.* the use of a telephone system for sending messages.

telephotography *tel-i-fȯ-tog'rȧ-fi*, *n.* the photographing of distant objects using a **tel'ephō'to lens** that enlarges them.

teleprinter *tel'i-prin-tėr*, *n.* a telegraph system in which messages are sent out at one place, and received and printed at another, by instruments resembling typewriters.

teleprompter *tel'i-promp'tėr*, *n.* a device that projects, in front of a television speaker, the text of what he is to say.

telescope *tel'i-skōp*, *n.* an instrument using a lens or a mirror to make distant things seem larger and nearer.—*v.t.* **1** to push together so that one thing slides inside another as do parts of a small jointed telescope. **2** to crush together with force: *The crash telescoped the rear coaches.* **3** to run together in thought, etc.: *His memory telescoped events really separated by several years.*—*v.i.* to be pushed, crushed, or run, together:—*pr.p.* **tel'escoping**.

telescop'ic *(-skop') adj.*

teletext *tel'i-tekst*, *n.* business news, etc., transmitted by television companies, that, with a special adaptor, can be read on an ordinary television.

television *tel-i-vizh'ȯn*, *n.* **1** the sending from a distance, and reproduction as pictures on a screen, of view(s) of still or moving objects. **2** (material sent by) this system. **3** a television receiving set.

tel'evise *(-vīz) v.t.* to send out a view of (e.g. a golf match) by television:—*pr.p.* **tel'evising**.

telex *tel'eks*, *n.* **1** the use of teleprinters hired from the Post Office for sending messages. **2** such a teleprinter. **3** a message sent by this service.—*v.t.* to send (someone a message) by telex.

tell *tel*, *v.t.* **1** to say in words (e.g. the truth, a lie). **2** to give the facts of (a story). **3** to make known: *to tell what has happened.* **4** to inform (e.g. person). **5** to order, command (e.g. person). **6** to make out, distinguish: *I cannot tell what it is, tell one from the other*; *I can tell him by his footsteps.* **7** to count, calculate: *to tell one's beads*; *to tell the time*—*v.i.* **1** to make known something one should not. **2** to have a marked effect or result: *Perseverance tells*:—*pa.p.* **told** *(tōld)*.

tell'er *n.* **1** one who tells. **2** a bank clerk who receives and pays out money. **3** one who counts votes in a election, etc.

tell'ing *adj.* having a marked effect.

tell'tale *n.* one who gives away private information about others.—*adj.* giving information not intended to be given: *tell-tale jam on the child's face*.

all told counting all: *an audience of nine persons all told.*

tell off **1** to count off. **2** to choose for duty. **3** (*coll.*) to scold (*n.* **tell'ing-off'**).

tell on **1** to have an effect on: *The strain told on him.* **2** to betray, give away secrets about.

telly *tel'i*, (*coll*) *n.* short for **television**:—*pl.* **tell'ies**.

temerity *ti-mer'i-ti*, *n.* rashness.

temp *temp*, (*coll.*) *n.* a *temp*orarily-employed secretarial worker.

temper *tem'pėr*, *v.t.* **1** to bring to the right degree of hardness, etc. by heating and cooling: *to temper steel.* **2** to make less severe, modify: *to temper justice with mercy.*—*n.* **1** the amount of hardness, etc., of a material such as metal, glass. **2** disposition, usual state of mind. **3** mood. **4** a fit of anger. **5** tendency to anger.

tem'pered *adj.* **1** brought to a certain

temper, as steel. **2** (as part of a word) having a particular disposition: *a good-tempered man*.
in a temper angry.
lose one's temper to show anger.
out of temper irritable, impatient.

temperament *tem'pėr-ȧ-mėnt*, *n.* natural quality of mind and feeling, disposition: *The deer had a nervous temperament*.
temperament'al *adj.* **1** having to do with temperament. **2** showing quick changes of mood. **3** excitable, irritable.
temperament'ally *adv.* **1** in an excitable way. **2** by temperament: *She is excitable and therefore temperamentally unfit to be a nurse*.

temperance *tem'pėr-ȧns*, *n.* **1** moderation and self-control in action or speech (e.g. in eating, criticism). **2** moderation in taking alcoholic drinks; also the habit of never taking them.
temperate *tem'pėr-it*, *adj.* **1** moderate in passions or appetites (*opp.* **intemperate**.) **2** not extremely hot or cold: *Britain has a temperate climate*.
tem'perately *adv.* **tem'perateness** *n.*
tem'perature *(-pri-chůr) n.* **1** degree of heat or cold. **2** a body heat above normal.
temperate zones the parts of the earth's surface between the Tropic of Cancer and the Arctic Circle and between the Tropic of Capricorn and the Antarctic Circle.

tempest *tem'pėst*, *n.* a violent storm with high wind.
tempes'tūous *adj.* **1** very stormy. **2** violently emotional or passionate.
tempes'tūously *adv.*
tempes'tūousness *n.*

template *tem'plāt*, *n.* a pattern, usu. cut from a thin plate, by means of which the shape of something to be made can be marked out.—Also **templet** *(-plit)*.

temple[1] *tem'pl*, *n.* a building in which people, esp. of a non-Christian religion, worship.

temple[2] *tem'pl*, *n.* either of the flat parts of the head above the cheekbones.

templet. See **template**.

tempo *tem'pō*, *n.* **1** the speed at which a piece of music should be or is played (*pl.* **tem'pi** *-pi*). **2** the speed of any activity (*pl.* **tem'pos**).

temporal *tem'pȯ-rȧl*, *adj.* **1** belonging to time. **2** concerned with this life, not eternity. **3** secular, not spiritual.
temporary *adj.* lasting, used, only for a time.
tem'porarily *adv.* for the time being: *The line is temporarily out of order*.
tem'porise *(-īz) v.i.* to speak or act vaguely, evasively, avoid deciding or promising anything:—*pr.p.* **tem'porising**.

tempt *tem(p)t*, *v.t.* **1** to try and persuade, or to entice, esp. to evil. **2** to attract.
temptā'tion *n.* **1** the act of tempting. **2** the state of being tempted. **3** something that tempts. **4** temptingness.
temp'ter, temp'tress (*fem.*) *ns.*
temp'ting *adj.* attractive.
temp'tingly *adv.* **temp'tingness** *n.*

ten *ten*, *n.* **1** the number next above nine (10 or X). **2** a set of ten things or persons. **3** the tenth hour after midday or midnight. **4** the age of ten years. **5** any thing (e.g. a shoe) denoted by ten.—*adj.* **1** 10 in number. **2** ten years old.
tenn'er (*coll.*) *n.* a ten-pound note.
tenth *adj.* **1** next after the ninth. **2** equal to one of ten equal parts.—Also *n.*
ten'fold *(-fōld) adj., adv.* (so as to be) ten times as much or as many: *a tenfold increase*; *It increased tenfold*.
ten'-pence' (**piece**) a coin worth ten pence.
ten'pin bowling a game similar to ninepins using ten skittles.

tenable *ten'ȧ-bl*, *tēn'*, *adj.* (of position, theory) able to be held or defended.

tenacious *ten-ā'shůs*, *adj.* **1** keeping a firm hold (often with *of*). **2** (of memory) holding facts for a long time. **3** determined, persevering, obstinate.
tenā'ciously *adv.*
tenā'ciousness, tenacity *(-as'-) ns.*

tenant *ten'ȧnt*, *n.* one who pays rent to another for the use of a house, building, land, etc.
ten'ancy *n.* **1** the holding of a house, etc., by a tenant. **2** the period of this:—*pl.* **ten'ancies**.
ten'anted *adj.* occupied.
ten'antless *adj.* without a tenant.
ten'antry *n.* all the tenants on an estate:—*pl.* **ten'antries**.

tench *tensh*, *-ch*, *n.* a freshwater fish.

tend[1] *tend*, *v.t.* to take care of, look after.
tender *n.* **1** one who tends. **2** a small craft that carries stores, etc., for a larger one. **3** a truck with coal and water attached to steam railway engine.

tend[2] *tend*, *v.i.* **1** to move, lean, slope, in a certain direction (with *towards*). **2** to be inclined, likely (to have a certain result, or to end in a certain way): *His actions tend to cause trouble*; *a course tending to disaster*. **3** to have a leaning, natural readiness (to): *He tends to take a gloomy view*.
ten'dency *n.* (*pl.* **-ies**).

tender[1]. See **tend**[1].

tender[2] *ten'dėr, v.t.* **1** to offer. **2** to present formally (e.g. one's resignation).—*v.i.* to make an offer (for work, a contract): *Several firms tendered for the contract to build the hospital.*—*n.* an offer.
legal tender coins which must be accepted when offered in payment: *Sixpences are no longer legal tender*; *Small coins are legal tender for small sums only.*

tender[3] *ten'dėr, adj.* **1** soft, not hard or tough. **2** easily hurt or damaged. **3** hurting when touched. **4** very young. **5** easily moved to feel pity, love, etc. **6** showing care, love, etc.; gentle.
ten'derise *v.t.* to make (meat) tender e.g. by beating:—*pr.p.* **ten'derising.**
ten'derly *adv.* **ten'derness** *n.*
ten'derfoot *n.* a beginner.
ten'der-hear'ted *adj.* full of kind feeling and sympathy.

tendon *ten'dȯn, n.* a sinew, a tough cord or band joining a muscle to a bone or other part.
ten'dinous *adj.*

tendril *ten'dril, n.* a thin curling part of a plant by which it holds to a support.

tenement *ten'i-mėnt, n.* **1** property (piece of land, house, flat). **2** a high building divided into flats, each occupied by a different tenant.

tenet *tē'nėt, ten', n.* political, religious, etc., belief held by person, group.

tenfold, **tenner**. See **ten**.

tennis *ten'is, n.* a game for two to four persons, using a ball, rackets, and net, orig. one played in a building of special shape, now usu. one played outside on a lawn or hard surface (also **lawn tennis**).
tenn'is-court *n.* a place prepared for tennis.

tenon *ten'ȯn, n.* a projection at the end of a piece of wood, etc. shaped to fit a mortise (see this).

tenor *ten'ȯr, n.* **1** the general course: *the even tenor of country life.* **2** the general meaning: *the tenor of his remarks.* **3** the highest singing voice in the normal range for men. **4** a musical part for such a voice. **5** a man who sings this part.—Also *adj.*

tense[1] *tens, n.* the form of a verb that shows time of action: *'I am' is in the present tense*; *'I was' is in the past tense.*

tense[2] *tens, adj.* **1** (of e.g. rope) tightly stretched. **2** (of the body, muscles) stiffened; prepared for action. **3** nervous, strained: *tense with excitement*; *a tense moment.*—*v.t.* and *v.i.* to make or become tense:—*pr.p.* **ten'sing.**
tense'ly *adv.* **tense'ness** *n.*
ten'sile *(-sīl), adj.* of, or capable of, stretching.
ten'sion *n.* **1** the act of stretching or stiffening. **2** tenseness. **3** mental strain.

tent *tent, n.* a movable shelter made usu. of canvas supported by pole(s) and ropes.
tent'-peg *n.* a strong peg of wood or iron fixed in the ground to which a tent rope is fastened.

tentacle *ten'tȧ-kl, n.* a long thin flexible part of an animal, used to feel, etc. (e.g. an arm of an octopus), or something that suggests it.

tentative *ten'tȧ-tiv, adj.* made, etc., as a trial, as something that can be withdrawn if not approved of: *a tentative offer, suggestion.* **2** uncertain, hesitating.
ten'tatively *adv.* **ten'tativeness** *n.*

tenterhook *ten'tėr-hook, n.* a sharp hooked nail used to hold cloth stretched.
be on tenterhooks to be in a state of great anxiety about what will happen.

tenth. See **ten**.

tenuous *ten'ū-ůs, adj.* thin or weak: *the tenuous threads of the spider's web*; *a tenuous hold on life.*

tenure *ten'ūr, n.* **1** the holding of property, or of an office or employment. **2** the conditions, or the period, of this.

tepee *tē'pē, n.* an American Indian tent of skins over a conical framework.

tepid *tep'id, adj.* **1** slightly warm, lukewarm. **2** not enthusiastic: *a tepid welcome.*
tep'idly *adv.*
tepid'ity, **tep'idness** *ns.*

tercentenary *tûr-sen-tē'nȧ-ri*, or *-ten'*, the 300th anniversary:—*pl.* **tercenten'aries.** —Also *adj.*

term *tûrm, n.* **1** a length of time: *his term of office*; *a term of three years.* **2** certain days on which rent is paid. **3** a division of a school, etc., year. **4** a word or expression: *a scientific term.* **5** (usu. in *pl.*) a condition: *the terms of the agreement.* **6** (in *pl.*) fixed charges. **7** (in *pl.*) footing, nature of relationship between persons, etc.: *on friendly, good, bad, terms*; *equal terms*, i.e. neither party having an advantage.—*v.t.* to name, call.
terminol'ogy *n.* the special words and expressions used in a particular art, science, etc.
terminolog'ical *adj.*
terms of reference see **reference.**
in terms of from the point of view of: *He judged everything in terms of profit and loss, not in terms of human happiness.*
come to terms **1** to reach an agreement. **2** (with *with*) to find a way of living with

or tolerating (inconvenience, illness, etc.).
make terms to reach an agreement.

termagant *tûr'mȧ-gȧnt, n.* a bad-tempered, violent woman.

terminable, etc. See **terminate**.

terminate *tûr'mi-nāt, v.t.* **1** to put an end to (e.g. a discussion, treaty, life). **2** to be, or be at, the end or limit of.—*v.i.* to come to an end either in space or in time:—*pr.p.* **ter'minating**.
ter'minable *adj.* (of agreement, etc.) that may come, be brought, to an end.
ter'minal *adj.* **1** having to do with, or growing at, the end. **2** (of a fatal illness) reaching its last stages.—*n.* **1** an end. **2** a point of connection in an electric circuit. **3** a terminus. **4** an airport when considered as the end of a long-distance flight.
ter'minally *adv*.
terminā'tion *n.* **1** the act of ending. **2** an end.
ter'minus *n.* **1** the end. **2** one of the end places or points on a railway or bus route:—*pl.* **ter'minuses**, **ter'minī**.
See also **interminable**.

termite *tûr'mīt, n.* (also **white ant**) a pale insect a little like an ant which eats wood, etc.

tern *tûrn, n.* a sea bird, smaller than a gull, with forked tail.

terrace *ter'ȧs, n.* **1** a raised level bank of earth. **2** any raised flat place. **3** a (esp. connected) row of houses.—*v.t.* to form into a terrace or terraces:—*pr.p.* **terr'acing**.

terra-cotta *ter'ȧ-cot'ȧ, n.* **1** clay burned in a kiln, brownish-red in colour, used for statues, tiles, etc. **2** a brownish-red colour.—Also *adj*.

terra firma *ter'ȧ fûr'mȧ, n.* land as opposed to water.

terrain *tė̇r'ān, n.* **1** a stretch of land, esp. considered with reference to its physical features, or to its suitability for e.g. a battle. **2** field of activity or experience.

terrapin *ter'ȧ-pin, n.* a tortoise of N. America.

terrestial *tė-res'tri-ȧl, adj.* **1** having to do with, or existing on, the earth. **2** living on the ground.

terrible. See **terror**.

terrier *ter'i-ėr, n.* a name given to many kinds of small dog (orig. to one that hunted burrowing animals).

terrific, terrify. See **terror**.

territory *ter'i-tȯ-ri, n.* **1** a stretch of land, region. **2** the land under the control of a ruler or state. **3** an area, as that given by a firm to a salesman to be worked by him. **4** field of activity:—*pl.* **terr'itories**.
territo'rial (*-ō'* or *-ö'*) *adj*.
territorial waters seas close to the shores of a country and considered as belonging to it.

terror *ter'ȯr, n.* **1** very great fear. **2** anything that causes great fear.
terr'ible *adj.* **1** causing great fear. **2** causing great hardship or distress: *a terrible disaster.* **3** (*coll.*) bad; unpleasant. **4** (*coll.*) remarkable.
terr'ibly *adv.* **1** frighteningly. **2** (*coll.*) extremely, greatly, very.
terr'ify *v.t.* to frighten greatly:—*pr.p.* **terr'ifying**; *pa.p.* **terr'ified**.
terrif'ic *adj.* **1** (*old*) causing terror. **2** (*coll.*) huge, very great. **3** (*coll.*) very good.
terrif'ically *adv*.
terr'ifying *adj*.
terr'orise *v.t.* **1** to terrify. **2** to compel to obey by making oneself greatly feared:—*pr.p.* **terr'orising**.
terrorisā'tion *n*.
terr'orism *n.* use of terrorist methods.
terr'orist *n.* one who tries to frighten people into some action by e.g. bomb explosions, murders.—Also *adj*.
terr'or-strick'en, **-struck** *adj.* seized by great fear.

terse *tûrs, adj.* **1** (of e.g. statement) short and well put. **2** (of style, person) using such statements.
terse'ly *adv.* **terse'ness** *n*.

tertiary *tûr'shi-ȧ-ri, adj.* of or at a third level, degree, stage, etc.

tessera *tes'ė-rȧ, n.* a small square or rectangular piece used in forming a mosaic design:—*pl.* **tess'erae** *(-rī)*.
tess'ellated *adj.* made of tesserae.

test *test, n.* **1** something done to find out whether a thing is good, etc.: *Tests were carried out on the new plane.* **2** a happening that shows up good or bad quality: *This was a test of his courage.* **3** (with *for*) a means of finding the presence of: *a test for radioactivity.* **4** a set of questions or exercises.—*v.t.* to try, carry out test(s) on.
test case a law case that may settle similar future cases.
test match in cricket, etc., one of a series of matches between two countries.
test pilot *n.* one who tests new aircraft.
test'-tube *n.* a glass tube closed at one end, used in chemistry tests.
put to the test to test, try.

testament *tes'tȧ-mėnt, n.* **1** a solemn written statement, esp. of what one desires to be done with one's personal property after death. **2** a covenant between God and man, as in the Bible—the **Old Testament** dealing with the covenant made by God with Moses, and the **New Testament** dealing with the promises of God through Christ.

testā'tor *n.* one who makes and leaves a will:—*fem.* **testā'trix**.

See also **intestate**.

testicle *tes'ti-kl, n.* (usu. in *pl.*) one of the two glands in the male body that produce sperm.

testis *tes'tis, n.* a testicle:—*pl.* **tes'tes** *(-tēz)*.

testify *tes'ti-fī, v.i.* **1** to give evidence, esp. in a law court. **2** to give evidence (against person). **3** (with *to*) to support the truth or reality of: *He will testify to my presence in the house.* **4** (with *to*) to show, be, evidence of.—*v.t.* **1** to declare, esp. solemnly: *I testify my willingness.* **2** to say in evidence (that):—*pr.p.* **tes'tifying**; *pa.p.* **tes'tified**.

testimony *tes'ti-mȯ-ni, n.* **1** evidence. **2** a statement to prove a fact. **3** an open statement of belief:—*pl.* **tes'timonies**.

testimō'nial *n.* **1** a written statement telling what one knows of a person's character, abilities. **2** something given to a person to show respect or thanks for services.

testy *tes'ti, adj.* **1** easily made angry. **2** peevish:—*comp.* **tes'tier**; *superl.* **tes'tiest**.

tes'ily *adv.*

tetanus *tet'ȧ-nu̇s, n.* a serious disease caused by a bacillus, entering usu. through a wound, which makes muscles rigid.

tête-à-tête *tet'-ȧ-tet', n.* a private talk usu. between two people.—*adv.* together in private conversations:—*pl.* **tête'-à-têtes'** *(-tets')*.

tetchy *tech'i, adj.* irritable.

tether *teTH'ėr, n.* a rope or chain for tying an animal, allowing it to feed within a certain area only.—*v.t.* **1** to tie with a tether. **2** to keep from moving beyond certain limits.

at the end of one's tether in a position where one has used up all strength, patience, resources, etc.

tetr(a)- *tet-r(ȧ)-*, (as part of a word) four.

tetrarch *tet'rärk, n.* in Roman times, orig., ruler of fourth part of province; a subordinate ruler.

Teuton *tū'tȯn, n.* one of a N. European race, including Germans.

Teuton'ic *adj.* **1** of Germans. **2** (of language) Germanic (see this).

text *tekst, n.* **1** the main part of a book, not drawings, notes, etc. **2** the words of an author as opp. to e.g. comments by another. **3** a passage from the Bible on which a sermon is preached. **4** the theme of a writing or speech.

tex'tūal *adj.* having to do with, or found in, the text.

text'book *n.* a book used in teaching, giving the main facts of a subject.

textile *teks'tīl, n.* a cloth or fabric formed by weaving.

texture *teks'chu̇r, n.* **1** the quality in a material produced by the manner in which threads are woven in it: *This tweed has a loose texture.* **2** quality to touch, taste, of a substance resulting from the way particles are arranged: *the texture of wood, stone, an apple, a date.*

than *THan, THȧn, conj.* a word placed after the comparative of an adjective or adverb to introduce the second part of a comparison: *This is better than that*; *It is easier than I thought*; *more carefully than usual.*

(no, none) other than see **other**.

thane *thān, n.* in England before the Norman Conquest, one, between earl and freeman in rank, who held land from the king or a higher noble.

thank *thangk, v.t.* **1** to express appreciation and gratitude to (someone) for a favour. **2** to admit that one owes a result to: *He has to thank calm weather for his safe return*; *He has himself to thank for this disaster.*—*n.* (usu. in *pl.*) expression of gratitude.

thank'ful *adj.* **1** grateful. **2** relieved and glad.

thank'fully *adv.* **1** gratefully. **2** (*coll.*) it is a relief that.

thank'fulness *n.*

thank'less *adj.* not winning thanks or achieving good results: *a thankless task.*

thank'lessly *adv.* **thank'lessness** *n.*

thanks'giving *n.* **1** act of giving thanks. **2** a church service giving thanks to God. **3** (with *cap.*) a day set apart for this, esp., in the United States, the fourth Thursday in November.

thanks, thank you I thank you.

thanks to 1 as a result of. **2** because of the action of.

give thanks to express gratitude (to).

that *THat, pron.* or *adj.* used to point out a person, thing, etc., esp. one more distant or mentioned earlier (*opp.* to *this*): *Don't take that, take this*; *On that occasion we were less well prepared than we are today*:—*pl.* **those**.—*pron.* (also *THȧt*) used in dependent clauses in place of *who(m), which*: *We hired the horses that we rode.*—*conj.* (also *THȧt*) used with various meanings to introduce a clause **1** showing indirect speech, etc.: *I said that I knew.* **2** (*old*) for the purpose of achieving a result: *These* *things have I spoken unto you that in me ye might have peace.* **3** with a certain result: *He whispered so loudly*, or *made such a noise, that I heard.* **4** because: *It is not that I mind personally, but for your own sake don't go*.

thatch *thach, v.t.* to cover with straw, reeds, etc.—*n.* straw, etc. used to cover e.g. roofs.
thatched *adj.* **thatch'ing** *n.*

thaw *thö, v.i.* **1** to melt or grow liquid, as ice. **2** to become less stiff, more friendly, in manner.—*v.t.* to cause to melt.—*n.* **1** the melting of ice or snow by heat. **2** the change of weather that causes it.

the TH*ė* (before words starting with the sound of a consonant, e.g. *the dog, the year, the ewe*), TH*ē* (before words starting with the sound of a vowel, e.g. *the ear, the honour*; also for emphasis), *adj.* the definite article. **1** used to point to a particular person, thing, etc.: *Find the thief*; *the dress I bought*; *the idea that came to me*; *the night of the party.* **2** also used in reference to any or all of a kind or species: *The rich man usually has rich friends*; *The elephant is an animal with a trunk*; *Do you play the piano?—adj., adv.* used with superl. adjs. and advs.: *the tallest of their three sons*; *I like him the best.—adv.* in phrases such as: *to be the better for a rest* (i.e. 'by that much better'); *Preach a short sermon, the shorter the better*.

theatre *thē'ȧ-tėr, n.* **1** a place where public performances, mainly drama, are seen. **2** any place in which the seats rise by steps as in a theatre. **3** a room for surgical operations. **4** scene of action: *The theatre of war was in France.* **5** the profession or life of actors. **6** drama; plays.
theat'rical *adj.* **1** having to do with a theatre or actors. **2** (of person) behaving as if in a play. **3** (of action, etc.) suited to stage, not real life.
theat'rically *adv.*
the'atre-in-the-round' *n.* use of a stage which has audience all round it.

thee. See **thou**.

theft. See **thief**.

their(s). See **they**.

theism *thē'izm, n.* belief in the existence of God or a god.
the'ist *n.* **thēist'ic** *adj.*
thēoc'racy *n.* a state which regards God or god(s) as its head, the laws as divine commands, and is governed by priests:—*pl.* **thēoc'racies**.
thēol'ogy *n.* the science that deals with the study of God and of man's duty to Him:—*pl.* **thēol'ogies**.
thēolog'ian *(-lōj')* *n.* one who makes a study of theology.
thēolog'ical *adj.*
thēos'ophy *(-ȯ-fi)* *n.* any of various systems of belief which claim that one can obtain knowledge of God through direct inspiration.
thēos'ophist *n.*
See also **atheism**.

them. See **they**.

theme *thēm, n.* **1** a subject for discussion, or on which a person speaks or writes. **2** (*music*) a subject, a short melody which may be repeated in different forms.
theme song, tune a melody that is repeated often in a musical drama, film, or radio or television series, and is connected with a certain character, idea, etc.
thēmat'ic *adj.* **thēmat'ically** *adv.*

themselves. See **they**.

then TH*en, adv.* **1** at that time. **2** after that. **3** in addition: *There'll be three of us—and then there's my mother.* **4** in that case: *'I'm not ill.' 'Why are you so cross, then?'* **5** as a result, therefore: *If the sides are equal, then the angles must be equal.* **6** often used in expressions that call for a response: *What do you think of that, then?*

thence TH*ens, adv.* **1** from that time or place. **2** for that reason.
thence'forth, thencefor'ward *advs.* from that time forward.

theocracy. See **theism**.

theodolite *thē-od'ȯ-līt, n.* an instrument for measuring angles used in surveying land.

theologian, theology, etc. See **theism**.

theorem *thē'ȯ-rėm, n.* something (to be) proved true by a series of steps in reasoning.
thē'ory *n.* **1** an explanation that one thinks is correct but which has not been tested. **2** the principles or methods of a branch of knowledge: *He knew a lot about the theory of music but he was a poor performer*:—*pl.* **thē'ories**.
theoret'ic(al) *adjs.* **1** (opp. of *practical*) having to do with theory, or with theory only. **2** not learned from experience: *theoretical knowledge.* **3** (of a result) arrived at by calculation, not experiment.
theoret'ically *adv.* in, according to, theory.
thē'orise *v.i.* to form a theory or theories (about something) without experiment or experience:—*pr.p.* **thē'orising**.
thē'orist *n.*

theosophy, etc. See **theism**.

therapeutic *ther-ȧ-pū'tik, adj.* having to do with healing or curing.
therapeu'tically *adv.*

therapeu'tics *n. sing.* the branch of medicine concerned with the treatment and cure of diseases.

ther'apy *n.* treatment of disease, or of a bad condition:—*pl.* **ther'apies**.

ther'apist *n.*

there THā̆r, THėr, *adv.* **1** (opp. to *here*) in that place. **2** at that point (in e.g. a speech, events). **3** to that place or point. **4** in that matter: *You are wrong there.*—Also used as a subject when the real subject follows the verb: *There is no one at home.*—*n.* that place or point.—Also *interj*.

there'about(s) *advs.* **1** about, near, that place. **2** near that number or degree.

thereaft'er *adv.* after that.

there'by' *adv.* **1** by that means. **2** as a result of that.

there'fore *(-fōr) adv.* **1** for that or this reason. **2** as a result.

therein' *adv.* **1** in that place. **2** in that fact or circumstance: *Therein lies the difficulty*.

thereon' *adv.* on that or it.

there'upon *adv.* **1** following that. **2** because of that. **3** immediately.

therewith' *adv.* **1** with that. **2** thereupon.

therm- *thûrm-*, **thermo-** *thûr-mō-, -o-, -ȯ-*, (as part of a word) heat.

therm *thûrm*, *n.* a measure of heat, used in the measurement of gas.

ther'mal *adj.* **1** having to do with heat, or with hot springs. **2** (of clothing) made to give special warmth.—*n.* a rising column of warm air.

thermion'ic *adj.* relating to, containing, **ther'mions** *(-mi-ȯnz)*, electrically charged particles given off from extremely hot substances.

thermodynam'ics *n. sing.* the science of the relation of heat to mechanical and other forms of energy.

thermometer *thėr-mom'i-tėr*, *n.* an instrument for measuring temperature.

thermonū'clear *adj.* having to do with the fusion of atomic nuclei at very high temperatures, as in the hydrogen bomb.

Thermos (flask) *thûr'mȯs (fläsk)*, *n.* (*orig.* a trademark) a flask or bottle with a vacuum jacket, for keeping liquids hot or cold.

ther'mostat *n.* an automatic device for controlling temperature.

thesaurus *thi-sö'rus*, *n.* a storehouse esp. of knowledge, a dictionary, etc.

these. See **this**.

thesis *thē'sis*, *n.* **1** a view, assertion, esp. one put forward for discussion. **2** a long essay, report, etc. on a subject set for study, esp. done for a university degree:—*pl.* **theses** *thē'sēz*.

they THā, *pron. pl.* **1** the people referred to. **2** some people, people in general: *They say bread is fattening.* **3** widely used instead of 'he or she': *If I say hello to someone, they usually say hello to me*:—*objective* **them** *(*THem*)*; *possessive* **their** (THār; sometimes described as possessive *adj.*), **theirs** *(*THārz*)*: *They—the two boys—left their skates in the pile, and afterwards were not sure which were theirs*.

themselves' *(-selvz') pron. pl.* the emphatic, or reflexive form of *they*, *them*: *They themselves thought so*; *They cut themselves with the razor*.

thick *thik*, *adj.* **1** not thin. **2** having a certain, or a considerable distance through: *It's two inches thick*; *a thick slice*, *body.* **3** (of e.g. paste, soup) fairly solid or firm. **4** (of e.g. a wood, a crowd) dense, difficult to pass through. **5** difficult to see through. **6** (of speech) not clear. **7** (*coll.*; of person, mind) stupid. **8** (*coll.*) very friendly, or working closely together.—*n.* the thickest, most crowded or active part: *in the thick of the fight*.

thick'ly *adv.* **thick'ness** *n.*

thick'en *v.t.*, *v.i.* to make, or become, thick or thicker.

thick'ening *n.* something used to thicken sauce, etc.

thick'et *thik'ėt* *n.* a group of trees or shrubs set close together.

thick'-head'ed, **-witt'ed** *adj.* stupid.

thickset' *adj.* **1** closely planted. **2** having a short, thick body.

thick'-skinned' *adj.* not sensitive or easily hurt (e.g. by insults).

a bit thick (*coll.*) going too far, more than one can be expected to stand.

thick and fast frequently and in great numbers.

through thick and thin in spite of all difficulties, without wavering.

thief *thēf*, *n.* one who steals or takes unlawfully what is not his own:—*pl.* **thieves**.

thieve *v.i.* to be a thief.—*v.t.* to take (something) unlawfully:—*pr.p.* **thiev'ing**.

thiev'ing *n.* and *adj.*

thiev'ery *n.* act, or practice, of a thief:—*pl.* **thiev'eries**.

thiev'ish *adj.* **1** inclined to thieve. **2** of a thief: *thievish acts*.

theft *theft*, *n.* **1** thievery. **2** an instance of stealing.

thigh *thī*, *n.* the thick fleshy part of the leg from the knee to the trunk.

thimble *thim'bl*, *n.* a small cap to protect the finger and push the needle in sewing.

thim'bleful *n.* a small quantity:—*pl.* **thim'blefuls**.

thin *thin*, *adj.* **1** having little distance through: *a thin slice, rope.* **2** slim, not fat. **3** not set close or crowded together: *a thin crop*; *The crowd was thin in that corner.* **4** (of e.g. soup) lacking strength, watery. **5** not dense. **6** not difficult to see through. **7** poor in quality. **8** (of e.g. voice) lacking in fullness or power. **9** not convincing: *a thin excuse*:—*comp.* **thinn'er**; *superl.* **thinn'est.**—*adv.* **1** not thickly. **2** in a scattered state:—*v.t.*, *v.i.* to make, or become, thin, thinner, or less close or crowded (with *away*, *out*, etc.):—*pr.p.* **thinn'ing**; *pa.p.* **thinned**.
thin'ly *adv.* **thin'ness** *n.*
thinn'ish *adj.*
thin'-skinned' *adj.* **1** having a thin skin. **2** sensitive, easily hurt.
a thin time (*coll.*) a time of little enjoyment.

thine. See **thy**.

thing *thing*, *n.* **1** an object that is not living. **2** a living being: *She is a nice old thing.* **3** (in *pl.*) belongings, esp. clothes. **4** any individual object, fact, circumstance, action, quality, or idea of which one may think or to which one may refer.
be a good (bad) thing to be a wise (unwise) action, or fortunate (unfortunate) happening.
have a thing about to be inclined to be worried or upset by.
just one of those things just something that has to be accepted, a happening that one can do nothing about.
make a thing of to make a fuss about.
see, hear things to see, hear things that are not there.
the thing the proper or right thing.

think *thingk*, *v.i.* **1** to turn over ideas, or to reason, in the mind. **2** to form a picture, idea, in the mind (of): *to think of past happiness.* **3** to intend (with *of*): *She is thinking of going.*—*v.t.* **1** to form (a thought). **2** to judge, believe or consider. **3** to expect:—*pa.p.* **thought** *(thöt)*.
think'er *n.* one who thinks, esp. one who is capable of fruitful thought.
think'ing *adj.* inclined to think deeply.
think'ing-cap *n.* one that one metaphorically puts on to solve a problem.
think'-tank *n.* a group of experts with the job of considering a problem, etc.
think fit to to choose to (do something).
think little, nothing, of 1 to have a poor opinion of. **2** not to regard as difficult.
think out 1 to make in detail (a plan). **2** to solve by careful thought.
think over, through to consider thoroughly.
think up to invent.
See also **thought**[2].

third *thûrd*, *adj.* **1** next after the second (also *n.*). **2** equal to one of three equal parts (also *n.*).—*n.* a major third (see this under **major**).
third'ly *adv.* in the third place (see **firstly**).
third degree see **degree**.
third-par'ty *adj.* having to do with a third person or party, as in *third-party insurance* (where the first party is the insured person, e.g. the car owner, the second the insurance company, and the third, say, a passenger in the car).
third'-rate' *adj.* of poor quality.
Third World the poorer, less developed countries of Asia, Africa and S. America, that are not politically aligned with the two main, communist and capitalist, groups.

thirst *thûrst*, *n.* **1** the dry feeling in the mouth and general discomfort caused by want of drink. **2** an eager desire (for e.g. information, power).—*v.i.* **1** to feel thirst. **2** to have a great desire (for).
thirst'y *adj.* **1** suffering from thirst. **2** (of earth) dry, parched. **3** eager (for):—*comp.* **thirst'ier**; *superl.* **thirst'iest**.
thirst'ily *adv.* **thirst'iness** *n.*

thirteen *thûr'tēn*, *-tēn'*, *n.* and *adj.* three and ten (13 or XIII).
thir'teenth (also *-tēnth'*) *adj.* **1** next after the twelfth. **2** equal to one of thirteen equal parts.—Also *n.*
thir'ty *n.* and *adj.* three times ten (30 or XXX).
thir'ties *n. pl.* the numbers thirty to thirty-nine.
thir'tieth *(-ti-ėth) adj.* **1** next after the twenty-ninth. **2** equal to one of thirty equal parts.—Also *n.*
See also **three**.

this TH*is*, *pron.* or *adj.* used to point out a person, thing, etc., esp. one near or being spoken about at the time (opp. to *that*): *This is more suitable than that*; *I am glad to be present on this occasion*:—*pl.* **these**.

thistle *this'l*, *n.* a prickly plant with purple heads of flowers.
this'tledown *n.* the light feathery bristles of the seeds of a thistle.

thither TH*i*TH'*ėr*, *adv.* **1** to that place. **2** to that end or result.

thole *thōl*, *n.* a pin in the side of a boat to keep the oar in place.

thong *thong*, *n.* **1** a piece of leather to fasten anything. **2** the lash of a whip.

thorax *thō'raks*, *thö'*, *n.* **1** the part of the body between the neck and the belly, the chest. **2** the middle section of an insect's body.

thorac'ic *(-as'ik), adj.*

thorn *thörn, n.* **1** a sharp, woody part sticking out from the stem of a plant; a prickle (as on a rose). **2** a shrub or small tree having thorns.

thor'ny *adj.* **1** full of thorns; prickly. **2** difficult, causing argument: *a thorny problem, subject:—comp.* **thor'nier**; *superl.* **thor'niest.**

thor'niness *n.*

a thorn in the flesh a cause of constant irritation.

thorough *thur'ȯ, adj.* **1** complete: *a thorough rogue, master of his trade.* **2** (of a person, manner of working, something done) very careful, covering every detail.

thor'oughly *adv.* **thor'oughness** *n.*

thor'oughbred *adj.* and *n.* **1** (a horse, etc.) bred from a dam and sire of the best blood. **2** (a person) well bred and spirited.

thor'oughfare *n.* **1** a public road, street. **2** a passage through, or right to use it: *a notice saying 'No Thoroughfare'.*

thor'oughgo'ing *adj.* thorough, complete: *a thoroughgoing nuisance.*

those. See **that.**

thou TH*ow, pron.* 2nd person *sing.*, now replaced by **you** except in solemn language as in church:—*objective* **thee**; *possessive* **thy** (TH*ī*; sometimes described as possessive *adj.*), **thine** *(*TH*īn).*

thyself' *pron.* the emphatic or reflexive form of *thou, thee.*

though TH*ō, conj.* **1** although. **2** if: *as though; even though.—adv.* however: *I wish I had not said it, though.*

thought[1]. See **think.**

thought[2] *thöt, n.* **1** the act or process of thinking. **2** something that one thinks, an idea. **3** an opinion, or opinions as a whole: *the political thought on this subject.* **4** consideration: *after much thought.* **5** (often in *pl.*) intention (of): *I had no thought, thoughts, of going.* **6** expectation (of): *I had no thought of failing.*

thought'ful *adj.* **1** deep in thought. **2** showing thought. **3** thinking of others, considerate.

thought'fully *adv.*

thought'fulness *n.*

thought'less *adj.* **1** not thinking what the results of one's actions may be. **2** showing such lack of thought: *She was hurt, was warned, by the other's thoughtless words.*

thought'-reading *n.* knowing what is passing in another's mind by watching his expressions, or by telepathy.

second thoughts see **second.**

take thought **1** to consider (how to). **2** take care about (with *for*).

See also **think.**

thousand *thow'zȧnd, n.* **1** ten times a hundred (1,000 or M). **2** a great number:—*pl.* **thousands**, or (after another number) **thousand.**—Also *adj.*

thou'sandth *n.* and *adj.*

one in a thousand rare and excellent.

thrall *thröl, n.* **1** a slave. **2** slavery.

thral'dom *n.* slavery.

thrash *thrash, v.t.* **1** to beat out (grain) from the straw by e.g. flail, machinery (more often **thresh**). **2** to beat soundly. **3** (with *out*) to discuss thoroughly, so as to reach agreement.—*v.i.* **1** to thresh grain. **2** to move, toss, violently (about).

thrash'er, thresh'er *n.*

thrash'ing, thresh'ing *n., adj.*

thread *thred, n.* **1** a very thin line or cord of any substance, esp. one twisted and drawn out. **2** the line, ridge, round a screw. **3** a connected series of details in proper order, or an awareness of this: *I lost the thread of his story, argument.—v.t.* **1** to pass a thread through the eye of (a needle). **2** to put (e.g. beads) on a thread. **3** to make (one's way) where the passage is narrow: *He threaded his way among the trees, through the crowd.*

thread'bare *adj.* **1** worn to the bare thread. **2** (of e.g. excuse) used too often.

threat *thret, n.* **1** a warning that one intends to punish or to hurt. **2** a warning of something bad that may come: *a threat of rain.* **3** something likely to cause harm etc: *His presence is a threat to the success of our plot.*

threat'en *v.t.* **1** to utter threats to harm (someone, etc.). **2** to be a threat to. **3** to suggest the approach of (something unpleasant). **4** to state one's intention (to do).—Also *v.i.*

threat'ening *adj.*

three *thrē, adj.* and *n.* **1** the number next above two (3 or III). **2** a set of three things or persons. **3** the third hour after midday or midnight. **4** the age of three years. **5** anything (e.g. a shoe, a playing-card) denoted by three.—*adj.* **1** 3 in number. **2** three years old.

third, thirteen, thrice see these words.

three'fold *adj.* **1** having three parts. **2** three times as great or as much.—Also *adv.: It repaid him threefold.*

three'some *(-sum) n.* a group of three.

threepence *thrip'ens, threp'ens (old) n.* three old pennies:—*pl.* **threep'ences.**

threepenny piece, bit *(thrip', threp') n.* an old coin of the value of three pence.

three-quar'ter (length) not quite full-

length: *three-quarter (length) sleeves.*
three'score' *n.* and *adj.* three times twenty, sixty.

thresh *thresh.* See **thrash**.

threshold *thresh'(h)ōld, n.* **1** the piece of timber or stone under the door of a building. **2** a doorway, entrance. **3** the place or point of entering or beginning: *at the threshold of his career.*

threw. See **throw**.

thrice *thrīs, adv.* three times.

thrift *thrift, n.* careful management of money or goods in order to save.
thrif'ty *adj.* showing thrift:—*comp.* **thrif'tier**; *superl.* **thrif'tiest**.
thrif'tily *adv.* **thrif'tiness** *n.*
thrift'less *adj.* not thrifty; spending carelessly, extravagant.

thrill *thril, v.i., v.t.* to feel, or make feel, keen emotion or excitement.—*n.* **1** an excited feeling. **2** vibration, quivering.
thrill'ing *adj.*
thrill'er *n.* an exciting novel, play, etc. esp. about crime and detection.

thrive *thrīv, v.i.* **1** to prosper, gain wealth. **2** to be successful. **3** to grow strong, flourish:—*pr.p.* **thri'ving**; *pa.t.* **throve, thrived**; *pa.p.* **thriv'en** *(thriv')*, **thrīved**.
thri'ving *adj.* **1** successful. **2** growing well.

throat *thrōt, n.* **1** the front part of neck, where gullet and windpipe are. **2** the back part of the mouth, connecting the openings of the nose, lungs and stomach.
throat'y *adj.* (of the voice) deep and hoarse:—*comp.* **throat'ier**; *superl.* **throat'iest**.
throat'ily *adv.* **throat'iness** *n.*

throb *throb, v.i.* **1** (of e.g. heart) to beat with more than usual force. **2** (of e.g. engine) to beat regularly. **3** (of a painful part of the body) to hurt rhythmically, in time with the pulse:—*pr.p.* **throbb'ing**; *pa.p.* **throbbed**.—Also *n.*

throes *thrōz, n.pl.* suffering, pain, great effort or struggle.
in the throes of engaged in, struggling with (e.g. revolution, moving house).

thrombosis *throm-bō'sis, n.* the forming of a clot in a blood-vessel:—*pl.* **thrombō'ses** *(-sēz)*.

throne *thrōn, n.* **1** the seat of a king or a bishop. **2** the king or his power.—*v.t.* to place on a royal seat:—*pr.p* **thron'ing**.

throng *throng, n.* **1** a crowd. **2** a great number.—*v.t.* **1** to fill (a place) with a crowd. **2** (of a crowd) to fill very full.—*v.i.* to crowd (together).

throttle *throt'l, n.* **1** the throat or windpipe. **2** (in engines) a device by which steam or petrol can be turned on or off.—*v.t.* **1** to choke by gripping the throat. **2** to shut off (e.g. steam) from an engine. **3** to slow (engine) by reducing flow of fuel. **4** to silence, suppress:—*pr.p.* **thrott'ling**.

through *thrōō, prep.* **1** from end to end, or from side to side, of. **2** into and out of at the other end. **3** from beginning to end of. **4** by means of: *He got the job through his uncle's influence.* **5** as a result of: *through his own stupidity.*—Also *adv.*—*adj.* **1** going from starting-point to destination without break or change: *a through train.* **2** *(coll.)* finished.
throughout' *prep.* **1** everywhere in. **2** from one end to the other of.—Also *adv.*
through and through thoroughly.
through with 1 finished with. **2** no longer willing to associate with.

throve. See **thrive**.

throw *thrō, v.t.* **1** to send through the air with force, hurl, fling, cast, propel. **2** to cause to fall to the ground. **3** to construct (a bridge across a river). **4** to make (pottery) on a wheel. **5** to upset, disconcert. **6** *(coll.)* to hold, give (a party).—Also *v.i.*:—*pa.t.* **threw** *(thrōō)*; *pa.p.* **thrown** *(thrōn)*.—*n.* **1** an act of throwing. **2** the distance to which anything is or may be thrown: *a stone's-throw.*
throw'away *adj.* **1** for throwing away as rubbish. **2** (of a remark) casual.
throw'back *n.* a person, etc. seeming to belong to an earlier stage in his ancestry, development, etc.
throw away 1 to get rid of (rubbish). **2** to waste.
throw in 1 to add, give, as a free gift. **2** to make (a comment) casually, in passing.
throw off 1 to cast off hastily. **2** to get rid of (e.g. a cold, depression).
throw on, to put on (e.g. clothes) quickly or carelessly.
throw over to reject, abandon (a fiancé, etc.).
throw oneself into to play one's part in heartily, with energy.
throw up 1 to give up, abandon (a job). **2** *(slang)* to vomit.

thrush[1] *thrush, n.* a singing bird with brown back and spotted under parts.

thrush[2] *n.* an infection causing a rash in the mouth, throat or vagina.

thrust *thrust, v.t.* **1** to push or drive with force. **2** to press (in). **3** to stab, pierce. **4** to force (oneself, one's company, on someone).—Also *v.i.*:—*pa.t., pa.p.* **thrust**.—*n.* **1** a stab. **2** pushing force or pressure. **3** the forward force developed by a propeller, high speed jet, etc. **4** an advance into an enemy's territory, etc.

thud *thud*, *n.* a dull, hollow sound of a blow or of a heavy body falling.—*v.i.* to move, fall, with such a sound:—*pr.p.* **thudd'ing**; *pa.p.* **thudd'ed**.

thug *thug*, *n.* a ruffian, a man who lives by violence.
thugg'ery *n.* the conduct of thug(s).

thumb *thum*, *n.* **1** the short, thick finger of the human hand. **2** what corresponds to it on other animals. **3** the part of a glove covering the thumb.—*v.t.* to turn over, or to soil (pages) with the thumb or fingers—Also *v.i.* (with *through*).
thumb'nail *n.* the nail on the thumb.—*adj.* small but complete: *a thumbnail sketch*.
thumb'screw *n.* old instrument of torture screwed tight on thumb(s).
thumb'tack (*U.S.*) *n.* a drawing pin.
rule of thumb a rough-and-ready practical method, found by experience to work.
under someone's thumb completely under someone's influence.

thump *thump*, *n.* a heavy blow.—*v.t.*, *v.i.* to beat, fall, or move, with a dull, heavy blow or sound.
thump'ing *adj.* (*coll.*) very big.

thunder *thun'dėr*, *n.* **1** the deep rumbling sound heard after a flash of lightning. **2** any loud, rumbling noise.—*v.i.* **1** (with *it* as subject) to give out thunder. **2** to sound like thunder. **3** to storm, threaten. —*v.t.* to say loudly and angrily.
thun'dery *adj.* **thun'deriness** *n.*
thun'dering *adj.* (*coll.*) very big or great.
thun'derous *adj.* **1** making a sound like thunder. **2** angry-looking.
thun'derbolt *n.* **1** a flash of lightning and peal of thunder. **2** a very great and sudden surprise.
thun'derclap *n.* a sudden crash of thunder.
thun'derstruck *adj.* overcome, made silent, by surprise.
steal someone's thunder to take away someone's chance of producing an effect by taking his idea, information, etc. and using it first.

Thursday *thûrz'di*, *n.* fifth day of week.

thus TH*us*, *adv.* **1** in this or that manner. **2** to this degree or extent (e.g. *thus far*). **3** because of this.

thwack *thwak*, *v.t.* to strike with something flat.—Also *n.*

thwart *thwört*, *v.t.* **1** to hinder (a person) from carrying out a plan, or from doing what he wants. **2** to frustrate (e.g. a purpose).

thy. See **thee**.

thyme *tīm*, *n.* a sweet-smelling herb used for seasoning.

thymus *thī'mus*, *n.* a gland near the base of the neck.

thyroid *thī'roid*, *adj.* having to do with a large gland in the neck which has great influence on growth of body.

thyself. See **thee**.

tiara *tē-ä'rȧ*, *n.* **1** a jewelled ornament for the head. **2** the pope's headdress, surrounded by three crowns.

tibia *tib'i-ȧ*, *n.* the larger of the two bones between knee and ankle.

tic *tik*, *n.* a twitching motion of certain muscles, esp. of the face.

tick¹ *tik*, *n.* a blood-sucking mite-like animal.

tick² *tik*, *n.* the case or cover in which feathers, etc. are put to make e.g. a mattress.
tick'ing *n.* the cloth of which ticks are made.

tick³ *tik*, *n.* a light, angular mark used to show that something is correct, has been dealt with, etc.—*v.t.* **1** (often with *off*) to put this mark beside (an item in a list, etc.) **2** (with *off*; *coll.*) to scold.
tick'ing-off' *n.* a scolding.

tick⁴ *tik*, *v.i.* to make a small, quick noise, esp. regularly as a watch.—*n.* **1** the sound of a watch or clock. **2** a moment.
tick'ing *n.* and *adj.*
tick'er-tape *n.* paper ribbon used in an automatic machine (**tick'er**) which receives by telegraph and prints the latest stock exchange prices, etc.
tick over (of an engine, etc.) to run, work, at a gentle pace.

tick⁵ *tik*, *n.*: **on tick** (*coll.*) on credit, with time allowed for payment.

ticket *tik'it*, *n.* **1** a marked card, esp. one giving the owner a right to travel, to be admitted, etc. **2** a certificate, e.g. of release from the armed forces. **3** a paper giving notification of a driving-offence, etc. **4** a label attached to something, e.g. giving its price. **5** (esp. *U.S.*) a list of candidates proposed by a political party; the party's principles.—*v.t.* to put a label on.

ticking. See **tick²**, **⁴**.

tickle *tik'l*, *v.t.* **1** to touch in a sensitive part of the body lightly and cause to laugh. **2** to please, amuse: *This story tickled the old man*.
tick'lish *adj.* **1** easily tickled. **2** (of e.g. a

person, problem, situation) difficult to handle:—*pr.p.* **tick'ling**.

tiddler *tid'lėr n.* a small fish.

tiddly *tid'li*, (*coll.*), *adj.* slightly drunk:—*comp* **tidd'lier**; *superl.* **tidd'liest**.

tiddlywinks *tid'li-wingks*, *n. sing.* a game in which small discs are flipped into a cup.

tide *tīd*, *n.* **1** the rise and fall of the sea which happens regularly twice each day. **2** (in e.g. *Whitsuntide*) season.—*v.t.* to carry (a person over a difficulty, difficult time) as if by the tide:—*pr.p.* **tid'ing**.

tī'dal *adj.* **1** having to do with tides. **2** affected by tides: *a tidal river*.

tide'mark *n.* **1** a high-water mark. **2** a line of dirt left round the inside of a bath, etc.

tidal wave a great wave caused by the tide or an earthquake.

tidier, etc. See **tidy**.

tidings *tī'dingz*, *n. pl.* news (of something).

tidy *tī'di*, *adj.* **1** neat. **2** in good order. **3** (*coll.*) fairly big (e.g. *a tidy sum of money*):—*comp.* **ti'dier**; *superl.* **ti'diest**.—*v.t.* to make neat, put in good order:—*pr.p.* **ti'dying**; *pa.p.* **ti'died**.

ti'dily *adv.* **ti'diness** *n.*

tie *tī*, *v.t.* **1** to fasten with string, etc. **2** to make a bow or knot in. **3** to form (a knot). **4** to join, unite. **5** (esp. with *down*) to bind or oblige (a person to take some action). **6** to limit, restrict.—*v.i.* **1** to score the same number of points. **2** to link, connect (with *in*):—*pr.p* **ty'ing** *(tī')*; *pa.p* **tied** *(tīd)*.—*n.* **1** a knot, bow, etc. **2** a shaped strip of fabric worn tied round the neck under the collar of a shirt. **3** a close connection. **4** a hindrance, restriction. **5** a state of being equal in number of e.g. votes or points. **6** one game or match in a series. **7** (*music*) a curved line drawn over notes of the same pitch to show they are to be treated as one note the length of both, or all, together.

tied *adj.* (of a dwelling) reserved for a person doing a particular job, e.g. on the landlord's farm.

tie'-break, **tie'-breaker** *ns.* an extra game that decides which of the competitors is to win a match which has ended in a draw.

tie'-dye'ing *n.* a method of producing designs in fabrics by knotting or tying them, then dyeing them.

tie'-pin, **-clip** *ns.* an ornamental clasp for a tie.

See also **untie**.

tier *tēr*, *n.* a row, esp. when several rows are placed one above another.

tiff *tif*, *n.* a slight quarrel.

tiger *tī'gėr*, *n.* a large, striped, fierce, cat-like animal from Asia:—*fem.* **tī'gress**.

ti'ger-lil'y *n.* a lily with large spotted or streaked flowers.

tight *tīt*, *adj.* **1** (of e.g. rope) firmly stretched, not loose. **2** packed or wedged closely. **3** (of e.g. lid) fitting closely. **4** (of e.g. clothes) fitting too closely. **5** (esp as part of a word) sealed so as to keep something in or out; not leaky: *airtight*; *watertight*. **6** (*coll.*) tipsy, drunk. **7** (of e.g. money) not easy to obtain. **8** difficult to get through or out of: *a tight place*. **9** (*coll.*) stingy.

tight'ly *adv.* **tight'ness** *n.*

tight'en *v.t.*, *v.i.* to make, or become, tight or tighter.

tights *n.pl.* a skin-tight garment for the legs and body up to the waist.

tight'rope *n.* a tightly stretched rope on which acrobats perform.

tile *tīl*, *n.* a piece of baked clay, etc. used in covering floors, roofs, etc.—*v.t.* to cover with tiles:—*pr.p.* **ti'ling**.

ti'ling *n.* the tiles of a floor, roof, etc.

till[1] *til*, *n.* a container or drawer in, or on, a counter, etc. in which money is put and registered.

till[2] *til*, *prep.* to the time of: *till death*, *till Sunday*.—*conj.* to the time when: *till I am forced to stop*.

till[3] *til*, *v.t.* **1** to prepare (land) and raise crops. **2** to plough.

till'age *n.* **1** the act of tilling. **2** tilled land.

till'er *n.*

tiller[1] *til'ėr*, *n.* the handle or lever for turning a rudder from side to side.

tiller[2]. See **till**[3].

tilt *tilt*, *v.i.* **1** (*history*) to joust (see this). **2** to thrust (at), attack in words. **3** to fall into a sloping position, or be raised at an angle.—*v.t.* **1** to slant. **2** to raise one end of.—*n.* **1** a thrust (at). **2** a state of sloping; dip, slant.

(at) full tilt with full speed and force.

timber *tim'bėr*, *n.* **1** wood for building, etc. **2** trees suitable for this; woods. **3** a wooden beam for the framework of a house or ship.

timber line *n.* on a mountain or in cold regions, the line beyond which there are no trees.

timbre *tan*^{g}*br'* or *tim'bėr*, *n.* the quality of a musical sound or voice.

timbrel *tim'brėl*, *n.* an ancient instrument like a tambourine.

time *tīm*, *n.* **1** the hour of the day: *What time is it?* **2** a point at which, or period during which, something happens. **3** the passage of days, years, events, etc.: *She recovered as time went by.* **4** (often in *pl.*) a period marked off from others in some way: *in the time of King John*; *in modern, future, hard, times*; *I enjoyed my time in Paris.* **5** an interval, space: *There is no time between trains.* **6** the quantity of minutes, hours, etc. spent in, or available for, an activity, etc.: *The work took a long time*; *I'll do it when I have time.* **7** a suitable season or moment: *Now is the time to make a change.* **8** one of a number of occasions or repetitions: *four guests at a time*; *He won four times.* **9** (in *pl.*) used in stating a multiplication sum: *Four times twenty-one*=4 × 21=84. **10** (*music*) grouping of notes in bars of equal duration according to position of principal accents; also, rate of performance.—*adj.* **1** having to do with time. **2** arranged to go off, etc., at a particular time: *a time bomb*; *a time switch.*—*v.t.* **1** to measure the minutes, seconds, etc., taken, or to be taken, by: *I timed the race, work.* **2** to choose the time for (well, badly, etc.): *He timed his intervention perfectly*:—*pr.p.* **tim'ing**.

time'less *adj.* **1** never ending. **2** not belonging, etc., to any particular time.

time'ly *adj.* coming at the right moment: *timely help*.

time'liness *n.*

tim'er *n.* a person or device that records time taken.

time bomb a bomb that has been set to explode at a particular time.

time'-consuming *adj.* taking up a lot of or too much time.

time'-hon'oured *adj.* (of a custom, etc.) respected because it has lasted a long time.

time'keeper *n.* **1** a timepiece. **2** one who keeps a record of time taken to do something, etc.

time limit a fixed period within which a thing must be completed.

time'piece *n.* a watch or clock.

time'server *n.* one who meanly suits his opinions or actions to the circumstances or to the person in power.

time'serving *adj.* and *n.*

time'-sharing *n.* **1** a system of using a computer so that it can deal with several programmes at the same time. **2** a scheme by which a person buys the right to use a holiday home for the same specified period of time each year for a specified number of years.

time'-signal *n.* (on the radio, etc.) a signal for giving the exact time.

time'table *n.* a table or list showing the times of e.g. school classes, the arrival and departure of trains, etc.

time'worn *adj.* **1** worn by long use. **2** old.

time zone one of 24 longitudinal divisions of the world, each having a standard time.

at times occasionally, now and then.

do time (*coll.*) to serve a prison sentence.

from time to time occasionally.

have no time for to despise.

(in) no time (in) a very short time.

in time early enough.

on time up to time.

take one's time to spend as long as one needs, or an unnecessarily long time, doing something.

the time being the present time.

time and (time) again repeatedly, over and over.

time and motion study an investigation of the motions performed and the time taken in industrial work with a view to cutting out unnecessary movement and so speeding up production.

time off, out time spent away from one's work.

up to time punctual(ly), (in a place) at the time fixed, stated.

timid *tim'id*, *adj.* **1** shy. **2** easily frightened. **3** cautious.

timid'ity *n.*

tim'idly *adv.* **tim'idness** *n.*

timorous *tim'ȯr-ůs*, *adj.* **1** very easily frightened, very timid. **2** full of fears.

timpani *tim'păn-i*, *n.pl.* kettledrums.

tim'panist *n.* one who plays these.

See also **tympanum**.

tin *tin*, *n.* **1** a silvery-white metal, an element. **2** a box or can made of **tinplate**, i.e. thin iron covered with tin, or other metal. **3** a sealed metal can containing food.—Also *adj.*—*v.t.* to cover with tin:—*pr.p.* **tinn'ing**; *pa.p.* **tinned**.

tinned *adj.* (of food) sealed in a tin for preservation.

tinn'y *adj.* **1** like tin. **2** (of sound) thin, like that of a tin being struck:—*comp.* **tinn'ier**; *superl.* **tinn'iest**.

tin'smith *n.* a worker in tin.

tin'foil tin or other metal in thin leaves for wrapping articles.

tin'-opener *n.* any of several devices for opening tins of food.

tin'pot *adj.* worthless.

tincture *tingk'chůr*, *n.*

tinkle *ting'kl*, *v.i.*, *v.t.* to make, or cause to make, little light sounds (as of small bells); to clink, jingle:—*pr.p.* **tink'ling**.—Also *n.*

tinned, tinning, tinny, etc. See **tin**.

tinsel *tin'sėl*, *n.* **1** a shiny, glittering substance or cloth, used for decoration. **2** anything showy but of little value.

tint *tint*, *n.* a variety of a colour, esp. one diluted and made lighter.—*v.t.* to give a slight colouring to.

tiny *tī'ni*, *adj.* very small:—*comp.* **ti'nier**; *superl.* **ti'niest**.

tip[1] *tip*, *n.* the small top, point, end, esp. of anything long.—*v.t.* (usu. in *pass.*) **1** to form a point to. **2** to cover the end of:—*pr.p.* **tipp'ing**; *pa.p.* **tipped**.

on the tip of one's tongue not quite within one's ability to recall and say.

tip[2] *tip*, *v.t.* **1** to strike lightly. **2** to cause to slant. **3** (with *over*) to overturn: *He tips over his chair.* **4** to empty (out, into, etc.). **5** (esp. with *off*) to give a hint to, private information to. **6** to give a small gift of money to (e.g. a waiter).—*v.i.* **1** to slant. **2** to give tips:—*pr.p.* **tipp'ing**; *pa.p.* **tipped**.—*n.* **1** a tap or light stroke. **2** a dump for rubbish. **3** a piece of private information, a hint. **4** a small gift of money.

tip'ster *n.* one whose business is to give special information supposed to be useful to gamblers, etc.

tip'-off *n.* a warning, hint.

straight tip a hint that can be depended upon in betting, etc.

tip someone the wink to give someone a useful hint.

tip the scale 1 to make one side of the scale go down. **2** to prove to be the important factor in a decision: *This fact tips the scale in his favour*.

tipple *tip'l*, *v.i.*, *v.t.* to drink (alcoholic drinks) in small quantities and often:—*pr.p.* **tipp'ling**.—*n.* an alcoholic drink.

tipp'ler *n.* a constant drinker.

tipsy *tip'si*, *adj.* rather drunk:—*comp.* **tip'sier**; *superl.* **tip'siest**.

tip'sily *adv.* **tip'siness** *n.*

tiptoe *tip'tō*, *v.i.* to walk on the toes, usu. in order to be quiet:—*pr.p.* **tip'toeing**; *pa.p.* **tip'toed**.—*adv.* on tiptoe.

on tiptoe (walking, standing) on one's toes.

tiptop *tip'top'*, *adj.* extremely good.

tirade *tī-rād'*, or *ti-*, *n.* a long, bitter scolding speech.

tire[1]. See **tyre**.

tire[2] *tīr*, *v.t.*, *v.i.* to make, or become, weary, without strength or without patience or interest to go on:—*pr.p.* **tir'ing**.

tired *adj.* **1** wearied, needing rest. **2** (with *of*) bored with.

tired'ness *(tīrd')* *n.*

tire'less *adj.* never becoming weary, never resting.

tire'some *adj.* **1** long and dull. **2** annoying.

tir'ing *adj.* causing tiredness.

tiro. See **tyro**.

tissue *tis'ū*, or *tish'ōō*, *n.* **1** very finely woven cloth. **2** substance of which organs of the body are made. **3** a connected series: *a tissue of lies*.

tissue paper a thin, soft almost transparent paper, used in wrapping, etc.

tit[1] *tit*, *n.* any of several kinds of small bird.

tit[2] *tit*: **tit for tat** (orig. *tip* for *tap*), blow for blow, repayment of injury with injury.

tit[3] *tit*, (*impolite slang*) *n.* a woman's breast.

Titan *tī'tȧn*, *n.* **1** one of the giants in Greek myth. **2** (without *cap.*) a person of great power, ability, or size.

titan'ic *adj.* **1** huge. **2** very strong.

titanium *ti'tā'ni-ŭm*, *n.* an element, a metal used in aircraft, steel industry, etc.

titbit *tit'bit*, *n.* a choice little bit.

tithe *tīTH*, (esp. *history*) *n.* **1** a tenth part. **2** a small part. **3** (usu. in *pl.*) money, land, or stock paid over for support of church and clergy.

titillate *tit'i-lāt*, *v.t.* to excite pleasurably:—*pr.p.* **tit'illating**.

titivate *tit'i-vāt*, *v.t.* and *v.i.* to decorate, make smart:—*pr.p.* **tit'ivating**.

titivā'tion *n.*

title *tī'tl*, *n.* **1** a name or phrase placed over, or at the beginning of a thing, by which that thing is known: *'Great Expectations' is the title of a book.* **2** a name showing rank or honour, or office held, or used in ordinary formal address (e.g. *Lord* Chatham, *Cardinal* Wolsey, *Mrs* Pankhurst). **3** legal right (to e.g. an estate); a just claim.

tī'tled *adj.* having a title.

tit'ūlar *adj.* having the title of an office but not the actual authority or duties: *He is titular head of the organisation*.

title deed a document that proves a right to ownership.

title page page of a book containing its title and usu. the author's name.

title role the part in a play of the character named in the title: *He plays Macbeth, the title role in 'Macbeth'*.

titter *tit'ėr*, *v.i.* to laugh with little noise, nervously or half secretly.

tittle *tit'l*, *n.* a very small part.

tittle-tattle *tit'l-tat'l*, *n.* idle gossip.

T-junction *tē'-jungk'-sh(ȯ)n*, *n.* a road junction in the shape of a T.

titular. See **title**.

to *too*, *tȯ*, or *to͞o*, *prep.* **1** in the direction of: *facing to the east.* **2** as far as: *to town, to the end.* **3** until: *from midday to four o'clock.* **4** showing the purpose of an action: *I came to his assistance.* **5** showing the result: *I tore it to shreds.* **6** used as the sign of the infinitive: *He knew how to sing.* **7** introducing the indirect object of a verb: *He gave the letter to her.* **8** showing belonging: *the key to the door, problem.* **9** compared with: *This selfish act is nothing to his selfish actions in the past.*—*adv.* **1** into a closed position: *Pull the door to.* **2** with various other uses (e.g. *to come to*, to recover from fainting, etc.; *to heave to* (see **heave**); *to set to*, to begin.).
to and fro see **fro**.

toad *tōd*, *n.* reptile like a large frog.
toad'y *n.* a mean hanger-on and flatterer:—*pl.* **toad'ies.**—*v.i.* to give way to person's wishes and flatter him in order to gain his favour: *Do not toady to the rich man*:—*pr.p.* **toad'ying**; *pa.p.* **toad'ied**.
toad'stool *n.* an umbrella-shaped fungus esp. the poisonous kinds of mushroom.

toast *tōst*, *v.t.* **1** to brown by means of the heat of fire, gas flame, or electricity. **2** to warm (e.g. feet). **3** to drink to the health, success, of (a person, etc.).—*n.* **1** bread toasted. **2** the person, thing, to whom a toast is drunk. **3** an act of drinking a toast, a call to drink a toast.
toas'ter *n.* one who, or something that, toasts, esp. now a machine.
toast'master *n.* the announcer of toasts at a public dinner.
toast'-rack *n.* a stand with partitions for slices of toast.
drink a toast to to toast.

tobacco *tȯ-bak'ō*, *n.* (a type of plant, native to America that has) leaves that are dried and used for smoking, chewing, or as snuff:—*pl.* **tobacc'os**.
tobacc'onist *n.* one who sells tobacco.

toboggan *tȯ-bog'ȧn*, *n.* kind of sled turned up at the front for sliding down snow-covered slopes, etc.—*v.i.* to slide over snow on such a sled.
tobogg'aning *n.*

toccata *tȯ-kä'tȧ*, *n.* a keyboard composition intended to show off the performer's skill.

today, **to-day** *too-dā'*, *tȯ-*, *n.* **1** this day. **2** the present time.—*adv.* **1** on the present day. **2** nowadays.

toddle *tod'l*, *v.i.* to walk with short, unsteady steps, as a child does:—*pr.p.* **todd'ling**.
todd'ler *n.* a young child.

toddy *tod'i*, *n.* a mixture of spirits, sugar, and hot water:—*pl.* **todd'ies**.

to-do *too-do͞o'*, *n.* bustle, stir, uproar:—*pl.* **to-dos'**.

toe *tō*, *n.* **1** one of the five end parts of the foot. **2** the part of a sock, shoe, etc. covering the toes. **3** the front of an animal's hoof, a golf club, etc.—*v.t.* **1** to touch or strike with the toe(s). **2** to put toe(s) on:—*pr.p.* **toe'ing**; *pa.p.* **toed.**
toed *tōd*, *adj.* having toes, usu. of a certain kind or number: *square-toed*; *a three-toed animal.*
toe'nail *n.* the nail on a toe.
on one's toes ready to act.
toe the line to act as one ought, esp. according to a rule laid down.

toff *tof*, (*coll.*) *n.* an aristocratic, refined, or well-dressed person.

toffee *tof'i*, *n.* a sweet made of sugar and butter.
toff'ee-apple *n.* a toffee-coated apple on a stick.
toff'ee-nosed (*coll.*) *adj.* conceited.

tog *tog*, *n.* (*slang*) a garment (usu. in *pl.*).

toga *tō'gȧ*, *n.* the loose outer garment worn by a Roman citizen.

together *too-geTH'ėr*, *tȯ-*, *adv.* **1** in or into one place, time, company, mass, etc. **2** in or into union: *to nail the planks together.* **3** by joint action: *Together we persuaded him.*

toggle *tog'l*, *n.* a short piece of wood, etc. passed through a loop of string, used as a button.

toil *toil*, *v.i.* **1** to work hard and long. **2** to move, travel, with effort.—*n.* work of a very tiring kind.
toil'worn *adj.* worn with hard work.

toilet *toi'lit*, *n.* **1** (*old*) the act of washing, dressing, making up: *to make a hasty toilet.* **2** a lavatory.
toi'letries *n.pl.* things used in washing oneself, etc., as soap, toothpaste.
toi'let-paper *n.* soft paper for use in the lavatory.
toi'let-roll *n.* a roll of toilet-paper.
toi'let-water *n.* perfumed liquid for the skin.

toils *toilz*, *n.pl.*: **in the toils of** snared by, under power, fascination, of.

token *tō'kėn*, *n.* **1** a visible sign, evidence: *Please accept this book as a token, in token, of my gratitude.* **2** a keepsake. **3** a card, piece of metal, etc. for use in place of money.—*adj.* acting as a symbol or sign of one's opinion, feeling, intentions: *a token strike, payment.*
by the same token as further supporting evidence or an additional point.

told. See **tell**.

tolerable *tol'ėr-ȧ-bl, adj.* **1** able to be borne, endured (*opp.* **intolerable**). **2** fairly good or pleasant.
tol'erably *adv.* **tol'erableness** *n.*
tol'erance *n.* **1** putting up with and being fair to people whose ways, opinions, etc. are different from one's own. **2** ability to take (e.g. a drug), endure (bad conditions, etc.) without effect, esp. bad effect:—*opp.* **intolerance.**
tol'erant *adj.* **tol'erantly** *adv.*
tol'erāte *v.t.* **1** to bear, endure. **2** to put up with. **3** to allow by not hindering:—*pr.p.* **tol'erating.**
tolerā'tion *n.* **1** the act of tolerating. **2** permitting by a government of religious freedom. **3** tolerance.

toll[1] *tōl, v.t.* to sound (a large bell) slowly and regularly, as for a funeral.—*v.i.* to be sounded thus.

toll[2] *tōl, n.* **1** a tax paid on crossing a bridge, using a road, etc. **2** loss inflicted by disaster: *a heavy toll of human lives.*

tomahawk *tom'ȧ-hök, n.* a light axe—weapon and tool—of North American Indians.

tomato *tȯ-mä'tō, n.* a juicy fruit, usu. red, sometimes yellow:—*pl.* **toma'toes.**

tomb *tōōm, n.* a hole in earth or rock, or a vault, etc., in which a dead body is placed.
tomb'stone *n.* a stone put up over a tomb in memory of the dead.

tombola *tom-bō'lȧ, n.* a kind of lottery, with prizes to be won.

tomboy *tom'boi, n.* a girl who prefers boyish games to games usu. thought suitable for girls.
tom'cat *n.* a full-grown male cat.
tomfool *tom'fōōl, n.* a great fool.—*adj.* foolish.
tomfool'ery *n.* **1** silly actions. **2** nonsense.
tom'tit' *n.* a small bird, a tit.
Tom, Dick, and Harry any persons taken at random.

tome *tōm, n.* a book, esp. a large heavy, or learned one.

tomfool. See **tomboy.**

tomorrow, to-morrow *too-mor'ō, tȯ-, n.* and *adv.* **1** (on) the day after today. **2** (in) the future.

tomtit. See **tomboy.**

tom-tom *tom'tom, n.* a drum orig. used in India, beaten by the hands.

ton *tun, n.* **1** a varying measure of space available, or of volume, used in speaking of a ship's cargo or of amount of sea water displaced by ship. **2** a measure of weight, usu. 2240 pounds (1016 kg.). **3** (*slang*) a speed of 100 m.p.h., or a score, total, etc. of 100.
tonn'age *n.* **1** the space available in a ship, measured in tons. **2** total amount of merchant shipping reckoned by its carrying capacity. **3** total weight in tons.
tonne *tun, n.* (also **metric ton**) a measure of weight, 1000 kg.

tone *tōn, n.* **1** a musical sound. **2** the quality of a sound: *a harsh tone.* **3** rising or falling of the voice, or sharpness or softness of its sound, by which a speaker's meaning, feelings, mood, are shown: *a tone of command*; *a tender tone.* **4** a shade of colour: *a light tone of pink.* **5** (good or stylish) quality: *to give tone to the party.* **6** firmness of body or muscle.—*v.t.* **1** to give the proper tone to. **2** to change the colour of.—*v.i.* to fit (in with), blend (with):—*pr.p.* **ton'ing.**
tō'nal *adj.* (esp. *music*) of tone.
tōnal'ity *n.*
tone'less *adj.* lacking tone or expression.
tonic *ton'ik, adj.* **1** having to do with tones. **2** relating to a keynote. **3** giving or increasing strength.—*n.* **1** a medicine that gives one strength and energy. **2** anything that does this. **3** (also **ton'ic-water**) water containing quinine, drunk with gin, etc. **4** a keynote, first note of a scale.
tone down to make or become softer, less strong, less extreme (e.g. colour, sound, an exaggerated statement).
tone up to give strength to (e.g. muscles).

tongs *tongz, n.pl.* an instrument for lifting and grasping, made of two movable metal arms joined at one end.

tongue *tung, n.* **1** the fleshy organ in the mouth, used in tasting, swallowing, and speaking. **2** a language: *speaking in strange tongues.* **3** an animal's tongue served as food. **4** something like a tongue in shape, e.g. a jet (of flame), a strip of leather under the laces in a shoe, a point of land.
tongu'ing *(tung'), n.* use of the tongue in playing a wind instrument.
tongue'-tied *adj.* not able to speak freely, from shyness, etc.
tongue'-twister *n.* a word, phrase, sentence, difficult to say clearly: *'She sells sea shells' is a popular tongue-twister.*

tonic. See **tone.**

tonight, to-night *too-nīt', tȯ-, n.* and *adv.* (on) the night of the present day.

tonnage, tonne. See **ton.**

tonsil *ton'sil, n.* either of two masses of tissue at the back of the throat.
tonsillī'tis *n.* reddening and painfulness of tonsil(s).

tonsure *ton'shür*, *n.* **1** the shaving of the head by priests and monks. **2** the part of the head so shaven.

too *tōō*, *adv.* **1** over; extremely: *too much.* **2** also: *I want to come too.*

took. See **take**.

tool *tōōl*, *n.* **1** an instrument for doing work, esp. by hand. **2** an instrument for carrying out a purpose: *Advertising is a powerful tool in increasing sales.* **3** a person used by another in gaining his own ends.—*v.t.* to work or mark with a tool, esp. to put designs on (e.g. a book cover).
tool'kit *n.* a set of tools.

toot *tōōt*, *v.i.* **1** to make short unmusical sounds on a flute or horn. **2** to sound a motor horn.—Also *v.t.* and *n.*
too'tle *v.i.* to make weak sounds on a flute, etc.—Also *v.t.*:—*pr.p.* **toot'ling**.

tooth *tōōth*, *n.* **1** one of the hard bodies in two rows in the mouth, used for biting and chewing. **2** anything tooth-like. **3** one of the points on a saw, comb, cogwheel, etc.:—*pl.* **teeth**.
teethe *tēTH*, *v.i.* (of a baby) to grow first teeth:—*pr.p.* **teeth'ing**.
toothed *adj.* having teeth.
tooth'less *adj.* having no teeth.
tooth'ache *n.* a pain in a tooth.
tooth'brush *n.* one for cleaning the teeth.
tooth'paste *n.* a kind of paste for cleaning the teeth.
tooth'pick *n.* an instrument for picking out anything in or between the teeth.
a sweet tooth a love of sweet things.
in the teeth of 1 straight against: *to walk in the teeth of the wind.* **2** in defiant resistance to.
long in the tooth (*coll.*) elderly.
show one's teeth to show one's anger and power to injure.
tooth and nail with all one's strength.

tootle. See **toot**.

top[1] *top*, *n.* **1** the highest part of anything. **2** the upper surface. **3** the highest place or rank. **4** the part of a plant above ground. **5** a lid. **6** (*coll.*) a (woman's) garment for the upper part of the body. **7** a circus tent.—*adj.* highest, chief.—*v.t.* **1** to cover on the top. **2** to rise above. **3** to do better than. **4** to reach the top of. **5** to take off the top of:—*pr.p.* **topp'ing**; *pa.p.* **topped**.
top'less *adj.* **1** very high. **2** (of a woman's dress) leaving the breasts uncovered.
top'most *adj.* highest; uppermost.
topp'er (*coll.*) *n.* a top hat.
topp'ing *n.* something, e.g. cream, a sauce, added on top of food.
top'-boots *n.pl.* long-legged boots with a showy band of leather round the top.
top'coat *n.* an overcoat.
top dog the leader; the boss.
top'-dress'ing *n.* a dressing of manure laid on the surface of the land.
topgallant. See **mast**.
top hat a tall silk hat.
top'-heav'y *adj.* having the upper part too heavy for the lower.
top'knot *n.* a tuft or bun on top of the head.
topmast. See **mast**.
top'notch *adj.* of highest quality.
top'-sec'ret *adj.* (of information) very secret because of highest importance.
in the top flight among those of the highest quality or position.
top up to refill to the top.

top[2] *top*, *n.* a child's toy set spinning by a string, whip, or spring.

topaz *tō'paz*, *n.* a precious stone of many different shades.

topcoat, etc. See **top**[1].

tope *tōp*, *v.i.* to drink heavily:—*pr.p.* **top'-ing**.

topi, **topee** *tō'pi*, *n.* helmet-like hat used in hot countries to protect from sun.

topiary *tō'pi-à-ri*, *n.* the art of cutting bushes, hedges, etc. into decorative shapes.

topic *top'ik*, *n.* a subject spoken, written, or argued about.
top'ical *adj.* **1** having to do with a topic or subject. **2** of interest at the moment, concerned with current events.

topmost, etc. See **top**[1].

topography *tò-pog'rà-fi*, *n.* (the description of) the features of the land in a certain region.
topog'rapher *n.* one skilled in topography.
topol'ogy *n.* a branch of geometry concerned with those properties of a figure that remain unchanged when the figure is bent, stretched, etc.

topper, **topping**. See **top**[1].

topple *top'l*, *v.i.* to fall forward, to tumble (down, over).—*v.t.* to cause to fall over:—*pr.p.* **topp'ling**.

topsyturvy *top'si-tûr'vi*, *adv.* **1** turned upside down. **2** in confusion.—Also *adj.*

tor *tör*, *n.* a hill, rocky hilltop.

torch *törch*, *n.* **1** (*history*) a piece of flaming twisted tow carried as a light. **2** a small hand light with switch and electric battery.

tore. See **tear**[2].

toreador *tor'i-à-dör*, *n.* a bullfighter, esp. on horseback.

torment *tör'ment*, *n.* **1** very great suffering, distress, or worry. **2** something that causes such pain.—*v.t.* (*tȯr-ment'*) **1** to torture, put to very great pain, physical or mental. **2** to worry. **3** to tease.

tormen'tor *n.* one who torments.

torn. See **tear²**.

tornado *tör-nā'dō*, *n.* a whirling wind that causes great damage:—*pl.* **tornā'does**.

torpedo *tör-pē'dō*, *n.* **1** a type of fish with organs on the head that give an electric shock. **2** a large cigar-shaped self-propelled missile, fired from ships or planes, which explodes when it hits its mark:—*pl.* **torpe'does**.—*v.t.* to attack with, damage or destroy by means of, torpedo(es):—*pr.p.* **torpe'doing**; *pa.p.* **torpe'doed**.

torpe'do-boat *n.* a small swift warship which attacks with torpedoes.

torpid *tör'pid*, *adj.* slow, sluggish.

torpid'ity, **tor'por** *ns.*

torque *törk*, *n.* **1** a twisting or rotating force in a machine, etc. **2** (esp. *archaeology*) a necklace formed from a twisted metal band.

torrent *tor'ėnt*, *n.* **1** a rushing stream (of water, lava, etc.). **2** a violent flow (of e.g. rain, words, insults).

torren'tial (*-shȧl) adj.* like a torrent.

torrid *tor'id*, *adj.* **1** burning hot. **2** parched by heat. **3** (*coll.*) full of violent passion.

torrid zone a broad band round the earth on either side of the equator, between the tropics of Cancer and Capricorn.

torsion *tör'sh(ȯ)n*, *n.* act of twisting or turning an object.

torso *tör'sō*, *n.* the trunk without head or limbs, esp. of a statue:—*pl.* **tor'sos**.

tortilla *tör-tēl'yȧ*, *n.* a Latin-American round flat maize cake.

tortoise *tör'tus*, *n.* a slow-moving reptile covered with a hard shell (a turtle or, more usu., a land type of turtle).

tor'toise-shell *tör'tė-shel*, *n.* the shell of a type of sea turtle.—*adj.* of the colour of this shell, mixed red, yellow, and black.

tortuous *tör'tū-u̇s*, *adj.* **1** twisting, winding. **2** (of e.g. methods) deceitful, crooked.

torture *tör'chu̇r*, *n.* **1** severe pain inflicted as a punishment or to force a confession. **2** great suffering of body or mind.—*v.t.* **1** to inflict torture on. **2** to twist out of the natural shape, position, or meaning, etc.:—*pr.p.* **tor'turing**.

Tory *tō'ri*, *tö'*, *n.* a Conservative (see this word) in English politics:—*pl.* **Tor'ies**.

toss *tos*, *v.t.* **1** to throw lightly or carelessly. **2** to throw about lightly or restlessly. **3** to throw up (a coin) to see which side is uppermost when it falls. **4** to toss up with: *I'll toss you for the seat.* **5** to throw up with force or with a jerk: *The bull tossed its master*; *She tossed her head in scorn.*—*v.i.* **1** to throw oneself from side to side restlessly. **2** (of e.g. ship) to be thrown about.—Also *n.*

toss'-up *n.* **1** the tossing of a coin to decide something. **2** something not settled, an even chance: *It is a toss-up whether we can catch the train.*

take a toss 1 to be thrown by a horse. **2** to suffer defeat, etc.

toss off 1 to drink off. **2** to produce quickly and easily (e.g. rhymes).

toss up to stake e.g. money, or make a choice depend, on which side of a tossed coin falls uppermost.

win, lose, the toss to guess rightly, wrongly, which side of a coin will fall uppermost.

tot¹ *tot*, *n.* **1** a small child. **2** a small amount of a liquor.

tot² *tot*, *v.t.* to add (up):—*pr.p.* **tott'ing**; *pa.p.* **tott'ed**.—*n.* an addition of a long column.

total *tō'tȧl*, *adj.* **1** whole: *The total number, loss, was four cows.* **2** complete: *The burned ship was a total loss*; *a total rejection of the offer.*—*n.* **1** the sum. **2** the entire amount.—*v.t.* **1** to add up. **2** to amount to: *The bill totalled fifty pounds*:—*pr.p.* **to'talling**; *pa.p.* **to'talled**.

to'tally *adv.* completely.

total'ity *n.* the whole sum, amount.

to'talīsātor *n.* a machine recording number and nature of bets, so that winners may share total stakes.—*Coll. abbrev.* **tote** (*tōt*).

totalitā'rian *adj.* belonging to a system of government by one party that allows no rivals.

in total counting everything.

tote¹ *tōt*, (*coll.*) *v.t.* to carry:—*pr.p.* **to'ting**.

tote bag a large bag for shopping.

tote². See **totalisator** under **total**.

totem *tō'tėm*, *n.* **1** an animal, plant, or object taken as the badge or sign of a tribe, etc. esp. among American Indians. **2** an image of this.

totem pole a large wooden post set up by American Indians, on which totems were carved and painted.

totter *tot'ėr*, *v.i.* **1** to walk unsteadily. **2** to be unsteady, shake as if about to fall: *The house, his empire, is tottering.*

tott'ery *adj.* shaky. **tott'eriness** *n.*

totting, etc. See **tot²**.

toucan *tōō'kȧn*, *n.* a South American bird with a huge beak.

touch *tuch*, *v.t.* **1** to be, or to come, in contact with, to lay hand, etc. against. **2** to reach as high as. **3** to call at (port). **4** to handle, move, etc., slightly. **5** to mark slightly (with e.g. colour). **6** to come up to (another) in goodness, skill, etc. **7** to play on (a musical instrument). **8** to speak of (a subject) in passing: *He touched that point briefly.* **9** to concern, affect (a person). **10** to move, make feel pity, etc. **11** (*coll.*) to persuade (someone) to give or lend money: *I touched him for £1.* **12** used esp. with 'not' or 'if' in various senses: *I did not touch it* (steal it), *touch him* (strike, etc., him); *I will not touch it* (have anything to do with it); *He won't touch fruit* (eat fruit).—*v.i.* **1** to be in contact. **2** to call (at a port). **3** to speak of (with *on*).—*n.* **1** act of touching. **2** the sense by which one becomes aware of contact. **3** communication: *I am in touch with the owner.* **4** sympathy, understanding: *out of touch with present taste in art.* **5** a slight quantity or degree: *a touch of salt*, *of imagination*, *of cold.* **6** skill in, or style of, handling a musical instrument. **7** (*football*, etc.) the part of the field outside the lines (**touch'-lines**) marking sides of area of play.

touché *tōō-shā'*, *interj.* acknowledging a hit in fencing, or a point scored in argument, etc.

touched *adj.* **1** stirred to gentle emotion. **2** (*coll.*; of person) slightly crazy.

touch'ing *adj.* moving, causing emotion.—*prep.* concerning.

touch'ingly *adv*.

touch'y *adj.* easily offended:—*comp.* **touch'ier**; *superl.* **touch'iest**.

touch'iness *n.*

touch'-and-go' *adj.* very uncertain: *It was touch-and-go whether he would recover*.

touch'-down *n.* **1** the touching to the ground behind the goal line of a football by a player. **2** the alighting of an aircraft on ground (*v.i.* **touch down**).

touchlines. See **touch** (*n.*) above.

touch'paper *n.* slow-burning paper soaked in saltpetre, used in igniting fireworks.

touch'stone *n.* **1** a stone used in testing purity of gold and silver. **2** anything used as a test.

touch'type *v.i.* to type without looking at the keys of the typewriter:—*pr.p.* **touch'-typing**.

touch off to cause to explode, or to become active: *A spark touched off the gunpowder*; *His remark touched off an argument*.

touch up to improve (e.g. a drawing) by a number of small touches.

touch wood. See **wood**.

tough *tuf*, *adj.* **1** not easily broken. **2** not easily chewed. **3** able to stand hardship or strain. **4** hardened in wrongdoing. **5** difficult. **6** (*coll.*; of luck) hard, bad.—*n.* (*coll.*) a rough, bully.

tough'en *v.t.* or *v.i.* to make, or become, tough.

toupee *tōō'pā*, *n.* a small wig or patch of false hair.

tour *tōōr*, *n.* **1** a going round. **2** a journey to various places and back, made for pleasure, or to give entertainment as a performer, or to give lectures, play matches, etc.—*v.t.*, *v.i.* to go on a tour (around).

tour'ism *n.* **1** touring for pleasure. **2** tourists in general.

tour'ist *n.* **1** one who travels for pleasure and sight-seeing. **2** a member of a touring team.

tourist class a type of less expensive accommodation on ships and aircraft.

tour de force *tōōr dė fōrs*, *n.* a feat of strength or skill.

tournament *tōōr'nȧ-mėnt*, *n.* **1** (also **tourney** *tōōr'ni*) in the Middle Ages, a sport in which knights fought on horseback. **2** any contest in skill consisting of a series of games in which a number of people take part: *a tennis*, *chess*, *tournament*.

tourniquet *tōōr'ni-kā*, *n.* a bandage or other device for pressing tightly on the main artery of thigh or arm to prevent great loss of blood.

tousle *tow'zl*, *v.t.* to make untidy, tangle (esp. hair):—*pr.p.* **tous'ling**.

tout *towt*, *v.i.* (*coll.*) to go about seeking custom, support, votes, etc.—*n.* **1** one who does this. **2** one who obtains secretly, or gives, information for betting.

tow[1] *tō*, *n.* coarse part of flax or hemp.

tow'-headed *adj.* having thick fair hair.

tow[2] *tō*, *v.t.* to pull (a vessel) through water, or pull (e.g. a vehicle), with a rope.—*n.* **1** a rope for towing with. **2** an act of towing.

tow'line *n.* a rope, etc., used in towing.

tow'path *n.* a path alongside a canal or river where a horse can walk while towing (a barge etc.).

have, take, in tow have, take under one's guidance or protection.

on tow (of vehicles), **under tow** (of vessels) being towed.

toward(s) *tō-wörd(z)'*, *prep.* **1** (moving, facing, etc.) in the direction of. **2** as regards: *his attitude towards his son*, *towards the plan.* **3** as part of, a help to: *toward the cost of.* **4** near, about (in e.g. time, number).

towel *tow'ėl*, *n.* a cloth or paper for wiping e.g. the skin after washing.—*v.t.* to rub with a towel:—*pr.p.* **tow'elling**; *pa.p.* **tow'elled.**

tow'elling *n.* a cloth for towels.

tower *tow'ėr*, *n.* **1** a high narrow building, standing alone or forming part of another. **2** a fortress.—*v.i.* to rise above surrounding things or people (with *over, above*).

tow'ering *adj.* **1** very high. **2** very violent: *a towering rage*.

tower block a tall block of flats or offices.

tower of strength a very reliable person.

towline. See **tow²**.

town *town*, *n.* **1** a place larger than a village. **2** the people living in it.

town centre *n.* the most important shopping area of a town.

town council the governing body in a town, elected by the ratepayers.

town councillor a member of a town council.

town hall a public hall for the official business of a town.

town planning the planning of the future development of a town.

towns'folk, towns'people *ns. pl.* the people of a town.

go to town **1** to go to London or nearest large town. **2** (*coll.*) to let oneself go, act freely, spend freely.

tox- *toks-*, (as part of a word) poison.

toxaemia *tok-sē'mi-ȧ n.* blood-poisoning (see **blood**).

tox'ic *adj.* **1** caused, or affected, by a poison. **2** poisonous.

toxicology, *tok-si-kol'ȯ-ji*, *n.* the science of poisons.

tox'in *n.* naturally produced poison (e.g. that of a snake).

toy *toi*, *n.* **1** an object made for a child to play with. **2** a thing for amusement only.—Also *adj.*—*v.i.* to trifle, play: *He toyed with his food, with the idea*.

toy dog a dog of a very small kind—of various breeds.

trace¹ *trās*, *n.* **1** a mark left. **2** a line of footprints. **3** a small amount. **4** the line drawn by an instrument recording a changing quantity (e.g. a temperature).—*v.t.* **1** to follow the tracks of, or the course of: *He traced the deer*; *traced the river to the sea, to its source*; *traced the trouble to its source*; *traced the course of Roman history.* **2** to find after a search. **3** to copy (map, etc.) through thin paper (and transfer it to a new sheet). **4** to make (e.g. letters) with care:—*pr.p.* **tra'cing.**

trace'able *adj.* able to be traced (to), or shown to be due (to).

tra'cery *n.* delicate work in interlacing lines, e.g. decorative stonework holding the glass in some church windows, or frost patterns:—*pl.* **tra'ceries.**

tra'cing *n.* copy made by tracing.

trace elements substances that are needed in small quantities for the growth and development of animal and plant life.

tra'cing-paper *n.* thin paper used for tracing.

trace² *trās*, *n.* one of the straps by which a carriage or cart is drawn.

kick over the traces. See **kick.**

trachea *trȧ-kē'ȧ*, *n.* the windpipe.

tracing. See **trace¹**.

track *trak*, *v.t.* to follow by marks, footsteps, evidence, etc.—*n.* **1** a mark left. **2** (in *pl.*) footprints. **3** a beaten path. **4** a course laid out for races. **5** a line of rails. **6** the belt round the wheels of a caterpillar vehicle. **7** the groove cut in a gramophone record. **8** a section of recorded matter on record, tape, etc.

track'less *adj.* without a path.

track event in a sports competition, a race of any kind.

track record a record of past (athletic) performance.

track'-suit a warm suit worn by athletes, etc. when exercising.

keep (lose) track of to keep (not to keep) oneself aware of the whereabouts or progress of.

make tracks (for) to go off (towards), esp. hastily.

track down to find after a search.

tract *trakt n.* **1** a region, stretch of land. **2** parts forming a bodily system: *the digestive tract.* **3** a short essay or pamphlet, esp. on a religious subject.

tractable *trak'tȧ-bl*, *adj.* **1**easily worked. **2** (of person) easily managed or led:—*opp.* **intractable.**

tractabil'ity, trac'tableness *ns.*

trac'tion *n.* the act of dragging or pulling, or state of being pulled.—Also *adj.*

trac'tor *n.* a motor vehicle used for pulling loads, working ploughs, etc.

trade *trăd*, *n.* **1** buying and selling. **2** an occupation, craft, job: *He is a mason by trade.* **3** people engaged in the same kind of work.—*v.i.* **1** to buy and sell. **2** to have dealings (with a person). **3** to run a business (in certain goods).—*v.t.* (orig. *U.S.*) to exchange, barter:—*pr.p* **tra'ding.**

tra'der *n.* **1** one who trades. **2** a merchant ship.

trade'mark, trade'(-)mark *n.* a registered mark or name belonging to a firm or person (others being forbidden to use it) put on goods to show that they were made by him or it.

trade secret a secret formula or process known to only one manufacturer.

trades'man *n.* **1** a shopkeeper. **2** a workman in a skilled trade:—*pl.* **trades'men**.

trades'people *n.pl.* tradesmen.

trade union workers of the same trade who join together so that they can bargain about wages, conditions, hours, etc.

trade unionism **1** the system of joining in trade unions. **2** trade unions as a whole.

trade unionist **1** a believer in trade unionism. **2** member of trade union.

trade wind a wind blowing steadily towards the equator.

trade in to give in part payment.

trade on to take advantage of unfairly: *He traded on the fact that the manager was his cousin.*

tradition *trȧ-dish'(ȯ)n*, *n.* **1** the handing down of stories, opinions, practices, from earlier to later generations. **2** a belief or custom handed down in this way.

tradi'tional *adj.* **trad'itionally** *adv.*

traduce *trȧ-dūs'*, *v.t.* to speak evil falsely about:—*pr.p.* **tradu'cing**.

traffic *traf'ik*, *n.* **1** trade. **2** dealings (esp. when dishonest). **3** passing to and fro. **4** the vehicles, etc., using road(s), railway(s), waterway(s), airway(s).—*v.i.* to trade; to deal (in).—*v.t.* to exchange:—*pr.p.* **traff'icking**; *pa.p.* **traff'icked**.

traffic jam a queue of vehicles that cannot move.

traffic lights lights of changing colour for controlling traffic at street crossings.

traffic warden an official controlling traffic, esp. the parking of vehicles.

tragedy *traj'i-di*, *n.* **1** a play about unhappy event(s) and with a sad ending. **2** a very sad happening, or one with very unfortunate results:—*pl.* **trag'edies**.

tragē'dian, **tragēdienne** *(-di-en')*, *ns.* an actor (or a writer), actress, of tragedies.

trag'ic *adj.* **1** having to do with tragedy. **2** sorrowful. **3** terrible.

trag'ically *adv.*

trag'icom'edy *n.* a play, or events, both sad or serious and funny:—*pl.* **trag'icomedies**.

trail *trāl*, *v.t.* **1** to draw (along, behind, in, through): *He trailed his foot along the sand, in, through the water*; *The aircraft trailed white vapour.* **2** to hunt by tracking. **3** to follow.—*v.i.* **1** to hang down (from), or be dragged loosely (behind). **2** (of e.g. smoke) to stream, float (from and behind). **3** to walk slowly and wearily. **4** (of a plant) to creep, spread or hang.—*n.* **1** the track followed by a hunter. **2** a track or path through a wild region. **3** something left stretching behind: *a trail of smoke*, *of debts*, *of misery*.

trail'er *n.* **1** one who trails. **2** a trailing plant. **3** a vehicle drawn behind another. **4** a series of extracts from a forthcoming film, etc. shown, broadcast, etc. in advance to advertise it.

trailing edge the rearmost edge of an aeroplane wing or propeller blade (opp. to **leading edge**).

train *trān*, *v.t.* **1** to educate: *to train a child in good habits.* **2** to tame and teach (an animal). **3** to cause (a plant) to grow in a particular way. **4** to prepare (a person) for a sport, a trade, war, etc., or (horse) for racing. **5** to aim, point at (with *on*): *They trained the gun on the hill.*—*v.i.* to make oneself ready (for something) by practice, etc.—*n.* **1** a part of a dress that trails behind the wearer. **2** the attendants who follow an important person. **3** a line of animals carrying people and baggage. **4** a line of linked carriages behind a railway engine. **5** a series (e.g. of incidents), line (e.g. of thought).

trained *adj.* skilled through training.

trainee' *n.* one who is being trained.

train'er *n.* **1** one who prepares men for sport or horses for a race. **2** (*pl.*) light canvas, etc. shoes with rubber, etc. soles for running, exercising, etc.

train'ing *n.* **1** preparation for a sport. **2** teaching in the practical side of a profession, craft, etc.—Also *adj.*

train'-bear'er *n.* one who holds up the train of a robe or gown on a formal occasion.

train'-ferry *n.* a ship that carries railway trains across water, e.g. across the Channel.

in train in order, ready (for).

traipse, **trapes** *trāps*, *v.i.* to walk about idly, wearily or looking untidy:—*pr.p.* **traip'sing**, **trape'sing**.

trait *trāt*, or *trā*, *n.* a noticeable feature of a person's character or mind: *Willingness to listen is one of his good traits.*

traitor *trā'tȯr*, *n.* **1** one who betrays when he has been trusted. **2** one who betrays his country, goes over to the enemy.

trai'torous *adj.* **trai'torously** *adv.*

See also **treason**.

trajectory *trȧ-jek'tȯ-ri*, *n.* the curved path of a body (e.g. bullet) propelled through air:—*pl.* **trajec'tories**.

tram(car) *tram('-kar)*, *n.* a car running on rails and driven usu. by electricity, used to

carry passengers along streets.
tram'way, -line *n.* rails for tramcars.

trammel *tram'l, n.* **1** type of net. **2** (often in *pl.*) anything that hinders movement.—*v.t.* to keep back, hinder:—*pr.p.* **tramelling**; *pa.t.* **tramm'elled**.

tramp *tramp, v.i.* **1** to walk with heavy footsteps. **2** to go on foot. **3** to wander about as a tramp.—*v.t.* to travel over on foot.—*n.* **1** a journey on foot. **2** a heavy tread or footstep. **3** a cargo boat with no fixed trade route. **4** a person who wanders with no fixed home, usu. begging, a vagrant.
trample *tram'pl, v.t.* **1** to tread under foot, stamp on. **2** to treat roughly, unfeelingly.—*v.i.* **1** to tread heavily. **2** to walk (over, on). **3** (with *on*) to treat with cruelty or contempt: *to trample on someone's feelings*:—*pr.p.* **tramp'ling**.

trampoline *tram'pò-lēn, n.* an elastic mattress-like piece of apparatus for gymnasts, acrobats, etc., to jump on.

tramway. See **tram**.

trance *träns, n.* **1** a sleeplike or half-conscious state. **2** a state in which one is not aware of one's surroundings because lost in thought.

tranquil *trang'kwil, adj.* quiet, peaceful.
tran'quillise *v.t.* to make quiet:—*pr.p* **tran'quillising**.
tran'quilliser *n.* a drug to calm nerves or cause sleep.
tranquill'ity, tran'quilness *ns.*
tran'quilly *adv.*

trans- *tränz-, träns-, pfx.* across, through, on the other side of.

transact *tränz-akt', träns-, v.t.* to carry through (business)—Also *v.i.*
transac'tion *n.* (the act of carrying through) a deal, piece of business.

transatlantic *tränz-, träns-àt-lan'tik, adj.* **1** crossing the Atlantic Ocean. **2** beyond, on the other side of, it.

transcend *trän-send', v.t.* **1** to rise, be, above or beyond. **2** to do, be, better than.
transcen'dent *adj.* supreme or very high in excellence, etc.: *transcendent goodness, importance*.
transcen'dence, transcend'ency *ns.*
transcenden'tal *adj.* going beyond or outside normal experience (**transcendental meditation** a type of meditation intended to detach one from one's problems and remove one's anxiety).

transcontinental *tränz-kon-ti-nen'tàl, adj.* crossing a continent.

transcribe *trän-skrīb', v.t.* **1** to write out a copy of. **2** to write out, changing from one form to another (e.g. shorthand into ordinary lettering); to transliterate. **3** to make an arrangement (see this word) of (a musical composition). **4** to record for future broadcasting, etc.:—*pr.p.* **transcrib'ing**.
tran'script *n.* **1** something transcribed. **2** a written copy.
transcrip'tion *n.* **1** the act of transcribing. **2** a transcript.

transept *trän'sept, n.* part of a cruciform (cross-shaped) church at right angles to the main part or nave.

transfer *träns-fûr', v.t.* **1** to carry, send, etc., from one place to another. **2** to hand over to another person, esp. legally. **3** to move (someone) to another department, football club, etc. **4** to convey (e.g. a design) from one surface to another.—*v.i.* to move oneself from one place, vehicle, job (to another):—*pr.p.* **transferr'ing**; *pa.p.* **transferred'**.—*n.* *(träns')* **1** act of transferring. **2** something transferred. **3** a design, etc. that can be transferred from one surface to another.
transfer'able (or *träns'*) *adj.* that may be transferred from one place or person to another.
trans'ference *n.* the act of transferring from one person or place to another.

transfigure *träns-fig'ėr, v.t.* to transform in appearance to something finer, more beautiful, etc.:—*pr.p.* **transfig'uring**.
transfiguration *-fig-ū-rā'sh(ȯ)n, n.*

transfix *träns-fiks', v.t.* **1** to pierce through. **2** (of horror, surprise, etc.) to make unable to move, act, think.

transform *träns-förm', v.t.* to change the appearance, nature, character of.—*v.i.* to be changed in appearance, etc.
transformā'tion *n.*
transform'er *n.* a device for changing electrical energy from one voltage to another.

transfuse *träns-fūz', v.t.* **1** to transfer (the blood of one person) to the body of another. **2** to put (another's blood) into the body of:—*pr.p.* **transfū'sing**.
transfū'sion *n.* act of transfusing.

transgress *tränz-gres', träns-, v.t.* **1** to go beyond: *This, he, transgresses the bounds of common sense.* **2** to break (a law, command).—Also *v.i.* (with *against*).
transgress'ion *(-gresh'(ȯ)n), n.* **1** breaking of a law or command. **2** a fault; a sin.
transgress'or *n.* **1** one who breaks a law. **2** a sinner.

tranship. Same as **trans-ship**.

transient *trän'zi-ėnt, trän'si-, tran', adj.* **1** passing, not lasting: *a transient feeling of annoyance.* **2** (of a person) passing

through a place, not staying long.
tran'sience, **tran'sientness** *ns*.

transistor *trän-sis'tȯr*, *n*. **1** a small electronic device that controls the flow of an electric current. **2** (also **transistor radio**) a portable radio that uses these.
transis'torised *adj*. having transistors.

transit *trän'sit*, *-zit*, *n*. **1** the carrying or passing of people or things from one place to another: *The parcel was lost in transit*. **2** the passing of a planet between the earth and the sun.
transi'tion *n*. change from one place, state, subject, etc. to another: *a quick transition from anger to amusement*.
transi'tional *adj*. relating to transition; intermediate.
tran'sitive *adj*. (of verb) that has an object (e.g. *to hit*, *to save*, in *to hit the ball*, *to save money*):—*opp*. **intransitive**.
tran'sitory *adj*. **1** passing away. **2** lasting only for a short time.
tran'sitorily *adv*. **tran'sitoriness** *n*.
transit camp a camp for soldiers, refugees, etc. who are in transit from one place to another.
transit lounge an area in an airport where passengers who are catching a connecting flight can wait.
transit visa a visa allowing a person to pass through a country but not to stop in it.

translate *träns-lāt'*, *tränz-*, *v.t.* **1** to remove to another place or state. **2** to put into another language: *Translate this English book*, *the remark*, *into Russian*:—*pr.p* **translat'ing**.
translā'tion *n*. **1** the act of translating. **2** a version in another language.
translā'tor *n*.

transliterate *träns-lit'ėr-āt*, *tränz-*, *v.t.* to write in letters of another alphabet, etc.:—*pr.p.* **translit'erating**.

translucent *träns-lo͞o'sėnt*, *-lū'*, *tränz-*, *adj*. allowing light to pass, but not transparent (see this).
translu'cence, **translu'cency** *ns*.

transmigrate *tränz'mī-grāt*, *träns-*, *v.i.* (of the soul) to pass into another body after death:—*pr.p.* **transmigrat'ing**.
transmigrā'tion *n*.

transmission. See **transmit**.

transmit *tränz-mit'*, *träns-*, *v.t.* **1** to pass on to another person, part or place. **2** to be the means of passing on (e.g. heat, light, news, message).—*v.i.* to send out radio or other signals:—*pr.p.* **transmitt'ing**; *pa.p.* **transmitt'ed**.
transmiss'ion *n*. **1** the sending from one place or person to another. **2** something transmitted. **3** (sending out of) radio signals or a programme.
transmitt'er *n*. **1** one who, or that which, transmits. **2** a set or station sending out radio waves for conversion into sound or pictures by a receiving set or station.

transmute *tränz-mūt'*, *träns-*, *v.t.* to change, transform, esp. to another substance or nature:—*pr.p.* **transmu'ting**.
transmutā'tion *n*.

transom *trän'sȯm*, *n*. a beam across a window or the top of a door.

transparency *träns-par'ėn-si*, *-pār'*, *n*. **1** the quality of being transparent. **2** a picture on semi-transparent material seen by light shining through:—*pl*. **transpar'encies**.
transpar'ent *adj*. **1** (of material, or of pretence, disguise, etc.) that can be seen through easily: *Ordinary glass is transparent*; *transparent lies*. **2** clear, obvious: *her transparent honesty*.

transpire *trän-spīr'*, *v.t.*, *v.i.* to pass out (moisture, etc.) through pores of the skin, or through surface of leaves.—*v.i.* **1** (of e.g. facts kept secret) to become known. **2** (*wrongly*) to happen:—*pr.p.* **transpir'ing**.
transpirā'tion *n*.

transplant *träns-plänt'*, *v.t.* **1** to remove and plant in another place. **2** to remove and re-settle. **3** to remove (skin) and graft it in another place, (an organ) and graft it in another individual.—*v.i.* to (be able to) survive transplantation.—*n*. *(träns')* a plant, organ, etc., transplanted.
transplantā'tion *n*.

transport *träns-pōrt'*, *-pört'*, *v.t.* **1** to carry (goods, passengers) from one place to another. **2** (*history*) to send (a convicted prisoner) to another land. **3** (of strong emotion) to carry away, overcome: *Joy transported him*; *He was transported with grief*.—*n*. *(träns')* **1** carrying of goods, people, from one place to another. **2** means of doing this. **3** a ship, truck, etc. for carrying troops and their stores. **4** a strong attack of emotion: *a transport of rage*; *transports of joy*.
transportā'tion *n*. **1** the act of transporting. **2** sending of convicts overseas. **3** (*U.S.*) means of transport.
transport'er *n*. someone or something that transports, esp. a large vehicle for carrying heavy goods.

transpose *tränz-pōz'*, *v.t.* **1** to cause (two or more things) to change places. **2** to alter the order of. **3** (*music*) to change the key of:—*pr.p.* **transpos'ing**.
transposi'tion, **transpō'sal** *ns*.

trans-ship *träns-ship'*, *tränz-*, *v.t.*, *v.i.* to change from one ship, etc., to another:—*pr.p.* **trans-shipp'ing**; *pa.p.* **trans-shipped'**.

transverse *tränz-vûrs'*, *träns'*, *adj.* lying across.
transverse'ly *adv.*

transvestite *tränz-ves'tīt*, *träns-*, *n.* a person who likes to dress in the clothes of the opposite sex.

trap *trap*, *n.* **1** an instrument for catching animals. **2** a plan or trick for catching a person unawares. **3** a bend in a pipe always full of water, for preventing escape of air, gas. **4** a light carriage, drawn by a pony, etc., with two wheels. **5** (*offensive*) a mouth.—*v.t.* to catch in a trap, or by a trick:—*pr.p.* **trapp'ing**; *pa.p.* **trapped**.
trapp'er *n.* one who traps animals for their fur.
trap'-door *n.* a door in a floor.

trapes. See **traipse**.

trapeze *trȧ-pēz'*, *n.* a swing-like apparatus, with a bar instead of a seat, used by acrobats.
trapē'zium *n.* a quadrilateral with only one pair of parallel sides.

traps *traps*, *n. pl.* personal belongings, luggage.
trapp'ings *n. pl.* **1** fine or dignified clothes or ornaments proper to a person or an occasion. **2** ornaments, etc. put on horses.

trash *trash*, *n.* something of little worth or use, rubbish.
trash'y *adj.*:—*comp.* **trash'ier**; *superl.* **trash'iest**.
trash'iness *n.*

trauma *trö'mȧ*, *n.* **1** a condition caused by violent injury. **2** a shock, distressing experience, having a lasting effect.
traumat'ic *adj.* **traumat'ically** *adv.*
traumatise *trö'mȧ-tīz*, *v.t.* to wound physically or emotionally:— *pr.p.* **trau'matising**.

travail *trav'āl*, *n.* (*old*) **1** very hard, esp. painful, work. **2** pain suffered during childbirth.—Also *v.i.*

travel *trav'ėl*, *v.i.* **1** to move. **2** to go on a journey. **3** to work as a firm's traveller.—*v.t.* to journey along, through: *He will travel the roads of, travel, Germany*:—*pr.p.* **trav'elling**; *pa.p.* **trav'elled**.—*n.* **1** the act of passing from place to place. **2** (often in *pl.*) journeys, esp. in foreign lands. **3** (*pl.*) a written account of such journeys.
trav'elled *adj.* having done much varied travelling.
trav'eller *n.* **1** one who travels. **2** a travelling representative of business firm.
travelogue *trav'ė-log*, *n.* a talk, article, or esp. motion picture with commentary, about travels.
travel agency a place where one can arrange travel, book tickets, etc.
travel agent a person in charge of a travel agency.
traveller's cheque a cheque issued by a bank, that can be cashed into the currency of the country one is visiting.

traverse *trav'ėrs*, *n.* **1** anything laid or built across. **2** sideways course in rock climbing. **3** zigzag track of ship.—*v.t.* (also *trȧ-vûrs'*) **1** to pass over, across, or through. **2** to move sideways, or from side to side, over.

travesty *trav'is-ti*, *n.* a grotesque, bad, imitation: *He sat proudly in a travesty of an armchair*; *The trial was a travesty of justice*:—*pl.* **trav'esties**.—*v.t.* to imitate badly:—*pr.p.* **trav'estying**; *pa.p.* **trav'estied**.

trawl *tröl*, *v.i.* to fish by dragging a trawl along the bottom of the sea.—*n.* an open-mouthed bag-shaped net.
traw'ler *n.* **1** one who trawls. **2** a boat used in trawling.

tray *trā*, *n.* a flat board or sheet of metal, wood, or plastic, with low edge, for carrying or holding articles.

treachery *trech'ėr-i*, *n.* (an act of) betraying the trust another has put in one; disloyalty, unfaithfulness:—*pl.* **treach'eries**.
treach'erous *adj.* **1** guilty of treachery, or liable to betray. **2** (of memory) untrustworthy. **3** (of e.g. ice, bog) dangerous.
treach'erously *adv.* **treach'erousness** *n.*

treacle *trē'kl*, *n.* a dark sticky liquid that drains from sugar at different stages in its manufacture, molasses.
treac'ly *adj.*:—*comp.* **treac'lier**; *superl.* **treac'liest**.

tread *tred*, *v.i.* **1** to set the foot down (on). **2** to walk or go.—*v.t.* **1** to walk on, along. **2** to crush under foot, trample: *Passers-by will tread it into the ground.* **3** to wear (a path, etc.) by walking:—*pa.t.* **trod**; *pa.p.* **trod** or **trodd'en**.—*n.* **1** a step, way of stepping. **2** the part of a shoe, wheel, or tyre, that touches the ground.
tread'le *n.* a part of a machine moved by the foot.
tread'mill *n.* **1** (*history*) a device turned by the weight of e.g. person(s) made to walk on steps fixed round a large cylinder (used in prisons). **2** any unchanging, wearisome routine.
tread on someone's toes to offend someone, hurt his feelings (see also **corn**[2]).

tread water to keep an upright position in deep water.

treason *trē'zn*, *n.* **1** disloyalty to ruler or government by trying to overthrow him, it, giving information to enemy, etc. (also called **high treason**). **2** (*rarely*) treachery.
trea'sonable *adj.* (of action) consisting of, or involving, treason.

treasure *trezh'ůr*, *n.* **1** money, jewels or other wealth stored up. **2** anything greatly valued.—*v.t.* to store, store (up), or keep in mind (something that one values): *The old woman treasures her possessions, memories, your visits*:—*pr.p.* **treas'uring**.
treas'urer *n.* one who has charge of collected funds (e.g. of a club).
treas'ury *n.* **1** a place where money is kept. **2** (*cap.*) a department of a government which has charge of the finances:—*pl.* **treas'uries**.
treas'ure-trove *(-trōv)* *n.* treasure or money found in the earth, the owner being unknown.

treat *trēt*, *v.t.* **1** to handle, use, deal with, act towards (in a certain manner): *to treat with care, kindly.* **2** to try to cure or give relief to: *He treated her for rheumatism, treated her chilblains.* **3** to put (something) through a process: *The wood has been specially treated.* **4** to write or speak about: *She treated this subject fully in her lecture.* **5** to pay for a meal, drink, etc. for (another person).—*v.i.* **1** to deal (with), try to arrange a settlement (with e.g. an enemy). **2** (*old*; with *of*) to speak or write about: *The second book treats of insects.*—*n.* **1** an entertainment. **2** a cause of special enjoyment or pleasure: *It was a treat to see her so happy.*
treat'ise *(-is)* *n.* a long, formal, detailed, carefully arranged essay.
treat'ment *n.* **1** the act, or manner, of treating. **2** remedies (for disease). **3** (with of) behaviour to (a person): *Her treatment of her mother was cruel.*
treat'y *n.* a formal agreement between states (about e.g. alliance, terms of peace):—*pl.* **treat'ies**.
treat as to consider to be, deal with as if: *Do not treat the matter, him, as unimportant.*

treble *treb'l*, *adj.* **1** triple, threefold: *walls of treble thickness.* **2** high in pitch.—*n.* **1** the highest part in singing (soprano), or for or of an instrument. **2** (a singer, usu. a boy, with) a high voice.—*v.t.*, *v.i.*, to make, or become, three times as much:—*pr.p.* **treb'ling**.
treb'ly *adv.*

tree *trē*, *n.* **1** a large plant with a single firm woody trunk, from which grow woody branches. **2** a piece of wood shaped for a special purpose: *a shoe-tree.*—*v.t.* **1** to drive into or up a tree. **2** to force into a hopeless situation:—*pr.p.* **tree'ing**; *pa.p.* **treed'**.
tree'less *adj.* **tree'lessness** *n.*
tree'top *n.*
genealogical (or **family**) **tree**. See **genealogy** under **gene**.

trefoil *trē'foil*, *tre'*, *n.* **1** any plant whose leaves are divided into three leaflets (e.g. the clovers). **2** an ornament or shape (e.g. in stone tracery) suggesting a three-part leaf.

trek *trek*, *v.i.* **1** to journey by ox-drawn wagon. **2** to migrate. **3** to make a long hard journey:—*pr.p.* **trekk'ing**; *pa.p.* **trekked**.—*n.* **1** a journey by wagon. **2** a long or tiresome journey.

trellis *trel'is*, *n.* a structure of crossed strips usu. of wood (**trell'is-work**), for holding up growing plants, etc.

tremble *trem'bl*, *v.i.* **1** to shake, shiver, from fear, cold, or weakness. **2** to fear greatly: *I tremble for Mary if she disobeys; tremble at the sight, to think what will happen.*—*n.* act of, or fit of, trembling:—*pr.p.* **tremb'ling**.
trem'ūlous *adj.* **1** trembling. **2** shaking. **3** showing fear, etc.: *a tremulous voice.*
tremor *trem'ȯr*, *n.* **1** a shaking, quivering, vibration. **2** a thrill (of e.g. excitement).
earth tremor a slight earthquake.

tremendous *trė-men'dus*, *adj.* very large, great, or powerful.
tremen'dously *adv.* (*coll.*) very.

tremolo *trem'ȯ-lō* *n.* (*music*) a trembling effect in singing or playing an instrument:—*pl.* **trem'olos**.

tremor, **tremulous**. See **tremble**.

trench *trench*, or *-sh*, *v.t.* **1** to dig a ditch in. **2** to dig (ground) deeply with the spade or plough.—*v.i.* to make trench(es).—*n.* **1** a long narrow cut in the earth. **2** one dug by soldiers as a shelter from enemy fire.
tren'cher *n.* one who digs trenches.
trench'-coat *n.* a lined, belted waterproof overcoat, esp. military.

trenchant *tren'chȧnt*, *-shȧnt*, *adj.* (orig. of weapon, now of e.g. remark, style of writing or speaking, policy) cutting straight to the point, vigorous, effective.

trencher[1]. See **trench**.

trencher[2] *tren'chėr*, *-shėr*, *n.* (*history*) a wooden plate or tray for cutting meat on, or serving food, at meals.

trend *trend, n.* a general direction, course (of e.g. a river, events, opinion, fashion).
tren'dy (*coll.*) *adj.* fashionable:—*comp.* **tren'dier**; *superl.* **tren'diest**.
trend-sett'er *n.* someone who starts off a fashion.

trepidation *trep-i-dā'sh(ȯ)n, n.* nervousness, flurry, fear of what is coming.
See also **intrepid**.

trespass *tres'pȧs, v.i.* **1** to enter unlawfully (on another's land, etc.). **2** (with *on*) to take or demand too much of: *He trespasses on your time, kindness.* **3** to sin.—*n.* **1** act of trespassing on property, rights, generosity, etc. **2** a sin.
tres'passer *n.*

tress *tres, n.* **1** a plait or lock of hair. **2** (in *pl.*) hair, usu. long.

trestle *tres'l, n.* a wooden support, usu. a bar with legs, for a table, platform, etc.

trews *trōōz, n. pl.* trousers of tartan cloth.

tri- *trī-, tri-*, (as part of a word) **1** three. **2** thrice. **3** in three parts.

trial. See **try**.

triangle *trī'ang-gl, n.* **1** a figure with three angles and three sides. **2** a musical instrument of this shape, played by striking with a small rod. **3** an emotional situation in which three people are involved with each other.
triang'ūlar *adj.*

tribe *trīb, n.* **1** a race or family who all come from the same ancestor. **2** a group of families, usu. of primitive or wandering people, under the government of a chief.
trīb'al *adj.*
trib'alism *n.* **1** state of existing as a separate tribe. **2** tribal life or feeling.
tribes'man *(trībz') n.*

tribulation *trib-ū-lā'sh(ȯ)n, n.* trouble, hardship, or an instance of it.

tribune *trib'ūn, n.* a high official elected by the common people in ancient Rome to defend their rights.
tribunal *trī-bū'nȧl, n.* **1** a court of justice. **2** a group of persons appointed to give judgment esp. on appeals against official decisions, etc.

tribute *trib'ūt, n.* **1** (*history*) money paid at intervals by one ruler or nation to another in return for peace or protection. **2** an expression, in word or action, of thanks, respect, praise: *many and varied tributes to his great courage—speeches, gifts, tears rejoicing*.
trib'ūtary *adj.* **1** paying tribute. **2** contributory.—*n.* a stream that flows into another:—*pl.* **trib'utaries**.
be a tribute to (of something good) to be a result of: *This success is a tribute to his careful planning*.
pay tribute to to express respect, etc., for.

trice *trīs*: **in a trice** in an instant.

trick *trik, n.* **1** a cunning action taken to cheat or deceive, or to surprise and annoy. **2** skilful action intended to puzzle or amuse: *a conjuring trick.* **3** skill, knack: *He had not learned the trick of getting the old machine to work.* **4** a habit: *He has a trick of pulling his ear when thinking.* **5** the cards falling to the winner at the end of a round.—*adj.* used to deceive e.g. the eye: *trick photography.*—*v.t.* **1** to cheat. **2** to deceive by skilful action. **3** to dress, decorate (with *out, up*).
trick'ery *n.* act or practice of trying to cheat by trick(s):—*pl.* **trick'eries**.
trick'y *adj.* **1** cunning, crafty. **2** requiring skill, not easy to do or to handle:—*comp.* **trick'ier**; *superl.* **trick'iest**.
trick'iness *n.*
trick'ster *n.* a cheat.

trickle *trik'l, v.i.* **1** to flow gently or in a small stream. **2** to drip. **3** to come, go, etc. slowly and in small numbers:—*pr.p.* **trick'ling**.—Also *n.*

tricky. See **trick**.

tricolour, **tricolor** *tri'kul-ȯr, trī-, n.* the flag of France, which has three upright stripes—red, white, and blue.

tricycle *trī'si-kl, n.* a vehicle with three wheels and a seat.

trident *trī'dėnt, n.* any three-pronged instrument, as spear or sceptre.

tried, trier. See **try**.

triennial *trī-en'yal, -i-ȧl, adj.* **1** lasting three years. **2** happening every third year.

tries. See **try**.

trifle *trī'fl, v.i.* (with *with*) **1** to amuse oneself in an idle way with. **2** to act towards without sufficient respect: *Never trifle with explosives*; *I am in no mood to be trifled with.* **3** to act, or to talk, idly, without seriousness:—*pr.p.* **tri'fling**.—*n.* **1** anything of little value or importance. **2** a small amount or sum. **3** pudding of sponge cake, sherry, whipped cream, etc.
tri'fler *n.* one who trifles.
tri'fling *adj.* **1** of small value or importance. **2** acting or talking without seriousness.—Also *n.*

trigger *trig'ėr, n.* **1** a catch on a gun which when pulled causes the weapon to fire. **2** something that starts a series of events.—*v.t.* (often with *off*) (of a small event) to start (a violent or important happening).

trigonometry *trig-ȯ-nom'i-tri, n.* the branch of mathematics which studies the

relationship between the sides and angles of triangles.
trigonomet'ric, -al *adjs.*

trilateral *trī-lat'ėr-ȧl, adj.* **1** having three sides. **2** involving three people or parties.

trilby *tril'bi, n.* a type of soft felt hat for a man:—*pl.* **tril'bies**.

trill *tril, v.t.* and *v.i.* **1** to sing or play with a quivering sound. **2** to utter with vibration of e.g. the tip of the tongue against the gums of the upper teeth: *Only some people trill every r.*—*n.* a trilled sound or letter.

trillion *tril'yȯn, n.* **1** a million multiplied twice by itself, written as 1 followed by 18 noughts. **2** (*U.S.*) ten thousand multiplied twice by itself, 1 followed by 12 noughts.

trilobite *trī'lȯ-bīt, n.* a jointed fossil animal having its body divided lengthways into three sections.

trilogy *tril'ȯ-ji, n.* a group of three related plays, novels, etc., intended to be seen, read, as one whole.

trim *trim, adj.* in good order, tidy, neat:—*comp.* **trimm'er**; *superl.* **trimm'est**.—*v.t.* **1** to make trim by cutting or clipping (e.g. hair, a hedge). **2** to decorate, esp. round the edge. **3** to arrange (sails, cargo) for sailing. **4** to adjust the balance of (a ship or aircraft). **5** to alter (one's opinions) to suit the circumstances (also *v.i.*):—*pr.p.* **trimm'ing**; *pa.p* **trimmed**.—*n.* **1** an act of trimming. **2** state or degree of readiness or fitness: *in fine trim for the battle of wills*; *in poor trim after illness.* **3** (*old*) dress, clothes.
trim'ly *adv.*
trimm'er *n.* one who trims.
trimm'ing *n.* **1** something fancy used to trim e.g. clothes. **2** something clipped off.
trim'ness *n.*

trimaran *trī'mȧ-ran, n.* a sailing-boat with three hulls.

trinitrotoluene *trī-nī-trō-tol'ū-ēn, n.* a powerful explosive (abbrev. **T.N.T.**).

trinity *trin'i-ti, n.* **1** a group of three. **2** (*cap.*) (the union in one God of) Father, Son, and Holy Ghost.

trinket *tring'kit, n.* a small ornament, esp. if of little value.

trio *trē'ō, n.* **1** a set of three. **2** (*music*) (a piece of music for) three performers. **3** the middle section of a minuet, etc.:—*pl.* **tri'os**.

trip *trip, v.i.* **1** to move with short, light steps. **2** to stumble (and fall). **3** (often with *up*) to make a mistake.—*v.t.* **1** (often with *up*) to cause (a person) to stumble (and fall). **2** (often with *up*) to cause to make, or to catch in, an error: *If I can trip him up over the details of the scene, I can prove he was not there*:—*pr.p.* **tripp'ing**; *pa.p.* **tripped**.—*n.* **1** a false step, a stumble. **2** a short voyage or journey. **3** (*coll.*) a hallucination, etc. experienced under the influence of a drug.
tripp'er *n.* one who makes, goes on, a popular trip or outing.
trip'wire *n.* a wire laid so that it operates an explosive device, etc. when disturbed.

tripartite *trī-pär'tīt, adj.* **1** divided into three parts. **2** having to do with, binding, three countries, etc.: *a tripartite agreement.*

tripe *trīp, n.* **1** parts of stomach, esp. of sheep or cattle, prepared as food. **2** (*coll.*) rubbish, poor stuff.

triple *trip'l, adj.* **1** made up of three. **2** three times as large.—*v.t., v.i.* to make, become, three times as large, to treble:—*pr.p.* **trip'ling**.
trip'let *n.* **1** three of a kind. **2** three lines rhyming together. **3** a group of three notes played, etc., in the time of two. **4** one of three children born at one birth.
in triplicate in three copies exactly alike.

tripod *trī'pod, n.* a stand, e.g. for a camera, that has three feet or legs.

tripos *trī'pos, n.* an examination for honours at Cambridge University.

tripper, etc. See **trip**.

triptych *trip'tich, n.* a set of three painted or carved panels hinged together.

trireme *trī'rēm,* (*history*) *n.* a galley with three rows of oars.

trite *trīt, adj.* (of e.g. a saying, remark) used so often that all interest is gone from it.
trite'ly *adv.* **trite'ness** *n.*

triumph *trī'ŭmf, n.* **1** in ancient Rome, a procession in honour of a victorious general. **2** victory. **3** success. **4** a state of great joy over success.—*v.i.* **1** to win a great victory or success. **2** to rejoice over this. **3** openly to show one's rejoicing (over the person one has defeated).
trium'phal *adj.* **1** having to do with triumph. **2** used in celebrating triumph.
trium'phant *adj.* **1** celebrating, showing joy over, success. **2** victorious.

triumvirate *trī-um'vir-it, n.* a group of three, esp. of men sharing power.

trivet *triv'it, n.* a small stand with three feet or one for hooking on to a grate.

trivia *triv'i-ȧ, n. pl.* trifles; unimportant matters.
trivial *triv'i-ȧl, adj.* of little importance; trifling.
triv'ially *adv.* **triv'ialness** *n.*

trivial'ity *n.* **1** trivialness. **2** something unimportant:—*pl.* **trivial'ities.**

trod, trodden. See **tread.**

troglodyte *trog'lō-dīt*, *n.* a (esp. prehistoric) dweller in caves.

Trojan *trō'jȧn*, *adj.* having to do with ancient Troy.—*n.* **1** one who lived in ancient Troy. **2** (*coll.*) one who shows pluck and endurance.

trolley *trol'i*, *n.* **1** a small cart or truck. **2** a small table, or shelved stand, on wheels, used e.g. for serving tea, etc. **3** the wheel or other device, on e.g. an overhead pole, through which electricity passes from a live wire to an electric street-car, bus, etc. **4** in a supermarket, a large basket on wheels. **5** in hospitals, a kind of bed on wheels, used for transporting patients.

troll'ey-bus *n.* a bus that receives power from an overhead wire by a trolley.

trollop *trol'ȯp*, *n.* **1** a careless, untidy woman. **2** a loose woman.

trombone *trom-bōn'*, *n.* a musical wind instrument, a tube twice bent back in U shape and flaring out at the end, with a slide (see this).

troop *trōōp*, *n.* **1** a crowd of people, etc. **2** a unit in cavalry, etc. **3** (in *pl.*) soldiers.—*v.i.* **1** to collect in numbers. **2** to go in a crowd: *The children trooped after him through the house.*

troop'er *n.* a soldier in the cavalry or in an armoured unit.

troop'ship, -carrier *ns.* a ship carrying soldiers.

trooping the colour carrying the flag ceremonially along ranks of Guards.

trophy *trō'fi*, *n.* **1** anything taken from an enemy and kept as a memorial of victory. **2** anything won by skill. **3** a prize (e.g. a cup) for winning in a sport, etc.:—*pl.* **tro'phies.**

tropic *trop'ik*, *n.* **1** either of two imaginary circles about 23 (about 1600 miles) north (*Tropic of Cancer*) and south (*Tropic of Capricorn*) of the equator above which the sun appears to turn at midsummer and midwinter. **2** (in *pl.*) the hot region between these circles.

trop'ical *adj.* **1** having to do with the tropics. **2** very hot. **3** growing in hot countries.

trot *trot*, *v.i.* **1** (of a horse) to go forward, lifting the feet quicker and higher than in walking. **2** to move fast with short steps.—*v.t.* to make (a horse) trot:—*pr.p* **trott'ing**; *pa.p.* **trott'ed.**—*n.* the pace of a horse, or of a person, when trotting.

trott'er *n.* a pig's foot.

trot out 1 to bring forward (usu. something already well known) for admiration. **2** to offer (e.g. an old or not very good excuse).

troth *trōth*, *troth*: **plight one's troth** to pledge one's word to marry a certain person.

troubadour *trōō'bȧ-dōōr*, *n.* a wandering poet or singer in France in the Middle Ages.

trouble *trub'l*, *v.t.* **1** to disturb, stir up (e.g. water). **2** to cause worry, uneasiness, sorrow, or inconvenience, to. **3** to make an effort, take pains (to do, etc.) (also *v.i.*):—*pr.p.* **troub'ling.**—*n.* **1** worry, uneasiness. **2** difficulty. **3** disturbance. **4** something that causes worry or difficulty. **5** a disease. **6** care taken in, effort given to, doing something.

troub'lesome *adj.* causing difficulty or inconvenience.

troub'le-shoot'er *n.* one who detects and puts right any trouble, mechanical or other.

trough *trof*, *n.* **1** a long, open container for water or other liquid, e.g. one from which animals feed. **2** a long hollow or narrow channel, e.g. the dip between two sea waves. **3** an area of low pressure.

trounce *trowns*, *v.t.* **1** to punish or beat severely. **2** (*coll.*) to defeat:—*pr.p.* **troun'cing.**

troupe *trōōp*, *n.* a company, esp. of dancers, actors, etc.

troup'er *n.* **1** a member of such a group. **2** a game, staunch person.

trousers *trow'zėrz*, *n. pl.* an outer garment for lower part of body and each leg separately.

trous'er- (as part of a word) of trousers: *trouser-leg.*

trous'er-suit *n.* a woman's suit with jacket and trousers.

trousseau *trōō'sō*, *n.* a bride's outfit of clothes, etc:—*pl.* **trou'sseaux** *(-sōz)*, **trou'sseaus.**

trout *trowt*, *n.* types of fish related to the salmon, most living wholly in fresh water.

trowel *trow'ėl*, *n.* a tool used in spreading plaster, paint, etc. and in gardening.

truck[1] *truk*: **have no truck with** to have nothing to do with, refuse to deal with.

truck[2] *truk*, *n.* **1** an open railway wagon for goods. **2** a wheeled barrow for luggage, used by porters. **3** a transport motor vehicle, a lorry.

truck'er (*coll.*) *n.* a driver of lorries.

truckle *truk'l*, *v.i.* to yield too humbly to the will of another (with *to*):—*pr.p.* **truck'ling.**

truck'le-bed *n.* a low bed that could be pushed under a larger one.

truculent *truk'ū-lėnt, adj.* threatening, very aggressive, in manner.

truc'ulently *adv.* **truc'ulence** *n.*

trudge *truj, v.i.* and *v.t.* to travel on foot, esp. with labour or weariness:—*pr.p.* **trud'ging.**—*n.* a heavy, tired walk.

true *tro͞o, adj.* **1** agreeing with fact: *a true story.* **2** accurate, correct: *a true copy; a true idea of its importance.* **3** properly so called: *The spider is not a true insect.* **4** placed, fitted, etc., accurately. **5** perfectly in tune. **6** rightful: *the true heir.* **7** sincere. **8** loyal.

true'ness *n.*

truism *tro͞o'izm, n.* a truth so obvious or plain that it is not worth stating.

tru'ly *adv.* **1** faithfully. **2** sincerely. **3** truthfully. **4** accurately. **5** really, geninuely.

truth *tro͞oth, n.* **1** trueness: *the truth of this statement.* **2** a true statment. **3** the facts. **4** an accepted principle, something acknowledged by all:—*pl.* **truths** *(tro͞o*THz*, tro͞oths).*

truth'ful *adj.* **truth'fully** *adv.*

truth'fulness *n.*

true'-love *n.* a sweetheart.

come true actually to happen.

out of true not fitting, placed, etc. accurately.

truffle *truf'l, troof'l, n.* **1** a round fungus (see this) found underground, used in cookery. **2** a rich sweet made with chocolate, butter, etc.

truism. See **true**.

trump[1]. See **trumpery**.

trump[2] *trump, n.* **1** in some card games, (a card of) a suit (chosen by chance or deliberately) which has more value than (cards of) the other suits. **2** (*coll.*) a good, trusty fellow.—*v.t.* to play a trump card on.—Also *v.i.*

trump card **1** a card from the suit chosen as trumps. **2** a means of winning, esp. something held in reserve until the crucial moment.

turn up trumps to provide generous and unexpected help.

trump[3] *trump (old) n.* (a blast on) a trumpet.

trumpery *trum'pėr-i, n.* **1** something showy but worthless. **2** nonsense:—*pl.* **trum'peries.**—Also *adj.*

trump up to make up falsely (e.g. evidence, a charge) (*adj.* **trumped'-up**).

trumpet *trum'pit, n.* **1** a brass musical instrument, a long tube, usu. bent once or twice in U-shape, and flaring out at the end. **2** something shaped like the end of a trumpet.—*v.t.* **1** to proclaim loudly. **2** to sound the praises of.—*v.i.* to sound a trumpet, or to make a sound that suggests one.

trum'peter *n.*

blow one's own trumpet to sound one's own praises.

truncate *trung-kāt', v.t.* to cut the top or end off; to shorten:—*pr.p.* **truncat'ing.**

trun'cated *adj.*

truncheon *trun'ch(ȯ)n, -sh(ȯ)n, n.* a short heavy staff or baton such as that used by policemen.

trundle *trun'dl, v.t., v.i.* to roll along as a wheel, or on wheels:—*pr.p.* **trund'ling.**

trunk *trungk, n.* **1** the main stem of a tree. **2** the body of a man or an animal apart from the limbs. **3** the main body of anything. **4** the long snout of an elephant. **5** a box or chest for clothes, esp. on a journey. **6** (in *pl.*) short, light pants, for e.g. running, swimming.

trunk call a long-distance telephone message sent by a main or trunk line.

trunk line a main line of a railway, canal, telephone system, etc.

trunk road a main road.

truss *trus, n.* **1** a bundle (e.g. of hay). **2** a combination of beams, etc., forming a rigid framework. **3** (*medical*) a bandage or support for patients suffering from hernia.—*v.t.* **1** to bind, tie tightly (up). **2** to skewer (a bird) for cooking.

trust *trust, n.* **1** confidence, belief, in the reality, truth, etc. of something, or goodness, etc. of someone (with *in*): *trust in his friendship, promises, in one's leaders* (*opp.* **distrust**). **2** something (e.g. a duty) given one in the belief that one will carry it out, etc. faithfully. **3** charge, keeping. **4** an arrangement by which property is given to a person, in the confidence that he will use it for a stated purpose. **5** in modern business, a number of firms working together as if they were one.—*adj.* **1** held in trust; administered, etc. by trustees: *a trust fund.* **2** acting as a trustee: *a trust company.*—*v.t.* **1** to put one's faith or confidence in (*opp.* **distrust**). **2** to give (something to a person) so that he may take care of it. **3** to supply (a person with something) expecting him to behave sensibly, etc. with it. **4** to hope confidently.—*v.i.* **1** to feel trust (in). **2** (with *to*) to depend on: *Don't trust to luck.*

trustee' *(-tē') n.* **1** one who holds property in trust for another or others. **2** a member of a body to whom the management of an organisation is entrusted.

trustee'ship *n.*

trust'ful, **trust'ing** *adjs.* ready to trust, not inclined to be suspicious.
trust'fully *adv.* **trust'fulness** *n.*
trus'ty *adj.* **1** honest. **2** strong, firm:—*comp.* **trus'tier**; *superl.* **trus'tiest**.—*n.* a well-behaved prisoner who has earned privileges:—*pl* **trus'ties**.
trus'tily *adv.* **trus'tiness** *n.*
trust territory a territory which does not govern itself but is ruled by a country chosen by the Trusteeship Council of the United Nations.
trust'worthy *adj.* worthy of trust, able to be depended upon.
on trust **1** allowing credit. **2** (accepted) without proof or checking.
See also **entrust**.

truth. See **true**.

try *trī*, *v.t.* **1** to make an attempt or effort (to do, etc.) (also *v.i.*). **2** to test the qualities of by experiment or use: *to try a new soap.* **3** (of experience) to test the strength of: *disasters that try one's courage, faith.* **4** to test too severely, strain: *I think the strong light will try my eyes*; *The children try her, her patience.* **5** to attempt to use, open, etc.: *Try the other path, the door.* **6** to put (a person or case) on trial in a court of law.:—*3rd pers. pr.t.* **tries**; *pr.p.* **try'ing**; *pa.p.* **tried** *(trīd)*.—*n.* **1** an attempt, effort. **2** in Rugby football, (a score of three points for) a touch-down:—*pl.* **tries**.
trial *trī'ȧl*, *n.* **1** act of testing or trying: *the trial of a new method, of the strength of someone's loyalty.* **2** act of straining severely. **3** a test. **4** a strain. **5** the judging of a prisoner in a court of law. **6** an attempt, effort. **7** an affliction, trouble.—*adj.* done, etc. for the sake of testing.
tried *adj.* tested, proved to be good.
tri'er *n.* one who tries, keeps on trying.
try'ing *adj.* **1** testing. **2** causing strains, discomfort, or irritation.
on trial being tried, or tested.
trial and error a type of learning in which several methods are tried until one is found that gives the result desired.
try on **1** to put on (e.g. clothes) to see the effect. **2** (*slang*) to attempt (an action) in the hope that it will be permitted (*n.* **try'-on**).
try one's hand at to have a go, an attempt, at.
try out to test by using.

tryst *trīst*, *trist*, (chiefly *Scot.*) *n.* an appointment to meet at an arranged place.

tsar, tzar, czar *tsär*, *n.* title of the former emperors of Russia.
tsarina *(-ē'nȧ) n.* a Russian empress.

tsetse (fly) *tset'si (flī)*, *n.* any of a number of small flies found in Africa which by their bite pass on to men and animals parasites which cause fatal diseases (in man, sleeping-sickness).

T-shirt. Same as **tee-shirt**.

T-square *tē'-skwār*, *n.* a T-shaped ruler.

tub *tub*, *n.* **1** an open wooden container for water. **2** a fixed basin used for washing clothes. **3** a bath. **4** a small cask. **5** a clumsy boat.
tubb'y *adj.* plump, round:—*comp.* **tubb'ier**; *superl.* **tubb'iest**.

tuba *tū'bȧ*, *n.* large brass wind instrument with deep tone.

tube *tūb*, *n.* **1** a long, hollow, esp. flexible cylinder, used to contain, or allow flow of, liquid, etc. **2** an organ of this kind in animal or plant. **3** a container from which a substance (e.g. paint, toothpaste) can be squeezed. **4** a cathode ray tube. **5** an underground railway in a tube-shaped tunnel.
tū'bing *n.* **1** tubes as a whole. **2** material for tubes.
tū'būlar *adj.* tube-shaped.

tuber *tū'bėr*, *n.* a swelling in an underground stem of a plant where food is stored: *The potato is a tuber*.
tuberous root a thickened root suggesting a tuber.

tubercle *tū'bėr-kl*, *n.* a small swelling.
tuber'cular *adj.* **1** like, or having, tubercles. **2** tuberculous.
tuber'culous *adj.* affected with, or caused by, tuberculosis.
tuberculō'sis *n.* an infectious disease, esp. of the lungs, in which tubercles form.
tubercle bacillus the organism that causes tuberculosis.

tuberous. See **tuber**.

tubing, tubular. See **tube**.

tuck *tuk*, *v.t.* **1** to press, push (in to a place). **2** to fold (under). **3** to gather (up). **4** to press clothes closely round (e.g. a child in bed; with *in* or *up*).—*v.i.* **1** (*slang*; with *into*) to eat with enjoyment or greedily. **2** (with *in*) to feed oneself enthusiastically.—*n.* **1** a fold stitched in a piece of cloth. **2** (*old coll.*) sweets, etc.

Tudor *tū'dȯr*, *adj.* having to do with the royal line of the *Tudors* (1485–1603), or with their time, or with the style of building common then.

Tuesday *tūz'di*, *n.* third day of week.

tuft *tuft*, *n.* a small bunch of grass, hair, feathers, etc.
tuf'ted *adj.* having, made of, growing in, tufts.

tug *tug*, *v.t.* **1** to pull hard. **2** to drag along.—*v.i.* to pull with great effort:—

pr.p. **tugg'ing**; *pa.p.* **tugged.**—*n.* **1** a strong pull. **2** a tugboat.
tug'boat *n.* a strongly-built powerful ship for towing larger ships.
tug'-of-war' *n.* **1** a contest in strength between teams pulling at opposite ends of a rope. **2** a hard struggle between opposing persons, etc.

tuition *tū-ish'(ȯ)n*, *n.* **1** teaching. **2** private coaching or instruction.

tulip *tū'lip*, *n.* a plant with a bulb and bell-shaped flowers of various colours.

tulle *tūl*, *tōōl*, *n.* a material of thin silk or rayon net.

tumble *tum'bl*, *v.i.* **1** to fall, to come down suddenly and violently. **2** to roll, toss (about). **3** to act, move, in a hurried, clumsy way. **4** to do acrobatic tricks.—*v.t.* **1** to throw over or down. **2** to throw carelessly. **3** to throw into disorder:—*pr.p.* **tumb'ling.**—*n.* **1** a fall. **2** a somersault. **3** a confused state.
tum'bler *n.* **1** one who tumbles, does acrobatic tricks. **2** a large drinking-glass. **3** a moving part in a lock or similar mechanism.
tum'ble-down *adj.* (of e.g. a house) shabby, falling to pieces.
tum'ble-dri'er, -dry'er *n.* a machine for drying clothes by tumbling them about and blowing hot air into them.
tumble to (*coll.*) to understand suddenly without explanation.

tumbrel, tumbril *tum'bril*, *n.* in the French Revolution, a cart with two wheels used to take victims to the guillotine.

tumid *tū'mid*, *adj.* swollen.
tūmesc'ent *(-es'ėnt) adj.* swelling.

tummy *tum'i*, *n.* (*childish*) stomach, belly:—*pl.* **tumm'ies.**

tumour *tū'mȯr*, *n.* a swelling, growth of abnormal tissue, in the body.

tumult *tū'mult*, *n.* **1** uproar made by a crowd. **2** confusion with loud sounds. **3** high excitement or agitation.
tumultuous *tū-mul'tū-ůs*, *adj.*

tumulus *tū'mū-lůs*, *n.* an artificial mound of earth, esp. over a tomb:—*pl.* **tu'mulī.**

tun *tun*, *n.* a large cask, esp. for wine.

tuna *tōō'nȧ*, *n.* a tunny, or fish like it.

tundra *tun'*, *toon'drȧ*, *n.* a level treeless Arctic plain with permanently frozen subsoil.

tune *tūn*, *n.* **1** notes arranged in pleasing order, an air, melody. **2** the state of giving a sound or sounds of the correct pitch or of the same pitch as something else: *to be in tune*; *Sing in tune with the piano*; or of giving correct vibrations.—*v.t.* **1** to put (a musical instrument) in tune (also *v.i.* with *up.*) **2** to adjust (a radio) so that it receives a particular station (also *v.i.* with *in, in to*). **3** to adjust (an engine, etc.) to one's satisfaction:—*pr.p.* **tun'ing.**
tune'ful *adj.* **tune'fully** *adv.*
tune'fulness *n.* **tune'less** *adj.*
tu'ner *n.* **tu'ning** *n.* and *adj.*
tu'ning-fork *n.* a steel instrument with two prongs which, when struck, gives a musical sound of a certain pitch.
call the tune (*coll.*) to give the orders.
change one's tune to change one's attitude, or way of talking.
to the tune of (*coll.*) to the amount of.

tungsten *tung'stėn*, *n.* an element, a bright grey metal.

tunic *tū'nik*, *n.* **1** a garment reaching to knees worn e.g. in ancient Greece and Rome. **2** a short, loose, usu. belted, often sleeveless or short-sleeved, garment. **3** a close-fitting jacket worn by soldiers and policemen.

tuning. See **tune.**

tunnel *tun'ėl*, *n.* an underground passage, esp. one by which a road or railway is carried under a hill, etc.—*v.i.* **1** to make a tunnel. **2** (of animal) to burrow.—*v.t.* to make a tunnel, burrow, in (e.g. a hill):—*pr.p.* **tunn'elling**; *pa.p.* **tunn'elled.**

tunny *tun'i*, *n.* a large sea fish:—*pl.* **tunn'-ies.**

turban *tûr'bȧn*, *n.* a head-covering worn by men of certain Eastern nations, a long sash wound round the head or round a cap.

turbid *tûr'bid*, *adj.* **1** (of liquid, etc.) muddy, clouded. **2** (of thought, etc.) confused.

turbine *tûr'bīn*, *-bin*, *n.* an engine, usu. with curved blades, turned by the action of water, steam, or gas, etc.
turbo- *tûr-bō-*, (as part of word) turbine; used in naming engines of which a turbine forms a part, or aeroplanes having such engines.

turbot *tûr'bȯt*, *n.* a large, flat fish used as food.

turbulent *tûr'bū-lėnt*, *adj.* **1** (of e.g. times, place, conditions) disturbed, tumultuous. **2** (of person, conduct) inclined to cause disturbance or riot.
tur'bulence *n.*

turd *tûrd*, (usu. *offensive*) *n.* a lump of excrement.

tureen *tu-rēn'*, *tū-*, *n.* a large dish for holding soup at table.

turf *tûrf*, *n.* **1** earth on the surface of land matted with roots of grass, etc. **2** a cake of turf cut off, sod. **3** in Ireland, peat. **4** (**the turf**) horse-racing, the racecourse:—*pl.* **turfs, turves.**—*v.t.* **1** to cover with turf.

2 (*coll.*) to throw (*out*, etc.).
turf accountant a bookmaker (see this).

turgid *tûr'jid*, *adj.* **1** swollen. **2** (of language, style) pompous, sounding grand but meaning very little.
turgid'ity, tur'gidness *ns.*
tur'gidly *adv.*

Turk *tûrk*, *n.* a native of Turkey.
Turk'ish *adj.* having to do with the Turks or Turkey.—*n.* the language of the Turks.
Turkish bath a kind of hot-air bath, the patient being sweated, rubbed down, and then cooled.
Turkish delight a sticky, jelly-like sweet, orig. from Turkey.

turkey *tûrk'i*, *n.* a large farmyard bird, native of America, so called through confusion with the guinea-fowl thought to have come from *Turkey*.

turmeric *tûr'mėr-ik*, *n.* the underground part of a plant grown in India; used in curry powder, etc.

turmoil *tûr'moil*, *n.* state of confusion, commotion, agitation: *the turmoil of war*; *The city was, his thoughts were, in a turmoil.*

turn *tûrn*, *v.i.* **1** to go round, revolve: *The wheel turns.* **2** to move round something as centre (with *on*): *The door turns on its hinges.* **3** to move so as to face in, or to go in, the opposite direction. **4** to take a different direction: *His thoughts turned to supper.* **5** to change (to, into): *The ice turned to water*; *Her hair has turned white*; *The leaves turn in autumn.* **6** (of milk, etc.) to sour. **7** (of head, brain) to become dizzy.—*v.t.* **1** to cause to go round, revolve completely or partly. **2** to reach and go round: *The ship turned the headland.* **3** to reach and pass (a certain age, etc.): *He turned thirty last month.* **4** to aim, point: *He turned the hose on the men.* **5** to direct, apply: *He turned his attention to painting.* **6** to change (often with *into*): *He was turned into a frog*; *The shock turned his hair white.* **7** to make sour. **8** to confuse (the wits). **9** to shape in a lathe.—*n.* **1** an act of turning. **2** a new direction. **3** a winding, bend. **4** a turning-point. **5** a manner, way, habit: *a strange turn of expression.* **6** a walk to and fro. **7** a spell (of e.g. work). **8** a short act in a programme of several. **9** one's chance to do, have, something shared with others: *It is my turn to bat now, my turn of the arm-chair.* **10** requirement at the moment: *This will serve our turn.* **11** an act of helpfulness or the opposite: *She did him a good turn.* **12** (*coll.*) a nervous shock.
tur'ner *n.* one who uses a lathe.
turn'ing *n.* **1** act of going round, revolving, or of going in a different direction. **2** a winding. **3** a street corner. **4** act of shaping.
turn'coat *n.* one who deserts his party.
tur'ning-point *n.* a point at which a turn is made, or at which an important change takes place.
turn'key *n.* one who keeps the keys in a prison.
turn'-out *n.* **1** a crowd, gathering, for a special purpose. **2** clothes, kind of dress. **3** output (of e.g. a factory).
turn'over *n.* **1** rate of change or replacement. **2** the total amount of the sales in a business during a certain time. **3** a pie made by folding the pastry over the contents.
turn'pike *n.* **1** (*history*) a gate set across a road which is opened when the traveller has paid a toll or fee. **2** (*U.S.*) a main road where a toll is collected.
turn'stile *n.* a gate which turns round and allows one person only to pass at a time.
turn'table *n.* **1** a revolving platform for turning a railway engine round. **2** the revolving plate for supporting a gramophone record in a record-player.
turn'-up *n.* **1** (*coll.*) a disturbance. **2** (*coll.*) an unexpected happening. **3** a piece of material folded up.
at every turn everywhere, at every stage, etc.
by turns one after another.
in turn in order, one after the other.
not turn a hair to be quite calm and untroubled.
out of turn **1** not in turn. **2** (*coll.*) impertinently.
take one's turn **1** to follow an arrangement which allows others to have a fair chance. **2** to take one's part, with others, e.g. in a task.
take turns to do (e.g. to work) one after the other.
to a turn exactly, perfectly.
turn against to become dissatisfied with or hostile to.
turn (and turn) about in turn, taking one's turn.
turn down to say no to (e.g. an offer).
turn in (*coll.*) **1** to go to bed. **2** to hand over to person(s) in authority.
turn off **1** to dismiss, get rid of. **2** to shut off (e.g. water from a tap). **3** to put out (a light). **4** (*coll.*) to disgust.
turn on **1** to set running (e.g. water). **2** to put on (a light, charm). **3** (*coll.*) to please, fascinate. **4** to move round. **5** to depend on: *What we do next turns on the success of the first step.* **6** to face angrily and unexpectedly.
turn one's hand to **1** to apply oneself

to. **2** to work at with some skill.

turn out 1 (*old*) to drive out. **2** to empty. **3** to make for selling or for use. **4** (esp. *pass.*) to dress, clothe: *She's always nicely turned out.* **5** to get out of bed, or out of the house. **6** to come or gather: *A crowd turned out for the match in spite of rain.* **7** to put out (e.g. a light). **8** to prove to be the fact: *It turned out that he had done it.*

turn someone's head to fill someone with pride or conceit.

turn the scale to be the fact, etc., that causes the decision or result.

turn the scale at to weigh: *to turn the scale at 17 stone.*

turn the stomach to disgust.

turn to 1 to set to work. **2** to change to. **3** to go to for help, etc.

turn up 1 to appear, arrive. **2** to be found. **3** to happen. **4** to look up in e.g. a book. **5** to discover.

turnip *tûr'nip*, *n.* a plant or its large round root used as vegetable and for feeding cattle.

turnpike, turnstile, turntable. See **turn**.

turpentine *tûr'pėn-tīn*, *n.* colourless inflammable oil obtained from resin of certain trees, used in paint and varnish, etc.—*abbrev.* **turps** *(tûrps)*.

turpitude *tûr'pi-tūd*, *n.* wickedness.

turquoise *tûr'kwäz, -k(w)oiz*, *n.* a greenish-blue precious stone.—*adj.* made of, of the colour of, this stone.

turret *tur'it*, *n.* **1** a small tower on a building. **2** a tower, often revolving, within which guns are mounted, as on a warship.

turr'eted *adj.* having turrets.

turtle *tûr'tl*, *n.* **1** a tortoise, esp. one found in water (esp. ocean). **2** the flesh of certain turtles used for making soup.

turt'leneck *adj.* (of a garment) having a high, close-fitting neck.

turn turtle (of e.g. boat) to capsize, turn bottom up.

turtle-dove *tûr'tl-duv*, *n.* a beautiful, softly-cooing dove.

tusk *tusk*, *n.* a large tooth sticking out of the mouth of certain animals (e.g. elephant, walrus), usu. one of a pair.

tussle *tus'l*, *n.* a struggle.—*v.i.* to struggle, wrestle:—*pr.p.* **tuss'ling**.

tussock *tus'ȯk*, *n.* a tuft of grass.

tutelage *tū'ti-lij*, *n.* **1** guardianship. **2** the state of being under a guardian.

tu'telary *adj.* having charge of a person or place.

tutor *tū'tȯr*, *n.* **1** one who has charge of the education of another. **2** one who teaches and examines students. **3** a book of lessons e.g. in music.—*v.t.* **1** to teach. **2** to direct the studies of.

tutō'rial *adj.* having to do with a tutor.—*n.* a meeting for study between a tutor and student(s).

See also **tuition**.

tutu *tōō'tōō*, *n.* a ballet dancer's short, stiff, spreading skirt.

tuxedo *tuk-sē'dō*, *n.* a dinner-jacket:—*pl.* **tuxe'do(e)s**.

twaddle *twod'l*, *n.* silly talk or writing.

twain *twān*, (*old*) *n.* two people, things.

in twain in two, asunder.

twang *twang*, *n.* **1** a sound as of a tight string of a musical instrument pulled and let go. **2** a sharp, nasal tone of voice.—*v.i.*, *v.t.* to have, make, or cause to make, one of these sounds.

tweak *twēk*, *v.t.* to pull or squeeze sharply.—*n.* an act of tweaking.

tweed *twēd*, *n.* **1** a kind of woollen cloth with rough surface, in various patterns. **2** (in *pl.*) garments of tweed.—Also *adj.*

tweezers *twēz'ėrz*, *n. pl.* small pincers for pulling out hairs, holding small things, etc.

twelve *twelv*, *n.* **1** the number next above eleven (12 or XII). **2** a set of twelve things or people. **3** the twelfth hour of the day or night, midday or midnight. **4** any thing (e.g. a shoe) denoted by twelve.—*adj.* **1** 12 in number. **2** twelve years old.

twelfth *twelfth*, *adj.* **1** next after the eleventh. **2** equal to one of twelve equal parts.—Also *n.*

Twelfth'-night *n.* eve of January 6th, which is the twelfth day after Christmas.

twelve'month (*old*) *n.* a year.

twenty *twen'ti*, *adj.* and *n.* two times ten (20 or XX).

twen'ties *n. pl.* the numbers twenty to twenty-nine.

twen'tieth *(-ti-ėth)* *adj.* **1** next after the nineteenth. **2** equal to one of twenty equal parts.—Also *n.*

twerp *twûrp*, (*slang*) *n.* a despicable person.

twi- *twī-*, (as part of a word; *old*) **1** two. **2** double. **3** twice.

twice *twīs*, *adv.* two times.

think twice to exercise caution.

twiddle *twid'l*, *v.t.* to play with, twirl idly:—*pr.p.* **twidd'ling**.

twiddle one's thumbs 1 to turn one's thumbs round each other. **2** to be idle.

twig^1 *twig*, *n.* a small shoot or branch.

twig^2 *twig*, (*coll.*) *v.t.* and *v.i.* to understand:—*pr.p.* **twigg'ing**; *pa.p.* **twigged**.

twilight *twī'līt*, *n.* **1** the faint light after sunset, and before sunrise. **2** a state or time before or esp. after full brightness or strength: *the twilight of the dictator's power*.

twī'lit *adj.* dimly lit, as by twilight.

twilight zone an intermediate or indefinite area or state.

twill *twil, n.* (woven fabric with) a ridged appearance.—*v.t.* to weave in this way.

twin *twin, n.* **1** one of two children or animals born at one birth. **2** one very like another.—*adj.* **1** being two, or one of two, born at a birth. **2** very like another. **3** double. **4** consisting of two similar parts.

twinned *adj.* (esp. of towns) paired.

twin bed one of a matching pair of beds.

twin'-en'gined *adj.* having two engines.

twin'-screw' *adj.* having two parallel propellers, on separate shafts.

twin'set *n.* a matching sweater and cardigan.

twin town a town paired with a foreign town of similar size, for the purpose of social, cultural and commercial exchanges.

twine *twīn, n.* **1** a cord made of two or more threads twisted together. **2** a coil, twist.—*v.t.* **1** to twist (together). **2** to wind (about, round something).—*v.i.* **1** to wind together, join closely. **2** to wind oneself (about, round):—*pr.p.* **twi'ning**.

twinge *twinj, n.* a sudden, sharp pain.

twinkle *twing'kl, v.i.* **1** (of e.g. star) to shine with a slightly trembling light. **2** (of eyes) to shine with amusement:—*pr.p.* **twink'-ling**.—*n.* **1** an act of twinkling. **2** an expression of amusement.

twink'ling *n.* an instant.

twirl *twûrl, v.t.* to turn round rapidly, esp. with the fingers.—*v.i.* to be whirled round.—*n.* a whirl, motion in a circle.

twist *twist, v.t.* **1** to wind together (two or more threads). **2** to form (e.g. rope) in this way. **3** to wind (about, round, something). **4** to form into a coil. **5** to bend out of shape: *The fire twisted the girders.* **6** to wrench round painfully (e.g. the arm). **7** to sprain (e.g. the ankle). **8** in reporting, to alter or distort (facts, etc.) unfairly.—*v.i.* to move, turn, be bent, etc., round something, or this way and that: *The vine twists round the post*; *The road twists up the hill.*—*n.* **1** an act of twisting. **2** a wrench, violent turn. **3** something that is twisted. **4** a roll of tobacco.

twis'ter *n.* **1** person or thing that twists. **2** (*coll.*) a dishonest person.

round the twist (*slang*) crazy.

twist someone round one's (little) finger to be able to make someone do what one wants.

twist someone's arm (*coll.*) to persuade, esp. forcefully.

twit[1] *twit, v.t.* to remind (a person) laughingly of a fault, etc., to tease:—*pr.p.* **twitt'ing**; *pa.p.* **twitt'ed**.

twit[2] *twit, (slang) n.* a fool.

twitch *twich, v.t.* to pull with a sudden jerk, snatch.—*v.i.* to move jerkily.—*n.* **1** a sudden, quick pull. **2** a jerking of the muscles.

twitter *twit'ėr, n.* **1** a chirp, of e.g. a bird. **2** slight nervous excitement.—*v.i.* **1** to chirp, make small noises. **2** to be excited.

twitt'ering *n.* **twitt'ery** *adj.*

two *tōō, n.* **1** the number next above one (2 or II). **2** a set of two things or persons. **3** the second hour after midday or midnight. **4** the age of two years. **5** any thing (e.g. a shoe, a playing-card) denoted by two.—*adj.* **1** 2 in number. **2** two years old.

two'-faced *adj.* deceitful, insincere.

two'fold *adj.* double (in senses of 'in two parts', 'two times as great or as much').—Also *adv.*

two'-hand'ed *adj.* **1** having, or used with, two hands. **2** to be used, played, by two persons.

twopence *tup'ėns, n.* the sum of two (esp. old) pennies.

twopenny *(tup') adj.* costing twopence.

two'some *(-sum) n.* **1** a group of two. **2** a match between two.—Also *adj.*

two'-time' (*slang*) *v.t.* to deceive:—*pr.p.* **two'-tim'ing**.

two'-tim'er *n.*

in two (broken) in two pieces.

two'-pence' (piece) a coin worth two pence.

See also **second, twice**.

tycoon *tī-kōōn', (coll.) n.* a businessman of great wealth and power.

tying. See **tie**.

tyke *tīk, (coll.)* n. a rough, unruly person.

tympanum *tim'pȧ-num, n.* **1** the eardrum. **2** a drum:—*pl.* **tym'panums, tym'pana**.

tym'pani *n.* timpani.

tym'panist *n.* a timpanist.

type *tīp, n.* **1** a sort, kind: *a new type of farming.* **2** a pattern, example, showing the normal or standard characteristics. **3** a rectangular block, usu. of metal, on one end of which is cast a letter, sign, etc. used in printing. **4** a set of these.—*v.t.* **1** to produce a copy of by means of a typewriter (also *v.i.*). **2** (*coll.*) to make (e.g. an actor) always play the same sort of part:—*pr.p* **ty'ping**.

typ'ical *(tip') adj.* **1** having to do with type. **2** having, or showing, the usual characteristics: *a typical athlete*; *It was typical of him to take all the credit* (*opp.*

atypical).
typ'ically *adv.* **typ'icalness** *n.*
typ'ify *(tip')* *v.t.* to serve as the type, or an example, of:—*pr.p.* **typ'ifying**; *pa.p.* **typ'ified**.
ty'pist *(tī')* *n.* one who uses a typewriter.
typog'raphy *(tī-)* *n.* **1** the art of printing. **2** the general appearance of printed matter.
typecast *tīp'kâst*, *v.t.* to cast (an actor) in the part of a character very like himself.
type'face *n.* (the style of the character on) the printing surface of a type.
type'script *n.* **1** a copy of a book, etc., made by a typewriter. **2** typewriting.
type'writer *n.* a machine which puts letters on a sheet of paper when its keys are struck.
type'writing *n.* **type'written** *adj.*

typhoid *tī'foid*, *adj.* *n.* (having to do with) a fever caused by a bacillus in bad food or drinking water.

typhoon *tī-fōōn'*, *n.* a violent storm of wind in the Chinese seas.

typhus *tī'fus*, *n.* a dangerous, quick-spreading fever, with dark rash, stupor, etc.

typical, **typify**, **typist**, **typography,** etc. See **type**.

tyrant *tī'ránt*, *n.* one who uses his power harshly or cruelly.
tyrann'ical, **tyrannous** *tir'á-nus*, *adjs.* cruel, unjustly severe.
tyr'annise *(tir'-)* *v.i.* **1** to act as a tyrant. **2** to rule (over) harshly:—*pr.p.* **tyr'annising.**
tyr'anny *(tir'-)* *n.* **1** the rule of a tyrant. **2** complete power used unfairly, or cruelly. **3** harshness:—*pl.* **tyr'annies**.

tyre, tire *tīr*, *n.* **1** a metal hoop that binds the rim of a wheel. **2** a hoop of thick rubber, solid or filled with air, fitted round a wheel rim.

tyro, tiro *tī'rō*, *n.* a person only learning an art or skill:—*pl.* **tyros, ti'ros**.

tzar. See **tsar**.

U

U-bend *ū'bend, n.* a bend making the shape of the letter U.

ubiquitous *ū-bi'kwi-tus, adj.* present everywhere.
ubi'quity, ubi'quitousness *ns.*

udder *ud'ėr, n.* the milk bag of a cow, sheep, etc.

ugh *ug, interj.* expressing disgust.

ugli *ug'li, n.* a cross between the grapefruit and the tangerine.

ugly *ug'li, adj.* **1** unpleasant to look at. **2** hateful: *an ugly deed.* **3** dangerous: *an ugly situation:—comp.* **ug'lier**; *superl.* **ug'liest**.
ug'liness *n.*
ugly duckling despised member of a family who later proves the most successful.

ukulele, ukelele *ū-ku-lā'li, n.* a small, usually four-stringed guitar.

ulcer *ul'sėr, n.* an open sore, a break in skin or mucous membrane, often with pus.
ulcerā'tion *n.* the formation of ulcers.
ul'cerous *adj.*

ulna *ul'nȧ, n.* the inner and larger bone of the forearm.

ult. See **ultimo** (under **ultimate**).

ulterior *ul-tē'ri-ȯr, adj.* beyond what is seen or admitted (*an ulterior motive*, a hidden, usu. bad, motive).

ultimate *ul'ti-mit, adj.* **1** farthest. **2** final. **3** most important.
ul'timately *adv.* in the end.
ultimatum *ul-ti-mā'tum, n.* a final demand made by one party to another, containing a threat to break off peaceful discussion.
ul'timo *(-mō) n.* in the month just past: *on the 30th ultimo:—abbrev.* **ult**.

ultra- *ul'trȧ-, pfx.* (1) beyond in place (e.g. **ultraviolet**); (2) beyond in degree (e.g. **ultramicroscopic**); (3) extreme(ly), excessive(ly) (e.g. **ultra-careful**).

ultramarine *ul-trȧ-mȧ-rēn', adj.* **1** situated beyond the sea. **2** of a deep sky-blue colour.—*n.* blue colouring matter.

ultramicroscopic *ul'trȧ-mī-krō-skop'ik, adj.* smaller than microscopic, too small to be seen with an ordinary microscope.

ultrasonic *ul-trȧ-son'ik, adj.* beyond the range of human hearing.

ultraviolet *ul'trȧ-vī'ȯ-lit, adj.* (of rays) beyond the violet end of the visible spectrum.

umbel *um'bėl, n.* a flower head in which a number of stalks, each bearing flowers, branch out from one centre.
umbellif'erous *adj.* bearing umbels.

umber *um'bėr, n.* a brown pigment or colouring material.

umbilical *um-bil'i-kl, adj.* of the navel.
umbilical cord a tube connecting the foetus to the placenta.

umbrage *um'brij, n.* a sense of injury or offence: *to take, give, umbrage.*

umbrella *um-brel'ȧ, n.* **1** a folding shelter against rain, carried in the hand. **2** a protective force of aircraft. **3** general cover or protection: *This action was taken under the umbrella of the United Nations.*

umpire *um'pīr, n.* **1** a judge called in to settle a dispute. **2** (in cricket, etc.) a person who enforces the rules and decides doubtful points.—Also *v.i.* and *v.t.:—pr.p* **um'piring**.

umpteen *um(p)'tēn, (coll.) adj.* an indefinitely large number.
umpteenth' *adj.* latest or last of many.

un-[1] *un-, pfx.* (a) used to make verbs showing the reversal of an action (e.g. **unfasten**). (b) Sometimes the *pfx.* merely strengthens the meaning (e.g. **unloose**).

un-[2] *un-, pfx.* not; used to indicate the opposite of the word to which it is attached (e.g. **unequal**, not equal; **unconsciousness**, lack of consciousness).

unable *un-ā'bl, adj.* without sufficient strength, power, skill, or opportunity. See also **inability**.

unaccountable *un-ȧ-kown'tȧ-bl, adj.* **1** not to be explained or accounted for. **2** not to be held responsible.
unaccount'ably *adv.*

unadulterated *un-ȧ-dul'tėr-āt-id, adj.* **1** not adulterated. **2** unmixed.

unadvised *un-ȧd-vīzd', adj.* **1** not advised. **2** not prudent, rash.
unadvīs'edly *(-id-li) adv.*

unaffected *un-ȧ-fek'tid, adj.* **1** not acted on or changed. **2** not influenced (by something). **3** without artificiality of manner: *a frank, unaffected girl.* **4** sincere.
unaffect'edly *adv.*

unalloyed *un-ȧ-loid', adj.* not alloyed or mixed, pure.

unanimity. See **unanimous**.

unanimous *ū-nan'i-mus, adj.* **1** agreeing, one and all, in opinion or resolve.

2 agreed to by all: *a unanimous decision.* **unanim'ity, unan'imousness** *ns.* **unan'imously** *adv.*

unanswerable *un-än'sėr-ȧ-bl, adj.* not able to be answered, or to be proved false: *an unanswerable argument.*

unapproachable *un-ȧ-prōch'ȧ-bl, adj.* **1** impossible to reach. **2** stiff and unfriendly. **3** that cannot be equalled.

unarmed *un-ärmd', adj.* without weapons, defenceless.

unasked'-for *adj.* not sought or invited.

unassuming *un-ȧ-sūm'ing,* or *-sōōm', adj.* modest.

unattached *un-ȧ-tacht', adj.* **1** not belonging to a particular regiment, etc. **2** not engaged to be married, or married.

unattended *un-ȧ-ten'did, adj.* **1** not accompanied. **2** not in the care of an attendant.

unauthorised *un-öth'ȯr-īzd, adj.* not having the permission of the people in authority: *unauthorised use of the firm's equipment.*

unavailing *un-ȧ-vāl'ing, adj.* achieving nothing, useless: *unavailing efforts.*

unavoidable *un-ȧ-void'ȧ-bl, adj.* that cannot be avoided. **unavoid'ably** *adv.*

unaware *un-ȧ-wār', adj.* not aware, ignorant (usu. with *of*).—*adv.* (also **unawares**) **1** without warning. **2** unconsciously, unintentionally.
take (someone) unawares to surprise or startle (someone): *The news took us unawares.*

unbalanced *un-bal'ȧnst, adj.* **1** disordered in mind. **2** not taking into account all the facts: *an unbalanced view.* **3** (*book-keeping*) not made up to show balance of debtor and creditor.

unbar *un-bär', v.t.* **1** to remove a bar from. **2** to open:—*pr.p.* **unbarr'ing**; *pa.p.* **unbarred'** *(-bärd').*

unbearable *un-bār'ȧ-bl, adj.* too painful to bear, or to tolerate: *unbearable toothache, injustice.*

unbecoming *un-bi-kum'ing, adj.* **1** (of clothes) not suited to the wearer. **2** (of behaviour) not what should be expected from the person or in the circumstances.

unbeknown *un-bi-nōn', adj.* without being known, unobserved.

unbelief *un-bi-lēf', n.* want of belief.
unbeliev'able **1** incredible. **2** (*coll.*) astonishing, remarkable.
unbeliev'ably *adv.*
unbeliev'er *n.* one who does not believe.
unbeliev'ing *adj.*

unbend *un-bend', v.t.* **1** to straighten (something with bend in it). **2** to slacken the string on (a bow).—*v.i.* to behave in a friendly, not formal, way:—*pa.p.* **unbent'**.
unben'ding *adj.* **1** not bending. **2** not changing purpose or opinion. **3** stiff and formal.—*n.* **1** straightening. **2** slackening.

unbias(s)ed *un-bī'ȧst, adj.* free from bias, not showing prejudice or favouritism, etc.

unbidden *un-bid'n, adj.* **1** without being told to. **2** uninvited.

unblushing *un-blush'ing, adj.* without shame.

unbolt *un-bōlt', v.t.* to open the bolt of (e.g. a door):—*pa.p.* and *adj.* **unbol'ted**.

unbosom *un-bōōz'ȯm, v.t.* (with *oneself*) or *v.i.* to tell freely one's troubles, etc.

unbound *un-bownd', adj.* not bound; loose.

unbounded *un-bown'did, adj.* **1** not limited. **2** very great.

unbridled *un-brīd'ld, adj.* **1** without a bridle. **2** not held in check: *unbridled rage.*

unbuckle *un-buk'l, v.t.* to undo the buckle or buckles of:—*pr.p.* **unbuck'ling**.

unburden *un-bûr'dn, v.t.* **1** to take a load off. **2** (with *oneself*) to tell one's secrets freely (also *v.i.*).

unbutton *un-but'n, v.t.* to unfasten the buttons of.

uncalled-for *un-köld'-fȯr, adj.* **1** quite unnecessary. **2** rude: *That criticism is uncalled-for.*

uncanny *un-kan'i, adj.* **1** strange, full of mystery. **2** more than human: *uncanny skill.*
uncann'ily *adv.* **uncann'iness** *n.*

uncared-for *un'kārd'-fȯr, adj.* not taken care of, neglected.

unceremonious *un-ser-i-mō'ni-ủs, adj.* **1** informal. **2** rudely abrupt.

uncertain *un-sûr't(i)n, adj.* **1** not knowing definitely: *I am uncertain of his whereabouts.* **2** not definitely known: *His whereabouts are uncertain.* **3** depending on chance. **4** changeable: *uncertain weather.* **5** vague. **6** hesitating.

unchain *un-chān', v.t.* to free from chain(s).

uncharted *un-chärt'id, adj.* **1** not shown on a chart or map. **2** of which a detailed map has never been made.

uncivil *un-siv'il, adj.* not courteous, rude.
unciv'illy *adv.* **unciv'ilness** *n.*
See also **incivility**.

unclassified *un-klas'i-fīd adj.* **1** not on the security list. **2** (of a road) not in a class entitled to a government grant.

For words in *un-* not found above, see **un-**[1] or **un-**[2], page 639.

uncle *ung'kl, n.* **1** the brother of one's father or mother. **2** an aunt's husband.
unclean *un-klēn', adj.* **1** dirty. **2** vile.
unclose *un-klōz', v.t.* to open:—*pr.p.* **unclos'ing**.
unclothe *un-klō*TH*', v.t.* to take the clothes off:—*pr.p.* **uncloth'ing**.
uncoil *un-koil', v.t., v.i.* to unwind.
uncoloured *un-kul'ȯrd, adj.* **1** not coloured, undyed. **2** truthful, not exaggerated.
uncommitted *un-kȯ-mit'id, adj.* not pledged to support any party or policy.
uncommon *un-kom'ȯn, adj.* **1** rare. **2** unusual.
uncommonly *adv.* very.
uncompromising *un-kom'prȯ-mīz-ing, adj.* **1** (of a person) not willing to compromise or give in. **2** very emphatic: *an uncompromising refusal.*
unconcern *un-kȯn-sûrn', n.* lack of interest or anxiety.
unconditional *un-kȯn-dish'ȯn-ȧl, adj.* made without conditions or stipulations, complete: *unconditional surrender*; *an unconditional promise.*
uncondi'tionally *adv.*
unconfirmed *un-kȯn-fûrmd', adj.* **1** not confirmed. **2** (of e.g. rumour) not as yet shown to be true.
unconscionable *un-kon'sh(ȯ)n-ȧ-bl, adj.* **1** without conscience (of e.g. a rascal). **2** excessive: *unconscionable demands.*
unconscious *un-kon'shu̇s, adj.* **1** not aware (of). **2** having lost consciousness, senseless, stunned. **3** not present to the conscious mind: *an unconscious prejudice.*—*n.* the deepest level of mind.
uncon'sciously *adv.*
uncon'sciousness *n.*
unconventional *un-kȯn-ven'sh(ȯ)n-ȧl, adj.* **1** not bound by accepted standards of conduct, manners or taste. **2** not customary.
unconven'tionally *adv.*
uncouple *un-kup'l, v.t.* to disconnect (e.g. railway wagons):—*pr.p.* **uncoup'ling**.
uncouth *un-ko͞oth', adj.* **1** clumsy, awkward. **2** rude. **3** odd in appearance.
uncover *un-kuv'ėr, v.t.* **1** to remove the cover of. **2** to lay open.—*v.i.* to take off one's hat.
uncrowned *un-krownd', adj.* (in *uncrowned king*) having power like a king's without the title.
unction *ungk'sh(ȯ)n, n.* **1** an anointing. **2** divine grace. **3** too great warmth or earnestness of manner.
unctuous *ungk'tū-u̇s, adj.* **1** oily. **2** making a false, unpleasant show of holiness, earnestness, sympathy, etc.
extreme unction praying over and anointing a person who is near death.
uncurl *un-kûrl', v.t.* to straighten out.—*v.i.* to relax, unwind.
uncut *un'kut', adj.* **1** not cut. **2** (of gem) not shaped by cutting.
undaunted *un-dawn'tid, adj.* **1** not discouraged. **2** fearless.
undeceive *un-di-sēv', v.t.* to free from a mistaken belief, tell the truth to (someone):—*pr.p.* **undeceiv'ing**.
undecided *un-di-sī'did, adj.* **1** not having the mind made up. **2** not settled.
undefiled *un-di-fīld', adj.* **1** pure. **2** not stained, or spoiled in any way.
undeniable *un-di-nī'ȧ-bl, adj.* **1** not able to be denied. **2** obviously true.
under *un'dėr, prep.* **1** in a position lower than or beneath. **2** less than. **3** subject to the authority of: *working under a new boss.* **4** beneath the weight of: *He sank under his burden.* **5** going through, suffering (e.g. attack). **6** having, using (a name, title). **7** in accordance with: *under this agreement.*—*adv.* in, or to, a lower place or condition.— *adj.* lower in position, rank, amount, etc.
under age still too young (for some legal or other purpose).
un'derarm *adj., adv.* (of action) with arm below shoulder.
under arms ready for battle.
under canvas in tents.
under fire **1** exposed to enemy attack. **2** receiving severe criticism.
under one's breath in a low voice.
under one's (very) nose right in front of one and in plain view: *He took my paper under my very nose.*
under way (of ship, etc.) in motion.
under-, *un'dėr-, pfx.* (1) beneath (e.g. **underlie**); (2) too little (e.g. **underpay**); (3) lower in position (e.g. **undercurrent**); (4) less in rank (e.g. **Under-secretary**).
undercarriage *un'dėr-kar-ij, n.* **1** the supporting framework, of e.g. a wagon. **2** the landing-gear of an aircraft.
underclothes *un'dėr-klō*TH*z, n.pl.* clothes worn under the outer garments.—Also **un'derclōthing**.
undercover *un'dėr-kuv'ėr, adj.* working or done in secret.
undercurrent *un'dėr-kur'ėnt, n.* flow or movement under the surface.
undercut *un-dėr-kut', v.t.* **1** to strike a blow upward. **2** to sell at a lower price than (a competitor):—*pr.p.* **undercutt'ing**; *pa.p.* **undercut'**.

For words in *un-* not found above, see **un-¹** or **un-²**, page 639.

un'dercut *n.* **1** a blow struck upward. **2** under side of a sirloin.

underdeveloped *un'dėr-di-vel'ȯpt, adj.* **1** not well grown. **2** (*photography*) not sufficiently developed. **3** (of country) not having efficient modern agriculture and industry or high standard of living.

underdo *un-dėr-dōō', v.t.* to do, cook, etc., less than is needed:—*pr.p.* **underdo'ing**; *pa.t.* **underdid'**; *pa.p.* **underdone'**.
underdone' *(-dun') adj.* incompletely cooked.

underdog *un'dėr-dog, n.* **1** the loser in a struggle (e.g. for existence). **2** one dominated, or likely to be beaten, by another.

underestimate *un-dėr-es'ti-māt, v.t.* **1** to estimate at less than the real value or amount. **2** to think less strong, great, etc., than he, it, really is: *to underestimate an opponent*:—*pr.p.* **underest'imating.**—*n.* *(-mit)* an estimate that is too low.

under-exposed *un-dėr-eks-pōzd', adj.* (*photography*) not exposed long enough to light.

underfed *un-dėr-fed', adj.* not given enough to eat.

underfoot *un-dėr-foot', adv.* **1** under the feet. **2** on the ground.

undergarment *un'dėr-gär-mėnt, n.* any article of clothing habitually worn under others.

undergo *un-dėr-gō', v.t.* **1** to endure. **2** to experience. **3** to go through (a process, e.g. repair):—*pr.p.* **undergo'ing**; *pa.t.* **underwent'**; *pa.p.* **undergone'**.

undergraduate *un-dėr-grad'ū-it, n.* a student who has not taken his or her first degree.

underground *un'dėr-grownd, adj.* **1** below the surface of the ground. **2** secret.—*n.* **1** a railway operating beneath the streets. **2** a secret movement against a ruling power.

undergrowth *un'dėr-grōth, n.* low woody plants growing among trees.

underhand *un'dėr-hand, adj.* **1** with the hand on a lower level than the shoulder. **2** (also **underhan'ded**) sly, mean.

underhung *un-dėr-hung', adj.* **1** (of e.g. sliding door) supported from below. **2** (of lower jaw) sticking out beyond upper.

underlie *un-dėr-lī', v.t.* **1** to lie under. **2** to be the hidden cause or source of:—*pr.p.* **underly'ing**; *pa.t.* **underlay'**; *pa.p.* **underlain'**.
underly'ing *adj.*
un'derlay *n.* material (e.g. felt or rubber) laid under a carpet, esp. to preserve it.

underline *un-dėr-līn', v.t.* **1** to draw a line under. **2** to emphasise:—*pr.p.* **underlin'ing.**

underling *un'dėr-ling, n.* **1** a subordinate. **2** an inferior in rank.

undermentioned *un-dėr-men'sh(ȯ)nd, adj.* mentioned below or in the text following.

undermine *un-dėr-mīn', v.t.* **1** to make a passage under. **2** to make insecure. **3** to weaken (e.g. health, authority). **4** to do so by underhand means:—*pr.p.* **undermīn'ing.**

undermost *un'dėr-mōst, adj.* lowest in place or condition.

underneath *un-dėr-nēth', adv.* beneath, in a lower place.—Also *prep.*

underpants *un'dėr-pants, n.pl.* undergarment for buttocks and thighs.

underpass *un'dėr-päs, n.* a road passing under another road, a railway, etc.

underpay *un-dėr-pā', v.t.* to pay too little:—*pa.p.* and *adj.* **underpaid'**.
underpay'ment *n.*

underpin *un-dėr-pin', v.t.* to put something under (e.g. a building) for support:—*pr.p.* **underpinn'ing**; *pa.p.* **underpinned'**.

underprivileged *un-dėr-priv'i-lijd, adj.* not enjoying normal social and economic rights.

underrate *un-dėr-rāt', v.t.* to think too little of:—*pr.p.* **underrat'ing.**

under-secretary *un'dėr-sek'ri-tȧ-ri, n.* an official next in rank below a Secretary of State.

undersell *un-dėr-sel', v.t.* to sell at a lower price than (a competitor).

underside *un'dėr-sīd, n.* the side lying underneath, often hidden.

undersign *un-dėr-sīn', v.t.* to sign one's name at the foot of.
the un'dersigned the person or persons whose names are signed below.

undersized *un'dėr-sīzd, adj.* below the usual size.

underskirt *un'dėr-skûrt, n.* a petticoat.

understand *un-dėr-stand', v.t.* **1** to see the meaning of. **2** to know thoroughly. **3** to gather (that). **4** to take for granted as part of an agreement. **5** to take (something) as meant though not expressed:—*pa.t.* and *pa.p.* **understood'**.
understand'ing *n.* **1** the act or power of grasping meaning. **2** intelligence. **3** an informal agreement. **4** appreciating another's feelings, point of view.—Also *adj.*

understate *un-dėr-stāt', v.t.* **1** to state at too low an amount, etc. **2** to state less than the truth about (something):—*pr.p.* **un-derstat'ing.**

understate'ment *n.*

understood. See **understand.**

understudy *un'dėr-stud-i, v.t.* and *v.i.* **1** to study (a dramatic part) so as to be able to take the place of another actor. **2** to learn the part of (another actor) for this purpose:—*pr.p.* **un'derstudying**: *pa.p.* **un'derstudied.**—*n.* an actor who learns a part thus:—*pl.* **un'derstudies.**

undertake *un-dėr-tāk', v.t.* **1** to take upon oneself (a duty, task, etc.). **2** to promise (to do something):—*pr.p.* **undertak'ing**; *pa.t.* **undertook'**; *pa.p.* **undertak'en.**

un'dertaker *n.* a manager of funerals.

undertak'ing *n.* **1** a project, task taken on, business. **2** a pledge, promise. **3** *(un'-dėr-)* conducting funerals.

undertone *un'dėr-tōn, n.* **1** a low tone of voice. **2** partly hidden emotion, meaning quality.

undertow *un'dėr-tō, n.* a current below the surface, in a different direction from the surface movement.

undervalue *un-dėr-val'ū, v.t.* to value below the real worth:—*pr.p.* **underval'uing.**

undervaluā'tion *n.*

underwear *un'dėr-wār, n.* underclothes.

underwent. See **undergo.**

underworld *un'dėr-wûrld, n.* **1** the place of evil spirits, or of the dead. **2** the habitual lawbreakers, esp. when banded together.

underwrite *un'dėr-rīt', v.t.* **1** to accept for insurance. **2** to guarantee (money or shares). **3** to accept liability for:—*pr.p.* **underwrit'ing**; *pa.t.* **underwrote'**; *pa.p.* **underwritt'en.**

un'derwriter *n.* one who insures, e.g. shipping.

undesirable *un-di-zīr'ȧ-bl, adj.* **1** not to be wished for. **2** objectionable.

undid. See **undo.**

undistinguished *un-dis-ting'gwisht, adj.* ordinary, commonplace.

undo *un-do͞o', v.t.* **1** to reverse, wipe out the effect of (what has been done). **2** to unfasten. **3** to ruin:—*pr.p.* **undo'ing**; *pa.t.* **undid'**; *pa.p.* **undone'.**

undo'ing *n.* ruin.

undone' *adj.*

undoubted *un-dowt'id, adj.* not doubted or denied: *the undoubted excellence of the work.*

undoubt'edly *adv.* without doubt, certainly.

undress *un-dres', v.t.* and *v.i.* to take the clothes off.—*n. (un')* **1** plain dress (not uniform). **2** scanty or inadequate dress.

undressed' *adj.* **1** not dressed. **2** not bandaged. **3** not prepared (for use, display, etc.).

undue *un-dū', adj.* too great, more than is necessary.

undu'ly *adv.*

undulate *un'dū-lāt, v.i.* **1** to move as waves do. **2** to have a rolling appearance: *There low hills and valleys undulate*:—*pr.p* **un'-dulating.**

un'dulating *adj.* **undulā'tion** *n.*

unduly. See **undue.**

unearned *un-ûrnd', adj.* **1** not gained by work. **2** not deserved.

unearned income income from money invested.

unearth *un-ûrth', v.t.* **1** to bring out from the earth, or from a place of hiding. **2** to bring to light (e.g. facts, a plot).

unearthly *un-ûrth'li, adj.* **1** supernatural, weird. **2** (*coll.*) absurdly early, loud, etc.

uneasy *un-ē'zi, adj.* **1** restless. **2** anxious. **3** not certain to last: *an uneasy peace*:—*comp.* **uneas'ier**; *superl.* **uneas'iest.**

unea'sily *adv.* **unea'siness** *n.*

unemployed *un-em-ploid', adj.* **1** not put to use. **2** out of work.

unemploy'ment *n.*

unequal *un-ē'kwȧl, adj.* **1** differing in quantity or quality: *an unequal division of the spoils.* **2** unfair. **3** varying. **4** not having enough strength or ability for (with *to*): *unequal to the task.*

une'qualled *adj.* without equal: *He was unequalled as a mimic; a landscape unequalled for beauty.*

une'qually *adv.* **une'qualness** *n.*

See also **inequality.**

unerring *un-ûr'ing, adj.* never making a mistake, always right or accurate: *unerring skill at darts.*

unerr'ingly *adv.*

uneven *un-ē'vn, adj.* **1** not smooth or level. **2** irregular, not uniform. **3** not divisible by two without remainder.

une'venly *adv.* **une'venness** *n.*

unexampled *un-ėg-zäm'pld, adj.* not following any example, alone of its kind: *unexampled courage, stupidity.*

unexceptionable *un-ėk-sep'sh(ȯ)n-ȧ-bl, adj.* in which one can find nothing to criticise, without fault.

unexpected *un-ėk-spek'tid, adj.* not expected, sudden.

unexpec'tedly *adv.*

unfailing *un-fā'ling, adj.* **1** never giving out: *unfailing supplies, courage.* **2** sure, to be counted on.

unfail'ingly *adv.*

For words in *un-* not found above, see **un-**[1] or **un-**[2], page 639.

unfair *un-fār'*, *adj.* not fair or just.
unfair'ly *adv.*

unfaithful *un-fāth'fool*, *-fl*, *adj.* **1** disloyal. **2** adulterous.
unfaithfully *adv*.

unfasten *un-fäs'n*, *v.t.* to undo, unfix.

unfathomable *un-fa*TH*'om-à-bl*, *adj.* too deep to be plumbed, or to be understood.

unfeeling *un-fē'ling*, *adj.* hard-hearted.
unfeel'ingly *adv*.

unfeigned *un-fānd'*, *adj.* sincere.

unfettered *un-fet'ėrd*, *adj.* free, not restrained or checked.

unfilial *un-fil'yȧl*, *-i-ȧl*, *adj.* (of a child's behaviour to a parent) not what it should be, not dutiful.

unfit *un-fit'*, *adj.* **1** not suitable. **2** not good enough, or not in a suitable state (to, for): *unfit to travel*; *food unfit for humans.* **3** not in full vigour of body or mind.—*v.t.* to make unfit or unsuitable:—*pr.p* **unfitt'ing**; *pa.p.* **unfitt'ed**.
unfit'ness *n*.

unfix *un-fiks'*, *v.t.* **1** to undo the fixing of. **2** to unsettle.

unflagging *un-flag'ing*, *adj.* not tiring or losing vigour.

unflappable *un-flap'ȧ-bl*, (*coll.*) *adj.* imperturbable.

unflinching *un-flinch'ing*, or *-sh'*, *adj.* not flinching or shrinking because of pain, danger, or opposition.

unfold *un-fōld'*, *v.t.* **1** to spread out. **2** to give details of (e.g. a plan).

unforgettable *un-fȯr-get'ȧ-bl*, *adj.* never to be forgotten, because of beauty, or horror, etc.

unfortunate *un-för'chu̇-nit*, *adj.* unlucky.
unfor'tunately *adv.* **1** in an unlucky way. **2** I'm sorry to say.

unfounded *un-fown'did*, *adj.* not based on facts or reality: *unfounded rumours, fears, hopes*.

unfrequented *un'fri-kwen'tid*, *adj.* not often visited, lonely.

unfrock *un-frok'*, *v.t.* to depose from the priesthood.

unfruitful *un-froot'fool*, *-fl*, *adj.* not producing fruit, results, etc.

unfurl *un-fûrl'*, *v.t.* and *v.i.* to unfold, shake out (a sail, a flag).

ungainly *un-gān'li*, *adj.* awkward, clumsy: —*comp.* **ungain'lier**; *superl.* **ungain'liest**.
ungain'liness *n*.

ungetatable *un-get-at'ȧ-bl*, *adj.* **1** in a place where it cannot be reached. **2** hard to reach.

ungodly *un-god'li*, *adj.* **1** not godly, sinful. **2** (*coll.*) outrageous: *at the ungodly hour of 3 a.m.*
ungod'liness *n*.

ungovernable *un-guv'ėr-nȧ-bl*, *adj.* uncontrollable.

ungracious *un-grā'shu̇s*, *adj.* **1** not showing appreciation. **2** rude, surly.

ungrammatical *un-grȧ-mat'i-kȧl*, *adj.* not according to the rules of grammar.

ungrateful *un-grāt'fool*, *-fl*, *adj.* not thankful.
See also **ingratitude**

ungrounded *un-grown'did*, *adj.* unfounded, groundless.

ungrudging *un-gruj'ing*, *adj.* giving, or given, freely.

unguarded *un-gär'did*, *adj.* **1** without protection. **2** careless, not prudent: *an unguarded remark*; *in an unguarded moment*.

unguent *ung'gwėnt*, *n.* ointment.

unhallowed *un-hal'ōd*, *adj.* **1** unholy. **2** very wicked.

unhappy *un-hap'i*, *adj.* **1** not happy, miserable. **2** not fortunate:—*comp.* **unhapp'ier**; *super.* **unhapp'iest**.
unhapp'ily *adv*. **unhapp'iness** *n*.

unharness *un-här'nis*, *v.t.* to take the harness off.

unhealthy *un-hel'thi*, *adj.* **1** not healthy. **2** sickly. **3** morally undesirable:—*comp.* **unheal'thier**; *superl.* **unheal'thiest**.
unheal'thily *adv.* **unheal'thiness** *n*.

unheard-of *un-hûrd'-ȯv*, *adj.* **1** not (yet) heard about. **2** unexampled, esp. in a bad way.

unhinge *un-hinj'*, *v.t.* **1** to take from the hinges. **2** to derange (the mind):—*pr.p.* **unhin'ging**.

unholy *un-hō'li*, *adj.* **1** not sacred or hallowed. **2** sinful. **3** (*coll.*) excessive (esp. of noise):—*comp.* **unhol'ier**; *superl.* **unhol'iest**.

unhook *un-hook'*, *v.t.* **1** to take down from a hook. **2** to unfasten the hooks of (e.g. a dress).

unhorse *un-hörs'*, *v.t.* to throw from a horse:—*pr.p.* **unhors'ing**.

uni- *ū-ni-*, *pfx.* one, single.

unicorn *ū'ni-körn*, *n.* an animal in myth, like a horse, but with one straight horn on the forehead.

unification, **unified**. See **unify**.

uniform *ū'ni-förm*, *adj.* not varying, the same always or in all parts: *a uniform flow of water*; *a uniform custom.*—*n.* the dress worn by soldiers, etc.
unifor'mity, **u'niformness** *ns*.

unify *ū'ni-fī, v.t.* to make into one:—*pr.p.* **u'nifying**; *pa.p.* **u'nified**.
unificā'tion *n.*

unilateral *ū'ni-lat'ė-răl, adj.* **1** one-sided. **2** on one side only. **3** (of e.g. a legal or other act) carried out by, affecting or binding, one side only.
unilat'erally *adv.*

unimpeachable *un-im-pēch'ȧ-bl, adj.* **1** not liable to be doubted: *an unimpeachable witness.* **2** blameless.

uninhibited *un-in-hib'i-tid, adj.* not repressed, unrestrained.

unintelligible *un-in-tel'i-ji-bl, adj.* not able to be understood.

uninterested *un-int'ris-tid, adj.* not having or showing any interest.
See also **disinterested**.

uninterrupted *un-in-tė-rup'tid, adj.* **1** not interrupted. **2** continuing without stoppage or break. **3** (of view) not blocked in any way.

uninvited *un-in-vīt'id, adj.* **1** without an invitation. **2** not asked for or encouraged.

union *ūn'yȯn, n.* **1** a joining together. **2** the state of being united. **3** marriage. **4** states joined together. **5** an association of persons for common purposes. **6** a trade union.
Un'ionist *n.* **1** orig. one opposed to 'Home Rule' (self-government) for Ireland. **2** a Conservative.
Union Jack the national flag of the United Kingdom.

unique *ū-nēk', adj.* without a like or equal.

unisex *ū'ni-seks, adj.* able to be used, worn, etc. by men and women.

unison *ū'ni-sȯn, n.* **1** identity, exact sameness, of pitch: *singing not in harmony but in unison.* **2** agreement.

unit *ū'nit, n.* **1** a single thing or person. **2** a fixed quantity by which other quantities of the same kind are measured. **3** a group within a larger body: *an army unit.*
u'nitary *adj.* **1** existing as a unit, not divided. **2** using unit(s).
unit trust a type of investment trust in which given amounts of different securities form a unit and units are sold to the public.
See also **unity**.

Unitarian. See **unity**.

unite *ū-nīt', v.t.* to join into one.—*v.i.* **1** to become one. **2** to act together:—*pr.p.* **unī'ting**.
unī'ted *adj.* **1** joined. **2** acting together, or thinking, feeling, alike.

unity *ū'ni-ti, n.* **1** state of being one. **2** state of being in complete agreement. **3** the number one.
Unitā'rian one who rejects the idea of the Trinity and believes that God the Father alone is divine.

universal. See **universe**.

universe *ū'ni-vûrs, n.* **1** all created things together with the earth and the heavenly bodies. **2** mankind. **3** the world.
universal *ū-ni-vûr'săl, adj.* **1** affecting or including all mankind. **2** in general use.
universal'ity, univer'salness *ns.*
univer'sally *adv.*

university *ū-ni-vûr'si-ti, n.* a centre of learning having power to grant degrees:—*pl.* **univer'sities**.

unjust *un-just', adj.* not just, unfair.

unkempt *un-kemt', adj.* untidy.

unkind *un-kīnd', adj.* not kind; harsh.

unknot *un-not', v.t.* to free from knots:—*pr.p.* **unknott'ing**; *pa.p.* **unknott'ed**.

unlace *un-lās', v.t.* to undo the lace in (a shoe, etc.):—*pr.p.* **unlāc'ing**.

unladen *un-lād'n, adj.* without a load.

unlearned *un-lûr'nid, adj.* **1** ignorant, not scholarly. **2** *(-lûrnd')* never learned, or known without learning.

unless *un-les', conj.* if not, supposing that not: *Do not speak unless he does* (i.e. if he does not speak).

unlike *un-līk', adj.* **1** not like, different. **2** not characteristic of: *It was unlike Mary to say anything cruel.*

unlikely *un-līk'li, adj.* not probable.

unload *un-lōd', v.t.* to take the load from.—*v.i.* to discharge a load.

unlock *un-lok', v.t.* **1** to open (something locked). **2** to reveal (e.g. hidden fact, facts, or feeling).

unlooked-for *un-lookt'-fŏr, adj.* not expected.

unloosen *un-lōōs'en, v.t.* to make loose:—*pr.p.* **unloos'ening**.
unloose' *v.t.* to unloosen:—*pr.p.* **unloos'ing**.

unlucky *un-luk'i, adj.* not lucky:—*comp.* **unluck'ier**; *superl.* **unluck'iest**.
unluck'ily *adv.*

unmanly *un-man'li, adj.* weak, cowardly:—*comp.* **unman'lier**; *superl.* **unman'liest**.

unmanned *un-mand', adj.* **1** not supplied with men. **2** overcome by emotion.

unmask *un-mäsk', v.t.* **1** to take a mask off (someone). **2** to show (someone) in his true character. **3** to lay bare.

unmatched *un-macht', adj.* without equal.

unmeaning *un-mē'ning, adj.* **1** having no meaning. **2** not intentional.

For words in *un-* not found above, see **un-¹** or **un-²**, page 639.

unmeasured *un-mezh'ůrd*, *adj.* **1** boundless, limitless. **2** unrestrained.

unmentionable *un-men'sh(ȯ)n-ȧ-bl*, *adj.* scandalous, indecent.

unmistakable *un-mis-tā'kȧ-bl*, *adj.* very clear, very obvious.
unmistāk'ably *adv*.

unmitigated *un-mit'i-gā-tid*, *adj.* complete: *an unmitigated nuisance*.

unmoved *un-mōōvd'*, *adj.* **1** firm. **2** calm.

unnatural *un-nach'ů-rȧl*, *adj.* **1** strange. **2** artificial. **3** cruel, wicked.

unnecessary *un-nes'i-sȧ-ri*, *adj.* **1** not necessary. **2** that might have been avoided.

unnerve *un-nûrv'*, *v.t.* to weaken, frighten, make irresolute:—*pr.p.* **unnerv'ing**.

unnumbered *un-num'bėrd*, *adj.* countless, in very great number.

unobtrusive *un-ob-trōō'siv*, *adj.* **1** not obvious. **2** modest, quiet.
unobtrus'ively *adv*.

unoccupied *un-ok'ū-pīd*, *adj.* **1** not occupied, vacant. **2** idle, not doing anything.

unpack *un-pak'*, *v.t.* **1** to take out of packing. **2** to open (luggage) and remove clothes, etc.—Also *v.i.*

unparalleled *un-par'ȧ-leld*, *adj.* **1** having no equal. **2** unexampled.

unpick *un-pik'*, *v.t.* to take out stitches of (knitting, sewing).

unpleasant *un-plez'ȧnt*, *adj.* disagreeable.

unplumbed *un-plumd'*, *adj.* **1** of unknown depth. **2** not tested or explored.

unpopular *un-pop'ū-lȧr*, *adj.* generally disliked.
unpopular'ity *n*.

unpractical *un-prak'ti-kȧl*, *adj.* (of person, method) not practical.

unprecedented *un-pres'i-den-tid*, *-prēs'*, or *-den'*, *adj.* never known before, unexampled, novel, unique.

unpremeditated *un-prē-med'i-tā-tid*, *adj.* not planned beforehand.

unprepossessing *un-prē-pȯ-zes'ing*, *adj.* unattractive.

unpretentious *un-pri-ten'shus*, *adj.* (of persons or things) modest, not showy, not affected.

unprincipled *un-prin'sip-ld*, *adj.* without moral principles.

unprofessional *un-prō-fesh'ȯn-ȧl*, *adj.* (of a person's conduct) not in keeping with standards of his profession.

unpromising *un-prom'is-ing*, *adj.* not likely to bring enjoyment, success, etc.

unqualified *un-kwol'i-fīd*, *adj.* **1** not having essential qualifications (e.g. for a post). **2** complete: *unqualified praise*.

unquestionable *un-kwes'ch(ȯ)n-ȧ-bl*, *adj.* not doubtful, certain, beyond dispute.

unquiet *un-kwī'ėt*, *adj.* **1** not at rest. **2** anxious.

unquote *un-kwōt'*, *interj.* word used to show the end of a passage quoted.

unravel *un-rav'ėl*, *v.t.* **1** to disentangle. **2** to solve (problem, mystery):—*pr.p.* **unrav'elling**; *pa.p.* **unrav'elled**.

unreadable *un-rēd'ȧ-bl*, *adj.* **1** illegible. **2** too boring to read.

unreal *un-rē'ȧl*, *adj.* not real.
unreal'ity *n*:—*pl.* **unreal'ities**.
unre'alised *adj.* not realised (in any sense of the verb).
unrealis'able *adj*.

unreasonable *un-rē'zȯn-ȧ-bl*, *adj.* **1** not guided by reason. **2** not moderate or sensible.
unrea'soning *adj.* not using reason.

unregenerate *un-ri-jen'ėr-it*, *adj.* **1** not having repented. **2** wicked.

unremitting *un-ri-mit'ing*, *adj.* never ceasing: *unremitting efforts*.

unrequited *un-ri-kwī'tid*, *adj.* **1** not paid (back). **2** not given in return: *unrequited love*.

unreserved *un-ri-zûrvd'*, *adj.* **1** not reserved. **2** complete: *unreserved approval*. **3** frank.
unreser'vedly *(-vid-li-) adv.* completely.

unrest *un-rest'*, *n.* **1** uneasiness. **2** rebellious feeling among a number of people: *political unrest*.

unrivalled *un-rī'vȧld*, *adj.* matchless.

unroll *un-rōl'*, *v.t.* to open out (something rolled).—Also *v.i.*

unruly *un-rōō'li*, *adj.* **1** not obeying the law or rules. **2** disorderly.
unru'liness *n*.

unsaddle *un-sad'l*, *v.t.* to take the saddle off:—*pr.p.* **unsadd'ling**.

unsaid *un-sed'*, *adj.* not said.

unsavoury *un-sā'vȯ-ri*, *adj.* **1** disgusting. **2** immoral.

unscathed *un-skā*THd*'*, *adj.* not harmed.

unscramble *un-skram'bl*, *v.t.* to decode (a message), or make clear the words of (a telephone message):—*pr.p.* **unscram'bling**.

unscrew *un-skrōō'*, *v.t.* to unfasten by loosening screws.

unscrupulous *un-skrōō'pū-lus*, *adj.* without scruples, unprincipled.

unseal *un-sēl'*, *v.t.* **1** to remove the seal of. **2** to open.

unseasonable *un-sē'z(ȯ)n-ȧ-bl*, *adj.* **1** (of weather) not suitable for the time of year.

For words in *un-* not found above, see **un-¹** or **un-²**, page 639.

2 not well timed: *the unseasonable arrival of guests.* **3** unsuitable: *at unseasonable hours.*

unseat *un-sēt'*, *v.t.* **1** to throw from a seat. **2** to remove from an official position.

unseen *un-sēn'*, *adj.* not seen.—*n.* an unfamiliar passage for translation.

unsettle *un-set'l*, *v.t.* to disturb, upset:—*pr.p.* **unsett'ling.**

unsett'led *adj.* **1** (of weather) changeable. **2** disturbed. **3** not decided. **4** (of e.g. a bill) unpaid.

unsheathe *un-shē*TH*'*, *v.t.* to draw from the sheath or scabbard:—*pr.p.* **unsheath'ing.**

unship *un-ship'*, *v.t.* to take out of a ship:—*pr.p.* **unshipp'ing**; *pa.p* **unshipped'**.

unsightly *un-sīt'li*, *adj.* ugly.

unskilled *un'skild'*, *adj.* **1** (of a worker) not trained for a particular job. **2** (of a job) not requiring special skill.

unsophisticated *un-sȯ-fis'ti-kā-tid*, *adj.* **1** simple. **2** not worldly-wise.

unsound *un-sownd'*, *adj.* **1** (of fruit, etc.) not in good condition. **2** (of reasoning, etc.) not correct. **3** (of mind) not sane.

unsparing *un-spār'ing*, *adj.* **1** giving freely. **2** never weakening: *unsparing efforts.* **3** merciless: *unsparing criticism.*

unspeakable *un-spē'kȧ-bl*, *adj.* too good or too bad to be put into words.

unstable *un-stā'bl*, *adj.* **1** not standing or fixed firmly. **2** having poor control over emotions or behaviour.

unstrung *un-strung'*, *adj.* **1** with strings removed or slackened. **2** having poor control over emotions or behaviour.

unstudied *un-stud'id*, *adj.* **1** not studied. **2** natural, easy.

unsuspected *un-sus-pek'tid*, *adj.* not imagined or known to exist.

unthinkable *un-thingk'ȧ-bl*, *adj.* **1** very unlikely indeed. **2** too bad to be thought of.

unthink'ing *adj.* showing lack of thought.

untidy *un-tī'di*, *adj.* not tidy, neat, etc.:—*comp.* **unti'dier**; *superl.* **unti'diest.**

unti'dily *adv.* **unti'diness** *n.*

untie *un-tī'*, *v.t.* to loosen, unfasten:—*pr.p.* **unty'ing**; *pa.p.* **untied'**.

until *un-til'*, *prep.*, *conj.* same as **till**[2].

untimely *un-tīm'li*, *adj.* **1** happening too soon. **2** not suitable to the occasion: *untimely mirth.*

untiring *un-tīr'ing*, *adj.* **1** not wearying. **2** (of e.g. effort) not slackening.

untold *un-tōld'*, *adj.* **1** not told. **2** too great to be counted, measured.

untoward *un-tō'ȧrd*, *un-tȯ-wörd'*, *adj.* unfortunate, inconvenient: *untoward circumstances.*

untried *un-trīd'*, *adj.* **1** not attempted. **2** not tested by experience.

untrodden *un-trod'n*, *adj.* seldom or never trodden: *untrodden paths.*

untroubled *un-trub'ld*, *adj.* **1** not anxious. **2** calm.

untrue *un-trōō'*, *adj.* **1** false. **2** disloyal.

untruth' *n.* **1** falseness. **2** a lie.

untwist *un-twist'*, *v.t.* to straighten out (something twisted).

untying. See **untie**.

unusual *un-ū'zhū-ȧl*, *adj.* **1** not usual. **2** rare, uncommon.

unū'sually *adv.*

unutterable *un-ut'ėr-ȧ-bl*, *adj.* **1** too great to be expressed. **2** very horrible.

unvarnished *un-vär'nisht*, *adj.* **1** not varnished. **2** plain, straightforward: *the unvarnished truth.*

unveil *un-vāl'*, *v.t.* **1** to remove a veil from. **2** to uncover ceremonially (e.g. a new statue).—*v.i.* to remove one's veil.

unwary *un-wā'ri*, *adj.* not cautious.

unwā'rily *adv.* **unwa'riness** *n.*

unwelcome *un-wel'kȯm*, *adj.* received unwillingly or with disappointment.

unwell *un-wel'*, *adj.* not in good health.

unwieldy *un-wēl'di*, *adj.* awkward to handle.

unwiel'diness *n.*

unwilling *un-wil'ing*, *adj.* not willing, reluctant.

unwind *un-wīnd'*, *v.t.*, *v.i.* to wind down or off:—*pa.p.* **unwound'**.

unwise *un-wiz'*, *adj.* not wise; foolish.

unwitting *un-wit'ing*, *adj.* **1** not aware. **2** unintentional.

unwonted *un-wōn'tid*, *adj.* unaccustomed, not usual.

unworthy *un-wûr'*TH*i*, *adj.* **1** not worthy. **2** base, discreditable. **3** not deserving: *unworthy of notice.* **4** less good than one would expect (of): *This drawing is unworthy of you*:—*comp.* **unwor'thier**; *superl.* **unwor'thiest.**

unwor'thily *adv.* **unwor'thiness** *n.*

unwound. See **unwind**.

unwrap *un-rap'*, *v.t.* to open (something wrapped or folded):—*pr.p.* **unwrapp'ing**; *pa.p.* **unwrapped'**.

unwritten *un-rit'n*, *adj.* **1** not written. **2** (of a rule, etc.) not recorded in writing.

up *up*, *adv.* **1** towards a higher place. **2** on high. **3** from a lower to a higher position. **4** towards a city, esp. London (with *to*).

For words in *un-* not found above, see **un-**[1] or **un-**[2], page 639.

5 at a college or university. **6** to, as far as, the place where one is, the stopping-place, etc.: *The bus came up*:—*superl.* **upp'ermost.**—*prep.* **1** to a higher level on (e.g. a hill). **2** towards the source of (a river). **3** into a stretch of: *to go up country.*—*adj.* **1** top: *the up side.* **2** going up. **3** risen. **4** (of time) ended. **5** wrong, amiss: *What's up?*:—*comp.* **upp'er**; *superls.* **upp'ermost, up'most.**

upp'er *comp. adj.* higher in position, dignity, etc.—*n.* the part of a boot or shoe above the sole and welt.

upp'er-class *adj.* of a high rank in society.

upp'ercut *n.* a swinging blow aimed upwards.—Also *v.t.* and *v.i.*

upp'ermost *adv.* and *adj.* See above.

the upper hand superiority, control.

ups and downs turns of good and bad fortune.

up to (*coll.*) **1** engaged in doing. **2** able and ready for. **3** the duty or responsibility of (a person): *It is up to me.*

up(-)to(-)date. See **date**[1].

up- *pfx.* has *adj.*, *adv.*, or *prep.* sense, as shown in examples below.

upbraid *up-brād'*, *v.t.* to reproach.

upbringing *up'bring-ing*, *n.* the rearing and training given to, received by, a child.

update *up-dāt'*, *v.t.* to bring up to date:—*pr.p.* **updāt'ing.** *n.* *(up')* **1** the act of updating. **2** new information: *We have an update on yesterday's report.*

up-grade *up'grād*, *n.* a rising slope.—*v.t.* (**upgrade'**) **1** to raise to a position of greater importance in e.g. a business. **2** to improve the quality of:—*pr.p.* **up-grād'ing.**

upheaval *up-hē'vȧl*, *n.* **1** a violent shaking. **2** a great disturbance.

upheld. See **uphold.**

uphill *up'hil'*, *adj.* **1** rising. **2** difficult.—*adv.* upwards.

uphold *up-hōld'*, *v.t.* **1** to support (a person or something he does). **2** to maintain (e.g. a view, tradition):—*pr.p.* **uphold'ing**; *pa.p.* **upheld'.**

upholster *up-hōl'stėr*, *v.t.* to fit (seats) with springs, stuffing, covers, etc.

uphōl'sterer *n.* one who makes, repairs or sells, upholstered furniture.

uphōl'stery *n.* covers, cushions, etc.

upkeep *up'kēp*, *n.* keeping a house, car, etc. in repair, or cost of this.

upland *up'lȧnd*, *n.* high ground.—Also *adj.*

uplift *up-lift'*, *v.t.* **1** to lift up, raise. **2** to improve morally, etc. **3** to raise the spirits of.—*n.* *(up'lift)* (something that gives) strong mental or moral encouragement.

upmost. See **up.**

upon *ů-pon'*, *prep.* on the top of.

upper, uppermost. See **up.**

upright *up'rīt*, *adj.* **1** standing straight up. **2** just and honest.—*n.* a vertical post.

up'rightly *adv.* **up'rightness** *n.*

uprising *up-rīz'ing*, *n.* **1** act of rising against government, etc. **2** a revolt.

uproar *up'rōr, -rör*, *n.* **1** noise and shouting. **2** a noisy disturbance.

uproar'ious *adj.* very noisy.

uproar'iously *adv.* **uproar'iousness** *n.*

uproot *up-rōōt'*, *v.t.* to tear up by the roots.

upset *up-set'*, *v.t.* **1** to turn upside-down. **2** to overturn. **3** to put out of order. **4** to distress:—*pr.p.* **upsett'ing**; *pa.t.* and *pa.p.* **upset'.**—*adj.* **1** worried, anxious. **2** ill.—*n.* *(up')* distress or its cause.

up'set price the price at which the bidding starts at an auction sale.

upshot *up'shot*, *n.* **1** (*orig.*, at archery) the last shot. **2** the result or end of a matter.

upside-down *up'sīd-down'*, *adv.* **1** with the top part underneath. **2** in confusion.

upstage *up'stāj'*, *adv.* away from the footlights.—*v.t.* *(-stāj')* (*coll.*) to divert interest, attention from (person or thing) to oneself:—*pr.p.* **upstag'ing.**

upstairs *up'stārz'*, *adv.* in or to an upper storey.—Also *n.* and *adj.*

upstanding *up-stan'ding*, *adj.* **1** standing up. **2** robust. **3** worthy, honest.

upstart *up'stärt*, *n.* one who has risen quickly to wealth or power, but seems to lack dignity or ability.

upstream *up'strēm'*, *adv.* towards the upper part of a stream.

up-to-date. See **date**[1].

upward *up'wȧrd*, *adj.* **1** going up. **2** directed up: *an upward glance.*

up'ward, up'wards *advs.*

uranium *ū-rā'ni-ům*, *n.* an element, a radioactive metal.

Uranus *ū-rā'nůs*, *n.* **1** in Greek myth, the personification of the heavens. **2** a large planet, seventh in order from the sun.

urban *ûr'bȧn*, *adj.* of, consisting of, or living in, city or town.

urbane *ûr-bān'*, *adj.* smoothly polite.

urban'ity *(-ban')* *n.* highly civilised politeness: (in *pl.*, **-ies**) polite actions.

urchin *ûr'chin*, *n.* **1** orig., a hedgehog. **2** a small child. **3** a dirty or ragged child.

Urdu *ōō r'dōō*, *n.* form of Hindustani with many Persian and Arabic words, the official language of Pakistan.

urge *ûrj*, *v.t.* **1** to drive (on). **2** to try to persuade:—*pr.p.* **ur'ging.**—*n.* a strong

impulse.
ur'gency *n.*
ur'gent *adj.* **1** requiring immediate attention. **2** eagerly pressing for action.

urine *ū'rin*, *n.* the fluid passed out of the body of human beings and animals.
u'rinate *(-āt) v.i.* to discharge urine:—*pr.p.* **u'rinating**.

urn *ûrn*, *n.* **1** a vessel used for keeping the ashes of the dead. **2** a large metal can, with tap, for making tea, etc.

us. See **we**.

usage. See **use**[1].

use[1] *ūz*, *v.t.* **1** to employ as an instrument: *to use a fork.* **2** to bring into action: *to use common sense.* **3** (often with *up*) to spend, consume, all of. **4** to treat: *to use him well*:—*pr.p.* **us'ing**.—Also *v.i.*; now only in *pa.t.* **used** *ūst*: *I used to go often.*—*n.* *(ūs)*; see **use**[2].
us'able *adj.*
usage *ū'zij*, *n.* **1** act or manner of using. **2** custom, habit. **3** treatment: *rough usage.*
used *ūzd*, *adj.* **1** employed, put to a purpose. **2** not new. **3** accustomed through experience: *used to hardship.*
user *n.*
user-friendly *adj.* easily understood, easy to use.
See also **use**[2], **usual**, **utility**.

use[2] *ūs*, *n.* **1** act of using or putting to a purpose. **2** suitability for a purpose: *of no practical use.* **3** practice, custom.—*v.t.* *(ūz)*; see **use**[1].
use'ful *adj.* **1** helpful. **2** serving a practical purpose.
use'fully *adv.* **use'fulness** *n.*
use'less *adj.* having no use or effect.
have no use for 1 to have no need for. **2** to disapprove of (e.g. a person).
make use of 1 to employ. **2** to treat (a person) as a means to one's own gain.
(of) no use useless.
use and wont customary practice.
See also **disuse**.

used. See **use**[1] (*pa.t.* of *v.i.*; also *adj.*).

usher *ush'ėr*, *n.* one who shows people to their seats in a theatre, etc.:—*fem.* **usherette'**.—*v.t.* to lead (in, into, to).

usual *ū'zhū-ȧl*, *adj.* **1** done, happening, etc., most often: *the usual routine*; *This result is usual.* **2** customary, habitual: *his usual carelessness.*
u'sually *adv.* on most occasions.

usurer. See **usury**.

usurp *ū-zûrp'*, *v.t.* to seize (power or rights belonging to another).
usurpā'tion *n.* **usur'per** *n.*

usury *ū'zhů-ri*, *n.* taking of interest on money, esp. if rate of interest is high.
u'surer *n.* a grasping moneylender.

utensil *ū-ten'sil*, *n.* an instrument or vessel used in everyday life.

uterus *ū'tėr-ůs*, *n.* the womb.
ū'terine *(-īn) adj.*

utilise *ū'ti-līz*, *v.t.* to make use of (something available, at hand):—*pr.p.* **u'tilising**.
utilisā'tion *n.*

utility *ū'til'i-ti*, *n.* **1** usefulness. **2** a useful service:—*pl.* **util'ities**.
utilitā'rian *adj.* useful (often in contrast to ornamental).

utmost *ut'mōst*, or *-mȯst*, *adj.* **1** most distant. **2** greatest possible: *Take the utmost care.*
to do one's utmost to make the greatest possible effort.
See also **utter**[1].

Utopian *ū-tō'pi-ȧn*, *adj.* ideally perfect.—*n.* one who tries to plan a perfect society.

utter[1] *ut'ėr*, *adj.* extreme, complete.
utt'erly *adv.* completely.
utt'ermost *adj.* utmost.

utter[2] *ut'ėr*, *v.t.* **1** to give out (words, cries, etc.). **2** to make public (a libel). **3** to put into circulation (e.g. counterfeit money).
utt'erance *n.* **1** way of speaking. **2** something said.

uttermost. See **utter**[1].

U-turn *ū'tûrn*, *n.* **1** a turn making the shape of the letter U. **2** a reversal of direction.

uvula *ū'-vū-lȧ*, *n.* the small piece of flesh which hangs down the back of the throat.

uxorious *uk-sōr'i-ůs*, *-sör'*, *adj.* excessively fond of one's wife.

V

vacant *vā'kȧnt, adj.* **1** empty. **2** unoccupied. **3** showing no intelligence or no interest: *a vacant stare*.
vā'cancy *n.* **1** emptiness. **2** empty space. **3** an unoccupied post: *a vacancy for a typist*:—*pl.* **vā'cancies**.
vacate *vȧ-kāt', v.t.* to leave empty, cease to occupy or own:—*pr.p.* **vacāt'ing**.
vacā'tion *n.* a holiday.

vaccinate *vak'si-nāt, v.t.* to protect against smallpox or other diseases by inoculation:—*pr.p.* **vac'cinating**.
vaccinā'tion *n.*
vaccine *vak'sēn, n.* **1** a preparation containing the virus (see this word) of cowpox. **2** disease germ prepared for inoculation (see this word).

vacillate *vas'i-lāt, v.i.* **1** to sway to and fro. **2** to waver, show indecision:—*pr.p.* **vac'illating**.
vacillā'tion *n.*

vacuous *vak'ū-ủs, adj.* empty, silly, stupid.
vacū'ity *n.* **1** emptiness. **2** emptiness of mind.
vac'uousness *n.*
vac'ūum *(-ū-ủm) n.* **1** a space empty of all matter. **2** (in practice) a space from which almost all air or other gas has been removed. **3** a vacuum-cleaner:—*pl.* **vac'ua** or **vac'uums** (*defs. 1, 2*), **vac'uums** (*def. 3*).—*v.t.* to use a vacuum-cleaner (on).
vac'ūum-brake *n.* a brake system which works quickly and strongly by withdrawal of air from brake cylinders.
vac'ūum-cleaner *n.* an apparatus for removing dust by suction.
vac'ūum-flask *n.* a vessel with double walls, which have a vacuum between them, to keep the contents from losing or gaining heat.
vac'ūum-packed *adj.* packed in a container from which most of the air has been removed.

vagabond *vag'ȧ-bond, adj.* **1** wandering. **2** having no settled home.—*n.* **1** one who has no settled home. **2** a rascal: *rogues and vagabonds*.

vagary *vāg'ȧ-ri, vȧ-gā'ri, n.* **1** a queer fancy. **2** odd or unexpected behaviour (often in *pl.* **vagaries**.)

vagina *vȧ-jīn'ȧ, n.* (in the female of humans and other mammals) the passage connecting the genital area to the womb.
vagī'nal *adj.*

vagrant *vā'grȧnt, adj.* unsettled, wandering: *a vagrant life*.—*n.* **1** one who has no fixed home. **2** a tramp.
vā'grancy *n.* the state of being a tramp.

vague *vāg, adj.* **1** not definite: *a vague statement*. **2** indistinct. **3** not clear or forceful in thinking or character
vāgue'ly *adv.* **vāgue'ness** *n.*

vain *vān, adj.* **1** unavailing, unsuccessful: *vain efforts, a vain attempt*. **2** empty, worthless: *vain threats, boasts, promises*. **3** conceited.
vain'ly *adv.* **vain'ness** *n.*
van'ity *(van') n.* **1** empty pride. **2** worthlessness. **3** something worthless, as empty pleasure:—*pl.* **van'ities**.
in vain with no success: *He tried in vain*.
take someone's name in vain to use someone's (*esp.* God's) name in an insulting or blasphemous way.

vainglory *vān-glō'ri, -glö', n.* boastful pride.
vainglō'rious *adj.*

valance *val'ȧns, n.* hanging drapery for a bed, etc.

vale *vāl, n.* a tract of low ground, esp. between hills, a valley.

valediction *val-i-dik'sh(ȯ)n, n.* a farewell.
valedic'tory *adj.* saying farewell.

valency *vā'lėn-si, n.* (*chemistry*) the combining power of an atom or group: *In water, H_2O, oxygen shows valency two*:—*pl.* **vā'lencies**.

valentine *val'ėn-tīn, n.* a sweetheart chosen, or a love-letter, etc., sent, on *St Valentine's Day*, 14th February.

valet *val'it,* or *val'ā, n.* a manservant, one who looks after his master's clothes, etc.—*v.t.* and *v.i.* to serve as a valet:—*pr.p.* **val'eting**; *pa.t.* **val'eted**.

valetudinarian *val-i-tū-di-nā'ri-ȧn, n.* and *adj.* **1** (a person) in poor health. **2** (one) too much concerned about his health.

valiant *val'yȧnt, adj.* **1** (of a deed, etc.) brave, heroic. **2** bold in danger.
val'iancy, val'iantness *ns.*

valid *val'id, adj.* **1** sound, reasonable, acceptable: *That is not a valid excuse, objection, proof.* **2** legally in force: *He has a valid passport*.
valid'ity, val'idness *ns.*

valley *val'i, n.* **1** low land between hills or mountains. **2** a region drained by a river and its tributaries:—*pl.* **vall'eys**.

valour *val'ȯr, n.* **1** courage, stoutness of heart. **2** bravery in battle.
val'orous *adj.* **val'orously** *adv.*

value *val'ū, n.* **1** worth. **2** importance. **3** usefulness. **4** price. **5** purchasing power (e.g. of a coin). **6** a fair return: *value for one's money.* **7** length of a musical note: *The value of a quaver is an eighth of the value of a semibreve.* **8** a particular number, quantity, put as equal to an expression in algebra: *In this case the value of y is 9.* **9** (in *pl.*) moral principles, standards, etc.—*v.t.* **1** to put a price on. **2** to prize, regard as good or important:—*pr.p.* **val'uing**; *pa.p.* **val'ued**.
val'uable *adj.* having considerable value.—*n.* (often in *pl.*) thing(s) of special value.
valuā'tion *n.* **1** act of valuing. **2** estimated price.
val'uator, **val'uer** *ns.* one who has been trained to estimate the value of property.
value-added tax (*abbrev.* **VAT**) a tax calculated on the basis of the increase in value of a product at each stage of its manufacture or marketing, or charged on certain services, etc.
value judgement an assessment of worth based on personal opinion.

valve *valv, n.* **1** a device for allowing a liquid or gas to pass through an opening in one direction only (e.g. the valve of a bicycle tyre). **2** a structure with the same effect in an animal body (e.g. controlling flow of blood). **3** a part of a wireless or television set. **4** one of the separate parts of the shell of animal such as oyster. **5** a device for varying the length of the tube, and therefore the pitch, in a brass musical instrument.
valvular *val'vū-lȧr, adj.* of valve(s).

vamp[1] *vamp, n.* **1** front part of upper of boot or shoe. **2** a patch. **3** a simple musical accompaniment.—*v.t., v.i.* **1** to patch. **2** to play (a simple type of accompaniment.)

vamp[2] *vamp, n.* (*disrespectfully*) a woman who seduces and exploits men.—*v.t.* to act (towards) like such a woman.

vampire *vam'pīr, n.* **1** a dead person imagined to rise by night and suck the blood of sleeping people. **2** one who extorts money from others.
vampire bat a blood-sucking bat.

van[1] *van, n.* **1** the front (formerly of an army or fleet). **2** the leaders in any movement.

van[2] *van, n.* a covered vehicle for carrying goods on road or rail.

vanadium *vȧn-ā'di-ủm, n.* an element, a hard silvery metal, used in strengthening steel.

vandal *van'dȧl, n.* **1** a person who carelessly spoils natural beauty. **2** one who damages a public building or other property.
van'dalise *v.t.* to damage public property intentionally:—*pr.p.* **van'dalising**.
van'dalism *n.* behaviour of a vandal.

vane *vān, n.* **1** a weathercock. **2** one of the blades of a windmill or propeller, etc.

vanguard *van'gärd, n.* **1** the part of an army going in front of the main body. **2** the front line. **3** leaders in any movement.

vanilla *vȧ-nil'ȧ, n.* a flavouring obtained from a tropical orchid.

vanish *van'ish, v.i.* **1** to go out of sight. **2** to fade away to nothing.

vanity. See **vain**.

vanquish *vangk'wish, v.t.* to defeat.

vantage ground, **point** *vän'tij grownd, point,* a position favourable for success in a contest, or from which one has a clear view.

vapid *vap'id, adj.* (of wine, talk, etc.) flat, uninteresting.

vapour *vā'pȯr, n.* **1** the gaseous (gas-like) state of a substance that is normally liquid or solid: *water vapour, mercury vapour.* **2** mist or smoke in the air.
vā'porise *(-īz) v.t.* and *v.i.* to (cause to) change into vapour:—*pr.p.* **vā'porising**.
vā'porīser *n.* an apparatus for sending liquid out in a fine spray.
vāporous *adj.*

variable, **variation**, etc. See **vary**.

varicose *var'i-kōs, adj.* permanently enlarged, as in **varicose veins**, a condition in which veins, usu. of the leg, are swollen.

variegate *vā'ri-ė-gāt, v.t.* **1** to mark with different colours. **2** to give variety to:—*pr.p.* **va'riegating**.
variegā'tion *n.*

variety *vȧ-rī'ė-ti, n.* **1** the quality of being of many kinds, or of being varied. **2** a mixed collection: *a variety of toys for sale, of excuses.* **3** sort, kind. **4** mixed theatrical entertainment including dances, songs, short sketches, etc.:—*pl.* **vari'eties**.
various *vā'ri-ủs, adj.* **1** varied, different, unlike each other. **2** several: *Various people have said it.*
vā'riously *adv.*
variety show a programme of variety.
variety theatre one which presents variety shows.
See also **variegate**, **vary**.

varlet *vär'lit, n.* a rascal, low fellow.

varnish *vär'nish, n.* a sticky liquid which gives a glossy surface to wood, paper, etc.—*v.t.* **1** to cover with varnish. **2** to give a falsely good appearance to.

varsity *vär'si-ti*, *n.* short for 'university':—*pl.* **var'sities**.

vary *vā'ri*, *v.t.* **1** to make different. **2** to free from sameness or monotony.—*v.i.* **1** to be, or become, different. **2** to differ (from):—*pr.p.* **va'rying**; *pa.p.* **va'ried**.

va'riable *adj.* **1** that may be varied. **2** changeable:—*opp.* **invariable**.—*n.* something that varies, e.g. in value.

variabil'ity, **va'riableness** *ns.*

va'riance *n.* **1** a change of condition. **2** a difference. **3** state of disagreement.

va'riant *n.* a different form or version.—Also *adj.*

variā'tion *n.* **1** the act, or process, of varying. **2** an instance of this. **3** extent to which a thing changes: *Farther from the sea the variation in temperature is greater.* **4** one of a series of musical changes made on a basic theme or melody. **5** (*ballet*) a solo dance.

at variance in disagreement: *The two men, their views, were at variance*; *A was at variance with B about the plan.*

vascular *vas'kū-lȧr*, *adj.* relating to the blood vessels of animals or the sap-conducting tissues of plants.

vase *väz*, or *vāz*, *n.* a jar, used in ancient days for domestic purposes and in sacrifices, but now mainly as an ornament or for holding cut flowers.

vasectomy *vȧs-ek'tȯ-mi*, *n.* male sterilisation by cutting of the sperm-carrying tubes:—*pl.* **vasec'tomies**.

Vaseline® *vas'ė-lēn*, *n.* an ointment made from petroleum.

vassal *vas'ȧl*, *n.* **1** under the feudal system, one who held land from, and paid homage to, a superior. **2** a dependant, retainer.

vast *väst*, *adj.* of very great size or amount.

vast'ly *adv.* **vast'ness** *n.*

vat *vat*, *n.* a large vessel or tank, esp. one for holding liquors.

VAT. See **value-added tax**.

Vatican *vat'i-kȧn*, *n.* **1** the palace of the Pope, standing on the Vatican Hill in Rome, in independent territory (**the Vatican City**). **2** the government or authority of the Pope.

vaudeville *vō'dė-vil*, *n.* an entertainment with songs and dances, usu. comic.

vault[1] *völt*, *n.* **1** an arched roof. **2** an underground room, a cellar.—*v.t.* to cover with an arched roof.

vaul'ted *adj.* having an arched roof.

vaul'ting *n.* arched ceiling(s), etc.

vault[2], *völt*, *n.* a leap aided by the hands or by a pole.—*v.t.* to leap, leap (over).

vaunt *vönt*, *v.i.* to boast, brag.—*v.t.* to boast about (e.g. one's success).

VDU. See **visual display unit**.

veal *vēl*, *n.* the flesh of a calf.

vector *vek'tȯr*, *n.* a straight line drawn from a given point to represent both the direction and the size of a quantity such as a velocity or a force.

veer *vēr*, *v.i.* **1** (of the wind) to change direction. **2** to change course. **3** to change in mood or outlook: *to veer away from opinions formerly held.*

vegan *vē'gȧn*, *n.* a vegetarian who uses no animal produce at all.—Also *adj.*

vegetable *vej'i-tȧ-bl*, *n.* **1** a plant. **2** a plant grown for food. **3** a person who exists but has little or no mental or physical capabilities.—*adj.* **1** belonging to plants. **2** obtained from, or consisting of, plants: *vegetable dyes, oils*; *a vegetable diet.*

vegetār'ian *adj.* consisting of vegetables: *a vegetarian diet.*—*n.* a person who believes it right to eat no flesh, but vegetable food only.

vegetār'ianism, *n.*

veg'etāte *v.i.* **1** to grow by roots and leaves. **2** to live an idle, aimless life:—*pr.p.* **veg'etating**.

vegetā'tion *n.* **1** plants in general. **2** the plants of a particular region: *the dense vegetation of a jungle.*

vegetable marrow the fruit of a kind of gourd.

the vegetable kingdom all the plants of the world.

vehement *vē'(h)i-mėnt*, *adj.* very eager, violent, passionate: *a vehement person*; *vehement arguments, denials.*

vē'hemence *n.* **vē'hemently** *adv.*

vehicle *vē'i-kl*, *n.* **1** any means of transport on wheels or runners. **2** a means of conveying information, etc.: *The daily papers, TV, and radio are vehicles for the spread of news.* **3** a substance not itself active used in making up medicine or paints.

vehicular *(vė-hik'ū-lȧr) adj.*

veil *vāl*, *n.* **1** anything that hides an object. **2** a piece of cloth or netting worn to shade or hide the face. **3** a nun's headdress (hence **take the veil**, to become a nun). **4** a deceptive appearance, or something (e.g. mystery, silence) that hides facts.—*v.t.* **1** to cover with a veil. **2** to hide.

vein *vān*, *n.* **1** one of the tubes that carry the blood back to the heart. **2** a small rib in a leaf. **3** a thin seam of mineral: *a vein of gold in quartz.* **4** a streak of different colour. **5** a strain in character: *He has a vein of stubbornness.* **6** manner, style: *in a humorous vein.*

vein'ing *n.* **1** the arrangement of veins in a leaf. **2** vein-like markings.

venous *vē'nus, adj.* **1** of vein(s). **2** flowing in veins: *venous blood.*

Velcro® *vel'kro, n.* a type of fastener for clothing, etc. made of two strips of specially treated fabric.

veld(t) *felt, velt, n.* (South Africa) unforested, or thinly forested, grass country.

vellum *vel'um, n.* a fine parchment made from the skin of calves, kids, or lambs, or an imitation of this.

velocity *vė-los'i-ti, n.* **1** rate of movement: *wind velocity.* **2** speed in a stated direction (e.g. that of a body falling vertically). **3** swiftness:—*pl.* **veloc'ities.**

velour(s) *vė-lōōr', n.* **1** a velvet-like material. **2** a hat made of such material.

velvet *vel'vit, n.* a cloth made from silk, etc., with a soft, thick surface.—*adj.* **1** made of velvet. **2** soft like velvet.

velveteen' *n.* a material resembling, but cheaper than, velvet.

venal *vē'nàl, adj.* **1** able to be bought (used of one who can be bribed). **2** disreputable and done for a bribe: *a venal act.*

vend *vend, v.t.* to sell.

ven'dor *n.* one who sells (e.g. *a street vendor,* one who sells in the streets).—Also **ven'der.**

vending machine a slot-machine.

vendetta *ven-det'à, n.* **1** a feud started by a murder. **2** a quarrel long pursued.

vendor. See **vend.**

veneer *vi-nēr', v.t.* **1** to cover wood with a thin piece of wood of finer quality. **2** to give a good appearance to what is really not good.—*n.* **1** a thin coating, as of wood. **2** false show: *a veneer of good manners hiding brutality.*

venerable *ven'ėr-à-bl, adj.* worthy of great respect because of age, or for special goodness.

ven'erāte *v.t.* **1** to honour greatly. **2** to regard with religious awe:—*pr.p.* **ven'erating.**

venerā'tion *n.* **1** the act of venerating. **2** reverence, great respect: *His pupils regarded him with veneration.*

venereal disease *vi-nē'ri-àl diz-ēz',* (*abbrev.* **VD**) any of various contagious diseases transmitted by sexual intercourse.

Venetian *vė-nē'sh(à)n, adj.* of or belonging to *Venice.*

Venetian blind a window blind made of thin movable strips of wood, metal, or plastic.

vengeance *ven'jàns, n.* punishment for an injury carried out by the sufferer or his friends.

venge'ful *adj.* eager for vengeance.

with a vengeance in a very great or unexpected degree: *This was generosity with a vengeance.*

venial *vē'ni-àl, adj.* pardonable: *a venial fault, not a deadly sin.*

venison *ven'zn, ven'i-zn, ven'i-sn, n.* flesh of deer.

venom *ven'òm, n.* **1** poison. **2** spite, malice.

ven'omous *adj.* **1** poisonous. **2** full of malice.

ven'omously *adv.* **ven'omousness** *n.*

venous. See **vein.**

vent[1] *vent, n.* **1** a small opening. **2** a hole to allow air, smoke, etc. to pass out. **3** outlet, expression: *He gave vent to his rage.*—*v.t.* **1** to let out (e.g. smoke). **2** to give outlet or expression to: *He vented his rage in a sneer, on his son.*

ventilate *ven'ti-lāt, v.t.* **1** to allow fresh air to enter (e.g. a room). **2** to expose (a subject) to discussion. **3** to give utterance to: *to ventilate one's grievances.*

ventilā'tion *n.*

ven'tilātor *n.* a device for bringing in fresh air.

vent[2] *vent, n.* a slit in the back of a coat.

ventilate, etc. See **vent**[1].

ventral *ven'tràl, adj.* belonging to the belly.—*n.* a fin on the lower side of a fish's body.

ven'tricle *n.* a small cavity, esp. in the brain or heart.

ventriloquist *ven-tril'ò-kwist, n.* one who can speak so that his voice seems to come from some other person or place.

ventril'oquism *n.*

venture *ven'chur, n.* an undertaking, scheme that involves some risk.—*v.t.* to do or say (something when one is not sure what the effect will be): *I ventured a remark,* or *to remark:*—*pr.p.* **ven'turing.**

ven'turous, ven'turesome *adjs.* daring.

at a venture at random.

venue *ven'ū, n.* the scene of an action or event.

Venus *vē'nus, n.* **1** Roman goddess of beauty and love. **2** a beautiful woman. **3** brightest of the planets.

veracious *vė-rā'shus, adj.* **1** truthful (esp. habitually). **2** true.

verā'ciously *adv.*

veracity *(-ras'i-ti),* **vera'ciousness** *ns.*

veranda(h) *vė-ran'dà, n.* a kind of covered balcony, with a roof sloping beyond the main building, supported by light pillars.

verb *vûrb, n.* a word used to state what a person or thing does, experiences, etc. (e.g.

He *ran*; I *have* a feeling; What *is* this?)

ver'bal *adj.* **1** connected with verbs: *verbal endings, such as '-fy', '-ise'.* **2** having to do with words: *to make verbal changes in a document.* **3** spoken, not written: *a verbal message.*

ver'bally *adv.* in or by speech.

verbā'tim *adj.* and *adv.* word for word.

ver'biage *n.* use of many unnecessary words, or an instance of this.

verbose' *(-bōs') adj.* (of a person or a statement, etc.) using too many words.

verbos'ity *(-bos') n.* **1** wordiness. **2** love of talking.

verdant *vûr'dȧnt, adj.* green with grass and/or leaves.

ver'dūre *n.* green vegetation.

verdict *vûr'dikt, n.* **1** the finding or decision of a jury at the end of a trial. **2** decision, opinion given.

verdigris *vûr'di-grēs, n.* the greenish rust of copper, brass, or bronze.

verdure. See **verdant**.

verge *vûrj, n.* **1** the brink, extreme edge. **2** the grass edging of a garden bed or border.

ver'ger *n.* **1** an official in church who shows people to seats, etc. **2** an official who carries a symbol of office, e.g. a staff, before a bishop, etc.

on the verge of on the point of.

verify *ver'i-fī, v.t.* to confirm the truth or correctness of (something) by considering evidence, looking up facts, etc.:—*pr.p.* **ver'ifying**; *pa.p.* **ver'ified**.

ver'ifīable *adj.* able to be verified.

verificā'tion *(-if-i-) n.*

verily *ver'i-li, adv.* truly, certainly.

verisimilitude *ver-i-sim-il'i-tūd, n.* **1** appearance of truth. **2** likeness to life.

ver'itable *adj.* genuine, real: *a veritable triumph.*

ver'itably *adv.*

verity *ver'i-ti, n.* truth:—*pl.* **ver'ities**.

vermicelli *vûr-mi-sel'i,* or *-chel'i, n.* stiff paste of hard wheat-flour made into small worm-like rolls—smaller than spaghetti.

vermicide, vermiform. See **vermin**.

vermilion *vėr-mil'yȯn, n.* a bright red paint.—*adj.* of a beautiful red colour.

vermin *vûr'min, n.* **1** pests, such as fleas, rats, worms, etc. **2** persons considered worthless and hateful.

ver'minous *adj.* full of vermin: *verminous clothing.*

vermicide *vûr'mi-sīd, n.* a killer of worms, esp. in the intestines.

ver'miform *adj.* having the shape of a worm.

vermouth *vûr'mȯth, -mōōth, -mōōt', n.* a drink containing white wine flavoured with wormwood.

vernacular *vėr-nak'ū-lȧr, n.* **1** the native speech of a country. **2** the native dialect of a region. **3** spoken language as opposed to literary.—Also *adj.*

vernal *vûr'nȧl, adj.* **1** belonging to spring. **2** appearing or occurring in spring.

vernier *vûr'ni-ėr, n.* a scale for measuring parts of the divisions of a larger scale.

verruca *vė-rōō'kȧ, n.* a wart.

versatile *vûr'sȧ-tīl,* or *-til, adj.* **1** able to turn easily and successfully from one task or pursuit to another. **2** capable of being used for many purposes.

versatil'ity *(-til') n.*

verse *vûrs, n.* **1** a line of poetry. **2** also a stanza of several lines. **3** a short section in a chapter of the Bible. **4** poetry as distinct from prose.

ver'sify *v.i.* to make verses.—*v.t.* to turn into verse:—*pr.p.* **ver'sifying**; *pa.p.* **ver'sified**.

versificā'tion *n.* **1** the writing of verses. **2** the scheme of feet and lines followed in a poem.

ver'sion *n.* **1** a translation, as in the 1611 *Authorised Version* of the Bible. **2** an account from one point of view: *The boy gave his version of what had occurred.*

versed *vûrst, adj.* thoroughly acquainted, skilled: *versed in the affairs of the village; versed in carpentry.*

versus *vûr'sus, prep.* against; shortened to **v.** or **vs.**

vertebra *vûr'tė-brȧ, n.* a bone of the spine:—*pl.* **vertebrae** *(vûr'tė-brē).*

ver'tebrate *n.* an animal having a backbone.—Also *adj.*:—*opp.* **invertebrate**.

vertex *vûr'teks, n.* **1** the top or summit. **2** the point of a cone, pyramid, or angle: —*pl.* **vertices** *(vûr'ti-sēz).*

ver'tical *adj.* **1** standing upright. **2** straight up and down.

ver'tically *adv.*

vertigo *vûr'ti-gō, vėr-tī'gō, n.* giddiness.

vertig'inous *(-tij') adj.* causing giddiness (used of e.g. height, a high place).

verve *vûrv, n.* lively spirit: *The musical performance lacked verve.*

very *ver'i, adv.* to a great degree.—*adj.* exact: *the very person I want to see.*
See also **verity**.

Very light *vē'ri, ver'i līt,* a flare for signalling, fired from a pistol.

vesicle *ves'i-kl, n.* **1** a small bladder-like cavity in the body. **2** a blister.

vesper *ves'pėr*, *n.* **1** (*cap.*) the evening star. **2** (in *pl.*) evening service.

vessel *ves'ėl*, *n.* **1** a container, usu. for liquid. **2** a ship. **3** a tube (as in *blood-vessel*).

vest *vest*, *n.* **1** a waistcoat. **2** an undergarment worn next to the skin.—*v.t.* to grant (authority, power) to: *They vested all power in him*; *They vested him with all power*.

vested interests, **rights 1** rights held by certain bodies or groups of people, often for a long time, and difficult to take away. **2** the people enjoying such rights and benefits.

vestibule *ves'ti-būl*, *n.* an entrance hall.

vestige *ves'tij*, *n.* **1** a footprint. **2** a trace.

vestig'ial *adj.* surviving only as a trace.

vestment *vest'mėnt*, *n.* **1** a garment. **2** (in *pl.*) articles of dress worn by the clergy during divine service.

vestry *ves'tri*, *n.* **1** a room in or near a church where vestments are kept. **2** a number of persons, in an English parish, appointed to share in the management of church affairs:—*pl.* **vest'ries**.

ves'tryman *n.* a member of a vestry.

vesture *ves'chůr*, *n.* **1** clothing. **2** a covering.

vet. See **veterinary**.

vetch *vech*, *n.* a plant of the pea kind.

veteran *vet'ė-rȧn*, *adj.* old, experienced.—*n.* **1** one who has given long service. **2** an old soldier. **3** (*U.S.*) anyone who has served in the armed forces.

veterinarian. See **veterinary**.

veterinary *vet'ė-ri-nȧ-ri*, *adj.* having to do with the curing of diseases in animals.

vet *v.t.* to check and pass as correct (e.g. *to vet a report*):—*pr.p.* **vett'ing**; *pa.p.* **vett'ed**.

vet'erinary surgeon a doctor for animals—often shortened to **vet**. Also **veterinā'rian**.

veto *vē'tō*, *n.* **1** the power or right to forbid. **2** an act of forbidding:—*pl.* **ve'toes**.—*v.t.* **1** to forbid. **2** refuse to consent to:—*pr.p.* **vē'toing**; *pa.p.* **vē'toed** *(-tōd)*.

vex *veks*, *v.i.* **1** to annoy. **2** to grieve.

vexā'tion *n.* **1** state of being vexed. **2** a cause of annoyance or trouble.

vexā'tious *(-shůs) adj.* causing annoyance; troublesome.

via *vī'ȧ* or *vē'ȧ*, *prep.* by way of: *to Exeter via London*.

viable *vī'ȧbl*, *adj.* **1** capable of living and developing. **2** (of e.g. a scheme) workable.

viaduct *vī'ȧ-dukt*, *n.* a long bridge carrying a road or railway.

vial *vī'ȧl*, *n.* a small bottle.

vibes. Short for **vibrations**.

vibrate *vī'brāt*, *-brāt'*, *v.i.* **1** to shake, tremble. **2** to swing to and fro.—*v.t.* to cause to shake:—*pr.p.* **vībrāting**.

vī'brant *adj.* **1** thrilling. **2** full of energy.

vībrā'tion *n.* a rapid to-and-fro motion, as of a plucked string. **2** (in *pl.*; *coll.*) feelings communicated to or aroused in a person (often shortened to **vibes**).

vī'bratory *adj.* having to do with vibration.

vicar *vik'ȧr*, *n.* **1** one who holds authority as delegate or substitute for another. **2** a clergyman of the Church of England.

vic'arage *n.* the house of a vicar.

vicā'rious (*vī*, or *vi-*) *adj.* **1** filling the place of another person. **2** endured on another person's behalf, in his place: *vicarious suffering*, *punishment*. **3** experienced through another person: *vicarious pleasure*.

vice[1], **vise** *vīs*, *n.* an instrument for holding an object firmly, usu. between two metal jaws.

vice[2] *vīs*, *n.* **1** a serious moral fault. **2** a bad habit.

vicious *vish'ůs*, *adj.* **1** having bad faults. **2** evil. **3** full of malice: *vicious comments*. **4** of a horse, etc., fierce.

vic'iously *adv.* **vic'iousness** *n.*

vicious circle a series, e.g. of causes and results, in which the last leads back to the first again (for instance, worry makes a person feel tired and tiredness makes him worry more.)

vice[3] *vī'si*, *prep.* in place of.

vice versa *vī'si vûr'sȧ*, the other way round: *John will take Jim's place, and vice versa*, i.e. and Jim will take John's; *I needed his help, and vice versa*, i.e. and he needed mine.

vice- *vīs-*, *pfx.* indicating a person second in rank of importance, who acts, when necessary, in place of his chief, as **vice-president**, etc.

vicinity *vi-sin'i-ti*, *n.* **1** neighbourhood. **2** nearness:—*pl.* **vicin'ities**.

vicious. See **vice**[2].

vicissitude *vi-sis'i-tūd*, *n.* **1** change from one state to another. **2** (in *pl.*) changes of fortune, ups and downs.

victim *vik'tim*, *n.* **1** an animal offered as a sacrifice. **2** a person who is killed or seriously harmed, intentionally or by accident.

vic'timise *v.t.* **1** to make (a person) suffer in some undeserved way. **2** to swindle:—*pr.p.* **vic'timising**.

victimīsā'tion *n.*

victor *vik'tȯr*, *n.* one who wins a battle or other contest.
victō'rious *adj.* successful in a contest.
victo'riously *adv.*
vic'tory *n.* the defeat of an enemy or rival:—*pl.* **vic'tories**.

Victorian *vik-tō'ri-ȧn*, *adj.* **1** having to do with the reign of Queen Victoria. **2** (of outlook on morals, etc.) strict, conventional, prudish.

victorious, etc. See **victor**.

victual *vit'l*, *n.* (usu. in *pl.*) food for human beings.—*v.t.* to supply with food:—*pr.p.* **vict'ualling**; *pa.p.* **vict'ualled**.
victualler *vit'lėr*, *n.* one who supplies provisions.

vicuna *vi-kōōn'yȧ*, *-kūn'ȧ*, *n.* S. American animal, related to the llama, which yields a fine wool.

video *vid'i-ō*, *n.* and *adj.* (having to do with) the recording or broadcasting of television pictures and sound:—*pl.* **vid'eos**:—*v.t.*, *v.i.* to record (a film, television broadcast, etc.) on videotape:—*pr.p.* **vid'eoing**; *pa.p.* **vid'eoed**.
video game an electronically operated game played on eg. a computer.
video recorder a machine for recording on videotape and playing back television broadcasts or films.
vid'eotape *n.* magnetic tape carrying pictures and sound.

vie *vī*, *v.i.* to contend as rivals: *They vied with each other in attempts to help*:—*pr.p.* **vy'ing**; *pa.p.* **vied**.

Viennese *vē-ė-nēz'*, *adj.* of Vienna.—*n. sing.* and *pl.* inhabitant(s) of Vienna.

view *vū*, *n.* **1** sight. **2** a scene, or a picture of one. **3** opinion: *Give me your view, views, on the subject.*—*v.t.* **1** to look at. **2** to watch (television programmes; also *v.i.*). **3** to see in the mind: *I view the problem in a different way.* **4** to consider (as): *I view it as a joke.*
view'er *n.*
view'data *n* a communications system by which information can be received and requested via a telephone line and presented on a television or other screen.
view'point *n.* **1** point from which a scene is viewed. **2** attitude to a subject.
in view 1 in sight. **2** before one as an aim, or as something likely to happen.
in view of taking into consideration.
on view ready to be looked at and examined.
with a view to with one's thoughts or aim directed towards: *with a view to cutting down expenses.*

vigil *vij'il*, *n.* keeping awake, esp. on the night before a religious feast.
vig'ilance *n.* watchfulness, alertness to danger.
vig'ilant *adj.* **vig'ilantly** *adv.*
vigilan'te *(-ti)* *n.* a member of a group carrying out rough justice in an unsettled country, or watching over the morals or welfare of a community.

vignette *vin-yet'*, *n.* **1** a small design or portrait, not enclosed by a definite border. **2** a character sketch.

vigour *vig'ȯr*, *n.* strength and energy.
vig'orous *adj.* strong, forceful.

viking *vī'king* (also *vik'ing*), *n.* a Norse invader of western Europe (8th–10th centuries).

vile *vīl*, *adj.* **1** wicked. **2** very bad or objectionable.
vile'ly *adv.* **vile'ness** *n.*
vil'ify *(vil')* *v.t.* to speak evil of:—*pr.p.* **vil'ifying**; *pa.p.* **vil'ified**.

villa *vil'ȧ*, *n.* a house, esp. in suburbs (often used to distinguish any house with a garden from a flat or apartment).
vill'age *vil'ij*, *n.* a group of houses, etc. smaller than a town.
vill'ager *n.* one who lives in, and has most of his interests in, a village.

villain *vil'ȧn*, *n.* **1** a man of very bad character. **2** (*playfully*) a rascal.
vill'ainous *adj.* **1** wicked. **2** (*coll.*) ugly, or very bad.
vill'ainy *n.* **1** wickedness. **2** a wicked action:—*pl.* **vill'ainies**.

vim *vim*, *n.* (*coll.*) energy, vigour.

vinaigrette *vin-ā-gret'*, *n.* a mixture of oil, vinegar and seasoning used as a salad dressing.

vindicate *vin'di-kāt*, *v.t.* **1** to defend successfully. **2** to clear from blame:—*pr.p.* **vin'dicating**.
vindicā'tion *n.* **vin'dicator** *n.*
vindic'tive *adj.* **1** revengeful. **2** spiteful, anxious to hurt.

vine *vīn*, *n.* **1** a plant bearing grapes. **2** a climbing or trailing plant.
vī'nery *n.* glasshouse for vines:—*pl.* **vī'neries**.
vin'iculture *n.* cultivation of grapes for wine.
vintage *vin'tij*, *n.* **1** the gathering of grapes. **2** wine of a particular year or region. **3** wine of good quality.—Also *adj.* **vint'ner** *(vint')* *n.* a wine seller.
vine'-dresser *n.* one who tends vines.
vineyard *vin'yȧrd*, *n.* a plantation of grape vines.
vintage car one of a very early model, still able to run.

vinegar *vin'i-gȧr, n.* a sour liquid used in preparing food, made from e.g. wine.

vinery, viniculture, vintage, etc. See **vine**.

vinyl *vī'nil, n.* a type of plastic, used e.g. in making gramophone records.

viola[1] *vē-ō'lȧ, vī', n.* a kind of large violin.

viola[2] *vī'ō-lȧ,* or *-ō', n.* **1** a member of the plant group which includes violets and pansies. **2** a single-coloured pansy.

violate *vī'ō-lāt, v.t.* **1** to break (an oath, a law etc.). **2** to treat with disrespect (a sacred place, e.g. temple, or object). **3** to disturb roughly (e.g. someone's privacy or peace). **4** to rape (a person):—*pr.p.* **vi'olāting.**
vīolā'tion *n.* **vī'olātor** *n.*

violent *vī'ȯ-lėnt, adj.* **1** acting with great force: *a violent storm, blow,* etc. **2** caused by force: *a violent death.* **3** powerful, uncontrollable: *violent behaviour, a violent temper.*
vī'olence *n.* great roughness and force.
vī'olently *adv.*
acts of violence those in which force is used illegally.

violet *vī'ȯ-lit, n.* **1** a plant of the kind to which pansies belong, esp. one of the smaller ones, such as the familiar **dog violet**. **2** a colour, bluish or light purple, esp. that seen at the end of the spectrum (or display of rainbow colours) opposite to the red.

violin *vī-ȯ-lin'* or *vī', n.* a musical instrument of four strings played with a bow.
vī'olinist (or *-lin'*) *n.* a violin player.

violoncello *vī-ȯ-lȯn-chel'ō* or *vē-, n.* a large musical instrument of the violin class:—*pl.* **violoncellos.**—See also **cello.**
violoncell'ist *n.* a violoncello player.

viper *vī'pėr, n.* **1** a kind of poisonous snake, esp. the common adder. **2** a base, malicious person.

virago *vi-rä'gō, vi-rā'gō, n.* **1** a bold, heroic woman. **2** a bad-tempered, nagging woman:—*pl.* **vira'gos.**

viral. See **virus.**

virgin *vûr'jin, n.* a person who has had no sexual intercourse.—*adj.* new, unused, unspoilt: *virgin soil.*
vir'ginal *adj.* **1** of or befitting a virgin. **2** maidenly, pure.
virgin'ity *n.* the state of maidenhood.
the Virgin Mary, the mother of Christ.

virginal[1]. See **virgin.**

virginal[2] *vûr'jin-ȧl, n.* a keyboard instrument earlier than the piano.

virile *vir'īl,* or *-il, adj.* **1** manly. **2** vigorous.
viril'ity *n.* **1** manhood. **2** manliness.

virtual. See **virtue.**

virtue *vûr'tū, n.* **1** moral goodness. **2** a particular merit, such as 'truthfulness'. **3** a good quality: *the virtues of nylon.*
vir'tual *adj.* not actually but having the same effect, power, etc: *the virtual end of the attempt; the virtual ruler of the country.*
vir'tually *adv.* in effect though not strictly speaking: *He was virtually penniless.*
vir'tuous *(-tū-ůs) adj.* morally good.
vir'tuously *adv.* **vir'tuousness** *n.*
by (or **in**) **virtue of** because of: *By virtue of the position he held, he was able to move about freely.*

virtuoso *vûr-tū-ōz'ō, -ōs'ō, n.* **1** one who knows much about e.g. music, painting. **2** a skilled performer:—*pl.* **virtuō'sos.**
virtuosity *(-os'i-ti) n.* unusual skill in one of the fine arts.

virtuous, etc. See **virtue.**

virulent *vir'ū-lėnt, adj.* **1** full of poison. **2** bitter in dislike or hatred.
vir'ulently *adv.* **vir'ulence** *n.*

virus *vī'rus, n.* **1** poison. **2** something which is smaller than known bacteria, can grow on body cells, and is a cause of disease: *Different viruses cause influenza, mumps, smallpox, etc.*
viral *adj.* caused by a virus.

visa *vē'zȧ, n.* a mark or stamp put on a passport by the authorities of a country to show that the bearer may travel in that country.

visage *viz'ij, n.* the face or look.

vis-à-vis *vēz-ȧ-vē, adj.* face to face, opposite:—*prep.* with regard to.

viscera *vis'ė-rȧ, n.pl.* the inner parts of the body.

viscid *vis'id, adj.* sticky.

viscose, viscosity. See **viscous.**

viscount *vī'kownt, n.* a title of nobility next below an earl.
viscountess *vī'kownt-es, n. fem.*

viscous *vis'kůs, adj.* sticky, not flowing readily.
viscos'ity *(-kos')* **vis'cousness** *ns.*
vis'cose *(-kōs), n.* a syrupy liquid made from wood pulp, one stage in the manufacture of rayon.

vise. See **vice**[1].

visible *viz'i-bl, adj.* able to be seen.
visibil'ity *n.* the clearness with which objects may be seen.
vis'ibly *adv.*
vision *vizh(ȯ)n, n.* **1** the act or sense of seeing. **2** something seen in the imagination (in the 'mind's eye'). **3** a supernatural appearance. **4** the power of imagining,

hence of foreseeing events, consequences, etc.
vis'ionary *adj.* seen in imagination only, not real.—*n.* one who forms plans that are difficult or impossible to carry out:—*pl.* **vis'ionaries.**
See also **visual.**

visit *viz'it, v.t.* **1** to go to see. **2** to inspect (an institution such as a school). **3** to come upon, attack: *Epidemics visited the shattered city.* **4** to inflict (on): *He visited his anger, grief, on them.*—*n.* **1** a call at a person's house. **2** a short stay.
visitā'tion *n.* **1** a formal visit by a superior. **2** a great calamity, viewed as a warning or punishment: *These visitations of disease seemed punishment for their sins.*
vis'itor *n.* one who makes a visit.—Also (*poetical*) **vis'itant.**

visor *vīz'ȯr, n.* **1** the part of a helmet covering the face. **2** a mask. **3** an eye-shade.

vista *vis'tȧ, n.* **1** a view, esp. one seen along an avenue of trees. **2** a picture in the mind: *a long vista of past events.*

visual *viz'ū-ȧl, adj.* belonging to, concerned with, received through, sight.
vis'ualise *(-īz) v.t.* to form a clear picture of (something) in the mind:—*pr.p.* **vis'ualising.**
vis'ually *adv.* by sight.
visual aids pictures, films, etc. used in learning.
visual display unit (abbrev. **VDU**) a device like a television set, on which data from a computer's memory can be displayed.

vital *vī'tȧl, adj.* **1** having to do with life. **2** necessary to life. **3** showing life and vigour. **4** essential, of the greatest importance: *Speed is vital to the success of our plan.*
vī'talise *(-īz) v.t.* to give life or vigour to:—*pr.p* **vī'talising.**
vītal'ity *n.* **1** life. **2** liveliness. **3** ability to go on living.
vī'tals *n. pl.* the organs of the body essential to life.
vital statistics **1** tables of figures dealing with population and its changes from year to year. **2** (*coll.*) female bust, waist, and hip measurements.

vitamin *vit'ā-min, vīt', n.* any of a group of substances necessary for healthy life, different ones occurring in different natural foods such, e.g., as raw fruit.

vitiate *vish'i-āt, v.t.* to spoil, to make impure or faulty:—*pr.p.* **vit'iating.**
vitiā'tion *n.*

viticulture *vit'i-kul-chůr, n.* cultivation of vine.—See also **viniculture (vine).**

vitreous *vit'ri-ůs, adj.* glass-like.
vit'rify *v.t., v.i.* to make, or become, glass-like:—*pr.p.* **vit'rifying;** *pa.p.* **vit'rified.**
vitrified fort an ancient fort in which the stones have been made glassy by fire.

vitriol *vit'ri-ȯl, n.* **1** sulphuric acid. **2** bitter criticism, etc.
vitriol'ic *adj.* biting, scathing: *vitriolic abuse.*

vituperate *vi-tū'pė-rāt,* or *vī-, v.t.* to abuse, revile.—Also *v.i.*:—*pr.p.* **vitū'perating.**
vitūperā'tion *n.* **vitū'perative** *adj.*

vivacious *vi-vā'shůs,* or *vī-, adj.* lively, sprightly.
vivac'ity *(-vas'),* **viva'ciousness** *ns.*
viva'ciously *adv.*

vivarium *vī-vā'ri-ům,* or *vi-, n.* an enclosure, tank, etc. for keeping living creatures.

viva voce *vī'vȧ vō'si, adv.* by word of mouth.—*n.* (also **vī'va**) an oral examination.

vivi- *viv-i-,* (as part of a word) alive.

vivid *viv'id, adj.* **1** life-like. **2** brilliant, striking.
viv'idly *adv.* **viv'idness** *n.*
viv'ify *v.t.* to make vivid, give life to:—*pr.p.* **viv'ifying;** *pa.p.* **viv'ified.**

viviparous *vi-vip'ȧ-růs,* or *vī-, adj.* producing young alive (i.e. not in eggs.).

vivisection *viv-i-sek'sh(ȯ)n, n.* the performance of experiments on living animals.

vixen *vik'sn, n.* **1** a female fox. **2** an ill-tempered woman.
vix'enish *adj.*

viz. *viz, adv.* meaning (and usu. read as) 'namely': *three boys, viz. John, James, and Peter.*

vizier *vi-zēr', vi'zi-ėr, n.* a minister of state, etc. in some Muslim countries.

vocabulary *vȯ-kab'ū-lȧ-ri,* or *vō-, n.* **1** a list of words in alphabetical order, with meanings. **2** the stock of words which a person knows and can use:—*pl.* **vocab'ularies.**

vocal *vō'kȧl, adj.* **1** having to do with the voice. **2** talkative, esp. about views, grievances, etc.
vō'calist *n.* a singer.
vocal cords folds of membrane in the larynx which vibrate and produce sounds.

vocation *vō-kā'sh(ȯ)n, n.* **1** a calling: *He had a sense of vocation, of being called by God to do this work.* **2** a profession or other way of living.

vocā'tional *adj.* (of training, etc.) preparing for a trade or business.

vociferate *vō-sif'ė-rāt, v.i.* to shout.—*v.t.* to utter with a loud voice:—*pr.p.* **vocif'erating**.
vocif'erous *adj.* loud of voice, noisy.
vocif'erously *adv.*
vocif'erousness *n.*

vodka *vod'kȧ, n.* a spirit made from grain, sometimes from potatoes.

vogue *vōg, n.* **1** the current fashion. **2** popularity.

voice *vois, n.* **1** sound from the mouth. **2** (quality of) singing sound. **3** expressed opinion, vote: *the voice of the people.* **4** right to express an opinion: *I had no voice in the matter.*—*v.t.* to give expression to (an opinion, etc.):—*pr.p.* **voic'ing**.
voice'-over *n.* the voice of an unseen narrator in a film, advertisement or television programme.
lower, raise one's voice to speak more softly (e.g. to avoid being overheard), or more loudly (e.g. in anger).

void *void, adj.* **1** empty. **2** not valid or binding (see **null**). **3** lacking entirely (with *of*): *a statement void of meaning.*—*n.* empty space.—*v.t.* to empty.

volatile *vol'ȧ-tīl, adj.* **1** (of a liquid) changing quickly to vapour. **2** lively but changeable in feeling: *She is volatile, has a volatile nature.*
vol'atilise (or *-at'-*) *v.t.* to cause to evaporate:—*pr.p.* **volatilising**.

vol-au-vent *vol'ō-vong, n.* a small pastry case filled with chicken, fish, etc.

volcano *vol-kā'nō, n.* usu. a cone-shaped mountain, through which molten rock, hot ash and other material reaches the earth's surface:—*pl.* **volca'noes**.
volcan'ic *(-kan') adj.* **1** having to do with a volcano. **2** caused or produced by the heat inside the earth.

vole *vōl, n.* any of a number of small animals with gnawing teeth, including the **water vole**, often called the 'water rat', some field-mice, etc.

volition *vō-lish'(ȯ)n, n.* will, act of willing: *No one told him to; he did it of his own volition.*
See also **voluntary**.

volley *vol'i, n.* **1** a flight of missiles. **2** in some games, the playing of a ball before it touches the ground:—*pl.* **voll'eys**.—*v.t.* **1** to shoot in a volley. **2** to play (a ball) before it bounces.

volt *vōlt, n.* the unit used in measuring the force driving electricity through a circuit.
vōl'tage *n.* force measured in volts: *Low voltage reduces current, causing lights to burn dimly.*

volte-face *vōlt-fäs' n.* sudden and complete change of opinion.

voluble *vol'ū-bl, adj.* (speaking) with too great a flow of words.
volubil'ity *n.* **vol'ubly** *adv.*

volume *vol'ūm, -yŭm, n.* **1** a book. **2** one of a series of connected books. **3** extent of space occupied: *the volume of a solid.* **4** amount: *the volume of trade.* **5** fullness (of sound).
volu'minous *adj.* **1** able to fill many volumes: *voluminous correspondence.* **2** (of a writer) producing many books. **3** large and full: *a voluminous dress.*
speak volumes to have much meaning: *Her frown spoke volumes.*

voluntary *vol'ŭn-tȧ-ri, adj.* done by choice, not by accident or under compulsion:—*opp.* **involuntary**.—*n.* a piece of music played (at his own choice) by an organist:—*pl.* **vol'untaries**.
vol'untarily *adv.* **vol'untariness** *n.*
volunteer *vol-ŭn-tēr', v.i.* to offer oneself for a service or duty.—*v.t.* to offer (e.g. an opinion, information).—*n.* one who offers service of his own accord.

voluptuous *vȯ-lup'tū-ŭs, adj.* **1** causing, or filled with, pleasure. **2** too much given to bodily pleasure.

vomit *vom'it, v.i.* to throw up the contents of the stomach.—*v.t.* to throw out: *The blaze vomited flame and smoke.*—*n.* matter ejected from the stomach.

voodoo *vōō'dōō, n.* (one who practises) a West Indian type of religious witchcraft.

voracious *vȯ-rā'shŭs, vō-, adj.* **1** very greedy, difficult to satisfy: *a voracious animal, appetite.* **2** very eager: *a voracious reader; voracious for pleasure.*
vora'city *(-ra'si-),* **vora'ciousness** *ns.*
vora'ciously *adv.*

vortex *vör'teks, n.* **1** a whirlpool. **2** a whirlwind:—*pl.* **vor'tices** *(-ti-sēz)*, **vor'texes**.

votary *vō'tȧ-ri, n.* **1** a person bound by a vow, or devoted to a service. **2** a believer in, supporter or admirer (of):—*pl.* **vo'taries**.

vote *vōt, n.* **1** a formal expression of a wish or opinion, esp. at an election or in a debate. **2** a sum of money granted by Parliament for a certain purpose.—*v.i.* (with *for*) to support (a candidate, a proposal):—*pr.p.* **vō'ting**.
vō'ter *n.* one who votes.

vouch *vowch, v.i.* **1** (with *for*) to say one is sure something is fact or truth: *I can vouch for his honesty, for the truth of the statement.* **2** (with *for*) to guarantee the honesty, etc. of (a person).

vouch'er *n.* a paper which confirms that a sum of money has been, or will be, paid.

vouchsafe *vowch-sāf', v.t.* to be good enough to give: *He vouchsafed a reply, a nod, information:—pr.p.* **vouchsaf'ing**.

vow *vow, n.* a solemn promise, esp. one made to God.—*v.t.* **1** to make a solemn promise (that). **2** to threaten: *to vow revenge.* **3** to assert solemnly (that).

vowel *vow'ėl, n.* **1** a simple sound made by the voice with no interruption by movement of tongue, teeth, or lips. **2** a letter used to represent such a sound, as *a, e, i, o, u*.

voyage *voi'ij, n.* a journey, esp. one made by sea.—*v.i.* to make a journey:—*pr.p.* **voy'aging**.

voy'ager *n.* a traveller making a journey (usu. a long one).

vulcanise *vul'kȧ-nīz, v.t.* to strengthen rubber by combining it with sulphur by heat:—*pr.p.* **vul'canising**

vulgar *vul'gȧr, adj.* **1** having to do with the common people: *the vulgar tongue is the language commonly spoken in a country.* **2** ill-mannered. **3** coarse.

vul'garise *v.t.* **1** to make common or ordinary. **2** to make unrefined, coarse:—*pr.p.* **vul'garising**.

vul'garism *n.* an expression not used in careful, educated speech.

vulgar'ity *n.* coarseness:—*pl.* **-ies**.

Vul'gate *n.* an ancient (4th century) Latin version of the Bible.

vulgar fractions common (i.e. not decimal) fractions.

vulnerable *vul'nėr-ȧ-bl, adj.* **1** exposed to attack: *The enemy's position was vulnerable* (*opp.* **invulnerable**). **2** liable to be hurt in body or feelings. **3** open to temptation or influence.

vulnerabil'ity, vul'nerableness *ns.*

vulpine *vul'pīn, adj.* **1** of, or like, a fox. **2** cunning.

vulture *vul'chůr, n.* **1** a large bird of prey, living chiefly on dead bodies. **2** a rapacious, merciless person.

vulva *vul'vȧ, n.* the opening of the female genitals.

vying. See vie.

W

wad *wod*, *n.* **1** a pack of loose material stuffed in to aid packing. **2** a bundle (esp. of bank notes).—*v.t.* to pad:—*pr.p.* **wadd'ing**; *pa.p.* **wadd'ed**.
wadd'ing *n.* **1** materials for wads. **2** cotton wool.

waddle *wod'l*, *v.i.* to take short steps and move from side to side in walking (as a duck does):—*pr.p.* **wadd'ling**.—*n.* a clumsy, rocking way of walking.

wade *wād*, *v.t.* **1** to walk through something that yields to the feet (e.g. water). **2** to make one's way with difficulty: *to wade through a book*.—*v.t.* to cross by wading:—*pr.p.* **wā'ding**.
wā'der *n.* **1** one who wades. **2** a bird that wades in search of food (also **wading bird**). **3** (in *pl.*) high waterproof boots used by anglers.

wafer *wā'fėr*, *n.* **1** a thin biscuit. **2** a thin disc of unleavened bread used at Holy Communion. **3** a thin disc or slice.

waffle[1] *wof'l*, *n.* a kind of batter cake cooked in a **waffle-iron**, a special metal utensil for this purpose.

waffle[2] *wof'l*, *v.i.* **1** to waver. **2** to talk on and on foolishly:—*pr.p.* **waff'ling**.—Also *n.*

waft *wäft*, *wöft*, *v.t.* to bear lightly through e.g. air or water.—*v.i.* to float or drift lightly.—*n.* a breath, puff.

wag[1] *wag*, *v.t.* and *v.i.* to move (e.g. one's head) from side to side, or up and down:—*pr.p.* **wagg'ing**; *pa.p.* **wagged**.—*n.* a single wagging movement.

wag[2] *wag*, *n.* **1** an amusing person, one who is always joking. **2** a wit.
wagg'ery *n.* **1** mischievous fun. **2** a joke showing this:—*pl.* **wagg'eries**.
wagg'ish *adj.* roguish.
wagg'ishly *adv.* **wagg'ishness** *n.*

wage *wāj*, *v.t.* to carry on (e.g. war):—*pr.p.* **wā'ging**.—*n.* payment for work (also **wag'es** *n.pl.*).
wa'ger *n.* a bet.—*v.t.* and *v.i.* to bet on the result of anything.

waggery, etc. See **wag**[2].

waggle *wag'l*, *v.t.* and *v.i.* to wag, esp. in an uncertain, irregular way:—*pr.p.* **wagg'ling**.
wagg'ly *adj.*:—*comp.* **wagg'lier**; *superl.* **wagg'liest**.
wagg'liness *n.*

wagon, waggon *wag'ȯn*, *n.* a four-wheeled vehicle for carrying heavy loads.
wag(g)'oner *n.* driver of a wagon.

wagtail *wag'tāl*, *n.* a small bird with a long tail which it flicks up and down.

waif *wāf*, *n.* an uncared-for child.
waifs and strays persons without homes or possessions.

wail *wāl*, *v.i.* to give sad or complaining cries.—*n.* **1** a cry of woe. **2** loud weeping.
wail'ing *n.* and *adj.*

wain *wān*, *n.* a wagon.

wainscot *wān'skȯt*, *n.* a wooden lining applied to the (lower part of the) walls of rooms.
wain'scoting, wain'scotting *n.* materials for making a wainscot.

waist *wāst*, *n.* **1** the narrow part of the human body between ribs and hips. **2** the part of a garment covering this area.
waist'coat *(wās', wāst')* *n.* a short, usu. sleeveless, jacket worn immediately under the outer jacket.

wait *wāt*, *v.i.* **1** to remain in the same place, or without acting (for, until): *to wait for a sign from the leader.* **2** to act as a waiter at table.—*v.t.* **1** to await, or be on the watch for (e.g. an opportunity). **2** to serve as a waiter at (table).—*n.* **1** a delay. **2** (in *pl.*) singers who go from house to house at Christmas. **3** ambush (in phrases —*to lay wait, lie in wait, for*; see **lay**[2], **lie**[2]).
wait'er *n.* **1** one who waits. **2** a man who serves at table (*fem.* **wait'ress**).
waiting room a room in which people wait (e.g. at a station).
wait (up)on **1** to pay a formal visit to. **2** to serve (a person) at table. **3** to serve as attendant to.

waive *wāv*, *v.t.* to give up, not insist upon (e.g. a claim, a right):—*pr.p.* **waiv'ing**.

wake[1] *wāk*, *v.i.* **1** to cease from sleep, idleness, indifference, etc. **2** to be awake.—*v.t.* to arouse from sleep, etc.:—*pr.p.* **wak'ing**; *pa.t.* **waked** *(wākt)* or **wōke**; *pa.p.* **waked, wō'ken**.—*n.* watching all night, esp. beside a corpse.
wake'ful *adj.* **1** not asleep. **2** not able to sleep. **3** watchful.
wake'fully *adv.* **wake'fulness** *n.*
wa'ken *v.t., v.i.* to wake, arouse or be aroused.

wake[2] *wāk*, *n.* a streak of smooth-looking or foamy water left in the track of a ship.

in the wake of immediately behind or after.

walk *wök*, *v.i.* to move, or to travel, on foot.—*v.t.* **1** to cause to walk. **2** to move or travel along (the streets, the plank, etc.).—*n.* **1** act of walking. **2** way of walking. **3** distance walked over. **4** place for walking (e.g. a path). **5** social position or the sphere in which one lives or works: *one's walk of life*.

walk'er *n.* **walk'ing** *n.* and *adj.*

walk'ie-talk'ie *n.* a wireless set for sending and receiving messages, carried on the body.

walk'ing-stick *n.* a stick used when walking.

walk'out *n.* a sudden departure esp. of a workforce.

walk'over *n.* an easy victory.

walk the plank to walk along a plank placed across a ship's side and fall into the sea (old pirate method of putting to death).

wall *wöl*, *n.* **1** an erection of brick, stone, etc. used to separate or to enclose. **2** the side of a building. **3** a surface forming the outside of something: *the wall of a plant cell.*—*v.t.* to enclose with, or as if with, a wall.

wall'flower *n.* a spring flower, sometimes growing on old walls.

wall'paper *n.* paper used in house decorating.

Wall Street New York location of chief U.S. financial market.

go to the wall (esp. of a firm or enterprise) to fail, be unsuccessful.

with one's back to the wall in a desperate situation, at bay.

wallaby *wol'ȧ-bi*, *n.* a small kind of kangaroo:—*pl.* **wall'abies**, **-by**.

wallet *wol'it*, *n.* a small case for holding money, papers, etc.

wallop *wol'ȯp*, (*slang*) *v.t.* to beat, flog.—*n.* a blow.

wallow *wol'ō*, *v.i.* **1** to roll about with enjoyment in mud etc. as an animal does. **2** to live in filth or vice.

wallow in money to be very rich.

walnut *wöl'nut*, *n.* **1** a tree, the wood of which is used for making furniture etc. **2** its nut.

walrus *wöl'rus*, or *wol'*, *n.* a large sea animal related to seals.

waltz *wöl(t)s*, *n.* **1** a dance with a whirling motion, performed by couples. **2** music for this.—Also *v.i.*

wan *won*, *adj.* pale and sickly looking:—*comp.* **wann'er**; *superl.* **wann'est**.

wan'ly *adv.* **wan'ness** *n.*

wand *wond*, *n.* a long slender rod e.g. as used by conjurors.

wander *won'dėr*, *v.i.* **1** to ramble, stroll, with no definite object. **2** to go astray, move away (from the subject, the point, the present scene): *His mind wanders.*—*v.t.* to ramble over.

wan'derer *n.*

wanderlust *vän'der-loost*, *won'dėr-lust*, *n.* a thirst for travel.

wane *wān*, *v.i.* **1** to become smaller, esp. of the moon—*opp.* to **wax**. **2** to lose power or importance:—*pr.p.* **wā'ning**.—*n.* decrease.

on the wane becoming less, declining.

wangle *wang'gl*, (*coll.*) *v.t.* to get or achieve by trickery, etc.:—*pr.p.* **wang'ling**.—Also *v.i.* and *n.*

wanly, **wanness**. See **wan**.

want *wont*, *n.* **1** poverty. **2** scarcity. **3** need. —*v.t.* **1** to lack. **2** to feel the need of. **3** to wish for.—*v.i.* **1** to be in need. **2** to be without something desired or necessary.

wan'ted *adj.* sought for (e.g. by the police or in order to speak to someone).

wan'ting *adj.* **1** absent. **2** lacking (in): *wanting in taste.* **3** not good, etc., enough: *found wanting.*—*prep.* without.

wanton *won'tȯn*, *adj.* **1** playful, irresponsible. **2** not chaste. **3** without motive: *wanton destruction.* **4** not provoked: *a wanton assault.*—*n.* **1** a trifler. **2** one who is wanton in morals.

wan'tonly *adv.* **wan'tonness** *n.*

war *wör*, *n.* **1** an open armed struggle esp. between nations. **2** a concerted effort against e.g. crime, disease.—*v.i.* **1** to make war. **2** to fight (against):—*pr.p.* **warr'ing**; *pa.p.* **warred**.

war'like *adj.* **1** fond of war. **2** threatening war: *warlike preparations.* **3** of war.

warr'ior *n.* a fighting man (or woman) in any kind of conflict.

war cry **1** cry of encouragement, threat, etc., before or during battle. **2** slogan.

war'fāre *n.* armed contest.

war'head *n.* the section of a torpedo or other missile containing the explosive.

war'monger *wör'mung-gėr*, *n.* one who encourages war, esp. for personal gain.

war'ship *n.* a vessel for war.

war'time *n.* time of war.—Also *adj.*

cold war a struggle for the upperhand by all means short of actual fighting.

on the warpath in fighting mood.

war of nerves attempts to lower morale by means of threats, rumours, etc.

warble *wör'bl*, *v.i.* **1** to sing in a quavery manner. **2** to sing sweetly as birds do:—*pr.p.* **war'bling**.—Also *v.t.*—*n.* the act of warbling.

war'bler *n.* **1** a singer. **2** a small singing bird.

ward *wörd, v.t.* **1** to guard or take care of. **2** to keep away (with *off*): to ward off danger, a blow, a cold.—*n.* **1** one who is under a guardian. **2** a division of a city for local election purposes. **3** a room with several beds, in a hospital, etc.

war'den *n.* **1** a man who guards a game reserve. **2** the head of certain colleges. **3** one appointed to look after the civil population in case of e.g. air raids. **4** a traffic warden.

war'der *n.* one who guards, esp. one in charge of prisoners:—*fem.* **ward'ress**.

ward'ship *n.* the state of being, or being under, a guardian.

ward'robe *n.* **1** a cupboard for clothes. **2** a stock of clothing.

ward'room *n.* a room used by officers of a warship for meals.

ware *wār, n.* **1** manufactured articles esp. pottery; often used as part of a word: *ironware.* **2** (in *pl.*) goods for sale.

ware'house *n.* a store for goods.—*v.t.* to put in a warehouse:—*pr.p.* **ware'housing**.

warfare, warhead, etc. See **war**.

warily, wariness. See **wary**.

war'lock *n.* a wizard.

warm *wörm, adj.* **1** moderately hot. **2** having, showing, strong emotions, sympathies, etc. **3** enthusiastic. **4** angry.—*v.t.* and *v.i.* to make, or become, warm.—*n.* act of warming.

warm'ly *adv.* **warm'er** *n.*

warm'ness, warmth *ns.*

warm'-blood'ed *adj.* **1** having a blood temperature greater than that of the surrounding atmosphere and changing little. **2** passionate.

warm front the surface of an advancing mass of warm air where it meets a mass of colder air.

warm'heart'ed *adj.* kind, affectionate.

warm up to exercise the body gently in preparation for a strenuous work-out, contest, etc. (*n.* **warm'-up**).

warmonger. See **war**.

warn *wörn, v.t.* **1** to give (a person) notice of danger. **2** to caution (against). **3** to urge or advise: *I warned him not to be late.* **4** to tell (a person) beforehand.

war'ning *n.*

warp *wörp, v.t.* **1** to twist out of shape. **2** to cause to think, reason, choose, etc., wrongly: *His experiences had warped his judgment, mind.*—*v.i.* to become twisted out of the straight.—*n.* **1** the threads stretched lengthwise in a loom, to be crossed by a weft or woof. **2** a crookedness, distortion, etc.

warped *adj.* **1** twisted. **2** embittered in outlook: *a warped nature.*

warrant *wor'ȧnt, v.t.* **1** to guarantee. **2** to justify: *A slight cold does not warrant your staying off work.*—*n.* **1** something that justifies, or that guarantees. **2** something that gives authority, esp. a writ for arresting a person.

warr'antable *adj.* justifiable.

warr'anter, warr'antor *n.*

warr'anty *n.* a guarantee of fitness for use, etc.:—*pl.* **warr'anties.**

warrant officer an officer holding a warrant (lower in rank than a commissioned officer).

warren *wor'ėn, n.* **1** (also **rabbit-warren**) a place where many rabbits have their burrows, or where people live crowded together. **2** a building with many passages.

warrior. See **war**.

wart *wört, n.* small hard growth on the skin.

war'ty *adj.*:—*comp.* **war'tier**; *superl.* **war'tiest**.

wary *wā'ri, adj.* cautious, on one's guard:—*comp.* **wā'rier;** *superl.* **wā'riest**.

wā'rily *adv.* **wā'riness** *n.*

was. See **be**.

wash *wosh, v.t.* **1** to wet with, or clean with, water or other liquid. **2** to flow against. **3** to sweep (away, along, etc.) by the action of water. **4** to cover with a thin coat e.g. of paint.—*v.i.* **1** to clean oneself, clothes, etc., with water. **2** to flow (over, against, along). **3** (*coll.*) to stand the test: *This statement will not wash.*—*n.* **1** a washing. **2** the breaking of waves e.g. on shore. **3** the rough water left by a moving boat. **4** a liquid with which anything is washed. **5** a thin coat of paint, etc.

wash- (as part of a word) for washing in, with, etc. (e.g. **wash'bowl**).

wash'able *adj.* able to be washed.

wash'er *n.* **1** a person, thing, that washes. **2** a flat ring of rubber, metal, etc., to keep nuts or joints tight, etc.

wash'ing *n.* **1** the act of cleaning by water. **2** clothes washed or to be washed.

washed'-up' (*slang*) *adj.* exhausted, at the end of one's resources.

wash'erwoman, -man *ns.* one who is paid to wash clothes.

washhand basin a basin in which to wash face and hands.

wash'ing-machine *n.* a machine, driven e.g. by electricity, for washing clothes.

wash up to wash dishes, etc. after a meal.

wasp *wosp, n.* a stinging winged insect with slender waist.
was'pish *adj.* **1** like a wasp. **2** spiteful.
was'pishly *adv.* **was'pishness** *n.*

wassail *wos'āl, v.i.* to hold a merry drinking meeting.—Also *n.*
wass'ailer *n.* **wass'ailing** *n.*

waste *wāst, adj.* **1** rejected as useless or worthless: *waste paper*; *waste materials from manufacture.* **2** uncultivated (e.g. ground). **3** desert, desolate.—*v.t.* **1** to make ruined and desolate. **2** to wear out gradually. **3** to use with too little result or return (e.g. money, time, effort).—*v.i.* to decay gradually:—*pr.p.* **wāst'ing.**—*n.* **1** loss, destruction. **2** extravagant use, bringing too poor a result. **3** uncultivated country. **4** an unbroken expanse (of e.g. water, snow).
wās'tage *n.* **1** loss by use, decay, etc. **2** an amount lost, wasted.
waste'ful *adj.* **1** involving or causing waste. **2** extravagant.
waste'fully *adv.* **waste'fulness** *n.*
wās'ter, wās'trel *ns.* a ne'er-do-well.
waste'basket, waste'paper basket one for paper being thrown away.
waste pipe a pipe to carry off water from e.g. a sink.

watch *woch, n.* **1** close observation. **2** guard. **3** one who is, or those who are, on guard or lookout. **4** a sailor's period of duty on deck (usu. four hours). **5** a small instrument for telling the time by, carried in the pocket, or worn on the wrist, etc.—*v.i.* **1** to look with attention. **2** to keep guard.—*v.t.* **1** to observe closely. **2** to wait for (e.g. one's opportunity.)
watch'er *n.*
watch'ful *adj.* **1** on the alert. **2** cautious.
watch'fully *adv.* **watch'fulness** *n.*
watch'-dog *n.* **1** a dog kept to guard premises and property. **2** a person or organisation monitoring government or commercial operations to guard against inefficiency or illegality.
watch'man *n.* one who guards (esp. premises).
watch'word *n.* a slogan, motto: *The watchword of the party was 'Opportunity for all'.*
watch over to keep guard over, care for and protect.

water *wö'tėr, n.* **1** a clear liquid without taste or smell, which falls as rain, etc. **2** any collection of it, as an ocean, lake, river, etc. **3** saliva. **4** urine.—*v.t.* **1** to supply with water. **2** to weaken by adding water.—*v.i.* **1** to gather saliva: *At the sight of food his mouth watered.* **2** to take in water.
wa'tery *adj.* **1** like water. **2** thin. **3** threatening rain: *a watery sky.*
wa'teriness *n.*
water buffalo the common domestic buffalo of hot Eastern countries.
water butt a large barrel for rainwater.
wa'ter-closet *n.* a place for discharging urine and excrement, in which a rush of water is provided for carrying waste away through pipes.—Also **W.C.**
water colour **1** a colour thinned down with water instead of oil. **2** a painting in such colours.
wa'tercourse *n.* a channel for water, bed of stream, etc.
wa'tercress *n.* a perennial plant with sharp-tasting leaves that are used in salads and soups.
wa'terfall *n.* a fall of water from a height.
wa'terfowl *n.* birds, esp. game birds, that live on, or beside, water.
water ga(u)ge an instrument for measuring the quantity or height of water.
wa'terhen *n.* **1** the moorhen. **2** (*rarely*) the coot.
wa'ter-ice *n.* an ice-cream made with water rather than cream, etc.
watering place **1** place where water may be obtained. **2** holiday resort where people drink mineral water, bathe, etc.
water line the line on a ship to which water rises.
wa'terlogged *adj.* **1** (of ship, etc.) unmanageable because flooded with water. **2** (of ground) saturated.
water main a large underground pipe carrying a public water supply.
wa'terman *n.* a boatman, a ferryman.
wa'termark *n.* **1** a tide mark. **2** a mark worked into paper to show its size or its manufacturer.
water melon a type of melon with green skin and red flesh.
wa'termill *n.* a mill driven by water.
water polo a ball game played by two teams of swimmers.
water power the power of water used to move machinery, etc.
wa'terproof *adj.* not allowing water to soak through.—*n.* a garment made of a waterproof material.—*v.t.* to make proof against water.
water rat the water vole (see **vole**).
wa'tershed *n.* **1** the line separating two river basins. **2** a district from which several rivers rise.
wa'terspout *n.* **1** a pipe from which water spouts. **2** a moving column of water, caused by storm wind, seen at sea.
water supply **1** obtaining of, and distribution of, water for a community. **2** the amount of water so supplied.
wa'tertight *adj.* **1** so tightly made that

water cannot pass through. **2** in which no fault can be found: *a watertight excuse*.

wa'terway *n.* a channel along which ships can sail.

wa'terwheel *n.* a wheel moved by water.

wa'terworks *n.pl.* **1** (also *n.sing.*) the apparatus by which water is collected and supplied e.g. to a town. **2** (*coll.*) tears.

like water very freely, in great quantity: *He spent money like water*.

watt *wot*, *n.* a unit of power.

watt'age *n.* power in watts.

wattle *wot'l*, *n.* **1** an Australian acacia. **2** a structure made of twigs and branches. **3** the fleshy part hanging from the throat of e.g. a turkey.

wave *wāv*, *n.* **1** a surge travelling on the surface of water. **2** a vibrating disturbance travelling e.g. through the air. **3** a succession of curves in the hair. **4** a rise, increase for a time (of e.g. emotion, crime, prosperity). **5** a gesture with e.g. one's hand.—*v.i.* **1** to move backwards and forwards, flutter. **2** to curve first one way then the other.—Also *v.t.*:—*pr.p.* **wā'ving**.

wā'vy *adj.*:—*comp.* **wā'vier**; *superl.* **wā'viest**.

wā'viness *n.*

wave'length *n.* a distance in the line of advance of a wave from one point to next similar point (e.g. in wave in water, from one highest point to the next).

wā'ver *v.i.* to falter, be irresolute.

wā'verer *n.*

wave aside to dismiss (a suggestion, etc.).

wax[1] *waks*, *n.* **1** beeswax (see this word). **2** any substance like it, as that in the ear. **3** sealing-wax.—Also *adj.*—*v.t.* to smear or rub with wax.

wax'en, **wax'y** (*comp.* **wax'ier**; *superl.* **wax'iest**), *adjs.* **1** resembling wax. **2** pale, pasty.

wax'works *n.sing.* an exhibition of figures (usu. of well-known people) made of wax.

wax[2] *waks*, *v.i.* to grow, increase (esp. of the moon)—*opp.* to **wane**.

way *wā*, *n.* **1** passage. **2** road. **3** room to go forward or to pass. **4** direction. **5** distance: *a long way*. **6** condition: *He is in a bad way*. **7** means: *Find a way to do this*. **8** manner: *in a polite way*. **9** habitual manner: *He thanked them warmly, as was his way*. **10** the course of action one prefers: *to have one's way*, *own way*.

way'fārer *n.* a traveller esp. on foot.

way'fāring *adj.* and *n.*

waylay' *v.t.* to lie in ambush for, or in wait for, and stop (a person):—*pr.p.* **waylay'ing**; *pa.p.* **waylaid'** (*-lād'*).

way'side *n.* the side of a road, path, etc.—Also *adj.*

way'ward *adj.* **1** wilful, following one's own inclinations or whims. **2** turning and changing in unexpected ways.

way'wardness *n.*

by the way incidentally, in passing.

by way of **1** by the route passing, or through. **2** for, as if for, the purpose of: *He did it by way of helping me*.

get, **have**, **one's own way** to do, get, etc. what one wants.

give way. See **give**.

have a way with one to have an attractive manner.

make one's way **1** to go (to). **2** to make progress, be successful.

on the way out becoming unpopular, unfashionable.

ways and means **1** resources. **2** methods (e.g. of raising money).

W.C. See **water-closet**.

we *wē*, *pron. pl.* I and another or others:—*objective* **us**; *possessive* **our** (*owr*; sometimes described as *possessive adj.*), **ours**: *We—Mary and I—are glad you can meet us and give us a good map for our journey*; *ours is very old*.

ourselves' (*-selvz'*) *pron. pl.* the emphatic or reflexive form of *we*, *us*: *We ourselves are going*; *We hid ourselves when we saw him*.

weak *wēk*, *adj.* **1** lacking strength of body, mind, or character. **2** easily led or influenced. **3** (of e.g. resistance) easily overcome.

weak'en *v.t.* and *v.i.* to make or become weak(er).

weak'ling *n.* a weak person, animal, or plant.

weak'ly *adv.* **weak'ness** *n.*

weak'-kneed' (*-knēd'*) *adj.* **1** having weak knees. **2** lacking firm will, too ready to give in.

weak'-min'ded *adj.* **1** having little intelligence. **2** too easily persuaded.

weal[1] *wēl*, *n.* a raised mark on the skin caused by e.g. a blow with a whip.

weal[2] *wēl*, *n.* welfare, good fortune.

wealth *welth*, *n.* **1** riches. **2** a great quantity (of).

weal'thy (*wel'*) *adj.*:—*comp.* **weal'thier**; *superl.* **weal'thiest**.

weal'thiness *n.*

wean *wēn*, *v.t.* **1** to accustom (a child, young animal) to food other than the mother's milk. **2** to turn away the interest or attachment of: *We must wean Mary from this bad habit*.

weapon *wep'ŏn*, *n.* any instrument or means of offence or defence.

wear *wār*, *v.t.* **1** to be dressed in. **2** to arrange (clothes, hair, in a particular way). **3** to have on the face (e.g. a beard). **4** to have, show: *She wears a pleased expression.* **5** to damage, eat away, make gradually less, by use or exposure. **6** to make (a hole) in this way. **7** to exhaust, tire.—*v.i.* **1** to be damaged or made less by use. **2** to last when used: *This material wears well*:—*pa.t.* **wore** *(wōr, wör)*; *pa.p.* **worn** *(wōrn, wörn)*.—*n.* **1** act of wearing. **2** damage by use. **3** durability. **4** articles worn.

wear'able *adj.* fit to be worn.

wear'er *n.*

wear'ing *adj.* **1** made for wear. **2** exhausting: *I find her chatter most wearing.*

wear and tear damage by ordinary use.

wear out **1** to become unfit for further use. **2** to exhaust (**worn'-out'** *adj.*).

weary *wē'ri*, *adj.* **1** tired, with strength or patience exhausted. **2** tiring, boring: *a weary job*:—*comp.* **wea'rier**; *superl.* **wea'riest**.—*v.t.* and *v.i.* **1** to tire. **2** to make, or become, bored or impatient:—*pr.p.* **wea'rying**; *pa.p.* **wea'ried**.

wea'rily *adv.* **wea'riness** *n.*

wea'risomely *adv.* **wea'risomeness** *n.*

weasel *wē'zl*, *n.* **1** a small flesh-eating animal with long slender body. **2** a cunning, treacherous person.

weather *weTH'ėr*, *n.* condition of the atmosphere (heat, coldness, cloudiness, etc.).—*v.t.* and *v.i.* to affect, or to be affected, by exposure to the air (to dry, discolour, wear away, etc.).—*v.t.* to come safely through (storm, difficulty).

weath'er-beaten *adj.* showing effects of exposure to the weather.

weath'ercock *n.* **1** a flat piece of metal (often in the form of a cock) turning and showing the direction of the wind. **2** one who changes his opinion often and easily.

weather glass a barometer.

weather report a statement about and forecast of the weather.

keep one's weather eye open to be alert, on one's guard.

make heavy weather of (something) to find it (unnecessarily) difficult.

under the weather indisposed, ill.

weave[1] *wēv*, *v.t.* **1** to interlace (threads, etc. as in a loom to form cloth). **2** to make (something) in this way. **3** to put details together to make (a story). **4** (with *together*) to unite.—Also *v.i.*:—*pr.p.* **weav'ing**; *pa.t.* **wōve**; *pa.p.* **wō'ven**.

wea'ver *n.* **wea'ving** *n.*

weave[2] *wēv*, *v.i.* to move in and out, or to and fro, in a fight, in a dance, or through traffic:—*pr.p.* **wea'ving**; *pa.p.* **weaved**.

web *web*, *n.* **1** something that is woven. **2** the fine snare for flies, etc., spun by a spider, etc. **3** the skin between the toes of a waterfowl.

webbed *adj.* with toes joined by web.

webb'ing *n.* a rough strong woven fabric of hemp.

web'-foot'ed *adj.* having webbed feet.

wed *wed*, *v.t.*, *v.i.* to marry:—*pr.p.* **wedd'ing**; *pa.p.* **wedd'ed**.

wedd'ing *n.* **1** marriage. **2** marriage ceremony.

wedlock *wed'lok*, *n.* **1** matrimony. **2** married state.

born in, or **out of, wedlock** legitimate, or illegitimate.

we'd *wēd*, *abbrev.* we had, we should or we would.

wedge *wej*, *n.* **1** a piece of wood or metal, thick at one end and sloping to a thin edge at the other, used in splitting, or in fixing tightly. **2** anything shaped like a wedge.—*v.t.* **1** to fix with a wedge or wedges. **2** to press, thrust (in) tightly: *He wedged himself in among the crowd at the door.*—*v.i.* to become fixed or jammed by, or as if by, a wedge:—*pr.p.* **wedg'ing**.

the thin end of the wedge a small beginning that will lead to larger and (worse) developments.

wedlock. See **wed**.

Wednesday *wenz'di*, *wednz'di*, *n.* the fourth day of the week.

wee *wē*, *adj.* small, tiny:—*comp.* **wee'(e)r**; *superl.* **wee'(e)st**.

weed[1] *wēd*, *n.* **1** any useless troublesome plant. **2** a worthless person.—*v.t.* **1** to free from weeds. **2** (with *out*) to remove (anything offensive or useless).—*v.t.* to remove weeds.

weed'er *n.*

weed'y *adj.* **1** weed-like. **2** full of weeds. **3** lanky:—*comp.* **weed'ier**; *superl.* **weed'iest**.

weed'iness *n.*

weed[2] *wēd*, *n.* (in *pl.*) mourning garments.

week *wēk*, *n.* **1** the space of seven days, esp. from Sunday to Saturday. **2** the (five) six days of the week leaving out (Saturday and) Sunday.

week'ly *adj.* happening, or done, once a week.—*adv.* once a week.—*n.* a publication coming out once a week:—*pl.* **week'lies**.

week'day *n.* any day except (Saturday and) Sunday.

week'end, **week'-end** (or *-end'*) *n.* the period including the end of one week and the beginning of the next.

this day week a week from today.

weep *wēp, v.i.* **1** to shed tears. **2** to drip, ooze.—Also *v.t.*:—*pa.t., pa.p.* **wept**.
wee'ping *adj.* **1** shedding tears. **2** (of trees) with drooping branches: *a weeping willow*.
weevil *wē'vil, n.* any beetle that damages stored grain.
wee'viled, wee'villed, wee'vily, wee'villy *adjs.* infested by weevils.
weft *weft, n.* in making cloth in a loom, thc threads woven into, and crossing the warp.—Also **woof**.
weigh *wā, v.t.* **1** to find the heaviness of (something). **2** to be equal to in heaviness: *This parcel weighs 1 lb.* **3** to measure (out). **4** to raise (ship's anchor). **5** (of burden, cares, etc.) to press heavily (down). **6** to ponder, consider (arguments, etc.).—*v.i.* **1** to have heaviness. **2** to be considered of importance. **3** to press heavily (on).
weight *wāt, n.* **1** the amount which anything weighs. **2** a piece of metal of a standard weight: *a ½ lb. weight, a 7 lb. weight.* **3** pressure. **4** importance: *a matter of some weight.*—*v.t.* **1** to attach, or add, a weight or weights to. **2** to hold down in this way.
weigh'ting *n.* extra pay to compensate for e.g. working in a particular area.
weight'less *adj.* **1** weighing nothing. **2** (of astronauts etc.) not subject to the Earth's gravity.
weigh'ty *adj.* **1** heavy. **2** important:—*comp.* **weigh'tier**; *superl.* **weigh'tiest**.
weigh'tily *adv.* **weigh'tiness** *n.*
weigh'bridge *n.* a machine for weighing vehicles and their loads.
weight'lifting *n.* the sport or exercise of lifting heavy weights.
weigh in 1 to find one's weight before a fight, or after a horse-race (**weigh out** before a race). **2** to join in a project.
weigh up to calculate or assess a probability, etc.
weir *wēr, n.* **1** a dam across a river. **2** a fence of stakes set in a stream for catching fish.
weird *wērd, adj.* **1** mysterious, supernatural. **2** odd, very queer.
weird'ō (*coll.*) *n.* an odd, eccentric person:—*pl.* **weird'ōs**.
welcome *wel'kom, adj.* **1** received with gladness. **2** causing gladness.—*n.* **1** reception. **2** kindly reception.—*v.t.* **1** to receive with kindness or pleasure. **2** to accept, or undergo, gladly:—*pr.p.* **wel'coming**.
welcome to given permission and encouragement to take, etc. (something): *You are welcome to the strawberries in the garden as long as you cut the grass.*
weld *weld, v.t.* **1** to join together (e.g. metal) by pressure with or without heat, or by fusion. **2** to unite closely (e.g. different groups of people).—*n.* a welded joint.
welfare *wel'fār, n.* **1** the state of faring well. **2** condition as regards health, etc. **3** money given by the state to the poor, the sick, etc.
welfare state a country with a public health service, insurance against unemployment, pensions, etc.
welfare work efforts to improve the living conditions of c.g. thc nccdy, or employees or workers.
well[1] *wel, n.* **1** a spring. **2** a lined shaft made in the earth so as to obtain water, oil, etc. **3** any similar walled space, e.g. the space round which a staircase winds.—*v.i.* (of water from the earth, tears) to rise, gush (often *up*, *out*, or *forth*).
well[2] *wel, adj.* **1** in health. **2** (used in predicate) fortunate: *It was well that you saw him coming*:—**bett'er** used as *comp.*—*adv.* **1** properly. **2** thoroughly. **3** successfully. **4** conveniently. **5** with good reason: *You may well be annoyed at his behaviour.* **6** with praise, approval: *He speaks well of you.* **7** to a great extent: *She is well over fifty*:—**bett'er** used as *comp.*; *superl.* **best**.—*interj.* expressing surprise, etc.
well'-advised' *adj.* wise, prudent: *You would be well-advised to sell now.*
well'-bal'anced *adj.* sane and stable.
well'-being *n.* welfare.
well'-born' *adj.* born into a good or noble family.
well'-bred' *adj.* **1** having good manners. **2** of good parentage.
well'-built' *adj.* muscular.
well'-conduc'ted *adj.* **1** properly managed. **2** behaving properly.
well'-disposed'. See **dispose**.
well'-earned' *adj.* thoroughly deserved.
well'-found'ed, -ground'ed *adjs.* justified by facts or events.
well'-groomed' *adj.* smart, tidy in appearance.
well'-heeled' (*coll.*) *adj.* rich.
well'-informed' *n.* having, or based on, wide information.
well'-known' *adj.* **1** familiar. **2** celebrated.
well'-mann'ered *adj.* polite.
well'-mean'ing *adj.* (of person, action) having good intentions.—Also (of action) **well'-meant'**.
well off. See **off**.
well'-read' *adj.* having read much and profitably.
well'-spō'ken *adj.* refined, pleasing or correct in one's speech.
well'-timed' *adj.* done, said, etc., at a suitable time.
well'-to-do' *adj.* having enough money

to live comfortably.
well'-wisher *n.* one who wishes success, etc., to person(s) or cause.
well'-worn' *adj.* that has been worn or used often, or too often: *a well-worn excuse.*
as well in addition.
as well as 'both ... and'.

wellingtons *wel'ing-tȯnz*, *n.pl.* rubber boots loosely covering calves of legs.

Welsh *welsh*, *adj.* of Wales or its inhabitants.—*n.pl.* **1** (**the Welsh**) the inhabitants of Wales. **2** (in *sing.*) their Celtic language.
Welsh'man *n.* a native of Wales:—*pl.* **Welsh'men.**
Welsh rarebit melted cheese on toast.

welsh *welsh*, *v.i.* to cheat by dodging payment or not carrying out an obligation.

welt *welt*, *n.* **1** a band or strip fastened to an edge, for strength or for ornament. **2** a narrow strip of leather used in one method of sewing the upper to the sole of a shoe.

welter *wel'tėr*, *v.i.* **1** (of e.g. sea) to roll, heave. **2** to roll about (in), or be drenched (in e.g. dirt, blood).—*n.* **1** state of confusion. **2** confused mass.

welterweight *wel'tėr-wāt*, *n.* (a boxer of) weight between *light* and *middle.*

wench *wench*, *-sh*, *n.* a girl.

wend *wend*, *v.i.* to go, wind:—*pa.t.* **wen'ded** (*old pa.t.* **went**; see **go**).
wend one's way to follow the road in leisurely fashion.

went. See **go**.

wept. See **weep**.

were. See **be**.

we're *wēr*, *abbrev.* we are.

wer(e)wolf *wēr'woolf*, *wûr'woolf*, *n.* a person supposed to change into a wolf at certain times:—*pl.* **wolves**.

west *west*, *n.* **1** one of the four chief points of the compass. **2** the region where the sun sets. **3** the region in the west of any country. **4** (*cap.*) Europe, or Europe and America, as opposed to Asia, the East.—*adj.* situated towards, or (of wind) coming from, the west.—*adv.* towards the west.
wes'tering *adj.* going towards the west.
wes'terly *adj.* **1** living or situated in, or moving towards, the west. **2** (of wind) from the west.—*adv.* towards the west.
wes'tern *adj.* situated in, or belonging to the west.—*n.* a film or novel about the Wild West (see below).
wes'terner *n.* a person belonging to the west.
west'(ern)most *adj.* most westerly.
west'ward *adj.* and (also **west'wards**) *adv.* towards the west.
West End the fashionable district in the west of London, or of other large towns.
go west **1** to die. **2** to become useless.
Wild West the western United States, before the establishment of law and order.

wet *wet*, *adj.* **1** containing water. **2** having water on the surface. **3** rainy:—*comp.* **wett'er**; *superl.* **wett'est.**—*n.* (*coll.*) a weak, ineffectual, irresolute person.—*v.t.* to make wet:—*pr.p.* **wett'ing**; *pa.p.* **wet**, **wett'ed**.
wett'ed.
wet'ness *n.* **wett'ish** *adj.*
wet blanket **1** a cause of discouragement. **2** a depressing companion.
wet dock a dock for floating ships at all states of the tide.
wet'-nurse *wet'nûrs*, *n.* a woman employed to breastfeed another's baby.
wet suit a tight-fitting rubber suit that is worn by divers etc.
in the wet in the rain, or other wet conditions.

we've *wēv*, *abbrev.* we have.

whack *hwak*, *wak*, *v.t.* and *v.i.* to strike smartly, making a sound in doing so.—*n.* **1** a blow. **2** an attempt. **3** a share.
whack'ing *adj.* very large.—*n.* a beating.

whale *hwāl*, *wāl*, *n.* a large sea mammal (animal that suckles its young).—*v.i.* to catch whales:—*pr.p.* **whāl'ing.**
whal'er *n.* a ship, or a person, engaged in whale fishing.
whal'ing *n.* and *adj.*
whale'bone *n.* a light bendable substance got from the upper jaw of certain whales.
whale oil oil obtained from the blubber of a whale.
bull, **cow**, or **calf**, **whale** an adult male, female, or a young, whale.

wharf *hwörf*, *wörf*, *n.* a landing-stage for loading, unloading, ships:—*pl.* **wharfs**, **wharves.**—*v.t.* to fasten up beside a wharf.
wharf'age *n.* the dues paid for using a wharf.

what *hwot*, *wot*, used as *pron.* or *adj.* in questions: *What are you hiding?*; *What book is that?*—and also in dependent (i.e. not main) clauses: *Give me what you have*; *Give me what money you have.*—*interj.* expressing astonishment: *What!*
whatev'er *pron.* **1** anything that. **2** no matter what (also *adj.*).
whatsoev'er *adj.* of whatever kind.
what's what the true state of affairs.

whatnot *hwot'not*, *wot'*, *n.* **1** such things: *books, magazines and whatnot.* **2** a piece of furniture used for holding books, ornaments, china, etc.

whatsoever. See **what**.

wheat *hwēt*, *wēt*, *n.* grain from which flour, much used in making bread, cakes, etc., is obtained.

wheat'en *adj.* **1** made of wheat. **2** wholemeal (see this).

wheedle *hwēd'l*, *wēd'l*, *v.t.* **1** to entice by soft words, cajole (into doing something). **2** to coax (something out of a person):—*pr.p.* **wheed'ling**.

wheed'ler *n.* **wheed'ling** *n.*, *adj.*

wheel *hwēl*, *wēl*, *n.* **1** a circular frame turning on an axle. **2** anything similar in shape or purpose, as a steering-wheel, potter's wheel.—*v.t.* to move or convey on wheels.—*v.i.* **1** to turn about a centre. **2** to turn. **3** (of e.g. birds) to move in a curving course.

wheel(ed) *adjs.* having wheel(s).

wheel'barrow *n.* a barrow with one wheel in front, and two handles and legs behind.

wheel'chair *n.* a chair with wheels, used by invalids, etc.

wheel'house *n.* the shelter in which a ship's steering-wheel is placed.

wheel'wright *n.* a craftsman who makes wheels and wheeled carriages.

wheels within wheels a situation in which many different influences are at work.

wheeze *hwēz*, *wēz*, *v.i.* **1** to breathe with a hissing sound and with difficulty. **2** to make a noise of this kind.—Also *n.*

whee'zy *adj.*:—*comp.* **whee'zier**; *superl.* **whee'ziest**.

whee'zily *adv.* **whee'ziness** *n.*

whelk *hwelk*, *welk*, *n.* a small shellfish with a spiral shell, used as food.

whelp *hwelp*, *welp*, *n.* **1** the young of dogs, lions, etc. **2** (in contempt) a young man.—*v.i.*, *v.t.* (of female dog, etc.) to give birth to young.

when *hwen*, *wen*, *adv.* and *conj.* **1** at what time: *When did he leave?*; *I know when to say nothing.* **2** at the time that: *when he came here.* **3** while: *when I was abroad.* **4** even though: *He bought it when he was told not to.* **5** considering that: *Why walk when you have a car?* **6** and then: *He waited until dark, when he unwillingly went home.*—*pron.* at which: *at the moment when he arrived.*

whence (also **from whence**) *adv.* and *conj.* from what place, source, etc.

whenev'er *conj.* at any, every, time.

where *hwār*, *wār*, *adv.* and *conj.* **1** at or in what place. **2** at or in what place? **3** and in that place: *He went to London, where he set up in business.*—*pron.* **1** in which: *He could not find the place where he had left it.* **2** to which.

whereabout(s)' *advs.* and *conjs.* **1** about where. **2** near what?—*n.* (**where'abouts**) place (roughly indicated) where person, thing, is: *his whereabouts*; *the whereabouts of his new house*.

whereas' *conj.* **1** when in fact. **2** but, on the other hand.

whereby' *adv.* and *conj.* by which.

where'fore *adv.*, *conj.* **1** (*old-fashioned*) why? **2** why. **3** and for this reason.—*n.* the cause.

where'upon *adv.* and *conj.* in, at, or to, any place no matter what.

wherev'er *adv.* and *conj.* in, at, or to, any place no matter what.

where'withal *n.* the means: *He had not the wherewithal to buy food.*

wherry *(h)wer'i*, *n.* a shallow, light boat:—*pl.* **wherr'ies**.

whet *hwet*, *wet*, *v.t.* **1** to sharpen (a tool) by rubbing. **2** to make keen: *to whet the appetite*:—*pr.p.* **whett'ing**; *pa.p.* **whett'ed**.—*n.* **1** act of sharpening. **2** something that sharpens e.g. appetite, desire.

whet'stone *n.* a stone for sharpening edged instruments.

whether *hwe*TH'*ėr*, *we*TH', *conj.* **1** if: *I don't know whether I'll go.* **2** introducing the first of two alternative words, phrases, or clauses, the second being introduced by *or*, or (in the case of clauses) sometimes by *or whether*: *whether I should go or whether I should stay*.

whether or no 1 whether or not. **2** whatever the circumstances.

whey *hwā*, *wā*, *n.* the watery part of milk separated from the curd (the thick part), esp. in making cheese.

which *hwich*, *wich*, used as a *pron.* or *adj.* in questions: *Which do you mean?*; *Which cup shall I take?*—and also in dependent (i.e. not main) clauses: *Tell me which you prefer*; *Say which road is prettier*; *The road which I took was rough*:—*objective* **which**; *possessive* **whose** (*hōōz*; often replaced by **of which**).

whichev'er *pron.* and *adj.* any(one), no matter which.

which is which which is the one and which is the other: *The twins are Mary and Anne, but I do not know which is which.*

whiff *hwif*, *wif*, *n.* a sudden puff (of air, smoke, smell, shot, etc.).

Whig *hwig*, *wig*, *n.* a member of one of the two English political parties in late 17th century, 18th, and early 19th; later known as Liberal.

while *whīl*, *wīl*, *n.* **1** space of time. **2** time and trouble spent (only in **worth (one's) while**).—*conj.* **1** during the time that. **2** although.—*v.t.* (with *away*) to cause (time) to pass without weariness: *He read to while away the time*:—*pr.p.* **whīl'ing**.
whilst *conj.* while.

whim *hwim*, *wim*, *n.* an odd, absurd fancy or sudden desire or change of mind.
whim'sical *adj.* **1** (of a person) full of whims. **2** quaintly humorous. **3** odd, fanciful: *The story was full of whimsical ideas*.
whim'sically *adv.*
whim'sicalness, **whimsical'ity** *ns.*
whim'sy, **whim'sey** *n.* **1** a whim. **2** quaint, fanciful humour:—*pl.* **whim'sies**, **-seys**.

whimper *hwim'pėr*, *wim'*, *v.i.* to cry with low whining voice.—*n.* a peevish cry.

whin *hwin*, *win*, *n.* a prickly shrub, gorse, furze.

whine *hwīn*, *wīn*, *v.i.* **1** to utter a complaining cry. **2** to complain in a feeble way or unnecessarily:—*pr.p.* **whīn'ing**.—*n.* a plaintive cry.
whī'ner *n.* **whī'ningly** *adv.*
whinn'y *(hwin', win')* *v.i.* to neigh:—*pr.p.* **whinn'ying**; *pa.p.* **whinn'ied**.—Also *n.*:—*pl.* **whinn'ies**.

whip *hwip*, *wip*, *n.* **1** a lash with a handle, for punishing or driving. **2** a stroke given as by a whip. **3** in parliament, a member chosen by his party to make sure that no one fails to vote in important divisions. **4** a notice sent out by a parliamentary whip.—*v.t.* **1** to lash. **2** to drive or punish with lashes. **3** to beat into a froth (eggs, cream, etc.). **4** to snatch (with *up*, *away*, *out*).—*v.i.* **1** to move nimbly. **2** to move in the manner of a whip lash:—*pr.p.* **whipp'ing**; *pa.p.* **whipped**.
whipp'ing *n.* and *adj.*
whip hand the hand that holds the whip in driving (**have the whip hand over someone** to be in a position to compel someone).
whip'lash *n.* the lash of a whip, or a similar sudden rapid movement.
whipp'er-snapp'er *n.* a boastful but unimportant person.
whipp'ing-boy *n.* someone punished for the faults of another, a scapegoat.
whip'-round (*coll.*) *n.* an informal appeal for, and collection of, financial contributions.

whippet *hwip'it*, *wip'*, *n.* a racing dog like a small greyhound.

whir(r) *hwûr*, *wûr*, *n.* a sound from rapid whirling.—*v.i.* to make such a sound.—*v.t.* and *v.i.* to move with a whirring, buzzing sound:—*pr.p.* **whirr'ing**; *pa.p.* **whirred**.

whirl *hwûrl*, *wûrl*, *n.* **1** a rapid turning. **2** an excited confusion (of emotion, activity, etc.) **3** commotion.—*v.i.* to go round rapidly.—*v.t.* **1** to turn (round) rapidly. **2** to carry (away) rapidly.
whirl'pool *n.* a circular current in a river or sea, caused by opposing tides, winds, or currents.
whirl'wind *n.* a violent current of wind with a whirling motion.

whisk *hwisk*, *wisk*, *v.t.* to move, sweep, or stir, rapidly.—*v.i.* to move nimbly and rapidly.—*n.* **1** a rapid, sweeping motion. **2** a kitchen tool for beating eggs, cream, etc. **3** implement for flapping flies away.
whis'ker *n.* **1** something that whisks. **2** (usu. in *pl.*) hair on the side of a man's face (**side whiskers**). **3** a long bristle on the upper lip of a cat, etc. **4** (*coll.*) a small amount, distance, etc.
whis'kered *adj.*

whisky, (*Ir.* and *U.S.*) **whiskey** *hwis'ki*, *wis'*, *n.* an alcoholic drink made from grain:—*pl.* **whis'kies**, (*Ir.* and *U.S.*) **whis'keys**.

whisper *hwis'pėr*, *wis'*, *v.i.* **1** to speak very softly. **2** (of trees, etc.) to make a soft sound. **3** to spread rumours.—*v.t.* **1** to say very softly. **2** to spread (a rumour).—*n.* **1** a sound made very softly. **2** a secret hint. **3** a rumour.
whis'perer *n.*
whispering campaign an attack made by secretly spreading rumours.

whist *hwist*, *wist*, *n.* a card game played by two against two.

whistle *hwis'l*, *wis'*, *v.i.* **1** to make a sound by forcing breath through lips or teeth. **2** to make such a sound with an instrument. **3** to sound shrill. **4** to whizz (through the air).—*v.t.* **1** to make, produce (a sound, tune, etc.) by whistling. **2** to call by a whistle:—*pr.p.* **whis'tling**.—*n.* **1** the sound made by whistling. **2** an instrument for whistling.
whis'tler *n.*
whis'tle-stop *adj.* having a lot of very brief stops: *a whistle-stop tour*.

whit *hwit*, *wit*, *n.* a very small particle or amount.

Whit. See **Whitsun**.

white *hwīt*, *wīt*, *adj.* **1** of the colour of pure snow. **2** pure. **3** bright. **4** light-coloured: *white wine*. **5** pale, wan. **6** of light complexion (as Europeans).—*n.* **1** the colour of snow. **2** something white (e.g. a white man, the part of an egg surrounding the yolk).

whī'ten *v.t.*, *v.i.* to make, or become, white or whiter.

white'ness *n.* **whī'tish** *adj.*

whī'ting[1] *n.* a small sea fish related to the cod.

whī'ting[2], **white'ning** *ns.* ground chalk free from stony matter.

white ant a termite (see this).

white'bait *n.* fry of herring and sprat.

white'-coll'ar *adj.* (of jobs, workers) not involving, or involved in, manual labour.

white corpuscle one of the colourless cells in blood plasma, etc.

white elephant, **feather**. See under **elephant**, **feather**.

white flag a sign of truce or of surrender.

white heat the degree of heat at which bodies become white.

white'-hot' *adj.*

white horse a white-topped wave.

White House official residence of the President of U.S.A. at Washington.

white lie a not very serious lie.

white meat flesh of poultry, and rabbit, veal, pork.

white paper a statement printed on white paper, issued by government for the information of parliament.

white sauce a sauce made of flour, melted butter, milk or lightly-flavoured stock and other desired flavourings.

white'wash *n.* **1** a mixture of whiting or lime and water, used for whitening walls. **2** anything that conceals a stain.—*v.t.* **1** to cover with whitewash. **2** to cover up faults, etc. in (e.g. conduct). **3** to attempt to clear (a reputation).

Whitehall *hwīt'höl'*, *wīt'*, *n.* **1** the offices or policy of the British Government. **2** the Civil Service.

whither *hwi*TH*'ėr*, *wi*TH, *adv.* and *conj.* **1** to what place? **2** to which place.

whitlow *hwit'lō*, *wit'*, *n.* inflammation and usu. suppuration, of finger or toe, esp. near nail.

Whitsun *hwit'sůn*, *wit'*, **Whit** *adjs.* of **Whitsuntide**, the week beginning with **Whit Sunday** (or **Whitsunday**), the seventh after Easter.

whittle *hwit'l*, *wit'*, *v.t.* **1** to pare or cut off with a knife. **2** to shape (e.g. a twig) with a knife. **3** (with *away*, *down*) to make gradually less:—*pr.p.* **whitt'ling**.

whiz(z) *hwiz*, *wiz*, *v.i.* **1** to make a hissing sound like an arrow flying through the air. **2** to move rapidly:—*pr.p.* **whizz'ing**; *pa.p.* **whizzed**.

whizz'-kid (*slang*) *n.* a very intelligent or brash, etc. person who achieves rapid success while relatively young.

who *hōō*, *pron.* **1** what person(s)? **2** also used in dependent (i.e. not main) clauses: *The man, men, who came, took it away*:—*objective* **whom** *(hōōm)*: *The man whom I saw, and to whom I gave the note*; *possessive* **whose** *(hōōz)*: *I saw someone whose face was familiar*.

whoev'er, (*old-fashioned*) **whosoev'er** *prons.* whatever person.

whole *hōl*, *adj.* **1** consisting of all. **2** complete. **3** not broken. **4** sound in health.—*n.* **1** a single unit, made up of parts. **2** the entire thing.

whole'ness *n.*

wholly *(hōl'li, hō'li) adv.* completely, altogether.

whole'food *n.* food produced without the use of artificial fertilisers, etc., and processed as little as possible.

whole'hear'ted *adj.* generous, sincere, enthusiastic: *His plan had my wholehearted support*.

whole'meal *n.* flour made from the entire wheat grain or seed.

whole'sale *n.* the sale of goods in large quantity to a retailer.—*adj.* **1** buying and selling thus. **2** on a large scale: *wholesale slaughter*.

whole'some *adj.* healthy, sound.

whole'somely *adv.* **whole'someness** *n.*

(up)on the whole taking everything into consideration.

who'll, *hōōl*, *abbrev.* who will.

whom. See **who**.

whoop *hwōōp*, *hōōp*, **hoop** *hōōp*, *ns.* **1** a loud eager shout. **2** the noisy sound of breathing-in heard in whooping-cough.—*v.i.* to give a loud cry, of delight, triumph, scorn, etc.

whoop'er *n.* a kind of swan.

whoop'ing-cough, **hoop'ing-cough** *ns.* an infectious disease with a violent cough and whoop.

whopper *hwop'ėr*, *wop'*, (*coll.*) *n.* anything very large, esp. a lie.

whore *hōr*, *hör*, *n.* a prostitute.

whorl *hwörl*, *hwûrl*, *wörl*, *wûrl*, *n.* **1** a number of leaves in a circle round the stem. **2** a turn in a spiral shell.

whorl'ed *adj.* having whorls.

whortleberry *hwûr'tl-ber-i*, *wûr'*, *hûr'*, *n.* bilberry:—*pl.* **whor'tleberries**.

whose. See **who** and **which**.

why *hwī*, *wī*, *adv.* for what cause or reason: *Why did you go?*; *Tell me why you went.*—*pron.* on account of which: *the reason why I came.*—*interj.* expressing surprise or protest.

the why and the wherefore the whole reason.

wick *wik, n.* the twisted threads of cotton, etc. in a candle, lamp, etc. which draw up the liquid that burns.

wicked *wik'id, adj.* **1** evil in behaviour, sinful. **2** mischievous and spiteful. **3** roguish. **4** (*coll.*) very bad.—*n.* (as *pl.*) wicked persons.
wick'edly *adv.* **wick'edness** *n.*

wicker *wik'ėr, n.* a small twig (e.g. a willow twig) that will bend easily.—*adj.* (of e.g. a table, basket) made of twigs.
wick'erwork *n.* basketwork.

wicket *wik'it, n.* **1** a small door or gate, esp. one forming part of a larger one. **2** (*cricket*) a set of three upright stumps at which the bowler aims the ball. **3** one of these stumps. **4** the ground between the bowler and the batsman. **5** a batsman's innings.
wick'et-keeper *n.* the fielder who stands immediately behind the wicket.

wide *wīd, adj.* **1** broad, not narrow. **2** stretching far: *wide estates.* **3** opened as far as possible: *with wide eyes*; *The window is wide.* **4** far apart. **5** far from the point aimed at (with *of*): *wide of the mark.*—*n.* a ball bowled beyond the batsman's reach.
wide, wide'ly *advs.*
wide'ness, width *(width), ns.*
wi'den *v.t., v.i.* to make, or become, wide or wider.
wide'-awake' *adj.* **1** fully awake. **2** on the alert. **3** not easily cheated or misled.
wide'spread *adj.* spread over a large area or among many people.

widow *wid'ō, n.* a woman whose husband is dead.—Also *v.t.* to take a husband away from (someone).
wi'dower *n.* a man whose wife is dead.
wid'owhood *n.* the state of being a widow or (*rarely*) a widower.

wield *wēld, v.t.* **1** to exercise (authority, power). **2** to manage, use (e.g. sword, pen).
wiel'der *n.*
wiel'dy *adj.* manageable:—*comp.* **wield'ier**; *superl.* **wield'iest**.

wife *wīf, n.* **1** a married woman. **2** the woman to whom one is married. **3** a woman:—*pl.* **wives** *(wīvz).*
wife'ly *adj.*
old wives' tale a superstitious and often misleading story.

wig *wig, n.* an artificial covering of hair for the head.
wigged *adj.* wearing a wig.

wigeon *wij'ŏn, n.* a kind of wild duck.

wiggle *wig'l, v.i.* and *v.t.* to move, or cause to move, irregularly from side to side:—*pr.p.* **wigg'ling**.
wigg'ly *adj.*:—*comp.* **wigg'lier**; *superl.* **wigg'liest**.
wigg'liness *n.*

wigwam *wig'wam, -wom, n.* Indian hut of skins, etc., usu. rounded in shape.

wild *wīld, adj.* **1** not tamed. **2** not cultivated. **3** uncivilised. **4** lawless. **5** violent. **6** distracted: *wild with anxiety.* **7** very stormy: *a wild night.* **8** rash. **9** wide of the mark: *a wild guess.*—*n.* (also in *pl.*) an uncultivated region.
wild'ly *adv.* **wild'ness** *n.*
wild'cat *adj.* unreliable, rash: *a wildcat scheme.*
wil'derness *(wil')* *n.* **1** desert or wild country. **2** an empty, unhappy place. **3** a wild part of a garden. **4** a large confused mass: *a wilderness of old car bodies.*
wild'fire *n.* **1** formerly, name of material burning strongly, used in war (still found in **spread like wildfire**—of e.g. news). **2** lightning without thunder.
wild'fowl *n.* wild birds, esp. water birds shot as game.
wild'life *n.* wild animals, birds, etc. regarded collectively.
wild-goose chase an absurd attempt to catch or find something one cannot possibly obtain.

wile *wīl, n.* **1** a trick, deceitful move. **2** (in *pl.*) persuasive manner: *She used her wiles to get her own way.*
wily *wī'li, adj.* crafty, artful, sly:—*comp.* **wī'lier**; *superl.* **wī'liest**.
wī'lily *adv.* **wī'liness** *n.*

will *wil, n.* **1** the power to choose or decide. **2** desire: *against one's will.* **3** determination: *the will to succeed.* **4** feeling towards someone or something: *good will*; *ill will.* **5** (document containing) a formal statement about what is to be done with one's property after one's death.—*v.t.* **1** to desire, intend, to (e.g. *I will speak out*), be willing to (e.g. *I will go if you ask me*). **2** (to try) to influence by exerting the will: *She willed him to pick it up.* **3** to bequeath, hand down, by will.—Also *v.i.*:—*pa.t.* **willed** (in sense 1, **would** *wood, wŭd, wd*).—Also used to form future tenses of other verbs when the subject is *he, she, it, you,* or *they*: *He, you, they, will certainly arrive late*; also used in requests or commands: *Will you please stop talking!*; also used to form a *pr.t.* describing a habit: *Each morning he will go for a walk*:—*pr.t. 2nd person* (thou) **wilt** (*old-fashioned*); *pa.t.* **would**. There is also a conditional form **would**: *He would be foolish if he did not go, or foolish not to go.*
See also **shall** and **should**.
wil'ful *adj.* **1** obstinate, set on one's own

way. **2** intentional: *wilful damage*.
wil'fully *adv.* **wil'fulness** *n.*
will'ing *adj.* **1** ready to agree (to do something). **2** eager.
will'ingly *adv.* **will'ingness** *n.*
will'power *n.* the power or determination to do something.
at will as, or when, one chooses.
with a will 1 eagerly. **2** energetically.

will-o'-the-wisp *wil'-ȯ-thi-wisp'*, *n.* **1** a pale light seen over marshes at night, supposed to be due to burning marsh gas. **2** an aim that one is always trying to achieve and that can never be accomplished: *Poor Jack was always chasing the will-o'-the-wisp of success.*

willow *wil'ō*, *n.* **1** a tree with slender, easily bent branches. **2** the wood of the willow. **3** a cricket bat.
will'owy *adj.* **1** easily bent. **2** slender, graceful. **3** with many willows.
willow pattern a blue design of Chinese style used on china made in England.

willy-nilly *wil'i-nil'i*, *adv.* whether one wishes it or not: *He must go, willy-nilly.*

wilt¹ *wilt*, *v.i.* **1** (of flowers) to droop. **2** to lose energy.

wilt². See **will**.

wily. See **wile**.

wimp *wimp*, (*slang*) *n.* an ineffectual person.

win *win*, *v.t.* **1** to gain, obtain, by contest (e.g. a victory), by luck (e.g. a prize in a lottery), by effort (e.g. love, consent, a wife). **2** to succeed in making (one's way). **3** to reach (a place).—Also *v.i.*:—*pr.p.* **winn'ing**; *pa.t.*, *pa.p.* **won** *(wun)*.—*n.* a victory, success.
winn'er *n.*
winn'ing *n.* **1** the act of one who wins. **2** (in *pl.*) something (esp. money) that is won.—*adj.* **1** victorious, successful. **2** attractive, charming: *She has winning ways.*
winn'ingly *adv.* **winn'ingness** *n.*
winn'ing-post *n.* post marking place where a race finishes.
win the day. See **day**.

wince *wins*, *v.i.* **1** to shrink or start back quickly in pain. **2** to be hurt (e.g. by an unkind remark):—*pr.p.* **win'cing**.

winch *winch*, *-sh*, *n.* **1** a crank or handle for turning a wheel. **2** a hoisting machine, windlass.—*v.t.* to raise, haul, etc. with such a machine.

wind¹ *wind*, *n.* **1** air in motion. **2** a current of air (gale, etc.). **3** air bearing the scent e.g. of game. **4** breath. **5** flatulence. **6** empty, unimportant words. **7** the wind instruments in an orchestra. **8** the players of these instruments.—*v.t.* to put out of breath.
win'ded *adj.* out of breath.
wind'ward *n.* the point from which the wind blows.—Also *adj.* and *adv.*
win'dy *adj.* **1** exposed to the wind: *a windy corner.* **2** tempestuous: *a windy day.* **3** (*coll.*) nervous, scared:—*comp.* **win'dier**; *superl.* **win'diest**.
win'diness *n.*
wind'bag *n.* a very talkative person.
wind'break *n.* something, e.g. a group of trees, sheltering from wind.
wind'cheater *n.* a type of close-fitting jacket.
wind'fall *n.* **1** fruit blown from a tree. **2** any unexpected gain or advantage.
wind instrument a musical instrument sounded by wind, esp. by the breath.
wind'jammer *(-jam-)* *n.* a large sailing vessel.
wind'mill *n.* a machine for grinding grain or pumping water worked by wind.
wind'pipe *n.* the passage for the breath between mouth and lungs, the trachea.
wind'screen *n.* a transparent screen above the dashboard in a car.
wind'sock *n.* airfield device for showing wind direction and strength.
wind'-swept *adj.* exposed to wind and showing effects of it.
close to, near, the wind 1 near the danger point. **2** near the limit of what may be said with propriety.
get the wind up to become nervous or anxious.
get wind of to get a hint of, hear indirectly about.
in the wind afoot, about to happen.
second wind natural breathing recovered after breathlessness.

wind² *wīnd*, *v.t.* **1** to turn, twist, coil. **2** to screw the mechanism of (e.g. a clock). **3** to make (one's, its, way) by turning and twisting (also *v.i.*).—*v.i.* **1** to turn completely or often. **2** to turn (round something):—*pr.p.* **wīn'ding**; *pa.p.* **wound** *(wownd)*.
wīn'der *n.* **1** one who winds. **2** an instrument for winding.
wīn'ding *adj.* **1** curving. **2** full of bends.—*n.* **1** a turning. **2** a twist.
wind down 1 to slow down and stop. **2** to relax.
wind up 1 to coil completely. **2** to wind the spring or mechanism of (e.g. a watch) completely. **3** to excite very much (usu. in *pass.*): *He was wound up about something.* **4** to bring or come to an end (e.g. a meeting, business).

windlass *wind'lȧs, n.* a machine for raising weights by winding a rope round a revolving cylinder.

windjammer. See **wind**[1].

window *win'dō, n.* **1** an opening in a wall of a building, etc. for air and light, fitted with a wooden or metal frame, and usu. glass. **2** something similar in shape or purpose.

window dressing **1** arranging goods in a shop window effectively. **2** giving an unduly attractive or favourable appearance to something (e.g. a plan, cause, or situation).

windpipe, etc. See **wind**[1].

wine *wīn, n.* **1** a drink made from the fermented juice of grapes or other fruit. **2** a rich, red colour.

wine'press *n.* a machine in which grapes are pressed in making wine.

wing *wing, n.* **1** the limb of a bird, bat, or insect, by which it flies. **2** a limb in the same position of certain birds that do not fly. **3** (in football, etc.) a player at the edge of the field. **4** a section with specific opinions, etc., of a political party. **5** a side structure on a stage, aeroplane, building, etc. **6** (in *pl.*) a badge worn by flying members of the Royal Air Force—*v.t.* **1** to give speed to. **2** to wound in the wing, or in the arm or shoulder.—*v.i.* to soar.

winged *wingd* or *wing'id, adj.* **1** having wings. **2** swift. **3** *(wingd)* wounded in the wing, shoulder, or arm.

wing'er *n.* a player at either end of the forward line in football, etc.

wing commander a rank in the Royal Air Force, or a person of this rank.

wing'span, -spread *ns.* distance from tip to tip of fully extended (bird or aeroplane) wings.

take wing to fly off, flee, depart.

under one's wing under one's protection, guidance.

wink *wingk, v.i.* **1** to shut and open an eye quickly. **2** to give a hint by winking. **3** (of e.g. lights) to flicker, twinkle.—*v.t.* to close and open (eye) quickly.—*n.* **1** act of winking. **2** a hint given by winking.

easy as winking very easy or easily.

forty winks a short sleep.

wink at purposely to take no notice of (action that is e.g. against rules).

winkle *wing'kl, n.* same as **periwinkle**[2].

winkle out to force out gradually and with difficulty:—*pr.p.* **win'kling out**.

winning, winner. See **win**.

winnow *win'ō, v.t.* **1** to separate the chaff from (the grain) by wind. **2** to separate, sift: *to winnow the truth from a mass of statements.*—Also *v.i.*

winsome *win'sȯm, adj.* charming.

win'somely *adv.* **win'someness** *n.*

winter *win'tėr, n.* **1** the cold season of the year—in the northern temperate regions (Europe, etc.) from November or December to January or February. **2** any cheerless time.—Also *adj.*—*v.i.* to pass the winter.—*v.t.* to keep, feed (cattle, etc.) during winter.

win'try *adj.* **1** like winter, cold, stormy. **2** (of e.g. a smile) dreary, not warm or cheerful:—*comp.* **win'trier**; *superl.* **win'triest**.

win'triness *n.*

winter quarters lodging, place of stay (esp. of soldiers) during the winter.

winter sports skiing, tobogganing, etc.

wipe *wīp, v.t.* **1** to clean or dry by rubbing. **2** (with *away, off, out, up*) to clear away:—*pr.p.* **wī'ping**.—*n.* act of cleaning by rubbing.

wī'per *n.* **wī'ping** *n.*

wipe out **1** to remove, get rid of. **2** to destroy completely.

wire *wīr, n.* **1** a thread of metal. **2** a metal string of a musical instrument. **3** the metal thread used in telegraphy, etc. **4** a telegram.—*adj.* formed of wire.—*v.t.* **1** to supply (e.g. a building) with wire necessary for carrying an electric current. **2** to send by, or to inform by, telegraph.—*v.i.* to telegraph:—*pr.p.* **wīr'ing**.

wire'less *adj.* without wires, esp. of telegraphy and telephony.—*n.* **1** wireless telegraphy or telephony. **2** a message sent by one of these. **3** a radio. **4** sound broadcasting generally.

wir'ing *n.*

wīr'y *adj.* **1** made of, or like, wire. **2** lean and strong: *his wiry body*:—*comp.* **wīr'ier**; *superl.* **wīr'iest**.

wīr'ily *adv.* **wīr'iness** *n.*

wire'-nett'ing *n.* material with wide mesh woven of wire.

wire'puller *n.* one who influences the actions of others by secret means (as if making puppets move), an intriguer.

wire'pulling *n.*

wisdom. See **wise**[1].

wise[1] *wīz, adj.* **1** learned. **2** able to use knowledge well, judging rightly: *He is wise—ask his advice.* **3** prudent, sensible: *a wise decision.*

wise'ly *adv.*

wise'ness, wis'dom *(wiz'), ns.*

wisdom tooth one of four back teeth cut after childhood, usu. about the age of twenty.

wise'crack (*coll.*) *n.* a joke, smart remark.—Also *v.i.*

be wise to to be aware of or know the purpose of.

wise² *wīz*, *n.* way, manner; used as sfx: *crosswise*.

in any (**no**) **wise** in any (no) way.

wiseacre *wīz'ā-kėr*, *n.* **1** one who puts on an air of great wisdom. **2** a simpleton, unconscious of being one.

wish *wish*, *v.i.* **1** to have a desire (for). **2** to express a desire.—*v.t.* **1** to desire or long for. **2** to express a desire (that, to do, etc). **3** to hope for on behalf of (someone): *I wish you luck.*—*n.* **1** desire, longing. **2** thing desired. **3** expression of desire.

wish'er *n.* **wish'ing** *n.* and *adj.*

wish'ful *adj.* **wish'fully** *adv.*

wish'bone *n.* a V-shaped bone in a chicken, etc.; when it is pulled apart, the longer part is supposed to indicate the fulfilment of a wish.

wishful thinking 1 belief that something will happen arising merely from a wish that it should. **2** wishing for something that is unlikely to happen.

wishy-washy *wish'i-wosh'i*, *adj.* **1** (of liquid) and thin and weak. **2** feeble, of poor quality.

wisp *wisp*, *n.* a small tuft or thin strand: *a wisp of hair.*

wistful *wist'fool*, *-fl*, *adj.* **1** thoughtful and rather sad. **2** yearning with little hope.

wist'fully *adv.* **wist'fulness** *n.*

wit¹ *wit*, *v.t.* and *v.i.* to know—an old verb now used in:—

witt'ingly *adv.* knowingly.

to wit that is to say.

wit² *wit*, *n.* **1** understanding. **2** (in *pl.*) natural mental ability. **3** common sense. **4** expression of ideas in a lively amusing way. **5** a person who expresses himself thus.

wit'less *adj.* **wit'lessness** *n.*

witt'ed *adj.* having wit or understanding—usu. with another *adj.*, as *quick-witted.*

witt'icism *n.* a witty remark.

witt'y *adj.* clever and amusing:—*comp.* **witt'ier**; *superl.* **witt'iest**.

witt'ily *adv.* **witt'iness** *n.*

at one's wits' end utterly perplexed and desperate.

have, **keep**, **one's wits about one** to be cautious, alert and watchful.

live by one's wits to live by cunning rather than by hard work.

witch *wich*, *n.* **1** a woman supposed to have powers of magic through being in league with the devil. **2** a hag. **3** (*coll.*) a fascinating woman.

witch'ery *n.* **1** witchcraft. **2** fascination.

witch'craft *n.* **1** the magic practised by a witch. **2** power like that of a witch or magician. **3** fascination.

witch'-doctor *n.* in African tribes, one whose profession is to cure illness and keep away evil magical influences.

witch'-hunt *n.* search for and persecution of people with unpopular or unorthodox views, etc.

with *wi*TH, *with*, *prep.* **1** against: *to fight with a rival.* **2** in the company of. **3** on the side of. **4** in the same direction as: *to drift with the stream.* **5** by, by means of: *Cut it with a knife.* **6** having: *a man with a ladder.* **7** in the keeping of: *Leave the coat with me.*

feel, to be, or **to think**, **with** (**someone**) to feel as, be of same opinion as, the other person concerned.

with it (*coll.*) up to date, fashionable.

with that at that point.

with- *wi*TH-, or *-th-*, *pfx.* against.

withdraw *wi*TH-*draw'* (or *with-*), *v.t.* **1** to draw back or away. **2** to take away: *to withdraw one's support for a plan.* **3** to take back (something one has said).—*v.i.* to retire, to go away:—*pa.p.* **withdrew'**; *pa.p.* **withdrawn'**.

withdraw'al *n.*

withdrawn' *adj.* **1** (of place) isolated, lonely. **2** (of manner) not responsive or friendly.

withe *wi*TH, **withy** *wi*TH'*i*, *ns.* **1** a bendable twig, esp. of willow. **2** a band of twisted twigs:—*pls.* **withes**, **with'ies**.

wither *wi*TH'*ėr*, *v.t.*, *v.i.* **1** to fade, dry up, decay. **2** to feel, or to make to feel, embarrassed or very unimportant: *She withered him with a look.*

withers *wi*TH'*ėrz*, *n.pl.* the ridge between the shoulder bones of a horse.

withhold *wi*TH-*hōld'* (or *with-*), *v.t.* **1** to hold back. **2** to refuse to give:—*pr.p.* **withheld'**.

within *wi*TH-*in'* (-or *with-*), *prep.* **1** inside. **2** in the limits of, not going beyond: *within sight*; *within one's rights.*—*adv.* **1** in, or into, the inner part. **2** inwardly.

without *wi*TH-*owt'* (or *with-*), *prep.* **1** outside of. **2** not having, free from, in absence of.—*adv.* on, or to, the outside.

withstand *wi*TH-*stand'* (or *with-*), *v.t.* to oppose or resist successfully:—*pa.p.* **withstood'**.

withy. See **withe**.

witness *wit'nis*, *n.* **1** a person who sees or has direct knowledge of a thing. **2** one who gives evidence. **3** testimony, evidence.—*v.t.* **1** to see, be present at. **2** to sign one's name to show one knows (another's sig-

nature), on e.g. a will, is genuine. **3** to bear witness (that). **4** to be evidence or proof of.—*v.i.* to give evidence.
witness box, **stand** the stand from which a witness gives evidence in a court of law.
bear witness (of person, fact, etc.) to give or be evidence (with *to*, *that*): *to bear witness to his honesty*, *that he is honest*.
witticism, **witty**, etc. See **wit**[2].
wittingly. See **wit**[1].
wives. See **wife**.
wizard *wiz'ȧrd*, *n.* **1** a man who practises magic. **2** one who works wonders.
wiz'ardry *n.*
wizened *wiz'nd*, *adj.* dried up, shrivelled.
wiz'en *v.i.*, *v.t.* to become, make, dry.
woad *wōd*, *n.* **1** plant yielding blue dye. **2** dyestuff made from its leaves.
wobble *wob'l*, *v.i.* **1** to rock unsteadily from side to side. **2** to waver:—*pr.p.* **wobb'ling**.
wobb'ly *adj.*:—*comp.* **wobb'lier**; *superl.* **wobb'liest**.
wobb'liness *n.*
woe *wō*, *n.* **1** grief, misery. **2** an affliction, trouble.
woe'ful *adj.* **woe'fully** *adv.*
woe'fulness *n.*
woe'begone *(-bi-gon) adj.* dismal looking.
wok *wok*, *n.* a hemispherical frying-pan used in Chinese cookery.
woke, **woken**. See **wake**[1].
wold *wōld*, *n.* open uncultivated country.
wolf *woolf*, *n.* **1** a beast of prey, of the dog family, that goes round with others in a pack. **2** a greedy and cruel person:—*pl.* **wolves** *(woolvz)*.—*v.t.* to eat greedily.
wolf'ish *adj.* like a wolf.
wolf'ishly *adv.* **wolf'ishness** *n.*
cry wolf to give a false alarm.
keep the wolf from the door to keep away hunger or want.
woman *woom'ȧn*, *n.* **1** an adult human female. **2** human females considered together. **3** a domestic help:—*pl.* **women** *(wim'in)*.
wom'anhood *n.* the state, or qualities, of a woman.
wom'anise *v.i.* to pursue women for sexual purposes:—*pr.p.* **wom'anising**.
wom'aniser *n.* **wom'anising** *n.*
wom'ankind, **wom'enkind**, **wom'enfolk** *ns.* women generally.
wom'anlike *adj.* and *adv.*
wom'anly *adj.* **1** natural, suitable, to a woman. **2** showing qualities of a woman.
wom'anliness *n.*
womens' lib(eration) a movement of feminists trying to achieve equality with men with regard to pay, legal status, etc.
womb *wōōm*, *n.* **1** the organ in which the young of mammals are developed and kept until birth. **2** any deep cavity.
wombat *wom'bat*, *n.* an Australian pouched animal.
women, etc. See **woman**.
won. See **win**.
wonder *wun'dėr*, *n.* **1** the state of mind produced by something unexpected or extraordinary. **2** a strange thing. **3** quality of being strange or unexpected: *the wonder of the discovery*.—*v.i.* **1** to be surprised (at, that). **2** to feel curiosity or doubt (about).—*v.t.* to feel curiosity about, or desire to know: *I wonder what the news is*.
won'derful *adj.* **1** arousing wonder, strange. **2** (*coll.*) superb, excellent.
won'derfully *adv.* **won'deringly** *adv.*
won'derment *n.* wonder (*def. 1*).
won'drous *adj.* wonderful (*def. 1*).
won'derland *n.* a land of wonders.
wonky *wong'ki*, *adj.* unsound, shaky, etc.:—*comp.* **wonk'ier**; *superl.* **wonk'iest**.
wont *wōnt*, *n.* habit, custom.
won'ted *adj.* usual, accustomed.
won't *wōnt*, will not.
woo *wōō*, *v.t.* **1** to seek in marriage, court. **2** to seek to win over (a person), or to gain (e.g. success):—*pr.p.* **woo'ing**; *pa.p.* **wooed** *(wōōd)*.
woo'er *n.* **woo'ing** *n.*
wood *wood*, *n.* **1** the hard part of a tree. **2** trees cut or sawn, timber. **3** a group of growing trees (also in *pl.*). **4** something made of wood.
wood'ed *adj.* covered with trees.
wood'en *adj.* **1** made of, or like, wood. **2** (of e.g. face, manner) stiff, dull, without liveliness or charm.
wood'y *adj.* **1** having many woods. **2** like or composed of wood:—*comp.* **wood'ier**; *superl.* **wood'iest**.
wood'enness *n.* **wood'iness** *n.*
woodchuck. See **marmot**.
wood'craft *n.* skill in everything to do with life in forests.
wood'cut *n.* an engraving cut on wood, or an impression from it.
wood'cutter *n.* one who cuts wood.
wood'land *n.* land covered with woods.
wood'pecker *n.* a bird that pecks holes in the bark of trees in search of insects.
wood pulp wood fibre reduced to a pulp, used in making paper.
wood spirit an alcohol obtained from wood, etc.
wood'wind *n.* **1** the section of an orchestra in which wind instruments of wood,

and also some of e.g. silver, etc., are played. **2** any such instrument.

wood'work *n.* **1** the wooden part of any structure. **2** carpentry.

wood'worm *n.* a beetle larva that bores in wood.

not to be able to see the wood for the trees not to understand exactly the nature and purpose of a situation, etc. because of too much concern with the details of it.

out of the wood(s) out of danger.

touch wood (also used as *interj.*), **knock on wood** to touch something wooden superstitiously, to avoid bad luck.

wooer, wooing. See **woo**.

woof *wōōf*, *n.* same as **weft**.

wool *wool*, *n.* **1** the soft hair of sheep and other animals. **2** yarn made of wool. **3** fabric of wool. **4** any light, fleecy or fibrous substance resembling wool.

wooll'en *adj.* **1** made of wool. **2** dealing in wool.

wooll'ens *n.pl.* garments made of wool.

wooll'y *adj.* **1** made of, or like, wool. **2** vague, hazy:—*comp.* **wooll'ier**; *superl.* **wooll'iest**.—*n.* a knitted garment:—*pl.* **wooll'ies**.

wooll'iness *n.*

wool'-gathering *n.* **1** absent-mindedness. **2** inattentive state.

wool'sack *n.* the seat of the Lord Chancellor in the House of Lords, a large square sack covered with scarlet.

word *wûrd*, *n.* **1** a spoken or written sign denoting a thing, an idea, etc. **2** (in *pl.*) speech, talk. **3** a brief conversation: *to have a word with someone.* **4** (in *pl.*) a quarrel. **5** news: *word of his arrival.* **6** a rumour. **7** a promise. **8** a password.—*v.t.* to express in words: *You must word the message more plainly*.

wor'dy *adj.* containing too many words:—*comp.* **wor'dier**; *superl.* **wor'diest**.

wor'dily *adv.* **wor'diness** *n.*

wor'ding *n.* the manner of expressing in words, choice of words.

word'-blindness *n.* dyslexia.

word'-per'fect *adj.* having memorised (and produced) precisely the correct words.

word processor an electronic machine (sometimes with a screen) which performs the tasks of typing, data-recording, dictating, etc.

break one's word to fail to keep one's promise.

eat one's words to admit humbly that one was mistaken in saying something.

hard words harsh, angry words.

in a word 1 in short. **2** to sum up.

say, etc., **a good word for 1** to defend, support. **2** to recommend.

take someone's word for it to assume that what someone says is correct (without checking).

the last word 1 the limit, the worst. **2** the very latest, most up-to-date.

word for word in the exact words: *He repeated the message word for word.*

wore. See **wear**.

work *wûrk*, *n.* **1** effort put out to make or to achieve something. **2** toil, labour. **3** employment. **4** a task. **5** anything made or done. **6** a fortification. **7** a building, etc. **8** needlework. **9** a production of art (a book, painting, piece of music, etc.). **10** manner of working, workmanship: *This is good work.* **11** (in *pl.*) a factory, workshop. **12** (in *pl.*) the mechanism e.g. of a watch.—*v.i.* **1** to make efforts (to achieve something). **2** to toil, labour. **3** to be employed. **4** (of a machine) to act, or be in action. **5** to produce results: *if the plan works.* **6** to make one's, its, way, carefully or with effort. **7** to ferment, boil, bubble.—*v.t.* **1** to make by labour. **2** to bring about by action. **3** to solve (e.g. a problem). **4** to manage, control. **5** to keep going (e.g. a machine). **6** to embroider. **7** to excite gradually (into a feeling): *He worked himself into a rage*:—*pa.p.* **worked** (also **wrought**; see this word).

work'able *adj.* which may be carried out, practical: *a workable plan*.

work'ing *n.* **1** action, operation. **2** (in *pl.*) the parts of a mine, etc., where work is, or has been, carried on.

work'aday *adj.* ordinary, unexciting.

workahol'ic *n.* one addicted to work.—Also *adj.*

working class(es) manual workers.

working day 1 a day on which work is done, as distinguished from a holiday. **2** the period of actual work each day.

working man member of working class.

working order the condition in which something is capable of, or ready to, work.

working party a group of people appointed to investigate a particular matter.

working week Monday to Friday inclusive.

work'man *n.* one who works with hands.

work'manlike *adj.* **1** befitting a skilled workman. **2** well performed.

work'manship *n.* **1** the skill of a workman. **2** manner of making.

work'shy *adj.* avoiding work; lazy.

work study time and motion study (see

time).

have one's work cut out to be faced with a difficult task.

work off to get rid of.

work out 1 to solve fully. **2** to come out by degrees. **3** to turn out in the end.

work to rule to keep all the regulations very carefully with the deliberate intention of slowing down work.

work up 1 to excite, rouse. **2** to make by degrees.

world *wûrld*, *n.* **1** the earth and its inhabitants. **2** the universe. **3** any planet or heavenly body. **4** state of existence, present or to come: *the next world.* **5** public life or society. **6** sphere of life or activity: *in my world*; *the insect world.* **7** sphere of particular interests: *the literary world.* **8** a great deal: *The holiday did him a world of good.*

world'ly *adj.* **1** belonging to this world. **2** having a fondness for material good things, not spiritual.—Also *adv.*

world'liness *n.*

world'ly-wise' *adj.* showing the wisdom of those experienced in the ways of the world.

world'-wide' *adj.* extending over, or found everywhere in the world.

all the world 1 everybody. **2** everything.

for all the world exactly, quite, etc.: *He looked for all the world like a film star.*

on top of the world feeling very well and happy.

out of this world unbelievably marvellous.

the New World the western hemisphere, the Americas.

the Old World the eastern hemisphere, Europe, Africa, Asia.

the ways of the world the way people behave, etc.

think the world of to have a very high opinion of.

worm *wûrm*, *n.* **1** an earthworm (see this word), or any invertebrate creature resembling it. **2** anything spiral e.g. the thread if a screw. **3** a mean grovelling person. **4** (in *pl.*) any disease caused by worms in the intestines.—*v.i.* to make one's way, or to work, slowly or secretly.—*v.t.* **1** to treat for, rid of, worms. **2** to work (oneself into a position) slowly or secretly. **3** to work (one's way) thus. **4** to obtain (information) by slow or indirect means: *to worm the facts out of someone.*

wor'my *adj.* **1** like a worm. **2** having worms:—*comp.* **wor'mier**; *superl.* **wor'miest**.

wor'miness *n.*

worm'-eaten *adj.* **1** eaten into by woodworms. **2** old. **3** worn-out.

worn, worn-out. See **wear**.

worry *wur'i*, *v.t.* **1** to shake, tear with the teeth, etc. as a dog does its prey. **2** to annoy, pester. **3** to cause anxiety to.—*v.i.* **1** to be too anxious. **2** to get (along) in spite of difficulties:—*pr.p.* **worr'ying**; *pa.p.* **worr'ied.**—*n.* anxiety, uneasiness, or a cause of this:—*pl.* **worr'ies**.

worse. See **bad** and **ill**.

wor'sen *(wûr')* *v.i.*, *v.t.* to grow, or make, worse.

worship *wûr'ship*, *n.* **1** religious service. **2** deep reverence. **3** adoration. **4** a title of honour (*your*, *his*, etc., *Worship*) e.g. in addressing the mayor of certain English cities.—*v.t.* **1** to pay honour to: *to worship God.* **2** to adore or admire deeply.—*v.i.* **1** to show deep reverence. **2** to take part in religious service:—*pr.p.* **wor'shipping**; *pa.p.* **wor'shipped**.

wor'shipful *adj.* **1** worthy of honour, used as a term of respect. **2** full of reverence.

wor'shipper *n.*

worst *wûrst*, *adj.* and *adv.* See **bad** and **ill**.—*n.* **1** the highest degree of badness. **2** the least good part (esp. of news). **3** one's utmost in evil or mischief: *to do one's worst.*—*v.t.* to defeat:—*pa.p.* **worst'ed**.

worsted[1] *woost'id*, *woorst'*, *n.* **1** a firm woollen fabric. **2** twisted yarn spun out of long, combed wool.—Also *adj.*

worsted[2]. See **worst**.

worth *wûrth*, *n.* **1** value. **2** price. **3** importance. **4** excellence of character.—*adj.* **1** equal in value to: *worth a penny.* **2** good enough for: *worth considering.*

worth'less *adj.* of no value or merit.

worth'lessly *adv.* **worth'lessness** *n.*

worthy *wûr'*THi, *adj.* **1** good, deserving: *a worthy cause.* **2** deserving (of). **3** suited to, in keeping with. **4** of sufficient merit (to do):—*comp.* **worth'ier**; *superl.* **worth'iest.**—*n.* a notable person, esp. local:—*pl.* **wor'thies**.

worth'ily (-TH-) *adv.* **worth'iness** *n.*

worthwhile' *adj.* deserving attention, time and effort, etc.

would. See **will**.

would'-be *adj.* trying, or merely pretending, to be.

wound[1]. See **wind**[2].

wound[2] *wōōnd*, *n.* **1** any cut or injury caused by force. **2** a hurt to feelings.—*v.t.* **1** to make a wound in. **2** to injure in feelings.

wove, woven. See **weave**.

wrack *rak*, *n.* **1** seaweed cast up on the shore. **2** destruction.

wraith *rāth*, *n.* an apparition, esp. of a living person.

wrangle *rang'gl*, *v.i.* to dispute noisily:—*pr.p.* **wrang'ling.**—*n.* an angry argument.
wrang'ler *n.*

wrap *rap*, *v.t.* **1** to roll or fold (round something). **2** to cover by folding or winding something round (often with *up*):—*pr.p.* **wrapp'ing**; *pa.p.* **wrapped.**—*n.* a covering e.g. a shawl.
wrapp'er *n.* **1** a garment likc a dressing-gown. **2** a loose· paper book-cover. **3** a paper band, e.g. on newspaper for post.
under wraps secret, concealed.
wrapped up in devoted to, giving all one's affection or attention to

wrath *röth*, *roth*, *räth*, *n.* violent anger.
wrath'ful *adj.* **wrath'fully** *adv.*

wreak *rēk*, *v.t.* **1** to act as prompted by: *to wreak one's anger.* **2** to carry out (e.g. vengeance).

wreath *rēth*, *n.* **1** a garland of flowers or leaves. **2** a drift or curl of smoke, mist, etc.:—*pl.* **wreaths** *(rē* TII*z)*.
wreathe *rē* TH, *v.t.*, *v.i.* to twine about.—*v.t.* to encircle, decorate with, a wreath or wreaths:—*pr.p.* **wreath'-ing.**

wreck *rek*, *n.* **1** a very badly damaged ship. **2** the remains of anything ruined. **3** a person ruined mentally or physically. **4** destruction (of something).—*v.t.*, *v.i.* to destroy, or be destroyed.
wreck'age *n.* remains of something wrecked.
wreck'er *n.* a person who destroys, esp. who purposely wrecks a ship for plunder.

wren *ren*, *n.* a very small song bird.

wrench *rench*, or *-sh*, *v.t.* **1** to pull with a twist. **2** to force by violence. **3** to sprain.—*v.i.* to undergo a violent twist.—*n.* **1** a violent twist. **2** an instrument for turning nuts, bolts, etc. **3** pain at parting from someone or something.

wrest *rest*, *v.i.* **1** to twist, or take away, by force (from). **2** to get by toil: *to wrest a living from the soil.*

wrestle *res'l*, *v.i.* **1** to struggle with someone, trying to bring him down. **2** to struggle (with): *to wrestle with a problem.*
wrest'ler *n.* **wrest'ling** *n.*

wretch *rech*, *n.* **1** a miserable, unhappy creature. **2** a worthless person.
wretch'ed *adj.* **1** very miserable. **2** worthless.
wretch'edly *adv.* **wretch'edness** *n.*

wrier, wriest. See **wry.**

wriggle *rig'l*, *v.i.* **1** to twist to and fro. **2** to move forward by doing this (as a worm does). **3** to escape by cunning: *to wriggle out of a difficulty*:—*pr.p.* **wrigg'ling.**
wrigg'ler *n.* **wrigg'ling** *n.* and *adj.*

wright *rīt*, *n.* a maker (used as part of words): *shipwright*, *wheelwright.*

wring *ring*, *v.t.* **1** to twist. **2** to force water from (material) by twisting or by pressure. **3** to clasp and unclasp (one's hands) in an agitated manner, e.g. in grief. **4** to force from, out of: *to wring a confession from someone.* **5** to distress: *to wring one's heart*:—*pa.p.* **wrung.**
wring'er *n.* a machine for forcing water from wet clothes.
wringing (wet) soaked through.

wrinkle *ring'kl*, *n.* a small crease on a surface (e.g. on one's face).—*v.t.* to make wrinkles or creases in.—*v.i.* to shrink into ridges:—*pr.p.* **wrink'ling.**
wrink'ly *adj.* full of wrinkles:—*comp.* **wrink'lier**; *superl.* **wrink'liest.**

wrist *rist*, *n.* the joint which joins the hand to the arm.
wrist'watch watch worn on wrist.

writ *rit*, *n.* (*law*) a document by which one is summoned, or required to do something.
Holy Writ the Scriptures.

write *rīt*, *v.t.* **1** to form letters with a pen, pencil, etc. **2** to put into writing. **3** to compose (e.g. a poem).—*v.i.* to send a letter (to someone):—*pa.p.* **wrī'ting**; *pa.t.* **wrote** *(rōt)*; *pa.p.* **writt'en.**
wrī'ter *n.*
wrī'ting *n.* **1** putting down in letters. **2** something composed and written.
write down **1** to record. **2** to write slightingly about. **3** to write so as to be understood or appreciated by: *He wrote down to readers he considered to have no intelligence and no taste.*
write off **1** to cancel (esp. in book-keeping). **2** to regard as lost for ever.
write out to copy.
write up **1** to bring (a record) up to date. **2** to write a description of. **3** to write in praise of.

writhe *rī* TH, *v.i.* **1** to twist violently this way and that. **2** to squirm (under, at):—*pr.p.* **wrīth'ing.**

written. See **write.**

wrong *rong*, *adj.* **1** not right. **2** evil. **3** not correct. **4** not what is intended or suitable. **5** mistaken: *You are wrong in thinking he left.*—*n.* **1** whatever is not right or just. **2** an injury done to another.—*adv.* **1** not correctly. **2** astray: *to go wrong.*—*v.t.* to do wrong to, treat unfairly, harm.
wrong'ful *adj.* not lawful.
wrong'fully *adv.* **wrong'fulness** *n.*
wrong'ly *adv.*

wrong'doer *n.* one who does wrong.
wrong'doing *n.*
wrong'head'ed *adj.* obstinately holding to wrong ideas or to an unwise course.
in the wrong guilty of error or injustice.
put in the wrong to cause to seem to be in the wrong.

wrote. See **write**.

wrought *röt*, *adj.* (an old *pa.t.* and *pa.p.* of **work**) made, manufactured.
wrought'-i'ron *n*, iron containing only small amounts of other materials.

wrung. See **wring**.

wry *rī*, *adj.* **1** twisted or turned to one side. **2** (of e.g. smile, remark) slightly bitter or mocking. **3** (of humour) having a clever twist:—*comp.* **wri'er, wry'er**; *superl.* **wri'est, wry'est.**
wry'ly *adv.* **wry'ness** *n.*

wynd *wīnd*, *n.* a narrow lane in a town.

X

xeno- *zen-ō-*, (as part of a word) stranger.
xenophobia *zen-ō-fō'bi-à*, *n.* hatred of strangers.

xero- *zer-ō-*, (as part of a word) dry.
xerography *zer-og'rà-fi*, *n.* a photographic process in which the plate is sensitised electrically and developed by dusting with electrically charged fine powder.
xerograph'ic *adj.*
Xerox® *zē'roks*, *n.***1** a registered trademark used for, among other things, copying-machines operating with a xerographic method of reproduction. **2** a copy so produced.—*v.t.* to copy by this method.

Xmas *eks'màs*, *kris'màs*, *n.* short for **Christmas**.

X-ray *eks'rā*, *n.* **1** (in *pl.*) powerful invisible rays which can go through matter that light rays cannot penetrate. **2** a photograph taken by X-rays.—*v.t.* to photograph by means of X-rays.

xylo- *zī-lō*, (as part of a word) wood.
xylophone *zīlō-fōn*, *n.* a musical instrument consisting of a series of bars which are struck by wooden hammers held in the hands.
xyloph'onist *(-lof')* *n.*

Y

yacht *yot, n.* a vessel fitted for racing, or for pleasure trips.—*v.i.* to sail in a yacht.
yacht'ing *n.* **yachts'man** *n.*

yack, yak *yak, (coll.) v.i.* to talk at length, esp. foolishly, to chatter:—*pr.p.* **yack'ing, yakk'ing**; *pa.p.* **yacked, yakked.**

yak *yak, n.* a long-haired ox found in Tibet.

yam *yam, n.* the potato-like tuber of several tropical plants.

yank *yangk, (coll.) v.t.* to pull sharply.—Also *v.i.* and *n.*

Yankee *yang'ki, n.* a citizen of the New England states of U.S.A., or of the northern states (as opp. to the southern), or simply a citizen of U.S.A.—Also **Yank**.

yap *yap, v.i.* to bark sharply:—*pr.p.* **yapp'-ing**; *pa.p.* **yapped.**—Also *n.*

yard[1] *yärd, n.* **1** a measure of length, 3 feet (0.9114 metre). **2** a long beam on a mast for spreading sails.
yard'arm *n.* either end (right or left) of a ship's yard.
yard'stick *n.* **1** a stick one yard long, for measuring. **2** any standard for measuring or comparison.

yard[2] *yärd, n.* **1** an enclosed place, esp. near a building. **2** one used for special work: *dockyard, railway yard, wood-yard.*
the Yard Scotland Yard, headquarters of the London Metropolitan Police.

yarn *yärn, n.* **1** spun thread. **2** one of the threads of a rope. **3** a story, esp. a sailor's.—*v.i.* to tell stories.

yarrow *yar'ō, n.* a strongly scented plant with flat-topped clusters of small flowers.

yashmak *yash'mak,* or *-mak', n.* a veil worn by Muslim women, covering the face below the eyes.

yawl *yöl, n.* **1** a ship's small boat. **2** a small fishing or sailing boat.

yawn *yön, v.i.* **1** to open the mouth wide and take a deep breath, without meaning to do so, as a result of sleepiness or boredom. **2** to gape: *A great hole yawned in his path.*—*n.* **1** the act of yawning. **2** (*coll.*) a boring person, event, etc.
yawn'ing *n.* and *adj.*

yaws *yöz, n. sing.* a skin disease of hot countries.

ye. See **you**.

yea *yā, (old) adv.* yes.

yeah *ye, ye'ȧ, yä, (coll.) adv.* yes.

year *yēr, n.* **1** the time taken by the earth to go once round the sun. **2** January 1 to December 31. **3** (in *pl.*) age: *wise for his years.* **4** (in *pl.*; *coll.*) a long time. **5** students, etc. as a group at the same stage of their education: *He was in my year at school*; *He's in third year*.
year'ling *n.* an animal a year old.
year'ly *adj.* **1** happening every year. **2** lasting a year.—Also *adv.*
year'-book *n.* a book published annually giving events of the previous twelve months.
financial year. See **finance**.

yearn *yûrn, v.i.* **1** to feel great desire (for). **2** to feel pity or tenderness.
yearn'ing *n., adj.* **yearn'ingly** *adv.*

yeast *yēst, n.* a substance which causes fermentation used in brewing and baking.
yeas'ty *adj.* frothy:—*comp.* **yeas'tier**; *superl.* **yeas'tiest**.
yeas'tiness *n.*

yell *yel, v.i., v.t.* to howl or cry with a sharp noise.—Also *n.*

yellow *yel'ō, adj.* **1** of the colour of gold or of the primrose. **2** (*slang*) cowardly.—Also *n.*—*v.i.* to become yellow(ish), e.g. with age.
yell'ow-hammer *n.* a yellow bunting, a sparrow-like bird with yellow head and front.
yellow pages the part or volume of a telephone directory, printed on yellow paper, which lists subscribers according to their trade or profession or the service they offer.

yelp *yelp, v.i.* to utter a sharp bark or cry.—Also *n.*

yen[1] *yen, n.* the basic unit of currency in Japan.

yen[2] *yen, (coll.) n.* a yearning.

yeoman *yō'mȧn, n.* a small farmer or land-owner:—*pl.* **yeo'men**.
yeo'manry *n.* **1** yeomen. **2** a volunteer cavalry force.
yeoman of the guard one of a company forming part of the king's or queen's bodyguard on certain occasions.

yes *yes, adv.* a word showing agreement or consent.
yes'-man *n.* an obedient follower who never disagrees with his chief.

yesterday *yes'tėr-di, n.* the day just past.—Also *adv.*
yes'teryear *n.* the past.

yet *yet, adv.* **1** in addition, besides: *yet another mistake.* **2** up to the present time:

Have you heard yet? **3** before the matter is finished: *I will get even with him yet.* **4** even: *a yet more terrible experience.*—*conj.* **1** nevertheless. **2** however.

as yet up to the time referred to.

yeti *yet'i*, *n.* an abominable snowman.

yew *ū*, *n.* **1** an evergreen tree, once planted in graveyards. **2** its wood, used for making bows.

Yiddish *yid'ish*, *n.* a language that grew out of old German, with Hebrew and Slavonic words, spoken by some Jews.—Also *adj.*

yield *yēld*, *v.t.* **1** to give up. **2** to grant. **3** to give out, produce: *The seeds yield oil.*—*v.i.* **1** to submit, admit that one's opponent has won. **2** to give way under pressure: *At last the door yielded.*—*n.* the amount produced: *the yield of ground under wheat, of a mine.*

yiel'ding *adj.* and *n.*

yob *yob*, **yobbo** *yob'ō*, (*slang*) *ns.* a lout:—*pl.* **yobs**, **yobb'os**.

yodel *yō'dėl*, *v.i.*, *v.t.* to sing changing often from ordinary voice to falsetto and back again:—*pr.p.* **yo'del(l)ing**; *pa.p.* **yo'del(l)ed**.—Also *n.*

yoga *yō'gȧ*, *n.* **1** a Hindu philosophy teaching how to bring about the union of the soul with God. **2** a system of physical and mental exercises and discipline leading to such union. **3** one such system, common in the West, which stresses the importance of physical exercises, etc. in promoting physical and mental well-being.

yo'gi *n.* a Hindu who practises yoga.

yog(h)urt, **yoghourt** *yō'gu̇rt*, *yog'*, *n.* a slightly acid curdled milk.

yoke *yōk*, *n.* **1** something that joins together. **2** a frame of wood joining oxen pulling e.g. a cart, or one for carrying pails, etc. **3** a pair (e.g. of oxen). **4** a mark of slavery. **5** part of a garment that fits the shoulders.—*v.t.* **1** to put a yoke on. **2** to join together:—*pr.p.* **yok'ing**.

yokel *yō'kl*, *n.* a country man or boy.

yolk *yōk*, *n.* the yellow part of an egg.

yonder *yon'dėr*, *adv.* in that place (at a distance but within sight).—Also *adj.*

yore *yōr*, *yör*, *n.* used in phrase **of yore**, in times past.

yorker *yör'kėr*, *n.* (*cricket*) a ball pitching just under the bat.

Yorkshire pudding *yörk'shir pood'ing*, a pudding made with unsweetened batter, baked, and eaten usu. with roast beef.

you *ū*, *pron.* 2nd person *pl.* and *sing.*, the word used in referring to person(s) to whom one is speaking or writing:—*objective* **you**; *possessive* **your** (sometimes described as *possessive adj.*), **yours**: *Give me your book*; *this one is not yours.* (**Ye** is an older form, no longer used, for *you* (as subject, not object).)

yourself' *pron.* the emphatic or reflexive form of *you*: *You yourself said so*; *Don't blame yourself.*

you'd *ūd*, **1** you would. **2** you had.

you'll *ūl*, you will, shall.

young *yung*, *adj.* **1** in early life. **2** in the first part of growth.—*n.* **1** the offspring of the animals. **2** (with *the*) young people.

young'ster *n.* a young person, not yet grown-up.

youth *yōōth*, *n.* **1** the state of being young. **2** the early part of life. **3** a young man. **4** young people as a group.

youth'ful *adj.* **1** young. **2** fresh and vigorous.

youth'fulness *n.*

youth hostel a hostel, inexpensive and with simple accomodation, for hikers, etc. provided by the Youth Hostels Association.

you're *yör*, *ūr*, you are.

yule *yūl*, *n.* (also with *cap.*) the season, or feast, of Christmas.

yule'tide *n*, (also with *cap.*) the Christmas season.

yuppie or **yuppy** *yup'i*, *n.* a young well-paid ambitious urban professional person:—*pl.* **yuppies**.

Z

zabaglione *zä-bäl-yō'ni, n.* a pudding of whipped egg yolks, wine and sugar.

zany *zā'ni, adj.* amusingly crazy, like a clown:—*comp.* **za'nier**; *superl.* **za'niest**.

zeal *zēl, n.* **1** warm enthusiasm. **2** eager, energetic support (for).
zealot *zel'ot, n.* **1** one full of zeal, an enthusiast. **2** a fanatic. **3** (with *cap.*; *history*) a member of a militant Jewish group vigorously opposing the Roman domination of Palestine.
zealous *(zel') adj.* full of enthusiasm and energy in support of something.
zeal'ously *adv.* **zeal'ousness** *n.*

zebra *zē'bra, zeb', n.* a striped African animal of the horse kind.
zebra crossing a street pedestrian crossing marked with stripes.

zebu *zē'bū, -bōō, n.* a type of domesticated ox found in India, East Africa, China, etc.

Zen *zen, n.* an orig. Japanese Buddhist sect which holds that the truth is not in scriptures but in man's own heart and that one must find it by meditation and intuition.

zenana *zi-nä'na, n.* in India and Iran, the women's apartments.

zenith *zen'ith, n.* **1** the point of the sky which is exactly overhead. **2** the highest point (of e.g. one's career).

zephyr *zef'ir, n.* **1** the west wind. **2** a soft wind.

zero *zē'rō, n.* **1** nothing, or the sign for it. **2** the point from which a scale begins:—*pl.* **zē'rōs**.
zero hour the exact time fixed for an attack or the beginning of some other operation.
zero in (on) (*slang*) **1** to direct oneself straight towards a target. **2** to focus one's attention, or energy on. **3** to aim for, move towards.
zero'-option *n.* a proposal to limit or abandon the deployment of (medium range) nuclear missiles if the opposing side does likewise.

zest *zest, n.* enthusiasm and pleasure.
zest'ful *adj.*

zigzag *zig'zag, n.* a line, or road, with sharp angles.—*adj.* having sharp turns.—*v.i.* to have, or to go forward making, sharp turns:—*pr.p.* **zig'zagging**; *pa.p.* **zig'-zagged**.—Also *adv.*

Zimmer® *zim'ėr, n.* a metal frame held in front of one, used as an aid to walking.

zinc *zingk, n.* an element, a bluish-white metal.

zing *zing, n.* **1** zest. **2** a short, shrill, humming sound, as made by a bullet, etc.—Also *v.i.*

zinnia *zin'i-a, n.* a tropical American plant of the thistle family.

Zionism *zī'on-izm, n.* the movement which got national privileges and territory in Palestine for the Jews.
zī'onist *n.* and *adj.*

zip *zip, n.* **1** a whizzing sound. **2** a zip-fastener.—*v.i., v.t.* **1** to whizz. **2** to fasten with a zip-fastener. **3** to proceed quickly and energetically:—*pr.p.* **zipp'ing**; *pa.p.* **zipped**.
zipp'er *n.* a zip-fastener.
zip'-fastener *n.* a device for fastening in which two sets of teeth are made to fit into each other by pulling a slide.

zip code *zip kōd,* in the U.S.A., the postal code.

zircon *zûr'kon, n.* a gemstone.

zither *ziTH'ėr, th-, n.* a flat musical instrument with many strings.

zodiac *zō'di-ak, n.* an imaginary belt in the heavens, divided into twelve equal parts, called the **signs of the zodiac**, each part named from a group of stars.

zombie *zom'bi, n.* **1** a dead body brought to life again by sorcery. **2** a stupid, very slow-moving, or apathetic person.

zone *zōn, n.* **1** one of the five great belts into which the surface of the earth is divided according to temperature. **2** any belt-like area. **3** a region in which all parts have the same characteristics.—*v.t.* to divide into zones:—*pr.p.* **zon'ing**.

zoo- *zō-o-,* (as part of a word) animal.
zoo *zōō, n.* a zoological garden.
zoology *zō-ol'o-ji, zōō-, n.* the science that studies animal life.
zoolog'ical *adj.* having to do with animals, or with a zoo.
zoolog'ically *adv.*
zool'ogist *n.* one who studies animal life.
zoological garden a place where wild animals are kept and shown.

zoom *zōōm, v.i.* **1** to make a long, loud, deep, buzzing noise. **2** to move with this noise. **3** to move, progress, very quickly.—Also *n.* and *v.t.*

zoom lens a type of camera lens which can make a distant object appear gradually closer without the camera being moved.

zoom in (on) to use a zoom lens to make what one isfilming appear to come closer: *Film the whole building first, then zoom in on the door.*

American English and British English

Standard American English differs from standard British English in various ways – in pronunciation, in grammar, in vocabulary, in spelling, even in punctuation. This appendix provides an overview of the most important or noticeable differences between the two standard languages.

Pronunciation

General differences in pronunciation

British English /ah/
In many words that have an /ah/ sound in British English followed by /f/, /s/, /th/, /n/ or /m/ sound, American English has an /a/, as in *after*, *banana*, *can't*, *dance*, *half*, *laugh*, *pass*, and *rather*.

British English /i/
Where British English has /i/ in final position in words such as *city* and *happy*, American English has /ee/.

British English /o/
In American English, words such as *block*, *got*, *pond*, *probable* and *top* are pronounced with an /ah/ sound. In words in which the vowel is followed by /f/, /s/, /th/, /r/, /g/ or /ng/ (eg in *coffee*, *dog*, *cross*, *forest* and *long*) a longer vowel similar to /aw/ is also common.

British English /yoo/, /yuu/
After /t/, /d/, /n/, /l/, /s/ and /th/, American English generally has /oo/ rather than /yoo/ if the vowel is stressed, eg in *duty*, *lurid*, *new*, *suit* and *tune*, but the /y/ sound is retained in unstressed syllables (eg in *menu* and *value*).

British English /iy/
In most words ending in *-ile*, American English generally pronounces the final syllable as /il/ rather than /iyl/ as in British English, eg in *futile* and *fragile*. In some words, /iyl/ is possible or required, eg in *juvenile* and *prehensile*. In general, the longer or more technical a word is, the more likely it is to be pronounced /iyl/.

British English /t/
In words such as *latter*, *metal* and *writing*, the *-tt-*/*-t-* is pronounced in American English with the same sound as that of the *-dd-*/*-d-* of *ladder*, *medal* and *riding*.

British English /r/
In most accents of American, /r/ is pronounced at the ends of words and before consonants. However, even in *r*-pronouncing accents, the *r* is often not pronounced when it follows an unstressed vowel and is itself followed by another *r*, eg in *governor*.

British English /ahr/ spelt -er-
In words such as *clerk* and *Derby*, where British English preserves an older pronunciation with /ahr/, American speech has /uhr/.

British English /-a-ri/
American English tends to give greater prominence than British English does to the suffixes *-ary*, *-ory* and often also *-ery*; as for example in *monetary* (BrE /*-ta*-ri/ or /-tri/, AmE /-te-ri/), *confectionery* (BrE /*-na*-ri/, AmE /-na-ri/), *obligatory* (BrE /*-to*-ri/, AmE /-taw-ri/).

British English /nt/
In American English, /t/ is often not pronounced after /n/ when what follows is an unstressed vowel, as for example in *Atlantic*, *gentleman*, *international* and *plenty*.

Pronunciation differences in individual words
There are also many differences between British English and American English in the pronunciation of individual words. A selection of such words follows:

anti-	BrE /**an**-ti/	AmE often /**an**-tiy/
depot	BrE /**de**-poh/	AmE /**dee**-poh/
epoch	BrE /**ee**-pok/	AmE /**e**-pok/
lever	BrE /**lee**-ver/	AmE usually /**le**-ver/
leisure	BrE /**le**-zhur/	AmE usually /**lee**-zhur/
lieutenant	BrE /lef-**te**-nant/	AmE /luu-**te**-nant/
moustache	BrE /mus-**tahsh**/	AmE /**mus**-tash/
schedule	BrE /**she**-dyool/	AmE /**ske**-jool/
simultaneous	BrE /si-mul-/	AmE usually /siy-mul-/
suggest	BrE /su-**jest**/	AmE usually /sug-**jest**/
tomato	BrE /to-**mah**-toh/	AmE /to-**may**-toh/
vase	BrE /vahz/	AmE usually /vays/
vitamin	BrE /**vi**-ta-min/	AmE /**viy**-ta-min/
z	BrE /zed/	AmE /zee/
zenith	BrE /**ze**-nith/	AmE /**zee**-nith/

Grammar

collective nouns
A singular verb is normally used with collective nouns in American English, where British English allows either a singular or a plural verb: *Our staff monitors the latest developments in language daily.*

do
American English does not use *do* as British English does in the following examples:

> *We don't have to go but we can do if you want* (AmE *we can if you want*)
> *'Will you fix that for me?' 'I have done.'* (AmE *I have*)

gotten
Gotten now exists in British English only in expressions such as *ill-gotten gains*. In other cases, the past participle is *got*. In American English, *gotten* is used when a process is involved (*he's gotten a new car*), but *got* when a state of possession is implied (*he's got a car*). As in British English, *he's got to go* means 'he must go', whereas *he's gotten to go* means 'he has received permission to go'.

have
The question form *Has she enough money?* is not used in American English, which uses the forms, also possible in British English, *Does she have enough money?* and *Has she got enough money?* The same applies to the negative statement form *She hasn't enough money,* as opposed to *She doesn't have enough money* and *She hasn't got enough money.*

past tense
The simple past-tense form of a verb is often used in American English where British English would use a perfect tense: *Did she leave yet?*

subjunctive verbs
After verbs, nouns and adjectives which denote requiring, demanding, ordering, urging, etc, the subjunctive is more extensively used in American English than in British English: *We demand that she be dismissed at once*; *his demand that she leave immediately!*; *It is vital that she leave tomorrow.*

will/shall
Will is used rather than shall to form the simple future tense with first-person pronouns: *We will come back again soon.*

Vocabulary

There are many differences in vocabulary between British English and American English, of which the following is a selection:

BrE	*aubergine*	AmE	*eggplant*
BrE	*autumn*	AmE	*fall*
BrE	*biscuit*	AmE	*cookie*
BrE	*bonnet* (*of car*)	AmE	*hood*
BrE	*boot* (*of car*)	AmE	*trunk*
BrE	*candy floss*	AmE	*cotton candy*
BrE	*caravan*	AmE	*trailer*
BrE	*car park*	AmE	*parking lot*
BrE	*chips*	AmE	*French fries*
BrE	*condom*	AmE	*rubber*
BrE	*cot*	AmE	*crib*
BrE	*courgettes*	AmE	*zucchini*
BrE	*crisps*	AmE	*chips*
BrE	*cupboard*	AmE	*closet*
BrE	*drawing-pin*	AmE	*thumb tack*
BrE	*dual carriageway*	AmE	*divided highway*
BrE	*first floor*	AmE	*second floor*
BrE	*garden*	AmE	*yard*
BrE	*grill*	AmE	*broil*
BrE	*ground floor*	AmE	*first floor*
BrE	*guard* (*on train*)	AmE	*conductor*
BrE	*handbag*	AmE	*purse*
BrE	*holiday*	AmE	*vacation*
BrE	*lift*	AmE	*elevator*
BrE	*paraffin*	AmE	*kerosene*
BrE	*pavement*	AmE	*sidewalk*
BrE	*petrol*	AmE	*gas*
BrE	*suppose*	AmE	*guess*
BrE	*sweets*	AmE	*candy*
BrE	*tap*	AmE	*faucet*
BrE	*tights*	AmE	*pantyhose*
BrE	*trousers*	AmE	*pants*
BrE	*vest*	AmE	*undershirt*
BrE	*waistcoat*	AmE	*vest*

Spelling

General differences between British and American spelling

i) British English **-*our***
American English **-*or***

American English has **-*or*** in words such as *color*, *flavor* and *humor*. (*Glamour* and *saviour* may be spelt as in British English, however.)

ii) British English **-*re***
American English **-*er***

American English has **-*er*** in words such as *center*, *fiber*, *meter* and *theater*. But to show the hard /g/ and /k/ sounds, *acre*, *massacre*, *ogre*, etc. (Note, however, *meager*, not *meagre*.)

iii) British English **-*ll*-**, **-*pp*-**, **-*tt*-**
American English **-*l*-**, **-*p*-**, **-*t*-**

In inflections and derivations of words ending in *l*, *p*, or *t* not immediately followed by a single stressed vowel, American English generally does not double the final letter as British English does:

British English: *cancelled*, *counsellor*, *equalled*, *kidnapped*, *traveller*

American English: *canceled*, *counselor*, *equaled*, *kidnaped*, *traveler*

(but American English spells *formatting* as in British English)

Note also British English *carburettor* and *woollen*, American English *carburetor* and *woolen*.

iv) British English **-*l***
American English **-*ll***

At the ends of certain two-syllable words, American English generally has a double *l* where British English has a single *l*:

British English: *appal*, *enrol*, *fulfil*, *instil*, *skilful*
American English: *appall*, *enroll*, *fulfill*, *instill*, *skilfull*

v) British English ***ae/oe*** or ***e***
American English ***e***

The tendency to replace *ae* and *oe* by *e* in words from Latin and Greek is more strongly developed in American English than in British English:

British English: *aesthetic*, *amoeba*, *diarrhoea*, *foetus*, *haemoglobin*, *oesophagus*

American English (more often): *esthetic*, *ameba*, *diarrhea*, *fetus*, *hemoglobin, esophagus*

(but *aerobics* and *aerosol* are spelt as in British English)

vi) British English **-*ize*** or **-*ise***
American English **-*ize***

In verbs that can be spelt either *-ise* or *-ize*, the use of *-ize* is now standard in American English. Note also the spellings *analyze*, *paralyze*, etc as opposed to the British English *analyse*, *paralyse*, etc.

vii) As a rule, hyphens are used less frequently in American English than in British English, eg *dining room* rather than *dining-room*.

Spelling differences in individual words

British English: *axe*, *catalogue*, *cheque*, *cosy*, *defence*, *draught*, *grey*, *jewellery*, *licence*, *moustache*, *offence*, *pyjamas*, *practice/practise*, *pretence*, *sceptic*, *sulphur*, *storey*, *tyre*.

American English: *ax*, *catalog*, *check*, *cozy*, *defense*, *draft*, *gray*, *jewelery*, *license*, *mustache*, *offense*, *pajamas*, *practise*, *pretense*, *skeptic*, *sulfur*, *story*, *tire*.

Punctuation

The main differences in punctuation between American and British practices are as follows:

i) **Commas between clauses:**
American English prefers some punctuation (usually a comma) between clauses in compound sentences where there is none in British English:
British English: *I was late home on Monday because I couldn't start the car.*
American English: *I was late home on Monday, because I couldn't start the car.*

ii) **Commas in lists:**
In American English, a comma is inserted before *and* in lists:
British English: *x,y and z*
American English: *x,y, and z*

iii) **Quotation marks:**
The American preference is for double quotation marks rather than single (and therefore for single quotation marks within double quotation marks for quotes within quotes). American practice also places commas and full stops (but not other punctuation marks) before quotation marks rather than after them.

British punctuation: *By an 'abstract object', McArthur means something which is 'neither spatial nor temporal'.*
American punctuation: *By an "abstract object," McArthur means something which is "neither spatial nor temporal."*

Dates

An important difference between American and British English is the way of writing dates.
In British English, '6/11/95' would mean '6 November 1995', whereas in American practice, it denotes '11 June 1995'.

Spelling rules

Verbs

In most cases, you can add **-ing** and **-ed** without changing the spelling of the first part of the verb:

walk	walk*ing*	walk*ed*
stay	stay*ing*	stay*ed*
pick	pick*ing*	pick*ed*

But if a verb consists of only one syllable, with a single short vowel, and ends in a consonant, double this final letter before adding **-ing** and **-ed**:

stop	stopp*ing*	stopp*ed*
grin	grinn*ing*	grinn*ed*
hum	humm*ing*	humm*ed*

If a verb has two or more syllables, and the last one contains a single short vowel and ends in a consonant, double this final letter, but only if the stress comes on the last syllable:

pre'fer	pre'ferr*ing*	pre'ferr*ed*
ad'mit	ad'mitt*ing*	ad'mitt*ed*
e'quip	e'quipp*ing*	e'quipp*ed*

But if the stress is *not* on the last syllable, the final letter is not doubled:

enter	'enter*ing*	'enter*ed*
'gossip	'gossip*ing*	'gossip*ed*

If the last syllable has a short vowel and ends in **-l**, double the **l**, regardless of where the stress comes:

'equal	'equall*ing*	'equall*ed*
re'pel	re'pell*ing*	re'pell*ed*

If the verb ends in **-c**, add a **k** before adding **-ing** or **-ed**:

picnic	picnick*ing*	picnick*ed*
panic	panick*ing*	panick*ed*

If the verb ends in **-e**, you remove the **e** before adding **-ing**. Instead of adding **-ed**, just add **-d**:

stare	star*ing*	stare*d*
bake	bak*ing*	bake*d*

issue	issu*ing*	issue*d*
refine	refin*ing*	refine*d*

But notice that verbs ending in **-oe**, **-ee** and **-ye** are exceptions to this rule:

agree	agree*ing*	agree*d*
dye	dye*ing*	dye*d*
hoe	hoe*ing*	hoe*d*
eye	eye*ing*	eye*d*

If the verb ends in **-y**, and there is no vowel before the **y**, change the **y** to **i** before adding **-es** or **-ed**:

cry	cry*ing*	cri*es*	cri*ed*
hurry	hurry*ing*	hurri*es*	hurri*ed*

But if a verb has a vowel before the **y**, keep the **y** when you add **-es** and **-ed**:

stay	stay*ing*	stay*s*	stay*ed*
play	play*ing*	play*s*	play*ed*

but watch out for these:

lay	lay*ing*	lai*d*
pay	pay*ing*	pai*d*
say	say*ing*	sai*d*

If the verb ends in **-ie**, you change **ie** to **y** before adding **-ing**:

tie	ty*ing* tie*d*	
die	dy*ing*	die*d*

Adjectives

In general, **-er** and **-est** are added to adjectives to form comparatives and superlatives. There are, however, rules to be observed in certain cases as follows:

If an adjective ends in **-e**, just add **-r** for the comparative and **-st** for the superlative:

white	white*r*	white*st*
simple	simple*r*	simple*st*
free	free*r* free*st*	

If the adjective is only one syllable long, with a single short vowel, and ends in a consonant, double this final letter before adding **-er** and **-est**.

red	redd*er*	redd*est*
big	bigg*er*	bigg*est*

If an adjective has two syllables and ends in **-y**, you change the **y** to **i** before adding **-er** or **-est**:

angry	angri*er*	angri*est*
funny	funni*er*	funni*est*

But note these one-syllable adjectives ending in **-y**:

dry	dri*er*	dri*est*
sly	sly*er*	sly*est*
shy	shi*er* or shy*er*	shi*est* or shy*est*

Adverbs

Most adverbs are formed by adding **-ly** to the adjective:

foolish	foolish*ly*
strange	strange*ly*
initial	initial*ly*

Note that adjectives ending in **-e** keep the **e** before adding **-ly**, but in the following four cases, it is removed:

true	tru*ly*
due	du*ly*
whole	whol*ly*
eerie	eeri*ly*

If the adjective ends in **-ic**, you add **-ally** to form the adverb:

basic	basic*ally*
economic	economic*ally*

An exception to this rule is:

public	public*ly*

If the adjective ends in **-y**, you change the **y** to **i** before adding **-ly**:

happy	happi*ly*
hungry	hungri*ly*

If the adjective ends in **-le**, you remove the **e** and add **-y**:

simple	simpl*y*
double	doubl*y*

Adjectives ending in a **-y** that is pronounced [ī], often have two possible adverb forms:

dry	dri*ly* or dry*ly*
shy	shi*ly* or shy*ly*

IE or EI?

A well-known and useful way of remembering this rule is the rhyme *i before e, except after c.*
This means that the order is **ie** except when a **c** comes first – then the order is **ei**. Have a look at these words:

ch*ie*f	br*ie*f	conc*ei*t
s*ie*ge	gr*ie*f	dec*ei*ve
ach*ie*ve	th*ie*f	dec*ei*t
bel*ie*f	c*ei*ling	rec*ei*ve
rel*ie*ve	conc*ei*ve	rec*ei*pt

A few common words pronounced with an [ē] sound have *ei* where *ie* would be expected:

s*ei*ze	n*ei*ther
w*ei*rd	prot*ei*n
*ei*ther	caff*ei*ne
counterf*ei*t	h*ei*nous

Singular and Plural

To form a plural noun, it is usually sufficient to add **-s** to the singular noun:

car	car*s*
house	house*s*
monkey	monkey*s*

If the singular form of the noun ends in **-s**, **-ss**, **-x**, **-z**, **-sh**, or **-ch** (when it is pronounced **ch** and not **k**) you form the plural by adding **-es**:

gas	gas*es*
kiss	kiss*es*
box	box*es*
waltz	waltz*es*
bush	bush*es*
church	church*es*

But notice the plural if **-ch** is pronounced **k**. You add only **-s** to form the plural:

stomach	stomach*s*
monarch	monarch*s*

Words ending in a consonant followed by a **-y** usually take **-es** as their plural form, the **y** being changed to **i**.

fly	fli*es*

ally	alli*es*
fairy	fairi*es*
butterfly	butterfli*es*

The plural of nouns that have a vowel before the **y** are simply formed with **-s**.

boy	boy*s*
day	day*s*

For some nouns ending in **-f** and **-fe** the plurals are formed by changing **-f** or **-fe** to **-ves**:

calf	calv*es*
knife	kniv*es*
loaf	loav*es*
thief	thiev*es*

But there are some exceptions which add only **-s** to form the plural.

belief	belief*s*
chief	chief*s*
proof	proof*s*
roof	roof*s*
safe	safe*s*

For most nouns ending in **-o**, you just add **-s** to form the plural.

piano	piano*s*
radio	radio*s*
yoyo	yoyo*s*
zoo	zoo*s*

But certain nouns have plurals ending in **-oes**.

potato*es*	hero*es*
tomato*es*	veto*es*
echo*es*	Negro*es*
domino*es*	embargo*es*

Some nouns change their vowels to form the plural.

foot	f*ee*t
goose	g*ee*se
tooth	t*ee*th
man	m*e*n
mouse	m*ic*e

There is also a plural formed by adding **-en**

child	childr*en*
ox	ox*en*

American spelling

Below are some of the common differences between British and American spelling:

British English	American English
-our as in **colour**, **humour**	**-or** as in **color**, **humor**
-re as in **centre**, **theatre**, **metre**	**-er** as in **center**, **theater**, **meter**
-ae- as in **haemoglobin**, **anaemia**	**-e-** as in **hemoglobin**, **anemia**
NOTE: There is a growing tendency in British English for the **ae** in such words to become **e** as in **medieval**, **encyclop(a)edia.**	
-ogue as in **catalogue**	**-og** as in **catalog**
NOTE: Many words of this type can be spelt either **-ogue** or **-og** in American English as in **prologue/prolog**, **dialogue/dialog**.	
-ll- as in **travelling**, **equalled**	**-l-** as in **traveling**, **equaled**
-pp- as in **kidnapped**, **worshipping**	**-p-** as in **kidnaped**, **worshiping**
-l- as in **skilful, wilful**	**-ll-** as in **skillful, willful**

Words which may be confused

a
an

aboard
abroad

accept
except

access
excess

acme
acne

ad
add

adapter
adaptor

addition
edition

adverse
averse

advice
advise

aesthetic
ascetic

affect
effect

affluent
effluent

ail
ale

air
heir

aisle
isle

ale
ail

all
awl

allay
alley

allegory
allergy

alley
allay

alliterate
illiterate

allude
elude

allusion
delusion
illusion

altar
alter

alteration
altercation

alternately
alternatively

amateur
amateurish

amend
emend

amiable
amicable

among
between

amoral
immoral
immortal

an
a

angel
angle

annals
annuals

annex
annexe

annuals
annals

ant
aunt

antiquated
antique

arc
ark

arisen
arose

arose
arisen

artist
artiste

ascent
assent

ascetic
aesthetic

assay
essay

assent
ascent

astrology
astronomy

ate
eaten

aunt
ant

aural
oral

averse
adverse

awl
all

axes
axis

bad
bade

bade
bid

bail
bale
bale out

baited
bated

bale
bale out
bail

ball
bawl

ballet
ballot

banns
bans

bare
bear

barn
baron
barren

base
bass

bass
(pl) basses

bated
baited

bath
bathe

baton
batten

bawl
ball

bazaar
bizarre

be
bee

beach
beech

bean
been
being

bear
bare

beat
beaten

beat
beet

beau
bow

became
become

bee
be

beech
beach

been
bean
being

beer
bier

beet
beat

befallen
befell

began
begun

being
bean
been

belief
believe

bell
belle

bellow
below

beret
berry
bury

berth
birth

beside
besides

between
among

bid
bade

bier
beer

bight
bite

birth
berth

bit
bitten

bite
bight

bizarre
bazaar

blew
blown

blew
blue

bloc
block

blond
blonde

blown
blew

blue
blew

boar
boor
bore

board
bored

boast
boost

bonny
bony

bookie
bouquet

boor
boar
bore

boost
boast

bootee
booty

bore
boar
boor

bore
born
borne

borough
burgh

bough
bow

bound
bounded

bouquet
bookie

bow
beau

bow
bough

boy
buoy

brae
bray

brake
break

brassiere
brazier

bray
brae

brazier
brassiere

breach
breech

bread
bred

break
brake

breath
breathe

bred
bread

breech
breach

bridal
bridle

broach
brooch

broke
broken

brooch
broach

buffet ['*bufit*]
buffet ['*bo͞ofā*]

buoy
boy

burgh
borough

bury
beret
berry

but
butt

buy
by
bye

cache
cash

caddie
caddy

calf
calve

callous
callus

calve
calf

came
come

canned
could

cannon
canon

can't
cant

canvas
canvass

carat
carrot

carpal
carpel

cart
kart

cartilage
cartridge

carton
cartoon

cartridge
cartilage

cash
cache

cast
caste

cavalier
cavalry

ceiling
sealing

cell
sell

cellular
cellulose

censor
censure

cent
scent
sent

centenarian
centenary

cereal
serial

chafe
chaff

charted
chartered

chased
chaste

cheap
cheep

check
cheque

checked
chequered

cheep
cheap

cheque
check

chilli
chilly

choir
quire

choose
chose
chosen

chord
cord

chose
choose
chosen

chute
shoot

cite
sight
site

clothes
cloths

coarse
course

collage
college

coma
comma

come
came

comma
coma

commissionaire
commissioner

complement
compliment

complementary
complimentary

concert
consort

confidant
confidante
confident

conscience
conscientious
conscious

consort
concert

consul
council
counsel

continual
continuous

coop
coup

coral
corral

cord
chord

co-respondent
correspondent

cornet
coronet

cornflour
cornflower

coronet
cornet

corps
corpse

corral
coral

correspondent
co-respondent

cost
costed

could
canned

council
counsel
consul

councillor
counsellor

coup
coop

course
coarse

courtesy
curtsy

creak
creek

crevasse
crevice

crochet
crotchet

cue
queue

curb
kerb

currant
current

curtsy
courtesy

cygnet
signet

cymbal
symbol

dairy
diary

dam
damn

dammed
damned

damn
dam

dear
deer

decry
descry

deer
dear

delusion
allusion
illusion

dependant
dependent

deprecate
depreciate

descendant
descendent

descry
decry

desert
dessert

device
devise

devolution
evolution

dew
due
Jew

diary
dairy

did
done

die
dye

died
dyed

dinghy
dingy

disbelief
disbelieve

discreet
discrete

discus
discuss

doe
dough

doily
dolly

done
did

dough
doe

draft
draught

dragon
dragoon

draught
draft

drawn
drew

drank
drunk

drew
drawn

driven
drove

drunk
drank

dual
duel

dudgeon
dungeon

due
dew
Jew

duel
dual

dully
duly

dungeon
dudgeon

dye
die

dyed
died

dyeing
dying

earthly
earthy

easterly
eastern

eaten
ate

eclipse
ellipse

economic
economical

edition
addition

eerie
eyrie

effect
affect

effluent
affluent

elder
eldest

elicit
illicit

eligible
legible

ellipse
eclipse

elude
allude

emend
amend

emigrant
immigrant

emigration
immigration

emission
omission

emphasis
emphasize

employee
employer

ensure
insure

entomologist
etymologist

envelop
envelope

epigram
epitaph
epithet

cre
err

erotic
erratic

err
ere

erratic
erotic

escapement
escarpment

essay
assay

etymologist
entomologist

evolution
devolution

ewe
yew
you

except
accept

excess
access

executioner
executor

exercise
exorcise

expand
expend

expansive
expensive

expatiate
expiate

expend
expand

expensive
expansive

expiate
expatiate

extant
extinct

eyrie
eerie

faerie
fairy

fain
feign

faint
feint

fair
fare

fairy
faerie

fallen
fell
felled

fare
fair

fate
fête

faun
fawn

feat
feet

feign
fain

feint
faint

fell
fallen
felled

ferment
foment

fête
fate

fiancé
fiancée

filed
filled

final
finale

fir
fur

fission
fissure

flair
flare

flammable
inflammable

flare
flair

flea
flee

flew
flu
flue

flew
flown

flocks
phlox

floe
flow

flour
flower

floury
flowery

flow
floe

flower
flour

flowery
floury

flown
flew

flu
flue
flew

foment
ferment

font
fount

forbade
forbidden

fore
four

foregone
forgone

foresaw
foreseen

foreword
forward

forgave
forgiven

forgone
foregone

forgone
forwent

forgot
forgotten

forsaken
forsook

forswore
forsworn

fort
forte
forty

forth
fourth

forty
fort
forte

forward
foreword

forwent
forgone

foul
fowl

found
founded

fount
font

four
fore

fourth
forth

fowl
foul

franc
frank

freeze
frieze

froze
frozen

funeral
funereal

fur
fir

gabble
gable

gaff
gaffe

gait
gate

galleon
gallon

gamble
gambol

gaol
goal

gate
gait

gave
given

genie
genius
genus

genteel
gentile
gentle

genus
genie
genius

gild
guild

gilt
guilt

given
gave

glacier
glazier

goal
gaol

gone
went

gorilla
guerrilla

gourmand
gourmet

gradation
graduation

grate
great

grew
grown

grief
grieve

grill
grille

griped
gripped

grisly
gristly
grizzly

grope
group

ground
grounded

grown
grew

guerrilla
gorilla

guild
gild

guilt
gilt

hail
hale

hair
hare

half
halve

hallo
hallow
halo

halve
half

hangar
hanger

hanged
hung

hanger
hangar

hare
hair

hart
heart

heal
heel

hear
here

heart
hart

heel
heal

heir
air

here
hear

heron
herring

hew
hue

hewed
hewn

hid
hidden

higher
hire

him
hymn

hire
higher

hoar
whore

hoard
horde

hoarse
horse

hole
whole

honorary
honourable

hoop
whoop

hoped
hopped

horde
hoard

horse
hoarse

hue
hew

human
humane

humiliation
humility

hung
hanged

hymn
him

idle
idol

illegible
ineligible

illicit
elicit

illiterate
alliterate

illusion
allusion
delusion

immigrant
emigrant

immigration
emigration

immoral
amoral
immortal

immorality
immortality

impetuous
impetus

impracticable
impractical

in
inn

inapt
inept

incredible
incredulous

indigenous
indigent

industrial
industrious

ineligible
illegible

inept
inapt

inflammable
flammable

ingenious
ingenuous

inhuman
inhumane

inn
in

insure
ensure

intelligent
intelligible

interment
internment

invertebrate
inveterate

isle
aisle

it's
its

jam
jamb

Jew
dew
due

jib
jibe

judicial
judicious

junction
juncture

kart
cart

kerb
curb

key
quay

knave
nave

knead
kneed
need

knew
known

knew
new

knight
night

knightly
nightly

knit
nit

knot
not

knotty
naughty

know
no

known
knew

lade
laid
lay
lied

lain
lane

lair
layer

lama
llama

lane
lain

laterally
latterly

lath
lathe

latterly
laterally

lay
lade
laid
lied

layer
lair

lea
lee

lead
led

leak
leek

led
lead

lee
lea

leek
leak

legible
eligible

lemming
lemon

leopard
leper

lessen
lesson

liable
libel

liar
lyre

libel
liable

licence
license

lied
lade
laid
lay

lightening
lightning

lineament
liniment

liqueur
liquor

literal
literary
literate

llama
lama

load
lode

loan
lone

loath
loathe

local
locale

lode
load

lone
loan

looped
loped
lopped

loose
lose

loot
lute

loped
lopped
looped

lose
loose

loth
loathe

lumbar
lumber

lute
loot

lyre
liar

macaroni
macaroon

made
maid

magnate
magnet

maid
made

mail
male

main
mane

maize
maze

male
mail

mane
main

maniac
manic

manner
manor

mare
mayor

marina
merino

marshal
martial

marten
martin

martial
marshal

martin
marten

mask
masque

mat
matt

mayor
mare

maze
maize

mean
mien

meat
meet
mete out

medal
meddle

mediate
meditate

meet
meat
mete out

merino
marina

metal
mettle

mete out
meat
meet

meter
metre

mettle
metal

mews
muse

mien
mean

might
mite

miner
minor

minister
minster

missal
missile

mistaken
mistook

mite
might

moat
mote

modal
model
module

momentary
momentous
momentum

moose
mouse
mousse

moped
mopped

moral
morale

morality
mortality

mote
moat

motif
motive

mouse
moose
mousse

mucous
mucus

multiple
multiply

muscle
mussel

muse
mews

mussel
muscle

mystic
mystique

naught
nought

naughty
knotty

naval
navel

nave
knave

navel
naval

navvy
navy

nay
née
neigh

need
knead
kneed

negligent
negligible

neigh
nay
née

net
nett

new
knew

night
knight

nightly
knightly

nit
knit

no
know

northerly
northern

not
knot

nougat
nugget

nought
naught

nugget
nougat

oar
ore

of
off

official
officious

omission
emission

oral
aural

ore
oar

organism
orgasm

outdid
outdone

overcame
overcome

overdid
overdone

overran
overrun

overtaken
overtook

overthrew
overthrown

packed
pact

pail
pale

pain
pane

pair
pare
pear

palate
palette
pallet

pale
pail

palette
palate
pallet

pane
pain

par
parr

pare
pear
pair

parr
par

passed
past

pastel
pastille

pate
pâté
patty

peace
piece

peak
peek
pique

peal
peel

pear
pair
pare

pearl
purl

peasant
pheasant

pedal
peddle

peek
peak
pique

peel
peal

peer
pier

pence
pennies

pendant
pendent

pennies
pence

perquisite
prerequisite

personal
personnel

petrel
petrol

pheasant
peasant

phlox
flocks

piazza
pizza

piece
peace

pier
peer

pined
pinned

piped
pipped

pique
peak
peek

pistil
pistol

pizza
piazza

place
plaice

plain
plane

plaintiff
plaintive

plait
plate

plane
plain

plate
plait

plum
plumb

politic
political

pool
pull

poplar
popular

pore
pour

pored
poured

poser
poseur

pour
pore

poured
pored

practicable
practical

practice
practise

pray
prey

precede
proceed

premier
première

prerequisite
perquisite

prey
pray

price
prise
prize

principal
principle

prise
price
prize

private
privet

prize
prise
price

proceed
precede

profit
prophet

program
programme

proof
prove

property
propriety

prophecy
prophesy

prophet
profit

propriety
property

prostate
prostrate

prove
proof

pull
pool

purl
pearl

put
putt

quash
squash

quay
key

queue
cue

quiet
quite

quire
choir

quite
quiet

racket
racquet

radar
raider

raged
ragged

raider
radar

rain
reign
rein

raise
raze

rampant
rampart

ran
run

rang
ringed
rung

rap
wrap

raped
rapped

rapped
rapt
wrapped

rated
ratted

raze
raise

read
red

read
reed

real
reel

red
read

reed
read

reel
real

refuge
refugee

regal
regale

reign
rain
rein

relief
relieve

reproof
reprove

respectful
respective

rest
wrest

retch
wretch

review
revue

rhyme
rime

ridden
rode

right
rite
write

rime
rhyme

ring
wring

ringed
rang
rung

risen
rose

rite
right
write

road
rode
rowed

rode
ridden

roe
row

rôle
roll

rose
risen

rote
wrote

rough
ruff

rout
route

row
roe

rowed
road
rode

ruff
rough

run
ran

rung
wrung

rye
wry

sail
sale

salon
saloon

sang
sung

sank
sunk
sunken

saviour
savour

saw
seen

sawed
sawn

scared
scarred

scene
seen

scent
cent
sent

sceptic
septic

scraped
scrapped

sculptor
sculpture

sea
see

sealing
ceiling

seam
seem

sear
seer
sere

secret
secrete

see
sea

seem
seam

seen
saw

seen
scene

seer
sear
sere

sell
cell

sensual
sensuous

sent
cent
scent

septic
sceptic

sere
sear
seer

serial
cereal

series
serious

sew
so
sow

sewed
sewn

sewer
sower

sewn
sewed

sewn
sown

sextant
sexton

shaken
shook

shear
sheer

sheared
sheered
shorn

shelf
shelve

shoe
shoo

shook
shaken

shoot
chute

shorn
sheared
sheered

showed
shown

shrank
shrunk

sight
cite
site

signet
cygnet

silicon
silicone

singeing
singing

sinuous
sinus

site
cite
sight

skies
skis

slain
slew

slated
slatted

slay
sleigh

slew
slain

sloe
slow

sloped
slopped

slow
sloe

smelled
smelt

sniped
snipped

so
sew
sow

soar
sore

sociable
social

solder
soldier

sole
soul

some
sum

son
sun

soot
suit

sore
soar

soul
sole

southerly
southern

sow
sew
so

sowed
sown

sower
sewer

sown
sewn

spared
sparred

speciality
specialty

species
specious

sped
speeded

spoke
spoken

sprang
sprung

squash
quash

staid
stayed

stair
stare

stake
steak

stalk
stock

stanch
staunch

stank
stunk

stare
stair

stared
starred

stationary
stationery

statue
statute

staunch
stanch

stayed
staid

steak
stake

steal
steel

step
steppe

stile
style

stimulant
stimulus

stock
stalk

stocked
stoked

storey
story

straight
strait

straightened
straitened

stratum
stratus

strewed
strewn

strife
strive

striped
stripped

strive
strife

striven
strove

stunk
stank

sty
stye

style
stile

suede
swede

suit
soot

suite
sweet

sum
some

summary
summery

sun
son

sundae
Sunday

sung
sang

sunk
sank
sunken

super
supper

surplice
surplus

swam
swum

swede
suede

sweet
suite

swelled
swollen

swingeing
swinging

swollen
swelled

swore
sworn

swum
swam

symbol
cymbal

tacks
tax

tail
tale

taken
took

tale
tail

taped
tapped

taper
tapir

tapped
taped

tare
tear

taught
taut

tax
tacks

tea
tee

team
teem

tear
tare

tear
tier

tee
tea

teem
team

teeth
teethe

temporal
temporary

tendon
tenon

tenor
tenure

testimonial
testimony

their
there
they're

thorough
through

thrash
thresh

threw
through

threw
thrown

throes
throws

throne
thrown

through
thorough

through
threw

thrown
threw

thrown
throne

throws
throes

thyme
time

tic
tick

tier
tear

tiled
tilled

timber
timbre

time
thyme

tire
tyre

to
too
two

toe
tow

tomb
tome

ton
tonne
tun

too
to
two

took
taken

topi
toupee

tore
torn

tortuous
torturous

tow
toe

trait
tray

treaties
treatise

trod
trodden

troop
troupe

tun
ton
tonne

turban
turbine

two
to
too

tycoon
typhoon

tyre
tire

unaware
unawares

unconscionable
unconscious

undid
undone

unwanted
unwonted

urban
urbane

vacation
vocation

vain
vane
vein

vale
veil

venal
venial

veracity
voracity

vertex
vortex

vigilant
vigilante

vocation
vacation

voracity
veracity

vortex
vertex

wafer
waver

waged
wagged

waif
waive
wave

waist
waste

want
wont

warden
warder

ware
wear

waste
waist

wave
waif
waive

waver
wafer

way
weigh

weak
week

wear
ware

weekly
weakly

weigh
way

went
gone

westerly
western

wet
whet

whit
wit

whole
hole

whoop
hoop

whore
hoar

willed
would

winded
wound

wit
whit

withdrawn
withdrew

wittily
wittingly

woe
woo

woke
woken

wont
want

woo
woe

wore
worn

would
willed

would
wood
wooed

wove
woven

wrap
rap

wrapped
rapped
rapt

wreak
wreck

wreath
wreathe

wrest
rest

wretch
retch

wring
ring

write
right
rite

wrote
rote

wrote
written

wrung
rung

wry
rye

yew
ewe
you

yoke
yolk

yore
your